MW00723688

Educators
Resource
Directory

L901 E443

LEARNING RESOURCE CENTER
ALAMANCE COMMUNITY COLLEGE
P.O. BOX 8000
GRAHAM, NC 27253-8000

2005/06
Sixth Edition

Educators
Resource
Directory

- *No Child Left Behind* Resources
- Associations & Organizations
- Professional Development
- Consultants
- Financial Resources
- Conferences & Trade Shows
- Opportunities Abroad
- Statistics & Rankings

LEARNING RESOURCE CENTER
ALAMANCE COMMUNITY COLLEGE
P.O. BOX 8000
GRAHAM, NC 27253-8000

A SEDGWICK PRESS Book

Grey House
Publishing

PUBLISHER: Leslie Mackenzie
EDITORIAL DIRECTOR: Laura Mars-Proietti
ASSOCIATE EDITOR: David Garoogian

PRODUCTION MANAGER: Gabby Templet
PRODUCTION ASSISTANTS: Amy Adams, Vicki Barker, Stephanie Capozzi, Carrie Wessel

MARKETING DIRECTOR: Jessica Moody

A Sedgwick Press Book
Grey House Publishing, Inc.
185 Millerton Road
Millerton, NY 12546
518.789.8700
FAX 518.789.0545
www.greyhouse.com
e-mail: books @greyhouse.com

While every effort has been made to ensure the reliability of the information presented in this publication, Grey House Publishing neither guarantees the accuracy of the data contained herein nor assumes any responsibility for errors, omissions or discrepancies. Grey House accepts no payment for listing; inclusion in the publication of any organization, agency, institution, publication, service or individual does not imply endorsement of the editors or publisher.

Errors brought to the attention of the publisher and verified to the satisfaction of the publisher will be corrected in future editions.

Except by express prior written permission of the Copyright Proprietor no part of this work may be copied by any means of publication or communication now known or developed hereafter including, but not limited to, use in any directory or compilation or other print publication, in any information storage and retrieval system, in any other electronic device, or in any visual or audio-visual device or product.

This publication is an original and creative work, copyrighted by Grey House Publishing, Inc. and is fully protected by all applicable copyright laws, as well as by laws covering misappropriation, trade secrets and unfair competition.

Grey House has added value to the underlying factual material through one or more of the following efforts: unique and original selection; expression; arrangement; coordination; and classification.

Grey House Publishing, Inc. will defend its rights in this publication.

Copyright © 2005 Grey House Publishing, Inc.
All rights reserved

First edition 1994
Sixth edition

Printed in the USA

ISBN 1-59237-080-2 softcover

Table of Contents

***NO CHILD LEFT BEHIND* RESOURCES**

SECTION ONE: RESOURCES

1.   Associations & Organizations

General 1
Administration...14
Early Childhood Education 16
Elementary Education 17
Employment 18
Guidance & Counseling 19
International 20
Language Arts 27
Library Services 28
Mathematics 29
Music & Art 29
Physical Education 31
Reading..31
Secondary Education...32
Science 33
Social Studies 34
Technology in Education...35
State Listings 37

2.   Conferences & Trade Shows

International..57
National 59
Regional: Northeast 77
Northwest 78
Southeast..79
Southwest 79

3.   Consultants...81

4.   Teaching Opportunities Abroad
See also **Publications, Employment** *for additional resources*

Africa..95
Asia, Pacific Rim & Australia 100
Central & South America 116
Eastern Europe...125
Middle East..127
Western Europe 133
West Indies & Caribbean...161
US Branches 162
International...178

5. Financial Resources

Grant Foundations, State Listings 181
Grants, Federal & Private...227
Fundraising...229
Scholarships & Financial Aid......................................231

6. Government Agencies

Federal Listings..233
State Listings 235

7. Professional Development

Associations..258
Awards & Honors..260
Conferences..261
Directories & Handbooks 273
Periodicals 279
Software, Hardware and Internet Resources 285
Training Materials 287
Workshops & Programs 292

8. Publications

Directories & Handbooks

General 303
Administration...316
Early Childhood Education 321
Elementary Education 321
Employment 322
Financial Aid 326
Guidance & Counseling 332
Language Arts 334
Library Services..335
Music & Art...336
Physical & Education 337
Reading...337
Secondary Education...338
Science..339
Social Studies 340
Technology in Education..341

Periodicals

General 343
Administration...363
Early Childhood Education 370
Elementary Education 373
Employment 374
Financial Aid 376
Guidance & Counseling 377
Language Arts 382
Library Services..386
Mathematics 388
Music & Art...389
Physical Education 392

Reading...393

Secondary Education..395

Science...396

Social Studies...399

Technology in Education......................................402

9.   Publishers...406

10.   Research Centers..431

11.   School Supplies

Audio Visual Materials...439

Classroom Materials..444

Electronic Equipment..458

Furniture & Equipment...462

Maintenance...468

Scientific Equipment...472

Sports & Playground Equipment..........................479

12.   Software, Hardware & Internet Resources

General...483

Administration...493

Early Childhood Education...................................497

Elementary Education..498

Employment..499

Guidance & Counseling.......................................499

International...500

Language Arts...501

Library Services...502

Mathematics...505

Music & Art...506

Physical Education..507

Reading..507

Secondary Education..507

Science...507

Social Studies...508

Technology in Education......................................509

13.   Testing Resources

Elementary Education..513

Language Arts...513

Mathematics...513

Music & Art...514

Reading..515

Secondary Education..515

SECTION TWO: STATISTICS & RANKINGS

14.   **Adult Education**...519

15   **College & University Education**...523

16.   **Educational Attainment**...555

17.   **Elementary & Secondary Education**..................................561

18.   **Federal Programs for Education & Related Activities**.......629

19.   **International Comparisons of Education**............................639

20.   **Learning Resources & Technology**....................................648

21.   **Opinions on Education**..649

22.   **Outcomes of Education**..651

SECTION THREE: INDEXES

Entry & Publisher Index..655
Geographic Index..697
Subject Index..714
Web Sites Index...720

Introduction

Welcome to the sixth edition of *Educators Resource Directory*, a comprehensive resource designed to provide educators, administrators, and other education professionals with immediate access to a unique combination of over 6,200 educational information resources, and more than 130 charts of education statistics and rankings.

This new and improved edition is reorganized to focus on Professional Development. This chapter has been expanded to include associations, publications, trade shows, workshops and training programs dedicated to help educators not only advance on a professional level, but also meet qualifications set forth in the *No Child Left Behind Act of 2001* (*NCLB*). This edition includes a special *NCLB* section that describes definitions and criteria used by *NCLB* at the federal, state and local level, and is just in time to assist teachers of core subjects meet the *NCLB* 2005-2006 "highly qualified" teacher designation.

This special section includes directory entries relating to *NCLB* regulations, in addition to a definition of *NCLB* terms. Also new to this edition of *Educators Resource Directory*, is a new Subject Index, that arranges relevant listings by *NCLB* certification areas: Arts; Civics & Government; Economics: English; Foreign Language; Geography; History; Math; Reading or Language Arts; and Science. It also includes Special Education, Technology and entries related to *NCLB* reform.

Our updated data expands professional horizons by providing new tools for classroom and career management, and resources that truly make a difference in job and school performance. Users will find 22 carefully organized chapters that include dozens of resources from associations to classroom suppliers. This one, easy-to-use volume replaces the hours it would take searching through multiple resources to uncover all the information presented here.

This edition includes thousands of updates and hundreds of new entries – every association, organization and agency has been updated or verified. In addition, chapters on Professional Development, Financial Resources and Publications & Periodicals have been thoroughly researched. The 6,263 listings in *Educators Resource Directory* include not only current name, address, phone numbers, and key contacts, but more than 5,500 fax numbers, 2,200 e-mail addresses and 3,000 web sites.

SECTION ONE: RESOURCES

Associations & Organizations disseminate information, host seminars, provide educational literature and promote study councils. The nearly 650 associations in this edition are consolidated in this chapter, and are further organized into 16 distinct categories. New to the state association listings are web sites with *NCLB* certification requirements for teachers.

The chapter on **Conferences & Trade Shows** lists everything from huge conventions of classroom resource and equipment suppliers to small, specialized conferences that target rural education and specific teaching challenges. Events are listed regionally.

Consultants listings offer information on companies that provide educational consulting services, including curriculum-building guidance, school district organizations, and facility format.

Teaching Opportunities Abroad includes not only US government schools, but also all American schools overseas. The chapter is divided by world region, and provides contact information, grade level and enrollment numbers on more than 1,200 schools.

Details on nearly 650 grants, foundations and scholarships can be found in the **Financial Resources** chapter. Here you will find information on how to obtain funds for individual professional advancement, schools, programs, students, and education districts and communities.

The new and improved **Professional Development** chapter offers hundreds of associations, awards & honors, conferences, career-advancement summer programs, educator workshops, handbooks and periodicals, software, Internet resources, and training materials.

The chapter on **Publications** includes nearly 1,400 directories, magazines and journals that are subdivided into 17 subject areas. Here the education professional will find support for everything from doing research, to getting published, to buying classroom materials.

Publishers include 350 publishers of textbooks, testing resources and classroom curriculums.

For those seeking research on general learning and training issues, or data on specific subjects, like *Gifted & Talented, Educational Media*, or *Scientific Learning, Educators Resource Directory* offers nearly 100 **Research Centers** throughout the country.

The chapter on **School Supplies** focuses on *Audio Visual, Electronic* and *Scientific Equipment*, plus *Classroom Materials, Furniture* and *Sports & Playground Equipment*.

Software, Hardware & Internet Resources now are combined in their own chapter, which includes 18 subchapters from *Administration* to *Technology in Education* for easy access to the exact resources you are looking for. Here you will find educational computer programs, and web sites with information on classroom resources for every level and subject.

Finally, **Testing Resources** includes resources for written materials and web sites in 10 categories.

SECTION TWO: STATISTICS & RANKINGS

This section offers 136 tables and charts -- 40 more than last edition -- in nine categories: **Adult Education, College & University Education; Educational Attainment; Elementary & Secondary Education; Federal Programs for Education & Related Activities; International Comparisons of Education; Learning Resources & Technology; Opinions on Education; Outcomes of Education.** Specific topics include degrees, enrollment, completions, dropouts, faculty, revenues, expenditures, and student behavior. Many tables offer state-by-state rankings.

Using the most current data available (December 2004), this section helps to complete the picture for educators making career development decisions, for school administrators interested in comparing fiscal health and educational scores, and for anyone doing educational research.

SECTION THREE: INDEXES

Four indexes offer users access to the information in this Directory via several ways:

Entry & Publisher Name Index -- alphabetical list of both entry names and the companies that publish the listed material. Publishers are listed in boldface type.

Geographic Index -- state by state listing of all entries.

Web Sites Index -- list of all the web site addresses in the Directory, with company name, organized by chapter.

New to this edition*: Subject Index* organizes entries by *NCLB* designated core subjects (Arts, Civics & Government, Economics, English, Foreign Language, Geography, History, Math, Reading or Language Arts, and Science) plus the categories of special education and technology.

Educators Resource Directory is also available in an Online Database. Subscribers can access this via the Internet and do customized searches that instantly locate needed sources of information. Visit www.greyhouse.com and explore the site free, or call 800-562-2139 for more information.

The 2005/06 edition of *Educators Resource Directory* and its *Online Database* offer the invaluable combination of educational resources with statistics and rankings, to give users the full educational picture of any given city or state. Either format is sure to be an indispensable reference for seasoned education professionals, for teachers just beginning their education career, and for all those who service and support the education industry.

11234

1 ➤ **Gifted Children's Association**
2 ➤ 70 International Road
PO Box 594
Anytown, NY 00000

3 ➤ 001-111-1113

4 ➤ 800-000-0000

5 ➤ 001-111-1112

6 ➤ info@GCA.com

7 ➤ www.GCA.com

8 ➤ Provides enrichment and support for gifted children through various national programs.

9 ➤ Director: Gina Thorson
Marketing Manager: Todd Fasco
Production Manager: Sally Felder

10 ➤ **Year Founded:** 1953

User Key

1 ➤ **Entry/Title:** Primary company or product name.

2 ➤ **Address:** Location or permanent mailing address of the company.

3 ➤ **Phone Number:** The listed phone number is usually for the main office, but may also be for sales, marketing, or public relations as provided by the company.

4 ➤ **Toll Free Number:** This is listed when provided by the company.

5 ➤ **Fax Number:** This is listed when provided by the company.

6 ➤ **E-Mail:** Listed when provided by the company, and is usually the main office e-mail

7 ➤ **Web Site:** Listed when provided by the company, and is also referred to as an URL address. To access through the Internet, type http:// before the URL address.

8 ➤ **Title/Entry Description:** This information is provided directly by the company, or abridged from data on their web site or in their literature.

9 ➤ **Key Executives:** Names of key executives in the company.

10 ➤ **Year Founded:** Year company was established.

No Child Left Behind (NCLB)

The *No Child Left Behind Act of 2001 (NCLB)* redefines the federal role in K-12 education and has been called the most sweeping reform of the *Elementary and Secondary Education Act (ESEA)* since it was enacted in 1965. It embodies four basic principles: stronger accountabilty for results; expanded flexibility and local control; expanded options for parents; and an emphasis on teaching methods that have been proven to work. A major focus of *NCLB* is naturally on educators — not only encouraging them to employ proven teaching methods, but also holding those educators accountable for results achieved with those methods. In fact, *NCLB* includes criteria for the "highly qualified" teacher, which we offer below, all in the name of Professional Development — the focus of this 6th edition of *Educators Resource Directory*.

NCLB Related Entries

Accreditation Fact Sheet, 4322

American Association School Administrators National Conference on Education, 658

American Association of Colleges for Teacher Education, 3262

American Association of School Administrators Annual Convention, 666

Annual Building Championship Schools Conference, 3303

Annual Effective Schools Conference, 688

Association for Supervision & Curriculum Development Annual Conference, 699

Center for Professional Development & Services, 858

Committee on Continuing Education for School Personnel, 3270

Council of Chief State School Officers, 158

Curriculum Associates, 6201

Directory of State Education Agencies, 3877

EDUCAUSE Quarterly, 4701

ERIC Clearinghouse on Assessment & Evaluation, 49
continued

Who defines "highly qualified" teacher?

Federal
NCLB sets the minimum requirements:
- A bachelor's degree.
- Full state certification, as defined by the state.
- Demonstrated competency, as defined by the state, in each core academic subject the teacher teaches.

NCLB sets a deadline:
- All new teachers of core academic subjects in Title I schools/programs hired beginning with the 2002–03 school year must meet the requirements before entering the classroom.
- All teachers of core academic subjects hired before the 2002–03 school year must meet the requirements by the end of the 2005–06 school year. (Special considerations may apply for multi-subject teachers in eligible small, rural schools.)

The secretary of education is responsible for monitoring state plans and providing assistance to states as they seek to meet these requirements.

State
States define "highly qualified teacher" according to the requirements of NCLB.

States may develop this definition according to their own unique needs. States determine what is meant by "full state certification."They may streamline requirements to make it less burdensome for talented individuals to enter the profession.

States develop a plan with goals for their districts, detailing how they will ensure that all teachers of core academic subjects will be highly qualified by the end of the 2005-06 school year.

States determine ways in which teachers can demonstrate competency in the subjects they teach, according to the requirements in NCLB. (For example, states choose whether or not to adopt their own high, objective, uniform state standard of evaluation [HOUSSE] for current teachers.)

Education Budget Alert, 3880

Education Personnel Update, 4339

Education Week, 4169

Educational Testing Service, 6240

Effective Strategies for School Reform, 3644

Guide to Federal Funding for Education, 4344

Harvard Seminar for Superintendents, 3656

Improving Student Performance, 729

Integrated/Thematic Curriculum and Performance Assessment, 734

International Congress for School Effectiveness & Improvement, 644

Journal of Curriculum & Supervision, 4347

Lilly Conferences on College and University Teaching, 3337

NEA Higher Education Advocate, 4240

National Association for Supervision and Curriculum Development, 163

National Association of Federal Education Program Administrators, 165

National Association of Federally Impacted Schools, 90

National Association of Secondary School Principals Annual Convention and Exposition, 3354

National Association of State Boards of Education, 91

National Association of State Boards of Education Conference, 3355

National Association of State Directors of Teacher Education & Certification, 3277

continued

Local
Local Districts ensure that newly hired teachers in Title I schools/programs meet their state's definition of "highly qualified teacher."

Districts work with states to communicate with current teachers regarding the "highly qualified" teacher definition, and provide a way for teachers to determine whether or not they meet the state definition of "highly qualified teacher."

Districts work with states to support teachers who do not meet the "highly qualified" teacher definition in the subjects they teach, providing opportunities or options for them to meet the requirements by the end of the 2005–06 school year.

Who determines what is high-quality professional development?

Federal
In NCLB, the term "high-quality professional development" refers to the definition of professional development in Title IX, Section 9101(34). It includes, but is not limited to, activities that:
- Improve and increase teachers' knowledge of academic subjects.
- Are integral to broad schoolwide and districtwide educational improvement plans.
- Give teachers and principals the knowledge and skills to help students meet challenging state academic standards.
- Improve classroom management skills.
- Are sustained, intensive and classroom-focused and are not one-day or short-term workshops.
- Advance teacher understanding of effective instructional strategies that are supported by scientifically based research.
- Are developed with extensive participation of teachers, principals, parents and administrators.

State
States report to the secretary of education the percentage of teachers involved in high-quality professional development.

States monitor the districts' use of professional development dollars provided by Title II grants, as well as by other federal and state funds.

States must use a minimum of 5 percent of their Title I funds for professional development for teachers and other school-level employees.

Local
To receive federal funds for improving teacher quality (Title II, Part A), districts must perform a needs assessment and use data to make decisions regarding the type of high-quality professional development to be provided for teachers. **Teachers must be involved in this process.**

National Coalition of Title 1-Chapter 1 Parents Conference, 768

National School Boards Association, 121

National Study of School Evaluation, 6205

National Survey of Course Offerings and Testing in Social Studies K-12, 6248

No Child Left Behind Web Site, 2894

Preventing School Failure, 6252

Principal, 4363

Public Education Alert, 4268

Recruiting New Teachers, 3284

Research in the Schools, 4278

Restructuring Curriculum Conference, 3398

Retaining Great Teachers, 3521

Scholastic Testing Service, 6259

School Administrator, 4369

Superintendents Only, 4380

TestSkills, 6263

Three R'S for Teachers: Research, Reports & Reviews, 4307

Title I Handbook, 4385

Title I Monitor, 4386

Twenty First Century Teachers Network: The McGuffey Project, 410

USC Summer Superintendents' Conference, 804

Updating School Board Policies, 4388

WCER Highlights, 4312

Districts and schools look at student achievement levels and set professional development goals for teachers.

Who defines and determines adequate yearly progress (AYP)?

Federal

NCLB sets requirements for state definitions of AYP, which is the progress that schools and districts must show in educating all students to grade-level standards, as reflected in student assessments.

NCLB requires subgroup accountability: English language learners, students with disabilities, economically disadvantaged youth, and breakouts by race and ethnicity.

NCLB sets a goal for AYP—100 percent proficiency for all students and each subgroup by the end of the 2013–14 school year.

The secretary of education approves and monitors each state's accountability plan, ensuring that it meets the NCLB minimum requirements.

State

States use assessment data to set benchmarks and determine a trajectory for meeting the goal of 100 percent proficiency by the end of the 2013–14 school year.

States use their own reading and math tests, participation rates in testing and at least one other academic indicator (such as performance on science assessments or graduation rate) when determining AYP.

States must provide assistance to districts in need of improvement and may choose to implement supports for districts, such as professional development, targeting of funds and other assistance.

States oversee districts' actions to help support schools identified as in need of improvement.

Local

Districts provide information to the state about performance on all indicators—math and reading assessments, assessment participation rates, and others.

Districts use this information, as well as determinations of achievement gaps in subgroups of students, to inform decision making at the district and school levels.

At the school level, principals and teachers use assessment data, participation rates and other indicators to help improve student achievement.

Source: U.S. Department of Education, Office of the Deputy Secretary, No Child Left Behind: A Toolkit for Teachers, Washington, D.C., 2004

Definition of Terms

Accountability System
Each state sets academic standards for what every child should know and learn. Student academic achievement is measured for every child, every year. The results of these annual tests are reported to the public.

Achievement Gap
The difference between how well low-income and minority children perform on standardized tests as compared with their peers. For many years, low-income and minority children have been falling behind their white peers in terms of academic achievement.

Adequate Yearly Progress (AYP)
An individual state's measure of yearly progress toward achieving state academic standards. "Adequate Yearly Progress" is the minimum level of improvement that states, school districts and schools must achieve each year.

Alternative Certification
Most teachers are required to have both a college degree in education and a state certification before they can enter the classroom. No Child Left Behind encourages states to offer other methods of qualification that allow talented individuals to teach subjects they know.

Assessment
Another word for "test." Under No Child Left Behind, tests are aligned with academic standards. Beginning in the 2002-03 school year, schools must administer tests in each of three grade spans: grades 3-5, grades 6-9, and grades 10-12 in all schools. Beginning in the 2005-06 school year, tests must be administered every year in grades 3 through 8 in math and reading. Beginning in the 2007-08 school year, science achievement must also be tested.

Charter School
Charter schools are independent public schools designed and operated by educators, parents, community leaders, educational entrepreneurs, and others. They are sponsored by designated local or state educational organizations, who monitor their quality and effectiveness but allow them to operate outside of the traditional system of public schools.

Comprehension
The ability to understand and gain meaning from what has been read.

Corrective Action
When a school or school district does not make yearly progress, the state will place it under a "Corrective Action Plan." The plan will include resources to improve teaching, administration, or curriculum. If a school continues to be identified as in need of improvement, then the state has increased authority to make any necessary, additional changes to ensure improvement.

Disaggregated Data
"Disaggregate" means to separate a whole into its parts. In education, this term means that test results are sorted into groups of students who are economically disadvantaged, from racial and ethnic minority groups, have disabilities, or have limited English fluency. This practice allows parents and teachers to see more than just the average score for their child's school. Instead, parents and teachers can see how each student group is performing.

Distinguished Schools
Awards granted to schools when they make major gains in achievement.

Early Reading First
A nationwide effort to provide funds to school districts and other public or private organizations that serve children from low-income families. The Department of Education will make competitive 6-year grants to local education agencies to support early language, literacy, and pre-reading development of preschool-age children, particularly those from low-income families.

Elementary and Secondary Education Act (ESEA)
ESEA, which was first enacted in 1965, is the principal federal law affecting K-12 education. The No Child Left Behind Act is the most recent reauthorization of the ESEA.

Flexibility

Refers to a new way of funding public education. The No Child Left Behind Act gives states and school districts unprecedented authority in the use of federal education dollars in exchange for strong accountability for results.

Fluency

The capacity to read text accurately and quickly.

Local Education Agency

(LEA) is a public board of education or other public authority within a State which maintains administrative control of public elementary or secondary schools in a city, county, township, school district, or other political subdivision of a state.

National Assessment of Educational Progress

An independent benchmark, NAEP is the only nationally representative and continuing assessment of what American students know and can do in various subject areas. Since 1969, The National Center for Education Statistics has conducted NAEP assessments in reading, mathematics, science, writing, U.S. history, geography, civics, and the arts.

Phonemic Awareness

The ability to hear and identify individual sounds—or phonemes—in spoken words.

Phonics

The relationship between the letters of written language and the sounds of spoken language.

Public School Choice

Students in schools identified as in need of improvement will have the option to transfer to better public schools in their districts. The school districts will be required to provide transportation to the students. Priority will be given to low-income students.

Reading First

A bold new national initiative aimed at helping every child in every state become a successful reader.

State Educational Agency

(SEA) is the agency primarily responsible for the State supervision of public elementary and secondary schools.

Supplemental Services

Students from low-income families who are attending schools that have been identified as in need of improvement for two years will be eligible to receive outside tutoring or academic assistance. Parents can choose the appropriate services for their child from a list of approved providers. The school district will purchase the services.

Teacher Quality

To ensure that every classroom has a highly qualified teacher, states and districts around the country are using innovative programs to address immediate and long-term needs, including alternative recruitment strategies, new approaches to professional development, financial incentive programs, partnerships with local universities, and much more.

Title I

The first section of the ESEA, Title I refers to programs aimed at America's most disadvantaged students. Title I Part A provides assistance to improve the teaching and learning of children in high-poverty schools to enable those children to meet challenging State academic content and performance standards. Title I reaches about 12.5 million students enrolled in both public and private schools.

Transferability

A new ESEA flexibility authority that allows states and local educational agencies (LEAs) to transfer a portion of the funds that they receive under certain Federal programs to other programs that most effectively address their unique needs to certain activities under Title I.

Unsafe School Choice Option

Students who attend persistently dangerous public schools or have been victims of violent crime at school are allowed to transfer to a safer public school.

Vocabulary

The words students must know to read effectively.

Source: U.S. Department of Education, Office of the Deputy Secretary, No Child Left Behind: A Toolkit for Teachers, Washington, D.C., 2004

General

1 ACCESS ERIC
1600 Research Boulevard
#5F
Rockville, MD 20850-3172

301-251-5789
800-LET-ERIC
Fax: 301-309-2084
http://http://ericec.org

Coordinates outreach, dissemination and system wide activities; develops new publications and provides reference and referral services. Staffs toll-free information line to 16 subject-specific ERIC Clearinghouses and more than 350 education organizations. Free brochures on themes such as parent involvement available.

Lynn Smarte, Director

2 ACTION
1100 Vermont Avenue NW
Suite 5200
Washington, DC 20005-3504

202-638-4840

Supports the development of creative, effective and lasting solutions to the challenges of crime, hunger, poverty, illiteracy and homelessness. Action's mission is to stimulate and expand voluntary citizen participation through the coordination of efforts with public and private organizations and other government agencies.

3 ASPIRA Association
1444 Eye Street NW
Suite 800
Washington, DC 20005-6543

202-835-3600
Fax: 202-835-3613
E-mail: info@aspira.org
http://www.aspira.org

Founded in 1961 ASPIRA promotes Latino youth leadership and education. Through its associate ASPIRA organizations and national demonstration projects, it provides a host of leadership development and education programs for Puerto Rican and other Latino youth.

Ronald Blackburn-Moreno, President & CEO
John Villamil-Casanova, Executive Vice President

4 Academy for Educational Development
1825 Connecticut Avenue
Washington, DC 20009-5746

202-884-8000
Fax: 202-884-8400
E-mail: communicationsmail@aed.org
http://www.aed.org

Assists schools, colleges and other educational institutions of developing countries in researching, planning, designing, implementing and evaluating development programs. In the US, manages the Center for Youth Development and Policy Research (disadvantaged youth), Disabilities Studies and Services Center (clearinghouse on special education and children with disabilities), National Institute for Work and Learning (school-to-work transition), and schools and Community Services Department.

Stephen Moseley, Director
Peter B. Johnson, Senior Vice President

5 Advance Program for Young Scholars
Louisiana Scholar's College
Northwestern State University
110 Morrison Hall
Natchitoches, LA 71497

318-357-4500
800-838-2208
Fax: 318-357-4547
E-mail: palmerh@nsula.edu
http://www.nsula.edu/scholars

From chemistry to history, from foreign languages to ecology, the program offers a broad spectrum of academic opportuities to the qualified 12-17 year old student.

David Wood PhD, Director
Harriette Palmer, Assistant Director

6 Alliance for Parental Involvement in Education
PO Box 59
East Chatham, NY 12060-0059

518-392-6900
E-mail: allpie@taconic.net

Seeks to nurture parents' natural teaching abilities and offer tools and resources, public, private and home in becoming active participants in the education of their children.

Katharine Houk, Executive Director

7 Alliance for Schools That Work
Education Alternatives, Inc. (EAI)
1300 Xerxes Avenue N
Minneapolis, MN 55411-2848

612-832-0092

Seeks to improve the results of education through proven financial, educational and facilities programs by forming public-private partnerships with local school boards and communities.

William F Goins, CEO

8 American Academy of Pediatrics
141 NW Point Boulevard
Elk Grove Village, IL 60007-1098

847-434-4000
Fax: 847-434-8000
E-mail: kidsdoc@aap.org
http://www.aap.org

Committed to the attainment of optimal physical, mental and social health for all infants, children, adolescents and young adults.

Eileen M Ouellette, MD, President
Errol R Alden, MD, Executive Director

9 American Association for Vocational Instructional Materials
220 Smithonia Road
Winterville, GA 30683-1418

706-742-5355
800-228-4689
Fax: 706-742-7005
E-mail: ksseab@aavim.com
http://www.aavim.com

Develops, publishes and distributes instructional materials for career education instructors, students, and administrators.

Karen S Seabaugh, Director
Frank Flanders, President

10 American Association of Specialized Colleges
825 S Pennsylvania Street
Marion, IN 46953-2408

An umbrella for non-tax supported colleges that maintain programs for various degrees and certificates.

Associations & Organizations / General

Assists members in securing monies, promotes educational standards and raises funds.

Founded: 1967

11 American Business Communication Association
University of Illinois
911 S 6th Street
Champaign, IL 61820-6206

217-333-1006

Members are varied, with teachers from the management fields and business communication programs, as well as training directors, public writers and copywriters. Bestows awards.

12 American Council for Drug Education
164 W 74th Street
New York, NY 10023

646-505-2060
800-488-3784
Fax: 212-595-2553
E-mail: acde@phoenixhouse.org

Distributes packaged information about drugs and the consequences of their use and identifies effective community programs to address the drug problem in the country.

Stacey J Reynolds, Executive Director

13 American Council on Education
1 Dupont Circle NW
Suite 800
Washington, DC 20036-1193

202-939-9300
Fax: 202-833-4760
E-mail: comments@ace.nche.edu
http://www.acenet.edu

Represents accredited degree-granting colleges and universities directly and through national and regional higher education associations. Seeks to advance education and serves as an advocate for adult education.

David Ward, President
Yvonne Wills, Director of Finance

14 American Council on Rural Special Education
Kansas State University/College of Education
2323 Anderson Avenue
Suite 226
Manhattan, KS 66502-2912

785-532-2737
Fax: 785-532-7732
E-mail: acres@ksu.edu
http://www.ksu.edu/acres

The organization is comprised of special educators, general educators, related service providers, administrators, teacher trainers, researchers, and parents committed to the enhancement of services to students and individuals living in rural America.

Ronda Menlove, Chair
Kevin Miller, Chair Elect

15 American Council on Schools and Colleges
13014 N Dale Mabry Highway 363
Suite 363
Tampa, FL 33618-2808

813-926-5446
don-tpu-bfax
Fax: 813-926-5446
E-mail: fredrick@corpmgttrust.com
http://www.corpmgttrust.com

Promotes ethical business practices and sound educational standards.

Dr. Fredrick O'Keefe, Executive Director

16 American Federation of Teachers
555 New Jersey Avenue NW
Washington, DC 20001

202-879-4400
Fax: 202-879-4556
E-mail: online@aft.org
http://www.aft.org

The AFT represents one million teachers, school support staff, higher education faculty and staff, health care professionals, and state and municipal employees. AFT is an affiliated international union of the AFL-CIO.

Sandra Feldman, President

17 American Montessori Society
281 Park Avenue South
New York, NY 10010-6102

212-358-1250
Fax: 212-358-1256
E-mail: east@amshq.org
http://www.amshq.org

Promotes quality Montessori education for all children from birth to 18 years of age.

Marie M Dugan, Interim Executive Director
Martha Torrence, President

18 American Public Human Services Association
810 1st Street NE
Suite 500
Washington, DC 20002-4207

202-682-0100
Fax: 202-289-6555
http://www.aphsa.org

Promotes effective policies and programs to benefit low-income and disabled individuals. Members include all state and many territorial human service agencies, more than 150 local agencies, and several thousand individuals who work in or otherwise have an interest in human service programs.

Jerry W Friedman, Executive Director
Susan Christie, Deputy Executive Director

19 American School Health Association
7263 State Route 43
PO Box 708
Kent, OH 44240-0013

330-678-1601
Fax: 330-678-4526
E-mail: asha@ashaweb.org
http://www.ashaweb.org

A nonprofit organization founded to protect and improve the health and well-being of children and youth by supporting comprehensive, preschool-12 school health programs.

David K Lohrmann, President
Phyllis J Lewis, President-Elect

20 Association for Community-Based Education
1806 Vernon Street NW
Washington, DC 20009-1217

202-462-6333

Offers technical assistance on planning, management and program development for community-based education.

Christofer Zachariadis, Executive Director

21 Association for Disabled Students
PO Box 21192
Columbus, OH 43221-0192

614-488-4972

Represents professionals working on college campuses with disabled students.

22 Association for Gender Equity Leadership in Education
317 S Division PMB 54
Ann Arbor, MI 48104

734-769-2456
Fax: 734-769-2456
E-mail: agelebusiness@yahoo.com
http://www.agele.org

A national organization for gender equity specialists and educators. Individuals and organizations committed to reducing sex role stereotyping for females and males. Services include an annual national training conference, a quarterly newsletter and a membership directory. Members may join task forces dealing with equity related topics such as computer/technology issues, early childhood, male issues, sexual harassment prevention, sexual orientation and vocational issues.

Marta Larson, Business Manager

23 Association for Integrative Studies
School of Interdisciplinary Studies
Miami University
Oxford, OH 45056

513-529-1809
Fax: 513-529-5849
E-mail: newellwh@muohio.edu
http://www.muohio.edu

Documents the importance of higher education and integrative studies.

William H Newell, Executive Director
Cheryl Jacobson, President

24 Association for Play Therapy
2050 N Winery Avenue
Suite 101
Fresno, CA 93703-2831

559-252-2278
Fax: 559-252-2297
E-mail: info@a4pt.org
http://www.a4pt.org

Founded in 1982 APT is interdisciplinary and defines play therapy as a distinct group of interventions which use play as an integral component of the therapeutic process.

Lisa Saldana, President
Bill Burns, Executive Director

25 Association for Supervision & Curriculum Development
1703 N Beauregard Street
Alexandria, VA 22311-1714

703-578-9600
800-933-2723
Fax: 703-575-5400
E-mail: member@ascd.org
http://www.ascd.org

Unique international, nonprofit, nonpartisan association of professional educators whose jobs cross all grade levels and subject areas.

Martha Bruckner, President

26 Association for the Care of Children's Health
19 Mantua Road
Mount Royal, NJ 08061-1006

609-224-1742
Fax: 609-423-3420
E-mail: amkent@tmg.smarthub.com

Offers books, journals, assistive technology, support, information and referrals for professionals and parents. With a network of over 3,000 members, ACCH strives to include parents and professionals in a united effort to affect positive outcomes for children. The organization takes a leading role in defining, promoting, implementing, and supporting standards and policy in family-centered healthcare for children and youth.

William Sciarillo, ScD, Executive Director

27 Association of Boarding Schools
4455 Connecticut Avenue NW
Suite A200
Washington, DC 20008-5695

202-966-8705
800-541-5908
Fax: 202-966-8708
E-mail: tabs@schools.com

A marketing consortium founded in 1975 of 300 boarding schools that seeks to increase the applicant pool of member schools by increasing public awareness of benefits and advantages of boarding school education.

Founded: 1975

Drew Casertano, Director
Steven D Ruzicka, Executive Director

28 Association of Educators in Private Practice
104 W Main Street, Suite 101
PO Box 348
Watertown, WI 0348

800-252-3280
Fax: 920-206-1475
E-mail: cyelich@aepp.org
http://www.aepp.org

Represents individuals and small firms with products and services for elementary and secondary schools.

29 Attention Deficit Disorder Association
P.O. Box 543
Pottstown, PA 19464

484-945-2101
Fax: 610-970-7520
E-mail: http://www.add.org

Provides a national network for all ADD support groups and individuals. The international organization has been in existence since 1989. The mission of ADDA is to provide information, resources and networking to adults with AD/HD and to the professionals who work with them. ADDA generates hope, awareness, empowerment and connections worldwide in the field of AD/HD.

David Giwerc, President
Linda Anderson, Vice President

30 Awards and Recognition Association
4700 W Lake Avenue
#500
Glenview, IL 60025

847-375-4800
800-344-2148
Fax: 877-734-9380
E-mail: info@ara.org
http://www.ara.org

The Awards and Recognition Association is a membership organization devoted to the awards engraving and recognition industry. Dedicated to advancing the image, capabilities and business growth of recognition specialists, ARA is committed to delivering educational programs that enhance technical and business skills.

Ralph Bloch, Director
Jim Weir, Executive Director

31 Better Chance
240 West 35th Street
Floor 9
New York, NY 10001-2506

646-346-1310
800-562-7865
Fax: 646-346-1311
http://www.betterchance.org

Identifies, recruits and places academically talented and motivated minority students into leading independent secondary schools and selected public high schools.

Sandra Timmons, President
Colin Lord, Director

32 CHADD: Children & Adults with Attention Deficit/Hyperactivity Disorder
8181 Professional Place
Suite 150
Landover, MD 20785

301-306-7070
800-233-4050
Fax: 301-306-7090
http://www.chadd.org

National nonprofit organization which offers advocacy, information and support for patients and parents of children with attention deficit disorders. Maintains support groups, provides a forum for continuing education about ADHD, andmaintains a national resource center for information about ADD.

Russ Shipley, Chief Development Officer
E Clarke Ross, CEO

33 Center for Adult Learning and Educational Credentials
1 Dupont Circle NW
Washington, DC 20036-1110

202-939-9475

Evaluates learning acquired in various non-college settings; monitors educational credit and credentialing policies and provides guidance to postsecondary education institutions for developing policies and procedures for evaluatingextra-institutional learning.

Henry A Spill, Director

34 Center for Civic Education
5145 Douglas Fir Road
Calabasas, CA 91302-1440

818-591-9321
Fax: 818-591-9330
E-mail: cce@civiced.org
http://www.civiced.org

Non-profit, nonpartisan educational corporation dedicated to fostering the development of informed, responsible participation in civic life by citizens committed to values and principles fundamental to American constitutionaldemocracy.

Dick Kean, Director Publication Service

35 Center for Educational Policy Studies
University of Minnesota
159 Pillsbury Drive SE
Minneapolis, MN 55455-0208

612-624-3377

Promotes, coordinates and conducts research and development activities pertaining to educational policy issues.

Karen J Hesla, Secretary

36 Center on Human Policy
805 S Crouse Avenue
Syracuse, NY 13244-2280

315-443-3851
800-894-0826
Fax: 315-443-4338
E-mail: thechp@sued.syr.edu

Promotes the integration of individuals with disabilities into the mainstream of society.

Steven J Taylor, Director

37 Civic Practices Network
Florence Heller School for Advanced
Studies in Social Welfare, Brandeis Univ
Waltham, MA 02154

617-736-4890
Fax: 617-736-4891
E-mail: cpn@cpn.org
http://www.cpn.org

Collaborative and nonpartisan project bringing together a diverse array of organizations and perspectives within the new citizenship movement.

Carmen Sirianni, Editor-in-Chief
Lewis Friedland, Research Director

38 Clearinghouse for Immigrant Education
100 Boylston Street
Suite 737
Boston, MA 02116-4610

617-357-8507
800-441-7192
Fax: 617-359-9549
E-mail: ncasmfe@aol.com
http://www.mcas1.org

Seeks to assist schools, parents, advocates and others who support the school success of immigrant students.

Jan Buettner, Resource Center Coordinator

39 Constitutional Rights Foundation
601 S Kingsley Drive
Los Angeles, CA 90005

213-487-5590
Fax: 213-386-0459
http://www.crf-usa.org

Seeks to instill in our nation's youth a deeper understanding of citizenship through values expressed in our Constitution and its Bill of Rights, and educate them to become active and responsible participants in our society. Dedicatedto assuring our country's future by investing in our youth today.

Todd Clark, Executive Director
JoAnn Burton, Director

40 Council for Advancement & Support of Education
1307 New York Avenue NW
Suite 1000
Washington, DC 20005-4701

202-328-2273
Fax: 202-387-4973
E-mail: MemberServiceCenter@case.org
http://www.case.org

Professional organization for advancement of professionals who work in alumni relations, public relations, publications, government relations, and fund raising at schools, colleges and universities worldwide.

John Lippincott, President

41 Council for Exceptional Children
1110 N Glebe Road
Suite 300
Arlington, VA 22201-5704

703-620-3660
888-232-7733
Fax: 703-264-9494
E-mail: cec@cec.sped.org
http://www.cec.sped.org

A non-profit association whose mission is to improve educational outcomes for individuals with exceptionalities.

Jacquelyn Alexander, President
Dr Drew Allbritten, Executive Treasurer

42 Council for Jewish Education
426 W 58th Street
New York, NY 10019-1102

212-245-8200
Fax: 212-247-1957

Promotes Jewish education and conducts programs to strengthen and improve Jewish life.

Philip Gorodetzer, Executive Secretary

43 Council of Graduate Schools
1 Dupont Circle NW
Suite 430
Washington, DC 20036-1173

202-223-3791
Fax: 202-331-7157

Founded in 1961 members comprise graduate schools in the US and Canada.

Nancy A Goffney, Administrator

44 Council on Postsecondary Accreditation
1 Dupont Circle NW
Suite 430
Washington, DC 20036-1173

202-223-3791
Fax: 202-331-7157
http://www.cgsnet.org

Supports, coordinates and improves all voluntary accrediting activities conducted at the postsecondary educational level in the United States.

Debra Syverson, President

45 Disability Rights Education & Defense Fund
2212 6th Street
Berkeley, CA 94710-2219

510-644-2555
Fax: 510-841-8645
E-mail: dredf@dredf.org
http://www.dredf.org

Promotes the full integration of people with disabilities into the mainstream of society. DREDF was founded in 1979.

Beverly Bertaina, President
Kim Connor, Secretary

46 Division for Learning Disabilities
The Council for Exceptional Children
1920 Association Drive
Reston, VA 20191-1545

703-620-3660
Fax: 703-264-9494

The Division for Learning Disabilities founded in 1983 represents professional personnel, students, parents and others interested in promoting the education and general welfare of children and adults with learning disabilities. Offers a journal and newsletter. A full schedule of sessions focusing on learning disabilities at the CEC convention.

47 Drug Information & Strategy Clearinghouse
PO Box 6424
Rockville, MD 20849-6424

301-251-5123
800-245-2691
Fax: 301-251-5747

Provides housing officials, residents and community leaders with information and assistance on drug abuse prevention and trafficking control techniques.

Nancy Kay, Director

48 EF Educational Tours
1 Education Street
Cambridge, MA 02141-1803

800-782-2076
Fax: 617-619-1803
http://www.eftours.com

Provides international travel for teachers and students. More than three million people have traveled on an EF tour since 1965.

49 ERIC Clearinghouse on Assessment & Evaluation
University of Maryland
1129 Shriver Lab
College Park, MD 20742-5701

301-405-7449
800-464-3742

Fax: 301-405-8134
E-mail: ericae@ericae.net
http://www.ericae.net

Disseminates education information on topics pertaining to tests and other measurement devices, research design and methodology.

Dr. Lawrence Rudner, Director
Carol Boston, Associate Director

50 ERIC Clearinghouse on Disabilities and Gifted Education
The Council for Exceptional Children
1920 Association Drive
Reston, VA 20191-1545

703-620-3660
800-328-0272
Fax: 703-264-9494
E-mail: askeric@ericir.syr.educ
http://www.cec.sped.org/ericec.htm

Addresses prevention, identification and assessment, intervention and enrichment, both in special settings within the mainstream of special/gifted education and produces publications on current research, programs, and practices.

Dr. Sheila Mingo, Director

51 ERIC Clearinghouse on Rural Education & Small Schools
AEL, Inc.
1031 Quarrier Street
Charleston, WV 25301-2337

304-347-0428
800-624-9120
Fax: 304-347-0467
E-mail: ericrc@ael.org
http://www.ael.org/eric

Economic, cultural, social or other factors related to educational programs and practices for rural residents.

Robert Hagerman, User Services

52 ERIC Clearinghouse on Urban Education
Teachers College, Columbia University
PO Box 40
New York, NY 10027-0040

212-678-3433
800-601-4868
Fax: 212-678-4012
E-mail: eric-cue@columbia.edu
http://http://eric-web.tc.columbia.edu

Collects and abstracts documents about urban and minority education, published and unpublished, for inclusion in the ERIC database. Includes topics of urban schools and students, African Americans, Hispanic Americans, Asian Americans, equity issues and multicultural education.

Dr. Erwin Flaxman, Director
Dr. Larry Yates, Associate Director

53 Easter Seals Communications
Easter Seals
230 W Monroe Street
Suite 1800
Chicago, IL 60606-4703

312-726-6200
800-221-6827
Fax: 312-726-1494
E-mail: info@easter-seals.org
http://www.easterseals.com

One of the nation's largest networks for medical rehabilitation and educational services, offering physical and occupational therapy, speech language services, home health, and specialized therapy and support programs for spinal cordinjuries, stroke, post-polio and disabilities that occur as a part of aging.

Vocational training and employment provided for young people.

Sara E Brewster, VP Marketing/Communications
Andrea D Knudsen, Communications Specialist

54 Education Commission of the States
700 Broadway
#1200
Denver, CO 80203-3460

303-299-3600
Fax: 303-296-8332
E-mail: ecs@ecs.org
http://www.ecs.org

Provides a forum for the discussion of major educational issues, and education, research and service function to the member states.

Ted Sanders, President
Mike Huckabee, Chairman

55 Education Development Center
55 Chapel Street
Newton, MA 02458-1060

617-969-7100
Fax: 617-969-5979
http://http://main.edc.org

A nonprofit institution financed by the US government, private educational foundations, foreign governments, and sales of materials for the purpose of comprehensive educational improvement.

Janet Ehitla, President

56 Education Extension
Oklahoma State University-Stillwater
106 Willard
Stillwater, OK 74078-4034

405-744-6254
800-765-8933
Fax: 405-744-7713
E-mail: edext@okstate.edu
http://www.okstate.edu/education/outreach

Provides outreach services to students, teachers and service organizations on a local, state and national basis.

Kenneth A Stern, Director
Adrienne Hyle, Associate Dean

57 Education, Training and Research Associates
4 Carbonero Way
Scotts Valley, CA 95066

831-438-4060
Fax: 831-439-9651
http://www.etr.org

Provides information, resources, training and research to enhance the quality of health and family through education.

Michael Bird, MSW, MPH
John Casken, PhD

58 Educational Equity Concepts
100 5th Avenue
8th Floor
New York, NY 10011

212-243-1110
Fax: 212-627-0407
E-mail: information@edequity.org
http://www.edequity.org

Founded in 1982, promotes bias-free learning through innovative programs and materials.

Merle Froschl, Co-Foundes and Co-Director

59 Educational Register
Vincent-Curtis
29 Simpson Lane
Falmouth, MA 02540-2230

508-457-6473
Fax: 508-457-6499
http://www.vincentcurtis.com

Designed specifically to introduce parents with children 8-18 to the advantages of independent education.

60 Equity Clearinghouse
Mid-Continent Regional Educational Laboratory
2550 S Parker Road
Suite 500
Aurora, CO 80014-1622

303-337-0990
Fax: 303-337-3005
http://www.mcrel.org

Provides information and literature on the topics of desegregation as it relates to education.

Timothy Waters, President
Louis Cicchinelli, Executive Vice President

61 Facing History & Ourselves
16 Hurd Road
Brookline, MA 02445-6919

617-232-1595
Fax: 617-232-0281
http://www.facinghistory.org

Facing History is an international nonprofit that helps teachers and students link the past to moral choices they face today.

Margot Strom, President

62 Family Centered Learning Alternatives
PO Box 236
Ocean Park, WA 98640-0236

425-665-4577

Supports parents' right to choose the educational environment best suited for their children's needs and to promote homeschooling as a legal nationwide learning alternative.

Mary Tufts, Administrator

63 Foundation for Student Communication
Princeton University
305 Aaron Burr Hall
Princeton, NJ 08544

609-258-1111
Fax: 609-258-1222
E-mail: fscint@princeton.edu
http://www.princeton.edu/~fscint

Student subscribers and conference participants who promote communication among students and business persons.

Grethen Roeder, President

64 Friends Council on Education
1515 Cherry Street
Philadelphia, PA 19102-1403

215-241-7245
Fax: 215-241-7299

Founded in 1931 the Friends Council on Education acts as a clearinghouse for information on Quaker schools and colleges.

Founded: 1931

Kay M Edstene, Executive Director

65 Gifted Child Society
190 Rock Road
Glen Rock, NJ 07452-1736

201-444-6530
Fax: 201-444-9099

E-mail: admin@gifted.org
http://www.gifted.org

Provides educational enrichment and support for gifted children through national advocacy and various programs.

Janet L Chen, Executive Director

66   Girls Incorporated
120 Wall Street
New York, NY 10005-3902

800-374-4475
Fax: 212-509-8708
http://www.girlsinc.org

Represents girls on issues of equality and works to create an environment in which girls can learn and grow to their fullest potential.

Val Ackerman, President

67   HEATH Resource Center
2121 K Street NW
Suite 220
Washington, DC 20037

202-973-0904
800-544-3284
Fax: 202-973-0908
E-mail: askheath@gwu.edu
http://www.heath.gwu.edu

The national clearinghouse on post-secondary education for individuals with disabilities. Support from the US Department of Education enables HEATH to serve as an information exchange for support services, policies, procedures andeducation opportunities.

Dr Pamela Ekpone, Director
Zavolia Willis, Assistant Director

68   Human Resources Center
201 I U Willets Road
Albertson, NY 11507-1516

516-747-5400
Fax: 516-393-2668

A pioneer in rehabilitation and special education fields, this nonprofit organization is dedicated to providing educational, vocational, social and recreational opportunities.

69   Independent Living
PO Box 486
Earlville, NY 13332-0486

212-254-5000

Information center dealing with family education for children based in the home and community environment.

Harold W Ingraham, Executive Officer

70   Institute for Development of Educational Activities
259 Regency Ridge Drive
Dayton, OH 45459-4221

937-434-6969
Fax: 937-434-5203

Action-oriented research and development organization.

John M Bahner, President
Jon S Paden, VP

71   Institute for Educational Leadership
1001 Connecticut Avenue NW
Suite 310
Washington, DC 20036-5541

202-822-8405
Fax: 202-872-4050
E-mail: iel@IEL.ORG
http://www.iel.org

The Institute's list of publications on educational trends and policies is available to the public.

Elizabeth Hale, President

72   International Society for Performance Improvement
1400 Spring Street
Suite 260
Silver Spring, MD 20910

301-587-8570
Fax: 301-587-8573
E-mail: info@ispi.org
http://www.ispi.org

Founded in 1962, the International Society for Performance Improvement is dedicated to improving productivity and performance in the workpalce.

Donald Tosti, President

73   Jewish Education Service of North America JESNA
111 8th Avenue
Suite 11E
New York, NY 10011-5201

212-284-6950
Fax: 212-284-6951
E-mail: info@jesna.org
http://www.jesna.org

Created in 1981 as the Jewish Federation system's educational coordinating, planning and development agency. JESNA is widely recognized for its leadership in six different areas, including media and technology, reasearch andevaluation, engaging and empowering Jewish youth, educator recruitment and development, day school education, and congregational and communal education.

Jonathan Woocher, President
Amy Amiel, Director/Project Development

74   Jewish Educators Assembly
300 Forest Drive
East Hills, NY 11548

516-484-9585
Fax: 516-484-9586
E-mail: jewisheducators@aol.com
http://wwww.jewisheducators.org

Professional educators who are affiliated and functioning within the Conservative movement. A source of trained, experienced and qualified personnel to administer, supervise and instruct on a professionally competent and effectivelevel. Members are professional colleagues dedicated to the perpetuation of Judaism and Jewish life.

Steve Freedman, President

75   Jewish Teachers Association
45 E 33rd Street
Room 310
New York, NY 10016-5336

212-684-0556

Focuses on the welfare and goodwill of Jewish educators in America.

Phyllis L Pullman, President

76   John Dewey Society for the Study of Education & Culture
1801 NW 11th Road
Gainesville, FL 32605-5323

352-378-7365
http://www.johndeweysociety.org

Founded in 1935, John Dewey's commitment to the use of critical and reflective intelligence in the search for solutions to crucial problems in education and cuture.

David Hansen, President
Jeanne Connell, Secretary/Treasurer

77   LAUNCH
Department of Special Education
Commerce, TX 75428

972-886-5932

Associations & Organizations / General

An organization that provides resources for learning disabled individuals, coordinates efforts of other local, state and national LD organizations.

78   Learning Disabilities Association of America
Learning Disabilities Association of America
4156 Library Road
Pittsburgh, PA 15234-1349

412-341-1515
888-300-6710
Fax: 412-344-0224
E-mail: info@ldaamerica.org
http://www.ldanatl.org

Has 50 state affiliates with more than 300 local chapters. The national office has a resource center of over 500 publications for sale.

Jane Browning, Executive Director

79   Lutheran Education Association
7400 Augusta Street
River Forest, IL 60305-1402

708-209-3343
Fax: 708-209-3458
E-mail: lea@crf.cuis.edu
http://www.lea.org

Seeks to spark ideas, thoughts and practices among Lutherans.

Dr Jonathan Laabs, Executive Director
Kathy Slupik, Executive Assistant

80   MATRIX: A Parent Network and Resource Center
94 Galli Drive
Suite C
Novato, CA 94949

415-884-3535
800-578-2592
Fax: 415-884-3555
E-mail: info@matrixparnets.org
http://www.matirxparents.org

For parents whose child has a special need or disability. Emotional support and information from parents who have been there.

81   National Academy of Education
School of Education
726 Broadway 5th Floor
New York, NY 10003-9580

212-998-9035
Fax: 212-995-4435
E-mail: nae.info@nyc.edu
http://www.nae.nyu.edu

Offers the Spencer Postdoctoral Fellowship which is designed to promote scholarship in the United States and abroad on matters relevant to the improvement of education in all its forms.

Debbie Leong-Childs, Executive Director

82   National Alliance for Safe Schools
Ice Mountain
PO Box 290
Slanesville, WV 25444-0290

304-496-8100
888-510-6500
Fax: 304-496-8105
E-mail: NASS@raven-villages.net
http://www.safeschools.org

Founded in 1977 NASS a non-profit corporation, ascribes to the belief that schools need to take back control and identify what the local issues are that may be causing fear and anxiety on the part of the students and staff. Once localissues have been identified, school administrators, working with students, teachers, parents and support staff, are able to effect change.

Peter D Blauvelt, CEO/President

83   National Association for Asian and Pacific American Education
310 8th Street
Suite 301
Oakland, CA 94607-4253

Objectives are to enhance awareness of multicultural studies in the United States as well as promoting inclusion of Asian and Pacific American culture and history into the school curricula.

Dr. Sau-Lim Tsang, President

84   National Association for Developmental Education
Northeastern Illinois University
5500 N Street Louis Avenue
Chicago, IL 60625-4679

773-583-4050

Improves the theory and performance at all academic levels.

Dr. Harold Hild, President

85   National Association for Industry-Education Cooperation
235 Hendricks Boulevard
Buffalo, NY 14226-3304

716-834-7047
Fax: 716-834-7047
E-mail: naiec@pcom.net
http://www2.pcom.net/naiec

Founded in 1964 advocates for business/industry education collaboration in continuous school improvement, workforce preparation and economic development. Serves as the national clearinghouse for information on industry involvement ineducation.

Dr. Donald M Clark, President/CEO
Dr. Vito R Pace, Editor

86   National Association for Legal Support of Alternative Schools
PO Box 2823
Santa Fe, NM 87504-2823

505-471-6928

Information and legal service center designed to research, coordinate, and support legal actions involving nonpublic educational alternatives.

Ed Nagel, Coordinator

87   National Association for Year-Round Education
PO Box 711386
San Diego, CA 92171-1386

619-276-5296
Fax: 858-571-5754
E-mail: info@nayre.org
http://www.NAYRE.org

Founded in 1972 NAYRE fosters and disseminates information about year-round education as a way to improve educational programs.

Marsha Speck, President

88   National Association of Boards of Education
1077 30th Street NW
Suite 100
Washington, DC 20007-3852

202-337-6232
Fax: 202-333-6706
E-mail: nceaadmin@ncea.org
http://www.ncea.org

Provides leadership for groups and individuals who are responsible for policy formation and decision making in Catholic education.

Michael Guerra, President
Claire Helm, Vice President/Operations

8

89   National Association of Catholic School Teachers
1700 Sansom Street
Suite 903
Philadelphia, PA 19103-5234
215-665-0993
Fax: 215-568-8270
Unifies, advises and assists Catholic school teachers in matters of collective bargaining.
John J Reilly, President

90   National Association of Federally Impacted Schools
Hall of the States, Suite 419
444 N Capitol Street NW
Washington, DC 20001-1512
202-624-5455
Fax: 202-624-5468
E-mail: nafis@sso.org
http://www.sso.org/nafis/
Public school districts receiving federal aid.
John Forkenbrock, Executive Director
Barbara Balduman, Associate Director

91   National Association of State Boards of Education
277 S Washington Street
Suite 100
Alexandria, VA 22314
703-684-4000
Fax: 703-836-2313
E-mail: boards@nasbe.org
http://www.nasbe.org
Aims are to study problems of mutual interest and concern, improve communication among state boards, and exchange and collect information concerning all aspects of education.
Brenda L Welburn, Executive Director

92   National Association of Student Activity Advisers
1904 Association Drive
Reston, VA 20191-1557
703-860-0200
800-253-7746
Fax: 703-476-5432
E-mail: nhs@nassp.org
http://http://nasccms.principals.org/s_nasc
Promotes leadership training for students involved in the creative process.

93   National Association of Student Councils
1904 Association Drive
Reston, VA 20191-1502
703-860-0200
800-253-7746
Fax: 703-620-6534
Supports student councils, relations between teachers and students, as well as directing student-sponsored activities.
Scott D Thompson, Executive Officer

94   National Association of Trade & Industrial Instructors
Canadian Valley Vo Tech
6505 E Highway 66
El Reno, OK 73036-0579
405-262-2629
Fax: 405-422-2354
Founded in 1965 the National Association of Trade and Industrial Instructors seeks to improve communication among members and to support the needs of classroom teachers.
Carol McNish, President

95   National Black Alliance for Graduate Level Education
Black Cultural Center
Akron, OH 44325-0001
330-375-7030
Advocates on behalf of black students, faculty and administrators providing the opportunity to discuss and resolve problems and issues affecting blacks in graduate and professional schools.
Dr. John W Wilson, President

96   National Catholic Educational Association
1077 30th Street NW
Suite 100
Washington, DC 20007-3852
202-337-6232
Fax: 202-333-6706
E-mail: nceaadmin@ncea.org
http://www.ncea.org
Conducts research, works with voluntary groups and government agencies on educational problems, conducts seminars and workshops for educators at all levels.
Catherine T McNamee CSJ, President

97   National Center for Learning Disabilities
381 Park Avenue S
Room 1401
New York, NY 10016-8806
212-545-7510
888-575-7373
Fax: 212-545-9665
http://www.ncld.org
Provides information, referral, public education and outreach programs on learning disabilities. Provides technical assistance on school to work transition, and referral to state employment services, job training partnership actprograms and rehabilitation services.
Frederic Poses, Chairman of the Board

98   National Coalition of Advocates for Students
556 Cambridge Street
Boston, MA 02134
617-746-9995
Fax: 617-746-9997
E-mail: ncasmfe@mindspring.com
http://www.ncasboston.org
NCAS is a national education advocacy organization with 21 member groups in 14 states that works to achieve equal access to a quality public education for the most vulnerable students those who are poor, children of color, recentlyimmigrated, or children with disabilities. Focusing on kindergarten through grade 12, NCAS informs and mobilizes parents, concerned educators, and communities to help resolve critical education issues. NCAS raises concerns that otherwise might not beaddressed.
Judge Nancy Francis, Chairperson

99   National Coalition of Alternative Community Schools
1266 Rosewood Unit 1
Ann Arbor, MI 48104-6205
888-771-9171
888-771-9171
E-mail: ncacs1@earthlink.net
http://www.ncacs.org
A clearinghouse for information regarding alternatives in education for all ages, including home education. Yearly conference, newsletters, mentored Teacher Education Program.
Ed Nagel, National Office Manager

100 National Coalition of Independent Scholars
PO Box 5743
Berkeley, CA 94705-0743

510-704-0990
http://www.ncis.org

Founded in 1989 the National Coalition of Independent Scholars is comprised of independent teachers and homeschooling professionals.

Founded: 1989

101 National Commission for Cooperative Education
360 Huntington Avenue
Suite 384CP
Boston, MA 02115-5096

617-373-3770
Fax: 617-373-3463
E-mail: ncce@neu.edu
http://www.co-op.edu

Founded in 1962 the national commission for Cooperative Education offers brochures and publications describing the structure and benefits of cooperative education. Co-op is an academic program which integrates classroom studies withpaid work experience in a field related to a student's goals.

Founded: 1962

Paul Stonely, President

102 National Conference on Parent Involvement
579 W Iroquois Road
Pontiac, MI 48341-2024

313-334-5887

Founded in 1977 the Natioal Conference on Parent Involvement builds skills, shares information and brings people together who are advocates of parent involvement in schools.

Marie Johnson, Executive Director

103 National Congress for Educational Excellence
11524 E Ricks Circle
Dallas, TX 75230-3030

214-368-3449

Dedicated to improving the educational system through a back-to-basics program.

Joanne McAuley, President

104 National Council for Black Studies
Georgia State University
PO Box 4109
Atlanta, GA 30302-4109

404-463-9483
Fax: 404-651-4883
E-mail: info@nationalcouncilforblackstudies.com
http://www.nationalcouncilforblackstudies.com

Established in 1975 the NCBS promotes and strengthens academic and community programs in black and/or African-American studies.

Dr. Shirley N Weber, President
Dr. Charles E Jones, VP

105 National Council of Higher Education
National Education Association (NEA)
1201 16th Street NW
Washington, DC 20036-3207

202-833-4000
Fax: 202-822-7624
E-mail: nche@nea.org
http://www.nea.org/he/nche

Founded in 1964 the National Council of Higher Education seeks to resolve problems related to quality higher education; promotes collaborations between K-12 and higher education; provides training for members and serves as a vehiclefor local input to the National Education Association.

Kathy Sproles, President

106 National Council of Urban Education Associations
National Education Association (NEA)
1201 16th Street NW
Suite 410
Washington, DC 20036-3207

202-822-7364
Fax: 202-822-7624
E-mail: ncuea@nea.org
http://www.nea.org/ncueahome

Founded in 1964 the National Council of Urban Education Association seeks to resolve urban problems related to quality education; promotes improved relations between local and state authorities; provides training for members andserves as a vehicle for local input to the National Education Association.

Susie Jablinske, President
Leon Horne, Vice President

107 National Council on Measurement in Education
1230 17th Street NW
Washington, DC 20036-3078

202-223-9318
Fax: 202-775-1824
E-mail: mwhite@area.net
http://www.ncme.org

Interested in the measurement and use of human abilities, personality characteristics and educational achievement.

Felice Levine, Executive Director
Gerald Sroufe, Administrative Officer

108 National Council on Rehabilitation Education
Emporia State University
1200 Commercial-VH 334
Emporia, KS 66801

316-343-5220

Promotes the improvement of rehabilitation services available to people with disabilities through quality education and rehabilitation research.

109 National Council on Student Development
New Mexico Junior College
5317 Lovington Highway
Hobbs, NM 88240

505-392-4510
Fax: 505-392-2526
http://www.wjcac.com/directory

Offers information and provides a forum for members and professionals involved in student development.

Dr. Steve McCleery, President

110 National Dissemination Center for Children with Disabilities
PO Box 1492
Washington, DC 20013-1492

202-884-8200
800-695-0285
Fax: 202-884-8441
E-mail: nichcy@aed.org
http://www.nichey.org

Services include personal responses, referrals to other organizations, information packets, publications on current issues, technical assistance to family and professional groups. Provides free information to assist parents,educators, caregivers, advocates and others in helping children and youth with disabilities become participating members of the community.

Lisa Savard, Sales/Marketing Director

111 National Education Association
1201 16th Street NW
Washington, DC 20036-3290

202-833-4000
Fax: 202-822-7974
E-mail: ncuea@nea.org
http://www.nea.org

Advocates for the education profession and the well-being of children; supports campaigns designed to improve the teaching profession and teachers in their efforts to improve teaching; training programs; safe schools; and betterworking conditions.

Reg Weaver, President
Dennis Van Roekel, Vice President

112 National Education Association Student Program
National Education Association (NEA)
1201 16th Street NW
Washington, DC 20036-3290

202-822-7364
Fax: 202-822-7624
E-mail: ncuea@nea.org
http://www.nea.org

Seeks to improve education and work with and for the student body of America.

113 National Education Association-Retired
National Education Association (NEA)
1201 16th Street NW
Washington, DC 20036-3207

202-822-7125
Fax: 202-822-7624
http://www.nea.org/retired

Serves as a resource in the maintenance of quality public education, promotes improved services and legislation for seniors, provides training for members and serves as a vehicle for local input to the National Education Association.

Jim Sproul, President
Barbara Matteson, Vice President

114 National Education Policy Institute
National Alliance of Black School Educators
2816 Georgia Avenue NW
Washington, DC 20001-3819

202-608-6310
800-221-2654
Fax: 202-608-6319
E-mail: nabse@nabse.org
http://www.nabse.org

Offers a wide array of professional development and information sharing programs for its growing membership of concerned educators. These programs offer hands-on learning opportunities as well as invaluable informational resources forAfrican American educators.

Deloris Saunders, President

115 National Educational Service
304 W Kirkwood Avenue
Suite 2
Bloomington, IN 47404-5132

812-336-7700
800-733-6786
Fax: 812-336-7790
E-mail: nes@nesonline.com
http://www.nesonline.com

Founded in 1989 the National Edcucational Service provides tested and proven resources to help those who work with youth create safe and caring schools, agencies, and communities where all children succeed.

Founded: 1989

116 National Homeschool Association
PO Box 290
Hartland, MI 48353-0290

513-772-9580

Advocates individual choice and freedom in education.

Sydney Mathis, Director

117 National Lekotek Center
3204 W Armitage Avenue
Chicago, IL 60647

773-276-5164
800-366-PLAY
Fax: 773-276-8644
E-mail: lekotek@lekotek.org
http://www.lekotek.org

Provides play-centered programs for children with disabilities and their families. In 50 US centers children with learning disabilities, Down Syndrome, Cerebral Palsy and developmental delay use play sessions, toy libraries, playgroups, computer programs and training. Also provides play experiences through adapted hardware.

Joyce Morimoto, Author
Beth Boosals Davis, Executive Director

118 National Middle School Association
4151 Executive Parkway
Suite 300
Westerville, OH 43081

614-895-4730
800-528-6672
Fax: 614-895-4750
E-mail: info@NMSA.org
http://www.nmsa.org

Resource centers, conferences, professional development, and more.

Kathy McAvoy, President

119 National Network of Learning Disabled Adults
808 N 82nd Street
Suite F2
Scottsdale, AZ 85257

602-941-5112
http://www.nifl.gov/nalld/resource.html

Organization formed to provide support, assistance and information to learning disabled adults and self-help groups for learning disabled adults nationwide.

120 National Organization on Disability
910 16th Street NW
Suite 600
Washington, DC 20006-2988

202-293-5960
800-248-ABLE
Fax: 202-293-7999
E-mail: ability@nod.org
http://www.nod.org

Administers a community-based network of more than 2,200 towns, cities, and counties established to improve the participation of people with disabilities in community life.

Alan Reich, President
Michael Deland, Board Chairman

121 National School Boards Association
1680 Duke Street
Alexandria, VA 22314-3455

703-838-6722
Fax: 703-683-7590
E-mail: info@nsba.org
http://www.nsba.org

A nationwide advocacy organization for the public school governance.

Anne Bryant, Executive Director

122 National School Public Relations Association
15948 Denwood Road
Rockville, MD 20855-1109

301-519-0436
Fax: 301-519-0494
E-mail: nspra@nspra.org
http://www.nspra.org

Seeks to further public understanding of its schools.

Jim Dunn, President

123   National Society for Experiential Education
515 King Street
Suite 420
Alexandria, VA 22314

703-706-9552
Fax: 703-684-6048
E-mail: info@nsee.org
http://www.nsee.org

Founded in 1971 the National Society for Experiential Education supports learning through experience for intellectual development, civic and social responsibility, career exploration and global awareness.

Dennis Boyd, Executive Director

124   National Society for the Study of Education
5835 S Kimbark Avenue
Chicago, IL 60637-1635

773-702-1582

Promotes the investigation and discussion of educational problems.

Kenneth J Rehage, Secretary

125   National Student Exchange
4656 W Jefferson Boulevard
Suite 140
Fort Wayne, IN 46804-6839

260-436-2634
Fax: 260-436-5676
E-mail: bworley@fwi.com
http://www.buffalostate.edu/~nse

A cooperative program that allows undergraduate students access to different United States universities.

Bette Worley, Presdient

126   National Student Program
National Education Association (NEA)
1201 16th Street NW
Washington, DC 20036-3207

202-822-7364
Fax: 202-822-7624
E-mail: ncuea@nea.org
http://www.nea.org

Promotes quality pre professional education and training; innovation in teacher training; local and state affiliates and colleges/universities provides training for members and serves as a vehicle for local input to the NationalEducation Association.

Herb Levitt, President
Katrina Thompson, Manager

127   National Telemedia Council
120 E. Wilson Street
Madison, WI 53703

608-257-7712
Fax: 608-257-7714
E-mail: ntc@danent.wicip.org
http://http://danenet.wicip.org/ntc/

Distributes information on education.

128   National Women's Student Coalition
University of Colorado
PO Box 206
Boulder, CO 80309-0206

303-492-7473

Lobbies for women students' concerns.

Elizabeth Burpe, Co-Chair

129   National Women's Studies Association
7100 Baltimore Ave.
University of Maryland
College Park, MD 20740

301-403-0524
Fax: 301-403-4137
E-mail: nwsaoffice@nwsa.org
http://www.nwsa.org

Founded in 1977 the National Women's Studies Association works to further the social, political and professional development of women's studies programs and projects.

Jacquelyn Zita, President

130   Native American Homeschool Association
PO Box 979
Fries, VA 24330

540-636-1020
Fax: 540-636-1464
http://www.expage.com/page/nahomeschool

Association of Native American homeschoolers.

131   North American Association for Environmental Education
410 Tarvin Road
Rock Spring, GA 30739-5708

706-764-2926
Fax: 706-764-2094
E-mail: email@naaee.org
http://www.naaee.org

Founded in 1974 the North American Association for Enviromental Education is a network of professionals and students working in the field of environmental education throughout North America and 45 other countries. The Association haspromoted environmental education and supported the work of environmental educators for over 25 years.

Elaine Andrews, President

132   North American Association of Educational Negotiators
PO Box 1068
Salem, OR 97308

503-588-2800
E-mail: naem@osba.org
http://www.naen.org/

Founded in 1966 the North American Association of Educational Negotiators purpose is to promote and unite those who negotiate on behalf of school boards into a single, strong body and to provide a facility for the effectivecommunication and exchange of information among these individuals.

Mark Pettitt, President

133   North American Professional Driver Education Association
4935 W Foster Avenue
Chicago, IL 60630-1635

773-777-9605

Focuses on the safety and correct procedures of driving education.

134   North American Students of Cooperation
PO Box 7715
Ann Arbor, MI 48107-7715

734-663-0889
Fax: 734-663-5072
E-mail: info@nasco.coop
http://www.nasco.coop

Founded in 1968 the North American Students of Cooperation supports student cooperatives and offers leadership training in the field.

James Jones, Executive Director
Anjanette Bunce, Director of Operations

135 Northwest Association of Schools & Colleges
1910 University Drive
Boise, ID 83725-1060

208-426-5727
Fax: 208-334-3228
E-mail: sclemens@boisestate.edu
http://www2.boisestate.edu/nasc

Seeks to advance the concept of education as well as addresses the educational opportunities and services available among schools and colleges. Publishes a 163 page annual paperback, Administrator, Steering Comittee, and Response TeamManual.

Shelli Clamens, Editor

136 Odyssey of the Mind
Creative Competitions, Inc.
1325 Route 130 S
Suite F
Gloucester City, NJ 08030

856-456-7776
Fax: 856-456-7008
E-mail: info@odysseyofthemind.com
http://www.odysseyofthemind.com

Founded in 1979 the Odyssey of the Mind teaches students to learn creative problem-solving methods while having fun in the process; also teaches students how to think divergently by providing open-ended problems that appeal to a widerange of people.

137 Outdoor Education Association
143 Fox Hill Road
Denville, NJ 07834-3013

973-627-7214

Supports people interested in promoting outdoor and environmental education.

Dr. Edward J. Ambry, President

138 PACER Center
8161 Normandale Boulevard
Minneapolis, MN 55437

952-838-9000
888-248-0822
Fax: 952-838-0919
E-mail: pacer@pacer.org
http://www.pacer.org

Founded in 1977 PACER a coalition of organizations founded on the concept of Parents Helping Parents. PACER strives to improve and expand opportunities that enhance the quality of life for children and young adults with disabilitiesand their families. Helps parents become informed and effective representatives for their children in early childhood, school-age and vocational settings through agencies and appropriate service.

Founded: 1977

Paula Goldberg, Executive Director

139 Parents Rights Organization
12571 Northwinds Drive
Saint Louis, MO 63146-4503

314-434-4171
Fax: 314-434-6995
E-mail: Martinmaeduggan@juno.com
http://www.educational-freedom.org

Founded in 1959 the Parents Rights Organization secures legal recognition for the right of parents to direct and control the education of their children; secures freedom of choice in education of their children, including analternative to the government-established school system.

Founded: 1959

Mae Duggan, President/CEF

140 Parents, Let's Unite for Kids
516 N 32nd Street
Billings, MT 59101-6003

406-255-0540
800-222-7585
Fax: 406-255-0523
E-mail: plukinfo@pluk.org
http://www.pluk.org

Formed in 1984 PLUNK informs parents of various resources, workshops, parent training and information in the education field.

141 People United for Rural Education
PO Box 35
Kamrar, IA 50132-0001

515-325-6059

Determined to preserve and improve educational opportunities in rural schools.

Claudia Jones, President

142 Public Relations Student Society of America
33 Maiden Lane
11th Floor
New York, NY 10038-5150

212-460-1474
Fax: 212-995-0757
E-mail: prssa@prsa.org
http://www.prssa.org

Cultivates cooperation between students and professional public relations practitioners.

Sarah Yeaney, National President

143 Religious Education Association of the US & Canada
409 Prospect Street
New Haven, CT 06511-2167

203-865-6141

Seeks to encourage and bring together various religions in the United States and Canadian educational system.

144 Renew America
1200 18th Street NW
Suite 1100
Washington, DC 20036

202-721-1545
Fax: 202-467-5780
E-mail: renewamerica@counterpart.org
http://www.sol.crest.org/enviroment/renew_america

Works to identify, verify, and recognize successful environmental programs that measurably protect, restore or enhance the environment. Honors successful environmental sustainability projects across the nation through Nation Awardsfor Environmental Sustainability.

Anna Slafer, Executive Director

145 Schiller Center
801 Duke Street
Alexandria, VA 22314-3623

703-684-4735
Fax: 703-684-4738
E-mail: schiller@schillercenter.org
http://www.schiller.org

Works extensively with businesses, state, local and national governments and education groups to assist in long-range and strategic planning.

Sherry L Schiller, President

146 Sexuality Information & Education Council of the US
130 W 42nd Street
Suite 350
New York, NY 10036-7802

212-819-9770
Fax: 212-819-9776
E-mail: siecus@siecus.org
http://www.siecus.org

Associations & Organizations / Administration

Develops, collects and disseminates information, promotes comprehensive education about sexuality, and advocates the right of individuals to make responsible sexual choices.

Joseph DiNorcia, President/CEO

147 Society for the Advancement of Education
99 West Hawthorne Avenue
Suite 518
Valley Stream, NY 11580-6101
516-568-9191

Comprised of educators on all levels.

Stanley Lehrer, President

148 Southwest Independent Schools Association
PO Box 52297
Tulsa, OK 74152-0297
918-749-5927

Supports and maintains the independent school system in the Southwestern United States.

149 Students Forum
CompuServe Information Services
5000 Arlington Centre Boulivard
Columbus, OH 43220-2913
614-457-8600
800-848-8199
Fax: 614-457-0348

Provides conferences with guest speakers for elementary and junior high school classes.

150 Summit Vision
5640 Lynx Drive
Westerville, OH 43081
614-645-5972
Fax: 614-645-8903
E-mail: tmcbane@wideopenwest.com
http://www.summit-vision.com

Provides specialized programs and activities designed to focus on proficiency objectives, conflict resolution, making smart choices and linking academic concepts to adventure activities.

Trey McBane, Contact
Penn Mallon, Contact

151 Wilderness Education Association
900 East 7th Street
Bloomington, IN 47405
812-855-4095
Fax: 812-855-8697
E-mail: wes@indiana.edu
http://www.weainfo.org

Promotes environmental, outdoor and wilderness education.

Dene Bermani, President

152 Women Educators
University of North Carolina, School of Education
Greensboro, NC 27412
919-334-5100

Promotes equal opportunities for women educators.

Marilyn Haring-Hidore, Chairman

153 Women's Educational & Industrial Union
One Washington Mall
Boston, MA 02108
617-536-5651
Fax: 617-247-8826
E-mail: infor@weiu.org
http://www.weiu.org

Recognizes, supports, maintains and strives to better women's educational opportunities.

Administration

154 American Association of Collegiate Registrars & Admissions Officers
1 Dupont Circle NW
Suite 520
Washington, DC 20036-1137
202-293-9161
Fax: 202-872-8857
http://www.aacrao.org

Promotes higher education and furthers the professional development of members working in admissions, enrollment management, financial aid, institutional research, records and registration.

Jerry Sullivan, Executive Director
Martha Henebry, Publications Manager

155 American Association of School Administrators
1801 N Moore Street
Arlington, VA 22209-1813
703-528-0700
Fax: 703-841-1543
E-mail: webmaster@aasa.org
http://www.aasa.org

Ensures high quality education systems through support and development of leadership on the building, district and state levels.

Paul D Houston, Executive Director

156 American Education Finance Association
5249 Cape Leyte Drive
Sarasota, FL 34242-1805
941-349-7580
Fax: 941-349-7580
E-mail: www.edu/aefa

Founded in 1976 the American Education Finance Association fosters communication among groups in educational finance. Interested in public policy, emerging issues and finance concepts and conducting workshops and conventions on thesesubjects.

Founded: 1976

George R Babigian, Executive Director

157 Association of School Business Officials International
ASBO International Annual Meetings and Exhibits
11401 N Shore Drive
Reston, VA 20190-4200
703-478-0405
Fax: 703-478-0205
E-mail: asboreg@asbointl.org
http://http://asbointl.org

Promotes improvement and advancement of school business management and provides a forum for the exchange of information and ideas among professionals.

John Frombach, President
Anne Miller, Exective Director

158 Council of Chief State School Officers
1 Massachusetts Avenue NW
Suite 700
Washington, DC 20001-1431
202-336-7000
Fax: 202-408-8072
http://www.ccsso.org

Organization of public officials who head state departments of education.

David Driscoll, President

159 **ERIC Clearinghouse on Educational Management**
University of Oregon
5207 University of Oregon
Eugene, OR 97403-5207

541-346-5044
800-438-8841
Fax: 541-346-2334
E-mail: sales@cepm.uoregon.edu
http://www.eric.uoregon.edu

Collects and publishes educational information and materials on topics dealing with all aspects of educational administration and management.

Dr. Philip Piele, Director
Stuart C Smith, Associate Director

160 **ERIC Clearinghouse on Languages and Linguistics**
4646 40th Street NW
Washington, DC 20016-1859

202-362-0700
800-276-9834
Fax: 202-362-3740
E-mail: eric@cal.org
http://www.cal.org

Provides a wide range of services and materials for language educators, most of them free of charge.

161 **Independent Schools Association of the Central States**
1550 North Dearborn Parkway
Chicago, IL 60610

312-255-1244
Fax: 312-255-1278
E-mail: info@isacs.org
http://www.isacs.org

Founded in 1908 the Independent Schools Association of the Central States provides curricular and research information for private schools on all levels in the midwest. Evaluation/accreditation of independent private schools in afifteen state region.

John Braman, President

162 **International Association of Pupil Personnel Workers**
114 W Church Street
Frederick, MD 21701-5411

301-831-4455

Dedicated to improving school attendance, helping administrators, parents, and teachers, enforcing compulsory objectives set forth in laws and increasing educational opportunities for children.

William E Myer, Executive Director

163 **National Association for Supervision and Curriculum Development**
ASCD
1703 N Beauregard Street
Alexandria, VA 22311-1714

703-578-9600
800-933-2723
Fax: 703-575-5400
E-mail: member@ascd.org
http://www.ascd.org

Represents administrators of pupil services, promotes the concept of pupil personnel services in school systems to serve the needs of children and youth. Provides communication and professional growth for members.

Dr. Charles M Wilson, Executive Director

164 **National Association of Elementary School Principals**
1615 Duke Street
Alexandria, VA 22314-3483

703-684-3345
800-386-2377
Fax: 800-396-2377

E-mail: naesp@naesp.org
http://www.naesp.org

To lead in the advocacy and support for elementary and middle level principals and other education leaders in their commitment to all children.

Rosemarie Young, President

165 **National Association of Federal Education Program Administrators**
1801 N Moore Street
Arlington, VA 22209-1813

703-528-0700
Fax: 703-841-1543

Supplies members with current information relative to compensatory, supplementary and exemplary programs, changes in rules, regulations and funding requirements.

Stanley J McFarland, Executive Director

166 **National Association of Principals of Schools for Girls**
4050 Little River Road
Hendersonville, NC 28739-8317

828-693-8248
Fax: 828-693-1490

Founded in 1921 the association consists of principals and deans of private and secondary schools for girls.

167 **National Association of Private Schools for Exceptional Children**
1522 K Street NW
Suite 1032
Washington, DC 20005-1211

202-408-3338
Fax: 202-408-3340
E-mail: napsec@aol.com
http://www.napsec.com

Strives to ensure access to special education for individuals as a vital component of the continuum of appropriate placements and services in American education.

Sherry L Kolbe, Executive Director/CEO
Sherry DeGroot, Manager

168 **National Association of Secondary School Principals**
1904 Association Drive
Reston, VA 20191-1537

703-860-0200
Fax: 703-476-5432
http://http://nasspcms.principals.org

To promote excellence in school leadership and to provide members with a wide variety of programs and services to assist them in administration, supervision, curriculum planning, and effective staff development.

Cynthia Rudrud, President

169 **National Association of State Directors of Special Education**
1800 Diagonal Road
Suite 320
Alexandria, VA 22314

703-519-3800
Fax: 703-519-3808
E-mail: east@nasdse.org
http://www.nasdse.org

A nonprofit corporation that promotes and supports education programs for students with disabilities in the United States and outlying areas.

Doug Cox, President

170 National Association of Student Financial Aid Administrators
1129 20th Street NW
Suite 400
Washington, DC 20036-3453

202-785-0453
Fax: 202-785-1487
E-mail: ask@nasfaa.org
http://www.nasfaa.org

A nonprofit corporation of postsecondary institutions, individuals, agencies and students interested in promoting the effective administration of student financial aid in the United States.

A Dallas Martin Jr, President

171 National Association of Student Personnel Administrators
1875 Connecticut Avenue NW
Suite 418
Washington, DC 20009-5737

202-265-7500
Fax: 202-797-1157
E-mail: office@naspa.org
http://www.naspa.org/

Serves chief student affairs officers of higher education institutions.

Pegke Blake, President
Gwen Dungy, Executive Director

172 National Council of Administrative Women in Education
1151 Ossipee Road
West Hempstead, NY 11552-3934

516-764-3169

Works to eliminate discrimination against women in educational administration, prepares and encourages careers for women in educational institutions, systems and schools.

Carol M Poteat, President

173 National Council of State Directors of Adult Education
444 North Capitol Street
Suite 422
Washington, DC 20001

202-624-5250
Fax: 202-624-1497
E-mail: dc1@naepdc.org
http://www.ncsdae.org

Comprised of state level leaders of adult education from each of the state adult education agencies.

174 National Data Bank for Disabled Student Services University of Maryland
Room 0126, Shoemaker Building
College Park, MD 20742

301-314-7682
Fax: 301-405-0813
http://www.inform.umd.edu/

Provides assessment of statistics related to services, staff, budget and other components of disabled student services programs across the country.

Dr. Vivian S Boyd, Director
Dr. William Scales, Assistant Director, DSS

175 National Institute for School and Workplace Safety
257 Plaza Drive
Suite B
Oviedo, FL 32765-6457

407-366-4878
Fax: 407-977-1210
http://www.nisws.com

Believes that every school and workplace must implement school and workplace safety standards. Committed to enhance school and workplace safety and to increase awareness of school and workplace safety issues.

Steven Burhoe, CEO

176 National School Safety Center
141 Duesenberg Drive
Suite 11
Westlake Village, CA 91362

805-373-9977
Fax: 805-373-9277
E-mail: info@nssc1.org
http://www.nssc1.org

Serves as a catalyst and advocate for the prevention of school crime and violence by providing information and resources and identifying strategies and promising programs which support safe schools for school children worldwide.

Dr. Ronald D Stephens, Executive Director
June Lane Arnette, Associate Director

177 Office of Juvenile Justice and Delinquency Prevention
810 7th Street NW
Washington, DC 20531

202-307-5911
Fax: 202-307-2093
E-mail: askjj@ojp.usdoj.gov
http://www.ojjdp.ncjrs.org

To provide national leadership, coordination, and resources to prevent and respond to juvenile delinquency and victimization.

178 Psychological Corporation Harcourt Brace Jovanovich
555 Academic Court
San Antonio, TX 78204-2498

800-211-8378
800-228-0752
Fax: 800-232-1223
http://www.hbem.com

Support to program teachers and administrators.

179 Safe Schools America
5180 Roswell Road
S Building, Suite 205
Atlanta, GA 30342

877-516-5283
Fax: 404-252-1047
E-mail: ssa@bellsouth.net
http://www.safeschoolsamerica.com

Dedicated to helping people create the safest and most secure environment for learning possible in any given situation. The consultants work with schools staff, parents, students and community agencies to develop safety solutions thataddress the needs and utilize the resources of each school and community.

Early Childhood Education

180 Child Care Information Exchange
PO Box 3249
Redmond, WA 98073-3249

800-221-2864
Fax: 425-861-9386
E-mail: infor@ChldCareExchange.com
http://www.ccie.com

Exchange has promoted the exchange of ideas among leaders in early childhood programs worldwide through its magazine, books, training products, trainig seminars, and international conferences for 27 years.

Kay Albrecht, Director

181 Dimensions of Early Childhood
Southern Early Childhood Association
PO 55930
Little Rock, AR 72215-5930
501-221-1648
800-305-SECA
Fax: 501-227-5297
E-mail: info@southernearlychildhood.org
http://www.southernearlychildhood.org

Provides opportunities in professional development, leadership and advocacy for early childhood educators, child development specialists and program administrators.

Glenda Bean, Executive Director

182 Division for Early Childhood
The Council for Exceptional Children
1920 Association Drive
Reston, VA 20191-1545
888-232-7733
Fax: 703-264-9494

Association for individuals who work with or on behalf of children with special needs, birth through age 8, and their families. Includes early childhood intervention professionals as well as parents of children who have disabilities,are gifted, or are at risk.

Barbara Smith, Executive Director

183 Education Advisory Group
6239 Woodlawn Avenue North
Seattle, WA 98810
206-323-1838
Fax: 206-267-1325
E-mail: info@eduadvisory.com
http://www.eduadvisory.com

Specializes in matching children with learning environments. Helps families identify concerns and establish priorities about their child's education.

184 National Early Childhood Technical Assistance Center
Campus Box 8040 UNC-CH
Chapel Hill, NC 27599-8040
919-962-2001
Fax: 919-966-7463
E-mail: nectac@unc.edu
http://www.nectas.unc.edu

Assists states and other designated governing jurisdictions as they develop multidisciplinary, coordinated and comprehensive services for children with special needs.

Pascal Trohanis, Director

185 National Educational Systems
6333 DeZavaia
Suite 106
San Antonio, TX 78249
800-231-4380

Offers products and services in parental involvement, bilingual/ESL materials, early childhood development curriculum, multiculturally diverse literature, meeting all new program performance standards and more. Partners with NationalHead Start Association in serving children, families, communities and our world.

186 National Head Start Association
1651 Prince Street
Alexandria, VA 22314-2818
703-739-0875
Fax: 703-739-0878
http://www.nhsa.org

Dedicated to promoting and protecting the Head Start program. Advocates on the behalf of America's low-income children and families. Publishes many books, periodicals and resource guides. Offers a legislative hotline as well astraining programs through the NHSA Academy.

Ron Herndon, President

Elementary Education

187 Center for Play Therapy
University of North Texas
PO Box 310829
Denton, TX 76203-0829
940-565-3864
Fax: 940-565-4461
E-mail: cpt@unt.edu
http://www.coe.unt.edu./cpt/prosindex.html

Encourages the unique development and emotional growth of children through the process of play therapy, a dynamic interpersonal relationship between a child and a therapist trained in play therapy procedures. Provides training,research, publications, counseling services and acts as a clearinghouse for literature in the field.

Garry Landreth PhD, Founder
Sue Bratton PhD, Director

188 ERIC Clearinghouse on Elementary & Early Childhood Education
University of Illinois at Urbana
51 Gerty Drive
Champaign, IL 61820-7453
217-333-1386
Fax: 212-678-4012
E-mail: ericeece@uius.edu
http://www.ericeece.org

Offers information on topics relating to the physiological, psychological and cultural development of children from birth through early adolescence.

Dr. Lilian Katz, Director
Dianne Rothenberg, Associate Director

189 Elementary School Center for Advocacy & Policy on Behalf of Children
2 E 103rd Street
New York, NY 10029-5207
212-732-4392
Fax: 212-766-5895

Fosters the optimal development and learning of every child and reaffirms the pivotal role of the elementary school.

Allan Sheldin, Jr, Executive Director

190 National Association for the Education of Young Children
1509 16th Street NW
Washington, DC 20036
202-232-8777
800-424-2460
Fax: 202-328-1846
E-mail: naeyc@naeyc.org
http://www.naeyc.org

Supports those interested in serving and acting on behalf of the needs and rights of the education of young children.

Dr. Mark Ginsberg, Executive Director

191 National Association of Elementary School Principals
1615 Duke Street
Alexandria, VA 22314-3483
703-684-3345
800-386-2377
Fax: 703-548-6021
E-mail: naesp@naesp.org
http://www.naesp.org

To lead in the advocacy and support for elementary and middle level principals and other education leaders in their commitment to all children.

Dr. Vincent L Ferrandino, Executive Director

192   Voyager Expanded Learning
One Hickory Center
1800 Valley View Suite 400
Dallas, TX 75234-8923

214-932-3213
888-399-1995
Fax: 214-631-0176
E-mail: jnowakowski@voyagerlearning.com
http://www.voyagerlearning.com

Founded in 1997 Voyager Expanded Learning is a national education initiative that provides learning programs to public schools.

Jeri Nowakowski, Executive VP

Employment

193   AAA Teacher's Agency
177 Main Street
Suite 364
Fort Lee, NJ 07024-2540

718-548-3267
Fax: 718-548-3315

A placement agency for teachers, administrators and others in the field of education.

Daniel Shea, Director/Owner

194   Aerospace Industries Association of America
1000 Wilson Boulevard
Suite 1700
Arlington, VA 22209-3901

703-358-1000
E-mail: sager@aia-aerospace.org
http://www.aia-aerospace.org

Offers a series of booklets for students and educators, available by email, regarding employment oppuortunities in the industry.

John W Douglas, AIA President/CEO

195   Association for Suppliers of Printing & Publishing Technologies
1899 Preston White Drive
Reston, VA 20191-4367

703-264-7200
Fax: 703-620-0994
E-mail: npes@npes.org
http://www.npes.org

Services include career placement.

Regis Delmontagne, President
Kathryn Marx, Vice President

196   Aviation Information Resources
1001 Riverdale Court
Atlanta, GA 30337

800-AIR-APPS
Fax: 404-592-6515
http://www.airapps.com

Services include career placement.

Kit Darby, President

197   English Teaching Fellow Program
US Information Agency
400 C Street SW
Washington, DC 20024-2800

202-619-4700

Career placement services.

198   Graphic Arts Education & Research Foundation
1899 Preston White Drive
Reston, VA 20191

703-264-7200
866-381-9839
Fax: 703-620-3165
E-mail: gaerf@npes.org
http://www.npes.org

Services include career placement.

Regis Delmontagne, President

199   Graphic Arts Technical Foundation
200 Deer Run Road
Sewickley, PA 15143

412-741-6860
Fax: 412-741-2311
E-mail: gatf@piagatf.org
http://www.gatf.org

Services include career placement.

200   Health Occupations Students of America
6021 Morriss Road
Suite 111
Flower Mound, TX 75028

972-874-0062
800-321-HOSA
Fax: 972-874-0063
http://www.hosa.org

Provides health occupations educators with a student organization used to recruit and develop a competent and motivated work force for the health care field.

Lauren Sheldon, Director

201   Interlocken Center for Experiential Learning
Interlocken
RR 2 Box 165
Hillsboro, NH 03244-9506

603-478-3166
Fax: 603-478-5260

Agency offering teachers the opportunity to lead educational travel programs for high school students.

Judi Wisch

202   International Graphic Arts Education Association
1899 Preston White Drive
Reston, VA 20191-4367

703-758-0595
http://www.igaea.org

Services include career placement.

203   Mainstream
6930 Carroll Avenue
#240
Takoma Park, MD 20912-4423

031-891-8777

Provides on-site accessibility surveys and job analyses, and offers advice on cost-effective training for employers and assists in the development of nondiscriminatory employment policies.

204   NASW Job Link: The Social Work Employment Line
750 First Stret NW
Suite 700
Washington, DC 20002-4241

Fax: 800-595-2929
http://www.socialworkers.org

Practical, convenient, and cost effective way to recruit professional social workers.

Gary Bailey, President
Elizabeth Clark, Executive Director

205 **National Association of Teachers' Agencies**
National Association of Teachers' Agencies
799 Kings Highway
Fairfield, CT 06432

203-333-0611
Fax: 203-334-7224
E-mail: fairfieldteachers@snet.net
http://www.jobsforteachers.com

Provides placement services for those seeking professional positions at all levels of teaching/administration/support services worldwide.

Mark King, Secretary/Treasurer

206 **National Business Education Association**
1914 Association Drive
Reston, VA 20191-1596

703-860-8300
Fax: 703-620-4483
http://www.nbea.org

Offers professional service to identify institutions at all educational levels that have positions open, register candidates who are seeking positions, and establish contact between candidates and representatives of the schools withvacancies.

Mary Ann Lammers, President

207 **National Teachers Clearinghouse**
PO Box 1257
Boston, MA 02118

617-267-3204

National job network for teachers and principals.

208 **Printing Industries of America**
100 Dangerfield Road
Alexandria, VA 22314

703-519-8100
Fax: 703-548-3227
E-mail: llarson@piagatf.org
http://www.gain.net

The world's largest graphic arts trade associations. Promotes the interest of more that 14,000 member companies, including career placement support.

Jana Cary, Senior Manager

209 **Western Association of Colleges & Employers**
16 Santa Ana Place
Walnut Creek, CA 94598

925-934-3877
Fax: 925-906-0922
E-mail: info@WACE.net
http://wwww.wace.net

Professional association of approximately 500 college career planning and placement offices and representatives from business, industry and government who recruit, employ and train graduates of colleges and universities in the westernstates and Canada.

Carl Martellino, President

210 **Women's International League for Peace & Freedom**
U.S. Section
1213 Race Street
Philadelphia, PA 19107-1691

215-563-7110
Fax: 215-563-5527
http://www.wilpf.org

Agency offering internships in the United States.

Marilyn Clement

Guidance & Counseling

211 **American Association of Sex Educators, Counselors & Therapists**
PO Box 5488
Richmond, VA 23220-0488

804-644-3288
Fax: 804-644-3290
E-mail: aasect@aasect.org
http://www.aasect.org

Certifies professionals as sex educators, counselors and therapists. Acts as a general referral service to the general public. Provides education and training in all areas of sexual health.

Stephen Conley, Executive Director
Jennifer Metze, Database Administrator

212 **American Counseling Association**
5999 Stevenson Avenue
Alexandria, VA 22304-3302

703-823-9800
800-347-6647
Fax: 703-823-0252
http://www.counseling.org

Founded in 1952 the American Counseling Association supports counselors working in higher education settings. Categories include research studies, professional issues and innovative practice.

Samuel Gladding, President

213 **American School Counselor Association**
1101 King Street
Suite 625
Alexandria, VA 22314

703-683-2722
800-306-4722
Fax: 703-683-1619
http://www.schoolcounselor,org

Promotes human rights and child welfare, as well as educational rights for children.

Richard Wong, Executive Director

214 **Association for Measurement & Evaluation in Counseling & Development**
American Association for Counseling & Development
5999 Stevenson Avenue
Alexandria, VA 22304-3302

703-823-9800
Fax: 703-823-0252

Founded in 1965 the Association supports increasing competency in assessment, testing, measurement and evaluation of professional counselors.

Dr. Theodore P. Remley, Jr, Executive Director

215 **Association of Educational Therapists**
1804 W Burbank Boulevard
Burbank, CA 91506-1315

800-286-4267
Fax: 818-843-7423
E-mail: aetaet@aol.com
http://www.aetonline.org

Founded in 1979 the Association of Educational Therapists establishes professional standards and defines roles, responsibilities and ethics of educational therapists; studies techniques, technologies, philosophies and research relatedto educational therapy; represents/defines educational therapy to the community, school and professional group; provides opportunities for continued professional growth.

Linda Schwarz, President

216 Counseling Association
5999 Stevenson Avenue
Alexandria, VA 22304-3302

703-823-9800
800-347-6647
Fax: 703-823-0252
E-mail: jmaedonald@counseling.org
http://www.counseling.org

Supports counselors from educational and social service settings across the country.

Samuel Gladding, President

217 ERIC Clearinghouse on Counseling & Student Services
University of North Carolina at Greensboro
1000 Spring Garden Street
Greensboro, NC 27412

800-414-9769
Fax: 336-334-4114
E-mail: eric-cue@columbia.edu

Collects and disseminates information on counseling, guidance and student services.

Dr. Garry Walz, Director
Dr. Jeanne Bleue, Associate Director

218 International Association of Counseling Services
101 S Whiting Street
Suite 211
Alexandria, VA 22304-3302

703-823-9840
Fax: 703-823-9843
E-mail: iacsinc@earthlink.net
http://www.iacsinc.org

Accreditation association for university, college and private counseling services.

Dan Jones, President

219 National Association of School Psychologists
4340 E West Highway
Suite 402
Bethesda, MD 20814

301-657-0270
Fax: 301-657-0275
E-mail: center@naspweb.org
http://www.masponline.org

Founded in 1977 the National Association of School Psychologists is a professional association representing over 22,000 school psychologists and related professionals.

Leland Huff, President

220 National Association of Social Workers
750 1st Street NE
Suite 700
Washington, DC 20002-4241

202-408-8600
800-638-8799
Fax: 202-336-8313
E-mail: naswfoudation@naswdc.org
http://www.naswdc.org

Founded in 1955 the Natioanl Association of Social Workers offers legislative action, professional programs, information through publications, and current developments in their field.

Gary Bailey, President
Stacie Hiramoto, Vice President

221 National Association of Substance Abuse Trainers & Educators
1521 Hillary Street
New Orleans, LA 70118-4007

504-286-5000

Sustains an information network of substance abuse/chemical dependency training programs in higher education.

Thomas Lief, Director

International

222 Academic Travel Abroad
1920 N Street NW
Suite 200
Washington, DC 20036

202-785-9000
800-556-7896
Fax: 202-342-0317
http://www.academic-travel.com/ata

Seeks to foster intercultural relations and educational cooperation between institutions of higher learning.

David Parry, President

223 Agency for International Development
International Development Intern Program
Recruitment Division M Pm R
Washington, DC 20523-0001

202-663-1451

Agency offering study abroad programs, exchange programs and international internships, financed and unfinanced.

224 American Friends Service Committee
Human Resources
1501 Cherry Street
Philadelphia, PA 19102-1429

215-241-7000
Fax: 215-241-7275
E-mail: afscinfo@afsc.org
http://www.afsc.org

Agency offering study abroad programs, exchange programs and international internships, financed and unfinanced.

Paul Lacey, Presiding Clerk

225 American Jewish Congress
Government & Public Affairs Office
2027 Massachusetts Avenue NW
Washington, DC 20036-1029

212-879-4500
Fax: 212-249-3672
E-mail: washrep@ajcongress.org
http://www.ajcongress.org

Offers study abroad programs, exchange programs and international internships.

Paul Miller, President

226 American Schools Association of Central America, Columbia-Caribbean and Mexico
Unit 5372-Box 004
Quito, APO aA 34039-3420
Ecuador

593-2-247-7534
Fax: 593-2-243-4985
E-mail: marsanc@uio.satnet.net
http://www.tri-association.org

Established to provide information to three regional educational associations: Association of American Schools of Central America, Association of Colombian-Caribbean American Schools, Association of Americann Schools of Mexico.

Mary Virginia Sanchez, Executive Director

227 American Society of International Law
2223 Massachusetts Avenue NW
Washington, DC 20008-2864
202-939-6000
Fax: 202-797-7133
http://www.asil.org

Agency offering study abroad programs, exchange programs and international internships, financed and unfinanced.

Charlotte Ku, Executive Director

228 Aprovecho Institute
80574 Hazelton Road
Cottage Grove, OR 97424-9747
503-942-9434

Agency offering study abroad programs, exchange programs and international internships, financed and unfinanced.

229 Associated Schools Project Network
UNESCO
7, place de Fontenoy
75352 Paris 07 SP
Paris, France
331-45681089
Fax: 331-43067925
http://http://portal.unesco.org

Founded in 1953 the Associated Schools Project Network is of schools designed to conduct pilot projects in favor of a culture of peace.

230 Association for Asian Studies
1021 E Huron Street
Ann Arbor, MI 48104
734-665-2490
Fax: 734-665-3801
http://www.aasianst.org

Founded in 1941 the Association for Asian Studies sponsors research through conferences, administers special projects and maintains placement services.

Mary Berry, President
Barbara Andaya, Vice President

231 Association for Canadian Studies in the US
1424 16th Street NW
Suite 502
Washington, DC 20036
202-332-1151
Fax: 202-462-2420
E-mail: info@acsus.org
http://www.acsus.org

Devoted to the encouragement and support of the study of Canada and the United States-Canada bilateral relationship. Publishes a quarterly journal, American Review of Canadian Studies.

George Sulzner, President
Diddy Hitchins, Vice President

232 Association for International Practical Training
10400 Little Patuxent Parkway
Suite 250
Columbia, MD 21044-3519
410-997-2200
Fax: 410-992-3924
E-mail: aipt@aipt.org
http://www.aipt.org

Non-profit association offering international internships and work-based training for both students and professionals.

Elizabeth Chazottes, Executive Director/CEO

233 Association for World Travel Exchange
38 W 88th Street
New York, NY 10024-2502
212-787-706

Sponsors a camp counselor program and low-cost, home-study tours.

Robert L Esdell, Executive Director

234 Association of American International Colleges & Universities
27 place de l'Universite, 13625
Aix-en-Provence
France
33-4-42-23-39-35
Fax: 33-4-42-21-11-38
http://www.aaicu.org

Founded in 1971 the Association of American International Colleges and Universities provides a unified source of information regarding accredited independent institutions in Europe and the Middle East offering a liberal arts ortechnical education.

Founded: 1971

John Bailey, President

235 Association of American Schools of Brazil
SGAS 605 Bloco E Lotes
34/37 CEP 70 200-650, Brasilia DF
Brazil
55-61-442-9700
Fax: 55-61-244-4303
E-mail: olmrio@ibm.br

Supports and encourage academic, artistic, athletic and cultural interaction between international schools that offer a US type education in Brazil.

Charles Lyndaker, President

236 Association of American Schools of Central America
US Embassy Quito
Unit 5372 Box 004
APO AA 34024
593-2-477-534
Fax: 502-369-8335
Fax: 593-2-434-985
E-mail: marysanc@uio.satnet.net
http://www.american-schools.com.mx

Supports and encourage academic, artistic, athletic and cultural interaction between international schools that offer a US type education in Central America.

Mary Sanchez, Executive Director

237 Association of American Schools of South America
14750 NW 77th Court Avenue
Suite 210
Miami Lakes, FL 33016-1507
305-821-0345
593-2-477-534
Fax: 305-821-4244
Fax: 593-2-434-985
E-mail: info@aassa.com
http://www.aassa.com

Non-profit organization works to explore ways to achieve better understanding through international education and improve the quality of teaching and learning in member schools. Strives to provide an avenue for communication andcooperation among member institutions and to facilitate cooperation with national, state and local governmental and non-governmental agencies in the field of international education.

James Morris, Executive Director

238 Association of British Schools in Spain
c/o Urbanizacion Los Pinos
S-N 18690, Almunecar, Granada
Spain

34-958-639-003
Fax: 34-958-639-003
http://www.nabss.org

Founded in 1978 to promote, uphold and defend British education in Spain.

Anne Farre, President

239 Association of Christian Schools International
PO Box 65130
731 Chapel Hills Drive
Colorado Springs, CO 80920-1027

719-528-6906
800-367-0798
Fax: 719-531-0716
E-mail: info@acsi.org
http://www.acsi.org

Founded in 1978 the Association of Christian Schools International represents members in legislative efforts and legal confrontations with the government.

Dr. Ken Smitherman, President

240 Association of International Educators
1307 New York Avenue NW
8th Floor
Washington, DC 20005

202-737-3699
800-836-4994
Fax: 202-737-3657
E-mail: inbox@nafsa.org
http://www.nafsa.org

A nonprofit membership association that provides training, information and other services to professionals in the field of international education and exchange.

John Greisberger, President

241 Association of International Schools in Africa
PO Box 14103
Nairobi
Kenya 00800

254-2-58257
Fax: 254-2-580596
E-mail: asia@isk.ac.ke
http://www.aisa.or.ke

Facilitates communications, cooperation, and professional growth among member schools. Promotes intercultural understanding and friendships as well as serves as a liaison between its members, host country schools, and other regionaland professional groups.

Areta Williams, Chairperson
Rob Ambrogi, Vice Chairperson

242 British American Educational Foundation
PO Box 33
Larchmont, NY 10538

914-834-2064
Fax: 914-833-3718
E-mail: scholars@baef.org
http://www.baef.org

Offers qualified American secondary school graduates the opportunity to spend a year at an independent boarding school in the United Kingdom.

Edwin Sheffield, Chairman

243 CARE
151 Ellis Street NE
Atlanta, GA 30303-2400

404-681-2552
Fax: 404-589-2651
E-mail: info@care.org

Agency offering study abroad programs, exchange programs and international internships, financed and unfinanced.

Peter Bell, President/CEO

244 CDS International
871 United Nations Plaza
1st Avenue at 49th Street
New York, NY 10017-1814

212-497-3500
Fax: 212-497-3535
E-mail: info@cdsintl.org
http://www.cdsintl.org

Founded in 1968 the CDS is a non-profit organization dedicated to developing and enhancing opportunities for Americans to participate in meaningful, practical training opportunities abroad. Offers students, recent graduates and youngprofessionals visa sponsorship and internship placement services, as well as study tours and seminars, in a variety of business, engineering and other technical fields in Germany, Argentina, Ecuador, Switzerland and Turkey. Most internships are paidand last 3-18 mo

Robert Fenstermacher, Executive Director

245 Canadian Association of Independent Schools
PO Box 820
Lakefield, ON

705-652-1745
514-935-9352
Fax: 705-652-1935
E-mail: admin@cais.ca
http://www.cais.ca

CAIS is a membership association for independent schools in Canada and abroad that offer a Canadian curriculum.

Susan Hazell, Executive Director

246 Casa del Pueblo Community Program
1459 Columbia Road NW
Washington, DC 20009-4705

202-332-1094
Fax: 202-667-7783

Offers internships and study abroad programs for fully-enrolled students.

Christian Delatosa

247 Catholic Medical Mission Board
10 W 17th Street
New York, NY 10011-5765

212-242-7757
800-678-5659
Fax: 212-807-9161
E-mail: info@cmmb.org
http://www.cmmb.org

Offers volunteer placement in developing countries involved in Health Care Delivery and Medical Education. All levels of health providers needed: MDs, surgeons, specialists, nurses, midlevel clinicians, PTs, etc.

John Galbraith, President/CEO

248 Center for Strategic & International Studies
1800 K Street NW
Suite 400
Washington, DC 20006-2202

202-887-0200
Fax: 202-775-3199
E-mail: books@csis.org
http://www.csis.org

Agency offering exchange programs and international internships, as well as a publication program.

John Hamre, President/CEO

249 **Central and Eastern European Schools Association**
American School of Warsaw
Verhulstlaan
3055 WJ Rotterdam
The Netherlands

31-10-202-1805
Fax: 31-10-202-1507
E-mail: office@ceesa.org
http://www.ceesa.org

Represents international schools in Central and Eastern Europe and the former Soviet Union. The purpose of the association is to provide educational programs of the kind which member schools can not provide for themselves in a costeffective manner.

David M Cobb, Executive Director

250 **Communicating for Agriculture**
112 E Lincoln Avenue
PO Box 677
Fergus Falls, MN 56538-0677

218-739-3241
800-432-3276
Fax: 218-739-3832
E-mail: peter@cainc.org
http://www.selfemployedcountry.org

Agency offering international internships, financed and unfinanced, in agriculture, horticulture, equine and ecology of Western Europe, Eastern Europe, Australia, New Zealand, South America and South Africa.

Wayne Nelson, President

251 **Concern-America Volunteers**
2015 N Broadway Avenue
PO Box 1790
Santa Ana, CA 92706-1790

714-953-8575
800-266-2376
Fax: 714-953-1242
E-mail: concamerinc@earthlink.net
http://www.concernamerica.org

Agency offering study abroad programs, exchange programs and international internships, financed and unfinanced.

Marianne Loewe, Director

252 **Cooperative International Pupil-to-Pupil Program**
3229 Chestnut Street NE
Washington, DC 20018-4004

202-529-2161

Individuals, schools and charitable organizations interested in fostering peace and goodwill in developing nations.

Louise C Dale, Secretary

253 **Cordell Hull Foundation for International Education**
116 West 23rd Street
New York, NY 10011

646-375-2023
E-mail: CordellHull@aol.com
http://http://payson.tulane.edu/cordellhull

Develops understanding among the United States and the rest of the hemisphere in the general interest of international education, the arts and sciences.

Marianne Mason, President

254 **Council of British Independent Schools in the European Communities**
14 Fernham Road
Farindon Oxon SN7 7JY

44-1303-260857
Fax: 44-1303-260857

E-mail: general.secretary@cobisec.org
http://www.cobisec.org

Supports british international schools of quality, Europe and worldwide, provide an English education. Affiliated to The Independent School Council of the United Kingdom.

Roger Fry CBE, Chairman
Sybil Melchers MBE, Honorary Secretary

255 **Council of Education Facility Planners-International**
9180 E Desert Cove
Suite 104
Scottsdale, AZ 85260

480-391-0840
Fax: 480-391-0940
E-mail: contact@cefpi.org
http://www.cefpi.com

Committed to facilitating creative and responsible planning, design, construction and renovation of schools and colleges, which will provide the most effective learning environments for students of all ages.

Dr Clacy Williams, President

256 **Council on Foreign Relations**
58 E 68th Street
New York, NY 10021-5939

212-434-9400
Fax: 212-434-9800
http://www.cfr.org

Agency offering study abroad programs, exchange programs and international internships, financed and unfinanced.

Richard Haass, President
Michael Peters, Executive Vice President

257 **Council on Hemisphere Affairs**
1250 Connecticut Avenue NW
Suite 1C
Washington, DC 20036

202-223-4975
888-922-9261
Fax: 202-223-4979
E-mail: coha@coha.org
http://www.coha.org

Offers internships for 14 weeks in the summer; 18 weeks during the rest of the year. Provides a way to participate in panel discussions on inter-America themes.

Larry Birns, Director

258 **Council on International Educational Exchange**
7 Custom House Street
3rd Floor
Portland, ME 04101

207-553-7600
800-40S-TUDY
Fax: 207-553-7699
http://www.ciee.org

Academic institutions and youth-serving agencies that actively promote and sponsor international educational exchange.

Jack Egle, Executive Director

259 **Council on Islamic Education**
9300 Gardenia Avenue
#B3
Fountain Valley, CA 92728-0186

714-839-2929
Fax: 714-839-2714
E-mail: info@cie.org
http://www.cie.org

Dedicated to provide academic Muslim resources such as professors of history and Islamic Studies, educational consultants, curriculum specialists, textbook publishers.

Provides information and reference materials to teachers, educators and others in this field.

Shabbir Mansuri, Founding Director

260 Division of International Special Education & Services
The Council for Exceptional Children
1920 Association Drive
Reston, VA 20191-1545

703-620-3660
888-232-7733
Fax: 703-264-9494

Focuses on special education programs and services in countries outside the United States. Members include teachers, students, administrators, faculty members and others.

261 East Asia Regional Council of Overseas Schools
Barangay Mamplasan
Binan, Laguna
4024 Philippines

63-49-511-5993
Fax: 63-49-511-4694
E-mail: earcos@mozcom.com
http://www.earcos.org

EARCOS is open to elementary and secondary schools in East Asia which offer an educational program using English as the primary language.

Harlan Lyso, President
Robert Gross, Vice President

262 Foreign Student Service Council
2263 12th Place NW
Washington, DC 20009-4405

202-232-4979

Over 500 local volunteers supported by private contributions, government grants and home hospitality for foreign students.

Frances Bremer, Executive Director

263 Global Learning
1018 Stuyvesant Avenue
Union, NJ 07083-6000

908-964-1114
Fax: 908-964-6334

Founded in 1995 Global Learning translates the world's interdependence into educational activities for teachers, students and educational systems from elementary through college levels.

Jeffrey Brown, Director
Paula Gotsch, Associate Director

264 Institute of Cultural Affairs
4750 N Sheridan Road
Chicago, IL 60640-5082

312-769-6363
Fax: 773-769-1144

Agency offering study abroad programs, exchange programs and international internships.

265 Institute of International Education
809 United Nations Plaza
New York, NY 10017-3503

212-883-8200
Fax: 212-984-5452

Seeks to develop better understanding between the people of the US and the peoples of other countries through educational exchange programs for students, scholars and specialists.

Richard Krasno, President

266 Inter-Regional Center
PO Box 020470
Tuscaloosa, AL 35402

205-391-0727
Fax: 205-391-0927

Dr. Burton Fox, Director

267 International Association for Continuing Education & Training
1620 I Street NW
Suite 615
Washington, DC 20006

202-463-2905
Fax: 202-463-8497
E-mail: iacet@moinc.com
http://www.iacet.org

Founded in 1978 the International Association for Continuing Education and Training is a non-profit association dedicated to quality continuing education and training programs.

Doug Yeager, President

268 International Association for the Exchange of Students for Technical Experience
10400 Little Patuxent Parkway
Suite 250
Columbia, MD 21044-3510

410-997-3068
Fax: 410-997-5186
E-mail: info@iaeste.org
http://www.iaeste.org

Offers paid summer internships in science and technology fields. Exchange programs and international internships are available. Fully-enrolled students at time of application are accepted. Also places international technical students with US employers.

Melissa Michel, Program Specialist

269 International Association of Students in Economics & Business Management
135 W 50th Street
Floor 20
New York, NY 10020-1201

212-757-3774
Fax: 212-757-4062

Agency offering study abroad programs, exchange programs and international internships, financed and unfinanced.

270 International Baccalaureate North America
475 Riverside Drive
Suite 1600
New York, NY 10115

212-696-4464
Fax: 212-889-9242
E-mail: ibna@ibo.org
http://www.ibo.org

Paul Campbell, Deputy Regional Director

271 International Baccalaureate Organization
Route des Morillons 15
1218 Grand-Saconnex, Geneva
Switzerland

41-22-791-7740
Fax: 41-22-791-0277
E-mail: ibhq@ibo.org
http://www.ibo.org

Non-profit educational foundation based in Geneva, Switzerland. Concentrates in the las two years of school before university studies in order to build a curriculum (Baccalaureate), administered in any country, recognized by universities around the world.

George Walker, Director General

**272 International Educational Exchange
Teacher Exchange, Off. of International Education**
US Department of Education
Washington, DC 20202

202-708-5366

Offers educational information on student and teacher
exchanges abroad.

273 International Graphic Arts Education Association
425 22nd Street
Glenellyn, IL 60137

630-942-2040
http://www.igaea.org

Services include career placement.

274 International Institutional Services
850 3rd Avenue
Floor 18
New York, NY 10022-6222

212-319-2924

American-sponsored educational institutions overseas
offering administrative support services to nonprofit
organizations.

Walter Prosser, Director

275 International Monetary Fund
700 19th Street NW
Washington, DC 20431-0002

202-623-7634
Fax: 202-623-4661

Agency offering exchange programs and international
internships, financed for fully enrolled students.

**276 International Physicians for the Prevention of
Nuclear War**
727 Mass Avenue
Cambridge, MA 02139-1024

617-868-5050
Fax: 617-868-2560
E-mail: ippnwbos@ippnw.org
http://www.ippnw.org

Agency offering non profit organization working to ban
nuclear weapons and exchange programs and
international internships, and unfinanced.

**277 International Research and Exchanges Board
IREX**
2121 K Street NW
Suite 700
Washington, DC 20037

202-628-8188
Fax: 202-628-8189
E-mail: irex@irex.org
http://www.irex.org

IREX is an international nonprofit oraganization
specializing in education, independent media, Internet
development and civil society programs.

Michelle Duplissis, Senior Program Office

278 International Schools Services
15 Roszel Road
PO Box 5910
Princeton, NJ 08543-5910

609-452-0990
Fax: 609-452-2690
E-mail: iss@iss.edu
http://www.iss.edu

Founded in 1955 the International Schools Services has
been an integral part of the international education
community, providing a broad range of services to
schools throughout the world, serves many international
schools andmultinational corporations.

John M Nicklas, President
Jane Larsson, Director

**279 International Society for Business Education
US Chapter**
1914 Association Drive
Reston, VA 20191-1538

703-860-8300
Fax: 703-620-4483

Focuses on developing and improving the area of
business education.

Dr. Janet Treichel, Executive Director

**280 International Studies Association
University of Pittsburgh**
Pittsburgh, PA 15260

412-648-7640
Fax: 412-648-7641

Encourages research, upgrades teaching and emphasizes
a multidisciplinary approach to international dilemmas.

**281 Mediterranean Association of International
Schools**
Apartado 80, 28080 Madrid
Spain

34-91-357-2154
Fax: 34-91-357-2678
E-mail: rohale@mais-web.org
http://www.mais-web.org

Professional organization that strives to improve the
quality of education in its Member Schools through
several venues. It promotes the professional
development of faculty, administrators and school board
members; effectscommunication and interchange and
creates international understanding.

Reina O'Hale, Executive Director

282 National Council on US-Arab Relations
1140 Connecticut Avenue NW
Suite 1210
Washington, DC 20036-2402

202-293-0801
Fax: 202-293-0903

Agency offering study abroad programs, exchange
programs and international internships, financed and
unfinanced.

Linda Kresge

283 National Registration Center for Study Abroad
PO Box 1393
Milwaukee, WI 53201-1393

414-278-0631
Fax: 414-271-8884
E-mail: info@nrcsa.com
http://www.nrcsa.com

Founded in 1968 the National Registration Center for
Study Abroad provides information about member
institutions programs and establishes standards for
treatment of visitors from abroad including the
appointment of bilingual housingofficers and counselors
to deal with culture shock.

Mike Wittig, General Manager

284 Near East-South Asia Council of Overseas Schools
The American Colleges of Greece
Gravias 6 St., Aghia Paraskevi 153-42
Athens, Greece

30-210-600-9821
Fax: 30-210-600-9928
E-mail: nesa@ath.forthnet.gr
http://www.nesacenter.org

To serve member school by being the catalyst for their
continous improvement and for on-going innovation
based in the best practices of American education.

David J Chojnacki, Executive Director

285 Northwest International Education Association
Whiteworth College
Spokane, WA 99251-0001

509-777-1000
Fax: 509-777-3786

Agency offering study abroad programs, exchange programs and international internships, financed and unfinanced.

Sue Jackson, Director

286 Operation Crossroads Africa
475 Riverside Drive
Suite 830
New York, NY 10115-0899

212-870-2106

Agency offering study abroad programs, exchange programs and international internships, financed and unfinanced.

287 Opportunities Industrialization Centers International
240 W Tulpehocken Street
Philadelphia, PA 19144-3295

215-236-7700
Fax: 215-236-8970

Offers study abroad programs, exchange programs and international internships.

Adrienne Robinson, Director

288 Organization of American States
1889 F Street NW
Washington, DC 20006-4413

202-458-3000
Fax: 202-458-3967

Study abroad programs, exchange programs and international internships.

Mary Baldwin, Director

289 People to People International
501 E Armour Boulevard
Kansas City, MO 64109-2200

816-531-4701
Fax: 816-561-7502
E-mail: ptpi@ptpi.org
http://www.ptpi.org

Various study abroad programs and international internships.

Mary Eisenhower, President/CEO

290 Phi Delta Kappa
408 N Union Street
Po Box 789
Bloomington, IN 47402-0789

812-339-1156
800-766-1156
Fax: 812-339-0018
E-mail: administration@pdkintl.org
http://www.pdkintl.org

Offers various international travel seminars, curriculum materials and international exchange programs.

Sherry Morgan, President

291 Population Institute
107 2nd Street NE
Washington, DC 20002-7303

202-544-3300
Fax: 202-544-0068

Agency offering exchange programs and international internships.

Werner Fornos, President

292 Service Civil International
5505 Walnut Level Road
Crozet, VA 22932-1633

804-823-1826

Agency offering study abroad programs, exchange programs and international internships, financed and unfinanced.

293 Teach Overseas
International Schools Services
PO Box 5910
Princeton, NJ 08540-6729

609-452-0990
Fax: 609-452-2690
E-mail: edustaffing@iss.edu
http://www.iss.edu

Placed over 17,000 K-12 teachers and administrators in overseas schools since 1955. Most candidates attend US-based International Recruitment Centers where ISS candidates interview with overseas school heads seeking new staff.

Jane Larsson, Director of Education

294 Teachers of English to Speakers of Other Languages
700 S Washington Street
Alexandria, VA 22314

703-836-0774
888-547-3369
Fax: 703-836-7864
E-mail: info@tesol.org
http://www.tesol.org

TESOL is an international professional organization whose mission is to ensure excellence in English language to speakers of other languages.

Susan Bayley, Executive Director

295 United Nations Development Program
1 United Nations Plaza
New York, NY 10017-3515

212-906-5364
Fax: 212-906-5307
http://www.undp.org

Agency offering study abroad programs, exchange programs and international internships, financed and unfinanced.

Djibril Diallo, Contact

296 Visions in Action
2710 Ontario Road NW
Washington, DC 20009-2154

202-625-7402
Fax: 202-588-9344
E-mail: visions@visionsinaction.org
http://www.visionsinaction.org

One year volunteer positions in African and Latin American counties, as well as an additional six month position in South Africa. Volunteers select positions within their area of preference. Internships are also available in thefields of international administration, public relations, fundraising and special projects.

Shaun Skelton PhD, Director

297 World Association of Publishers, Manufacturers & Distributors
Worlddidac
Bollwerk 21, PO Box 8866 CH-3001
Berne
Switzerland

41-31-3121744
Fax: 41-31-3121744
E-mail: info@worlddidac.org

Founded in 1996 the World Association of Publishers, Manufacturers and Distributors is a worldwide listing of over 330 publishers, manufacturers and distributors of educational materials. Listings include all contact information,products and school levels/grades.

Beat Jost, Coordinating Education

Language Arts

298 American Association of Schools & Departments of Journalism
Northern Illinois University
102 Reavis Hall
DeKalb, IL 60115-3084
815-753-0150
Fax: 815-753-0606

Founded in 1917 the American Association of Schools and Departments of Journalism compiles statistics for journalism education. Holds annual convention and publishes various journals.

299 American Association of Teachers of French
Southern Illinois University
Mailcode 4510
Carbondale, IL 62901-4510
618-453-5731
Fax: 618-453-5733
E-mail: abrate@siu.edu
http://www.frenchteachers.org

Founded in 1927, AATF is the largest national association of French teachers in the world.

Dr. Jayne Abrate, Executive Director

300 American Business Communication Association
University of Illinois
911 S 6th Street
Champaign, IL 61820-6206
217-333-1006

Members are varied, with teachers from the management fields and business communication programs, as well as training directors, public writers and copywriters. Bestows awards.

301 American Council on Education for Journalism
University of Missouri
School of Journalism
Columbia, MO 65201
573-882-4821

Promotes cooperation between the media and colleges. Accredits professional programs in schools and departments.

302 American Council on the Teaching of Foreign Languages
700 S Washington Street
Suite 210
Alexandria, VA 22314
703-894-2900
Fax: 703-894-2905
E-mail: headquarters@actfl.org
http://www.actfl.org/

National organization dedicated to the improvement and expansion of the teaching and learning of all languages at all levels of instruction. Individual membership organization of more than 7,000 foreign language educators andadministrators from elementary through graduate education, as well as government industry.

Audrey Heining-Boynton, President

303 American Speech-Language-Hearing Association
10801 Rockville Pike
Rockville, MD 20852-3226
301-897-5700
800-498-2071
Fax: 301-571-0454
E-mail: actioncenter@asha.org
http://www.asha.org

Certifies professionals providing speech, language and hearing services to the public. It is an accrediting agency for college and university graduate programs in speech-language pathology and audiology.

304 Center for Applied Linguistics
4646 40th Street NW
Washington, DC 20016-1859
202-362-0700
Fax: 202-362-3740
E-mail: info@cal.org
http://www.cal.org

Aims to promote and improve the teaching and learning of languages, identify and solve problems related to language and culture, and serve as a resource for information about language and culture.

Donna Christian, President
Joy Peyton, Vice-President

305 ERIC Clearinghouse on Languages and Linguistics
4646 40th Street NW
Washington, DC 20016-1859
202-362-0700
800-276-9834
Fax: 202-362-3740
E-mail: eric@cal.org
http://www.cal.org/ericcll/

Supports all aspects of second language instruction and learning in all commonly and uncommonly taught languages including English as a second language. Reference and referral service; searches of ERIC database.

Dr. Craig Packard, User Services Coordinator
Laurel Winston, User Services Associate

306 International Dyslexia Association
8600 LaSalle Road
Chester Building, Suite 382
Baltimore, MD 21286-2044
410-296-0232
800-223-3123
Fax: 410-321-5069
E-mail: info@interdys.org
http://www.interdys.org

Committed to the advancement of the study and treatment of specific language disability, or developmental dyslexia. Sponsors research and encourages successful and appropriate teaching. Offers a strong voice in developing theworld-wide understanding of the illness.

Nancy Hennessy, President

307 Journalism Education Association
Kansas State University
103 Kedzie Hall
Manhattan, KS 66506-1505
785-532-5532
Fax: 785-532-5563
E-mail: lindarp@ksu.edu
http://www.jea.org

An organization of about 2,300 journalism teachers and advisers, offers two national teacher-student conventions a year, quarterly newsletter and magazines, bookstore and national certification program. This association serves as aleader in scholastic press freedom and media curriculum.

Ann Visser, President
Jack Kennedy, Vice President

308 National Association for Bilingual Education
National Education Association (NEA)
1030 15th Street NW
Suite 470
Washington, DC 20005
202-898-1829
Fax: 202-789-2866
E-mail: nabe@nabe.org
http://www.nabe.org

Recognizes, promotes and publicizes bilingual education.

Zaida Cintron, President
Marcia Vargas, Vice President

309 National Council of Teachers of English
1111 W Kenyon Road
Urbana, IL 61801-1096

217-328-3870
877-369-6283
Fax: 217-328-9645
E-mail: public_info@ncte.org
http://www.ncte.org

Founded in 1911 the National Council of Teachers of English is devoted to the advancement of English language and literature studies at all levels of education. Publishes 12 periodicals, a member newspaper, and 20-25 books a year, andholds conventions and workshops.

Lori Bianchini, Public Affairs

310 National Federation of Modern Language Teachers Association
659 N 57th Avenue
Omaha, NE 68132-2037

402-551-6290

Encourages research and study in foreign language education.

311 National Foundation for Dyslexia
4801 Hermitage Road
Richmond, VA 23227-3332

804-262-0586
800-SOS-READ

Provides screenings for schools or individuals and assists individuals with IEP's. Provides information about support groups and organizations and teacher training workshops.

Jo Powell, Executive Director

312 National Network for Early Language Learning (NELL)
Center for Applied Linguistics
4646 40th Street NW
Washington, DC 20016

202-362-0700
Fax: 202-362-3740
E-mail: nnell@cal.org
http://www.educ.iastate.edu/nnell/

An organization for educators involved in teaching foreign languages to children. To promote opportunities for all children to develop a high level of competence in at least one language in addition to their own. Provides leadership,suport, and service to those committed to early language learning and coordinates efforts to make language learning in programs of excellence a reality for all children.

Janis Jensen, Pesident
Terry Caccavale, VP

313 National Research Center on English Learning and Achievement
School of Education
University of Albany
1400 Washington Avenue
Albany, NY 12222-0100

518-442-5026
Fax: 518-442-5933
E-mail: cela@albany.edu
http://www.cela.albany.edu

Offers information, newsletter, educational materials, download research reports.

Janet I Angelis, Associate Director

314 Sigma Tau Delta
Northern Illinois University
English Department
DeKalb, IL 60115

815-753-1612
http://www.english.org

An honor society for English that offers awards and sponsors competitions.

315 Teachers & Writers Collaborative
5 Union Square W
New York, NY 10003-3306

212-691-6590
888-BOO-KSTW
Fax: 212-675-0171
E-mail: info@twc.org
http://www.twc.org

Brings writers and educators together in collaborations that explore the connections between writing and reading literature and that generate new ideas and materials.

Nancy Shapiro, Director

Library Services

316 American Library Association
50 E Huron Street
Chicago, IL 60611-2795

312-944-6780
800-545-2433
http://www.ala.org

With a membership of over 34,000 across the United States, this Association is the main representative of libraries, school, public and private in the world.

Carol Brey-Casiano, President

317 Asian American Curriculum Project
529 East Third Avenue
San Mateo, CA 94401

650-375-8286
800-874-2242
Fax: 650-375-8797
E-mail: aacpinc@asianamericanbooks.com
http://www.asianamericanbooks.com

Develops, promotes and disseminates Asian-American books to schools, libraries and Asian-Americans. Over 1,500 titles.

Florence M Hongo, General Manager

318 Association for Library & Information Science Education
1009 Commerce Park Drive
PO Box 4219
Oak Ridge, TN 37830

865-425-0155
Fax: 865-481-0390
E-mail: contact@alise.org
http://www.alise.org

Promotes excellence in education for library and information sciences as a means of increasing library services.

Ken Haycock, President

319 Council on Library Technical Assistants
Kennedy-King College
6800 S Wentworth Avenue
Chicago, IL 60621-3728

773-602-5000
Fax: 773-602-5103

320 International Association of School Librarianship
PMB 292
1903 W 8th Street
Erie, PA 16505

Fax: 604-925-0566
E-mail: iasl@kb.au
http://www.ias-slo.org

Provides an international forum for those people interested in promoting effective school library media programmes as viable isntruments in the educational process. Also provides guidance and advice for the development of schoollibrary profession.

Peter Genco, President

321 Pacific Northwest Library Association
PO Box 7220
Olympia, WA 98507-7220

425-753-2916
http://www.pnla

Organization of people who work in, with, and for libraries. Provides opportunities in communication, education and leadership that transcend political boundaries.

322 Pro Libra
6 Inwood Place
Maplewood, NJ 07040

973-762-0070
800-262-0070
Fax: 973-763-6500
E-mail: staffing@prolibra.com
http://www.prolibra.com

Library management to academic institutions.

M Bennett Livingston

323 Society of School Librarians International
19 Savage Street
Charleston, SC 29401

843-661-1310
E-mail: ramseyil@jmu.edu
http://http://facon.jmu.edu/~ramseyil/sslihome.htm

An organization promoting information literacy.

Jeanne Schwartz, Executive Director

Mathematics

324 Association for Advancement of Computing in Education
PO Box 3728
Norfolk, VA 23514

757-623-7588
Fax: 703-997-8760
E-mail: info@aace.org
http://www.aace.org

Offers support materials and conferences on educational multimedia and hypermedia, mathematics, science education and technology. Conferences are held in March, June and July.

Angela Bradley, Conference Contact

325 Eisenhower National Clearinghouse for Mathematics and Science Education
1929 Kenny Road
Columbus, OH 43210-1079

614-292-7784
800-621-5785
Fax: 614-292-2066
E-mail: info@enc.org
http://www.enc.org

Designed for educators concerned about creating equitable classroom conditions. Provides math and science equity materials to help teachers and administrators acknowledge children's diverse strengths, identify inequities, and improvethe ways students with varied needs are served.

Len Simutis, Executive Director

326 Equity 2000
College Board Publications
45 Columbus Avenue
New York, NY 10023-6917

212-713-8000
800-323-7155
Fax: 212-307-5694
http://www.collegeboard.org

A six-year, national education-reform project designed to improve minority preparation for, and success in, college by using mathmatics to leverage access to a rigorous college-prep curriculum. Located at six demonstration sites,Equity 2000 is a model of systemic reform designed to be replicated throughout the nation.

Vinetta Jones, President

327 Mathematical Association of America
1529 18th Street NW
Washington, DC 20036-1358

202-387-5200
800-741-9415
Fax: 202-265-2384
E-mail: maahq@maa.org
http://www.maa.org

Founded in 1915 the Mathematical Association of America advances the mathematical sciences, especially at the collegiate level.

Carl Cowen, President

328 National Council of Teachers of Mathematics
1906 Association Drive
Reston, VA 20191-1502

703-620-9840
800-235-7566
Fax: 703-476-2970
E-mail: nctm@nctm.org
http://www.nctm.org

Dedicated to the improvement of mathematics education and to meeting the needs of Pre K-12 mathematics teaching. Conferences, journals and a collection of educational materials for teacher development.

Cathy Seeley, President

Music & Art

329 American Art Therapy Association
1202 Allanson Road
Mundelein, IL 60060-3808

847-949-6064
888-290-0878
Fax: 847-566-4580
E-mail: info@arttherapy.org
http://www.arttherapy.org

Seeks to improve the standards of art therapy training and practice and to widen employment opportunities for art therapists.

Edward Stygar, Executive Director

330 American Council on Industrial Arts Teacher Education
Arizona State University
Division of Technology
Tempe, AZ 85281

480-727-1874
Fax: 480-727-1089

Represents individuals committed to industrial arts teaching and education.

331 American Dance Therapy Association
2000 Century Plaza
Suite 108
Columbia, MD 21044-3273

410-997-4040
Fax: 410-997-4048
E-mail: info@adta.org
http://www.adta.org

Offers free information on educational programs, guidelines for dance therapy training and internship, professional registration requirements and regional professional contacts.

Elissa White, President
Robyn Cruz, Vice President

332 American Musicological Society
201 S 34th Street
Philadelphia, PA 19104-6313

215-898-8698
888-611-4267
Fax: 215-573-3673
E-mail: ams@sas.upenn.edu
http://www.ams-net.org

Founded in 1934 the American Musicological Society advances research and scholarship in music education and its related fields. Bestows awards and publishes journals.

Robert Judd, Executive Director

333 Future Music Oregon
School of Music
1225 University of Oregon
Eugene, OR 97403-1225

541-346-3761
Fax: 541-346-0723
http://http://darkwing.uoregon.edu/~fmo

Educational Institute dedicated to the exploration of sound and its creation, and to the innovative use of computers and other recent technologies to create expressive music and media composition.

Jeffrey Stolet, Director
Gary Martin, Associate Dean

334 International Thespian Society
Educational Theatre Association
2343 Auburn Avenue
Cincinnati, OH 45219-2819

513-421-3900
Fax: 513-421-7077
http://www.edta.org

Serves as an honor society for middle school and high school drama students.

335 Kennedy Center Alliance for Arts Education
John F Kennedy Center for the Performing Arts
2700 F Street NW
Washington, DC 20566-0001

202-416-8000
Fax: 202-416-8802
E-mail: kcaaen@kennedy-center.org
http://www.kennedy-center.org/education/kcaaen

Advances education in the arts, collects and disseminates information about arts education, offers technical assistance on arts education to general public and education field.

Nancy Welch w/Andrea Greene, Author
Michael Kaiser, President

336 Music Teachers National Association
441 Vine Street
Suite 505
Cincinnati, OH 45202-2811

513-421-1420
888-512-5278
Fax: 513-421-2503

E-mail: mtnanet@mtna.org
http://www.mtna.org

Founded in 1876, the Music Teachers National Association is a nonprofit association of independent and collegiate music teachers committed to furthering the art of music through teaching, performance, composition and scholarlyresearch.

Gary Ingle, Executive Director

337 National Art Education Association
1916 Association Drive
Reston, VA 20191-1590

703-860-8000
Fax: 703-860-2960
E-mail: naea@dgs.dgsys.com
http://www.naea-reston.org

Founded in 1947 the National Art Education Associationh promotes art education through professional development, service, advancement of knowledge and leadership.

Thomas A Hatfield, Executive Director

338 National Association for Music Education
1806 Robert Fulton Drive
Reston, VA 20191

703-860-4000
800-336-3768
Fax: 703-860-1531
http://www.menc.org

A voluntary, nonprofit organization representing all phases of music education in schools, colleges, universities, and teacher-education institutions.

David Circle, President

339 National Association of Schools of Music
11250 Roger Bacon Drive
Suite 21
Reston, VA 20190

703-437-0700
Fax: 703-437-6312
E-mail: info@arts-accredit.org
http://www.arts-accredit.org/nasm.htm

Founded in 1924 the National Association of Schools of Music interested in promoting and funding music schools and conservatories.

340 National Guild of Community Schools of the Arts
520 8th Avenue
Suite 302, 3rd Floor
New York, NY 10018

212-268-3337
Fax: 212-268-3995
E-mail: info@natguild.org
http://www.nationalguild.org

A nationwide service and educational organization that fosters the growth and development of nonprofit, nondegree-granting community schools offering instruction in the performing and visual arts to students of all ages.

Jonathan Herman, Executive Director
Kenneth Cole, Program Director

341 National Institute of Art and Disabilities
551 23rd Street
Richmond, CA 94804-1626

510-620-0290
Fax: 510-620-0326
E-mail: admin@niadart.org
http://www.niadart.org

An organization which operates a demonstration visual arts program, provides professional training and consultations, helps establish art centers and art programs for children and adults with disabilities, and conducts research.Books, videos, artwork and other items available.

Amanda Cauldwell, Executive Director
Elias Katz, President

Physical Education

342 American Alliance for Health, Physical Educatiion, Recreation and Dance
1900 Association Drive
Reston, VA 20191-1598

703-476-3400
800-213-7193
Fax: 703-476-9527
http://www.aahperd.org

Membership organization in the fields of physical education, recreation, health, safety and dance.

Michael G Davis, CEO

343 American Sports Education Institute
200 Castlewood Drive
North Palm Beach, FL 33408-5666

561-842-3600
Fax: 561-863-8984
E-mail: mmsgma@aol.com

Boosts amateur sports and physical education at all levels.

Mike May, Executive Director

344 International Council for Health, Physical Education and Recreation
1900 Association Drive
Reston, VA 20191-1598

703-476-3462
Fax: 703-476-9527
E-mail: ichperaahperd.org
http://www.ichpersd.org

Concerned with health and physical education issues related to child development and education.

Dr. Dong Ja Yang, Secretary General

345 National Association for Girls and Women in Sports
1900 Association Drive
Reston, VA 20191-1598

703-476-3400
800-213-7193
Fax: 703-476-4566
E-mail: nagws@aahperd.org
http://www.aahperd.org/nagws

An association of information for girls and women in sports.

Sharon Shields, President

346 National Association of Academic Advisors for Athletics
PO Box A-7
College Station, TX 77844-9007

979-862-4310
Fax: 979-862-2461
E-mail: N4A@athletics.tamu.edu
http://www.nfoura/org

Aim is to promote academic achievement and personal development among student athletes.

Steve McDonnell, President

347 National Athletic Trainers' Association
2952 Stemmons Freeway
Dallas, TX 75247-6196

214-637-6282
800-879-6282
Fax: 214-637-2206

E-mail: ebd@nata.org
http://www.nata.org

Offers advertising, corporate membership, exhibiting, list rental and sponsorship opportunities.

Teresa Welch, Assistant Executive Director

348 President's Council on Physical Fitness & Sports
200 Independence Avenue SW
Room 738-H
Washington, DC 20201-0004

202-690-9000
Fax: 202-690-5211
http://www.fitness.gov

Promotes and encourages the development of physical activity fitness and sports programs for all Americans.

Joey Kung, Director Communications
Janice Meer, Public Affairs Specialist

Reading

349 ERIC Clearinghouse on Reading, English & Communication
2805 E 10th Street
Suite 150
Bloomington, IN 47408-2601

212-678-3433
800-759-4723
Fax: 212-678-4012
E-mail: eric-cue@columbia.edu

Concerned with the acquisition of functional competence in reading, writing, speaking and listening at all educational levels in all social contexts. Catalogue of publications available for free, ERIC bibliographic searches performedfor clients for a small fee.

Jim Sizemore, User Services Coordinator
Ellie Macfarlane, Associate Director

350 International Reading Association
800 Barksdale Road
Newark, DE 19714-8139

302-731-1600
800-336-7323
Fax: 302-731-1057
E-mail: customerservice@reading.org
http://www.reading.org

Proffesional organization dedicated to promoting high levels of literacy for all by improving the quality of reading instruction, disseminating research and information about reading, and encouraging the lifetime reading habit.

Mary Ellen Vogt, President
Richard Allington, President-Elect

351 National Center for ESL Literacy Education
4646 40th Street NW
Washington, DC 20016-1859

202-362-0700
Fax: 202-363-7204
E-mail: ncle@cal.org

National clearinghouse for adult English as a second language and literacy information.

352 National Contact Hotline Contact Center, Inc.
PO Box 81826
Lincoln, NE 68501-1826

800-228-8813

A 25-year-old information and referral agency, to help individuals with literacy problems. Maintains a database of over 7,000 literacy programs across the country and the 7-day hotline.

353 ProLiteracy Worldwide
1320 Jamesville Avenue
Syracuse, NY 13210

315-422-9121
888-528-2224
Fax: 315-422-6369
E-mail: info@proliteracy.org
http://www.proliteracy.org

Now the oldest and largest non-governmental literacy organization in the world and pursues a mission of sponsoring educational programs that help adults and their families acquire the literacy practices and skills they need to function more effectively in their dialy lives.

M Shan Atkins, Chairperson
Walter H Curchack, Secretary

354 Reading Recovery Council of North America
1929 Kenny Road
Suite 100
Columbus, OH 43210-1069

614-292-7111
Fax: 614-292-4404
E-mail: jjohnson@readingrecovery.org
http://www.readingrecovery.org

An early intervention program for children in the primary grades who are having difficulty learning to read and write.

Jady Johnson, Executive Director

Secondary Education

355 American Board of Master Educators
300 25th Avenue N
Suite 10
Nashville, TN 37203-1510

615-327-2984
Fax: 615-327-9235

Founded in 1983 the American Board of Master Educators promotes high standards of education in secondary and college level public and private institutions.

Dr. Jack Allen, Executive Director

356 American Driver & Traffic Safety Education Association
National Education Association (NEA)
1201 16th Street NW
Washington, DC 20036-3207

202-822-7634
Fax: 202-822-7624
http://http://144.80.48.9/adtsea/default.aspx

Professional association which represents traffic safety educators throughout the United States and abroad. Serves as a national advocate for quality traffic safety education, conducts conferences, workshops and seminars and provides consultative services.

Elizabeth Weaver-Shepard, President
James Gibb, President-Elect

357 Association for Institutional Research
Florida State University
222 Stone Building
Tallahassee, FL 32306

850-644-4470
Fax: 850-644-8824
E-mail: trussell@mailer.fsu.edu
http://www.airweb.org

Membership includes individuals interested in policy research, management, education and statistical information for high schools.

358 Close-Up Foundation
44 Canal Center Plaza
Alexandria, VA 22314-1592

703-706-3300
800-336-5479
Fax: 703-706-0001
http://www.closeup.org

Offers government studies programs for high school students, educators and older Americans.

Barbara Krebs, Director

359 College Board
45 Columbus Avenue
New York, NY 10023-6992

212-713-8000
Fax: 212-713-8282
http://www.collegeboard.org

Champions educational excellence for all students through the ongoing collaboration of nearly 3,000 member schools, colleges, universities, education systems and organizations. Promotes research, programs, policy development, universal access to high standards of learning, equity of opportunity and financial support.

Gaston Caperton, President

360 National Business Education Association
1914 Association Drive
Reston, VA 20191-1596

703-860-8300
Fax: 703-620-4483
E-mail: nbea@nbea.com
http://www.nbea.com

Administers student keyboarding tests and National Business Competency Tests for high school and college students.

Mary Ann Lammers, President
Cynthia Green, President-Elect

361 National Middle School Association
4151 Executive Parkway
Suite 300
Westerville, OH 43081

614-895-4730
800-528-6672
Fax: 614-895-4750
E-mail: info@nmsa.org
http://www.nmsa.org

Promotes the development and growth of middle schools.

Sue Swaim, Executive Director

Science

362 Academy of Applied Science
Washington Street
Concord, NH 03301

603-228-4530
Fax: 603-228-4730
E-mail: info@aas-world.org
http://www.aas-world.org

Founded in 1952 the Academy of Applied Science is dedicated to the advancement of scientific endeavors. Members are active contributors to the applied science field. Sponsors programs and offers research grants.

Robert Rines, President
Joanne Hayes-Rines, Vice-President

363 Aerospace Education Foundation
1501 Lee Highway
Arlington, VA 22209-1198

703-247-5839
800-291-8480

Fax: 703-247-5853
E-mail: aefstaff@aef.org
http://www.aef.org

Dedicated to ensuring America's aerospace excellence through public awareness programs, education and financial assistance.

Danny D Marrs, Managing Director

364 Association for Advancement of Computing in Education
PO Box 2966
Charlottesville, VA 22902-2966

757-623-7588
Fax: 757-623-7221

Offers support materials and conferences on educational multimedia and hypermedia, mathematics, science education and technology. Conferences are held in March, June and July.

Angela Bradley, Conference Contact

365 Association for Science Education Teachers
Old Dominion University
Curriculum & Instruction
Norfolk, VA 23508

757-683-3283
Fax: 757-683-5862
http://http://theaste.org

Promotes leadership in the professional development of teachers in science, including science teacher educators, staff developers, college-level science instructors, education policy makers, instructional material d e v e l o p e r s , sciencesupervisors/specialists/coordinators, lead/mentor teachers, and all interested in promoting the development of teachers in science.

Kathy Norman, President
Jon Pedersen, Director

366 Association of Science-Technology Centers
1025 Vermont Avenue NW
Suite 500
Washington, DC 20005-3516

202-783-7200
Fax: 202-783-7207
E-mail: info@astc.org
http://www.astc.org

Founded in 1973 the Association of Science Technology Centers include science centers and museums dedicated to furthering public understanding of science. ASTC encourages excellence and innovation in informal science learning byserving and linking its members worldwide.

Per-Edvin Persson, President
Lesley Lewis, Vice-President

367 California Biomedical Research Association
1008 10th Street
Suite 328
Sacramento, CA 95814-3502

916-558-1515
Fax: 916-558-1523

Educational materials designed to assist teachers in addressing issues of animal research in the classroom.

Linda Cork, Chair
Desiree Glaspey, Secretary

368 ERIC Clearinghouse for Science, Math & Environmental Education
Ohio State University
1929 Kenny Road
Columbus, OH 43210-1080

614-292-6717
800-276-0462
Fax: 614-292-0263
E-mail: eric-cue@columbia.edu

Collects and disseminates information on topics pertaining to science, math and environmental education issues at all levels.

Dr. David Haury, Director
Linda A Milbourne, Associate Director

369 Eisenhower National Clearinghouse for Mathematics and Science Education
Ohio State University
1929 Kenny Road
Columbus, OH 43210-1079

800-621-5785
Fax: 614-292-2066
E-mail: info@enc.org
http://www.enc.org

Designed for educators concerned about creating equitable classroom conditions. Provides math and science equity materials to help teachers and administrators acknowledge children's diverse strengths, identify inequities, and improvethe ways students with varied needs are served.

Len Simutis, Executive Director
Thomas Gadsden, Associate Director

370 Geothermal Education Office
664 Hilary Drive
Tiburon, CA 94920-1446

415-435-4574
800-866-4436
Fax: 415-435-7737
E-mail: geo@marin.org
http://http://geothermal.marin.org

Provides a resource for user-friendly information about geothermal energy for teachers and students.

Marliyn Nemzer, Executive Director

371 History of Science Society
3310 Turlington Hall
University of Florida
Gainesville, FL 32611-7360

352-392-1677
Fax: 352-392-2795
http://www.hssonline.org

Professional society focusing on the influence of science throughout history and culture.

Michael Sokal, President
Joan Cadden, Vice President

372 Institute for Earth Education
Institute for Earth Education
Cedar Cove
PO Box 115
Greenville, WV 24945

304-832-6404
Fax: 304-832-6077
E-mail: iee1@aol.com
http://www.eartheducation.org

International, nonprofit educational organization made up of a volunteer network of individuals and member organizations committed to fostering earth education programs throughout our societies. IEE develops and disseminateseducational programs that will help people build an understanding of appreciation for, and harmony with the earth and its life.

Steve Van Matre, Chairman

373 International Council of Scientific Unions
Committee on Science Teaching
Western Michigan University
Department of Geography
Kalamazoo, MI 49008

616-387-3429
Fax: 616-387-0958

Promotes the teaching and learning of science from elementary through university levels internationally.

David Waddington, Director

374 National Association for Research in Science Teaching
179 Chambers Building
University Park, PA 16802-3205

614-292-3339
Fax: 614-292-0263

Promotes and educates science teachers in new research findings as well as providing grants for study.

Dr. Art White

375 National Association of Biology Teachers
12030 Sunrise Valley Drive
Suite 110
Reston, VA 20191

703-264-9696
800-406-0775
Fax: 703-264-7778
E-mail: wcarley@nabt.org
http://www.nabt.org

Interested in the advancement of biology education and awareness of new developments in the biology field by educators.

Rebecca Ross, President
Wayne Carley, Executive Director

376 National Center for Science Education
420 40th Street Suite 2
Oakland, CA 94609-2509

510-601-7203
800-290-6006
Fax: 510-601-7204
E-mail: ncseoffice@ncseweb.org
http://www.ncseweb.org

Engages in a number of activities advancing two primary goals: improving and supporting evolution education, and assuring inclusion of evolution (and not sectarian creation science) in public school curricula. This work is supportedprimarily by membership contributions, with some additional assistance from grants.

Josephine Borgeson, Project Director
Glenn Branch, Deputy Director

377 National Institute for Science Education
1025 W Johnson Street
Suite 753
Madison, WI 53706-1706

608-263-4200
E-mail: niseinfo@education.wisc.edu
http://www.wcer.wisc.edu/nise

A partnership of the University of Wisconsin-Madison and the National Center for Improving Science Education, Washington, DC, with funding from the National Science Foundation. Strives to strengthen the nation's science enterprise byhelping to extend science, mathematics, engineering and technology literacy to all students.

Andrew Porter, Director
Norman Webb, Associate Director

378 National Science Teachers Association
1840 Wilson Bulivard
Arlington, VA 22201-3000

703-243-7100
800-782-6782
Fax: 703-243-7177
E-mail: publicinfo@nsta.org
http://www.nsta.org

Seeks to improve all aspects of science education at all grade levels. Provides award-winning journals for every level of science teaching, special publications, awards and competitions for students and teachers.

Michael Padilla, President

379 Science Service
1719 N Street NW
Washington, DC 20036-2888

202-785-2255
Fax: 202-785-1243
E-mail: sciedu@sciserv.org
http://www.sciserv.org

Offers a variety of services to teachers and students, including Intel Science Talent Search Scholarship competition, science fairs and publications.

Donald Harless, President

Social Studies

380 African-American Institute
420 Lexington Avenue
Suite 1706
New York, NY 10170

212-949-5666
Fax: 212-682-6174
E-mail: aainy@aaionline.org
http://www.aaionline.org

Committed to developing African-American understanding and providing Americans with information regarding Africa. Offices in New York and Washington, D.C. lead a team in over 50 African countries.

Mora McLean, President
Kofi A Boateng, COO

381 American Association for Chinese Studies
The City College-CUNY
NAC R4/116
New York, NY 10031

212-650-8268
Fax: 212-650-8287
E-mail: clarkcm@mail.auburn.edu
http://www.ccny.cuny.edu/aacs

Promotes the development of Chinese culture in American studies. AACS, founded in 1959, is the only academic society in America devoted exclusively to the general area of Chinese studies.

Cal Clark, President
Peter Chow, Executive Secretary

382 Center for Education Studies
American Textbook Council
475 Riverside Drive
Room 1948
New York, NY 10115-0599

212-870-2760
Fax: 212-870-3112
http://www.historytextbooks.org

Conducts independent reviews and studies of schoolbooks in the humanities and publishes a quarterly bulletin providing commentary and reviews of social studies textbooks for leading historians, educators and public officials.

Gilbert T Sewall, President

383 Council for Indian Education
1240 Burlington Avenue
Billings, MT 59102-4224

406-252-7451
E-mail: cie@cie-mt.org
http://www.cie-mt.org

Founded in 1965 the Council for Indian Education publishes small books of Native American life and culture. Offers workshops for teachers, conference speeches and University Extension Courses on teaching Native American students.

Dr. Hap Gilliland, President

384 ERIC Clearinghouse for Social Studies Education
Indiana University, Social Studies Dev. Center
2805 E 10th Street
Suite 120
Bloomington, IN 47408-2601

812-855-3838
800-266-3815
Fax: 812-855-0455
E-mail: eric-cue@columbia.edu

Collects and disseminates information on social studies/social sciences fields art and music; produces ERIC Digests and answers questions related to the field.

Dr John J Patrick, Co-Director
Jane E Henson, Co-Director

385 National Council for the Social Studies
8555 Sixteenth Street
Suite 500
Silver Spring, MD 20910

301-588-1800
800-683-0812
Fax: 301-588-2049
E-mail: essp@ncss.org
http://www.ncss.org

Defines social studies as the integrated study of the social studies and humanities to promote civic competence, engages and supports educators in strengthening and advocating social studies. Founded in 1921, NCSS has grown to be the largest association in the country devoted solely to social studies education. The membership is organized into a network of over 110 affiliated state, local, and regional councils, associated groups and special interest groups.

Jesus Garcia, President
Jeff Passe, President-Elect

386 New England History Teachers Association
Bentley College
Waltham, MA 02154

Association devoted to the knowledge and scholarship of history and its teachers.

387 North American Association for Environmental Education
2000 P Street NW
Suite 540
Washington, DC 20036-5708

202-419-0412
Fax: 202-419-0415
E-mail: email@naaee.org
http://http://naaee.org

Founded in 1974 the North American Association for Environmental Education is a network of professionals and students working in the field of environmental education throughout North America and 45 other countries. The Association has promoted environmental education and supported the work of environmental educators for over 25 years.

Abigail Ruskey, President
Joseph Baust, President-Elect

388 Society for History Education
California State University, Dept. of History
1250 N Bellflower Boulevard
Long Beach, CA 90840-0006

562-985-4431
Fax: 562-985-5431

Serves as a network for those interested in history and its importance in the classroom.

389 Teachers' Committee on Central America
657 Neilson Street
Berkeley, CA 94707-1504

650-525-9616

Teachers and educators working to develop a curriculum on Central America for use in American public schools.

Rob Kessler, Executive Officer

390 Western History Association
University of New Mexico
MSC06 3770
Albuquerque, NM 87131-0001

505-277-5234
Fax: 505-277-6023
E-mail: wha@unm.edu
http://www.unm.edu/~wha

Founded in 1962 the Western History Association promotes the teaching of Western history.

Peter Iverson, President
Walter Nugent, President-Elect

Technology in Education

391 Agency for Instructional Technology
Box A
1800 North Stonelake Drive
Bloomington, IN 47402-0120

812-339-2203
800-457-4509
Fax: 812-333-4218
E-mail: info@ait.net
http://www.ait.net

Seeks to strengthen education through electronic technologies. Develops, produces and distributes instructional materials in a variety of media, including online instruction, CDs, DVDs, and instructional software.

392 Alliance for Technology Access Conference
Alliance for Technology Access
1304 Southpoint Boulevard
Suite 240
Petaluma, CA 94954

707-778-3011
Fax: 707-765-2080
E-mail: ATAinfo@ATAaccess.org
http://www.ataccess.org

Providing technology information to children and adults with disabilities, and increasing their use of standard, assistive, and information technologies.

Russ Holland, Program Director
Libbie Butler, Program Coordinator

393 Association for Advancement of Computing in Education
PO Box 3728
Norfolk, VA 23514

757-623-7588
Fax: 703-997-8760
http://www.aace.org

Offers support materials and conferences on educational multimedia and hypermedia, mathematics, science education and technology. Conferences are held in March, June and July.

394 Association for Career and Technical Education
1410 King Street
Alexandria, VA 22314-2749

703-683-3111
800-826-9972
Fax: 703-683-7424
E-mail: sackley@acteonline.org
http://www.acteonline.org

Founded in 1924 the Association for Career and Technical Education represents education professionals dedicated to developing programs for advancement and improvement in vocational and business schools.

James Comer, President-Elect
Margaret Hess, Vice-President

395 **Association for Educational Communications & Technology**
1800 N Stonelake Drive
Suite 2
Bloomington, IN 47404

812-335-7675
877-677-2328
Fax: 812-335-7678
E-mail: aect@aect.org
http://www.aect.org/

Provide leadership in educational communications and technology by linking a wide range of professionals holding a common interest in the use of educational technology and its application learning process.

Sharon Smaldino, President
Wes Miller, President-Elect

396 **Center for Educational Technologies**
Wheeling Jesuit University
316 Washington Ave
Wheeling, WV 26003-6243

304-243-2388
Fax: 304-243-2497
E-mail: judih@cet.edu
http://www.cet.edu

To enhance lifelong learning and teaching through the effective use of technology. Provides turn-key solutions to schools, school districts, state departments of education, federal agencies, foundations, businesses, andindustry—solutions for planning, developing, and implementing advances in educational technologies.

397 **Computer Using Educators, Inc (CUE)**
2150 Mariner Square Drive
Suite 100
Alameda, CA 94501

510-814-6630
Fax: 510-814-0195
E-mail: cueinc@cue.org
http://www.cue.org

Promotes and develops insructional uses of technology in all disciplines and at all educational levels from preschool through college.

Mike Lawrence, Executive Director
Marisol Valles, Conference Manager

398 **Consortium for School Networking**
1710 Rhode Island Ave, NW
Suite 900
Washington, DC 20036-3007

202-861-2676
866-267-8747
Fax: 202-861-0888
E-mail: membership@cosn.org
http://www.cosn.org

Promotes the use of telecommunications to improve K-12 learning.

Keith Krueger, CEO
Irene Spero, Vice President

399 **EDUCAUSE**
4772 Walnut Street
Suite 206
Boulder, CO 80301-2538

303-449-4430
Fax: 303-440-0461
E-mail: info@educause.edu
http://www.educause.edu

A nonprofit association whose mission is to advance higher education by promoting the intelligent use of information technology.

Perry Hanson, Chair

400 **Educational Technology Center**
Harvard Graduate School of Education
Nichols House, Appian Way
Cambridge, MA 02138

617-495-9373
Fax: 617-495-0540
http://http://edetc1.harvard.edu

Investigates and develops methods for using computers and other information technologies to teach K-12 science, mathematics and computing.

401 **International Society for Technology in Education**
480 Charnelton Street
Eugene, OR 97401-2626

800-336-5191
Fax: 541-302-3778
E-mail: iste@iste.org
http://www.iste.org

Promotes appropriate uses of information technology to support and improve learning, teaching, and administration in K-12 education and teacher education. Provides information on networking oppportunities and guidance on thechallenges of incorporating computers, the Internet, and other new technologies into their schools.

Kurt Steinhaus, President-Elect
Jan Van Dam, Board President

402 **Learning Independence Through Computers**
LINC
1001 Eastern Avenue
#3
Baltimore, MD 21202-4325

410-659-5462
800-772-7372
Fax: 410-659-5472
http://www.linc.org

Offers specially adapted computer technology and quarterly newsletter to children and adults with a variety of disabilities. State-of-the-art systems allow consumers to achieve their potential for productivity and independence athome, school, work and in the community.

Mary Salkever, Executive Director
Susan Pomp, Associate Director

403 **MarcoPolo**
WorldCom Foundation
14200 Park Meadow Drive
Stamford, CT 06905

215-579-8590
Fax: 215-579-8589
E-mail: oposewa@edumedia.com
http://www.marcopolo-education.org

A non-profit consortium of premier national and international education organizations and the MCI Foundation dedicated to providing high quality internet and professional development to teachers and students throughout the UnitedStates.

Oksana Posewa, Project Manager
Della Cronin, Prog Officer Communications

404 **National Association of Media and Technology Centers**
PO Box 9844
Cedar Rapids, IA 52409

319-654-0608
Fax: 319-654-0609
http://www.namtc.org

Committed to promoting leadership among its membership through networking, advocacy, and support activities that will enhance the equitable access to media, technology, and information services to educational communities.

Ron Enger, President
Ricki Chowning, President-Elect

405 National Institute on Disability and Rehabilitation Research
U.S. Department of Education
400 Maryland Avenue SW
Washington, DC 20202-2572

202-205-8134
800-872-5327
Fax: 202-401-0689
http://www.ed.gov/about/offices/list/osers/nidrr

Funds 31 state technology assistance projects providing information and technical assistance on technology, related services and devices for individuals with disabilities.

Margaret Spellings, Secretary
Edward R McPherson, Under Secretary

406 Technology & Media Division
The Council for Exceptional Children
1110 North Glebe Road
Arlington, VA 22201

703-620-3660
888-232-7733
Fax: 703-264-9494
http://www.tamcec.org

Association promoting availability and effective use of technology and media for individuals with disabilities and/or who are gifted. The membership is comprised of special education teachers, speech and language therapists, rehabilitation therapists, counselors, researchers, teacher educators and others.

John Castellani, President
Joy Zabala, President-Elect

407 Technology Student Association
1914 Association Drive
Reston, VA 20191-1538

703-860-9000
Fax: 703-758-4852
http://www.tsaweb.org

A student organization devoted to the needs of technology education students. TSA is composed of over 100,000 elementary, middle, and high school students in 2,000 schools spanning 45 states; supported by educators, parents, and business leaders who believe in the need for a technologically literate society.

Mike Amrhein, President
Steve Price, President-Elect

408 Technology and Children
International Technology Education Association
1914 Association Drive
Suite 201
Reston, VA 20191-1539

703-860-2100
Fax: 703-860-0353
E-mail: itea@iris.org
http://www.iteawww.org

The largest professional education association devoted to technology education. Technology educators teach students to use their ingenuity with tools, materials, processes, and resources to create solutions and opportunities that relate to medical, agricultural and related biotechnologies, energy and power, information and communication, transportation, manufacturing, and construction technologies.

Kendall Starkweather, Executive Director
Barry Burke, CATTS Director

409 Telemetrics
6 Leighton Place
Mahwah, NJ 07430-3198

201-848-9818
Fax: 201-848-9819
http://www.telemetrics.com

Telecommunication network for schools, camera remote control systems and robotics.

Anthony Cuomo, President
Jim Wolfe, Sales Manager

410 Twenty First Century Teachers Network: The McGuffey Project
888 17th Street NW
12th Floor
Washington, DC 20006

202-429-0572
Fax: 202-296-2962
E-mail: info@mcguffey.org
http://www.21ct.org/

A nationwide, non-profit initiative of the McGuffey Project, dedicated to assisting K-2 teachers learn, use and effectively integrate technology in the curriculum for improved student learning.

Wade D Sayer, Project Director
Kristina S Ellis, Director Program Development

Alabama

411 Alabama Business Education Association
A&M University
PO Box 429
School of Business
Normal, AL 35762

256-858-4799
Fax: 256-851-5568
E-mail: aampiw01@asnaam.aamu.edu
http://http://abea2000.tripod.com

Foster business education in the state of Alabama.

Roslyn Moore, President

412 Alabama Education Association
422 Dexter Avenue
Montgomery, AL 36104-3743

334-834-9790
800-392-5839
Fax: 334-262-8377
http://www.myaea.org

Serves as an advocate for Alabama teachers and leads in the advancement of equitable and quality public education.

413 Alabama Library Association
400 S Union Street
Suite 395
Montgomery, AL 36104

334-263-1272
877-563-5146
Fax: 334-265-1281
E-mail: mdginc@bellsouth.com
http://www.akla.org/akasl/home.com

Non-profit corporation formed to encourage and promote the welfare of libraries and professional interests of librarians in Alabama.

Karen Davis, President
Valerie Oliver, President-Elect

Alaska

414 Alaska Association of School Librarians
615 Cedar Drive
Kenai, AK 99611

E-mail: lweatherman@kpbsd.k12.ak.us

School librarians.

Lesley Weatherman, Membership Chairman

415 Alaska Business Education Association
Colony High School
PO Box 2626
Palmer, AK 99645

907-746-6544
Fax: 907-746-9509

Foster business education in the state of Alaska.

Barbara Mabry, Contact

416 Alaska Library Association
P.O. Box 81084
Fairbanks, AK 99708

907-459-1020
Fax: 907-459-1024
E-mail: mcgeemb@yahoo.com
http://www.akla.org

Holds a conference in March and publishes a journal.

Mary H McGee, President
Mary Jennings, Executive Officer

Arizona

417 Arizona Association of Independent Academic Schools
4832 E Weldon Avenue
Phoenix, AZ 85018-5518

602-959-2042

Organization of independent schools.

418 Arizona Library Association
14449 N 73rd Street
Scottdale, AZ 85260

480-998-1954
Fax: 480-998-7838
E-mail: meetmore@aol.com

Holds a conference in November/December and publishes a newsletter.

Courtney Gilstrap, Administrator
Christine Bailey, Conference Administrator

419 Arizona School Boards Association
2100 North Central Ave
Suite 200
Phoenix, AZ 85004-1441

602-254-1100
800-238-4701
Fax: 602-254-1177
http://www.azsba.org

Non-profit, non-partisan organization representing more that 225 all-volunteer school district governing boards of Arizona's public school district.

Joan Fleming, President
Rae Waters, President Elect

420 Professional Office Instruction & Training
1325 W 16th Street
Suite 5
Yuma, AZ 85364

928-343-3076
Fax: 520-782-3211
E-mail: rthomp@c2i2.com

Computer software applications training.

Rochelle Thompson, Owner

421 Southeastern Library Association
31 Forest Court
Conway, AR 72032

501-450-5248
Fax: 501-450-5208
E-mail: ellenj@mail.uca.edu

Holds a conference in October and publishes a journal.

Barry Baker, President
Ellen Johnson, Executive Secretary

Arkansas

422 Arkansas Business Education Association
Bryant Junior High School
201 Sullivan
Bryant, AR 72022

501-847-5620
Fax: 501-847-5627
E-mail: vmcgohan@bjhs1.dsc.k12.ar.us

Foster business education in the state of Arkansas.

Vicky McGohan, Contact

423 Arkansas Education Association
1500 W 4th Street
Little Rock, AR 72201

501-375-4611
Fax: 501-375-4620
E-mail: ttalbot@nea.org

Promotes the cause of public education in Arkansas.

Sid Johnson, President

424 Arkansas Library Association
9 Shackleford Plaza
Little Rock, AR 72211

501-228-0775
Fax: 501-228-5535
E-mail: jcolelo145@aol.com

Holds a conference in October and publishes a journal.

Kaye Talley, President
Jennifer Coleman, Executive Director

425 Southeastern Library Association
1438 W Peachtree Street NW
Suite 200
Atlanta, GA 30309-2955

770-939-5080

Association of libraries in the Southeast

California

426 California Business Education Association
P.O. Box 2804
San Marcos, CA 92079-2804

760-489-6471
Fax: 760-598-0990
E-mail: cbeasdi@cox.net
http://www.cbeaonline.org

Fosters business education in the state of California.

Rhonda James, President
Joseph Otto, Treasurer

427 California Classical Association-Northern Section
San Francisco State University
Department of Classics
San Francisco, CA 94132

415-253-2267
Fax: 415-338-2514
http://http://userwww.sfsu.edu/~barbaram/cca.htm

Supports programs to enrich and promote Classics.

Michelle Discher, President
Dobbie Nicholls, Vice President

428 California Foundation for Agriculture in the Classroom
2300 River Plaza Drive
Sacramento, CA 95833-3293

916-561-5625
800-700-2482
Fax: 916-561-5697
E-mail: cfaitc@cfaitc.org
http://www.cfaitc.org

Our mission is to increase awarenes and understanding of agriculture among California's educators and students. Our vision is an appreciation of agriculture by all.

Judy Culbertson, Executive Director

429 California Library Association
717 20th Street
Suite 200
Sacramento, CA 95814

916-447-8541
Fax: 916-447-8394
E-mail: info@cla-net.org
http://www.cla-net.org

Provides leadership for the development, promotion, and improvement of library services, librarianship, and the library community. A resource for learning about new ideas and technology.

Susan E Negreen, Executive Director

430 California Reading Association
3186 D-1 Airway
Costa Mesa, CA 92626

714-435-1983
Fax: 714-435-0269
E-mail: kathy@californiareads.org
http://www.californiareads.org

CRA is an independent, self-governing organization dedicated to increasing literacy in California.

Kathy Belanger, Administrative Director

431 California School Library Association
717 K Street
Suite 515
Sacramento, CA 95814-3477

916-447-2684
E-mail: csla@pacbell.net
http://www.schoolibrary.org

Organized of library media teachers, classroom teachers, paraprofessionals, district and county coordinators of curriculum, media and technology and others committed to enriching student learning by building a better future for schoollibraries.

Penny Kastanis, Executive Director
Sue Dalrymple, Office Manager

432 California Teachers Association
1705 Murchison Drive
Burlingame, CA 94010-4583

650-697-1400
Fax: 650-552-5002
E-mail: webmaster@cta.org
http://www.cta.org

Protects and promotes the well-being of California teachers by improving the conditions of teaching and learning and advancing the cause of universal education.

Barbara Kerr, President
David Sanchez, Vice President

433 Northern California Comprehensive Assistance Center
300 Lakeside Drive
18th Floor
Oakland, CA 64612

415-565-3000
877-493-7833
Fax: 415-565-3012
E-mail: plloyd@wested.com
http://www.wested.org/cs/we/view/pj/224

One of 15 comprehensive assistance centers in the country, the Region XI Comprehensive Center is prepared to provide technical assistance to schools, districts, the State Department of Education, community-based organizations, andother entities participating in the implementation of the Improving America's Schools Act of 1994.

Fred Tempes, Director
Rose Owens-West, Assistant Director

434 WestEd
730 Harrison Street
San Francisco, CA 94107-1242

415-615-3144
877-493-7833
Fax: 415-512-2024
E-mail: dtorres@WestEd.org
http://www.WestEd.org

Nonprofit research, development and service agency working with education and other human services communities across the country. As one of the nation's Regional Educational Laboratories, WestEd also has a special relationshipserving the states of Arizona, California, Nevada, and Utah. For complete listings of all WestEd developed resources visit us online at www.WestEd.org/catalog.

Danny Torres, Publications Coordinator
Liza Cardinal-Hand, Information/Outreach Manager

Colorado

435 Colorado Association of Libraries
12081 W. Alameda Pkwy
Suite 427
Lakewood, CO 80228

303-463-6400
Fax: 303-431-9752
http://www.cal-webs.org

Association of Colorado libraries.

Ellen Greenblatt, President
Judy Barnett, VP

436 Colorado Business Educators
Prairie High School
300 Thomas
Box 82
New Rayemr, CO 80742

970-437-5386
Fax: 970-437-5732
E-mail: caroll@csn.net

Association of Colorado Business Educators.

437 Colorado Community College & Occupational Education System
1391 Speer Boulevard
Suite 600
Denver, CO 80204-2554

303-620-4000
Fax: 303-620-4030

The Colorado Community College System compries the state's largest system of higher education serving more than 117,000 students annually.

Jerome F Wartgow, President

438 Colorado Congress of Parents, Teachers & Students
3460 W 38th Avenue
Denver, CO 80211-1912

303-458-1210

Parent, teachers and student organization.

439 Colorado Education Association
1500 Grant Street
Denver, CO 80203

303-837-1500
800-332-5939
Fax: 303-837-9006

Advances education in the state of Colorado.

Ron Brady, President
Jane Goff, Vice President

440 Colorado Library Association
4350 Wadsworth Boulevard
Suite 340
Wheat Ridge, CO 80033

303-463-6400
Fax: 303-431-9752
E-mail: officemanager@cla-web.org
http://www.coloradoea.org

Holds a conference in the fall and publishes one journal and one newsletter.

Tom Fry, President
Kathleen Sagee, Executive Director

Connecticut

441 Connecticut Business Education Association
Farmington High School
10 Monteith Drive
Farmington, CT 06032

860-673-2514
Fax: 860-673-7284

Fosters business education in the state of Connecticut.

Mari-Jo Scandura, Contact

442 Connecticut Education Association
21 Oak Street
Suite 500
Hartford, CT 06106-8001

860-525-5641
800-842-4316
Fax: 860-725-6323

Represents teachers.

Robert F Eagan, President
Daria M Plummer, Vice President

443 Connecticut Educational Media Association
25 Elmwood Avenue
Trumbull, CT 06611-3594

203-372-2260
Fax: 203-377-2239
E-mail: aweimann@snet.net
http://www.ctcema.org

Professional association of Connecticut school library media specialist.

Jerilyn Van Leer, President
Dianne Kimball, VP

444 Connecticut School Library Association
New Haven Free Library
133 Elm Street
New Haven, CT 06510-2003

203-946-8130

New Haven Free Public Library provides free and equal access to knowledge and information in an environment conducive to study and resource sharing. Through its collection of media, services and programs, the library promotesliteracy, reading, personal development and cultural understanding for the individual and the community at large.

Delaware

445 Delaware Business Education Association
Delcastle High School
1417 Newport Road
Wilimington, DE 19804

302-994-8580
Fax: 302-831-6081
E-mail: jlm@strauss.udel.edu

Fosters business education in the state of Delaware.

Jane Trochimowicz, Contact

446 Delaware Library Association
PO Box 816
Dover, DE 19903-0816

302-831-8085
Fax: 302-831-1631
E-mail: dla@dla.lib.de.us
http://www.dla.lib.de.us

This union of public school employees advocates for the rights and interests of its members and outstanding public education for all students.

Barbara Grogg, President
Diane Donohue, Vice President

447 Delaware State Education Association
136 E Water Street
Dover, DE 19901-3630

302-734-5834
Fax: 302-674-8499

Represents teachers.

Earlene Gillan-Smith, President
Mary Ann Pry, VP

District of Columbia

448 American Council on Education Library & Information Service
American Council on Education
1 Dupont Circle NW
Suite 1B-20
Washington, DC 20036-1110

202-939-9300
Fax: 202-833-4730
http://www.acenet.edu

A special collection of books, journals and nonprint materials devoted to the study of higher education. Library services are available to selected education associations in the greater Washington, DC area. Open to the public foron-site use only.

William Kirwan, Chair
M Lee Pelton, Vice Chair

449 Associates for Renewal in Education
The Slater/ Langston Community Complex
45 P Street NW
Washington, DC 20001-1133

202-483-9424
Fax: 202-667-5299
E-mail: AREinc@crls.com

A multi project agency working to improve the quality of life and education of the young people of the District of Columbia, with an emaphasis on youth-at risk and under served populations.

450 District of Columbia Business Education Association
3606 Burleigh Drive
Mitchellville, MD 20721

202-872-1112
http://www.dcla.org

Fosters business education in the District of Columbia.

Calvin Street, Contact
Jureen Benjamin, Membership Director

451 District of Columbia Library Association
Benjamin Franklin Station
PO Box 14177
Washington, DC 20044

202-628-8410
Fax: 202-628-8419
E-mail: cwtc@ala.org

Publishes a journal.

Claudette Tennant, President
Gail W Avery, Chapter Councilor

452 Office of District of Columbia Affairs
1201 16th Street NW
Washington, DC 20036-3207

202-822-7123

Dale A Robinson, Co-Director
Patrice R Gancie, Co-Director

Florida

453 Florida Association for Media in Education
P.O. Box 560787
Orlando, FL 32856

407-275-3777
Fax: 407-275-3667
E-mail: gthomas@mailer.fsu.edu
http://www.floridamedia.org

Florida Association for Media in Education is to promote and publicize the library media specialist's role in Florida. FAME participates in the initiative to develop and implement statewide guidelines for teacher library specialistsand media specialists. FAME is an efficient, effective, and influential organization that cooperates and collaborates with related professional groups. We care about our libraries, our media centers, and our students. FAME...it's all about the kids

Glenn Thomas, Director/CEO
Eileen McDaniel, Research Director

454 Florida Business Education Association
Robert Morgan Vocational Tech.
18180 SW 122nd Avenue
Miami, FL 33177

954-431-6379

Fosters business education in the state of Florida.

Virginia Calehuff, Contact
Carol Bourke, Contact

455 Florida Education Association
213 South Adams Street
Tallahassee, FL 32301-1700

850-201-2800
888-807-8007
Fax: 850-222-1840
http://www.feaweb.org

Represents teachers.

456 Florida Library Association
1133 W Morse Boulevard
Winter Park, FL 32789

407-647-8839
Fax: 407-629-2502
E-mail: mjs@crowsegal.com

Holds a conference in April and publishes a journal.

Betty Johnson, President
Marjorie Stealey, Executive Secretary

457 Florida Teaching Profession-National Association
213 S Adams Street
Tallahassee, FL 32301-1720

850-222-4702
Fax: 850-222-1840

Advocate the right to a free, quality public education for all, Empower and support local affiliates. Advance professional growth, development and status of all who serve the students in Florida's public schools. Engage our membersand communities to ensure that all students learn and succeed in a diverse world.

Jeff Wright, President
Aaron Wallace, Vice President

Georgia

458 Georgia Association of Educators
3951 Snapfinger Parkway
Decatur, GA 30035-3203

678-837-1100
Fax: 678-837-1110

Educators organization.

Carolyn Lee Hart, President

459 Georgia Business Education Association
Etowah High School
6565 Putnam Ford Drive
Woodstock, GA 30189

770-926-4411
Fax: 770-926-4157
http://www.georgiagbea.org

Fosters business education in the state of Georgia.

Stephanie Hezekiah, President
Connie Zachary, Vice President

460 Georgia Library Association
P.O. Box 793
Rex, GA 30273

770-961-3520
800-999-8558
Fax: 770-961-3712
E-mail: bobfox@mail.clayton.edu

Holds a conference in October and publishes a journal.

Grace McLeod, President
Ralph E Russell, Chapter Councilor

461 **Georgia Parents & Teachers Association**
114 Baker Street NE
Atlanta, GA 30308-3366

404-659-0214
Fax: 404-525-0210
E-mail: gapta@bellsouth.net
http://www.georgiapta.org

Parent-teacher organizations.

Hawaii

462 **Hawaii Business Education Association**
Employment Training Center, Community College
Leeward Community College
96-045 Ala Ike
Pearl City, HI 96782-3393

808-455-0344
Fax: 808-453-6735
E-mail: jhara@hawaii.edu
http://www.geocites.com

HBEA is devoted exclusivlely to serving individuals and groups engaged in instruction, administration, research, and dissemination of information for and about business and technology. Hosts conferences and other professionalimprovement opportunities.

Jean Hara, Publicity Director
Kay Fujimoto Ono, President

463 **Hawaii Education Association**
Jolani School
563 Kamoku Street
Honolulu, HI 96826-5245

808-949-6657
Fax: 808-944-2032

Represents teachers.

464 **Hawaii Library Association**
PO Box 4441
Honolulu, HI 96814-4441

808-292-2068
Fax: 808-956-5968
E-mail: worldlibrary@usa.net
http://www.hlaweb.org

Holds a conference in November and publishes a journal and a newsletter.

A Lee Adams, President
Carol Kellett, Vice President

465 **Hawaii State Teachers Association**
1200 Ala Kapuna Street
Honolulu, HI 96819

800-833-2711
Fax: 808-839-7106
http://www.hsta.org

State teachers organization.

Roger Takabayashi, President
Joan Lee Husted, Executive Director

Idaho

466 **Idaho Education Association**
P.O.Box 2638
Boise, ID 83702-5542

208-344-1341
Fax: 208-336-6967
E-mail: info@idahoea.org
http://www.idahoea.org

Advocates the professional and personal well-being of its members and the vision of excellence in public education.

Diana Mikesell, VP
Kathy Phelan, President

467 **Idaho Library Association**
PO Box 8533
Moscow, ID 83843-1033

208-334-2150
Fax: 208-334-4016
http://www.idaholibraries.org

Holds a conference in October.

Larry Almeida, President

468 **Pacific Northwest Library Association**
Boise Public Library
715 Capitol Boulevard
Boise, ID 83702

208-384-4026
Fax: 208-384-4156
E-mail: sprice@pobox.ci.boise.id.us
http://www.iapsec.org

Holds a conference in August and publishes a journal.

Jan Zauha, President
Charlotte Glover, Vice President

Illinois

469 **Illinois Affiliation of Private Schools for Exceptional Children**
Lawrence Hall Youth Services
4833 N Francisco Avenue
Chicago, IL 60625-3640

773-769-3500
http://www.iapsec.org

A non-profit organization consisting of private schools serving Illionis children with exceptional needs and the quality of special education made available to them.

Pamela Barnet, Division Director

470 **Illinois Association of School Business Officials**
Northern Illinois University
108 Carroll Ave
DeKalb, IL 60115

815-753-1276
Fax: 815-753-9367

Association of school business officials.

Allen Albus, President
R.E. Everett, Executive Director

471 **Illinois Business Education Association**
Southern Illinous University
Pulliam 212-Mailcode 4605
Carbondale, IL 62901-4605

618-650-2522
Fax: 618-650-3979
E-mail: cmbaker@siu.edu

Fosters business education in the state of Illinois.

Clora Mae Baker, Contact

472 **Illinois Citizens' Education Council**
100 East Edwards Street
Springfield, IL 62704-1999

217-544-0706
Fax: 217-333-2736

Association of 120,000 members composed of Illinois elementary and secondary teachers, higher education faculty and staff, educational support professionals, retired educators, and college students preparing to become teachers.

Anne Davis, President
Ken Swanson, Vice President

473 Illinois Education Association
33 W Grand Avenue
Suite 301
Chicago, IL 60610-4306

312-644-1896
Fax: 312-644-1899
http://www.ila.org

Represents public, academic, and special libraries as well as librarians, library assistants, trustees, students and library vendors.

Allen Lanham, President
Dianne Harmon, Vice President

474 Illinois Library Association
33 W Grand Avenue
Suite 301
Chicago, IL 60610-4306

312-644-1896
Fax: 312-644-1899
E-mail: ila@ila.org
http://www.ila.org

The Illinois Library Association is the voice for Illinois libraries and the millions who depend on them.

Syliva Murphy Williams, President
Robert P Doyle, Executive Director

475 Illinois School Library Media Association
PO Box 598
Canton, IL 61520

309-649-0911
Fax: 309-649-0916
E-mail: islma@islma.com
http://www.islma.org

Promotes student interaction, continuing education of school library media specialists, and collaboration among parents, community members, teachers and administrators to prepare students for life-long learning.

Lou Ann Jacobs, President
David Little, Secretary

Indiana

476 Indiana Association of School Business Officials
1 North Capital Avenue
Suite 1215
Indianapolis, IN 46204-2095

765-289-1241
Fax: 765-285-1516
E-mail: dcosterison@indiana-asbo.org
http://www.indiana-asbo.org

Association of school business officials.

Eric Rody, President
Mark Miller, Vice President

477 Indiana Business Education Association
South Putnam High School
1780 E US Highway 40
Greencastle, IN 46135-9768

765-653-3149
Fax: 317-232-9121
E-mail: rokickph@sputnam.k12.in.us
http://http://ind-ibea.org

Fosters business education in the state of Indiana.

Nona Mortensen, President
Greg Valentine, Vice President

478 Indiana Library Federation
941 E 86th Street
Suite 260
Indianapolis, IN 46240-1853

317-257-2040
Fax: 317-257-1389
http://www.ilfonline.org

Holds a conference in April and publishes two journals.

John Robson, President
Wendy Phillips, Vice President

479 Indiana State Teachers Association
150 W Market Street
Suite 900
Indianapolis, IN 46204-2806

317-263-3400
800-382-4037
Fax: 317-655-3700
http://www.istain.org

With nearly 50,000 members, ISTA is committed to great public schools across Indiana.

Judith Briganti, President
Michael Zulich, Vice President

Iowa

480 Iowa Business Education Association
Cental Decatur
1201 NE Poplar
Leon, IA 52761

515-471-8005
Fax: 515-446-7990
E-mail: teacher2@netins.net

Foster business education in the state of Iowa.

Kimberly Schultz, Contact

481 Iowa Educational Media Association
Iowa State University
Media Resources Center
Ames, IA 50011-0001

515-294-4111

Promotes the use of media in education.

482 Iowa Library Association
3636 Westown
Suite 202
West Des Moines, IA 50266

515-273-5322
800-452-5507
Fax: 515-309-4576
http://www.iowalibraryassociation.org

Holds a conference in October and publishes a journal.

Katherine Martin, President
Susan Craig, VP

483 Iowa State Education Association
777 Third Street
Des Moines, IA 50309

515-471-8000
800-445-9358
http://www.isea.org

Committed to quality public education in Iowa.

Linda Nelson, President
Bruce Jensen, Vice President

Kansas

484   Association for Individually Guided Education
Hutchinson United School District #308
PO Box 1908
Hutchinson, KS 67504-1908

316-662-4461

Disseminates education research information and provides methods to teachers faced with situations such as declining test scores and mainstreaming.

Shirley Hutcherson, Executive Director

485   Kansas Association of School Librarians
8517 W Nothridge
Wichita, KS 67205

Association of school librarians in the state of Kansas.

Judy Eller, Contact

486   Kansas Business Education Association
Fory Hays State University
600 Park Street
Hays, KS 67601

785-628-4019
Fax: 785-628-5398
http://www.ksbea.org

Fosters business education in the state of Kansas.

Jean Anna Sellers, Contact

487   Kansas Education Association
715 SW 10th Avenue
Topeka, KS 66612-1686

785-232-8271
Fax: 785-232-6012
http://www.knea.org

Empowers its members to promote quality public schools, strenghthen the teaching profession, and improve the well-being of members.

Christy Levings, President
Blake West, Vice President

488   Kansas Library Association
1020 SW Washburn
Topeka, KS 66604

785-235-1383
Fax: 866-552-4636
E-mail: kansaslibraryassociation@yahoo.com
http://http://skyways.lib.ks.us.kla

Holds a conference in April and publishes a newsletter.

Patti Butcher, President
Rosanne Siemens, Executive Director

Kentucky

489   Kentucky Business Education Association
Jefferson Community College
109 E Broadway
Louisvelle, KY 40202

502-584-0181
Fax: 606-783-5025
E-mail: palderdi@pop.jcc.uky.edu

Fosters business education in the state of Kentucky.

Phyllis Alderdice, Contact
Jack Henson, Contact

490   Kentucky Library Association
1501 Twilight Trail
Frankfort, KY 40601

502-223-5322
Fax: 502-223-4937

E-mail: kylibasn@mis.net
http://www.kylibasn.org

Holds a conference in October and publishes a journal.

Linda Kompanik, President
John Underwood, Executive Secretary

491   Kentucky School Media Association
Scott County School
1080 Cardinal Driove
Georgtown, KY 40324

E-mail: mroberts@scott.k12.ky.us
http://www.kysma.org

Promotes the use of media in schools.

Lisa Hughes, President
Pat Hall, Secretary

Louisiana

492   Louisiana Association of Business Educators
Alfred M Barbe High School
2200 W McNeese Street
Lake Charles, LA 70615

337-478-3628
Fax: 337-474-6782

Foster business education in the state of Louisiana.

Rebecca St. Cyr, President
Melissa Boudreaux, Vice President

493   Louisiana Association of Educators
PO Box 479
Baton Rouge, LA 70821

225-343-9243
Fax: 225-343-9272
http://www.lae.org

Dedicated to improving the education profession and the quality of education. Affiliated with National Education Association.

Carol Davis, President
Gene Neely, Executive Director

494   Louisiana Association of School Business Officials
915 S Main Street
Homer, LA 71040-3819

318-927-3376

Organization of school business officials.

495   Louisiana Library Association
421 South 4th Street
Eunice, LA 70535

337-550-7890
877-550-7890
Fax: 337-550-7846
E-mail: office@llaonline.com
http://www.llaonline.org

Holds a conference in March and publishes a journal.

Terry Thibodeaux, President
Jackie Choate, Vice President

Maine

496   Maine Association of School Libraries
Maine State Library
64 State House Station
Augusta, ME 04333-0064

207-287-5620
Fax: 207-287-5624
E-mail: edna.comstock@state.me.us
http://www.maslibraries.org

Sponsors two state-wide conferences, publishes literature and provides annual scholarships.

Gretchen Asam, President

497 Maine Business Education Association
RR5 Box 1010
Augusta, ME 04330

207-626-5666
Fax: 207-721-0907
E-mail: jhunter@ime.net

Foster business education in the state of Maine.

Leila G Ealker, Contact

498 Maine Education Association
35 Community Drive
Augusta, ME 04330-9412

207-622-5866
800-452-8709
Fax: 207-623-2129

Advance the cause of public education, protect human and civil rights, advocate for professional excellence and autonomy of the profession. To guarantee the independence of the profession ane protect the rights of educators andadvance their interest and welfare.

Rob Walker, President
Chris Galgay, Vice President

499 Maine Library Association
Maine Municipal Association
Community Drive
Augusta, ME 04330

207-623-8428
Fax: 207-626-5947
E-mail: jscherma@thomas.lib.me.us
http://http://mainelibraries.org

Holds a conference in May and publishes two journals.

Jay Scherma, President
Joan Kiszely, Executive Secretary

Maryland

500 Maryland Educational Media Organization
PO Box 21127
Baltimore, MD 21228

http://www.tcps.md.us

Brings students and information regarding educational media together.

Dorothy D'Ascanio, President
Patricia Goff, Secretary

501 Maryland Library Association
1401 Hillins Street
Baltimore, MD 21223

410-947-5090
Fax: 410-947-5089
E-mail: mla@pratt.lib.md.us
http://www.mdlib.org

Holds a conference in May and publishes a journal.

Dolores Mamunski, President
Margaret Carty, Executive Director

502 Maryland State Teachers Association
140 Main Street
Annapolis, MD 21401-2003

410-263-6600
Fax: 410-263-3605

Organization representing 60,000 Maryland teachers, support professionals, retired educators, school

administers, higher education faculty, and future educators.

Patricia Foerster, President
Clara Floyd, Vice President

Massachusetts

503 Massachusetts Business Educators Association
Amherst Regional High School
21 Mattoon Street
Amherst, MA 01002

413-549-9700
Fax: 413-549-9704

Fosters business education in the state of Massachusetts.

Mary Ann Shea, Contact

504 Massachusetts Library Association
P.O. Box 1445
Marston Mills, MA 02648

508-428-5865
Fax: 508-428-5865
E-mail: malibraries@comcast.com
http://www.masslib.org

Holds conferences in April and May.

Carolyn Noah, President
Katie Baxter, Vice President

505 Massachusetts Teachers Association
20 Ashburton Place
Boston, MA 02108-2727

617-878-8000
800-392-6175
Fax: 617-742-7046
http://www.massteacher.org

A member driven organization that supports the interdependence of professionals and unionism.

Catherine Bourdreau, President
Anne Wass, Vice President

506 New England Library Association
14 Pleasant Street
Gloucester, MA 01930

978-282-0787
Fax: 978-282-1304
E-mail: office@nelib.org

Holds conferences in September and October, also publishes a journal. Members have access to educational and professional development, scholarship opportunities, leadership training, mentoring and participation in a variety ofspecialized committees and sections, reduced registration fees to the annual conference, access to an online distribution list devoted to library issues and information related to libraries on local, regional, state, and national levels.

Joanne Lamothe, President
Janice Wilbur, Vice President

Michigan

507 Michigan Association for Media in Education
1407 Rensen Street
Suite 3
Lansing, MI 48910

517-394-2808
Fax: 517-394-2096
http://www.mame.gen.mi.us

Promotes the use of media in education and library science.

Roger Ashley, Executive Director
Diane Nye, President

508 Michigan Association of School Administrators
1001 Centennial Way
Suite 300
Lansing, MI 48917-9279

517-327-5910
Fax: 517-327-0771
E-mail: jscofield@gomasa.org

Professional organization serving superintendents and their first line of assistants.

Dan Pappas, Associate Executive Director
Jon Tomlanovich, Associate Executive Director

509 Michigan Education Association
1216 Kendale Boulevard
P.O. Box 2573
E Lansing, MI 48826-2573

517-332-6551
800-292-1934
Fax: 517-337-5598

A self-governing education association, representing more than 157,000 teaches, faculty, and education support staff throughout the state.

Julius Maddox, President
Lynn Larson, Vice President

510 Michigan Elementary & Middle School Principals Association
1980 N. College Road
Mason, MI 48854

517-694-8955
800-227-0824
Fax: 517-694-8945
E-mail: info@memspa.org

Membership association of 1,600 Michigan elementary and middle school principals; sponsoring workshops, conferences, resource materials, job security, networking services to members. Affiliated with National Association of ElementarySchool Principals.

Joanne Welihan, Executive Director

511 Michigan Library Association
1407 Rensen Street
Suite 2
Lansing, MI 48910

517-394-2774
Fax: 517-394-2675
E-mail: mla@mlcnet.org
http://www.mla.lib.mi.us

Holds a conference in October and November, also publishes a newsletter.

Linda Farynk, President
Michael McGuire, President-Elect

Minnesota

512 Education Minnesota
41 Sherburne Avenue
St. Paul, MN 55103-2196

651-227-9541
800-652-9073
Fax: 651-292-4802
http://www.educationminnesota.org

Includes 70,000 educators working in the state's largest education organization.

Judy L Schaubach, President
Marc Doepner-Hove, Vice President

513 Minnesota Business Educators
2620 Eleventh Avenue NW
Rochester, MN 55901-7722

507-389-6116
Fax: 507-389-5074
http://http://mbei.gen.mn.us

Fosters business education in the state of Minnesota.

Jeanette Karjala, President
Coralie Fiegel, Secretary

514 Minnesota Congress of Parents, Teachers & Students
55 Sherburne Avenue
Saint Paul, MN 55103-2119

612-224-4841

Parent-teacher-student organization.

515 Minnesota Library Association
1619 Dayton Avenue
Suite 314
St. Paul, MN 55104

651-641-0982
877-867-0982
Fax: 651-649-3169
E-mail: alison@mnlibraryassociation.org
http://www.mnlibraryassociation.org

Holds a conference in September and publishes newsletter.

Nancy Hegdahl, Chair-Elect
Rita Schultz, Vice-Chair

516 Minnesota School Boards Association
1900 W Jefferson Avenue
St. Peter, MN 56082-3015

507-934-2450
800-324-4459
Fax: 507-931-1515
http://www.mnmsba.org

Association of Minnesota school boards.

Jack Williams, President
Barbara Klaas, President-Elect

Mississippi

517 Mississippi Advocate For Education
775 N State Street
Jackson, MS 39202-3086

601-354-4463
800-530-7998
Fax: 601-352-7054
E-mail: mmarks@nea.org

Member-driven organization dedicated to promoting and strengthening public education by advocating for students and members.

Beverly Brahan, President
Rena Butler, Vice President

518 Mississippi Business Education Association
Itawamba Community College
2176 S Eason Boulevard
Tupelo, MS 38801

662-620-5001
Fax: 601-982-5801
E-mail: coverby@tsixroads.com

Fosters business education in the state of Mississippi.

519 Mississippi Library Association
PO Box 20448
Jackson, MS 39289-1448

601-352-3917
Fax: 601-352-4240
E-mail: info@misslib.org
http://www.misslib.org

Provides professional leadership for the development, promotion, and the improvement of library and information services and the profession of librarianship in order to enhance learning and ensure access to information for all.

Susan Cassagne, President
Catherine Nathan, Vice President

Missouri

520 Missouri Association of Elementary School Principals
398 Dix Road
Suite 201
Jefferson City, MO 65109
573-556-6272
Fax: 573-556-6270
E-mail: maesp@mcsa.org

Organization of elementary school principals.

521 Missouri Association of Secondary School Principals
2409 West Ash Street
Columbia, MO 65203
573-445-5071
E-mail: mass@moassp.org
http://www.moassp.org

Organization of secondary school principals.

Steve Jurkins, President
Bill Scully, President Elect

522 Missouri Business Education Association
Jackson Senior High School
315 S Missouri
Jackson, MO 63755
573-243-9513
Fax: 573-243-9524
E-mail: twg018@mail.connect.more.net

Foster business education in the state of Missouri.

Janet L Ludwig, Contact

523 Missouri Congress of Parents & Teachers
2101 Burlington Street
Columbia, MO 65202-1997
573-474-8631
Fax: 573-886-0693

Parent-teacher organization.

524 Missouri Library Association
1306 Business 63 S
Suite B
Columbia, MO 65201
573-449-4627
Fax: 573-449-4655
E-mail: jmccartn@mail.more.net
http://http://molib.org

A non-profit, educational organization operating to promote library service, the profession of librarianship, and cooperation among all types of libraries and organizations concerned with library service in Missouri.

Ann Campion Riley, President
Margaret Booker, Executive Director

525 Missouri National Education Association
1810 E Elm Street
Jefferson City, MO 65101-4174
573-634-3202
Fax: 573-634-5646
http://www.mnea.org

Membership of 30,000+ teachers and other school employees located in school districts and on college campuses throughout Missouri.

Peggy Cochran, Executive Director
Greg Jung, President

526 Missouri State Teachers Association
407 S 6th Street
Columbia, MO 65201-4201
573-442-3127
800-392-0532
Fax: 573-443-5079
http://www.msta.org

A grassroots organization made up of local community teachers associations in each school district.

Tami Pasley, President
Valerie Moats, Vice President

Montana

527 Montana Association of County School Superintendents
1134 Butte Avenue
Helena, MT 59601
406-442-2510
http://www.sammt.org/macss

Organization of school superintendents.

Darrell Rud, Executive Director
Julia Sykes, Associate Director

528 Montana Association of School Librarians
1522 Rue Riviera
Bonne Terre, MO 63628-9349

School librarians organizations.

529 Montana Business Education Association
Three Forks High School
PO Box 1491
Poplar, MT 59255
406-768-3736
Fax: 406-768-5510

Fosters business education in the state of Montana.

Toby Bowling, Contact

530 Montana Library Association
510 Arbor Drive
Missoula, MT 59802-3126
406-721-3347
Fax: 406-243-2060
http://www.mtlib.org

Holds a conference in April and publishes a journal.

Karen A Hatcher, Executive Director
Richard Wojtowicz, President

Nebraska

531 Nebraska Library Association
PO Box 98
Crete, NE 68333-0098
402-826-2636
Fax: 402-471-6244
http://www.nol.org/home/nla

Supports and promotes all libraries, library media centers and library services in Nebraska.

Brenda Ealey, President
Joan Birnie, Vice President

532 Nebraska State Business Education Association
UNL-Independent Study High School
Office 295C NCCE
Lincoln, NE 68583-9800
402-472-4338
Fax: 402-472-1901
E-mail: lbourlie@unlinfo.edu

Foster business education in the state of Nebraska.

Lisa Bourlier, Contact

533 Nebraska State Education Association
605 S 14th Street
Lincoln, NE 68508-2726

402-475-7611
800-742-0047
Fax: 402-475-2630
http://www.nsea.org

Member-direct union of professional educators dedicated to providing quality education for students of Nebraska.

Carolyn Grice, Director
Art Tanderup, Director

Nevada

534 Nevada Library Association
N Las Vegas Library District
2300 Civic Center Drive
North Las Vegas, NV 89030

702-633-1070
Fax: 702-649-2576
http://www.nevadalibraries.org

Holds a conference in October and publishes a journal.

Susan Graf, President
Nadine Phinney, Executive Secretary

535 Nevada State Education Association
1890 Donald Street
Reno, NV 89502-5237

775-828-6732
800-232-6732
Fax: 775-828-6745
http://www.nsea.nv.org

Represents more than 22,000 members advocating professional rights and economic security for those working in public education in Nevada.

Terry Hickman, President
Barbara Clark, Vice President

New Hampshire

536 New Hampshire Business Education Association
Newfound Regional High School
150 Newfound Road
Bristol, NH 03222

603-926-3395
Fax: 603-926-5418
http://rhill@newfound.k12.nh.us

Fosters business education in the state of New Hampshire.

Ruby Hill, Contact

537 New Hampshire Education Association
103 N State Street
Concord, NH 03301-4334

603-224-7751
Fax: 603-224-2648
http://www.neanh.org

Represents teachers in New Hampshire.

Karen McDonough, President
Terry Shumaker, Executive Director

538 New Hampshire Library Association
PO Box 2332
Concord, NH 03302

603-863-3430
Fax: 603-863-3022
http://www.state.nh.us/nhla

Holds a conference in May and publishes a newsletter.

Catherine Redden, President
Doris Mitton, Vice President

New Jersey

539 Educational Media Association of New Jersey
PO Box 610
Trenton, NJ 08607

609-394-8032
Fax: 609-394-8164
http://www.emanj.org

Promotes the use of media in education.

Sue Henis, President

540 New Jersey Education Association
180 W State Street
PO Box 1211
Trenton, NJ 08607

609-599-4561
800-359-6049
Fax: 609-599-1201
http://www.njea.org

NJEA represents active and retired teaching staff members, support staff, and other staff in New Jersey public schools and colleges.

Edithe Fulton, President
Joyce Powell, Vice President

541 New Jersey Library Association
PO Box 1534
Trenton, NJ 08607

609-394-8032
Fax: 609-394-8164
E-mail: berger@princetonlibrary.org

Holds a conference and publishes a newsletter.

Leslie Burger, President
Patricia A Tumulty, Executive Director

542 New Jersey State Department of Education
Resource Center
240 S Harrison Street
East Orange, NJ 07018-1411

973-414-4491
http://www.state.nj.us/education

Works to provide special education information to New Jersey residents.

Donna Bogart, President

New Mexico

543 National Education Association of New Mexico
130 S Capitol Place
Santa Fe, NM 87501-2698

505-982-1916
Fax: 505-982-6719
http://www.nea-nm.org

Advocated for New Mexico public schools and their students and employees.

Eduardo Hoiguin, President
Sharon Morgan, Vice President

544 **New Mexico Business Education Association**
Tularosa High School
1305 8th Street
Tularosa, NM 88352

505-585-2282
Fax: 505-585-8112
E-mail: gecgec@juno.com

Fosters business education in the state of New Mexico.

Elaine Chestnut, Contact

545 **New Mexico Library Association**
c/o NMLA
PO Box 26074
Albuquerque, NM 87125

505-899-3516
Fax: 505-899-7600
E-mail: nmla@rt66.com

Holds a conference in April and publishes a newsletter.

Kay Krehbiel, President
Linda O'Connell, Administrative Assistant

New York

546 **Business Education Association of Metro New York**
Edward R. Murrow High School
1600 Avenue L
Brooklyn, NY 11230

718-258-9283
Fax: 718-252-2611

Fosters business education in the New York metro area.

Dominick Rivalan, Contact

547 **Business Teachers Association of New York State**
PO Box 434
Old Forge, NY 13420

315-369-6133
Fax: 315-369-6216
E-mail: jlphelan@telenet.net

Fosters business education in the state of New York.

Patricia Phela, Contact

548 **Martin De Porress**
OASES
13625 218th Street
Springfield Gardens, NY 11413-2226

718-525-3414
Fax: 718-525-0989
http://www.mdp.org

We believe that all youngsters who have been entrusted to our care have the capacity, to learn and to achieve no matter how severe their needs or problems, we teach all who have been entrusted to our care that they are lovable and worthwhile persons capable of making responsible choices based upon respect for themselves and for the other persons in their lives and capable of establishing relationships of trust among our diverse community of adults and peers.

Thomas Darnowski, Division Director

549 **National Education Association of New York**
217 Lark Street
Albany, NY 12210-1192

518-462-6451
Fax: 518-462-1731

Represents teachers.

Gregory Nash, President
Robin Rapaport, Vice President

550 **New York Library Association**
252 Hudson Avenue
Albany, NY 12210-1802

518-432-6952
800-252-NYLA
Fax: 518-427-1697
E-mail: john@northnet.org

Holds conferences in October and November, also publishes a journal.

John Hammond, President
Susan L Keitel, Executive Director

North Carolina

551 **North Carolina Association for Career and Technical Education**
PO Box 25159
Raleigh, NC 27611-5159

919-782-0708
Fax: 919-782-8096
http://www.ncacte.org

A professional organization for educators in career and technical education. Publishes quarterly newsletter.

Paul Heiderpiem, Author
Dr. Clifton Belcher, Conference Contact

552 **North Carolina Association of Educators**
700 S Salisbury Street
Raleigh, NC 27601-2264

919-832-3000
Fax: 919-829-1626
http://www.ncae.org

NCAE's mission is to advocate for members and students, to enhance the education profession, and to advance public education.

Rose Marie Lowry, President
Cecil S Banks, President-Elect

553 **North Carolina Business Education Association**
King's College
322 Lamar Avenue
Charlotte, NC 28204

704-372-0266
Fax: 704-348-2029

Fosters business education in the state of North Carolina.

Becky Mashburn, Contact

554 **North Carolina Department of Public Instruction**
301 N Wilmington Street
Education Building, Suite 5540
Raleigh, NC 27601-2825

919-807-3430
Fax: 919-807-3445
E-mail: hsparlin@dpi.state.nc.us

Serves as a professional reference library for the North Carolina State Department of Public Instruction and the state education community.

Michael E Ward, Superintendent

555 **North Carolina Library Association**
4646 Mail Service Center
Raleigh, NC 27699-4646

919-839-6252
Fax: 919-839-6253
E-mail: ncla@ibiblio.org

Holds conferences in September and October and publishes a journal.

Ross Holt, President
Maureen Costello, Administrative Assistant

North Dakota

556 North Dakota Business and Office Education Association
Richardton High School
PO Box 289
Richardton, ND 58652-0289

701-974-2111
Fax: 701-974-2161
E-mail: haag@sendit.nodak.edu

Fosters business education in the state of North Dakota.

Laurie Haag, Contact

557 North Dakota Education Association
PO Box 5005
Bismarck, ND 58502-5005

701-223-0450
Fax: 701-224-8535

Advocated to North Dakota students and teachers.

Bill Lipp, President
Jane Rupprecht, Vice President

558 North Dakota Library Association
Chester Fritz Library
University of North Dakota, Box 9000
Grand Forks, ND 58202-9000

701-777-4640
Fax: 701-777-3319
E-mail: sally_dockter@mail.und.nodak.edu

Holds conferences in September and October and publishes a journal.

Sally Dockter, President
LaDean Moen, Vice President

Ohio

559 Association for Technology Educators
Owens Community College
PO Box 10000 Oregon Road
Toledo, OH 43699

419-661-7224
Fax: 419-661-7174
E-mail: rkuceyeski@owens.cc.oh.us
http://www.rwc.uc.edu/obta

Technology aducators organization.

Dr. Rose M Kuceyeski, Contact
Mark Williams, President

560 Ohio Association of School Business Officials
750 Brooksedge Boulevard
Westerville, OH 43081-2881

614-431-9116
Fax: 614-431-9137

School businees officials organizations.

561 Ohio Association of Secondary School Administrators
750 Brooksedge Boulevard
Westerville, OH 43081-2881

614-430-8311
Fax: 614-430-8315

A trade organization of secondary school administrators offering staff development opportunities, consultation concerning day-to-day problems, lobbying efforts on behalf of the membership and limited help on status and welfare issues.Sponsors limited opportunities for student development of extracurricular activities.

Donald G Wynkoop, President

562 Ohio Library Council
35 E Gay Street
Suite 305
Columbus, OH 43215-3138

614-221-9057
Fax: 614-221-6234
E-mail: fhaley@olc.org

Holds a conference in October and publishes a journal.

James Switzer, President
Frances Haley, Executive Director

Oklahoma

563 Oklahoma Education Association
323 E Madison Avenue
Suite 18485
Oklahoma City, OK 73105-3190

402-528-7785
Fax: 405-524-0350
http://www.okea.org

Represents teachers.

Carolyn Crowder, President
Roy Bishop, Vice President

564 Oklahoma Library Association
300 Hardy Drive
Edmond, OK 73013

405-348-0506
Fax: 405-348-7027
E-mail: kboies@ionet.net

Holds a conference in April and publishes a journal.

Wayne Hanway, President
Kay Boies, Executive Director

Oregon

565 Oregon Association of Student Councils
PO Box 771
Salem, OR 97308-0771

503-286-0477

Organization made up of Oregon students councils.

566 Oregon Education Association
1 Plaza SW
6900 SW Atlanta
Portland, OR 97223

503-684-3300
Fax: 503-684-8063

Represents teachers.

James Sager, President
Kris Kain, Vice President

567 Oregon Educational Media Association
PO Box 277
Terrebonne, OR 97760

503-625-7820
E-mail: agriffen@teleport.com
http://www.teleport.com

Conferences, resources for members, newsletters and promotions.

Jim Hayden, Executive Director

568 Oregon Federation of Teachers
811 NW 23rd Avenue
Portland, OR 97210-3069

503-221-0548

Teachers organization

569 Oregon Library Association
PO Box 2042
Salem, OR 97308-2042

503-370-7019
Fax: 541-867-0105
E-mail: janet.webster@orst.edu

Holds a conference in March and publishes two journals.

Janet Webster, President
Deborah Carver, Chapter Councilor

Pennsylvania

570 Pennsylvania Library Association
3905 N Front Street
Harrisburg, PA 17110

717-233-3113
Fax: 717-233-3121
E-mail: jsulzer@psu.edu

Holds conferences in September and October, also publishes a journal.

Jack Sulzer, President
Glenn R Miller, Executive Director

571 Pennsylvania School Librarians Association
9 Saint James Avenue
Somerville, MA 02144

617-628-4451
http://www.plsa.org

Organization of school librarians.

Molly Moyer, Membership Chairman

572 Pennsylvania State Education Association
400 N 3rd Street
Harrisburg, PA 17101-1346

717-255-7000
Fax: 717-255-7124
http://www.psea.org

Represents teachers.

Rhode Island

573 Rhode Island Association of School Business Officials
Hayes Street
Room B-4
Providence, RI 02908

401-222-2651

Organization of school business officials.

574 Rhode Island Educational Media Association
PO Box 470
East Greenshich, RI 02818

401-295-9200
Fax: 401-295-8101
http://www.ri.net

Conferences, newsletters and updates on new technologies.

Mike Mello, Membership Chairman

575 Rhode Island Library Association
PO Box 7858
Warwick, RI 02887-7858

401-943-9080
Fax: 401-946-5079
E-mail: davidmm@lori.state.ri.us

Holds a conference and publishes a journal.

David Macksam, President
Kathy Ellen Bullard, Chapter Councilor

576 Rhode Island National Education Association
99 Bald Hill Road
Cranston, RI 02920-2648

401-463-9630
Fax: 401-463-5337
http://www.neari.org

The NEA Rhode Island is both a union and a professional organization. As a union, it provides traditional collective bargaining assistance to its 74 local associations, and representation to its 11,000 members in work-related issues.Members include teachers, education employees, higher education faculty and staff, state and municipal employees, and retirees.

Harvey B Press, President
Lawrence Purtill, Vice President

South Carolina

577 South Carolina Education Association
421 Zimalcrest Drive
Columbia, SC 29210-6899

803-772-6553
Fax: 803-772-0922

Represent teachers.

James A Gilstrap, Jr, President
Betty Morris, Vice President

578 South Carolina Library Association
PO Box 1763
Columbia, SC 29202

803-252-1087
Fax: 803-252-0589
E-mail: scla@capconsc.com
http://www.scla.org

Informes members of issues and to provide training and networking opportunities.

Tom Gilson, President

South Dakota

579 Mountain Plains Library Association
University of South Dakota
ID Weeks Library
Vermillion, SD 57069-2390

605-677-6082
Fax: 605-677-5757
E-mail: jedelen@usd.edu

Holds conferences in September, October and November. Also publishes a newsletter.

Linda M Rae, President
Joe Edelen, Executive Secretary

580 South Dakota Education Association
441 E Capitol Avenue
Pierre, SD 57501-3100

605-224-9263
Fax: 605-224-5810

Represents teachers.

Clyde Clauson, President
Dave Dangel, Vice President

581 South Dakota Library Association
c/o Deveraux Library
501 E St. Joseph Street
Rapid City, SD 57701

605-394-1258
Fax: 605-642-6298
E-mail: Brenda.Standiford@sdsmt.edu

Holds a conference in October and publishes a journal.

Mary Caspers-Graper, President
Brenda Standiford, Executive Secretary

Tennessee

582 Tennessee Association of Secondary School Principals
University of Tennessee
Henson Hall
Room 224
Knoxville, TN 37916

865-974-1000
Fax: 865-974-6146

Organization of secondary school principals.

583 Tennessee Library Association
PO Box 158417
Nashville, TN 37215-8417

615-297-8316
Fax: 615-269-1807
E-mail: foldredge@mail.state.tn.us

Holds a conference in April and publishes a journal and a newsletter.

Faith Holdredge, President
Betty Nance, Executive Secretary

584 Tennessee School Boards Association
1130 Nelson Merry Street
Nashville, TN 37203-2884

615-741-0666
800-448-6465
Fax: 615-741-2824
http://www.tsba.net

Organization of school boards.

Tammy Grissom, Assistant Executive

Texas

585 Texas Association of Secondary School Principals
316 W 12th Street
Austin, TX 78701-1840

512-443-2100
Fax: 512-442-3343

Organization of secondary school principals.

586 Texas Library Association
3355 Bee Cave Road
Suite 401
Austin, TX 78746-6763

512-328-1518
800-580-2852
Fax: 512-328-8852
E-mail: pats@txla.org
http://www.txla.org

Holds conferences in March or April, also publishes a quarterly journal and a bimonthly newsletter.

Herman L Totten, President
Patricia H Smith, Executive Director

Utah

587 Utah Education Association
875 E 5180 S
Murray, UT 84107-5218

801-266-4461
Fax: 801-265-2249

Represents teachers.

Phyllis Sorensen, President
Pat Rusk, Vice President

588 Utah Library Association
543 N 1000 E
Orem, UT 84097

801-378-4433
Fax: 801-378-6708
E-mail: shannon_reid@byu.edu

Holds a conference and publishes a journal.

Susan Hamada, President
Shannon Reid, Executive Secretary

Vermont

589 Vermont Education Association
10 Wheelock Street
#567
Montpelier, VT 05602-3737

802-223-6375
Fax: 802-223-1253

Represents teachers.

Marlene R Burke, President
Charles Duzinski, Vice President

590 Vermont Library Association
PO Box 803
Burlington, VT 05402-0803

802-388-3845
Fax: 802-388-4367
E-mail: vlaorg@sover.net
http://www.vermontlibraries.org

Holds a conference in May and publishes a quarterly newsletter.

Karen Lane, President
David Clark, Chapter Councilor

591 Volunteers for Peace
1034 Tiffany Road
Belmont, VT 05730

802-259-2759
Fax: 802-259-2922
E-mail: vfp@vfp.org
http://www.vfp.org

Vermont non-profit membership organization promoting over 2,800 international workcamps in 90 countries.

288 pages Paperback/Annually
ISBN: 0-945617-22-4
ISSN: 0896-565X

Peter Coldwell, Director

Virginia

592 Action Alliance for Virginia's Children and Youth
701 E Franklin Street
Richmond, VA 23219-2226

804-649-0184
Fax: 804-649-0161
http://www.vakids.org

Nonprofit and non-partisan, Voices for Virginia's Children is a persistent voice of reason in advocating for better lives and futures for children. The Commonwealth's only statewide multi-issue organization advocating for childrenand youth, Voices promotes sound, far-reaching program and policy solutions, focusing on early care and education, health care, family economic success, and foster care and adoption.

Bennet Greenberg, Division Director

593 Division of Student Leadership Services
PO Box K 170
Richmond, VA 23288-0001
804-285-2829
Fax: 804-285-1379
http://www.vaprincipals.org

Organization that sponsors the Virginia Student Councils Association; the Virginia Association of Honor Societies; and the Virginia Association of Student Activity Advisers.

Dr. Randy Barrack, Executive Director

594 Organization of Virginia Homeschoolers
PO Box 5131
Charlottesville, VA 22905
866-513-6173
Fax: 804-946-2263
http://www.vahomeschoolers.org

The Organization of Virginia Homeschoolers' most effective action is screening legislation for potential impact on homeschoolers. We pay attention to a large list of topics: home instruction statute, tutor provision, religiousexemption provision, driver training, truancy, curfews, tax credits, and more.

John Haugherty, President
Kenneth L Payne, Executive Director

595 Southern Association of Colleges & Schools Virginia Secondary & Middle School Committee
PO Box 7007
Radford, VA 24142-7007
540-831-5399
Fax: 540-831-6309
E-mail: mdalderm@runet.edu

Public and private school accreditation organization. 12,000 member schools in 11 southern state regions. 430 middle and secondary SACS member schools in Virginia.

Dr. Emmett Sufflebarger, President
Lanny Holsinger, President-Elect

596 Virginia Alliance for Arts Education
PO Box 70232
Richmond, VA 23255-0232
804-740-7865
Fax: 804-828-2335

To promote aesthetic and creative art education for the development of the individual at all levels in the commonwealth of Virginia. To assist teachers in improving the quality of art education. To organize and conduct panels, forums,lectures, and tours for art educators and the general public on art and art instruction. To keep the public informed of the arts through whatever means are available.

Margaret Edwards, Division Director

597 Virginia Association for Health, Physical Education, Recreation & Dance
817 W Franklin Street
Box 842037
Richmond, VA 23284-2037
800-918-9899
Fax: 800-918-9899

VAHPERD is a professional association of educators that advocate quality programs in health, physical education, recreation, dance and sport. The association seeks to facilitate the professional growth and educational practices andlegislation that will impact the profession.

Judith Clark, President

598 Virginia Association for Supervision and Curriculum Development
106 Yorkview Road
Yorktown, VA 23692
757-898-4434
Fax: 757-898-6674
E-mail: jbyrne@visi.net

The Virginia affiliate of the Association for Supervision and Curriculum Development (ASCD).

Gail L Pope, President
Joan S Byrne, Executive Director

599 Virginia Association for the Education of the Gifted
PO Box 26212
Richmond, VA 23260-6212
804-355-5945
Fax: 804-355-5137
E-mail: vagifted@comcast.net
http://www.vagifted.org

The Virginia Association for the Gifted supports research in gifted education and advocates specialized preparation for educators of the gifted. The association disseminates information, maintains a statewide network of communication,and cooperates with organizations and agencies to improve the quality of education in the Commonwealth of Virginia.

Liz Nelson, Executive Director

600 Virginia Association of Elementary School Principals
2116 Dabney Road
Suite A-4
Richmond, VA 23230-5017
804-355-6791
Fax: 804-355-1196

Nonprofit professional association advocating for public education and equal educational opportunities. Promotes leadership of school administrators, principals as educational leaders, and provides professional developmentopportunities.

Thomas L Shortt, Executive Director
Judy Grady, Financial

601 Virginia Association of Independent Specialized Education Facilities
118 N 8th Street
Richmond, VA 23219-2306
804-649-4978

Mary R Simmons, Executive Director
Pam Alteresca, President

602 Virginia Association of Independent Schools
8001 Franklin Farms Drive
Suite 100
Richmond, VA 23229-5108
804-282-3592
Fax: 804-282-3596
E-mail: director@vais.org
http://www.vais.org

The Virginia Association of Independent Schools is a service organization that promotes educational, ethical and professional excellence. Through its school evaluation/accreditation program, attention to professional development andinsistence on integrity, the Association safeguards the interests of its member schools.

Andrew A Zvara, Professional Development
Dr. Sally K Boese, Executive Director

603 Virginia Association of School Superintendents
405 Emmet Street
Charlottesville, VA 22903
434-924-0538
Fax: 434-982-2942

The Virginia Association of School Superintendents (VASS) is a professional organization dedicated to the mission of providing leadership and advocacy for public school education throughout the Commonwealth of Virginia.

J Andrew Stamp, Division Director

604 Virginia Association of School Business Officials
Williamsburg-James City County Public Schools
PO Box 8783
Williamsburg, VA 23187-8783

757-253-6748
Fax: 757-253-0173

The mission of the Virginia Association of School Business Officials is to promote the highest standards of school business practices for its membership through professional development, continuing education, networking, andlegislative impact.

David C Papenfuse, Division Director

605 Virginia Association of School Personnel
Administrators
800 E City Hall Avenue
Norfolk, VA 23510-2723

757-340-1217
Fax: 757-340-1889
E-mail: aaspa@aaspa.org
http://www.aaspa.org

AASPA is the only organization that specifically targets and represents school personnel professionals. If you are a personnel / human resource administrator, personnel support staff, superintendent, principal, or graduate studentinterested in this field, you will benefit from AASPA membership. The association provides research, reports, professional development activities, and networking opportunities to help you do your job efficiently, legally, and effectively.

Eddid P Antoine II, Division Director

606 Virginia Congress of Parents & Teachers
1027 Wilmer Avenue
Richmond, VA 23227

804-264-1234
Fax: 804-264-4014
E-mail: info@vapta.org
http://www.vapta.org

To promote the welfare of the children and youth in home, school, community, and place of worship.To raise the standards of home life, to secure adequate laws for the care and protection of children and youth, to bring into closerrelation the home and the school, that parents and teachers may cooperate intelligently in the education of children and youth.

Sue Glasco, President
Eugene A Goldberg, Executive Director

607 Virginia Consortium of Administrators for
Education of the Gifted
RR 5 Box 680
Farmville, VA 23901-9011

804-225-2884
Fax: 814-692-3163

Catherine Cottrell, Division Director

608 Virginia Council for Private Education
8001 Franklin Farms Drive
Suite 100
Richmond, VA 23229-5108

804-282-8273
Fax: 804-282-3596
E-mail: kimfailen@vcpe.org
http://www.vcpe.org

VCPE provides a statewide framework for communications and cooperation among private elementary and secondary schools, between such schools and their public school counterparts, and among private schools and state and localgovernments and other agencies and organizations. In legislative or policy matters, VCPE is available to members of the legislature, to the Board of Education, and to the Department of Education to furnish information about, and to articulate theprivate school viewpoint.

George McVey, President
Kimberly Failon, Vice President

609 Virginia Council of Administrators of Special
Education
Franklin County Public Schools
25 Bernard Road
Rocky Mount, VA 24151

703-493-0280
Fax: 540-483-5806
E-mail: mflora@frlo.k12.va.us
http://www.vcase.org

The Virginia Council of Administrators of Special Education is a professional organization that promotes professional leadership through the provision of collegial support and current information on recommended instructional practicesas well as local, state and national trends in Special Education for professionals who serve students with disabilities in order to improve the quality and delivery of special education services in Virginia's public Schools

Patricia Addison, President

610 Virginia Council of Teachers of Mathematics
1033 Backwoods Road
Virginia Beach, VA 23455-6617

757-671-7316

The purpose of the Virginia Council of Teachers of Mathematics is to stimulate an active interest in mathematics, to provide an interchange of ideas in the teaching of mathematics, to promote the improvement of mathematics educationin Virginia, to provide leadership in the professional development of teachers, to provide resources for teachers and to facilitate cooperation among mathematics organizations at the local, state and national levels

Ellen Smith Hook, Division Director

611 Virginia Council on Economic Education
1015 Floyd Avenue #844000
Richmond, VA 23284-4000

804-828-1627
Fax: 804-828-7215
E-mail: ed.miller@vcu.edu
http://www.vcee.org

Goal is for students to understand our economy and develop the life-long decision-making skills they need to be effective, informed citizens, consumers, savers, investors, producers and employees.

G Edward Miller, President

612 Virginia Education Association
116 S 3rd Street
Richmond, VA 23219-3744

804-648-5801
Fax: 804-775-8379

Represents teachers.

Jerry Caruthers, Executive Director
Jean Bankos, President

613 Virginia Educational Media Association
PO Box 2743
Fairfax, VA 22031-0743

703-764-0719
Fax: 703-764-0719
E-mail: jremler@pen.k12.va.us
http://www.vema.gan.va.us

Aim is to promote literacy, information access and evaluation, love of literature, effective use of technology, collaboration in the teaching and learning process, intellectual freedom, professional growth, instructional leadershipand lifelong learning.

Roxanne Mills, President

614 Virginia Educational Research Association
305 Fairway Drive
Radford, VA 24142

540-639-1263
Fax: 540-831-6441

The mission of the Educational Research Service is to improve the education of children and youth by providing educators and the public with timely and reliable research and information.

Dr. Edith Carter, Assistant Professor

615 Virginia High School League
1642 State Farm Boulevard
Charlottesville, VA 22911-8609

804-225-2884
Fax: 804-692-3163

Craig Barbrow, President
Ken Tilley, Executive Director

616 Virginia Library Association
PO Box 8277
Norfolk, VA 23503-0277

757-583-0041
Fax: 757-583-5041
E-mail: hahne@bellatlantic.net

Holds a conference in October and publishes a journal and a newsletter.

Cy Dillon, President
Linda Hahne, Executive Director

617 Virginia Middle School Association
11138 Marsh Road
Bealeton, VA 22712-9360

703-439-3207
Fax: 540-439-2051

Mary Barton, Division Director

618 Virginia School Boards Association
2320 Hunters Way
Charlottesville, VA 22911-7931

434-295-8722
800-446-8722
Fax: 434-295-8785
http://www.vsba.org

State school boards association.

Gina Patterson, Assistant Executive Director

619 Virginia Student Councils Association
8001 Franklin Farms Drive
Suite 114
Richmond, VA 23229-5108

804-288-2777
Fax: 804-285-1379

Statewide association of elementary, middle and high school student cuoncils.

Anthony S Morris, Director

620 Virginia Vocational Association
10259 Lakeridge Square Court #G
Ashland, VA 23005-8159

804-365-4556

Jean Holbrook, President
Kathy Williams, Executive Director

Washington

621 Washington Education Association
33434 8th Avenue S
Federal Way, WA 98003-6397

253-941-6700
Fax: 253-946-4735

Represents teachers.

CT Purdom, President
Leeann Prielipp, VP

622 Washington Library Association
4016 1st Avenue NE
Seattle, WA 98105-6502

206-545-1529
Fax: 206-545-1543
E-mail: washla@wla.org

Holds a conference in April, also publishes a journal and a newsletter.

Carol Gill Schuyler, President Elect
Gail Willis, Association Coordinator

West Virginia

623 Appalachia Educational Laboraory
1031 Quarrier Street
PO Box 1348
Charleston, WV 25301-1348

304-347-0400
800-624-9120
Fax: 304-347-0487
E-mail: link@ael.org
http://www.ael.org

Educational research and development organization supported by contracts with the US Education Department, Office of Educational Research and Improvement. Specialty area: emerging technologies in education.

Nancy Balow, Author
Carolyn Luzader, Communications Associate

624 West Virginia Education Association
1558 Quarrier Street
Charleston, WV 25311-2497

304-346-5315
Fax: 304-346-4325

Represents teachers.

Kayetta Meadows, President
Mary Carden, Vice President

625 West Virginia Library Association
1900 Kanawha Boulevard E
Charleston, WV 25305

304-558-2045
Fax: 304-558-2044
E-mail: goffk@wvlc.wvnet.edu

Holds conferences in October and November, also publishes a journal.

Dottie Thomas, President
Monica Garcia Brooks, Chapter Councilor

Wisconsin

626 Wisconsin Education Association Council
33 Nob Hill Drive
#8003
Madison, WI 53713-2199

608-276-7711
Fax: 608-276-8203

Advocates the ideas of a diverse, democratic society and quality public education.

Mary Lou Zuege, President

627 Wisconsin Educational Media Association
1300 Industrial Drive
Fennimore, WI 53809

http://www.wemaonline.org

Promotes the use of media in education.

628 Wisconsin Library Association
5250 E Terrace Drive
Suite A
Madison, WI 53718-8345

608-245-3640
Fax: 608-245-3646
E-mail: strand@scls.lib.wi.us

Holds conferences in October and November, also publishes a newsletter.

Michael Gelhausen, President
Lisa Strand, Executive Director

Wyoming

629 Wyoming Education Association
115 E 22nd Street
Cheyenne, WY 82001-3758

307-634-7991
Fax: 307-778-8161

Represents teachers.

Jim Fotter, President
Holly Thompson, Vice President

630 Wyoming Library Association
PO Box 1387
Cheyenne, WY 82003

307-632-7622
Fax: 307-638-3469
E-mail: lgrott@wyld.state.wy.us

Holds a conference in September and publishes a newsletter.

Vickie Hoff, President
Laura Grott, Executive Secretary

631 Wyoming School Boards Association
PO Box 3274
Laramie, WY 82071-3274

307-766-2389
Fax: 307-766-5544

Organization of school boards.

International

632 Association for Childhood Education International Annual Conference
Assn for Childhood Educational International
17904 Georgia Avenue
Suite 215
Olney, MD 20832

301-570-2111
800-423-3563
Fax: 301-570-2212
E-mail: conference@acei.org
http://www.acei.org

Symposium focusing on education for bi-lingual and culturally diverse children. International issues and over 200 workshops.

April
50 booths with 1000 attendees

Lisa Wenger, Director Conferences
Gerald C Odland, Executive Director

633 Association for Experiential Education Annual Conference
3775 Iris Avenue
Suite 4
Boulder, CO 80301-1043

303-440-8844
866-522-8337
Fax: 303-440-9581
E-mail: conferences@aee.org
http://www.aee.org

Annual international and regional conference dedicated to promoting, defining, developing, and applying the theories and practices of experiential education.

November
1,200 attendees

Evan Narotsky, Conference & Events Manager
Amy Green, Membership Coordinator

634 Bienvenue Annual Conference
Council on International Educational Exchange
633 3rd Avenue
20th Floor
New York, NY 10017-6706

212-822-2625
800-407-8839
Fax: 212-822-2779
E-mail: conference@ciee.org
http://www.ciee.org

Open to study-abroad advisors, administrators, faculty and other international education professionals. The conference is an opportunity to share ideas, keep up with developments in the field, and meet with colleagues from around theworld.

635 Center for Critical Thinking and Moral Critique Annual International
Po Box 220
Dillon Beach, CA 94929

707-878-9100
Fax: 707-878-9111
E-mail: cct@criticalthinking.org
http://www.criticalthinking.org

Over 1,200 educators participate to discuss critical thinking and educational change.

Dr Linda Elder, President

636 Childhood Education Association International
17904 Georgia Avenue
Suite 215
Olney, MD 20832-2277

301-570-2111
800-423-3563
Fax: 301-570-2212
E-mail: aceihq@aol.com
http://wwwacei.org

To promote and support in the global community the optimal education and development of children, from birth through early adolescence, and to influence the professional growth of educators and the efforts of others who are committedto the needs of children in a changing society.

35 booths

Lisa Wenger, Director of Conference
Jana Pauldin, Public Relations Manager

637 Council for Learning Disabilities International Conference
PO Box 40303
Overland Park, KS 66204-4303

913-492-8755
Fax: 913-492-2546
http://www.cldinternational.org

Intensive interaction with and among professional educators and top LD researchers. Concise, informative and interesting forums on topics from effective instruction to self-reliance are presented by well-known professionals fromacross the country and around the world.

October
35 booths with 800 attendees

Kirsten McBride, Conference Contact

638 Council of British Independent Schools in the European Communities Annual Conference
14 Fernham Road
Faringdon Oxon SN7—7JY

44-1303-260857
Fax: 44-1303-260857
E-mail: general.secretary@cobisec.org
http://www.cobisec.org

Conference for Heads, Governors and members of Senior Management Teams of schools. Assurance of quality in member schools.

May
75 attendees and 20 exhibits

639 European Council of International Schools
21B Lavant Street
Petersfield, Hampshire GU32 3EL
United Kingdom

44-1730-268-244
Fax: 44-1730-267-914
E-mail: ecis@ecis.org
http://www.ecis.org

Support professional development, curriculum and instruction, leadership and good governance in international schools located in Europe and around the world.

Michelle Daughtry, Events Manager
Peter Price, Executive Officer

640 Hort School: Conference of the Association ofAmerican Schools
International School of Panama
PO Nox 6-7589
El Dorado
Panama

507-266-7037
Fax: 507-266-7808
E-mail: isp@isp.edu.pa
http://www.isp.edu.pa

Founded in 1982 by a group of interested parents from the Panamanian and International community. ISP is a private, independent, non-profit educational institution providing instruction in English for the multinational and Panamanianpopulation residing in Panama City, Panama.

October
600 attendees and 35 exhibits

Dr. Mark G Mend, Director
Laurie Lewter, Business Manager

641 International Association of Teachers of English as a Foreign Language
Darwin College
University of Kent
Canterbury, Kent, UK CT2-7NY

44-1227-276528
Fax: 44-1227-274415
E-mail: generalenquires@iatefl.org
http://www.iatefl.org

Plenary sessions by eminent practitioners, a large number of workshops, talks and round tables given by other speakers, an ELT Resources Exhibition and Pre-Conference Events organised by Special Interest Groups.

April
80 booths with 1500 attendees

Alison Medland, Conference Organizer
Glenda Smart, Executive Officer

642 International Awards Market
Awards and Recognition Association
4700 W Lake Avenue
Glenview, IL 60025

847-375-4800
800-344-2148
Fax: 877-734-9380
E-mail: info@ara.org
http://www.ara.org

Providing outstanding business and educational opportunities for both retailers and suppliers. Retailers can view the latest industry products, take advantage of special show offers and benefit from a full educational program.

Feb, March, Nov
200 booths with 6,000 attendees

Brian Martin, President

643 International Conference
World Associaiton for Symphonic Bands & Ensembles
1037 Mill Street
San Luis Obispo, CA 93401

805-541-8000
Fax: 805-543-9498
E-mail: admin@wasbe2005.com
http://www.wasbe.org/en/conferences/index.html

WASBE is a nonprofit, international association open to individuals, institutions, and industries interested in symphonic bands and wind ensembles. Dedicated to enhancing the quality of the wind band throughout the world and exposingits members to new worlds of repertoire, musical culture, people and places.

Twice a Year

Dennis Johnson, President

644 International Congress for School Effectiveness & Improvement
International Congress Secretariat
PO Box 527-Frankston, VC 3199
Australia

61-037844230
http://www.icsei.net

The purpose of building and using an expanded base for advancing research, practice and policy in the area of school effectiveness and improvement. The Congress offers the opportunity to exchange information and networking for theeducational community.

500 attendees

Lejf Moos, President

645 International Dyslexia Association Annual Conference
8600 LaSalle Road
Chester Building, Suite 382
Baltimore, MD 21286-2044

410-296-0232
800-ABC-D123
Fax: 410-321-5069
E-mail: info@interdys.org
http://www.interdys.org

Provide the most comprehensive range of information and services that address the full scope of dyslexia and related difficulties in learning to read and write.

3000 attendees

Margaret Palmer, Conferences Coordinator
Noreen A Frohme, Conference Director

646 International Exhibit
National Institute for Staff & Organizational Dev.
University of Texas
1 University Station
Austin, TX 78712

512-471-7545
Fax: 512-471-9426
E-mail: mpg@mail.utexas.edu
http://www.nisod.org

The largest international conference to focus specifically on the celebration of teaching, learning, and leadership excellence. This conference has enjoyed steady growth since its inception in 1978.

1500 attendees

Margot Perez-Greene, Conference Director

647 International Listening Association Annual Convention
Center for Information & Communication
Ball State University
BC 221
Muncie, IN 47306-0001

765-285-1889
Fax: 765-285-1516
http://www.bsu.edu/cics

Geared toward the teaching of listening in the classroom and various techniques for increasing effectiveness in the classroom setting.

March

Barbara B Nixon, Conference Contact

648 International Reading Association Annual Convention
800 Barksdale Road
PO Box 8139
Newark, DE 19714-8139

302-731-1600
800-336-7323
Fax: 302-731-1057
E-mail: conferences@reading.org
http://www.reading.org

Contains exhibitors involved in various lectures and workshops dealing with illiteracy, literature and some library science courses.

May
800 booths with 13M attendees

Maryellen Vogt, President

649 International Symposium
American Association of University Women
1111 16th Street NW
Washington, DC 20036

800-326-2289
Fax: 202-872-1425
E-mail: convention@aauw.org
http://www.aauw.org

The nation's leading voice promoting education and equity for women and girls.

Ashleyr Carr, Media Relations
Christy Jones, Membership Director

650 International Technology Education Association Conference
1914 Association Drive
Suite 201
Reston, VA 20191-1539

703-860-2100
Fax: 703-860-0353
E-mail: itea@iris.org
http://www.iteawww.org

Provides teachers with new and exciting ideas for educating students of all grade levels. The conference gives educators an opportunity for better understanding of the constant changes that take place in technology education.

April
150 booths with 2,200+ attendees

Katie de la Paz, Communications Coordinator

651 International Trombone Festival
International Trombone Association
1 Broomfield Road
Conventry, UK CV5-6JW

903-886-8711
Fax: 903-886-7975
http://www.trombone.net

This annual festival takes place at The Crane School of Music, State University of New York College at Potsdam.

June

Tony Baker, Festival Director
Jon Bohls, ITF Exhibits Coordinator

652 Learner-Centered
Improving Learning and Teaching
8510 49th Avenue
College Park, MD 20740-2412

Fax: 301-474-3473
E-mail: iut2000@aol.com
http://www.iut2000.org

Provides a forum in which participants from across the globe share discoveries, practices and challenges relating to improving the effectiveness of postsecondary teaching and learning. The conference will be held in Johannesburg, South Africa.

July

653 Learning Disabilities Association of America International Conference
4156 Library Road
Pittsburgh, PA 15234-1349

412-341-1515
Fax: 412-344-0224
E-mail: info@ldaamerica.org
http://www.ldaamerica.org

The largest meeting on learning disabilities (LD) in the world. Disabled, parents, various educators and administrators. The conference follows a general theme set by LDAA.

Febuary, March
95 booths with 2600 attendees and 300 exhibits

Andrea Turkheimer, Conference Coordinator

National

654 ACSI Teachers' Convention
Assocation of Christian Schools International
731 Chapel Hills Drive
Colorado City, CO 80920

719-528-6906
800-367-0798
Fax: 562-690-6234
E-mail: exhibitors@acsi.org
http://www.acsi.org

Educational convention for administrators, school board members, and early educators to assist and encourage staff and volunteer development throughout the year.

50000 attendees

Ken Smitherman, President
Janet Stump, Public Relations

655 ASCD Annual Conference & Exhibit Show
Association for Supervision & Curriculum
1703 N Beauregard Street
Alexandria, VA 22311

703-578-9600
800-933-2723
Fax: 703-575-5400
E-mail: member@ascd.org
http://www.ascd.org

Explore the big ideas in education today, or examine new developments in your content area or grade level. Stretch your professional development learning into new areas, or pick an issue you care about most and examine it in depth.

April
12000 attendees

Barbara Gleason, Public Information Director
Christy Guilfoyle, Public Relations Specialist

656 AZLA/MPLA Conference
Arizona Library Association
14449 N 73rd Street
Scottdale, AZ 85260

480-998-1954
Fax: 480-998-7838
E-mail: meetmore@aol.com
http://www.azla.org

Advance the education advantages of the state through libraries, and to promote general interest in library extension (traveling libraries).

October
90+ booths with 2,000 attendees

Christine Bailey, Conference Administrator
Deanna Anderson, Exhibitor & Registration Mgn

657 Advocates for Language Learning Annual Meeting
Kansas City School District
301 E Armour Boulevard #620
Kansas City, MO 64111-1259

301-808-8291

Designed for both language instruction and language learning, the Conference is attended by language teachers, school administrators, directors, principals and parents at the elementary level.

October

Pat Barr-Harrison, Conference Contact

658 American Association School Administrators National Conference on Education
801 N Quincy Street
Suite 700
Arlington, VA 22203

703-528-0700
Fax: 703-841-1543
E-mail: info@aasa.org
http://www.aasa.org

For school superintendents, assistant superintendents, central office staff and those aspiring to the superintendency.

Paul Houston, Executive Director
Marilyn Maury, Conference Assist. Director

659 American Association for Employment in Education Annual Conference
American Association for Employment in Education
3040 Riverside Drive
Suite 125
Columbus, OH 43221

614-485-1111
Fax: 614-485-9609
E-mail: aaee@osu.edu
http://www.aaee.org

Disseminate information on the educational marketplace, and job search process. Promote ethical standards and practices in the employment process. Promote dialogue and cooperation among institutions

which prepare educators andinstitutions which provide employment opportunities.

November
20 booths with 150-200 attendees

BJ Bryant, Executive Director
Chris Barton, Project Coordinator

660 American Association for Higher Education: Annual Assessment Conference
American Associations for Higher Education
1 Dupont Circle NW
Suite 360
Washington, DC 20036-1137

202-293-6440
Fax: 202-293-0073
E-mail: info@aahe.org
http://www.aahe.org

Bringing together trendsetters - the individuals, institutions, and coalitions in North America and beyond - who demonstrates the courage and imagination to act on the pressing issues of our time.

20 booths with 1700 attendees

Joyce DePass, Conference Director
Robert Mundhenk, Assessment Director

661 American Association for Higher Education: Learning to Change Conference
American Associations for Higher Education
1 Dupont Circle NW
Suite 360
Washington, DC 20036-1137

202-293-6440
Fax: 202-293-0073
E-mail: info@aahe.org
http://www.aahe.org

Widens the circle of faculty and administrators interested in higher education.You will be engaged and excited by a rich mix of learning and networking events.

March
20 booths with 1000 attendees

Joyce DePass, Conference Director
Clara Lovett, President

662 American Association for Higher Education: Summer Academy, Organizing for Learning
American Associations for Higher Education
1 Dupont Circle NW
Suite 360
Washington, DC 20036-1137

202-293-6440
Fax: 202-293-0073
E-mail: info@aahe.org
http://www.aahe.org

Team-based, project-centered experience focused on undergraduate change initiatives that enhance student learning.

July
300 attendees

Joyce DePass, Convention Director

663 American Association of Colleges for TeacherEd Annual Meeting and Exhibits
1307 New York Avenue NW
Suite 300
Washington, DC 20005-4701

202-293-2450
Fax: 202-457-8095

E-mail: aacte@aacte.org
http://www.aacte.org

Identifying and meeting the learning needs of teacher education deans and faculty.

Feb
75 booths with 2400 attendees

Sharon P Robinson, President/CEO
Judy A Beck, VP Professional Development

664 American Association of French Teachers Conference
American Association of French Teachers
Mailcode 4510
Southern Illinois University
Carbondale, IL 62901-4510

618-453-5731
Fax: 618-453-5733
E-mail: aatf@frenchteachers.org
http://www.frenchteachers.org/convention

Takes place in French-speaking areas where our members can benefit from immersion in a French-speaking culture. Representing the French language in North America and to encourage the dissemination, both in the schools and in thegeneral public, of knowledge concerning all aspects of the culture and civilization of France and the French-speaking world.

July
1100 attendees

Dr Jayne Abrate, Executive Director

665 American Association of Physics Teachers National Meeting
One Physics Ellipse
College Park, MD 20740-4129

301-209-3300
Fax: 301-209-0845
E-mail: aapt-meet@aapt.org
http://www.aapt.org

Gives members the opportunity to network, discuss innovations in teaching methods and share the results of research about teaching and learning.

January & August

Carol Heimpel, Director of Meetings
Maria Elena Khoury, Program Director

666 American Association of School Administrators Annual Convention
American Association of School Administrators
801 N Quincy Street
Suite 700
Arlington, VA 22203-1730

703-528-0700
Fax: 703-528-2146
E-mail: info@aasa.org
http://www.aasa.org

To support and develop effective school system leaders who are dedicated to the highest quality public education for all children.

Marilynn Maury, Conference Assist. Director
Paul Houston, Executive Director

667 American Association of School Librarians National Conference
American Library Association
50 E Huron Street
Chicago, IL 60611

312-280-4386
800-545-2433
Fax: 312-664-7459

E-mail: aasl@ala.org
http://www.ala.org/aasl

An open conference holding seminars, workshops and tours of local libraries and facilities.

October
3,000 attendees

Laura Hayes, Conference Program Officer
Stephanie Hoerner, Conference Services Manager

668 American Association of Sex Educators, Counselors & Therapists Conference
PO Box 5488
Richmond, VA 23220-0488

804-644-3288
Fax: 804-644-3290
E-mail: aasect@aasect.org
http://www.aasect.org

For professionals and affiliated groups with a focus on continuing education for license renewal.

May
50 booths with 400-500 attendees

Helen Bush, Conference Co-Chair
William Finger, Conference Co-Chair

669 American Camping Association National Conference
American Camping Association
5000 State Road 67 N
Martinsville, IN 46151-7902

765-342-8456
Fax: 765-342-2065
E-mail: conference@ACAcamps.org
http://www.acaamps.org

Each year our community comes together to share the work we do and to explore opportunities for the future. With new directions, exciting and creative improvements, and added value for all attendees, the 2005 ACA National Conferenceoffers you essential opportunities.

Februrary
175 booths with 1500 attendees

Peg Smith, CEO
Kim Bruno, Marketing Manager

670 American Council on Education Annual Meeting
American Council on Education
1 Dupont Circle NW
Washington, DC 20036-1110

202-939-9410
Fax: 202-833-4760
E-mail: annualmeeting@ace.nche.edu
http://www.acenet.edu/meeting/index.cfm

The social compact that has governed and financed U.S. higher education for more than 50 years. A compact among government, citizens, and institutions has made postsecondary education broadly accessible. Join us as we explore theimplications behind this highly politicized and provocative topic.

February
74 booths

Stephanie Marshall, Meeting Services Director
Wendy Bresler, Program Planning

671   American Council on the Teaching of Foreign Languages Annual Conference
700 S Washington Street
Suite 210
Alexandria, VA 22314

703-894-2900
Fax: 703-894-2905
E-mail: morehouse@actfl.org
http://www.actfl.org

Annual convention, the largest meeting of second language educators in the US and the only national convention in the continental US for teachers of Chinese, French, Russian, German, Italian, Japanese, Spanish and other languages. Itis the professional forum for all languages, and all levels of instruction and the largest exhibition of teaching materials and technology in support of foreign language instruction in the US.

November
250 booths with 5,000+ attendees

Roberta Morehouse, Convention Coordinator
Bret Lovejoy, Executive Director

672   American Counseling Association Annual Convention
American Counseling Association
5999 Stevenson Avenue
Alexandria, VA 22304-3302

703-823-9800
800-347-6647
Fax: 703-823-0252
E-mail: rhayes@counseling.org
http://www.counseling.org

Counseling: A Creative Force in the Fabric of Life. Development of professional counselors, advancing the counseling profession, and using the profession and practice of counseling to promote respect for human dignity and diversity.

March, April

Robin Hayes, Convention & Meeting Contact
Dawn Tullis, Convention & Meeting Contact

673   American Education Finance Association Annual Conference & Workshop
American Education Finance Association
5249 Cape Leyte Drive
Sarasota, FL 34242-1805

941-349-7580
Fax: 941-349-7580
http://www.aefa.cc

Information and discussion relating to critical issues in education finance for administrators, directors and principals.

March
3000 attendees

Marge Plecki, President
Ed Steinbrecher, Executive Director

674   American Educational Research Association Annual Meeting
1230 17th Street NW
Washington, DC 20036-3078

202-223-9485
Fax: 202-775-1824
E-mail: 2005annualmtg@aera.net
http://www.aera.net

Contains exhibiting college and secondary school text publishers, software and hardware manufacturers that emphasize such applications as test development, test scoring and applications.

April
120 booths with 12M attendees

James Mears, Meetings Manager
Robert Smith, Director

675   American Educational Studies Association
Tennessee Technical University
PO Box 5193
Cookeville, TN 38505-0001

931-372-3101
Fax: 931-372-6319

Encourages research and the improvement of teaching in various curriculum areas.

November

Harvey Neufeldt, Conference Contact

676   American Indian Science & Engineering Society Annual Conference
AISES
PO Box 9828
Albuquerque, NM 87106

505-765-1052
Fax: 505-765-5608
E-mail: info@aises.org
http://www.aises.org

Issues of science and technological advances in regard to the various American Indian cultures and possible opportunities in North America. Workshops, seminars, cultural ceremonies, and a job fair with opportunities for employment orreceiving scholarships for future academics.

November
3000 attendees

Cristy Davies, Events Coordinator
Pamela Silas, Executive Director

677   American Library Association Annual Conference
American Library Association
50 E Huron Street
Chicago, IL 60611-2795

312-280-3219
800-545-2433
E-mail: ala@ala.org
http://www.ala.org

Bi-Annual conference for librarians.

June/January

Yvonne McLean, Conference Coordinator
Keith Michael Fiels, Executive Director

678   American Mathematical Society
American Mathematical Society
201 Charles Street
Providence, RI 02904

401-455-4000
800-321-4267
Fax: 401-331-3842
E-mail: meet@ams.org
http://www.ams.org

Information on joint mathematics meetings, publications, and professional services of the American Mathematical Society.

January

Diane Saxe, Meetings Director

679 **American Montessori Society Conference**
281 Park Avenue S
6th Floor
New York, NY 61020

212-358-1250
Fax: 212-358-1256
E-mail: east@amshq.org
http://www.amshq.org

Promotes quality Montessori education for all children from birth to 18 years of age.

May
75 booths with 1000 attendees

Richard A Ungerer, Executive Director
Marcy K Krever, Communication Director

680 **American Psychological Association Annual Conference**
750 1st Street NE
Washington, DC 20002-4241

202-336-6020
800-374-2721
Fax: 202-336-5919
E-mail: convention@apa.org
http://www.apa.org/convention05

A national conference attended by psychologists from around the world. The conference has workshops, lectures, discussions, roundtables and symposiums.

August

13,000 attendees

Ronald F LeVant, President

681 **American Public Health Association Annual Meeting**
American Public Health Association
800 I Street NW
Washington, DC 20001

202-777-2742
Fax: 202-777-2534
E-mail: edward.shipley@alpha.org
http://www.apha.org/meetings

The premier platform to share successes and failures, discover exceptional best practices and learn from expert colleagues and the latest research in the field.

November
650 booths with 13000 attendees

Diane Lentini, Meeting Information Contact
Karla Pearce, Meeting Information Contact

682 **American School Health Association's National School Conference**
7263 State Route 43
PO Box 708
Kent, OH 44240-5960

330-678-1601
Fax: 330-678-4526
E-mail: asha@ashaweb.org
http://www.ashaweb.org

Attendees include school nurses, health educators, health counselors, physicians and students. During the five-day conference, presentations are made by ASHA members, government officials and health education professionals.

October
40 booths with 700 attendees

Mary Bamer Ramsier, Meeting Planner
Susan F Wooley, Executive Director

683 **American Speech-Language-Hearing Association Annual Convention**
ASHA
10801 Rockville Pike
Rockville, MD 20852-3226

301-897-5700
800-638-8255
Fax: 301-571-0457
E-mail: convention@asha.org
http://www.asha.org

A scientific and professional conference of speech-language pathology, audiology and other professionals.

Annual
November
400 booths with 12,000 attendees

Arlene A Pietranton, Executive Director

684 **American Technical Education Association Annual Conference**
American Technical Education Association
800 6th Street N
Wahpeton,, ND 58076-0002

701-671-2240
Fax: 701-671-2260
E-mail: betty-krump@ndscs.nodak.edu
http://www.ateaonline.org

Over 350 administrators/directors and faculty of various technical institutes, junior colleges, universities and colleges, with 40 exhibitors. Topics cover all aspects of computer assisted instruction, distance education and technicaleducation.

March
35 booths with 700 attendees and 75 exhibits

Betty Krump, Executive Director

685 **Annual Academic-Vocational Integrated Curriculum Conference**
National School Conference Institute
2525 East Arizona
Biltmore Circle, Suite 240
Phoenix, AZ 85069-7527

602-778-1030
800-242-3419
Fax: 602-778-1032
http://www.nscinet.com

Two pre-conference workshops: Comprehensive Career Guidance K-12, and Curriculum Integration: A New Level of Learning. Conference will also hold over 50 breakout sessions.

March

686 **Annual Challenging Learners with Untapped Potential Conference**
National School Conference Institute
2525 East Arizona
Biltmore Circle, Suite 240
Phoenix, AZ 85016

602-778-1030
800-242-3419
Fax: 602-778-1032

Two pre-conference workshops: The necessary ingredients for success, and Trends; identification strategies. Conference will also hold over 60 breakout sessions.

February

Carl Boyd, President

687   Annual Conference on Hispanic American Education
National School Conference Institute
2525 East Arizona
Biltmore Circle, Suite 240
Phoenix, AZ 85016

> 602-778-1030
> 800-242-3419
> Fax: 602-778-1032

Two pre-conference workshops: Hispanic educational success: What schools can do to meet the challenge, and Closing the Hispanic achievement gap: A K-16 strategy using real data and standards-based professional development. Conferencewill also hold over 60 breakout sessions.

April

688   Annual Effective Schools Conference
National School Conference Institute
2525 East Arizona
Biltmore Circle, Suite 240
Phoenix, AZ 85069-7527

> 602-778-1030
> 800-242-3419
> Fax: 602-778-1032

Two pre-conference workshops: Making the right changes at the district level to assure successful, sustainable school reform, and The challenges of high standards, accurate assessments, and meaningful accountability. Conference willalso hold over 70 breakout sessions.

Bill Daggett

689   Annual Ethics & Technology Conference
Loyola University
820 N Michigan Avenue
School of Business
Chicago, IL 60611-2103

> 312-915-7394
> E-mail: rkizior@luc.edu
> http://www.ethicstechconference.org

The primary goal of the conference is to continue the interdisciplinary dialogue about ethical and social challenges triggered by the rapid diffusion of information technology.

June

Dr Ronald Kizior, Conference Chair
Dr Mary Malliaris, Program Chair

690   Annual Microcomputers in Education Conference
Arizona State University
PO Box 870101
Tempe, AZ 85287-0908

> 480-965-9700
> Fax: 480-965-4128
> E-mail: info@mec.asu.edu
> http://mec.asu.edu

The conference provides a forum to explore emerging educational technology and draws administrators, teachers, researchers, professionals and technology specialists from Arizona and throughout the country. Conference sessions coverK-12 through university-level applications, and target beginner through experienced users.

March
81 booths with 1,200+ attendees and 80+ exhibits

Dr Gary Bitter, Conference Director
Julie Solomon, Event Coordinator, Sr

691   Annual NCEA Convention & Exposition
National Catholic Educational Association
1077 30th Street NW
Suite 100
Washington, DC 20007-3852

> 202-337-6232
> Fax: 202-333-6706
> E-mail: convasst@ncea.org
> http://www.ncea.org

For all Catholic educators. 700 special exhibits, 400 engaging sessions and dozens of outstanding speakers.

Annually
April

Sue Arvo, Convention/Exposition Dir.
Stacey Svendgard, Exposition Coordinator

692   Annual Technology & Learning Conference
National School Boards Association
1680 Duke Street
Alexandria, VA 22314

> 703-838-6722
> 800-950-6722
> Fax: 703-683-7590
> E-mail: info@nsba.org
> http://www.nsba.org

The latest education technology and the most innovative programming.

October

Anne L Bryant, Executive Director
Sandy Folks, General Conference Contact

693   Association for Advancement of Behavior Therapy Annual Convention
305 7th Avenue
New York, NY 10001-6008

> 212-647-1890
> Fax: 212-647-1865
> E-mail: mebrown@aabt.org
> http://www.aabt.org

Psychologists, psychology faculty and students, and counselors with information on behavior modification, counseling and guidance and mental health issues.

November
2,000 attendees

Mary Ellen Brown, Convention Manager
Mary Jane Eimer, Executive Director

694   Association for Behavior Analysis Annual Convention
Association for Behavior Analysis
1219 South Park Street
Kalamazoo, MI 49001

> 269-492-9310
> Fax: 269-492-9316
> E-mail: convention@abainternational.org
> http://www.abainternational.org

Psychologists, psychology faculty and students, counselors and social workers are among the attendees of this conference offering over 25 exhibitors. The conference is research and education oriented.

43 booths
Maria E Malott, PhD, Conference Contact

695 Association for Education in Journalism and Mass Communication Convention
AEJMC
234 Outlet Pointe Boulevard
Columbia, SC 29210-5667

803-798-0271
http://www.aejmc.org/convention

Featuring the latest in technology as well as special sessions on teaching, research and public service in the various components of journalism and mass communication — from advertising and public relations to radio and televisionjournalism to media management and newspapers.

August
1,500 attendees

Fred Williams, Convention Manager
Jennifer McGill, Executive Director

696 Association for Persons with Severe Handicaps Annual Conference
29 W Susquehanna Avenue
Suite 210
Baltimore, MD 21204

410-828-8274
Fax: 410-828-6706
E-mail: info@tash.org
http://www.tash.org

Provides a forum for individuals with disabilities, families, researchers, educators, scholars, and others to create dialogue around creating action for social and systems reform.

December
2,500 attendees

Kelly Nelson, Conference Coordinator
Nancy Weiss, Executive Director

697 Association for Play Therapy Conference
Association for Play Therapy
2050 N Winery Avenue
Suite 101
Fresno, CA 93703-2831

559-252-2278
Fax: 559-252-2297
E-mail: info@a4pt.org
http://www.a4pt.org

Dedicated to the advancement of play therapy. APT is interdisciplinary and defines play therapy as a distinct group of interventions which use play as an integral component of the therapeutic process.

October
1000 attendees

Kathryn Lebby, Events Coordinator
Bill Burns, Executive Director

698 Association for Science Teacher Education Science Annual Meeting
The Association For Science Teacher Education
5040 Haley Center
Auburn, AL 36849

972-690-2496
http://www.aste.chem.pitt.edu

Offers programs in science, mathematics and environmental education with a wide variety of teachers and professors attending.

January

Paul Kuerbis, Conference Chair

699 Association for Supervision & Curriculum Development Annual Conference
ASCD
1703 N Beauregard Street
Alexandria, VA 22311-1717

703-578-9600
800-933-2723
Fax: 703-575-5400
E-mail: member@ascd.org
http://www.ascd.org

Explore the big ideas in education today, or examine new developments in your content area or grade level. Stretch your professional development learning into new areas, or pick an issue you care about most and examine it in depth.

300 booths with 1,100+ attendees

Barbara Gleason, Public Information Director
Christy Guilfoyle, Public Relations

700 Association for the Advancement of International Education
San Diego State University
College of Extended Studies
5250 Campanile Drive
San Diego, CA 92182

619-594-2877
Fax: 619-594-3648
E-mail: ajenkins@mail.sdsu.edu
http://www.aaie.org

Provides the organizational leadership to initiate and promote an understanding of the need for and the support of American/International education.

February
70 booths with 550 attendees

Annie Jenkins, Executive Assistant
Richard Krajcar, Executive Director

701 Association for the Education of Gifted Underachieving Students Conference
PO Box 221
Mountain Lakes, NJ 07046

651-962-5385
http://www.aegus1.org

Attended by teachers, professors, administrators and social workerss, this conference deals with cultural awareness and education of the disabled and gifted students.

April

Lois Baldwin, President
Terry Neu, Vice President

702 Association for the Study of Higher Education Annual Meeting
Michigan State University
424 Erickson Hall
East Lansing, MI 48824

517-432-8805
Fax: 517-432-8806
E-mail: ashemsu@msu.edu
http://www.ashe.ws/index.htm

Promotes collaboration among its members and others engaged in the study of higher education.

November

Gary Rhoades, President

703 **Association of American Colleges & Universities Annual Meeting**
Association of American Colleges & Universities
1818 R Street NW
Washington, DC 20009-1604
202-387-3760
Fax: 202-265-9532
http://www.aacu-edu.org

Bringing together college educators from across institutional types, disciplines, and departments. Providing participants with innovative ideas and practices, and shaping the direction of their educational reform efforts.

January
1,200 attendees

Carol Geary, President
Ross Miller, Director of Programs

704 **Association of Community College TrusteesConference**
1233 20th Street NW
Suite 605
Washington, DC 20036-2907
202-775-4667
Fax: 202-223-1297
http://www.acct.org

Exists to develop effective lay governing board leadership to strengthen the capacity of community colleges to achieve their missions on behalf of their communities.

1000 attendees

Ray Taylor, President/CEO
Lila Farmer, Conference Logistics Coord.

705 **Association of Science-Technology Centers Incorporated Conference**
Association of Science-Technology Centers Incorp.
1025 Vermont Avenue NW
Suite 500
Washington, DC 20005-3516
202-783-7200
Fax: 202-783-7207
E-mail: conference@astc.org
http://www.astc.org

An organization of science centers and museums dedicated to furthering the public understanding of science. ASTC encourages excellence and innovation in informal science learning by serving and linking its members worldwide andadvancing the common goals.

October
165 booths with 1600 attendees

Cindy Kong, Meetings/Conference Director
Gareth Rees, Meetings/Conference Coord.

706 **CHADD: Children & Adults with Attention Deficit/Hyperactivity Disorder**
CHADD
8181 Professional Place
Suite 150
Landover, MD 20785
301-306-7070
800-233-4050
Fax: 301-306-7090
http://www.chadd.org

National non-profit organization which offers advocacy, information and support for patients and parents of children with attention deficit disorders. Maintains support groups, provides a forum for continuing education about ADHD, andmaintains a national resource center for information about ADD.

October
60 booths with 1,500 attendees

Alison Harris, Conference Coordinator
Peg Nichols, Communications Director

707 **Center for Appalachian Studies & Services Annual Conference**
East Tennessee University
PO Box 70556
Johnson City, TN 37614-0918
423-439-7865
Fax: 423-439-7870
E-mail: asa@marshal.edu
http://www.cass.etsu.edu/

Sponsor educational programs and public service activities that enhance the quality of life in Appalachia and that empower people to live more effectively within the region.

March

Elizabeth Fine, Conference Contact

708 **Center for Applications of PsychologicalType Biennial Education Conference**
2815 NW 13th Street
Suite 401
Gainesville, FL 32609
352-375-0160
800-777-2278
Fax: 352-378-0503
E-mail: fields@capt.org

Promotes the practical application and ethical use of psychological type. Conference sponsored by Center for Applications of Psychological Type (CAPT).

July

Jim Weir, Executive Director

709 **Center for Gifted Education and Talent Development Conference**
University of Connecticut
2131 Hillside Road
Unit 3007
Storrs Mansfield, CT 06269-3007
860-486-4826
Fax: 860-486-2900
http://www.gifted.uconn.edu

Conducts research on methods and techniques for teaching gifted and talented students.

Annual

Sally M Reis, Professor

710 **Center for Rural Education and Small Schools Annual Conference**
College of Education
124 Bluemont Hall
1100 Mid-Campus Drive
Manhattan, KS 66506
785-532-5886
Fax: 785-532-7304
E-mail: barbhav@ksu.edu
http://www.coe.ksu.edu/CRESS/conference.html

Annual conference is held which includes over 200 administrators, directors, principals, teachers and

Conferences & Trade Shows / National

university faculty discussing all aspects of education in rural areas.

October
200 attendees and 20 exhibits

Barbara Havlicek, Assistant Director
Robert Newhouse, Director

711 Center on Disabilities Conference
Students with Disabilities Resources
1811 Nordhoff
Northridge, CA 91330-8264

818-677-2684
Fax: 818-677-4932
E-mail: sdr@csun.edu
http://www.csun.edu/cod

This is a comprehensive, international conference, where all technologies across all ages; disabilities; levels of education and training; employment; and independent living are addressed. It is the largest conference of its kind!

March
130 booths with 4,000+ attendees

Marina Sanchez, Participant Coordinator
Sonya Hernandez, Speakers Coordinator

712 Choristers Guild's National Festival & Directors'
Conference
Choristers Guild
2834 W Kingsley Road
Garland, TX 75041-2498

972-271-1521
Fax: 972-840-3113
E-mail: conferences@mailcg.org
http://www.choristersguild.org

Enables leaders to nurture the spiritual and musical growth of children and youth.

September

Jim Rindelaub, Director

713 Closing the Gap
526 Main Street
PO Box 68
Henderson, MN 56044-0068

507-248-3294
Fax: 507-248-3810
E-mail: info@closingthegap.com
http://www.closingthegap.com

Provides information on the use of computer technology by and for persons with disabilities and the opportunities available for education and independent learning.

October
150+ booths with 2400 attendees

Maryann Harty, Advertising/Exhibits Manager
Connie Kneip, VP/General Manager

714 Computers on Campus National Conference
University of South Carolina
937 Assembly Street
Suite 108
Columbia, SC 29208

803-777-2260
Fax: 803-777-2663
E-mail: confs@rcce.scarolina.edu
http://www.rcce.sc.edu/coc

This conference provides a national forum for showcasing computer-based instructional models, discussing successful experiences in computer networking, making effective use of computer support in

academic assessment, and usingcomputer technology to enhance total student development.

November

Dr Andrew A Sorensen, President
Margaret M Lamb, Media Relations Director

715 Conference for Advancement of Mathematics
Teaching
Texas Education Agency
William Travis Building
1701 N Congress Avenue
Austin, TX 78701-1402

512-463-9734
Fax: 512-463-9838
http://www.tea.state.tx.us

Exhibits educational materials useful to mathematics teachers.

July
175 booths with 7.5M-8M attendees

Anita Hopkins, Conference Contact

716 Conference on Information Technology
League for Innovation in the Community College
4505 East Chandler Boulevard
Suite 250
Phoenix, AZ 85048

480-705-8200
Fax: 480-705-8201
E-mail: harris@league.org
http://www.league.org

The premier showcase of the use of information technology to improve teaching and learning, student services, and institutional management. Celebrating 18 years of excellence, CIT features a technologically sophisticated and topicallydiverse program that enables educators to explore and expand their use of technology.

October
3,000 attendees

Mary K Harris, Conference Manager
Robin Piccilliri, Conference Specialist

717 Council for Advancement and Support of
Education
1307 New York Avenue NW
Suite 1000
Washington, DC 20005-4701

202-328-2273
Fax: 202-387-4973
E-mail: conference@case.org
http://www.case.org

Offers numerous opportunities in the United States, Canada, Mexico, mainland Europe, the United Kingdom, and even online, to network with colleagues and learn about Institutional Advancement.

Fall/Winter

Lucinda Lyon-Vaiden, Sr Conference Program Coord.
Richard Salatiello, Sr Conference Program Coord.

718 Council for Exceptional Children Annual
Convention
The Council for Exceptional Children
1110 N Glebe Road
Suite 300
Arlington, VA 22201-5704

703-620-3660
800-224-6830
Fax: 703-264-1637
E-mail: victore@cec.sped.org
http://www.cec.sped.org

largest profesional orgenization dedicated to improving educationl results of individuals with disabilities and the gifted. 50,000 members

April
437 booths with 6541 attendees and 299 exhibits
Victor Erickson, Marketing Manager

719 EDUCAUSE
4772 Walnut Street
Suite 206
Boulder, CO 80301-2408

303-449-4430
Fax: 303-440-0461
E-mail: bwilliams@educause.edu
http://www.educause.edu

EDUCAUSE is an international, nonprofit association whose mission is to help shape and enable tranformational change in higher education through the introduction, use, and management of information resources and technologies inteaching, learning, scholarship, research, and institutional management. EDUCAUSE publishes books, magazines, monographs, executive briefings, white papers, and other materials that provide thoughtful leadership to effect transformational change inhigher education.

October
4,000+ attendees and 180 exhibits
Brian L Hawkins, President
Beverly Williams, Conference Director

720 Education Technology Conference
Society for Applied Learning Technology
50 Culpeper Street
Warrenton, VA 20186

540-347-0055
800-457-6812
Fax: 540-349-3169
E-mail: info@lti.org
http://www.salt.org

For over 30 years the Society has sponsored conferences which are educational in nature and cover a wide range of application areas such as distance learning, interactive multimedia in education and training, development ofinteractive instruction materials, performance support systems applications in education and training, interactive instruction delivery, and information literacy.

August
20 booths with 400 attendees
Raymond G Fox, President

721 Educational Publishing Summit: Creating Managing & Selling Content
Association of Educational Publishers
510 Heron Drive
Suite 201
Logan Township, NJ 08085

856-241-7772
Fax: 856-241-0709
E-mail: mail@edpress.org
http://www.edpress.org

Offers diverse sessions about the latest publishing educational and technology trends and an incomparable opportunity for those in every avenue of the educational publishing community, at every career level, to network with peers.

June
Charlene F Gaynor, Executive Director
Stacey Pusey, Communications Manager

722 Educational Theatre Association Conference
Educational Theatre Association
2343 Auburn Avenue
Cincinnati, OH 45219-2815

513-421-3900
Fax: 513-421-7055
E-mail: mpeitz@edta.org
http://www.edta.org

Promotes and strengthens theatre in education-primarily middle school and high school. Sponsors an honor society, various events, numerous publications, and arts education advocacy activities.

September
220 attendees
Michael J Peitz, Executive Director
Christopher Hunt, Marketing Director

723 Embracing an Inclusive Society: The Challenge for the New Millennium
National Multicultural Institute
3000 Connecticut Avenue NW
Suite 438
Washington, DC 20008-2556

202-483-0700
Fax: 202-483-5233
E-mail: nmci@nmci.org
http://www.nmci.org

Brings together practitioners from across the country and around the world to explore diversity and multiculturalism in both personal and professional contexts. Leaders from academia, business, and government present the latestthinking and action on diversity issues to conference participants.

June
Maria Morukian, Conference Coordinator
Elizabeth P Salett, President

724 Foundation for Critical Thinking Regional Workshop & Conference
Foundation for Critical Thinking
PO Box 220
Dillon Beach, CA 94929

800-833-3645
Fax: 707-878-9111
E-mail: cct@criticalthinking.org
http://www.criticalthinking.org

Investigates and reports on the value and use of analytical thinking programs and curriculum in the classroom.

July
Dr Linda Elder, President

725 Gifted Child Society Conference
190 Rock Road
Glen Rock, NJ 07452-1736

201-444-6530
Fax: 201-444-9099
E-mail: admin@gifted.org
http://www.gifted.org

Provides educational enrichment and support for gifted children through national advocacy and various programs.

September
250 attendees
Janet L Chen, Executive Director

726 High School Reform Conference
National School Conference Institute
PO Box 37527
Phoenix, AZ 85069-7527

602-371-8655
Fax: 602-371-8790
http://www.nscinet.com

Conference will cover restructuring the high school schedule, designing curriculum and instruction, assessments and student motivation, and information and communication technology. Being held in Las Vegas, Nevada.

April
Robert Lynn Canady
Rick Stiggins

727 Hitting the High Notes of Literacy
Proliteracy Volunteers of America
1320 Jamesville Avenue
Syracuse, NY 13210

315-422-9121
Fax: 315-422-6369
E-mail: lvanat@aol.com
http://www.literacyvolunteers.org

Conference dealing with literacy issues.

November
50 booths with 1,000 attendees

Peggy May, Conference Manager

728 INFOCOMM Tradeshow
8401 Eagle Creek Parkway
Suite 700
Savage, MN 55378

952-894-6280
800-582-6480
Fax: 877-894-6918
E-mail: chief@chiefmfg.com
http://www.chiefmfg.com

Chief Manufacturing is the leader in total mounting solutions for presentation systems. Based in Minnesota, Chief designs, manufactures and distributes worlwide, a full line of mounts, lifts and accessories for LCD/DLP/CRT projectors,large flat panel displays and small flat panel displays.

Cristy Sabatka, Sales Admin. Coordinator

729 Improving Student Performance
National Study of School Evaluation
1699 E Woodfield Road
Suite 406
Schaumburg, IL 60173-4958

847-995-9080
Fax: 847-995-9088
E-mail: schoolimprovement@nsse.org
http://www.nsse.org

A comprehensive guide for data-driven and research-based school improvement planning.

November

730 Increasing Student Achievement in Reading, Writing, Mathematics, Science
National School Conference Institute
PO Box 37527
Phoenix, AZ 85069-7527

602-371-8655
Fax: 602-371-8790
http://www.nscinet.com

March
Orlando Taylor
George Nelson

731 Independent Education Consultants Association Conference
3251 Old Lee Highway
Suite 510
Fairfax, VA 22030-1504

703-591-4850
800-888-4322
Fax: 703-591-4860
E-mail: requests@IECAonline.com
http://www.IECAonline.com

National professional association of educational counselors working in private practice. Provides counseling in college, secondary schools, learning disabilities and wilderness therapy programs. Publishes a monthly newsletter called'Insight'.

Spring & Fall
400 booths with 800 attendees

Mark H Sklarow, Executive Director
Susan Millburn, Conference Manager

732 Infusing Brain Research, Multi-Intelligence, Learning Styles and Mind Styles
National School Conference Institute
Crowne Plaza Hotel
Phoenix, AZ 85069-7527

602-371-8655
Fax: 602-371-8790
http://www.nscinet.com

Two pre-conference workshops: Intelligences in the curriculum and classroom, and What do educators need to know about the human brain? Conference will also hold over 50 breakout sessions.

February
Geoffrey Caine
Renate Caine

733 Instant Access: Critical Findings from the NRC/GT
University of Connecticut
362 Fairfield Road
Storrs, CT 06269

860-486-4826
Fax: 860-486-2900
http://www.gifted.uconn.edu

Conference sponsored by the National Research Center on the Gifted and Talented.

March

734 Integrated/Thematic Curriculum and Performance Assessment
National School Conference Institute
Hyatt Regency Hotel
Phoenix, AZ 85069-7527

602-371-8655
Fax: 602-371-8790
http://www.nscinet.com

Two pre-conference workshops: The door to restructuring, aligning, and integrating the curriculum for the 21st century, and Moving assessment to the top of the charts. Conference will also hold over 50 breakout sessions.

February
Heidi Hayes Jacobs
Roger Taylor

**735   International Performance Improvement
Conference Expo
International Society for Performance**
1400 Spring Street
Suite 260
Silver Spring, MD 20910

301-587-8570
Fax: 301-587-8573
E-mail: info@ispi.org
http://www.ispi.org

April
60 booths with 1500 attendees
Ellen Kaplan, Conference Manager

**736   Iteachk
Society for Developmental Education**
10 Sharon Road
PO Box 577
Peterborough, NH 03458

800-462-1478
Fax: 800-337-9929
http://www.iteachk.com

National conference for kindergarten teachers.

**737   Journalism Education Association
Kansas State University**
103 Kedzie Hall
Manhattan, KS 66506-1505

785-532-5532
Fax: 785-532-5563
E-mail: lindarp@ksu.edu
http://www.jea.org/

An organization of about 2,300 journalism teachers and
advisers, offers two national teacher-student
conventions a year, quarterly newsletter and magazines,
bookstore and national certification program. This
association serves as aleader in scholastic press freedom
and media curriculum.

Linda Puntrey, Executive Director

**738   Literacy Volunteers of America National
Conference**
5795 Widewaters Parkway
Syracuse, NY 13214-1846

315-472-0001
Fax: 315-422-6369

Workshops to promote literacy and reading.

November
30 booths with 1000+ attendees
Peg Price, Conference Contact

**739   Lutheran Education Association Convention
Lutheran Education Association**
7400 Augusta Street
River Forest, IL 60305-1402

708-209-3343
Fax: 708-209-3458
E-mail: lea@crf.cuis.edu
http://www.lea.org

Equip, and affirms educators in Lutheran ministries,
helping them become excellent educators.

Kathy Slupik, Executive Assistant
Jonathan C Laabs, Executive Director

740   Master Woodcraft Inc.
1312 College Street
Oxford, NC 27565

919-693-8811
800-333-2675
Fax: 919-693-1707

Announcement and classroom chalkboards, arts and craft
supplies. Cork bulletin boards, dry erase melamine

boards, easels, floor, table top, lap boards (white
melamine dry erase, chalkboard and magnetic).

2 booths with 6 exhibits
Louis B Moss, Manager

741   Meeting the Tide of Rising Expectations
39 Nathan Ellis Highway
PMB #134
Mashpee, MA 02649-3267

508-539-8844
Fax: 508-539-8868
E-mail: nasdtec@attbi.com
http://www.nasdtec.org

NASDTEC is the National Association of State Directors
of Teacher Education and Certification. It is the
organization that represents professional standards
boards and commissions and state departments of
education in all 50 states.

October
Roy Einreinhofer, Executive Director

**742   Modern Language Association Annual
Conference**
10 Astor Place
New York, NY 10003-6935

646-576-5260

Promotes and explains the role of language, specifically
second language training, in education.

December
Maribeth Kraus, Conference Contact

743   Music Educators National Conference
1806 Robert Fulton Drive
Reston, VA 20191-4348

703-860-4000
Fax: 703-860-2652
http://www.menc.org

Provides a forum for music educators and other musical
development in the school setting.

April

**744   Music Teachers Association National Conference
Music Teachers National Association**
441 Vine Street
Suite 505
Cincinnati, OH 45202-2811

513-421-1420
888-512-5278
Fax: 513-421-2503
E-mail: mtnanet@mtna.org
http://www.mtna.org

Supports and supplies music teachers with information
on development and training.

March
160 booths with 2000 attendees
Rachel Kramer, Assistant Executive Director

745   NAAEE Member Services Office
410 Tarvin Road
Rock Spring, GA 30739

706-764-2926
Fax: 706-764-2094
E-mail: csmith409@aol.com
http://www.naaee.org

Exhibitors seeking to integrate and expand
environmental education in school systems and in
nonformal settings as well.

September

746 NAFSA: National Association of International Educators
1875 Connecticut Avenue NW
Suite 1000
Washington, DC 20009-5747

202-737-3699
800-836-4994
Fax: 202-737-3657

Annual meeting of professionals in the field of international education, with exhibits of services and products relating to international education.

May
150 booths with 5,500 attendees

Marlene M Johnson, Director/CEO

747 NSTA Educational Workshops
National Science Teachers Association
1840 Wilson Boulevard
Arlington, VA 22201-3000

703-522-5413
888-400-6782
Fax: 703-522-5413
http://www.nsta.org/programs/new

To promote excellence and innovation in science teaching and learning for all.

748 National Academy Foundation Annual Institute for Staff Development
National Academy Foundation
39 Broadway
Sutie 1640
New York, NY 10006

212-635-2400
Fax: 212-635-2409
http://www.naf-education.org

Features several days of intensive peer training, industry presentations, and networking opportunities, with the goal of ensuring that Academy programs are seccessful, focused on the improvement of public education, and dedicatedtoward helping young people of all backgrounds continue their education as a step toward building careers.

July

749 National Alliance of Black School Educators Conference
2816 Georgia Avenue NW
Washington, DC 20001-3819

202-483-1549
800-221-2654
Fax: 202-608-6319
E-mail: nabse@nabse.org
http://www.nabse.org

Teachers, principals, specialists, superintendents, school board members and higher education personnel. Workshops, plenary sessions, public forums, networking and fellowship.

November
300 booths with 3,500 attendees

Quentin R Lawson, Conference Manager

750 National Art Education Association Annual Convention
National Art Education Association
1916 Association Drive
Reston, VA 20191-1590

703-860-8000
Fax: 703-860-2960
E-mail: naea@dgs.dgsys.com
http://www.naea-reston.org

Containing booths of art education products and services. New art techniques, skills, and knowledge; renowned speakers and teachers; new ideas for art instruction and curriculum.

March
171 booths with 5,000 attendees

Kathy Duse, Conference Manager

751 National Association for Bilingual Education
1030 15th Street NW
Suite 470
Washington, DC 20005-4018

202-898-1829
Fax: 202-789-2866
E-mail: nabe@nabe.org
http://www.nabe.org

Contains publishers and Fortune 500 companies displaying educational materials and multi-media products.

March
350 booths with 8,000 attendees

Delia Pompa, Executive Director
Josephina Velasco, Conference Manager

752 National Association for College Admission Counseling Conference
Nat'l Association for College Admission Counseling
1631 Prince Street
Alexandria, VA 22314-2818

703-836-2222
Fax: 703-836-8015
http://www.nacac.com

Membership association offering information to counselors and guidance professionals working in the college admissions office.

September
142 booths with 4,000 attendees

Shanda T Ivory, Chief Officer Communications
Amy C Vogt, Assistant Director

753 National Association for Girls and Womenin Sports Yearly Conference
1900 Association Drive
Reston, VA 20191-1599

703-476-3450
800-213-7193
Fax: 703-476-4566
E-mail: nagws@aahperd.org
http://www.aahperd.org/nagws/nagws

An association providing information for girls and women in sports.

March/April
280 booths with 6,000 attendees

Sandra Sumner, Director

754 National Association for Multicultural Education
NAME National Office
1511 K Street NW
Suite 430
Washington, DC 20005

202-628-6263
Fax: 202-628-6264
E-mail: nameorg@erols.com
http://www.inform.umd.edu/name

Keynote speakers and presenters are individuals and educators who value and appreciate diversity and multiculturalism, seek creative approaches to educative practices, and strive to promote social justice through education andtraining.

755 **National Association for Year-Round Education Annual Conference**
5404 Napa Street
Suite A
San Diego, CA 92110-7319

619-276-5296
Fax: 858-571-5754
E-mail: info@nayre.org
http://www.NAYRE.org

Fosters the study of year-round education as a way to improve educational programs in terms of providing quality education and adapting the school calendar to community and family living patterns Disseminates information aboutyear-round education.

February
60 booths with 1200 attendees

Marilyn J Stenvall, Executive Director
Don Jeffries, Exhibit Coordinator

756 **National Association of Biology Teachers Conference**
12030 Sunrise Valley Drive
Sutie 110
Reston, VA 20191

703-264-9696
800-406-0775
Fax: 703-264-7778
E-mail: office@nabt.org
http://www.nabt.org

Contains textbooks, laboratory and classroom supplies and equipment.

November
140 booths with 1,700 attendees

Lisa Walker, Director of Conventions

757 **National Association of Elementary School Principals Conference**
1615 Duke Street
Alexandria, VA 22314-3406

703-684-3345
Fax: 703-518-6281
E-mail: lburnett@naesp.org
http://www.naesp.org

Products and services in the educational market shopping area. Industry leaders offer practical ways from curriculum resources and instructional aids to fundraising ideas and playground equipment.

April
300 booths

Marguerite Leishman, Director
Lani Burnett, Exhibit Manager

758 **National Association of Independent Schools Conference**
1620 L Street NW
11th Floor
Washington, DC 20036-5695

202-973-9700
Fax: 202-973-9790
E-mail: bassett@nais.org
http://www.nais.org

Publications, statistics, professional development for independent schools.

February/March
166 booths

Peter D Relic, President

759 **National Association of Private Schools for Exceptional Children Conference**
1522 K Street NW
Suite 1032
Washington, DC 20005-1211

202-408-3338
Fax: 202-408-3340
E-mail: napsec@aol.com
http://www.napsec.com

This in an annual conference that is held for administrators/directors/principals and private school educators.

January
300 attendees and 8 exhibits

Barb DeGroot, Manager

760 **National Association of School Psychologists Annual Convention**
4340 EW Highway
Suite 402
Bethesda, MD 20814

301-657-0270
Fax: 301-657-0275
E-mail: center@naspweb.org
http://www.nasponline.org

Gathering of school psychologists and related professionals, offering over 500 workshops, seminars, symposia, papers, presentations and exhibits.

April
100 booths with 4000 attendees

Glenn Reighart, Director Meeting/Conference

761 **National Association of Student Financial Aid Administrators**
1129 20th Street NW
Suite 400
Washington, DC 20036-5020

202-785-0453
Fax: 202-785-1487

Exhibits computer hardware and software and banks participating in student loan programs.

July
105 booths

Babara Kay Gordon, Conference Contact

762 **National Association of Teachers' Agencies Conference**
National Association of Teachers' Agencies
799 Kings Highway
Fairfield, CT 06432

203-333-0611
Fax: 203-334-7224
E-mail: fairfieldteachers@snet.net
http://www.jobsforteachers.com

Mark King, Secretary/Treasurer

763 **National Black Child Development Institute Annual Conference**
1101 15th Street NW
Suite 900
Washington, DC 20005-2618

202-833-2220
800-556-2234
Fax: 202-833-8222
E-mail: moreinfo@ndcdi.orh
http://www.nbcdi.org

Offers information to counselors and social service workers on African-American Children.

October

Vicki Pinkston, Vice President
Derrell Winder, Program Associate

764 National Catholic Education Association Annual Convention & Exposition
National Catholic Educational Association
1077 30th Street NW
Suite 100
Washington, DC 20007-3852

202-337-6232
Fax: 202-333-6706
http://www.ncea.org

The convention features general sessions with outstanding speakers, special convention liturgies, and a large exposition of many products and services to benefit the educator.

April
675 booths
Leonard DeFiore, President

765 National Center for Montessori Education Conference
PO Box 1543
Roswell, GA 30077-1543

770-434-1128

Focuses on developing and maintaining the Montessori Education system.

March
Kristen Cook, Conference Contact

766 National Coalition for Sex Equity in Education
PO Box 534
Annandale, NJ 08801

908-735-5045
Fax: 908-735-9674
E-mail: info@ncsee.org
http://www.ncsee.org

The only national organization for gender equity specialists and educators. Individuals and organizations committed to reducing sex role stereotyping for females and males. Services include an annual national training conference, aquarterly newsletter and a membership directory. Members may join task forces dealing with equity related topics such as computer/technology issues, early childhood, male issues, sexual harassment prevention, sexual orientation and vocational issues.

September
200 attendees
Theodora Martin, Business Manager

767 National Coalition of Alternative Community Schools
PO Box 15036
Santa Fe, NM 87506-5036

505-474-4312
888-771-9171

A clearinghouse for information regarding alternatives in education for all ages, including home education. Yearly conference, newsletters, mentored Teacher Education Program.

April
Ed Nagel, National Office Manager

768 National Coalition of Title 1-Chapter 1 Parents Conference
Edmonds School Building
9th & D Streets NE
#201
Washington, DC 20002

202-547-9286

Provides lectures and presentations aimed at Chapter 1 parents and professionals.

October

769 National Conference on Student Services
Magna Publications
2718 Dryden Drive
Madison, WI 53704

608-227-8109
800-206-4805
Fax: 608-246-3597
E-mail: carriej@magnapubs.com
http://www.magnapubs.com

Target hard to reach college audiences, and attract campus leaders. Each 4-day conference has potential for the right exhibitor. A second conference will be held in Boston.

October
15 booths with 500 attendees
Carrie Jenson, Conference Manager
David Burns, Associate Publisher

770 National Congress on Aviation and Space Education
Omni Rosen Hotel
Orlando, FL

334-953-5095
E-mail: bspick@cap.af.mil
http://www.cap.af.mil

Provides educators with the tools that make classroom learning fun.

April

771 National Council of Higher Education
National Education Association (NEA)
1201 16th Street NW
Washington, DC 20036-3207

202-822-7162
Fax: 202-822-7624
E-mail: nche@nea.org
http://www.nea.org

Assessing a 20 year journey of the academy.

February, March
400 attendees
Rachel Hendrickson, Coordinator

772 National Council on Alcoholism & Drug Abuse
8790 Manchester Road
Saint Louis, MO 63144

314-962-3456
Fax: 314-968-7394
E-mail: ncada@ncada-stl.org
http://www.ncada-stl.org

A not-for-profit community health agency serving the metropolitian St. Louis area, provides educational materials on substance abuse and addiction, information and referral services, prevention and intervention.

Harriet Kopolow, Director Prevention

773 National Dropout Prevention Center/Network Conference
205 Martin Street
Clemson, SC 29631-1555

864-656-2599
800-443-6392
Fax: 864-656-0136
E-mail: ndpc@clemson.edu
http://www.dropoutprevention.com

Concentrating on programs and services for educators and counselors who deal with at-risk students.

October
100 booths with 1000 attendees

Jay Smink, Executive Director
John Peters, Network Coordinator

774 National Education Association-Retired
National Education Association (NEA)
1201 16th Street NW
Washington, DC 20036-3207

202-822-7125
Fax: 202-822-7624
http://www.nea.org/retired

Serves as a resource in the maintenance of quality public education, promotes improved services and legislation for seniors, provides training for members and serves as a vehicle for local input to the National Education Association.

150 attendees

Deborah C Jackson, Manager
Todd Crenshaw, Coordinator

775 National Guild of Community Schools of theArts
Conference
520 8th Avenue
Suite 302, 3rd Floor
New York, NY 10018

212-268-3337
Fax: 212-268-3995
E-mail: info@natguild.org
http://www.nationalguild.org

The National Guild of Community Schools of the Arts fosters and promotes the creation and growth of high-quality arts education in communities across the country. The Guild provides community arts organizations with multiple levelsof support, including training, advocacy, information resources, and high-profile leadership in arts education.

November
15 booths with 300 attendees and 15 exhibits

Noah Xifr, Director Membership/Oper.

776 National Head Start Association Annual
Conference
1651 Prince Street
Alexandria, VA 22314-2818

703-739-0875
Fax: 703-739-0878
http://www.nhsa.org

Seeks to advance program development, policy and promote training of the Head Start program professionals.

May

A Renee Battle, CMP, Conference Contact
Ruby Lewis-Riar, Conference Assistant

777 National Institute for School and Workplace
Safety Conference
160 Internation Parkway
Suite 250
Heathrow, FL 32746

407-804-8310
Fax: 407-804-8306
http://www.nisws.com/

Believes that every school and workplace must implement school and workplace safety standards.

April
80 attendees

Wolfgang Halbig, CEO/Manager

778 National Parent-Teacher Association Annual
Convention & Exhibition
1787 Agate Street
Eugene, OR 97403-1923

503-346-4414

Addresses parent-teacher involvement in education. Includes lectures, workshops and seminars for parents and professionals.

June

779 National Reading Styles Institute Conference
179 Lafayette Drive
Syosset, NY 11791-3933

512-224-4555

This conference addresses reading instruction and the problems of illiteracy.

July

Juliet Carbo, Conference Contact

780 National Rural Education Annual Convention
National Rural Education Association
230 Education
Colorado State University
Fort Collins, CO 80523-0001

970-491-1101
Fax: 970-491-1317

Exchanges ideas, practices and better ways to enhance rural educational school systems.

October
30 booths with 400 attendees

Joseph T Newlin, PhD, Conference Contact

781 National Rural Education AssociationAnnual
Convention
National Rural Education Association
820 Van Vleet Oval
Room 227
Norman, OK 73019

Fax: 405-325-7959
E-mail: bmooney@ou.edu
http://www.nrea.net

The NREA will be the leading national organization providing services which enhance educational opportunities for rural schools and their communities.

October
35 booths with 400 attendees

Bob Mooneyham, Executive Director

782 National School Boards Annual Conference
1680 Duke Street
Alexandria, VA 22314-3493

703-838-6722
Fax: 703-683-7590
http:// ww.nsba.org/itte

The nation's largest policy and training conference for local education officials on national and federal issues affecting public schools in the U.S.

March
7,000 attendees and 300 exhibits
Sandra Folks, Conference/Meetings Coord.
Karen Miller, Exhibit Services Manager

783 National School Conference Institute
11202 N 24th Street
Suite 103
Phoenix, AZ 85029
602-371-8655
888-399-8745
Fax: 602-371-8790
http://www.nscinet.com

Our purpose is to increase every student's opportunity for academic success.

784 National School Supply & Equipment Association
NSSEA Essentials
8380 Colesville Road
Suite 250
Silver Spring, MD 20910-3297
301-495-0240
800-395-9350
Fax: 301-495-3330
E-mail: awatts@nssea.org
http://www.nessa.org

Features exhibits of school supplies, instructional materials, and equipment.

March
1200 booths with 5,000 attendees and 700 exhibits
Desnuna Spencer, Author
Tim Holt, President/CEO

785 National Society for Experiential Education Conference
National Society for Experiential Education
3509 Haworth Drive
Suite 207
Raleigh, NC 27609-7235
919-787-3263
Fax: 919-787-3381
E-mail: info@nsee.org
http://www.nsee.org

To foster the effective use of experience as an integral part of education, in order to empower learners and promote the common good.

October
600-700 attendees

786 National Student Assistance Conference
1270 Rakin Drive
Suite F
Troy, MI 48033-2843
800-453-7733
Fax: 800-499-5718

Learn to maintain and improve safe, drug free schools, student assistance programs. Develop skills to implement the Principles of Effectiveness. Choose from workshops and skill building sessions.

787 National Women's History Project Annual Conference
7738 Bell Road
Windsor, CA 95492-8518
707-838-6000
Fax: 707-838-0478
http://www.nwhp.org

Posters, reference books, curriculum materials and biographies of American women in all subjects for grades K-12.

July
72 attendees
Molly Murphy MacGregor, Conference Manager

788 New Learning Technologies
Society for Applied Learning Technology
50 Culpeper Street
Warrenton, VA 20186
540-347-0055
800-457-6812
Fax: 540-349-3169
E-mail: info@lti.org
http://www.salt.org

To provide a comprehensive overview of the latest in research, design, and development in order to furnish attendees information on systems that are applicable to their organizations.

789 North American Montessori Teachers' Association
13693 Butternnut Road
Burton, OH 44021
440-834-4011
Fax: 440-834-4016
E-mail: staff@montessori-namta.org
http://www.montessori-namta.org/

Professional organization for Montessori teachers and administrators. Services include The NAMTA Journal and other publications, videos and slide shows. Conferences in January and March.

David J Kahn, Executive Director

790 Parents as Teachers National Center Conference
2228 Ball Drive
Saint Louis, MO 63146
314-432-4330
Fax: 314-432-8963
E-mail: patnc@patnc.org
http://www.patnc.org

An international early childhood parent education and family support program designed to enhance child development and school achievement through parent education accessible to all families. Serves families throughout pregnancy anduntil their child enters kindergarten, usually age 5.

April-May
40 booths with 1400+ attendees
Susan S Stepleton, President/CEO
Cheryl Dyle-Palmer, Director Operations

791 Retention in Education Today for All Indigenous Nations
National Conference Logistics Center
University of Oklahoma
555 E Constitution Street, Suite 208
Norman, OK 73072-7820
405-325-3760
800-203-5494
Fax: 405-325-7075
E-mail: tmonnard@ou.edu
http://www.conferencepros.com

National conference designed to disscuss and share retention strategies for indigenous students.

Theresa Monnard, Program Coordinator

792 SERVE Conference
SERVE
PO Box 5367
Greensboro, NC 27435
336-315-7400
800-755-3277
Fax: 336-315-7457
E-mail: jsanders@serve.org
http://www.serve.org

The Regional Educational Laboratories are educational research and development organizations supported by contracts with the US Education Department, National Insitiute for Education Sciences. Specialty area: Expanded LearningOpportunities.

October-November

Jack Sanders, Executive Director

793 School Equipment Show
830 Colesville Road
Suite 250
Silver Spring, MD 20910-3297
301-495-0240
Fax: 301-495-3330

Annual show featuring exhibits from manufacturers of school equipment such as bleachers, classroom furniture, lockers, playground and athletic equipment, computer hardware, software, etc.

February

Elizabeth Bradley, Conference Contact

794 Sexual Assault and Harassment on Campus Conference
c/o Sexual Conference
PO Box 1338
Holmes Beach, FL 34218-1338
800-537-4903
http://www.ed.mtu.edu/safe

Topics include gender based hate crime, sexual assault investigators, generational legacy of rape, innovations in the military, sexual harrassment in K-12, updates on date-rape drugs and many more. Hosted by the Hyatt Orlando Hotel inKissimmee, Florida.

Karen McLaughlin, Conference Co-Chair
Alan McEvoy, Conference Co-Chair

795 Society for Research in Child Development Conference
5720 S Woodlawn Avenue
Chicago, IL 60637-1603
773-702-7700
Fax: 773-702-9756

Working to further research in the area of child development and education.

March/April
40 booths

Barbara Kahn, Conference Contact

796 Teacher Link: An Interactive National Teleconference
Center for the Study of Small/Rural Schools
555 E Constitution Street
Room 138
Norman, OK 73072-7820
405-325-1450
Fax: 405-325-7075
E-mail: jcsimmons@ou.edu
http://cssrs.ou.edu

Prevention Series

Spring
5 booths with 100 attendees

Jan C Simmons, Director

797 Teachers of English to Speakers of Other Languages Convention and Exhibit
700 S Washington Street
Alexandria, VA 22314
703-836-0774
Fax: 703-836-6447
http://www.tesol.org

Leading worldwide professional development opportunity. Simulating program of presentations sponsored by nineteen interest sections, a half-dozen caucus groups and TESOL's advocacy division as well as sessions invited especially fortheir relevance to our work and our students.

March
245 booths with 8000 attendees

Bart Ecker, Manager

798 Teaching for Intelligence Conference
SkyLight
2626 S Clearbrook Drive
Arlington Heights, IL 60005
847-290-6600
800-348-4474
Fax: 877-260-2530
E-mail: info@irisskylight.com
http://www.iriskylight.com

Focuses on student achievement, brain-based learning and multiple intelligences.

April

799 Technology & Learning Schooltech Exposition & Conference
212-615-6030
http://www.SchoolTechExpo.com

Over 150 targeted sessions specifically designed for all education professionals: technology directors, teachers, principals, superintendents and district administrators.

800 Technology Student Conference
Technology Student Association
1914 Association Drive
Reston, VA 20191-1538
703-860-9000
Fax: 703-758-4852
http://www.tsawww.org

Devoted to the needs of technology education students and supported by educators, parents, and business leaders who believe in the need for a technologically literate society.

June
2,500 attendees

Rosanne White, Conference Manager

801 Technology in 21st Century Schools
National School Conference Institute
PO Box 37527
Phoenix, AZ 85069-7527
602-371-8655
Fax: 602-371-8790
http://www.nscinet.com

Conference will cover managing the Internet, literacy skills, Web Site designs, short and long term planning, creating curriculum, and staff development. Being held at the Boston Park Plaza Hotel in Boston, Massachusetts.

July
Alan November

802 Technology, Reading & Learning Difficulties Conference
International Reading Association
19 Calvert Court
Piedmont, CA 94611

510-594-1249
888-594-1249
Fax: 510-594-1838
http://www.trld.com

Focuses on ways to use technology for reading, learning difficulties, staff development, adult literacy, and more.

January

803 Training of Trainers Seminar
Active Parenting Publishers
810 Franklin Court SE
Suite B
Marietta, GA 30067-8943

770-429-0565
800-825-0060
Fax: 770-429-0334
E-mail: cservice@activeparenting.com
http://www.activeparenting.com

Delivers quality education programs for parents, children and teachers to schools, hospitals, social services organizations, churches and the corporate market.

Dana McKie, Training Coordinator

804 USC Summer Superintendents' Conference
University of Southern California, School of Ed.
Waite Room 901
Los Angeles, CA 90089-0001

213-740-2182
Fax: 213-749-2707
E-mail: lpicus@bcf.usc.edu

A select group of educational leaders nationwide engaged in reform practices offer discussions with nationally renowned speakers; tour innovative schools; and network with colleagues from the United States, Great Britain and Australia.

Lawrence O Picus, Conference Director
Carolyn Bryant, Conference Coordinator

Northeast

---

805 Clonlara School Annual Conference Home Educators
Clonlara Home Based Education Programs
1289 Jewett Street
Ann Arbor, MI 48104-6201

734-769-4511
Fax: 734-769-9629
E-mail: info@clonlara.org
http://www.clonlara.org

Clonlara School is committed to illuminating educational rights and freedoms through our actions and deep dedication to human rights and dignity.

June
300 attendees
Terri Wheeler, Associate Director

806 Connecticut Library Association
PO Box 85
Williamantic, CT 06226-0085

860-465-5006
Fax: 860-465-5004
E-mail: kmcnulty@avon.lib.ct.us

Holds a conference in April and publishes a journal.

April
1000 attendees and 100 exhibits

Karen McNulty, President
Mary Rupert, Manager

807 Hoosier Science Teachers Association Annual Meeting
5007 W 14th Street
Indianapolis, IN 46224-6503

317-244-7238
Fax: 317-486-4838

Papers, workshops, demonstrations and presentations in each area of science.

February
78 booths

Edward Frazer, Conference Contact

808 Illinois Library Association Conference
Illinois Library Association
33 W Grand Avenue
Suite 301
Chicago, IL 60610-4306

312-644-1896
Fax: 312-644-1899
E-mail: ila@ila.org
http://www.ila.org

More than 70 program sessions, exploring nearly every facet of library services, from building projects and professional recruitment to storytelling and the latest revisions of AACR2.

September
2,400+ attendees

Cyndi Robinson, Conference Manager
Bob Doyle, Executive Director

809 Illinois Vocational Association Conference
230 Broadway
Suite 150
Springfield, IL 62701-1138

217-585-9430
Fax: 217-544-0208
E-mail: iva@eosinc.com

Equipment and supplies, publications, teaching aids, computers and food services.

February
75 booths with 600 attendees

Karen Riddle, Conference Contact

810 National Association of Student Financial Aid Administrators
1129 20th Street NW
Suite 400
Washington, DC 20036-3453

202-785-0453
Fax: 202-785-1487

Exists to promote the professional preparation, effectiveness, and mutual support of persons involved in student financial aid administration.

May
40 booths
Suzy Allen, President

811 New Jersey School Boards Association Annual Meeting
413 W State Street
PO Box 909
Trenton, NJ 08605-0909
609-278-5233
Fax: 609-695-0413

School/office supplies, furniture, equipment, counseling services and more.

October
630 booths with 9,000 attendees

Wendy L. Wilson, Conference Contact

812 New York State Council of Student Superintendents Forum
111 Washington Avenue
Suite 104
Albany, NY 12210-2210
518-449-1063
Fax: 518-426-2229

Offers educational products and related services.

February
12 booths

Dr. Claire Brown, Conference Contact

813 Northeast Regional Christian Schools International Association
845 Silver Spring Plaza
Suite B
Lancaster, PA 17601-1183
717-285-3022
Fax: 717-285-2128

40 booths.

November

Alan Graustein, Conference Contact

814 Ohio Library Council Trade Show
35 E Gay Street
Suite 305
Columbus, OH 43215-3138
614-221-9057
Fax: 614-221-6234

Exhibits will offer products and services for library administrators and professionals.

May

Lori Hensley, Exhibits Manager

815 Ohio School Boards Association Capital Conference & Trade Show
700 Brooksedge Boulevard
Westerville, OH 43081-2820
614-891-6466

Provides school officials from Ohio an opportunity to gain information about products, equipment, materials and services.

November
425 booths

Richard Lewis, Conference Contact

816 Satellites and Education Conference
189 Schmucker Science Center
W Chester University
West Chester, PA 19383
610-436-1000
Fax: 610-436-2790
http://www.sated.org/eceos

The Satellite Educators Association was established in 1988 as a professional society to promote the innovative use of satellite technology in education and disseminate information nationally to all members.

March
15 booths with 200 attendees

Nancy McIntyre, Director

817 UNI Overseas Recruiting Fair
University of Northern Iowa
SSC #19
Cedar Falls, IA 50614-0390
319-273-2083
Fax: 319-273-6998
E-mail: overseas.placement@uni.edu
http://www.uni.edu/placement/overseas

About 160 recruiters from 120 schools in 80 countries recruit at this fair for certified K-12 educators.

February

Tracy Roling, Coordinator

818 Wisconsin Vocational Association Conference
44 E Mifflin Street
Suite 104
Madison, WI 53703-2800
608-283-2595
Fax: 608-283-2589

Trade and industry vendor equipment and book publishers.

April
50 booths

Linda Stemper, Conference Contact

Northwest

819 Montana High School Association Conference
1 S Dakota Street
Helena, MT 59601-5111
406-442-6010

School athletic merchandise.

January
15 booths

Dan Freund, Conference Contact

820 Nebraska School Boards Association Annual Conference
140 S 16th Street
Lincoln, NE 68508-1805
402-475-4951
Fax: 402-475-4961

60 booths exhibiting products and services directed at the public school market.

November

Burma Kroger, Conference Contact

821 North Dakota Vocational Educational Planning Conference
State Capitol
15th Floor
Bismarck, ND 58505
701-231-6032
Fax: 701-231-6052

August
30 booths

Ernest Breznay, Conference Contact

822 Pacific Northwest Library Association
Boise Public Library
715 Capitol Boulevard
Boise, ID 83702

208-384-4026
Fax: 208-384-4156
E-mail: sprice@pobox.ci.boise.id.us

Holds a conference in August and publishes a journal.

Susannah Price, President
Colleen Bell, Secretary

823 WA-ACTE Career and Technical Exhibition for Career and Technical Education
Washington Association for Career & Tech Education
PO Box 315
Olympia, WA 98507-0315

360-786-9286
Fax: 360-357-1491
E-mail: kal@wa-acte.org
http://www.wa-acte.org

August
40 booths with 1,000 attendees

Kathleen Lopp, Executive Director

Southeast

824 Association for Continuing Higher Education Conference
Trident Technical College
PO Box 118067
Charleston, SC 29423-8067

843-722-5546
Fax: 843-574-6470

15 tabletops.

October

Dr. Wayne Whelan, Executive VP

825 Center for Play Therapy Summer Institute
University of North Texas
PO Box 311337
Denton, TX 76203

940-565-3864
Fax: 940-565-4461
E-mail: cpt@coefs.coe.unt.edu
http://www.centerforplaytherapy.com

Encourage the unique development and emotional growth of children through the process of play therapy, a dynamic interpersonal relationship between a child and a therapist trained in play therapy procedures. The therapist provides the child with selected play materials and facilitates a safe relationship to express feelings, thoughts, experiences and behaviors through play, the child's natural medium of communication.

July
500 attendees

Garry Landreth PhD, Director

826 Missouri Library Association Conference
1306 Business 63 S
Suite B
Columbia, MO 65201

573-449-4627
Fax: 573-449-4655
E-mail: jmccartn@mail.more.net
http://www.mlnc.com/~mla/

The mission of the Missouri Library Network Corporation (MLNC) is to organize and deliver to its member libraries and other contracting entities OCLC-based information services, related electronic services and content, and training in the management and use of information.

October
75 booths with 400 attendees

Margaret Conroy, President
Jean Ann McCartney, Executive Director

827 National Youth-At-Risk Conference
Georgia Southern University
PO Box 8124
Statesboro, GA 30460

912-681-5557
Fax: 912-681-0306

Stresses education and development for professionals working with at-risk students.

February

Sybil Fickle, Conference Contact

828 Technology and Learning Conference
National School Boards Association
1680 Duke Street
Alexandria, VA 22314

703-838-6722
Fax: 703-683-7590
E-mail: info@nsba.org
http://www.nsba.org

This conference offers programs, equipment, services, and ideas. It will be held at the Dallas Convention Center.

Southwest

829 Children's Literature Festival
Department of Library Science
Sam Houston State University
PO Box 2236
Huntsville, TX 77341-2236

936-294-1614
Fax: 936-294-3780

This annual event is sponsored by the Department of Library Science at Sam Houston State University.

830 Colorado Library Association Conference
4350 Wadsworth Boulevard
Suite 340
Wheat Ridge, CO 80033

303-463-6400
Fax: 303-431-9752
E-mail: officemanager@cla-web.org

October
60 booths with 450 attendees

Tom Fry, President
Lorena Mitchell, Manager

831 Phoenix Learning Resources Conference
12 W 31st Street
New York, NY 10001-4415

212-629-3887
800-221-1274
Fax: 212-629-5648

Supplemental and remedial reading and language arts programs for early childhood, K-12, and adult literacy programs.

Alexander Burke, President
John Rothermich, Executive VP

832 **Southwest Association College and University Housing Officers**
Sam Houston State University
PO Box 2416
Huntsville, TX 77341-2416

936-294-1812
Fax: 936-294-1920

Products and services for college and university housing.

Febuary/March
45 booths

E Thayne King, Conference Contact

833 **Texas Classroom Teachers Association Conference**
PO Box 1489
Austin, TX 78767-1489

512-477-9415
Fax: 512-469-9527

Educational materials, fundraising and jewelry.

February
150 booths

Jan Lanfear, Conference Contact

834 **Texas Library Association Conference**
3355 Bee Cave Road
Suite 401
Austin, TX 78746-6763

512-328-1518
800-580-2852
Fax: 512-328-8852
E-mail: pats@txla.org
http://www.txla.org

Established in 1902 to promote and improve library services in Texas.

March
750 booths with 6,000 attendees

Herman L Totten, President
Kathy Pustyovsky, Meetings Manager

835 **Texas Vocational Home Economics Teachers Association Conference**
3737 Executive Center Drive
Suite 210
Austin, TX 78731-1633

512-794-8370

July/August

Terry Green, Conference Contact

836 **Western History Association Annual Meeting**
University of New Mexico
Mesa Room 1080
Albuquerque, NM 87131-0001

505-277-5234
Fax: 505-277-6023

Exhibits by book sellers.

October
45 booths

Paul Hutton, Conference Contact

General

837 **Accuracy Temporary Services Incorporated**
1431 E 12 Mile Road
Madison Hieghts, MI 48071-2653
248-399-0220

Educational consultant for public and private schools.

Howard Weaver, President

838 **Add Vantage Learning Incorporated**
5430 LB Freeway
Suite 210
Dallas, TX 75240
214-503-6800
Fax: 214-503-6800

Management and educational consultant for the general public.

Jim Pepitone, Chairman

839 **Advance Infant Development Program**
2232 D Street
Suite 203
LaVerne, CA 91750-5409
909-593-3935
Fax: 909-593-7969

Business and educational consultant for general trade.

840 **Aguirre International Incorporated**
480 E 4th Avenue
Unit A
San Mateo, CA 94401-3349
650-373-4900
Fax: 650-348-0260

Educational, data, market analysis, statistical and research consultants for US Government Agencies.

Edward Aguirre, President

841 **American International Schools**
2203 Franklin Road SW
Roanoak, VA 24014-1109
405-343-3719

Educational and marketing consulting for colleges and universities.

Andrew Hurst, President
Lewis C Smith Jr, Executive VP

842 **Area Cooperative Educational Services**
350 State Street
North Haven, CT 06473-3108
203-498-6836
Fax: 203-498-6890

Educational consultant for school systems.

Alfred H Hopkins, Jr, COO

843 **Aspira of Penna**
2726 N 6th Street
Philadelphia, PA 19133-2714
215-229-1226

Educational consultant for educational institutions.

Oscar Cardona, President

844 **Association for Refining Cross-Cultured International**
Japanese American Cultural Center
442 S San Pedro Street
Suite 402
Los Angeles, CA 90012
213-620-0696
800-304-0018
Fax: 213-620-0930
E-mail: info@arcint.com
http://www.arcint.com

Educational consultants for international studies.

Chiey Nomura, Director

845 **Association of Christian Schools International**
PO Box 35097
Colorado Springs, CO 80935-3509
719-594-4612
Fax: 719-531-0631
E-mail: david_wilcox@acsi.org
http://www.acsi.org

Educational consultant for Christian Schools.

Ken Smitherman, President

846 **Auerbach Central Agency for Jewish Education Incorporated**
7607 Old York Road
Elkins Park, PA 19027-3010
215-635-8940
Fax: 215-635-8946

Educational consultants.

Helene Tigay, Executive Director

847 **Basics Plus**
921 Aris Avenue
Suite C
Metairie, LA 70005-2200
504-832-5111
Fax: 504-832-5110

Educational consultants.

Scott Green, President

848 **Beacon Education Management**
112 Turnpike Road
Suite 107
Westborough, MA 01581
508-836-4461
800-789-1258
Fax: 508-836-2604
http://www.beaconedu.com

A K-12, education services company that offers contracted management services to public schools and charter school boards. Currently operating 27 charter schools in Massachusetts, Michigan, Missouri and North Carolina.

849 **Beverly Celotta**
13517 Haddonfield Lane
Gaitherburg, MD 20878
301-330-8803
E-mail: beverly.celotta@internet.mci.com

Provides psycological and educational services to organizations that serve children and parents.

850 **Bluegrass Regional Recycling Corporation**
360 Thompson Road
Lexington, KY 40508-2045
859-233-7300
Fax: 859-233-7787

Consultants for educational, training, and services for governments and school systems.

Douglas Castle, Chairman

851 CPM Educational Program
1233 Noonan Drive
Sacramento, CA 95822-2569
916-446-9936
Fax: 916-444-5263
Educational and training consultants for school districts.

Brian Hoey, Executive Director

852 Caldwell Flores Winters
2187 Newcastle Avenue
Suite 201
Cardiff, CA 92007-1848
760-634-4239
800-273-4239
Fax: 760-436-7357
E-mail: cfw@cts.com
Offers educational counsel to school districts.

853 Career Evaluation Systems
1024 N Oakley Boulevard
Chicago, IL 60622-3586
773-645-1363
800-448-7552
Fax: 773-772-5010
Testing instruments for vocational evaluation.

854 Carnegie Foundation for the Advancement of Teaching
555 Middlefield Road
Menlo Park, CA 94025-3443
650-566-5100
Fax: 650-326-0278
Educational consultant for the educational field.

Jacquelyn Tate, Assistant to President

855 Carney Sandoe & Associates
136 Bolyston Street
Boston, MA 02116-4608
617-542-0260
Fax: 617-542-9400
Educational consultant for private schools.

James H Carney, Chairman/President

856 Carter/Tardola Associates
419 Pleasant Street
Suite 307
Beloit, WI 53511
608-365-3163
Fax: 608-365-5961
E-mail: tardola@tucm.net
Evaluates program, administration, staff, resource and time organization, and utilization of resources. Proposal development, language skills development, diversity training.

H Elizabeth Tardola, Educational Consultant

857 Center for Educational Innovation
28 W 44th Street
New York, NY 10036-6600
212-302-8800
Fax: 212-302-0088

Educational consultant for private and commercial accounts.

Steven Kaln, Director

858 Center for Professional Development & Services
PO Box 789
Bloomington, IN 47402-0789
812-339-1156
800-766-1156
Fax: 812-339-0018
E-mail: curriculumaudit@pdkintl.org
http://www.pdkintl.org
Examines school district curriculum management system. Determines how effectively a school district designs and delivers its curriculum.

859 Center for Resource Management
2 Highland Road
East Kingston, NH 03827-3607
603-427-0206
Fax: 603-427-6983

Employment, human resources, educational, development, training, computer software, organizational and management consultants for Human Service Agencies and Educational Institutions/ Schools.

Mary Ann Lachat, Chairman

860 Child Like Consulting Limited
82 Santa Monica Avenue
Royal Palm Beach, FL 33411
800-487-6725
Fax: 561-795-0228
E-mail: clinic@aol.com
Training in literacy, music, classroom and learning center management.

861 Children's Educational Opportunity Foundation
901 McClain Road
Suite 802
Bentonville, AR-9242
479-273-6957
Fax: 479-273-9362
Educational consultant for institutions.

Fritz Steiger, President

862 Childs Consulting Associates
29516 Southfield Road
Southfield, MI 48076
248-569-2355
Fax: 248-569-2232
E-mail: info@childes.com
http://www.childs.com
Educational, schools and technology consultants for schools, banking and automotive industries.

Jeff Wale, President

863 Classroom
245 5th Avenue
Room 1901
New York, NY 10016-8728
212-545-8400
Fax: 212-481-7178
http://www.classroominc.org
Technology based curriculum and teacher professional development for middle school and high school use.

Shari Bloom, VP

864 Coalition of Essential Schools
1814 Franklin Street
Suite 700
Oakland, CA 94612

510-433-1451
Fax: 510-433-1455

The Coalition of Essential Schools (CES) is a leading comprehensive school reform organization, fundamentally changing the way people think about teaching and learning and transforming American education.

Hudi Podolsky, Executive Director

865 College Bound
18000 Studebaker Road
Cerritos, CA 90703-2679

562-860-2127
Fax: 562-860-1957

Educational consultants.

Johnnie Savoy, President

866 College Entrance Examination Board
45 Columbus Avenue
New York, NY 10023-6917

212-713-8215
Fax: 212-713-8304
E-mail: claire_jackson@brookline.mec.edu

Educational, research, testing and financial consultant for learning institutions and students.

867 Community Connections
2030 Sea Level Drive
Suite 350
Ketchikan, AK 99901-6057

907-225-5396
Fax: 907-225-1541

Educational consultant for the general public.

Bess Clark, Director

868 Community Foundation for Jewish Education
618 S Michigan Avenue
10th Floor
Chicago, IL 60605-1901

312-913-1818
Fax: 312-913-1763

Educational consultant for the general public and schools.

Howard Swibel, President

869 Connecting Link
387 Coopers Pond Drive
Siute 1
Lawrenceville, GA 30044-5231

770-979-5804
Fax: 770-931-6831

Business and educational consultants for teachers.

Dr. Bernard F Cleveland, President

870 Conover Company
2926 Hidden Hollow Road
Oshkosh, WI 54904

920-231-4667
Fax: 920-231-4809
E-mail: conover@execpc.com
http://www.conovercompany.com

Training and setting up workplace literacy programs; emotional intelligence assesment and skill enhancement; functional literacy software, career exploration and assessment software

Rebecca Schmitz, Member

871 Consortium on Reading Excellence
5855 Christie Avenue
Suite A
Emeryville, CA 94608-1923

510-595-4803

Educational consultant for public and private schools.

Bill Honing, President

872 Continuous Learning Group Limited Liability Company
Route 12
Box 245
Morgantown, WV 26505

304-284-0570
Fax: 304-599-7806
E-mail: clginfo@clg-online.com
http://www.clg-online.com

Educational consultants.

873 Corporate Design Foundation
20 Park Plaza
Suite 21
Boston, MA 02116

617-350-7097
Fax: 617-451-6355

Educational consultant for universities and colleges.

Peter G Lawrence, Chairman

874 Corporate University Enterprise
1483 Chain Bridge Road
McLean, VA 22102-5703

703-848-0070
Fax: 703-848-0071

Educational consultant for government concerns.

John H. Wells, President

875 Council for Aid to Education
342 Madison Avenue
Room 1532
New York, NY 10173-1599

212-661-5800
Fax: 212-661-9766

Non-profit educational consultant for government and commercial concerns.

Roger Benjamin, President

876 Council on Occupational Education
41 Perimeter Center E
North East
Atlanta, GA 30346-1903

770-396-3898
800-917-2081
Fax: 770-396-3790
E-mail: bowmanh@council.org
http://www.council.org

Managerial and educational consultant for post secondary technical education institutions.

Dr. Harry Bowman, President
Cindy Sheldon, Manager

877 Creative Learning Consultants
1610 Brook Lynn Drive
Dayton, OH 45432-1906

937-427-0530

Educational consulting for school districts, teachers, book stores and parents.

Nancy Johnson, President
Kathy Balsamo, VP

878 Creative Learning Systems
16510 Via Esprillo
San Diego, CA 92127-1708

858-592-7050
Fax: 858-675-7707

Educational consulting firm.

879 Dawson Education Cooperative
711 Clinton Street
Suite 201
Arkadelphia, AR 71923-5921

870-246-3077
Fax: 870-246-5892
E-mail: rds@dawson.dsc.k12.ar.us

Educational consulting group.

880 Dawson Education Service Cooperative
711 Clinton Street
Suite 201
Arkadelphia, AR 71923-5921

870-246-3077
Fax: 870-246-5892

Educational and organizational consultants for school districts

Patricia Lamb, Contact

881 Designs for Learning
1745 University Avenue W
St. Paul, MN 55104-3613

651-645-0200
Fax: 651-649-5490

Educational consultants for primary schools and the private sector.

J David Alley, President

882 Direct Instructional Support Systems
623 High Street
Worthington, OH 43085-4146

614-846-8946
Fax: 614-846-1794

Educational consultant for public and private agencies.

Dr Charles L Mand, President

883 Dr. Anthony A Cacossa
4300 N Charles Street
Apartment 9B
Baltimore, MD 21218-1052

410-889-1806
Fax: 410-889-1806

Assists schools in marketing academic programs that offer internship opportunities.

884 EPPA Consulting
1116 Comanche Trail
Georgetown, KY 40324-1071

502-867-0157
Fax: 502-867-0157
E-mail: eppa@juno.com

Strategic and operational planning.

Theo R Leverenz, PhD, Contact

885 East Bay Educational Collaborative
2658 E Main Road
Portsmouth, RI 02871-2608

401-245-4998

Business and educational consultant for member school districts.

Gerald Kowalczyk, Executive Director

886 East Central Educational Service Center
1601 Indiana Avenue
Connersville, IN 47331

765-825-1247
Fax: 765-825-2532
E-mail: harrison@ecesc.k12.in.us
http://www.ecesc.k12.in.us

Educational services for school districts in East Central Indiana.

William J Harrison, Executive Director

887 Edge Learning Institute
2217 N 30th Street 200
Tacoma, WA 98403-3320

253-272-3103
Fax: 253-572-2668

Educational consultants for the general public, commercial concerns, government agencies and school districts.

Shauni Rock, Contact

888 Edison Schools
521 5th Avenue
15th Floor
New York, NY 10175

212-419-1600
Fax: 212-419-1604
http://www.edisonschools.com

The country's largest private manager of public schools. Implemented its design in 79 public schools, including 36 charter schools, which it operates under mangement contracts with local school districts and charter school boards.

889 Education Concepts
9861 Strausser Street
Canal Fulton, OH 44614

330-497-1055
Fax: 330-966-8000
E-mail: info@ed-concepts.com
http://www.ed-concepts.com

Professional development programs for early childhood educators.

890 Education Data
1305 E Waterman
Witchata, KS 67211

800-248-4135

Expertise in organizational needs assessments.

891 Education Development Center
55 Chapel Street
Newton, MA 02158

617-969-7100
Fax: 617-244-3436
http://www.edc.org

Developing programs in science, mathematics, reading, writing, health and special education.

892 Education Management Consulting LLC
Diamond Silver Office Complex
24 Arnett Avenue, Suite 102
Lambertville, NJ 08530

609-397-8989
800-291-0199
Fax: 609-397-1999

E-mail: edragan@edmgt.com
http://www.edmgt.com

Consultation for schools on special education and administration consultation for lawyers working on education and school related issues.

Dr. Edward F Dragon, President

893 Educational Consultants of Oxford
10431 Highway 51 S
Courtland, MS 38620

601-563-8954

All areas of educational information services, tutoring, scholarship information, and non-traditional and overseas training.

894 Educational Credential Evaluators
PO Box 514070
Milwaukee, WI 53202-3470

414-289-3400
Fax: 414-289-3411
E-mail: eval@ece.org
http://www.ece.org

Evaluates foreign educational credentials.

895 Educational Data Service
236 Midland Avenue
Saddle Brook, NJ 07663-4604

973-340-8800
Fax: 973-340-0078

Educational and school consulting for Boards of Education.

Robert F O'Connor, President
Gilbert Wohl, VP

896 Educational Information & Resource Center
606 Delsea Drive
Sewell, NJ 08080

856-582-7000
Fax: 856-582-4206
E-mail: info@eirc.org
http://www.eirc.org

Programs and consulting services for schools, on many topics from teaching techniques to technical assistance.

897 Educational Resources
8910 W 62nd Terrace
Shawnee Mission, KS 66202-2814

913-362-4600
Fax: 913-362-4627

Educational consulting for colleges.

Michael Frost, President
Karen Harrison, VP

898 Educational Services Company
5730 W 74th Street
Indianapolis, IN 43278-1754

317-290-4100

Educational and management consulting for primary and secondary schools.

Douglas Cassman, President
William McMaster, Secretary

899 Educational Specialties
9923 S Wood Street
Chicago, IL 60643-1809

773-445-1000
Fax: 773-445-5574

Educational consultant for schools.

Elois W Steward, President

900 Educational Systems for the Future
14650 Viburnum Drive
Dayton, MD 21036

410-531-3737
Fax: 410-531-3939

E-mail: info@esf-protainer.com
http://www.esf-protainer,com

Development of teaching skills, training needs analysis, and training management.

901 Educational Technology Design Consultants
100 Allentown Parkway
Suite 110
Allen, TX 75002

972-727-1234
Fax: 972-727-1491
http://www.etdc.com/html/about_us.html

Developing system design for virtual campus control and support.

902 Educational Testing Service
Rosedale Road
Princeton, NJ 08541-0001

609-921-9000

Educational and professional consulting for schools.

Nancy S Cole, President
Sharon Robison, COO, Senior VP

903 Edusystems Export
820 Wisconsin Street
Walworth, WI 53184-9765

262-275-5761
Fax: 262-275-2009
E-mail: sales@edusystems.com;admin@edusystems.com

Expertise in educational systems.

904 Effective Schools Products
2199 Jolly Road
Suite 160
Okemos, MI 48864-5983

517-349-0941
Fax: 517-349-8852

Publishing consultants for schools, teachers, directors of planning and others in this field.

Ruth Lezotte, PhD, President

905 Effective Training Solutions
39355 California Street
Suite 207
Fremont, CA 94538-1447

510-797-6806
800-949-5035
Fax: 510-797-6805
E-mail: boris@trainingsuccess.com
http://www.trainingsucess.com

Design and implementation of training strategies. Proficiency training-performance improvement training.

Boris Levitsky, VP Marketing

906 Efficacy Institute
182 Felton Street
Waltham, MA 02453-4134

781-547-6060
Fax: 781-547-6077
E-mail: info@efficacy.org
http://www.efficacy.org

Non-profit, educational consultants for educational and community service institutions.

Jeff P Howard, President

907 Emerging Technology Consultants
216 Heritage Lane
New Brighton, MN 55112

651-639-3973
Fax: 651-639-3973

Consultants / General

Serves as a connection between technology producers
and the education and training industries.

Richard Pollak, Chief Executive Officer
Rubyanna Pollak, President

908 Epie Institute
103 Montauk Highway
Suite 3
Hampton Bays, NY 11946-4006

631-728-9100
Fax: 631-728-9228
E-mail: epie_inst@aol.com

Curriculum development, training and evaluation of
education products.

909 Epistemological Engineering
5269 Miles Avenue
Oakland, CA 94618-1044

510-653-3377
Fax: 510-428-1120
E-mail: publications@eeps.com

Educational consultants.

910 Examiner Corporation
1327 Delaware Avenue
St. Paul, MN 55118-1911

651-451-7360
800-395-6840
Fax: 651-451-6563
E-mail: examine@xmn.com
http://www.xmn.com

Educational and certification evaluation instruments.

911 Excell Education Centers
3807 Wilshire Boulevard
Los Angeles, CA 90010-3101

213-386-1953

Educational and planning consultants.

Raymond Hahl, Owner

912 FPMI Communications
707 Fiber Street NW
Huntsville, AL 35801-5833

256-539-1850
Fax: 256-539-0911
http://www.fmpi.com

Educational management consulting.

913 First District Resa
110 Zetterower Road
Statesboro, GA 30458-4257

912-842-5000
Fax: 912-842-5161

Educational consultants for the general public and
commercial concerns.

Kay Brown, Executive Director

914 Foundation for Educational Innovation
401 M Street SW
2nd Floor, Suite 1
Washington, DC 20024-2610

202-554-7400
Fax: 202-554-7401

Educational consultant for educational/school systems.

Archie Prioleau, President

915 George Dehne & Associates
203 Overlook Drive
Brewster, NY 10509-3836

845-279-6674

Educational and business consultants for commercial
concerns and colleges.

George Dehne, President

916 Health Outreach Project
825 Cascade Avenue
Atlanta, GA 30331-8362

404-755-6700

Educational consultants.

Sandra McDonald, President

917 Higher Education Consortium
2233 University Avenue W
Suite 210
St. Paul, MN 55104-1205

651-646-8831
Fax: 651-659-9421

Educational consultants.

Amy Sunderland, Executive Director

918 Highlands Program
1708 Peachtree Street NW
Atlanta, GA 30309-3915

404-872-9974
Fax: 404-872-9974

Educational consultants for educational institutions,
corporations and consumers.

Don Hutcheson, President

919 Howard Greene Associates
60 Post Road W
Westport, CT 06880-4208

203-226-4257
Fax: 203-226-5595

Educational consultants for school systems and
individuals.

Howard Greene, President

920 Huntley Pascoe
19125 N Creek Parkway
Bothel, WA 98011-8035

425-485-0900
Fax: 425-487-1825

Educational consultant for architects, utility companies,
computer facilities, school districts and hospitals.

Roger Huntley, President

921 Ingraham Dancu Associates
1265 Lakevue Drive
Butler, VA 16002

724-586-8761
Fax: 724-586-6638
E-mail: dedance@msn.com

Development planning for educational and industrial
clients.

Dr. Daniel Dancu, Contact

922 Innovative Learning Group
410 Elgin Avenue
Suite F
Forest Park, IL 60130-1780

708-488-1099

Educational consultants for schools and the general public.

Joseph Elliott, President

923 Innovative Programming Systems
9001poplar Bridge Road
Bloomington, MN 55437
612-835-1290

Development of instructional and training programs.

924 Insight
12 S 6th Street
Suite 510
Minneapolis, MN 55402-1510
612-338-5777

Educational consultants for commercial concerns.

Mark Kovatch, President

925 Institute for Academic Excellence
901 Deming Way
Suite 101
Madison, WI 53717-1964
608-664-3880
Fax: 608-664-382

Educational consultants for K-12 schools.

Terrance D Paul, Chairman

926 Institute for Development of Educational Activities
259 Regency Ridge
Dayton, OH 45459
937-434-6969
Fax: 937-434-5203
E-mail: ideadayton@aol.com
http://www.idea.com

Assistance for administrators and teachers of elementary and secondary schools.

927 Institute for Global Ethics
11 Main Street
PO Box 563
Camden, ME 04843-1703
207-236-6658
Fax: 207-236-4014
E-mail: ethics@globalethics.org
http://www.globalethics.org

Educational consultants for the general public, corporations and educators.

Rushworth Kidder, President

928 Interface Network
321 SW 4th Avenue
Suite 502
Portland, OR 97204-2323
503-222-2702
Fax: 503-222-7503
E-mail: www.daggettt.com
http://info@leaderEd.com

Educational consultant for the United States Department of Education, businesses, school districts and other governmental agencies.

929 International Center for Leadership in Education
219 Liberty Street
Schenectady, NY 12305-1803
518-377-6878

Educational consultants for educational institutions, governments and commercial concerns.

Willard R Daggett, President

930 International Schools Association
CIC Case 20, Ch-1211 Geneva 20
Switzerland
39-011-645-967
Fax: 39-011-643-298
E-mail: acatist@hotmail.com

Provides advisory and consultative services to its international and internationally minded member schools, as well as to other organizations in the field of education, such as UNESCO. The Association promotes innovations ininternational education, conducts conferences and workshops and publishes various educational materials.

John Mores, Headmaster

931 J&Kalb Associates
300 Pelham Road
Suite 5K
New Rochelle, NY 10805
914-636-6154

Consulting experience to school districts.

932 JCB/Early Childhood Education Consultant Service
813 Woodchuck Place
Bear, DE 19701
302-836-8505

Program design and cross-cultural staff development through seminars.

933 JJ Jones Consultants
1206 Harrison Avenue
Oxford, MS 38655-3904
662-234-6755

Educational consultant for high school and college students.

JJ Jones, Owner

934 JP Associates Incorporated
131 Foster Avenue
Valley Stream, NY 11580-4726
516-561-7803
Fax: 516-561-4066

Educational consultant for schools.

Jane Dinapoli, President

935 Janet Hart Heinicke
1302 W Boston Avenue
Indianola, IA 50125
515-961-8933
Fax: 515-961-8903
E-mail: heinicke@simpson.edu

Development of new programs and maintenance strategies.

936 Jobs for California Graduates
2525 O Street
Merced, CA 95340-3634
209-385-8466

Educational consultants for high school students.

Obie Obrien, Director

Consultants / General

937 John McLaughlin Company
122 S Phillips Avenue
Suite 200
Sioux Falls, SD 57104
605-332-4900
Fax: 605-339-1662
http://www.mclaughlincompany.com
Advises companies regarding private-sector activities in K-12 and higher education.

938 Johnson & Johnson Associates
3970 Chain Bridge Road
Fairfax, VA 2030-3316
703-359-5969
Educational consultants for governmental agencies and commercial concerns.

Dr. Johnson Edosomwan, President/CEO

939 Joseph & Edna Josephson Institute
4640 Admiralty Way
Marina Del Ray, CA 90292-6621
310-306-1868
Fax: 310-827-1864
Educational consultant for organizations, government, businesses and the general public.

Michael Josephson, President

940 Kaludis Consulting Group
1050 Thomas Jefferson Street NW
Washington, DC 20007
800-345-0907
Fax: 202-298-2804
E-mail: info@kcg.com
http://www.kcg.com
Educational consultants for colleges and universities.

941 Kentucky Association of School Administrators
152 Consumer Lane
Suite 154
Frankfort, KY 40601-8489
502-875-3411
Fax: 502-875-4634
Educational consultant for school administrators.

V Wayne Young, Director

942 Kleiner & Associates
8441 SE 68th Street
Suite 296
Mercer Island, WA 98040-5235
206-236-0608
Educational consultants for public and private institutions.

Charles Kleiner, Owner

943 Lawrence A Heller Associates
7625 W Hutchinson Avenue
Pittsburgh, PA 15218-1248
412-820-0670
Fax: 412-820-0669
E-mail: lawhel@aol.com
Development and implementation of educational programs.

944 Leona Group
4660 S Hagadorn Road
Suite 500
East Lansing, MI 48823-5353
517-333-9030
Fax: 517-333-4559
http://www.leonagroup.com
Currently manages more than 40 school sites in Michigan, Arizona, Ohio and Indiana

945 Linkage
One Forbes Road
Lexington, MA 02421-7305
781-862-4030
Fax: 781-862-2355
E-mail: info@linkage-inc.com
http://www.linkageinc.com
Educational consultants for commercial concerns and educational institutions.

Philip Harkins, President

946 Logical Systems
411 E 2nd Street
Rome, GA 30161-3109
706-234-9896
Fax: 706-290-0998
Educational consultants for school districts.

Francis Ranwez, President

947 Los Angeles Educational Alliance for Restructuring Now
300 S Grand Avenue
Suite 1160
Los Angeles, CA 91071-3118
323-255-3276
Educational consulting for school systems.
Marcy Chambers, President
Michael Roos, Director

948 Louisiana Children's Research Center for Development & Learning
208 S Tyler Street
Suite A
Covington, LA 70433-3036
504-893-7777
Fax: 985-893-5443
Educational consultants for the general public.

Alice P Thomas, Executive Director

949 MK & Company
132 Bronte Street
San Francisco, CA 94110
415-826-5923
Program development and project management for educational products, services and organizations.

950 MPR Associates
2150 Shattuck Avenue
Suite 800
Berkeley, CA 94704-1321
510-849-4942
Fax: 510-849-0794
Educational consultants for governmental, educational and commercial concerns including law firms.

E Gareth Hoachlander, President

951 Magi Educational Services Incorporated
7-11 Broadway
Suite 402
White Plains, NY 10601-3546

914-682-1969
Fax: 914-682-1760
http://www.westchesterinst.org

Educational consultant for educational institutions.

Dr. Ronald Szczypkowski, President

952 Management Concepts
8230 Leesburg Pike
Suite 800
Vienna, VA 22182-2639

703-790-9595
Fax: 703-790-1371
E-mail: csmith@managementconcepts.com
http://www.managementconcepts.com

Educational consultants for commercial and governmental concerns.

Cynthia E Smith, Corporate Director Marketing

953 Management Simulations
540 W Frontage Road
Winnetka, IL 60093-1250

847-441-9041
Fax: 847-441-9044

Educational consultants for comercial concerns and universities.

Daniel Smith, President

954 Marketing Education Resource Center
1375 King Avenue
PO Box 12279
Columbus, OH 43212-2220

800-448-0398
Fax: 614-486-1819
http://www.mark-ed.com

Educational, development and curriculum consulting for high schools and post secondary schools.

955 Maryland Educational Opportunity Center
2700 Gwynns Falls
Baltimore, MD 21216

410-728-3400
800-636-6396
Fax: 410-523-6340

Consultant services for educational institutions.

956 Maryland Elco Incorporated Educational Funding Company
4740 Chevy Chase Drive
Chevy Chase, MD 20815-6461

301-654-8677
Fax: 301-654-7750

Educational, accounting and billing consultants for service and vocational schools and businesses.

Nicholas Peter Cokinos, Chairman

957 Mason Associates
142 N Mountain Avenue
Montclair, NJ 07042

201-744-9143

Educational services for independent secondary schools, colleges and universities.

958 Matrix Media Distribution
28310 Roadside Drive
Suite 237
Agoura, CA 91301-4951

818-865-3470

Educational consultant for the educational market.

Paul Luttrell, President

959 McKenzie Group
1100 17th Street NW
Suite 1100
Washington, DC 20036-4638

202-466-1111
Fax: 202-466-3363

Educational consultant for commercial concerns and government.

Floretta D McKenzie, President

960 Measurement
423 Morris Street
Durham, NC 27701-2128

919-683-2413
Fax: 919-683-1531

Educational, research, testing and printing consultant for schools, state governments and private businesses.

Henry H Scherich, President/CEO

961 Measurement Learning Consultants
80920 Highway 10
Tolovana Park, OR 97145

503-436-1464

Business, educational, testing and development consultants for the general public and commercial concerns such as schools.

Albert G Bennyworth, Partner

962 Merrimack Education Center
101 Mill Road
Chelmsford, MA 01824-4844

978-256-3985
Fax: 978-256-6890

Educational consultant for educational facilities.

John Barranco, Executive Director

963 Michigan Education Council
40440 Palmer Road
Canton, MI 48188-2034

734-729-1000

Educational consultant for individuals.

Dawud Tauhidi, Director

964 Midas Consulting Group
600 E Ocean Boulevard
Long Beach, CA 90802-5013

562-495-2700
Fax: 562-628-0466

Educational consultant for schools, universities, training centers and government agencies.

Kary Seeney, President/Treasurer

965 Miller, Cook & Associates
1316 2nd Street SW
Roanoke, VA 24016-4923

540-345-4393

Educational consultants for colleges and universities.

William B Miller, President

966 Model Classroom
4095 173rd Place SW
Bellvue, WA 98008-5929
425-746-0331

Educational consultant for school districts, commercial concerns and the Department of Education.

Cheryl Avena, Owner

967 Modern Educational Systems
15 Limestone Terrace
Ridgefield, CT 06877-2621
203-431-4144

Educational consultant for schools.

Edward T McCormick, President

968 Modern Red Schoolhouse Institute
208 23rd Avenue
2nd Floor
Nashville, TN 37203-1502
615-320-8804
Fax: 615-320-5366

Educational consultant for school districts.

Sally B Kilgore, President

969 Montana School Boards Association
1 S Montana Avenue
Helena, MT 59601-5156
406-442-2180
Fax: 406-442-2194

Training, educational and school districts consultant for school boards.

Karen Richardson, President

970 Montgomery Intermediate Unit 23
1605 W Main Street
Suite B
Norristown, PA 19403-3268
610-539-8550
Fax: 610-539-7411

Educational consultants for professional associations, groups and student organizations.

Len Gircoski

971 Moore Express
1940 International Way
Idaho Falls, ID 83402-4908
800-380-6296
Fax: 406-442-7174

Educational consultant for public school districts, state and local governments and commercial concerns.

Lawry Wilde, President

972 Mosaica Education
2 Penn Plaza
Suite 1500
New York, NY 10121
212-292-5080
Fax: 212-232-0309
http://www.mosaicaeducation.com

Manages public schools either under contract with local school districts or funded directly by states under charter school laws that permit private management.

973 Multicorp
1912 Avenue K
Suite 210
Plano, TX 75074-5960
972-551-8899

Computer and educational consultant.

Fred Sammet, Chairman

974 National Center on Education & the Economy
700 11th Street NW
Suite 750
Washington, DC 20001-4507
202-783-3668
Fax: 202-783-3672

Educational consultant for schools.

Marc S Tucker, President

975 National Evaluation Systems
30 Gatehouse Road
PO Box 226
Amherst, MA 01004
Fax: 413-256-8221

Educational testing, test development, and assessment for education agencies.

976 National Heritage Academies
989 Spaulding Avenue SE
Grand Rapids, MI 49546
616-222-1700
800-699-9235
Fax: 616-222-1701
E-mail: info@heritageacademics.com
http://www.heritageacademies.com

Manages 22 charter academies (K-8) in Michigan and North Carolina.

977 National Reading Styles Institute
179 Lafayette Drive
Syosset, NY 11791-3933
516-921-5500
Fax: 516-921-5591
E-mail: readingsstyle@nrsi.com
http://www.nrsi.com

Educational consultants for schools and educators.

Marie Carbo, President
Carol McLaughlin, Staff Development Coord

978 National School Safety and Security Services
PO Box 110123
Cleveland, OH 44111
216-251-3067
E-mail: kentrump@aol.com
http://www.schoolsecurity.org

National consulting firm specializing in school security and crisis preparedness training, security assessments, and related safety consulting for K-12 schools, law enforcement, and other youth safety providers.

Kenneth S Trump, President/CEO

979 Noel/Levitz Centers
2101 Act Circle
Iowa City, IA 52245-9581
319-337-4700
Fax: 319-337-5274

Educational consultant for colleges and universities.

Tom Williams, President/CEO

980 Ome Resa
2023 Sunset Boulevard
Steubenville, OH 43952-1349
740-283-2050
Fax: 740-283-2709

Educational consultants for school districts.

Craige Klausser, Executive Director

981 Oosting & Associates
200 Seaboard Lane
Franklin, TN 37067-8237
615-771-7706
Fax: 615-771-7810

Educational consultants for colleges and universities.

Dr. Kenneth Oosting, President

982 Pamela Joy
1049 Whipple Avenue
Suite A
Redwood City, CA 94062-1414
650-368-9968
Fax: 650-368-2794

Educational consultants for schools.

Pamela Joy, Owner

983 Parsifal Systems
311 S Craig Street
Suite 2a
Pittsburgh, PA 15213-3731
412-682-8080

Educational consultants for commercial concerns and schools.

Marcia Morton, President

984 Paul H Rosendahl, PHD
204 Waianuenue Avenue
Hilo, HI 96720-2445
808-935-5233
Fax: 808-961-6998

Science, archaeology, historical, resouces and management consultant for developers, government agencies, educational institutions, groups and individuals.

Paul H Rosendahl, Owner

985 Perfect PC Technologies
15012 Red Hill Avenue
Tustin, CA 92780-6524
714-258-0800

Computer consultants for commercial concerns, schools and institutions.

Neil Lin, President

986 Performa
301 N Broadway
De Pere, WI 54115-2557
920-336-9929
Fax: 920-336-2899
E-mail: tang@performainc.com
http://www.performainc.com

Planning and facility consultants for higher education, manufacturing and government agencies.

Tom Gavic, President Higher Education

987 Poetry Alive
20 Battery Park Avenue
Asheville, NC 28801-2720
828-255-7636
800-476-8172
Fax: 828-232-1045
E-mail: poetry@poetryalive.com
http://www.poetryalive.com

Educational consultants for commercial concerns and school systems.

Bob Falls, President

988 Post Secondary Educational Assistance
1210 20th Street S
Suite 200
Birmingham, AL 35205-3814
205-930-4900
Fax: 205-930-4905

Educational consultant for commercial concerns.

John K Jones, President

989 Prevention Service
7614 Morningstar Avenue
Harrisburg, PA 17112-4226
717-651-9510

Educational consultant for corporations, private health clubs, school districts and other organizations.

Mark Everest, President

990 Princeton Review
2315 Broadway
2nd Floor
New York, NY 10024-4332
212-874-8282
Fax: 212-874-0775

Educational consultants for commercial concerns.

John Katzman, President

991 Priority Computer Services
1001 N Hickory Road
Suite 9b
South Bend, IN 46615-3700
219-236-5979
Fax: 219-287-8884
E-mail: priority@pcserv-inc.com

Computer consultant for commercial education.

Ben Hahaj, President

992 Prism Computer Corporation
2 Park Plaza
Suite 1060
Irvine, CA 92614-8520
949-553-6550
Fax: 949-553-6559

Educational consultant for manufacturers, government agencies and colleges.

Micheal A Ellis, President

993 Professional Computer Systems
849 E Greenville Avenue
Winchester, IN 47394-8441
765-584-2288
Fax: 765-584-1283

Computer consultants for businesses, schools and municipalities.

Mark Burkhardt, President

994 Professional Development Institute
280 S County Road
Suite 427
Longwood, FL 32750-5468
407-834-5224

Educational consultants for US Department of Transportation and commercial concerns.

Elsom Eldridge, Jr, President

995 Profiles
507 Highland Avenue
Iowa City, IA 52240-4516
319-354-7600
Fax: 319-354-6813

Educational consultants for school districts and commercial concerns.

Douglas Paul, President

996 Pyramid Educational Consultants
226 W Park Place
Suite 1
Newark, DE 19711-4565
302-368-2515
Fax: 302-368-2516

Educational consultant for general trade, historical commissions and other public bodies.

Andrew Bondy, President

997 Quality Education Development
41 Central Park West
New York, NY 10023
212-724-3335
800-724-2215
Fax: 212-724-4913
E-mail: info@qedconsulting.com

Structures courses that promote knowledge and understanding through interactive learning, and communication programs.

998 Quantum Performance Group
5050 Rushmore Road
Palmyra, NY 14522-9414
315-986-9200

Educational consultant for commercial concerns, including schools.

Dr. Mark Blazey, President

999 Rebus
4111 Jackson Road
Ann Arbor, MI 48103-1827
734-668-4870
Fax: 734-913-4750

Educational consultant for schools and school districts.

Linda Borgsdorf, President

1000 Records Consultants
10826 Gulfdale Street
San Antonio, TX 78216-3607
210-366-4127
Fax: 210-366-0776

Educational consultant for school districts and municipalities.

Lang Glotfelty, President

1001 Regional Learning Service of Central New York
3049 E Genesee Street
Suite 211
Syracuse, NY 13224-1644
315-446-0500
Fax: 315-446-5869

Educational consultants for commercial concerns.

Rebecca Livengood, Executive Director

1002 Reinventing Your School Board
Aspen Group International,Inc
PO Box 260301
Highlands Ranch, CO 80163-0301
303-478-0125
Fax: 208-248-6084

Linda Dawson, Contact
Dr. Randy Quinn, Contact

1003 Relearning by Design
447 Forcina Hall
PO Box 7718
Ewing, NJ 08628-0718
609-771-2921
Fax: 609-637-5130
E-mail: info@relearning.org
http://www.relearning.org

Grant Wiggins, Author/Editor
Julia Meneghin, Operations Manager

1004 Research Assessment Management
816 Camarillo Springs Road
Camarillo, CA 93012-9441
805-987-5538
Fax: 805-987-2868

Educational consultants for governmental agencies and commercial concerns.

Adrienne McCollum, PhD, President

1005 Robert E Nelson Associates
120 Oak Brook Center
Suite 208
Oak Brook, IL 60523
630-954-5585
Fax: 630-954-5606

Consulting for private colleges, universities and secondary schools.

1006 Rookey Associates
1740 Little York Xing
Little York, NY 13087
607-749-2325

Educational consultant for school districts, public utility companies and the government.

Ernest J Rookey, President

1007 Root Learning
810 W S Boundary Street
Perrysburg, OH 43551-5200
419-874-0077
Fax: 419-874-4801
Business, educational, employment consultant for commercial concerns.

Randall Root, Chairman/CEO

1008 School Management Study Group
860 18th Avenue
Salt Lake City, UT 84103-3719
801-532-5340
Organization seeking to promote improvement of schools and to involve educators in critical school problems.
Donald Thomas, Executive Secretary

1009 School March by Public Priority Systems
Blendonview Office Park
5027 Pine Creek Drive
Westerville, OH 43081
614-890-1573
Fax: 614-890-3294
E-mail: bainbridge@schoolmatch.com
http://www.schoolmatch.com
Stategies and information systems for working with public and private schools.
William L Bainbridge, President/CEO
William R Masco Jr, VP

1010 Sensa of New Jersey
110 Mohawk Trail
Wayne, NJ 07470-5030
973-831-1757
An educational consultant for private and public schools.

John Pinto, President

1011 Shirley Handy
19860 Bloss Avenue
Hilmar, CA 95324-8308
209-668-4142
Fax: 209-668-1855
Educational consultants for school districts and teachers.

Shirley Handy, Owner

1012 Sidney Kreppel
704 E Benita Boulevard
Vestal, NY 13850-2629
607-754-6870
Educational consultants.

Sidney Kreppel, Owner

1013 Solutions Skills
519 1/2 E Tennessee Street
Tallahassee, FL 32308-4981
850-681-6543
Fax: 850-681-6543
Business and educational consultants for state and governments, educational, medical and legal publishing companies.

Randall Vickers, President

1014 Special Education Service Agency
2217 E Tudor Road
Suite 1
Anchoage, AK 99507-1068
907-562-7372
Fax: 907-562-0545
http://www.isbe.net
Educational consultant for school districts.

Anthony Sims, State Director Special Edu

1015 Sports Management Group
2240 4th Street
Suite 200
Oakland, CA 94607-4335
510-251-1280
Educational consulting for universities.
Lauren Livingston, President

1016 Stewart Howe Alumni Service of New York
317 W State Street
Ithaca, NY 14850-5431
607-273-2717
Educational consultants for college organizations.

Peter McChesney, Director

1017 Strategies for Educational Change
11 Whitby Court
Mount Holly, NJ 08060
609-261-1702
E-mail: barbd@prodigy.net
Development of programs for youths at risk.

1018 Success for All Foundation
200 W Towsontown Boulevard
Baltimore, MD 21204-5200
410-616-2372
800-548-4998
Fax: 410-324-4444
E-mail: sfainfo@successforall.net
http://www.successforall.net
A not-for-profit organization dedicated to the development, evaluation and dissemination of proven reform models for preschool, elementary and middle schools.

Mary Thuman, Contact

1019 Teachers Curriculum Institute
E170 E Meadow Drive
Palo Alto, CA 94303-4234
650-856-0565
Fax: 800-343-6828
Educational consultant for schools and teachers.

Bert Bower, President

1020 Teachers Service Association
1107 E Lincoln Avenue
Orange, CA 92865-1939
714-282-6342
Educational consultants for schools and teachers.

Richard Ghysels, Secretary Treasurer

1021 Tech Ed Services
8255 Firestone Boulevard
Downey, CA 90241-4800
562-869-1913
Fax: 562-869-5673

Consultants / General

Computer, planning and training consultant for k-12 educators and adult educators.

Patricia K Sanford, President

1022 Technical Education Research Centers
2067 Massachusetts Avenue
Cambridge, MA 02140-1340
617-547-0430
Fax: 617-349-3535

Educational consultant for the National Science Foundation and the Department of Education.

Arthur Nelson, Chairman

1023 Tesseract Group
3820 E Ray Raod
Suite 2
Phoenix, AZ 85044
480-706-2500
http://www.tesseractgroup.org

An integrated education management company, serving private and public charter elementary, middle and high schools in six states.

1024 Timothy Anderson Dovetail Consulting
936 Nantasket Avenue
Hull, MA 02045-1453
781-925-3078
Fax: 781-925-9830

Educational consultant for businesses.

Eric Anderson, Owner

1025 University Research
7200 Wisconsin Avenue
Bethesda, MD 20814-4811
301-654-8338
Fax: 301-941-8427

Educational consultants for the federal government along with other government and private sectors.

Melvin Estrin, CEO

1026 University of Georgia-Instructional Technology
607 Aderhold Hall
Athens, GA 30602
706-542-3810
Fax: 706-542-4032
E-mail: instech@uga.cc.uga.edu
http://http//itechl.coe.uga.edu

Instructional design and development.

1027 Uplinc
104 Damon Road
Northampton, MA 01060-1818
413-586-3210
Fax: 413-586-5760
E-mail: sales@uplinc.com
http://www.uplinc.com

Computer consultants for commercial, general public and educational concerns.

Ron Marino, President

1028 William A Ewing & Company
505 S Main Street
Suite 700
Orange, CA 92868
714-245-1850
Fax: 714-456-1755
E-mail: ewingo@aol.com
http://www.members.aol.com/ewingo

Expertise in compensation and classification.

1029 Wisconsin Technical College System Foundation
1 Foundation Circle
Waunakee, WI 53597-8914
608-849-2424
Fax: 608-849-2468

Educational consultant for educational institutions and businesses.

Loren Brumm, Executive Director

Africa

1030 Alexandra House School
King George V Avenue
Floreal
Mauritius

230-696-4108

Alexandra House is an English language primary school following British/international curriculum catering for Expatriate and Mauritian pupils. Enrollment consists of 100 day students (50 boys; 50 girls), in grades K-6.

M Wrenn-Beejadhur, Principal

1031 American International School-Dhaka
United Nations Road
Dhaka
Bangladesh

880-2-882-2414
Fax: 880-2-883-3175
E-mail: info@ais-dhaka.net
http://www.ais-dhaka.net

An independent, coeducational day school which offers an educational program from prekindergarten through grade 12 for students of all nationalities.

Michael D Popinchalk, Superintendent

1032 American International School-Johannesburg
Plot 160, Diepsloot
Gauteng
South Africa

27-11-464-1505
Fax: 27-11-464-1327
E-mail: info@aisj-jhb.com
http://www.aisj-jhb.com

An independent, coeducational, multiracial day school which offers an educational program from kindergarten through grade 12 for children of all nationalities residing in the Republic of South Africa.

Dr. Leo A Ruberto, Director

1033 American International School-Lom,
35 Rue Kayigan Lawson Avenue
Duisburg, Kodjoviakope BP 852
Lome Togo

228-221-30-00
Fax: 228-221-79-52
E-mail: aisl@cafe.tg

Grade levels N-12, school year August-June

Geri Branch, Director

1034 American International School-Zambia
PO Box 31617
Lusaka
Zambia

260-1-260-509
Fax: 260-1-260-538
E-mail: aesl@zamnet.zm
http://www.aesl.sch.zm

Grade levels prekindergarten through twelfth/ enrollment total 220.

Helen Jeffery, Secondary Principal
Walker Plotkin, Director

1035 American School of Kinshasa
TASOK/Kinshasa,c/o Panalpina World
Transport, Bldg 743,Zone Brucargo, 1931
Zaventem, Brussels, Belguim

243-884-6619
Fax: 243-884-1161
E-mail: bertpbedford@yahoo.com

Grade levels K-12, school year August-June

Bert Bedford, Superintendent
Fiona M Merali, Business Manager

1036 American School-Tangier
Rue Christophe Colomb
Tangier 9000
Morocco

212-39 93 98 27/28
Fax: 212-39 94 75 35
E-mail: ast@tangeroise.net.ma

An independent, coeducational day and boarding school which offers an educational program from prekindergarten through grade 12 for students of all nationalities.

1037 American School-Yaounde
BP 7475
Yaounde
Cameroon

237-230-421
Fax: 237-236-011
E-mail: asoy@camnet.cm

Grade levels Pre-K through 12, school year August - June

Areta Williams, Director

1038 Arundel School
PO Box MP 91 Mount Pleasant
Harere
Zimbabwe

263-14-30-2121
E-mail: arundel@samara.co.zw

Grade levels K-12

G Alcock, Principal

1039 Arusha International School
PO Box 2691
Arusha
Tanzania

255-27-250-5029
Fax: 255-27-250-5031

Grade levels K-12

R Redding, Principal

1040 Asmara International Community School
PO Box 4941
Asmara
Eritrea

291-1-161-705
Fax: 291-1-161-705
E-mail: aics@eol.com.er

Grade levels pre K-12.

Scott Newland, Director

1041 Banda School
PO Box 24722
Nairobi
Kenya

254-891220

Teaching Opportunities Abroad / Africa

Fax: 254-890004
E-mail: bandaschool@swiftkenya.com

School for children kindergarten to the age of 13.

Norman Farmer, Principal

1042 Bishop Mackenzie International Schools
PO Box 102
Lilongwe
Malawi

265-1-756-364
Fax: 265-1-751-374
E-mail: bmiss@unima.wn.apc.org

International, coeducational day schools which offer an educational program from kindergarten through grade 11 for pupils of all nationalities.

Graham Burgess, Principal

1043 Braeburn High School
PO Box 16944
Nairobi
Kenya

254-2-861144
Fax: 254-2-862450
E-mail: ken@bhs.braeburn.ac.uk

Boarding school

Ivor Dougan, Principal

1044 Braeburn School
PO Box 45112
Nairobi
Kenya

254-2-572572
Fax: 254-2-572310
E-mail: primary@braeburn.ac.ke

Provides opprtunities for all children from the early years to the age of 8.

RE Diaper, Principal

1045 British International School Cairo
PO Box 9057
Nasr City, Cairo
Egypt

002-02-758-2881
Fax: 002-02-758-1390
E-mail: ncbis_rc@intouch.com

Prepares international students for grade level A exams ages 16-18.

Aleen Cooper, Principal

1046 British School-Lom,
Residence du Benin
Lome
Togo

228-226-46-06
Fax: 228-226-49-89
E-mail: bsl@cafe.tg
http://www.bsl.tg

This school offers an English based curriculum for 120 day students and 95 boarding students (110 boys; 105 girls), ages 4-18. The school is an independent, co-educational day and boarding school. External exams from the Universityof London and Cambridge-UK plus International Baccalaureate (IB) is offered. Applications needed to teach include science, pre-school, French, math, social sciences, administration, Spanish, reading, German, English and physical education.

Ian Sayer, Headmaster

1047 British Yeoward School
Parque Taoro Puerto de la Cruz
Tenerife
Canary Islands

34-22-38-46-85
Fax: 34-22-37-35-65
E-mail: bys@jct.cs

British curriculum for pupils from3 to 18 years of age.

Martin Weston, Principal

1048 Broadhurst Primary School
Pvt Bag BR 114 Broadhurst
Garborone
Botswana

267-371221
Fax: 267-307987
E-mail: headmaster@botsnet.bw

International primary school which children can develop to their full potenial and aquire the knowledge and skills to equip them for living.

HJA Brown, Principal

1049 Brookhouse Preparatory School
PO Box 24468
Nairobi
Kenya

254-89-46-41-89
E-mail: headmaster@brookschool.com

School follows British curriculum.

RJH Seaman, Principal

1050 Cairo American College
PO Box 39
Digla, Maadi, 11431 Cairo
Egypt

20-2-519-6665
Fax: 20-2-519-6584
E-mail: support@tc.cac.edu.eg
http://www.cac.edu.eg

Grade levels K-12, school year August-June

Robert Hetzel PhD, Superintendent
Drew Alexander, HS Principal

1051 Casablanca American School
Route de la Meque
Casablanca 20150
Morocco

212-2-221-4115
Fax: 212-2-221-2488
E-mail: cas@cas.ac.ma
http://www.cas.ac.ma

An independent, university-preparatory, coeducational day school which offers American and International Baccalaureate oriented education from nursery through grade 12.

Anne Asman, Director

1052 Cavina School
PO Box 43090
Nairobi
Kenya

254-2-560081
Fax: 254-2-566676

British preparatory school for children aged 3 to thirteen.

RA Massie-Blomfield, Principal

1053 Dakar Academy
BP 3189, Rue des Maristes
Dakar
Senegal

221-832-0682
Fax: 221-832-1721
E-mail: daoffice@telecomplus.sn
http://www.dakaracademy.com

Grade levels kindergarten through twelfth, enrollment 160.

Floyd Celi, Director

1054 Greensteds School
Private Bag
Nakuru
Kenya

037-850024
Fax: 037-851248

An international school for boys and girls.

R Albon, Principal

1055 Harare International School
66 Pendennis Road
Harare
Zimbabwe

263-4-883-336
Fax: 263-4-883-371
E-mail: his@his.ac.zw
http://www.his.ac.zw

Grade levels prekindergarten through twelfth, with enrollment of 376.

Paul Poore, Director

1056 Hillcrest Secondary School
PO Box 24819
Nairobi
Kenya

254-882222
Fax: 254-882350

Mixed boarding school.

David Marshall, Principal

1057 International Community School-Addis Ababa
PO Box 70282
Addis Adaba
Ethiopia

251-1-710-870
Fax: 251-1-710-722
E-mail: ICS@telecom.net.et
http://www.icsaddisababa.org

An independent, coeducational day school which offers an educational program from prekindergarten through grade 12 for students of all nationalities.

Paul Olson, Director

1058 International School-Kenya
PO Bxo 14103
Nairobi
Kenya

254-2-582-224
Fax: 254-2-582-272
E-mail: isk_admin@isk.ac.ke
http://www.isk.ac.ke

grade levels K-12.

Monica N Greeley, Superintendent

1059 International School-Moshi
PO Box 733
Moshi
Tanzania

255-27-275-5004
Fax: 255-27-250-5031
E-mail: ismoshi@maf.org
http://www.ecis.org

This international school offers a curriculum in English for 360 day students and 70 boarding students (215 boys and 215 girls), in grades K-12. Teaching applications must be received by January for an August start date. The length ofstay is two years and housing is provided. Applications needed to teach include science, math, social sciences, French, English and physical education. Student/teacher ratio is 10:1.

Geoff Lloyd, Headmaster
Keiron White, Deputy Head

1060 International School-Tanganyika
United Nations Road
PO Box 2651, Dar es Salaam
Tanzania

255-51-151-817-8
Fax: 255-51-152-077
E-mail: ist@raha.com
http://www.istafrica.com

A private, coeducational school which offers PreK-12 and hosts 1,071 students. Offers language courses in French, Kiswahili, Spanish and German.

Simon Leslie, CEO

1061 John F Kennedy International School
PO Box 232 Warri Delta
Nigeria
Africa

234-58-231-286

Boarding day school for boys and girls aged 5-14 years.

VOM Omonuwa, Principal

1062 Kabira International School
PO Box 2020
Kampala
Uganda

256-41-530472
Fax: 256-41-543444
E-mail: kisu@imul.com
http://www.kabiraschool.com

Grade levels Pre-K through 8, school year - September - July

Rob Freeth, Head Teach
Glyn Lewis, Deputy Head Teacher

1063 Kestrel Manor School
Ring Road Westlands
PO Box 14489, Nairobi
Kenya

254-2-3740-311
http://www.kestrelmanorschool.com

Coeducational school for children Kindergarten through secondary schooling.

J O'Connor, Principal

Teaching Opportunities Abroad / Africa

1064 Khartoum American School
PO Box 699
Khartoum
Sudan

249-11-427-593
Fax: 249-11-427-592
E-mail: kas@sudanmail.net

An independent, coeducational day school which offers an educational program from prekindergarten through grade 12 for students of all nationalities.

Melissa Hicks, Superintendent

1065 Kigali International School
BP 1375
Kigali
Rwanda

Fax: 250-72128

Jennifer G Sevier, Principal

1066 Kingsgate English Medium Primary School
Box 169
Mafeteng, 900 Lesotho
Africa

Kingsgate is the only non-denominational primary school in the district. The curriculum is English-based offered to a total of 460 day students (240 boys; 220 girls), PreK-7. Overseas teachers are welcome with the length of stay beingone year, with housing provided. Applications needed to teach include pre-school and reading.

M Makhothe, Principal

1067 Kisumu International School
PO Box 1276
Kisumu
Kenya

254-35-21678

This school is located on the shores of Lake Victoria and offers a unique education to students of all nationalities and cultural backgrounds. The total enrollment of the school is 35 day students, in grades K-7. The school doesparticipate in the teacher exchange programs, with the length of stay being two years with housing provided by the school. Applications needed to teach include science, preschool, math, social sciences, English and physical education.

Neena Sharma, Principal

1068 Lincoln Community School
American Embassy Accra
Washington
Accra
Ghana

233-21-774-018
Fax: 233-21-774-018
E-mail: lincoln@lincoln.edu.gh
http://www.lincoln.edu.gh

Grade levels preK thru 12.

Don Groves, PhD, Superintendent

1069 Lincoln International School of Uganda
PO Box 4200
Kampala
Uganda

251-41-200374/8/9
Fax: 256-41-200303
E-mail: gmail@lincoln.ac.ug
http://www.lincoln.ac.ug

Grade levels Pre-K through 12, school year August - June

Peter Todd, Director
Mary-Lily Foster, Business Manager

1070 Lincoln International School-Uganda
PO Box 4200
Kampala
Uganda

256-41-200374
Fax: 256-41-200303
E-mail: gmail@lincoln.ac.ug
http://www.lincoln.ac.ug

Peter Todd, Director

1071 Maru A Pula School
Mara a Pula Way
Gaborone
Botswana

267-312953
Fax: 267-373338
http://www.map.ac.bw

independent co-educational secondary school offering international reconized classes.

Neil Smooker, Principal

1072 Mombasa Academy
PO Box 86487
Mombasa
Kenya

254-11-471629
Fax: 254-11-221484
E-mail: msaacademy@swiftmombasa.com

Private school, pupils ranging in the ages of 3-18 years old.

PR Uppal, Principal

1073 Northside Primary School
PO Box 897
Gaborone
Botswana

00-267-395-2440
Fax: 09-267-395-3573

International school that strives to improve the educatin offered to pupils. For boys and girls of all nationalities.

Mandy Watson, Headteacher

1074 Nsansa School
PO Box 70322
Ndola
Zambia

26-2-611753
Fax: 26-2-618465

This school offers an English curriculum to 185 day students (96 boys; 124 girls), in grades K-7. Length of stay for overseas teachers is one year with housing provided. Student/teacher ratio is 20:1.

Nel Mather, Principal

1075 Peterhouse
Private Bag 3741
Marondera
Zimbabwe

263-79-24951

This Anglican school offers an English based curriculum for 19 day students and 790 boarding students (535 boys; 255 girls), in Form I-Form VI. The school is willing to participate in a teacher exchange program with the length

98

of staybeing one year, with housing provided. Applications needed to teach include science, math, and physical education.

MW Bawden, Principal

1076 Rabat American School
American Embassy Rabat
PSC 74, Box 010
Morocco

212-3-767-1476
Fax: 212-3-767-0963
E-mail: info@ras.edu.ac.ma
http://www.ras.edu.ac.ma

An independent, coeducational day school which offers an American educational program from prekindergarten through grade 12 for students of all nationalities.

David A Randall, Director

1077 Rift Valley Academy
PO Box 80
Kijabe
Kenya

254-154-64646
Fax: 254-154-64412

Grade levels 1-12.

Roy E Entwistle, Principal

1078 Rosslyn Academy
PO Box 14146
Nairobi
Kenya

570-995-9248
Fax: 570-995-5142
E-mail: rosslyn@maf.org

Grade levels 1-12.

Jim Richardson, Principal

1079 Sandford English Community School
PO Box 30056 MA
Addis Adaba
Ethiopia

251-1-557-613
Fax: 251-1-551-945

Grade levels N-13.

Micheal Thompson, Headmaster

1080 Schutz American School
PO Box 1000
Alexandria
Egypt 2111

20-3-576-2205
Fax: 20-3-576-0229
E-mail: 103375.1022@compuserve.com

An independent, coeducational day school which offers an educational program from prekindergarten through grade 12 for students of all nationalities.

Robert Woods, Head of School

1081 Sifundzani School
PO Box A286
Mbabane
Swaziland

268-404-2465
Fax: 268-404-0320
E-mail: sifundzani@realnet.co.sz

A coeducational day school which offers an educational program from grades 1 through 10 for students of all nationalities.

Mary Fraser, Principal

1082 Sir Harry Johnston Primary School
Kalembuka Road
PO Box 52, Zomba
Malawi

RN Wells, Principal

1083 St. Barnabas College
PO Box 88188
Newclare 2112, Johannesburg
South Africa

474-2055
Fax: 474-2249

Co-educational secondary school. Grade levels 7-12.

Michael Corke, Principal

1084 St. Mary's School
PO Box 40580
Nairobi
Kenya

254-02-444569
Fax: 254-02-444754

Grade levels 6-12.

Rev. Tom Hogan, CSSP, Principal

1085 St. Paul's College
Gobabis Road 63, PO Box 11736
Windhoek 9000, Namibia
Africa

CP Sexon, Principal

1086 Tigoni Girls Academy
Box 10
Limuru
Kenya

This Academy is a small, closely knit community of individuals from different cultures in which physical, emotional, creative and intellectual development is fortified in all aspects of daily life. Total enrollment is 40 boardingstudents, ages 11-16. Applications from overseas include science, math, social sciences, French, Spanish and English. Length of stay for overseas teachers is 2 years with housing provided. The Academy is affiliated with the Church of England.

Duncan Kelly, Principal

1087 Waterford-Kamhlaba United World College
World College
PO Box 52, Mbabane
Swaziland

00268-42966

This school offers a curriculum based in English for 181 day students and 295 boarding (251 boys; 226 girls), in grades 6-12. Overseas teachers length of stay is three years with housing provided. Applications needed to teach includemath, English, and physical education.

PJ Midermott, Principal
P Rose, Faculty Head

1088 Westwood International School
PO Box 2446
Gabarone
Botswana

267-306736
Fax: 267-306734
E-mail: westwood@info.bw

This International school offers an English based curriculum to 420 day students (210 boys; 210 girls), in grades K-11. Applications needed to teach include science, math, English and physical education. The overall purpose of theschool is to provide an international standard of education for boys and girls of all ethnic, national and religious backgrounds, enabling them to re-enter their educational systems of origin.

Robert Sylvester, Principal

1089 Windhoek International School
Private Bag 16007
Windhoek
Namibia

264-61-241-783
Fax: 264-61-243-127
E-mail: kjarman@wis.edu.na
http://www.wis.edu.na

A coeducational day school which offers educational programs from preschool through grade 11.

Ken Jarman, Director

Asia, Pacific Rim & Australia

1090 Aiyura International Primary School
PO Box 407
Ukarumpa Papua
New Guinea

Perry Bradford, Principal

1091 Ake Panya International School
158/1 Moo 3 Hangdong-Samoeng Road
Banpong, Hangdong, Chiang Mai 50230
Thailand

66-53-36-5303
Fax: 66-53-365-304
E-mail: akepanya@cm.ksc.co.th
http://www.akepanya.co.th

Grade levels 1-12, school year August - June

Barry Sutherland, Headmaster
Holly Shaw, Director of Studies

1092 Alotau International Primary School
PO Box 154
Alotau MBP, Papua
New Guinea

Martha Barss, Principal

1093 Amelia Earhart Intermediate School
Unit 5166
APO Kadena
Okinawa, AP 96368-5166

Rosemarie Arnestad, Principal

1094 American International School-Dhaka
PO Box 6106
Gulshan, Dhaka 1212
Bangladesh

880-2-882-2452
Fax: 880-2-882-3175
E-mail: info@ais-dhaka.net
http://www.ais-dhaka.net

Grade levels Pre-K through 12, school year August-June

Richard Detwiler, Superintendent

1095 American International School-Guangzhou
3 Yan Yu Street S
Ersha Island, Dongshan District
Guangdong, 510620, China

86-20-8735-3392
Fax: 86-20-8735-3339
E-mail: info@aisgz.edu.cn
http://www.aisgz.edu.cn

Grade levels Pre-K through 12, school year September-June

David Shawver, PhD, Director

1096 American School-Bombay
SF 2 G Block
Bandra Kurla Complex Road
Mumbai, India 400 051

91-22-652-1837
Fax: 91-22-652-1838
E-mail: asbadmin@bom3.vsnl.net.in
http://www.asbindia.org

Grade levels Pre-K through 13, school year August - June

James Mains, Superintendent

1097 American School-Guangzhou (China)
N Yan Yu Street S
Ersha Island, Dongshan District
Guangzhou 510105, China

8620-8735-3393
Fax: 8620-8735-3339
E-mail: info@aisgz.edu.cn
http://www.aisgz.edu.cn

An independent, coeducational day school which offers an educational program from kindergarten through grade 12.

David Shawver PhD, Director

1098 American School-Japan
1-1 Nomizu 1-chome
Chofu-shi, Tokyo 182-0031
Japan

81-422-34-5300
Fax: 81-422-34-5301
E-mail: info@asij.ac.jp
http://www.asij.ac.jp

The American School in Japan is a private, coeducational day school which offers an educational program from nursery through grade 12 for students of all nationalities, but it primarily serves the American community living in theTokyo area. The school was founded in 1902. The school year comprises 2 semesters extending from September to January and January to June.

Peter R Cooper, Headmaster

1099 Aoba International School
2-10-34 Aobadai
Meguro-Ku, Tokyo 153
Japan

81334611441
Fax: 81334639873

This boys school operates as a US bilingual (English and Japanese) multicultural. Languages taught-English and Japanese. Special programs include ESL, JSL, PE, swimming, soroban (abacus). Extra activities include field trips, yearbook, graduation trips-downtown Tokyo.

Total enrollment is 142 day students in nursery, kindergarten and preschool with the student/teacher ratio is 8:1.

Regina M Doi, Headmistress
Belen Tolentino, VP

1100 Ashgabat International School
Berzengi, Ataturk Street
Ashgabat
Turkmenistan

993-12-489027
Fax: 993-12-489028
E-mail: tomcrosby@qsi.org
http://www.qsi.org

Grade levels N-12, school year September - June

Thomas Crosby, Director

1101 Bali International School
PO Box 3259
Denpasar, Bali
Indonesia

62-361-288-467
Fax: 62-361-288-770
E-mail: bisadmin@poboxes.com
http://www.bdg.centrin.net.id/~bis

William D Robertson, Principal

1102 Bandung Alliance International School
Jalan Gunung Agung 14
Bandung, 40142 Java
Indonesia

022-203-1844
Fax: 022-203-4202
http://www.baisedu.org

English based curriculum for grades n-12.

John Havill, Principal

1103 Bandung International School
Kotak Pos 132
Jl Drg Suria Suman, Bandung
Indonesia

62-22-201-4995
Fax: 62-22-201-2688
E-mail: bisadmin@poboxes.com

Grade level preK through 8.

Angus Ogilvy, Head of Schools

1104 Bangalore International School
14 Benson Cross Road
Bangalore 560 046
India

91-912-57-4007

Grades levels K-12.

Meera Menon, BA, BEd., Principal

1105 Bangkok Patana School
2/38 Soi La Salle
Sukhumbit 105, Bangkok 10260
Thailand

662-398-0200
Fax: 662-399-3179
E-mail: pabe@pantana.ac.th
http://www.patana.com

Language of instruction English. Offers UK National Curriculum, IGCSE and IB examination courses.

Accredited by NEASC and ECIS. Currently enrolls 1,950 students and teaches grades N-12.

Paul Beresford-Hill, Headmaster
Anna Whitcraft, Business Manager

1106 Beacon Hill School
23 Ede Road
Kowloon Tong, Hong Kong
China

233-65-221
Fax: 233-87-895
E-mail: bhs@bhs.esf.edu.hk
http://www.asioonline.net.hk/beacon

Aim to provide each child with a safe and secure schoool where everyone, irrespective of ability, is an valued individual.

RP Lyden, Principal

1107 Beijing BISS International School
#17, Area 4, An Zhen Xi Li
Chao Yang District, Beijing 100029
China

8610-6443-3151
Fax: 8610-6443-5156
E-mail: istirling@biss.com.cn
http://www.biss.com.cn

Grade levels K-12, school year August-June

Iain Stirling, Headmaster
Daren Woo, Admissions Manager

1108 Bob Hope Primary School
Unit 5166
APO, Kadena
Okinawa

634-0093
Fax: 634-1236

Grade levels K-3.

Elaine Grande, Principal

1109 Bogor Expatriate School
PO Box 160
JL Papandayan 7, Bogar 16001
Indonesia

62-251-324360
Fax: 62-251-328512

Mission is to provide oportunities to foster positive attitdes towards learning.

Paul Kenworthy, Principal

1110 Bontang International School
Vico 9 Penang Road 07-08
Park Mall 0923
Singapore

62-548551176

An international school with an English/Japanese based curriculum for twenty day students (6 boys; 14 girls), grades PreK-8. Student/teacher ration 5:1.

Barry Benger, Principal

1111 Brent International School-Manila
UL Complex, Meralco Avenue
1603 Pasig City
Philippines

632-631-1265
Fax: 632-633-8420
E-mail: bism@brentmanila.edu.ph
http://www.brentmanila.edu.ph

Grade levels N-12, enrollment 966.

Dick B Robbins, Headmaster

1112 Brent School
PO Box 35
Baguio City 2600
Philippines

63-74-442-2260
Fax: 63-74-442-3638
E-mail: brentreg@bgo.cyber-space.com.ph
http://www2.mozcom.com/~brent

Coeducational boarding and day college-preparatory school, affiliated with Church of England.

Don Holmes, Headmaster

1113 British International School
PO Box 4120
Jakarta 12041 Indonesia

62-21-745-1670
Fax: 62-21-745-1671
E-mail: bisnet@rad.net.id

Grade level preK through 13.

John Birchill, Principal

1114 British School Manila
PO Box 873
Makati, Metro Manila
Philippines

632-840-1561
Fax: 632-840-1520

School offers education that nurtures the different strengths and talents of the students.

Vanessa Cloutt, BEd, Principal

1115 British School-Muscat
PO Box 1907
Post Code 112
Ruwi Sultanate of Oman

968-600-842
Fax: 968-601-062
E-mail: admin@britishschool.edu.om

Dr. John Scarth, Principal
Ian Forster, Director Finance/Personnel

1116 Calcutta International School Society
18 Lee Road
Calcutta 700 020
India

This school offers an English-based curriculum to 480 day students (230 boys; 250 girls), grades Nursery-12. CIS follows GCE London Curriculum. The cultures represented by the student body include expatriates, NRIs, local children. The student body is mainly Indians. Highly qualified individuals offering excellent results. The school is willing to participate in a teacher exchange program with the length of stay being 1-2 years, with no housing provided.

N Chatterjee, Principal
L Chaturvedi, Faculty Head

1117 Caltex American School
CPI Rumbal
Pekanbaru, Sumatra Riau
Indonesia

62-765-995-501
Fax: 62-765-996-321

Grade level preK through 8.

Daniel Hovde, Superintendent

1118 Camberwell Grammar School
55 Mout Albert Road
Canterbury 3126, Victoria
Australia

03-9836-6266
http://www.asap.unimelb.edu.au/asa/directory/data/342

Independent boys school.

CF Black, Principal

1119 Canadian Academy
4-1 Koyo Cho Naka
Higashinada-Ku, Kobe 658-0032
Japan

81-78-857-0100
Fax: 81-78-857-3250
E-mail: hdmstr@canacad.ac.jp
http://www.canacad.ac.jp/canacad/welcome.html

Grade levels Pre-K through 12, school year August - June

David A Ottaviano EdD, Headmaster
Charles Kite, Assistant Headmaster

1120 Canadian School-India
14/1 Kodigehalli Main Road
Sahakar Nagar, Bangalore 560 092
India

91-80-343-8414
Fax: 91-80-343-6488
E-mail: csib@vsnl.com
http://www.canschoolindia.org

Grade levels K-13, school year August - June

T Alf Mallin, Principal

1121 Canberra Grammar School
Monaro Crescent
Red Hill, Canberra 2603
Australia

02-6260-9700
Fax: 02-6260-9701
E-mail: canberra.grammar@cgs.act.edu.au
http://www.cgs.act.edu.au

International boys school.

Timothy C Murray, BA, Principal

1122 Carmel School-Hong Kong
10 Borrett Road
Mid Levels, SAR, Hong Kong
China

852-2964-1600
Fax: 852-2813-4121
E-mail: admin@carmel.edu.hk
http://www.carmel.edu.hk

Grade levels N-7, school year September - June

Edwin Epstein, Head of School
Chris Wee, School Manager

1123 Casa Montessori Internationale
17 Palm Avenue Forbes Park Makati
Etro Manila D-3117
Philippines

Pre-nursery, nursery and kindergarten classes.

Carina Lebron, Principal

1124 Cebu International School
Banilad Road
PO Box 735, Cebu City 6401
Philippines

632-32-417-6327
Fax: 632-32-417-6332
E-mail: markb@mozcom.com
http://www2.mozcom.com/~cisram

Grade levels kindergarten through twelfth, enrollment 337.

Mark Bretherton, Superintendent

1125 Central Java Inter-Mission School
PO Box 142
Salatiga 50711, Jaleng
Indonesia

62-298-311-673
Fax: 62-298-321-609
E-mail: cjims@xc.org
http://www.geocities.com

Grade level K-12.

Ona L Liles, Superintendent

1126 Central Primary School
Port Vila Private Mail Bag 016
Republic of Vanuatu

ID Kay, Principal

1127 Chiang Mai International School
2686 Minamihara
Nakashidami, Moriyama-Ku, Nagoya 463
Japan

81-52-736-2025
Fax: 81-52-736-3883
E-mail: nisinfo@tcp-ip.or.jp

A private, coeducational day school which offers an educational program from preschool through grade 12 for students of all nationalities. The school year comprises 2 semesters extending from the first week of September to mid-Januaryand from mid-January to the third week of June.

Kamol Boonprohm, Principal

1128 Chinese International School
1 Hau Yuen Path
Braemar Hill, Hong Kong
China

852-251-25918
Fax: 852-251-07378
E-mail: cis_info@cis.edu.hk
http://www.cis.edu.hk

Grade levels Pre-K through 12, school year August - June

Richard Blumenthal, Headmaster

1129 Chittagong Grammar School
39 Fazlul Kader Road
Chiottagong
Bangladesh

880-31-654-191
Fax: 880-31-657-189
E-mail: cgs@gononet.com

Grade levels Pre-K through 10, school year September - June

Fazle Allem, Principal

1130 Colombo International School
28, Gregory's Road
Colombo 7, Sri Lanka

94-1-697-587
Fax: 94-1-699-592
E-mail: principal@cis.lk
http://www.cis.lk

An independent, coeducational day school which offers an educational program from preschool through grade 12 for students of all nationalities.

David Sanders, Principal

1131 Concordia International School-Shanghai
999 Mingyue Road, Jinqiao,Pudong
Shanghai
201206, China

86-21-5899-0380
Fax: 86-21-5899-1685
E-mail: headofschool@ciss.com.cn
http://www.ciss.com.cn

Preschool through grade 12; school year August-June; WASC accredited pP-12 through June 2008; American cirrculum.

David Rittmann, Head of School

1132 Cummings Elementary School
Unit 5039
APO Misawa
Japan, AP 96319-5039

81-3117-66-2226
Fax: 81-3117-62-5110

Commited to guideing students to become successful learners and responsible citizens.

Dr. Frank Vohovich, Principal

1133 Dalat School
Tanjung Bunga 11200 Penang
Malaysia

60-4-899-2105
Fax: 60-4-890-2141
E-mail: office@dalat2.po.my

Offers American style college preparatory curriculum.

Dwight Carlblom, Director

1134 Dover Court Prep School
Dover Road
Singapore 0513
Singapore

Maureen Roach, Principal

1135 Ela Beach International School
PO Box 282
Port Moresby, Papua
New Guinea

This school consists of 262 boys and 222 girl day students in PreK-Grade 6. The length of stay for overseas teachers is three years with housing provided. School enrollment is made up of 260 PNG children, 224 non PNG children,overseas and PNG staff team teaching in mixed age group classrooms.

Bruce E Mackinlay, Principal

1136 Elsternwick Campus-Wesley College
577 St. Kilda Road
Prahran 3181, Victoria 9185
Australia

03-9510-8694

Fax: 03-9521-3164
E-mail: principal@wesley.vic.edu.ar

This college is affiliated with the United Church in Australia and offers an English curriculum to 450 day students (250 boys and 220 girls), in pre-preparatory to year ten. The student/teacher ratio currently being 11:1, the schoolis willing to participate in a teacher exchange program. The length of stay for overseas teachers is one year and the housing provided is exchange housing only.

Rev. Robert W Renton, Principal

1137 Faisalabad Grammar School
Kohinoor Nagar
Faisalabad 728593
Pakistan

This Islamic school offers a curriculum taught in both English and Urdu to 2,000 day students (1,000 boys; 1,000 girls), in Junior Nursery up to eighteen years of age. The school runs 50% of classes in Matriculation Streams Local, and50% in 'O' and 'A' level University of Cambridge UK examinations. Applications needed to teach include science, math, English and computers, with the length of stay for overseas teachers being one year.

RY Saigol Sarfraz, Principal
N Akhtar MSc (Bio), VP

1138 Faith Academy
PO Box 2016 MCPO
0706 Makati City
Philippines

63-2-658-0048
Fax: 63-2-658-0026
E-mail: vanguard@faith.edu.ph
http://www.faith.edu.ph

Grade levels kindergarten through twelfth, enrollment 630 students.

Craig Cook, Superindentent
Martha Macomber, Deputy Superindentent

1139 French International School
165 Blue Pool
Happy Valley, SAR, Hong Kong
China

852-257-76217
Fax: 852-257-79658
E-mail: fis@lfis.edu.hk

Grade levels Pre-K through 13, school year September - June

Pascal Panthene, Headmaster

1140 Fukuoka International School
3-18-50 Momochi
Sawara-ku, Fukuoka 814-0006
Japan

81-92-841-7601
Fax: 81-92-841-7602
E-mail: adminfis@fka.att.ne.jp
http://www.worldwide.edu/japan/fukuoka

Prekindergarten through grade 12 for English-speaking students of all nationalities. There are English-as-a-Second-Language classes available throughout the grades. The school year comprises 2 semesters extending approximately fromSeptember 1 to June 15.

Barry Clough, Headmaster

1141 Garden International School
#16 Jalan 1/61Aoff Jalan Bukit
Kiara, PO Box 13056, 50798 Kuala Lumpur
Malaysia

603-6201-8988
Fax: 603-6201-2467
E-mail: admin@gardenschool.edu.my
http://www.gardenschool.edu.my

Grade levels preK through eleventh.

Raymond Davis, Principal

1142 Geelong Grammar School-Glamorgan
50 Biddlecomb Avenue
Corio, Victoria 3142
Australia

61-3-5273-9200
Fax: 61-3-5274-1695

Boarding day school for girls and boys Nursery to 12.

IL Sutherland, Principal

1143 German Swiss International School
11 Guildford Road, The Peak
Hong Kong
China

852-849-6216
Fax: 852-2849-6347

Grades levels K-12.

E Schierschke, Principal

1144 Glenunga International High School
Le Strange Street
Glenuga 5064
Australia

Grade levels 8-12.

Robert Knight, Principal

1145 Good Hope School-Kowloon
303clear Water Bay Road
Kowloon
Hong Kong

852-2321-0250
Fax: 850-2324-8242
E-mail: goodhope@ghs.edu.uk

1146 Goroka International School
PO Box 845
Goroka Ehp Papua
New Guinea

675-732-1466
Fax: 675-732-2146
E-mail: gorokais@global.net.pg
http://www.ieapng.com

Grade levels prekindergarten through tenth.

Gaven Hogan, Principal

1147 Hebron School-Lushington Hall
Ootacamund, Lushington Hall
643 001 Nilgris
India

91-423-244-2587
Fax: 91-423-244-1295

Independent, international Christain school.

Rod L Gilbert, BEd, Principal

1148 Hillcrest International School
PO Box 249
Sentani 99352
Indonesia

62-967-591-460
Fax: 62-967-591-673
E-mail: his-pos7@maf.org

HIS is a Christian international school. Teachers must raise their own support, normally with a mission. Enrollment consists of 97 day students and 24 boarding (53 boys; 68 girls), in grades K-12.

Dr. Kenneth Schmitt, Principal

1149 Hiroshima International School
3-49-1 Kurakake
Asakita-Ku, Hiroshima 739-1743
Japan

81-82-843-4111
Fax: 81-82-843-6399
E-mail: hishead@orange.ocn.ne.jp
http://http://hiroshima-is.ac.jp

The Hiroshima International School is an independent, coeducational day school which offers educational programs from preschool through grade 12. The school year comprises 2 semesters extending from early September to mid-June.

Paul Ketkok, Principal

1150 Hokkaido International School
1-55, 5-Jo, 19-Chome
Hirahishi, Toyohira-Ku
Sapporo, Hokkaido 062, Japan

81-11-816-5000
Fax: 81-11-816-2500
E-mail: his@his.ac.jp
http://http://his.ac.jp

A private, coeducational day and boarding school which offers an America-style education from preschool through grade 12.

Wayne Rutherford, Headmaster

1151 Hong Kong International School
1 Red Hill Road
Tai Tam, Hong Kong
China

852-3149-7816
Fax: 852-281-38740
E-mail: csteinbach@hkis.edu.hk
http://www.hkis.edu.hk

The Hong Kong International School is a private, Christian, coeducational day school which offers an educational program from pre-primary through grade 12 for students of all nationalities and religious backgrounds. The school yearcomprises 2 semesters extending approximately from August 19 to January 16 and from January 19 to June 12.

William Wehrenberg, Head of School
Jan Westrick, Deputy Head of School

1152 Ikego Elementary School
PSC 473 Box 96
APO, Yokosuka
Japan, AP 96349-0005

81-468-72-8320
E-mail: IKEG_ESprincipal@pac.odedodea.edu

Grade levels K-6.

1153 Indianhead School
523-1, Saengyon 1 Dong
Tongduchon City 483-031
Korea

82-2-999-4707
Fax: 82-31-826-3476
E-mail: indian@soback.kornet.nm.kr

Myungsin Park, President

1154 International Christian School
PO Box 89009
Kowloon City, SAR Hong Kong
China

852-2304-6808
Fax: 852-2336-6114
E-mail: admin@ics.edu.hk
http://www.ics.edu.hk

Grade levels Pre-K through 12, school year August - June

Robert Morgan, Headmaster
Michael Bevis, HS Principal

1155 International Community School
72 Soi Prong Jai
Thungmahmek, Sathorn, Bangkok 10120
Thailand

662-679-7175
Fax: 662-287-4530
E-mail: info@icsbangkok.com
http://www.ICSBangkok.com

Grade levels K-12, school year August - June

James Bedford, Headmaster
Orrin Everhat, Financial Manager

1156 International School Manila
University Parkway
Fort Bonifacio, Taguig 1634 Metro Manila
Philippines

63-2-840-8400
Fax: 63-2-899-3964
E-mail: superintendent @ismanila.com
http://www.ismanila.com

Grades K-12, enrollment 1,868.

Dr. Donald Bergman, Superintendent

1157 International School of the Sacred Heart
4-3-1 Hiroo
Shibuya-Ku, Tokyo 150
Japan

81-3-3400-3951
Fax: 81-3-3400-3496
E-mail: issh@gol.com
http://http://iac.co.jp/~issh3

This catholic girls school offers an English curriculum to 600 day students in grades K-12.

Masako Egawa, Headmaster

1158 International School-Bangkok
39/7 Soi Nichada Thani
Samakee Road, Nonthaburi 11120
Thailand

66-2-963-5800
Fax: 66-2-583-5432
E-mail: revadik@isb.ac.th
http://www.isb.ac.th

Grade levels K-1, school year August - June

Stepehn Conner, Chairman

1159 International School-Beijing

10 An Hua Street
Shunyi District, Beijing 100004
China

8610-8149-2345
Fax: 8610-8046-2002
E-mail: addmissions@isb.bj.edu.cn
http://www.isb.bj.edu.cn

Jointly sponsored by the governments of Australia, Canada, New Zealand and the United States, as the successor to the American Educational Association and the former australian, Canadian, and British schools. ISB is an Eglishlanguage, private, nonsectarian college preparatory, coeducational day school offering a program ranging from prekindergarten through grade 12.

Paul Dulac, Director

1160 International School-Eastern Seaboard

PO Box 6
Banglamung, Chonburi 20150
Thailand

038-345-556-9
Fax: 038-345-156-038
E-mail: ise@loxinfo.co.th
http://www.ise.ac.th

Grade levels Pre-K through 12, school year August - June

Bruce Hovbert, Superintendent

1161 International School-Fiji

PO Box 10828
Laucala Beach Estate, Suva
Fiji

679-393-560
Fax: 679-393-300
E-mail: info@international.school.fj
http://www.internationalschool.fj

David Hill, Principal

1162 International School-Ho Chi Minh City

649A Vo Truong Toan
An Phu, District 2, Ho Ci Minh City
Vietnam

84-8-898-9100
Fax: 84-8-887-4022
E-mail: ishcmc@hcm.vnn.vn
http://www.ishcmc.com

Grade levels Pre-K through 12, school year August - June

Sean O'Maonaigh, Headmaster
Alice Walker, President

1163 International School-Kuala Lumpur

PO Box 12645
50784 Kuala Lumpar
Malaysia

603-4259-5600
Fax: 603-4257-9044
E-mail: ISKL@iskl.edu.my
http://www.iskl.edu.my

Grades PK-12, enrollment 1,116.

William Powell, Headmaster

1164 International School-Lae

PO Box 2130
Lea Papua
New Guinea

Bruce Knox, Principal

1165 International School-Manila

Univeristy Parkway
Metro Manila
Philippines

632-840-8400
Fax: 632-899-3964
E-mail: addmissions@ismanila.com
http://www.ismanila.com

Multicultural based curriculum to 2200 day students (1100 boys; 1100 girls), in grades K-12.

David Toze, Superintendent

1166 International School-Penang-Uplands

Kelawei Road
10250 Penang
Malaysia

This school provides education to the children of expatriates working in the region. Students sit for IGCSE and GCE A Level examinations. Total enrollment of the school is 415 day students and 55 boarding (250 boys; 220 girls), gradesNursery through year thirteen. Student/teacher ratio is currently 12:1, and the applications needed to teach include Science, French, Math, Social Sciences, Spanish, German, English and Physical Education.

Ian J Kerr, Principal

1167 International School-Phnom Penh, Cambodia

PO Box 138
Phnom Penh
RK of Cambodia

855-23-213-103/5
Fax: 855-23-361-002
E-mail: ispp@bigpond.com.kh
http://www.cambodia-web.net/education.ispp

Grades PS-12, enrollment 313.

Dr. Michael Francis, Director

1168 International School-Phnom Penh-Cambodia

PO Box 138
Phnom Penh
Cambodia

855-23-213-103
Fax: 855-23-361-002
E-mail: ispp@bigpond.com.kh
http://www.ispp.edu.kh

The International School of Phnom Penh is a private, non-profit, English language, coeducational day school which offers and educational program from preschool through grade 12. The school year consists of 2 semesters, each of 2terms.

Terry Hamilton, Director

1169 International School-Pusan

PO Box 77 Nam Pusan Post Office
Sooyoung-Ku, Pusan
Korea

82-51-742-3332
Fax: 82-51-742-3375
E-mail: ispusan@ispusan.co.kr
http://www.ispusan.co.kr

Grade levels prekindergarten through eighth.

Hugh Younger, Headmaster

1170 International School-Singapore
21 Preston Road
109355
Singapore

65-475-4188
Fax: 65-27-37-065
E-mail: hmiss@mbox5.singnet.com.sg
http://www.iss.edu.sg

ISS offers an integrated curriculum combining an American style high school diploma with the British Examination System. Total enrollment of the school is 650 day students (330 boys; 320 girls), in grades PreK-12.

Margaret Alvarez, Principal

1171 International School-Ulaanbaatar
PO Box 49/564
Ulaanbaatar
Mongolia

976-11-452-839
Fax: 976-11-450-340
E-mail: inschool@magicnet.mn
http://www.mongol.net/inschool

A private, coeducational day school which offers an educational program from preschool through grade 8 for students of all nationalities. The School also offers a grade 9-12 correspondence program.

Anne Fowles, Principal

1172 Island School
20 Borrett Road
Hong Kong, SAR
China

852-252-47135
Fax: 852-284-01673
E-mail: school@is.esf.edu.hk
http://www.island.edu.hk

Grade levels 7 - 13, school year September - June

David James, Principal
Rebecca Yip, Business Manager

1173 Ivanhoe Grammar School
PO Box 91
The Ridgeway, Ivanhoe, Victoria 3079
Australia

61-3-9490-3426
Fax: 61-3-9490-3539
E-mail: enrol@igs.vic.edu.au
http://www.igs.vic.edu.au

An international grammar school.

Charles Sligo BA, Principal

1174 JN Darby Elementary School
PSC 485 Box 99
96321 FPO, AP
Japan

81-6160-52-8800
E-mail: principal_darby_es@pac.odedodea.edu
http://www.darby-es.pac.odedodea.edu

Promote academic excellence so all students will become productive citizens.

1175 Jakarta International School
PO Box 1078/JKS
Jakarta 12010
Indonesia

62-21-769-2555
Fax: 62-21-765-7852
E-mail: jcornacc@jisedu.org
http://www.jisedu.org

Coeducational day school which draws on North American and other curriculum models from preparatory through grade 12.

Niall Nelson, Headmaster

1176 Japan International School
5-20 Kamiyama-cho
Shibuya-Ku, Tokyo 150
Japan

03-3461-1442
Fax: 03-3463-9873

Student of all nationalitites, and religions are welcome.

Regina Doi, BA, Principal

1177 John McGlashan College
2 Pilkington Street
Maori Hill, Dunedin
New Zealand

03-467-6620
Fax: 03-467-6622

An all boys college.

AA Paulin, Principal

1178 Kansai Christian School
951 Tawaraguchi Cho Ikoma Shi
Nara Ken 630-02
Japan

KCS was established to provide Christian instruction for children of evangelical missionaries. Children from Christian homes are welcome to attend, and children from non-Christian homes may enter on a limited basis. The school's enrollment consists of 15 day students (7 boys; 8 girls), in grades 1-8. Applications needed to teach include math, social sciences, science, reading, and English.

David Verwey, Principal

1179 Kaohsiung American School
96 Fu-Teh 3rd Road
Kaohsiung 802
Taiwan

886-7-716-2270
Fax: 886-7-716-2295

This school offers an English based curriculum for a total of 180 day students (65 boys; 65 girls), in PreK-12. The school is willing to participate in a teacher exchange program with the length of stay being one year. Applications needed to teach include science, math, social sciences, reading and physical education.

Dr. Rupert Bale, Principal

1180 Kellett School
2 Wah Lok Path
Wah Fu, Pokfulam, Hong Kong
China

Grades 6-12.

Vivienne E Steer, Principal

Teaching Opportunities Abroad / Asia, Pacific Rim & Australia

1181 Kilmore International School
40 White Street
Kilmore, Victoria 3764
Australia

61-357-822-211
Fax: 61-357-822-525
E-mail: tkisadmn@kilmore.vic.edu.au
http://www.kilmore.vic.edu.au

This school offers an English curriculum for 29 day students and 121 boarding (100 boys and 50 girls), grades 7-12. The applications needed to teach include science, math, social sciences, English and physical education. The length ofstay for teachers is one year, and housing is only provided if the teacher wishes to be involved in boarding. Student/teacher ratio is 5:1.

John Settle, Principal

1182 Kinabalu International School
PO Box 12080
88822 Kota Kinabalu, Sabah
Malaysia

This school offers an English-based curriculum for 100 day students (50 boys; 50 girls), ages 3-13 years.

1973 pages

Barbara D. Abidin, Principal

1183 King George V School
2 Tin Kwong Road
Kowloon
China

852-2711-3028
Fax: 852-276-07116
E-mail: kgvsch@hk.net

Non selective secondary school which provides a broad.

Michael Behennah, Principal

1184 Kitakyushu International School
Yahata Higashi-ku Takami 2
Shinnittetsu Shijo
Japan

093-652-0682

This school offers an English based curriculum for 8 day students (2 boys; 6 girls), in kindergarten through elementary. The school is always looking for dedicated and qualified teachers to teach children and adults in school andpreschool (especially female teachers). Applications needed include preschool and English.

Ann Ratnayake, Principal

1185 Kodaikanal International School
PO Box 25
7 Roads Junction, 624-101 Kodaikanal
India

91-4542-41104
Fax: 91-4542-41109
E-mail: principal@kis.ernet.in
http://www.kis.ernet.in

Grade levels Pre-K through 12, school year July - May

Sara Lockwood, Addmissions Officer

1186 Kooralbyn International School
Ogilvie Place-Kooralbyn
Queensland 4285
Australia

07-5544-6288

Fax: 07-5544-6108
http://www.isd.com.au/schools/q7209

Aims to provide students with a broad liberal education.

Robyn Collins, Principal

1187 Kowloon Junior School
20 Perth Street
Kowloon
China

Primary students learn English, maths, science, technology, history, geography, art, music and physical education.

GT Davies, Principal

1188 Kyoto International School
317 Kitatawara-cho, Yoshiyamachi-dori, Nakadachiuri-sagaru, Kamigyo-ku
Kyoto, 602 8247, Japan

81-75-451-1022
Fax: 81-75-451-1023
E-mail: hellokis@mbox.kyoto-inet.or.jp
http://www.kyoto-is.org

Grade levels Pre-K through 8, school year September - June

Gerry Moran, Headmaster

1189 Lahore American School
American Consulate General Lahore
LAS
APO, Unit 62216 09812 2216
Pakistan

92-42-576-2406
Fax: 92-42-571-1901
E-mail: las@las.edu.pk

An independent, coeducational day school which offers an educational program from nursery through grade 12 for students of all nationalities.

Everett McGlothin, Superintendent

1190 Lanna International School Thailand
300 Grandview Moo 1
Chiang-Mai to Hang Dong Road, Chiang Mai
50100, Thailand

66-53-806-231
Fax: 66-53-271-159
E-mail: lannaist@loxinfo.co.th

Grade levels Pre-K through 12, school year August - June

Robert Lewis, Head of School
Rachanee Puangwong, Thai Headmistress

1191 Lincoln School
GPO 2673
Kathmandu
Nepal

977-1-270-482
Fax: 977-1-272-685
E-mail: info@lsnepal.com.np
http://www.lsnepal.com

Grade levels preschool - 12, school year August - June

Barbara Butterworth, PhD, Director

1192 Makassar International School
Jalan Andi Mappanyukki
Makassar, Sulawesi Selatan 90125
Indonesia

62-411-872-591
Fax: 62-411-873-035
E-mail: mischool@indosat.net.id
http://www.crosswinds.net\-mischool

Grade levels Pre-K through 7, school year August - June

Andrew Etheridge, Principal

1193 Malacca Expatriate School
2443-C Jalan Batang Tiga
Malacca
Malaysia

06-315-4970

Mission is provide a high standard of learning.

Neil Jackson, Principal

1194 Marist Brothers International School
1-2-1 Chimori-cho
Suma-ku, Kobe 654-0072
Japan

078-732-6266
Fax: 078-732-6268
E-mail: info@marist.ac.jp
http://www.marist.ac.jp

Grade levels Pre-K through 12, school year September - June

Mary Fyfe, Headmistress
Kevin Roxas, HS Principal

1195 Matthew C Perry Elementary School
PSC 561 Box 1874
FPO Iwakuni 96310 1874
Japan

81-611-753-3447
Fax: 81-611-753-6490

Committed to promoting student achievement in a postive safe enviroment.

David Crittenden, Principal

1196 Matthew C Perry Middle & High School
PSC 561 Box 1874
FPO Iwakuni 96310 1874
Japan

Lawrence Wolfe, Principal

1197 Mentone Boys Grammar School
63 Venice St. Mentone
Melbourne 3196
Australia

03-9584-4211
Fax: 03-9581-3290
E-mail: admin@mentonegs.vic.edu.au
http://www.mentonegs.vic.edu.au

Neville J Clark, Principal

1198 Mercedes College
540 Fullarton Road
Springfield 5063
South Australia

61-8-379-6844
Fax: 61-8-379-9540

This Catholic school offers a curriculum based in English for 901 day students (407 boys; 494 girls) in grades Reception-12. The school is willing to participate in a teacher exchange program with the length of stay being one to twoyears, housing not provided.

Chris McCabe, BA, MA, Principal

1199 Methodist Ladies College
207 Barkers Road Kew Victoria
3101 Victoria
Australia

03-9274-6333
Fax: 03-9819-2345
E-mail: shane@mlc.vic.edu.au
http://www.mlc.vic.edu.au

This college prepares its students for the world of tomorrow by liberating their talents through challenge, enrichment, and opportunity in a supportive Christian environment. Committed to technology and to student initiated learningso each girl from year five onward works with her personal computer to understand the present and shape the future. Total enrollment: 2,135 day students; 105 boarding. Grade range K-12. The school is willing to participate in a teacher exchangeprogram.

David Loader, Principal

1200 Minsk International School
DOS/Administrative Officer
7010 Minsk Place
Washington, DC 20521-7010

375-172-343-035
Fax: 375-172-343-035
E-mail: mis@open.by

An independent, coeducational day school which offers an educational program from kindergarten through grade 8 for students of all nationalities. Enrollment 11.

Lisa Cummins, Director

1201 Moreguina International Primary School
PO Box 438
Konedobu Papua
New Guinea

Wayne Coleman, Principal

1202 Morrison Christian Academy
136-1 Shui Nan Road
Taichung 406
Taiwan

886-4-2292-1171
Fax: 886-4-2295-6140
E-mail: morrison@mknet.org
http://www.morrison.mknet.org

This academy offers Chinese and Spanish to 769 students in K-12.

Gregory Meeks, Superintendent
Tim McGill, Business Manager

1203 Mount Hagen International School
PO Box 1050
Mount Hagen
New Guinea

CM White, Principal

1204 Mt Zaagham International School
PT Freeport
Timika Irian Joya 9920
Indonesia

62-9-014-07641

Fax: 62-901-403-170
E-mail: joecuthbertson@efmi.com

Grade levels Pre-K through 98, school year September - June. Two campuses Tembagapura and Kula Kencanna

Dr. Joe Cuthbertson, Superintendent
Richard Ledger, Principal

1205 Murray International School
PO Box 1137
Boroko Papua
New Guinea

Maureen Stubberfield, Principal

1206 Murree Christian School
Jhika Gali
Murree, 47180
Pakistan

This school offers an English-based curriculum for 20 day students and 140 boarding students (75 boys; 85 girls), in grades K-12. Murree Christian School educates the children of missionaries from 14 different countries working inPakistan and the region. Living allowances rather than salaries are awarded. Overseas teacher stay is two years with housing provided by the school.

Phil Billing, Director
Linda Fisher, HS Faculty Head

1207 Mussoorie International School
Srinagar Estate
Mussoorie Up
India

HK Rawal, Principal

1208 Nagoya International School
2686 Minamihara, Nakashidami
Moriyama-ku, Nagoya, 463-0002
Japan

81-52-736-2025
Fax: 81-52-736-3883
E-mail: nisinfo@kr.tep-ip.or.jp
http://www.nisjapan.net

Grade levels Pre-K through 12, school year August - June

1209 Narrabundah College
Jerrabomberra Avenue
Kingston, Canberra
Australia

This college offers an English based curriculum for 930 total day students (558 boys; 372 girls), in grades 11 and 12. The school is willing to participate in a teacher exchange program with the length of stay being one year, with nohousing provided. This is a secondary college with teaching specialities: International Baccalaureate, foreign language, performing arts, creative arts, sciences and ESL.

Jeff Mason, Principal

1210 New International School of Thailand
Un Building
Rajadamnern Avenue, 10200 Bangkok
Thailand

Harry Deelman, Principal

1211 Nile C Kinnick High School
PSC 473 Box 95
FPO Yokosuka 96349 0005
Japan

Bruce Derr, Principal

1212 Nishimachi International School
2-14-7 Moto Azabu, Minato-ku
Tokyo
Japan

81-3-3451-5520
Fax: 81-3-3456-0197
E-mail: info@nishimachi.ac.jp
http://www.nishimachi.ac.jp

Offers a dual-language, multicultural program ro 430 student k-9.

Thomas Walters, Headmaster

1213 Okinawa Christian School International
PO Box 6, Yomitan
Okinawa 904-0391
Japan

81-98-958-3000
Fax: 81-98-958-6279
E-mail: ocschool@ii-okinawa.ne.jp
http://www.ocsi.org

Grade levels K-12, school year August - June

Cullen Ohashi, Superintendent

1214 Osaka International School
4-4-16 Onohara-nishi
Mino-shi, Osaki-Fu 562 0032
Japan

81-727-275-050
Fax: 81-727-275-055
E-mail: addmissions@senri.ed.jp
http://www.senri.ed.jp

Grade levels Pre-K through 13, school year September - June

Julie Wagner, Head

1215 Osaka YMCA International High School
1-5-6 Tosabori Nishi-ku
Osaka 550
Japan

Katsushigo Majima, Principal

1216 Osan Elementary School
Unit 2037
APO Osan 96278 0005
Korea

Ronald Warner, Principal

1217 Osan High School
Unit 2037
APO Osan 96278 0005
Korea

Ronald Warner, Principal

1218 Overseas Children's School
Pellawatte PO Box 9
Battaramulla, Sri Lanka

Dennis MacKinnon, BA, MA, Principal

1219 Overseas Family School
25 F Paterson Road
238515
Singapore

65-738-0211
Fax: 65-733-8825
E-mail: executive_director@ofs.edu.sg
http://www.ofs.edu.sg

Grade levels prekindergarten through 13, enrollment 1,660.

David Perry, Chairman

1220 Overseas School of Colombo
Pelawatte
PO Box 9, Battarandulla
Sri Lanka

94-1-864-920
Fax: 94-1-864-999
E-mail: admin@osc.lk
http://www.osc.lk

Grades preSchool-12, enrollment 313.

Peter Gittins, Head of School

1221 Pacific Harbour International School
PO Box 50
Pacific Harbour, Deuba
Fiji Islands

Janet Tuni, Principal

1222 Pasir Ridge International
Unocal-po Box 3-tampines S
Balikpapan 9152
Singapore

62-542-543-474
Fax: 62-542-767-126
http://prschool@bpp.mega.net.id

Grade levels preK through 8.

Kathryn Carter-Golden PhD, Principal

1223 Peak School
20 Plunketts Road
Hong Kong
China

PL Young, Principal

1224 Phuket International Preparatory School
PO Box 432
Phuket 83000
Thailand

Agnes Hebler, Principal

1225 Popondetta International School
PO Box 10
Popondetta, Papua
New Guinea

Michael Whitting, Principal

1226 Prahram Campus-Wesley College
577 St. Kilda Road-Prahran
Victoria 3181 Australia

AB Conabere, Principal

1227 Pusan American School
Do DOS
Pusan 96259
South Korea

82-51-801-7528
Fax: 82-51-803-1729

E-mail: pas@pac.odedodea.edu
http://www.210.107.81.252

Alexia Venglek, Principal

1228 Pusan Elementary & High School
Unit 15625
APO AP 96259-0005, Pusan
Korea

82-52-801-7528
Fax: 82-51-803-1729

1229 QSI International School-Phuket
PO Box 432
Phuket, 83000
Thailand

66-76-354076
Fax: 66-76-354077
E-mail: pkt@qsi.org
http://www.phuketschl.com

Grade levels N-12, school year August-June

Khun Janrita Hnobnorb, Administrative Coordinator

1230 QSI International School-Zhuhai
22 Longxing Street
Zhuhai 519020
China

86-756-815-6134
Fax: 86-756-889-6758
http://www.qsi.org

Grade levels N-8, school year September-June

Bruce Wood, Director

1231 Quarry Bay School
6 Hau Yuen Braemar Hill
North Point, Hong Kong
China

DJ Harrison, Principal

1232 Rabaul International School
PO Box 571
Rabaul Enbp, Papua
New Guinea

Ian Smith, Principal

1233 Richard E Byrd Elementary School
PSC 472 Box 12
FPO Yokohama 96348 0005
Japan

Milton Halloran, Principal

1234 Robert D Edgren High School
Unit 5040
APO Misawa 96319 5040
Japan

Daborah Berry, Principal

1235 Ruamrudee International School
42 Moo 4
Ramkamhaeng 184 Road
Minburi, Bangkok, 10510

66-2-518-0320
Fax: 66-2-518-0334
E-mail: director@rism.ac.th
http://www.rism.ac.th

Grade levels K-12, school year August - June

Fr. Leo Travis, Director
Dave Parsons HS Principal

1236 Saigon South International School
Saigon S Parkway, Tan Phu Ward
Ho Chi Minh City
Vietnam

84-8-873-1375
Fax: 84-8-873-1375
E-mail: ssischool@hcm.vnn.vn
http://www.web.cybercon.com/SSIS
Grade levels Pre-K through 7, school year August - June

Robert Crowther, Headmaster

1237 Sancta Maria International School
41 Karasawa Minami-ku
Yokohama
Japan

Sr Mary Elizabeth Doll, Principal

1238 School at Tembagapura
PO Box 616 Cairns
Queensland 4870
Australia

Bruce Goforth, Principal

1239 Scots PGC College
60 Oxenham Street
Warwick, QLD 4370
Australia

61-7-4666-9922
Fax: 61-7-4666-9999
E-mail: postbox@scotspgc.qld.edu.au
http://www.scotspgc.qld.edu.au

Neil O Bonnell MEd, Principal

1240 Seisen International School
12-15 Yoga 1-chome
Setagaya-Ku, Tokyo 158
Japan

03-3704-2661
Fax: 033701-1033
E-mail: sisinfo@seisen.com
http://www.seisen.com
Grade levels pre-K through twelfth.

Concesa Martin, Headmistress

1241 Semarang International School
Jl Jangli 37, Semarang
Semarang 50254, Central Java
Indonesia

62-24-8311-424
Fax: 62-24-8311-994

E Fitzgerald DipEd, Principal

1242 Seoul Academy
Young Dong
PO Box 85, Seoul
Korea

82-2-562-1690
Fax: 82-2-562-0451
E-mail: unicorn@uriel.net
http://www.uriel.net/~unicorn
Grade levels pre-K through eighth.

Thomas O'Connor, Director

1243 Seoul British School
55 Yonhi Dong Sudaemun Ku
Seoul
Korea

Philip Mayor-Smith, Principal

1244 Seoul Elementary School
Unit 15549
APO, Seoul 96205 0005
Korea

John Blom, Principal

1245 Seoul Foreign School
55 Yonhi-Dong
Seoul 120-113
Korea

82-2-330-3100
Fax: 82-2-335-1857
E-mail: sfsoffice@sfs.or.kr
http://www.sfs-h.ac.kr
Grade levels preK through 12. Offering IB diploma st the HS and both North American and British programs at the Elementary and Middle Schools.
Harlan Lyso PhD, Headmaster
Steven Nurre, Director Human Resources

1246 Seoul High School
Unit 15549
APO, Seouls 96205 0005
South Korea

Dr. Benjamin Briggs, Principal

1247 Shanghai American School
258 Jin Feng Lu
Zhudi Town, Minhang District, Shanghai
201107 China

86-21-6221-1445
Fax: 86-21-6221-1269
E-mail: info@saschina.org
http://www.saschina.org
Grade levels Pre-K through 12, school year August - June

Anthony Horton PhD, Superintendent

1248 Shatin College
3 Lai Wo Lane
Fo Tan, Shatin, Hong Kong
China

This mixed international school provides high quality education through the medium of English, leading to GCSE and A-level examinations. The student body of 900 day students is comprised of 450 boys and 450 girls in grades 7-13.Applications from overseas needed to teach at the school include science, French, math, social sciences, Spanish, German, English and physical education. The student/teacher ratio is 14:1, with a curriculum in English.

David Cottam, MA, MSc, Principal

1249 Shatin Junior College
3A Lai Wo Lane
Sha Tin, Hong Kong
China

BG Lewis, Principal

1250 Shirley Lanham Elementary School
PSC 477 Box 38
FPO Atsugi 96306 0005
Japan

Susan Jackson, Principal

1251 Singapore American School
40 Woodlands Street 41
Singapore 738547
Singapore

65-6360-6309
Fax: 65-6363-3408
E-mail: sasinfo@sas.edu.sg
http://www.sas.edu.sg

Day school which offers an educational program from preschool through grade 12 for students of all nationalities. The school year comprises 2 semesters extending from approximately August 17 to December 18, and from January 11 to June4.

Bob Gross, Superintendent

1252 Sollars Elementary School
Unit 5041
APO Misawa 96319 5041
Japan

Scarlett Rehrig, Principal

1253 South Island School
50 Nam Fung Road
Hong Kong
China

RE Brookin, Principal

1254 St. Andrews International School-Bangkok
9 Soi Pridi Banomyong 20
Sukhumvit Soi 71, Prakanong, Bangkok
10110, Thailand

2381-2387
Fax: 2390-1780
E-mail: bangkok@at-andrews.ac
http://www.st-andrews.ac

Grade levels N-5, school year September - July

Mary Gibb, Head of School
Janet Gigler, Deputy Head

1255 St. Christopher's School
10 Nunn Road
10350 Penang
Malaysia

JM Wrench, Principal

1256 St. John's International School
1110/1-11 Bipavadee-Rungsit Road
Jatujak, Bangkok 10900
Thailand

662-938-7058-65
Fax: 662-513-8588
E-mail: info@stjohn.ac.th

Chainarong Monthienvic, Principal

1257 St. Joseph International School
85 Yamate-cho Naka-ku
Yokohama 231
Japan

45-641-0065
E-mail: sjislib@gol.com

Coeducational day/boarding school, preschool through grade 12.

James Mueller, Principal

1258 St. Joseph's International Primary School
PO Box 5784
Boroko Papua
New Guinea

Barbara D'Arbon, Principal

1259 St. Mark's College
46 Penntington Tce
North Adelaide
South Australia 5006

08-8334-5600
Fax: 08-8267-4694
E-mail: manager@atmarkscollege.com.au
http://www.stmarkscollege.com.au

Grade levels Pre-K through 12, school year March - December

Gabriela de Martin, Principal
Alejandra Rubio, Vice Head

1260 St. Mary's International School
1-6-19 Seta Setagaya-ku
Tokyo 158
Japan

This international school for boys in grades K-12 offers an America curriculum and international baccalaureate program. The enrollment of the catholic school includes 920 day students with the student/teacher ratio being 20:1.Overseas teachers are welcome for an indefinite time period with the applications needed to teach being science, pre-school, French, math, social sciences, administration, reading, English and physical education.

Michel Jutras, Principal

1261 St. Maur International School
83 Yamate-cho Naka-ku
Yokohama 231-8654
Japan

45-641-5751

This Roman Catholic affiliated school offers an English-based curriculum to 500 day students in grades PreK-12. This is a co-ed K-12 college preparatory catholic international school. Teachers are from US, Canada, UK, Australia and SAfrica. Overseas teachers are offered an annual contract that is renewable each year. Housing is provided but deduction from pay is made. Applications needed to teach include science, Montessori preschool, French, math, Spanish and English

Jeanette Thomas, Headmistress
Richard B Rucci, Principal

1262 St. Michael's International School
3-17-2 Nakayamate-Dori
Chuo-ku, Kobe, Hyoyo-Ken 650-0004
Japan

81-78-231-8885
Fax: 81-78-231-8899
E-mail: smis@movenet.or.jp

This Anglican school offers an English curriculum for 95 day students (45 boys; 30 girls), in grades pre-school through 6th.

Aileen Pardon, Principal

1263 St. Stephen's International School
Viphavadi Rangsit Road
Lad Yao, Chatuchak, Bangkok 10900
Thailand

66-2-5130270
Fax: 66-2-9303307
E-mail: info@sis.edu
http://www.sis.edu

Grade levels N-2, enrollment 205

Richard A Ralphs, School Director
Amara Sawasidevi, School Head

1264 St. Xavier's Greenherald School
Asad Ave-Mohammedpur
Dhaka 1207
Bangladesh

Mary Imelda, Principal

1265 Stearley Heights Elementary School
Unit 5166
APO Kadena 96368 5166
Okinawa

Thomas Godbold, Principal

1266 Sullivans Elementary School
PSC 473, Box 96
Yokosuka 96349 0005
Japan

Dr. Carol Cressy, Principal

1267 Surabaya International School
CitraRaya International Village
Tromol Pos 2/SBDK
Surabaya 60225
Indonesia

62-31-741-4300
Fax: 62-31-741-4334
E-mail: Incsupt@rad.net.id

Private, coeducational day school which offers an educational program from preschool through grade 12.

Larry Crouch, Superintendent

1268 TEDA International School-Tianjin
Wei Shan Road, Shuang Gang
Tianjin 300350
China

86-22-2859-2001
Fax: 86-22-2859-2007
E-mail: tist_development@yahoo.com
http://www.tistschool.org

Grade levels N-10, school year August - June

Nick Bowley, Director

1269 Tabubil International School
PO Box 408 Tabubil
W Province, Papua
New Guinea

SE Walker, Principal

1270 Taegu Elementary & High School
Unit 15623
APO Taegu 96218 0005
Korea

Leon Rivers, Principal

1271 Taipei American School
800 Chung Shan N Road
Section 6, Shin Lin 111, Taipei
Taiwan

886-2-287-39900
Fax: 886-2-287-31641
E-mail: mainadmn@tas.edu.tw
http://www.tas.edu.tw

An independent, coeducational school, which offers K-12 for students of all nationalities. Hosts 2,142 students. Offers Mandarin, French, Spanish and Japanese language courses.

Mark Ulfers, Superintendent
Ira B Weislow, Business Manager

1272 Tanglin Trust Schools
Portsdown Road
Songapore 0513
Singapore

65-67780711
Fax: 65-67775862
E-mail: dvmt@tt.edu.sg
http://www.tts.edu.sg

Gade levels prekindergarten through eleventh, enrollment 1550.

Ronald Stones, Head of School

1273 Thai-Chinese International School
Prasertsin Road, Bangplee-Yai
Bangplee, Sumut Prakarm 10540
Thailand

66-2-260-8202
E-mail: tcis@schoolmail.com

Grade levels Pre-K through 12, school year August - June

1274 Timbertop Campus
Timbertop PB-Mansfield
Victoria 3722
Australia

S Leslie, Principal

1275 Traill Preparatory School
34-36 S01
18 Ramkhamheng Road, Huamark Bangkok
Thailand

AM Traill, Principal

1276 Ukarumpa High School
PO Box 406
Ukarumpa Via Lae, Papua
New Guinea

Steve Walker, Principal

1277 United Nations International School-Hanoi
2C Van Phuc Diplomatic Compound
Kima Ma Road, Hanoi
Veitnam

84-0-4846-1284
Fax: 84-0-4846-2967

E-mail: postmaster@unishanoi.netnam.vn
http://www.unishanoi.org

A private, nonprofit, English language, coeducational day school which offers an educational program from prekindergarten through grade 12 for the expatriate community of Hanoi.

Frances Rhodes PhD, Director

1278 United World College-SE Asia
Pasir Panjang
PO Box 15, Singapore 9111
Singapore

65-775-5344
Fax: 65-778-5846
E-mail: uwcsea@singnet.com.sg
http://www.uwcsea.edu.sg

Grade levels k-12, enrollment 2,358.

Andrew Bennet, Head of College

1279 University Vacancies in Australia
Australian Vice-Chancellors' Committee
PO Box 1142
Canberra City
Australia

61-02-6285-8200
Fax: 60-02-6285-8211
E-mail: enquiries@avcc.edu.au
http://www.avcc.edu.au

1280 Vientiane International School
PO Box 3180
Vientianne
Laos PDR

856-21-313-606
Fax: 856-21-315-008
E-mail: dragon@laotel.com
http://www.vis.laopdr.com

Grades PS-9, enrollment 159.

John Ritter, Director

1281 Wellesley College
PO Box 41037
Eastbourne, Wellington
New Zealand

G Dreadon, Principal

1282 Wesley International School
Kotak Pos 275
Jalan Simpang Kwoka 1, Malang 65101
Indonesia

62-341-586410
Fax: 62-341-586413
E-mail: wesley@mlg.mega.net.id
http://www.weleyinterschool.org

Grade levels K-12, school year August - May

Paul Richardson, HS Principal

1283 Western Academy of Beijing
PO Box 8547
Chao Yong District, Beijing 100102
China

86-10-8456-4155
Fax: 86-10-6432-2440
E-mail: wabinfo@westernacademy.com
http://www.wab.edu

Grade levels N-8, school year August - June

John McBryde, Director

1284 Wewak International Primary School
PO Box 354
Wewak Esp, Papua
New Guinea

Darian Sullavan, Principal

1285 Woodstock School
Mussoorie 248 179
Uttar Pradesh
India

91-135-632-610
Fax: 91-135-632-885
http://www.woodstock.ac.in

Woodstock is an international Christian boarding school, for grades preK-12.

David Jeffery, Principal

1286 Xiamen International School
Jiu Tian Hu, Xinglin District
Xiamen 361022
China

86-592-625-6581
Fax: 86-592-625-6584
E-mail: JDFISCH47@yahoo.com
http://www.xischina.com

Grade levels Pre-K through 12, school year August - June

Rob Leveillee PhD, Headmaster

1287 Yew Chung Shanghai International School
11 Shui Cheng Road
20036 Shanghai
China

8621-6242-3243
Fax: 8621-6242-7331
E-mail: inquiry@ycef.com
http://www.ycef.com

Grade levels Pre-K through 12, school year September - July

Wayne McCullar PhD, Co-Principal
James O'Connor, Co-Principal

1288 Yogyakarta International School
Jl Kaliurang KM5
Pogung Baru Block
Indonesia

62-274-586-067
Fax: 62-274-586-067
E-mail: yisworld@indosat.net.id

Grade levels Pre-K through 6, school year August - June

Mark Massion, Principal

1289 Yokohama International School
258 Yamate-cho Naka-ku
Yokohama 241
Japan

81-45-622-0084
Fax: 81-45-621-0379
E-mail: yis@yis.ac.jp
http://www.yis.ac.jp

Grade levels N through 12.

Neil Richards, Headmaster

1290 Yokota East Elementary School
DoDDS P J YE Unit 5072
APO, Yokota 96328 5072
Japan

81-3117-55-5503
Fax: 81-3117-55-5502

Yokota East Elementary School is located on Yokota Air Force Base near Tokyo, Japan. There are approximately 900 students grades K-6.

Charles Yahres, Principal

1291 Yokota High School
DoDDS P J YH Unit 5072
APO, Yokota 96328 5072
Japan

Dr. Edward Davies, Principal

1292 Yokota West Elementary School
DoDDS P J YW Unit 5072
APO, Yokota 96328 5072
Japan

James Bowers, Principal

1293 Yonggwang Foreign School
Ceii Site Office
PO Box 9, Yonggwang-Kun 513-880
Korea

Eleanor Jones, Principal

1294 Zama Junior High & High School
USA Garrison, Camp Zama
APO, Honshu 96343 0005
Japan

Samuel Menniti, Principal

1295 Zukeran Elementary School
Unit 35017
FPO 96373 5017
Japan

011-81-611-7452576
Fax: 011-81-611-7457662
E-mail: zessac@hotmail.com
http://www.oki-dso.odedodea/okinawa/schools/zes/zes.html

Sharon Carter, Principal

Central & South America

1296 Academia Cotopaxi American International School
De las Higuerillas y Alondras
Quito, Ecuador, Casilla 1701-199
Ecuador

593-2-246-7373
Fax: 593-2-244-5195
E-mail: director@cotopaxi.k12.ec
http://www.cotopaxi.k12.ec

Grade levels Pre-K through 12, school year August - June

F Joseph Stucker, Director

1297 American Cooperative School
Lawton 20
Paramarobo
Suriname

597-49-9461
Fax: 597-498-853
E-mail: acs_suriname@sil.org

A private, coeducational day school which offers an educational program from prekindergarten through grade 12 for students of all nationalities.

Frank Martens, Administrator

1298 American Elementary & High School
Caixa Postal 7432
01064-970, Sao Paulo
Brazil

55-11-3842-2499
Fax: 55-11-3842-9358
E-mail: graded@eagle.aegsp.br

A private, coeducational day school which offers a full college-preparatory educational program from preschool through grade 12 for students of all nationalities.

Dr. Gunther Brandt, Principal

1299 American International School-Bolivia
PO Box 5309
Cochabamba
Bolivia

591-42-88-577
Fax: 591-42-88-576
E-mail: dsmith@mail.aisb.edu.bo
http://www.aisb.edu.bo

Kathleen Asbun, Director General

1300 American International School-Lincoln Buenos Aires
Andr,s Ferreyra 4073 La Lucila
1636 La Lucila, Buenos Aires
Argentina

54-11-479-49400
Fax: 54-11-479-02117
E-mail: lincoln@lincoln.edu.ar
http://www.lincoln.edu.ar

Grade levels K-12, school year August-June

Philip Joslin, Superintendent

1301 American School
Final Calle La Mascotta #3
Colonia La Mascota, San Salvador
El Salvador

503-26-38-330
Fax: 503-26-38-385
E-mail: llarsen@ns.amschool.edu.sv
http://www.amschool.edu.sv

Leslie Larsen, General Director

1302 American School Foundation AC
Bondojito #215
Colonia Las Americas, Delegacion Alvaro
Mexico DF, Mexico 01120

52-55-5227-4900
Fax: 52-55-5273-4357
E-mail: asf@www.asf.edu.mx
http://www.asf.edu.mx

Dr. Joyce Lujan Martinez, Head of School

1303 American School Foundation-Guadalajara
Colomos 2100, Col. Providencia
Guadalajara, Jalisco 44640
Mexico

52-3-817-3377
Fax: 52-3-817-3356
E-mail: asfg@warrior.asfg.mx

A private, coeducational day school which offers an educational program from prekindergarten to grade 12.

Charles E Prince, Principal

1304 American School Foundation-Monterrey
Rio Missouri 555 Ote
Coronel del Valle, Garza Garcia
Nuevo Leon 66220, Mexico

52-81-8153-4400
Fax: 52-81-8378-2535
E-mail: jeff.keller@asfm.edu.mx
http://www.asfm.edu.mx

A private, nonprofit, coeducational day school which offers an educational program from nursery through grade 12 for students of all nationalities.

Dr. Jeffrey Keller, Superintendent

1305 American School-Belo Horizonte
Avenida Deputado Cristovan Chiaradia 120
Caixa Postal 1701
Bairro Buritis, Belo Horizonte 30575-440
Brazil

55-31-378-6700
Fax: 55-31-378-6878
E-mail: eabhawk@bhnet.br

A coeducational, private day school which offers an educational program from prekindergarten through grade 12 for students of all nationalities.

Sid Stewart, Principal

1306 American School-Brasilia
Avenicla L-2 Sul
SGAS Q-605-E Brasilia
Brazil

55-61-443-3237
Fax: 55-61-244-4303
E-mail: rwernen@bus.eabdf.br
http://www.eabdf.br

A private, coeducational day school which offers an educational program from prekindergarten through grade 12 for students of all nationalities.

Raymond Lauk PhD, Headmaster

1307 American School-Campinas
Caixa Postal 1183
13100 Campinas Sp, Brazil

55-19-754-1200
Fax: 55-19-754-1212

David Cardenas, Superintendent

1308 American School-Durango
Francisw Sarabia #416 Pte
Durango 34000
Mexico

52-181-33-636
Fax: 52-181-12-839

Dr. Jorge O Nelson, Principal

1309 American School-Guatemala
US Embassy, Unit 3325
APO AA 34024
Guatemala

502-369-8334
Fax: 502-369-8335
E-mail: cagadm@cag.edu.gt
http://www.colegioamericanoguatemula.com

Grade levels K-12, school year January - October

Barbara Barillas, General Director

1310 American School-Guayaquil
PO Box 3304
Guayaquill
Ecuador

593-4-255-503
Fax: 593-4-250-453
E-mail: dir_asg@gye.satnet.net

Grade levels K-12, school year April - January

Francisco Andrade, Interim General Director
Patricia Ayala de Coronel, HS Principal

1311 American School-Laguna Verde
Veracruz, Mexico

Maurice H Blum, Principal

1312 American School-Lima
Apartado 18-0977 Miraflores
Lima 18
Peru

51-14-35-0890
Fax: 51-14-36-0927
E-mail: drandall@amersol.edu.pe

This school offers an English curriculum (with some classes in Spanish) to 741 boys and 565 girls in grades EC2-12. Teacher exchanges are welcome with the length of stay being two years, with an allowance for housing.

David Randall, Principal

1313 American School-Pachuca
Boulevard Valle De San Javier S/N
Pachuca, Hidalgo
Mexico

52-771-39608
Fax: 52-771-85077
E-mail: amerpach@compaq.net.mx

Grade levels prekindergarten through ninth.

Andrew Sherman, General Director

1314 American School-Puebla
Apartado 665
Puebla
Mexico

Dr. Arthur W Chaffee, Principal

1315 American School-Puerto Vallarta
PO Box 275-B
Puerto Vallarta, Jalisco 48300
Mexico

52-3-221-1525
Fax: 52-3-221-1996
E-mail: gsel@pvnet.com.mx
http://www.americanschool-pv.com.mx

Gerald Selitzer, Director

1316 American School-Recife
Rua Sa e Souza, 408
Boa Viagem, Recife
Brazil

55-81-341-4716
Fax: 55-81-341-0142
E-mail: hgueiros@ear.com.br
http://www.ear.com

A private, coeducational day school which offers an instructional program from prekindergarten through grade 12 for students of all nationalities.

Helen Gueiros, Superindendent

1317 American School-Tampico
Hidalgo S/N
Col. Tancol, Tamaulipas
Mexico

52-12-272-081
Fax: 52-12-280-080
E-mail: ast@tamnet.com.mx
http://www.ats.edu.mx

Grade levels N through tenth.

Emma deSalazar, Headmaster

1318 American School-Torreon
Avenue Mayran Y Nogal Col Jardin
27200 Coahula
Mexico

52-8717-135-389
Fax: 52-8717-173-155
E-mail: lsynder@cat.mx
http://www.cat.mx

Larry F Snyder, Director General

1319 Anglo American School
PO Box 3188-1000
San Jose
Costa Rica

506-279-2626
Fax: 506-279-7894
E-mail: angloam@racsa.co.cr

Grade levels Pre-K through 6, school year February - November

Virginia Hine Barrantes, Principal

1320 Anglo Colombian School
Apaptado Aereo 253393
Bogota
Colombia

David Toze, Principal

1321 Anglo-American School
Calle 37
Avenida Central, 1000 San Jose
Costa Rica

E-mail: angloam@sd.racsa.co.cr

Virginia Hine, Principal

1322 Antofagasta International School
Avenida Angamos 587
Antofagasta
Chile

56-55-256-613
Fax: 56-55-256-628
E-mail: ais@ais.cl
http://www.ais.cl

Grade levels Pre-K through 8, school year February - December

Bryan Lewallen, Principal

1323 Asociacion Colegio Granadino
AA 2138
Manizales, Caldas
Colombia

57-68-745-774
Fax: 57-68-746-066
E-mail: granadino@emtelsa.multi.net.co
http://www.granadino.com

Grade levels Pre-K through 12, school year August - June

Gonzalo Arango, General Director

1324 Asociacion Escuelas Lincoln
Andres Ferreyra 4073
1636 La Lucila, Buenos Aires
Argentina

54-11-4794-9400
Fax: 54-11-4790-2117
E-mail: joslin_p@lincoln.edu.ar
http://www.lincoln.edu.ar

Phil Joslin, Superintendent

1325 Balboa Elementary School
Unit 9025
APO Balboa 34002
Panama

Susan Beattie, Principal

1326 Balboa High School
Unit 9025
APO Balboa 34002
Panama

Ernest Holland, Principal

1327 Barker College
Avenida Meeks 337
Lomas de Zamora, Buenos Aires
Argentina

Jimmy Cappanera, Principal

1328 Belgrano Day School
Juramento 3035
1428 Capital Federal, Buenos Aires
Argentina

E-mail: rrpp@bds.esc.edu.ar

This Roman Catholic affiliated school offers an English/Spanish curriculum for 1,002 day students (570 boys and 432 girls) in grades K-12.

Bernard Green, Principal
Carol Halle, Faculty Head

1329 Bilingue School Isaac Newton
Chihuahua, Mexico

Lauya Gonzalez Valenzula, Principal

1330 British American School
AA 4368
Barranquilla
Colombia

Rafael Ortegon Rocha, Principal

1331 British School-Costa Rica
PO Box 8184-1000
San Jose
Costa Rica

David John Lloyd, Principal

1332 British School-Rio de Janeiro
Rua Real Grandeza 87-Cep 22281
Botafogo, Rio de Janeiro
Brazil

55-21-2539-2717
Fax: 55-21-2266-4060
E-mail: wiseman@britishschool.g12.br

David Morley, Principal

1333 British School-Venezuela
Apartado 61.161
Caracas 1060A
Venezuela

JH Sidwell, Principal

1334 Buenos Aires International Christian Academy
Chile 343
1642 San Isidro, Buenos Aires
Argentina

54-114-4732-1914
Fax: 54-114-4732-3329
E-mail: baica@ciudad.com.ar
http://www.baica.com
Grade levels Pre-K through 10, school year August - June

Eric Sticker, Director
Guillermo Larzabal, Principal

1335 Caribbean International School
Box 1594
Cristobal Colon
Panama

Yolanda Anderson, Principal

1336 Centro Cultural Brazil-Elementary School
Rua Jorge Tibirica 5
11100 Santos, Sao Paulo
Brazil

Newton Antonio Martin, Principal

1337 Cochabamba Cooperative School
Casilla 1395
Cochabamba
Bolivia

591-42-987-61
Fax: 591-42-329-06
E-mail: ccs@bo.net

Howard Robertson, Director

1338 Colegio Abraham Lincoln
Calle 170, #50-25
Bos 90339, Bogota
Columbia

Dr. Luis Hernando Ramir, Principal

1339 Colegio Alberto Einstein
PO Box 5018
Quito
Ecuador

Benjamin Tobar, Principal

1340 Colegio Americano De Guayaquil
PO Box 3304
Guayaquil
Ecuador

593-4-255-03
Fax: 593-4-250-453
E-mail: amschool@gye.satnet.net

Stanley Whitman, Principal

1341 Colegio Anglo Colombiano
PO Box 253393
Bogota
Colombia

David Toze, Principal

1342 Colegio Bilingue Juan Enrigue
Pestalozzi AC
Veracruz
Mexico

Michael S Garber, Principal

1343 Colegio Bolivar
Apartado Aereo 26300
Cali
Colombia

57-2-555-2039
Fax: 57-2-555-2041
E-mail: admisiones@colegiobolivar.edu.co
http://www.colegiobolivar.edu.co
Grade levels Pre-K through 12, school year August-June

Martin Felton, PhD, Director

1344 Colegio Columbo Britanico
Apartado Aereo 5774
Cali
Colombia

Ian Watson, Principal

1345 Colegio Gran Bretana
Carrera 51 #215-20
Bogota
Colombia

57-1-615-0391
Fax: 57-1-676-0426
E-mail: cgbdirector@bigfoot.com
http://www.colgranbret.edu.co
Grade levels N-10, school year August-June

Daryl Barker, Director
David Simpson, Deputy Director

1346 Colegio Granadino
AA 2138 Manizales
Colombia

57-6-874-57-74
Fax: 57-6-874-60-66
E-mail: granadino@emtelsa.multi.net.com

Gonzalo Arango, Principal

1347 Colegio Interamericano de la Montana
Moulevard La Montana
Finca El Socorro, Zona 16
Guatemala City, Guatemala

502-3-641-803
Fax: 502-3-641-779

Dr. Bert Webb, General Director

1348 Colegio Jorge Washington
Apartado Aereo 1899
Cartagena
Colombia

> 57-5-665-3136
> Fax: 57-5-665-6447
> E-mail: director@cojowa.edu.co

Grade levels Pre-K through 12, school year August-June

Pete Nonnenkamp, Director

1349 Colegio Karl C Parrish
AA 52962
Barranquilla
Colombia

> 57-5-359-9484
> Fax: 57-5-359-8828
> E-mail: drfarr@col13.telecom.com.co
> http://www.kcparrish.edu.co

Grade levels N-12, school year August-June

Michael Farr, PhD, Director

1350 Colegio Montelibano
AA 6823 Cerromatoso
Montelibano, Bogota
Colombia

Francisco Cajiao, Principal

1351 Colegio Nueva Granada
AA 51339
Santa Fe de Bogota
Colombia

> 57-1-235-5350
> Fax: 57-1-211-3720
> E-mail: sngrana@COL1.telecom.com.co
> http://www.cng.edu

A private, coeducational day school which offers an educational program from prekindergarten through grade 12 for students of all nationalities.

Barry McCombs PhD, Director

1352 Colegio Peterson SC
Apartado Postal 10-900
DF 11000
Mexico

> 52-5-81-30-11-4
> Fax: 52-5-81-31-38-5
> E-mail: kapm@mail.internet.com.mx

Marvin Peterson, Principal

1353 Colegio San Marcus
Jorges Miles 153
1842 Monte Grande, Buenos Aires
Argentina

Susana Raffo, Principal

1354 Colegio Ward
Hector Coucheiro 599
1706 DF Sarmiento, Ramos Mejia
Buenos Aires, Argentina

Ruben Carlos Urcola, Principal

1355 Costa Rica Academy
Apartado Postal 4941
San Jose 1000
Costa Rica

> 506-239-03-76
> Fax: 506-239-06-25

A private, coeducational school which offers an educational program from prekindergarten through grade 12 for students of all nationalities.

William D Rose, BS, MEd, Principal

1356 Cotopaxi Academy
Casilla 17.01-199
Quito
Ecuador

> 593-2-246-7411
> Fax: 593-2-244-5195
> E-mail: director@cotopaxi.kl2.ec

A private, independent, coeducational day school which offers an American program of studies from play group through grade 12 for students of all nationalities.

Arthur Pontes, Principal

1357 Country Day School
Apartado 1139
1250 Escazu, Escazu, Costa Rica
Central America

> 506-289-8406
> Fax: 506-228-2076
> E-mail: codasch@sol.racsa.co.cr
> http://www.cds.ed.cr

Grade levels through 12, school year August-June.

Timothy Carr, Director

1358 Crandon Institute
Casilla Correo 445
Montevideo
Uruguay

This school offers a curriculum taught in Spanish for 2,000 day students (700 boys; 1,300 girls), in high school through junior college level (home economics, commercial). The school, affiliated with the Methodist church, employs 300teachers.

Marcos Rocchietti, Principal

1359 Curundu Elementary School
Unit 0925
APO Curundu 34002 0005
Panama

Clifford Drexler, Principal

1360 Curundu Junior High School
Unit 0925
APO Curundu 34002 0005
Panama

Charles Renno, Principal

1361 Edron Academy-Calz Al Desierto
Desierto de los Leones 5578
Mexico City 01740
Mexico

> 5-585-30-49
> Fax: 5-585-28-46

Richard Gilby Travers, Principal

1362 El Abra School
Phelps Dodge Corporation
Calama
Chile

56-55-313-600
Fax: 56-55-315-182
E-mail: elabraschool@hotmail.com
Grade levels K-11, school year August - June

Margaret Maclean, Head Of School

1363 English School
AA 51284
Bogota
Colombia

Leonard Mabe, Principal

1364 Escola Americana do Rio de Janeiro
Estrada Da Gavea 132
Rio de Janeiro 22451-260
Brazil

55-21-512-9830
Fax: 55-21-259-4722
E-mail: americanrio@ax.apc.org
A private coeducational day school which offers an educational program from nursery through grade 12 for students of all nationalities.

Dr. Dennis Klumpp, Principal

1365 Escola Maria Imaculada
Caixa Postal 21293 Brooklin
Sao Paulo 04698
Brazil

Gerald Gates, Principal

1366 Escuela Anaco
Apartado 31
Anaco
Venezuela

Francene Conte, Principal

1367 Escuela Bilingue Santa Barbara
Apartado 342-El Marchito
San Pedro Sila
Honduras

504-659-3053
Fax: 504-659-3059
E-mail: mochitoschool@breakwater.hn
Grade levels preK through 8.

John P Leddy, Principal

1368 Escuela Bilingue Valle De Sula
Apartado 735
San Pedro Sula
Honduras

Carole A Black, Principal

1369 Escuela International Sampedrana
Apartado Postal 565
San Pedro Sula
Honduras

504-566-2722
Fax: 504-566-1458
E-mail: scis@netsys.hn

Gregorg E Werner, Principal

1370 Escuela Las Palmas
Apartdo 6-2637
Panama

Aleida Molina, Principal

1371 Foreign Students School
Avenue Station B
#6617-6615 Esquina 70
Miramar Havana City, Cuba

Gillian P Greenwood, Principal

1372 Fort Clayton Elementary School
Unit 0925
APO, Fort Clayton 34004 0005
Panama

Barbara Seni, Principal

1373 Fort Kobbe Elementary School
Unit 0714
APO, Fort Kobbe 34001 0005
Panama

Dr. Vinita Swenty, Principal

1374 Fundacion Colegio Americano de Quito
Manuel Benigno Cueva N 80-190
Carcelen, Quito
Ecuador

593-2-472-974
Fax: 593-2-472-972
E-mail: dirgeneral@fcaq.k12.ec
http://www.fcaq.k12.ec
Grade levels Pre-K through 12, school year September - June.

Susan Barbara, Director General

1375 George Washington School
Apartado Aereo 2899
Cartagena
Colombia

57-5-665-3396
Fax: 57-5-665-6447
A private, coeducational day school which offers and educational program from prekindergarten through grade 12 for students of all nationalities.

Steven Fields, Principal

1376 Grange School
Casilla 218
Correo 12, Santiago
Chile

56-2-396-0101
Fax: 56-2-227-1204
E-mail: admissions@grange.cl
http://www.grange.cl
Grade levels Pre-K through 12, school year March - December

John Mackenzie, Headmaster
James Cowan, Deputy Headmaster

1377 Greengates School
Circumbalacion Pte 102
Baliones De San Mateo, Naucalpah
Mexico 53200

52-55-5373-0088
Fax: 52-55-5373-0765
E-mail: sarav@greengates.edu.mx

Grade levels prekindergarten through twelfth.
Susan E Mayer, Principal

1378 Howard Elementary School
Unit 0713
APO, Howard AFB 34001 0005
Panama

Jean Lamb, Principal

1379 Inst Tecnologico De Estudios
Apartado Postal 28B
Chihuahua
Mexico

Hector Chavrez Barron, Principal

1380 International Preparatory School
PO Box 20015-LC
Santiago
Chile

56-2-321-5800
Fax: 56-2-321-5821
E-mail: info@tipschool.com
http://www.tipschool.com

Grade levels Pre-K through 12, school year March - December

Lesley Easton-Allen, Headmistress
Pamela Thomson, Curriculum Coordinator

1381 International School Nido de Aguilas
Casilla 27020
Correo 27, Santiago
Chile

56-2-216-6842
Fax: 56-2-216-7603
E-mail: mail@nido.cl
http://www.nido.cl

A private, coeducational day school which offers a comprehensive educational program from prekindergarten through grade 12 for students of all nationalities.

Dr. Clifford Strommen, Headmaster
Joe McDonald, HS Principal

1382 International School-Curitiba
PO Box 7004
80520 Curitiba
Brazil

Ronald James Mccluskey, Principal

1383 International School-La Paz
CC1075870 Villa Dolores
La Paz, Cordoba
Argentina

LH Sullivan, Principal

1384 International School-Panama
PO Box 6-7589
El Dorado
Panama

507-266-7037
Fax: 507-266-7808
E-mail: isp@isp.edu.pa
http://www.isp.edu.pa

A private, coeducational day school which offers an educational program from prekindergarten through grade 12 for students of all nationalities.
Dr. Mary G Mend, Director
Laurie Lewter, Business Manager

1385 Karl C Parrish School
3598629 AA 52962
Barranquilla
Colombia

57-5-3598590
Fax: 57-5-3598828
E-mail: kcparrish@rnd.net
http://www.kcparrish.edu.co

This school offers a curriculum of English/Spanish to 806 day students (455 boys; 351 girls), in grades 1-12. The length of stay for overseas teachers is two years, with housing provided. Applications needed to teach include science, social sciences, math, reading, English, and physical education. Other criteria include a BA Degree, two years of successful experience in grade/subject for which applying. Overseas experience, preferred Spanish language.

Michael Farr, PhD, Director

1386 Liceo Pino Verde
Kilometro 6
Via Cerritos, Pereira Rda
Colombia

963-379368

This school teaches English as a second language; builds strong human values; develops logical thinking skills and prepares students for the world of technology and communication. Enrollment consists of 110 day students (57 boys; 53girls, in grades PK-12. Overseas teachers are welcome to apply with the length of stay being two years, with housing provided. Applications needed to teach include science, math and English.

Luz Stella Rios Patino, Principal

1387 Limon School
Apartado 565
Limon
Costa Rica

Elexer Arava, Principal

1388 Lincoln International Academy
PO box 20000
Correo 20, Santiago
Chile

56-2-217-1907
Fax: 56-2-215-1080
E-mail: lintac@entelchile.net
http://www.lintac.com

Grade levels Pre-K through 12, school year March - December

Veronica Caroca, Headmistress
John F Seaquist, Director

1389 Mackay School
Vicuna Mackenna 700 Renaca
Vina del Mar
Chile

Nigel William Blackbur, Principal

1390 Marian Baker School
Apartado 4269
7an Jose
Costa Rica

560-273-3426
Fax: 506-273-4609
E-mail: mbschool@sol.racsa.co.cr
http://www.marianbakerschool.com

Grade level pre-k through 12.

Linda Niehaus, Director

1391 Marymount School
Apartado Aereo #1912
Barranquilla
Colombia

Dr. Kathleen Cunniffe, Principal

1392 Metropolitan School
Tegucigalpa, Honduras

Bertha DeFlores, Principal

1393 Modern American School
Cerro del Hombre #18
Coyoacan CP 04310
Mexico

1394 Northlands Day School
Roma 1210
1636 Olivos, Buenos Aires
Argentina

This bilingual day school for girls offers modern facilities, sports, etc. on a spacious campus. Languages spoken include English and Spanish and total enrollment is 1,100 students, ranging in grade from K1-12. Overseas teachers areaccepted, with the length of stay being 2-6 years with housing provided.

Susan Brooke Jackson, MA, Principal

1395 Our Lady of Mercy School
48 Visconde De Caravelas
Botafoga ZC02 Rio de Janeiro
Brazil

Charles Lyndaker, Principal

1396 Pan American Christian Academy
Caixa Postal 12491
04798 Sao Paulo
Brazil

55-11-5929655
Fax: 55-11-59289591
http://www.paca.com.br

Micheal Epp, Superintendent

1397 Pan American School-Bahia
Caixa Postal 231
Salvador Bahia 40901-970
Brazil

55-71-367-9099
Fax: 55-71-367-9090
E-mail: epaba@svn.com.br

A private, coeducational day school which offers a program from preschool through grade 12 for students of all nationalities.

Mary Jo Heatherington, PhD, Superintendent

1398 Pan American School-Costa Rica
Apartado 118-1150, La Uruca
Monterrey, San Jose
Costa Rica

52-8-342-0778
Fax: 52-8-340-2749
E-mail: dadmission@pas.edu.mx
http://www.pas.edu.mx

Grade levels prekindergarten through eleventh.

Robert Arpee, Director

1399 Pan American School-Monterrey
Hidalgo 656 Pte
Apartado Postal 474, Monterrey 64000
Mexico

52-83-404176

This school offers an English curriculum for 1,393 day students and 100 boarding students (709 boys; 684 girls), grades preschool through nine. The school is willing to participate in a teacher exchange program with the length of staybeing one year. Applications needed to teach include science, preschool, math, reading, English, and physical education.

Tobert L Arpee, Principal
Lenor Arpee, Faculty Head

1400 Pan American School-Porto Alegre
Rua Joao Paetzel 440
91 330 Porto Alegre
Brazil

Jennifer Sughrue, Principal

1401 Panama Canal College
Unit 0925
APO Balboa 34002 0005
Panama

1402 Prescott Anglo American School
PO Box 1036
Arequipa
Peru

This school offers a Spanish/English curriculum for 1,050 day students (450 boys; 600 girls) in grades K-12. Students are taught English three hours a day, so they can reach an intermediate level in grade 9, and high intermediate ingrades 11-12.

Jorge Pachecot, Principal

1403 Redland School
Camino El Alba 11357
Santiago
Chile

This school offers an English/spanish curriculum to 820 day students (420 boys; 400 girls), in grades PreK-12. The student body is mostly Chilean and 90% of the teachers are Chilean. However, overseas teachers are welcome, with theapplications being pre-school and English.

Richard Collingwood-Selby, Principal

1404 Reydon School for Girls
5178 Cruz Chica
Sierras de Cordoba, Cordoba
Argentina

NJ Milman, Principal

1405 Saint George's School
Apartado Aereo 51579
Bogota
Colombia

Mary De Acosta, Principal

1406 Santa Cruz Cooperative School
Casilla 753
Santa Cruz
Bolivia

591-3-530-8080
Fax: 591-3-352-6993
E-mail: wmck@hotmial.com
http://www.sccs.edu.bo

A private, coeducational day school which offers an educational program from prekindergarten through grade 12 for students of all nationalities.

William McKelligott, Director General

1407 Santa Margarita School
Avenue Manuel Olguin 961 El Derby
Surco, Lima
Peru

Guillermo Descalzi, Principal

1408 St. Albans College
R Falcon 250
1832 Lomas de Zamora, Buenos Aires
Argentina

This school offers courses to 702 day students (383 boys and 319 girls) in grades K through twelve. The school does participate in teacher exchange programs with the length of stay for teachers being one year. Applications fromoverseas needed to teach include science, pre-school, math, social sciences, administration, reading, German, English, and physical education.

John R Vibart, Headmaster
Carlos Palermo, Faculty Director

1409 St. Andrew's Scots School
Ruque Sanez Pena
1636 Olivos, Buenos Aires
Argentina

54-114-799-8318
Fax: 54-114-799-8318
E-mail: johntaylor@sanandres.esc.edu.ar
http://www.sanandres.esc.edu.ar

Grades K-12, school year February - December

John Taylor, Headmaster
Ana Repila, Admissions Director

1410 St. Catherine's School
Carbajal 3250
1426 Capital Federal, Buenos Aires
Argentina

54-114-552-4353
Fax: 54-114-554-4113
E-mail: stcath@ciudad.com.ar
http://www.redeseducacion.com.ar

Pre-K through 12, school year March-December

Mabel Manzitti, Principal

1411 St. George's College
Casilla de Correo No 2
1878 Quilmes, Bunos Aires
Argentina

54-11-425-73472
Fax: 54-11-425-30030
E-mail: info@stgeorge.com.ar
http://www.stgeorge.com.ar

Grade levels N-12, school year February - December

James Batten, Headmaster
Peter Ashton, Deputy Headmaster

1412 St. Hilda's College
Cowley Palce
Oxford OX4 1DY
Argentina

44-1865-276884
Fax: 44-1865-276816

Martin Garvie, Principal

1413 St. John School
Casilla 284
Concepcion
Chile

St. John School is a bilingual school that caters to children from PK through grade twelve. The student body includes 1,170 day students (580 boys and 590 girls). The school does participate in teacher exchange programs with thelength of stay for teachers being two years. The languages spoken include Spanish and English and the student/teacher ratio is 10:1.

Chris Pugh, Principal

1414 St. Margaret's British School-Girls
Casilla 392-5 Norte
1351 Vina del Mar
Chile

Margery Byrne, Principal

1415 St. Paul's School
Caixa Postal 3472 Cep 01051
Sao Paulo
Brazil

Richardo Pons, Principal

1416 St. Pauls School
5178 Cruz Grande
Cordoba
Argentina

AH Thurn, Principal

1417 St. Peter's School
Pacheco 715
1640 Martinez, Buenos Aires
Argentina

Joy Headland, Principal

1418 Teaching Opportunities in Latin America for US Citizens
Organization of American States
17th & Constitution Avenue NW
Washington, DC 20036

202-458-3000
Fax: 202-458-3967

Supports teaching abroad opportunities.

1419 The American School Foundation of Monterrey
R¡o Missouri, 555 Ote
Garza Garc¡a, Nuevo Leon 66220
Mexico

52-8-158-4409
Fax: 52-8-378-2535
E-mail: jeff.keller@missouri.asfm.edu.mx

Private international day school founded in 1928 to provide students with a US type of education.

Dr. Jeff Keller, Superintendent

1420 Uruguayan American School
1785 Dublin
Montevideo 11500
Uruguay

598-2-600-7681
Fax: 598-2-606-1935
E-mail: info@uas.edu.uyuy
http://www.uas.edu.uy

Grade level N through twelfth, with enrollment of 207 students.

David Deuel, Director

1421 William T Sampson
Elementary & High School
PSC 1005 Box 49
FPO, Guantanamo Bay 09593 0005
Cuba

Eastern Europe

1422 American Academy Larnaca
PO Box 112-Gregory Afxentious Ave
Larnaca
Cyprus

Maurice Holt, Principal

1423 American College-Sofia
PO Box 873
Sofia 1000
Bulgaria

359-2-975-3695
Fax: 359-2-934-3129
E-mail: acs@acs.bg
http://www.acs.acad.bg

This school offers an English-based curriculum to 530 day students (250 boys; 280 girls), in grades 8-12. This is the oldest American educational institution outside of the United States. The school is very selective regarding the student body and the faculty is 30% American. Student/teacher ratio is 8.5:1. Students are admitted to the best US Universities: Harvard, MIT, Colgate, Cornell, Brown, etc.

Louis J Perske, President

1424 American International School-Bucharest
Sos Pipera-Tunari 196
Com Voluntari-Pipera, Bucharest
Romania

40-1-211-0102/3
Fax: 40-1-211-0104
E-mail: director@aisb.ro
http://www.aisb.ro

Grades preK-12, enrollment 387.

Frederic F Wesson, Director

1425 American International School-Budapest
PO Box 53
Budapest 1525
Hungary

36-1-395-2176
Fax: 36-1-395-2179
http://www.aisb.hu

Grade levels Pre-K through 13, school year August-June

John Johnson, School Director

1426 American International School-Cyprus
PO Box 23847, 11 Kansas Street
1086 Nisocia
Cyprus

357-2-316-345
Fax: 357-2-316-549
E-mail: aisc@aisc.ac.cy
http://www.aisc.ac.cy

Grade levels Pre-K through 12, school year August-June

Joanna Ramos, Director

1427 American International School-Krakow
ul Warnenczyka 14
30-520 Krakow
Poland

48-12-656-3617
Fax: 48-12-656-4952
E-mail: aisk@kompit.com.pl
http://www.aisk.kompit.com.pl

Affiliated with the American School of Warsaw, AISK is an independent, coeducational day school which offers an educational program from preschool through grade 8 for students of all nationalities.

Brain J Marquano, Director

1428 American International School-Vienna
Salmannsdorfer Strasse 47
A-1190 Vienna
Austria

43-1-40-132-0
Fax: 43-1-40-132-5
E-mail: info@ais.at
http://www.ais.at

Grades PK-12, PG Enrollment 750.

Dr. Richard Spradling, Director

1429 American School of Bucharest
Sos Pipera-Tunari 196arest
Com Voluntari-Pipera, Bucharest
Romania

40-21-2044300
Fax: 40-21-2044306
E-mail: fwesson@asb.kappa.ro

An independent, international, coeducational day school which offers an educational program from prekindergarten through grade 12 for students of all nationalities.

F Wesson, Director

1430 Asuncion Christian Academy
American Embassy
APO, Unit #4751 34036 4751

011-595-21-607-378
Fax: 011-595-21-604-855
E-mail: aca@uninet.com.py

A co-educational Christian day school that is interdenominational and international and accredited through both Southern Association of Colleges and Associations of Christian Schools International (ACSI).

Bethany Abreu, Director

1431 Falcon School
PO Box 3640
Nicosia
Cyprus

Nikolas Michael Ieride, Principal

1432 Gimnazija Bezigrad
Periceva 4
61000 Ljublijana Slovenia

Barbara Costisa, Principal

1433 International Elementary School-Estonia
Kannu 67
13418 Tallinn
Estonia

372-660-6072
Fax: 372-660-6128
E-mail: iese@online.ee
http://www.online.ee/~iese

An independent, coeducational day school which offers an educational program for students aged 3 to 14 of all nationalities. Grades PS-10, enrollment 83.

George Lumm, Director

1434 International School-Belgrade
American Embassy Belgrade
Pariska 7, 11001 Belgrade
Yugoslavia

381-11-651-832
Fax: 381-11-652-619
E-mail: isb@eunet.yu
http://www.isb.co.yu

An independent, coeducational day school which offers an edcuational program from kindergarten through grade 8 for students of all nationalities.

Dr. Nikola P Kodzas, Director

1435 International School-Budapest
H-1121
Budapest, Kolkoly-Thege
Hungary

36-1-395-9312
Fax: 36-1-395-9310
E-mail: isb@okk.szamalk.hu

Grade levels N-8, school year August - June

Zsuzsanna Flachner, Headmaster

1436 International School-Estonia
Juhkentali 18 Tallinn
Tallinn 10132
Estonia

372-6-606-072
Fax: 372-6-606-128
E-mail: iese@online.ee
http://www.online.ee/~iese

Grade levels Pre-K through 10, school year August - June

1437 International School-Latvia
Viestura Iela 6A
Jurmala LV2010
Latvia

371-775-5146
Fax: 371-775-5009
E-mail: isl@latnet.lv
http://www.isl.edu.lv

Grades preSchool-12, enrollment 160.

Sally Hadden, Director

1438 International School-Paphos
PO Box 2018, 22-26 Hellas Avenue
Paphos
Cyprus

061-32236
Fax: 061-34090

Anton Floyd, Principal

1439 International School-Prague
Bohumila Limova
Prague 6 164 00
Czech Republic

420-2-2038-4215
Fax: 420-2-2038-4555
E-mail: ispmail@isp.cz
http://www.isp.cz

Educational program from prekindergarten through grade 12 for students of all nationalities.

Robert Landau, Director

1440 International Teachers Service
47 Papakyriazi Street
Larissa, Greece

41-253856
Fax: 41-251022

A recruitment service for teachers of English in Greece. Must have a BA/BS in education preferably English and/or EFL training or past experience in EFL and be a native speaker of English.

Fani Karatzou

1441 Kiev International School
3A Svyatoshinskiy Provilok
Kyiv 03115
Ukraine

380-44-452-2792
Fax: 380-44-452-2998
E-mail: kisukr@sovamua.com
http://www.qsi.org

Grade levels N-12, school year September-June

Michael Tewalthomas, Director
David Pera, Director Instruction

1442 Limassol Grammar-Junior School
Homer St. Ayios Nicolaos
Limassol
Cyprus

EWP Foley, Principal

1443 Logos School of English Education
33-35 Yialousa Street
PO Box 51075 3501 Limassol
Cyprus

357-25336061
Fax: 357-25335578
E-mail: rsee@spidernet.com.cy
http://www.hlogos.ac.cy

Peter Ross, Principal

1444 Magyar British International School
H-1519 Budapest
PO Box 219, Budapest
Hungary

Mary E Pazsit, Principal

1445 Melkonian Educational Institute
PO Box 1907
Nicosia
Cyprus

An Armenian boarding school with high academic standards.

S Bedikan, Principal

1446 Private English Junior School
PO Box 2262
Nicosia
Cyprus

Vassos Hajierou, BA, Principal

1447 QSI International School-Bratislava
Karloveska 64
Bratislava
Slovak Republic

421-2-6542-2844
Fax: 421-2-6541-1646
E-mail: phillipsylla@qsi.org
http://www.qsi.org

Grade levels N-12, school year September-June

Philip Sylla, Director
Margaret Davis, Director Instruction

1448 QSI International School-Ljubljana
Puharjehva Ulica 10
100n Ljubljana
Solvenia

386-01-4396300
Fax: 386-01-4396305
E-mail: qsisln@siol.net
http://www.qsi.org

Grade levels N-9, school year September-June

Peter Janda, Director

1449 QSI International School-Tbilisi
10 Topuria Street
Tbilisi
Republic of Georgia

995-32-982909
Fax: 995-32-322607
E-mail: qsi@access.sanet.ge
http://www.qsi.org

Grade levels N-10, school year September-June

Antonio Trujillo, Director

1450 QSI International School-Yerevan
PO Box 82
375010 Yerevan
Republic of Armenia

374-1-391030
Fax: 374-1-284913

Grade levels N-8, school year September-June

Randy Speer, Director

Middle East

1451 ACI & SEV Elementary School
Inonu Cad. #476
Goztepe, Izmir
Turkey

90-232-285-3401
Fax: 90-232-246-1674
E-mail: school@aci.k12.tr
http://www.aci.k12.tr

Grade levels Pre-K through 12, school year September - June

Kenneth Frank, Superintendent
Kenneth Frank, Turkish First VP

1452 Abdul Hamid Sharaf School
PO Box 6008
Amman
Jordan

Sue Dahdah, Principal

1453 Abquaiq Academy
Box 5150
Abqaiq
Saudi Arabia

Bob Herman, Principal

1454 Al Ain English Speaking School
PO Box 1419 Al Ain
Abu Dhabi
United Arab Emirates

00971-3-7678636
Fax: 00971-3-767-1973

James G Crawford, Principal

1455 Al Bayan Bilingual School
PO Box 24472
Safat 13105
Kuwait

965-531-5125
Fax: 965-533-2836
E-mail: bbsadm@ncc.moc.lcw
http://www2.kems.net/users/bbs

Grade levels N through twelfth.

Lance C Curlin, Sr, PhD, Director

1456 Al Khubairat Community School
PO Box 4001
Abu Dhabi
United Arab Emirates

DJ Holford, Principal

1457 Al Rabeeh School
PO Box 138
Abu Dhabi
United Arab Emirates

HJ Kadri, Principal

1458 Al-Nouri English School
PO Box 46901
Fahaheel
Kuwait

PD Oldfield, Principal

Teaching Opportunities Abroad / Middle East

1459 Al-Worood School
PO Box 46673
Abu Ghabi
United Arab Emirates

971-2-444-7655
Fax: 971-2-444-9732
E-mail: alworood@emirates.net.ae
http://www.alworood.sch.ae

Grade levels N-12, school year September - June

Nazmieh Al-Abed, Principal

1460 American Collegiate Institute
Inonu Caddesi #476 Hatay
Izmir
Turkey

90-232-285-3401
Fax: 90-232-246-4128
E-mail: school@aci.k12.tr
http://www.aci.k12.tr

Fredrick L Thompson, PhD, Superintendent

1461 American Community School
PO Box 8129
Beirut
Lebanon

961-1-374-370
Fax: 961-1-366-050
E-mail: acs@acs.edu.lb
http://www.acs.edu.lb

Grades N-12, enrollment 997.

Catherine Bashshur, Head of School

1462 American Community School-Abu Dhabi
PO Box 42114
Abu Dhabi
United Arab Emirates

971-2-681-5115
Fax: 971-2-681-6006
E-mail: acs@acs.sch.ae
http://www.acs.sch.ae

An independent, coeducational day school which offers
an educational program from preschool through grade 12
for English-speaking students of all nationalities.

Dr. David Cramer, Superintendent

1463 American Community School-Beirut
Avenue de Paris JelEl-Bahr
PO Box 11-8129, Riad El Solh, Beirut
Lebanon 11072260

961-1-374-370
Fax: 961-1-366-050
E-mail: acs@acs.edu.lb
http://www.acs.edu.lb

The American Community School at Beruit is an
independent, not-for-profit, non-sectarian,
coeducational preschool through secondary school
serving the international and Lebanese communities.

Catherine Bashshur, Head of School

1464 American International School
PO Box 22090
Doha
Qatar

Dr. Brian J Jones, Principal

1465 American International School-Abu Dhabi
PO Box 5992
Abu Dhabi
United Arab Emirates

971-2-444-4333
Fax: 971-2-444-4005
E-mail: aisa@emirates.net.ae
http://www.aisa.sch.ae

Grade levels kindergarten through twelfth, with
enrollment of 750 students.

Peter J McMurray, Director

1466 American International School-Israel
PO Box 9005
Kfar Shmaryahu
Israel

972-9-961-8100
Fax: 972-9-961-8111
E-mail: aisrael@american.hasharon.k12.il

An independent, coeducational day school which offers
an educational program from kindergarten through grade
12 for students of all nationalities.

Richard Detwiler, Principal

1467 American International School-Kuwait
PO Box 3267
Salmiya 23033
Kuwait

965-564-5083
Fax: 965-564-5089
E-mail: admin@aiskuwait.org
http://www.aiskuwait.org

Grade levels kindergarten through twelfth.

Samera Al Rayes, Owner/Director
Noreen Hawley, Superintendent

1468 American International School-Muscat
PO Box 584
Azaiba, PC 130, Muscat
Sultanate of Oman

968-595-180
Fax: 968-503-815
E-mail: taism@omantel.net.com
http://www.taism.com

Grades preK-12, enrollment 172.

Kevin Schafer, Director

1469 American International School-Riyadh
PO Box 990
Riyadh 11412
Saudi Arabia

966-1-491-4270
Fax: 966-1-491-7101
E-mail: registration@ais-r.edu.sa
http://www.aisr.org

Grades KindergartenI-11, enrollment 1,463.

Dr. Dennis Larkin, Superintendnet

1470 American School-Doha
PO Box 22090
Doha
Qatar

974-442-1377
Fax: 974-442-0885
E-mail: info@asdqatar.org
http://www.asdqatar.org

Grades preK-12, enrollment 470.

Ronald H Schultz, PhD, Director

1471 American School-Kuwait
PO Box 6735
32040 Hawalli
Kuwait

965-266-4341
Fax: 965-265-0438
E-mail: askkewt@kuwait.net
http://www.ask.edu.kw/index1

Founded by a group of American and Kuwaiti citizens for students who wanted to attend American colleges and universities. The comprehensive American curriculum has remained to characteristic to atrract students to ASK. Provides asolid foundation in essential learning skills preparatory to higher edudation.

Dr. Peter Nanos, Superintendent

1472 American-British Academy
PO Box 372
Medinat al Sultan Qaboos, 115
Sultanate of Oman

968-603-646
Fax: 968-603-544

An independent, coeducational day school with an educational program from kindergarten through grade 12 for students of all nationalities.

Philippa MC Leggate, BA, Principal

1473 Amman Baccalaureate School
PO Box 441
Sweileh Amman 11910
Jordan

962-6-541-1191/7
Fax: 962-6-541-2603
E-mail: abs@go.com.jo
http://www.arabia.com/ABS

School offers Arabic and English language curriculum for grade levels kindergarten through twelfth.

Samia Al Farra, Principal

1474 Anglican International School-Jerusalem
82 Prophet Street
Jerusalem 91001
Israel

972-2-567-7200
Fax: 972-2-538-474
E-mail: aisj@netvision.net.il

This Anglican school offers a curriculum based in English to 320 day students, in grades K-12. The length of stay for overseas teachers is four years, with some on-site housing available.

David Jeffery, Principal

1475 Ankara Elementary & High School
PSC 89 Unit 7010
APO, Ankara 09822 7010
Turkey

Robert Marble, Principal

1476 Arab Unity School
PO Box 10563
Rashidiya, Dubai
United Arab Emirates

971-4-886-226
Fax: 971-4-859-885
E-mail: auschool@amirates.net.ae

This school has grown to one of the leading institutions of learning in the UAE. It has about 2,700 day students (1,400 boys; 1,300 girls), grades LKG to Senior-6, of various nationalities drawn from expatriate and local population. The teaching staff of 120 is also multinational. The school follows IGCSE and AICE and A-Level curriculum of University of Cambridge.

Zainab A Taher

1477 Baghdad International School
PO Box 571
Baghdad
Iraq

Amen A Rihani, Principal

1478 Bahrain Bayan School
PO Box 32411
Isa Town
Bahrain

973-682-227
Fax: 973-780-019
E-mail: bayanschool@bayan.edu.bh
http://www.bayan.edu.bh

Grade levels N-12, school year September-June.

Nabil Sukhun, Director General

1479 Bahrain Elementary & High School
Psc 451
FPO Bahrain
Bahrain 09834-5200

Grade levels K-12.

Dr. Gilbert Fernandes, Principal

1480 Bahrain School
PO Box 934
Juffair
Bahrain

973-727828
Fax: 973-725714

Frithjof R Wannebo, PhD, Principal

1481 Bilkent University Preparatory School-Bilkent International School
E Campus 06533
Bilkent, Ankara 06533
Turkey

90-312-266-4961
Fax: 90-312-266-4963
E-mail: school@bups.bilkent.edu.tr
http://www.bupsbis.bilkent.edu.tr

Grade levels Pre-K through 12, school year September - June

Roy Lewis, Director

1482 Bishop's School
PO Box 2001
Amman
Jordan

962-6-653668

This Episcopal boy's school, founded in 1936, teaches both the Jordanvian Curricula and the London University General Certification of Education Curriculum. Total enrollment is 855 day students in grades 1-12. Length of stay forteachers is one year with no housing provided. Languages spoken are English and Arabic.

Najib F Elfarr, Principal
Jamil Ismair, Faculty Head

1483 British Aircraft Corp School
PO Box 3843
Riyadh
Saudi Arabia

MR Pound, Principal

1484 British Embassy Study Group
Sehit Ersan Caddesi 46Å, 06680
Cankaya Ankara
Turkey

127-43-10

T Gray, Principal

1485 British International School-Istanbul
Dilhayat Sok, #3 Etiler 80600
Istanbul
Turkey

212-265-2558
Fax: 212-257-8842

This international school offers an English based curriculum for 490 day students and 7 boarding (251 boys and 246 girls), ages 2 1/2 to nineteen. Applications needed include science, pre-school, French, math, social sciences, reading, German, English and physical education, with the student/teacher ratio being 14:1.

Graham Pheby, Principal

1486 Cairo American College
PO Box 39
Maadi 11431, Cairo
Egypt

20-2-519-6665
Fax: 20-2-519-6584
E-mail: support@tc.cac.edu.eg
http://www.cac.edu.eg

An independent, coeducational day school which offffers an educational program from kindergarten through grade 12 for students of all nationalities.

Dr. Robert Hetzel, Superintendent

1487 Cambridge High School
PO Box 3004
Dubai
United Arab Emirates

T Jackson, Principal

1488 Continental School (Sais British)
PO Box 6453
Jeddah 21442
Saudi Arabia

Chris Spedding, Principal

1489 Dhahran Academy International School Group
PO Box 31677
Al Khobar 31952
Saudi Arabia

966-3-330-0555
Fax: 966-3-330-2450
E-mail: isg@isgdh.org

Grades preSchool-11, enrollment 994.

Dr. Fred Bowen, Superintendent

1490 Dhahran Central School
Box 73
Dhahran 31311
Saudi Arabia

Jess Arceneaux, Principal

1491 Dhahran Hills School
Box 73
Dhahran 31311
Saudi Arabia

William Parks, Principal

1492 Doha College-English Speaking
PO Box 22090
Doha Qatar
Arabian Gulf

974-806-770
Fax: 974-806-311
E-mail: asdoha@qatar.net.qa

An independent, coeducational day school which offers an educational program from children of all nationalities from kindergarten through grade12.

E Goodwin, Principal

1493 Doha English Speaking School
PO Box 7660
Doha Qatar
Arabian Gulf

GB Savage, Principal

1494 Doha Independent School
PO Box 5404
Doha Qatar
Arabian Gulf

SJ Williams, Principal

1495 Emirates International School
PO Box 6446
Dubai
United Arab Emirates

971-4-348-9804
Fax: 971-4-348-2813
E-mail: eischool@emirates.net.ae
http://www.eischool.com

Grade levels Pre-K through 12, school year September - June

Daryle Russell, EdD, Headmaster
David A Shore, HS Principal

1496 English School-Fahaheel
PO Box 7209
64003 Fahaheel
Kuwait

This school offers English for the British national curriculum, also Arabic language and Islamic studies for 518 day students (298 boys and 220 girls) in grades K-11. The school offers a teacher exchange program with the length of stay being two years (3+ years for heads). The student/teacher ratio is 19:1 and the applications needed include science, pre-school, math, reading, social sciences, English and physical education.

Ibrahim J Shuhaiber, MSc, Chairman
John J MacGregor, Principal

1497 English School-Kuwait
PO Box 379
Safat 13004
Kuwait

William James Strath, Principal

1498 English Speaking School
PO Box 2002, Dubai
United Arab Emirates

Bernadette McCarty, Principal

1499 Enka Okullari-Enka Schools
Sadi Gulcelik Spor Sitesi
Istinye, Istanbul 80860
Turkey

90-212-276-05-4547
Fax: 90-212-286-59-3035
E-mail: mailbox@enkaschools.com
http://www.enkaschools.com
Grade levels N-5, school year September-June.

Andrew Homden, Director

1500 Gulf English School
PO Box 6320
32068 Hawalli
Kuwait

The school, offers an English based curriculum to 1,406 day students (830 boys; 576 girls), in grades KG through university entrance. The school recruits UK trained teachers every February. The length of stay is one year, withhousing provided by the school.

Paul Andrews, Principal
Tim Brosnan, Faculty Head

1501 Habara School
PO Box 26516
Bahrain

PM Wrench, Principal

1502 IBN Khuldoon National School
Po Box 20511
Isa Town
Bahrain

973-780-661
Fax: 973-689-028
E-mail: president.office@ikns.edu.bh

This IBN school is a private, fee paying, non-profit, coeducational, accredited middle states school. The curriculum offered to the 1,210 day students (630 boys and 580 girls) in grades K-12, is English/Arabic. The school is willingto participate in a teacher exchange program with the applications needed being science, math, social sciences, pre-school and English.

Samir J Chammaa, President
Ghada R Bou Zeineddine, Principal

1503 Incirlik Elementary School
PSC 94
APO, Incirlik 09827 0005
Turkey

Mary Davis, Principal

1504 Incirlik High School
PSC 94
APO, Incirlik 09824 0005
Turkey

Dr. Donald Torrey, Principal

1505 Infant School-House #45
Khalil Kando Gardens Road, 5651
Manama
Bahrain

Maria Stiles, Principal

1506 International Community School
PO Box 2002
Amman
Jordan

Wendy Bataineh, Principal

1507 International School of Choueifat
PO Box 7212, Abu Dhabi
United Arab Emirates

971-2-446-1444
Fax: 971-2-446-1048
E-mail: iscad@sabis.net
http://www.iscad-sabis.net/
Grade levels Pre-K through 13, school year September - June

Marilyn Abu-Esber, Acting Director

1508 Istanbul International Community School
Karaagac Koyu
Hadimkoy, Istanbul 34866
Turkey

90-212-857-8264
Fax: 90-212-857-8270
E-mail: headmaster@iics.k12.tr
http://www.iics.k12.tr
Grade levels Pre-K through 12, school year August - June

Kenneth Hillmann, Headmaster
Eileen Freely Baker, Primary Principal

1509 Izmir Elementary & High School
PSC 88
APO, Izmir 09821 0005
Turkey

Terry Emerson, Principal

1510 Jeddah Preparatory School
British Consulate, Box 6316
Jeddah 21442 Saudi Arabia

John GF Parsons, Principal

1511 Jubail British Academy
PO Box 10059 Madinat Al Jubail
Al Sinaiyah 31961
Arabia

Norman Edwards, Principal

1512 Jumeirah English Speaking School
PO Box 24942, Dubai
United Arab Emirates

971-4-394-5515
Fax: 971-4-394-3531
E-mail: jumeng@emirates.net.ac

CA Branson, Headmaster

1513 King Faisal School
PO Box 94558, Riyadh 11614
Saudia Arabia

966-1-482-0802

Fax: 966-1-482-1521
E-mail: dgkfs@kff.com

Grade levels preK-12, enrollment 600.

Mohammed Al-Humood, Director General

1514 Koc School
PK 60-Tuzla
Istanbul 34941
Turkey

90-216-304-1003
Fax: 90-216-304-1048
E-mail: info@kocschool.k12.tr
http://www.kocschool.k12.tr

Grade levels K-12, school year September - June

John Chandler, General Director
Jale Onur, Provost

1515 Kuwait English School
PO Box 8640
Salmiya 22057
Kuwait

Rhoda Elizabeth Muhmoo, Principal

1516 Mohammed Ali Othman School
PO Box 5713
Taiz Yeman
Arab Republic

Saleh Zokari, Principal

1517 Nadeen Nursery & Infant School
PO Box 26367
Adliya
Bahrain

Pauline Puri, Principal

1518 New English School
PO Box 6156
32036 Hawalli
Kuwait

Arthur Rodgers, Principal

1519 Pakistan International School-Peshawar
PO Box 3797
Riyadh
Saudi Arabia

92-441-4428
Fax: 92-441-7272

An independent, coeducaional day school which offers an educaional program from prekindergarten through grade 8 and supervised correspondence study for the high school grades for all expatriate nationalities.

Angela Coleridge, Principal

1520 Rahmaniah-Taif-Acad International School
American Consulate General, Dhahran
District Saudi Arabia

Dean May, Principal

1521 Ras Al Khaimah English Speaking School
PO Box 975
Ras Al Khaimah
United Arab Emirates

971-7-362-441
Fax: 971-7-362-445

Deryck M Wilson, Principal

1522 Ras Tanura School
Box 6140
Ras Tanura
Saudi Arabia

Kent Larson, Principal

1523 Sanaa International School
Box 2002
Sanaa
Yemen

967-1-370-191
Fax: 967-1-370-193
E-mail: gordonblackie@qsi.org
http://www.qsi.org

Grade levels N-12, school year September - June

James Gilson, Director

1524 Saudi Arabian International British School
PO Box 85769
Riyadh 11612
Saudi Arabia

Don Martin, Principal

1525 Saudi Arabian International School-Dhahran
SAIS-DD, Box 677
Dhahran International Airport
Dhahran 31932, Saudi Arabia

996-3-330-0555
Fax: 966-3-330-0555
E-mail: brent_mutsch%sais@macexpress.org

Dr. Leo Ruberto, Principal

1526 Saudi Arabian International School-Riyadh
PO Box 990
Riyadh 11421
Saudi Arabia

966-1-491-4270
Fax: 966-1-491-7101
E-mail: superintendent@saisras.org

An independent, coeducational day school which offers an educational program from kindergarten through grade 9.

Daryle Russell, EdD, Principal

1527 Saudia-Saudi Arabian International School
PO Box 167, CC 100
Jeddah 21231
Saudi Arabia

John Hazelton, Principal

1528 Sharjah English School
PO Box 1600, Sharjah
United Arab Emirates

David Rowlands, Principal

1529 Sharjah Public School
PO Box 6125, Sharjah
United Arab Emirates

Nazim Khan, Principal

1530 St. Mary's Catholic High School
PO Box 1544, Dubai
United Arab Emirates

Fosca Berardi, Principal

1531 Sultan's School
PO Box 9665
Seeb Sultanate of Oman

Alan Henderson, Principal

1532 Sunshine School
PO Box 26922
13130 Safat
Kuwait

David Brinded, Principal

1533 Tarsus American College and SEV Primary
PK 6
33401 Tarsus
Turkey

90-324-613-5402
Fax: 90-324-624-6347
E-mail: school@tac.k12.tr
http://www.tac.k12.tr

This school is a highly competitive international school for Turkish children seeking admission to universities here and abroad. It has a total of 815 day students in grades six through twelve and participates in a teacher exchangeprogram with the length of stay two years, and housing is provided. The applications from overseas that are required to teach at the school are science, French, math, administration, reading, German, and English.

Bernard Mitchell, PhD, Superintendent
Jale Sever, Primary School Principal

1534 Universal American School
PO Box 17035
72451 Khaldiya
Kuwait

965-562-0297/561
Fax: 965-562-5343
E-mail: uas@qualitynet.net

Grade levels N-12.

Nora Al-Ghanim, Administrative Director

1535 Uskudar American Academy
Vakif Sokak Number 1
Baglarbasi, Istanbul 81130
Turkey

90-216-310-6823
Fax: 90-216-333-1818
E-mail: wshepard@uaa.k12.tr
http://www.uaa.k12.tr

Grade levels K-12, school year September - June

Whitman Shepard, Director
Dilek Yakar, Primary Principal

1536 Walworth Barbour American International School in Israel
PO Box 9005
Kfar Shmaryahu
Israel

972-9-961-8100
Fax: 972-9-961-8111
E-mail: aisrael@wbais.org
http://www.american.hasharon.k12.il

Grades K-12, enrollment 619.

Robert A Sills, Superintendent

Western Europe

1537 AC Montessori Kids
Route De Renipont 4
Lasne B-1380
Belgium

32-2-633-6652
Fax: 32-2-633-6652
E-mail: info@acmontessorikids.com
http://www.acmontessorikids.com

Grade levels 1 1/2 years - 9 years, school year September - June

Laurence Randoux, Headmaster
Mark Ciepers, Administrator

1538 AFCENT Elementary & High School
Unit 21606
APO Brunssum 09703 0005
Netherlands

1539 Abbotsholme School
Rocester (Uttoxeter, Staffordshire)
ST14 5BS
England

01889-590217
Fax: 01889-590001

This interdenominational school offers an English-based curriculum for 78 day students and 166 boarding (152 boys; 92 girls), in grades 7-13.

Darrell J Farrant, MA, FRSA, Principal

1540 Academy-English Prep School
Apartado 1300 Palma D Mallorca
07080 Palma de Mallorca
Spain

CA Walker, Principal

1541 Ackworth School, Ackworth
Pontefract, West Yorkshire
WF7 7LT
England

0977-611401

This school offers an English-based curriculum to 264 day students and 111 boarding students (180 boys; 195 girls), ages 11-18 years of age.

Martin J Dickinson, Principal

1542 Alconbury Elementary School
10 CSG CCSH Unit 5570 Box 50
APO, Alconbury 09470 0005
Great Britain

011-44-1480-843620
Fax: 011-44-1480-843172
http://www.alco-hs.odedodea.edu/aes

William Ramos, Principal

1543 Alconbury High School
10 Csg CCSH Unit 5570 Box 60
APO, Alconbury 09470 0005
Great Britain

Darryl Maenpaa, Principal

1544 Alexander M Patch Elementary School
Unit 30401 Box 4003
APO, Vaihingen (Stuttgart) 09131
Germany

Louis Hughes, Principal

1545 Alexander M Patch High School
Unit 30401
APO, Vaihingen 09131 0005
Germany

John Brokaw, Principal

1546 Alfred T Mahan Elementary School
PSC 1003 Box 48
FPO Keflavik 09728
Iceland

Jan Long, Principal

1547 Alfred T Mahan High School
PSC 1003 Box 52
FPO Keflavik 09728 0352
Iceland

M Deatherage, Principal

1548 Amberg Elementary School
CMR 414
APO, Amberg 09173 0005
Germany

Letcher Connell, Principal

1549 Ambrit Rome International School
Via Filippo Tajani, 50
Rome 00149
Italy

39-06-559-5305
Fax: 39-06-559-5309
E-mail: ambrit@email.telpress.it
http://www.ambrit-rome.com

Grade levels Pre-K through 8, school year September - June

Bernard Mullane, Director
Loretta Nannini, Assistant Director

1550 American College-Greece
6 Gravias Street
GR-153 42 Aghia Paraskevi, Athens
Greece

30-1-600-9800
Fax: 30-1-600-9811
E-mail: acgadm@proetheus.hol.gr
http://www.acg.edu

Grae levels 7-12, school year September - June

John Bailey, EdD, President

1551 American Community School-Cobham
Heywood, Portsmouth Road
Cobham, Surrey, KT11 1BL
United Kingdom

44-1932-869-744
Fax: 44-1932-869-789
E-mail: hmulkey@acs-england.co.uk
http://www.acs-england.co.uk

Grade levels N-13, school year August - June

Thomas Lehman, Head of School
Malcolm Kay, Superintendent

1552 American Community School-Egham
Woodlee London Road (A30)
Egham, Surrey, TW20 OHS
United Kingdom

44-1784-430-611
Fax: 44-1784-430-626
E-mail: abarker@acs-england.co.uk
http://www.acs-england.co.uk

Grade levels Pre-K through 11, school year August - June

Malcom Kay, Superintendent
Moyra Hadley, Head of School

1553 American Community School-Hillingdon
108 Vine Lane
Hillingdon, Middlesex, UB10 OBE
United Kingdom

44-189-581-3734
Fax: 44-189-581-0634
E-mail: hillingdonadmissions@acs-england.co.uk
http://www.acs-england.co.uk

Grade levels Pre-K through 13, school year August - June

Ginger Apple, Head of School
Rebecca Duesenberg, Dean Addmissions

1554 American Community Schools
108 Vine Court
Hillingdon, Uxbridge, Middlesex UB100BE
England

44-189-581-3734
Fax: 44-189-581-0634
E-mail: hmulkey@acs-england.co.uk

This school serves the needs of the international business families in Greater London. Programs are nonsectarian, coeducational day schools with lower, middle and high school divisions offering coordinate college preparatory curricula from pre-kindergarten through grade twelve.

Paul Berg, Headmaster

1555 American Community Schools-Athens
129 Aghias Paraskevis Street
152 34 Halandri, Athens
Greece

301-639-3200
Fax: 301-639-0051
E-mail: acs@acs.gr
http://www.acs.gr

Grades preSchool-12, enrollment 718.

Dr. George Besculides, Superintendent

1556 American Embassy School-Reykjavik
American Embassy
PSC 1003 Box 40
Iceland

202-261-8223
Fax: 202-261-8224
E-mail: aes@islandia.is
http://www.state.gov/m/a/os/1438.htm

Grade levels K-6, school year August - May

Barbara Sigurbjornsson, Principal

1557 American International School-Carinthia
Friesacher Strasse 3 Audio ICC
A-9330 Althofen
Austria

Ron Presswood, Principal

1558 American International School-Florence
Via del Carota 23/25
Bagno a Ripoli, Florence 50012
Italy

39-055-646-1007
Fax: 39-055-644-226
E-mail: adminaisf@interbusiness.it
http://www.aisfitaly.org

Grade levels Pre-K through 12, school year
September-June

Laura Mongiat, Head of School
Paul Cook, Deputy Head

1559 American International School-Genoa
Via Quarto 13-C
16148 Genova
Italy

39-010-386-528
Fax: 39-010-398-700
E-mail: aisgdirector@libero.it
http://www.space.tin.it/internet/elrosser

Grade levels Pre-K through 9, school year
September-June

Gary Crippin PhD, Director

1560 American International School-Lisbon
Rua Antonio Dos Reis, 95
Linho, 2710-301 Sintra
Portugal

351-21-923-98-00
Fax: 351-21-923-98-26
E-mail: tesc0893@mail.telepac.pt
http://www.ecis.org/aislisbon/index.html

An independent, coeducational day school which offers
an educational program from early childhood through
grade 12 for student of all nationalities.

Blannie M Curtis, Director

1561 American International School-Rotterdam
Verhulstlaan 21
3055 WJ Rotterdam
Netherlands

31-10-422-5351
Fax: 31-10-422-4075
E-mail: information@aisr.nl
http://www.aisr.nl

Grades preK-12, enrollment 205.

Alan Conkey, Director

1562 American International School-Salzburg
Moosstrasse 106
Salzburg A-5020
Austria

43-662-824-617
Fax: 43-662-824-555
E-mail: office@ais.salzburg.at
http://www.ais.salzburg.at

Grade levels 7-13, school year September-May

Paul McLean, Headmaster
Harold Morgan, Academic Dean

1563 American International School-Vienna
Salmannsdorfer Strasse 47
Vienna A-1190
Austria

43-1-401-320
Fax: 43-1-401-325
E-mail: info@ais.at
http://www.ais.at

Grade level Pre-K through 12, school year August-June

Richard Spradling, PhD, Director
Alan Benson, HS Principal

1564 American Overseas School-Rome
Via Cassia, 811
Rome 00189
Italy

39-06-3326-4841
Fax: 39-06-3326-2608
E-mail: aosr@aosr.org
http://www.aosr.org

An independent, coeducational day school for students
of all nationalities in prekindergarten through grade 13
and offers a boarding program for select students in
grades 9-12.

Dr. Larry W Dougherty, Headmaster

1565 American School of the Hague
Rijksstraatweg 200
2241 BX Wassenaar
The Netherlands

31-70-512-1060
Fax: 31-70-511-2400
E-mail: Gerritz@ash.nl
http://www.ash.nl

Grades preK-12, enrollment 1,020.

Paul De Minico, Superintendent

1566 American School-Barcelona
Balmes, 7
Esplugues de Llobregat, Barcelona 08950
Spain

34-93-371-4016
Fax: 34-93-473-4787
E-mail: info@a-s-b.com
http://www.a-s-b.com

Grade levels Pre-K through 12, school year September -
June

Nancy Boyd, Elementary School Principal
Bill Volckok, Secondary School Principal

1567 American School-Bilbao
Soparda Bidea 10
Berango, Bizkaia 48640
Spain

34-94-668-0860
Fax: 34-94-668-0452
E-mail: asb@asb.saranet.es
http://www.saranet.es/asb

This school offers a curriculum in Spanish and English
for 275 day students (137 boys; 138 girls), in grades
PreK-10. Length of stay for overseas teachers is two

years with no housing provided. Applications needed to teach includemath, social sciences and physical education.

Richard Pacheco, Director

1568 American School-Las Palmas
Apartado 15-Tafira Alta
35017 Las Palmas
Spain

34-928-430-023
Fax: 34-928-430-017
E-mail: info@dns.aslp.org
http://www.aslp.org
Grade levels N-12, school year September - June

Carmen Ana Perez, Director
Conchita Neyra, Assistant Director

1569 American School-London
1-8 Loudoun Road
London, NW8 0NP
United Kingdom

44-207-449-1200
Fax: 44-207-449-1350
E-mail: admissions@asl.org
http://www.asl.org
Grade levels Pre-K through 12, school year September - June

William Mules, EdD, Head of School

1570 American School-Madrid
Apartado 80
Madrid 28080
Spain

34-91-740-1900
Fax: 34-91-357-2678
E-mail: asmadm@amerschmad.org
http://www.amerschmad.org
Grade levels Pre-K through 12, school year September - June

Robert Thompson, Director

1571 American School-Milan
Villaggio Mirasole
Noverasco di Opera, Milan 20090
Italy

39-02-530-001
Fax: 39-02-576-06274
E-mail: director@asmilan.org
http://www.asmilan.org
Grade levels N-13, school year September - June

Shirley Grover, Director

1572 American School-Paris
41, rue Pasteur
Saint Cloud, 92210 Paris
France

33-1-411-28282
Fax: 33-1-460-22390
E-mail: admissions@asparis.org
http://www.asparis.org

Grade levels Pre-K through 13, school year August - June

Pilar Cabeza de Vaca, Headmistress

1573 American School-Valencia
Avenida Sierra Calderona 29
Urb. Los Monasterios, Puzol
Spain

34-96-140-5412
Fax: 34-96-140-5039
E-mail: lalfonso@asvalencia.org
http://www.ecis.org/valencia
Grade levels include N-12 with a total enrollment of 745.
Luis Alfonso, Director

1574 American School-the Hague
Rijksstraatweg 200
2241 BX Wassenaar
Netherlands

31-70-514-0113
Fax: 31-70-511-2400
E-mail: gerritz@ash.nl
An independent, coeducational day school which offers an educational program from prekindergarten through grade 12 for students of all nationalities.

William H Gerritz, PhD, Principal

1575 Anatolia College
PO Box 21021
Pylea, Thessaloniki 55510
Greece

30-31-398-201
Fax: 30-31-327-500
E-mail: jpg@ac.anatolia.edu.gr
http://www.anatolia.edu.gr
Grade levels 7-12, school year September - June

Richard Jackson, President

1576 Anglo-American School-Moscow
American Embassy
Box M, Helsinki 00140
Finland

7-095-231-4488
Fax: 7-095-231-4477
E-mail: director@aas.ru
http://www.aas.ru
An independent, coeducational day school that offers an educational program from First Steps through grade 12.
Ellen Deitsch Stern, Director,   4177650

1577 Anglo-American School-St. Petersburg
US Consulate Box L
00140 Helsinki
Finland

7-812-320-8925
Fax: 7-812-320-8926
E-mail: aassp@glas.apc.prg
Grades K-12, enrollment 104.
Nancy Hope, Principal
Ellen D Stren, Director

1578 Ansbach Elementary School
CMR 454 Box 3616
APO, Ansbach 09250 0005
Germany

Wayne Dozark, Principal

1579 Ansbach High School
Unit 28614
APO, 09250 0005
Germany

49-9802-223
Fax: 49-9802-1496

Dr. Larry E Sessions, Principal

1580 Antwerp International School
Veltwijcklaan 180
B-2180 Ekeren-Antwerpen
Belgium

32-3-543-9300
Fax: 32-3-541-8201
E-mail: ais@ais-antwerp.be
http://www.ais-antwerp.be

Grade levels Pre-K through 12, school year August - June

Robert Schaecher, Headmaster

1581 Argonner Elementary School
Unit 20193 Box 0015
APO, Hanau 09165 0015
Germany

Christine Holsten, Principal

1582 Athens College
PO Box 65005
154 10 Psychico
Greece

Walter McCanny Eggleston, Principal

1583 Aviano Elementary School
PSC 1
APO, Aviano 09601 0005
Italy

011-39-0434-660921
E-mail: joel_hansen@odedodea.edu

Joel K Hansen, Principal

1584 Aviano High School
Unit 6210 Box 180
APO, Aviano 09601 0005
Italy

Robert Bennett, Principal

1585 BEPS 2 Limal International School
13 Rue Leon Deladriere
Limal 1300
Belgium

32-10-417-227
Fax: 32-2-687-2968
E-mail: info@beps.com
http://www.beps.com

Grade levels Pre-K through 6, school year September - June

Charles Gellar, Head
Henny de Waal, Headmistress

1586 Babenhausen Elementary School
CMR 426 Unit 20219
APO, Babenhausen 09089 0005
Germany

Ida Rhodes, Principal

1587 Bad Kissingen Elementary School
CMR 464
APO, Bad Kissingen 09226 0005
Germany

Beatrice McWaters, Principal

1588 Bad Kreuznach Elementary School
CMR 441
APO, Bad Kreuznach 09525 0005
Germany

Peter Grenier, Principal

1589 Bad Kreuznach High School
Unit 24324
APO, Bad Kruznach 09252 0005
Germany

Jennifer Beckwith, Principal

1590 Bad Nauheim Elementary School
Unit 21103
APO, Bad Nauheim 09074 0005
Germany

Raymond Burkard, Principal

1591 Badminton School
Westbury-on-Trym, Bristol
BS9 3BA
England

0272-623141

A non-denominational boarding and day school for girls ages seven to eighteen. Enrollment consists of 163 day students and 195 boarding.

CJT Gould, MA, Principal

1592 Bamberg Elementary School
Unit 27539
APO, Bamberg 09139 0005
Germany

John G Rhyne, Principal

1593 Bamberg High School
Unit 27539
APO, Bamberg 09139 0005
Germany

Lewis Johnson, Principal

1594 Barrow Hills School
Roke Lane
Witley Godalming GU8 5NY
England

01428-683639
Fax: 01428-683639
E-mail: barhills@netcomuk.co.uk
http://www.haslemere.com

Michael Connolly, Headmaster

1595 Baumholder High School
Unit 23816
APO, Baumholder 09034 3816
Germany

William Diesselhorst, Principal

1596 Bavarian International School
Haputstrasse 1
Schloss Haimbausen, Bavaria D-85778
Germany

49-8133-9170

Fax: 49-8133-917-135
E-mail: e.werner@bix-school.com
http://www.bis-school.com
Grade levels Pre-K through 12, school year August - June

Anne Ponisch, Director

1597 Bedales School
Petersfield (Hampshire)
GU32 2DG
England

01730-300100
Fax: 01730-300500
http://www.bedales.org.uk

A Willcocks, MA, Headmaster

1598 Bedford School
De Parys Avenue
Bedford MK40 2TU
England

44-0-1234-362200
Fax: 44-0-1234-362283
E-mail: registar@bedfordschool.beds.org.uk
http://www.bedfordschool.beds.org.uk/info/contac

This Bedford school provides an English curriculum for 850 day students and 250 boarding students. The all boy school is involved in the teacher exchange program with the length of stay being one year, with housing provided.

Dr. IP Evans, Principal

1599 Bedgebury School
Bedgebury Park, Goudhurst (Kent)
TN17 2SH
England

0580-211954

Boarding school for girls ages eight to eighteen; and day school for girls ages three to eighteen.

ME Anne Kaye, MA, Headmaster

1600 Belgium Antwerp International School
Veltwijcklaan 180
B-2180
Belgium

32-3-543-9300
Fax: 32-3-541-8201
E-mail: ais@ais-antwerp.be
http://www.ais-antwerp.be

Coeducational day school meeting the needs of the international community of Antwerp, with approximately 45 percent of the enrollment from the United States. Grades PS-12, enrollment 588.

Robert F Schaecher, BS, MS, Headmaster

1601 Benjamin Franklin International School
Martorell i Pena 9
08017 Barcelona
Spain

34-93-434-2380
Fax: 34-93-417-3633
E-mail: bfranklin@bfis.org
http://www.bfis.org
Grade levels N-12, school year September - June

Mark Klimesh, Director
Cindy Moyer, Assistant Director

1602 Berlin International School
K"rnerstrasse 11
Berlin 12169
Germany

49-30-790-00370
Fax: 49-30-3790-00370
E-mail: office@berlin-international-school.de
http://www.berlin-international-school.de
Grade levels N-12, school year August - July

Andreas Wegener, Administrative Director

1603 Berlin Potsdam International School
Am Hochwald 30, Haus 2
14 532 Kleinmachnow
Germany

49-332-086-760
Fax: 49-332-086-7612
E-mail: office@bpis.de
http://www.bpis.de
Grade levels N-12, school year August - June

Stephen Middlebrook, Director

1604 Bitburg Elementary School
52 SPTG CCSE B Unit 3820 Box 45
APO, Bitburg 09126 2045
Germany

Joseph Kane, Principal

1605 Bitburg High School
52 SUG CCSH, Unit 3820 Box 50
APO, Bitburg 09126 2050
Germany

Henry Demps, Principal

1606 Bitburg Middle School
52 SPTG CCSM B, Unit 3820 Box 55
APO, Bitburg 09132
Germany

James Lawther, Principal

1607 Bjorn's International School
Gartnerivej 5
2100 Copenhagen
Denmark

Lea Kroghly, Principal

1608 Black Forest Academy
Postfach 1109
79396 Kandern
Germany

49-7626-91610
Fax: 49-7626-8821
http://www.bfacademy.com

This Academy is a private residential Christian school providing 1-12 education. Admission is conditional upon agreement with the school educational philosophy and preference is given to the children of missionaries. Total enrollmentis 115 day students and 100 total boarding (100 boys; 115 girls).

George Durance, Principal
Dave Jones, Faculty Head

1609 Bloxham School
Bloxham (Nr Banbury, Oxfordshire)
OX15 4PE
England

01295-720206
Fax: 01295-721897
E-mail: registar@bloxhamschool.co.uk
http://www.bloxhamschool.com

Boarding and day school for boys ages thirteen to eighteen and girls ages sixteen to eighteen.

MW Vallance, MA, Headmaster

1610 Blue Coat School
Somerset Road, Edgbaston Birmingham
B17 0HR
England

0121-456-3966
E-mail: bcs@argonet.co.uk
http://www.bluecoatschool.org

Brian Bissell, Principal

1611 Boeblingen Elementary School
CMR 445
APO, Boeblingen 09046 0004
Germany

Janette Johnson, Principal

1612 Bonn International School
Martin Luther King Strasse 14
Bonn 53175
Germany

49-228-308-540
Fax: 49-228-308-5420
E-mail: admin@bis.bonn.org
http://www.bis.bonn.org

Grade levels Pre-K through 12, school year August - June

Tom Ulmer, Director

1613 Bordeaux International School
53 Rue De Laseppe
33000 Bordeaux
France

33-557-870-211
Fax: 33-556-790-047
E-mail: bis@easynet.fr
http://http://bordeaux-intl-school.com

Grade levels k-13.

Christine Cussac, Directrice

1614 Brillantmont International School
Avenue Secretan 16
Lausanne, Vaud 1005
Switzerland

41-21-310-0400
Fax: 41-21-320-8417
E-mail: info@brillantmont.ch
http://www.brillantmont.ch

Grade levels include 9-13 with a total enrollment of 130.

Francoise Frei-Huguenin, Headmistress

1615 British Council School-Madrid
Po General Martinez Campos 31
28010 Madrid
Spain

34-91-337-3500
Fax: 34-91-337-3573
E-mail: madris@britishcouncil.com

Jack Cushman, Principal

1616 British Kindergarten
Ctra Del La Coruna Km 17
Las Rozas, 28230 Madrid
Spain

Mary Jane Maybury, Principal

1617 British Primary School
Stationsstraat 3
3080 Brussels
Belgium

32-2-767-3098
Fax: 32-2-767-0351
E-mail: info@britishprimary.com
http://www.britishprimary.com

Grade levels N-4, school year September - July

Dorothy Guy, Headmistress
Bruce Guy, Finacial Manager

1618 British Primary School-Stockholm
Ostra Valhallavagen 17
S182 62 Djursholm
Sweden

Gaye Elliot, Principal

1619 British School-Amsterdam
PO Box 920
1180 AX Amsterdam
Netherlands

31-20-347-1111
Fax: 31-20-347-1222

An independent, coeducational day school which offers an educaitonal program from preschool through grade 13 for students of all nationalities.

MWG Roberts, Principal

1620 British School-Bern
Mattenstrasse 3
3073 Gumligen
Switzerland

41-31-951-2358
Fax: 41-31-951-1710
E-mail: isbern@ibm.net

An independent, coeducational day school which offers and educational program from prekindergarten through grade 12 for students of all nationalities.

Enid Potts, BEd, Principal

1621 British School-Brussels
Leuvensesteenweg 19
B-3080 Tervuren
Belgium

322-767-4700
Fax: 322-767-8070
E-mail: admissions@britishschool.be
http://www.britishschool.be

Coeducational day program, ages three to eighteen.

1622 British School-Netherlands
Tarwekamp 3
2595 XG, Den Haag
Netherlands

071-616958
Fax: 071-617144
E-mail: foundation@britishschool.nl
http://www.britishschool.nl

Michael J Cooper, Principal

1623 British School-Oslo
PO Box 7531, Skillebekk 0205
Oslo 2
Norway

Margaret Stark, Principal

1624 British School-Paris
38 Quai De l'Ecluse, 78290
Croissy-sur-Seine
France

01-34-80-45-94
Fax: 01-39-76-12-69
E-mail: bsprincipal@wanadoo.fr
http://www.ecis.org

Alan Livingston-Smith, Principal

1625 Bromsgrove School
Worcester Road
Bromsgrove Worcestershire B617DU
England

44-0-1527-579679
Fax: 44-0-1527-576177
E-mail: marketing@bromsgrove-school.co.uk
http://www.bromit.demon.co.uk

This school offers an English curriculum to 840 day students and 350 boarding (700 boys; 490 girls), ages 3 to 18. The curriculum is English based but french, german and Spanish are also taught. Teachers from overseas are welcome withthe length of stay being 1-2 years. Applications needed to teach include science, French, math, Spanish, reading, German, English and physical education.

Timothy Malcolm Taylor, Headmaster
John Rogers, Faculty Head

1626 Brooke House College
Leicester Road gh (Leicestershire)
Market Harbourough, Leicestershire
England

44-0-1852-462452
Fax: 44-0-1858-462487

Brooke House is a non-denominational school with an enrollment of twenty day students and seventy boarding students (45 boys and 45 girls), age thirteen to nineteen years.

F Colyer, Headmaster
FJ Colombo, Faculty Head

1627 Brussels American School
PSC 79 Box 003
APO, Brussels 09724 0005
Belgium

Dennis Mcguane, Principal

1628 Brussels English Primary School
13 Rue Leon Deladrire
1300 Limal
Belgium

62-010-41-72-27
Fax: 62-010-40-10-43
E-mail: hdewaal@beps.com
http://www.beps.com

Coeducational day school for ages three to twelve, with the student body representing over 45 countries.

Henny de Waal, Head

1629 Bryanston School
Blandford (Dorset)
DT11 0PX
England

0258-452411

Coeducational boarding school for ages thirteen to eighteen.

Thomas D Wheare, MA, Principal

1630 Buckswood Grange International School
Uckfield (East Sussex)
E Sussex TN22 3PG
United Kingdom

44-182-574-7000
Fax: 44-182-576-5010
E-mail: admissions@buckswood.co.uk
http://www.buckswood.co.uk

A multinational boarding school for British and foreign students which combines the British curriculum with specialist EFL tution and close attention to social skills in an international environment.

Michael Reiser, Principal

1631 Butzbach Elementary School
CMR 452 Box 5500
APO, Butzbach 09045 0005
Germany

Carl Ford, Principal

1632 Byron Elementary School
Via San Zeno 17
Pisa
Italy

Chiara Bernieri, Principal

1633 CIV International School-Sophia Antipolis
BP 97, 190 rue Frederic Mistral
Sophia Antipolis 06902
France

33-4-929-65224
Fax: 33-4-936-52215
E-mail: secretary@civissa.org
http://www.civissa.org

Grade levels 1-12, school year September-June

Andrew Derry, Head of Section

1634 Calpe College International School
Cta. de Cadiz Km 171
29670 Malaga
Spain

95-278-1479
Fax: 95-278-9416
E-mail: calpe@activanet.es

Luis Proetta, Principal

1635 Campion School
PO Box 67484
Pallini GR-15302
Greece

301-813-5901
Fax: 301-813-6492
E-mail: dbaker@hol.gr

Dennis MacKinnon, Principal

1636 Canadian College Italy-The Renaissance School
59 Macamo Courte
Maple, Ontario L6A 1G1
Canada

905-508-7180
800-422-0548
Fax: 905-508-5480
E-mail: cciren@rogers.com
http://www.ccilanciano.com

Grae levels 11-13, school year September - June

1637 Cascais International School
Rua Das Faias, Lt 7 Torre
2750 Cascais
Portugal

An international nursery school, founded in 1996, that caters to children ages 1-6 years on a fulltime or part-time basis. The first language of the school is English and Portuguese is the second. Many other languages are spokenthroughout the school. Offers an individual approach, flexible hours and transport. Total enrollment is 75 day students (45 boys; 30 girls).

Evan Lerven Sixma, Principal

1638 Castelli Elementary School
Via Dei Laghi, 8.60
Ligetta Di Marinus, Ag, 00047 Marina
Italy

39-06-9366-1311
Fax: 39-06-9366-1311

Diana Jaworska, Principal

1639 Castelli International School
Via Degli Scozzesi 13
Grottaferrata, Rome 00046
Italy

39-06-943-15779
Fax: 39-06-943-15779
E-mail: maryac@pcg.it
http://www.pcg.it/CIS

Grade levels 1-6, school year September - June

Marianne Palladino, BA, MA, PhD, Director of Studies

1640 Casterton School
Kirkby Lonsdale, Carnforth
LA6 2SG
England

052-42-71202

AF Thomas, MA, Headmaster

1641 Caxton College
Ctra De Barcelona S/N 46530
Puzol Valencia
Spain

34-96-146-4500
Fax: 34-96142-0930
E-mail: oaxton@camerdata.es

Amparo Gil Marques, Principal

1642 Center Academy
92 St. John's Hill Battersea
London SW11 1SH
England

071-821-5760

Robert Detweiler, Principal

1643 Centre International De Valbonne
Civ-bp 097 06902 Sophia
Antipolis Cedex
France

33-4-929-652-24
Fax: 33-4-936-522-15
E-mail: issaciv@riviera.net

Ian Hill, Principal

1644 Charters-Ancaster School
Penland Road, Bexhill on Sea
TN40 2JQ
England

0424-730499

Boarding girls ages eleven to eighteen; day school for boys three to eight and girls three-eighteen.

K Lewis, MA, Headmaster

1645 Children's House
Kornbergvegen 23-4050 Sola
Stavanger
Norway

Christine Grov, Principal

1646 Cite Scolaire International De Lyon
2 Place De Montreal
69007 Lyon
France

33-04-78-69-60-06
Fax: 33-04-78-69-60-36
E-mail: csi-lyon-gerland@ac-lyon.fr

Grade levels 1-12.

Donna Galiana, Director

1647 Cobham Hall
Cobham (Nr Gravesend, Kent)
DA12 3BL
England

0474-82-3371

Rosalind McCarthy, BA, Headmaster

1648 Colegio Ecole
Santa Rosa 12
PO Box 88-Lugone, 33690 Llanera
Spain

Patrick Wilson, Principal

1649 Colegio International-Meres
Apartado 107
33080 Oviedo, Asturias
Spain

Belen Orejas Fernandez, Principal

1650 Colegio International-Vilamoura
Apt 856, 8125 Vilamoura
Loule Algarve
Portugal

Lawrence James, Principal

1651 College Du Leman International School
74 Route De Sauverny
Versoix/Geneva, CH-1290
Switzerland

41-22-775-5555
Fax: 41-22-775-5559
E-mail: info@cdl.ch
http://www.cdl.ch

Grade levels include N-13 with an enrollment of 1700.

Francis Clivaz, General Director

1652 College International-Fontainebleau
48 Rue Guerin 77300
Fontainebleau
France

01-64-22-11-77
Fax: 01-64-23-43-17
E-mail: glenyskennedy@compuserve.com

Mrs. G. Kennedy, Principal

1653 College Lycee Cevenol International
43400 Le Chambon sur Lignon
France

04-71-59-72-52
Fax: 04-71-65-87-38
E-mail: lecevenol@aol.com

Christiane Minssen, Principal

1654 Copenhagen International School
Hellerupvej 22-26
2900 Hellerup
Denmark

45-39-463-300
Fax: 45-39-612-230
E-mail: cis@cisdk.dk
http://www.cis-edu.dk

Coeducational day school which offers an educational program from prekindergarten through grade 12 for students of all nationalities.

Christopher Bowman, Director

1655 Croughton High School
Unit 5485 Box 15
APO Croughton, 09494 0005
Great Britain

Dr. Charles Recesso, Principal

1656 Danube International School
Josef Gall-Gassee 2
A-1020 Vienna
Austria

00-43-1-720-3110
Fax: 43-1-720-3110-40
http://www.danubeschool.at

Peter Harding, Director

1657 Darmstadt Elementary School
CMR 431
APO, Darmstadt 09175 0005
Germany

Sherry Templeton, Principal

1658 Darmstadt Junior High School
CMR 431
APO, Darmstadt 09175 0005
Germany

Daniel Basarich, Principal

1659 De Blijberg
Postbus 27518-3003 MA
Rotterdam
Netherlands

I Van Der Voordt, Principal

1660 Dean Close School
Shelburne Road, Cheltenham
GL51 6HE
England

0242-522640
E-mail: 9166035.c_57323@clialnet.ls.uk

This school offers an English based curriculum for 157 day students and 279 boarding students (246 boys; 190 girls), ages 13-18 years. The curriculum offered at the coeducational school is an up-to-date balanced curriculum with a widerange of options which aim to outdo the requirements of the national Curriculum. The school is a Church of England foundation and the Evangelical tradition is maintained.

Christopher J. Bacon, MA, Headmaster
Anthony R Barchand, Faculty Head

1661 Dexheim Elementary School
Unit 24027
APO, Dexheim 09110 0005
Germany

Gary Waltner, Principal

1662 Downside School
Stratton-on-the-Fosse, Bath (Avon)
BA3 4RJ
England

0761-232-206

This Roman Catholic boys school offers an English curriculum for 310 boarding students, ages 10-19. Applications needed to teach include science, French, math, social sciences, German, Spanish, English and physical education. manyother languages including Mandarin and Arabic are also offered, and the school boasts superb music, drama and sports facilities.

Dom Antony Sutch, MA, Principal

1663 Dresden International School
Goetheallee 18
Dredsen 01309
Germany

49-351-3400428
Fax: 49-351-3400430
E-mail: dis@dredsen-is.de
http://www.dresden-is.de

Grade levels Pre-K through 9, school year August - June

Don Vinge, Director

1664 ECC International School
Jacob Jordaensstraat 85-87
2018 Antwerp
Belgium

Dr. X Nieberding, Principal

1665 Ecole Active Bilingue
70 rue du Theatre
75105 Paris
France

01-44-37-00-80
Fax: 01-45-79-06-66
E-mail: nhourcade@lcnet.fr

Danielle Monod, Principal

1666 Ecole Active Bilingue Jeannine Manuel
70 rue du Theatre
75015 Paris
France

33-1-443-70080
Fax: 33-1-457-90666
http://www.eabjm.com

Grade levels k-12.

Elizabeth Zeboulon, Directrice

1667 Ecole D'Humanite
CH-6085 Hasliberg-Goldern
Switzerland

41-33-972-9292
Fax: 41-33-972-9211

150 boys and girls, aged 6 to 20 and faculty live in small family-style groups. International, inter-racial student body. Main language is German, with special classes for beginners.

A Luethi-Peterson, Principal

1668 Ecole Des Roches & Fleuris
3961 Bluche
Valais
Switzerland

Marcel Clivez, Principal

1669 Ecole Lemania
Ch. de Preville 3
1001 Lausanne
Switzerland

41-0-21-350-15-01
Fax: 41-0-21-312-67-00

This international college represents over 65 nationalities offering French and English intensive courses, summer programs, American academic studies at graduate and undergraduate levels, sports and cultural activities, andaccommodation in boarding school. Total enrollment: 800 day students; 100 boarding (450 boys; 450 girls), in grades 1-10.

M JP du Pasquier, Principal

1670 Ecole Nouvelle Preparatoire
Route Du Lac 22, Ch-1094
Paudex
Switzerland

Marc Desmet, Principal

1671 Ecole Nouvelle de la Suisse Romande
Rovereaz 20, CH-161
1000 Lausanne
Switzerland

41-21-654-65-00
Fax: 41-21-654-65-05

Francois Zbinden, Principal

1672 Edinburgh American School
29 Chester Street
Edinburgh EH37EN
Scotland

AW Morris, Principal

1673 Edradour School
Edradour House - Pitlochry
Perthshire PH165JW,
Scotland

JPA Romanes, Principal

1674 El Plantio International School Valencia
Urbanizacion. El Plantio
Calle 233, X36, La Canada, Valencia
Spain

96-132-14-10
Fax: 96-132-18-41

Anthony C Nelson, Principal

1675 Ellerslie School
Abbey Road, Malvern
WR14 3HF
England

0684-575701

Elizabeth M Baker, BA, Headmaster

1676 English Junior School
Lilla Danska Vagen 1
412 74 Gothenburg
Sweden

31-401819

Patricia Gabrielsson, Principal

1677 English Kindergarten
Valenjanpolku 2
05880 Hyvinkaa
Finland

Riva Rentto, Principal

1678 English Montessori School
Avda La Salle S/N Aravaca
Madrid 28023
Spain

91-357-26-67
Fax: 91-307-15-43
E-mail: english@acade.es
http://www.emeg.home.ml.org

Norman Roddom, Principal

1679 English School-Helsinki
Selkamerenkatu 11
00180 Helinski
Finland

358-9-686-6160
Fax: 358-9-685-6699
E-mail: mainoffice@ish.edu.hel.fi

An independent, coeducational day school which offers an educational program from kindergarten through grade 12 for students of all nationalities. The school year comprises 2 semesters extending from August to December and fromJanuary to June.

Mary Venard, Principal

1680 English School-Los Olivos
Avda Pino Panera 25, 46110 Godella
Valencia
Spain

96-363-99-38
Fax: 96-364-48-63

Jane Rodriguez, Principal

1681 European Business & Management School
Jacob Jordaensstraat 77
2018 Antwerp
Belgium

323-218-8182
Fax: 323-218-5868
E-mail: info@ebms.edu
http://www.ebms.edu

Provides international education in small classes, individual attention and international awareness. Bachelor and Master.

Luc Van Meli

1682 European School Culham
Abingdon Oxfordshire
OX14 3DZ
Great Britain

T Hyem, Principal

1683 European School-Brussels I
Avenue Du Vert Chasseur 46
1180 Brussels
Belgium

02-374-58-44

J Marshall, Principal

1684 European School-Italy
Via Montello 118
21100 Varese
Italy

Jorg Hoffman, Principal

1685 Evangelical Christian Academy
Calle Talia 26
Madrid 28022
Spain

34-91-741-2900
Fax: 34-91-320-8606
E-mail: ECA_Madrid@compuserve.com
http://http://ourworld.compuserve.com/homepages/eca_ma-drid

This academy offers an English-based curriculum to 75 day students (45 boys; 30 girls), in grades K-12. The length of stay for overseas teachers is one, two or more years with no housing provided. Applications from overseas needed toteach include science, administration, math, English and physical education.

Beth Hornish, Principal
Scot Musser, Business Manager

1686 Feltwell Elementary School
CCSE F Unit 5185 Box 315
APO Feltwell 09461 5315
Grest ritain

Myron Caylor, Principal

1687 Frankfurt International School
An der Waldlust
61440 Frankfurt
Germany

49-6171-2020
Fax: 49-6171-202384
http://www.fis.edu

An independent, coeducational day school which offers an educational program from preprimary through grade 12 for students of all nationalities.

Jutta Kuehne, Director

1688 Frederiksborg Gymnasium
Carlsbergvej 15
3400 Hillerod
Denmark

Peter Kuhlman, Principal

1689 Friends School
Saffron Walden, Essex
CB11 3EB
England

0642-722141

Boarding coed school for ages eleven to eighteen and day coed for ages seven to eighteen.

David G Cook, BEd, Headmaster

1690 Gaeta Elementary & Middle School
PSC Box 811
FPO Gaeta 09609 0005
Italy

Dr. Robert Kirkpatrick, Principal

1691 Garmisch Elementary School
Unit 24511
APO, Garmisch 09053 0005
Germany

Russell Mcclain, Principal

1692 Geilenkirchen Elementary School
Unit 8045
APO, Geilenkirchen 09104 0005
Germany

James Van Dierendonck, Principal

1693 Gelnhausen Elementary School
CMR 465
APO, Gelnhausen 09076 0005
Germany

Jim Harrison, Principal

1694 Geneva English School
36, route de Malagny
1294 Genthod, Geneva
Switzerland

41-22-755-18-55
Fax: 41-22-779-14-29
E-mail: gesadmin.n@iprolink.ch
http://www.geneva-english-school.ch

A private, nonprofit primary school that is owned and managed by an association which is composed of parents whose children attend the school. The main objective of the school is to offer education on British lines for children ofprimary school age living in or near Geneva, and to prepare them for secondary education in any English-speaking school.

Denis Unsworth, Principal

1695 Giessen Elementary School
414th BSB GSN, Unit 20911
APO, Giessen 09169 0005
Germany

Mary Ann Burkard, Principal

1696 Giessen High School
414th BSB GSB, Unit 20911
APO, Giessen 09169 0005
Germany

Gordon Gartner, Principal

1697 Grafenwoehr Elementary School
Unit 28127
APO, Grafenwoehr 09114 0005
Germany

Richard Sagerman, Principal

1698 Greenwood Garden School
Via Vito Sinisi 5
00189 Rome
Italy

39-06-332-66703
Fax: 39-06-332-66703
E-mail: donnase@tin.it

Donna Seibert Ricci, BA, Principal

1699 Gstaad International School
Ahorn, 3780
Gstaad
Switzerland

41-33-744-2373
Fax: 41-33-744-3578
E-mail: gis@gstaad.ch
http://www.gstaadschool.ch

This school addresses the academic needs of 24 boarding students (15 boys and 9 girls) in grades eight through twelve. Overseas teachers are welcome for a length of three years, with housing provided. Applications from overseas neededto teach are science, math, social studies, reading, English, economics and business.

Alain Souperbiet, Director

1700 Haagsche School Vereeniging
Nassaulaan 26-2514jt
The Hague
Netherlands

HM Jongeling, Principal

1701 Hainerberg Elementary School
Unit 29647
APO, Wiesbaden 09096 0005
Germany

Maren James, Principal

1702 Halvorsen Tunner Elementary and Middle School
Unit 7565
APO, Rhein Main 09050 0005
Germany

Julie Gaski, Principal

1703 Hanau High School
Unit 20235
APO, Hanau 09165 0005
Germany

Allen Davenport, Principal

1704 Hanau Middle School
Unit 20193
APO, Hanau 09165 0016
Germany

Robert Sennett, Principal

1705 Harrow School
5 High Street
Harrow on the Hill, HA1 3HP
England

01-423-2366
E-mail: hm.harrowschool@cwcom.net

IDS Beer, MA, Headmaster

1706 Hatherop Castle School
Hatherop, Cirencester
GL7 3NB
England

028-575-206

Brian W Forster, BA, MA, Headmaster

1707 Heidelberg High School
Unit 29237
APO, Heidelberg 09102 0005
Germany

Robert Briton, Principal

1708 Heidelberg Middle School
Unit 29237
APO, Heidelberg 09102 0005
Germany

Donald Johnson, Principal

1709 Hellenic College-London
67 Pont Street
London SWIX OBD
England

0171-581-5044
Fax: 0171-589-9055
E-mail: hellenic@rmplc.co.uk
http://www.rmplc.co.uk/eduweb/sites/hellenic

James Wardrobe, Principal

1710 Hellenic-American Education Foundation Athens College-Psychico College
PO Box 65005
Palaio Psychico, 154 10
Greece

30-1-671-2771
Fax: 30-1-674-8156
E-mail: acpresoff@hol.gr
http://www.haef.gr

Grade levels 1-12, school year September - June

Dennis Skiotis, PhD, President

1711 Helsingin Suomalainen
Yhteiskoulu-Isonnevantie 8
00300 Helinski
Finland

Vesa Nikunen, Principal

1712 Het Nederlands Lyceum
Theo Mann-Bouwmeesterlaan 75
2597GV The Hague
Netherlands

Bryan G Morland, Principal

1713 Het Rijnlands Lyceum
Appollolaan 1 2341 BA
Oegstgeest Zh,
Netherlands

31-3771-5155640

Lyceum is a state subsidized school with an international department offering IBMYP and IB. Offers an English/Dutch spoken curriculum to 1,190 day students and 60 boarding (650 boys; 600 girls), in grades 6 through 12. Student/teacherratio is 15:1, and the school is willing to participate in a teacher exchange program, however, housing will not be provided by the school.

Drs LE Timmerman, Principal

1714 Hillhouse Montessori School
Avenida Alfonso Xiii 30 Y 34
Madrid 2
Spain

Judy Amick, Principal

1715 Hohenfels Elementary School
Unit 28214
APO, Hohenfels 09173 0005
Germany

Susan Somani, Principal

1716 Hohenfels High School
Unit 28214
APO, Hohenfels 09173 0005
Germany

Susan Somani, Principal

1717 Holmwood House
114 Holgate Road, York
(Essex) CO3 5ST
England

44-0-1904-626183
Fax: 44-0-1904-670899
E-mail: holmwood.house@dial.pipex.com

Holmwood House is an independent coeducational day
and boarding preparatory school. The total enrollment of
the school is 310 day students and 50 boarding students
(240 boys and 120 girls), ages 4 1/2 to 13 1/2.

HS Thackrah, Principal

1718 Hvitfeldtska Gymnasiet
Rektorsgatan 2, SE-411 33
Goteborg
Sweden

46-31-367-0623
Fax: 46-31-367-0602
E-mail: agneta.santesson@educ.goteborg.se
http://www.hvitfeldt.educ.goteborg.se

State school, founded 1647, offers the International
Baccalaureate curriculum to a total enrollment of 90 girls
and 90 boys, in grades 10-12.

Christen Holmstrom, Principal
Agneta Santesson, Deputy Headmaster

1719 Illesheim Elementary and Middle School
CMR 416 Box J
APO, Hohenfels 09140 0005
Germany

49-9841-8408
Fax: 49-9841-8987

Donald J Ness, Principal

1720 Independent Bonn International School
Tulpenbaumweg 42
Bonn 53177
Germany

49-228-32-31-66
Fax: 49-228-32-39-58
E-mail: ibis@ibis-school.com
http://www.ibis-school.com

Grade levels Pre-K through 7, school year September -
July

Graham Fenner, Headmaster

1721 Independent Schools Information Service
Grosveror Gardens House 35-37
Frosvernor Gardens, London SW1W 0BS
England

020-77981575
Fax: 020-77981561
E-mail: national@isis.org.uk
http://www.isis.org.uk

Provides information on 1400 elementary and secondary
schools in the United Kingdom and Ireland.

David J Woodhead

1722 Innsbruck International High School
Schonger, Austria A-6141

0-5225-4201
Fax: 0-5225-4202

An accredited coeducational boarding and day school.
The school offers an American college preparatory high
school curriculum for grades 9-12.

Gunther Wenko, Director
John E Wenrick, Headmaster

1723 Institut Alpin Le Vieux Chalet
1837 Chateau D'oex
Switzerland

Jean Bach, Principal

1724 Institut Auf Dem Rosenberg
Hohenweg 60-9000 St. Gallen
Switzerland

Felicitas Scharli, Principal

1725 Institut Chateau Beau-Cedre
57 Av De Chillion
CH-1820 Territet Montreux
Switzerland

41-21-963-5341
Fax: 41-21-963-4783
E-mail: info@monterosaschool.com

This Institut is an exclusive boarding and finishing
international school for girls. American high school with
a general culture section for 30 boarding students in
grades 9 through twelve. Languages spoken include
French and Englishand the student/teacher ratio is 1:6.

Pierre Gay, Principal

1726 Institut Le Champ Des Pesses
1618 Chatel-st-denis
Montreux
Switzerland

PL Racloz, Principal

1727 Institut Le Rosey
Chateau du Rosey
CH-1180 Rolle
Switzerland

41-21-822-5500
Fax: 41-21-822-5555
E-mail: rosey@rosey.ch
http://www.rosey.ch

Grade levels include 2-13 with a total enrollment of 340.

Philippe Gudin, General Director

1728 Institut Montana Bugerbug-American Schools
Zugerberg
CH 6300 Zug
Switzerland

41-41-711-1722
Fax: 41-41-711-5465
E-mail: kob@montana.zug.ch
http://www.montana.zug.ch

Grade levels include 7-13 with a total enrollment of 111.

Daniel Fredez, Director

1729 Institut Monte Rosa
57, Ave de Chillon,
Montreux/VD CH-1820
Switzerland

021-963-5341
Fax: 021-963-4783

Bernhard Gademann, BS, MS, Principal

1730 Inter-Community School
Strubenacher 3, CH-8126
Zumikon
Switzerland

41-1-919-8300
Fax: 41-1-919-8320
http://www.icsz.ch

This school offers a curriculum in English, Italian, German and French. Grades N-12, enrollment is 659.

John Young, Headmaster
Gary Winning, Principal

1731 International Academy
Via di Grottarossa 295
00189 Rome
Italy

39-340-731-4195

Joan Bafaloukas Bulgarini, Principal

1732 International College Spain
Vereda Norte 3
Lamoraleja, 28109 Aclobendas, Madrid
Spain

34-91-650-2398
Fax: 34-91-650-1035
E-mail: icsmadrid@compuserve.com
http://www.icsmadric.com

An international school with over forty different nationalities among students and fifteen among staff. Programs lead to the International Baccalaureate. Total enrollment is 497 day students; 8 boarding (249 boys; 256 girls), ingrades K-12. Applications needed to teach include science, pre-school, French, math, social sciences, administration, Spanish, English, physical education, art and music.

Terry Hedger, Director
Hubert Keulers, Head of Primary School

1733 International Management Institute
Jacob Jordaensstraat 77
2018 Antwerp
Belgium

32-3-21-85-431
Fax: 32-3-21-85-868
E-mail: info@timi.edu
http://www.timi.edu

Bachelor and Master degrees, small classes, individual touch.

Luc Van Mele

1734 International Preparatory School
Rua Do Boror 12 Carcavelos
2775 Parede
Portugal

56-2-321-5800
Fax: 56-2-321-5821
E-mail: info@tipschool.com
http://www.tipschool.com

1735 International School Beverweerd
Beverweerdseweg 60, 3985 RE
Werkhoven
Netherlands

03437-1341
Fax: 03437-2079

Ray Kern, BA, MA, Principal

1736 International School-Aberdeen
296 N Deeside Road
Milltimber, Aberdeen AB13 OAB
England

44-1224-732267
Fax: 44-1224-735648
E-mail: admin@isa.abdn.sch.uk
http://www.isa.abdn.sch.uk

Dan Hovde, Director

1737 International School-Algarve
Apartado 80 Porches 8400
Lagoa Algarve
Portugal

Peter Maddison, Principal

1738 International School-Amsterdam
PO Box 920
1180 AX Amstelveen
The Netherlands

31-20-347-1111
Fax: 31-20-347-1222
E-mail: info@isa.nl
http://www.isa.nl

This school's total enrollment is 573 day students (260 boys; 313 girls), ages toddler through thirteen.

Steve Bannell, Director

1739 International School-Basel
Schulstrasse 5
Bottminger, Ch-4103
Switzerland

41-61-426-96-26
Fax: 41-61-426-96-25

Geoff Tomlinson, Principal

1740 International School-Bergen
Vilhelm Bjerknesvei 15
5081 Landas
Norway

47-55-30-63-30
Fax: 47-55-30-63-31
E-mail: murison@isb.gs.hl.no
http://www.isb.gs.hl.no

Grade levels prekindergarten through tenth.

June Murison, Director

1741 International School-Berne
Mattenstrasse 3
3073 Gumligen
Switzerland

41-31-951-2358
Fax: 41-31-951-1710
E-mail: rosemary.schelker@isberne.ch
http://www.isberne.ch

Grades preK-12, enrollment 290

David Gatley, Director

1742 International School-Brussels
Kattenberg 19
Brussels 1170
Belguim

32-2-661-4211
Fax: 32-2-661-4200
E-mail: admissions@isb.be
http://www.isb.be

Coeducational day school for ages three to eighteen.

Richard P Hall, BA, Director

1743 International School-Cartagena
Manga Club Cp 30385 Cartagena
Los Belones Murcia
Spain

34-68-175000
E-mail: isc@sendanet.es

Robert Risch, Principal

1744 International School-Curacao
PO Box 3090
Koninginnelaan Emmastad, Cuavao
Netherlands Antilles

599-9-737-3633
Fax: 599-90737-3142
E-mail: iscmec@attglobal.net
http://www.isc.an

Margie Elhage, Director

1745 International School-Dusseldorf
Niederrheinstrasse 336
40489 Dusseldorf
Germany

49-211-94066-799
Fax: 49-211-4080-744
E-mail: nmcw@isdedu.de
http://www.isdedu.com

Grade levels preK-13.

Neil McWilliam, Director

1746 International School-Eerde
Kasteellaan 1, 7731 PJ
Ommen
Netherlands

031-0529-451452
Fax: 031-0529-456377
E-mail: ise@landstede.nl

B Schollema, Headmaster

1747 International School-Friuli
Via Delle Grazie 1/A
Pordenone 33170
Italy

Susan Clarke, Principal

1748 International School-Geneva
62 route de Chene
CH-1208 Geneva
Switzerland

41-22-787-2400
Fax: 41-22-787-2410

A coeducational international general academic and college preparatory school.

George Walker, Director General

1749 International School-Hamburg
Holmbrook 20
Hamburg 22605
Germany

49-40-883-1101
Fax: 49-40-1881-1405
E-mail: info@ish.intrasat.org
http://www.ish.intrasat.org

Grade levels Pre-K through 12, school year August - June

Geoffrey Clark, Headmaster

1750 International School-Hannover Region
Bruchmeisterstrasse 16
Hannover, Lower Saxony 30169
Germany

49-511-27041650
Fax: 49-511-557934
E-mail: IntSchoolH@aol.com
http://www.is-hr.de

Grade levels K-11, school year August - June

Derek Malpass, Director

1751 International School-Helsinki
Selk,,merenkatu 11
Helsinki 00180
Finland

358-9-686-6160
Fax: 358-9-685-6699
E-mail: mainoffice@ish.edu.hel.fi
http://www.ish.edu.hel.fi

Grade levels K-12, school year August - June

Peter Ostrom, Headmaster

1752 International School-Iita
Carolyn House 26 Dingwall Road
Croydon CR9 3EE
England

Neil Jackson, Principal

1753 International School-Lausanne
73 av CF Ramuz
Pully/Lausanne, VD, 1009
Switzerland

41-21-728-1733
Fax: 41-21-728-7868
E-mail: isl@span.ch
http://www.isl.ch

This International School is Lausanne's only accredited co-educational day school for children ages three to eighteen in grades Nursery through twelth. ESL, French as foreign and second language are taught with a wide range of extraactivities. The IB Diploma provides a sound college preparatory program for students in

Grades 11 and 12. The total enrollment currently 425 students.

Simon G Taylor, Director
John Ivett, Assistant Director

1754 International School-Le Chaperon Rouge
3963 Crans Sur Sierre
Crans/Montana
Switzerland

41-27-4812-500
Fax: 41-27-4812-502

Prosper Bagnoud, Principal

1755 International School-London
139 Gunnersbury Avenue
London W3 8LG
England

44-20-8992-5823
Fax: 44-20-8993-7012
E-mail: islondon@dial.pipex.com
http://www.islondon.com

Grade levels R-13, school year September - June

Ian Hackett, Headmaster
Rita Ward, Deputy Head

1756 International School-Lyon
Ave Tony Garnier
69007 Lyon
France

John Larner, Principal

1757 International School-Naples
Viale della Liberazione, 1
Bagnoli, Napoli 80125
Italy

39-081-721-2037
Fax: 39-081-570-0248
E-mail: isn@na.cybernet.it
http://www.intschoolnaples.it

Grade levels Pre-K through 12, school year September - June

Josephine Sessa, Principal
Patricia Montesano, VP

1758 International School-Nice
15 Avenue Claude Debussy
Nice 02600
France

33-493-210-400
Fax: 33-493-216-911
E-mail: robert.silvetz@cote-azur.cci.fr

Grade levels Pre-K through 12, school year September - June

Robert Silvetz, Director

1759 International School-Paris
6, rue Beethoven
75016 Paris
France

33-1-422-40954
Fax: 33-1-452-71593
E-mail: info@isparis.edu
http://www.isparis.edu

A coeducational elementary and secondary day school founded as a non-profit association. Emphasizing individual attention, the class size is limited to approximately twenty students.

Gareth Jones, Headmaster

1760 International School-Sotogrande
Apartado 15
11310 Sotogrande Pcia de Cadiz
Spain

34-956-79-59-02
Fax: 34-956-79-48-16
E-mail: director@sis.ac
http://www.sis.ac

This school offers various classes to 250 day students and 10 boarding students made up of 138 boys and 122 girls. The grade range covered is K-12 with the student/teacher ratio being 10:1.

Geroge O'Brien, Headmaster

1761 International School-Stavanger
Treskeveien 3
4042 Hafrsfjord
Norway

47-51-559-100
Fax: 47-51-552-962
E-mail: intschol@iss.stavanger.rl.no
http://www.iss.stavager.rl.no

An English language international school providing educaion from preschool up to and including high school graduation.

Linda Duevel, PhD, Director

1762 International School-Stockholm
Johannesgatan 18
Stockholm SE-111 34
Sweden

46-8-412-4000
Fax: 46-8-412-4001
E-mail: admin@intsch.se
http://www.intsch.se

Grade levels include preK-10 with an enrollment of 340.

Claes-Goran Widlund, Principal

1763 International School-Stuttgart
Sigmaringerstr 2578
70 597 Stuttgart-Degerlock
Germany

49-7-11-76-9600-0
Fax: 49-7-11-76-9600-0
E-mail: iss@iss.s.bw.schule.de
http://www.ecis.org/iss

Thomas Schaedler, Director

1764 International School-Trieste
Via Conconello 16 (Opicina)
34016 Trieste
Italy

39-040-211-452
Fax: 39-040-213-122
E-mail: istrieste@interbusiness.it
http://www.geocities.com/athens/oracle/1329

This school offers a curriculum taught in English and Italian to 230 day students (115 boys; 115 girls) in grades PreK-8. Applications needed to teach include science, preschool, French, math, social sciences, reading, German,English and physical education.

Peter Metzger, Principal

1765 International School-Turin
Vicolo Tiziano 10
10024 Moncalieri
Italy

George Selby, BA, MA, Principal

1766 International School-Venice
The British Center, San Marco
4267A Venice
Italy

John Millerchip, Principal

1767 International School-Zug
Walterswil
Baar 6340
Switzerland

41-41-768-1188
Fax: 41-41-768-1189
E-mail: office@isoz.ch

Grade levels include preK-8 with a total enrollment of 354.

Martin Latter, Head of School

1768 International Schule-Berlin, Potsdam
Seestrasse 45
14467 Potsdam
Germany

49-332-086-760
Fax: 49-332-086-7612
E-mail: office@isbp.p.bb.schule.de
http://www.shuttle.de/p/isbp

This school offers an English curriculum to 157 day students (87 boys and 64 girls) in grades PreK-12. Applications needed to teach include science, pre-school, math, social sciences, reading, English and physical education.

Matthias Truper, Principal

1769 International Secondary School-Eindhoven
Jerusalemlaan 1, 5625 PP Eindhoven
Netherlands

040-413600

JM Westerhout, Principal

1770 Internationale Schule Frankfurt-Rhein-Main
Albert-Blank-Strasse 50
65931 Frankfurt
Germany

49-69-954-3190
Fax: 49-69-954-31920
E-mail: isf@sabis.net
http://www.isf-net.de

Grade levels Pre-K through 13, school year September - June

Richard Long, School Director

1771 Interskolen
Engtoften 22
DK-8260 Viby J
Denmark

45-8611-4560

Fax: 45-8614-9670
http://www.interskolen.com

Coeducational day program for ages five to seventeen.

Tommy Schou Christesen, Principal

1772 John F Kennedy International School
Kirchgasse
CH-3792 Saanen
Switzerland

41-33-744-1372
Fax: 41-33-744-8982
E-mail: lovell@jfk.ch
http://wwwjfk.ch

Grade levels include K-8 with an enrollment of 60.

William M Lovell, Directorl

1773 John F Kennedy School-Berlin
Teltower Damm 87-93
Berlin 14167
Germany

49-30-6321-5711
Fax: 49-30-6321-6377
E-mail: school/ad@jfks.de
http://www.jfks.de

Grade levels K-13, school year August - July

Charles Hanna, Managing Prnicipal

1774 Joppenhof/Jeanne D'arc Clg
PO Box 4050, 6202 Rb Maastricht
Netherlands

L Spronck, Principal

1775 Kaiserslautern Elementary School
86 SPTG CCSE K Unit 3240 Box 425
APO, Kaiserslautern 09094 0005
Germany

Les Haney, Principal

1776 Kaiserslautern High School
86 SPTG CCSH K Unit 3240, Box 440
APO, Kaiserslautern 09094 0005
Germany

William Leclair, Principal

1777 Kaiserslautern Middle School
86 SPTG CCSM K Unit 3240 Box 450
APO, Kaiserslautern 09094 0005
Germany

Richard Nielsen, Principal

1778 Kendale Primary International School
Via Gradoli 86, Via Cassia Km 10300
00189 Rome
Italy

39-06-332-676-08
Fax: 39-06-332-676-08
E-mail: kendale@diesis.com
http://www.diesis.com/kendale

Veronica Said Tani, Principal

1779 Kensington School
Carrer Dels Cavallers 31-33
Pedralbes 08034, Barcelona
Spain

EP Giles, Principal

1780 King Fahad Academy
Bromyard Avenue
London W3 7HD
England

020-7259-3350

Dr. Ibtissam Al-Bassam, Principal

1781 King's College
Paseo de los Andes
Soto De Vinuelas, 28761 Madrid
Spain

91-803-48-00
Fax: 91-803-65-57
E-mail: soto@kingsgroup.com
http://www.kingsgroup.com/idik

CA Clark, Principal

1782 Kitzingen Elementary School
Unit 26124
APO, Kitzingen 09031 0005
Germany

Fred Paesel, Principal

1783 Kleine Brogel Elementary School
58 MUNSS, Unit 21903
kleine Brogel 09713
Belgium

Robert Nance, Principal

1784 La Chataigneraie International School
Geneva La Chataigneraie, 1297
Founex Vaud
Switzerland

Michael Lee, Principal

1785 La Maddalena Elementary School
PSC 816 Box 1755
FPO, La Maddalena, Sardinia 09612 0005
Italy

Janice Barber, Principal

1786 Lajes Elementary School
Unit 7725
APO, Lajes, The Azores 09720 0005
Portugal

David Trukositz, Principal

1787 Lajes High School
Unit 7725
APO, Lajes, The Azores 09720 7725
Portugal

Ira Scheier, Principal

1788 Lakenheath Elementary School
Unit 5185 Box 40
APO, Lakenheath, 09464
Great Britain

Wolfgang Plakinger, Principal

1789 Lakenheath High School
Unit 5185 Box 45
APO, Lakenheath, 09464 8545
Great Britain

Dr. Joan Halloran, Principal

1790 Lakenheath Middle School
Unit 5185 Box 40
APO, Feltwell 09464 8555
Great Britain

Georgia Williams, Principal

1791 Lancing College
Lancing (West Sussex)
BN15 0RW
England

0273-452213
Fax: 01273-464720

JS Woodhouse, MA, Headmaster

1792 Landstuhl Elementary and Middle School
CMR 402
APO, Ladstuhl 09180 0005
Germany

James Parker, Principal

1793 Leighton Park School
Shinfield Road
Reading RG2 7DH
England

4-118-987-9600
Fax: 44-118-987-9625
E-mail: info@leightonparkreading.sch.uk
http://www.leightonparkreading.sch.uk

Co-educational day and boarding school for pupils aged 11-18 years.

John Dunston, Headmaster

1794 Leipzig International School
Konneritzstrasse 47
D-04229 Leipzig
Germany

49-341-421-0574
Fax: 49-341-421-2154
E-mail: admin@intschool-leipzig.com
http://www.intschool-leipzig.com

An independent, coeducational day school which offers and educational program from kindergarten through grade 12 for students of all nationalities. We offer the IGCSE and IB diploma program.

Michael Webster, Headmaster

1795 Lennen Bilingual School
65 Quai d'Orsay
75007 Paris
France

01-47-05-66-55
Fax: 01-47-05-17-18

This school teaches a curriculum in English and French to 120 day students. The school is willing to participate in a teacher exchange program with the length of stay being one year, with no housing provided by the school. Bilingualeducation is offered in the preschool and grade school (until Grade 3).

Michelle Lennen, Principal

1796 Leys School
Cambridge
CB2 2AD England

44-1223-508-900
Fax: 44-1223-505-333
E-mail: office@theleys.cambs.sch.uk
http://www.theleys.cambs.sch.uk

Teaching Opportunities Abroad / Western Europe

Boarding and day school for boys ages eleven to eighteen and girls ages eleven to eighteen.

Rev Dr John Barrett, Headmaster

1797 Leysin American School
The Savoy, Leysin CH 1864
Switzerland

> 41-24-493-3777
> Fax: 41-24-493-3790
> E-mail: admissions@las.ch
> http://www.las.ch

The only American boarding school in Switzerland accredited by the European Council of International Schools and the Middle States Association for College and Secondary Schools.

Steven Oh, Executive Director

1798 Livorno Elementary School
Unit 31301 Box 65
APO, Livorno 09613 0005
Italy

Dr. Robert Kethcart, Principal

1799 Livorno High School
Unit 31301 Box 65
APO, Livorno 09613 0005
Italy, AE 09613-0005

Dr. Frank Calvano, Principal

1800 London Central High School
PSC 821 Box 119
APO, High Wycombe 09421 0005
Great Britain, AE 09421-0005

Dr. Charles Recesso, Principal

1801 Lorentz International School
Groningensingel 1245, 6835HZ
Arnhem
Netherlands

> 31-26-320-0110
> Fax: 31-26-320-0113

Jan M Meens, Principal

1802 Lusitania International College Foundation
Apartado 328
8600 Lagos
Portugal

Krisine Byrne, Principal

1803 Lycee Francais De Belgique
9 Avenue Du Lycee Francais
1180 Brussels
Belgium

> 02-374-58-78

Jean-Claude Giudicelli, Principal

1804 Lycee International-American Section
 Rue du Fer a Cheval
BP 230 Germain En Laye
France

> 33-34-51-74-85
> Fax: 33-30-87-00-49
> E-mail: american.lycee.intl@wanadoo.fr
> http://www.lycee-intl-american.org

Yves Lemarie, Head of School
Ted Fauance, Head of Section

1805 Lyc,e International-American Section
BP 230, rue du Fer A Cheval
St. Germain-En-Laye, 78104 Cedex
France

> 33-1-345-17485
> Fax: 33-1-308-70049
> E-mail: american.lycee@wanadoo.fr
> http://http://lycee-intl-american.org

Grade levels Pre-K through 12, school year September - June

Theodore Faunce, PhD, Director

1806 Malvern College
College Road, Malvern
Worcestershire WR14 3DF
England

> 01684-581-500
> E-mail: inquiry@malcol.org
> http://www.malcol.org

Roy de C Chapman, MA, Headmaster

1807 Mannheim Elementary School
Unit 29938
APO, Mannheim 09086
Germany

> 380-4705
> Fax: 0621-723-905
> E-mail: mann-es@odedodea.edu
> http://www.mann-es.odedodea.edu

Dr. Ardelle Hamilton PhD, Principal
Dr. Ellen Minette, Assisantant Principal

1808 Mannheim High School
Unit 29939
APO, Mannheim 09086 0005
Germany

Barbara Axton, Principal

1809 Margaret Danyers College
N Downs Road, Cheadle Hulme
Cheadle SK8 5HA
England

> 061-485-4372

Harry Tomlinson, BA, MA, MS, Headmaster

1810 Mark Twain Elementary School
Unit 29237
APO, Heidelberg 09102 0005
Germany

Joseph Newbury, Principal

1811 Marymount International School-Rome
Via di Villa Lauchli 180
00191 Rome
Italy

> 33-1-462-41051
> Fax: 33-1-463-70750
> E-mail: school@ecole-marymount.fr

A coeducational, day school for grades prek-12.

Anne Marie Clancy, Headmistress

1812 Marymount International School-United Kingdom
George Road
Kingston upon Thames, Surrey, KT2 7PE
United Kingdom

> 44-20-8949-0571
> Fax: 44-20-8336-2485

E-mail: admissions@marymount.kingston.sch.uk
http://www.marymount.kingston.sch.uk

Grade levels 6-12, school year September - June

Rosaleen Sheridan, Principal

1813 Mattlidens Gymnasium
Mattgardsvagen 20
02230 Esbo
Finland

Hilding Klingenberg, Principal

1814 Mayenne English School
Chateau les Courges 53420
Chailland
France

J Braillard, Principal

1815 Menwith Hill Estates & Middle School
PSC 45 Unit 8435
APO, High Wycombe 09468 0005
Great Britain

Dr. Arnold Watland, Principal

1816 Millfield School
Street, Somerset, BA16 0YD
Glastonbury, Somerset
England

145-844-2291

A coeducational boarding/day school with over 1,250 pupils and 165 members of staff.

CS Martin, Contact

1817 Monkton Combe School
Bath (Avon) BA2 7HG
England

01225-721102
Fax: 01225-721208
E-mail: addmissions@monkton.org.uk
http://www.monktoncombesschool.com

Boarding and day school for girls and boys ages two to nineteen.

Michael J Cuthberton, Head Master
Rus P Neaverson, Registrar

1818 Monti Parioli English School
Via Monti Parioli 50
00197 Rome
Italy

Lynette Surtees, Principal

1819 Mougins School
615 Avenue Drive, Maurice Donat
BP 401, 06251 Mougins Cedex
France

33-4-93-90-15-47
Fax: 33-4-93-75-31-40
E-mail: information@mougins-school.com
http://www.mougins-school.com

International school for Pre-K to Form 13 teaching the British curriculum leading to IGCSE and A Level examinations.

Brian G Hickmore, Headmaster
Sue Dunnachie, Marketing Coordinator

1820 Mountainview School
Bosch 35-6331 Hunenberg
Switzerland

Brenda Moors, Principal

1821 Munich International School
Schloss Buchhof
Starnberg, Munich D82319
Germany

49-8151-366-100
Fax: 49-8151-366-109
E-mail: adminssions@mis-munich.de
http://www.mis-munich.de

Grade levels Pre-K through 12, school year August - June

Ray Taylor, Head of School

1822 Naples Elementary School
PSC 808 Box 39
FPO, Aversa 09618 0039
Italy

Dr. Jacqueline Hulbert, Principal

1823 Naples High School
PSC 808 Box 15
FPO, Aversa 09618 0015
Italy

Carl Albrecht, Principal

1824 Neubruecke Elementary School
Unit 23825
APO, Neubruecke 09034 0005
Germany

Margaret Hoffman-Otto, Principal

1825 Neuchatel Junior College
Cret-Taconnet 4
2002 Neichatel
Switzerland

038-25-27-00
Fax: 038-24-42-59

This school offers an English based curriculum for 80 day students (30 boys; 50 girls) in the pre-university year. The length of stay for overseas teachers is three to five years. Applications needed to teach include science, French, math, social sciences, German, English.

Nancy Edwards, BA, BEd, Principal

1826 New School Rome
Via Della Camilluccia 669
00135 Rome
Italy

39-329-4269

Josette Fusco, Principal

1827 Newton College
Empedrat 4 Elche
Alicante
Spain

David Few, Principal

1828 Norra Reals Gymnasium
Roslagsgatan 1
S-113 55 Stockholm
Sweden

Curt Lagergren, Principal

1829 Numont School
Calle Parma 16
28043 Madrid
Spain

Margaret Ann Swanson, Principal

1830 Oak House School
San Pedro Claver 12-18
08017 Barcelona
Spain

Pauline Ernest, Principal

1831 Oakham School
Chapel Close, Oakham
Rutland, LE15 6DT
England

44-0-1572-758758
Fax: 44-0-1572-758595
E-mail: registrar@oakham.rutland.sch.uk

Graham Smallbone, Headmaster

1832 Oporto British School
Rua Da Cerca 326/338
Oporto 4100
Portugal

Mark Rogers, Principal

1833 Oslo American School
Gml Ringeriksv 53, 1340 Bekkestua
Oslo
Norway

James Mcneil, Principal

1834 Panterra American School
Via Ventre D'oca 41, Fontanella
Pescara 65131
Italy

Virginia Simpson, Principal

1835 Paris American Academy
9, rue Des Ursulines
75005 Paris
France

Enrolls students from sixteen years of age who are
interested in studying the French language and culture.

Richard Roy, Headmaster

1836 Patrick Henry Elementary School
Unit 29237
APO, Heidelberg 09102 0005
Germany

Phillip Crooks, Principal

1837 Perse School
Hills Road
Cambridge CB2 2QF
England

0223-248127

GM Stephen, Headmaster

1838 Pinewood Schools of Thessaloniki
PO Box 21001
555 10 Pilea
Greece

30-31-301-221

Fax: 30-31-323-196
E-mail: pinewood@spark.net.gr

Independent, coeducational schools which offer an
educational program from prekindergarten through
grade 12 and boarding facilities from grade 7 though
grade 12 for students of all nationalities. The school year
comprises 2 semestersextending from September to
January and from January to June.

Peter B Baiter, Director

1839 Pordenone Elementary School
PSC 1
Aviano
Italy

39-0434-28462
Fax: 39-0434-28761

D Jean Waddell, Principal

1840 Priory School
West Bank, Dorking
Surrey RH4 3DG
England

130-688-7337
Fax: 130-688-8715
E-mail: priory.surrey.ss@connect.bt.com

A voluntary aided Church of England School.

A Sohatski, Headteacher

1841 Queen Elizabeth School
Rua Filipe Magalhaes 1
1700 Lisbon
Portugal

Susan Van Den Berg, Principal

1842 Queens College the English School
Juan De Saridakis 64
Palma de Malorca
Spain

809-393-2153

This Methodist affiliated school offers an English-based
curriculum to a total of 1,200 female students, grades
K1-12. The school does recruit from overseas, offering
three year contracts with housing provided for one week
at thebeginning of the contract, while they find
accommodations. Applications needed to teach include
science, pre-school, French, math, Spanish, English and
physical education.

Philip Cash, Principal

1843 Rainbow Elementary School
Unit 28614 Box 0040
APO, Ansbach 09177 0005
Germany

Thomas Murdock, Principal

1844 Ramstein Elementary School
86 SPTG CCSE R, Unit 3240 Box 430
APO, Unit 3240 Box 430 09094 0005
Germany

Robin Gartner, Principal

1845 Ramstein High School
86 SPTG CCSH R, Unit 3240 Box 445
APO, Ramstein 09094 0005
Germany

Douglas Kelsey, Principal

1846 Ramstein Intermediate School
86 SPTG CCSI R, Unit 3240 Box 600
APO, Ramstein 09094 0005
Germany

Richard Snell, Principal

1847 Ramstein Junior High School
86 SPTG CCSI R, Unit 3240 Box 455
APO, Ramstein 09094 0005
Germany

Richard Snell, Principal

1848 Rathdown School
Glenageary
Dublin
Ireland

01-853133

Stella G Mew, MA, Principal

1849 Regionale Internationale School
Humperdincklaan 4, 5654 PA
Eindhoven
Netherlands

040-2519437

This school teaches a curriculum in Dutch, English, and French for 360 day students (180 boys; 180 girls), 4-12 years of age. The enrollment and teaching staff represent 43 nationalities, and the student/teacher ratio is 14:1.

HA Schol, Principal

1850 Rikkyo School in England
Guildford Road Rudgwick, Sussex
RH12 3BE
Great Britain

M Usuki, Principal

1851 Riverside School
The Salesianum
Arthestrass 55, Zug, 6300
Switzerland

41-41-724-5690
Fax: 41-41-724-5692
E-mail: david.brooks@riverside.ch
http://www.riverside.ch

Grade levels include 7-12 with a total enrollment of 65.

David Brooks, Director

1852 Robinson Barracks Elementary School
CMR 477 Box 2231
APO, Stuttgart 09154 0005
Germany

Clarence Allen, Principal

1853 Rome International School
Via Morgagni 25
00161 Rome
Italy

Gillian Bennett, Principal

1854 Rosall School
Fleetwood
Lancashire FY7 8JW
United Kingdom

Rosall is an anglican school situated on 220 miles N.W. of London in a self-contained campus of 150 acres. The school offers an English based curriculum to 350 day students and 250 boarding students (350 boys; 250 girls), ages 2-19. Teachers are accepted from overseas with housing provided by the school. Applications needed to teach include science, math, and physical education.

RDW Rhodes, Principal
GSH Penelley, Faculty Head

1855 Rosemead
East Street, Littlehampton
BN17 6AL
England

0903-716065

J Bevis, BA, Headmaster

1856 Rota Elementary School
PSC 819 Box 19
FPO Rota 09645 0005
Spain

Charles Callahan, Principal

1857 Rota High School
PSC 819 Box 63
FPO, Rota 09645 0005
Spain

Dr. Robert Jones, Principal

1858 Roudybush Foreign Service School
Place des Arcades, Sauveterre de
Rouergue (Averyon)
France

This European school prepares men for the foreign service.

Franklin Roudybush, AB, MA, Headmaster

1859 Rugby School
Lawrence Sheriff Street
Rugby, Warwickshire CV22 5EH
United Kingdom

44-178-854-3465
Fax: 44-178-856-9124
E-mail: postmaster@rugby-school.warwks.sch.uk
http://www.rugby-school.co.uk

MB Mavot, MA, Headmaster

1860 Runnymede College School
Salvia 30
28109 La Moraleja, Madrid
Spain

34-91-650-8302
Fax: 34-91-650-8236
E-mail: mail@runnymede-college.com
http://www.runnymede-college.com

Grade levels include N-13 with a total enrollment of 409.

Frank M Powell, Headmaster

1861 Rygaards International School
Bernstorffsvej 54, DK-2900
Hellerup
Denmark

45-39-62-10-53
Fax: 45-39-62-10-81
E-mail: paulinebrroks@rygaards.com

Coeducational day school for ages five to sixteen.

Mathias Jepsen, Principal

1862 Salzburg International Preparatory School
Moosstrasse 106
A-5020 Salzburg
Austria

662-844485
Fax: 662-847711

A coeducational boarding school offering an American college preparatory high school curriculum for grades 7 to 12 as well as a post graduate course.

1863 Schiller Academy
51-55 Waterloo Road
London, SE1 8TX
United Kingdom

44-207-928-1372
Fax: 44-207-928-8089
E-mail: office@schiller-academy.org.uk
http://www.schiller-academy.org.uk

Grade levels 9-12, school year August - June

George Selby, Headmaster
Renee Miller, Director Studies

**1864 Schools of England, Wales, Scotland & Ireland
J. Burrow & Company**
Imperial House, Lypiatt Road
Cheltenham 50201
England

1865 Schweinfurt American Elementary School
CMR 457
APO, Schweinfurt 09033 0005
Germany

09721-81893
Fax: 09721-803905
http://www.schw-es.odedodea.edu

Grades Pre-k to 5th, fully accredited Department of Defense Education Activity school.

Michael Diekmann, Principal

1866 Schweinfurt Middle School
CMR 457
APO, Schweinfurt 09033 0005
Germany

EB Stafford, Principal

1867 Sembach Elementary School
Unit 4240 Box 325
APO, Sembach 09136 0005
Germany

Marlene Knudson, Principal

1868 Sembach Middle School
Unit 4240 Box 320
APO, Sembach 09136 0005
Germany

Shelley Rucker, Principal

1869 Sevenoaks School
Sevenoaks
TN13 IHU
Great Britain

RP Barker, Principal

1870 Sevilla Elementary & Junior High School
496 ABS DODDS Unit 6585
APO Moron AB 09643 0005
Spain

Robert Ludwig, Principal

1871 Shape Elementary School
CMR 451 Box 0005
APO, Shape 09713 0005
Belgium

Judith Mayo, Principal

1872 Shape High School
CMR 451 Box 0005
APO, Shape 09708 0005
Belgium

Dr. Juliana Cardone, Principal

1873 Shape International School
General Services Section
Building 717, 7010 Shape
Belgium

65-44-52-83

Jacques Laurent, Principal

1874 Sherborne School
Abbey Road
Sherborne, Dorset DT9 4AP
England

44-193-581-2249
Fax: 44-193-581-6628
E-mail: enquiries@sherborne.cix.co.uk

Ralph Mowat, Principal

1875 Sidcot School
Winscombe
North Somerset BS25 1PD
England

44-193-484-3102
Fax: 44-193-484-4181
E-mail: addmissions@sidcot.org.uk
http://www.sidcot.org.uk

This friendly school with an international enrollment of 277 day students and 149 boarding students (255 boys; 171 girls), in grades K-12, is set in over one hundred acres of Somerset countryside. The school offers an English-basedcurriculum and the student/teacher ratio is 10:1.

John Walmsley, Headteacher

1876 Sierra Bernia School
La Caneta s/n
San Rafael 03580
Spain

96-687-51-49
Fax: 96-687-36-33
E-mail: duncan@ctv.es

Duncan M Allan, Principal

1877 Sigonella Elementary & High School
PSC 824 Box 2630
FPO Signoella, Sicily 09627 2630
Italy

Dr. Peter Price, Principal

1878 Sigtunaskolan Humanistiska Laroverket
Manfred Bjorkquists Alle 6-8
Sigtuna S-193 28
Sweden

46-8-592-57100
Fax: 46-8-592-57250
E-mail: info@sshl.se
http://www.sshl.se
Grade levels include 7-12 with an enrollment of 543.

Ingrid Karlsson, Principal

1879 Sir James Henderson School
Via Pisani Dossi 16
Milano 20134
Italy

39-02-264-13310
Fax: 39-02-264-13515
E-mail: sirjames@bbs.infosquare.it
http://www.sirjameshenderson.com
Grade levels N-13, school year September - June

Stephen Anson, Principal

1880 Skagerak Gymnas
PO Box 1545-Veloy
3206 Sandefjord
Norway

Elisabeth Norr, Principal

1881 Smith Elementary School
Unit 23814
APO, Baumholder 09034 0005
Germany

Edward Drozdowski, Principal

1882 Southlands English School
Via Teleclide 20, Casalpalocco
00124 Rome
Italy

Vivien Franceschini, DipEd, Principal

1883 Spangdahlem Elementary School
52 SPTG CCSE S, Unit 3640 Box 50
APO, Spangdahlem 09126 0005
Germany

Lynda Simmons, Principal

1884 Spangdahlem Middle School
52 CSG CCSM, Unit 3640 Box 45
APO, Spangdahlem
Germany 09126-0005

Catherine Ake, Principal

1885 Sportfield Elementary School
Unit 20193 Box 0014
APO, Hanau
Germany, AE 09165-0014

John O'Reilly, Jr, Principal

1886 St. Andrew's College
PO Box 56
Marayong NSW 2148
Ireland

02-9626-1999
E-mail: admin@standrews.nsw.edu.au

Arthur Godsil, Principal

1887 St. Anne's School
Jarama 9
Madrid 2
Spain

Margaret Raines, Principal

1888 St. Anthony's International College
Carretera De Cadiz Km 217
Fuengriola Malaga
Spain

1889 St. Catherine's British School
British Embassy Ploutarchou 1
Athens 106/75
Greece

Michael Toman, Principal

1890 St. Christopher School
Letchworth
Hertfordshire SG6 3JZ
England

0462-679301
Fax: 0462-481578

Colin Reid, MA, Headmaster

1891 St. Clare's Oxford
139 Banbury Road
Oxford OX2 7AL
England

44-186-555-2031
Fax: 44-186-551-3359
E-mail: admissions@stclares.ac.uk

Margaret Skarland, Principal

1892 St. David's School
Justin Hall, Beckenham Road
West Wickham BR4 0QS
England

01784-252494
Fax: 01784-252494
E-mail: office@stdavidsschool.com
Boarding school for girls ages nine to eighteen; day school for girls ages four to eighteen.

Judith G Osborne, BA, Headmaster

1893 St. Dominic's International School
Outeiro de Polima-Arneiro
2775 Sao Domingos da Rana
Lisbon
Portugal

351-21-448-0550
Fax: 351-21-444-3027
E-mail: adm@dominic.mailpac.pt
School offers a curriculum in English to 466 day students (237 boys; 229 girls), in nursery, kindergarten, transitionary, and Grades 1-12.

Maria R Empis, Principal

1894 St. Dominic's Sixth Form College
Mount Park Ave, Harrow on the Hill
Middlesex HA1 3HX
England

020-84228084
Fax: 020-8422-3759

Reformed in 1979, this school offers an English based curriculum to a total of 600 day students (300 boys; 300 girls), in the last two years of high school (pre-university). The school is Roman Catholic affiliated.

John L Lipscomb, Principal

1895 St. Georges English School
Via Cassia Km 16
00123 Rome
Italy

06-3790141
Fax: 06-3792490

Colin Niven, MA, DipEd, Principal

1896 St. Georges School
Vila Goncalve, Quinta Loureiras
2750 Cascais
Portugal

MPB Hoare, Principal

1897 St. Georges School-Switzerland
1815 Clarens-Montreux
Switzerland

21-964-34-11
Fax: 21-964-49-32

A British International School which operates a joint British/U.S. system of secondary boarding school education for girls between the ages of 11-19 years, Grades 7-13.

Alan Locke, MA, Principal

1898 St. Gerard's School
Thornhill Road, Bray Co Wicklow
Republic of Ireland

Michael O'Horan, Principal

1899 St. Helen's School
Eastbury Road
Northwood (Middleeast) HA6 3AS
England

09274-28511
Fax: 0923-835824

YA Burne, Principal

1900 St. John's International School
Dreve Richelle 146
Waterloo 1410
Belguim

32-2-352-0610
Fax: 32-2-352-0630
E-mail: admissions@stjohns.be
http://www.stjohns.be

Grade levels Pre-K through 13, school year August - June

Joseph Doenges, Director
Judith Hoskins, Director Addmissions

1901 St. Mary's School
Ascot (Berkshire)
SL5 9JF
England

0990-23721

Boarding and day school for girls ten to eighteen.
M Mark Orchard, IBVM, BA, Principal

1902 St. Michael's School
St. Michael's Drive
Otford TN14 5SA
England

095-92-2137

Rev. Paul G Cox, BA, Headmaster

1903 St. Stephen's School
Via Aventina 3
00153 Rome
Italy

39-06-575-0605
Fax: 39-06-574-1941
E-mail: ststephens@mclink.it
http://www.ststephens.it

A nonsectarian, coeducational college preparatory school which serves the American and international communities from Rome.

Philip Allen, Headmaster

1904 Stavenger British School
Gauselbakken 107
4032 Gausel
Norway

Zelma Roisli, Principal

1905 Stover School
Newton Abbot (Devon)
TQ12 6QG
England

0626-54505

WE Lunel, BA, Principal

1906 Stowe School
Stowe (Buckingham)
MK18 5EH
England

44-1280-818000
Fax: 44-1280-818181
E-mail: enquiries@stowe.co.uk

Stowe is a leading independent boarding school for boys (13-18) and girls (16-18). It is situated in magnificent country surroundings. Over 90% of its pupils go on to higher education. Around 20% are from expatriate and non-Britishfamilies. Total enrollment consists of 32 day students and 518 boarding (450 boys; 100 girls), in grades 9-13. The length of stay for overseas teachers is one year, with housing provided by the school.

JGL Nichols, Headmaster
GM Hornby, Faculty Head

1907 Summerfield School SRL
Via Tito Poggi 21 Divino Amore
00134 Rome
Italy

Vivien Franceschini, Principal

1908 Summerhill School
Westward Ho., Leiston (Suffolk)
IP16 4HY
England

0728-830540

Zoe Readhead

1909 Sunny View School
Apartado 175 Cerro De Toril
Torremolinos Malaga
Spain

Jane Barbadillo, Principal

1910 Sutton Park School
St. Fintan's Road, Sutton
Dublin 13
Ireland

353-1-832-2940
Fax: 353-1-832-5929
E-mail: info@suttonpark.ie
http://www.suttonpoark.ie

Grade levels K-12, school year September - June

Laurence J Finnegan, Chief Executive

1911 Sutton Valence School
Sutton Valence, Maidstone (Kent)
ME17 3HL
England

0622-842281

Michael R Haywood, MA, Headmaster

1912 Swans School
Capricho 2, Marbella
29600 Malaga
Spain

TJ Swan, Principal

1913 TASIS Hellenic International School
PO Box 51051
Kifissia Gr-145 10
Greece

30-1-623-3888
Fax: 30-1-623-3160
E-mail: info@tasis.edu.gr
http://www.tasis.com

Grade levels Pre-K through 12, school year September - June

Basile Daskalakis, President

1914 TASIS The American School in England
Coldharbour Lane
Thorpe, Surrey, TW20 8TE
England

44-1932-565-252
Fax: 44-1932-564-644
E-mail: ukadmissions@tasis.com
http://www.tasis.com

Grade levels Pre-K through 12, school year August - June

Barry Breen, Headmaster

1915 Taunus International Montessori School
Altkonigstrasse 1 6370
Oberursel
Germany

Kathleen Hauer, Principal

1916 Teach in Great Britain
5 Netherhall Gardens
London, NW3, England

**1917 Thessaloniki International High School &
Pinewood Elementary School**
PO Box 21001
555 10 Pilea, Thessaloniki
Greece

30-31-301-221
Fax: 30-31-323-196
E-mail: pinewood@spark.net.gr
http://www.users.otenet.gr/~pinewood

Grades preK-12, enrollment 256.

Peter B Baiter, Director

1918 Thomas Jefferson School
13 rue de la Clef
75005 Paris
France

William Wheeler, Principal

1919 United Nations Nursery School
40 Rue Pierre Guerin
75016 Paris
France

33-1-452-72024
Fax: 33-1-428-87146

Pre-K and kindergarten levels.

Brigitte Weill, Directrice

1920 United World College-Adriatic
Via Trieste 29 34013 Duino
Trieste
Italy

DB Sutcliffe, Principal

1921 United World College-Atlantic
St. Donats Castle Llantwit
Major S Glamorgan
United Kingdom

Colin Jenkins, Principal

1922 Vajont Elementary School
PSC 1
Aviano
Italy

427-701553

Nick Suida, Principal

1923 Verdala International School
Fort Pembroke
Pembroke, STJ 14
Malta

356-332-361
Fax: 356-372-387
E-mail: vis@maltanet.net
http://www.verdala.org

An independent, coeducational day and boarding school which offers an educational program from play school through grade 12 for students of all nationalities.

Adam Pleasance, Headmaster

1924 Verona Elementary School
CMR 428
APO, Verona 09628 0005
Italy

Wilma Holt, Principal

1925 Vicenza Elementary School
Unit 31401 Box 11
APO, Vicenza 09630 0005
Italy

Cathy Magni, Principal

1926 Vicenza High School
Unit 31401 Box 11
APO, Vicenza 09630 0005
Italy

Arnold Goldstein, Principal

1927 Vicenza International School
Viale Trento 141
Vicenza 36100
Italy

39-0444-288-475
Fax: 39-0444-963-633
E-mail: vix-ib@vip.it

Grade levels 11-13, school year September - June

Dionigio Tanello, PhD, Director

1928 Vienna Christian School
Wagramerstrasse 175
A-1220 Wien
Austria

43-1-25122-501
E-mail: 100337.1501@compuserve.com
http://www.vienna-christian-sch.org

Grade levels 1-12, school year August - June

Phillip Paden, Directorl
Nancy L Deibert, Principal

1929 Vienna International School
Strasse der Menschenrechte 1
Vienna 1220
Austria

43-1-203-5595
Fax: 43-1-203-0366
E-mail: info@vis.ac.at
http://www.vis.ac.at

Academic curriculum designed to meet the needs of the international community, therefore offering special emphasis to the mastery of languages.

Walther Hetzer, PhD, Director
Malcolm Davis, Head Primary School

1930 Vilseck Elementary School
Unit 28040
APO, Vilseck 09112 0014
Germany

Martin Kinney, Principal

1931 Vilseck High School
Unit 20841
APO, Vilseck 09112 0005
Germany

Andrew Zacharias, Principal

1932 Violen School, International Department
Violenstraat 3, 1214
CJ Hilversum
Netherlands

This school offers an enrollment of 240 day students (125 boys and 115 girls), in grades K through 6. The primary education is in the English language for international mobile families, set up and supported by the Dutch government.

Atse R Spoor, Principal

1933 Vogelweh Elementary School
86 SPTG CCSE V, Unit 3240 Box 435
APO, Kaiserslautern 09094 0005
Germany

Susan Kraebber, Principal

1934 Volkel Elementary School
752 MUNSS Unit 6790
APO, Volkel 09717 5018
Netherlands

Claudia Holtzclaw, Principal

1935 Westwing School
Kyneton House
Thornbury BS122JZ
England

0454-412311

Marjorie Crane, MA, Headmaster

1936 Wetzel Elementary School
Unit 23815
APO, Baumholder 09034 0005
Germany

Robert Richards, Principal

1937 Wiesbaden Middle School
Unit 29647
APO, Wiesbaden 09096 0005
Germany

Patricia Smith, Principal

1938 Wolfert Van Borselen
Bentincklaan 280-3039 KK
Rotterdam
Netherlands

Gilles Schuilenburg, Principal

1939 Worksop College
Worksop (Nottinghamshire)
S80 3AP
England

0909-472391

A Hugh Monro, MA, Headmaster

1940 Worms Elementary School
CMR 455
APO, Worms 09058 0005
Germany

Charles Raglan, Principal

1941 Wuerzburg Elementary School
CMR 475 Box 6
APO, Wuerzburg 09244 6627
Germany

Dee Ann Edwards, Principal

1942 Wuerzburg High School
CMR 475 Box 8
APO, Wuerzburg 09036 0005
Germany

Robert Kubarek, Principal

1943 Wuerzburg Middle School
CMR 475 Box 7
APO, Wuerzburg 09036 0005
Germany

Karen Kroon, Principal

1944 Zurich International School
Steinacherstrasse 140
8820 Wadenswill
Switzerland

41-43-833-2222
Fax: 41-43-833-2223
E-mail: zis@zis.ch
http://www.zis.ch

Day school for grades Pre-School through 12 serving the Zurich international community. Total enrollment is 900 students.

Peter C Mott, BA,MA, Director
Jennifer Saxe, Director Development

West Indies & Carribean

1945 American School-Santo Domingo
Apartado 20212
Santo Domingo
Dominican Republic

809-565-7946
809-549-5841
E-mail: a.school@codetel.net.do

Grade levels Pre-K through 12, school year August - June

Joseph Dunham, Director

1946 Aquinas College
PO Box N-7540
Nassau
Bahamas

Vincent Ferguson, Principal

1947 Belair School
PO Box 156
Mandeville
Jamaica

1-876-962-2168
Fax: 1-876-962-3396
E-mail: belair.school@cwjamaica.com

Grade levels K-12, school year September - June

Sylvan Shields, Director

1948 Bermuda High School
27 Richmond Road
Pembroke HM 08
Bermuda

1-441-295-6153
Fax: 1-441-295-2754

This girls school offers an English-based curriculum for 620 total day students in grades 1-12.

Eleanor W Kingsbury, Principal

1949 Bermuda Institute-SDA
PO Box SN 114
Southampton SNBX
Bermuda

441-238-1566

A Seventh-day Adventist school that offers an English curriculum for 489 day students (239 boys; 250 girls), in grades K-12.

Sheila Holder, Principal

1950 Bishop Anstey Junior School
Ariapita Road St. Ann's
Port of Spain
Trinidad and Tobago

Joyce Kirton, Principal

1951 Capitol Christian School
C-11 #3 Urb Real Santo Domingo
Dominican Republic

Stacy Lee Blossom, Principal

1952 Ecole Flamboyant
PO Box 1744-A Schweitzer Hosp.
Port-au-Prince
Haiti

509-381-141/2
Fax: 509-381-141
E-mail: has-pap@acn.com

William Dunn, Principal

1953 International School-Aruba
Seroe Colorado
Aruba
Dutch Caribbean

297-845-365
Fax: 297-847-341
E-mail: intschool@satarnet.aw

A nonprofit, coeducational English-speaking day school serving students from prekindergarten to grade 12.

Dennis Klumpp, Headmaster
Violet Marin, Guidance Counselor

1954 International School-Curacao
PO Box 3090
Williamstad
Curacao

5-999-737-3633
Fax: 5-999-737-3142
E-mail: ismec@attglobal.ne

A private, coeducational day school which offers an educational program from kindergarten through grade 12.

Margie Elhage PhD, Director

1955 International School-West Indies
PO Box 278 Leeward
Providenciales
British West Indies

Alison Hodges, Principal

1956 Kingsway Academy
PO Box N4378, Bernard Road
Nassau
Bahamas

Carol Harrison, Principal

Teaching Opportunities Abroad / U.S. Branches

1957 Mount Saint Agnes Academy
99 Dundonald Street W
Hamilton HMDX
Bermuda

Judith Marie Rollo, Principal

1958 Queens College
PO Box N7127
Nassau
Bahamas

Rev. Charles Sweeting, Principal

1959 Saltus Cavendish School
Middle Road
Devonshire
Bermuda

Susan Furr, Headteacher

1960 St. Andrew's School
16 Valleton Avenue
Marraval, Port of Spain
Trinidad and Tobago

Peter Harding, Principal

1961 St. Anne's Parish School
PO Box SS6256
Nassau
Bahamas

Rev. Patrick Adderley, Principal

1962 St. John's College
PO Box N4858
Nassau
Bahamas

Arlene Ferguson, Principal

1963 St. Paul's Methodist College
PO Box F897
Freeport
Grand Bahamas

Annette Poitier, Principal

1964 Sunland Lutheran School
PO Box F2469
Freeport
Bahamas

J Pinder, Principal

1965 Tapion School
PO Box 511 Castries
St. Lucia
West Indies

This school offers an English based curriculum to 130 day students (64 boys; 66 girls), in grades 1 to 3. The length of stay for overseas teachers are two years or longer, and the applications needed to teach include French, Spanishand reading.

Wilbert Pickett, Principal

U.S. Branches

1966 Aisha Mohammed International School
Washington, DC 20521-0001

Daryl Barker, Principal

1967 Albania Tirana International School
DOS/Administrative Officer
9510 Tirana Place
Washington, DC 20521-9510

355-42-27734
Fax: 355-42-37734
E-mail: qsialb@albaniaonline.net

An independent, coeducational day school which offers an educational program from kindergarten through grade 10 for students of all nationalities. The school comprises 3 trimesters extending from early September to mid-June.Enrollment 30.

Glenn H Mosher, Director

1968 Alexander Muss High School Israel
12550 Biscayne Boulevard
Suite 604
North Miami, FL 33181

305-891-8868
800-327-5980
Fax: 305-891-8806
E-mail: amhsi1@aol.com
http://www.amhsi.com

8-week intensive academic program for 11th and 12th graders which uses Israel as a living classroom. HS and 6 college credits. Scholarships available.

Joseph E Breman, CEO
Chaim Fischgrund, Headmaster

1969 Almaty International School
DOS/Administrative Officer
7030 Almaty Place
Washington, DC 20521-7030

7-3272-409-412
Fax: 7-3272-409-622
E-mail: director@ais.almaty.kz
http://www.state.gov/www/about_state/schools/oalmaty.html

Grades preK-12, enrollment 169.

Dr. David Pera, Director

1970 American School
DOS/Administrive Officer
3480 Tegucigalpa Place
Washington, DC 20521-3480

504-239-3333
Fax: 504-239-6162
E-mail: info@amschool.org
http://www.amschool.org

Liliana Jenkins, Superintendent

1971 American Cooperative School
DOS/Administrive Officer
3220 La Paz Place
Washington, DC 20521-3220

519-2-792-302
Fax: 591-2-797-218
E-mail: acs@ns.acslp.org
http://www.acslp.org

Dennis Sheehan, Superintendent

1972 American Cooperative School of Tunis
6360 Tunis Place
Washington, DC 20521-6360

216-71-760-905
Fax: 216-71-761-412
E-mail: acst@acst.intl.tn
http://www.acst.net

Dennis Sheehan, Superintendent

1973 American Embassy School
Department of State/AES
9000 New Delhi Place
Washington, DC 20521-9000

91-11-611-7140
Fax: 91-11-687-3320
E-mail: aesindia@aes.ac.in
http://www.serve.com/aesndi
Grade levels Pre-K through 12, school year August - May

Rob Mochrish, PhD, Director

1974 American Embassy School of New Delhi
American Embassy New Delhi
Department of State
Washington, DC 20521-9000

202-234-1494
91-11-611-7140
Fax: 202-234-3159
Fax: 91-11-687-3320
E-mail: aesindia@del2.vsnl.net.in
An independent, coeducational day school which offers an educational program from prekindergarten through grade 12 for all non-Indian students.

Stephen Kapner, Principal

1975 American International School of Nouakchott
DOS/Administrative Officer
2430 Nouakchott Place
Washington, DC 20521-2430

222-2-52967
Fax: 222-2-52967
E-mail: sharon_sperry@opt.mr

Sharon A Sperry, Director

1976 American International School-Abuja
DOS/Administrative Officer
8300 Abuja Place
Washington, DC 20521-8300

234-9-413-4464
Fax: 234-9-413-4464
E-mail: stanjacobsen60@hotmail.com
A coeducational international day school which offers an educational program from preschool to grade 8 for English-speaking students of all nationalities.

Amy Uzoewulu, Superintendent

1977 American International School-Bamako
DOS/Administrative Officer
2050 Bamako Place
Washington, DC 20521

223-222-4738
Fax: 223-222-0853
E-mail: aisb@aisb-ml.org
http://www.aisbmali.org
An independent, coeducational day school which offers an educational program from prekindergarten through grade 10. Supervised study using the University of Nebraska High School correspondence courses for grades 12 may also bearranged.

Irene Epp, Director

1978 American International School-Chennai
DOS/Administrative Officer
6260 Chennai Place
Washington, DC 20521-6260

91-44-499-0881
Fax: 91-44-466-0636
E-mail: officemanager@aisch.org
http://www.aisch.org

Grades preSchool-12, enrollment 160.

Barry Clough, Head of School

1979 American International School-Costa Rica
Interlink 249
PO Box 02-5635
Miami, FL 33102

Fax: 503-239-0625
E-mail: aiscr@cra.ed.cr
http://www.cra.ed.cr

Glenn Grieshaber, Headmaster

1980 American International School-Freetown
2160 Freetown Place
Washington, DC 20521-2160

232-22-232-480
Fax: 232-22-225-471
E-mail: jacquelinejleigh@yahoo.com
A private, coeducational day school which traditionally offers an educational program from preschool through grade 8 to students of all nationalities. Instruction is in English.

1981 American International School-Kingston
DOS/Administrative Officer
3210 Kingston Place
Washington, DC 20521-3210

876-977-3625
Fax: 876-977-3625
E-mail: aiskoff@cwjamaica.com

Eugene Vincent, Principal

1982 American International School-Lesotho
DOS/Administrative Officer
2340 Maseru Place
Washington, DC 20521-2340

266-322-987
Fax: 266-311-963
E-mail: aisl@lesoff.co.za
http://www.aisl.lesoff.co.za

An independent, coeducational day school which offers an American education from preschool through grade 8. The school was founded in 1991 to serve the needs of the American community and other students seeking an English-languageeducation.

Harvey Cohen, Principal

1983 American International School-Libreville
2270 Libreville Place
Washington, DC 20521-2270

241-76-20-03
Fax: 241-74-55-07
E-mail: aisl@internetgabon.com

Paul Sicard, Director

1984 American International School-Lome
DOS/Administrative Officer
2300 Lome Place
Washington, DC 20521-2300

228-221-3000
Fax: 228-221-7952
E-mail: aisl@cafe.tg
http://www.membres.lycos.fr

Geri Branch, Director

1985 American International School-Lusaka
DOS/Administrative Officer
2310 Lusaka Place
Washington, DC 20521-2310

260-1-260-509
Fax: 260-1-260-538

E-mail: aesl@zamnet.zm
http://www.aislusaka.org

An independent, coeducational day school which offers a preschool program for 2-4 year olds and an educational program from prekindergaretn through grade 10.

Walter Plotkin, Director

1986 American International School-Mozambique
DOS/Administrative Officer
2330 Maputo Place
Washington, DC 20521-2330

258-1-49-1994
Fax: 258-1-49-0596
E-mail: aism@aism-moz.com

Don Reeser, Director

1987 American International School-N'Djamena
DOS/Administrative Officer
2410 N'Djamena Place
Washington, DC 20521-2410

235-52-2103
Fax: 235-51-5654
E-mail: aisn@intent.td

Gay Mickle, Director

1988 American International School-Nouakchott
2430 Nouakchott Place
Washington, DC 20521-2430

222-2-52967
Fax: 222-2-52967
E-mail: aisnsahara@yahoo.com

Founded in 1978, a nonprofit, private, coeducational day school which offers an educational program to students from prekindergarten through grade 8 and independent study 9.

1989 American Nicaraguan School
American Embassy Managua
Unit No 2710 Box 7
Washington, DC 20521-3240

505-278-2565
Fax: 505-267-3088
E-mail: director@ans.edu.ni
http://www.ans.edu.ni

A private, nonsectarian coeducaitonal day school which offers an educaional program from prekindergarten through grade 12 for students of all nationalities.

Marvin Happel, Principal

1990 American Samoa Department of Education
Pago Pago
American Samoa 96799

011-684-633-5237
Fax: 011-684-633-5733

For certification information visit www.doe.as or contact (011) 684-633-5237.

Sili K Sataua

1991 American School Honduras
American Embassy Tegucigalpa
Department of State
Washington, DC 20521-3480

504-239-333
Fax: 504-239-6162

A private, coeducational day school which offers an educational program from nursery through grade 12 for students of all nationalities.

James Szoka, Principal

1992 American School-Algiers
American Embassy Algiers
Washington, DC 20520-0001

202-265-2800
Fax: 202-667-2174

Richard Gillogly, Principal

1993 American School-Antananarivo
DOS/Administrative Officer
2040 Antananarivo Place
Dulles, VA 20189-2040

261-20-22-420-39
Fax: 261-20-22-345-39
E-mail: asamad@dts.mg
http://www.asa.blueline.mg

Jay Long, Director

1994 American School-Asuncion
DOS/Administrative Officer
3020 Asuncion Place
Washington, DC 20521-3020

595-21-600-476
Fax: 595-21-603-518
E-mail: asagator@asa.edu.py
http://www.asa.edu.py

Elsa Lamb, Director

1995 American School-Dschang
Washington, DC 20521-0001

Jane French, Principal

1996 American School-Guatemala
DOS/Administrative Officer
3190 Guatemala Place
Washington, DC 20521-3190

502-369-0791
Fax: 502-369-8335
E-mail: bbarilla@shamballa.cag.edu.gt
http://www.cag.edu.gt

Barbara Barillas, General Director

1997 American School-Niamey
DOS/Administrative Officer
2420 Niamey Place
Washington, DC 20521-2420

227-723-942
Fax: 227-723-457
E-mail: asniger@bow.intnet.ne

A coeducational day school offering an educational program from prekindergarten through grade 9, and 10-12 correspondence.

Sharon Sperry, Director

1998 American School-Port Gentil
1100 Louisiana Street
Suite 2500
Houston, TX 77002-5215

Keith Marriott, Principal

1999 American School-Tegucigalpa
American Embassy
Washington, DC 20521-0001

James Shepherd, Principal

2000 American School-Warsaw
DOS/Administrative Officer
5010 Warsaw Place
Washington, DC 20521-5010

48-22-651-9611
Fax: 48-22-642-1506

E-mail: admissions@asw.waw.pl
http://www.asw.waw.pl

An independent, coeducational day school which offers an educational program from prekindergarten through grade 12 for students of all nationalities.

Charles P Barder, Director

2001 American School-Yaounde
BP 7475
Yaounde Place Camaroon
Washington, DC 20521-2520

234-223-0421
Fax: 237-223-6011
E-mail: school@asoy.org

An independent, coeducational day school founded in 1964 which offers an educational program from prekindergarten through grade 12.

Areta Williams, Director

2002 American-Nicaraguan School
DOS/Administrative Officer
3240 Managua Place
Washington, DC 20521-3240

505-2-782-565
Fax: 505-2-673-088
E-mail: msacasa@nicanet.com.ni
http://www.ans.edu.ni

Mary Ellen Normandin, Director

2003 Amoco Galeota School
PO Box 4381
Houston, TX 77210-4381

Barbara Punch, Principal

2004 Andersen Elementary & Middle School
Unit 14057
APO, Mariana Islands 96543 4057
Guam

2005 Anzoategui International School
PO Box 020010, M-42
Jet Cargo International
Miami, FL 33102-0010

58-82-22683
Fax: 58-82-22683
E-mail: aishead@telcel.net.ve
http://www.anaco.net

Grade levels Pre-K through 12, school year August - June

Jorge Nelson EdD, Superintendent

2006 Armenia QSI International School-Yerevan
DOS/Administrative Officer
7020 Yerevan Place
Washington, DC 20521-7020

374-1-391-030
Fax: 374-1-151-438
E-mail: qsiy@arminco.com

An independent, coeducational day school which offers an educational program from preschool (3-4 years) through grade 12 for students of all nationalities. Enrollment 45.

Arthur W Hudson, Director

2007 Atlanta International School
2890 N Fulton Drive
Atlanta, GA 30305

404-841-3840
Fax: 404-816-3060

E-mail: info@aischool.org
http://www.aischool.org

Grade levels prekindergarten through twelfth, with total enrollment of 805 students.

David Hawley,PhD, Headmaster

2008 Awty International School
7455 Awty School Lane
Houston, TX 77055

713-686-4850
Fax: 713-686-4956
E-mail: admin@awty.org
http://www.awty.org

Grade level prekindergarten through twelfth, with total enrollment of 900 students.

David Watson, Headmaster

2009 Azerbaijan Baku International School
DOS/Administrative Officer
Department Of State
Washington, DC 20521-7050

994-12-90-63-52
Fax: 994-12-90-63-51
E-mail: qsi@bis.baku.az
http://www.qsi.org

An independent, coeducational day school which offers an educational program from prekindergarten through grade 10 for students of all nationalities. Enrollment 45.

Beverly McAloon, Director

2010 Baku International School
Administrative Officer
Department of State
Washington, DC 20521-7050

994-12-656352
Fax: 991-12-4105951
E-mail: qsi@bis.baku.az
http://www.qsi.org

Grade levels N-8, school year September - June

Phil Dale, irector

2011 Ball Brothers Foundation
222 S Mulberry Street #1408
Muncie, IN 47305-2802

765-741-5500
Fax: 765-741-5518

Offers support in the areas of higher and other education including health and medical education.

ouglas A Bakken, Executive Director

2012 Banjul American Embassy School
DOS/Administrative Officer
2070 Banjul Place
Washington, DC 20521-2070

220-495-920
Fax: 220-497-181
E-mail: baes@qanet.gm
http://www.baes.gm

Earl Ballard, Headmaster

2013 Bingham Academy Ethiopia
SIM International
PO Box 7900
Charlotte, NC 28241-7900

Harold Jongeward, BAEd, Principal

Teaching Opportunities Abroad / U.S. Branches

2014 Bishkek International School
DOS/Administrative Officer
7040 Bishkek Place
Washington, DC 20521-7040

996-312-66-35-03
Fax: 996-312-66-35-03
E-mail: qsibis@elcat.kg
http://www.qsi.org

Grades K-11, enrollment 26.
Gordon Stands, Director

**2015 Bosnia-Herzegovina QSI International
School-Sarajevo**
DOS/Administrative Officer
7130 Sarajevo Place
Washington, DC 20521-7130

387-33-434-756
Fax: 387-33-434-756
E-mail: qsi@bih.net.ba
http://www.qsi.org

An independent, coeducational day school which offers an educational program from preschool (3 and 4 year old class) through grade 8 (13 year old class) for students of all nationalities. Enrollment 53.
Ralph A Reed, Director

**2016 Bratislava American International School
American Embassy Bratislava**
Department of State
Washington, DC 20521-5850

202-885-1600
421-7-722-844
Fax: 202-885-2494
Fax: 721-7-722-844
E-mail: qsi@ba.sanet.sk

An independent, coeducational day school wich offers an educational program from prekindergarten through grade 12 for students of all nationalities.
Ronald Adams, Principal

**2017 Bulgaria Anglo-American School-Sofia
DOS/Administrative Officer**
5740 Sophia Place
Washington, DC 20521-5740

359-2-974-4575
Fax: 359-2-974-4483
E-mail: aasregist@infotel.bg
http://www.geocities.com/angloamericanschool

An independent, coeducational day school which offers an educational program from prekindergarten through grade 8 for students of all nationalities. The school year comprises 2 semesters extending from August to December and fromJanuary to June. Enrollment 140.

Brian M Garton, Director

2018 Burma International School Yangon
DOS/Administrative Officer
4250 Rangoon Place
Washington, DC 20521-4250

95-1-512-793/795
Fax: 95-1-525-020
E-mail: ISYDIRECTOR@mptmail.net.mm
Grades PK-12, enrollment 331.
Merry Wade, Director

2019 Burns Family Foundation
410 N Michigan Avenue
Room 1600
Chicago, IL 60611-4213

Offers support in secondary school education, higher education and youth services.

2020 Caribbean American School
5 Gates Court
Cranbury, NJ 08512-2926

Ernestine Rochelle, Principal

2021 Caribbean-American School
PO Box 407139
Lynx Air
Ft Lauderdale, FL 33340-7139

509-257-7961
Grade levels Pre-K through 12, school year September - June

Ernestine Roche Robinson, Director

2022 Chinese American International School
150 Oak Street
San Francisco, CA 94102

415-865-6000
Fax: 415-865-6089
E-mail: caishead@aol.com
http://www.cie-cais.org

Grade level preK-8, with total enrollment of 353 students.
David Haack, Principal

2023 Colegio Albania
PO Box 25573
Miami, FL 33102-5573

Eric Spindler, Principal

2024 Colegio Corazon de Maria
Ferrer y Ferrer-Santiago Igles
San Juan 00921
Puerto Rico

M Cyril Stauss, Principal

2025 Colegio De Parvulos
263 Calle San Sebastian
San Juan 00901-1205
Puerto Rico

Maria Dolores Vice, Principal

2026 Colegio Del Buen Pastor
Camino Alejandrino Km 3.4
Rio Piedras 00927
Puerto Rico

Adria M Borges, Principal

2027 Colegio Del Sagrado Corazon
Obispado Final Urb La Alhambra
Ponce 00731
Puerto Rico

Joan G Dedapena, Principal

2028 Colegio Espiritu Santo
PO Box 1715
Hato Rey 00918
Puerto Rico

Carmen Jovet, Principal

2029 Colegio Inmaculada
Carr Militar 2 Km 49.6
Manati 00674
Puerto Rico

Sor Nichlasa Maderea, Principal

2030 Colegio Inmaculada Concepcion
2 Calle Isabela
Guayanilla 00656-1703
Puerto Rico

Sor Alejandrina Torres, Principal

2031 Colegio Internacional-Carabobo
VLN 1010
PO Box 025685
Miami, FL 33102-5685

58-41-421-807
Fax: 58-41-426-510
E-mail: CICadm@telcel.net.ve
http://www.aassa.com
Grade levels Pre-K through 12, school year August-June

Frank Anderson, Superintendent

2032 Colegio Internacional-Caracas
PAKMAIL 6030
PO Box 025323
Miami, FL 33102-5323

58-2-945-0444
Fax: 58-2-945-0533
E-mail: cic@cic-caracas.org
http://www.cic-caracas.org
Grade levels N-12, school year August-June

Winthrop Sargent Jr, Superintendent

2033 Colegio Internacional-Puerto La Cruz
2010 NW 84th Avenue
Suite 8403
Miami, FL 33122

58-281-277-6051
Fax: 58-281-274-1134
E-mail: ciplc@telcel.net.ve
http://www.ciplc.net
Grade levels Pre-K through 12, school year August-June

Dan McClain, Superintendent
Frank Capuccio, Administrative Assistant

2034 Colegio La Inmaculada
1711 Ave Ponce De Leon
San Juan 00909-1905
Puerto Rico

Sor Teresa Del Rio, Principal

2035 Colegio La Milagrosa
107 Calle De Diego
San Juan 00925-3303
Puerto Rico

Maria Flores, Principal

2036 Colegio Lourdes
PO Box 847
Hato Rey 00919
Puerto Rico

Maria Paz Asiain, Principal

2037 Colegio Madre Cabrini
1564 Calle Encarnacion
San Juan 00920-4739
Puerto Rico

Anne Marie Gavin, Principal

2038 Colegio Maria Auxiliadora
PO Box 797
Carolina 00986-0797
Puerto Rico

Leles Rodriguez, Principal

2039 Colegio Marista
Final Santa Ana Alt Torrimar
Guaynabo 00969
Puerto Rico

Hilario Martinez, Principal

2040 Colegio Marista El Salvador
PO Box 462
Manati 00674-0462
Puerto Rico

Hnio Efrain Romo, Principal

2041 Colegio Mater Salvatoris
RR 3 Box 3080
San Juan 00926-9601
Puerto Rico

Maria Luisa Benito, Principal

2042 Colegio Notre Dame Nivel
PO Box 967
Caguas 00726-0967
Puerto Rico

Francisca Suarez, Principal

2043 Colegio Nuestra Senora de La Caridad
PO Box 1164
Caparra Heigh 00920
Puerto Rico

Madre Esperanza Sanchez, Principal

2044 Colegio Nuestra Senora de La Merced
PO Box 4048
San Juan 00936-4048
Puerto Rico

Ivette Lopez, Principal

2045 Colegio Nuestra Senora de Lourdes
1050 Demetrio Odaly-Country Club
Rio Piedras 00924
Puerto Rico

Rita Manzano, Principal

2046 Colegio Nuestra Senora de Valvanera
53 Calle Jose I Quinton # 53
Coamo 00769-3108
Puerto Rico-

Cruz Victor Colon, Principal

2047 Colegio Nuestra Senora del Carmen
RR 2, Box 9KK, Carr Trujillo Alt
Rio Piedras 00721
Puerto Rico

Candida Arrieta, Principal

2048 Colegio Nuestra Senora del Pilar
PO Box 387
Canovanas 00729-0387
Puerto Rico

Sor Leonilda Mallo, Principal

2049 Colegio Nuestra Senora del Rosario
Aa7 Calle 5
Bayamon 00959-3719
Puerto Rico

Theresita Miranda, Principal

2050 Colegio Nuestra Sra del Rosario
PO Box 1334
Ciales 00638-0414
Puerto Rico

787-871-1318
Fax: 787-871-5797

Parrochial School - Prekindergarten to 9th grade.

Angel Mendoza, Principal
Padre Gabriel M Jorres, Director

2051 Colegio Padre Berrios
PO Box 7717
San Juan 00916-7717
Puerto Rico

Sor Enedina Santos, Principal

2052 Colegio Parroquial San Jose
PO Box 1386
Aibonito 00705-1386
Puerto Rico

Maria Maria Malave, Principal

2053 Colegio Ponceno
Coto Laurel, Puerto Rico 00644

809-848-2525

Rev. Jose A Basols, MA, Principal

2054 Colegio Puertorriqueno de Ninas
Urb. Golden Gate
Turquesa Street, Guaynabo 00968
Puerto Rico

787-782-2618
Fax: 787-782-8370
E-mail: cpn@coqui.net

Ivette Nater Prieto, School Director

2055 Colegio Reina de Los Angeles
M19 Frontera Urb Vl Andalucia
San Juan 00926
Puerto Rico

Victorina Ortega, Principal

2056 Colegio Rosa Bell
PO Box 1789
Guaynabo 00970-1789
Puerto Rico

Rose Rodriquez, Principal

2057 Colegio Sacred Heart
Palma Real Urb, Univ. Gardens
San Juan 00927
Puerto Rico

Paul Marie, CSB, Principal

2058 Colegio Sagrada Familia
7 Hostos
Ponce
Puerto Rico 00731

Sor Pilar Becerra, Principal

2059 Colegio Sagrados Corazones
A Esmeralda Urb, Ponce De Leon
Guaynabo 00969
Puerto Rico

Ana Arce de Marrer, Principal

2060 Colegio San Agustin
PO Box 4263
Bayamon 00958-1263
Puerto Rico

Georgina Ortiz, Principal

2061 Colegio San Antonio
PO Box 21350
San Juan 00928-1350
Puerto Rico

809-764-0090

Rev. Paul S Brodie, Principal

2062 Colegio San Antonio Abad
PO Box 729
Humacao 00792-0729
Puerto Rico

Padre Eduardo Torrella, Principal

2063 Colegio San Benito
PO Box 728
Humacao 00792-0728
Puerto Rico

Hermana Carmen Davila, Principal

2064 Colegio San Conrado (K-12)
PO Box 7111
Ponce 00732-7111
Puerto Rico

Fax: 787-841-7303
E-mail: sanconrado@pucpr.edu

Sister Nildred Rodriguez, Principal
Sister Wilma de Echevarria, Assistant Principal

2065 Colegio San Felipe
566 Ave San Luis # 673
Arecibo 00612-3600
Puerto Rico

809-878-3532

Veronica Oravec, Principal

2066 Colegio San Francisco De Asis
PO Box 789
Barranquitas 00794-0789
Puerto Rico

Hermana Maria Carbonell, Principal

2067 Colegio San Gabriel
Gpo Box 347
San Juan 00936
Puerto Rico

Sor Antonia Garatachea, Principal

2068 Colegio San Ignacio de Loyola
Sauco Final Urb Santa Maria
Rio Piedras 00927
Puerto Rico

Rev. Thomas H Feely, Principal

2069 Colegio San Jose
PO Box 21300
San Juan 00928-1300
Puerto Rico

809-751-8177

Rev. Joaquin Suarez SM, Principal

2070 Colegio San Juan Bautista
PO Box E
Orocovis 00720
Puerto Rico

Sor Maria Antonia Miya, Principal

2071 Colegio San Juan Bosco
PO Box 14367
San Juan 00916-4367
Puerto Rico

Rev. P Jose Luis Gomez, Principal

2072 Colegio San Luis Rey
43 Final SE, Urb Reparto Metro
San Juan 00921
Puerto Rico

Rosario Maria, Principal

2073 Colegio San Miguel
GPO Box 1714
San Juan 00936
Puerto Rico

Elvira Gonzalez, Principal

2074 Colegio San Rafael
PO Box 301
Quebradillas 00678-0301
Puerto Rico

2075 Colegio San Vicente Ferrer
PO Box 455
Catano 00963-0455
Puerto Rico

Maria Soledad Colon, Principal

2076 Colegio San Vicente de Paul
PO Box 8699
Santurce 00909
Puerto Rico

Sor Luz Maria Arzuago, Principal

2077 Colegio Santa Clara
Via 14-2JL-456 Villa Fontana
Carolina 00983
Puerto Rico

Elsie Mujica, Principal

2078 Colegio Santa Cruz
PO Box 235
Trujillo Alto 00977-0235
Puerto Rico

Maria Ramon Santiago, Principal

2079 Colegio Santa Gema
PO Box 1705
Carolina 00984-1705
Puerto Rico

Lilia Luna De Anaya, Principal

2080 Colegio Santa Rita
Calle 9, Apartado 1557
Bayamon 00958
Puerto Rico

Elba N Villalba, Principal

2081 Colegio Santa Rosa
Calle Marti, 15 Esquina Maceo
Bayamon 00961
Puerto Rico

Ana Josefa Colon, Principal

2082 Colegio Santa Teresita
342 Victoria
Ponce 00731
Puerto Rico

Mary Terence, Principal

2083 Colegio Santiago Apostol
Calle Celis Aguilera
Fajardo 00738
Puerto Rico

Hilda Velazquez, Principal

2084 Colegio Santisimo Rosario
PO Box 26
Yauco 00698-0026
Puerto Rico

Judith Negron, Principal

2085 Colegio Santo Domingo
192 Calle Comerio
Bayamon 00959-5358
Puerto Rico

Pura Huyke, Principal

2086 Colegio Santo Nino de Praga
PO Box 25
Penuelas 00624-0025
Puerto Rico

Aminta Santos, Principal

2087 Colegio Santos Angeles Custod
3 Sicilia Urb, San Jose
San Juan 00923
Puerto Rico

Roberto Rivera, Principal

2088 Colegio de La Salle
PO Box 518
Bayamon 00960-0518
Puerto Rico

Wilfredo Perez De, Principal

2089 Commandant Gade Special Education School
St. Thomas, Virgin Islands 00801

Miss Jeanne Richards, Principal

2090 Community United Methodist School
PO Box 681
Frederiksted 00841-0681
Virgin Islands

Marva Oneal, Principal

2091 Country Day
RR 1 Box 6199
Kingshill 00850-9803
Virgin Islands

809-778-1974

This school offers an English based curriculum for 440 day students (215 boys; 225 girls) in grades nursery through twelve. The school does participate in teacher exchange programs. Currently all but the PE position is filled.(Position includes coaching).

James Sadler, Principal
Patricia Bessette, Faculty Head

2092 Croatia American International School-Zagreb
DOS/Administrative Officer
5080 Zagreb Place
Washington, DC 20521-5080

385-1-4680-133
Fax: 385-1-4680-171
E-mail: asz@asz.tel.hr
http://www.asz.tel.hr/asz

Grades K-8, enrollment 112.

Gloria Doll, Director

2093 Dallas International School
6039 Churchill Way
Dallas, TX 75230

972-991-6379
Fax: 972-991-6608
E-mail: rwkdis@metronet.com
http://http://dis.pvt.k12.tx.us

Grade levels prekindergarten through twelfth, with total enrollment of 255 students.

Noelle Delhomme, Headmaster

2094 Dominican Child Development Center
PO Box 5668
Agana
Guam 96910

617-477-7228
Fax: 671-472-4782

Kindergarten and nursery school.

Lednor Flores, Principal

2095 Dorado Academy
PO Box 969
Dorado 00646-0969
Puerto Rico

Liutma Caballero, Principal

2096 Dwight School
291 Central Park W
New York, NY 10024

212-724-2146
Fax: 212-724-2539
E-mail: admissions@dwight.edu
http://www.dwight.edu

Grade levels kindergarten through twelfth, with total enrollment of 425 students.

Susan Hurroit, Director Admissions
Vimmi Snroff, Director Admissions

2097 Educare
3 Storre Gronne Gade
St. Thomas 00802
Virgin Islands

Sara Connell, Principal

2098 Episcopal Cathedral School
PO Box 13305
San Juan 00908-3305
Puerto Rico

787-721-5478
Fax: 787-724-6668
http://www.episcopalcathedralschool.com

Rev. Gary J DeHope, BS, MS, Headmaster

2099 Escole Tout Petit
PO Box 1248
San Juan 00902
Puerto Rico

Vivian Aviles, Principal

2100 Escuela Beata Imelda
PO Box 804
Guanica 00653-0804
Puerto Rico

P Salvador Barber, Principal

2101 Escuela Bella Vista
C-MAR-P 1815
PO Box 02-8537
Miami, FL 33102-8537

58-61-966-696
Fax: 58-61-969-417
E-mail: newtonr@ebv.org.ve
http://www.ebv.org.ve

Grade levels K-12, school year August - June

Valyn Anderson, Superintendent

2102 Escuela Campo Alegre
8424 NW 56th Street
Suite CCS 00007
Miami, FL 33166

58-2-993-3230
Fax: 58-2-993-0219
E-mail: info@eca.com.ve
http://www.eca.com.ve

Grade levels N-12, school year August - June.

Bambi Betts, Director

2103 Escuela Campo Alegre-Venezuela
8424 NW 56th Street
Suite CCS00007
Miami, FL 33166

58-2-993-7135
Fax: 58-2-993-0219
E-mail: info@eca.com.ve

A private, coeducational day school offering a program for students from prekindergarten through grade 12.

Dr. Forest Broman, Principal

2104 Escuela Caribe Vista School
New Horizon-100 S & 350 E
Marion, IN 46953

765-668-4009

Phil Redwine, Principal

2105 Escuela Las Morochas
Intercomunal, Sector Las Morochas
Zulia, Venezuela
Miami, FL 33152

58-265-6315-539
Fax: 58-265-6315-539
E-mail: sseb@iamnet.com

Grade levels Pre-K through 12, school year August - June.

Stephen Sibley, Director

2106 Escuela Nuestra Senora Del Carmen
PO Box 116, Playa De Ponce
Ponce 00731
Puerto Rico 00731

Paquita Alvarado, Principal

2107 Escuela Superior Catolica
PO Box 4245
Bayamon 00958-1245
Puerto Rico

Eledis Diaz, Principal

2108 Evangelical School for the Deaf
PO Box 7111
Luquillo 00773
Puerto Rico 00773

Pamela Eadie, Principal

2109 Fajardo Academy
55 Calle Federico Garcia
PO Box 1146, Fajardo 00648
Puerto Rico

809-863-1001

Miguel A Rivera, BA, MA, MEd, Principal

2110 Freewill Baptist School
PO Box 6265
Christiansted 00823-6265
Virgin Islands

Joe Postlewaite, Principal

2111 French-American International School
150 Oak Street
San Francisco, CA 94102

415-558-2000
Fax: 415-558-2024
E-mail: fais@fais-ihs.org
http://www.fais-ihs.org

Grade levels preK-12, with total student enrollment of 813.

Jane Camblin, Head of School

2112 George D Robinson School
5 Nairn Condado
Santurce 00907
Puerto Rico

Daniel W Sheehan, Principal

2113 Georgetown American School
3170 Georgetown Place
Washington, DC 20521-3170

592-225-1595
Fax: 592-226-1459
E-mail: admin@amschoolguyana.net
http://www.geocities.com/Athens/Atlantis/6811

Thurston Riehl, Director

2114 Georgia QSI International School-Tbilisi
DOS/Administrative Officer
7060 Tbilisi Place
Washington, DC 20521-7060

995-32-982909

Fax: 995-32-322-607
E-mail: qsi@access.sanet.ge

An independent, coeducational day school which offers an educational program for students of all nationalities grades PK-12. Enrollment 68.

Anthony Trujillo, Director

2115 Glynn Christian School
Club 6, Christian Hill
St. Croix, Kingshill 00851
Virgin Islands

Muriel Francis, Principal

2116 Good Hope School-St. Croix
Estate Good Hope Frederiksted
St. Croix 00840
Virgin Islands

Tanya L Nichols, Principal

2117 Good Shepherd School
PO Box 1069
St. Croix, Kingshill 00851
Virgin Islands 00851

340-772-2280
Fax: 340-772-1021

Mary Ellen Mcencil, Director
Susan P Eversley, Assistant Director

2118 Grace Baptist Academy
PO Box 7490
Christoansted 00823-7490
Virgin Islands

Helen Yasper, Principal

2119 Guam Adventist Academy
1200 Aguilar Road
Taldfofo
Guam 96930

617-789-1515
Fax: 617-789-3547
E-mail: sdagaaguam@netpci.guam
http://www.tagnet.org/gaa

Grade levels K-12.

Murray Cooper, Principal

2120 Guam Department of Education
PO Box DE
Hagatna, Guam 96932

011-671-475-0457
Fax: 011-671-472-5003

For certification information visit www.guam.net/gov/doe/fpd.

Rosie R Tainatongo, Director

2121 Guam High School
PSC 455 Box 192
FPO, Mariana Islands 96540 1192
Guam

2122 Guam S Elementary & Middle School
PSC 455 Box 168
FPO
Mariana Islands, Guam 96540-1054

2123 Guamani School
3 Los Veteranos Km 141.3
Guayama 00787
Puerto Rico 00784

Eduardo Delgado, Principal

2124 Harvest Christian Academy
PO Box 23189
Barrigada
Guam 96921

671-477-6341
Fax: 671-477-7136
http://www.harvestministries.net

Harvest Christian Academy is a K-12th grade school. It is a ministry of Harvest Baptist Church.

John McGraw, Principal

2125 Hogar Colegio La Milagrosa
Ave Cotto 987 Barrio Cotto
Arecibo 00612
Puerto Rico 00612

Sor Trinidad Ibizarry, Principal

2126 India American Embassy School-New Delhi
DOS/Administrative Officer
9000 New Delhi Place
Washington, DC 20521-9000

91-11-611-7140
Fax: 91-11-687-3320
E-mail: aesindia@aes.ac.in
http://www.serve.com/aesndi

Grades preK-12, enrollment 944.

Robert M Mockrish Jr, Director

2127 India American International School-Bombay
DOS/Administrative Officer
6240 Mumbai Place
Washington, DC 20521-6240

91-22-652-1837
Fax: 91-22-652-1838
E-mail: asbadmin@vsnl.com
http://www.asbindia.org

Grades N-12, enrollment 291.

James A Mains, Director

2128 Inter-American Academy
Suite 8227
6964 N.W. 50th Street
Miami, FL 33166-5632

593-4-871-790
Fax: 593-4-873-358
E-mail: bgoforth@acig.k12.ec
http://www.acig.k12.ec

Dr. Bruce Goforth, Executive Director

2129 International Community School-Abidjan
DOS/Administrative Officer
2010 Abidjan Place
Washington, DC 20521-2010

225-22-47-11-52
Fax: 225-22-47-19-96
E-mail: rmockrish@icsa.ac.ci
http://www.icsa.ac.ci

American style curriculum from kindergarten through grade 12 for children of all nationalities.

Rob Mockrish, Director

2130 International High School-Yangon
4250 Rangoon Place
Department of State
Washington, DC 20521-4250

95-1-512-793
Fax: 95-1-525-020
E-mail: isydirector@mptmail.net.mm

Merry Wade, Director

2131 International School of Port-of-Spain
POS 1369
1601 NW 97th Avenue
Miami, FL 33166

868-632-4591
Fax: 868-632-4595
E-mail: biatham@isps.edu.ttu.tt
http://www.isps.edu.tt

J Barney Latham, Director

2132 International School-Conakry
DOS/Administrative Officer
2110 Conakry Place
Washington, DC 20521-2110

224-12-661-535
Fax: 224-41-15-22
E-mail: iscgeckos@yahoo.com

Steven Asp-Schussheim, Director

2133 International School-Dakar
DOS/Administrative Officer
2130 Dakar Place
Washington, DC 20521-2130

221-825-0871
Fax: 221-825-5030
E-mail: isd@enda.sn

The only nonsectarian English language school in Kakar. ISD is an independent coeducational day school offering an enriched American educational program to reflect the diverse international background of the student body and thefaculty.

Ron Halsey, Director

2134 International School-Grenada
Washington, DC 20521-0001

Mary Delaney Dunn, Principal

**2135 International School-Havana
Department of State**
Havana Office
Washington, DC 20520-0001

Linda Daly, Principal

2136 International School-Islamabad
DOS/Administrative Officer
8100 Islamabad Place
Washington, DC 20521-8100

92-51-434-950
Fax: 92-51-440-193
E-mail: school@isoi.edu.pkom
http://www.isoi.edu.pk

An independent, coeducational day school which offers an educational program from nursery through grade 12 for students of all nationalities.

Dr. Robert E Ambrogi, Superintendent

2137 International School-Ouagadougou
DOS/Administrative Officer
Ambassade des Etats Unis
Washington, DC 20521-2440

226-36-21-43
Fax: 226-36-22-28
E-mail: isouaga@fasonet.bf
http://http://iso.htmlplanet.com

Patrick M Meyer, Director

2138 International School-Port of Spain
1601 NW 97th Avenue
PO Box 025307h Street
Miami, FL 33102-5307
868-633-4777
Fax: 868-632-4595
E-mail: blatham@isps.edu.tt
http://www.isps.edu.tt
Grade levels Pre-K through 12, school year August - June

Barney Latham, Headmaster

2139 International School-Sfax
Brit Gas 1100 Louisiana
Houston, TX 77002

Sidney Norris, Principal

2140 International School-Yangon
Washington, DC 20521-0001

Dr. David Shawver, Principal

2141 Izmir American Institute
Friends-850 Third Avenue
18th Floor
New York, NY 10022

Richard Curtis, Principal

2142 John F Kennedy School-Queretaro
Cahm 8535 San Gabriel Drive
Laredo, TX 78041
956-580-5401
Fax: 956-580-5415

Dr. Francisco Galicia, Principal

2143 Jordan American Community School
DOS/Administrative Officer
6050 Amman Place
Washington, DC 20521-6050
962-6-581-3944
Fax: 962-6-582-3357
E-mail: school@acsamman.edu.jo
http://www.acsamman.edu.jo
Grades preK-12, enrollment 355.

Dr. Gray Duckett, Superintendent

2144 Karachi American Society School
American Consulate General Karachi
6150 Karachi Place
Washington, DC 20521-6150
92-21-453-909619
Fax: 92-21-453-7305

David Holmer, Principal

2145 Kongeus Grade School
44-46 Gade
St. Thomas 00802
Virgin Islands 00802

Veronica Miller, Principal

2146 Lincoln International School-Kampala
Co of State
Washington, DC 20521-0001

Margaret Bell, Principal

2147 Lincoln School
PO Box 025216
Miami, FL 33102-5216
305-643-4888
Fax: 305-642-8402
E-mail: director@ns.lincoln.ed.cr
A private coeducational day school which offers an educational program from prekindergarten through grade 12 for students of all nationalities.

Dr. Gilbert Brown, Principal

2148 Lincoln-Marti Schools
904 SW 23rd Avenue
Miami, FL 33135
305-643-4200
877-874-1999
Fax: 305-649-2767
E-mail: main@lincoln-marti.com
http://www.lincolnmarti.com
Bilingual private educational institution serving children from birth through 12th grade; offering an exceptional Student Education program as well as accredited childcare programs and K-12 private schooling.

Demitrio Perez, President

2149 Little People's Learning Center
PO Box 12354
St. Thomas 00801-5354
Virgin Islands

Daphne Maynard, Principal

2150 Little School House
47 Kongens Gade
St. Thomas 00802
Virgin Islands

Carol Struiell, Principal

2151 Luanda International School
DOS/Administrative Officer
2550 Luanda Place
Washington, DC 20521-2550
244-2-44-3416
Fax: 244-2-44-3416
E-mail: lis@netangola.com

Ken Hillamn, Director

2152 Lutheran Parish School
#1 Lille Taarne Gade
Charlotte Aml 00802
Puerto Rico 00802

Nancy Gotwalt, Principal

2153 Manor School
236 La Grande Princesse
Christiansted 00820
Virgin Islands 00820

Judith C Gadd, Principal

2154 Maranatha Christian Academy
HC00867, Box 17945, Km 50.3
Fajardo 00738
Puerto Rico 00738

Rev. Gary Sprunger, Principal

2155 Montessori House of Children
PO Box 805
Frederiksted 00841-0805
Virgin Islands

William Myers, Principal

2156 Moravian School
PO Box 1777
Chrisyiansted 00821-1777
Virgin Islands

809-773-8921

This Moravian affiliated school offers a curriculum based in English for 200 day students (96 boys; 104 girls), in grades K-6. The school is willing to participate in a teacher exchange program, with the length of stay being one year, with housing provided. Applications include science, Spanish and computer skills.

Condon L Joseph, Principal

2157 Morrocoy International
MUN 4051
PO Box 025352
Miami, FL 33102-5352

58-286-9520016
Fax: 58-286-9521861
E-mail: kempenich@telcel.net.ve
http://www.geocities.com/minaspov

Grade levels Pre-K through 10, school year August - June

Michael Kempenich, Headmaster

2158 Mount Carmel Elementary School
PO Box 7830
Agat 96928 0830
Guam-b830

This Catholic school offers an English (primary) curriculum for 206 day students (100 boys; 106 girls), in Kinder 4 - 8th grade. Overseas teachers are accepted, with the length of stay being one year. Applications needed to teach include reading, English and counseling/counselor.

Bernadette Quintanilla, Sr, SSND, Principal
Augustin Gumataotao, Administrator

2159 Nazarene Christian School
#55 Golden Rock
C'sted, St. Croix 00820
Virgin Islands

Pastor Hugh Connor, Principal

2160 Nepal Lincoln School
DOS/Administrative Officer
6190 Kathmandu Place
Washington, DC 20521-6190

977-1-270-482
Fax: 977-1-272-685
E-mail: info@lsnepal.com.np
http://www.lsnepal.com

Grades preschool - 12, enrollment 235.

Dr. Barbara Butterworth, Director

2161 Northern Mariana Islands Department of Education
PO Box 501370 CK
Siapan, MP 96950

011-670-664-3720
Fax: 011-670-664-3798

Rita Hocog Inos, Commissioner

2162 Notre Dame High School
480 S San Miguel Street
Talofofo
Guam 96930-4699

671-789-1676

Notre Dame is a co-educational, year-round high school run by the School Sisters of Notre Dame. This Roman Catholic affiliated school offers a curriculum in English for 191 day students and 9 boarding (32 boys; 168 girls), in grades 9-12. Student/teacher ratio is 10:1, and the applications needed to teach include science, math, social sciences, and English.

Regina Paulino, SSND, Principal

2163 Nuestra Senora de La Altagracia
672 Calle Felipe Gutierrez #672
San Juan 00924-2225
Puerto Rico

2164 Nuestra Senora de La Providencia
PO Box 11610
San Juan 00922-1610
Puerto Rico

2165 Okinawa Christian School
PO Box 14250
Gainesville, FL 32604-2250

Paul Gieschen, Principal

2166 Open Classroom
PO Box 4046
St. Thomas 00803
Virgin Islands 00803

Janie Lang, Principal

2167 Osaka International School
International Schools Services
PO Box 5910
Princeton, NJ 08543-5910

James Wiese, Principal

2168 Palache Bilingual School
PO Box 1832
Arecibo 00613-1832
Puerto Rico

Rev. David Valez, Principal

2169 Peace Corp
11 20th Street NW
Washington, DC 20526

202-692-2000
800-424-8580
Fax: 202-692-1897
http://www.peacecorps.gov

2170 Pine Peace School
PO Box 361
Cruz Bay 00830
Virgin Islands

Katharine Hilliard, Principal

2171 Ponce Baptist Academy
72 Calle 1 Belgica
Ponce 00731
Puerto Rico

Vivian Medina, Principal

2172 Prophecy Elementary School
PO Box 10497
APO St. Thomas 00801-3497
Virgin Islands

Verona Rogers, Principal

2173 Puerto Rico Department of Education
Hato Rey 00919
PO Box 190759
San Juan, Puerto Rico 00919

787-763-2171
http://www.de.gobierno.pr

Cesar A Rey-Hernandez, Secretary

2174 QSI International School-Chisinau
DOS/Administrative Officer
7080 Chisinau Place
Washington, DC 20521-7080

373-24-2366
E-mail: qsimdv@qsi.moldline.net

Grades preK-12, enrollment 29.

Mary Kay Smith, Director

2175 QSI International School-Skopje
DOS/Administrative Officer
7120 Skopje Place
Washington, DC 20521-7120

389-91-367-678
Fax: 389-91-362-250
E-mail: qsisk@mt.com.mk

Grades preSchool-8, enrollment 47.

David Dutson, Director

2176 QSI International School-Vladivostok
DOS/Administrative Officer
5880 Vladivostok Place
Washington, DC 20521-5880

7-4232-321-292
Fax: 7-4232-313-684
E-mail: qsiisv@fastmail.vladivostok.ru

Grades preK-9, enrollment 18.

Harold M Strom Jr, Director

2177 Rainbow Development Center
PO Box 7618
Christiansted 00823-7618
Virgin Islands

Gloria Henry, Principal

2178 Rainbow Learning Institute
PO Box 75
Christiansted 00821-0075
Virgin Islands

Alda Lockhart, Principal

2179 Rainbow School
PO Box 422
Charlotte Aml 00801
Virgin Islands

Louise Thomas, Principal

2180 Robinson School
5 Nairn Street
Condado 00907
Puerto Rico

1-787-728-6767
Fax: 1-787-727-7736
E-mail: robinson_school@hotmail.com
http://www.geocities.com

Grade level prekindergarten through twelfth, with enrollment of 445.

Giberto Quintana, Executive Director

2181 Roosevelt Roads Elementary School
PO Box 420132
Roosevelt Roads 00742-0132
Puerto Rico

787-865-3073
Fax: 787-865-4891
http://www.netdial.caribe.net

2182 Roosevelt Roads Middle & High School
PO Box 420131
Roosevelt Roads 00742-0131
Puerto Rico

787-865-4000
Fax: 787-865-4893
E-mail: wjames@caribe.net
http://www.antilles.ododedoa.edu

Waynna James, Principal

2183 Saint Anthony School
529 Chalan San Antonio
Tamuning 96911 3600
Guam

Sor Mary Kathleen Sarmi, Principal

2184 Saint Eheresas Elementary School
Leone
Pago Apgo 96799
American Samoa

Sister Katherine, Principal

2185 Saint Francis Elementary School
520130 Lepua
Pago Pago 96799
American Samoa

Sister Gaynor Ana, Principal

2186 Saint John's School
911 N Marine Drive
Tumon Bay 96911
Guam

671-646-8080
Fax: 617-649-1055
E-mail: info@stjohns.edu.gu
http://www.stjohns.edu.gu

PreK-12th grade college preparatory school.

2187 Saint John's School, Puerto Rico
1466 Ashford Condado
Santurce 00907
Puerto Rico

Louis R Christiansen, Principal

2188 Saints Peter & Paul High School
Box 1706
Charlotte Aml 00801
Virgin Islands

Diana Parker, Principal

2189 Samoa Baptist Academy
Tafuna
Pago Pago 96799
American Samoa

Janice Yerton, Principal

2190 San Carlos & Bishop McManus High School
PO Box Loo 9, Yumet
Aguadilla 00605
Puerto Rico

Nydia U Nieves, Principal

2191 San Vincente Elementary School
San Vincente School Drive
Barrigada 96913
Puerto Rico 96913

671-734-4242

This campus is on five acres of outside Barrigada Village. The average enrollment of 460 students consists of 234 boys and 226 girls in grades PreK-8. SVS holds a Certificate of Accreditation from the Western Association of Schoolsand Colleges until 1998. Length of stay for overseas teachers is two years, with housing provided. Applications needed to teach include English and physical education.

Adrian Cristobal, Principal
Tarcisia Sablan SSND, Faculty Head

2192 Santa Barbara School
274A W Santa Barbara Avenue
Dededo 96912 1308
Guam

2193 Santiago Christian School
PO Box 5600
Fort Lauderdale, FL 33310-5600

Lloyd Haglund, Principal

2194 School of the Good Shepherd
1069 Kinghill
St. Croix 00851
Virgin Islands 00851

Linda Navarro, Principal

2195 Seventh Day Adventist
PO Box 7909
St. Thomas 00801-0909
Virgin Islands

Josiah Maynard, Principal

2196 Shekou International School
PO Box 4381
Houston, TX 72210-4381

86-755-2669-3669
Fax: 86-755-2667-4099
E-mail: sis@sis.org.cn
http://www.sis.org

Grade levels PK-9, school year August - June

Eleanor Jones, Director
Jennifer Lees, Curriculum Coordinator

2197 Slovak Republic QSI International School of Bratislava
DOS/Administrative Officer
5850 Bratislava Place
Washington, DC 20521-5840

421-2-6541-1636
Fax: 421-2-6541-1646
E-mail: director@qsi.sk
http://www.qsi.sk

Grades preK-12, enrollment 140.
Phil Sylla, Director

2198 Slovenia QSI International School-Ljubljana
DOS/Administrative Officer
7140 Ljubljana Place
Washington, DC 20521-7140

386-1-439-6300
Fax: 386-1-439-6305
E-mail: qsisln@siol.net
http://www.qsi.org

Grades K-8, enrollment 26.
Peter Janda, Director

2199 South Pacific Academy
PO Box 520
Pago Pago 96799 0520
American Samoa

Tina Senrud, Principal

2200 Southern Peru Staff Schools-Peru
180 Maiden Lane
New York, NY 10038-4925

John Dansdill, Principal

2201 St. Croix Christian Academy
PO Box 712
Christiansted 00850
Virgin Islands

Randolph Lockhart, Principal

2202 St. Croix Country Day School
Rt-01, Box 6199
Kingshill 00850
Virgin Islands

1-340-778-1974
Fax: 1-340-779-3331

Grade levels N-12, school year August - June

James Sadler, Headmaster
Susan Gibbons, Business Manager

2203 St. Croix Moravian School
PO Box 117
St. Thomas 00801
Virgin Islands

Condon L Joseph, Principal

2204 St. Croix SDA School
PO Box 930
Kingshill 00851-0930
Virgin Islands

Peter Archer, Principal

2205 St. Joseph High School
PO Box 517
Frederiksted 00841-0517
Virgin Islands

Kevin Marin, Principal

2206 St. Patrick School
PO Box 988
Frderiksted 00841-0988
Virgin Islands

Juliette Clarke, Principal

2207 St. Peter & Paul Elementary School
PO Box 1706
St. Thomas 00803
Virgin Islands

Annamay Komment, Principal

2208 Sunbeam
36 Hospital Ground
St. Thomas 00803
Virgin Islands

Ione Leonard, Principal

2209 Syria Damascus Community School
DOS/Administrative Officer
6110 Damascus Place
Washington, DC 20521-6110

963-11-333-0331
Fax: 963-11-332-1457
E-mail: dcs-dam@net.sy
http://www.syria-guide.com/school/dcs

An independent, coeducational day school which offers an American educational program from preschool through grade 12 for students of all nationalities.

Dr. James L Liebzeit, Director

2210 Tashkent International School
ADM/2 TIS
Dept. of State, 7110 Tashkent Place
Washington, DC 20521-7110

998-71-191-9671
Fax: 998-71-120-6621
E-mail: office@tis.uz

Grade levels K-12, school year August - June

John Thomas, Director

2211 Teaching in Austria
Austrian Institute
11 E 52nd Street
New York, NY 10022-5301

212-579-5165

2212 Temple Christian School
PO Box 3009
Agana 96910
Guam 96910

Rev. Ray Fagan, Principal

2213 Tirana International School-Albania
9510 Tirana Place
Washington, DC 29521-9510

355-4-365-239
Fax: 335-4-227-734
E-mail: qsialb@albaniaonline.net
http://www.qsi.org

Grade levels K-8, school year September - June

Glenn Mosher, Director

2214 Trinity Christian School
PO Box 11343
Yiga 96929 0343
Guam

Craig A Fletcher, Principal

2215 Turkmenistan Ashgabat International School
Box 2002
7070 Ashgabat Place
Washington, DC 20521-7070

967-1-234-437
Fax: 967-1-234-438
E-mail: director@ais.cat.glasnet.ru

Grades K-11, enrollment 75.

Scott Root, Director

2216 Ukraine Kiev International School-An American Institution
EOS/Administrative Officer
5850 Kiev Place
Washington, DC 20521-5850

380-44-452-2792
Fax: 380-44-452-2998
E-mail: kisukr@sovamua.com

An independent, coeducational day school which offers an educational program from prekindergarten through high school for students of all nationalities.

E Michael Tewalthomas, Director

2217 United Nations International School
24-50 FDR Drive
New York, NY 10010

212-684-7400
Fax: 212-779-2259
E-mail: administration@unis.org
http://www.unis.org

Grade levels kindergarten through twelfth, with total enrollment of 1440 students.

Kenneth Wrye, EdD, Director

2218 University del Sagrado Corazon
PO Box 12383
San Juan 00917-8505
Puerto Rico

2219 Uruguayan American School
1785 Dublin Montevideo
Department of State
Washington, DC 20521-3360

598-2-600-7681
Fax: 598-2-600-1935
E-mail: amschool@chasque.apc.org

A private, nonsectarian, coeducational day school which offers an educational program from nursery through grade 12 for students of all nationalities.

Larry Synder, Principal

2220 Uruguayan American School-Montevideo
DOS/Administrative Officer
3360 Montevideo Place
Washington, DC 20521-3360

598-2-600-7681
Fax: 598-2-606-1935
E-mail: amschool@chasque.apc.org
http://www.uas.edu.uy

David Deuel, Director

2221 Uzbekistan Tashkent International School
DOS/Administrative Officer
7110 Tashkent Place
Washington, DC 20521-7110

998-71-191-9671
Fax: 998-71-120-6621
E-mail: office@tis.uz

Grades K-12, enrollment 138.

John Thomas, Director

Teaching Opportunities Abroad / International

2222 Venezuela Colegio Internacional-Carabobo
VLN 1010
PO Box 025685
Miami, FL 33102-5685

58-41-426-551
Fax: 58-41-426-510
E-mail: admin@cic-valencia.org.ve

Grades K-12, enrollment 417.

Frank Anderson, Superintendent

2223 Venezuela Escuela Campo Alegre
8424 NW 56th Street
Suite CCS 00007
Miami, FL 33166

58-2-993-7135
Fax: 58-2-993-0219
E-mail: info@eca.com.ve
http://www.internet.ve/eca

Grades N-12, enrollment 803.

Bambi Betts, Superintendent

2224 Venezuela International School-Caracas
PO Box 025323
CCS 10249
Miami, FL 33102-5323

58-2-945-0422
Fax: 58-2-945-0533
E-mail: wsargent@ciccaracas.com.ve
http://www.cic-caracus.org

Grades PK-12, enrollment 450.

Winthrop Sargent Jr, Headmaster

2225 Virgin Island Montessori School
Vessup Bay Star Route
Charlotte Aml 00801
Virgin Islands 00801

Shournagh Mcweeney, Principal

2226 Virgin Islands Department of Education
44-46 Kongens Gade
Saint Thomas, Virgin Islands 00802

340-774-2810
Fax: 340-774-7153
http://www.networkvi.com/education

Ruby Simmonds, Commissioner

2227 Washington International School
3100 Macomb Street NW
Washington, DC 20008-3324

202-243-1800
Fax: 202-243-1695
E-mail: admissions@wis.edu
http://www.wis.edu

Grade levels preK-12, with total student enrollment of 800.

Anne-Marie Pierce, Head of School

2228 We Care Child Development Center
PO Box 818
Christiansted 00821-0818
Virgin Islands

Pauline Canton, Principal

2229 Wesleyan Academy
PO Box 1489
Guaynabo 00970-1489
Puerto Rico

Jack Mann, Principal

2230 Yakistan International School-Karachi
DOS/Administrative Officer
6150 Karachi Place
Washington, DC 20521-6150

92-21-453-9096
Fax: 92-21-454-7305
E-mail: ameschl@cyber.net.pk
http://www.isk.edu.pk

Grades N-12, enrollment 338.

Glen Shapin, Superintendent

2231 Zion Academy
PO Box 10141
St. Thomas 00801-3141
Virgin Islands

Evelyn Williams, Principal

International

2232 Council for International Exchange of Scholars
3007 Tilden Street NW
Suite 5-L
Washington, DC 20008-3008

202-686-8664
Fax: 202-362-3442
E-mail: scholars@cies.iie.org
http://www.cies.org

Announces each year approximately 1,000 Fulbright awards for Americans to teach or conduct research at universities in about 134 countries.

Patti McGill Peterson, Executive Director
Judy Pehrson, Director External Relations

2233 Defense Language Institute-English Language Branch
US Civil Service Commission, San Antonio Area
8610 Broadway Street
San Antonio, TX 78217-6352

512-229-6622

Employs English language instructors at the school and in numerous overseas locations.

2234 Education Information Services which Employ Americans
Education Information Services
PO Box 620662
Newton, MA 02462-0662

781-433-0125
Fax: 781-237-2842

Devoted to helping Americans who wish to teach in American overseas schools and International Schools in which English is the primary teaching language. Supports those wishing to teach English as a second language. Publish paperscovering every country in the world, list of recruiting fairs, internships, volunteers, jobs, summer overseas jobs.

Frederic B Viaux, President

2235 Educational Information Services
PO Box 662
Newtown Lower Falls, MA 02162

617-964-4555

Offers information on employment opportunities including books, periodicals and more for the teaching professional who wishes to teach in American overseas schools, international schools, language (ESL) schools, and Department ofDefense Dependencies Schools (DODDS).

Frederick B Viaux, President
Michelle V Curtin, Editor

178

2236 **Educational Placement Sources-US**
Education Information Services/Instant Alert
PO Box 620662
Newton, MA 02462-0662

617-433-0125

Lists 100 organizations in the United States that find positions for teachers, educational administrators, counselors and other professionals. Listings are classified by type, listed alphabetically and offer all contact information.

4 pages Annual

FB Viaux, President

2237 **Educational Staffing Program**
International Schools Services
PO Box 5910
Princeton, NJ 08543

609-452-0990
Fax: 609-452-2690
E-mail: edustaffing@iss.edu

The Educational Staffing Program has placed almost 15,000 K-12 teachers and administrators in overseas schools since 1955. Most candidates obtain their overseas teaching positions by attending our US-based International RecruitmentCenter where ISS candidates have the potential to interview with overseas school heads seeking new staff. You must be an active ISS candidate to attend an IRC. Applicants must have a bachelor's degree and two years of current relevant experience.

2238 **European Council of International Schools**
21 Lavant Street
Petersfield, Hampshire GU3 23EL
United Kingdom

44-0-1730-268244
Fax: 44-0-1730-267914
E-mail: ecis@ecis.org
http://www.ecis.org

Provides a variety of services to its 150 member schools in Europe and over 120 associate member schools worldwide: conducts professional conferences, evaluates and accredits international schools, assists schools with staffing,offers placement assistance to teaching candidates and provides comprehensive consultative services.

T Michael Maybury, Executive Secretary

2239 **FRS National Teacher Agency**
PO Box 298
Seymour, TN 37865-0298

865-577-8143

Offers employment options to educators in the United States and abroad.

2240 **Foreign Faculty and Administrative Openings**
Education Information Services
PO Box 620662
Newton, MA 02462-0662

617-433-0125

150 specific openings in administration, counseling, library and other professional positions for American teachers in American schools overseas and in international schools in which teaching language is English.

15 pages Every 6 Weeks

FB Viaux, Coordinating Education

2241 **Fulbright Teacher Exchange**
600 Maryland Avenue SW
Room 235
Washington, DC 20024-2520

800-726-0479
http://www.grad.usda.gov

An organization that offers opportunities for two-year college faculty and secondary school teachers who would like to exchange with teachers in Eastern or Western Europe, Latin America, Australia, Africa, and Canada. To qualify,teachers must be US citizens, have three years full-time teaching experience and be employed in a full-time academic position.

2242 **International Educators Cooperative**
212 Alcott Road
East Falmouth, MA 02536-6803

508-540-8173
Fax: 508-540-8173

In addition to year round recruitment, International Educators Cooperative hosts Recruitment Centers in the United States each year.

Dr. Lou Fuccillo, Director

2243 **National Association of Teachers' Agencies**
National Association of Teachers' Agencies
799 Kings Highway
Fairfield, CT 06432

203-333-0611
Fax: 203-334-7224
E-mail: fairfieldteachers@snet.net
http://www.jobsforteachers.com

Provides placement services for those seeking professional positions at all levels of teaching/administration/support services worldwide.

Mark King, Secretary/Treasurer

2244 **National Council of Independent Schools'**
Associations
Curtin ACT 2605
PO Box 324
Australia

06-282-3488
Fax: 06-282-2926

Services include career placement.

Fergus Thomson

2245 **Overseas Employment Opportunities for**
Educators
Department of Defense, Office of Dependent Schools
2461 Eisenhower Avenue
Alexandria, VA 22331-3000

703-325-0867

This publication tells about teaching jobs in 250 schools operated for children of US military and civilian personnel stationed overseas. Applicants usually must qualify in two subject areas.

2246 **Recruiting Fairs for Overseas Teaching**
Education Information Services/Instant Alert
PO Box 620662
Newton, MA 02462-0662

781-433-0125
Fax: 781-237-2842

Recruiting fairs and sponsors in the US and elsewhere for American educators who wish to teach outside of the United States.

FB Viaux, Coordinating Education

2247 UNI Overseas Recruiting Fair
University of Northern Iowa
SSC #19
Cedar Falls, IA 50614-0390

                                    319-273-2083
                              Fax: 319-273-6998
                E-mail: overseas.placement@uni.edu
                http://www.uni.edu/placement/overseas

About 160 recruiters from 120 schools in 80 countries
recruit at this fair for certified K-12 educators.

February

Tracy Roling, Coordinator

2248 US College-Sponsored Programs Abroad
Institute of International Education
809 United Nations Plaza
New York, NY 10017-3503

                                    212-883-8200
                              Fax: 212-984-5325

Offers learning and teaching abroad opportunities.

2249 WorldTeach
Center for International Development
Harvard University
79 John F Kennedy Street
Cambridge, MA 02138-5705

                                    617-495-5527
                                    800-483-2240
                              Fax: 617-495-1599
                E-mail: info@worldteach.org
                http://www.worldteach.org

Agency offering volunteers teaching placements in
developing countries for English, math, science, and
computer education. Summer teaching internships or on
a-year programs.

Robin Teater, Executive Director
Harriet Wong, Program Manager

Alabama

2250 Auburn University at Montgomery Library
PO Box 244023
Montgomery, AL 36124-4023

334-244-3649
Fax: 334-244-3720
http://www.aumnicat.aum.edu

Member of The Foundation Center network, maintaining a collection of private foundation tax returns which provide information on the scope of grants dispensed by that particular foundation.

R Best, Dean Administration
T Bailey, ILL/ Reference

2251 Benjamin & Roberta Russell Educational and Charitable Foundation
PO Box 272
Alexander City, AL 35010-0272

256-329-4224

Offers giving in the areas of higher and public education, youth programs and a hospital.

James D Nabors, Executive Director

2252 Birmingham Public Library
Government Documents
2100 Park Place
Birmingham, AL 35203-2794

205-226-3600
Fax: 205-226-3729
http://www.bplonline.org/resources/subjects/gov/deault

Member of The Foundation Center network, maintaining a collection of private foundation tax returns which provide information on the scope of grants dispensed by that particular foundation.

2253 Carolina Lawson Ivey Memorial Foundation
PO Box 340
Smiths, AL 36877-0340

334-826-5760

Scholarships are offered to college juniors and seniors who are pursuing careers of teaching social studies in middle or secondary grades. The grants are also offered to teachers in Alabama and west Georgia for curriculum planning anddevelopment, in-service training, the development of instructional materials for use in elementary and secondary schools, and other projects that focus on the cultural approach method of teaching.

2254 Huntsville Public Library
915 Monroe Street SW
Huntsville, AL 35801-5007

256-532-5940
http://www.hpl.lib.al.us/

Member of The Foundation Center network, maintaining a collection of private foundation tax returns which provide information on the scope of grants dispensed by that particular foundation.

Donna B Schremser, Library Director

2255 JL Bedsole Foundation
PO Box 1137
Mobile, AL 36633-1137

251-432-3369
Fax: 251-432-1134
http://www.jlbedsolefoundation.org

The foundation's primary interest is the support of educational institutions within the state of Alabama and civic and economic development which is limited to the geographical area of Southwest Alabama. The arts, social service andhealth programs receive limited grants.

Organizations or projects outside of the State of Alabama are not considered for funding by the Foundation.

Mabel B Ward, Executive Director
Scott A Morton, Assistant Director

2256 Mildred Weedon Blount Educational and Charitable Foundation
PO Box 607
Tallassee, AL 36078-0007

334-283-4931

Support for Catholic schools, public schools and a scholarship fund for secondary school students.

Arnold B Dopson, Executive Director

2257 Mitchell Foundation
PO Box 1126
Mobile, AL 36633

251-432-1711
Fax: 334-432-1712

Places an emphasis on secondary and higher education, social services programs, youth agencies, and aid for the handicapped.

Augustine Meaher, Executive Director

2258 University of South Alabama
307 University Boulevard
Mobile, AL 36688-0002

251-460-7025
Fax: 251-460-7636
http://http://library.southalabama.edu

Richard Wood, Dean Of Libraries

Alaska

2259 University of Alaska-Anchorage Library
3211 Providence Drive
Anchorage, AK 99508-8000

907-786-1848
Fax: 907-786-6050
http://www.lib.uaa.alaska.edu/

Member of The Foundation Center network, maintaining a collection of private foundation tax returns which provide information on the scope of grants dispensed by that particular foundation.

Stephen J Rollins, Dean Of Library

Arizona

2260 Arizona Department of Education
1535 W Jefferson Street
Phoenix, AZ 85007

602-542-5393
800-352-4558
Fax: 602-542-5440
http://www.ade.state.az.us

Implements procedures that ensure the proper allocation, distribution, and expenditure of all federal and state funds administerd by the department. The following links to our web pages contain information pertaining to educationalgrants funded from the state or federal programs.

Tom Horne, Superintendent

2261 Arizona Governor's Committee on Employment of People with Disabilities
Samaritan Rehabilitation Institute
1012 E Willetta Street
Phoenix, AZ 85006-3047

602-239-4762
Fax: 602-239-5256

Jim Bruzewski, Executive Director

2262 Education Services
Arizona Department of Education
1535 W Jefferson Street
Phoenix, AZ 85007-3280

602-364-1961
Fax: 602-542-5440
http://www.ade.state.az.us/edservices

Provides quality services and resources to schools, parent groups, government agencies, and community groups to enable them to achieve their goals.

Lillie Sly, Associate Superintendent

2263 Evo-Ora Foundation
2525 E Broadway Boulevard
Suite 111
Tucson, AZ 85716-5398

Giving is primarily aimed at education, especially Catholic high schools and universities.

2264 Flinn Foundation
1802 N Central Avenue
Suite 2300
Phoenix, AZ 85012-2513

602-744-6800
Fax: 602-744-6815
http://www.flinn.org

Supports nonprofit organizations in the state of Arizona for programs in health care, as well as an annual awards competition for Arizona's principal arts institutions and a college scholarship program for Arizona high schoolgraduates. Scholarship provides expenses for four years, two summers of study-related travel abroad and other benefits.

John W Murphy, Executive Director

2265 Phoenix Public Library
Business & Sciences Department
12 E McDowell Road
Phoenix, AZ 85004-1627

602-262-4636
Fax: 602-261-8836
http://www.phxlib.org

Member of The Foundation Center network, maintaining a collection of private foundation tax returns which provide information on the scope of grants dispensed by that particular foundation.

2266 Special Programs
Arizona Department of Education
1535 W Jefferson Street
Phoenix, AZ 85007-3280

602-542-5393
Fax: 602-542-5440

Tom Horne, Superintendent

2267 Support Services
Arizona Department of Education
1535 W Jefferson Street
Phoenix, AZ 85007-3280

602-542-5393
Fax: 602-542-5440

Rachel Arroyo, School Finance

2268 Vocational Technological Education
Arizona Department of Education
1535 W Jefferson Street
Phoenix, AZ 85007-3280

602-542-5393
Fax: 602-542-5440

Tom Horne, Superintendent

Arkansas

2269 Charles A Frueauff Foundation
900 S Shackleford Road
Suite 300
Little Rock, AR 72211-3848

501-219-1410
http://www.frueauffoundation.com

Will review proposals from private four-year colleges and universities.

Zoe Cole Galloway

2270 Roy and Christine Sturgis Charitable and Educational Trust
PO Box 92
Malvern, AR 72104-0092

501-337-5109

Giving is offered to Baptist and Methodist organizations, including schools, churches and higher and secondary education.

Katie Speer, Executive Director

2271 The Jones Center For Families
922 East Emma Avenue
Springdale, AR 72765

479-756-8090

Focuses funds on education, medical resources and religious organizations in Arkansas.

HG Frost Jr, Executive Director
Grace Donoho, Director Of Education

2272 Walton Family Foundation
125 W Central Avenue
Room 217   Po Box 2030
Bentonville, AR 72712-5248

479-464-1570
Fax: 479-464-1580
http://www.wffhome.com

Offers giving for systemic reform of primary education (K-12) and early childhood development.

Stewart T Springfield, Executive Director

2273 Westark Community College
Borham Library
5210 Grand Avenue
Fort Smith, AR 72904-7397

479-788-7200
Fax: 479-788-7209

Member of The Foundation Center network, maintaining a collection of private foundation tax returns which provide information on the scope of grants dispensed by that particular foundation.

2274 William C & Theodosia Murphy Nolan Foundation
200 N Jefferson Avenue
Suite 308
El Dorado, AR 71730-5853

870-863-7118
Fax: 870-863-6528

Supports education and the arts (historic preservation, arts centers) as well as religious welfare and youth organizations in Northern Louisiana and Southern Arkansas.

William C Nolan, Executive Director

2275 Winthrop Rockefeller Foundation
308 E 8th Street
Little Rock, AR 72202-3999

501-376-6854
Fax: 501-374-4797

Dedicated to improving the quality of life and education in Arkansas. Grants go to schools that work to involve teachers and parents in making decisions; to universities and local schools to strengthen both levels of education; andfor projects that promote stakeholder participation in the development of educational policy.

Mahlon Martin, President
Jackie Cox-New, Sr Program Officer

California

2276 Ahmanson Foundation
9215 Wilshire Boulevard
Beverly Hills, CA 90210-5538
310-278-0770

Concentrates mainly on education, health and social services in Southern California.

Lee E Walcott, Executive Director

2277 Alice Tweed Tuohy Foundation
205 E Carrillo Street
Suite 219
Santa Barbara, CA 93101-7186
805-962-6430

Priority consideration is given to applications from organizations serving: young people; education; selected areas of interest in health care and medicine; and community affairs.

Harris W Seed, President
Eleanor Van Cott, Executive VP

2278 Arrillaga Foundation
2560 Mission College Boulevard
Suite 101
Santa Clara, CA 95054-1217
408-980-0130
Fax: 408-988-4893

Giving is aimed at secondary schools and higher education in the state of California.

John Arrillaga, Executive Director

2279 Atkinson Foundation
1100 Grundy Lane
Suite 140
San Bruno, CA 94066-3030
650-876-0222
Fax: 650-876-0222

Provides opportunities for people in San Mateo County, California to reach their highest potential and to improve the quality of their lives and to assist educational institutions and supporting organizations with the implementationof effective programs that reach and serve their target populations.

Elizabeth Curtis, Executive Director

2280 BankAmerica Foundation
Bank of America Center
PO Box 37000
San Francisco, CA 94137-0001
415-953-3175
Fax: 415-622-3469
E-mail: bacef@consumer-action.org

Fields of interest include arts/cultural programs, higher education, community development and general federated giving programs.

Elizabeth Nachbaur, Program Director

2281 Bechtel Group Corporate Giving Program
Po Box 193965
San Francisco, CA 94119-3965
415-768-5974

Offers support for higher education and programs related to engineering and construction, math and science in grades K-12 and general charitable programs.

Kathryn M Bandarrae, Executive Director

2282 Bernard Osher Foundation
909 Montgomery
#300
San Francisco, CA 94133
415-861-5587
Fax: 415-677-5868
E-mail: nagle@osherfoundation.org

Funds in the arts, post-secondary education and environmental education on San Francisco and Alameda Counties.

Patricia Nagle, Sr VP

2283 Boys-Viva Supermarkets Foundation
955 Carrillo Drive
Suite 103
Los Angeles, CA 90048-5400

Wide range of support for education of school-aged children, especially the at-risk population, tutoring, and social opportunities.

Fred Snowden, Executive Director

2284 California Community Foundation
445 South Figueroa Street
Suite 3400
Los Angeles, CA 90071-1638
210-413-4130
Fax: 213-622-2979
http://www.calfund.org

Improving human condition through nonprofit agencies in Los Angeles County. Integral parts of eligible proposals are, hosting conferences, incurring debt, individuals, sectarian purposes or regranting.

Judy Spiegel, Sr VP of Programs
Antonia Hernandez, President/CEO

2285 Carrie Estelle Doheny Foundation
707 Wilshire Boulevard
Suite 4960
Los Angeles, CA 90017-2659
213-488-1122
Fax: 213-488-1544
http://www.dohenyfoundation.org

This foundation funds a myriad of organizations ranging from the education and medicine field to public health and science areas.

Robert A Smith III, Executive Director

2286 Dan Murphy Foundation
PO Box 711267
Los Angeles, CA 90071-9767
213-623-3120
Fax: 213-623-1421

Funds Roman Catholic institutions, with a primary interest in religious orders and schools.

Daniel J Donohue, Executive Director

2287 David & Lucile Packard Foundation
300 2nd Street
Suite 200
Los Altos Hills, CA 94022-3643
650-948-7658
Fax: 650-941-3151
http://www.packard.org

Concentrates on four categories: education, the arts, conservation and child health. Also allocates funds to companies interested in public improvement and public policy.

Colburn S Wilbur, Executive Director

2288 Evelyn & Walter Haas Jr Fund
One Market Landmark
Suite 400
San Francisco, CA 94105
415-856-1400
Fax: 415-856-1500

Interested in strengthening neighborhoods, communities, and human services. Funds mainly in San Francisco Bay Area.

Ira Hirschfield, President
Clayton Juan, Grants Administrator

2289 Foundation Center-San Francisco
312 Sutter Street
Suite 606
San Francisco, CA 94108-4323

415-397-0902
Fax: 415-397-7670
http://www.fdncenter.org

One of five Foundation Centers nationwide, the Foundation Center - San Francisco is a library which collects information on private foundations, corporate philanthropy, nonprofit management, fundraising and other topics of interest tononprofit organization representatives.

2290 Foundations Focus
Marin Community Foundation
5 Hamilton Landing
Suite 200
Novato, CA 94949

415-464-2500
Fax: 415-464-2555
http://www.marincf.org

Grants support projects that benefit residents of Marin County, CA.

Don Jen, Program Officer/Education
Thomas Peters, President/CEO

2291 Francis H Clougherty Charitable Trust
500 Newport Center Drive
Suite 720
Newport Beach, CA 92660-7007

Offers grants in the areas of elementary, secondary school and higher education in Southern California.

2292 Freitas Foundation
C/O Fiduciary Resources
1120 Nye Street
Suite 320
San Rafael, CA 94901-2945

Offers giving in the areas of elementary and secondary education, as well as theological education.

Margaret Boyden, Executive Director

2293 Fritz B Burns Foundation
4001 W Alameda Avenue
Suite 201
Burbank, CA 91505-4338

818-840-8802
Fax: 818-840-0468

Grants are primarily focused on education, hospitals and medical research organizations.

Joseph E Rawlinson, Executive Director

2294 George Frederick Jewett Foundation
235 Montgomery Street
Suite 612
San Francisco, CA 94104-2909

415-421-1351
Fax: 415-421-1351

Concerns itself mainly with voluntary, nonprofit organizations that promote human welfare.

2295 Grant & Resource Center of Northern California
2280 Benton Drive, Building C
Suite A
Redding, CA 96003

530-244-1219
Fax: 530-244-0905
E-mail: library@grcnc.org

Member of The Foundation Center network, maintaining a collection of private foundation tax returns which provide information on the scope of grants dispensed by that particular foundation.

2296 Greenville Foundation
283 2nd Street E
Suite A
Sonoma, CA 95476-5708

707-938-9377
Fax: 707-939-9311

This foundation focuses its support on education, the environment and human rights. The main focus of the educational grants lie within the areas of elementary, secondary and higher education.

Virginia Hubbell, Executive Director

2297 HN & Frances C Berger Foundation
PO Box 3064
Arcadia, CA 91006

626-447-3351

Provides scholarships and endowments to colleges and universities.

2298 Harry & Grace Steele Foundation
441 Old Newport Boulevard
Suite 301
Newport Beach, CA 92663-4231

949-631-0418

Grants are given in the areas of secondary education, including scholarship funds in the fine arts and youth agencies.

Marie F Kowert, Executive Director

2299 Henry J Kaiser Family Foundation
Quadrus
2400 Sand Hill Road
Menlo Park, CA 94025-6941

650-854-9400
Fax: 650-854-4800
http://www.kff.org

Concentrates on health care, minority groups and South Africa.

Drew Altman, President/CEO

2300 Hon Foundation
25200 La Paz Road
Suite 210
Laguna Hills, CA 92653-5110

949-586-4400

Offers giving in the areas of elementary, secondary and higher education in the states of Hawaii and California.

2301 Hugh & Hazel Darling Foundation
520 S Grand Avenue
7th Floor
Los Angeles, CA 90071-2645

213-683-5200
Fax: 213-627-7795

Supports education in California with special emphasis on legal education; no grants to individuals; grants only to 501(c)(3) organizations.

Richard L Stack, Trustee

2302 Ingraham Memorial Fund
C/O Emrys J. Ross
301 E Colorado Boulevard
Suite 900
Pasadena, CA 91101-1916

Offers giving in the areas of elementary, secondary and higher education, as well as theological education in Claremont and Pasadena, California.

2303 James G Boswell Foundation
101 W Walnut Street
Pasadena, CA 91103-3636
626-583-3000
Fax: 626-583-3090

Funds hospitals, pre-college private schools, public broadcasting and youth organizations.

James G Boswell II, Chairman
Sherman Railsback, EVP/COO

2304 James Irvine Foundation
1 Market, Steuart Tower
Suite 2500
San Francisco, CA 94105-1017
415-777-2244
Fax: 415-777-0869

Giving is primarily aimed at the areas of education, youth and health.

James E Canales, President/CEO
Kristin Nelson, Executive Assistant

2305 James S Copley Foundation
7776 Ivanhoe Avenue #1530
La Jolla, CA 92037-4520
858-454-0411
Fax: 858-729-7629

Support is offered for higher and secondary education, child development, cultural programs and community services.

Anita A Baumgardner, Executive Director

2306 John Jewett & H Chandler Garland Foundation
PO Box 550
Pasadena, CA 91102-0550

Support given primarily for secondary and higher education, social services and cultural and historical programs.

GE Morrow, Executive Director

2307 Joseph Drown Foundation
1999 Avenue of the Stars
Suite 2330
Los Angeles, CA 90067-4611
310-277-4488
Fax: 310-277-4573
http://www.jdrown.org

The Foundation's goal is to assist individuals in becoming successful, self-sustaining, contributing citizens. The foundation is interested in programs that break down any barrier that prevents a person from continuing to grow andlearn.

Norman Obrow, Executive Director

2308 Jules & Doris Stein Foundation
PO Box 30
Beverly Hills, CA 90213-0030
213-276-2101

Supports charitable organizations.

2309 Julio R Gallo Foundation
PO Box 1130
Modesto, CA 95353-1130
209-579-3373

Offers grants and support to secondary schools and higher education universities.

Sam Gallo, Chairman

2310 Kenneth T & Eileen L Norris Foundation
11 Golden Shore Street
Suite 450
Long Beach, CA 90802-4214
562-435-8444
Fax: 562-436-0584
E-mail: gerringer@ktn.org
http://www.norrisfoundation.org

Funding categories include medical, education/science, youth, cultural and community.

Ronald Barnes, Executive Director

2311 Koret Foundation
33 New Montgomery Street
Suite 1090
San Francisco, CA 94105-4526
415-882-7740
Fax: 415-882-7775
E-mail: sandyedwards@koretfoundation.org
http://www.koretfoundation.org

Funding includes; public policy and selected programs in K-12 public education, higher education, youth programs, Jewish studies at colleges and universities, and Jewish education. The geographical area for grant-making is the SanFrancisco Bay area.

Tad Taube, President

2312 Lane Family Charitable Trust
500 Almer Road
Apartment 301
Burlingame, CA 94010-3966

Offers giving in the areas of secondary schools and higher education facilities in California.

Ralph Lane, Trustee
Joan Lane, Trustee

2313 Levi Strauss Foundation
1155 Battery Street
Floor 7
San Francisco, CA 94111-1230
415-501-6000
Fax: 415-501-7112
http://www.levistrauss.com

Grants are made in four areas: AIDS prevention and care; economic empowerment; youth empowerment; and social justice. Grants are limited to communities where Levi Strauss and Company has plants or customer service centers.

Theresa Fay-Buslillos, Executive Director

2314 Louise M Davies Foundation
580 California Street
Suite 1800
San Francisco, CA 94104-1039

Offers giving in the areas of elementary, secondary and higher education, as well as scholarship funding for California students.

Donald Crawford Jr, Executive Director

2315 Lowell Berry Foundation
3685 Mount Diablo Boulevard
Lafayette, CA 94549
925-284-4427
Fax: 925-284-4332

Assists Christian ministry at local church levels.

Debbie Coombe, Office Manager

2316 Luke B Hancock Foundation
360 Bryant Street
Palo Alto, CA 94301-1409

650-321-5536
Fax: 650-321-0697
E-mail: lhancock@lukebhancock.org
http://www.fdcenter.org/grantmaker/hancock

Provides funding for programs which promote the well being of children and youth. Priority is given to programs which address the needs of youth who are at risk of school failure. Additional funding is provided for early childhood development, music education and homeless families.

Ruth M Ramel, Executive Director

2317 Margaret E Oser Foundation
1911 Lyon Court
Santa Rosa, CA 95403-0974

949-553-4202

Offers grants in the areas of elementary and secondary and higher education, which will benefit women.

Carl Mitchell, Executive Director

2318 Marin Community Foundation
17 E Sir Francis Drake Boulevard
Suite 200
Larkspur, CA 94939-1736

415-461-3333
Fax: 415-464-2555
http://www.marincf.org

Established as a nonprofit public benefit corporation to engage in educational and philanthropic activities in Marin County, California.

2319 Mary A Crocker Trust
233 Post Street
Floor 2
San Francisco, CA 94108-5003

415-982-0138
Fax: 415-982-0141
http://www.mactrust.org

Giving is aimed at precollegiate education, as well as conservation and environmental programs.

Barbaree Jernigan, Executive Director

2320 Maurice Amado Foundation
3940 Laurel Canyon Boulevard
Suite 809
Studio City, CA 91604

818-980-9190
Fax: 818-980-9190
E-mail: pkaizer@mauriceamadofdn.org

Concentrates on the Jewish heritage.

Pam Kaizer, Executive Director

2321 McConnell Foundation
PO Box 492050
Redding, CA 96049-2050

530-226-6200
Fax: 530-226-6210
http://www.mcconnellfoundation.org

Interested in cultural, community and health care related projects.

Ana Diaz, Program Assistant

2322 McKesson Foundation
1 Post Street
San Francisco, CA 94104-5203

415-983-8300
http://www.mckesson.com/foundation.html

Giving is primarily to programs for junior high school students and for emergency services such as food and shelter.

Marcia M Argyris, Executive Director

2323 Milken Family Foundation
C/O Foundations of the Milken Families
1250 4th Street
Floor 6
Santa Monica, CA 90401-1350

310-570-4800
http://www.mff.org

Offers support to the educational community to reward educational innovators, stimulate creativity among students, involve parents and other citizens in the school system, and help disadvantaged youth.

Dr. Julius Lesner, Executive Director

2324 Miranda Lux Foundation
57 Post Street
Suite 510
San Francisco, CA 94104-5020

415-981-2966
http://ww.mirandalux.org

Offers support to promising proposals for pre-school through junior college programs in the fields of pre-vocational and vocational education and training.

Kenneth Blum, Executive Director

2325 Northern California Grantmakers
625 Market Street
15th Floor
San Francisco, CA 94105

415-777-4111
Fax: 415-777-1741
E-mail: ncg@ncg.org

Northern California Grantmakers is an association of foundations, corporate contributions programs and other private grantmakers. Its mission is to jpromote the well being of people and their communities in balance with a healthyenvironment by the thoughtful and creative use of private wealth and resources for the public benefit. To this end, NCG works to enhance the effectiveness of philanthropy, including nonprofit organizations, government, business, media, academia andthe public at large.

Colin Lacon, President

2326 Pacific Telesis Group Corporate Giving Program
130 Kearny Street
San Francisco, CA 94108-4818

415-394-3000

Primary areas of interest include K-12 education reform, education of minorities, women and disabled individuals in the math, science, engineering, education and MBA fields; and specific K-12 issues such as dropouts, informationtechnology and parent involvement.

Jere A Jacobs, Executive Director

2327 Peninsula Community Foundation
1700 S El Camino Real
Suite 300
San Mateo, CA 94402-3049

650-358-9369
Fax: 650-358-9817
http://www.pcf.org

Serving a population from Daly City to Mountain View, the foundations focus is on children and youth, adult services, programs serving homeless families and children, prevention of homelessness and civic and public benefit grants.

Sterling K Speirn, Executive Director

2328 Peter Norton Family Foundation
225 Arizona Avenue
Floor 2
Santa Monica, CA 90401-1243

310-576-7700
Fax: 310-576-7701

Offers giving in the areas of early childhood education, elementary school education, higher education, childrens services and AIDS research.

Anne Etheridge, ED, Executive Director

2329 RCM Capital Management Charitable Fund
4 Embarcadero Center
Suite 2900
San Francisco, CA 94111-4189
415-954-5474
Fax: 415-954-8200

Giving is offered in many areas including youth development, early childhood education and elementary education.

Jami Weinman, Executive Director

2330 Ralph M Parsons Foundation
1055 Wilshire Boulevard
Suite 1701
Los Angeles, CA 90017-5600
213-482-3185
Fax: 213-482-8878
http://www.rmpf.org

Giving is focused on higher and pre-collegiate education, with an emphasis on engineering, technology, and science; social impact programs serving families, children and the elderly; health programs targeting underserved populations;civic and cultural programs.

Wendy G Hoppe, Executive Director

2331 Riordan Foundation
300 S Grand Avenue
Suite 29
Los Angeles, CA 90071-3110
213-229-8402
Fax: 213-229-5061
http://www.riordanfoundation.org

Priorities of the foundation include early childhood literacy, youth programs, leadership programs, job training, direct medical services to young children, and cyclical, targeted mini-grants. When determining levels of support,priority is always given to programs which impact young children.

Nike Irvin, President

2332 Royal Barney Hogan Foundation
PO Box 193809
San Francisco, CA 94119-3809

Offers grants specifically for secondary education in the state of California.

2333 SH Cowell Foundation
120 Montgomery Street
Suite 2570
San Francisco, CA 94104-4303
415-397-0285
Fax: 415-986-6786
http://www.shcowell.org

Offers support for educational programs, including pre-school and primary public educational programs.

JD Erickson, Executive Director
Mary S Metz, President

2334 Sacramento Regional Foundation
555 Capitol Mall
Suite 550
Sacramento, CA 95814-4502
916-492-6510
Fax: 916-492-6515
http://www.sacregfoundation.org

Primary interests of this foundation include the arts, humanities and education.

Stephen F Boutin, President
Janice Gow Pettey, CEO

2335 San Diego Foundation
1420 Kettner Boulevard
Suite 500
San Diego, CA 92101-2434
619-235-2300
Fax: 619-239-1710
E-mail: info@sdfoundation.org
http://www.sdfoundation.org

Offers grants in the areas of social services with emphasis on children and families, education and health for San Diego County.

Robert A Kelly, President/CEO
Rebecca Reichmann, VP Programs

2336 San Francisco Foundation
225 Bush Street
Suite 500
San Francisco, CA 94104-4224
415-733-8500
Fax: 415-477-2783
E-mail: rec@sff.org
http://www.sff.org

Addresses community needs in the areas of community health, education, arts and culture, neighborhood revitalization, and environmental justice. Works to support families and communities to help children and youth succeed in schooland provide opportunities for them to become confident, caring and contributing adults.

Sandra R Hernandez MD, CEO
Sara Ying Kelley, Director Public Affairs

2337 Santa Barbara Foundation
15 E Carrillo Street
Santa Barbara, CA 93101-2780
805-963-1873
Fax: 805-966-2345
http://www.sbfoundation.org

Offers a student aid program with no interest-1/2 loan and 1/2 scholarship. Funding limited to long-term Santa Barbara County residents.

Claudia Armann, Program Officer
Charles O Slosserm, President/CEO

2338 Sega Youth Education & Health Foundation
255 Shoreline Drive
Suite 200
Redwood City, CA 94065-1428

Offers support only to organizations that address and promote youth education and health issues.

Trizia Carpenter, Executive Director

2339 Sidney Stern Memorial Trust
PO Box 893
Pacific Palisades, CA 90272-0893
310-459-2117

Funding offered includes education, community action groups, the arts and the disabled.

2340 Sol & Clara Kest Family Foundation
5150 Overland Avenue
Culver City, CA 90230-4914
213-204-2050

Offers support for Jewish organizations in the areas of education.

Sol Kest, Executive Director

2341 Szekely Family Foundation
3232 Dove Street
San Diego, CA 92103
619-295-2372

Offers giving in the areas of early childhood education, child development, elementary education, higher education, and adult and continuing education.

Deborah Szekely, Executive Director

2342 Thomas & Dorothy Leavey Foundation
10100 Santa Monica Boulevard
Suite 610
Los Angeles, CA 90067

310-551-9936

Focus is placed on college scholarships, medical research, youth groups and programs, and secondary and higher education purposes.

J Thomas McCarthy, Executive Director

2343 Times Mirror Foundation
202 West First Street
Los Angeles, CA 90012

213-237-3945
Fax: 213-237-2116
http://www.timesmirrorfoundation.org

Giving is largely for higher education purposes including liberal arts and business education.

Cassandra Malry, Executive Director

2344 Timken-Sturgis Foundation
7421 Eads Avenue
La Jolla, CA 92037-5037

619-454-2252

Offers support for education in Southern California and Nevada.

Joannie Barrancotto, Executive Director

2345 Toyota USA Foundation
19001 S Western Avenue
Torrance, CA 90501-1106

310-715-7486
Fax: 310-468-7809
E-mail: b_pauli@toyota
http://www.toyota.com/foundation

Supports K-12 education programs, with strong emphasis on math and science.

William Pauli, National Manager

2346 Turst Funds Incorporated
100 Broadway Street
Floor 3
San Francisco, CA 94111-1404

415-434-3323

Offers grants for Catholic Schools, including elementary and secondary education, in the San Francisco Bay Area.

James T Healy, President

2347 Ventura County Community Foundation
Funding & Information Resource Center
1317 Del Norte Road
Suite 150
Camarillo, CA 93010-8504

805-988-0196
Fax: 805-485-5537
http://www.vccf.org

Member of The Foundation Center network, maintaining a collection of private foundation tax returns which provide information on the scope of grants dispensed by that particular foundation.

Hugh J Ralston, President/CEO
Virginia Weber, Program Officer

2348 WM Keck Foundation
550 South Hope Street
Suite 2500
Los Angeles, CA 90071

213-680-3833
Fax: 213-614-0934

E-mail: info@wmkeck.org
http://www.wmkeck.org

The Foundation also gives some consideration, limited to Southern California, for the support of arts and culture, civic and community services, health care and precollegiate education. The foundation's grant-making is focusedprimarily on pioneering research efforts in the areas of science, engineering and medical research, and on higher education, including liberal arts.

Maria Pellegrini, Program Director

2349 Walter & Elise Haas Fund
1 Lombard Street
Suite 305
San Francisco, CA 94111-1130

415-398-4474
Fax: 415-986-4779
http://www.haassr.org

Supports education, arts, environment, human services, humanities and public affairs; is especially in projects which have a wide impact within their respective fields through enhancing public education and access to information,serving a central organizing role, addressing public policy, demonstrating creative approaches toward meeting human needs, or supporting the work of a major institution in the field.

Pamela H David, Executive Director
Peter E Hass Jr, President

2350 Walter S Johnson Foundation
525 Middlefield Road
Suite 160
Menlo Park, CA 94025-3447

650-326-0485
Fax: 650-326-4320
http://www.wsjf.org

Giving is centered on education in public schools and social service agencies concerned with the quality of public education in Northern California and Washoe County, Nevada.

Pancho Chang, Executive Director

2351 Wayne & Gladys Valley Foundation
1939 Harrison Street
Suite 510
Oakland, CA 94612-3535

510-466-6060
Fax: 510-466-6067

Supports four areas: education, medical research, community services and special projects.

Michael D Desler, Executive Director

2352 Weingart Foundation
1055 W 7th Street
Suite 3050
Los Angeles, CA 90017-2509

213-688-7799
Fax: 213-688-1515
http://www.weingartfnd.org

Offers support for community services including a student loan program.

William D Schulte, Chairman & CEO
Fred J Ali, President/Chief Adm. Officer

2353 Wells Fargo Foundation
550 California Street
7th Floor MAC A0112-073
San Francisco, CA 94104

415-396-5830
Fax: 415-975-6260
http://www.wellsfargo.com

Offers support for elementary school education, secondary school education and community development.

Tim Hanlon, Executive Director

2354 Wilbur D May Foundation
C/O Brookhill Corporation
2716 Ocean Park Boulevard
Suite 2011
Santa Monica, CA 90405

Gives to youth organizations and hospitals.

2355 William & Flora Hewlett Foundation
2121 Sand Hill Road
Menlo Park, CA 94025-3448

650-234-4500
Fax: 650-234-4501
http://www.hewlett.org

The Hewlett Foundation concentrates its resources on the performing arts, education, population issues, environmental issues, conflict resolution and family and community development. Grants in the education program, specifically the elementary and secondary education part of it, are limited to K-12 areas in California programs, with primary emphasis on public schools in the San Francisco Bay area. The program favors schools, school districts and universities.

Paul Brest, President

2356 William C Bannerman Foundation
9255 Sunset Boulevard
Suite 400
West Hollywood, CA 90069

310-273-9933
Fax: 310-273-9931

Offers grants in the fields of elementary school, secondary schools, education, human services and youth programs K-12 in Los Angeles County, Adult Education and Vocational Training.

Elliot Ponchick, President

2357 Y&H Soda Foundation
2 Theatre Square
Suite 211
Orinda, CA 94563-3346

925-253-2630
Fax: 925-253-1814
E-mail: jNM@silcom.com

Offers support in the areas of early childhood education, child development, elementary education and vocational and higher education.

Judith Murphy, Executive Director

2358 Zellerbach Family Fund
120 Montgomery Street
Suite 1550
San Francisco, CA 94104-4318

415-421-2629
Fax: 415-421-6713

Provides funds to nonprofit organizations in the San Francisco Bay Area.

Cindy Rambo, Executive Director
Linda Avidan, Program Director

Colorado

2359 Adolph Coors Foundation
4100 East Mississippi Avenue
Suite 1850
Denver, CO 80246

303-388-1636
Fax: 303-388-1684
http://www.adolphcoors.org

Giving is primarily offered for programs with an emphasis on education, human services, youth and health.

Sally W Rippey, Executive Director
Jeanne L Bistranin, Program Officers

2360 Boettcher Foundation
600 17th Street
Suite 2210
Denver, CO 80202-5402

303-534-1937
800-323-9640
http://www.boettcherfoundation.org

Offers grants to educational institutions, with an emphasis on scholarships and fellowships.

Timothy W Schultz, President/Executive Director

2361 Denver Foundation
950 South Cherry Street
Suite 200
Denver, CO 80246

303-300-1790
Fax: 303-300-6547
http://www.denverfounation.org

The Foundation serves as the steward and the administrator of the endowment, charged with investing its earned income in programs that meet the community's growing and changing needs. The Foundation has a solid history of supporting abroad array of community efforts. Grants are awarded to nonprofit organizations that touch nearly every meaningful artistic, cultural, civic, educational, human service and health interest of metro Denver's citizens.

David Miller, President/CEO
Betsy Mangone, VP Philanthropic Services

2362 El Pomar Foundation
10 Lake Circle
Colorado Springs, CO 80906-4201

719-633-7733
800-554-7711
Fax: 719-577-5702
http://www.elpomar.org

Founded in 1937, the philosophy of this foundation is simply to help foster a climate for excellence in Colorado's third sector, the nonprofit community, as well as the foundation's own responsibility to improve the quality of life for all residents of Colorado. The foundation gives grants to the arts and humanities, civic and community, education, health, human services, and youth in community service.

William J Hybl, Executive Director

2363 Gates Foundation
3575 Cherry Creek N Drive
Suite 100
Denver, CO 80209-3247

303-722-1881
Fax: 303-698-9031

The purpose of this foundation is to aid, assist, encourage, initiate, or carry on activities that will promote the health, well-being, security and broad education of all people. Because of a deep concern for and confidence in the future of Colorado, the foundation will invest primarily in institutions and programs that will enhance the quality of life for those who live and work in the state.

Thomas C Stokes, Executive Director

2364 Ruth & Vernon Taylor Foundation
518 17th Street
Suite 1670
Denver, CO 80202

303-893-5284
Fax: 303-893-8263

Offers support for education, the arts, human services and conservation.

Friday A Green, Executive Director

2365 US West Foundation
7800 E Orchard Road
Suite 300
Englewood, CO 80111-2526

303-799-3852

Grants are given in the areas of health and human services, including programs for youth, early childhood, elementary, secondary, higher and other.

Janet Rash, Executive Director

Connecticut

2366 Aetna Foundation
151 Farmington Avenue
Hartford, CT 06156-0001

860-273-0123
Fax: 860-273-4764
http://www.aetna.com/foundation/

Aetna gives grants in various areas that improve the community and its citizens. Certain areas include; children's health, education for at-risk students, and community initiatives. Geographic emphasis is placed on organizations andinitiatives in Aetna's Greater Hartford headquarters communities; organizations in select communities across the country where Aetna has a significant local presence; and national organizations that can influence state, local or federal policies andprograms.

Marilda L Gandara, President
Dave Wilmont, Executive Assistant

2367 Community Foundation of Greater New Haven
70 Audubon Street
New Haven, CT 06510-1248

203-777-2386
Fax: 203-787-6584
http://www.cfgnh.org

Offers a wide variety of giving with an emphasis on social services, youth services, AIDS research and education.

William W Ginsberg, President/CEO
Ronda Maddox, Administrative Assistant

2368 Connecticut Mutual Financial Services
140 Garden Street
Hartford, CT 06154-0200

860-987-6500

Giving is aimed at education, primarily higher education, equal opportunity programs and social services.

Astrida R Olds, Executive Director

2369 Hartford Foundation for Public Giving
85 Gillett Street
Hartford, CT 06105-2693

860-548-1888
Fax: 860-524-8346
E-mail: www.hfpg.org

Offers grants for demonstration programs and capital purposes with emphasis on educational institutions, social services and cultural programs.

Michael R Bangser, Executive Director

2370 Loctite Corporate Contributions Program
Hartford Square North
10 Columbus Boulevard
5th Floor
Hartford, CT 06106-1976

860-571-5100
Fax: 860-571-5430

Offers support in various fields of interest including funding for educational programs for inner city youths in grades K-12.

Kiren Cooley, Corporate Contributions

2371 Louis Calder Foundation
175 Elm Street
New Canaan, CT 06840

203-966-8925
Fax: 203-966-5785
http://www.louiscalderfdn.org

Offers support to organizations who promote education, health and welfare of children and youth in New York City.

Holly Nuechterlein, Program Manager

2372 Sherman Fairchild Foundation
71 Arch Street
Greenwich, CT 06830-6544

203-661-9360
Fax: 203-661-9360

Offers grants in higher education, fine arts and cultural institutions.

Patricia A Lydon, Executive Director

2373 Smart Family Foundation
74 Pin Oak Lane
Wilton, CT 06897-1329

203-834-0400
Fax: 203-834-0412

The foundation is interested in educational projects that focus on primary and secondary school children.

Raymond Smart, Executive Director

2374 Worthington Family Foundation
411 Pequot Avenue
Southport, CT 06490-1386

203-255-9400

Offers grants in the areas of elementary school education and secondary school education in Connecticut.

Worthington Johnson, Executive Director

Delaware

2375 Crystal Trust
Po Box 39
Montchanin, DE 19710-0039

302-651-0533

Grants are awarded for higher and secondary education and social and family services.

Stephen C Doberstein, Executive Director

2376 HW Buckner Charitable Residuary Trust
JP Morgan Services
PO Box 8714
Wilmington, DE 19899-8714

302-633-1900

Focuses giving on educational and cultural organizations in New York, Rhode Island and Massachusetts.

2377 Longwood Foundation
100 W 10th Street
Suite 1109
Wilmington, DE 19801-1694

302-654-2477
Fax: 302-654-2323

Limited grants are offered to educational institutions and cultural programs.

David D Wakefield, Executive Director

District of Columbia

2378 Abe Wouk Foundation
3255 N Street NW
Washington, DC 20007-2845

Offers grants in elementary, secondary education and federated giving programs.

Herman Wouk, Executive Director

2379 Eugene & Agnes E Meyer Foundation
1400 16th Street NW
Suite 360
Washington, DC 20036-2215
202-483-8294
Fax: 202-328-6850
http://www.meyerfoundation.org

Offers grants in the areas of development and housing, education and community services, arts and humanities, law and justice, health and mental health.

Julie L Rogers, President

2380 Foundation Center-District of Columbia
1627 K Street NW
3rd Floor
Washington, DC 20006-1708
202-331-1400
Fax: 202-331-1739
http://www.fdncenter.org/washington/index.jhtml

Member of The Foundation Center network, maintaining a collection of private foundation tax returns which provide information on the scope of grants dispensed to nonprofit organizations by those particular foundations.

2381 Foundation for the National Capitol Region
1201 15th Street NW
Suite 420
Washington, DC 20005
202-955-5890
Fax: 202-955-8084
http://www.cfncr.org

Grants are focused on organization strengthening and regional collaboration. The Foundation wishes to foster collaborations that identify, address, and increase awareness of regional issues, as well as help strengthen the region's existing nonprofit organizations to improve their financial stability. The Foundation welcomes requests from organizations serving the Greater Washington area that are tax-exempt under Section 501(c)(3) of the Internal Revenue Code.

Terry Lee Freeman, President

2382 Gilbert & Jaylee Mead Family Foundation
2700 Virginia Avenue NW #701
Washington, DC 20037-1908
202-338-0208

Offers support for education (K-12), the performing arts and community service programs for Washington, DC, Montgomery County, Maryland, and Geneva, Switzerland.

Linda Smith, Executive Director

2383 Hitachi Foundation
1509 22nd Street NW
Washington, DC 20037-1073
202-457-0588
Fax: 202-296-1098
http://www.hitachi.org

The majority of projects supported by the foundation: promote collaboration across sectors and among institutions, organizations and individuals; reflect multi-or-interdisciplinary perspectives; respect and value diversity of thought, action, and ethnicity. Grants are given in the areas of community development, education, global citizenship and program related investments.

Barbara Dyer, President/CEO

2384 Morris & Gwendolyn Cafritz Foundation
1825 K Street NW
Suite 1400
Washington, DC 20006-1202
202-223-3100
Fax: 202-296-7567
http://www.cafritzfoundation.org

Gives grants to organizations in the metropolitan area, focusing on arts, humanities and scholarships.

Sara Cofrin, Program Assistant

2385 Public Welfare Foundation
1200 U Street NW
Washington, DC 20009-4443
202-965-1800
Fax: 202-265-8851
http://www.publicwelfare.org

Offers grants to grass roots organizations in the US and abroad with emphasis on the environment and education.

Larry Kressley, Executive Director
Teresa Langston, Director Of Programs

2386 Washington Post Company Educational Foundation
1150 15th Street NW
Washington, DC 20071-0002
202-334-6000

Offers support for pre-college and higher education including student scholarships and awards for academic excellence.

Eric Grant, Director Contributions

Florida

2387 Applebaum Foundation
1111 Biscaynees Boulevard
Tower 3, Room 853
North Miami, FL 33181

Offers an emphasis on higher education.

2388 Benedict Foundation for Independent Schools
607 Lantana Lane
Vero Beach, FL 32963-2315

Support is offered primarily for independent secondary schools that have been members of the National Association of Independent Schools for ten consecutive years.

Nancy H Benedict, Executive Director

2389 Chatlos Foundation
PO Box 915048
Longwood, FL 32791-5048
407-862-5077
Fax: 407-862-0708
http://www.chatlos.org

Bible colleges and seminaries, liberal arts colleges, vocation and domestic education, medical education; children, elderly, disabled and learning disabled. The Foundation is non-receptive to primary or secondary education, the arts, medical research, individual churches. No direct scholarship support to individuals.

William J Chatlos, Executive Director

2390 Citibank of Florida Corporate Giving Program
8750 Doral Boulevard
7th Floor
Miami, FL 33718

305-599-5775
Fax: 305-599-5520

Offers support for K-12 education for at-risk children. Funding is also available through the program for housing and community development in the state of Florida.

Susan Yarosz, Executive Director

2391 Dade Community Foundation
200 S Biscayne Boulevard
Suite 505
Miami, FL 33131-2343

305-371-2711
Fax: 305-371-5342
http://www.dadecommunityfoundation.org

Offers support for projects in the fields of education, arts and culture.

Ruth Shack, Executive Director

2392 Innovating Worthy Projects Foundation
Lakeview Corporate Center
6415 Lake Worth Road
Suite 208
Lake Worth, FL 33463-2904

561-439-4445

Offers grants and support for education in the areas of childhood education and elementary education.

Dr. Irving Packer, Executive Director

2393 Jacksonville Public Library
Business, Science & Documents
122 N Ocean Street
Jacksonville, FL 32202-3374

904-630-1994
Fax: 904-630-2431
http://www.neflin.org/members/libraries/jackspub.htm

Member of The Foundation Center network, maintaining a collection of private foundation tax returns which provide information on the scope of grants dispensed by that particular foundation.

Gretchen Mitchell, Business/Science Department

2394 Jessie Ball duPont Fund
One Independent Drive
Suite 1400
Jacksonville, FL 32202-5011

904-353-0890
800-252-3452
Fax: 904-353-3870
E-mail: smagill@dupontfund.org
http://www.dupontfund.org

Grants limited to those institutions to which the donor contributed personally during the five year period ending December 31, 1964. Among the 325 institutions eligible to recieve funds are higher and secondary education intitutions,cultural and historic preservation programs, social services organizations, hospitals, health agencies, churches and church-related organizations and youth agencies.

Dr. Sherry P Magill, President
JoAnn Bennett, Director Administration

2395 Joseph & Rae Gann Charitable Foundation
10185 Collins Avenue
Apartment 317
Bal Harbour, FL 33154-1606

Offers support in the areas of elementary, secondary and theological education.

2396 Orlando Public Library-Orange County Library System
Social Sciences Department
101 E Central Boulivard
Orlando, FL 32801-2471

407-835-7323
Fax: 407-835-7646
E-mail: ajacobe@ocls.lib.fl.us
http://www.ocls.lib.fl.us

Member of The Foundation Center network, maintaining a collection on microfiche of Florida private foundation tax returns which provide information on the scope of grants dispensed by that particular foundation. Other availableresources include directories of foundations, guide to funding, and materials on successful grant acquisition. FC Search Foundation Center CD Rom.

Angela C Jacobe, Head Social Science Dpt

2397 Peter D & Eleanore Kleist Foundation
12734 Kenwood Lane
Suite 89
Fort Myers, FL 33907-5638

Support is given to secondary school education and higher education.

Peter D Kleist, Executive Director

2398 Robert G Friedman Foundation
76 Isla Bahia Drive
Fort Lauderdale, FL 33316-2331

Giving is offered to elementary and high schools, with minor support to indigent individuals and charitable activities.

Robert G Friedman, Executive Director

2399 Southwest Florida Community Foundation
8260 College Parkway
Suite 101
Fort Myers, FL 33919

239-274-5900
Fax: 239-274-5930
E-mail: swflcfo@earthlink.net
http://www.floridacommunity.com

Offers grants and support in the areas of education, higher education, children and youth services and general charitable giving to Lee, Charlotte, Hendry, Glades, and Collier Counties, Florida.

Paul B Flynn, Executive Director
Carol McLaughlin, Program Director

2400 Student Help and Assistance Program to Education
C/O Michael Bienes
141 Bay Colony Drive
Fort Lauderdale, FL 33308-2024

Offers grants and support in the areas of elementary and secondary education, music and dance.

2401 Thomas & Irene Kirbo Charitable Trust
1112 W Adams Street
Suite 1111
Jacksonville, FL 32202

904-354-7212

Favors smaller colleges in Florida and Georgia.

Murray Jenks, Executive Director

2402 Thompson Publishing Group
PO Box 26185
Tampa, FL 33623

800-876-0226
http://www.thompson.com or www.grantsandfunding.com

Assists education administrators and grant seekers in successful fundraising in the public and private sectors.

Joel M Drucker, Executive Director

Georgia

2403 Atlanta-Fulton Public Library
Foundation Collection/Ivan Allen Department
1 Margaret Mitchell Square NW
Atlanta, GA 30303-1089

404-730-1700
Fax: 404-730-1990
http://www.af.public.lib.ga.us

Member of The Foundation Center network, maintaining a collection of private foundation tax returns which provide information on the scope of grants dispensed by that particular foundation.

2404 BellSouth Foundation
C/O BellSouth Corporation
1155 Peachtree Street NE
Sutie 7H08
Atlanta, GA 30309-3600

404-249-2396
Fax: 404-249-5696
http://www.bellsouthfoundation.org

The foundation's purpose is to improve education in the South and to address the problem of the inadequate schooling in the region.

Mary D Boehm, President
Beverly Fleming, Administrative Assistant

2405 Bradley Foundation
PO Box 1408
Savannah, GA 31402-1408

404-571-6040

Focuses on higher educational facilities, elementary and secondary education, human services and federated giving programs.

2406 Callaway Foundation
209 W Broome Street
#790
Lagrange, GA 30240-3101

706-884-7348
Fax: 706-884-0201

Offers giving in the areas of elementary, higher and secondary education, including libraries and community giving.

JT Gresham, Executive Director

2407 Coca-Cola Foundation
Po Box 1734
Atlanta, GA 30301

404-676-2568
Fax: 404-676-8804
http://www.thecoca-colacompany.com

Committed to serving communities through education. The foundation supports programs for early childhood education, elementary and secondary schools, public and private colleges and universities, teacher training, adult learning andglobal education programs, among others.

Donald R Greene, Executive Director

2408 J Bulow Campbell Foundation
50 Hurt Plaza
Suite 312
Atlanta, GA 30303

404-658-9066
Fax: 404-659-4802

The purpose of this foundation is to offer grants and support to privately supported education, human welfare, youth services and the arts in the state of Georgia.

John W Stephenson, Executive Director

2409 JK Gholston Trust
C/O NationsBank of Georgia
PO Box 992
Athens, GA 30603-0992

706-357-6271

Support is offered to elementary school and higher education facilities in the Comer, Georgia area.

Janey M Cooley, Executive Director

2410 John & Mary Franklin Foundation
C/O Bank South N.A.
PO Box 4956
Atlanta, GA 30302

404-521-7397

Offers grants in secondary school/education, higher education and youth services.

Virlyn Moore Sr, Executive Director

2411 John H & Wilhelmina D Harland Charitable
Foundation
2 Piedmont Center NE
Suite 106
Atlanta, GA 30305-1502

404-264-9912
Fax: 404-266-8834

Children and higher education.

2412 Joseph B Whitehead Foundation
50 Hurt Plaza SE
Suite 1200
Atlanta, GA 30303-2916

404-522-6755
Fax: 404-522-7026
http://www.jbwhitehead.org

Offers grants in education, cultural programs, the arts and civic affairs.

Charles H McTier, Executive Director

2413 Lettie Pate Evans Foundation
50 Hurt Plaza SE
Suite 1200
Atlanta, GA 30303-2916

404-522-6755
Fax: 404-522-7026
http://www.lpevans.org

Offers grants in the areas of higher education, and support for educational and cultural institutions.

Charles H McTier, Executive Director
Russell Hardin, Vice President/Secretary

2414 McCamish Foundation
1 Buckhead Loop NE #3060
Atlanta, GA 30326-1528

Offers grants for conservation and educational institutions.

2415 Metropolitan Atlanta Community Foundation
50 Hurt Plaza
Suite 449
Atlanta, GA 30303

404-688-5525
Fax: 404-688-3060
http://www.atlcf.org

This foundation was organized for the administration of funds placed in trust for the purposes of improving education, community development and civic health of the 19-county metropolitan area of Atlanta.

Winsome Hawkins Sr, Executive Director
Alicia Phillip, President

2416 Mill Creek Foundation
PO Box 190
115 North Racetrack Street
Swainsboro, GA 30401-0190

478-237-0101
Fax: 478-237-6187

The foundation's primary interests are educational programs in all levels of study in Emanuel County, Georgia.

James H Morgan, Executive Director

2417 Mills Bee Lane Memorial Foundation
Nations Bank of Georgia
PO Box 9626
Savannah, GA 31412-9626

Offers support in various areas of education, including higher, secondary, and elementary.

2418 Peyton Anderson Foundation
577 Mulberry Street
Suite 105
Macon, GA 31201

478-743-5359
Fax: 912-742-5201

Supports organizations and programs that center on elementary education, higher education, adult education, literacy and basic skills and youth services, in Bibb County, Georgia only.

Juanita T Jordan, Executive Director

2419 Rich Foundation
11 Piedmont Avenue NE
Atlanta, GA 30303

404-262-2266

Funds are allocated to social services, health, the arts and education.

Anne Berg, Executive Director

2420 Robert & Polly Dunn Foundation
PO Box 723194
Atlanta, GA 31139-0194

404-816-2883
Fax: 404-237-2150

Offers support in the areas of child development, education, higher education, and children and youth services.

Karen C Wilbanks, Executive Director

2421 Sapelo Foundation
1712 Ellis Street
2nd Floor
Brunswick, GA 31520

912-265-0520
Fax: 912-265-1888

The Sapelo Foundation's scholarship program, The Richard Reynolds Scholarship Program offers college scholarships only to students who are legal residents of McIntosh County, Georgia.

Phyllis Bowen, Administrative Assistant
Alan McGregor, Executive Director

2422 Tull Charitable Foundation
50 Hurt Plaza SE
Suite 1245
Atlanta, GA 30303-2916

404-659-7079
http://www.tullfoundation.org

Offers support to secondary schools, elementary schools and higher education facilities in the state of Georgia.

Barbara Cleveland, Executive Director

2423 Warren P & Ava F Sewell Foundation
PO Box 645
Bremen, GA 30110-0645

Offers support in elementary school, secondary school education and religion.

Jack Worley, Executive Director

Hawaii

2424 Barbara Cox Anthony Foundation
1132 Bishop Street #120
Honolulu, HI 96813-2807

Offers support to secondary schools, higher education, and human service organizations in Hawaii.

Barner Anthony, Executive Director

2425 Cooke Foundation
1164 Bishop Street
Suite 800
Honolulu, HI 96813

808-566-5524
888-731-3863
Fax: 808-521-6286
E-mail: foundations@hcf-hawaii.org
http://www.hawaiicommunityfoundation.org

The environment, the arts, education and social services are the priority areas for this foundation.

Lisa Schiff, Private Foundation Service
Samuel Cooke, President & Trustee

2426 Harold KL Castle Foundation
146 Hekili Street
Suite 203A
Kailua, HI 96734-2835

808-262-9413
http://www.castlefoundation.org

Grants are given in the area of education, community and cultural/community affairs.

Terrence R George, Executive Director
H Mitchell D'Olier, President

2427 Hawaiian Electric Industries Charitable Foundation
PO Box 730
Honolulu, HI 96808-0730

808-532-5862
http://www.hei.com/heicf/heicf.html

Offers support for education, including higher education, business education, educational associations and secondary schools.

Scott Shirai, Executive Director
Robert F Clark, President

2428 James & Abigail Campbell Foundation
1001 Kamokila Boulevard
Kapolei, HI 96707-2014

808-674-6674
888-322-2232
Fax: 808-674-3111

Offers support in education for schools and educational programs related to literacy or job training in Hawaii.

Theresia McMurdo, Public Relations

2429 Oceanic Cablevision Foundation
200 Akamainui Street
Mililani, HI 96789-3999

808-625-8359

Offers support in a variety of areas with an emphasis on education, especially early childhood and cultural programs.

Kit Beuret, Executive Director

2430 Samuel N & Mary Castle Foundation
733 Bishop Street
Suite 1275
Honolulu, HI 96813-2912

808-522-1101
Fax: 808-522-1103
E-mail: acastle@aloha.net
http://www.fdncenter.org

Funding is offered in the areas of education, human services and the arts for the state of Hawaii.

Annually

Al Castle, Executive Director

2431 University of Hawaii
Hamilton Library
2550 The Mall
Honolulu, HI 96822-2233

808-956-7214
Fax: 808-956-5968
http://www.libweb.hawaii.edu/uhmlib

Member of The Foundation Center network, maintaining a collection of private foundation tax returns which provide information on the scope of grants dispensed by that particular foundation.

Idaho

2432 Boise Public Library
715 S Capitol Boulevard
Boise, ID 83702-7115

208-384-4076
http://www.boisepubliclibrary.org

Member of The Foundation Center network, maintaining a collection of private foundation tax returns which provide information on the scope of grants dispensed by that particular foundation.

2433 Claude R & Ethel B Whittenberger Foundation
PO Box 1073
Caldwell, ID 83606-1073

208-459-0091
E-mail: whittfnd@cableone.net
http://www.whittenberger.org

Offers support for youth and children in higher and secondary education.

William J Rankin, Executive Director

2434 Walter & Leona Dufresne Foundation
1150 W State Street
Boise, ID 83702-5327

Offers support in the areas of secondary school education and higher education.

Royce Chigbrow, Executive Director

Illinois

2435 Ameritech Foundation
30 S Wacker Drive
Floor 34
Chicago, IL 60606-7487

312-750-5223
Fax: 312-207-1098
http://www.ntlf.com

A foundation that offers grants to elementary school/education, secondary school/education and higher education.

Michael E Kuhlin, Executive Director

2436 Carus Corporate Contributions Program
315 5th Street
Peru, IL 61354-2859

815-223-1500

Offers support for higher, secondary, elementary and early childhood education.

Robert J Wilmot, Executive Director

2437 Chauncey & Marion Deering McCormick
Foundation
410 N Michigan Avenue
Suite 590
Chicago, IL 60611-4220

312-644-6720

Preschool education, journalism and the improvement of socio-economic condition of Metropolitan Chicago are the main areas of giving for this foundation.

Charles E Schroeder, Executive Director

2438 Chicago Community Trust
11 East Wacker Drive
Suite 1400
Chicago, IL 60601-1088

312-616-8000
Fax: 312-616-7955
E-mail: sandy@cct.org
http://www.cct.org

A community foundation that offers support for general operating projects and specific programs and projects in areas including child development, education and higher education.

Sandy Chears, Grants Manager
Terry Mazany, President

2439 Coleman Foundation
575 W Madison Street
Suite 4605-Ii
Chicago, IL 60661-2515

312-902-7120
Fax: 312-902-7124
http://www.colemanfoundation.org

A nonprofit, private foundation established in the state of Illinois in 1951. Major areas of support include health, educational, cultural, scientific and social programs. Grants generally focus on organizations within the Midwest andparticularly within the state of Illinois and the Chicago Metropolitan area. No grants are made for programs outside of the United States. Ongoing support is not available, continuing programs must indicate how they will be sustained in the future.

Rosa Janus, Program Manager
Michael W Hennessy, President/CEO

2440 Dellora A & Lester J Norris Foundation
PO Box 4325
Saint Charles, IL 60174-9075

630-377-4111

Education, health and social services are the main concerns of this foundation, with Illinois, Colorado and Florida being their priority.

Eugene W Butler, Executive Director

2441 Dillon Foundation
2804 West Le Fevre Road
Sterling, IL 61081-0537

815-626-9000

Offers support for educational purposes, including higher education and community services.

Peter W Dillon, Executive Director

2442 Dr. Scholl Foundation
1033 Skokie Boulevard
Suite 230
Northbrook, IL 60062

847-559-7430
http://www.drschollfoundation.com

Applications for grants are considered in the following areas: private education at all levels including elementary, secondary schools, colleges and universities and medical and nursing institutions; general charitable organizationsand programs, including grants to hospitals and programs for children, developmentally disabled and senior citizens; civic, cultural, social services, health care, economic and religious activities.

Pamela Scholl, Executive Director

2443 Evanston Public Library
1703 Orrington Avenue
Evanston, IL 60201-3886

847-866-0300
Fax: 847-866-0313
http://www.evanston.lib.il.us

Member of The Foundation Center network, maintaining a collection of private foundation tax returns which provide information on the scope of grants dispensed by that particular foundation.

Neal J Ney, Director

2444 Farny R Wurlitzer Foundation
PO Box 418
Sycamore, IL 60178-0418

Offers support in the areas of education, including programs for minorities, early childhood, elementary and secondary institutions, music education and organizations.

William A Rolfing, Executive Director

2445 Grover Hermann Foundation
1000 Hill Grove
Suite 200
Western Springs, IL 60558-6306

708-246-8331

Focus of giving is on higher education and private schooling activities.

Paul K Rhoads, Executive Director

2446 Joyce Foundation
70 W Madison Street
Suite 2750
Chicago, IL 60602

312-782-2464
Fax: 312-782-4160
E-mail: info@joycefdn.org
http://www.joycefdn.org

Based in Chicago with assets of $1 billion, the Joyce foundation supports efforts to strengthen public policies in ways that improve the quality of life in the Great Lakes region. Last year the foundation made nearly $17 million ingrants to groups working to inprove public education in Chicago, Cleveland, Detroit and Milwaukee.

Ellen Alberding, President

2447 Lloyd A Fry Foundation
120 S Lasalle Street
Suite 1950
Chicago, IL 60603-4204

312-580-0310
Fax: 312-580-0980
http://www.fryfoundation.org

The foundation primarily supports education, higher education, the performing arts, and social service organizations.

Unmi Song, Executive Director

2448 Northern Trust Company Charitable Trust Community Affairs Division
50 S Lasalle Street
Chicago, IL 60603-1006

312-630-6000
http://www.ntrs.com

Offers grants in the areas of community development, education and early childhood education.

Marjorie W Lundy, Executive Director

2449 Palmer Foundation
C/O Jay L. Owen
824 N Western Avenue
Lake Forest, IL 60045-1703

Offers grants in elementary and secondary education, as well as youth services and Protestant churches.

2450 Philip H Corboy Foundation
33 North Dearborn Street
Chicago, IL 60602-2502

312-346-3191
http://www.corboydemetrio.com

Offers grants in the areas of elementary, secondary, law school education and health care.

2451 Polk Brothers Foundation
20 W Kinzie Street
Suite 1100
Chicago, IL 60610-4600

312-527-4684
Fax: 312-527-4681
http://www.polkbrosfdn.org

Offers grants for new or ongoing programs to organizations whose work is based in the areas of education, social services and health care.

Nikki W Stein, Executive Director
Shiela A Robinson, Grants Administrator

2452 Prince Charitable Trust
303 West Madison Street
Suite 1900
Chicago, IL 60606-7407

312-419-8700
Fax: 312-419-8558
http://www.fdncenter.org/grantmaker/prince/chicago.html

Offers support for cultural programs, public school programming and social service organizations.

Benna B Wilde, Managing Director
Sharon L Robison, Grants Manager

2453 Regenstein Foundation
8600 W Bryn Mawr Avenue
Suite 705N
Chicago, IL 60631-3579

773-693-6464
Fax: 773-693-2480

Offers grants for educational and general charitable institutions within the metropolitan Chicago area and the state of Illinois.

Joseph Regenstein Jr, Executive Director

2454 Richard H Driehaus Foundation
77 W Wacker Drive
Chicago, IL 60601-1604

312-641-5772
Fax: 312-641-5736

Offers support in elementary, secondary and higher education in the state of Illinois.

Susan M Levy, Executive Director

2455 Robert R McCormick Tribune Foundation
435 N Michigan Avenue
Suite 770
Chicago, IL 60611-4066

312-222-3512
Fax: 312-222-3523
http://www.rrmtf.org

Offers contributions for private higher education and rehabilitation services.

Nicholas Goodban, Senior VP/Philanthropy
Richard A Behrenhausen, President/CEO

2456 Sears-Roebuck Foundation
Sears Tower
Department 903-BSC 51-02
Chicago, IL 60684

312-875-8337

The foundation focuses its giving primarily on projects that address education and volunteerism.

Paula A Banke, Executive Director

2457 Spencer Foundation
875 North Michigan Avenue
Suite 3930
Chicago, IL 60611-1803

312-337-7000
Fax: 312-337-0282
http://www.spencer.org

Supports research aimed at the practice of understanding and expanding knowledge in the area of education.

Michael McPherson, President

2458 Sulzer Family Foundation
1940 W Irving Park Road
Chicago, IL 60613-2437

312-321-4700

Offers giving for education, including higher, secondary, elementary and adult education in the areas of Chicago, Illinois.

John J Hoellen, Executive Director

2459 United Airlines Foundation
PO Box 66919
Chicago, IL 60666-0919

847-952-5714

Offers a wide variety of support programs with an emphasis on education and educational reform.

Eileen Younglove, Executive Director

2460 Valenti Charitable Foundation
Valenti Builders
225 Northfield Road
Northfield, IL 60093-3311

847-446-2200
Fax: 847-446-2610

Offers support in elementary education, secondary school education, higher education and children and youth services.

Valenti Sr Trustee, Executive Director

Indiana

2461 Allen County Public Library
Po Box 2270
Fort Wayne, IN 46802-3699

260-421-1200
Fax: 260-421-1386
http://www.acpl.lib.in.us

Member of The Foundation Center network, maintaining a collection of private foundation tax returns which provide information on the scope of grants dispensed by that particular foundation.

2462 Arvin Foundation
1 Noblitt Plaza #3000
Columbus, IN 47201-6079

812-379-3207
Fax: 812-379-3688

Giving is offered primarily to primary, secondary and higher education and technical training.

E Fred Meyer, Executive Director

2463 Clowes Fund
320 N Meridian Street Suite 316
The Chamber of Commerce Building
Indianapolis, IN 46204-1722

800-943-7209
Fax: 800-943-7286
http://www.clowesfund.org

Offers giving for higher and secondary education; the performing arts; marine biology and social service organizations.

Elizabeth Casselman, Executive Director

2464 Dekko Foundation
PO Box 548
Kendallville, IN 46755-0548

260-347-1278
Fax: 260-347-7103

Offers support for all levels of education and human service organizations.

Linda Speakman, Executive Director

2465 Eli Lilly & Company Corporate Contribution Program
Lilly Corporate Center D.C. 1627
Indianapolis, IN 46285

317-276-2000

Offers support in the areas of secondary school/education, higher education and health care programs.

Thomas King, President

2466 Foellinger Foundation
520 E Berry Street
Fort Wayne, IN 46802-2002

260-422-2900
Fax: 260-422-9436
http://www.foellinger.org

Giving is aimed at higher education and other secondary and elementary projects, community programs and social service organizations.

Harry V Owen, Executive Director

2467 Indianapolis Foundation
615 N Alabama Street
Suite 119
Indianapolis, IN 46204-1498

317-634-2423
Fax: 317-684-0943
http://www.indyfund.org

Offers support in the areas of education and neighborhood services.

Kenneth Gladish, Executive Director

2468 John W Anderson Foundation
402 Wall Street
Valparaiso, IN 46383-2562

219-462-4611
Fax: 219-531-8954

Offers grants in the areas of higher education, youth programs, human services, and arts and humanities. Grants are limited primarily to Northwest Indian organizations.

William Vinovich, Vice Chairman/Trustee

2469 Lilly Endowment
2801 N Meridian Street
Indianapolis, IN 46208-4712

317-924-5471
Fax: 317-926-4431
http://www.lillyendowment.org

Supports the causes of religion, education and community development. Although the Endowment supports efforts of national significance, especially in the field of religion, it is primarily committed to its hometown, Indianapolis, and home state, Indiana.

Sue Ellen Walker, Communications Associate

2470 Moore Foundation
9100 Keystone Xing
Suite 390
Indianapolis, IN 46240-2158

317-848-2013
Fax: 317-571-0744

Offers support in elementary school and secondary school education, higher education, business school education and youth services in Indiana.

Eileen C Ryan, Executive Director

2471 W Brooks Fortune Foundation
7933 Beaumont Green W Drive
Indianapolis, IN 46250-1652

317-842-1303

Support is limited to education-related programs in Indiana.

William Brooks Fortune, Executive Director

Iowa

2472 Cedar Rapids Public Library
Funding Information Center
500 1st Street SE
Cedar Rapids, IA 52401-2095

319-398-5123
Fax: 319-398-0476
http://www.crlibrary.org

Member of The Foundation Center network, maintaining a collection of private foundation tax returns which provide information on the scope of grants dispensed by that particular foundation.

Tamara Glise, Public Services Manager
Eileen C Ryan, Executive Director

2473 RJ McElroy Trust
425 Cedar Street
Suite 312
Waterloo, IA 50701

319-287-9102
312
Fax: 319-287-9105
http://www.mcelroytrust.org

The trust funds grants to educational youth programs in the northeast quarter of Iowa. The trust guidelines do not include grants to individuals.

Linda L Klinger, Executive Director

Kansas

2474 Mary Jo Williams Charitable Trust
PO Box 439
Garden City, KS 67846-0439

Offers support in the areas of early childhood education, higher education, and children and youth services.

Michael E Collins, Executive Director

2475 Sprint Foundation
2330 Shawnee Mission Parkway
Westwood, KS 66205-2090

913-624-3343

Offers grants in a variety of areas with an emphasis on education, including business education, secondary education and higher education.

Don G Forsythe, Executive Director

2476 Wichita Public Library
223 S Main Street
Wichita, KS 67202-3795

316-261-8500
Fax: 316-262-4540
http://www.wichita.lib.ks.us

Member of The Foundation Center network, maintaining a collection of private foundation tax returns which provide information on the scope of grants dispensed by that particular foundation.

Kentucky

2477 Ashland Incorporated Foundation
50 E River Center Boulevard
Covington, KY 41012

859-815-3630
Fax: 859-815-4496
http://www.ashland.com

Offers support to educational organizations, colleges and universities, as well as giving an employee matching gift program to higher education and community funding.

James O'Brien, CEO

2478 Gheens Foundation
One Riverfront Plaza
Suite 705
Louisville, KY 40202

502-584-4650
Fax: 502-584-4652

The foundation's support is aimed at higher and secondary education, ongoing teacher education, and social service agencies.

James N Davis, Executive Director

2479 James Graham Brown Foundation
4350 Brownsboro Road
Suite 200
Louisville, KY 40207

502-896-2440
Fax: 502-896-1774
http://www.jgbf.org

Offers grants in the areas of higher education and social services.

Mason Rummel, Executive Director
Dodie L McKenzie, Program Officer

2480 Louisville Free Public Library
301 York Street
Louisville, KY 40203-2257

502-574-1611
Fax: 502-574-1657
http://www.lfpl.org

Member of The Foundation Center network, maintaining a collection of private foundation tax returns which provide information on the scope of grants dispensed by that particular foundation.

2481 Margaret Hall Foundation
291 S Ashland Avenue
Lexington, KY 40502-1727

859-269-2236
http://www.margarethallfoundation.org

Awards grants and scholarships to private, nonprofit secondary schools for innovative programming.

Helen R Burg, Executive Director

2482 VV Cooke Foundation Corporation
220 Mount Mercy Drive
Pewee Valley, KY 40056

502-241-0303

Offers support in education and youth services with an emphasis on Baptist church and school support.

John B Gray, Executive Director

Louisiana

2483 Baton Rouge Area Foundation
406 N 4th Street
Baton Rouge, LA 70802

225-387-6126
877-387-6126
Fax: 225-387-6153

Offers grants in the area of elementary and secondary education and health.

John G Davies, President

2484 Booth-Bricker Fund
826 Union Street
Suite 300
New Orleans, LA 70112-1421

504-581-2430
Fax: 504-566-4785

Does not have a formal grant procedure or grant application form; nor does it publish an annual report. The Booth-Bricker Fund makes contributions for the purposes of promoting, developing and fostering religious, charitable,scientific, literary or educational programs, primarily in the state of Louisiana. It does not make contributions to individuals.

Gray S Parker, Chairman

2485 East Baton Rouge Parish Library
Centroplex Branch Grants Collection
7711 Goodwood Boulevard
Baton Rouge, LA 70806

225-231-3750

Member of The Foundation Center network, maintaining a collection of private foundation tax returns which provide information on the scope of grants dispensed by that particular foundation.

2486 Fred B & Ruth B Zigler Foundation
PO Box 986
Zigler Building
Jennings, LA 70546-0986

337-824-2413
Fax: 337-824-2414
http://www.ziglerfoundation.org

Offers support to higher, secondary and primary education.

Julie G Berry, President

2487 New Orleans Public Library
Business & Science Division
219 Loyola Avenue
New Orleans, LA 70112-2044

504-529-7323
Fax: 504-596-2609

Member of The Foundation Center network, maintaining a collection of private foundation tax returns which provide information on the scope of grants dispensed by that particular foundation.

2488 Shreve Memorial Library
424 Texas Street
Shreveport, LA 71101-5452

318-226-5897
Fax: 318-226-4780
http://www.shreve-lib.org

Member of The Foundation Center network, maintaining a collection of private Louisiana foundation tax returns which provide information on the scope of grants dispensed by that particular foundation.

Carlos Colon, Reference Supervisor

Maine

2489 Clarence E Mulford Trust
PO Box 290
Fryeburg, ME 04037-0290

207-935-2061
Fax: 207-935-3939

Offers grants to charitable, educational and scientific organizations for the purpose of improving education.

David R Hastings II, Executive Director

2490 Harold Alfond Trust
C/O Dexter Shoe Company
PO Box 353
Dexter, ME 04930-0353

Grants are offered to secondary and higher education in Maine and Maryland.

Keith Burden, Executive Director

Maryland

2491 Abell Foundation
111 S Calvert Street
Suite 2300
Baltimore, MD 21202-6182

410-547-1300
Fax: 410-539-6579
http://www.abell.org

The foundation supports education with an emphasis on public education, including early childhood and elementary, research, and minority education.

Robert C Embry Jr, Executive Director

2492 Aegon USA
1111 N Charles Street
Baltimore, MD 21201-5505

410-576-4571
Fax: 410-347-8685
http://www.aegonins.com

Offers grants in elementary school, secondary school, higher education and medical school education.

Larry G Brown, Executive Director

2493 Clarence Manger & Audrey Cordero Plitt Trust
C/O First National Bank of Maryland
PO Box 1596
Baltimore, MD 21203-1596

410-566-0914

Offers grants to educational institutions for student loans and scholarships.

Mary M Kirgan, Executive Director

2494 Clark-Winchcole Foundation
Air Rights Building
3 Bethesda Metro Center
Suite 550
Bethesda, MD 20814

301-654-3607
Fax: 301-654-3140

Offers grants in the areas of higher education and social service agencies.

Laura E Philips, Executive Director

2495 Commonwealth Foundation
9737 Colesville Road
Suite 800
Silver Spring, MD 20910

301-495-4400

Offers grants in the areas of early childhood education, child development, elementary schools, secondary schools and youth services.

Barbara Bainum, Executive Director

2496 Dresher Foundation
4940 Campbell Boulevard
Suite 110
Baltimore, MD 21236

410-933-0384
http://www.jdgraphicdesign.com/dresher/dresherfoundation/

Offers giving in the areas of elementary school, early childhood education, meals on wheels, and food distribution.

2497 Edward E Ford Foundation
1122 Kenilworth Drive
Suite 105
Towson, MD 21204

410-823-2201
Fax: 410-823-2203
http://www.eeford.org

Offers giving to secondary schools and private education in the US and its protectorates.

Robert Hallett, Executive Director

2498 Enoch Pratt Free Library
Social Science & History Department
400 Cathedral Street
Baltimore, MD 21201-4484

301-396-5430
http://www.pratt.lib.md.us

Member of The Foundation Center network, maintaining a collection of private foundation tax returns which provide information on the scope of grants dispensed by that particular foundation.

2499 France-Merrick Foundation
The Exchange
1122 Kenilworth Drive
Suite 118
Baltimore, MD 21204-2139

410-832-5700
Fax: 410-832-5704

Offers grants in the areas of public education, private and higher education, health, social services and cultural activities.

Frederick W Lafferty, Executive Director

2500 Grayce B Kerr Fund
117 Bay Street
Easton, MD 21601-2769

410-822-6652
Fax: 410-822-4546
E-mail: gbkf@bluecrab.org

The major area of interest to the fund is education, including higher, elementary and early childhood education for the state of Maryland with focus on the Eastern Shore Counties.

Margaret van den Berg, Administrative Assistant

2501 Henry & Ruth Blaustein Rosenberg Foundation
Blaustein Building
10 East Baltimore Street
Suite 1111
Baltimore, MD 21202

410-347-7201
Fax: 410-347-7210
http://www.blaufund.org

Offers grants in the areas of secondary and higher education.

Betsy F Ringel, Executive Director
Henry A Rosenberg Jr, President

2502 James M Johnston Trust for Charitable and Educational Purposes
2 Wisconsin Circle
Suite 600
Chevy Chase, MD 20815-7003

301-907-0135

Grants are given to higher and secondary educational institutions located in Washington, DC and North Carolina.

Julie Sanders, Executive Director

2503 John W Kluge Foundation
6325 Woodside Court
Columbia, MD 21046-1017

Offers grants in higher education and secondary education.

2504 Marion I & Henry J Knott Foundation
3904 Hickory Avenue
Baltimore, MD 21211-1834

410-235-7068
Fax: 410-889-2577
http://www.knottfoundation.org

Grantmaking limited to private nonsectarian schools and Catholic schools geographically located within the Archdiocese of Baltimore, Maryland.

Greg Cantori, Executive Director

2505 Robert G & Anne M Merrick Foundation
The Exchange
1122 Kenilworth Drive
Suite 118
Baltimore, MD 21204-2142

410-832-5700
Fax: 410-832-5704

Offers grants for public education, higher education and social services.

Frederick W Lafferty, Executive Director

Massachusetts

2506 Associated Grantmakers of Massachusetts
55 Court Street
Suite 520
Boston, MA 02108-4304

617-426-2606
Fax: 617-426-2849
http://www.agmconnect.org

Member of The Foundation Center network, maintaining a collection of private foundation tax returns which provide information on the scope of grants dispensed by that particular foundation.

Ron Ancrum, President
Martha Moore, Director Center Philanthropy

2507 Boston Foundation
75 Arlington Street
10th Floor
Boston, MA 02108-4407
617-338-1700
Fax: 617-338-1604
http://www.tbf.org

Supports local educational, social and housing programs and institutions.

Paul Grogan, President

2508 Boston Globe Foundation II
135 Morrissey Boulevard
Boston, MA 02107
617-929-2895
Fax: 617-929-7889
http://www.bostonglobe.com/community/foundation/partner.stm

The foundation's highest priority is community based agencies which understand, represent and are part of the following populations; children and youth with disabilities, children and youth with AIDS, refugees, low-birth weightbabies, pregnant and nursing mothers and incarcerated youth.

Suzanne W Maas, Executive Director
Leah P Bailey

2509 Boston Public Library
Social Sciences Reference
700 Boylston Street
Boston, MA 02116-2813
617-536-5400
http://www.bpl.org

Member of The Foundation Center network, maintaining a collection of private foundation tax returns which provide information on the scope of grants dispensed by that particular foundation.

Bernard Margolis, President

2510 Dean Foundation for Little Children
C/O Boston Safe Deposit & Trust Company
1 Boston Pl
Boston, MA 02108-4407

Giving is centered on little children age twelve and under for the care and relief of destitute children. Provides support for preschools, day care, summer camps and other programs.

Nancy Criscitiello, Executive Director

2511 Hyams Foundation
175 Federal Street
Floor 14
Boston, MA 02110-2210
617-426-5600
Fax: 617-426-5696
http://www.hyamsfoundation.org

The foundation seeks to promote understanding and appreciation of diversity, including race, ethnicity, gender, sexual orientation, age, physical ability, class and religion. The foundation's primary objective is to meet the needs oflow-income and other underserved populations, striving to address the causes of those needs, whenever possible. Foundation supports low-income communities in their efforts to identify their own problems, solve these problems and improve people'slives.

Elizabeth B Smith, Executive Director

2512 Irene E & George A Davis Foundation
C/O Ann T Keiser
1 Monarch Place
Suite 1450
Springfield, MA 01144-1450
413-734-8336
Fax: 413-734-7845
http://www.davisfdn.org

Education and social service organizations and programs in Western Massachusetts are the primary concern of this foundation.

Mary E Walachy, Executive Director

2513 James G Martin Memorial Trust
122 Pond Street
Jamaica Plain, MA 02130-2714

Giving is centered on elementary education and higher education in Massachusetts.

Ms Martin, Executive Director

2514 Jessie B Cox Charitable Trust
Grants Management Association
60 State Street
Boston, MA 02109-1899
617-227-7940
Fax: 617-227-0781
http://www.hemenwaybarnes.com/selectsrv/jbcox/cox.html

This trust makes grants for projects which will address important social issues in the trust's fields of interest and for which adequate funding from other sources cannot be obtained. The trust funds projects in New England in theareas of health, education and the environment. The trustees look to support special projects which will assist the applicants to achieve their long-range organizational goals.

Michaelle Larkins, Executive Director
Susan M Fish, Grants Administrator

2515 LG Balfour Foundation
Fleet Bank of Massachusetts
75 State Street
Boston, MA 02109-1775
617-346-4000

Offers support for scholarships and innovative projects designed to eliminate barriers and improve access to education for all potentially qualified students.

Kerry Herliney, Executive Director

2516 Little Family Foundation
33 Broad Street
Suite 10
Boston, MA 02109-4216
617-723-6771
Fax: 617-723-7107

Offers scholarships at various business schools and Junior Achievement programs in secondary schools.

Arthur D Little, Executive Director

2517 Rogers Family Foundation
29 Water Street
Newburyport, MA 01950-4501
978-465-6100
Fax: 978-685-1588

Offers support in the areas of secondary and higher education in the Lawrence, Massachusetts area.

Stephen Rogers, President

2518 State Street Foundation
225 Franklin Street
12th Floor
Boston, MA 02110
617-664-1937
http://www.statestreet.com

Offers grants to organizations that help improve the quality of life in the greater Boston area. Interest includes human services, public and secondary education, vocational education, and arts and culture programs.

Madison Thompson, Executive Director

2519 Sudbury Foundation
278 Old Sudbury Road
Sudbury, MA 01776-1843

> 978-443-0849
> Fax: 978-579-9536
> http://www.sudburyfoundation.org

Offers college scholarships to local high school seniors who meet eligibility criteria.

Fredericka Tanner, Executive Director
Marilyn Martino, Program Officer

2520 Trustees of the Ayer Home
PO Box 1865
Lowell, MA 01853-1865

> 978-452-5914
> Fax: 978-452-5914

Funding (greater Lowell, MA only) educational programs (RLF, SMARTS). Primary interests are women and children.

D Donahue, Assistant Treasurer

2521 Weld Foundation
Peter Loring/Janice Palumbo
Loring, Wolcott & Coolidge
30 Congress Street
Boston, MA 02110-2409

> 617-523-6531
> Fax: 617-523-6535

Grants are offered in the areas of elementary, secondary and higher education in Massachusetts.

2522 Western Massachusetts Funding Resource Center
65 Elliot Street
Springfield, MA 01105-1713

> 413-732-3175
> Fax: 413-452-0618
> http://www.diospringfield.org/wmfrc.html

Member of The Foundation Center network, maintaining a collection of private foundation tax returns which provide information on the scope of grants dispensed by that particular foundation.

Kathleen Dowd, Director
Jean Los, Administrative Assistant

2523 William E Schrafft & Bertha E Schrafft
Charitable Trust
1 Financial Center
Floor 26
Boston, MA 02111-2621

> 617-457-7327

Giving is primarily allocated to educational programs in the Boston metropolitan area.

2524 Woodstock Corporation
Woodstock Corporation
27 School Street
Suite 200
Boston, MA 02108-2301

> 617-227-0600
> Fax: 617-523-0229

Offers support in the area of secondary school education in the state of Massachusetts.

2525 Worcester Public Library
Grants Resource Center
Salem Square
Worcester, MA 01608

> 508-799-1655
> Fax: 508-799-1652
> http://www.worcpublib.org

Member of The Foundation Center network, maintaining a collection of private foundation tax returns which provide information on the scope of grants dispensed by that particular foundation.

J Peck, Director Grants Resource

Michigan

2526 Alex & Marie Manoogian Foundation
21001 Van Born Road
Taylor, MI 48180-1340

> 313-274-7400
> Fax: 313-792-6657

Supports higher and secondary education, cultural programs and human service organizations.

Alex Manoogian, Executive Director

2527 Charles Stewart Mott Foundation
Office of Proposal Entry
503 S Saginaw Street
Suite 1200
Flint, MI 48502-1851

> 810-238-5651
> 800-645-1766
> Fax: 810-237-4857
> E-mail: infocenter@mott.org
> http://www.mott.org

Grants are given to nonprofit organizations with an emphasis on programs of volunteerism, at-risk youth, environmental protection, economic development and education.

2528 Chrysler Corporate Giving Program
12000 Chrysler Drive
Detroit, MI 48288-0001

> 810-576-5741

Offers support for education, especially secondary education and leadership development.

Lynn A Feldhouse, Executive Director

2529 Community Foundation for Southeastern
Michigan
333 W Fort Street
Suite 2010
Detroit, MI 48226-3134

> 313-961-6675
> Fax: 313-961-2886
> http://www.cfsem.org

Supports projects in the areas of education, culture and social services.

Mariam C Noland, President

2530 Community Foundation of Greater Flint
502 Church Street
Flint, MI 48502-2013

> 810-767-8270
> Fax: 810-767-0496
> E-mail: cfgf@cfgf.org
> http://www.cfgf.org

A community foundation that makes grants to benefit residents of Genessee County, Michigan. Areas of interest include: arts, education, environment, community services and health and social services.

Kathi Horton, President
Evan M Albert, VP Program

2531 Cronin Foundation
203 E Michigan Avenue
Marshall, MI 49068-1545

> 616-781-9851
> Fax: 616-781-2070

Offers support to expand educational, social and cultural needs of the community within the Marshall, Michigan school district.

Joseph E Schroeder, Executive Director

2532 Detroit Edison Foundation
2000 2nd Avenue
Room 1046
Detroit, MI 48226-1279

313-235-9271
Fax: 313-237-9271
http://www.my.dteenergy.com

Offers support for all levels of education, and local community social services and cultural organizations in Southeast Michigan.

Katharine W Hunt, Executive Director

2533 Ford Motor Company Fund
One American Road
PO Box 1899
Dearborn, MI 48126-2798

888-313-0102
Fax: 313-337-6680
http://www.ford.com

Ford Motor Company Fund continues the legacy of Henry Ford's commitment to innovative education at all levels. We remain dedicated to creating and enriching educational opportunities, especially in the areas of science, engineering, math and business, while promoting diversity in education.

Sandra E Ulsh, President
Jim Graham, Manager Education Programs

2534 Frey Foundation
40 Pearl Street NW
Suite 1100
Grand Rapids, MI 49503-3023

616-451-0303
Fax: 616-451-8481
http://www.freyfdn.org

Awards grants and supports the needs of children in their early years, support for environmental education and protection of our natural resources.

Milton W Rohwer, President
Teresa J Crawford, Grants Manager

2535 General Motors Foundation
13-145 General Motors Building
Detroit, MI 48202

313-556-4260
http://www.gm.com/company/gmability/philanthropy

Offers support for higher education, cultural programs and civic affairs.

Ronald L Theis, Executive Director

2536 Grand Rapids Foundation
209-C Water Building
161 Ottawa Avenue NW
Grand Rapids, MI 49503

616-454-1751
Fax: 616-454-6455
E-mail: mrapp@grfoundation.org
http://www.grfoundation.org

A community foundation established in 1922. The foundation actively serves the people of Kent County by administering funds it receives and by making philanthropic grants to non-profit organizations in response to community needs. Various educational scholarships are offered on the basis of a competitive process which considers academic achievement, extracurricular activities, a statement of one's own personal aspirations and educational goals, and financial need. Kent County Residency required.

Ruth Bishop, Program Associate-Education
Diana Sieger, President

2537 Harry A & Margaret D Towsley Foundation
3055 Plymouth Road
Suite 200
Ann Arbor, MI 48105-3208

312-662-6777

Areas of support include pre-school education, social services, and continuing education.

Margaret Ann Riecker, Executive Director

2538 Henry Ford Centennial Library
Adult Services
16301 Michigan Avenue
Dearborn, MI 48126-2792

313-943-2330
Fax: 313-943-3063
http://www.dearborn.lib.mi.us/aboutus/adult.htm

Member of The Foundation Center network, maintaining a collection of private foundation tax returns which provide information on the scope of grants dispensed by that particular foundation.

2539 Herbert H & Grace A Dow Foundation
1018 W Main Street
Midland, MI 48640

989-631-3699
Fax: 989-631-0675
http://www.hhdowfdn.org

Limited to organizations within Michigan. Has charter goals to improve the educational, religious, economic and cultural lives of Michigan's people.

Margaret Ann Riescker, President
Elysa M Rogers, Assistant VP

2540 Herrick Foundation
150 W Jefferson Avenue
Suite 2500
Detroit, MI 48226-4415

313-496-7585

Offers grants to colleges and universities, health agencies and social service organizations.

Dolores de Galleford, Executive Director

2541 Kresge Foundation
2701 Troy Center Drive
Suite 150
Troy, MI 48084

248-643-9630
Fax: 313-643-0588
http://www.kresge.org

Giving is aimed at areas of interest including arts and humanities, social services and public policy.

John E Marshall III, Executive Director
Sandra McAlister Ambrozy, Senior Program Officer

2542 Malpass Foundation
PO Box 1206
East Jordan, MI 49727-1206

Offers giving in the areas of education and community development.

William J Lorne, Executive Director

2543 McGregor Fund
333 W Fort Street
Suite 2090
Detroit, MI 48226-3134

313-963-3495
Fax: 313-963-3512
http://www.mcgregorfund.org

Social services, health and education grants awarded to organizations located in Ohio, primarily the Detroit area.

C David Campbell, President
Kate Levin Markel, Program Officer

2544 Michigan State University Libraries
Social Sciences/Humanities
Main Library
East Lansing, MI 48824

517-353-8700
Fax: 517-432-3532
http://www.lib.msu.edu

Member of The Foundation Center network, maintaining a collection of private foundation tax returns which provide information on the scope of grants dispensed by that particular foundation.

2545 Richard & Helen DeVos Foundation
190 Muncie NW
Suite 500
Grand Rapids, MI 49503

616-454-4114
Fax: 616-454-4654

Strong geographical preference to Western Michigan. Funding includes Christian education, cultural, community, education (not an individual basis) and government services. Donations are also made on a national level to organizationsbased in Washington, DC.

Stephanie Roy, Executive Director

2546 Rollin M Gerstacker Foundation
PO Box 1945
Midland, MI 48641-1945

989-631-6097
Fax: 517-832-8842
http://www.tamu.edu/baum/gerstack.html

Primary purpose of this foundation is to carry on, indefinitely, financial aid to charities concentrated in the states of Michigan and Ohio. Grants are given in the areas of community support, schools, education, social services,music and the arts, youth activities, health care and research, churches and other areas.

Carl A Gerstacker, Executive Director

2547 Steelcase Foundation
PO Box 1967, CH-4E
Grand Rapids, MI 49501-1967

616-246-4695
Fax: 616-475-2200
E-mail: sbroman@steelcse.com
http://www.steelcase.com

Offers support for human services and education, to improve the quality of life for children, the elderly and the disabled in the areas where there are manufacturing plants.

Susan Broman, Executive Director

2548 Wayne State University
Purdy-Kresge Library
5265 Cass Avenue
Detroit, MI 48202-3930

313-577-6424
http://www.lib.wayne.edu

Member of The Foundation Center network, maintaining a collection of private foundation tax returns which provide information on the scope of grants dispensed by that particular foundation.

2549 Whirlpool Foundation
2000 N M 63
Benton Harbor, MI 49022-2632

269-923-5580
Fax: 269-925-0154

Giving centers on learning, cultural diversity, adult education, and scholarships for children of corporation employees.

Ddaniel Hopp, President & Chairman
Barbara Hall, Program Officer

Minnesota

2550 Andersen Foundation
Andersen Corporation
100 4th Avenue N
Bayport, MN 55003-1096

651-264-5150
Fax: 651-264-5537

Grants are given in the areas of higher education, health, youth and the arts in Minnesota.

2551 Bush Foundation
E-900 First National Bank Building
332 Minnesota Street
Saint Paul, MN 55101-1314

651-227-0891
Fax: 651-297-6485
http://www.bushfoundation.org

The foundation is predominantly a regional grantmaking foundation, with broad interests in education, human services, health, arts and humanities and in the development of leadership.

Anita M Pampusch, President
John Archabal, Senior Program Officer

2552 Cargill Foundation
PO Box 9300
Minneapolis, MN 55440-9300

952-742-4311
Fax: 612-742-7224
http://www.cargill.com

Offers grants in the areas of education, health, human service organizations, arts and cultural programs and social service agencies.

Audrey Tulberg, Executive Director

2553 Charles & Ellora Alliss Educational Foundation
332 Minnesota Street #64704
Saint Paul, MN 55101-1314

651-244-4581
Fax: 651-244-0860

The foundation is organized exclusively for support of the education of young people, up to and including the period of postgraduate study. As a matter of policy, the foundation generally has limited its program to universities andcolleges located in Minnesota. Grants are made to such institutions in support of undergraduate scholarship programs administered by their student aid offices. The foundation makes no direct grants to individuals.

John Bultena, Executive Director

2554 Duluth Public Library
520 W Superior Street
Duluth, MN 55802-1578

218-723-3802
Fax: 218-723-3815
http://www.duluth.lib.mn.us

Member of The Foundation Center network, maintaining a collection of private foundation tax returns which provide information on the scope of grants dispensed by that particular foundation.

Elizabeth Kelly, Library Director

2555 FR Bigelow Foundation
600 Fifth Street
Center 55th Street East
St. Paul, MN 55101-1797

651-224-5463
Fax: 651-224-8123
http://www.frbigelow.org

Offers support in early childhood education, elementary and secondary education, higher and adult education and human services.

Jon A Theobald, Chair
Carleen K Rhodes, Secretary

2556 First Bank System Foundation
PO Box 522
Minneapolis, MN 55480-0522

612-973-2440

Offers support for public elementary and secondary education, arts and cultural programs.

Cheryl L Rantala, Executive Director

2557 Hiawatha Education Foundation
360 Vila Street
Winona, MN 55987-1500

507-453-5550

Giving is centered on Catholic high schools and colleges, as well as awarding scholarships to college-bound high school graduates.

Robert Kierlin, Executive Director

2558 IA O'Shaughnessy Foundation
First Trust
PO Box 64704
Saint Paul, MN 55164-0704

612-291-5164

Giving is centered on cultural programs, secondary and higher education, human services and medical programs.

John Bultena, Executive Director

2559 Marbrook Foundation
730 2nd Avenue
1450 US Trust Building
Minneapolis, MN 55402

612-752-1783
Fax: 612-752-1780
E-mail: marbrook@brooksinc.net

Offers grants in the areas of the environment, the arts, social empowerment, spiritual endeavors, basic human needs and health.

Annual Report

Conley Brooks Jr, Executive Director
Julie S Hara, Program Officer

2560 Medtronic Foundation
7000 Central Avenue NE
Minneapolis, MN 55432-3576

763-514-4000
800-328-2518
Fax: 763-514-8410
http://www.medtronic.com

Offers grants in the areas of education (especially at the pre-college level), community funding and social services.

Penny Hunt, Executive Director

2561 Minneapolis Foundation
800 Ids Center 80 South 8th Street
Minneapolis, MN 55402

612-672-3878
Fax: 612-672-3846
http://www.minneapolisfoundation.org

The foundation strives to strengthen the community for the benefit of all citizens. Grants are awarded for the purposes of achieving this goal in the areas of early childhood education, child development, and education.

Karen Kelley-Ariwoola, VP Community Philanthropy

2562 Minneapolis Public Library
Music, Art, Sociology & Humanities
250 S Marquette
Minneapolis, MN 55401-2188

612-630-6000
Fax: 612-630-6220
http://www.mplib.org

Member of The Foundation Center network, maintaining a collection of private foundation tax returns which provide information on the scope of grants dispensed by that particular foundation.

Katherine G Hadle, Director

2563 Otto Bremer Foundation
445 Minnesota Street
Suite 2250
Saint Paul, MN 55101-2135

651-227-8036
Fax: 651-312-3665
http://www.fdncenter.org/grantmaker/bremer/

Offers support for post-secondary education, human services and community affairs.

John Kostishack, Executive Director
Karen Starr, Senior Program Officer

2564 Saint Paul Foundation
55 Fifth Street East
Suite 600
St. Paul, MN 55101-1797

651-224-5463
Fax: 651-224-8123
http://www.saintpaulfoundation.org

Offers support for educational, charitable and cultural purposes of a public nature.

Carleen K Rhodes, President
Mindy K Molumby, Grants Administrator

2565 TCF Foundation
Code EXO-02-C
200 Lake Street
East Wayzata, MN 55391-1693

952-745-2757
Fax: 612-661-8554
http://www.tcfexpress.com

Giving is primarily for education through grants and employee matching gifts, including secondary schools, higher education and organizations that increase public knowledge.

Neil I Whitehouse, Executive Director

Mississippi

2566 Foundation for the Mid South
1230 Raymond Road
Box 700
Jackson, MS 39204

601-355-8167
Fax: 601-355-6499
http://www.fndmidsouth.org

Makes grants in the area of education, as well as economic development and families and children.

George Penick, Executive Director

2567 Jackson-Hinds Library System
300 N State Street
Jackson, MS 39201-1705

601-968-5803
http://www.jhlibrary.com

Member of The Foundation Center network, maintaining a collection of private foundation tax returns which

Financial Resources / Missouri

provide information on the scope of grants dispensed by that particular foundation.

Carolyn McCallum, Executive Director

2568 Mississippi Power Foundation
PO Box 4079
Gulfport, MS 39502-4079

228-864-1211
http://www.southerncompany.com/mspower/edufound

The foundation is dedicated to the improvement and enhancement of education in Mississippi from kindergarten to twelfth grade.

Huntley Biggs, Executive Director

2569 Phil Hardin Foundation
Citizens National Bank
1921 24th Avenue
Meridian, MS 39301-5800

601-483-4282
Fax: 601-483-5665
http://www.philhardin.org

Offers giving in Mississippi for schools and educational institutions and programs.

C Thompson Wacaster, Executive Director

Missouri

2570 Ameren Corporation Charitable Trust
Ameren Corporation
PO Box 66149
MC 100
Saint Louis, MO 63166-6149

314-554-2789
877-426-3736
Fax: 314-554-2888
E-mail: sbell@ameren.com
http://www.ameren.com

Offers giving in the areas of education, environment, youth and seniors; giving restricted to nonprofits located in Ameren service area in Missouri and Illinois.

Annually

Susan M Bell, Sr Community Relations
Otis Cowan, Community Relations Manger

2571 Clearinghouse for Midcontinent Foundations
University of Missouri
5110 Cherry Street
Suite 310
Kansas City, MO 64110-2426

816-253-1176
Fax: 816-235-5727

Member of The Foundation Center network, maintaining a collection of private foundation tax returns which provide information on the scope of grants dispensed by that particular foundation.

2572 Danforth Foundation
211 N Broadway
Suite 2390
Saint Louis, MO 63102-2733

314-588-1900
Fax: 314-588-0035
E-mail: banderson@info.csd.org
http://www.orgs.muohio.edu/forumscp/indez.html

This foundation is aimed at enhancing human life through activities which emphasize the theme of improvement in teaching and learning. Serves the pre-collegiate education through grantmaking and program activities.

Dr. Bruce J Anderson, President

2573 Enid & Crosby Kemper Foundation
C/O UMB Bank, N.A.
PO Box 419692
Kansas City, MO 64141-6692

816-860-7711
Fax: 816-860-5690

Giving is primarily allocated to organizations and programs focusing on educational and cultural needs.

Stephen J Campbell, Executive Director

2574 Hall Family Foundation
Charitable & Crown Investment - 323
PO Box 419580
Kansas City, MO 64141-8400

816-274-8516
Fax: 816-274-8547

Offers grants in the areas of all levels of education, performing and visual arts, community development, and children, youth and families.

Wendy Burcham, Program Officer
Peggy Collins, Program Officer

2575 James S McDonnell Foundation
1034 S Brentwood Boulevard
Suite 1850
Saint Louis, MO 63117-1284

314-721-1532
Fax: 314-721-7421
http://www.jsmf.org

Foundation Program, Cognitive Studies for Educational Practice, funding available through competition in broadly announced requests for proposals. Program grant guidelines are announced in 3 year cycles.

John T Bruer, President
Cheryl A Washington, Grants Manager

2576 Kansas City Public Library
14 West 10th Street
Kansas City, MO 64105

816-701-3400
Fax: 816-701-3401
http://www.kclibrary.org

Member of The Foundation Center network, maintaining a collection of private foundation tax returns which provide information on the scope of grants dispensed by that particular foundation.

2577 Mary Ranken Jordan & Ettie A Jordan
Charitable Foundation
Mercantile Bank
PO Box 387
Saint Louis, MO 63166-0387

314-231-7626

Giving is limited to charitable institutions with an emphasis on secondary education and cultural programs, as well as higher education and social services.

Fred Arnold, Executive Director

2578 McDonnell Douglas Foundation
PO Box 516
MC S100-1510
Saint Louis, MO 63166-0516

314-234-0360
Fax: 314-232-7654

Offers various grants with an emphasis on higher and other education and community funding.

AM Bailey, Executive Director

2579 Monsanto Fund
800 N Lindbergh Boulevard
Saint Louis, MO 63167-0001

314-694-1000
Fax: 314-694-7658
E-mail: monsanto.fund@monsanto.com

http://www.monsanto.com/monsanto/about_us/monsanto_f
und

Giving is offered primarily in the area of education, specifically science and math.

Deborah J Patterson, President

Montana

2580 Eastern Montana College Library
Special Collections-Grants
1500 N 30th Street
Billings, MT 59101-0245

406-657-1662
Fax: 406-657-2037
http://www.msubillings.edu/library

Member of The Foundation Center network, maintaining a collection of private foundation tax returns which provide information on the scope of grants dispensed by that particular foundation.

Joan Bares, Grants Manager

2581 Montana State Library
Library Services
1515 E 6th Avenue
Helena, MT 59601-4542

406-444-3115
Fax: 406-444-5612
http://www.msl.state.mt.us/

Member of The Foundation Center network, maintaining a collection of private foundation tax returns which provide information on the scope of grants dispensed by that particular foundation.

Barbara Duke, Administrative Assistant

Nebraska

2582 Dr. CC & Mabel L Criss Memorial Foundation
US Bank
1700 Farnam Streets
Omaha, NE 68102

800-441-2117
Fax: 402-348-6666

Offers support for educational and scientific purposes, including higher education.

2583 Thomas D Buckley Trust
PO Box 647
Chappell, NE 69129-0647

308-874-2212
Fax: 308-874-3491

Offers giving in the areas of education, health care and youth and religion. Grants awarded in Chappell, NE, community and surrounding area.

Connie Loos, Secretary

2584 W Dale Clark Library
Social Sciences Department
215 S 15th Street
Omaha, NE 68102-1601

402-444-4826
Fax: 402-444-4504
http://www.omahapubliclibrary.org

Member of The Foundation Center network, maintaining a collection of private foundation tax returns which provide information on the scope of grants dispensed by that particular foundation.

Angela Green-Garland, President

Nevada

2585 Conrad N Hilton Foundation
100 W Liberty Street
Suite 840
Reno, NV 89501-1988

775-323-4221
Fax: 775-323-4150
http://www.hiltonfoundation.org

Founded in 1944 as a Trust, this foundation is dedicated to fulfilling and expanding Conrad Hilton's philanthropic vision by carrying out grantmaking activities. The foundation's giving is focused primarily in two areas: the alleviation of human suffering, particularly among disadvantaged children; and the human services works of the Catholic Sisters through a separate entity as described under Major Projects (supportive housing, disabled, education and prevention of domestic violence).

Donald H Hubbs, Executive Director
Steven M Hilton, President

2586 Cord Foundation
E.L. Cord Foundation Center For Learning Literacy
College Of Education/Mail Stop 288
University Of Nevada, Reno
Reno, NV 89557-0215

775-784-4951
Fax: 775-784-4758
http://www.unr.edu/cll

Offers support for secondary and higher education, including youth organizations and cultural programs.

Donald Bear, Director/Professor

2587 Donald W Reynolds Foundation
1701 Village Center Circle
Las Vegas, NV 89134

702-804-6000
Fax: 702-804-6099
E-mail: generalquestions@dwrf.org
http://www.dwreynolds.org

Devotes funds to further the cause of free press and journalism education.

Fred Smith, Chairman

2588 EL Wiegand Foundation
Wiegand Center
165 W Liberty Street
Reno, NV 89501-1915

775-333-0310
Fax: 775-333-0314

Offers grants in of culture and the arts, organizations, health and medical institutions, with an emphasis on Roman Catholic organizations.

Kristen A Avansino, Executive Director

2589 Las Vegas-Clark County
Library District
833 Las Vegas Boulevard N
Las Vegas, NV 89101-2030

702-382-5280
Fax: 702-382-5491
http://www.lvccld.org

Member of The Foundation Center network, maintaining a collection of private foundation tax returns which provide information on the scope of grants dispensed by that particular foundation.

Daniel L Walters, Executive Director

Financial Resources / New Hampshire

2590 Washoe County Library
301 S Center Street
Reno, NV 89501-2102

775-327-8349
Fax: 775-327-8341
http://www.washoe.lib.nv.us/

Member of The Foundation Center network, maintaining a collection of private foundation tax returns which provide information on the scope of grants dispensed by that particular foundation.

New Hampshire

2591 Lincolnshire
Liberty Lane
Hampton, NH 03842

Giving is primarily for secondary school education, business school education and recreation.

William Coffey, Executive Director

2592 New Hampshire Charitable Foundation
37 Pleasant Street
Concord, NH 03301-4005

603-225-6641
Fax: 603-225-1700
E-mail: scg@nhcf.org
http://www.nhcf.org

Offers grants for charitable and educational purposes including college scholarships, existing charitable organizations, child welfare, community services, health and social services and new programs that emphasize programs ratherthan capital needs.

Racheal Stuart, VP Program

2593 Plymouth State College
Herbert H. Lamson Library
Highland Street MSC #47
Plymouth, NH 03264

603-535-2258
Fax: 603-535-2445
http://www.plymouth.edu/psc/library

Member of The Foundation Center network, maintaining a collection of private foundation tax returns which provide information on the scope of grants dispensed by that particular foundation.

New Jersey

2594 Community Foundation of New Jersey
Knox Hill Road
PO Box 338
Morristown, NJ 07963-0338

973-267-5533
Fax: 973-267-2903
E-mail: cfnj@bellatlantic.net
http://www.cfnj.org

Offers support for programs that offer a path of solution of community problems in the areas of education, leadership development and human services.

Hans Dekker, President

2595 Fund for New Jersey
Kilmer Square
94 Church Street
Suite 303
New Brunswick, NJ 08901-1242

732-220-8656
Fax: 732-220-8654
http://www.fundfornj.org

Offers grants on projects which provide the basis of action in education, AIDS research, minorities/immigrants, public policy and community development.

Mark M Murphy, Executive Director

2596 Hoechst Celanese Foundation
Route 202-206 N
PO Box 2500
Somerville, NJ 08876

908-522-7500
Fax: 908-598-4424

Provides support for education, particularly in the sciences.

Lewis F Alpaugh, Executive Director

2597 Honeywell Foundation
101 Columbia Road
Morristown, NJ 07960-4658

973-455-2000
Fax: 973-455-4807
http://www.honeywell.com/about/foundation.html

Offers support for education, including fellowship and scholarship aid to colleges.

2598 Hyde & Watson Foundation
437 Southern Boulevard
Chatham, NJ 07928-1454

973-966-6024
Fax: 973-966-6404
http://www.fdncenter.org/grantmaker/hydeandwatson

Support of capital projects of lasting value which tend to increase quality, capacity, or efficiency of a grantee's programs or services, such as purchase or relocation of facilities, capital equipment, instructive materialsdevelopment, and certain medical research areas. Broad fields include health, education, religion, social services, arts, and humanities. Geographic areas served include the New York City Metropolitan region and primarily Essex, Union, and MorrisCounties in New Jersey.

Hunter W Corbin, President

2599 Mary Owen Borden Memorial Foundation
160 Hodge Road
Princeton, NJ 08540-3014

609-924-3637
Fax: 609-252-9472
E-mail: tborden@ibm.net
http://www.fdncenter.org/grantmaker/borden/index.htm

Offers grants in the areas of childhood education, child development, education, conservation and health and human services.

Thomas Borden, Executive Director

2600 Merck Company Foundation
1 Merck Drive #100
Whitehouse Station, NJ 08889-3400

908-423-2042
http://www.merck.com

Offers support of education, primarily medical through community programs, grants and matching gift programs for colleges and secondary education.

John R Taylor, Executive Director

2601 Prudential Foundation
Prudential Plaza
751 Broad Street
Floor 15
Newark, NJ 07102-3714

973-802-4791
http://www.prudential.com

Focus is on children and youth for services that can better their lives. Grants are made in the areas of education, health and human services, community and urban development, business and civic affairs, culture and the arts. Emphasisis placed on programs that serve the city of Newark and the surrounding New Jersey urban centers, programs in cities where The Prudential has a substantial presence and national programs that further the company's objectives.

Barbara L Halaburda, Executive Director

2602 Turrell Fund
21 Van Vleck Street
Montclair, NJ 07042-2358

201-783-9358
Fax: 973-783-9283
E-mail: turrell@bellatlantic.net
http://www.fdncenter.org/grantmaker/turrell

Offers grants to organizations and agencies that are dedicated to the care of children and youth under twelve years of age, with an emphasis on education, early childhood education, delinquency prevention and child and youth services.

E Belvin Williams, Executive Director

2603 Victoria Foundation
946 Bloomfield Avenue
Glen Ridge, NJ 07028

973-748-5300
Fax: 973-748-0016
E-mail: cmcfarvic@aol.com
http://www.victoriafoundation.org

Grants are limited to Newark, New Jersey in the following areas: elementary and secondary education, after school enrichment programs, teacher training and academic enrichment.

Catherine M McFarland, Executive Officer
Nancy K Zimmerman, Senior Program Officer

2604 Warner-Lambert Charitable Foundation
201 Tabor Road
Morris Plains, NJ 07950-2614

212-573-2323
Fax: 212-573-7851

Grants are given in the areas of education, health care, culture and the arts. Supports higher institutions of learning which concentrate on pharmacy, medicine, dentistry, the sciences and mathematics. Current support is aimed at thehigher levels of education, but the foundation has begun to place more of its attention on the growing needs that impact elementary and secondary training.

Evelyn Self, Community Affairs
Richard Keelty, VP Investor Affair

2605 Wilf Family Foundation
820 Morris Tpke
Short Hills, NJ 07078-2619

973-467-5000

Awards grants in the areas of Jewish higher education and religion.

Joseph Wilf, Executive Director

New Mexico

2606 Dale J Bellamah Foundation
PO Box 36600
Albuquerque, NM 87176-6600

858-756-1154
Fax: 858-756-3856

Offers grants for higher education including military academies, hospitals and social service organizations.

AF Potenziani, Executive Director

2607 New Mexico State Library
Information Services
1209 Camino Carlos Rey
Santa Fe, NM 87507

505-476-9700
Fax: 505-476-9701
http://www.stlib.state.nm.us

Member of The Foundation Center network, maintaining a collection of private foundation tax returns which provide information on the scope of grants dispensed by that particular foundation.

2608 RD & Joan Dale Hubbard Foundation
PO Box 1679
Ruidoso Downs, NM 88346-1679

505-378-4142

Giving is offered in the areas of childhood education, elementary, secondary and higher education as well as other cultural programs.

Jim Stoddard, Executive Director

New York

2609 Achelis Foundation
767 3rd Avenue
4th Floor
New York, NY 10017

212-644-0322
Fax: 212-759-6510
E-mail: achelis@aol.com
http://fdncenter.org/grantmaker/achelis-bodman

Grants include biomedical research at Rockefeller University, rebuilding the Hayden Planetarium at the American Museum of Natural History, support for the arts and culture, the charter school movement, youth organizations, and specialefforts to curb father absence and strengthen family life with awards.

Russell P Pennoyer, President
Joseph S Dolan, Executive Director

2610 Adrian & Jessie Archbold Charitable Trust
401 East 60th Street
New York, NY 10022

212-371-1152

Eastern United States educational institutions and health care service organizations are the main recipients of the Trust.

Myra Mahon, Executive Director

2611 Alfred P Sloan Foundation
630 5th Avenue
Suite 2550
New York, NY 10111-0100

212-649-1649
Fax: 212-757-5117
E-mail: www.sloan.org

A nonprofit foundation offering Sloan Research Fellowships which are awarded in chemistry, computer science, economics, mathematics, neuroscience and physics. These are competitive grants given to young faculty members with highresearch potential on the recommendation of department heads and other senior scientists.

Ralph E Gomory, President

2612 Altman Foundation
521 5th Avenue
35th Floor
New York, NY 10175

212-682-0970
http://www.altmanfoundation.org

In education, the Altman Foundation supports programs that identify, sponsor and tutor talented disadvantaged youngsters and help them to obtain educations in non-public and independent schools. The Foundation awards grants only in New York State with an almost-exclusive focus on the five boroughs of New York City. The Foundation does not award grants or scholarships to individuals.

Karen L Rosa, VP/Executive Director

2613 Ambrose Monell Foundation
C/O Fulton, Duncombe & Rowe
1 Rockefeller Plaza
Room 301
New York, NY 10020-2002

212-586-0700
Fax: 212-245-1863
http://www.monellvetlesen.org

Broad range of allocation including education, social service, cultural organizations and the environment.

Ambrose K Monell, Executive Director

2614 American Express Foundation
American Express Company
World Financial Center
New York, NY 10285

212-640-5661
http://www.home3.americanexpress.com/corp/philanthropy/contacts.asp

The foundation's giving focuses on three areas including community service, education and employment.

Mary Beth Salerno, Executive Director
Angela Woods, Philanthropic Program

2615 Andrew W Mellon Foundation
140 E 62nd Street
New York, NY 10021-8187

212-838-8400
Fax: 212-223-2778
http://www.mellon.org

Offers grants in the areas of higher education, cultural affairs and public affairs.

William G Bowen, President

2616 Arnold Bernhard Foundation
220 E 42nd Street
Floor 6
New York, NY 10017-5806

212-907-1500

Offers funding in the areas of education with the emphasis placed on college and universities as well as college preparatory schools.

Jean B Buttner, Executive Director

2617 Atran Foundation
23-25 East 21st Street
3rd Floor
New York, NY 10010

212-505-9677

Offers grants and funding to nonprofit educational and religious organizations.

2618 Beatrice P Delany Charitable Trust
The Chase Manhattan Bank
1211 Avenue of the Americas
34th Floor
New York, NY 10036

212-935-9935

Giving is offered for education, especially higher education and religion.

John HF Enteman, Executive Director

2619 Bodman Foundation
767 3rd Avenue
4th Floor
New York, NY 10017

212-644-0322
Fax: 212-759-6510
E-mail: bodmanfnd@aol.com

Grants include biomedical research at Rockefeller University, building the Congo Gorilla Forest Education Center at the Bronx Zoo through the Wildlife Conservation Society, rebuilding of the Hayden Planetarium for Science and Technology at the American Museum of Natural History, support for Symphony Space, the charter school movement, youth organizations, and the Rutgers University Foundation.

John N Irwin III, President
Joseph S Dolan, Executive Director

2620 Bristol-Myers Squibb Foundation
345 Park Avenue
Floor 43
New York, NY 10154-0004

212-546-4331
http://www.bms.com

Offers support for elementary and secondary school, math and science education reform, civic affairs and health care.

Cindy Johnson, Executive Director

2621 Buffalo & Erie County Public Library
History Department
Lafayette Square
Buffalo, NY 14203

716-858-8900
Fax: 716-858-6211
http://www.buffalolib.org/libraries/central

Member of The Foundation Center network, maintaining a collection of private foundation tax returns which provide information on the scope of grants dispensed by that particular foundation.

Michael C Mahaney, Director

2622 Caleb C & Julia W Dula Educational &
Charitable Foundation
C/O Chemical Bank
270 Park Avenue
Floor 21
New York, NY 10017-2014

212-270-9066

Offers grants to charities with an emphasis on secondary and higher education.

G Price-Fitch, Executive Director

2623 Capital Cities-ABC Corporate Giving Program
77 W 66th St
New York, NY 10023-6201

212-456-7498
Fax: 212-456-7909

Offers support in adult education, literary and basic skills, reading, and AIDS research.

Bernadette Longford Williams, Executive Director

2624 Carl & Lily Pforzheimer Foundation
476 5th Avenue
New York, NY 10018

212-764-0655

Offers support primarily for higher and secondary education, cultural programs, public administration, and health care.

Carl H Pforzheimer III, Executive Director

2625 Carnegie Corporation of New York
437 Madison Avenue
New York, NY 10022-7001
212-374-3200
Fax: 212-754-4073
http://www.carnegie.org

The foundation has several program goals including education and healthy development of children and youth, including early childhood health and education, early adolescence educational achievement, science education and educationreform.

Vartan Gregorian, President

2626 Chase Manhattan Corporation Philanthropy Department
1 Chase Manhattan Plaza
Floor 9
New York, NY 10005-1401
212-552-7087

Offers support to various organizations to enhance the well-being of the communities Chase Manahattan serves. Grants are awarded in the areas of education, youth services, community and economic development, homeless, library science,health care and housing development.

Steven Gelston, Executive Director

2627 Christian A Johnson Endeavor Foundation
1060 Park Avenue
New York, NY 10128-1008
212-534-6620
http://www.csuohio.edu/uored/funding/johnson.htm

Offers support to private institutions of higher education at the baccalaureate level and on educational outreach programs.

Wilmot H Kidd, Executive Director

2628 Cleveland H Dodge Foundation
670 W 247th Street
Bronx, NY 10471-3292
212-543-1220
Fax: 718-543-0737
http://www.chdodgefoundation.org

Bestows funding for nonprofit organizations aimed at improving higher education and youth organizations.

William D Rueckert, President

2629 Cowles Charitable Trust
630 5th Avenue
Suite 1612
New York, NY 10111-0100
212-765-6262

Funding for higher education and cultural organizations.

2630 Daisy Marquis Jones Foundation
1600 S Avenue
Suite 250
Rochester, NY 14620
585-461-4950
Fax: 585-461-9752
http://www.dmjf.org

Offers grants for nonprofit organizations focusing on improving the lives of children, youth and the elderly, in Monroe and Yates counties in New York State.

Roger L Gardner, President
Marless A Honan, Administrative Assistant

2631 DeWitt Wallace-Reader's Digest Fund
2 Park Avenue
Floor 23
New York, NY 10016-9301
212-251-9700
Fax: 212-679-6990
E-mail: www.wallacefoundation.org

The mission of this foundation is to invest in programs and projects that enhance the quality of educational and career development opportunities for all school-age youth.

M Christine De Vita, President

2632 Edna McConnell Clark Foundation
415 Madison Avenue
10th Floor
New York, NY 10017
212-551-9100
Fax: 212-421-9325
http://www.emcf.org

Supports select youth, serving organizations working with children 9-24 during the non-school hours.

Michael Bailin, President

2633 Edward John Noble Foundation
32 E 57th Street
Floor 19
New York, NY 10022-2513
212-759-4212
Fax: 212-888-4531

Offers grants to major cultural organizations in New York City, especially for arts educational programs and management training internships.

June Noble Larkin, Chairman

2634 Edward W Hazen Foundation
90 Broad Street
Suite 604
New York, NY 10004
212-889-3034
E-mail: hazen@hazenfoundation.org
http://www.hazenfoundation.org

The foundation focuses giving on public education and youth development in the area of public education.

Lori Bezahler, President

2635 Edwin Gould Foundation for Children
126 East 31st Street
New York, NY 10016
212-251-0907
Fax: 212-982-6886

Supports projects that promote the welfare and education of children. Interests lies in early childhood education, higher education, children and youth services and family services.

Michael W Osheowitz, Executive Director

2636 Elaine E & Frank T Powers Jr Foundation
81 Skunks Misery Road
Locust Valley, NY 11560-1306

Offers support in the areas of secondary and higher education as well as youth services.

2637 Elmer & Mamdouha Bobst Foundation
Elmer Holmes Bobst Library, NYU
70 Washington Square S
New York, NY 10012-1019
212-998-2440
Fax: 212-995-4070

Offers grants and funding in the areas of youth, community development and the arts.

2638 Equitable Foundation
787 7th Avenue
Floor 39
New York, NY 10019-6018
212-554-3511

Offers grants in the areas of secondary school education, arts, community services, art and cultural programs, and higher education.

Kathleen A Carlson, Executive Director

2639 Ford Foundation
320 E 43rd Street
New York, NY 10017-4890

212-573-5000
Fax: 212-351-3677
E-mail: offsec@fordfound.rog
http://www.fordfound.org

Offers grants to advance public well-being and educational opportunities. Grants are given in the areas of education, secondary school/education, early childhood education, development services, human services, citizenship, academicsand more.

Barron M Tenny, Secretary

2640 Frances & Benjamin Benenson Foundation
708 3rd Avenue
Floor 28
New York, NY 10017-4201

212-867-0990

Offers grants in elementary/secondary education, higher education and human services.

Charles B Benenson, Executive Director

2641 George F Baker Trust
477 Madison Avenue
New York, NY 10022

212-755-1890
Fax: 212-319-6316

Offers giving in the areas of higher and secondary education, social services, civic affairs and international affairs.

Rocio Suarez, Executive Director

2642 George Link Jr Foundation
C/O Emmet, Marvin & Martin
120 Broadway
32nd Floor
New York, NY 10271

212-238-3000
Fax: 212-238-3100

Giving is primarily centered on higher education, secondary school/education and medical research.

Michael J Catanzaro, Executive Director

2643 Gladys & Roland Harriman Foundation
63 Wall Street
Floor 23
New York, NY 10005-3001

212-493-8182
Fax: 212-493-5570

Giving is centered on education and support for youth and social service agencies.

William F Hibberd, Executive Director

2644 Gladys Brooks Foundation
1055 Franklin Avenue
Garden City, NY 11530

212-943-3217
http://www.gladysbrooksfoundation.org

The purpose of this foundation is to provide for the intellectual, moral and physical welfare of the people of this country by establishing and supporting nonprofit libraries, educational institutions, hospitals and clinics. In thearea of education, grant applications will be considered generally for (a) educational endowments to fund scholarships based solely on leadership and academic ability of the student; (b) endowments to support salaries of educators.

Harman Hawkins, Chairman
Robert E Hill, Executive Director

2645 Green Fund
14 E 60th Street
Suite 702
New York, NY 10022-1006

212-755-2445
Fax: 212-755-0021

Offers grants in the area of higher and secondary education.

Cynthia Green Colin, Executive Director

2646 Hagedorn Fund
C/O JPMorgan Private Bank
Global Foundations Group
345 Park Avenue 4th Floor
New York, NY 10154

212-473-1587
http://www.fdncenter.org/grantmaker/hagedorn/

Offers support for higher and secondary education, youth agencies and social service agencies.

Monica J Neal, Vice President

2647 Hasbro Children's Foundation
10 Rockefeller Plaza
16th Floor
New York, NY 10020

212-713-7654
Fax: 212-645-4055
http://www.hasbro.org

Offers support to improve the quality of life for children. Areas of interest include education, AIDS research, literacy, special education, and youth services.

Eve Weiss, Executive Director

2648 Henry Luce Foundation
111 W 50th Street
Room 3710
New York, NY 10020-1202

212-489-7700
Fax: 212-581-9541
http://www.hluce.org

Offers grants for specific programs and projects in the areas of higher education and scholarship, social sciences at private colleges and universities, American arts and public affairs.

Michael Gilligan, President

2649 Herman Goldman Foundation
61 Broadway
Floor 18
New York, NY 10006-2701

212-797-9090
Fax: 212-797-9161

This foundation offers grants in the areas of social, legal and organizational approaches to aid for deprived or handicapped people; education for new or improved counseling for effective pre-school, vocational, and paraprofessionaltraining; and the arts.

Richard K Baron, Executive Director

2650 Hess Foundation
1185 Avenue of the Americas
New York, NY 10036-2601

212-997-8500
Fax: 212-536-8390
E-mail: webmaster@hess.com
http://www.hess.com

Offers grants that focus on higher education, performing arts, and welfare organizations.

Leon Hess, Executive Director

2651 Horace W Goldsmith Foundation
375 Park Avenue
Suite 1602
New York, NY 10152-1699
                    212-319-8700
                    800-319-2881
                    Fax: 212-319-2881

Offers giving and support for education, higher
education, cultural programs and museums.

James C Slaughter, Executive Director

2652 IBM Corporate Support Program
Old Orchard Road
Armonk, NY 10504
                    914-765-1900

The mission of this fund is to improve the areas and the
communities that IBM operates in. Grants are awarded in
various areas including early childhood education,
elementary education, secondary education, business
school/education,and engineering school/education.

Stanley Litow, Executive Director

2653 JI Foundation
C/O Patterson, Belknap, Webb & Tyler
1133 Avenue of the Americas
New York, NY 10036
                    212-336-2000

Offers grants in the areas of elementary education, higher
education, and general charitable giving.

2654 JP Morgan Charitable Trust
60 Wall Street
Floor 46
New York, NY 10005-2836
                    212-648-9673

Offers support in the area of education, housing,
economic development, advocacy and international
affairs.

Roberta Ruocco, Executive Director

2655 Joukowsky Family Foundation
410 Park Avenue
Suite 1610
New York, NY 10022-4407
                    212-355-3151
                    Fax: 212-355-3147
                    http://www.joukowsky.org

Giving is focused on higher and secondary education.

Nina J Koprulu, Director/President
Emily R Kessler, Executive Director

2656 Julia R & Estelle L Foundation
1 HSBC Center
Suite 3650
Buffalo, NY 14203-1217
                    716-856-9490
                    Fax: 716-856-9493
                    http://www.oisheifdt.org

This fund offers grants in the areas of higher and
secondary education, medical research, social services
and support agencies.

Thomas E Baker, President

2657 Leon Lowenstein Foundation
575 Madison Avenue
New York, NY 10022-3613
                    212-605-0444
                    Fax: 212-688-0134

Support is given for New York City public education and
medical research.

John F Van Gorder, Executive Director

2658 Levittown Public Library
1 Bluegrass Lane
Levittown, NY 11756-1292
                    516-731-5728
                    Fax: 516-735-3168
                    http://www.nassaulibrary.org/levtown/

Member of The Foundation Center network, maintaining
a collection of private foundation tax returns which
provide information on the scope of grants dispensed by
that particular foundation.

Margaret Santer, President

2659 Louis & Anne Abrons Foundation
C/O First Manhattan Company
437 Madison Avenue
New York, NY 10022-7001
                    212-756-3376
                    Fax: 212-832-6698

Offers support in the areas of education, improvement
programs, environmental and cultural projects.

Richard Abrons, Executive Director

2660 Margaret L Wendt Foundation
40 Fountain Plaza
Suite 277
Buffalo, NY 14202-2200
                    716-855-2146
                    Fax: 716-855-2149

Offers various grants with an emphasis on education, the
arts and social services in Buffalo and Western New
York.

Robert J Kresse, Executive Director

2661 McGraw-Hill Foundation
1221 Avenue of the Americas
Room 2917
New York, NY 10020
                    212-512-6113
                    800-442-9685

Offers support to educational organizations in the areas
of company operations or to national organizations.

Susan A Wallman, Executive Director

2662 New York Foundation
350 5th Avenue
Suite 2901
New York, NY 10118-2996
                    212-594-8009
                    Fax: 212-594-5918
                    http://www.nyf.org

Provides support for the implementation of programs
that offer support for the quality of life including
educational services, health organizations, centers and
services, civil rights, public policy, research and more.

Madeline Lee, Executive Director

2663 Palisades Educational Foundation
C/O Gibney, Anthony & Flaherty
665 5th Avenue
Floor 2
New York, NY 10022-5305

Offers support for secondary and higher education in
New York, New Jersey and Connecticut.

Ralph F Anthony, Executive Director

2664 Robert Sterling Clark Foundation
135 E 64th Street
New York, NY 10021-7307
                    212-288-8900
                    Fax: 212-288-1033
                    http://www.rsclark.org

For more than 15 years, this foundation has provided
support to New York City's cultural community. During
this time, the Foundation has tried to structure a grants

program so that it is flexible and meets the needs of theinstitutions and organizations. Grants are given in the areas of cultural institutions, arts advocacy, family planning services and supporting new initiatives in the area of arts and education.

Winthrop R Munyan, President
Margaret C Ayers, Executive Director

2665 Rochester Public Library
Business, Economics & Law
115 S Avenue
Rochester, NY 14604-1896

585-428-8045
Fax: 585-428-8353
http://www.rochester.lib.ny.us/central

Member of The Foundation Center network, maintaining a collection of private foundation tax returns which provide information on the scope of grants dispensed by that particular foundation.

Emeterio M Otero, President

2666 Ronald S Lauder Foundation
767 5th Avenue
42nd Floor
New York, NY 10153-0023

212-572-6966

Offers giving in the areas of elementary/secondary education, human services and religion.

Marjorie S Federbush, Executive Director

2667 SH & Helen R Scheuer Family Foundation
350 5th Avenue
Suite 3410
New York, NY 10118-0110

212-947-9009
Fax: 212-947-9770

Offers support in the areas of higher education, welfare funding and cultural programs.

2668 Samuel & May Rudin Foundation
345 Park Avenue
New York, NY 10154-0004

212-407-2544
Fax: 212-407-2540

Offers support for higher education, social services, religious welfare agencies, hospitals and cultural programs.

Susan H Rapaport, Executive Director

2669 Seth Sprague Educational and Charitable Foundation
C/O U.S. Trust Company of New York
114 W 47th Street
New York, NY 10036-1510

212-852-3683
Fax: 212-852-3377

Offers support in the areas of education, culture, the arts, human services, community development and government/public administration.

Maureen Augusciak, Executive Director

2670 Starr Foundation
70 Pine Street
New York, NY 10270-0002

212-770-6881
Fax: 212-425-6261
http://www.fdncenter.org/grantmaker/starr

Support is given for educational projects with an emphasis on higher education, including scholarships under specific programs.

Ta Chun Hsu, Executive Director

2671 Tiger Foundation
101 Park Avenue
47th Floor
New York, NY 10178-0002

212-984-2565
Fax: 212-949-9778
http://www.tigerfoundation.org

Support is given primarily for early childhood education, youth programs and job training.

Phoebe Boyer, Executive Director

2672 Tisch Foundation
667 Madison Avenue
New York, NY 10021-8029

212-545-2000

Support is given in the area of education, especially higher education, and includes institutions in Israel and research-related programs.

Laurence A Tisch, Executive Director

2673 Travelers Group
388 Greenwich Street
New York, NY 10013-2375

212-816-8000
Fax: 212-816-5944

The main purpose of this foundation is to support public education, offering grants in the communities that the company serves.

Dee Topol, Executive Director

2674 White Plains Public Library
100 Martine Avenue
White Plains, NY 10601-2599

914-422-1400
Fax: 914-422-1462
http://www.whiteplainslibrary.org

Member of The Foundation Center network, maintaining a collection of private foundation tax returns which provide information on the scope of grants dispensed by that particular foundation.

2675 William Randolph Hearst Foundation
888 7th Avenue
Floor 45
New York, NY 10106-0001

212-586-5404
Fax: 212-586-1917
http://www.hearstfdn.org

Offers support to programs that aid priority-level and minority groups, educational programs especially private secondary and higher education, health systems and cultural programs.

Robert M Frehse Jr, Executive Director
Ilene Mack, Senior Program Officer

2676 William T Grant Foundation
570 Lexington Avenue
Floor 18
New York, NY 10022-6837

212-752-0071
Fax: 212-752-1398
E-mail: info@wtgrantfdn.org
http://www.wtgrantfoundation.org

The goal of the foundation is to help create a society that values people and helps them to reach their potenial. The Foundation is interested in environmentally friendly approaches

Edward Seidman, Senior VP Programs
Robert Granger, President

North Carolina

2677 **AE Finley Foundation**
1151 Newton Road
Raleigh, NC 27615

919-782-0565
Fax: 919-782-6978

Private foundation contributing and supporting to charitable, scientific, literary, religious and educational organizations. It endeavors to contribute to soundly managed and operated qualifying organizations which fundamentally giveservice with a broad scope and impact, aid all kinds of people and contribute materially to the general welfare.

Robert C Brown, Executive Director

2678 **Cannon Foundation**
PO Box 548
Concord, NC 28026-0548

704-786-8216
Fax: 704-785-2052
http://www.thecannonfoundationinc.org

Offers support for higher and secondary education, cultural programs, and grants to social service and youth agencies.

Frank Davis, Executive Director
William C Cannon Jr, President

2679 **Dickson Foundation**
301 S Tryon Street
Suite 1800
Charlotte, NC 28202

704-372-5404
Fax: 704-372-6409

Main focus is on areas of education & healthcare. Considers funding programs in the Southeast.

Susan Patterson, Secretary/Treasurer

2680 **Duke Endowment**
100 N Tryon Street
Suite 3500
Charlotte, NC 28202-4012

704-376-0291
Fax: 704-376-9336
http://www.dukeendowment.org

Support is given to higher education, children and youth services, churches and hospitals.

Eugene W Cochrane Jr, Executive Director

2681 **First Union University**
Two 1st Union Center
Charlotte, NC 28288

704-374-6868
Fax: 704-374-4147

Offers support for higher education and special programs for public elementary and secondary schools.

Ann D Thomas, Executive Director

2682 **Foundation for the Carolinas**
PO Box 3479
Charlotte, NC 28234

704-973-4500
800-973-7244
Fax: 704-376-1243
http://www.fftc.org

Offers support for education, the arts and health in North Carolina and South Carolina.

Michael Marsicano, President/CEO

2683 **Kathleen Price and Joseph M Bryan Family Foundation**
3101 N Elm Street
Greensboro, NC 27408-3184

336-288-5455

Grants are primarily offered in the fields of higher, secondary, and early childhood education.

William Massey, Executive Director

2684 **Mary Reynolds Babcock Foundation**
2920 Reynolda Road
Winston Salem, NC 27106-4618

336-748-9222
Fax: 336-777-0095
http://www.mrbf.org

This foundation traditionally provides funds to programs in education, social services, the environment, the arts and citizen participation in the development of public policy. The foundation prefers to fund programs of two kinds:those particularly sensitive to the changing and emerging needs of society and those addressing society's oldest needs in new and imaginative ways.

Gayle W Dorman, Executive Director
Sandra H Mikush, Assitant Director

2685 **Non-Profit Resource Center/Pack Memorial Library**
Learning Resources Center
67 Haywood Street
Asheville, NC 28801-4897

828-254-4960
Fax: 828-251-2258
http://www.buncombecounty.org

Cooperating collection of the Foundation Center. Other resources for non-profit organizations are also available.

Ed Sheary, Library Director

2686 **State Library of North Carolina**
Government & Business Services
109 E Jones Street
Raleigh, NC 27601-2806

919-807-7450
Fax: 919-733-5679
http://www.statelibrary.dcr.state.nc.us

Member of The Foundation Center network, maintaining a collection of private foundation tax returns which provide information on the scope of grants dispensed by that particular foundation.

2687 **William R Kenan Jr Charitable Trust**
Kenan Center
PO Box 3858
Chapel Hill, NC 27515-3858

919-962-0343
Fax: 919-962-3331

The focus of this foundation is on education, primarily at private institutions in the US. The emphasis now is on national literacy and the importance of early childhood education. Grants have just established an institute for thearts and an institute for engineering, technology and science. No grants are given to individuals for scholarships, for research or other special projects or for medical, public health or social welfare projects. This Trust does not acceptunsolicited requests.

William C Friday, Executive Director

2688 **Winston-Salem Foundation**
860 W 5th Street
Winston Salem, NC 27101-2506

336-725-2382
Fax: 336-727-0581
http://www.wsfoundation.org

Educational grants and loans to residents of Forsyth County, North Carolina in most areas.

Scott Wierman, President
Donna Rader, VP Grants & Programs

Financial Resources / North Dakota

2689 Z Smith Reynolds Foundation
147 S Cherry Street
Suite 200
Winston Salem, NC 27101

336-725-7541
800-443-8319
Fax: 336-725-6069
http://www.zsr.org

Grants are limited to the state of North Carolina. General purpose foundation provides for their current priorities including community economic development, women's issues, minority issues, environment and pre-collegiate education.No grants are given to individuals.

Thomas W Ross, Executive Director

North Dakota

2690 Myra Foundation
PO Box 13536
Grand Forks, ND 58208-3536

701-775-9420

Offers grants in the areas of secondary school, and higher education to residents of Grand Forks County, North Dakota.

Edward C Gillig, Executive Director

2691 Tom & Frances Leach Foundation
PO Box 1136
Bismarck, ND 58502-1136

701-255-0479

Offers grants in the areas of higher and other education in North Dakota.

Clement C Weber, Executive Director

Ohio

2692 Akron Community Foundation
345 W Cedar Street
Akron, OH 44307-2407

330-376-8522
Fax: 330-376-0202
E-mail: acf_fund@ix.netcom.com
http://www.akroncommunityfdn.org

The foundation receives donations to permanent endowment and makes grants to qualified nonprofit organizations within Summit County, Ohio.

Jody Bacon, President

2693 American Foundation Corporation
720 National City Bank Building
Cleveland, OH 44114

216-241-6664
Fax: 216-241-6693

Offers support in the areas of higher and secondary education, the arts and community funds.

Maria G Muth, Executive Director

2694 Burton D Morgan Foundation
PO Box 1500
Akron, OH 44309-1500

330-258-6512
Fax: 330-258-6559
http://www.bdmorganfdn.org

The foundation's present areas of interest include economics, education, mental health and organizations principally located in Northeast Ohio. No grants are made to individuals and few grants are made to social service organizations.

John V Frank, President

2695 Dayton Foundation
2300 Kettering Tower
Dayton, OH 45423-1395

937-222-0410
Fax: 937-222-0636
http://www.daytonfoundation.org

Educational and community service grants.

Michael M Parks, President

2696 Eva L & Joseph M Bruening Foundation
1422 Euclid Avenue
Suite 627
Cleveland, OH 44115-1952

216-621-2632
Fax: 216-621-8198
http://www.fmscleveland.com/bruening

Support is offered in the fields of education, early childhood education, education fund-raising, higher education, youth services and health agencies.

Janet E Narten, Executive Director

2697 GAR Foundation
50 S Main Street #1500
Akron, OH 44308-1828

330-643-0201
800-686-2825
Fax: 330-252-5584
http://www.garfdn.org

Established in 1967 as a charitable trust, the foundation offers grants to organizations located primarily in Akron, Ohio area or, secondarily, in Northeastern Ohio or elsewhere in the United States at the discretion of theDistribution Committee. Grants for research projects of educational or scientific institutions, capital improvement projects, or matching campaigns are the priorities of this foundation.

Richard A Chenoweth, Executive Director
Robert W Briggs, Co-Trustee

2698 George Gund Foundation
1845 Guildhall Building
45 Prospect Avenue
West Cleveland, OH 44115

216-241-3114
Fax: 216-241-6560
E-mail: info@gundfdn.org
http://www.gundfdn.org

The primary interest of this foundation is in educational projects, with an emphasis on inventive movements in teaching and learning, and on increasing educational opportunities for the disadvantaged.

David Abbott, Executive Director
Marcia Egbert, Senior Program Officer

2699 Hoover Foundation
101 E Maple Street
North Canton, OH 44720-2517

330-499-9200
Fax: 330-966-5433

Offers grants for elementary education, secondary and higher education and youth agencies.

LR Hoover, Executive Director

2700 Kettering Fund
40 N Main Street
Suite 1440
Dayton, OH 45423-1001

937-228-1021

Support is offered for social and educational studies and research as well as community development and cultural programs.

Richard F Beach, Executive Director

2701 Kulas Foundation
Tower City Center
50 Public Square
Suite 924
Cleveland, OH 44113-2203
216-623-4770
Fax: 216-623-4773
http://www.fdncenter.org/grantmaker/kulas/

A major general interest foundation, but with an emphasis on music. Giving is limited to Cuyahuga County and its surrounding area. Provides support to musical educational programs at Baldwin Wallace College, Case Western ReserveUniversity and Cleveland Institute of Music. Also provides tickets to cultural programs to students in 16 colleges and universities in the area. The Foundation does not provide grants or loans to individuals. Support is geared to local primary andsecondary schools.

Nancy W McCann, President/Treasurer

2702 Louise H & David S Ingalls Foundation
20600 Chagrin Boulevard
Suite 301
Shaker Heights, OH 44122-5334
216-921-6000

Offers support to organizations whose primary interest in the improvement of the educational, physical and mental condition of humanity throughout the world. Grants are given in secondary, elementary, and educational research.

Jane W Watson, Executive Director

2703 Louise Taft Semple Foundation
425 Walnut Street
Suite 1800
Cincinnati, OH 45202-3948
513-381-2838
Fax: 513-381-0205

Support is offered in the areas of secondary school/education, higher education, human services and health care organizations.

Dudley S Taft, Executive Director

2704 Martha Holden Jennings Foundation
Advisory & Distribution Committee Office
1228 Euclid Avenue
Suite 710
Cleveland, OH 44115-1831
216-589-5700
Fax: 216-589-5730
http://mhjf.org

The purpose of this foundation is to foster the development of young people to the maximum possible extent through improving the quality of teaching in secular elementary and secondary schools.

William T Hiller, Executive Director
Kathy L Kooyman, Grants Manager

2705 Mead Corporation Foundation
Courthouse Plz NE
Dayton, OH 45463-0001
937-495-3883
Fax: 937-495-4103

Grants are given to elementary, secondary, higher and minority education.

Ronald F Budzik, Executive Director

2706 Nord Family Foundation
747 Milan Avenue
Amherst, OH 44001
440-984-3939
Fax: 440-984-3934
http://www.nordff.org

Offers support for a variety of programs, including giving for early childhood, secondary, and higher education, social services, cultural affairs and civic activities.

David R Ashenhurst, Executive Director

2707 Ohio Bell Telephone Contribution Program
45 Erieview Plaza
Room 870
Cleveland, OH 44114-1814
216-822-4445
800-257-0902

Offers support of elementary school/education, secondary school/education, higher education, literacy and basic skills.

William W Boag Jr, Executive Director

2708 Ohio State Library Foundation Center
Kent H. Smith Library
1422 Euclid Avenue
Suite 1356
Cleveland, OH 44115-2001
216-861-1933
Fax: 216-861-1936

Member of The Foundation Center network, maintaining a collection of private foundation tax returns which provide information on the scope of grants dispensed by that particular foundation.

2709 Owens-Corning Foundation
PO Box 1688
Toledo, OH 43603-1688
419-248-8000
Fax: 419-325-4273

Offers support for education, including religious schools and science and technology programs.

Emerson J Ross, Executive Director

2710 Procter & Gamble Fund
PO Box 599
Cincinnati, OH 45201-0599
513-983-1100
Fax: 513-983-8250

Always considers the interests of the company's employees helping in the community, the arts, improving of schools and universities and to meet the needs of the less-fortunate neighbors. Some donations into the education programinclude grants to the United Negro College Fund, The National Hispanic Scholarship Fund, The Leadership Conference on Civil Rights Education Fund and more than 600 colleges and universities.

RL Wehling, President
G Talbot, VP

2711 Public Library of Cincinnati
Grants Resource Center
800 Vine Street #Library
Cincinnati, OH 45202-2009
513-369-6940
Fax: 513-369-6993
http://www.cincinnatilibrary.org

Member of The Foundation Center network, maintaining a collection of private foundation tax returns which provide information on the scope of grants dispensed by that particular foundation.

Kimber L Fender, Director

2712 Thomas J Emery Memorial
Frost & Jacobs
201 E 5th Street
Suite 2500
Cincinnati, OH 45202-4113
513-621-3124

Offers support in secondary school/education, higher education, health care, human services and arts/cultural programs.

Henry W Hobson Jr, Executive Director

2713 Timken Foundation of Canton
200 Market Avenue N
Suite 210
Canton, OH 44702-1622

330-452-1144
Fax: 330-455-1752

Offers support to promote the broad civic betterment including the areas of education, conservation and recreation. Grants restricted to caption projects only.

Don D Dickes, Secretary
Nancy Kuvdsen

2714 Wolfe Associates
34 S 3rd Street
Columbus, OH 43215-4201

614-461-5220
Fax: 614-469-6126

The foundation supports those organizations whose programs educate the individual and cultivate the individual's ability to participate in and contribute to the community or which enhance the quality of life which the community canoffer to its citizens. The foundation has six general program areas in which it focuses its support: health and medicine, religion, education, culture, community service and environment.

AK Pierce Jr, Executive Director

Oklahoma

2715 Grace & Franklin Bernsen Foundation
15 W 6th Street
Suite 1308
Tulsa, OK 74119-5407

918-584-4711
Fax: 918-584-4713
E-mail: gfbersen@aol.com
http://www.bernsen.org

The foundation is limited by its policies to support of nonprofit organizations within the metropolitan area of Tulsa. The foundation discourages applications for general support or reduction of debt or for continuing or additionalsupport for the same programs, although a single grant may cover several years. No grant is made to individuals or for the benefit of specific individuals and the applications must be received before the twelfth of each month.

John Strong Jr, Trustee

2716 Mervin Bovaird Foundation
100 W 5th Street
Suite 800
Tulsa, OK 74103-4291

918-583-1777
Fax: 918-592-5809

Awards scholarships to the University of Tulsa. Recipients are selected by Tulsa Area high schools and by Tulsa Junior College. No individual grants are made.

R Casey Cooper, President

2717 Oklahoma City University
Dulaney Brown Library
2501 N Blackwelder Avenue
Oklahoma City, OK 73106-1493

405-521-5000
Fax: 405-521-5291

Member of The Foundation Center network, maintaining a collection of private foundation tax returns which provide information on the scope of grants dispensed by that particular foundation.

Victoria Swinney, Director

2718 Public Service Company of Oklahoma Corporate Giving Program
212 E 6th Street #201
Tulsa, OK 74119-1295

918-586-0420

Offers support in the areas of elementary, secondary and higher education.

Mary Polfer, Executive Director

2719 Samuel Roberts Noble Foundation
PO Box 2180
Ardmore, OK 73402-2180

580-223-5810
Fax: 580-224-6380
http://www.noble.org

Offers support in the areas of higher education, agricultural research, human services and educational grants for health research pertaining to degenerative diseases, cancer and for health delivery systems.

Michael A Cawley, Executive Director

Oregon

2720 Collins Foundation
1618 SW 1st Avenue
Suite 305
Portland, OR 97201-5708

503-227-7171
Fax: 503-295-3794
http://www.collinsfoundation.org

Offers general support with an emphasis on higher education, hospices and health agencies, youth programs and arts and culture.

Jerry E Hudson, Executive Vice President
Cynthia G Adams, Director Of Programs

2721 Ford Family Foundation
1600 NW Stewart Parkway
Roseburg, OR 97470-0252

541-957-5574
Fax: 541-957-5720
E-mail: info@tfff.org
http://www.tfff.org

Giving is centered on education, youth organizations and human service programs in Oregon and Siskiyou County in California.

Bart Howard, Director Scholarship Program
Sarah Reeve, Scholarship Program Officer

2722 Meyer Memorial Trust
425 NW 10th Avenue
Suite 400
Portland, OR 97209

503-228-5512
Fax: 503-228-5840
E-mail: mmt@mmt.org
http://www.mmt.org

The Trust operates three different funding programs, all of which are restricted primarily to Oregon: 1) a broad-based General Purpose program that provides funds for education, arts, and humanities, health, social welfare, communitydevelopment, and other activities; 2) a Small Grants program that provides up to $12,000 for small projects in the general purpose categories; and 3) the Support for Teacher Initiatives program, which provides grants of up to $7,000- to teachers.

Doug Stamm, Executive Director

**2723 Multnomah County Library
Government Documents**
801 SW 10th Avenue
Portland, OR 97205-2597

503-988-5123
Fax: 503-988-8014
http://www.multcolib.org

Member of The Foundation Center network, maintaining a collection of private foundation tax returns which provide information on the scope of grants dispensed by that particular foundation.

2724 Oregon Community Foundation
1221 SW Yamhill
Suite 100
Portland, OR 97205

503-227-6846
Fax: 503-274-7771
http://www.ocfl.org

The purpose of this foundation is to improve the cultural, educational and social needs in all levels of society throughout the state of Oregon.

Gregory A Chaille, Executive Director

2725 Tektronix Foundation
PO Box 1000
Wilsonville, OR 97070-1000

503-627-7111
http://www.tek.com

Offers support for education, especially science, math and engineering, and some limited art grants.

Jill Kirk, Executive Director

Pennsylvania

2726 Alcoa Foundation
201 Isabella Street
Pittsburgh, PA 15212-5858

412-553-2348
Fax: 412-553-4498
http://www.alcoa.com

Grants are given for education, arts and cultural programs.

F Worth Hobbs, Executive Director

**2727 Annenberg Foundation
St. David's Center**
150 N Radnor Chester Road
Suite A200
Saint Davids, PA 19087-5293

610-341-9066
Fax: 610-964-8688
E-mail: info@annenbergfoundation.org
http://www.annenbergfoundation.org

Primary support is given to childhood and K-12 education.

Dr. Gail C Levin Sr, Executive Director

2728 Arcadia Foundation
105 E Logan Street
Norristown, PA 19401-3058

215-275-8460

Gives only in Eastern Pennsylvania, no personal scholarships, accepts proposals only between June 1-August 15. These will be considered for the following calendar year. Proposal has to be no more than 2 pages long and longer submissions will be discarded. Must have a copy of the IRS tax-identified letter with no other enclosures.

Marilyn Lee Steinbright, Executive Director

2729 Audrey Hillman Fisher Foundation
2000 Grant Building
Pittsburgh, PA 15219

412-338-3466
Fax: 412-338-3463

Offers support for secondary school/education, higher education, rehabilitation, science and engineering.

Ronald W Wertz, Executive Director

2730 Bayer Corporation
100 Bayer Court
Pittsburgh, PA 15205

412-777-2000
Fax: 412-777-3468
http://www.bayerus.com/about/community/

Support is given primarily in education, especially science programs, chemistry and the arts.

Rebecca Lucore, Executive Director

2731 Buhl Foundation
650 Smithfield Street
Pittsburgh, PA 15222-1207

412-566-2711
Fax: 412-566-2714

Grants are given to colleges and universities, secondary schools and educational associations, community educational and training programs, and other community programs offering health and education to the community. Grants are not made for building funds, overhead costs, accumulated deficits, ordinary operating budgets, general fund-raising campaigns, loans, scholarships and fellowships, other foundations, nationally funded organized groups or individuals.

Dr. Doreen Boyce, President

2732 Connelly Foundation
One Tower Bridge
Suite 1450
West Conshohocken, PA 19428

610-834-3222
Fax: 610-834-0866
http://www.connellyfdn.org

Offers support for education, health, human service, culture and civic programs to nonprofit organizations located in the city of Philadelphia and the greater Delaware Valley region.

Victoria K Flaville, VP Administration
Josephine C Mandeville, President/CEO

**2733 Eden Hall Foundation
Pittsburgh Office And Research Park**
600 Grant Street
Suite 3232
Pittsburgh, PA 15219

412-642-6697
Fax: 412-642-6698
http://www.edenhallfdn.org

This foundation offers support for higher education, social welfare and the improvement of conditions of the poor and needy.

Sylvia V Fields, Program Director
George C Greer, Chairman/President

2734 Erie County Library System
160 E Front Street
Erie, PA 16507-1554

814-451-6927
Fax: 814-451-6969
http://www.ecls.lib.pa.us

Member of The Foundation Center network, maintaining a collection of private foundation tax returns which provide information on the scope of grants dispensed by that particular foundation.

2735 Foundation Center-Carnegie Library of Pittsburgh
Foundation Collection
4400 Forbes Avenue
Pittsburgh, PA 15213-4080

412-281-7143
Fax: 412-454-7001
E-mail: foundati@carnegielibrary.org
http://www.clpgh.org/clp/Foundation

Member of the Foundation Center network, of cooperating collections; providing current, factual information about grants and grantmaking organizations, and other aspects of philanthropy to the local nonprofit community.

Jim Lutton, Manager
Herb Elish, Director

2736 HJ Heinz Company Foundation
PO Box 57
Pittsburgh, PA 15230-0057

412-456-5772
Fax: 412-456-7859
E-mail: heinz.foundation@hjheinz.com
http://www.heinz.com/jsp/foundation.jsp

Offers support for higher education, employee matching gifts, social service agencies and cultural programs.

Loretta M Oken, Executive Director

2737 John McShain Charities
540 N 17th Street
Philadelphia, PA 19130-3988

215-564-2322

Offers support for higher and secondary education, Roman Catholic church support and social welfare.

Mary McShain, Executive Director

2738 Mary Hillman Jennings Foundation
625 Stanwix Street
Apt 2203
Pittsburgh, PA 15222-1408

412-434-5606
Fax: 412-434-5907

Offers grants to schools, youth agencies, and hospitals and health associations.

Paul Euwer Jr, Executive Director

2739 McCune Foundation
750 Six PPG Place
Pittsburgh, PA 15222

412-644-8779
Fax: 412-644-8059
http://www.mccune-db.mccune.org

The foundation provides support to independent higher education and human services.

Henry S Beukema, Executive Director

2740 Pew Charitable Trusts
One Commerce Square
2005 Market Street
Suite 1700
Philadelphia, PA 19103-7077

215-575-9050
Fax: 215-575-4939
http://www.pewtrusts.com

Offers support for education (including theology), arts culture, as well as public policy and religion.

Rebecca W Rimel, Executive Director

2741 Richard King Mellon Foundation
One Mellon Bank Center
500 Grant Street
Suite 4106
Pittsburgh, PA 15219-2502

412-392-2800
Fax: 412-392-2837
http://fdncenter.org/grantmaker/rkmellon/

Offers local grant programs with an emphasis on education, social services and the environment.

Seward Prosser Mellon, Trustee/President

2742 Rockwell International Corporation Trust
625 Liberty Avenue
Pittsburgh, PA 15222-3110

414-212-5200
Fax: 414-212-5201

Offers support in the areas of K-12 math and science education, and higher education in the field of engineering and science.

William R Fitz, Executive Director

2743 Samuel S Fels Fund
1616 Walnut Street
Suite 800
Philadelphia, PA 19103-5308

215-731-9455
Fax: 215-731-9457
http://www.samfels.org

Offers grants in continuing support that help prevent, lessen or resolve contemporary social problems including education, arts/cultural programs, and community development.

Helen Cunningham, Executive Director
Nell Williams, Office Administrator

2744 Sarah Scaife Foundation
Three Mellon Bank Center
301 Grant Street
Suite 3900
Pittsburgh, PA 15219-6402

412-392-2900
http://www.scaife.com

Offers grants in the areas of education and community development.

Joanne B Beyer, Executive Director
Michael W Gleba, Executive Vice President

2745 Shore Fund
C/O Melton Bank N.A.
PO Box 185
Pittsburgh, PA 15230-0185

412-234-4695
Fax: 412-234-3551

Although the foundation appreciates funding opportunities within the field of education, most grants given out have been to schools with which the foundation's trustees have been personally involved.

Helen M Collins, Executive Director

2746 Stackpole-Hall Foundation
44 S Saint Marys Street
Saint Marys, PA 15857-1667

814-834-1845
Fax: 814-834-1869

Offers support for higher education and secondary education, literacy and vocational projects, social services, arts and cultural programs, and community development.

William C Conrad, Executive Director

2747 United States Steel Foundation
600 Grant Street
Suite 639
Pittsburgh, PA 15219-2800

412-433-5237
Fax: 412-433-2792
http://www.psc.uss.com/usxfound

Grants are awarded for capital development, special projects or operating needs. Support is limited to organizations within the United States, with preference to those in the US Steel Corporation's operating areas. US Steel does notaward grants for religious purposes. Additionally, grants are not awarded for conferences, seminars or symposia, travel, publication of papers, books or magazines, or production of films, videotapes or other audiovisual materials.

Craig D Mallick, General Manager
Pamela E DiNardo, Program Administrator

2748 William Penn Foundation
2 Logan Square11th Floor
100 North 18th Street
Philadelphia, PA 19103-2757

215-988-1830
Fax: 215-988-1823
http://www.williampennfoundation.org

The foundation supports culture, environment, human development, including programs for youth and elderly, education, including early childhood, secondary, elementary and higher.

Kathryn J Engebretson, President

Rhode Island

2749 Champlin Foundations
300 Centerville Road
Suite 300 S
Warick, RI 02868

401-736-0370
Fax: 401-736-7248
E-mail: champlinfons@worldnet.att.net
http://www.fdncenter.org/grantmaker/champlin

Offers giving in the areas of higher, secondary and other education. Exclusively in Rhode Island.

David A King, Executive Director

2750 Providence Public Library
Reference Department
150 Empire Street
Providence, RI 02903-3219

401-455-8005
http://www.provlib.org

Member of The Foundation Center network, maintaining a collection of private foundation tax returns which provide information on the scope of grants dispensed by that particular foundation.

Dale Thompson, Director

2751 Rhode Island Foundation
One Union Station
Providence, RI 02903-4630

401-274-4564
Fax: 401-331-8085
http://www.rifoundation.org

Promotes charitable activities which tend to improve the living conditions and well-being of the residents of Rhode Island.

Ronald V Gallo, President

South Carolina

2752 Charleston County Library
68 Calhoun Street
Charleston, SC 29401

843-805-6801
Fax: 843-727-3741
http://www.ccpl.org

Member of The Foundation Center network, maintaining a collection of private foundation tax returns which provide information on the scope of grants dispensed by that particular foundation.

Jan Buvinger, Director

2753 South Carolina State Library
1500 Senate Street
Columbia, SC 29201-3815

803-734-8666
Fax: 803-734-8676
http://www.state.sc.us/scsl/

Member of The Foundation Center network, maintaining a collection of private foundation tax returns which provide information on the scope of grants dispensed by that particular foundation.

James B Johnson Jr, Director

South Dakota

2754 South Dakota Community Foundation
207 E Capitol Avenue
Suite 296
Pierre, SD 57501-3159

605-224-1025
800-888-1842
Fax: 605-224-5364
http://www.sdcommunityfoundation.org

The mission of the foundation is to promote philanthropy, receive and administer charitable gifts and invest in a wide range of programs promoting the social and economic well being of the people of the South Dakota. Grants given inSouth Dakota only.

Bob Sutton, Executive Director

2755 South Dakota State Library
Reference Department
800 Governors Drive
Pierre, SD 57501-2294

605-773-5070
Fax: 605-773-4950
http://www.sdstatelibrary.com

Member of The Foundation Center network, maintaining a collection of private foundation tax returns which provide information on the scope of grants dispensed by that particular foundation.

Tennesse

2756 Benwood Foundation
736 Market Street
Chattanooga, TN 37402-4803

423-267-4311
Fax: 423-267-9049

The general purpose of this foundation is to support such religious, charitable, scientific, literary and educational activities as will promote the advancement of mankind in any part of the United States of America. It should berecognized by all prospective grantees that while the foundation is not limited to the Chattanooga, Tennessee area, the bulk of the grants are made to organizations in the immediate area.

Jean R McDaniel, Executive Director

2757 Christy-Houston Foundation
1296 Dow Street
Murfreesboro, TN 37130-2413

615-898-1140
Fax: 615-895-9524

Offers grants for education, arts, culture and health care to residents and organizations of Rutherford County, Tennessee.

James R Arnhart, Executive Director

2758 Frist Foundation
3100 West End Avenue
Suite 1200
Nashville, TN 37203

615-292-3868
Fax: 615-292-5843
http://www.fristfoundation.org

Broad general-purposed charitable foundation whose grants are restricted primarily to Nashville.

Peter F Bird Jr, President/CEO

2759 JR Hyde Foundation
First Tennessee Bank
PO Box 84
Memphis, TN 38101-0084

901-523-4883
Fax: 901-523-4266

Offers grants for higher education, including scholarships for the children of Malone and Hyde employees, community funds, secondary education and youth services.

JR Hyde III, Executive Director

2760 Lyndhurst Foundation
517 E 5th Street
Chattanooga, TN 37403

423-756-0767
Fax: 423-756-0770
http://www.lyndhurstfoundation.org

Support local arts and culture and downtown revitalzation efforts in Chattanooga. Support the protection and enhancement of the natural environment of the Southern Appalachian Region. Support the elementary and secondary publicschools in Chattanooga.

Jack E Murrah, President

2761 Nashville Public Library
Business Information Division
615 Church Street
Nashville, TN 37219

615-862-5800
http://www.library.nashville.org

Member of The Foundation Center network, maintaining a collection of private foundation tax returns which provide information on the scope of grants dispensed by that particular foundation.

2762 Plough Foundation
6410 Poplar Avenue
Suite 710
Memphis, TN 38119-5736

901-761-9180
Fax: 901-761-6186

Offers grants for community projects, including a community fund, early childhood and elementary education, social service agencies and the arts.

Noris R Haynes Jr, Executive Director

2763 RJ Maclellan Charitable Trust
Provident Building
Suite 501
Chattanooga, TN 37402

423-755-1366

Supports higher and theological education, social services and youth programs.

Hugh O Maclellan Jr, Executive Director

Texas

2764 Albert & Ethel Herzstein Charitable Foundation
6131 Westview Drive
Houston, TX 77055-5421

713-681-7868
Fax: 713-681-3652
http://www.herzsteinfoundation.org

Concentrates support on temples and medical research with grants offered to medical schools.

L Michael Hajtman, President

2765 Burlington Northern Foundation
3800 Continental Plaza
777 Main Street
Fort Worth, TX 76102

817-352-6425
Fax: 817-352-7924

The major channel of philanthropy for Burlington Northern and its subsidiaries. The foundation administers a consistent contribution program in recognition of the company's opportunity to support and improve the general welfare andquality of life in communities it serves.

Beverly Edwards, President
Becky Blankenship, Grant Administrator

2766 Burnett Foundation
801 Cherry Street
Suite 1400
Fort Worth, TX 76102-6814

817-877-3344
Fax: 817-338-0448

Focus is on Fort Worth and Santa Fe, NM, seeking to be a positive force in the community, supporting the energy and creativity that exist in the nonprofit sector, and building capacity in organizations and people in the fields ofeducation, health, community affairs, human services and arts and humanities.

Thomas F Beech, Executive Director

2767 Cooper Industries Foundation
PO Box 4446
Houston, TX 77210-4446

713-209-8607
Fax: 713-209-8982
E-mail: evans@cooperindustries.com
http://www.cooperindustries.com

The policy of this foundation is to carry out the responsibilities of corporate citizenship, by supporting nonprofit organizations in areas where employees are located, which best serve the educational, health, welfare, civic,cultural and social needs of the foundation's communities. All gifts are consistent with the company's objectives to enhance the quality of life and to honor the principles and freedoms that have enabled the company to prosper and grow. AverageGrant: $5,000.

Victoria Guennewig, President
Jennifer L Evans, Secretary

2768 Corpus Christi State University
Library-Reference Department
805 Comanche
Corpus Christi, TX 78401

361-880-7000
Fax: 361-880-7005
http://www.library.ci.corpus-christi.tx.us

Member of The Foundation Center network, maintaining a collection of private foundation tax returns which provide information on the scope of grants dispensed by that particular foundation.

Denise Landry

2769 Cullen Foundation
601 Jefferson Street
Floor 40
Houston, TX 77002-7900

713-651-8837
Fax: 713-651-2374
http://www.cullenfdn.org

Supports educational, medical purposes, community funds and conservation.

Alan M Stewart, Executive Director
Sue A Alexander, Grants Administrator

2770 Dallas Public Library
Urban Information
1515 Young Street
Dallas, TX 75201-5499

214-670-1487
Fax: 214-670-1451
http://www.dallaslibrary.org

Member of The Foundation Center network, maintaining a collection of private foundation tax returns which provide information on the scope of grants dispensed by that particular foundation.

2771 El Paso Community Foundation
Historic Cortez Building
310 North Mesa 10th Floor
El Paso, TX 79901

915-533-4020
Fax: 915-532-0716
http://www.epcf.org

Grants to 501(c)(3) organizations in the El Paso geographic area. Fields of interest are arts and humanities, education, environment, health and disabilities, human services and civic benefits. No grants to individuals are offered.

Janice Windle, President
Virginia Martinez, Executive VP

2772 Ellwood Foundation
PO Box 52482
Houston, TX 77052-2482

713-739-0763

Scholarships for social services and education.

H Wayne Hightower, Executive Director

2773 Eugene McDermott Foundation
3808 Euclid Avenue
Dallas, TX 75205-3102

214-521-2924

Offers support primarily for higher and secondary education, health, cultural programs, and general community interests.

Eugene McDermott, Executive Director

2774 Ewing Halsell Foundation
711 Navarro Street
Suite 535
San Antonio, TX 78205-1786

210-223-2649
Fax: 210-271-9089

Offers grants in the areas of art and cultural programs, education, medical research, human services and youth services.

2775 Exxon Education Foundation
5959 Las Colinas Boulevard
Irving, TX 75039-2298

972-444-1106
Fax: 972-444-1405
http://www.exxon.mobile.com

Grants are given in the areas of environment, education, public information and policy research, united appeals and federated drives, health, civic and community service organizations, minority and women-oriented serviceorganizations, arts, museums and historical associations. In the education area grants are awarded to mathematics education programs, elementary and secondary school improvement programs, undergraduate general education programs, research, trainingand support programs.

EF Ahnert, Executive Director

2776 Fondren Foundation
7 TCT 37
PO Box 2558
Houston, TX 77252

713-236-4403

Provides support in various areas of interest with an emphasis on higher and secondary education, social services and cultural organizations.

Melanie Scioneaus, Executive Director

2777 George Foundation
310 Morton Street
PMB Suite C
Richmond, TX 77469-3135

281-342-6109
Fax: 281-341-7635
http://www.thegeorgefoundation.org

Offers giving for religious, educational, charitable or scientific purposes.

Roland Adamson, Executive Director

2778 Gordon & Mary Cain Foundation
8 E Greenway Plaza
Suite 702
Houston, TX 77046-0892

713-960-9283
Fax: 713-877-1824

The foundation is not limited to education but does contribute a large amount to that area. For a company to apply for a grant they must offer a statement of purpose or a summary of the project needing funding; budget with balancesheet, fund balance, distribution of funds, audited statement and number of employees; latest copy of IRS tax-exempt status letter 501(c)(3); current projects needing funding with amounts needed for entire project and the amount of the grant beingrequested.

James D Weaver, Executive Director

2779 Haggar Foundation
6113 Lemmon Avenue
Dallas, TX 75209-5715

214-352-8481
Fax: 214-956-4446

Offers support in various areas with an emphasis on higher and secondary education, including a program for children of company employees.

Mary Vaughan Rumble, Executive Director

2780 Hobby Foundation
2131 San Felipe Street
Houston, TX 77019-5620

713-521-4694
Fax: 713-521-3950

Offers grants to educational facilities in the state of Texas.

Oveta Culp Hobby, Executive Director

2781 Houston Endowment
600 Travis Street
Suite 6400
Houston, TX 77002-3000
713-238-8100
Fax: 713-238-8101
E-mail: info@houstonendowment.org
http://www.houstonendowment.org

Offers support for charitable, religious or educational organizations.

H Joe Nelson III, Executive Director

2782 Houston Public Library
Bibliographic Information Center
500 McKinney Street
Houston, TX 77002-2534
832-238-9640
Fax: 832-393-1383
http://www.hpl.lib.tx.us/hpl/hplhome

Member of The Foundation Center network, maintaining a collection of private foundation tax returns which provide information on the scope of grants dispensed by that particular foundation.

2783 James R Dougherty Jr Foundation
PO Box 640
Beeville, TX 78104-0640
361-358-3560
Fax: 361-358-9693

Offers support for Roman Catholic church-related industries including education, higher, secondary and other education.

Hugh Grove Jr, Executive Director

2784 Leland Fikes Foundation
3050 Lincoln Plaza
500 N Akard
Dallas, TX 75201
214-754-0144
Fax: 214-855-1245

Giving is focused on education, youth services, family planning, public interest and cultural programs.

Nancy Solana, Executive Director

2785 MD Anderson Foundation
PO Box 2558
Houston, TX 77252-2558
713-658-2316

The purpose of this foundation is to improve lives in the areas of health care, education, human service, youth and research.

John W Lowrie, Executive Director

2786 Meadows Foundation
3003 Swiss Avenue
Wilson Historic Block
Dallas, TX 75204-6049
214-826-9431
800-826-9431
Fax: 214-824-0642
E-mail: besterline@mfi.org
http://www.mfi.org

Support is given in the area of arts and culture, civic and public affairs , education, health, including mental health, and human services.

Bruce Esterline, VP Grants
Carol Stabler, Director Communications

2787 Moody Foundation
2302 Post Office Street
Suite 704
Galveston, TX 77550-1994
409-763-5333
Fax: 409-763-5564
http://www.moodyf.org

Provides major support for two foundation-initiated projects: the Transitional Learning Center, a residential rehabilitation and research facility for the treatment of traumatic brain injury, and Moody Gardens, a world-class educationand recreation complex that includes a 1-acre enclosed rainforest, the area's largest aquarium, a space museum, IMAX theater, and the Moody Hospitality Institute.

Peter M Moore, Grants Director

2788 Paul & Mary Haas Foundation
PO Box 2928
Corpus Christi, TX 78403-2928
361-887-6955

Offers scholastic grants to graduating high school seniors from Corpus Christi, Texas. The student must have above average grades and ability to prove financial need. The Foundation asks that the senior contact them in the Fall ofhis/her senior year in order to begin the in-house application process. The grant is a maximum of $1,500 per semester and is renewable for a total of eight semesters if the student maintains a 3.0 GPA. The student may attend college or university ofhis choice.

Karen Wesson, Executive Director

2789 Perot Foundation
12377 Merit Drive
Suite 1700
Dallas, TX 75251-2239
972-788-3000
Fax: 972-788-3091

Educational grants, medical research funding and grantmaking for the arts and cultural organizations.

Bette Perot, Executive Director

2790 RW Fair Foundation
PO Box 689
Tyler, TX 75710-0689
903-592-3811

Grants are given for secondary and higher education, church-related programs and legal education.

Wilton H Fair, Executive Director

2791 Sid W Richardson Foundation
309 Main Street
Fort Worth, TX 76102-4006
817-336-0494
Fax: 817-332-2176
E-mail: www.sidrichardson.org

This foundation was established for the purpose of supporting organizations that serve the people of Texas. Grants are given in the areas of education, health, the arts and human services.

Valleau Wilkie Jr, Executive Director

2792 Strake Foundation
712 Main Street
Suite 3300
Houston, TX 77002-3210
713-546-2400
Fax: 713-216-2401

Foundation gives primarily in Texas in the areas of operating budgets, continuing support, annual campaigns, special projects, research, matching funds and general purposes.

George W Strake Jr, Executive Director

2793 Trull Foundation
404 4th Street
Palacios, TX 77465-4812

361-972-5241
Fax: 361-972-1109
E-mail: trullfdn@ncnet.net
http://www.trullfoundation.org

1. A concern for the needs of the Palacios, Matagorda county are, where the foundation has its roots. Local health care, the senior center, and other local projects were considered and supported. 2. A concern for children and families. Grants are given to direct and channel lives away from child abuse, neglect from hunger, and poverty. 3. A concern for those persons and families devastated by the effects of substance abuse.

Gail Purvis, Executive Director
Lucja White, Administrative Assistant

Utah

2794 Marriner S Eccles Foundation
79 S Main Street
Salt Lake City, UT 84111-1901

801-246-5155

General support for Utah's human services, education and the arts programs.

Erma E Hogan, Executive Director

2795 Ruth Eleanor Bamberger and John Ernest Bamberger Memorial Foundation
136 South Main Street
Salt Lake City, UT 84101

801-364-2045
Fax: 801-322-5284

Offers support for secondary education, especially undergraduate scholarships for student nurses and for schools.

William H Olwell, Executive Director

2796 Salt Lake City Public Library
210 East 400 south
Salt Lake City, UT 84111-3280

801-524-8200
Fax: 801-524-8272
http://www.slcpl.lib.ut.us

Member of The Foundation Center network, maintaining a collection of private foundation tax returns which provide information on the scope of grants dispensed by that particular foundation.

Dana Tumtowsky, Comm Relations Coordinator
Nancy Tessman, Director

Vermont

2797 Vermont Community Foundation
PO Box 30
Three Court Street
Middlebury, VT 05753-0030

802-388-3355
Fax: 802-388-3398
http://www.vermontcf.org

Offers support for the arts and education, the environment, preservation of the community, public affairs and more for the betterment of Vermont.

Brian T Byrnes, President/CEO
Mary Conlon, Program Director

2798 Vermont Department of Libraries
Reference Services
109 State Street
Montpelier, VT 05609-0001

802-828-3268
Fax: 802-828-2199
http://www.dol.state.vt.us

Member of The Foundation Center network, maintaining a collection of private foundation tax returns which provide information on the scope of grants dispensed by that particular foundation.

2799 William T & Marie J Henderson Foundation
PO Box 600
Stowe, VT 05672-0600

Offers grants in the areas of elementary and secondary education.

William T Henderson, Executive Director

Virginia

2800 Beazley Foundation
3720 Brighton Street
Portsmouth, VA 23707-3902

757-393-1605
Fax: 757-393-4708
http://www.beazleyfoundation.org

The purpose of this foundation to further the causes of charity, education and religion. Offers support for higher, secondary and medical education, youth agencies, community agencies and development.

Richard Bray, President
Donna Russell, Associate Director

2801 Flagler Foundation
PO Box 644
Richmond, VA 23205

804-648-5033

Offers support for secondary and higher education, cultural programs and restoration.

Lawrence Lewis Jr, Executive Director

2802 Hampton Public Library
4207 Victoria Boulevard
Hampton, VA 23669-4200

757-727-1154
Fax: 757-727-1152
http://www.hampton.va.us

Member of The Foundation Center network, maintaining a collection of private foundation tax returns which provide information on the scope of grants dispensed by that particular foundation.

2803 Jeffress Memorial Trust
Bank Of America Private Bank
Po Box 26688
Richmond, VA 23261-6688

804-788-3698
Fax: 804-788-2700
http://www.wm.edu/grants/opps/jeffress.htm

Funds research in higher education.

Richard B Brandt, Advisor

2804 Kentland Foundation
PO Box 837
Berryville, VA 22611-0837

540-955-1082

Focuses on civic affairs organizations and education.

Helene Walker, Executive Director

Financial Resources / Washington

2805 Longview Foundation for Education in World Affairs/International Understanding
8639 B Sixteenth Street
Box 211
Silver Spring, MD 20910
301-681-0899
Fax: 301-681-0925
http://www.fdncenter.org/grantmaker/longview/index.html
Offers grants and scholarships with an emphasis on pre-collegiate education, primarily elementary education, and also supports teacher education.

Betsy Devlin-Foltz, Director

2806 Richmond Public Library
Business, Science & Technology Department
101 E Franklin Street
Richmond, VA 23219-2193
804-646-7223
Fax: 804-646-4757
http://www.richmondpubliclibrary.org
Member of The Foundation Center network, maintaining a collection of private foundation tax returns which provide information on the scope of grants dispensed by that particular foundation.

2807 Virginia Foundation for Educational Leadership
2204 Recreation Drive
Virginia Beach, VA 23456-6178
757-430-2412
Fax: 757-430-3247

George E McGovern, Division Director

Washington

2808 Comstock Foundation
S 2607 SE Boulevard #B115
Spokane, WA 99223
509-534-6499
The Foundation contributes only to 501(c)(3) organizations, limited to Spokane County and its environs. In the field of general education, Comstock Foundation favors grants only to private institutions of higher learning, and nogrants are made to individuals.

Horton Herman, Trustee
Charles M Leslie, Trustee

2809 Foster Foundation
1201 3rd Avenue
Suite 2101
Seattle, WA 98101-3086
206-624-5200
Offers support in art, culture, higher education, adult education, literacy and basic reading, health care and children and youth services.

Jill Goodsell, Executive Director

2810 MJ Murdock Charitable Trust
703 Broadway Street
Suite 701
Vancouver, WA 98660-3308
360-694-8415
Fax: 360-694-1819
http://www.murdock-trust.org
Offers support primarily for special projects of private organizations in the areas of education, higher education, human services and program development.

John Van Zytveld, Senior Program Director

2811 Seattle Foundation
200 5th Avenue
Suite 1300
Seattle, WA 98101-3151
206-622-2294
Fax: 206-622-7673
http://www.seattlefoundation.org
A community foundation that facilitates charitable giving; administers charitable funds, trusts and bequests; and distributes grants to non-profit organizations that are making a positive difference in our community. Grants areawarded to organizations working in areas that include social service, children and youth, civic, culture, elderly, conservation, education and health/rehabilitation.

Phyllis J Campbell, President/CEO
Molly Stearns, Senior Vice President

2812 Seattle Public Library
Science, Social Science
1000 4th Avenue
Seattle, WA 98104-1193
206-386-4636
Fax: 206-386-4634
http://www.spl.org
Member of The Foundation Center network, maintaining a collection of private foundation tax returns which provide information on the scope of grants dispensed by that particular foundation.

2813 Spokane Public Library
Funding Information Center
906 West Main Street
Spokane, WA 99201-0903
509-444-5300
Fax: 509-444-5364
http://www.spokanelibrary.org
Member of The Foundation Center network, maintaining a collection of private foundation tax returns which provide information on the scope of grants dispensed by that particular foundation.

Jan Sanders, Director

West Virginia

2814 Clay Foundation
1426 Kanawha Boulevard E
Charleston, WV 25301-3084
304-344-8656
Fax: 304-344-3805
Private charitable foundation making grants for health, education and programs for the aging or disadvantaged children.

Charles M Avampao, Executive Director

2815 Kanawha County Public Library
123 Capitol Street
Charleston, WV 25301-2686
304-343-4646
Fax: 304-348-6530
http://www.kanawha.lib.wv.us
Member of The Foundation Center network, maintaining a collection of private foundation tax returns which provide information on the scope of grants dispensed by that particular foundation.

2816 Phyllis A Beneke Scholarship Fund
Security National Bank & Trust Company
PO Box 511
Wheeling, WV 26003-0064

226

Offers support and scholarships for secondary education.

GP Schramm Sr, Executive Director

Wisconsin

2817 Faye McBeath Foundation
1020 N Broadway
Suite 112
Milwaukee, WI 53202-3157

414-272-2626
Fax: 414-272-6235
http://www.fayemcbeath.org

The purpose of the foundation is to provide Wisconsin people the best in education, child welfare, homes and care for the elderly and research in civics and government.

Scott E Gelzer, Executive Director
Aileen Mayer, Executive Assistant

2818 Lynde & Harry Bradley Foundation
1241 North Franklin Place
Milwaukee, WI 53202-2901

414-291-9915
Fax: 414-291-9991
http://www.bradleyfdn.org

The Foundation encourages projects that focus on cultivating a renewed, healthier and more vigorous sense of citizenship among the American people, and among peoples of all nations, as well. Grants are awarded to organizations andinstitutions exempt from federal taxation under Section 501(c)(3) and publicly supported under section 509(a), favor projects which are not normally financed by public tax funds, consider requests from religious organizations and institutions aswell.

Michael W Grebe, President/CEO
Terri L Famer, Director Of Administration

2819 Marquette University Memorial Library
1415 W Wisconsin Avenue
Milwaukee, WI 53233-2287

414-288-1515
Fax: 414-288-5324
http://www.marquette.edu/library/

Member of The Foundation Center network, maintaining a collection of private foundation tax returns which provide information on the scope of grants dispensed by that particular foundation.

2820 Siebert Lutheran Foundation
2600 N Mayfair Road
Suite 390
Wauwatosa, WI 53226-1392

414-257-2656
Fax: 414-257-1387
E-mail: rdjslf@execpc.com
http://www.siebertfoundation.org

Offers support in elementary and secondary, higher education and early childhood education.

Ronald D Jones, President
Deborah Engel, Administrative Assistant

2821 University of Wisconsin-Madison Memorial Library
728 State Street
Madison, WI 53706-1418

608-262-3242
Fax: 608-262-8569
E-mail: grantsinfo@library.wisc.edu
http://www.grants.library.wisc.edu

Member of The Foundation Center network, maintaining a collection of private foundation tax returns which provide information on the scope of grants dispensed by that particular foundation.

Wyoming

2822 Natrona County Public Library
307 E 2nd Street
Casper, WY 82601-2598

307-237-4935
Fax: 307-266-3734
http://www.library.natrona.net

Member of The Foundation Center network, maintaining a collection of private foundation tax returns which provide information on the scope of grants dispensed by that particular foundation.

Grants, Federal & Private

2823 American Honda Foundation
PO Box 2205
Torrance, CA 90509-2205

310-781-4090
Fax: 310-781-4270
http://www.hondacorporate.com/community

Offers support for national organizations whose areas of interest include youth and scientific education. Grants reach private elementary, secondary, higher, vocational and scientific education.

Kathryn A Carey, Manager

2824 Awards for University Administrators and Librarians
Association of Commonwealth Universities
John Foster House
36 Gordon Square
London WC1H OPF, England

171 3878572
Fax: 171 3872655
E-mail: pubinfo@acu.ac.uk; acusales@acu.ac.uk

Lists approximately 40 sources of financial assistance for administrative and library staff for universities worldwide. Includes name, address, phone, fax, tenure place and length, amount of aid, requirements for eligibility andapplication procedure, and frequency and number of grants available.

40 pages Biennial
ISSN: 0964-2714

Moira Hunter, Editor

2825 Awards for University Teachers and Research Workers
Association of Commonwealth Universities
36 Gordon Square
London
WC1H OPF, England

44-20-7380-6700
Fax: 44-20-7387-2655
E-mail: info@devry.edu
http://www.devry.edu

Lists approximately 740 awards open to university teachers and research workers in one country for research, study visits or teaching at a university in another country. Offers fellowships, visiting professorships and lectureships andtravel grants.

364 pages Biennial
ISSN: 0964-2706

2826 Educational Foundation of America
35 Church Lane
Westport, CT 06880-3515

203-226-6498
Fax: 203-227-0424
http://www.efaw.org

Funds projects in arts, education and programs benefiting Native Americans.

Diane M Allison, Executive Director

2827 Foundation Center
79 5th Avenue
Floor 8
New York, NY 10003-3076

212-620-4230
Fax: 212-807-3677
http://www.fdncenter.org

A national service organization which disseminates information on private giving through public service programs, publications, and through a national network of library reference collections for free public use. Over 100 networkmembers have sets of private foundation information returns, and the New York, Washington, DC, Cleveland and San Francisco reference collections operated by the Foundation offer a wide variety of services and collections of information on foundationsand grants.

Cheryl Loe, Director Of Communications
Laura Cascio, Fulfillment Management

2828 GTE Foundation
PO Box 152257
Irving, TX 75015-2257

972-507-5434
Fax: 972-615-4310
http://www.gte.com

The emphasis of giving for the foundation is on higher education in math, science and technology. It also sponsors scholarships and supports community funds and social service agencies that emphasize literacy training.

Maureen Gorman, VP

2829 George I Alden Trust
370 Main Street
Worcester, MA 01608-1714

508-798-8621
Fax: 508-791-6454
http://www.aldentrust.org

Gives to higher education organizations and facilities with an emphasis on scholarship endowments.

Francis H Dewey III, Executive Director

2830 Gershowitz Grant and Evaluation Services
505 Merle Hay Tower
Des Moines, IA 50310

515-270-1718
Fax: 515-270-8325
E-mail: gershowitz@netins.net

To give schools an edge in funding their technology programs

Michael V Gershowitz, PhD
Steve Panyan, PhD

2831 Grants and Awards for K-12 Students: 80 Sources of Funding
Aspen Publishing
1101 King Street
Suite 444
Alexandria, VA 22314-2944

800-638-8437
Fax: 301-417-7650

Offers information on what types of organizations fund K-12 students' activities and why; how to apply for grants and awards and contests; and more about grant and award opportunities for students in math, art, electronic networking,geography, civics and many other areas.

2832 Grants and Contracts Service
Department of Education/Regional Office Building
7th & D Streets
Suite 3124
Washington, DC 20202-0001

202-401-2000
Fax: 202-260-7225

To support improvements in teaching and learning and to help meet special needs of schools and students in elementary and secondary education

Gary J Rasmussen, Director

2833 Grantsmanship Center
PO Box 17220
Los Angeles, CA 90017-0220

213-482-9860
Fax: 213-482-9863
E-mail: norton@tgci.com
http://www.tgci.com

The world's oldest and largest training organization for the nonprofit sector. Since it was founded in 1972, the has trained trains more than 75,000 staff members of public and private agencies; training provided includesgrantsmanship, program management and fundraising. Center also produces publications on grantsmanship, fundraising, planning, management and personnel issues for nonprofit agencies.

Norton Kiritz, President

2834 John S & James L Knight Foundation
Wachovia Financial Center
Suite 3300
200south Biscayne Boulevard
Miami, FL 33131-2349

305-908-2635
http://www.knightfdn.org

The foundation makes national grants in journalism, education and the field of arts and culture. It also supports organizations in communities where the Knight brothers were involved in publishing newspapers but is wholly separatefrom and independent of those newspapers.

James D Spaniolo, Executive Director

2835 National Academy of Education
School of Education
Ceras 108
Stanford, CA 94305

212-998-9035
Fax: 212-995-4435

Offers the Spencer Postdoctoral Fellowship which is designed to promote scholarship in the United States and abroad on matters relevant to the improvement of education in all its forms.

Debbie Leong-Childs, Executive Director

2836 National Science Foundation
4201 Wilson Boulevard
Arlington, VA 22230

703-292-5111
Fax: 703-292-9184
http://www.nsf.gov

Offers grants, workshops and curricula for all grade levels.

Arden L Bement Jr, Director

2837 Trust to Reach Education Excellence
1904 Association Drive
Reston, VA 20191-1537

703-860-0200
800-253-7746
Fax: 703-476-5432

E-mail: tree@principals.org
http://http://tree.principals.org

Founded to make grants to educators and students who would ordinarily not have access to outstanding NASSP programs, such as camps, programs and workshops on leadership, technology and school reform.

Dr. Anne Miller, Executive Director

2838 Union Carbide Foundation
39 Old Ridgebury Road
Danbury, CT 06817-0001

203-794-6945
Fax: 203-794-7031

Offers grants in the areas of elementary and secondary education, with an emphasis on systemic reform; higher education with a focus on science and engineering; and environmental protection awareness.

Nancy W Deibler, Executive Director

2839 United States Institute of Peace
1200 17th Street NW
Washington, DC 20036

202-457-1700
Fax: 202-429-6063
http://www.usip.org

Includes grants, fellowships, a National Peace Essay Contest for high school students and teacher training institutes.

Richard H Solomon, President

2840 United States-Japan Foundation
145 E 32nd Street
Floor 12
New York, NY 10016-6055

212-481-8753
Fax: 212-481-8762
E-mail: info@us-jf.org
http://www.us-jf.org

A nonprofit, philanthropic organization with the principal mission of promoting a greater mutual knowledge between United States and Japan and to contribute to a strengthened understanding of important public policy issues ofinterest to both countries. Currently the focus is on precollegiate education, policy studies, and communications and public opinion.

2841 Westinghouse Foundation
Westinghouse Electric Corporation
Po Box 355
ECE 575C
Pittsburgh, PA 15230-0355

412-374-6824
Fax: 412-642-4874
http://www.westinghousenuclear.com

Makes charitable contributions to community priorities primarily where Westinghouse has a presence. Areas of emphasis include: education, health and welfare, culture and the arts and civic and social grants. Support for education iscentral to Westinghouse's contributions program, particularly higher education in the areas of engineering, applied science and business. Also encourages educational programs that strengthen public schools through enhanced student learningopportunities.

G Reynolds Clark, Executive Director

2842 Xerox Foundation
800 Long Ridge Road #1600
Stamford, CT 06902-1227

203-968-3445
http://www.xerox.com

Offers giving in the areas of higher education to prepare qualified men and women for careers in business, government and education.

Joseph M Cahalan, Executive Director

Fundraising

2843 A&L Fund Raising
95 Leggett Street
East Hartford, CT 06108-1140

860-242-2476
800-286-7247

Offers many successful fundraising programs including Christmas gifts, designer gift wraps from Ashley Taylor and Geoffrey Boehm chocolates. A&L sells only the highest quality items at affordable prices with great service to schoolsand organizations.

Anita Brown

2844 A+ Enterprises
1426 Route 33
Hamilton Square, NJ 08690-1704

609-587-1765
800-321-1765

A promotional corporation offering a variety of fundraising programs for schools and educational institutions, ranging from Christmas campaigns to chocolates, as well as magnets and gift campaigns.

2845 Aid for Education
CD Publications
8204 Fenton Street
Sliver Spring, MD 20910

301-588-6380
800-666-6380
Fax: 301-588-0519
E-mail: afe@cdpublications.com
http://cdpublications.com

18 pages Newsletter
ISSN: 1058-1324

Frank Kimko, Editor

2846 All Sports
21 Round Hill Road
Wethersfield, CT 06109

860-721-0273
800-829-0273
Fax: 860-257-9609
http://www.graduationshirts.com

Fundraising and school promotion company offering crew sweatshirts, hoods, tees, jackets, caps, gymwear and specialty signature shirts for graduating classes.

Wally Schultz, Owner

2847 Art to Remember
5535 Macy Drive
Indianapolis, IN 46236

317-826-0870
800-895-8777
Fax: 317-823-2822
E-mail: brackney@arttoremember.com
http://www.arttoremember.com

Raises funds for art departments and special school programs.

2848 Childrens Youth Funding Report
CD Publications
8204 Fenton Street
Sliver Spring, MD 20910

301-588-6380
800-666-6380
Fax: 301-588-0519
E-mail: cye@cdpublications.com
http://cdpublications.com

Detailed coverage of federal and private grant opportunities and legislative initiatives effecting childrens programs in such areas as child welfare, education healthcare.

18 pages Monthly

Steve Albright, Editor

2849 Dutch Mill Bulbs
25 Trinidad Avenue
PO Box 407
Hershey, PA 17033-1386

717-534-2900
800-533-8824
Fax: 800-556-0539
E-mail: info@dutchmillbulbs.com
http://www.dutchmillbulbs.com

Fundraising with flower bulbs since 1960. 50% profit-no hidden costs. Guaranteed to bloom. Free shipping. No cash up front.

Jeffrey E Ellenberger, President

2850 E-S Sports Screenprint Specialists
47 Jackson Street
Holyoke, MA 01040-5512

413-534-5634
800-833-3171
Fax: 413-538-8648

Scholastic Spirit Division offers screenprinted T-shirts, sweatshirts, shorts and apparel. This program offers schools and organizations an easy way to increase school spirit with no risk, no minimum orders and prompt delivery.

Aaron Porchelli, Division Director

2851 Fundraising USA
1395 State Route 23
Butler, NJ 07405-1736

973-283-1946
800-428-6178

Fundraiser offering a variety of programs for schools and organizations including Walk-A-Thons. This program is fast becoming the most popular way for schools to raise money. The walks are designed to take place at your own school,and children are not responsible for collecting any money. Fundraising USA collects all donations through the mail.

2852 Gold Medal Products
10700 Medallion Drive
Cincinnati, OH 45241-4807

513-769-7676
800-543-0862
Fax: 513-769-8500
E-mail: info@gmpopcorn.com
http://www.gmpopcorn.copm

Offers a full line of fundraising products popcorn poppers and supplies and programs including candy, clothing and sports programs for schools and colleges.

Chris Petroff
Dan Kroeger, President

2853 Human-i-Tees
400 Columbus Avenue
Valhalla, NY 10595-1335

800-275-2638
Fax: 914-745-1799
http://www.humanitees.com

Environmental T-shirt fundraisers that provide large profits while raising environmental awareness for thousands of school, youth and service organizations across the country.

2854 Hummel Sweets
PO Box 232
Forestville, MD 20747

800-998-8115

Offer fundraising programs with 45% to 50% profit.

2855 M&M Mars Fundraising
800 High Street
Hackettstown, NJ 07840-1552

908-852-1000
Fax: 908-850-2734

Offers America's favorite candies for fundraising programs throughout the year.

2856 QSP
Subsidiary of the Reader's Digest Association
PO Box 2003
Ridgefield, CT 06877-0903

203-756-3022

For twenty-seven years, this fundraiser has helped students raise more than $900,000,000 for extracurricular programs and projects that are essential to a meaningful, well-rounded education. With QSP programs, students earn money tofund worthwhile projects and learn about the business world at the same time. QSP offers various fundraising programs including: Family Reading Programs; The Music Package; Delightful Edibles; and The Parade of Gifts.

Robert L Metivier, Sales Manager

2857 Sally Foster Gift Wrap
PO Box 539
Duncan, SC 29334-0539

800-552-5875
Fax: 800-343-0809

Fundraiser offers gift wrap packages to schools. Offers high quality merchandise, including the heaviest papers and foils available. This proven two-week program is quick, easy and profitable offering your school or organization theopportunity to raise thousands of dollars to buy computers, books, athletic equipment and more. Organizations and schools keep 50% of all the profits, and there are no up-front costs or risks.

Mark Metcalfe, Sr VP

2858 School Identifications
Chas. E. Petrie Comapny
PO Box 12
Long Beach, CA 90801-0012

562-591-0666
800-772-0798
Fax: 562-591-0071
E-mail: info@schoolidents.com
http://www.schoolidents.com

An easy fundraising project for schools, offering school identification cards and tags for students.

2859 School Memories Collection
Fundcraft Publishing
PO Box 340
Collierville, TN 38027

901-853-7070
800-390-2129
Fax: 901-853-6196
E-mail: info@schoolplanners.com
http://www.schoolmemories.com

Memory books with games and activities.

Chris Bradley, Marketing Director

2860 Sports Shoes & Apparel
3 Moulton Drive
Londonderry, NH 03053-4061

603-437-7844
800-537-7844
Fax: 603-437-2300

Offers customized sweatshirts, T-shirts and beach towels at group discount, with several complete fund raising programs being available as well. Beach towels for fundraising.

Bill McMahon, Regional Manager

2861 Steve Wronker's Funny Business
39 Boswell Road
W Hartford, CT 06107-3708

860-233-6716
800-929-swfb
Fax: 860-561-8910
http://www.swfb.net/swfb.htm

Comedy and educational magic shows available for preschool and elementary school aged children. Award winning programs such as The Magic of Books and Magic from Around the World are available for any size audience. For middle schoolsand high schools, comedy hypnosis is a perfect venue for entertainment as a fundraising program, for high school after-prom parties, graduation parties, or just for an evening's entertainment.

Steve Wronker

2862 T-Shirt People/Wearhouse
10722 Hanna Street
Beltsville, MD 20705-2123

301-937-4843
800-638-7070
Fax: 301-937-2916

Fundraiser offering customized T-shirts to boost school spirit, raise funds, instill school pride and save money.

2863 Troll Book Fairs
100 Corporate Drive
Mahwah, NJ 07430-2041

201-529-4000
Fax: 201-529-8282

A profit-making program designed to introduce children to the wonderful world of books.

2864 Union Pen Company
70 Riverdale Avenue
Greenwich, CT 06831

800-846-6600
Fax: 800-688-4877
E-mail: unionpen@aol.com
http://www.unionpen.com

This company offers advertising gifts including customized pens and key chains that will increase confidence, school spirit and community goodwill in education. Group discounts are available.

Matt Roberts, General Manager
Morton Tenny, President

2865 www.positivepins.com
802 E 6th Streetve
PO Box 52528
Tulsa, OK 74152

918-587-2405
800-282-0085
Fax: 918-382-0906
E-mail: pinrus@aol.com
http://www.thepinman-pins.com

Fundraising organization used by educational organizations. Designer and manufacturer of lapel pins used for employee service, appreciation, volunteer recognition, donor incentives and recognition, public relations and spirit.

Bern L Gentry, President
Michelle Anderson, VP

Scholarships & Financial Aid

2866 AFL-CIO Guide to Union Sponsored Scholarships, Awards & Student Aid
AFL-CIO
815 16th Street NW
Suite 407
Washington, DC 20006-4104

202-637-5000
http://www.unionplus.org

Lists international and national unions, local unions, state federations and labor councils offering scholarships, awards or financial aid to students.

100 pages Annual

2867 American-Scandinavian Foundation
58 Park Avenue
New York, NY 10016

212-879-9779
Fax: 212-249-3444
E-mail: info@amscan.org
http://www.amscan.org

The Foundation provides information, scholarships and grants on the study programs in Scandinavia.

Andrey Henkin, Assistant Fellowship/Grant

2868 Arts Scholarships
Jewish Foundation for Education of Women
135 E 64th Street
New York, NY 10019-1827

212-288-3931
Fax: 212-288-5798
E-mail: fdnscholar@aol.com
http://www.jfew.org

These scholarships are being offered at the Julliard School, Tisch School, of the Arts at New York University, and the Manhattan School of Music to qualified students enrolled in their programs. Faculty members will select recipients.

Marge Goldwater, Executive Director

2869 CUNY Teacher Incentive Program
Jewish Foundation for Education of Women
135 E 64th Street
New York, NY 10019-1827

212-288-3931
Fax: 212-288-5798
E-mail: fdnscholar@aol.com
http://www.jfew.org

Provide stipends to CUNY graduates who are studying for a master's degree in education and interested in a teaching career in the New York City public school system. Contact the office of the Vice Chancellor for Academic Affairs atCUNY for further information.

Marge Goldwater, Executive Director

2870 College Board
45 Columbus Avenue
New York, NY 10023-6992

212-713-8000
Fax: 212-713-8282
http://www.collegeboard.org

The College Board is a national, nonprofit membership association that supports educational transitions through programs and services in assessment, guidance, admission, placement, financial aid, and educational reform.

2871 Dissertation Fellowships in the Humanities
Jewish Foundation for Education of Women
330 W 58th Street
New York, NY 10019-1827

212-883-9315
Fax: 212-288-5798

E-mail: fdnscholar@aol.com
http://www.jfew.org

A small number of fellowships will be awarded through the CUNY Graduate Center to qualified applicants.

Marge Goldwater, Executive Director

2872 George & Mary Kremer Foundation
1100 5th Avenue S
Suite 411
Naples, FL 34102-7415

941-261-2367
Fax: 941-261-1494

Provides scholarship funding for needy children in elementary Catholic schools throughout the Continental United States.

Mary Anderson Goddard, Director
Sister MT Ballrach, Assistant Director

2873 Intel Science Talent Search Scolarship
1719 N Street NW
Washington, DC 20036-2888

202-785-2255
Fax: 202-785-1243
E-mail: sciedu@sciserv.org
http://www.sciserv.org

Offers a variety of services to teachers and students, including Intel Science Talent Search Scholarship competition, science fairs and publications.

2874 Jewish Foundation for Education of Women
330 W 58th Street
New York, NY 10019-1827

212-288-3931
Fax: 212-288-5798
E-mail: fdnscholar@aol.com
http://www.jfew.org

The Jewish Foundation for Education of Women is a private, nonsectarian foundation providing scholarships to women for higher education in the New York City area. A variety of specific programs are available. Most programs areadministered collaboratively with area schools and organizations; the Foundation's mission is to help women of all ages attain the education and training needed to make them productive, economically independent members of the community.

Marge Goldwater, Executive Director

2875 Octameron Associates
1900 Mount Vernon Avenue
Alexandria, VA 22301-0748

703-836-5480
Fax: 703-836-5650
E-mail: info@octameron.com
http://www.octameron.com

Octameron is a publishing and consulting firm with over 25 years experience in financial aid and admissions.

2876 Scholarship America
One Scholarship Way
Saint Peter, MN 56082-1556

507-931-1682
800-537-4180
Fax: 507-931-9250
E-mail: dsnatoff@aol.com
http://dollarsforscholars.org

Provides community volunteers with the tools and support to create, develop and sustain legally constituted community-based scholarship foundations. Over 15,000 volunteers are active on 760 Dollars for Scholars chapter boards andcommittees throughout the United States. In addition, 20,000 high school youth and community residents are active in fund-raising events and academic support programs. Since the late 1950's, over 155,000 students have received Dollars for Scholarsscholarships.

David Bach, VP

2877 Scholarships in the Health Professions
Jewish Foundation for Education of Women
135 E 64th Street
New York, NY 10021

212-288-3931
Fax: 212-288-5798
E-mail: fdnscholar@aol.com
http://www.jfew.org

Provides scholarships to emigres from the former Soviet Union who are studying medicine, dentistry, nursing, pharmacy, OT, PT, dental hygiene, and physician assistanceship.

Marge Goldwater, Executive Director

Federal Listings

2878 Accounting & Financial Management Services
Department of Education/1175 Main Building
400 Maryland Avenue SW
Washington, DC 20202-0001

Fax: 202-401-0207

Mitchell L Laine, Chief Officer

2879 Assistance to States Division
Department of Education/3042 Mary E. Switzer Bldg.
330 C Street
Washington, DC 20202

202-401-2000
Fax: 202-260-7225

Tom Irvin, Acting Director

2880 Civil Rights
Department of Education/Mary E. Switzer Building
330 C Street
Suite 50001
Washington, DC 20202

202-205-5413
Fax: 202-260-7225

Norma Y Canto, Assistant Secretary

2881 Compensatory Education Program
US Department of Education
400 Maryland Avenue SW
Washington, DC 20202

202-260-0826
Fax: 202-260-7764

Mary Jean LeTendre, Director

2882 Elementary & Secondary Education
Department of Education/4000 Portals Building
1250 Maryland Avenue SW
Washington, DC 20024-2141

202-401-0113
Fax: 202-205-0303

Thomas W Payzant, Assistant Secretary

2883 Elementary Secondary Bilingual & Research Branch
Department of Education/Regional Office Bldg.
7th & D Streets
Suite 3653
Washington, DC 20202

202-401-0113
Fax: 202-260-7225

Queenola Tyler, Bureau Chief

2884 Elementary, Secondary & Vocational Analysis
Department of Education
400 Maryland Avenue SW
3043 Main Building
Washington, DC 20202-0001

202-401-0318
Fax: 202-260-7225

Thomas Corwin, Division Director

2885 Human Resources and Administration
Department of Education/3181 Main Building
400 Maryland Avenue SW
Washington, DC 20202-0001

202-401-0470
Fax: 202-260-7225

Rodney A McCowan, Assistant Secretary

2886 International Educational Exchange
Teacher Exchange, Off. of International Education
US Department of Education
Washington, DC 20202

202-708-5366

Offers educational information on student and teacher exchanges abroad.

2887 Legislation & Congressional Affairs
Department of Education/3153 Main Building
400 Maryland Avenue SW
Washington, DC 20202-0001

202-401-0020
Fax: 202-260-7225

Kay Casstevens, Assistant Secretary

2888 Library Programs
Department of Education
402 Capitol Place
555 New Jersey
Washington, DC 20202

202-219-2293
Fax: 202-260-7225

Inez Frazier, Administrative Officer

2889 Management Services
Department of Education/3005 Main Building
400 Maryland Avenue SW
Washington, DC 20202-0001

202-401-0500
Fax: 202-260-7225

2890 National Center for Education Statistics
Department of Education
400 Capitol Place
555 New Jersey
Washington, DC 20202

202-401-2000
Fax: 202-260-7225

Emerson J Elliott, Commissioner

2891 National Council on Disability
1331 F Street
Suite 1050
Washington, DC 20004-1107

202-272-2004
Fax: 202-272-2022
E-mail: mquighley@ncd.gov
http://www.ncd.gov/

An independent federal agency comprised of 15 members appointed by the President and confirmed by the Senate.

2892 National Institute of Child Health and Human Development
Office of Research Reporting
Building 31 Room 2A32
MSC 2425
Bethesda, MD 20892-2425

301-496-5133
Fax: 301-496-7101
http://www.nichd.nih.gov

Develops research to solve problems in the physical and mental evolution of development. Including some of the most emotionally draining disorders, learning disabilities, behavioral disabilities, birth defects and infant mortality. Acts as a clearinghouse of materials, information and referrals and more.

Duane Alexander, Director
Yvonne Thompson Maddox, Deputy Director

2893 **National Trust for Historic Preservation: Office of Education Initiatives**
1785 Massachusetts Avenue NW
Washington, DC 20036-2117
202-588-6296
http://www.nationaltrust.org

Teaching with Historic Places, a program offered by the National Park Service's National Register of Historic Places, and the National Trust for Historic Preservation Press.

2894 **No Child Left Behind**
Department of Education
400 Maryland Avenue, SW
Washington, DC 20202
202-401-2000
800-872-5327
Fax: 202-401-0689
http://www.ed.gov/nclb

Margaret Spelling, Secretary of Education

2895 **Office of Bilingual Education and Minority Language Affairs**
Department of Education/5082 Mary E. Switzer Bldg.
330 C Street
Washington, DC 20202
202-205-5463
Fax: 202-260-7225

Eugene E Garcia, Division Director

2896 **Office of Indian Education**
Department of Education/4300 Portals Building
1250 Maryland Avenue SW
Washington, DC 20024-2141
202-260-3774
Fax: 202-260-7225

John Wade, Division Director

2897 **Office of Migrant Education**
Department of Education/4100 Portals Building
1250 Maryland Avenue SW
Washington, DC 20024-2141
202-260-1164
Fax: 202-260-7225

Francis Corrigan, Division Director

2898 **Office of Overseas Schools**
US Department of State
US Department of State
Room H 328, SA 1
Washington, DC 20522-0132
202-261-8200
Fax: 202-261-8224
E-mail: OverseasSchools@state.gov
http://www.state.gov

Maintains detailed information on 190 overseas elementary and secondary schools which receive some assistance from the US Department of State. These schools provide an American-type education which prepares students for schools,colleges and universities in the United States.

Dr. Keith D Miller, Director

2899 **Office of Public Affairs**
Department of Education/4181 Main Building
400 Maryland Avenue SW
Washington, DC 20202-0001
202-401-3026
Fax: 202-260-7225

Kay Kahler, Division Director

2900 **Office of Special Education Programs**
Department of Education/3086 Mary E. Switzer Bldg.
600 Independence Avenue SW
Washington, DC 20202-2570
202-205-5507
Fax: 202-260-7225
E-mail: thomas_hehir@ed.gov
http://www.ed.gov./offices/osers/idea/index.htm

Thomas Hehir, Director

2901 **Office of Student Financial Assistance Programs**
Department of Education/5102 Regional Office Bldg.
7th & D Sts
Washington, DC 20202-0001
202-401-2000
Fax: 202-260-7225

Leo Kornfeld, Deputy Assistant

2902 **Planning & Evaluation Service**
Department of Education
Elementary Secondary Division
3127 Main Building, 400 Maryland
Washington, DC 20202
202-401-1968
Fax: 202-260-7225

Val Ptisko, Division Director

2903 **Policy, Planning & Management Services**
Department of Education
330 C Street SW
Suite 4022
Washington, DC 20201-0001
202-205-9960
Fax: 202-260-7225

Gen. John P Higgins Jr, Assistant Inspector

2904 **Programs for the Improvement of Practice**
Department of Education
500 N Capitol Street NW
Suite 555
Washington, DC 20001-1531
202-219-2164
Fax: 202-260-7225

Ronald W Cartwright, Sr Program Manager

2905 **Rehabilitation Services Administration**
Department of Education/3028 Mary E. Switzer Bldg.
330 C Street
Washington, DC 20202
202-205-5482
Fax: 202-260-7225
E-mail: fredric_schroeder@ed.gov

Fredric K Schroeder, Commissioner

2906 **Research to Practice Division**
Department of Education/3530 Mary E. Switzer Bldg.
330 C Street
Washington, DC 20202
202-205-9864
Fax: 202-260-7225
http://www.ed.gov/offices/osers/osef

Louis Danielson, Director

2907 **School Assistance Division**
Department of Education/4200 Portals Building
1250 Maryland Avenue SW
Washington, DC 20024-2141
202-260-2270
Fax: 202-260-7225

Catherine Schagh, Division Director

2908 School Improvement Programs-Drug Free Schools & Communities Division
Department of Education/4500 Portals Building
1250 Maryland Avenue SW
Washington, DC 20024-2141
202-260-3693
Fax: 202-260-7225

2909 School Improvement Programs-Equity and Educational Excellence Division
Department of Education/4500 Portals Building
1250 Maryland Avenue SW
Washington, DC 20024-2141
202-260-3693
Fax: 202-260-7225

Janice Williams-Madison, Division Director

2910 School Improvement Programs-School Effectiveness Division
Department of Education/4500 Portals Building
1250 Maryland Avenue SW
Washington, DC 20024-2141
202-260-3693
Fax: 202-260-7225

Daniel F Bonner, Division Director

2911 Training & Development Programs
Bureau of National Affairs
1231 25th Street NW
Washington, DC 20037-1157
202-452-4200
800-452-7773
Fax: 202-822-8092

Covers various types of employer-sponsored training programs, remedial education, program administration and more.

2912 US Department of Defense Dependents Schools
2461 Eisenhower Avenue
Alexandria, VA 22331-3000
571-325-0867

Marilyn Witcher

2913 US Department of Education
400 Maryland Avenue SW
Washington, DC 20202
800-872-5327
Fax: 202-401-0689
E-mail: customerservice@inet.ed.gov
http://www.ed.gov

Ensures equal access to education and promotes educational excellence for all Americans.

Margaret Spellings, Secretary of Education

2914 Vocational & Adult Education
Department of Education/4090 Mary E. Switzer Bldg.
330 C Street
Washington, DC 20202
202-205-5451
Fax: 202-260-7225

Augusta Souza Kappner, Assistant Secretary

2915 Washington DC Department of Education
825 N Capitol Street NE
Suite 900
Washington, DC 20202-4210
202-442-5885
Fax: 202-442-5026

Paul L Varce, Superintendent

Alabama

2916 Alabama State Department of Education
50 N Ripley Street
PO Box 302101
Montgomery, AL 36130-2101
334-242-9700
Fax: 334-242-9708
http://www.alsde.edu

Mission is to provide a state system of education which is committed to academic excellence and which provides education of the highest quality to all Alabama students, preparing them for the 21st century. For certification information contact the Alabama certification office at 334-242-9977.

Edward R Richardson, Superintendent

2917 Assistant Superintendent & Financial Services
Alabama Department of Education
50 N Ripley Street
Montgomery, AL 36130-0624
334-242-9741
Fax: 334-242-9708

William C Berryman, Division Director

2918 Deputy Superintendent
Alabama Department of Education
50 N Ripley Street
Montgomery, AL 36130-0624
334-242-9700
Fax: 334-242-9708

Thomas Ingram, Assistant Superintendent

2919 Disability Determination Division
Alabama Department of Education
50 N Ripley Street
Montgomery, AL 36130-0624
205-989-2100
Fax: 800-524-6489

Tommy Warren, General Counsel

2920 General Administrative Services
Alabama Department of Education
50 N Ripley Street
Montgomery, AL 36130-0624
334-242-9700
Fax: 334-242-9708

William J Rutherford, Assistant Superintendent

2921 General Counsel
Alabama Department of Education
50 N Ripley Street
Montgomery, AL 36130-0624
334-242-9700
Fax: 334-242-9708

Richard N Meadows, General Counsel

2922 Instructional Services
Alabama Department of Education
50 N Ripley Street
Montgomery, AL 36130-0624
334-242-9700
Fax: 334-242-9708

Charlie G Williams, Assistant Superintendent

2923 Professional Services
Alabama Department of Education
50 N Ripley Street
Montgomery, AL 36130-0624
334-242-9700
Fax: 334-242-9708

Eddie R Johnson, Assistant Superintendent

2924 Rehabilitation Services
Alabama Department of Rehabilitation Services
2129 E South Boulevard
PO Box 11586
Montgomery, AL 36111-0586

334-281-8780
800-441-7607
Fax: 334-281-1973
http://www.rehab.state.al.us

State agency that provides and services and assistance to Alabama's children and adults with disabilities and their families.

Steve Shrivers, Commissioner

2925 Special Education Services
Alabama Department of Education
50 N Ripley Street
Montgomery, AL 36130-0624

334-242-8114
Fax: 334-242-9192

Bill East, Division Director

2926 Student Instructional Services
Alabama Department of Education
50 N Ripley Street
Montgomery, AL 36130-0624

334-242-8256
Fax: 334-242-9708

Martha V Beckett, Assistant Superintendent

2927 Superintendent
Alabama Department of Education
50 N Ripley Street
Montgomery, AL 36130-0624

334-242-9700
Fax: 334-242-9708

Ed Richardson, Superintendent

2928 Vocational Education
Alabama Department of Education
50 N Ripley Street
Montgomery, AL 36130-0624

334-242-9111
Fax: 334-353-8861

Stephen B Franks, Division Director

Alaska

2929 Alaska Commission on Postsecondary Education
Alaska Department of Education & Early Development
3030 Vintage Boulevard
Juneau, AK 99801-7100

907-465-2962
800-441-2962
Fax: 907-465-5316
E-mail: custsvc@acpe.state.ak.us
http://www.state.ak.us/acpc

This state agency coordinates administration of state-funded education financial assistance for students and their families. This agency is also responsible for licensing and regulating postsecondary institutions to operate in Alaska.

Diane Barrans, Executive Director
Dennis Watson, SFA Director

2930 Alaska Department of Education Administrative Services
801 W 10th Street
Suite 200
Juneau, AK 99801-1894

907-465-2802
Fax: 907-465-4156

For certification information visit www.eed.state.ak.us/TeacherCertification/ or contact 907-465-2831.

Shirley J Halloway, Commissioner

2931 Alaska Department of Education & Early Development
801 W 10th Street
Suite 200
Juneau, AK 99801

907-465-2800
Fax: 907-465-3452
http://www.educ.state.ak.us

Gerald Covey, Commissioner

2932 Education Program Support
Alaska Department of Education
801 W 10th Street
Suite 200
Juneau, AK 99801-1878

907-465-2800
Fax: 907-465-4156

Harry Gamble, Information Officer

2933 Libraries, Archives & Museums
Alaska Department of Education & Energy Developmnt
PO Box 110571
Juneau, AK 99811

907-465-2910
Fax: 907-465-2151
E-mail: ase@eed.state.ak.us
http://www.energy.state.ak.us

Karen Crane, Division Director

2934 School Finance & Data Management
Alaska Department of Education
801 W 10th Street
Suite 200
Juneau, AK 99801-1878

907-465-2800
Fax: 907-465-3452

Duane Guiley, Division Director

2935 Vocational Rehabilitation
Alaska Department of Labor & Workforce Development
801 W 10th Street
Suite A
Juneau, AK 99801-1878

907-465-2814
Fax: 907-465-2856
http://www.labor.state.ak.us/dur/home.htm

Duane French, Division Director

Arizona

2936 National Council of State Supervisors of Music
Arizona Department of Education
1535 W Jefferson Street
Phoenix, AZ 85007-3209

602-542-5393
800-352-4558
Fax: 602-542-3590
E-mail: mgiffor@mail1.ade.state.az.com
http://http://ade.state.az.us/

Strives to improve the supervision and education of music on the state level and to encourage coordination between states.

Arkansas

2937 Arkansas Department of Education
4 State Capitol Mall
Room 304A
Little Rock, AR 72201-1071
501-682-4475
Fax: 501-682-1079
http://http://arkedu.state.ar.us

Mission is to provide the highest quality leadership, service, and support to school districts and schools in order that they may provide equitable, quality education for all to ensure that all public schools comply with theStandards. For certification information visit http://arkedu.state.us/teachers/index.html or contact 501-371-1580.

T.Kenneth James, Education Director

2938 Arkansas Department of Education: Special Education
4 State Capitol Mall
Room 105C
Little Rock, AR 72201-1071
501-682-4221
Fax: 501-682-5159
E-mail: mharding@arkedu.k12.ar.us
http://http://arkedu.state.ar.us

Marcia Harding, Associate Director

2939 Federal Programs
Arkansas Department of Education
4 State Capitol
Room 304A
Little Rock, AR 72201-1011
501-682-4268
Fax: 501-682-5010

Clearence Lovell, Associate Director

2940 Human Resources Office
Arkansas Department of Education
4 State Capitol
Room 304A
Little Rock, AR 72201-1011
501-682-4210
Fax: 501-682-1193

Clemetta Hood, Personnel Manager

California

2941 California Department of Education
721 Capitol Mall
1430 N Street
Sacramento, CA 95814-4702
916-657-4766
Fax: 916-657-4975
http://www.cde.ca.gov

For certification information visit www.ctc.ca.gov or contact 916-445-8778.

Delaine A Easton, Superintendent

2942 California Department of Education Catalog
CDE Books & Videos
PO Box 271
Sacramento, CA 95812-0271
916-323-4583
800-995-4099
Fax: 916-323-0823

Offers new techniques and fresh perspectives in handbooks, guides, videos and more.

2943 California Department of Special Education
721 Capitol Mall
Sacramento, CA 95814-4702
916-445-4613
Fax: 916-327-3516

Alice Parker, Director

2944 Curriculum & Instructional Leadership Branch
California Department of Education
721 Capitol Mall
Sacramento, CA 95814-4702
916-657-3043

Harvey Hunt, Deputy

2945 Department Management Services Branch
California Department of Education
721 Capitol Mall
Sacramento, CA 95814-4785
916-657-5474
Fax: 916-319-0106

Diane Kirkham, Deputy

2946 Executive Office & External Affairs
California Department of Education
721 Capitol Mall
Sacramento, CA 95814-4702
916-657-3027
Fax: 916-657-4975

Susie Lange, Division Director

2947 Field Services Branch
California Department of Education
721 Capitol Mall
Sacramento, CA 95814-4702
916-657-4748
Fax: 916-319-0155

Robert W Agee, Division Director

2948 Governmental Policy Branch
California Department of Education
721 Capitol Mall
Sacramento, CA 95814-4702
916-657-5461

Joe Holsinger, Deputy

2949 Legal & Audits Branch
California Department of Education
1430 N Street
Suite 5319
Sacramento, CA 95814-4702
916-319-0860
Fax: 916-319-0155

Marsha Bedwell, General Counsel

2950 Region 9: Education Department
50 United Nations Plaza
San Francisco, CA 94102-4912
415-556-4920

2951 Specialized Programs Branch
California Department of Education
721 Capitol Mall
Sacramento, CA 95814-4702
916-657-2642
Fax: 916-319-0155

Shirley A Thornton, Chief Counsel

Colorado

2952 Colorado Department of Education
201 E Colfax Avenue
Denver, CO 80203-1799

303-866-6600
Fax: 303-866-6938
http://www.cde.state.co.us

For certification information visit
www.cde.state.co.us/index_license.htm or contact
303-866-6628.

William T Moloney, Commissioner

2953 Educational Services
Colorado Department of Education
201 E Colfax Avenue
Denver, CO 80203-1704

303-866-6600
Fax: 303-866-6811

Arthur J Ellis, Commissioner

2954 Federal Program Services
Colorado Department of Education
201 E Colfax Avenue
Denver, CO 80203-1704

303-866-6782
Fax: 303-866-6647

Betty Hinkle, Executive Director

2955 Management, Budget & Planning
Colorado Department of Education
201 E Colfax Avenue
Denver, CO 80203-1704

303-866-6822
Fax: 303-866-6938

Karen Stroup, Division Director

2956 Public School Finance
Colorado Department of Education
201 E Colfax Avenue
Denver, CO 80203-1704

303-866-6845

Dan Stewart, Division Director

2957 Special Services
Colorado Department of Education
201 E Colfax Avenue
Denver, CO 80203-1704

303-866-6782
Fax: 303-866-6785

Brian McNulty, Assistant Commissioner

2958 State Library
Colorado Department of Education
201 E Colfax Avenue
Denver, CO 80203-1704

303-866-6900
Fax: 303-866-6940

Nancy Bolt, Assistant Commissioner

2959 Teacher Certification & Professional Education
Colorado Department of Education
201 E Colfax Avenue
Denver, CO 80203-1704

303-866-6851
Fax: 303-866-6968

Gene Campbell, Assistant Commissioner

2960 US Department of Education: Region VIII
1244 Speer Boulevard
Suite 310
Denver, CO 80204-3582

303-844-3544
Fax: 303-844-2524
http://www.ed.gov

Helen Littlejohn, Public Affairs Officer

Connecticut

2961 Connecticut Department of Education
165 Capitol Avenue
Hartford, CT 06106

860-713-6500
Fax: 860-713-7001
E-mail: thomas.murphy@po.state.ct.us
http://www.state.ct.us/sde

For certification information visit www.state.ct.us/sde
or contact 860-713-6969.

Betty Sternberg, Commissioner

2962 Connecticut Early Childhood Unit
Department of Education
PO Box 2219
Hartford, CT 06145

860-566-5497

Offers programs for children, infants and toddlers with
disabilities.

Kay Halverson, Coordinator

2963 Connecticut Governor's Committee on
Employment of the Handicapped
Labor Department Building
200 Folly Brook Boulevard
Wethersfield, CT 06109-1153

860-263-6000
Fax: 860-263-6216

2964 Education Programs & Services
Connecticut Department of Education
25 Industrial Park Road
Middletown, CT 06457-1520

860-807-2005
Fax: 860-635-7125

Theodore S Sergi, Division Director

2965 Finance & Administrative Services
Connecticut Department of Education
165 Capitol Avenue Office Building
Hartford, CT 06106-1659

860-566-4879
Fax: 860-713-7011

John G Coroso, Division Director

2966 Human Services
Connecticut Department of Education
165 Capitol Avenue Office Building
Hartford, CT 06106-1659

860-713-6690
Fax: 860-713-7011

Dick Wilber, Division Director

2967 Information Systems
Connecticut Department of Education
165 Capitol Avenue Office Building
Hartford, CT 06106-1659

860-647-5064
Fax: 860-647-5027

Greg Vassar, Division Director

2968 Office of State Coordinator of Vocational Education for Disabled Students
Vocational Prgs. for the Disabled & Disadvantaged
PO Box 2219
Hartford, CT 06145
860-807-2001
Fax: 860-807-2196

2969 Teaching & Learning Division
Connecticut Department of Education
165 Capitol Ave Ofc Building
Hartford, CT 06106-1659
203-566-8113

Betty J Sternberg, Division Director

2970 Vocational-Technical School Systems
Connecticut Department of Education
25 Industrial Park Road
Middletown, CT 06457-1520
860-822-6832
Fax: 860-807-2196

Delaware

2971 Assessments & Accountability Branch Delaware Department of Education
Federal & Lockerman Streets
#279
Dover, DE 19903
302-739-6700
Fax: 302-739-3092

Marsha DeLain, Associate Supervisor

2972 Delaware Department of Education
401 Federal Street
PO Box 1402
Dover, DE 19903-1402
302-739-4601
Fax: 302-739-4654
E-mail: dedoe@doe.k12.de.us
http://www.doe.state.de.us

Our mission is to promote the highest quality education for every Delaware student by providing visionary leadership and superior service. For certification information visit www.doe.state.de.us or contact 302-739-4686.

Joseph A Pika PhD, President State Board of Ed.
Valerie A Woodruff, Executive Secretary

2973 Delaware Department of Education: Administrative Services
Townsend Building, Suite 2
PO Box 1402
Dover, DE 19903-1402
302-739-4601
Fax: 302-739-4654
E-mail: dedoe@doe.k12.de.us
http://www.doe.state.de.us

Valerie Woodroff, Secretary

2974 Improvement & Assistance Branch Delaware Department of Education
Federal & Lockerman Streets
#279
Dover, DE 19903
302-739-3772
Fax: 302-739-7645

Valerie Woodruff, Associate Superintendent

District of Columbia

2975 DC Division of Special Education
10th & H Streets NW
Washington, DC 20001
202-724-4800
Fax: 202-442-5517

Doris Woodson, Superintendent

2976 District of Columbia Department of Education
415 APO Street NW
Presidential Building
Washington, DC 20004
204-724-4222

For certification information visit www.k12.dc.us.

Franklin L Smith, Superintendent

2977 Grants Administration Branch
District of Columbia
415 12th St NW, Presidential Building
Washington, DC 20004
202-274-5597
Fax: 202-274-5264

Barbara Jackson, Division Director

2978 Management Systems & Technology Services Division
District of Columbia
415 12th St NW, Presidential Building
Washington, DC 20004
202-724-4062

Ulysses Keyes, Division Director

2979 State Services Division District of Columbia
415 12th Street NW
Presidential Building
Washington, DC 20004
202-624-5490
Fax: 202-624-8588

Andrew E Jenkins, Division Director

Florida

2980 Florida Department of Education
Turlington Building Suite 1514
325 West Gaines Street
Tallahassee, FL 32399
850-245-0505
Fax: 850-245-9667
E-mail: mccueq@mail.doe.state.fl.us
http://www.firn.edu/doe/

Offers information on community colleges, vocational education, public schools, human resources, financial assistance, adult education and more. For certification information visit www.fldoe.org or contact 850-488-2317.

John Winn, Commissioner

Georgia

2981 Georgia Department of Education
2066 Twin Towers E
Atlanta, GA 30334
404-656-2800
877-729-7867
Fax: 404-651-6867
E-mail: help.desk@doe.k12.ga.us
http://www.gadoe.org

Among many other features, this organization offers agriculture education, federal programs, Leadership

Development Academy, school and community nutrition progams, Spanish language and cultural program, technology/career (vocational)education and more. For certification information visit www.gapsc.com or contact 404-657-9000.

Ron Newcomb, Commission Staff Director
Kathy Cox, Superintendent

Hawaii

2982 Business Services Office
Hawaii Department of Education
1390 Miller Street
Honolulu, HI 96813-2418
808-586-3444
Fax: 808-586-3445

Alfred Suga, Division Director

2983 Hawaii Department of Education
PO Box 2360
1390 Miller Street
Honolulu, HI 96804
808-586-3349
Fax: 808-586-3234
E-mail: boe_hawaii@notes.k12.hi.us
http://www.k12.hi.us

For certification information visit http://doe.k12.hi.us.

Patricia Hamamoto, Superintendent

2984 Information & Telecommunications Services
Hawaii Department of Education
1390 Miller Street
Honolulu, HI 96813-2418
808-586-3307
Fax: 808-586-3645

Philip Bossert, Division Director

2985 Instructional Services
Hawaii Department of Education
1390 Miller Street
Honolulu, HI 96813-2418
808-586-3446
Fax: 808-586-3429

Mildred Higashi, Division Director

2986 Office of the State Director for Career & Technical Education
University of Hawaii
Lower Campus Road
Lunalilo Freeway Portable 1
Honolulu, HI 96822-2489
808-956-7461
Fax: 808-956-9096
E-mail: kjones@hawaii.edu
http://www.hawaii.edu/cte

Karla Jones, State Director

2987 Personnel Services
Hawaii Department of Education
1390 Miller Street
Honolulu, HI 96813-2418
808-586-3400
Fax: 808-586-3419

Donald Nugent, Division Director

2988 State Public Library System
Hawaii Department of Education
1390 Miller Street
Honolulu, HI 96813-2418
808-586-3704
Fax: 808-586-3715

Batholomew Kane, State Librarian

Idaho

2989 Idaho Department of Education
PO Box 83720-0027
650 West State Street
Boise, ID 83702-0027
208-332-6800
Fax: 208-334-2228
E-mail: mhoward@sde.state.id.us
http://www.sde.state.id.us

For certification information visit www.sde.state.id.us/certification or contact 808-586-2616.

Marilyn Howard, Superintendent

2990 Vocational Education Division
Idaho State Department of Education
605 W State Street
Boise, ID 83702-0096
208-334-3390
Fax: 208-334-5305
http://www.sde.state.id.us

Committed to empower people with disabilities with appropriate resources to make informed choices about their futures.

Dr.Michael Graham, Administrator

Illinois

2991 Executive Deputy Superintendent
Illinois Department of Education
100 N 1st Street
Springfield, IL 62777
217-782-0342
Fax: 217-782-5333

2992 Finance & Support Services
Illinois Department of Education
100 N 1st Street
Springfield, IL 62777
217-782-5596
Fax: 217-782-4550

Karol Richardson, Division Director

2993 Illinois Department of Education
100 N 1st Street
Springfield, IL 62777
217-782-2221
Fax: 217-785-8585
http://www.isbe.state.il.us

For certification information visit www.isbe.state.il.us/teachers/default.htm.

Ernest R Wish, Superintendent

2994 Planning, Research & Evaluation
Illinois Department of Education
100 N 1st Street
Springfield, IL 62702-5199
217-782-3950
Fax: 217-524-7784

Connie Wise, Division Director

2995 Programs & Accountability
Illinois Department of Education
100 N 1st Street
Springfield, IL 62702-5199
217-782-2221
Fax: 217-524-4928

2996 Recognition & Supervision of Schools
Illinois Department of Education
100 N 1st Street
Springfield, IL 62702-5199
217-782-4123
Fax: 217-524-6125

Dick Haney, Division Director

2997 Region 5: Education Department
6130 W Walcott Avenue
Chicago, IL 60636
773-535-9570
Fax: 773-535-9582

2998 School Finance
Illinois Department of Education
100 N 1st Street
Springfield, IL 62702-5199
217-782-5439
Fax: 217-785-7650

Gary Ey, Division Director

2999 School Improvement & Assessment Services
Illinois Department of Education
100 N 1st Street
Springfield, IL 62702-5199
217-782-5439
Fax: 217-785-7650

Tom Kerins, Division Director

3000 Special Education
Illinois State Board of Education
100 N 1st Street
Springfield, IL 62702-5199
217-782-5589
Fax: 217-782-0372
E-mail: asims@isbe.net
http://www.isbe.net

Anthony Sims, Manager Special Education

3001 Specialized Programs
Illinois Department of Education
100 N 1st Street
Springfield, IL 62702-5199
312-814-2223
Fax: 312-814-2282

Brenda Heffner, Division Director

3002 Student Development Services
Illinois Department of Education
100 N 1st Street
Springfield, IL 62702-5199
217-782-0995
Fax: 217-785-7849

Frank Llano, Division Director

3003 Teacher Education & Certification
Illinois Department of Education
100 N 1st Street
Springfield, IL 62702-5199
217-782-3774
Fax: 217-524-1289

Sue Bentz, Division Director

Indiana

3004 Administration & Financial Management Center
Indiana Department of Education
100 N Capitol Avenue, Room 229
Indianapolis, IN 46204-2203
317-232-0808
Fax: 317-233-6326

Patty Bond, Director

3005 Center for School Assessment & Research
Indiana Department of Education
100 N Capitol Avenue, Room 229
Indianapolis, IN 46204-2203
317-232-9050
Fax: 317-233-2196

Wes Bruce, Director

3006 Community Relations & Special Populations
Indiana Department of Education
100 N Capitol Avenue, Room 229
Indianapolis, IN 46204-2203
317-232-0520
Fax: 317-233-6502

Linda Miller, Senior Officer

3007 External Affairs
Indiana Department of Education
100 N Capitol Avenue, Room 229
Indianapolis, IN 46204-2203
317-232-6614
Fax: 317-232-8004

Joe DiLaura, Division Director

3008 Indiana Department of Education
200 W Washington Street
State House, Room 229
Indianapolis, IN 46204-2798
317-232-6665
Fax: 317-232-8004
http://www.doe.state.in.us

For certification information visit www.in.gov/psb or contact 866-542-3672.

Suellen K Reed, Superintedent

3009 Office of the Deputy Superintendent
Indiana Department of Education
100 N Capitol Avenue, Room 229
Indianapolis, IN 46204-2203
317-232-0510
Fax: 317-232-0589

Robert Dalton, Division Director

3010 Policy & Planning
Indiana Department of Education
100 N Capitol Avenue
Room 229
Indianapolis, IN 46204-2203
317-232-6648

Evelyn Sayers, Policy Analyst

3011 School Improvement & Performance Center
Indiana Department of Education
100 N Capitol Avenue, Room 229
Indianapolis, IN 46204-2203
317-232-9100
Fax: 317-232-9121

Phyllis Land Usher, Division Director

3012 State Board Relations & Legal Services
Indiana Department of Education
100 N Capitol Avenue, Room 229
Indianapolis, IN 46204-2203
317-232-6622
Fax: 317-232-8004

Jeffrey Zaring, Administrator

Iowa

3013 Community Colleges Division
Iowa Department of Education
14th E & Grand Streets
Des Moines, IA 50319-0001
515-281-8260

Harriet Custer, Division Director

3014 Division of Library Services
Iowa Department of Education
14th E & Grand Streets
Des Moines, IA 50319-0001
515-281-4105

Sharman B Smith, Administrator

3015 Educational Services for Children & Families
Iowa Department of Education
14th E & Grand Streets
Des Moines, IA 50319-0001
515-281-3575

Susan J Donielson, Administrator

3016 Elementary & Secondary Education
Iowa Department of Education
14th E & Grand Streets
Des Moines, IA 50319-0001
515-281-3333

Ted Stilwill, Administrator

3017 Financial & Information Services
Iowa Department of Education
Grimes State Office Buildings
Des Moines, IA 50319-0001
515-281-5293
Fax: 515-242-5988
E-mail: lee.tack@ed.state.ia.us
http://www.state.ia.us/educate

Leland Tack, Administrator

3018 Iowa Department of Education
Grimes State Office Building
400 E 14th & Grand Streets
Des Moines, IA 50319-0146
515-281-5294
Fax: 515-281-5988
E-mail: webmaster@ed.state.ia.us
http://www.state.ia.us/educate

Serves the students of Iowa by providing leadership and resources for schools, area education agencies and community colleges. For certification information visit www.state.ia.us/boee or contact 515-281-3245.

Ted Stilwill, Director

3019 Iowa Public Television
Iowa Department of Education
14th E & Grand Streets
Des Moines, IA 50319-0001
515-242-3150

David Bolender, Executive Director

3020 Vocational Rehabilitation Services
Iowa Department of Education
14th E & Grand Streets
Des Moines, IA 50319-0001
515-281-6731

Margaret Knudsen, Administrator

Kansas

3021 Assistant Commissioner's Office
Kansas Department of Education
120 SE 10th Avenue
Topeka, KS 66612
785-296-2303
Fax: 785-296-1413
E-mail: sfreden@ksbe.state.ks.us
http://www.ksbe.state.ks.us

Sharon Freden, Assistant Commissioner

3022 Fiscal Services & Quality Control
Kansas Department of Education
120 SE 10th Avenue
Topeka, KS 66612
785-296-3871
Fax: 785-296-0459

Dale M Dennis, Deputy Commissioner

3023 Kansas Department of Education
120 SE Tenth Avenue
Topeka, KS 66612-1182
785-296-3201
Fax: 785-796-7933
http://www.ksbe.state.ks.us

For certification information visit www.ksde.org or contact 785-291-3678.

John A Tompkins, Commissioner

3024 Kansas Division of Special Education
120 E 10th Street
Topeka, KS 66612
785-296-4945
Fax: 785-296-1413

Kentucky

3025 Chief of Staff Bureau
Kentucky Department of Education
500 Mero Street, 19th Floor
Frankfort, KY 40601-1957
502-564-3141
Fax: 502-564-6470

Hunt Helm, Office Communications

3026 Communications Services
Kentucky Department of Education
500 Mero Street
19th Floor
Frankfort, KY 40601-1957
502-564-3421
Fax: 502-564-6470
http://www.kde.state.ky.us

Hunt Helm, Associate Commissioner

3027 Curriculum, Assessment & Accountability Services
Kentucky Department of Education
500 Mero Street, 19th Floor
Frankfort, KY 40601-1957
502-564-4394
Fax: 502-564-7749

Neal Klingston, Division Director

3028 Education Technology Office
Kentucky Department of Education
500 Mero Street, 19th Floor
Frankfort, KY 500 M-1957
502-564-6900
Fax: 502-564-4695

Don Coffman, Division Director

3029 Kentucky Department of Education
500 Mero Street
Capitol Plaza Tower
Frankfort, KY 40601-1957
502-564-3141
Fax: 502-564-5680
http://www.kde.state.ky.us

For certification information visit www.kyepsb.net or contact 502-573-4606.

Gene Wilhoit, Commissioner

3030 Learning Results Services Bureau
Kentucky Department of Education
500 Mero Street, 19th Floor
Frankfort, KY 40601-1957
502-564-2256
Fax: 502-564-7749

Vickie Basham, Division Director

3031 Office of Learning Programs Development
Kentucky Department of Education
500 Mero Street, 19th Floor
Frankfort, KY 40601-1957
502-564-3010
Fax: 502-564-6952

Linda Hargan, Division Director

3032 Regional Services Centers
Kentucky Department of Education
500 Mero Street
19th Floor
Frankfort, KY 40601-1957
502-564-9850
Fax: 502-564-9848
E-mail: svice@kde.state.ky.us
http://www.kde.state.ky.us

Sheila Vice, Principal Assistant

3033 Special Instructional Services
Kentucky Department of Education
500 Mero Street, 19th Floor
Frankfort, KY 40601-1957
502-564-4970
Fax: 502-564-6721

Ken Warlick, Division Director

3034 Support Services Bureau on Learning
Kentucky Department of Education
500 Mero Street, 19th Floor
Frankfort, KY 40601-1957
502-564-3301
Fax: 502-564-6952

Lois Adams-Rodgers, Division Director

3035 Teacher Education & Certification
Kentucky Department of Education
500 Mero Street, 19th Floor
Frankfort, KY 40601-1957
502-564-4606

Roland Goddu, Division Director

Louisiana

3036 Academic Programs Office
Louisiana Department of Education
626 N 4th Street
Baton Rouge, LA 70802-5363
225-342-4411
Fax: 225-342-0193

Moselle Dearborne, Division Director

3037 Educational Support Programs
Louisiana Department of Education
626 N 4th Street
Baton Rouge, LA 70802-5363
225-342-4411
Fax: 225-342-0781

Gayle Neal, Division Director

3038 Louisiana Department of Education
2758-D Brightside Drive
PO Box 94064
Baton Rouge, LA 70804-9064
504-342-3607
Fax: 504-342-7316
http://www.doe.state.la.us

Provides leadership and enacts policies that result in improved academic achievement and responsible citizenship for all students. For certification information visit www.louisianaschools.net or contact 225-342-3490.

Cecil J Picard, Superintendent

3039 Management & Finance Office
Louisana State Department of Education
PO Box 64064
Baton Rouge, LA 70804-9064
225-342-3617
877-453-2721
Fax: 225-219-7538
E-mail: mlangley@doe.state.la.us
http://www.doe.state.la.us

Marlyn J Langley, Deputy Superintendent

3040 Office of Vocational Education
Louisiana Department of Education
626 N 4th Street
Baton Rouge, LA 70802-5363
225-342-4411
Fax: 225-342-0781

Chris Strother, Division Director

3041 Research & Development Office
Louisiana Department of Education
626 N 4th Street
Baton Rouge, LA 70802-5363
225-342-4411
Fax: 225-342-0781

Mari Ann Fowler, Division Director

3042 Special Education Services
Louisiana Department of Education
626 N 4th Street
Baton Rouge, LA 70802-5363
225-342-4411
Fax: 225-342-0781

Leon L Borne Jr, Division Director

Maine

3043 Applied Technology & Adult Learning
Maine Department of Education
23 State House Station
Augusta, ME 04333-0023
207-287-5854

Chris Lyons, Division Director

3044 Division of Compensatory Education
Maine Department of Education
23 State House Station
Augusta, ME 04333-0023
207-624-6705
Fax: 207-624-6706

Kathryn Manning, Division Director

3045 Maine Department of Education
23 State House Station
Augusta, ME 04333-0023
207-624-6620
Fax: 207-624-6601
http://www.state.me.us/education

Susan Gendron, Commissioner

Maryland

3046 Career Technology & Adult Learning
Maryland Department of Education
200 W Baltimore Street
Baltimore, MD 21201-2502
410-767-0158

Katharine Oliver, Division Director

3047 Certification & Accreditation
Maryland Department of Education
200 W Baltimore Street
Baltimore, MD 21201-2502
410-333-2141

A Skipp Sanders, Division Director

3048 Compensatory Education & Support Services
Maryland Department of Education
200 W Baltimore Street
Baltimore, MD 21201-2502
410-333-2400

Ellen Gonzales, Division Director

3049 Division of Business Services
Maryland Department of Education
200 W Baltimore Street
Baltimore, MD 21201-2502
410-333-2648

Raymond H Brown, Division Director

3050 Instruction Division
Maryland Department of Education
200 W Baltimore Street
Baltimore, MD 21201-2502
410-767-0316

Colleen Seremet, Assistant Superintendent

3051 Library Development & Services
Maryland Department of Education
00 W Baltimore Street
Baltimore, MD 21201-2502
410-333-2113

Irene Padilla, Division Director

3052 Maryland Department of Education
200 W Baltimore Street
Baltimore, MD 21201-2502
410-767-0600
888-246-0016
Fax: 410-333-6033
http://www.msde.state.md.us

Mission of MSDE is to provide leadership, support, and accountability for effective systems of public education, library services and rehabilitation services. For certification information visit www.certification.msde.state.md.us orcontact 410-767-0412.

Nancy S Grasmick, Superintendent

3053 Planning, Results & Information Management
Maryland Department of Education
200 W Baltimore Street
Baltimore, MD 21201-2502
410-333-2045

Mark Moody, Division Director

3054 Rehabilitation Services Division
Maryland Department of Education
200 W Baltimore Street
Baltimore, MD 21201-2502
410-554-3276

James S Jeffers, Division Director

3055 Special Education
Maryland Department of Education
200 W Baltimore Street
Baltimore, MD 21201-2502
410-767-0261
800-535-0182
Fax: 410-333-8166

Richard J Steinke, Division Director

Massachusetts

3056 Massachusetts Department of Education
350 Main Street
Malden, MA 02148-5023
781-338-3000
Fax: 781-338-3770
http://www.doe.mass.edu

David P Driscoll, Commissioner

3057 Massachusetts Department of Educational Improvement
350 Main Street
Malden, MA 02148-5089
781-388-3300

Andrea Perrault, Division Director

3058 Region 1: Education Department
J.W. McCormick Post Office & Courthouse
540 McCormick Courthouse
Boston, MA 02109-4557
617-223-9317
Fax: 617-223-9324

Michael Sentance

Michigan

3059 Administrative Services Office
Michigan Department of Education
608 W Allegan Street
Lansing, MI 48933-1524
517-373-3324
Fax: 517-335-4565
http://www.michigan.gov

Calvin C Cupidore, Director

3060 Adult Extended Learning Office
Michigan Department of Education
608 W Allegan Street
Lansing, MI 48933-1524
517-373-3324
Fax: 517-335-4565
http://www.michigan.gov

Ronald Gillum, Director

3061 Career & Technical Education
Michigan Department of Education
608 W Allegan Street
Lansing, MI 48933-1524
517-373-3324
Fax: 517-373-8776
http://www.michigan.gov

William Welsgerber, Director

3062 Higher Education Management Office
Michigan Department of Education
608 W Allegan Street
Lansing, MI 48933-1524
517-373-3324
Fax: 517-373-2759
http://www.michigan.gov

Ronald L Root, Director

3063 Instructional Programs
Michigan Department of Education
608 W Allegan Street
Lansing, MI 48933-1524

517-373-3324
Fax: 517-335-4565
http://www.michigan.gov

3064 Michigan Department of Education
608 W Allegan Street
PO Box 30008
Lansing, MI 48909

517-373-3324
Fax: 517-335-4565
E-mail: MDEweb@michigan.gov
http://www.michigan.gov/mde

Thomas D Watkins, Superintendent

3065 Office of School Management
Michigan Department of Education
608 W Allegan Street
Lansing, MI 48933-1524

517-373-3324
Fax: 517-335-4565
http://www.michigan.gov

Roger Lynas, Director

3066 Office of the Superintendent
Michigan Department of Education
608 W Allegan Street
Lansing, MI 48933-1524

517-373-3324
Fax: 517-335-4565
http://www.michigan.gov

3067 Postsecondary Services
Michigan Department of Education
608 W Allegan Street
Lansing, MI 48909

517-373-3324
Fax: 517-335-4565
http://www.michigan.gov

3068 School Program Quality
Michigan Department of Education
608 W Allegan Street
Lansing, MI 48933-1524

517-373-3324
Fax: 517-373-4565
http://www.michigan.gov

Anne Hansen, Division Director

3069 Special Education
Michigan Department of Education
608 W Allegan Street
Lansing, MI 48933-1524

517-373-3324
Fax: 581-733-5456

Richard Baldwin, Director

3070 Student Financial Assistance
Michigan Department of Education
608 W Allegan Street
Lansing, MI 48933-1524

517-373-3324
Fax: 517-335-4565

Jack Nelson, Director

3071 Teacher & Administrative Preparation
Michigan Department of Education
608 W Allegan Street
Lansing, MI 48933-1524

514-373-3324
Fax: 517-335-4565
http://www.michigan.gov

Carolyn Logan, Director

Minnesota

3072 Data & Technology
Minnesota Department of Education
550 Cedar Street
Saint Paul, MN 55101-2233

612-297-3151

Mark Manning, Division Director

3073 Data Management
Minnesota Department of Education
1500 Highway 39 W
Roseville, MN 55113

651-582-8296
Fax: 651-582-8873

Carol Hokenson, Manager Data Management

3074 Education Funding
Minnesota Department of Education
550 Cedar Street
Saint Paul, MN 55101-2233

651-297-2194

Tom Melcher, Division Director

3075 Financial Conditions & Aids Payment
Minnesota Department of Education
550 Cedar Street
Saint Paul, MN 55101-2233

612-296-4431

Gary Farland, Division Director

3076 Government Relations
Minnesota Department of Education
550 Cedar Street
Saint Paul, MN 55101-2233

612-296-5279

Sliv Carlson, Division Director

3077 Human Resources Office
Minnesota Department of Education
550 Cedar Street
Saint Paul, MN 55101-2233

651-582-8200

William O'Neill, Division Director

3078 Minnesota Department of Children, Families & Learning
1500 Highway 36 W
Roseville, MN 55113-4266

651-582-8204
Fax: 651-582-8724
http://cfl.state.mn.us

Works to help communities to measurably improve the well-being of children through programs that focus on education, community services, prevention, and the preparation of young people for the world of work. All department effortsemphasize the achievement of positive results for children and their families.

Dr.Cheri Pierson, Commissioner

3079 Minnesota Department of Education
1500 Highway 36 W
Roseville, MN 55113-4266

651-582-8204
Fax: 651-582-8724
http://www.education.state.mn.us

Christine Jax, Commissioner

3080 Residential Schools
Minnesota Department of Education
550 Cedar Street
Saint Paul, MN 55101-2233

507-332-3363

Wade Karli, Division Director

Mississippi

3081 Community Outreach Services
Mississippi Department of Education
PO Box 771
Jackson, MS 39205-1113
601-359-3513
Fax: 601-359-3033

Sarah Beard, Division Director

3082 Educational Innovations
Mississippi Department of Education
PO Box 771
Jackson, MS 39205-0771
601-359-3499
Fax: 601-359-2587

David Robinson, Division Director

3083 External Relations
Mississippi Department of Education
PO Box 771
372 Central High Building
Jackson, MS 39201
601-359-3515
Fax: 601-359-3033

Andrew P Mullins, Division Director

3084 Management Information Systems
Mississippi Department of Education
PO Box 771
Jackson, MS 39205
601-359-3487
Fax: 601-359-3033

Rusty Purvis, Division Director

3085 Mississippi Department of Education
359 NW Street
PO Box 771
Jackson, MS 39205-0771
601-359-3512
Fax: 601-359-3242
http://www.mde.k12.ms.us

Dr.Henry Johnson, Superintendent

3086 Mississippi Employment Security Commission
PO Box 1699
Jackson, MS 39215-1699
601-961-7400
Fax: 601-961-7405
http://www.mesc.state.ms

3087 Office of Accountability
Mississippi Department of Education
PO Box 771
Jackson, MS 39205
601-359-2038
Fax: 601-359-1748

Judy Rhodes, Division Director

3088 Vocational Technical Education
Mississippi Department of Education
359 NW Street
PO Box 771
Jackson, MS 39292
601-359-3090
Fax: 601-359-3989

Samuel McGee, Division Director

Missouri

3089 Deputy Commissioner
Missouri Department of Education
205 Jefferson Street
PO Box 480 Floor 6
Jefferson City, MO 65101-2901
573-751-3503
Fax: 573-751-1179

Dr.Bert Schulte, Deputy Commissioner

3090 Division of Instruction
Missouri Department of Education
205 Jefferson Street
Floor 6
Jefferson City, MO 65101-2901
573-751-4234
Fax: 573-751-8613

Otis Baker, Division Director

3091 Missouri Department of Education
205 Jefferson Street, 6th Floor
PO Box 480
Jefferson City, MO 65102-0480
573-751-4212
Fax: 573-751-8613
E-mail: pubinfo@mail.dese.state.mo.us
http://www.dese.state.mo.us

A team of dedicated individuals working for the continuous improvement of education and services for all citizens. We believe that we can make a positive difference in the quality of life for all Missourians by providing exceptionalservice to students, educators, schools and citizens.

D Kent King, Commissioner

3092 Region 7: Education Department
10220 NW Executive Hills Boulevard
Kansas City, MO 64153-2312
816-891-7972
Fax: 816-891-7972

3093 Special Education Division
Missouri Department of Education
205 Jefferson Street
PO Box 480 Floor 6
Jefferson City, MO 65102-2901
573-751-5739
Fax: 573-526-4404

John F Allan, Division Director

3094 Urban & Teacher Education
Missouri Department of Education
205 Jefferson Street
Floor 6
Jefferson City, MO 65101-2901
573-751-2931
Fax: 573-751-8613

L Celestine Ferguson, Division Director

3095 Vocational & Adult Education
Missouri Department of Education
205 Jefferson Street, 5th Floor
PO Box 480
Jefferson City, MO 65102-0480
573-751-2660
Fax: 573-526-4261
E-mail: nheadrick@mail.dese.state.mo.us
http://www.dese.state.mo.us

Nancy J Headrick, Assistant Commissioner

3096 **Vocational Rehabilitation**
Missouri Department of Education
3024 Dupont Circle
Jefferson City, MO 65109-0525
573-751-3251
Fax: 573-751-1441

Don L Gann, Division Director

Montana

3097 **Accreditation & Curriculum Services Department**
Montana Department of Education
106 State Capitol
Helena, MT 59620
406-444-5726
Fax: 406-444-2893

Dr.Linda Vrooman, Administrator

3098 **Division of Information-Technology Support**
Montana Department of Education
106 State Capitol
Helena, MT 59620
406-444-4326
Fax: 406-444-2893

Scott Buswell, Division Director

3099 **Montana Department of Education**
1227 11th Avenue
PO Box 202501
Helena, MT 59620-2501
406-444-3095
Fax: 406-444-2893
http://www.opi.state.mt.us

For certification information visit www.opi.state.mt.us or contact 406-444-3150.

Linda McCulloch, Superindtendent

3100 **Operations Department**
Montana Department of Education
106 State Capitol
Helena, MT 59620
406-444-3095
Fax: 406-444-2893

Nebraska

3101 **Administrative Services Office**
Nebraska Department of Education
301 Centennial Mall S
Lincoln, NE 68508-2529
402-471-2295
Fax: 402-471-6351
http://www.nde.state.ne.us/ADSS/index.html

To provide quality services and support in the areas of finance human resource management continuous quality improvement, office/building services,and technical assistant.

Mike Stefkovich, Division Director

3102 **Division of Education Services**
Nebraska Department of Education
301 Centennial Mall S
Lincoln, NE 68508-2529
402-471-2783
Fax: 402-471-0117

Marge Harouff, Division Director

3103 **Nebraska Department of Education**
301 Centennial Mall S
PO Box 94987
Lincoln, NE 68509-4987
402-471-5020
Fax: 402-471-4433
http://www.nde.state.ne.us

Douglas D Christensen, Commissioner

3104 **Rehabilitation Services Division**
Nebraska Department of Education
301 Centennial Mall S 6th Floor
PO Box 94987
Lincoln, NE 68509-2529
402-471-3649
877-637-3422
Fax: 402-471-0788
http://www.bocrehab.state.ne.us

Frank C Lloyd, Director

Nevada

3105 **Administrative & Financial Services**
Nevada Department of Education
400 W King St
Carson City, NV 89703-4204
775-687-9102
888-590-6726
Fax: 702-486-5803

Douglas Thunder

3106 **Instructional Services Division**
Nevada Department of Education
400 W King St
Carson City, NV 89703-4204
775-687-3104

Mary L Peterson, Division Director

3107 **Nevada Department of Education**
700 E 5th Street
Carson City, NV 89701-5096
775-687-9200
Fax: 775-687-9101
http://www.nsn.k12.nv.us

Mission is to lead Nevada's citizens in accomplishing lifelong learning and educational excellence.

Jack McLaughlin, Superintendent

New Hampshire

3108 **Information Services**
New Hampshire Department of Education
101 Pleasent Street
Concord, NH 03301-3852
603-271-2778
Fax: 603-271-1953
http://www.ed.state.nh.us

New Hampshire schools enrollment, financial, assessment information.

Dr.Judith Fillion, Division Director

3109 **New Hampshire Department of Education**
101 Pleasant Street
State Office Park S
Concord, NH 03301-3860
603-271-3494
800-339-9900
Fax: 603-271-1953
E-mail: llovering@ed.state.nh.us
http://www.state.nh.us/doe

Mission is to provide educational leadership and services which promote equal educational opportunities and quality practices and programs than enable New Hampshire residents to become fully productive members of society.

Nicholas C Donohue, Commissioner

3110 New Hampshire Division of Instructional Services
101 Pleasant Street
Concord, NH 03301-3852

603-271-3880

William B Evert, Division Director

3111 Standards & Certification Division
New Hampshire Dept of Education
101 Pleasant St
Concord, NH 03301-3852

603-271-3453
Fax: 603-271-8709

Judith D Fillion, Divisions Director

New Jersey

3112 New Jersey Department of Education
100 Riverview Plaza
PO Box 500
Trenton, NJ 08625-0500

609-292-4450
Fax: 609-777-4099
http://www.state.nj.us/education

Develops and implements policies that address the major education issues in New Jersey. The State Board will engage in an effort to ensure that all children receive a quality public education that prepares them to succeed asresponsible, productive citizens in a global society.

William L Librera, Commissioner

3113 New Jersey Department of Education: Finance
100 Riverview Plaza
PO Box 500
Trenton, NJ 08625-0500

609-292-4421
Fax: 609-292-6794
http://www.state.nj.us/education

Richard Rosenberg, Assistant Commissioner

3114 New Jersey Division of Special Education
100 Riverview Plaza
PO Box 500
Trenton, NJ 08625

609-292-0147
Fax: 609-984-8422

Jeffrey Osowski, Divsion Director

3115 New Jersey State Library
PO Box 520
Trenton, NJ 08625-0520

609-292-6200
Fax: 609-292-2746
E-mail: nblake@njstatelib.org
http://www.njstatelib.org

Norma E Blake, State Librarian

3116 Professional Development & Licensing
New Jersey Department of Education
100 Riverview Plaza, PO Box 500
Trenton, NJ 08625

609-292-2070
Fax: 609-292-3768

Hilda Hidalgo, Division Director

3117 Urban & Field Services
New Jersey Department of Education
100 Riverview Plaza, PO Box 500
Trenton, NJ 08625

609-292-4442
Fax: 609-292-3830

Elena Scambio, Division Director

New Mexico

3118 Agency Support
New Mexico Department of Education
300 Don Gaspar, Education Building
Santa Fe, NM 87501-2786

505-827-6330

Tres Giron, Division Director

3119 Learning Services
New Mexico Department of Education
300 Don Gaspar, Education Building
Santa Fe, NM 87501

505-827-6508
Fax: 505-827-6689

Albert Zamora, Division Director

3120 New Mexico Department of Education
300 Don Gaspar
Education Building
Santa Fe, NM 87501-2786

505-827-6688
Fax: 505-827-6520
http://www.sde.state.nm.us

Michael J Davis, Superintendent

**3121 New Mexico Department of
School-Transportation & Support Services**
300 Don Gaspar, Education Building
Santa Fe, NM 87501

505-827-6683

Susan Brown, Division Director

3122 School Management Accountability
New Mexico Department of Education
300 Don Gaspar, Education Building
Santa Fe, NM 87501

505-827-3876
Fax: 505-827-6689

Michael J Davis, Division Director

3123 Vocational Education
New Mexico Department of Education
300 Don Gaspar, Education Building
Santa Fe, NM 87501

505-827-6511

Tom Trujillo, Division Director

New York

3124 Cultural Education
New York Department of Education
Madison Avenue
Albany, NY 12230

518-474-5976
Fax: 518-474-2718
E-mail: CISINFO@mail.nysed.gov

Carole F Huxley, Division Director

3125 Elementary, Middle & Secondary Education
New York Department of Education
89 Washington Avenue
Room 875 EBA
Albany, NY 12234-0001
518-474-5915
Fax: 518-474-2718
E-mail: emscgen@mail.nysed.gov

James Kadamus, Deputy

3126 Higher & Professional Education
New York Department of Education
111 Education Avenue W Mezzanine
2nd Floor
Albany, NY 12234-0001
518-474-5851
Fax: 518-474-2718

Johanna Duncan-Poitier, Deputy Commissioner

3127 New York Department of Education
89 Washington Avenue
Education Building, Room 111
Albany, NY 12234
518-474-5844
Fax: 518-473-4909
E-mail: rmills@mail.nysed.gov
http://www.nysed.gov

Richard P Mills, President

3128 Professional Responsibility Office
New York Department of Education
89 Wolf Road Suite 204
Albany, NY 12205-2643
518-485-9350
Fax: 518-485-9361

3129 Region 2: Education Department
75 Park Place
New York, NY 10007
212-264-7005
Fax: 212-264-4427

3130 Vocational & Educational Services for Disabled
New York Department of Education
80 Wolf Road Suite 200
Albany, NY 12205
518-473-8097
800-272-5448
Fax: 518-457-4562

David Segalla, Regional Coordinator

North Carolina

3131 Auxiliary Services
North Carolina Department of Education
301 N Wilmington Street
Raleigh, NC 27601-2825
919-733-1110
Fax: 919-733-5279

Charles Weaver, Division Director

3132 Financial & Personnel Services
North Carolina Department of Education
301 N Wilmington Street
Raleigh, NC 27601-2825
919-807-3600

James O Barber, Division Director

3133 North Carolina Department of Education
301 N Wilmington Street
Raleigh, NC 27601-2825
919-715-1299
Fax: 919-807-3279
http://www.ncpublicschools.org

Bob R Etheridge, Division Director

3134 North Carolina Department of Instructional Services
301 N Wilmington Street
Raleigh, NC 27601-2825
919-715-1506
Fax: 919-807-3279

Henry Johnson, Division Director

3135 Staff Development & Technical Assistance
North Carolina Department of Education
301 N Wilmington Street
Raleigh, NC 27601-2825
919-715-1315

Nancy Davis, Division Director

North Dakota

3136 North Dakota Department of Education
600 E Boulevard Avenue
State Capitol Building, Floor 11
Bismarck, ND 58505-0440
701-328-4572
Fax: 701-328-2461
http://www.state.nd.us/espb

Wayne G Sanstead, Superintendent

3137 North Dakota Department of Public Instruction Division
600 E Boulevard Avenue, Dept. 201
Floor 9,10, & 11
Bismarck, ND 58505-0440
701-328-2260
Fax: 701-328-2461
E-mail: wsanstea@mail.dpi.state.nd.us
http://www.dpi.state.nd.us/dpi/index.htm

Dr. Wayne G Sanstead, State Superintendent

3138 North Dakota State Board for Vocational & Technical Education
600 E Boulevard Avenue
Floor 15
Bismarck, ND 58505-0660
701-224-2259
Fax: 701-328-2461

Reuben Guenthner, Division Director

3139 Study & State Film Library
North Dakota Department of Education
600 E Boulevard Avenue
Floor 11
Bismarck, ND 58505-0660
701-237-7282

Robert Stone, Division Director

Ohio

3140 Blind School
Ohio Department of Education
65 S Front Street
Columbus, OH 43215-4131
614-466-3641
Fax: 614-752-1713

Dennis Holmes, Division Director

3141 Curriculum, Instruction & Professional Development
Ohio Department of Education
65 S Front Street
Columbus, OH 43215-4131
614-466-2761
Fax: 704-992-5168

Nancy Eberhart, Division Director

3142 Early Childhood Education
Ohio Department of Education
65 S Front Street
Columbus, OH 43215-4131
614-466-0224
Fax: 614-728-2338

Jane Wiechel, Division Director

3143 Federal Assistance
Ohio Department of Education
65 S Front Street
Columbus, OH 43215-4131
614-466-4161
Fax: 704-992-5168

William Henry, Division Director

3144 Ohio Department of Education
25 S Front Street
7th Floor
Columbus, OH 43215-4183
614-466-7578
877-644-6338
Fax: 614-728-4781
http://www.ode.state.oh.us

Works in partnership with school districts to assure high achievements for all learners, promote a safe and orderly learning environment, provide leadership, support, and build capacity, and provide support to school districtsparticularly those who need it most.

Susan T Zelman, Superintendent

3145 Personnel Services
Ohio Department of Education
65 S Front Street
Columbus, OH 43215-4131
614-466-3763
Fax: 704-992-5168

Larry Cathell, Division Director

3146 School Finance
Ohio Department of Education
65 S Front Street
Columbus, OH 43215-4131
614-466-6266
Fax: 704-992-5168
E-mail: sf_tavakolia@ode.ohio.gov
http://www.ode.state.ohio.us/foundation/www_.html

Susan Tavakolian, Division Director

3147 School Food Service
Ohio Department of Education
65 S Front Street
Columbus, OH 43215-4131
614-466-2945
Fax: 704-992-5168

Lorita Myles, Division Director

3148 School for the Deaf
Ohio Department of Education
65 S Front Street
Columbus, OH 43215-4131
614-466-3641
Fax: 704-992-5168

Edward C Corbett Jr, Division Director

3149 Special Education
Ohio Department of Education
933 High Street
Worthington, OH 43085
614-466-2650
Fax: 704-992-5168
E-mail: se_herner@ode.ohio.gov

John Herner, Director Special Education

3150 Student Development
Ohio Department of Education
65 S Front Street
Columbus, OH 43215-4131
614-466-3641
Fax: 704-992-5168

Hazel Flowers, Division Director

3151 Teacher Education & Certification
Ohio Department of Education
65 S Front Street
Columbus, OH 43215-4131
614-466-3430
Fax: 704-992-5168

Darrell Parks, Division Director

3152 Vocational & Career Education
Ohio Department of Education
65 S Front Street
Columbus, OH 43215-4131
614-466-3430
Fax: 704-992-5168

Darrell Parks, Division Director

Oklahoma

3153 Accreditation & Standards Division
Oklahoma Department of Education
2500 N Lincoln Boulevard
Oklahoma City, OK 73105-4503
405-521-3333
Fax: 405-521-6205

Sharon Lease, Division Director

3154 Federal/Special/Collaboration Services
Oklahoma Department of Education
2500 N Lincoln Boulevard
Oklahoma City, OK 73105-4503
405-521-4873
Fax: 405-522-3503

Sid Hudson, Division Director

3155 Oklahoma Department of Career and Technology Education
1500 W 7th Avenue
Stillwater, OK 74074-4398
405-743-5444
Fax: 405-743-5541

Roy Peters Jr, Division Director

3156 Oklahoma Department of Education
2500 N Lincoln Boulevard
Hodge Education Building
Oklahoma City, OK 73105-4599
405-521-4485
Fax: 405-521-6205
http://http://sde.state.ok.us

Sandy Garrett, Superindentdent

3157 Oklahoma Department of Education; Financial Services
Oklahoma Department of Education
2500 N Lincoln Boulevard
Oklahoma City, OK 73105-4503
405-521-3371
Fax: 405-521-6205

Don Shive, Division Director

3158 Professional Services
Oklahoma Department of Education
2500 N Lincoln Boulevard
Oklahoma City, OK 73105-4503
405-521-4311
Fax: 405-521-6205

Paul Simon, Division Director

3159 School Improvement
Oklahoma Department of Education
2500 N Lincoln Boulevard
Oklahoma City, OK 73105-4503
405-521-4869
Fax: 405-521-6205

Hugh McCrabb, Division Director

Oregon

3160 Assessment & Evaluation
Oregon Department of Education
255 Capitol Street NE
Salem, OR 97310-0203
503-378-3600
Fax: 503-378-5156
E-mail: firstname.lastname@state.or.us
http://www.ode.state.or.us

Doug Kosty, Assistant Superintendent

3161 Community College Services
Oregon Department of Education
225 Capitol Street NE
Salem, OR 97310-1341
503-378-3600
Fax: 503-378-5156

Stan Bunn, Superintendent

3162 Compensatory Education Office
Oregon Department of Education
225 Capitol Street NE
Salem, OR 97310-1341
503-378-3569
Fax: 503-378-5156

Jerry Fuller, Division Director

3163 Deputy Superintendent Office
Oregon Department of Education
225 Capitol Street NE
Salem, OR 97310-1341
503-378-3573
Fax: 503-378-5156

Bob Burns, Division Director

3164 Early Childhood Council
Oregon Department of Education
225 Capitol Street NE
Salem, OR 97310-1341
503-378-5585
Fax: 503-378-5156

Judy Miller, Division Director

3165 Government Relations
Oregon Department of Education
225 Capitol Street NE
Salem, OR 97310-1341
503-378-8549
Fax: 503-378-5156

Greg McMurdo, Division Director

3166 Management Services
Oregon Department of Education
225 Capitol Street NE
Salem, OR 97310-1341
503-378-8549
Fax: 503-378-5156

Chris Durham, Division Director

3167 Office of Field, Curriculum & Instruction Services
Oregon Department of Education
225 Capitol Street NE
Salem, OR 97310-1341
503-378-8004
Fax: 503-378-5156

Roberta Hutton, Division Director

3168 Oregon Department of Education
225 Capitol Street NE
Salem, OR 97310-0203
503-378-3569
Fax: 503-378-5156
E-mail: ode.frontdesk@ode.state.or.us
http://www.ode.state.or.us

Susan Castillo, Superintendent

3169 Professional Technical Education
Oregon Department of Education
225 Capitol Street NE
Salem, OR 97310-1341
503-378-3584
Fax: 503-378-5156

JD Hoye, Division Director

3170 Special Education
Oregon Department of Education
225 Capitol Street NE
Salem, OR 97310-1341
503-378-3600
Fax: 503-378-5156
http://www.ode.state.or.us

Steve Johnson, Division Director

3171 Student Services Office
Oregon Department of Education
225 Capitol Street NE
Salem, OR 97310-1341
503-378-5585
Fax: 503-378-5156

Judy Miller, Division Director

3172 Twenty First Century Schools Council
Oregon Department of Education
225 Capitol Street NE
Salem, OR 97310-1341
503-378-3600
Fax: 503-378-5156

Joyce Reinke, Division Director

Pennsylvania

3173 Chief Counsel
Pennsylvania Department of Education
333 Market Street
Harrisburg, PA 17101-2210
717-787-5500
Fax: 717-783-0347

Jeffrey Champagne, Division Director

3174 Chief of Staff Office
Pennsylvania Department of Education
333 Market Street
Harrisburg, PA 17101-2210
717-787-9744
Fax: 717-787-7222

Terry Dellmuth, Chief of Staff

3175 Higher Education/Postsecondary Office
Pennsylvania Department of Education
333 Market Street
Harrisburg, PA 17101-2210
717-787-5041
Fax: 717-783-0583

Charles Fuget, Division Director

3176 Office of Elementary and Secondary Education
Pennsylvania Department of Education
333 Market Street
5th Floor
Harrisburg, PA 17101
717-787-2127
Fax: 717-783-6802
E-mail: dhaines@state.pa.us
http://www.pde.state.pa.us

Debra Haines, Executive Secretary

3177 Office of the Comptroller
Pennsylvania Department of Education
333 Market Street
Harrisburg, PA 17101-2210
717-787-5506
Fax: 717-787-3593

William Hardenstine, Division Director

3178 Pennsylvania Department of Education
333 Market Street
Harrisburg, PA 17126
717-783-6788
Fax: 717-787-7222
http://www.teaching.state.pa.us

Charles B Zogby, Secretary

3179 Region 3: Education Department
3535 Market Street
Philadelphia, PA 19104-3309
215-596-1001

Rhode Island

3180 Career & Technical Education
Rhode Island Department of Education
255 Westminster Street
Providence, RI 02903-3414
401-222-4600
Fax: 401-222-2537
http://www.ridoe.net

Frank M Santoro, Division Director

3181 Equity & Access Office
Rhode Island Department of Education
255 Westminster Street
Providence, RI 02903-3414
401-222-4600
Fax: 401-222-2537
http://www.ridoe.net

Frank R Walker III, Division Director

3182 Human Resource Development
Rhode Island Department of Education
255 Westminster Street
Providence, RI 02903-3414
401-222-4600
Fax: 401-222-2537
http://www.ridoe.net

Paula A Rossi, Division Director

3183 Instruction Office
Rhode Island Department of Education
255 Westminster Street
Providence, RI 02903-3414
401-222-4600
Fax: 401-222-2537
http://www.ridoe.net

Marie C DiBiasio, Division Director

3184 Office of Finance
Rhode Island Department of Education
255 Westminster Street
Providence, RI 02903-3414
401-222-4600
Fax: 401-222-2537
http://www.ridoe.net

Frank A Pontarelli, Division Director

3185 Outcomes & Assessment Office
Rhode Island Department of Education
255 Westminster Street
Providence, RI 02903-3414
401-222-4600
Fax: 401-222-2537
http://www.ridoe.net

Pasquale J DeVito, Division Director

3186 Resource Development
Rhode Island Department of Education
255 Westminster Street
Providence, RI 02903-3414
401-222-4600
Fax: 401-222-6033
http://www.ridoe.net

Edward T Costa, Division Director

3187 Rhode Island Department of Education
255 Westminster Street
Providence, RI 02903
401-222-4600
Fax: 401-222-6178
E-mail: ride0001@ride.ri.net
http://www.ridoe.net

Goal of all our work is to improve student performance and help all students meet or exceed a high level of performance. Standards, instruction, and assessment intertwine to provide a system that ensures a strong education for ourstudents.

Peter McWalters, Commissioner

3188 School Food Services Administration
Rhode Island Department of Education
255 Westminster Street
Providence, RI 02903-3414
401-222-4600
Fax: 401-222-3080
http://www.ridoe.net

Virginia da Mora, Dir Integrated Soc Service

3189 Special Needs Office
Rhode Island Department of Education
255 Westminster Street
Providence, RI 02903-3414
401-456-9331
Fax: 401-456-8699
http://www.ridoe.net

Dr.Frances Gallo, Acting Dirctor

3190 Teacher Education & Certification Office
Rhode Island Department of Education
255 Westminster Street
Providence, RI 02903-3414
401-222-4600
Fax: 401-222-2048
http://www.ridoe.net

Louis E DelPapa, Division Director

South Carolina

3191 Budgets & Planning
South Carolina Department of Education
1201 Main Street
Suite 950
Columbia, SC 29201-3730
803-734-2280
Fax: 803-734-0645

Les Boles, Division Director

3192 Communications Services
South Carolina Department of Education
1429 Senate Street
Columbia, SC 29201-3730
803-734-8500
Fax: 803-734-3389

Jerry Adams, Division Director

3193 General Counsel
South Carolina Department of Education
1429 Senate Street
Columbia, SC 29201-3730
803-734-8500
Fax: 803-734-4384

Shelly Carrigg, Esq, Division Director

3194 Internal Administration
South Carolina Department of Education
1429 Senate Street
Columbia, SC 29201-3730
803-734-8500
Fax: 803-734-6225

Jackie Rosswurm, Division Director

3195 Policy & Planning
South Carolina Department of Education
1429 Senate Street
Columbia, SC 29201-3730
803-734-8500
Fax: 803-734-8624

Valerie Truesdale, Division Director

3196 South Carolina Department of Education
1429 Senate Street
Columbia, SC 29201
803-734-8492
Fax: 803-734-3389
http://www.state.sc.us

Provides leadership and services to ensure a system of public education in which all students become educated, responsible, and contributing citizens. For certification information visit www.myscschools.com or contact 803-734-5280.

Inez M Tenenbaum, Superintendent

3197 Support Services
South Carolina Department of Education
1429 Senate Street
Columbia, SC 29201-3730
803-734-8500
Fax: 803-734-8254

Donald Tudor, Division Director

South Dakota

3198 Finance & Management
South Dakota Department of Education
700 Governors Drive
Pierre, SD 57501-2291
605-773-3248
Fax: 605-773-6139

Stacy Krusemark, Division Director

3199 Services for Education
South Dakota Department of Education
700 Governors Drive
Pierre, SD 57501-2291
605-773-4699
Fax: 605-773-3782

Donlynn Rice, Division Director

3200 South Dakota Department of Education & Cultural Affairs
700 Governors Drive
Pierre, SD 57501-2291
605-773-2291
Fax: 605-773-6139
E-mail: ray.christensen@state.sd.us
http://www.state.sd.us/deca/

Advocates for education, facilitate the delivery of statewide educational and cultural services, and promote efficient, appropriate, and quality educational opportunities for all persons residing in South Dakota.

Ray Christensen, Secretary
Patrick Keating, Division Director

3201 South Dakota State Historical Society
South Dakota Dept of Education & Cultural Affairs
900 Governors Drive
Pierre, SD 57501-2291
605-773-3458
Fax: 605-773-6041
E-mail: jay.vogt@state.sd.us
http://www.state.sd.us/deca/

Program areas: Archaeology, archives, historic preservation, museum, research, and publishing

Jay D Vogt, History Manager

3202 Special Education Office
South Dakota Department of Education
700 Governors Drive
Pierre, SD 57501-2291
605-773-3678
Fax: 605-773-3782

Michelle Powers, Division Director

Government Agencies / Texas

Tennessee

3203 Special Education
Tennessee Department of Education
710 John Robertson Parkway
6th Floor
Nashville, TN 37243
615-741-2851
Fax: 615-532-9412

Joe Fisher, Division Director

3204 Teaching and Learning
Tennessee Department of Education
710 James Robertson Parkway
5th Floor
Nashville, TN 37243
615-532-6195
Fax: 615-741-1837
E-mail: wprotoe@mail.state.tn.us
http://www.state.tn.us/education

Wilma Protoe, Assitant Commissioner

3205 Tennessee Department of Education
710 James Robertson Parkway
6th Floor
Nashville, TN 37243-0375
615-741-2731
Fax: 615-741-6236
E-mail: jwalters@mail.state.tn.us
http://www.state.tn.us/education

Lana Seivers, Commissioner

3206 Vocational Education
Tennessee Department of Education
710 John Robertson Parkway
4th Floor
Nashville, TN 37243-0383
615-532-2800
Fax: 615-532-8226

Ralph Barnett, Assistant Commissioner

Texas

3207 Accountability Reporting and Research
Texas Education Agency
1701 Congress Avenue
WBT Building Room 3-111
Austin, TX 78701-1494
512-475-3523
Fax: 512-475-0028
E-mail: ccloudt@tmail.tea.state.tx.us
http://www.tea.state.tx.us

Criss Cloudt, Associate Commissioner

3208 Chief Counsel
Texas Department of Education
1701 Congress Avenue
Austin, TX 78701-1402
512-463-9720
Fax: 512-463-9838

Kewin O'Hanlon, Division Director

3209 Continuing Education
Texas Education Agency
1701 Congress Avenue
Austin, TX 78701-1402
512-463-9322
Fax: 512-463-6782
E-mail: wtillian@tea.state.tx.us

Walter Tillian, Manager

3210 Curriculum Development & Textbooks
Texas Department of Education
1701 Congress Avenue
Austin, TX 78701-1402
512-463-9581
Fax: 512-463-8057

Ann Smisko, Division Director

3211 Curriculum, Assessment & Professional Development
Texas Department of Education
1701 Congress Avenue
Austin, TX 78701-1402
512-463-9328
Fax: 512-475-3640

Linda Cimusz, Division Director

3212 Curriculum, Assessment and Technology
Texas Department of Education
1701 Congress Avenue
Austin, TX 78701-1402
512-463-9087
Fax: 512-475-3667
E-mail: asmisko@tea.tetn.net

Ann Smisko, Associate Commissioner

3213 Education of Special Populations & Adults
Texas Department of Education
1701 Congress Avenue
Austin, TX 78701-1402
512-463-8992
Fax: 512-463-9176

Jay Cummings, Division Director

3214 Field Services
Texas Department of Education
1701 Congress Avenue
Austin, TX 78701-1402
512-463-9354
Fax: 512-463-9227

3215 Internal Operations
Texas Department of Education
1701 Congress Avenue
Austin, TX 78701-1402
512-463-9437
Fax: 512-475-4293

3216 Operations & School Support
Texas Department of Education
1701 Congress Avenue
Austin, TX 78701-1494
512-463-8994
Fax: 512-463-9227

Roberto Zamora, Division Director

3217 Permanent School Fund
Texas Department of Education
1701 Congress Avenue
Room 5-120
Austin, TX 78701-1402
512-463-9169
Fax: 512-463-9432

Carlos Resendez, Division Director

3218 Region 6: Education Department
1200 Main Tower
Dallas, TX 75202-4325
214-767-3626

3219 Texas Department of Education
1701 N Congress Avenue
William B Travis Building
Austin, TX 78701-1494

512-463-8985
Fax: 512-463-9008
http://www.sbec.state.tx.us

Dr.Shirley Neeley, Commissioner

Utah

3220 Applied Technology Education Services
Utah Department of Education
250 E 500 S
Salt Lake City, UT 84111-4200

801-538-7840
Fax: 801-538-7868
E-mail: rbrems@usoe.kiz.ut.us
http://www.usoe.k12.ut.us

State agency for career and technical education.

Rod Brems, Associate Superintendent
Leslee Andelean, Administrative Assistant

3221 Instructional Services Division
Utah Department of Education
250 E 500 S
Salt Lake City, UT 84111-3204

801-538-7515
Fax: 801-538-7768

Jerry P Peterson, Division Director

3222 Schools for the Deaf & Blind
Utah Department of Education
250 E 500 S
Salt Lake City, UT 84111-3204

801-629-4700
Fax: 801-629-4896

Wayne Glaus, Division Director

3223 Utah Office of Education
250 E 500 South
PO Box 144200
Salt Lake City, UT 84111

801-538-7510
Fax: 801-538-7768
http://www.usoe.k12.ut.us

Steven O Laing, Superintendent

3224 Utah Office of Education; Agency Services
Division
250 E 500 S
PO Box 144200
Salt Lake City, UT 84114-4200

801-538-7500
Fax: 801-538-7768
http://www.usoe.k12.ut.us

Patrick Ogden, Associate Superintendent

Vermont

3225 Career & Lifelong Learning
Vermont Department of Education
120 State Street
Montpelier, VT 05620-0001

802-828-3101
Fax: 802-828-3146

Charles Stander, Division Director

3226 Core Services
Vermont Department of Education
120 State Street
Montpelier, VT 05620-0001

802-828-3135
Fax: 802-828-3140

Eleanor Perry, Division Director

3227 Family & School Support
Vermont Department of Education
120 State Street
Montpelier, VT 05620-0001

802-828-2447
Fax: 802-828-3140

Jo Busha, Division Director

3228 Financial Management Team
Vermont Department of Education
120 State Street
Montpelier, VT 05620-0001

802-828-3155
Fax: 802-828-3140

Mark O'Day, Division Director

3229 School Development & Information
Vermont Department of Education
120 State Street
Montpelier, VT 05620-0001

802-828-2756
Fax: 802-828-3140

Douglas Chiappetta, Division Director

3230 Teaching & Learning
Vermont Department of Education
120 State Street
Montpelier, VT 05620-0001

802-828-3111
Fax: 802-828-3140

Marguerite Meyer, Division Director

3231 Vermont Department of Education
120 State Street
Montpelier, VT 05620-2501

802-828-3135
Fax: 802-828-3140
http://Vermont.gov

For certification information visit www.pen.k12.va.us
or contact 804-225-2022.

Richard Cate, Commissioner

3232 Vermont Special Education
120 State Street
Montpelier, VT 05602-2703

802-828-3141

Theodore Riggen, Division Director

Virginia

3233 Administrative Services
Virginia Department of Education
14th & Franklin Streets
PO Box 2120
Richmond, VA 23216

804-225-3252
Fax: 804-786-5828

Edward W Carr, Division Director

3234 Policy, Assessment, Research & Information Systems
Virginia Department of Education
101 N 4th Street
PO Box 2120
Richmond, VA 23218-2120

804-225-2102
800-292-3820
Fax: 804-371-8978
E-mail: charris@pen.k12.va.us
http://www.pen.k12.va.us

Anne Wescott, Assistant Superintendent

3235 Student Services
Virginia Department of Education
14th & Franklin Streets
PO Box 2120
Richmond, VA 23216

804-225-2757
Fax: 804-786-5828

Dr.Cynthia Cave, Division Director

3236 Virginia Centers for Community Education
Virginia Department of Education
PO Box 2120
Richmond, VA 23218-2120

804-225-2293
Fax: 804-786-5828

Dr. Lenox L McLendon, Division Director

3237 Virginia Department of Education
James Monroe Building
101 N 14th Street
Richmond, VA 23219

804-225-2023
800-292-3820
Fax: 804-371-2099
E-mail: rlayman@pen.k12.va.us
http://www.pen.k12.va.us

Jo Lynne DeMary, Superintendent

Washington

3238 Region 10: Education Department
915 2nd Avenue
Room 3362
Seattle, WA 98174-1001

206-220-7800
Fax: 202-220-7806
http://www.ed.gov

3239 Washington Department of Education
PO Box 47200
Olympia, WA 98504-7200

360-725-6000
Fax: 360-753-6712
http://www.k12.wa.us

Theresa Bergeson, Superintendent

3240 Washington Department of Education; Instruction Program
PO Box 47200
Olympia, WA 98504-7200

206-753-1545
Fax: 360-586-0247

John Pearson, Division Director

3241 Washington Department of Education; Commission on Student Learning Administration
PO Box 47200
Olympia, WA 98504-7200

360-664-3155
Fax: 360-664-3028

Terry Bergeson, Division Director

3242 Washington Department of Education; Executive Services
PO Box 47200
Olympia, WA 98504-7200

360-586-9056
Fax: 360-753-6754

Ken Kanikeberg, Division Director

3243 Washington Department of Education; School Business & Administrative Services
PO Box 47200
Olympia, WA 98504-7200

206-753-6742

David Moberly, Division Director

West Virginia

3244 Division of Administrative Services
West Virginia Department of Education
1900 Kanawha Boulevard E
Building 6
Charleston, WV 25305-0009

304-558-2441
Fax: 304-558-8867

Carolyn Arrington, Division Director

3245 Research, Accountability & Professional
West Virginia Department of Education
1900 Kanawha Boulevard E
Building 6
Charleston, WV 25305-0009

304-558-3762
Fax: 304-558-8867

William J Luff Jr, Division Director

3246 Student Services & Instructional Services
West Virginia Department of Education
1900 Kanawha Boulevard E
Building 6
Charleston, WV 25305-0009

304-558-2691
Fax: 304-558-8867

Keith Smith, Division Director

3247 Technical & Adult Education Services
West Virginia Department of Education
1900 Kanawha Boulevard E
Building 6
Charleston, WV 25305-0009

304-558-2346
Fax: 304-558-8867

Adam Sponaugle, Division Director

3248 West Virginia Department of Education
1900 Kanawha Boulevard E
Building 6, Room B-358
Charleston, WV 25305-0330

304-558-2681
Fax: 304-558-0048
http://www.wvde.state.wv.us

The constitutional mission is to provide supervision of the K-12 education system.

David Stewart, Superintendent
Audrey Horne, President

Wisconsin

3249 Division for Learning Support: Equity & Advocacy
Wisconsin Department of Education
125 S Webster Street
PO Box 7841
Madison, WI 53707-7841

608-266-1649
Fax: 608-267-3746
http://www.dpi.state.wi.us

Carolyn Stanford-Taylor, Division Director

3250 Instructional Services Division
Wisconsin Department of Education
125 S Webster Street
PO Box 7841
Madison, WI 53707-7841

608-266-3361
Fax: 608-267-3746
http://www.dpi.state.wi.us

Pauline Nikolay, Division Director

3251 Library Services Division
Wisconsin Department of Education
125 S Webster Street
PO Box 7841
Madison, WI 53707-7841

608-266-2205
Fax: 608-267-3746
http://www.dpi.state.wi.us

William Wilson, Division Director

3252 School Financial Resources & Management
Wisconsin Department of Education
125 S Webster Street
PO Box 7841
Madison, WI 53707-7841

608-266-3851
Fax: 608-267-3746
http://www.dpi.state.wi.us

Bambi Statz, Division Director

3253 Wisconsin College System Technical
310 Price Place
PO Box 7874
Madison, WI 53707-7874

608-266-1770
Fax: 608-266-1285
E-mail: wtcsb@board.tec.wi.us
http://www.board.tec.wi.us

Richard Carpenter, President

3254 Wisconsin Department of Public Instruction
125 S Webster Street
PO Box 7841
Madison, WI 53707-7841

608-266-1771
800-441-4563
Fax: 608-266-5188
http://www.dpi.state.wi.us

Elizabeth Burmaster, Superintendent

Wyoming

3255 Accounting, Personnel & School Finance Unit
Wyoming Department of Education
2300 Capitol Avenue
Floor 2
Cheyenne, WY 82001-3644

307-777-6392
Fax: 307-777-6234

Barry Nimmo, Division Director

3256 Applied Data & Technology Unit
Wyoming Department of Education
2300 Capitol Avenue
Floor 2
Cheyenne, WY 82001-3644

307-777-6213
Fax: 307-777-6234

Steven King, Division Director

3257 Services for Individuals with Hearing Loss
Wyoming Department of Education
2300 Capitol Avenue
Floor 2
Cheyenne, WY 82001-3644

307-777-4686
Fax: 307-777-6234

Tim Sanger, Division Director

3258 Support Programs & Quality Results Division
Wyoming Department of Education
2300 Capitol Avenue
Floor 2
Cheyenne, WY 82001-3644

307-777-6213
Fax: 307-777-6234

Dr. Alan Sheinker, Division Director

3259 Wyoming Department of Education
2300 Capitol Avenue
Hathaway Building, 2nd Floor
Cheyenne, WY 82002-0050

307-777-7675
Fax: 307-777-6234
http://www.k12.wy.us

Dr. Trent Blankenship, Superintendent

Associations

3260 Academic Alliances
American Association of Higher Education
1 Dupont Circle NW
Suite 360
Washington, DC 20036-1143
202-293-6440
Fax: 202-293-0073
E-mail: info@aahe.net
http://www.aahe.org

Encourages quality education and the professional development of all teachers and educators.

J.Michael Ortiz, Chair Elect

3261 Agency for Instructional Technology
1800 N StoneLake Drive
Box A
Bloomington, IN 47402-0120
812-339-2203
800-457-4509
Fax: 812-333-4218
E-mail: info@ait.net
http://www.ait.net

Professional development, school-to-career, employability skills of problem solving, self management and teamwork.

George Turner, Chair
Sandra McBrayer, Vice Chair

3262 American Association of Colleges for Teacher Education
1307 New York Avenue NW
Suite 300
Washington, DC 20005-4701
202-293-2450
Fax: 202-457-8095
E-mail: aacte@aacte.org
http://www.aacte.org

Colleges and universities concerned with the preparation and development of professionals in education.

Sharon Robinson, President/CEO

3263 American Educational Research Association
1230 17th Street NW
Washington, DC 20036-3078
202-223-9485
Fax: 202-775-1824
E-mail: aera@gmu.edu
http://www.aera.net

Supports improvement of the educational process through the encouragement of scholarly inquiry related to education, the dissemination of research results, and their practical application. Holds a conference and publishes books,videos, and magazines.

Marilyn Cochran-Smith, President

3264 American Educational Studies Association
302 Buchtel Mall
Akron, OH 44325
330-972-7111
http://www.uakron.edu/aesa

Encourages research and the improvement of teaching in various curriculum areas.

Kathleen Bennett deMarrais, President

3265 American Foundation for Negro Affairs
117 S 17th Street
Suite 1200
Philadelphia, PA 19103-5011
215-854-1470
Fax: 215-854-1487

Offers a model for educational programs preparing minority students for professional careers.

Samuel L Evans, President

3266 American Society for Training and Development Information Center
1640 Duke Street
Alexandria, VA 22314-3407
703-683-8100
Fax: 703-683-8103

Serves as the educational society for persons engaged in training and development of business, industry, education and government personnel.

Edith Allen, Director

3267 American Speech-Language-Hearing Association
10801 Rockville Pike
Rockville, MD 20852-3226
301-897-5700
800-638-8255
Fax: 301-571-0457
E-mail: actioncenter@asha.org
http://www.asha.org

Certifies professionals providing speech, language and hearing services to the public. It is an accrediting agency for college and university graduate programs in speech-language pathology and audiology.

3268 Association of Teacher Educators
1900 Association Drive
Sute Ate
Reston, VA 20191-1502
703-620-3110
Fax: 703-620-9530
E-mail: ATE@aol.com
http://www.ate1.org/pubs/home.cfm

Found in 1920 ATE, promotes quality teacher education programs.

Ed Pultorak, President

3269 Center for Rural Studies
University of Vermont, College of Agriculture
108 Morrill Hall
146 University Place
Burlington, VT 05405-0106
802-656-3021
Fax: 802-656-0290
http://crs.uvm.edu

Disseminates information on social, economic, organizational and natural resource aspects of rural life and conducts training and workshops for the professional.

Jane Kolodinsky, Co-Director
Fred Schmidt, Co-Director

3270 Committee on Continuing Education for School Personnel
Kean College of New Jersey
Academic Services
Union, NJ 07083
908-737-5326
Fax: 908-737-5845

Develops activities for professional and personal growth among teachers and educators.

George Sisko, Director

3271 Council for Learning Disabilities
PO Box 4014
Leesburg, VA 20177

571-258-1010
Fax: 571-258-1011
http://www.cldinternational.org

Provides services to professionals who work with individuals with learning disabilities including conferences and publications.

Kirsten McBride, Executive Director

3272 Council of Administrators of Special Education
The Council for Exceptional Children
Fort Valley State University
1005 State University Drive
Fort Valley, GA 31030

478-825-7667
888-232-7733
Fax: 478-825-7811
E-mail: lpurcell@bellsouth.net
http://www.casecec.org

Promotes professional leadership and opportunities for personal and professional advancement. CASE's 5,400 members include administrators, directors and supervisors of special education programs and services.

Steve Milliken, President

3273 Distance Education & Training Council
1601 18th Street NW
Washington, DC 20009-2529

202-234-5100
Fax: 202-332-1386
E-mail: detc@detc.org
http://www.detc.org

A voluntary association of accredited distance education institutions.

Henry Spille, Chair

3274 ERIC Clearinghouse on Teaching and Teacher Education
American Association of Colleges for Teacher Ed.
1307 New York Avenue NW
Suite 300
Washington, DC 20055-4701

202-293-2450
Fax: 202-457-8095
E-mail: aacte@aacte.org
http://www.aacte.org

Teacher recruitment, selection, licensing, certification, training, preservice and inservice preparation, evaluation, retention and retirement. Includes theory, philosophy and teaching practice.

Dr. Mary Dilworth, Director
Deborah Newby, Associate Director

3275 Educational Leadership Institute
4455 Connecticut Avenue NW
Suite 310
Washington, DC 20008

202-822-8405
Fax: 202-872-4050
E-mail: iel@iel.org
http://www.iel.org

Seeks to improve the quality of educational leadership at all levels through field-level research and training programs.

Elizabeth Hale, President

3276 International Council on Education for Teaching
1000 Capitol Drive
Wheeling, IL 60090

847-465-0191
Fax: 847-465-5617
E-mail: icet@nl.edu
http://www.nl.edu

International association dedicated to the improvement of teacher education and all forms of education and training related to national development.

Darrell Bloom, Executive Director
Barbara Spence, Administrative Assistant

3277 National Association of State Directors of Teacher Education & Certification
22 Bates Road
PMB #134
Mashpee, MA 02649-3267

508-539-8844
Fax: 508-539-8868
E-mail: nasdtec@attbi.com
http://www.nasdtec.org

Provides leadership in matters related to the preparation and certification of professional school personnel.

Roy Einreinhofer, Executive Director

3278 National Center for Community Education
1017 Avon Street
Flint, MI 48503-2797

810-238-0463
800-811-1105
Fax: 810-238-9211
E-mail: nccenet@earthlink.net
http://www.nccenet.org

Provides short term training workshops for persons entering and/or working in the field of community education.

Duane R Brown, Director

3279 National Council for the Accreditation of Teacher Education
2010 Massachusetts Avenue NW
Washington, DC 20036-1023

202-466-7496
Fax: 202-296-6620
E-mail: ncate@ncate.org
http://www.ncate.org

Professional accrediting organization for schools, colleges, and departments of education in the United States.

Arthur E Wise, President
Donna M Gollnick, Sr VP

3280 National Education Association
1201 16th Street NW
Washington, DC 20036-3290

202-833-4000
Fax: 202-822-7974
E-mail: ncuea@nea.org
http://www.nea.org

Advocates for the education profession and the well-being of children; supports campaigns designed to improve the teaching profession, teachers in their efforts to improve teaching; training programs, safe schools and better workingconditions.

Reg Weaver, President
Dennis Van Roekel, Vice President

3281 National Middle School Association
4151 Executive Parkway
Suite 300
Westerville, OH 43081

614-895-4730
800-528-6672
Fax: 614-895-4750
E-mail: info@NMSA.org
http://www.nmsa.org

Resource centers, conferences, professional development, and more.

Kathy McAvoy, President

3282 National Staff Development Council
5995 Fairfield Road
Suite 4
Oxford, OH 45056

513-523-6029
Fax: 513-523-0638
http://www.nsdc.org

Researches and organizes staff development theories and practices for various school districts.

Dennis Sparks, Executive Director

3283 National Women's Studies Association
7100 Baltimore Boulevard
University of Maryland
College Park, MD 20740

301-403-0524
Fax: 301-403-4137
E-mail: nwsa@umail.umd.edu
http://www.nwsa.org

Works to further the social, political and professional development of women's studies programs and projects.

Jacquelyn Zita, President

3284 Recruiting New Teachers
385 Concord Avenue
Suite 103
Belmont, MA 02478-3037

617-489-6000
800-45 -EACH
Fax: 617-489-6005
E-mail: rnt@rnt.org
http://www.rnt.org/channels/clearinghouse

Conducts public service advertising campaign encouraging people to consider teaching careers.

Mildred Hudson, CEO/RNT

3285 Search Associates
PO Box 636
Dallas, PA 18612-0636

570-696-5400
Fax: 570-696-9500

Sponsors recruiting fairs across the country.

Dr. John Magagna

3286 Teacher Education Division
The Council for Exceptional Children
1920 Association Drive
Reston, VA 20191-1545

703-620-3660
888-232-773
Fax: 703-264-9494

Association promoting preparation and continuing development of effective professionals in special education and related fields such as general education, allied health, speech and language pathology, rehabilitation, legal servicesand more.

Awards & Honors

3287 Apple Education Grants
Apple Computer
2420 Ridge Point Drive
Austin, TX 78754

800-800-2775
Fax: 512-919-2992
http://www.apple.com

Awarded each year to teams of K-12 educators working on educational technology plans. Potential awardees find innovative uses of technology in the classroom and come

from schools that would otherwise have limited access to technology.

3288 Bayer/NSF Award for Community Innovation
105 Terry Drive
Suite 120
Newtown, PA 18940

215-579-8590
800-291-6020
Fax: 215-579-8589
E-mail: success@edumedia.com
http://www.bayernsfaward.com

A community-based science and technology competition to give all sixth, seventh and eighth-graders a hands-on experience with real-world problems using the scientific method.

Stephanie Hallman, Program Manager
Stacey Gall, Competition Coordinator

3289 Excellence in Teaching Cabinet Grant
Curriculm Associates
PO Box 2001
North Billericka, MA 01862

800-225-0248
Fax: 800-366-1158
http://www.curriculumassociates.com

Awarded to educators who wish to implement unique educational projects. Potential awardees propose projects using a variety of teaching tools, including technology and print.

3290 Magna Awards
American School Board Journal
1680 Duke Street
Alexandria, VA 22314

703-549-6719
Fax: 703-549-6719

Recognizes local school boards that are putting student achievement and community engagement at the center of their work. October 31st deadline.

Annual

3291 NSTA Award for Principals
National Science Teachers Association
1840 Wilson Boulevard
Arlington, VA 22201

703-243-7100
888-400-NSTA
Fax: 703-243-7177
E-mail: lpinson@nsta.org
http://www.nsta.org

The 1999 Exemplary Middle Level and High School Principal Awards recognizes one middle level and one high school principal who have demonstrated leadership in developing, implementing, and maintaining an outstanding science progam;supported staff development; promoted positive relationships, and served as an advocate and leader.

3292 NSTA Awards
National Science Teachers Association
1840 Wilson Boulevard
Arlington, VA 22201-3000

703-243-7100
Fax: 703-243-7177

Awards for excellence in dozens of fields and programs.

3293 National Teachers Hall of Fame
1320 C of E Drive
Emporia, KS 66801

620-341-9131
800-968-3224
Fax: 620-341-5912
E-mail: hallfame@emporia.edu
http://www.nthf.org

Founded for the purpose of recognizing the exceptional qualities possessed by our nation's teachers. Candidates eligible for induction must have at least 20 years of full-time classroom teaching in grades pre-kindergarten through highschool. Candidates may be active or retired.

David John, President
Cora Hedstrom, Coordinator/Teacher

3294 Presidential Awards for Excellence in Mathematics and Science Teaching
National Science Foundation
4201 Wilson Boulevard
Arlington, VA 22230

703-292-8620
Fax: 703-292-9044
E-mail: msaul@nsf.gov
http://www.ehr.nsf.gov

This award is the nation's highest commendation for K-12 math and science teachers. Approximately 108 teachers are recognized annually with this prestigious award.

Mark Saul, Director

3295 Senior Researcher Award
Music Education Research Council
Deptartment of Music
138 Fine Arts Center
Columbia, MO 65211

573-884-1604
Fax: 573-884-7444

For recognition of a significant scholarly achievement maintained over a period of years.

3296 Toyota Tapestry Grants for Teachers
National Science Teachers Association
1840 Wilson Boulevard
Arlington, VA 22201-3000

800-807-9852
Fax: 703-522-6193
E-mail: tapestry@nsta.org
http://www.nsta.org/programs/tapestry

Sponsored by Toyota Motor Sales USA, this offers a minimum of 70 grants totaling $550,000 each year to K-12 teachers of science who wish to implement an innovative, community based science project. 50 large grants of up to $10,000each will be available as well as a minimum of 20 mini-grants of up to $2,500 each. Categories include Physical Science, Environmental Science and Literacy and Science.

Eric Crossley, Industry/Education Programs

Conferences

3297 ACE Fellows Program
American Council on Education
1 Dupont Circle NW
Washington, DC 20036-1193

202-939-9420
Fax: 808-785-8056
E-mail: fellows@ace.nche.edu
http://www.acenet.edu

Provides comprehensive leadership development for senior faculty and administrators of universities and colleges. Offers mentor-intern relationships programs. Special institutional grants available for candidates from communitycolleges, tribal colleges and private historical black universities and colleges.

3298 ASQ Annual Koalaty Kid Conference
ASQ
611 E Wisconsin Avenue
Milwaukee, WI 53201

414-272-8717
Fax: 414-272-1247
http://www.asq.org

A professional association headquartered in Milwaukee, Wisconsin, creates better workplaces and communities worldwide by advancing learning, quality improvement, and knowledge exchange.

April
Andrew Hohensee

3299 Alaska Department of Education Bilingual & Bicultural Education Conference
University of Alaska, Conference & Special Events
117 Eielson Building
Fairbanks, AK 99775

907-474-7396

Stresses the importance of literacy and multicultural education for Alaskan educators.

February

3300 American Association of Collegiate Registrars & Admissions Officers
1 Dupont Circle NW
Suite 520
Washington, DC 20036-1137

202-293-9161
Fax: 202-872-8857
http://www.aacrao.org

Promotes higher education and furthers the professional developmentof members working in admissions, enrollment management, financial aid, institutional research, records and registration.

April
125 booths with 2500 attendees
Jerry Sullivan, Executive Director
Martha Henebry, Publications Manager

3301 American Federation of Teachers Biennial Convention & Exhibition
AFL-CIO
555 New Jersey Avenue NW
Washington, DC 20001-2029

202-879-4400
Fax: 202-879-4558
E-mail: online@aft.org
http://www.aft.org

represent the economic, social and professional interests of classroom teachers

Edward McElroy, President

3302 American Society for Training-Development International Conference
1640 King Street
Po Box 1443
Alexandria, VA 22313-2043

703-683-8100
800-628-2783
Fax: 703-683-1523
http://www.astd.org/astd/conferences/about_conferences

Explore the newest training theories and models. ASTD conferences ensure that you're up-to-date with the latest thinking and trends affecting workplace learning and

Professional Development / Conferences

performance. Attended by international teachers and professors,counselors and human relations personnel.

May

Tony Bingham, President/CEO
Christopher Palazio, Advertising Coordinator

3303 Annual Building Championship Schools Conference
Center for Peak Performing Schools
2021 Clubhouse Drive
Greeley, CO 80634

970-339-9277

Interested in curriculum development and instructional assessment. Members include administrators at all levels of education.

February

3304 Annual Convention
New York School Board Association
24 Century Hill Drive
Suite 200
Latham, NY 12210-2125

518-783-0200
Fax: 518-783-0211
E-mail: info@nyssba.org
http://www.nyssba.org

Contains exhibitors representing various educational industries including: buses, athletic and recreational services, school furnishings and public utilities.

October
240 booths with 3,000 attendees

Cheryl Brenn, Marketing Manager

3305 Annual New England Kindergarten Conference
Lesley University
29 Everett Street
Cambridge, MA 02138

617-349-8922
800-999-1959
Fax: 617-349-8125
E-mail: kindconf@mail.lesley.edu
http://www.lesley.edu

November
1000 attendees

Mary Mindess, Conference Coordinator
Kari Nygaard, Conference Manager

3306 Annual State Convention of Association of Texas Professional Educators
305 E Huntland Drive
Suite 300
Austin, TX 78752

512-467-0071
800-777-2873
Fax: 512-467-2203
E-mail: atpe@atpe.org
http://www.atpe.org

Professional association for Texas public school educators.

March
100 booths with 1,300 attendees

Doug Rogers, Executive Director
Kara Lacke, Conference Manager

3307 Association for Educational Communications & Technology Annual Convention
AECT
1800 North Stonelake Drive
Suite 2
Bloomington, IN 47404

812-335-7675
Fax: 812-335-7678
E-mail: aect@aect.org
http://www.aect.org/Events/default.htm

Offers training tracks focusing on a variety of special interest areas. Special sessions examine such topics as hypermedia, TQM, school reform, and advanced telecommunications. Half-day workshops offer in-depth training on the latesttechnology applications for education.

Dr Phillip Harris, Executive Director
Ned Shaw, Mktg & Communications Dir.

3308 Association for Library & Information Science Education Annual Conference
ALISE
1009 Commerce Park Drive
Suite 150
Oak Ridge, TN 37830

865-425-0155
Fax: 865-481-0390
E-mail: contact@alise.org
http://www.alise.org

An annual conference attended by over 250 university/college faculty librarians with over 10 co-sponsors. Although a special interest conference, it has open registration and includes a job placement service.

January

Deborah York, Executive Director
Lance Vowell, Information Management

3309 California Council for Adult Education
1006 4th Street
Suite 260
Sacramento, CA 95814-3314

916-444-3323
Fax: 916-557-1152

A state conference of adult educators representing school districts, community colleges and related products and services to the education field.

April
40 booths

Richard Whiteman, Conference Contact

3310 California Kindergarten Association Annual Conference
California Kindergarten Association
1710 S Amphlett Boulevard
Suite 117
San Mateo, CA 94402-2704

650-286-0167
Fax: 916-780-5330

Caters to childhood education professionals, preschool, kindergarten and day care center workers.

January

3311 California School Boards Association Conference
PO Box 1660
West Sacramento, CA 95691-6660

916-371-4691
Fax: 916-371-3407
E-mail: colcese@csba.org
http://www.csba.org

Products and services targeted to the California public schools.

December
200 booths

Chris Olcese, Conference Contact

3312 Careers Conference
Center on Education and Work
964 Educational Sciences Building
1025 W. Johnson Street
Madison, WI 53706-1706
608-263-4779
800-446-0399
Fax: 608-262-3063
E-mail: cewconf@education.wisc.edu
http://www.cew.wisc.edu

Designed to serve all practitioners concerned with career development and education for work. This annual conference presents learning opportunities at all levels, from a basic introduction to keeping current with the very latest in advanced practices.

Jan - Feb
40 booths with 1500 attendees

Carol Edds, Conference Director

3313 Center for Play Therapy Fall Conference
University of North Texas
PO Box 311337
Denton, TX 76203
940-565-3864
Fax: 940-565-4461
E-mail: cpt@coefs.coe.unt.edu
http://www.centerforplaytherapy.com

October
4 booths with 350 attendees

Garry Landreth PhD, Director

3314 Central States Conference on the Teaching of Foreign Languages
University of Nebraska at Omaha
Omaha, NE 68182
402-554-2403

Offers various information, updates and programs to advance the teaching of foreign languages and foreign language educators.

3315 Chicago Principals Association Education Conference
221 N Lasalle Street
Suite 3316
Chicago, IL 60601-1505
312-263-7767
Fax: 312-263-2012

Educational or fund raising products including copy machines, computers, book companies, etc.

February

Beverly Tunney, Conference Contact

3316 Classroom Connect
8000 Marina Boulevard
Suite 400
Brisbane, CA 94005
650-351-5100
800-638-1639
Fax: 650-351-5300
E-mail: conect@classroom.com
http://www.classroom.com

A leading provider of professional development programs and online instructional content for K-12 education.

October

3317 Colorado Association of School Executives Conference
4101 S Bannock Street
Englewood, CO 80110-4605
303-762-8762
Fax: 303-762-8697

47 booths exhibiting school administration and education/construction related products.

August

Janice Hartmangruber, Conference Contact

3318 Education Conference
International Honor and Professional Association
PO Box 6626
Bloomington, IN 47407-6626
812-339-3411
800-487-3411
Fax: 812-339-3462
E-mail: office@pilambda.org
http://www.pilambda.org

Honor outstanding educators and inspire them to be effective leaders who address critical issues in education.

400 attendees

Juli Knutson, Conference Manager

3319 Florida Elementary School Principals Association Conference
206 S Monroe Street
Suite B
Tallahassee, FL 32301-1801
800-593-3626
Fax: 850-224-3892

Exhibitors from fundraisers to computer companies.

November
50 booths

Lisa Begue, Conference Contact

3320 Florida School Administrators Association Summer Conference
206 S Monroe Street
Suite B
Tallahassee, FL 32301-1801
850-224-3626
800-593-3626
Fax: 850-224-3892
E-mail: sgray@fasa.net

Exhibits include computer software, textbooks and school supplies, fundraising companies, schoolyear book and ring companies, video and audio companies, furniture suppliers and other school related products.

Jan./June/Nov.
700/300 attendees and 100/85 exhibits

Sharon Gray, Conference Coordinator
Kim Beaty, Director Communications

3321 Florida Vocational Association Conference
1420 N Paul Russell Road
Tallahassee, FL 32301-4835
850-878-6860
Fax: 850-878-5476

Curriculum materials, industrial equipment and supplies, computer hardware and software, medical

Professional Development / Conferences

equipment and other materials utilized by vocational educators.

July
150 booths

Donna Harper, Conference Contact

3322 Illinois Assistant Principals Conference
2990 Baker Drive
Springfield, IL 62703-2800

217-525-1383
Fax: 217-525-7264
http://http://ipa.vsat.net

Professional member association dedicated to the improvement of elementary and secondary education.

February
120 booths with 200 attendees

David Turner, Executive Director
Pam Burdine, Exhibit Contact

3323 Illinois Principals Professional Conference
2990 Baker Drive
Springfield, IL 62703-2800

217-525-1383
Fax: 217-525-7264
http://http:ipa.vsat.net

Professional member association dedicated to the improvement of elementary and secondary education.

October
120 booths with 800 attendees

Julie Weichert, Associate Director
David Turner, Executive Director

3324 Illinois Resource Center Conference of Teachers of Linguistically Diverse Students
Illinois Resource Center
1855 S Mount Prospect Road
Des Plaines, IL 60018-1805

847-803-3112
Fax: 847-803-2828

A conference that caters to those educators involved with teaching multi-licensed pupils.

March

3325 Illinois School Boards Association
430 E Vine Street
Springfield, IL 62703-2236

217-528-9688
Fax: 217-528-2831

School equipment, supplies, building maintenance, insurance and bond sales programs, supplies and equipment.

November
235 booths

Sandra Boston, Conference Contact

3326 Indiana School Boards Association Annual Conference
1 N Capitol Avenue
Suite 1215
Indianapolis, IN 46204-2095

317-639-0330

Educational products and services.

September/October
158 booths

Mary A. Chapman, Conference Contact

3327 International Association for Social Science Information Service & Technology
Institute for Social Science Research/UCLA Archive
405 Hilgard Avenue
Attn: Wendy Treadwell
Los Angeles, CA 90095-9000

612-624-4389
Fax: 612-626-9353
http://www.iassistdata.org/conferences

Conference for association members offering the latest information on research and technology in the social sciences fields.

May
May

Ann Green, President

3328 Iowa Council Teachers of Math Conference
1712 55th Street
Des Moines, IA 50310-1548

515-242-7846

Math teachers conference.

February
48 booths

Michael Link, Conference Contact

3329 Iowa Reading Association Conference
512 Lynn Avenue
Ames, IA 50014-7320

515-292-0126

100 tabletops.

April

Evelyn Beavers, Conference Contact

3330 Iowa School Administrators Association Annual Convention
4500 Westown Parkway
Suite 140
West Des Moines, IA 50266-6717

515-267-1115
Fax: 515-267-1066

150 booths.

August

Gaylord Tryon, Conference Contact

3331 Iowa School Boards Association
700 2nd Avenue
Suite 100
Des Moines, IA 50309-1713

515-288-1991

November
135 booths

Wayne R Beal, Conference Contact

3332 Kansas School Boards Association Conference
1420 SW Arrowhead Road
Topeka, KS 66604-4001

785-273-3600
Fax: 785-273-7580

Wide variety of school district vendors and contacts for products and services.

December
70 booths

3333 Kansas United School Administrators Conference
820 SE Quincy Street
Suite 200
Topeka, KS 66612-1158

785-232-6566
Fax: 785-232-9776
E-mail: usakl@ink.org

Exhibits of the latest educational goods and services.

January
180 booths

Brilla Highfill Scott, Conference Contact

3334 Kentucky School Boards Association Conference
260 Democrat Drive
Frankfort, KY 40601-9214

502-695-4630
Fax: 502-695-5451

February
45 booths

Ann Booten, Conference Contact

3335 Kentucky School Superintendents Association Meeting
154 Consumer Lane
Frankfort, KY 40601-8489

502-875-3411
Fax: 502-875-4634

A variety of education services and sales, and products from architecture to computers.

June
36 booths

Dr. Roland Haun, Conference Contact

3336 Lilly Conference on College Teaching
Miami University
102 Roudebush Hau
Oxford, OH 45056

513-529-6648
Fax: 513-529-3762
E-mail: lillyconference@muohio.edu
http://www.muohio.edu/lillyconference/

Celebrating 23 years of presenting the Scholarship of Teaching. The Lilly Conference specializes in training and teaching methodology for higher education professionals through approximately 160 sessions by over 150 presenters. Manyof the presenters are nationally or internationally known experts in Scholarship of Teaching.

November
660 attendees

Melody Barton, Conference Manager
Milton Cox, Conference Director

3337 Lilly Conferences on College and University Teaching
International Alliance of Teacher Scholars
Box 1000
Claremnont, CA 91711

800-718-4287
Fax: 909-621-8270
E-mail: alliance@iats.com
http://www.iats.com

Lilly Conferences are retreats that combine workshops, discussion sessions and major addresses, with opportunities for informal discussion about excellence in college and university teaching and learning. Internationally knownscholars join new and experienced faculty members and administrators from all over the world.

November

Laurie Richlin, Director

3338 Louisiana School Boards Association Conference
7912 Summa Avenue
Baton Rouge, LA 70809-3416

504-769-3191

60 booths of school and classroom related products and/or services.

February

James V Soileau, Conference Contact

3339 Maine Principals Association Conference
PO Box 2468
Augusta, ME 04338-2468

207-622-0217

50 booths.

April

Barbara Proko, Conference Contact

3340 Massachusetts Elementary School Principals Association Conference
28 Lord Road
Suite 125
Marlborough, MA 01752-4548

508-624-0500
Fax: 508-485-9965

Educational products, texts and fundraising products.

May
100 booths

Nadya Aswad Higgins, Conference Contact

3341 Massachusetts School Boards Association Meeting
90 Topsfield Road
Ipswich, MA 01938-1650

978-356-5453

May
100 booths

Capt. Edward Bryant, NCCC, Conference Contact

3342 Michigan Association of Elementary and Middle School Principals Conference
1405 S Harrison Road
Suite 210
East Lansing, MI 48823-5245

517-353-8770
Fax: 517-432-1063

Exhibits offer books, fundraisers, camps, insurance groups and non-profit organizations.

October
100 booths

William Hays, Jr, Conference Contact

3343 Michigan School Boards Association Fall Leadership Conference
1001 Centennial Way
#400
Lansing, MI 48917-9279

517-327-5900
Fax: 517-327-0775
E-mail: mkreh@masb.org
http://www.masb.org

Exhibits flooring, buses, school supplies, computer hardware and software.

October
150 booths with 800 attendees

Matt Kreh, Projects Directort

3344 Michigan Science Teachers Association Annual Conference
Western Michigan University
Office of Conferences
Kalamazoo, MI 49008

616-387-4174
Fax: 616-387-4189

A conference that aims to supply science teachers with information and research.

February

3345 Mid-South Educational Research Association Annual Meeting
Louisiana State University, School of Dentistry
1100 Florida Avenue
#223
New Orleans, LA 70119-2714

504-619-8700
Fax: 504-619-8740

Focuses on assessment and involvement in education by releasing research and statistics.

November

Diana Gardiner PhD, Conference Contact

3346 Middle States Council for the Social Studies Annual Regional Conference
Rider College
2083 Lawrenceville Road
Lawrenceville, NJ 08648-3001

717-865-2117

Seeks to develop and implement new curriculum into the social studies area.

April

Dan Sidelnick, Conference Contact

3347 Minnesota Leadership Annual Conference
Minnesota School Boards Association
1900 W Jefferson Avenue
St. Peter, MN 56082-3014

507-934-2450
800-324-4459
Fax: 507-931-1515
http://www.mnmsba.org

A prime networking opportunity combined with sessions discussing the latest information and ideas in school governance and operations.

January
200+ booths with 2,000+ attendees

Mike Torkelson, Deputy Executive Director
Tiffany Rodning, Coordinator Finance

3348 Minnesota School Administrators Association
1884 Como Avenue
Saint Paul, MN 55108-2715

651-645-7231
Fax: 651-645-7518
E-mail: members@mnasa.org
http://wwwmnasa.org

Educational materials and school building products.

October
70 booths

Charles Kyle, Executive Director
Mia Vrick, Conference Contact

3349 Minnesota School Boards Association Annual Meeting
1900 W Jefferson Street
Saint Peter, MN 56082-3014

507-931-2450
Fax: 507-931-1515

School supplies and services as diverse as buses and architectural services.

January
190 booths

Mike Torkelson, Conference Contact

3350 Missouri National Education Association Conference
1810 E Elm Street
Jefferson City, MO 65101-4174

573-634-3202
Fax: 573-634-5646
http://www.mo.nea.org

November annual
95 booths with 1,500 attendees

Carol Schmoock, Conference Manager
Ann Claypool, Conference Manager

3351 Missouri School Boards Association Annual Meeting
2100170 Drive SW
Columbia, MO 65203

573-445-9920
Fax: 573-445-9981

Education-related products and services.

October
125 booths

Evelyn Graham, Conference Contact

3352 Missouri State Teachers Association Conference
PO Box 458
Columbia, MO 65205-0458

573-442-3127
Fax: 573-443-5079

Educational materials.

November
280 booths

Kent King, Conference Contact

3353 Montana Association of Elementary School Principals Conference
1134 Butte Avenue
Helena, MT 59601-5178

406-442-2510
Fax: 406-442-2518

January/Febuary
20 booths

Loran Frazier, Conference Contact

3354 National Association of Secondary School Principals Annual Convention and Exposition
1904 Association Drive
Reston, VA 22019

703-860-0200
800-253-7746
Fax: 703-620-6534
http://www.nasspconvention.org

Offers workshops for principals on leadership training, student personnel services, and how to deal with at-risk students. Convention highlights include more than 200 educational sessions, special interest forums and luncheons andspotlights on the latest education products and services.

Phoenix
March
290 booths

Gayle Mercer, Conference Contact

3355 National Association of State Boards of Education Conference
277 S Washington Street
Suite 100
Alexandria, VA 22314

703-684-4000
Fax: 703-836-2313

E-mail: boards@nasbe.org
http://www.nasbe.org

October
24 booths with 150 attendees
Doris Cruel, Conference Contact

3356 National Career Development Association Conference
4700 Reed Road
Suite M
Columbus, OH 43220-3074

703-823-9800
Fax: 703-823-0252

Supplies information and guidance for vocational-technical and career development professionals.

January

3357 National Conference on Education
American Association of School Administrators
1801 N Moore Street
Arlington, VA 22209-1813

703-528-0700
Fax: 703-841-1543
http://www.aasa.org

Ensures the highest quality education systems for all learners through the support and development of leadership on the building, district and state levels. Containing 5,000 attendees.

March

Andrea Saris, Manager

3358 National Conference on Standards and Assessment
National School Conference Institute
Riviera Hotel
Las Vegas, NV 89101

602-371-8655
Fax: 602-371-8790
http://www.nscinet.com

Two pre-conference workshops: The five most important things that educators need to know when using information for continuous program improvement, and The key to sustained leadership effectiveness. Conference will also hold over 60breakout sessions.

April

Bill Daggett
Bob Marzano

3359 National Council for Geographic Education Annual Meeting
700 Pelham Road N
Jacksonville, AL 36265

256-782-5293
Fax: 256-782-5336
E-mail: ncge@jsucc.jsu.edu
http://www.nege.org

Stresses the essential value of geographic education and knowledge in schools.

October
45 booths with 800 attendees

Michael LeVasseur, Executive Director
Angelia Mance, Associate Director

3360 National Council for History Education Conference
National Council for History Education
26915 Westwood Road
Suite B-2
Westlake, OH 44145-4657

440-835-1776
Fax: 440-835-1295
E-mail: nche@nche.net
http://www.history.org/nche

Discovering history, places, documents and artifacts.

October
750 attendees and 75 exhibits

Elaine W Reed, Manager

3361 National Council for Social Studies Annual Conference
3501 Newark Street NW
Washington, DC 20016-3100

202-966-7840
Fax: 202-966-2061

Focuses on social studies educators.

November
150 booths

Peter Stavros, Conference Contact

3362 National Council of English Teachers Conference
National Council of Teachers of English
1111 W Kenyon Road
Urbana, IL 61801-1010

217-328-3870
800-369-6283
Fax: 217-328-9645
http://www.ncte.org

Jacqui Joseph-Biddle, Conference Manager

3363 National Council of Teachers of Mathematics Annual Meeting
1906 Association Drive
Reston, VA 20191-1593

703-620-9840
Fax: 703-476-2970
E-mail: annimtg@nctm.org
http://www.nctm.org

Elementary school teachers at a school that is an NCTM member are entitled to a special individual member registration fee at our conferences. Consult your school administration about the Title II Dwight D. Eisenhower funds earmarkedfor teacher training. Ask us about group discounts.

April
620 booths with 18M attendees

Patty Markusson, Conference Manager

3364 National Council of Teachers of English Annual Convention
1111 W Kenyon Road
Urbana, IL 61801-1010

217-328-3870
800-369-6283
Fax: 217-278-3763
E-mail: public_info@ncte.org
http://www.ncte.org

Provides a forum for English educators of all grade levels.

November
290+ booths with 6500 attendees

Jacqui Joseph-Biddle, Conference Contact

3365 National Council of Teachers of Mathematics Conference
1906 Association Drive
Reston, VA 20191-9988

703-620-9840
800-235-7566
Fax: 703-476-2970
E-mail: nctm@nctm.org
http://www.nctm.org

Dedicated to the improvement of mathematics education and to meeting the needs of Pre K-12 mathematics teaching. Conferences, journals and a collection of educational materials for teacher development.

January

Cynthia Rosse, Directorf Marketing Services
Barbara Thode, Conference Manager

3366 National Education Association Annual Meeting
National Education Association (NEA)
1201 16th Street NW
Washington, DC 20036-3290

202-822-7364
Fax: 202-822-7624
E-mail: ncuea@nea.org
http://www.nea.org

A general conference that addresses all facets and concerns of the educator.

July

Gloria Durgin, Conference Contact

3367 National Educational Computing Conference
Washington State Convention & Trade Center
800 Convention Place
Seattle, WA 98101-2350

206-694-5000
Fax: 206-694-5399
E-mail: info@wsctc.com
http://www.neccsite.com

Strengthen the role of technology in education by sharpening your skills, learning new ones, sharing with colleagues, and becoming involved.

June
417 booths with 12,500 attendees
Dr Heidi Rogers, First Executive Director

3368 National Middle School Association's Annual Conference and Exhibition
National Middle School Association
4151 Executive Parkway
Suite 300
Westerville, OH 43081

800-528-6672
E-mail: info@nmsa.org
http://www.nmsa.org

Provides professional development, journals, books, research and other valuable information to assist educators on an ongoing basis.

October

3369 National Occupational Information Coordinating Committee Conference
2100 M Street NW
Suite 156
Washington, DC 20037-1207

202-653-7680

Focuses on policy, social issues and social services addressing career development and occupational information.

August
Mary Susan Vickers, Conference Contact

3370 National School Boards Association Annual Conference & Exposition
1680 Duke Street
Alexandria, VA 22314-3455

703-838-6788
Fax: 703-549-6719

Distributes information on issues confronting school administration today.

Februrary
550 booths
Teresaa Dumochelle, Conference Contact

3371 National Science Teachers Association Area Convention
1840 Wilson Boulevard
Arlington, VA 22201-3000

703-243-7100
800-782-6782
Fax: 703-243-7177

Three area conventions are held in Portland, Minneapolis and Las Vegas.

March/April
Sallie Snyder, Conference Contact

3372 New England Kindergarten Conference
Lesley University
29 Everett Street
Cambridge, MA 02138-2702

617-349-8922
800-233-1636
Fax: 617-349-8125
E-mail: kinconf@mail.lesley.edu
http://www.lesley.edu/kc

100 booths consisting of materials and products that help educators work more effectively with children.

November
100 booths with 2000 attendees
Kerri Schmidt, Conference Manager

3373 New England League of Middle Schools
New England League of Middle Schools
460 Boston Street
Suite 4
Topsfield, MA 01983-1223

978-887-6263
Fax: 978-887-6504
E-mail: nelms@nelms.org
http://www.nelms.org

Offers vendors the opportunity to showcase educationally supportive ideas and meet one-on-one with professionals who are resources for advice on new products appropriate to the middle level.

March
160+ booths with 3800+ attendees
Jeannette Southall, Exhibit Manager
Adrian Aleckna, Conference Planner

**3374 New Mexico School Boards Association
Conference Annual Meeting**
300 Galisteo Street
Suite 204
Santa Fe, NM 87501-2606
505-983-5041
Fax: 505-983-2450

December
20 booths
Wesley H Lane, Conference Contact

**3375 New York School Superintendents Association
Annual Meeting**
111 Washington Avenue
Suite 404
Albany, NY 12210-2210
518-449-1063
Fax: 518-426-2229

Provides leadership and membership services through a
professional organization of school superintendents.

October
50 booths
Dr. Claire Brown, Conference Contact

**3376 New York Science Teachers Association Annual
Meeting**
2449 Union Boulevard
Apartment 20B
Islip, NY 11751-3117
516-783-5432
Fax: 516-783-5432

Education related publications, equipment, supplies and
services.

November
110 booths
Harold Miller, Conference Contact

3377 New York State United Teachers Conference
159 Wolf Road
Albany, NY 12205-1106
518-213-6000
Fax: 518-213-6415

February
40 booths
Anthony Bifaro, Conference Contact

3378 New York Teachers Math Association Conference
92 Governor Drive
Scotia, NY 12302-4802
518-399-0149

October-November
50 booths
Phil Reynolds, Conference Contact

**3379 North American Association for Environmental
Education**
1825 Connecticut Avenue NW
Suite 800
Washington, DC 20009-5708
202-884-8942
Fax: 202-884-8455
E-mail: email@naaee.org
http://www.naaee.org

A network of professionals and students working in the
field of environmental education throughout North
America and 45 other countries. The Association
promotes environmental education and supports the
work of environmental educatorsfor over 25 years.

October
Elaine Andrews, President

**3380 North Carolina Association for Career and
Technical Education Conference**
PO Box 25159
Raleigh, NC 27611-5159
919-782-0708
Fax: 919-782-8096
http://www.ncacte.org

Educational books, supplies, materials, interactive
video, computers, lasers, robotics, child care equipment
and hand tools.

July
110 booths with 3000 + attendees
Dr. Clifton Belcher, Conference Contact

**3381 North Carolina School Administrators
Conference**
PO Box 1629
Raleigh, NC 27602-1629
919-828-1426
Fax: 919-828-6099

March
40 booths
Joyce Myers, Conference Contact

**3382 North Central Association Annual Meeting
North Central Association Commission on Accred.**
Arizona State University
PO Box 874705
Tempe, AZ 85287-4705
303-722-6019
Fax: 303-593-2849
http://www.ncacasi.org

Sponsored by the North Central Association
Commission on Accreditation and School Improvement.

April
30 booths with 1,800 attendees
Teri Schwindt, Conference Contact
Ron Stastney, Conference Manager

**3383 North Central Conference on Summer Schools
Summer School**
University of Wisconsin
410 S 3rd Street
River Falls, WI 54022
715-425-3851
Fax: 715-425-3785
E-mail: roger.a.swanson@uwrf.edu
http://www.conted.ufuc.edu

The NCCSS is an organization of colleges and
universities offering undergraduate and/or graduate
programs in the summer months. The organization's
boundries roughly coincide with those of North Central
Association of Colleges andSchools. The NCCSS is able
to address concerns unique to this area and is dedicated to
maintaining high standards in summer programs.

March
Dr. Roger Swanson, Manager

Professional Development / Conferences

3384 Northeast Conference on the Teaching of Foreign Languages
Northeast Conference at Dickinson College
PO Box 1773
Carlisle, PA 17013-2896
717-245-1977
Fax: 717-245-1976
E-mail: nectfl@dickinson.edu
http://www.dickinson.edu/nectfl
Annual conference on the teaching of foreign languages; juried periodical, advocacy, information clearinghouse.

April
160 booths with 2500 attendees
Rebecca Kline, Executive Director

3385 Northeast Teachers Foreign Language Conference
St. Michael's College
29 Ethan Allen Avenue
Dupont Building
Colchester, VT 05446
802-654-2000
Fax: 802-654-2595
Foreign language textbooks, supplementary materials, audio equipment, computer software, travel abroad program materials and other related teaching aids and publications.

April
130 booths
Elizabeth L Holekamp, Conference Contact

3386 Northwest Association of Schools & Colleges Annual Meeting
1910 University Drive
Boise, ID 83725-1060
208-426-5727
Fax: 208-334-3228
http://www2.idbsu.edu/nasc
Serves the educational administration community by addressing topics that concern colleges, schools and other educational institutions.

December
120 attendees
Shelli D Clemens, Manager

3387 Northwest Regional Educational Laboratory Conference
101 SW Main Street
Suite 500
Portland, OR 97204-3297
800-547-6339
Concentrates on career education and educational change for professionals in vocational education, counseling and social work.

October/November
Francie Lindner, Conference Contact

3388 Ohio Business Teachers Association
Wright State University, Lake Campus
7600 State Route 703
Celina, OH 45822-2921
419-586-0337
Fax: 419-586-0368

October
40 booths
Roger Fulk, Conference Contact

3389 Ohio Public School Employees Association Convention
6805 Oak Creek Drive
Columbus, OH 43229
614-890-4770
Fax: 614-890-3540

May
15 booths
Joe Rugola, Conference Contact

3390 Ohio Secondary School Administrators Association Fall Conference
750 Brooksedge Boulevard
Westerville, OH 43081-2881
614-430-8311
Fax: 614-430-8315
Ring companies, furniture, computer software and fundraising companies.

October
42 booths
Jo Anne Rubsam, Conference Contact

3391 Oklahoma School Boards Association & School Administrators Conference
2801 N Lincoln Boulevard
Oklahoma City, OK 73105-4223
405-528-3571
Fax: 405-528-5695
School-related products and/or services.

August
195 booths
Joann Yandell, Conference Contact

3392 Oregon School Boards Association Annual Convention
PO Box 1068
Salem, OR 97308-1068
503-588-2800
Fax: 503-588-2813
This convention addresses various issues emerging in the Oregon school system.

November
Pat Fitzwater, Conference Contact

3393 Pacific Northwest Council on Languages Annual Conference
PO Box 4649
Portland, OR 97208-4649
503-287-8539
E-mail: reverzasconi@uswest.net
http://www.isu.edu/~nickcrai/pncfl
Focuses on learning, instruction and training practices in second language development.

April
Ray Verzasconi, Conference Contact

3394 Pennsylvania Council for the Social Studies Conference
Pennsylvania Council for the Social Studies
1212 Smallman Street
Senator John Heinz Regional Histiry Cnt.
Pittsburgh, PA 15222-4200
717-238-8768
E-mail: lguru1@aol.com
http://www.pcss.org

Committed to the promotion of the teaching and learning of the Social Studies in the Commonwealth of Pennsylvania.

October
50 booths with 500 attendees
Stephen Bullick, President Elect

3395 Pennsylvania School Boards Association Annual Meeting
774 Limekiln Road
New Cumberland, PA 17070-2315
717-774-2331
Fax: 717-774-0718

School\office products, services and information for public education systems.

October
140 booths
Wayne W Updegraff, Conference Contact

3396 Pennsylvania Science Teachers Association Center for Science & Technology Education
PO Box 330
Shippenville, PA 16254-0330
814-782-6301

December
70 booths
Dr. Ken Mechling, Conference Contact

3397 Principals' Center Spring Institute Conference Harvard Graduate School of Education
6 Appian Way
#336
Cambridge, MA 02138-3704
617-495-1825
Fax: 617-495-5900

Administrative professionals get together to discuss issues, policy and procedures.

April
Nindy Leroy, Conference Contact

3398 Restructuring Curriculum Conference National School Conference Institute
PO Box 35099
Phoenix, AZ 85069-5099
602-674-8990

Presents research, studies, and new information relevant to curriculum development.

January

3399 SchoolTech Forum Miller Freeman
600 Harrison Street
San Francisco, CA 94109
415-947-6657
Fax: 415-947-6015

National forum for educational technology professional development and exhibits, devoted to intensive instruction by today's leading practitioners, eye-opening special events, unparalleled networking opportunities, and exposure to products and services.

3400 Sonoma State University Annual Conference
1801 E Colati Avenue
Sonoma State University, Carson Hall 65
Rohnert Park, CA 94928-3613
707-664-2940
800-833-3645
Fax: 707-878-9111
E-mail: cct@criticalthinking.org
http://www.criticalthinking.org

Participants to discuss promoting critical thinking and educational change.

July-August
1200 attendees
Paul Binker, Author

3401 South Carolina Library Association Conference
PO Box 1763
Columbia, SC 29202
803-252-1087
Fax: 803-252-0589
E-mail: scla@capconsc.com
http://www.scla.org

October
125 booths with 350 attendees
Tom Gilson, President

3402 Southern Association Colleges & Schools
1866 Southern Lane
Decatur, GA 30033-4033
404-679-4500
Fax: 404-679-4556
http://www.saes.org

Exhibits publications, data and word processing equipment, school photography, charter bus services and more.

December
50 booths with 3700 attendees
Dr. James Rogers, Chhief Academic Officer

3403 Southern Early Childhood Annual Convention Southern Early Childhood Association
PO Box 55930
Little Rock, AR 72215-5930
501-663-0353
800-305-SECA
Fax: 501-227-5297
E-mail: seca@aristotle.net
http://www.seca50.org

April
2,500 attendees
Sherry Hamilton, Dir Administrative Services

3404 Suburban Superintendents Conference American Association of School Administrators
1801 N Moore Street
Arlington, VA 22209-1813
800-458-9383
Fax: 301-206-9789
http://www.aasa.org

Speakers will include prominent superintendents, cutting-edge reformers and others concerned about increasing achievement in high-achieving districts.

July

3405 Superintendents Work Conference Teachers College, Columbia University
525 W 120th Street
PO Box 7
New York, NY 10027-6696
212-678-3783
Fax: 212-678-3682
E-mail: TCSuper@columbia.edu
http://www.conference.tc.columbia.edu

Offers practicing school superintendents a unique opportunity for professional growth in stimulating surroundings.

July
60 attendees

Thomas Sobol, Conference Chair
Gibran Matdalany, Associate Chair

3406 Teacher Educators Association
1900 Association Drive
Reston, VA 20191-1502

703-620-3110
Fax: 703-620-9530

Exhibits publications, teaching materials, model programs, and other related merchandise.

February
25 booths

Dr. Gloria Chernay, Conference Contact

3407 Teachers Association in Instruction Conference
150 W Market Street
Indianapolis, IN 46204-2806

317-634-1515

Exhibits a wide variety of teaching materials and information from Grades K-12.

October
150 booths

Barbara Stainbrook, Conference Contact

3408 Tennessee School Boards Association Conference
1130 Nelson Merry Street
Nashville, TN 37203-2884

615-741-0666
800-448-6465
Fax: 615-741-2824
http://www.tsba.net

Contains exhibiting equipment, materials and services used by schools and selected by boards of education.

November
60 booths with 1,000 attendees

Tammy Grissom, Conference Manager

3409 Texas Middle School Association Conference
PO Box 18896
Austin, TX 78760-8896

512-462-1105

25 booths.

February

Cecil Floyd, Conference Contact

3410 Texas School Boards Association Conference
7620 Guadalupe Street
Austin, TX 78752-1348

512-467-0222
Fax: 512-483-7100

275 booths exhibiting sports equipment, computers, and more.

September

Susan Bell, Conference Contact

3411 Texas State Teachers Association
318 W 12th Street
Austin, TX 78701-1815

512-476-5355
Fax: 512-476-9555

April
120 booths

Carla Bond, Conference Contact

3412 Training & Presentations
Chief Manufacturing, Inc.
14310 Ewing Avenue S
Burnsville, MN 55306-4839

612-894-6280
800-582-6480
Fax: 877-894-6918
E-mail: chief@chiefmfg.com
http://www.chiefmfg.com

Chicago, Illinois
February

Liz Sorensen, Marketing Assistant
Sharon McCubbin, Marketing Manager

3413 University Continuing Education Association
Annual Conference
Leadership for Lifelong Learning
1 Dupont Circle NW
Suite 615
Washington, DC 20036-1134

202-659-3130
Fax: 202-785-0374

Focuses on life-long training and postgraduate work.

70 booths with 1,000 attendees

Frances Glover, Conference Manager

3414 Virginia Association of Elementary School
Principals Conference
2116 Dabney Road
Suite A-4
Richmond, VA 23230

804-355-6791
Fax: 804-355-1196
E-mail: vaesp@earthlink.net
http://www.vaesp.org

Nonprofit professional association advocating for public education and equal educational opportunities. Promotes leadership of school administrators, principal as educational leaders, and provides professional developmentopportunities.

October
50 booths with 300 attendees

Thomas L Shortt, Executive Director
Judy Grady, Financial Director

3415 Virginia Association of Independent
Schools-Conference
8001 Franklin Farms Drive
Suite 100
Richmond, VA 23229-5108

804-282-3592
Fax: 804-282-3596
E-mail: director@vais.org
http://www.vais.org

November
1,500 attendees

Andrew A Zvara, Manager

3416 Virginia Educators Annual Conference
Virginia ASCD
106 Yorkview Road
Yorktown, VA 23692

757-898-4434
Fax: 757-898-4344
E-mail: jbyrne@visi.net

December
30 booths with 600 attendees

Joan S Byrne, Executive Director

3417 Virginia School Boards Association Conference
2320 Hunters Way
Charlottesville, VA 22911-7931
434-295-8722
800-446-8722
Fax: 434-295-8785
http://www.vsba.org

State school boards association.

Barbara Coyle, Conference Manager

3418 Wisconsin Association of School Boards Annual Conference
Wisconsin Association of School Boards
122 W Washington Avenue
#400
Madison, WI 53703-2718
608-257-2622
Fax: 608-257-8386
E-mail: info@wasb.org
http://www.wasb.org

Contains sports equipment, textbooks, computers, office equipment and management, architects, contractors, food service and more.

January
370 booths with 3,000 attendees

Dianne Calgaro, Conference Contact
Carrie Tobin, Exhibit Show Manager

3419 Wisconsin Association of School District Administrators Conference
4797 Hayes Road
Madison, WI 53704-3288
608-242-1090
Fax: 608-242-1290

Annual convention featuring exhibits of school equipment, supplies and services.

April/May
70 booths

Miles Turner, Conference Contact

3420 Wisconsin School Administrators Association Conference
4797 Hayes Road Stop 1
Madison, WI 53704-3288
608-241-0300
Fax: 608-249-4973

School equipment, supplies and services including books, fundraising and computers.

October
60 booths

Charles R Hilston, Conference Contact

Directories & Handbooks

3421 American Association of Colleges for Teacher Education-Directory
American Association of Colleges for Teacher Ed.
1307 New York Avenue NW
Suite 300
Washington, DC 20005-4701
202-293-2450
Fax: 202-457-8095
E-mail: aacte@aacte.org
http://www.aacte.org

Offers listings of over 750 member schools, colleges and departments of education offering programs in teacher education, including more than 6,300 academic administrators and faculty. Publishes a paperback book annually.

144 pages Annual
ISSN: 0516-9313

Kristin McCabe, Publications Manager/Editor
Brinda Albert, Conference Manager

3422 American Society for Training/Development-Training Video
American Society for Training & Development
1640 King Street
Alexandria, VA 22314-2746
703-683-8100
Fax: 703-683-1523

Two volumes listing producers and distributors of about 22,000 training videos covering management, career development and technical skills.

3423 Appropriate Inclusion and Paraprofessionals
National Education Association (NEA)
1201 16th Street NW
Washington, DC 20036-3207
202-822-7364
Fax: 202-822-7624
E-mail: ncuea@nea.org
http://www.nea.org

A book offering information on mainstreaming disabled students and the work of paraprofessionals in the education process.

10 pages

3424 Assessing Student Performance
Jossey-Bass Publishers
989 Market Street
San Francisco, CA 94104-1342
415-433-1740
Fax: 415-433-0499

A powerful and well-written work, which begins by raising a fundamental question: What is assessment and how does testing differ from it?

336 pages Softcover
ISBN: 0-7879-5047-5

3425 Association for Continuing Higher Education Directory
Trident Technical College, CE-M
PO Box 118067
Charleston, SC 29423-8067
843-574-6658
800-807-ACHE
Fax: 843-574-6470
E-mail: zpbarrineau@al.trident.tec.sc.us
http://charleston.net/org/ache/

Directory includes information on 500 individual education professionals and approximately 300 member institutions. Includes name, address, titles and phone numbers of institutions and name, title, address and phone numbers of individuals.

102 pages Annual/March
10 booths with 250 attendees

Wayne L Whelan, Executive VP

3426 Before the School Bell Rings
Phi Delta Kappa Educational Foundation
408 N Union Street
PO Box 789
Bloomington, IN 47402-0789
812-339-1156
800-766-1156
Fax: 812-339-0018
http://www.pdkintl.org

Early childhood teachers and administrators, childcare providers and parents will enjoy and learn from this practical, insightful book.

84 pages Paperback
ISBN: 0-87367-476-6

Carol B Hillman, Author
George Kersey, Executive Director
Donovan R Walling, Editor, Special Publications

3427 Beyond Tracking: Finding Success in Inclusive Schools
Phi Delta Kappa Educational Foundation
PO Box 789
Bloomington, IN 47402-0789
812-339-1156
800-766-1156
Fax: 812-339-0018
http://www.pdkintl.org

Research data, practical ideas and reports from educators involved in untracking schools make this an authoritative and useful collection of important articles.

293 pages Hardcover
ISBN: 0-87367-470-7

Harbison Pool and Jane A Page, Author
George Kersey, Executive Director
Donovan R Walling, Dir Publications/Research

3428 Book of Metaphors, Volume II
AEE and Kendall/Hunt Publishing Company
4050 Westmark Drive
Dubuque, IA 52004-1840
563-589-1000
800-228-0810
Fax: 800-772-9165
http://www.kendallhunt.com

A compilation of presentations designed to enhance learning for those participating in adventure-based programs. Practitioners share how they prepare experiences for presentations.

256 pages Paperback
ISBN: 0-7872-0306-8

AEE, Author
Karen Berger, Customer Service Assistant

3429 Brief Legal Guide for the Independent Teacher
441 Vine Street
Suite 505
Cincinnati, OH 45202-2811

Offering insights into the most common legal issues faced by independent music teachers.

28 pages

3430 Building Life Options: School-Community Collaborations
Academy for Educational Development
1255 23rd Street NW
Washington, DC 20037-1125
202-884-8800
Fax: 202-884-8400

A handbook for family life educators on how to prevent pregnancy in the middle grades.

3431 Closing the Achievement Gap
Master Teacher
PO Box 1207
Manhattan, KS 66505-1207
785-539-0555
800-669-9633
Fax: 785-539-7739
http://www.masterteacher.com

A complete step-by-step approach to building a system that narrows the gap between student potenial and student performance— between success and failure.

162 pages
ISBN: 0-914607-73-1

Kristy Meeks, Author

3432 Coming Up Short? Practices of Teacher Educators Committed to Character
Character Education Partnership
1025 Connecticut Avenue NW
Suite 1011
Washington, DC 20036
202-296-7743
800-988-8081
Fax: 202-296-7779
http://www.character.org

Henry Huffman, Author
Andrea Grenadier, Director Communications
Esther Schaeffer, CEO/Executive Director

3433 Competency-Based Framework for Professional Development of Certified Health Specialists
Nat'l Health Education Credentialing
Columbia University
Department of Health Education
New York, NY 10027
212-854-1754
Fax: 212-678-4048

Aims to help the health education profession provide the leadership necessary for improving health in a rapidly changing, culturally pluralistic and technologically complex society. Provides universities, professional organizations,and accreditation a common basis of skills for the development, assessment, and improvement of professional preparation for health educators.

3434 Contracting Out: Strategies for Fighting Back
National Education Association (NEA)
1201 16th Street NW
Washington, DC 20036-3207
202-822-7364
Fax: 202-822-7624
E-mail: ncuea@nea.org
http://www.nea.org

Offers information for teachers and administration on how to stop contracting out, subcontracting, and other forms of privatization of public services that are a threat to school employees and the communities they serve.

3435 Directory of Curriculum Materials Centers
Association of College & Research Libraries
50 E Huron Street
Chicago, IL 60611-5295
312-280-2517
Fax: 312-280-2520

Listing of over 275 centers that have collections of curriculum materials to aid in elementary and secondary teaching preparation.

200 pages

3436 Distance Learning Directory
Virginia A Ostendorf
PO Box 2896
Littleton, CO 80161-2896
303-797-3131
Fax: 303-797-3524
E-mail: ostendorf@vaostendorf.com

Comprehensive list of distance learning practitioners and vendors. Each listing includes names, addresses, e-mail, fax and phones, credits awarded, program content, peripherals and technologies used, class configurations and more.Includes a lists of vendors offering descriptions of distance learning products, services and programming.

308 pages Annual

Virginia A Ostendorf, President
Ronald Ostendorf, VP

3437 Ethical Issues in Experiential Education
AEE and Kendall/Hunt Publishing Company
4050 Westmark Drive
Dubuque, IA 52002-2624

319-589-1000
800-228-0810
Fax: 800-772-9165
http://www.kendallhunt.com

An examination of ethical issues in the field of adventure programming and experiential education. Topics include ethical theory, informed consent, sexual issues, student rights, environmental concerns and programming practices.

144 pages
ISBN: 0-7872-93083

Karen Berger, Customer Service Assistant

3438 Finishing Strong: Your Personal Mentoring & Planning Guide for the Last 60 Days of Teaching
Master Teacher
PO Box 1207
Manhattan, KS 66505-1207

785-539-0555
800-669-9633
Fax: 785-539-7739
http://www.masterteacher.com

In this book we've selected from the 32 years of The Master Teacher, the writings we know you would most like your teachers to have to support that last 60 days of the school year.

132 pages
ISBN: 1-58992-095-3

Robert L De Bruyn, Author

3439 How to Plan and Develop a Career Center
Center on Education and Work
964 Educational Sciences Building
1025 W Johnson Street
Madison, WI 53706-1796

800-446-0399
Fax: 608-262-9197
E-mail: cewmail@soemadison.wisc.edu
http://www.cew.wisc.edu

High school, postsecondary, adult, and virtual career centers-a comprehensive blueprint that covers all the bases.

3440 How to Raise Test Scores
Skylight Professional Development
1900 E Lake Avenue
Glenview, IL 60025

847-657-7450
800-348-4474
Fax: 847-486-3183
E-mail: info@skylightedu.com
http://www.skylightedu.com

Addresses the teaching and learning process at its most basic and important level-the classroom.

30 pages Softcover
ISBN: 1575171635

Robin Fogarty, Author

3441 Inclusion: The Next Step
Master Teacher
PO Box 1207
Manhattan, KS 66505-1207

785-539-0555
800-669-9633
Fax: 785-539-7739
http://www.masterteacher.com

Offers practical help for regular classroom teachers and special education teachers in meeting the challenges of inclusion.

225 pages
ISBN: 0-914607-69-3

Wendy Dover, Author

3442 Law of Teacher Evaluation: A Self-Assestment Handbook
Phi Delta Kappa Educational Foundation
PO Box 789
Bloomington, IN 47402-0789

812-339-1156
800-766-156
Fax: 812-339-0018
http://www.pdkintl.org

This handy guidebook provides a concise, authoritative overview of US state statutes, regulations and guidelines regarding the performance evaluation of educators.

51 pages Paperback
ISBN: 0-87367-488-X

Perry A. Zirkel, Author
DR Walling, Dir Publications/Research

3443 Learning for Life
1325 W Walnut Hill Lane
PO Box 152079
Irving, TX 75015-2079

972-580-2433
Fax: 972-580-2137
http://www.learning-for-life.org

Emphasizes respect, responsibility, honesty, and kindness from the very start.

3444 Lesson Plans for the Substitue Teacher:
Elementary Edition
Master Teacher
PO Box 1207
Manhattan, KS 66505-1207

785-539-0555
800-669-9633
Fax: 785-539-7739
http://www.masterteacher.com

Gives you more than 100 lessons developed and tested by teachers across the curriculum and at all grade levels.

145 pages
ISBN: 1-58992-107-0

Robert L DeBruyn, Author

3445 Life Skills Training
711 Westchester Avenue
White Plains, NY 10604

914-421-2525
800-293-4969
Fax: 914-683-6998
E-mail: lstinfo@nhpanet.com
http://www.LifeSkillsTraining.com

A powerful prevention program with a proven record of effectiveness.

3446 List of Regional, Professional & Specialized Accrediting Association
Educational Information Services
PO Box 662
Newton Lower Falls, MA 02162
617-964-4555

A list of those associations involved in accreditation for the education fields.

3447 MacMillan Guide to Correspondence Study
MacMillan Publishing Company
1633 Broadway
New York, NY 10019
212-512-2000
Fax: 800-835-3202

Listing of 175 colleges, accredited trade, technical and vocational schools that offer home study courses.

500 pages

3448 Middle Grades Education in an Era of Reform
Academy for Educational Development
1255 23rd Street NW
Washington, DC 20037-1125
202-884-8800
Fax: 202-884-8400

Reviews middle-grades educational reform policies and practices.

3449 Middle School Teachers Guide to FREE Curriculum Materials
Educators Progress Service
214 Center Street
Randolph, WI 53956-1408
920-326-3126
888-951-4469
Fax: 920-326-3127
E-mail: epsinc@centurytel.net
http://www.freeteachingaids.com

Lists and describes free supplementary teaching aids for the middle school and junior high level.

290 pages Annual
ISBN: 87708-401-7

Kathy Nehmer, President

3450 NASDTEC Knowledge Base
22 Bates Road
PMB #134
Mashpee, MA 02649-3267
508-539-8844
Fax: 508-539-8868
E-mail: nasdtec@comcast.com
http://www.nasdtec.org

Annually
ISBN: 0-9708628-3-0
June
10 booths with 275 attendees and 10 exhibits

Roy Einreinhofer, Executive Director

3451 Orators & Philosophers: A History of the Idea of Liberal Education
College Board Publications
45 Columbus Avenue
New York, NY 10023-6917
212-713-8165
800-323-7155
Fax: 800-525-5562
http://www.collegeboard.org

A cogent study of the historical evolution of the idea of liberal education. Clearly and forcefully argued, the book portrays this evolution as a struggle between two contending points of view, one oratorical and the otherphilosophical.

308 pages
Bruce A Kimball, Author

3452 Parent Training Resources
PACER Center
8161 Normandale Boulevard
Minneapolis, MN 55437
952-838-9000
800-537-2237
Fax: 952-838-0199
E-mail: pacer@pacer.org
http://www.pacer.org

Booklets, information handouts, videotapes, newsletters and training materials for parents of children and adults with disabilities, individuals with disabilities, educators and other professionals.

130 pages
Paula Goldberg, Executive Director

3453 Personal Planner and Training Guide for the Paraprofessional
Master Teacher
PO Box 1207
Manhattan, KS 66505-1207
785-539-0555
800-669-9633
Fax: 785-539-7739
http://www.masterteacher.com

Includes numerous forms which allow each para to keep track of vital information he or she will need in working with specific teachers and their special students.

128 pages
ISBN: 0-914607-39-1

Wendy Dover, Author

3454 Practical Handbook for Assessing Learning Outcomes in Continuing Education
International Association for Continuing Education
Departmant #3087
Washington, DC 20042-0001
202-463-2905
Fax: 202-463-8498

Innovative guide offers readers a series of steps to help select an assessment plan which will work for any organization.

3455 Principles of Good Practice in Continuing Education
International Association for Continuing Education
Department #3087
Washington, DC 20042-0001
202-463-2905
Fax: 202-463-8498

Principles from many sources for the field of continuing education, placing a pervasive emphasis on learning outcomes for the individual learner.

3456 Professional Learning Communities at Work
National Educational Service
304 W Kirkwood Avenue
Suite 2
Bloomington, IN 47404-5132
812-336-7700
800-733-6786
Fax: 812-336-7790
E-mail: nes@nesonline.com
http://www.nesonline.com

This publication provides specific, practical, how-to information on the best practices in use in schools through the US and Canada for curriculum development, teacher preparation, school leadership, professional development programs, school-parent partnerships, assessment practices and much more.

3457 Programs for Preparing Individuals for Careers in Special Education
The Council for Exceptional Children
1920 Association Drive
Reston, VA 20191-1545

703-620-3660
800-232-7323
Fax: 703-264-1637

This directory offers over 600 colleges and universities with programs in special education. Information includes institution name, address, contact person, telephone, fax, Internet, accreditation status, size of faculty, level of program, and areas of specialty.

256 pages

3458 Quality School Teacher
National Professional Resources
25 S Regent Street
Port Chester, NY 10573-8295

914-937-8897
800-453-7461
Fax: 914-937-9327
E-mail: info@nprinc.com
http://www.nprinc.com

Provides the specifics that classroom teachers are asking for as they begin the move to quality schools. It is written for educators who are trying to give up the old system of boss-managing, and to create classrooms that produce quality work.

144 pages
ISBN: 0060-952857

William Glasser, Author
Robert Hanson, President
Helene Hanson, VP

3459 Requirements for Certification of Teachers & Counselors
University of Chicago Press
5801 S Ellis Avenue
Floor 4
Chicago, IL 60637-5418

312-702-7700
800-621-2736
Fax: 800-621-8476

A list of state and local departments of education for requirements including teachers, counselors, librarians, and administrators for elementary and secondary schools.

256 pages Annual
ISBN: 0-226-42850-8

Elizabeth Kaye, Author
John Tryneski, Coordinating Education

3460 Research for Better Schools Publications
444 N 3rd Street
Philadelphia, PA 19123

215-574-9123
Fax: 215-574-0133
E-mail: maguire@rbs.org
http://www.rbs.org

Offers a variety of books on thinking skills, classroom materials, school and student assessment, at-risk students, school restructuring and improvement. As well as professional development resources for students.

Louis M Maguire, Executive Director

3461 Resources for Teaching Middle School Science
National Academy Press
Arts & Industries Bldg Room 1201
900 Jefferson Drive SW
Washington, DC 20560-0403

202-287-2063
Fax: 202-287-2070
E-mail: outreach@nas.edu
http://www.si.edu/nsrc

Second in a series of resource guides for elementary, middle school, and high school science teachers, this book is an annotated guide to hands-on, inquiry-centered curriculum materials and sources of help in teaching science in grades six through eight. Produced by the National Science Resources Center.

496 pages

National Science Resources Center, Author
Douglas Lapp, Executive Director

3462 Restructuring in the Classroom
Jossey-Bass Publishers
989 Market Street
San Francisco, CA 94104-1304

415-433-1740
800-956-7739
Fax: 415-433-0499
http://www.josseybass.com

Teaching, learning and school organization.

288 pages Hardcover
ISBN: 0-7879-0239-X

Riched Elmore, Penelope Peterson & Sara McCarthey, Author

3463 Revolution Revisited: Effective Schools and Systemic Reform
Phi Delta Kappa Educational Foundation
PO Box 789
Bloomington, IN 47402-0789

812-339-1156
800-766-1156
Fax: 812-339-0018
http://www.pdkintl.org

The authors examine the Effective Schools movement of the past quarter century as a school reform philosophy and renewal process for today and for the coming years.

132 pages Paperback
ISBN: 0-873674-83-9

BO Taylor and P Bullard, Author
Donovan R Walling, Dir Publications/Research

3464 Seminar Information Service
17752 Sky Park Circle
Suite 210
Irvine, CA 92614-4469

949-261-9104
877-SEM-INFO
Fax: 949-261-1963
E-mail: info@seminarinformation.com
http://www.seminarinformation.com

Offers information on over 700 sponsors of more than 100,000 business and technical seminars.

1,000 pages Annual

Mona Pointkowski, VP

3465 Service-Learning and Character Education: One Plus One is More Than Two
Character Education Partnership
1025 Connecticut Avenue NW
Suite 1011
Washington, DC 20036

202-296-7743
800-988-8081

Fax: 202-296-7779
http://www.character.org

Andrea Grenadier, Director Communications
Esther Schaeffer, CEO/Executive Director

3466 Teacher Ideas Press Libraries Unlimited
PO Box 6633
Englewood, CO 80155-6633

303-770-1220
800-237-6124
Fax: 303-220-8843

Publisher of resource books written by educators for educators. The books offer innovative ideas, practical lessons, and classroom-tested activities in the areas of math, science, social studies, whole language literature and libraryconnections.

3467 Teacher-Created Materials
6421 Industry Way
Westminster, CA 92683-3652

714-891-7895
800-662-4321
Fax: 714-892-0283
E-mail: tcminfo@teachercreated.com
http://www.teachercreated.com

Publishes supplementary materials for Pre-K to grade 12 educators in the areas of language arts, social studies, science, math, and classroom management. Submissions should include tentative table of contents or outline, introductionand 8-12 sample pages. Conducts public, on-site and online seminars in many areas of education.

Sharon Coan, Editor-in-Chief

3468 Teachers as Educators of Character: Are the Nations Schools of Education Coming Up Short?
Character Education Partnership
1025 Connecticut Avenue NW
Suite 1011
Washington, DC 20036

202-296-7743
800-988-8081
Fax: 202-296-7779
http://www.character.org

Henry Huffman, Author
Andrea Grenadier, Director Communications
Esther Schaeffer, CEO/Executive Director

3469 Teachers as Leaders
Phi Delta Kappa Educational Foundation
PO Box 789
Bloomington, IN 47402-0789

812-339-1156
800-766-1156
Fax: 812-339-0018
http://www.pdkintl.org

Examines teacher recruitment, retention, professional development and leadership. The central theme of these twenty essays is excellence in education and how to achieve it.

320 pages Hardcover
ISBN: 0-873674-68-5

Donovan R Walling, Author
Donovan R Walling, Dir Publications/Research

3470 Teachers in Publishing
Pike Publishing Company
221 Town Center W
Suite 112
Santa Maria, CA 93458-5083

Editorial, research, sales, consulting, in office positions or travel to learn teachers' needs and instruct new texts.

3471 Teaching About Islam & Muslims in the Public School Classroom
9300 Gardenia Avenue
#B3
Fountain Valley, CA 92708-2253

714-839-2929
Fax: 714-839-2714

117 pages
ISBN: 1-930109-008

Susan Douglas, Author
Shabbir Mansuri, Founding Director

3472 Teaching as the Learning Profession: Handbook of Policy and Practice
Jossey-Bass Publishers
PO Box 411
Annapolis Junction, MD 20701-0411

301-617-7802
888-782-2272
Fax: 301-206-9789

Provides the best essays about the status of teaching, and the contributing writers are among the best thinkers in education today.

426 pages Hardcover

Linda Darling-Hammond, Editor

3473 Teaching for Results
Master Teacher
PO Box 1207
Manhattan, KS 66505-1207

785-539-0555
800-669-9633
Fax: 785-539-7739
http://www.masterteacher.com

An easy-to-implement powerful method for helping to ensure sucess in the classroom.

45 pages
ISBN: 1-58992-120-8

3474 Their Best Selves: Building Character Education and Service Learning Together
Character Education Partnership
1025 Connecticut Avenue NW
Suite 1011
Washington, DC 20036

202-296-7743
800-988-8081
Fax: 202-296-7779
http://www.character.org

Andrea Grenadier, Director Communications
Esther Schaeffer, CEO/Executive Director

3475 Theory of Experiential Education
AEE and Kendall/Hunt Publishing Company
4050 Westmark Drive
Dubuque, IA 52002-2624

319-589-1000
800-228-0810
Fax: 800-772-9165
http://www.kendallhunt.com

This groundbreaking resource looks at the theoretical foundations of experiential education from philosophical, historical, psychological, social and ethical perspectives.

496 pages
ISBN: 0-7872-0262-2

AEE, Author
Karen Berger, Customer Service Assistant

3476 Time to Teach, Time to Learn: Changing the Pace of School
Northeast Foundation for Children
39 Montague City Road
Greenfield, MA 01301

413-772-2066
800-360-6332
Fax: 413-774-1129
E-mail: info@responsiveclassroom.org

Giving students the chance to learn and their teachers the chance to teach.

322 pages Softcover

Chip Wood, Author

3477 Top Quality School Process (TQSP)
National School Services
390 Holbrook Drive
Wheeling, IL 60090-5812

847-541-2768
800-262-4511
Fax: 847-541-2553

A customized School Improvement Program that incorporates input from all stakeholders in the educational process to establish baseline data, implement a continuous process of school improvement, and select quality programs for professional development.

3478 US Department of Education: Office of Educational Research & Improvement
National Library of Education
555 New Jersey Avenue NW
Washington, DC 20001-2029

877-433-7827
800-424-1616
Fax: 202-401-0457

Offers a variety of publications for professional development. The list of sources includes statistical reports, topical reports and effective programs, schools and practices.

John Blake, Reference/Information
Nancy Cavanaugh, Collection Development

3479 Understanding and Relating To Parents Professionally
Master Teacher
PO Box 1207
Manhattan, KS 66505-1207

785-539-0555
800-669-9633
Fax: 785-539-7739
http://www.masterteacher.com

Gives teachers both the perspective and the techniques to relate to parents professionally to secure the maximum benefit for students.

70 pages
ISBN: 0-914607-65-0

Robert L DeBruyn, Author

3480 Welcome to Teaching and our Schools
Master Teacher
PO Box 1207
Manhattan, KS 66505-1207

785-539-0555
800-669-9633
Fax: 785-539-7739
http://www.masterteacher.com

Sets the stage for teachers so that they can have an enthusiastic and successful year in the classroom.

50 pages
ISBN: 0-914607-49-9

Robert L DeBryon, Author

3481 World Exchange Program Directory
Center for U.N. Studies, GPO Box 2786
Ramna
Dacca 1000, Bangladesh

Offers listings, by geographical location, of exchange programs available to United States and abroad students. Listings include all contact information, schedules, fields and levels of study and bilingual information.

Biennial

3482 You Can Handle Them All
Master Teacher
PO Box 1207
Manhattan, KS 66505-1207

785-539-0555
800-669-9633
Fax: 785-539-7739
http://www.masterteacher.com

Encyclopedia of student misbehaviors offering answers that work. one hundred seventeen student misbehaviors are covered.

320 pages
ISBN: 0-914607-04-9

Robert L DeBruyn, Author

3483 Your Personal Mentoring & Planning Guide for the First 60 Days of Teaching
Master Teacher
PO Box 1207
Manhattan, KS 66505-1207

785-539-0555
800-669-9633
Fax: 785-539-7739
http://www.masterteacher.com

In this book we've selected from 32 years of The Master Teacher, the writings we know you would most like your teachers to have to support the first 60 days of the school year.

116 pages
ISBN: 1-58992-056-2

Periodicals

3484 AACTE Briefs
American Association of Colleges for Teacher Ed.
1307 New York Avenue NW
Suite 300
Washington, DC 20005-4701

202-293-2450
Fax: 202-457-8095
E-mail: aacte@aacte.org
http://www.aacte.org

Covers current events in teacher education including public policy, research and programs. Publishes a newsletter and there is a conference.

4-12 pages Monthly
ISSN: 0731-602x

Kristin McCabe, Publications Manager/Editor
Brinda Albert, Conference Manager

3485 ATEA Journal
American Technical Education Association
800 N 6th Street N
Wahpeton, ND 58076-0002

701-671-2240
Fax: 701-671-2260
E-mail: charles_losh@msn.com
http://www.ateaonline.org

Dedicated to excellence in the quality of postsecondary technical education, with an emphasis on professional development.

32 pages Quarterly
ISSN: 0889-6488

Betty M Krump, Executive Director
Dr. Charles Losh, Editor

3486 Action in Teacher Education
University of Georgia, College of Education
427 Aderhold Hall
Athens, GA 30602

706-542-4238
Fax: 706-542-4277

The official publication of the Association of Teacher Educators, serving as a forum for the exchange of information and ideas related to the improvement of teacher education at all levels.

Quarterly

Brenda H Manning, Editor
H James McLaughlin, Editor

3487 American Educational Research Journal
Columbia University Teachers College
PO Box 51
New York, NY 10027-0051

212-678-3498
Fax: 212-678-4048

Focuses on teaching development and human resource training.

Quarterly

Lyn Corno, Co-Editor
Gary Natriello, Co-Editor

3488 American Educator
American Federation of Teachers
555 New Jersey Avenue NW
Washington, DC 20001-2029

202-879-4420

Contains articles on education, politics, media and social commentary.

Quarterly

Elizabeth McPike, Editor
Mary Kearney, Advertising/Sales

3489 Arts Management in Community Institutions: Summer Training
National Guild of Community Schools of the Arts
520 8th Avenue
Suite 302, 3rd Floor
New York, NY 10018

212-268-3337
Fax: 212-268-3995
E-mail: info@natguild.org
http://www.nationalguild.org

June

Noah Xifr, Director Membership/Oper.

3490 Balance Sheet
ITP South-Western Publishing
5101 Madison Road
Cincinnati, OH 45227-1427

513-271-8811
800-824-5179
Fax: 800-487-8488

Informational publication for high school accounting educators. Articles contain information about innovations in teaching accounting, producing an extensive line of educational texts and software for K-postsecondary markets.

2x Year

Larry Qualls, Editor
Carol Bross-McMahon, Coordinating Editor

3491 Better Teaching
The Parent Institute
PO Box 7474
Fairfax Station, VA 22039-7474

703-323-9170
Fax: 703-323-9173
http://www.parent-institute.com

Newsletter for teachers (grades 1-12) that offers tips and techniques to improve student learning.

Monthly
ISSN: 1061-1495

John Wherry, Publisher

3492 Board
Master Teacher
PO Box 1207
Manhattan, KS 66505-1207

785-539-0555
800-669-9633
Fax: 785-539-7739
http://www.masterteacher.com

Helps to train the entire board in the fundamental concepts of board work.

2 pages

3493 C/S Newsletter
Center for Instructional Services
Purdue University
W. Lafayette, IN 47907

317-494-9454

Contains descriptions of CIS services and articles about instructional techniques.

4 pages 7x Year

Vickie Lojek

3494 Curriculum Brief
International Technology Education Association
1914 Association Drive
Reston, VA 20191-1538

703-860-2100
Fax: 703-860-0353

Seeks to advance technological literacy through professional development activities and publications.

4x Year

Kendall Starkweather, Executive Director

3495 Cut & Paste, Master Teacher
Master Teacher
PO Box 1207
Manhattan, KS 66505-1207

785-539-0555
800-669-9633
Fax: 800-669-1132
http://www.masterteacher.com

The publication that provides you with great articles to complete your in-house newsletters and newsletters to parents, without fear of copyright violations.

1 pages Monthly Newsletter

Tracey H DeBruyn, Executive Editor

3496 Education & Treatment of Children
Pressley Ridge School
530 Marshall Avenue
Pittsburgh, PA 15214-3016
412-321-6995
Fax: 412-321-5313

A journal devoted to the dissemination of information concerning the development and improvement of services for children and youth. Its primary criterion for publication is that the material be of direct value to educators and otherchild care professionals in improving their teaching/training effectiveness. Various types of material are appropriate for publication including original experimental research, experimental replications, adaptations of previously reported researchand reviews.

Quarterly

Bernie Fabry, Managing Editor

3497 Educational Placement Sources-US
Education Information Services/Instant Alert
PO Box 620662
Newton, MA 02462-0662
617-433-0125

Lists 100 organizations in the United States that find positions for teachers, educational administrators, counselors and other professionals. Listings are classified by type, listed alphabetically and offers all contact information.

4 pages Annual

FB Viaux, President

3498 Exceptional Child Education Resources
The Council for Exceptional Children
1920 Association Drive
Reston, VA 20191-1545
703-620-3660
800-328-0272
Fax: 703-264-1637
E-mail: askeric@ericir.syr.edu

A quarterly abstract journal that helps teachers stay abreast of the book, nonprint media, and journal literature in special and gifted education.

Quarterly
ISSN: 0160-4309

3499 Extensions - Newsletter of the High/Scope Curriculum
High/Scope Educational Research Foundation
600 N River Street
Ypsilanti, MI 48198-2821
734-485-2000
800-40P-RESS
Fax: 734-485-0704
E-mail: lynnt@highscopes.org
http://www.highscope.org

Teacher guide for users of the High/Scope curriculum. Articles on classroom strategies, training techniques, problem-solving ideas, and news from the field. Also includes updated training data.

8 pages BiMonthly
ISSN: 0892-5135

Lynn Taylor, Editor
Kathleen Woodard, Marketing/Sales Director

3500 Guild Notes Bi-Monthly Newswletter
National Guild of Community Schools of the Arts
520 8th Avenue
Suite 302, 3rd Floor
New York, NY 10018
212-268-3337
Fax: 212-268-3995
E-mail: info@natguild.org
http://www.nationalguild.org

Bi-Monthly

Noah Xifr, Director Membership/Oper.

3501 In-Box Master Teacher
Master Teacher
PO Box 1207
Manhattan, KS 66505-1207
785-539-0555
800-669-9633
Fax: 800-669-1132
http://www.masterteacher.com

Loaded with practical information that professionals can immediately use to become more effective in their school or district.

1 pages Monthly Newsletter

Tracey H DeBruyn, Executive Editor

3502 Infocus: A Newsletter of the University Continuing Education Association
University Continuing Education Association
1 Dupont Circle NW
Suite 615
Washington, DC 20036-1134
202-659-3130
Fax: 202-785-0374
E-mail: postmaster@nucea.edu
http://www.nucea.edu

Reports on higher education activities, federal legislation and government agencies, innovative programming at institutions across the country; member institutions; trends in continuing and part-time education; resources; professionaldevelopment opportunities within the field; and changes in member personnel.

12-20 pages Monthly

Susan Goewey, Contact

3503 Innovator
University of Michigan Association
4001 School of Education Building
Ann Arbor, MI 48104
734-764-0394
Fax: 734-763-6934

For professional educators and alumni of University of Michigan's School of Education.

20 pages Quarterly

Eric Warden, Contact

3504 International Journal of Instructional Media
Westwood Press
149 Goose Lane
Tolland, CT 06084-3822
860-875-5484

A professional journal directly responsive to the need for precise information on the application of media to your instructional and training needs.

Quarterly

Dr. Phillip J. Sleeman, Editor

3505 Intervention in School and Clinic
Pro-Ed., Inc.
8700 Shoal Creek Boulevard
Austin, TX 78757-6816

512-451-3246
800-897-3202
Fax: 512-302-9129
http://www.proedinc.com

The hands-on how-to resource for teachers and clinicians working with students (especially LD and BD) for whom minor curiculum and environmental medications are ineffective.

64 pages 5x Year Magazine
ISSN: 1053-4512

Judith K Voress, Periodicals Director
Brenda Smith Myles, Editor

3506 Journal of Classroom Interaction
University of Houston-University Park
Farish Hall
Room 240
Houston, TX 77004

713-743-5919
Fax: 713-743-8664
E-mail: jci@bayou.uh.edu
http://www.coe.uh.edu

Reports on student and teacher rapport as well as classroom activities that promote interaction.

Bi-Annually

Dr. Jerome Freiberg, Editor

3507 Journal of Economic Education
Heldref Publications
1319 18th Street NW
Washington, DC 20036-1802

202-296-6267
800-365-9753
Fax: 202-296-5149
http://www.heldref.org

The Journal of Economic Education offers original articles on innovations and evaluations of teaching techniques, materials, and programs in economics. Articles, tailored to the needs of instructors of introductory throughgraduate-level economics, cover content and pedagogy in a variety of mediums.

Quarterly

William E Becker, Editor

3508 Journal of Experiential Education
Association for Experiental Education
2305 Canyon Boulevard
Suite 100
Boulder, CO 80302-5651

303-440-8844
Fax: 303-440-9581
E-mail: ED@aee.org
http://www.aee.org

A professional journal that publishes a diverse range of articles in such subject areas as outdoor adventure programming, service learning, experiential school based programming, environmental education, cultural journalism,internships, therapeutic applications, research and theory, the creative arts, etc.

64 pages 3x Year
ISSN: 1053-8259

Alan Ewert, Coordinating Editor
Sue Beggs, Executive Director

3509 Journal on Excellence in College Teaching
Miami University
109 Bonham House
Oxford, OH 45056

513-529-7224
Fax: 513-529-3762
E-mail: wentzegw@muohio.edu
http://http://ject.lib.muohio.edu/

A peer-reviewed journal published by and for faculty at colleges and universities to increase student learning through effective teaching, interest in and enthusiasm for the profession of teaching, and communication among facultyabout their classroom experiences. The Journal provides a scholarly forum for faculty to share proven, innovative pedagogies and thoughtful, inspirational insights about teaching.

Journal 3x/Yr

Gregg Wentzell, Managing Editor
Milton Cox, Editor-in-Chief

3510 Journalism Education Association
Kansas State University
103 Kedzie Hall
Manhattan, KS 66506-1505

785-532-5532
Fax: 785-532-5563
E-mail: lindarp@ksu.edu
http://www.jea.org/

An organization of about 2,300 journalism teachers and advisers, offers two national teacher-student conventions a year, quarterly newsletter and magazines, bookstore and national certification program. This association serves as aleader in scholastic press freedom and media curriculum.

April & November
25-30 booths with 4700 attendees

Linda Puntrey, Executive Director

3511 NCRTL Special Report
National Center for Research on Teacher Education
Michigan State University
East Lansing, MI 48824

517-355-9302
E-mail: floden@msu.edu
http://www.ncrtb.msu.edu

Membership news and updates.

3512 NCSIE Inservice
National Council of States on Inservice Education
Syracuse University
402 Huntington Hall
Syracuse, NY 13244

315-443-1870
Fax: 315-443-9082

Professional development, staff development and inservice education.

20 pages Quarterly

James Collins

3513 Paraeducator's Guide to Instructional &
Curricular Modifications
Master Teacher
PO Box 1207
Manhattan, KS 66505-1207

785-539-0555
800-669-9633
Fax: 785-539-7739
http://www.masterteacher.com

An indispensible tool your paras can use to understand, plan for and carry out appropriate modification for students with all types of special needs.

100 pages
ISBN: 0-914607-88-X

Wendy Dover, Author

3514 Pennsylvania Education
Pennsylvania Department of Education
333 Market Street
Harrisburg, PA 17101-2210

717-783-9802
Fax: 717-783-8230

A newsletter to keep educators informed on activities of the state education department, schools and other educational institutions. Also contains information on conferences and workshops on relevant educational topics.

8-10 pages 8x Year

Gary Tuma, Press Secretary
Beth Boyer, Information Specialist

3515 Performance Improvement Journal
International Society for Performance
1400 Spring Street
Suite 260
Silver Spring, MD 20910

301-587-8570
Fax: 301-587-8573
E-mail: info@ispi.org
http://www.ispi.org

48 pages Monthly
ISSN: 1090-8811

April Davis, Publications Director

3516 Preventing School Failure
Heldref Publications
1319 18th Street NW
Washington, DC 20036-1826

202-296-6267
800-365-9753
Fax: 202-296-5149
E-mail: psf@heldref.org
http://www.heldref.org

The journal for educators and parents seeking strategies to promote the success of students who have learning and behavior problems. It includes practical examples of programs and practices that help children and youth in schools,clinics, correctional institutions, and other settings. Articles are written by educators and concern teaching children with various kinds of special needs.

48 pages Quarterly
ISSN: 1045-988X

Mary O'Donnell, Managing Editor

3517 Prevention Researcher
Integrated Research
66 Club Road
Suite 370
Eugene, OR 97401

541-683-9278
800-929-2955
Fax: 541-683-2621
E-mail: orders@TPRonline.org
http://www.TPRonline.org

Quarterly newsletter for professionals who work with youth. Each issue addresses a single topic, such as gun violence, dating violence, eating disorders, and drug abuse. Annual resource issue included

24 pages Magazine/Quarterly
ISSN: 1086-4385

Steven Ungerleider PhD, Editor

3518 Professional Vision Master Teacher
Master Teacher
PO Box 1207
Manhattan, KS 66505-1207

785-539-0555
800-669-9633
Fax: 800-669-1132
http://www.masterteacher.com

Positive, practical, and successful insights and techniques to help you manage and work with your support staff.

1 pages Monthly Newsletter

Tracey H DeBruyn, Executive Editor

3519 Professor Master Teacher
Master Teacher
PO Box 1207
Manhattan, KS 66505-1207

785-539-0555
800-669-9633
Fax: 800-669-1132
http://www.masterteacher.com

Designed for college faculties, this program provides ideas and suggestions to improve instructional techniques and student learning.

1 pages Monthly Newsletter

Tracey H DeBruyn, Executive Editor

3520 Progressive Teacher
Progressive Publishing Company
2678 Henry Street
Augusta, GA 30904-4656

770-868-1691

Offers new information and updates for the improvement and development of higher education.

Quarterly
ISSN: 0033-0825

MS Adcock

3521 Retaining Great Teachers
Master Teacher
PO Box 1207
Manhattan, KS 66505-1207

785-539-0555
800-669-9633
Fax: 785-539-7739
http://www.masterteacher.com

This book will help you and your staff reconize the common dilemmas new teachers face and will empower you, lead teachers, and mentors with practical solutions to help new teachers over the hurdles.

85 pages
ISBN: 1-58992-097-X

Michael J Lovett PhD, Author

3522 Rural Educator-Journal for Rural and Small Schools
National Rural Education Association
246 E Ed Building
Colorado State University
Ft. Collins, CO 80523-1588

970-491-7022
Fax: 970-491-1317

E-mail: jnewlin@lamar.colostate.edu
http://www.colostate.edu

Official journal of the NREA. A nationally recognized publication that features timely and informative articles written by leading rural educators from all levels of education. All NREA members are encouraged to submit researcharticles and items of general information for publication.

40 pages Quarterly Magazine
ISSN: 0273-446X

Joseph T Newlin, Editor

3523 TED Newsletter
The Council for Exceptional Children
1920 Association Drive
Reston, VA 20191-1545

703-620-3660
888-232-7733
Fax: 703-264-9494

Newsletter of the Teacher Education Division offering information about TED activities, upcoming events, current trends and practices, state and national legislation, recently published materials and practical information of interestto persons involved in the preparation and continuing professional development of effective professionals in special education and related service fields.

3x Year

Diana Hammitte, Co-Editor
Laurence O'Shea, Editor

3524 TESOL Journal: A Journal of Teaching and Classroom Research
Teachers of English to Speakers of Other Languages
1600 Cameron Street
Suite 300
Alexandria, VA 22314-2705

703-836-0774
Fax: 703-836-7864
E-mail: tescol@tesol.edu
http://www.tesol.edu

TESOL's mission is to develop the expertise of its members and others involved in teaching English to speakers of other languages to help them foster communication in diverse settings. The association advances standards forprofessional preparation and employment, continuing education, and student programs, produces programs, services, and products, and promotes advocacy to further the profession. TESOL has 91 affiliates worldwide.

50 pages Quarterly

Christian J Faltis, Editor
Marilyn Kupetz, Managing Editor

3525 Teacher Education Reports
Feistritzer Publishing
4401-A Connecticut Avenue NW
#212
Washington, DC 20008-2302

202-362-3444
Fax: 202-362-3493

Covers the field of teacher education for elementary and secondary schools, including pre-service preparation, in-service training and professional development, related federal programs, legislation and funding.

8 pages BiWeekly

David T Chester, Editor

3526 Teacher Education and Special Education
The Council for Exceptional Children
1920 Association Drive
Reston, VA 20191-1545

703-620-3660
Fax: 352-392-7159

Contains information on current research, exemplary practices, timely issues, legislation, book reviews, and new programs and materials relative to the preparation and continuing professional development of effective professionals inspecial education and related service fields.

Quarterly

Vivian Correa, Editor

3527 Teacher Magazine
6935 Arlington Road
Suite 100
Bethesda, MD 20814

301-280-3100
800-346-1834
Fax: 301-280-3250
E-mail: ads@epe.org
http://www.edweek.org

Articles for educators.

3528 Teacher's Guide to Classroom Management
Economics Press
12 Daniel Road
Fairfield, NJ 07004-2507

973-227-1224

Bulletins showing teachers how to solve problems and avoid problematic situations.

BiWeekly

Robert Guder

3529 Teachers in Touch
ISM Independent School Management
1316 N Union Street
Wilmington, DE 19806-2534

302-656-4944
800-955-4944
Fax: 302-656-0647

Faculty professional development publication with strategies for career satisfaction, good teaching practices and stress-reducing techniques. The forum for professional sharing for private-independent school educators.

4 pages 5x Year

Rozanne S Elliott, Publisher
Kelly Rawlings, Editor

3530 Teaching Education
University of South Carolina, College of Education
Wardlaw College
Room 231
Columbia, SC 29208-0001

803-777-6301
Fax: 803-777-3068

Focuses on the actual profession of teaching and new methodology by which to learn.

2x Year

James T. Sears, PhD, Editor

3531 Teaching Exceptional Children
The Council for Exceptional Children
1920 Association Drive
Reston, VA 20191-1545

703-620-3660
800-232-7323
Fax: 703-264-1637

A practical classroom-oriented magazine that explores instructional methods, materials and techniques for working with children who have disabilities or who are gifted.

BiMonthly
ISSN: 0040-0599

H William Heller, Editor
Fred Spooner, Editor

3532 Techniques-Connecting Education and Careers
Association for Career and Technical Education
1410 King Street
Alexandria, VA 22314-2749

703-683-3111
800-826-9972
Fax: 703-683-7424
E-mail: sackley@acteonline.org
http://www.acteonline.org

Each issue is packed with information on subjects of successful partnerships, new education models, career exploration, balancing work and family responsibilities, adapting to new workplace practices and technologies, positioning in the global market, teaching approaches and safety issues.

Newsletter/Magazine

Steve Ackley, Asst Exec Dir Communications

3533 Technology Pathfinder for Teachers Master Teacher
Master Teacher
PO Box 1207
Manhattan, KS 66505-1207

785-539-0555
800-669-9633
Fax: 800-669-1132
http://www.masterteacher.com

Full of short technology articles for classroom teachers including how-to's, tips, curriculum ideas, and useful internet hints.

Monthly Newsletter

Tracey H DeBruyn, Executive Editor

3534 Three Rs Master Teacher
Master Teacher
PO Box 1207
Manhattan, KS 66505-1207

785-539-0555
800-669-9633
Fax: 800-669-1132
http://www.masterteacher.com

A quarterly publication that synthesizes the most recent educational research for classroom teachers.

Quarterly Newsletter

Tracey H DeBruyn, Executive Editor

3535 Today's Catholic Teacher
330 Progress Road
Dayton, OH 45449-2322

937-847-5900
800-523-4625
Fax: 937-847-5910
E-mail: mnoschang@peterli.com
http://www.catholicteacher.com

The voice of Catholic education for over a quarter of a century. Lists teaching suggestions, curriculum strategies and ready-to-use classroom ideas. Editorial and special columns are also included in each issue.

72 pages Bimonthly
ISSN: 0040-8441

Mary C Noschang, Editor

3536 Training Research Journal: The Science and Practice of Training
Educational Technology Publications
700 Paliside Avenue
Englewood Cliffs, NJ 07632

Fax: 201-871-4009

Peer-reviewed publication, published once yearly by Educational Technology Publications, is now in its fourth volume. Provides a high-quality, peer-reviewed forum for theoretical and empirical work relevant to training.

Annually

3537 What's New Magazine
1429 Walnut Street
Philadelphia, PA 19102-3218

215-563-6005
800-555-5657
Fax: 215-587-9706
http://www.media-methods.com

Professional source publication dedicated to the needs of home economics/family and consumer sciences, health and guidance educators. Full of creative lesson ideas, resources and industry highlights. Timely and application oriented-articles.

BiMonthly
ISSN: 1097-5616

Michele Sokoloff, Publisher
Christine Weiser, Editor

Software, Hardware & Internet Resources

3538 Analog & Digital Peripherals
251 S Mulberry Street
Troy, OH 45373-3585

937-339-2241
800-758-1041
Fax: 937-339-0070

Rewritable optical desk systems with storage from 128 meg. to 1.3 Gig for all operating systems. Backup systems for all operating systems, one system backs up all PC's.

Lyle Ellicott

3539 E-Z Grader Software
E-Z Grader Company
PO Box 23608
Chagrin Falls, OH 44023

800-432-4018
http://www.ezgrader.com

Electronic guidebook designed by teachers for teachers.

3540 Education Index
H.W. Wilson Company
950 University Avenue
Bronx, NY 10452-4224

718-588-8400
800-367-6770
Fax: 718-590-1617

Contains more than 456,000 citations to articles, interviews, editorials and letters, reviews of books, educational films, and software for approximately 427 English-language periodicals, monographs and yearbooks in the field of education. Available electronically in Windows and Web formula with index abstracts and full text versions.

Monthly

Barbara Barry, Author

3541 Educational Administration Resource Centre Database
University of Alberta
Department of Chemistry
Edmonton, AB, Canada, T6 G 2G2
780-492-3254
Fax: 780-492-8231

Over 3,650 bibliographic descriptions of the Centre's collection of educational administration print and audiovisual materials.

3542 KidsCare Childcare Management Software
770 Cochituate Road
Framingham, MA 01701-4672
508-875-3451

Sells software programs to education professionals involved in childcare to aid their development and understanding.

3543 Mental Edge
Learning ShortCuts
PO Box 382367
Germantown, TN 38183-2367
901-755-4732
E-mail: learning@learningshortcuts.com
http://www.learningshortcuts.com

A teacher information network.

3544 http://www.gsn.org
Global Schoolhouse

http://www.gsn.org

Collaborative projects, communication tools and professional development.

3545 http://www.usajobs.opm.gov/b1c.htm
Institute of Int'l Education Overseas Employment
Info-Teachers United States Office
of Personnel Management

3546 www.K12jobs.com

E-mail: info@k12jobs.com

Concentrates in posting job opportunities available at elementary, junior high, high schools and vocational schools.

3547 www.aasa.org
American Association of School Administrators

Leadership news online.

3548 www.cftl.org
Center for the Future of Teaching & Learning

A not-for-profit organization with roots in California's education reform movement. Our primary focus is strengthening California's teacher workforce.

3549 www.classbuilder.com

Free teachers toolbox! Grade book, Create tests, Reports, Lessons, Distance Learning Courseware, and more.

3550 www.ed.gov/free
Federal Resources for Educational Excellence

Provides hundreds of searchable teaching and learning resources from across 35 federal government agencies. Links to 30 offerings on physics, language, arts, history, current events and other areas. Publishes input from teachers, students and parents.

3551 www.eduverse.com
eduverse.com

Leading Internet e-Knowledge software developer building core technologies for powering international distance education.

3552 www.freeteachingaids.com
Free Teaching Aids.com

Guides for finding free resources for teachers.

3553 www.imagescape.com/helpweb/www/oneweb.html
An Overview of the World Wide Web
A New Surfer's Guide

Let this Web site, ease you gently into World Wide Web vocabulary and history. Click Index to find A Guide to Getting Started on the Internet.

3554 www.learningpage.com

http://www.sitesforteachers.com

A wealth of resource links to teacher organizations, sites to recommend to parents, administrators, and students.

3555 www.mmhschool.com
McGraw Hill School Division

A collection of some Web links that offer basic information to guide you. From simple definitions, to a brief description of the history of the Wide Web, to a list of ways to use Web technology with students.

3556 www.nprinc.com
National Professional Resources

Major distributor of professional development materials to support our nation's teachers in the field of education.

3557 www.onlinelearning.net
OnlineLearning.net

Leading online supplier of instructor-led continuing/adult education.

3558 www.pagestarworld.com
Pagestar

Software products that are specifically designed for teachers. Over 600 electronic forms that are commonly used by teachers for planning, administering, delivering and assessing student learning.

3559 www.pbs.org
PBS TeacherSource

Quick access to a collection of resources for teachers including more than 1,400 lesson plans, teacher's guides and online student activities.

3560 www.pbs.org/uti/quicktips.html
QuickTips

On understanding and using the Internet, you'll find tips on navigating the Web.

3561 www.rhlschool.com
RHL School

Free worksheets for english basics, math computation, math problem solving, reading comprehension and research skills.

3562 www.sanjuan.edu/select/structures.html
San Juan Select - Structures

A Web site that examines various ways to structure and facilitate student projects using Internet capabilities. Each suggestion is accompanied by a specific example of how that structure can be or is being used on the Internet.

3563 www.schoolrenaissance.com
School Renaissance Model

The School Renaissance Model combines the #1 software in education with professional development and consulting services to help you dramatically improve student performance.

3564 www.teachingjobs.com
The Teachers Employment Network

http://

Leading resource for education employment.

3565 www.usajobs.opm.gov/b1c.htm
Overseas Employment Info- Teachers
US Office of Personnel Management

Covers eligibility, position categories and special requirements, application procedures, program information and entitlement, housing, living/working conditions, shipment of household goods, and complete application forms andguidance.

3566 www.webworkshops.com
Web Work Shops

A series of on-line courses, designed to prepare teachers to integrate both the Internet and classroom computer applications into daily lessons.

Training Materials

3567 At-Risk Students: Identification and Assistance Strategies
Center for the Study of Small/Rural Schools
555 E Constitution Street
Room 138
Norman, OK 73072-7820

405-325-1450
Fax: 405-325-7075
E-mail: jcsimmons@ou.edu
http://cssrs.ou.edu

Series II

Video

Jan C Simmons, Director

3568 Character Education: Making a Difference
Character Education Partnership
1025 Connecticut Avenue NW
Suite 1011
Washington, DC 20036

202-296-7743
800-988-8081
Fax: 202-296-7779
http://www.character.org

Andrea Grenadier, Director Communications
Esther Schaeffer, CEO/Executive Director

3569 Character Education: Restoring Respect & Responsibility in our Schools
Master Teacher
PO Box 1207
Manhattan, KS 66505-1207

785-539-0555
800-669-9633
Fax: 785-539-7739
http://www.masterteacher.com

Provides a comprehensive model for character education in our nations schools. Specific classroom stategies as well as school wide approaches are outlines in a clear and compelling fashion.

ISBN: 1-887943-08-0

Thomas Lickona PhD, Author

3570 Cisco Educational Archives
University of North Carolina at Chapel Hill
CB# 3456, Manning Hall
Chapel Hill, NC 27599-3455

http://www.sunsite.unc.edu/cisco/cisco-home

Resource for education programs, discounts and special offers.

3571 Classroom Teacher's Guide for Working withParaeducators Video Set
Master Teacher
PO Box 1207
Manhattan, KS 66505-1207

785-539-0555
800-669-9633
Fax: 785-539-7739
http://www.masterteacher.com

Covers a range of nuts-and-bolts topics including why the job duties of paras have changed so much over the years, what a classroom teacher needs to know to get started working effectively with a para. Useful tips for managing anotheradult, and how para factor into the planning process.

ISBN: 0-91407-80-4

Wendy Dover, Author

3572 Clinical Play Therapy Videos: Child-Centered Developmental & Relationship Play Therapy
University of North Texas
PO Box 311337
Denton, TX 76203

940-565-3864
Fax: 940-565-4461
E-mail: cpt@coefs.coe.unt.edu
http://www.centerforplaytherapy.com

Garry Landreth PhD, Director

3573 Conferencing with Students & Parents Video Series
Master Teacher
PO Box 1207
Manhattan, KS 66505-1207

785-539-0555
800-669-9633
Fax: 785-539-7739
http://www.masterteacher.com

Will help teachers turn both formal and informal conferences with students and parents into opportunities for student success.

ISBN: 1-58992-069-4

3574 Conflict Resolution Strategies in Schools
Center for the Study of Small/Rural Schools
555 E Constitution Street
Room 138
Norman, OK 73072-7820

405-325-1450
Fax: 405-325-7075
E-mail: jcsimmons@ou.edu
http://cssrs.ou.edu

Series IV

Video

Jan C Simmons, Director

3575 Conover Company
2926 Hidden Road
Oshkosh, WI 54902

920-231-4667
Fax: 920-231-4809
E-mail: conover@execpc.com
http://www.conovercompany.com

Emotional intelligence related to learning, leadership, teamwork and change, anger management, violence prevention; functional literary, career exploration and assessment.

3576 Cooperative Learning Strategies
Center for the Study of Small/Rural Schools
555 E Constitution Street
Room 138
Norman, OK 73072-7820

405-325-1450
Fax: 405-325-7075
E-mail: jcsimmons@ou.edu
http://cssrs.ou.edu

Series I

Video

Jan C Simmons, Director

3577 Creating Schools of Character Video Series
Master Teacher
PO Box 1207
Manhattan, KS 66505-1207

785-539-0555
800-669-9633
Fax: 785-539-7739
http://www.masterteacher.com

Visit a Blue Ribbon School of excellence and hear staff and others discuss how to create or improve a whole school charecter education program.

ISBN: 0-914607-90-1

3578 Crisis Management in Schools
Center for the Study of Small/Rural Schools
555 E Constitution Street
Room 138
Norman, OK 73072-7820

405-325-1450
Fax: 405-325-7075
E-mail: jcsimmons@ou.edu
http://cssrs.ou.edu

Series IV

Video

Jan C Simmons, Director

3579 Critical Thinking Video Set
Master Teacher
PO Box 1207
Manhattan, KS 66505-1207

785-539-0555
800-669-9633
Fax: 785-539-7739
http://www.masterteacher.com

Will help teachers challange students to think in a new way. Research shows that when we engage students in critical and creative though, retention increases tremendously.

ISBN: 1-58992-079-1

3580 Curriculum Alignment: Improving Student Learning
Center for the Study of Small/Rural Schools
555 E Constitution Street
Room 138
Norman, OK 73072-7820

405-325-1450
Fax: 405-325-7075
E-mail: jcsimmons@ou.edu
http://cssrs.ou.edu

Series I

Video

Jan C Simmons, Director

3581 Datacad
20 Tower Lane
Avon, CT 06001

860-677-4004
800-394-2231
Fax: 860-677-2610
E-mail: info@datacad.com
http://www.datacad.com

Software for AKC professionals.

Mark F Madura, President/CEO

3582 Discipline Techniques you can Master in a Minute Video Series
Master Teacher
PO Box 1207
Manhattan, KS 66505-1207

785-539-0555
800-669-9633
Fax: 785-539-7739
http://www.masterteacher.com

Key attitudes and strategies for maximizing your options, handle chronic and habitual discipline problems, approaches and actions to get the responses you want, critical mistakes that cause or perpetuate misbehavior.

ISBN: 1-58992-040-6

3583 Eleven Principals of Effective Character Education
Master Teacher
PO Box 1207
Manhattan, KS 66505-1207

785-539-0555
800-669-9633
Fax: 785-539-7739
http://www.masterteacher.com

Takes you to schools in Maryland, New York, and Missouri, where quality character education programs are being implemented by skilled and resourceful staff.

ISBN: 1-887943-13-7
Thomas Lickona PhD, Author

3584 Eleven Principles of Effective Character Educaion
Character Education Partnership
1025 Connecticut Avenue NW
Suite 1011
Washington, DC 20036

202-296-7743
800-988-8081
Fax: 202-296-7779
http://www.character.org

Andrea Grenadier, Director Communications
Esther Schaeffer, CEO/Executive Director

3585 Eye on Education
6 Depot Way W
Larchmont, NY 10538

914-833-0551
Fax: 914-833-0761
http://www.eyeoneducation.com

Books on performance-based learning and assessment.

3586 Great Classroom Management Series
Master Teacher
PO Box 1207
Manhattan, KS 66505-1207

785-539-0555
800-669-9633
Fax: 785-539-7739
http://www.masterteacher.com

Effestive classroom management is getting more difficult everday. teachers face increasing demands and expectations in ebery aspect of their jobs.

ISBN: 0-914607-90-1

3587 Great Classroom Management Video Series
Master Teacher
PO Box 1207
Manhattan, KS 66505-1207

785-539-0555
800-669-9633
Fax: 785-539-7739
http://www.masterteacher.com

Effective classroom management is getting more difficult everyday. teachers face increasing demands and expectations in everyday. Teachers face increasing demands and expectations in every aspect of their jobs.

ISBN: 1-58992-121-6

3588 Handling Chronically Disruptive Students at Risk Video Series
Master Teacher
PO Box 1207
Manhattan, KS 66505-1207

785-539-0555
800-669-9633
Fax: 785-539-7739
http://www.masterteacher.com

Implement and utlize a CARE couscil, develop and individual Action plan, strategies for enhancing individual action plan.

ISBN: 1-58992-031-7

3589 Hearlihy & Company
714 W Columbia Street
Springfield, OH 45504

800-622-1000
Fax: 800-443-2260
E-mail: hearlihy@hearlihy.com
http://www.hearlihy.com

Training and installation for schools purchasing modular labratories.

Chuck Young, Contact

3590 Improving Parent/Educator Relationships
Center for the Study of Small/Rural Schools
555 E Constitution Street
Room 138
Norman, OK 73072-7820

405-325-1450
Fax: 405-325-7075
E-mail: jcsimmons@ou.edu
http://cssrs.ou.edu

Series I

Video

Jan C Simmons, Director

3591 Improving Student Thinking in the Content Area
Center for the Study of Small/Rural Schools
555 E Constitution Street
Room 138
Norman, OK 73072-7820

405-325-1450
Fax: 405-325-7075
E-mail: jcsimmons@ou.edu
http://cssrs.ou.edu

Series II

Video

Jan C Simmons, Director

3592 Inclusion: The Next Step the Video Series
Master Teacher
PO Box 1207
Manhattan, KS 66505-1207

785-539-0555
800-669-9633
Fax: 785-539-7739
http://www.masterteacher.com

Will help you propel your inclusion efforts to a new level of success giving you the necessary insights and stategies for building consensus; weighing your program, curriculum, and instructional options.

ISBN: 1-58992-012-0

Wendy Dover, Author

3593 Integrating Technology into the Classroom Video Series
Master Teacher
PO Box 1207
Manhattan, KS 66505-1207

785-539-0555
800-669-9633
Fax: 785-539-7739
http://www.masterteacher.com

Gives teachers the tools and strategies they need to make information technology work for then and for students while empowering then to teach the skills necessary for students to be productive in a technology driven world.

ISBN: 1-58992-007-Y

3594 International Clearinghouse for the Advancement of Science Teaching
University of Maryland
Benjamin Building
Room 226
College Park, MD 20742-1100

301-405-3161
Fax: 301-314-9055

Provides curriculum information about science and mathematics teaching.

Dr. David Lockard, Director

3595 Lesson Plans and Modifications for Inclusion and Collaborative Classrooms
Master Teacher
PO Box 1207
Manhattan, KS 66505-1207

785-539-0555
800-669-9633
Fax: 785-539-7739
http://www.masterteacher.com

Discover specific strategies lesson plans and activity modifications to enhance learning for all students in the inclusive classroom.

ISBN: 1-58992-022-8

3596 Managing Students Without Coercion
Center for the Study of Small/Rural Schools
555 E Constitution Street
Room 138
Norman, OK 73072-7820

405-325-1450
Fax: 405-325-7075
E-mail: jcsimmons@ou.edu
http://cssrs.ou.edu

Series II

Video

Jan C Simmons, Director

3597 Master Teacher
PO Box 1207
Manhattan, KS 66505-1207

785-539-0555
800-669-9633
Fax: 785-539-7739
http://www.mastertcacher.com

Program of staff development and leadership. It provides a continuous inspiration each week to correspond to the mood and activities present in schools.

2 pages Weekly

3598 Mentoring Teachers to Mastery
Master Teacher
PO Box 1207
Manhattan, KS 66505-1207

785-539-0555
800-669-9633
Fax: 785-539-7739
http://www.masterteacher.com

This 5 tape set will provide your staff with the focus, ideas, and stategies necessary for developing the skills of a Master Teacher.

ISBN: 1-58992-001-5

3599 Motivating Students in the Classroom Video Series
Master Teacher
PO Box 1207
Manhattan, KS 66505-1207

785-539-0555
800-669-9633
Fax: 785-539-7739
http://www.masterteacher.com

Will help teachers with the tough job of motivating students to want to learn.

ISBN: 1-58992-074-0

3600 Multicultural Education: Teaching to Diversity
Center for the Study of Small/Rural Schools
555 E Constitution Street
Room 138
Norman, OK 73072-7820

405-325-1450
Fax: 405-325-7075
E-mail: jcsimmons@ou.edu
http://cssrs.ou.edu

Series II

Video

Jan C Simmons, Director

3601 Outcome-Based Education: Making it Work
Center for the Study of Small/Rural Schools
555 E Constitution Street
Room 138
Norman, OK 73072-7820

405-325-1450
Fax: 405-325-7075
E-mail: jcsimmons@ou.edu
http://cssrs.ou.edu

Series III

Video

Jan C Simmons, Director

3602 Overview of Prevention: A Social Change Model
Center for the Study of Small/Rural Schools
555 E Constitution Street
Room 138
Norman, OK 73072-7820

405-325-1450
Fax: 405-325-7075

E-mail: jcsimmons@ou.edu
http://cssrs.ou.edu

Prevention Series

Video

Jan C Simmons, Director

3603 Personal Planner & Traning Guide for theParaeducator Video Set
Master Teacher
PO Box 1207
Manhattan, KS 66505-1207

785-539-0555
800-669-9633
Fax: 785-539-7739
http://www.masterteacher.com

A 3 tape series to take paras through all the important aspects of what they need to know to become vital contributions in the school setting.

ISBN: 1-58992-127-5

Wendy Dover, Author

3604 Quality School
Center for the Study of Small/Rural Schools
555 E Constitution Street
Room 138
Norman, OK 73072-7820

405-325-1450
Fax: 405-325-7075
E-mail: jcsimmons@ou.edu
http://cssrs.ou.edu

Series II

Video

Jan C Simmons, Director

3605 SAP Today
Performance Resource Press
1270 Rankin Drive
Suite F
Troy, MI 48083-2843

800-453-7733
Fax: 800-499-5718

Overview offers the basics of student assistance.

3606 School-Wide Stratigies for Retaining Great Teachers
Master Teacher
PO Box 1207
Manhattan, KS 66505-1207

785-539-0555
800-669-9633
Fax: 785-539-7739
http://www.masterteacher.com

You will hear proven strategies for supporting new teachers through all those typical expirences that cansabatage their efforts and cause them to leave your district or even abandon teaching all together.

ISBN: 1-58992-098-8

3607 Site-Based Management
Center for the Study of Small/Rural Schools
555 E Constitution Street
Room 138
Norman, OK 73072-7820

405-325-1450
Fax: 405-325-7075
E-mail: jcsimmons@ou.edu
http://cssrs.ou.edu

Series III

Video

Jan C Simmons, Director

3608 Strategic Planning for Outcome-Based Education
Center for the Study of Small/Rural Schools
555 E Constitution Street
Room 138
Norman, OK 73072-7820

405-325-1450
Fax: 405-325-7075
E-mail: jcsimmons@ou.edu
http://cssrs.ou.edu

Series II

Video

Jan C Simmons, Director

3609 Strengthening the Family: An Overview of a Holistic Family Wellness Model
Center for the Study of Small/Rural Schools
555 E Constitution Street
Room 138
Norman, OK 73072-7820

405-325-1450
Fax: 405-325-7075
E-mail: jcsimmons@ou.edu
http://cssrs.ou.edu

Prevention Series

Video

Jan C Simmons, Director

3610 Students-at-Risk Video Series
Master Teacher
PO Box 1207
Manhattan, KS 66505-1207

785-539-0555
800-669-9633
Fax: 785-539-7739
http://www.masterteacher.com

Gives you specific stategies for reaching those students who are giving up.

ISBN: 1-58992-060-0

Mildred Odom Bradley, Author

3611 Superintendent/School Board Relationships
Center for the Study of Small/Rural Schools
555 E Constitution Street
Room 138
Norman, OK 73072-7820

405-325-1450
Fax: 405-325-7075
E-mail: jcsimmons@ou.edu
http://cssrs.ou.edu

Series I

Video

Jan C Simmons, Director

3612 TQM: Implementing Quality Management in Your School
Center for the Study of Small/Rural Schools
555 E Constitution Street
Room 138
Norman, OK 73072-7820

405-325-1450
Fax: 405-325-7075
E-mail: jcsimmons@ou.edu
http://cssrs.ou.edu

Series III

Video

Jan C Simmons, Director

3613 Teachers as Heros
Center for the Study of Small/Rural Schools
555 E Constitution Street
Room 138
Norman, OK 73072-7820

405-325-1450
Fax: 405-325-7075
E-mail: jcsimmons@ou.edu
http://cssrs.ou.edu

Series IV

Video

Jan C Simmons, Director

3614 Teaching for Intelligent Behavior
Center for the Study of Small/Rural Schools
555 E Constitution Street
Room 138
Norman, OK 73072-7820

405-325-1450
Fax: 405-325-7075
E-mail: jcsimmons@ou.edu
http://cssrs.ou.edu

Series IV

Video

Jan C Simmons, Director

3615 Training Video Series for the Substitute Teacher
Master Teacher
PO Box 1207
Manhattan, KS 66505-1207

785-539-0555
800-669-9633
Fax: 785-539-7739
http://www.masterteacher.com

Will help you provide the consistent direction and training for substitute teachers.

ISBN: 0-914607-95-2

3616 Voices in the Hall: High School Principals at Work
Phi Delta Kappa Educational Foundation
PO Box 789
Bloomington, IN 47402-0789

812-339-1156
800-766-1156
Fax: 812-339-0018
http://www.pdkintl.org

William E Webster's visits to more than 150 schools for this three-year study yield insights into the new roles of the high school principal in American education.

William E Webster, Author
Donovan R Walling, Dir Publications/Research

3617 Wavelength
4753 N Broadway
Suite 808
Chicago, IL 60640

Fax: 773-784-1079
E-mail: winwave@aol.com
http://www.wavelengthinc.com

Humorous programs and videos cover a variety of topics including team building, motivation, diversity, mentoring, brain research and character education.

3618 You Can Handle Them All Discipline Video Series
Master Teacher
PO Box 1207
Manhattan, KS 66505-1207

785-539-0555
800-669-9633
Fax: 785-539-7739
http://www.masterteacher.com

Based upon the best selling books You Can Handle Them All and BEfore you can Discipline by Robert L Debruyn. It contains the vital professional foundations that must underpin and solid philosophy of discipline.

ISBN: 1-58992-035-X

Robert L DeBruyn, Author

Workshops & Programs

3619 ACE Fellows Program
American Council on Education
1 Dupont Circle NW
Washington, DC 20036-1193

202-939-9300
Fax: 202-785-8056
E-mail: fellows@ace.nche.edu
http://www.acenet.edu/programs/fellows

Providing senior faculty and administrators with the knowledge, skills, and experience to manage change.

William Kirwan, Chair
M Lee Pelton, Vice Chair

3620 ART New England Summer Workshops
Art New England Workshops
425 Washington Street
Brighton, MA 02135

617-879-7175
E-mail: nmccarthy@massart.edu
http://www.massart.edu/at_massart/academic_prgms/continuing/

Offers painting, drawing, photography, jewelry making, sculpting, computer imaging and ceramics.

Nancy McCarthy, Administrator

3621 Annual Conductor's Institute of South Carolina
University of South Carolina
School of Music
Columbia, SC 29208

803-777-7500
Fax: 803-777-9774
E-mail: CI@mozart.sc.edu
http://www.conductorsinstitute.com

Since its inception, more than 600 conductors have traveled to Columbia to study with guest conductors and composers. Academic credit is available.

Donald Portnoy, Director

3622 Annual Summer Institute for Secondary Teachers
Rock and Roll Hall of Fame

E-mail: soehler@rockhall.org
http://www.rockhall.com/programs/institute.asp

The institute provides teachers with the knowledge and tools needed to bring popular music into the curriculum. The program includes a rock and roll history survey; guest speakers; discussions and workshops.

June

Susan Oehler, Education Programs Manager

3623 Ball State University
Department of Industry & Technology
Applied Technology Building 131
Muncie, IN 47306-0255

765-285-5641
Fax: 765-285-2162
http://www.bsu.edu/cast/itech

Summer programs in manufacturing, printing, graphic arts, technology education, industrial vocational/technical education.

3624 Bryant and Stratton College
200 Bryant and Stratton Way
Williamsville, NY 14231-0142

716-821-9331
Fax: 716-821-9343
http://www.bryantstratton.edu

Summer programs in information technology, data communications and networking, logic and program design.

3625 Center for Educational Leadership Trinity University
Trinity University
715 Stadium Drive
San Antonio, TX 78212-7200

210-999-7501
Fax: 210-999-7696
E-mail: paul.kelleher@trinity.edu
http://http://carme.cs.trinity.edu/education/index.asp

Offers three Masters degree programs for Arts, Teaching, Psychology and School Administration. The school also offers summer institutes and training programs for educators and administrators. Also see information regarding the Masterof Education: School Administration at http://carme.cs.trinity.edu/education/graduate/medschoolleadership.htm

3626 Center for Global Education
Augsbury College
2211 Riverside Avenue
Minneapolis, MN 55454-1350

612-330-1159
800-299-8889
Fax: 612-330-1695
E-mail: globaled@augsburg.edu
http://www.augsburg.edu/global

Offers travel seminars for educators, 7-21 day programs to Mexico, Central America, Southern Africa and Cuba. Explores social change, human rights, development and US policy. Educators reflect upon teaching goals, methods andcurricula and discover new models of teaching.

3627 Center for Image Processing in Education
PO Box 13750
Tucson, AZ 85732-3750

520-322-0118
800-322-9884
Fax: 520-327-0175
E-mail: kRISR@evisual.org
http://www.evisual.org

Disseminates curriculum materials and in-service workshops for using digital image processing in classroom applications. The materials are designed for hands-on, open-ended exploration and discovery, using professional scientificsoftware. Workshops provide the needed background and training for teachers to effectively implement image processing.

Steve Moore, Executive Director
Kristine Rees, Business Operations Director

3628 Center for Learning Connections
Highline Community College 25-55A
PO Box 98000
Des Moines, IA 98198-9800

206-870-3783
Fax: 206-870-3787
http://www.learningconnections.org

Workshops, seminars, conferences, focus groups and retreats; education reform, school-to-career, project design and management.

3629 Center for Occupational Research & Development
601 Lake Air Drive
Waco, TX 76710

800-231-3015
Fax: 254-776-3906
E-mail: twarner@cord.org
http://www.cord.org

Workshops, onsite workshops and video conferencing courses in education technology applications.

Teemus Warner, Training Coordinator

3630 Center for Play Therapy
University of North Texas
PO Box 311337
Denton, TX 76203

940-565-3864
Fax: 940-565-4461
E-mail: cpt@unt.edu
http://www.centerforplaytherapy.com

Encourages the unique development and emotional growth of children through the process of play therapy, a dynamic interpersonal relationship between a child and a therapist trained in play therapy procedures. Provides training,research, publications, counseling services and acts as a clearinghouse for literature in the field.

Sue Bratton, Director

3631 Classroom Connect
8000 Marina Boulevard
Suite 400
Brisbane, CA 94005

650-351-5100
800-638-1639
Fax: 650-351-5300
E-mail: conect@classroom.com
http://www.classroom.com

A leading provider of professional development programs and online instructional content for K-12 education.

Jim Bowler, President
Melinda Cook, Vice President Sales

3632 College of the Ozarks
PO Box 17
Point Lookout, MO 65726

417-334-6411
Fax: 417-335-2618
E-mail: divine@cofd.edu
http://www.cofo.edu

Summer programs in CAD, welding, woodworking, machine tool processes, CNC.

3633 Connect
Synergy Learning
116 Birge Street
PO Box 60
Brattleboro, VT 05302-0060

802-257-2629
800-769-6199
Fax: 802-254-5233
E-mail: casey@synergylearning.org
http://www.synergylearning.org

Sponsors literature teacher institutes and on-site workshops in math, science and design technology.

Publishes Connect magazine for teachers of grades K-8 focusing on Math, Science and technology.

28 pages
ISSN: 1041-682X

Casey Murrow, Director
Susan Hathaway, Circulation Manager

3634   Critical Issues in Urban Special Education: The Implications of Whole-School Change
Harvard Graduate School of Education
Programs in Professional Education
339 Gutman Library
Cambridge, MA 02138

617-495-3572
800-545-1849
Fax: 617-496-8051
E-mail: ppe@harvard.edu
http://www.gse.harvard.edu/~ppe

A one-week summer seminar that examines the implications of whole-school change on students with disabilities, policy, procedure, and practice. The program will clarify competing agendas, illuminate various models, and identifyunified approaches to ensuring measurable benefits to all children.

Genet Jeanjean, Program Coordinator

3635   Critical and Creative Thinking in the Classroom
National Center for Teaching Thinking
815 Washington Street
Suite 8
Newtonville, MA 02460

617-965-4604
Fax: 617-965-4674

A unique summer program of courses for K-12 teachers, curriculum developers, staff-development specialists, school/district administrators, teacher educators and college faculty.

3636   Curriculum Center - Office of Educational Services
3430 Constitution Drive
Suite 114
Springfield, IL 62707-9402

217-786-3010
Fax: 217-786-3020
E-mail: oesiscc@siu.edu
http://www.oes.siu.edu

Programs in vocational areas, career awareness, career development, integration, technology, tech preparation.

3637   Darryl L Sink & Associates
60 Garden Court
Suite 101
Monterey, CA 93940

831-649-8384
800-650-7465
Fax: 831-649-3914
E-mail: info@dsink.com
http://www.dsink.com

Three-day workshop based on proven instructional design principles adapted for web-based training.

3638   DeVry University
1 Tower Lane
Oakbrook Terrace, IL 60181

630-571-7700
800-295-8694
Fax: 630-574-1973
http://www.devry.edu

Subjects include communications, computer technology, electronics, graphic communications, and training and development.

3639   Delmar Thomson Learning
3 Columbia Circle
Albany, NY 12212

518-464-3500
Fax: 518-464-7000
E-mail: info@delmar.com
http://www.delmar.com

Subjects include welding, HVAC-R, electrical, electronics, automotive, CADD and drafting, construction, blueprint reading, and fire science.

3640   Depco
3305 Airport Drive
PO Box 178
Pittsburg, KS 66762

620-231-0019
800-767-1062
Fax: 620-231-0024
E-mail: sales@depcoinc.com
http://www.depcoinc.com

Subjects include technology service, linear and non-linear video production, and autodesk product training.

3641   Eastern Illinois University School of Technology
600 Lincoln Avenue
Charleston, IL 61920

217-581-3226
Fax: 217-581-6607
http://www.eiu-edu/~tech1

Subjects include manufacturing, construction, electronics, graphic communications, training and development.

3642   Edison Welding Institute
EWI
1250 Arthur E Adams Drive
Columbus, OH 42321

614-688-5000
Fax: 614-688-5001
E-mail: ewi@ewi.org
http://www.ewi.org

Welding courses taught by world experts in materials joining.

3643   Educational Summit
The Principals' Center
20 Nassau Street
Suite 211
Princeton, NJ 08542-4509

609-497-1907
Fax: 609-497-1927

An educational summit held in August for school principals to explore, debate and design new models for schooling in America with implications for choice, charters and the community.

3644   Effective Strategies for School Reform
Harvard Graduate School of Education
Programs in Professional Education
339 Gutman Library
Cambridge, MA 02138

617-495-3572
800-545-1849
Fax: 617-496-8051
E-mail: ppe@harvard.edu
http://www.gse.harvard.edu/~ppe

A two-week residential program on the Harvard campus for leadership teams from school districts that are involved in the process of school reform or restructuring. Participants will gain practical skills for leading change in theirdistricts, and will forge effective action plans for school reform to take back to their districts.

Genet Jeanjean, Program Coordinator

3645 Electronics Industries Alliance/CEA
2500 Wilson Boulevard
Arlington, VA 22201-3834

703-907-7670
Fax: 703-907-7968
http://www.CEMAweb.org

Electronics workshops.

**3646 Elementary Education Professional
DevelopmentSchool
Pennsylvania State University**

148 Chambers Building
Pennsylvania State University
University Park, PA 16802

814-865-2243
E-mail: n78@psu.edu
http://www.ed.psu/pds

Through courses and training seminars teachers can engage in research and rethinking of pracice, thus creating an opportunity for the profession to expand its knowledge base.

James Nolan, Professor of Education

3647 Emco Maier Corporation
2757 Scioto Parkway
Columbus, OH 43221

614-715-991
Fax: 614-771-5990
E-mail: training@emcomaier-usa.com
http://www.emcomaier-usa.com

Subjects include CNC training - turning and milling.

3648 Energy Concepts
404 Washington Boulevard
Mundelein, IL 60060

847-837-8191
800-621-1247
Fax: 847-837-8171
http://www.energy-concepts-inc.com

Subjects include material science technology, principles of technology year I&II.

3649 Fastech
1750 Westfield Drive
Findlay, OH 45840

419-425-2233
Fax: 419-425-9431
E-mail: info@fastechinc.net
http://www.fastechinc.net

Subjects include mastercam training, and FMMT CD's.

3650 Festo Corporation
395 Moreland Road
Hauppauge, NY 11788

631-435-0800
Fax: 631-435-3847
E-mail: fred_zieran@festo.com
http://www.festo-usa.com

Subjects include fluid power, PLC, industrial automation.

3651 Foundation for Critical Thinking
PO Box 7087
Dillon Beach, CA 94929

707-878-9100
E-mail: cct@criticalthinking.org
http://www.criticalthinking.org

Nonprofit organization which distributes books, videotapes, audiotapes and micropublications on critical thinking. Also hosts regional workshops which are geared toward educators.

**3652 Four State Regional Technology Conference
Pittsburg State University**
College of Technology
1701 S Broadway
Pittsburg, KS 66762

620-235-4365
800-854-7488
Fax: 620-235-4343
E-mail: tbaldwin@pittstate.edu
http://www.pittstate.edu

Subjects include educational technology and technology management.

November
30 booths with 250 attendees
Tom Baldwin, Dean College of Technology

**3653 Graduate Programs for Professional Educators
North Central Association of Colleges & Schools**
Walden University
155 5th Avenue S
Minneaoplis, MN 55401

800-444-6795
Fax: 941-498-4266
E-mail: request@waldenu.edu

Both the MS and PhD in Education allow study from home or work. The Master of Science in Education serves classroom teachers and the PhD in education serves the advanced learning needs of educators from a wide range that servespractice fields and levels.

3654 Grand Canyon University College of Education
30 N LaSalle Street
Chicago, IL 60602

312-263-0456
800-621-7440
Fax: 312-263-7462
http://www.ncahigherlearningcommission.org

A program created specifically to answer the needs of teachers with practical application of teaching strategies based on theory and research; work at your own pace within term deadlines.

**3655 Harvard Institute for School Leadership
Harvard Graduate School of Education**
14 Story Street
4th Floor
Cambridge, MA 02138

617-495-3572
800-545-1849
Fax: 617-496-8051
E-mail: ppe@harvard.edu
http://www.gse.harvard.edu/~ppe

An intensive residential program for leadership teams from school districts. Participants will gain new perspectives on the processes and goals of school reform and practical skills for leading change in their districts.

July

**3656 Harvard Seminar for Superintendents
Harvard Graduate School of Education**
Programs in Professional Education
339 Gutman Library
Cambridge, MA 02138

617-495-3572
800-545-1849
Fax: 617-496-8051
E-mail: ppe@harvard.edu
http://www.gse.harvard.edu/~ppe

Veteran superintendents from around the country participate in a week of intellectually stimulating conversations with Harvard faculty and networking with colleagues. Topics discussed include the arts, science, social science, and current events.

July

Valencia Miner, Program Assistant

3657 Hobart Institute of Welding Technology
400 Trade Square East
Troy, OH 45373

800-332-9448
Fax: 937-332-5200
http://www.welding.org

Preparation course for CWI/CWE exams. Instructor course devoted to welding theory and hand-son practice.

Elmer Swank, Contact

3658 Indiana University-Purdue University of Indianapolis, IUPUI
Department of Construction Technology
799 W Michigan Street
ET 309
Indianapolis, IN 46202-5160

317-274-2413
Fax: 317-278-3669
E-mail: dilpatto@iupui.edu
http://www.engr.iupui.edu/cnt

Subjects include architectural technology, civil engineering technology, construction technology, interior design.

E Sener, Chairman
Diane Patton, Administative Assistant

3659 Industrial Training Institute
3385 Wheeling Road
Lancaster, OH 43130

740-687-5262
800-638-4180
Fax: 740-687-5262
E-mail: drbillstevens1@msn.com
http://www.trainingrus.com

Subjects include basic electricity, motors, controls, PLC's, NEC and process control; custom designed training and consulting.

3660 Institute of Higher Education
General Board of Higher Education & Ministry/UMC
1001 Nineteenth Avenue
PO Box 340007
Nashville, TN 37203-0007

615-340-7406
Fax: 615-340-7379
E-mail: scu@gbhem.org
http://www.gbhem.org/highed.html

An annual seminar for administrators and faculty of United Methodist-related educational institutions addressing current themes related to the college's mission.

June
125 attendees

Dr. James A Noseworthy, Assistant General Secretary

3661 International Curriculum Management Audit Center
Phi Delta Kappa International
Professional Development & Services
PO Box 789
Bloomington, IN 47402-0789

812-339-1156
800-776-1156
Fax: 812-339-0018
E-mail: cpds@pdkintl.org
http://www.pdkintl.org

Training in the curriculum audit process empowers you to look objectively at the entire curriculum management system.

3662 International Graduate School
Berne University
35 Center Street
Suite 18
Wolfeboro Falls, NH 03896-1080

603-569-8648
866-755-5557
Fax: 603-569-4052
E-mail: berne@berne.edu
http://www.berne.edu

Doctoral Degrees in one to two years, Specialist Diplomas in six to twelve months in: business, education (all specialties), government, health services, international relations, psychology, religion, social work and human services.

3663 International Workshops
187 Aqua View Drive
Cedarburg, WI 53012

262-377-7062
Fax: 262-377-7096
E-mail: thintz@execpc.com
http://www.internationalworkshops.org

Music education, accompanying, chamber music, improvisation, jazz, technique, pedagogy, storing and piano repertoire and chorus.

400 attendees
Tori Hintz, Manager

3664 Island Drafting & Technical Institute
128 Broadway
Amityville, NY 11701

631-691-8733
Fax: 631-691-8738
E-mail: info@islanddrafting.com
http://www.islanddrafting.com

Subjects include CAD, drafting, computer repair, electronics technology, novel CNE, microsoft MSCE, and networking. Degree and non-degree programs.

John G Diliberto, VP

3665 Janice Borla Vocal Jazz Camp
N Central College, Music Department
30 N Brainard
Naperville, IL 60566

630-416-3911
Fax: 630-416-6249
E-mail: jborla@aol.com
http://www.janiceborlavocaljazzcamp.org

Solo vocal jazz workshops, music education, vocal jazz history, improvisation, repertoire, technique and theory.

Janice Borla, Director

3666 Jefferson State Community College
2601 Carson Road
Birmingham, AL 35215

205-856-8517
Fax: 205-856-8572
E-mail: alfie@jscc.cc.al.us
http://www.jeffstateonline.com

Certificate and degree programs in automated manufacturing, electromechanical systems, industrial maintenance, and CAD.

3667 July in Rensselaer
St. Joseph's College, Graduate Dept
PO Box 984
Rensselaer, IN 47978

219-866-6352
Fax: 219-866-6102
E-mail: jamesc@saintjoe.edu

Solo, ensemble, liturgy, accompanying, history, improvision, private lessons, technique, repertoire, sight reading, workshops, theory and sacred choral music.

Rev. James Challancin, Director

3668 K'nex Education Division
2990 Bergey Road
PO Box 700
Hatfield, PA 19440

888-ABC-KNEX
Fax: 215-996-4222
E-mail: abcknex@knex.com
http://www.knexeducation.com

Introductory, set specific, regional and design your own professional development programs offered for any/all K-12 technology, math and science sets.

3669 Kaleidoscope
Consulting Psychologists Press
3803 E Bayshore Road
Palo Alto, CA 94303-4300

800-624-1765
Fax: 650-969-8608

An institute for educators that develops insights into teaching styles and learning styles; administers and interprets the Myers-Briggs Type Indicator (personality inventory); learn new techniques to help children understand and valuetheir unique qualities; create and deliver lessons that enlighten all students and more.

July

3670 Kent State University
School of Technology
117 Van Deusen Hall
Kent, OH 44242-0001

330-672-2892
Fax: 330-672-2894
http://www.tech.kent.edu

Subjects include aeronautics, electronics, manufacturing engineering, computer technology, and automotive engineering technology.

3671 Kentucky State University
Department of Industrial Technology
East Main Street, Shauntee Hall
Frankfort, KY 40601

502-597-6897
Fax: 502-227-6236
http://www.kysu.edu

Associates in applied science in drafting and design technology and applied science in electronics technology.

3672 Kodaly Teaching Certification Program
DePaul University, School of Music
804 West Belden Avenue
Chicago, IL 60614

773-325-4355
Fax: 773-325-7263

Music education, pedagogy and workshops.

Robert Krueger, Director Operations

3673 Lab Volt Systems
1710 Highway 34 N
Wall, NJ 07727

732-938-2000
800-522-2658

Fax: 732-774-8573
E-mail: us@labvolt.com
http://www.labvolt.com

Hands-on training in the concepts, skills and procedures that work best in modular, multimedia technology education programs.

Eric Maynard, Contact

3674 Leadership and the New Technologies
Harvard Graduate School of Education
Programs in Professional Education
339 Gutman Library
Cambridge, MA 02138

617-495-3572
800-545-1849
Fax: 617-496-8051
E-mail: ppe@harvard.edu
http://www.gse.harvard.edu/~ppe

Programs designed to help teams of school leaders anticipate the far-reaching impacts that new technologies can have on students, teachers, curriculum, and communication. Participants make long-term plans for the use of technology intheir schools and districts and learn how to take advantage of federal and state technology initiatives.

July

Ann Doyle, Program Coordinator

3675 Learning & The Enneagram
National Enneagram Institute at Milton Academy
230 Atherton Street
Milton, MA 02186-2424

617-898-1798
Fax: 617-898-1712

An educational enterprise dedicated to guiding individuals and organizations in the most responsible and effective format for their needs. Programs include exploration of what every educator needs to know; why we learn in the way wedo; and how we teach.

July

Regina Pyle, Coordinator

3676 Learning Materials Workshop
274 N Winooski Avenue
Burlington, VT 05401-3621

802-802-8399
800-693-7164
Fax: 802-862-0794
E-mail: mail@learningmaterialswork.com
http://www.learningmaterialswork.com

Designs and produces open-ended blocks and construction sets for early childhood classrooms. An education guide and video, as well as training workshops are offered.

Karen Hewitt, President

3677 Light Machines

http://www.lmcorp.com/_vti_bin/shtml.exe/search/in-dex.html

Subjects include demonstrations and comprehensive training on CNC routers, turning machines and milling machines, and CAD/CAM software.

3678 Marcraft International Corporation
100 N Morain Street
Suite 302
Kennwick, WA 99336

800-441-6006
Fax: 509-374-9250
E-mail: mcraft@mic-inc.com
http://www.eclassrooms.net

Subjects include A+ certification, network+ certification, i-net+ certification and copper and optical cabling certifications.

3679 Maryland Center for Career and Technology Education
1415 Key Highway
Baltimore, MD 21230

410-685-1648
Fax: 410-685-0032

Subjects include technology education and occupational education certification.

**3680 Media and American Democracy
Harvard Graduate School of Education**
Programs in Professional Education
339 Gutman Library
Cambridge, MA 02138

617-495-3572
800-545-1849
Fax: 617-496-8051
E-mail: ppe@harvard.edu
http://www.gse.harvard.edu/~ppe

Participants learn about the interaction between the media and American democratic process, develop curriculum units, and examine ways to help students become thoughtful consumers of media messages about politics. Designed forsecondary school teachers of history, social studies, English, journalism, and humanities.

August

Tracy Ryder, Program Assistant

3681 Miller Electric Manufacturing Company
1635 W Spencer Street
Appleton, WI 54914

800-426-4553
Fax: 877-327-8132
http://www.millerwelds.com

Subjects include welding.

3682 Millersville University
Department of Industry & Technology
PO Box 1002, Osborn Hall
Millersvile, PA 54914

800-426-4553
Fax: 877-327-8132
http://www.millersv.edu

Subjects include continuing education in technology education, computers, internet for educators, aerospace/aviation, and websites for classroom use.

3683 Morehead State University
Dept. of Industrial Ed. & Tech
210 Loyd Cassity Building, MSU
Morehead, KY 40651

606-783-2418
Fax: 606-783-5030
E-mail: r.hayes@morehead-st.edu
http://www.morehead-st.edu/colleges/science/iet

AAS and BS in Industrial Technology, BS in Industrial Education, MS in Vocational Education and Technology.

3684 Mpulse Maintenance Software
PO Box 22906
Eugene, OR 97402

800-944-1796
Fax: 541-302-6680
E-mail: info@mpulsecmms.com
http://www.mpulsecmms.com

Subjects include maintenance and facility management software.

3685 Musikgarten
507 Arlington Street
Greensboro, NC 27406

336-272-5303
800-216-6864
Fax: 336-272-0581
E-mail: musgarten@aol.com
http://www.musikgarten.org

Early childhood music education workshops teaching music and understanding children.

Lorna Heyge, Speaker

**3686 NASA Educational Workshop
NSTA**
1840 Wilson Boulevard
Arlington, VA 22201-3000

888-400-6782
Fax: 703-522-5413
http://www.nsta.org/programs/new.htm

Two week workshop at a NASA Center, professional development opportunity for K-12 teachers in mathematics, science, and technology, teachers and curriculum specialists at the K-12 levels; media specialists, resource teachers,elementary curriculum developers, counselors, and others with special interest in mathematics, science, technology, and geography.

**3687 NCSS Summer Professional Development Programs
National Council for the Social Studies**
3501 Newark Street NW
Washington, DC 20016-3100

202-966-7840
Fax: 202-966-2061

Offers independent workshops and conferences concentrating on the social studies classroom.

July

Susan Griffin

3688 National Center for Construction Education & Research
PO Box 141104
Gainsville, FL 32614-1104

352-334-0911
Fax: 352-334-0932
E-mail: info@nccer.org
http://www.nccer.org

Subjects include industry-developed standardized craft training program covering more than 25 craft trades. Accredited, competency-based, task driven, and modular in format.

3689 National Computer Systems
4401 L Street NW
Suite 550
Edina, MN 55435

612-995-8997
800-328-6172
Fax: 952-830-8564
http://www.ncs.com

Programs offer skills to teach technology in the classroom.

3690 National Head Start Association
1651 Prince Street
Alexandria, VA 22314-2818

703-739-0875
Fax: 703-739-0878
http://www.nhsa.org

Dedicated to promoting and protecting the Head Start program. Advocates on the behalf of America's low-income children and families. Publishes many books, periodicals and resource guides. Offers a legislative hotline as well astraining programs through the NHSA Academy.

Ron Herndon, President
Blanche Russ-Glover, VP

3691 Northern Arizona University
AZTEC Lab
Box 6025
Flagstaff, AZ 86011

928-523-9011
Fax: 520-523-6395
E-mail: nicole.snow@nau.edu
http://www.nau.edu/~ifwfd/aztec

Offers computer and technology workshops on site or off. Lab available for rental for training.

3692 Orff-Schulwerk Teacher Certification Program
DePaul University, School of Music
804 West Belden Avenue
Chicago, IL 60614

773-325-7260
Fax: 773-325-7264
E-mail: ahutchen@wppost.depaul.edu.

Music education, pedagogy and workshops.

Judy Bundra, Associate Dean

3693 Owens Community College
PO Box 10000
Toledo, OH 43699

419-661-7459
Fax: 419-661-7664
E-mail: ddevier@owens.cc.oh.us
http://www.owens.cc.oh.us

Subjects include welding, machining, electronics, automotive, diesel, environmental, quality, and mechanical and digital media.

3694 Paideia Group
PO Box 3423
Chapel Hill, NC 27515-3423

919-929-0600
Fax: 919-932-3905
E-mail: paideiapgi@aol.com
http://http://hometown.aol.com/paideiapgi/webpage.html

Programs are designed with options for beginner and advanced levels. Activities include seminars and sessions that focus on socratic teaching, coaching, evaluation and curriculum design.

March
150 attendees

Patricia Weiss, PhD, President

3695 Pamela Sims & Associates
54 Mozart Crescent
Brampton, Ontario
Canada L6Y 2W7

905-455-7331
888-610-7467
Fax: 905-455-0207
E-mail: loveofkids@aol.com
http://www.pamelasims.com

Seminars and workshops for educators and parents.

Pamela Sims, President
Kelly Smith, Marketing Director

3696 Pennsylvania State University-Workforce Education & Development Program
301 Keller Building
University Park, PA 16802-1303

814-863-2584
Fax: 814-863-7532
http://www.ed.psu.edu/wfed

Subjects include educational, business, and industrial for vocational instructors, counselors, administrators, and students.

3697 Performance Learning Systems
466 Old Hood Road
Suite 25-26
Emerson, NJ 07630

270-522-2000
Fax: 270-522-2010
E-mail: plsnj@aol.com

Training programs with a specialization in teacher education.

3698 Piano Workshop
Goshen College, Music Department
1700 S Main Street
Goshen, IN 46526

574-535-7364
Fax: 574-535-7949
E-mail: beverlykl@goshen.edu

Solo, ensemble, music education, technique, pedagogy, repertoire, workshops and master classes.

Beverly Lapp

3699 Pittsburg State University
College of Technology
1701 S Broadway
Pittsburg, KS 66762

620-235-4365
800-854-7488
Fax: 620-235-4343
E-mail: tbaldwin@pittstate.edu
http://www.pittstate.edu

Subjects include educational technology and technology management. Hosts a regional conference in November.

Tom Baldwin, Dean College of Technology

3700 Polaroid Education Program
565 Technology Square
#3B
Cambridge, MA 02139-3539

781-386-2000
Fax: 781-386-3925

This program offers workshops for professional educators, preK-12; the Visual Learning Workshop and an Instant Image Portfolio Workshop.

3701 Professional Development Institutes
Center for Professional Development & Services
Phi Delta Kappa International
PO Box 789
Bloomington, IN 47402-0789

812-339-1156
800-766-1156
Fax: 812-339-0018
E-mail: cpds@pdkintl.org
http://www.pdkintl.org

Offers programs such as active learning strategies for extended blocks of time; block scheduling; efficacy in action/working to get smart.

3702 Professional Development Workshops
Rebus
4111 Jackson Road
Ann Arbor, MI 48103

734-668-4870
800-435-3085
Fax: 734-668-4728
http://www.rebusinc.com

Workshops that promote success by assessing children in the context of active learning.

June/July

Sam Meisels, CEO
Linda Borgsdorf, President

3703 Project Zero Classroom
Harvard Graduate School of Education
Programs in Professional Education
339 Gutman Library
Cambridge, MA 02138

617-495-3572
800-545-1849
Fax: 617-496-8051
E-mail: ppe@harvard.edu
http://www.gse.harvard.edu/~ppe

Renowned educators Howard Gardner and David Perkins and their Project Zero colleagues work with K-12 educators to help them reshape their classroom practices to promote student understanding. The week focuses on five concepts:teaching for understanding, multiple intelligences, the thinking classroom, authentic assessment, and learning with and through the arts.

July

Deana Tassi, Program Assistant

3704 Robert McNeel & Associates
3670 Woodland Park Avenue N
Seattle, WA 98103

206-545-7000
Fax: 206-545-7321
E-mail: bob@mcneelcom
http://www.rhino3d.com

3D modeling workshop for design, drafting, graphics, and technology educators.

3705 Rockford Systems
4620 Hydraulic Road
Rockford, IL 61109-2695

815-874-7891
800-922-7533
Fax: 815-874-6144
E-mail: sales@rockfordsystems.com
http://www.rockfordsystems.com

Machine safegaurding seminar for technology educators.

3706 SUNY College at Oswego
Department of Technology
Oswego, NY 13126

315-312-2500
Fax: 315-312-2863
E-mail: techdept@oswego.edu
http://www.oswego.edu

Subjects include technical and computer drafting, CADD, design, energy technology, materials processing, and manufacturing systems.

October
26 booths with 350-400 attendees

P Gaines, Chair

3707 School of Music
Georgia State University
PO Box 4097
Atlanta, GA 30302-4097

404-651-1720

Offers high school piano camp,music education leadership, summer opera workshops, and much more.

3708 Southern Polytechnic State University
1100 S Marietta Parkway
Marietta, GA 30060

770-528-7240
Fax: 770-528-7490
E-mail: coned@spsu.edu
http://www.spsu.edu/oce

Information technology continuing education.

3709 Southwestern Oklahoma State University
100 Campus Drive
Weatherford, OK 73096

580-774-3162
Fax: 580-774-7028
E-mail: bellg@swosu.edu
http://www.swosu.edu

Subjects include technology education, engineering technology and industrial technology.

3710 Specialized Solutions
338 E Lemon Street
Tarpon Springs, FL 34689

727-287-1070
Fax: 727-287-1080
E-mail: pr@specializedsolutions.com
http://www.specializedsolutions.com

Technology based training and certification self study programs.

3711 Staff Development Workshops & Training Sessions
National School Conference Institute
PO Box 37527
Phoenix, AZ 85069-7527

602-371-8655
Fax: 602-371-8790

Offers twenty relevant and leading edge programs including curriculum instruction assessment, restructuring your school, improving student performance and gifted at-risk students. Ten monthly sessions of each program are available,with monthly feedback to follow-up. Accelerates restructuring efforts and also offers graduate credit.

3712 Standards and Accountability: Their Impact on Teaching and Assessment
Harvard Graduate School of Education
Programs in Professional Education
339 Gutman Library
Cambridge, MA 02138

617-495-3572
800-545-1849
Fax: 617-496-8051
E-mail: ppe@harvard.edu
http://www.gse.harvard.edu/~ppe

Examines educational and policy issues by new approaches to standards, assessment, and accountability. Focuses on issues of excellence and equity, aligning assessments with standards, strengthening professional development, impacts ofchallenges on school communities, and political and legal issues surrounding standards and forms of accountability. Designed for public school leaders whose responsibilities include evaluation and testing.

July

Tracy Ryder, Program Assistant

3713 Storytelling for Educational Enrichment The Magic of Storytelling
2709 Oak Haven Drive
San Marcos, TX 78666-5065

512-392-0669
800-322-3199
Fax: 512-392-9660
E-mail: krieger@corridor.net

Teacher in-service and training in storytelling and puppetry for teachers of Pre-K through third grades. The Magic of Storytelling is for all ages and levels, specializing in original stories of enlightenment and environmentaleducation. Over ten years experiences with many national and regional conferences and training.

Cherie Krieger, President

3714 Summer Institute in Siena
University of Siena-S/American Universities
Music Director
595 Prospect Road
Waterbury, CT 06706

203-754-5741
Fax: 203-753-8105
http://www.sienamusic.org

Programs offered in cooperation with the University of Siena-S and American Universities and Colleges. The program in Siena Italy is open to qualified graduates, undergraduates, professionals, teachers, 19 years of age or above. Special diploma; credit or non-credit; in-service credit; auditions; trips to Rome, Florence, Assisi, Venice, Pisa, three days in Switzerland; a Puccini Opera.

3715 Summer Programs for School Teams
National Association of Elementary School Principa
1615 Duke Street
Alexandria, VA 22314-3406

703-684-3345
800-386-2377
Fax: 703-518-6281
http://www.naesp.org

Events focused on the key to exceptional instruction. Effective teaching and learning for school teams, must include the principal.

Ann R Walker, Assistant Executive Director
Herrie Hahn, Director Programs

3716 Supplemental Instruction, Supervisor Workshops
University of Missouri-Kansas City
5100 Rockhill Road
SASS 210
Kansas City, MO 64110-2499

816-235-1178
Fax: 816-235-5156
E-mail: arendaled@umkc.edu
http://www.umkc.edu/cad

Training dates in February, April, June, July, September and November.

3717 THE Institute & Knowvation

800-840-0003
http://www.thejournal.com/institute

Online courses helping educators become comfortable with technology tools, integrating technology into their classroom and delivering high quality content for their professional growth.

3718 TUV Product Service
5 Cherry Hill Drive
Danvers, MA 01923

800-TUV-0123
Fax: 978-762-7637
E-mail: info@tuvps.com
http://www.tuvglobal.com

Subjects include ISO 9000:2000, ISO 14001, SEMI, and CE Marking.

3719 Teacher Education Institute
1079 W Morse Boulivard
Winter Park, FL 32789-3751

407-629-4877
800-331-2208
Fax: 407-740-8177
E-mail: tei@tish.net

Programs and courses needed by educators and administrators.

Ken Miller, President

3720 Teachers College: Columbia University
Center for Technology & School Change
Teachers College
Box 8, 525 W 120th Street
New York, NY 10002

212-678-3773
Fax: 212-678-4048
E-mail: hb50@columbia.edu
http://www.tc.columbia.edu/~academic/ctsc

Earn an MA degree in Computing and Education or Instructional Technology in 2 or 3 July sessions in New York, plus independent study. Concentrate in: multimedia design, technology leadership and teaching and learning with technology.

Howard Budin, Contact

3721 Technology Training for Educators
Astronauts Memorial Foundation

321-452-2887
800-792-3494
Fax: 321-452-6244
http://www.amfcse.org

Microsoft NT Administration; Technology Specialist; Management of Technology; Advanced Technology Specialist.

3722 Tooling University
15700 S Waterloo Road
Cleveland, OH 44110

866-706-8665
Fax: 216-706-6601
E-mail: info@toolingu.com
http://www.toolingu.com

Offers online training for manufacturing via the website.

Gene Jones, Director Marketing

3723 Total Quality Schools Workshop
Pennsylvania State University
302F Rackley Building
University Park, PA 16802

814-843-3765
E-mail: hli@psu.edu
http://www.ed.psu.edu/ctqs/index.html

Designed for public school educators at the state, national, and international level, this training program provides information in the philosophy, tools, and techniques of total quality management in education. The three day-six weekprogram focuses on leadership, reform models, and education decision making.

William Hartman, Director

3724 University of Arkansas at Little Rock
2801 S University Avenue
Little Rock, AR 72204

501-569-8222
Fax: 501-569-8206
E-mail: mdstewart@ualr.edu
http://www.ualr.edu/~autocad

Computer aided design training classes on autodesk products; autoCAD 2000, mechanical desktop R4, and inventor R2.

Mike Stewart, Contact

3725 University of Central Florida
12424 Research Parkway
Suite 264
Orlando, FL 32826-3271

407-823-4908
Fax: 407-270-4911
http://www.distrib.ucf.edu

Web-based vocational teacher education courses.

Professional Development / Workshops & Programs

3726 University of Michigan-Dearborn Center for Corporate & Professional Development
4901 Evergreen Road
CCPD-2000
Dearborn, MI 48128

313-593-5000
Fax: 313-593-5111
E-mail: sjmull@umich.edu
http://www.umich.edu

Over 230 professional development seminars, workshops, and conferences targeted for line-managers to mid- and senior-level management.

Saundra Mull, Assitant Director

3727 Wavelength
4753 N Broadway
Suite 808
Chicago, IL 60640

Fax: 773-784-1079
E-mail: winwave@aol.com
http://www.wavelengthinc.com

Humorous programs and videos cover a variety of topics including team building, motivation, diversity, mentoring, brain research and character education.

3728 Wids Learning Design System
One Foundation Circle
Waunakee, WI 53597

800-821-6313
Fax: 608-849-2468
E-mail: wids_team@wids.org
http://www.wids.org

Subjects include instructional design, developing outcomes, designing assessments and assessing standards.

3729 Workforce Education and Development Southern Illinois University Carbondale
Pulliem Hall
Carbondale, IL 62901-4603

618-453-3321
Fax: 618-453-1934
E-mail: wed@siu.edu
http://www.siu.edu/~wed01/OCDP/OCDPFrame.htm

Students majoring in workforce education and development are prepared as instructors and instructional support personnel in education, business, industry, labor, and government training organizations.

Directories & Handbooks
General

3730 A Personal Planner & Training Guide for the Substitute Teacher
Master Teacher
PO Box 1207
Manhattan, KS 66505-1207

785-539-0555
800-669-9633
Fax: 785-539-7739
http://www.masterteacher.com

Helps substitute teachers set the tone for a positive experience.

90 pages
ISBN: 0-914607-89-8
John Eller, Author

3731 A Principal's Guide to Creating and Building Climate for Inclusion
Master Teacher
PO Box 1207
Manhattan, KS 66505-1207

785-539-0555
800-669-9633
Fax: 785-539-7739
http://www.masterteacher.com

Provides an educational foundation, comprehensive presentations, and follow up activities that can be used to assist faculty members in exploring issues related to the inclusion of special needs students.

115 pages
ISBN: 6-914607-36-7
Teresa VanDover, Author

3732 Academic Year & Summer Programs Abroad
American Institute for Foreign Study
102 Greenwich Avenue
Greenwich, CT 06830-5504

203-869-9090
800-727-2437
Fax: 203-399-5590
E-mail: college.info@aifs.com
http://www.aifs.com

Offers school names, addresses, courses offered, tuition and fee information.

224 pages Annual

3733 Accredited Institutions of Postsecondary Education
MacMillan Publishing Company
1633 Broadway
New York, NY 10019

212-654-8500
Fax: 800-835-3202

Lists over 5,000 accredited institutions and programs for postsecondary education in the United States.

600 pages Annual

3734 Activities and Strategies for Connecting Kids with Kids: Elementary Edition
Master Teacher
PO Box 1207
Manhattan, KS 66505-1207

785-539-0555
800-669-9633
Fax: 785-539-7739
http://www.masterteacher.com

Activities, lesson plans, and strategies that celebrate each student's individual differences while developing cooperation, tolerance, understanding, sharing and caring.

159 pages
ISBN: 0-914607-74-X

3735 Activities and Strategies for Connecting Kids with Kids: Secondary Edition
Master Teacher
PO Box 1207
Manhattan, KS 66505-1207

785-539-0555
800-669-9633
Fax: 785-539-7739
http://www.masterteacher.com

Activities, lesson plans, and strategies that celebrate each student's individual differences while developing cooperation, tolerance, understanding, sharing and caring.

136 pages
ISBN: 0-914607-75-8

3736 American School Directory
PO Box 20002
Murfreesboro, TN 37129

866-273-2797
Fax: 800-929-3408
E-mail: asdwebmaster@asd.com
http://www.asd.com

More than 104,000 school sites are loaded with pictures, art, calendars, menus, local links and notes from students, parents and alumni. Choose the school by name, state list, or by ASD number.

3737 Amusing and Unorthodox Definitions
Careers/Consultants Consultants in Education
3050 Palm Aire Drive N
#310
Pompano Beach, FL 33069

954-974-5477
Fax: 954-974-5477
E-mail: carconed@aol.com

Collection of amusing and unorthodox definitions. The meanings, purposes and implications assigned to the words appearing here will delight audiences, enliven conversations and keep you chuckling.

ISBN: 0-7392-0089-5
ISSN: 99-94623
Dr. Robert M Bookbinder, President

3738 Associated Schools Project in Education for International Co-operation
UNESCO Associated Schools Project Network
7 Place de Fontenoy
F-75700 Paris
France

1-45681000

Lists 1,970 secondary and primary schools, teacher training institutions and nursery schools in 95 countries that participate in the UNESCO Associated School Project.

200 pages Annual

3739 Association for Community-Based Education Directory of Members
Association for Community Based Education
1805 Florida Avenue NW
Washington, DC 20009-1708
202-462-6333

Offers information on 100 private community organizations concerned with alternative education including colleges that award degrees without residency requirements and more.

115 pages Annual

3740 Authentic Jane Williams' Home School Market Guide
Bluestocking Press
PO Box 2030
Department ERD
Shingle Springs, CA 95682-2030
530-621-1123
800-959-8586
Fax: 530-642-9222

Listing of over 500 companies, publishers of books and magazines, conferences, reviewers, catalogers, seminar speakers and more who concern themselves with the home school market. Includes many indexes to help locate home schoolconferences, magazines, publishers, organizations, mailing lists, stores, consultants and more. Gives information on the size of the home school market, how much parents spend, how to locate them and get products reviewed.

Publication Date: 1996 368 pages Annually
ISBN: 0-942617-33-9
ISSN: 1080-4730

Jane A Williams, Coordinating Editor

3741 Awakening Brilliance: How to Inspire Children to Become Successful Learners
Pamela Sims & Associates
54 Mozart Crescent
Brampton, Ontario
Canada L6Y 2W7
905-455-7331
888-610-7467
Fax: 905-455-0207
E-mail: loveofkids@aol.com
http://www.pamelasims.com

Seminars and workshops for educators and parents. Upcoming workshops include themes of awakening students' potential, team leadership skills, and creativity at work.

248 pages Paperback
ISBN: 0-9651126-0-8

Pamela Sims, Author/Editor
Kelly Smith, Marketing Director

3742 Beyond the Bake Sale
Master Teacher
PO Box 1207
Manhattan, KS 66505-1207
785-539-0555
800-669-9633
Fax: 785-539-7739
http://www.masterteacher.com

A notebook containing 101 detailed plans that not only provide you with fundraising ideas, but get you started, keep you on track, and lead your team through the finishing touches.

101 pages
ISBN: 1-58992-119-4

3743 Biographical Membership Directory
American Educational Research Association
1230 17th Street NW
Washington, DC 20036-3078
202-223-9485
Fax: 202-775-1824

Membership directory of more than 23,000 persons involved in education research and development, including the names, addresses, phone numbers, highest degree held and year received, occupational specialization areas, e-mail addressesand more.

420 pages Bi-Annual
Thomas J Campbell, Director Publications

3744 CASE Directory of Advancement Professionals in Education
Council for Advancement & Support of Education
1307 New York Avenue NW
Suite 1000
Washington, DC 20005-4701
202-328-2273
Fax: 202-387-4973
E-mail: info@case.org
http://www.case.org

Membership directory of 16,000 professionals in alumni relations, communications and fund raising at educational institutions worldwide.

Publication Date: 1995 200 pages Annual
ISBN: 0-899643-10-8

Cedric Calhoun, Membership Director

3745 Cabells Directory of Publishing Opportunities in Educational Curriculum & Methods
Cabell Publishing Company
Box 5428
Tobe Hahn Station
Beaumont, TX 77726
409-898-0575
Fax: 409-866-9554
E-mail: publish@cabells.com
http://www.cabells.com

Provides information on editor's contact information, manuscript guidelines, acceptance rate, review information and circulation data for over 350 academic journals.

799 pages Annual
ISBN: 0-911753-27-3

David WE Cabell, Editor
Deborah L English, Editor

3746 Cadet Gray: Your Guide to Military Schools-Military Colleges & Cadet Programs
Reference Desk Books
PO Box 22925
Santa Barbara, CA 93121
805-772-8806

This is a comprehensive reference book which describes 55 American military schools, grade schools, high schools, junior colleges, senior colleges, and the federal service academies. Descriptions include school histories, academicrequirements, military environment, extracurricular activities and costs.

Publication Date: 1990 212 pages
ISBN: 0-962574-90-2

3747 Character Education Evaluation Tool Kit
Character Education Partnership
1025 Connecticut Avenue NW
Suite 1011
Washington, DC 20036
202-296-7743
800-988-8081

Fax: 202-296-7779
http://www.character.org

Julea Posey, Matthew Davison, Meg Korpi, Author
Andrea Grenadier, Director Communications
Esther Schaeffer, CEO/Executive Director

3748 Character Education Kit: 36 Weeks of Success: Elementary Edition
Master Teacher
PO Box 1207
Manhattan, KS 66505-1207

785-539-0555
800-669-9633
Fax: 785-539-7739
http://www.masterteacher.com

Takes the guesswork out of delivering your character education message by providing you with all the pieces of a well-rounded program including important components for 36 character traits.

428 pages
ISBN: 1-58992-096-1

3749 Chinese Universities & Colleges
Institute of International Education
809 United Nations Plaza
New York, NY 10017-3580

301-617-7804
800-455-0443
Fax: 301-206-9789
E-mail: iiebooks@pmds.com
http://www.iie.org

Profiles higher education institutions in China. Contains contact information, Chinese character equivalents to all institutional names and an alphabetical index.

3750 Choosing Your Independent School in the United Kingdom & Ireland
Independent Schools Information Service
56 Buckingham Gate
London SW1E 6AG
England

71-63087934

1,400 independent schools in the United Kingdom and Ireland with contact information, entry requirements, fees, scholarships available, subjects and exam boards.

293 pages Annual/September

3751 Classroom Teacher's Guide for Working with Paraeducators
Master Teacher
PO Box 1207
Manhattan, KS 66505-1207

785-539-0555
800-669-9633
Fax: 785-539-7739
http://www.masterteacher.com

This workbook includes numerous forms that allow teachers to communicate more effectively to paras the vital information they will need in working with special students.

60 pages
ISBN: 1-58992-127-5

Wendy Dover, Author

3752 Commonwealth Universities Yearbook
Association of Commonwealth Universities
36 Gordon Square
London WC1H 0PF
England

44-20-7380-6700
Fax: 44-20-738-2655

E-mail: info@acu.ac.uk
http://www.acu.ac.uk

Offers information on over 700 university institutions of recognized academic standing in 36 Commonwealth countries or regions, including Africa, Asia, Australia, Britain, Canada and the Pacific.

2,600 pages Annual
ISBN: 0-85143-188-7
ISSN: 0069-7745

3753 Complete Learning Disabilities Directory
Grey House Publishing
185 Millerton Road
Millerton, NY 12546

518-789-8700
800-562-2139
Fax: 518-789-0545
E-mail: books@greyhouse.com
http://www.greyhouse.com

A one-stop sourcebook for people of all ages with learning disabilities and those who work with them. This comprehensive database in print includes information about associations and organizations, schools, government agencies, testing materials, camps, books, newsletters and more.

800 pages Annual/Softcover
ISBN: 1-59237-049-7

Leslie Mackenzie, Publisher
Richard Gottlieb, Editor

3754 Computer and Web Resources for People with Disabilities
Alliance for Technology Access/Hunter House
1304 Southpoint Boulevard
Suite 240
Petaluma, CA 94954

707-778-3011
Fax: 707-765-2080
E-mail: atainfo@ataccess.org
http://www.ataccess.org

This directory shows how America's forty-five million people with disabilities can potentially benefit from using computer technology to achieve goals and change their lives. Written by experts in the field, this important work provides a comprehensive, step-by-step guide to approaching computer innovations. It explains how to identify the appropriate technology, how to seek funding, how to set it up and what to consider.

Publication Date: 1996 256 pages
Paperback/CD ROM
ISBN: 0-897931-23-8

Mary Lester, Executive Director/Editor

3755 Contemporary World Issues: Public Schooling in America
ABC-CLIO
130 Cremona Drive
#1911
Santa Barbara, CA 93117-5599

805-963-4221
800-368-6868
Fax: 805-685-9685

Offers information on organizations and agencies involved with public education systems.

3756 Cornocopia of Concise Quotations
Careers/Consultants Consultants in Education
3050 Palm Aire Drive N
#310
Pompano Beach, FL 33069

954-974-5477
Fax: 954-974-5477
E-mail: carconed@aol.com

Wealth of practical reminders of the enduring ideas. The book furthers humane understandings by gathering and preserving the wisdom of the wise and experienced.

ISBN: 0-7392-0275-8
ISSN: 99-95201

Dr. Robert M Bookbinder, President

3757   Council for Educational Development and Research Directory
National Education Association (NEA)
1201 16th Street NW
Washington, DC 20036-3290

202-833-4000
Fax: 202-822-7974
E-mail: ncuea@nea.org
http://www.nea.org

Offers 15 member educational research and development institutions.

50 pages Annual

3758   Digest of Supreme Court Decisions
Phi Delta Kappa Educational Foundation
PO Box 789
408 N Union Street
Bloomington, IN 47402-0789

812-339-1156
800-786-1156
Fax: 812-339-0018
http://www.pdkintl.org

Designed as a ready reference, this edition of a popular digest provides a concise set of individual summaries of cases decided by the Supreme Court. Fully indexed.

256 pages Paperback
ISBN: 0-87367-835-4

Perry A Zirkel, Author
George Kersey, Executive Director
Donovan R Walling, Dir Publications/Research

3759   Directory for Exceptional Children
Porter Sargent Publishers, Inc.
11 Beacon Street
Suite 1400
Boston, MA 02108-3028

617-523-1670
800-342-7470
Fax: 617-523-1021
E-mail: info@portersargent.com
http://www.portersargent.com

A comprehensive survey of 2,500 schools, facilities and organizations across the country serving children and young adults with developmental, physical and medical disabilities. With 15 distinct chapters covering a range of disabilities, this work is an invaluable aid to parents and professionals seeking the optimal environment for special-needs children. Hardcover.

Publication Date: 1994 1152 pages BiAnnual
ISBN: 0-875581-41-2

J Yonce, General Manager
Daniel McKeever, Sr Editor

3760   Directory of Catholic Schools & Colleges in the UK
State Mutual Book & Periodical Service
521 5th Avenue
Floor 17
New York, NY 10175-1799

718-261-1704
Fax: 631-537-0412

Offers information on the current superintendents, enrollments, cost and fees.

Publication Date: 1990 120 pages

3761   Directory of Catholic Special Educational Programs & Facilities
National Catholic Educational Association
1077 30th Street NW
Suite 100
Washington, DC 20007-3829

202-337-6232
Fax: 202-333-6706

Lists approximately 950 Catholic schools and day and residential school programs for children and adolescents with special education needs.

Publication Date: 1989 100 pages

3762   Directory of Central Agencies for Jewish Education
Jewish Education Service of North America
111 8th Avenue
Suite 11E
New York, NY 10011

212-284-6950
Fax: 212-284-6951
E-mail: info@jesna.org
http://www.jesna.org

Offers educational resources in Israel, including general education information, materials and services.

3763   Directory of College Cooperative Education Programs
National Commission for Cooperative Education
360 Huntington Avenue
#384CP
Boston, MA 02115-5096

617-373-3770
Fax: 617-373-3463
E-mail: ncce@neu.edu
http://www.co-op.edu

A publication providing detailed information on cooperative education programs at 460 colleges throughout the United States.

Publication Date: 1962 219 pages
ISBN: 0-89774-998-4

Polly Hutcheson, VP
Paul Stonely, President

3764   Directory of ERIC Information Service Providers
Educational Resources Information Ctr./Access ERIC
1600 Research Boulevard
Rockville, MD 20850-3172

301-656-9723

Offers information on more than 1,000 government agencies, nonprofit and profit organizations, individuals and foreign organizations that provide access to ERIC microfiche collections, search services and abstract journal collections.

100 pages Biennial

3765   Directory of Graduate Programs
Graduate Record Examinations Program/ ETS
PO Box 6014
Princeton, NJ 08541-6014

609-951-1542

Accredited institutions that offer graduate degrees.

1,400 pages 4 Volumes

3766   Directory of Indigenous Education
Floyd Beller - Wested
730 Harrison Street
San Francisco, CA 94107

415-565-3000
877-4we-sted
Fax: 415-565-3012

E-mail: fbeller@WestEd.org
http://www.wested.org

This revised and expanded edition incorporates a wider scope of information, including a list of Head Start, Child Care and Title IX programs and JOM contractors, which enhances our principal goal of improving educational services tonative students and communities.

Publication Date: 1998   94 pages

Floyd Beller, Research Associate

3767 Directory of International Internships: A World of Opportunities
International Studies & Programs

209 International Center
Michigan State University
East Lansing, MI 48824-1035

517-353-5589
Fax: 517-353-7254
E-mail: gliozzo@msu.edu
http://www.isp.msu.edu

A directory containing information about a wide range of overseas internship oppotunities. Over 500 entries of international internships sponsored by educational institutions, government agencies, and private organizations. There areindexes of topics in geographical areas listed by countries and geographical areas listed by topic.

Charles Gliozzo

3768 Directory of Member Institutions and Institutional Representatives
Council of Graduate Schools

1 Dupont Circle NW
Suite 430
Washington, DC 20036-1136

202-223-3791
Fax: 202-331-7157

Offers listings of over 400 member graduate schools in the US and Canada.

85 pages Annually

Nancy A Goffney, Administrator/Editor
Kathy Baker, Assistant

3769 Directory of Overseas Educational Advising Centers
College Board Publications

45 Columbus Avenue
New York, NY 10023-6917

212-713-8165
800-323-7155
Fax: 800-525-5562
http://www.collegeboard.org

This directory has been developed as a means through which institutions of higher education can communicate directly with overseas education advisers and through which advisers can communicate more directly with each other.

Publication Date: 1995   165 pages

3770 Directory of Postsecondary Institutions
National Center for Education Statistics

K Street NW
Washington, DC 20006

202-502-7300
877-4ED-PUBS
Fax: 301-470-1244
E-mail: edpubs@inet.ed.gov
http://www.ed.pubs/

Postsecondary institutions in the US, Puerto Rico, Virgin Islands and territories in the Pacific United States. Two volumes: Volume I Degree-Granting Institutions, Volume II Non-Degree-Granting Institutions.

Publication Date: 1990   500 pages Biennial

3771 Directory of Public School Systems in the United States
American Association for Employment in Education

3040 Riverside Drive
Suite 125
Columbus, OH 43221

614-485-1111
Fax: 614-485-9609
E-mail: aaee@osu.edu
http://www.aaee.org

Lists 15,000 public school systems in the United States, their administrative personnel and size/type of district.

212 pages Bi-Annually

BJ Bryant, Executive Director

3772 Directory of Resources & Exchange Programs
ERIC Document Reproduction Service

7420 Fullerton Road
Suite 110
Springfield, VA 22153-2852

703-440-1400
800-443-3742
Fax: 703-440-1408
E-mail: service@erds.com
http://www.erds.com

A directory of organizations that sponsor international cultural and educational exchange programs. Includes name, address, phone number of the organization and description.

130 pages

3773 Directory of Youth Exchange Programs
UN Educational, Scientific & Cultural Association

Youth Division, 1 Rue Miollis
Paris F-75015
France

1-4563842

Offers about 370 nonprofit organizations and governmental agencies in 95 countries that organize youth and student exchanges, study tours and correspondence exchanges.

Publication Date: 1992   225 pages

3774 Diversity, Accessibility and Quality
College Board Publications

45 Columbus Avenue
New York, NY 10023-6917

212-713-8165
800-323-7155
Fax: 800-525-5562
http://www.collegeboard.org

Primarily for non-Americans, this overview is designed to examine aspects of US education that have particular importance in programs of student exchange.

Publication Date: 1995   47 pages
ISBN: 0-874474-24-8

Clifford F Sjogren, Author

3775 Education Sourcebook: Basic Information about National Education Expectations and Goals
Omnigraphics

615 Griswold Street
Detroit, MI 48226

313-961-1340
800-234-1340
Fax: 313-961-1383
E-mail: info@omnigraphics.com
http://www.omnigraphics.com

A collection of education-related documents and articles for parents and students.

1123 pages
ISBN: 0-7808-0179-2

Jeanne Gough, Author
Paul Rogers, Publicity Associate

3776 Educational Placement Sources-Abroad
Education Information Services/Instant Alert
PO Box 620662
Newton, MA 02462-0662

617-433-0125

Lists 150 organizations, arranged by type, in the United States and abroad that place English-speaking teachers and education administrators in positions abroad.

19 pages Annual

FB Viaux, President

3777 Educational Rankings Annual
Gale Group
27500 Drake Road
Farmington Hills, MI 48331-3535

248-699-GALE
800-414-5043
Fax: 248-699-8069
E-mail: galeord@galegroup.com
http://www.galegroup.com

Top 10 lists from popular and scholarly periodicals, government publications, and others. The lists cover all facets of education.

890 pages Annual Hardcover
ISBN: 0-7876-7419-2

Lynn C Hattendorf Westney, Author
Kathleen Maki Petts, Coordinating Editor

3778 Educational Resources Catalog
CDE Press
PO Box 271
Sacramento, CA 95812-0271

916-445-1260
800-995-4099
Fax: 916-323-0823
http://www.cde.ca.gov/cdepress

Resource catalog from the California Department of Education.

3779 Educator's Desk Reference: A Sourcebook of Educational Information & Research
MacMillan Publishing Company
1633 Broadway
New York, NY 10019

212-654-8500
Fax: 800-835-3202

Directory includes national and regional education organizations.

Publication Date: 1989

3780 Educator's Scrapbook
Careers/Consultants Consultants in Education
3050 Palm Aire Drive N
#310
Pompano Beach, FL 33069

954-974-5477
Fax: 954-974-5477
E-mail: carconed@aol.com

Collection of education morsels offered to those who who would seek to redefine and clarify the aims and purposes of today's education. The book attepts to help

its readers refocus upon the real purposes of education and theirrelationships to current education practices.

ISBN: 0-9703623-0-7
ISSN: 00-93185

Dr. Robert M Bookbinder, President

3781 Educators Guide to FREE Computer Materials and Internet Resources
Educators Progress Service
214 Center Street
Randolph, WI 53956-1408

920-326-3126
888-951-4469
Fax: 920-326-3127
E-mail: epsinc@centurytel.net
http://www.freeteachingaids.com

Lists and describes almost 2000 web sites of educational value. Available in two grade specific editions.

317 pages Annual
ISBN: 87708-362-2

Kathy Nehmer, President

3782 Educators Guide to FREE Films, Filmstrips and Slides
Educators Progress Service
214 Center Street
Randolph, WI 53956-1408

920-326-3126
888-951-4469
Fax: 920-326-3127
E-mail: epsinc@centurytel.net
http://www.freeteachingaids.com

Lists and describes free and free-loan films, filmstrips, slides, and audiotapes for all age levels.

135 pages Annual
ISBN: 87708-400-9

Kathy Nehmer, President

3783 Educators Guide to FREE Multicultural Material
Educators Progress Service
214 Center Street
Randolph, WI 53956-1408

920-326-3126
888-951-4469
Fax: 920-326-3127
E-mail: epsinc@centurytel.net
http://www.freeteachingaids.com

Lists and describes FREE films, videotapes, filmstrips, slides, web sites, and hundreds of free printed materials in the field of multicultural and diversity education for all age levels.

198 pages Annual
ISBN: 87708-412-2

Kathy Nehmer, President

3784 El-Hi Textbooks and Serials in Print
RR Bowker Reed Reference
121 Chanlon Road
New Providence, NJ 07974-1541

908-464-6800
Fax: 908-665-6688

Listing of about 995 publishers of elementary and secondary level textbooks and related teaching materials.

Annual

3785 Exceptional Children Education Resources
The Council for Exceptional Children
110 N Glebe Road
Suite 300
Arlington, VA 22201-5704
703-620-3660
800-232-7323
Fax: 703-264-9494
E-mail: cec@cec.sped.org
http://www.cec.sped.org/bk/catalog/journals.htm

A proprietary database that includes bibliographic data and abstract information on journal articles, and audiovisual materials in special education, and gifted education.

ISSN: 0160-4309

3786 Family Services Report
CD Publictions
8204 Fenton Street
Sliver Spring, MD 20910
301-588-6380
301-666-6380
Fax: 301-588-0519
E-mail: fsr@cdpublications.com
http://cdpublications.com

Private grants for family service programs

18 pages
ISSN: 1524-9484

Ray Sweeney, Editor

3787 Fifty State Educational Directories
Career Guidance Foundation
8090 Engineer Road
San Diego, CA 92111-1906
619-560-8051

A collection on microfiche consisting of reproductions of the state educational directories published by each individual state department of education.

3788 Funny School Excuses
Careers/Consultants Consultants in Education
3050 Palm Aire Drive N
#310
Pompano Beach, FL 33069
954-974-5477
Fax: 954-974-5477
E-mail: carconed@aol.com

Collection of illustrations, cartoons and excuses gathered from authentic notes written by parents and sometimes their children. The book is wonderfully entertaining and recommended for its unusual humor, variety, and revelations of human nature.

ISBN: 0-7392-0309-6
ISSN: 99-95349

Dr. Robert M Bookbinder, President

3789 Ganley's Catholic Schools in America
Fisher Publishing Company
PO Box 15070
Scottsdale, AZ 85267-5070
800-759-7615
Fax: 480-657-9422
E-mail: publisher@ganleyscatholicschools.com
http://www.ganleyscatholicschool.com

Comprehensive listings on all Catholic Schools in America. Listings include phone numbers, addresses, names of administrators, number of students, complete diocesan, state, regional and national statistics. Includes an extensiveanalysis of demographic trends within

Catholic elementary and secondary education, prepared by the National Catholic Education Association.

450+ pages Annual/June
ISBN: 1-558331-59-0

Millard T Fischer, Publisher

3790 Graduate & Undergraduate Programs & Courses in Middle East Studies in the US, Canada
Middle East Studies Association of North America
University of Arizona
1643 E Helen Street
Tucson, AZ 85721
520-621-5850
Fax: 520-626-9095
E-mail: mesana@u.arizona.edu
http://www.acls.org

3791 Guide to International Exchange, Community Service & Travel for Persons with Disabilities
Mobility International USA
45 W Broadway Suite 202
PO Box 10767
Eugene, OR 97401
541-343-1284
Fax: 541-343-6812
E-mail: info@miusa.org
http://www.miusa.org

This directory lists an impressive array of information regarding international study, living, travel, funding and contact organizations for people with disabilities.

Publication Date: 1997
ISBN: 1-880034-24-7

Christa Bucks, Editor

3792 Guide to Schools and Departments of Religion and Seminaries
MacMillan Publishing Company
1633 Broadway
New York, NY 10019
800-858-7674
Fax: 201-767-5029

Over 700 accredited programs and institutions granting degrees in theology, divinity and religion.

3793 Guide to Summer Camps & Schools
Porter Sargent Publishers
11 Beacon Street
Suite 1400
Boston, MA 02108-3028
617-523-1670
800-342-7470
Fax: 617-523-1021
E-mail: info@portersargent.com
http://www.portersargent.com

Covers the broad spectrum of recreational and educational summer opportunities. Current facts from 1,500 camps and schools, as well as programs for those with special needs or learning disabilities, makes the guide a comprehensive andconvenient resource.

816 pages Biannual
ISBN: 0-875581-33-1

HJ Lane Coordinating Editor, Author
J Yonce, General Manager
Daniel McKeever, Sr Editor

3794 Guidelines for Effective Character Education Through Sports
Character Education Partnership
1025 Connecticut Avenue NW
Suite 1011
Washington, DC 20036
202-296-7743
800-988-8081

Fax: 202-296-7779
http://www.character.org

Guidelines for turning sports and physical education programs into the powerful, positive forces they should be.

Andrea Grenadier, Director Communications
Esther Schaeffer, CEO/Executive Director

3795 Handbook of Private Schools
Porter Sargent Publishers
11 Beacon Street
Suite 1400
Boston, MA 02108-3028

617-523-1670
800-342-7470
Fax: 617-523-1021
E-mail: info@portersargent.com
http://www.portersargent.com

Continuing a tradition that began in 1915, this handbook provides optimal guidance in the choice of educational environments and opportunities for students. Totally revised and updated, this 83rd edition presents current facts on1,700 elementary and secondary boarding and day schools across the United States. Complete statistical data on enrollments, tuition, graduates, administrators and faculty have been compiled and objectively reported. Hardcover.

1472 pages Annual
ISBN: 0-875581-44-7

J Yonce, General Manager
Daniel McKeever, Sr Editor

3796 Handbook of United Methodist-Related Schools,
Colleges, Universities & Theological Schools
General Board of Higher Education &
Ministry/UMC
1001 19th Avenue
PO Box 340007
Nashville, TN 37203-0007

615-340-7406
Fax: 615-340-7379
E-mail: scu@gbhem.org
http://www.gbhem.org/highed.html

Includes two pages of information about each of United Methodist's 123 institutions, a chart indicating major areas of study, information about United Methodist loan and scholarship programs, as well as information about how to selecta college. Published every four years.

344 pages Paperback

Dr. James A Noseworthy, Assistant General Secretary

3797 Hidden America
Place in the Woods
3900 Glenwood Avenue
Golden Valley, MN 55422-5302

763-374-2120
Fax: 952-593-5593
E-mail: placewoods@aol.com

Set of five reference-essay books on American minorities (African America; Hispanic America, the People (Native Americans); American women; My Own Book! classroom reference for elementary through secondary).

36+ pages Paperback Book

Roger Hammer, Publisher

3798 Higher Education Directory
Higher Education Publications
6400 Arlington Boulevard
Suite 648
Falls Church, VA 22042-2342

703-532-2300
888-349-7915
Fax: 703-532-2305

E-mail: info@hepinc.com
http://www.hepinc.com

Lists over 4,364 degree granting colleges and universities accredited by approved agencies, recognized by the US Secretary of Education successor to the Department of Education's: Education Directory, Colleges and Universities andCouncil for Higher Education Accreditation (CHEA).

Publication Date: 1994   1,040 pages
Annual/Paperback
ISBN: 0-914927-44-2
ISSN: 0736-0197

Jeanne Burke, Editor
Fred Hafner JR, Vice President Operations

3799 Higher Education Opportunities for Women &
Minorities: Annotated Selections
U.S. Office of Postsecondary Education
400 Maryland Avenue SW
Room 3915
Washington, DC 20202-0001

202-708-9180

Programs of public and private organizations and state and federal government agencies that offer loans, scholarships and fellowship opportunities for women and minorities.

143 pages Biennial

3800 Home from Home (Educational Exchange
Programs)
Central Bureau for Educational Visits & Exchanges
10 Spring Gardens
London, SW1A 2BN, England

171-389-4004
Fax: 171-389-4426

150 organizations and agencies worldwide that arrange stays with families for paying guests or on an exchange basis. Organizations are geographically listed including a description of program, costs, insurance information, overseasrepresentation and language instruction.

216 pages

3801 Homeschooler's Guide to FREE Teaching Aids
Educators Progress Service
214 Center Street
Randolph, WI 53956-1408

920-326-3126
888-951-4469
Fax: 920-326-3127
E-mail: epsinc@centurytel.net
http://www.freeteachingaids.com

Lists and describes free print materials specifically available to homeschoolers with students of all age levels.

277 pages
ISBN: 87708-375-4

Kathy Nehmer, President

3802 Homeschooler's Guide to FREE Videotapes
Educators Progress Service
214 Center Street
Randolph, WI 53956-1408

920-326-3126
888-951-4469
Fax: 920-326-3127
E-mail: epsinc@centurytel.net
http://www.freeteachingaids.com

Lists and describes free and free-loan videotapes specifically available to homeschoolers with students of all age levels.

248 pages Annual
ISBN: 87708-411-4

Kathy Nehmer, President

3803 IIE Academic Year Abroad
Institute of International Education
809 United Nations Plaza
New York, NY 10017-3503

412-741-0930
Fax: 212-984-5496
E-mail: iiebooks@abdintl.com
http://www.iiebooks.org

Over 3,100 undergraduate and graduate study-abroad programs conducted worldwide during the academic year by United States and foreign colleges, universities, and private organizations.

Publication Date: 1994 540 pages Annual
ISBN: 87206-279-1

Marie O'Sullivan, Author
Daniel Obst, Sr Editor

3804 ISS Directory of Overseas Schools
International Schools Services
15 Roszel Road
PO Box 5910
Princeton, NJ 08540-6729

609-452-0990
Fax: 609-452-2690
E-mail: jlarsson@iss.edu
http://www.iss.edu

The only comprehensive guide to American and international schools around the world. The Directory is carefully researched and compiled to include current and complete information on over 600 international schools.

590 pages Paperback
ISBN: 0-913663-13-1

Jane Larsson, Director Of Education

3805 Inclusion Guide for Handling Chronically
Disruptive Behavior
Master Teacher
PO Box 1207
Manhattan, KS 66505-1207

785-539-0555
800-669-9633
Fax: 785-539-7739
http://www.masterteacher.com

A comprehensive process for ensuring that no disruptive behavior is tolerated, no student is turned away, and all students are served.

150 pages
ISBN: 0-914607-40-5

Teresa VanDover, Author

3806 Incorporating Multiple Intelligences into the
Curriculum and into the Classroom: Elementary
Master Teacher
PO Box 1207
Manhattan, KS 66505-1207

785-539-0555
800-669-9633
Fax: 785-539-7739
http://www.masterteacher.com

Contains lesson plans and teaching methods that address the needs of students and help them identify their strengths according to the domains of multiple intelligences.

181 pages
ISBN: 0-914607-63-4

3807 Incorporating Multiple Intelligences into the
Curriculum and into the Classroom: Secondary
Master Teacher
PO Box 1207
Manhattan, KS 66505-1207

785-539-0555
800-669-9633
Fax: 785-539-7739
http://www.masterteacher.com

Contains lesson plans and teaching methods that address the needs of students and help them identify their strengths according to the domains of multiple intelligences.

147 pages
ISBN: 0-914607-64-2

3808 Independent Schools Association of the
Southwest-Membership List
Independent Schools Association of the Southwest
PO Box 52297
Tulsa, OK 74152-0297

817-569-9200
Fax: 817-569-9103

A geographical index of 65 independent elementary and secondary schools accredited by the association.

5 pages Annual/August

Richard W Ekdahl, Coordinating Education

3809 Independent Study Catalog
Peterson's Guides
PO Box 2123
Princeton, NJ 08543-2123

800-338-3282
Fax: 609-896-4531

A comprehensive listing of over 10,000 correspondence course offerings at 100 accredited colleges and universities nationwide, for those seeking the flexibility and convenience of at-home study.

293 pages
ISBN: 1-560794-60-7

3810 Industry Reference Handbooks
Gale Group
27500 Drake Road
Farmington Hills, MI 48331

248-699-4253
Fax: 248-699-8064
http://www.galegroup.com

Brings together and supplements Gale and D&B data on specific industries for reference use in public and academic libraries.

Hardcover
ISBN: 0787639567

Alen W Paschal, President

3811 International Federation of Organizations for
School Correspondence/Exchange
FIOCES
29, rue d'ulm, F-75230 Paris
F-75230 Paris
France

Publications / Directories & Handbooks

Governmental agencies and other organizations concerned with scholastic correspondence and student exchange programs.

Publication Date: 1991   3 pages

3812   International Schools Directory
European Council of International Schools
21B Lavant Street, Petersfield,
Hampshire GU3 23EL
United Kingdom

1730-268244
Fax: 1730-267914
E-mail: 100412.242@compuserve.com

Over 420 ECIS schools in more than 90 countries; 300 affiliated colleges and universities worldwide; educational publishers and equipment suppliers.

550 pages   Annual

JS Henleu, Coordinating Education

3813   International Study Telecom Directory
WorldWide Classroom
PO Box 1166
Milwaukee, WI 53201-1166

414-224-3476
Fax: 414-224-3466
E-mail: info@worldwide.edu
http://www.worldwide.edu

Comprehensive directory for locating educational resources both internationally and throughout the US Provides contact information on educational institutions including address, phone, fax, e-mail and URL. New icon system offersadditional information on the type of programs offered. Resource guide at beginning includes useful web sites, airline and car rental contact numbers, currency converters, international organizations and international publications.

Mike Witley, President
Stacy Hargarten, Classroom Publications

3814   International Who's Who in Education
International Biographical Centre/Melrose Press
3 Regal Lane, Soham, Ely
Cambridgeshire CB7 5BA
United Kingdom

353-721091

Lists about 5,000 persons at all levels of teaching and educational administration.

1,000 pages

3815   International Workcamp Directory
Volunteers for Peace
1034 Tiffany Road
Belmont, VT 05730

802-259-2759
Fax: 802-259-2922
E-mail: vfp@vfp.org
http://www.vfp.org

Comprehensive listing of over 2,200 workcamps in 80 countries around the world. Organized by country.

289 pages   Annual
ISBN: 0-945617-20-B

Peter Coldwell, Director

3816   International Yearbook of Education: Education in the World
UN Educational, Scientific & Cultural Assn.
7, place de Fontenoy
F-75700 Paris
France

1-45681000

Describes and offers information on educational systems worldwide.

Publication Date: 1989   200 pages

3817   Legal Basics: A Handbook for Educators
Phi Delta Kappa International
408 N Union Street
PO Box 789
Bloomington, IL 47402-0789

812-339-1156
800-766-1156
Fax: 812-339-0018
http://www.pdkintl.org

Superintendents, principals, counselors, teachers, and paraprofessionals need to pay close attention to their actions in schools and classrooms because, from a legal standpoint, those settings may contain hazardous conditions. LegalBasics points out the pitfalls and how to avoid them.

Publication Date: 1998   120 pages   Paperback
ISBN: 0-8736-806-0

Evelyn B Kelly, Author
DR Walling, Dir Publications/Research

3818   Lesson Plans and Modifications for Inclusion and Collaborative Classrooms
Master Teacher
PO Box 1207
Manhattan, KS 66505-1207

785-539-0555
800-669-9633
Fax: 785-539-7739
http://www.masterteacher.com

Each modification is a complete lesson plan that gives the teacher a description of the activity and objetive the materials need and a step-by-step guide of how to carry out the learning process.

Publication Date: 0 242 pages
ISBN: 0-914607-37-5

3819   Lesson Plans for Character Education: Elementary Edition
Master Teacher
PO Box 1207
Manhattan, KS 66505-1207

785-539-0555
800-669-9633
Fax: 785-539-7739
http://www.masterteacher.com

Gives you more than 140 practical lessons developed and tested by teachers across the curriculum and in all grade levels.

207 pages
ISBN: 0-914607-53-7

3820   List of Over 70 Higher Education Association
Educational Information Services
PO Box 662
Newton Lower Falls, MA 02162

617-964-4555

Provides descriptions and contact information on associations for individuals in higher education.

3821   List of State Boards of Higher Education
Educational Information Services
PO Box 662
Newton Lower Falls, MA 02162

617-964-4555

A compilation of the boards of education for all the states in the union.

3822 List of State Community & Junior College Board Offices
Educational Information Services
PO Box 662
Newton Lower Falls, MA 02162
617-964-4555

A list of the board officers and state officers within community, junior and university institutions.

3823 MDR School Directory
Market Data Retrieval
1 Forest Parkway
Shelton, CT 06484-6216
203-926-4800
800-333-8802
Fax: 203-929-5253
E-mail: msubrizi@dnb.com

MDR's school directories provide comprehensive data on every public school district and school, Catholic and other independent schools, regional and county centers in all fifty states and the District of Columbia. Updated each year,each state directory contains current names and job titles of key decision makers, school and district addresses, phone numbers, current enrollments and much more. Also available on CD-ROM and diskette.

51 Volume Set

Mike Subrizi, Director Marketing

3824 Minority Student Guide to American Colleges
Paoli Publishing
1708 E Lancaster Avenue
Suite 287
Paoli, PA 19301-1553
215-640-9889

Covers colleges, military schools, and financial aid information for minority students.

89 pages

3825 NAFSA's Guide to Education Abroad for Advisers & Administrators
NAFSA: Association of International Educators
1307 New York Avenue NW
8th Floor
Washington, DC 20005-4701
202-737-3699
800-836-4994
Fax: 202-737-3657
E-mail: inbox@nafsa.org
http://www.nafsa.org

Marlene M Johnson, Director/CEO

3826 NEA Almanac of Higher Education
National Education Association (NEA)
1201 16th Street NW
Washington, DC 20036-3207
202-833-4000
Fax: 202-822-7624
E-mail: nche@nea.org
http://www.nea.org

Annually
ISSN: 0743-670X

Con Lehane, Author

3827 National Association for Women in Education Directory
1325 18th Street NW
Suite 210
Washington, DC 20036-6502
202-376-1038
Fax: 202-457-0946

2,000 American and foreign members listed alphabetically including all contact information, education, position and committee membership.

Annual

3828 National Directory of Children, Youth & Families Services
14 Inverness Drive E
Suite D-144
Englewood, CO 80112
800-343-6681
Fax: 800-845-6452

Social/human services, health/mental health services, juvenile justice agencies, state by state educational departments, treatment centers, hospitals, interstate compact, child protectional services CASA's and advocacy and territorialagencies.

Publication Date: 0

3829 National Guide to Educational Credit for Training Programs
American Council on Education
1 Dupont Circle NW
Suite 535
Washington, DC 20036-1110
202-939-9430
Fax: 202-833-4762

More than 4,500 courses offered by over 280 government agencies, business firms and nonprofit groups.

1,018 pages Annual

3830 National Reference Directory of Year-Round Education Programs
National Association for Year-Round Education
PO Box 711386
San Diego, CA 92171-1386
619-276-5296
Fax: 858-571-5754
E-mail: info@nayre.org
http://www.nayre.org

Six hundred fifty school districts in the US with year-round programs are covered in this directory, listed by geographical location, including all contact information and descriptions.

178 pages Annual Paperback

Shirley Jennings, Directory Editor
Samuel Pepper, Executive Director

3831 National Schools of Character: Best Practices and New Perspectives
Character Education Partnership
1025 Connecticut Avenue NW
Suite 1011
Washington, DC 20036
202-296-7743
800-988-8081
Fax: 202-296-7779
http://www.character.org

Andrea Grenadier, Director Communications
Esther Schaeffer, CEO/Executive Director

3832 National Schools of Character: Practices to Adopt & Adapt
Character Education Partnership
1025 Connecticut Avenue NW
Suite 1011
Washington, DC 20036
202-296-7743
800-988-8081
Fax: 202-296-7779
http://www.character.org

Andrea Grenadier, Director Communications
Esther Schaeffer, CEO/Executive Director

3833 National Society for Experiential Education
515 King Street
Suite 420
Alexandria, VA 22314

703-706-9552
Fax: 703-684-6048
E-mail: info@nsee.org
http://www.nsee.org

28 pages Quarterly

Linda Goff, Author

3834 New England Association of Schools and Colleges
New England Association of Schools and Colleges
209 Burlington Road
Bedford, MA 01730-1433

781-271-0022
Fax: 781-271-0950

Listing of over 1,575 institutions of higher education, public and independent schools and vocational-technical schools in New England.

65 pages Annual

3835 One Hundred Ways Parents Can Help Students Achieve
American Association of School Administrators
801 N Quincy Street
Arlington, VA 22203-1730

703-528-0700
888-782-2272
Fax: 703-841-1543
http://www.aasa.org

Provides parents with useful information about the importance of parental involvement, concrete ways to work with children and schools to promote success, and a list of resources for further reading.

3836 Overseas American-Sponsored Elementary and Secondary Schools
US Department of State, Office Overseas Schools
Room 245, SA-29
Washington, DC 20522

202-647-4000
Fax: 202-261-8224

Lists nearly 180 independent schools overseas and 10 regional associations of schools.

30 pages Annual

3837 Paradigm Lost: Reclaiming America's Educational Future
American Association of School Administrators
1801 N Moore Street
Arlington, VA 22209-1813

703-875-0759
888-782-2272
Fax: 703-841-1543
http://www.aasa.org

Explores the beliefs and assumptions upon which schools operate, provides powerful and practical insights and improvement strategies.

158 pages Softcover
ISBN: 0-87652-230-0

William G Spady, Editor

3838 Patterson's American Education
Educational Directories
PO Box 199
6828 W 171st Street
Mount Prospect, IL 60056-0199

847-459-0605
800-357-6183
Fax: 847-891-0945

Lists more than 11,000 public school districts; 300 parochial superintendents; 400 territorial schools; 400 state department of education personnel; and 400 educational associations in one easy to use consistent format. Arrangedalphabetically by state then by city. City listings include the city name, telephone area code, city population, county name, public school district name, enrollment, grade range, superintendent's name, address and phone number. Index of secondaryschools included.

Publication Date: 1994 850 pages Annual
ISBN: 0-910536-58-9

Douglas Moody, Coordinating Education

3839 Patterson's Schools Classified
Educational Directories
PO Box 199
Mount Prospect, IL 60056-0199

847-459-0605
Fax: 847-459-0608

Contains 7,000 accredited postsecondary schools, the broadest assortment available in a single directory. Universities, colleges, community colleges, junior colleges, career schools and teaching hospitals are co-mingled under 50academic disciplines but retain their school type identification. School professional accreditation is shown in 32 classifications. The basic entry includes school name, mailing address and contact person, with additional descriptive materialsupplied by the school.

Publication Date: 1993 314 pages Annual
ISBN: 0-910536-60-0

Wayne Moody, Coordinating Education

3840 Persons as Resources
World Council for Curriculum & Instruction
School of Education
Indiana University
Bloomington, IN 47405

812-336-4702
Fax: 812-856-8088

Listing of about 600 member individuals and institutions concerned with curriculum and instruction in schools, colleges, universities and non-school agencies.

75 pages Triennial

3841 Peterson's Competitive Colleges
Peterson's Guides
PO Box 2123
Princeton, NJ 08543-2123

609-243-9111
800-338-3282
Fax: 609-243-9150

The most trusted source of advice for excellent students searching for high-quality schools. Provides objective criteria to compare more than 350 leading colleges and universities.

432 pages
ISBN: 1-560795-98-0

3842 Peterson's Guide to Four-Year Colleges
Peterson's Guides
PO Box 2123
Princeton, NJ 08543-2123

609-896-1800
800-338-3282
Fax: 609-896-1811

Includes descriptions of over 2,000 colleges, providing guidance on selecting the right school, getting in and financial aid.

3,000 pages

3843 Peterson's Guide to Two-Year Colleges
Peterson's Guides
PO Box 2123
Princeton, NJ 08543-2123
609-243-9111
800-338-3282
Fax: 609-243-9150

The only two-year college guide available, this new and expanded directory is the most complete source of information on institutions that grant an associate as their highest degree.

752 pages
ISBN: 1-560796-05-7

3844 Peterson's Regional College Guides
Peterson's Guides
PO Box 2123
Princeton, NJ 08543-2123
609-243-9111
800-338-3282
Fax: 609-243-9150

Six individual regional guides that help students compare colleges in a specific geographic area.

3845 Power of Public Engagement Book Set
Master Teacher
PO Box 1207
Manhattan, KS 66505-1207
785-539-0555
800-669-9633
Fax: 785-539-7739
http://www.masterteacher.com

Learn how to engage your community to make the changes needed to ensure the best education for its children.

ISBN: 1-58992-128-3

William G O'Callaghan Jr, Author

3846 Private Independent Schools
Bunting & Lyon
238 N Main Street
Wallingford, CT 06492-3728
203-269-3333
Fax: 203-269-5697
E-mail: BuntingandLyon@aol.com
http://www.buntingandlyon.com

Provides information on more than 1,100 elementary and secondary private schools and summer programs in the United States and abroad. This annual guide, now in its 56th edition, is the most concise, current resource available onprivate school programs.

Publication Date: 1996 644 pages Annual
Hardcover
ISBN: 0-913094-56-0
ISSN: 0079-5399

Peter G Bunting, Publisher

3847 Private School Law in America
Oakstone Publishing
PO Box 381687
Birmingham, AL 35238-1687
205-437-9515
800-365-4900
Fax: 205-995-4651

An up-to-date compilation of summarized federal and state appellate court decisions which affect private education. The full legal citation is supplied for each case. A brief introductory note on the American judicial system isprovided along with updated appendices of recent US Supreme Court cases and recently published law review articles. Also included are portions of the US

Constitution which are most frequently cited in private education cases.

Publication Date: 1996 500 pages Annually
ISBN: 0-939675-80-3

3848 Public Schools USA: A Comparative Guide to School Districts
Peterson's Guides
PO Box 2123
Princeton, NJ 08543-2123
609-243-9111
800-338-3282
Fax: 609-243-9150

Lists over 400 school districts in 52 metropolitan areas throughout the United States.

490 pages Annual

3849 School Foodservice Who's Who
Information Central
PO Box 3900
Prescott, AZ 86302-3900
520-778-1513

Listing of over 2,500 food service programs in public and Catholic school systems.

110 pages Triennial

3850 School Guide
School Guide Publications
210 N Avenue
New Rochelle, NY 10801-6402
914-632-7771
800-433-7771
Fax: 914-632-3412
E-mail: info@schoolguides.com
http://schoolguides.com

Listing of over 3,000 colleges, vocational schools and nursing schools in the US.

280 pages Annual/Paperback
ISBN: 1-893275-30-2

Janette Aiello, Editor

3851 Schools Abroad of Interest to Americans
Porter Sargent Publishers
11 Beacon Street
Suite 1400
Boston, MA 02108-3028
617-523-1670
800-342-7470
Fax: 617-523-1021
E-mail: info@portersargent.com
http://www.portersargent.com

Lists and authoritatively describes 800 elementary and secondary schools in 130 countries. Written for the educator, personnel advisor, student and parent as well as diplomatic and corporate officials, this unique guide is anindispensable reference for American students seeking preparatory schooling overseas. Hardcover.

Publication Date: 1991 544 pages BiAnnual

J Yonce, General Manager
Daniel McKeever, Sr Editor

3852 Schools-Business & Vocational Directory
American Business Directories
5711 S 86th Circle
Omaha, NE 68127-4146
402-593-4600
888-999-1307
Fax: 402-331-5481

A complete listing of business and vocational schools nationwide. Includes phone numbers, contact names, employee sizes and more.

Annual

Jerry Venner, Coordinating Education

3853 Treasury of Noteworthy Proverbs
Careers/Consultants Consultants in Education
3050 Palm Aire Drive N
#310
Pompano Beach, FL 33069

954-974-5477
Fax: 954-974-5477
E-mail: carconed@aol.com

Tapestry of maxims, aphorisims, and pithy sayings. A revealing picture of the wisdom, philosophy, and humor of the people of this and many other nations throughout the world.

ISBN: 0-7392-0208-1
ISSN: 99-943-75

Dr. Robert M Bookbinder, President

3854 US Supreme Court Education Cases
Oakstone Publishing
PO Box 381687
Birmingham, AL 35238-1687

205-437-9515
800-365-4900
Fax: 205-995-4651

A compilation of summarized US Supreme Court decisions since 1954 which affect education. The full legal citation is supplied for each case. Also included are portions of the US Constitution which are most frequently cited ineducation cases.

Publication Date: 1996   275 pages Annually
ISBN: 0-939675-78-1

3855 Vincent-Curtis Educational Register
Vincent-Curtis
29 Simpson Lane
Falmouth, MA 02540-2230

508-457-6473
Fax: 508-457-6499
http://www.vincentcurtis.com

Hundreds of illustrated announcements describing a variety of private boarding schools and resident summer programs in the United States, Canada and Europe, together with articles by school heads and camp directors of interest toparents of students 10-18.

Publication Date: 1994   236 pages Annual/June

Stanford B Vincent, Coordinating Education

3856 Western Association of Schools and Colleges
Western Association of Schools and Colleges
3060 Valencia Avenue
#70
Aptos, CA 95003-4126

831-688-7575

Listing of schools and colleges in California, Hawaii, Guam, American Samoa and East Asia.

130 pages Annual

3857 Whole Nonprofit Catalog
Grantmanship Center
PO Box 17720
Los Angeles, CA 90017

Offers information on training programs offered by the Center, publications and other services available to the nonprofit sector.

3858 Working Together: A Guide to Community-Based Educational Resources
Research, Advocacy & Legislation/Council of LaRaza
810 1st Street NE
Suite 300
Washington, DC 20002-4227

202-289-1380

Listing of about 30 community-based organizations nationwide providing educational services to Hispanic Americans.

35 pages

3859 World of Learning
Gale Group
27500 Drake Road
Farmington Hills, MI 48331

248-699-4253
800-877-4253
Fax: 248-699-8064
E-mail: galeord@galegroup.com
http://www.galegroup.com

Contains information for over 26,000 universities, colleges, schools of art and music, libraries, archives, learned societies, research institutes, museums and art galleries in more than 180 countries.

ISBN: 0-7876-5004-8

Allen W Paschal, President

Directories & Handbooks
Administration

3860 American Association of Collegiate Registrars & Admissions Officers
American Association of Collegiate Registrars
1 Dupont Circle NW
Suite 330
Washington, DC 20036-1137

202-293-9161
Fax: 202-872-8857

Offers more than 2,300 member institutions and 8,400 college and university registrars, financial aid information and admissions officers.

Publication Date: 1995   224 pages Annual

3861 American School & University - Who's Who Directory & Buyer's Guide
Intertec Publishing
9800 Metcalf Avenue
Overland Park, KS 66212-2286

913-967-1960
Fax: 913-967-1905

Comprehensive directory of suppliers and products for facility needs; listings of architects by region; listing of associations affiliated with the education industry; article index for quick and easy reference; in-depth calendar ofevents.

Annual

Joe Agron, Coordinating Education

3862 Bricker's International Directory
Peterson's Guides
PO Box 2123
Princeton, NJ 08543-2123

609-243-9111
800-338-3282
Fax: 609-243-9150

Offers over 400 residential management development programs at academic institutions in the United States and abroad.

600 pages Annual

3863 Cabells Directory of Publishing Opportunities in Educational Psychology and Administration
Cabell Publishing Company
Box 5428
Tobe Hahn Station
Beaumont, TX 77726

409-898-0575
Fax: 409-866-9554
E-mail: publish@cabells.com
http://www.cabells.com

Provides information on editor contact information, manuscript guidelines, acceptance rate, review information and circulation data for over 225 academic journals.

799 pages Annual
ISBN: 0-911753-28-1

David WE Cabell, Editor
Deborah L English, Associate Editor

3864 Character Education Questions & Answers
Character Education Partnership
1025 Connecticut Avenue NW
Suite 1011
Washington, DC 20036

202-296-7743
800-988-8081
Fax: 202-296-7779
http://www.character.org

Andrea Grenadier, Director Communications
Esther Schaeffer, CEO/Executive Director

3865 Character Education Resource Guide
Character Education Partnership
1025 Connecticut Avenue NW
Suite 1011
Washington, DC 20036

202-296-7743
800-988-8081
Fax: 202-296-7779
http://www.character.org

Andrea Grenadier, Director Communications
Esther Schaeffer, CEO/Executive Director

3866 Character Education: The Foundation for Teacher Education
Character Education Partnership
1025 Connecticut Avenue NW
Suite 1011
Washington, DC 20036

202-296-7743
800-988-8081
Fax: 202-296-7779
http://www.character.org

Andrea Grenadier, Director Communications
Esther Schaeffer, CEO/Executive Director

3867 Continuing Education Guide
International Association for Continuing Education
Department #3087
Washington, DC 20042-0001

202-463-2905
Fax: 202-463-8498

Explores how to interpret and use the Continuing Education Unit or other criteria used for continuing education programs. This guide, written by continuing education and training consultant, Louis Phillips, is a reference sourcecomplete with sample forms, charts, checklists and everything you need to plan, develop and evaluate your school's continuing education program.

3868 Creating High Functioning Schools : Practice and Research
Charles C Thomas, Publisher
2600 S 1st Street
Springfield, IL 62704

800-258-8980
Fax: 217-789-9130
E-mail: books@ccthomas.com
http://www.ccthomas.com

Publication Date: 1998 283 pages Paperback
ISBN: 0-98-06859-3

3869 Creating Quality Reform: Programs, Communities and Governance
Pearson Education Communications
1 Lake Street
Upper Saddle River, NJ 07458

201-236-7000
Fax: 515-284-6719

Publication Date: 2002

J Thomas Owens, Editor
Jan C Simmons, Editor

3870 Creating the Quality School
Magna Publications
2718 Dryden Drive
Madison, WI 53704

608-246-3590
Fax: 608-246-3597
http://www.magnapubs.com

Publication Date: 1995 530 pages Paperback
ISBN: 0-912150-36-X
November
1000 attendees and 10+ exhibits

David Burns, Publisher

3871 Designing & Implementing a Leadership Academy in Character Education
Character Education Partnership
1025 Connecticut Avenue NW
Suite 1011
Washington, DC 20036

202-296-7743
800-988-8081
Fax: 202-296-7779
http://www.character.org

Andrea Grenadier, Director Communications
Esther Schaeffer, CEO/Executive Director

3872 Deskbook Encyclopedia of American School Law
Oakstone Publishing
PO Box 381687
Birmingham, AL 35238-1687

205-437-9515
800-365-4900
Fax: 205-995-4651

An up-to-date compilation of summarized federal and state appellate court decisions which affect education. The full legal citation is supplied for each case with a brief introductory note on the American judicial system is providedalong with updated appendices of recent US Supreme Court cases and recently published law review articles.

Publication Date: 1996 600 pages Annually
ISBN: 0-939675-79-X

3873 Developing a Character Education Program
Character Education Partnership
1025 Connecticut Avenue NW
Suite 1011
Washington, DC 20036

202-296-7743
800-988-8081
Fax: 202-296-7779
http://www.character.org

Henry Huffman, Author
Andrea Grenadier, Director Communications
Esther Schaeffer, CEO/Executive Director

3874 Development Education: A Directory of
Non-Governmental Practitioners
U.N. Non-Governmental Liaison Service
Palais des Nations, CH 1211
Geneva 10
Switzerland

Lists about 800 national non-governmental organizations in industrialized countries and international non-governmental networks concerned with developmental education.

Publication Date: 1992   400 pages

3875 Directory of Chief Executive Officers of United
Methodist Schools, Colleges & Universities
General Board of Higher Education &
Ministry/UMC
1001 19th Avenue
PO Box 340007
Nashville, TN 37203-0007

615-340-7406
Fax: 615-340-7379
E-mail: scu@gbhem.org
http://www.gbhem.org/highed.html

123 United Methodist educational institutions including theology schools, professional schools, two year colleges and colleges and universities with all contact information arranged by institution type. Paperback.

32 pages Annual
Dr. James A Noseworthy, Assistant General Secretary

3876 Directory of Organizations in Educational
Management
ERIC Clearinghouse on Educational Management
1787 Agate Street
Eugene, OR 97403-1923

541-346-5043
800-438-8841
Fax: 541-346-2334
E-mail: sales@oregon.uoregon.edu
http://www.eric.uoregon.edu

Offers listings of 163 organizations in the field of educational management at the elementary and secondary school levels.

Dr. Philip Piele, Director
Stuart C Smith, Associate Director

3877 Directory of State Education Agencies
Council of Chief State School Officers
1 Massachusette Avenue NW
Suite 700
Washington, DC 20001-1431

202-336-7000
Fax: 202-408-8072
http://www.ccsso.org

A reference to state and national education agency contracts. Arranged state-by-state, it includes state education agency personnel titles, addresses, phone numbers, and fax numbers when applicable. National information includes keycontacts and information for 33 national education associations and 5 pages of names,

titles, addresses, and numbers for the US Department of Education.

103 pages
ISBN: 1-884037-66-6
Kathleen Neary, Editor

3878 Educating for Character
Master Teacher
PO Box 1207
Manhattan, KS 66505-1207

785-539-0555
800-669-9633
Fax: 785-539-7739
http://www.masterteacher.com

Dr. Licona has developed a 12 point program that offers practical strategies designed to create a working coalition of parents, teachers and communities.

428 pages
ISBN: 0-553-37052-9
Thomas Lickona PhD, Author

3879 Educating for Character: How Our Schools Can
Teach Respect and Responsibility
Character Education Partnership
1025 Connecticut Avenue NW
Suite 1011
Washington, DC 20036

202-296-7743
800-988-8081
Fax: 202-296-7779
http://www.character.org

Tom Likona, Author
Andrea Grenadier, Director Communications
Esther Schaeffer, CEO/Executive Director

3880 Education Budget Alert
Committee for Education Funding
122 C Street NW
Suite 280
Washington, DC 20001-2109

202-383-0083
Fax: 202-383-0097
E-mail: jchang@cef.org
http://www.cef.org

Federal programs currently help over 63 million Americans to engage in formal learning. This guidebook explains what these programs do, what types of activities are supported, the reasons the federal government initiated theseprograms, and their level at funding.

150 pages Annually
Jennifer Chang, Administrative Assistant
Michael Pons, Editor

3881 Educational Consultants Directory
American Business Directories, Inc.
5711 S 86th Circle
PO Box 27347
Omaha, NE 68127

402-593-4600
800-555-6124
Fax: 402-331-5481
E-mail: directory@abi.com

A list of more than 5,000 entries, including name, address, phone, size of advertisement, name of owner or manager and number of employees.

3882 Educational Dealer-Buyers' Guide Issue
Fahy-Williams Publishing
171 Reed Street
Geneva, NY 14456-2137

315-789-0458
Fax: 315-789-4263

List of approximately 2,000 suppliers of educational materials and equipment.

Annual

3883 Executive Summary Sets
Master Teacher
PO Box 1207
Manhattan, KS 66502

785-539-0555
800-669-9633
Fax: 785-539-7739
http://www.masterteacher.com

An easy, effective and practical way to orient new board members before they attend their first meeting. Executive Summary Sets cover the vital information board members must have in eight areas: tenets of education; powers andresponsibilities; decision making; communication for maximum results; resource management; assessment of programs; assessment of personnel and conflict resolution.

Robert DeBruyn, Editor

3884 Grants and Contracts Handbook
Association of School Business Officials Int'l
11401 N Shore Drive
Reston, VA 20190-4232

703-478-0405
Fax: 703-478-0205

This is a basic reference for grant applicants, executors, project managers, administrators and staff. The ideas are school-tested and based on information gathered from institutions and agencies over the past two decades.

32 pages
ISBN: 0-910170-52-5

Peg D Kirkpatrick, Editor/Publisher
Robert Gluck, Managing Editor

3885 Guidelines for Contracting with Private Providers for Educational Services
American Association of School Administrators
1801 N Moore Street
Arlington, VA 22209-1813

301-617-7802
888-782-2722
Fax: 301-206-9789
http://www.aasa.org

3886 Hispanic Yearbook-Anuario Hispano
TIYM Publishing
6718 Whittier Avenue
Suite 130
McLean, VA 22101

703-734-1632
Fax: 703-356-0787
E-mail: TIYM@aol.com
http://www.tiym.com

This guide lists Hispanic organizations, publications, radio and TV stations, through not specifically for grant-giving purposes.

Annually

John O Zavala, COO
Ramon Palencia, Director PR

3887 Leading to Change
Jossey-Bass Publishers
989 Market Street
San Francisco, CA 94104-1304

415-433-1740
800-956-7739
Fax: 415-433-0499
http://www.josseybass.com

The challenge of the new superintendency.

352 pages
ISBN: 0-7879-0214-4

Susan Moore Johnson, Author

3888 Legal Basics: A Handbook for Educators
Phi Delta Kappa International
PO Box 789
Bloomington, IL 47402-0789

812-339-1156
Fax: 812-339-0018
http://www.pdkintl.org

Superintendents, principals, counselors, teachers, and paraprofessionals need to pay close attention to their actions in schools and classrooms because, from a legal standpoint, those settings may contain hazardous conditions. LegalBasics points out the pitfalls and how to avoid them.

120 pages Paperback
ISBN: 8-87367-806-0

Evelyn B Kelly, Author
DR Walling, Dir Publications/Research

3889 Legal Issues and Education Technology
National School Board Association
PO Box 161
Annapolis Junction, MD 20701

800-706-6722
Fax: 703-683-7590

Helps administrators craft an acceptable-use policy.

Publication Date: 1999
ISSN: 0314510

3890 Lifeworld of Leadership
Jossey-Bass Publishers
989 Market Street
San Francisco, CA 94104-1342

415-433-1740
Fax: 415-433-0499
http://www.josseybass.com

Explores the crucial link between school improvement and school character.

Publication Date: 1999   240 pages Paperback
ISBN: 0-7879-7277-0

Thomas J Sergiovanni

3891 Looking at Schools: Instruments & Processes for School Analysis
Research for Better Schools
112 N Broad Street
Philadelphia, PA 19102

215-586-6150
Fax: 215-568-7260
http://www.rbs.org

Thirty-five institutions that offer instruments and processes to assess the performance of students, teachers and administrators, school climate effectiveness and school-community relations.

Publication Date: 1991   140 pages

Louis Maguire, Executive Co-Director

3892 Market Data Retrieval-National School Market Index
Market Data Retrieval
1 Forest Parkway
Shelton, CT 06484-0947

203-926-4800
800-333-8802

Fax: 203-929-5253
E-mail: msubrizi@dnb.com

An annual report on school spending patterns for instructional materials in the United States. The Index now in its twenty-fifth year of publication, lists the expenditures for instructional materials for all 15,000 US seniordistricts.

Publication Date: 1996
ISBN: 0-897708-25-3

Mike Subrizi, Marketing Director

3893 National Association of Principals of Schools for Girls Directory
National Association of Principals/Girls Schools
4050 Little River Road
Hendersonville, NC 28739-8317

828-693-8248
Fax: 828-693-1490

List of 575 principals and deans of private and secondary schools for girls and coeducational schools, colleges and admissions officers.

Annual

3894 National School Public Relations Association Directory
National School Public Relations Association
1501 Lee Highway
Arlington, VA 22209-1109

703-528-6713

Lists over 2,800 school system public relations directors and school administration officers.

100 pages Annual

3895 National School Supply & Equipment Association Membership/Buyers' Guide Directory
National School Supply & Equipment Association
830 Colesville Road
Suite 250
Silver Spring, MD 20910

301-495-0240
800-395-5550
Fax: 301-495-3330
E-mail: awatts@nssea.org
http://www.nssea.org

Lists 1,500 member dealers, manufacturers and manufacturers' representatives for school supplies, equipment and instructional materials.

200 pages Annual

Adrienne Watts, Author
Adrienne Watts, VP Marketing
Kathy Jentz, Director Communications

3896 National Schools of Character
Character Education Partnership
1025 Connecticut Avenue NW
Suite 1011
Washington, DC 20036

202-296-7743
800-988-8081
Fax: 202-296-7779
http://www.character.org

Andrea Grenadier, Director Communications
Esther Schaeffer, CEO/Executive Director

3897 Proactive Leadership in the 21st Century
Master Teacher
PO Box 1207
Manhattan, KS 66505-1207

785-539-0555
800-669-9633
Fax: 785-539-7739
http://www.masterteacher.com

Contain the laws and principals of leadership and people management as they had never been defined and described before giving school administrators a set of guidelines that if followed would guarantee success.

ISBN: 0-914607-44-8

Robert L DeBruyn, Author

3898 Public Relations Starter Pacs Notebook
Master Teacher
PO Box 1207
Manhattan, KS 66505-1207

785-539-0555
800-669-9633
Fax: 785-539-7739
http://www.masterteacher.com

Will give you the exact steps to follow to initiate the ideas in your own school setting.

ISBN: 1-58992-129-1

3899 QED's State School Guides
Quality Education Data
1625 Broadway Street
Suite 250
Denver, CO 80203

303-860-1832
800-525-5811
Fax: 303-209-9444
E-mail: info@qeddata.com
http://www.qeddata.com

Complete directories of every US school district and public, Catholic and private school. Directories are available for individual states, geographic regions and the entire United States. Each directory includes names of districtadministrators, school principals and school librarians, as well as addresses, phone numbers and enrollment information. QED's State school guide also includes key demographic and instructional technology data for each district and school.

Publication Date: 1993 Yearly
ISBN: 0-887476-49-0

Liz Stephens, Marketing

3900 School Promotion, Publicity & Public Relations: Nothing but Benefits
Master Teacher
PO Box 1207
Manhattan, KS 66505-1207

785-539-0555
800-669-9633
Fax: 785-539-7739
http://www.masterteacher.com

Contains the vital foundations an administrator must have to understand and implement a program of publicity, promotion and public relations, in a school or school district.

327 pages
ISBN: 0-914607-25-1

Tracey H DeBruyn, Author

3901 Schoolwide Discipline Strategies that Make a Difference in Teaching & Learning
Master Teacher
PO Box 1207
Manhattan, KS 66505-1207

785-539-0555
800-669-9633
Fax: 785-539-7739
http://www.masterteacher.com

This approach to discipline will help your school or district eliminate the dependecy on one individual, provide guidance for present and new teachers, allow disipline to become a K-12 program, an bring about consistancy in thehandling of all student misbehaviors.

150 pages
ISBN: 1-58992-000-7

Larry Dixon, Author

Directories & Handbooks
Early Childhood Education

3902 Nursery Schools & Kindergartens Directory
American Business Directories
5711 S 86th Circle
Omaha, NE 68127-4146

402-593-4600
888-999-1307
Fax: 402-331-5481

A geographical listing of 34,900 nursery schools and kindergartens including all contact information, first year in Yellow Pages and descriptions. Also available are regional editions and electronic formats.

Annual

Jerry Venner, Coordinating Education

Directories & Handbooks
Elementary Education

3903 Educational Impressions
PO Box 77
Hawthorne, NJ 07507-0077

973-423-4666
800-451-7450
Fax: 973-423-5569
E-mail: awpeller@worldnet.att.net

Educational workbooks, activity books, literature guides, and audiovisuals. Grades K-8, with emphasis on intermediate and middle grades.

Paperback/Video/Audi

Neil Peller, Marketing Director
Lori Brown, Sales/Marketing

3904 Educators Guide to FREE Videotapes-Elementary/ Middle School Edition
Educators Progress Service
214 Center Street
Randolph, WI 53956-1408

920-326-3126
888-951-4469
Fax: 920-326-3127
E-mail: epsinc@centurytel.net
http://www.freeteachingaids.com

Lists and describes free and free-loan videotapes for the elementary and middle school level.

Annual
ISBN: 0-877082-67-7

Kathy Nehmer, President

3905 Educators Guide to FREE Videotapes-Secondary Edition
Educators Progress Service
214 Center Street
Randolph, WI 53956-1408

920-326-3126
888-951-4469
Fax: 920-326-3127
E-mail: epsinc@centurytel.net
http://www.freeteachingaids.com

Lists and describes free and free-loan videotapes for the elementary and middle school level.

Annual
ISBN: 0-877082-67-7

Kathy Nehmer, President

3906 Elementary Teachers Guide to FREE Curriculum Materials
Educators Progress Service
214 Center Street
Randolph, WI 53956-1408

920-326-3126
888-951-4469
Fax: 920-326-3127
E-mail: epsinc@centurytel.net
http://www.freeteachingaids.com

Lists and describes free supplementary teaching aids for the elementary level.

Annual
ISBN: 0-877082-64-2

Kathy Nehmer, President

3907 KIDSNET Media Guide and News
KIDSNET
6856 Eastern Avenue NW
Suite 208
Washington, DC 20012

202-291-1400
Fax: 202-882-7315
E-mail: kidsnet@kidsnet.org
http://www.kidsnet.org

Contains children's television, radio and video listings. Also lists related teaching materials and copyright guidelines.

150 pages Monthly

3908 Lesson Plans for Problem-Based Learning, Elementary Edition
Master Teacher
PO Box 1207
Manhattan, KS 66505-1207

785-539-0555
800-669-9633
Fax: 785-539-7739
http://www.masterteacher.com

An instructional technique which organizes the curriculum around a major problem that students work to solve over the weeks or months.

129 pages
ISBN: 0-914607-86-3

3909 Lesson Plans, Integrating Technology into the Classroom: Elementary Edition
Master Teacher
PO Box 1207
Manhattan, KS 66505-1207

785-539-0555
800-669-9633
Fax: 785-539-7739
http://www.masterteacher.com

Gives teachers practical lessons developed and tested by teachers across the curriculum, with students of all levels of ability in using technology.

130 pages
ISBN: 0-914607-59-6

3910 Parent Involvement Facilitator: Elementary Edition
Master Teacher
PO Box 1207
Manhattan, KS 66505-1207

785-539-0555
800-669-9633
Fax: 785-539-7739
http://www.masterteacher.com

Packed with ideas for you and your teachers to implement along with the exact steps for you to follow.

169 pages
ISBN: 0-914607-45-6

3911 Patterson's Elementary Education
Educational Directories
PO Box 199
Mount Prospect, IL 60056-0199

847-459-0605
800-357-6183
Fax: 847-459-0608

A directory to more than 13,000 public school districts; 71,000 public, private and Catholic elementary and middle schools; 1,600 territorial schools; and 400 state department of education personnel in one easy to use consistentformat. Arranged alphabetically by state then city. City listings include city name, telephone area code, city population, county name, public school district name, enrollment, grade range, superintendent's name, address and phone number.

Publication Date: 1994 870 pages Annual
ISBN: 0-910536-59-7

Douglas Moody, Coordinating Education

3912 Teaching Our Youngest-A Guide for PreschoolTeachers and Child Care and Family Providers
PO Box 1398
Jessup, MD 20794-1398

877-4ED-PUBS
Fax: 301-470-1244
E-mail: edpubs@inet.ed.gov
http://www.edpubs.org

This booklet draws from scientifically based research about what can be done to help children develop their language abilities, increase their knowledge, become familiar with books and other printed materials,learn letters and sounds,recognize numbers and learn to count.

Directories & Handbooks
Employment

3913 AAEE Job Search Handbook for Educators
American Association for Employment in Education
3040 Riverside Drive
Suite 125
Columbus, OH 43221

614-485-1111
Fax: 614-485-9609
E-mail: aaee@osu.edu
http://www.aaee.org

Information for those pursuing work as educators.

72 pages Annually
BJ Bryant, Executive Director

3914 Cabell's Directory of Publishing Opportunities in Education
Cabell Publishing
Box 5428
Tobe Hahn Station
Beaumont, TX 77726-5428

409-898-0575
Fax: 409-866-9554
E-mail: publish@cabells.com
http://www.cabells.com

Includes list of more than 430 education journals that consider manuscripts for publication. Includes contact names and addresses for submitting manuscripts, topics considered, publication guidelines, fees, and circulationinformation.

1,200 pages

David WE Cabell, Editor
Deborah L English, Associate Editor

3915 Cabell's Directory of Publishing Opportunities in Accounting
Cabell Publishing Company
Box 5428
Tobe Hahn Station
Beaumont, TX 77726

409-898-0575
Fax: 409-866-9554
E-mail: publish@cabells.com
http://www.cabells.com

Contains information on 130 journal. Entries include manuscript guidelines for authors: editor's address, phone, fax and e-mail. Review process and the time required, acceptance rates, readership circulation and subscription prices.The Index classifies journals by 15 topics areas and provides information on type of review, acceptance rate and review time.

425 pages Annual
ISBN: 0-911753-13-3

David WE Cabell, Editor
Deborah L English, Editor

3916 Cabell's Directory of Publishing Opportunities in Economics & Finance
Cabell Publishing Company
Box 5428
Tobe Hahn Station
Beaumont, TX 77726-5428

409-898-0575
Fax: 409-866-9554
E-mail: publish@cabells.com
http://www.cabells.com

Contains information on 350 journals. Each journal entry includes manuscript guidelines for authors: editor's address, phone, fax and e-mail, review process and time required, acceptance rates, readership, circulation and subscriptionprices. The Index classifies journals by 15 topic areas and provides information on type of review, acceptance rate and review time.

Publication Date: 1995 1100 pages Annual
ISBN: 0-911753-14-1

David WE Cabell, Editor
Deborah L English, Associate Editor

3917 Cabells Directory of Publishing Opportunities in Management
Cabell Publishing Company
Box 5428
Tobe Hahn Station
Beaumont, TX 77726
409-898-0575
Fax: 409-866-9554
E-mail: publish@cabells.com
http://www.cabells.com

Provides editor contact information, acceptance rates, review information, manuscript guidelines and circulation data for over 540 academic journals.

Publication Date: 1973   648 pages
ISBN: 0-911753-15-X

David WE Cabell, Editor
Deborah L English, Associate Editor

3918 Career Book
VGM Career Books
4255 W Touhy Avenue
Lincolnwood, IL 60712
732-329-6991
Fax: 732-329-6994

Offers information on educational employment opportunities in America and abroad.

BiAnnual Hard/Paper

Joyce Lain Kennedy & Darryl Laramore, Author

3919 Career Development Activities for Every Classroom
University of Wisconsin-Madison
1025 W Johnson Street
Madison, WI 53706-1796
608-263-3696
800-446-0399
Fax: 608-262-9197
E-mail: cewmail@soemadison.wisc.edu
http://www.cew.wisc.edu

Four volumes containing hundreds of career development activities, and separate activity masters to duplicate. All lessons are keyed to National Career Development Guidelines Competencies and subject matter areas. Each volume isavailable individually.

3920 Career Guide to Professional Associations
Directory of Organizations
Sulzburger & Graham Publishing
165 W 91st Street
New York, NY 10024-1708
212-947-0100
800-366-7087
Fax: 212-947-0360

Lists over 2,500 organizations which are concerned with specific occupations; coverage includes Canada.

Publication Date: 1980   300 pages

3921 Career Information Center; 13 Volumes
MacMillan Publishing Company
1633 Broadway
New York, NY 10019
212-512-2000
Fax: 800-835-3202

13 volumes covering 3,000 careers, 633 job summaries with 800 photos. Up-to-date information on salaries and occupational outlooks for nearly 3,000 careers.

2.6M pages Triennial
ISBN: 0-028974-52-2

3922 Careers Information Officers in Local Authorities
Careers Research & Advisory Centre/Hobsons Pub.
Bateman Street
Cambridge CB2 1LZ England
223-354551

1,100 United Kingdom institutions offering collections of career information and audio-visual materials covering career opportunities and current job markets. Arranged alphabetically listing address, phone, contact name and titles,type of materials held and a description of the facilities.

165 pages 12.95 pounds

3923 Certification and Accreditation Programs Directory
Gale Research
27500 Drake Road
Farmington Hills, MI 48331-3535
248-699-4253
800-877-4253
Fax: 248-699-8064
E-mail: galeord@gale.com
http://www.galegroup.com

Directory of private organizations that offer more than 1,700 voluntary certification programs and approximately 300 accreditation programs. Also on CD-ROM.

Publication Date: 1995   620 pages
ISSN: 1084-2128

Allen W Paschal, President

3924 Complete Guide to Work, Study & Travel Overseas
Transitions Abroad
PO Box 1300
Amherst, MA 01004-1300
413-256-3414
800-293-0373
Fax: 413-256-0373
E-mail: info@TransitionsAbroad.org
http://www.transitionsabroad.org

A resource for those interested in work, study or travel abroad.

3925 Council of British Independent Schools in the European Communities-Members Directory
Lucy's Hill
Hythe, Kent CT21 5ES
England
44-1303-260857
Fax: 44-1303-260857
E-mail: secretariat@cobisec.org
http://www.cobisec.org

Annual

Roger Fry CBE, Chairman
Sybil Melchers MBE, Honorary Secretary

3926 Directory of English Language Schools in Japan
Hiring English Teachers
Information Career Opportunities Research Center
Box 1100, Station F
Toronto M4Y 2T7
Canada
416-925-8878

English-language schools in Japan.

15 pages Annual

3927 Directory of International Internships Michigan State University
MSU: Dean's Office of Int'l Studies and Programs
209 International Center
East Lansing, MI 48824

517-355-2350
Fax: 517-353-7254
E-mail: gliozzo@pilot.msu.edu
http://www.isp.msu.edu

International internships sponsored by academic institutions, private corporations and the federal government.

Publication Date: 1994   168 pages   Paperback

Charles A Gliozzo, Coordinating Editor

3928 Directory of Schools, Colleges, and Universities Overseas
Overseas Employment Services
EBSCO Industries
PO Box 1943
Birmingham, AL 35201

205-991-1330
Fax: 205-995-1582

Directory of 300 educational institutions worldwide that hire teachers to teach different subjects in English.

21 pages   Annual

Leonard Simcoe, Editor

3929 Directory of Work and Study in Developing Countries
Vacation-Work Publishers
9 Park End Street
Oxford OX1 1HJ
England

865-241978

Offers information on about 420 organizations worldwide offering employment and study opportunities in over 100 developing countries.

215 pages

3930 Earn & Learn: Cooperative Education Opportunities
Octameron Associates
1900 Mount Vernon Avenue
PO Box 2748
Alexandria, VA 22301-0748

703-836-5480
Fax: 703-836-5650
E-mail: info@octameron.com
http://www.octameron.com

Explains how students may participate in cooperative work-study education programs with federal government agencies.

Publication Date: 1997   48 pages   BiAnnual
ISBN: 1-57509-023-6

3931 English in Asia: Teaching Tactics for New English Teachers
Global Press
697 College Parkway
Rockville, MD 20850-1135

303-393-7645

Directory covering 1,000 private English-language schools in Asia, to which applications can be sent to teach.

Publication Date: 1992   180 pages

3932 European Council of International Schools Directory
European Council of International Schools
21 Lavant Street, Petersfield
Hampshire GU3 23EL
United Kingdom

44-1730-26-8244
Fax: 44-1730-267914
E-mail: 100412.242@compuserve.com

More than 420 member elementary and secondary international schools in Europe and worldwide.

480 pages   Annual

JS Henley, President

3933 Faculty Exchange Center Directory and House Exchange Supplement
Faculty Exchange Center
962 Virginia Avenue
Lancaster, PA 17603-3116

717-393-1130

Offers information for college and faculty members wishing to exchange positions and/or homes temporarily with faculty members at other institutions.

35 pages   Annual

3934 Foreign Faculty and Administrative Openings
Education Information Services
PO Box 620662
Newton, MA 02462-0662

617-433-0125

150 specific openings in administration, counseling, library and other professional positions for American teachers in American schools overseas and in international schools in which teaching language is English.

15 pages   Every 6 Weeks

FB Viaux, Coordinating Education

3935 Guide to Educational Opportunities in Japan
Embassy of Japan
2520 Massachusetts Avenue NW
Washington, DC 20008

202-238-6700
Fax: 202-328-2187
http://www.embjapan.org

This guide describes opportunities for study in Japan and outlines different forms of financial assistance.

3936 How to Create a Picture of Your Ideal Job or Next Career
Ten Speed Press
PO Box 7123
Berkeley, CA 94707-0123

415-845-8414
800-841-BOOK
Fax: 510-524-4588

Offers handy tips on how to choose the right career, and then go out and get it.

Publication Date: 1989

Richard Nelson Bolles, Author

3937 How to Plan and Develop a Career Center
Center on Education and Work
964 Educational Sciences Building
1025 W Johnson Street
Madison, WI 53706-1796

800-446-0399
Fax: 608-262-9197
E-mail: cewmail@soemadison.wisc.edu
http://www.cew.wisc.edu

High school, postsecondary, adult, and virtual career centers-a comprehensive blueprint that covers all the bases.

3938 Jobs in Russia & the Newly Independent States
Impact Publications
9104 Manassas Drive
Sutie N
Manassas Park, VA 20111-5211

703-361-7300
Fax: 703-335-9486
E-mail: info@impactpublications.com
http://www.impactpublications.com

This guide provides background information on the Russian Federation, the Baltics, the Eastern Slavic Republics, the Transcaucasian Republics and the Asiatic Republics.

3939 Leading Educational Placement Sources in the US
Educational Information Services
PO Box 662
Newton Lower Falls, MA 02162

617-964-4555

An index of the host placement agencies in America for education professionals.

3940 List of Over 200 Executive Search Consulting Firms in the US
Educational Information Services
PO Box 662
Newton Lower Falls, MA 02162

617-964-4555

Covers companies with active search committees in America.

3941 List of Over 600 Personnel & Employment Agencies
Educational Information Services
PO Box 662
Newton Lower Falls, MA 02162

617-964-4555

Contains information on personnel and employment agencies.

3942 Living in China: A Guide to Studying, Teaching & Working in the PRC & Taiwan
China Books & Periodicals
360 Swift Avenue Suite 48
South San Francisco, CA 94080

650-872-7076
800-818-2017
Fax: 650-872-7808
E-mail: info@chinabooks.com
http://www.chinabooks.com

America's #1 source of publications about China since 1960.

284 pages Paperback
ISBN: 25823
November

Tracy Lin, Marketing Director

3943 National Association of Teachers' Agencies Membership Directory
National Association of Teachers' Agencies
524 S Avenue E
Cranford, NJ 07016-3298

908-272-2080
Fax: 908-272-2962

Listing of over 20 private employment agencies engaged primarily in the placement of teaching and administrative personnel in education.

Annual

3944 National Directory of Internships
National Society for Experiential Education
3509 Haworth Drive
Suite 207
Raleigh, NC 27609-7235

631-728-9100
Fax: 631-728-9228
E-mail: info@nsee.org
http://www.nsee.org

Directory contains internship descriptions for hundreds of organizations in 85 fields in nonprofit organizations, government and corporations. Lists work and service experiences for high school, college and graduate students, peopleentering the job market, mid-career professionals and retired persons. Includes indexes by field of interest, location and host organization.

Publication Date: 1995 703 pages
ISBN: 0-536-01123-0

3945 Opening List in US Colleges, Public & Private Schools
Education Information Services/Instant Alert
PO Box 620662
Newton, MA 02462-0662

617-433-0125

Offers about 150 current professional openings in US colleges and public and private schools.

10 pages Every 6 weeks

FB Viaux, Coordinating Education

3946 Opening List of Professional Openings in American Overseas Schools
Education Information Services/Instant Alert
PO Box 620662
Newton, MA 02462-0662

617-433-0125

About 150 current professional openings for teachers, administrators, counselors, librarians and educational specialists in American overseas schools and international schools at which the teaching language is primarily English.

FB Viaux, Coordinating Education

3947 Overseas Employment Opportunities for Educators
Department of Defense, Office of Dependent Schools
2461 Eisenhower Avenue
Alexandria, VA 22331-3000

703-325-0867

This publication tells about teaching jobs in 250 schools operated for children of US military and civilian personnel stationed overseas. Applicants usually must qualify in two subject areas.

3948 Private School, Community & Junior College Four Year Colleges & Universities
Educational Information Services
PO Box 662
Newton Lower Falls, MA 02162

617-964-4555

Names, addresses and phones for any state or region in the United States offering employment opportunities.

3949 Research, Study, Travel, & Work Abroad
US Government Printing Office
732 N Capitol Street NW
Washington, DC 20401

202-512-1999
Fax: 202-512-1293
E-mail: admin@access.gpo.gov
http://www.access.gpo.gov

3950 Teaching Overseas
KSJ Publishing Company
PO Box 2311
Sebastopol, CA 95473-2311

A directory of information on how to find jobs teaching overseas.

> *Publication Date: 1992   89 pages 2nd Edition*
> *ISBN: 0-962044-55-5*

3951 Thirty-Four Activities to Promote Careers in
Special Education
The Council for Exceptional Children
1920 Association Drive
Reston, VA 20191-1545

> 703-620-3660
> 800-232-7323
> Fax: 703-264-1637

This guide introduces individuals to the opportunities, rewards and delights of working with children with exceptionalities. It provides directions on how to plan, develop, and implement activities in the school and community thatwill increase people's awareness of careers in special education and related services.

> *Publication Date: 1996   120 pages*
> *ISBN: 0-865862-77-0*

3952 VGM's Careers Encyclopedia
VGM Career Books/National Textbook Company
4255 W Touhy Avenue
Lincolnwood, IL 60646-1933

> 708-679-5500

A list of over 200 professional associations that provide career guidance information.

3953 Women's Job Search Handbook
Williamson Publishing Company
Church Hill Road
PO Box 185
Charlotte, VT 05445-0185

> 802-425-2102
> 800-234-8791
> Fax: 802-425-2199
> E-mail: info@williamsonbooks.com

Offers creative self-assessment, positioning and mapping out job search with help from two knowledgeable career consultants.

> *264 pages*
> *ISBN: 0-913589-49-7*

Gerri Bloomberg & Margaret Holden, Author
June C Roelle, Marketing Specialist

3954 Workforce Preparation: An International
Perspective
PO Box 8623
Ann Arbor, MI 48107-8623

> 800-530-9673
> Fax: 734-975-2787

Excellent collection of material by 20 prominent educators describes efforts in developed and developing countries worldwide to prepare youth and adults for work.

3955 Working Holidays: The Complete Guide to
Finding a Job Overseas
Transitions Abroad
PO Box 1300
Amherst, MA 01004-1300

> 413-256-3414
> 800-293-0373
> Fax: 413-256-0373
> E-mail: info@TransitionsAbroad.org
> http://www.transitionsabroad.org

Resource for finding both short- and long-term jobs abroad. Organized by region and country, includes websites and phone numbers.

3956 World of Learning
Europa Publications
18 Bedford Square
London WC1B 3JN
England

> 171-580-8236
> Fax: 171-636-1664

Details over 26,000 educational, cultural and scientific institutions throughout the world, together with an exhaustive directory of over 150,000 people active within them.

> *2,072 pages Annual*
> *ISBN: 0-946653-92-5*

Directories & Handbooks
Financial Aid

3957 Annual Register of Grant Support
RR Bowker, Reed Reference
630 Central Avenue
New Providence, NJ 07974

> 908-665-6770
> 888-269-5372
> Fax: 908-665-2895
> E-mail: info@bowker.com
> http://www.bowker.com

Offers information on both traditional (corporate, private and public) and nontraditional (educational associations and unions) sources of funding.

3958 Catalog of Federal Domestic Assistance
Office of Management & Budget
Washington, DC 20402

Offers information from all federal agencies that have assistance programs (loans, scholarships and technical assistance as well as grants) and compiles these into the CFDA. The individual entries are grouped by Department of Agencyand includes an excellent set of instructions and several indices. Indices allow the user to search for grants by subject matter, agency, deadline date or eligibility criteria.

3959 Catalog of Federal Education Grants
Aspen Publishing, Inc.
1101 King Street
Suite 444
Alexandria, VA 22314-2944

> 800-638-8437
> Fax: 301-417-7650

Offers professionals instant access to background research of hundreds of pertinent federal programs that could fund the next education project. Offers regular monthly updates and a hotline for up-to-date, daily information. Offersinformation on the grant program, objectives, programs, updates, news and what the agencies are willing to fund.

3960 Chronicle Financial Aid Guide
Chronicle Guidance Publications
66 Aurora Street
Moravia, NY 13118-3576

> 315-497-0330
> 800-622-7284
> Fax: 315-497-3359
> E-mail: customerservice@chronicleguidance.com
> http://www.chronicleguidance.com

Financial aid programs offered primarily by noncollegiate organizations, independent and AFL-CIO affiliated labor unions and federal and state governments for high school seniors and undergraduate and graduate students.

476 pages Annual
ISBN: 1-5563-310-1

Janet Seemann, Author

3961 College Costs and Financial Aid Handbook
College Board Publications
PO Box 869010
Plano, TX 75074-6917

800-323-7155
Fax: 888-321-7183
http://www.collegeboard.org

A step-by-step guide providing the most up-to-date facts on costs plus financial aid and scholarship availability at 3,200 two- and four-year institutions.

Publication Date: 2003
ISBN: 0-874476-83-6

3962 College Financial Aid Annual
Arco/Macmillan
1633 Broadway
Floor 7
New York, NY 10019-6708

212-654-8933

Lists of private businesses, academic institutions and other organizations that provide awards and scholarships for financial aid; guide to federal and state financial aid.

3963 Directory of Educational Contests for Students K-12
ABC-CLIO
130 Cremona Drive
#1911
Santa Barbara, CA 93117-5599

805-968-1911
800-368-6868
Fax: 805-685-9685

Offers about 200 competitive scholarship programs and other educational contests for elementary and secondary school students.

Publication Date: 1991 253 pages

3964 Directory of Financial Aid for Women
Reference Service Press
5000 Windplay Drive
Suite 4
El Dorado Hills, CA 95762

916-939-9620
Fax: 916-939-9626
E-mail: rspinfo@aol.com
http://www.rspfunding.com

Offers information on more than 1,500 scholarships, fellowships, loan sources, grants, awards and internships.

490 pages

3965 Directory of Institutional Projects Funded by Office of Educational Research
U.S. Office of Educational Research & Improvement
555 New Jersey Avenue NW
Washington, DC 20001-2029

202-219-2050

Publication Date: 1990 60 pages

3966 Directory of International Grants & Fellowships in the Health Sciences
National Institutes of Health
31 Center Drive MSC 2220
Building 31, Room B2C29
Bethesda, MD 20892-2220

301-496-2075
Fax: 301-594-1211
E-mail: ficinfo@nih.gov
http://www.nih.gov/fic

Fellowships and grants listed separately in this guide. Each listing includes a complete program description with contact information.

3967 Don't Miss Out: The Ambitous Students Guide to Financial Aid
Octameron Associates
1900 Mt Vernon Avenue
Alexandria, VA 22301-0748

703-836-5480
Fax: 703-836-5650
E-mail: info2octameron.com
http://www.octameron.com

Publication Date: 0   192 pages Anually

3968 Fellowships in International Affairs-A Guide to Opportunities in the US & Abroad
Lynne Rienner Publishing
1800 30th Street
Suite 314
Boulder, CO 80301

303-444-6684
Fax: 303-444-0824
E-mail: questions@rienner.com
http://www.rienner.com

This guide lists fellowships meant to encourage women to pursue careers in international security.

3969 Fellowships, Scholarships and Related Opportunities
Center for International Ed./University of TN
201 Aconda Court
Knoxville, TN 37996

865-974-1000
Fax: 865-974-2985

140 grants, scholarships and fellowships available to citizens of the United States for study or research abroad.

50 pages Biennial

3970 Financial Aid for Research & Creative Activities Abroad
Reference Service Press
5000 Windplay Drive
Suite 4
El Dorado Hills, CA 95762

916-939-9620
Fax: 916-939-9626
E-mail: webagent@rspfunding.com
http://www.rspfunding.com

This book lists opportunities fir high school students and undergraduates, graduates, postdoctoral students, professionals and others.

432 pages
ISBN: 1588410625

Gail Schlachter, Author
R.David Weber, Author

3971 Financial Aid for Study Abroad: a Manual for Advisers & Administrators
NAFSA: Association of International Educators
1307 New York Avenue NW
8th Floor
Washington, DC 20005-4701

202-737-3699
800-836-4994
Fax: 202-737-3657
E-mail: inbox@nafsa.org
http://www.nafsa.org

Publication Date: 1989   105 pages

Marlene M Johnson, Director/CEO

3972 Financial Resources for International Study
Peterson's Guides
PO Box 2123
Princeton, NJ 08543-2123

609-243-9111
800-338-3282
Fax: 609-243-9150

More than 500 grants of at least $500 for US undergraduates, graduates and postgraduates who wish to study abroad.

Publication Date: 1989   250 pages

3973 Financial Resources for International Study
Institute of International Education
809 United Nations Plaza
New York, NY 10017-3580

212-883-8200
800-445-0443
Fax: 212-984-5452
E-mail: iiebooks@pmds.com
http://www.iie.org

Directory of more than 600 awards that can be used for international study.

Publication Date: 1996   320 pages
ISBN: 087206-220-1

3974 Financing Graduate School
Peterson's Guides
PO Box 2123
Princeton, NJ 08543-2123

609-243-9111
800-338-3282
Fax: 609-243-9150

In-depth answers to the most frequently asked questions about sources of graduate financial aid.

208 pages
ISBN: 1-560791-47-0

Patricia McWade, Author

3975 Foundation Grants to Individuals
Foundation Center
79 Fifth Avenue
New York, NY 10003-3076

212-260-4230
Fax: 212-807-3677

Features current information for grant seekers.

3976 Free Money for College: Fifth Edition
Facts On File
132 West 31st Street
17th Floor
New York, NY 10001

800-678-3633
E-mail: llikoff@factsonfile.com
http://www.factsonfile.com

1,000 grants and scholarships.

Publication Date: 1999   240 pages Annual
Hardcover
ISBN: 081603947X

Laurie Blum, Author
Laurie Likoff, Editorial Director

3977 Free Money for Foreign Study: A Guide to 1,000 Grants for Study Abroad
Facts On File
132 West 31st Street
17th Floor
New York, NY 10001

800-678-3633
E-mail: llikoff@factsonfile.com
http://www.factsonfile.com

Lists organizations and institutions worldwide offering scholarships and grants for study outside the United States.

262 pages

Laurie Likoff, Editorial Director

3978 Fulbright and Other Grants for USIA Graduate Study Abroad
U.S. Student Programs Division
809 United Nations Plaza
New York, NY 10017-3503

212-984-5330
Fax: 212-984-5325
http://www.iie.org

Mutual educational exchange grants for pre-doctoral students offered by foreign governments.

90 pages Annual

3979 Fund Your Way Through College: Uncovering 1,100 Opportunities in Aid
Visible Ink Press/Gale Research
830 Penobscot Building
Detroit, MI 48226

313-961-2242

1,100 scholarships, grants, loans, awards and prizes for undergraduate students.

470 pages

3980 German-American Scholarship Guide-Exchange Opportunities for Historians and Social Scientist
German Historical Institute
1607 New Hampshire Avenue NW
Washington, DC 20009-2562

202-387-3355
Fax: 202-483-3430
http://www.ghi-dc.org

This guide is divided into two sections: scholarships for study and research in the US and scholarships for study and research in Germany.

3981 Getting Funded: The Complete Guide to WritingGrant Proposals
Continuing Education Press
PO Box 1394
Portland, OR 97207-1394

503-725-4891
866-647-7377
Fax: 503-725-4840
E-mail: press@pdx.edu
http://www.cep.pdx.edu

A step-by-step guide to writing successful grants and proposals. An indispensible reference for experienced and first-time grant writers alike.

180 pages Paperback
ISBN: 0-87678-071-0

Mary Hall, Author
Alba Scholz, Manager
Martha Ketchum, Customer Service

3982 Graduate Scholarship Book
Pearson Education
1 Lake Street
Upper Saddle River, NJ 07458

201-909-6200
Fax: 201-767-5029

A complete guide to scholarships, grants and loans for graduate and professional study.

441 pages Biennial

3983 Grant Opportunities for US Scholars & Host Opportunities for US Universities
International Research & Exchange Board
2121 K Street NW
Suite 700
Washington, DC 20037

202-628-8188
Fax: 202-628-8189
E-mail: irex@irex.org
http://www.irex.org

This pamphlet lists programs in advanced research, language and development, short-term travel, special projects and institutional opportunities.

3984 Grant Writing Beyond The Basics: Proven Strategies Professionals Use To Make Proposals Work
Continuing Education Press
PO Box 1394
Portland, OR 97207-1394

503-725-4891
866-647-7377
Fax: 503-725-4840
E-mail: press@pdx.edu
http://www.cep.pdx.edu

Designed to inspire those with grant writing experience who want to take their development strategies to the next level.

128 pages Paperback
ISBN: 0-87678-117-2

Michael K Wells, Author
Alba Scholz, Manager
Martha Ketchum, Customer Service

3985 Grants & Awards Available to American Writers
PEN American Center
588 Broadway
Suite 303
New York, NY 10012

212-334-1660
Fax: 212-334-2181
E-mail: ftw@pen.org
http://www.pen.org

Includes a full program description and is then broken down by type of writing. Awards for work in a particular country are listed alphabetically by country.

340 pages Paperback
ISBN: 0-934638-20-9

3986 Grants Register
St. Martin's Press
175 5th Avenue
New York, NY 10010

212-674-5151
888-330-8477
Fax: 800-672-2054
E-mail: firstname.lastname@stmartins.com
http://www.vhpsva.com

This directory offers a comprehensive list of programs organized alphabetically with special attention to eligibility requirements. Index by subject.

3987 Grants, Fellowships, & Prizes of Interest to Historians
American Historical Association
400 A Street SE
Washington, DC 20003-3889

202-544-2422
Fax: 202-544-8307
E-mail: aha@theaha.org
http://www.theaha.org

This guide offers information on awards for historians from undergraduate to postgraduate grants, fellowships, prizes, internships and awards.

3988 Guide to Department of Education Programs
US Department of Education
400 Maryland Avenue SW
Washington, DC 20202-0001

202-401-0765

Programs of financial aid offered by the Department of Education.

35 pages Annual

3989 Guide to Federal Funding for Education
Education Funding Research Council
PO Box 22782
Tampa, FL 33622-2782

703-528-1000
800-876-0226
Fax: 800-926-2012

Two hundred fifty federal programs that offer financial aid for state and local educational agencies, colleges and universities.

1,047 pages

3990 Harvard College Guide to Grants
Office of Career Services
Harvard University
54 Dunster Street
Cambridge, MA 02138

617-495-2595
Fax: 617-496-6880
http://www.ocs.fas.harvard.edu

This guide describes national and regional grants and fellowships for study in the US, study abroad and work and practical experience.

234 pages Paperback

3991 How to Find Out About Financial Aid & Funding
Reference Service Press
5000 Windplay Drive
Suite 4
El Dorado Hills, CA 95762

916-939-9620
Fax: 916-939-9626
E-mail: rspinfo@aol.com
http://www.rspfunding.com

Over 700 financial aid directories and Internet sites described and evaluated.

432 pages Hardcover
ISBN: 1588410935

Gail A Schlachter, Author

3992 International Foundation Directory
Europa Publications
11 New Fetter Lane
London
England EC4P 4EE

44-0-20-7842-2110
Fax: 44-0-20-7842-2249
http://www.europapublications.co.uk

A world directory of international foundations, trusts and similar non-profit institutions. Provides detailed information on over 1,200 institutions in some 70 countries throughout the world.

Publication Date: 1994 736 pages
ISBN: 1-857430-01-8

Paul Kelly, Editorial Director

3993 International Scholarship Book: The Complete Guide to Financial Aid
Pearson Education
1 Lake Street
Upper Saddle River, NJ 07458

201-909-6200
Fax: 201-767-5029

Offers information on private organizations providing financial aid for university students interested in studying in foreign countries.

335 pages Cloth

3994 Journal of Student Financial Aid
University of Notre Dame
Office of Financial Aid
Notre Dame, IN 46556

574-631-6436

Offers a listing of private and federal sources of financial aid for college bound students.

3x Year

Joseph A Russo, Editor

3995 Loans and Grants from Uncle Sam
Octameron Associates
1900 Mount Vernon Avenue
PO Box 2748
Alexandria, VA 22301-0748

703-836-5480
Fax: 703-836-5650
E-mail: info@octameron.com
http://www.octameron.com

Offers information on federal student loan and grant programs and state loan guarantee agencies.

72 pages Annual
ISBN: 1-57509-097-X

Anna Leider, Author

3996 Money for Film & Video Artists
American for the Art
1000 Vermont Avenue NW
6th Floor
Washington, DC 20005

202-371-2830
Fax: 202-371-0424
http://www.artsusa.org

The listings are organized by sponsoring organization and entries include basic application and program information.

3997 Money for International Exchange in the Arts
American for the Art
1000 Vermont Avenue NW
12th Floor
Washington, DC 20005

202-371-2830
Fax: 202-371-0424
http://www.artsusa.org

A guide to the various resources available to support artists and arts organizations in international work.

3998 Money for Visual Artists
America for the Art
1000 Vermont Avenue NW
6th Floor
Washington, DC 20005

202-371-2830
Fax: 202-371-0424
http://www.artsusa.org

Programs are listed alphabetically by sponsor with detailed program description.

3999 National Association of State Scholarship and Grant Program Survey Report
National Association of State Scholarship Programs
660 Boas Street
Harrisburg, PA 17102-1324

717-257-2794

Listing of over 50 member state agencies administering scholarship and grant programs for student financial aid.

150 pages

4000 National Association of Student Financial Aid Administrators Directory
1129 20th Street NW
Suite 400
Washington, DC 20036-5001

202-785-0453
Fax: 202-785-1487

Offers information on over 3,000 institutions of postsecondary education and their financial aid administrators.

230 pages Annual

4001 Need A Lift?
The American Legion
700 North Pennsylvania Street
PO Box 1055
Indianapolis, IN 46206-1050

317-630-1200
888-453-4466
Fax: 317-630-1223
http://www.EMBLEM.legion.org

Sources of career, scholarship and loan information or assistance.

144 pages Annual/Paperback

Robert Caudell, Author

4002 Paying Less for College
Peterson's Guides
PO Box 2123
Princeton, NJ 08543-2123

609-243-9111
800-338-3282
Fax: 609-243-9150

A comprehensive information resource and financial aid adviser featuring in-depth financial aid data and money-saving options at more than 1,600 accredited US four-year colleges.

720 pages 14th Edition
ISBN: 1-560796-50-2

4003 Peterson's Grants for Graduate and Postdoctoral Study
Peterson's Guides
PO Box 2123
Princeton, NJ 08543-2123

609-243-9111
800-338-3282
Fax: 609-243-9150

Only comprehensive source of current information on grants and fellowships exclusively for graduate and postdoctoral students.

526 pages 4th Edition
ISBN: 1-560794-01-1

4004 Peterson's Guide to Four-Year Colleges
Peterson's Guides
PO Box 2123
Princeton, NJ 08543-2123

609-896-1800
800-338-3282
Fax: 609-896-1811

Includes descriptions of over 2,000 colleges, providing guidance on selecting the right school, getting in and financial aid.

3,000 pages

4005 Peterson's Sports Scholarships and College Athletic Programs
Peterson's Guides
PO Box 2123
Princeton, NJ 08543-2123

609-243-9111
800-338-3282
Fax: 609-243-9150

A college-by-college look at scholarships designated exclusively for student athletes in 32 men's and women's sports.

822 pages 2nd Edition
ISBN: 1-560794-83-6

4006 Scholarship Handbook
The College Board
45 Columbus Avenue
New York, NY 10023

800-323-7155
http://www.collegeboard.org

Useful text for college-bound students, their families and guidance counselors. Offers more than 2,000 descriptions of national and state level award programs, public and private education loan programs, intership opportunities and more.

4007 Scholarships for Emigres Training for Careers in Jewish Education
Jewish Foundation for Education of Women
135 E 64th Street
New York, NY 10021

212-288-3931
Fax: 212-288-5798
E-mail: fdnscholar@aol.com
http://www.jfew.org

Open to emigres from the former Soviet Union who are pursuing careers in Jewish education. Candidates in Jewish education, rabbinical and cantorial studies, and Jewish studies are invited to write the Foundation.

Marge Goldwater, Executive Director

4008 Scholarships, Fellowships and Loans
Gale Research
PO Box 33477
Detroit, MI 48232-5477

800-877-GALE
Fax: 800-414-5043
http://www.galegroup.com

Written especially for professionals, students, counselors, parents and others interested in education. This resource provides more than 3,700 sources of education-related financial aid and awards at all levels of study.

Publication Date: 1995 1,290 pages Annual
ISBN: 0-810391-14-7

4009 Student Guide
Federal Student Aid Information Center
PO Box 84
Washington, DC 20044-0084

800-433-3243
800-433-3243

Describes the federal student aid programs, and general information about the eligibility criteria, application procedures and award levels, and lists important deadlines and phone numbers.

54 pages

John J McCarthy, Director

4010 Study Abroad
U.N. Educational, Scientific & Cultural Assn.
7, place de Fontenoy
F-75700 Paris
France

1-45681123

Listing of over 200,000 scholarships, fellowships and educational exchange opportunities offered for study in 124 countries.

1,300 pages Biennial

4011 USA Today Financial Aid for College
Peterson's Guides
PO Box 2123
Princeton, NJ 08543-2123

609-243-9111
800-338-3282
Fax: 609-243-9150

Explains the types of aid available and tells how to qualify for aid, and includes the 1996 Financial Aid Profile forms. Covers the most commonly asked questions, and answers, from USA Today's Financial Aid Hotline.

160 pages
ISBN: 1-560795-68-9

Pat Ordovensky, Author

4012 Winning Federal Grants: A Guide to the Government's Grant-Making Process
Aspen Publishing
1101 King Street
Suite 444
Alexandria, VA 22314-2944

800-638-8437
Fax: 301-417-7650

This book shows grant-seekers how the federal government is structured and what areas and issues the various federal agencies fund. It also speaks on how Congress creates grant programs and how individuals can monitor its activities to learn more about the grant programs that best meet their needs. Information can also be found on how agencies review proposals and make grant awards.

4013 Winning Money for College: The High School Student's Guide to Scholarships
Peterson's Guides
PO Box 2123
Princeton, NJ 08543-2123

609-243-9111
800-338-3282
Fax: 609-243-9150

The first complete guide to the more than $40 million awarded in non-need scholarship competitions, including valuable tips from previous scholarship winners.

362 pages 3rd Edition
ISBN: 1-560790-59-8

Alan Deutschman, Author

4014 Write Now: A Complete Self-Teaching Program Foor Better Handwriting
Continuing Education Press
PO Box 1394
Portland, OR 97207-1394

503-725-4891
866-647-7377
Fax: 503-725-4840
E-mail: press@pdx.edu
http://www.cep.pdx.edu

A step-by-step guide to improving one's handwriting. Develop clean and legible italic handwriting with regular practice.

128 pages Paperback
ISBN: 0-87678-089-3

Barbara Getty & Inga Dubay, Author
Alba Scholz, Manager
Martha Ketchum, Customer Service

Directories & Handbooks
Guidance & Counseling

4015 Accredited Institutions of Postsecondary Education
MacMillan Publishing Company
1633 Broadway
New York, NY 10019

212-512-2000
Fax: 800-835-3202

Lists over 5,000 accredited institutions and programs for postsecondary education in the United States.

600 pages Annual

4016 Adolescent Pregnancy Prevention Clearinghouse
Children's Defense Fund Education & Youth Develop.
122 C Street NW
#400
Washington, DC 20001-2109

202-628-8787
Fax: 202-662-3560

Provides information and clarification on the connection between pregnancy and broader life questions for youth.

Marian Wright Edelman, Coordinating Education

4017 COLLEGESOURCE
Career Guidance Foundation
8090 Engineer Road
San Diego, CA 92111-1906

800-854-2670
Fax: 858-278-8960
http://www.collegesource.org

CD-ROM and Web College Catalog Collection. Contains colleges and universitie's catalogs from throughout the US, over 2,600. Also a college search program that can be searched by major, tuition costs, and more. Foreign catalogsavailable.

Annette Crone, Account Coordinator
David Hunt, Account Coordinator

4018 Cabells Directory of Publishing Opportunities in Educational Psychology and Administration
Cabell Publishing Company
Box 5428
Tobe Hahn Station
Beaumont, TX 77726

409-898-0575
Fax: 409-866-9554
E-mail: publish@cabells.com
http://www.cabells.com

Provides information on editor contact information, manuscript guidelines, acceptance rate, review information and circulation data for over 225 academic journals.

799 pages Annual
ISBN: 0-911753-19-2

David WE Cabell, Editor
Deborah L English, Associate Editor

4019 Career & Vocational Counseling Directory
American Business Directories
5711 S 86th Circle
Omaha, NE 68127-4146

402-593-4600
888-999-1307
Fax: 402-331-5481

Nationwide listing of 3,300 companies/consultants available in print, computer magnetic tape and diskette, mailing labels, and index cards listing the name, address, phone, size of advertisement, contact person and number ofemployees.

Annual

Jerry Venner, Coordinating Education

4020 College Handbook
College Board Publications
45 Columbus Avenue
New York, NY 10023-6992

212-713-8000
Fax: 800-525-5562
E-mail: puborderinfo@collegeboard.org
http://www.collegeboard.org

Descriptions of 3,200 colleges and universities.

Publication Date: 1994 1728 pages Annually
Kea Waithe, Director Customer Service

4021 College Handbook Foreign Student Supplement
College Board Publications
45 Columbus Avenue
New York, NY 10023-6917

212-713-8000
Fax: 800-525-5562

Lists about 2,800 colleges and universities that are open to foreign students.

Publication Date: 1994 288 pages Annual
ISBN: 0-877474-83-3

4022 College Transfer Guide
School Guide Publications
210 N Avenue
New Rochelle, NY 10801-6402

914-632-7771
800-433-7771
Fax: 914-632-3412

Five hundred four-year colleges in the Northeast and Midwest that accept transfer students listing transfer requirements, deadlines, fees, enrollment, costs and contact information. Circulation, 60,000.

125 pages Annual/January

4023 Community College Exemplary Instructional Programs
Massachusetts Bay Community College Press
50 Oakland Street
Wellsley Hills, MA 02181

781-237-1100
Fax: 781-237-1061

Community college programs identified as outstanding by the National Council of Instructional Administrators.

4024 Comparative Guide to American Colleges for Students, Parents & Counselors
HarperCollins
10 E 53rd Street
New York, NY 10022-5244

212-207-7000
Fax: 212-207-7145

Accredited four-year colleges in the United States.

800 pages Cloth

4025 Directory of Play Therapy Training
University of North Texas
PO Box 310829
Denton, TX 76203-0829

940-565-3864
Fax: 940-565-4461
E-mail: cpt@coefs.coe.unt.edu
http://www.centerforplaytherapy.com

Paperback
Garry Landreth PhD, Director

4026 Educators Guide to FREE Guidance Materials
Educators Progress Service
214 Center Street
Randolph, WI 53956-1408

920-326-3126
888-951-4469
Fax: 920-326-3127
E-mail: epsinc@centurytel.net
http://www.freeteachingaids.com

Lists and describes free films, videotapes, filmstrips, slides, web sites, and hundreds of free printed materials in the field of career education and guidance for all age levels.

190 pages Annual
ISBN: 87708-406-8

Kathy Nehmer, President

4027 Index of Majors and Graduate Degrees
College Board Publications
45 Columbus Avenue
New York, NY 10023-6992

212-713-8000
Fax: 800-525-5562
http://www.collegeboard.org

Includes descriptions of over 600 majors and identifies the 3,200 colleges, universities, and graduate schools that offer them.

Annual
ISBN: 0-87447-592-9

4028 National Association of School Psychologist Directory
National Association of School Psychologists
8455 Colesville Road
Suite 1000
Silver Spring, MD 20910-3392

301-608-0500
Fax: 301-608-2514

Listing of over 15,000 members and officers of NASP and 50 affiliated state organizations of school psychologists. Includes geographical and alphabetical indexes. Available to members only.

Publication Date: 1990   210 pages

4029 Tests: a Comprehensive Reference for Psychology, Education & Business
PRO-ED
8700 Shoal Creek Boulevard
Austin, TX 78757-6897

512-451-3246
800-897-3202
Fax: 800-397-7633
E-mail: info@proedinc.com
http://www.proedinc.com

This fifth edition groups updated information on approximately 2,000 assessment instruments into three primary classifications-psychology, education, and business-and 89 subcategories, enabling users to readily identify the tests thatmeet their assessment needs. Each entry contains a statement of the instrument's purpose, a concise description of the instrument, scoring procedures, cost, and publisher information.

Publication Date: 1991   809 pages
Paperback/Hardcover
ISBN: 0-89079-709-9

Taddy Maddox, General Editor

4030 Vocational Biographies
PO Box 31
Sauk Centre, MN 56378-0031

320-352-6516
800-255-0752
Fax: 320-352-5546
E-mail: careers@vocbio.com
http://www.vocbio.com

Real life career success stories of persons in every walk of life that allow students to see a career through the eyes of a real person. New for 2005: Internet Access to 1001 Career Success Stories.

Toby Behnen, President
Roxann Behnen, Customer Service/Sales

4031 What Works and Doesn't With at Risk Students
BKS Publishing
3109 150th Place SE
Mill Creek, WA 98012-4864

425-745-3029
Fax: 425-337-4837
E-mail: DocBlokk@aol.com
http://www.literacyfirst.com

Publication Date: 1919   162 pages Paperback
ISBN: 0-9656713-0-5

Jan Glaes, Author
Bill Blokker, Owner

4032 World of Play Therapy Literature
Center for Play Therapy
PO Box 311337
Denton, TX 76203

940-565-3864
Fax: 940-565-4461
E-mail: cpt@coefs.coe.unt.edu
http://www.centerforplaytherapy.com

Author and topical listings of over 6,000 books, dissertations, documents, and journal articles on play therapy, updated every two years.

Publication Date: 1995 306 pages

Landreth, Homeyer, Bratton, Kale, Hipl, Schumann, Author

Directories & Handbooks
Language Arts

4033 Classroom Strategies for the English Language Learner
Master Teacher
PO Box 1207
Manhattan, KS 66505-1207

785-539-0555
800-669-9633
Fax: 785-539-7739
http://www.masterteacher.com

A practical model for accelerating both oral language and literacy development, based on the latest research for effective instruction of both Native English speakers and English language learners.

266 pages
ISBN: 1-58992-068-6

Socrro Herrera EdD, Author

4034 Italic Handwriting Series-Book A
Continuing Education Press
PO Box 1394
Portland, OR 97207-1394

503-725-4891
866-647-7377
Fax: 503-725-4840
E-mail: press@pdx.edu
http://www.cep.pdx.edu

Book A is the first workbook of a seven-part series. Designed for the beginning reader and writer, it introduces the alphabet one letter at a time. Illustrated.

64 pages Paperback
ISBN: 0-87678-092-3

Barbara Getty & Inga Dubay, Author
Alba Scholz, Manager

4035 Italic Handwriting Series-Book B
Continuing Education Press
PO Box 1394
Portland, OR 97207-1394

503-725-4891
866-647-7377
Fax: 503-725-4840
E-mail: press@pdx.edu
http://www.cep.pdx.edu

Book B is the second workbook of a seven-part series. Designed for the beginning reader and writer. Introduces

words and sentences, lowercase and capitol print script, one letter per page. Illustrated.

59 pages Paperback
ISBN: 0-87678-093-1

Barbara Getty & Inga Dubay, Author
Alba Scholz, Manager

4036 Italic Handwriting Series-Book C
Continuing Education Press
PO Box 1394
Portland, OR 97207-1394

503-725-4891
866-647-7377
Fax: 503-725-4840
E-mail: press@pdx.edu
http://www.pdx.edu

Book C is the third workbook of a seven-part series. Covers basic italic and introduces the cursive. Words and sentences include days of week, months of year, modes of transportation, and tongue twisters. Illustrated.

60 pages Paperback
ISBN: 0-87678-094-X

Barbara Getty & Inga Dubay, Author
Alba Scholz, Manager

4037 Italic Handwriting Series-Book D
Continuing Education Press
PO Box 1394
Portland, OR 97207-1394

503-725-4891
866-647-7377
Fax: 503-725-4840
E-mail: press@pdx.edu
http://www.cep.pdx.edu

Book D is the fourth workbook of a seven-part series. Reviews basic italic and covers the total cursive program. Includes prefixes, suffixes, capitalization, and playful poems. Explores history of the alphabet. Illustrated.

80 pages Paperback
ISBN: 0-87678-095-8

Barbara Getty & Inga Dubay, Author
Alba Scholz, Manager

4038 Italic Handwriting Series-Book E
Continuing Education Press
PO Box 1394
Portland, OR 97207-1394

503-725-4891
866-647-7377
Fax: 503-725-4840
E-mail: press@pdx.edu
http://www.cep.pdx.edu

Book E is the fifth workbook of a seven-part series. Reviews basic italic and covers the total cursive program. Writing practice covers natural history—plants, volcanoes, cities. Explores history of the alphabet. Illustrated.

56 pages Paperback
ISBN: 0-87678-096-6

Barbara Getty & Inga Dubay, Author
Alba Scholz, Manager

4039 Italic Handwriting Series-Book F
Continuing Education Press
PO Box 1394
Portland, OR 97207-1394

503-725-4891
866-647-7377
Fax: 503-725-4840
E-mail: press@pdx.edu
http://www;.cep.pdx.edu

Book F is the sixth workbook of a seven-part series. Reviews basic italic and covers the total cursive program. Writing practice emphasizes figures of speech (e.g. homophones, puns, metaphors, acronyms). Explores history of thealphabet. Illustrated.

56 pages Paperback
ISBN: 0-87678-097-4

Barbara Getty & Inga Dubay, Author
Alba Scholz, Manager

4040 Italic Handwriting Series-Book G
Continuing Education Press
PO Box 1394
Portland, OR 97207-1394

503-725-4891
866-647-7377
Fax: 503-725-4840
E-mail: press@pdx.edu
http://www.cep.pdx.edu

Book G is the seventh workbook of a seven-part series. A comprehensive self-instruction program in basic and cursive italic. Writing content follows a central theme-the history of our alphabet. Suitable for older students.Illustrated.

56 pages Paperback
ISBN: 0-87678-098-2

Barbara Getty & Inga Dubay, Author
Alba Scholz, Manager

4041 Language Schools Directory
American Business Directories
5711 S 86th Circle
Omaha, NE 68127-4146

402-593-4600
888-999-1307
Fax: 402-331-5481

A listing of language schools, arranged by geographic location, offering contact information which is updated on a continual basis, and printed on request. Directory is also available in electronic formats.

Jerry Venner, Coordinating Education

4042 Picture Book LearningVolume-1
Picture Book Learning Inc.
PO Box 270075
Louisville, CO 80027

303-548-2809
E-mail: todd@picturebooklearning.com
http://www.picturebooklearning.com

Teachers can use this fun method of teaching elementary children basic language arts skills through the use of picture books.

60 pages
ISBN: 0-9760725-0-5

Todd Osborne, Co-President
Corinne Osborne, Editor

4043 Process of Elimination - a Method of Teaching and Learning Basic Grammar
Scott & McCleary Publishing Company
2482 11th Street SW
Akron, OH 44314-1712

702-566-8756
800-765-3564
Fax: 702-568-1378
E-mail: jscott7576@aol.com
http://www.scottmccleary.com

Series of 7 steps designed to teach basic grammar skills to students in middle grades through college. Available in a teacher edition and a student workbook.

50 pages
ISBN: 0-9636225-2-8
ISSN: 0-9636225-

Milton Metheny, Author
Janet Scott, President
Sheila McCleary, Vice President

4044 Put Reading First: The Research BuildingBlocks For Teaching Children To Read
PO Box 1398
Jessup, MD 20794-1398

877-4ED-PUBS
Fax: 301-470-1244
E-mail: edpubs@inet.ed.gov
http://www.edpubs.org

Provides analysis and discussion in five areas of reading instruction: phonemic awareness, phonics, fluency, vocabulary and text comprehension.

4045 Write Now: A Complete Self Teaching Program for Better Handwriting
Continuing Education Press
PO Box 1394
Portland, OR 97207-1394

503-725-4891
866-647-7377
Fax: 503-725-4840
E-mail: press@pdx.edu
http://www.cep.pdx.edu

Finally, a handwriting improvement book for adults. Teach yourself to write legibly and retain it over time using this step-by-step guide to modern italic handwriting with complete instructions as well as practice exercises and tips.The secret to legible handwriting is the absence of loops in letterform, making it easier to write and easier to read.

96 pages Paperback
ISBN: 0-87678-089-3

Barbara Getty & Inga Dubay, Author
Alba Scholz, Manager
Wendi Johnson, Customer Service

Directories & Handbooks
Library Services

4046 Directory of Manufacturers & Suppliers
Special Libraries Association
331 South Patrick Street
Alexandria, VA 22314-3501

703-647-4900
Fax: 703-647-4901
E-mail: sla@sla.org
http://www.sla.org

The SLA network consists of nearly 15,000 librarians and information professionals who specialize in the arts, communication, business, social science, biomedical sciences, geosciences and environmental studies, and industry,business, research, educational and technical institutions, government, special departments of public and university libraries, newspapers, museums, and public or private organizations that provide or require specialized information.

4047 Directory of Members of the Association for Library and Information Science Education
1009 Commerce Park Drive Suite 150
PO Box 4219
Oak Ridge, TN 37830

865-425-0155
Fax: 865-481-0390
E-mail: contact@alise.org
http://www.alise.org

The Directory is designed to serve as a handbook for the association, including a list of officers, committees, and interest groups and strategic planning information for the association. Also listed are graduate schools of libraryand information science and their faculty.

Annual Paperback

Rand Price, Executive Director
Maureen Thompson, Administrator

4048 Libraries Unlimited Academic Catalog
88 Post Road W
Westport, CT 06881

203-226-3571
Fax: 203-222-1502
E-mail: lu-books@lu.com
http://www.lu.com

Catalog includes reference, collection development, library management, cataloging, and technology.

4049 Managing Info Tech in School Library Media Center
Libraries Unlimited
88 Post Road W
Westport, CT 06881

203-226-3571
Fax: 203-222-1502
E-mail: lu-books@lu.com
http://www.lu.com

Hardcover
ISBN: 1-56308-724-3

L Anne Clyde

4050 Managing Media Services Theory and Practice
Libraries Unlimited
PO Box 6633
Englewood, CO 80155-6633

303-770-1220
800-237-6124
Fax: 303-220-8843
E-mail: lu-books@lu.com
http://www.lu.com

Cloth
ISBN: 1-56308-530-5

L Anne Clyde

Directories & Handbooks
Music & Art

4051 Community Outreach and Education for the Arts Handbook
Music Teachers National Association
441 Vine Street
Suite 505
Cincinnati, OH 45202-2811

513-421-1420
888-512-5278
Fax: 513-421-2503
E-mail: mtnanet@mtaa.org
http://www.mtaa.org

Resource booklet for independent music teachers.

Paperback
April
170 booths with 2000 attendees and 100 exhibits
Brian Shepard, Director of Marketing

4052 Italic Letters
Continuing Education Press
PO Box 1394
Portland, OR 97207-1394

503-725-4891
866-647-7377
Fax: 503-725-4840
E-mail: press@pdx.edu
http://www.cep.pdx.edu

Italic Letters is for professional and amateur calligraphers, art teachers, and enthusiasts of the book arts. Numerous tips on letter shapes, spacing, slant, pen edge angle, and other secrets to handsome writing.

128 pages Paperback
ISBN: 0-87678-091-5

Barbara Getty & Inga Dubay, Author
Alba Scholz, Manager

4053 Money for Film & Video Artists
American for the Art
1000 Vermont Avenue NW
6th Floor
Washington, DC 20005

202-371-2830
Fax: 202-371-0424
http://www.artsusa.org

The listings are organized by sponsoring organization and entries include basic application and program information.

4054 Money for Visual Artists
America for the Art
1000 Vermont Avenue NW
12th Floor
Washington, DC 20005

202-371-2830
Fax: 202-371-0424
http://www.artsusa.org

Programs are listed alphabetically by sponsor with detailed program description.

4055 Music Teachers Guide to Music Instructional Software
Music Teachers National Association
441 Vine Street
Suite 505
Cincinnati, OH 45202-2811

888-512-5278
Fax: 513-421-2503
E-mail: mtnanet@mtna.org
http://www.mtna.org

Evaluations of music software for the macintosh and PC, including CD-ROMs, music skills and keyboard technique drill software, sequencers and soundequipment controllers.

4056 Peterson's Guide to Professional Degree Programs in the Visual Arts
Peterson's Guides
PO Box 2123
Princeton, NJ 08543-2123

609-243-9111
800-338-3282
Fax: 609-243-9150

Offers descriptions of over 700 accredited US colleges and universities, music conservatories, and art/design schools that grant undergraduate degrees in the areas of studio art.

559 pages
ISBN: 1-560795-36-0

4057 Resource Booklet for Independent Music Teachers
Music Teachers National Association
441 Vine Street
Suite 505
Cincinnati, OH 45202-2811

888-512-5278
Fax: 513-421-2503
E-mail: mtnanet@mtna.org
http://www.mtna.org

A booklet for organizing information about community resources.

4058 School Arts
50 Portland Street
Worcester, MA 01608

800-533-2847
Fax: 508-753-3834

Companies offering products, materials, and art education resources or programs that focus on the history of art, multicultural resources such as Fine Art, reproductions, CD-Roms, museum education, programs, slides, books, videos,exhibits, architecture, timelines, and resource kits.

Directories & Handbooks
Physical Education

4059 Educators Guide to FREE HPER Materials
Educators Progress Service
214 Center Street
Randolph, WI 53956-1408

920-326-3126
888-951-4469
Fax: 920-326-3127
E-mail: epsinc@centurytel.net
http://www.freeteachingaids.com

Lists and describes free films, videotapes, filmstrips, slides, web sites, and hundreds of free printed materials in the field of health, physical education, and recreation for all age levels.

184 pages Annual
ISBN: 87708-407-6

Kathy Nehmer, President

4060 Schools & Colleges Directory
Association for Experiential Education
3775 Iris Avenue
Suite 4
Boulder, CO 80301-2043

303-440-8844
Fax: 303-440-9581
E-mail: publications@aee.org
http://www.aee.org

Provides information about many schools, colleges and universities that have programs or offer degrees related to the field of outdoor/experiential education. Listings include programs in high schools and independent organizations aswell as institutions of higher learning. Paperback.

Publication Date: 1995 Paperback

Natalie Kurylke, Publications Manager

Directories & Handbooks
Reading

4061 Diagnostic Reading Inventory for Bilingual
Students in Grades K-8
Scott & McCleary Publishing Company
2482 11th Street SW
Akron, OH 44314-1712

702-566-8756
800-765-3564
Fax: 702-568-1378
E-mail: jscott7576@aol.com
http://www.scottmccleary.com

Series of 13 tests designed to access reading performance. IRI, spelling, phonics, visual and auditory discrimination and listening comprehension are just some of the tests included.

155 pages
ISBN: 0-9636225-1-X

Janet M Scott, Co-Author
Sheila C McCleary, Co-Author

4062 Diagnostic Reading Inventory for Primary and
Intermediate Grades K-8
Scott & McCleary Publishing Company
2482 11th Street SW
Akron, OH 44314-1712

702-566-8756
800-765-3564
Fax: 702-568-1378
E-mail: jscott7576@aol.com
http://www.scottmccleary.com

Designed to assess reading performance in grades K-8. Tests include: word recognition, oral reading inventory, comprehension, listening comprehension, auditory and visual discrimination, auditory and visual memory, learning modalitiesinventory, phonics mastery tests, structural analysis, word association and a diagnostic spelling test.

260 pages
ISBN: 0-9636225-4-4

Janet M Scott, Co-Author
Sheila C McCleary, Co-Author

4063 Educational Leadership
Assn. for Supervision & Curriculum Dev. (ASCD)
1703 N Beauregard Street
Alexandria, VA 22311-1714

703-578-9600
800-933-2723
Fax: 703-575-5400
E-mail: el@ascd.org
http://www.ascd.org

For educators by educators. With a circulation of 175,000, Educational Leadership is acknowledged throughout the world as an authoritative source of information about teaching and learning, new ideas and practices relevant topracticing educators, and the latest trends and issues affecting prekindergarten through higher education.

Marge Scherer, Executive Editor

4064 Everything You Need for Reading
ESP Publishers, Inc.
5200 S Jules Verne
Tampa, FL 33611

813-242-0655
800-643-0280
Fax: 813-837-1043
E-mail: e.espbooks@verizon.net
http://www.espbooks.com

Publishers of full curriculum workbooks.

Derek Brooks, CEO
Dan Broks, President

4065 Laubach Literacy Action Directory
Laubach Literacy Action
1320 Jamesville Avenue
Syracuse, NY 13210

315-422-9121
888-528-2224
Fax: 315-422-6369
E-mail: info@laubach.org
http://www.laubach.org

Listing of over 1,100 local literacy councils and associates who teach the Laubach Method.

90 pages Annual

4066 Ready to Read, Ready to Learn
PO Box 1398
Jessup, MD 20794-1398

877-4ED-PUBS
Fax: 301-470-1244
E-mail: edpubs@inet.ed.gov
http://www.edpubs.org

4067 Tips for Reading Tutors
PO Box 1398
Jessup, MD 20794-1398

877-4ED-PUBS
Fax: 301-470-1244
E-mail: edpubs@inet.ed.gov
http://www.edpubs.org

Basic tips for reading tutors

Directories & Handbooks
Secondary Education

4068 College Board Guide to High Schools
College Board Publications
45 Columbus Avenue
New York, NY 10023-6917

212-713-8165
800-323-7155
Fax: 800-525-5562
http://www.collegeboard.org

Offers listings and information on over 25,000 public and private high schools nationwide.

Publication Date: 1994 2,024 pages
ISBN: 0-874474-66-3

4069 Compendium of Tertiary & Sixth Forum Colleges
SCOTVIC: S McDonald, Principal
Ridge College
Manchester
England

61-4277733

Offers listings of over 200 Sixth Form and Tertiary Colleges in the United Kingdom offering courses preparing secondary students for university study.

Publication Date: 1990 200 pages Biennial

4070 Consider a Christian College
Peterson's Guides
PO Box 2123
Princeton, NJ 08543-2123

609-243-9111
800-338-3282
Fax: 609-243-9150

Seventy eight accredited four-year liberal arts colleges representing the Christian philosophy of higher education choices in the members of the Christian College Coalition. Each college listing includes all contact information, school denomination and affiliation, academic programs, student activities, fees and expenses and financial aid information.

149 pages 4th Edition

4071 Directory of Public Elementary and Secondary Education Agencies
US National Center for Education Statistics
555 New Jersey Avenue NW
Washington, DC 20208-5651

202-219-1916
800-424-1616
Fax: 202-502-7466

Directory of approximately 17,000 local education agencies that operate their own schools or pay tuition to other local education agencies.

400 pages Annual

John Sietsema, Statistician
Lena McDowell, Contact

4072 Educators Guide to FREE Family and Consumer Education Materials
Educators Progress Service
214 Center Street
Randolph, WI 53956-1408

920-326-3126
888-951-4469
Fax: 920-326-3127
E-mail: epsinc@centurytel.net
http://www.freeteachingaids.com

Lists and describes free films, videotapes, filmstrips, slides, web sites, and hundreds of free printed materials in the field of home econominics and consumer education for all age levels.

161 pages Annual
ISBN: 87708-408-4

Kathy Nehmer, President

4073 Focus on School
ABC-CLIO
130 Cremona Drive
#1911
Santa Barbara, CA 93117-5599

805-968-1911
800-368-6868
Fax: 805-685-9685

Hotlines, print and nonprint resources on education for young adults.

Publication Date: 1990

4074 Great Source Catalog
Great Source Education Group
PO Box 7050
Wilmington, MA 01887

800-289-4490
Fax: 800-289-3994
http://www.greatsource.com

Alternative, affordable, student-friendly K-12 materials to make teaching and learning fun for educators and students.

4075 Lesson Plans for Integrating Technology into the Classroom: Secondary Edition
Master Teacher
PO Box 1207
Manhattan, KS 66505-1207

785-539-0555
800-669-9633

Fax: 785-539-7739
http://www.masterteacher.com

Gives teachers practical lessons developed and tested by teachers across the curriculum, with students of all levels of ability in using technology.

104 pages
ISBN: 1-58992-152-6

4076 Lesson Plans for Problem-Based Learning: Secondary Edition
Master Teacher
PO Box 1207
Manhattan, KS 66505-1207

785-539-0555
800-669-9633
Fax: 785-539-7739
http://www.masterteacher.com

An instructional technique which organizes the curriculum around a major problem that students work to solve over the weeks or months.

117 pages
ISBN: 0-914607-87-1

4077 Lesson Plans for the Substitute Teacher: Secondary Edition
Master Teacher
PO Box 1207
Manhattan, KS 66505-1207

785-539-0555
800-669-9633
Fax: 785-539-7739
http://www.masterteacher.com

Gives you more than 100 lessons developed and tested by teachers across the curriculum and at all grade levels.

177 pages
ISBN: 1-58992-108-9

4078 Parent Involvement Facilitator: Secondary Edition
Master Teacher
PO Box 1207
Manhattan, KS 66505-1207

785-539-0555
800-669-9633
Fax: 785-539-7739
http://www.masterteacher.com

Ideas for you and your teachers to implement along with the exact steps for you to follow.

115 pages
ISBN: 0-914607-46-4

4079 Peterson's Guide to Independent Secondary Schools
Peterson's Guides
PO Box 2123
Princeton, NJ 08543-2123

609-243-9111
800-338-3282
Fax: 609-243-9150

Listing of over 1,400 accredited and state-approved private secondary schools in the US and abroad.

1,300 pages Annual

4080 Secondary Teachers Guide to FREE Curriculum Materials
Educators Progress Service
214 Center Street
Randolph, WI 53956-1408

920-326-3126
888-951-4469
Fax: 920-326-3127
E-mail: epsinc@centurytel.net
http://www.freeteachingaids.com

Lists and describes free supplementary teaching aids for the high school and college level.

296 pages Annual
ISBN: 87708-399-1

Kathy Nehmer, President

Directories & Handbooks
Science

4081 Earth Education: A New Beginning
Institute for Earth Education
Cedar Cove
PO Box 115
Greenville, WV 24945

304-832-6404
Fax: 304-832-6077
E-mail: iee1@aol.com
http://www.eartheducation.org

This book proposes another direction-an alternative that many environmental leaders and teachers around the world have already taken. It is called The Earth Education Path, and anyone can follow it in developing a genuine program madeup of magical learning adventures.

334 pages Paperback
ISBN: 0917011023

Steve Van Matre, Chairman

4082 Earthkeepers
Institute for Earth Education
Cedar Cove
PO Box 115
Greenville, WV 24945

304-832-6404
Fax: 304-832-6077
E-mail: iee1@aol.com
http://www.eartheducation.org

This book will give you the best picture of what a complete earth education program involves. Even if you can't set up the complete Earthkeepers program, there are many activities you can use to build an earth education program inyour own settting and situation.

108 pages Paperback
ISBN: 0917011015

Bruce Johnson, Chairman

4083 Educators Guide to FREE Science Materials
Educators Progress Service
214 Center Street
Randolph, WI 53956-1408

920-326-3126
888-951-4469
Fax: 920-326-3127
E-mail: epsinc@centurytel.net
http://www.freeteachingaids.com

Lists and describes free films, videotapes, filmstrips, slides, web sites, and hundreds of free printed materials in the field of science for all age levels.

Annual

Kathy Nehmer, President

4084 K-6 Science and Math Catalog
Carolina Biological Supply Co.
2700 York Road
Burlington, NC 27215-3398

336-584-0381
800-334-5551
Fax: 800-222-7112
http://www.carolina.com

Service teaching materials for grades Pre K through 8, including charts, computers, software, books, living animals and plants, microscopes, microscope slides, models, teaching kits and more.

4085 **Science for All Children; A Guide to Improving Science Education**
National Academy Press
Arts & Industries Bldg Room 1201
900 Jefferson Drive SW
Washington, DC 20560-0403

202-287-2063
Fax: 202-287-2070
E-mail: outreach@nas.edu
http://www.si.edu/nsrc

Provides concise and practical guidelines for implementing science education reform at local level, including the elements of an effective, inquiry-based, hands-on science program. Produced by the National Science Resources Center. Published by National Academy Press.

240 pages
ISBN: 0-309-05297-1

National Science Resources Center, Author
Douglas Lapp, Executive Director

4086 **Sunship Earth**
Institute for Earth Education
Cedar Cove
PO Box 115
Greenville, WV 24945

304-832-6404
Fax: 304-832-6077
E-mail: iee1@aol.com
http://www.eartheducation.org

Contains clear descriptions of key ecological concepts and concise reviews of important learning principals, plus over 200 additional pages of ideas, activities and guidelines for setting up a complete Sunship Earth Study Station.

265 pages Paperback
ISBN: 0876030460

Bruce Johnson, Chairman

4087 **Sunship III**
Institute for Earth Education
Cedar Cove
PO Box 115
Greenville, WV 24945

304-832-6404
Fax: 304-832-6077
E-mail: iee1@aol.com
http://www.eartheducation.org

Examines perception and choice in our daily habits and routines. It is about exploration and discovery in the larger context of where and how we live, and examining alteratives and making sacrifices on behalf of a healthier homeplanet.

133 pages Paperback
ISBN: 0917011031

Bruce Johnson, Chairman

4088 **Top Colleges for Science**
Peterson's Guides
PO Box 2123
Princeton, NJ 08543-2123

609-243-9111
800-338-3282
Fax: 609-243-9150

A guide to the leading four-year programs in the biological, chemical, geological, mathematical and physical sciences.

292 pages
ISBN: 1-560793-90-2

4089 **UNESCO Sourcebook for Out-of-School Science & Technology Education**
U.N. Educational, Scientific & Cultural Assn.
7, place de Fontenoy
F-75700 Paris
France

Offers information on science clubs, societies and congresses, science fairs and museums.

145 pages

Directories & Handbooks
Social Studies

4090 **Directory of Central America Classroom Resources**
Central American Resource Center
317 17th Avenue SE
Minneapolis, MN 55414-2012

612-627-9445

Offers information on suppliers of education resource materials about Central America, including curricula, materials, directories and organizations providing related services.

Publication Date: 1990   200 pages

4091 **Educators Guide to FREE Social Studies Materials**
Educators Progress Service
214 Center Street
Randolph, WI 53956-1408

920-326-3126
888-951-4469
Fax: 920-326-3127
E-mail: epsinc@centurytel.net
http://www.freeteachingaids.com

Lists and describes free films, videotapes, filmstrips, slides, web sites, and hundreds of free printed materials in the field of social studies for all age levels.

287 pages Annual
ISBN: 87708-405-X

Kathy Nehmer, President

4092 **Geography: A Resource Guide for Secondary Schools**
ABC-CLIO
130 Cremona Drive
#1911
Santa Barbara, CA 93117-5599

805-968-1911
800-368-6868
Fax: 805-685-9685

List of organizations and associations to use as resources for secondary education geography studies.

4093 **Who's Who in the Social Studies Annual Directory**
National Council for the Social Studies
3501 Newark Street NW
Washington, DC 20016-3100

202-966-7840
Fax: 202-966-2061

This directory provides up-to-date listings of state, local, and regional social studies organizations that are a part of the NCSS network. This resource includes addresses and phone numbers for key contacts in each council, servingas an essential tool within the social studies community.

Directories & Handbooks
Technology in Education

4094 American Trade Schools Directory
Croner Publications
10951 Sorrento Valley Road
Suite 1D
San Diego, CA 92121

858-546-1954
800-441-4033
Fax: 858-546-1955
E-mail: paul@croner.com
http://ww.croner.com

Loose leaf binder directory listing trade and technical schools throughout the United States, in alphabetical order, by state, then city, then school name.

411 pages
ISBN: 0-875140-02-5

Rosa Padilla, Office Manager

4095 Association for Educational Communications & Technology: Membership Directory
Association for Educational Communications & Tech.
1025 Vermont Avenue NW
Suite 820
Washington, DC 20005-3516

202-965-2059

Five thousand audiovisual and instructional materials specialists and school media specialists, with audio-visual and TV production personnel. Also listed are committees, task force divisions, auxiliary affiliates, stateorganizations and directory of corporate members.

200 pages Annual/Spring

4096 Chronicle Vocational School Manual
Chronicle Guidance Publications
66 Aurora Street
Moravia, NY 13118-3569

315-497-0330
800-899-0454
Fax: 315-497-3359
E-mail: customerservice@chronicleguidance.com
http://www.chronicleguidance.com

A geographical index of more than 3,500 vocational schools including all contact information, programs, admissions requirements, costs, financial aid programs and student services.

Publication Date: 1996 300 pages Annual
ISBN: 1-556312-50-4

Patricia F Hammon, Research Associate
Stephen Thompson, Managing Editor

4097 Directory of Public Vocational-Technical Schools & Institutes in the US
Media Marketing Group
PO Box 611
DeKalb, IL 60115-0611

360-576-5864

Offers information on over 1,400 post secondary vocational and technical education programs in public education; private trade and technical schools are not included.

Publication Date: 1994 400 pages Biennial
ISBN: 0-933474-51-2

4098 Directory of Vocational-Technical Schools
Media Marketing Group
PO Box 611
DeKalb, IL 60115-0611

360-576-5864

Offers information on public, postsecondary schools offering degree and non-degree occupational education.

Publication Date: 1996 450 pages Biennial
ISBN: 0-933474-52-0

4099 Educational Film & Video Locator
RR Bowker Reed Reference
121 Chanlon Road
New Providence, NJ 07974-1541

908-464-6800
Fax: 908-665-6688

Producers and distributors of educational films.

Publication Date: 1990

4100 Guide to Vocational and Technical Schools East & West
Peterson's Guides
PO Box 2123
Princeton, NJ 08543-2123

609-243-9111
800-338-3282
Fax: 609-243-9150

These two directories cover the full range of training programs in over 240 career fields divided into the categories of Business, Technology, Trade, Personal Services, and Health Care. East edition covers East of Mississippi; Westedition covers West of the Mississippi.

Per Volume

4101 Industrial Teacher Education Directory
National Assn. of Industrial Teacher Educators
University of Northern Iowa
Cedar Falls, IA 50614-0001

319-273-2753
Fax: 319-273-5818

Listing of about 2,800 industrial education faculty members at 250 universities and four-year colleges in the United States, Canada, Australia, Japan and Taiwan.

108 pages Annual
Dr. EA Dennis, Professor, Coordinating Education

4102 Information Literacy: Essential Skills for the Information Age
Syracuse University
4-194 Center for Science & Tech.
Syracuse, NY 13244-0001

315-443-3640
800-464-9107
Fax: 315-443-5448
E-mail: eric@ericir.sye.edu

Traces history, development, and economic necessity of information literacy. Reports on related subject matter standards. Includes reports on the National Educational Goals (1991), the Secretary's Commission on Achieving NecessarySkills Report (1991), and the latest updates from ALA's Information Power (1998).

377 pages
ISBN: 0-937597-44-9

Kathleen L Spitzer, Editor

4103 Internet Resource Directory for Classroom Teachers
Regulus Communications
140 N 8th Street
Suite 201
Lincoln, NE 68508-1358
402-432-2680

Directory offering information on all resources available on-line for classroom teachers, including e-mail addresses, Home Page URL's, phone and fax numbers, surface-mail addresses, classroom contacts and teaching resources.Available in paper and electronic formats.

Publication Date: 1996   272 pages   Paper Format

Jane A Austin, Coordinating Education

4104 K-12 District Technology Coordinators
Quality Education Data
1625 Broadway
Suite 250
Denver, CO 80202-4715
303-860-1832
800-525-5811
Fax: 303-209-9444
E-mail: info@qeddata.com
http://www.qeddata.com

The first in QED's National Educator Directories, this comprehensive directory of technology coordinators combines QED's exclusive database of technology and demographic data with names of technology coordinators in the 7,000 largestUS school districts. The directory includes district phone number, number of students in the district, number of computers, student/computer ratio and predominant computer brand.

Publication Date: 1994   400 pages

Laurie Christensen, Coordinating Education

4105 Multimedia and Videodisc Compendium for Education and Training
Emerging Technology Consultants
2819 Hamline Avenue N
Saint Paul, MN 55113-7118
651-639-3973
Fax: 651-639-0110
E-mail: sales@emergingtechnology.com
http://www.emergingtechnology.com

Nationally acclaimed as the most comprehensive guide to interactive media available today. Over 3,000 tiles of laserdisc, CD and multimedia software produced by 300 companies, make this award-winning publication an essential resourcefor professionals in the education and training industries. Each listing contains a detailed product description, hardware requirements, cost, subject area, grade level, publisher name and phone number.

Publication Date: 1994   140 pages
ISBN: 0-922649-24-3

Richard Pollak, CEO
Rubyanna Pollak, President

4106 NetLingo Internet Directory
PO Box 627
Ojai, CA 93024
805-640-3754
Fax: 805-640-3654
E-mail: info@netlingo.com
http://www,netlingo.com

A smart looking easy-to-understand dictionary of 3000 internet terms, 1200 chat acronyms, and much more. Modem reference book for international students, educators, industry professionals and online businesses and organizations.

Publication Date: 0   528 pages
ISBN: 0-9706396-7-8

Erin Jansen, Author

4107 Quick-Source
AM Educational Publishing
3745 Suffolk Drive
Suite D
Tallahassee, FL 32308-3048
850-668-4148

Educational technology directory with over 1,100 names, addresses, phones/faxes, and brief descriptions of the products/services of companies/organizations; supports major works/word processors (MS-DOS/MAC); conferences and othereducational technology listings.

Annual/September

4108 Schools Industrial, Technical & Trade Directory
American Business Directories
5711 S 86th Circle
Omaha, NE 68127-4146
402-593-4600
888-999-1307
Fax: 402-331-5481

A geographical listing of over 3,750 schools with all contact information, size of advertisement and first year in Yellow Pages. Also available in electronic formats.

Annual

Jerry Venner, Coordinating Education

4109 TESS: The Educational Software Selector
EPIE Institute
103 W Montauk Highway
Suite 3
Hampton Bays, NY 11946-4003
631-728-9100
Fax: 631-728-9228

A list of over 1,200 suppliers of educational software and over 18,000 educational software products (on CD-ROM) for pre-school through college information. Includes description of program, grade level data, price, platform and reviewcitations.

BiAnnual

Nancy Boland, Coordinating Education

4110 Tech Directions-Directory of Federal & Federal and State Officials Issue
Prakken Publications
416 Longshore Drive
Ann Arbor, MI 48105-1624
313-577-4042
Fax: 313-577-1672

Listing of federal and state officials concerned with vocational, technical, industrial trade and technology education in the United States and Canada.

Annual

4111 Technology in Public Schools
Quality Education Data
1624 Broadway
Suite 250
Denver, CO 80202-4715
303-860-1832
800-525-5811
Fax: 303-209-9444
E-mail: info@qeddata.com
http://www.qeddata.com

Annual survey of instructional technology represents more than 67% of all US K-12 students. Includes computer brand and processor type market share, CD-ROM, networks, LAN, modem, cable and in-depth internet access installed baseinformation.

Publication Date: 1994   160 pages   Yearly
ISBN: 0-88947-925-1

Liz Stephens, Marketing Coordinator

Periodicals
General

4112   AACS Newsletter
American Association of Christian Schools
4500 S Selsa Road
Blue Springs, MO 64015-2221
　　　　　　　　　　　　　816-252-9900
　　　　　　　　　　　Fax: 703-252-6700
Association news offering the most up-to-date information relating to Christian education.

4 pages   Monthly
Dr. Carl Herbster, Contact

4113   AACSB Newsline
American Assembly/Collegiate Schools of Business
600 Emerson Road
Suite 300
Saint Louis, MO 63141-6762
　　　　　　　　　　　　　314-872-8481
　　　　　　　　　　　Fax: 314-872-8495
Covers assembly activities as well as trends and issues in management education.

32 pages   Quarterly
Sharon Barber, Contact

4114   AAHE Bulletin
American Association for Higher Education
1 Dupont Circle
Suite 360
Washington, DC 20036
　　　　　　　　　　　　　202-293-6440
　　　　　　　　　　　Fax: 202-293-0073
　　　　　　　　http://www.aahebulletin.com
Electronic newsletter

16 pages   Monthly
Vicky Hendly Dobin, Manager

4115   ACJS Today
Academy of Criminal Justice Services
7339 Hanover Parkway
Suite A
Greenbelta, MD 20770
　　　　　　　　　　　　　301-446-6300
　　　　　　　　　　　　　800-757-2257
　　　　　　　　　　　Fax: 301-446-2819
　　　　　　　　　　　http://www.acjs.org
Provides upcoming events, news releases, ACJS activities, ads, book reviews and miscellaneous information.

24-32 pages   Quarterly
Laura Myers, Editor
Laura Monaco, Association Manager

4116   ASCD Update
Assn. for Supervision & Curriculum Development
1703 N Beauregard Street
Alexandria, VA 22311
　　　　　　　　　　　　　703-578-9600
　　　　　　　　　　　Fax: 703-575-5400
News on contemporary education issues and information on ASCD programs.

Ronald Brandt, Publisher
John O'Neil, Editor

4117   ASSC Newsletter
Arkansas School Study Council
255 Graduate Education Building
Fayetteville, AR 72701
　　　　　　　　　　　　　479-442-8464
　　　　　　　　　　　Fax: 479-442-2038
Monthly up-date on education, finance, new legislation, mandates for Arkansas public schools.

3-10 pages
Martin Schoppmeyer, Editor

4118   AV Guide Newsletter
Educational Screen
380 E NW Highway
Des Plaines, IL 60016-2201
　　　　　　　　　　　　　847-298-6622
　　　　　　　　　　　Fax: 847-390-0408
Provides concise and practical information on audiovisually oriented products with an emphasis on new ideas and methods of using learning media, including educational computer software.

Monthly
ISSN: 0091-360X

HS Gillette, Publisher
Natalie Ferguson, Editor

4119   Academe
American Association of University Professors
1012 14th Street NW
Suite 500
Washington, DC 20005-3406
　　　　　　　　　　　　　202-737-5900
　　　　　　　　　　　Fax: 202-737-5526
　　　　　　　　E-mail: academe@aaup.org
　　　　　　　　　　　http://www.aaup.org
A thoughtful and provocative review of developments affecting higher education faculty. With timely features and informative departments, Academe delivers the latest on the state of the profession, legal and legislative trends, andissues in academia.

BiMonthly

Lawrence Hanley, Editor, Author
Gwendolyn Bradley, Managing Co-Director
Wendi Maloney, Managing Editor

4120   Advocate
National Education Association of New York
217 Lark Street
Albany, NY 12210-1101
　　　　　　　　　　　　　518-462-6451
　　　　　　　　　　　Fax: 518-462-1731
The official newsletter of the NEA of New York. The Advocate features news and photos of organizational events and activities, legislative and political developments, professional issues and other items affecting public educationemployees.

12-16 pages   9x Year

Gregory S Nash, President
Mollie T Merchiane, Editor

4121 Aero Gramme
Alternative Education Resource Organizations
417 Roslyn Road
Roslyn Heights, NY 11577-2620
516-621-2195
800-769-4171
Fax: 516-625-3257

Networks all forms of educational alternatives, from public and private alternative schools to homeschooling.

Quarterly
Jerry Mintz, Editor

4122 Agenda: Jewish Education
Jewish Education Service of North America
111 Eighth Avenue
Suite 11E
New York, NY 10011
212-284-6950
Fax: 212-284-6951
E-mail: info@jesna.org
http://www.jesna.org

Seeks to create a community of discourse on issues of Jewish public policy dealing with Jewish education and the indications of policy options for the practice of Jewish education.

Quarterly
ISSN: 1072-1150

Amy Skin, Dir Marketing/Communication

4123 American Council on Education: GED Testing Service
American Council on Education
1 Dupont Circle NW
Suite 800
Washington, DC 20036-1193
202-939-9300
Fax: 202-833-4760

Information relating to GED items and testing.

8 pages 5x Year
Colleen Allen, Contact

4124 American Journal of Education
University of Chicago
5835 S Kimbark Avenue
Chicago, IL 60637
773-702-1555
Fax: 773-702-6207
E-mail: aje@uchicago.edu

Quarterly

Robert Dreeben and Zalman Usiskin, Author
John E Craig, Editor
Susan S Stodolsky, Editor

4125 American Scholar
1785 Massachusetts Avenue NW
4th Floor
Washington, DC 20036-2117
202-265-3808

A general interest magazine that includes articles on science, literature, and book reviews.

Quarterly
Anne Fadiman, Editor

4126 American Students & Teachers Abroad
US Government Printing Office
732 North Capitol Street NW
Washington, DC 20401
202-512-0000
Fax: 202-512-1293
E-mail: admin@access.gpo.gov
http://www.access.gpo.gov

4127 Annual Report & Notes from the Field
Jessie Ball duPont Fund
One Dependent Drive
Suite 1400
Jacksonville, FL 32202-5011
904-353-0890
800-252-3452
Fax: 904-353-9870
E-mail: smagill@dupontfund.org
http://www.dupontfund.org

Focused on a variety of good work aimed at growing the capacity of the nonprofit sector.

Publication Date: 0 Annually

4128 Association of Orthodox Jewish Teachers of the New York Public Schools
Association of Orthodox Jewish Teachers of the NY
1577 Coney Island Avenue
Brooklyn, NY 11230
718-258-3585
Fax: 718-258-3586
E-mail: aojt@juno.com

Newsletter representing observant Jewish teachers in the New York City Public Schools.

8-12 pages Quarterly Newsletter
Max Zakon, Executive Director

4129 Between Classes-Elderhostel Catalog
Elderhostel
75 Federal Street
Boston, MA 02110-1913
617-426-7788
Fax: 617-426-8351
http://www.elderhostel.org

Seasonal listings of elderhostel educational programs offered by educational cultural institutions in the US and 60 countries overseas.

120 pages Quarterly
Heather Baynes, Contact

4130 Blumenfeld Education Newsletter
PO Box 45161
Boise, ID 83711-5161

Providing knowledge to parents and educators who want to save children of America from destructive forces that endanger them. Children in public schools are at grave risk in 4 ways: academically, spiritually, morally, physically, andonly a well-informed public will be able to reduce these risks.

8 pages
Peter F Watt, Publisher
Samuel L Blumenfeld, Editor

4131 Brighton Times
Brighton Academy/Foundation of Human Understanding
1121 NE 7th Street
Grants Pass, OR 97526-1421
541-474-6865
Fax: 541-474-6866

Home schooling information.

Monthly
Cynthia Coumoyer, Contact

4132 **Brochure of American-Sponsored Overseas Schools**
Office of Overseas Schools, Department of State
Room 245
SA-29
Washington, DC 20522
202-261-8200
Fax: 202-261-8224

4133 **Business-Education Insider**
Heritage Foundation
214 Massachusetts Avenue NE
Washington, DC 20002-4958
202-546-4400
Fax: 202-546-8328

Deals with issues relating to the corporate/business world, and the effects it has on education.

Monthly

Jeanne Allen, Contact

4134 **CBE Report**
Association for Community Based Education
1806 Vernon Street NW
Washington, DC 20009-1217
202-462-6333

Educational institutions covering news, workshops and resources.

Monthly

4135 **CEDS Communique**
The Council for Exceptional Children
1920 Association Drive
Reston, VA 20191-1545
703-620-3660
888-232-7733
Fax: 703-264-9494

Reports on the activities of the Council for Educational Diagnostic Services and information about special programs, upcoming events, current trends and practices, and other topical matters.

Quarterly

Lamoine Miller, Contact

4136 **Catalyst for Change**
Texas A & M University- Commerce
Dept. of Education Administration
Commerce, TX 75429
903-886-5521
Fax: 903-886-5507
E-mail: anita_pankake@tamu-commerce.edu

A referred educational journal featuring articles on a variety of current educational topics.

36 pages 3x Year
ISSN: 0739-2532

Anita Pankake, Author
Stacey Edmonson, Editor
Anita Pankake, Editor

4137 **Center Focus**
Center of Concern
1225 Otis Street NE
Washington, DC 20017-2516
202-635-2757
Fax: 202-832-9494
E-mail: coc@coc.org
http://www.coc.org

Newsletters addressing the everchanging needs and concerns in the education field.

6 pages BiMonthly

Jane Deren, Publisher/Editor

4138 **Center for Continuing Education of Women Newsletter**
University of Michigan
Ann Arbor, MI 48109
734-763-1400
Fax: 734-936-1641

Association news focusing on the concerns of women in education.

4 pages

4139 **Center for Parent Education Newsletter**
81 Wyman Street
Wapham, MA 02160
617-964-2442

Offers information and tips to address parent involvement in the education of their children.

BiMonthly

4140 **Change**
Heldref Publications
1319 18th Street NW
Washington, DC 20036-1802
202-296-6267
800-365-9753
Fax: 202-296-5149
http://www.heldref.org

Perspectives on the critical issues shaping the world of higher education. It is not only issue-oriented and reflective, but challenges the status quo in higher education.

BiMonthly

Margaret A Miller, President
Theodore J Marchese, VP/Editor

4141 **Clearing House: A Journal of Educational Research**
Heldref Publications
1319 18th Street NW
Washington, DC 20036-1826
202-296-6267
800-365-9753
Fax: 202-296-5149
E-mail: tch@heldfred.org

Each issue offers a variety of articles for teachers and administrators of middle schools and junior and senior high schools. It includes experiments, trends and accomplishments in courses, teaching methods, administrative proceduresand school programs.

4 pages BiMonthly
ISSN: 0009-8655

Deborah N Cohen, Promotions Manager
Judy Cusick, Managing Editor

4142 **Commuter Perspectives**
National Clearinghouse for Commuter Programs
1195 Stamp Union
College Park, MD 30314-9634
301-405-0986
Fax: 301-314-9874
E-mail: nccp@accmail.umd.edu
http://www.umd.edu/NCCP

A quarterly newsletter published by the National Clearinghouse for Commuter Programs for professionals who work for, with, and on behalf of commuter students.

8 pages Quarterly

Barbara Jacoby, Contact

Publications / Periodicals

4143 Contemporary Education
Indiana State University, School of Education
SE 1005th
Terre Haute, IN 47809-0001

877-856-8005
Fax: 812-856-8088

A readable and currently informative journal of topics in the mainstream of educational thought.

Quarterly
ISSN: 0010-7476

Todd Whitaker, Editor
Beth Whitaker, Editor

4144 Counterpoint
LRP Publications
747 Dresher Road
PO Box 980
Horsham, PA 19044-0980

215-784-0941
800-341-7874
Fax: 215-784-9639
E-mail: custserve@lrp.com
http://www.lrp.com

Offers its readers concise, informative and timely articles covering innovative practices in special education. Covers: special education news from the states; updates on curriculum; developments in special education technology;classified ads; descriptions of new products and publications; and more.

Quarterly

Gary Bagin, Director Communications
Ann Checkosky, Editor

4145 Creative Child & Adult Quarterly
Nat'l Assn. for Creative Children & Adults
8080 Springvalley Drive
Cincinnati, OH 45236-1352

513-631-1777

Quarterly
Anne Fabe Isaacs, Editor

4146 Creativity Research Journal
Lawrence Erlbaum Associates
10 Industrial Avenue
Mahwah, NJ 07430-2262

201-258-2200
800-926-6579
Fax: 201-236-0072
E-mail: journals@erlbaum.com
http://www.erlbaum.com

A peer-reviewed journal covering a full range of approaches including behavioral, cognitive, clinical developmental, educational, social and organizational. Online access is available by visiting LEAonline.com

Quarterly
ISSN: 1040-0419

Mark A Runco, PhD., Editor

4147 Currents
Council for Advancement & Support of Education
1307 New York Avenue NW
Suite 1000
Washington, DC 20005-4726

703-379-4611

A how-to magazine covering educational fund raising and public relations publications.

Monthly
Sue Partyke, Editor

4148 DCDT Network
The Council for Exceptional Children
1920 Association Drive
Reston, VA 20191-1545

703-620-3660
888-232-7733
Fax: 703-264-9494

Newsletter of the Division on Career Development and Transition. Provides the latest information on legislation, projects, resource materials and implementation strategies in the field of career development and transition for personswith disabilities and/or who are gifted. Carries information about Division activities, upcoming events, announcements and reports of particular interest to DCDT members.

3x Year

Sherrilyn Fisher, Contact

4149 DECA Dimensions
1908 Association Drive
Reston, VA 20191-1503

703-860-5000
Fax: 703-860-4013
http://www.deca.org

An educational nonprofit association news management for marketing education students across the country, Canada, Guam and Puerto Rico. Offers information on DECA activities, leadership, business and career skills, which help developfuture leaders in business, marketing and management.

36 pages Quarterly
ISSN: 1060-6106

Carol Lund, Author

Carol Lund, Editor

4150 DLD Times
The Council for Exceptional Children
1920 Association Drive
Reston, VA 20191-1589

703-620-3660
800-CEC-SPED
Fax: 703-264-1637

Information concerning education and welfare of children and youth with learning disabilities.

8 pages TriQuarterly
Katherine Garnett

4151 Decision Line
Decision Sciences Institute
University Plaza
Atlanta, GA 30303

404-651-4000
Fax: 404-651-2896

Contains articles on education, business and decision sciences as well as available positions and textbook advertising.

32 pages 5x Year
K Roscoe Davis

4152 Desktop Presentations & Publishing
Doron & Associates
1213 Ridgecrest Circle
Denton, TX 76205-5421

940-320-0068
Fax: 940-591-9586

Computer generated presentations and visual aids for education and business.

16 pages BiMonthly
Tom Doron, Contact

4153 Development and Alumni Relations Report
LRP Publications
747 Dresher Road
PO Box 980
Horsham, PA 19044-0980
215-784-0941
800-341-7874
Fax: 215-784-0870
E-mail: custserve@lrp.com
http://www.lrp.com

Provides colleges and universities with innovative ideas for improving: alumni relations; the involvement of alumni in clubs and chapters; annual giving; endowment and capital campaigns; and planned giving. Plus, you can recieve free e-mail updates on crucial news affecting your job with your paid subscription.

Monthly Newsletter

Kate Rago, Director Customer Service
Edward Filo, Editor

4154 Different Books
Place in the Woods
3900 Glenwood Avenue
Golden Valley, MN 55422-5302
763-374-2120
Fax: 952-593-5593
E-mail: differentbooks@aol.com

Special imprint of books by, for and about persons on a different path. Features main characters with disabilities as heroes and heroines in storyline. For hi-lo reading in early elementary grades (3-7).

Paperback

Roger Hammer, Publisher

4155 Directions
AFS Intercultural Programs USA
198 Madison Avenue
Floor 8
New York, NY 10016
212-299-9000
Fax: 212-299-9090

News of AFS US volunteers.

6 pages Monthly

Pedro Valez, Contact

4156 Disability Compliance for Higher Education
LRP Publications
747 Dresher Road
PO Box 980
Horsham, PA 19044-0980
215-784-0941
800-341-7874
Fax: 215-784-9639
E-mail: custserve@lrp.com
http://www.lrp.com/ed

Newsletter helps colleges determine if they're complying with the Americans with Disabilities Act (ADA) and Section 504 of the Rehabilitation Act- so they can avoid costly litigation. Gives tips on how to provide reasonable accommodations in test-taking, grading, admissions, and accessibility to programs and facilities.

Monthly
ISSN: 1086-1335

Edward Filo, Author
Gary Bagin, Director Communications
Edward Filo, Editor

4157 Diversity 2000
Holocaust Resource Center
Kean College
1000 Morris Avenue
Union, NJ 07083

Offers ideas and issues on multicultural school education programs.

BiMonthly

J Preill, Contact

4158 ERIC/CRESS Bulletin
AEL, Inc.
PO Box 1348
Charleston, WV 25325-1348
304-347-0437
800-624-9120
Fax: 304-347-0467
E-mail: ericrc@ael.org

Announces new developments in the ERIC system nationally, and publications and events relevant to American Indians, Alaska Natives, Mexican Americans, migrants, outdoor education and rural, small schools.

3x Year Newsletter

Patricia Hammer Cahape, Associate Director

4159 Eagle Forum
Eagle Education Fund
8383 E 123rd Avenue
Brighton, CO 80601-8110

News on the Eagle Education Fund.

Quarterly

Jayne Schindler, Editor

4160 EdPress News
Association of Educational Publishers
510 Heron Drive
Suite 201
Logan Township, NJ 08085
856-241-7772
Fax: 856-241-0709
E-mail: mail@edpress.org
http://www.edpress.org

The Association supports the growth of educational publishing and it's positive effects on learning and teaching. EdPress provides information and analysis of markets and trends, education and legislative policy, learning and teaching research, and intellectual property. The Association also provides training and staff development programs, promotes supplemental learning resources as essential curriculum materials, and advocates on issues relevant to its constituents.

Charlene F Gaynor, Executive Director
Stacey Pusey, Communications Director

4161 Education
Project Innovation
1362 Santa Cruz Court
Chula Vista, CA 91910-7114
760-630-9938
E-mail: rcassel5@aol.com
http://www.rcassel.com

Original investigations and theoretical articles dealing with education. Preference given to innovations, real or magical, which promise to improve learning.

160 pages Quarterly
ISSN: 0013-1172

Dr. Russell Cassel, Editor
Lan Mieu Cassel, Managing Editor

4162 Education Digest
Prakken Publications
PO Box 8623
3970 Varsity Drive
Ann Arbor, MI 48107-8623
734-975-2800
800-530-9673

Fax: 734-975-2787
E-mail: publisher@techdirectories.com
http://www.eddigest.com

Offers outstanding articles condensed for quick review from over 200 magazines, monthlies, books, newsletters and journals, timely and important for professional educators and others interested in the field.

80 pages Monthly
ISSN: 0013-127X

George F Kennedy, Publisher
Kenneth Schroeder, Managing Editor

4163 Education Hotline
6935 Arlington Road
Suite 100
Bethesda, MD 20814

301-280-3100
800-346-1834
Fax: 301-280-3250
E-mail: ads@epe.org
http://www.edweek.org

Education newsletter.

4164 Education Newsline
National Association of Christian Educators
PO Box 3200
Costa Mesa, CA 92628-3200

949-251-9333

Articles pertinent to public education for teachers and parents, current trends and solutions and the work of Citizens for Excellence in Education.

8 pages BiMonthly

Robert Simonds, Publisher
Kathi Hudson, Editor

4165 Education Now and in the Future
Northwest Regional Educational Laboratory
101 SW Main Street
Suite 500
Portland, OR 97204-3213

503-275-9500
800-597-6339
Fax: 503-275-0458
E-mail: info@nwrel.org
http://www.nwrel.org

Contains articles about products, events, research and publications produced or sponsored by the NW Regional Educational Laboratory, a private nonprofit educational institution whose mission is to help schools improve outcomes for allstudents.

Carol F Thomas, CEO

4166 Education Quarterly
New Jersey State Department of Education
100 Riverview Plaza
PO Box 500
Trenton, NJ 08625

609-292-4040

New Jersey education information and updates.

6 pages Quarterly

Richard Vespucci, Contact

4167 Education USA
Aspen Publishing, Inc.
1101 King Street
Suite 444
Alexandria, VA 22314-2944

703-683-4100
800-638-8437
Fax: 301-417-7650

Offers information on court decisions, federal funding, the national debate over standards, education research, school finance, and more. Subscribers receive biweekly reports on Education Department policies on Title I, specialeducation, bilingual education, drug-free schools and other issues affecting schools nationwide.

8-10 pages BiWeekly

Cynthia Carter, Contact

4168 Education Update
Heritage Foundation
214 Massachusetts Avenue NE
Washington, DC 20002-4958

202-546-4400
Fax: 202-544-7330
http://www.heritage.org

Contains analyses of policy issues and trends in US education.

4169 Education Week
6935 Arlington Road
Suite 100
Bethesda, MD 20814

301-280-3100
800-346-1834
Fax: 301-280-3250
E-mail: ads@epe.org
http://www.edweek.org

For principals, superintendents, director, managers and other administrators.

4170 Education in Focus
Books for All Times
PO Box 2
Alexandria, VA 22313-0002

703-548-0457
E-mail: jdavid@bfat.com

Examines failures and successes of public and private education by looking beneath the surface for answers and explanations.

6 pages BiAnnually
ISSN: 1049-7250

Joe David, Editor

4171 Educational Forum
University of Colorado-Denver, School of Education
PO Box 173364
Denver, CO 80217-3364

303-556-3402
Fax: 303-556-4479

Quarterly

4172 Educational Freedom Spotlight On Homeschooling
Clonlara Home Based Education Programs
1289 Jewett Street
Ann Arbor, MI 48104-6201

734-769-4511
Fax: 734-769-9629
E-mail: clonlara@wash.k12.mi.us
http://www.clonlara.org

Clonlara School is committed to illuminating educational rights and freedoms through our actions and deep dedication to human rights and dignity.

12 pages Monthly

Susan Andrews, Editor
Carmen Amabile, Coordinator

4173 Educational Horizons
P. Lambda Theta, Int'l Honor & Professional Assn.
PO Box 6626
Bloomington, IN 47407-6626

812-339-3411
Fax: 812-339-3462
E-mail: root@pilambda.org
http://www.pilambda.org

Founded in the spirit of academic excellence in order to provide leadership in addressing educational, social and cultural issues of national and international significance and to enhance the status of educators by providing arecognized forum for sharing new perspectives, research findings and scholarly essays.

48 pages Quarterly
ISSN: 0013-175X

Juli Knutson, Editor

4174 Educational Research Forum
American Educational Research Association
1230 17th Street NW
Washington, DC 20036-3078
202-223-9485
Fax: 202-775-1824
E-mail: aera@gmu.edu

Contains news and information on educational research, teaching, counseling and school administration.

4175 Educational Researcher
American Educational Research Association
1230 17th Street NW
Washington, DC 20036-3078
202-223-9485
Fax: 202-775-1824
E-mail: aera@gmu.edu

Publishes research news and commentary on events in the field of educational research and articles of a wide interest to anyone involved in education.

9x Year

Robert Donmoyer, Editor
Leannah Harding, Managing Editor

4176 Educational Theory
University of Illinois at Urbana
1310 S 6th Street
Champaign, IL 61820-6925
217-333-3003
Fax: 217-244-3711
E-mail: edtheory@uiuc.edu
http://www.ed.uiuc.edu/educational-theory

The purpose of this journal is to foster the continuing development of educational theory and encourage wide and effective discussion of theoretical problems with the educational profession. Publishes articles and studies in thefoundations of education and in related disciplines outside the field of education which contribute to the advancement of education theory.

570 pages Quarterly
ISSN: 0013-2004

Nicholas C Burbules, Editor
Diane E Beckett, Business Manager

4177 Exceptional Children
The Council for Exceptional Children
1920 Association Drive
Reston, VA 20191-1545
703-620-3660
800-232-7323
Fax: 703-264-1637

Informs readers through research studies, articles by authorities in the field of special education, and discussions of current issues and problems.

Quarterly
ISSN: 0014-4029

Bob Algozzine, Editor
Martha Thurlow, Editor

4178 Focus
Florida Education Association
118 N Monroe Street
Tallahassee, FL 32301-1531
850-224-1161
Fax: 850-681-2905

Emphasizes such issues as education, unionism and politics.

8 pages Quarterly

Pat Tomillo, Publisher
Frank Ciarlo, Editor

4179 Focus on Autism
Pro-Ed., Inc.
8700 Shoal Creek Boulevard
Austin, TX 78757-6816
512-451-3246
800-897-3202
Fax: 512-302-9129
http://www.proedinc.com

Hands-on tips, techniques, methods and ideas from top authorities for improving the quality of assessment, instruction and management.

Brenda Smith Myles, PhD, Editor

4180 Focus on Research
The Council for Exceptional Children
1920 Association Drive
Reston, VA 20191-1545
703-620-3660
888-232-7733
Fax: 703-264-9494

Contains member opinion articles, debates on research issues, descriptions and dates of specific projects, notices of funded program priorities in special education, the availability of research dollars, and the discussion of emergingissues that may affect research in special education.

3x Year

Mavis Donahue, Co-Editor
Eileen Ball, Co-Editor

4181 Foreign Student Service Council
2263 12th Place NW
Washington, DC 20009-4405
202-232-4979

Non-profit organization dedicated to promoting understanding between international students and Americans.

Quarterly

4182 Fortune Education Program
105 Terry Drive
Suite 120
Newtown, PA 18940-1872
800-448-3399
Fax: 215-579-8589

Professional program that offers 75% off the cover price of Fortune magazine, a free educator's desk reference, a free 2-page teaching guide, fast delivery, choice of billing options. Plus quality customer service.

Pat Sproehnle, Editor

4183 Forum
Educators for Social Responsibility
23 Garden Street
Cambridge, MA 02138-3623
617-492-1764
Fax: 617-864-5164
E-mail: educators@esrnational.org
http://www.esrnational.org

Edited for educators concerned with teaching in the nuclear age.

12 pages Quarterly

Susan Pittman, Contact

4184 Foundation for Exceptional Children: Focus
The Council for Exceptional Children
1920 Association Drive
Reston, VA 20191-1545

703-620-3660
888-232-7733
Fax: 703-264-9494

Membership and association news.

6 pages TriQuarterly

Ken Collins, Contact

4185 Fulbright News
Metro International Program Services of New York
285 W Broadway
Room 450
New York, NY 10013-2269

212-431-1195
Fax: 212-941-6291

A four page newsletter distributed 5 times a year to visiting Fulbright scholars in the New York area. Contains a scholar profile, information about activities, tips for living in the United States, events in the New York area, andrelevant announcements.

4 pages

Kristen Pendleton, Publisher

4186 GED Items
Center for Adult Learning & Education Credentials
1 Dupont Circle NW
Washington, DC 20036-1110

202-939-9490

Newsletter of the GED Testing Service with articles focusing on adult education programs, teaching tips, GED graduate success stories and administration of GED testing.

12 pages BiMonthly

4187 Gifted Child Society Newsletter
190 Rock Road
Glen Rock, NJ 07452-1736

201-444-6530
Fax: 201-444-9099
E-mail: admin@gifted.org
http://www.gifted.org

Provides educational enrichment and support for gifted children through national advocacy and various programs.

Bi-Annual

Janet L Chen, Executive Director

4188 Harvard Education Letter
8 Story Street
5th Floor
Cambridge, MA 02138

617-495-3432
800-513-0763
Fax: 617-496-3584
E-mail: editor@edletter.org
http://www.edletter.org

Published by the Harvard Graduate School of Education and reports on current research and innovative practice in PreK-12.

8 pages Bi-Monthly
ISSN: 8755-3716

Douglas Clayton, Publisher
David T Gordon, Editor

4189 Health in Action
American School Health Association
PO Box 708
Kent, OH 44240-0013

330-678-1601
800-445-2742
Fax: 330-678-4526
E-mail: asha@ashaweb.org
http://www.ashaweb.org

24 pages Quarterly
ISSN: 1540-2479

Tom Reed, Assistant Executive Director

4190 Higher Education & National Affairs
American Council on Education
1 Dupont Circle NW
Suite 800
Washington, DC 20036-1132

202-939-9365

National newsletter with Capitol Hill and Administration updates on issues that affect colleges and universities. Includes stories on the federal budget, student financial aid, tax laws, Education Department regulations and research,legal issues and minorities in higher education.

Janetta Hammock, Contact

4191 History of Education Quarterly
Indian University
School of Education
Bloomington, IN 47405

812-855-9334
Fax: 812-855-3631

Discusses current and historical movements in education.

Quarterly

Amy Schutt, Editor

4192 Homeschooling Marketplace Newsletter
13106 Patrici Circle
Omaha, NE 68164

Offers information, strategies and tips for homeschooling.

Clarice Routh, Contact

4193 IDRA Newsletter
Intercultural Development Research Association
5835 Callaghan Road
Suite 350
San Antonio, TX 78228-1125

210-444-1710
Fax: 210-444-1714
E-mail: idra@txdirect.net
http://www.idra.org

Mini-journal covering topics in the education of minority, poor and language-minority students in public institutions. It provides research-based solutions and editorial materials for education.

Monthly

Maria Robledo Montecel, Executive Director

4194 IEA Reporter
Idaho Education Association
620 N 6th Street
Boise, ID 83702-5542

208-344-1341
Fax: 208-336-6967
http://www.idahoea.org

Quarterly

Diana Mikesell, VP
Kathy Phelan, President

4195 Inclusive Education Programs
LRP Publications
747 Dresher Road
PO Box 980
Horsham, PA 19044-0980
215-784-0941
800-341-7874
Fax: 215-784-0870
E-mail: custserve@lrp.com
http://www.lrp.com/ed

Newsletter covers the legal and practical issues of educating children with disabilities in regular education environments. It provides practical, how-to-advice, real life examples, and concise case summaries of the most recentjudicial case laws.

Monthly
ISSN: 1076-8548

Gary Bagin, Director Communications
Lisa Lombardo, Editor

4196 Independent Scholar
National Coalition of Independent Scholars
PO Box 5743
Berkeley, CA 94705-0743
510-704-0990

A newsletter for independent scholars and their organizations.

Quarterly

Murray Wax, Contact

4197 Innovative Higher Education
Kluwer Academic/Human Sciences Press
233 Spring Street
New York, NY 10013
212-620-8000
800-221-9369
Fax: 212-463-0742
http://www.wkpa.nl

Provides educators and scholars with the latest creative strategies, programs and innovations designed to meet contemporary challenges in higher education. Professionals throughout the world contribute high-quality papers on thechanging rules of vocational and liberal arts education, the needs of adults reentering the education process, and the reconciliation of faculty desires to economic realities, among other topics.

Quarterly
ISSN: 0742-5627

Carol Bischoff, Publisher
Ronald Simpson, Editor

4198 Insight
Independent Education Consultants Association
3251 Old Lee Highway
Suite 510
Fairfax, VA 22030-1504
703-591-4850
800-888-4322
Fax: 703-591-4860
E-mail: requests@IECAonline.com
http://www.IECAonline.com

Publication of national professional association of educational counselors working in private practice. Association provides counseling in college, secondary schools, learning disabilities and wilderness therapy programs.

Rebecca Peek, Author
Mark H Sklarow, Executive Director

4199 International Education
University of Tennessee
College of Education
Health & Human Services
Knoxville, TN 37996-3400
865-974-5252
Fax: 865-974-8718
E-mail: scarey@utk.edu

Publishes articles related to various international topics.

Publication Date: 1997   BiAnnual/Paperback
ISSN: 0160-5429

Sue Carey, Managing Editor

4200 International Journal of Qualitive Studies in Education
Sanchez 310
University of Texas at Austin
Austin, TX 78712
512-232-1552
Fax: 512-471-5975
E-mail: 8se@uts.cc.utexas.edu
http://www.tandF.co.uk/journals

Aims to enhance the theory of qualitative research in education.

6 Issues Per Year

Jim Scheurich, Editor
Angela Valenzuela, Editor

4201 International Volunteer
Volunteers for Peace
1034 Tiffany Road
Belmont, VT 05730-9988
802-259-2759
Fax: 802-259-2922
E-mail: vfp@vfp.org
http://www.vfp.org

Newsletter of Volunteers for Peace, which provides intercultural education and community services.

8 pages Annual

Peter Coldwell, Author

4202 It Starts in the Classroom
National School Public Relations Association
1501 Lee Highway
Suite 201
Arlington, VA 22209-1109
703-528-5840

Devoted to classroom and teacher public relations techniques and ideas.

8 pages Monthly

Joseph Scherer, Publisher
Judi Cowan, Editor

4203 Journal of Behavioral Education
Kluwer Academic/Human Sciences Press
233 Spring Street
New York, NY 10013
212-620-8000
800-221-9369
Fax: 212-463-0742
http://www.wkpa.nl

Provides the first single-source forum for the publication of research on the application of behavioral principles and technology to education. Publishes original empirical research and brief reports covering behavioral education inregular, special and adult education settings.

Subject populations include handicapped, at-risk, and non-handicapped students of all ages.

Quarterly
ISSN: 1053-0819

Carol Bischoff, Publisher
Christopher Skinner, Co-Editor

4204 **Journal of Creative Behavior**
Creative Education Foundation
1050 Union Road
Suite 4
Buffalo, NY 14224-3402

716-675-3181
Fax: 716-675-3209
E-mail: cefhq@cef-cpsi.org
http://www.cef-cpsi.org

Devoted to the serious general reader with vocational/avocational interests in the fields of creativity and problem solving. Its articles are authored not only by established writers in the field, but by up-and coming contributors aswell. The criteria for selecting articles include reference, clarity, interest and overall quality.

Publication Date: 1995 80 pages Quarterly
ISSN: 0022-0175

Grace A Guzzetta, Managing Editor
Mary Pokojowczyk, Circulation Manager

4205 **Journal of Curriculum Theorizing**
Colgate University
Department of Education
Hamilton, NY 13346

315-228-1000
Fax: 315-228-7998

Analyzes and provides insights to curriculum movements and evolution.

Quarterly

JoAnne Pagano, Editor

4206 **Journal of Disability Policy Studies**
Pro-Ed., Inc.
8700 Shoal Creek Boulevard
Austin, TX 78757-6816

512-451-3246
800-897-3202
Fax: 512-302-9129
E-mail: proed1@aol.com
http://www.proedinc.com

Devoted exclusively to disability policy topics and issues.

Quarterly Magazine
ISSN: 1044-2073

Craig R Fiedler, JD, PhD, Editor
Billie Jo Rylance, PhD, Editor

4207 **Journal of Educational Research**
Heldref Publications
1319 18th Street NW
Washington, DC 20036-1826

202-296-6267
800-365-9753
Fax: 202-296-5149
http://www.heldref.org

Since 1920, this journal has contributed to the advancement of educational practice in elementary and secondary schools. Authors experiment with new procedures, evaluate traditional practices, replicate previous research forvalidation and perform other work central to understanding and improving the education of today's students and teachers. This Journal is a valuable resource for teachers, counselors, supervisors, administrators, planners and educational researchers.

64 pages BiMonthly
ISSN: 0022-0671

Deborah Cohen, Promotions Editor

4208 **Journal of Experimental Education**
Heldref Publications
1319 18th Street NW
Washington, DC 20036-1826

202-296-6267
800-365-9753
Fax: 202-296-5149
E-mail: jxe@heldref.org
http://www.heldref.org

Aims to improve educational practice by publishing basic and applied research studies using the range of quantitative and qualitative methodologies found in the behavioral, cognitive and social sciences. Published studies address alllevels of schooling, from preschool through graduate and professional education, and various educational context, including public and private education in the United States and abroad.

96 pages Quarterly

Paige Jackson, Managing Editor

4209 **Journal of Law and Education**
University of South Carolina Law School
Columbia, SC 29208

803-777-4155
Fax: 803-777-9405

A periodical offering information on the newest laws and legislation affecting education.

Quarterly

Eldon D Wedlock Jr, Editor

4210 **Journal of Learning Disabilities**
Pro-Ed., Inc.
8700 Shoal Creek Boulevard
Austin, TX 78757-6816

512-451-3246
800-897-3202
Fax: 512-302-9129
E-mail: proed1@aol.com
http://www.proedinc.com

Special series, feature articles and research articles.

Bi-Monthly Magazine
ISSN: 0022-2194

Wayne P Hresko, PhD, Editor-in-Chief

4211 **Journal of Negro Education**
Howard University
PO Box 311
Washington, DC 20059-0001

202-806-8120
Fax: 202-806-8434
E-mail: jne@howard.edu

A Howard University quarterly review of issues incident to the education of Black people; tracing educational developments and presenting research on issues confronting Black students in the US and around the world.

120+ pages Quarterly
ISSN: 0022-2984

D. Kamili Anderson, Associate Editor
Dr. Sylvia T. Johnson, Editor-in-Chief

4212 Journal of Positive Behavior Interventions
Pro-Ed., Inc.
8700 Shoal Creek Boulevard
Austin, TX 78757-6816

512-451-3246
800-897-3202
Fax: 512-302-9129
http://www.proedinc.com

Sound, research-based principles of positive behavior support for use in home, school and community settings for people with challenges in behavioral adaptation.

Glen Dunlap, PhD, Editor
Robert L Koegel, PhD, Editor

4213 Journal of Research and Development in Education
University of Georgia, College of Education
427 Tucker Hall
Athens, GA 30602

404-542-1154

A magazine offering insight and experimental and theoretical studies in education.

Quarterly

4214 Journal of Research in Character Education
Character Education Partnership
1025 Connecticut Avenue NW
Suite 1011
Washington, DC 20036

202-296-7743
800-988-8081
Fax: 202-296-7779
http://www.character.org

Andrea Grenadier, Director Communications
Esther Schaeffer, CEO/Executive Director

4215 Journal of Research in Rural Education
University of Maine, College of Education
5766 Shibles Hall
Orono, ME 04469-5766

207-581-2493
Fax: 207-581-2423
http://www.umaine.edu

Publishes the results of educational research relevant to rural settings.

3x Year Journal

Theodore Coladarci, Editor
Sara Sheppard, Managing Editor

4216 Journal of School Health
American School Health Association
PO Box 708
Kent, OH 44240-0013

330-678-1601
800-445-2742
Fax: 330-678-4526
E-mail: asha@ashaweb.org
http://www.ashaweb.org

Contains material related to health promotion in school settings. A non-profit organization founded in 1927, ASHA's mission is to protect and improve the health and well-being of children and youth by supporting comprehensive,preschool-12 school health programs. ASHA and its 4,000 members (school nurses, health educators, and physicians) work to improve school health services and school health environments.

40 pages Monthly
ISSN: 0022-4391

Tom Reed, Assistant Executive Director

4217 Journal of Special Education
Pro-Ed., Inc.
8700 Shoal Creek Boulevard
Austin, TX 78757-6816

512-451-3246
800-897-3202
Fax: 512-302-9129
http://www.proedinc.com

Timely, sound special education research.

Lynn S Fuchs, PhD, Editor
Douglas Fuchs, PhD, Editor

4218 Journal of Urban & Cultural Studies
University of Massachusetts at Boston
Department of English
Harbor Campus
Boston, MA 02125

617-287-5760
Fax: 617-287-6511

Explores various issues in education that deal with urban and cultural affairs.

Donaldo Macedo, Editor

4219 Kaleidoscope
Evansville-Vanderburgh School Corporation
1 SE 9th Street
Evansville, IN 47708-1821

812-435-8453

A staff publication for and about employees of the Evansville-Vanderburgh School Corporation.

8 pages Monthly

Patti S Coleman, Contact

4220 LD Forum
Council for Learning Disabilities
PO Box 40303
Overland Park, KS 68204

913-492-8755
Fax: 913-492-2546

Provides updated information and research on the activities of the Council for Learning Disabilities.

60 pages Quarterly
ISSN: 0731-9487

4221 Learning Disability Quarterly
Council for Learning Disabilities
PO Box 40303
Overland Park, KS 66204-4303

913-492-8755
Fax: 913-492-2546

Aimed at learning disabled students, their parents and educators. Accepts advertising.

Quarterly

4222 Learning Point MagazineLaboratory
North Central Regional Educational Laboratory
1900 Spring Road
Suite 300
Oak Brook, IL 60523-1447

630-649-6500
Fax: 630-649-6700
E-mail: info@ncrel.org
http://www.ncrel.org

Applies research and technology to learning.

16 pages Quarterly
Jeri Nowakowski, Director

4223 Learning Unlimited Network of Oregon
31960 SE Chin Street
Boring, OR 97009-9708

503-663-5153

Cuts through all barriers to communication and learning; institutional, personal, physical, psychological, spiritual. It focuses on basic communication/language skills but sets no limits on means or tools, subjects or participants inseeking maximum balance and productivity for all.

10 pages 9x Year

Gene Lehman, Contact

4224 Liaison Bulletin
National Assn. of State Directors of Special Ed.
1800 Diagonal Road
Suite 320
Alexandria, VA 22314-2840

703-519-3800
Fax: 703-519-3808

Membership news for persons affiliated with the National Association of State Directors of Special Education.

BiWeekly

Dr. William Schipper

4225 Liberal Education
Association of American Colleges & Universities
1818 R Street NW
Washington, DC 20009-1604

202-387-3760
Fax: 202-265-9532
http://www.aacu-edu.org

Concentrates on issues currently affecting American higher education. Promotes and strengthens undergraduate curriculum, classroom teaching and learning, collaborative leadership, faculty leadership, diversity. Other publications onhigher education include books, monographs, peer review, and on campus with women.

64 pages Quarterly
ISSN: 0024-1822

Bridget Puzon, Editor
Debra Humphreys, Comm/Public Affairs VP

4226 Link
AEL, Inc.
PO Box 1348
Charleston, WV 25325-1348

304-347-0400
800-624-9120
Fax: 304-347-0487
E-mail: aelinfo@ael.org
http://www.ael.org

A newsletter for educators providing research summaries, education news, and news of AEL products, services and events.

12 pages Quarterly Newsletter
Carolyn Luzader, Communications Associate

4227 Lisle-Interaction
433 W Sterns Street
Temperance, MI 48182-9568

734-847-7126
800-477-1538
Fax: 512-259-0392

Reports on domestic and international programs, annual meetings and board meetings of the Lisle Fellowship which seeks to broaden global awareness and appreciation of different cultures. Occasional special articles on topics such asracism, book reviews. News of members are also included.

16 pages Quarterly

Mark Kinney, Executive Director
Dianne Brause, VP

4228 MEA Today
Montana Education Association
1232 E 6th Avenue
Helena, MT 59601-3927

406-442-4250
Fax: 406-443-5081

National and state association news, legislative policies, and classroom features.

8 pages Monthly

Nancy Robbins

4229 Massachusetts Home Learning Association Newsletter
23 Mountain Street
Sharon, MA 02067-2234

781-784-8006

A source for information gleaned from all the major national magazines and many state newsletters. Calendar of events for Massachusetts homeschooling and several feature articles on legal, educational or familial issues.

24 pages Quarterly

Sharon Terry, Editor
Patrick Terry, Editor

4230 Mel Gabler's Newsletter
Educational Research Analysts
PO Box 7518
Longview, TX 75607-7518

972-753-5993

Educational information pertaining to curricula used in schools.

8 pages SemiAnnually

Mel Gabler, Publisher
Chad Rosenberger, Editor

4231 Minnesota Education Update
Office of Library Development & Services
440 Capital Square
550 Cedar Street
St. Paul, MN 55101

651-296-2821

Policies and activities in elementary and secondary education in the state of Minnesota.

8 pages Monthly

James Lee

4232 Missouri Schools
Missouri Department of Education
PO Box 480
Jefferson City, MO 65102-0480

573-751-3469
Fax: 573-751-8613

State education policy.

28 pages BiMonthly

James L Morris

4233 Momentum
National Catholic Educational Association
1077 30th Street NW
Suite 100
Washington, DC 20007-3852

202-337-6232
Fax: 202-333-6706
http://www.ncea.org

The association offers a quarterly publication, conducts research, works with voluntary groups and government agencies on educational problems, conducts seminars and workshops for all levels of educators.

Quarterly

Catherine T McNamee, CSJ, President

4234 Montana Schools
Montana Office of Public Instruction
State Capitol
Helena, MT 59620

406-444-3095
Fax: 406-444-2893

Information about people and programs in the Montana education system.

12 pages 5x Year

Ellen Meloy

4235 Montessori Observer
International Montessori Society
912 Thayer Avenue
Suite 207
Silver Spring, MD 20910-4570

301-589-1127
800-301-3131
Fax: 301-589-0733
E-mail: havis@erols.com
http://www.wdn.com/trust/ims

Provides news and information about Montessori teaching and the work of the International Montessori Society.

ISSN: 0889-5643

Lee Havis, Editor

4236 NAEIR Advantage
Nat'l Assn. for Exchange of Industrial Resources
560 McClure Street
Galesburg, IL 61401-4286

309-343-0704
800-562-0955
Fax: 309-343-3519
E-mail: member.naeir@misslink.net
http://www.freegoods.com

News of the National Association for the Exchange of Industrial Resources, which collects donations of new excess inventory from corporations and redistributes them to American schools and nonprofits.

8 pages BiMonthly

Gary C Smith, President/CEO
Jack Zavada, Communications Director

4237 NAFSA Newsletter
NAFSA: Association of International Educators
1875 Connecticut Avenue NW
8th Floor
Washington, DC 20009-5728

202-737-3699
800-836-4994
Fax: 202-737-3657
E-mail: inbox@nafsa.org
http://www.nafsa.org

Publishes news and information related to international education and exchange.

40 pages Weekly & Quarterly

Marlene M Johnson, Director/CEO

4238 NAIEC Newsletter
National Association for Industry-Education Co-op
235 Hendricks Boulevard
Buffalo, NY 14226-3304

716-834-7047
Fax: 716-834-7047
E-mail: naiec@pcom.net
http://www2.pcom.net/naiec

Has served as a clearinghouse for information on industry involvement in education for the past 30 years.

Advocates for substantive industry-education collaboration.

4 pages BiMonthly

Dr. Donald M. Clark, President/CEO

4239 NAPSEC News
Assn. of Private Schools for Exceptional Children
1522 K Street NW
Suite 1032
Washington, DC 20005-1202

202-408-3338
Fax: 202-408-3340

Association news and events.

8-12 pages Quarterly

Sherry L Kolbe, Executive Director/CEO
Barb DeGroot, Manager

4240 NEA Higher Education Advocate
National Education Association (NEA)
1201 16th Street NW
Washington, DC 20036-3207

202-822-7364
Fax: 202-822-7624
E-mail: ncuea@nea.org
http://www.nea.org

Reports on NEA and general higher education news.

4 pages Monthly

Alicia Sandoual, Publisher
Rebecca Robbins, Editor

4241 NEA Today
National Education Association (NEA)
1201 16th Street NW
Washington, DC 20036-3290

202-822-7364
Fax: 202-822-7624
E-mail: ncuea@nea.org
http://www.nea.org

Contains news and features of interest to classroom teachers and other employees of schools.

8x Year

Bill Fischer, Editor
Suzanne Wade, Advertising Coordinator

4242 NEWSLINKS
International Schools Services
15 Roszel Road
Princeton, NJ 08540-6248

609-452-0990
Fax: 609-452-2690
E-mail: newslinks@iss.edu
http://www.iss.edu

Regularly published newspaper of International Schools Services that is distributed free of charge to overseas teachers, school administrators and libraries, US universities, educational organizations, multinational corporations, school supply companies and educational publishers.

32-40 pages Quarterly

Judy Seltz, Director Communications

4243 NJEA Review
New Jersey Education Association
180 W State Street
PO Box 1211
Trenton, NJ 08607

609-599-4561
Fax: 609-392-6321

Monthly educational journal of the New Jersey Education Association which focuses on educational news and issues related to New Jersey public schools. Its

Publications / Periodicals

readers are active and retired teaching staff members and support staff, administrators, board members, teacher education students, and others in New Jersey public schools and colleges.

80 pages Monthly
ISSN: 0027-6758

Martha O DeBlieu, Editor
Rosemary Kaub, Conference Manager

4244 NREA News
National Rural Education Association
Education Room 246
Fort Collins, CO 80523-0001

Fax: 970-491-1317
E-mail: jnewlin@lamar.colostate.edu
http://www.colostate.edu

Keeps all members up-to-date on Association activities, events, rural education conferences and meetings, and research projects in progress.

8 pages Quarterly Newsletter
ISSN: 0273-4460

Joseph T Newlin, Editor

4245 National Accrediting Commission of Cosmetology, Arts and Sciences
National Accrediting Commission of Cosmetology
901 N Stuart Street
Suite 900
Arlington, VA 22203-1816

703-527-7600
Fax: 703-379-2200
E-mail: naccas@naccas.org
http://www.naccas.org

Information on accreditation, cosmetology schools and any federal regulations affecting accreditation and postsecondary education.

20 pages 6x Year

Clifford A Culbreath, Editor

4246 National Alliance of Black School Educators (NABSE)
2816 Georgia Avenue NW
Washington, DC 20001-3819

202-483-1549
800-221-2654
Fax: 202-608-6319
E-mail: nabse@nabse.org
http://www.nabse.org

For teachers, principals, specialists, superintendents, school board members and higher education personnel.

15-25 pages 3x Year

4247 National Homeschool Association Newsletter
National Homeschool Association
PO Box 290
Hartland, MI 48353-0290

425-432-1544

Information on what's happening in the homeschooling community.

28 pages Quarterly

4248 National Monitor of Education
CA Monitor of Education
1331 Fairmount Avenue
Suite 61
El Cerrito, CA 94530

510-527-4430
Fax: 510-528-9833
E-mail: jsod@aol.com
http://www.e-files.org

Supports traditional moral and academic values in education. Reports on litigation and reviews various education publications. Issues reported on include parents' rights and movement to restore basic academics.

8 pages Bi-Monthly/Paperback

Susan O'Donnell, Publisher
Susan Sweet, Newsletter Design

4249 New Hampshire Educator
National Education Association, New Hampshire
103 N State Street
Concord, NH 03301-4334

603-224-7751
Fax: 603-224-2648

Reports on the advancements in education in the state and nation and promotes the welfare of educators.

10 pages Monthly

Carol Carstarphen

4250 New Images
METCO
55 Dimock Street
Boston, MA 02119-1029

617-427-1545

Mailed to METCO parents and educational institutions local and national.

4 pages Quarterly

JM Mitchell

4251 New York Teacher
New York State United Teachers
PO Box 15008
Albany, NY 12212-5008

518-213-6000
800-342-9810
Fax: 518-213-6415

Edited primarily for teaching personnel in elementary, intermediate and high schools and colleges. News and features cover organizations' development, progress of legislation affecting education at local state and national levels and news of the labor movement.

BiWeekly

Nicki Rhue, Advertising Director
Bob Fitzpatrick, Production Manager

4252 News N' Notes
NTID at Rochester Institute of Technology
LBJ 2264
Box 9687
Rochester, NY 14623

716-475-6201

Convention news, membership information, education legislation advocacy and personal contributions to the scholarly society.

12 pages Quarterly

Judy Egleston

4253 Non-Credit Learning News
Learning for All Seasons
6 Saddle Club Road
#579X
Lexington, MA 02420-2115

781-861-0379

Marketing information for directors and marketers of non-credit programs.

8 pages 10x Year

Susan Capon

4254 North American Association of Educational Negotiators News
122 White Pine Drive
Springfield, IL 62707-8760
217-529-7802
Fax: 217-529-7904

Association news and notes.

25 pages BiMonthly

Lyn King

4255 Occupational Programs in California Community Colleges
Leo A Myer Associates/LAMA Books
20956 Corsair Boulevard
Hayward, CA 94545-1002
510-785-1091
Fax: 510-785-1099
E-mail: lama@lmabooks.com

Writers and publishers of HVAC books.

186 pages
ISBN: 0-88069-025-9

Barbara Ragura, Marketing Assistant

4256 Options in Learning
Alliance for Parental Involvement in Education
PO Box 59
East Chatham, NY 12060-0059
518-392-6900
Fax: 518-392-6900

A newsletter published by the Alliance for Parental Involvement in Education, a nonprofit organization which assists parents of children in public or private school or involved in homeschooling. Options In Learning includes letters, articles, resources and book reviews, calendar of events and announcements.

16-28 pages Quarterly

Katharine Houk

4257 Our Children: The National PTA Magazine
330 N Wabash Avenue
Suite 2100
Chicago, IL 60611-3603
312-670-6782
Fax: 312-670-6783
http://www.pta.org

Written by, for and about the National PTA. A nonprofit organization of parents, educators, students, and other citizens active in their schools and communities.

5x Year

Douglas Seibold, Editor
Laura Martinelli, Graphic Designer

4258 PTA National Bulletin
National Association of Hebrew Day School PTA'S
160 Broadway
New York, NY 10038-4201
212-227-1000
Fax: 212-406-6934

Educational events in day school relating to PTA movement. News of national and regional groups.

Quarterly

4259 PTA in Pennsylvania
Pennsylvania PTA
4804 Derry Street
Harrisburg, PA 17111-3440
717-564-8985
Fax: 717-564-9046
E-mail: infopta717@aol.com
http://www.papta.org

Topical articles about issues affecting education and children, such as safety and health, AIDS, parents involvement and guidance, environmental concerns and special education.

Quarterly

Kera Daily, Office Administrator

4260 Parents as Teachers National Center
2228 Ball Drive
Saint Louis, MO 63146
314-432-4330
Fax: 314-432-8963
E-mail: patnc@patnc.org
http://www.patnc.org

Provides information, training and technical assistance for those interested in adopting the home-school-community partnership program. Offers parents the information and support needed to give their children the best possible startin life.

Quarterly

Julie Robbens, Editor, Author
Susan S Stepleton, President/CEO
Cheryl Dyle-Palmer, Director Operations

4261 Passing Marks
San Bernadino City Unified School District
777 N F Street
San Bernardino, CA 92410-3017
909-381-1250
Fax: 909-388-1451

Educational resume of school activities, covering instruction, personnel, administration, board of education, etc.

12 pages Monthly

Jan Bell

4262 Pennsylvania Home Schoolers Newsletter
RR 2 Box 117
Kittanning, PA 16201-9311
724-783-6512
Fax: 724-783-6512

A support newsletter directed to homeschooling families in Pennsylvania. Articles, reviews of curriculum, advice, calendar, support group listing, children's writing section.

32 pages Quarterly

Howard Richman, Publisher
Susan Richman, Editor

4263 Pennsylvania State Education Association
400 N 3rd Street
Harrisburg, PA 17101-1346
717-255-7000
Fax: 717-255-7124
http://www.psea.org

16 pages 9x Year
ISSN: 0896-6605

William H Johnson, Editor

4264 Phi Delta Kappa Educational Foundation
PO Box 789
Bloomington, IN 47402-0789
812-339-1156
800-766-1156
Fax: 812-339-0018
E-mail: information@pdkintl.org
http://www.pdkintl.org

Articles concerned with educational research, service, and leadership; issues, trends and policy are emphazied.

350 pages 10x Year
ISBN: 0-87367-835-4

November
600 attendees and 30 exhibits

Perry A. Zirkel, Author
William Bushaw, Executive Director
Donovan Walling, Director Publications

4265 Planning for Higher Education
Society for College and University Planning (SCUP)
399 East Liberty Street
Suite 300
Ann Arbor, MI 48104

734-998-7832
Fax: 734-998-6532
E-mail: info@scup.org
http://www.scup.org/phe

A quarterly, peer-reviewed journal devoted to the advancement and application of the best planning practices for colleges and universities.

70+ pages Quarterly Journal
ISSN: 0736-0983
July
150 booths with 1,200 attendees and 150 exhibits

Tom Longin, Executive Editor
Chantelle Neumann, Managing Editor

4266 Policy & Practice
American Public Human Services Association
810 1st Street NE
Suite 500
Washington, DC 20002-4207

202-682-0100
Fax: 202-289-6555
http://www.aphsa.org

This quarterly magazine presents a comprehensive look at issues important to public human services administrators. It also features a wide spectrum of views by the best thinkers in social policy.

52 pages Quarterly
ISSN: 1520-801X

Sybil Walker Barnes, Editor

4267 Population Educator
Population Connection
1400 16th Street NW
Suite 320
Washington, DC 20036-2215

202-332-2200
800-767-1956
Fax: 202-332-2302
E-mail: poped@populationconnection.org
http://www.populationeducation.org

Offers population education news, classroom activities and workshop schedules for grades K-12.

4 pages Quarterly
Pamela Wasseman

4268 Public Education Alert
Public Education Association
39 W 32nd Street
New York, NY 10001-3803

212-868-1640
Fax: 212-302-0088
E-mail: info@peaonline
http://www.pea-online.org

Provides information and consumer-oriented analysis of law policy issues and current developments in New York City public education. PEA Alert back issues; e-guide to New York City's public high school offering comparative data.

Ray Domanico, Publisher
Jessica Wolfe, Editor

4269 QEG
Friends Council on Education
1507 Cherry Street
Philadelphia, PA 19102-1403

215-241-7245

Informal news sheet for Quaker schools.

4 pages BiMonthly
Irene McHenry

4270 QUIN: Quarterly University International News
University of Minnesota, Office in Education
149 Nicholson Hall
Minneapolis, MN 55455

612-625-1915
Fax: 612-624-6839

International campus update for students, faculty, staff and the community.

TriQuarterly
Gayla Marty

4271 Reclaiming Children and Youth
Pro-Ed., Inc.
8700 Shoal Creek Boulevard
Austin, TX 78757-6816

512-451-3246
800-897-3202
Fax: 512-302-9129
E-mail: proed1@aol.com
http://www.proedinc.com

Provides positive, creative solutions to professionals serving youth in conflict.

Quarterly Magazine
Nicholas J Long, PhD, Editor
Larry K Brendtro, PhD, Editor

4272 Recognition Review
Awards and Recognition Association
4700 W Lake Avenue
Glenview, IL 60025

847-375-4800
Fax: 877-734-9380
E-mail: rbloch@accessgroup.com
http://www.ara.org

Published monthly by the Awards and Recognition Association. Recognition Review is the leading voice of the awards, engraving and recognition industry.

Monthly
Stacy McTaggert, Editor

4273 Regional Spotlight
Southern Regional Education Board
592 10th Street NW
Atlanta, GA 30318-5776

404-875-9211

News of educational interest directed to 15 SREB-member states.

9 pages
Margaret Sullivan

4274 Remedial and Special Education
Pro-Ed., Inc.
8700 Shoal Creek Boulevard
Austin, TX 78757-6816

512-451-3246
800-897-3202
Fax: 512-302-9129
E-mail: proed1@aol.com
http://www.proedinc.com

Highest-quality interdisciplinary scholarship that bridges the gap between theory and practice involving the education of individuals for whom typical instruction is not effective.

Bi-Monthly Magazine
ISSN: 0741-9325

Edward A Polloway, EdD, Editor-in-Chief

4275 Renaissance Educator
Renaissance Educational Associates
4817 N County Road 29
Loveland, CO 80538-9515

970-679-4300

Quarterly publication highlighting educators around the world who are revealing the effectiveness of integrity in education.

8 pages Quarterly

Kristy Clark

4276 Report on Education Research
Captiol Publications
1101 King Street
Suite 444
Alexandria, VA 22314-2944

703-739-6490
800-655-5597
Fax: 800-392-7886

This report pinpoints the latest findings in both basic and applied research to refine schools' programs; finds funding sources to keep the lifeblood of those programs flowing; stays plugged into Washington to see what's coming downthe pike; and networks with colleagues on the forefront of school improvement across the nation.

10 pages BiWeekly

Cynthia Carter

4277 Research in Higher Education
Kluwer Academic/Human Sciences Press
233 Spring Street
New York, NY 10013

212-620-8000
800-221-9369
Fax: 212-463-0742
http://www.wkpa.nl

Essential source of new information for all concerned with the functioning of postsecondary educational institutions. Publishes original, quantitative research articles which contribute to an increased understanding of an institution,aid faculty in making more informed decisions about current or future operations, and improve the efficiency of an institution.

Bimonthly
ISSN: 0361-0365

Carol Bischoff, Publisher
John C Smart, Editor

4278 Research in the Schools
Mid-South Educational Research Association
University of Alabama
Tuscaloosa, AL 35487-0001

Fax: 205-348-6873

A nationally refereed journal sponsored by the Mid-South Educational Research Association and the University of Alabama. RITS publishes original contributions in the following areas: 1) Research in practice; 2) Topical Articles; 3)Methods and Techniques; 4) Assessment and 5) Other topics of interest dealing with school-based research. Contributions should follow the guidelines in the latest edition of the Publications Manual of the American Psychological Association.

James E McLean, Co-Editor
Alan S Kaufman, Co-Editor

4279 Roeper Review: A Journal on Gifted Education
Roeper Institute
PO Box 329
Bloomfield Hills, MI 48303-0329

248-203-7321
Fax: 248-203-7310
E-mail: tcross@bsu.edu
http://www.roeperreview.org

A journal that focuses on gifted and talented education, the Roeper Review applies the highest standards of peer review journalism to cover a broad range of issues. For professionals who work with teachers and for professionals whowork directly with gifted and talented children and their families, the journal provides readable coverage of policy issues. Each issue covers one or more subjects. Regular departments include research reports and book reviews.

60-80 pages Quarterly
ISSN: 0278-3193

Tracy L Cross PhD, Editor
Vicki Rossbach, Subscription

4280 Rural Educator: Journal for Rural and Small Schools
National Rural Education Association
246 E Ed Building
Colorado State University
Fort Collins, CO 80523-1588

970-491-7022
Fax: 970-491-1317
E-mail: jnewlin@lamar.colostate.edu
http://www.colostate.edu

Official journal of the NREA. A nationally recognized publication that features timely and informative articles written by leading rural educators from all levels of education. All NREA members are encouraged to submit researcharticles and items of general information for publication.

40 pages TriAnnual

Joseph T Newlin, Editor

4281 SKOLE: A Journal of Alternative Education
Down-To-Earth Books
72 Philip Street
Albany, NY 12202-1729

518-432-1578

Publishes articles, poems, and research by people engaged in alternative education.

200 pages SemiAnnually

Mary Leue

4282 SNEA Impact: The Student Voice of the Teaching Profession
National Education Association (NEA)
1201 16th Street NW
Washington, DC 20036-3207

202-822-7131
Fax: 202-822-7624

Offers articles and views on current events and the educational system through students' eyes for education professionals.

7x Year

4283 Safety Forum
Safety Society
1900 Association Drive
Reston, VA 20191-1502

703-476-3440

Offers articles and up-to-date information on school safety.

4 pages TriQuarterly

Linda Moore

4284 **School Bulletin**
Independent School District #709
Lake Ave & 2nd Street
Duluth, MN 55802

218-723-4150
Fax: 218-723-4195

Reports to school district staff and the community on issues concerning education in Duluth and throughout the state of Minnesota.

8 pages BiWeekly

Charles Anderson, Publisher
Glenn Sandvik, Editor

4285 **School Bus Fleet**
Bobit Publishing Company
PO Box 2703
Torrance, CA 90509-2703

310-533-2400
Fax: 310-533-2503

Coverage of federal vehicle and education regulations that affect pupil transportation, policy and management issues and, of course, how to improve the safety of children riding yellow buses. Special sections include how to transportstudents with disabilities, a state report on regulations and legislation, and various other departments. School officials that manage finance operations at school districts, private contractors, school bus manufacturers are the audience.

4286 **School Foodservice & Nutrition**
1600 Duke Street
Floor 7
Alexandria, VA 22314-3421

703-739-3900
800-877-8822
Fax: 703-739-3915

For foodservice professionals presenting current articles on industry issues, management events, legislative issues, public relations programs and professional development news.

11x Year

Adrienne Gall Tufts, Editor

4287 **School Law Bulletin**
Quinlan Publishing
23 Drydock Avenue
Boston, MA 02210-2336

617-542-0048

Covers cases and laws pertaining to schools.

8 pages Monthly

4288 **School Safety**
National School Safety Center
141 Duesenberg Drive
Suite 11
Westlake Village, CA 91362-3815

805-373-9977
800-453-7461
Fax: 805-373-9277
E-mail: rstephens@nssc1.org
http://www.nssc1.org

For educators, law enforcers, judges and legislators on the prevention of drugs, gangs, weapons, bullying, discipline problems and vandalism; also on-site security and character development as they relate to students and schools.

Monthly

Dr. Ronald D Stephens, Executive Director
June Lane Arnette, Editor

4289 **School Transportation News**
STN Media Company Inc.
700 Torrance Boulevard
Suite C
Redondo Beach, CA 90277

310-792-2226
Fax: 310-792-2231
E-mail: bpaul@stnonline.com
http://www.stnonline.com

Covers school district and contractor fleets, special needs and prekindergarten transportation, Head Start, and more on a monthly basis. Reports developments affecting public school transportation supervisors and directors, statedirectors of school transportation, school bus contractors, special needs transportation, Head Start transportation, private school transportation, school business officials responsible for transportation and industry suppliers.

Magazine/Monthly
100 booths

Bill Paul, Author
Colette Paul, VP
Bill Paul, Publisher/Editor

4290 **School Zone**
West Aurora Public Schools, District 129
80 S River Street
#14
Aurora, IL 60506-5178

630-844-4400

Informs the community of what is happening in their schools, with their students, and with their tax dollars.

4 pages 5x Year

Laurel Chivari

4291 **Shaping the Future**
Lutheran Education Association
7400 Augusta Street
River Forest, IL 60305-1402

708-209-3343
Fax: 708-209-3458
E-mail: lea@lea.org
http://www.lea.org

Newsletter for LEA members to focus on the unique spiritual and professional needs of church workers and to celebrate life in the ministry. Resource information for the organization, upcoming events, encouragement for pre-planning.

Dr. Johnathan Laabs, Contact

4292 **Sharing Space**
Creative Urethanes, Children's Creative Response
PO Box 271
Nyack, NY 10960-0271

845-358-4601

Trains all those working with children to communicate positivity and cooperation.

12 pages TriAnnually

4293 **Southwest Educational Development Laboratory Letter**
211 E 7th Street
Austin, TX 78701-3218

512-476-6861
800-476-6861
Fax: 512-476-2286
E-mail: whoover@sedl.org
http://www.sedl.org

32 pages Tri-Annually

Lesile A Blair, Editor, Author

4294 Special Education Leadership
LifeWay Church Resources
One LifeWay Plaza
Nashville, TN 37234
615-251-2000
Fax: 615-251-5933

Covers special education issues relating to religious education.

52 pages Quarterly

Ben Garner, Editor-in-Chief
Ellen Beene, Editor

4295 Special Educator
LRP Publications
747 Dresher Road
PO Box 980
Horsham, PA 19044-0980
215-784-0941
800-341-7874
Fax: 215-784-0870
E-mail: custserve@lrp.com
http://www.lrp.com

Covers important issues in the field of special education, including such topics as law and administrative policy.

22 pages BiWeekly
ISSN: 1047-1618

Stephen Bevilacqua, Editor

4296 Star News
Jefferson Center for Character Education
PO Box 1283
Monrovia, CA 91017-1283
949-770-7602
Fax: 949-450-1100

Mission is to produce and promote programs to teach children the concepts, skills and behavior of good character, common core values, personal and civic responsibility, workforce readiness and citizenship.

Quarterly

Robert Jamieson, CEO
Sharon McClenahan, Administrative Assistant

4297 Statewise: Statistical & Research Newsletter
State Board of Education, Planning & Research
PO Box 1402
Dover, DE 19903-1402
302-736-4601
Fax: 302-739-4654

Statistical data relating to Delaware public schools.

2 pages

4298 Street Scenes
(APO Street College of Education
610 W 112th Street
New York, NY 10025-1898
212-222-6700
Fax: 212-222-6700

New ideas in education.

8 pages SemiAnnually

Renee Creange

4299 Student Travels Magazine
Council on International Educational Exchange
Attention: Membership Services
633 Third Avenue, 20th Floor
New York, NY 10017
212-822-2625
800-407-8839
Fax: 212-822-2779
E-mail: studyinfo@ciee.org
http://www.ciee.org

This publication contains articles by students on traveling abroad as well as information on CIEE's travel, work, study, teaching and volunteer abroad service programs.

4300 Taylor Law Update
NYPER Publications
PO Box 662
Latham, NY 12110-0662
518-786-1654
Fax: 518-456-8582
E-mail: nyper@capital.net

Summarizes important court and administrative rulings of interest to employees, union officials, and attorneys.

Publication Date: 1980 Monthly Newsletter
ISSN: 1071-7404

Harvey Randall, Editor

4301 Teacher$ Talk
Teachers Insurance and Annuity Association
730 3rd Avenue
New York, NY 10017-3206
212-490-9000
Fax: 800-914-8922

Offers timely information and helpful hints about savings, investments, finance and insurance for teachers and educators.

Quarterly

Robert D Williams, Editor

4302 Telluride Newsletter
217 W Avenue
Ithaca, NY 14850-3980
607-273-5011
Fax: 607-272-2667

News of interest to alumni of Telluride Association sponsored programs.

8 pages TriQuarterly
Eric Lemer

4303 Tennessee Education
University of Tennessee
College of Education
Knoxville, TN 37996-0001
865-974-5252
Fax: 865-974-8718
E-mail: scarey@utk.edu

Publishes articles on topics related to K through higher education.

BiAnnually
ISSN: 0739-0408

Sue Carey, Editor

4304 Tennessee School Board Bulletin
Tennessee School Boards Association
500 13th Avenue N
Nashville, TN 37203-2884

Articles of interest to boards of education.

6 pages

Daniel Tollett, Publisher
Holly Hewitt, Editor

4305 Theory Into Practice
Ohio State University, College of Education
341 Ramseyer Hall
29 W Woodruff Avenue
Columbus, OH 43210-1120
614-292-3407
888-678-3382
Fax: 614-292-7020

E-mail: tip@osu.edu
http://www.coe.ohio-state.edu

Nationally recognized for excellence in educational journalism; thematic format, providing comprehensive discussion of single topic with many diverse points of view.

80+ pages Quarterly
ISSN: 0040-5841

Anita Woolfolk Hay, Author
Sue Gabel, Editorial Assistant

4306 This Active Life
National Education Association (NEA)
1201 16th Street NW
Washington, DC 20036-3207
202-822-7125
Fax: 202-822-7624
http://www.nea.org/retired

Serves as a resource in the maintenance of quality public education.

20 pages Bi-Monthly
ISSN: 1526-9342

John O'Neil, Editor

4307 Three R'S for Teachers: Research, Reports & Reviews
Master Teacher
PO Box 1207
Manhattan, KS 66502
785-539-0555
800-669-9633
Fax: 785-539-7739
http://www.masterteacher.com

Developed to help provide teachers with up-to-date information on the most current data, thoughts, trends and instructional strategies occurring in education. Synthesizing the most recent research done by some of the most renownedresearchers and practitioners in the field of education.

4 pages Quarterly

4308 Tidbits
Assn. for Legal Support of Alternative Schools
PO Box 2823
Santa Fe, NM 87504-2823
505-471-6928

Information and legal advice to those involved in non-public educational facilities.

12 pages Quarterly

Ed Nagel

4309 Transitions Abroad: The Guide to Learning, Living, & Working Abroad
Transitions Abroad Publishing
PO Box 1300
Amherst, MA 01004-1300
413-256-3414
800-293-0373
Fax: 413-256-0373
E-mail: info@TransitionsAbroad.com
http://www.transitionsabroad.com

This magazine contains articles and bibliographies on travel, study, teaching, internships and work abroad. Published annually.

4310 Unschoolers Network
2 Smith Street
Farmingdale, NJ 07727-1006
732-938-2473

Information and support for families teaching their children at home.

14 pages Monthly

Nancy Plent

4311 VSBA Newsletter
Vermont School Boards Association
2 Prospect Street
Montpelier, VT 05602-3555
802-223-3580

General information.

16 pages Monthly

Donald Jamieson

4312 WCER Highlights
Wisconsin Center for Education Research
1025 W Johnson Street
Suite 785
Madison, WI 53706-1706
608-263-8814
Fax: 608-263-6448

News about research conducted at the Wisconsin Center for Education Research.

8 pages Quarterly
ISSN: 1073-1882

Paul Baker, Editor

4313 WestEd: Focus
730 Harrison Street
San Francisco, CA 94107-1242
415-615-3144
877-493-7833
Fax: 415-512-2024
E-mail: dtorres@WestEd.org
http://www.WestEd.org

Improving education through research, development and service.

Danny Torres, Publications Coordinator
Liza Cardinal-Hand, Information/Outreach Manager

4314 Western Journal of Black Studies
Washington State University
Heritage House
Pullman, WA 99164-0001
509-335-8681
Fax: 509-335-8338

A journal which canvasses topical issues affecting Black studies and education.

Quarterly

Talmadge Anderson, Editor

4315 World Gifted
World Council for Gifted & Talented Children
Purdue University
1446 S Campus
West Lafayette, IN 47907

Offers information and articles on gifted education for the professional.

4316 Young Audiences Newsletter
115 E 92nd Street
New York, NY 10128-1688
212-831-8110
Fax: 212-289-1202

Organization news of performing arts education programs in schools and communities.

Annual

Jane Bak

Periodicals
Administration

4317 AACRAO Data Dispenser
American Association of Collegiate Registrars
1 Dupont Circle NW
Suite 330
Washington, DC 20036-1137

202-293-9161
Fax: 202-872-8857

Association newsletter for US and foreign postsecondary education institution professionals involved in admissions, records and registration.

12 pages 10x Year

Eileen Kennedy

4318 AASA Bulletin
American Association of School Administrators
1801 N Moore Street
Arlington, VA 22209-1813

703-875-0759
888-782-2272
Fax: 703-841-1543
http://www.aasa.org

The AASA Bulletin is a supplement to The School Administrator. It contains the Job Bulletin and information for school leaders about the many products, services and events available to them from AASA.

Ginger O'Neil, Editor
Kari Arfstrom, Project Director

4319 ACCT Advisor
Association of Community College Trustees
1233 20th Street NW
Suite 605
Washington, DC 20036-2907

202-775-4667
Fax: 202-223-1297
http://www.acct.org

Provides news of association events, federal regulations, activities, state activities, legal issues and other news of interest to community college governing board members.

Ray Taylor, ACCT President
Alvin Major II, Director Mktg/Communications

4320 ADA Update
NYPER Publications
PO Box 662
Latham, NY 12110-0662

518-786-1654
Fax: 518-456-8582
E-mail: nyper@capital.net

Covers significant court rulings on the Americans with Disabilities Act.

Publication Date: 1919 Monthly Newsletter
ISSN: 1071-7388

Harvey Randall, Editor

4321 AVA Update
Association for Volunteer Administration
PO Box 4584
Boulder, CO 80306-4584

303-447-0558

Information of value to administrators of volunteer services.

4 pages BiMonthly

Martha Martin

4322 Accreditation Fact Sheet
NAPNSC Accrediting Commission for Higher Education
182 Thompson Road
Grand Junction, CO 81503-2246

970-243-5441
Fax: 970-242-4392
E-mail: director@napnsc.org
http://www.napnsc.org

Newsletter reporting on the origin, history, developments, procedures and changes of educational institution accreditation.

Annually

H. Earl Heusser, Author
H Earl Heusser, Executive Director

4323 Administrative Information Report
Nat'l Association of Secondary School Principles
1904 Association Drive
Reston, VA 20191-1502

703-860-0200
800-253-7746
Fax: 703-620-6534

Offers school statistics and administrative updates for secondary school principals and management officers.

4 pages Monthly

Thomas Koerner

4324 American School & University Magazine
Intertec Publishing
PO Box 12960
Overland Park, KS 66282-2960

913-967-1960
Fax: 913-967-1905

Directed at business and facilities administrators in the nation's public and private schools.

Monthly

Joe Agron, Editor

4325 American School Board Journal
National School Boards Association
1680 Duke Street
Alexandria, VA 22314-3455

703-838-6722
Fax: 703-549-6719
E-mail: editor@asbj.com

Published primarily for school board members and school system superintendents serving public elementary and secondary schools in the United States and Canada.

Monthly

Anne L Bryant, Executive Publisher
Harold P Seamon, Deputy Executive Publisher

4326 Board
Master Teacher
PO Box 1207
Manhattan, KS 66502

785-539-0555
800-669-9633
Fax: 785-539-7739
http://www.masterteacher.com

Designed to be a continuous form of communication to help board members know and understand the duties, responsibilities, and commitments of the office; view the superintendent of schools as the educational leader; improve administrator-board working relationships; better understand the purpose of education; and work at their responsibilities in a prudent, calm, and rational manner.

Monthly

Robert DeBruyn, Editor

4327 Building Leadership Bulletin
2990 Baker Drive
Springfield, IL 62703-2800

217-525-1383
Fax: 217-525-7264
http://www.ipa.vsta.net

Topical, timely issues.

8 pages 11x Year

Julie Weichert, Associate Director

4328 Business Education Forum
National Business Education Association
1914 Association Drive
Reston, VA 20191-1538

703-860-8300
Fax: 703-620-4483

A journal of distinctive articles dealing with current issues and trends, future directions and exemplary programs in business education at all instructional levels. Articles focus on international business, life-long learning, cultural diversity, critical thinking, economics, state-of-the-art technology and the latest research in the field.

200 pages Quarterly

Janet M Treichel, Executive Director
Regina McDowell, Editor

4329 CASE Currents
1307 New York Avenue NW
Suite 1000
Washington, DC 20036-1226

202-328-2273
Fax: 202-387-4973

Covers the world of fund raising, alumni administration, public relations, periodicals, publications and student recruitment in higher education.

10x Year

Karla Taylor, Editor

4330 CASE Newsletter
The Council for Exceptional Children
1920 Association Drive
Reston, VA 20191-1545

703-620-3660
888-232-7733
Fax: 703-264-9494

News about CASE activities, upcoming events, current trends and practices, state and national legislation, and other practical information relevant to the administration of special education programs.

5x Year

Jo Thomason

4331 CASE in Point
The Council for Exceptional Children
1920 Association Drive
Reston, VA 20191-1545

703-620-3660
888-232-7733
Fax: 703-264-9494

A journal reporting on emerging promising practices, current research, contact points for expanded information, and field-based commentary relevant to the administration of special education programs.

BiAnnual

Donnie Evans, Editor

4332 California Schools Magazine
California School Boards Association
3100 Beacon Boulevard
West Sacramento, CA 95691

916-371-4691
Fax: 916-372-3369

For school board members, superintendents and school business managers, responsible for the operation of California's public schools. Articles of interest to parents, teachers, community members and anyone else concerned with publiceducation.

20 pages Quarterly
ISSN: 1081-8936

Mina G Fasulo, Executive Editor

4333 Clearing House: A Journal of Educational Research
Heldref Publications
1319 18th Street NW
Washington, DC 20036-1826

202-296-6267
800-365-9753
Fax: 202-296-5149
E-mail: tch@heldfred.org

Each issue offers a variety of articles for teachers and administrators of middle schools and junior and senior high schools. It includes experiments, trends and accomplishments in courses, teaching methods, administrative proceduresand school programs.

4 pages BiMonthly
ISSN: 0009-8655

Deborah N Cohen, Promotions Manager
Judy Cusick, Managing Editor

4334 Connection
National Association of State Boards of Education
277 S Washington Street
Suite 100
Alexandria, VA 22314

703-684-4000
Fax: 703-836-2313

Quarterly magazine for state board of education members.

10 pages

David Kysilko, Editor

4335 Developer
National Staff Development Council
PO Box 240
Oxford, OH 45056-0240

513-523-6029
Fax: 513-523-0638

Devoted to staff development for educational personnel.

8 pages 10x Year

Dennis Sparks

4336 Discrimination Law Update
NYPER Publications
PO Box 662
Latham, NY 12110-0662

518-786-1654
Fax: 518-456-8582
E-mail: nyper@capital.net

Summarizes important court and administrative rulings concerning civil rights, equal employment and affirmative action of interest to personnel administrators and attorneys.

Publication Date: 1919 Monthly Newsletter
ISSN: 1522-4023

Harvey Randall, Editor

4337 ERS Spectrum
Educational Research Service
2000 Clarendon Boulevard
Arlington, VA 22201-2908

703-243-2100
800-791-9308
Fax: 703-243-1985
E-mail: editor@ers.org
http://www.ers.org

A quarterly journal of school research and information. Publishes practical research and information for school decisions. Authors include practicing administrators and other educators in local school districts.

48 pages Quarterly
ISSN: 0740-7874

Deborah Perkins-Gough, Editor-in-Chief, Editor

4338 Education Daily
Aspen Publishing, Inc.
1101 King Street
Suite 444
Alexandria, VA 22314-2944

800-638-8437
Fax: 301-417-7650

News on national education policy. Offers daily reports of Education Department policies, initiatives and priorities— how they are developed and how they affect school programs.

6-8 pages Daily

Cynthia Carter, Contact

4339 Education Personnel Update
NYPER Publications
PO Box 662
Latham, NY 12110-0662

518-786-1654
Fax: 518-456-8582
E-mail: nyper@capital.net

Summarizes important court and administrative decisions of interest to educators.

Monthly

Harvey Randall, Editor

4340 Educational Administration Quarterly
University of Wisconsin, Milwaukee
PO Box 413
Milwaukee, WI 53201-0413

414-229-4740
Fax: 414-229-5300

Deals with administrative issues and policy.

Quarterly

Dr. James Cibulka, Editor

4341 Electronic Learning
Scholastic
555 Broadway
New York, NY 10012-3919

212-343-6100
800-724-6527
Fax: 212-343-4801

Published for the administrative level, education professionals who are directly responsible for the implementing of electronic technology at the district, state and university levels.

8x Year

Lynn Diamond, Advertising Director
Therese Mageau, Editor

4342 Enrollment Management Report
LRP Publications
747 Dresher Road
PO Box 980
Horsham, PA 19044-0980

215-784-0941
800-341-7874
Fax: 215-784-0870
E-mail: custserve@lrp.com
http://www.lrp.com

Provides colleges and universities with solutions and strategies for recruitment, admissions, retention and financial aid. Reviews the latest trends, research studies and their findings and gives a profile on how other institutionsare handling their enrollment management issues.

Monthly
ISSN: 1094-3757

Gary Bagin, Director Communications
Jay Margolis, Editor

4343 Executive Session
NYPER Publications
PO Box 662
Latham, NY 12110-0662

518-786-1654
Fax: 518-456-8582
E-mail: nyper@capital.net

Focuses on New York State: the summaries of decisions made by the Commission of Education, State and Federal Courts, that would affect school policies and operations.

Publication Date: 1919 Monthly Newsletter
ISSN: 1092-4041

Harvey Randall, Editor

4344 Guide to Federal Funding for Education
Education Funding Research Council
1725 K Street NW
7th Floor
Washington, DC 20006

202-872-4000
800-876-0226
Fax: 202-739-9578
http://www.grantsandfunding.com

Two-volume looseleaf provides complete, up-to-date coverage of federal education grants for schools, colleges, universities, technical schools and job training organizations. Updated quarterly with new and revised program descriptionswritten in easy-to-understand language.

1,500 pages Quarterly

Helen Kim, Jessica Gowan, Ann Fishback, Author
Charles J Edwards, Sr Managing Editor

4345 HR on Campus
LRP Publications
747 Dresher Road
PO Box 980
Horsham, PA 19044-0980

215-784-0941
800-341-7874
Fax: 215-784-0870
E-mail: custserve@lrp.com
http://www.lrp.com

This monthly newsletter provides coverage of the latest and most inovative programs higher education institutions use to handle their human resource challenges. Plus, you can recieve free e-mail updates on crucial news affecting yourjob with your paid subscription.

Monthly
ISSN: 1098-9293

Gary Bagin, Director Communications
Jay Margolis, Editor

4346 IPA Newsletter
2990 Baker Drive
Springfield, IL 62703-2800
217-525-1383
Fax: 217-525-7264
http://www.ipa.vsta.net

Provides current information on Illinois principals and the profession.

8 pages 11x Year

David Turner, Author
Julie Weichert, Associate Director

4347 Journal of Curriculum & Supervision
Association for Supervision & Curriculum Develop.
1703 N Beauregard Street
Alexandria, VA 22311-1714
512-471-4611
Fax: 512-471-8460
E-mail: oldavisjr@mail.uteyas.edu
http://www.ascd.org/framejcs.html

Offers professional updates and news as well as membership/association information.

Quarterly Paperback

OL Davis Jr, Editor

4348 Journal of Education for Business
Heldref Publications
1319 18th Street NW
Washington, DC 20036-1802
202-296-6267
800-365-9753
Fax: 202-296-5149
http://www.heldref.org

Offers information to instructors, supervisors, and administrators at the secondary, postsecondary and collegiate levels. The journal features basic and applied research-based articles in accounting, communications, economics,finance, information systems, management, marketing and other business disciplines.

BiMonthly

4349 Keystone Schoolmaster Newsletter
Pennsylvania Assn. of Secondary School Principals
PO Box 953
Easton, PA 18044-0953
215-253-8516

Reports achievements, honors, problems and innovations by officers and established authorities.

4 pages Monthly

Joseph Mamana, Contact

4350 LSBA Quarter Notes
Louisiana School Boards Association
7912 Summa Avenue
Baton Rouge, LA 70809-3416

News articles relative to the association, feature stories on research.

6 pages BiMonthly

Victor Hodgkins

4351 Legal Notes for Education
Oakstone Publishing, Inc.
PO Box 381687
Birmingham, AL 35238-1687
205-437-9515
800-365-4900
Fax: 205-995-4651

Reports the latest school law cases and late-breaking legislation along with the most recent law review articles affecting education. Federal and state appellate court decisions are summarized and the full legal citation is suppliedfor each case.

12 pages Monthly
ISSN: 0093-397X

4352 Maintaining Safe Schools- School Violence Alert
LRP Publications
747 Dresher Road
PO Box 980
Horsham, PA 19044-0980
215-784-0941
800-341-7874
Fax: 215-784-0870
E-mail: custserve@lrp.com
http://www.lrp.com/ed

Focuses on the legal and practical issues involved in preventing and responding to violent acts by students in schools, and highlights successful violence prevention programs in school districts across the country. Offers strategiesfor mediation, discipline and crisis managment.

Monthly
ISSN: 1082-4774

Gary Bagin, Director Communications
Caroline Ryan, Editor

4353 Managing School Business
LRP Publications
747 Dresher Road
PO Box 980
Horsham, PA 19044-0980
215-784-0941
800-341-7874
Fax: 215-784-9639
E-mail: custserve@lrp.com
http://www.lrp.com

Newsletter provides school business managers with tips on how to solve the problems they face in managing finance, operations, personnel, and their own career.

Biweekly
ISSN: 1092-2229

Angela Childers, Author
Gary Bagin, Director Communications
Angela Childers, Editor

4354 Memo to the President
American Assn. of State Colleges & Universities
1307 New York Avenue
Washington, DC 20005
202-293-7070
Fax: 202-296-5819
http://www.aascu.org

Monitors public policies at national, state and campus level on higher education issues. Reports on activities of the Association and member institutions.

20 pages Monthly
November

Susan Chilcott, Director Communications

4355 NASPA Forum
National Assn. of Student Personnel Administrators
1875 Connecticut Avenue NW
Suite 418
Washington, DC 20009-5737
202-265-7500
Fax: 202-797-1157

Offers information for personnel administrators and strategies, updates and tips on the education system.

Monthly
Sybil Walker

4356 NY School Boards
New York State School Boards Association
119 Washington Avenue
Albany, NY 12210-2204
518-465-3474
800-342-3360
Fax: 518-465-3481
E-mail: info@nssba.org
http://www.nyssba.org

Contains general educational news, state and federal legislative activity, legal and employee relations issues, commentary, issues in education, and successful education programs around the state.

10x Year
Eric Randall, Editor

4357 National Faculty Forum
National Faculty of Humanities, Arts & Sciences
1676 Clifton Road NE
Atlanta, GA 30329-4050
404-727-5788

Offers administrative news and updates for persons in higher education.

TriQuarterly

4358 Network
National School Public Relations Association
1501 Lee Highway
Suite 201
Arlington, VA 22209-1109
301-519-0496
Fax: 301-519-0494
E-mail: nspra@nspra.org
http://www.nspra.org

Monthly newsletter for and about our members. Some articles about school public relations, issues that affect school public relations people.

Andy Grunig, Editorial Coordinator
Tommy Jones, Advertising/Sales

4359 New York Education Personnel Update
NYPER Publications
PO Box 662
Latham, NY 12110-0662
518-786-1654
Fax: 518-456-8582
E-mail: nyper@capital.net

Summarizes important court and administrative discussions of interest to educators.

Publication Date: 1919 Monthly Newsletter
ISSN: 1071-7420

Harvey Randall, Editor

4360 OASCD Journal
Oklahoma Curriculum Development
3705 S. 98th East Avenue
Tulsa, OK 74146
918-627-4403
Fax: 918-627-4433

A refereed journal which prints contributions on curriculum theory and practices, leadership in education, staff development and supervision. The Editorial Board welcomes photographs, letters to the editor, program descriptions, interviews, research reports, theoretical pieces, reviews of books and non-print media, poetry, humor, cartoons, satire and children's art and writing, as well as expository articles.

Annual
Blaine Smith, Executive Secretary

4361 Perspectives for Policymakers
New Jersey School Boards Association
413 W State Street
#909
Trenton, NJ 08618-5617
609-695-7600

Each issue focuses on a specific topic in education providing background, activities and resources.

8 pages SemiAnnually
Missy Martin

4362 Planning & Changing
Illinois State University
Dept. of Ed. Admin. & Foundations
Normal, IL 61790-5900
309-438-2399
Fax: 309-438-8683
http://http://coe.ilstu.edu/eafdept/pandc.htm

An educational leadership and policy journal. This journal attempts to disseminate timely and useful reports of practice and theory with particular emphasis on change, and planning in K-12 educational settings and higher education settings. Paperback.

64 pages Quarterly
ISSN: 0032-0684

Judith Mogilka, Editor
Lilly J Meiner, Publications Manager

4363 Principal
Nat'l Association of Elementary School Principals
1615 Duke Street
Alexandria, VA 22314-3406
703-684-3345
Fax: 800-396-2377

A professional magazine edited for elementary and middle school principals and others interested in education.

5x Year
Leon E Greene, Editor
Louanne M Wheeler, Production Manager

4364 Principal Communicator
National School Public Relations Association
15948 Derwood Road
Rockville, MD 20855
301-519-0496
Fax: 301-519-0494
E-mail: nspra@nspra.org
http://www.napra.org

Tips for building public relations people.

6 pages Monthly
Andy Grunig, Manager of Communications

4365 Private Education Law Report
Oakstone Publishing, Inc.
PO Box 381687
Birmingham, AL 35238-1687
205-437-9515
800-365-4900
Fax: 205-995-4651

Reports the latest school law cases and late-breaking legislation along with the most recent law review articles affecting private education. Federal and state appellate court decisions are summarized and the full legal citation issupplied for each case.

Monthly
ISSN: 0890-121X

4366 Public Employment Law Notes
NYPER Publications
PO Box 662
Latham, NY 12110-0662

518-786-1654
Fax: 518-456-8582
E-mail: nyper@capital.net

Summarizes important court and administrative decisions of interest to administrators, union officials and attorneys involved in public personnel administration.

Publication Date: 1919   Monthly Newsletter
ISSN: 0809-9789

Harvey Randall, Editor

4367 Public Personnel Management
International Personnel Management Association
1617 Duke Street
Alexandria, VA 22314-3406

703-549-7100
Fax: 703-684-0948

Caters to those professionals in human resource management.

Quarterly
Sarah Al Shiffert, Editor

4368 Rural Educator-Journal for Rural and Small Schools
National Rural Education Association
246 E Ed Building
Colorado State University
Ft. Collins, CO 80523-1588

970-491-7022
Fax: 970-491-1317
E-mail: jnewlin@lamar.colostate.edu
http://www.colostate.edu

Official journal of the NREA. A nationally recognized publication that features timely and informative articles written by leading rural educators from all levels of education. All NREA members are encouraged to submit researcharticles and items of general information for publication.

40 pages   Quarterly Magazine
ISSN: 0273-446X

Joseph T Newlin, Editor

4369 School Administrator
American Association of School Administrators
1801 N Moore Street
Arlington, VA 22209-1813

703-528-0700
888-782-2722
Fax: 703-841-1543
E-mail: magazine@aasa.org
http://www.aasa.org

Ensures the highest quality education systems for all learners through the support and development of leadership on the building, district and state levels.

52 pages Monthly

Paul D Houston, Executive Director

4370 School Business Affairs
Association of School Business Officials Int'l
11401 N Shore Drive
Reston, VA 20190-4232

703-478-0405
Fax: 703-478-0205

For school business administrators responsible for the administration and purchase of products and services for the schools.

Monthly

Peg D Kirkpatrick, Editor/Publisher
Robert Gluck, Managing Editor

4371 School Executive
1429 Walnut Street
Philadelphia, PA 19102

215-563-6005
Fax: 215-587-9706
http://www.media-methods.com

Published as an educational service to foster the exchange of information for administrators about the creative uses of technology and presentation tools in K-12 school districts nationwide.

Quarterly

Michele Sokoloff, Publisher/Editorial Director
Christine Weiser, Editor

4372 School Law Briefings
LRP Publications
747 Dresher Road
PO Box 980
Horsham, PA 19044-0980

215-784-0941
800-341-7874
Fax: 215-784-9639
E-mail: custserve@lrp.com
http://www.lrp.com

Gives you summaries of general education, special education, and early childhood court cases, as well as administrative hearings.

Monthly
ISSN: 1094-3749

Gary Bagin, Director Communications
John Norlin, Editor

4373 School Law News
Aspen Publishing, Inc.
1101 King Street
Suite 44
Alexandria, VA 22314-2944

800-638-8437
Fax: 301-417-7650

Advises administrators to avoid legal pitfalls by monitoring education-related court action across the nation. With School Law News, administrators receive the latest information on issues like sexual harassment liability, specialeducation, religion in the schools, affirmative action, youth violence, student-faculty rights, school finance, desegregation and much more.

8-10 pages BiWeekly

Cynthia Carter

4374 School Planning & Management
Peter Li Education Group
330 Progress Road
Dayton, OH 45449-2322

937-293-1415
800-523-4625
Fax: 415-626-0554

For the business needs of school administrators featuring issues, ideas and technology at work in public, private and independent schools.

Monthly
ISSN: 1086-4628

Peter J Li, Publisher
Deborah Moore, Editor

4375 Section 504 Compliance Advisor
LRP Publications

747 Dresher Road
PO Box 980
Horsham, PA 19044-0980

215-784-0941
800-341-7874
Fax: 215-784-0870
E-mail: custserve@lrp.com
http://www.lrp.com/ed

Newsletter examines the requirements of Section 504 of the Rehabilitation Act and analyzes their impact on disciplining students. Provides educators and administrators with detailed tips and advice to help them solve the disciplineproblems they face everyday and keep their policies and programs in compliance.

Monthly
ISSN: 1094-3730

Gary Bagin, Director Communications
Brian Caruso, Editor

4376 Special Education Law Monthly
LRP Publications

747 Dresher Road
PO Box 980
Horsham, PA 19044-0980

215-784-0941
800-341-7874
Fax: 215-784-0870
E-mail: custserve@lrp.com
http://www.lrp.com/ed

Covers court decisions and administrative rulings affecting the education of students with disabilities.

Monthly
ISSN: 1094-3773

Ken Ronenberger, Director Communications
Patty Grzywacz, Esq, Editor

4377 Special Education Law Update
Oakstone Publishing, Inc.

PO Box 381687
Birmingham, AL 35238-1687

205-437-9515
800-365-4900
Fax: 205-995-4651

Reports the latest school law cases and late-breaking legislation along with the most recent law review articles affecting special education. Federal and state appellate court decisions are summarized and the full legal citation issupplied for each case.

Monthly
ISSN: 8756-3746

4378 Special Education Report
Aspen Publishing, Inc.

1101 King Street
Suite 444
Alexandria, VA 22314-2944

800-638-8437
Fax: 301-417-7650

The special education administrator's direct pipeline to federal legislation, regulation and funding of programs for children and youths with disabilities.

6-8 pages BiWeekly

Cynthia Carter

4379 Student Affairs Today
LRP Publications

747 Dresher Road
PO Box 980
Horsham, PA 19044-0980

215-784-0941
800-341-7874
Fax: 215-784-0870
E-mail: custserve@lrp.com
http://www.lrp.com

Newsletter provides strategies and tips for handling higher education institutions' student affairs challenges and problems involving: sexual harassment, binge drinking, fraternity and sorority activities, student housing and more.Gives profiles of other colleges programs.

Monthly
ISSN: 1098-5166

Gary Bagin, Director Communications
Marsha Jaquays, Editor

4380 Superintendents Only
Master Teacher

PO Box 1207
Manhattan, KS 66502

785-539-0555
800-669-9633
Fax: 785-539-7739
http://www.masterteacher.com

Offers superintendents hundreds of solid ideas to help their jobs run more smoothly. Written by practicing superintendents and business executives, this publication saves hundreds of hours of anguish over the course of the year.

Monthly

4381 Superintendents Only Master Teacher
Master Teacher

PO Box 1207
Manhattan, KS 66505-1207

785-539-0555
800-669-9633
Fax: 800-669-1132
http://www.masterteacher.com

An invaluable resource for generating ideas, planning effective strategies, solving problems, and balancing responsibilites.

1 pages Monthly Newsletter

Tracey H DeBruyn, Executive Editor

4382 THE Journal
17501 17th Street
Suite 230
Tustin, CA 92780

714-730-4011
Fax: 714-730-3739
E-mail: editorail@thejournal.com
http://www.thejournal.com

A forum for administrators and managers in school districts to share their experiences in the use of technology-based educational aids.

Monthly

Wendy LaDuke, Publisher/CEO
Matthew Miller, Editor

4383 Technology Pathfinder for Administrators Master Teacher
Master Teacher
PO Box 1207
Manhattan, KS 66505-1207

785-539-0555
800-669-9633
Fax: 800-669-1132
http://www.masterteacher.com

Relevant, concise technology information and tips to help school administrators catch up and stay ahead.

Monthly Newsletter

Tracey H DeBruyn, Executive Editor

4384 Thrust for Educational Leadership
Association of California School Administrators
1517 L Street
Sacramento, CA 95814-4004

916-444-3216
Fax: 916-444-3245

Designed for school administrators who must stay abreast of educational developments, management and personnel practices, social attitudes and issues that impact schools.

7x Year

Tom DeLapp, Communications Director
Susan Davis, Editor

4385 Title I Handbook
Education Funding Research Council
1725 K Street NW
7th Floor
Washington, DC 20006

202-872-4000
800-876-0226
Fax: 202-739-9578
http://www.TitleIonline.com

Two-volume looseleaf provides complete, up-to-date coverage of Title I, the largest federal program of aid for elementary and secondary education. The book contains all the laws, regulations and guidance needed to sucessfully operatethe grant program, and insightful articles on key Title I topics, ongoing budget coverage, and special reports on issues like Title I testing, schoolwide programs, and audits. Also included is a compilation of official Title I policy letters, foundnowhere else.

1,500 pages Quarterly

Cheryl L. Sattler, Author

4386 Title I Monitor
Education Funding Research Council
1725 K Street NW
7th Floor
Washington, DC 20006

202-872-4000
800-876-0226
Fax: 202-739-9578
http://www.TitleIonline.com

This newsletter provides continuing coverage of Title I, the largest federal program of aid for elementary and secondary education. Title I is at the heart of the debate over education reform, and the Monitor ensures that educatorshave the most up-to-date information about developments in this ever-changing program. Breaking news about the Title I budget, new legislation and regulations, court cases and other issues.

30 pages Monthly
ISSN: 1086-2455

Cheryl L Sattler, Author

4387 Training Magazine
Lakewood Publications
50 S 9th Street
Minneapolis, MN 55402-3118

612-333-0471
800-328-4329
Fax: 612-333-6526

Focuses on corporate training and employee development, as well as management and human performance issues.

Monthly

Jack Gordon, Editor

4388 Updating School Board Policies
National School Boards Association
1680 Duke Street
Alexandria, VA 22314-3455

703-838-6722
Fax: 703-683-7590

Offers information and statistics for school boards and administrative offices across the country.

16 pages BiMonthly
ISSN: 1081-8286

Michael Wessely

4389 VIP Views, Ideas & Practical Solutions
Master Teacher
PO Box 1207
Manhattan, KS 66505-1207

785-539-0555
800-669-9633
Fax: 800-669-1132
http://www.masterteacher.com

A newsletter offering practical information, strategies and solutions for district and school administrators.

8 pages Monthly

Tracey H DeBruyn, Executive Editor

4390 Your School and the Law
LRP Publications
747 Dresher Road
PO Box 980
Horsham, PA 19044-0980

215-784-0941
800-341-7874
Fax: 215-784-0870
E-mail: custserve@lrp.com
http://www.lrp.com/ed

This newsletter analyzes how current judicial decisions affect schools. Each issue tells where new problems are arising and why, how legal controversies are being resolved, and why these new actions and interpretations influence aschool district's operations and policies.

Biweekly
ISSN: 0094-0399

Gary Bagin, Director Communications
Steve D'Olivera, Editor

Periodicals
Early Childhood Education

4391 Child Development
Arizona State University
Department of Psychology
Tempe, AZ 85287

480-965-3326
Fax: 480-965-8544
http://www.asu.edu

Offers professionals working with children news on childhood education, books, reviews, questions and answers and professional articles of interest.

BiMonthly
Susan C Somerville

4392 Child Study Journal
Buffalo State College
1300 Elmwood Avenue
#306
Buffalo, NY 14222-1004
716-878-5302

Articles of interest related to childhood education.

Quarterly
Donald E Carter

4393 Children Today
ACF Office of Public Affairs
370 Lenfant Plaza SW
Floor 7
Washington, DC 20560-0002
202-401-9218
Fax: 202-205-9688

An interdisciplinary magazine published by the Administration for Children and Families (ACF). The content is a mix of theory and practice, research and features, news and opinions for its audience.

Quarterly

4394 Children and Families
National Head Start Association
1651 Prince Street
Alexandria, VA 22314-2818
703-739-0875
Fax: 703-739-0878
http://www.nhsa.org

Designed to support the Head Start programs, directors, staff, parents and volunteers.

Quarterly
ISSN: 1091-7578
Julie Konieczny, Editor

4395 Division for Children with Communication Disorders Newsletter
The Council for Exceptional Children
1920 Association Drive
Reston, VA 20191-1545
703-620-3660
800-232-7323
Fax: 703-264-1637

Information concerning education and welfare of children with communication disorders.

12 pages SemiAnnually
Christine DeSouza, Editor

4396 Early Childhood Education Journal
Kluwer Academic/Human Sciences Press
233 Spring Street
New York, NY 10013
212-620-8000
Fax: 212-463-0742
http://www.wkpa.nl

Provides professional guidance on instructional methods and materials, child development trends, funding and administrative issues and the politics of day care.

Quarterly
ISSN: 1082-3301
Carol Bischoff, Publisher
Mary Renck Jalongo, Editor

4397 Early Childhood Report: Children with Special Needs and Their Families
LRP Publications
747 Dresher Road
PO Box 980
Horsham, PA 19044-0980
215-784-0941
800-341-7874
Fax: 215-784-0870
E-mail: custserve@lrp.com
http://www.lrp.com

Educational newsletter for parents and professionals involved at the local state and federal levels responsible for the design and implementation of early childhood programs.

Monthly
ISSN: 1058-6482
Scott Kraft, Editor

4398 Early Childhood Research Quarterly
Department of Individuals & Family Syudies
111 Alison Annex
University of Delaware
Newark, DE 19716
302-831-8552
Fax: 302-831-8776

Addresses various topics in the development and education of young children.

Quarterly
Dr. Marion Hyson, Editor

4399 Early Childhood Today
Scholastic
555 Broadway
New York, NY 10012
212-343-6100
800-724-6527
Fax: 212-343-4801
E-mail: ect@scholastic.com
http://www.scholastic.com

The magazine for all early childhood professionals working with infants to six-year-olds. Each issue provides child development information resources, staff development information and parent communication information.

8x Year
ISSN: 1070-1214
Ellen Christian, Publisher
Jill Strauss, Managing Editor

4400 Highlights for Children
PO Box 269
Columbus, OH 43216-0269
800-255-9517
Fax: 614-876-8564

Magazine featuring Fun with a Purpose, to all children preschool to preteen. Features stories, hidden pictures, reading and thinking exercises, crafts, puzzles, and more.

4401 Journal of Early Intervention
The Council for Exceptional Children
1920 Association Drive
Reston, VA 20191-1545
703-620-3660
800-232-7323
Fax: 703-264-1637

Quarterly
ISSN: 0885-3460

Publications / Periodicals

4402 Journal of Research in Childhood Education
Association for Childhood Education International
17904 Georgia Avenue
Suite 215
Olney, MD 20832
301-570-2111
800-423-3563
Fax: 301-570-2212

Current research in education and related fields. It is intended to advance knowledge and theory of the education of children, from infancy through early adolescence. The journal seeks to stimulate the exchange of research ideasthrough publication of: reports of empirical research; theroetical articles; ethnographic and case studies; cross-cultural studies and studies addressing international concerns; participant observation studies and, studies, deriving data collected.

142 pages BiAnnual
ISSN: 0256-8543

4403 NHSA Journal
National Head Start Association
1651 Prince Street
Alexandria, VA 22314-2818
703-739-0875
Fax: 703-739-0878

Edited for Head Start communities serving children 3 to 5 years of age throughout the country. The journal is an invaluable resource containing current research, innovative programming ideas, details on the Head Start conferences andtraining events.

Quarterly
Ethan Salwen, Editor

4404 National Guild of Community Schools of the Arts
National Guild of Community Schools of the Arts
520 8th Avenue
Suite 302, 3rd Floor
New York, NY 10018
212-268-3337
Fax: 212-268-3995
E-mail: info@natguild.org
http://www.nationalguild.org

National association of community based arts education institutions employment opportunities, guildnotes newsletter, publications catalog. See www.nationalguild.org.

Monthly
Noah Xifr, Director Membership/Oper.

4405 Parents Make the Difference!: School Readiness Edition
The Parent Institute
PO Box 7474
Fairfax Station, VA 22039-7474
703-323-9170
Fax: 703-323-9173
http://www.parent-institute.com

Newsletter focusing on parent involvement in education. Focuses on parents of children ages infant to five.

Monthly
ISSN: 1089-3075
John Wherry, Publisher

4406 Pre-K Today
Scholastic
555 Broadway
New York, NY 10012-3919
212-343-6100
800-724-6527
Fax: 212-343-4801

Edited to serve the needs of early childhood professionals, owners, directors, teachers and administrators in preschools and kindergarten.

8x Year
Ellen Christian, Editor

4407 Report on Preschool Programs
Business Publishers
8737 Colesville Road
Suite 1100
Silver Spring, MD 20910-3928
301-587-6300
800-274-6737
Fax: 301-585-9075
E-mail: bpinews@bpinews.com
http://www.bpinews.com

Reports on information about Head Start regulations, federal funding policies, state trends in Pre-K and research news. Also covers information on grant and contract opportunities.

8 pages BiWeekly
Eric Easton, Publisher
Chuck Devarics, Editor

4408 Topics in Early Childhood Special Education
Pro-Ed
8700 Shoal Creek Boulevard
Austin, TX 78757-6816
512-451-3246
800-897-3202
Fax: 512-302-9129
http://www.proedinc.com

Provides program developers, advocates, researchers, higher education faculty and other leaders with the most current, relevant research on all aspects of early childhood education for children with special needs.

Judith J Carta, PhD, Editor

4409 Totline Newsletter
Frank Schaffer Publications
23740 Hawthorne Boulevard
Torrance, CA 90505
310-378-1137
800-421-5533
Fax: 800-837-7260
E-mail: fspcustsrv@aol.com
http://www.frankschaffer.com

Creative activities for working with toddlers and preschool children.

32 pages BiMonthly

4410 Vision
SERVE
PO Box 5367
Greensboro, NC 27435
336-315-7400
800-755-3277
Fax: 336-315-7457
E-mail: cahearn@serve.org
http://www.serve.org

Publication of the Regional Educational Laboratories, an educational research and development organization supported by contracts with the US Education Department, National Institute for Education Sciences. Specialty area: ExtendedLearning Opportunity including Before and After School programs and Early Childhood.

Quarterly
Charles Ahearn, Author
Jack Sanders, Executive Director

Periodicals
Elementary Education

4411 Children's Literature in Education
Kluwer Academic/Human Sciences Press
233 Spring Street
New York, NY 10013

212-620-8000
Fax: 212-463-0742
http://www.wkpa.nl

Source for stimulating articles and interviews on noted children's authors, incisive critiques of classic and contemporary writing for young readers, and original articles describing successful classroom reading projects. Offerstimely reviews on a variety of reading-related topics for teachers and teachers-in-training, librarians, writers and interested parents.

Quarterly
ISSN: 0045-6713

Margaret Mackey & Geoff Fox, Editors, Author
Carol Bischoff, Publisher

4412 Creative Classroom
Creative Classroom Publishing
149 5th Avenue
12th Floor
New York, NY 10010

212-353-3639
Fax: 212-353-8030
http://www.creativeclassroom.com

A magazine for teachers of K-8, containing innovative ideas, activities, classroom management tips and information on contemporary social problems facing teachers and students.

BiMonthly

Susan Eveno, Editorial Director
Laura Axler, Associate Editor

4413 Dragonfly
National Science Teachers Association
1840 Wilson Boulevard
Arlington, VA 22201-3000

703-243-7100
800-782-6782
Fax: 703-243-7177
http://www.nsta.org

A fun-filled interdisciplinary magazine for children grades 3-6. A teacher's companion is also available. The teacher's companion is designed to help you integrate Dragonfly into your curriculum.

Dr. Gerald Wheeler, Executive Director
Shelley Johnson Carey, Managing Editor

4414 Educate@Eight
US Department of Education, Region VIII
1244 Speer Boulevard
Suite 310
Denver, CO 80204-3582

303-844-3544
Fax: 303-844-2524
http://www.ed.gov

8 pages
Helen Littlejohn, Author

4415 Elementary School Journal
University of Missouri
1507 E Broadway
Hillcrest Hall
Columbia, MO 65211

573-882-7889

Academic journal publishing primarily original studies but also reviews of research and conceptual analyses for researchers and practitioners interested in elementary schooling. Emphasizes papers dealing with educational theory andresearch and their implications.

5x Year

Thomas L Good, Editor
Gail M Hinkel, Managing Editor

4416 Elementary Teacher's Ideas and Materials Workshop
Princeton Educational Publishers
117 Cuttermill Road
Great Neck, NY 11021-3101

516-466-9300

Articles on teaching for elementary schools.

16 pages 10x Year

Barry Pavelec

4417 Helping Your Child Succeed in Elementary School
American Association of School Administrators
1801 N Moore Street
Arlington, VA 22209-1813

888-782-2272
Fax: 301-206-9789
http://www.aasa.org

Provides parents with useful information about the importance of parental involvement, concrete ways to work with children and schools to promote success, and a list of resources for further reading.

4418 Highlights for Children
PO Box 269
Columbus, OH 43216-0269

800-255-9517
Fax: 614-876-8564

Magazine featuring Fun with a Purpose, to all children preschool to preteen. Features stories, hidden pictures, reading and thinking exercises, crafts, puzzles, and more.

4419 Independent School
National Association of Independent Schools
75 Federal Street
Boston, MA 02110-1913

617-451-2444

Contains information and opinion about secondary and elementary education in general and independent education in particular.

TriAnnually

Thomas W Leonhardt, Editor
Kurt R Murphy, Advertising/Editor

4420 Instructor
Scholastic
555 Broadway
New York, NY 10012-3919

212-343-6100
800-724-6527
Fax: 212-343-4801
http://www.scholastic.com/instructor

Edited for teachers, curriculum coordinators, principals and supervisors of primary grades through junior high school.

Monthly

Claudia Cohl, Publisher
Lynn Diamond, Advertising Director

4421 Journal of Research in Childhood Education
Association for Childhood Education International
17904 Georgia Avenue
Suite 215
Olney, MD 20832
301-570-2111
800-423-3563
Fax: 301-570-2212

Current research in education and related fields. It is intended to advance knowledge and theory of the education of children, from infancy through early adolescence. The journal seeks to stimulate the exchange of research ideasthrough publication of: reports of empirical research; theroretical articles; ethnographic and case studies; cross-cultural studies and studies addressing international concerns; participant observation studies and, studies, deriving data collected.

142 pages BiAnnual
ISSN: 0256-8543

4422 Montessori LIFE
American Montessori Society
281 Park Avenue S
6th Floor
New York, NY 10010
212-358-1250
Fax: 212-358-1256
E-mail: kate@amshq.org
http://www.amshq.org

Magazine for parents and educators.

Quarterly
ISSN: 1054-0040

Joy Turner, Author
Eileen Roper, Executive Assistant

4423 Parents Make the Difference!
The Parent Institute
PO Box 7474
Fairfax Station, VA 22039-7474
703-323-9170
Fax: 703-323-9173
http://www.parent-institute.com

Newsletter focusing on parent involvement in children's education. Focuses on parents of preschool-aged children.

9x Year

John Wherry, Publisher

4424 Teaching K-8 Magazine
Early Years
40 Richards Avenue
Norwalk, CT 06854-2319
203-855-2650
800-249-9363
Fax: 203-855-2656
E-mail: patricia@teachingk-8.com
http://www.teachingk-8.com

Written for teachers in the elementary grades, kindergarten through eighth, offering classroom tested ideas and methods.

Monthly Magazine
ISSN: 0891-4508
November-December

Allen A Raymond, Publisher
Patricia Broderick, Editorial Director

Periodicals
Employment

4425 AACE Careers Update
American Association for Career Education
2900 Amby Place
Hermosa Beach, CA 90254-2216
310-376-7378
Fax: 310-376-2926

Connects careers, education and work through career education for all ages. Career awareness, exploration, decision making, and preparation. Employability, transitions, continuing education, paid and nonpaid work, occupations, careertips, resources, partnerships, conferences and workshops. Awards and recognition, trends and futures. A newsletter is published.

8+ pages Quarterly/Newsletter
ISBN: 1074-9551

Dr.Pat Nellor Wickwire, Author
Dr. Pat Nellor Wickwire, President

4426 Career Development for Exceptional Individuals
The Council for Exceptional Children
1920 Association Drive
Reston, VA 20191-1545
703-620-3660
888-232-7733
Fax: 703-264-9494

Contains articles dealing with the latest research activities, model programs, and issues in career development and transition planning for individuals with disabilities and/or who are gifted.

2x Year

Gary Greene, Executive Editor

4427 Career Education News
Diversified Learning
72300 Vallat Road
Rancho Mirage, CA 92270-3906
619-346-3336

Reports on programs, materials and training for career educators.

4 pages BiWeekly

Webster Wilson Jr, Publisher
Webster Wilson, Editor

4428 Careers Bridge Newsletter
St. Louis Public Schools
901 Locust Street
Saint Louis, MO 63101-1401
314-231-3720

Available to educators and business/community persons on collaborative activities and promotion of career and self-awareness education in preschool to grade 12.

BiMonthly

Susan Katzman, Contact

4429 Chronicle of Higher Education
Subscription Department
PO Box 1955
Marion, OH 43305-1955
800-347-6969

Newspaper published weekly advertising many teaching opportunities overseas.

Weekly

4430 Current Openings in Education in the USA
Education Information Services
PO Box 620662
Newton, MA 02462-0662
617-433-0125

This publication is a booklet listing about 140 institutions or school systems, each with one to a dozen or more openings for teachers, librarians, counselors and other personnel.

15 pages Every 6 Weeks

F Viaux, Coordinating Education

4431 Educating for Employment
LRP Publications
747 Dresher Road
PO Box 980
Horsham, PA 19044-0980
215-784-0941
800-341-7874
Fax: 215-784-0870
E-mail: custserve@lrp.com
http://www.lrp.com/ed

This newsletter helps educators, directors, and coordinators prepare students for work and obtain funding to establish effective school-to-work programs. Covers legal issues surrounding students in the workforce and provides a business viewpoint, so educators know what companies look for.

BiMonthly
ISSN: 1082-4456

Gary Bagin, Director Communications
Brian Caruso, Editor

4432 Education Jobs
National Education Service Center
PO Box 1279
Riverton, WY 82501-1279
307-856-0170

Offers information on employment in the education field.

Weekly

Lucretia Ficht, Contact

4433 Employment Opportunities
National Guild of Community Schools of the Arts
520 8th Avenue
Suite 302, 3rd Floor
New York, NY 10018
212-268-3337
Fax: 212-268-3995
E-mail: info@natguild.org
http://www.nationalguild.org

Monthly

Noah Xifr, Director Membership/Oper.

4434 Faculty, Staff & Administrative Openings in US Schools & Colleges
Educational Information Services
PO Box 662
Newton Lower Falls, MA 02162
617-964-4555

A listing of available positions in the educational system in the United States.

Monthly

4435 International Educator
PO Box 513
Cummaquid, MA 02637-0513
508-580-1880

A newspaper listing over 100 teaching positions overseas.

Quarterly

4436 Jobs Clearinghouse
Association for Experiential Education
2305 Canyon Boulevard
Suite 100
Boulder, CO 80302-5651
303-440-8844
Fax: 303-440-9581
E-mail: jch@aee.org
http://www.aee.org

A newsletter that is one of the most comprehensive and widely-used monthly listings of full-time, part-time, and seasonal employment and internship opportunities in the experiential/adventure education field for both employers and jobseekers.

Monthly

Kristen Cherry

4437 Journal of Cooperative Education
University of Waterloo
200 University Avenue
Waterloo, ON N2L 3G1 Canada
519-888-4567
519-885-1211
Fax: 519-746-8631

Dedicated to the publication of thoughtful and timely articles concerning work-integrated education. It invites manuscripts which are essays that analyze issues, reports of research, descriptions of innovative practices.

3x Year

Patricia M Rowe, Editor

4438 Journal of Vocational Education Research
Colorado State University
202 Education
Fort Collins, CO 80523-0001
970-491-6835
Fax: 970-491-1317

Publishes refereed articles dealing with research and research-related topics in vocational education. Manuscripts based on original investigations, comprehensive reviews of literature, research methodology and theoretical constructs in vocational education are encouraged.

Quarterly

Brian Cobb, Editor

4439 New Jersey Education Law Report
Whitaker Newsletters
313 South Avenue
#340
Fanwood, NJ 07023-1364
908-889-6336
800-359-6049
Fax: 908-889-6339

Court decisions and rulings on employment in New Jersey schools.

8 pages
ISSN: 0279-8557

Joel Whitaker, Publisher
Fred Rossu, Editor

4440 SkillsUSA Champions
Vocational Industrial Clubs of America
PO Box 3000
Leesburg, VA 20177-0300
703-777-8810
Fax: 703-777-8999
E-mail: anyinfo@skillsusa.org
http://www.skillsusa.org

To individuals interested in cultivating leaderships skills, SkillsUSA is a dynamic resource that inspires and connects all members creating a virtual community through its revalent and useful content.

28 pages Quarterly
ISSN: 1040-4538

E Thomas Hah, Director Office Publications
Timothy W Lawrence, Executive Director

4441 VEWAA Newsletter
Vocational Evaluation & Work Adjustment Assn.
1234 Haley Circle
Auburn University
Auburn, AL 36849

334-844-3800

News and information about the practice of vocational evaluation and work adjustment.

8 pages Quarterly

Ronald Fru, Publisher
Clarence D Brown, Editor

4442 Views & Visions
Wisconsin Vocational Association
44 E Mifflin Street
Suite 104
Madison, WI 53703-2800

608-283-2595
Fax: 608-283-2589

For teachers of vocational and adult education.

8 pages BiMonthly

Linda Stemper

4443 Vocational Training News
Aston Publications
701 King Street
Suite 444
Alexandria, VA 22314-2944

703-683-4100
800-453-9397
Fax: 703-739-6517

Contains timely, useful reports on the federal Job Training Partnership Act and the Carl D Perkins Vocational Education Act. Other areas include literacy, private industry councils and training initiatives.

10 pages Weekly

Cynthia Carter, Publisher
Matthew Dembicki, Editor

Periodicals
Financial Aid

4444 American-Scandinavian Foundation Magazine
American-Scandinavian Foundation
58 Park Avenue
New York, NY 10016-5025

212-879-9779
Fax: 212-686-1157
E-mail: info@amscan.org
http://www.amscan.org

Covers politics, culture and lifestyles of Denmark, Finland, Iceland, Norway and Sweden.

100 pages Quarterly Magazine

Richard J Litell, Editor

4445 Aspen Publishers
Aspen Publishing
200 Orchard Ridge Drive
Gaithsburg, MD 20878

800-638-8437

Fax: 301-417-7650
E-mail: christine.gilstrap@aspenpubl.com

Discover new grants from all federal agencies, plus the best from private funding sources. From the departments of education, health and human services, agriculture and transportation to the National Endowment for Humanities, NationalInstitutes of Health and more. This newsletter offers inside information for persons to obtain a grant and learn of other grant programs that are not widely publicized.

8 pages Weekly

Christine Gilstrap, Account Manager

4446 Education Grants Alert
Aspen Publishing, Inc.
1101 King Street
Suite 444
Alexandria, VA 22314-2944

800-638-8437
Fax: 301-417-7650

Dedicated to helping schools increase funding for K-12 programs. This newsletter will uncover new and recurring grant competitions from federal agencies that fund school projects, plus scores of corporate and foundation sources.

Weekly

Cynthia Carter, Publisher

4447 Federal Research Report
Business Publishers
8737 Colesville Road
Suite 1100
Silver Spring, MD 20910-3928

301-587-6300
800-274-6737
Fax: 301-585-9075
E-mail: bpinews@bpinews.com
http://www.bpinews.com

Identifies critical funding sources supplying administrator's with contact names, addresses, telephone numbers, RFP numbers and other vital details.

8 pages Weekly

Eric Easton, Publisher
Leonard Eiserer, Editor

4448 Foundation & Corporate Grants Alert
Aspen Publishing, Inc.
1101 King Street
Suite 444
Alexandria, VA 22314-2944

800-638-8437
Fax: 301-417-7650

Offers information on funding trends, new foundations and hard-to-find regional funders. You'll also get to foundation and corporate funders from the inside, with foundation profiles and interviews with program officers.

Monthly

4449 Grants for School Districts Monthly
Quinlan Publishing
23 Drydock Avenue
Boston, MA 02210-2336

617-542-0048

Listing of grants available for schools across the country.

Monthly

4450 **Grantsmanship Center Magazine**
PO Box 17220
Los Angeles, CA 90017-0220

213-482-9860
Fax: 213-482-9863
E-mail: green@tgci.com
http://www.tgci.com

Information on nonprofit fund development, management, etc.

Quarterly

Marc Green, Author

4451 **Informativo**
LASPAU (Latin America Scholarship Program)
25 Mount Auburn Street
Cambridge, MA 02138-6028

617-495-5255

Administers scholarships for staff members nominated by Latin American and Caribbean education and development organizations and other public and private sector entities.

8 pages SemiAnnually

Carole Biederman, Contact

4452 **NASFAA Newsletter**
National Assn. of Student Financial Aid Admin.
1920 L Street NW
Suite 200
Washington, DC 20036-5010

202-785-0453
Fax: 202-785-1487

News covering student financial aid legislation and regulations.

24 pages SemiMonthly

Madeleine McLean

4453 **Student Aid News**
Captiol Publications
1101 King Street
Suite 444
Alexandria, VA 22314-2944

703-683-4100
800-655-5597
Fax: 800-392-7886

Offers comprehensive coverage of new and proposed eligibility requirements, new federal regulations and policies, annual federal funding battles, default reduction mandates, major student aid conferences and conventions.

10 pages BiWeekly

Cynthia Carter

4454 **United Student Aid Funds Newsletter**
PO Box 6180
Indianapolis, IN 46206-6180

317-578-6094

USA Funds Education Loan products and services information.

8 pages BiMonthly

Nelson Scharadin, Publisher
Dena Weisbard, Editor

Periodicals
Guidance & Counseling

4455 **ASCA Counselor**
American Counseling Association
5999 Stevenson Avenue
Alexandria, VA 22304-3302

703-823-9800
Fax: 703-823-0252

Aimed at the guidance counselor.

16 pages BiMonthly

Dolores Ehrlich

4456 **Adolescence**
Libra Publishers
3089C Clairemont Drive
PNB 383
San Diego, CA 92117-6802

858-571-1414
Fax: 858-571-1414

Articles contributed by professionals spanning issues relating to teenage education, counseling and guidance. Paperback.

256 pages Quarterly
ISSN: 0001-8449

William Kroll, Editor

4457 **Association for Play Therapy Newsletter**
2050 N Winery Avenue
Suite 101
Fresno, CA 93703-2831

559-252-2278
Fax: 559-252-2297
E-mail: info@a4pt.org
http://www.a4pt.org

Dedicated to the advancement of play therapy. APT is interdisciplinary and defines play therapy as a distinct group of interventions which use play as an integral component of the therapeutic process.

Quarterly

William S Burns CAE, Executive Director
Kathryn Lebby MS, General Manager

4458 **Attention**
8181 Professional Place
Suite 201
Landover, MD 20785

301-306-7070
800-233-4050
Fax: 301-306-7090
http://www.chadd.org

Magazine for children and adults with Attention Deficit/Hyperactivity Disorder, and their families.

45 pages Bi-Monthly

E Clarke Ross, CEO

4459 **Before You Can Discipline**
Master Teacher
PO Box 1207
Manhattan, KS 66505-1207

785-539-0555
800-669-9633
Fax: 785-539-7739
http://www.masterteacher.com

Understand exactly how student's primary and secondary needs can and do influence acceptable and unacceptable behavior. Develop professional attitudes toward discipline problems and learn the laws and principals of managing people.

170 pages
ISBN: 0-914607-03-0

Robert L DeBruyn, Author

4460 Child Psychiatry & Human Development
Kluwer Academic/Human Sciences Press
233 Spring Street
New York, NY 10013

212-620-8000
800-221-9369
Fax: 212-463-0742
http://www.wkpa.nl

Interdisciplinary international journal serving the groups represented by child and adolescent psychiatry, clinical child/pediatric/family psychology, pediatrics, social science, and human development. Publishes research on diagnosis, assessment, treatment, epidemiology, development, advocacy, training, cultural factors, ethics, policy, and professional issues as related to clinical disorders in children, adolescents and families.

Quarterly
ISSN: 0009-398X

Carol Bischoff, Publisher
Kenneth J Tarnowski, Editor

4461 Child Welfare
Child Welfare League of America
440 1st Street NW
Suite 310
Washington, DC 20001-2085

202-638-2952
Fax: 202-638-4004

BiMonthly

Eve Klein, Editor

4462 Child and Adolescent Social Work Journal
Kluwer Academic/Human Sciences Press
233 Spring Street
New York, NY 10013

212-620-8000
800-221-9369
Fax: 212-463-0742
http://www.wkpa.nl

Features original articles that focus on clinical social work practice with children, adolescents and their families. The journal addresses current issues in the field of social work drawn from theory, direct practice, research, and social policy, as well as focuses on problems affecting specific populations in special settings.

Bimonthly
ISSN: 0738-0151

Carol Bischoff, Publisher
Thomas Kenemore, Editor

4463 College Board News
College Board Publications
45 Columbus Avenue
New York, NY 10023-6992

212-713-8165
800-323-7155
Fax: 800-525-5562
http://www.collegeboard.org

Sent free to schools and colleges several times a year, the News reports on the activities of the College Board. Its articles inform readers about the Board's services in such areas as high school, guidance, college admission, curriculum and placement, testing, financial aid, adult education and research.

4464 College Board Review
College Board Publications
45 Columbus Avenue
New York, NY 10023-6992

212-713-8165
800-323-7155
Fax: 800-525-5562
http://www.collegeboard.org

Each issue of the Review probes key problems and trends facing education professionals concerned with student transition from high school to college.

4465 College Times
College Board Publications
45 Columbus Avenue
New York, NY 10023-6917

212-713-8165
800-323-7155
Fax: 800-525-5562
http://www.collegeboard.org

This annual magazine is a one-stop source to college admission. It provides valuable advice to help students through the complex college selection, application and admission process.

Publication Date: 1995   32 pages Package of 50

4466 Communique
National Association of School Psychologists
4340 EW Highway
Suite 402
Bethesda, MD 20814

301-657-0270
Fax: 301-657-0275
E-mail: center@naspweb.org
http://www.nasponline.org

50 pages 8x Year
ISSN: 0164-775X

4467 Counseling & Values
American Counseling Association
5999 Stevenson Avenue
Alexandria, VA 22304-3302

703-823-9800
Fax: 703-823-0252

Editorial content focuses on the roles of values and religion in counseling and psychology.

3x Year

Stephen Brooks, Advertising Director
Susan Lausch, Advertising/Sales

4468 Counseling Today
American Counseling Association
5999 Stevenson Avenue
Alexandria, VA 22304-3302

703-823-9800
Fax: 703-823-0252

Covers national and international counseling issues and reports legislative and governmental activities affecting counselors.

Monthly

Kathy Maguire, Advertising Director
Mary Morrissey, Editor-in-Chief

4469 Counselor Education & Supervision
American Counseling Association
5999 Stevenson Avenue
Alexandria, VA 22304-3302

703-823-9800
Fax: 703-823-0252

Covers counseling theories, techniques and skills, teaching and training.

Quarterly

Stephven Brooks, Advertising Director
Susan Lausch, Advertising/Sales

4470 ERIC Clearinghouse on Counseling & Student Services
201 Ferguson Building UNCG
Greensboro, NC 27402-6171
336-334-4114
800-414-9769
Fax: 336-334-4116
E-mail: ericcass@uncg.edu.edu
http://ericcass.uncg.edu

Covers news about ERIC and the counseling clearinghouse and developments in the fields of education and counseling.

4 pages Quarterly

Garry R Walz, Co-Director
Jeanne C Bleuer, Co-Director

4471 Educational & Psychological Measurement
Sage Publications
2455 Telle Road
Thousand Oaks, CA 91320
805-499-9774
Fax: 805-375-1700
E-mail: order@sagepub.com
http://www.sagepub.com

Quarterly

4472 Elementary School Guidance & Counseling
American Counseling Association
5999 Stevenson Avenue
Alexandria, VA 22304-3300
703-823-9800
Fax: 703-823-0252
http://www.counseling.org

Journal concerned with enhancing the role of the elementary, middle school and junior high school counselor.

Quarterly
ISSN: 0013-5976

Michael Comlish, Editor

4473 Family Relations
Miami University
Family & Child Studies Center
Oxford, OH 45056
513-529-4909
Fax: 513-529-7270

Quarterly

Timothy H Brubaker, Editor

4474 Family Therapy: The Journal of the California Graduate School of Family Psychology
Libra Publishers
3089C Clairemont Drive
PNB 383
San Diego, CA 92117-6802
858-571-1414
Fax: 858-571-1414

Articles contributed by professionals spanning issues relating to teenage education, counseling and guidance. Paperback.

96 pages Quarterly
ISSN: 0091-6544

William Kroll, Editor

4475 Health & Social Work
National Association of Social Workers
750 First Street NE
Suite 700
Washington, DC 20002-4241
202-408-8600
800-638-8799
Fax: 202-336-8311
http://www.socialworkers.org

Covers practice, innovation, research, legislation, policy , planning, and all the professional issues relevant to social work services in all levels of education.

Mal Milburn, Marketing/Sales Associate
Lyn Carter, Advertising Specialist

4476 ICA Quarterly
Western Illinois University
Counseling Center
Memorial Hall
Macomb, IL 61455
309-298-2453
Fax: 309-298-3253

Official publication of the Illinois Counseling Association. Focus is on material of interest and value to professional counselors.

Quarterly

Michael Illovsky, Editor

4477 International Journal of Play Therapy
2050 N Winery Avenue
Suite 101
Fresno, CA 93703-2831
559-252-2278
Fax: 559-252-2297
E-mail: info@a4pt.org
http://www.a4pt.org

Dedicated to the advancement of play therapy. APT is interdisciplinary and defines play therapy as a distinct group of interventions which use play as an integral component of the therapeutic process.

Publication Date: 1982 BiAnnual

William S Burns CAE, Executive Director
Kathryn Lebby MS, General Manager

4478 Journal for Specialists in Group Work
American Counseling Association
5999 Stevenson Avenue
Alexandria, VA 22304-3302
703-823-9800
Fax: 703-823-0252

Contains theory, legal issues and current literature reviews.

Quarterly

Stephven Brooks, Editor

4479 Journal of At-Risk Issues
Clemson University
209 Martin Street
Clemson, SC 29631-1555
864-656-2599
800-443-6392
Fax: 864-656-0136
E-mail: NDPC@clemson.edu
http://www.dropoutprevention.org

36 pages
ISBN: 1098-1608

Dr. Judy Johnson, Author
Dr. Judy Johnson, Author
Dr. Alice Fisher, Editor

4480 Journal of Child and Adolescent Group Therapy
Kluwer Academic/Human Sciences Press
233 Spring Street
New York, NY 10013

212-620-8000
800-221-9369
Fax: 212-463-0742
http://www.wkpa.nl

Addresses the whole spectrum of professional issues relating to juvenile and parent group treatment. Promotes the exchange of new ideas from a wide variety of disciplines concerned with enhancing treatments for this specialpopulation. The multidisciplinary contributions include clinical reports, illustrations of new technical methods, and studies that contribute to the advancement of therapeutic results, as well as articles on theoretical issues, applications, and thegroup process.

Quarterly
ISSN: 1053-0800

Carol Bischoff, Publisher
Edward S Soo, Editor

4481 Journal of College Admission
Nat'l Association for College Admission Counseling
1631 Prince Street
Alexandria, VA 22314-2818

703-836-2222
Fax: 703-836-8015
http://www.nacac.com

Membership association offering information to counselors and guidance professionals working in the college admissions office.

32 pages Quarterly
ISSN: 0734-6670

Elaina Loveland, Author
Shanda T Ivory, Chief Officer Communications
Amy C Vogt, Assistant Director

4482 Journal of Counseling and Development
American Counseling Association
5999 Stevenson Avenue
Alexandria, VA 22304-3302

703-823-9800
Fax: 703-823-0252

Edited for counseling and human development specialists in schools, colleges and universities.

Monthly

Stephven Brooks, Editor

4483 Journal of Drug Education
California State University
Department of Health Science
Northridge, CA 91330-8285

818-677-3101
Fax: 818-677-2045

Offers information to counselors and guidance professionals dealing with areas of drug and substance abuse education in the school system.

Quarterly

Robert Huff, Contact

4484 Journal of Emotional and Behavioral Disorders
Pro-Ed
8700 Shoal Creek Boulevard
Austin, TX 78757-6816

512-451-3246
800-897-3202
Fax: 512-302-9129
http://www.proedinc.com

Presents high-quality interdisciplinary scholarship in the area of emotional and behavioral disabilities. Explores issues including youth violence, emotional problems among minority children, long-term foster care placement, mentalhealth services, social development and educational strategies.

Michael H Epstein, EdD, Editor
Douglas Cullinan, EdD, Editor

4485 Journal of Employment Counseling
American Counseling Association
5999 Stevenson Avenue
Alexandria, VA 22304-3302

703-823-9800
Fax: 703-823-0252

Editorial content includes developing trends in case studies and newest personnel practices.

Quarterly

Stephven Brooks, Editor

4486 Journal of Humanistic Education and
Development
Ohio University
201 McCracken Hall
Athens, OH 45701

740-593-4000
Fax: 740-593-0569

Focuses on the humanities and promotes their place in the educational system.

Quarterly

4487 Journal of Multicultural Counseling &
Development
American Counseling Association
5999 Stevenson Avenue
Alexandria, VA 22304-3302

703-823-9800
Fax: 703-823-0252

Contains articles with focus on research, theory and program application related to multicultural counseling.

Quarterly

Stephven Brooks, Editor

4488 Journal of Sex Education & Therapy
American Association of Sex Educators
PO Box 5488
Richmond, VA 23220-0488

804-644-3288
Fax: 804-644-3290
E-mail: aasect@worldnet.att.net
http://www.aasect.org

Provides education and training in all areas of sexual health.

110 pages Quarterly
ISSN: 0161-4576

Michael Plant, Author

4489 Measurement & Evaluation in Counseling and
Development
American Counseling Association
5999 Stevenson Avenue
Alexandria, VA 22304-3302

703-823-9800
Fax: 703-823-0252

Editorial focuses on research and applications in counseling and guidance.

Quarterly

Stephven Brooks, Advertising Director
Susan Lausch, Advertising/Sales

4490 NACAC Bulletin
Nat'l Association for College Admission Counseling
1631 Prince Street
Alexandria, VA 22314-2818
703-836-2222
Fax: 703-836-8015
http://www.nacac.com

Membership association offering information to counselors and guidance professionals working in the college admissions office.

Monthly

Shanda T Ivory, Chief Officer Communications
Amy C Vogt, Assistant Director

4491 NASW News
National Association of Social Workers
PO Box 431
Annapolis Junction, MD 20701-0431
301-317-8688
800-638-8799
Fax: 301-206-7989

Features in-depth coverage of developments in social work practice, news of national social policy developments, political and legislative news in social services, noteworthy achievements of social workers and association news.

Monthly

Scott Moss

4492 National Coalition for Sex Equity in Education
PO Box 534
Annandale, NJ 08801
908-735-5045
Fax: 908-735-9674
E-mail: info@ncsee.org
http://www.ncsee.org

The only national organization for gender equity specialists and educators. Individuals and organizations committed to reducing sex role stereotyping for females and males. Services include an annual national training conference, aquarterly newsletter and a membership directory. Members may join task forces dealing with equity related topics such as computer/technology issues, early childhood, male issues, sexual harassment prevention, sexual orientation and vocational issues.

Quarterly Newsletter

Theodora Martin, Business Manager

4493 New Horizons
National Registration Center for Study Abroad
PO Box 1393
Milwaukee, WI 53201-1393
414-278-0631
Fax: 414-271-8884
E-mail: info@nrcsa.com
http://www.nrcsa.com

Provides information about member institution's programs and establishes standards for treatment of visitors from abroad including the appointment of bilingual housing officers and counselors to deal with culture shock.

16 pages Quarterly
ISBN: 1-977864-43-3

Anne Wittig, Author
Mike Wittig, General Manager

4494 Rehabilitation Counseling Bulletin
Pro-Ed
8700 Shoal Creek Boulevard
Austin, TX 78757-6816
512-451-3246
800-897-3202
Fax: 512-302-9129

E-mail: proed1@aol.com
http://www.proedinc.com

International journal providing original empirical research, essays of a theoretical nature, methodological treatises and comprehensive reviews of the literature, intensive case studies and research critiques.

Quarterly Magazine
ISSN: 0034-3552

Douglas Strohmer, PhD, Editor

4495 School Counselor
American Counseling Association
5999 Stevenson Avenue
Alexandria, VA 22304-3302
703-823-9800
Fax: 703-823-0252

Includes current issues and information affecting teens and how counselors can deal with them.

5x Year

Stephven Brooks, Advertising Director
Susan Lausch, Advertising/Sales

4496 School Psychology Review
National Association of School Psychologists
4340 EW Highway
Suite 402
Bethesda, MD 20814
301-657-0270
Fax: 301-657-0275
E-mail: center@naspweb.org
http://www.nasponline.org

170 pages Quarterly
ISSN: 0279-6015

4497 Social Work Research Journal
National Association of Social Workers
750 1st Street NE
Suite 700
Washington, DC 20002-4241
202-408-8600
800-638-8799
Fax: 202-336-8311
http://www.socialworkers.org

Contains orginal research papers that contribute to knowledge about social work issues and problems. Topics include new technology, strategies and methods, and resarch results.

Quarterly
ISSN: 1070-5309

Stuart A Kirk, Editor

4498 Social Work in Education
National Association of Social Workers
750 1st Street NE
Suite 700
Washington, DC 20002-4241
202-408-8600
Fax: 202-336-8310
http://www.socialworkers.org

Covers practice, innovation, research, legislation, policy, planning, and all the professional issues relevant to social work services in all levels of education.

Mal Milburn, Marketing/Sales Associate
Lyn Carter, Advertising Specialist

4499 SocialWork
National Association of Social Workers
750 1st Street NE
Suite 700
Washington, DC 20002-4241
202-408-8600
800-638-8799

Fax: 202-336-8311
http://www.socialworkers.org

Covers important research findings, critical analyses, practice issues, and information on current social issues such as AIDS, homelessness, and federal regulation of social programs. Case management, third-party reimbursement, credentialing, and other professional issues are addressed.

Mal Milburn, Marketing/Sales Associate
Lyn Carter, Advertising Specialist

4500   Today's School Psychologist
LRP Publications
747 Dresher Road
PO Box 980
Horsham, PA 19044-0980

215-784-0941
800-341-7874
Fax: 215-784-0870
E-mail: custserve@lrp.com
http://www.lrp.com/ed

An in-depth guide to a school psychologist's job, offering practical strategies and tips for handling day-to-day responsibilites, encouraging change, and improving professional standing and performance.

Monthly
ISSN: 1098-9277

Gary Bagin, Director Communications
Ann Checkosky, Editor

4501   Washington Counseletter
Chronicle Guidance Publications
66 Aurora Street
Moravia, NY 13118-1190

315-497-0330
800-622-7284
Fax: 315-497-3359
E-mail: customerservice@chronicleguidance.com
http://www.chronicleguidance.com

Monthly report highlighting federal, state, and local developments affecting the counseling and education professions. Items list events, programs, activities and publications of interest to counselors and educators.

8 pages 8x Year

Gary Fickeisen, President
Priscilla Lorah, Coordinator

Periodicals
Language Arts

4502   AATF National Bulletin
American Association of Teachers of French
2324 Avenue
Suite 34
Cincinnati, OH 45206

513-861-6928
Fax: 513-861-5572
E-mail: jbg@2fuse.net
http://www.frenchteachers.org

Announcements and short articles relating to the association on French language and cultural activities.

30-50 pages 5x Year

Jane Black Goepper, Editor

4503   ACTFL Newsletters
American Council on the Teaching of Foreign Lang.
6 Executive Plaza
Yonkers, NY 10701-6832

914-963-8830
Fax: 914-963-1275

A quarterly newsletter containing topical and timely information on matters of interest to foreign language educators. Regular columns include Languages in the News and Washington Watch.

20 pages Quarterly

C Edward Scebold, C-Editor
Jamie Draper, Co-Editor

4504   ADE Bulletin
Association of Departments of English
26 Broadway
Third Floor
New York, NY 10004-1789

646-576-5133
Fax: 646-458-0033
http://www.ade.org

This bulletin concentrates on developments in scholarship, curriculum and teachers in English.

64 pages
ISSN: 0001-0888

4505   Beyond Words
1534 Wells Drive NE
Albuquerque, NM 87112-6383

505-275-2558

Offers information on literature, language arts and English for the teaching professional.

10x Year

4506   Bilingual Research Journal
National Association for Bilingual Education
1030 15th Street NW
Suite 470
Washington, DC 20005-4018

202-898-1829
Fax: 202-789-2866
E-mail: nabe@nabe.org
http://www.nabe.org

Journal published by National Association for Bilingual Education.

Quarterly
8,000 attendees

Delia Pompa, Executive Director
Alicia Sosa, Membership Director

4507   Bilingual Review Press
Arizona State University
Hispanic Research Center
Tempe, AZ 85287

480-965-3990
Fax: 480-965-0315

Offers information and reviews on books, materials and the latest technology available to bilingual educators.

3x Year

Gary D Keller, Editor

4508   CEA Forum
College English Association
English Department
Youngstown State University
Youngstown, OH 44555-0001

330-941-3415
Fax: 330-941-2304
E-mail: Daniel.Robinson@widener.edu
http://www.as.ysu.edu/~english/cea/forum1.htm

Publishes articles on professional issues and pedagogy related to the teaching of English. Subscription includes CEA Critic, a scholarly journal that appears 3x annually.

Newsletter
ISSN: 0007-8034

Daniel Robinson, Editor

4509 Classroom Notes Plus
National Council of Teachers of English
1111 W Kenyon Road
Urbana, IL 61801-1010
217-328-3870
800-369-6283
Fax: 217-278-3761
E-mail: notesplus@ncte.org
http://www.ncte.org

Secondary periodical for English/Language Arts featuring usable teaching ideas for teachers by teachers.

16 pages Quarterly

Felice Kaufmann, Communications Director

4510 Communication Disorders Quarterly
Pro-Ed., Inc.
8700 Shoal Creek Boulevard
Austin, TX 78757-6816
512-451-3246
800-897-3202
Fax: 512-302-9129
E-mail: proed1@aol.com
http://www.proedinc.com

Research, intervention and practice in speech, language and hearing.

Quarterly Magazine
ISSN: 1525-7401

Alejandro Brice, Editor

4511 Communication: Journalism Education Today
Truman High School
3301 S Noland Road
Independence, MO 64055-1318
816-521-2710
Fax: 816-521-2913

A quarterly journal for the Journalism Education Association, based at Kansas State University, Manhattan, KS. Most articles are designed to relate to a theme. The magazine focuses on secondary and collegiate journalism educators.

Quarterly

Molly J Clemons, Editor

4512 Composition Studies Freshman English News
De Paul University
802 W Belden Avenue
Chicago, IL 60614
312-362-8000
Fax: 773-325-7328

Theoretical and practical articles on rhetorical theory.

44 pages SemiAnnually
Peter Vandenberg, English Department

4513 Council-Grams
National Council of Teachers of English
1111 W Kenyon Road
Urbana, IL 61801-1010
217-328-3870
800-369-6283
Fax: 217-328-9645
http://www.ncte.org

Offers information and updates in the areas of English, language arts and reading.

16 pages 5x Year
Michael Spooner

4514 Counterforce
Society for the Advancement of Good English
4501 Riverside Avenue
#30
Anderson, CA 96007-2759
530-365-8026

Offers updates and information for English teachers and professors.

Quarterly

4515 English Education
New York University
635 E Building
New York, NY 10003
212-998-8857
Fax: 212-995-4376

Offers updates and information for reading and English teachers, and professors.

Quarterly
Gordon M Pradl, Editor

4516 English Journal
National Council of Teachers of English
1111 W Kenyon Road
Urbana, IL 61801-1010
217-328-3870
800-369-6283
Fax: 217-328-9645
http://www.ncte.org

An ideal magazine for middle school, junior and senior high school English teachers.

Biannual
ISSN: 0013-8274

Carrie Stewart, Editor

4517 English Leadership Quarterly
National Council of Teachers of English
1111 W Kenyon Road
Urbana, IL 61801-1010
217-328-3870
800-369-6283
Fax: 217-328-9645
http://www.ncte.org

Teaching of English for secondary school English Department chairpersons.

12 pages Quarterly
James Strickland

4518 English for Specific Purposes
University of Michigan
Ann Arbor, MI 48109
619-594-6331
Fax: 619-594-6530

Concerned with English education and its importance to the developing student.

3x Year
John Swales, Editor

4519 Foreign Language Annals
American Council on the Teaching of Foreign Lang.
6 Executive Plaza
Yonkers, NY 10701-6832
914-963-8830
Fax: 914-963-1275

Dedicated to advancing all areas of the profession of foreign language teaching. It seeks primarily to serve the interests of teachers, administrators and researchers, regardless of educational level of the language with which theyare concerned. Preference is given in this scholarly journal to articles that describe innovative and successful teaching methods, that report educational research or experimentation, or that are relevant to the concerns and problems of theprofession.

128 pages Quarterly

C Edward Scebold, Executive Director

4520 Journal of Basic Writing
City University of NY, Instructional Resource Ctr.
535 E 80th Street
New York, NY 10021-0767
212-794-5445
Fax: 212-794-5706

Publishes articles of theory, research and teaching practices related to basic writing. Articles are referred by members of the Editorial Board and the editors.

Spring & Fall

Karen Greenberg, Editor
Trudy Smoke, Editor

4521 Journal of Children's Communication Development
The Council for Exceptional Children
1920 Association Drive
Reston, VA 20191-1545
703-620-3660
800-232-7323
Fax: 703-264-1637

Provides in-depth research and practical application articles in communication assessment and intervention. The journal frequently contains a practitioner's section that addresses professional questions, reviews tests and therapymaterials, and describes innovative programs and service delivery models.

2x Year
ISSN: 0735-3170

Richard Nowell, Editor

4522 Journal of Teaching Writing
Indiana University-Purdue University/Indianapolis
425 University Boulevard
Indianapolis, IN 46202-5148
317-274-0092
Fax: 317-274-2347

A refereed journal for classroom teachers and researchers at all academic levels whose interest or emphasis is the teaching of writing. Appearing semiannually, JTW publishes articles on the theory, practice, and teaching of writingthroughout the curriculum. Each issue covers a range of topics, from composition theory and discourse analysis to curriculum development and innovative teaching techniques. Contributors are reminded to tailor their writing for a diverse readership.

12-20 pages Semiannually

4523 Journalism Quarterly
George Washington University
School of Journalism
Washington, DC 20052-0001
202-994-6227
Fax: 202-994-5806

Information on all facets of writing and journalism for the student and educator.

Quarterly

Jean Folkerts, Editor

4524 Language & Speech
Kingston Press Services, Ltd.
43 Derwent Road, Whitton
Twickenham, Middlesex TW2 7HQ
United Kingdom
0-20-8893-3015
Fax: 208-893-3015
E-mail: sales@kingstonepress.com
http://www.kingstonepress.com

Psychological research articles, speech perception, speech production, psycholinguistics and reading.

Quarterly

4525 Language Arts
National Council of Teachers of English
1111 W Kenyon Road
Urbana, IL 61801-1010
217-328-3870
800-369-6283
Fax: 217-328-9645
http://www.ncte.org

Edited for instructors in language arts at the elementary level.

Monthly

Kent Williamson, Editor

4526 Language, Speech & Hearing Services in School
Ohio State University
110 Pressey Hall
1070 Carmack Road
Columbus, OH 43210
614-292-8207
Fax: 614-292-7504

Interested in innovative technology and growth in language development in schools.

Wayne A Secord, PhD, Editor

4527 Merlyn's Pen: Fiction, Essays and Poems by America's Teens
PO Box 910
East Greenwich, RI 02818-0964
401-885-5175
800-247-2027
Fax: 401-885-5199
E-mail: merlynspen@aol.com
http://www.merlynspen.com

Merlyns' Pen magazine is a selective publisher of model writing by America's students in grades 6-12. Products include Merlyn's Pen magazine (a reproducible annual magazine) and the American Teen Writer Series, collections ofanthologized short fiction and nonfiction by brilliant teen writers. Used for models, inspiration, and instruction in literature and writing.

100 pages Annually
ISSN: 0882-2050

Jim Stahl, Editor

4528 Modern Language Journal
Case Western Reserve University
Department of Modern Languages
Cleveland, OH 44106
216-368-2000
Fax: 216-368-2216

Quarterly

David P Benseler, Editor

4529 NABE News
National Association for Bilingual Education
1030 15th Street NW
Suite 470
Washington, DC 20005-4018
202-898-1829
Fax: 202-789-2866
E-mail: nabe@nabe.org
http://www.nabe.org

Magazine published by the National Association for Bilingual Education.

Bi-Monthly

Delia Pompa, Executive Director
Alicia Sosa, Membership Director

4530 NASILP Journal
National Assn. of Self-Instructional Language
Temple University
Philadelphia, PA 19122
215-204-7000

Articles, news and book reviews on language instructional methodology.

12 pages SemiAnnually

Dr. John Means

4531 National Clearinghouse for Bilingual Education Newsletter
George Washington University
2121 K Street NW
Suite 260
Washington, DC 20037-1214
202-467-0867
800-321-6223
E-mail: askncbe@ncbe.gwu.edu
http://www.ncbe.gwu.edu

Provides information to practitioners on the education of language minority students.

Weekly

Dr. Minerva Gorena, Director

4532 PCTE Bulletin
Pennsylvania Council of Teachers of English
Williamsport Area Community College
Williamsport, PA 17701

Focuses on Pennsylvania literacy issues.

SemiAnnually

Robert Ulrich

4533 Quarterly Journal of Speech
National Communication Association
1765 N Street NW
Washington, DC 20036
202-464-4622
Fax: 202-464-4600
http://www.natcom.org

Main academic journal in the speech/communication field of education.

Quarterly

James Gaudino, Executive Director

4534 Quarterly Review of Doublespeak
National Council of Teachers of English
1111 W Kenyon Road
Urbana, IL 61801-1010
217-328-3870
800-369-6283
Fax: 217-328-9645
http://www.ncte.org

Provides information on the misuses and abuse of language.

8 pages Quarterly

Harry Brent

4535 Quarterly of the NWP
National Writing Project
2105 Bancroft Way
Suite 1042
Berkeley, CA 94720-1042
510-642-0963
Fax: 510-642-4545
E-mail: writingproject.org
http://www.writingproject.org

Journal on the research in and practice of teaching writing at all grade levels.

40 pages Quarterly Magazine
ISSN: 0896-3592

Art Peterson, Amy Bauman; Editors, Author
Art Peterson, Senior Editor
Amy Bauman, Managing Editor

4536 Quill and Scroll
University of Iowa
School of Journalism
Iowa City, IA 52242
319-335-5795
Fax: 319-335-5210

Founded and distributed for the purpose of encouraging and rewarding individual achievements in journalism and allied fields. This magazine is published bimonthly during the school year and has a variety of pamphlets and lists of publications available as resources.

BiMonthly

Richard P Johns, Editor

4537 Research in the Teaching of English
Harvard Graduate School of Education
Larsen Hall
Appian Way
Cambridge, MA 02138
617-495-3521
Fax: 617-495-0540

A research journal devoted to original research on the relationships between teaching and learning for language development in reading, writing and speaking at all age levels.

Quarterly

Sandra Stotsky, Editor

4538 Rhetoric Review
University of Arizona
Department of English
Tucson, AZ 85721-0001
520-621-3371
Fax: 520-621-7397
http://http://members.aol.com/sborrowman/rr/html

A journal of rhetoric and composition publishing scholarly and historical studies, theoretical and practical articles, views of the profession, review essays of professional books, personal essays about writing and poems.

200+ pages Quarterly
ISSN: 0735-0198

Theresa Enos, Editor

4539 Slate Newsletter
National Council of Teachers of English
1111 W Kenyon Road
Urbana, IL 61801-1010
217-328-3870
800-369-6283
Fax: 217-328-9645
http://www.ncte.org

Short articles on topics such as censorship, trends and issues and testing.

4540 Studies in Second Language Acquisition
Cambridge University Press
1105 Atwater
Bloomington, IN 47401-5020

812-855-6874
Fax: 812-855-2386
E-mail: ssla@indiana.edu
http://www.indiana.edu/~ssla

Referred journal devoted to problems and issues in second and foreign language acquisition of any language.

140 pages Quarterly Paperback
ISSN: 0272-2631

Albert Valdman, Editor

4541 TESOL Journal: A Journal of Teaching and Classroom Research
Teachers of English to Speakers of Other Languages
1600 Cameron Street
Suite 300
Alexandria, VA 22314-2705

703-836-0774
Fax: 703-836-7864
E-mail: tesol@tesol.edu
http://www.tesol.edu

TESOL's mission is to develop the expertise of its members and others involved in teaching English to speakers of other languages to help them foster communication in diverse settings. The association advances standards forprofessional preparation and employment, continuing education, and student programs, produces programs, services, and products, and promotes advocacy to further the profession. TESOL has 91 affiliates worldwide.

50 pages Quarterly

Christian J Faltis, Editor
Marilyn Kupetz, Managing Editor

4542 TESOL Quarterly
Teachers of English to Speakers of Other Languages
1600 Cameron Street
Suite 300
Alexandria, VA 22314-2705

703-836-0774
Fax: 703-836-7864
E-mail: tesol@tesol.edu
http://www.tesol.com

TESOL Quarterly is our scholarly journal containing articles on academic research, theory, reports, reviews. Articles about linguistics, ethnographies, and more describe the theoretic basis for ESL/EFL teaching practices. Readershipis approximately 23,400.

830 pages Quarterly

Carol Chapelle, Editor

4543 Writing Lab Newsletter
Purdue University, Department of English
500 Oval Drive
W. Lafayette, IN 47907-2038

765-494-7268
Fax: 765-494-3780
E-mail: wln@purdue.edudue.edu
http://www.owl.english.purdue.edu/lab/newsletter/index.html

Monthly newsletter for readers involved in writing centers and/or one-to-one instruction in writing skills.

16 pages Monthly/Newsletter
ISSN: 1040-3779

Muriel Harris, Editor
Shawna McCaw, Managing Editor

Periodicals
Library Services

4544 ALA Editions Catalog
Membership Services American Library Association
50 E Huron Street
Chicago, IL 60611

800-545-2433
Fax: 312-836-9958
http://www.ala.org

Contains over 1,000 job listings, news and reports on the latest technologies in 11 issues annually. Also scholarships, grants and awards are possibilities.

Annually

4545 American Libraries
American Library Association
50 E Huron Street
Chicago, IL 60611-2795

312-944-6780
Fax: 312-440-9374

A news magazine covering library development today. Includes news on trends, recent developments and subjects of interest to modern library professionals.

Monthly

Tom Gaughan, Editor

4546 Booklist
American Library Association
50 E Huron Street
Chicago, IL 60611-5295

312-944-6780
Fax: 312-440-9374
http://www.ala.org/booklist

A guide to current print and audiovisual materials worthy of consideration for purchase by small and medium-sized public libraries and school library media centers.

Semimonthly

Bill Ott, Editor

4547 Catholic Library World
Catholic Library Association
461 W Lancaster Avenue
Haverford, PA 19041-1412

734-722-7185

A periodical geared toward the professional librarian in order to keep them abreast of new publications, library development, association news and technology.

Quarterly

Allen Gruenke, Executive Director

4548 Choice
Current Reviews for Academic Libraries
100 Riverview Center
Middletown, CT 06457-3445

860-347-6933
Fax: 860-346-8586
E-mail: adsales@ala-choice.org
http://www.ala.org/acrl/choice

A magazine distributed to librarians and other organizations that analyzes various materials, offers book reviews and information on the latest technology available for the library acquisitions departments.

11x Year

Steven Conforti, Subscriptions Manager
Stuart Foster, Advertising Manager

4549 Emergency Librarian
Ken Haycock and Associates
101-1001 W Braodway
Vancouver
British Columbia
604-925-0266
604-925-056

Professional journal targeted to the specific needs and concerns of teachers and teacher-librarians.

5x Year

Dr. Ken Haycock

4550 ILA Reporter
33 W Grand Avenue
Suite 301
Chicago, IL 60610-4306
312-644-1896
Fax: 312-644-1899
E-mail: ila@ila.org
http://www.ila.org

30 pages
ISSN: 0018-9979

Robert P Doyle, Arthor

4551 Information Technology & Libraries
University of the Pacific
William Knox Holt Library
Stockton, CA 95211-0001
209-946-2434
Fax: 209-946-2805

Offers information on the latest technology, systems and electronics offered to the library market.

Quarterly

Thomas W Leonhardt, Editor
Karen Hope

4552 Journal of Education for Library and Information Sciences
Kent State University
School of Library Science
Kent, OH 44242-0001
330-672-2782
Fax: 330-672-7965

The latest information on books, publications, electronics and technology for the librarian.

Quarterly

4553 Libraries & Culture
University of Texas at Austin/Univ. of Texas Press
PO Box 7819
Austin, TX 78713-7819
512-232-7618
Fax: 512-232-7178
E-mail: dgdavis@gslis.utexas.edu

An interdisciplinary journal that explores the significance of collections of recorded knowledge. Scholarly articles and book reviews cover international topics dealing with libraries, books, reviews, archives, personnel, and theirhistory; for scholars, librarians, historians, readers interested in the history of books and libraries.

100 pages Quarterly
ISSN: 0894-8631

Dr. Donald G Davis Jr, Editor
Colleen Daly, Assistant Editor

4554 Library Collections, Acquisitions & Technical Services
Pergamon Press, Elsevier Science
The Boulevard, Lanngford Lane
Kidlington, Oxford
United Kingdom
614-292-4738
Fax: 614-292-7859
E-mail: deidrichs.1@osu.edu
http://www.elsvier.com

Offers information on policy, practice, and research on the collection management and technical service areas of libraries.

500 pages Quarterly
ISSN: 1464-9055

Carol Pitts Diedrichs, Editor

4555 Library Issues: Briefings for Faculty and Administrators
Mountainside Publishing Company
PO Box 8330
Ann Arbor, MI 48107-8330
734-662-3925
Fax: 734-662-4450
E-mail: apdougherty@compuserve.com
http://www.libraryissues.com

Offers overviews of the trends and problems affecting campus libraries. Explained in layman's terms as they relate to faculty, administrators and the parent institution.

4-6 pages Bi-Monthly
ISSN: 0734-3035

Dr. Richard M Dougherty, Editor
Ann Dougherty, Managing Editor

4556 Library Quarterly
Indiana University, School of Library Science
Lib 013
Bloomington, IN 47405
812-855-5113
Fax: 812-855-6166

Updates, information, statistics, book reviews and publications for librarians.

Quarterly

Stephen P Harter, Editor

4557 Library Resources & Technical Services
Columbia University, School of Library Sciences
516 Butler Library
New York, NY 10027
212-854-3329
Fax: 212-854-8951

Quarterly

Richard P Smirgalia, Editor

4558 Library Trends
Grad. School Library & Info. Science
501 E Daniel Street
Champaign, IL 61820
217-333-1359
Fax: 217-244-7329
E-mail: puboff@alexia.lis.uiuc.edu
http://www.edfu.lis.uiuc.edu/puboff

A scholarly quarterly devoted to invited papers in library and information science. Each issue is devoted to a single theme.

208 pages Quarterly

FW Lancaster, Editor
James Dowling, Managing Editor

Publications / Periodicals

4559 Media & Methods Magazine
American Society of Educators
1429 Walnut Street
Philadelphia, PA 19102-3218

215-563-6005
800-555-5657
Fax: 215-587-9706
http://www.media-methods.com

Leading pragmatic magazine for K-12 educators and administrators. The focus is on how to integrate today's technologies and presentation tools into the curriculum. Very up-to-date and well respected national source publication. Loyalreaders are media specialists, school librarians, technology coordinators, administrators and classroom teachers.

5x School Year

Michele Sokoloff, Publisher
Christine Weiser, Editor

4560 Read, America!
Place in the Woods
3900 Glenwood Avenue
Golden Valley, MN 55422-5302

763-374-2120
Fax: 952-593-5593
E-mail: readamerica10732@aol.com

News, book reviews, ideas for librarians and reading program leaders; short stories and poetry pages for adults and children; and an annual Read America! collection with selections of new books solicited from 350 publishers.

12 pages Quarterly Newsletter
ISSN: 0891-4214

Roger Hammer, Editor/Publisher

4561 School Library Journal
245 W 17th Street
New York, NY 10011

212-463-6759
Fax: 212-463-6689
E-mail: slj@cahners.com
http://www.slj.com

For children, young adults and school librarians.

Bruce Barnet, President/CEO
Renee Olson, Editor-in-Chief

4562 School Library Media Activities Monthly
LMS Associates
17 E Henrietta Street
Baltimore, MD 21230-3910

301-685-8621

Monthly
Paula Montgomery, Editor

4563 School Library Media Quarterly
American Library Association
50 E Huron Street
Chicago, IL 60611-5295

312-944-6780
Fax: 312-280-3255

For elementary and secondary building level library media specialists, district supervisors and others concerned with the selection and purchase of print and nonprint media.

Quarterly
Judy Pitts, Editor
Barbara Stripling, Editor

4564 Special Libraries
Special Libraries Association
1700 18th Street NW
Washington, DC 20009-2514

202-234-4700
Fax: 202-265-9317

Includes information and manuscripts on the administration, organization and operation of special libraries.

Quarterly
Maria Barry, Editor

4565 Specialist
Special Libraries Association
1700 18th Street NW
Washington, DC 20009-2514

202-234-4700
Fax: 202-265-9317

Contains news and information about the special library/information field.

Monthly
Alisa Nesmith Cooper, Editor

Periodicals
Mathematics

4566 Focus on Learning Problems in Math
Center for Teaching/Learning Math
PO Box 3149
Framingham, MA 01701-3149

508-877-7895
Fax: 508-788-3600
E-mail: msharma@rea.com

An interdisciplinary journal. Edited jointly by the Research Council for Diagnostic and Prescription Mathematics and the Center for Teaching/Learning of Mathematics. The objective of focus is to make available the current research, methods of identification, diagnosis, and remediation of learning problems in mathematics. Contribution from the fields of education psychology and mathematics having the potential to import on classroom or clinical practice are valued.

64-96 pages Quarterly
Mahesh Sharma, Editor

4567 Journal for Research in Mathematics Education
National Council of Teachers of Mathematics
1906 Association Drive
Reston, VA 20191-1502

703-620-9840
Fax: 703-476-2970
E-mail: nctm@nctm.org
http://www.nctm.org

A forum for disciplined inquiry into the teaching and learning of math at all levels— from preschool through adult. Available in print or online version.

5x Year
ISSN: 0021-8251

Harry B Tunis, Publications Director
Rowena G Martelino, Promotions Manager

4568 Journal of Computers in Math & Science
PO Box 2966
Charlottesville, VA 22902-2966

804-973-3087
Fax: 703-997-8760

Quarterly

4569 Journal of Recreational Mathematics
4761 Bigger Road
Kettering, OH 45440-1829
631-691-1470
Fax: 631-691-1770

Promotes the creative practice of mathematics for educational learning.

Quarterly

Joseph S Madachy, Editor

4570 Math Notebook
Center for Teacher/Learning Math
PO Box 3149
Framingham, MA 01705-3149
508-877-7895
Fax: 508-788-3600

A publication for teachers and parents to improve mathematics instruction.

4x/5x Year

Mahesh Sharma, Editor

4571 Mathematics & Computer Education
MAYTC Journal
PO Box 158
Old Bethpage, NY 11804-0158
516-822-5475

Contains a variety of articles pertaining to the field of mathematics.

TriAnnually

George Miller, Editor

4572 Mathematics Teacher
National Council of Teachers of Mathematics
1906 Association Drive
Reston, VA 20191-1502
703-620-9840
Fax: 703-295-0973
E-mail: nctm@nctm.org
http://www.nctm.org

Devoted to the improvement of mathematics instruction in grades 9 and higher.

Monthly
ISSN: 0025-5769

Harry B Tunis, Publications Director
Rowena G Martellino, Promotions Manager

4573 Mathematics Teaching in the Middle School
National Council of Teachers of Mathematics
1906 Association Drive
Reston, VA 20191-1593
703-620-9840
Fax: 703-476-2970
E-mail: nctm@nctm.org
http://www.nctm.org

Addresses the learning needs of students in grades 5-9.

Monthly
ISSN: 1072-0839

Harry B Tunis, Publications Director
Rowena G Martelino, Promotions Manager

4574 NCTM News Bulletin
National Council of Teachers of Mathematics
1906 Association Drive
Reston, VA 20191-9988
703-620-9840
Fax: 703-476-2970
E-mail: nctm@nctm.org
http://www.nctm.org

Publication that reaches all of NCTM's individual and institutional members of more than 107,000 math teachers and school personnel.

Harry B Tunis, Director Publications
Krista Hopkins, Director Marketing Services

4575 Notices of the American Mathematical Society
American Mathematical Society
PO Box 6248
Providence, RI 02940-6248
401-455-4000
Fax: 401-331-3842

Announces programs, meetings, conferences and symposia of the AMS and other mathematical groups.

10x Year

Dr. John S Bradley, Managing Editor
Anne Newcomb, Avertising Coordinator

4576 SSMart Newsletter
School Science & Mathematics Association
Curriculum & Foundations
Bloomsburg, PA 17815
570-389-3894
Fax: 570-389-3894

Membership news offering information, updates, reviews, articles and association news for professionals in the science and mathematics fields of education.

8 pages Quarterly

Darrel Fyffe, Publisher
Norbert Kuenzi, Editor

4577 Teaching Children Mathematics
National Council of Teachers of Mathematics
1906 Association Drive
Reston, VA 20191-1502
703-620-9840
Fax: 703-476-2970
E-mail: nctm@nctm.org
http://www.nctm.org

Concerned primarily with the teaching of mathematics from Pre-K through grade 6.

Monthly
ISSN: 1073-5836

Harry B Tunis, Publications Director
Rowena G Martelino, Promotions Manager

Periodicals
Music & Art

4578 American Academy of Arts & Sciences Bulletin
Norton Woods, 136 Irving Street
Cambridge, MA 02138
617-576-5000
Fax: 617-576-5050

Covers current news of the Academy as well as developments in the arts and sciences.

Alexandra Oleson

4579 Art Education
National Art Education Association
1916 Association Drive
Reston, VA 20191-1590
703-860-8000
Fax: 703-860-2960

A professional journal in the field of art education devoted to articles on all education levels.

6x Year

Thomas A Hatfield, Editor
Beverly Jeanne Davis, Managing Editor

4580 Arts & Activities
Publishers' Development Corporation
591 Camino de la Reina
Suite 200
San Diego, CA 92108-3102

619-297-8520
Fax: 619-297-5353
http://www.artsandactivities.com

For classroom teachers, art teachers and other school personnel teaching visual art from kindergarten through college levels.

76 pages Monthly
ISSN: 0004-3931

Tom von Rosen, Publisher
Maryellen Bridge, Editor in Client

4581 Arts Education Policy Review
Heldref Publications
1319 18th Street NW
Washington, DC 20036-1826

202-296-6267
800-365-9753
Fax: 202-296-5149
http://www.heldref.org

Discusses major policy issues concerning K-12 education in the various arts. The journal presents a variety of views rather than taking sides and emphasizes analytical exploration. Its goal is to produce the most insightful,comprehensive and rigorous exchange of ideas ever available on arts education. The candid discussions are a valuable resource for all those involved in the arts and concerned about their role in education.

40 pages BiWeekly
ISSN: 1063-2913

Leila Saad, Managing Editor

4582 CCAS Newsletter
Council of Colleges of Arts & Sciences
186 University Hall
Columbus, OH 43210

614-292-1882
Fax: 614-292-8666

Membership newsletter to inform deans about arts and sciences issues in education.

4-10 pages BiMonthly

Richard J Hopkins, Contact

4583 Choral Journal
American Choral Directors Association
PO Box 6310
Lawton, OK 73506-0310

903-935-7963
Fax: 903-934-8114
E-mail: jmoore@etbu.edu

Publishes scholarly, practical articles and regular columns of importance to professionals in the fields of choral music and music education. Articles explore conducting teachnique, rehearsal strategies, historical performancepractice, choral music history and teaching materials.

Monthly

James A Moore, President

4584 Clavier
200 Northfield Road
Northfield, IL 60093

847-446-5000
Fax: 847-446-6263

Published 10 times each year for piano and organ teachers, with issues in all months except June and August.

Monthly

4585 Dramatics
Educational Theatre Association
2343 Auburn Avenue
Cincinnati, OH 45219-2815

513-421-3900
Fax: 513-421-7055
E-mail: info@etassoc.org
http://www.etassoc.org

Magazine published by Educational Theatre Association, a professional association for theatre educators/artists.

Monthly

David LaFleche, Dir Membership/Leadership

4586 Flute Talk
200 Northfield Road
Northfield, IL 60093

847-446-5000
Fax: 847-446-6263

Published 10 times each year for flute teachers and intermediate or advanced students, with issues every month except June and August.

Monthly

4587 Instrumentalist
200 Northfield Road
Northfield, IL 60093

847-446-5000
Fax: 847-446-6263

Published 12 times each year for band and orchestra directors and teachers of instruments in these groups.

Monthly

4588 Journal of Experiential Education
Association of Experiential Education
2305 Canyon Boulevard
Suite 100
Boulder, CO 80302

303-440-8844
Fax: 303-440-9581
E-mail: aewert@indiana.edu
http://www.aee.org

A professional journal that publishes articles in outdoor adventure programming, service learning, environmental education, therapeutic applications, research and theory, the creative arts, and much more. An invaluable reference toolfor anyone in the field of experiential education.

3x Year
ISSN: 1053-8259

Alan Ewert, Editor

4589 Music Educators Journal
National Association for Music Education
1806 Robert Fulton Drive
Reston, VA 20191-4348

703-860-4000
Fax: 703-860-1531
http://www.menc.org

Offers informative, timely and accurate articles, editorials, and features to a national audience of music educators.

BiMonthly
ISSN: 0027-4321

Frances Ponick, Editor, Author

4590 Music Educators Journal and Teaching Music
National Association for Music Education
1806 Robert Fulton Drive
Reston, VA 20191-4348
703-860-4000
Fax: 703-860-4826
http://www.menc.org

Informative, timely and accurate articles, editorials, and features to a national audience of music educators.

BiMonthly
ISSN: 1069-7446

Jeanne Spaeth, Editor

4591 NAEA News
National Art Education Association
1916 Association Drive
Reston, VA 20191-1502
703-860-8000
Fax: 703-860-2960
E-mail: naea@dgs.dgsys.com
http://www.naea-reston.org

National, state and local news affecting visual arts education.

24 pages BiMonthly

Dr. Thomas Hatfield, Executive Director

4592 National Guild of Community Schools of the Arts
National Guild of Community Schools of the Arts
520 8th Avenue
Suite 302, 3rd Floor
New York, NY 10018
212-268-3337
Fax: 212-268-3995
E-mail: info@natguild.org
http://www.nationalguild.org

National association of community based arts education institutions employment opportunities, guildnotes newsletter, publications catalog. See www.nationalguild.org.

Monthly

Noah Xifr, Director Membership/Oper.

4593 Oranatics Journal
Educational Theatre Association
2343 Auburn Avenue
Cincinnati, OH 45219-2815
513-451-3900
Fax: 513-421-7077
http://www.etassoc.org

Promotes and strengthens theatre in education - primarily middle school and high school. Sponsors an honor society, various events, numerous publications, and arts education advocacy activities.

9x Year

David LaFleche, Director Membership

4594 SchoolArtsDavis Publications
50 Portland Street
Worcester, MA 01682
800-533-2847
Fax: 508-791-0779
http://www.davis-art.com/

Davis has promoted and advocated for art education at both the local and national levels, providing good ideas for teachers and celebrating cultural diversity and the contributions of world cultures through a wide range of art forms.

Wyatt Wade, Publisher
Claire Mowbray Golding, Managing Editor

4595 SchoolArts Magazine
Davis Publications
50 Portland Street
Worcester, MA 01608-2013
508-754-7201
800-533-2847
Fax: 508-791-0779

Aimed at art educators in public and private schools, elementary through high school. Articles offer ideas and information involving art media for the teaching profession and for use in classroom activities.

Monthly
ISSN: 0036-3463

Wyatt Wade, Publisher
Eldon Katter, Editor

4596 Studies in Art Education
Louisiana State University, Dept. of Curriculum
Baton Rouge, LA 70803-0001
225-578-3202
Fax: 225-578-9135

Reports on developments in art education.

Quarterly

Karen A Hamblen, Editor

4597 Teaching Journal
Educational Theatre Association
2343 Auburn Avenue
Cincinnati, OH 45219-2815
513-421-3900
Fax: 513-421-7055
E-mail: info@etassoc.org
http://www.etassoc.org

Journal published by Educational Theatre Association, a professional association for theatre educators/artists.

Quarterly

David LaFleche, Dir Membership/Leadership

4598 Teaching Music
National Association for Music Education
1806 Robert Fulton Drive
Reston, VA 20191-4348
703-860-4000
Fax: 703-860-4826
http://www.menc.org

Offers informative, timely and accurate articles, editorials, and features to a national audience of music educators.

BiMonthly
ISSN: 1069-7446

Christine Stinson, Editor

4599 Ultimate Early Childhood Music Resource
Miss Jackie Music Company
10001 El Monte Street
Shawnee Mission, KS 66207-3631
913-381-3672

Designed to assist parents and teachers engaged in early childhood.

16 pages Quarterly

Jackie Weissman, Publisher
Emily Smith, Editor

Periodicals
Physical Education

4600 Athletic Director
National Association for Sport & Physical Ed.
1900 Association Drive
Reston, VA 20191-1502
703-476-3410
Fax: 703-476-8316

Of interest to athletic directors and coaches.

4 pages SemiAnnually

4601 Athletic Management
College Athletic Administrator
2488 N Triphammer Road
Ithaca, NY 14850-1014
607-272-0265
Fax: 607-273-0701

Offers information on how athletic managers can improve their operations, focusing on high school and college athletic departments.

BiMonthly

Mark Goldberg, Publisher
Eleanor Frankel, Editor

4602 Athletic Training
National Athletic Trainers' Association
2952 N Stemmons Freeway
Dallas, TX 75247-6103
214-637-6282
800-879-6282
Fax: 214-637-2206
http://www.nata.org

Edited for athletic trainers.

100 pages Quarterly Magazine

4603 Athletics Administration
NACDA
PO Box 16428
Cleveland, OH 44116-0428
440-892-4000
Fax: 440-892-4007
E-mail: lgarrison@nacda.com
http://www.nacda.com

The official publication of the National Association of Collegiate Directors of Athletics (NACDA), Athletics Administration focuses on athletics facilities, new ideas in marketing, promotions, development, legal ramifications and other current issues in collegiate athletics administrations.

44-48 pages BiMonthly
ISSN: 0044-9873

Laurie Garrison, Editor
Jude Killy, Associate Editor

4604 Journal of Environmental Education
Heldref Publications
1319 18th Street NW
Washington, DC 20036-1826
202-296-6267
800-365-9753
Fax: 202-296-5149
E-mail: jee@heldref.org
http://www.heldref.org

An excellent resource for department chairpersons and directors of programs in environmental, resources, and outdoor education.

48 pages Quarterly
ISSN: 0095-8964

B Alison Panko, Managing Editor

4605 Journal of Experiential Education
Association for Experiential Education
2305 Canyon Boulevard
Suite 100
Boulder, CO 80302
303-440-8844
800-787-7979
Fax: 303-440-9581
E-mail: simps_sv@mail.uwlax.edu
http://www.aee.org

A professional journal that publishes articles in outdoor adventure programming, service learning, environmental education, therapeutic applications, research and theory, the creative arts, and much more. An invaluable reference tool for anyone in the field of experiential education.

3x Year

Steve Simpson, Editor

4606 Journal of Physical Education, Recreation and Dance
American Alliance for Health, Phys. Ed. & Dance
1900 Association Drive
Reston, VA 20191-1502
703-476-3495
Fax: 703-476-9527

Presents new books, teaching aids, facilities, equipment, supplies, news of the profession and related groups.

9x Year

Fran Rowan, Editor

4607 Journal of Teaching in Physical Education
Human Kinetics Publishers
1607 N Market Street
Champaign, IL 61820-2220
217-351-5076
800-747-4457
Fax: 217-351-2674

Journal for in-service and pre-service teachers, teacher educators, and administrators, that presents research articles based on classroom and laboratory studies, descriptive and survey studies, summary and review articles, as well as discussions of current topics.

132 pages Quarterly
ISSN: 0273-5024

G Jake Jaquet, Director Journal Division
Peg Goyette, Managing Editor

4608 Marketing Recreation Classes
Learning Resources Network
1550 Hayes Drive
Manhattan, KS 66502-5068
785-539-5376
800-678-5376

Successful new class ideas and promotion techniques for recreation instructors.

8 pages Monthly

William Draves, Publisher
Julie Coates, Production Manager

4609 **National Association for Sport & Physical Education News**
National Association for Sport & Physical Ed.
1900 Association Drive
Reston, VA 20191-1502
703-476-3410
800-321-0789
Fax: 703-476-8316

News of conventions, new publications, workshops, and more, all tailored for people in the field of sports, physical education, coaching, etc. Legislative issues are covered as well as news about the over 20 structures in NASPE.

12 pages Monthly
Paula Kun

4610 **National Standards for Dance Education News**
National Dance Association
1900 Association Drive
Reston, VA 20191-1502
703-476-3400
Fax: 703-476-9527
E-mail: nda@aahperd.org
http://www.aahperd.org/nda

News of the National Dance Association activities, national events in dance education and topics of interest to recreation and athletic directors.

12 pages Quarterly
Barbara Hernandez, Executive Director

4611 **Physical Education Digest**
11 Cerilli Crescent
Sudbury
Ontario, Canada P3E5R5
705-523-3331
800-455-8782
Fax: 705-523-3331
E-mail: coach@pedigest.com
http://www.pedigest.com

Edited for physical educators and scholastic coaches. Condenses practical ideas from periodicals and books.

36 pages Quarterly
ISSN: 0843-2635

Dick Moss, Editor

4612 **Physical Educator**
Arizona State University
Editorial Office
Department of ESPE
Tempe, AZ 85287
480-965-3875
Fax: 480-965-2569

Offers articles for the physical educator.

Quarterly
Robert Pangrazi, Editor

4613 **Quest**
Louisiana State University/Dept. of Kinesiology
Huey Room 112
Baton Rouge, LA 70803-0001
225-388-2036
Fax: 225-388-3680

Publishes articles concerning issues critical to physical education in higher education. Its purpose is to stimulate professional development within the field.

Quarterly

4614 **Teaching Elementary Physical Education**
Human Kinetics Publishers
1607 N Market Street
Champaign, IL 61820-2220
217-351-5076
800-747-4457
Fax: 217-351-2674

A resource for elementary physical educators, by physical educators. Each 32-page issue includes informative articles on current trends, teaching hints, activity ideas, current resources and events, and more.

32 pages BiMonthly Magazine
ISSN: 1045-4853

G Jake Jaquet, Director Journal Division
Margery Robinson, Managing Editor

Periodicals
Reading

4615 **Beyond Words**
1534 Wells Drive NE
Albuquerque, NM 87112-6383
505-275-2558

Offers information on literature, language arts and English for the teaching professional.

10x Year

4616 **Christian Literacy Outreach**
Christian Literacy Association
541 Perry Highway
Pittsburgh, PA 15229-1851
412-364-3777

Association news offering membership information, convention news, books and articles for the Christian education professional.

4 pages Quarterly
Joseph Mosca

4617 **Exercise Exchange**
Appalachian State University
222 Duncan Hall
Boone, NC 28608-0001
828-262-2234
Fax: 828-262-2128

Bi-annual journal which features classroom-tested approaches to the teaching of English language arts from middle school through college; articles are written by classroom practitioners.

BiAnnual
ISSN: 0531-531X

Charles R Duke, Editor

4618 **Forum for Reading**
Fitchburg State College, Education Department
160 Pearl Street
Fitchburg, MA 01420-2631
978-343-2151

Offers articles, reviews, question and answer columns and more for educators and students.

2x Year
Rona F Flippo, Editor

4619 **Journal of Adolescent & Adult Literacy**
International Reading Association
800 Barksdale Road
#8139
Newark, DE 19714

302-731-1600
800-336-7323
Fax: 302-731-1057
E-mail: journals@reading.org
http://www.reading.org

Carries articles and departments for those who teach reading in adolescent and adult programs. Applied research, instructional techniques, program descriptions, training of teachers and professional issues.

80-96 pages 8x Year
ISSN: 1081-3004

John Elleins, Editor

4620 **Laubach LitScape**
Laubach Literacy Action
1320 Jamesville Avenue
Syracuse, NY 13210

315-422-9121
888-528-2224
Fax: 315-422-6369
E-mail: info@laubach.org
http://www.laubach.org

Includes articles about national literacy activities as well as support and information on tutoring, resources, training, new readers, program management, and recruitment and retention of students and volunteers.

12 pages Quarterly

Linda Church, Managing Editor

4621 **Literacy Advocate**
Laubach Literacy Action
1320 Jamesville Avenue
Syracuse, NY 13210

315-422-9121
888-528-2224
Fax: 315-422-6369
E-mail: info@laubach.org
http://www.laubach.org

Covers United States and international programs and membership activities.

8 pages Quarterly

Beth Kogut, Editor

4622 **News for You**
Laubach Literacy Action
1320 Jamesville Avenue
Syracuse, NY 13210

315-422-9121
888-528-2224
Fax: 315-422-6369
E-mail: info@laubach.org
http://www.laubach.org

A newspaper for older teens and adults with special reading needs. Includes US and world news written at a 4th to 6th grade reading level.

4 pages Weekly
ISSN: 0884-3910

Heidi Stephens, Editor

4623 **Phonics Institute**
PO Box 98785
Tacoma, WA 98498-0785

253-588-3436
E-mail: mah@readingstore.com
http://www.readingstore.com

Restoration of intensive phonics to beginning reading instruction.

8 pages 5x Year

4624 **RIF Newsletter**
Smithsonian Institution
900 Jefferson Drive SW
Washington, DC 20560-0004

202-357-2888
Fax: 202-786-2564

Describes RIF's nationwide reading motivation program.

TriQuarterly

4625 **Read, America!**
Place in the Woods
3900 Glenwood Avenue
Golden Valley, MN 55422-5302

763-374-2120
Fax: 952-593-5593
E-mail: readamerica10732@aol.com

News, book reviews, ideas for librarians and reading program leaders; short stories and poetry pages for adults and children; and an annual Read America! collection with selections of new books solicited from 350 publishers.

12 pages Quarterly Newsletter
ISSN: 0891-4214

Roger Hammer, Editor/Publisher

4626 **Reading Improvement**
Project Innovation of Mobile
PO Box 8508
Mobile, AL 36689-0508

334-633-7802

A journal dedicated to improving reading and literacy in America.

Quarterly

Dr. Phil Feldman, Editor

4627 **Reading Psychology**
Texas A&M University, College of Education
Department of Education
College Station, TX 77843-0001

979-845-7093
Fax: 979-845-9663

Quarterly

Dr. William H. Rupley, Editor

4628 **Reading Research Quarterly**
Ohio State University
1945 N High Street
Columbus, OH 43210-1120

614-292-8054
Fax: 614-292-1816

Delves into reading ratings and special concerns in the field of literacy.

Quarterly

Dr. Robert Tierney, Editor

4629 **Reading Research and Instruction**
Appalachian State University, College of Education
Dept. of Curriculum & Instruction
Boone, NC 28608-0001

828-262-6055

Quarterly

William E Blanton, Editor

4630 Reading Teacher
International Reading Association
800 Barksdale Road
#8139
Newark, DE 19711-3204

302-731-1600
800-336-READ
Fax: 301-731-1057

Carries articles and departments for those who teach reading in preschool and elementary schools. Applied research, instructional techniques, program descriptions, the training of teachers, professional issues and special featurereviews of children's books and ideas for classroom practice.

8x Year

Dr. James Baumann, Journal Editor
Linda Hunter, Advertising Manager

4631 Reading Today
International Reading Association
800 Barksdale Road
#8139
Newark, DE 19711-3204

302-731-1600
800-336-READ
Fax: 302-731-1057

Edited for IRA individual and institutional members offering information for teachers, news of the education profession and information for and relating to parents, councils and international issues.

36-44 pages BiMonthly

Linda Hunter, Advertising Manager
John Mickles, Editor

4632 Recording for the Blind & Dyslexic
20 Roszel Road
Princeton, NJ 08540

609-452-0606
Fax: 609-520-8041
http://www.rfbd.org

Textbooks on tape for students who cannot read standard print.

4633 Report on Literacy Programs
Business Publishers
8737 Colesville Road
Suite 1100
Silver Spring, MD 20910-3928

301-587-6300
800-274-6737
Fax: 301-585-9075
E-mail: bpinews@bpinews.com
http://www.bpinews.com

Reports on the efforts of business and government to provide literacy training to adults— focusing on the effects of literacy on the workforce.

8-10 pages BiWeekly

Eric Easton, Publisher
Dave Speights, Editor

4634 Visual Literacy Review & Newsletter
International Visual Literacy Association
Virginia Tech
Old Security Building
Blacksburg, VA 24061

540-231-8992

Forum for sharing research and practice within an educational context in the area of visual communication.

8 pages BiMonthly

Richard Couch

4635 WSRA Journal
University of Wisconsin - Oshkosh
1863 Doty Street
Oshkosh, WI 54901-6978

920-424-7231
Fax: 920-326-6280
E-mail: wsra@centurytel.net

A quarterly publication of the Wisconsin State Reading Association that publishes articles about literacy for academicians, teachers, libraries and literary workers.

Quarterly

Dr. Margaret Humadi Genisio, Editor

4636 What's Working in Parent Involvement
The Parent Institute
PO Box 7474
Fairfax Station, VA 22039-7474

703-323-9170
Fax: 703-323-9173
http://www.parent-institute.com

Focuses on parent involvement in children's reading education.

10x Year

John Wherry, Publisher

Periodicals
Secondary Education

4637 ACTIVITY
American College Testing
2201 Dodge
Iowa City, IA 52243-0001

319-337-1410
Fax: 319-337-1014

Distributed free of charge to more than 100,000 persons concerned with secondary and postsecondary education. ACT, an independent nonprofit organization provides a broad range of educational programs and services throughout thiscountry and abroad.

Quarterly

Dan Lechay, Editor

4638 Adolescence
Libra Publishers
3089C Clairemont Drive
PNB 383
San Diego, CA 92117-6802

858-571-1414
Fax: 858-571-1414

Articles contributed by professionals spanning issues relating to teenage education, counseling and guidance. Paperback.

256 pages Quarterly
ISSN: 0001-8449

William Kroll, Editor

4639 American Secondary Education
Bowling Green State University
Education Room 531
Bowling Green, OH 43403-0001

419-372-7379
Fax: 419-372-8265

Serves those involved in secondary education— administrators, teachers, university personnel and others. Examines and reports on current issues in secondary education and provides readers with information on a wide range of topicsthat impact secondary education professionals. Professionals are provided with the most up-to-date theories and practices in their field.

Quarterly

Gregg Brownell, Editor
Madu Ireh, Graduate Editor

4640 Child and Youth Care Forum
Kluwer Academic/Human Sciences Press
233 Spring Street
New York, NY 10013

212-620-8000
800-221-9369
Fax: 212-463-0742
http://www.wkpa.nl

Independent, professional publication committed to the improvement of child and youth care practice in a variety of day and residential settings and to the advancement of this field. Designed to serve child and youth carepractitioners, their supervisors, and other personnel in child and youth care settings, the journal provides a channel of communication and debate including material on practice, selection and training, theory and research, and professional issues.

Bimonthly
ISSN: 1053-1890

Carol Bischoff, Publisher
Doug Magnuson, Co-Editor

4641 Family Therapy: The Journal of the California Graduate School of Family Psychology
Libra Publishers
3089C Clairemont Drive
PNB 383
San Diego, CA 92117-6802

858-571-1414
Fax: 858-571-1414

Articles contributed by professionals spanning issues relating to teenage education, counseling and guidance. Paperback.

96 pages Quarterly
ISSN: 0091-6544

William Kroll, Editor

4642 High School Journal
University of North Carolina
212-D #3500
Chapel Hill, NC 27599-0001

919-962-1395
Fax: 919-962-1533

The Journal publishes articles dealing with adolescent growth, development, interests, beliefs, values, learning, etc., as they effect school practice. In addition, it reports on research dealing with teacher, administrator andstudent interaction within the school setting. The audience is primarily secondary school teachers and administrators, as well as college level educators.

60 pages Quarterly
ISSN: 0018-1498

Dr. George Noblit, Editor

4643 Independent School
National Association of Independent Schools
75 Federal Street
Boston, MA 02110-1913

617-451-2444

Contains information and opinion about secondary and elementary education in general and independent education in particular.

TriAnnually

Thomas W Leonhardt, Editor
Kurt R Murphy, Advertising/Editor

4644 Journal of At-Risk Issues
Clemson University
209 Martin Street
Clemson, SC 29631-1555

864-656-2599
800-443-6392
Fax: 864-656-0136
E-mail: NDPC@clemson.edu
http://www.dropoutprevention.org

Publication Date: 0 36 pages
ISBN: 1098-1608

Dr. Judy Johnson, Author
Dr. Judy Johnson, Author
Dr. Alice Fisher, Editor

4645 NASSP Bulletin
National Assn. of Secondary School Principals
1904 Association Drive
Reston, VA 20191-1537

703-860-0200
800-253-7746
Fax: 703-620-6534
E-mail: nassp@nassp.org

For administrators at the secondary school level dealing with subjects that range from the philosophical to the practical.

TriAnnual

Eugenia Cooper Potter, Editor

4646 Parents Still Make the Difference!
The Parent Institute
PO Box 7474
Fairfax Station, VA 22039-7474

703-323-9170
Fax: 703-323-9173
http://www.parent-institute.com

Newsletter focusing on parent involvement in children's education. Focuses on parents of children in grades 7-12.

Monthly
ISSN: 1523-2395

Betsie Millar, Author
John Wherry, Publisher

4647 Parents Still Make the Difference!: Middle School Edition
The Parent Institute
PO Box 7474
Fairfax Station, VA 22039-7474

703-323-9170
Fax: 703-323-9173
http://www.parent-institute.com

Newsletter focusing on parent involvement in children's education. Focuses on parents of children in grades 7-12.

Monthly
ISSN: 1071-5118

John Wherry, Publisher

Periodicals
Science

4648 American Biology Teacher
National Association of Biology Teachers
12030 Sunrise Valley Drive
Suite 110
Reston, VA 20191

703-264-9696
800-406-0775
Fax: 703-264-7778

E-mail: office@nabt.org
http://www.nabt.org

Edited for elementary, secondary school, junior college, four-year college and university teachers of biology.

80 pages 9 times a year
Wayne Carley, Publisher
Christine Chantry, Managing Editor

4649 AnthroNotes
Smithsonian Anthropology Outreach Office
PO Box 37012
Washington, DC 20013-7012

202-633-1917
Fax: 202-357-2208
http://www.nmnsi.edu/anthro

Offers archeological, anthropological research in an engaging style.

Ann Krupp, Managing Editor

4650 Appraisal: Science Books for Young People
Children's Science Book Review Committee
Boston University
School of Education
Boston, MA 02215

617-353-4150

This is a journal dedicated to the review of science books for children and young adults. Now in its 27th year of publication, Appraisal reviews nearly all of the science books published yearly for pre-school through high-school ageyoung people. Each book is examined by a children's librarian and by a specialist in its particular discipline.

Quarterly
Diane Holzheimer, Editor

4651 Association of Science-Technology Centers
Dimensions
1025 Vermont Avenue NW
Suite 500
Washington, DC 20005-3516

202-783-7200
Fax: 202-783-7207
E-mail: info@astc.org
http://www.astc.org

20 pages
ISSN: 1528-820X

Carolyn Sutterfield, Author
Bonnie VanDorn, Executive Director
Wendy Pollock, Dir Communication/Research

4652 CCAS Newsletter
Council of Colleges of Arts & Sciences
186 University Hall
Columbus, OH 43210

614-292-1882
Fax: 614-292-8666

Membership newsletter to inform deans about arts and sciences issues in education.

4-10 pages BiMonthly
Richard J Hopkins, Contact

4653 Journal of College Science Teaching
National Science Teachers Association
1840 Wilson Boulevard
Arlington, VA 22201-3000

703-243-7100
800-782-6782
Fax: 703-243-7177
http://www.nsta.org

Professional journal for college and university teachers of introductory and advanced science with special emphasis on interdisciplinary teaching of nonscience

majors. Contains feature articles and departments including a sciencecolumn, editorials, lab demonstrations, problem solving techniques and book reviews.

6x Year
Dr. Gerald Wheeler, Executive Director
Michael Byrnes, Managing Editor

4654 Journal of Environmental Education
Heldref Publications
1319 18th Street NW
Washington, DC 20036-1826

202-296-6267
800-365-9753
Fax: 202-296-5149

A vital research journal for everyone teaching about the environment. Each issue features case studies of relevant projects, evaluation of new research, and discussion of public policy and philosophy in the area of environmentaleducation. The Journal is an excellent resource for department chairpersons and directors of programs in outdoor education.

Quarterly
Kerri P Kilbane, Editor

4655 Journal of Research in Science Teaching
Louisiana State University, Dept. of Curriculum
223-E Peabody
Baton Rouge, LA 70803-0001

504-388-2442
Fax: 225-388-3680

10x Year
Dr. Ronald Good, Editor

4656 NSTA Reports!
National Science Teachers Association
1840 Wilson Boulevard
Arlington, VA 22201-3000

703-243-7100
800-782-6782
Fax: 703-243-7177
http://www.nsta.org

The association's timely source of news on issues of interest to science teachers of all levels. Includes national news, information on teaching materials, announcements of programs for teachers and students, and advance notice aboutall NSTA programs, conventions and publications.

52 pages BiMonthly
Dr. Gerald Wheeler, Executive Director
Jodi Peterson, Editor

4657 Odyssey
Cobblestone Publishing
30 Grove Street
Suite C
Peterborough, NH 03458-1453

603-924-7209
800-821-0115
Fax: 603-924-7380
E-mail: custsvc@cobblestonepub.org
http://www.odysseymagazine.com

Secrets of science are probed with each theme issues's articles, interviews, activities and math puzzles. Astronomical concepts are experienced with Jack Horkheimer's Star Gazer cartoon and Night-Sky Navigation.

48 pages Monthly
ISSN: 0163-0946

Elizabeth E Lindstrom, Editor

Publications / Periodicals

4658 Physics Teacher
American Association of Physics Teachers
Suny Stony Brook
Stony Brook, NY 11794-0001
631-689-6000
Fax: 516-632-8167

Published by the American Association of Physics Teachers and dedicated to the improvement of the teaching of introductory physics at all levels.

9x Year

Clifford Swartz, Editor

4659 Quantum
National Science Teachers Association
1840 Wilson Boulevard
Arlington, VA 22201-3000
703-243-7100
800-782-6782
Fax: 703-243-7177
http://www.nsta.org

Illustrated magazine containing material translated from Russian magazine Kvant as well as original material specifically targeted to American students. In addition to feature articles and department pieces, Quantum offersolympiad-style problems and brainteasers. Each issue also contains an answer section.

BiMonthly

Dr. Gerald Wheeler, Executive Director
Mike Donaldson, Managing Editor

4660 Reports of the National Center for Science Education
National Center for Science Education
925 Kearney Street
El Cerrito, CA 94530-2810
510-601-7203
800-290-6006
Fax: 510-601-7204
E-mail: ncse@ncseweb.org
http://www.ncseweb.org

An examination of issues and current events in science education with a focus on evolutionary science, and the evolution/creation controversy.

36-44 pages BiMonthly Newsletter
ISSN: 1064-2358

Eugenie C Scott, PhD, Publisher
Andrew J Petto PhD, Editor

4661 Science Activities
Heldref Publications
1319 18th Street NW
Washington, DC 20036-1826
202-296-6267
800-365-9753
Fax: 202-296-5149
E-mail: sa@heldref.org
http://www.heldref.org

A storehouse of up-to-date creative science projects and curriculum ideas for the K-12 classroom teacher. A one-step source of experiments, projects and curriculum innovations in the biological, physical and behavioral sciences, thejournal's ideas have been teacher tested, providing the best of actual classroom experiences. Regular departments feature news notes, computer news, book reviews and new products and resources for the classroom.

48 pages Quarterly
ISSN: 0036-8121

Betty Bernard, Managing Editor

4662 Science News Magazine
1719 N Street NW
Washington, DC 20036-2888
202-785-2255
Fax: 202-659-0365

Information and programs in all areas of science.

Weekly

4663 Science Scope
National Science Teachers Association
1840 Wilson Boulevard
Arlington, VA 22201-3000
703-243-7100
800-782-6782
Fax: 703-243-7177
http://www.nsta.org

Specifically for middle-school and junior-high science teachers. Science Scope addresses the needs of both new and veteran teachers. The publication includes classroom activities, posters and teaching tips, along with educationaltheory on the way adolescents learn.

8x Year

Dr. Gerald Wheeler, Executive Director
Ken Roberts, Managing Editor

4664 Science Teacher
National Science Teachers Association
1840 Wilson Boulevard
Arlington, VA 22201-3000
703-243-7100
800-782-6782
Fax: 703-243-7177
http://www.nsta.org

Professional journal for junior and senior high school science teachers. Offers articles on a wide range of scientific topics, innovative teaching ideas and experiments, and current research news. Also offers reviews, posters,information on free or inexpensive materials, and more.

9x Year

Dr. Gerald Wheeler, Executive Director
Shelley Johnson Carey, Managing Editor

4665 Science and Children
National Association of Science Teachers
1840 Wilson Boulevard
Arlington, VA 22201-3000
703-243-7100
800-782-6782
Fax: 703-243-7177
http://www.nsta.org

Dedicated to preschool through middle school science teaching provides lively how-to articles, helpful hints, software and book reviews, colorful posters and inserts, think pieces and on-the-scene reports from classroom teachers.

8x Year

Dr. Gerald Wheeler, Executive Director
Linda L Roswog, Managing Editor

4666 Sea Frontiers
International Oceanographic Foundation
4600 Rickenbacker Causeway
Key Biscayne, FL 33149-1031
305-361-4888

A general interest magazine about science education including underwater studies.

BiMonthly

Bonnie Gordon, Editor

4667 Universe in the Classroom
Astronomical Society of the Pacific
390 Ashton Avenue
San Francisco, CA 94112-1722
415-337-1100
Fax: 415-337-5205
E-mail: service@astrosociety.org
http://www.astrosociety.org

On teaching astronomy in grades 3-12, including astronomical news, plain-English explanations, teaching resources and classroom activities.

8 pages Quarterly

Noel Encaracian, Customer Service

Periodicals
Social Studies

4668 Alumni Newsletter
Jewish Labor Committee
25 E 21st Street
Floor 2
New York, NY 10010-6207
212-477-0707
Fax: 212-477-1918

Newsletter of American public secondary school teachers who teach about the Holocaust and Jewish Resistance to the Nazis during World War II.

8 pages SemiAnnually

Arieh Lebowitz

4669 American Sociological Review
Pennsylvania State University
206 Oswald Tower, Sociology Dept
University Park, PA 16802
814-865-5021
Fax: 814-865-0705

Addresses most aspects of sociology in a general range of categories for academic and professional sociologists.

Bimonthly

Glenn Firebaugh, Editor

4670 AnthroNotes
Anthropology Outreach Office
PO Box 37012
Washington, DC 20013-7012
202-357-1592
Fax: 202-357-2208

Offers archeological, anthropological research in an engaging style.

4671 AppleSeeds
Cobblestone Publishing
30 Grove Street
Suite C
Peterborough, NH 03458-1453
603-924-7209
800-821-0115
Fax: 603-924-7380
E-mail: custsvc@cobblestonepub.com
http://www.cobblestonepub.com

A delightful way to develop love of non-fiction reading in grades 2-4. Full color articles, photographs, maps, activities that grab student and teacher interest. Children's doings and thinking around the world in Mail Bag.

32 pages Monthly
ISSN: 1099-7725

Susan Buckey, Barb Burt, Editors, Author
Lou Waryncia, Managing Editor

4672 Boletin
Center for the Teaching of the Americas
Immaculata College
Immaculata, PA 19345
610-647-4400

School teaching of the Americas.

Quarterly

Sr. Mary Consuela

4673 California Weekly Explorer
California Weekly Reporter
285 E Main Street
Suite 3
Tustin, CA 92780-4429
714-730-5991
Fax: 714-730-3548

Resources, events, awards and reviews relating to California history.

16 pages Weekly

Don Oliver

4674 Calliope
Cobblestone Publishing
30 Grove Street
Suite C
Peterborough, NH 03458-1453
603-924-7209
800-821-0115
Fax: 603-924-7380
E-mail: custsvc@cobblestonepub.com
http://www.cobblestonepub.com

Invests in world history with reality not only through articles, stories and maps but also current events and resource lists. Calliope's themes are geared to topics studied in world history classrooms.

48 pages Monthly
ISSN: 1058-7086

Lou Waryncia, Managing Editor
Charles F Baker, Editors

4675 Cobblestone
Cobblestone Publishing
30 Grove Street
Suite C
Peterborough, NH 03458-1445
603-924-7209
800-821-0115
Fax: 603-924-7380
E-mail: custsvc@cobblestonepub.com
http://www.cobblestonepub.com

Blends sound information with excellent writing, a combination that parents and teachers appreciate. Cobblestone offers imaginative approaches to introduce young readers to the world of American history.

48 pages Monthly
ISSN: 0199-5197

Lou Waryncia, Managing Editor
Meg Chorlian, Editor

4676 Colloquoy on Teaching World Affairs
World Affairs Council of North California
312 Sutter Street
Suite 200
San Francisco, CA 94108-4311
415-982-3263
Fax: 415-982-5028

Offers information, articles and updates for the history teacher.

3x Year

Cassie Todd

Publications / Periodicals

4677 Faces
Cobblestone Publishing
30 Grove Street
Suite C
Peterborough, NH 03458-1453

603-924-7209
800-821-0115
Fax: 603-924-7380
E-mail: custsvc@cobblestonepub.com
http://www.cobblestonepub.com

The world is brought to the classroom through the faces of its people. World culture encourages young readers' perspectives through history, folk tales, news and activities.

48 pages Monthly
ISSN: 0749-1387

Lou Waryncia, Managing Editor
Elizabeth Crooker Carpentiere, Editor

4678 Focus
Freedoms Foundation at Valley Forge
PO Box 706
Valley Forge, PA 19482-0706

215-933-8825
800-896-5488
Fax: 610-935-0522
E-mail: tsueta@ffvf.org
http://www.ffvf.org

Strives to teach America and promote responsible citizenship through educational programs and awards designed to recognize outstanding Americans.

6 pages Quarterly

Thomas M Sueat, Editor

4679 Footsteps
Cobblestone Publishing
30 Grove Street
Suite C
Peterborough, NH 03458-1453

603-924-7209
800-821-0115
Fax: 603-924-7380
E-mail: custsvc@cobblestonepub.com
http://www.cobblestonepub.com

Celebrates heritage of African Americans and explores their contributions to culture from colonial times to present. Courage, perserverance mark struggle for freedom and equality in articles, maps, photos, etc.

48 pages 9x Year
ISSN: 1521-5865

Lou Waryncia, Managing Editor
Charles Baker, Editor

4680 Freedom & Enterprise
National Schools Community for Economic Education
PO Box 295
Cos Cob, CT 06807-0295

203-869-1706
Fax: 203-869-1707
E-mail: nscee@aol.com
http://www.nscee.org

Nonprofit educational organization specializing in supplementary enterprise economic education teaching aides for grades K-8.

John Murphy, President

4681 History Matters Newsletter
National Council for History Education
26915 Westwood Road
Suite B-2
Westlake, OH 44145-4657

440-835-1776
Fax: 440-835-1295
E-mail: nche@nche.nett
http://www.history.org/nche

Serves as a resource to help members improve the quality and quantity of history learning.

8 pages Monthly
ISSN: 1090-1450

Elaine W Reed, Executive Director

4682 History Teacher
California State University - Long Beach
History Department
Long Beach, CA 90840-0001

213-985-4432
Fax: 562-985-5431

Quarterly

Edward Gosselin, Editor
Troy Johnson

4683 Inquiry in Social Studies: Curriculum, Research & Instruction
University of North Carolina-Charlotte
Dept of Curriculum & Instruction
Charlotte, NC 28223

704-547-4500
Fax: 704-547-4705

An annual journal of North Carolina Council for the Social Studies with a readership of 1,400.

Annual

John A Gretes, Editor
Jeff Passe, Editor

4684 Journal of American History
Organization of American Historians
121 N Bryan Street
Bloomington, IN 47408-4136

812-855-7311
800-446-8923
Fax: 812-855-0696

Contains articles and essays concerning the study and investigation of American history.

Quarterly

Tamzen Meyer, Editor

4685 Journal of Economic Education
Heldref Publications
1319 18th Street NW
Washington, DC 20036-1826

202-296-6267
800-365-9753
Fax: 202-296-5149

Offers original articles on innovations in and evaluations of teaching techniques, materials and programs in economics.

Quarterly
ISSN: 0022-4085

4686 Journal of Geography
National Council for Geographic Education
700 Pelham Road N
Jacksonville, AL 36265

256-782-5293
Fax: 256-782-5336
E-mail: ncge@jsu.edu
http://www.ncge.org

Stresses the essential value of geographic education and knowledge in schools.

Quarterly
ISSN: 0022-1341

Michal LeVasseur, Executive Director
Allison Newton, Associate Director

4687 Magazine of History
Organizations of American History
112 N Bryan Avenue
Bloomington, IN 47408-4199

812-855-7311
800-446-8923
Fax: 812-855-0696
E-mail: oah@oah.org
http://www.oah.org

Includes informative articles, lesson plans, current historiography and reproducible classroom materials on a particular theme. In addition to topical articles, such columns as Dialogue, Studentspeak and History Headlines allow forthe exchange of ideas from all levels of the profession.

70-90 pages Quarterly Magazine
ISSN: 0882-228X

Michael Regoli, Managing Editor

4688 New England Journal of History
Bentley College
Dept of History
Waltham, MA 02254

781-891-2509
Fax: 781-891-2896

Covers all aspects of American history for the professional and student.

3x Year

Joseph Harrington, Editor

4689 News & Views
Pennsylvania Council for the Social Studies
11533 Clematis Boulevard
Pittsburgh, PA 15235-3105

717-238-8768
E-mail: lguru1@aol.com
http://www.pcss.org

Offers news, notes, and reviews of interest to social studies educators.

20 pages 5x Year
ISSN: 0894-8712

Jack Suskind, Executive Secretary
Leo R West, Editor

4690 Perspective
Association of Teachers of Latin American Studies
PO Box 620754
Flushing, NY 11362-0754

718-428-1237
Fax: 718-428-1237

Promotes the teaching of Latin America in US schools and colleges.

10 pages BiMonthly

Daniel Mugan

4691 Social Education
National Council for the Social Studies
3501 Newark Street NW
Washington, DC 20016-3100

202-966-7840
Fax: 202-966-2061
E-mail: socialed@ncss.org
http://www.ncss.org

Journal for the social studies profession serves middle school, high school and college and university teachers. Social Education features research on significant topics relating to social studies, lesson plans that can be applied tovarious disciplines, techniques for using teaching materials in the classroom and information on the latest instructional technology.

7x Year
ISSN: 0337-7724

Michael Simpson, Editor
Robin Hayes, Manager

4692 Social Studies
Heldref Publications
1319 18th Street NW
Washington, DC 20036-1826

202-296-6267
800-365-9753
Fax: 202-296-5149

Offers K-12 classroom teachers, teacher educators and curriculum administrators an independent forum for publishing their ideas about the teaching of social studies at all levels. The journal presents teachers' methods andclassroom-tested suggestions for teaching social studies, history, geography and the social sciences.

48 pages BiMonthly

Helen Kress, Managing Editor

4693 Social Studies Journal
Pennsylvania Council for the Social Studies
11533 Clematis Boulevard
Pittsburgh, PA 15235-3105

717-238-8768
E-mail: lguru1@aol.com
http://www.pcss.org

Delves into matters of social studies, history, research and statistics for the education professional and science community.

80 pages Annual

Leo R West, Editor
Dr. Saundra McKee, Editor

4694 Social Studies Professional
National Council for the Social Studies
3501 Newark Street NW
Washington, DC 20016-3100

202-966-7840
Fax: 202-966-2061
E-mail: essp@ncss.org
http://www.ncss.org

Newsletter focusing on strategies, tips and techniques for the social studies educator. New product announcements, professional development opportunities, association news, state and regional meetings.

6 Times

Terri Ackermann, Editor

4695 Social Studies and the Young Learner
National Council for the Social Studies
3501 Newark Street NW
Washington, DC 20016-3100

202-966-7840
Fax: 202-966-2061

This publication furthers creative teaching in grades K-6, meeting teachers' needs for new information and effective teaching activities.

Quarterly

Martharose Laffey, Editor

4696 Teaching Georgia Government Newsletter
Carl Vinson Institute of Government
201 N Milledge Avenue
Athens, GA 30602-5027

706-542-2736
Fax: 706-542-6239

Substantive and supplementary material for social studies teachers in Georgia. Topics of government, history, archaeology, geography, citizenship, etc. are covered. Publications available and upcoming social studies meetings in thestate are also announced.

8 pages TriAnnually

Inge Whittle, Editor
Ed Jackson, Editor

4697 Theory and Research in Social Education
National Council for the Social Studies
3501 Newark Street NW
Washington, DC 20016-3100

202-966-7840
Fax: 202-966-2061

Features articles covering a variety of topics: teacher training, learning theory, and child development research; instructional strategies; the relationship of the social sciences, philosophy, history and the arts to socialeducation; models and theories used in developing social studies curriculum; and schemes for student participation and social action.

4698 Wall Street Journal - Classroom Edition
11 Piedmont Center NW
Suite 318
Atlanta, GA 30305-1738

404-240-1331
800-439-9843
Fax: 404-240-1355
E-mail: nancyschwartzmiller@dowjones.com

Monthly student newspaper, with stories drawn from the daily journal that show international, business, economic, and social issues affect students' lives and futures. The newspaper is supported by posters, monthly teacher guides, andvideos. Regular features on careers, enterprise, marketing, personal finance and technology. Helps teachers prepare students for the world of work by combining timely articles with colorful graphics, etc.

Monthly

Nancy Schwartzmiller

4699 Women's History Network News
National Women's History Network
7738 Bell Road
Windsor, CA 95492-8518

707-838-6000
Fax: 707-838-0478

Quarterly newsletter about US women's history, for educators, researchers, program planners, and general women's history enthusiasts.

8 pages Quarterly
ISSN: 1097-0657

Mary Ruthsdotter, Coordinator/Editor

LEARNING RESOURCE CENTER
ALAMANCE COMMUNITY COLLEGE
P.O. BOX 8000
GRAHAM, NC 27253-8000

Periodicals
Technology in Education

4700 Cable in the Classroom
CCI/Crosby Publishing
214 Lincoln Street
Suite 112
Boston, MA 02134

617-254-9481
Fax: 617-254-9776
http://www.ciconline.org

Most comprehensive guide to integrating educational video with the Internet and other curriculum resources for K-12 educators.

54 pages Monthly
ISSN: 1054-5409

Stephen P Crosby, Publisher
Al Race, Executive Editor

4701 EDUCAUSE Quarterly
EDUCAUSE
4772 Walnut Street
Suite 206
Boulder, CO 80301-2538

303-544-5665
Fax: 303-440-0461
E-mail: pdeblois@educause.edu
http://www.educause.edu

Strategic policy advocacy; teaching and learning initiatives; applied research; special interest collaboration communities; awards for leadership and exemplary practices; and extensive online information services.

Quarterly Magazine
ISSN: 1528-5324

Nancy Hays, Author
Peter DeBlois, Director Communications

4702 EDUCAUSE Review
EDUCAUSE
4772 Walnut Street
Suite 206
Boulder, CO 80301-2408

303-544-5665
Fax: 303-440-0461
E-mail: pdeblois@educause.edu
http://www.educause.edu

Strategic policy advocacy; teaching and learning initiatives applied research; special interest collaboration communities; awards for leadership and exemplary practices; and extensive online information services.

Monthly
ISSN: 1527-6619

Nancy Hays, Author
Peter DeBlois, Director Communications

4703 Education Technology News
Business Publishers
8737 Colesville Road
Suite 1100
Silver Spring, MD 20910-3928

301-587-6300
800-274-6737
Fax: 301-585-9075
E-mail: bpinews@bpinews.com
http://www.bpinews.com

Offers information on computer hardware, multimedia products, software applications, public and private funding and integration of technology into K-12 classrooms.

8 pages BiWeekly

Eric Easton, Publisher
Brian Love, Editorial Coordinato

4704 Educational Technology
700 E Palisade Avenue
Englewood Cliffs, NJ 07632-3040

201-871-4007
800-952-BOOK
Fax: 201-871-4009

Published since 1961, periodical covering the entire field of educational technology. Issues feature essays by leading authorities plus a Research Section. With many special issues covering aspects of the field in depth. Readers arefound in some 120 countries.

9x Year

Lawrence Lipsitz, Editor

4705 Electronic Learning
Scholastic
555 Broadway
New York, NY 10012-3919

212-343-6100
800-724-6527
Fax: 212-343-4801

Published for the administrative level, education professionals who are directly responsible for the implementing of electronic technology at the district, state and university levels.

8x Year

Lynn Diamond, Advertising Director
Therese Mageau, Editor

4706 Electronic School
1680 Duke Street
Alexandria, VA 22314

703-838-6722
Fax: 703-683-7590
E-mail: cwilliams@nsba.org
http://www.electronic-school.com

The school technology authority.

Cheryl S Williams, Director
Ann Lee Flynn, Director Ed/Technology Part

4707 Information Searcher
Datasearch Group
14 Hadden Road
Scarsdale, NY 10583-3328

914-723-1995
Fax: 914-723-1995
http://www.infosearcher.com

Quarterly newsletter for the Internet and curriculum-technology integration in school.

32 pages

Pam Berger, President
Bill Berger, Treasurer

4708 Journal of Computing in Childhood Education
AACE
PO Box 2966
Charlottesville, VA 22902-2966

757-623-7588
Fax: 703-997-8760

Discusses the realm of software and technology now merging with primary education.

Quarterly

4709 Journal of Educational Technology Systems
58 New Mill Road
Smithtown, NY 11787-3342

516-632-8767

A compendium of articles submitted by professionals regarding the newest technology in the educational field.

Quarterly

Dr. Thomas Liao, Editor

4710 Journal of Information Systems Education
Bryant University
1150 Douglas Pike
Smithfield, RI 02917-1291

401-232-6393
Fax: 401-232-6319

Publishes original articles on current topics of special interest to Information Systems Educators and Trainers. Focus is applications-oriented articles describing curriculum, professional development or facilities issues. Topicsinclude course projects/cases, lecture materials, curriculum design and/or implementation, workshops, faculty/student intern/extern programs, hardware/software selection and industry relations.

Quarterly

Richard Glass, Contact

4711 Journal of Research on Computing in Education
International Society for Technology in Education
480 Charnelton Street
Eugene, OR 97401-2626

541-302-3777
800-336-5191
Fax: 541-302-3778
E-mail: cust_serv@ccmail.uoregon.edu
http://www.iste.org

A quarterly journal of original research and detailed system and project evaluations. It also defines the state of the art and future horizons of educational computing.

Quarterly

Diane McGrath, Editor

4712 Journal of Special Education Technology
The Council for Exceptional Children
1920 Association Drive
Reston, VA 20191-1545

703-620-3660
888-232-7733
Fax: 703-264-9494

Provides professionals in the field with information on new technologies, current research, exemplary practices, relevant issues, legislative events and more concerning the availability and effective use of technology and media forindividuals with disabilities and/or who are gifted.

Quarterly

Herbert Rieth, Editor

4713 Matrix Newsletter
Department of CCTE, Teachers
College/Communication
PO Box 8
New York, NY 10027-0008

212-678-3344
Fax: 212-678-8227

Newsletter describing activities and interests of Department of Communication, Computing and Technology.

14 pages SemiAnnually

Marie Sayer

4714 **Media & Methods Magazine**
American Society of Educators
1429 Walnut Street
Philadelphia, PA 19102-3218

215-563-6005
800-555-5657
Fax: 215-587-9706
http://www.media-methods.com

Leading pragmatic magazine for K-12 educators and administrators. The focus is on how to integrate today's technologies and presentation tools into the curriculum. Very up-to-date and well respected national source publication. Loyalreaders are media specialists, school librarians, technology coordinators, administrators and classroom teachers.

5x School Year

Michele Sokoloff, Publisher
Christine Weiser, Editor

4715 **MultiMedia Schools**
Information Today
143 Old Marlton Pike
Medford, NJ 08055-8750

609-654-6266
800-300-9868
Fax: 609-654-4309
E-mail: custserv@infotoday.com
http://www.infotoday.com

A practical journal of multimedia, CD-Rom, online and Internet in K-12.

Thomas H Hogan, Publisher
Ferdi Serim, Editor

4716 **National Forum of Instructional Technology Journal**
McNeese State University
324 Prewitt Street
Lake Charles, LA 70601-5915

337-475-5000
Fax: 318-475-5467

Dr. J Mark Hunter, Editor

4717 **Society for Applied Learning Technology**
50 Culpeper Street
Warrenton, VA 20186

540-347-0055
800-457-6812
Fax: 540-349-3169
E-mail: info@lti.org
http://www.salt.org

Quarterly

4718 **TAM Connector**
The Council for Exceptional Children
1920 Association Drive
Reston, VA 20191-1545

703-620-3660
888-232-7733
Fax: 703-264-9494

Contains information about upcoming events, current trends and practices, state and national legislation, recently published materials and practical information relative to the availability and effective use of technology and mediafor individuals who are gifted or are disabled.

Quarterly

Cynthia Warger

4719 **TECHNOS Quarterly for Education & Technolgy**
Agency for Instructional Technology
PO Box A
Bloomington, IN 47402-0120

812-339-2203
Fax: 812-333-4218

E-mail: info@technos.net
http://www.technos.net

TECHNOS Quarterly is a forum for the discussion of ideas about the use of technology in education, with a focus on reform.

36 pages Quarterly
ISSN: 1060-5649

Michael F Sullivan, Executive Director
Carole Novak, Manager TECHNOS Press

4720 **THE Journal**
17501 17th Street
Suite 230
Tustin, CA 92780

714-730-4011
Fax: 714-730-3739
E-mail: editorail@thejournal.com
http://www.thejournal.com

A forum for administrators and managers in school districts to share their experiences in the use of technology-based educational aids.

Monthly

Wendy LaDuke, Publisher/CEO
Matthew Miller, Editor

4721 **Tech Directions**
Prakken Publications
275 Meity Drive
Suite 1
Ann Arbor, MI 48107

734-975-2800
Fax: 734-975-2787
E-mail: publisher@techdirections.com
http://www.eddigest.com

Issues programs, projects for educators in career-technical and technology education and monthly features on technology, computers, tech careers.

Monthly
ISSN: 1062-9351

Tom Bowden, Managing Editor

4722 **Technology & Learning**
CMP Media
600 Harrison Street
San Francisco, CA 94107

516-562-5000
800-607-4410
Fax: 516-562-7013
http://www.techlearning.com

Product reviews; hard-hitting, straightforward editorial features; ideas on challenging classroom activities; and more. Tailor made to the special needs of a professional and an educator.

60-80 pages Monthly Magazine
ISSN: 1053-6728
March & October

Susan McLester, Author
Judy Salpeter, Editor-in-Chief
Jo-Ann McDevitt, Publisher

4723 **Technology Pathfinder for Administrators Master Teacher**
Master Teacher
PO Box 1207
Manhattan, KS 66505-1207

785-539-0555
800-669-9633
Fax: 800-669-1132
http://www.masterteacher.com

Relevant, concise technology information and tips to help school administrators catch up and stay ahead.

Monthly Newsletter

Tracey H DeBruyn, Executive Editor

4724 Technology Pathfinder for Teachers
Master Teacher
PO Box 1207
Manhattan, KS 66505-1207

785-539-0555
800-669-9633
Fax: 785-539-7739
http://www.masterteacher.com

4 pages Monthly

4725 Technology Pathfinder for Teachers Master Teacher
Master Teacher
PO Box 1207
Manhattan, KS 66505-1207

785-539-0555
800-669-9633
Fax: 800-669-1132
http://www.masterteacher.com

Full of short technology articles for classroom teachers including how-to's, tips, curriculum ideas, and useful internet hints.

Monthly Newsletter

Tracey H DeBruyn, Executive Editor

4726 Technology Teacher
International Technology Education Association
1914 Association Drive
Suite 201
Reston, VA 20191-1538

703-860-2100
Fax: 703-860-0353
E-mail: itea@iris.org
http://www.iteawww.org

Seeks to advance technological literacy through professional development activities and publications.

40 pages 8x Year

Kendall Starkweather, Executive Director
Kathleen de la Paz, Editor

4727 Technology in Education Newsletter
111 E 14th Street
#140
New York, NY 10003-4103

800-443-7432

This newsletter for K-12 educators and administrators, covers national trends of technology in education.

4728 Web Feet Guides
RockHill Communications
14 Rock Hill Road
Bala Cynwyd, PA 19004

610-667-2040
888-762-5445
Fax: 610-667-2291
http://www.webfeetguides.com

The premier subject guides to the Internet, rigorously reviewed by librarians and educators, fully annotated, expanded and updated monthly. Appropriate for middle school through adult. Available in print, online, or MARC records. Formore information, free trials and free samples.

Monthly

Linda Smith, General Manager
Sophie Socha, Executive V

4729 eSchool News
7920 Norfolk Avenue
Suite 900
Bethesda, MD 20814

301-913-0115
800-394-0115
Fax: 301-913-0119
http://www.eschoolnews.com

Monthly newspaper dedicated to providing news and information to help educators use technology to improve education.

Monthly

Gregs Downey, Publisher

General

4730 ABC Feelings Adage Publications
PO Box 2377
Coeur D Alene, ID 83816-2377

208-762-3177
800-745-3170
Fax: 208-772-0411
E-mail: feelings@iea.com
http://www.abcfeelings.com

Interactive line of children's products that relate feelings to each letter of the alphabet. Encourages dialogue, understanding, communication, enhances self-esteem. Books, audiotape, poster, placemats, charts, activity cards, t-shirts and multicultural activity guides, floor puzzles, feelings dictionary, carpets.

Ages 3-10

Dr. Alexandra Delis-Abrams, President
Gene Abrams, VP

4731 ABDO Publishing Company
4940 Viking Drive
Suite 622
Edina, MN 55435-5300

452-831-2120
800-800-1312
Fax: 952-831-1632
E-mail: info@abdopub.com
http://www.abdopub.com

K-8 nonfiction books, including Abdo and Daughters imprint, high/low books for reluctant readers and Checkerboard Library with K-3 science, geography, and biographics for beginning readers. Sand Castle for pre-K to second grade, graduated reading program.

Jill Abdo Hansen, President
James Abdo, Publisher

4732 AGS
4201 Woodland Road
Circle Pines, MN 55014-1796

763-786-4343
800-328-2560
Fax: 800-471-8457

Major test publisher and distributor of tests for literature, reading, English, mathematics, sciences, aptitude, and various other areas of education. Includes information on timing, scoring, teacher's guides and student's worksheets.

4733 AIMS Education Foundation
1595 S Chestnut Avenue
Fresno, CA 93702-4706

559-255-4094
888-733-2467
Fax: 559-255-6396
E-mail: aimsed@fresno.edu
http://www.aimsedu.org

A nonprofit educational foundation that focuses on preparing materials for science and mathematics areas of education.

4734 Ablex Publishing Corporation
PO Box 811
Stamford, CT 06904-0811

201-767-8450
Fax: 201-767-8450

Publishes academic books and journals dealing with many different subject areas. Some of these include: education, linguistics, psychology, library science, computer and cognitive science, writing research and sociology.

Kristin K Butter, President

4735 Acorn Naturalists
155 El Camino Real
PO Box 2423
Tustin, CA 92780

714-838-4888
800-422-8886
Fax: 714-838-5309
http://www.acornnaturalists.com

Publishes and distributes science and environmental education materials for teachers, naturalists and outdoor educators. A complete catalog is available.

World Wildlife Fund, Author
Jennifer Rigby, President

4736 Active Child
PO Box 2346
Salem, OR 97308-2346

503-371-0865

Publishes creative curriculum for young children.

4737 Active Learning
10744 Hole Avenue
Riverside, CA 92505-2867

909-689-7022
Fax: 909-689-7142

Interactive learning center publishing materials for childhood education.

4738 Active Parenting Publishers
810 Franklin Court SE
Suite B
Marietta, GA 30067-8943

770-429-0565
800-825-0060
Fax: 770-429-0334
E-mail: cservice@activeparenting.com
http://www.activeparenting.com

Produces and sells books and innovative video-based programs for use in parent education, self-esteem education and loss education groups/classes.

4739 Addison-Wesley Publishing Company
2725 Sand Hill Road
Menlo Park, CA 94025-7019

650-854-0300

Publisher and distributor of a wide range of fiction, nonfiction and textbooks for grades K-12 in the areas of mathematics, reading, language arts, science, social studies and counseling.

4740 Advance Family Support & Education Program
301 S Frio Street
Suite 103
San Antonio, TX 78207-4422

210-270-4630
Fax: 210-270-4612

Offers books and publications on counseling and support for the family, student and educator.

4741 Alarion Press
PO Box 1882
Boulder, CO 80306-1882

303-443-9039
800-523-9177
Fax: 303-443-9098
E-mail: info@alarion.com
http://www.alarion.com

Video programs, posters, activities, manuals and workbooks dealing with History Through Art and Architecture for grades K-12.

4742 Albert Whitman & Company
6340 Oakton Street
Morton Grove, IL 60053-2723

847-581-0033

Children's books.

4743 Allyn & Bacon
160 Gould Street
Needham Heights, MA 02194

781-455-1250
Fax: 781-455-1220

Publisher of college textbooks and professional reference books.

4744 Alpha Publishing Company
1910 Hidden Point Road
Annapolis, MD 21401-6002

410-757-5404

Educational materials for K-12 curricula.

4745 American Association for State & Local History
1717 Church Street
Nashville, TN 37203-2921

615-320-3203
Fax: 615-327-9013

How-to books for anyone teaching history or social studies.

4746 American Association of School Administrators
1801 N Moore Street
Arlington, VA 22209-1813

703-528-0700
Fax: 703-528-2146
http://www.aasa.org

Paul Houston, Executive Director

4747 American Guidance Service
4201 Woodland Road
Circle Pines, MN 55014-1796

612-786-4343
800-328-2560
Fax: 763-783-4658

Largest distributor of educational materials focusing on guidance counselors and educators in the field of counseling. Materials include books, pamphlets, workshops and information on substance abuse, childhood education, alcoholism,inner-city subjects and more.

Matt Keller, Marketing Director

4748 American Institute of Physics
500 Sunnyside Boulevard
Woodbury, NY 11797-2999

516-576-2200
Fax: 516-349-9704

Physics books.

4749 American Nuclear Society
Outreach Department
555 N Kensington Avenue
La Grange Park, IL 60526-5592

708-352-6611
800-323-3044
Fax: 708-352-0499
E-mail: outreach@ans.org
http://www.aboutnuclear.com

Nuclear science and technology, supplemental educational materials for grades K-12. ReActions newsletters.

Chuck Vincent, Communications Administrator

4750 American Physiological Society
9050 Rockville Pike
Bethesda, MD 20814

301-530-7132
Fax: 301-634-7098

Videotapes, tracking materials and free teacher resource packets.

4751 American Technical Publishers
1155 W 175th Street
Homewood, IL 60430-4600

708-957-1100
800-323-3471
Fax: 708-957-1101
E-mail: service@americantech.net
http://www.go2atp.com

Offers instructional materials for a variety of vocational and technical training areas.

4752 American Water Works Association
6666 W Quincy Avenue
Denver, CO 80235-3098

303-794-7711
Fax: 303-795-1989

Activity books, teacher guides and more on science education.

4753 Ampersand Press
750 Lake Street
Port Townsend, WA 98368

360-379-5187
800-624-4263
Fax: 360-379-0324
E-mail: info@ampersandpress.com
http://www.ampersandpress.com

Nature and science educational games.

Lou Haller, Owner

4754 Amsco School Publications
315 Hudson Street
New York, NY 10013-1009

212-675-7000
Fax: 212-675-7010

Basal textbooks, workbooks and supplementary materials for grades 7-12.

4755 Anderson's Bookshops
PO Box 3832
Naperville, IL 60567-3832

630-355-2665

The very latest and best trade books to use in the classroom.

4756 Annenberg/CPB Project
901 E Street NW
Washington, DC 20004-2037

202-393-7100
Fax: 202-879-6707

Offers teaching resources in chemistry, geology, physics and environmental science.

4757 Art Image Publications
PO Box 568
Champlain, NY 12919-0568

800-361-2598
Fax: 800-559-2598

Offers various products including art appreciation kits, art image mini-kits and visual arts programs for grades K-12.

Rachel Ross, President

4758 Art Visuals
PO Box 925
Orem, UT 84059-0925

801-226-6115
Fax: 801-226-6115
E-mail: artvisuals@sisna.com
http://www.members.tripod.com

Social studies and art history products including an Art History Timeline, 20 feet long that represents over 50 different styles, ranging from prehistoric to contemporary art; Modern Art Styles, set of 30 posters depicting 20thcentury styles; Multicultural Posters, Africa, India, China, Japan and the World of Islam, with

Publishers / General

18 posters in each culture. Sets on women artists and African American Artists. Each set is printed on hard cardstock, laminated and ultravioletprotected.

Diane Asay, Owner

4759 Asian American Curriculum Project
83-37th Avenue
San Mateo, CA 94403

650-357-1088
800-874-2242
Fax: 650-357-6908
E-mail: aacpinc@best.com
http://www.asianamericanbooks.com

Develops, promotes and disseminates Asian-American books to schools, libraries and Asian-Americans. Over 1,500 titles.

Florence M Hongo, General Manager

4760 Association for Science Teacher Education
University of Florida
11000 University Parkway
Pensacola, FL 32514-5732

850-474-2000
Fax: 850-474-3205

Yearbooks, journals, newsletters and information on AETS.

4761 Association for Supervision & Curriculum
Development
ASCD
1703 N Beauregard Street
Alexandria, VA 22311-1717

703-578-9600
800-933-2723
Fax: 703-575-5400
E-mail: member@ascd.org
http://www.ascd.org

Publishers of educational leadership books, audios and videos focusing on teaching and learning in all subjects and grade levels.

4762 Association of American Publishers
71 5th Avenue
Floor 12
New York, NY 10003

212-255-0200
Fax: 212-255-7007

Association for the book publishing industry.

4763 Atheneum Books for Children
MacMillan Publishing Company
1633 Broadway
New York, NY 10019

212-512-2000
Fax: 800-835-3202

Hardcover trade books for children and young adults.

4764 Australian Press-Down Under Books
15235 Brand Boulevard
Suite A107
Mission Hills, CA 91345-1423

818-837-3755

Big Books, models for writing, small books and teacher's ideas books from Australia.

4765 Avon Books
1350 Avenue of the Americas
New York, NY 10019-4702

212-481-5600
Fax: 212-532-2172

Focuses on middle grade paperbacks for the classroom and features authors such as Cleary, Avi, Borks, Hous, Reeder, Hobbs, Hahn, Taylor and Prish.

4766 Awiley Company
Jossey-Bass Publishers
989 Market Street
San Francisco, CA 94104-1304

415-433-1740
800-956-7739
Fax: 415-433-0499
http://www.josseybass.com

Creating educational incentives that work.

Adrianne Biggs, Publicity/Manager
Jennifer A O'Day, Editor

4767 Ballantine/Del Rey/Fawcett/Ivy
201 E 50th Street
New York, NY 10022-7703

212-782-9000
800-638-6460
Fax: 212-782-8438

Offer paperback books for middle school and junior and senior high.

4768 Barron's Educational Series
250 Wireless Boulevard
Hauppauge, NY 11788-3924

631-434-3311
800-645-3476
Fax: 631-434-3217
E-mail: barrons@barronseduc.com
http://www.barronseduc.com

Educational books, including a full line of juvenile fiction and non-fiction, and titles for test prep and guidance, ESL, foreign language, art history and techniques, business, and reference.

Frederick Glasser, Director School/Library Sale

4769 Baylor College of Medicine
1709 Dryden Road
Suite 519
Houston, TX 77030-2404

713-798-4951
Fax: 713-798-6521

Offers materials and programs in the scientific area from Texas Scope, Sequence and Coordination projects.

4770 Beech Tree Books
1350 Avenue of the Americas
New York, NY 10019-4702

212-261-6500
Fax: 212-261-6518

Curriculum offering reading materials, fiction and nonfiction titles.

4771 Black Butterfly Children's Books
625 Broadway
Floor 10
New York, NY 10012-2611

212-982-3158

A wide variety of books focusing on children, hardcover and paperback.

4772 Blake Books
2222 Beebee Street
San Luis Obispo, CA 93401-5505

805-543-7314
800-727-8550
Fax: 805-543-1150

Photo books on nature, endangered species, habitats, etc. for ages 10 and up.

Paige Torres, President

4773 Bluestocking Press Catalog
Bluestocking Press
PO Box 2030 Dept. ERD
Shingle Springs, CA 95682-2030

530-621-1123
800-959-8586

Fax: 530-642-9222
E-mail: uncleric@jps.net
http://www.bluestockingpress.com

Approximately 800 items with a concentration in American History, economics and law. That includes fiction, nonfiction, primary source material, historical documents, facsimile newspapers, historical music, hands-on-kits, audiohistory, coloring books and more.

Jane A Williams, Coordinating Editor

4774 Boyds Mill Press
815 Church Street
Honesdale, PA 18431-1889

570-253-1164
Fax: 570-253-0179

Publishes books for children from preschool to young adult.

4775 BridgeWater Books
100 Corporate Drive
Mahwah, NJ 07430-2041

Distinctive children's hardcover books featuring award-winning authors and illustrators, including Laurence Yep, Babette Cole, Joseph Bruchac and others. An imprint of Troll Associates.

4776 Bright Ideas Charter School
2507 Central Freeway East
Wichita Falls, TX 76302-5802

940-767-1561
Fax: 940-767-1904
E-mail: lydiaplmr@aol.com

K-12 curriculum framework for educators struggling to move toward a global tomorrow.

Lynda Plummer, President

4777 Brown & Benchmark Publishers
25 Kessel Court
Madison, WI 63711

608-273-0040

College textbooks in language arts and reading.

4778 Bureau for At-Risk Youth Guidance Channel
Guidance Channel
135 Dupont Street
PO Box 760
Plainview, NY 11803-0760

516-349-5520
800-999-6884
Fax: 800-262-1886
E-mail: info@at-risk.com
http://www.at-risk.com

Publisher and distributor of educational curriculums, videos, publications and products for at-risk youth and the counselors and others who work with them. Bureau products focus on areas such as violence and drug prevention, charactereducation, parenting skills and more.

Sally Germain, Editor-in-Chief

4779 Business Publishers
8737 Colesville Road
Suite 1100
Silver Spring, MD 20910-3928

301-587-6300
800-274-6737
Fax: 301-585-9075
E-mail: bpinews@bpinews.com
http://www.bpinews.com

Publishes education related materials.

4780 CLEARVUE/eav
6465 N Avondale Avenue
Chicago, IL 60631

773-775-9433
800-253-2788
Fax: 773-775-9855
E-mail: slucas@clearvue.com
http://www.clearvue.com

CLEARVUE/eav offers educators the largest line of curriculum-oriented media in the industry. CLEARVUE/eav programs have, and will continue to enhance students' interest, learning, motivation and skills.

Sarah M Lucas, Communications Coordinator
Kelli Campbell, VP

4781 Calculators
7409 Fremont Avenue S
Minneapolis, MN 55423-3971

800-533-9921
Fax: 612-866-9030

Calculators and calculator books for K thru college level instruction. Calculator products by Texas Instruments, Casio, Sharp and Hewlett-Packard.

Richard Nelson, President

4782 Cambridge University Press
Edinburgh Building
Shaftesbury Road
Cambridge, England CB22RU

http://www.cup.cam.ac.uk

Curriculum materials and textbooks for science education for grades K-12.

4783 Candlewick Press
2067 Massachusetts Avenue
Cambridge, MA 02140-1340

617-661-3330
Fax: 617-661-0565

High quality trade hardcover and paperback books for children and young adults.

4784 Capstone Press
151 Good Counsel Drive
Mankato, MN 56001-3143

952-224-0529
888-262-6135
Fax: 888-262-0705
E-mail: timadsen@capstone-press.com
http://www.capstonepress.com

PreK-12 Nonfiction publisher

Tim Mandsen, Director Marketing

4785 Careers/Consultants in Education Press
3050 Palm Aire Drive N
#310
Pompano Beach, FL 33069

954-974-5477
Fax: 954-974-5477
E-mail: carconed@aol.com

Current education job lists for teacher and administrator positions in schools and colleges. Plus nine differently titled desk/reference paperback books.

Dr. Robert M Bookbinder, President

4786 Carolrhoda Books
A Division of Lerner Publishing Group
241 1st Avenue N
Minneapolis, MN 55401-1607

612-332-3344
800-328-4929
Fax: 612-332-7615
http://www.lernerbooks.com

Fiction and nonfiction for readers K through grade 6. List includes picture books, biographies, nature and science titles, multicultural and introductory geography books, and fiction for beginning readers.

Rebecca Poole, Submissions Editor

4787 Carson-Dellosa Publishing Company
4321 Piedmont Parkway
Greensboro, NC 27410-8114
336-632-0084
Fax: 800-535-2669

Textbooks, manuals, workbooks and materials aimed at increasing students reading skills.

4788 Center for Play Therapy
University of North Texas
PO Box 311337
Denton, TX 76203
940-565-3864
Fax: 940-565-4461
E-mail: cpt@coefs.coe.unt.edu
http://www.centerforplaytherapy.com

Encourages the unique development and emotional growth of children through the process of play therapy, a dynamic interpersonal relationship between a child and a therapist trained in play therapy procedures. Provides training,research, publications, counseling services and acts as a clearinghouse for literature in the field.

Garry Landreth PhD, Director

4789 Central Regional Educational Laboratory
2550 S Parker Road
Suite 500
Aurora, CO 80014
303-337-0990
Fax: 303-337-3005
E-mail: twaters@mcrel.org

The Regional Educational Laboratories are educational research and development organizations supported by contracts with the US Education Department, Office of Educational Research and Improvement. Specialty area: curriculum, learningand instruction.

Dr. J Timothy Waters, Executive Director

4790 Charles Scribner & Sons
MacMillan Publishing Company
1633 Broadway
New York, NY 10019
212-632-4944
Fax: 800-835-3202

Hardcover trade books for children and young adults.

4791 Chicago Board of Trade
141 W Jackson Boulevard
Chicago, IL 60604-2992
312-435-3500

Educational materials including a new economics program entitled Commodity Challenge.

4792 Children's Book Council
12 W 38th Street
2nd Floor
New York, NY 10018
212-966-1990
Fax: 212-966-2073
E-mail: staff@cbcbooks.org
http://www.cbcbooks.org

Offers a variety of modestly priced reading encouragement materials and multi-publisher bibliographies for science, social studies, language arts and reading teachers. Publishes FEATURES, a semi-annual publication on items of interestto professionals working with children.

JoAnn Sabatino-Falkenstein, VP Marketing

4793 Children's Press
Grolier Publishing
90 Sherman Turnpike
Danbury, CT 06816
800-621-1115
Fax: 800-374-4329
http://publishing.grolier.com

Leading supplier of reference and children's nonfiction and fiction books.

4794 Children's Press/Franklin Watts
PO Box 1330
Danbury, CT 06813-1330
203-797-3500
Fax: 203-797-3197

K-12 curriculum materials.

4795 Children's Television Workshop
1 Lincoln Plaza
New York, NY 10023-7129
212-875-6809
Fax: 212-875-7388

Hands-on books for elementary school use in the area of science education.

Brenda Pilson, Review Coordinator
Elaine Israel, Editor-in-Chief

4796 Chime Time
2440-C Pleasantdale Road
Atlanta, GA 30340-1562
770-662-5664

Early childhood products and publications.

4797 Choices Education Project
Watson Institute for International Studies
Brown University
PO Box 1948
Providence, RI 02912-1948
401-863-3155
Fax: 401-863-1247
E-mail: choices@brown.edu
http://www.choices.edu

Develops interactive, supplementary curriculum resources on current and historical international issues. Makes complex current and historic international issues accessible for secondary school students. Materials are low-cost,reproducible, updated annually.

Annually

4798 Close Up Publishing
44 Canal Center Plaza
Alexandria, VA 22314-1592
800-765-3131
Fax: 703-706-3564

Offers textbooks, workbooks and other publications focusing on self-esteem, learning and counseling.

4799 Cognitive Concepts
PO Box 1363
Evanston, IL 60204-1363
888-328-8199
Fax: 847-328-5881
http://www.cogcon.com

Leading provider of language and literacy software, books, internet services and staff development. Specialize in integrating technology with scientific principles and proven instructional methods to offer effective and affordablelearning solutions for educators, specialists and families.

4800 College Board
45 Columbus Avenue
New York, NY 10023-6992
212-713-8000
Fax: 212-713-8282
http://www.collegeboard.org

Publishers of books of interest to educational researchers, policymakers, students, counselors, teachers; products to prepare students for college and test prep materials.

4801 Coloring Concepts
1732 Jefferson Street
Suite 7
Napa, CA 94559-1737
707-257-1516
800-257-1516
Fax: 707-253-2019
E-mail: chris@coloringconcepts.com
http://www.coloringconcepts.com

Colorable active learning books for middle school through college that combine scientifically correct text with colorable illustrations to provide an enjoyable and educational experience that helps the user retain more informationthan during normal reading. Subjects include Anatomy, Marine Biology, Zoology, Botany, Human Evolution, Human Brain, Microbiology and biology.

Christopher Elson, Operations

4802 Comprehensive Health Education Foundation
22323 Pacific Hwy S
Seattle, WA 98198-5104
206-824-2907

Primarily Health gives K-3 kids a dynamic, hands-on health program while teaching academic skills.

4803 Computer Learning Foundation
PO Box 60007
Palo Alto, CA 94306-0007
408-720-8898
Fax: 408-730-1191
E-mail: clf@computerlearning.org
http://www.computerlearning.org

Publishes books and videos on using technology.

4804 Computer Literacy Press
Computer Literacy Press
11584 Goldcoast Drive
Cincinnati, OH 45249-1640
513-530-5100
888-833-5413
Fax: 513-530-0110
E-mail: info@complitpress.com
http://www.complitpress.com

Instructional materials using hands-on, step-by-step format, appropriate for courses in adult and continuing education, business education, computer literacy and applications, curriculum integration, Internet instruction, and trainingand staff development. Products are available for ranging from middle school through high school as well as post secondary, teacher training and adult/senior courses.

Robert First

4805 Concepts to Go
PO Box 10043
Berkeley, CA 94709-5043
510-848-3233
Fax: 510-486-1248

Develops and distributes manipulative activities for language arts and visual communications for ages 3-8.

4806 Congressional Quarterly
1414 22nd Street NW
Washington, DC 20037-1003
202-887-8500
Fax: 202-293-1487

Comprehensive publications and reference and paperback books pertaining to Congress, US Government and politics, the presidency, the Supreme Court, national affairs and current issues.

4807 Continental Press
520 E Bainbridge Street
Elizabethtown, PA 17022-2299
717-367-1836
800-233-0759
Fax: 717-367-5660
E-mail: cpeducation@continentalpress.com
http://www.continentalpress.com

Publisher of print for PreK-12 (plus adult education). Programs relate to skill areas in reading, math, comprehension, phonics, etc. Producers of Testlynx Software.

4808 Cottonwood Press
107 Cameron Drive
Suite 398
Fort Collins, CO 80525
970-204-0715
800-864-4297
Fax: 970-204-0761
E-mail: cottonwood@cottonwwodpress.com
http://www.cottonwoodpress.com

Publishes books focusing on teaching language arts and writing, grades 5-12.

Cheryl Thurston

4809 Council for Exceptional Children
The Council for Exceptional Children
1920 Association Drive
Reston, VA 20191-1589
703-620-3660
800-232-7323
Fax: 703-264-9494
E-mail: cec@cec.sped.org
http://www.cec.sped.org

The Council for Exceptional Children is a major publisher of special education literature and produces a catalog semiannually.

4810 Creative Teaching Press
10701 Holder Street
Cypress, CA 90630-4809
714-895-5047
800-287-8879
Fax: 714-895-6547
http://www.creativeteaching.com

Offers language and literature-based books including Teaching Basic Skills through Literature, Literature-Based Homework Activities, I Can Read! I Can Write!, Multicultural Art Activities, Responding to Literature, and Linking Mathand Literature.

4811 Cricket Magazine Group
315 5th Street
Peru, IL 61354-2859
815-223-1500

Magazines of high quality children's literature.

4812 Curriculum Associates
PO Box 2001
North Billerica, MA 01862-0901
978-667-8000
800-225-0248
Fax: 800-366-1158
E-mail: cainfo@curriculumassociates.com
http://www.curriculumassociates.com

Supplementary educational materials; cross-curriculum, language arts, reading, study skills, test preparation, diagnostic assessments, emergent readers, videos, and software.

4813 DC Heath & Company
125 Spring Street
Lexington, MA 02421-7801
781-862-6650

Publishes resources for all academic levels ranging from textbooks, fiction and nonfiction titles to business and college guides.

4814 DLM Teaching Resources
PO Box 4000
Allen, TX 75013-1302
972-248-6300
800-527-4747

Offers a variety of teacher's resources and guides for testing in all areas of education.

4815 Dawn Publications
14618 Tyler Foote Road
Nevada City, CA 95959-9316
530-478-7540
800-545-7475
Fax: 530-478-0112

Specializes in nature, children and health and healing books, tapes and videos and dedicated to helping people experience unity and harmony.

Bob Rinzler, Publisher
Glenn Hoveman, Editor

4816 Delta Education
PO Box 950
Hudson, NH 03051-0950
800-442-5444
Fax: 800-282-9560

Science programs, materials and curriculum kits.

4817 Dial Books for Young Readers
345 Hudson Street
New York, NY 10014-3658
212-366-2800
Fax: 212-366-2938
http://www.penguinputnam.com

General hardcover, children's books, from toddler through young adult, fiction and nonfiction.

4818 Didax Educational Resources
PO Box 507
Rowley, MA 01969-0907
978-948-2340
800-458-0024
Fax: 978-948-2813
E-mail: info@didaxinc.com
http://www.didaxinc.com

High quality educational materials featuring Unifix and hundreds of math and reading supplements.

Brian Scarlett, President
Martin Kennedy, VP

4819 Dinah-Might Activities
PO Box 39657
San Antonio, TX 78218-6657
210-698-0123
Fax: 210-698-0095

Learn how to integrate language arts, math, map and globe skills and more into a science curriculum. Books include The Big Book of Books and Activities, Organizing the Integrated Classroom, Write Your Own Thematic Units and Readingand Writing All Day Long.

4820 Dinocardz Company
146 5th Avenue
San Francisco, CA 94118-1310
415-751-5809

Dinosaur curriculums for grades 1-3 and 4-6.

4821 Disney Press
Disney Juvenile Publishing
114 5th Avenue
New York, NY 10011-5604
212-633-4400
Fax: 212-633-5929

Hardcover trade and library editions and paperback books for children, grades K-12.

Liisa-Ann Fink, President

4822 Dominic Press
1949 Kellogg Avenue
Carlsbad, CA 92008-6582
619-481-3838

Offers a range of materials for the Reading Recovery Program and Chapter 1 programs.

4823 Dorling Kindorley Company
95 Madison Avenue
New York, NY 10016
212-213-4800
Fax: 212-689-5254

Science books for all grade levels.

4824 Dover Publications
31 E 2nd Street
Mineola, NY 11501
516-294-7000
Fax: 516-742-6953

Fun and educational storybooks, coloring, activity, cut-and-assemble toy books, science for children.

Clarence Strowbridge, President

4825 Dutton Children's Books
375 Hudson Street
New York, NY 10014-3658
212-366-2000
Fax: 212-366-2948

General hardcover children's books from toddler through young adult, fiction and nonfiction.

4826 DynEd International
1350 Bayshore Highway
Suite 850
Burlingame, CA 94010
800-765-4375
Fax: 650-375-7017
http://www.dyned.com

Pre-K-adult listening and speaking skill development English language acquisition software.

Steven Kearney, Sales
Sue Young, Operations

4827 ETA - Math Catalog
620 Lakeview Parkway
Vernon Hills, IL 60061-1828
847-816-5050
800-445-5985
Fax: 847-816-5066
E-mail: info@etauniverse.com
http://www.etauniverse.com

Offers a full line of mathematics products, materials, books, textbooks and workbooks for grades K-12.

Mary Cooney, Product Development Manager
Monica Butler, Director Marketing

4828 ETR Associates
PO Box 1830
Santa Cruz, CA 95061-1830
800-321-4407
Fax: 800-435-8433
http://www.etr.org

Videos and booklets on health issues for grades K-12.

4829 EVAN-Motor Corporation
18 Lower Ragsdale Drive
Monterey, CA 93940-5728
831-649-5901
Fax: 800-777-4332

Resource materials for K-6 science educational programs.

4830 Early Start-Fun Learning
PO Box 350187
Jacksonville, FL 32235-0187
904-641-6138

Preschool materials for the educator.

4831 Earth Foundation
5151 Mitchelldale
B11
Houston, TX 77092-7200
713-686-9453
Fax: 713-686-6561

Join the largest active network of educators working to save endangered ecosystems and their species! Multi-disciplinary, hands-on curriculum and videos for the classroom.

Cynthia Everage, President

4832 Editorial Projects in Education
4301 Connecticut Avenue NW
Suite 432
Washington, DC 20008-2362
202-364-4114

Publishes various newsletters and publications in the fields of history and education.

4833 Edmark
6727 185th Avenue NE
PO Box 97021
Redmond, WA 98052
800-691-2986
Fax: 425-556-8430
http://www.edmark.com

Develops innovative and effective educational materials for children.

4834 Education Center
3515 W Market Street
Greensboro, NC 27403-1309
336-273-9409

Publishers of the Mailbox, teacher's helper magazines, learning centers clubs, classroom beautiful bulletin board clubs, the storybook club and more.

4835 Educational Marketer
SIMBA Information
11 Riverbend Drive
PO Box 4234
Stamford, CT 06907-0234
800-307-2529
Fax: 203-358-5824

Contains a range of print and electronic tools, including software and multimedia materials for educational institutions.

4836 Educational Press Association of America
Glassboro State College
Glassboro, NJ 08028
609-445-7349

Offers various publications and bibliographic data focusing on all aspects of education.

4837 Educational Productions
9000 SW Gemini Drive
Beaverton, OR 97008
503-644-7000
800-950-4949
Fax: 503-350-7000
E-mail: custserv@edpro.com
http://www.edpro.com

Video training programs that help increase parenting skills and help every teacher meet performance standards. Offers training on preventing discipline problems, increasing parenting skills, supporting literacy efforts and more.

4838 Educational Teaching Aids
620 Lakeview Pkwy
Vernon Hills, IL 60061-1838
847-816-5050
800-445-5985
Fax: 847-816-5066
E-mail: info@etauniverse.com
http://www.etauniverse.com

Manipulatives to enhance understanding of basic concepts and to help bridge the gap between the concrete and the abstract.

4839 Educators Progress Service
214 Center Street
Randolph, WI 53956
920-326-3127
888-951-4469
Fax: 920-326-3126
http://www.freeteachingaids.com

A complete spectrum of curriculum and mixed media resources for allgrade levels.

4840 Educators Publishing Service
31 Smith Place
Cambridge, MA 02138-1089
617-547-6706
800-225-5750
Fax: 617-547-0412
http://www.epsbooks.com

Supplementary workbooks and teaching materials in reading, spelling, vocabulary, comprehension, and elementary math, as well as materials for assessment and learning differences.

4841 Edumate-Educational Materials
2231 Morena Boulevard
San Diego, CA 92110-4134
619-275-7117

Multicultural and multilingual materials in the form of toys, puzzles, books, videos, music, visuals, games, dolls and teacher resources. Special emphasis on Spanish and other languages. Literature offered from North and SouthAmerica.

Gustavo Blankenburg, President

4842 Ellis
406 W 10600 S
Suite 610
Salt Lake City, UT 84003
801-374-3424
888-756-1570
Fax: 801-374-3495
http://www.ellis.com

Publish software that teaches English.

4843 Encyclopaedia Britannica
310 S Michigan Avenue
Chicago, IL 60604-4207
312-347-7900
800-323-1229
http://www.britannica.com

Books and related educational materials.

4844 Energy Learning Center
USCEA
1776 I Street NW
Suite 400
Washington, DC 20006-3700
703-741-5000
Fax: 703-741-6000

Energy learning materials.

4845 Essential Learning Products
PO Box 2590
Columbus, OH 43216-2590
800-357-3570
Fax: 614-487-2272

Publishers of phonics workbooks.

4846 Ethnic Arts & Facts
PO Box 20550
Oakland, CA 94620-0550
510-465-0451
888-278-5652
Fax: 510-465-7488
E-mail: eaf@ethnicartsnfacts.com
http://www.ethnicartsnfacts.com

Kit titles include: Traditional Africa, Urban Africa, China, Guatemala, Peru, Huichol Indians of Mexico, Chinese Shadow Puppet Kit. African-American Music History Mini-Kit. Artifact kits/resource booklets designed to enhanceappreciation of cultural diversity, improve geographic literacy and sharpen critical thinking and writing skills.

Susan Drexler, Curriculum Specialist

4847 Evan-Moor Corporation
18 Lower Ragsdale Drive
Monterey, CA 93940-5728

How to Make Books with Children and other fine teacher resources and reproducible materials for all curriculum areas grades PreK-6.

4848 Everyday Learning Corporation
PO Box 812960
Chicago, IL 60681-2960
800-382-7670
Fax: 312-233-7860

University of Chicago school mathematics project. Everyday Mathematics enriched curriculum for grades K-6.

4849 Exploratorium
3601 Lyon Street
San Francisco, CA 94123-1099
415-563-7337
Fax: 415-561-0307
http://www.exploratorium.edu

Exploratorium is dedicated to the formal and informal teaching of science using innovative interactive methods of inquiry. It publishes materials for educators and provides professional development opportunities both in print andonline.

Quarterly/Monthly

4850 Extra Editions K-6 Math Supplements
PO Box 38
Urbana, IL 61803-0038
Fax: 614-794-0107

Special needs math supplements offering 70 single-topic units from K-6 that reach students your basic math program misses. Extra Editions newspaper-like format uses animation with a hands-on approach to show real life necessity forcomputational skills, time, money, problem solving, critical thinking, etc. Ideal for Chapter One,

Peer-Tutoring, Parental Involvement, Home Use, and more.

Craig Rucker, General Manager
Earl Ockenga, Author/Owner

4851 F(G) Scholar
Future Graph
75 James Way
Southampton, PA 18966-3858
215-396-0720
Fax: 215-396-0724

A revolutionary program for teaching, learning and using math. This single program allows students and teachers easy answers to Algebra, Trigonometry, Pre-Calculus, Calculus, Statistics, Probability and more. It combines all of thepower of a graphing calculator, spreadsheet, drawing tools, mathematics and programming/scripting language and much more, and makes it simple and fun to use.

4852 Facts on File
11 Penn Plaza
New York, NY 10001
212-967-8800
800-322-8755
Fax: 212-967-9196
E-mail: llikoff@factsonfile.com
http://www.factsonfile.com

Reference books for teacher education, software, hardware and educational computer systems.

9 Hardcover Books

Laurie Likoff, Editorial Director

4853 Farrar, Straus & Giroux
19 Union Square W
New York, NY 10003-3304
212-741-6900
Fax: 212-633-9385

Children's, young adult and adult trade books in hardcover and paperback, including Sunburst Books, Aerial Miraso/libros juveniles and Hill and Wang.

4854 First Years
1 Kiddie Drive
Avon, MA 02322-1171
508-588-1220

Early childhood books, hardcover and paperback.

4855 Forbes Custom Publishing
60 5th Avenue
New York, NY 10011-8802
513-229-1000
800-355-9983
Fax: 800-451-3661
E-mail: fcpinfo@forbes.com
http://www.forbescp.com

Offers educators and teachers the opportunity to select unique teaching material to create a book designed specifically for their courses.

4856 Formac Distributing
5502 Atlantic Street
Halifax, NS E3HIG-4
902-421-7022
800-565-1905
Fax: 902-425-0166

Contemporary and historical fiction for ages 6-15. Multicultural themes featuring Degrassi Y/A series; first novel chapter books.

4857 Frank Schaffer Publications
23740 Hawthorne Boulevard
Torrance, CA 90505-5927
310-378-1133
800-421-5565
Fax: 800-837-7260

Best-selling supplemental materials including charts, literature notes, resource materials and more.

4858 Franklin Watts
Grolier Publishing
Sherman Turnpike
Danbury, CT 06816

800-621-1115
800-843-3749
Fax: 800-374-4329

Publisher of library bound books, paperback and Big Books for literature based, multicultural classrooms and school libraries.

4859 Free Spirit Publishing
400 1st Avenue N
Suite 616
Minneapolis, MN 55401-1730

612-338-2068
Fax: 612-337-5050

Creative learning materials to help young people develop self-esteem, manage stress, succeed in school, and more.

4860 Frog Publications
PO Box 280996
Tampa, FL 33682

813-935-5845
Fax: 813-935-3764
http://www.frog.com

An organized system of cooperative games for K-5 reading, language arts, thinking skills, math, social studies, Spanish and multicultural studies. Parental Involvement Program, Learning Centers, Test Preperation, Afterschool ProgramMaterials. Drops in the Bucket daily practice books.

4861 Gareth Stevens
330 W Olive Street
Suite 100
Milwaukee, WI 53212

414-332-3520
800-542-2595
Fax: 414-336-0156
E-mail: info@gsinc.com
http://garethstevens.com

Complete display of supplemental children's reading material for grades K-6, including our New World Almanac Library imprint grades 6-12.

Bi-Annually
ISSN: 0-8368

Mark Sachner, Author
Juanita Jones, Marketing Manager
Jonathan Strickland, National Sales Manager

4862 Glencoe/Div. of Macmillan/McGraw Hill
936 Eastwind Drive
Westerville, OH 43081-3329

708-615-3360
800-442-9685
Fax: 972-228-1982

Secondary science programs.

4863 Goethe House New York
1014 5th Avenue
New York, NY 10028-0104

Teaching materials on Germany for the social studies classroom in elementary, middle and high schools.

4864 Goodheart-Willcox Publisher
18604 W Creek Drive
Tinley Park, IL 60477-6243

800-323-0440
Fax: 888-409-3900
E-mail: custerv@goodheartwillcox.com
http://www.goodheartwillcox.com

Comprehensive text designed to help young students learn about themselves, others, and the environment. Readers will develop skills in clothing, food, decision making, and life management. Case studies throughout allow students toapply learning to real-life situations.

4865 Greenhaven Press
10911 Technology Place
San Diego, CA 92127-1811

800-231-5163
Fax: 248-699-8035

Publishers of the Opposing Viewpoints Series, presenting viewpoints in an objective, pro/con format on some of today's controversial subjects.

4866 Greenwillow Books
1350 Avenue of the Americas
New York, NY 10019-4702

212-261-6500
Fax: 212-261-6518

Offers publications for all reading levels.

4867 Grolier Publishing
90 Sherman Turnpike
Danbury, CT 06816

203-797-3500
800-621-1115
Fax: 203-797-3197
http://www.publishing.grolier.com

Publisher of library bound and paperback books in the areas of social studies, science, reference, history, and biographies for schools and libraries for grades K-12.

4868 Gryphon House
Gryphon House
PO Box 275
Mount Rainier, MD 20712-0275

301-779-6200
Fax: 301-595-0051
E-mail: info@ghbooks.com
http://www.ghbooks.com

Resource and activity books for early childhood teachers and directors.

Cathy Callootte, Marketing Director

4869 Hands-On Prints
PO Box 5899-268
Berkeley, CA 94705

510-601-6279
Fax: 510-601-6278

Specializes in cultural and language materials for children with an emphasis on internationalism and multiculturalism.

Christina Cheung, President

4870 Hardcourt Religion Publishers
1665 Embassy W Drive
Suite 200
Dubuque, IA 52002-2259

563-557-3700
800-922-7696
Fax: 563-557-3719
E-mail: hardcourtreligion.com

Publishers of religion education materials for schools and parishes.

4871 Hazelden Educational Materials
PO Box 176
Center City, MN 55012-0176

651-257-4010
Fax: 651-213-4590

Educational publisher of materials supporting both students and faculty in areas of substance abuse and related topics.

4872 Heinemann
361 Hanover Street
Portsmouth, NH 03801-3959
603-431-7894
Fax: 203-750-9790

Holistic/student-centered publications, videotapes and workshops for parents, teachers and administrators.

4873 Henry Holt & Company
115 W 18th Street
New York, NY 10011-4113
800-628-9658
Fax: 212-633-0748

Books and materials for classroom teachers, grades 6-adult, including programs on science literacy.

4874 Henry Holt Books for Young Readers
115 W 18th Street
New York, NY 10011-4113
800-628-9658
Fax: 212-647-0490

Hardcover and paperback trade books for preschool through young adult, fiction and nonfiction. Also, big books and promotional materials are available.

4875 High Touch Learning
PO Box 754
Houston, MN 55943-0754
507-896-3500
800-255-0645
Fax: 507-896-3243

Classroom interactive learning maps promoting the hands-on approach to the teaching of social studies.

4876 High/Scope Educational Research Foundation
600 N River Street
Ypsilanti, MI 48198-2821
734-485-2000
800-40 -RESS
Fax: 734-485-4467

Early childhood, elementary, movement and music, and adolescent materials. Over 300 titles of books, videos, cassettes and CDs from which to choose. Research and training materials as well as curriculum and development materials arebased on the acclaimed High/Scope active learning approach.

Emily Koepp, President

4877 Holiday House
425 Madison Avenue
New York, NY 10017-1110
212-688-0085
Fax: 212-688-0395

Hardcover and paperback children's books. General fiction and nonfiction, preschool through high school.

4878 Hoover's
5800 Airport
Dallas, TX 78752-3812
512-374-4500
Fax: 512-374-4501

Everything educational, for the early childhood and K-12 market. As a partner for over 100 years, the company is eager to extend their commitment to produce quality, timely shipping and customer service to the public. Offer over10,000 products for infants, toddlers, pre-school and school age educational needs.

4879 Horn Book Guide
Horn Book
56 Roland Street
Suite 200
Boston, MA 02129
617-628-0225
800-325-1170
Fax: 617-628-0882
E-mail: info@hbook.com
http://http://www.hbook.com

The most comprehensive review source of children's and young adult books available. Published each spring and fall, the Guide contains concise, critical reviews of almost every hardcover trade children's and young adult book publishedin the United States - nearly 2,000 books each issue.

BiAnnually
ISSN: 1044-405X

Anne Quirk, Marketing Manager
Roger Sutton, Editor

4880 Houghton Mifflin Books for Children
222 Berkeley Street
Boston, MA 02116-3748
617-351-5000
800-225-3362
Fax: 617-351-1111
http://www.hmco.com

Wide variety of children's and young adult books, fiction and nonfiction.

4881 Houghton Mifflin Company: School Division
222 Berkeley Street
Boston, MA 02116-3748
617-351-5000
Fax: 617-651-1106

Children's literature; K-12 reading and language arts print and software programs; and testing and evaluation for K-12.

4882 Hyperion Books for Children
114 5th Avenue
New York, NY 10011-5604
212-633-4400
Fax: 212-633-5929

Children's books in paperback and hardcover editions.

4883 ITP South-Western Publishing Company
5101 Madison Road
Cincinnati, OH 45227-1427
800-824-5179
Fax: 800-487-8488

Innovative instructional materials for teaching integrated science.

4884 Idea Factory
10710 Dixon Drive
Riverview, FL 33569-7406
813-677-6727

Teacher resource books, science project ideas, materials and more for elementary and middle school teachers.

4885 Institute for Chemical Education
University of Wisconsin
1101 University Avenue
Madison, WI 53706-1322
608-262-3033
800-991-5534
Fax: 608-265-8094
E-mail: ice@chem.wisc.edu
http://ice.chem.wisc.edu

Hands-on activities, publications, kits and videos.

4886 Institute for Educational Leadership
1001 Connecticut Avenue NW
Suite 310
Washington, DC 20036-5541
202-822-8405
Fax: 202-872-4050

The Institute's list of publications on educational trends and policies is available to the public.

Michael C Usdan, President

4887 IntelliTools
1720 Corporate Circle
Petaluma, CA 94954

707-773-2000
800-899-6687
Fax: 707-773-2001
http://www.intellitools.com

Provider of hardware and software giving students with special needs comprehensive access to learning.

4888 Intellimation
130 Cremona Drive
Santa Barbara, CA 93117-5599

805-968-2291
800-346-8355
Fax: 805-968-8899

Educational materials in all areas of curriculum for early learning through college level. Over 400 titles are available in video, and software and multimedia exclusively for the Macintosh. Free catalogs avaiable.

Karin Fisher, Marketing Associate
Marlene Carlyle, Marketing Supervisor

4889 Intercultural Press
PO Box 700
Yarmouth, ME 04096

207-846-5168
800-370-2665
Fax: 207-846-5181
E-mail: books@interculturalpress.com
http://www.interculturalpress.com

Publishes over 100 titles.

Judy Carl-Hendrick, Managing Editor

4890 J Weston Walch, Publisher
321 Valley Street
PO Box 658
Portland, ME 04104-0658

207-722-846
800-341-6094
Fax: 207-772-3105
http://www.walch.com

Supplemental publications for grades 6 through adult.

4891 Jacaranda Designs
3000 Jefferson Street
Boulder, CO 80304-2638

707-374-2543
Fax: 707-374-2543

Authentic African children's books from Kenya, including modern concept stories for K-3 in bilingual editions, folktales, and traditional cultural stories for older readers. All books are written and illustrated by African Kenyans.

Carrie Jenkins Williams, President

4892 Jarrett Publishing Company
19 Cross Street
Lake Ronkonkoma, NY 11779-4363

631-981-4248
Fax: 631-588-4722

Offers a wide range of books for today's educational needs.

4893 JayJo Books
Guidance Channel
135 Dupont Street
PO Box 760
Plainview, NY 11803

516-349-5520
800-999-6884
Fax: 516-349-5521

E-mail: jayjobooks@guidancechannel.com
http://www.jayjo.com

Publisher of books to help teachers, parents and children cope with chronic illnesses, special needs and health education in classroom, family and social settings.

Sally Germain, Editor-in-Chief

4894 John Wiley & Sons
605 3rd Avenue
New York, NY 10158-0180

212-850-6000

Publish science and nature books for children and adults.

4895 Junior Achievement
1 Education Way
Colorado Springs, CO 80906-4477

719-540-8000
Fax: 719-540-6127

Provides business and economics-related materials and programs to students in grades K-12. All programs feature volunteers from the local business community. Materials are free, but available only from local Junior Achievementoffices.

4896 Kaeden Corporation
PO Box 16190
19915 Lake Road
Rocky River, OH 44116

440-356-0030
800-890-7323
Fax: 440-356-5081
E-mail: lcowan@kaedeen.com
http://www.kaeden.com

Books for emergent readers at the K, 1 and 2 levels, ideal for Title 1 and Reading Recovery and other at-risk reading programs.

Laura Cowan, Sales Manager
Joan Hoyer, Office Manager

4897 Kane/Miller Book Publishers
PO Boxn 8515
La Jolla, CA 92038-0529

858-456-0540
Fax: 858-456-9641
E-mail: info@kanemiller.com
http://www.kanemiller.com

English translation of foreign children's picture books. Distributors of Spanish language children's books.

Byron Parnell, Sales Manager
Kira Lynn, President

4898 Keep America Beautiful
1010 Washington Boulevard
Stamford, CT 06901

203-323-8987
Fax: 203-325-9199
E-mail: info@kab.org
http://www.kab.org

K-12 curriculum specializing in litter prevention and environmental education. Education posters with lesson plans printed right on the back of each poster and school recycling guides.

4899 Kendall-Hunt Publishing Company
4050 Westmark Drive
Dubuque, IA 52002-2624

319-589-1000
800-228-0810
Fax: 800-772-9165
E-mail: webmaster@kendallhunt.com
http://www.kendallhunt.com

A leading custom publisher in the United States with over 6,000 titles in print. Kendall/Hunt publishes educational materials for kindergarten through college to continuing education creditation and distance learning courses.

Karen Berger, Customer Service Assistant

4900 Knowledge Adventure
19840 Pioneer Avenue
Torrance, CA 90503

310-431-4000
800-545-7677
Fax: 310-342-0533
http://www.education.com

Develops, publishes, and distributes best-selling multimedia educational software for use in both homes and schools.

4901 Knowledge Unlimited
PO Box 52
Madison, WI 53701-0052

800-356-2303
Fax: 608-831-1570
http://www.newscurrents.com

NewsCurrents, the most effective current events programs for grades 3-12. Now available on DVD or Online.

4902 Kraus International Publications
358 Saw Mill River Road
Millwood, NY 10546-1035

914-762-2200
800-223-8323
Fax: 914-762-1195

Offers teacher resource notebooks with complete resource information for teachers and administrators at all levels. Great for program planning, quick reference, inservice training. Also offers books on early childhood education,English/language arts, mathematics, science, health education and visual arts.

Barry Katzen, President

4903 Lake Education
AGS/Lake Publishing Company
500 Harbor Boulevard
Belmont, CA 94002-4075

650-592-1606
800-328-2560
Fax: 800-471-8457

Alternative learning materials for underachieving students grades 6-12, RSL and adult basic education. High interest, low readability fiction, adapted classic literature, lifeskills and curriculum materials to supplement and supportmany basal programs.

Phil Schlenter
Carol Hegarty, VP Editorial

4904 Landmark Editions
PO Box 270169
Kansas City, MO 64127-0169

816-241-4919

Books written and illustrated by children.

4905 Langenseheidt Publishing
515 Valley Street
Maplewood, NJ 07040-1337

800-526-4953
Fax: 908-206-1104
E-mail: edusales@hammond.com
http://www.hammondmap.com

World maps, atlases, general reference guides and CD-Roms.

4906 Lawrence Hall of Science
University of California
Berkeley, CA 94720

510-642-5132
Fax: 510-642-1055

E-mail: lhsinfo@uclink.berkeley.edu
http://www.lawrencehallofscience.org

Offers programs and materials in the field of science and math education for teachers, families and interested citizens. Exhibits include Equals, Family Math, CePUP and FOSS.

Linda Schneider, Marketing Manager
Mike Salter, Marketing/PR Associate

4907 Leap Frog Learning Materials
PO Box 534
Crandall, TX 75114-0534

972-472-6896

Learning materials, books, posters, games and toys for children.

4908 Learning Connection
19 Devane Street
Frostproof, FL 33843-2017

863-635-5610
800-338-2282
Fax: 863-635-4676

Thematic, literature-based units with award-winning books, media and hands-on for PK-12 including parent involvement, early childhood, bilingual, literacy, math, writing, science and multicultural.

4909 Learning Disabilities Association of America
Learning Disabilities Association of America
4156 Library Road
Pittsburgh, PA 15234-1349

412-341-1515
888-300-6710
Fax: 412-344-0224
E-mail: info@ldaamerica.org
http://www.ldaamerica.org

Has 50 state affiliates with more than 300 local chapters. The national office has a resource center of over 500 publications for sale.

4910 Learning Links
2300 Marcus Avenue
New Hyde Park, NY 11042-1083

516-437-9075
800-724-2616
Fax: 516-437-5392
E-mail: learningLx@aol.com
http://www.learinglinks.com

All you need for literature based instruction; Noveltie, study guides, thematic units books and more.

4911 Lee & Low Books
95 Madison Avenue
Suite 606
New York, NY 10016-3303

212-779-4400
Fax: 212-683-1894
E-mail: info@leeandlow.com
http://www.leeandlow.com

A multicultural children's book publisher. Our primary focus is on picture books, especially stories set in contemporary America. Spanish language titles are available.

Craig Low, VP Publisher
Louise May, Executive Editor

4912 Leo A Myer Associates/LAMA Books
20956 Corsair Boulevard
Hayward, CA 94545-1002

510-785-1091
Fax: 510-785-1099
E-mail: lama@lmabooks.com

Writers and publishers of HVAC books.

Barbara Ragura, Marketing Assistant

4913 Lerner Publishing Group
A Division Lerner Publications Group
241 1st Avenue N
Minneapolis, MN 55401-1607
612-332-3344
800-328-4929
Fax: 612-332-7615
http://www.lernerbooks.com

Primarily nonfiction for readers of all grade levels. List includes titles encompassing nature, geography, natural and physical science, current events, ancient and modern history, world art, special interests, sports, world cultures,and numerous biography series. Some young adult and middle grade fiction.

Jennifer Martin, Submissions Editor

4914 Linden Tree Children's Records & Books
170 State Street
Los Altos Hills, CA 94022-2863
650-949-3390
Fax: 650-949-0346

Offers a wide variety of books, audio cassettes and records for children.

4915 Listening Library
One Park Avenue
Old Greenwich, CT 06870-1727
203-637-3616
800-243-4504
Fax: 800-454-0606
E-mail: moreinfo@listeninglib.com
http://www.listeninglib.com

A producer of quality unabridged audiobooks for listeners of all ages. Specializing in children's literature and adult classics.

BiAnnually

Annette Imperati, Director Sales/Marketing

4916 Little, Brown & Company
3 Center Plaza
Boston, MA 02108-2084
617-227-0730
Fax: 617-263-2854

Trade books for children and young adults, hardcover and paper, including Sierra Club Books for Children.

4917 Lodestar Books
375 Hudson Street
New York, NY 10014-3658
212-366-2000

General hardcover children's books from toddler through young adult, fiction and nonfiction.

4918 Lothrop, Lee & Shepard Books
1350 Avenue of the Americas
New York, NY 10019-4702
212-261-6500
Fax: 212-261-6518

Children's books.

4919 Lynne Rienner Publishing
1800 30th Street
Suite 314
Boulder, CO 80301
303-333-3003
800-803-8488
Fax: 303-333-4037
E-mail: karen-hemmes@mindspring.com
http://www.fireflybooks.com

Publishes academic-level books with a focus on international and domestic social sciences.

Karen Hemmes, Publicist
Mary Kay Opicka, Publicist

4920 MHS
908 Niagara Boulevard
North Tonawanda, NY 14120-2060
416-492-2627
800-456-3003
Fax: 416-492-3343
E-mail: customer_service@mhs.com
http://www.mhs.com

Publishers and distributors of professional assessment materials.

Steven J Stein, PhD, President

4921 MacMillan Children's Books
1633 Broadway
New York, NY 10019
212-512-2000
Fax: 800-835-3202

Hardcover trade books for children and young adults.

4922 MacMillan Reference
1633 Broadway
New York, NY 10019
212-512-2000
Fax: 800-835-3202

A wide variety of titles for students and teachers of all grade levels.

4923 Macmillan/McGraw-Hill School Division
1633 Broadwaty
New York, NY 10019
212-654-8500
800-442-9685
Fax: 800-835-3202

Quality literature for the student and excellent support for the teacher. Programs and educational materials for all grade levels.

4924 Macro Press
18242 Peters Court
Fountain Valley, CA 92708-5873
310-823-9556
Fax: 310-306-2296

Includes resources to conduct thematic hands-on science lessons and integrated curriculum; and, student materials offering a Scientist's Notebook and reading materials to integrate hands-on (grade specific) scientific thinking,problem solving and documenting skills to benefit all students. Nine award-winning K-6 teachers (200+ years combined experience) joined together to address the real needs of today's high student load.

Leigh Hoven Swenson, President

4925 Magna Publications
2718 Dryden Drive
Madison, WI 53704
608-227-8109
800-206-4805
Fax: 608-246-3597
E-mail: carriej@magnapubs.com
http://www.magnapubs.com

Produces eight subscriptions newsletters in the field of higher education.

Carrie Jenson, Conference Manager
David Burns, Associate Publisher

4926 Major Educational Resources Corporation
10153 York Road
Suite 107
Hunt Valley, MD 21030-3340
800-989-5353

Multimedia curriculum tools for educators.

4927 Margaret K McElderry Books
1633 Broadway
New York, NY 10019
212-512-2000
Fax: 800-835-3202

Hardcover trade books for children and young adults.

4928 Mari
3215 Pico Boulevard
Santa Monica, CA 90405-4603
310-829-2212
800-955-9494
Fax: 310-829-2317
http://www.mariinc.com

The best literature learning materials for K-12. Offers Mini-Units for writing and critical thinking skills, Literature Extenders that extend literature across the curriculum and Basic Skills Through Literature that combine literature and skill work.

4929 MasterTeacher
PO Box 1207
Manhattan, KS 66505-1207
785-539-0555
800-669-9633
Fax: 785-539-7739
http://www.masterteacher.com

A publisher of videotapes for the professional. Offers programs on inclusion, tests and testing, student motivation, discipline and more.

4930 MathSoft
101 Main Street
Cambridge, MA 02142
617-577-1017
800-628-4223
Fax: 617-577-8829
http://www.mathsoft.com

Provider of math, science and engineering software for business, academia, research and government.

4931 McCracken Educational Services
PO Box 3588
Blaine, WA 98231
360-332-1881
800-447-1462
Fax: 360-332-7332
E-mail: mes@mccrackened.com
http://www.mccrackened.com

Materials for beginning reading, writing and spelling. Big Books, manipulative materials, teacher resource books, spelling through phonics, posters and both audio and video tapes.

Robert & Marlene McCracken, Author

4932 McGraw Hill Children's Publishing
PO Box 1650
Grand Rapids, MI 49501-1650
616-363-1290
Fax: 800-543-2690

New self-esteem literature based reading and multicultural literature based reading.

4933 Mel Bay Publications
4 Industrial Drive
PO Box 66
Pacific, MO 63069-0066
637-257-3970
800-863-5229
Fax: 636-257-5062
E-mail: email@melbay.com
http://www.melbay.com

Music supply distributors.

Sheri Stephens, Customer Service Supervisor

4934 Merriam-Webster
47 Federal Street
#281
Springfield, MA 01105-3805
413-734-3134
Fax: 413-734-0257

A wide variety of titles for students and teachers of all grade levels.

4935 Millbrook Press
2 Old New Milford Road
Brookfield, CT 06804-2426
203-740-2220
800-462-4703
Fax: 203-740-2526
http://www.millbrookpress.com

Exceptional nonfiction juvenile and young adult books for schools and public libraries.

4936 Milton Roy Company
820 Linden Avenue
Rochester, NY 14625-2710
716-248-4000

Teacher support materials, scientific kits and manuals.

4937 Mimosa Publications
90 New Montgomery Street
San Francisco, CA 94105-4501
415-982-5350

A language based K-3 math program featuring big books, language and activity based math topics and multicultural math activities.

4938 Model Technologies
2420 Van Layden Way
Modesto, CA 95356-2454
209-575-3445

Curriculum guides and scientific instruction kits.

4939 Mondo Publishing
One Plaza Road
Greenvale, NY 11548
800-242-3650
Fax: 212-268-3561
E-mail: mondopub@aol.com
http://www.mondopub.com

Offers multicultural big books and music cassettes: Folk Tales from Around the World series; Exploring Habitats series; and, Let's Write and Sing a Song, whole language activities through music.

4940 Morning Glory Press
6595 San Haroldo Way
Buena Park, CA 90620-3748
714-828-1998
888-612-8254
Fax: 714-828-2049
E-mail: info@morningglorypress.com
http://www.morningglorypress.com

Publishes books and materials for teenage parents.

Quarterly

Jeanne Lindsay, President
Carole Blum, Promotion Director

4941 Music for Little People
PO Box 1460
Redway, CA 95560-1460
707-923-3991
Fax: 707-923-3241

Science and environmental education materials set to music for younger students.

4942 N&N Publishing Company
18 Montgomery Street
Middletown, NY 10940-5116

Low-cost texts and workbooks.

4943 NASP Publications
National Association of School Psychologists
4340 EW Highway
Suite 402
Bethesda, MD 20814
301-657-0270
Fax: 301-657-0275
E-mail: center@naspweb.org
http://www.naspionline.org

Over 100 hard-to-find books and videos centering on counseling, psychology and guidance for students.

Betty Somerville, President

4944 NCTM Educational Materials
National Council of Teachers of Mathematics
1906 Association Drive
Reston, VA 20191-1502
703-620-9840
Fax: 703-476-2970
E-mail: nctm@nctm.org
http://www.nctm.org

Publications, videotapes, software, posters and information to improve the teaching and learning of mathematics.

Harry B Tunis, Publications Director
Cynthia C Rosso, Director Marketing Services

4945 NYSTROM
3333 N Elston Avenue
Chicago, IL 60618-5898
773-463-1144
800-621-8086
Fax: 773-463-0515

Maps, globes, hands-on geography and history materials.

4946 Narrative Press
PO Box 2487
Santa Barbara, CA 93120
805-966-2186
800-315-9005
Fax: 805-456-3915
E-mail: sje@narrativepress.com
http://www.narrativepress.com

Publisher of first person narratives of adventure and exploration.

Sara Ellsworth, President

4947 National Aeronautics & Space Administration
NASA Headquarters
300 E Street SW
Washington, DC 20546
202-358-0000
Fax: 202-358-3251

Over 10 different divisions offering a wide variety of classroom and educational materials in the areas of science, physics, aeronautics and more.

4948 National Center for Science Teaching &
Learning/Eisenhower Clearinghouse
1929 Kenny Road
Columbus, OH 43210-1015

Collects and creates the most up-to-date listing of science and mathematics curriculum materials in the nation.

4949 National Council for the Social Studies
3501 Newark Street NW
Washington, DC 20016-3100
202-966-7840
Fax: 202-966-2061

Publishes books, videotapes and journals in the area of social education and social studies.

4950 National Council of Teachers of English
1111 W Kenyon Road
Urbana, IL 61801-1096
217-328-3870
800-369-6283
Fax: 217-328-9645
E-mail: public_info@ncte.org
http://www.ncte.org

Devoted to the advancement of English language and literature studies at all levels of education. Publishes 12 periodicals, a member newspaper, and 20-25 books a year, and holds conventions and workshops.

Lori Bianchini, Public Affairs

4951 National Council on Economic Education
1140 Avenue of the Americas
New York, NY 10036-5803
212-730-7007

Offers various programs including their latest, US History: Eyes on the Economy, a council program for secondary education teachers.

4952 National Geographic School Publishing
1145 17th Street NW
Washington, DC 20036
800-368-2728
Fax: 515-362-3366

Books, magazines, videos, and software in the areas of science, geography and social studies.

4953 National Geographic Society
PO Box 10041
Des Moines, IA 50340-0597
800-548-9797
Fax: 301-921-1575
http://www.nationalgeographic.com

Science materials, videos, CD-ROM's and telecommunications program.

4954 National Head Start Association
1651 Prince Street
Alexandria, VA 22314-2818
703-739-0875
Fax: 703-739-0878
http://www.nhsa.org

Dedicated to promoting and protecting the Head Start program. Advocates on the behalf of America's low-income children and families. Publishes many books, periodicals and resource guides. Offers a legislative hotline as well astraining programs through the NHSA Academy.

Ron Herndon, President
Blanche Russ-Glover, VP

4955 National Textbook Company
4255 W Touhy Avenue
Lincolnwood, IL 60646-1975
847-679-5500
800-323-4900
Fax: 847-679-2494

Offers various textbooks for students grades K-college level.

4956 National Women's History Project
7738 Bell Road
Windsor, CA 95492-8518
707-838-6000
Fax: 707-838-0478

E-mail: nehp@aol.com
http://www.nwhp.org

Non-profit organization, the clearinghouse for information about multicultural US women's history. Initiated March as National Women's History Month; issues a catalog of women's history materials. Provides teacher-training nationwide;coordinates the Women's History Network; produces videos, posters, curriculum units and other curriculum materials.

Molly Murphy Margregorer, President

4957 National Writing Project
University of California, Berkeley
2105 Bancroft Way
#1042
Berkeley, CA 94720-1042

510-642-6096
Fax: 510-642-4545
http://www.writingproject.org

Technical reports and occasional paper series: a series of research reports and essays on the research in and practice of teaching writing at all grade levels.

4958 New Canaan Publishing Company
PO Box 752
New Canaan, CT 06840

203-966-3408
800-705-5698
Fax: 203-966-3408
http://www.newcanaanpublishing.com

Children's publications.

4959 New Press
450 W 41st Street
New York, NY 10036-6807

212-629-8802
Fax: 212-629-8617

Multicultural teaching materials, focusing on the social studies.

4960 NewsBank
5020 Tamiami Trail N
Suite 110
Naples, FL 34103-2837

941-263-6004

Electronic information services that support the science curriculum.

4961 North South Books
11 E 26th Street
17 Floor
New York, NY 10010-2007

212-706-4545
Fax: 212-706-4544

Publisher of quality children's books by authors and illustrators from around the world.

4962 Nystrom, Herff Jones
3333 N Elston Avenue
Chicago, IL 60618-5811

913-432-8100
Fax: 913-432-3958

Charts for earth, life and physical science for upper elementary and high school grades.

4963 Options Publishing
PO Box 1749
Merrimack, NH 03054

603-429-2698
800-782-7300
Fax: 603-424-4056
E-mail: serviceoptionspublishing.com m
http://www.optionspublishing.com

Publishers of supplemental materials in reading, math and language arts.

Marty Furlong, VP

4964 Organization of American Historians
112 N Bryan Avenue
Bloomington, IN 47408-4136

812-855-7311
800-446-8923
Fax: 812-855-0696
E-mail: oah@oah.org
http://www.oah.org

Offers various products and literature dealing with American history, as well as job registries, Magazine of History, Journal of American History, OAH Newsletter, and more.

Damon Freeman, Marketing Manager
Michael Regoli, Publications Director

4965 PF Collier
1315 W 22nd Street
Suite 250
Oak Brook, IL 60523-2061

A leading educational publisher for more than 110 years, creating the home learning center. Products include: Collier's Encyclopedia, Quickstart and Early Learning Fun.

4966 PRO-ED
8700 Shoal Creek Boulevard
Austin, TX 78757-6897

512-451-3246
800-897-3202
Fax: 800-397-7633
E-mail: info@proedinc.com
http://www.proedinc.com

A leading publisher of assessments, therapy materials and resource/reference books in the areas of speech, language, and hearing; psychology; special education; and occupational therapy.

4967 Parenting Press
PO Box 75267
11065 5th Avenue NE
Seattle, WA 98125-0267

206-364-2900
800-992-6657
Fax: 206-364-0702
E-mail: office@ParentingPress.com
http://www.ParentingPress.com

Publishes books for parents, children, and professionals who work with them. Nonfiction books include topics on parenting, problem solving, dealing with feelings, safety, and special issues.

Carolyn J Threadgill, Publisher

4968 Penguin USA
375 Hudson Street
New York, NY 10014-3658

212-366-2000
Fax: 212-366-2934
http://www.penguinputnam.com

Children's and adult hardcover and paperback general trade books, including classics and multiethnic literature.

4969 Perfection Learning Corporation
Perfection Learning
10520 New York Avenue
Des Moines, IA 50322

303-333-3003
800-803-8488
Fax: 303-333-4037
E-mail: karen-hemmes@mindspring.com
http://www.fireflybooks.com

Perfection Learning publishes high interest-low reading level fiction and non-fiction books for young adults.

Karen Hemmes, Publicist
Mary Kay Opicka, Publicist

4970 Perma Bound Books
E Vandalia Road
Jacksonville, IL 62650
217-243-5451
800-637-6581
Fax: 800-551-1169

Thematically arranged for K-12 classroom use with 480,000 titles available in durable Perma-Bound bindings; related library services also available.

Ben Mangum, President

4971 Personalizing the Past
1534 Addison Street
Berkeley, CA 94703-1454
415-388-9351

Museum quality artifact history kits complete with integrated lesson plan teachers guide. Copy-ready student worksheets, literature section, videos and audio tapes. United States and ancient world history.

4972 Perspectives on History Series
Discovery Enterprises, Ltd.
31 Laurelwood Drive
Carlisle, MA 01741
978-287-5401
800-729-1720
Fax: 978-287-5402
E-mail: ushistorydocs@aol.com
http://www.ushistorydocs.com

Primary and secondary source materials for middle school to college levels; bibliographies; plays for grades 5-9 on American history topics. Educators curriculum guides for using primary source documents. 75-volumes of primary sourcedocuments on American history may be purchased individually or in sets. New Researching American History Series presents documents with summaries and vocabulary on each page (20 volumes) sold individually or in sets.

JoAnne Deitch, President

4973 Peytral Publications
PO Box 1162
Minnetonka, MN 55345
877-739-8725
Fax: 952-906-9777
http://www.peytral.com

Books and videos for educators.

4974 Phelps Publishing
PO Box 22401
Cleveland, OH 44122
216-752-4938
Fax: 216-752-4941
E-mail: earl@phelpspublishing.com
http://www.phelpspublishing.com

Publisher of art instruction books for ages 8 to 108.

4975 Phoenix Learning Resources
12 W 31st Street
New York, NY 10001-4415
212-629-3887
800-221-1274
Fax: 212-629-5648

Supplemental and remedial reading and language arts programs for early childhood, K-12, and adult literacy programs.

Alexander Burke, President
John Rothermich, Executive VP

4976 Pleasant Company Publications
8400 Fairway Pl
Middleton Branch, WI 53562-2554
608-836-4848
800-233-0264
Fax: 800-257-3865

The American Girls Collection historical fiction series.

4977 Pocket Books/Paramount Publishing
1230 Avenue of the Americas
New York, NY 10020-1513
212-698-7000

Books for children and young adults in hardcover and paperback originals and reprints of bestselling titles.

4978 Population Connection
1400 16th Street NW
Suite 320
Washington, DC 20036-2290
800-767-1956
Fax: 202-332-2302
E-mail: poped@populationconnection.org
http://www.populationconnection.org

Curriculum materials for grades K-12 to teach students about population dynamics and their social, political and environmental effects in the United States and the world.

Pamela Wasserman, Director Education

4979 Prentice Hall School Division
340 Rancheros Drive
Suite 160
San Marcos, CA 92069
760-510-0222
Fax: 760-510-0230

Superb language arts textbooks and ancillaries for students grades 6-12.

4980 Prentice Hall School Division - Science
1 Lake Street
Upper Saddle River, NJ 07458
201-236-7000
Fax: 201-236-3381

Science textbooks and ancillaries for grades 6-12 and advanced placement students.

4981 Prentice Hall/Center for Applied Research in Education
1 Lake Street
Upper Saddle River, NJ 07458
201-236-7000
Fax: 201-236-3381

Publisher of practical, time and work saving teaching/learning resources for PreK-12 teachers and specialists in all content areas.

4982 Project Learning Tree
American Forest Foundation
1111 19th Street NW
Suite 780
Washington, DC 20036-3603
202-463-2462
Fax: 202-463-2461

Pre-K through grade 12 curriculum materials containing hundreds of hands-on science activities. PLT uses the forest as a window into the natural world to increase students' understanding of our complex environment. Stimulates criticaland creative thinking; develops the ability to make informed decisions on environmental issues; and instills the confidence and commitment to take action on them.

Kathy McGlauflin, President

4983 Prufrock Press
PO Box 8813
Waco, TX 76714

800-998-2208
Fax: 800-240-0333
http://www.prufrock.com

Exciting classroom products for gifted and talented education.

4984 Puffin Books
375 Hudson Street
New York, NY 10014-3658

212-366-2819
Fax: 212-366-2040

Offers the Puffin Teacher Club set.

Lisa Crosby, President

4985 Quality Education Data
1700 Lincoln Street
Suite 3600
Denver, CO 80203

303-209-9328
800-525-5811
Fax: 303-209-9444
E-mail: qedinfo@qeddata.com
http://www.qeddata.com

Gathers information about K-12 schools, colleges and other educational institutions, offers an on-line database on education, directories of public and nonpublic schools and research reports.

Jeanne Hayes, President

4986 RR Bowker
Reed Reference Publishing Company
121 Chanlon Road
New Providence, NJ 07974-1541

908-464-6800
Fax: 908-665-6688

A leading information provider to schools and libraries for over one hundred years, RR Bowker provides quality resources to help teachers and librarians make informed reading selections for children and young adults.

4987 Raintree/Steck-Vaughn
PO Box 26015
Austin, TX 78755-0015

800-531-5015
http://www.steck-vaughn.com

Reference materials for K-8 students and texts for underachieving students K-12.

4988 Rand McNally
8255 Central Park Avenue
Skokie, IL 60076-2970

847-674-2151

Cross-curricular products featuring reading/language arts in the social studies.

4989 Random House
201 E 50th Street
New York, NY 10022-7703

212-751-2600
Fax: 212-572-8700

Offers a line of science trade books for grades K-8.

4990 Random House/Bullseye/Alfred A Knopf/Crown Books for Young Readers
201 E 50th Street
New York, NY 10022-7703

212-751-2600
Fax: 212-572-8700

Publisher of hardcover books, paperbacks, books and cassettes and videos for children.

4991 Recorded Books
270 Skipjack Road
Prince Frederick, MD 20678-3410

800-638-1304

Professionally narrated, unabridged books on standard-play audio cassettes, classroom ideas and combinations of print book, cassettes and teacher's guides.

Linda Hirshman, President

4992 Redleaf Press
450 Syndicate Street N
Suite 5
Saint Paul, MN 55104-4127

800-428-8309
Fax: 800-641-0115
http://www.redleafpress.org

Publisher of curriculum, activity, and childrens books for early childhood professionals.

4993 Reference Desk Books
430 Quintana Road
Suite 146
Morro Bay, CA 93442-1948

805-772-8806

Offers a variety of books for the education professional.

4994 Rhythms Productions
PO Box 34485
Los Angeles, CA 90034-0485

310-836-4678
800-544-7244
Fax: 310-837-1534

Producer and publisher of songs and games for learning through music. Cassettes, CDs, books for birth through elementary featuring rhythms, puppet play, art activities, and more. Titles include Lullabies, Singing Games, Watch Me Grow series, Mr. Windbag concept stories, phonics, First Reader's Kit, Hear-See-Say-Do Musical Math series, Themes, and more. Also publishes a line of folk dances from elementary through adult.

Audio

Ruth White, President

4995 Richard C Owen Publishers
PO Box 585
Katonah, NY 10536

914-232-3903
800-336-5588
Fax: 914-232-3977
E-mail: mfrund@rcowen.com
http://www.rcowen.com

Focus child-centered learning, Books for Young Learners, professional books, the Learning Network and Meet the Author series.

Mary Frundt, Marketing

4996 Riverside Publishing Company
425 Spring Lake Drive
Ithaca, IL 60143

630-467-7000
800-323-9540
Fax: 630-467-7192
http://www.riverpub.com

Offers a full line of reading materials, including fiction and nonfiction titles for all grade levels.

4997 Roots & Wings Educational Catalog-Australia for Kids
PO Box 19678
Boulder, CO 80308-2678

303-776-4796
800-833-1787
Fax: 303-776-6090

E-mail: roos@boulder.net
http://www.rootsandwingscatalog.com/
www.australiaforkids.com

Catalog company providing materials for the education of the young child, specializing in the following topics: Australia, multiculturalism, parenting and families, teaching, special needs, environment and peace.

Susan Ely, President/Sales
Anne Wilson, VP/Marketing

4998 Rosen Publishing Group
29 E 21st Street
New York, NY 10010-6209

212-777-3017
800-237-9932
Fax: 888-436-4643

Nonfiction books on self-help and guidance for young adults. Books also available for reluctant readers on self-esteem, values and drug abuse prevention.

4999 Routledge/Europa Library Reference
Taylor & Francis Books
29 W 35 Street
New York, NY 10001-2299

212-216-7800
800-634-7064
Fax: 212-564-7854
E-mail: reference@routledge-ny.com
http://www.reference.routlege-ny.com

Publisher of a wide range of print and online library reference titles, including the renowned Europa World Yearbook and the award-winning Routledge Encyclopedia of Philosophy (both available in online and print formats), GarlandEncyclopedia of World Music, Routledge Religion and Society Encyclopedias, Chronological History of US Foreign Relations, and many other acclaimed resources.

Koren Thomas, Sr Marketing/Library Ref
Elizabeth Sheehan, Marketing/Library Reference

5000 Runestone Press
A Divisions of Lerner Publishing Group
241 1st Avenue N
Minneapolis, MN 55401-1607

612-332-3344
800-328-4929
Fax: 612-332-7615
http://www.lernerbooks.com

Nonfiction for readers in Grades 5 and up. Newly revised editions of previously out-of-print books. List includes Buried Worlds archaeology series and titles of Jewish and Native American interest. Complete catalog is available.

Harry J Lerner, President
Mary M Rodgers, Editorial Director

5001 Saddleback Educational
3505 Cadillac Avenue
Suite F9
Costa Mesa, CA 92626-1443

800-637-8715
Fax: 888-734-4010

Supplementary curriculum materials for K-12 and adult students.

5002 SafeSpace Concepts
1424 N Post Oak Road
Houston, TX 77055-5401

713-956-0820
800-622-4289
Fax: 713-956-6416
E-mail: safespacec@aol.com
http://www.safespaceconcepts.com

Manufactures young children's play equipment and furnishings.

Barbara Carlson, PhD, President
Jerry Johnson, Marketing Director

5003 Sage Publications
Sage Publications
2455 Teller Road
Thousand Oaks, CA 91320

303-333-3003
800-803-8488
Fax: 303-333-4037
E-mail: karen-hemmes@mindspring.com
http://www.fireflybooks.com

Sage Publications publishes handbooks and guides with a focus on research and science.

Karen Hemmes, Publicist
Mary Kay Opicka, Publicist

5004 Santillana Publishing
901 W Walnut Street
Compton, CA 90220-5109

310-763-0455
800-245-8584
Fax: 305-591-9145

Publishers of K-12 and adult titles in Spanish.Imprints include: Altea, Alfagunea, Taurus and Aguilar.

Marla Norman, Publisher/Trade Book
Antonio de Marco, President

5005 Scholastic
555 Broadway
New York, NY 10012

212-343-6100
800-724-6527
Fax: 212-343-4801
http://www.scholastic.com

Publisher and distributor of children's books. Provides professional and classroom resources for K-12.

5006 School Book Fairs
PO Box 25558
Tampa, FL 33622-5558

813-578-7600

A children's book publisher that provides distribution of leisure reading materials to elementary and middle schools through book fair fund-raising events via a North American network with 97 locations.

5007 Science Inquiry Enterprises
14358 Village View Lane
Chino Hills, CA 91709-1706

530-295-3338
Fax: 530-295-3334

Selected science teaching materials.

5008 Scott & McCleary Publishing Company
2482 11th Street SW
Akron, OH 44314-1712

702-566-8756
800-765-3564
Fax: 702-568-1378
E-mail: jscott7576@aol.com
http://www.scottmccleary.com

Diagnostic reading and testing material.

Janet M Scott, Publisher
Sheila C McCleary, Publisher

5009 Scott Foresman Company
1900 E Lake Avenue
Glenview, IL 60025-2086

800-554-4411
Fax: 800-841-8939

Science tests and reading/language arts materials for teachers and students. Celebrate Reading! is the K-8 literature-based reading/integrated language arts program designed to meet the needs of all children. Book Festival is aliterature learning center that offers teachers a collection of trade books for independent reading.

Bert Crossland, Reading Product Manager
Jim Fitzmaurice, VP Editor Group

5010 Sharpe Reference
M.E. Sharpe, Inc.
80 Business Park Drive
Armonk, NY 10504

914-273-1800
800-541-6563
Fax: 914-273-2106
E-mail: custserv@mesharpe.com
http://www.mesharpe.com

Historical, political, geographical and art reference books.

Diana McDermott, Director Marketing

5011 Signet Classics
375 Hudson Street
New York, NY 10014-3658

212-366-2000
Fax: 212-366-2888

Publishes books on literature, poetry and reading.

5012 Silver Moon Press
160 5th Avenue
Suite 622
New York, NY 10010-7003

212-242-6499
800-874-3320
Fax: 212-242-6799

Informational and entertaining books for young readers. Subjects include history, multiculturalism and science.

5013 Simon & Schuster Children's Publishing
1230 Avenue of the Americas
New York, NY 10020

212-698-7000
Fax: 212-698-7007
http://www.simonsayskids.com

Fiction and nonfiction, in hardcover and paperback editions, for preschool through young adult.

5014 Social Issues Resources Series
1100 Holland Drive
Boca Raton, FL 33487-2701

561-994-0079
Fax: 561-994-2014

Provides information systems in print format and CD-ROM format.

5015 Social Science Education Consortium
Box 21270
Boulder, CO 80308-4270

303-492-8154
Fax: 303-449-3925
E-mail: singletl@stripe.colorado.edu
http://www.ssecinc.org

Produces curriculum guides, instructional units and collections of lesson plans on US history, law-related education, global studies, public issues and geography. Develops projects for social studies teachers and evaluates socialstudies programs.

James Cooks, Executive Director
Laurel Singleton, Associate Director

5016 Social Studies School Service
10200 Jefferson Boulevard
Culver City, CA 90232-3598

310-839-2436
800-421-4246
Fax: 310-839-2249
E-mail: access@socialstudies.com
http://www.socialstudies.com

Supplemental materials in all areas of social studies, language arts.

5017 Special Education & Rehabilitation Services
330 C Street
Washington, DC 20202

202-205-5465
Fax: 202-260-7225

Judith E Heuman, Assistant Secretary

5018 Speech Bin
1965 25th Avenue
Vero Beach, FL 32960-3000

561-770-0007
800-477-3324
Fax: 561-770-0006

Publisher and distributor of books and materials for professionals in rehabilitation, speech-language pathology, occupational and physical therapy, special education, and related fields. Major product lines include professional andchildren's books, computer software, diagnostic tests.

Jan J Binney, VP

5019 Stack the Deck Writing Program
PO Box 429
Tinley Park, IL 60477-0429

708-429-2100
Fax: 708-429-9516

Composition textbooks, grades 1-12, plus computer software.

5020 Stenhouse Publishers
477 Congress Street
Suite 4B
Portland, ME 04101-3417

888-363-0566
Fax: 800-833-9164
http://www.stenhouse.com

Professional materials for teachers by teachers.

5021 Story Teller
PO Box 921
Salem, UT 84653-0921

801-423-2560
Fax: 801-423-2568
E-mail: patti@thestoryteler.com
http://www.thestoryteller.com

Felt board stories books and educational sets.

Patti Gardner, VP Sales

5022 Summit Learning
PO Box 493
Fort Collins, CO 80522-0493

800-777-8817
Fax: 800-317-2194
http://www.summitlearning.com

Manipulatives for teaching math to grade K-9. Manipulatives include pattern blocks, decimal squares, rulers, books, balances and more.

Gary Otto, Marketing Manager

5023 Sunburst Technology
101 Castleton Street
Pleasantville, NY 10570

914-747-3310
800-338-3457
Fax: 914-747-4109
http://www.sunburst.com

K-12 educational software, guidance and health materials, and online teacher resources.

5024 Sundance Publishing
234 Taylor Street
PO Box 1326
Littleton, MA 01460

978-486-9201
800-343-8204
Fax: 978-486-8759
E-mail: kjasmine@sundancepub.com
http://www.sindancepub.com

A supplementary educational publisher of instructional materials for shared, guided, and independent reading, phonics, and comprehension skills for grades K-9. Some of its programs include AlphKids, SunLit Fluency, Popcorns and LittleReaders. Its Second Chance Reading Program for below-level readers features high-interest titles, written for upper elementary/middle school students. It also distributes paperback editions of some of the most widely taught literature titles forgrades K-1

Katherine Jasmine, VP Marketing

5025 Synergistic Systems
2297 Hunters Run Drive
Reston, VA 20191-2834

703-758-9213

Science education curriculum materials.

5026 TASA
PO Box 382
Brewster, NY 10509-0382

845-277-8100
800-800-2598
Fax: 845-277-3548

Degrees of Literacy Power Program; English Language Profiles, primary, standard and advanced DRP tests, Degrees of World Meaning Tests.

5027 TL Clark Incorporated
5111 SW Avenue
St. Louis, MO 63110

314-865-2525
800-859-3815
Fax: 314-865-2240
E-mail: general@tlclarkinc.com
http://www.tlclarkinc.com

Educational products for grades Pre-K-3. Rest time products including cots and mats, sand and water play tubs, active play items including tunnels, tricycles and foam play items.

Jim Fleminla, President

5028 TMC/Soundprints
353 Main Avenue
Norwalk, CT 06851-1508

203-846-2274
800-228-7839
Fax: 203-846-1776
E-mail: sndprnts@ixinctcom.com
http://www.soundprints.com

Children's story books for children ages 4 through 8 under the license of the Smithsonian Institute and the National Wildlife Federation. Each 32 page four color book highlights a unique aspect of the animal featured in the book so asto provide education while still being entertaining. Each book can be bought with an audiocassette read-a-long and plush toy. Over 80 books in print.

Ashley Anderson, Associate Publisher
Chelsea Shriver

5029 Tambourine Books
1350 Avenue of the Americas
New York, NY 10019-4702

212-261-6500
Fax: 212-261-6518

A wide variety of books to increase creativity and reading skills in students.

5030 Taylor & Francis Publishers
7625 Empire Drive
Florence, KY 41042

800-624-7064
Fax: 800-248-4724

Publisher of professional texts and references in several fields including the behavioral sciences; arts, humanities, social sciences, science technology and medicine.

Chris Smith, Customer Service Manager

5031 Teacher's Friend Publications
3240 Trade Center Drive
Riverside, CA 92507

909-682-4748
800-343-9680
Fax: 909-682-4680

Complete line of the original monthly and seasonal Creative Idea Books. Plus, two new cooperative-learning language series and much more.

Karen Sevaly, Author
Richard Sevaly, President/CEO
Kim Marsh, National Sales Manager

5032 Theme Connections
Perfection Learning
PO Box 500
Logan, IA 51546-0500

800-831-4190
Fax: 712-644-2392

Features 135 best-selling literature titles and related theme libraries for students to develop lifelong learning strategies.

5033 Ther-A-Play Products
PO Box 2030
Lodi, CA 95241-2030

209-368-6787
800-308-6749
Fax: 209-365-2157
E-mail: madgic@attbi.com

Children's books, play therapy books, sandplay and sandtray manipulatives, puppets, games, doll houses and furniture. Playmobile and educational toys, specializing in counselors' tools. Books on abuses, illness, death, behavior andparenting.

Madge Geiszler, Owner

5034 Thomson Learning
115 5th Avenue
New York, NY 10003-1004

212-979-2210
800-880-4253
Fax: 248-699-8061

Book publisher of library and classroom-oriented educational resources for children and young adults. Over 200 books are available in 30 different subjects.

5035 Time-Life Books
2000 Duke Street
Alexandria, VA 22314-3414

703-838-7000
Fax: 703-838-7166

A wide-ranging selection of quality reference and supplemental books for students from elementary to high school.

5036 Tiny Thought Press
1427 S Jackson Street
Louisville, KY 40208-2720

502-637-6916
Fax: 502-634-1693

Children's books that build character and self-esteem.

5037 **Tom Snyder Productions**
80 Coolidge Hill Road
Watertown, MA 02472

800-342-0236
Fax: 800-304-1254
E-mail: ask@tomsynder.com
http://www.tomsynder.com

Developer and publisher of educational software.

John McAndrews, Contact

5038 **Tor Books/Forge/SMP**
175 5th Avenue
New York, NY 10010-7703

212-388-0100
Fax: 212-388-0191

Science-fiction and fantasy children's books, mysteries, Westerns, general fiction and classics publications.

5039 **Tricycle Press**
PO Box 7123
Berkeley, CA 94707-0123

510-559-1600
800-841-2665
Fax: 510-559-1637

Publisher of books and posters for children ages 2-12 and their grown-ups. Catalog available.

Christine Longmuir, Publicity/Marketing

5040 **Troll Associates**
100 Corporate Drive
Mahwah, NJ 07430-2322

201-529-4000
Fax: 201-529-8282

Publisher of children's books and products, including paperbacks and hardcovers, special theme units, read-alongs, videos, software and big books.

5041 **Trumpet Club**
1540 Broadway
New York, NY 10036-4039

212-492-9595

School book club featuring hardcover and paperback books, in class text sets and author video visits.

5042 **Turn-the-Page Press**
203 Baldwin Avenue
Roseville, CA 95678-5104

916-786-8756
800-959-5549
Fax: 916-786-9261
E-mail: mleeman@ibm.net
http://www.turnthepage.com

Books, cassettes and videos focusing on early childhood education.

Michael Leeman, President

5043 **USA Today**
1000 Wilson Boulevard
Arlington, VA 22209-3901

703-276-3400
Fax: 703-854-2103

Educational programs focusing on social studies.

5044 **Upstart Books**
PO Box 800
Fort Atkinson, WI 53538-0800

920-563-9571
800-558-2110
Fax: 920-563-7395
http://www.hpress.highsmith.com

Publishes teacher activity resources, reading activities, library and information seeking skills, Internet.

Matt Mulder, Director
Virginia Harrison, Editor

5045 **Useful Learning**
711 Meadow Lane Court
Apartment 12
Mount Vernon, IA 52314-1549

319-895-6155
800-962-3855

The Useful Spelling Textbook series for Grades 2-8, represents a curriculum based upon the scientific knowledge of research studies conducted during the past 80 years at The University of Iowa, Iowa City, IA. Incorporates the NewIowa Spelling Scale and is composed of qualitative curriculum, qualitative learning practices and qualitative instructional procedures.

Larry D. Zenor, PhD, President
Bradley M Loomer, PhD, Board Chairman

5046 **VIDYA Books**
PO Box 7788
Berkeley, CA 94707-0788

510-527-9932
Fax: 510-527-2936

Supplemental materials about India and the surrounding region for K-12 lesson plans.

5047 **Viking Children's Books**
375 Hudson Street
New York, NY 10014-3658

212-941-8780

General hardcover children's books, from toddler through young adult, fiction and nonfiction.

5048 **Vision 23**
Twenty-Third Publications
185 Willow Street
Mystic, CT 06355-2636

860-536-2611
Fax: 800-572-0788

A wide variety of children's products including books, games, clothing and toys.

5049 **WH Freeman & Company**
41 Madison Avenue
New York, NY 10010-2202

212-576-9400
Fax: 212-481-1891

Books relating to the world of mathematics.

5050 **WORLD OF DIFFERENCE Institute**
Anti-Defamation League
823 United Nations Plaza
New York, NY 10017-3518

212-490-2525
Fax: 212-867-0779
E-mail: webmaster@adl.org
http://www.adl.org

Materials and training, as well as Pre K-12 curriculum resources, Anti-bias and diversity.

Lindsay J Friedman, Director

5051 **Wadsworth Publishing School Group**
10 Davis Drive
Belmont, CA 94002-3002

650-595-2350
Fax: 800-522-4923

College and advanced placement/honors high school materials in biology, chemistry and environmental science.

5052 Walker & Company
435 Hudson Street
New York, NY 10014-3941
212-727-8300
800-289-2553
Fax: 212-727-0984
http://www.walkerbooks.com

Hardcover and paperback trade titles for Pre-K-12th grade, including picture books, photo essays, fiction and nonfiction titles appropriate for every curriculum need.

5053 Warren Publishing House
11625-G Airport Road
Everett, WA 98204-3790
425-353-3100

New Totline Teaching Tales with related activities plus quality whole language teacher activity books including Alphabet Theme-A-Saurus and Piggyback Songs.

5054 Waterfront Books
85 Crescent Road
Burlington, VT 05401-4126
802-658-7477
800-639-6063
Fax: 802-860-1368
E-mail: helpkids@waterfrontbooks.com
http://www.waterfrontbooks.com

Publishes and distributes books on special issues for children: barriers to learning, coping skills, mental health, prevention strategies, family/parenting, etc. for grades K-12. Titles include: The Divorce Workbook; Josh, a Boy with Dyslexia; What's a Virus, Anyway? The Kids' Book About AIDS and more.

Sherrill N Musty, Publisher
Michelle Russell, Order Fulfillment

5055 Web Feet Guides
Rock Hill Communications
14 Rock Hill Road
Bala Cynwyd, PA 19004
610-667-2040
888-762-5445
Fax: 610-667-2291
E-mail: info@rockhillcommunications.com
http://www.webfeetguides.com

The premier subject guides to the Internet, rigorously reviewed by librarians and educators, fully annotated, expanded and updated monthly. Appropriate for middle school through adult. Available in print, online, or marc records. For more information, free trials and Web casts, and free interactive Web Quests for your K-8 students, visit our Web site.

Linda Smith, Marketing Coordinator

5056 West Educational Publishing
620 Opperman Drive
#645779
Saint Paul, MN 55123-1340

A leader in quality social studies textbooks and ancillaries for grades K-12.

5057 Western Psychological Services
12031 Wilshire Boulevard
Los Angeles, CA 90025-1251
310-478-2061
800-648-8857
Fax: 310-478-7838
http://www.wpspublish.com

Assessment tools for professionals in education, psychology and allied fields. Offer a variety of tests, books, software and therapeutic games.

5058 Wildlife Conservation Society
Bronx Zoo
Education Department
2300 Southern Boulevard
Bronx, NY 10460
718-220-5131
800-937-5131
Fax: 718-733-4460
E-mail: sscheio@wes.org
http://www.wcs.com

Environmental science and conservation biology curriculum materials and information regarding teacher training programming for Grades K-12, on site or off site, nationally and locally. Science programming for grades pre-K-12 available on site.

Sydell Schein, Manager/Program Services
Ann Robinson, Director National Programs

5059 William Morrow & Company
1350 Avenue of the Americas
New York, NY 10019-4702
212-261-6500
Fax: 212-261-6518

High quality hardcover and paperback books for children.

5060 Winston Derek Publishers
101 French Landing Drive
Nashville, TN 37228-1511
615-321-0535

A cross section of African American books and educational materials, including preschool and primary grade books.

5061 Wolfram Research
100 Trade Centre Drive
Champaign, IL 61820-7237
800-441-MATH
Fax: 217-398-1108

Offers mathematics publications, statistics and information to educators of grades K-12.

5062 Workman Publishing
708 Broadway
New York, NY 10003-9508
212-254-5900
Fax: 212-254-8098

Children's curriculum, books, textbooks, workbooks, fiction and nonfiction titles.

5063 World & I
News World Communications
2800 New York Avenue NE
Washington, DC 20002-1945
202-636-3365
800-822-2822
Fax: 202-832-5780
E-mail: ckim@worldandimag.com
http://www.worldandi.com

With over 40 articles each month, The World & I presents an enlightening look at our changing world through the eyes of noted scholars and experts covering current issues, the arts, science, book reviews, lifestyles, cultural perspectives, philosophical trends, and the millennium. For educators, students and libraries. Free teacher's guides year round. Also, online archives available at www.worldandi.com.

Charles Kim, Business Director

5064 World Association of Publishers, Manufacturers & Distributors
Worlddidac
Bollwerk 21, PO Box 8866 CH-3001
Berne
Switzerland

41-31-3121744
Fax: 41-31-3121744
E-mail: info@worlddidac.org

A worldwide listing of over 330 publishers, manufacturers and distributors of educational materials. Listings include all contact information, products and school levels/grades.

160 pages Annual
Beat Jost, Coordinating Education

5065 World Bank
1818 H Street NW
Room T-8061
Washington, DC 20433-0002

202-477-1234
Fax: 202-477-6391

Maps, poster kits, case studies and videocassettes that teach about life in developing countries.

5066 World Book Educational Products
525 W Monroe Street
20th Floor
Chicago, IL 60661

312-729-5800
Fax: 312-729-5600

Reference books and the World Book Encyclopedia on CD-Rom.

5067 World Eagle
111 King Street
Littleton, MA 01460-1527

978-486-9180
800-854-8273
Fax: 978-486-9652
E-mail: info@ibaradio.org
http://www.worldeagle.com

Publishes an online, social studies educational resource magazine: comparative data, graphs, maps and charts on world issues. Publishes world regional atlases, and supplies maps and curriculum materials.

Valentina Bardawil Powers, Author
Martine Crandall-Hollick, President

5068 World Resources Institute
1709 New York Avenue NW
Washington, DC 20006-5206

202-729-7600
Fax: 202-729-7610

Environmental education materials, including teachers' guides, research and reference materials and computer software.

5069 Worth Publishers
33 Irving Plaza
New York, NY 10003-2332

212-475-6000
Fax: 212-689-2383

A balanced and comprehensive account of the U.S. past is accompanied by an extensive set of supplements.

5070 Wright Group
19201 120th Avenue NE
Bothell, WA 98011-9507

800-523-2371
Fax: 425-486-7704
http://www.wrightgroup.com

Supplementary program materials for reading education.

5071 Write Source Educational Publishing House
PO Box 460
Burlington, WI 53105-0460

262-763-8258
Fax: 262-763-2651

Publishes Writers Express, a writing, thinking and learning handbook series for grades 4 and 5. Also offer the latest editions of Write Source 2000 and Writers INC for grades 6-8 and 9-12.

5072 Zaner-Bloser K-8 Catalog
2200 W 5th Avenue
Columbus, OH 43215

614-486-0221
800-421-3018
Fax: 614-487-2699
http://www.zaner-bloser.com

Publisher of handwriting materials and reading, writing, spelling and study skills programs.

Robert Page, President

5073 Zephyr Press
PO Box 66006
Tucson, AZ 85728-6006

520-322-5090
800-232-2187
Fax: 520-323-9402
E-mail: neways2learn@zephyrpress.com
http://www.zephyrpress.com

Zephyr Press publishes effective, state-of-the-art-teaching materials for classroom use.

Joey Tanner MEd, President

5074 ZooBooks
ZooBooks/Wildlife Education. Ltd.
12233 Thatcher Court
Poway, CA 92064-6880

619-513-7600
800-477-5034
Fax: 858-513-7660
E-mail: animals@zoobooks.com
http://www.zoobooks.com

Reference books offering fascinating insights into the world of wildlife. Created in collaboration with leading scientists and educators, these multi-volume Zoobooks make important facts and concepts about nature, habitat and wildlifeunderstandable to children. From alligators to zebras, aquatic to exotic, each Zoobook is colorful, scientifically accurate and easy to read.

General

5075 AVKO Dyslexia Research Foundation
3084 W Willard Road
Clio, MI 48420-7801

810-686-9283
Fax: 810-686-1101
E-mail: avkomail@aol.com
http://www.avko.org

Comprised of teachers and individuals interested in helping others learn to read and spell. Develops reading training materials for individuals with dyslexia or other learning disabilities using a method involving audio, visual,kinesthetic and oral diagnosis and remediation. Conducts research into the causes of reading, spelling and writing disabilities.

Donald J McCabe, Executive Director

5076 Assistive Technology Clinics
Children's Hospital
1056 E 19th Avenue
#030
Denver, CO 80218-1007

303-861-6250
Fax: 303-764-8214

A diagnostic clinic providing evaluation, information and support to families with children with disabilities in the areas of seating and mobility. Offers augmentative communication and assistive technology access.

Tracey Kovach, Coordinator

5077 Center for Equity and Excellence in Education
George Washington University
1730 N Lynn Street
Suite 401
Arlington, VA 22209

703-528-3588
Fax: 703-528-5973
E-mail: ceeeinfo@ceee.gwu.edu
http://www.ceee.gwu.edu

Mission is to advance education reform so that all students achieve high standards. Operates under the umbrella of the Institute for Education Policy Studies within the Graduate School of Education and Human Development. Designs andconducts program evaluation for states, districts and schools and conducts program evalutaion, policy and applied research effecting equitable educational opportunities for all students.

Dr. Charlene Rivera, Director/Research Professor

5078 Center for Learning
The Center for Learning
24600 Detroit Road
Suite 201
Westlake, OH 44145

440-250-9341
800-767-9090
Fax: 440-250-9715
E-mail: customerservice@centerforlearning.org
http://www.centerforlearning.org

Sopplementary curriculum units for all grade levels in English, Language Arts, Novel-Dramas, and Social Studies.

JoAnn Wagner, Office Administrator

5079 Center for Research on the Context of Teaching
Stanford University
School of Education, CERAS Building
Stanford, CA 94305

650-723-4972
Fax: 650-723-7578

Conducts research on ways in which secondary school teaching and learning are affected by their contexts.

5080 Center for Research on the Education of Students Placed at Risk
Johns Hopkins University
3003 N Charles Street
Baltimore, MD 21218-2404

410-516-8800
Fax: 410-516-8890
http://www.csos.jhu.edu

Conducts research, development, evaluation and dissemination to transform schooling for students placed at risk, especially by supporting a talent development model of school organization and instruction.

James McPortland, Director
Marc Cutright, Communication Director

5081 Center for Social Organization of Schools
Johns Hopkins University
3003 N Charles Street
Suite 200
Baltimore, MD 21218-3888

410-516-0370
Fax: 410-516-8890
E-mail: jmcpartland@csos.jhu.edu

Explores how schools can foster growth in student learning and development.

James McPartland, Director
Joyce Epstein, Director

5082 Center for Technology in Education
Bank Street College of Education
610 W 112th Street
New York, NY 10025-1898

212-875-4467
Fax: 212-875-4753

Studies and demonstrates the role technology can play in improving student learning and achievement in schools.

Jan Hawkins, Director

5083 Center for the Study of Reading
University of Illinois
175 Children's Research Center
Champaign, IL 61820

217-333-2552
Fax: 217-244-4501

Conducts basic and applied research on the better understanding of reading.

Richard C Anderson, Director

5084 Center for the Study of Small/Rural Schools
University of Oklahoma
555 E Constitution Street
Room 138
Norman, OK 73072-7820

405-325-1450
Fax: 405-325-7075
E-mail: jcsimmons@ou.edu
http://cssrs.ou.edu

Provides services to small and/or rural schools while conducting research projects that generate knowledge to improve the quality of education.

Jan C Simmons, Director

5085 Center on Families, Schools, Communities & Children's Learning
Northeastern University
50 Nightingale Hall
Boston, MA 02215

617-373-2595
Fax: 617-373-8924

Examines how families, communities and schools can work in partnership to promote children's motivation, learning and development, including disseminating information.

Don Davies, Co-Director

5086 Center on Organization & Restructuring of Schools
1025 W Johnson Street
Madison, WI 53706-1706
608-263-7575
Fax: 608-263-6448

Focuses on restructuring K-12 schools in various areas of student development and progress.

Fred M Newman, Director

5087 Cirriculum Research and Development Group
1776 University Avenue
Honolulu, HI 96822-2463
808-956-4949
800-799-8111
Fax: 808-956-6730
E-mail: crdg@hawaii.edu
http://www.hawaii.edu/crdg

Develops new curricular and instructional materials for K-12. Professional development for teachers and ongoing assistance to schools that adopt our programs is also offered.

Lani Abrigana, Marketing Manager
Glen Schmitt, Marketing Specialist

5088 Council for Educational Development and Research
National Education Association (NEA)
1201 16th Street NW
Washington, DC 20036-3207
202-822-7364
Fax: 202-822-7624
E-mail: ncuea@nea.org
http://www.nea.org

Advances research and development in education.

E Joseph Schneider, Executive Director

5089 Division for Research
The Council for Exceptional Children
1920 Association Drive
Reston, VA 20191-1545
703-620-3660
888-232-7733
Fax: 703-264-9494

Association devoted to the advancement of research in the education of individuals with disabilities and/or who are gifted. Members include university personnel, teachers, researchers, administrators and others.

5090 Educational Information & Resource Center
Research Department
606 Delsea Drive
Sewell, NJ 08080-9399
856-582-7000
Fax: 856-582-4206

Provides information on education-related services and programs to parents, schools and communities.

Art Rainear, Director

5091 Educational Products Information Exchange Institute
103 W Montauk Highway
Suite 3
Hampton Bays, NY 11946-4003
631-728-9100
Fax: 631-728-9228

Analyzes all types of teaching materials such as textbooks, tests and computer software.

Ken Komoski, Director

5092 Educational Research Service
2000 Clarendon Boulevard
Arlington, VA 22201-2908
703-243-2100
800-759-9308
Fax: 703-243-1985
E-mail: ers@ers.org
http://www.ers.org

ERS is an independent, nonprofit research organization founded in 1973 by seven national education assocations of school management. Offers objective research and information to school district administrators. Publishes reports andperiodicals dealing with issues in school management, instruction, curriculum and compensation.

Dr. John Forsyth, President
Katherin A Behmens, Sr Director Marketing

5093 Educational Testing Service
Rosedale Road
MS 26-C
Princeton, NJ 08541
609-921-9000
Fax: 609-734-5410

Private educational measurement institution and a leader in educational research.

Susan Keipper, Program Director

5094 Florida Atlantic University-Multifunctional Resource Center
1515 W Commercial Boulevard
Suite 303
Boco Raton, FL 33309-3095
561-297-3000
800-328-6721
Fax: 561-297-2141

Provides training and technical assistance to Title VII-funded classroom instructional projects and other programs serving limited-English proficient students.

Dr. Ann C Willig, Director
Elaine Sherr, Research Assistant

5095 Higher Education Center
National Education Association (NEA)
1201 16th Street NW
Washington, DC 20036-3207
202-822-7162
Fax: 202-822-7624
E-mail: ncuea@nea.org
http://www.nea.org

The center provides data and other research products to NEA higher education affiliates. The Research Advisory Group, composed of higher education leaders and staff, meets twice a year to review products from the NEA Research Centerfor Higher Education and make recommendations about additional research needs. The center currently provides salary reports, Higher Education Contract Analysis System, and budget analysis.

5096 Information Center on Education
Eba Room 385
Albany, NY 12234-0001
518-474-8716
Fax: 518-473-7737

Coordinates data collection procedures within the New York State Education Department.

Leonard Powell, Director

5097 Information Exchange
Maine State Library
64 State House Station
Augusta, ME 04333-0064
207-287-5620
800-322-8899
Fax: 207-287-5624

Provides access to the latest education research and information for teachers.

Edna M Comstock, Director

5098 Institute for Research in Learning Disabilities
The University of Kansas
3060 Robert
Lawrence, KS 66045-0001
785-864-4780
Fax: 785-864-5728

Although the focus of the Institute's research is children, they have a sizeable publication list with some of their research having relevance for adults.

5099 Instructional Materials Laboratory
University of Missouri-Columbia
8 London Hall
Columbia, MO 65211-2230
314-882-2884

Prepares and disseminates instructional materials for the vocational education community.

Dr. Harley Schlichting, Director

5100 Learning Research and Development Center
University of Pittsburgh
3939 O'Hara Street
Pittsburgh, PA 15260
412-624-7020
Fax: 412-624-9149
E-mail: asklrdc@vms.cis.pitt.edu
http://www.lrdc.pitt.edu

Interdisciplinary center conducting fundamental and applied research in learning in schools, workplaces, and other institutions, investigates cognitive processes involved in learning and instruction; engages in analysis and design ofteaching and training programs; and disseminates findings to other researchers, practitioners, and policy makers.

Lauren Resnick, Director
Alan Lesgold, Executive Associate

5101 Life Lab Science Program
1156 High Street
Santa Cruz, CA 95064-1077
831-459-2001
Fax: 831-459-3483
E-mail: lifelab@zzyx.ucsc.edu
http://www.lifelab.org

Develops and provides garden-centered educational programs connecting science to all other areas of learning.

Jane Delgado, Director

5102 Merrimack Education Center
101 Mill Road
Chelmsford, MA 01824-4899
978-256-3985
Fax: 978-256-6890

Offers programs and services to teachers and students with a special focus on technology.

Richard Lavin, Director

5103 Mid-Atlantic Regional Educational Laboratory
13th & Cecil B Moore
933 Ritter Annex
Philadelphia, PA 19122
215-204-3030
Fax: 215-204-5130

E-mail: mmurphy@vum.temple.edu
http://www.temple.edu/lss

The Regional Educational Laboratories are educational research and development organizations supported by contracts with the US Education Department. Specialty area: Education Leadership.

JoAnn Manning, Executive Director
Marilyn Murphy, Outreach/Dissemination

5104 Mid-Continent Regional Educational Laboratory
2550 S Parker Road
Suite 500
Aurora, CO 80014-1678
303-337-0990
Fax: 303-337-3005

Focuses on improvement of education practices in Colorado, Kansas, Missouri, Nebraska, Wyoming, North Dakota and South Dakota.

C. Lawrence Hutchins, Director

5105 Midwestern Regional Educational Laboratory
1900 Spring Road
Suite 300
Oak Brook, IL 60521
630-649-6500
Fax: 630-649-6700
E-mail: nowakows@ncrel.org

The Regional Educational Laboratories are educational research and development organizations supported by contracts with the US Education Department, Office of Educational Research and Improvement. Specialty area: Technology.

Dr. Jeri Nowakowski, Executive Director

5106 Missouri LINC
401 E Stewart Road
Columbia, MO 65211
573-882-2733
800-392-0533
Fax: 573-882-5071

Serves students with special needs through a resource and technical assistance center.

Linda Bradley, Director

5107 Music Teachers National Association
441 Vine Street
Suite 505
Cincinnatti, OH 45202
513-421-1420

Research reports dealing with any aspects of music, music teaching, music learning and related subjects.

Rachel Kramer, Executive Director Programs

5108 NEA Foundatrion for tHe Improvement of Education
1201 16th Street NW
Washington, DC 20036-3207
202-822-7840
Fax: 202-822-7779
E-mail: info@nfie.org
http://www.nife.org

Works through grants, publications and reports to give educators the resources they need to create better learning environments for students.

5109 National Black Child Development Institute
1101 15th Street NW
Suite 900
Washington, DC 20005-2618
800-556-2234
Fax: 202-833-8222
E-mail: moreinfoe@nbcdi.org
http://www.nbcdi.org

Offers information and training to advocates, educators, and childcare professionals on African American children.

Vicki D Pinkston, VP
Cerrell Winder, Program Associate

5110 National Center for Improving Science Education
2000 L Street NW
Suite 616
Washington, DC 20036-4917
202-467-0652
Fax: 202-467-0659

Promotes change in state and local policies and practices in science curricula, teaching, and assessment.

Senta A Raizen, Director

5111 National Center for Research in Mathematical Sciences Education
University of Wisconsin-Madison
1025 W Johnson Street
#557
Madison, WI 53706-1706
608-263-4285
Fax: 608-263-3406

Provides a research base for the reform of school mathematics.

Thomas A Romberg, Director

5112 National Center for Research in Vocational Education
University of California, Berkeley
2030 Addison Street
Suite 500
Berkeley, CA 94720-1674
510-642-0323
800-762-4093
E-mail: NCRVE@berkeley.edu
http://http://vocserve.berkeley.edu

Enables educators, employers, researchers and policymakers to stay up-to-date on work-related education reform. Offers hands-on guides for educators interested in developing or redesigning a career development system.

5113 National Center for Research on Teacher Learning
Michigan State University, College of Education
116 Erickson Hall
East Lansing, MI 48824-1034
517-355-9302
Fax: 517-432-2795

Researches the development of elementary and secondary teacher expertise in teaching the subjects of the curriculum.

Bob Fludon, Director

5114 National Center for Science Teaching & Learning
Ohio State University
1314 Kinnear Road
Columbus, OH 43212-1156
614-292-3339
Fax: 614-292-0263

Seeks to understand how non-curricular factors affect how science is taught in grades K-12.

Arthur L White, Director

5115 National Center for the Study of Privatization in Education
525 West 120th Street
Box 181
New York, NY 10027
212-678-3259
Fax: 212-678-3474
E-mail: ncspe@columbia.edu

An independent research center.

5116 National Center on Education & the Economy
39 State Street
Suite 500
Rochester, NY 14614-1312
888-361-6233
Fax: 585-482-1284
http://www.ncee.org

Develops proposals for building a world-class education and training system.

Marc S Tucker, Director

5117 National Center on Education in the Inner Cities
Temple University
13th Street & Cecil B Moore Avenue
Philadelphia, PA 19122
215-893-8400
Fax: 215-735-9718

Conducts systematic studies of innovative initiatives for improving the quality and outcomes of schooling and broad-based efforts to strengthen and improve education.

Margaret C Wang, Director

5118 National Child Labor Committee
1501 Broadway
Suite 1111
New York, NY 10036-5592
212-840-1801
Fax: 212-768-0963

Produces and disseminates information on youth employment and child labor laws with the aim of advocating the rights and dignity of youth.

Jeffrey Newman, Director

5119 National Clearinghouse for Alcohol & Drug Information
PO Box 2345
Rockville, MD 20847-2345
301-468-2600
800-729-6686
Fax: 301-468-6433
http://health.org

Serves to collect, disseminate and exchange alcohol and drug information.

John Noble, Director

5120 National Clearinghouse for Bilingual Education
George Washington University
2121 K Street NW
Suite 260
Washington, DC 20037-1214
202-467-0867
800-321-6223
E-mail: askncbe@ncbe.gwu.edu
http://www.ncbe.gwu.edu

Provides information to practitioners on the education of language minority students. Operates a web site, sponsors discussion groups and an electronic newsletter.

Dr. Minerva Gorena, Director

5121 National Clearinghouse for Information on Business Involvement in Education
National Association for Industry-Education Co-op
235 Hendricks Boulevard
Buffalo, NY 14226-3304
716-834-7047
Fax: 718-834-7047
E-mail: www2.pecom/naiec
http://www2.pecom.net/naiec

Seeks to foster industry-education cooperation in the US and Canada in the areas of school improvement, career education and human resource/economic development.

Dr. Donald Clark, Director

5122 National Dropout Prevention Center
Clemson University
209 Martin Street
Clemson, SC 29631-1555

864-656-2599
800-443-6392
Fax: 864-656-0136
E-mail: NDPC@clemson.edu
http://www.dropoutprevention.org

Seeks to reduce America's dropout rate significantly by fostering public-private partnerships in local school districts and communities throughout the nation.

Dr. Jay Smink, Director
Mary Reimen, Information Resource

5123 National Early Childhood Technical Assistance System
137 E Franklin Street
Room 500
Chapel Hill, NC 27514

919-962-2001
Fax: 919-966-7463
http://www.nectas.unc.edu

Provides technical assistance to state agencies and model projects sponsored by the US Dept of Education in the development of services for children with special needs and their families.

Pascal Trohanis, Director

5124 National Information Center for Educational Media
PO Box 8640
Albuquerque, NM 87198-8640

505-265-3591
800-926-8328
Fax: 505-256-1080
E-mail: nicem@nicem.com
http://www.nicem.com

Maintains the world's largest database of information about educational media and materials and makes the information available on CD-rom and the Internet.

Marjorie Hlava, President
Lisa Savard, Sales/Marketing Director

5125 National Research Center on the Gifted & Talented
University of Connecticut
362 Fairfield Road
Unit U-7
Storrs Mansfield, CT 06269-2007

860-486-4826
Fax: 860-486-2900

Conducts research on methods and techniques for teaching gifted and talented students.

Joseph S Renzulli, Director
Phillip E Austin, President

5126 National Resource Center on Self-Care & School-Age Child Care
American Home Economics Association
1555 King Street
Alexandria, VA 22314-2738

703-706-4620
800-252-SAFE
Fax: 703-706-4663

Provides materials to parents, educators, child care professionals and others concerned about the number of latchkey children and about quality school-age child care.

Dr. Margaret Plantz, Director

5127 National School Boards Association Library
1680 Duke Street
Alexandria, VA 22314-3455

703-838-6731
Fax: 703-683-7590

Maintains up-to-date collection of resources concerning education issues, with an emphasis on school board policy issues.

Adria Thomas, Director

5128 National School Safety Center
14 Duesenberg Drive
Suite 11
Westlake Village, CA 91362-3815

805-373-9977
Fax: 805-373-9277

Provides training, technical assistance and resources on school safety and school crime prevention.

Dr. Ronald Stephens, Executive Director
June Arnette, Editor

5129 National Science Resources Center
901 D Street Sw
Suite 704B
Washington, DC 20024

202-633-2792
Fax: 202-287-2070
E-mail: nsrcinfo@si.edu
http://www.nsrconline.org

Works to improve teaching of science in the nation's schools. Through national outreach to build consensus, dissemination of information on resources for teaching science, and development of curriculum materials. NSRC offers strategicplanning institutes for school district teams every summer. Operated by the Smithsonian Institution and the National Academies.

Sally Shuler, Executive Director

5130 North Central Regional Educational Laboratory
1120 E Diehl Drive
Suite 200
Naperville, IL 60563

630-649-6500
Fax: 630-649-6700
E-mail: info@ncrel.org
http://www.ncrel.org

Applies research and technology to learning. Makes connections between researchers and educators on a wide variety of topics.

Gina Burkhard, Executive Director

5131 Northeast Regional Center for Drug-Free Schools & Communities
12 Overton Avenue
Sayville, NY 11782-2437

718-340-7000
Fax: 516-589-7894

Works to support the prevention of alcohol and other drug use in the northeast region of the United States.

Dr. Gerald Edwards, Director

5132 Northeast and Islands Regional Educational Laboratory
222 Richmond Street
Suite 300
Providnce, RI 02903

401-274-9548
800-521-9550
Fax: 401-421-7650
E-mail: info@lab.brown.edu
http://www.lab.brown.edu

The LAB at Brown University is one of ten federally funded labs performing applied research and development to improve teaching and learning and promote effective school reform. We focus on education issues in New England, New York,Puerto Rico and the

Virgin Islands. Our national leadership area is teaching diverse learners. We examine ways that learning standards, portfolio assessment systems and math and science instructional practices can be revised to more effectivelychallenge students.

Lisa DiMartino, Administrative Assistant
Eileen Harrington, Public Information Associate

5133 Northwest Regional Educational Laboratory
101 SW Main Street
Suite 500
Portland, OR 97204-3297

503-275-9500
800-547-6339
Fax: 503-275-0458
E-mail: info@nwrel.org
http://www.nwrel.org

The Regional Educational Laboratories are educational research and development organizations supported by contracts with the US Education Department, Office of Educational Research and Improvement. Specialty area: school changeprocesses.

Carol F Thomas, CEO

5134 Pacific Regional Educational Laboratory
1099 Alakea Street
Suite 2500
Honolulu, HI 96813

808-969-3482
Fax: 808-969-3483
E-mail: kofelj@prel.hawaii.edu

The Regional Educational Laboratories are educational research and development organizations supported by contracts with the U.S. Education Department, Office of Educational Research and Improvement. Specialty area: Language andCultural Diversity.

Dr. John Kofel, Executive Director

5135 Parent Educational Advocacy Training Center
10340 Democracy Lane
Fairfax, VA 22030

703-923-0010
800-869-6782
Fax: 703-923-0030
E-mail: partners@peatc.org
http://www.peatc.org

Serves parents and professionals in translating the legal rights of children with disabilities into opportunities for participation in the school and community.

Deidre Hayden, Director

5136 Parents as Teachers National Center
2228 Ball Drive
Saint Louis, MO 63146

314-432-4330
Fax: 314-432-8963
E-mail: patnc@patnc.org
http://www.patnc.org

Provides information about PAT, plus training and technical assistance for those interested in adopting the program. PAT is a home-school-community partnership designed to provide all parents from birth, (or prenatally) tokindergarten entry the information and support needed to give their children the best possible start in life. Independent evaluations show strong positive outcomes for children and parents. Publishes a quarterly newsletter.

Susan S Stepleton, President/CEO
Cheryl Dyle-Palmer, Director Operations

5137 Public Education Fund Network
601 13th Street NW
Suite 209
Washington, DC 20005-3807

202-628-7460
Fax: 202-628-1893

Dedicated to improving public education, especially for disadvantaged children.

Wendy D Puriefoy, Director

5138 Quality Education Data
1700 Lincoln Street
Suite 3600
Denver, CO 80203

303-209-9328
800-525-5811
Fax: 303-209-9444
E-mail: qedinfo@qeddata.com
http://www.qeddata.com

Gathers information about K-12 schools, colleges and other educational institutions, offers an on-line database on education, directories of public and nonpublic schools and research reports.

Jeanne Hayes, President

5139 Regional Laboratory for Educational Improvement of the Northeast
300 Brickstone Square
Suite 900
Andover, MA 01810-1435

800-347-4200
Fax: 781-481-1120

Seeks to improve education in Connecticut, Maine, Massachusetts, New Hampshire, New York, Rhode Island, Vermont, Puerto Rico and the Virgin Islands.

David P Crandall, Director

5140 Research for Better Schools
1818 N Street NW
Suite 350
Washington, DC 20036-2471

215-574-9300
Fax: 215-574-0133

Seeks to improve schools and classroom instruction in Delaware, the District of Columbia, Maryland, New Jersey and Pennsylvania.

Peter J Donahoe, Director

5141 SERVE
PO Box 5367
Greensboro, NC 27435

336-315-7400
800-755-3277
Fax: 336-315-7457
E-mail: info@serve.org
http://www.serve.org

Regional Educational Laboratories is an educational research and development organization supported by contracts with the US Education Department, National Institute for Education Sciences. Specialty area: Extended Learning Opporunityincluding Before and After School programs and Early Childhood.

Jack Sanders, Executive Director

5142 SIGI PLUS
Educational Testing Service
105 Terry Drive
Suite 120
Newtown, PA 18940-1872

800-257-7444
Fax: 215-579-8589

A computerized career guidance program developed by Educational Testing Service. Covers all the major aspects of career decision making and planning through a carefully constructed system of nine separate but interrelated sections,including a Tech Prep module and Internet Hydrolink Connectivity.

Annie Schofer, Sales Manager

5143 Satellite Educational Resources Consortium
939 S Stadium Road
Columbia, SC 29201-4724
803-252-2782
Fax: 803-252-5320

Seeks to expand educational opportunities by employing the latest telecommunication technologies to make quality education in math, science, and foreign languages available equally and cost-effectively to students regardless of theirgeographic location.

John Chambers, Director Education Services

5144 Scientific Learning
1995 University Avenue
Suite 400
Berkeley, CA 94704
888-665-9707
Fax: 510-874-1884
http://www.scientificlearning.com

Scientific Learning bases their products and services on neuroscience research and scientifically validated efficacy and deliver them using the most efficient technologies. We also provide beneficial products and services to ourcustomers that are easy to use and access.

Cynthia Myers, VP Public Affairs

5145 Smithsonian Institution/Office of Elementary & Secondary Education
PO Box 3701263
Washington, DC 20560-0001
202-357-2700
Fax: 202-357-2116
E-mail: info@si.edu

Helps K-12 teachers incorporate museums and other community resources into their curricula.

Ann Bay, Director

5146 Society for Research in Child Development
University of Chicago Press
5720 S Woodlawn Avenue
Chicago, IL 60637-1603
773-702-7700
Fax: 773-702-9756

Works to further research in the area of child development.

Barbara Kahn, Business Manager

5147 Southeast Regional Center for Drug-Free Schools & Communities
Spencerian Office Plaza
Louisville, KY 40292-0001
502-588-0052
800-621-7372
Fax: 502-588-1782

Works to support the prevention of alcohol and drug use among youth in the Southeast region.

Nancy J Cunningham, Director

5148 Southern Regional Education Board
592 10th Street NW
Atlanta, GA 30318-5790
404-875-9211
Fax: 404-872-1477

Identifies and directs attention to key education issues.

Mark D Musick, Director

5149 Southwest Comprehensive Regional Assistance Center-Region IX
New Mexico Highlands University
121 Tijeras Avenue NE
Suite 2100
Albuquerque, NM 87102-3461
800-247-4269
Fax: 505-243-4456

National network of 15 technical assistance centers, funded through the US Department of Education, designed to support federally funded educational programs. Specifically, these centers will provide comprehensive training andtechnical assistance under the Improving America's Schools Act (IASA) to States, Tribes, community based organizations, local education agencies, schools and other recipients of funds under the Act.

Paul E Martinez EdD, Director

5150 Southwestern Educational Development Laboratory
211 E 7th Street
Austin, TX 78701
512-476-6861
800-476-6861
Fax: 512-476-2286
E-mail: whoover@sedl.org
http://www.sedl.org

SEDL is a private not-for-profit corporation that conducts education research, development, technical assistance, and professional development. SEDL holds contracts with the US Education Department for the Regional EducationalLaboratory, the Eisenhower Math & Science Consortium, and the Regional Technology on Education Consortium serving Arkansas, Louisiana, New Mexico, Oklahoma and Texas.

Dr. Wesley A Hoover, Executive Director
Dr. Joyce S Pollard, Director Institutional Comm.

5151 Special Interest Group for Computer Science Education
Computer Science Department
University of Texas at Austin
Austin, TX 78712
512-471-9539
Fax: 512-471-8885

Provides a forum for solving problems common in developing, implementing and evaluating computer science education programs and courses.

Nell B Dale, Director

5152 TACS/WRRC
University of Oregon
1268 University of Oregon
Eugene, OR 97403
541-346-5641
Fax: 541-346-0322
E-mail: wrrc@oregon.uoregon.edu
http://http://interact.uoregon.edu/wrrc/wrrc.html

Supports state education agencies in their task of ensuring quality programs and services for children with disabilities and their families.

Richard Zeller, Co-Director
Caroline Moore, Co-Director

5153 TERC
2067 Massachusetts Avenue
Cambridge, MA 02140-1340
617-547-0430
Fax: 617-349-3535
E-mail: communications@terc.edu
http://www.terc.edu

Researches, develops, and disseminates innovative programs in science, mathematics and technology for educators, schools and other learning environments.

24 pages
ISSN: 0743-0221

Kenneth Mayer, Author
Peggy Kapisovsky, Communications Director

5154 UCLA Statistical Consulting
University of California, Los Angeles
8130 MSB, UCLA
PO Box 951554
Los Angeles, CA 90095-1554

310-825-8299
Fax: 310-206-5658

Provides statistical consulting services to UCLA and off-campus students. The staff is faculty members, graduate students and the Department of Statistics. Specializes in the quantitative analysis of research problems in a widevariety of fields.

Debbie Barrera, Administrator
Richard Berk, Director

Audio Visual Materials

5155 AGC/United Learning
Discovery Education
1560 Sherman Avenue
Suite 100
Evanston, IL 60201

847-328-6700
800-323-9084
Fax: 847-328-6706
http://www.discoveryed.com

A publisher/producer of educational videos and digital content K-College curriculum based.

Coni Rechner, Director Marketing
Ronald Reed, Sr. Vice President

5156 Active Parenting Publishing
810 Franklin Court
Suite B
Marietta, GA 30067

800-825-0060
Fax: 770-429-0334
E-mail: cservice@activeparenting.com
http://www.activeparenting.com

Videos and books on parenting, character education, substance abuse prevention, divorce and step-parenting, ADHD and more.

5157 Agency for Instructional Technology/AIT
PO Box A
Bloomington, IN 47402-0120

800-457-4509

Videodiscs, videocassettes, films and electronics.

5158 Allied Video Corporation
PO Box 702618
Tulsa, OK 74170-2618

918-587-6477
800-926-5892
Fax: 918-587-1550
E-mail: allied@farpointer.net
http://www.alliedvd.com

Produces the educational video series, The Assistant Professor. Animations and three-dimensional graphics clearly illustrate concepts in mathematics, science and music. Companion supplementary materials are also available.

Video

Charles Brown, President

5159 Altschul Group Corporation
1560 Sherman Avenue
Suite 100
Evanston, IL 60201-4817

800-323-9084

Video and film educational programs.

5160 Ambrose Video Publishing Inc
145 West 45th Street
New York, NY 10036

212-768-7373
800-526-4663
Fax: 212-768-9282
http://www.ambrosevideo.com

A leading distributor of broadcast quality documentation/educational videos to individuals (in the home) and schools, libraries and other institutions. The company also sells through catalog, sales staff and television advertising.

5161 Anchor Audio
3415 Lomita Boulevard
Torrance, CA 90505-5010

310-784-2300
800-262-4671
Fax: 310-784-0533
http://www.anchoraudio.com

Various audio visual products for the school and library.

5162 Association for Educational Communications & Technology
1025 Vermont Avenue NW
Suite 820
Washington, DC 20005-3516

202-347-7834

Offers a full line of videotapes and films for the various educational fields including language arts, science and social studies.

5163 BUILD Sucess Through the Values of Excellence
Center for the Study of Small/Rural Schools
555 E Constitution Street
Room 138
Norman, OK 73072-7820

405-325-1450
Fax: 405-325-7075
E-mail: jcsimmons@ou.edu
http://cssrs.ou.edu

Series IV

Video

Jan C Simmons, Director

5164 Bergwall Productions
540 Baltimore Pike
Chadds Ford, PA 19317-9304

800-645-3565

Educational videotapes and films.

5165 Cedrus
1420 Buena Vista Avenue
McLean, VA 22101-3510

703-883-0986

Videodiscs, videocassettes and filmstrips for educational purposes.

5166 Character Education
Center for the Study of Small/Rural Schools
555 E Constitution Street
Room 138
Norman, OK 73072-7820

405-325-1450
Fax: 405-325-7075
E-mail: jcsimmons@ou.edu
http://cssrs.ou.edu

Series IV

Video

Jan C Simmons, Director

5167 Chip Taylor Communications
2 E View Drive
Derry, NH 03038-5728

603-434-9262
800-876-2447
Fax: 603-432-2723
E-mail: sales@chiptaylor.com
http://www.chiptaylor.com

Quality educational videotapes and DVDs and multimedia in all areas of interest.

Video

Chip Taylor, President

5168 Churchill Media
6677 N NW Highway
Chicago, IL 60631-1304

310-207-6600
800-334-7830
Fax: 800-624-1678

Videos, videodiscs and curriculum packages for schools and libraries.

5169 College Board Publications
College Board Publications
45 Columbus Avenue
New York, NY 10023-6992

212-713-8165
800-323-7155
Fax: 800-525-5562
http://www.collegeboard.org

Offers a variety of educational videotapes and publications focusing on college issues.

5170 Computer Prompting & Captioning Company
1010 Rockville Pike
Suite 306
Rockville, MD 20852-3035

301-738-8487
800-977-6678
Fax: 301-738-8488
E-mail: info@cpcweb.com
http://www.cpcweb.com

Closed captioning systems and service.

Sid Hoffman, Project Manager

5171 Concept Media
2493 Du Bridge Avenue
Irvine, CA 92606-5022

949-660-0727
800-233-7078
Fax: 949-660-0206
E-mail: info@conceptmedia.com
http://www.conceptmedia.com

Videos for students and professionals focused on child development, early childhood education, and the challenges facing many young children. Effective educational media for development specialists, regular and special education staffin elementary school, preschool teachers, childcare providers, health care workers and parents.

Dennis Timmerman, Sr Account Executive

5172 Crystal Productions
PO Box 2159
Glenview, IL 60025-6159

847-657-8144
800-255-8629
Fax: 800-657-8149
E-mail: custserv@crystalproductions.com
http://www.crystalproductions.com

Producer and distributor of educational resource material in art and sciences. Resources include videotapes, posters, books, videodiscs, CD-Rom, reproductions, games.

132 pages

Amy Woodworth, President

5173 Dukane Corporation
Audio Visual Products Division
2900 Dukane Drive
St Charles, IL 60174-3395

630-584-2300
Fax: 630-584-5156

Full line of audio visual products, LCD display panels, computer data projectors, overhead projectors, microfilm readers and silent and sound filmstrip projectors.

Stew deLacey

5174 Early Advantage
270 Monroe Turnpike
PO Box 4063
Monroe, CT 06468-4063

888-999-4670
Fax: 800-301-9268
E-mail: customerservice@early-advantage.com
http://www.earlyadvantage.com

Features the Muzzy video collection for teaching children beginning second language skills.

5175 Educational Video Group
291 S Wind Way
Greenwood, IN 46142-9190

317-888-6581
Fax: 317-888-5857
E-mail: evg@insightbb.com
http://www.evgonline.com

Award-winning video programs and textbooks in education, presenting new offerings in speech, government and historic documentaries.

Roger Cook, President

5176 English as a Speech Language Video Series
Master Teacher
PO Box 1207
Manhattan, KS 66505-1207

785-539-0555
800-669-9633
Fax: 785-539-7739
http://www.masterteacher.com

Assessing the needs of culturally diverse learners, you will learn what must be done to evaluate the learning needs and progress of ESL students.

ISBN: 1-58992-045-7

5177 Fase Productions
4801 Wilshire Boulevard
Suite 215
Los Angeles, CA 90010-3813

213-965-8794

Educational videotapes and films.

5178 Films for Humanities & Sciences
PO Box 2053
Princeton, NJ 08543-2053

609-419-8000
800-257-5126
Fax: 609-419-8071

A leading publisher/distributor of over four thousand educational programs, including NOVA and TV Ontario, for school and college markets. Also a leader in the production and distribution of videotapes and videodiscs to theeducational, institutional and government markets.

5179 First Steps/Concepts in Motivation
18105 Town Center Drive
Olney, MD 20832-1479

301-774-9429
800-947-8377

Educational videotapes and accessories promoting physical fitness for preschoolers and young children. Using choreographed dance movement, familiar and fun children's music, colorful mats, bean bags and rhythm sticks, First Stepsteaches balance, gross and fine motor skills, rhythm, coordination, and primary learning skills.

Dale Rimmey, Marketing Director
Larry Rose, President/Owner

5180 Future of Rural Education
Center for the Study of Small/Rural Schools
555 E Constitution Street
Room 138
Norman, OK 73072-7820
405-325-1450
Fax: 405-325-7075
E-mail: jcsimmons@ou.edu
http://cssrs.ou.edu

Series I

Video

Jan C Simmons, Director

5181 GPN Year 2005 Literacy Catalog
GPN Educational Media
PO Box 80669
Lincoln, NE 68501-0669
402-472-2007
800-228-4630
Fax: 402-472-4076
E-mail: gpn@unl.edu
http://www.gpn.unl.edu

DVD, VHS, CD-ROM and slides for K-12 libraries and higher education. Free previews and satisfaction guaranteed. The sole source of Reading Rainbow and many other quality programs seen on PBS.

Annually/Video

Stephen C Lenzen, Executive Director
John Vondracek, Director Marketing

5182 Gangs in Our Schools: Identification, Response, and Prevention Strategies
Center for the Study of Small/Rural Schools
555 E Constitution Street
Room 138
Norman, OK 73072-7820
405-325-1450
Fax: 405-325-7075
E-mail: jcsimmons@ou.edu
http://cssrs.ou.edu

Series III

Video

Jan C Simmons, Director

5183 Guidance Associates
PO Box 1000
Mount Kisco, NY 10549-7000
800-431-1242
Fax: 914-666-5319
E-mail: sales@guidanceassociates.com
http://www.guidanceassociates.com

Curriculum based videos in health/guidance, social studies, math, science, English, the humanities and career education.

Will Goodman, President

5184 Health Connection
55 W Oak Ridge Drive
Hagerstown, MD 21740
800-548-8700
Fax: 888-294-8405
E-mail: sales@healthconnection.org
http://www.healthconnection.org

Tools for freedom from tobacco and other drugs.

5185 Human Relations Media
175 Tompkins Avenue
Pleasantville, NY 10570-3144
800-431-2050
Fax: 914-244-0485

Offers a wide variety of videotapes and videodiscs in the areas of guidance, social services, human relations, self-esteem and student services.

5186 IIE Passport: Short Term Study Abroad
Institute of International Education
809 United Nations Plaza
New York, NY 10017-3503
412-741-0930
Fax: 212-984-5496
E-mail: iiebooks@abdintl.com
http://www.iiebooks.org

Over 2,900 short-term study abroad programs offered by universities, schools, associations and other organizations.

Daniel Obst, Sr Editor

5187 INSIGHTS Visual Productions
374-A N Highway 101
Encinitas, CA 92024-2527
760-942-0528
Fax: 760-944-7793

Science video for K-12 and teacher training.

5188 INTELECOM Intelligent Telecommunications
150 E Colorado Boulevard
Suite 300
Pasadena, CA 91105-3710
626-796-7300
Fax: 626-577-4282

Videos and educational films.

Bob Miller, VP Marketing/Sale

5189 In Search of Character
Performance Resource Press
1270 Rankin Drive
Suite F
Troy, MI 48083-2843
800-453-7733
Fax: 800-499-5718
http://www.pronline.net

Character education videos.

5190 Instructional Resources Corporation
1819 Bay Ridge Avenue
Annapolis, MD 21403-2835

American History Videodisc.

5191 Intermedia
1165 Eastlake Ave East
Suite 400
Seattle, WA 98109-3571
206-284-2995
800-553-8336
Fax: 206-283-0778
http://www.intermedia-inc.com

Distributes a wide range of high-quality, social interest videos on topics such as teen pregnancy prevention, substance abuse prevention, domestic violence, sexual harassment, dating violence, date rape, gang education, culturaldiversity, AIDS prevention and teen patenting. Offer free 30 day previews of the programs which are developed to address the needs of educators who must deal with the pressing social problems of today.

Paperback/Video

Susan Hoffman, President
Ted Fitch, General Manager

5192 International Historic Films
3533 S Archer Avenue
Chicago, IL 60609-1135

773-927-2900
Fax: 773-927-9211
E-mail: info@ihffilm.com
http://www.ihffilm.com

Military, political and social history of the 20th century.

Video/Audio

5193 January Productions
PO Box 66
Hawthorne, NJ 07507-0066

973-423-4666
800-451-7450
Fax: 973-423-5569
E-mail: anpeller@worldnet.att.net

Educational videotapes, read-a-long books, and CD-Rom.

Paperback/Video/Audi

Lori Brown, Sales/Marketing

5194 Karol Media
350 N Pennsylvania Avenue
Wilkes Barre, PA 18702-4415

570-822-8899
Fax: 570-822-8226

Science videos.

5195 Kimbo Educational
PO Box 477
Long Branch, NJ 07740-0477

800-631-2187

Manufacturer of children's audio-musical learning fun. Also offers videos and music by other famous children's artists such as Raffi, Sharon, Lois and Bram.

5196 Leadership: Rethinking the Future
Center for the Study of Small/Rural Schools
555 E Constitution Street
Room 138
Norman, OK 73072-7820

405-325-1450
Fax: 405-325-7075
E-mail: jcsimmons@ou.edu
http://cssrs.ou.edu

Series IV

Video

Jan C Simmons, Director

5197 MPC Multimedia Products Corp
1010 Sherman Avenue
Hamden, CT 06514

203-407-4623
800-243-2108
Fax: 203-407-4636
E-mail: sales@800-pickmpc.com
http://www.800-pickmpc.com

Over 5,000 most frequently requested high quality audio, visual and video products and materials offered at deep discount prices. Manufacturer of high quality tape records,CD's record players, PA systems, headphones

148 pages BiAnnual

T. Guercia, Author
T Guercia, VP
A Melillo, Sales Manager

5198 Main Street Foundations: Building Community Teams
Center for the Study of Small/Rural Schools
555 E Constitution Street
Room 138
Norman, OK 73072-7820

405-325-1450
Fax: 405-325-7075
E-mail: jcsimmons@ou.edu
http://cssrs.ou.edu

Prevention Series

Video

Jan C Simmons, Director

5199 Marshmedia
Marsh Media
8025 Ward Parkway Plaza
Kansas City, MO 64114

816-523-1059
800-821-3303
Fax: 816-333-7421
E-mail: order@marshmedia.com
http://www.marshmedia.com

Children's educational videotapes, books and teaching guides.

32 pages Bi-Annual
ISBN: 1-55942-xxx

Joan K Marsh, President

5200 Media Projects
5215 Homer Street
Dallas, TX 75206-6623

214-826-3863
Fax: 214-826-3919
E-mail: mediaprojects@noval.net
http://www.mediaprojects.org

Educational videotapes in all areas of interest, including drug education, violence prevention, women's studies, history, youth issues and special education.

5201 Middle School: Why and How
Center for the Study of Small/Rural Schools
555 E Constitution Street
Room 138
Norman, OK 73072-7820

405-325-1450
Fax: 405-325-7075
E-mail: jcsimmons@ou.edu
http://cssrs.ou.edu

Series III

Video

Jan C Simmons, Director

5202 Multicultural Educations: Valuing Diversity
Center for the Study of Small/Rural Schools
555 E Constitution Street
Room 138
Norman, OK 73072-7820

405-325-1450
Fax: 405-325-7075
E-mail: jcsimmons@ou.edu
http://cssrs.ou.edu

Series I

Video

Jan C Simmons, Director

5203 NUVO, Ltd.
PO Box 1729
Chula Vista, CA 91912

619-426-8440
Fax: 619-691-1525
E-mail: nuvoltd@aol.com

Produces and distributes how-to videotapes for teens and adults on beginning reading and decorative napkin folding useful in classroom instruction and individual practice. Also distributes two bilingual (Spanish/English) books bypsychologist Dr. Jorge Espinoza.

5204 National Film Board
1251 Avenue of the Americas
New York, NY 10020-1104

800-542-2164
Fax: 845-774-2945

Educational films and videos ranging from documentaries on nature and science to social issues such as teen pregnancy.

5205 National Geographic School Publishing
PO Box 10579
Washington, DC 20090-8019

800-368-2728
Fax: 515-362-3366

Offers a wide variety of videodiscs, videotapes and educational materials in the area of social studies, geography, science and social sciences.

5206 PBS Video
1320 Braddock Pl
Alexandria, VA 22314-1649

703-739-5380
800-424-7963
Fax: 703-739-5269

Award-winning programs from PBS, public television's largest video distributors. Video and multimedia programming including interactive videodiscs for schools, colleges and libraries. The PBS Video Resource Catalog is organized intodetailed subject categories.

5207 PICS Authentic Foreign Video
University of Iowa
270 International Center
Iowa City, IA 52242-1802

319-335-2335
800-373-PICS
Fax: 319-335-0280

Provides educators with authentic foreign language videos in French, German and Spanish on videotapes and videodisc. Also offers software to accompany the videodiscs as well as written materials in the form of transcripts andvideoguides with pedagogical hints and tips.

Becky Bohde, German Coll Editor
Anny Ewing, French Coll Editor

5208 Penton Overseas
2470 Impala Drive
Carlsbad, CA 92008-7226

800-748-5804
Fax: 760-431-8110

Educational videotapes and videodiscs in a wide variety of interests for classroom use.

5209 Phoenix Films/BFA Educ Media/Coronet/MII
Phoenix Learning Group
2349 Chaffee Drive
St. Louis, MO 63146

314-569-0211
800-777-8100
Fax: 314-569-2834
E-mail: phoenixdealer@aol.com
http://www.phoenixlearninggroup.com

Educational multi-media - VHS, CD-Rom, DVD, streaming & broadcast.

Video

Kathy Longsworth, Vice President, Market Dev

5210 Presidential Classroom
119 Oronoco Street
Alexandria, VA 22314-2015

703-683-5400
800-441-6533
Fax: 703-548-5728
E-mail: eriedel@presidentialclassroom.org
http://www.presidentialclassroom.org

Video of civic education programs in Washington, DC for high school juniors and seniors. Each one week program provides students with an inside view of the federal government in action and their role as responsible citizens and futureleaders.

Annual
400 attendees

Jack Buechner, President/CEO
Emily Davisriedel, Director Marketing

5211 Rainbow Educational Media Charles Clark Company
4540 Preslyn Drive
Raleigh, NC 27616

919-954-7550
800-331-4047
Fax: 919-954-7554
E-mail: karencf@rainbowedumedia.com
http://www.rainbowedumedia.com

Educational videocassettes and CD-Roms.

Karen C Francis, Business Analyst

5212 Rainbow Educational Video
170 Keyland Court
Bohemia, NY 11716-2638

800-331-4047

Producer and distributor of educational videos.

Wesley Clark, Marketing Director

5213 Reading & O'Reilly: The Wilton Programs
PO Box 302
Wilton, CT 06897-0302

800-458-4274

Producers and distributors of award-winning audiovisual educational programs in art appreciation, history, multicultural education, social studies and music. Titles include: African-American Art and the Take-a-Bow, musical productionseries. Free catalog is available of full product line.

Lee Reading, President
Gretchen O'Reilly, VP

5214 SAP Today
Performance Resource Press
1270 Rankin Drive
Suite F
Troy, MI 48083-2843

800-453-7733
Fax: 800-499-5718

Overview offers the basics of student assistance.

5215 SVE: Society for Visual Education
55 E Monroe Street
Suite 3400
Chicago, IL 60603-5710

312-849-9100
800-829-1900
Fax: 800-624-1678

Producer and distributor of curriculum based instructional materials including videodisc, microcomputer software, video cassettes and filmstrips for grade levels PreK-12.

5216 Slow Learning Child Video Series
Master Teacher
PO Box 1207
Manhattan, KS 66505-1207

785-539-0555
800-669-9633
Fax: 785-539-7739
http://www.masterteacher.com

Provides a full understandging of the slow learning child and allows all educators to share in the excitment of teaching this invidual in ways that develop his or her emerging potenial to the fullest.

ISBN: 1-58992-157-0

Mildred Odom Bradley, Author

5217 Spoken Arts
PO Box 100
New Rochelle, NY 10802-0100

727-578-7600

Literature-based audio and visual products for library and K-12 classrooms.

5218 Teacher's Video Company
8150 S Krene Road
Tempe, AZ 85284

800-262-8837
Fax: 800-434-5638
http://www.teachersvideo.com

Video for teachers.

5219 Teen Court: An Alternative Approach to Juvenile Justice
Center for the Study of Small/Rural Schools
555 E Constitution Street
Room 138
Norman, OK 73072-7820

405-325-1450
Fax: 405-325-7075
E-mail: jcsimmons@ou.edu
http://cssrs.ou.edu

Prevention Series

Video

Jan C Simmons, Director

5220 Tools to Help Youth
529 S 7 Street
Suite 570
Minneapolis, MN 55415

800-328-0417
Fax: 612-342-2388
http://www.communityintervention.com

Books and videos on counseling, character education, anger management, life skills, and achohol, tobacco and other drug uses.

5221 Training Video Series for the Professional School Bus Driver
Master Teacher
PO Box 1207
Manhattan, KS 66505-1207

785-539-0555
800-669-9633
Fax: 785-539-7739
http://www.masterteacher.com

Will help you provide bus drivers with consistent direction and training for the many situations thay will encounter beyond driving safety.

ISBN: 1-58992-082-1

5222 True Colors
Center for the Study of Small/Rural Schools
555 E Constitution Street
Room 138
Norman, OK 73072-7820

405-325-1450
Fax: 405-325-7075
E-mail: jcsimmons@ou.edu
http://cssrs.ou.edu

Series III

Video

Jan C Simmons, Director

5223 United Transparencies
435 Main Street
Johnson City, NY 13790-1935

607-729-6368
800-477-6512
Fax: 607-729-4820

A full line of overhead transparencies for Junior-Senior high school and colleges and technical programs.

D Hetherington

5224 Video Project
200 Estates Drive
Ben Lomond, CA 95005

800-475-2638
Fax: 905-278-2801
E-mail: videoproject@igc.org
http://www.videoproject.org

Distributor of environmental videos with a collection of over 500 programs for all grade levels, including Oscar and Emmy award winners. Many videotapes come with teacher's guides. Free catalogs available.

Terry Thiermann, Administrative Director
Ian Thiermann, Executive Director

5225 Weston Woods Studios
265 Post Road West
Westport, CT 06880

203-845-0197
800-243-5020
Fax: 203-845-0498
E-mail: wstnwoods@aol.com

Audiovisual adaptations of classic children's literature.

Video

Cindy Cardozo, Marketing Coordinator

Classroom Materials

5226 ABC School Supply
3312 N Berkeley Lake Road NW
Duluth, GA 30096-3024

Instructional materials and supplies.

5227 ADP Lemco
5970 W Dannon Way
West Jordan, UT 84088

801-280-4000
800-575-3626
Fax: 801-280-4040
E-mail: sales@adplemco.com
http://www.adplemco.com

Announcement boards, schedule boards, chalkboards, tackboard, marker boards, trophy cases, athletic equipment, gym divider curtains and basketball backstops.

David L Hall, Sr VP

5228 APCO
388 Grant Street SE
Atlanta, GA 30312-2227

404-688-9000
Fax: 404-577-3847

Classroom supplies including announcement and chalkboards.

Anne M Gallup

5229 AbleNet
1081 Tenth Avenue SE
Minneapolis, MN 55414-1312

800-322-0956
Fax: 612-379-9143
http://www.ablenet.com

Adaptive devices for students with disabilities from Pre-K through adult, as well as activities and games for students of all abilities.

5230 Accounter Systems USA
1107 S Mannheim Road
Suite 305
Westchester, IL 60154-2560

800-229-8765

Sports timers and clocks and classroom supplies.

5231 Accu-Cut Systems
1035 E Dodge Street
Fremont, NE 68025

402-721-4134
800-288-1670
Fax: 402-721-5778
E-mail: info@accucut.com
http://www.accucut.com

Manufacturer of die cutting machines dies.

5232 Airomat Corporation
2916 Engle Road
Fort Wayne, IN 46809-1198

260-747-7408
800-348-4905
Fax: 260-747-7409
E-mail: airomat@airomat.com
http://www.airomat.com

Mats and matting.

Jody Feasel, VP
Janie Feasel, President/CEO

5233 Airspace USA
89 Patton Avenue
Asheville, NC 28801

828-258-1319
800-872-1319
Fax: 828-258-1390
E-mail: sales@airspace-usa.com
http://www.airspacesolutions.com

Airspace Soft Center Play and Learn Systems provide a comprehensive range of play, learning and physical development opportunities using commercial grade and foam filled play equipment. Play manual provided.

Daniel Brenman, VP Sales/Marketing
Tracy Syxes, Administrator

5234 All Art Supplies
Art Supplies Wholesale
4 Enon Street
North Beverly, MA 01915

800-462-2420
Fax: 800-462-2420
E-mail: info@allartsupplies.com
http://www.allartsupplies.com

Art supplies at wholesale prices.

5235 American Foam
HC 37 Box 317 H
Lewisburg, WV 24901

304-497-3000
800-344-8997
Fax: 304-497-3001
http://www.bfoam.com

Carving blocks of foam.

5236 American Plastics Council
1300 Wilson Boulevard
Arlington, VA 22209

800-243-5790
http://www.plastics.org

Offers classroom materials on recycling and environmental education.

5237 Anatomical Chart Company
8221 Kimball Avenue
Skokie, IL 60076-2956

847-679-4700
http://www.anatomical.com

Maps and charts for educational purposes.

5238 Angels School Supply
600 E Colorado Boulevard
Pasadena, CA 91101-2006

626-584-0855
Fax: 626-584-0888
http://www.angelschoolsupply.com

School and classroom supplies.

Jennifer , Sales Representitive

5239 Aol@School
22070 Broderick Drive
Dulles, VA 20166

888-468-3768
E-mail: aol at school@aol.com
http://www.school.aol.com

Age-appropriate, high-quality educational content tailored for K-12 students and educators. Aol@School focuses and filters the Web for us, providing appropriate, developmental access to the vast educational resources on the internet.

5240 Armada Art Materials
Armada Art Inc.
142 Berkeley Street
Boston, MA 02116

617-859-3800
800-435-0601
Fax: 617-859-3808
E-mail: info@armadaart.com
http://www.armadaart.com

5241 Art Materials Catalog
United Art and Education
PO Box 9219
Fort Wayne, IN 46899

800-322-3247
Fax: 800-858-3247
http://www.unitednow.com

Art materials.

5242 Art Supplies Wholesale
4 R Enon Street
N Beverly, MA 01915

800-462-2420
Fax: 978-922-1495
E-mail: info@allartsupplies.com
http://www.allartsupplies.com

Wholesale art supplies.

5243 Art to Remember
10625 Deme Drive
Unit E
Indianapolis, IN 46236

317-826-0870
800-895-8777
Fax: 317-823-2822
http://www.arttoremember.com

A unique program that encourages your students' artisic creativity while providing an opportunity to raise funds for schools.

5244 Artix
PO Box 25008
Kelowna, BC V1W3Y

250-861-5345
800-665-5345
http://www.artix.bc.ca

Papermaking kits.

5245 Assessories by Velma
PO Box 2580
Shasta, CA 96087-2580

Multicultural education-related products.

5246 At-Risk Resources
135 Dupont Street
PO Box 760
Plainview, NY 11803-0706

800-999-6884
Fax: 800-262-1886

Dealing with drug violence prevention, character education, self-esteem, teen sexuality, dropout prevention, safe schoolks, career development, parenting crisis and trauma, and professional development.

5247 Atlas Track & Tennis
19495 SW Teton Avenue
Tualatin, OR 97062-8846

800-423-5875
Fax: 503-692-0491

Specialty sport surfaces; synthetic running tracks, tennis courts, and athletic flooring for schools.

5248 Audio Forum
69 Broad Street
Guildford, CT 06437

203-453-9794
Fax: 203-453-9774
E-mail: info@audioforum.com
http://www.audioforum.com

Cassettes, CD's and books for language study.

5249 Badge-A-Minit
PO Box 800
La Salle, IL 61301-0800

815-883-8822
800-223-4103
Fax: 815-883-9696
E-mail: questions@badgeaminit.com
http://www.badgeaminit.com

Awards, trophies, emblems and badges for educational purposes.

5250 Bag Lady School Supplies
9212 Marina Pacifica Drive N
Long Beach, CA 90803-3886

Classroom supplies.

5251 Bale Company
PO Box 6400
Providence, RI 02940-6400

800-822-5350
Fax: 401-831-5500
http://www.bale.com

Awards, medals, pins, plaques and trophies.

5252 Bangor Cork Company
William & D Streets
Pen Argyl, PA 18072

610-863-9041
Fax: 610-863-6275

Announcement boards.

Janice Cory, Customer Services Rep

5253 Baumgarten's
144 Ottley Drive
Atlanta, GA 30324-4016

404-874-7675
800-247-5547
Fax: 800-255-5547
E-mail: mlynch@baumgartens.com
http://www.baumgartens.com

Products available include pencil sharpeners, pencil grips, pocket binders, disposable aprons, American flags, practical colorful clips, fastening devices in a variety of shapes and sizes, identification security items, lamination,magnifiers and key chains.

Michael Lynch, National Sales Manager

5254 Best Manufacturing Sign Systems
PO Box 577
Montrose, CO 81402-0577

970-249-2378
800-235-2378
Fax: 970-249-0223
E-mail: sales@bestsigns.com
http://www.bestsigns.com

Architectural and ADA signs, announcement boards.

Mary Phillips, Sales Manager

5255 Best-Rite
201 N Crockett Avenue
#713
Cameron, TX 76520-3376

254-778-4727
800-749-2258
Fax: 866-888-7483
E-mail: boards@bestrite.com
http://www.bestrite.com

Quality visual display products which include a complete line of chalk, marker, tack, bulletin, fabric and projection boards. Display and trophy cases, beginner boards, reversible boards, mobile easels, desk-top and floor carrels andearly childhood products are also manufactured.

Bob Wilson, VP
Greg Moore, Executive VP

5256 Binney & Smith
1100 Church Lane
Easton, PA 18044

610-253-6271
800-CRA-YOLA
Fax: 610-250-5768
http://www.crayola.com

Crayons.

5257 Black History Month
Guidance Channel
135 Dupont Street
PO Box 760
Plainview, NY 44803-0706

800-999-6884
Fax: 800-262-1886

Products to celebrate Black history, multicultutral resources.

5258 Blackboard Resurfacing Company
50 N 7th Street
Bangor, PA 18013-1731

610-588-0965
Fax: 610-863-1997

Chalk and announcement boards.

Karin Karpinski, Administrative Assistant

5259 Bob's Big Pencils
1848 E 27th Street
Hays, KS 67601-2108

Large novelty pencils, plaques, bookends and many pencil related items.

5260 Book It!/Pizza Hut
9111 E Douglas Avenue
Wichita, KS 67207-1205

316-687-8401

National reading incentive program with materials, books and incentive display items to get students interested in reading.

5261 Borden
Home & Professional Products Group
180 E Broad Street
Columbus, OH 43215-3799

614-225-7479
Fax: 614-225-7167

Arts and crafts supplies, maintenance and repair supplies.

5262 Bulman Products
1650 McReynolds NW
Grand Rapids, MI 49504

616-363-4416
Fax: 616-363-0380
E-mail: bulman@macatawa.com

Art craft paper.

5263 Bydee Art
8603 Yellow Oak Street
Austin, TX 78729-3739

512-474-4343
Fax: 512-474-5749

Prints, books, T-shirts with the Bydee People focusing on education.

5264 C-Thru Ruler Company
6 Britton Drive
Bloomfield, CT 06002-3632

860-243-0303
Fax: 860-243-1856
http://www.CThruRuler.com

Arts, crafts and classroom supplies.

Ross Zachs, Manager

5265 CHEM/Lawrence Hall of Science
University of California
Berkeley, CA 94720

510-642-6000
Fax: 510-642-1055
E-mail: lhsinfo@uclink.berkley.edu
http://www.lawrencehallofscience.org

Activities for grades 5-6 and helps students understand the use of chemicals in our daily lives.

Linda Schnieder, Marketing Manager
Mike Slater, Marketing/PR Associate

5266 CORD Communications
324 Kelly Street
Waco, TX 76710-5709

254-776-1822
Fax: 254-776-3906

Instructional materials for secondary and postsecondary applications in science education.

5267 Califone International
21300 Superior Street
Chatsworth, CA 91311-4328

818-407-2400
800-722-0500
Fax: 818-407-2491
http://www.califone.com

Multisensory, supplemental curricula on magnetic cards for use with all Card Reader/Language master equipment.

Nelly Spievak, Sales Coordinator

5268 Cardinal Industries
PO Box 1430
Grundy, VA 24614-1430

276-935-4545
800-336-0551
Fax: 276-935-4970

Awards, emblems, trophies and badges.

5269 Carousel Productions
1100 Wilcrest Drive
Suite 100
Houston, TX 77042-1642

281-568-9300
Fax: 281-568-9498

Moments in History T-shirts, as well as other various educational gifts and products.

5270 Cascade School Supplies
1 Brown Street
PO Box 780
North Adams, MA 01247

800-628-5078
Fax: 413-663-3719

Offers a variety of school supplies and more.

5271 Celebrate Diversity
Guidance Channel
135 Dupont Street
PO Box 760
Plainview, NY 44803-0706

800-999-6884
Fax: 800-262-1886

Educational resources that celebrate diversity.

5272 Celebrate Earth Day
Guidance Channel
135 Dupont Street
PO Box 760
Plainview, NY 44803-0706

800-999-6884
Fax: 800-262-1886

Educational resources for celebrating earth day.

5273 Center Enterprises
PO Box 33161
West Hartford, CT 06110

860-953-4423
Fax: 800-373-2923

Clifford individual curriculum and storybook stamp sets, individual, grading, curriculum based and Sweet Arts rubber stamp line, stamp pads, embossing inks and powders.

5274 Center for Learning
21590 Center Ridge Road
Rocky River, OH 44116-3963

440-331-1404
800-767-9090
Fax: 888-767-8080
E-mail: cfl@stratos.net
http://www.centerforlearning.org

Supplementary curriculum units for all grade levels in biography, language arts, novel/drama and social studies.

5275 Center for Teaching International Relations
University of Denver
Denver, CO 80208

303-871-3106

Reproducible teaching activities and software promoting multicultural understanding and international relations in the classroom for grades K-adult.

5276 Childcraft Education Corporation
20 Kilmer Avenue
Edison, NJ 08817

732-572-6100

Distributes children's toys, products, materials and publications to schools.

5277 Childswork/Childsplay
The Guidence Channel
135 Dupont Street
PO Box 760
Plainview, NY 11803-0760

800-962-1141
Fax: 800-262-1886
http://www.childswork.com

Contains over 450 resources to address the social and emotional needs of children and adolescents.

Lawrence C Shapiro, PhD, President
Constance H Logan, Development Coordinator

5278 Chroma
205 Bucky Drive
Lititz, PA 17543

717-626-8866
800-257-8278
Fax: 717-626-9292
http://www.chromaonline.com

Tempera and acrylic paints.

5279 Chroma-Vision Sign & Art System
PO Box 434
Greensboro, NC 27402-0434

336-275-0602

Refillable and renewable felt tip markers used with non-toxic, water soluable, fast drying colors for making signs, posters, and general art work with no messy cleanup.

S Gray, President

5280 Citizenship Through Sports and Fine Arts
Curriculum
National Federation of State High School Assoc.
PO Box 20626
Kansas City, MO 64195-0626

816-464-5400
800-776-3462
Fax: 816-891-2414
http://www.nfhs.org

High school activities curriculum package that includes an introductory video, Rekindling the Spirit, along with the Overview booklet, plus two insightful books covering eight targets of the curriculum.

5281 Claridge Products & Equipment
Claridge Products & Equipment
601 Highway 62-65 S
PO Box 910
Harrison, AR 72601-0910

870-743-2200
Fax: 870-743-1908
E-mail: claridge@claridgeproducts.com
http://www.claridgeproducts.com

Claridge manufactures chalkboards, markerboards, bulletin boards, display and trophy cases, bulletin and directory board cabinets, easels, lecterns, speakers' stands, wood lecture units with matching credenzas and much more.

Terry McCutchen, Sales Manager

5282 Collins & Aikman Floorcoverings
311 Smith Industrial Boulevard
Dalton, GA 30722

800-248-2878
Fax: 706-259-2666
E-mail: tellis@powerbond.com
http://www.powerbond.com

An alternative to conventional carpet to improve indoor air quality and reduce maintenance cost. Powerboard floor covering.

T Ellis, General Manager/Edu Markets

5283 Columbia Cascade Company
1975 SW 5th Avenue
Portland, OR 97201-5293

503-223-1157
Fax: 503-223-4530
E-mail: hq@timberform.com
http://www.timberform.com

Playground equipment and site furniture.

Dale Gordon, Sales Manager

5284 Creative Artworks Factory
19031 McGuire Road
Perris, CA 92570-8305

909-780-5950

Screenprinted T-shirts, posters and gifts for educational purposes.

5285 Creative Educational Surplus
9801 James Avenue S
#C
Bloomington, MN 55431-2919

Art and classroom materials.

5286 Crizmac Art & Cultural Education Materials Inc
PO Box 65928
Tucson, AZ 85728

520-323-8555
800-913-8555
Fax: 520-323-6194
E-mail: customerservice@crizmac.com
http://www.crizmac.com

Publisher of art and cultural education materials includes curriculum, books, music,and folk art.

Stevie Mack, President

5287 Crown Mats & Matting
2100 Commerce Drive
Fremont, OH 43420-1048

419-332-5531
800-628-5463
Fax: 800-544-2806
E-mail: sales@crown-mats.com
http://www.crown-mats.com

Mats, matting and flooring for schools.

5288 Dahle USA
375 Jaffrey Road
Peterborough, NH 03458

603-924-0003
800-243-8145
Fax: 603-924-1616
E-mail: info@dahleusa.com
http://www.dahleusa.com

Arts and crafts supplies, school and office products, office shreddars and more.

5289 Designer Artwear I
8475 C-1 Highway 6 N
Houston, TX 77095

281-446-6641

Specialty clothing, accessories, etc. all educationally designed.

5290 Dexter Educational Toys
Dexter Educational Toys, Inc.
PO Box 630861
Aventura, FL 33163-0861

305-931-7426
Fax: 305-931-0552

Manufacturer and distributor of education material. Dress-ups for children 2-7 years. Multicultural hand puppets, finger puppets, head masks puppet theaters, rag dolls, dress-ups for teddy bears and dolls, cloth books, exportmanufacturing under special designs and orders.

Genny Silverstein, VP Secretary

5291 Dick Blick Art Materials
PO Box 1267
Galesburg, IL 61402

800-828-4584
Fax: 800-621-8293
E-mail: info@dickblick.com
http://www.dickblick.com

Classroom art supplies.

5292 Dinorock Productions
407 Granville Drive
Silver Spring, MD 20901-3238

301-588-9300

Musical, Broadway puppet shows for early childhood fun and education.

5293 Discovery Toys
12443 Pine Creek Road
Cerritos, CA 90703-2044

562-809-0331
Fax: 562-809-0331
http://www.discoverytoyslink.com/elizabeth

Emphasizes child physical, social and educational development through creative play. Educational toys, games and books are available for all ages. Services include home demonstrations, fund raisers, phone and catalog orders. New Bookof Knowledge Encyclopedia and patenting video tapes are also available.

5294 Disney Educational Productions
500 S Buena Vista Street
Burbank, CA 91521-0001

800-777-8100

Creates and manufactures classroom aids for the educational field.

5295 Dixie Art Supplies
2612 Jefferson Highway
New Orleans, LA 70121

800-783-2612
Fax: 504-831-5738
http://www.dixieart.com

Fine art supplier.

5296 Dr. Playwell's Game Catalog
Guidance Channel
135 Dupont Street
PO Box 760
Plainview, NY 44803-0706

800-999-6884
Fax: 800-262-1886

Games that develop character and life skills.

5297 Draper
125 S Pearl Street
Spiceland, IN 47385

765-987-7999
800-238-7999
Fax: 765-987-7142
E-mail: draper@draper.com
http://www.draperinc.com

Projection screens, video projector mounts and lifts, plasma display mounts, presentation easels, window shades and gymnasium equipment.

Chris Broome, Contract Market Manager
Bob Mathes, AV/Video Market Manager

5298 Draw Books
Peel Productions
PO Box 546
Columbus, NC 28722-0546

828-859-3879
800-345-6665
Fax: 801-365-9898
http://www.drawbooks.com

How-to-draw books for elementary and middle school.

Paperback
ISBN: 0-939217

5299 Dupont Company
Corlan Products
CRP-702
Wilmington, DE 19880

302-774-1000
800-436-7426
Fax: 800-417-1266

Arts and crafts supplies.

5300 Durable Corporation
75 N Pleasant Street
Norwalk, OH 44857-1218

419-668-8138
800-537-1603
Fax: 419-668-8068

Furniture, classroom supplies, arts and crafts and educational products.

5301 EZ Grader
PO Box 23608
Chagrin Falls, OH 44023

800-732-4018
Fax: 800-689-2772

Electronic gradebook designed by teachers for teachers. It is an incredible time saver and computes percentage scores accurately, quickly and easily.

5302 Early Ed
3110 Sunrise Drive
Crown Point, IN 46307-8905

Teacher sweatshirts, cardigans, T-shirts, tote bags and jewelry.

5303 Education Department
Wildlife Conservation Society
2300 Southern Boulevard
Bronx, NY 10460

718-220-5131
800-937-5131
Fax: 718-733-4460
http://www.wcs.com

Year round programs for school and general audience. Teacher training, grades K-12.

Sydell Schein, Manager/Program Services
Ann Robinson, Director/National Programs

5304 Educational Equipment Corporation of Ohio
845 Overholt Road
Kent, OH 44240-7529

330-673-4881
Fax: 330-673-4915
E-mail: mkaufman@mkco.com

Chalkboards, tackboards, trophy cases, announcement boards.

Michael Kaufman, General Manager
Eric Baughman, Sales Manager

5305 Electronic Book Catalog
Franklin Learning Resources
1 Franklin Plaza
Burlington, NJ 08016-4908

800-BOO-MAN
Fax: 609-387-1787

Electronic translation machines, calculators and supplies.

5306 Ellison Educational Equipment
25862 Commercentre Drive
Lake Forest, CA 92630-8804

800-253-2238
Fax: 888-270-1200
E-mail: info@ellison.com
http://www.ellison.com

Serves the educational and craft community with time-saving equipment, supplies and ideas.

5307 Endura Rubber Flooring
2 University Office Park
Waltham, MA 02453-3421

781-647-5375
Fax: 781-647-4543

Floorcoverings, mats and matting for schools.

5308 Fairgate Rule Company
22 Adams Avenue
Cold Spring, NY 10516-1501

845-265-3677
Fax: 845-265-4128

Arts and crafts supplies.

5309 Family Reading Night Kit
Renaissance Learning
PO Box 8036
Wisconsin Rapids, WI 54495-8036

715-424-3636
800-338-4204
Fax: 715-424-4242
E-mail: answers@renlearn.com
http://www.renlearn.com

Kit to start a family reading night where parents and children spent quality time together sharing enthusiasm over books.

5310 Fascinating Folds
PO Box 10070
Glendale, AZ 85318

602-375-9979
Fax: 602-375-9978
http://www.fascinating-folds.com

World's large supplier of origami and paper arts products.

5311 Fiskars Corporation
636 Science Drive
Madison, WI 53711

608-233-1649
Fax: 608-294-4790
http://www.fiskars.com

School scissors.

5312 Fox Laminating Company
84 Custer Street
W Hartford, CT 06110-1955

860-953-4884
800-433-2468
Fax: 860-953-1277
E-mail: sales@foxlam.com
http://www.foxlam.com

Easy, simple, and inexpensive do-it-yourself laminators. A piece of paper can be laminated for just pennies. Badges, ID's and luggage tags can also be made. Also laminated plaques for awards, diplomas, and mission statements.

Joe Fox, President
John Mills, Marketing Manager

5313 George F Cram Company
PO Box 426
Indianapolis, IN 46206-0426

317-635-5564
Fax: 317-687-2845

Classroom geography maps, state maps, social studies skills and globes.

5314 Gift-in-Kind Clearinghouse
PO Box 850
Davidson, NC 28036-0850

704-892-7228
Fax: 704-892-3825

Educational and classroom supplies, computers and gifts for teachers.

5315 Gold's Artworks
2100 N Pine
Lumberton, NC 28358

910-739-9605
800-356-2306

Fax: 910-739-9605
http://www.goldsartworks.20m.com
Papermaking supplies.

5316 Golden Artist Colors
188 Bell Road
New Berlin, NY 13411-9527

800-959-6543
E-mail: goldenart@goldenpaints.com
http://www.goldenpaints.com
Acrylic paints.

5317 Graphix
19499 Miles Road
Cleveland, OH 44128-4109

216-581-9050
Fax: 216-581-9041
E-mail: sales@grafixarts.com
http://www.grafixarts.com
Art and crafts supplies and a source for creative plastic films.
Tanya Lutz, National Sales Manager

5318 Grolier Multimedial Encyclopedia
Grolier Publishing
PO Box 1716
Danbury, CT 06816

203-797-3703
800-371-3908
Fax: 203-797-3899
Encyclopedia software.

5319 Hands-On Equations
Borenson & Associates
PO Box 3328
Allentown, PA 18106

800-993-6284
Fax: 610-398-7863
http://www.borenson.com
System to teach algebraic concepts to elementary and middle school students.

5320 Harrisville Designs
Center Village
PO Box 806
Harrisville, NH 03450

603-827-3333
800-938-9415
Fax: 603-827-3335
http://www.harrisville.com
Award-winning weaving products for children.

5321 Hayes School Publishing
321 Penwood Avenue
Pittsburgh, PA 15221

800-245-6234
Fax: 800-543-8771
E-mail: info@hayespub.com
http://www.hayespub.com
Suppliers of certificates and awards.

5322 Henry S Wolkins Company
605 Myles Standish Boulevard
Taunton, MA 02780

800-233-1844
Fax: 877-965-5467
http://www.wolkins.com
Art and craft materials, teaching aids, early learning products, furniture, general school equipment.

5323 Hooked on Phonics Classroom Edition
665 3rd Street
Suite 225
San Francisco, CA 94107

714-437-3450
800-222-3334
E-mail: customerservice@hop.com
http://www.hop.com
Program that teaches students to learn letters and sounds to decoding words, and then reading books.

5324 Hydrus Galleries
PO Box 4944
San Diego, CA 92164-4944

800-493-7299
Fax: 619-283-7466
E-mail: info@hydra9.com
http://www.hydra9.com
Curriculum-based classroom activities including papyrus outlines for students to paint.

5325 Insect Lore
PO Box 1535
Shafter, CA 93263

800-548-3284
Fax: 661-746-0334
E-mail: livebug@insectlore.com
http://www.insectlore.com
Science materials for elementary and preschool students.

5326 J&A Handy-Crafts
165 S Pennsylvania Avenue
Lindenhurst, NY 11757-5058

631-226-2400
888-252-1130
Fax: 631-226-2564
E-mail: info@jacrafts.com
http://www.jacrafts.com
Arts, crafts and educational supplies.
Paul Siegelman, Marketing

5327 Jiffy Printers Products
35070 Maria Road
Cathedral City, CA 92234

760-321-7335
Fax: 760-770-1955
E-mail: jiffyprod@aol.com
Adhesive wax sticks.
Ivan Zwelling, Owner

5328 Key-Bak
Division of West Coast Chain Manufacturing Co.
4245 Pacific Privado
Ontario, CA 91761

909-923-7800
800-685-2403
Fax: 800-565-6202
E-mail: sales@keybak.com
http://www.keybak.com
Badges, awards and emblems for educational purposes.

5329 Keyboard Instructor
Advanced Keyboard Technology, Inc.
PO Box 2418
Paso Robles, CA 93447-2418

805-237-2055
Fax: 805-239-8973
http://www.keyboardinstructor.com
Mobile keyboarding lab with individualized instruction.

5330 Kids Percussion Buyer's Guide
Percussion Marketing Council

818-753-1310
E-mail: DLevine360@aol.com
http://www.playdrums.com

This guide is divided into two sections- recreational instruments and those for beginning traditional drummers.

5331 Kids at Heart & School Art Materials
PO Box 94082
Seattle, WA 98124-9482

Classroom and art materials.

5332 Kidstamps
PO Box 18699
Cleveland Heights, OH 44118-0699

216-291-6884
Fax: 216-291-6887
E-mail: kidstamps@apk.net
http://www.kidstamps.com

Rubber stamps, T-shirts, bookplates and mugs designed by leading children's illustrators.

5333 Knex Education Catalog
Knex Education

2990 Bergey Road
PO Box 700
Hatfield, PA 19440-0700

888-ABC-KNEX
E-mail: abcknex@knex.com
http://www.knexeducation.com

Hands-on, award-winning curriculum supported K-12 math, science and technology sets.

5334 Lauri
PO Box 0263
Smethport, PA 16749

800-451-0520
Fax: 207-639-3555

Lacing puppets craft kits, crepe rubber picture puzzles, phonics kits and math manipulatives for pre- K and up. Catalog offers 200 manipulatives for early childhood.

5335 Learning Materials Workshop
274 N Winooski Avenue
Burlington, VT 05401-3621

802-802-8399
800-693-7164
Fax: 802-862-0794
E-mail: mail@learningmaterialswork.com
http://www.learningmaterialswork.com

Designs and produces open-ended blocks and construction sets for early childhood classrooms. An education guide and video, as well as training workshops are offered.

Karen Hewitt, President

5336 Learning Needs Catalog
Riverdeep Interactive Learning
PO Box 97021
Redmond, WA 98073-9721

800-362-2890
http://www.learningneeds.com

Hardware, software and print products designed for specialized student needs for Pre-K to grade 12.

5337 Learning Power and the Learning Power Workbook
Great Source Education Group
181 Ballardvale
Willmington, MA 01887

800-289-4490

Student materials for 8th and 9th grade critical thinking, study skills, life management, and other student success course.

218 pages
ISBN: 0-963813-33-1

5338 Learning Well
111 Kane Street
Baltimore, MD 21224-1728

800-645-6564
Fax: 800-413-7442
E-mail: learningwell@wclm.com

Drawing compass/ruler.

5339 Linray Enterprises
167 Corporation Road
Hyannis, MA 02601-2204

800-537-9752

Mats and matting for gym classes.

5340 Loew-Coenell
563 Chestnut Avenue
Teaneck, NJ 07666-2491

201-836-8110
Fax: 201-836-7070
E-mail: sales@loew-cornell.com
http://www.loew-cornell.com

Leader in art and craft brushes, painting accessories and artists'tools.

5341 Longstreth
PO Box 475
Parker Ford, PA 19457-0475

610-495-7022
Fax: 610-495-7023

Awards, emblems, badges and trophies, sports timers and clocks.

5342 Love to Teach
693 Glacier Pass
Westerville, OH 43081-1295

614-899-2118
800-326-8361
Fax: 614-899-2070
http://www.lovetoteach.com

Gifts for teachers.

Linda Vollmer, Contact

5343 Lyra
78 Browne Street
Suite 3
Brookline, MA 02146

888-PEN-LYRA
E-mail: mshoham@aol.com

Drawing supplies.

5344 MPI School & Instructional Supplies
PO Box 24155
Lansing, MI 48909-4155

517-393-0440
Fax: 517-393-8884

School and classroom supplies, arts and crafts.

5345 Magnetic Aids
133 N 10th Street
Paterson, NJ 07522-1220
                                973-790-1400
                                800-426-9624
                           Fax: 973-790-1425
           E-mail: magneticaids@worldnet.att.com
                      http://www.magneticaids.com

Announcement and chalkboards, office supplies and equipment. Magnetic book supports.

Paul Pecka, VP Sales

5346 Mailer's Software
970 Calle Negocio
San Clemente, CA 92673-6201
                                949-492-7000
                           Fax: 949-589-5211

Charts, maps, globes and software for the classroom.

5347 Marsh Industries
Div. of Marsh Lumber Company
PO Box 509
Dover, OH 44622-1935
                                330-343-8825
                                800-426-4244
                           Fax: 330-343-9515
           E-mail: wdsinghaus@marsh-ind.com
                      http://www.marsh-ind.com

Marker boards chalkboards, and tacknoards for new rennovative construction projects. Glass enclosed bulletin and directory boards. Map rail and accessories.

William Singhaus, Sales Manager

5348 Master Woodcraft
1312 College Street
Oxford, NC 27565
                                919-693-8811
                                800-333-2675
                           Fax: 919-693-1707

Announcement and classroom chalkboards, arts and craft supplies. Cork bulletin boards, dry erase melamine boards, easels, floor and table top.

J Moss, VP

5349 Material Science Technology
Energy Concepts
595 Bond Street
Lincolnshire, IL 60069

                                800-621-1247
                      http://www.energy-concepts-inc.com

Provides practical knowledge of the use and development of materials in todays world. Each unit combines theory with hands-on experience.

5350 Midwest Publishers Supply
4640 N Olcott Avenue
Harwood Heights, IL 60706

                                800-621-1507
                           Fax: 800-832-3189
                E-mail: info@mps-co.com
                      http://www.mps-co.com

Arts and crafts supplies.

Bonnie Cready, Sales Manager

5351 Miller Multiplex
1555 Larkin Williams Road
Fenton, MO 63026-3008
                                636-343-5700
                                800-325-3350
                           Fax: 636-326-1716
                E-mail: info@millermultiplex.com

Announcement boards, classroom displays, charts and photography, books towers, posters, frames, kiosk displays, presentation displays.

12 pages Annually
Kathy Webster, Director Marketing

5352 Monsanto Company
800 N Lindbergh Boulevard
Saint Louis, MO 63167-0001
                                314-694-3902
                           Fax: 314-694-7625

Arts and crafts supplies.

5353 Morrison School Supplies
304 Industrial Road
San Carlos, CA 94070-6285
                                650-592-3000
                           Fax: 650-592-1679

School supplies, classroom equipment, furniture and toys.

5354 Names Unlimited
2300 Spikes Lane
Lansing, MI 48906-3996

Chalkboard and markerboard slates and tablets.

5355 Nasco Arts & Crafts Catalog
Nasco
901 Janesville Avenue
PO Box 901
Fort Atkinson, WI 53538-0901
                                920-563-2446
                                800-558-9595
                           Fax: 920-563-8296
                      http://www.eNASCO.com

Complete line of arts and craft materials for the art educator and individual artist.

Kris Bakke, Arts & Crafts Director

5356 Nasco Early Learning & Afterschool Essential Catalogs
Nasco
901 Janesville Avenue
PO Box 901
Fort Atkinson, WI 53538-0901
                                920-563-2446
                                800-558-9595
                           Fax: 920-563-8296
                E-mail: info@enasco.com
                      http://www.eNasco.com

Features low prices on classroom supplies, materials, furniture and equipment for early childhood and afterschool programs.

Scott J Beyer, Director, Sales & Marketing

5357 Nasco Math Catalog
Nasco
901 Janesville
PO Box 901
Fort Atkinson, WI 53538-0901
                                920-563-2446
                                800-558-9595
                           Fax: 920-563-8296
                      http://www.nascofa.com

Features hands-on manipulatives and real-life problem-solving projects.

5358 National Teaching Aids
PO Box 2121
Fort Collins, CO 80522
                                970-484-7445
                                800-289-9299
                           Fax: 970-484-1198

E-mail: bevans@amep.com
http://www.hubbardscientific.com

Learning math, alphabet, and geography skills is easy with our Clever Catch Balls. These colorful 24" inflatable vinyl balls provide an excellent way for children to practice math, alphabet and geography skills. Excellent learningtool in organized classroom activities, on the playground, or at home.

Barbara Evans, Customer Service Manager
Candy Coffman, National Sales Manger

5359 New Hermes
2200 Northmont Parkway
Duluth, GA 30096

770-623-0331
800-843-7637
Fax: 800-533-7637
E-mail: sales@newhermes.com
http://www.newhermes.com

Announcement boards, trophies, badges, emblems.

5360 Newbridge Discovery Station
PO Box 5267
Clifton, NH 07015

Monthly quick tips and activities for teachers.

5361 Newbridge Jumbo Seasonal Patterns
PO Box 5267
Clifton, NJ 07015

Art projects, games, bulletin boards, flannel boards, story starters, learning center displays, costumes, masks and more for grades Pre K-3.

5362 NewsCurrents
Knowledge Unlimited
PO Box 52
Madison, WI 53701

800-356-2303
Fax: 608-831-1570
E-mail: sales@newscurrents.com
http://www.newscurrents.com

Current issues discussion programs for grades 3 and up.

5363 Partners in Learning Programs
1065 Bay Boulevard
Suite H
Chula Vista, CA 91911-1626

619-407-4744
Fax: 619-407-4755

Manufacturers and produces books, manuals, materials, supplies and gifts, such as banners for classroom purposes.

5364 Pearson Education Technologies
827 W Grove Avenue
Mesa, AZ 85210

520-615-7600
800-222-4543
Fax: 520-615-7601
http://www.pearsonedtech.com

SuccessMaker is a multimedia K-Adult learning system which includes math, reading, language arts and science courseware.

5365 Pentel of America
2805 Columbia Street
Torrance, CA 90509-3800

310-320-3831
800-421-1419
Fax: 310-533-0697
http://www.pentel.com

Office supplies and equipment.

5366 Pin Man
Together Inc.
802 E 6th Street
P.O. Box 52528
Tulsa, OK 74105-3264

918-587-2405
800-282-0085
Fax: 918-382-0906
http://www.thepinmanok.com

Manufacturer of custom designed lapel pins, totes for Chapter 1, reading, scholastic achievement, honor roll, parent involvement, staff awards and incentives with over 25,000 items available for imprint.

Bern Gentry, CEO

5367 PlayConcepts
2275 Huntington Drive
#305
San Marino, CA 91108-2640

800-261-2584
Fax: 626-795-1177

Creative, 3-D scenery that stimulates dramatic play. The scenes complement integrated curriculum. They are age and developmentally appropriate, non-biased, and effective for groups or individuals.

5368 Polyform Products Company
1901 Estes Avenue
Elk Grove Village, IL 60007

847-427-0020
Fax: 847-427-0020
E-mail: polyform@sculpey.com
http://www.sculpey.com

Manufacturer of sculpey modeling clay.

5369 Presidential Classroom
119 Oronoco Street
Alexandria, VA 22314-2015

703-683-5400
800-441-6533
Fax: 703-548-5728
E-mail: eriedel@presidentialclassroom.org
http://www.presidentialclassroom.org

Civic education programs in Washington, DC for high school juniors and seniors. Each one week program provides students with an inside view of the federal government in action and their role as responsible citizens and future leaders.

Jan-March, June+July
400 attendees

Jack Buechner, President/CEO
Ginger King, Dean

5370 Professor Weissman's Software
Professor Weissman's Software
246 Crafton Avenue
Staten Island, NY 10314-4227

718-698-5219
Fax: 718-698-5219
E-mail: mathprof@hotmail.com
http://www.math911.com

Algebra comic books, learn by example algebra flash cards, step-by-step software tutorials for algebra, trigonometry, precalculus, statistics, network versions for all software.

Martin Weissman, Owner
Keith Morse, VP

5371 Pumpkin Masters
PO Box 61456
Denver, CO 80206-8456

303-860-8006
Fax: 303-860-9826

Classroom pumpkin carving kits featuring whole language curriculum with safer and easier carving tools and patterns.

5372 Puppets on the Pier
Pier 39
Box H4
San Francisco, CA 94133

415-781-4435
800-443-4463
Fax: 415-379-9544
E-mail: onepuppet@earthlink.net
http://www.puppetdream.com

Puppets, arts, crafts and other creative educational products for children.

Arthur Partner

5373 Qwik-File Storage Systems
1000 Allview Drive
Crozet, VA 22932-3144

804-823-4351

Schedule boards and classroom supplies.

5374 RC Musson Rubber Company
1320 E Archwood Avenue
Akron, OH 44306-2825

330-773-7651
800-321-3281
Fax: 330-773-3254
E-mail: info@mussonrubber.com
http://www.mussonrubber.com

Rubber floorcoverings, mats and athletic matting.

Mark Reese, Customer Service Manager
Robert Segers, VP

5375 RCA Rubber Company
1833 E Market Street
Akron, OH 44305-4214

330-784-1291
Fax: 330-784-2899

Floorcoverings, athletic mats and more for the physical education class.

5376 Reading is Fundamental
600 Maryland Avenue SW
Suite 600
Washington, DC 20024-2520

202-673-1641
Fax: 202-673-1633

Distributor of posters, bookmarks, and parent guide brochures.

5377 Reconnecting Youth
National Educational Service
304 W Kirkwood Avenue
Suite 2
Bloomington, IN 47404-5132

812-336-7700
800-733-6786
Fax: 812-336-7790
E-mail: nes@nesonline.com
http://www.nesonline.com

Curriculum to help discouraged learners achieve in school, manage their anger, and decrease drug use, depression, and suicide risk. The program was piloted for five years with over 600 urban Northwestern public high school studentswith funding from the National Institute on Drug Abuse and the National Institute of Mental Health, and has since been successful in many educational settings.

3 Ring Binder Circul
ISBN: 1-879639-42-4

Jane St. John, Sales Marketing Director

5378 Red Ribbon Resources
135 Dupont Street
PO Box 760
Plainview, NY 11803

800-646-7999
Fax: 800-262-1886
http://ww.redribbonresources.com

Over 250 low cost giveaways to promote your safe and drug-free school and community.

5379 Renaissance Graphic Arts
69 Steamwhistle Drive
Ivyland, PA 18974

888-833-3398
Fax: 215-357-5258
E-mail: pat@printmaking-materials.com
http://www.printmaking-materials.com

Tools, papers, plates, inks and assorted products necessary for printmaking.

5380 Rock Paint Distributing Corporation
PO Box 482
Milton, WI 53563

608-868-6873
Fax: 800-715-7625
E-mail: handyart@handyart.com
http://www.handyart.com

Tempera paint, India ink, acrylic paint, block inc, washable paint, fabric paint.

5381 S&S Worldwide
S&S Arts & Crafts
75 Mill Street
Department 2030
Colchester, CT 06415-1263

800-243-9232
Fax: 800-566-6678

Arts and crafts, classroom games and group paks.

5382 Safe & Drug Free Catalog
Performance Resource Press
1270 Rankin Drive
Suite F
Troy, MI 48083-2843

800-453-7733
Fax: 800-499-5718
http://www.pronline.net

Books, videos, CD-Roms, phamlets and posters toassist students with social skills, counseling, drug and violence prevention.

5383 Sakura of America
30780 San Clemente Street
Hayward, CA 94544-7131

510-475-8880
800-776-6257
Fax: 510-475-0973
E-mail: express@sakuraofamerica.com
http://www.gellyroll.com

Gelly Roll pens, Cray pas oil pastels, Fantasia watercolors, Pigma micron pens, Pentouch and Aqua Wipe markers and other art supplies for the classroom.

John Crook
Donna Wilson, Marketing Director

School Supplies / Classroom Materials

5384 Sanford Corporation
A Lifetime of Color
2711 Washington Boulevard
Bellwood, IL 60104-1970
708-547-6650
800-323-0749
Fax: 708-547-6719
E-mail: consumer.service@sanfordcorp.com
http://www.sanfordcorp.com
Writing instruments, art supplies.
Angela Nigl, Author
Sharon Meyers, PR Manager

5385 Sax Visual Art Resources
Sax Arts and Crafts
2725 S Moorland Road
bept. SA
New Berlin, WI 53151
800-558-6696
Fax: 800-328-4729
E-mail: catalog@saxfcs.com
http://www.saxfcs.com
Variety of resources for slides, books, videos, fine art posters and CD-Roms.

5386 School Mate
PO Box 2225
Jackson, TN 38302
731-935-2000
Fax: 800-668-7610
E-mail: school@schoolmateinc.com
Pre-school and elementary art products.

5387 SchoolMatters
Current
The Current Building
Colorado Springs, CO 80941-0001
800-525-7170
Fax: 800-993-3232
Offers a variety of creative classroom ideas including stickers, mugs, posters, signs and more for everyday and holidays and everyday of the year.

5388 Scott Sign Systems
PO Box 1047
Tallevast, FL 34270-1047
941-355-5171
800-237-9447
Fax: 941-351-1787
E-mail: mail@scottsigns.com
http://www.scottsigns.com
Educational supplies including announcement, letters, signs, graphics and chalkboards.

5389 Scratch-Art Company
PO Box 303
Avon, MA 02322
508-583-8085
800-377-9003
Fax: 508-583-8091
E-mail: info@scratchart.com
http://www.scratchart.com
Offers materials for drawing, sketching and rubbings.

5390 Sea Bay Game Company
PO Box 162
Middletown, NJ 07748-0162
732-583-7902
Fax: 732-583-7284
Manufacturer and distributor of products, games and creative play to nursery schools and preschools.

5391 Seton Identification Products
20 Thompson Road
PO Box 819
Branford, CT 06405
203-488-8059
800-243-6624
Fax: 203-488-4114
http://www.seton.com
Manufacturer of all types of identification products including signs, tags, labels, traffic control, OSHA, ADA and much more.

5392 Shapes, Etc.
PO Box 400
Dansville, NY 14437-0400
585-335-6619
Fax: 585-335-6070
Notepads and craft materials for creative writing projects. Coordinates with literature themes. Perfect for storystarters, bulletin boards, awards and motivators.

5393 Sign Product Catalog
Scott Sign Systems, Inc.
PO Box 1047
Tallevast, FL 34270-1047
845-355-5171
800-237-9447
Fax: 941-351-1787
E-mail: scottsigns@mindspring.com
http://www.scottsigns.com
Educational supplies including announcement, letters, signs, graphics and chalkboards.
Robert Lew, Account Executive

5394 Small Fry Originals
2700 S Westmoreland Road
Dallas, TX 75233-1312
214-330-8671
800-248-9443
Children's original artwork preserved in plastic plates and mugs.

5395 Southwest Plastic Binding Corporation
109 Millwell Drive
Maryland Heights, MO 63043-2509
800-986-2001
Fax: 800-942-2010
Overhead transparencies, maps, charts and classroom supplies.

5396 Spectrum Corporation
10048 Easthaven Boulevard
Houston, TX 77075-3298
800-392-5050
Fax: 713-944-1290
Announcement boards, scoreboards and sports equipment, sports timers and clocks.

5397 Speedball Art Products Company
2226 Speedball Road
PO Box 5157
Statesville, NC 28687
704-838-1475
800-898-7224
Fax: 704-838-1472
E-mail: tonyahill@speedballart.com
http://www.speedballart.com
Art products for stamping, calligraphy, printmaking, drawing and painting.
Rita Madsen, Manager
Tonya Hill, Director of Sales

5398 Sponge Stamp Magic
525 S Anaheim Hills Road
Apartment C314
Anaheim, CA 92807-4726

Rubber stamps and games for classroom use.

5399 Staedtler
PO Box 2196
Chatsworth, CA 91313-2196

818-882-6000
800-776-5544
Fax: 818-882-3767
E-mail: rhoye@staedtler-usa.com
http://www.staedtler-usa.com

Arts and crafts supplies, office supplies and equipment.

Dick Hoye, National Sales Manager

5400 Sylvan Learning Systems
1000 Lancaster Street
Baltimore, MD 21202

410-843-6828
888-779-5826
Fax: 410-783-3832
http://www1.sylvan.net

Provides public school academic programs that are traditional sylvan programs modified to fit the needs of individual school districts and performance guarantees.

Jody Madron, Contact

5401 Tandy Leather Company
PO Box 791
Fort Worth, TX 76101-0791

817-451-1480
Fax: 817-451-5254

Arts and crafts supplies, computer peripherals and systems.

5402 Teacher Appreciation
Guidance Channel
135 Dupont Street
PO Box 760
Plainview, NY 44803-0706

800-999-6884
Fax: 800-262-1886

Products for celebrating teacher appreciation week.

5403 Teachers Store
PO Box 24155
Lansing, MI 48909-4155

517-393-0440
Fax: 517-393-8884

School and classroom supplies, arts and crafts.

5404 Texas Instruments
12500 TI Boulevard
Dallas, TX 75243-4136

800-336-5236
Fax: 972-995-4360
http://www.ti.com

Manufacturer of calculators.

5405 Triarco Arts & Crafts
14650 28th Avenue N
Plymouth, MN 55447

763-559-5590
800-328-3360
Fax: 736-559-2215
E-mail: info@triarcoarts.com

Art supplies.

5406 Vanguard Crafts
1081 E 48th Street
Brooklyn, NY 11234

718-377-5188
800-662-7238
Fax: 888-692-0056

Arts and crafts supplier.

5407 Wagner Zip-Change
3100 W Hirsch Avenue
Melrose Park, IL 60160-1741

800-323-0744
Fax: 708-681-4165

Non-lighted changeable letter message activity signs, changeable letters in all sizes and colors.

CJ Krasula, Marketing VP
Jim Leone, Sales Manager

5408 Walker Display
6520 Grand Avenue
Duluth, MN 55807-2242

218-624-8990
Fax: 888-695-4647

Arts, crafts, classroom supplies and displays.

5409 Wellness Reproductions
Guidance Channel
135 Dupont Street
PO Box 760
Plainview, NY 44803-0706

800-999-6884
Fax: 800-262-1886

Mental and life skills educational materials.

5410 Wikki Stix One-of-a-Kind Creatables
Omnicor
2432 W Peoria Avenue #1188
Suite 1188
Phoenix, AZ 85029-4735

602-870-9937
800-869-4554
Fax: 602-870-9877
E-mail: info@wikkistix.com
http://www.wikkistix.com

Unique, one-of-a-kind twistable, stickable, creatable, hands-on teaching tools. Ideal for Pre-K through 8 for science, language arts, math, arts and crafts, positive behavior rewards, rainy day recess, classroom display, diagrams and3-D work. Self-stick; no glue needed.

Kem Clark, President

5411 Wilson Language Training
175 W Main Strete
Millbury, MA 01527-1441

508-865-5699
Fax: 508-865-9644

Multisensory language program.

5412 Wilton Art Appreciation Programs
Reading & O'Reilley
PO Box 646
Botsford, CT 06404

203-270-6336
800-458-4274
Fax: 203-270-5569
E-mail: ror@wiltonart.com
http://www.wiltonart.com

Materials for art appreciation including CD-ROMS, videos, fine art prints, slides, workbooks, teacher' guides, lessons, puzzles and games.

Diana O'Neill, President
Linda Hood, VP/Secretary

5413 Young Explorers
1810 E Eisenhower Boulevrd
Loveland, CO 80539

800-239-7577
Fax: 888-876-8847
http://www.youngexplorers.com

Educational material for children.

Electronic Equipment

5414 AIMS Multimedia
9710 De Soto Avenue
Chatsworth, CA 91311-4409

818-773-4300
800-367-2467
Fax: 818-341-6700
E-mail: info@aimsmultimedia.com
http://www.aimsmultimedia.com

Film, video, laserdisc producer and distributor, offering a free catalog available materials. Also provides internet video streaming via www.digitalcurriculum.com.

David Sherman, President
Biff Sherman, President

5415 Advance Products Company
1101 E Central Avenue
Wichita, KS 67214-3922

316-263-4231
Fax: 316-263-4245

Manufacturer of steel mobile projection and television tables, video cabinets, easels, computer furniture, wall and ceiling TV mounts, and study tables and carrels.

Paul Keck

5416 All American Scoreboards
Everbrite
401 S Main Street
Pardeeville, WI 53954

608-429-2121
800-356-8146
Fax: 608-429-9216
E-mail: score@everbrite.com
http://www.allamericanscoreboards.com

Scoreboards.

Doug Winkelmann, Product Manager

5417 American Time & Signal Company
140 3rd Avenue S
Dassel, MN 55325

800-328-8996
Fax: 800-789-1882

Sports timers and clocks.

5418 Arts & Entertainment Network
235 E 45th Street
Floor 9
New York, NY 10017-3354

212-210-1400
Fax: 212-210-9755

Cable network offering free educational programming to schools.

5419 Barr Media/Films
12801 Schabarum Avenue
Irwindale, CA 91706-6808

626-338-7878

K-12 film, video and interactive Level I and III laserdisc programs.

5420 Buhl Optical Company
1009 Beech Avenue
Pittsburgh, PA 15233-2013

412-321-0076
Fax: 412-322-2640

Overhead projectors and transparencies.

5421 C-SPAN Classroom
4000 N Capitol Street NW
Washington, DC 20001

800-523-7586
Fax: 202-737-6226

C-SPAN School Bus travels through more than 80 communities during each school year. This bus is a mobile television production studio and learning center designed to give hands-on experience with C-SPAN's programming.

5422 CASIO
570 Mount Pleasant Avenue
Dover, NJ 07801-1631

973-361-5400
Fax: 570-868-6898

Cameras, overhead projectors and electronics.

5423 CASPR
100 Park Center Plaza
Suite 550
San Jose, CA 95113-2204

800-852-2777
http://www.caspr.com

Leader in the field of library automation for schools. Integrated library automation-cross platforms: Macintosh, Windows, Apple IIe/IIGS. Multimedia source.

Norman Kline, President

5424 Cable in the Classroom
1800 N Beauregard Street
Suite 100
Alexandria, VA 22311-1710

703-845-1400
Fax: 703-845-1409
http://www.ciconline.org

Represents the cable tele-communications industry's commitment to improving teaching and learning for children in schools, at home and in their communities.

5425 Canon USA
1 Canon Plaza
New Hyde Park, NY 11042-1198

516-488-1400
Fax: 516-328-5069

School equipment and supplies including a full line of electronics, cameras, calculators and other technology.

5426 Caulastics
5955 Mission Street
Daly City, CA 94014-1397

415-585-9600

Overhead projectors, transparencies and electronics.

5427 Cheshire Corporation
Cheshire Corporation
PO Box 61109
Denver, CO 80206-8109

303-333-3003
Fax: 303-333-4037
E-mail: karen-hemmes@mindspring.com

Cheshire corporation is a publicist for book, video, CD-ROM and internet publishers in the school and library market.

Karen Hemmes, Publicist
Mary Kay Opicka, Publicist

5428 Chief Manufacturing
14310 Ewing Avenue S
Burnsville, MN 55306-4839

612-894-6280
800-582-6480
Fax: 877-894-6918
E-mail: chief@chiefmfg.com
http://www.chiefmfg.com

Manufacturer of Communications Support Systems for audio visual and video equipment. Chief's product includes a full-line of mounts, electric lifts, carts, and accessories for LCD/DLP projectors, plasma displays and TV/monitors.

Liz Sorensen, Marketing Assistant
Sharon McCubbin, Marketing Manager

5429 Chisholm
7019 Realm Drive
San Jose, CA 95119-1321

800-888-4210

Computer peripherals, overhead projectors and overhead transparencies.

5430 Daktronics
331 32nd Avenue
Brookings, SD 57006-4704

605-697-4300
888-325-8766
Fax: 605-697-4300
E-mail: sales@daktronics.com
http://www.daktronics.com

Scoreboards, electronic message displays statistics software.

Gary Gramm, HSPR Market Manager

5431 Depco- Millennium 3000
3305 Airport Drive
PO Box 178
Pittsburg, KS 66762

316-231-0019
800-767-1062
Fax: 316-231-0024
E-mail: sales@depcoinc.com
http://www.depcoinc.com

Program tracks and schedules for you, the test taker delivers tests electronically, as well as, automatic final exams. There are workstation security features to help keep students focused on their activities.

5432 Discovery Networks
7700 Wisconsin Avenue
Bethesda, MD 20814-3578

301-986-0444

Manages and operates The Discovery Channel, offering the finest in nonfiction documentary programming, as well as The Learning Channel, representing a world of ideas to learners of all ages.

5433 Echolab
175 Bedford Street
Burlington, MA 01803-2794

781-273-1512
Fax: 978-250-3335

Cameras, equipment, projectors and electronics.

5434 Eiki International
Audio Visual/Video Products
26794 Vista Terrace Drive
Lake Forest, CA 92630

949-457-0200
Fax: 949-457-7878

Video projectors, overhead projectors and transparencies.

5435 Elmo Manufacturing Corporation
1478 Old Country Road
Plainview, NY 11803-5034

516-501-1400
800-654-7628
Fax: 516-501-0429

Overhead projectors and transparencies.

5436 Fair-Play Scoreboards
1700 Delaware Avenue
Des Moines, IA 50317-2999

800-247-0265
Fax: 515-265-3364
E-mail: sales@fair-play.com
http://www.fair-play.com

Scoreboards and sports equipment.

5437 Festo Corporation
395 Moreland Road
PO Box 18023
Hauppauge, NY 11788

631-435-0800
Fax: 631-435-3847
http://www.festo-usa.com

5438 General Audio-Visual
333 W Merrick Road
Valley Stream, NY 11580-5219

516-825-8500
Fax: 516-568-2057

Offers a full line of audio-visual equipment and supplies, cameras, projectors and various other electronics for the classroom.

5439 Hamilton Electronics
2003 W Fulton Street
Chicago, IL 60612-2365

312-421-5442
Fax: 312-421-0818

Electronics, equipment and supplies.

5440 JR Holcomb Company
3205 Harvard Avenue
Cleveland, OH 44101

216-341-3000
800-362-9907
Fax: 216-341-5151

A full line of electronics including calculators, overhead projectors and overhead transparencies.

5441 JVC Professional Products Company
41 Slater Drive
Elmwood Park, NJ 07407-1311

201-794-3900

Electronics line including cameras, projectors, transparencies and other technology for the classroom.

5442 Labelon Corporation
10 Chapin Street
Canandaigua, NY 14424-1589

585-394-6220
800-428-5566
Fax: 585-394-3154

Electronics, supplies and equipment for schools.

5443 Learning Channel
7700 Wisconsin Avenue
Bethesda, MD 20814

800-346-0032

Offers educational programming for schools.

5444 Learning Station/Hug-a-Chug Records
3950 Bristol Court
Melbourne, FL 32904-8712

321-728-8773
800-789-9990
Fax: 321-722-9121
http://www.learningstationmusic.com

Early childhood products including OMH, cassettes, CD's and videos. Also, the Learning Station performs children and family concerts and are internationally acclaimed for their concert/keynote presentations for early childhoodconferences and other educational organizations.

Don Monopoli, President
Laurie Monopoli, VP

5445 Learning Well
2200 Marcus Avenue
#3759
New Hyde Park, NY 11042-1042

800-645-6564
Fax: 800-638-6499

Instructional material including computer and board games, videos, cassettes, audio tapes, theme units, manipulatives for grades PreK-8.

Mona Russo, President

5446 Leightronix
2330 Jarco Drive
Holt, MI 48842-1210

517-694-5589
Fax: 517-694-1600

Educational cable programming for schools and institutions.

5447 MCM Electronics
650 Congress Park Drive
Centerville, OH 45459

800-543-4330
Fax: 800-765-6960
http://www.mcmelectronics.com

Offers a full line of electronics products and components for use in the classroom or at home. Over 40,000 parts.

5448 Magna Plan Corporation
1320 Route 9
Champlain, NY 12919-5007

518-298-8404
800-361-1192
Fax: 518-298-2368
E-mail: info@visualplanning.com
http://www.visualplanning.com

Overhead projectors.

Joseph P Josephson, Managing Director
Joel Boloten, Manager Consultation Service

5449 Mitsubishi Professional Electronics
200 Cottontail Lane
Somerset, NJ 08873-1231

732-563-9889

Video projectors and electronics.

5450 Multi-Video
PO Box 35444
Charlotte, NC 28235-5444

704-563-4279
800-289-0111
Fax: 704-568-0219

Cameras, projectors and equipment.

5451 Naden Scoreboards
505 Fair Avenue
PO Box 636
Webster City, IA 50595-0636

515-832-4290
800-467-4290
Fax: 515-832-4293
E-mail: naden@ncn.net
http://www.naden.com

Electronic scoreboards for sports.

Russ Naden, President

5452 Neumade Products Corporation
30 Pecks Lane
Newtown, CT 06470-2361

203-270-1100
Fax: 203-270-7778
E-mail: neumadeGJ@aol.com
http://www.neumade.com

Overhead projectors, overhead transparencies, video projectors and electronics.

Gregory Jones, VP Sales

5453 Nevco Scoreboard Company
301 E Harris Avenue
Greenville, IL 62246-2151

618-664-0360
800-851-4040
Fax: 618-664-0398
E-mail: info@nevco.com
http://www.nevco.com

Nevco is a premier manufacturer and distributor of scoreboards, message centers and video displays.

Phil Robertson, Sales Manager

5454 Panasonic Communications & System Company
1 Panasonic Way
Secaucus, NJ 07094-2917

201-392-4818
800-524-1064
Fax: 201-392-4044

Cameras, projectors, equipment, players, CD-ROM equipment and school supplies.

5455 Quickset International
3650 Woodhead Drive
Northbrook, IL 60062-1895

800-247-6563
Fax: 847-498-1258

Telecommunication equipment, cameras, projectors and electronics.

5456 RMF Products
PO Box 520
Batavia, IL 60510-0520

630-879-0020
Fax: 630-879-6749
E-mail: mail@rmfproducts.com
http://www.rmfproducts.com

Complete line of slide-related products including two and three-projector dissolve controls, programmers, multi-track tape recorders, audio-visual cables, remote controls and slide mounts.

Richard Frieders, President

5457 RTI-Research Technology International
4700 W Chase Avenue
Lincolnwood, IL 60646-1608

800-323-7520
Fax: 800-784-6733

TapeChek Videotape Cleaner/Inspector/Rewinders make videotapes last longer and perform better. Find damage before tape is circulated. Also available is videotape/laser disc storage, shipping and care products.

Bill Wolavka, Marketing Director

5458 Recreation Equipment Unlimited
PO Box 4700
Pittsburgh, PA 15206-0700

412-731-3000
Fax: 412-731-3052

Scoreboards and sports/recreation equipment.

5459 Reliance Plastics & Packaging
25 Prospect Street
Newark, NJ 07105-3300

973-473-7200
Fax: 973-589-6440

Vinyl albums for audio or video cassettes, video discs, slides, floppy disks, CDs Protect, store and circulate valuable media properly.

5460 Resolution Technology
26000 Avenida Aeropuerto Spc 22
San Juan Capistrano, CA 92675-4736

949-661-6162
Fax: 949-661-0114

Video systems and videomicroscopy equipment.

5461 RobotiKits Direct
17141 Kingsview Avenue
Suite B
Carson, CA 90746

310-515-6800
877-515-6652
Fax: 310-515-0927
E-mail: info@owirobot.com
http://www.robotikitsdirect.com

New science and robotic kits for the millenium.

Craig Morioka, President
Armer Amante, General Manger

5462 S'Portable Scoreboards
3058 Alta Vista Drive
Fallbrook, CA 92028-8738

800-323-7745
Fax: 270-759-0066

Portable scoreboards, manual and electronic, sports timers and clocks.

5463 SONY Broadcast Systems Product Division
1 Sony Drive
Park Ridge, NJ 07656

800-472-SONY

Interactive videodisc players for multimedia applications, VTRs, monitors, projection systems, video cameras, editing systems, printers and scanners, video presentation stands, audio cassette duplicators and video library systems.

5464 Scott Resources/ Hubbard Scientific
National Training Aids
PO Box 2121
Fort Collins, CO 80522-2121

970-484-7445
800-289-9299
Fax: 970-484-1198
E-mail: sgranger@amep.com
http://www.hubbardscientific.com

Microslide system is a comprehensive, classroom-ready to help students learn. The microslide system combines superb photo-materials with detailed curriculum material and reproducible student activity sheets at an affrdable price.

Shelley Granger, OEM/Retail Sales Manager
Candy Coffman, National Sales Manager

5465 Shure Brothers
222 Hartrey Avenue
Evanston, IL 60202-3696

847-866-2200
Fax: 847-866-2551

Electronics, hardware and classroom supplies.

5466 Swift Instruments
1190 N 4th Street
San Jose, CA 95112

408-293-2380
800-523-4544
Fax: 408-292-7967
http://www.swiftmicroscope.com

Capture live or still microscopic images through your compound or stereo microscope and background sound images through your VCR or computer.

5467 Tech World
Lab-Volt
PO Box 686
Farmingdale, NJ 07727

732-938-2000
800-522-8658
Fax: 732-774-8573
E-mail: us@labvolt.com
http://www.labvolt.com

Tech World provides superior hands-on instruction using state-of-the-art technology and equipment. Lab-Volt also offers a full line of attractive, durable, and flexible modular classroom furniture.

5468 Technical Education Systems
814 Chestnut Street
PO Box 1203
Rockford, IL 61102

815-966-2525
800-451-2169
Fax: 815-965-4836
http://www.tii-tech.com

Hands-on application-oriented training systems integrating today's real world technologies in a flexible and easy-to-understand curriculum format.

5469 Telex Communications
12000 Portland Avenue S
Burnsville, MN 55337

952-884-4051
800-828-6107
Fax: 952-884-0043
http://www.telex.com

Telex manufactures a variety of products for the educational market, including multimedia headphones, headsets and microphones; LCD computer and multimedia projection panels, group listening centers, video projectors, slideprojectors, portable sound systems, wired and wireless intercoms, and wired and wireless microphones.

Dawn Wiome, Marketing Coordinator

5470 Three M Visual Systems
3M Austin Center
6801 River Place Boulevard
Austin, TX 78726-4530

800-328-1371
Fax: 512-984-6529

Overhead projectors, audiovisual carts and tables, and overhead transparencies.

5471 Tom Snyder Productions
80 Coolidge Hill Road
Watertown, MA 02472-7013

617-926-6000
800-342-0236
Fax: 800-304-1254

E-mail: ask@tpmsnyder.com
http://www.tomsnyder.com

Educational videotapes, videodiscs and computer programs.

5472 Varitronics Systems
PO Box 234
Minneapolis, MN 55440

800-637-5461
Fax: 800-543-8966

Computer electronics, hardware, software and systems.

5473 Wholesale Educational Supplies
PO Box 120123
East Haven, CT 06512-0123

800-243-2518
Fax: 800-452-5956
E-mail: wes4@snet.net
http://www.discountav.com

Over 5,000 audio visual and video equipment and supplies offered at deep discount prices. Free 148 page catalog.

J Fields, President

Furniture & Equipment

5474 ASRS of America
225 W 34th Street
Suite 1708
New York, NY 10122-0049

212-760-1607
Fax: 212-714-2084
E-mail: elecompack@erols.com
http://www.elecompack.com

Offers Elecompack, high density compact shelving which offers double storage capacity, automatic passive safety systems and custom front panels.

Walter M Kaufman

5475 Adden Furniture
26 Jackson Street
Lowell, MA 01852-2199

978-454-7848
800-625-3876
Fax: 978-453-1449
E-mail: fsafran@addenfurniture.com
http://www.addenfurniture.com

Manufacturer of dormitory furniture, bookcases and shelving products.

Frank Safran, Education/Sales Director

5476 Air Technologies Corporation
27130 Paseo Espada
Suite 1405-A
San Juan Capistrano, CA 92675

949-661-5060
800-759-5060
Fax: 949-661-2454
E-mail: sales@airtech.net
http://www.airtech.net

Develop and manufacture professional ergonomic computer products.

5477 Alma Industries
1300 Prospect Street
High Point, NC 27260-8329

336-578-5700
Fax: 336-578-0105

Bookcases and shelving for educational purposes.

5478 Angeles Group
Dailey Industrial Park
9 Capper Drive
Pacific, MO 63069

636-257-0533
Fax: 636-257-5473
http://www.angeles-group.com

Housekeeping furniture and children play kitchen's made of durable and sturdy molded polyethylene. Baseline Furniture: tables, chairs, lockers, cubbies, bookcases, bookracks, silver rider trikes, spaceline cots, basic trikes, and byebye buggies.

Dianna Pritcjett, Customer Service Manager
Tami Warren, Customer Service Manager

5479 Anthro Corporation Technology Furniture
10450 SW Manhasset
Tualatin, OR 97062

503-691-2556
800-325-3841
Fax: 800-325-0045
http://www.anthro.com

Durable computer workstations and accessories; educational discounts; and dozens of shapes and sizes.

Mila Graham, Educational Sales

5480 Architectural Precast
10210 Winstead Lane
Cincinnati, OH 45231

513-772-4670
Fax: 513-772-4672

Furniture, tables, playground equipment, desks.

5481 Blanton & Moore Company
PO Box 70
Barium Springs, NC 28010-0070

704-528-4506
Fax: 704-528-6519
http://www.blantonandmoore.com

Standard and custom library furniture crafted from fine hardwoods.

Billy Galliher, Manager Sales Administration

5482 Borroughs Corporation
3002 N Burdick Street
Kalamazoo, MI 49004-3483

616-342-0161
800-627-6767

Bookcases and shelving products for educational purposes.

5483 Brady Office Machine Security
11056 S Bell Avenue
Chicago, IL 60643-3935

773-779-8349
800-326-8349
Fax: 773-779-9712
E-mail: b.brady1060@aol.com

The Brady Office Machine Security physically protects all office machines, computer components, faxes, printers, VCRs, have wall and ceiling mounts for TVs.

Bernadette Brady, President
Don Brady, VP

5484 Bretford Manufacturing
9715 Soreng Avenue
Schiller Park, IL 60176-2186

540-678-2545

Manufacturer of a full line of AV and computer projection screens, television mounts, wood office furniture and a full line of combination wood shelving and steel library shelving.

5485 Brixey
30414 Ganado Drive
Suite A
Palos Verdes Estates, CA 90275-6221
310-544-6098

Furniture for the classroom.

5486 Brodart Company, Automation Division
500 Arch Street
Williamsport, PA 17701
570-326-2461
800-233-8467
Fax: 570-327-9237
E-mail: salesmkt@brodart.com
http://www.brodart.com

Brodart's Automation Division has been providing library systems, software, and services for over 25 years. Products include: library management systems, media management systems, Internet solutions, cataloged web sites, catalogingresource tools, union catalog solutions, public access catalogs, and bibliographic services.

Kasey Dibble, Marketing Coordinator
Sally Wilmoth, Director Marketing/Sales

5487 Buckstaff Company
Buckstaff Company
1127 S Main Street
PO Box 2506
Oshkosh, WI 54902
920-235-5890
800-755-5890
Fax: 920-235-2018
E-mail: tmugerauer@buckstaff.com
http://www.buckstaff.com

The premier manufacturer of library furniture in the United States. Quality and durability has been the Buckstaff trademark for 150 years.

Tom Mugerauer, Sales Manager, National

5488 Carpets for Kids Etc...
115 SE 9th Avenue
Portland, OR 97214-1301
503-232-1203
Fax: 503-232-1394
http://www.carpetforkids.com

Carpets, flooring and floorcoverings for educational purposes.

5489 Children's Factory
505 N Kirkwood Road
Saint Louis, MO 63122-3913
314-821-1441
Fax: 877-726-1714

Manufactures children's indoor play furniture.

5490 Children's Furniture Company
Gressco Ltd.
328 Moravian Valley Road
Waunakee, WI 53597
800-697-3408
Fax: 608-849-6300
E-mail: caroline@gresscoltd.com
http://www.gressco.com

Commercial quality furniture for children of all ages.

Robert Childers, President
Caroline Ashmore, Marketing/Sales

5491 Community Playthings
PO Box 901
Rifton, NY 12471-0901
800-777-4244
Fax: 800-336-5948
E-mail: sales@bruderhof.com

Unstructured maple toys and furniture including innovative products, especially for infants and toddlers.

5492 Continental Film
PO Box 5126
Chattanooga, TN 37406-0126
423-622-1193
888-909-3456
Fax: 423-629-0853
E-mail: cfpc@chattanooga.net
http://www.continentalfilm.com

LCD projectors, distance learning systems, interactive white boards, document cameras.

Jim Webster, President
Courtney Sisk, VP

5493 Counterpoint
17237 Van Wagoner Road
Spring Lake, MI 49456-9702
800-628-1945
Fax: 616-847-3109

Audiovisual carts and tables.

5494 CyberStretch By Jazzercise
2460 Impala Drive
Carlsbad, CA 92008
760-476-1750
Fax: 760-602-7180
E-mail: cyberstretch@cyberstretch.com
http://www.jazzercize.com

To foster and promote wellness through the production of free interactive software programs for business, government, educational and personal use.

Kathy Missett, Contact

5495 Da-Lite Screen Company
3100 N Detroit Street
Warsaw, IN 46582
574-267-8101
800-622-3737
Fax: 574-267-7804
E-mail: info@dalite.com
http://www.da-lite.com

Projection screens, monitor mounts, audiovisual carts and tables, overhead projectors and transparencies.

5496 DeFoe Furniture 4 Kids
910 S Grove Avenue
Ontario, CA 91761-8011
909-947-4459
Fax: 909-947-3377

Furniture, floorcoverings, toys, constructive playthings and more for children grades PreK-5.

5497 Decar Corporation
7615 University Avenue
Middleton Branch, WI 53562-3142
606-836-1911

Library shelving, storage facilities and furniture.

5498 DecoGard Products
Construction Specialties
Route 405
PO Box 400
Muncy, PA 17756
570-546-5941
Fax: 570-546-5169

Physical fitness and athletic floorcoverings and mats.

5499 Engineering Steel Equipment Company
1307 Boissevain Avenue
Norfolk, VA 23507-1307
757-627-0762
Fax: 757-625-5754

Audiovisual carts and tables, bookcases and library shelving.

5500 Environments
PO Box 1348
Beaufort, SC 29901-1348

843-846-8155
800-348-4453
Fax: 843-846-2999

Publishes a catalog featuring equipment and materials for child care and early education. Offers durable and easy-to-maintain products with values that promote successful preschool, kindergarden, special needs and multi-age programs.

5501 Flagship Carpets
PO Box 1189
Chatsworth, GA 30705-1189

Carpets, flooring and floorcoverings.

5502 Fleetwood Group
PO Box 1259
Holland, MI 49422-1259

616-396-1142
800-257-6390
Fax: 616-820-8300
E-mail: www.fleetwoodfurniture.com

Offers library and school furniture including shelving, check out desks and multimedia units.

5503 Fordham Equipment Company
3308 Edson Avenue
New York, NY 10469

718-379-7300
800-249-5922
Fax: 718-379-7312
E-mail: alrobbi@attglobal.net
http://www.fordhamequip.com

Distributor and manufacturer of complete line of library supplies. Specialize in professional library shelving and furniture (wood and metal), mobile shelving and displayers. Catalog on request.

Al Robbins, President

5504 Good Sports
6031 Broad Street Mall
Pittsburgh, PA 15206-3009

412-661-9500

Mats, matting, floorcoverings and athletic training mats.

5505 Grafco
ERD
PO Box 71
Catasauqua, PA 18032-0071

800-367-6169
Fax: 610-782-0813
E-mail: info@grafco.com
http://www.grafco.com

GRAFCO manufacturers sturdy and durable computer furniture and tables designed for the educational environment.

Art Grafenberg, President

5506 Grammer
6989 N 55th Street
Suite A
Oakdale, MN 55128

651-770-6515
800-367-7328
http://www.grammerusa.com

Leading manufacturer and designer of ergonomically sound seating. Offers a chair designed especially for children.

5507 Greeting Tree
2709 Oak Haven Drive
San Marcos, TX 78666

512-392-0669
800-322-3199
Fax: 512-392-9660
E-mail: krieger@corridor.net
http://www.greetingtree.com

Solid wood furniture for Reading Recovery, Reading Library, Primary and Early Childhood. Specializes in quality and customized furniture for today's classroom. Kitchen learning centers, storage units of all sizes and sorts, easelswith over fourteen different display front possibilities.

BiAnnually

Cherie Krieger, Owner

5508 Gressco Ltd.
Gressco
328 Moravian Valley Road
PO Box 339
Waunakee, WI 53597

608-849-6300
800-345-3480
Fax: 608-849-6304
E-mail: custserv@gresscoltd.com
http://www.gressco.com

Gressco is a supplier of a complete line of commercial children's HABA furniture and library displays for all types of medias. Kwik-case for the security protection of CDs, videos, and audiocassettes. Catalog available.

Caroline Ashmore, Marketing/Sales

5509 H Wilson Company
555 W Taft Drive
South Holland, IL 60473-2071

708-339-5111
800-245-7224
Fax: 800-245-8224
E-mail: sales@wilson.com
http://www.hwilson.com

Manufacturer of furniture for audio, video, and computers. Complete line of TV wall and ceiling mounts. Makers of the famous Tuffy color carts.

Matthew Glowiak, Director Sales/Marketing

5510 HON Company
200 Oak Street
#769
Muscatine, IA 52761-4341

563-264-7100
Fax: 563-264-7505

Bookcases and shelving units.

5511 Haworth
One Haworth Center
Holland, MI 49423-9570

616-393-3000
800-344-2600
Fax: 616-393-1570
http://www.haworth.com

Steel and wood desks, systems furniture, seating, files, bookcases, shelving units, and tables.

5512 Joy Carpets
104 W Forrest Road
Fort Oglethorpe, GA 30742-3675

706-866-3335
800-645-2787
Fax: 706-866-7928
E-mail: joycarpets@joycarpets.com
http://www.joycarpets.com

Manufacturer of recreational and educational carpet for the classroom, home, or business. With a 10 year wear warranty, Class #1 Flammability rating, anti-stain and anti-bacterial treatment.

Joy Dobosh, Director Marketing

5513 KI
PO Box 8100
Green Bay, WI 54308-8100

920-468-8100
Fax: 920-468-2232

Library shelving, furniture, bookcases and more.

5514 Kensington Technology Group
2855 Campus Drive
San Mateo, CA 94403

650-572-2700
Fax: 650-572-9675
http://www.kensington.com

Offers several ergonomic mice.

5515 Kimball Office Furniture Company
1600 Royal Street
Jasper, IN 47549-1022

812-482-1600
Fax: 812-482-8300

Bookcases, office equipment and shelving units for educational institutions.

5516 Lee Metal Products
PO Box 6
Littlestown, PA 17340-0006

717-359-4111
Fax: 717-359-4414
http://www.leemetal.com

Carts, tables, bookcases and storage cabinets.

Richard Kemper, President

5517 Library Bureau
172 Industrial Road
Fitchburg, MA 01420

978-345-7942
800-221-6638
Fax: 978-345-0188
E-mail: melvil@librarybureau.com
http://www.librarybureau.com

Library shelving, bookcases, cabinets, circulation desks, carrels, computer workstations, upholstered seating.

Dennis Ruddy, Sr Project Manager

5518 Library Store
Library Store
112 E South Street
PO Box 964
Tremont, IL 61568

309-925-5571
800-548-7204
Fax: 800-320-7706
E-mail: libstore@thelibrarystore.com
http://www.thelibrarystore.com

The Library Store offers through its full-line catalog, supplies and furniture items for librarians, schools, and churches. Free catalog available containing special product discounts.

Janice Smith, Marketing Director

5519 Little Tikes Company
2180 Barlow Road
Hudson, OH 44236-4199

330-656-3906
800-321-4424
Fax: 330-650-3221

Offers a wide variety of furniture, educational games and toys and safety products for young children.

5520 Lucasey Manufacturing Company
2744 E 11th Street
Oakland, CA 94601-1429

510-534-1435
800-582-2739
Fax: 510-534-6828
E-mail: janrence@lucasey.com

Audiovisual carts , tables, and TV mounts

Jan RenceTurnbull, National Accountant

5521 Lundia
600 Capitol Way
Jacksonville, IL 62650-1096

800-726-9663
Fax: 800-869-9663

Bookcases and shelving products, as well as furniture for educational institutions.

5522 Lyon Metal Products
PO Box 671
Aurora, IL 60507-0671

630-892-8941
Fax: 630-892-8966

Bookcases and library shelving.

5523 Mateflex-Mele Corporation
1712 Erie Street
Utica, NY 13502-3337

315-733-4600
800-926-3539
Fax: 315-733-3183
http://www.mateflex.com

Manufacturers of Mateflex gymnasium flooring for basketball/gym courts. Mateflex II tennis court surfaces and Mateflex/Versaflex gridded safety floor tiles.

Gabe Martini, Sales Manager

5524 Microsoft Corporation
One Microsoft Way
Redmond, WA 98502-6399

425-882-8080
Fax: 206-703-2641
http://www.microsoft.com

Strives to produce innovative products and services that meet our costomers' evolving needs.

5525 Miller Multiplex
1555 Larkin Williams Road
Fenton, MO 63026-3008

636-343-5700
800-325-3350
Fax: 636-326-1716
E-mail: info@millermultiplex.com

Announcement boards, classroom displays, charts and pghtography, books towers, posters, frames, kiosk displays, presentation displays.

12 pages

Kathy Webster, Director Marketing

5526 ModuForm
ModuForm, Inc.
172 Industry Road
Fitchburg,, MA 01420

978-345-7942
800-221-6638
Fax: 978-345-0188
E-mail: guestlog@moduform.com
http://www.moduform.com

Residence hall furniture, loung seating, tables, stacking chairs, fully upholstered seating.

Robert Kushnir, Nationals Sales Manager
Darlene Bailey, VP Sales/Marketing

5527 Morgan Buildings, Pools, Spas, RV's
PO Box 660280
Dallas, TX 75266-0280

972-864-7300
800-935-0321
Fax: 972-864-7382
E-mail: rmoran@morganusa.com
http://www.morganusa.com

Classrooms, campus and other buildings custom designed to meet your projects needs. Permanent and relocatable modular classrooms or complete custom facilities. Rent, lease or purchase options available.

5528 Norco Products
Division of USA McDonald Corporation
PO Box 4227
Missoula, MT 59806

406-251-3800
800-662-2300
Fax: 406-251-3824
E-mail: john@norcoproducts.com
http://www.norcoproducts.com

Mobile cabinets, YRE funiture, tables, science labs, home economics displays, bookcases and shelving units, laboratory equipment, casework, cabinets, computer labs, podiums, award display cabinets, flags and flag poles.

Jim McDonald, President
John Schrom, Office Manger

5529 Nova
421 W Industrial Avenue
PO Box 725
Effingham, IL 62401

800-730-6682
Fax: 800-940-6682
E-mail: novadesk@effingham.net
http://www.novadesk.com

Patented furniture solution for computer mounting incorporates the downward gaze, our visual system's natural way of viewing close objects. Scientific evidence indicates that viewing a computer monitor at a downward gaze angle is abetter solution than with traditional monitor placement.

5530 Oscoda Plastics
5585 N Huron Avenue
PO Box 189
Oscoda, MI 48750

989-739-6900
800-544-9538
Fax: 800-548-7678
E-mail: sales@oscodaplastics.com
http://www.oscodaplastics.com

Oscoda Plastics manufactures Protect-All Specialty Flooring from 100% recycled post-industrial vinyls. Protect-All is perfect for use in locker rooms, kitchen/walk-in cooler floors, fitness areas, weight rooms, gym floors, or as atemporary gym floor cover.

Joe Brinn, National Sales Manager
Rick Maybury, Sales Coordinator

5531 Palmer Snyder
201 High Street
Conneautville, PA 16406

814-587-6313
800-762-0415
Fax: 814-587-2375

Tables are built with the highest quality materials for long life and low maintenance. A complete range of rugged options.

5532 Paragon Furniture
2224 E Randol Mill Road
Arlington, TX 76011

817-633-3242
800-451-8546
Fax: 817-633-2733
E-mail: customerservice@paragoninc.com
http://www.paragoninc.com

Offers a line of furniture for classroom, labs, science, and libraries.

Carl Brockway, VP Sales
Mark Hubbard, President

5533 Pawling Corporation
Borden Lane
Wassaic, NY 12592

845-373-9300
800-431-3456
Fax: 800-451-2200
E-mail: sales@pawling.com

Pawling is an approved manufacturer by E&I cooperative buying for athletic flooring, traffic safety products, wall and corner protection and entrance mat systems.

Richard Meyer, Sales Manager

5534 Peerless Sales Company
1980 N Hawthorne Avenue
Melrose Park, IL 60160-1167

708-865-8870
Fax: 708-865-2941

Auidovisual carts and tables.

5535 RISO
300 Rosewood Drive
Suite 210
Danvers, MA 01923-4527

978-777-7377
800-876-7476
Fax: 978-777-2517

The Risograph digital printer offers high speed copy/duplicating at up to 130 pages per minute. A 50-sheet document feeder lets people print multi-page documents quickly and inexpensively. Specifically designed to handle medium runlength jobs that are too strenuous for copiers. Offers various other products and office equipment available to the education community.

5536 Research Technology International
4700 Chase Avenue
Lincolnwood, IL 60646-1689

847-677-3000
800-323-7520
Fax: 847-677-1311
E-mail: sales@rtico.com
http://www.ritco.com

Tape check, Video tape cleaner, disk chack optical, disc rejestor.

5537 Russ Bassett Company
8189 Byron Road
Whittier, CA 90606-2615

800-350-2445
Fax: 562-689-8972

Shelving units, furniture and bookcases for educational institutions.

5538 SNAP-DRAPE
2045 Westgate
Suite 100
Carrollton, TX 75006-5116

972-466-1030
800-527-5147
Fax: 800-230-1330
E-mail: mecton@snapdrape.com
http://www.snapdrape.com

Table and stage skirting

Melissa Acton, Marketing/Sales Assistant

5539 Screen Works
2201 W Fulton Street
Chicago, IL 60612

312-243-8265
800-294-8111
Fax: 312-243-8290
E-mail: daveh@thescreenworks.com
http://www.thescreenworks.com

Manufacturers the E-Z Fold brand of portable projection screens and offers a full line of portable presentation accessories and services, including: an extensive screen rental inventory; audio-visula roll carts; lecterns andPaperStand flip charts. Custom screen sizes, screen surface cleaning and frame repair service also available.

David Hull, National Sales Manager

5540 Spacemaster Systems
155 W Central Avenue
Zeeland, MI 49464-1601

616-772-2406
Fax: 616-772-2100

Standard and Custom Shelving Systems and USEFUL AISLE Storage Systems.

5541 Spacesaver Corporation
1450 Janesville Avenue
Fort Atkinson, WI 53538-2798

920-563-6362
800-492-3434
Fax: 920-563-2702
E-mail: ssc@spacesaver.com
http://www.spacesaver.com

Flexible Spacesaver custom designs high-density mobile storage systems. Will double your storage and filing capacity while increasing usable floor space. Store files, supplies, manuals, books, drawings, multi-media, etc.

5542 Synsor Corporation
1920 Merrill Creek Pkwy
Everett, WA 98203-5859

800-426-0193
Fax: 425-551-1313

Offers a full line of educational furniture.

5543 Tab Products Company
1400 Page Mill Road
Palo Alto, CA 94304-1124

800-672-3109
Fax: 920-387-1802

Bookcases and shelving products for library/media centers.

5544 Tepromark International
206 Mosher Avenue
Woodmere, NY 11598-1662

516-569-4533
800-645-2622
Fax: 516-295-5991

Trolley Rail wall guards, corner guards, wall guards with hand rails, door plates, chair rolls, kick plates, vinyl floor mats and carpet mats. All mats promote safety from slipping in wet areas.

Robert Rymers

5545 Tesco Industries
1038 E Hacienda Street
Bellville, TX 77418-2828

979-865-3176
Fax: 979-865-9026

Bookcases and shelving units.

5546 Texwood Furniture
1353 N 2nd Street
Taylor, TX 76574

512-352-3000
888-878-0000
Fax: 512-352-3084
E-mail: ajohnson@texwood.com
http://www.texwood.com

Wood library furniture, shelving, computer tables and circulation desks and early childhood furniture.

Andrea Johnson, Director Marketing
Dave Gaskers, VP Sales/Marketing

5547 Tot-Mate by Stevens Industries
704 W Main Street
Teutopolis, IL 62467-1212

217-857-6411
800-397-8687
Fax: 217-857-3638
E-mail: timw@stevens.com

Early learning furniture manufactured by Stevens Industries. Features include 16 color choices, plastic laminate surfacing, rounded corners, beveled edges, safe and strong designs. Items offered include change tables, storageshelving, book displays, teacher cabinets, housekeeping sets and locker cubbies.

Randy Ruholl, Sales Representative
Paul Jones, Customer Service

5548 University Products
University Products
517 Main Street
PO Box 101
Holyoke, MA 01041-0101

413-532-3372
800-628-1912
Fax: 413-532-9281
E-mail: info@universityproducts.com
http://www.universityproducts.com

University Products specializes in top-quality archival materials for conservation and preservation as well as library and media centers supplies, equipment, and furnishings.

John A Dunphy

5549 W. C. Heller & Company
Heller
201 W Wabash Avenue
Montpelier, OH 43543

419-485-3176
Fax: 419-485-8694
E-mail: wcheller@hotmail.com

Complete line of wood library furniture in oak and birch, custom cabinetry and special modifications. Over 110 years in business.

Robert L Heller II, VP Sales

5550 Wheelit
PO Box 352800
Toledo, OH 43635-2800

419-531-4900
800-523-7508
Fax: 419-531-6415

Carts and storage containers.

5551 White Office Systems
50 Boright Avenue
Kenilworth, NJ 07033-1015

908-272-8888
Fax: 908-931-0840

Shelving, bookcases, furniture and products for libraries, media centers, schools and offices.

5552 Whitney Brothers Company
PO Box 644
Keene, NH 03431-0644

603-352-2610
Fax: 603-357-1559

Manufactures children's furniture products for preschools and day care centers.

5553 Winsted Corporation
10901 Hampshire Avenue S
Minneapolis, MN 55438-2385

952-944-9050
800-447-2257
Fax: 800-421-3839
E-mail: racks@winsted.com
http://www.winsted.com

Video furniture, accessories, tape storage systems and lan rack systems.

Randy Smith, President

5554 Wood Designs
PO Box 1308
Monroe, NC 28111-1308

704-283-7508
800-247-8465
Fax: 704-289-1899
E-mail: p.schneider@tip-me-not.com

Manufactures wooden educational equipment and teaching toys for early learning environments. Sold through school supply dealers and stores.

Dennis Gosney, President
Paul Schneider, VP Sales/Marketing

5555 Worden Company
199 E 17th Street
Holland, MI 49423-4298

800-748-0561
Fax: 616-392-2542

Furniture for office, business, school or library.

Maintenance

5556 American Locker Security Systems
608 Allen Street
Jamestown, NY 14701-3966

716-664-9600
800-828-9118
Fax: 716-664-2949
E-mail: 103303.1432@compuserve.com
http://www.americanlocker.com

Lockers featuring coin operated lockers.

David L Henderson, VP/General Manager

5557 Atlantic Fitness Products
PO Box 300
Linthicum Hts, MD 21090-0300

800-445-1855

School lockers and fitness/physical education products and equipment.

5558 Barco Products
11 N Batavia Avenue
Batavia, IL 60510-1961

800-338-2697

Maintenance and safety products made from recycled materials.

Kitt Pittman, Office Manager
Judy Leonard, Marketing Manager

5559 Blaine Window Hardware
17319 Blaine Drive
Hagerstown, MD 21740-2394

800-678-1919
Fax: 301-797-2510
E-mail: user533955@aol.com
http://www.blainewindow.com

Window and door parts including window repair hardware, custom screens locker hardware, chair glides, panic exit hardware, balance systems, door closers and motorized operators.

William Pasquerette, VP
Robert Slick, Purchasing Agent

5560 Bleacherman, M.A.R.S.
105 Mill Street
Corinth, NY 12822-1021

518-654-9084

School lockers.

5561 Burkel Equipment Company
14670 Hanks Drive
Red Bluff, CA 96080-9475

800-332-3993

School lockers, hardware and security equipment, maintenance and repair supplies.

5562 Chemtrol
Santa Barbara Control Systems
5375 Overpass Road
Santa Barbara, CA 93111-5879

800-621-2279
Fax: 805-683-1893
E-mail: chemtrol@slocontrol.com
http://www.chemtrolcontrol.com

Maintenance supplies for educational institutions.

Kevin R Smith, Sales Manager

5563 Contact East
335 Willow Street S
N Andover, MA 01845-5995

978-682-2000
800-225-5370
Fax: 978-688-7829
E-mail: sales@contacteast.com
http://www.contacteast.com

Maintenance supplies and equipment.

5564 DeBourgh Manufacturing Company
27505 Otero Avenue
La Junta, CO 81050-9403

719-384-8161
Fax: 719-384-7713

Security equipment, hardware, storage and school lockers.

5565 Dow Corning Corporation
PO Box 0994
Midland, MI 48686-0001

989-496-4000
Fax: 989-496-4572

Maintenance supplies and equipment.

5566 Dri-Dek Corporation
2706 Horseshoe Drive S
Naples, FL 34104-6142

941-643-0578
800-348-2378
Fax: 800-828-4248
E-mail: dri-dek@kictr.com
http://www.dri-dek.com

Oxy-BI vinyl compound in the Dri-Dek flooring systems helps halt the spread of infectious fungus and bacteria in areas with barefooted traffic. This compound makes Dri-Dek's anti-skid, self-draining surface ideal for use in thewettest conditions.

5567 Esmet
Tufloc Group
1406 5th Street SW
Canton, OH 44702-2062
330-452-9132
Fax: 330-452-2557

Lockers for the educational institution.

5568 Ex-Cell Metal Products
11240 Melrose Avenue
Franklin, IL 60131
847-451-0451
Fax: 847-451-0458

Maintenance supplies and repair equipment.

5569 Facilities Network
PO Box 868
Mahopac, NY 10541-0868
845-621-1664

School lockers and security system units.

5570 Fibersin Industries
37031 E Wisconsin Avenue
Oconomowoc, WI 53066
262-567-4427
Fax: 262-567-4814

School lockers and maintenance supplies. Desks, cradenzas, bookcases for school adm. Tables for cafeteria and adm.

5571 Flagpole Components
4150A Kellway Circle
Addison, TX 75001-4205
972-250-0893
800-634-4926
Fax: 972-380-5143

Maintenance and repair supplies and equipment.

5572 Flexi-Wall Systems
PO Box 89
Liberty, SC 29657-0089

Maintenance and repair supplies for educational institutions.

5573 Flo-Pac Corporation
700 Washington Avenue N
Suite 400
Minneapolis, MN 55401-1130
612-332-6240
Fax: 612-344-1663

Maintenance and repair supplies.

5574 Four Rivers Software Systems
2400 Ardmore Boulevard
7th Floor
Pittsburgh, PA 15221-1451
412-273-6400
Fax: 412-273-6420

Maintenance and repair supplies, business and administrative software and supplies.

5575 Friendly Systems
3878 Oak Lawn Avenue
#1008-300
Dallas, TX 75219-4460
972-857-0399

Maintenance and repair supplies.

5576 GE Capitol Modular Space
40 Liberty Boulevard
Malvern, PA 19355
610-225-2836
800-523-7918
Fax: 610-225-2762

School lockers, shelving and storage facilities.

5577 Glen Products
13765 Alton Parkway
Suite A
Irvine, CA 92618-1627
800-486-4455

Storage facilities, lockers and security systems.

5578 Global Occupational Safety
22 Harbor Park Drive
Port Washington, NY 11050-4650
516-625-4466

Safety storage facilities, shelving, lockers and hardware.

5579 Graffiti Gobbler Products
6428 Blarney Stone Court
Springfield, VA 22152-2106
800-486-2512

Educational maintenance and repair supplies and equipment.

5580 H&H Enterprises
PO Box 585
Grand Haven, MI 49417-9430
616-846-8972
800-878-7777
Fax: 616-846-1004
E-mail: hhenterprises@novagate.com

Maintenance and repair supplies.

5581 HAZ-STOR
2454 Dempster Street
Des Plaines, IL 60016
217-345-4422
800-727-2067
Fax: 217-345-4475
E-mail: info@hazstor.com
http://www.hazstor.com

Manufacturer of pre-fabricated steel structures including hazardous material storage buildings and outdoor flammables lockers as well as waste compactors and drum crushers, secondary containment products and process shelters.

Roger Quinlan, National Sales Manager
Antoinette Balthazor, Marketing Coordinator

5582 HOST/Racine Industries
1405 16th Street
Racine, WI 53403-2249
800-558-9439
Fax: 262-637-1624

Maintenance and repair supplies.

5583 Hako Minuteman
111 S Rohlwing Road
Addison, IL 60101-4244
630-627-6900
Fax: 630-627-1130

Maintenance and repair supplies for educational institutions.

5584 Haws Corporation
PO Box 2070
Sparks, NV 89432-2070
775-359-4712
Fax: 775-359-7424

E-mail: haws@hawsco.com
http://www.hawsco.com

Manufacturer of drinking fountains, electric water coolers, emergency drench showers and eyewashes.

Jim Bowers, Marketing Manager

5585 Honeywell
Home & Building Control
PO Box 524
Minneapolis, MN 55440-0524

973-455-2001
Fax: 973-455-4807

Maintenance and cleaning products for educational purposes.

5586 Insta-Foam Products
2050 N Broadway Street
Joliet, IL 60435-2571

800-800-FOAM
Fax: 800-326-1054

Maintenance supplies, cleaning products and repair hardware.

5587 Interstate Coatings
1005 Highway 301 S
Wilson, NC 27895

800-533-7663

Hardware, repair, maintenance and cleaning supplies.

5588 J.A. Sexauer
PO Box 1000
White Plains, NY 10602-1000

800-431-1872
Fax: 856-439-1333

Cleaning and maintenance supplies for educational institutions.

5589 Karnak Corporation
330 Central Avenue
Clark, NJ 07066-1199

732-388-0300
800-526-4236
Fax: 732-388-9422

Maintenance and cleaning supplies.

5590 Kool Seal
Unifex Professional Maintenance Products
1499 Enterprise Pkwy
Twinsburg, OH 44087-2241

800-321-0572
Fax: 330-425-9778

Maintenance, repair and cleaning supplies.

5591 LDSystems
9535 Monroe Road
Suite 140
Charlotte, NC 28270

704-847-1338
Fax: 704-847-1354
E-mail: ds@starkpr.com
http://www.bottompump.com

Environmentally-safe bottom pump air powered spray containers to dispense cleaning supplies such as window sprays, for cooling during workouts and general storage containers.

Dick Stark

5592 List Industries
401 NW 12th Avenue
Deerfield Beach, FL 33442-1707

954-429-9155
Fax: 954-428-3843

School lockers and storage facilities.

5593 Maintenance
1051 W Liberty Street
Wooster, OH 44691-3307

330-264-6262
800-892-6701
Fax: 800-264-2578

Provides pavement maintenance products for parking lots, driveways, tennis courts, etc.

Robert E Huebner

5594 Master Bond
PO Box 522
Teaneck, NJ 07666-0522

201-343-8983
Fax: 201-343-2132
E-mail: main@masterbond.com
http://www.masterbond.com

Repair hardware, maintenance and cleaning products for schools.

5595 Master Builders
Admixture Division
23700 Chagrin Boulevard
Cleveland, OH 44122-5554

216-831-5500
Fax: 216-839-8815

School hardware, maintenance and repair supplies and equipment.

5596 Medart
Division of Carriage Industries
PO Box 435
Garrettsville, OH 44231-0435

662-453-2506

School lockers.

5597 Modular Hardware
8190 N Brookshire Court
Tucson, AZ 85741-4037

520-744-4424
800-533-0042
Fax: 800-533-7942

School hardware, for repair and maintenance purposes.

5598 Penco Products
99 Brower Avenue
PO Box 378
Oaks, PA 19456-0378

610-666-0500
800-562-1000
Fax: 610-666-7561
E-mail: general@pencoproducts.com
http://www.pencoproducts.com

School lockers.

5599 Permagile Industries
910 Manor Lane
Bay Shore, NY 11706-7512

516-349-1100

Maintenance and cleaning products and supplies.

5600 Powr-Flite Commercial Floor Care Equipment
3301 Wichita Court
Fort Worth, TX 76140

817-551-0700
800-880-2913
Fax: 817-551-0719
http://www.powrflite.com

School maintenance supplies focusing on floor care equipment products, accessories and parts.

Curtis Walton, Contact

5601 ProCoat Products
260 Centre Street
Suite D
Holbrook, MA 02343-1074

781-767-2270
Fax: 781-767-2271
E-mail: info@procoat.com
http://www.procoat.com

Designed to restore aged and discolored acoustical ceiling tiles. Acoustical and fire retarding qualities are maintained. Ceiling restoration is cost effective, time efficient and avoids solid waste disposal. Products available alsofor preventative maintenance programs.

Kenneth Woolf, President

5602 Rack III High Security Bicycle Rack Company
675 Hartz Avenue
Suite 306
Danville, CA 94526-3859

800-733-1971

Lockers, bicycle racks, storage facilities and hardware.

5603 Republic Storage Systems Company
1038 Belden Avenue NE
Canton, OH 44705-1454

330-438-5800
Fax: 330-452-5071

Storage facilities, containers, maintenance products, shelving and lockers.

5604 Safety Storage
2301 Bert Drive
Hollister, CA 95023-2547

800-344-6539
Fax: 831-637-7405

Equipment, supplies and storage containers for maintenance and educational purposes.

5605 Salsbury Industries
1010 E 62nd Street
Los Angeles, CA 90001-1598

800-624-5269
Fax: 800-624-5299
E-mail: salsbury@mailboxes.com
http://www.mailboxes.com

School lockers, maintenance products and storage facilities.

5606 Servicemaster
Education Management Services
One Servicemaster Way
Downers Grove, IL 60515

800-926-9700
http://www.servicemaster.com

A provider of facility management support services to education.

5607 Sheffield Plastics
DSM Engineered Plastics Company
119 Salisbury Road
Sheffield, MA 01257-9706

413-229-8711

Maintenance and cleaning products for schools.

5608 Southern Sport Surfaces
PO Box 1817
Cumming, GA 30028-1817

770-887-3508
800-346-1632

Maintenance and cleaning products for schools.

5609 System Works
3301 Windy Ridge Parkway
Marietta, GA 30067

770-952-8444
800-868-0497
Fax: 770-955-2977

Addresses the capacity, quality and safety requirements of maintenance operations. Comprehensive and interactive it maximizes maintenance resources, people, tools and replacement parts, for increased productivity and equipmentreliability, reduced inventories and accurate cost accounting.

Karen Kharlead

5610 TENTEL Corporation
4475 Golden Foothill Parkway
El Dorado Hills, CA 95762-9638

800-538-6894
Fax: 916-939-4114

Cleaning, repair and maintenance products for educational institutions.

5611 Tiffin Systems
450 Wall Street
Tiffin, OH 44883-1366

419-447-8414
800-537-0983
Fax: 419-447-8512
E-mail: tiffin@bpsom.com
http://www.tiffinmetal.com

Lockers, storage containers and shelving.

5612 Topog-E Gasket Company
1224 N Utica Avenue
Tulsa, OK 74110-4682

918-587-6649
Fax: 918-587-6961

Maintenance supplies and products.

5613 Tru-Flex Recreational Coatings
Touraine Paints
1760 Revere Beach Pkwy
Everett, MA 02149-5906

800-325-0017

Maintenance, floor care, coatings and repair supplies for upkeep of schools and institutions.

5614 Wagner Spray Tech Corporation
1770 Fernbrook Lane N
Plymouth, MN 55447-4663

763-553-7000
Fax: 763-553-7288

Maintenance supplies, floor care, cleaning and repair products and equipment.

5615 Wilmar
303 Harper Drive
Moorestown, NJ 08057

609-439-1222
800-523-7120
Fax: 800-220-3291

Maintenance and repair products, hardware and supplies.

5616 Witt Company
4454 Steel Place
Cincinnati, OH 45209-1184

513-979-3127
800-543-7417
Fax: 513-979-3134

Lockers, maintenance supplies and storage containers for educational purposes.

5617 Zep Manufacturing
1310 Seaboard Industrial Blvd NW
Atlanta, GA 30318-2807

404-352-1680

Maintenance and cleaning supplies.

Scientific Equipment

5618 Adventures Company
435 Main Street
Johnson City, NY 13790-1935

607-729-6512
800-477-6512
Fax: 607-729-4820

A full line of supplies and equipment for science and technology education.

D Hetherington

5619 Alfa Aesar
30 Bond Street
Ward Hill, MA 01835-8042

800-343-0660

Laboratory equipment and supplies.

5620 American Chemical Society
1155 16th Street NW
Washington, DC 20036-4800

202-872-4600
800-ACS-5558
Fax: 202-833-7732

Exhibits hands-on activities and programs for K-12 and college science curriculum.

5621 Arbor Scientific
PO Box 2750
Ann Arbor, MI 48106-2750

800-367-6695
Fax: 734-477-9570
E-mail: mail@arborsci.com
http://www.arborsci.com

Innovative products for Science Education.

56 pages Bi-Annual Catalog

Dave Barnes, Marketing Director

5622 Astronomy to Go
1115 Melrose Avenue
Melrose Park, PA 19027-3017

215-782-8970
Fax: 215-831-0486
E-mail: astro2go@aol.com
http://www.astronomytogo.com

Programs include Starlab Planetarium presentations, hands-on demonstrations, slides and lecture shows and energy observing sessions with our many telescopses. We are funded through our traveling museum shop which carries a largeassortment of t-shirts, jewelry, gifts, books, and teaching supplies as well as an extensive selection of meterorites.

Bob Summerfield, Director

5623 CEM Corporation
3100 Smith Farm Road
Matthews, NC 28104-5044

704-821-7015
Fax: 704-821-7894

Laboratory and scientific supplies, furniture, casework and equipment.

5624 Carolina Biological Supply Company
2700 York Road
Burlington, NC 27215-3398

336-584-0381
800-334-5551
Fax: 800-222-7112
E-mail: carolina@carolina.com
http://www.carolina.com

Educational products for teachers and students of biology, molecular biology, biotechnology, chemistry, earth science, space science, physics, and mathematics. Carolina serves elementary schools through universities with living andpreserved animals and plants, prepared microscope slides, microscopes, audiovisuals, books, charts, models, computer software, games, apparatus, and much more.

5625 Challenger Center for Space Science Education
1250 N Pitt Street
Alexandria, VA 22314

703-683-9740
Fax: 703-683-7546
E-mail: mail@challenger.org
http://www.challenger.org

Is a global not-for-profit education organization created in 1986 by familes of the astronauts tragically lost during the last flight of the Challenger Space Shuttle. Dedicated to the educaltional spirit of that mission, Challengercenter develops Learning Centers and othe educational programs worldwide to continue the mission to engage students in science and math education

Glenn Ono, Marketing/Communications
Tracy Martin, Marketing Assistant

5626 ChronTrol Corporation
9975 Businesspark Avenue
San Diego, CA 92131-1644

619-282-8686
Fax: 619-563-6563

Scientific equipment, laboratory supplies and furniture.

5627 Classic Modular Systems
1911 Columbus Street
Two Rivers, WI 54241-2898

920-793-2269
800-558-7625
Fax: 920-793-2896
E-mail: cms@dataplusnet.com
http://www.dct.com/cms

Laboratory equipment, shelving, cabinets and markerboards.

Cathy Albers, Advertising Manager

5628 Columbia University's Biosphere 2 Center
Highway 77 & Biosphere Road
Oracle, AZ 85623

520-896-6200
Fax: 520-896-6471

Educational programs and products.

5629 Connecticut Valley Biological Supply Company
82 Valley Road
PO Box 326
Southampton, MA 01073-9536

413-527-4030
800-628-7748
Fax: 800-355-6813
E-mail: connval@ctvalleybio.com

Cultures and specimens, instruments, equipment, hands-on kits, books, software, audiovisuals, models and charts for teaching botany, zoology, life science, anatomy, physiology, genetics, astronomy, entomology, microscopy, AP Biology,microbiology, horticulture, biotechnology, earth science, natural history and environmental science.

5630 Crow Canyon Archaeological Center
23390 County Road K
Cortez, CO 81321-9408
970-565-8975
800-422-8975
Fax: 970-565-4859
E-mail: jsimpson@crowcanyon.org
http://www.crowcanyon.org

Experiential education programs in archaeology and Native American history. Programs offered for school groups, teachers and other adults.

ISBN: 0-7872-6748-1

M Elaine Davis and Marjorie R Connelly, Author
Joyce Simpson, Director Marketing
Elaine Davis, Director Education

5631 Cuisenaire Company of America
10 Bank Street
#5026
White Plains, NY 10606-1933
914-997-2600
Fax: 914-684-6137

Science materials and equipment.

5632 DISCOVER Science Program
105 Terry Drive
Suite 120
Newtown, PA 18940-1872
800-448-3399
Fax: 215-579-8589

Features the newest developments in a wide range of science topics and provides an easy way for teachers to stay current and up-to-date in the world of science. The DISCOVER Program offers the DISCOVER magazine at the lowest possible price.

5633 Delta Biologicals
PO Box 26666
Tucson, AZ 85726-6666
520-790-7737
800-821-2502
Fax: 520-745-7888
E-mail: sales@deltabio.com
http://www.deltabio.com

Products and supplies for science and biology educators for over 30 years. Preserves specimens, laboratory furniture, microscopes, anatomy models, balances and scales, dissection supplies, lab safety supplies, multimedia, plantpresses.

Lynn Hugins, Marketing
Darlene Harris, Customer Service Manager

5634 Delta Biologicals Catalog
PO Box 26666
Tucson, AZ 85726-6666
520-790-7737
800-821-2502
Fax: 520-745-7888
E-mail: sales@deltabio.com
http://www.deltabio.com

96 pages

Lynn Hugins, Marketing
Darlene Harris, Customer Service Manager

5635 Detecto Scale Corporation
203 E Daugherty Street
Webb City, MO 64870-1929
417-673-4631
800-641-2008
Fax: 417-673-5001
E-mail: detecto@cardet.com
http://www.detectoscale.com

Scientific equipment and supplies for educational laboratories.

5636 Dickson Company
930 S Westwood Avenue
Addison, IL 60101-4997
630-543-3747

Laboratory instruments, electronics, furniture and equipment.

5637 Donald K. Olson & Associates
PO Box 858
Bonsall, CA 92003-0858

Mineral and fossil samples for educational purposes.

5638 Dranetz Technologies
1000 Durham Road
Edison, NJ 08818
732-287-3680
Fax: 732-287-9014

Laboratory instruments, equipment and supplies.

5639 Edmund Scientific - Scientifics Catalog
E726 Edscorp Building
Department 16A1
Barrington, NJ 08007
856-547-3488
Fax: 856-573-6295

Over 5,000 products including a wide selection of microscopes, telescopes, astronomy aids, fiber optic kits, demonstration optics, magnets and science discover products used in science fair projects.

Nancy McGonigle, President

5640 Educational Products
1342 N I35 E
Carrollton, TX 75006
972-245-9512
Fax: 972-245-5468

Science display boards, workshop materials and science fair accessories.

5641 Edwin H. Benz Company
73 Maplehurst Avenue
Providence, RI 02908-5324
401-331-5650
Fax: 401-331-5685
E-mail: sales@benztesters.com
http://www.benztesters.com

Laboratory equipment.

5642 Electro-Steam Generator Corporation
1000 Bernard Street
Alexandria, VA 22314-1299
703-549-0664
800-634-8177
Fax: 703-836-2581
E-mail: jharlinelectrosteam.com
http://www.electrosteam.com

Laboratory equipment and supplies. Manufacture steam generators for sterilizers, autoclaves, clean rooms, pure steam humidification, laboratories, steam rooms, and cleaning of all kinds.

Jack Harlin, Sales/Marketing Associate

5643 Estes-Cox Corporation
1295 H Street
Penrose, CO 81240-9676
719-372-6565
800-820-0202
Fax: 719-372-3217
E-mail: info@esteseducator.com
http://www.esteseducator.com

Supplier of model rockets, engines and supporting videos, curriculums and educational publications for K-12.

Ann Grimm, Director Education

5644 FOTODYNE
950 Walnut Ridge Drive
Hartland, WI 53029-9388

262-369-7000
800-362-3642
Fax: 262-369-7017

Biotechnology curriculum equipment.

5645 First Step Systems
PO Box 2304
Jackson, TN 38302-2304

800-831-0877
Fax: 216-361-0829

Developed an effective, safe and less expensive approach to blood exposure safety for schools and classrooms that both help comply with OSHA requirements and is easy to purchase and resupply.

Susan Staples, Account Manager
Renee Carr, Bid Support

5646 Fisher Scientific Company
1410 Wayne Avenue
Indiana, PA 15701-3940

724-357-1000
Fax: 724-357-1019

A full line of laboratory and scientific supplies and equipment for educational institutions.

5647 Fisher Scientific/EMD
3970 John Creek Court
Suite 500
Suwanee, GA 30024

770-871-4500
800-766-7000
Fax: 800-926-1166

Supplier of chemistry, biology and physics laboratory supplies and equipment.

5648 Fisons Instruments
8 Forge Parkway
Franklin, MA 02038-3157

978-524-1000

Laboratory equipment and instruments for the scientific classroom.

5649 Flinn Scientific
PO Box 219
Batavia, IL 60510-0219

630-879-6900
800-452-1261
Fax: 630-879-6962

Laboratory safety supplies.

5650 Forestry Supplies
PO Box 8397
Jackson, MS 39284-8397

601-354-3565
800-647-5368
Fax: 800-543-4203
E-mail: fsi@forestry-suppliers.com
http://www.forestry-suppliers.com

Field and lab equipment for earth, life and environmental sciences.

Ken Peacock, VP Marketing
Debbie Raddin, Education Specialist

5651 Frank Schaffer Publications
23740 Hawthorne Boulevard
Torrance, CA 90505-5927

310-378-1133
800-421-5565
Fax: 800-837-7260

Charts, animal posters, floor puzzles, resource books and more.

5652 Frey Scientific
905 Hickory Lane
Mansfield, OH 44905-2862

800-225-FREY
Fax: 419-589-1522

Name brand scientific products including Energy Physics, Earth Science, Chemistry and Applied Science. Over 12,000 products and kits for grades 5-14 are available.

5653 Great Adventure Tours
1717 Old Topanga Canyon Road
Topanga, CA 90290-3934

800-642-3933

Educational science field trips and adventures.

5654 Guided Discoveries
PO Box 1360
Claremont, CA 91711-1360

Outdoor educational science programs.

5655 HACH Company
PO Box 389
Loveland, CO 80539-0389

970-669-3050
Fax: 970-669-2932

Water and soil test kits for field and laboratory work.

5656 Heathkit Educational Systems
455 Riverview Drive
Benton Harbor, MI 49022-5015

616-925-6000
800-253-0570
Fax: 616-925-3895

Electronics educational products from basic electricity to high-tech lasers and microscopes and beyond. Comprehensive line of different media to fit varied applications. Including Computer-Aided Instruction and Computer-AidedTroubleshooting services and Heathkit's PC Servicing, Troubleshooting and Networking courses.

Carolyn Feltner, Sales Coordinator
Patrick Beckett, Marketing Manager

5657 Holometrix
25 Wiggins Avenue
Bedford, MA 01730-2314

781-275-3300
Fax: 781-275-3705

Laboratory instruments.

5658 Howell Playground Equipment
1714 E Fairchild Street
Danville, IL 61832-3616

217-442-0482
800-637-5075
Fax: 217-442-8944
E-mail: howellequipment@aol.com
http://www.primestripe.com

Playground equipment and bicycle racks.

Nina Payne, President

5659 Hubbard Scientific
PO Box 2121
Fort Collins, CO 80522-2121

Earth science and life science models, kits, globes and curriculum materials.

5660 Innova Corporation
115 George Lamb Road
Bernardston, MA 01337-9742

Science kits and globes.

5661 Insect Lore
PO Box 1535
Shafter, CA 93263-1535

661-746-6047
800-548-3284
Fax: 661-746-0334
E-mail: orders@insectlore.com
http://www.insectlore.com

Science and nature materials for preschool through grade 6. Raises butterflies, frogs, ladybugs and more. Features books, curriculum units, videos, puppet, posters, and other nature oriented products.

5662 Insights Visual Productions
PO Box 230644
Encinitas, CA 92023-0644

800-942-0528

Laboratory instruments, manuals, and supplies.

5663 Instron Corporation
100 Royall Street
Canton, MA 02021-1089

781-828-2500
Fax: 781-575-5776

Laboratory and scientific equipment, supplies and furniture.

5664 Johnsonite
16910 Munn Road
Chagrin Falls, OH 44023-5493

800-899-8916
Fax: 440-632-5643

Physical education mats, matting and floors.

5665 Justrite Manufacturing Company
2454 E Dempster Street
Des Plaines, IL 60016-5315

847-298-9250
Fax: 847-298-3429
E-mail: justrite@justritemfg.com
http://www.justritemfg.com

Supplies and equipment aimed at the scientific classroom or laboratory.

5666 KLM Bioscientific
8888 Clairemont Mesa Boulevard
Suite D
San Diego, CA 92123

858-571-5562
Fax: 858-571-5587

A mail order company that provides high quality, reasonably priced, on time living and preserved biological specimens. The Biology Store also carries a wide range of instructional materials including books, charts, models and videos. Also available is a wide range of general labware.

Loli Victorio, President

5667 Ken-a-Vision Manufacturing Company
5615 Raytown Road
Kansas City, MO 64133-3388

816-353-4787
Fax: 816-358-5072
E-mail: info@ken-a-vision.com
http://www.ken-a-vision.com

Video Flex, Vison Viewer, Pupil CAM, Microscopes and Microrojectors

Steve Dunn, Domestic/International Op.
Ben Hoke, Sales Manger

5668 Kepro Circuit Systems
3640 Scarlet Oak Boulevard
Kirkwood, MO 63122-6606

800-325-3878
Fax: 636-861-9109

Laboratory equipment.

5669 Kewaunee Scientific Corporation
2700 W Front Street
Statesville, NC 28677-2894

704-873-7202
Fax: 704-873-1275
E-mail: humanresources@kewaunee.com
http://www.kewaunee.com

Science and laboratory supplies.

Bob Neals, Human Resources

5670 Knex Education Catalog
Knex Education
2990 Bergey Road
PO Box 700
Hatfield, PA 19440-0700

888-ABC-KNEX
E-mail: abcknex@knex.com
http://www.knexeducation.com

Hands-on, award-winning curriculum supported K-12 math, science and technology sets.

5671 Koffler Sales Company
100A Oakwood Road e
Lake Zurich, IL 60047-1524

847-438-1152
800-323-0951
Fax: 847-438-1514
http://www.kofflersales.com

Floor mats, Matting and stair treads.

5672 Komodo Dragon
PO Box 822
The Dalles, OR 97058-0822

541-773-5808

Museum-quality fossils and minerals.

5673 Kreonite
715 E 10th Street N
Wichita, KS 67214-2918

316-263-1111
Fax: 316-263-6829

Laboratory equipment, furniture and hardware.

5674 Kruger & Eckels
1406 E Wilshire Avenue
Santa Ana, CA 92705-4423

714-547-5165
Fax: 714-547-2009

Laboratory and scientific instruments for institutional or educational use.

5675 LEGO Data
PO Box 1600
Enfield, CT 06083-1600

860-749-2291
Fax: 860-763-7477

Curriculum programs and materials for science education.

5676 LINX System
Science Source
PO Box 727
Waldoboro, ME 04572-0727

207-832-6344
800-299-5469
Fax: 207-832-7281
E-mail: info@thesciencesource.com
http://www.thesciencesource.com

A building system that integrates science, mathematics and technology at the K-9 level.

5677 Lab Safety Supply
PO Box 1368
Janesville, WI 53547-1368

608-754-2345
Fax: 800-543-9910

Extensive variety of school products, including lab and safety apparel and floorcoverings.

5678 Lab Volt Systems
PO Box 686
Farmingdale, NJ 07727-0686

Educational materials and equipment for the science educator.

5679 Lab-Aids
17 Colt Center
Ronkonkoma, NY 11779-6949

631-737-1133
800-381-8003
Fax: 631-737-1286
E-mail: mkt@lab-aids.com
http://www.lab-aids.com

Science kits, published curriculum materials.

John Weatherby, Sales/Marketing Director
David M Frank, President

5680 Labconco Corporation
8811 Prospect Avenue
Kansas City, MO 64132-2696

816-333-8811
Fax: 816-363-0130

Laboratory equipment and supplies.

5681 Lakeside Manufacturing
1977 S Allis Street
Milwaukee, WI 53207-1295

414-481-3900
Fax: 414-481-9313

Laboratory and scientific instruments, equipment, furniture and supplies.

5682 Lane Science Equipment Company
225 W 34th Street
Suite 1412
New York, NY 10122-1496

212-563-0663
Fax: 212-465-9440

Scientific equipment, technology and supplies.

5683 Lasy USA
1309 Webster Avenue
Fort Collins, CO 80524-2756

800-444-2126
Fax: 970-221-4352

Building sets that encourage children to encounter technology through problem solving activities, planning, co-operation and perseverance. Allows students to build and learn programming skills in areas of communication, construction, manufacturing and transportation.

Dave Nayak

5684 Learning Technologies
40 Cameron Avenue
Somerville, MA 02144-2404

617-628-1459
800-537-8703
Fax: 617-628-8606
E-mail: starlab@starlab.com
http://www.starlab.com

STARLAB portable planetarium systems and the Project STAR hands-on science materials.

Jane Sadler, President

5685 Leica Microsystems EAD
PO Box 123
Buffalo, NY 14240-0123

716-686-3000
Fax: 716-686-3085

Educational microscopes for elementary through university applications.

5686 Life Technologies
7335 Executive Way
Suite A
Frederick, MD 21704-8354

716-774-6700
800-952-9166
Fax: 716-774-6727

Supplier of biology and cell culture products.

5687 Lyon Electric Company
1690 Brandywine Avenue
Chula Vista, CA 91911-6021

619-216-3400
Fax: 619-216-3434

Electrical tabletop incubators for science classrooms and tabletop animal intensive care units, hatchers and brooders.

Caroline Vazquez, Sales Manager
Jose Madrigal, Marketing Manager

5688 Magnet Source
607 S Gilbert Street
Castle Rock, CO 80104-2221

303-688-3966
888-293-9190
Fax: 303-688-5303
E-mail: magnet@magnetsource.com
http://www.magnetsource.com

Educational magnetic products and magnetic toys designed to stimulate creativity and encourage exploration of science with fun magnets. Kits include experiments, fun games, activities and powerful magnets. Moo Magnets, rare earthmagnets, horseshoes, and bulk magnets.

Jim Madsen, Sales Manager

5689 Meiji Techno America
Meiji Techno America
2186 Bering Drive
San Jose, CA 95131-2041

408-428-9654
800-832-0060
Fax: 408-428-0472
http://www.meijitechno.com

A full line of elementary, secondary, grade school and college-level microscopes and accessories.

James J Dutkiewicz, General Manager

5690 Metrologic Instruments
Coles Road at Route 42
Blackwood, NJ 08012

800-436-3876
Fax: 856-228-0653

Manufactures low-power lasers and laser accessories for the classroom, a range of helium-neon lasers, a modulated VLD laser, optics lab, sandbox holography kit, speed of light lab, optics bench system and digital laser power meter, aswell as a selection of pin carriers, mounting pins, lenses and mirrors. Sponsors the Physics Bowl, a yearly national physics competition for high school students by the American Association of Physics Teachers.

Betty Williams

5691 Modern School Supplies
PO Box 958
Hartford, CT 06143-0958

860-243-9565
Fax: 800-934-7206

Products for hands-on science education.

5692 Mohon International
1600 Porter Court
Paris, TN 38242

731-642-4251
Fax: 731-642-4262

Classroom equipment and supplies, directed at the scientific classroom and laboratory.

5693 Museum Products Company
84 Route 27
Mystic, CT 06355-1226

860-536-6433
800-395-5400
Fax: 860-572-9589
E-mail: museumprod@aol.com
http://www.museumproducts.net

Field guides, rock collections, environmental puzzles, posters, charts, books, magnets, magnifiers, microscopes and other lab equipment. Also weather simulators, physics demonstration, games, toys in space, animal track replicas andfossils. Free catalog.

John Bannister, President

5694 Nalge Company
PO Box 20365
Rochester, NY 14602-0365

585-586-8800
800-625-4327
Fax: 585-586-8987

Plastic labware and safety products for the scientific classroom.

5695 National Instruments
6504 Bridge Point Parkway
Austin, TX 78730-5039

512-794-0100
Fax: 512-683-5794

Laboratory/scientific instruments.

5696 National Optical & Scientific Instruments
11113 Landmark 35 Drive
San Antonio, TX 78233-5786

210-590-7010
800-275-3716
Fax: 210-590-1104
E-mail: natlopt@sbcglobal.net
http://www.nationaloptical.com

Wholesale distributor of national comppound, stero and digital miocroscopes for K-12 and college.

Michael Hart, Director Sales/Marketing

5697 Ohaus Corporation
19 A Chapin Road
Pine Brook, NJ 07058-1408

973-377-9000
800-672-7722
Fax: 973-593-0359

Scientific supplies and equipment for the classroom or laboratory.

5698 PASCO Scientific
10101 Foothills Boulevard
Roseville, CA 95747-7100

916-786-3800
800-772-8700
Fax: 916-786-7565
E-mail: jbrown@pasco.com
http://ww.pasco.com

US manufacturers of physics apparatus and probe warer that enable teachers to improve science literacy and meet the standards

Justine Brown, Copy Writer

5699 Quest Aerospace Education
350 E 18th Street
Yuma, AZ 85364

602-595-9506
Fax: 520-783-9534

A complete line of model rockets and related teaching materials.

5700 Resources for Teaching Elementary School Science
National Academy Press
Arts & Industries Bldg Room 1201
900 Jefferson Drive SW
Washington, DC 20560-0403

202-287-2063
Fax: 202-287-2070
E-mail: outreach@nas.edu
http://www.si.edu

Resource guides for elementary, middle school, and high school science teachers. Annotated guides to hands-on, inquiry-centered curriculum materials and sources of help in teaching science from kindergarten through sixth grades.Produced by the National Science Resources Center.

National Science Resources Center, Author
Douglas Lapp, Executive Director

5701 Rheometrics
1 Possumtown Road
Piscataway, NJ 08854-2100

732-560-8550

Laboratory/science supplies and equipment.

5702 SARUT
107 Horatio Street
New York, NY 10014-1569

212-691-9453

Science and nature-related educational tools.

5703 Safe-T-Rack Systems
4325 Dominguez Road
Suite A
Rocklin, CA 95677-2146

916-632-1121
Fax: 916-632-1173

Laboratory furniture, safety storage containers and equipment.

5704 Sargent-Welch Scientific Company
911 Commerce Court
Buffalo Grove, IL 60089-2375

847-459-6625

Models, books and instruments for the scientific classroom.

5705 Science Instruments Company
6122 Reisterstown Road
Baltimore, MD 21215-3423
410-358-7810

Develops, manufactures and markets unique hands-on programs in biotechnology, biomedical instrumentation, telecommunications, electronics and industrial controls.

5706 Science Source
PO Box 727
Waldoboro, ME 04572-0727
207-832-6344
800-299-5469
Fax: 207-832-7281
E-mail: info@thesciencesource.com
http://www.thesciencesource.com

Design technology books, teacher resource and student books on design and technology, design technology materials, equipment and supplies used in the construction of design challenges.

Michelle Winter, Sales/Marketing Support
Rudolf Graf, President

5707 Science for Today & Tomorrow
1840 E 12th Street
Mishawaka, IN 46544
574-258-5397
Fax: 574-258-5594

Hands-on science activities packaged for K-3 students.

5708 Scientific Laser Connection, Incorporated
5021 N 55th Avenue
Suite 10
Glendale, AZ 85301-7535
623-939-6711
877-668-7844
Fax: 623-939-3369
E-mail: sales@slclaser.com
http://www.slclasers.com

Laser education modules.

Don Morris, President
Travis Gatrin, Service

5709 Shain/Shop-Bilt
509 Hemlock Street
Philipsburg, PA 16866-2937
814-342-2820
Fax: 814-342-6180

Laboratory casework and cabinets.

5710 Sheldon Lab Systems
PO Box 836
Crystal Springs, MS 39059-0836
601-892-2731
Fax: 601-892-4364

Laboratory casework and technical equipment for K-12, college and university level.

5711 Skilcraft
CRAFT House Corporation
328 N Westwood Avenue
Toledo, OH 43607-3317
419-537-9090
Fax: 419-537-9160

Microchemistry sets.

5712 Skullduggery Kits
624 S B Street
Tustin, CA 92780-4318
800-336-7745
Fax: 714-832-1215

Social studies kits offers hands-on learning, art projects, complete lesson plans, authentic replicas, and challenging products designed for small groups of students with increasing levels of difficulty.

5713 Skulls Unlimited International
10313 S Sunnylane Road
Oklahoma City, OK 73160
405-794-9300
800-659-SKUL
Fax: 405-794-6985
E-mail: sales@skullsunlimited.com
http://www.skullsunlimited.com

Leading supplier of specimen supplies to the educational community.

5714 Society of Automotive Engineers
400 Commonwealth Drive
Warrendale, PA 15086-7511
724-776-4841
877-606-7323
Fax: 724-776-5760
E-mail: info@sae.org
http://www.sae.org

Award-winning science unit for grades 4-6.

Steve Yaeger, Corporate PR Manager
Kathleen O'Conner, K-12 Education Program Mgr

5715 Southern Precision Instruments Company
3419 E Commerce Street
San Antonio, TX 78220-1322
210-212-5055
800-417-5055
Fax: 210-212-5062
E-mail: spico@flash.net
http://www.flash.net/spico

Microscopes and microprojectors for grades K-1-K-12 and college levels. Stereo and compound microscopes, along with CCTV color systems.

Victor Spiroff, VP/General Manager

5716 Southland Instruments
17741 Metzler Lane
Unit A
Huntington Beach, CA 92647-6246
714-847-5007
Fax: 714-893-3613

Microscopes.

5717 Spectronics Corporation
956 Brush Hollow Road
Westbury, NY 11590-1714
516-333-4840
800-274-8888
Fax: 800-491-6868
E-mail: vvvv@aol.com
http://www.spectroline.com

Laboratory and scientific classroom equipment, hardware and shelving.

Gloria Blusk, Manager Customer Service
Vincent McKenna, Publicist

5718 Spitz
Transnational Industries
PO Box 198
Chadds Ford, PA 19317-0198
215-459-5200

Offers scientific and laboratory instruments and accessories.

5719 Swift Instruments
1190 N 4th Street
San Jose, CA 95112-4946
408-293-2380

Educational microscopes and other laboratory instruments.

5720 TEDCO
498 S Washington Street
Hagerstown, IN 47346-1596
765-489-4527
800-654-6357
Fax: 765-489-5752
E-mail: sales@tedcotoys.com
http://www.tedcotoys.com

Bill Nye Extreme Gyro, Prisms, Educational Toys Solar Science Kit.

Jane Shadle

5721 Telaire Systems
6489 Calle Real
Goleta, CA 93117-1538
805-964-1699
Fax: 805-964-2129

Laboratory instruments and hardware.

5722 Tooltron Industries
103 Parkway
Boerne, TX 78006-9224
830-249-8277
800-293-8134
Fax: 830-755-8134
E-mail: easyleut@gvtc.comt
http://www.tooltron.com

Scientific hardware and laboratory equipment, including instruments and accessories. School scissors and craft supplies.

Thomas Love, Owner/VP Marketing

5723 Triops
PO Box 10852
Pensacola, FL 32524-0852
850-479-4415
800-200-DINO
Fax: 850-479-3315
E-mail: triopsinc@aol.com
http://www.triops.com

Classroom activities and kits in environmental, ecological and biological sciences.

Dr. Eugene Hull, President
Peter Bender, Office Manager

5724 Trippense Planetarium Company
Science First
95 Botsford Place
Buffalo, NY 14216
716-874-0133
800-875-3214
Fax: 716-874-9853
E-mail: info@sciencefirst.com
http://www.sciencefirst.com

Astronomy and earth science models and materials, including the Trippense planetarium, Elementary planetarium, Copernican and Ptolemic solar systems, Milky Way model, Explore Celestial Globes and the patented top quality educationalastronomy models since 1905.

Kris Spors, Customer Service Manager
Nancy Bell, President

5725 Unilab
967 Mabury Road
San Jose, CA 95133
800-288-9850
Fax: 408-975-1035
E-mail: unilab@richnet.net
http://www.unilabinc.com

Designs and manufactures products for teaching science and technology.

Gerald A Beer, VP

5726 Vibrac Corporation
16 Columbia Drive
Amherst, NH 03031-2304
603-882-6777
Fax: 603-271-3454

Scientific instruments and hardware.

5727 Wild Goose Company
5181 S 300 W
Murray, UT 84107-4709
801-466-1172

Hands-on science kits for elementary-aged students 3 and up and resource books for all levels of general science.

5728 Wildlife Supply Company
95 Botsford Place
Buffalo, NY 14216-d
716-877-9518
800-799-8301
Fax: 716-874-9853
E-mail: goto@wildco.com
http://www.wildco.com

Aquatic sampling equipment including Fieldmaster Field Kits, Water Bottle Kits, Secchi Disks, line and messengers and a NEW Mini Ponar bottom grab. Also, a variety of professional Wildco bottom grabs, water bottles, plankton nets,hand corers and other materials.

Aaron Bell, Product Manager
Bruce Izard, Customer Service Manager

5729 WoodKrafter Kits
PO Box 808
Yarmouth, ME 04096-0808
207-846-3722
Fax: 207-846-1019

Science kits, hands-on curriculum-based science kits for ages 4 and up, classroom packs, supplies and science materials also available.

Sports & Playground Equipment

5730 ACT Success
Peterson's Guides
PO Box 2123
Princeton, NJ 08543-2123
609-243-9111
800-338-3282
Fax: 609-243-9150

Familiarizes students with the test's format, reviews skills, and provides the all-important practice that helps build confidence.

416 pages Book & Disk
ISBN: 1-560796-07-3

Elaine Bender, Mark Weinfeld, et al., Author

5731 American Playground Corporation
6406 Production Drive
Anderson, IN 46013-9408
765-642-0288
800-541-1602
Fax: 765-649-7162
E-mail: sales@american-playground.com
http://www.american-playground.com

Playground equipment and supplies.

Julie Morson, Inside Sales Manager
Marty Bloyd, General Manager

5732 American Swing Products
2533 N Carson Street
Suite 1062
Carson City, NV 89706-0147

800-433-2573
800-433-2573
Fax: 775-883-4874
E-mail: play@americanswing.com
http://www.americanswing.com

Replacement playground parts, including commercial and residential swing sets, swing hangers for pipes and wood beams, spring animals, S-hooks, spring connectors, and more.

Susan Watson, President

5733 BCI Burke Company
660 Van Dyne Road
Fond Du Lac, WI 54937-1447

920-921-9220
Fax: 920-921-9566

Playground equipment.

5734 Belson Manufacturing
111 N River Road
North Aurora, IL 60542-1396

800-323-5664

Playground equipment.

5735 Colorado Time Systems
1551 E 11th Street
Loveland, CO 80537-5056

970-667-1000
800-279-0111
Fax: 970-667-5876
E-mail: sales@colooradotimes.com
http://www.coloradotime.com

Been the system of choice for sports timing and scoring. Has a timing system for almost every sport including swimming, basketball, football, baseball, track, soccer and most others. Has a wide variety of displays ranging from fixeddigit scoreboards to animation LED boards to fullcolor video displays and ribbon boards.

Randy Flint, Sr Sales Representative
Rick Connell, CDS Sales Manager

5736 Constructive Playthings
1227 E 119th Street
Grandview, MO 64030-1178

Playground, recreational and indoor fun equipment for children grades PreK-3.

5737 Creative Outdoor Designs
142 Pond Drive
Lexington, SC 29073-8009

803-957-9259
Fax: 803-957-7152

Playground equipment.

5738 Curtis Marketing Corporation
2550 Rigel Road
Venice, FL 34293-3200

941-493-8085

Playground equipment.

5739 GameTime
PO Box 680121
Fort Payne, AL 35968-0099

256-845-5610
800-235-2440
Fax: 256-845-9361
E-mail: info@gametime.com
http://www.gametime.com

Playground equipment.

Doris Dellinger, Marketing Service Manager

5740 Gared Sports
707 N 2nd Street
Suite 220
Saint Louis, MO 63102

800-325-2682
Fax: 314-421-6014
E-mail: laura@garedsports.com
http://www.garedsports.com

Basketball, Volleyball, Soccer, Equipment and training aids for indoor and outdoor facilities.

Laura St George, Sales/Marketing Manager

5741 Gerstung/Gym-Thing
6308 Blair Hill Lane
Baltimore, MD 21209-2102

800-922-3575

Physical education mats, matting and floorcoverings.

5742 Grounds for Play
1401 E Dallas Road
Mansfield, TX 76063

817-477-5482
800-552-7529
Fax: 817-477-1140
E-mail: jimdempsey@groundsforplay.com
http://www.groundsforplay.com

Playground equipment, flooring, floorcoverings, play eviroment design, lanscape architecure, insatllation, and safety insepection.

Jim Dempsey, Senior VP
Emily Smith, Office Manager

5743 Iron Mountain Forge
One Iron Mountain Drive
Farmington, MO 63640

800-325-8828
Fax: 573-760-7441

Playground equipment.

5744 JCH International
978 E Hermitage Road NE
Rome, GA 30161-9641

800-328-9203

Coverings, mats and physical education matting.

5745 Jaypro
Jaypro Sports
976 Hartford Tpke
Waterford, CT 06385-4002

860-447-3001
800-243-0533
Fax: 860-444-1779
E-mail: info@jaypro.com
http://www.jaypro.com

Sports equipment.

Linda Andels, Marketing Manager
Bill Wild, VP Sales/Marketing

5746 Kidstuff Playsystems
5400 Miller Avenue
Gary, IN 46403-2844

800-255-0153
Fax: 219-938-3340
E-mail: rhagelberg@kidstuffplaysystems.com
http://www.fun-zone.com

Preschool and grade school playground equipment, Health Trek Fitness Course, park site furnishings.

Dick Hagelberg, CEO

School Supplies / Sports & Playground Equipment

5747 Kompan
7717 New Market Street
Olympia, WA 98501

360-943-6374
800-426-9788
Fax: 360-943-5575
http://www.kompan.com

Unique playgrond equipment.

Tom Grover, Marketing Director

5748 LA Steelcraft Products
1975 Lincoln Avenue
Pasadena, CA 91103-1395

626-798-7401
800-371-2438
Fax: 626-798-1482
E-mail: info@lasteelcraft.com
http://www.lasteelcraft.com

Manufacturer of quality athletic, park and playground equipment for schools, parks and industry. Features indoor/outdoor fiberglass furniture, court and field equipment, site furnishings, bike racks, flagpoles, baseball andbasketball backstops.

James D Holt, President
John C Gaudesi, COO

5749 Landscape Structures
PO Box 198
Delano, MN 55328-0198

612-972-3391

Playground equipment.

5750 MMI-Federal Marketing Service
PO Box 241367
Montgomery, AL 36124-1367

334-286-0700
Fax: 334-286-0711

Playground equipment, sports timers, clocks and school supplies.

5751 Matworks
Division of Janitex Rug Service Corporation
11900 Old Baltimore Pike
Beltsville, MD 20705-1265

800-523-5179
Fax: 301-595-0740

Mats, matting and floorcoverings for entrances, gymnasiums, and all other facilities where the potential for slip and fall exists.

5752 Miracle Recreation Equipment Company
PO Box 420
Monett, MO 65708-0420

417-235-6917
Fax: 417-235-6816

Playground and recreation equipment.

5753 National Teaching Aids
PO Box 2121
Fort Collins, CO 80522

970-484-7445
800-289-9299
Fax: 970-484-1198
E-mail: bevans@amep.com
http://www.hubbardscientific.com

Learning math, alphabet, and geography skills is easy with our Clever Catch Balls. These colorful 24" inflatable vinyl balls provide an excellent way for children to practice math, alphabet and geography skills. Excellent learningtool in organized classroom activities, on the playground, or at home.

Barbara Evans, Customer Service Manager
Candy Coffman, National Sales Manger

5754 New Braunfels General Store International
3150 Interstate H 35 S
New Braunfels, TX 78130-7927

830-620-4000
Fax: 830-620-0598

Playground equipment, supplies and classroom supplies.

5755 Outback Play Centers
1280 W Main Street
Sun Prairie, WI 53590-0010

608-825-2140
800-338-0522
Fax: 608-825-2114
http://www.outbackplaycenters.com

Playground equipment.

Jack Garczynskl, President

5756 PlayDesigns
1000 Buffalo Road
Lewisburg, PA 17837-9795

800-327-7571
Fax: 570-522-3030
E-mail: webmaster@playdesigns.com
http://www.playdesigns.com

Playground and recreational equipment, flooring and matting.

5757 Playground Environments
22 Old Country Road
PO Box 578
Quogue, NY 11959

631-231-1300
800-662-0922
Fax: 631-231-1329
E-mail: peplay@mindspring.com

Designs and manufactures integrated play and recreational areas for children, providing them with new experiences in a safe, accessible, educationally supportive and fun environment.

5758 Playnix
3530 S Logan Street
Englewood, CO 80110-3731

303-761-5630
Fax: 303-781-6749

Wood products and playground equipment.

5759 Playworld Systems
1000 Buffalo Road
Lewisburg, PA 17837-9795

570-522-9800
800-233-8404
Fax: 570-522-3030
E-mail: webmaster@playworldsystems.com
http://www.playworldsystems.com

Playground and recreational equipment.

5760 Porter Athletic Equipment Company
Porter Athletic Equipment Company
2500 S 25th Avenue
Broadview, IL 60155-3870

708-338-2000
800-947-6783
Fax: 708-338-2060
E-mail: porter@porter-ath.com
http://www.porter-ath.com

Athletic equipment, floorcoverings, mats and supplies.

Dan Morgan, VP Sales/Marketing

5761 Quality Industries
PO Box 765
Hillsdale, MI 49242-0765

800-766-9458
Fax: 517-439-1878

Recycled plastic park and playground equipment.

5762 Recreation Creations
PO Box 955
Hillsdale, MI 49242-0955

517-439-0300
800-888-0977
Fax: 517-439-0303

Heavy duty park and playground equipment for school and public use. Equipment is both colorful and safe.

DC Shaneour

5763 Roppe Corporation
1602 N Union Street
Fostoria, OH 44830-1958

419-435-8546
Fax: 419-435-1056

Floorcoverings, mats and matting.

5764 Safety Play
10460 Roosevelt Boulevard
#295
St Petersburgh, FL 33716-3818

727-522-0061
888-878-0244
Fax: 727-522-0061
http://www.mindspring.com

Playground and recreational accident consultants. Experienced in insepctions, design, expert witness. Creators of Playground Safety Signs as required to be on the playground.

Scott Burmon, Contact

5765 Sport Court
939 S 700 W
Salt Lake City, UT 84104-1504

801-972-0260
800-421-8112
Fax: 801-975-7752
E-mail: info@sportcourt.com
http://www.sportcourt.com

Sport flooring, portable flooring, outdoor-indoor educational institutions.

Finnika Lundmark, Director Marketing

5766 Sport Floors
PO Box 1478
Cartersville, GA 30120-1478

800-322-3567
Fax: 574-293-2381

Sport floors, flooring, floorcoverings, mats and matting.

5767 Sportmaster
6031 Broad Street Mall
Pittsburgh, PA 15206-3009

412-243-5100
Fax: 412-731-3052

Playground equipment, sports timers and clocks.

5768 Stackhouse Athletic Equipment Company
1505 Front Street NE
Salem, OR 97303-6949

503-363-1840
Fax: 503-363-0511
E-mail: bob@stackhouseathletic.com
http://www.stackhouseathletic.com

Volleyball, soccer, football and baseball hardgoods.

Greg Henshaw, VP Marketing

5769 Swedes Systems - HAGS Play USA
2180 Stratingham Drive
Dublin, OH 43016-8907

Fax: 614-889-9026

Playground safety consultants.

5770 Ultra Play Systems
Parek Stuff
425 Sycamore Street
Anderson, IN 46016-1000

800-45 -LTRA

Playground and recreational equipment.

5771 Wausau Tile
PO Box 1520
Wausau, WI 54402-1520

715-359-3121
800-388-8728
Fax: 715-355-4627
E-mail: wtile@wausautile.com
http://www.wausautile.com

Playground and recreation equipment.

Rob Geurink, Furnishings Division Manager

5772 Wear Proof Mat Company
2156 W Fulton Street
Chicago, IL 60612-2392

312-733-4570
Fax: 800-322-7105
http://www.notracks.com

Mats, matting and floorcoverings for the physical education class.

5773 Wolverine Sports
745 State Circle
Ann Arbor, MI 48108-1647

734-761-5690
Fax: 800-654-4321

Playground, sports and physical fitness furniture and equipment.

General

5774 A-V Online
National Information Center for Educational Media
PO Box 8640
Albuquerque, NM 87198
505-265-3591
800-926-8328
Fax: 505-256-1080
E-mail: nicem@nicem.com
http://www.nicem.com

A CD-ROM that contains over 400,000 citations with abstracts, to non-print educational materials for all educational levels. It is available on an annual subscription basis and comes with semiannual updates.

Lisa Savard, Marketing and Sales

5775 ACT
2201 N Dodge Street
PO Box 168
Iowa City, IA 52243-0168
319-337-1000
Fax: 319-339-3021
http://www.act.org

Help individuals and organizations make informed decisions about education and work.

5776 AMX Corporation
11995 Forestgate Drive
Dallas, TX 75243-5481
972-644-3048
Fax: 972-624-7153

Multiple products, equipment and supplies.

5777 ASC Electronics
2 Kees Pl
Merrick, NY 11566-3625
516-623-3206
Fax: 516-378-2672

High tech multimedia system. Completely software driven, featuring interactive video, audio and data student drills. Novell network. System includes CD-ROM, laserdisc and digital voice card technology.

5778 Accelerated Math
Renaissance Learning
PO Box 8036
Wisconsin Rapids, WI 54495-8036
715-424-3636
800-338-4204
Fax: 715-424-4242
E-mail: answers@renlearn.com
http://www.renlearn.com

Math management software that helps teachers increase student math achievement in grades 1 through calculus.

5779 Accelerated Reader
Renaissance Learning
PO Box 8036
Wisconsin Rapids, WI 54495-8036
715-424-3636
800-338-4204
Fax: 715-424-4242
E-mail: answers@renlearn.com
http://www.renlearn.com

Software program that helps teachers manage literature-based reading.

5780 Actrix Systems
6315 San Ignacio Avenue
San Jose, CA 95119-1202
800-422-8749
Fax: 509-744-2851

Computer networks.

5781 Allen Communications
5 Triac Center
5th Floor
Salt Lake Cty, UT 84180
801-537-7800
Fax: 801-537-7805

Software.

5782 Alltech Electronics Company
602 Garrison Street
Oceanside, CA 92054-4865
760-721-0093
Fax: 760-732-1460

Computer hardware.

5783 Anchor Pad Products
Anchor Pad Products
11105 Dana Circle
Cypress, CA 90630-5133
714-799-4071
800-626-2467
Fax: 714-799-4094
E-mail: kris@anchor.com
http://www.anchorpad.com

Cost effective physical security systems for computers, computer peripherals and office equipment.

Kris Jones, Marketing Associate
Melanie Rustle, Marketing Associate

5784 Apple Computer
1 Infinite Loop
Cupertino, CA 95014-2084
408-996-1010
Fax: 408-974-2786

Offers a wide selection of software systems and programs for the student, educator, professional and classroom use. Program areas include reading, science, social studies, history, language arts, mathematics and more.

5785 Ascom Timeplex
400 Chestnut Ridge Road
Woodcliff Lake, NJ 07675-7604
201-646-1571
Fax: 201-646-0485

Computer networks.

5786 BGS Systems
128 Technology Drive
Waltham, MA 02453-8909
617-891-0000

Facility planning and evaluation software.

5787 BLS Tutorsystems
5153 W Woodmill Drive
Wilmington, DE 19808-4067
800-545-7766

Computer software.

5788 Broderbund Software
500 Redwood Boulevard
Novato, CA 94947-6921
319-395-9626
800-223-8941
Fax: 319-395-7449

Educational software.

5789 Bulletin Boards for Busy Teachers

http://www.geocities.com/VisionTeacherwv/
Bulletin board tips and education links.

5790 CASL Software
6818 86th Street E
Puyallup, WA 98371-6450

206-845-7738

Educational software for schools and institutions in all areas of interest.

5791 CCU Software
PO Box 6724
Charleston, WV 25362-0724

800-843-5576
Fax: 800-321-4297

Educational software.

5792 CCV Software
5602 36th Street S
Fargo, ND 58104-6768

800-541-6078
Fax: 800-457-6953

All varieties of software and hardware for the educational fields of interest including language arts, math, social studies, science, history and more.

5793 Cambridge Development Laboratory
86 West Street
Waltham, MA 02451-1110

800-637-0047
Fax: 781-890-2894
E-mail: customerservice@edumatch.com
http://www.edumatch.com

Meets all educational software needs in language arts, mathematics, science, social studies early learning and special education.

5794 Chariot Software Group
123 Camino De La Reina W Building
San Diego, CA 92108-3002

619-298-0202
800-242-7468
Fax: 619-491-0021
E-mail: info@chariot.com
http://www.chariot.com

Academic software.

5795 Child's Play Software
5785 Emporium Square
Columbus, OH 43231-2802

614-833-1836
Fax: 614-833-1837

Markets learning games and creative software to schools.

5796 Claris Corporation
5201 Patrick Henry Drive
Santa Clara, CA 95054-1171

800-747-7483

Educational software.

5797 Classroom Direct
20200 E 9 Mile Road
Saint Clair Shores, MI 48080-1791

800-777-3642
Fax: 800-628-6250

Full line of hardware and software for Mac, IBM and Apple II at discount prices.

5798 College Board/SAT
45 Columbus Avenue
New York, NY 10023-6992

217-713-8000
http://http://sat.org/

5799 Computer City Direct
2000 Two Tandy Center
Fort Worth, TX 76102

800-538-0586

Hardware.

5800 Computer Friends
10200 SW Eastridge Street
Portland, OR 97225

800-547-3303
Fax: 503-643-5379
E-mail: cfi@cfriends.com
http://www.cfriends.com

Computer hardware, software and networks, printer support products.

Jimmy Moglia, Marketing Director

5801 Conference Daily Newspaper Online
American Association of School Administrators
1801 N Moore Street
Arlington, VA 22209-1813

800-458-9383
Fax: 301-206-9789
http://www.aasa.org

Jay Goldman, Editor

5802 Data Command
PO Box 548
Kankakee, IL 60901-0548

800-528-7390

Educational software.

5803 Davidson & Associates
19840 Pioneer Avenue
Torrance, CA 90503-1690

800-545-7677

Educational software and systems.

5804 Dell Computer Corporation
9595 Arboretum Boulevard
Austin, TX 78759-6337

512-338-4400
800-388-1450

Hardware.

5805 Digital Divide Network

http://www.digitaldividenetwork.org
Knowledge to help everyone succeed in the digital age.

5806 Digital Equipment Corporation
Educational Computer Systems Group
2 Iron Way
Marlboro, MA 01752

Computer hardware and networks.

5807 Don Johnston Developmental Equipment
1000 N Rand Road
Suite 115
Wauconda, IL 60084-1190

847-526-2682
800-999-4660

Develops educational software for special needs. Products include the Ukandu Series for emergent literacy, LD, ESL, students Co-Writer and Write: OutLoud.

5808 Edmark Corporation
6727 185th Avenue NE
PO Box 97021
Redmond, WA 98052-5037

425-556-8400
800-691-2986
Fax: 425-556-8430

Markets educational software.

5809 EduQuest, An IBM Company
PO Box 2150
Atlanta, GA 30301-2150

Offers exciting educational software in various fields of interest including history, social studies, reading, math and language arts, as well as computers.

5810 Educational Activities
1937 Grand Avenue
Baldwin, NY 11510-2889

516-223-4666
800-645-3739
Fax: 516-623-9282
http://www.edact.com

Supplemental materials.

Roni Hofbauer, Office Manager
Carol Stern, VP

5811 Educational Resources
1550 Executive Drive
Elgin, IL 60123-9330

630-213-8681
Fax: 630-213-8681

The largest distributor of educational software and technology in the education market. Features Mac, APL, ligs and IBM school versions, lab packs, site licenses, networking and academic versions. Hardware, accessories and multimediais also available.

5812 Electronic Specialists Inc.
PO Box 389
Natick, MA 01760-0004

508-655-1532
810-225-4876
Fax: 508-653-0268
E-mail: esp@elect-spec.com
http://www.elect-spec.com

Computer and electronics, including networks and computer systems plus transformers and power converters.

F Stifter, President

5813 Environmental Systems Research Institute
380 New York Street
Redlands, CA 92373-8118

Demonstrates a full range of geographic information system software products.

5814 Eversan Inc.
34 Main Street
Whitesboro, NY 13492

800-383-6060
Fax: 315-736-4058
E-mail: sales&eversan.com
http://www.eversan.com

Announcement boards, scoreboards and classroom supplies, sports timers and clocks.

Michelle Moran, Sales Representative
Elsa Kucherna, Sales Representative

5815 GAMCO Educational Materials
PO Box 1911
Big Spring, TX 79721-1911

800-351-1404

Publishes software in math, language arts, reading, social studies, early childhood education and teacher tools for Macintosh, Apple, IBM and MS-DOS compatible.

5816 Games2Learn
1936 East Deere Avenue
Suite 120
Santa Ana, CA 92705

714-751-4263
888-713-4263
Fax: 714-442-0869
E-mail: CustomerService@Games2Learn.com
http://www.games2learn.com

Develops, markets and provides children and adults with quality, fun, interactive educational products designed to increase their skills in language, math and general knowledge. Creator of The Phonics Game.

5817 Gateway Learning Corporation
665 3rd Street
Suite 225
San Francisco, CA 94107

800-544-7323
http://www.hop.com

Develop and sell innovative educational products for home learning.

5818 Greene & Associates
1834 E Manhatton Drive
Tempe, AZ 85282-5857

480-491-1151

Educational software.

5819 Grolier
PO Box 1716
Danbury, CT 06816

800-371-3908
Fax: 800-456-4402

Multimedia software for education.

5820 Hubbell
Kellems Division
14 Lords Hill Road
Stonington, CT 06378-2604

860-535-5350
Fax: 860-535-1719

Computer hardware, software, systems, and networks.

5821 Indiana Cash Drawer
1315 S Miller Street
Shelbyville, IN 46176-2424

317-398-6643
Fax: 317-392-0958

Computer peripherals.

5822 Ingenuity Works
1123 Fir Avenue
Blaine, WA 98230-9702

604-412-1555
800-665-0667
Fax: 604-431-7996
E-mail: info@ingenuityworks.com
http://www.ingenuityworks.com

Publishes K-12 educational software for classroom use. Key curriculum areas include geography, keyboarding, and math (K-9). Network and district licenses are available.

Brigetta , Director Marketing

5823 Instructional Design
WIDS-Worldwide Instructional Design System
1 Foundation Circle
Waunakee, WI 53597-8914

608-849-2411
800-677-9437
Fax: 608-849-2468
E-mail: info@wids.org
http://www.wids.org

Performance-based curriculum design software and professional devlopment tools. Use software to write curriculum, implement standards, create assessments, and build in learning styles. Excellent upfront online design tool.

Robin Nickel, Associate Director

5824 Instructor
Scholastic
555 Broadway
New York, NY 10012-3919

212-343-6100
800-724-6527
Fax: 212-343-4801
http://www.scholastic.com/instructor

Edited for teachers, curriculum coordinators, principals and supervisors of primary grades through junior high school.

Monthly

Claudia Cohl, Publisher
Lynn Diamond, Advertising Director

5825 Jostens Learning Corporation
4920 Pacific Heights Boulevard
Suite 500
San Diego, CA 92121

858-587-0087
800-521-8538
Fax: 858-587-1629

Educational software and CD-ROM's.

5826 Journey Education
1325 Capital Parkway
Suite 130
Carrollton, TX 75006

800-874-9001
Fax: 972-245-3585
E-mail: sales@journeyed.com
http://www.journeyed.com

Software for students.

5827 Ken Cook Education Systems
9929 W Silver Spring Drive
PO Box 25267
Milwaukee, WI 53225-1024

800-362-2665
Fax: 414-466-0840

Classroom curricular software.

5828 Kensington Microwave
2855 Campus Drive
San Mateo, CA 94403-2510

650-572-2700
800-535-4242
Fax: 650-572-9675
http://www.kensington.com

Computer systems and peripherals.

5829 Lapis Technologies
1100 Marina Village Parkway
Alameda, CA 94501-1043

510-748-1600

Computer peripherals.

5830 Laser Learning Technologies
120 Lakeside Avenue
#3240
Seattle, WA 98122-6533

800-722-3505

Educational CD-ROM's and interactive videos.

5831 Lawrence Productions
1800 S 35th Street
Galesburg, MI 49053-9687

800-421-4157
Fax: 616-665-7060

More than 60 proven software titles for PreK to adult, covering problem solving, early learning and leadership skills.

5832 Learning Company
500 Redwood Boulevard
Novato, CA 94947

800-825-4420
Fax: 877-864-2275
http://www.learningcompanyschool.com

School educational software.

5833 Library Corporation, Sales & Marketing
1501 Regency Way
Woodstock, GA 30189-5487

Computer networks.

5834 LinkNet
Introlink
1400 E Touhy Avenue
Suite 260
Des Plaines, IL 60018-3339

847-390-8700
Fax: 847-390-9435

Computer networks.

5835 MECC
6160 Summit Drive N
Minneapolis, MN 55430-2100

800-685-MECC

Educational software, hardware and overhead projectors.

5836 Mamopalire of Vermont
PO Box 24
Warren, VT 05674

802-496-4095
888-496-4094
Fax: 802-496-4096
E-mail: bethumpd@wcvt.com
http://www.bethumpd.com

Provides quality educational books and board games for the whole family.

Rebecca Cahilly, President
Glenn Cahilly, CEO

5837 McGraw-Hill Educational Resources
11 W 19th Street
New York, NY 10011-4209

800-442-9685
Fax: 972-228-1982

Educational software for all areas of interest including social studies, science, mathematics and reading.

5838 Microsoft Corporation
1 Microsoft Way
Redmond, WA 98052-8300

425-882-8080
Fax: 425-936-7329

One of the largest publishers and distributors of educational software, hardware, equipment and supplies.

5839 Misty City Software
11866 Slater Avenue NE
Kirkland, WA 98034-4103
206-820-2219
800-795-0049
Fax: 425-820-4298

Publisher of Grade Machine, gradebook software for Macintosh, MS-DOS, and Apple II. Grade Machine used by thousands of teachers in hundreds of schools worldwide. Grade Machine has full-screen editing, flexible reports, large classcapacity, excellent documentation and reasonable cost.

Roberta Spiro, Business Manager
Russell Cruickshanks, Sales Manager

5840 NCR Corporation
1700 S Patterson Boulevard
Dayton, OH 45479-0002
937-445-5000

Computer networks, systems (large, mini, micro, medium and personal).

5841 NetLingo The Internet Dictionary
PO Box 627
Ojai, CA 93024
805-640-3754
Fax: 805-640-3654
E-mail: info@netlingo.com
http://www.NetLingo.com

A smart-looking and easy to understand dictionary of 3000 internet terms, 1200 chat acronyms, and much more. NetLingo is a modern reference book fo international students, educators, industry professionals, and online businesses andorganizations.

528 pages Paperback
ISBN: 0-9706396-7-8

Erin Jansen, Author
Erin Jansen, Author/Publisher

5842 NetZero
2555 Townsgate Road
Westlake Village, CA 91361-2650
805-418-2020
Fax: 805-418-2075
http://www.netzero.com

Free Internet access.

5843 New Century Education Corporation
220 Old New Brunswick Road
Piscataway, NJ 08854
732-981-0820
800-833-6232
Fax: 732-981-0552
E-mail: jharrison@ncecorp.com
http://www.ncecorp.com

ILS systems.

Janice Harrison, Marketing Representative

5844 OnLine Educator
http://faldo.atmos.uiuc.edu/CLA

A comprehensive archive of educational sites with useful search capabilities and descriptions of the sites.

5845 Online Computer Systems
1 Progress Drive
Horsham, PA 19044-3502

CD-ROM networking, CD-ROM titles and CD-ROM tower units.

5846 PBS TeacherSource
http://www.pbs.org/teachersource

Includes an on-line inventory of more than 1,000 free lesson plans, teacher guides and other activities designed to complement PBS television programs.

5847 Parent Link
Parlant Technology
290 N University Avenue
Provo, UT 84601
801-373-9669
800-735-2930
Fax: 801-373-9697
E-mail: info@parlant.com
http://www.parlant.com

School to home communication systems allow scholls to create messages — emails, telephone calls, web content, printed letters, about student information, grades, attendance, homework, and activities. Also provides inbound access viainternet and telephone.

George Joeckel, Marketing

5848 Peopleware
1621 114th Avenue SE
Suite 120
Bellevue, WA 98004-6905
425-454-6444
Fax: 425-454-7634

Classroom curricular software.

5849 Phillips Broadband Networks
100 Fairgrounds Drive
Manlius, NY 13104-2437
315-682-9105
Fax: 315-682-1022

Computer networks.

5850 Pioneer New Media Technologies
2265 E 220th Street
Long Beach, CA 90810-1639
800-LAS-R ON

DRM-604X CD-ROM mini-changer, world's fastest CD-ROM drive for multimedia. Also offers special packages including The Mystery Reading Bundle, CLD-V2400RB which includes the CLD-V2400 LaserDisc player, educator's remote control,UC-V109BC barcode reader and membership in the Pioneers in Learning Club and The Case of the Missing Mystery Writer videodisc from Houghton Mifflin.

5851 Polaroid Corporation
575 Tech Square
Cambridge, MA 02139
781-386-2000
Fax: 781-386-3925

Computer repair, hardware and peripherals, equipment and various size systems.

5852 Power Industries
37 Walnut Street
Wellsley Hills, MA 02181
800-395-5009

Educational software.

5853 Quetzal Computers
1708 E 4th Street
Brooklyn, NY 11223-1925
718-375-1186

Computer systems and networks, peripherals and hardware.

Software, Hardware & Internet Resources / General

5854 RLS Groupware
Realtime Learning Systems
2700 Connecticut Avenue NW
Washington, DC 20008-5330
202-483-1510

Classroom curricular software.

5855 Radio Shack
100 Throckmorton Street
Suite 1800
Ft. Worth, TX 76102
817-415-3700
Fax: 817-415-2335

Computer networks and peripherals.
Laura Moore, Sr VP Public Relations

5856 Rose Electronics
10850 Wilcrest Drive
Suite 900
Houston, TX 77099-3599
281-933-7673
Fax: 281-933-0044

Computer peripherals and hardware.

5857 STAR Reading & STAR Math
Renaissance Learning
PO Box 8036
Wisconsin Rapids, WI 54495-8036
715-424-3636
800-338-4204
Fax: 715-424-4242
E-mail: answers@renlearn.com
http://www.renlearn.com

Computer-adaptive tests provide instructional levels, grade equivalents and percentile ranks.

5858 SVE & Churchill Media
6677 N Northwest Highway
Chicago, IL 60631
773-775-9550
800-829-1900
Fax: 773-775-5091
E-mail: slucas@svemedia.com
http://www.svemedia.com

Has brought innovative media technology into america's pre-K through high school classrooms. By producing programs to satisfy state curriculum standards, SVE consistently provides educators with high-quality and award-winning videos,CD-ROMs, eLMods, and DVDs in science, social studies, english and health/guidance.

Sarah M Lucas, Communications Coordinator
Kelli Campbell, VP Marketing/Development

5859 School Cruiser
Time Cruiser Computing Corporation
9 Law Drive
3rd Floor, Ottawa, Ontario
Canada K1N 7G1
613-562-9847
877-450-9482
Fax: 613-562-4768
http://www.epals.com

School Cruiser provides online tools and resources to promote academic and community interaction. It lets you access and share school calenders, lesson plans, homework assignments, announcements and other school related information.

5860 SchoolHouse

http://www.encarta.msn.com/schoolhouse/maincontent.asp
The Encarta Lesson Collection and other educational resources.

5861 Seaman Nuclear Corporation
7315 S 1st Street
Oak Creek, WI 53154-2095
414-762-5100
Fax: 414-762-5106

Facility planning and evaluation software.

5862 Skills Bank Corporation
7104 Ambassador Road
Suite 1
Baltimore, MD 21244-2732
800-451-5726

Educational manufacturing company offering computer and electronic resources, software, programs and systems focusing on home education and tutoring.

5863 Sleek Software Corporation
2404 Rutland Drive
Suite 600
Austin, TX 78758
800-337-5335
Fax: 888-353-2900
http://www.sleek.com

Specializes in Algorithm-Based tutorial and test-generating software.

5864 Smartstuff Software
PO Box 82284
Portland, OR 97282-0284
415-763-4799
800-671-3999
Fax: 877-278-7456
E-mail: info@smartstuff.com
http://www.smartstuff.com

Foolproof Security is a dual platform desktop security product that prevents unwanted changes to the desktop and a product line for the internet that protects browser settings, filters content, and allows guided activities.

5865 Society for Visual Education
1345 W Diversey Parkway
Chicago, IL 60614-1249
773-775-9550
Fax: 800-624-1678

Educational software dealing specifically with special education.

5866 SofterWare
540 Pennsylvania Avenue
Suite 200
Fort Washington, PA 19034-3388
215-628-0400
800-220-4111
Fax: 215-628-0585
E-mail: info@softerware.com
http://www.softerware.com

Offers software, support and administrative solutions to four markets: childcare centers, public and private schools, nonprofit organizations and institutions, and camps.

5867 SpecialNet
GTE Educational Network Services
5525 N Macarthur Boulevard
Suite 320
Irving, TX 75038-2600
214-518-8500
800-927-3000
Fax: 757-852-8277

Contains news and information on trends and developments in educational services and programs. Databases, bulletin boards, school packages, student/teacher packages, online magazines, distance learning, vocational education, schoolhealth, educational laws, and more.

5868 Student Software Guide

800-874-9001
E-mail: journey.com

Discounts on a variety of software materials.

5869 Sun Microsystems
2550 Garcia Avenue
#6-13
Mountain View, CA 94043-1100

714-643-2688
800-555-9786
Fax: 650-934-9776

Computer networks and peripherals.

5870 Sunburst/Wings for Learning
101 Castleton Street
Pleasantville, NY 10570-3405

914-747-3310
800-338-3457
Fax: 914-747-4109

Educational materials, including software, print materials, videotapes, videodisc and interdisciplinary packages.

5871 Support Systems International Corporation
136 S 2nd Street
Richmond, CA 94804-2110

510-234-9090
800-777-6269
Fax: 510-233-8888
E-mail: info@support-systems-intl.com
http://www.fiberopticcableshop.com

Fiber optic patch cables, converters, and switches.

Ben Parsons, General Manager

5872 Surfside Software
PO Box 1112
East Orleans, MA 02643-1112

800-942-9008

Educational software.

5873 Target Vision
1160 Pittsford Victor Road
Suite K
Pittsford, NY 14534-3825

800-724-4044
Fax: 585-248-2354

TVI DeskTop expands your show directly to desktop PC utilizing existing LANS. View information by topics or as a screen saver. Features: graphic importing, VCR interface, advanced scheduling and more.

5874 Teacher Universe
5900 Hollis Street
Suite A
Emeryville, CA 94608

877-248-3224
Fax: 415-763-4917
E-mail: info@teacheruniverse.com
http://www.teacheruniverse.com

Creates technology-rich solutions for improving the quality of life and work for teachers worldwide.

5875 Technolink Corporation
24 Depot Square
Tuckahoe, NY 10707-4004

914-961-1900

Computer systems and electronics.

5876 Tom Snyder Productions
80 Coolidge Hill Road
Watertown, MA 02472

800-342-0236
Fax: 800-304-1254
E-mail: ask@tomsnyder.com
http://www.tomsnyder.com

Educational CD-ROM products and Internet services for schools.

5877 Tripp Lite
500 N Orleans Street
Chicago, IL 60610-4117

312-329-1601

Peripherals, hardware and computer systems.

5878 True Basic
12 Commerce Avenue
West Lebanon, NH 03784-1669

800-436-2111
Fax: 603-298-7015
E-mail: john@truebasic.com
http://www.truebasic.com

Educational software.

5879 U.S. Public School Universe Database
U.S. National Center for Education Statistics
555 New Jersey Avenue NW
Washington, DC 20001-2029

202-219-1335

85,000 public schools of elementary and secondary levels, public special education, vocational/technical education and alternative education schools.

5880 USA CityLink Project
USA CityLink Project
Floppies for Kiddies
4060 Highway 59
Mandevelle, LA 70471

985-898-2158
Fax: 985-892-8535

Collects used and promotional diskets from the masses for redistribution to school groups and nonprofits throughout the county.

Carol Blake, Contact

5881 Unisys
PO Box 500
Blue Bell, PA 19424-0001

215-986-3501
Fax: 215-986-3279

A full line of computers (sizes ranging from mini/micro to medium/large and personal).

5882 Ventura Educational Systems
910 Ramona Avenue
Suite E
Grover Beach, CA 93433-2154

805-473-7383
800-336-1022
Fax: 805-473-7382
E-mail: sales@venturaes.com
http://www.venturaes.com

Publishers of curriculum based educational software for all grade levels, specializing in interactive math and science software. Programs include teacher's guide with student worksheets.

5883 Viziflex Seels
16 E Lafayette Street
Hackensack, NJ 07601-6895

201-487-8080

Peripherals, hardware and electronics, floorcoverings, mats and matting.

5884 Waterford Institute
1590 E 9400 S
Sandy, UT 84093-3009

800-767-9976
Fax: 801-572-1667

Produces children's educational software for math and reading.

5885 Web Connection
Education Week

301-280-3100
E-mail: ads@epe.org
http://www.edweek.org

Information about education suppliers.

5886 Wiremold Company
60 Woodlawn Street
W Hartford, CT 06110-2383

800-243-8421

Computer networks and peripherals.

5887 Wisconsin Technical College System Foundation
1 Foundation Cir
Waunakee, WI 53597-8914

800-821-6313
Fax: 608-849-2468
E-mail: foundation@wtcsf.tec.wi.us

Interactive videodiscs, self-paced instruction or with barcodes. Students learn faster, become more motivated and retain more information. Math, algebra and electronics courseware are also available.

5888 Word Associates
3226 Robincrest Drive
Northbrook, IL 60062-5125

847-291-1101
Fax: 847-291-0931
E-mail: microlrn@aol.com
http://www.wordassociates.com

Software tutorials featuring lessons in question format, with tutorial and test mode. 15 titles include Math SAT, 2 English SAT; US Constitution Tutor; Phraze Maze; Geometry: Planely Simple, Concepts and Proofs, Right Triangles; LifeSkills Math; Algebra; Reading: Myths and More Myths, Magic and Monsters; Economics; American History. Windows, Macintosh, CD's or disks.

Software

Myrna Helfand, President
Sherry Azaria, Marketing

5889 Ztek Company
PO Box 11768
Lexington, KY 40577-1768

859-281-1611
800-247-1603
Fax: 859-281-1521
E-mail: cs@ztek.com
http://www.ztek.com

Offers physics multimedia lessons on CD-ROM, DVD, videodisc and videotape. Also, carries Pioneer New Media DVD and videodisc players as well as Bretford Manufacturing's line of audio-visual furniture.

5890 ePALS.com
Classroom Exchange

http://www.epals.com

World's largest online classroom community, connecting over 3 million students and teachers through 41,044 profiles.

5891 http://ericir.syr.edu
AskERIC

Ask a question about education and receive a personalized e-mail response in two business days.

5892 http://gsn.bilkent.edu.tr
Ballad of an EMail Terrorist
Global SchoolNet Foundation

One pitfall of the internet is danger of vulgarity and/or obscenity to a child via e-mail.

5893 http://suzyred.home.texas.net
The Little Red School House

Offers sections on music, writing, quotes, web quests, jokes, poetry, games, activities and more.

5894 www.FundRaising.Com
FundRaising.Com

800-443-5353

Internet fundraising company.

5895 www.abcteach.com

E-mail: sandkems@abcteach.com

Offers ideas and activities for kids, parents, students and teachers. Features section on many topics in education, including writing, poetry, word searches, crosswords, games, maps, mazes and more.

5896 www.abctooncenter.com
ABC Toon Center

This family orientated site offers games, cartoons, storybook, theater, information stations and more. This site is open to children of differnt languages. Can be translated into Italian, French, Spanish, German and Russian.

5897 www.americatakingaction.com
America Taking Action

Provides every school with a free, 20 page website with resources for teachers, parents, students and the community. Created entirely by involved parents, teachers and community leaders as a public service.

5898 www.awesomelibrary.org
Awesome Library

Organizes the Web with 15,000 carefully reviewed resources, including the top 5 percent in education. Offers sections of mathematics, science, social studies, english, health, physical education, technology, languages, specialeducation, the arts and more. Features a section involved with today's current issues facing our world, like pollution, gun control, tobacco, and other changing 'hot' topics. Site can be browsed in English, German, Spanish, French or Portuguese.

5899 www.bigchalk.com
Big Chalk-The Education Network

Educational web site tailored to fit teachers' and students' needs.

5900 www.brunchbunch.org
Brunch Bunch

The foundation names all of the grants it makes after teachers who have demonstrated excellence. The foundation regularly makes significant grants to aid teachers' efforts.

5901 www.busycooks.com
BusyCooks.com

A hit with home economics teachers, enjoying free recipes and online cooking shows. Tapping into the experience of thousands to nuture your culinary creativity.

5902 www.chandra.harvard.edu
Chandra X-ray Observatory Center

Find teacher-developed, classroom-ready materials based on results from the Chandra mission. Classroom-ready activities, interactive games, activities, quizzes, and printable activities which will keep students absorbed with interest.

5903 www.cherrydale.com
Cherrydale Farms

Website offers company information, fund raising products and information, online mega mall, card shop, career opportunities and much more. Produces fine chocolates and confections. Many opportunities for schools to raise funds with various Cherrydale programs.

5904 www.cleverapple.com
Education Station

Offers links to many sites involved with education.

5905 www.edhelper.com
edhelper.com

Keeps you up to date with the latest educational news.

5906 www.education-world.com
Education World

Features and education-specific search engine with links to over 115,000 sites. Offers monthly reviews of other educational web sites, and other original content on a weekly basis.

5907 www.eduverse.com

Software developer building core technologies for powering international distance education. Features an online distance education engine, product information, news releases and more.

5908 www.efundraising.com
efundraising.com

Provides non-profit groups with quality products, low prices and superior service. Helping thousands of schools, youth sports teams and community groups reach their fundraising goals each year.

5909 www.embracingthechild.com
Embracing the Child

Educational resource for teachers and parents that provides a structural resource for home and classroom use, lesson planning, as well as a child-safe site, for children's research, classroom use and homework fulfillment.

5910 www.enc.org
Eisenhower National Clearinghouse

For math and science teachers-anywhere in the K-12 spectrum. This organization contains a wealth of information, activities, resources, and demonstrations for the sciences and math.

5911 www.englishhlp.com
English Help

E-mail: englishhlpr@hotmail.com
This page is a walk through of Microsoft Power Point. The goal is to show in a few simple steps how to make your own website. Created by Rebecca Holland.

5912 www.expage.com/Just4teachers
Just 4 Teachers

The ultimate website for educators! Teaching tips, resources, themeunits, search engines, classroom management and sites for kids.

5913 www.fraboom.com
Fraboom

This site's tools let you specify areas within your state's standards and search for a list of 'Flying Rhinoceros' lessons that meet your criteria. Offers other information sources for teachers and students.

5914 www.globalschoolnet.org
Global Schoolhouse

Connects teachers, administrators, and parents with options and possibilities the Internet has to offer the schools of the world.

5915 www.gradebook.org/
The Classroom

Dedicated to the students and teachers of the world.

5916 www.homeworkspot.com
HomeworkSpot

A free online homework resource center developed by educators, students, parents and journalists for K-12 students. It simplifies the search for homework help, features a top-notch reference cetner, current events, virtual field tripsand expeditions, extracurricular activities and study breaks, parent and teacher resources and much more.

5917 www.iearn.org
iEARN USA

Utilizes projects for students ages 6 through 19. Projects are concerned with the environment as well as arts, politics, and the health and welfare of all the Earth's citizens.

5918 www.jasonproject.org
Jason Project

Founded in 1989 as a tool for live, interactive programs for students in the fourth through eighth grades. Annual projects are funded through a variety of public corporations and governmental organizations.

5919 www.junebox.com
JuneBox.com

A classroom superstore that features the leading suppliers of educational products and services. A gateway to project ideas and educational links.

5920 www.k12planet.com
Chancery Software

Chancery Software is announcing a new school to home extension that will provide student information systems to give parents, students, and educators access to accurate information about students in one, easy-to-use website.

5921 www.kiddsmart.com
Institute for Child Development

E-mail: dcornell@kiddsmart.com
The ICD develops educational materials and resources designed to facilitate children's social and emotional development. Offers the previous materials as well as research summaries, lesson plans, training, workshops, games,multi-cultural materials and other resources to teachers, educational centers, parents, counselors, corporations, non-profits and others involved in the child-care professions.

5922 www.lessonplansearch.com
Lesson Plan Search

220 lesson plans from cooking to writing.

5923 www.lessonplanspage.com
lessonplanspage.com

A collection of over 1,000 free lesson plans for teachers to use in their classrooms. Lesson plans are organized by subject and grade level.

5924 www.library.thinkquest.org
Think Quest Library of Entries

The Arti FAQS 2100 Project is designed to predict how art will influence our lives in the next hundred years. Students can use available data to make reasonable predictions for the future.

5925 www.ncspearson.com
NCS Pearson

E-mail: info@ncs.com
NCS Pearson is at the forefront of the education space with curriculum, contant, tools, assessment, and interface to enterprise systems

5926 www.negaresa.org
LearningGate

For teachers, electronic web-based grade book aplication eGRader 2000. Many educational resource links as well has discussion groups, a news and events section, and even links to online shopping.

5927 www.netrover.com/~kingskid/108.html
Room 108

An educational activity center for kids. Offers lots of fun for children with educational focus; like songs, art, math, kids games, children's stories and much more. Sections with pen pal information, puzzles, crosswords, teachersstore, spelling, kids sites, email, music, games and more.

5928 www.pcg.cyberbee.com
Postcard Geography

Offered to classes all over the world via the internet. Your class commits to exchanging picture postcards with all other participants. Appropriate for all ages, for public and private schools, for youth groups and for home-schools.

5929 www.pitt.edu
EdIndex

E-mail: poole@pitt.edu
A web resource for teachers and students, offers course information, MS Office tutorials, personal and professional pages, and more.

5930 www.riverdeep.net
Riverdeep Interactive Learning

Riverdeep's interactive science, language and math arts programs deliver high quality educational experiences.

5931 www.safedayeducation.com
Safe Day Education

The leader in bully prevention and street proofing education for kids; safe dating preparation programs for teens; and re-empowerment and assault prevention training for women.

5932 www.safekids.com/child_safety.htm
SafeKids.Com

Cyberspace is a fabulous tool for learning, but some of it can be exploitative and even criminal.

5933 www.sdcoe.k12.ca.us

Researches a coral reef and creates a diorama for The Cay by Theodore Taylor.

5934 www.shop2gether.com
Collective Publishing Service

We are committed to helping all schools buy better by shopping together. Building upon a scalable, dynamic procurement platform and group buying technology, we also provide a unique ecommerce system, delivering next generationprocurement services over the Internet.

5935 www.spaceday.com
Space Day

Program engineered to build problem-solving and teamwork skills.

5936 www.specialednews.com
Special Education News

E-mail: info@specialednews.com
Consists of breaking news stories from Washington and around the country. These stories are compliled together in the Special Education News letter is sent via e-mail once a week.

5937 www.straightscoop.org
Straight Scoop News Bureau

SSNB increases the frequency of anti-drug themes and messages in junior high and high school student media.

5938 www.tcta.org
Texas Classroom Teachers Association

Compromised of Texas educators, provides interest for teachers everywhere. Education laws and codes are presented here.

5939 www.teacherszone.com
TeachersZone.Com

Lesson plans, free stuff for teachers, contests, sites for kids, conferences and workshops, schools and organizations, job listings, products for school.

5940 www.teacherweb.com
TeacherWeb

TeacherWeb, your free personal website that's as easy to use as the bulletin board in your classroom. This site offers a secure, password-protected service.

5941 www.teachingheart.com
Teaching is A Work of Heart

Chock-full of ideas, projects, motivational thoughts, behavior ideas.

5942 www.thelearningworkshop.com
Learning Workshop.com

Services for teachers, students, and parents. For teachers online gradebooks and grade tracking, students can check their grades online, parents enjoy articles written expressly for them and a tutor search by zip code.

5943 www.tutorlist.com
TutorList.com

Offers information on tips on how to find and choose a tutor, what a tutor does, educational news and more.

5944 www.worksafeusa.org
WorkSafeUSA

Addresses the alarming injury and death rates experienced by America's adolescent workers. This non-profit site publishes and distributes A Teen Guide to Workplace Safety, available in English and Spanish.

5945 www1.hp.com
Compaq Computer Corporation

Compaq is one of the leading corporations in educational technology, working on developing solutions that will connect students, teachers and the community.

Administration

5946 ASQC
611 E Wisconsin Avenue
Milwaukee, WI 53202-4695

800-248-1946
Fax: 414-272-1734

Business and administrative software.

5947 Anchor Pad
Anchor Pad Products
11105 Dana Cir
Cypress, CA 90630-5133

714-799-4071
800-626-2467
Fax: 714-799-4094
E-mail: anchor@anchor.com
http://www.anchorpad.com

Computer and office security
Caroline Jones, COO
Melanie Ruste, Sales/Marketing Associate

5948 Applied Business Technologies
4631 W Chester Pike
Newtown Square, PA 19073-2225

610-359-0700
800-220-2281
Fax: 610-359-9420

Computer networks and administrative software.

5949 AskSam Systems
121 S Jefferson Street
Perry, FL 32347-3232

850-584-6590
800-800-1997
Fax: 850-584-7481
E-mail: info@asksam.com
http://www.asksam.com

Business and administrative free form database software.

Dottie Sheffield, Sales Manager

5950 Autodesk Retail Products
1725 220th Street
Suite C101
Bothell, WA 98021-8809

425-487-2233
Fax: 425-486-1636

Administrative and business software.

5951 Avcom Systems
250 Cox Lane
PO Box 977
Cutchogue, NY 11935-1303

631-734-5080
800-645-1134
Fax: 631-734-7204

Supplies for making and mounting transparencies. Products includes economy and self-adhesive mounts; transparent rolls and sheets; markers, pens and cleaners; thermo, computer graphics and plain-paper copier transparency films andlaminating supplies.

Joseph K Lukas

5952 Bobbing Software
67 Country Oaks Drive
Buda, TX 78610-9338

800-688-6812

Administrative software and systems.

5953 Bull HN Information Systems
Technology Park
Billerica, MA 01821

978-294-6000
Fax: 978-294-7999

Computer networks, computers (large, medium, micro and mini), and supplies.

5954 Bureau of Electronic Publishing
745 Alexander Road
#728
Princeton, NJ 08540-6343

973-808-2700

Administrative software, hardware and systems.

5955 CRS
17440 Dallas Parkway
Suite 120
Dallas, TX 75287-7307

800-433-9239

Administrative software and systems.

5956 Campus America
900 E Hill Avenue
Suite 205
Knoxville, TN 37915-2580

865-523-4477
877-536-0222
Fax: 617-492-9081
http://www.campus.com

Computer supplies, equipment, systems and networks.

5957 Century Consultants
150 Airport Road
Suite 1500
Lakewood, NJ 08701-3309

732-363-9300
Fax: 732-363-9374
E-mail: marketing@centuryltd.com
http://www.centuryltd.com

Develops, markets, and services Oracle based web-enabled Management software, STAR_BASE, for school districts K-12.

5958 Computer Resources
PO Box 60
Barrington, NH 03825-0060

603-664-5811
Fax: 603-664-5864

The Modular Management System for Schools is a school administrative software system designed to handle all student record keeping and course scheduling needs. A totally integrated modular system built around a central Student MasterFile. Additional modules handle student scheduling, grades, attendance and discipline reporting.

Raymond J Perreault, VP Marketing
Robert W Cook, National Sales Manager

5959 Cyborg Systems
2 N Riverside Plaza
Chicago, IL 60606-2600

312-454-1865

Administrative and business software programs.

5960 Diskovery Educational Systems
1860 Old Okeechobee Road
Suite 105
West Palm Beach, FL 33409-5281

561-683-8410
800-331-5489
Fax: 561-683-8416
http://www.diskovery.com

Computer supplies, equipment, and various size systems.

5961 Doron Precision Systems
Doron Precision Systems
174 Court Street
PO Box 400
Binghamton, NY 13902-0400

607-772-1610
Fax: 607-772-6760
http://www.doronprecision.com

Business and classroom curriculum software. Driving Simulation Systems and Entertainment Simulation Systems.

5962 Educational Data Center
180 De La Salle Drive
Romeoville, IL 60446-1895

800-451-7673
Fax: 815-838-9412

Administration software.

5963 EnrollForecast: K-12 Enrollment Forecasting Program
Association of School Business Officials Int'l
11401 N Shore Drive
Reston, VA 20190-4232

703-478-0405
Fax: 703-478-0205

A powerful planning tool that helps project student enrollment.

Peg D Kirkpatrick, Editor/Publisher
Robert Gluck, Managing Editor

5964 Epson America
20770 Madrona Avenue
Torrance, CA 90503-3778

800-289-3776

Computer repair and peripherals.

5965 FMJ/PAD.LOCK Computer Security Systems
741 E 223rd Street
Carson, CA 90745-4111

310-549-3221
800-322-3365
Fax: 310-549-2921
E-mail: info@fmjpadlock.com

Computer peripherals, supplies and equipment.

Tom Separa

5966 Geist
Geist Manufacturing
1821 Yolande Avenue
Lincoln, NE 68521-1835

402-474-3400
Fax: 402-474-4369
E-mail: products@geistmfg.com
http://www.geistmfg.com

Power distribution for racks, cabinets and data centers.

Terri Rockeman, Customer Service Supervisor

5967 Global Computer Supplies
11 Harbor Park Drive
Port Washington, NY 11050-4622

516-625-6200
Fax: 516-484-8533

Computer supplies, equipment, hardware, software and systems.

5968 Harrington Software
658 Ridgewood Road
Maplewood, NJ 07040-2536

201-761-5914

Administrative and business software.

5969 Information Design
7009 S Potomac Street
Suite 110
Englewood, CO 80112

303-792-2990
800-776-2469
Fax: 303-792-2378
E-mail: sales@idesgninc.com
http://www.idesigninc.com

Administrative and business software including systems focusing on payroll, personnel, financial accounting, purchasing, budgeting, fixed asset accounting and salary administration.

5970 International Rotex
7171 Telegraph Road
Los Angeles, CA 90040-3227

800-648-1871

Computer supplies.

5971 Jay Klein Productions Grade Busters
1695 Summit Point Court
Colorado Springs, CO 80919-3444

719-599-8786
Fax: 719-599-8312

A line of teacher productivity tools, the most highly recognized integrated gradebooks, attendance records, seating charts and scantron packages in K-12 education today (Mac, DOS, Windows, Apple II).

Jay A Klein, President
Angela C Wormley, Office Manager

5972 Jostens Learning Corporation
5521 Norman Center Drive
Minneapolis, MN 55437-1040

800-635-1429

The leading provider of comprehensive multimedia instruction, including hardware, software and service.

5973 MISCO Computer Supplies
1 Misco Plaza
Holmdel, NJ 07733-1033

800-876-4726

Computer supplies, networks, equipment and accessories.

5974 Mathematica
Wolfram Research
100 Trade Centre Drive
Champaign, IL 61820-7237

217-398-0700
800-441-6284
Fax: 217-398-0747
E-mail: info@wolfram.com
http://www.wolfram.com

Classroom curricular software and business/administrative software.

5975 Media Management & Magnetics
N94W14376 Garwin Mace Drive
Menomonee Falls, WI 53051-1629

262-251-5511
800-242-2090
Fax: 262-251-4737
E-mail: medmgt@execpc.com
http://www.computersupplypeople.com

Computer supplies, equipment and systems, Koss headphones.

John Schimberg, Education Sales

5976 MicroAnalytics
Student Transportation Systems
2300 Clarendon Boulevard
Suite 404
Arlington, VA 22201-3331

703-841-0414
Fax: 703-527-1693

Automates bus routing and scheduling for school districts with fleets of 5 to 500 buses. BUSTOPS is flexible, affordable and easy to use. Offers color maps and graphics, efficient routing, report writing, planning and more toimprove your pupil transportation system.

Mary Buchanan, Sales Manager

5977 MicroLearn Tutorial Series
Word Associates
3226 Robincrest Drive
Northbrook, IL 60062-5125

847-291-1101
Fax: 847-291-0931
E-mail: microlrn@aol.com
http://www.wordassociates.com

Software tutorials featuring lessons in question format, with tutorial and test mode. 15 titles include Math SAT, 2 English SAT; US Constitution Tutor; Phraze Maze; Geometry: Planely Simple, Concepts and Proofs, Right Triangles; LifeSkills Math; Algebra; Reading: Myths and More Myths, Magic and Monsters; Economics; American History. Windows, Macintosh, CD's or disks.

Software

Myrna Helfand, President

5978 NCS Marketing
11000 Prairie Lakes Drive
Eden Prairie, MN 55344-3885

800-447-3269
Fax: 612-830-7788
http://www.ncspearson.com

OpScan optical mark reading scanners from NCS process data at speeds of up to 10,000 sheets per hour for improved accuracy and faster turnaround. Also provides software and scanning applications and services that manage student, financial, human resources, instructional and assessment information.

Sheryl Kyweriga

5979 National Computer Systems
11000 Prairie Lakes Drive
Minneapolis, MN 55440

800-447-3269
Fax: 952-830-8564

Administrative software and systems.

5980 Parlant Technologies
290 N University Avenue
Provo, UT 84601-2821

800-735-2930
Fax: 801-373-9697

Administrative software and systems.

5981 Quill Corporation
100 Schelter Road
Lincolnshire, IL 60069-3621

847-634-4800
Fax: 847-634-5708

Computer and office supplies and equipment.

5982 Rauland Borg
3450 Oakton Street
Skokie, IL 60076-2958

847-679-0900
Fax: 800-217-0977

Administrative software and systems.

5983 Rediker Administration Software
2 Wileraham Road
Hampden, MA 01036-9685

800-882-2994
Fax: 413-566-2274
E-mail: sales@rediker.com

School administrative software for the teaching professional.

5984 Scantron Corporation
PO Box 2411
Tustin, CA 92781-2411

714-259-8887

Computer peripherals, administrative software and services.

5985 SourceView Software International
PO Box 578
Concord, CA 94522-0578

925-825-1248

Classroom curricular, business and administrative software.

5986 Systems & Computer Technology Services
4 Country View Road
Malvern, PA 19355-1408

610-647-5930
Fax: 610-578-7778

Administrative hand business software programs and services.

5987 Trapeze Software
23215 Commerce Park Drive
Suite 200
Beachwood, OH 44122

216-595-3100
Fax: 216-595-3113
E-mail: clint@mail.trapezesoftware.com
http://www.trapezesoftware.com

Computerized bus routing, boundary planning and redistricting software and services, and AVL (automatic vehicle locator software).

Clint Rooley, Director of Sales

5988 University Research Company
4724 W 2100 N
Cedar City, UT 84720-7846

800-526-4972

Supplies Quiz-A-Matic electronics for quiz competitions.

5989 Velan
4153 24th Street
Suite 1
San Francisco, CA 94114-3667

415-949-9150

Administrative software and systems.

5990 WESTLAW
West Group
610 Opperman Drive
Eagan, MN 55123-1340

612-687-7000
800-757-9378
Fax: 651-687-5827
http://www.westlaw.com

Online service concerning the complete text of U.S. federal court decisions, state court decisions from all 50 states, regulations, specialized files, and texts dealing with education.

5991 http://teacherfiles.homestead.com/index~ns4

Offers sections on clip art, quotes, slogans, lesson plans, organizations, web quests, political involvement, grants, publications, special education, professional development, humor and more.

5992 www.abcteach.com
Abcteach

E-mail: sandkems@abcteach.com

Free printable materials for kids, parents, student teachers and teachers. Theme units, spelling word searches, research help, writing skills and much more.

5993 www.apple.com
PowerSchool

PowerSchool's web-based architecture makes it easy to learn and easy to use.

5994 www.atozteacherstuff.com
A to Z Teacher Stuff

E-mail: webmaster@atozteacherstuff.com

Features quick indexes to online lesson plans and teacher resources, educational sites for teachers, articles, teacher store and more.

5995 www.awesomelibrary.org
Awesome Library

Organizes the Web with 15,000 carefully reviewed resources, including the top 5 percent in education. Offers sections of mathematics, science, social studies, english, health, physical education, technology, languages, specialeducation, the arts and more. Features a section involved with today's current issues facing our world, like pollution, gun control, tobacco, and other changing 'hot' topics. Site can be browsed in English, German, Spanish, French or Portuguese.

5996 www.easylobby.com
EasyLobby

The complete electronic visitor management system.

5997 www.fraboom.com
Stan D. Bird's WhizBang Thang

This site's tools let's you specify areas within your state's standards and search for a list of 'Flying Rhinoceros' lessons that meet your criteria. Offers other information sources for teachers and students.

5998 www.fundraising.com

800-443-5353
http://www.fundraising.com
Internet fundraising company.

5999 www.hoagiesgifted.org
Hoagies Gifted Education Page

Features the latest research on parenting and educating gifted children. Offers ideas, solutions and other things to try for parents of gifted children. Sections with world issues facing children and other important social topics.

6000 www.kiddsmart.com
Institute for Child Development

E-mail: dcornell@kiddsmart.com
The ICD develops educational materials and resources designed to facilitate children's social and emotional development. Offers the previous materials as well as research summaries, lesson plans, training, workshops, games,multi-cultural materials and other resources to teachers, educational centers, parents, counselors, corporations, non-profits and others involved in the child-care professions.

6001 www.nycteachers.com
NYCTeachers.com

Designed for NYC teachers that work within public school systems. Speaks out on controversial issues facing the broadening, funding, development, staffing and other concerns about public schools. Welcomes your suggestions and commentsabout the site and the issues involved.

6002 www.songs4teachers.com
O'Flynn Consulting

E-mail: oflynn4@home.com

Offers many resources for teachers including songs made especially for your classroom. Sections with songs and activities for holidays, seasons and more. Features books and audios with 101 theme songs for use in the classroom oranywhere children gather to sing.

6003 www.thecanadianteacher.com
Free Stuff for Canadian Teachers

Site where educators can find the latest links to free resources, materials, lesson plans, software, samples and computers. Some links are for Canadians only.

6004 www.welligent.Com
Welligent

A web-based software program that improves student health management and your school's finances at the same time.

Early Childhood Education

6005 Jump Start Math for Kindergartners
Knowledge Adventure
Torrance, CA

800-545-7677
http://www.knowledgeadventure.com
The program covers important and essential kindergarten math skills such as, writing numbers, sorting, and problem solving/following directions.

6006 Mindplay
160 W Fort Lowell Road
Tucson, AZ 85705

520-888-1800
800-221-7911
Fax: 520-888-7904
E-mail: mail@mindplay.com
http://www.mindplay.com
Educational software focusing on early childhood education and adult literacy.

Stacie Johnson, Communication Coordinator

6007 Nordic Software
PO Box 5403
Lincoln, NE 68505

402-489-1557
800-306-6502
Fax: 402-489-1560
E-mail: info@nordicsoftware.com
http://www.nordicsoftware.com
Specializes in developing and publishing educational software titles. Well-known for its software titles that make it easy for children to learn while playing on the computer. Develops and publishes elementary software products forthe Macintosh and Windows platforms. Products include Turbo Math Facts, Clock Shop, Coin Critters, Language Explorer and Preschool Parade, and more.

Tammy Hurlbut, Finance/Operations

6008 Personalized Software
PO Box 359
Phoenix, OR 97535

541-535-8085
Fax: 541-535-8889
Offers a full line of childcare management and development software programs.

6009 Science for Kids
9950 Concord Church Road
Lewisville, NC 27023-9720
336-945-9000
800-572-4362
Fax: 336-945-2500
E-mail: sci4kids@aol.com
http://www.scienceforkids.com

Developers and publishers of CD-ROM science and early learning programs for children ages 5-14; for Macintosh and Windows computers; school and home programs available.

Charles Moyer, Executive VP

6010 http://daycare.about.com/parenting/daycare
About Parenting/Family Daycare

6011 www.booksofwonder.com

New and vintage childrens books.

6012 www.lil-fingers.com
Lil' Fingers

A computer storybook site for toddlers. Parents and children are encouraged to enjoy the colorful drawings and animations. Offers games, storybooks, coloring pages, the Lil' Store and more.

Elementary Education

6013 Educational Institutions Partnership Program
Defense Information Systems Agency
Automation Resources Information
701 S Courthouse Road
Arlington, VA 22204-2199
703-607-6900
Fax: 703-607-4371

Makes available used computer equipment for donation of transfer to eligible schools, including K-12 schools recognized by the US Department of Education, Universities, colleges, Minority Institutions and nonporfit groups.

6014 Houghton Mifflin Company
222 Berkeley Street
Boston, MA 02116-3748
617-351-5000
Fax: 617-351-1106

Offers literature-based technology products for grades K-8 including CD's Story Time, a Macintosh based CD-ROM programs for grades 1 and 2 and Channel R.E.A.D., a videodisc series for grades 3-8.

6015 Kid Keys 2.0
Knowledge Adventure
800-545-7677

Keyboarding for grades K-2.

6016 Kinder Magic
1680 Meadowglen Lane
Encinitas, CA 92024-5652
760-632-6693
Fax: 760-632-9995

Educational software for ages 4-11.
Dr. Ilse Ortabasi, President

6017 Micrograms Publishing
9934 N Alpine Road
Suite 108
Machesney Park, IL 61115-8240
800-338-4726
Fax: 815-877-1482
http://www.micrograms.com

Micrograms develops educational software for schools and homes.

6018 Tudor Publishing Company
17218 Preston Road
Suite 400
Dallas, TX 75252-4018

Grade level evaluation (GLE) is a computer-adaptive assessment program for elementary and secondary students.

6019 Wordware Publishing
2320 Los Rios Boulevard
#200
Plano, TX 75074-8157
214-423-0090
Fax: 972-881-9147

Publisher of computer reference tutorials, regional Texas and Christian books. Educational division produces a diagnostic and remediation software for grade levels 3-8. Content covers over 3,000 objectives in reading, writing andmath. Contact publisher for dealer information.

Eileen Schnett, Product Manager

6020 World Classroom
Global Learning Corporation
PO Box 201361
Arlington, TX 76006-1361
214-641-3356
800-866-4452

An educational telecommunications network that prepares students, K-12 to use real-life data to make real-life decisions about themselves and their environment. Participating countries have included Argentina, Australia, Belgium,Canada, Denmark, France, Germany, Hungary, Iceland, Indonesia, Kenya, Russia, Lithuania, Mexico, Singapore, Taiwan, the Netherlands, the United States and Zimbabwe.

6021 http://k-6educators....education/k-6educators
About Education Elementary Educators

6022 http://www.etacuisenaire.com/index.htm
ETA Cuisenaire

Over 5,000 manipulative-based education and supplemental materials for grades K-12.

6023 http://www.wnet.org/wnetschool
wNet School
212-560-2713

Helps K-12 teachers by providing free standards based lesson plans, classroom activities, multimedia primers, online mentors, links to model technology schools, and more. Online workshops are also included in the WNET TV site.

6024 www.cherrydale.com/
Cherrydale Farms

Website offers company information, fund raising products and information, online mega mall, card shop, career opportunities and much more. Produces fine chocolates and confections. Many opportunities for schools to raise funds with various Cherrydale programs.

6025 www.efundraising.com
eFundraising

Provides non-profit groups with quality products, low prices and superior service. Helping thousands of schools, youth sports teams and community groups reach their fundraising goals each year.

6026 www.hoagiesgifted.org
Hoagies' Gifted Education Page

Features the latest research on parenting and educating gifted children. Offers ideas, solutions and other things to try for parents of gifted children. Sections with world issues facing children and other important social topics.

6027 www.netrover.com/~kingskid/108.html
Room 108

An educational activity center for kids. Offers lots of fun for children with educational focus; like songs, art, math, kids games, children's stories and much more. Sections with pen pal information, puzzles, crosswords, teachersstore, spelling, kids sites, email, music, games and more.

6028 www.netrox.net
Dr. Labush's Links to Learning

General links for teachers with internet help, coloring pages, and enrichment programs.

6029 www.primarygames.com
PrimaryGames.com

Contains educational games for elementary students.

6030 www.usajobs.opm.gov/b1c.htm
Overseas Employment Info-Teachers

Employment

6031 **Educational Placement Service**
90 S Cascade
Suite 1110
Colorado Springs, CO 80903

http://www.teacherjobs.com
Largest teacher placement service in the U.S.

6032 **Job Bulletin**
American Association of School Administrators
1801 N Moore Street
Arlington, VA 22209-1813

800-458-9383
Fax: 301-206-9789
http://www.aasa.org
The Job Bulletin was made to help employers and job candidates save time finding one another.

Jay Goldman, Editor

6033 **Teachers@Work**
PO Box 430
Vail, CO 81658

970-476-5008
Fax: 970-476-1496
http://www.teachersatwork.com
Electronic employment service designed to match the professional staffing needs of schools with teacher applicants.

6034 www.SchoolJobs.com
SchoolJobs.com

Provides principals, superintendents and other administrators the ability to market their job openings to a national pool of candidates, also gives educational professionals the chance to search for opportunities matching theirskills.

6035 www.aasa.org
American Association of School Administrators

Leadership news online.

Guidance & Counseling

6036 **Alcohol & Drug Prevention for Teachers, Law Enforcement & Parent Groups**
PO Box 4656
Reading, PA 19606

610-582-2090
Fax: 610-404-0406
E-mail: nodrugs@earthlink.net
http://www.nodrugs.com
Local organizations and international groups against drugs.

6037 **Live Wire Media**
3450 Sacramento Street
619
San Francisco, CA 94118

800-359-5437
Fax: 415-665-8006
E-mail: info@livewiremedia.com
http://www.livewiremedia.com/
Videos for youth guidance and character development, and teacher training.

Christine Hollander, Director Marketing

6038 **Phillip Roy Multimedia Materials**
PO Box 130
Indian Rocks Beach, FL 34635

727-593-2700
800-255-9085
Fax: 727-595-2685
E-mail: info@philliproy.com
http://www.philliproy.com

Multimedia materials for use with alternative education, Chapter 1, dropout prevention, Even Start, Head Start, JTPA/PIC, special education students, at-risk students, transition to work programs. Focuses on basic skills, conflictresolution, remediation, vocational education, critical thinking skills, communication skills, reasoning and decision making skills. Materials can be duplicated networked at no cost.

Phil Padol, Consultant
Regina Jacques, Customer Support

6039 www.goodcharacter.com
Character Education

Teaching guides for k-12 character education, packed with discussion questions, assignments, and activities that you can use as your own lesson plans.

International

6040 www.aed.org
Academy for Educational Development

The site provides information on international exchange, fellowshipand training.

6041 www.asce.org
American Society of Civil Engineers

This site lists scholarships and fellowships available only to ASCE members.

6042 www.cie.uci.edu
International Opportunities Program

Valuable links for exploring opportunities for study and research abroad.

6043 www.ciee.org
Council on International Educational Exchange

Study abroad programs by region, work abroad opportunities, international volunteer projects and Council-administered financial aid and grant information .

6044 www.cies.org
Council for International Exchange of Scholars

Information on the Fulbright Senior Scholar Program which is made available to Fulbright alumni,grantees, prospective applicants and public at large.

6045 www.daad.org
German Academic Exchange Service (DADD)

Promotes international academic relations and contains links to research grants, summer language grants,annual grants, grants in German studies andspecial programs.

6046 www.ed.gov
US Department of Education
Office of Higher Education Programs

This site describes programs and fellowships offered by the International Education and Graduate Programs office of the US Department of Education.

6047 www.finaid.org
FinAid

A free, comprehensive, independent and ojective guide to student financial aid.

6048 www.iie.org
Institute of International Education

The largest not-for-profit international educational organization in the United States. This site provides information regarding IIE's programs, services and resources, including the Filbright Fellowship.

6049 www.iiepasspport.org
Institute of International Education
IIE Passport: Living and Learning Aboard

A student guide on the web to 5,000 learning oppurtunities worldwide.

6050 www.irex.org
International Research and Exchange Board

Academic exchanges between the United States and Russia. Lists a variety of programs as well as grant and fellowship oppurtunities.

6051 www.isp.msu.edu/ncsa
Michigan State University
National Consortium for Study in Africa

Provides a comprehensive lists of sponsors for African exchange.

6052 www.istc.umn.edu/
University of Minnesota
International Study and Travel Center

Comprehensive and searchable links to study, work and travel abroad opportunities.

6053 www.languagetravel.com
Language Travel Magazine

Resource for finding study abroad language immersion courses.

6054 www.nsf.gov/
National Science Foundation

Encourages exchange in science and engineering. The site has inter-national component, providing links with valuable information on fellowships grants and awards, summer institutes, workshops,research and education projects andinternational programs.

6055 **www.si.edu/**
Smithsonian Institution

Fellowships link to Smithsonian Oppurtunities for research and study.

6056 **www.studiesinaustralia.com/study**
Studies in Australia

Listing of study abroad oppurtunities in Australia, providing details of academic and training institutions and the programs they offer to prospective international students and education professionals.

6057 **www.studyabroad.com/**
Educational Directories Unlimited, Inc.

Study abroad information resource listing study abroad programs worldwide.

6058 **www.studyabroad.com/.**
StudyAbroad.com

A commercial site with thousands of study abroad programs in over 100 countries with links to study abroad program home pages.

6059 **www.ucis.pitt.edu/crees**
University of Pittsburgh
Center for Russian/European Studies

Index of electronic resources for the student interested in Russian and European language and culture study.

6060 **www.upenn.edu/oip/scholarships.html**
University of Pennsylvania
Scholarships/Graduate Study Abroad

Provides links for graduate study abroad and scholarship opportunities.

6061 **www.usc.edu**
University of Southern California
Resources for Colleges and
Universities in International Exchange

Links for browsing all aspects of international exchange, including study, research, work and teaching abroad, financial aid, grants and scholarships.

6062 **www.usinfo.state/gov**
US Department of State International
Information Programs

Comprehensive desriptions of all IIP programs, sections on policy issues, global and regional issues and IIP publications.

6063 **www.wes.org**
World Education Services

Features information on WES' foreign credentials evaluation services, world education workshops, and the journals World Education and News Reviews.

6064 **www.world-arts-resources.com/**
World Wide Arts Resources

Focuses solely on the arts, this site provides links for funding sources, university programs and arts organizations all over the world.

6065 **www.yfu.org/**
Youth for Understanding (YFU)

Oppurtunities for young people around the world to spend a summer, semester or year with a host family in another country.

6066 **wwww.sas.upenn.edu**
African Studies Center, University of Pennsylvania
African Studies WWW

Links to Africa-related internet sources, African Studies Association and UPenn African Studies Center.

Language Arts

6067 **Advantage Learning Systems**
Renaissance Learning
PO Box 8036
Wisconsin Rapids, WI 54495-8036

715-424-3636
800-338-4204
Fax: 715-424-4242
E-mail: answers@renlearn.com
http://www.renlearn.com

Accelerated Reader software and manuals that motivate K-12 students to read more and better books. The program boosts reading scores and library circulation. Lets educators quickly and accurately assess student reading whilemotivating students to read more and better books.

6068 **Bytes of Learning Incorporated**
150 Consumers Road
Suite 2021
Willowdale, ON, Canada, M2 J 1P9

800-465-6428

Single and site licensed software for Macintosh, Apple II, DOS and Windows-network compatible too. Keyboarding, language arts, career exploration and more on diskette and CD-ROM.

6069 **Humanities Software**
408 Columbia Street
#950
Hood River, OR 97031-2044

503-386-6737
800-245-6737
Fax: 541-386-1410

Over 150 whole language, literature-based language arts software titles for grades K-12.

Karen Withrow, Marketing Assistant
Charlotte Arnold, Marketing Director

6070 **Teacher Support Software**
3542 NW 97th Boulevard
Gainesville, FL 32606-7322

352-332-6404
800-228-2871

Fax: 352-332-6779
E-mail: tss@tssoftware.com
http://www.tssoftware.com

Language arts, Title 1, special ed, at-risk and ESL, curriculum-based networkable software for grades K-12. Vocabulary software that develops sight word recognition, provides basal correlated databases, tests reading comprehension, tracks student's progress and provides powerful teacher tools.

6071 Weaver Instructional Systems
6161 28th Street SE
Grand Rapids, MI 49546-6931

616-942-2891
Fax: 616-942-1796

Reading and language arts computer software programs for K-college.

6072 www.caslt.org
Canadian Association of Second Language Teachers

Promotes the advancement of second language education throughout Canada.

6073 www.riverdeep.net
Riverdeep Interactive Learning

Riverdeep's interactive science, language and math arts programs deliver high quality educational experiences.

6074 www.signit2.com
Aylmer Press

Website hosted by Aylmer Press which produces video's to teach kids sign language as well as music.

6075 www.usajobs.opm.gov/b1c.htm1
Overseas Employment Info- Teachers
US Office of Personnel Management

Library Services

6076 American Econo-Clad Services
2101 N Topeka
Topeka, KS 66601

800-255-3502
Fax: 785-233-3129

A full service supplier of educational materials for the library, curriculum and software resource needs including MatchMaker, CD-ROM and ABLE (Analytically Budgeted Library Expenditures) computer systems.

6077 Anchor Audio
3415 Lomita Boulevard
Torrance, CA 90505-5010

310-784-2300
800-262-4671
Fax: 310-784-0533
http://www.anchoraudio.com

Various audio visual products for the school and library.

6078 Baker & Taylor
8140 Lehigh Avenue
Morton Grove, IL 60053-2627

847-965-8060

Nation's leading wholesale supplier of audio, computer software, books, videocassettes and other accessories to schools and libraries.

6079 Brodart Company, Automation Division
500 Arch Street
Williamsport, PA 17701

570-326-2461
800-233-8467
Fax: 570-327-9237
E-mail: salesmkt@brodart.com
http://www.brodart.com

Brodart's Automation Division has been providing library systems, software, and services for over 25 years. Products include: library management systems, media management systems, Internet solutions, cataloged web sites, catalogingresource tools, union catalog solutions, public access catalogs, and bibliographic services.

Kasey Dibble, Marketing Coordinator
Sally Wilmoth, Director Marketing/Sales

6080 Catalog Card Company
12219 Nicollet Avenue
Burnsville, MN 55337-1650

612-882-8558
800-442-7332
Fax: 785-290-1223

MARC records compatible with all software for retrospective conversions and new book orders. Catalog Card's conversion services include barcode labels to complement circulation software. MARC records generated from Dewey/Sears andLibrary of Congress databases are in standard USMARC or MicroLIF format.

6081 Chancery Student Management Solutions
3001 Wayburne Drive
Burnbay
Canada V5G 4W3

604-294-1233
800-999-9931
Fax: 604-294-2225
http://www.chancery.com

Online catalog searches and checking materials in and out.

6082 Data Trek
5838 Edison Place
Carlsbad, CA 92008-6519

800-876-5484

Turn-key library automation systems and computer networks.

6083 Demco
PO Box 7488
Madison, WI 53707-7488

800-356-1200
Fax: 608-241-1799

A leader in educational and library supplies for more than 80 years, Demco offers library audio and visual supplies and equipment plus display furniture.

6084 Dewey Decimal Classification
OCLC Forest Press
6565 Frantz Road
Dublin, OH 43017-3395

800-848-5878
Fax: 888-339-3921
E-mail: orders@oclc.org
http://www.oclc.org/fp

OCLC Forest Press publishes the Dewey Decimal Classification (DDC) system and many related print and CD-ROM products that teach librarians and library users about the DDC.

Libble Clawford, Marketing Manager

6085 Ebsco Subscription Services
International Headquarters
PO Box 1943
Birmingham, AL 35201-1943

205-991-1480
Fax: 205-980-6700

Periodical subscription and ordering and customer service equipment, computer and CD-ROM supplies, products and hardware for libraries.

Shannon Hayslip

6086 Electronic Bookshelf
5276 S Country Road, 700 W
Frankfort, IN 46041

765-324-2182
Fax: 765-324-2183

Reading motivation, testing management system and various computer systems and networks for educational purposes.

Rosalie Carter

6087 Filette Keez Corporation/Colorworks Diskette Organizing System
3204 Channing Lane
Bedford, TX 76021-6506

817-283-5428

Produces ten filing inventions for classroom library, lab and district technology resources management. SelecTsideS folders store multimedia in Press-an-Inch Technology Slings and keep instruction, printouts, pamphlets andblackliners altogether. The diskette/CD portfolio color coordinates with the student/magazine Spbinder, plastic LaceLox fastener and all systems paper supplies: CD envelopes, storage box dividers, sheeted cards, perforated tractor labels and keys,available in 7 tech colors.

Roxanne Kay Harbert, Founder/President
Ray L Harbert, VP

6088 Follett Software Company
1391 Corporate Drive
McHenry, IL 60050

815-344-8700
800-323-3397
Fax: 815-344-8774
E-mail: marketing@fsc.follett.com
http://www.fsc.follett.com

Helping K-12 schools and districts create a vital library-to-classroom link to improve student achievement. FSC combines award-winning library automation with practical applications of the Internet. From OPAC data enhancement andeasy-to-implement Internet technology to innovative information literacy solutions, FSC helps simplify resource management, increase access to resources inside and outside your collection and provide tools to integrate technology into the curriculum.

Patricia Yonushonis, Marketing Manager
Ann Reist, Conference Manager

6089 Foundation for Library Research
1200 Bigley Avenue
Charleston, WV 25302-3752

304-343-6480
Fax: 304-343-6489

The Automated Library Systems integrated library automation software.

Robert Evans

6090 Gaylord Brothers
PO Box 4901
Syracuse, NY 13221-4901

800-448-6160
Fax: 315-457-8387

Library, AV supplies and equipment; security systems; and library furniture.

Tim Krein

6091 Highsmith Company
W5527 Highway 106
Fort Atkinson, WI 53538

414-563-9571

Catalog of microcomputer and multimedia curriculum products and software.

Barbara R Endl

6092 Information Access Company
362 Lakeside Drive
Foster City, CA 94404-1171

800-227-8431

Offers automation products and electronics for library/media centers.

6093 LePAC NET
Brodart Automation
500 Arch Street
Williamsport, PA 17705

570-326-2461
800-233-8467
Fax: 570-327-9237
E-mail: salesmkt@brodart.com
http://www.brodart.com

Software for searching thousands of library databases with a single search. Schools can use to take multiple individual library databases and consolidate them, while deleting duplicate listings, into a union database.

Shawn Knight, Assistant Marketing Manager
Denise Macafee, Marketing Manager

6094 Library Corporation
Library Corporation
Research Park
Inwood, WV 25428-9733

800-325-7759
http://www.tlcdelivers.com

Web-based library management systems allows patrons to have easy and immediate access to books and other library resources.

6095 Lingo Fun
International Software
PO Box 486
Westerville, OH 43086-0486

800-745-8258

Providers of microcomputer software including CD-ROM's for Macintosh and MPC, on-line dictionaries, translation assistants; teaching programs for elementary presentation, review and reinforcement, test preparation, and literaryexploration.

6096 MARCIVE
PO Box 47508
San Antonio, TX 78265-7508

210-646-6161
800-531-7678
Fax: 210-646-0167
E-mail: info@marcive.com
http://www.marcive.com

Economical, fast 100% conversion. Full MARC records with SEARS or LC headings. Free authorities processing smart barcode labels, reclassification, MARC Record enrichment

6097 Medianet/Dymaxion Research Limited
5515 Cogswell Street
Halifax, Nova Scotia, B3 J 1R2
902-422-1973
Fax: 902-421-1267
E-mail: info@medianet.ns.ca
http://www.medianet.ns.ca

Medianet is the scheduling system for equipment and media that has consistently been rated as best in its class. Features include book library system integration, time-of-day booking, catalog production, WWW and touch tone phonebooking by patrons.

Peter Mason, President

6098 Mitinet/Marc Software
6409 Odana Road
Madison, WI 53719-1125
800-824-6272
Fax: 608-270-1107

Import/export USMARC, MICROLIF to USMARC conversions.

6099 Orange Cherry Software
69 Westchester Avenue
PO Box 390
Pound Ridge, NY 10576-1702
914-764-4104
800-672-6002
Fax: 914-764-0104
http://www.orangecherry.com

Educational software products for libraries and media centers.

Biannual

Nicholas Vazzana, President

6100 Right on Programs
778 New York Avenue
Huntington, NY 11743-4240
631-424-7777
Fax: 631-424-7207
E-mail: friends@rightonprograms.com
http://www.rightonprograms.com

Computer software for Windows and networks for library management including circulation, cataloging, periodicals, catalog cardmaking, inventory and thirty more. Used in more than 24,000 schools and libraries of all sizes.

D Farren, VP

6101 SOLINET, Southeastern Library Network
1438 W Peachtree Street NW
Suite 200
Atlanta, GA 30309-2955
404-892-0943
800-999-8558
Fax: 404-892-7879
E-mail: information@solinet.net
http://www.solinet.net

SOLINET provides access, training and support for OCLC products and services; offers discounted library products and services, including licensed databases; provides electronic information solutions; workflow consulting, training andcustomized workshops; and supports a regional preservation of materials program.

Cathie Gharing, Marketing Coordinator
Liz Hornsby, Editor

6102 Sirsi Corporation
101 Washington Street SE
Huntsville, AL 35801-4827
256-704-7000
800-917-4774
Fax: 256-704-7007
E-mail: sales@sirsi.com
http://www.sirsi.com

Unicorn Collection Management Systems are fully integrated UNIX-based library systems, automating all of a library's operation. Modules include: cataloging, authority control, public access, materials booking, circulation, academicreserves, acquisitions, serials control, reference database manager and electronic mail. Modules can be configured for all types and sizes of libraries.

Vicki Smith, Communication Specialist

6103 Social Issues Resources Series
PO Box 2348
Boca Raton, FL 33427
561-994-0079
800-232-SIRS
Fax: 561-994-4704

Publisher of CD-ROM reference systems for PC and Macintosh computers. Databases of full-text articles carefully selected from 1,000 domestic and international sources. Also provides PC-compatible and stand-alone and networkpackages.

Paula Jackson, Marketing Director
Suzanne Panek, Customer Service

6104 TekData Systems Company
1111 W Park Avenue
Libertyville, IL 60048-2952
847-367-8800
Fax: 847-367-0235
E-mail: tekdata@tekdata.com
http://www.tekdata.com

Scheduling and booking systems for intranets and internets.

Randy Kick, Sales Manager

6105 Three M Library Systems
Three M Center
Building 225-4N-14
St. Paul, MN 55144
800-328-0067
Fax: 800-223-5563

Materials Flow Management system is the first comprehensive system for optimizing the handling, processing and security of your library materials - from processing to checkout to check-in. The SelfCheck System and Staff Workstationautomate the processing of virtually all of your library materials, while the Tattle-Tape Security Strips and Detection Systems help ensure the security of those materials.

6106 UMI
300 N Zeeb Road
Ann Arbor, MI 48103-1553
800-521-0600
Fax: 800-864-0019

Information products in microform, CD-ROM, online and magnetic tape.

6107 University Products
517 Main Street
#101
Holyoke, MA 01040-5514
413-532-3372
800-628-1912
Fax: 413-452-0618

Complete selection of library and media center supplies and equipment.

Juhn Dunpay

6108 WLN
PO Box 3888
Lacey, WA 98509-3888

360-923-4000
800-342-5956
Fax: 360-923-4009

School and media librarians experience 95% hit rates with WLN's LaserCat, CD-ROM database, a cataloging product and MARC record service.

6109 Winnebago Software Company
457 E South Street
Caledonia, MN 55921-1356

800-533-5430
Fax: 507-725-2301
E-mail: sales@winnebago.com
http://www.winnebago.com

Comprehensive, user-friendly circulation and catalog software for Windows, Mac OS, and MS-DOS systems-plus Internet technology, online periodical databases, outstanding customer support, and retrospective conversion services-alldeveloped within the quality guidelines of Winnebago's ISO 9001 certification with TickIT accreditation.

6110 www.awesomelibrary.org
Awesome Library

Organizes the Web with 15,000 carefully reviewed resources, including the top 5 percent in education. Offers sections of mathematics, science, social studies, english, health, physical education, technology, languages, specialeducation, the arts and more. Features a section involved with today's current issues facing our world, like pollution, gun control, tobacco, and other changing 'hot' topics. Site can be browsed in English, German, Spanish, French or Portuguese.

6111 www.techlearning.com
Technology & Learning

Open 24 hours, every day of the week, with an extensive and up-to-date catalog of over 53,000 software and hardware products. Powerful search engine will help you find the right education-specific products.

Mathematics

6112 Accelerated Math
Renaissance Learning
PO Box 8036
Wisconsin Rapids, WI 54495-8036

715-424-3636
800-338-4204
Fax: 715-424-4242
E-mail: answers@renlearn.com
http://www.renlearn.com

Accelerated Math provides 17 different reports, providing individualized, constructive feedback to students, parents, and teachers.

6113 Applied Mathematics Program
Prime Technology Corporation
PO Box 2407
Minneola, FL 34755-2407

352-394-7558
Fax: 352-394-3778
http://www.primetechnology.net

Provides students with comprehensive instruction in 11 math areas. In working with this program, students develop employment and life skills. The program will

also lead the student to greater success on the mathematics sections of anystandardized test.

Paul Scime, President

6114 CAE Software
3608 Shepherd Street
Chevy Chase, MD 20815-4132

301-907-9845
800-354-3462

Provides educational software for mathematics, grades 3-12. Simulations, tutorials, games, and problem solving. Titles include Mathematics Life Skills Services, Reading and Making Graphs Series, MathLab Series, Meaning of Fractions,Using Fractions and Using Decimals, ALG Football, GEO Pool and GEO Billiards, Paper Route, Mathematics Achievement Project, and others.

Alan R Chap, President

6115 EME Corporation
PO Box 1949
Stuart, FL 34995-1949

800-848-2050
Fax: 561-219-2209
E-mail: emecorp@aol.com
http://www.emescience.com

Publishers of award-winning science and math software, elementary through high school levels.

6116 Logal Software
125 Cambridgepark Drive
Cambridge, MA 02140-2329

617-491-4440
Fax: 617-491-5855

Math and science products for high school through college.

Martha Cheng, President

6117 MathType
Design Science
4028 E Broadway
Long Beach, CA 90803-1502

562-433-0685
800-827-0685
Fax: 562-433-6969
http://www.mathtype.com

Designed to make the creation of complex equations on a computer simple and fast. It works in conjunction with the software applications you already own, such as word processing programs, graphics programs, presentation programs, andweb-authoring applications. Create research papers, tests, slides, books or web pages quickly and easily. MathType is the powerful, professional version of the Equation Editor in Microscoft Word, and Wordperfect.

Bruce Virga, VP Sales/Marketing
Nicole Jessey, Sale/Marketing Coordinator

6118 Mathematica
Wolfram Research

877-239-7149
http://www.wolfram.com

Mathematica is an indispensable tool for finding and communicating solutions quickly and easily.

6119 MindTwister Math
Edmark Corporation
PO Box 97021
Redmond, WA 98073-9721

425-556-8400
800-691-2986
Fax: 425-556-8430

E-mail: edmarkteam@edmark.com
http://www.edmark.com

Software to help students in grade 3 and 4 build math fact fluency, practice mental math and improve estimating skills as they compete in a series of math challenges.

6120 Multimedia - The Human Body
Sunburst Technology
101 Castleton Street
Pleasantville, NY 10570

914-747-3310
800-321-7511
Fax: 914-747-4109
http://www.sunburst.com

Multimedia production of the intricate workings of the human body.

6121 Texas Instruments
Consumer Relations
PO Box 53
Lubbock, TX 79408-0053

800-842-2737
Fax: 972-917-0874

Instructional calculators offer features matched to math concepts taught at each of conceptional development. Classroom accessories and teacher support programs that support the Texas Instruments products enhance instruction andlearning. TI also offers a complete range of powerful notebook computers and laser printers for every need.

6122 William K. Bradford Publishing Company
35 Forest Ridge Road
Concord, MA 01742-5414

800-421-2009
Fax: 978-318-9500
http://www.wkbradford.com

Educational software for grades K-12. Especially math and grade book.
Hal Wexler, VP

6123 www.mathgoodies.com
Mrs. Glosser's Math Goodies

Free educational site featuring interactive math lessons. Use a problem-solving approach and actively engage students in the learning process.

6124 www.mathstories.com
MathStories.com

The goal of this site is to help grade school children improve their math problem-solving and critical thinking skills. Offers over 4000 math word problems for children.

6125 www.riverdeep.net
Riverdeep Interactive Learning

Riverdeep's interactive science, language and math arts programs deliver high quality educational experiences.

6126 www.themathemagician.8m.com
The Mathemagician

Offers the help of a real live person to help students correct and understand math and other home work problems.

Music & Art

6127 Harmonic Vision
68 E Wacker Place
Chicago, IL 60610

312-332-9200
800-474-0903
http://www.harmonicvision.com

Leading musical education software to teach effectiveness of music in the home, school and studio.

6128 Midnight Play
Simon & Schuster Interactive

800-793-9972
http://www.simonandschuster.com

Electronic picture book with an unusual look at creativity.

6129 Music Teacher Find
33 W 17th Street
10th Floor
New York, NY 10011

212-242-2464
http://www.MusicTeacherFind.com

Comprehensive Music Teacher Database designed to help music students find quality teachers in their neighborhood.

6130 Music and Guitar

http://www.nl-guitar.com

Original music programs for schools, courses and encounterswith music.

6131 Pure Gold Teaching Tools
PO Box 16622
Tuscon, AZ 85732

520-747-5600
866-692-6500
Fax: 520-571-9077
E-mail: info@puregoldteachingtools.com
http://www.puregoldteachingtools.com

Exciting teaching methods and fabulous gifts for teachers, parents, students, pre-schoolers, homeschoolers and music therapists.
Heidi Goldman, President

6132 http://library.thinkquest.org
Think Quest

The Arti FAQS 2100 Project is designed to predict how art will influence our lives in the next hundred years. Students can use available data to make reasonable predictions for the future.

6133 http://members.truepath.com/headoftheclass
Head of The Class

Offers three galleries with clip art for teachers and children, several lesson plans, teaching tips, songs for teachers, lounge laughs, teacher tales and more.

6134 www.billharley.com
BillHarley.com

Humerous, yet meaningful songs which chronicle the lives of children at school and at home. His recordings of songs and stories can be used most effectively in the classroom as inspirational tools for the motivation of learning.

6135 www.sanford-artedventures.com
Sanford- A Lifetime of Color

800-323-0749

Teaches students about art and color theory while they play a game. Lessons plans, newsletter and product information.

6136 www.songs4teachers.com
O'Flynn Consulting

E-mail: oflynn4@home.com

Offers many resources for teachers including songs made especially for your classroom. Sections with songs and activities for holidays, seasons and more. Features books and audios with 101 theme songs for use in the classroom oranywhere children gather to sing.

6137 www.ushistory.com
History Happens

Teaches integrating art, music, literature, science, math, library skills, and American history. The Primary source is stories from American history presented in musci video style.

Physical Education

6138 InfoUse
2560 9th Street
Suite 216
Berkeley, CA 94710-2557

510-549-6520
Fax: 510-549-6512

An award-winning, multimedia development and products firm, features CD-ROM, websites on health, education and disability. For training, education or presentations, our services include: research, instructional design, interfacedesign, graphics, animation, content acquisition, videoing, analog and digital editing and evaluation. Products include SafeNet, (HIV prevention for fifth and sixth grade children), Place Math and Math Pad (math tools and lessons for students withdisabilities).

Lewis E Kraus, VP
Susan Stoddard, President

6139 www.sports-media.org
Sports Media

A tool for p.e. teachers, coaches, students and everyone who is interested in p.e./fitness and sports. Interactive p.e. lesson plans, sports pen-apls for the kids, European p.e. mailing list, and developing teaching skills in physicaleducation.

Reading

6140 Accelerated Reader
Renaissance Learning
PO Box 8036
Wisconsin Rapids, WI 54495-8036

715-424-3636
800-338-4204
Fax: 715-424-4242
E-mail: answers@renlearn.com
http://www.renlearn.com

Helps teachers increase literature-based reading practice for all k-12 students

Secondary Education

6141 New York Times
New York, NY

646-698-8000
Fax: 646-698-8344
http://www.nytimes.com/learning

A resource for educators, parents and students in grades six through 12. Provides a daily lesson plan and comprehensive interactive resources based on newspaper content.

Rob Larson, Education Editor
Diane Morgan, Director Marketing

6142 Wm. C. Brown Communications
2460 Kerper Boulevard
Dubuque, IA 52001-2224

College textbooks, software, CD-ROM and more for grades 10-12.

6143 http://adulted.about.com/education/adulted
Adult/Continuing Education

6144 http://englishhlp.www5.50megs.com
English Help

E-mail: englishhlpr@hotmail.com

This page is a walk through of Microsoft Power Point. The goal is to show in a few simple steps how to make your own website. Created by Rebecca Holland.

6145 www.number2.com
Number2.com

Currently offer SAT and GRE prep along with a vocabulary builder. Practice questions and word drill are adapted to the ability level of the user.

Science

6146 Academic Software Development Group
University of Maryland
University of Maryland
Computer Science Center
College Park, MD 20742-0001

301-405-5100
Fax: 301-405-0726

Offers BioQuest Library which is a set of peer-reviewed resources for science education.

6147 Accu-Weather
385 Science Park Road
State College, PA 16803-2215
814-237-0309
Fax: 814-238-1339

Offers a telecommunications weather and oceanography database.

6148 AccuLab Products Group
614 Senic Drive
Suite 104
Modesto, CA 95350
209-522-8874
Fax: 209-522-8875

Science laboratory software.

6149 Learning Team
10 Long Pond Road
Armonk, NY 10504-2625
914-273-2226
800-793-TEAM
Fax: 914-273-2227

Offers CD-ROM, including MathFinder, Science Helper and Small Blue Planet and Redshift, the Learning Team edition.

Thomas Laster

6150 Problem Solving Concepts
611 N Capitol Avenue
Indianapolis, IN 46204-1205
317-267-9827
800-755-2150
Fax: 317-262-5044

Pro Solv provides students with a new approach to learning introductory physics problem solving techniques. Multi-experiential exercises with supporting text introduce students to relevant variables and their interrelations,principles, graphing and the development of problem solving skills through the quiz/tutorial mode.

Thomas D Feigenbaum, President
Gean R Shelor, Administrative Assistant

6151 Quantum Technology
PO Box 8252
Searcy, AR 72145-8252

A microcomputer database collection system that allows users to perform experiments in chemistry, biology and applied physics.

6152 SCI Technologies
SCI Technologies
105 Terry Drive
Suite 120
Newtown, PA 18940
215-579-8590
800-421-9881
Fax: 215-579-8589
E-mail: cgreenblatt@scitechnologies.com
http://www.scitechnologies.com

A computer-based interface with an integrated hardware and software package that allows the focus of a science lab to shift from data collection to data analysis and experiment design.

Colleen Greenblatt, Sales Manager
Michelle Trexler, Event Coordinator

6153 Videodiscovery
1700 Westlake Avenue N
Suite 600
Seattle, WA 98109-3040
206-285-5400
800-548-3472
Fax: 206-285-9245

Publishers of award winning science videodiscs and multimedia software for kindergarten through post-secondary classes.

6154 www.kidsastronomy.com
KidsAstronomy.com

Offers information on astronomy, deep space, the solar system, space exploration, a teachers corner and more.

6155 www.riverdeep.net
Riverdeep Interactive Learning

Riverdeep's interactive science, language and math arts programs deliver high quality educational experiences.

Social Studies

6156 AccuNet/AP Multimedia Archive
AccuWeather, Inc.
385 Science Park Road
State College, PA 16803
814-235-8600
800-566-6606
Fax: 814-231-0453
E-mail: salesmail@accuwx.com
http://www.ap.accuweather.com

The Photo Archive is an on-line database containing almost a half-million of Associated Press's current and historic images for the last 150 years.

Michael Warfield, Southeastern Sales Manager
Richard Towne, Northeastern Sales Manager

6157 Gale Research
PO Box 33477
Detroit, MI 48232-5477
800-877-GALE
Fax: 800-414-5043

Offers CD-Rom information that offer students contextual understanding of the most commonly-studies persons, events and social movements in U.S. history; concepts, theories, discoveries and people involved in the study of science;current geopolitical data with cultural information on 200 nations of the world as well as all U.S. states and dependencies; poetry and literary information; and more in various databases for education.

6158 World Geography Web Site
ABC-CLIO Schools
130 Cremona Drive
#1911
Santa Barbara, CA 93117-5599
805-968-1911
800-368-6868
Fax: 805-685-9685

Provides convenient internet access to curriculum-based reference and research materials for media specialist, educators and students.

CD-ROM

Judy Fay, Managing Editor
Valerie Mercado, Customer Service

6159 WorldView Software
76 N Broadway
Suite 4009
Hicksville, NY 11801-4241
516-681-1773
800-347-8839

Fax: 516-681-1775
E-mail: history@worldviewsoftware.com

WorldView Software's interactive social studies programs for middle school and high school are comprehensive, curriculum-based tools that may be used along with or in place of textbooks. Each dynamic program contains Socratic learningsessions, writing activities and exams with instant feedback. Resource materials in every program include sketches and artwork. Used nationallly in classrooms, computer labs and learning centers.

Grades 7-12

Jerrold Kleinstein, President

6160 http://faculty.acu.edu
M.I. Smart Program

Site designed for teacher and students. Offers electronic resources for historical and cultural geography. Features games, quizzes, trivia and virtual tours for students and thier teachers.

Technology in Education

6161 BLINKS.Net
PO Box 79321
Atlanta, GA 30357

404-243-5202
Fax: 404-241-4992
E-mail: info@blinks.net
http://www.blinks.net

Fastest growing free Internet service provider and community portal for information and resources for the African American, Caribbean, Latino, and African markets.

6162 Boyce Enterprises
360 Sharry Lane
Santa Maria, CA 93455

805-937-4353
Fax: 805-934-1765

Development of computer-based vocational curriculums.

6163 Center for Educational Outreach and Innovation
Teachers College-Columbia University
525 W 120th Street
Box 132
New York, NY 10027

212-678-3987
800-209-1245
Fax: 212-678-8417
E-mail: ceoi-mail@tc.columbia.edu
http://www.tc.columbia.edu

Lifelong learning programs, including distance learning courses, certificates and workshoops in education related topics.

6164 Depco
3305 Airport Drive
PO Box 178
Pittsburg, KS 66762

316-231-0019
800-767-1062
Fax: 316-231-0024
E-mail: sales@depcoinc.com
http://www.depcoinc.com

Program tracks and schedules for you, the test taker delivers tests electronically, as well as, automatic final exams. There are workstation security features to help keep students focused on their activities.

6165 Dialog Information Services
Worldwide Headquaters
3460 Hillview Avenue
#10010
Palo Alto, CA 94304-1338

415-858-3785
800-334-2564
Fax: 650-858-7069

The world's most comprehensive online information source offering over 450 databases containing over 330 million articles, abstracts and citations - covering an unequaled variety of topics, with particular emphasis on news, business,science and technology. Dialog has offices throughout the United States and around the world.

6166 Distance Education Database
International Centre for Distance Learning
Open University, Walton Hall
Milton Keynes
England

441-085-3537
Fax: 441-086-4173

Contains information on distance education, including more than 22,000 distance-taught programs and courses in the Commonwealth of Learning, an organization created by the Commonwealth Heads of Government. On-line and CD-Rom versionsof the database contain detailed information on over 30,000 distance-taught courses, 900 distance teaching instructions, and nearly 9,000 books, journals, reports and papers.

Keith Harry, Director

6167 EDUCAUSE
1112 16th Street NW
Suite 600
Washington, DC 20036-4822

202-872-4200
Fax: 202-872-4318
http://www.educause.edu

Aims to link practitioners in primary and secondary education through computer-mediated communications networks.

John Clement, Director

6168 Educational Structures
NCS Pearson
827 W Grove Avenue
Mesa, AZ 85210

800-736-4357
http://www.ncspearson.com

Features complete lesson plans and resources in social studies, mathematics, science, and language arts.

6169 Gibson Tech Ed
1216 S 1580 West
Building C
Orem, UT 84058

800-422-1100
Fax: 800-470-1606
E-mail: gary@gibsonteched.com
http://www.gibsonteched.com

Educational materials to teach electronics, from middle, junior, high school and college.

Gary Gibson, Manager
Tim Gibson, President

6170 Grolier Interactive
Grolier Publishing
90 Sherman Turnpike
Danbury, CT 06816

800-371-3908

Fax: 800-456-4402
http://http://publishing.grolier.com

Instructional software including reference, science, mathematics, music, social studies, early learning, art and art history, language arts/literature.

6171 Heifner Communications
4451 Interstate 70 Drive NW
Columbia, MO 65202-3271

573-445-6163
800-445-6164
Fax: 512-527-2395

Offers educational-merit, cable-programming available via satellite. HCI Distance Learning systems are designed for dependable services and ease of operation and competitive prices.

Vicky Roberts

6172 In Focus
27700 B SW Parkway Avenue
Wilsonville, OR 97070-9215

503-685-8887
800-294-6400
Fax: 503-685-8887

LCD panels, video projectors and systems.

6173 JonesKnowledge.com
9697 E Mineral Avenue
Englewood, CO 80112

800-701-6463

For administrators, that means and integrated solution-with no minimum commitment, or upfront investment. For instructors, it means getting your course online your way, without being a web expert, and for students it means, anaccessible and convenient online experience.

6174 Mastercam
CNC Software
5717 Wollochet Drive NW
Suite 2A
Gig Harbor, WA

800-275-6226
Fax: 253-858-6737
E-mail: mcinfo@mastercam.com
http://www.mastercamedu.com

6175 Merit Audio Visual
Merit Software
132 W 21st Street
New York, NY 10011-3203

212-675-8567
800-753-6488
Fax: 212-675-8607
E-mail: sales@meritsoftware.com
http://www.merutsoftware.com

Easy to use, interactive basic skills software for Windows 9x/ME/NT/2000/XP computers. Lessons for reading, writing, grammar and math with appropriate graphics for teens and adults.

Ben Weintraub, Marketing Manager

6176 National Information Center for Educational Media
PO Box 8640
Albuquerque, NM 87198

505-265-3591
800-926-8328
Fax: 505-256-1080
E-mail: nicem@nicem.com
http://www.nicem.com

NICEM maintains a comprehensive database describing educational media materials for all ages and subjects. It is available on CD-ROM and online.

Lisa Savard, Sales/Marketing Director

6177 NoRad Corporation
4455 Torrance Boulevard
#2806513
Torrance, CA 90503-4398

310-605-0808
Fax: 323-934-2101

Mini, personal, medium and large computer systems for educational institutions.

6178 Proxima Corporation
9440 Carroll Park Drive
San Diego, CA 92121

858-457-5500
800-294-6400
Fax: 503-685-7239
http://www.proxima.com

Proxima Corporation is a global leader in the multimedia projection market, providing world class presentation solutions to corporate enterprises, workgroups, mobile professionals, trainers, and professional public speakers.

Kim Gallagher, Public Relations Manager
Kathy Bankerd, Director Marketing Programs

6179 RB5X: Education's Personal Computer Robot
General Robotics Corporation
760 S Youngfield Court
Suite 8
Lakewood, CO 80228-2813

303-988-5636
800-422-4265
Fax: 303-988-5303
E-mail: cbrown@generalrobotics.com
http://www.edurobot.com

RB5X: Education's Personal Computer Robot. All grade levels. Self learn, self teach, hands on modular system. Problem solving, basic learning skills, increases self-esteem. Expanable open-ended, motivation at its best.

Constant Brown, President

6180 SEAL
550 Spring Street
Naugatuck, CT 06770-1906

203-729-5201

Complete line of systems and electronics for schools.

6181 Sharp Electronics Corporation
LCD Products Group
Sharp Plaza
Mall Stop One
Mahwah, NJ 07430

201-529-8731
Fax: 201-529-9636
E-mail: prolcd@sharpsec.com
http://www.sharplcd.com

Offers a full line of LCD-based video and computer multimedia projectors and projection panels for use in a wide range of educational applications. Sharp's product line also includes industrial VHS format VCRs, color TV monitors.

J Ganguzza, Director/Marketing

6182 Valiant
PO Box 3171
S Hackensack, NJ 07606-1171

800-631-0867
Fax: 201-814-0418

Distributors of LCD projection panels, P/A systems, overhead/slide and filmstrip projectors, cassette recorders, classroom record players, laser pointers, laminating equipment, lecturns, listening centers and headphones.

Sheldon Goldstein

6183 Vernier Software
8565 SW Beaverton Hillsdale Hwy
Portland, OR 97225-2429

Laboratory interacting software for the Macintosh, IBM and Apple II.

6184 Websense
10240 Sorrento Valley Road
San Diego, CA 92121

858-320-8000
800-723-1166
Fax: 858-458-2950
http://www.websense.com

Internet filtering.

**6185 http://di...elearn/cs/eductechnology/index.htm
About Education Distance Learning**

**6186 http://futurekids.com
FUTUREKIDS School Technology Solutions**

http://www.futurekids.com
Helping schools use technology to transform education.

**6187 http://online.uophx.edu
University of Phoenix Online**

Offers you the convenience and flexibility of attending classes from your personal computer. Students are discussing issues, sharing ideas, testing theories, essentially enjoying all of the advantages of an on-campus degree programs.Interaction is included like e-mail, so you practice at your convenience.

**6188 http://www.crossteccorp.com
NetOp**

800-675-0729
Fax: 561-391-5820
http://www.crossteccorp.com
A powerful combination of seven essential tools for networked classrooms. Based on the award winning technology of NetOp Remote Control and is easy-to-use software only solution.

**6189 http://www.growsmartbrains.com
GrowSmartBrains.com**

Website for parents and educators who want research based information and practical stradegies for raising children in a media age.

**6190 http://www.zdnet.com
ZDNet**

Full-service destination for people looking to buy, use and learn more about technology.

**6191 www.21ct.org
Twenty First Century Teachers Network**

A nationwide, non-profit initiative of the McGuffey Project, dedicated to assisting k-12 teachers learn, use and effectively integrate technology in the curriculum for improved student learning.

**6192 www.aboutonehandtyping.com/
One Hand Typing and Keyboarding Resources**

This site dishes up a blend of messages and stories, resources for one-hand typists, links to alternative keyboards, teaching links, and more.

**6193 www.digitaldividenetwork.org
Digital Divide Network**

E-mail: ddivide@benton.org
The goal of bridging the divide is to use communications technology to help improve the quality of life of all communities and their citizens; provide them with the tools, skills and information they need to help them realize theirsocioeconomic, educational and cultural potential.

**6194 www.getquizzed.com
GetQuizzed**

Designed as a free service that provides a database that allows users to create, store and edit Multiple Choice or Question and Answer quizzes, under password protected conditions.

**6195 www.guidetogeekdom.com
Guide to Geekdom**

E-mail: info@guidetogeekdom.com
Designed especially for Homeschoolers, step-by-step lessons teach students how to use the computer and troubleshoot computer problems. Offers workbooks, sample lesson and more.

**6196 www.happyteachers.com
HappyTeachers.com**

Information about technical and vocational education programs, products and curriculum.

**6197 www.integratingit.com
Integrating Information Technology for the**
Classroom, School, & District

Dedicated to providing the education community a place to find real world strategies, solutions, and resources for integrating technology. Organized by the perspective of the classroom teacher, the school administrator, and thedistrict.

**6198 www.livetext.com
LiveText Curriculum Manager**

Provides tools for engaged learning classroom projects and provides online professional development for teachers.

**6199 www.ncrel.org
North Central Regional Educational Laboratory**

Offers research results regarding the effective use of technology.

6200 **www.ncrtec.org**
North Central Regional Technology
in Education Consortiums

Provides a variety of tools and information to improve technology-related professional development programs.

Elementary Education

6201 Curriculum Associates
153 Rangeway Road
No. Billerica, MA 01862

800-225-0248
Fax: 800-366-1158
http://www.curriculumassociates.com

Test preparation material with a guarantee of success; skill instruction and assessment.

6202 Diagnostic Reading Inventory for Primary and Intermediate Grades K-8
Scott and McCleary Publishing Co.
2482 11th Street SW
Akron, OH 44314-1712

702-566-8756
800-765-3564
Fax: 702-568-1378
E-mail: jscott7576@aol.com
http://www.scottmccleary.com

A series of 13 tests at each grade level, 10 can be given in a group setting. 3 Forms of the IRI teacher friendly. Easy to administer.

Spiral Paperback
ISBN: 0-9636225-4-4

Janet M. Scott and Sheila C. McCeary, Author
Janet Scott, Co-Author
Sheila McCleary, Co-Author

6203 Lexia Learning Systems
PO Box 466
Lincoln, MA 01773-0466

781-259-8752
Fax: 781-259-1349
E-mail: info@lexialearning.com
http://www.lexialearning.com

Reading software and assessment programs for children and adults, professional development programs for teachers, principals and administrators.

6204 LinguiSystems
3100 4th Avenue
East Moline, IL 61244-9700

800-776-4332
Fax: 800-577-4555
E-mail: service@linguisystems.com
http://www.linguisystems.com

Offers tests and print materials for speech language pathologists, teachers of the learning disabled, middle school language arts and reading teachers.

6205 National Study of School Evaluation
1699 E Woodfield Road
Suite 406
Schaumburg, IL 60173-4958

847-995-9080
800-843-6773
Fax: 847-995-9088
E-mail: schoolimprovement@nsse.org
http://www.nsse.org

Provides educational leaders with state-of-the-art assessment and evaluation materials to enhance and promote student growth and school improvement.

Dr. Kathleen A. Fitzpatrick, Executive Director

6206 Testing Miss Malarky
Walker And Company
435 Hudson Street
New York, NY 10014

212-727-8300
800-289-2553
Fax: 212-727-0984
http://www.walkerbooks.com

Author and artist exploit the mania that accompanies the classes first standardized test.

32 pages
ISBN: 0-8027-8737-1

Judy Finchler, Contact

Language Arts

6207 CTB/McGraw-Hill
20 Ryan Ranch Road
Monterey, CA 93940-5703

831-393-0700
800-538-9547
Fax: 800-282-0266
http://www.ctb.com

K-12 achievement tests, early literacy assessment, language proficiency evaluation, adult basic skills tests, and test management and instructional planning software.

6208 SLEP Program Office
PO Box 6155
Princeton, NJ 08541-6155

Offers information on the Secondary Level English Proficiency Test.

Mathematics

6209 Psychological Assessment Resources
PO Box 998
Odessa, FL 33556

800-331-TEST
Fax: 800-727-9329
http://www.parinc.com

Catalog of professional testing resources.

6210 SAT Math Flash
Peterson's Guides
PO Box 2123
Princeton, NJ 08543-2123

609-243-9111
800-338-3282
Fax: 609-243-9150

Lets students work through 120 problems in two full tests, providing immediate feedback.

144 pages
ISBN: 1-560793-21-0

Michael R. Crystal, Author

6211 Summing It Up: College Board Mathematics Assessment Programs
College Board Publications
45 Columbus Avenue
New York, NY 10023-6917

212-713-8165
800-323-7155
Fax: 800-525-5562
http://www.collegeboard.org

An overview of SAT I: Reasoning Tests and PSAT/NMSQT, SAT II: Subject Tests, Descriptive Tests of Mathematical Skills (DTMS), CPTs in Mathematics, CLEP Mathematics Examinations, AP Exams in Mathematics, AP Exams in Computer Sciences,and Pacesetter Mathematics.

30 pages

Music & Art

6212 A&F Video's Art Catalog
PO Box 264
Geneseo, NY 14454

http://www.aandfvideo.com
New listing of titles for Art Teachers and Art Lovers.

6213 All Art Supplies
Art Supplies Wholesale
4 Enon Street
North Beverly, MA 01915

800-462-2420
http://www.allartsupplies.com
Art supplies at wholesale prices.

6214 American Art Clay Company
6060 Guion Road
Indianapolis, IN 46254

317-244-6871
800-374-1600
Fax: 317-248-9300
E-mail: catalog@amaco.com
http://www.amaco.com

Provides ceramic materials and equipment.

6215 Arnold Grummer
PO Box 13245
Milwaukee, WI 53213

800-453-1485
Fax: 414-453-1495
E-mail: webmaster@arnoldgrummer.com
http://www.arnoldgrummer.com

Products and information to meet most any papermaking need.

6216 Arrowmont School of Arts & Crafts
556 Parkway
Gainsburg, TN 37738

865-438-5860
Fax: 865-438-4101
http://www.arrowmont.org

The art school of tomorrow.

6217 Art & Creative Materials Institute
PO Box 479
Hanson, MA 02341

781-293-4100
Fax: 781-294-0808
E-mail: debbieg@acminec.org
http://www.acminec.org

A non-profit trade association whose memebers are manufacturers of art and creative materials. Sponsors a certification program to ensure that art materials are non-toxic or affixed with health warning labels where appropriate.Publishes a booklet on the safe use of art materials and a listing of products that are approved under its certification program. Both of these publications are free of charge.

Deborah Fanning, Executive Vice President
Deborah Gustafson, Associate Director

6218 Art Instruction Schools
3309 Broadway Street NW
Minneapolis, MN 55413

http://www.artists-ais.com

6219 Art to Remember
10625 Deme Drive
Unit E
Indianapolis, IN 46236

317-826-0870
800-895-8777
Fax: 317-823-2822
http://www.arttoremember.com

A unique program that encourages your students' artisic creativity while providing an oppurtunity to raise funds for schools.

6220 ArtSketchbook.com
487 Hulsetown Road
Campbell Hall, NY 10916

845-496-4709
http://www.artsketchbook.com

Provides instructions and work examples by an elementary student, secondary student and a professional artist.

6221 Arts Institutes International
Education Management Corporation
300 6th Avenue
Suite 800
Pittsburgh, PA 15222

800-275-2440

Post-secondary career education. Offers associate's, bachelor's and non-degree programs in design, media arts, technology, culinary arts and fashion.

6222 Museum Stamps
PO Box 356
New Canaan, CT 06840

800-659-2787
Fax: 203-966-2729
http://www.museumstamps.com

Rubber stamps of famous works of art, stamp accessories, classroom projects.

6223 Music Ace 2
Harmonic Vision
68 E Wacker Place
8th Floor
Chicago, IL 60610

312-332-9200
800-474-0903
Fax: 312-726-1946
http://www.harmonicvision.com

Introduces concepts such as standard notation, rhythm, melody, time signatures, harmony, intervals and more.

6224 http://www.ilford.com
Ilford

Partners in imaging.

6225 www.schoolrenaissance.com
School Renaissance Model

The School Renaissance Model combines the #1 software in education with professional development and consulting services to help you dramatically improve student performance.

6226 www.speedballart.com

Speedball lesson plans and teaching aids for calligraphy, stamping, printmaking, drawing, painting and more.

Reading

6227 Advantage Learning Systems
2911 Peach Street
PO Box 8036
Wisconsin Rapids, WI 54495-8036

800-338-4204
Fax: 715-424-4242
http://www.advlearn.com

New computer-adaptive tests that assess student reading and math levels in just 15 minutes or less.

6228 Educational Testing Service/Library
Test Collection
Rosedale Road
Princeton, NJ 08541

609-734-5686
Fax: 609-734-5410

Provides information on tests and related materials to those in research and advisory services and educational activities.

Janet Williams, President

6229 National Foundation for Dyslexia
4801 Hermitage Road
Richmond, VA 23227-3332

804-262-0586
800-SOS-READ

Provides screenings for schools or individuals and assists individuals with IEP's. Provides information about support groups and organizations and teacher training workshops.

Jo Powell, Executive Director

6230 Psychological Assessment Resources
PO Box 998
Odessa, FL 33556

800-331-TEST
Fax: 800-727-9329
http://www.parinc.com

Catalog of professional testing resources.

6231 www.schoolrenaissance.com
Renaissance Learning and School Renaissance Inst.

The School Renaissance Model combines the #1 software in education with professional development and consulting services to help you dramatically improve student performance.

6232 www.voyagerlearning.com
Voyager Expanded Learning

Improves students performance in reading for those at different grade levels.

Secondary Education

6233 ACT
PO Box 4060
Iowa City, IA 52243-0001

319-337-1000
800-498-6065

Offers a full-service catalog of tests for intermediate and secondary schools organized by assessment, career and educational planning, study skills, surveys and research services.

Catalog

6234 Admission Officer's Handbook for the New SAT
Program
College Board Publications
45 Columbus Avenue
New York, NY 10023-6917

212-713-8165
800-323-7155
Fax: 800-525-5562
http://www.collegeboard.org

Designed to help college admission staff quickly find information on the new SAT program, the Handbook has detailed descriptions of score reports and special services for colleges.

56 pages

6235 American College Testing
ACT
2201 Dodge
#168
Iowa City, IA 52243-0001

319-337-1028
Fax: 319-337-1014
E-mail: gullettk@act.org
http://www.act.org

Provides educational assessment services to students and their parents, high schools, colleges and professional associations. Also workforce development services, including a network of ACT Centers and the Workkeys program.

Ken Gullette, Director,Media Relations

6236 College-Bound Seniors
College Board Publications
45 Columbus Avenue
New York, NY 10023-6917

212-713-8165
800-323-7155
Fax: 800-525-5562
http://www.collegeboard.org

Profile of SAT and achievement test takers, national report.

13 pages

6237 CollegeChoice, StudentChoice
College Board Publications
45 Columbus Avenue
New York, NY 10023-6917

212-713-8165
800-323-7155
Fax: 800-525-5562
http://www.collegeboard.org

This video provides a reassuring perspective on the SAT's importance and how the college admission process really works. It shows how SAT scores are only one of many elements in the admission picture and emphasizes academicpreparation for college and discusses the SAT within the context of the entire admission process.

15 Minutes

6238 Counselor's Handbook for the SAT Program
College Board Publications
45 Columbus Avenue
New York, NY 10023-6917

212-713-8165
800-323-7155
Fax: 800-525-5562
http://www.collegeboard.org

Easy-to-use reference provides details on the new SAT program tests and services.

64 pages

6239 Destination College: Planning with the PSAT/NMSQT
College Board Publications
45 Columbus Avenue
New York, NY 10023-6917

212-713-8165
800-323-7155
Fax: 800-525-5562
http://www.collegeboard.org

This new video offers schools an ideal format for explaining the features and benefits of the PSAT/NMSQT Score Report to groups of students.

18 Minutes

6240 Educational Testing Service
Rosedale Road
MS 26-C
Princeton, NJ 08541

609-921-9000
Fax: 609-734-5410

Private educational measurement institution and a leader in educational research.

Susan Keipper, Program Director

6241 Focus on the SAT: What's on it, How to Prepare & What Colleges Look For
College Board Publications
45 Columbus Avenue
New York, NY 10023-6917

212-713-8165
800-323-7155
Fax: 800-525-5562
http://www.collegeboard.org

The authoritative video for students on how to prepare for the SAT and PSAT/NMSQT. It provides test-taking tips, sample test questions, and an explanation of how SAT is developed.

20 Minutes

6242 GED Testing Service
American Council on Education
1 Dupont Cir NW
Washington, DC 20036-1110

202-939-9490
Fax: 202-775-8578

The largest testing service in the United States. Maintains a full line of tests and testing resources for all areas of education and all grade levels K-college level testing.

6243 GMAT Success
Peterson's Guides
PO Box 2123
Princeton, NJ 08543-2123

609-243-9111
800-338-3282
Fax: 609-243-9150

Helps test takers get ready, develop test-preparation strategies and manage test anxiety constructively, whether they have seven weeks to prepare or just one day.

352 pages Book & Disk
ISBN: 1-560796-08-1

6244 Guide to the College Board Validity Study Service
College Board Publications
45 Columbus Avenue
New York, NY 10023-6917

212-713-8165
800-323-7155
Fax: 800-525-5562
http://www.collegeboard.org

The purpose of this manual is to assist Validity Study Service users in designing and interpreting validity studies. It provides design suggestions, sample admission and placement studies, advice on interpreting studies, and a discussion of basic statistical concepts.

60 pages

6245 Look Inside the SAT I: Test Prep from the Test Makers Video
College Board Publications
45 Columbus Avenue
New York, NY 10023-6917

212-713-8165
800-323-7155
Fax: 800-525-5562
http://www.collegeboard.org

Brings the College Board's test-taking tips to life through interviews with people from different backgrounds who recount their SAT experiences.

30 Minutes
ISBN: 0-874475-29-5

6246 National Center for Fair & Open Testing
342 Broadway
Cambridge, MA 02139-1843

617-864-4810
Fax: 617-497-2224

Dedicated to ensuring that America's students and workers are assessed using fair, accurate, relevant and open tests.

Cinthia Schuman, President

6247 National Study of School Evaluation
1699 E Woodfield Road
Suite 406
Schaumburg, IL 60173-4958

847-995-9080
800-843-6773
Fax: 847-995-9088
E-mail: schoolimprovement@nsse.org
http://www.nsse.org

Provides educational leaders with state-of-the-art assessment and evaluation materials to enhance and promote student growth and school improvement.

Dr. Kathleen A. Fitzpatrick, Executive Director

6248 National Survey of Course Offerings and Testing in Social Studies K-12
National Council for the Social Studies
3501 Newark Street NW
Washington, DC 20016-3100

202-966-7840
Fax: 202-966-2061

This resource provides a profile of social studies course offerings and requirements in grades K-12 for the fifty states and the District of Columbia, this resource includes an analysis of the state-by-state profiles and a summary of data.

Annual

6249 Official Guide to the SAT II: Subject Tests
College Board Publications
45 Columbus Avenue
New York, NY 10023-6917

212-713-8165
800-323-7155
Fax: 800-525-5562
http://www.collegeboard.org

The authoritative preparation guide for students taking the SAT II: Subject Tests. The guide includes full-length practice Subject Tests, along with answer sheets, answer keys, and scoring instructions for Writing, Literature, American History, World History, Math I, Math IIC, Biology, Chemistry and Physics. It also includes minitests in French (reading only), German (reading only), Italian, Latin, Modern Hebrew, and Spanish.

380 pages
ISBN: 0-874474-88-4

6250 One-On-One with the SAT
College Board Publications
45 Columbus Avenue
New York, NY 10023-6917

212-713-8165
800-323-7155
Fax: 800-525-5562
http://www.collegeboard.org

Gives students easy access to proven advice and test-taking strategies directly from the test makers, as well as a unique chance to take a real SAT on computer. This program also includes password protection for each student record and toll-free technical support.

Home License

6251 Panic Plan for the SAT
Peterson's Guides
PO Box 2123
Princeton, NJ 08543-2123

609-243-9111
800-338-3282
Fax: 609-243-9150

An excellent, two-week review, featuring actual questions from the SAT. Helps students make the most out of the limited time they have left to study.

200 pages
ISBN: 1-560794-32-1
Joan Davenport Carris with Michael R. Crystal, Author

6252 Preventing School Failure
Heldref Publications
1319 Eighteenth Street NW
Washington, DC 20036-1802

202-296-6267
800-365-9753
Fax: 202-296-5149
http://www.heldref.org

The articles cover a broad array of specific topics, from important technical aspects and adaptions of functional behavioral assessment to descriptions of projects in which functional behavioral assessment is being used to provide technical assistance to preschools, schools, and families who must deal eith children and adolescents who present serious challenging behaviors.

Quarterly
ISSN: 1045-988X

Sheldon Braaten, Executive Editor

6253 Psychological Corporation
555 Academic Court
San Antonio, TX 78204-2498

210-921-8701

Assessment materials for teachers in all areas of curricula.

6254 Psychometric Affiliates
PO Box 807
Murfreeboro, TN 37133

615-890-6296

Testing instruments for use by educational institutions.
Jeannette Heritage

6255 Real SAT's
College Board Publications
45 Columbus Avenue
New York, NY 10023-6917

212-713-8165
800-323-7155
Fax: 800-525-5562
http://www.collegeboard.org

The only preparation guide that contains actual scorable tests. It has been developed to help the millions of students taking the tests each year to do their best on the PSAT/NMSQT and SAT and to improve their scores.

396 pages
ISBN: 0-874475-11-2

6256 Registration Bulletin
College Board Publications
45 Columbus Avenue
New York, NY 10023-6917

212-713-8165
800-323-7155
Fax: 800-525-5562
http://www.collegeboard.org

Available in five regional and a New York State edition, the Bulletin provides information on how to register for the SAT I and SAT II, and on how to use the related services.

24 pages

6257 SAT Services for Students with Disabilities
College Board Publications
45 Columbus Avenue
New York, NY 10023-6917

212-713-8165
800-323-7155
Fax: 800-525-5562
http://www.collegeboard.org

Describes arrangements for students with physical, hearing, visual and learning disabilities who wish to take the SAT I and/or SAT II.

6 pages

6258 SAT Success
Peterson's Guides
PO Box 2123
Princeton, NJ 08543-2123

609-243-9111
800-338-3282
Fax: 609-243-9150

Features easily accessible Red Alert sections offering essential tips for test-taking success. Provides students with the critical skills they need to tackle the SAT.

512 pages Book & Disk
ISBN: 1-560796-06-5

John Davenport Carris with Michael R. Crystal, Author

6259 Scholastic Testing Service
480 Meyer Road
Bensenville, IL 60106-1617

630-766-7150
800-642-6STS
Fax: 630-766-8054
E-mail: stslh25@aol.com
http://www.ststesting.com

Publisher of assessment materials from birth into adulthood, ability and achievement tests for kindergarten through grade twelve. Tests are also constructed on contract for educational agencies and school districts. Publish theTorrance Tests of Creative Thinking, Thinking Creatively in Action and Movement, the STS High School Placement Test and Educational Development Series.

OF Anderhalter, President
John D Kauffman, VP Marketing

6260 TOEFL Test and Score Manual
College Board Publications
45 Columbus Avenue
New York, NY 10023-6917

212-713-8165
800-323-7155
Fax: 800-525-5562
http://www.collegeboard.org

Focuses on information that college admissions officers, foreign student advisers and other users of TOEFL score reports need to know about the operation of the TOEFL program, the test itself, and the interpretation of scores.

48 pages

6261 Taking the SAT I: Reasoning Test
College Board Publications
45 Columbus Avenue
New York, NY 10023-6917

212-713-8165
800-323-7155
Fax: 800-525-5562
http://www.collegeboard.org

A complete guide for students who plan to take the SAT I: Reasoning Test.

80 pages

6262 Taking the SAT II: The Official Guide to the SAT II: Subject Tests
College Board Publications
45 Columbus Avenue
New York, NY 10023-6917

212-713-8165
800-323-7155
Fax: 800-525-5562
http://www.collegeboard.org

Provides information about the content and format of each of the SAT II: Subject Tests, as well as test-taking advice and sample questions.

95 pages

6263 TestSkills
College Board Publications
45 Columbus Avenue
New York, NY 10023-6917

212-713-8165
800-323-7155

Fax: 800-525-5562
http://www.collegeboard.org

A preparation program for the PSAT/NMSQT that helps students, particularly those from minority and disadvantaged groups, sharpen skills and increase confidence needed to succeed on the tests.

Spiral-Bound

6264 Think Before You Punch: Using Calculators on the New SAT I and PSAT/NMSQT
College Board Publications
45 Columbus Avenue
New York, NY 10023-6917

212-713-8165
800-323-7155
Fax: 800-525-5562
http://www.collegeboard.org

This video looks at the pros and cons of calculators usage on a test. In it, students talk about using them, and College Board and ETS staff explain the new calculator policy. It works through math questions that may or may not bestbe answered with the help of a calculator.

12 Minutes

Participation of employed persons, 17 years old and over, in adult education during the previous 12 months, by selected characteristics of participants: 1995 and 1999

Characteristic of employed persons	Employed persons, in thousands	Adult education participants, in thousands	1995 — In any programs	In part-time higher education	Other personal courses	In career or job-related courses	Number of career or job-related courses taken, per employee	Percent of career or job-related courses provided by businesses	Employed persons, in thousands	Adult education participants, in thousands	1999 — In any programs	In part-time higher education	In career or job-related courses	In apprentice programs	Other personal courses	Number of career or job-related courses, taken in thousands	Number of career or job-related courses taken, per employee
1	2	3	4	5	6	7	8	9	10	11	12	13	14	15	16	17	18
Total	117,826	59,734	50.7	8.2	22.0	31.1	0.78	49.0	132,715	69,644	52.5 (1.3)	11.9 (0.8)	30.5 (1.1)	2.2 (0.4)	23.4 (1.1)	91,369	0.70 (0.03)
Sex																	
Men	63,127	29,346	46.5	7.0	17.9	29.0	0.70	46.7	69,950	33,671	48.1 (1.4)	11.6 (0.8)	28.3 (1.2)	3.0 (0.4)	18.2 (1.0)	43,645	0.62 (0.03)
Women	54,699	30,387	55.6	9.7	26.8	33.4	0.86	50.9	62,765	35,973	57.3 (1.3)	12.4 (0.8)	32.9 (1.1)	1.4 (0.3)	29.2 (1.1)	47,724	0.76 (0.03)
Age																	
17 to 24 years	15,104	7,653	50.7	14.2	21.8	18.6	0.39	53.8	16,697	8,412	50.4 (2.7)	16.2 (1.8)	19.1 (1.9)	4.4 (1.4)	19.8 (1.8)	6,836	0.41 (0.06)
25 to 29 years	14,207	7,746	54.5	12.5	22.2	31.2	0.76	51.3	15,352	8,871	57.8 (2.8)	20.2 (2.0)	34.3 (2.4)	3.7 (0.9)	23.4 (2.2)	11,862	0.77 (0.08)
30 to 34 years	16,291	8,323	51.1	8.4	22.8	31.6	0.78	49.7	16,343	9,556	58.5 (2.8)	14.2 (1.8)	34.4 (2.5)	2.9 (0.8)	26.0 (2.3)	12,675	0.78 (0.08)
35 to 39 years	17,595	9,361	53.2	8.0	21.8	35.1	0.91	51.8	20,041	10,309	51.4 (2.6)	11.8 (1.5)	29.2 (2.2)	1.6 (0.5)	25.1 (2.3)	14,192	0.71 (0.07)
40 to 44 years	16,049	8,906	55.5	8.0	26.0	36.6	0.93	44.9	18,392	10,126	55.1 (2.7)	10.7 (1.5)	36.4 (2.4)	1.5 (0.5)	25.6 (2.2)	15,415	0.84 (0.07)
45 to 49 years	13,743	7,586	55.2	6.3	23.0	39.6	1.03	44.8	14,944	8,231	55.1 (2.9)	9.8 (1.4)	30.4 (2.4)	1.8 (0.8)	27.7 (2.4)	9,886	0.66 (0.06)
50 to 54 years	10,408	5,222	50.2	4.9	20.9	34.4	0.87	49.2	12,820	6,658	51.9 (3.0)	6.2 (1.1)	34.7 (2.6)	1.3 (0.5)	23.1 (2.3)	9,820	0.77 (0.07)
55 to 59 years	6,698	2,667	39.8	2.3	18.0	26.7	0.66	46.8	9,672	4,319	44.7 (3.3)	7.9 (1.9)	30.3 (2.8)	0.8 (0.5)	16.7 (2.3)	6,135	0.63 (0.08)
60 to 64 years	4,435	1,394	31.4	0.6	15.3	21.1	0.49	58.6	4,526	1,900	42.0 (4.4)	4.6 (1.6)	27.2 (3.8)	0.8 (0.8)	18.1 (3.0)	3,004	0.66 (0.15)
65 and over	3,297	876	26.6	0.3	16.3	13.7	0.37	39.7	2,135	837	39.2 (6.0)	4.3 (2.5)	20.3 (4.2)	0.2 (0.3)	21.3 (5.0)	800	0.39 (0.08)
Racial/ethnic group																	
White, non-Hispanic	92,333	47,967	51.9	8.0	22.7	33.2	0.83	47.9	96,581	51,612	53.4 (1.1)	11.5 (0.6)	32.8 (1.0)	1.7 (0.3)	24.3 (0.9)	71,627	0.64 (0.03)
Black, non-Hispanic	11,577	5,800	50.1	10.5	23.1	26.2	0.67	58.4	15,227	8,160	53.6 (2.8)	13.0 (1.6)	28.1 (2.3)	4.1 (1.3)	26.2 (2.4)	9,754	0.96 (0.07)
Hispanic	8,980	3,627	40.4	6.7	15.1	18.1	0.37	46.8	13,805	6,107	44.2 (3.1)	10.6 (1.7)	16.4 (1.8)	4.3 (1.5)	15.9 (2.2)	5,061	0.53 (0.05)
Asian American/Pacific Islander	2,825	1,246	44.1	8.0	15.5	25.5	0.58	48.6	4,273	2,275	53.2 (5.5)	19.6 (4.3)	32.8 (4.8)	# (#)	20.5 (4.2)	3,135	0.37 (0.15)
American Indian/Alaska Native	663	329	49.6	13.9	25.2	34.0	0.86	54.6	667	350	52.5 (13.1)	20.9 (10.0)	29.5 (11.5)	6.8 (5.6)	10.0 (6.0)	642	0.73 (0.52)
Highest level of education completed																	
Less than high school completion	9,635	2,444	25.4	0.8	9.4	8.8	0.15	56.6	14,493	4,271	29.5 (8.8)	3.2 (2.0)	7.9 (2.3)	2.5 (1.7)	11.1 (3.1)	1,987	0.41 (0.05)
High school completion	38,071	14,639	38.5	4.9	16.5	20.9	0.45	56.7	37,383	15,037	40.2 (1.8)	8.9 (0.9)	21.4 (1.5)	2.4 (0.6)	16.2 (1.3)	15,250	0.82 (0.10)
Some vocational/technical	3,997	2,078	52.0	7.2	23.5	32.3	0.82	45.3	4,165	2,025	48.6 (15.5)	9.7 (3.5)	28.7 (5.8)	5.1 (3.2)	21.5 (5.7)	3,030	0.91 (0.17)
Some college	23,006	12,868	55.9	14.3	25.4	29.9	0.74	53.5	24,577	13,860	56.4 (2.1)	16.7 (1.5)	29.0 (1.8)	3.0 (0.7)	27.0 (1.8)	17,331	0.71 (0.06)
Associate degree	7,591	4,746	62.5	13.3	27.7	39.2	1.02	49.7	9,240	5,698	61.7 (3.3)	19.3 (2.4)	39.7 (3.1)	2.6 (0.9)	25.2 (2.8)	8,133	0.88 (0.09)
Bachelor's degree	20,602	12,948	62.8	8.3	26.5	44.6	1.17	47.2	23,943	15,377	64.2 (2.1)	12.5 (1.3)	43.8 (2.0)	1.0 (0.3)	29.8 (1.8)	24,068	1.01 (0.06)
Some graduate work (or study)	14,924	10,010	67.1	19.7	29.6	50.2	1.40	40.3	18,914	13,377	70.7 (19.4)	14.6 (3.1)	46.8 (2.0)	1.4 (1.0)	34.0 (4.3)	21,570	1.22 (0.14)
No degree	2,770	1,987	71.8	9.9	34.8	44.3	1.20	45.6	3,168	2,353	74.3 (4.5)	24.4 (4.1)	54.2 (4.9)	0.9 (0.7)	30.4 (4.3)	3,785	1.19 (0.14)
Master's	8,149	5,456	67.0	9.6	30.4	50.5	1.44	41.7	10,243	7,266	70.9 (2.9)	13.6 (2.0)	45.3 (3.0)	0.9 (0.4)	36.8 (2.9)	11,711	1.14 (0.11)
Doctor's	2,060	1,133	55.0	5.0	22.4	40.4	0.98	35.5	3,698	2,350	63.6 (5.3)	9.7 (2.6)	34.4 (4.8)	3.2 (1.5)	32.8 (5.6)	2,623	0.71 (0.12)
Professional	1,946	1,434	73.7	2.6	26.4	67.6	1.97	31.4	1,804	1,407	78.0 (6.6)	13.0 (7.1)	67.6 (7.0)	1.4 (1.4)	26.6 (5.7)	3,452	1.91 (0.31)
Metropolitan area																	
Inside metropolitan area	89,192	46,911	52.6	8.7	22.6	32.4	0.81	48.6	102,278	54,210	53.0 (1.9)	11.7 (1.0)	31.5 (1.7)	2.3 (0.5)	23.1 (1.5)	73,498	0.72 (0.05)
Inside central city	74,367	39,519	53.1	8.8	22.5	33.3	0.83	48.3	87,662	46,478	53.0 (1.8)	12.0 (0.7)	31.2 (1.0)	2.4 (0.4)	23.3 (0.9)	61,774	0.70 (0.03)
Outside central city	14,825	7,392	49.9	8.0	23.1	27.9	0.70	50.9	14,616	7,732	52.9 (2.8)	9.6 (1.5)	32.9 (2.5)	1.8 (0.6)	21.8 (2.1)	11,724	0.80 (0.08)
Outside metropolitan area	28,634	12,823	44.8	6.9	20.2	26.9	0.66	50.2	30,437	15,434	50.7 (2.1)	12.8 (1.3)	27.1 (1.7)	2.0 (0.7)	24.5 (1.7)	17,871	0.59 (0.05)
Occupation																	
Executive, administrative, or managerial	12,500	7,070	56.6	7.4	23.4	42.9	1.20	37.7	25,407	14,654	57.7 (2.2)	11.1 (1.2)	40.6 (2.1)	1.2 (0.4)	23.9 (1.7)	24,581	0.97 (0.07)
Engineers, surveyors, and architects	1,702	1,116	65.6	14.5	23.7	44.2	1.07	59.0	1,967	1,575	80.1 (6.2)	26.2 (5.7)	52.1 (5.0)	6.0 (4.3)	29.5 (6.0)	2,037	1.04 (0.16)
Natural scientists and mathematicians	1,648	1,211	73.5	10.4	25.6	59.7	1.75	44.0	2,180	1,379	63.2 (7.0)	13.7 (4.2)	46.0 (6.6)	1.4 (0.9)	26.5 (5.8)	1,782	0.82 (0.14)
Social scientists and workers, lawyers	2,438	1,873	76.8	11.7	32.4	59.5	1.77	35.6	2,295	1,831	79.8 (4.5)	10.8 (3.2)	56.9 (5.7)	0.7 (0.7)	41.3 (5.5)	4,893	1.70 (0.24)
Teachers, elementary/secondary	5,207	4,046	77.7	16.9	36.9	53.9	1.46	50.5	6,634	5,272	79.5 (3.2)	24.6 (3.0)	52.1 (3.5)	0.4 (0.2)	39.3 (3.4)	8,077	1.22 (0.11)
Teachers, postsecondary	1,175	657	55.9	4.4	26.1	41.6	1.03	53.5	1,941	1,286	66.3 (6.4)	13.1 (4.0)	35.6 (5.9)	2.1 (1.3)	41.0 (6.1)	1,427	0.74 (0.14)
Physicians, dentists, veterinarians	828	590	71.3	1.3	18.3	68.6	2.00	32.4	563	472	83.9 (8.6)	5.0 (4.9)	65.2 (12.0)	4.5 (4.5)	29.0 (11.8)	859	1.53 (0.50)
Registered nurses, pharmacists	2,143	1,896	88.5	11.2	34.6	72.8	2.24	45.6	3,051	2,654	87.0 (4.1)	16.6 (4.9)	72.2 (5.0)	0.2 (0.2)	47.9 (5.5)	5,639	1.85 (0.21)
Writers, artists, entertainers, and athletes	1,675	829	49.5	8.1	28.7	23.4	0.46	33.3	2,162	1,065	49.3 (7.5)	15.4 (4.8)	30.6 (6.2)	2.5 (1.3)	18.8 (5.0)	1,354	0.63 (0.18)

See notes at end of table.

Participation of employed persons, 17 years old and over, in adult education during the previous 12 months, by selected characteristics of participants: 1995 and 1999—Continued

	1995								1999								
			Percent of employed adults participating								Percent of employed adults participating						
Characteristic of employed persons	Employed persons, in thousands	Adult education participants, in thousands	In any programs	In part-time higher education	Other personal courses	In career or job-related courses	Number of career or job-related courses taken, per employee	Percent of career or job-related courses provided by businesses	Employed persons, in thousands	Adult education participants, in thousands	In any programs	In part-time higher education	In career or job-related courses	In apprentice programs	Other personal courses	Number of career or job-related courses, taken in thousands	Number of career or job-related courses taken, per employee
1	2	3	4	5	6	7	8	9	10	11	12	13	14	15	16	17	18
Health technologists and technicians ...	1,528	1,147	75.1	12.9	32.1	50.0	1.39	45.0	2,074	1,436	69.2 (6.4)	19.9 (4.5)	41.8 (6.0)	5.2 (3.5)	37.0 (6.0)	2,158	1.04 (0.19)
Technologists, except health ...	3,283	2,153	65.6	12.9	28.3	43.8	1.12	55.8	4,803	2,775	57.8 (5.3)	20.1 (3.8)	37.6 (4.9)	4.0 (2.8)	23.3 (4.1)	4,644	0.97 (0.15)
Marketing and sales occupations ...	15,666	7,131	45.5	6.6	20.2	25.2	0.55	51.2	11,699	5,019	42.9 (2.9)	9.9 (1.2)	21.1 (2.3)	1.7 (0.7)	23.8 (2.4)	5,033	0.43 (0.06)
Administrative support, including clerical ...	20,460	10,727	52.4	9.3	24.1	30.8	0.69	52.4	18,913	9,606	50.8 (2.4)	9.9 (1.2)	27.4 (2.0)	0.9 (0.3)	22.0 (1.9)	10,480	0.55 (0.05)
Service occupations ...	17,355	8,238	47.5	9.0	22.7	22.6	0.60	57.0	15,949	8,078	50.6 (3.0)	14.5 (2.0)	21.0 (2.2)	2.3 (0.7)	22.1 (2.5)	8,067	0.51 (0.07)
Agriculture, forestry, and fishing ...	1,908	500	26.2	1.8	14.8	12.4	0.26	—	2,297	927	40.4 (8.5)	11.2 (4.9)	12.4 (4.1)	6.9 (6.6)	13.0 (5.0)	475	0.21 (0.07)
Mechanics and repairers ...	4,266	2,129	49.9	7.6	16.6	29.1	0.73	57.2	4,736	2,087	44.1 (5.6)	15.2 (3.7)	15.0 (3.4)	6.1 (2.3)	23.0 (5.0)	1,640	0.35 (0.09)
Construction and extractive occupations ...	5,490	2,093	38.1	4.6	18.4	18.6	0.33	48.8	3,973	1,464	36.9 (5.2)	11.2 (3.2)	13.2 (3.2)	6.0 (2.4)	12.0 (3.3)	906	0.23 (0.06)
Precision production occupations ...	1,685	754	44.8	5.9	16.2	25.6	0.58	40.8	1,570	608	38.7 (8.8)	9.4 (4.4)	18.3 (6.5)	11.9 (5.3)	19.5 (6.5)	569	0.36 (0.12)
Production workers ...	8,309	2,515	30.3	5.9	10.1	14.8	0.27	58.5	9,346	3,681	39.4 (3.8)	6.7 (1.7)	23.0 (3.2)	2.4 (1.2)	14.8 (2.5)	4,220	0.45 (0.08)
Transportation, material moving ...	4,488	1,295	28.8	3.8	12.1	15.8	0.28	60.6	5,178	1,753	33.9 (4.6)	5.9 (1.8)	18.4 (3.6)	1.6 (1.0)	12.9 (2.9)	1,426	0.28 (0.06)
Handler, equipment, cleaners, helpers, and laborers ...	1,989	519	26.1	3.1	10.3	11.7	0.21	46.9	3,474	731	21.0 (5.1)	4.6 (2.2)	6.8 (3.5)	1.7 (1.4)	5.0 (2.3)	594	0.17 (0.12)
Miscellaneous occupations ...	2,022	1,194	59.0	8.5	22.1	38.8	1.03	51.8	1,923	828	43.0 (8.6)	9.9 (4.3)	14.2 (4.6)	3.7 (2.3)	23.9 (6.8)	509	0.26 (0.08)
Annual family income																	
$10,000 or less ...	9,776	3,224	33.0	6.1	15.6	12.6	0.25	50.9	5,248	1,646	31.4 (5.8)	7.8 (3.0)	9.5 (3.1)	1.9 (1.5)	13.2 (4.1)	787	0.15 (0.05)
$10,001 to $15,000 ...	6,183	2,389	38.6	7.2	19.5	15.1	0.37	59.1	5,281	1,597	30.2 (4.1)	8.3 (2.4)	8.3 (1.9)	2.5 (1.7)	12.9 (2.8)	751	0.14 (0.03)
$15,001 to $20,000 ...	7,321	3,040	41.5	8.0	18.2	20.1	0.42	52.8	6,061	2,511	41.4 (4.2)	8.2 (2.0)	16.3 (2.8)	1.9 (0.9)	17.1 (3.0)	1,705	0.28 (0.05)
$20,001 to $25,000 ...	7,832	3,164	40.4	7.4	19.3	20.4	0.48	53.1	8,595	3,618	42.1 (3.8)	8.4 (1.6)	18.8 (2.8)	4.4 (2.1)	19.8 (2.8)	3,568	0.42 (0.08)
$25,001 to $30,000 ...	10,133	4,803	47.4	8.8	21.4	24.7	0.54	55.8	11,848	4,863	41.0 (3.4)	9.8 (1.5)	22.2 (2.7)	2.7 (1.2)	15.3 (2.2)	5,396	0.46 (0.07)
$30,001 to $40,000 ...	19,617	9,734	49.6	8.9	21.9	30.2	0.76	50.2	18,961	9,589	50.6 (3.6)	15.2 (2.4)	26.6 (2.8)	2.3 (1.0)	21.3 (2.7)	11,137	0.59 (0.07)
$40,001 to $50,000 ...	15,115	8,127	53.8	8.0	22.9	34.7	0.82	48.3	16,577	9,005	54.3 (2.7)	14.7 (1.8)	32.3 (2.3)	2.6 (0.8)	24.9 (2.3)	11,569	0.70 (0.07)
$50,001 to $75,000 ...	23,006	13,288	57.8	8.9	23.7	40.0	1.02	48.3	28,433	17,356	61.0 (2.1)	13.1 (1.2)	36.6 (1.9)	2.5 (0.6)	31.4 (1.9)	24,629	0.87 (0.06)
More than $75,000 ...	18,843	11,964	63.5	8.6	26.5	45.2	1.25	45.0	31,711	19,458	61.4 (1.9)	11.2 (1.1)	42.5 (1.8)	1.2 (0.3)	31.4 (1.5)	31,828	1.00 (0.06)

—Not available.

#Rounds to zero.

NOTE: Percent of career or job-related courses provided by businesses are based on the respondent's reports of the first six work-related courses taken. Adult education is defined as all education activities, except full-time enrollment in higher education credential programs. Examples of adult education activities include part-time college attendance, classes or seminars given by employers, and classes taken for adult literacy purposes, or for recreation and enjoyment.

Includes adult basic education and English as a second language classes. Data are based upon a sample survey of the civilian noninstitutional population. Data revised from previously published figures. Detail may not sum to totals due to rounding and survey item nonresponse. Standard errors appear in parentheses.

SOURCE: U.S. Department of Education, National Center for Education Statistics, The Adult Education Survey of the National Household Education Surveys Program, (AR-NHES:1995) and (AR-NHES:1999). (This table was prepared June 2001.)

Participation in adult education during the previous 12 months by adults 17 years old and older, by selected characteristics of participants: 1991, 1995, and 1999

Characteristic of participants	Percent participating in any program, 1991 [1]	1995						1999								
		Population, in thousands	Adult education participants, in thousands [1]	Percent participating [2]				Population, in thousands	Adult education participants, in thousands [1]	Percent participating						
				In any program	In part-time postsecondary education	In career or job related courses	Personal development courses			In any program	In basic education [3]	In English as a second language	In part-time postsecondary education	In career or job related courses	In apprentice programs	Personal development courses
	2	3	4	5	6	7	8	9	10	11	12	13	14	15	16	17
Total	**33.0**	**189,543**	**76,261**	**40.2**	**6.1**	**20.9**	**19.9**	**194,559**	**86,593**	**44.5 (0.8)**	**1.1 (0.2)**	**0.9 (0.2)**	**9.3 (0.4)**	**22.1 (0.6)**	**1.8 (0.2)**	**22.2 (0.6)**
Sex																
Men	32.6	90,256	34,450	38.2	5.6	21.8	15.8	93,071	38,765	41.7 (1.2)	1.0 (0.2)	0.9 (0.2)	9.9 (0.6)	22.1 (0.9)	2.5 (0.4)	17.4 (0.9)
Women	33.2	99,287	41,811	42.1	6.5	20.2	23.5	101,488	47,828	47.1 (1.0)	1.1 (0.2)	1.0 (0.2)	8.8 (0.5)	22.2 (0.8)	1.1 (0.2)	26.7 (0.9)
Age																
17 to 24 years	37.8	22,407	10,539	47.0	12.6	14.7	21.5	23,372	11,673	49.9 (2.3)	4.9 (1.0)	1.1 (0.3)	13.6 (1.4)	16.4 (1.5)	4.0 (1.1)	22.8 (1.9)
25 to 29 years	40.0	18,988	9,420	49.6	10.9	25.5	21.0	18,427	10,406	56.5 (2.5)	1.2 (0.5)	2.5 (0.8)	18.6 (1.8)	30.0 (2.2)	3.4 (0.8)	23.8 (2.0)
30 to 34 years	37.6	21,338	10,088	47.3	8.0	26.1	23.3	19,423	10,908	56.2 (2.6)	1.0 (0.4)	1.6 (0.6)	13.0 (1.5)	29.4 (2.2)	3.0 (0.8)	26.5 (2.2)
35 to 39 years	42.1	22,494	10,737	47.7	7.5	29.1	20.9	23,183	11,622	50.1 (2.4)	0.6 (0.3)	1.4 (0.5)	10.9 (1.3)	26.2 (1.9)	1.7 (0.6)	25.4 (2.1)
40 to 44 years	49.2	19,810	10,078	50.9	7.1	31.2	24.9	22,116	11,159	50.5 (2.4)	0.7 (0.3)	0.3 (0.2)	10.2 (1.3)	31.3 (2.1)	1.7 (0.5)	24.7 (2.0)
45 to 49 years	40.0	17,463	8,499	48.7	5.7	32.5	21.1	18,299	9,116	49.8 (2.7)	0.7 (0.4)	0.8 (0.4)	9.4 (1.3)	26.0 (2.1)	1.5 (0.6)	25.5 (2.1)
50 to 54 years	26.8	14,344	6,093	42.5	3.9	26.3	19.7	16,893	7,966	47.2 (2.5)	0.4 (0.3)	0.2 (0.1)	5.8 (1.0)	28.2 (2.1)	1.1 (0.4)	23.5 (2.1)
55 to 59 years	29.0	11,096	3,577	32.2	1.7	17.8	17.3	13,450	5,107	38.0 (2.6)	0.3 (0.3)	0.1 (0.1)	6.7 (1.5)	23.3 (2.1)	0.5 (0.4)	16.2 (1.8)
60 to 64 years	17.4	10,728	2,540	23.7	0.6	10.6	15.2	10,718	3,368	31.4 (2.8)	# (#)	1.4 (1.4)	2.4 (0.7)	13.4 (1.8)	0.3 (0.4)	18.8 (2.2)
65 to 69 years	14.2	10,215	1,850	18.1	0.2	4.0	15.3	9,211	2,339	25.4 (2.5)	0.3 (0.3)	0.3 (0.3)	1.2 (0.6)	6.9 (1.2)	0.1 (0.1)	19.6 (2.3)
70 years and over	8.6	20,661	2,841	13.8	0.1	1.4	12.6	19,466	2,929	15.0 (1.4)	# (#)	# (#)	1.3 (0.5)	1.7 (0.5)	# (#)	12.2 (1.2)
Racial/ethnic group																
White, non-Hispanic	34.1	144,587	59,982	41.5	6.0	22.8	20.8	143,135	63,522	44.4 (0.9)	0.6 (0.1)	0.1 (0.1)	8.8 (0.5)	23.6 (0.7)	1.3 (0.2)	22.9 (0.7)
Black, non-Hispanic	25.9	20,806	7,704	37.0	7.3	16.2	18.9	22,129	10,241	46.3 (2.3)	2.7 (0.8)	0.2 (0.1)	11.0 (1.3)	20.2 (1.7)	2.9 (0.9)	23.6 (1.9)
Hispanic	31.4	15,689	5,281	33.7	4.8	11.8	13.8	19,491	8,045	41.3 (2.5)	2.4 (0.6)	6.5 (1.2)	8.6 (1.3)	12.5 (1.3)	3.7 (1.1)	16.2 (1.9)
Asian American/Pacific Islander	35.9	4,377	1,739	39.7	6.5	18.1	15.9	5,619	2,872	51.1 (4.6)	2.0 (1.1)	5.8 (2.2)	17.1 (3.4)	26.9 (3.8)	0.5 (0.5)	22.6 (3.6)
American Indian/Alaska Native	29.3	1,155	448	38.8	9.3	20.6	21.6	1,102	400	36.3 (9.2)	# (#)	# (#)	12.7 (6.2)	19.2 (7.4)	4.1 (3.4)	10.6 (4.7)
Highest level of education completed																
Eighth grade or less	7.7	12,808	1,283	10.0	0.1	1.9	4.9	11,438	1,680	14.7 (2.9)	0.9 (0.4)	5.0 (1.7)	0.2 (0.2)	1.4 (0.6)	0.4 (0.4)	6.6 (2.4)
9th to 12th grade, no completion	15.8	16,511	3,332	20.2	0.8	4.9	9.2	21,174	5,419	25.6 (2.6)	4.8 (1.0)	1.3 (0.5)	3.3 (1.1)	5.5 (1.2)	1.9 (0.9)	10.1 (1.9)
High school completion	24.1	62,956	19,341	30.7	3.6	13.9	15.4	55,553	19,356	34.8 (1.4)	1.1 (0.3)	0.6 (0.2)	6.9 (0.7)	15.5 (1.0)	1.9 (0.4)	16.9 (1.1)
Some vocational/technical	34.2	6,327	2,648	41.9	5.4	21.9	21.1	6,517	2,678	41.1 (4.0)	2.5 (1.1)	1.9 (1.0)	6.5 (1.7)	19.9 (3.1)	3.2 (1.5)	21.8 (3.2)
Some college	41.4	34,433	16,978	49.3	12.1	22.3	25.3	34,270	17,504	51.1 (1.8)	0.6 (0.2)	0.4 (0.2)	13.9 (1.1)	22.2 (1.4)	2.8 (0.6)	27.5 (1.5)
Associate degree	49.2	9,975	5,601	56.1	10.9	32.1	27.4	11,275	6,384	56.6 (2.9)	(¹)	0.2 (0.1)	17.4 (2.2)	33.3 (2.6)	2.4 (0.8)	24.2 (2.4)
Bachelor's degree	51.1	26,858	15,286	56.9	7.1	36.1	27.0	30,121	18,178	60.3 (1.8)	(¹)	0.5 (0.2)	11.2 (1.1)	36.7 (1.7)	0.9 (0.3)	31.1 (1.7)
Some graduate work (or study)	55.1	19,677	11,792	59.9	8.5	40.4	29.1	24,211	15,394	63.6 (2.0)	(¹)	0.8 (0.4)	12.8 (1.3)	38.9 (1.9)	1.2 (0.3)	33.0 (1.8)
No degree	—	4,123	2,563	62.2	15.2	32.5	33.5	4,083	2,640	64.7 (4.4)	(¹)	# (#)	20.9 (3.5)	45.1 (4.4)	1.1 (0.6)	28.1 (3.7)
Master's	—	10,522	6,219	59.1	8.1	41.0	29.0	12,715	8,357	65.7 (2.6)	(¹)	1.1 (0.7)	12.5 (1.7)	38.8 (2.6)	0.7 (0.4)	36.8 (2.6)
Doctor's	—	2,564	1,384	54.0	4.7	35.0	25.1	5,039	2,675	53.1 (4.7)	(¹)	1.0 (0.9)	7.9 (2.0)	26.7 (3.8)	2.7 (1.1)	28.5 (4.2)
Professional	—	2,467	1,626	65.9	3.0	56.6	26.0	2,374	1,722	72.5 (5.8)	(¹)	# (#)	10.9 (5.6)	54.7 (6.2)	1.1 (1.1)	31.0 (5.4)
Metropolitan area																
Inside metropolitan area	34.5	142,522	59,627	41.8	6.5	22.0	20.3	146,309	67,322	46.0 (0.9)	1.2 (0.2)	1.2 (0.2)	9.4 (0.5)	23.2 (0.7)	1.9 (0.2)	22.4 (0.7)
Inside central city	—	118,170	49,996	42.3	6.7	22.7	20.2	124,108	57,688	46.5 (1.0)	1.3 (0.2)	1.3 (0.2)	9.7 (0.5)	23.4 (0.7)	1.9 (0.3)	22.8 (0.8)
Outside central city	—	24,352	9,630	39.5	5.6	18.4	21.1	22,200	9,634	43.4 (2.2)	0.5 (0.2)	0.4 (0.3)	7.9 (1.1)	22.2 (1.7)	1.5 (0.4)	20.4 (1.8)
Outside metropolitan area	28.3	47,021	16,634	35.4	4.9	17.9	18.5	48,250	19,271	39.9 (1.6)	0.8 (0.3)	0.2 (0.1)	9.1 (0.9)	18.9 (1.2)	1.6 (0.4)	21.5 (1.3)
Labor force status																
In labor force	40.7	125,982	62,717	49.8	8.1	29.8	21.7	140,400	73,097	52.1 (0.9)	1.1 (0.2)	0.7 (0.1)	12.0 (0.5)	29.4 (0.8)	2.2 (0.3)	23.3 (0.8)
Employed	42.0	117,826	59,734	50.7	8.2	31.1	22.0	132,715	69,644	52.5 (1.0)	1.0 (0.2)	0.6 (0.1)	11.9 (0.5)	30.5 (0.8)	2.2 (0.3)	23.4 (0.8)
Unemployed	26.0	8,155	2,983	36.6	5.5	11.1	17.4	7,685	3,453	44.9 (4.6)	3.6 (1.7)	2.4 (1.2)	13.7 (2.8)	11.3 (2.4)	1.9 (0.9)	21.5 (4.1)
Not in labor force	15.7	63,562	13,544	21.3	2.2	3.4	16.2	54,159	13,496	24.9 (1.2)	0.9 (0.3)	1.5 (0.4)	2.3 (0.4)	3.3 (0.4)	0.7 (0.2)	19.4 (1.1)
Occupation																
Executive, administrative, or managerial	49.3	13,098	7,313	55.8	7.3	42.1	23.1	27,315	15,579	57.0 (2.1)	# (#)	0.2 (0.2)	10.9 (1.1)	38.7 (2.0)	1.2 (0.4)	24.6 (1.7)
Engineers, surveyors, and architects	62.6	1,756	1,150	65.5	14.1	44.6	23.3	2,042	1,629	79.8 (6.0)	# (#)	# (#)	27.9 (5.8)	52.4 (6.8)	5.8 (4.2)	28.8 (5.8)
Natural scientists and mathematicians	48.2	1,743	1,261	72.3	9.9	58.6	24.8	2,289	1,386	60.5 (6.7)	# (#)	# (#)	13.0 (4.0)	44.1 (6.3)	1.3 (0.9)	24.8 (5.5)

See notes at end of table.

Participation in adult education during the previous 12 months by adults 17 years old and older, by selected characteristics of participants: 1991, 1995, and 1999—Continued

Characteristic of participants	Percent participating in any program, 1991[1]	1995						1999								
		Population, in thousands	Adult education participants, in thousands[1]	Percent participating[2]				Population, in thousands	Adult education participants, in thousands[1]	Percent participating						
				In any program	In part-time post-secondary education	In career or job related courses	Personal development courses			In any program	In basic education[3]	In English as a second language	In part-time post-secondary education	In career or job related courses	In apprentice programs	Personal development courses
	2	3	4	5	6	7	8	9	10	11	12	13	14	15	16	17
Social scientists and workers, lawyers	55.6	2,530	1,938	76.6	11.5	59.4	32.3	3,069	2,433	79.3 (4.4)	# (#)	# (#)	10.4 (3.1)	56.6 (5.4)	0.6 (0.6)	42.0 (5.3)
Teachers, elementary and secondary	55.0	5,414	4,155	76.7	16.6	52.4	36.9	7,033	5,511	78.4 (3.1)	# (#)	# (#)	23.8 (2.8)	50.2 (3.4)	0.3 (0.2)	38.8 (3.3)
Teachers, postsecondary	45.5	1,254	687	54.8	4.1	40.8	26.0	2,214	1,472	66.5 (5.6)	0.4 (0.4)	# (#)	17.0 (5.0)	37.1 (5.8)	1.8 (1.1)	42.1 (5.9)
Physicians, dentists, veterinarians	67.1	859	611	71.1	1.2	67.1	19.0	610	487	79.8 (9.0)	# (#)	3.5 (3.4)	4.6 (4.5)	62.5 (11.5)	4.2 (4.2)	29.1 (11.2)
Registered nurses, pharmacists	59.6	2,337	2,026	86.7	10.6	71.3	33.6	3,210	2,741	85.4 (4.1)	# (#)	# (#)	16.0 (4.7)	71.1 (4.9)	0.2 (0.2)	46.0 (5.3)
Writers, artists, entertainers, and athletes	42.9	1,874	934	49.9	7.7	23.1	30.0	2,481	1,241	50.0 (6.9)	0.4 (0.4)	# (#)	13.4 (4.2)	29.1 (5.6)	2.2 (1.2)	21.4 (5.1)
Health technologists and technicians	68.6	1,697	1,270	74.8	12.8	47.5	33.0	2,190	1,465	66.9 (6.2)	1.7 (1.2)	0.6 (0.6)	19.1 (4.3)	40.6 (5.7)	4.9 (3.3)	35.5 (5.7)
Technologists, except health	55.4	3,543	2,279	64.3	13.5	41.3	28.7	5,090	3,032	59.6 (5.1)	# (#)	0.4 (0.4)	20.9 (3.8)	37.0 (4.7)	3.8 (2.7)	24.5 (4.0)
Marketing and sales occupations	34.4	18,174	8,038	44.2	6.8	23.2	20.4	13,578	6,022	44.4 (2.7)	1.4 (0.5)	0.1 (0.1)	6.1 (1.1)	20.7 (2.1)	1.6 (0.6)	25.1 (2.3)
Administrative support, including clerical	29.9	22,968	11,867	51.7	9.5	28.9	24.7	22,052	11,042	50.1 (2.3)	1.9 (0.7)	0.3 (0.2)	10.3 (1.2)	25.1 (1.8)	0.8 (0.3)	22.5 (1.8)
Service occupations	25.2	20,072	9,342	46.5	9.0	20.9	22.8	18,649	9,497	50.9 (2.7)	3.2 (0.9)	1.3 (0.5)	13.7 (1.8)	18.5 (1.9)	2.5 (0.7)	23.7 (2.4)
Agriculture, forestry, and fishing	14.3	2,336	616	26.4	1.6	11.5	15.6	2,809	964	34.3 (7.2)	2.0 (1.5)	2.0 (1.6)	9.2 (4.0)	10.5 (3.4)	6.4 (5.5)	11.2 (3.8)
Mechanics and repairers	32.1	4,692	2,231	47.6	7.1	27.7	15.6	4,964	2,097	42.2 (5.4)	2.1 (1.4)	# (#)	14.7 (3.5)	14.4 (3.3)	5.8 (2.2)	21.9 (4.8)
Construction and extractive occupations	21.9	6,100	2,319	38.0	4.3	17.6	18.0	4,734	1,634	34.5 (4.8)	0.7 (0.4)	2.5 (1.3)	10.4 (2.8)	12.0 (2.8)	7.0 (2.4)	11.1 (2.9)
Precision production occupations	31.2	1,875	807	43.0	5.5	23.2	16.1	1,638	628	38.3 (8.5)	1.2 (1.2)	1.9 (1.4)	9.0 (4.2)	17.5 (6.2)	11.4 (5.0)	19.9 (6.3)
Production workers	21.1	9,483	2,908	30.7	5.8	14.7	10.7	10,638	4,043	38.0 (3.5)	0.7 (0.4)	0.7 (0.3)	6.8 (1.6)	20.2 (2.8)	2.1 (1.0)	15.9 (2.4)
Transportation, material moving	20.7	5,311	1,507	28.4	3.5	15.5	11.9	5,829	1,941	33.3 (4.3)	2.8 (1.5)	0.9 (0.7)	5.9 (1.7)	17.1 (3.3)	2.5 (1.1)	11.8 (2.6)
Handler, equipment, cleaners, helpers, and laborers	20.8	2,456	617	25.1	3.1	11.1	9.7	3,981	781	19.6 (4.6)	# (#)	2.1 (1.5)	4.6 (2.0)	6.1 (3.0)	1.5 (1.2)	5.6 (2.2)
Miscellaneous occupations	—	2,311	1,308	56.6	7.9	35.4	22.6	2,150	925	43.0 (8.0)	# (#)	3.3 (1.9)	11.7 (4.6)	16.7 (5.0)	3.3 (2.1)	24.6 (6.5)
Annual family income																
$5,000 or less	13.6	12,638	2,689	21.3	3.3	4.1	11.8	5,198	1,092	21.0 (3.2)	2.0 (1.0)	1.2 (0.8)	3.0 (1.1)	5.0 (1.4)	0.5 (0.3)	11.9 (2.6)
$5,001 to $10,000	17.5	17,560	4,194	23.9	4.0	6.7	13.2	9,137	2,236	24.5 (3.4)	2.8 (1.4)	0.9 (0.4)	3.8 (1.2)	4.1 (1.1)	1.2 (0.6)	14.5 (3.0)
$10,001 to $15,000	22.8	13,523	3,610	26.7	4.0	8.7	14.8	11,263	2,564	22.8 (2.5)	2.4 (0.9)	2.3 (0.8)	6.1 (1.4)	4.3 (0.9)	1.5 (0.8)	11.5 (1.8)
$15,001 to $20,000	21.9	13,116	4,176	31.8	5.4	13.0	15.8	12,623	3,967	31.4 (2.8)	2.7 (0.9)	2.3 (0.7)	5.4 (1.2)	10.1 (1.6)	1.6 (0.7)	16.4 (2.2)
$20,001 to $25,000	26.7	13,812	4,339	31.4	4.8	13.3	17.0	13,663	4,885	35.8 (2.8)	1.5 (0.6)	1.7 (0.7)	7.8 (1.3)	12.7 (1.8)	3.1 (1.4)	17.5 (2.1)
$25,001 to $30,000	32.1	16,386	6,208	37.9	6.5	17.1	19.2	17,353	6,375	36.7 (2.6)	0.8 (0.3)	1.5 (0.7)	7.3 (1.0)	15.5 (1.9)	2.1 (0.9)	17.0 (1.9)
$30,001 to $40,000	35.6	28,628	12,220	42.7	6.9	22.1	22.0	27,715	12,524	45.2 (2.1)	0.3 (0.2)	0.9 (0.6)	11.7 (1.3)	20.0 (1.5)	1.6 (0.5)	22.4 (1.7)
$40,001 to $50,000	44.8	20,446	9,567	46.8	6.8	27.0	22.4	21,715	10,394	47.9 (2.3)	0.6 (0.4)	0.7 (0.4)	12.0 (1.4)	26.0 (1.9)	2.5 (0.7)	23.3 (1.9)
$50,001 to $75,000	46.6	29,161	15,169	52.0	7.6	32.8	23.6	35,984	19,828	55.1 (1.8)	0.5 (0.2)	0.2 (0.1)	11.2 (1.0)	30.6 (1.5)	2.1 (0.5)	29.8 (1.6)
More than $75,000	48.7	24,274	14,089	58.0	7.7	37.3	26.8	39,909	22,726	56.9 (1.7)	1.0 (0.4)	0.3 (0.2)	10.1 (1.0)	35.2 (1.2)	1.1 (0.3)	26.5 (1.4)

—Not available.

Rounds to zero.

[1] Adult education is defined as all education activities, except full-time enrollment in higher education credential programs. Examples of adult education activities include part-time college attendance, classes or seminars given by employers, and classes taken for adult literacy purposes, or for recreation and enjoyment.

[2] Any participation includes adult basic education, English as a second language, and apprentice programs not shown separately.

[3] The estimates of participation in basic education include only those participating in courses to improve "reading, writing, and math skills," and do not count participation in GED or other high-school equivalency courses.

NOTE: Data are based upon a sample survey of the civilian noninstitutional population. Data revised from previously published figures. Detail may not sum to totals due to rounding and survey item nonresponse. Standard errors appear in parentheses.

SOURCE: U.S. Department of Education, National Center for Education Statistics, The Adult Education Survey of the National Household Education Surveys Program, (AR–NHES:1991), (AR–NHES:1995), and (AR–NHES:1999). (This table was prepared June 2001.)

Earned degrees conferred by degree-granting institutions, by level of degree and sex of student: Selected years, 1869–70 to 2012–13

Year	Associate degrees			Bachelor's degrees			Master's degrees			First-professional degrees			Doctor's degrees [1]		
	Total	Men	Women	Total	Men	Women	Total	Men	Women	Total	Men	Women	Total	Men	Women
1	2	3	4	5	6	7	8	9	10	11	12	13	14	15	16
1869–70	—	—	—	[2]9,371	[2]7,993	[2]1,378	0	0	0	[3]	[3]	[3]	1	1	0
1879–80	—	—	—	[2]12,896	[2]10,411	[2]2,485	879	868	11	[3]	[3]	[3]	54	51	3
1889–90	—	—	—	[2]15,539	[2]12,857	[2]2,682	1,015	821	194	[3]	[3]	[3]	149	147	2
1899–1900	—	—	—	[2]27,410	[2]22,173	[2]5,237	1,583	1,280	303	[3]	[3]	[3]	382	359	23
1909–10	—	—	—	[2]37,199	[2]28,762	[2]8,437	2,113	1,555	558	[3]	[3]	[3]	443	399	44
1919–20	—	—	—	[2]48,622	[2]31,980	[2]16,642	4,279	2,985	1,294	[3]	[3]	[3]	615	522	93
1929–30	—	—	—	[2]122,484	[2]73,615	[2]48,869	14,969	8,925	6,044	[3]	[3]	[3]	2,299	1,946	353
1939–40	—	—	—	[2]186,500	[2]109,546	[2]76,954	26,731	16,508	10,223	[3]	[3]	[3]	3,290	2,861	429
1949–50	—	—	—	[2]432,058	[2]328,841	[2]103,217	58,183	41,220	16,963	[3]	[3]	[3]	6,420	5,804	616
1959–60	—	—	—	[2]392,440	[2]254,063	[2]138,377	74,435	50,898	23,537	[3]	[3]	[3]	9,829	8,801	1,028
1960–61	—	—	—	365,174	224,538	140,636	84,609	57,830	26,779	25,253	24,577	676	10,575	9,463	1,112
1961–62	—	—	—	383,961	230,456	153,505	91,418	62,603	28,815	25,607	24,836	771	11,622	10,377	1,245
1962–63	—	—	—	411,420	241,309	170,111	98,684	67,302	31,382	26,590	25,753	837	12,822	11,448	1,374
1963–64	—	—	—	461,266	265,349	195,917	109,183	73,850	35,333	27,209	26,357	852	14,490	12,955	1,535
1964–65	—	—	—	493,757	282,173	211,584	121,167	81,319	39,848	28,290	27,283	1,007	16,467	14,692	1,775
1965–66	111,607	63,779	47,828	520,115	299,287	220,828	140,602	93,081	47,521	30,124	28,982	1,142	18,237	16,121	2,116
1966–67	139,183	78,356	60,827	558,534	322,711	235,823	157,726	103,109	54,617	31,695	30,401	1,294	20,617	18,163	2,454
1967–68	159,441	90,317	69,124	632,289	357,682	274,607	176,749	113,552	63,197	33,939	32,402	1,537	23,089	20,183	2,906
1968–69	183,279	105,661	77,618	728,845	410,595	318,250	193,756	121,531	72,225	35,114	33,595	1,519	26,158	22,722	3,436
1969–70	206,023	117,432	88,591	792,316	451,097	341,219	208,291	125,624	82,667	34,918	33,077	1,841	29,866	25,890	3,976
1970–71	252,311	144,144	108,167	839,730	475,594	364,136	230,509	138,146	92,363	37,946	35,544	2,402	32,107	27,530	4,577
1971–72	292,014	166,227	125,787	887,273	500,590	386,683	251,633	149,550	102,083	43,411	40,723	2,688	33,363	28,090	5,273
1972–73	316,174	175,413	140,761	922,362	518,191	404,171	263,371	154,468	108,903	50,018	46,489	3,529	34,777	28,571	6,206
1973–74	343,924	188,591	155,333	945,776	527,313	418,463	277,033	157,842	119,191	53,816	48,530	5,286	33,816	27,365	6,451
1974–75	360,171	191,017	169,154	922,933	504,841	418,092	292,450	161,570	130,880	55,916	48,956	6,960	34,083	26,817	7,266
1975–76	391,454	209,996	181,458	925,746	504,925	420,821	311,771	167,248	144,523	62,649	52,892	9,757	34,064	26,267	7,797
1976–77	406,377	210,842	195,535	919,549	495,545	424,004	317,164	167,783	149,381	64,359	52,374	11,985	33,232	25,142	8,090
1977–78	412,246	204,718	207,528	921,204	487,347	433,857	311,620	161,212	150,408	66,581	52,270	14,311	32,131	23,658	8,473
1978–79	402,702	192,091	210,611	921,390	477,344	444,046	301,079	153,370	147,709	68,848	52,652	16,196	32,730	23,541	9,189
1979–80	400,910	183,737	217,173	929,417	473,611	455,806	298,081	150,749	147,332	70,131	52,716	17,415	32,615	22,943	9,672
1980–81	416,377	188,638	227,739	935,140	469,883	465,257	295,739	147,043	148,696	71,956	52,792	19,164	32,958	22,711	10,247
1981–82	434,526	196,944	237,582	952,998	473,364	479,634	295,546	145,532	150,014	72,032	52,223	19,809	32,707	22,224	10,483
1982–83	449,620	203,991	245,629	969,510	479,140	490,370	289,921	144,697	145,224	73,054	51,250	21,804	32,775	21,902	10,873
1983–84	452,240	202,704	249,536	974,309	482,319	491,990	284,263	143,595	140,668	74,468	51,378	23,090	33,209	22,064	11,145
1984–85	454,712	202,932	251,780	979,477	482,528	496,949	286,251	143,390	142,861	75,063	50,455	24,608	32,943	21,700	11,243
1985–86	446,047	196,166	249,881	987,823	485,923	501,900	288,567	143,508	145,059	73,910	49,261	24,649	33,653	21,819	11,834
1986–87	436,304	190,839	245,465	991,264	480,782	510,482	289,349	141,269	148,080	71,617	46,523	25,094	34,041	22,061	11,980
1987–88	435,085	190,047	245,038	994,829	477,203	517,626	299,317	145,163	154,154	70,735	45,484	25,251	34,870	22,615	12,255
1988–89	436,764	186,316	250,448	1,018,755	483,346	535,409	310,621	149,354	161,267	70,856	45,046	25,810	35,720	22,648	13,072
1989–90	455,102	191,195	263,907	1,051,344	491,696	559,648	324,301	153,653	170,648	70,988	43,961	27,027	38,371	24,401	13,970
1990–91	481,720	198,634	283,086	1,094,538	504,045	590,493	337,168	156,482	180,686	71,948	43,846	28,102	39,294	24,756	14,538
1991–92	504,231	207,481	296,750	1,136,553	520,811	615,742	352,838	161,842	190,996	74,146	45,071	29,075	40,659	25,557	15,102
1992–93	514,756	211,964	302,792	1,165,178	532,881	632,297	369,585	169,258	200,327	75,387	45,153	30,234	42,132	26,073	16,059
1993–94	530,632	215,261	315,371	1,169,275	532,422	636,853	387,070	176,085	210,985	75,418	44,707	30,711	43,185	26,552	16,633
1994–95	539,691	218,352	321,339	1,160,134	526,131	634,003	397,629	178,598	219,031	75,800	44,853	30,947	44,446	26,916	17,530
1995–96	555,216	219,514	335,702	1,164,792	522,454	642,338	406,301	179,081	227,220	76,734	44,748	31,986	44,652	26,841	17,811
1996–97	571,226	223,948	347,278	1,172,879	520,515	652,364	419,401	180,947	238,454	78,730	45,564	33,166	45,876	27,146	18,730
1997–98	558,555	217,613	340,942	1,184,406	519,956	664,450	430,164	184,375	245,789	78,598	44,911	33,687	46,010	26,664	19,346
1998–99	559,954	218,417	341,537	1,200,303	518,746	681,557	439,986	186,148	253,838	78,439	44,339	34,100	44,077	25,146	18,931
1999–2000	564,933	224,721	340,212	1,237,875	530,367	707,508	457,056	191,792	265,264	80,057	44,239	35,818	44,808	25,028	19,780
2000–01	578,865	231,645	347,220	1,244,171	531,840	712,331	468,476	194,351	274,125	79,707	42,862	36,845	44,904	24,728	20,176
2001–02	595,133	238,109	357,024	1,291,900	549,816	742,084	482,118	199,120	282,998	80,698	42,507	38,191	44,160	23,708	20,452
2002–03 [4]	662,000	246,000	416,000	1,311,000	548,000	763,000	492,000	210,000	282,000	80,400	42,300	38,100	43,300	22,900	20,400
2003–04 [4]	660,000	243,000	417,000	1,333,000	559,000	774,000	502,000	213,000	289,000	84,400	44,300	40,100	44,200	23,300	20,900
2004–05 [4]	669,000	243,000	426,000	1,352,000	578,000	774,000	506,000	213,000	293,000	87,800	46,300	41,500	44,600	23,600	21,000
2005–06 [4]	675,000	244,000	431,000	1,397,000	584,000	813,000	513,000	215,000	298,000	89,100	47,100	42,000	45,000	23,700	21,300
2006–07 [4]	676,000	243,000	433,000	1,413,000	585,000	828,000	519,000	217,000	302,000	90,100	47,300	42,800	45,300	23,800	21,500
2007–08 [4]	681,000	244,000	437,000	1,425,000	589,000	836,000	522,000	218,000	304,000	91,300	47,800	43,500	45,600	24,000	21,600
2008–09 [4]	684,000	244,000	440,000	1,441,000	594,000	847,000	526,000	219,000	307,000	92,200	48,300	43,900	45,700	24,100	21,600
2009–10 [4]	688,000	245,000	443,000	1,456,000	598,000	858,000	530,000	220,000	310,000	92,900	48,600	44,300	45,900	24,200	21,700
2010–11 [4]	692,000	246,000	446,000	1,469,000	603,000	866,000	536,000	222,000	314,000	93,600	48,800	44,800	46,200	24,400	21,800
2011–12 [4]	696,000	247,000	449,000	1,488,000	610,000	878,000	544,000	224,000	320,000	94,600	49,200	45,400	46,600	24,500	22,100
2012–13 [4]	699,000	248,000	451,000	1,509,000	616,000	893,000	556,000	228,000	328,000	95,900	49,600	46,300	47,300	24,700	22,600

—Not available.

[1] Includes Ph.D., Ed.D., and comparable degrees at the doctoral level. Excludes first-professional, such as M.D., D.D.S., and law degrees.

[2] Includes first-professional degrees.

[3] First-professional degrees are included with bachelor's degrees.

[4] Projected.

NOTE: Data for 1869–70 to 1994–95 are for institutions of higher education. Institutions of higher education were accredited by an agency or association that was recognized by the U.S. Department of Education, or recognized directly by the Secretary of Education. The new degree-granting classification is very similar to the earlier higher education classification, except that it includes some additional institutions, primarily 2-year colleges, and excludes a few higher education institutions that did not award associate or higher degrees. Data for 1998–99 were imputed using alternative procedures. (See Guide to Sources for details.) Some data have been revised from previously published figures. Detail may not sum to totals due to rounding.

SOURCE: U.S. Department of Education, National Center for Education Statistics, Earned Degrees Conferred, 1869–70 through 1964–65; *Projections of Education Statistics to 2013;* Higher Education General Information Survey (HEGIS), "Degrees and Other Formal Awards Conferred" surveys, 1965–66 through 1985–86; and Integrated Postsecondary Education Data System (IPEDS), "Completions" surveys, 1986–87 through 1998–99, and Fall 2000 through Fall 2002 surveys. (This table was prepared August 2003.)

Degrees awarded by degree-granting institutions, by control, level of degree, and state or jurisdiction: 2001–02

State or jurisdiction	Public					Private				
	Associate degrees	Bachelor's degrees	Master's degrees	Doctor's degrees (Ph.D., Ed.D., etc.)	First-professional degrees [1]	Associate degrees	Bachelor's degrees	Master's degrees	Doctor's degrees (Ph.D., Ed.D., etc.)	First-professional degrees [1]
1	2	3	4	5	6	7	8	9	10	11
United States	471,660	841,512	249,828	27,622	33,439	123,473	450,388	232,290	16,538	47,259
Alabama	6,677	16,757	7,740	482	640	1,250	3,557	544	45	426
Alaska	858	1,277	354	19	0	48	100	78	0	0
Arizona	7,980	16,123	5,836	798	456	5,028	5,891	5,412	11	257
Arkansas	4,007	8,009	2,286	165	490	206	2,069	184	0	0
California	70,271	96,179	21,455	2,733	2,125	13,938	34,973	26,244	2,798	5,931
Colorado	5,029	18,168	5,016	607	492	3,047	4,107	3,549	114	353
Connecticut	3,349	6,954	2,553	221	379	1,064	7,693	4,957	372	613
Delaware	919	3,879	712	137	0	244	1,057	837	21	291
District of Columbia	106	291	69	0	54	506	8,300	7,295	541	2,627
Florida	38,746	38,064	11,371	1,269	1,335	10,206	18,287	8,923	1,014	1,882
Georgia	7,297	20,517	7,645	855	796	1,764	9,482	4,407	307	1,530
Hawaii	2,204	2,910	838	110	130	1,105	1,991	705	20	1
Idaho	1,618	4,497	1,113	91	132	2,965	416	128	0	0
Illinois	21,791	31,821	10,473	1,087	1,133	4,133	25,609	18,056	1,448	3,368
Indiana	8,165	22,681	6,281	887	1,066	3,726	11,266	2,808	135	545
Iowa	8,702	10,366	2,501	571	668	1,237	9,022	1,377	8	912
Kansas	6,635	11,602	3,830	416	682	574	3,185	1,225	0	19
Kentucky	5,187	12,469	4,018	306	757	2,118	3,932	896	76	247
Louisiana	4,054	16,767	4,265	401	763	1,316	3,545	1,590	136	747
Maine	1,459	3,450	742	39	67	516	2,343	577	0	117
Maryland	7,305	17,136	6,009	585	922	445	5,194	5,582	387	207
Massachusetts	11,605	12,645	4,074	372	89	2,646	30,452	21,810	1,915	3,823
Michigan	15,202	35,784	15,455	1,432	1,506	3,566	12,145	6,614	65	934
Minnesota	9,169	15,250	4,089	560	673	2,673	9,456	4,288	313	848
Mississippi	6,934	10,021	2,751	334	420	668	1,878	635	0	121
Missouri	7,234	16,965	4,401	401	692	3,714	15,117	9,513	552	1,728
Montana	1,348	4,700	959	73	121	180	577	31	0	0
Nebraska	3,415	6,952	2,422	255	337	791	3,687	789	78	458
Nevada	1,974	4,175	1,131	107	152	418	314	370	0	0
New Hampshire	1,443	3,698	791	55	0	1,480	3,551	1,587	68	166
New Jersey	10,937	20,884	5,861	528	1,019	1,706	7,492	4,469	452	521
New Mexico	3,493	5,333	2,034	280	286	264	1,099	582	0	0
New York	37,483	41,519	13,436	1,008	1,279	13,665	56,813	37,485	2,456	7,198
North Carolina	13,936	24,066	6,751	844	833	803	12,005	2,626	270	998
North Dakota	1,737	4,045	722	54	181	147	765	191	0	0
Ohio	15,737	33,545	11,050	1,450	2,018	4,151	19,203	7,026	471	1,264
Oklahoma	6,766	12,783	4,008	365	688	484	3,449	1,217	74	337
Oregon	5,832	10,207	3,299	362	366	686	4,243	1,606	56	654
Pennsylvania	11,506	34,136	9,037	1,164	1,652	12,320	34,863	14,164	1,143	2,786
Rhode Island	1,205	2,971	884	81	78	2,352	5,874	1,195	161	171
South Carolina	6,267	12,391	3,548	433	589	865	4,495	607	16	188
South Dakota	1,487	3,215	802	69	138	369	1,150	141	4	25
Tennessee	6,072	14,983	5,038	476	700	2,013	8,497	2,933	305	735
Texas	27,633	61,210	19,256	2,233	3,118	4,198	18,385	6,160	327	1,992
Utah	8,276	10,277	2,158	287	240	884	7,911	1,508	63	153
Vermont	758	2,319	417	54	93	757	2,354	963	3	168
Virginia	9,747	25,249	8,440	1,016	1,306	2,508	7,699	2,249	151	907
Washington	18,540	18,635	4,285	613	642	1,495	5,827	3,266	41	554
West Virginia	2,074	7,433	2,094	146	407	852	1,589	151	0	0
Wisconsin	9,809	21,304	5,083	736	607	641	7,479	2,740	121	457
Wyoming	1,682	1,655	445	55	122	741	0	0	0	0
U.S. Service Schools [2]	0	3,245	0	0	0	0	0	0	0	0
Outlying areas	2,053	8,549	880	76	285	3,108	8,521	2,537	75	508
American Samoa	174	0	0	0	0	0	0	0	0	0
Federated States of Micronesia	176	0	0	0	0	0	0	0	0	0
Guam	125	354	131	0	0	25	0	0	0	0
Marshall Islands	35	0	0	0	0	0	0	0	0	0
Northern Marianas	82	27	0	0	0	0	0	0	0	0
Palau	32	0	0	0	0	0	0	0	0	0
Puerto Rico	1,382	7,957	720	76	285	3,083	8,521	2,537	75	508
Virgin Islands	47	211	29	0	0	0	0	0	0	0

[1] Includes degrees which require at least 6 years of college work for completion (including at least 2 years of preprofessional training). See Definitions for details.

[2] Excludes Uniformed Services University of the Health Sciences, National Defense University, Air Force Institute of Technology, Community College of the Air Force, Naval Postgraduate School, Joint Military Intelligence College, and the U.S. Army Command and General Staff College.

SOURCE: U.S. Department of Education, National Center for Education Statistics, Integrated Postsecondary Education Data System (IPEDS), Fall 2002 survey. (This table was prepared August 2003.)

Degrees conferred by degree-granting institutions, by control of institution, level of degree, and discipline division: 2001–02

Discipline division	Public institutions				Private institutions			
	Associate degrees	Bachelor's degrees	Master's degrees	Doctor's degrees [1]	Associate degrees	Bachelor's degrees	Master's degrees	Doctor's degrees [1]
1	2	3	4	5	6	7	8	9
Total	**471,660**	**841,512**	**249,828**	**27,622**	**123,473**	**450,388**	**232,290**	**16,538**
Agriculture and natural resources [2]	6,135	21,051	3,918	1,146	359	2,302	601	20
Architecture and related programs	353	6,770	2,944	123	90	2,038	1,622	60
Area, ethnic, and cultural studies	85	3,791	807	120	234	2,766	771	96
Biological sciences/life sciences	1,400	39,633	4,123	3,059	117	20,623	2,082	1,430
Business [3]	72,727	164,170	46,580	676	36,184	117,160	74,205	482
Communications	1,695	43,857	2,681	293	1,124	18,934	2,829	81
Communications technologies	1,516	528	110	0	505	582	439	9
Computer and information sciences	14,381	25,873	7,936	448	16,584	21,426	8,177	302
Construction trades	2,216	73	0	0	423	129	9	0
Education	7,927	76,042	75,485	4,798	1,340	30,341	61,094	2,169
Engineering	1,508	44,738	17,632	3,730	216	14,743	8,383	1,465
Engineering-related technologies	17,280	10,367	784	14	15,615	3,750	112	1
English language and literature/letters	813	36,435	5,221	1,066	51	16,727	2,047	380
Foreign languages and literatures	431	10,147	2,080	557	86	5,171	781	286
Health professions and related sciences	65,791	46,272	23,224	2,049	14,097	24,245	20,420	1,474
Home economics and vocational home economics	9,004	15,558	1,569	255	476	2,595	1,047	100
Law and legal studies	3,862	1,106	854	10	2,963	865	3,199	69
Liberal arts and sciences, general studies, and humanities	198,924	27,626	1,112	33	8,239	11,707	1,642	80
Library science	94	73	4,139	43	2	1	974	2
Mathematics	668	8,002	2,659	682	17	4,393	828	276
Mechanics and repairers	7,697	74	0	0	4,389	90	0	0
Multi/interdisciplinary studies	12,972	20,282	1,835	210	232	7,347	1,376	174
Parks, recreation, leisure, and fitness studies	657	15,127	2,189	138	173	5,427	565	13
Philosophy and religion	89	3,842	438	212	45	5,464	896	394
Physical sciences and science technologies	2,224	11,678	3,684	2,693	84	6,173	1,350	1,110
Precision production trades	6,968	356	0	0	3,850	112	2	0
Protective services	15,258	19,037	1,580	46	1,431	6,499	1,355	3
Psychology	1,526	51,095	5,881	1,742	179	25,576	9,007	2,599
Public administration and services	3,007	13,254	15,784	311	316	6,138	9,664	260
R.O.T.C. and military technologies	62	3	0	0	0	0	0	0
Social sciences and history	5,334	86,454	8,773	2,457	259	46,420	5,339	1,445
Theological studies/religious vocations	0	0	0	0	414	7,785	4,952	1,355
Transportation and material moving workers	741	1,649	74	0	418	2,371	635	0
Visual and performing arts	8,262	36,549	5,732	711	12,649	30,224	5,863	403
Not classified by field of study	53	0	0	0	312	264	24	0

[1] Includes Ph.D., Ed.D., and comparable degrees at the doctoral level. Excludes first-professional degrees, such as M.D., D.D.S., and law degrees.

[2] Includes "Agricultural business and production," "Agricultural sciences," and "Conservation and renewable natural resources."

[3] Includes "Business management and administrative services," "Marketing operations/marketing and distribution," and "Consumer and personal services."

SOURCE: U.S. Department of Education, National Center for Education Statistics, Integrated Postsecondary Education Data System (IPEDS), Fall 2002 survey. (This table was prepared August 2003.)

First-professional degrees conferred by degree-granting institutions in dentistry, medicine, and law, by number of institutions conferring degrees and sex of student: Selected years, 1949–50 to 2001–02

Year	Dentistry (D.D.S. or D.M.D.)				Medicine (M.D.)				Law (LL.B. or J.D.)			
	Number of institutions conferring degrees	Degrees conferred			Number of institutions conferring degrees	Degrees conferred			Number of institutions conferring degrees	Degrees conferred		
		Total	Men	Women		Total	Men	Women		Total	Men	Women
1	2	3	4	5	6	7	8	9	10	11	12	13
1949–50	40	2,579	2,561	18	72	5,612	5,028	584	—	—	—	—
1951–52	41	2,918	2,895	23	72	6,201	5,871	330	—	—	—	—
1953–54	42	3,102	3,063	39	73	6,712	6,377	335	—	—	—	—
1955–56	42	3,009	2,975	34	73	6,810	6,464	346	131	8,262	7,974	288
1957–58	43	3,065	3,031	34	75	6,816	6,469	347	131	9,394	9,122	272
1959–60	45	3,247	3,221	26	79	7,032	6,645	387	134	9,240	9,010	230
1961–62	46	3,183	3,166	17	81	7,138	6,749	389	134	9,364	9,091	273
1963–64	46	3,180	3,168	12	82	7,303	6,878	425	133	10,679	10,372	307
1965–66	47	3,178	3,146	32	84	7,673	7,170	503	136	13,246	12,776	470
1967–68	48	3,422	3,375	47	85	7,944	7,318	626	138	16,454	15,805	649
1969–70	48	3,718	3,684	34	86	8,314	7,615	699	145	14,916	14,115	801
1970–71	48	3,745	3,703	42	89	8,919	8,110	809	147	17,421	16,181	1,240
1971–72	48	3,862	3,819	43	92	9,253	8,423	830	147	21,764	20,266	1,498
1972–73	51	4,047	3,992	55	97	10,307	9,388	919	152	27,205	25,037	2,168
1973–74	52	4,440	4,355	85	99	11,356	10,093	1,263	151	29,326	25,986	3,340
1974–75	52	4,773	4,627	146	104	12,447	10,818	1,629	154	29,296	24,881	4,415
1975–76	56	5,425	5,187	238	107	13,426	11,252	2,174	166	32,293	26,085	6,208
1976–77	57	5,138	4,764	374	109	13,461	10,891	2,570	169	34,104	26,447	7,657
1977–78	57	5,189	4,623	566	109	14,279	11,210	3,069	169	34,402	25,457	8,945
1978–79	58	5,434	4,794	640	109	14,786	11,381	3,405	175	35,206	25,180	10,026
1979–80	58	5,258	4,558	700	112	14,902	11,416	3,486	179	35,647	24,893	10,754
1980–81	58	5,460	4,672	788	116	15,505	11,672	3,833	176	36,331	24,563	11,768
1981–82	59	5,282	4,467	815	119	15,814	11,867	3,947	180	35,991	23,965	12,026
1982–83	59	5,585	4,631	954	118	15,484	11,350	4,134	177	36,853	23,550	13,303
1983–84	60	5,353	4,302	1,051	119	15,813	11,359	4,454	179	37,012	23,382	13,630
1984–85	59	5,339	4,233	1,106	120	16,041	11,167	4,874	181	37,491	23,070	14,421
1985–86	59	5,046	3,907	1,139	120	15,938	11,022	4,916	181	35,844	21,874	13,970
1986–87	58	4,741	3,603	1,138	121	15,428	10,431	4,997	179	36,056	21,561	14,495
1987–88	57	4,477	3,300	1,177	122	15,358	10,278	5,080	180	35,397	21,067	14,330
1988–89	58	4,265	3,124	1,141	124	15,460	10,310	5,150	182	35,634	21,069	14,565
1989–90	57	4,100	2,834	1,266	124	15,075	9,923	5,152	182	36,485	21,079	15,406
1990–91	55	3,699	2,510	1,189	121	15,043	9,629	5,414	179	37,945	21,643	16,302
1991–92	52	3,593	2,431	1,162	120	15,243	9,796	5,447	177	38,848	22,260	16,588
1992–93	55	3,605	2,383	1,222	122	15,531	9,679	5,852	184	40,302	23,182	17,120
1993–94	53	3,787	2,330	1,457	121	15,368	9,544	5,824	185	40,044	22,826	17,218
1994–95	53	3,897	2,480	1,417	119	15,537	9,507	6,030	183	39,349	22,592	16,757
1995–96	53	3,697	2,374	1,323	119	15,341	9,061	6,280	183	39,828	22,508	17,320
1996–97	52	3,784	2,387	1,397	118	15,571	9,121	6,450	184	40,079	22,548	17,531
1997–98	53	4,032	2,490	1,542	117	15,424	9,006	6,418	185	39,331	21,876	17,455
1998–99	53	4,144	2,674	1,470	118	15,562	8,954	6,608	188	39,167	21,628	17,539
1999–2000	54	4,250	2,547	1,703	118	15,286	8,761	6,525	190	38,152	20,638	17,514
2000–01	54	4,391	2,696	1,695	118	15,403	8,728	6,675	192	37,904	19,981	17,923
2001–02	53	4,239	2,608	1,631	118	15,237	8,469	6,768	192	38,981	20,254	18,727

—Not available.

NOTE: Data for 1998–99 were imputed using alternative procedures. (See *Guide to Sources* for details.)

SOURCE: U.S. Department of Education, National Center for Education Statistics, *Earned Degrees Conferred;* Higher Education General Information Survey (HEGIS), "Degrees and Other Formal Awards Conferred" surveys; and Integrated Postsecondary Education Data System (IPEDS), "Completions" surveys, 1986–87 through 1998–99, and Fall 2000 through Fall 2002 surveys. (This table was prepared August 2003.)

Statistical profile of persons receiving doctor's degrees in education: Selected years, 1979–80 to 2000–01

Item	1979–80	1980–81	1985–86	1989–90	1990–91	1991–92	1992–93	1993–94	1994–95	1995–96	1996–97	1997–98	1998–99	1999–2000	2000–01
1	2	3	4	5	6	7	8	9	10	11	12	13	14	15	16
Number of doctorates	**7,576**	**7,489**	**6,649**	**6,510**	**6,454**	**6,677**	**6,689**	**6,708**	**6,649**	**6,772**	**6,497**	**6,559**	**6,557**	**6,420**	**6,324**
Sex (percent)															
Men	55.5	52.8	45.6	42.4	41.9	40.5	41.3	39.1	38.4	38.3	36.7	37.0	35.8	35.1	35.4
Women	44.5	47.2	54.4	57.6	58.1	59.5	58.7	60.9	61.6	61.7	63.3	63.0	64.2	64.9	64.6
Racial/ethnic group (percent)															
White, non-Hispanic	86.3	85.9	86.1	86.0	85.6	84.8	83.7	83.9	81.6	82.2	81.1	79.1	79.3	78.3	78.8
Black, non-Hispanic	9.1	9.1	8.1	8.2	7.9	8.4	9.4	8.6	10.4	10.1	10.2	11.6	11.7	12.6	12.6
Hispanic	2.4	2.5	3.7	3.3	3.3	3.5	3.7	4.0	4.4	3.6	4.6	5.1	4.8	5.1	5.1
Asian [1]	1.3	1.9	1.6	1.8	2.2	2.4	2.4	2.9	3.0	3.1	3.2	3.2	3.1	3.1	2.7
American Indian /Alaska Native	0.8	0.6	0.5	0.6	1.0	0.8	0.8	0.6	0.7	1.0	0.9	0.9	1.1	0.9	0.8
Citizenship (percent)															
United States	88.7	87.7	84.7	84.4	84.8	86.8	86.4	87.4	86.8	86.6	82.6	84.3	82.8	86.2	84.0
Foreign	8.2	8.8	9.6	9.7	10.2	10.7	10.8	11.0	11.0	9.9	8.2	9.1	10.6	10.3	9.7
Unknown	3.1	3.6	5.6	5.8	5.0	2.4	2.7	1.6	2.3	3.4	9.3	6.6	6.5	3.5	6.2
Median age at doctorate (years)	37.0	37.3	39.4	41.6	42.1	42.7	43.0	43.6	43.8	44.3	44.0	44.3	44.3	44.4	43.8
Percent with bachelor's degree in same field as doctorate	39.0	38.9	39.0	37.5	39.3	38.7	37.4	36.9	37.0	36.1	34.1	35.0	34.8	33.7	33.2
Median time lapse from bachelor's to doctorate (years)															
Total time	13.1	13.5	15.7	17.9	18.4	18.9	19.2	19.7	19.9	20.2	20.0	20.0	19.9	19.4	19.0
Registered time	6.9	7.0	7.8	8.1	8.1	8.2	8.2	8.1	8.2	8.2	8.4	8.4	8.2	8.1	8.3

[1] Does not include Native Hawaiians or other Pacific Islanders.

NOTE: Longitudinal comparisons by race/ethnicity should be done with extreme care, due to periodic changes in the survey. In particular, large numbers of Asians converted from temporary visas to permanent visas in the mid 1990s. Distribution by race/ethnicity based on U.S. citizens and those with permanent visas only. The classification of degrees by field used in this survey differs somewhat from that in most publications of the National Center for Education Statistics (NCES). The number of degrees also differs slightly from that reported in the NCES "Completions" survey. Detail may not sum to totals due to rounding.

SOURCE: *Survey of Doctorate Recipients from United States Universities,* various years, sponsored by the National Science Foundation, National Institutes of Health, U.S. Department of Education, National Endowment for the Humanities, U.S. Department of Agriculture, and the National Aeronautics and Space Administration. (This table was prepared June 2003.)

Total fall enrollment in degree-granting institutions, by attendance status, age, and sex: Selected years, 1970 to 2013

[In thousands]

Age and sex	1970[1]	1975[1]	1980[1]	1990[1]	1995[1]	1998[2]	1999[2]	2000[2]	Projected[2]			
									2002	2003	2010	2013
1	2	3	4	5	6	7	8	9	10	11	12	13
Men and women, total	**8,581**	**11,185**	**12,097**	**13,819**	**14,262**	**14,507**	**14,791**	**15,312**	**16,102**	**16,361**	**17,541**	**18,151**
14 to 17 years old	259	278	247	177	148	119	143	145	147	151	162	163
18 and 19 years old	2,600	2,786	2,901	2,950	2,894	3,382	3,414	3,531	3,580	3,631	4,002	3,921
20 and 21 years old	1,880	2,243	2,424	2,761	2,705	2,811	2,989	3,045	3,337	3,357	3,695	3,749
22 to 24 years old	1,457	1,753	1,989	2,144	2,411	2,377	2,435	2,617	2,888	3,014	3,231	3,511
25 to 29 years old	1,074	1,774	1,871	1,982	2,120	1,991	1,870	1,960	2,014	2,056	2,393	2,520
30 to 34 years old	487	967	1,243	1,322	1,236	1,195	1,145	1,265	1,295	1,304	1,326	1,471
35 years old and over	823	1,383	1,421	2,484	2,747	2,632	2,796	2,749	2,841	2,848	2,731	2,815
Men	**5,044**	**6,149**	**5,874**	**6,284**	**6,343**	**6,369**	**6,491**	**6,722**	**7,008**	**7,098**	**7,561**	**7,734**
14 to 17 years old	130	126	99	87	61	45	72	63	61	62	65	65
18 and 19 years old	1,349	1,397	1,375	1,421	1,338	1,535	1,541	1,583	1,624	1,637	1,780	1,733
20 and 21 years old	1,095	1,245	1,259	1,368	1,282	1,374	1,392	1,382	1,539	1,551	1,683	1,691
22 to 24 years old	964	1,047	1,064	1,107	1,153	1,127	1,090	1,293	1,355	1,405	1,490	1,601
25 to 29 years old	783	1,122	993	940	962	908	874	862	902	918	1,058	1,096
30 to 34 years old	308	557	576	537	561	463	517	527	535	536	541	591
35 years old and over	415	654	507	824	986	917	1,005	1,012	992	990	943	958
Women	**3,537**	**5,036**	**6,223**	**7,535**	**7,919**	**8,138**	**8,301**	**8,591**	**9,095**	**9,263**	**9,980**	**10,416**
14 to 17 years old	129	152	148	90	87	74	72	82	86	89	97	99
18 and 19 years old	1,250	1,389	1,526	1,529	1,557	1,847	1,874	1,948	1,956	1,994	2,222	2,188
20 and 21 years old	786	998	1,165	1,392	1,424	1,437	1,597	1,663	1,799	1,806	2,012	2,058
22 to 24 years old	493	706	925	1,037	1,258	1,250	1,344	1,324	1,533	1,609	1,741	1,910
25 to 29 years old	291	652	878	1,043	1,159	1,083	995	1,099	1,111	1,138	1,336	1,424
30 to 34 years old	179	410	667	784	675	732	627	738	760	768	785	880
35 years old and over	409	729	914	1,659	1,760	1,715	1,791	1,736	1,849	1,859	1,788	1,857
Full-time	**5,816**	**6,841**	**7,098**	**7,821**	**8,129**	**8,563**	**8,786**	**9,010**	**9,590**	**9,774**	**10,681**	**11,029**
14 to 17 years old	242	253	223	144	123	93	129	125	128	131	142	143
18 and 19 years old	2,406	2,619	2,669	2,548	2,387	2,794	2,848	2,932	2,968	3,015	3,330	3,274
20 and 21 years old	1,647	1,910	2,075	2,151	2,109	2,271	2,362	2,401	2,633	2,653	2,930	2,982
22 to 24 years old	881	924	1,121	1,350	1,517	1,564	1,662	1,653	1,894	1,978	2,127	2,325
25 to 29 years old	407	630	577	770	908	890	854	878	909	931	1,092	1,161
30 to 34 years old	100	264	251	387	430	367	338	422	440	444	456	512
35 years old and over	134	241	182	471	653	584	593	599	618	622	605	633
Men	**3,505**	**3,927**	**3,689**	**3,808**	**3,807**	**3,934**	**4,026**	**4,111**	**4,419**	**4,484**	**4,822**	**4,928**
14 to 17 years old	124	114	87	71	54	39	63	51	52	53	56	55
18 and 19 years old	1,265	1,329	1,270	1,230	1,091	1,240	1,271	1,250	1,326	1,337	1,454	1,420
20 and 21 years old	990	1,074	1,109	1,055	999	1,129	1,125	1,106	1,242	1,252	1,358	1,369
22 to 24 years old	650	633	665	742	789	777	788	839	932	966	1,023	1,104
25 to 29 years old	327	445	360	401	454	424	416	415	433	441	507	530
30 to 34 years old	72	181	124	156	183	141	149	195	199	199	200	221
35 years old and over	75	149	74	152	238	184	213	256	236	235	224	230
Women	**2,311**	**2,915**	**3,409**	**4,013**	**4,321**	**4,630**	**4,761**	**4,899**	**5,172**	**5,290**	**5,860**	**6,101**
14 to 17 years old	117	138	136	73	69	54	66	74	76	79	86	88
18 and 19 years old	1,140	1,290	1,399	1,318	1,296	1,555	1,577	1,682	1,643	1,677	1,876	1,854
20 and 21 years old	657	835	966	1,096	1,111	1,142	1,237	1,296	1,392	1,401	1,572	1,613
22 to 24 years old	231	291	456	608	729	787	875	814	962	1,011	1,104	1,221
25 to 29 years old	80	185	217	369	455	466	437	463	476	490	585	631
30 to 34 years old	28	83	127	231	247	226	190	227	241	245	256	291
35 years old and over	59	92	108	319	415	400	380	343	382	387	381	403
Part-time	**2,765**	**4,344**	**4,999**	**5,998**	**6,133**	**5,944**	**6,005**	**6,303**	**6,512**	**6,587**	**6,860**	**7,122**
14 to 17 years old	17	42	38	32	25	26	14	20	19	20	21	21
18 and 19 years old	194	340	418	402	507	588	566	599	612	616	672	647
20 and 21 years old	233	447	441	610	596	540	627	644	704	705	765	767
22 to 24 years old	576	717	844	794	894	813	772	964	994	1,036	1,104	1,186
25 to 29 years old	668	1,032	1,209	1,213	1,212	1,101	1,016	1,083	1,105	1,125	1,302	1,360
30 to 34 years old	388	670	905	935	805	828	806	843	855	859	870	959
35 years old and over	689	1,098	1,145	2,012	2,093	2,048	2,203	2,150	2,223	2,226	2,126	2,183
Men	**1,540**	**2,222**	**2,185**	**2,476**	**2,535**	**2,436**	**2,465**	**2,611**	**2,589**	**2,614**	**2,739**	**2,806**
14 to 17 years old	5	18	17	16	7	5	8	11	9	9	10	10
18 and 19 years old	84	153	202	191	246	296	269	333	298	300	326	313
20 and 21 years old	105	219	201	313	283	245	267	276	297	299	324	323
22 to 24 years old	314	358	392	365	365	350	302	454	422	438	468	497
25 to 29 years old	456	631	594	539	508	485	458	447	469	477	551	567
30 to 34 years old	236	361	397	381	378	322	369	332	337	337	340	370
35 years old and over	340	486	382	672	748	733	791	757	756	754	720	728
Women	**1,225**	**2,121**	**2,814**	**3,521**	**3,598**	**3,508**	**3,540**	**3,692**	**3,923**	**3,972**	**4,120**	**4,316**
14 to 17 years old	12	24	20	17	18	21	6	9	10	10	11	11
18 and 19 years old	110	188	215	211	261	292	297	266	314	316	345	334
20 and 21 years old	128	228	240	297	313	295	360	368	407	406	441	445
22 to 24 years old	262	359	452	429	529	463	470	510	571	597	636	689
25 to 29 years old	212	401	616	674	704	617	558	636	635	648	751	793
30 to 34 years old	151	309	507	554	427	506	438	511	519	522	529	589
35 years old and over	349	612	762	1,340	1,345	1,315	1,411	1,393	1,467	1,472	1,407	1,455

[1] Institutions that were accredited by an agency or association that was recognized by the U.S. Department of Education, or recognized directly by the Secretary of Education.

[2] Data are for 4-year and 2-year degree-granting institutions that were participating in Title IV federal financial aid programs.

NOTE: Distributions by age are estimates based on samples of the civilian noninstitutional population. Data for 1999 were imputed using alternative procedures. (See Guide to Sources for details.) Some data have been revised from previously published figures. Detail may not sum to totals due to rounding.

SOURCE: U.S. Department of Education, National Center for Education Statistics, Higher Education General Information Survey (HEGIS), "Fall Enrollment in Colleges and Universities" surveys, 1970 through 1980; Integrated Postsecondary Education Data System (IPEDS), "Fall Enrollment" surveys; *Projections of Education Statistics to 2013*; and U.S. Department of Commerce, Bureau of the Census, *Current Population Reports*, "Social and Economic Characteristics of Students," selected years. (This table was prepared November 2003.)

Total fall enrollment in degree-granting institutions, by attendance status, sex of student, and control of institution: 1947 to 2001

Year	Total enrollment	Attendance status		Sex of student		Control of institution			
		Full-time	Part-time	Men	Women	Public	Private		
							Total	Not-for-profit	For-profit
1	2	3	4	5	6	7	8	9	10
Institutions of higher education [1]									
1947 [2]	2,338,226	—	—	1,659,249	678,977	1,152,377	1,185,849	—	—
1948 [2]	2,403,396	—	—	1,709,367	694,029	1,185,588	1,217,808	—	—
1949 [2]	2,444,900	—	—	1,721,572	723,328	1,207,151	1,237,749	—	—
1950 [2]	2,281,298	—	—	1,560,392	720,906	1,139,699	1,141,599	—	—
1951 [2]	2,101,962	—	—	1,390,740	711,222	1,037,938	1,064,024	—	—
1952 [2]	2,134,242	—	—	1,380,357	753,885	1,101,240	1,033,002	—	—
1953 [2]	2,231,054	—	—	1,422,598	808,456	1,185,876	1,045,178	—	—
1954 [2]	2,446,693	—	—	1,563,382	883,311	1,353,531	1,093,162	—	—
1955 [2]	2,653,034	—	—	1,733,184	919,850	1,476,282	1,176,752	—	—
1956 [2]	2,918,212	—	—	1,911,458	1,006,754	1,656,402	1,261,810	—	—
1957	3,323,783	—	—	2,170,765	1,153,018	1,972,673	1,351,110	—	—
1959	3,639,847	2,421,016	[3] 1,218,831	2,332,617	1,307,230	2,180,982	1,458,865	—	—
1961	4,145,065	2,785,133	[3] 1,359,932	2,585,821	1,559,244	2,561,447	1,583,618	—	—
1963	4,779,609	3,183,833	[3] 1,595,776	2,961,540	1,818,069	3,081,279	1,698,330	—	—
1964	5,280,020	3,573,238	[3] 1,706,782	3,248,713	2,031,307	3,467,708	1,812,312	—	—
1965	5,920,864	4,095,728	[3] 1,825,136	3,630,020	2,290,844	3,969,596	1,951,268	—	—
1966	6,389,872	4,438,606	[3] 1,951,266	3,856,216	2,533,656	4,348,917	2,040,955	—	—
1967	6,911,748	4,793,128	[3] 2,118,620	4,132,800	2,778,948	4,816,028	2,095,720	—	—
1968	7,513,091	5,210,155	2,302,936	4,477,649	3,035,442	5,430,652	2,082,439	—	—
1969	8,004,660	5,498,883	2,505,777	4,746,201	3,258,459	5,896,868	2,107,792	—	—
1970	8,580,887	5,816,290	2,764,597	5,043,642	3,537,245	6,428,134	2,152,753	—	—
1971	8,948,644	6,077,232	2,871,412	5,207,004	3,741,640	6,804,309	2,144,335	—	—
1972	9,214,820	6,072,350	3,142,470	5,238,718	3,976,102	7,070,635	2,144,185	—	—
1973	9,602,123	6,189,493	3,412,630	5,371,052	4,231,071	7,419,516	2,182,607	—	—
1974	10,223,729	6,370,273	3,853,456	5,622,429	4,601,300	7,988,500	2,235,229	—	—
1975	11,184,859	6,841,334	4,343,525	6,148,997	5,035,862	8,834,508	2,350,351	—	—
1976	11,012,137	6,717,058	4,295,079	5,810,828	5,201,309	8,653,477	2,358,660	2,314,298	44,362
1977	11,285,787	6,792,925	4,492,862	5,789,016	5,496,771	8,846,993	2,438,794	2,386,652	52,142
1978	11,260,092	6,667,657	4,592,435	5,640,998	5,619,094	8,785,893	2,474,199	2,408,331	65,868
1979	11,569,899	6,794,039	4,775,860	5,682,877	5,887,022	9,036,822	2,533,077	2,461,773	71,304
1980	12,096,895	7,097,958	4,998,937	5,874,374	6,222,521	9,457,394	2,639,501	2,527,787	[4] 111,714
1981	12,371,672	7,181,250	5,190,422	5,975,056	6,396,616	9,647,032	2,724,640	2,572,405	[4] 152,235
1982	12,425,780	7,220,618	5,205,162	6,031,384	6,394,396	9,696,087	2,729,693	2,552,739	[4] 176,954
1983	12,464,661	7,261,050	5,203,611	6,023,725	6,440,936	9,682,734	2,781,927	2,589,187	192,740
1984	12,241,940	7,098,388	5,143,552	5,863,574	6,378,366	9,477,370	2,764,570	2,574,419	190,151
1985	12,247,055	7,075,221	5,171,834	5,818,450	6,428,605	9,479,273	2,767,782	2,571,791	195,991
1986	12,503,511	7,119,550	5,383,961	5,884,515	6,618,996	9,713,893	2,789,618	2,572,479	[5] 217,139
1987	12,766,642	7,231,085	5,535,557	5,932,056	6,834,586	9,973,254	2,793,388	2,602,350	[5] 191,038
1988	13,055,337	7,436,768	5,618,569	6,001,896	7,053,441	10,161,388	2,893,949	2,673,567	220,382
1989	13,538,560	7,660,950	5,877,610	6,190,015	7,348,545	10,577,963	2,960,597	2,731,174	229,423
1990	13,818,637	7,820,985	5,997,652	6,283,909	7,534,728	10,844,717	2,973,920	2,760,227	213,693
1991	14,358,953	8,115,329	6,243,624	6,501,844	7,857,109	11,309,563	3,049,390	2,819,041	230,349
1992	14,487,359	8,162,118	6,325,241	6,523,989	7,963,370	11,384,567	3,102,792	2,872,523	230,269
1993	14,304,803	8,127,618	6,177,185	6,427,450	7,877,353	11,189,088	3,115,715	2,888,897	226,818
1994	14,278,790	8,137,776	6,141,014	6,371,898	7,906,892	11,133,680	3,145,110	2,910,107	235,003
1995	14,261,781	8,128,802	6,132,979	6,342,539	7,919,242	11,092,374	3,169,407	2,929,044	240,363
1996	14,300,255	8,213,490	6,086,765	6,343,992	7,956,263	11,090,171	3,210,084	2,940,557	269,527
1997	14,345,416	8,322,362	6,023,054	6,329,960	8,015,456	11,146,155	3,199,261	2,961,714	237,547
Degree-granting institutions [6]									
1996	14,367,520	8,302,953	6,064,567	6,352,825	8,014,695	11,120,499	3,247,021	2,942,556	304,465
1997	14,502,334	8,438,062	6,064,272	6,396,028	8,106,306	11,196,119	3,306,215	2,977,614	328,601
1998	14,506,967	8,563,338	5,943,629	6,369,265	8,137,702	11,137,769	3,369,198	3,004,925	364,273
1999 [7]	14,791,224	8,786,494	6,004,730	6,490,646	8,300,578	11,309,399	3,481,825	3,051,626	430,199
2000	15,312,289	9,009,600	6,302,689	6,721,769	8,590,520	11,752,786	3,559,503	3,109,419	450,084
2001	15,927,987	9,447,502	6,480,485	6,960,815	8,967,172	12,233,156	3,694,831	3,167,330	527,501

—Not available.

[1] Institutions that were accredited by an agency or association that was recognized by the U.S. Department of Education, or recognized directly by the Secretary of Education.

[2] Degree-credit enrollment only.

[3] Includes part-time resident students and all extension students.

[4] Large increases are due to the addition of schools accredited by the Accrediting Commission of Career Schools and Colleges of Technology.

[5] Because of imputation techniques, data are not consistent with figures for other years.

[6] Data are for 4-year and 2-year degree-granting institutions that were participating in Title IV federal financial aid programs.

[7] Data were imputed using alternative procedures. (See Guide to Sources for details.)

NOTE: Trend tabulations of institutions of higher education data are based on institutions that were accredited by an agency or association that was recognized by the U.S.

Department of Education, or recognized directly by the Secretary of Education. As of 1996, the Department has been collecting data from Title IV participants. The new degree-granting classification is very similar to the earlier higher education classification, except that it includes some additional institutions, primarily 2-year colleges, and excludes a few higher education institutions that did not award associate or higher degrees.

SOURCE: U.S. Department of Education, National Center for Education Statistics, *Biennial Survey of Education in the United States; Opening Fall Enrollment in Higher Education,* various years; Higher Education General Information Survey (HEGIS), "Fall Enrollment in Colleges and Universities" surveys, 1966 through 1985; and Integrated Postsecondary Education Data System (IPEDS), "Fall Enrollment" surveys, 1986 through 1999, and Spring 2001 and Spring 2002 surveys. (This table was prepared August 2003.)

College enrollment and enrollment rates of recent high school completers, by sex: 1960 to 2002

[Numbers in thousands]

Year	High school completers [1]			Enrolled in college [2]					
	Total	Males	Females	Total		Males		Females	
				Number	Percent	Number	Percent	Number	Percent
1	2	3	4	5	6	7	8	9	10
1960	1,679 (44)	756 (32)	923 (30)	758 (41)	45.1 (2.1)	408 (30)	54.0 (3.2)	350 (28)	37.9 (2.8)
1961	1,763 (46)	790 (33)	973 (31)	847 (43)	48.0 (2.1)	445 (31)	56.3 (3.1)	402 (30)	41.3 (2.8)
1962	1,838 (44)	872 (32)	966 (30)	900 (43)	49.0 (2.0)	480 (31)	55.0 (3.0)	420 (30)	43.5 (2.8)
1963	1,741 (44)	794 (32)	947 (30)	784 (42)	45.0 (2.1)	415 (30)	52.3 (3.1)	369 (29)	39.0 (2.8)
1964	2,145 (43)	997 (32)	1,148 (28)	1,037 (46)	48.3 (1.9)	570 (33)	57.2 (2.8)	467 (31)	40.7 (2.5)
1965	2,659 (48)	1,254 (35)	1,405 (32)	1,354 (51)	50.9 (1.7)	718 (37)	57.3 (2.5)	636 (36)	45.3 (2.3)
1966	2,612 (45)	1,207 (34)	1,405 (29)	1,309 (50)	50.1 (1.7)	709 (36)	58.7 (2.5)	600 (35)	42.7 (2.3)
1967	2,525 (38)	1,142 (28)	1,383 (24)	1,311 (41)	51.9 (1.4)	658 (29)	57.6 (2.1)	653 (29)	47.2 (1.9)
1968	2,606 (37)	1,184 (28)	1,422 (24)	1,444 (42)	55.4 (1.4)	748 (30)	63.2 (2.0)	696 (29)	48.9 (1.9)
1969	2,842 (36)	1,352 (27)	1,490 (24)	1,516 (43)	53.3 (1.3)	812 (30)	60.1 (1.9)	704 (30)	47.2 (1.8)
1970	2,758 (37)	1,343 (26)	1,415 (27)	1,427 (42)	51.7 (1.4)	741 (30)	55.2 (1.9)	686 (30)	48.5 (1.9)
1971	2,875 (38)	1,371 (27)	1,504 (27)	1,538 (43)	53.5 (1.3)	790 (30)	57.6 (1.9)	749 (31)	49.8 (1.8)
1972	2,964 (38)	1,423 (27)	1,542 (26)	1,459 (43)	49.2 (1.3)	750 (30)	52.7 (1.9)	709 (30)	46.0 (1.8)
1973	3,058 (37)	1,460 (28)	1,599 (25)	1,424 (43)	46.6 (1.3)	730 (31)	50.0 (1.9)	694 (30)	43.4 (1.8)
1974	3,101 (39)	1,491 (28)	1,611 (27)	1,475 (44)	47.6 (1.3)	736 (31)	49.4 (1.8)	740 (31)	45.9 (1.8)
1975	3,185 (39)	1,513 (27)	1,672 (27)	1,615 (45)	50.7 (1.3)	796 (31)	52.6 (1.8)	818 (32)	49.0 (1.7)
1976	2,986 (40)	1,451 (29)	1,535 (27)	1,458 (44)	48.8 (1.3)	685 (30)	47.2 (1.9)	773 (31)	50.3 (1.8)
1977	3,141 (41)	1,483 (30)	1,659 (28)	1,590 (45)	50.6 (1.3)	773 (32)	52.1 (1.9)	817 (32)	49.3 (1.8)
1978	3,163 (40)	1,485 (29)	1,677 (27)	1,585 (45)	50.1 (1.3)	759 (32)	51.1 (1.9)	827 (32)	49.3 (1.8)
1979	3,160 (40)	1,475 (29)	1,685 (27)	1,559 (45)	49.3 (1.3)	744 (31)	50.4 (1.9)	815 (32)	48.4 (1.8)
1980	3,088 (39)	1,498 (28)	1,589 (27)	1,523 (45)	49.3 (1.3)	700 (31)	46.7 (1.9)	823 (32)	51.8 (1.8)
1981	3,056 (42)	1,491 (30)	1,565 (29)	1,648 (46)	53.9 (1.3)	817 (32)	54.8 (1.9)	831 (32)	53.1 (1.8)
1982	3,100 (40)	1,509 (29)	1,592 (28)	1,569 (47)	50.6 (1.4)	741 (33)	49.1 (2.0)	828 (34)	52.0 (1.9)
1983	2,963 (42)	1,389 (30)	1,573 (28)	1,562 (47)	52.7 (1.4)	721 (32)	51.9 (2.0)	841 (34)	53.4 (1.9)
1984	3,012 (37)	1,429 (29)	1,584 (22)	1,663 (46)	55.2 (1.4)	801 (33)	56.0 (2.0)	862 (32)	54.5 (1.9)
1985	2,668 (40)	1,287 (29)	1,381 (28)	1,540 (45)	57.7 (1.4)	755 (32)	58.6 (2.1)	785 (32)	56.8 (2.0)
1986	2,786 (39)	1,332 (28)	1,454 (26)	1,498 (45)	53.8 (1.4)	743 (32)	55.8 (2.1)	755 (32)	51.9 (2.0)
1987	2,647 (41)	1,278 (30)	1,369 (28)	1,503 (45)	56.8 (1.5)	746 (32)	58.3 (2.1)	757 (32)	55.3 (2.0)
1988	2,673 (47)	1,334 (34)	1,339 (32)	1,575 (50)	58.9 (1.6)	761 (36)	57.1 (2.2)	814 (35)	60.7 (2.2)
1989	2,450 (46)	1,204 (33)	1,246 (33)	1,460 (49)	59.6 (1.6)	693 (34)	57.6 (2.4)	767 (35)	61.6 (2.3)
1990	2,362 (43)	1,173 (31)	1,189 (30)	1,420 (46)	60.1 (1.6)	680 (32)	58.0 (2.3)	740 (33)	62.2 (2.2)
1991	2,276 (41)	1,140 (29)	1,136 (29)	1,423 (45)	62.5 (1.6)	660 (31)	57.9 (2.3)	763 (32)	67.1 (2.2)
1992	2,397 (40)	1,216 (29)	1,180 (28)	1,483 (45)	61.9 (1.6)	729 (32)	60.0 (2.2)	754 (32)	63.8 (2.2)
1993	2,342 (41)	1,120 (31)	1,223 (28)	1,467 (45)	62.6 (1.6)	670 (32)	59.9 (2.3)	797 (32)	65.2 (2.2)
1994	2,517 (38)	1,244 (28)	1,273 (26)	1,559 (43)	61.9 (1.4)	754 (31)	60.6 (2.0)	805 (30)	63.2 (2.0)
1995	2,599 (41)	1,238 (30)	1,361 (28)	1,610 (44)	61.9 (1.4)	775 (31)	62.6 (2.0)	835 (31)	61.3 (1.9)
1996	2,660 (41)	1,297 (29)	1,363 (28)	1,729 (46)	65.0 (1.4)	779 (32)	60.1 (2.1)	950 (32)	69.7 (1.9)
1997	2,769 (42)	1,354 (31)	1,415 (28)	1,856 (47)	67.0 (1.4)	860 (34)	63.6 (2.0)	995 (33)	70.3 (1.9)
1998	2,810 (44)	1,452 (31)	1,358 (31)	1,844 (48)	65.6 (1.4)	906 (34)	62.4 (2.0)	938 (34)	69.1 (1.9)
1999	2,897 (42)	1,474 (30)	1,423 (29)	1,822 (48)	62.9 (1.4)	905 (34)	61.4 (2.0)	917 (33)	64.4 (2.0)
2000	2,756 (45)	1,251 (34)	1,505 (30)	1,745 (48)	63.3 (1.4)	749 (33)	59.9 (2.1)	996 (34)	66.2 (1.9)
2001	2,545 (47)	1,275 (34)	1,270 (32)	1,569 (47)	61.7 (1.5)	762 (34)	59.7 (2.1)	808 (33)	63.6 (2.1)
2002	2,796 (45)	1,412 (33)	1,384 (31)	1,824 (49)	65.2 (1.4)	877 (35)	62.1 (2.0)	947 (34)	68.4 (1.9)

[1] Individuals age 16 to 24 who graduated from high school or completed a GED during the preceding 12 months.

[2] Enrollment in college as of October of each year for individuals age 16 to 24 who completed high school during the preceding 12 months.

NOTE: Data are based upon sample surveys of the civilian population. High school graduate data in this table differ from figures appearing in other tables because of varying survey procedures and coverage. High school graduates include GED recipients.

Some data revised from previously published figures. Standard errors appear in parentheses. Detail may not sum to totals due to rounding.

SOURCE: American College Testing Program, unpublished tabulations, derived from statistics collected by the U.S. Bureau of the Census; and U.S. Department of Labor, *College Enrollment of High School Graduates,* various years. (This table was prepared March 2004.)

Total undergraduate fall enrollment in degree-granting institutions, by attendance status, sex of student, and control of institution: 1969 to 2001

[In thousands]

Year	Total	Full-time	Part-time	Men	Women	Men Full-time	Men Part-time	Women Full-time	Women Part-time	Men Public	Men Private	Women Public	Women Private
1	2	3	4	5	6	7	8	9	10	11	12	13	14
Institutions of higher education													
1969	6,884	4,991	1,893	4,008	2,876	2,952	1,056	2,039	837	2,997	1,011	2,162	714
1970	7,376	5,280	2,096	4,254	3,122	3,097	1,157	2,183	939	3,241	1,013	2,387	735
1971	7,743	5,512	2,231	4,418	3,325	3,201	1,217	2,311	1,014	3,427	991	2,580	745
1972	7,941	5,488	2,453	4,429	3,512	3,121	1,308	2,367	1,145	3,467	962	2,756	756
1973	8,261	5,580	2,681	4,538	3,723	3,135	1,403	2,445	1,278	3,579	959	2,943	780
1974	8,798	5,726	3,072	4,765	4,033	3,191	1,574	2,535	1,498	3,799	966	3,232	801
1975	9,679	6,169	3,510	5,257	4,422	3,459	1,798	2,710	1,712	4,245	1,012	3,581	841
1976	9,429	6,030	3,399	4,902	4,527	3,242	1,660	2,788	1,739	3,949	953	3,668	859
1977	9,717	6,094	3,623	4,897	4,820	3,188	1,709	2,906	1,914	3,937	960	3,906	914
1978	9,691	5,967	3,724	4,766	4,925	3,072	1,694	2,895	2,030	3,812	954	3,974	951
1979	9,998	6,080	3,919	4,821	5,178	3,087	1,734	2,993	2,185	3,865	956	4,181	995
1980	10,475	6,362	4,113	5,000	5,475	3,227	1,773	3,135	2,340	4,014	985	4,427	1,048
1981	10,755	6,449	4,306	5,109	5,646	3,261	1,848	3,188	2,458	4,090	1,018	4,558	1,088
1982	10,825	6,484	4,341	5,170	5,655	3,299	1,871	3,184	2,470	4,140	1,031	4,573	1,081
1983	10,846	6,514	4,332	5,158	5,688	3,304	1,854	3,210	2,478	4,117	1,042	4,580	1,107
1984	10,618	6,348	4,270	5,007	5,611	3,195	1,812	3,153	2,459	3,990	1,017	4,504	1,107
1985	10,597	6,320	4,277	4,962	5,635	3,156	1,806	3,163	2,471	3,953	1,010	4,525	1,110
1986	10,798	6,352	4,446	5,018	5,780	3,146	1,871	3,206	2,575	4,002	1,015	4,658	1,122
1987	11,046	6,463	4,584	5,068	5,978	3,164	1,905	3,299	2,679	4,076	992	4,842	1,136
1988	11,317	6,642	4,674	5,138	6,179	3,206	1,931	3,436	2,743	4,113	1,024	4,990	1,189
1989	11,743	6,841	4,902	5,311	6,432	3,279	2,032	3,562	2,869	4,272	1,039	5,216	1,216
1990	11,959	6,976	4,983	5,380	6,579	3,337	2,043	3,639	2,940	4,353	1,027	5,357	1,223
1991	12,439	7,221	5,218	5,571	6,868	3,436	2,135	3,786	3,082	4,531	1,040	5,617	1,251
1992	12,538	7,244	5,293	5,583	6,955	3,425	2,158	3,820	3,135	4,537	1,046	5,679	1,275
1993	12,324	7,179	5,144	5,484	6,840	3,382	2,102	3,797	3,043	4,447	1,036	5,565	1,276
1994	12,263	7,169	5,094	5,422	6,840	3,342	2,081	3,827	3,013	4,394	1,028	5,551	1,290
1995	12,232	7,145	5,086	5,401	6,831	3,297	2,105	3,849	2,982	4,380	1,021	5,524	1,307
1996	12,259	7,211	5,049	5,411	6,848	3,304	2,107	3,907	2,942	4,368	1,043	5,537	1,311
1997	12,298	7,306	4,992	5,405	6,893	3,330	2,075	3,976	2,917	4,385	1,021	5,574	1,319
Degree-granting institutions													
1996	12,327	7,299	5,028	5,421	6,906	3,339	2,082	3,960	2,947	4,383	1,038	5,553	1,354
1997	12,451	7,419	5,032	5,469	6,982	3,380	2,089	4,039	2,943	4,408	1,060	5,599	1,383
1998	12,437	7,539	4,898	5,446	6,991	3,428	2,018	4,111	2,880	4,361	1,085	5,589	1,402
1999	12,681	7,735	4,946	5,559	7,122	3,516	2,044	4,219	2,903	4,431	1,128	5,679	1,443
2000	13,155	7,923	5,232	5,778	7,377	3,588	2,190	4,335	3,042	4,622	1,156	5,917	1,460
2001	13,716	8,328	5,388	6,004	7,711	3,769	2,236	4,559	3,152	4,804	1,200	6,182	1,529

NOTE: Data include unclassified undergraduate students. Trend tabulations of institutions of higher education data are based on institutions that were accredited by an agency or association that was recognized by the U.S. Department of Education, or recognized directly by the Secretary of Education. The new degree-granting classification is very similar to the earlier higher education classification, except that it includes some additional institutions, primarily 2-year colleges, and excludes a few higher education institutions that did not award degrees. Data for 1999 were imputed using alternative methods. (See *Guide to Sources* for details.) Detail may not sum to totals due to rounding.

SOURCE: U.S. Department of Education, National Center for Education Statistics, Higher Education General Information Survey (HEGIS), "Fall Enrollment in Colleges and Universities" surveys, 1969 through 1985; and Integrated Postsecondary Education Data System (IPEDS), "Fall Enrollment" surveys, 1986 through 1999, and Spring 2001 and Spring 2002 surveys. (This table was prepared August 2003.)

Total graduate fall enrollment in degree-granting institutions, by attendance status, sex of student, and control of institution: 1969 to 2001

[In thousands]

Year	Total	Full-time	Part-time	Men	Women	Men Full-time	Men Part-time	Women Full-time	Women Part-time	Men Public	Men Private	Women Public	Women Private
1	2	3	4	5	6	7	8	9	10	11	12	13	14
Institutions of higher education													
1969	955	363	593	590	366	252	338	111	255	393	197	273	93
1970	1,031	379	651	630	400	264	366	115	285	423	207	301	99
1971	1,012	388	621	615	394	269	346	119	275	415	200	296	100
1972	1,066	394	671	626	439	268	358	126	313	427	199	330	109
1973	1,123	410	715	648	477	273	375	137	340	442	206	358	119
1974	1,190	427	762	663	526	276	387	151	375	454	209	398	128
1975	1,263	453	810	700	563	290	410	163	400	481	219	425	138
1976	1,333	463	870	714	619	287	427	176	443	477	237	454	165
1977	1,319	473	845	700	617	289	411	184	434	458	243	443	174
1978	1,312	468	844	682	630	280	402	188	442	441	241	453	177
1979	1,309	476	833	669	640	280	389	196	444	427	242	457	182
1980	1,343	485	860	675	670	281	394	204	466	426	247	474	195
1981	1,343	484	859	674	669	277	397	207	462	419	255	468	201
1982	1,322	485	838	670	653	280	390	205	447	417	253	453	200
1983	1,340	497	843	677	663	286	391	211	452	418	259	454	209
1984	1,345	501	844	672	673	286	386	215	459	411	261	459	215
1985	1,376	509	867	677	700	289	388	220	479	414	263	477	223
1986	1,435	522	913	693	742	294	399	228	514	433	260	508	234
1987	1,452	527	925	693	759	294	400	233	525	429	264	516	243
1988	1,472	553	919	697	774	304	393	249	526	429	268	520	254
1989	1,522	572	949	710	811	309	401	263	548	437	273	541	271
1990	1,586	599	987	737	849	321	416	278	571	456	281	567	282
1991	1,639	642	997	761	878	341	419	300	578	471	290	580	299
1992	1,669	666	1,003	772	896	351	421	314	582	474	298	584	313
1993	1,688	688	1,000	771	917	355	416	334	584	473	298	590	327
1994	1,721	706	1,016	776	946	359	417	347	598	472	304	603	343
1995	1,732	717	1,015	768	965	356	412	361	604	464	304	610	355
1996	1,743	736	1,007	760	983	358	403	378	604	456	305	613	370
1997	1,751	750	1,000	756	994	359	398	392	603	452	304	618	377
Degree-granting institutions													
1996	1,742	737	1,005	759	983	358	401	379	604	456	303	613	370
1997	1,753	752	1,001	758	996	360	398	393	603	452	306	618	377
1998	1,768	754	1,014	754	1,013	355	399	398	615	444	310	623	390
1999	1,807	781	1,026	766	1,041	363	403	418	623	446	320	630	411
2000	1,850	813	1,037	780	1,071	377	402	436	635	447	332	642	428
2001	1,904	843	1,061	796	1,108	388	408	455	653	460	336	659	449

NOTE: Data include unclassified graduate students. Trend tabulations of institutions of higher education data are based on institutions that were accredited by an agency or association that was recognized by the U.S. Department of Education, or recognized directly by the Secretary of Education. The new degree-granting classification is very similar to the earlier higher education classification, except that it includes some additional institutions, primarily 2-year colleges, and excludes a few higher education institutions that did not award degrees. Data for 1999 were imputed using alternative methods. (See *Guide to Sources* for details.) Detail may not sum to totals due to rounding.

SOURCE: U.S. Department of Education, National Center for Education Statistics, Higher Education General Information Survey (HEGIS), "Fall Enrollment in Colleges and Universities" surveys, 1969 through 1985; and Integrated Postsecondary Education Data System (IPEDS), "Fall Enrollment" surveys, 1986 through 1999, and Spring 2001 and Spring 2002 surveys. (This table was prepared August 2003.)

Total fall enrollment in degree-granting institutions by state or jurisdiction: Selected years, 1970 to 2001

State or jurisdiction	Institutions of higher education [1]				Degree-granting institutions [2]						
	Fall 1970	Fall 1980	Fall 1990	Fall 1995	Fall 1996	Fall 1997	Fall 1998	Fall 1999 [3]	Fall 2000	Fall 2001	Percent change, 1996 to 2001
1	2	3	4	5	6	7	8	9	10	11	12
United States	**8,580,887**	**12,096,895**	**13,818,637**	**14,261,781**	**14,367,520**	**14,502,334**	**14,506,967**	**14,791,224**	**15,312,289**	**15,927,987**	**10.9**
Alabama	103,936	164,306	218,589	225,612	220,711	218,785	216,241	223,144	233,962	236,146	7.0
Alaska	9,471	21,296	29,833	29,348	28,806	27,915	27,652	26,948	27,953	27,756	−3.6
Arizona	109,619	202,716	264,148	273,981	288,036	292,730	302,123	326,159	342,490	366,485	27.2
Arkansas	52,039	77,607	90,425	98,180	108,636	112,342	113,751	115,092	115,172	122,282	12.6
California	1,257,245	1,790,993	1,808,740	1,817,042	1,900,099	1,958,200	1,949,508	2,017,483	2,256,708	2,380,090	25.3
Colorado	123,395	162,916	227,131	242,739	245,112	252,245	257,247	261,744	263,872	269,292	9.9
Connecticut	124,700	159,632	168,604	157,695	154,139	153,128	153,336	156,907	161,243	165,027	7.1
Delaware	25,260	32,939	42,004	44,307	44,838	44,890	46,260	46,613	43,897	47,104	5.1
District of Columbia	77,158	86,675	79,551	77,277	74,460	72,397	72,388	72,118	72,689	87,252	17.2
Florida	235,525	411,891	588,086	637,303	645,832	658,259	661,187	684,745	707,684	753,554	16.7
Georgia	126,511	184,159	251,786	314,712	300,795	306,238	303,685	311,812	346,204	376,098	25.0
Hawaii	36,562	47,181	56,436	63,198	62,844	61,514	61,615	62,578	60,182	62,079	−1.2
Idaho	34,567	43,018	51,881	59,566	60,411	61,641	63,085	64,661	65,594	69,674	15.3
Illinois	452,146	644,245	729,246	717,854	721,133	726,199	729,084	733,182	743,918	748,444	3.8
Indiana	192,668	247,253	284,832	289,615	290,184	295,517	299,176	304,725	314,334	338,715	16.7
Iowa	108,902	140,449	170,515	173,835	178,860	180,967	181,944	186,780	188,974	194,822	8.9
Kansas	102,485	136,605	163,733	177,643	173,865	177,544	177,561	176,737	179,968	184,943	6.4
Kentucky	98,591	143,066	177,852	178,858	178,904	178,924	180,550	181,626	188,341	214,839	20.1
Louisiana	120,728	160,058	186,840	203,935	213,993	219,196	221,110	221,348	223,800	228,871	7.0
Maine	34,134	43,264	57,186	56,547	56,017	56,368	56,986	57,822	58,473	61,127	9.1
Maryland	149,607	225,526	259,700	266,310	260,757	261,262	265,173	268,820	273,745	288,224	10.5
Massachusetts	303,809	418,415	417,833	413,794	411,676	412,620	415,501	419,695	421,142	425,071	3.3
Michigan	392,726	520,131	569,803	548,339	547,629	549,742	557,011	558,998	567,631	585,998	7.0
Minnesota	160,788	206,691	253,789	280,816	284,964	269,887	271,612	282,756	293,445	308,233	8.2
Mississippi	73,967	102,364	122,883	122,690	126,027	130,561	132,438	133,170	137,389	137,882	9.4
Missouri	183,930	234,421	289,899	291,536	293,584	302,896	310,507	317,480	321,348	331,580	12.9
Montana	30,062	35,177	35,876	42,674	43,550	44,141	44,150	43,114	42,240	44,932	3.2
Nebraska	66,915	89,488	112,831	115,718	120,689	111,542	111,123	110,806	112,117	113,817	−5.7
Nevada	13,669	40,455	61,728	67,826	73,970	76,417	83,120	89,711	87,893	93,368	26.2
New Hampshire	29,400	46,794	59,510	64,327	64,396	63,811	60,784	63,366	61,718	65,031	1.0
New Jersey	216,121	321,610	324,286	333,831	328,143	325,754	325,885	330,537	335,945	346,507	5.6
New Mexico	44,461	58,283	85,500	102,405	106,662	108,560	108,810	111,896	110,739	112,861	5.8
New York	806,479	992,237	1,048,286	1,041,566	1,028,351	1,024,498	1,014,220	1,020,991	1,043,395	1,057,794	2.9
North Carolina	171,925	287,537	352,138	372,030	372,993	373,717	387,407	395,907	404,652	427,784	14.7
North Dakota	31,495	34,069	37,878	40,399	41,142	38,937	39,441	40,348	40,248	42,843	4.1
Ohio	376,267	489,145	557,690	540,275	544,371	537,169	542,077	548,545	549,553	569,223	4.6
Oklahoma	110,155	160,295	173,221	180,676	177,166	177,157	178,507	179,055	178,016	189,785	7.1
Oregon	122,177	157,458	165,741	167,145	166,662	169,852	171,056	175,635	183,065	191,378	14.8
Pennsylvania	411,044	507,716	604,060	617,759	587,447	588,185	595,749	605,283	609,521	630,299	7.3
Rhode Island	45,898	66,869	78,273	74,100	72,432	72,078	73,970	74,821	75,450	77,235	6.6
South Carolina	69,518	132,476	159,302	174,125	174,303	176,278	181,353	183,626	185,931	191,590	9.9
South Dakota	30,639	32,761	34,208	36,695	39,820	39,042	41,545	42,147	43,221	45,534	14.3
Tennessee	135,103	204,581	226,238	245,962	247,637	249,805	251,319	252,915	263,910	258,534	4.4
Texas	442,225	701,391	901,437	952,525	959,698	969,283	978,550	990,587	1,033,973	1,076,678	12.2
Utah	81,687	93,987	121,303	147,324	152,262	157,891	151,232	161,591	163,776	177,045	16.3
Vermont	22,209	30,628	36,398	35,065	35,779	36,482	37,054	36,728	35,489	36,351	1.6
Virginia	151,915	280,504	353,442	355,919	355,190	364,904	370,142	377,970	381,893	389,853	9.8
Washington	183,544	303,603	263,384	285,819	303,450	315,281	298,974	306,723	320,840	325,132	7.1
West Virginia	63,153	81,973	84,790	86,034	87,099	87,965	88,107	88,657	87,888	91,319	4.8
Wisconsin	202,058	269,086	299,774	300,223	299,522	298,248	301,963	304,776	307,179	315,850	5.5
Wyoming	15,220	21,147	31,326	30,176	30,805	30,280	29,707	29,002	30,004	31,095	0.9
U.S. Service Schools [4]	17,079	49,808	48,692	88,451	81,669	83,090	13,991	13,344	13,475	14,561	−82.2
Outlying areas	**67,237**	**137,749**	**164,618**	**183,657**	**182,536**	**178,154**	**181,244**	**185,244**	**194,633**	**201,642**	**10.5**
American Samoa	0	976	1,219	1,232	1,239	1,248	909	1,172	297	1,178	−4.9
Federated States of Micronesia	0	224	975	1,296	1,396	1,372	772	1,506	1,576	2,243	60.7
Guam	2,719	3,217	4,741	6,010	5,335	5,533	5,758	5,727	5,215	4,869	−8.7
Marshall Islands	0	0	0	418	431	459	513	616	328	220	−49.0
Northern Marianas	0	0	661	959	1,096	1,136	1,239	1,080	1,078	982	−10.4
Palau	0	0	491	351	332	330	424	569	581	579	74.4
Puerto Rico	63,073	131,184	154,065	170,337	169,809	165,466	168,983	171,832	183,290	188,430	11.0
Virgin Islands	1,445	2,148	2,466	3,054	2,898	2,610	2,646	2,742	2,268	3,141	8.4

[1] Institutions that were accredited by an agency or association that was recognized by the U.S. Department of Education, or recognized directly by the Secretary of Education.

[2] Data are for 4-year and 2-year degree-granting institutions that participated in Title IV federal financial aid programs.

[3] Data were imputed using alternative procedures. (See Guide to Sources for details.)

[4] Data for 1998 and later years reflect substantial changes in survey coverage.

SOURCE: U.S. Department of Education, National Center for Education Statistics, Higher Education General Information Survey (HEGIS), "Fall Enrollment in Colleges and Universities" surveys, 1970 and 1980; and Integrated Postsecondary Education Data System (IPEDS), "Fall Enrollment" surveys, 1990 through 1999, and Spring 2001 and Spring 2002 surveys. (This table was prepared August 2003.)

533

Total fall enrollment in public degree-granting institutions, by state or jurisdiction: Selected years, 1970 to 2001

State or jurisdiction	Institutions of higher education [1]				Degree-granting institutions [2]						Percent change, 1996 to 2001
	Fall 1970	Fall 1980	Fall 1990	Fall 1995	Fall 1996	Fall 1997	Fall 1998	Fall 1999 [3]	Fall 2000	Fall 2001	
1	2	3	4	5	6	7	8	9	10	11	12
United States	6,428,134	9,457,394	10,844,717	11,092,374	11,120,499	11,196,119	11,137,769	11,309,399	11,752,786	12,233,156	10.0
Alabama	87,884	143,674	195,939	203,165	196,531	193,974	190,685	197,173	207,435	208,385	6.0
Alaska	8,563	20,561	27,792	28,368	27,828	26,717	26,296	25,687	26,559	26,550	−4.6
Arizona	107,315	194,034	248,213	254,530	259,163	260,832	268,102	276,268	284,522	294,174	13.5
Arkansas	43,599	66,068	78,645	87,067	97,405	100,855	102,264	103,326	101,775	108,950	11.9
California	1,123,529	1,599,838	1,594,710	1,564,230	1,625,021	1,664,478	1,646,329	1,692,607	1,927,771	2,043,182	25.7
Colorado	108,562	145,598	200,653	210,312	209,183	213,475	216,351	219,436	217,897	222,815	6.5
Connecticut	73,391	97,788	109,556	100,539	96,336	95,041	94,299	96,834	101,027	104,066	8.0
Delaware	21,151	28,325	34,252	36,204	36,579	36,495	37,362	36,895	34,194	36,510	−0.2
District of Columbia	12,194	13,900	11,990	9,663	7,736	4,887	5,410	5,349	5,499	5,589	−27.8
Florida	189,450	334,349	489,081	530,607	529,422	534,721	531,921	540,967	556,912	588,921	11.2
Georgia	101,900	140,158	196,413	248,682	230,204	235,011	229,928	237,411	271,755	298,215	29.5
Hawaii	32,963	43,269	45,728	50,198	47,370	45,542	45,270	46,479	44,579	45,994	−2.9
Idaho	27,072	34,491	41,315	48,986	49,806	50,233	51,330	52,615	53,751	56,673	13.8
Illinois	315,634	491,274	551,333	530,248	532,470	536,578	533,294	533,522	534,155	534,280	0.3
Indiana	136,739	189,224	223,953	224,795	220,967	224,522	228,450	230,810	240,023	259,258	17.3
Iowa	68,390	97,454	117,834	122,396	125,923	128,073	129,302	133,753	135,008	140,227	11.4
Kansas	88,215	121,987	149,117	160,449	156,446	159,955	158,594	157,088	159,976	164,173	4.9
Kentucky	77,240	114,884	147,095	148,808	147,423	146,295	146,344	146,558	151,973	178,349	21.0
Louisiana	101,127	136,703	158,290	174,873	185,223	189,179	189,896	188,573	189,213	194,790	5.2
Maine	25,405	31,878	41,500	38,195	38,260	38,010	38,636	40,349	40,662	42,425	10.9
Maryland	118,988	195,051	220,783	222,857	217,277	217,250	219,055	220,809	223,797	236,795	9.0
Massachusetts	116,127	183,765	186,035	176,777	173,854	174,694	178,376	181,514	183,248	186,891	7.5
Michigan	339,625	454,147	487,359	462,390	458,989	458,561	462,580	461,825	467,861	482,154	5.0
Minnesota	130,567	162,379	199,211	217,249	213,284	203,088	200,422	207,474	218,617	225,941	5.9
Mississippi	64,968	90,661	109,038	110,600	114,905	118,847	120,831	121,369	125,355	125,656	9.4
Missouri	132,540	165,179	200,093	189,993	189,851	190,608	194,462	199,324	201,509	206,721	8.9
Montana	27,287	31,178	31,865	37,435	38,000	38,702	38,768	38,336	37,387	39,368	3.6
Nebraska	51,454	73,509	94,614	95,599	99,717	89,414	89,040	88,386	88,531	89,639	−10.1
Nevada	13,576	40,280	61,242	66,683	71,925	73,309	79,147	85,270	83,120	86,790	20.7
New Hampshire	15,979	24,119	32,163	36,069	36,365	35,259	32,187	34,927	35,870	37,224	2.4
New Jersey	145,373	247,028	261,601	271,069	264,596	261,365	260,092	263,752	266,921	275,655	4.2
New Mexico	40,795	55,077	83,403	97,220	99,918	100,708	101,150	103,125	101,450	103,758	3.8
New York	449,437	563,251	616,884	588,491	572,482	567,893	567,202	566,306	583,417	584,607	2.1
North Carolina	123,761	228,154	285,405	303,099	302,939	302,033	314,110	321,311	329,422	350,684	15.8
North Dakota	30,192	31,709	34,690	36,810	36,765	35,037	35,264	35,940	36,014	38,560	4.9
Ohio	281,099	381,765	427,613	409,818	407,108	404,694	408,487	411,541	411,161	425,265	4.5
Oklahoma	91,438	137,188	151,073	158,026	154,381	154,572	155,796	155,361	153,699	163,336	5.8
Oregon	108,483	140,102	144,427	143,617	141,429	144,342	144,326	148,177	154,756	162,645	15.0
Pennsylvania	232,982	292,499	343,478	339,928	335,181	334,901	338,047	336,930	339,229	353,950	5.6
Rhode Island	25,527	35,052	42,350	38,653	37,487	37,251	38,368	38,650	38,458	39,149	4.4
South Carolina	47,101	107,683	131,134	148,706	148,363	148,694	152,542	153,496	155,519	158,661	6.9
South Dakota	23,936	24,328	26,596	29,693	32,861	32,863	34,088	34,197	34,857	37,310	13.5
Tennessee	98,897	156,835	175,049	193,136	194,138	193,516	193,393	193,646	202,530	194,696	0.3
Texas	365,522	613,552	802,314	836,851	838,943	845,686	849,075	862,271	896,534	935,826	11.5
Utah	49,588	59,598	86,108	110,560	113,696	118,619	111,315	120,558	123,046	133,790	17.7
Vermont	12,536	17,984	20,910	20,470	20,139	20,540	20,549	20,580	20,021	20,480	1.7
Virginia	123,279	246,500	291,286	293,127	292,412	301,594	305,455	311,536	313,780	326,758	11.7
Washington	162,718	276,028	227,632	246,635	262,359	274,705	257,047	263,415	273,928	277,023	5.6
West Virginia	51,363	71,228	74,108	74,857	75,116	76,078	76,322	76,777	76,136	78,304	4.2
Wisconsin	170,374	235,179	253,529	245,770	245,060	243,858	247,462	249,608	249,737	257,888	5.2
Wyoming	15,220	21,121	30,623	29,420	29,994	29,475	28,757	27,944	28,715	29,545	−1.5
U.S. Service Schools [4]	17,079	49,808	48,692	88,451	81,669	83,090	13,991	13,344	13,475	14,561	−82.2
Outlying areas	46,680	60,692	66,244	77,050	79,083	80,715	82,537	83,919	84,464	85,535	8.2
American Samoa	0	976	1,219	1,232	1,239	1,248	909	1,172	297	1,178	−4.9
Federated States of Micronesia	0	224	975	1,296	1,396	1,372	772	1,506	1,576	2,243	60.7
Guam	2,719	3,217	4,741	6,010	5,335	5,533	5,758	5,727	5,215	4,869	−8.7
Marshall Islands	0	0	0	418	431	459	513	616	328	220	−49.0
Northern Marianas	0	0	661	959	1,096	1,136	1,239	1,080	1,078	982	−10.4
Palau	0	0	491	351	332	330	424	569	581	579	74.4
Puerto Rico	42,516	54,127	55,691	63,730	66,356	68,027	70,276	70,507	73,121	73,173	10.3
Virgin Islands	1,445	2,148	2,466	3,054	2,898	2,610	2,646	2,742	2,268	2,291	−20.9

[1] Institutions that were accredited by an agency or association that was recognized by the U.S. Department of Education, or recognized directly by the Secretary of Education.
[2] Data are for 4-year and 2-year degree-granting institutions that participated in Title IV federal financial aid programs.
[3] Data were imputed using alternative procedures. (See Guide to Sources for details.)
[4] Data for 1998 and later years reflect substantial changes in survey coverage.

SOURCE: U.S. Department of Education, National Center for Education Statistics, Higher Education General Information Survey (HEGIS), "Fall Enrollment in Colleges and Universities" surveys, 1970 and 1980; and Integrated Postsecondary Education Data System (IPEDS), "Fall Enrollment" surveys, 1990 through 1999, and Spring 2001 and Spring 2002 surveys. (This table was prepared August 2003.)

Total fall enrollment in private degree-granting institutions, by state or jurisdiction: Selected years, 1970 to 2001

State or jurisdiction	Institutions of higher education [1]				Degree-granting institutions [2]						Percent change, 1996 to 2001
	Fall 1970	Fall 1980	Fall 1990	Fall 1995	Fall 1996	Fall 1997	Fall 1998	Fall 1999 [3]	Fall 2000	Fall 2001	
1	2	3	4	5	6	7	8	9	10	11	12
United States	**2,152,753**	**2,639,501**	**2,973,920**	**3,169,407**	**3,247,021**	**3,306,215**	**3,369,198**	**3,481,825**	**3,559,503**	**3,694,831**	**13.8**
Alabama	16,052	20,632	22,650	22,447	24,180	24,811	25,556	25,971	26,527	27,761	14.8
Alaska	908	735	2,041	980	978	1,198	1,356	1,261	1,394	1,206	23.3
Arizona	2,304	8,682	15,935	19,451	28,873	31,898	34,021	49,891	57,968	72,311	150.4
Arkansas	8,440	11,539	11,780	11,113	11,231	11,487	11,487	11,766	13,397	13,332	18.7
California	133,716	191,155	214,030	252,812	275,078	293,722	303,179	324,876	328,937	336,908	22.5
Colorado	14,833	17,318	26,478	32,427	35,929	38,770	40,896	42,308	45,975	46,477	29.4
Connecticut	51,309	61,844	59,048	57,156	57,803	58,087	59,037	60,073	60,216	60,961	5.5
Delaware	4,109	4,614	7,752	8,103	8,259	8,395	8,898	9,718	9,703	10,594	28.3
District of Columbia	64,964	72,775	67,561	67,614	66,724	67,510	66,978	66,769	67,190	81,663	22.4
Florida	46,075	77,542	99,005	106,696	116,410	123,538	129,266	143,778	150,772	164,633	41.4
Georgia	24,611	44,001	55,373	66,030	70,591	71,227	73,757	74,401	74,449	77,883	10.3
Hawaii	3,599	3,912	10,708	13,000	15,474	15,972	16,345	16,099	15,603	16,085	3.9
Idaho	7,495	8,527	10,566	10,580	10,605	11,408	11,755	12,046	11,843	13,001	22.6
Illinois	136,512	152,971	177,913	187,606	188,663	189,621	195,790	199,660	209,763	214,164	13.5
Indiana	55,929	58,029	60,879	64,820	69,217	70,995	70,726	73,915	74,311	79,457	14.8
Iowa	40,512	42,995	52,681	51,439	52,937	52,894	52,642	53,027	53,966	54,595	3.1
Kansas	14,270	14,618	14,616	17,194	17,419	17,589	18,967	19,649	19,992	20,770	19.2
Kentucky	21,351	28,182	30,757	30,050	31,481	32,629	34,206	35,068	36,368	36,490	15.9
Louisiana	19,601	23,355	28,550	29,062	28,770	30,017	31,214	32,775	34,587	34,081	18.5
Maine	8,729	11,386	15,686	18,352	17,757	18,358	18,350	17,473	17,811	18,702	5.3
Maryland	30,619	30,475	38,917	43,453	43,480	44,012	46,118	48,011	49,948	51,429	18.3
Massachusetts	187,682	234,650	231,798	237,017	237,822	237,926	237,125	238,181	237,894	238,180	0.2
Michigan	53,101	65,984	82,444	85,949	88,640	91,181	94,431	97,173	99,770	103,844	17.2
Minnesota	30,221	44,312	54,578	63,567	71,680	66,799	71,190	75,282	74,828	82,292	14.8
Mississippi	8,999	11,703	13,845	12,090	11,122	11,714	11,607	11,801	12,034	12,226	9.9
Missouri	51,390	69,242	89,806	101,543	103,733	112,288	116,045	118,156	119,839	124,859	20.4
Montana	2,775	3,999	4,011	5,239	5,550	5,439	5,382	4,778	4,853	5,564	0.3
Nebraska	15,461	15,979	18,217	20,119	20,972	22,128	22,083	22,420	23,586	24,178	15.3
Nevada	93	175	486	1,143	2,045	3,108	3,973	4,441	4,773	6,578	221.7
New Hampshire	13,421	22,675	27,347	28,258	28,031	28,552	28,597	28,439	25,848	27,807	−0.8
New Jersey	70,748	74,582	62,685	62,762	63,547	64,389	65,793	66,785	69,024	70,852	11.5
New Mexico	3,666	3,206	2,097	5,185	6,744	7,852	7,660	8,771	9,289	9,103	35.0
New York	357,042	428,986	431,402	453,075	455,869	456,605	447,018	454,685	459,978	473,187	3.8
North Carolina	48,164	59,383	66,733	68,931	70,054	71,684	73,297	74,596	75,230	77,100	10.1
North Dakota	1,303	2,360	3,188	3,589	4,377	3,900	4,177	4,408	4,234	4,283	−2.1
Ohio	95,168	107,380	130,077	130,457	137,263	132,475	133,590	137,004	138,392	143,958	4.9
Oklahoma	18,717	23,107	22,148	22,650	22,785	22,585	22,711	23,694	24,317	26,449	16.1
Oregon	13,694	17,356	21,314	23,528	25,233	25,510	26,730	27,458	28,309	28,733	13.9
Pennsylvania	178,062	215,217	260,582	277,831	252,266	253,284	257,702	268,353	270,292	276,349	9.5
Rhode Island	20,371	31,817	35,923	35,447	34,945	34,827	35,602	36,171	36,992	38,086	9.0
South Carolina	22,417	24,793	28,168	25,419	25,940	27,584	28,811	30,130	30,412	32,929	26.9
South Dakota	6,703	8,433	7,612	7,002	6,959	6,179	7,457	7,950	8,364	8,224	18.2
Tennessee	36,206	47,746	51,189	52,826	53,499	56,289	57,926	59,269	61,380	63,838	19.3
Texas	76,703	87,839	99,123	115,674	120,755	123,597	129,475	128,316	137,439	140,852	16.6
Utah	32,099	34,389	35,195	36,764	38,566	39,272	39,917	41,033	40,730	43,255	12.2
Vermont	9,673	12,644	15,488	14,595	15,640	15,942	16,505	16,148	15,468	15,871	1.5
Virginia	28,636	34,004	62,156	62,792	62,778	63,310	64,687	66,434	68,113	63,095	0.5
Washington	20,826	27,575	35,752	39,184	41,091	40,576	41,927	43,308	46,912	48,109	17.1
West Virginia	11,790	10,745	10,682	11,177	11,983	11,887	11,785	11,880	11,752	13,015	8.6
Wisconsin	31,684	33,907	46,245	54,453	54,462	54,390	54,501	55,168	57,442	57,962	6.4
Wyoming	0	26	703	756	811	805	950	1,058	1,289	1,550	91.1
Outlying areas	**20,557**	**77,057**	**98,374**	**106,607**	**103,453**	**97,439**	**98,707**	**101,325**	**110,169**	**116,107**	**11.4**
American Samoa	0	0	0	0	0	0	0	0	0	0	†
Federated States of Micronesia	0	0	0	0	0	0	0	0	0	0	†
Guam	0	0	0	0	0	0	0	0	0	0	†
Marshall Islands	0	0	0	0	0	0	0	0	0	0	†
Northern Marianas	0	0	0	0	0	0	0	0	0	0	†
Palau	0	0	0	0	0	0	0	0	0	0	†
Puerto Rico	20,557	77,057	98,374	106,607	103,453	97,439	98,707	101,325	110,169	115,257	11.4
Virgin Islands	0	0	0	0	0	0	0	0	0	850	†

† Not applicable.

[1] Institutions that were accredited by an agency or association that was recognized by the U.S. Department of Education, or recognized directly by the Secretary of Education.

[2] Data are for 4-year and 2-year degree-granting institutions that participated in Title IV federal financial aid programs.

[3] Data were imputed using alternative procedures. (See Guide to Sources for details.)

SOURCE: U.S. Department of Education, National Center for Education Statistics, Higher Education General Information Survey (HEGIS), "Fall Enrollment in Colleges and Universities" surveys, 1970 and 1980; and Integrated Postsecondary Education Data System (IPEDS), "Fall Enrollment" surveys, 1990 through 1999, and Spring 2001 and Spring 2002 surveys. (This table was prepared August 2003.)

Total fall enrollment in all degree-granting institutions, by attendance status, sex, and state or jurisdiction: 2000 and 2001

State or jurisdiction	Fall 2000					Fall 2001				
	Total	Full-time		Part-time		Total	Full-time		Part-time	
		Men	Women	Men	Women		Men	Women	Men	Women
1	2	3	4	5	6	7	8	9	10	11
United States	15,312,289	4,111,093	4,898,507	2,610,676	3,692,013	15,927,987	4,299,890	5,147,612	2,660,925	3,819,560
Alabama	233,962	67,698	87,437	32,625	46,202	236,146	68,967	88,840	32,177	46,162
Alaska	27,953	4,972	6,120	6,249	10,612	27,756	5,108	6,382	5,954	10,312
Arizona	342,490	80,237	82,962	75,531	103,760	366,485	89,645	97,221	74,053	105,566
Arkansas	115,172	33,663	44,778	14,236	22,495	122,282	34,922	46,487	15,804	25,069
California	2,256,708	474,814	578,823	535,032	668,039	2,380,090	501,915	613,370	563,150	701,655
Colorado	263,872	69,218	75,994	51,576	67,084	269,292	69,912	78,537	50,892	69,951
Connecticut	161,243	42,573	50,474	26,979	41,217	165,027	44,032	52,981	26,403	41,611
Delaware	43,897	12,002	16,350	5,496	10,049	47,104	12,410	16,952	6,464	11,278
District of Columbia	72,689	21,831	29,089	9,001	12,768	87,252	23,960	31,770	13,184	18,338
Florida	707,684	163,860	200,850	139,766	203,208	753,554	176,028	219,054	145,165	213,307
Georgia	346,204	99,097	124,694	48,303	74,110	376,098	106,003	135,456	52,929	81,710
Hawaii	60,182	16,416	20,675	9,963	13,128	62,079	16,413	21,112	10,557	13,997
Idaho	65,594	20,421	23,831	8,838	12,504	69,674	22,195	24,755	9,159	13,565
Illinois	743,918	184,758	213,345	141,716	204,099	748,444	187,707	218,762	139,038	202,937
Indiana	314,334	100,792	112,355	44,521	56,666	338,715	104,904	117,962	49,204	66,645
Iowa	188,974	62,886	69,248	22,707	34,133	194,822	64,819	71,697	23,620	34,686
Kansas	179,968	49,046	53,116	31,242	46,564	184,943	50,761	54,989	31,891	47,302
Kentucky	188,341	54,713	71,769	23,206	38,653	214,839	59,107	77,780	33,175	44,777
Louisiana	223,800	68,557	91,389	25,089	38,765	228,871	70,127	95,171	24,583	38,990
Maine	58,473	15,037	18,917	7,980	16,539	61,127	15,831	19,752	8,024	17,520
Maryland	273,745	62,820	78,312	50,152	82,461	288,224	66,274	82,536	52,834	86,580
Massachusetts	421,142	123,735	149,124	58,388	89,895	425,071	126,082	152,121	57,295	89,573
Michigan	567,631	138,966	169,279	107,807	151,579	585,998	146,596	179,468	106,577	153,357
Minnesota	293,445	85,015	97,977	48,868	61,585	308,233	90,259	104,684	47,717	65,573
Mississippi	137,389	43,101	57,606	13,197	23,485	137,882	45,043	61,979	10,726	20,134
Missouri	321,348	85,877	101,640	54,246	79,585	331,580	89,526	106,247	54,407	81,400
Montana	42,240	15,572	16,612	4,002	6,054	44,932	16,358	17,713	4,189	6,672
Nebraska	112,117	33,789	37,611	16,770	23,947	113,817	34,709	38,554	16,855	23,699
Nevada	87,893	14,753	18,429	23,667	31,044	93,368	16,616	21,721	23,718	31,313
New Hampshire	61,718	18,060	22,263	8,164	13,231	65,031	19,253	23,269	8,592	13,917
New Jersey	335,945	89,255	104,464	56,390	85,836	346,507	92,876	108,894	56,369	88,368
New Mexico	110,739	26,121	33,090	19,972	31,556	112,861	26,871	34,246	19,729	32,015
New York	1,043,395	310,984	386,912	130,201	215,298	1,057,794	321,297	399,430	124,836	212,231
North Carolina	404,652	110,582	141,602	59,693	92,775	427,784	117,829	152,358	60,726	96,871
North Dakota	40,248	16,508	15,727	3,430	4,583	42,843	17,502	16,369	3,818	5,154
Ohio	549,553	163,067	192,787	78,624	115,075	569,223	170,775	201,794	79,198	117,456
Oklahoma	178,016	54,273	59,281	26,735	37,727	189,785	57,926	63,834	27,698	40,327
Oregon	183,065	47,511	54,702	35,835	45,017	191,378	51,351	58,595	35,494	45,938
Pennsylvania	609,521	204,216	231,026	68,247	106,032	630,299	211,248	237,374	69,487	112,190
Rhode Island	75,450	23,620	26,864	9,531	15,435	77,235	24,468	28,193	9,204	15,370
South Carolina	185,931	52,308	67,636	24,255	41,732	191,590	53,412	70,398	24,230	43,550
South Dakota	43,221	14,217	15,443	4,874	8,687	45,534	14,603	15,819	5,241	9,871
Tennessee	263,910	78,876	99,630	34,379	51,025	258,534	79,674	101,182	30,390	47,288
Texas	1,033,973	269,098	310,096	195,780	258,999	1,076,678	281,344	326,638	198,149	270,547
Utah	163,776	51,621	50,481	30,972	30,702	177,045	56,308	52,972	34,151	33,614
Vermont	35,489	11,949	13,394	3,641	6,505	36,351	12,388	13,667	3,630	6,666
Virginia	381,893	98,046	121,508	65,784	96,555	389,853	101,492	125,280	65,780	97,301
Washington	320,840	87,841	103,680	54,827	74,492	325,132	90,872	107,673	51,980	74,607
West Virginia	87,888	30,018	33,636	9,191	15,043	91,319	31,074	35,221	9,764	15,260
Wisconsin	307,179	86,812	104,845	48,261	67,261	315,850	90,052	109,278	47,894	68,626
Wyoming	30,004	8,447	8,603	4,737	8,217	31,095	8,823	8,737	4,821	8,714
U.S. Service Schools	13,475	11,444	2,031	0	0	14,561	12,223	2,338	0	0
Outlying areas	194,633	58,071	89,604	19,148	27,810	201,642	60,953	93,378	18,828	28,483
American Samoa	297	69	103	47	78	1,178	269	388	182	339
Federated States of Micronesia	1,576	529	644	218	185	2,243	706	879	321	337
Guam	5,215	971	1,674	1,045	1,525	4,869	910	1,568	1,011	1,380
Marshall Islands	328	38	46	140	104	220	103	109	6	2
Northern Marianas	1,078	210	310	222	336	982	135	282	222	343
Palau	581	167	217	78	119	579	167	217	77	118
Puerto Rico	183,290	55,822	85,742	17,149	24,577	188,430	57,620	89,009	16,774	25,027
Virgin Islands	2,268	265	868	249	886	3,141	1,043	926	235	937

NOTE: Data are for 4-year and 2-year degree-granting institutions that participated in Title IV federal financial aid programs.

SOURCE: U.S. Department of Education, National Center for Education Statistics, Integrated Postsecondary Education Data System (IPEDS), Spring 2001 and Spring 2002 surveys. (This table was prepared August 2003.)

Total fall enrollment in public degree-granting institutions, by attendance status, sex and state or jurisdiction: 2000 and 2001

State or jurisdiction	Fall 2000					Fall 2001				
	Total	Full-time		Part-time		Total	Full-time		Part-time	
		Men	Women	Men	Women		Men	Women	Men	Women
1	2	3	4	5	6	7	8	9	10	11
United States	**11,752,786**	**2,899,900**	**3,471,326**	**2,232,507**	**3,149,053**	**12,233,156**	**3,043,734**	**3,643,971**	**2,283,877**	**3,261,574**
Alabama	207,435	57,839	74,666	31,028	43,902	208,385	58,998	75,372	30,556	43,459
Alaska	26,559	4,633	5,748	5,935	10,243	26,550	4,846	5,964	5,719	10,021
Arizona	284,522	52,866	61,626	70,981	99,049	294,174	56,452	64,971	71,480	101,271
Arkansas	101,775	28,477	38,090	13,609	21,599	108,950	29,578	40,078	15,212	24,082
California	1,927,771	353,280	444,427	501,518	628,546	2,043,182	378,231	472,245	530,200	662,506
Colorado	217,897	53,879	60,178	44,360	59,480	222,815	55,914	62,994	42,916	60,991
Connecticut	101,027	22,645	26,614	20,096	31,672	104,066	23,759	28,476	19,809	32,022
Delaware	34,194	10,049	13,634	3,876	6,635	36,510	10,373	13,899	4,653	7,585
District of Columbia	5,499	794	1,143	1,244	2,318	5,589	806	1,149	1,285	2,349
Florida	556,912	113,752	145,907	118,127	179,126	588,921	121,864	157,015	122,273	187,769
Georgia	271,755	72,412	90,879	42,265	66,199	298,215	78,434	98,732	47,306	73,743
Hawaii	44,579	11,342	13,893	8,157	11,187	45,994	11,589	14,246	8,313	11,846
Idaho	53,751	15,669	17,437	8,507	12,138	56,673	16,709	18,015	8,833	13,116
Illinois	534,155	119,060	136,320	114,200	164,575	534,280	120,597	139,265	112,324	162,094
Indiana	240,023	71,985	79,094	40,395	48,549	259,258	75,176	82,350	44,268	57,464
Iowa	135,008	44,624	46,587	18,398	25,399	140,227	46,154	48,186	19,240	26,647
Kansas	159,976	42,817	45,777	29,047	42,335	164,173	44,288	47,285	29,616	42,984
Kentucky	151,973	42,469	56,479	19,891	33,134	178,349	47,130	61,689	30,151	39,379
Louisiana	189,213	57,040	75,711	21,897	34,565	194,790	59,108	78,358	22,500	34,824
Maine	40,662	10,237	12,298	6,459	11,668	42,425	10,615	12,735	6,542	12,533
Maryland	223,797	50,462	62,472	41,988	68,875	236,795	52,990	66,081	44,108	73,616
Massachusetts	183,248	42,967	51,890	33,728	54,663	186,891	44,831	54,128	33,401	54,531
Michigan	467,861	113,752	133,762	92,857	127,490	482,154	120,128	140,967	91,568	129,491
Minnesota	218,617	61,088	67,068	40,938	49,523	225,941	64,856	70,588	39,304	51,193
Mississippi	125,355	39,545	51,723	12,421	21,666	125,656	41,397	55,861	9,975	18,423
Missouri	201,509	51,854	62,961	33,316	53,378	206,721	54,228	65,303	33,442	53,748
Montana	37,387	14,319	14,705	3,350	5,013	39,368	14,800	15,481	3,557	5,530
Nebraska	88,531	25,286	27,086	15,227	20,932	89,639	25,935	27,929	15,186	20,589
Nevada	83,120	12,914	15,981	23,551	30,674	86,790	14,536	18,066	23,544	30,644
New Hampshire	35,870	9,302	11,923	5,772	8,873	37,224	9,774	12,194	5,914	9,342
New Jersey	266,921	66,545	81,793	46,576	72,007	275,655	69,231	85,242	46,626	74,556
New Mexico	101,450	22,840	29,044	19,209	30,357	103,758	23,599	30,042	19,145	30,972
New York	583,417	157,724	199,159	85,585	140,949	584,607	161,581	203,973	81,477	137,576
North Carolina	329,422	81,900	105,989	55,597	85,936	350,684	88,997	116,322	56,009	89,356
North Dakota	36,014	14,927	13,480	3,325	4,282	38,560	15,878	14,033	3,720	4,929
Ohio	411,161	115,127	136,867	65,542	93,625	425,265	121,176	143,402	65,650	95,037
Oklahoma	153,699	43,622	49,387	24,907	35,783	163,336	46,559	53,316	25,392	38,069
Oregon	154,756	37,478	41,868	33,398	42,012	162,645	40,860	45,455	33,442	42,888
Pennsylvania	339,229	109,621	121,745	42,640	65,223	353,950	113,888	126,197	43,857	70,008
Rhode Island	38,458	8,236	11,794	6,377	12,051	39,149	8,504	12,252	6,254	12,139
South Carolina	155,519	41,611	53,185	22,328	38,395	158,661	41,943	54,195	22,455	40,068
South Dakota	34,857	11,897	11,972	3,843	7,145	37,310	12,477	12,342	4,189	8,302
Tennessee	202,530	54,652	70,835	31,151	45,892	194,696	54,684	70,978	27,124	41,910
Texas	896,534	220,548	259,303	177,633	239,050	935,826	231,188	273,657	180,771	250,210
Utah	123,046	34,375	32,812	27,944	27,915	133,790	38,178	34,823	30,393	30,396
Vermont	20,021	5,979	6,838	2,511	4,693	20,480	6,065	7,051	2,484	4,880
Virginia	313,780	76,731	93,059	57,765	86,225	326,758	79,690	97,002	60,506	89,560
Washington	273,928	74,182	85,130	47,695	66,921	277,023	76,398	88,545	45,321	66,759
West Virginia	76,136	25,835	27,595	8,707	13,999	78,304	26,396	28,594	9,204	14,110
Wisconsin	249,737	70,097	82,771	41,899	54,970	257,888	72,829	85,874	41,842	57,343
Wyoming	28,715	7,171	8,590	4,737	8,217	29,545	7,294	8,716	4,821	8,714
US Service Schools	13,475	11,444	2,031	0	0	14,561	12,223	2,338	0	0
Outlying areas	**84,464**	**25,652**	**41,037**	**6,613**	**11,162**	**85,535**	**25,520**	**41,377**	**6,979**	**11,659**
American Samoa	297	69	103	47	78	1,178	269	388	182	339
Federated States of Micronesia	1,576	529	644	218	185	2,243	706	879	321	337
Guam	5,215	971	1,674	1,045	1,525	4,869	910	1,568	1,011	1,380
Marshall Islands	328	38	46	140	104	220	103	109	6	2
Northern Marianas	1,078	210	310	222	336	982	135	282	222	343
Palau	581	167	217	78	119	579	167	217	77	118
Puerto Rico	73,121	23,403	37,175	4,614	7,929	73,173	22,954	37,091	4,925	8,203
Virgin Islands	2,268	265	868	249	886	2,291	276	843	235	937

NOTE: Data are for 4-year and 2-year degree-granting institutions that participated in Title IV federal financial aid programs.

SOURCE: U.S. Department of Education, National Center for Education Statistics, Integrated Postsecondary Education Data System (IPEDS), Spring 2001 and Spring 2002 surveys. (This table was prepared August 2003.)

Total fall enrollment in private degree-granting institutions, by attendance status, sex and state or jurisdiction: 2000 and 2001

State or jurisdiction	Fall 2000					Fall 2001				
	Total	Full-time		Part-time		Total	Full-time		Part-time	
		Men	Women	Men	Women		Men	Women	Men	Women
1	2	3	4	5	6	7	8	9	10	11
United States	**3,559,503**	**1,211,193**	**1,427,181**	**378,169**	**542,960**	**3,694,831**	**1,256,156**	**1,503,641**	**377,048**	**557,986**
Alabama	26,527	9,859	12,771	1,597	2,300	27,761	9,969	13,468	1,621	2,703
Alaska	1,394	339	372	314	369	1,206	262	418	235	291
Arizona	57,968	27,371	21,336	4,550	4,711	72,311	33,193	32,250	2,573	4,295
Arkansas	13,397	5,186	6,688	627	896	13,332	5,344	6,409	592	987
California	328,937	121,534	134,396	33,514	39,493	336,908	123,684	141,125	32,950	39,149
Colorado	45,975	15,339	15,816	7,216	7,604	46,477	13,998	15,543	7,976	8,960
Connecticut	60,216	19,928	23,860	6,883	9,545	60,961	20,273	24,505	6,594	9,589
Delaware	9,703	1,953	2,716	1,620	3,414	10,594	2,037	3,053	1,811	3,693
District of Columbia	67,190	21,037	27,946	7,757	10,450	81,663	23,154	30,621	11,899	15,989
Florida	150,772	50,108	54,943	21,639	24,082	164,633	54,164	62,039	22,892	25,538
Georgia	74,449	26,685	33,815	6,038	7,911	77,883	27,569	36,724	5,623	7,967
Hawaii	15,603	5,074	6,782	1,806	1,941	16,085	4,824	6,866	2,244	2,151
Idaho	11,843	4,752	6,394	331	366	13,001	5,486	6,740	326	449
Illinois	209,763	65,698	77,025	27,516	39,524	214,164	67,110	79,497	26,714	40,843
Indiana	74,311	28,807	33,261	4,126	8,117	79,457	29,728	35,612	4,936	9,181
Iowa	53,966	18,262	22,661	4,309	8,734	54,595	18,665	23,511	4,380	8,039
Kansas	19,992	6,229	7,339	2,195	4,229	20,770	6,473	7,704	2,275	4,318
Kentucky	36,368	12,244	15,290	3,315	5,519	36,490	11,977	16,091	3,024	5,398
Louisiana	34,587	11,517	15,678	3,192	4,200	34,081	11,019	16,813	2,083	4,166
Maine	17,811	4,800	6,619	1,521	4,871	18,702	5,216	7,017	1,482	4,987
Maryland	49,948	12,358	15,840	8,164	13,586	51,429	13,284	16,455	8,726	12,964
Massachusetts	237,894	80,768	97,234	24,660	35,232	238,180	81,251	97,993	23,894	35,042
Michigan	99,770	25,214	35,517	14,950	24,089	103,844	26,468	38,501	15,009	23,866
Minnesota	74,828	23,927	30,909	7,930	12,062	82,292	25,403	34,096	8,413	14,380
Mississippi	12,034	3,556	5,883	776	1,819	12,226	3,646	6,118	751	1,711
Missouri	110,839	34,023	38,679	20,930	26,207	124,859	35,298	40,944	20,965	27,652
Montana	4,853	1,253	1,907	652	1,041	5,564	1,558	2,232	632	1,142
Nebraska	23,586	8,503	10,525	1,543	3,015	24,178	8,774	10,625	1,669	3,110
Nevada	4,773	1,839	2,448	116	370	6,578	2,080	3,655	174	669
New Hampshire	25,848	8,758	10,340	2,392	4,358	27,807	9,479	11,075	2,678	4,575
New Jersey	69,024	22,710	22,671	9,814	13,829	70,852	23,645	23,652	9,743	13,812
New Mexico	9,289	3,281	4,046	763	1,199	9,103	3,272	4,204	584	1,043
New York	459,978	153,260	187,753	44,616	74,349	473,187	159,716	195,457	43,359	74,655
North Carolina	75,230	28,682	35,613	4,096	6,839	77,100	28,832	36,036	4,717	7,515
North Dakota	4,234	1,581	2,247	105	301	4,283	1,624	2,336	98	225
Ohio	138,392	47,940	55,920	13,082	21,450	143,958	49,599	58,392	13,548	22,419
Oklahoma	24,317	10,651	9,894	1,828	1,944	26,449	11,367	10,518	2,306	2,258
Oregon	28,309	10,033	12,834	2,437	3,005	28,733	10,491	13,140	2,052	3,050
Pennsylvania	270,292	94,595	109,281	25,607	40,809	276,349	97,360	111,177	25,630	42,182
Rhode Island	36,992	15,384	15,070	3,154	3,384	38,086	15,964	15,941	2,950	3,231
South Carolina	30,412	10,697	14,451	1,927	3,337	32,929	11,469	16,203	1,775	3,482
South Dakota	8,364	2,320	3,471	1,031	1,542	8,224	2,126	3,477	1,052	1,569
Tennessee	61,380	24,224	28,795	3,228	5,133	63,838	24,990	30,204	3,266	5,378
Texas	137,439	48,550	50,793	18,147	19,949	140,852	50,156	52,981	17,378	20,337
Utah	40,730	17,246	17,669	3,028	2,787	43,255	18,130	18,149	3,758	3,218
Vermont	15,468	5,970	6,556	1,130	1,812	15,871	6,323	6,616	1,146	1,786
Virginia	68,113	21,315	28,449	8,019	10,330	63,095	21,802	28,278	5,274	7,741
Washington	46,912	13,659	18,550	7,132	7,571	48,109	14,474	19,128	6,659	7,848
West Virginia	11,752	4,183	6,041	484	1,044	13,015	4,678	6,627	560	1,150
Wisconsin	57,442	16,715	22,074	6,362	12,291	57,962	17,223	23,404	6,052	11,283
Wyoming	1,289	1,276	13	0	0	1,550	1,529	21	0	0
Outlying areas	**110,169**	**32,419**	**48,567**	**12,535**	**16,648**	**116,107**	**35,433**	**52,001**	**11,849**	**16,824**
American Samoa	0	0	0	0	0	0	0	0	0	0
Federated States of Micronesia	0	0	0	0	0	0	0	0	0	0
Guam	0	0	0	0	0	0	0	0	0	0
Marshall Islands	0	0	0	0	0	0	0	0	0	0
Northern Marianas	0	0	0	0	0	0	0	0	0	0
Palau	0	0	0	0	0	0	0	0	0	0
Puerto Rico	110,169	32,419	48,567	12,535	16,648	115,257	34,666	51,918	11,849	16,824
Virgin Islands	0	0	0	0	0	850	767	83	0	0

NOTE: Data are for 4-year and 2-year degree-granting institutions that participated in Title IV federal financial aid programs.

SOURCE: U.S. Department of Education, National Center for Education Statistics, Integrated Postsecondary Education Data System (IPEDS), Spring 2001 and Spring 2002 surveys. (This table was prepared August 2003.)

Fall enrollment in degree-granting institutions, by race/ethnicity of student and state or jurisdiction: 2001

State or jurisdiction	Total	White, non-His-panic	Minority enrollment, by race/ethnicity					Non-resident alien	Percentage distribution of students							
			Total	Black, non-His-panic	Hispanic	Asian/ Pacific Islander	American Indian/ Alaska Native		Total	White, non-His-panic	Minority by race/ethnicity of students					Non-resi-dent alien
											Total	Black, non-His-panic	His-panic	Asian/ Pa-cific Is-lander	Amer-ican Indian/ Alaska Native	
1	2	3	4	5	6	7	8	9	10	11	12	13	14	15	16	17
United States	15,927,987	10,774,519	4,588,206	1,850,420	1,560,587	1,019,048	158,151	565,262	100.0	67.6	28.8	11.6	9.8	6.4	1.0	3.5
Alabama	236,146	157,489	72,583	65,280	2,475	3,055	1,773	6,074	100.0	66.7	30.7	27.6	1.0	1.3	0.8	2.6
Alaska	27,756	20,356	6,594	998	884	1,134	3,578	806	100.0	73.3	23.8	3.6	3.2	4.1	12.9	2.9
Arizona	366,485	252,108	103,778	16,027	59,736	13,450	14,565	10,599	100.0	68.8	28.3	4.4	16.3	3.7	4.0	2.9
Arkansas	122,282	93,970	25,499	21,008	1,711	1,579	1,201	2,813	100.0	76.8	20.9	17.2	1.4	1.3	1.0	2.3
California	2,380,090	1,096,589	1,207,781	178,091	574,549	430,861	24,280	75,720	100.0	46.1	50.7	7.5	24.1	18.1	1.0	3.2
Colorado	269,292	209,578	52,824	11,217	27,699	10,089	3,819	6,890	100.0	77.8	19.6	4.2	10.3	3.7	1.4	2.6
Connecticut	165,027	123,921	34,083	15,545	11,330	6,581	627	7,023	100.0	75.1	20.7	9.4	6.9	4.0	0.4	4.3
Delaware	47,104	35,067	10,936	8,179	1,341	1,210	206	1,101	100.0	74.4	23.2	17.4	2.8	2.6	0.4	2.3
District of Columbia	87,252	41,516	36,832	27,112	3,834	5,653	233	8,904	100.0	47.6	42.2	31.1	4.4	6.5	0.3	10.2
Florida	753,554	448,234	276,392	125,505	122,615	24,880	3,392	28,928	100.0	59.5	36.7	16.7	16.3	3.3	0.5	3.8
Georgia	376,098	232,837	131,789	110,516	7,338	12,831	1,104	11,472	100.0	61.9	35.0	29.4	2.0	3.4	0.3	3.1
Hawaii	62,079	15,948	40,767	1,747	1,792	36,909	319	5,364	100.0	25.7	65.7	2.8	2.9	59.5	0.5	8.6
Idaho	69,674	62,741	5,251	529	2,595	1,149	978	1,682	100.0	90.0	7.5	0.8	3.7	1.6	1.4	2.4
Illinois	748,444	493,721	230,786	99,984	83,860	44,581	2,361	23,937	100.0	66.0	30.8	13.4	11.2	6.0	0.3	3.2
Indiana	338,715	283,793	41,929	26,176	8,511	5,996	1,246	12,993	100.0	83.8	12.4	7.7	2.5	1.8	0.4	3.8
Iowa	194,822	171,005	15,647	6,219	4,017	4,472	939	8,170	100.0	87.8	8.0	3.2	2.1	2.3	0.5	4.2
Kansas	184,943	154,191	24,080	9,743	6,915	4,582	2,840	6,672	100.0	83.4	13.0	5.3	3.7	2.5	1.5	3.6
Kentucky	214,839	187,946	22,688	17,648	1,926	2,456	658	4,205	100.0	87.5	10.6	8.2	0.9	1.1	0.3	2.0
Louisiana	228,871	144,650	77,830	66,193	5,352	4,806	1,479	6,391	100.0	63.2	34.0	28.9	2.3	2.1	0.6	2.8
Maine	61,127	56,393	3,350	930	739	919	762	1,384	100.0	92.3	5.5	1.5	1.2	1.5	1.2	2.3
Maryland	288,224	173,274	102,387	74,165	9,367	17,739	1,116	12,563	100.0	60.1	35.5	25.7	3.2	6.2	0.4	4.4
Massachusetts	425,071	312,647	83,956	29,731	23,118	29,239	1,868	28,468	100.0	73.6	19.8	7.0	5.4	6.9	0.4	6.7
Michigan	585,998	453,825	106,985	69,655	14,056	18,638	4,636	25,188	100.0	77.4	18.3	11.9	2.4	3.2	0.8	4.3
Minnesota	308,233	264,997	33,920	13,872	4,875	11,554	3,619	9,316	100.0	86.0	11.0	4.5	1.6	3.7	1.2	3.0
Mississippi	137,882	84,419	51,433	48,888	870	1,085	590	2,030	100.0	61.2	37.3	35.5	0.6	0.8	0.4	1.5
Missouri	331,580	269,035	52,442	35,273	7,456	7,702	2,011	10,103	100.0	81.1	15.8	10.6	2.2	2.3	0.6	3.0
Montana	44,932	38,584	5,497	330	719	384	4,064	851	100.0	85.9	12.2	0.7	1.6	0.9	9.0	1.9
Nebraska	113,817	99,716	10,606	4,133	2,892	2,706	875	3,495	100.0	87.6	9.3	3.6	2.5	2.4	0.8	3.1
Nevada	93,368	63,118	28,012	7,113	11,196	8,206	1,497	2,238	100.0	67.6	30.0	7.6	12.0	8.8	1.6	2.4
New Hampshire	65,031	58,969	4,335	1,247	1,415	1,363	310	1,727	100.0	90.7	6.7	1.9	2.2	2.1	0.5	2.7
New Jersey	346,507	213,982	116,918	46,232	41,698	27,950	1,038	15,607	100.0	61.8	33.7	13.3	12.0	8.1	0.3	4.5
New Mexico	112,861	49,811	61,132	3,178	45,764	2,476	9,714	1,918	100.0	44.1	54.2	2.8	40.5	2.2	8.6	1.7
New York	1,057,794	661,498	337,773	144,170	111,302	78,543	3,758	58,523	100.0	62.5	31.9	13.6	10.5	7.4	0.4	5.5
North Carolina	427,784	298,827	117,883	94,954	8,302	9,618	5,009	11,074	100.0	69.9	27.6	22.2	1.9	2.2	1.2	2.6
North Dakota	42,843	37,982	3,556	504	314	366	2,372	1,305	100.0	88.7	8.3	1.2	0.7	0.9	5.5	3.0
Ohio	569,223	466,724	85,151	60,573	9,772	12,755	2,051	17,348	100.0	82.0	15.0	10.6	1.7	2.2	0.4	3.0
Oklahoma	189,785	137,130	43,677	15,802	5,933	4,489	17,453	8,978	100.0	72.3	23.0	8.3	3.1	2.4	9.2	4.7
Oregon	191,378	157,613	27,353	4,108	7,701	12,387	3,157	6,412	100.0	82.4	14.3	2.1	4.0	6.5	1.6	3.4
Pennsylvania	630,299	508,268	100,291	58,298	15,111	25,164	1,718	21,740	100.0	80.6	15.9	9.2	2.4	4.0	0.3	3.4
Rhode Island	77,235	61,984	12,289	4,313	4,394	3,246	336	2,962	100.0	80.3	15.9	5.6	5.7	4.2	0.4	3.8
South Carolina	191,590	130,386	57,458	51,648	2,517	2,676	617	3,746	100.0	68.1	30.0	27.0	1.3	1.4	0.3	2.0
South Dakota	45,534	40,378	4,276	455	374	293	3,154	880	100.0	88.7	9.4	1.0	0.8	0.6	6.9	1.9
Tennessee	258,534	197,569	54,974	46,206	3,507	4,509	932	5,991	100.0	76.4	21.3	17.8	1.4	1.7	0.4	2.3
Texas	1,076,678	598,471	434,717	121,090	254,848	53,182	5,597	43,490	100.0	55.6	40.4	11.2	23.7	4.9	0.5	4.0
Utah	177,045	158,038	13,607	1,122	6,166	4,649	1,670	5,400	100.0	89.3	7.7	0.6	3.5	2.6	0.9	3.1
Vermont	36,351	33,328	2,159	550	736	679	194	864	100.0	91.7	5.9	1.5	2.0	1.9	0.5	2.4
Virginia	389,853	272,762	105,524	71,242	11,844	20,321	2,117	11,567	100.0	70.0	27.1	18.3	3.0	5.2	0.5	3.0
Washington	325,132	250,677	64,175	12,987	14,911	30,262	6,015	10,280	100.0	77.1	19.7	4.0	4.6	9.3	1.9	3.2
West Virginia	91,319	82,780	6,367	4,327	711	966	363	2,172	100.0	90.6	7.0	4.7	0.8	1.1	0.4	2.4
Wisconsin	315,850	275,572	32,943	14,588	7,377	7,749	3,229	7,335	100.0	87.2	10.4	4.6	2.3	2.5	1.0	2.3
Wyoming	31,095	28,413	2,243	274	1,146	255	568	439	100.0	91.4	7.2	0.9	3.7	0.8	1.8	1.4
U.S. Service Schools	14,561	11,689	2,748	925	976	704	143	124	100.0	80.3	18.9	6.4	6.7	4.8	1.0	0.9
Outlying areas	201,642	1,474	199,595	2,009	188,166	9,395	25	573	100.0	0.7	99.0	1.0	93.3	4.7	0.0	0.3
American Samoa	1,178	3	1,036	0	1	1,034	1	139	100.0	0.3	87.9	0.0	0.1	87.8	0.1	11.8
Federated States of Micronesia	2,243	0	2,243	0	0	2,243	0	0	100.0	0.0	100.0	0.0	0.0	100.0	0.0	0.0
Guam	4,869	330	4,435	38	40	4,352	5	104	100.0	6.8	91.1	0.8	0.8	89.4	0.1	2.1
Marshall Islands	220	0	220	0	0	220	0	0	100.0	0.0	100.0	0.0	0.0	100.0	0.0	0.0
Northern Marianas	982	37	873	4	4	865	0	72	100.0	3.8	88.9	0.4	0.4	88.1	0.0	7.3
Palau	579	0	579	1	0	578	0	0	100.0	0.0	100.0	0.2	0.0	99.8	0.0	0.0
Puerto Rico	188,430	254	188,080	29	187,989	51	11	96	100.0	0.1	99.8	#	99.8	#	#	0.1
Virgin Islands	3,141	850	2,129	1,937	132	52	8	162	100.0	27.1	67.8	61.7	4.2	1.7	0.3	5.2

Rounds to zero.

NOTE: Data are for 4-year and 2-year degree-granting institutions that were partici-pating in Title IV federal financial aid programs. Detail may not sum to totals due to rounding.

SOURCE: U.S. Department of Education, National Center for Education Statistics, In-tegrated Postsecondary Education Data System (IPEDS), Spring 2002. (This table was prepared September 2003.)

Average salary of full-time instructional faculty on 9-month contracts in degree-granting institutions, by academic rank, sex, and type and control of institution: Selected years, 1980–81 to 2001–02

Academic year and type and control of institution	All faculty	Academic rank						Sex	
		Professor	Associate professor	Assistant professor	Instructor	Lecturer	No academic rank	Men	Women
1	2	3	4	5	6	7	8	9	10
1980–81									
All institutions	$23,302	$30,753	$23,214	$18,901	$15,178	$17,301	$22,334	$24,499	$19,996
4-year	23,693	31,016	23,265	18,867	15,056	17,375	17,380	24,909	19,809
University	25,949	33,622	24,392	19,684	15,530	17,327	17,856	27,206	20,736
Other 4-year	22,230	28,798	22,558	18,398	14,887	17,425	17,334	23,271	19,372
2-year	21,898	26,528	22,750	19,166	15,621	16,222	22,615	22,736	20,434
Public institutions	23,745	31,077	23,772	19,431	15,613	17,620	22,820	24,873	20,673
4-year	24,373	31,442	23,898	19,442	15,486	17,712	19,240	25,509	20,608
University	25,571	32,945	24,268	19,637	15,305	17,426	17,358	26,788	20,564
Other 4-year	23,500	30,097	23,639	19,315	15,567	17,997	19,798	24,499	20,633
2-year	22,177	26,880	22,947	19,370	15,928	16,458	22,875	22,965	20,778
Private institutions	22,093	29,994	21,833	17,767	14,192	15,899	15,946	23,493	18,073
4-year	22,325	30,089	21,887	17,816	14,316	15,971	16,706	23,669	18,326
University	26,897	35,227	24,730	19,792	16,197	16,956	18,933	28,251	21,176
Other 4-year	19,996	26,173	20,502	16,939	13,905	14,741	16,617	21,040	17,342
2-year	15,065	18,645	17,685	14,663	12,155	12,441	14,993	16,075	13,892
1990–91									
All institutions	42,165	55,540	41,414	34,434	26,332	30,097	36,395	45,065	35,881
4-year	43,693	56,485	41,811	34,657	25,772	30,209	31,494	46,519	36,574
University	49,430	63,437	44,877	37,838	27,105	31,748	31,533	52,426	39,788
Other 4-year	40,313	51,467	39,994	33,020	25,370	29,009	31,488	42,660	35,135
2-year	36,642	44,916	37,650	32,253	27,933	28,048	36,752	38,465	34,224
Public institutions	42,317	55,371	42,101	35,137	26,907	29,881	36,990	45,084	36,459
4-year	44,510	56,668	42,742	35,520	26,134	29,956	32,349	47,168	37,573
University	47,499	60,536	43,851	36,889	25,647	30,429	30,412	50,405	38,363
Other 4-year	42,499	53,704	41,969	34,680	26,316	29,664	33,507	44,804	37,147
2-year	37,055	45,411	38,051	32,673	28,389	28,780	37,096	38,787	34,720
Private institutions	41,788	55,911	39,983	33,116	24,928	30,864	28,523	45,019	34,359
4-year	42,224	56,127	40,122	33,235	25,159	31,053	31,122	45,319	34,898
University	53,875	69,732	47,405	40,013	31,239	34,444	36,211	56,989	43,273
Other 4-year	36,888	47,405	36,965	30,688	23,973	25,416	30,915	39,162	32,251
2-year	24,088	29,520	26,353	24,587	20,911	—	23,187	25,937	22,585
1995–96									
All institutions	49,309	64,540	47,966	39,696	30,344	34,136	42,996	52,814	42,871
4-year	51,044	65,866	48,432	39,991	29,941	34,082	35,657	54,520	43,702
University	58,173	74,650	51,993	43,838	30,689	35,272	36,818	61,972	48,011
Other 4-year	46,946	59,599	46,356	38,179	29,718	33,140	35,470	49,726	41,773
2-year	43,009	51,454	43,107	36,927	31,421	35,165	43,537	44,944	40,791
Public institutions	48,837	63,189	48,122	40,092	30,581	33,634	43,590	52,163	42,871
4-year	51,172	64,946	48,815	40,562	29,907	33,525	36,829	54,448	43,986
University	55,068	69,924	50,186	42,335	29,186	34,139	35,532	58,648	45,676
Other 4-year	48,566	61,076	47,850	39,544	30,178	33,134	37,266	51,375	43,063
2-year	43,295	51,679	43,389	37,241	31,805	35,244	43,754	45,209	41,086
Private institutions	50,466	67,457	47,654	38,964	29,701	35,792	34,599	54,364	42,871
4-year	50,819	67,598	47,760	39,071	30,002	35,810	35,098	54,649	43,236
University	65,405	84,970	56,517	47,387	35,782	37,516	38,649	69,579	53,717
Other 4-year	44,504	57,089	44,186	36,325	28,993	33,170	34,771	47,126	39,982
2-year	31,915	37,929	33,283	29,887	23,895	—	33,410	33,301	30,671
1999–2000									
All institutions	55,888	74,410	54,524	44,978	34,918	38,194	47,389	60,084	48,997
4-year	58,087	76,419	55,198	45,312	33,950	38,124	40,452	62,348	50,124
University	67,507	88,079	59,996	50,678	35,465	40,306	44,591	72,363	56,060
Other 4-year	52,716	67,985	52,404	42,902	33,479	36,295	39,851	55,908	47,454
2-year	48,012	57,677	47,844	41,730	37,433	39,928	48,012	49,819	46,096
Public institutions	55,011	72,475	54,641	45,285	35,007	37,403	47,990	58,984	48,714
4-year	57,950	75,204	55,681	45,822	33,528	37,261	40,579	62,030	50,168
University	63,595	82,344	57,984	48,671	33,230	38,576	41,147	68,135	53,216
Other 4-year	54,255	69,641	54,062	44,293	33,641	36,351	40,430	57,618	48,527
2-year	48,240	57,806	48,056	41,984	37,634	40,061	48,233	50,033	46,340
Private institutions	58,013	78,490	54,295	44,410	34,641	40,652	39,630	62,631	49,737
4-year	58,323	78,582	54,384	44,494	34,809	40,674	40,381	62,905	50,052
University	76,132	99,634	64,782	55,232	43,456	43,822	49,454	81,418	62,787
Other 4-year	50,415	65,277	50,087	40,971	33,197	36,056	39,572	53,271	45,926
2-year	35,925	39,454	36,349	31,499	27,178	25,965	37,532	38,636	32,951
2001–02									
All institutions	59,742	80,792	58,724	48,796	46,959	41,798	46,569	64,320	52,662
4-year	62,404	83,265	59,637	49,287	37,187	41,545	50,238	67,126	54,094
University	72,822	96,478	65,179	55,498	38,404	43,273	62,378	78,355	60,651
Other 4-year	56,384	73,571	56,436	46,461	36,810	40,117	42,130	59,801	51,067
2-year	50,636	60,415	50,206	44,168	52,273	45,479	45,675	52,164	49,088
Public institutions	58,524	78,387	58,663	48,956	48,279	40,809	46,772	62,835	52,123
4-year	62,013	81,726	60,041	49,697	36,820	40,361	53,777	66,577	53,895
University	68,510	89,888	62,886	53,138	36,733	41,300	64,351	73,658	57,585
Other 4-year	57,724	75,268	58,059	47,859	36,855	39,754	40,080	61,402	51,875
2-year	50,837	60,614	50,436	44,487	52,505	45,610	45,756	52,360	49,290
Private institutions	62,818	85,848	58,845	48,489	37,517	44,762	44,391	67,871	54,149
4-year	63,088	85,997	58,955	48,605	37,934	44,794	45,121	68,100	54,434
University	82,487	109,721	70,639	60,874	45,536	46,714	52,528	88,508	68,109
Other 4-year	54,331	70,811	54,159	44,435	36,735	41,697	43,674	57,294	49,867
2-year	33,139	39,811	37,879	30,892	30,404	23,484	32,985	33,395	32,921

—Not available

NOTE: Data for 1980–81 to 1995–96 are for institutions of higher education. Institutions of higher education were accredited by an agency or association that was recognized by the U.S. Department of Education, or recognized directly by the Secretary of Education. The new degree-granting classification is very similar to the earlier higher education classification, except that it includes some additional institutions, primarily 2-year colleges, and excludes a few higher education institutions that did not award associate or higher degrees.

SOURCE: U.S. Department of Education, National Center for Education Statistics, Higher Education General Information Survey (HEGIS), "Faculty Salaries, Tenure, and Fringe Benefits, 1980–81;" and Integrated Postsecondary Education Data System (IPEDS), "Salaries, Tenure, and Fringe Benefits of Full-Time Instructional Faculty" surveys, 1990–91, 1995–96, 1999–2000, and Winter 2001–02. (This table was prepared September 2003.)

Average salary of full-time instructional faculty on 9-month contracts in degree-granting institutions, by type and control of institution and state or jurisdiction: 2001–02

State or jurisdiction	All institutions	Public institutions					Private institutions				
		Total	4-year institutions			2-year	Total	4-year institutions			2-year
			Total	University	Other 4-year			Total	University	Other 4-year	
1	2	3	4	5	6	7	8	9	10	11	12
United States	$59,742	$58,524	$62,013	$68,510	$57,724	$50,837	$62,818	$63,088	$82,487	$54,331	$33,139
Alabama	49,572	50,250	53,084	58,687	49,466	43,501	46,039	46,412	†	46,412	28,249
Alaska	52,206	52,723	52,627	53,861	51,839	64,859	43,763	43,763	†	43,763	†
Arizona	61,190	61,586	65,830	69,758	54,526	54,662	50,850	50,850	†	50,850	†
Arkansas	46,128	46,220	49,667	60,322	46,636	36,777	45,628	45,867	†	45,867	25,435
California	70,342	69,973	75,180	95,519	71,292	64,334	71,992	72,145	89,713	62,348	47,338
Colorado	56,869	56,342	60,175	69,804	53,021	40,567	60,731	60,731	64,457	56,506	†
Connecticut	71,234	69,002	72,397	82,386	63,445	58,973	73,553	73,858	97,740	63,713	30,808
Delaware	67,193	67,880	70,844	73,271	54,496	52,119	60,140	60,140	†	60,140	†
District of Columbia	71,377	60,196	60,196	†	60,196	†	71,905	71,905	73,977	55,634	†
Florida	55,597	55,543	60,924	68,933	56,858	47,767	55,787	55,787	67,760	51,814	†
Georgia	56,926	57,112	59,747	69,740	57,486	43,685	56,408	57,098	89,687	48,490	37,709
Hawaii	57,401	57,364	62,403	64,829	49,895	49,071	57,555	57,555	†	57,555	†
Idaho	49,638	50,210	51,584	56,468	49,463	42,817	43,904	43,904	†	43,904	†
Illinois	62,075	59,507	61,528	65,788	57,643	55,782	66,423	66,581	87,658	52,845	32,172
Indiana	57,521	57,003	60,211	64,270	52,144	39,284	58,600	58,847	87,233	49,838	35,585
Iowa	54,857	60,129	67,947	71,935	56,549	40,431	46,269	46,314	56,174	45,145	22,478
Kansas	50,727	53,006	58,029	61,642	50,019	41,210	36,874	37,485	†	37,485	28,367
Kentucky	51,104	52,720	55,263	64,494	49,752	43,801	44,913	45,217	†	45,217	27,921
Louisiana	51,294	49,637	51,035	59,160	48,598	38,383	58,071	58,071	65,385	46,434	†
Maine	53,273	49,775	51,383	56,347	48,817	42,376	59,233	59,434	†	59,434	39,628
Maryland	61,539	60,752	65,095	77,823	58,786	53,435	64,178	64,178	80,429	54,266	†
Massachusetts	72,752	61,988	65,239	75,540	61,090	54,180	78,410	78,545	89,580	66,055	36,621
Michigan	63,146	65,167	65,977	76,728	57,943	62,254	50,459	50,548	52,607	50,305	27,242
Minnesota	56,398	57,820	63,264	81,494	54,271	49,784	52,985	53,034	†	53,034	31,588
Mississippi	46,211	46,984	50,697	54,383	47,979	42,256	39,871	41,141	†	41,141	25,237
Missouri	54,667	53,371	55,639	66,945	53,302	46,252	57,352	57,908	78,165	44,495	38,469
Montana	47,679	49,424	51,096	53,614	44,963	36,247	37,152	38,197	†	38,197	26,700
Nebraska	52,338	53,998	58,099	66,950	51,323	38,461	47,412	47,789	56,126	43,563	23,513
Nevada	62,183	62,407	67,349	70,241	65,625	52,133	44,654	44,654	†	44,654	†
New Hampshire	60,461	57,211	61,904	66,691	53,990	40,073	64,668	64,668	†	64,668	†
New Jersey	70,350	69,353	73,085	81,279	70,285	59,830	72,892	72,892	91,268	60,063	†
New Mexico	47,681	47,936	51,400	59,110	32,350	39,525	42,052	47,662	†	47,662	28,299
New York	65,946	61,341	63,641	73,966	62,177	56,445	70,783	70,984	83,383	61,606	35,822
North Carolina	52,055	49,931	61,356	74,778	55,884	36,117	59,052	59,277	88,976	45,130	33,134
North Dakota	43,049	43,845	46,739	49,326	40,884	35,317	37,291	39,502	†	39,502	28,389
Ohio	57,984	59,528	63,018	64,743	56,569	49,376	54,410	54,561	80,851	51,704	22,255
Oklahoma	49,294	49,564	52,180	58,577	46,042	40,594	48,174	48,174	62,942	41,923	†
Oregon	51,887	50,820	53,492	56,901	49,976	47,677	56,010	56,010	†	56,010	†
Pennsylvania	64,428	64,478	66,383	73,100	62,518	53,112	64,371	64,734	89,787	56,758	34,560
Rhode Island	64,875	61,413	65,248	70,970	55,565	49,953	67,593	67,593	†	67,593	†
South Carolina	50,891	51,942	58,027	66,675	49,243	39,994	46,519	46,774	†	46,774	33,882
South Dakota	44,930	46,159	48,258	50,135	46,169	36,857	39,530	39,530	†	39,530	†
Tennessee	51,804	51,499	55,680	65,341	52,570	38,800	52,452	52,650	79,455	43,474	26,284
Texas	55,113	54,098	58,919	66,671	52,785	45,432	59,498	59,692	71,042	50,610	29,852
Utah	56,940	53,788	56,214	62,686	48,086	42,440	66,253	66,567	68,536	50,209	44,528
Vermont	52,119	52,297	52,297	57,070	43,184	†	51,950	55,253	†	55,253	29,869
Virginia	59,123	60,747	64,846	71,399	60,784	46,679	53,356	53,356	†	53,356	†
Washington	57,480	58,135	64,981	68,748	55,677	45,911	54,004	54,004	†	54,004	†
West Virginia	48,311	49,744	50,412	58,693	46,798	40,145	40,349	40,349	†	40,349	†
Wisconsin	58,942	60,932	63,236	81,261	56,566	57,460	50,572	50,659	63,759	47,093	36,745
Wyoming	47,707	47,707	54,784	54,784	†	40,458	†	†	†	†	†
U.S. Service Schools	73,971	73,971	73,971	†	73,971	†	†	†	†	†	†
Outlying areas	**37,667**	**37,790**	**40,828**	**38,489**	**43,636**	**19,219**	**20,381**	**20,381**	†	**20,381**	†
American Samoa	26,037	26,037	†	†	†	26,037	†	†	†	†	†
Federated States of Micronesia	19,722	19,722	†	†	†	19,722	†	†	†	†	†
Guam	49,205	49,205	55,690	†	55,690	37,462	†	†	†	†	†
Marshall Islands	7,442	7,442	†	†	†	7,442	†	†	†	†	†
Northern Marianas	39,644	39,644	39,644	†	39,644	†	†	†	†	†	†
Palau	†	†	†	†	†	†	†	†	†	†	†
Puerto Rico	38,765	38,939	39,166	38,489	40,324	†	20,381	20,381	†	20,381	†
Virgin Islands	50,598	50,598	50,598	†	50,598	†	†	†	†	†	†

† Not applicable.

NOTE: Data include imputations for nonrespondent institutions.

SOURCE: U.S. Department of Education, National Center for Education Statistics, Integrated Postsecondary Education Data System (IPEDS), Winter 2001–02. (This table was prepared September 2003.)

Average salary of full-time instructional faculty on 9-month contracts in 4-year degree-granting institutions, by type and control of institution, rank of faculty, and state or jurisdiction: 2001–02

State or other area	Public university			Public other 4-year			Private university			Private other 4-year		
	Professor	Associate professor	Assistant professor	Professor	Associate professor	Assistant professor	Professor	Associate professor	Assistant professor	Professor	Associate professor	Assistant professor
1	2	3	4	5	6	7	8	9	10	11	12	13
United States	**$89,888**	**$62,886**	**$53,138**	**$75,268**	**$58,059**	**$47,859**	**$109,721**	**$70,639**	**$60,874**	**$70,811**	**$54,159**	**$44,435**
Alabama	76,836	57,075	46,807	64,233	51,597	44,856	†	†	†	60,808	45,761	39,885
Alaska	70,620	54,661	46,142	66,579	53,278	45,971	†	†	†	55,659	48,319	39,409
Arizona	88,215	62,725	54,392	71,344	56,177	44,727	†	†	†	61,255	58,619	43,893
Arkansas	80,324	60,882	53,341	61,076	52,361	43,172	†	†	†	55,325	46,511	40,350
California	115,841	73,894	65,950	86,742	65,598	53,166	115,769	76,948	66,657	79,816	59,185	48,407
Colorado	86,327	64,032	53,900	69,364	54,027	45,420	81,808	63,228	51,048	76,299	54,880	45,151
Connecticut	102,553	74,518	59,577	78,040	61,218	49,179	131,749	75,414	60,865	82,802	61,610	50,230
Delaware	98,897	69,029	56,473	68,506	56,474	47,858	†	†	†	77,334	62,956	39,731
District of Columbia	†	†	†	67,315	54,978	43,149	97,988	67,013	55,238	80,920	58,111	48,047
Florida	85,365	59,738	53,367	75,748	58,387	49,002	95,715	63,384	56,006	67,986	52,038	44,220
Georgia	92,320	62,877	53,373	80,058	60,042	48,590	118,542	74,929	64,284	56,501	50,547	41,998
Hawaii	79,946	60,269	52,793	60,966	48,884	45,720	†	†	†	81,038	65,734	51,872
Idaho	71,104	56,749	50,327	60,161	53,353	44,040	†	†	†	56,648	47,718	39,554
Illinois	92,683	63,666	53,806	77,539	59,864	49,759	117,968	71,576	63,150	66,278	54,982	44,618
Indiana	85,652	60,513	50,840	70,913	55,236	46,514	109,901	73,622	64,256	61,453	49,961	42,100
Iowa	91,695	63,531	54,188	73,885	57,520	47,909	71,895	50,890	44,903	57,531	45,256	38,986
Kansas	79,827	58,386	50,497	65,389	52,257	43,536	†	†	†	45,045	38,472	34,566
Kentucky	84,566	59,729	49,428	66,920	53,124	45,223	†	†	†	56,181	44,908	39,138
Louisiana	84,717	59,721	53,725	65,391	51,781	43,667	90,975	60,159	50,819	59,960	49,927	41,729
Maine	68,069	56,562	47,425	59,894	49,986	40,208	†	†	†	83,703	58,570	46,019
Maryland	101,718	72,697	68,356	79,082	61,816	51,091	105,800	71,478	61,830	68,883	55,169	44,818
Massachusetts	89,654	70,471	55,688	72,042	60,402	47,284	119,803	73,264	65,321	85,709	62,541	51,991
Michigan	99,570	71,125	58,828	73,713	59,201	48,149	68,371	55,120	40,988	60,853	50,788	41,228
Minnesota	99,446	69,112	58,725	66,242	55,620	45,944	†	†	†	69,857	52,949	43,601
Mississippi	74,503	58,740	48,021	62,755	50,446	43,254	†	†	†	53,691	42,323	37,689
Missouri	88,099	64,242	53,007	69,433	54,579	44,374	101,198	66,907	60,186	56,851	46,745	39,316
Montana	67,025	52,009	44,987	54,609	45,016	39,854	†	†	†	45,207	39,833	34,044
Nebraska	87,718	63,122	54,807	63,754	55,064	44,424	84,507	55,399	44,406	53,767	45,163	38,809
Nevada	91,558	66,611	52,938	82,077	67,149	52,717	†	†	†	69,909	52,250	35,245
New Hampshire	83,464	61,525	49,630	66,610	52,004	42,951	†	†	†	86,270	58,242	46,585
New Jersey	106,395	73,785	57,359	91,719	70,408	53,883	124,387	71,533	60,030	77,175	61,309	48,258
New Mexico	75,271	56,563	48,808	39,558	33,782	31,751	†	†	†	57,195	49,976	40,395
New York	94,727	67,413	55,743	80,839	62,110	48,126	108,259	73,037	62,237	82,730	61,328	49,278
North Carolina	98,273	68,556	59,833	73,411	58,103	49,741	113,105	77,205	61,911	55,543	47,078	39,257
North Dakota	61,323	51,999	45,959	50,297	44,417	38,856	†	†	†	46,903	39,976	38,563
Ohio	84,948	60,687	49,742	73,437	56,528	45,737	97,579	70,153	64,061	65,429	51,434	43,165
Oklahoma	80,130	56,871	48,105	58,049	50,194	42,847	83,273	60,078	50,441	53,850	43,286	36,483
Oregon	75,289	56,434	48,230	63,686	50,143	43,229	†	†	†	73,048	52,504	45,255
Pennsylvania	97,030	67,534	55,196	82,729	64,746	52,961	114,972	76,559	65,619	75,117	57,186	46,189
Rhode Island	82,417	62,663	50,454	62,931	53,778	46,037	†	†	†	91,719	61,765	51,698
South Carolina	84,000	61,812	52,078	60,904	51,017	43,108	†	†	†	60,539	47,953	40,319
South Dakota	62,776	50,779	43,614	62,776	43,909	43,929	†	†	†	50,255	42,586	35,644
Tennessee	80,834	62,148	50,115	66,306	51,308	44,220	106,773	70,481	59,347	54,018	44,764	38,842
Texas	90,455	60,739	52,802	69,125	55,283	47,397	96,463	65,970	57,556	65,624	50,843	41,436
Utah	81,534	57,154	50,231	58,837	49,978	43,607	84,864	64,629	55,060	60,448	50,559	45,958
Vermont	74,925	56,891	46,964	50,815	41,070	33,785	†	†	†	68,599	53,959	47,022
Virginia	94,894	67,742	55,002	79,662	60,869	48,171	†	†	†	67,246	52,291	43,090
Washington	85,647	62,148	55,669	64,552	53,924	47,795	†	†	†	68,100	53,403	44,959
West Virginia	74,487	55,750	45,317	57,397	47,431	39,891	†	†	†	49,583	42,210	35,635
Wisconsin	93,553	71,881	59,925	67,828	55,746	47,765	78,927	61,397	50,976	58,368	48,051	41,141
Wyoming	69,285	52,522	49,668	†	†	†	†	†	†	†	†	†
U.S Service Schools	†	†	†	88,901	70,471	56,051	†	†	†	†	†	†
Outlying areas	**43,089**	**37,058**	**31,614**	**56,840**	**48,113**	**39,396**	**†**	**†**	**†**	**†**	**†**	**†**
American Samoa	†	†	†	†	†	†	†	†	†	†	†	†
Federated States of Micronesia	†	†	†	†	†	†	†	†	†	†	†	†
Guam	†	†	†	71,980	57,289	44,710	†	†	†	†	†	†
Northern Marianas	†	†	†	†	†	†	†	†	†	†	†	†
Palau	†	†	†	†	†	†	†	†	†	†	†	†
Puerto Rico	43,089	37,058	31,614	52,632	43,692	36,877	†	†	†	†	†	†
Virgin Islands	†	†	†	66,710	53,926	43,575	†	†	†	†	†	†

† Not applicable.

NOTE: Data include imputations for nonrespondent institutions.

SOURCE: U.S. Department of Education, National Center for Education Statistics, Integrated Postsecondary Education Data System (IPEDS), Winter, 2001–02. (This table was prepared September 2003.)

Full-time instructional faculty with tenure for degree-granting institutions reporting tenure status, by academic rank, sex, and type and control of institution: Selected years, 1993–94 to 2001–02

Academic year and type and control of institution	All ranks			Professor			Associate professor			Assistant professor			Instructor	Lecturer	No academic rank
	Total	Men	Women	Total	Men	Women	Total	Men	Women	Total	Men	Women			
1	2	3	4	5	6	7	8	9	10	11	12	13	14	15	16
1993–94															
All institutions	56.2	62.6	42.7	91.9	92.8	87.7	76.8	77.5	75.1	14.4	13.6	15.5	38.3	10.8	26.0
4-year	54.0	61.0	38.0	93.0	93.5	90.6	76.2	77.0	74.3	12.1	11.5	12.9	4.8	9.6	9.4
University	54.3	61.0	35.8	94.1	94.5	91.3	78.0	78.6	76.4	6.6	6.2	7.3	5.7	10.5	9.9
Other 4-year	53.8	61.1	39.4	92.1	92.5	90.2	74.9	75.7	73.1	15.7	15.4	16.0	4.4	8.3	8.7
2-year	69.3	74.7	62.4	80.8	83.7	75.7	83.8	86.1	81.1	46.6	50.5	43.2	67.9	41.2	65.6
Public institutions	58.9	65.4	45.6	92.6	93.6	87.5	80.8	81.6	78.9	17.1	16.1	18.5	45.5	7.2	28.6
4-year	56.3	63.5	39.3	94.3	94.7	92.0	80.4	81.2	78.4	13.8	13.0	14.8	4.4	5.4	6.1
University	57.0	64.2	37.2	95.6	96.0	92.5	83.9	84.4	82.6	7.6	7.0	8.6	3.1	1.0	7.0
Other 4-year	55.7	62.9	40.8	93.2	93.5	91.7	77.5	78.3	75.5	18.1	17.6	18.7	5.1	9.8	4.9
2-year	69.9	75.4	63.0	80.7	83.7	75.5	84.2	86.4	81.5	47.7	51.1	44.6	68.9	39.9	65.7
Private institutions	49.5	56.0	35.4	90.3	90.8	88.1	67.6	68.1	66.5	9.0	8.7	9.4	6.8	21.9	18.8
4-year	49.5	56.0	35.4	90.3	90.8	88.0	67.6	68.1	66.5	9.0	8.7	9.4	5.5	21.6	15.7
University	48.4	54.1	32.9	90.8	91.1	89.1	63.2	64.1	60.6	4.7	4.8	4.7	10.4	30.0	15.4
Other 4-year	50.3	57.5	36.8	89.9	90.5	87.4	70.2	70.7	69.1	11.6	11.5	11.7	3.1	1.4	16.3
2-year	45.4	51.9	36.8	89.8	86.8	95.0	62.9	64.1	61.8	12.0	11.8	12.0	25.8	—	64.8
1997–98															
All institutions	55.9	62.2	44.3	92.6	93.1	90.4	78.6	79.0	78.0	14.0	13.2	14.9	32.0	4.6	20.6
4-year	53.5	60.6	39.3	92.5	93.0	89.9	78.0	78.5	77.1	10.8	10.4	11.4	3.5	2.8	3.5
University	52.5	59.6	35.4	91.8	92.6	86.5	79.5	79.9	78.7	5.4	5.2	5.8	2.2	0.8	1.3
Other 4-year	54.4	61.5	41.8	93.1	93.4	91.9	76.9	77.4	76.2	14.3	14.1	14.5	4.3	5.0	7.5
2-year	71.7	75.6	67.3	93.8	94.4	92.9	86.0	87.1	84.9	54.5	57.5	52.0	62.0	34.1	69.3
Public institutions	58.5	64.8	47.1	94.4	94.8	92.8	82.4	82.8	81.7	16.6	15.6	17.8	38.2	5.7	23.9
4-year	55.5	62.8	40.4	94.5	94.8	92.7	82.0	82.4	81.0	12.1	11.5	12.7	4.1	3.4	2.6
University	55.4	62.9	37.7	95.1	95.5	92.6	84.3	84.6	83.6	6.1	5.7	6.6	2.9	0.8	1.4
Other 4-year	55.5	62.7	42.3	94.0	94.2	92.8	80.0	80.5	79.2	16.0	15.7	16.5	4.8	5.7	4.7
2-year	72.0	75.9	67.7	93.8	94.4	92.9	86.3	87.2	85.2	54.9	57.8	52.3	62.3	34.4	70.1
Private institutions	49.7	56.1	37.0	88.4	89.3	84.7	70.1	70.2	69.8	8.8	8.5	9.1	3.3	1.2	7.7
4-year	49.7	56.1	37.0	88.4	89.3	84.6	70.1	70.3	69.8	8.7	8.4	9.1	2.4	1.2	5.8
University	46.2	52.7	30.4	84.9	86.6	75.9	67.7	68.3	66.2	4.1	4.1	4.1	0.6	0.9	1.1
Other 4-year	52.2	59.0	40.9	91.4	91.8	90.3	71.5	71.6	71.4	11.4	11.4	11.4	3.2	1.8	18.8
2-year	46.2	54.6	37.2	90.2	89.4	91.4	60.5	63.3	58.9	31.7	36.2	28.9	32.0	—	49.3
1999–2000															
All institutions	53.6	59.6	43.1	92.8	93.2	91.2	76.8	76.8	76.7	11.7	10.9	12.8	34.1	3.4	18.4
4-year	51.5	58.3	38.5	92.9	93.2	91.5	76.3	76.5	76.0	9.1	8.6	9.7	3.6	2.5	4.9
University	50.1	57.1	34.5	92.5	92.9	90.3	77.1	77.4	76.6	4.1	3.9	4.5	1.7	0.9	1.3
Other 4-year	52.6	59.4	41.1	93.2	93.5	92.2	75.7	75.8	75.7	12.4	12.1	12.8	4.7	4.4	11.6
2-year	67.7	70.6	64.6	91.3	92.3	89.9	83.2	83.3	83.1	53.5	55.9	51.6	60.9	21.1	64.5
Public institutions	55.9	61.9	45.5	92.9	93.4	91.9	81.0	81.2	80.7	14.0	13.0	15.2	39.9	4.1	21.2
4-year	53.1	60.3	39.3	94.2	94.6	92.5	80.8	81.0	80.3	10.0	9.6	10.6	3.9	3.0	4.0
University	53.0	60.4	36.7	94.2	94.7	91.4	83.0	83.2	82.7	4.6	4.3	5.1	2.3	0.7	1.7
Other 4-year	53.2	60.2	41.2	94.1	94.4	93.1	78.9	79.0	78.5	13.8	13.5	14.1	4.8	5.2	7.5
2-year	67.8	70.7	64.6	91.3	92.3	89.8	83.4	83.5	83.4	53.7	56.0	51.8	61.0	21.2	64.4
Private institutions	48.3	54.3	37.0	90.3	90.5	89.7	68.1	67.9	68.5	7.5	6.9	8.2	4.1	1.2	8.6
4-year	48.2	54.3	36.8	90.3	90.5	89.7	68.1	67.9	68.5	7.4	6.8	8.2	3.1	1.2	7.2
University	44.1	50.3	29.8	88.9	89.1	87.9	64.1	64.6	62.8	3.2	3.1	3.3	0.4	1.3	0.4
Other 4-year	51.4	57.7	41.1	91.4	91.7	90.6	70.6	70.2	71.3	10.1	9.6	10.6	4.6	1.0	28.3
2-year	59.9	60.3	59.6	95.9	92.0	100.0	60.0	66.7	55.8	33.8	40.0	30.0	50.5	—	68.8
2001–02															
All institutions	50.8	56.5	41.5	92.0	92.3	90.7	75.6	75.4	75.9	10.0	9.1	11.1	30.0	3.2	18.9
4-year	48.7	55.2	36.9	92.0	92.3	90.7	75.0	74.9	75.1	7.5	6.8	8.2	3.1	2.0	3.4
University	47.8	54.5	33.5	91.9	92.3	89.6	76.0	76.2	75.8	3.4	3.1	3.7	1.4	0.5	1.1
Other 4-year	49.4	55.8	39.2	92.1	92.4	91.3	74.1	73.9	74.6	10.2	9.6	10.9	4.0	3.8	7.4
2-year	64.2	66.6	61.8	91.8	92.2	91.2	84.0	83.9	84.0	49.6	51.5	48.0	53.0	31.5	67.8
Public institutions	52.6	58.2	43.5	93.2	93.6	91.8	79.4	79.3	79.5	11.9	10.8	13.3	34.4	3.9	22.1
4-year	49.8	56.6	37.4	93.4	93.7	92.0	78.9	78.9	78.8	8.1	7.5	9.0	2.5	2.4	2.4
University	50.2	57.3	35.5	93.7	94.2	91.4	81.3	81.6	80.6	3.6	3.2	4.1	1.8	0.6	0.8
Other 4-year	49.4	56.0	38.7	93.0	93.2	92.3	76.9	76.6	77.4	11.3	10.7	12.0	2.8	4.2	4.8
2-year	64.3	66.6	61.8	91.8	92.3	91.2	84.0	83.9	84.1	49.9	51.9	48.2	53.0	30.6	67.9
Private institutions	46.5	52.4	36.2	89.3	89.6	88.2	67.7	67.3	68.4	6.3	5.7	7.0	6.6	1.1	6.8
4-year	46.5	52.3	36.0	89.3	89.6	88.2	67.7	67.3	68.4	6.3	5.7	7.0	4.4	0.9	6.0
University	42.7	48.9	29.1	88.0	88.4	85.8	64.4	64.5	64.2	3.0	3.0	3.0	0.6	0.4	1.7
Other 4-year	49.4	55.2	40.3	90.4	90.7	89.6	69.7	69.2	70.4	8.4	7.7	9.0	6.3	2.1	18.6
2-year	61.0	63.0	58.1	88.7	86.5	91.1	80.4	81.0	80.0	24.2	17.1	30.0	57.8	—	65.6

—Not available.

NOTE: The coverage of this tabulation differs from similar tables published in earlier editions of the *Digest*. Previous tenure tabulations included only instructional staff classified as full-time faculty; this table includes all staff with full-time instructional duties, including faculty and other instructional staff. Data for 1993–94 are for institutions of higher education that were accredited by an agency or association that was recognized by the U.S. Department of Education, or recognized directly by the Secretary of Education. The new degree-granting classification is very similar to the earlier higher education classification, except that it includes some additional institutions, primarily 2-year colleges, and excludes a few higher education institutions that did not award associate or higher degrees.

SOURCE: U.S. Department of Education, National Center for Education Statistics, Integrated Postsecondary Education Data System (IPEDS), "Fall Staff" surveys, 1993–94, 1997–98, and 1999–2000, and Winter 2001–02 survey. (This table was prepared September 2003.)

543

Degree-granting institutions, by control and type of institution: 1949–50 to 2002–03

Year	All institutions			Public			Private		
	Total	4-year	2-year	Total	4-year	2-year	Total	4-year	2-year
1	2	3	4	5	6	7	8	9	10
Institutions of higher education [1] excluding branch campuses									
1949–50	1,851	1,327	524	641	344	297	1,210	983	227
1950–51	1,852	1,312	540	636	341	295	1,216	971	245
1951–52	1,832	1,326	506	641	350	291	1,191	976	215
1953–54	1,863	1,345	518	662	369	293	1,201	976	225
1955–56	1,850	1,347	503	650	360	290	1,200	987	213
1956–57	1,878	1,355	523	656	359	297	1,222	996	226
1957–58	1,930	1,390	540	666	366	300	1,264	1,024	240
1958–59	1,947	1,394	553	673	366	307	1,274	1,028	246
1959–60	2,004	1,422	582	695	367	328	1,309	1,055	254
1960–61	2,021	1,431	590	700	368	332	1,321	1,063	258
1961–62	2,033	1,443	590	718	374	344	1,315	1,069	246
1962–63	2,093	1,468	625	740	376	364	1,353	1,092	261
1963–64	2,132	1,499	633	760	386	374	1,372	1,113	259
1964–65	2,175	1,521	654	799	393	406	1,376	1,128	248
1965–66	2,230	1,551	679	821	401	420	1,409	1,150	259
1966–67	2,329	1,577	752	880	403	477	1,449	1,174	275
1967–68	2,374	1,588	786	934	414	520	1,440	1,174	266
1968–69	2,483	1,619	864	1,011	417	594	1,472	1,202	270
1969–70	2,525	1,639	886	1,060	426	634	1,465	1,213	252
1970–71	2,556	1,665	891	1,089	435	654	1,467	1,230	237
1971–72	2,606	1,675	931	1,137	440	697	1,469	1,235	234
1972–73	2,665	1,701	964	1,182	449	733	1,483	1,252	231
1973–74	2,720	1,717	1,003	1,200	440	760	1,520	1,277	243
1974–75	2,747	1,744	1,003	1,214	447	767	1,533	1,297	236
1975–76	2,765	1,767	998	1,219	447	772	1,546	1,320	226
1976–77	2,785	1,783	1,002	1,231	452	779	1,554	1,331	223
1977–78	2,826	1,808	1,018	1,241	454	787	1,585	1,354	231
1978–79	2,954	1,843	1,111	1,308	463	845	1,646	1,380	266
1979–80	2,975	1,863	1,112	1,310	464	846	1,665	1,399	266
1980–81	3,056	1,861	1,195	1,334	465	869	1,722	1,396	[2] 326
1981–82	3,083	1,883	1,200	1,340	471	869	1,743	1,412	[2] 331
1982–83	3,111	1,887	1,224	1,336	472	864	1,775	1,415	[2] 360
1983–84	3,117	1,914	1,203	1,325	474	851	1,792	1,440	352
1984–85	3,146	1,911	1,235	1,329	461	868	1,817	1,450	367
1985–86	3,155	1,915	1,240	1,326	461	865	1,829	1,454	375
Institutions of higher education, including branch campuses									
1974–75	3,004	1,866	1,138	1,433	537	896	1,571	1,329	242
1975–76	3,026	1,898	1,128	1,442	545	897	1,584	1,353	231
1976–77	3,046	1,913	1,133	1,455	550	905	1,591	1,363	228
1977–78	3,095	1,938	1,157	1,473	552	921	1,622	1,386	236
1978–79	3,134	1,941	1,193	1,474	550	924	1,660	1,391	269
1979–80	3,152	1,957	1,195	1,475	549	926	1,677	1,408	269
1980–81	3,231	1,957	1,274	1,497	552	945	1,734	1,405	[2] 329
1981–82	3,253	1,979	1,274	1,498	558	940	1,755	1,421	[2] 334
1982–83	3,280	1,984	1,296	1,493	560	933	1,787	1,424	[2] 363
1983–84	3,284	2,013	1,271	1,481	565	916	1,803	1,448	355
1984–85	3,331	2,025	1,306	1,501	566	935	1,830	1,459	371
1985–86	3,340	2,029	1,311	1,498	566	932	1,842	1,463	379
1986–87 [3]	3,406	2,070	1,336	1,533	573	960	1,873	1,497	376
1987–88 [3]	3,587	2,135	1,452	1,591	599	992	1,996	1,536	460
1988–89 [3]	3,565	2,129	1,436	1,582	598	984	1,983	1,531	452
1989–90 [3]	3,535	2,127	1,408	1,563	595	968	1,972	1,532	440
1990–91 [3]	3,559	2,141	1,418	1,567	595	972	1,992	1,546	446
1991–92 [3]	3,601	2,157	1,444	1,598	599	999	2,003	1,558	445
1992–93 [3]	3,638	2,169	1,469	1,624	600	1,024	2,014	1,569	445
1993–94 [3]	3,632	2,190	1,442	1,625	604	1,021	2,007	1,586	421
1994–95 [3]	3,688	2,215	1,473	1,641	605	1,036	2,047	1,610	437
1995–96 [3]	3,706	2,244	1,462	1,655	608	1,047	2,051	1,636	415
Title IV eligible degree-granting institutions									
1996–97	4,009	2,267	1,742	1,702	614	1,088	2,307	1,653	654
1997–98	4,064	2,309	1,755	1,707	615	1,092	2,357	1,694	663
1998–99	4,048	2,335	1,713	1,681	612	1,069	2,367	1,723	644
1999–2000	4,084	2,363	1,721	1,682	614	1,068	2,402	1,749	653
2000–01	4,182	2,450	1,732	1,698	622	1,076	2,484	1,828	656
2001–02	4,197	2,364	1,833	1,713	612	1,101	2,484	1,752	732
2002–03	4,168	2,324	1,844	1,712	611	1,101	2,456	1,713	743

[1] Institutions that were accredited by an agency or association that was recognized by the U.S. Department of Education, or recognized directly by the Secretary of Education.

[2] Large increases are due to the addition of schools accredited by the Accrediting Commission of Career Schools and Colleges of Technology.

[3] Because of revised survey procedures, data are not entirely comparable with figures for earlier years. The number of branch campuses reporting separately has increased since 1986–87.

SOURCE: U.S. Department of Education, National Center for Education Statistics, *Education Directory, Colleges and Universities*, 1949–50 through 1965–66; Higher Education General Information Survey (HEGIS), "Institutional Characteristics of Colleges and Universities" surveys, 1966–67 through 1985–86; and Integrated Postsecondary Education Data System (IPEDS), "Institutional Characteristics" surveys, 1986–87 through 2000–01, and Spring 2001 and Spring 2002 surveys. (This table was prepared November 2003.)

Degree-granting institutions and branches, by type and control of institution and state or jurisdiction: 2002–03

State or jurisdiction	Total	All public institutions	Public, 4-year institutions						Public 2-year	All private institutions	Private 4-year institutions						Private 2-year
			Total	Doctor's extensive [1]	Doctor's intensive [2]	Master's [3]	Baccalaureate [4]	Other 4-year [5]			Total	Doctor's extensive [1]	Doctor's intensive [2]	Master's [3]	Baccalaureate [4]	Other 4-year [5]	
1	2	3	4	5	6	7	8	9	10	11	12	13	14	15	16	17	18
United States	4,168	1,712	611	103	63	283	100	62	1,101	2,456	1,713	49	46	363	558	697	743
Alabama	75	47	18	3	3	11	1	0	29	28	17	0	0	4	9	4	11
Alaska	8	5	3	0	1	2	0	0	2	3	2	0	0	1	1	0	1
Arizona	71	25	5	2	1	1	0	1	20	46	21	0	0	6	1	14	25
Arkansas	46	33	10	1	1	5	2	1	23	13	10	0	0	1	8	1	3
California	400	144	33	8	2	20	1	2	111	256	176	4	9	31	26	106	80
Colorado	76	28	13	2	2	3	4	2	15	48	27	1	0	5	5	16	21
Connecticut	45	22	10	1	0	7	1	1	12	23	18	1	2	5	5	5	5
Delaware	10	5	2	1	0	1	0	0	3	5	4	0	1	0	1	2	1
District of Columbia	16	2	2	0	0	1	0	1	0	14	14	5	0	4	1	4	0
Florida	161	40	12	4	2	4	1	1	28	121	80	1	4	20	23	32	41
Georgia	124	74	19	3	0	13	1	2	55	50	38	1	1	5	17	14	12
Hawaii	20	10	3	1	0	0	2	0	7	10	7	0	0	3	1	3	3
Idaho	14	7	4	1	1	1	1	0	3	7	5	0	0	1	1	3	2
Illinois	175	60	12	4	1	7	0	0	48	115	92	3	3	15	24	47	23
Indiana	99	29	14	2	3	6	3	0	15	70	44	1	0	8	22	13	26
Iowa	62	18	3	2	0	1	0	0	15	44	36	0	0	4	22	10	8
Kansas	60	35	9	2	1	4	0	2	26	25	21	0	0	8	10	3	4
Kentucky	79	37	8	2	0	6	0	0	29	42	26	0	0	4	16	6	16
Louisiana	87	62	15	1	3	9	0	2	47	25	13	1	0	4	4	4	12
Maine	32	15	8	1	0	1	5	1	7	17	11	0	0	3	5	3	6
Maryland	63	29	13	2	1	9	1	0	16	34	28	1	0	4	7	16	6
Massachusetts	119	31	15	1	2	7	1	4	16	88	77	7	2	15	21	32	11
Michigan	109	44	15	4	3	8	0	0	29	65	59	0	1	9	23	26	6
Minnesota	113	52	11	1	0	7	3	0	41	61	39	0	3	6	13	17	22
Mississippi	41	26	9	3	1	3	1	1	17	15	11	0	0	2	5	4	4
Missouri	119	32	13	1	3	6	2	1	19	87	61	2	0	11	16	32	26
Montana	22	17	6	0	2	2	1	1	11	5	4	0	0	1	2	1	1
Nebraska	38	14	7	1	0	5	0	1	7	24	15	0	0	4	8	3	9
Nevada	14	6	2	1	1	0	0	0	4	8	3	0	0	1	2	0	5
New Hampshire	25	9	5	1	0	2	2	0	4	16	13	0	2	2	5	4	3
New Jersey	57	33	14	1	2	8	2	1	19	24	20	1	2	5	6	6	4
New Mexico	43	27	7	2	1	3	0	1	20	16	13	0	0	4	3	6	3
New York	310	80	41	6	1	20	7	7	39	230	167	9	7	32	35	84	63
North Carolina	126	75	16	2	2	8	3	1	59	51	44	1	1	7	29	6	7
North Dakota	22	16	7	0	2	1	3	1	9	6	4	0	0	1	1	2	2
Ohio	179	61	19	5	5	1	6	2	42	118	68	1	2	15	25	25	50
Oklahoma	53	29	14	2	0	7	3	2	15	24	17	0	1	5	7	4	7
Oregon	57	26	9	2	1	3	1	2	17	31	27	0	0	6	9	12	4
Pennsylvania	257	68	45	3	1	19	20	2	23	189	96	3	3	28	34	28	93
Rhode Island	13	3	2	1	0	1	0	0	1	10	9	1	0	4	1	3	1
South Carolina	63	33	12	2	1	5	3	1	21	30	23	0	0	3	15	5	7
South Dakota	27	14	9	0	2	2	2	3	5	13	12	0	0	3	5	4	1
Tennessee	89	22	9	2	3	4	0	0	13	67	47	1	0	11	17	18	20
Texas	200	109	42	6	6	20	2	8	67	91	55	2	2	14	19	18	36
Utah	25	10	5	2	0	2	1	0	5	15	6	1	0	2	1	2	9
Vermont	27	6	5	1	0	2	1	1	1	21	17	0	0	6	9	2	4
Virginia	100	38	14	4	2	5	3	0	24	62	46	0	0	9	18	19	16
Washington	78	45	11	2	0	8	1	0	34	33	27	0	0	11	4	12	6
West Virginia	37	15	12	1	0	1	9	1	3	22	10	0	0	2	6	2	12
Wisconsin	68	31	13	2	0	11	0	0	18	37	33	1	0	8	10	14	4
Wyoming	9	8	1	1	0	0	0	0	7	1	0	0	0	0	0	0	1
U.S. Service Schools	5	5	5	0	0	0	0	5	0	0	0	0	0	0	0	0	0
Outlying areas	83	29	15	0	1	4	7	3	14	54	40	0	0	7	18	15	14
American Samoa	1	1	0	0	0	0	0	0	1	0	0	0	0	0	0	0	0
Federated States of Micronesia	4	4	0	0	0	0	0	0	4	0	0	0	0	0	0	0	0
Guam	3	2	1	0	0	1	0	0	1	1	1	0	0	0	0	1	0
Marshall Islands	1	1	0	0	0	0	0	0	1	0	0	0	0	0	0	0	0
Northern Marianas	1	1	0	0	0	0	0	0	1	0	0	0	0	0	0	0	0
Palau	1	1	0	0	0	0	0	0	1	0	0	0	0	0	0	0	0
Puerto Rico	70	17	12	0	1	1	7	3	5	53	39	0	0	7	18	14	14
Virgin Islands	2	2	2	0	0	2	0	0	0	0	0	0	0	0	0	0	0

[1] Doctoral, extensive institutions are committed to graduate education through the doctorate, and award 50 or more doctor's degrees per year across at least 15 disciplines.

[2] Doctoral, intensive institutions are committed to education through the doctorate and award at least 10 doctor's degrees per year across 3 or more disciplines or at least 20 doctor's degrees overall.

[3] Master's institutions offer a full range of baccalaureate programs and are committed to education through the master's degree. They award at least 20 master's degrees per year.

[4] Baccalaureate institutions primarily emphasize undergraduate education.

[5] Other specialized 4-year institutions award degrees primarily in single fields of study, such as medicine, business, fine arts, theology and engineering. Includes some institutions which have 4-year programs, but have not reported sufficient data to identify program category. Also, includes institutions classified as 4-year under the IPEDS system, which had been classified as 2-year in the Carnegie classification system because they primarily award associate degrees.

NOTE: New institutions which do not have sufficient data to report by detailed level are included under "other 4-year" or 2-year depending on the level reported by the institution.

SOURCE: U.S. Department of Education, National Center for Education Statistics, Integrated Postsecondary Education Data System (IPEDS), Spring 2002. (This table was prepared November 2003.)

Scores on Graduate Record Examination (GRE) and subject matter tests: 1965 to 2000

Academic year ending	Number of GRE takers	GRE takers as a percent of bachelor's degrees	Verbal Mean	Verbal Standard deviation	Quantitative Mean	Quantitative Standard deviation	Analytical Mean	Analytical Standard deviation	Biology Mean	Biology Standard deviation	Chemistry Mean	Chemistry Standard deviation	Education Mean	Education Standard deviation	Engineering Mean	Engineering Standard deviation	Literature Mean	Literature Standard deviation	Psychology Mean	Psychology Standard deviation
1	2	3	4	5	6	7	8	9	10	11	12	13	14	15	16	17	18	19	20	21
1965	93,792	18.7	530	124	533	137	†	†	617	117	628	114	481	86	618	108	591	95	556	91
1966	123,960	23.8	520	124	528	133	†	†	610	115	618	110	474	87	609	106	588	94	552	91
1967	151,134	27.0	519	125	528	134	†	†	613	114	615	104	476	90	603	104	582	91	553	93
1968	182,432	28.8	520	124	527	135	†	†	614	114	617	104	478	87	601	105	572	91	547	93
1969	206,113	28.3	515	124	524	132	†	†	613	112	613	104	477	88	591	103	569	89	543	89
1970	265,359	33.5	503	123	516	132	†	†	603	111	613	113	462	92	586	110	556	90	532	91
1971	293,600	35.0	497	125	512	134	†	†	603	114	618	117	457	95	587	115	546	91	530	92
1972	293,506	33.1	494	126	508	136	†	†	606	115	624	124	446	93	594	119	544	96	528	92
1973	290,104	31.5	497	125	512	135	†	†	619	110	630	114	459	96	593	114	545	96	529	92
1974	301,070	31.8	492	126	509	137	†	†	624	110	634	115	452	93	591	121	547	99	530	95
1975	298,335	32.3	493	125	508	137	†	†	—	—	627	107	454	93	594	119	—	—	531	—
1976	299,292	32.3	492	127	510	138	†	†	627	112	630	109	453	93	592	115	539	101	532	93
1977	287,715	31.3	490	129	514	139	†	†	625	113	624	108	452	91	594	114	532	101	529	95
1978	286,383	31.1	484	128	518	135	†	†	622	113	623	104	451	89	592	115	530	102	530	97
1979	282,482	30.7	476	130	517	135	†	†	621	117	620	105	449	90	590	115	525	102	534	97
1980	272,281	29.3	474	131	522	136	†	†	619	115	618	103	453	90	590	116	521	105	532	98
1981	262,855	28.1	473	128	523	136	†	†	617	115	615	105	456	90	593	116	520	99	542	97
1982	256,381	26.9	469	130	533	137	498	126	616	114	616	105	459	89	599	115	521	100	543	97
1983	263,674	27.2	473	131	541	138	504	128	623	115	620	102	461	90	604	114	527	98	541	95
1984	265,221	27.2	475	130	541	139	512	129	622	115	619	101	459	90	615	114	530	97	542	96
1985	271,972	27.8	474	126	545	140	516	129	619	114	621	106	464	89	616	120	531	95	536	95
1986	279,428	28.3	475	126	552	140	520	128	612	114	628	104	465	87	619	119	527	96	537	97
1987	293,560	29.6	477	126	550	140	521	128	616	116	629	108	467	86	622	119	526	95	538	95
1988	303,703	30.5	483	123	557	140	528	128	615	114	631	117	465	85	626	120	525	94	537	94
1989	326,096	32.0	484	125	560	142	530	129	612	116	642	123	461	87	617	116	528	91	535	95
1990	344,572	32.8	486	123	562	143	534	128	612	114	662	123	457	84	611	111	523	92	536	92
1991	379,882	34.7	485	122	562	141	536	129	639	113	660	128	462	85	610	111	523	93	536	93
1992	411,528	36.2	483	120	561	140	537	129	635	113	654	133	462	82	602	117	525	92	538	92
1993	400,246	34.4	481	117	557	140	541	129	606	114	662	113	462	80	601	115	516	94	541	94
1994	[1]399,395	34.2	479	116	553	139	545	129	620	116	627	138	[2]493	104	596	115	517	95	542	95
1995	[1]389,539	33.6	477	115	553	140	544	131	622	116	675	135	[2]488	102	604	113	513	96	544	96
1996	[1]376,013	32.3	473	114	558	139	549	131	614	114	678	143	[2]489	104	602	119	512	97	547	99
1997	[1]376,062	32.1	472	113	562	139	548	129	620	115	684	137	[2]487	103	609	114	525	100	554	99
1998	[1]364,554	30.8	471	113	569	141	543	133	628	113	686	137	[2]477	100	604	118	530	100	563	100
1999[3]	396,330	33.0	468	114	565	143	542	133	626	114	684	137	—	—	604	115	527	100	559	99
2000[4]	363,932	29.4	465	116	578	147	562	141	629	114	686	133	—	—	—	—	530	99	563	98

† Not applicable.
— Not available.

[1] Total includes examinees who received no score on one or more General Test measures.

[2] Data reported for 1994 through 1998 are from the revised education test.

[3] Subject test score data for 1999 reflect the three-year average for all examinees who tested between October 1, 1996 and September 30, 1999, and are not directly comparable with previous years.

[4] Subject test score data for 2000 reflect the three-year average for all examinees who tested between October 1, 1997 and September 30, 2000, and are not directly comparable with previous years.

NOTE: GRE scores for the verbal, quantitative, and analytical sections range from 200 to 800. The range of scores is different for the various subject tests—from 200 to 990—although the range for any particular subject test is usually smaller. The education subject test was administered for the final time in April 2001. The engineering subject test was administered for the final time in April 1998. Some data have been revised from previously published figures.

SOURCE: Graduate Record Examination Board, *Examinee and Score Trends for the GRE General Test*, various years; and *A Summary of Data Collected From Graduate Record Examinations Test-Takers During 1986–87*; *Guide to the Use of Scores*, various years; *Sex, Race, Ethnicity, and Performance on the GRE General Test*, various years; unpublished data; and U.S. Department of Education, National Center for Education Statistics, Higher Education General Information Survey (HEGIS) "Degrees and Other Formal Awards Conferred" surveys, and Integrated Postsecondary Education Data System (IPEDS), "Completions" surveys. (This table was prepared July 2002.)

Percent of degree-granting institutions with first-year undergraduates using various selection criteria for admission, by type and control of institution: 2000–01, 2001–02, and 2002–03

Selection criteria	All institutions			Public institutions			Private institutions								
										Not-for-profit			For-profit		
	Total	4-year	2-year	Total	4-year	2-year	Total	4-year	2-year	Total	4-year	2-year	Total	4-year	2-year
1	2	3	4	5	6	7	8	9	10	11	12	13	14	15	16
Number of institutions with first-year undergraduates															
2000–01	3,717	2,034	1,683	1,647	580	1,067	2,070	1,454	616	1,383	1,247	136	687	207	480
2001–02	3,803	2,102	1,701	1,663	579	1,084	2,140	1,523	617	1,410	1,278	132	730	245	485
2002–03	3,796	2,105	1,691	1,655	577	1,078	2,141	1,528	613	1,392	1,268	124	749	260	489
Percent of institutions															
Open admissions															
2000–01	40.2	12.9	73.2	63.8	12.1	91.9	21.4	13.3	40.7	14.0	11.7	34.6	36.5	22.7	42.5
2001–02	42.3	14.8	76.2	65.5	11.4	94.5	24.2	16.2	44.1	14.2	11.7	37.9	43.6	39.2	45.8
2002–03	43.3	16.2	76.9	66.5	12.5	95.4	25.3	17.7	44.4	14.6	12.5	36.3	45.3	43.1	46.4
Some admission requirements [1]															
2000–01	58.4	85.8	25.1	35.4	87.4	7.1	76.6	85.2	56.3	84.5	86.8	63.2	60.7	75.4	54.4
2001–02	56.4	83.6	22.8	34.1	87.9	5.4	73.8	82.0	53.5	84.0	86.4	61.4	54.0	59.2	51.3
2002–03	55.4	82.5	21.6	33.2	87.0	4.5	72.5	80.8	51.9	84.0	86.1	62.1	51.1	54.6	49.3
Secondary grades															
2000–01	34.6	58.7	5.5	23.9	63.4	2.4	43.0	56.7	10.7	60.1	64.1	23.5	8.7	12.6	7.1
2001–02	34.3	58.0	4.9	24.4	65.8	2.3	42.0	55.1	9.6	59.7	63.4	24.2	7.7	11.8	5.6
2002–03	34.3	58.1	4.8	24.2	65.5	2.1	42.1	55.2	9.5	61.4	64.6	28.2	6.4	9.6	4.7
Secondary class rank															
2000–01	13.7	24.3	1.0	10.9	30.3	0.3	16.0	21.9	2.3	23.2	25.1	5.9	1.6	2.4	1.3
2001–02	13.1	23.1	0.7	10.6	30.2	0.2	15.0	20.4	1.6	22.1	23.8	6.1	1.1	2.4	0.4
2002–03	12.5	21.9	0.7	10.5	29.8	0.2	14.0	18.9	1.6	21.0	22.6	5.6	0.8	1.2	0.6
Secondary school record															
2000–01	45.8	70.3	16.2	29.4	72.9	5.8	58.7	69.2	34.1	73.2	75.5	52.2	29.5	30.6	29.0
2001–02	46.1	71.1	15.1	29.3	75.0	5.0	59.1	69.7	32.9	74.8	77.2	51.5	28.8	30.6	27.8
2002–03	48.3	73.1	17.4	29.2	75.7	4.4	63.0	72.1	40.3	76.4	78.3	57.3	38.1	41.9	36.0
College preparatory program															
2000–01	15.5	27.3	1.2	16.2	44.0	1.1	14.9	20.7	1.3	22.1	24.1	4.4	0.4	0.5	0.4
2001–02	15.6	27.5	1.0	17.0	46.6	1.1	14.6	20.2	0.8	22.1	23.9	3.8	0.1	0.4	#
2002–03	15.7	27.6	0.8	17.3	47.8	1.0	14.4	20.0	0.5	22.1	24.1	2.4	0.1	0.4	#
Recommendations															
2000–01	20.4	34.4	3.5	2.7	7.4	0.2	34.4	45.1	9.3	46.6	49.2	22.8	10.0	20.8	5.4
2001–02	19.9	33.3	3.2	3.0	8.1	0.3	32.9	42.9	8.3	47.5	50.2	22.0	4.8	5.3	4.5
2002–03	20.0	33.8	2.9	3.1	8.5	0.3	33.1	43.4	7.5	48.4	51.1	21.0	4.7	5.8	4.1
Demonstration of competencies [2]															
2000–01	8.0	12.1	3.0	2.2	5.0	0.7	12.7	15.0	7.1	12.1	12.7	7.4	13.7	29.0	7.1
2001–02	6.7	9.8	2.9	2.3	6.0	0.3	10.1	11.2	7.5	10.2	10.6	6.8	9.9	14.3	7.6
2002–03	7.0	9.5	3.8	2.5	6.8	0.3	10.4	10.5	10.1	9.8	10.2	5.6	11.6	12.3	11.2
Test scores [3]															
2000–01	47.2	72.5	16.7	33.2	83.4	5.8	58.5	68.2	35.6	70.3	73.4	41.9	34.6	36.7	33.8
2001–02	45.5	70.5	14.7	32.1	84.1	4.3	55.9	65.3	32.9	68.2	71.8	34.1	32.2	31.4	32.6
2002–03	43.3	69.1	11.2	31.5	83.5	3.7	52.5	63.7	24.5	67.2	71.3	25.0	25.1	26.5	24.3
TOEFL [4]															
2000–01	43.4	71.2	9.9	30.2	77.4	4.6	54.0	68.7	19.2	66.2	70.1	30.9	29.3	60.4	15.8
2001–02	42.1	68.7	9.3	29.8	78.1	4.0	51.7	65.1	18.6	65.5	69.2	29.5	25.1	43.7	15.7
2002–03	42.4	69.2	8.9	30.0	79.0	3.7	51.9	65.5	18.1	66.8	70.3	31.5	24.3	42.3	14.7
No admission requirements, only recommendations															
2000–01	1.4	1.2	1.7	0.8	0.5	0.9	1.9	1.5	2.9	1.5	1.4	2.2	2.8	1.9	3.1
2001–02	1.3	1.5	1.0	0.4	0.7	0.2	2.0	1.8	2.4	1.8	1.9	0.8	2.5	1.6	2.9
2002–03	1.4	1.3	1.5	0.3	0.5	0.2	2.2	1.6	3.8	1.4	1.4	1.6	3.6	2.3	4.3

Rounds to zero.
[1] Many institutions have more than one admission requirement.
[2] Formal demonstration of competencies (e.g. portfolios, certificates of mastery, assessment instruments).
[3] Includes SAT, ACT, or other admission tests.
[4] Test of English as a Foreign Language.

NOTE: Detail may not sum to totals due to rounding.
SOURCE: U.S. Department of Education, National Center for Education Statistics, Integrated Postsecondary Education Data System (IPEDS), "Institutional Characteristics, 2000–01 survey," and Spring 2001 and Spring 2002 surveys. (This table was prepared November 2003.)

Current-fund expenditures and expenditures per full-time-equivalent student in degree-granting institutions, by type and control of institution: Selected years, 1970–71 to 2000–01

Control of institution and year	All institutions			4-year institutions			2-year institutions		
	Current-fund expenditures, in millions		Current-fund expenditures per student, in constant 2000–01 dollars	Current-fund expenditures, in millions		Current-fund expenditures per student, in constant 2000–01 dollars	Current-fund expenditures, in millions		Current-fund expenditures per student, in constant 2000–01 dollars
	Unadjusted dollars	Constant 2000–01 dollars		Unadjusted dollars	Constant 2000–01 dollars		Unadjusted dollars	Constant 2000–01 dollars	
1	2	3	4	5	6	7	8	9	10
All institutions									
1970–71	$23,375	$103,029	$15,291	$21,049	$92,774	$18,030	$2,327	$10,255	$6,440
1975–76	38,903	122,825	14,485	33,811	106,749	18,092	5,092	16,076	6,233
1977–78	45,971	128,512	15,271	39,899	111,537	18,793	6,072	16,975	6,844
1978–79	50,721	129,647	15,529	44,163	112,885	19,029	6,558	16,763	6,938
1979–80	56,914	128,362	15,124	49,661	112,004	18,617	7,253	16,358	6,619
1980–81	64,053	129,468	14,681	55,840	112,868	18,319	8,212	16,600	6,246
1981–82	70,339	130,870	14,518	61,333	114,114	18,259	9,006	16,756	6,061
1982–83	75,936	135,463	14,900	66,238	118,164	18,910	9,697	17,299	6,085
1983–84	81,993	141,049	15,388	71,680	123,307	19,495	10,314	17,742	6,245
1984–85	89,951	148,910	16,635	78,744	130,357	20,715	11,207	18,553	6,978
1985–86	97,536	156,940	17,548	85,560	137,671	21,872	11,976	19,269	7,274
1986–87	105,764	166,483	18,367	92,985	146,367	23,013	12,779	20,115	7,440
1987–88	113,786	171,985	18,634	100,143	151,363	23,335	13,644	20,622	7,518
1988–89	123,867	178,957	18,909	109,141	157,681	23,661	14,726	21,276	7,598
1989–90	134,656	185,683	18,984	118,578	163,513	23,998	16,077	22,170	7,471
1990–91	146,088	191,005	19,132	128,594	168,133	24,129	17,494	22,872	7,585
1991–92	156,189	197,872	19,098	137,375	174,037	24,576	18,814	23,835	7,269
1992–93	165,241	202,999	19,450	145,300	178,501	25,037	19,941	24,498	7,407
1993–94	173,351	207,584	20,054	152,164	182,213	25,588	21,187	25,371	7,854
1994–95	182,969	212,996	20,583	160,891	187,295	26,242	22,078	25,701	8,005
1995–96	190,476	215,863	20,887	166,954	189,206	26,378	23,522	26,657	8,430
Public institutions									
1970–71	14,996	66,097	13,344	12,899	56,853	16,391	2,097	9,243	6,226
1975–76	26,184	82,668	12,675	21,392	67,538	16,649	4,792	15,130	6,136
1977–78	30,725	85,893	13,428	25,013	69,925	17,312	5,712	15,968	6,774
1978–79	33,733	86,224	13,732	27,600	70,549	17,654	6,132	15,675	6,866
1979–80	37,768	85,181	13,325	30,979	69,869	17,212	6,789	15,312	6,562
1980–81	42,280	85,459	12,866	34,677	70,092	16,856	7,602	15,366	6,186
1981–82	46,219	85,993	12,681	37,890	70,495	16,751	8,330	15,498	6,024
1982–83	49,573	88,434	12,909	40,616	72,455	17,167	8,957	15,979	6,076
1983–84	53,087	91,322	13,271	43,588	74,982	17,577	9,499	16,340	6,247
1984–85	58,315	96,537	14,442	48,017	79,490	18,757	10,298	17,047	6,967
1985–86	63,194	101,682	15,250	52,184	83,967	19,805	11,010	17,715	7,296
1986–87	67,654	106,494	15,712	56,003	88,154	20,522	11,651	18,340	7,388
1987–88	72,641	109,795	15,826	60,137	90,895	20,678	12,505	18,900	7,435
1988–89	78,946	114,057	16,071	65,349	94,413	20,954	13,597	19,644	7,581
1989–90	85,771	118,273	16,044	70,865	97,719	21,152	14,906	20,554	7,469
1990–91	92,961	121,544	16,081	76,722	100,311	21,163	16,239	21,232	7,535
1991–92	98,847	125,227	15,926	81,334	103,040	21,486	17,513	22,187	7,234
1992–93	104,570	128,464	16,237	86,065	105,731	22,037	18,505	22,734	7,301
1993–94	109,310	130,896	16,755	89,697	107,411	22,537	19,612	23,485	7,709
1994–95	115,465	134,414	17,267	94,895	110,468	23,259	20,570	23,946	7,890
1995–96	119,525	135,455	17,474	97,905	110,953	23,323	21,620	24,502	8,182
1996–97	125,429	138,203	17,730	103,069	113,566	23,823	22,360	24,637	8,137
1997–98	132,846	143,811	18,274	109,190	118,202	24,555	23,656	25,609	8,380
1998–99	140,539	149,550	18,978	115,158	122,542	25,168	25,381	27,008	8,969
1999–2000	152,325	157,544	19,644	124,878	129,156	26,121	27,447	28,388	9,230
2000–01	170,345	170,345	20,606	140,578	140,578	27,973	29,766	29,766	9,183
Private institutions									
1970–71	8,379	36,932	20,694	8,150	35,920	21,421	230	1,012	9,383
1975–76	12,719	40,157	20,516	12,419	39,210	21,265	300	947	8,343
1979–80	19,146	43,181	20,614	18,682	42,135	21,533	464	1,046	7,584
1980–81	21,773	44,009	20,218	21,163	42,776	21,355	610	1,233	7,103
1983–84	28,907	49,727	21,763	28,092	48,325	23,465	815	1,402	6,216
1984–85	31,637	52,373	23,102	30,727	50,867	24,755	910	1,506	7,097
1985–86	34,342	55,258	24,282	33,376	53,704	26,137	966	1,554	7,035
1986–87	38,110	59,989	26,240	36,982	58,213	28,193	1,128	1,775	8,022
1987–88	41,145	62,190	27,133	40,006	60,468	28,921	1,139	1,722	8,555
1988–89	44,922	64,900	27,415	43,792	63,268	29,313	1,130	1,632	7,808
1989–90	48,885	67,410	27,979	47,713	65,794	29,991	1,172	1,616	7,496
1990–91	53,127	69,461	28,639	51,872	67,821	30,441	1,255	1,640	8,306
1991–92	57,342	72,645	29,084	56,041	70,997	31,061	1,301	1,648	7,774
1992–93	60,671	74,534	29,518	59,235	72,770	31,212	1,436	1,764	9,112
1993–94	64,041	76,688	30,204	62,466	74,802	31,764	1,575	1,886	10,243
1994–95	67,504	78,582	30,652	65,996	76,827	32,175	1,508	1,755	9,980
1995–96	70,952	80,408	31,128	69,050	78,253	32,394	1,902	2,156	12,868

NOTE: Constant dollars based on the Consumer Price Index adjusted to a school year basis. Data for 1995–96 and earlier years are for institutions of higher education. Institutions of higher education were accredited by an agency or association that was recognized by the U.S. Department of Education, or recognized directly by the Secretary of Education. The new degree-granting classification is very similar to the earlier higher education classification, except that it includes some additional institutions, primarily 2-year colleges, and excludes a few higher education institutions that did not award associate or higher degrees. Private college data not collected on a basis consistent with public institutions after 1995–96. Detail may not sum to totals due to rounding.

SOURCE: U.S. Department of Education, National Center for Education Statistics, Higher Education General Information Survey (HEGIS), 'Financial Statistics of Institutions of Higher Education," 1970–71 through 1985–86, "Fall Enrollment in Colleges and Universities," 1970 through 1985; Integrated Postsecondary Education Data System (IPEDS), "Finance," 1986–87 through 1999–2000, and Spring 2002 survey, "Fall Enrollment," 1986 through 1999, and Spring 2001 survey; and Bureau of Labor Statistics, Consumer Price Index. (This table was prepared October 2003.)

Current-fund expenditures of public degree-granting institutions, by state or jurisdiction: Selected years, 1980–81 to 2000–01

[In thousands of dollars]

State or jurisdiction	Institutions of higher education [1]				Degree-granting institutions [2]						Percent change, 1995–96 to 2000–01
	1980–81	1985–86	1990–91	1994–95	1995–96	1996–97	1997–98	1998–99 [3]	1999–2000	2000–01	
1	2	3	4	5	6	7	8	9	10	11	12
United States	$42,279,806	$63,193,853	$92,961,093	$115,464,975	$119,524,500	$125,428,736	$132,846,205	$140,538,586	$152,324,948	$170,344,840	42.5
Alabama	839,366	1,324,774	2,054,798	2,648,077	2,715,643	2,840,619	3,013,873	3,202,503	3,337,958	3,508,298	29.2
Alaska	158,700	224,042	289,606	336,584	352,811	344,723	349,939	361,140	385,553	432,793	22.7
Arizona	691,481	1,017,203	1,586,891	1,854,180	1,976,169	2,070,170	2,232,166	2,350,274	2,508,136	2,677,742	35.5
Arkansas	340,621	528,831	797,291	1,070,668	1,181,083	1,247,987	1,318,057	1,430,166	1,528,643	1,636,672	38.6
California	5,775,482	8,515,440	12,023,304	13,899,338	14,284,348	15,489,455	16,349,033	17,894,180	20,204,478	22,674,570	58.7
Colorado	738,363	1,057,558	1,452,137	1,862,438	1,974,306	2,077,034	2,257,920	2,358,290	2,440,045	2,630,166	33.2
Connecticut	367,850	562,696	886,846	1,134,014	1,168,038	1,193,722	1,301,238	1,419,257	1,568,490	1,621,083	38.8
Delaware	158,332	229,377	367,012	469,085	491,597	510,290	542,429	578,210	606,042	625,737	27.3
District of Columbia	71,791	80,764	97,556	99,351	103,072	92,985	69,345	83,575	81,990	91,938	−10.8
Florida	1,170,305	1,782,180	2,896,046	3,549,470	3,714,984	3,968,197	4,235,932	4,634,378	4,947,847	5,442,666	46.5
Georgia	754,060	1,255,964	1,929,993	2,728,682	2,835,505	3,043,813	3,337,172	3,506,991	3,955,764	4,049,036	42.8
Hawaii	222,718	312,248	498,307	653,303	634,970	638,096	684,248	688,307	679,287	737,605	16.2
Idaho	166,844	238,438	353,561	473,733	510,601	530,013	556,349	603,889	626,644	685,758	34.3
Illinois	1,780,403	2,571,409	3,528,967	4,293,437	4,498,142	4,712,347	4,942,580	5,217,493	5,525,410	5,932,860	31.9
Indiana	1,064,395	1,602,203	2,391,173	2,967,184	2,783,027	3,021,556	3,298,268	3,429,404	3,633,100	3,852,626	38.4
Iowa	767,590	1,092,542	1,734,476	2,051,631	2,163,536	2,233,470	2,368,381	2,478,128	2,612,023	2,603,053	20.3
Kansas	579,857	848,602	1,190,573	1,495,926	1,547,154	1,587,212	1,692,700	1,687,445	1,734,127	1,830,606	18.3
Kentucky	673,775	898,718	1,400,529	1,663,738	1,779,945	1,994,760	2,061,525	2,235,257	2,442,117	2,589,557	45.5
Louisiana	716,702	1,039,177	1,439,415	1,909,675	1,970,177	2,056,770	2,890,392	3,051,898	3,236,605	3,293,683	67.2
Maine	153,658	216,737	355,074	391,269	407,819	431,850	442,573	475,783	507,930	549,851	34.8
Maryland	795,100	1,064,430	1,684,341	1,997,636	2,136,898	2,309,739	2,490,326	2,567,437	2,920,899	3,141,491	47.0
Massachusetts	553,019	980,585	1,435,063	1,557,225	1,647,254	1,739,959	1,915,680	1,992,772	2,149,182	2,337,046	41.9
Michigan	2,053,795	2,946,336	4,416,914	5,395,757	5,653,791	5,980,104	6,293,933	6,658,103	7,329,879	7,966,990	40.9
Minnesota	876,632	1,324,691	2,012,225	2,624,464	2,694,395	2,583,477	2,607,348	2,763,990	2,898,495	3,076,832	14.2
Mississippi	539,222	706,380	978,366	1,358,795	1,440,692	1,490,260	1,636,580	1,816,580	2,008,628	2,111,975	46.6
Missouri	687,643	999,869	1,453,608	1,836,878	1,994,150	2,117,072	2,257,626	2,402,362	2,617,736	2,836,688	42.3
Montana	121,894	182,102	254,175	376,618	402,792	443,314	450,665	474,278	507,851	552,708	37.2
Nebraska	378,928	537,858	848,778	1,076,670	1,143,547	1,218,570	1,089,700	1,158,111	1,225,449	1,259,443	10.1
Nevada	111,347	180,107	330,592	447,901	505,518	547,065	597,026	648,485	701,413	757,424	49.8
New Hampshire	134,391	183,959	281,542	371,554	390,816	405,304	424,077	439,768	469,642	500,329	28.0
New Jersey	903,169	1,406,490	2,309,968	2,982,535	3,064,901	3,147,805	3,276,738	3,479,536	3,853,074	4,127,205	34.7
New Mexico	325,960	456,600	896,299	1,278,741	1,329,422	1,372,587	1,439,205	1,502,684	1,609,904	1,727,683	30.0
New York	2,519,104	3,802,602	5,605,621	6,922,118	6,728,593	6,872,196	7,180,732	7,170,827	7,798,717	13,541,832	101.3
North Carolina	1,128,383	1,799,173	2,581,156	3,406,215	3,538,606	3,791,447	4,057,906	4,335,879	4,665,386	5,062,536	43.1
North Dakota	192,046	288,214	367,959	456,730	440,332	450,580	472,760	481,388	487,364	516,617	17.3
Ohio	1,784,754	2,718,408	4,084,840	4,907,686	4,818,930	4,880,235	5,248,688	5,521,383	6,010,509	6,433,761	33.5
Oklahoma	583,174	844,829	1,057,248	1,263,002	1,329,938	1,458,358	1,592,465	1,698,453	1,904,467	2,129,124	60.1
Oregon	642,411	880,696	1,329,794	1,756,424	1,815,638	1,984,619	2,107,519	2,270,364	2,503,013	2,699,552	48.7
Pennsylvania	1,544,586	2,392,145	3,602,685	4,506,833	4,781,347	4,919,829	4,961,929	5,303,351	5,678,716	6,454,947	35.0
Rhode Island	158,365	213,253	292,199	344,457	353,270	368,598	376,190	401,526	421,252	451,179	27.7
South Carolina	617,963	951,848	1,475,074	1,817,631	1,903,952	2,020,736	2,192,724	2,311,108	2,515,415	2,194,033	15.2
South Dakota	124,103	149,092	197,853	252,443	290,868	294,514	319,705	335,243	350,211	382,250	31.4
Tennessee	665,885	1,081,052	1,585,614	2,042,171	2,062,547	2,126,871	2,185,603	2,286,000	2,258,072	2,430,880	17.9
Texas	2,736,276	4,375,082	5,959,584	7,817,433	8,300,915	8,758,306	9,313,169	9,843,327	10,820,078	12,744,081	53.5
Utah	405,314	669,714	993,625	1,354,017	1,442,592	1,536,120	1,654,048	1,867,303	1,978,429	2,085,409	44.6
Vermont	122,708	188,112	274,746	316,455	329,457	347,605	355,673	374,752	411,271	426,370	29.4
Virginia	1,143,755	1,825,156	2,812,109	3,414,167	3,515,201	3,804,552	3,608,285	3,832,003	4,085,736	4,415,701	25.6
Washington	993,171	1,399,780	2,157,074	2,807,168	2,945,074	3,102,644	3,599,004	3,521,717	3,807,514	4,205,962	42.8
West Virginia	317,482	376,293	548,802	674,664	718,596	741,058	755,252	799,193	847,145	916,466	27.5
Wisconsin	1,208,396	1,754,395	2,469,260	2,941,034	3,024,877	2,827,128	3,088,341	3,255,308	3,512,443	3,814,064	26.1
Wyoming	126,082	203,307	240,216	294,334	291,864	296,393	305,567	314,762	333,127	354,195	21.4
U.S. Service Schools ..	592,454	912,393	1,150,209	1,313,438	1,394,800	1,406,676	1,047,619	1,024,025	1,081,740	1,223,770	−12.3
Outlying areas	268,310	451,370	516,958	727,524	809,779	864,454	924,241	940,891	975,025	1,048,185	29.4
American Samoa	1,609	1,092	3,187	3,483	15,486	6,462	7,532	7,103	7,289	3,994	−74.2
Federated States of Micronesia	†	†	3,777	5,056	8,442	7,381	6,949	7,288	9,111	11,031	30.7
Guam	16,100	31,310	57,645	81,148	68,230	69,168	73,311	73,140	73,052	74,747	9.6
Marshall Islands	†	†	†	1,237	1,282	1,566	1,781	3,143	3,453	1,478	15.2
Northern Marianas	†	1,350	2,798	12,366	15,029	16,393	16,536	13,557	14,759	342	−97.7
Palau	†	†	3,837	3,667	5,942	3,940	4,032	4,567	4,127	4,494	−24.4
Puerto Rico	237,319	394,046	385,511	586,910	659,617	724,397	780,586	793,069	825,102	902,747	36.9
Trust Territory of the Pacific	1,447	5,992	†	†	†	†	†	†	†	†	†
Virgin Islands	11,835	17,580	60,202	33,656	35,750	35,149	33,513	39,023	38,131	49,352	38.0

† Not applicable.

[1] Institutions that were accredited by an agency or association that was recognized by the U.S. Department of Education, or recognized directly by the Secretary of Education.

[2] Four-year and 2-year degree-granting institutions that were participating in Title IV federal financial aid programs.

[3] Data imputed using alternative procedures.

NOTE: Detail may not sum to totals due to rounding.

SOURCE: U.S. Department of Education, National Center for Education Statistics, Higher Education General Information Survey (HEGIS), "Financial Statistics of Institutions of Higher Education" surveys, 1980–81 and 1985–86; and Integrated Postsecondary Education Data System (IPEDS), "Finance" surveys, 1990–91 through 1999–2000, and Spring 2002 survey. (This table was prepared October 2003.)

Average undergraduate tuition and fees and room and board rates paid by full-time-equivalent students in degree-granting institutions, by type and control of institution: 1964–65 to 2002–03

	Total tuition, room, and board					Tuition and required fees (in-state)					Dormitory rooms					Board (7-day basis)[1]				
Year and control of institution	All institutions	4-year institutions			2-year	All institutions	4-year institutions			2-year	All institutions	4-year institutions			2-year	All institutions	4-year institutions			2-year
		All 4-year	Universities	Other 4-year			All 4-year	Universities	Other 4-year			All 4-year	Universities	Other 4-year			All 4-year	Universities	Other 4-year	
1	2	3	4	5	6	7	8	9	10	11	12	13	14	15	16	17	18	19	20	21
All institutions																				
1976–77	$2,275	$2,577	$2,647	$2,527	$1,598	$924	$1,218	$1,210	$1,223	$346	$603	$611	$649	$584	$503	$748	$748	$788	$719	$750
1977–78	2,411	2,725	2,777	2,685	1,703	984	1,291	1,269	1,305	378	645	654	691	628	525	781	780	818	752	801
1978–79	2,587	2,917	2,967	2,879	1,828	1,073	1,397	1,370	1,413	411	688	696	737	667	575	826	825	860	800	842
1979–80	2,809	3,167	3,223	3,124	1,979	1,163	1,513	1,484	1,530	451	751	759	803	729	628	895	895	936	865	900
1980–81	3,101	3,499	3,535	3,469	2,230	1,289	1,679	1,634	1,705	526	836	846	881	821	705	976	975	1,020	943	1,000
1981–82	3,489	3,951	4,005	3,908	2,476	1,457	1,907	1,860	1,935	590	950	961	1,023	919	793	1,083	1,082	1,121	1,055	1,094
1982–83	3,877	4,406	4,466	4,356	2,713	1,626	2,139	2,081	2,173	675	1,064	1,078	1,150	1,028	873	1,187	1,189	1,235	1,155	1,165
1983–84	4,167	4,747	4,793	4,712	2,854	1,783	2,344	2,300	2,368	730	1,145	1,162	1,211	1,130	916	1,239	1,242	1,282	1,214	1,208
1984–85	4,563	5,160	5,236	5,107	3,179	1,985	2,567	2,539	2,583	821	1,267	1,282	1,343	1,242	1,058	1,310	1,311	1,353	1,282	1,301
1985–86[2]	4,885	5,504	5,597	5,441	3,367	2,181	2,784	2,770	2,793	888	1,338	1,355	1,424	1,309	1,107	1,365	1,365	1,403	1,339	1,372
1986–87[3]	5,206	5,964	6,124	5,857	3,295	2,312	3,042	3,042	3,042	897	1,405	1,427	1,501	1,376	1,034	1,489	1,495	1,581	1,439	1,364
1987–88	5,494	6,272	6,339	6,226	3,263	2,458	3,201	3,168	3,220	809	1,488	1,516	1,576	1,478	1,017	1,549	1,555	1,596	1,529	1,437
1988–89	5,869	6,725	6,801	6,673	3,573	2,658	3,472	3,422	3,499	979	1,575	1,609	1,665	1,573	1,085	1,636	1,644	1,715	1,601	1,509
1989–90	6,207	7,212	7,347	7,120	3,705	2,839	3,800	3,765	3,819	978	1,638	1,675	1,732	1,638	1,105	1,730	1,737	1,850	1,663	1,622
1990–91	6,562	7,602	7,709	7,528	3,930	3,016	4,009	3,958	4,036	1,087	1,743	1,782	1,848	1,740	1,182	1,802	1,811	1,903	1,751	1,660
1991–92	7,077	8,238	8,390	8,142	4,092	3,286	4,385	4,368	4,394	1,189	1,874	1,921	1,996	1,875	1,240	1,918	1,931	2,026	1,872	1,692
1992–93	7,452	8,758	8,934	8,648	4,207	3,517	4,752	4,665	4,795	1,276	1,939	1,991	2,104	1,926	1,240	1,996	2,015	2,165	1,927	1,692
1993–94	7,931	9,296	9,495	9,186	4,449	3,827	5,119	5,104	5,127	1,399	2,057	2,111	2,190	2,068	1,332	2,047	2,067	2,201	1,992	1,718
1994–95	8,306	9,728	9,863	9,646	4,633	4,044	5,391	5,287	5,441	1,488	2,145	2,200	2,281	2,155	1,396	2,116	2,138	2,295	2,049	1,750
1995–96	8,800	10,330	10,560	10,195	4,725	4,338	5,786	5,733	5,812	1,522	2,264	2,318	2,423	2,260	1,473	2,199	2,226	2,404	2,123	1,730
1996–97	9,206	10,841	11,033	10,726	4,895	4,564	6,118	6,055	6,150	1,543	2,365	2,422	2,518	2,368	1,522	2,276	2,301	2,460	2,208	1,830
1997–98	9,588	11,277	11,382	11,205	5,192	4,755	6,351	6,232	6,408	1,695	2,444	2,507	2,575	2,469	1,598	2,389	2,419	2,576	2,327	1,900
1998–99	10,076	11,888	12,123	11,752	5,291	5,013	6,723	6,713	6,728	1,725	2,557	2,626	2,710	2,578	1,616	2,506	2,540	2,700	2,446	1,950
1999–2000	10,444	12,352	12,613	12,198	5,408	5,238	7,044	7,026	7,052	1,721	2,682	2,749	2,845	2,695	1,733	2,524	2,559	2,741	2,451	1,954
2000–01	10,818	12,922	13,177	12,775	5,460	5,377	7,372	7,360	7,377	1,698	2,819	2,893	2,999	2,833	1,744	2,622	2,658	2,818	2,565	2,017
2001–02	11,380	13,639	13,942	13,468	5,718	5,646	7,786	7,788	7,785	1,800	2,981	3,060	3,184	2,992	1,848	2,753	2,793	2,970	2,692	2,070
2002–03[4]	12,111	14,504	14,907	14,286	6,238	6,067	8,342	8,439	8,297	1,901	3,177	3,260	3,377	3,195	2,059	2,866	2,902	3,091	2,794	2,278
Public institutions																				
1964–65	950	—	1,051	867	638	243	—	298	224	99	271	—	291	241	178					
1965–66	983	—	1,105	904	670	257	—	327	241	109	281	—	304	255	194					
1966–67	1,026	—	1,171	947	710	275	—	360	259	121	294	—	321	271	213					
1967–68	1,064	—	1,199	997	789	283	—	366	268	144	313	—	337	292	243					
1968–69	1,117	—	1,245	1,063	883	295	—	377	281	170	337	—	359	318	278					
1969–70	1,203	—	1,362	1,135	951	323	—	427	306	178	369	—	395	346	308					
1970–71	1,287	—	1,477	1,206	998	351	—	478	332	187	401	—	431	375	338					
1971–72	1,357	—	1,579	1,263	1,073	376	—	526	354	192	430	—	463	400	366					
1972–73	1,458	—	1,668	1,460	1,197	407	—	566	455	233	476	—	505	464	398					
1973–74	1,517	—	1,707	1,506	1,274	438	—	581	463	274	480	—	527	497	409					
1974–75	1,563	—	1,760	1,558	1,339	432	—	599	448	277	506	—	573	533	424					
1975–76	1,666	—	1,935	1,657	1,386	433	—	642	469	245	544	—	614	572	442					
1976–77	1,789	1,935	2,067	1,827	1,491	479	617	689	564	283	582	592	649	616	465					
1977–78	1,888	2,038	2,170	1,931	1,590	512	655	736	596	306	621	631	689	641	486					
1978–79	1,994	2,145	2,289	2,027	1,691	543	688	777	622	327	655	664	750	703	527					
1979–80	2,165	2,327	2,487	2,198	1,822	583	738	840	662	355	715	725	827	796	574					
1980–81	2,373	2,550	2,712	2,421	2,027	635	804	915	722	391	799	811	970	885	642					
1981–82	2,663	2,871	3,079	2,705	2,224	714	909	1,042	813	434	909	925	1,072	993	703					
1982–83	2,945	3,196	3,403	3,032	2,390	798	1,031	1,164	936	473	1,010	1,030	1,131	1,092	755					
1983–84	3,156	3,433	3,628	3,285	2,534	891	1,148	1,284	1,052	528	1,087	1,110	1,237	1,200	801					
1984–85	3,408	3,682	3,899	3,518	2,807	971	1,228	1,386	1,157	584	1,196	1,217	1,290	1,240	921					
1985–86[2]	3,571	3,859	4,146	3,637	2,981	1,045	1,318	1,536	1,248	641	1,242	1,263	1,355	1,295	960					
1986–87[3]	3,805	4,138	4,469	3,891	2,989	1,106	1,414	1,651	1,407	660	1,301	1,323	1,410	1,409	979					
1987–88	4,050	4,403	4,619	4,250	3,066	1,218	1,537	1,726	1,515	706	1,378	1,410	1,483	1,506	943					
1988–89	4,274	4,678	4,905	4,526	3,183	1,285	1,646	1,846	1,608	730	1,457	1,496	1,561	1,554	965					
1989–90	4,504	4,975	5,324	4,723	3,299	1,356	1,780	2,035	1,707	756	1,513	1,557	1,658	1,655	962					
1990–91	4,757	5,243	5,585	5,004	3,467	1,454	1,888	2,159	1,931	824	1,612	1,657	1,789	1,782	1,050					
1991–92	5,138	5,693	6,050	5,458	3,623	1,628	2,117	2,409	2,192	936	1,731	1,785	1,856	1,787	1,074					
1992–93	5,379	6,020	6,442	5,740	3,799	1,782	2,349	2,604	2,360	1,025	1,756	1,816	1,897	1,958	1,106					
1993–94	5,694	6,365	6,710	6,146	3,996	1,942	2,537	2,820	2,499	1,125	1,873	1,934	1,992	2,044	1,190					
1994–95	5,965	6,670	7,077	6,409	4,137	2,057	2,681	2,977	2,660	1,192	1,959	2,023	2,104	2,133	1,232					
1995–96	6,256	7,014	7,448	6,730	4,217	2,179	2,848	3,151	2,778	1,239	2,057	2,121	2,187	2,232	1,297					
1996–97	6,530	7,334	7,792	7,035	4,404	2,271	2,987	3,323	2,877	1,276	2,148	2,214	2,285	2,312	1,339					
1997–98	6,813	7,673	8,210	7,318	4,509	2,360	3,110	3,486	2,974	1,314	2,225	2,301	2,408	2,410	1,401					
1998–99	7,107	8,027	8,625	7,631	4,604	2,430	3,229	3,640		1,327	2,330	2,409			1,450					

See notes at end of table.

Average undergraduate tuition and fees and room and board rates paid by full-time-equivalent students in degree-granting institutions, by type and control of institution: 1964–65 to 2002–03—Continued

	Total tuition, room, and board					Tuition and required fees (in-state)					Dormitory rooms					Board (7-day basis) [1]				
		4-year institutions					4-year institutions					4-year institutions					4-year institutions			
Year and control of institution	All institutions	All 4-year	Universities	Other 4-year	2-year	All institutions	All 4-year	Universities	Other 4-year	2-year	All institutions	All 4-year	Universities	Other 4-year	2-year	All institutions	All 4-year	Universities	Other 4-year	2-year
1	2	3	4	5	6	7	8	9	10	11	12	13	14	15	16	17	18	19	20	21
1999–2000	7,310	8,275	8,912	7,852	4,720	2,506	3,349	3,768	3,091	1,338	2,440	2,519	2,516	2,521	1,549	2,364	2,406	2,628	2,239	1,834
2000–01	7,586	8,653	9,321	8,218	4,839	2,562	3,501	3,979	3,208	1,333	2,569	2,654	2,657	2,652	1,600	2,455	2,499	2,686	2,358	1,906
2001–02	8,022	9,196	9,948	8,715	5,137	2,700	3,735	4,273	3,409	1,380	2,723	2,816	2,838	2,801	1,722	2,598	2,645	2,837	2,504	2,036
2002–03 [4]	8,556	9,828	10,660	9,302	5,596	2,928	4,059	4,698	3,675	1,479	2,925	3,022	3,023	3,022	1,943	2,702	2,747	2,939	2,605	2,174
Private institutions																				
1964–65	1,907	—	2,202	1,810	1,455	1,088	—	1,297	1,023	702	331	—	390	308	289	488	—	515	479	464
1965–66	2,005	—	2,316	1,899	1,557	1,154	—	1,369	1,086	768	356	—	418	330	316	495	—	529	483	473
1966–67	2,124	—	2,456	2,007	1,679	1,233	—	1,456	1,162	845	385	—	452	355	347	506	—	548	490	487
1967–68	2,205	—	2,545	2,104	1,762	1,297	—	1,534	1,237	892	392	—	455	366	366	516	—	556	501	504
1968–69	2,321	—	2,673	2,237	1,876	1,383	—	1,638	1,335	956	404	—	463	382	391	534	—	572	520	529
1969–70	2,530	—	2,920	2,420	1,993	1,533	—	1,809	1,468	1,034	436	—	503	409	413	561	—	608	543	546
1970–71	2,738	—	3,163	2,599	2,103	1,684	—	1,980	1,603	1,109	468	—	542	434	434	586	—	641	562	560
1971–72	2,917	—	3,375	2,748	2,186	1,820	—	2,133	1,721	1,172	494	—	576	454	449	603	—	666	573	565
1972–73	3,038	—	3,512	2,934	2,273	1,898	—	2,226	1,846	1,221	524	—	622	490	457	616	—	664	598	595
1973–74	3,164	—	3,717	3,040	2,410	1,989	—	2,375	1,925	1,303	533	—	622	502	483	642	—	720	613	624
1974–75	3,403	—	4,076	3,156	2,591	2,117	—	2,614	1,954	1,367	586	—	691	536	564	700	—	771	666	660
1975–76	3,663	—	4,467	3,385	2,711	2,272	—	2,881	2,084	1,427	636	—	753	583	572	755	—	833	718	712
1976–77	3,906	3,977	4,715	3,714	2,971	2,467	2,534	3,051	2,351	1,592	649	651	783	604	607	790	791	882	759	772
1977–78	4,158	4,240	5,033	3,967	3,148	2,624	2,700	3,240	2,520	1,706	698	702	850	648	631	836	838	943	800	811
1978–79	4,514	4,609	5,403	4,327	3,389	2,867	2,958	3,487	2,771	1,831	758	761	916	704	700	889	890	1,000	851	858
1979–80	4,912	5,013	5,891	4,700	3,751	3,130	3,225	3,811	3,020	2,062	827	831	1,001	768	766	955	957	1,078	912	923
1980–81	5,470	5,594	6,569	5,249	4,303	3,498	3,617	4,275	3,390	2,413	918	921	1,086	859	871	1,054	1,056	1,209	1,000	1,019
1981–82	6,166	6,330	7,443	5,947	4,746	3,953	4,113	4,887	3,853	2,605	970	1,039	1,229	970	1,022	1,175	1,178	1,327	1,124	1,119
1982–83	6,920	7,126	8,536	6,646	5,364	4,439	4,639	5,583	4,329	3,008	1,181	1,181	1,453	1,083	1,177	1,300	1,306	1,501	1,234	1,179
1983–84	7,508	7,759	9,308	7,244	5,571	4,851	5,093	6,217	4,726	3,099	1,278	1,279	1,531	1,191	1,253	1,380	1,387	1,559	1,327	1,219
1984–85	8,202	8,451	10,243	7,849	6,203	5,315	5,556	6,843	5,135	3,485	1,426	1,426	1,753	1,309	1,424	1,462	1,469	1,647	1,405	1,294
1985–86 [2]	8,885	9,228	11,034	8,551	6,512	5,789	6,121	7,374	5,641	3,672	1,553	1,557	1,940	1,420	1,500	1,542	1,551	1,720	1,490	1,340
1986–87 [3]	9,676	10,039	12,278	9,276	6,384	6,316	6,658	8,118	6,171	3,684	1,658	1,673	2,097	1,518	1,266	1,702	1,708	2,060	1,587	1,434
1987–88	10,512	10,659	13,075	9,854	7,078	6,988	7,116	8,771	6,574	4,161	1,748	1,760	2,244	1,593	1,380	1,775	1,783	2,063	1,687	1,537
1988–89	11,189	11,474	14,073	10,620	7,967	7,461	7,722	9,451	7,172	4,817	1,849	1,863	2,353	1,686	1,540	1,880	1,889	2,269	1,762	1,609
1989–90	12,018	12,284	15,098	11,374	8,670	8,147	8,396	10,348	7,778	5,196	1,923	1,935	2,411	1,774	1,663	1,948	1,953	2,339	1,823	1,811
1990–91	12,910	13,237	16,503	12,220	9,302	8,772	9,083	11,379	8,389	5,570	2,063	2,077	2,654	1,889	1,744	2,074	2,077	2,470	1,943	1,989
1991–92	13,892	14,258	17,572	13,201	9,632	9,419	9,759	12,037	9,060	5,754	2,221	2,241	2,825	2,042	1,788	2,252	2,257	2,709	2,098	2,090
1992–93	14,634	15,009	18,898	13,882	9,903	9,942	10,294	13,055	9,533	6,059	2,348	2,362	3,018	2,151	1,970	2,344	2,354	2,825	2,197	1,875
1993–94	15,496	15,904	20,097	14,640	10,406	10,572	10,952	13,874	10,100	6,370	2,490	2,506	3,277	2,261	2,067	2,434	2,445	2,946	2,278	1,970
1994–95	16,207	16,602	21,041	15,363	11,170	11,111	11,481	14,537	10,653	6,914	2,587	2,601	3,469	2,347	2,233	2,509	2,520	3,035	2,362	2,023
1995–96	17,208	17,612	22,502	16,198	11,563	11,864	12,243	15,605	11,297	7,094	2,738	2,751	3,680	2,473	2,371	2,606	2,617	3,218	2,429	2,098
1996–97	18,039	18,442	23,520	16,994	11,954	12,498	12,881	16,552	11,871	7,236	2,878	2,889	3,826	2,602	2,537	2,663	2,672	3,132	2,520	2,181
1997–98	18,516	19,070	24,116	17,717	12,921	12,801	13,344	17,229	12,338	7,464	2,954	2,964	3,756	2,731	2,672	2,762	2,761	3,132	2,648	2,785
1998–99	19,368	19,929	25,443	18,430	13,319	13,428	13,973	18,340	12,815	7,854	3,075	3,091	3,914	2,850	2,581	2,865	2,865	3,188	2,765	2,884
1999–2000	20,186	20,706	26,534	19,127	13,965	14,081	14,588	19,307	13,361	8,235	3,224	3,237	4,070	2,976	2,808	2,882	2,881	3,157	2,790	2,922
2000–01	21,368	21,856	27,676	20,247	14,788	15,000	15,470	20,106	14,233	9,067	3,374	3,392	4,270	3,121	2,722	2,993	2,993	3,300	2,893	3,000
2001–02	22,413	22,896	29,115	21,220	15,825	15,742	16,211	21,176	14,923	10,076	3,567	3,576	4,478	3,301	3,116	3,104	3,109	3,462	2,996	2,653
2002–03 [4]	23,503	23,940	31,052	22,103	17,760	16,517	16,948	22,686	15,532	10,755	3,750	3,762	4,712	3,476	3,184	3,236	3,229	3,653	3,095	3,821

—Not available.

[1] Data for 1986–87 and later years reflect 20 meals per week rather than meals 7 days per week.

[2] Room and board data are estimated.

[3] Because of revisions in data collection procedures, figures are not entirely comparable with those for previous years. In particular, data on board rates are somewhat higher than earlier years because they reflect a basis of 20 meals per week rather than meals served 7 days per week. Since many institutions serve fewer than 3 meals each day, the 1986–87 and later data reflect a more accurate accounting of total board costs.

[4] Preliminary data based on fall 2001 enrollment weights.

NOTE: Data are for the entire academic year and are average charges paid by students. Tuition and fees were weighted by the number of full-time-equivalent undergraduates, but were not adjusted to reflect student residency. Room and board were based on full-time students. The data have not been adjusted for changes in the purchasing power of the dollar over time. Data for 1976–77 to 1996–97 are for institutions of higher education were accredited by an agency or association that was recognized by the U.S. Department of Education, or recognized directly by the Secretary of Education. The new degree-granting classification is very similar to the earlier higher education classification, except that it includes some additional institutions, primarily 2-year colleges, and excludes a few higher education institutions that did not award associate or higher degrees. Some data have been revised from previously published figures. Because of their low response rate, data for private 2-year colleges must be interpreted with caution. Data for 1999 imputed using alternative procedures. (See Guide to Sources for details.) Some data have been revised from previously published figures. Detail may not sum to totals due to rounding.

SOURCE: U.S. Department of Education, National Center for Education Statistics, Higher Education General Information Survey (HEGIS), "Institutional Characteristics of Colleges and Universities" surveys, 1965–66 through 1985–86; and "Fall Enrollment in Institutions of Higher Education" surveys, 1965 through 1985; Integrated Postsecondary Education Data System (IPEDS), "Fall Enrollment" surveys, 1985 through 1999, and "Institutional Characteristics" surveys, 1986–87 through 2000–01, and Spring 2001 and Spring 2002 surveys. (This table was prepared November 2003.)

Average graduate and first-professional tuition and required fees in degree-granting institutions, by first-professional discipline and control of institution: 1987–88 to 2002–03

Year and control	Average full-time graduate tuition	Average full-time first-professional tuition									
		Chiro-practic	Dentistry	Medicine	Optometry	Osteopathic medicine	Pharmacy	Podiatry	Veterinary medicine	Law	Theology
1	2	3	4	5	6	7	8	9	10	11	12
All institutions											
1987–88	$3,599	$6,996	$9,399	$9,034	$7,926	$10,674	$5,201	$12,736	$4,503	$6,636	$3,572
1988–89	3,728	7,972	9,324	9,439	8,503	11,462	4,952	13,232	4,856	7,099	3,911
1989–90	4,135	8,315	10,515	10,597	9,469	11,888	5,890	14,611	5,470	8,059	4,079
1990–91	4,488	9,108	10,270	10,571	9,512	12,830	5,889	15,143	5,396	8,708	4,569
1991–92	5,116	10,226	12,049	11,646	9,610	13,004	6,731	16,257	6,367	9,469	4,876
1992–93	5,475	11,117	12,710	12,265	10,858	14,297	6,635	17,426	6,771	10,463	5,331
1993–94	5,973	11,503	14,403	13,074	10,385	15,038	7,960	17,621	7,159	11,552	5,253
1994–95	6,247	12,324	15,164	13,834	11,053	15,913	8,315	18,138	7,741	12,374	5,648
1995–96	6,741	12,507	15,647	14,860	11,544	16,785	8,602	18,434	8,208	13,278	5,991
1996–97	7,111	12,721	16,585	15,481	12,250	17,888	9,207	19,056	8,668	14,081	6,558
1997–98	7,246	13,131	17,393	16,075	12,685	18,654	9,544	19,355	9,013	14,877	6,761
1998–99	7,685	13,582	18,800	17,110	14,066	19,718	9,636	19,547	9,392	15,590	7,147
1999–2000	8,071	14,256	19,314	17,775	14,389	20,817	10,601	20,102	9,865	16,399	7,425
2000–01	8,429	15,092	21,696	18,935	15,360	21,685	11,175	20,313	10,365	17,659	10,100
2001–02 [1]	8,857	15,605	22,643	19,973	16,066	22,753	12,008	21,115	10,940	18,577	8,543
2002–03 [2]	9,264	—	—	—	—	—	—	—	—	—	—
Public [3]											
1987–88	1,827	†	4,614	5,245	2,789	5,125	2,462	†	3,523	2,810	†
1988–89	1,913	†	5,286	5,669	3,455	6,269	2,218	†	3,889	2,766	†
1989–90	1,999	†	5,728	6,259	3,569	6,521	2,816	†	4,505	3,196	†
1990–91	2,206	†	5,927	6,437	3,821	7,188	2,697	†	4,840	3,430	†
1991–92	2,524	†	6,595	7,106	4,161	7,699	2,871	†	5,231	3,933	†
1992–93	2,791	†	7,006	7,867	5,106	8,404	2,987	†	5,553	4,261	†
1993–94	3,050	†	7,525	8,329	5,325	8,640	3,567	†	6,107	4,835	†
1994–95	3,250	†	8,125	8,812	5,643	8,954	3,793	†	6,571	5,307	†
1995–96	3,449	†	8,806	9,585	6,130	9,448	4,100	†	6,907	5,821	†
1996–97	3,607	†	9,434	10,057	6,561	9,932	4,884	†	7,343	6,565	†
1997–98	3,744	†	9,657	10,501	7,366	10,358	5,065	19,541	7,742	7,004	†
1998–99	3,897	†	10,277	11,141	7,890	10,802	5,482	19,818	7,975	7,425	†
1999–2000	4,043	†	10,615	11,569	8,021	11,211	5,897	19,578	8,601	7,740	†
2000–01	4,243	†	11,574	12,074	8,302	11,516	6,245	20,228	8,964	8,326	†
2001–02 [1]	4,496	†	12,446	13,264	9,060	12,587	7,020	21,254	9,524	9,043	†
2002–03 [2]	4,855	†	—	—	—	—	—	—	—	—	†
Private											
1987–88	6,769	6,996	16,201	14,945	11,635	13,311	8,834	12,736	12,544	9,048	3,572
1988–89	6,945	7,972	16,127	15,610	12,050	13,536	9,692	13,232	13,285	9,892	3,911
1989–90	7,881	8,315	16,800	16,826	13,640	14,117	10,656	14,611	14,184	10,901	4,079
1990–91	8,507	9,108	18,270	17,899	13,767	15,009	11,546	15,143	14,159	12,247	4,569
1991–92	9,592	10,226	20,318	19,225	14,366	16,098	12,937	16,257	15,816	12,946	4,876
1992–93	10,008	11,117	21,309	19,585	14,459	17,098	13,373	17,426	17,103	13,975	5,331
1993–94	10,790	11,503	23,824	20,769	14,156	17,720	14,838	17,621	17,433	15,193	5,253
1994–95	11,338	12,324	24,641	21,819	14,497	18,422	14,894	18,138	17,940	16,201	5,648
1995–96	12,083	12,507	25,678	23,001	15,235	19,619	15,618	18,434	19,380	17,251	5,991
1996–97	12,537	12,721	26,618	24,242	15,949	20,714	15,934	19,056	19,526	18,276	6,558
1997–98	12,774	13,151	29,923	25,189	16,415	21,710	16,307	19,316	20,299	19,171	6,761
1998–99	13,299	13,582	31,659	26,502	17,848	22,796	16,905	19,492	21,286	20,154	7,147
1999–2000	13,782	14,256	32,268	27,694	18,087	23,838	18,091	20,193	21,772	21,081	7,425
2000–01	14,420	15,092	35,234	29,863	19,592	24,712	19,031	20,329	22,600	22,775	10,100
2001–02 [1]	15,165	15,605	36,207	30,485	20,463	25,779	20,459	21,089	23,303	23,911	8,543
2002–03 [2]	15,279	—	—	—	—	—	—	—	—	—	—

† Not applicable.

—Not available.

[1] Preliminary first-professional figures based on 2000–01 graduates.

[2] Preliminary data based on fall 2001 enrollment.

[3] Data are based on in-state tuition only.

NOTE: Average graduate student tuition weighted by fall full-time-equivalent graduate enrollment. Average first-professional tuition weighted by number of degrees conferred during the academic year. Some year-to-year fluctuations in tuition data may reflect non-reporting by individual institutions. Excludes institutions not reporting degrees conferred and institutions not reporting tuition. Some data have been revised from previously published figures. Data for 1987–88 to 1997–98 are for institutions of higher education. Institutions of higher education were accredited by an agency or association that was recognized by the U.S. Department of Education, or recognized directly by the Secretary of Education. The new degree-granting classification is very similar to the earlier higher education classification, except that it includes some additional institutions, primarily 2-year colleges, and excludes a few higher education institutions that did not award associate or higher degrees. Some data have been revised from previously published figures. Detail may not sum to totals due to rounding.

SOURCE: U.S. Department of Education, National Center for Education Statistics, Integrated Postsecondary Education Data System (IPEDS), "Fall Enrollment" surveys, 1987 through 1999, and "Institutional Characteristics" surveys, 1987–88 through 2000–01, and Spring 2001 and Spring 2002 surveys. (This table was prepared November 2003.)

Average undergraduate tuition and fees and room and board rates paid by full-time-equivalent students in degree-granting institutions, by type and control of institution and state: 2001–02 and 2002–03

State	Public 4-year, 2001–02		Public 4-year, 2002–03 [1]				Private 4-year, 2001–02		Private 4-year, 2002–03 [1]				Public 2-year, tuition only (in-state)	
	Total	Tuition and required fees (in-state)	Total	Tuition and required fees (in-state)	Room	Board	Total	Tuition and required fees	Total	Tuition and required fees	Room	Board	2001–02	2002–03 [1]
1	2	3	4	5	6	7	8	9	10	11	12	13	14	15
United States	$9,196	$3,735	$9,828	$4,059	$3,022	$2,747	$22,896	$16,211	$23,940	$16,948	$3,762	$3,229	$1,380	$1,479
Alabama	7,647	3,242	7,931	3,511	2,257	2,163	15,137	10,135	15,833	10,607	2,518	2,709	1,989	2,133
Alaska	9,260	3,062	9,457	3,162	3,074	3,221	16,179	10,161	17,697	11,108	3,018	3,571	1,706	1,748
Arizona	8,233	2,488	8,797	2,587	3,390	2,820	15,913	10,716	17,075	11,723	2,889	2,462	963	1,024
Arkansas	7,287	3,371	7,791	3,714	2,111	1,966	14,347	9,888	15,091	10,437	2,085	2,568	1,290	1,514
California	10,289	2,719	10,849	2,782	4,090	3,977	26,193	18,394	26,760	18,623	4,354	3,783	316	317
Colorado	8,815	3,166	9,179	3,102	2,814	3,263	25,038	16,917	24,425	16,461	4,059	3,904	1,693	1,728
Connecticut	11,066	4,780	11,805	5,142	3,553	3,110	29,008	21,016	30,634	22,257	5,040	3,337	1,889	2,008
Delaware	10,889	5,063	11,523	5,439	3,324	2,760	14,886	8,980	15,626	9,348	3,225	3,053	1,800	1,878
District of Columbia	†	2,070	†	2,070	†	†	26,977	18,751	28,053	19,595	5,407	3,051	†	†
Florida	8,364	2,555	8,762	2,594	3,391	2,777	20,287	13,988	21,216	14,675	3,506	3,035	1,494	1,496
Georgia	7,945	2,836	8,749	2,945	3,437	2,368	21,018	14,451	22,125	15,263	3,943	2,919	1,275	1,336
Hawaii	7,987	3,051	8,242	3,133	2,507	2,601	16,755	8,985	17,350	8,829	3,487	5,034	1,067	1,069
Idaho	7,162	2,859	7,585	3,033	2,048	2,504	10,116	5,278	10,643	5,542	2,045	3,057	1,410	1,542
Illinois	10,206	4,572	11,027	5,171	2,819	3,037	22,781	16,105	24,604	17,353	3,977	3,274	1,567	1,662
Indiana.	9,781	3,999	10,655	4,620	2,730	3,305	22,419	16,854	23,741	17,762	3,077	2,903	2,154	2,436
Iowa	8,251	3,470	9,185	4,140	2,657	2,389	20,289	15,332	21,392	16,201	2,393	2,799	2,359	2,559
Kansas	6,986	2,701	7,791	3,174	2,206	2,412	16,501	11,911	17,542	12,612	2,166	2,763	1,444	1,640
Kentucky	7,365	3,184	7,691	3,405	2,262	2,024	15,743	11,037	15,080	10,187	2,331	2,562	1,494	1,861
Louisiana	6,711	2,877	6,922	2,881	2,049	1,992	23,266	16,737	24,175	17,198	3,748	3,228	963	994
Maine	10,292	4,821	10,329	4,624	2,829	2,877	24,152	17,621	25,678	18,851	3,337	3,490	2,647	2,768
Maryland	11,372	4,966	12,332	5,406	3,906	3,020	26,936	19,606	27,668	20,156	4,279	3,233	2,238	2,358
Massachusetts	9,361	3,991	10,818	4,974	3,208	2,637	29,939	21,492	32,108	23,309	4,908	3,892	1,939	2,353
Michigan	10,551	5,042	11,408	5,494	2,934	2,979	16,843	11,600	17,770	12,109	2,815	2,846	1,779	1,810
Minnesota	9,065	4,483	9,983	5,036	2,682	2,265	22,349	16,918	23,517	17,900	2,825	2,792	2,749	2,880
Mississippi	7,613	3,417	8,039	3,716	2,358	1,965	14,342	10,106	15,223	10,612	2,344	2,268	1,362	1,453
Missouri	8,673	4,112	9,395	4,602	2,676	2,117	18,745	13,201	19,743	13,724	3,075	2,943	1,514	1,792
Montana	8,310	3,468	8,966	3,925	2,261	2,780	16,033	10,107	15,892	10,805	2,305	2,782	2,152	2,309
Nebraska	7,739	3,224	8,408	3,612	2,277	2,519	18,805	14,060	17,937	12,953	2,457	2,528	1,495	1,567
Nevada	8,575	2,450	9,001	2,529	3,781	2,692	19,482	13,273	17,811	10,956	3,530	3,325	1,410	1,454
New Hampshire	12,343	6,725	9,415	3,524	3,575	2,316	25,955	18,707	27,384	19,777	4,245	3,362	4,330	4,492
New Jersey	12,853	6,076	13,937	6,709	4,472	2,756	25,111	17,333	26,705	18,413	4,366	3,926	2,237	2,315
New Mexico	7,587	2,846	7,979	3,016	2,323	2,639	20,417	14,393	17,329	11,664	2,776	2,890	923	945
New York	10,739	4,119	10,984	4,220	3,762	3,003	26,419	18,275	27,812	19,272	4,995	3,544	2,594	2,729
North Carolina	7,655	2,640	8,350	3,097	2,791	2,462	21,054	15,143	22,248	16,079	2,979	3,190	1,015	1,112
North Dakota	6,844	3,128	7,388	3,401	1,551	2,435	11,853	8,379	12,551	8,947	1,565	2,039	2,104	2,230
Ohio	11,170	5,138	12,260	5,898	3,559	2,803	22,022	16,161	23,265	17,125	3,115	3,026	2,376	2,597
Oklahoma	6,295	2,373	6,832	2,612	1,962	2,258	16,311	11,218	16,778	11,609	2,444	2,725	1,209	1,301
Oregon	10,065	3,864	10,548	4,028	3,443	3,077	24,454	18,312	25,194	18,737	3,249	3,208	1,716	1,964
Pennsylvania	11,867	6,316	12,944	7,072	3,156	2,716	26,168	18,917	27,506	19,976	4,076	3,455	2,365	2,384
Rhode Island	11,575	4,689	12,266	5,072	3,866	3,328	27,172	19,142	27,827	20,007	4,229	3,591	1,854	2,014
South Carolina	10,038	5,448	11,139	6,306	2,650	2,183	18,009	13,041	18,934	13,708	2,634	2,591	1,791	2,182
South Dakota	7,544	3,787	7,724	3,971	1,568	2,186	16,306	12,023	16,806	12,287	2,045	2,474	2,969	3,167
Tennessee	7,780	3,339	8,349	3,589	2,303	2,457	19,161	13,692	20,134	14,384	3,078	2,672	1,652	1,751
Texas	8,057	2,967	8,661	3,318	2,839	2,504	18,160	12,673	19,708	13,970	2,907	2,832	977	1,023
Utah	7,411	2,389	7,410	2,638	1,961	2,812	8,947	3,969	9,237	4,250	2,455	2,533	1,676	1,798
Vermont	13,426	7,449	14,016	7,754	3,916	2,345	23,208	16,454	23,990	17,165	3,733	3,093	3,148	3,652
Virginia	8,989	3,770	9,538	4,087	2,922	2,529	20,096	14,429	21,584	15,754	2,938	2,893	1,133	1,275
Washington	9,994	3,790	10,816	4,288	3,031	3,497	22,690	16,706	23,720	17,264	3,216	3,241	1,884	2,095
West Virginia.	7,628	2,646	8,175	2,899	2,611	2,665	18,066	12,854	18,210	12,815	2,556	2,839	1,676	1,741
Wisconsin	7,788	3,693	8,204	3,965	2,382	1,856	21,234	15,829	22,402	16,724	2,909	2,768	2,310	2,555
Wyoming	7,421	2,807	7,977	2,997	2,182	2,798	†	†	†	†	†	†	1,493	1,561

† Not applicable.

[1] Preliminary data based on fall 2001 enrollments.

NOTE: Data are for the entire academic year and are average charges. Tuition and fees were weighted by the number of full-time-equivalent undergraduates in 2001, but are not adjusted to reflect student residency. Room and board are based on full-time students. (See Guide to Sources for details.) Data revised from previously published figures. Detail may not sum to totals due to rounding.

SOURCE: U.S. Department of Education, National Center for Education Statistics, Integrated Postsecondary Education Data System (IPEDS), Spring 2001 and Spring 2002. (This table was prepared November 2003.)

College & University Education / Student Charges & Financial Assistance

Percent of undergraduates receiving aid, by type and source of aid and selected student characteristics: 1999–2000

Selected student characteristic	Enrollment of undergraduates,[1] in thousands	Any aid			Grants			Loans			Work study	Other		
		Total[2]	Federal	Non-federal	Total	Federal	Non-federal	Total	Federal	Non-federal	Total[3]	Total	Federal	Non-federal
1	2	3	4	5	6	7	8	9	10	11	12	13	14	15
All undergraduates	16,539	55.3 (0.6)	40.5 (0.6)	36.8 (0.6)	44.4 (0.6)	23.1 (0.5)	34.0 (0.6)	28.8 (0.5)	27.9 (0.5)	3.9 (0.1)	5.4 (0.2)	6.9 (0.3)	2.9 (0.1)	1.6 (0.2)
Sex														
Men	7,231	52.5 (0.7)	37.7 (0.7)	34.7 (0.7)	40.3 (0.7)	19.4 (0.5)	31.7 (0.7)	27.3 (0.6)	26.4 (0.6)	4.0 (0.2)	4.7 (0.2)	8.8 (0.3)	3.1 (0.1)	1.7 (0.2)
Women	9,308	57.5 (0.7)	42.7 (0.7)	38.3 (0.7)	47.5 (0.6)	26.0 (0.6)	35.8 (0.7)	30.0 (0.6)	29.1 (0.6)	3.8 (0.2)	6.0 (0.2)	5.5 (0.3)	2.7 (0.1)	1.6 (0.2)
Race/ethnicity[4]														
White, non-Hispanic	11,074	53.3 (0.6)	37.5 (0.6)	36.7 (0.6)	41.4 (0.6)	17.7 (0.4)	34.0 (0.6)	29.1 (0.6)	28.2 (0.6)	4.2 (0.2)	5.5 (0.2)	7.1 (0.3)	3.2 (0.1)	1.5 (0.1)
Black, non-Hispanic	2,051	69.5 (1.4)	55.3 (1.5)	39.9 (2.0)	58.3 (1.5)	40.1 (1.2)	36.9 (2.1)	35.9 (1.9)	35.2 (1.8)	3.3 (0.3)	5.9 (0.5)	7.9 (0.7)	2.6 (0.3)	2.1 (0.5)
Hispanic	1,984	58.3 (1.6)	46.4 (1.7)	36.5 (1.3)	50.3 (1.6)	35.1 (1.7)	33.3 (1.3)	24.4 (1.2)	23.3 (1.2)	3.5 (0.4)	5.3 (0.5)	6.2 (0.7)	2.0 (0.2)	1.8 (0.6)
Asian American/ Pacific Islander	1,050	44.3 (1.7)	33.5 (1.4)	32.1 (1.4)	37.4 (1.5)	22.4 (1.2)	30.2 (1.3)	22.4 (1.3)	21.8 (1.3)	2.5 (0.3)	5.3 (0.6)	4.6 (0.5)	1.8 (0.3)	1.5 (0.3)
American Indian/ Alaska Native	170	56.5 (3.5)	44.0 (3.6)	36.9 (2.7)	50.0 (3.5)	33.7 (3.6)	33.9 (2.8)	23.3 (2.6)	22.5 (2.5)	2.4 (0.8)	3.0 (0.7)	8.7 (1.9)	1.2 (0.5)	3.7 (1.4)
Age														
23 years old or younger	9,462	58.9 (0.6)	44.7 (0.6)	40.6 (0.6)	47.1 (0.6)	22.9 (0.5)	37.8 (0.6)	33.8 (0.5)	32.8 (0.5)	5.2 (0.2)	8.1 (0.3)	7.3 (0.2)	5.0 (0.2)	1.2 (0.1)
24 to 29 years old	2,806	55.7 (1.1)	44.7 (1.0)	31.2 (1.0)	44.3 (1.0)	30.4 (0.9)	28.5 (1.0)	30.1 (0.9)	29.3 (0.9)	2.6 (0.2)	2.6 (0.2)	7.2 (0.5)	# (#)	1.6 (0.2)
30 years old or over	4,271	47.1 (1.0)	28.6 (0.8)	31.9 (1.1)	38.4 (0.9)	18.8 (0.6)	29.1 (1.0)	16.9 (0.6)	16.2 (0.6)	1.7 (0.1)	1.4 (0.2)	5.9 (0.6)	# (#)	2.6 (0.5)
Marital status														
Married	3,578	48.1 (1.0)	30.0 (0.8)	31.0 (0.9)	38.1 (0.9)	18.5 (0.6)	28.4 (0.9)	18.1 (0.7)	17.4 (0.6)	1.9 (0.2)	1.3 (0.2)	6.5 (0.5)	# (#)	2.1 (0.4)
Not married[5]	12,715	56.9 (0.6)	42.9 (0.6)	38.3 (0.6)	45.6 (0.6)	23.7 (0.5)	35.5 (0.6)	31.6 (0.5)	30.7 (0.5)	4.4 (0.2)	6.6 (0.2)	7.0 (0.3)	3.8 (0.1)	1.5 (0.2)
Separated	247	77.1 (2.4)	69.6 (2.7)	39.2 (2.6)	69.4 (2.5)	59.6 (2.8)	35.3 (2.7)	39.0 (2.4)	37.9 (2.3)	3.5 (0.8)	4.2 (0.9)	6.6 (1.3)	# (#)	2.6 (0.7)
Attendance status														
Full-time, full-year	6,364	72.5 (0.5)	57.7 (0.6)	51.8 (0.7)	58.6 (0.6)	30.3 (0.6)	48.3 (0.7)	45.4 (0.6)	44.3 (0.6)	6.8 (0.3)	11.2 (0.4)	9.6 (0.3)	5.6 (0.2)	1.9 (0.2)
Part-time and part-year	10,176	44.6 (0.8)	29.8 (0.7)	27.4 (0.8)	35.4 (0.7)	18.6 (0.5)	25.0 (0.7)	18.4 (0.6)	17.7 (0.6)	2.0 (0.1)	1.9 (0.1)	5.2 (0.4)	1.2 (0.1)	1.5 (0.3)
Dependency status and family income														
Dependent	8,126	58.9 (0.6)	44.2 (0 6)	41.8 (0.6)	46.1 (0.6)	20.1 (0.5)	38.9 (0.6)	34.9 (0.6)	33.8 (0.6)	5.6 (0.2)	8.9 (0.3)	7.8 (0.3)	5.8 (0.2)	1.1 (0.1)
Less than $20,000	1,079	77.4 (1.1)	70.3 (1.3)	50.2 (1.4)	75.0 (1.2)	65.9 (1.3)	47.8 (1.5)	35.8 (1.3)	35.2 (1.3)	4.6 (0.4)	12.2 (0.8)	5.1 (0.5)	2.8 (0.3)	1.3 (0.3)
$20,000–$39,999	1,686	67.6 (0.9)	56.8 (1.1)	49.3 (1.1)	61.1 (1.0)	43.6 (1.1)	47.0 (1.1)	38.8 (1.1)	37.9 (1.1)	5.5 (0.4)	11.9 (0.6)	6.6 (0.5)	4.4 (0.3)	1.3 (0.2)
$40,000–$59,999	1,755	57.5 (1.0)	41.5 (1.0)	43.0 (1.0)	42.7 (1.0)	8.8 (0.5)	40.2 (1.0)	38.1 (1.0)	36.9 (1.0)	5.8 (0.4)	9.9 (0.6)	8.3 (0.5)	6.0 (0.4)	1.3 (0.2)
$60,000–$79,999	1,394	53.8 (1.2)	37.2 (1.0)	37.6 (1.1)	34.7 (1.1)	1.4 (0.2)	34.4 (1.1)	36.6 (1.0)	35.4 (1.0)	6.7 (0.5)	8.0 (0.6)	9.4 (0.5)	8.2 (0.5)	0.9 (0.2)
$80,000–$99,999	901	52.3 (1.4)	33.1 (1.2)	36.8 (1.3)	33.2 (1.2)	0.5 (0.1)	33.0 (1.2)	32.6 (1.2)	31.1 (1.2)	6.4 (0.6)	5.5 (0.5)	8.8 (0.6)	7.1 (0.5)	0.8 (0.2)
$100,000 or more	1,312	44.4 (1.0)	25.3 (0.8)	31.7 (0.9)	28.7 (0.9)	0.4 (0.1)	28.7 (0.9)	24.4 (0.8)	23.3 (0.8)	4.4 (0.3)	4.2 (0.4)	8.3 (0.5)	6.5 (0.4)	0.9 (0.2)
Independent	8,414	51.9 (0.8)	51.9 (0.8)	31.9 (0.9)	42.7 (0.8)	26.0 (0.6)	29.2 (0.8)	23.0 (0.7)	22.3 (0.6)	2.2 (0.1)	2.1 (0.1)	6.1 (0.4)	0.1 (0.0)	2.1 (0.3)
Less than $10,000	1,668	74.0 (0.9)	66.4 (1.1)	41.5 (1.3)	69.4 (1.0)	61.5 (1.1)	38.1 (1.3)	39.7 (1.2)	39.0 (1.2)	3.1 (0.3)	6.1 (0.4)	6.6 (0.5)	0.3 (0.1)	3.1 (0.4)
$10,000–$19,999	1,610	63.5 (1.0)	53.5 (1.4)	35.3 (1.3)	52.6 (1.3)	38.6 (1.2)	32.3 (1.3)	33.2 (1.2)	32.6 (1.2)	2.9 (0.3)	2.5 (0.3)	6.9 (0.5)	0.1 (#)	2.5 (0.3)
$20,000–$29,999	1,343	51.9 (1.4)	38.0 (1.2)	30.4 (1.5)	41.1 (1.3)	24.8 (1.0)	27.9 (1.5)	22.1 (1.0)	21.4 (1.0)	2.1 (0.3)	1.3 (0.3)	6.8 (0.7)	# (#)	1.8 (0.3)
$30,000–$49,999	1,773	41.6 (1.2)	23.6 (1.0)	27.8 (1.1)	31.1 (1.1)	11.6 (0.6)	25.1 (1.1)	15.2 (0.8)	14.6 (0.8)	1.8 (0.2)	0.8 (0.3)	6.6 (0.7)	# (#)	2.0 (0.5)
$50,000 or more	2,020	33.4 (1.2)	10.4 (0.5)	25.8 (1.1)	23.9 (1.0)	0.2 (0.1)	23.9 (1.0)	8.4 (0.5)	7.7 (0.4)	1.3 (0.2)	0.1 (0.1)	4.2 (0.6)	# (#)	1.4 (0.5)
Housing status														
School-owned	2,600	73.1 (0.8)	57.0 (0.8)	57.2 (1.0)	60.4 (0.9)	22.9 (0.8)	53.8 (1.0)	52.1 (0.8)	50.8 (0.8)	9.0 (0.4)	18.0 (0.7)	12.5 (0.5)	10.0 (0.4)	1.4 (0.2)
Off-campus, not with parents	9,932	52.9 (0.7)	37.8 (0.6)	33.4 (0.8)	41.9 (0.7)	23.2 (0.5)	30.6 (0.7)	25.7 (0.6)	24.9 (0.6)	3.0 (0.2)	3.0 (0.1)	6.3 (0.3)	1.2 (0.1)	1.9 (0.3)
With parents	4,007	49.9 (0.9)	36.7 (1.0)	31.8 (0.8)	40.2 (0.9)	23.0 (0.9)	29.5 (0.8)	21.4 (0.7)	20.6 (0.7)	2.7 (0.2)	3.3 (0.3)	4.8 (0.3)	2.4 (0.2)	1.2 (0.2)

Rounds to zero.

[1] Numbers of undergraduates may not equal figures reported in other tables, since these data are based on a sample survey. Includes all postsecondary institutions.

[2] Includes students who reported they were awarded aid, but did not specify the source or type of aid.

[3] Details on federal and nonfederal work study participants are not available.

[4] Excludes persons not reported by race/ethnicity.

[5] Includes students who were single, divorced, or widowed.

NOTE: Rows may not sum to totals due to rounding and/or the fact that some students receive aid from multiple sources. Data include undergraduates in degree-granting and nondegree-granting institutions. Standard errors appear in parentheses.

SOURCE: U.S. Department of Education, National Center for Education Statistics, 1999–2000 National Postsecondary Student Aid Study (NPSAS:2000). (This table was prepared May 2002.)

Percent of persons age 25 and over and 25 to 29, by years of school completed, race/ethnicity, and sex: Selected years, 1910 to 2002

Age and year	Total — Less than 5 years of elementary school	Total — High school completion or higher[2]	Total — 4 or more years of college[3]	White, non-Hispanic[1] — Less than 5 years of elementary school	White, non-Hispanic[1] — High school completion or higher[2]	White, non-Hispanic[1] — 4 or more years of college[3]	Black, non-Hispanic[1] — Less than 5 years of elementary school	Black, non-Hispanic[1] — High school completion or higher[2]	Black, non-Hispanic[1] — 4 or more years of college[3]	Hispanic — Less than 5 years of elementary school	Hispanic — High school completion or higher[2]	Hispanic — 4 or more years of college[3]
1	2	3	4	5	6	7	8	9	10	11	12	13
25 and over					*Males and females*							
1910[4]	23.8	13.5	2.7	—	—	—	—	—	—	—	—	—
1920[4]	22.0	16.4	3.3	—	—	—	—	—	—	—	—	—
1930[4]	17.5	19.1	3.9	—	—	—	—	—	—	—	—	—
April 1940	13.7	24.5	4.6	10.9	26.1	4.9	41.8	7.7	1.3	—	—	—
April 1950	11.1	34.3	6.2	8.9	36.4	6.6	32.6	13.7	2.2	—	—	—
April 1960	8.3	41.1	7.7	6.7	43.2	8.1	23.5	21.7	3.5	—	—	—
March 1970	5.3	55.2	11.0	4.2	57.4	11.6	14.7	36.1	6.1	—	—	—
March 1975	4.2	62.5	13.9	2.6	65.8	14.9	12.3	42.6	6.4	18.2	38.5	6.6
March 1980	3.4 (0.08)	68.6 (0.20)	17.0 (0.16)	1.9 (0.07)	71.9 (0.21)	18.4 (0.18)	9.1 (0.40)	51.4 (0.69)	7.9 (0.38)	15.8 (0.74)	44.5 (1.01)	7.6 (0.54)
March 1985	2.7 (0.07)	73.9 (0.18)	19.4 (0.16)	1.4 (0.05)	77.5 (0.19)	20.8 (0.19)	6.1 (0.31)	59.9 (0.64)	11.1 (0.41)	13.5 (0.58)	47.9 (0.85)	8.5 (0.48)
March 1986	2.7 (0.07)	74.7 (0.18)	19.4 (0.16)	1.4 (0.05)	78.2 (0.19)	20.9 (0.19)	5.3 (0.29)	62.5 (0.62)	10.9 (0.40)	12.9 (0.55)	48.5 (0.83)	8.4 (0.46)
March 1987	2.4 (0.06)	75.6 (0.17)	19.9 (0.16)	1.3 (0.05)	79.0 (0.18)	21.4 (0.19)	4.9 (0.27)	63.6 (0.61)	10.8 (0.39)	11.9 (0.52)	50.9 (0.81)	8.6 (0.45)
March 1988	2.4 (0.06)	76.2 (0.17)	20.3 (0.16)	1.2 (0.05)	79.8 (0.18)	21.8 (0.19)	4.8 (0.27)	63.5 (0.60)	11.2 (0.40)	12.2 (0.52)	51.0 (0.79)	10.0 (0.47)
March 1989	2.5 (0.06)	76.9 (0.17)	21.1 (0.16)	1.2 (0.05)	80.7 (0.18)	22.8 (0.19)	5.2 (0.27)	64.7 (0.59)	11.7 (0.40)	12.2 (0.50)	50.9 (0.77)	9.9 (0.46)
March 1990	2.4 (0.06)	77.6 (0.17)	21.3 (0.16)	1.1 (0.05)	81.4 (0.17)	23.1 (0.19)	5.1 (0.27)	66.2 (0.58)	11.3 (0.39)	12.3 (0.50)	50.8 (0.75)	9.2 (0.44)
March 1991	2.4 (0.06)	78.4 (0.16)	21.4 (0.16)	1.1 (0.05)	81.9 (0.17)	23.3 (0.19)	4.7 (0.26)	66.8 (0.57)	11.5 (0.39)	12.5 (0.49)	51.3 (0.74)	9.7 (0.44)
March 1992	2.1 (0.06)	79.4 (0.16)	21.4 (0.16)	0.9 (0.04)	83.4 (0.16)	23.2 (0.19)	3.9 (0.23)	67.7 (0.56)	11.9 (0.39)	11.8 (0.47)	52.6 (0.73)	9.3 (0.42)
March 1993	2.1 (0.06)	80.2 (0.16)	21.9 (0.16)	0.8 (0.04)	84.1 (0.16)	23.8 (0.19)	3.7 (0.22)	70.5 (0.54)	12.2 (0.39)	11.8 (0.46)	53.1 (0.71)	9.0 (0.41)
March 1994	1.9 (0.06)	80.9 (0.15)	22.2 (0.16)	0.8 (0.04)	84.9 (0.16)	24.3 (0.19)	2.7 (0.19)	73.0 (0.52)	12.9 (0.39)	10.8 (0.42)	53.3 (0.67)	9.1 (0.39)
March 1995	1.8 (0.05)	81.7 (0.15)	23.0 (0.16)	0.7 (0.04)	85.9 (0.16)	25.4 (0.19)	2.5 (0.18)	73.8 (0.52)	13.3 (0.40)	10.6 (0.41)	53.4 (0.67)	9.3 (0.39)
March 1996	1.8 (0.05)	81.7 (0.16)	23.6 (0.17)	0.6 (0.04)	86.0 (0.16)	25.9 (0.20)	2.2 (0.18)	74.6 (0.53)	13.8 (0.42)	10.3 (0.42)	53.1 (0.69)	9.3 (0.40)
March 1997	1.7 (0.05)	82.1 (0.14)	23.9 (0.16)	0.6 (0.03)	86.3 (0.15)	26.2 (0.19)	2.0 (0.16)	75.3 (0.49)	13.3 (0.38)	9.4 (0.36)	54.7 (0.62)	10.3 (0.38)
March 1998	1.6 (0.05)	82.8 (0.14)	24.4 (0.16)	0.6 (0.03)	87.1 (0.14)	26.6 (0.19)	1.7 (0.15)	76.4 (0.47)	14.8 (0.40)	9.3 (0.35)	55.5 (0.60)	11.0 (0.38)
March 1999	1.6 (0.05)	83.4 (0.14)	25.2 (0.16)	0.6 (0.03)	87.7 (0.14)	27.7 (0.19)	1.7 (0.15)	77.4 (0.46)	15.5 (0.40)	9.0 (0.34)	56.1 (0.60)	10.9 (0.37)
March 2000	1.6 (0.05)	84.1 (0.13)	25.6 (0.16)	0.5 (0.03)	88.4 (0.14)	28.1 (0.19)	1.6 (0.14)	78.9 (0.45)	16.6 (0.41)	8.7 (0.33)	57.0 (0.58)	10.6 (0.36)
March 2001	1.6 (0.05)	84.3 (0.13)	26.1 (0.16)	0.5 (0.03)	88.7 (0.13)	28.6 (0.19)	1.3 (0.12)	79.5 (0.44)	16.1 (0.40)	9.3 (0.34)	56.5 (0.57)	11.2 (0.37)
March 2002	1.6 (0.03)	84.1 (0.09)	26.7 (0.11)	0.5 (0.02)	88.7 (0.10)	29.4 (0.14)	1.6 (0.10)	79.2 (0.32)	17.2 (0.30)	8.7 (0.22)	57.0 (0.39)	11.1 (0.25)
25 to 29												
1920[4]	5.9	38.1	—	12.9	22.0	4.5	44.6	6.3	1.2	—	—	—
April 1940	4.6	52.8	5.9	3.4	41.2	6.4	27.0	12.3	1.6	—	—	—
April 1950	2.8	60.7	7.7	3.3	56.3	8.2	16.1	23.6	2.8	—	—	—
April 1960	1.1	75.4	11.0	2.2	63.7	11.8	7.2	38.6	5.4	—	—	—
March 1970	1.0	83.1	16.4	0.9	77.8	17.3	2.2	58.4	10.0	—	—	—
March 1975	1.0	83.1	21.9	0.6	86.6	23.8	0.5	71.1	10.5	8.0	53.1	8.8
March 1980	0.8 (0.10)	85.4 (0.40)	22.5 (0.47)	0.3 (0.07)	89.2 (0.40)	25.0 (0.55)	0.6 (0.27)	76.7 (1.41)	11.6 (1.07)	6.7 (1.12)	58.0 (2.22)	7.7 (1.20)
March 1985	0.7 (0.09)	86.1 (0.37)	22.2 (0.45)	0.4 (0.06)	89.5 (0.38)	24.4 (0.53)	0.4 (0.20)	80.5 (1.22)	11.6 (0.99)	6.0 (0.91)	60.9 (1.86)	11.1 (1.20)
March 1986	0.9 (0.10)	86.1 (0.37)	22.4 (0.45)	0.4 (0.07)	89.6 (0.37)	25.2 (0.53)	0.5 (0.22)	83.5 (1.13)	11.8 (0.99)	5.6 (0.83)	59.1 (1.78)	9.0 (1.04)
March 1987	0.9 (0.10)	86.0 (0.37)	22.0 (0.44)	0.4 (0.08)	89.4 (0.38)	24.6 (0.53)	0.4 (0.20)	83.4 (1.13)	11.5 (0.97)	4.8 (0.76)	59.8 (1.75)	8.7 (1.01)
March 1988	1.0 (0.11)	85.9 (0.37)	22.7 (0.45)	0.3 (0.07)	89.7 (0.38)	25.1 (0.54)	0.3 (0.18)	80.9 (1.20)	12.0 (0.99)	6.0 (0.82)	62.3 (1.68)	11.3 (1.10)
March 1989	1.0 (0.11)	85.5 (0.38)	23.4 (0.45)	0.3 (0.07)	89.3 (0.38)	26.3 (0.55)	0.5 (0.23)	82.3 (1.16)	12.6 (1.01)	5.4 (0.76)	61.0 (1.65)	10.1 (1.02)
March 1990	1.2 (0.12)	85.7 (0.38)	23.2 (0.46)	0.3 (0.07)	90.1 (0.37)	26.4 (0.55)	1.0 (0.31)	81.7 (1.17)	13.4 (1.03)	7.3 (0.88)	58.2 (1.66)	8.1 (0.92)
March 1991	1.0 (0.11)	85.4 (0.39)	23.2 (0.46)	0.4 (0.08)	89.8 (0.39)	26.7 (0.56)	0.5 (0.22)	81.8 (1.17)	11.0 (0.97)	5.8 (0.80)	56.7 (1.69)	9.2 (0.99)
March 1992	0.9 (0.10)	86.3 (0.38)	23.6 (0.47)	0.3 (0.07)	90.7 (0.38)	27.2 (0.58)	0.8 (0.28)	80.9 (1.21)	13.3 (1.05)	5.2 (0.75)	60.9 (1.66)	9.5 (1.00)
March 1993	0.7 (0.09)	86.7 (0.38)	23.7 (0.48)	0.3 (0.07)	91.2 (0.37)	27.2 (0.58)	0.2 (0.15)	82.6 (1.17)	13.6 (1.06)	4.0 (0.65)	60.9 (1.64)	8.3 (0.93)
March 1994	0.8 (0.10)	86.1 (0.39)	23.3 (0.47)	0.2 (0.07)	91.1 (0.38)	27.1 (0.59)	0.6 (0.24)	84.1 (1.13)	15.4 (1.13)	3.6 (0.57)	60.3 (1.51)	8.0 (0.84)
March 1995	0.9 (0.11)	86.8 (0.39)	24.7 (0.49)	0.3 (0.08)	92.5 (0.36)	28.8 (0.62)	0.2 (0.14)	86.1 (1.06)	14.6 (1.16)	4.9 (0.67)	57.1 (1.55)	8.9 (0.89)
March 1996	0.8 (0.11)	87.3 (0.40)	27.1 (0.53)	0.2 (0.07)	92.6 (0.38)	31.6 (0.67)	0.4 (0.20)	86.0 (1.14)	14.2 (1.07)	4.3 (0.66)	61.1 (1.58)	10.0 (0.98)
March 1997	0.8 (0.10)	87.4 (0.37)	27.8 (0.50)	0.1 (0.05)	93.9 (0.35)	32.6 (0.63)	0.6 (0.23)	86.9 (1.03)	15.8 (1.11)	4.2 (0.59)	61.8 (1.42)	11.0 (0.91)
March 1998	0.7 (0.09)	88.1 (0.36)	27.3 (0.50)	0.1 (0.05)	93.6 (0.34)	32.3 (0.64)	0.4 (0.19)	88.2 (0.98)	15.0 (1.09)	3.7 (0.55)	62.8 (1.41)	11.0 (1.02)
March 1999	0.7 (0.09)	87.8 (0.37)	28.2 (0.51)	0.1 (0.05)	93.0 (0.35)	33.6 (0.66)	0.2 (0.15)	88.7 (0.97)	17.8 (1.20)	3.2 (0.52)	61.6 (1.44)	10.4 (0.89)
March 2000	0.6 (0.09)	88.1 (0.37)	29.1 (0.52)	0.1 (0.04)	94.0 (0.33)	34.0 (0.67)	#	86.8 (1.06)	17.8 (1.19)	3.8 (0.55)	62.8 (1.40)	8.9 (0.84)
March 2001	0.8 (0.11)	87.7 (0.38)	28.6 (0.52)	0.2 (0.06)	93.3 (0.36)	33.0 (0.68)	0.1 (0.09)	87.0 (1.05)	18.0 (0.88)	4.7 (0.62)	63.2 (1.41)	9.7 (0.85)
March 2002	1.1 (0.08)	86.4 (0.28)	29.3 (0.37)	0.1 (0.04)	93.0 (0.26)	35.9 (0.50)	0.6 (0.18)	87.6 (0.76)	18.0 (0.88)	4.7 (0.39)	62.4 (0.89)	8.9 (0.53)

See notes at end of table.

Percent of persons age 25 and over and 25 to 29, by years of school completed, race/ethnicity, and sex: Selected years,1910 to 2002—Continued

Age and year	Total			White, non-Hispanic [1]			Black, non-Hispanic [1]			Hispanic		
	Less than 5 years of elementary school	High school completion or higher [2]	4 or more years of college [3]	Less than 5 years of elementary school	High school completion or higher [2]	4 or more years of college [3]	Less than 5 years of elementary school	High school completion or higher [2]	4 or more years of college [3]	Less than 5 years of elementary school	High school completion or higher [2]	4 or more years of college [3]
1	2	3	4	5	6	7	8	9	10	11	12	13
Males												
25 and over												
April 1940	15.1 —	22.7 —	5.5 —	12.0 —	24.2 —	5.9 —	46.2 —	6.9 —	1.4 —	—	—	—
April 1950	12.2 —	32.6 —	7.3 —	9.8 —	34.6 —	7.9 —	36.9 —	12.6 —	2.1 —	—	—	—
April 1960	9.4 —	39.5 —	9.7 —	7.4 —	41.6 —	10.3 —	27.7 —	20.0 —	3.5 —	—	—	—
March 1970	5.9 —	55.0 —	14.1 —	4.5 —	57.2 —	15.0 —	17.9 —	35.4 —	6.8 —	—	—	—
March 1980	3.6 (0.12)	69.2 (0.30)	20.9 (0.26)	2.0 (0.10)	72.4 (0.31)	22.8 (C.29)	11.3 (0.67)	51.2 (1.06)	7.7 (0.56)	16.5 (1.11)	44.9 (1.49)	9.2 (0.87)
March 1990	2.7 (0.09)	77.7 (0.24)	24.4 (0.25)	1.3 (0.07)	81.6 (0.25)	26.7 (C.29)	6.4 (0.45)	65.8 (0.88)	11.9 (0.60)	12.9 (0.73)	50.3 (1.09)	9.8 (0.65)
March 1995	2.0 (0.08)	81.7 (0.22)	26.0 (0.25)	0.8 (0.06)	86.0 (0.22)	28.9 (0.29)	3.4 (0.32)	73.5 (0.78)	13.7 (0.61)	10.8 (0.59)	52.9 (0.95)	10.1 (0.57)
March 1996	1.9 (0.08)	81.9 (0.23)	26.0 (0.26)	0.7 (0.06)	86.1 (0.23)	28.8 (0.30)	2.9 (0.31)	74.6 (0.80)	12.5 (0.61)	10.1 (0.59)	53.0 (0.97)	10.3 (0.59)
March 1997	1.8 (0.07)	82.0 (0.21)	26.2 (0.24)	0.6 (0.05)	86.3 (0.21)	29.0 (0.28)	2.9 (0.28)	73.8 (0.75)	12.5 (0.56)	9.2 (0.50)	54.9 (0.87)	10.6 (0.54)
March 1998	1.7 (0.07)	82.8 (0.20)	26.5 (0.24)	0.7 (0.05)	87.1 (0.21)	29.3 (0.28)	2.3 (0.25)	75.4 (0.72)	14.0 (0.58)	9.3 (0.50)	55.7 (0.85)	11.1 (0.54)
March 1999	1.6 (0.07)	83.4 (0.20)	27.5 (0.24)	0.6 (0.05)	87.7 (0.20)	30.6 (0.28)	2.0 (0.24)	77.2 (0.70)	14.3 (0.58)	9.0 (0.49)	56.0 (0.85)	10.7 (0.53)
March 2000	1.6 (0.07)	84.2 (0.19)	27.8 (0.24)	0.6 (0.05)	88.5 (0.20)	30.8 (0.28)	2.1 (0.24)	79.1 (0.67)	16.4 (0.61)	8.2 (0.46)	56.6 (0.83)	10.7 (0.52)
March 2001	1.6 (0.07)	84.4 (0.19)	28.0 (0.24)	0.6 (0.05)	88.6 (0.19)	30.9 (0.28)	1.7 (0.21)	80.6 (0.65)	15.9 (0.60)	9.4 (0.48)	55.6 (0.82)	11.1 (0.52)
March 2002	1.7 (0.05)	83.8 (0.14)	28.5 (0.17)	0.5 (0.03)	88.5 (0.14)	31.7 (0.20)	1.9 (0.16)	79.0 (0.48)	16.5 (0.44)	9.0 (0.32)	56.1 (0.55)	11.0 (0.34)
Females												
25 and over												
April 1940	12.4 —	26.3 —	3.8 —	9.8 —	28.1 —	4.0 —	37.5 —	8.4 —	1.2 —	—	—	—
April 1950	10.0 —	36.0 —	5.2 —	8.1 —	38.2 —	5.4 —	28.6 —	14.7 —	2.4 —	—	—	—
April 1960	7.4 —	42.5 —	5.8 —	6.0 —	44.7 —	6.0 —	19.7 —	23.1 —	3.6 —	—	—	—
March 1970	4.7 —	55.4 —	8.2 —	3.9 —	57.7 —	8.6 —	11.9 —	36.6 —	5.6 —	—	—	—
March 1980	3.2 (0.11)	68.1 (0.28)	13.6 (0.21)	1.8 (0.09)	71.5 (0.30)	14.4 (0.23)	7.4 (0.49)	51.5 (0.94)	8.1 (0.52)	15.3 (1.03)	44.2 (1.42)	6.2 (0.69)
March 1990	2.2 (0.08)	77.5 (0.23)	18.4 (0.22)	1.0 (0.06)	81.3 (0.24)	19.8 (0.25)	4.0 (0.33)	66.5 (0.79)	10.8 (0.52)	11.7 (0.69)	51.3 (1.07)	8.7 (0.61)
March 1995	1.7 (0.07)	81.6 (0.21)	20.2 (0.22)	0.6 (0.05)	85.8 (0.22)	22.1 (0.26)	1.7 (0.21)	74.1 (0.69)	13.0 (0.53)	10.4 (0.58)	53.8 (0.94)	8.4 (0.52)
March 1996	1.7 (0.07)	81.6 (0.22)	21.4 (0.23)	0.5 (0.05)	85.9 (0.22)	23.2 (0.27)	1.6 (0.21)	74.6 (0.72)	14.8 (0.58)	10.5 (0.60)	53.3 (0.97)	8.3 (0.54)
March 1997	1.6 (0.06)	82.2 (0.20)	21.7 (0.21)	0.5 (0.04)	86.3 (0.20)	23.7 (0.25)	1.3 (0.17)	76.5 (0.64)	14.0 (0.52)	9.5 (0.51)	54.6 (0.87)	10.1 (0.53)
March 1998	1.6 (0.06)	82.9 (0.19)	22.4 (0.21)	0.6 (0.04)	87.1 (0.20)	24.1 (0.25)	1.2 (0.16)	77.1 (0.63)	15.4 (0.54)	9.2 (0.50)	55.3 (0.86)	10.9 (0.54)
March 1999	1.5 (0.06)	83.3 (0.19)	23.1 (0.22)	0.5 (0.04)	87.6 (0.19)	25.0 (0.26)	1.5 (0.18)	77.5 (0.62)	16.5 (0.55)	9.0 (0.48)	56.3 (0.83)	11.0 (0.53)
March 2000	1.5 (0.06)	84.0 (0.19)	23.6 (0.22)	0.4 (0.04)	88.4 (0.19)	25.5 (0.26)	1.1 (0.16)	78.7 (0.60)	16.8 (0.55)	9.3 (0.48)	57.5 (0.81)	10.6 (0.50)
March 2001	1.5 (0.06)	84.2 (0.18)	24.3 (0.22)	0.4 (0.04)	88.8 (0.19)	26.5 (0.26)	1.0 (0.15)	78.6 (0.60)	16.3 (0.54)	9.1 (0.47)	57.4 (0.80)	11.3 (0.51)
March 2002	1.5 (0.04)	84.4 (0.13)	25.1 (0.15)	0.5 (0.03)	88.9 (0.13)	27.3 (0.19)	1.4 (0.12)	79.4 (0.42)	17.7 (0.40)	8.3 (0.31)	57.9 (0.55)	11.2 (0.35)

\# Rounds to zero.

—Not available.

[1] Includes persons of Hispanic origin for years prior to 1980.

[2] Data for years prior to 1993 include all persons with at least 4 years of high school.

[3] Data for 1993 and later years are for persons with a bachelor's or higher degree.

[4] Estimates based on Bureau of the Census retrojection of 1940 Census data on education by age.

NOTE: Total includes other racial/ethnic groups not shown separately. Standard errors appear in parentheses.

SOURCE: U.S. Department of Commerce, Bureau of the Census, U.S. Census of Population, 1960, Volume 1, part 1; *Current Population Reports*, Series P-20 and previously unpublished tabulations; and 1960 Census Monograph, "Education of the American Population," by John K. Folger and Charles B. Nam. (This table was prepared October 2003.)

Persons age 18 and over who hold at least a bachelor's degree in specific fields of study, by sex, race/ethnicity, and age: 1996

[Numbers in thousands]

Field of study	Total	Sex		Race/ethnicity			Age		
		Males	Females	White, non-His-panic	Black [1]	Hispanic	18 to 29 years old	30 to 49 years old	50 years and over
1	2	3	4	5	6	7	8	9	10
Total population, 18 and over	196,121	94,092	102,029	148,397	22,813	18,081	43,775	83,107	69,238
Number of persons with bachelor's or higher degree	40,543	21,084	19,459	34,090	2,640	1,515	6,787	21,976	11,780
Percent of population	20.7	22.4	19.1	23.0	11.6	8.4	15.5	26.4	17.0
Agriculture	484	421	63	414	18	27	51	276	156
Architecture	1,118	490	627	960	27	50	236	601	281
Business	8,019	5,241	2,778	6,726	606	286	1,333	4,790	1,897
Communications	895	452	443	773	56	39	281	514	100
Computer	913	621	292	704	91	41	172	659	83
Education	6,785	1,737	5,049	5,806	553	281	701	3,315	2,768
Engineering	2,913	2,656	256	2,452	74	61	425	1,480	1,009
Literature	1,093	315	777	955	46	46	231	491	370
Foreign language	297	79	218	246	11	18	56	126	114
Health sciences	1,611	295	1,316	1,301	108	55	339	894	378
Law	1,127	889	237	1,024	47	29	85	691	351
Liberal arts	2,030	883	1,149	1,670	139	96	404	1,011	616
Mathematics	736	479	257	612	79	23	134	394	209
Medicine and dentistry	996	731	265	794	7	72	85	559	352
Natural science	1,928	1,092	835	1,599	81	61	413	990	525
Nursing, public health	424	65	359	377	23	5	18	245	160
Philosophy	610	489	121	532	30	18	88	260	260
Pre-professional	147	66	80	101	22	21	60	51	35
Psychology	1,350	493	857	1,130	110	51	319	735	295
Social sciences	1,795	815	979	1,494	173	49	364	944	485
Other fields	5,273	2,774	2,500	4,419	342	187	988	2,947	1,338
Percentage distribution of degree holders, by field									
Total	100.0	100.0	100.0	100.0	100.0	100.0	100.0	100.0	100.0
Agriculture	1.2	2.0	0.3	1.2	0.7	1.8	0.8	1.3	1.3
Architecture	2.8	2.3	3.2	2.8	1.0	3.3	3.5	2.7	2.4
Business	19.8	24.9	14.3	19.7	23.0	18.9	19.6	21.8	16.1
Communications	2.2	2.1	2.3	2.3	2.1	2.6	4.1	2.3	0.8
Computer	2.3	2.9	1.5	2.1	3.4	2.7	2.5	3.0	0.7
Education	16.7	8.2	25.9	17.0	20.9	18.5	10.3	15.1	23.5
Engineering	7.2	12.6	1.3	7.2	2.8	4.0	6.3	6.7	8.6
Literature	2.7	1.5	4.0	2.8	1.7	3.0	3.4	2.2	3.1
Foreign language	0.7	0.4	1.1	0.7	0.4	1.2	0.8	0.6	1.0
Health sciences	4.0	1.4	6.8	3.8	4.1	3.6	5.0	4.1	3.2
Law	2.8	4.2	1.2	3.0	1.8	1.9	1.3	3.1	3.0
Liberal arts	5.0	4.2	5.9	4.9	5.3	6.3	6.0	4.6	5.2
Mathematics	1.8	2.3	1.3	1.8	3.0	1.5	2.0	1.8	1.8
Medicine and dentistry	2.5	3.5	1.4	2.3	0.3	4.8	1.3	2.5	3.0
Natural science	4.8	5.2	4.3	4.7	3.1	4.0	6.1	4.5	4.5
Nursing, public health	1.0	0.3	1.8	1.1	0.9	0.3	0.3	1.1	1.4
Philosophy	1.5	2.3	0.6	1.6	1.1	1.2	1.3	1.2	2.2
Pre-professional	0.4	0.3	0.4	0.3	0.8	1.4	0.9	0.2	0.3
Psychology	3.3	2.3	4.4	3.3	4.2	3.4	4.7	3.3	2.5
Social sciences	4.4	3.9	5.0	4.4	6.6	3.2	5.4	4.3	4.1
Other fields	13.0	13.2	12.8	13.0	13.0	12.3	14.6	13.4	11.4

[1] Includes Black persons of Hispanic origin.

NOTE: Total includes other racial/ethnic groups not shown separately. Data are based on a sample survey of the civilian noninstitutional population. Detail may not sum to totals due to rounding.

SOURCE: U.S. Department of Commerce, Bureau of the Census, *Survey of Income and Program Participation*, unpublished data. (This table was prepared April 2001.)

Number of persons age 18 and over, by highest level of education attained, age, sex, and race/ethnicity: March 2002

[In thousands]

Age, sex, and race/ethnicity	Total	Elementary level — Less than 7 years	Elementary level — 7 or 8 years	High school — 1 to 3 years	High school — 4 years	High school — Completion	Some college	College — Associate degree	College — Bachelor's degree	College — Master's degree	College — Professional degree	College — Doctorate
1	2	3	4	5	6	7	8	9	10	11	12	13
Total												
18 and over	209,454	7,157	6,222	18,644	3,400	66,682 (241)	40,282	16,183	34,368 (189)	11,574 (115)	2,752	2,190
18 and 19 years old	7,909	74	96	2,806	501	2,276 (52)	2,097	50	6 (3)	2 (2)	#	#
20 to 24 years old	19,404	392	247	1,924	435	5,949 (84)	7,194	1,082	2,081 (50)	85 (10)	15	#
25 years old and over	182,142	6,690	5,880	13,914	2,464	58,456 (231)	30,991	15,051	32,282 (184)	11,487 (115)	2,737	2,190
25 to 29 years old	18,310	588	262	1,340	297	5,200 (78)	3,746	1,505	4,288 (71)	799 (31)	207	78
30 to 34 years old	20,360	649	327	1,317	292	5,789 (83)	3,653	1,873	4,694 (75)	1,295 (39)	274	199
35 to 39 years old	21,648	609	322	1,388	269	6,854 (90)	3,840	2,128	4,348 (72)	1,298 (39)	351	240
40 to 49 years old	43,624	1,104	648	2,544	524	14,219 (127)	7,738	4,324	8,251 (98)	2,990 (60)	731	550
50 to 59 years old	33,223	1,057	781	1,978	390	10,400 (110)	5,755	3,014	5,701 (82)	3,018 (60)	597	533
60 to 64 years old	11,208	450	454	1,029	161	4,070 (69)	1,753	666	1,506 (42)	738 (30)	189	193
65 years old and over	33,769	2,233	3,086	4,320	531	11,926 (117)	4,506	1,541	3,494 (64)	1,349 (40)	388	396
Males												
18 and over	100,701	3,648	3,013	9,132	1,857	31,234 (181)	19,078	7,005	16,801 (137)	5,620 (81)	1,801	1,514
18 and 19 years old	4,026	43	58	1,545	290	1,117 (37)	944	21	5 (2)	5 (2)	#	#
20 to 24 years old	9,679	245	114	989	270	3,169 (61)	3,473	517	871 (32)	23 (5)	7	#
25 years old and over	86,996	3,359	2,841	6,597	1,297	26,947 (170)	14,661	6,466	15,925 (134)	5,595 (81)	1,795	1,514
25 to 29 years old	9,150	354	135	730	179	2,767 (57)	1,843	684	2,012 (49)	313 (19)	93	39
30 to 34 years old	10,084	416	184	702	170	2,984 (60)	1,747	857	2,208 (51)	570 (26)	135	110
35 to 39 years old	10,698	323	177	743	143	3,466 (64)	1,843	919	2,095 (50)	644 (28)	208	138
40 to 49 years old	21,381	544	340	1,341	304	7,091 (91)	3,663	1,826	3,976 (69)	1,414 (41)	498	384
50 to 59 years old	16,166	529	406	897	219	4,643 (74)	2,802	1,332	3,009 (60)	1,524 (43)	431	384
60 to 64 years old	5,282	229	224	458	63	1,694 (45)	792	309	811 (31)	432 (23)	135	136
65 years old and over	14,235	973	1,374	1,725	219	4,303 (71)	1,971	540	1,816 (47)	698 (29)	295	322
Females												
18 and over	108,753	3,509	3,209	9,513	1,543	35,448 (191)	21,205	9,179	17,567 (140)	5,954 (84)	950	676
18 and 19 years old	3,883	31	38	1,260	211	1,159 (37)	1,154	29	1 (1)	# (#)	#	#
20 to 24 years old	9,724	147	132	935	165	2,780 (58)	3,721	565	1,210 (38)	62 (9)	8	8
25 years old and over	95,146	3,331	3,039	7,317	1,167	31,509 (182)	16,330	8,585	16,357 (136)	5,893 (83)	942	676
25 to 29 years old	9,159	234	127	610	117	2,433 (54)	1,903	821	2,276 (52)	486 (24)	114	39
30 to 34 years old	10,277	233	143	615	121	2,805 (58)	1,906	1,016	2,486 (54)	725 (30)	139	89
35 to 39 years old	10,950	286	144	644	126	3,388 (63)	1,997	1,210	2,253 (54)	655 (28)	144	102
40 to 49 years old	22,243	560	308	1,202	219	7,128 (91)	4,076	2,499	4,276 (71)	1,576 (43)	233	166
50 to 59 years old	17,057	537	375	1,080	172	5,757 (82)	2,952	1,681	2,693 (57)	1,494 (42)	166	149
60 to 64 years old	5,926	221	229	571	98	2,375 (53)	961	357	695 (29)	306 (19)	54	57
65 years old and over	19,534	1,260	1,712	2,595	313	7,623 (94)	2,535	1,001	1,678 (45)	651 (28)	93	74
White, non-Hispanic												
18 and over	150,443	1,573	3,880	11,075	1,701	49,114 (217)	29,677	12,529	27,364 (171)	9,514 (105)	2,249	1,767
18 and 19 years old	4,988	7	42	1,743	223	1,468 (42)	1,463	38	2 (2)	2 (2)	#	#
20 to 24 years old	12,038	23	78	881	151	3,648 (66)	4,836	757	1,585 (44)	67 (9)	12	#
25 years old and over	133,417	1,544	3,760	8,451	1,327	43,998 (208)	23,378	11,734	25,777 (167)	9,445 (105)	2,237	1,767
25 to 29 years old	11,252	41	92	554	104	3,062 (60)	2,325	1,037	3,217 (62)	603 (27)	150	69
30 to 34 years old	13,068	47	105	530	113	3,615 (66)	2,437	1,412	3,520 (65)	965 (34)	181	145
35 to 39 years old	14,760	62	103	658	121	4,786 (75)	2,644	1,589	3,384 (65)	978 (34)	280	154
40 to 49 years old	31,814	147	242	1,422	281	10,584 (98)	5,767	3,388	6,551 (88)	2,412 (54)	605	415
50 to 59 years old	25,674	246	454	1,141	232	8,161 (98)	4,670	2,435	4,722 (75)	2,642 (56)	506	466
60 to 64 years old	8,876	112	280	715	99	3,354 (63)	1,511	553	1,277 (39)	642 (28)	161	172
65 years old and over	27,973	889	2,483	3,432	378	10,437 (110)	4,023	1,321	3,107 (61)	1,203 (38)	355	346
Black, non-Hispanic												
18 and over	23,449	666	633	3,148	661	7,965 (87)	5,113	1,709	2,488 (55)	797 (32)	142	105
18 and 19 years old	1,147	5	12	446	93	371 (22)	215	6	3 (3)	# (#)	#	#
20 to 24 years old	2,661	4	14	388	87	927 (35)	972	108	150 (14)	8 (3)	#	#
25 years old and over	19,642	657	607	2,314	482	6,667 (82)	3,925	1,594	2,335 (54)	788 (32)	142	105
25 to 29 years old	2,303	18	23	197	59	787 (32)	632	182	360 (22)	43 (8)	13	16
30 to 34 years old	2,475	22	20	206	57	883 (34)	579	207	398 (23)	74 (10)	20	15
35 to 39 years old	2,628	20	30	224	54	984 (36)	581	249	352 (22)	109 (12)	18	29
40 to 49 years old	5,031	69	97	483	103	1,726 (47)	1,124	484	622 (29)	254 (19)	41	19
50 to 59 years old	3,378	88	96	460	80	1,175 (39)	605	294	378 (23)	163 (15)	20	19
60 to 64 years old	1,026	54	68	168	36	364 (22)	136	60	75 (10)	47 (8)	9	8
65 years old and over	2,801	386	322	576	94	748 (31)	269	119	150 (14)	98 (12)	21	18

See notes at end of table.

Number of persons age 18 and over, by highest level of education attained, age, sex, and race/ethnicity: March 2002—Continued
[In thousands]

Age, sex, and race/ethnicity	Total	Elementary level			High school				College			
		Less than 7 years	7 or 8 years	1 to 3 years	4 years	Completion	Some college	Associate degree	Bachelor's degree	Master's degree	Professional degree	Doctorate
1	2	3	4	5	6	7	8	9	10	11	12	13
Hispanic												
18 and over	24,550	4,490	1,430	3,729	846	6,977 (69)	3,584	1,189	1,710 (38)	384 (19)	143	68
18 and 19 years old	1,321	63	45	492	140	336 (17)	238	7	# (#)	# (#)	#	#
20 to 24 years old	3,559	355	145	611	181	1,147 (32)	855	141	118 (10)	4 (2)	1	#
25 years old and over	19,670	4,072	1,241	2,626	526	5,493 (63)	2,491	1,041	1,592 (37)	380 (19)	141	68
25 to 29 years old	3,537	528	154	535	114	1,112 (31)	565	213	267 (16)	36 (6)	11	1
30 to 34 years old	3,457	571	205	512	110	995 (30)	474	162	326 (17)	71 (8)	27	4
35 to 39 years old	2,953	508	178	432	75	798 (27)	421	183	277 (16)	52 (7)	17	14
40 to 49 years old	4,424	810	258	539	117	1,286 (34)	544	263	426 (20)	110 (10)	45	26
50 to 59 years old	2,564	626	166	285	56	669 (25)	313	150	178 (13)	76 (8)	29	14
60 to 64 years old	839	252	71	119	17	213 (14)	70	29	41 (6)	17 (4)	8	2
65 years old and over	1,896	777	208	204	37	420 (20)	104	40	76 (8)	19 (4)	3	7

Rounds to zero.

NOTE: Total includes other racial/ethnic groups not shown separately. Although cells with fewer than 75,000 weighted persons are subject to relatively wide sampling variation, they are included in the table to permit various types of aggregations. Detail may not sum to totals because of rounding. Standard errors appear in parentheses.

SOURCE: U.S. Department of Commerce, Bureau of the Census, Current Population Survey, previously unpublished tabulations. (This table was prepared May 2003.)

Educational Attainment

Educational attainment of persons 18 years old and over, by state: Selected years, 1990 to 2002

State	Percent of population, 25 years old and over, by education level, April 1990					Percent of population, 25 years old and over, by education level, 2002		Percent of 18- to 24-year-olds who are high school graduates [1]	
	Percent less than high school	Percent high school diploma or higher	Percent with bachelor's degree or higher			Percent with high school diploma or higher	Percent with bachelor's degree or higher	1993–95	1998–2000
			Total	Bachelor's degree	Graduate or professional degree				
1	2	3	4	5	6	7	8	9	10
United States	**24.8**	**75.2**	**20.3**	**13.1**	**7.2**	**84.1 (0.1)**	**26.7 (0.1)**	**85.3 (0.2)**	**85.7 (0.2)**
Alabama	33.1	66.9	15.7	10.1	5.5	78.9 (0.8)	22.7 (0.8)	84.0 (1.7)	81.6 (1.7)
Alaska	13.4	86.6	23.0	15.0	8.0	92.2 (0.6)	25.6 (1.0)	90.5 (3.9)	93.3 (3.2)
Arizona	21.3	78.7	20.3	13.3	7.0	84.6 (0.8)	26.3 (1.0)	84.0 (1.8)	73.5 (1.7)
Arkansas	33.7	66.3	13.3	8.9	4.5	81.0 (0.8)	18.3 (0.8)	88.4 (2.0)	84.1 (2.1)
California	23.8	76.2	23.4	15.3	8.1	80.2 (0.4)	27.9 (0.4)	78.9 (0.7)	82.5 (0.6)
Colorado	15.6	84.4	27.0	18.0	9.0	87.6 (0.5)	35.7 (0.8)	88.4 (1.6)	81.6 (1.8)
Connecticut	20.8	79.2	27.2	16.2	11.0	88.0 (0.5)	32.6 (0.8)	94.7 (1.3)	91.7 (1.6)
Delaware	22.5	77.5	21.4	13.7	7.7	88.5 (0.7)	29.5 (1.0)	93.3 (2.8)	91.0 (3.2)
District of Columbia	26.9	73.1	33.3	16.1	17.2	83.5 (0.9)	44.4 (1.1)	87.7 (4.1)	88.0 (3.8)
Florida	25.6	74.4	18.3	12.0	6.3	83.3 (0.4)	25.7 (0.5)	80.7 (1.0)	84.6 (0.9)
Georgia	29.1	70.9	19.3	12.9	6.4	82.9 (0.8)	25.0 (0.9)	80.3 (1.4)	83.5 (1.2)
Hawaii	19.9	80.1	22.9	15.8	7.1	87.9 (0.7)	26.8 (1.0)	92.0 (2.5)	91.8 (2.4)
Idaho	20.3	79.7	17.7	12.4	5.3	86.8 (0.7)	20.9 (0.9)	86.4 (3.0)	86.4 (2.6)
Illinois	23.8	76.2	21.0	13.6	7.5	85.9 (0.4)	27.3 (0.5)	86.7 (0.9)	87.1 (0.9)
Indiana	24.4	75.6	15.6	9.2	6.4	85.3 (0.6)	23.7 (0.7)	88.5 (1.2)	89.4 (1.2)
Iowa	19.9	80.1	16.9	11.7	5.2	88.3 (0.6)	23.1 (0.8)	93.2 (1.3)	90.8 (1.6)
Kansas	18.7	81.3	21.1	14.1	7.0	87.5 (0.5)	29.1 (0.8)	90.9 (1.7)	90.4 (1.6)
Kentucky	35.4	64.6	13.6	8.1	5.5	80.8 (0.8)	21.6 (0.8)	82.4 (2.0)	86.2 (1.7)
Louisiana	31.7	68.3	16.1	10.5	5.6	78.8 (0.9)	22.1 (0.9)	80.5 (1.9)	82.1 (1.6)
Maine	21.2	78.8	18.8	12.7	6.1	87.4 (0.5)	23.8 (0.7)	92.9 (2.3)	94.5 (2.0)
Maryland	21.6	78.4	26.5	15.6	10.9	87.5 (0.6)	37.6 (0.9)	93.6 (1.1)	87.4 (1.5)
Massachusetts	20.0	80.0	27.2	16.6	10.6	86.5 (0.5)	34.3 (0.8)	92.5 (1.1)	90.9 (1.1)
Michigan	23.2	76.8	17.4	10.9	6.4	86.5 (0.5)	22.5 (0.5)	88.7 (1.0)	89.2 (0.9)
Minnesota	17.6	82.4	21.8	15.6	6.3	92.2 (0.5)	30.5 (0.8)	93.3 (1.1)	91.9 (1.2)
Mississippi	35.7	64.3	14.7	9.7	5.1	79.1 (0.9)	20.9 (0.9)	83.9 (2.1)	82.3 (2.1)
Missouri.	26.1	73.9	17.8	11.7	6.1	88.1 (0.6)	26.7 (0.8)	90.3 (1.3)	92.6 (1.1)
Montana	19.0	81.0	19.8	14.1	5.7	89.7 (0.7)	23.6 (0.9)	89.8 (3.5)	91.1 (2.7)
Nebraska	18.2	81.8	18.9	13.1	5.9	89.8 (0.6)	27.1 (0.9)	94.5 (1.7)	91.3 (1.9)
Nevada	21.2	78.8	15.3	10.1	5.2	85.8 (0.7)	22.1 (0.9)	81.9 (3.4)	77.9 (2.9)
New Hampshire	17.8	82.2	24.4	16.4	7.9	90.2 (0.5)	30.1 (0.8)	86.9 (3.2)	85.1 (3.6)
New Jersey	23.3	76.7	24.9	16.0	8.8	85.9 (0.5)	31.4 (0.6)	91.8 (1.0)	90.1 (1.0)
New Mexico	24.9	75.1	20.4	12.1	8.3	81.6 (0.9)	25.4 (1.0)	82.4 (3.0)	83.0 (2.7)
New York	25.2	74.8	23.1	13.2	9.9	83.7 (0.4)	28.8 (0.5)	87.1 (0.8)	86.3 (0.8)
North Carolina	30.0	70.0	17.4	12.0	5.4	80.1 (0.7)	22.4 (0.7)	85.5 (1.3)	86.1 (1.2)
North Dakota	23.3	76.7	18.1	13.5	4.5	89.0 (0.6)	25.3 (0.8)	96.6 (2.1)	94.4 (2.7)
Ohio	24.3	75.7	17.0	11.1	5.9	87.3 (0.4)	24.5 (0.5)	88.4 (0.9)	87.7 (0.9)
Oklahoma	25.4	74.6	17.8	11.8	6.0	85.1 (0.7)	20.4 (0.7)	87.0 (1.9)	85.7 (1.8)
Oregon	18.5	81.5	20.6	13.6	7.0	87.7 (0.6)	27.1 (0.9)	82.7 (2.1)	82.3 (1.9)
Pennsylvania	25.3	74.7	17.9	11.3	6.6	86.1 (0.4)	26.1 (0.5)	89.5 (0.9)	89.0 (0.9)
Rhode Island	28.0	72.0	21.3	13.5	7.8	80.1 (0.7)	30.1 (0.8)	89.4 (3.3)	87.9 (3.2)
South Carolina	31.7	68.3	16.6	11.2	5.4	80.2 (0.9)	23.3 (0.9)	88.0 (1.6)	85.1 (1.7)
South Dakota	22.9	77.1	17.2	12.3	4.9	89.2 (0.5)	23.6 (0.7)	91.5 (3.3)	92.0 (2.8)
Tennessee	32.9	67.1	16.0	10.5	5.4	80.1 (0.7)	21.5 (0.9)	84.6 (1.5)	89.0 (1.3)
Texas	27.9	72.1	20.3	13.9	6.5	78.1 (0.5)	26.2 (0.5)	79.5 (0.9)	79.4 (0.8)
Utah	14.9	85.1	22.3	15.4	6.8	91.0 (0.7)	26.8 (1.0)	93.6 (1.5)	90.0 (1.6)
Vermont	19.2	80.8	24.3	15.4	8.9	87.4 (0.7)	30.8 (0.9)	88.1 (4.3)	90.8 (3.9)
Virginia	24.8	75.2	24.5	15.4	9.1	86.7 (0.7)	34.6 (0.9)	87.7 (1.2)	87.3 (1.3)
Washington	16.2	83.8	22.9	15.9	7.0	90.4 (0.6)	28.3 (0.9)	85.7 (1.4)	87.4 (1.3)
West Virginia	34.0	66.0	12.3	7.5	4.8	78.5 (0.7)	15.9 (0.6)	86.8 (2.4)	89.6 (2.2)
Wisconsin	21.4	78.6	17.7	12.1	5.6	86.8 (0.5)	24.7 (0.7)	93.7 (1.0)	90.0 (1.3)
Wyoming	17.0	83.0	18.8	13.1	5.7	91.6 (0.5)	19.6 (0.8)	90.8 (4.0)	86.5 (4.5)

[1] Excludes students still enrolled in high school. Data reflect 3-year averages.

NOTE: Standard errors appear in parentheses. Detail may not sum to totals due to rounding. Some data revised from previously published figures.

SOURCE: U.S. Department of Commerce, Bureau of the Census, *Current Population Reports,* "Educational Attainment in the United States," various years; and Decennial Census, *Minority Economic Profiles,* unpublished data; and National Center for Education Statistics, *Dropout Rates in the United States,* various years. (This table was prepared May 2003.)

Percent of 12- to 17-year olds reporting drug use during the past 30 days and past year, by drug used: Selected years, 1982 to 2001

Type of drug	1982	1985	1988	1990	1991	1992	1993	1994	1995	1996	1997	1998	1999	2000	2001
1	2	3	4	5	6	7	8	9	10	11	12	13	14	15	16
Percent reporting drug use during past 30 days															
Any illicit use [1]	—	13.2	8.1	7.1	5.8	5.3	5.7	8.2	10.9	9.0	11.4	9.9	9.8	9.7	10.8
Marijuana	9.9	10.2	5.4	4.4	3.6	3.4	4.0	6.0	8.2	7.1	9.4	8.3	7.2	7.2	8.0
Cocaine	1.9	1.5	1.2	0.6	0.4	0.3	0.4	0.3	0.8	0.6	1.0	0.8	0.5	0.6	0.4
Alcohol	34.9	41.2	33.4	32.5	27.0	20.9	23.9	21.6	21.1	18.8	20.5	19.1	16.5	16.4	17.3
Cigarettes	—	29.4	22.7	22.4	20.9	18.4	18.5	18.9	20.2	18.3	19.9	18.2	14.9	13.4	13.0
Percent reporting drug use during past year															
Any illicit use [1]	—	20.7	14.9	14.1	13.1	10.4	11.9	15.5	18.0	16.7	18.8	16.4	19.8	18.6	20.8
Marijuana	17.7	16.7	10.7	9.6	8.5	6.9	8.5	11.4	14.2	13.0	15.8	14.1	14.2	13.4	15.2
Cocaine	3.7	3.4	2.5	1.9	1.3	1.0	0.7	1.1	1.7	1.4	2.2	1.7	1.6	1.7	1.5
Alcohol	46.1	52.7	45.5	41.8	41.2	33.3	35.9	36.2	35.1	32.7	34.0	31.8	34.1	33.0	33.9
Cigarettes	—	29.9	26.8	26.2	23.7	21.4	22.5	24.5	26.6	24.2	26.4	23.8	23.4	20.8	20.0

—Not available.

[1] Includes other illegal drug use not shown separately.

NOTE: Marijuana includes hashish usage for 1996 and later years. Due to changes in the survey instrument and administration and to improve comparability with new data, estimates for 1982 through 1993 have been adjusted and may differ from those reported in previous years. Data for 1999 have been revised from previously published figures. Data for 1999 through 2001 were gathered using Computer Assisted Interviewing (CAI) and may not be directly comparable to previous years.

SOURCE: U.S. Department of Health and Human Services, Substance Abuse and Mental Health Services Administration, "National Household Survey on Drug Abuse," selected years 1982–2001. (This table was prepared June 2003.)

Percent of high school seniors reporting drug use, by type of drug and frequency of use: Selected years, 1975 to 2002

Type of drug and frequency of use	Class of 1975	Class of 1980	Class of 1985	Class of 1987	Class of 1988	Class of 1989	Class of 1990	Class of 1991	Class of 1992	Class of 1993	Class of 1994	Class of 1995	Class of 1996	Class of 1997	Class of 1998	Class of 1999	Class of 2000	Class of 2001	Class of 2002
1	2	3	4	5	6	7	8	9	10	11	12	13	14	15	16	17	18	19	20
Percent reporting having ever used drugs																			
Alcohol[1]	90.4	93.2	92.2	92.2	92.0	90.7	89.5	88.0	87.5	80.0	80.4	80.7	79.2	81.7	81.4	80.0	80.3	79.7	78.4
Any illicit drug	55.2	65.4	60.6	56.6	53.9	50.9	47.9	44.1	40.7	42.9	45.6	48.4	50.8	54.3	54.1	54.7	54.0	53.9	53.0
Marijuana only	19.0	26.7	20.9	20.8	21.4	19.5	18.5	17.2	15.6	16.2	18.0	20.3	22.3	24.3	24.7	25.3	25.0	23.2	23.5
Any illicit drug other than marijuana[2]	36.2	38.7	39.7	35.8	32.5	31.4	29.4	26.9	25.1	26.7	27.6	28.1	28.5	30.0	29.4	29.4	29.0	30.7	29.5
Use of selected drugs																			
Cocaine	9.0	15.7	17.3	15.2	12.1	10.3	9.4	7.8	6.1	6.1	5.9	6.0	7.1	8.7	9.3	9.8	8.6	8.2	7.8
Heroin	2.2	1.1	1.2	1.2	1.1	1.3	1.3	0.9	1.2	1.1	1.2	1.6	1.8	2.1	2.0	2.0	2.4	1.8	1.7
LSD	11.3	9.3	7.5	8.4	7.7	8.3	8.7	8.8	8.6	10.3	10.5	11.7	12.6	13.6	12.6	12.2	11.1	10.9	8.4
Marijuana/hashish	47.3	60.3	54.2	50.2	47.2	43.7	40.7	36.7	32.6	35.3	38.2	41.7	44.9	49.6	49.1	49.7	48.8	49.0	47.8
PCP	—	9.6	4.9	3.0	2.9	3.9	2.8	2.9	2.4	2.9	2.8	2.7	4.0	3.9	3.9	3.4	3.4	3.5	3.1
Percent reporting use of drugs in the past 12 months																			
Alcohol[1]	84.8	87.9	85.6	85.7	85.3	82.7	80.6	77.7	76.8	72.7	73.0	73.7	72.5	74.8	74.3	73.8	73.2	73.3	71.5
Any illicit drug	45.0	53.1	46.3	41.7	38.5	35.4	32.5	29.4	27.1	31.0	35.8	39.0	40.2	42.4	41.4	42.1	40.9	41.4	41.0
Marijuana only	18.8	22.7	18.9	17.6	17.4	15.4	14.6	13.2	12.2	13.9	17.8	19.6	20.4	21.7	21.2	21.4	20.5	19.8	20.1
Any illicit drug other than marijuana[2]	26.2	30.4	27.4	24.1	21.1	20.0	17.9	16.2	14.9	17.1	18.0	19.4	19.8	20.7	20.2	20.7	20.4	21.6	20.9
Use of selected drugs																			
Cocaine	5.6	12.3	13.1	10.3	7.9	6.5	5.3	3.5	3.1	3.3	3.6	4.0	4.9	5.5	5.7	6.2	5.0	4.8	5.0
Heroin	1.0	0.5	0.6	0.5	0.5	0.6	0.5	0.4	0.6	0.5	0.6	1.1	1.0	1.2	1.0	1.1	1.5	0.9	1.0
LSD	7.2	6.5	4.4	5.2	4.8	4.9	5.4	5.2	5.6	6.8	6.9	8.4	8.8	8.4	7.6	8.1	6.6	6.6	3.5
Marijuana/hashish	40.0	48.8	40.6	36.3	33.1	29.6	27.0	23.9	21.9	26.0	30.7	34.7	35.8	38.5	37.5	37.8	36.5	37.0	36.2
PCP	—	4.4	2.9	1.3	1.2	2.4	1.2	1.4	1.4	1.4	1.6	1.8	2.6	2.3	2.1	1.8	2.3	1.8	1.1
Percent reporting use of drugs in the past 30 days																			
Alcohol[1]	68.2	72.0	65.9	66.4	63.9	60.0	57.1	54.0	51.3	48.6	50.1	51.3	50.8	52.7	52.0	51.0	50.0	49.8	48.6
Any illicit drug	30.7	37.2	29.7	24.7	21.3	19.7	17.2	16.4	14.4	18.3	21.9	23.8	24.6	26.2	25.6	25.9	24.9	25.7	25.4
Marijuana only	15.3	18.8	14.8	13.1	11.3	10.6	9.2	9.3	8.1	10.4	13.1	13.8	15.1	15.5	14.9	15.5	14.5	14.7	14.1
Any illicit drug other than marijuana[2]	15.4	18.4	14.9	11.6	10.0	9.1	8.0	7.1	6.3	7.9	8.8	10.0	9.5	10.7	10.7	10.4	10.4	11.0	11.3
Use of selected drugs																			
Cocaine	1.9	5.2	6.7	4.3	3.4	2.8	1.9	1.4	1.3	1.3	1.5	1.8	2.0	2.3	2.4	2.6	2.1	2.1	2.3
Heroin	0.4	0.2	0.3	0.2	0.2	0.3	0.2	0.2	0.3	0.2	0.3	0.6	0.5	0.5	0.5	0.5	0.7	0.4	0.5
LSD	2.3	2.3	1.6	1.8	1.8	1.8	1.9	1.9	2.0	2.4	2.6	4.0	2.5	3.1	3.2	2.7	1.6	2.3	0.7
Marijuana/hashish	27.1	33.7	25.7	21.0	18.0	16.7	14.0	13.8	11.9	15.5	19.0	21.2	21.9	23.7	22.8	23.1	21.6	22.4	21.5
PCP	—	1.4	1.6	0.6	0.3	1.4	0.4	0.5	0.6	1.0	0.7	0.6	1.3	0.7	1.0	0.8	0.9	0.5	0.4

—Not available.

[1] Survey question changed in 1993; data are not comparable to figures for earlier years.

[2] Other illicit drugs include any use of LSD, other hallucinogens, crack, other cocaine, or heroin, or any use of other narcotics, amphetamines, barbiturates, or tranquilizers not under a doctor's orders.

NOTE: A revised questionnaire was used in 1982 and later years to reduce the inappropriate reporting of non-prescription stimulants. This slightly reduced the positive responses for some types of drug abuse.

SOURCE: University of Michigan, Institute for Social Research, "Monitoring the Future" Study, various years (This table was prepared June 2003.)

Percent of students in grades 9 through 12 who reported experience with drugs and violence on school property, by race/ethnicity, grade, and sex: 1997, 1999, and 2001

Type of violence or drug-related behavior	1997 Total	1999 Total	2001 Total	Race/ethnicity White, non-Hispanic	Race/ethnicity Black, non-Hispanic	Race/ethnicity Hispanic	Grade 9	Grade 10	Grade 11	Grade 12
1	2	3	4	5	6	7	8	9	10	11
Felt too unsafe to go to school [1]										
Total	4.0	5.2	6.6 (0.5)	5.0 (0.6)	9.8 (0.8)	10.2 (0.7)	8.8 (0.9)	6.3 (0.7)	5.9 (0.6)	4.4 (0.4)
Male	4.1	4.8	5.8 (0.6)	4.2 (0.7)	9.6 (1.0)	9.0 (0.8)	8.0 (1.0)	5.6 (0.8)	5.0 (0.8)	3.9 (0.6)
Female	3.9	5.7	7.4 (0.7)	5.6 (0.7)	10.0 (1.2)	11.4 (0.8)	9.6 (1.1)	7.0 (0.9)	6.8 (0.9)	5.0 (0.6)
Carried a weapon on school property [1,2]										
Total	8.5	6.9	6.4 (0.5)	6.1 (0.6)	6.3 (0.9)	6.4 (0.5)	6.7 (0.7)	6.7 (0.6)	6.1 (0.7)	6.0 (0.7)
Male	12.5	11.0	10.2 (0.9)	10.0 (1.1)	8.4 (1.5)	9.1 (0.9)	10.7 (1.1)	10.5 (1.0)	9.5 (1.3)	9.6 (1.1)
Female	3.7	2.8	2.9 (0.3)	2.3 (0.3)	4.2 (0.7)	3.8 (0.8)	2.9 (0.4)	2.9 (0.5)	2.9 (0.5)	2.7 (0.6)
Threatened or injured with a weapon on school property [3]										
Total	7.4	7.7	8.9 (0.6)	8.5 (0.7)	9.3 (0.7)	8.9 (1.1)	12.7 (0.9)	9.1 (0.8)	6.9 (0.7)	5.3 (0.5)
Male	10.2	9.5	11.5 (0.7)	11.1 (0.9)	11.9 (1.3)	11.3 (1.4)	15.7 (1.2)	11.9 (0.9)	9.1 (0.9)	7.7 (0.9)
Female	4.0	5.8	6.5 (0.5)	6.0 (0.6)	6.7 (0.8)	6.4 (1.2)	10.0 (1.0)	6.3 (0.8)	4.7 (0.7)	3.0 (0.5)
Engaged in a physical fight on school property [3]										
Total	14.8	14.2	12.5 (0.5)	11.2 (0.6)	16.8 (1.3)	14.1 (0.9)	17.3 (0.8)	13.5 (0.9)	9.4 (0.7)	7.5 (0.6)
Male	20.0	18.5	18.0 (0.8)	17.2 (0.9)	21.3 (1.6)	17.3 (1.4)	25.1 (1.3)	19.5 (1.5)	13.8 (1.1)	10.7 (1.1)
Female	8.6	9.8	7.2 (0.5)	5.4 (0.6)	12.7 (1.6)	11.0 (1.0)	10.2 (0.9)	7.7 (0.7)	5.1 (0.6)	4.4 (0.7)
Property stolen or deliberately damaged on school property [3]										
Total	32.9	—	— (—)	— (—)	— (—)	— (—)	— (—)	— (—)	— (—)	— (—)
Male	36.1	—	— (—)	— (—)	— (—)	— (—)	— (—)	— (—)	— (—)	— (—)
Female	29.0	—	— (—)	— (—)	— (—)	— (—)	— (—)	— (—)	— (—)	— (—)
Cigarette use on school property [1]										
Total	14.6	14.0	9.9 (0.6)	11.3 (0.8)	4.9 (1.0)	7.7 (1.0)	8.8 (0.9)	10.2 (0.8)	10.0 (0.9)	10.8 (1.3)
Male	15.9	14.8	11.3 (0.7)	12.8 (0.8)	7.2 (1.6)	7.5 (0.9)	11.1 (1.0)	10.7 (0.9)	11.8 (1.3)	12.1 (1.3)
Female	13.0	13.2	8.5 (0.7)	9.8 (0.9)	2.8 (0.9)	7.9 (1.5)	6.7 (1.0)	9.8 (1.2)	8.3 (0.8)	9.6 (1.6)
Smokeless tobacco use on school property [4]										
Total	5.1	4.2	5.0 (0.6)	6.2 (0.9)	1.1 (0.3)	2.7 (0.3)	3.8 (0.7)	5.9 (0.7)	5.1 (0.9)	5.3 (0.9)
Male	9.0	8.1	9.4 (1.2)	11.9 (1.6)	2.0 (0.6)	4.3 (0.8)	7.4 (1.3)	10.8 (1.4)	9.5 (1.6)	10.4 (1.6)
Female	0.4	0.3	0.7 (0.2)	0.7 (0.2)	0.3 (0.2)	1.0 (0.4)	0.4 (0.2)	1.2 (0.4)	0.8 (0.3)	0.4 (0.2)
Alcohol use on school property [1]										
Total	5.6	4.9	4.9 (0.3)	4.2 (0.3)	5.3 (0.7)	7.0 (0.7)	5.3 (0.5)	5.1 (0.5)	4.7 (0.5)	4.3 (0.5)
Male	7.2	6.1	6.1 (0.4)	5.3 (0.5)	7.5 (0.9)	6.9 (0.9)	6.3 (0.6)	5.4 (0.6)	6.5 (0.8)	6.1 (0.8)
Female	3.6	3.6	3.8 (0.4)	3.2 (0.5)	3.1 (0.6)	7.1 (0.9)	4.4 (0.7)	4.8 (0.7)	2.9 (0.5)	2.6 (0.7)
Marijuana use on school property [1]										
Total	7.0	7.2	5.4 (0.4)	4.8 (0.5)	6.1 (0.6)	7.4 (0.6)	5.5 (0.6)	5.8 (0.5)	5.1 (0.5)	4.9 (0.7)
Male	9.0	10.1	8.0 (0.6)	7.4 (0.7)	10.2 (1.1)	9.0 (1.0)	8.0 (1.1)	8.6 (0.9)	7.7 (0.8)	7.5 (1.1)
Female	4.6	4.4	2.9 (0.3)	2.2 (0.4)	2.3 (0.5)	5.8 (0.6)	3.0 (0.6)	3.2 (0.5)	2.5 (0.5)	2.4 (0.5)
Offered, sold, or given an illegal drug on school property [3]										
Total	31.7	30.2	28.5 (1.0)	28.3 (1.3)	21.9 (1.7)	34.2 (1.2)	29.0 (1.6)	29.0 (1.4)	28.7 (1.4)	26.9 (1.3)
Male	37.4	34.7	34.6 (1.2)	34.2 (1.5)	27.9 (2.4)	39.8 (1.9)	35.1 (2.3)	34.7 (1.7)	34.6 (1.8)	33.8 (1.7)
Female	24.7	25.7	22.7 (1.0)	22.7 (1.3)	16.2 (1.6)	28.7 (1.3)	23.4 (1.6)	23.6 (1.7)	22.8 (1.4)	20.4 (1.9)

—Not available.

[1] One or more times during the 30 days preceding the survey.

[2] Such as a gun, knife, or club.

[3] One or more times during the 12 months preceding the survey.

[4] Used chewing tobacco or snuff one or more times during the 30 days preceding the survey.

NOTE: Totals include other racial/ethnic groups not shown seperately. Standard errors appear in parentheses.

SOURCE: U.S. Department of Health and Human Services, Centers for Disease Control and Prevention, *CDC Surveillance Summaries*, MMWR 47(SS-03) and 51(SS-04). (This table was prepared July 2002.)

Suspensions and expulsions of public elementary and secondary school students, by state, sex, and percent of enrollment: 2000

State	Suspensions [1]			Suspensions as a percent of enrollment, by sex			Expulsions			Expulsions as a percent of enrollment, by sex		
	Total	Male	Female	Total	Male	Female	Total	Male	Female	Total	Male	Female
1	2	3	4	5	6	7	8	9	10	11	12	13
United States	3,053,449	2,182,273	871,176	6.6	9.2	3.9	97,177	74,852	22,325	0.21	0.31	0.10
Alabama	56,436	39,371	17,065	7.8	10.5	4.8	745	572	173	0.10	0.15	0.05
Alaska	7,324	5,315	2,009	5.5	7.8	3.1	261	212	49	0.20	0.31	0.08
Arizona	33,753	24,990	8,763	7.6	10.9	4.0	589	470	119	0.13	0.20	0.05
Arkansas	47,022	34,533	12,489	5.4	7.7	2.9	1,473	1,043	430	0.17	0.23	0.10
California	414,736	311,457	103,279	7.0	10.2	3.6	14,970	12,238	2,732	0.25	0.40	0.09
Colorado	44,419	32,406	12,013	6.3	8.9	3.5	1,904	1,561	343	0.27	0.43	0.10
Connecticut	38,305	26,744	11,561	7.2	9.8	4.4	669	530	139	0.13	0.19	0.05
Delaware	13,276	8,867	4,409	11.8	15.3	8.1	158	119	39	0.14	0.21	0.07
District of Columbia	3,838	2,402	1,436	6.1	7.7	4.5	0	0	0	0.00	0.00	0.00
Florida	198,801	139,323	59,478	8.4	11.4	5.2	872	665	207	0.04	0.05	0.02
Georgia	104,216	73,429	30,787	7.4	10.2	4.4	2,519	1,999	520	0.18	0.28	0.08
Hawaii	7,327	4,961	2,366	4.0	5.3	2.7	4	4	0	0.00	0.00	0.00
Idaho	8,144	6,124	2,020	3.4	4.9	1.7	308	248	60	0.13	0.20	0.05
Illinois	89,559	62,295	27,264	4.4	6.0	2.8	1,919	1,467	452	0.10	0.14	0.05
Indiana	87,535	62,935	24,600	8.8	12.3	5.1	7,792	5,601	2,191	0.78	1.10	0.45
Iowa	17,687	13,028	4,659	3.7	5.2	2.0	220	170	50	0.05	0.07	0.02
Kansas	25,458	18,443	7,015	5.6	7.8	3.2	878	704	174	0.19	0.30	0.08
Kentucky	40,131	29,208	10,923	6.5	9.1	3.6	740	574	166	0.12	0.18	0.06
Louisiana	77,945	52,776	25,169	10.8	14.3	7.2	5,549	3,887	1,662	0.77	1.06	0.47
Maine	10,546	7,802	2,744	4.9	7.0	2.6	175	135	40	0.08	0.12	0.04
Maryland	50,128	34,555	15,573	6.0	8.0	3.8	815	607	208	0.10	0.14	0.05
Massachusetts	51,662	36,615	15,047	5.4	7.5	3.3	777	633	144	0.08	0.13	0.03
Michigan	124,394	88,103	36,291	7.3	10.0	4.4	2,780	2,066	714	0.16	0.23	0.09
Minnesota	44,642	33,437	11,205	5.3	7.7	2.7	644	421	223	0.08	0.10	0.05
Mississippi	51,141	35,766	15,375	10.3	14.2	6.4	1,605	1,248	357	0.32	0.49	0.15
Missouri	55,889	40,747	15,142	6.3	9.0	3.5	795	591	204	0.09	0.13	0.05
Montana	6,189	4,493	1,696	4.0	5.6	2.3	208	143	65	0.13	0.18	0.09
Nebraska	11,188	7,949	3,239	4.0	5.5	2.4	553	425	128	0.20	0.30	0.09
Nevada	16,378	11,713	4,665	4.9	6.8	2.9	777	598	179	0.23	0.35	0.11
New Hampshire	12,407	8,940	3,467	5.7	8.0	3.2	180	156	24	0.08	0.14	0.02
New Jersey	74,123	52,090	22,033	5.8	8.0	3.6	508	402	106	0.04	0.06	0.02
New Mexico	21,935	15,615	6,320	7.0	9.7	4.1	470	379	91	0.15	0.24	0.06
New York	119,163	86,822	32,341	4.2	5.9	2.3	1,533	1,121	412	0.05	0.08	0.03
North Carolina	120,520	85,350	35,170	9.6	13.3	5.7	2,319	1,763	556	0.19	0.28	0.09
North Dakota	2,590	1,855	735	2.4	3.3	1.4	75	38	37	0.07	0.07	0.07
Ohio	146,062	101,488	44,574	7.9	10.7	5.0	7,614	5,604	2,010	0.41	0.59	0.23
Oklahoma	37,988	27,357	10,631	6.2	8.7	3.6	1,356	1,040	316	0.22	0.33	0.11
Oregon	32,702	24,595	8,107	6.0	8.8	3.1	1,897	1,525	372	0.35	0.55	0.14
Pennsylvania	117,654	81,017	36,637	6.5	8.7	4.2	2,034	1,539	495	0.11	0.17	0.06
Rhode Island	14,641	10,190	4,451	9.3	12.6	5.8	259	191	68	0.16	0.24	0.09
South Carolina	98,479	67,342	31,137	14.6	19.6	9.5	4,328	3,391	937	0.64	0.99	0.28
South Dakota	3,746	2,716	1,030	2.9	4.1	1.6	155	122	33	0.12	0.18	0.05
Tennessee	81,753	55,814	25,939	9.0	12.0	5.9	3,241	2,472	769	0.36	0.53	0.17
Texas	187,196	134,376	52,820	4.8	6.7	2.8	11,527	9,068	2,459	0.29	0.45	0.13
Utah	13,119	9,883	3,236	2.8	4.1	1.4	1,614	1,263	351	0.34	0.52	0.15
Vermont	5,254	3,835	1,419	4.9	7.0	2.7	128	108	20	0.12	0.20	0.04
Virginia	88,494	62,115	26,379	7.8	10.6	4.8	1,734	1,381	353	0.15	0.24	0.06
Washington	62,012	47,257	14,755	6.2	9.2	3.1	3,671	2,932	739	0.37	0.57	0.15
West Virginia	44,531	30,712	13,819	5.2	7.0	3.4	1,288	993	295	0.15	0.23	0.07
Wisconsin	26,615	19,928	6,687	9.5	13.7	4.9	402	313	89	0.14	0.22	0.07
Wyoming	4,398	3,190	1,208	4.9	6.9	2.8	145	119	26	0.16	0.26	0.06

[1] Student can be suspended more than once during the same year.

NOTE: Detail may not sum to totals due to rounding.

SOURCE: U.S. Department of Education, Office of Civil Rights, "OCR Elementary and Secondary Survey: 2000." (This table was prepared October 2003.)

Mathematics average scale score and performance and selected statistics on mathematics education for 4th-graders in public schools, by state or jurisdiction: 1992, 2000, and 2003

State or jurisdiction	Average scale score			Percent attaining mathematics achievement levels,[1] 2003				Percent of students with 3 or more hours of math instruction each week, 2003	Percent of students, 2003	
									Spending 30 minutes or more on math homework each day[5]	Watching 6 hours or more of television each day
	1992	2000	2003	Below basic	Basic or above[2]	Proficient or above[3]	Advanced[4]			
1	2	3	4	5	6	7	8	9	10	11
United States	**219 (0.8)**	**224 (1.0)**	**234 (0.2)**	**24 (0.3)**	**76 (0.3)**	**31 (0.3)**	**4 (0.1)**	**56 (1.0)**	**49**	**21 (0.2)**
Alabama	208 (1.6)	217 (1.2)	223 (1.2)	35 (1.7)	65 (1.7)	19 (1.5)	1 (0.2)	41 (4.7)	47	22 (1.1)
Alaska	— (—)	— (—)	233 (0.8)	25 (1.2)	75 (1.2)	30 (1.1)	4 (0.5)	68 (4.2)	—	— (—)
Arizona	215 (1.1)	219 (1.3)	229 (1.1)	30 (1.5)	70 (1.5)	25 (1.4)	2 (0.3)	70 (4.5)	52	19 (1.0)
Arkansas	210 (0.9)	216 (1.1)	229 (0.9)	29 (1.3)	71 (1.3)	26 (1.1)	2 (0.4)	57 (5.3)	51	24 (1.0)
California[6]	208 (1.6)	213 (1.6)	227 (0.9)	33 (1.1)	67 (1.1)	25 (1.3)	3 (0.5)	43 (5.1)	56	20 (0.7)
Colorado	221 (1.0)	— (—)	235 (1.0)	23 (1.3)	77 (1.3)	34 (1.5)	4 (0.5)	55 (4.5)	50	15 (0.8)
Connecticut	227 (1.1)	234 (1.1)	241 (0.8)	18 (0.9)	82 (0.9)	41 (1.5)	5 (0.5)	73 (3.8)	42	21 (0.8)
Delaware	218 (0.8)	— (—)	236 (0.5)	19 (1.1)	81 (1.1)	31 (0.9)	3 (0.4)	51 (0.6)	49	25 (0.7)
District of Columbia	193 (0.5)	192 (1.1)	205 (0.7)	64 (1.1)	36 (1.1)	7 (0.6)	1 (0.2)	54 (0.6)	52	32 (1.0)
Florida	214 (1.5)	— (—)	234 (1.1)	24 (1.4)	76 (1.4)	31 (1.3)	4 (0.5)	41 (5.3)	50	26 (1.0)
Georgia	216 (1.2)	219 (1.1)	230 (1.0)	28 (1.2)	72 (1.2)	27 (1.3)	3 (0.5)	42 (5.3)	48	23 (1.1)
Hawaii	214 (1.3)	216 (1.0)	227 (1.0)	32 (1.4)	68 (1.4)	23 (1.2)	2 (0.3)	63 (4.7)	58	23 (1.1)
Idaho[6]	222 (1.0)	224 (1.4)	235 (0.7)	20 (1.0)	80 (1.0)	31 (1.1)	2 (0.4)	66 (4.6)	49	14 (0.6)
Illinois[6]	— (—)	223 (1.9)	233 (1.1)	27 (1.2)	73 (1.2)	32 (1.6)	5 (0.7)	68 (4.2)	50	21 (0.9)
Indiana[6]	221 (1.0)	233 (1.1)	238 (0.9)	18 (1.0)	82 (1.0)	35 (1.4)	4 (0.5)	69 (4.8)	50	23 (0.9)
Iowa[6]	230 (1.0)	231 (1.2)	238 (0.7)	17 (1.0)	83 (1.0)	36 (1.2)	3 (0.5)	64 (4.5)	46	17 (1.0)
Kansas	— (—)	232 (1.6)	242 (1.0)	15 (1.2)	85 (1.2)	41 (1.6)	6 (0.8)	48 (4.8)	48	19 (1.1)
Kentucky	215 (1.0)	219 (1.4)	229 (1.1)	28 (1.6)	72 (1.6)	22 (1.4)	2 (0.3)	49 (5.3)	49	24 (0.8)
Louisiana	204 (1.5)	218 (1.4)	226 (1.0)	33 (1.8)	67 (1.8)	21 (1.2)	2 (0.4)	49 (5.6)	43	24 (1.2)
Maine[6]	232 (1.0)	230 (1.0)	238 (0.7)	17 (1.3)	83 (1.3)	34 (1.3)	3 (0.5)	72 (4.1)	46	15 (0.9)
Maryland	217 (1.3)	222 (1.2)	233 (1.3)	27 (1.4)	73 (1.4)	31 (1.7)	5 (0.8)	61 (4.1)	42	25 (1.1)
Massachusetts	227 (1.2)	233 (1.2)	242 (0.8)	16 (1.0)	84 (1.0)	41 (1.4)	6 (0.6)	67 (4.1)	47	19 (0.7)
Michigan[6]	220 (1.7)	229 (1.6)	236 (0.9)	23 (1.0)	77 (1.0)	34 (1.4)	5 (0.5)	75 (4.4)	46	22 (0.9)
Minnesota[6]	228 (0.9)	234 (1.3)	242 (0.9)	16 (0.9)	84 (0.9)	42 (1.6)	7 (0.8)	56 (5.1)	48	15 (0.8)
Mississippi	202 (1.1)	211 (1.1)	223 (1.0)	38 (2.0)	62 (2.0)	17 (1.1)	1 (0.2)	53 (5.1)	51	24 (1.0)
Missouri	222 (1.2)	228 (1.2)	235 (0.9)	21 (1.2)	79 (1.2)	30 (1.4)	3 (0.5)	68 (4.5)	49	21 (1.0)
Montana[6]	— (—)	228 (1.7)	236 (0.8)	19 (1.2)	81 (1.2)	31 (1.6)	2 (0.4)	70 (3.8)	49	13 (0.7)
Nebraska	225 (1.2)	225 (1.8)	236 (0.8)	20 (1.0)	80 (1.0)	34 (1.2)	3 (0.5)	71 (4.7)	51	19 (1.1)
Nevada	— (—)	220 (1.0)	228 (0.8)	31 (1.4)	69 (1.4)	23 (1.0)	1 (0.2)	65 (4.5)	47	19 (0.8)
New Hampshire	230 (1.2)	— (—)	243 (0.9)	13 (1.0)	87 (1.0)	43 (1.4)	6 (0.5)	74 (3.7)	45	15 (0.8)
New Jersey	227 (1.5)	— (—)	239 (1.1)	20 (1.4)	80 (1.4)	39 (1.4)	5 (0.8)	74 (4.0)	45	20 (1.1)
New Mexico	213 (1.4)	213 (1.5)	223 (1.1)	37 (1.8)	63 (1.8)	17 (1.1)	1 (0.3)	54 (5.1)	55	18 (0.8)
New York[6]	218 (1.2)	225 (1.4)	236 (0.9)	21 (1.0)	79 (1.0)	33 (1.4)	4 (0.5)	63 (4.2)	47	23 (1.0)
North Carolina	213 (1.1)	230 (1.1)	242 (0.6)	15 (0.8)	85 (0.8)	41 (1.4)	6 (0.6)	58 (4.8)	50	20 (0.8)
North Dakota	229 (0.8)	230 (1.2)	238 (0.7)	17 (1.1)	83 (1.1)	34 (1.1)	2 (0.4)	77 (3.4)	48	14 (0.7)
Ohio[6]	219 (1.2)	230 (1.5)	238 (1.0)	19 (1.4)	81 (1.4)	36 (1.7)	4 (0.5)	60 (4.7)	45	21 (1.0)
Oklahoma	220 (1.0)	224 (1.0)	229 (1.0)	26 (1.5)	74 (1.5)	23 (1.4)	1 (0.3)	64 (4.7)	48	21 (1.0)
Oregon[6]	— (—)	224 (1.8)	236 (0.9)	21 (1.2)	79 (1.2)	33 (1.4)	4 (0.5)	58 (4.6)	49	16 (0.8)
Pennsylvania	224 (1.3)	— (—)	236 (1.1)	22 (1.4)	78 (1.4)	36 (1.6)	4 (0.5)	68 (4.9)	41	23 (1.0)
Rhode Island	215 (1.5)	224 (1.1)	230 (1.0)	28 (1.4)	72 (1.4)	28 (1.4)	3 (0.5)	68 (4.7)	44	19 (1.0)
South Carolina	212 (1.1)	220 (1.4)	236 (0.9)	21 (1.2)	79 (1.2)	32 (1.5)	4 (0.5)	60 (5.0)	47	25 (0.9)
South Dakota	— (—)	— (—)	237 (0.7)	18 (1.0)	82 (1.0)	34 (1.3)	3 (0.4)	69 (3.2)	55	14 (0.8)
Tennessee	211 (1.4)	220 (1.4)	228 (1.0)	30 (1.6)	70 (1.6)	24 (1.1)	2 (0.4)	61 (4.4)	50	23 (0.9)
Texas	218 (1.2)	231 (1.1)	237 (0.9)	18 (1.2)	82 (1.2)	33 (1.4)	4 (0.5)	41 (4.6)	53	19 (0.9)
Utah	224 (1.0)	227 (1.3)	235 (0.8)	21 (1.1)	79 (1.1)	31 (1.3)	2 (0.4)	51 (5.4)	46	15 (0.8)
Vermont[6]	— (—)	232 (1.6)	242 (0.8)	15 (1.1)	85 (1.1)	42 (1.2)	5 (0.5)	71 (2.4)	47	14 (0.9)
Virginia	221 (1.3)	230 (1.0)	239 (1.1)	17 (1.2)	83 (1.2)	36 (1.8)	5 (0.8)	57 (5.0)	46	23 (1.0)
Washington	— (—)	— (—)	238 (1.0)	19 (1.1)	81 (1.1)	36 (1.5)	5 (0.6)	47 (4.6)	51	17 (0.9)
West Virginia	215 (1.1)	223 (1.3)	231 (0.8)	25 (1.4)	75 (1.4)	24 (1.2)	2 (0.4)	63 (4.9)	47	22 (0.9)
Wisconsin[6]	229 (1.1)	— (—)	237 (0.9)	21 (1.3)	79 (1.3)	35 (1.3)	4 (0.5)	71 (4.8)	49	17 (0.7)
Wyoming	225 (0.9)	229 (1.1)	241 (0.6)	13 (0.8)	87 (0.8)	39 (1.1)	4 (0.4)	64 (0.7)	56	15 (0.7)
Department of Defense dependents schools:										
Domestic schools	— (—)	228 (1.4)	237 (0.7)	16 (1.1)	84 (1.1)	30 (1.5)	2 (0.6)	75 (0.9)	51	21 (1.2)
Overseas schools	— (—)	226 (0.9)	237 (0.5)	16 (0.7)	84 (0.7)	31 (1.1)	2 (0.4)	75 (0.6)	52	18 (0.6)
Outlying areas										
American Samoa	— (—)	152 (2.5)	— (—)	— (—)	— (—)	— (—)	— (—)	— (—)	—	— (—)
Guam	193 (0.8)	184 (1.7)	— (—)	— (—)	— (—)	— (—)	— (—)	— (—)	—	— (—)
Virgin Islands	— (—)	181 (1.8)	— (—)	— (—)	— (—)	— (—)	— (—)	— (—)	—	— (—)

—Jurisdiction did not participate.

[1] Achievement levels are in trial status.

[2] This level denotes partial mastery of prerequisite knowledge and skills that are fundamental for proficient work at the 4th grade.

[3] This level represents solid academic mastery for 4th-graders. Students reaching this level have demonstrated competency over challenging subject matter, including subject-matter knowledge, application of such knowledge to real-world situations, and analytical skills appropriate to the subject matter.

[4] This level signifies superior performance.

[5] Percent of students who report spending 30 minutes, 45 minutes, 1 hour, and over 1 hour on mathematics homework each day.

[6] Did not meet one or more of the guidelines for school sample participation rates in 2000. Data are subject to appreciable nonresponse bias.

NOTE: Excludes students unable to be tested due to limited proficiency in English or due to a disability. These test scores are from the National Assessment of Educational Progress (NAEP). Forty-three jurisdictions (states, the District of Columbia, and Department of Defense Schools) participated in the 2000 State Assessment of 4th-graders and met student and school participation criteria for reporting results. Fifty-three jurisdictions participated in the 2003 state assessment and met student and school participation criteria for reporting results. Data for 2000 and 2003 are for situations where accommodations for the testing were permitted. Detail may not sum to totals due to rounding. Scale ranges from 0 to 500. Standard errors appear in parentheses.

SOURCE: U.S. Department of Education, National Center for Education Statistics, *National Assessment of Educational Progress (NAEP), The Nation's Report Card: Mathematics, 2000* and *2003*; and unpublished data, prepared by Educational Testing Service; NAEP Data Tool (http://nces.ed.gov/nationsreportcard/). (This table was prepared August 2004.)

Mathematics proficiency of 8th-graders in public schools, by state or jurisdiction: Selected years, 1990 to 2003

State or jurisdiction	Average scale score					Percent attaining mathematics achievement levels,[1] 2003				Average scale score, by highest level of education attained by parents,[2] 2003			
	1990	1992	1996	2000	2003	Below basic	Basic or above[3]	Proficient or above[4]	Advanced[5]	Did not finish high school	Graduated high school	Some education after high school	Graduated college
1	2	3	4	5	6	7	8	9	10	11	12	13	14
United States	262 (1.4)	267 (1.0)	271 (1.2)	272 (0.9)	276 (0.3)	33 (0.3)	67 (0.3)	27 (0.3)	5 (0.1)	256 (0.6)	267 (0.4)	280 (0.4)	287 (0.4)
Alabama	253 (1.1)	252 (1.7)	257 (2.1)	264 (1.8)	262 (1.5)	47 (1.7)	53 (1.7)	16 (1.4)	2 (0.5)	249 (2.7)	253 (1.7)	267 (2.0)	270 (2.2)
Alaska	— (—)	— (—)	278 (1.8)	— (—)	279 (0.9)	30 (1.4)	70 (1.4)	30 (1.1)	6 (0.6)	‡ (‡)	‡ (‡)	‡ (‡)	‡ (‡)
Arizona[6]	260 (1.3)	265 (1.3)	268 (1.6)	269 (1.8)	271 (1.2)	39 (1.6)	61 (1.6)	21 (1.2)	3 (0.3)	257 (2.1)	266 (1.7)	277 (1.8)	284 (1.3)
Arkansas	256 (0.9)	256 (1.2)	262 (1.5)	257 (1.5)	266 (1.2)	42 (1.6)	58 (1.6)	19 (1.2)	2 (0.4)	253 (3.1)	259 (1.8)	275 (1.8)	274 (2.1)
California[6]	256 (1.3)	261 (1.7)	263 (1.9)	260 (2.1)	267 (1.2)	44 (1.3)	56 (1.3)	22 (1.1)	4 (0.7)	246 (1.8)	255 (1.6)	275 (1.9)	282 (1.8)
Colorado	267 (0.9)	272 (1.0)	276 (1.1)	— (—)	283 (1.1)	26 (1.1)	74 (1.1)	34 (1.3)	8 (0.8)	254 (2.2)	270 (1.8)	282 (1.7)	295 (1.2)
Connecticut	270 (1.0)	274 (1.1)	280 (1.1)	281 (1.3)	284 (1.2)	27 (1.3)	73 (1.3)	35 (1.6)	8 (0.9)	259 (3.8)	273 (1.9)	280 (1.8)	295 (1.4)
Delaware	261 (0.9)	263 (1.0)	267 (0.9)	— (—)	277 (0.7)	32 (1.1)	68 (1.1)	26 (0.9)	4 (0.5)	258 (3.5)	271 (1.6)	278 (1.5)	286 (1.2)
District of Columbia	231 (0.9)	235 (0.9)	233 (1.3)	235 (1.1)	243 (0.8)	71 (1.1)	29 (1.1)	6 (0.6)	1 (0.3)	236 (3.1)	235 (1.3)	252 (2.0)	250 (1.6)
Florida	255 (1.2)	260 (1.5)	264 (1.8)	— (—)	271 (1.5)	38 (1.8)	62 (1.8)	23 (1.5)	4 (0.6)	255 (2.8)	264 (2.0)	280 (1.8)	280 (1.7)
Georgia	259 (1.3)	259 (1.2)	262 (1.6)	266 (1.2)	270 (1.2)	41 (1.4)	59 (1.4)	22 (1.2)	4 (0.6)	254 (2.2)	259 (1.6)	277 (1.8)	280 (1.5)
Hawaii	251 (0.8)	257 (0.9)	262 (1.0)	262 (1.4)	266 (0.8)	44 (1.0)	56 (1.0)	17 (1.0)	2 (0.4)	253 (2.8)	256 (1.3)	270 (1.5)	273 (1.3)
Idaho[6]	271 (0.8)	275 (0.7)	— (—)	277 (1.0)	280 (0.9)	27 (1.2)	73 (1.2)	28 (1.0)	4 (0.5)	260 (3.1)	269 (1.7)	283 (1.6)	291 (0.9)
Illinois[6]	261 (1.7)	— (—)	— (—)	275 (1.7)	277 (1.2)	34 (1.2)	66 (1.2)	29 (1.5)	6 (0.6)	256 (2.7)	271 (1.6)	278 (1.6)	288 (1.5)
Indiana[6]	267 (1.2)	270 (1.1)	276 (1.4)	281 (1.4)	281 (1.1)	26 (1.4)	74 (1.4)	31 (1.2)	5 (0.4)	265 (2.2)	274 (1.9)	284 (1.6)	290 (1.4)
Iowa	278 (1.1)	283 (1.0)	284 (1.3)	— (—)	284 (0.8)	24 (1.1)	76 (1.1)	33 (1.2)	5 (0.5)	255 (2.9)	272 (1.5)	288 (1.4)	294 (0.9)
Kansas[6]	— (—)	— (—)	— (—)	283 (1.7)	284 (1.3)	24 (1.5)	76 (1.5)	34 (1.5)	6 (0.6)	260 (2.5)	275 (2.0)	287 (1.5)	294 (1.3)
Kentucky	257 (1.2)	262 (1.1)	267 (1.1)	270 (1.3)	274 (1.2)	35 (1.5)	65 (1.5)	24 (1.3)	4 (0.5)	258 (2.3)	266 (1.8)	278 (1.6)	286 (1.7)
Louisiana	246 (1.2)	250 (1.7)	252 (1.6)	259 (1.5)	266 (1.5)	43 (1.8)	57 (1.8)	17 (1.3)	2 (0.5)	256 (3.2)	262 (1.9)	274 (1.9)	271 (2.1)
Maine[6]	— (—)	279 (1.0)	284 (1.3)	281 (1.1)	282 (0.9)	25 (1.1)	75 (1.1)	29 (1.2)	5 (0.6)	255 (3.0)	272 (1.5)	281 (1.4)	291 (1.0)
Maryland	261 (1.4)	265 (1.3)	270 (2.1)	272 (1.7)	278 (1.0)	33 (1.2)	67 (1.2)	30 (1.3)	7 (0.8)	259 (2.7)	265 (2.0)	281 (1.7)	288 (1.3)
Massachusetts	— (—)	273 (1.0)	278 (1.7)	279 (1.5)	287 (0.9)	24 (1.0)	76 (1.0)	38 (1.1)	8 (0.8)	262 (3.3)	271 (1.9)	281 (1.7)	298 (1.0)
Michigan[6]	264 (1.2)	267 (1.4)	277 (1.8)	277 (1.9)	276 (2.0)	32 (2.2)	68 (2.2)	28 (1.9)	5 (0.6)	253 (3.2)	268 (2.0)	280 (2.1)	284 (2.4)
Minnesota	275 (0.9)	282 (1.0)	284 (1.3)	287 (1.4)	291 (1.1)	18 (1.1)	82 (1.1)	44 (1.4)	9 (0.8)	262 (6.6)	279 (1.8)	295 (1.9)	298 (1.1)
Mississippi	— (—)	246 (1.2)	250 (1.2)	254 (1.1)	261 (1.1)	53 (1.4)	47 (1.4)	12 (1.1)	1 (0.3)	253 (2.3)	253 (1.7)	268 (1.9)	266 (1.6)
Missouri	— (—)	271 (1.2)	273 (1.4)	271 (1.5)	279 (1.1)	29 (1.4)	71 (1.4)	28 (1.2)	4 (0.5)	265 (2.6)	271 (1.7)	281 (1.5)	287 (1.5)
Montana[6]	280 (0.9)	— (—)	283 (1.3)	285 (1.4)	286 (0.8)	21 (1.0)	79 (1.0)	35 (1.2)	6 (0.6)	263 (4.8)	277 (1.8)	288 (1.7)	292 (0.9)
Nebraska	276 (1.0)	270 (1.1)	283 (1.0)	280 (1.2)	282 (0.9)	26 (1.1)	74 (1.1)	32 (1.4)	5 (0.6)	253 (3.8)	273 (1.7)	283 (1.7)	292 (1.1)
Nevada	— (—)	— (—)	— (—)	265 (0.8)	268 (0.8)	41 (1.3)	59 (1.3)	20 (0.7)	3 (0.3)	249 (2.7)	263 (1.9)	277 (1.6)	279 (1.3)
New Hampshire	273 (0.9)	278 (1.0)	— (—)	— (—)	286 (0.8)	21 (1.1)	79 (1.1)	35 (1.2)	7 (0.8)	260 (3.2)	276 (1.6)	287 (1.7)	295 (1.0)
New Jersey	270 (1.1)	272 (1.6)	— (—)	— (—)	281 (1.1)	28 (1.2)	72 (1.2)	33 (1.3)	6 (0.7)	260 (4.4)	269 (2.1)	280 (1.3)	292 (1.2)
New Mexico	256 (0.7)	260 (0.9)	262 (1.2)	259 (1.3)	263 (1.0)	48 (1.3)	52 (1.3)	15 (0.8)	2 (0.3)	246 (1.9)	254 (1.5)	268 (1.6)	277 (1.2)
New York[6]	261 (1.4)	266 (2.1)	270 (1.7)	271 (2.2)	280 (1.1)	30 (1.2)	70 (1.2)	32 (1.4)	6 (0.6)	259 (3.3)	270 (1.9)	282 (1.7)	289 (1.3)
North Carolina	250 (1.1)	258 (1.2)	268 (1.4)	276 (1.3)	281 (1.0)	28 (1.3)	72 (1.3)	32 (1.3)	7 (0.7)	264 (2.8)	270 (1.8)	283 (1.3)	291 (1.3)
North Dakota	281 (1.2)	283 (1.1)	284 (0.9)	282 (1.1)	287 (0.8)	19 (1.1)	81 (1.1)	36 (1.1)	5 (0.4)	257 (6.6)	278 (1.8)	290 (1.7)	293 (0.9)
Ohio	264 (1.0)	268 (1.5)	— (—)	281 (1.6)	282 (1.3)	26 (1.5)	74 (1.5)	30 (1.8)	5 (0.8)	260 (2.2)	276 (1.6)	281 (2.1)	291 (1.8)
Oklahoma	263 (1.3)	268 (1.1)	— (—)	270 (1.3)	272 (1.1)	35 (1.5)	65 (1.5)	20 (1.1)	2 (0.4)	254 (2.7)	262 (1.6)	275 (1.4)	282 (1.3)
Oregon[6]	271 (1.0)	— (—)	276 (1.5)	280 (1.5)	281 (1.3)	30 (1.3)	70 (1.3)	32 (1.5)	7 (0.8)	261 (2.6)	271 (1.9)	283 (1.8)	293 (1.4)
Pennsylvania	266 (1.6)	271 (1.5)	— (—)	— (—)	279 (1.1)	31 (1.5)	69 (1.5)	30 (1.3)	5 (0.5)	252 (3.2)	269 (1.7)	280 (1.8)	289 (1.3)
Rhode Island	260 (0.6)	266 (0.7)	269 (0.9)	269 (1.3)	272 (0.7)	37 (1.0)	63 (1.0)	24 (0.9)	3 (0.4)	249 (3.1)	264 (1.8)	271 (2.2)	284 (1.0)
South Carolina	— (—)	261 (1.0)	261 (1.5)	265 (1.5)	277 (1.3)	32 (1.5)	68 (1.5)	26 (1.3)	5 (0.5)	269 (2.2)	267 (1.9)	283 (1.5)	284 (1.5)
South Dakota	— (—)	— (—)	— (—)	— (—)	285 (0.8)	22 (1.3)	78 (1.3)	35 (1.1)	5 (0.5)	267 (3.7)	277 (1.7)	285 (1.7)	293 (0.8)
Tennessee	— (—)	259 (1.4)	263 (1.4)	262 (1.5)	268 (1.8)	41 (2.1)	59 (2.1)	21 (1.5)	3 (0.5)	253 (2.4)	258 (2.3)	274 (2.1)	280 (2.0)
Texas	258 (1.4)	265 (1.3)	270 (1.4)	273 (1.6)	277 (1.1)	31 (1.4)	69 (1.4)	25 (1.4)	4 (0.6)	265 (1.8)	271 (2.1)	282 (1.5)	286 (1.6)
Utah	— (—)	274 (0.7)	277 (1.0)	274 (1.2)	281 (1.0)	28 (1.1)	72 (1.1)	31 (1.5)	6 (0.7)	253 (3.7)	265 (1.7)	281 (1.5)	292 (1.1)
Vermont[6]	— (—)	— (—)	279 (1.0)	281 (1.5)	286 (0.8)	23 (0.9)	77 (0.9)	35 (1.1)	7 (0.7)	262 (2.8)	276 (1.4)	286 (1.3)	294 (1.0)
Virginia	264 (1.5)	268 (1.2)	270 (1.6)	275 (1.3)	282 (1.3)	28 (1.5)	72 (1.5)	31 (1.6)	6 (0.8)	262 (2.3)	271 (1.5)	282 (1.8)	291 (1.5)
Washington	— (—)	— (—)	276 (1.3)	— (—)	281 (0.9)	28 (1.2)	72 (1.2)	32 (1.3)	6 (0.8)	263 (2.0)	271 (1.7)	283 (1.6)	292 (1.4)
West Virginia	256 (1.0)	259 (1.0)	265 (1.0)	266 (1.2)	271 (1.2)	37 (1.8)	63 (1.8)	20 (1.3)	2 (0.3)	255 (3.0)	266 (1.8)	275 (1.6)	279 (1.4)
Wisconsin	274 (1.3)	278 (1.5)	283 (1.5)	— (—)	284 (1.3)	25 (1.4)	75 (1.4)	35 (1.4)	6 (0.6)	255 (4.5)	276 (1.6)	286 (1.9)	293 (1.5)
Wyoming	272 (0.7)	275 (0.9)	275 (0.9)	276 (1.0)	284 (0.7)	23 (1.0)	77 (1.0)	32 (1.0)	4 (0.5)	269 (2.6)	277 (1.5)	284 (1.2)	291 (1.0)
Department of Defense dependents schools:													
Domestic schools	— (—)	— (—)	269 (2.3)	274 (1.8)	282 (1.5)	22 (1.9)	78 (1.9)	27 (1.9)	5 (0.9)	‡ (‡)	273 (3.9)	283 (2.5)	285 (1.7)
Overseas schools	— (—)	— (—)	275 (0.9)	278 (1.1)	286 (0.7)	21 (1.0)	79 (1.0)	35 (1.2)	5 (0.7)	‡ (‡)	277 (2.3)	286 (1.3)	290 (0.9)
Outlying areas													
American Samoa	— (—)	— (—)	— (—)	192 (5.5)	— (—)	— (—)	— (—)	— (—)	— (—)	— (—)	— (—)	— (—)	— (—)
Guam	232 (0.7)	235 (1.0)	239 (1.7)	234 (2.6)	— (—)	— (—)	— (—)	— (—)	— (—)	— (—)	— (—)	— (—)	— (—)
Virgin Islands	219 (0.9)	223 (1.1)	— (—)	— (—)	— (—)	— (—)	— (—)	— (—)	— (—)	— (—)	— (—)	— (—)	— (—)

—Jurisdiction did not participate.

‡ Sample size is insufficient to permit a reliable estimate.

[1] Achievement levels are in trial status.

[2] Excludes students who responded "I don't know" to the question about educational level of parents.

[3] This level denotes partial mastery of prerequisite knowledge and skills that are fundamental for proficient work at the 8th grade.

[4] This level represents solid academic performance for 8th-graders. Students reaching this level have demonstrated competency over challenging subject matter, including subject-matter knowledge, application of such knowledge to real-world situations, and analytical skills appropriate to the subject matter.

[5] This level signifies superior performance.

[6] Did not meet one or more of the guidelines for school participation in 2000. Data are subject to appreciable nonresponse bias.

NOTE: Excludes persons not enrolled in school and those who were unable to be tested due to limited proficiency in English or due to a disability. These test scores are from the National Assessment of Educational Progress (NAEP). Fifty states, the District of Columbia, and two Department of Defense school systems participated in the 2003 State Assessment of 8th-graders and met student and school participation criteria for reporting results. Scale ranges from 0 to 500. Data for 2000 and 2003 are for situations where student accommodations were permitted. Detail may not sum to totals due to rounding. Standard errors appear in parentheses.

SOURCE: U.S. Department of Education, National Center for Education Statistics, *National Assessment of Educational Progress (NAEP), The Nations Report Card: Mathematics, 2003*; prepared by Educational Testing Service; and unpublished data, NAEP Data Tool (http://nces.ed.gov/nationsreportcard/naepdata). (This table was prepared August 2004.)

Average mathematics scale scores and achievement-level results, by gender, grade 4 public schools: By state, 2003

	Male				Female			
		Percentage of students				Percentage of students		
	Average scale scores	Below **Basic**	At or above **Basic**	At or above **Proficient**	Average scale scores	Below **Basic**	At or above **Basic**	At or above **Proficient**
Nation (public)	235	23	77	34	233	25	75	29
Alabama	223	35	65	19	223	36	64	18
Alaska	235	24	76	33	231	26	74	27
Arizona	231	28	72	28	227	32	68	23
Arkansas	228	30	70	27	230	27	73	25
California	229	31	69	28	225	35	65	22
Colorado	237	22	78	37	233	24	76	31
Connecticut	243	15	85	45	238	20	80	37
Delaware	237	20	80	34	235	19	81	29
Florida	235	24	76	33	233	25	75	29
Georgia	231	28	72	29	229	29	71	25
Hawaii	227	32	68	24	226	32	68	22
Idaho	237	19	81	34	233	22	78	27
Illinois	234	26	74	34	232	28	72	29
Indiana	239	17	83	37	237	18	82	34
Iowa	240	15	85	39	236	19	81	32
Kansas	244	14	86	44	240	17	83	39
Kentucky	230	26	74	24	227	30	70	20
Louisiana	227	33	67	22	226	33	67	20
Maine	239	16	84	37	236	19	81	31
Maryland	235	26	74	33	232	29	71	29
Massachusetts	244	14	86	44	239	18	82	38
Michigan	238	21	79	38	233	25	75	30
Minnesota	244	15	85	45	240	17	83	38
Mississippi	223	38	62	18	223	37	63	16
Missouri	235	22	78	30	235	20	80	29
Montana	236	19	81	33	235	19	81	29
Nebraska	238	19	81	36	235	22	78	31
Nevada	229	30	70	25	226	31	69	21
New Hampshire	246	11	89	46	240	15	85	39
New Jersey	240	19	81	41	237	20	80	36
New Mexico	224	36	64	21	221	39	61	14
New York	237	21	79	35	235	22	78	31
North Carolina	243	15	85	42	241	15	85	40
North Dakota	240	16	84	38	235	18	82	30
Ohio	239	19	81	37	237	19	81	34
Oklahoma	230	26	74	25	228	27	73	20
Oregon	237	20	80	35	235	22	78	31
Pennsylvania	238	21	79	39	234	23	77	32
Rhode Island	231	27	73	29	229	30	70	27
South Carolina	237	18	82	34	234	23	77	29
South Dakota	239	16	84	37	235	20	80	31
Tennessee	228	31	69	25	228	30	70	22
Texas	239	17	83	35	236	18	82	31
Utah	236	20	80	34	233	22	78	28
Vermont	244	14	86	44	240	17	83	39
Virginia	240	18	82	38	239	17	83	35
Washington	240	18	82	39	237	20	80	33
West Virginia	232	24	76	26	230	25	75	22
Wisconsin	238	20	80	38	235	21	79	32
Wyoming	242	12	88	41	240	14	86	36
Other jurisdictions								
District of Columbia	204	64	36	8	206	63	37	7
DDESS[1]	239	15	85	34	235	16	84	27
DoDDS[2]	239	14	86	34	236	18	82	29

[1]Department of Defense Domestic Dependent Elementary and Secondary Schools.
[2]Department of Defense Dependents Schools (Overseas).
SOURCE: U.S. Department of Education, Institute of Education Sciences, National Center for Education Statistics, National Assessment of Educational Progress (NAEP), 2003 Mathematics Assessment.

Average mathematics scale scores and achievement-level results, by gender, grade 8 public schools: By state, 2003

	Male				Female			
	Average scale scores	Percentage of students			Average scale scores	Percentage of students		
		Below *Basic*	At or above *Basic*	At or above *Proficient*		Below *Basic*	At or above *Basic*	At or above *Proficient*
Nation (public)	277	33	67	29	275	34	66	26
Alabama	263	45	55	18	261	49	51	14
Alaska	280	29	71	32	278	31	69	28
Arizona	271	39	61	21	271	38	62	21
Arkansas	265	43	57	19	267	41	59	18
California	268	43	57	23	266	45	55	21
Colorado	284	26	74	35	283	26	74	34
Connecticut	285	27	73	37	283	27	73	33
Delaware	278	30	70	27	276	33	67	25
Florida	273	36	64	26	269	41	59	21
Georgia	270	40	60	24	269	41	59	20
Hawaii	265	44	56	17	266	45	55	16
Idaho	281	27	73	30	279	28	72	27
Illinois	278	33	67	31	276	34	66	28
Indiana	282	25	75	33	280	28	72	29
Iowa	285	23	77	35	283	24	76	31
Kansas	284	25	75	34	284	24	76	34
Kentucky	275	35	65	25	274	34	66	23
Louisiana	267	42	58	19	266	44	56	15
Maine	283	24	76	31	281	26	74	28
Maryland	279	32	68	33	276	34	66	27
Massachusetts	289	22	78	42	284	26	74	35
Michigan	277	33	67	30	276	32	68	26
Minnesota	289	20	80	43	292	16	84	44
Mississippi	262	51	49	14	260	55	45	11
Missouri	280	29	71	30	278	30	70	26
Montana	286	21	79	36	286	20	80	34
Nebraska	284	25	75	35	281	27	73	30
Nevada	268	41	59	21	268	41	59	19
New Hampshire	287	21	79	36	286	22	78	33
New Jersey	282	28	72	34	281	29	71	33
New Mexico	264	47	53	16	263	49	51	15
New York	281	29	71	33	279	30	70	31
North Carolina	281	29	71	32	282	28	72	32
North Dakota	287	19	81	37	287	19	81	36
Ohio	283	25	75	32	281	27	73	29
Oklahoma	272	36	64	22	272	35	65	18
Oregon	282	29	71	33	280	30	70	30
Pennsylvania	280	30	70	33	277	32	68	27
Rhode Island	273	37	63	26	271	38	62	22
South Carolina	280	30	70	29	274	35	65	23
South Dakota	286	21	79	35	284	23	77	34
Tennessee	268	42	58	22	268	41	59	20
Texas	278	31	69	27	276	32	68	23
Utah	282	28	72	33	280	28	72	29
Vermont	286	23	77	35	286	22	78	35
Virginia	283	26	74	33	280	29	71	30
Washington	282	28	72	33	281	29	71	31
West Virginia	271	38	62	21	271	37	63	18
Wisconsin	284	25	75	36	284	24	76	34
Wyoming	284	24	76	34	283	22	78	30
Other jurisdictions								
District of Columbia	242	71	29	7	244	71	29	5
DDESS[1]	284	21	79	31	280	23	77	22
DoDDS[2]	287	20	80	37	284	22	78	32

[1]Department of Defense Domestic Dependent Elementary and Secondary Schools.
[2]Department of Defense Dependents Schools (Overseas).
SOURCE: U.S. Department of Education, Institute of Education Sciences, National Center for Education Statistics, National Assessment of Educational Progress (NAEP), 2003 Mathematics Assessment.

Average mathematics scale scores and achievement-level results, by race/ethnicity, grade 4 public schools: By state, 2003

	White					Black					Hispanic				
	Weighted percentage of students	Average scale scores	Below Basic	At or above Basic	At or above Proficient	Weighted percentage of students	Average scale scores	Below Basic	At or above Basic	At or above Proficient	Weighted percentage of students	Average scale scores	Below Basic	At or above Basic	At or above Proficient
Nation (public)	58	243	13	87	42	17	216	46	54	10	19	221	38	62	15
Alabama	61	232	22	78	27	36	208	59	41	5	1	‡	‡	‡	‡
Alaska	56	242	14	86	41	5	221	36	64	15	5	228	32	68	24
Arizona	50	241	15	85	39	4	215	48	52	11	38	217	44	56	11
Arkansas	69	237	17	83	34	25	206	61	39	5	4	221	38	62	15
California	32	243	14	86	42	7	213	49	51	9	49	216	47	53	11
Colorado	65	243	12	88	44	5	217	46	54	12	25	217	46	54	13
Connecticut	67	250	8	92	53	14	217	45	55	10	15	223	36	64	15
Delaware	56	244	9	91	43	33	223	34	66	12	7	226	31	69	17
Florida	50	243	13	87	43	25	215	48	52	8	21	232	26	74	27
Georgia	50	241	16	84	40	39	217	44	56	11	7	219	40	60	13
Hawaii	16	238	18	82	35	3	221	36	64	16	3	219	45	55	17
Idaho	83	238	16	84	34	1	‡	‡	‡	‡	13	217	45	55	11
Illinois	59	244	13	87	44	20	210	56	44	7	18	218	45	55	13
Indiana	80	242	13	87	40	12	215	46	54	7	4	226	31	69	18
Iowa	87	241	14	86	39	5	215	50	50	9	5	222	38	62	14
Kansas	78	246	10	90	47	11	217	45	55	13	8	230	22	78	19
Kentucky	85	231	25	75	24	12	214	47	53	8	1	‡	‡	‡	‡
Louisiana	44	242	12	88	39	53	213	51	49	6	1	‡	‡	‡	‡
Maine	97	238	17	83	34	1	‡	‡	‡	‡	1	‡	‡	‡	‡
Maryland	51	244	15	85	44	37	216	47	53	11	6	227	32	68	21
Massachusetts	73	247	9	91	49	11	222	38	62	13	12	222	37	63	13
Michigan	70	244	12	88	43	21	209	58	42	7	4	223	39	61	17
Minnesota	81	246	11	89	47	8	219	46	54	16	4	220	40	60	14
Mississippi	44	236	17	83	30	55	212	54	46	6	1	‡	‡	‡	‡
Missouri	77	240	14	86	35	18	216	47	53	9	3	220	43	57	14
Montana	86	238	16	84	34	1	‡	‡	‡	‡	2	236	17	83	25
Nebraska	80	241	13	87	39	7	211	56	44	7	9	213	49	51	9
Nevada	53	236	19	81	32	10	215	48	52	10	30	216	47	53	10
New Hampshire	94	244	12	88	43	2	‡	‡	‡	‡	3	225	35	65	19
New Jersey	58	248	10	90	51	18	217	45	55	11	16	224	33	67	18
New Mexico	31	237	18	82	33	3	216	44	56	10	53	217	45	55	10
New York	54	246	9	91	45	19	219	42	58	12	20	221	38	62	15
North Carolina	58	251	6	94	55	30	225	32	68	14	6	235	21	79	30
North Dakota	88	240	13	87	37	1	‡	‡	‡	‡	1	‡	‡	‡	‡
Ohio	77	243	13	87	42	19	217	46	54	10	2	225	34	66	16
Oklahoma	59	235	18	82	29	12	211	53	47	6	7	220	39	61	11
Oregon	75	240	16	84	36	3	223	39	61	20	14	218	46	54	15
Pennsylvania	74	243	13	87	44	20	212	52	48	8	5	216	48	52	12
Rhode Island	70	239	17	83	37	9	210	55	45	7	16	207	58	42	6
South Carolina	55	246	10	90	46	40	222	35	65	13	3	232	22	78	26
South Dakota	84	241	13	87	38	1	‡	‡	‡	‡	2	223	37	63	20
Tennessee	71	235	20	80	30	26	208	59	41	6	2	218	43	57	14
Texas	40	248	8	92	49	13	226	29	71	15	44	230	24	76	21
Utah	82	238	16	84	35	1	‡	‡	‡	‡	11	216	48	52	11
Vermont	95	242	15	85	42	2	‡	‡	‡	‡	1	‡	‡	‡	‡
Virginia	62	246	10	90	46	26	223	34	66	13	7	230	25	75	20
Washington	71	242	14	86	40	6	222	38	62	17	12	223	39	61	18
West Virginia	95	231	24	76	24	4	221	38	62	13	1	‡	‡	‡	‡
Wisconsin	76	243	12	88	43	12	209	59	41	8	8	221	37	63	13
Wyoming	86	243	11	89	42	1	‡	‡	‡	‡	8	229	24	76	20
Other jurisdictions															
District of Columbia	4	262	3	97	71	87	202	67	33	4	8	205	61	39	7
DDESS[1]	47	243	9	91	40	25	225	29	71	13	19	236	15	85	27
DoDDS[2]	48	241	12	88	38	22	227	25	75	15	11	233	21	79	25

See notes at end of table. ▶

Average mathematics scale scores and achievement-level results, by race/ethnicity, grade 4 public schools: By state, 2003—Continued

| | Asian/Pacific Islander | | | | | American Indian/Alaska Native | | | | |
| | | | Percentage of students | | | | | Percentage of students | | |
	Weighted percentage of students	Average scale scores	Below *Basic*	At or above *Basic*	At or above *Proficient*	Weighted percentage of students	Average scale scores	Below *Basic*	At or above *Basic*	At or above *Proficient*
Nation (public)	4	246	13	87	48	1	224	35	65	18
Alabama	1	‡	‡	‡	‡	1	‡	‡	‡	‡
Alaska	7	230	27	73	27	26	218	46	54	13
Arizona	2	244	11	89	41	6	210	56	44	8
Arkansas	1	‡	‡	‡	‡	#	‡	‡	‡	‡
California	11	246	13	87	49	#	‡	‡	‡	‡
Colorado	3	242	19	81	44	1	‡	‡	‡	‡
Connecticut	3	249	8	92	52	#	‡	‡	‡	‡
Delaware	3	250	13	87	59	#	‡	‡	‡	‡
Florida	2	249	10	90	53	#	‡	‡	‡	‡
Georgia	2	248	13	87	53	#	‡	‡	‡	‡
Hawaii	67	225	34	66	21	1	‡	‡	‡	‡
Idaho	1	‡	‡	‡	‡	1	‡	‡	‡	‡
Illinois	2	252	8	92	58	#	‡	‡	‡	‡
Indiana	1	‡	‡	‡	‡	#	‡	‡	‡	‡
Iowa	2	‡	‡	‡	‡	1	‡	‡	‡	‡
Kansas	2	‡	‡	‡	‡	1	‡	‡	‡	‡
Kentucky	1	‡	‡	‡	‡	#	‡	‡	‡	‡
Louisiana	1	‡	‡	‡	‡	1	‡	‡	‡	‡
Maine	1	‡	‡	‡	‡	#	‡	‡	‡	‡
Maryland	6	254	10	90	58	#	‡	‡	‡	‡
Massachusetts	4	248	11	89	49	#	‡	‡	‡	‡
Michigan	2	248	14	86	47	1	‡	‡	‡	‡
Minnesota	5	229	32	68	27	2	‡	‡	‡	‡
Mississippi	1	‡	‡	‡	‡	#	‡	‡	‡	‡
Missouri	1	‡	‡	‡	‡	#	‡	‡	‡	‡
Montana	1	‡	‡	‡	‡	10	217	45	55	11
Nebraska	1	‡	‡	‡	‡	2	219	39	61	11
Nevada	5	237	18	82	34	2	215	45	55	10
New Hampshire	1	‡	‡	‡	‡	#	‡	‡	‡	‡
New Jersey	7	256	5	95	61	1	‡	‡	‡	‡
New Mexico	1	‡	‡	‡	‡	11	210	55	45	7
New York	6	250	9	91	51	1	‡	‡	‡	‡
North Carolina	2	255	7	93	60	1	‡	‡	‡	‡
North Dakota	1	‡	‡	‡	‡	8	215	48	52	9
Ohio	1	‡	‡	‡	‡	#	‡	‡	‡	‡
Oklahoma	2	247	9	91	45	18	225	32	68	16
Oregon	4	245	12	88	46	2	‡	‡	‡	‡
Pennsylvania	2	‡	‡	‡	‡	#	‡	‡	‡	‡
Rhode Island	4	225	37	63	22	1	‡	‡	‡	‡
South Carolina	1	‡	‡	‡	‡	#	‡	‡	‡	‡
South Dakota	1	‡	‡	‡	‡	12	217	46	54	9
Tennessee	1	‡	‡	‡	‡	#	‡	‡	‡	‡
Texas	3	258	2	98	62	#	‡	‡	‡	‡
Utah	4	224	34	66	16	1	‡	‡	‡	‡
Vermont	2	‡	‡	‡	‡	#	‡	‡	‡	‡
Virginia	5	255	6	94	60	#	‡	‡	‡	‡
Washington	7	244	15	85	44	3	229	31	69	24
West Virginia	1	‡	‡	‡	‡	#	‡	‡	‡	‡
Wisconsin	3	230	28	72	26	2	224	41	59	17
Wyoming	1	‡	‡	‡	‡	3	221	37	63	16
Other jurisdictions										
District of Columbia	1	‡	‡	‡	‡	#	‡	‡	‡	‡
DDESS[1]	3	‡	‡	‡	‡	1	‡	‡	‡	‡
DoDDS[2]	10	240	14	86	38	1	‡	‡	‡	‡

#The estimate rounds to zero.

‡Reporting standards not met. Sample size is insufficient to permit a reliable estimate.

[1]Department of Defense Domestic Dependent Elementary and Secondary Schools.

[2]Department of Defense Dependents Schools (Overseas).

NOTE: Results are not shown for students whose race based on school records was "other" or, if school data were missing, who self-reported their race as "multiracial" but not "Hispanic," or did not self-report racial/ethnic information.

SOURCE: U.S. Department of Education, Institute of Education Sciences, National Center for Education Statistics, National Assessment of Educational Progress (NAEP), 2003 Mathematics Assessment.

Average mathematics scale scores and achievement-level results, by race/ethnicity, grade 8 public schools: By state, 2003

	White					Black					Hispanic				
			Percentage of students					Percentage of students					Percentage of students		
	Weighted percentage of students	Average scale scores	Below *Basic*	At or above *Basic*	At or above *Proficient*	Weighted percentage of students	Average scale scores	Below *Basic*	At or above *Basic*	At or above *Proficient*	Weighted percentage of students	Average scale scores	Below *Basic*	At or above *Basic*	At or above *Proficient*
Nation (public)	62	287	21	79	36	17	252	61	39	7	15	258	53	47	11
Alabama	62	274	32	68	23	36	240	73	27	3	1	‡	‡	‡	‡
Alaska	58	290	19	81	41	5	263	44	56	11	3	263	49	51	11
Arizona	50	284	22	78	32	4	256	55	45	7	37	258	55	45	9
Arkansas	72	275	31	69	24	24	239	74	26	3	3	248	63	37	7
California	37	283	26	74	34	9	246	65	35	6	39	250	63	37	8
Colorado	70	292	16	84	43	5	255	60	40	9	21	259	52	48	12
Connecticut	71	293	17	83	44	13	255	58	42	7	12	259	52	48	11
Delaware	60	287	19	81	35	31	260	52	48	8	6	257	53	47	11
Florida	50	286	22	78	34	27	249	64	36	7	19	264	47	53	16
Georgia	53	284	23	77	32	39	250	64	36	7	4	262	51	49	14
Hawaii	15	273	36	64	25	2	‡	‡	‡	‡	3	263	52	48	16
Idaho	85	284	23	77	31	1	‡	‡	‡	‡	11	251	61	39	7
Illinois	62	289	20	80	40	20	249	66	34	6	15	259	52	48	9
Indiana	82	286	21	79	35	12	251	60	40	7	3	261	51	49	9
Iowa	90	287	20	80	35	4	257	58	42	11	4	255	56	44	10
Kansas	79	290	17	83	39	9	252	65	35	8	9	263	51	49	16
Kentucky	88	277	32	68	25	9	250	62	38	5	1	‡	‡	‡	‡
Louisiana	51	281	25	75	28	46	250	64	36	5	2	‡	‡	‡	‡
Maine	97	282	25	75	30	1	‡	‡	‡	‡	1	‡	‡	‡	‡
Maryland	58	289	21	79	40	31	256	56	44	9	6	262	51	49	15
Massachusetts	77	292	17	83	44	8	260	52	48	10	10	255	59	41	9
Michigan	70	286	21	79	35	22	245	68	32	4	3	267	43	57	14
Minnesota	83	295	13	87	49	6	251	57	43	9	3	262	52	48	16
Mississippi	49	275	33	67	22	48	246	73	27	3	1	‡	‡	‡	‡
Missouri	82	284	23	77	32	15	250	65	35	6	2	‡	‡	‡	‡
Montana	87	289	17	83	37	1	‡	‡	‡	‡	2	‡	‡	‡	‡
Nebraska	84	287	20	80	36	5	247	65	35	7	7	255	60	40	10
Nevada	57	278	29	71	27	9	248	65	35	9	25	250	63	37	7
New Hampshire	95	287	20	80	35	1	‡	‡	‡	‡	2	‡	‡	‡	‡
New Jersey	61	292	16	84	42	18	253	59	41	7	14	262	50	50	14
New Mexico	34	282	24	76	31	3	254	60	40	5	51	254	59	41	7
New York	56	293	14	86	44	20	255	57	43	10	17	262	50	50	16
North Carolina	59	294	15	85	44	30	260	51	49	11	5	263	45	55	16
North Dakota	90	290	15	85	39	1	‡	‡	‡	‡	1	‡	‡	‡	‡
Ohio	79	287	20	80	35	17	257	55	45	8	2	270	42	58	18
Oklahoma	63	278	27	73	25	10	249	63	37	5	6	258	53	47	9
Oregon	79	284	25	75	35	3	265	47	53	17	10	258	58	42	12
Pennsylvania	80	285	24	76	35	15	247	68	32	4	3	253	58	42	6
Rhode Island	76	280	28	72	29	7	244	71	29	5	13	245	71	29	5
South Carolina	56	291	16	84	39	40	258	54	46	8	2	‡	‡	‡	‡
South Dakota	89	288	18	82	37	1	‡	‡	‡	‡	1	‡	‡	‡	‡
Tennessee	74	277	31	69	26	23	242	72	28	5	2	‡	‡	‡	‡
Texas	44	290	16	84	38	16	260	53	47	8	38	267	42	58	14
Utah	86	285	23	77	34	1	‡	‡	‡	‡	9	249	65	35	7
Vermont	97	286	22	78	35	1	‡	‡	‡	‡	#	‡	‡	‡	‡
Virginia	64	290	18	82	40	27	262	51	49	11	5	268	41	59	17
Washington	75	285	24	76	36	5	262	46	54	13	9	263	50	50	17
West Virginia	96	271	37	63	20	4	253	61	39	6	#	‡	‡	‡	‡
Wisconsin	84	290	18	82	40	8	241	76	24	5	4	262	50	50	16
Wyoming	89	286	20	80	35	1	‡	‡	‡	‡	7	265	46	54	13
Other jurisdictions															
District of Columbia	3	‡	‡	‡	‡	87	240	74	26	3	9	246	67	33	3
DDESS[1]	39	294	10	90	42	22	268	39	61	10	27	276	28	72	19
DoDDS[2]	48	292	14	86	42	21	270	37	63	15	10	280	28	72	29

See notes at end of table. ▶

Average mathematics scale scores and achievement-level results, by race/ethnicity, grade 8 public schools: By state, 2003—Continued

| | Asian/Pacific Islander | | | | | American Indian/Alaska Native | | | | |
| | | | Percentage of students | | | | | Percentage of students | | |
	Weighted percentage of students	Average scale scores	Below *Basic*	At or above *Basic*	At or above *Proficient*	Weighted percentage of students	Average scale scores	Below *Basic*	At or above *Basic*	At or above *Proficient*
Nation (public)	4	289	23	77	42	1	265	46	54	16
Alabama	1	‡	‡	‡	‡	#	‡	‡	‡	‡
Alaska	7	280	30	70	29	25	259	51	49	12
Arizona	2	‡	‡	‡	‡	7	254	61	39	7
Arkansas	1	‡	‡	‡	‡	#	‡	‡	‡	‡
California	13	287	26	74	39	1	‡	‡	‡	‡
Colorado	4	290	20	80	38	1	‡	‡	‡	‡
Connecticut	3	296	21	79	51	#	‡	‡	‡	‡
Delaware	2	‡	‡	‡	‡	#	‡	‡	‡	‡
Florida	2	287	25	75	41	#	‡	‡	‡	‡
Georgia	3	286	27	73	40	#	‡	‡	‡	‡
Hawaii	69	265	46	54	15	#	‡	‡	‡	‡
Idaho	1	‡	‡	‡	‡	1	‡	‡	‡	‡
Illinois	3	302	11	89	58	#	‡	‡	‡	‡
Indiana	1	‡	‡	‡	‡	#	‡	‡	‡	‡
Iowa	1	‡	‡	‡	‡	#	‡	‡	‡	‡
Kansas	2	284	21	79	34	1	‡	‡	‡	‡
Kentucky	1	‡	‡	‡	‡	#	‡	‡	‡	‡
Louisiana	1	‡	‡	‡	‡	#	‡	‡	‡	‡
Maine	1	‡	‡	‡	‡	#	‡	‡	‡	‡
Maryland	5	302	10	90	56	#	‡	‡	‡	‡
Massachusetts	4	304	12	88	57	#	‡	‡	‡	‡
Michigan	2	‡	‡	‡	‡	2	‡	‡	‡	‡
Minnesota	5	284	25	75	32	2	‡	‡	‡	‡
Mississippi	1	‡	‡	‡	‡	#	‡	‡	‡	‡
Missouri	1	‡	‡	‡	‡	#	‡	‡	‡	‡
Montana	1	‡	‡	‡	‡	9	260	52	48	15
Nebraska	2	‡	‡	‡	‡	2	‡	‡	‡	‡
Nevada	7	280	27	73	31	1	‡	‡	‡	‡
New Hampshire	1	‡	‡	‡	‡	#	‡	‡	‡	‡
New Jersey	6	306	10	90	61	#	‡	‡	‡	‡
New Mexico	1	‡	‡	‡	‡	10	245	70	30	3
New York	6	290	21	79	41	1	‡	‡	‡	‡
North Carolina	2	297	13	87	48	2	259	52	48	13
North Dakota	1	‡	‡	‡	‡	7	261	50	50	11
Ohio	1	‡	‡	‡	‡	#	‡	‡	‡	‡
Oklahoma	1	‡	‡	‡	‡	17	265	44	56	14
Oregon	4	292	22	78	41	2	263	50	50	14
Pennsylvania	2	‡	‡	‡	‡	#	‡	‡	‡	‡
Rhode Island	3	265	46	54	20	#	‡	‡	‡	‡
South Carolina	1	‡	‡	‡	‡	#	‡	‡	‡	‡
South Dakota	1	‡	‡	‡	‡	8	255	57	43	9
Tennessee	1	‡	‡	‡	‡	#	‡	‡	‡	‡
Texas	3	303	9	91	58	#	‡	‡	‡	‡
Utah	3	275	34	66	25	1	‡	‡	‡	‡
Vermont	1	‡	‡	‡	‡	1	‡	‡	‡	‡
Virginia	4	297	14	86	48	#	‡	‡	‡	‡
Washington	8	285	28	72	37	2	264	44	56	17
West Virginia	#	‡	‡	‡	‡	#	‡	‡	‡	‡
Wisconsin	4	273	33	67	17	1	‡	‡	‡	‡
Wyoming	1	‡	‡	‡	‡	3	261	52	48	14
Other jurisdictions										
District of Columbia	1	‡	‡	‡	‡	#	‡	‡	‡	‡
DDESS[1]	7	‡	‡	‡	‡	1	‡	‡	‡	‡
DoDDS[2]	11	288	18	82	38	1	‡	‡	‡	‡

#The estimate rounds to zero.
‡Reporting standards not met. Sample size is insufficient to permit a reliable estimate.
[1]Department of Defense Domestic Dependent Elementary and Secondary Schools.
[2]Department of Defense Dependents Schools (Overseas).
NOTE: Results are not shown for students whose race based on school records was "other" or, if school data were missing, who self-reported their race as "multiracial" but not "Hispanic," or did not self-report racial/ethnic information.
SOURCE: U.S. Department of Education, Institute of Education Sciences, National Center for Education Statistics, National Assessment of Educational Progress (NAEP), 2003 Mathematics Assessment.

Average scale score in reading for 4th-graders in public schools, by race/ethnicity and state or jurisdiction: Selected years, 1994 to 2003

State or jurisdiction	1994 Average	1998 Average	2002 Average	2003 Average	Race/ethnicity [1]				
					White, non-Hispanic	Black, non-Hispanic	Hispanic	Asian/Pacific Islander	American Indian/Alaska Native
1	2	3	4	5	6	7	8	9	10
United States [2]	**212 (1.1)**	**213 (1.2)**	**217 (0.5)**	**216 (0.3)**	**227 (0.2)**	**197 (0.4)**	**199 (0.6)**	**225 (1.3)**	**202 (1.4)**
Alabama	208 (1.5)	211 (1.9)	207 (1.4)	207 (1.7)	219 (1.5)	188 (2.5)	‡ (‡)	‡ (‡)	‡ (‡)
Alaska	— (—)	— (—)	— (—)	212 (1.6)	226 (1.2)	209 (3.5)	209 (3.0)	207 (4.5)	184 (2.5)
Arizona	206 (1.9)	206 (1.4)	205 (1.5)	209 (1.2)	223 (1.4)	196 (3.4)	195 (1.9)	225 (4.9)	182 (2.5)
Arkansas	209 (1.7)	209 (1.6)	213 (1.4)	214 (1.4)	223 (1.3)	190 (2.3)	204 (4.1)!	‡ (‡)	‡ (‡)
California [3,4]	197 (1.8)	202 (2.5)	206 (2.5)	206 (1.2)	224 (1.7)	193 (3.1)	191 (1.3)	224 (3.2)	‡ (‡)
Colorado	213 (1.3)	220 (1.4)	— (—)	224 (1.2)	232 (1.2)	208 (2.6)	205 (1.6)	225 (3.7)	‡ (‡)
Connecticut	222 (1.6)	230 (1.6)	229 (1.1)	228 (1.1)	238 (1.2)	201 (2.2)	206 (2.5)	231 (3.9)	‡ (‡)
Delaware	206 (1.1)	207 (1.7)	224 (0.6)	224 (0.7)	233 (0.7)	211 (1.1)	209 (3.0)	238 (3.5)	‡ (‡)
District of Columbia	— (—)	179 (1.2)	191 (0.9)	188 (0.9)	254 (2.6)	184 (0.8)	187 (2.8)	‡ (‡)	‡ (‡)
Florida	205 (1.7)	206 (1.4)	214 (1.4)	218 (1.1)	229 (1.3)	198 (1.9)	211 (2.2)	233 (6.2)	‡ (‡)
Georgia	207 (2.4)	209 (1.4)	215 (1.0)	214 (1.3)	226 (1.4)	199 (1.3)	201 (3.5)	233 (6.2)	‡ (‡)
Hawaii	201 (1.7)	200 (1.5)	208 (0.9)	208 (1.4)	221 (2.2)	211 (3.0)	204 (4.7)	205 (1.6)	‡ (‡)
Idaho	— (—)	— (—)	220 (1.1)	218 (1.0)	222 (0.9)	‡ (‡)	199 (2.1)	‡ (‡)	‡ (‡)
Illinois	— (—)	— (—)	— (—)	216 (1.6)	228 (1.8)	194 (1.8)	197 (3.1)	235 (4.9)	‡ (‡)
Indiana	220 (1.3)	— (—)	222 (1.4)	220 (1.0)	224 (1.0)	197 (3.9)	212 (3.1)!	‡ (‡)	‡ (‡)
Iowa [3,4]	223 (1.3)	220 (1.6)	223 (1.1)	223 (1.1)	226 (1.1)	196 (2.7)	205 (3.6)	‡ (‡)	‡ (‡)
Kansas [3,4]	— (—)	221 (1.4)	222 (1.4)	220 (1.2)	225 (1.3)	197 (2.9)	207 (2.5)	‡ (‡)	‡ (‡)
Kentucky	212 (1.6)	218 (1.5)	219 (1.1)	219 (1.3)	221 (1.2)	202 (3.3)	‡ (‡)	‡ (‡)	‡ (‡)
Louisiana	197 (1.3)	200 (1.6)	207 (1.7)	205 (1.4)	223 (1.4)	189 (1.6)	‡ (‡)	‡ (‡)	‡ (‡)
Maine	228 (1.3)	225 (1.4)	225 (1.1)	224 (0.9)	224 (0.9)	‡ (‡)	‡ (‡)	‡ (‡)	‡ (‡)
Maryland	210 (1.5)	212 (1.6)	217 (1.5)	219 (1.4)	231 (1.5)	200 (2.1)	209 (4.5)	237 (4.0)	‡ (‡)
Massachusetts [3]	223 (1.3)	223 (1.4)	234 (1.1)	228 (1.2)	234 (1.3)	207 (1.6)	202 (2.1)	229 (3.4)	‡ (‡)
Michigan	— (—)	216 (1.5)	219 (1.1)	219 (1.2)	228 (0.9)	189 (2.0)	205 (3.4)!	232 (8.4)!	‡ (‡)
Minnesota [3,4]	218 (1.4)	219 (1.7)	225 (1.4)	223 (1.1)	229 (1.0)	194 (3.4)	195 (3.7)	197 (2.8)	‡ (‡)
Mississippi	202 (1.6)	203 (1.3)	203 (1.3)	205 (1.3)	221 (1.3)	192 (1.7)	‡ (‡)	‡ (‡)	‡ (‡)
Missouri	217 (1.5)	216 (1.3)	220 (1.3)	222 (1.2)	227 (1.3)	203 (1.7)	218 (4.2)	‡ (‡)	‡ (‡)
Montana [3,4]	222 (1.4)	225 (1.5)	224 (1.8)	223 (1.2)	227 (1.0)	‡ (‡)	‡ (‡)	‡ (‡)	195 (4.0)
Nebraska [5]	220 (1.5)	— (—)	222 (1.5)	221 (1.0)	225 (1.1)	203 (2.9)	202 (2.7)	‡ (‡)	‡ (‡)
Nevada	— (—)	206 (1.8)	209 (1.2)	207 (1.2)	217 (1.5)	193 (3.0)	192 (2.0)	214 (2.6)	190 (6.0)!
New Hampshire [3]	223 (1.5)	226 (1.7)	— (—)	228 (1.0)	229 (0.9)	‡ (‡)	206 (4.5)	‡ (‡)	‡ (‡)
New Jersey	219 (1.2)	— (—)	— (—)	225 (1.2)	235 (1.4)	200 (3.3)	212 (2.1)	235 (3.3)	‡ (‡)
New Mexico	205 (1.7)	205 (1.4)	208 (1.6)	203 (1.5)	222 (2.0)	202 (5.2)	197 (1.9)	‡ (‡)	182 (2.6)
New York [3,4]	212 (1.4)	215 (1.6)	222 (1.5)	222 (1.1)	235 (1.3)	203 (1.9)	208 (1.9)	230 (2.5)	‡ (‡)
North Carolina	214 (1.5)	213 (1.6)	222 (1.0)	221 (1.0)	232 (1.1)	203 (1.2)	212 (2.8)	227 (3.8)	200 (5.5)!
North Dakota [4]	225 (1.2)	— (—)	224 (1.0)	222 (0.9)	224 (0.9)	‡ (‡)	‡ (‡)	‡ (‡)	202 (1.8)
Ohio	— (—)	— (—)	222 (1.3)	222 (1.2)	226 (1.3)	202 (2.4)	207 (5.7)	‡ (‡)	‡ (‡)
Oklahoma	— (—)	219 (1.2)	213 (1.2)	214 (1.2)	220 (1.3)	195 (2.5)	200 (3.0)	‡ (‡)	206 (2.9)
Oregon	— (—)	212 (1.8)	220 (1.4)	218 (1.3)	222 (1.2)	202 (5.1)	199 (2.3)	219 (4.0)	‡ (‡)
Pennsylvania [5]	215 (1.6)	— (—)	221 (1.2)	219 (1.3)	227 (1.2)	191 (2.3)	195 (4.4)!	‡ (‡)	‡ (‡)
Rhode Island [5]	220 (1.3)	218 (1.4)	220 (1.2)	216 (1.3)	224 (1.3)	196 (3.3)	196 (2.7)	221 (3.5)	‡ (‡)
South Carolina	203 (1.4)	209 (1.4)	214 (1.3)	215 (1.3)	226 (1.5)	199 (1.4)	205 (5.7)	‡ (‡)	‡ (‡)
South Dakota	— (—)	— (—)	— (—)	222 (1.2)	227 (0.9)	‡ (‡)	‡ (‡)	‡ (‡)	197 (3.4)
Tennessee [4,5]	213 (1.7)	212 (1.4)	214 (1.2)	212 (1.6)	220 (1.4)	188 (2.7)	206 (5.6)	‡ (‡)	‡ (‡)
Texas	212 (1.9)	214 (1.9)	217 (1.7)	215 (1.0)	227 (1.6)	202 (1.9)	205 (1.3)	229 (4.3)!	‡ (‡)
Utah	217 (1.3)	216 (1.2)	222 (1.0)	219 (1.0)	223 (1.0)	‡ (‡)	194 (2.7)	212 (5.1)	‡ (‡)
Vermont	— (—)	— (—)	227 (1.1)	226 (0.9)	226 (0.9)	‡ (‡)	‡ (‡)	‡ (‡)	‡ (‡)
Virginia	213 (1.5)	217 (1.2)	225 (1.3)	223 (1.5)	231 (2.0)	206 (2.1)	210 (3.0)	235 (4.5)	‡ (‡)
Washington [4]	213 (1.5)	218 (1.4)	224 (1.2)	221 (1.1)	226 (1.1)	212 (2.4)	201 (2.7)	218 (2.9)	208 (4.9)
West Virginia	213 (1.1)	216 (1.7)	219 (1.2)	219 (1.0)	220 (1.0)	203 (3.7)	‡ (‡)	‡ (‡)	‡ (‡)
Wisconsin [3,4,5]	224 (1.1)	222 (1.1)	— (—)	221 (0.8)	225 (1.0)	200 (2.5)	209 (3.5)!	213 (4.6)	211 (3.5)!
Wyoming	221 (1.2)	218 (1.5)	221 (1.0)	222 (0.8)	224 (0.8)	‡ (‡)	214 (2.5)	‡ (‡)	189 (3.5)
Department of Defense dependents schools:									
Domestic schools	— (—)	219 (1.6)	225 (0.7)	223 (1.2)	232 (1.6)	213 (2.1)	216 (3.0)	‡ (‡)	‡ (‡)
Overseas schools	218 (0.9)	221 (1.0)	224 (0.5)	225 (0.6)	230 (1.0)	215 (1.7)	220 (2.1)	223 (2.0)	‡ (‡)
Outlying Areas									
Guam	181 (1.2)	— (—)	185 (1.3)	— (—)	— (—)	— (—)	— (—)	— (—)	— (—)
Virgin Islands	— (—)	174 (2.2)	179 (1.9)	— (—)	— (—)	— (—)	— (—)	— (—)	— (—)

—Jurisdiction did not participate.

! Interpret data with caution.

‡ Sample size is insufficient to permit a reliable estimate.

[1] Based on school records.

[2] Based on nationally representative sample. Forty-one states and Guam participated in the test in 1994; 44 jurisdictions (state, territory, and Department of Defense schools) participated in 1998; 50 jurisdictions participated in 2002; and 53 participated in 2003.

[3] Did not satisfy one or more of the guidelines for school sample participation rates in 1998. Data are subject to appreciable nonresponse bias.

[4] Did not satisfy one or more of the guidelines for school sample participation rates in 2002. Data are subject to appreciable nonresponse bias.

[5] Did not satisfy one or more of the guidelines for school sample participation rates in 1994. Data are subject to appreciable nonresponse bias.

NOTE: These test scores are from the National Assessment of Educational Progress (NAEP). Excludes persons not enrolled in school and those who were unable to be tested due to limited proficiency in English or due to a disability. Scale ranges from 0 to 500. Unlike data for previous years, the 2002 and 2003 data are from samples where accommodations were permitted for special needs students. Standard errors appear in parentheses.

SOURCE: U.S. Department of Education, National Center for Education Statistics, *National Assessment of Educational Progress, NAEP 1998, 2002, and 2003 Reading Report Cards for the Nation and the States,* prepared by the Educational Testing Service. (This table was prepared August 2004.)

Average scale score in reading for 8th-graders in public schools, by locale and state or jurisdiction: 1998, 2002, 2003

State or jurisdiction	Average, 1998	2002				2003			
		Average	Locale			Average	Locale		
			Central city	Urban fringe/large town	Rural/small town		Central city	Urban fringe/large town	Rural/small town
1	2	3	4	5	6	7	8	9	10
United States [1]	261 (0.8)	263 (0.5)	254 (0.7)	266 (0.8)	266 (0.6)	261 (0.2)	253 (0.5)	265 (0.5)	264 (0.4)
Alabama	255 (1.4)	253 (1.3)	241 (3.1)	259 (2.0)	254 (1.8)	253 (1.5)	246 (3.3)	262 (2.7)	251 (1.7)
Alaska	— (—)	— (—)	— (—)	— (—)	— (—)	256 (1.1)	— (—)	— (—)	— (—)
Arizona	260 (1.1)	257 (1.3)	255 (1.5)	259 (3.3)	258 (2.7)	255 (1.4)	254 (1.8)	257 (2.4)	256 (3.7)
Arkansas	256 (1.3)	260 (1.1)	257 (3.3)	267 (2.8) !	259 (1.2)	258 (1.3)	257 (2.6)	263 (3.7)	257 (1.8)
California [2,3,4]	252 (1.6)	250 (1.8)	247 (2.7)	252 (2.3)	256 (7.5)	251 (1.3)	245 (2.2)	254 (1.8)	257 (3.4)
Colorado	264 (1.0)	— (—)	— (—)	— (—)	— (—)	268 (1.2)	264 (2.6)	268 (2.0)	270 (1.7)
Connecticut	270 (1.0)	267 (1.2)	246 (2.1)	273 (1.5)	276 (2.0)	267 (1.1)	250 (1.7)	270 (1.6)	277 (1.7)
Delaware	254 (1.3)	267 (0.5)	264 (1.9)	268 (0.6)	266 (1.0)	265 (0.7)	259 (2.6)	265 (1.0)	266 (1.4)
District of Columbia	236 (2.1)	240 (0.9)	240 (0.9)	‡ (‡)	‡ (‡)	239 (0.8)	239 (0.8)	‡ (‡)	‡ (‡)
Florida	255 (1.4)	261 (1.6)	262 (3.5)	260 (2.1)	264 (2.4)	257 (1.3)	256 (2.7)	257 (1.8)	258 (2.7)
Georgia	257 (1.4)	258 (1.0)	254 (3.1)	259 (2.0)	258 (1.6)	258 (1.1)	242 (2.8)	259 (1.9)	259 (1.7)
Hawaii	249 (1.0)	252 (0.9)	258 (1.3)	246 (1.3)	253 (1.4)	251 (0.9)	260 (1.6)	249 (1.5)	249 (1.1)
Idaho	— (—)	266 (1.1)	270 (3.1)	264 (2.1)	266 (1.0)	264 (0.9)	265 (2.3)	260 (1.9)	265 (1.3)
Illinois	— (—)	— (—)	— (—)	— (—)	— (—)	266 (1.0)	253 (1.8)	273 (1.6)	272 (1.8)
Indiana	— (—)	265 (1.3)	260 (2.5)	265 (1.7)	268 (2.0)	265 (1.0)	256 (2.0)	270 (1.7)	267 (1.6)
Iowa	— (—)	— (—)	— (—)	— (—)	— (—)	268 (0.8)	261 (1.8)	275 (2.6)	268 (1.0)
Kansas [2,3,4]	268 (1.4)	269 (1.3)	259 (3.4)	277 (2.6)	271 (1.7)	266 (1.5)	253 (3.2)	273 (2.5)	270 (1.5)
Kentucky	262 (1.4)	265 (1.0)	267 (3.0)	267 (2.1)	264 (1.3)	266 (1.3)	268 (3.1)	264 (3.2)	267 (1.2)
Louisiana	252 (1.4)	256 (1.5)	251 (3.7)	259 (2.1)	258 (1.9)	253 (1.6)	247 (2.7)	258 (3.4)	256 (2.0)
Maine	271 (1.2)	270 (0.9)	267 (3.4)	274 (2.6)	269 (1.1)	268 (1.0)	264 (2.8)	274 (2.4)	268 (1.1)
Maryland [3]	261 (1.8)	263 (1.7)	243 (3.0)	265 (2.1)	271 (2.4)	262 (1.4)	244 (3.8)	263 (1.6)	269 (4.0)
Massachusetts	269 (1.4)	271 (1.3)	253 (2.4)	276 (2.1)	281 (2.1)	273 (1.0)	256 (2.2)	279 (1.5)	279 (1.6)
Michigan	— (—)	265 (1.6)	246 (5.7)	270 (1.6)	268 (1.5)	264 (1.8)	253 (4.6)	266 (3.2)	269 (1.7)
Minnesota [7G52,3]	265 (1.4)	— (—)	— (—)	— (—)	— (—)	268 (1.1)	257 (5.1)	273 (1.3)	266 (1.3)
Mississippi	251 (1.2)	255 (0.9)	252 (3.3)	262 (2.7)	253 (1.5)	255 (1.4)	249 (5.7)	260 (2.3)	255 (2.3)
Missouri	262 (1.3)	268 (1.0)	259 (3.5)	270 (1.7)	270 (1.3)	267 (1.0)	256 (3.1)	271 (1.7)	268 (1.6)
Montana [2,3]	271 (1.4)	270 (1.0)	271 (1.3)	273 (2.1) !	270 (1.3)	270 (1.0)	271 (1.8)	271 (3.1)	269 (1.3)
Nebraska	— (—)	270 (0.9)	265 (1.3)	271 (2.6) !	272 (1.3)	266 (0.9)	264 (1.8)	269 (2.0)	267 (1.2)
Nevada	258 (1.0)	251 (0.8)	251 (1.2)	250 (1.4)	255 (2.4)	252 (0.8)	250 (1.1)	254 (1.4)	255 (3.1)
New Hampshire	— (—)	— (—)	— (—)	— (—)	— (—)	271 (0.9)	261 (3.1)	274 (1.2)	272 (1.3)
New Jersey	— (—)	— (—)	— (—)	— (—)	— (—)	268 (1.2)	250 (4.0)	269 (1.4)	274 (2.5)
New Mexico	258 (1.2)	254 (1.0)	258 (2.2)	255 (1.7)	250 (1.4)	252 (0.9)	253 (1.8)	253 (1.7)	250 (1.6)
New York [2,3]	265 (1.5)	264 (1.5)	251 (2.2)	275 (1.9)	271 (3.6)	265 (1.3)	252 (1.8)	277 (2.1)	270 (3.2)
North Carolina	262 (1.1)	265 (1.1)	264 (2.3)	265 (2.3)	265 (1.5)	262 (1.0)	265 (1.8)	262 (2.2)	260 (1.7)
North Dakota [3]	— (—)	268 (0.8)	264 (1.8)	264 (2.5) !	271 (1.1)	270 (0.8)	270 (2.0)	266 (2.1)	271 (0.9)
Ohio	— (—)	268 (1.6)	255 (4.6)	273 (1.6)	271 (1.7)	267 (1.0)	250 (1.9)	272 (2.3)	267 (1.8)
Oklahoma	265 (1.2)	262 (0.8)	258 (1.7)	265 (1.9)	262 (1.4)	262 (0.9)	257 (2.4)	267 (1.7)	261 (1.2)
Oregon [3]	266 (1.5)	268 (1.3)	268 (2.8)	270 (2.4)	266 (1.8)	264 (1.2)	260 (2.9)	268 (1.9)	263 (1.9)
Pennsylvania	— (—)	265 (1.0)	243 (2.8)	273 (1.2)	269 (1.6)	264 (1.2)	246 (4.0)	270 (1.3)	266 (2.1)
Rhode Island	264 (0.9)	262 (0.8)	249 (1.1)	269 (1.1)	269 (2.0)	261 (0.7)	247 (1.3)	268 (1.2)	269 (1.4)
South Carolina	255 (1.1)	258 (1.1)	257 (2.3)	264 (1.6)	254 (1.7)	258 (1.3)	258 (2.5)	263 (2.0)	254 (1.8)
South Dakota	— (—)	— (—)	— (—)	— (—)	— (—)	270 (0.8)	269 (1.1)	268 (2.6)	270 (1.1)
Tennessee [3]	258 (1.2)	260 (1.4)	251 (2.8)	268 (2.2)	262 (1.5)	258 (1.2)	250 (2.3)	265 (1.8)	260 (1.4)
Texas	261 (1.4)	262 (1.4)	256 (2.5)	268 (2.1)	266 (3.0)	259 (1.1)	255 (1.7)	264 (1.8)	258 (2.6)
Utah	263 (1.0)	263 (1.1)	262 (2.2)	264 (1.3)	261 (3.4)	264 (0.8)	263 (2.3)	266 (0.9)	261 (1.9)
Vermont	— (—)	272 (0.9)	— (—)	— (—)	— (—)	271 (0.8)	— (—)	— (—)	— (—)
Virginia	266 (1.1)	269 (1.0)	261 (2.3)	275 (1.5)	267 (1.9)	268 (1.1)	260 (1.4)	274 (1.3)	267 (2.2)
Washington [3]	264 (1.2)	268 (1.2)	264 (2.4)	270 (1.9)	268 (2.2)	264 (0.9)	265 (1.7)	267 (0.9)	261 (2.0)
West Virginia	262 (1.0)	264 (1.0)	261 (2.3)	265 (2.2)	264 (1.4)	260 (1.0)	261 (2.7)	260 (2.1)	259 (1.4)
Wisconsin [2,3]	265 (1.8)	— (—)	— (—)	— (—)	— (—)	266 (1.3)	255 (3.2)	275 (1.9)	268 (1.5)
Wyoming	263 (1.3)	265 (0.7)	265 (1.6)	261 (4.2)	265 (0.6)	267 (0.5)	264 (1.1)	274 (2.9)	268 (0.8)
Department of Defense dependents schools:									
Domestic schools	268 (4.5)	272 (1.0)	269 (2.3)	273 (2.3)	271 (2.4)	269 (1.4)	265 (3.6)	274 (1.9)	270 (3.3)
Overseas schools	269 1.0	273 (0.6)	— (—)	— (—)	— (—)	273 (0.7)	— (—)	— (—)	— (—)
Outlying areas									
American Samoa	— (—)	198 (1.7)	— (—)	— (—)	— (—)	— (—)	— (—)	— (—)	— (—)
Guam	— (—)	240 (1.2)	— (—)	— (—)	— (—)	— (—)	— (—)	— (—)	— (—)
Virgin Islands	231 (2.1)	241 (1.3)	— (—)	— (—)	— (—)	— (—)	— (—)	— (—)	— (—)

—Jurisdiction did not participate.

! Interpret data with caution.

‡ Sample size is insufficient to permit a reliable estimate.

[1] Based on nationally representative sample. Forty-four jurisdictions (state, District of Columbia, territory, and Department of Defense overseas schools) participated in 1998; 50 jurisdictions participated in 2002; and 53 participated in 2003.

[2] Did not satisfy one or more of the guidelines for school sample participation rates in 1998. Data are subject to appreciable nonresponse bias.

[3] Did not satisfy one or more of the guidelines for school sample participation rates in 2002. Data are subject to appreciable nonresponse bias.

[4] Did not satisfy one or more of the guidelines for school sample participation rates in 2003. Data are subject to appreciable nonresponse bias.

NOTE: These test scores are from the National Assessment of Educational Progress (NAEP). Excludes persons not enrolled in school and those who were unable to be tested due to limited proficiency in English or due to a disability. Scale ranges from 0 to 500. Standard errors appear in parentheses.

SOURCE: U.S. Department of Education, National Center for Education Statistics, *National Assessment of Educational Progress, NAEP 2002 and 2003 Reading Report Cards for the Nation and the States,* prepared by Educational Testing Service. (This table was prepared August 2004.)

Average reading scale scores and achievement-level results, by gender, grade 4 public schools: By state, 2003

| | Male | | | | Female | | | |
| | Average scale scores | Percentage of students | | | Average scale scores | Percentage of students | | |
		Below *Basic*	At or above *Basic*	At or above *Proficient*		Below *Basic*	At or above *Basic*	At or above *Proficient*
Nation (public)	213	42	58	26	220	35	65	33
Alabama	204	50	50	21	211	44	56	24
Alaska	205	48	52	23	218	36	64	33
Arizona	206	49	51	21	212	43	57	26
Arkansas	209	45	55	25	218	36	64	31
California	202	54	46	18	209	47	53	24
Colorado	220	33	67	32	227	28	72	41
Connecticut	224	30	70	38	232	23	77	47
Delaware	222	31	69	30	226	27	73	36
Florida	214	42	58	29	222	33	67	35
Georgia	210	45	55	24	218	37	63	30
Hawaii	202	53	47	17	215	39	61	26
Idaho	216	38	62	28	221	33	67	33
Illinois	214	41	59	28	219	37	63	33
Indiana	216	38	62	29	224	30	70	37
Iowa	220	33	67	31	227	26	74	38
Kansas	216	38	62	29	224	29	71	36
Kentucky	215	40	60	27	223	32	68	34
Louisiana	200	56	44	17	210	46	54	23
Maine	221	32	68	32	226	27	73	39
Maryland	215	42	58	29	222	34	66	36
Massachusetts	225	29	71	38	231	24	76	43
Michigan	216	39	61	30	222	33	67	34
Minnesota	216	37	63	31	229	25	75	44
Mississippi	202	55	45	17	209	48	52	20
Missouri	219	35	65	31	226	29	71	37
Montana	218	35	65	30	228	26	74	40
Nebraska	218	37	63	30	223	31	69	35
Nevada	202	54	46	16	211	42	58	24
New Hampshire	224	29	71	35	232	22	78	45
New Jersey	222	33	67	35	229	27	73	42
New Mexico	201	55	45	18	206	51	49	20
New York	218	37	63	30	226	28	72	38
North Carolina	216	40	60	27	227	29	71	38
North Dakota	218	35	65	28	225	28	72	36
Ohio	218	35	65	31	226	27	73	37
Oklahoma	210	43	57	23	217	37	63	29
Oregon	213	42	58	26	223	31	69	36
Pennsylvania	215	38	62	30	222	32	68	36
Rhode Island	213	41	59	26	220	34	66	33
South Carolina	211	45	55	22	219	36	64	30
South Dakota	220	34	66	31	225	28	72	36
Tennessee	208	47	53	22	217	38	62	30
Texas	212	44	56	24	218	38	62	29
Utah	215	38	62	28	224	30	70	36
Vermont	224	29	71	34	229	24	76	40
Virginia	219	36	64	32	228	27	73	39
Washington	216	37	63	27	226	28	72	39
West Virginia	215	40	60	25	223	30	70	32
Wisconsin	217	36	64	28	225	28	72	37
Wyoming	219	34	66	30	225	28	72	37
Other jurisdictions								
District of Columbia	182	74	26	8	195	64	36	13
DDESS[1]	218	37	63	28	229	25	75	42
DoDDS[2]	222	32	68	32	228	24	76	38

[1]Department of Defense Domestic Dependent Elementary and Secondary Schools.
[2]Department of Defense Dependents Schools (Overseas).
SOURCE: U.S. Department of Education, Institute of Education Sciences, National Center for Education Statistics, National Assessment of Educational Progress (NAEP), 2003 Reading Assessment.

575

Average reading scale scores and achievement-level results, by gender, grade 8 public schools: By state, 2003

	Male				Female			
	Average scale scores	Percentage of students			Average scale scores	Percentage of students		
		Below *Basic*	At or above *Basic*	At or above *Proficient*		Below *Basic*	At or above *Basic*	At or above *Proficient*
Nation (public)	256	33	67	25	267	23	77	35
Alabama	246	42	58	17	261	28	72	28
Alaska	250	39	61	22	263	28	72	32
Arizona	251	38	62	21	260	29	71	29
Arkansas	254	34	66	23	263	26	74	31
California	247	42	58	20	255	35	65	25
Colorado	262	27	73	29	274	18	82	43
Connecticut	262	28	72	31	273	19	81	43
Delaware	260	28	72	26	270	18	82	37
Florida	251	39	61	21	263	26	74	32
Georgia	253	37	63	22	263	24	76	30
Hawaii	245	46	54	17	258	32	68	26
Idaho	258	29	71	26	271	18	82	39
Illinois	264	25	75	31	269	21	79	38
Indiana	259	28	72	26	270	18	82	39
Iowa	261	26	74	28	273	15	85	43
Kansas	260	29	71	28	272	18	82	42
Kentucky	261	27	73	27	272	17	83	40
Louisiana	248	41	59	18	258	31	69	26
Maine	262	26	74	29	275	15	85	45
Maryland	255	35	65	24	269	23	77	37
Massachusetts	268	23	77	37	278	14	86	49
Michigan	259	30	70	27	270	20	80	38
Minnesota	261	27	73	29	274	16	84	46
Mississippi	249	41	59	16	260	28	72	26
Missouri	263	25	75	30	271	16	84	39
Montana	264	22	78	30	276	14	86	45
Nebraska	261	27	73	29	271	18	82	41
Nevada	246	43	57	15	258	31	69	26
New Hampshire	265	24	76	34	276	14	86	47
New Jersey	263	25	75	32	272	17	83	42
New Mexico	246	43	57	16	257	32	68	24
New York	259	31	69	28	271	19	81	42
North Carolina	256	33	67	23	267	22	78	34
North Dakota	264	22	78	31	275	15	85	46
Ohio	263	25	75	30	270	19	81	38
Oklahoma	256	32	68	24	268	20	80	35
Oregon	259	30	70	27	270	21	79	39
Pennsylvania	259	30	70	26	270	18	82	38
Rhode Island	256	34	66	25	266	23	77	34
South Carolina	253	36	64	19	263	26	74	29
South Dakota	265	23	77	32	275	14	86	45
Tennessee	252	38	62	21	265	24	76	31
Texas	253	35	65	21	265	24	76	31
Utah	259	28	72	26	269	19	81	38
Vermont	265	23	77	32	276	14	86	45
Virginia	263	25	75	31	272	18	82	41
Washington	258	30	70	27	271	19	81	39
West Virginia	254	35	65	20	265	22	78	30
Wisconsin	259	29	71	29	274	16	84	45
Wyoming	262	26	74	29	272	15	85	40
Other jurisdictions								
District of Columbia	231	62	38	8	245	45	55	13
DDESS[1]	261	27	73	28	278	11	89	47
DoDDS[2]	269	17	83	34	277	12	88	46

[1] Department of Defense Domestic Dependent Elementary and Secondary Schools.
[2] Department of Defense Dependents Schools (Overseas).
SOURCE: U.S. Department of Education, Institute of Education Sciences, National Center for Education Statistics, National Assessment of Educational Progress (NAEP), 2003 Reading Assessment.

Average reading scale scores and achievement-level results, by race/ethnicity, grade 4 public schools: By state, 2003

	White					Black					Hispanic				
			Percentage of students					Percentage of students					Percentage of students		
	Weighted percentage of students	Average scale scores	Below *Basic*	At or above *Basic*	At or above *Proficient*	Weighted percentage of students	Average scale scores	Below *Basic*	At or above *Basic*	At or above *Proficient*	Weighted percentage of students	Average scale scores	Below *Basic*	At or above *Basic*	At or above *Proficient*
Nation (public)	59	227	26	74	39	17	197	61	39	12	18	199	57	43	14
Alabama	60	219	34	66	30	37	188	69	31	9	1	‡	‡	‡	‡
Alaska	54	226	27	73	40	5	209	44	56	21	4	209	45	55	21
Arizona	50	223	29	71	35	5	196	59	41	13	36	195	62	38	12
Arkansas	69	223	30	70	35	25	190	68	32	10	4	204	52	48	18
California	34	224	31	69	36	8	193	63	37	11	47	191	67	33	9
Colorado	67	232	22	78	45	5	208	46	54	18	23	205	52	48	18
Connecticut	69	238	16	84	54	14	201	54	46	12	14	206	51	49	18
Delaware	56	233	18	82	44	33	211	46	54	16	8	209	47	53	20
Florida	51	229	25	75	42	23	198	60	40	13	21	211	45	55	24
Georgia	51	226	28	72	38	38	199	58	42	12	6	201	52	48	17
Hawaii	16	221	32	68	35	2	211	42	58	18	3	204	47	53	17
Idaho	84	222	31	69	33	1	‡	‡	‡	‡	13	199	61	39	12
Illinois	60	228	26	74	42	21	194	64	36	10	16	197	58	42	15
Indiana	80	224	29	71	36	12	197	62	38	11	5	212	42	58	26
Iowa	87	226	26	74	37	5	196	66	34	8	5	205	52	48	17
Kansas	78	225	29	71	37	10	197	60	40	14	8	207	49	51	19
Kentucky	85	221	33	67	33	12	202	56	44	16	1	‡	‡	‡	‡
Louisiana	44	223	30	70	34	53	189	70	30	8	1	‡	‡	‡	‡
Maine	95	224	29	71	36	2	‡	‡	‡	‡	1	‡	‡	‡	‡
Maryland	52	231	24	76	44	37	200	59	41	14	5	209	48	52	23
Massachusetts	74	234	19	81	48	10	207	50	50	15	11	202	57	43	15
Michigan	71	228	25	75	40	21	189	70	30	8	5	205	52	48	16
Minnesota	81	229	24	76	43	8	194	62	38	14	4	195	64	36	16
Mississippi	45	221	33	67	30	53	192	67	33	8	1	‡	‡	‡	‡
Missouri	78	227	27	73	39	18	203	54	46	14	3	218	39	61	30
Montana	85	227	26	74	38	1	‡	‡	‡	‡	2	‡	‡	‡	‡
Nebraska	81	225	29	71	36	6	203	53	47	17	9	202	56	44	14
Nevada	54	217	37	63	28	10	193	63	37	9	28	192	64	36	11
New Hampshire	94	229	24	76	41	2	‡	‡	‡	‡	2	206	52	48	19
New Jersey	58	235	18	82	49	18	200	59	41	14	16	212	44	56	21
New Mexico	32	222	33	67	34	3	202	55	45	18	51	197	59	41	13
New York	52	235	18	82	48	20	203	56	44	14	21	208	49	51	18
North Carolina	58	232	23	77	44	29	203	56	44	12	6	212	44	56	24
North Dakota	88	224	28	72	34	1	‡	‡	‡	‡	2	‡	‡	‡	‡
Ohio	78	226	26	74	39	17	202	56	44	16	2	207	52	48	23
Oklahoma	61	220	32	68	32	11	195	59	41	13	7	200	56	44	14
Oregon	76	222	32	68	34	3	202	52	48	19	14	199	57	43	15
Pennsylvania	74	227	25	75	40	19	191	68	32	9	4	195	59	41	10
Rhode Island	69	224	29	71	36	9	196	60	40	12	18	196	61	39	12
South Carolina	55	226	26	74	36	40	199	60	40	11	3	205	52	48	20
South Dakota	84	227	26	74	37	1	‡	‡	‡	‡	2	‡	‡	‡	‡
Tennessee	71	220	33	67	32	25	188	70	30	9	2	206	49	51	27
Texas	41	227	26	74	39	14	202	56	44	16	42	205	52	48	17
Utah	83	223	29	71	35	2	‡	‡	‡	‡	11	194	64	36	11
Vermont	95	226	27	73	37	2	‡	‡	‡	‡	1	‡	‡	‡	‡
Virginia	62	231	23	77	44	27	206	51	49	16	5	210	45	55	20
Washington	70	226	27	73	38	7	212	42	58	23	12	201	56	44	16
West Virginia	95	220	35	65	29	4	203	55	45	13	#	‡	‡	‡	‡
Wisconsin	79	225	27	73	36	9	200	58	42	13	6	209	46	54	20
Wyoming	86	224	29	71	36	1	‡	‡	‡	‡	8	214	41	59	23
Other jurisdictions															
District of Columbia	5	254	10	90	70	85	184	73	27	7	9	187	71	29	8
DDESS [1]	47	232	22	78	44	27	213	43	57	21	18	216	41	59	26
DoDDS [2]	49	230	22	78	43	21	215	38	62	22	12	220	34	66	29

See notes at end of table. ▶

Average reading scale scores and achievement-level results, by race/ethnicity, grade 4 public schools: By state, 2003—Continued

	Asian/Pacific Islander					American Indian/Alaska Native				
			Percentage of students					Percentage of students		
	Weighted percentage of students	Average scale scores	Below *Basic*	At or above *Basic*	At or above *Proficient*	Weighted percentage of students	Average scale scores	Below *Basic*	At or above *Basic*	At or above *Proficient*
Nation (public)	4	225	31	69	37	1	202	53	47	16
Alabama	1	‡	‡	‡	‡	1	‡	‡	‡	‡
Alaska	8	207	50	50	18	28	184	70	30	9
Arizona	2	225	32	68	38	7	182	75	25	6
Arkansas	1	‡	‡	‡	‡	1	‡	‡	‡	‡
California	10	224	32	68	37	#	‡	‡	‡	‡
Colorado	3	225	31	69	33	1	‡	‡	‡	‡
Connecticut	3	231	26	74	44	#	‡	‡	‡	‡
Delaware	3	238	14	86	48	#	‡	‡	‡	‡
Florida	2	233	21	79	44	#	‡	‡	‡	‡
Georgia	2	233	23	77	43	#	‡	‡	‡	‡
Hawaii	67	205	50	50	18	#	‡	‡	‡	‡
Idaho	1	‡	‡	‡	‡	2	‡	‡	‡	‡
Illinois	2	235	16	84	46	#	‡	‡	‡	‡
Indiana	1	‡	‡	‡	‡	#	‡	‡	‡	‡
Iowa	2	‡	‡	‡	‡	1	‡	‡	‡	‡
Kansas	2	‡	‡	‡	‡	1	‡	‡	‡	‡
Kentucky	1	‡	‡	‡	‡	#	‡	‡	‡	‡
Louisiana	1	‡	‡	‡	‡	1	‡	‡	‡	‡
Maine	1	‡	‡	‡	‡	1	‡	‡	‡	‡
Maryland	5	237	20	80	52	#	‡	‡	‡	‡
Massachusetts	4	229	26	74	40	#	‡	‡	‡	‡
Michigan	2	232	25	75	51	1	‡	‡	‡	‡
Minnesota	6	197	63	37	15	1	‡	‡	‡	‡
Mississippi	1	‡	‡	‡	‡	#	‡	‡	‡	‡
Missouri	1	‡	‡	‡	‡	#	‡	‡	‡	‡
Montana	1	‡	‡	‡	‡	11	195	62	38	15
Nebraska	1	‡	‡	‡	‡	2	‡	‡	‡	‡
Nevada	6	214	41	59	21	2	190	66	34	12
New Hampshire	1	‡	‡	‡	‡	#	‡	‡	‡	‡
New Jersey	7	235	21	79	47	#	‡	‡	‡	‡
New Mexico	2	‡	‡	‡	‡	13	182	75	25	6
New York	5	230	25	75	42	1	‡	‡	‡	‡
North Carolina	2	227	27	73	36	2	200	59	41	8
North Dakota	1	‡	‡	‡	‡	9	202	57	43	13
Ohio	1	‡	‡	‡	‡	#	‡	‡	‡	‡
Oklahoma	1	‡	‡	‡	‡	18	206	48	52	18
Oregon	4	219	39	61	33	2	‡	‡	‡	‡
Pennsylvania	1	‡	‡	‡	‡	#	‡	‡	‡	‡
Rhode Island	4	221	33	67	28	#	‡	‡	‡	‡
South Carolina	1	‡	‡	‡	‡	#	‡	‡	‡	‡
South Dakota	1	‡	‡	‡	‡	12	197	60	40	11
Tennessee	1	‡	‡	‡	‡	#	‡	‡	‡	‡
Texas	3	229	27	73	39	1	‡	‡	‡	‡
Utah	3	212	46	54	23	1	‡	‡	‡	‡
Vermont	2	‡	‡	‡	‡	1	‡	‡	‡	‡
Virginia	4	235	21	79	50	1	‡	‡	‡	‡
Washington	8	218	36	64	29	3	208	43	57	21
West Virginia	1	‡	‡	‡	‡	#	‡	‡	‡	‡
Wisconsin	3	213	46	54	27	2	211	42	58	25
Wyoming	1	‡	‡	‡	‡	4	189	70	30	10
Other jurisdictions										
District of Columbia	1	‡	‡	‡	‡	#	‡	‡	‡	‡
DDESS[1]	3	‡	‡	‡	‡	1	‡	‡	‡	‡
DoDDS[2]	10	223	30	70	31	1	‡	‡	‡	‡

#The estimate rounds to zero.
‡Reporting standards not met. Sample size is insufficient to permit a reliable estimate.
[1]Department of Defense Domestic Dependent Elementary and Secondary Schools.
[2]Department of Defense Dependents Schools (Overseas).
NOTE: Results are not shown for students whose race based on school records were "other" or, if school data were missing, who self-reported their race as "multiracial" but not "Hispanic," or did not self-report racial/ethnic information.
SOURCE: U.S. Department of Education, Institute of Education Sciences, National Center for Education Statistics, National Assessment of Educational Progress (NAEP), 2003 Reading Assessment.

Average reading scale scores and achievement-level results, by race/ethnicity, grade 8 public schools: By state, 2003

	White					Black					Hispanic				
			Percentage of students					Percentage of students					Percentage of students		
	Weighted percentage of students	Average scale scores	Below *Basic*	At or above *Basic*	At or above *Proficient*	Weighted percentage of students	Average scale scores	Below *Basic*	At or above *Basic*	At or above *Proficient*	Weighted percentage of students	Average scale scores	Below *Basic*	At or above *Basic*	At or above *Proficient*
Nation (public)	61	270	18	82	39	17	244	47	53	12	15	244	46	54	14
Alabama	63	262	25	75	30	35	237	54	46	9	1	‡	‡	‡	‡
Alaska	58	268	21	79	36	4	249	40	60	13	4	246	44	56	17
Arizona	51	268	20	80	36	5	245	48	52	16	36	240	49	51	12
Arkansas	73	266	21	79	33	22	232	58	42	6	3	257	32	68	25
California	35	265	24	76	34	9	239	52	48	12	41	237	54	46	11
Colorado	70	275	15	85	43	6	249	40	60	16	20	247	43	57	14
Connecticut	71	275	16	84	45	14	244	46	54	12	11	244	45	55	14
Delaware	63	273	15	85	40	27	248	40	60	13	6	246	40	60	13
Florida	51	268	21	79	37	27	239	52	48	11	19	251	38	62	19
Georgia	54	268	19	81	36	39	244	46	54	12	4	245	45	55	16
Hawaii	15	259	31	69	31	2	‡	‡	‡	‡	2	249	41	59	28
Idaho	87	267	21	79	35	#	‡	‡	‡	‡	10	242	47	53	12
Illinois	63	276	13	87	45	20	247	44	56	13	14	250	39	61	16
Indiana	82	269	19	81	36	12	244	46	54	13	3	247	43	57	16
Iowa	91	269	18	82	38	3	245	44	56	10	4	244	46	54	13
Kansas	80	271	18	82	40	9	243	47	53	10	7	245	45	55	17
Kentucky	87	269	19	81	36	10	245	46	54	14	1	‡	‡	‡	‡
Louisiana	49	267	20	80	33	46	238	54	46	9	2	‡	‡	‡	‡
Maine	96	269	21	79	37	2	‡	‡	‡	‡	1	‡	‡	‡	‡
Maryland	58	271	20	80	40	32	245	45	55	13	6	251	39	61	20
Massachusetts	78	278	14	86	49	8	252	38	62	18	9	246	44	56	14
Michigan	70	272	16	84	39	24	242	51	49	12	3	257	33	67	27
Minnesota	83	273	17	83	42	6	243	49	51	12	3	240	54	46	16
Mississippi	49	267	20	80	32	49	243	50	50	9	1	‡	‡	‡	‡
Missouri	82	272	15	85	39	15	243	48	52	10	1	‡	‡	‡	‡
Montana	87	273	15	85	40	#	‡	‡	‡	‡	2	‡	‡	‡	‡
Nebraska	84	271	18	82	39	5	239	53	47	10	7	241	51	49	11
Nevada	56	262	25	75	29	11	233	57	43	7	25	237	56	44	8
New Hampshire	94	272	18	82	41	2	‡	‡	‡	‡	2	‡	‡	‡	‡
New Jersey	60	277	12	88	46	20	248	42	58	15	14	248	39	61	17
New Mexico	34	268	20	80	35	3	246	45	55	14	52	243	47	53	12
New York	55	277	13	87	48	21	246	45	55	14	17	250	39	61	18
North Carolina	60	271	17	83	38	31	247	44	56	13	4	244	48	52	15
North Dakota	90	272	16	84	40	1	‡	‡	‡	‡	1	‡	‡	‡	‡
Ohio	78	271	18	82	39	18	249	40	60	13	2	268	19	81	37
Oklahoma	64	267	20	80	34	9	240	49	51	13	6	250	38	62	17
Oregon	80	267	23	77	36	3	251	39	61	18	9	249	40	60	18
Pennsylvania	80	268	19	81	36	15	243	48	52	11	3	257	36	64	24
Rhode Island	75	267	22	78	36	8	241	50	50	15	13	238	54	46	8
South Carolina	54	269	18	82	35	43	244	47	53	10	2	‡	‡	‡	‡
South Dakota	88	273	15	85	41	1	‡	‡	‡	‡	1	‡	‡	‡	‡
Tennessee	73	265	24	76	32	24	239	53	47	9	2	‡	‡	‡	‡
Texas	44	272	16	84	39	15	247	44	56	14	37	247	41	59	14
Utah	86	268	20	80	35	1	‡	‡	‡	‡	9	241	49	51	13
Vermont	96	271	18	82	39	1	‡	‡	‡	‡	1	‡	‡	‡	‡
Virginia	65	275	15	85	44	27	250	38	62	15	4	266	22	78	31
Washington	74	268	20	80	36	6	251	40	60	19	9	246	45	55	16
West Virginia	94	260	28	72	25	5	248	40	60	13	#	‡	‡	‡	‡
Wisconsin	84	271	17	83	41	9	234	60	40	8	3	244	49	51	17
Wyoming	88	269	18	82	36	2	‡	‡	‡	‡	6	255	34	66	20
Other jurisdictions															
District of Columbia	3	‡	‡	‡	‡	88	236	55	45	8	8	240	49	51	11
DDESS[1]	40	280	11	89	50	25	255	30	70	19	23	268	21	79	38
DoDDS[2]	51	277	10	90	46	19	260	25	75	22	10	269	19	81	35

See notes at end of table. ▶

Average reading scale scores and achievement-level results, by race/ethnicity, grade 8 public schools: By state, 2003—Continued

	Asian/Pacific Islander					American Indian/Alaska Native				
			Percentage of students					Percentage of students		
	Weighted percentage of students	Average scale scores	Below *Basic*	At or above *Basic*	At or above *Proficient*	Weighted percentage of students	Average scale scores	Below *Basic*	At or above *Basic*	At or above *Proficient*
Nation (public)	4	268	22	78	38	1	248	41	59	18
Alabama	1	‡	‡	‡	‡	1	‡	‡	‡	‡
Alaska	6	253	36	64	23	26	235	56	44	11
Arizona	2	‡	‡	‡	‡	6	238	55	45	8
Arkansas	1	‡	‡	‡	‡	1	‡	‡	‡	‡
California	13	266	24	76	37	1	‡	‡	‡	‡
Colorado	4	275	16	84	47	1	‡	‡	‡	‡
Connecticut	3	282	12	88	54	#	‡	‡	‡	‡
Delaware	3	281	13	87	52	#	‡	‡	‡	‡
Florida	2	‡	‡	‡	‡	#	‡	‡	‡	‡
Georgia	2	265	30	70	39	#	‡	‡	‡	‡
Hawaii	70	249	41	59	19	#	‡	‡	‡	‡
Idaho	1	‡	‡	‡	‡	1	‡	‡	‡	‡
Illinois	3	281	13	87	53	#	‡	‡	‡	‡
Indiana	1	‡	‡	‡	‡	#	‡	‡	‡	‡
Iowa	2	‡	‡	‡	‡	#	‡	‡	‡	‡
Kansas	3	266	25	75	35	1	‡	‡	‡	‡
Kentucky	1	‡	‡	‡	‡	#	‡	‡	‡	‡
Louisiana	1	‡	‡	‡	‡	1	‡	‡	‡	‡
Maine	1	‡	‡	‡	‡	#	‡	‡	‡	‡
Maryland	4	282	13	87	55	#	‡	‡	‡	‡
Massachusetts	4	281	13	87	52	#	‡	‡	‡	‡
Michigan	2	‡	‡	‡	‡	2	‡	‡	‡	‡
Minnesota	5	257	36	64	26	2	‡	‡	‡	‡
Mississippi	1	‡	‡	‡	‡	#	‡	‡	‡	‡
Missouri	1	‡	‡	‡	‡	#	‡	‡	‡	‡
Montana	1	‡	‡	‡	‡	10	247	40	60	13
Nebraska	1	‡	‡	‡	‡	2	‡	‡	‡	‡
Nevada	6	260	25	75	25	2	‡	‡	‡	‡
New Hampshire	1	‡	‡	‡	‡	#	‡	‡	‡	‡
New Jersey	6	289	8	92	62	#	‡	‡	‡	‡
New Mexico	1	‡	‡	‡	‡	9	242	48	52	11
New York	7	270	23	77	42	1	‡	‡	‡	‡
North Carolina	2	267	24	76	30	2	242	48	52	10
North Dakota	1	‡	‡	‡	‡	7	244	51	49	12
Ohio	1	‡	‡	‡	‡	#	‡	‡	‡	‡
Oklahoma	2	‡	‡	‡	‡	16	257	31	69	26
Oregon	4	265	28	72	34	2	‡	‡	‡	‡
Pennsylvania	1	‡	‡	‡	‡	#	‡	‡	‡	‡
Rhode Island	3	252	42	58	23	#	‡	‡	‡	‡
South Carolina	1	‡	‡	‡	‡	#	‡	‡	‡	‡
South Dakota	1	‡	‡	‡	‡	9	246	46	54	15
Tennessee	1	‡	‡	‡	‡	#	‡	‡	‡	‡
Texas	3	272	14	86	37	#	‡	‡	‡	‡
Utah	2	262	26	74	28	2	‡	‡	‡	‡
Vermont	1	‡	‡	‡	‡	1	‡	‡	‡	‡
Virginia	3	274	12	88	40	#	‡	‡	‡	‡
Washington	8	270	21	79	39	3	247	38	62	18
West Virginia	#	‡	‡	‡	‡	#	‡	‡	‡	‡
Wisconsin	3	253	39	61	24	1	‡	‡	‡	‡
Wyoming	1	‡	‡	‡	‡	3	242	52	48	8
Other jurisdictions										
District of Columbia	1	‡	‡	‡	‡	#	‡	‡	‡	‡
DDESS[1]	7	‡	‡	‡	‡	#	‡	‡	‡	‡
DoDDS[2]	10	272	14	86	38	1	‡	‡	‡	‡

#The estimate rounds to zero.
‡Reporting standards not met. Sample size is insufficient to permit a reliable estimate.
[1]Department of Defense Domestic Dependent Elementary and Secondary Schools.
[2]Department of Defense Dependents Schools (Overseas).
NOTE: Results are not shown for students whose race based on school records were "other" or, if school data were missing, who self-reported their race as "multiracial" but not "Hispanic," or did not self-report racial/ethnic information.
SOURCE: U.S. Department of Education, Institute of Education Sciences, National Center for Education Statistics, National Assessment of Educational Progress (NAEP), 2003 Reading Assessment.

Percent of students at or above selected writing proficiency levels, by grade level and selected characteristics of students: 2002

Selected characteristic of students	Percentage of 4th-graders				Percentage of 8th-graders				Percentage of 12th-graders			
	Below basic	At or above basic	At or above proficient	At advanced	Below basic	At or above basic	At or above proficient	At advanced	Below basic	At or above basic	At or above proficient	At advanced
1	2	3	4	5	6	7	8	9	10	11	12	13
All students	**14 (0.4)**	**86 (0.4)**	**28 (0.4)**	**2 (0.1)**	**15 (0.4)**	**85 (0.4)**	**31 (0.6)**	**2 (0.1)**	**26 (0.7)**	**74 (0.7)**	**24 (0.8)**	**2 (0.2)**
Sex												
Male	19 (0.5)	81 (0.5)	20 (0.5)	1 (0.1)	21 (0.6)	79 (0.6)	21 (0.6)	1 (0.1)	37 (1.0)	63 (1.0)	14 (0.8)	1 (0.1)
Female	9 (0.3)	91 (0.3)	36 (0.6)	3 (0.2)	9 (0.3)	91 (0.3)	42 (0.8)	3 (0.2)	15 (0.7)	85 (0.7)	33 (1.0)	3 (0.3)
Race/ethnicity												
White, non-Hispanic	9 (0.2)	91 (0.2)	35 (0.4)	3 (0.2)	9 (0.4)	91 (0.4)	39 (0.6)	3 (0.2)	20 (0.7)	80 (0.7)	28 (0.9)	2 (0.3)
Black, non-Hispanic	21 (0.6)	79 (0.6)	15 (0.7)	1 (0.2)	25 (1.0)	75 (1.0)	13 (0.6)	# (0.1)	41 (1.8)	59 (1.8)	9 (1.0)	# (#)
Hispanic	22 (1.1)	78 (1.1)	18 (0.7)	1 (0.2)	27 (0.8)	73 (0.8)	17 (0.9)	1 (0.2)	38 (1.5)	62 (1.5)	13 (1.2)	# (0.2)
Asian/Pacific Islander	7 (0.8)	93 (0.8)	42 (2.0)	4 (0.7)	10 (1.0)	90 (1.0)	42 (2.3)	3 (0.6)	24 (2.5)	76 (2.5)	26 (3.2)	3 (1.0)
American Indian/ Alaska Native	20 (1.2)	80 (1.2)	16 (1.0)	1 (0.3)	23 (2.5)	77 (2.5)	18 (2.9)	1 (#)	— (—)	— (—)	— (—)	— (—)
Parents' highest level of education												
Not high school graduate	— (—)	— (—)	— (—)	— (—)	26 (1.3)	74 (1.3)	14 (1.0)	# (#)	43 (2.1)	57 (2.1)	8 (1.4)	# (#)
Graduated high school ..	— (—)	— (—)	— (—)	— (—)	19 (0.7)	81 (0.7)	20 (0.6)	1 (0.2)	32 (1.2)	68 (1.2)	14 (1.1)	1 (0.2)
Some college	— (—)	— (—)	— (—)	— (—)	11 (0.6)	89 (0.6)	31 (0.8)	1 (0.2)	23 (1.0)	77 (1.0)	22 (1.3)	1 (0.2)
Graduated college	— (—)	— (—)	— (—)	— (—)	9 (0.4)	91 (0.4)	43 (0.8)	4 (0.2)	18 (0.9)	82 (0.9)	32 (1.0)	3 (0.4)
Free/reduced price lunch eligibility												
Eligible	22 (0.8)	78 (0.8)	15 (0.5)	1 (0.1)	26 (0.6)	74 (0.6)	16 (0.6)	1 (0.1)	40 (1.5)	60 (1.5)	11 (1.0)	1 (0.2)
Not eligible	8 (0.3)	92 (0.3)	36 (0.6)	3 (0.2)	9 (0.4)	91 (0.4)	39 (0.8)	3 (0.2)	23 (0.8)	77 (0.8)	26 (1.0)	2 (0.3)
Information not available	10 (1.1)	90 (1.1)	34 (1.6)	3 (0.3)	11 (0.7)	89 (0.7)	39 (1.7)	4 (0.6)	19 (1.3)	81 (1.3)	29 (1.6)	2 (0.4)

#Rounds to zero.
—Not available.

NOTE: Includes public and private schools. Excludes persons unable to be tested due to limited proficieny in English or due to a disability (and the accommodations provided were not sufficient to enable the test to properly reflect the students' writing proficiency). Beginning in 2002, the NAEP national sample was obtained by aggregating the samples from each state, rather than by obtaining an independently selected national sample. As a consequence, the size of the national sample increased, and smaller differences be-

tween years or between types of students were found to be statistically significant than would have been detected in previous assessments. Detail may not sum to totals due to rounding. Standard errors appear in parentheses.

SOURCE: U.S. Department of Education, National Center for Education Statistics, National Assessment of Educational Progress (NAEP), Main NAEP, *National Writing Results,* previously unpublished tabulations from the *NAEP Data Tool* (http://nces.ed.gov/nationsreportcard/naepdata). (This table was prepared August 2003.)

Percent of students at or above selected U.S. history proficiency levels, by grade level and selected characteristics of students: 2001

Selected characteristic of students	Percentage of 4th-graders				Percentage of 8th-graders				Percentage of 12th-graders			
	Below basic	At or above basic	At or above proficient	At advanced	Below basic	At or above basic	At or above proficient	At advanced	Below basic	At or above basic	At or above proficient	At advanced
1	2	3	4	5	6	7	8	9	10	11	12	13
All students	33 (1.1)	67 (1.1)	18 (1.0)	2 (0.5)	36 (0.9)	64 (0.9)	17 (0.8)	2 (0.3)	57 (1.2)	43 (1.2)	11 (0.9)	1 (0.4)
Sex												
Male	34 (1.3)	66 (1.3)	19 (1.2)	2 (0.7)	35 (1.1)	65 (1.1)	18 (1.0)	2 (0.3)	55 (1.6)	45 (1.6)	12 (1.1)	1 (0.5)
Female	32 (1.4)	68 (1.4)	17 (1.1)	2 (0.4)	37 (1.2)	63 (1.2)	15 (0.8)	1 (0.4)	59 (1.3)	41 (1.3)	10 (0.9)	1 (0.3)
Race/ethnicity												
White, non-Hispanic	21 (1.3)	79 (1.3)	24 (1.4)	3 (0.7)	25 (1.0)	75 (1.0)	21 (1.1)	2 (0.4)	51 (1.4)	49 (1.4)	13 (1.0)	1 (0.4)
Black, non-Hispanic	56 (2.1)	44 (2.1)	6 (1.0)	# (0.3)	62 (2.4)	38 (2.4)	4 (0.8)	# (—)	80 (1.5)	20 (1.5)	3 (0.6)	# (—)
Hispanic	58 (3.0)	42 (3.0)	7 (1.1)	1 (0.3)	60 (1.7)	40 (1.7)	5 (0.7)	# (0.2)	74 (2.4)	26 (2.4)	5 (1.1)	# (—)
Asian/Pacific Islander	29 (3.8)	71 (3.8)	19 (3.2)	3 (1.9)	32 (3.8)	68 (3.8)	20 (3.6)	2 (0.8)	47 (5.1)	53 (5.1)	21 (6.0)	5 (2.3)
American Indian/												
Alaska Native	47 (6.4)	53 (6.4)	12 (4.6)	4 (—)	50 (7.1)	50 (7.1)	8 (3.5)	1 (—)	66 (7.2)	34 (—)	1 (—)	# (—)
Region												
Northeast	27 (3.1)	73 (3.1)	23 (2.9)	3 (1.1)	28 (2.2)	72 (2.2)	22 (2.1)	2 (0.8)	55 (3.8)	45 (3.8)	13 (3.2)	2 (—)
Southeast	34 (2.7)	66 (2.7)	16 (2.2)	2 (1.2)	38 (2.3)	62 (2.3)	16 (1.3)	2 (0.4)	61 (2.3)	39 (2.3)	10 (1.3)	1 (0.3)
Central	25 (2.3)	75 (2.3)	24 (2.4)	3 (1.1)	29 (2.2)	71 (2.2)	19 (1.5)	2 (0.5)	54 (2.2)	46 (2.2)	11 (1.3)	1 (0.4)
West	41 (2.5)	59 (2.5)	13 (1.2)	1 (0.4)	45 (1.7)	55 (1.7)	12 (1.3)	1 (0.2)	58 (2.2)	42 (2.2)	11 (1.5)	1 (0.4)
Parents' highest level of education												
Not high school graduate	— (—)	— (—)	— (—)	— (—)	59 (3.3)	41 (3.3)	3 (1.8)	# (—)	80 (2.1)	20 (2.1)	2 (0.7)	# (—)
Graduated high school	— (—)	— (—)	— (—)	— (—)	48 (1.7)	52 (1.7)	7 (1.0)	# (—)	74 (1.3)	26 (1.3)	4 (0.8)	# (0.1)
Some college	— (—)	— (—)	— (—)	— (—)	30 (1.3)	70 (1.3)	14 (1.3)	1 (0.3)	61 (1.3)	39 (1.3)	8 (0.7)	1 (0.2)
Graduated college	— (—)	— (—)	— (—)	— (—)	22 (1.0)	78 (1.0)	27 (1.1)	3 (0.5)	42 (1.5)	58 (1.5)	18 (1.5)	2 (0.8)
Free/reduced price lunch eligibility												
Eligible	53 (1.7)	47 (1.7)	6 (0.8)	1 (0.2)	59 (1.4)	41 (1.4)	6 (0.7)	# (0.2)	77 (1.8)	23 (1.8)	3 (0.7)	# (—)
Not eligible	21 (1.7)	79 (1.7)	25 (1.6)	3 (0.8)	27 (1.2)	73 (1.2)	20 (1.2)	2 (0.3)	55 (1.5)	45 (1.5)	11 (1.1)	1 (0.6)
Not available	25 (2.8)	75 (2.8)	24 (2.9)	3 (1.1)	30 (2.4)	70 (2.4)	22 (2.1)	3 (0.6)	47 (2.9)	53 (2.9)	17 (2.3)	2 (0.6)

—Not available
Rounds to zero.

NOTE: Includes public and private schools. Excludes persons unable to be tested due to limited proficency in English or due to a disability (and the accommodations provided were not sufficient to enable the test to properly reflect the students' writing proficiency). Beginning in 2002, the NAEP national sample was obtained by aggregating the samples from each state, rather than by obtaining an independently selected national sample. As a consequence, the size of the national sample increased, and smaller differences between years or between types of students were found to be statistically significant than would have been detected in previous assessments. Detail may not sum to totals due to rounding. Standard errors appear in parentheses.

SOURCE: U.S. Department of Education, National Center for Education Statistics, National Assessment of Educational Progress (NAEP), *The Nation's Report Card: U.S. History 2001.* (This table was prepared May 2002.)

**Percent of students at or above selected geography proficiency levels, by grade level
and selected characteristics of students: 2001**

Selected characteristic of students	Percentage of 4th-graders				Percentage of 8th-graders				Percentage of 12th-graders			
	Below basic	At or above basic	At or above proficient	At advanced	Below basic	At or above basic	At or above proficient	At advanced	Below basic	At or above basic	At or above proficient	At advanced
1	2	3	4	5	6	7	8	9	10	11	12	13
All students	**26 (1.2)**	**74 (1.2)**	**21 (1.0)**	**2 (0.3)**	**26 (0.9)**	**74 (0.9)**	**30 (1.2)**	**4 (0.6)**	**29 (0.9)**	**71 (0.9)**	**25 (1.1)**	**1 (0.3)**
Sex												
Male	25 (1.3)	75 (1.3)	24 (1.4)	3 (0.5)	25 (1.0)	75 (1.0)	33 (1.5)	5 (0.7)	27 (1.1)	73 (1.1)	28 (1.5)	2 (0.4)
Female	28 (1.6)	72 (1.6)	18 (1.1)	1 (0.4)	27 (1.2)	73 (1.2)	26 (1.4)	3 (0.6)	30 (1.0)	70 (1.0)	21 (1.0)	1 (0.3)
Race/ethnicity												
White, non-Hispanic	13 (1.3)	87 (1.3)	29 (1.5)	3 (0.5)	14 (0.9)	86 (0.9)	39 (1.7)	5 (0.8)	19 (0.9)	81 (0.9)	31 (1.4)	2 (0.4)
Black, non-Hispanic	56 (2.1)	44 (2.1)	5 (0.9)	# (#)	60 (2.3)	40 (2.3)	6 (0.8)	# (#)	65 (2.3)	35 (2.3)	4 (0.7)	# (#)
Hispanic	51 (3.0)	49 (3.0)	6 (1.0)	# (#)	52 (1.9)	48 (1.9)	10 (1.0)	1 (0.2)	48 (2.6)	52 (2.6)	10 (1.4)	# (0.1)
Asian/Pacific Islander	23 (3.4)	77 (3.4)	25 (3.0)	1 (0.9)	21 (3.4)	79 (3.4)	32 (3.2)	4 (1.8)	28 (4.3)	72 (4.3)	26 (4.7)	1 (0.7)
Region												
Northeast	22 (3.7)	78 (3.7)	24 (2.2)	3 (0.9)	22 (2.5)	78 (2.5)	34 (3.3)	4 (1.3)	29 (2.3)	71 (2.3)	26 (4.1)	2 (1.1)
Southeast	28 (2.5)	72 (2.5)	18 (1.9)	1 (0.6)	27 (2.4)	73 (2.4)	26 (1.6)	3 (0.6)	33 (1.6)	67 (1.6)	21 (1.3)	1 (0.3)
Central	18 (1.7)	82 (1.7)	30 (2.5)	3 (0.7)	18 (2.3)	82 (2.3)	38 (3.7)	6 (1.3)	24 (1.8)	76 (1.8)	28 (1.9)	1 (0.5)
West	34 (2.7)	66 (2.7)	14 (1.7)	1 (0.3)	34 (1.7)	66 (1.7)	23 (1.7)	2 (0.6)	30 (1.9)	70 (1.9)	23 (1.8)	1 (0.4)
Free/reduced price lunch eligibility												
Eligible	49 (2.2)	51 (2.2)	6 (0.9)	# (#)	50 (1.8)	50 (1.8)	11 (1.2)	1 (0.3)	49 (2.3)	51 (2.3)	11 (1.6)	# (#)
Not eligible	14 (1.1)	86 (1.1)	29 (1.5)	3 (0.6)	17 (0.9)	83 (0.9)	37 (1.7)	5 (0.8)	25 (1.2)	75 (1.2)	26 (1.6)	1 (0.4)
Not available	16 (2.5)	84 (2.5)	27 (3.2)	3 (0.8)	21 (2.1)	79 (2.1)	33 (2.5)	4 (0.9)	24 (2.0)	76 (2.0)	31 (2.1)	2 (0.4)

—Not available.
Rounds to zero.

NOTE: Includes public and private schools. Excludes students unable to be tested due to limited proficiency in English or due to a disability (and the accommodations provided were not sufficient to enable the test to properly reflect the students' proficiency in geog-

raphy). Totals include other racial/ethnic groups not shown seperately. Detail may not sum to totals due to rounding. Standard errors appear in parentheses.

SOURCE: U.S. Department of Education, National Center for Education Statistics, National Assessment of Educational Progress (NAEP), *The Nation's Report Card: Geography 2001.* (This table was prepared July 2002.)

Scholastic Assessment Test (SAT) score averages, for college-bound seniors, by race/ethnicity: Selected years, 1986–87 to 2002–03

Racial/ethnic background	1986–87	1990–91	1995–96	1996–97	1999–2000	2000–01	2001–02	2002–03	Score change					
									1986–87 to 1996–97	1990–91 to 2000–01	1995–96 to 1996–97	1999–2000 to 2000–01	2000–01 to 2001–02	2001–02 to 2002–03
1	2	3	4	5	6	7	8	9	10	11	12	13	14	15
SAT-Verbal														
All students	**507**	**499**	**505**	**505**	**505**	**506**	**504**	**507**	**-2**	**7**	**0**	**1**	**-2**	**3**
White	524	518	526	526	528	529	527	529	2	11	0	1	-2	2
Black	428	427	434	434	434	433	430	431	6	6	0	-1	-3	1
Hispanic or Latino	464	458	465	466	461	460	458	457	2	2	1	-1	-2	-1
Mexican American	457	454	455	451	453	451	446	448	-6	-3	-4	-2	-5	2
Puerto Rican	436	436	452	454	456	457	455	456	18	21	2	1	-2	1
Asian American	479	485	496	496	499	501	501	508	17	16	0	2	0	7
American Indian	471	470	483	475	482	481	479	480	4	11	-8	-1	-2	1
Other	480	486	511	512	508	503	502	501	32	17	1	-5	-1	-1
SAT-Mathematical														
All students	**501**	**500**	**508**	**511**	**514**	**514**	**516**	**519**	**10**	**14**	**3**	**0**	**2**	**3**
White	514	513	523	526	530	531	533	534	12	18	3	1	2	1
Black	411	419	422	423	426	426	427	426	12	7	1	0	1	-1
Hispanic or Latino	462	462	466	468	467	465	464	464	6	3	2	-2	-1	0
Mexican American	455	459	459	458	460	458	457	457	3	-1	-1	-2	-1	0
Puerto Rican	432	439	445	447	451	451	451	453	15	12	2	0	0	2
Asian American	541	548	558	560	565	566	569	575	19	18	2	1	3	6
American Indian	463	468	477	475	481	479	483	482	12	11	-2	-2	4	-1
Other	482	492	512	514	515	512	514	513	32	20	2	-3	2	-1

NOTE: Scholastic Assessment Test was formerly known as the Scholastic Aptitude Test. Possible scores on each part of the SAT range from 200 to 800.

SOURCE: College Entrance Examination Board, *National Report on College-Bound Seniors*, selected years 1986–87 through 2002–03. (Copyright © 2003 by the College Entrance Examination Board. All rights reserved.) (This table was prepared August 2003.)

Scholastic Assessment Test score averages for college-bound seniors, by sex: 1966–67 to 2002–03

School year	Scholastic Assessment Test I [1] (recentered scale) [2]						Scholastic Aptitude Test (old scale)					
	Verbal score			Mathematical score			Verbal score			Mathematical score		
	Total	Male	Female	Total	Male	Female	Total	Male	Female	Total	Male	Female
1	2	3	4	5	6	7	8	9	10	11	12	13
1966–67	543	540	545	516	535	495	466	463	468	492	514	467
1967–68	543	541	543	516	533	497	466	464	466	492	512	470
1968–69	540	536	543	517	534	498	463	459	466	493	513	470
1969–70	537	536	538	512	531	493	460	459	461	488	509	465
1970–71	532	531	534	513	529	494	455	454	457	488	507	466
1971–72	530	531	529	509	527	489	453	454	452	484	505	461
1972–73	523	523	521	506	525	489	445	446	443	481	502	460
1973–74	521	524	520	505	524	488	444	447	442	480	501	459
1974–75	512	515	509	498	518	479	434	437	431	472	495	449
1975–76	509	511	508	497	520	475	431	433	430	472	497	446
1976–77	507	509	505	496	520	474	429	431	427	470	497	445
1977–78	507	511	503	494	517	474	429	433	425	468	494	444
1978–79	505	509	501	493	516	473	427	431	423	467	493	443
1979–80	502	506	498	492	515	473	424	428	420	466	491	443
1980–81	502	508	496	492	516	473	424	430	418	466	492	443
1981–82	504	509	499	493	516	473	426	431	421	467	493	443
1982–83	503	508	498	494	516	474	425	430	420	468	493	445
1983–84	504	511	498	497	518	478	426	433	420	471	495	449
1984–85	509	514	503	500	522	480	431	437	425	475	499	452
1985–86	509	515	504	500	523	479	431	437	426	475	501	451
1986–87	507	512	502	501	523	481	430	435	425	476	500	453
1987–88	505	512	499	501	521	483	428	435	422	476	498	455
1988–89	504	510	498	502	523	482	427	434	421	476	500	454
1989–90	500	505	496	501	521	483	424	429	419	476	499	455
1990–91	499	503	495	500	520	482	422	426	418	474	497	453
1991–92	500	504	496	501	521	484	423	428	419	476	499	456
1992–93	500	504	497	503	524	484	424	428	420	478	502	457
1993–94	499	501	497	504	523	487	423	425	421	479	501	460
1994–95	504	505	502	506	525	490	428	429	426	482	503	463
1995–96	505	507	503	508	527	492	—	—	—	—	—	—
1996–97	505	507	503	511	530	494	—	—	—	—	—	—
1997–98	505	509	502	512	531	496	—	—	—	—	—	—
1998–99	505	509	502	511	531	495	—	—	—	—	—	—
1999–2000	505	507	504	514	533	498	—	—	—	—	—	—
2000–01	506	509	502	514	533	498	—	—	—	—	—	—
2001–02	504	507	502	516	534	500	—	—	—	—	—	—
2002–03	507	512	503	519	537	503	—	—	—	—	—	—

—Not available.

[1] Formerly known as the Scholastic Aptitude Test.

[2] Data for 1967 to 1986 were converted to the recentered scale by using a formula applied to the original mean and standard deviation. For 1987 to 1995, individual student scores were converted to the recentered scale and recomputed. For 1996 to 2002, most students received scores on the recentered scale score. Any score on the original scale was converted to the recentered scale prior to recomputing the mean.

NOTE: Possible scores on each part of the SAT range from 200 to 800. Data for the years 1966–67 through 1970–71 are estimates derived from the test scores of all participants.

SOURCE: College Entrance Examination Board, *National Report on College-Bound Seniors,* selected years 1966–67 through 2002–03. (Copyright © 2003 by the College Entrance Examination Board. All rights reserved.) (This table was prepared August 2003.)

Scholastic Assessment Test score averages for selected student characteristics: Selected years, 1995–96 to 2002–03

Selected characteristic	1995–96			1997–98			1999–2000			2002–03 [2]	
	Verbal score	Mathematical score	Percentage distribution [1]	Verbal score	Mathematical score	Percentage distribution [1]	Verbal score	Mathematical score	Percentage distribution [1]	Verbal score	Mathematical score
1	2	3	4	5	6	7	8	9	10	11	12
All students	505	508	100	505	512	100	505	514	100	507	519
High school rank											
Top decile	591	606	22	590	607	‡	589	608	‡	585	607
Second decile	530	539	22	530	543	‡	528	543	‡	522	539
Second quintile	494	496	28	494	500	‡	493	500	‡	486	494
Third quintile	455	448	24	454	453	‡	455	453	‡	449	449
Fourth quintile	429	418	4	427	421	‡	425	419	‡	420	417
Fifth quintile	411	401	1	408	403	‡	408	401	‡	410	410
High school grade point average											
A+ (97–100)	617	632	6	613	629	7	610	628	7	607	625
A (93–96)	573	583	14	569	582	15	567	582	16	566	583
A– (90–92)	545	554	15	542	554	16	540	553	17	538	552
B (80–89)	486	485	49	483	487	48	482	486	47	480	485
C (70–79)	432	426	15	430	428	13	428	426	12	425	424
D, E, or F (below 70)	414	408	#	408	411	#	405	406	#	416	430
Intended college major											
Agriculture/natural resources	491	484	2	491	487	2	490	486	1	484	482
Architecture/environmental design ...	492	519	3	494	524	2	494	524	2	483	511
Arts: visual/performing	520	497	6	520	502	7	518	502	8	514	500
Biological sciences	546	545	6	545	546	6	544	548	5	543	553
Business and commerce	483	500	13	484	505	14	487	510	14	489	512
Communications	527	497	4	523	501	4	526	505	4	524	506
Computer or information sciences	497	522	3	500	529	5	499	533	6	503	535
Education	487	477	8	483	480	9	483	481	9	482	483
Engineering	525	569	8	525	571	9	523	573	8	525	574
Foreign/classical languages	556	534	#	552	538	1	558	539	1	564	545
General/interdisciplinary	576	553	#	568	549	#	562	545	#	547	539
Health and allied services	500	505	19	497	505	18	497	505	16	489	498
Home economics	458	452	#	458	459	#	462	462	#	462	462
Language and literature	605	545	1	605	549	1	608	552	1	603	550
Library and archival sciences	554	512	#	547	525	#	556	511	#	572	512
Mathematics	552	628	1	552	629	1	551	630	1	545	626
Military sciences	503	505	#	504	507	#	505	512	#	513	516
Philosophy/religion/theology	560	536	#	558	538	1	560	539	1	562	544
Physical sciences	575	595	1	571	592	1	569	592	1	563	588
Public affairs and services	458	448	3	459	453	3	459	454	3	462	458
Social sciences and history	532	509	11	531	512	11	532	513	11	531	514
Technical and vocational	435	441	1	440	448	1	442	452	1	441	450
Undecided	500	507	7	510	520	6	512	521	7	516	528
Degree level goal											
Certificate program	434	439	1	436	447	1	439	453	1	441	456
Associate degree	422	415	2	421	419	2	420	419	2	417	416
Bachelor's degree	476	476	23	475	480	23	478	483	25	475	481
Master's degree	514	518	29	513	523	31	515	526	31	513	524
Doctoral or related degree	548	552	24	548	554	23	547	554	22	542	552
Other	430	438	1	435	446	1	442	454	1	441	453
Undecided	502	503	20	505	510	19	508	514	19	514	523
Family income											
Less than $10,000	429	444	4	427	446	5	425	447	‡	420	444
$10,000, but less than $20,000	456	464	8	451	463	9	447	460	‡	437	452
$20,000, but less than $30,000	482	482	10	477	482	11	471	478	‡	460	467
$30,000, but less than $40,000	497	495	12	495	497	13	490	493	‡	480	484
$40,000, but less than $50,000	509	507	10	506	509	11	503	505	‡	495	498
$50,000, but less than $60,000	517	517	9	514	518	11	511	515	‡	504	508
$60,000, but less than $70,000	524	525	7	521	525	9	517	522	‡	511	514
$70,000, but less than $80,000	531	533	6	527	532	8	524	530	‡	518	523
$80,000 to $100,000	541	544	7	539	546	9	536	543	‡	529	536
More than $100,000	560	569	9	559	572	13	558	571	‡	555	568
Highest level of parental education											
No high school diploma	414	439	4	411	441	4	413	442	4	413	443
High school diploma	475	474	31	473	477	34	472	477	33	470	475
Associate degree	489	487	7	489	491	8	488	491	9	487	491
Bachelor's degree	525	529	25	525	532	28	525	533	29	525	534
Graduate degree	556	558	23	556	563	25	558	566	25	559	569

Rounds to zero.

‡ Reporting standards not met.

[1] Because of survey item nonresponse, percentage distributions may not add to 100 percent.

[2] Percentage distribution not reported since this year had less than 80 percent combined unit and item response rates.

NOTE: Scholastic Assessment Test was formerly known as the Scholastic Aptitude Test. Possible scores on each part of the SAT range from 200 to 800.

SOURCE: College Entrance Examination Board, *National Report on College-Bound Seniors*, selected years 1995–96 through 2002–03. (Copyright © 2003 by the College Entrance Examination Board. All rights reserved.) (This table was prepared August 2003.)

Scholastic Assessment Test score averages, by state: Selected years, 1987–88 to 2002–03

State	1987–88		1995–96		1999–2000		2000–01		2001–02		2002–03		Percentage of graduates taking SAT, 2001–02	Percentage of graduates taking SAT, 2002–03
	Verbal	Mathe-matical	Verbal	Mathe-matical	Verbal	Mathe-matical	Verbal	Mathe-matical	Verbal	Mathe-matical	Verbal	Mathe-matical		
1	2	3	4	5	6	7	8	9	10	11	12	13	14	15
United States	**505**	**501**	**505**	**508**	**505**	**514**	**506**	**514**	**504**	**516**	**507**	**519**	**46**	**48**
Alabama	554	540	565	558	559	555	559	554	560	559	559	552	9	10
Alaska	518	501	521	513	519	515	514	510	516	519	518	518	52	55
Arizona	531	523	525	521	521	523	523	525	520	523	524	525	36	38
Arkansas	554	536	566	550	563	554	562	550	560	556	564	554	5	6
California	500	508	495	511	497	518	498	517	496	517	499	519	52	54
Colorado	537	532	536	538	534	537	539	542	543	548	551	553	28	27
Connecticut	513	498	507	504	508	509	509	510	509	509	512	514	83	84
Delaware	510	493	508	495	502	496	501	499	502	500	501	501	69	73
District of Columbia	479	461	489	473	494	486	482	474	480	473	484	474	76	77
Florida	499	495	498	496	498	500	498	499	496	499	498	498	57	61
Georgia	480	473	484	477	488	486	491	489	489	491	493	491	65	66
Hawaii	484	505	485	510	488	519	486	515	488	520	486	516	53	54
Idaho	543	523	543	536	540	541	543	542	539	541	540	540	18	18
Illinois	540	540	564	575	568	586	576	589	578	596	583	596	11	11
Indiana	490	486	494	494	498	501	499	501	498	503	500	504	62	63
Iowa	587	588	590	600	589	600	593	603	591	602	586	597	5	5
Kansas	568	557	579	571	574	580	577	580	578	580	578	582	9	9
Kentucky	551	535	549	544	548	550	550	550	550	552	554	552	12	13
Louisiana	551	533	559	550	562	558	564	562	561	559	563	559	8	8
Maine	508	493	504	498	504	500	506	500	503	502	503	501	69	70
Maryland	509	501	507	504	507	509	508	510	507	513	509	515	67	68
Massachusetts	508	499	507	504	511	513	511	515	512	516	516	522	81	82
Michigan	532	533	557	565	557	569	561	572	558	572	564	576	11	11
Minnesota	546	549	582	593	581	594	580	589	581	591	582	591	10	10
Mississippi	557	539	569	557	562	549	566	551	559	547	565	551	4	4
Missouri	547	539	570	569	572	577	577	577	574	580	582	583	8	8
Montana	547	547	546	547	543	546	539	539	541	547	538	543	23	26
Nebraska	562	561	567	568	560	571	562	568	561	570	573	578	8	8
Nevada	517	510	508	507	510	517	509	515	509	518	510	517	34	36
New Hampshire	523	511	520	514	520	519	520	516	519	519	522	521	73	75
New Jersey	500	495	498	505	498	513	499	513	498	513	501	515	82	85
New Mexico	553	543	554	548	549	543	551	542	551	543	548	540	14	14
New York	497	495	497	499	494	506	495	505	494	506	496	510	79	82
North Carolina	478	470	490	486	492	496	493	499	493	505	495	506	67	68
North Dakota	572	569	596	599	588	609	592	599	597	610	602	613	4	4
Ohio	529	521	536	535	533	539	534	539	533	540	536	541	27	28
Oklahoma	558	542	566	557	563	560	567	561	565	562	569	562	8	8
Oregon	517	507	523	521	527	527	526	526	524	528	526	527	56	57
Pennsylvania	502	489	498	492	498	497	500	499	498	500	500	502	72	73
Rhode Island	508	496	501	491	505	500	501	499	504	503	502	504	73	74
South Carolina	477	468	480	474	484	482	486	488	488	493	493	496	59	59
South Dakota	585	573	574	566	587	588	577	582	576	586	588	588	5	4
Tennessee	560	543	563	552	563	553	562	553	562	555	568	560	14	14
Texas	494	490	495	500	493	500	493	499	491	500	493	500	55	57
Utah	572	553	583	575	570	569	575	570	563	559	566	559	6	7
Vermont	514	499	506	500	513	508	511	506	512	510	515	512	69	70
Virginia	507	498	507	496	509	500	510	501	510	506	514	510	68	71
Washington	525	517	519	519	526	528	527	527	525	529	530	532	54	56
West Virginia	528	519	526	506	526	511	527	512	525	515	522	510	18	20
Wisconsin	549	551	577	586	584	597	584	596	583	599	585	594	7	7
Wyoming	550	545	544	544	545	545	547	545	531	537	548	549	11	11

NOTE: Scholastic Assessment Test was formerly known as the Scholastic Aptitude Test. The percent of graduates taking the SAT is based on the projection of high school graduates by the Western Interstate Commission for Higher Education, and number of students in the graduating class who took the SAT I: Reasoning Test. Possible scores on each part of the SAT range from 200 to 800. Rankings of states based on SAT scores alone are invalid because of the varying proportions of students in each state taking the tests.

SOURCE: College Entrance Examination Board, "College-Bound Seniors: 2003 Profile of SAT Program Test Takers," (Copyright © 2003 by the College Entrance Examination Board. All rights reserved.) (This table was prepared August 2003.)

American College Testing (ACT) score averages and standard deviations, by sex: Selected years, 1995 to 2002

Type of test	Number							Standard deviation					
	1995	1997	1998	1999	2000	2001	2002	1997	1998	1999	2000	2001	2002
1	2	3	4	5	6	7	8	9	10	11	12	13	14
Participants:													
Total (in thousands)	945	959	995	1,019	1,065	1,070	1,116	†	†	†	†	†	†
	Average test score [1]												
Composite, total	20.8	21.0	21.0	21.0	21.0	21.0	20.8	4.7	4.7	4.7	4.7	4.7	4.8
Male	21.0	21.1	21.2	21.1	21.2	21.1	20.9	4.9	4.9	4.9	4.9	4.9	5.0
Female	20.7	20.8	20.9	20.9	20.9	20.9	20.7	4.6	4.6	4.6	4.6	4.6	4.7
English, total	20.2	20.3	20.4	20.5	20.5	20.5	20.2	5.4	5.4	5.5	5.5	5.6	5.8
Male	19.8	19.9	19.9	20.0	20.0	20.0	19.7	5.4	5.4	5.5	5.6	5.6	5.8
Female	20.6	20.7	20.8	20.9	20.9	20.8	20.6	5.4	5.4	5.5	5.5	5.6	5.7
Mathematics, total	20.2	20.6	20.8	20.7	20.7	20.7	20.6	5.0	5.1	5.0	5.0	5.0	5.0
Male	20.9	21.3	21.5	21.4	21.4	21.4	21.2	5.2	5.3	5.2	5.2	5.2	5.3
Female	19.7	20.1	20.2	20.2	20.2	20.2	20.1	4.7	4.8	4.7	4.8	4.7	4.8
Reading, total	21.3	21.3	21.4	21.4	21.4	21.3	21.1	6.1	6.0	6.0	6.1	6.0	6.1
Male	21.1	21.2	21.1	21.1	21.2	21.1	20.9	6.1	6.2	6.1	6.1	6.1	6.3
Female	21.4	21.5	21.6	21.6	21.5	21.5	21.3	6.0	5.9	5.9	6.0	6.0	6.1
Science reasoning, total	21.0	21.1	21.1	21.0	21.0	21.0	20.8	4.7	4.6	4.5	4.5	4.6	4.6
Male	21.6	21.7	21.8	21.5	21.6	21.6	21.3	4.9	4.9	4.8	4.8	4.9	4.9
Female	20.5	20.6	20.6	20.6	20.6	20.6	20.4	4.4	4.3	4.2	4.3	4.3	4.3
	Percent												
Obtaining composite scores of—													
27 or above [2]	12	10	10	10	10	10	10	†	†	†	†	†	†
18 or below [3]	35	26	25	25	25	25	27	†	†	†	†	†	†
Planned major field of of study													
Business [4]	13	12	12	12	11	11	10	†	†	†	†	†	†
Engineering [5]	8	8	8	8	8	7	7	†	†	†	†	†	†
Social science [6]	9	9	9	9	9	9	8	†	†	†	†	†	†
Education [7]	8	9	9	9	9	8	8	†	†	†	†	†	†

† Not applicable.

[1] Minimum score, 1; maximum score, 36.
[2] Beginning in 1997, data are for scores of 28 or higher.
[3] Beginning in 1997, data are for scores of 17 or lower.
[4] Includes business and management, business and office, and marketing and distribution.

[5] Includes engineering and engineering-related technologies.
[6] Includes social science and philosophy, religion, and theology.
[7] Includes education and teacher education.

SOURCE: The American College Testing program, *High School Profile Report,* selected years 1995 through 2002. (This table was prepared June 2003.)

Enrollment in public elementary and secondary schools, by state or jurisdiction: Fall 1988 to fall 2002

State or jurisdiction	Fall 1988 Total	Fall 1989 Total	Fall 1990 Total	Fall 1991 Total	Fall 1992 Total	Fall 1993 Total	Fall 1994 Total	Fall 1995 Total	Fall 1996 Total	Fall 1997 Total	Fall 1998 Total
1	2	3	4	5	6	7	8	9	10	11	12
United States	40,188,690	40,542,707	41,216,683	42,046,878	42,823,312	43,464,916	44,111,482	44,840,481	45,611,046	46,126,897	46,538,585
Alabama	724,751	723,743	721,806	722,004	731,634	734,288	736,531	746,149	747,932	749,207	747,980
Alaska	106,481	109,280	113,903	118,680	122,487	125,948	127,057	127,618	129,919	132,123	135,373
Arizona	574,890	607,615	639,853	656,980	673,477	709,453	737,424	743,566	799,250	814,113	848,262
Arkansas	436,387	434,960	436,286	438,518	441,490	444,271	447,565	453,257	457,349	456,497	452,256
California	4,618,120	4,771,978	4,950,474	5,107,145	5,254,844	5,327,231	5,407,475	5,536,406	5,686,198	5,803,887	5,926,037
Colorado	560,081	562,755	574,213	593,030	612,635	625,062	640,521	656,279	673,438	687,167	699,135
Connecticut	460,637	461,560	469,123	481,050	488,476	496,298	506,824	517,935	527,129	535,164	544,698
Delaware	96,678	97,808	99,658	102,196	104,321	105,547	106,813	108,461	110,549	111,960	113,262
District of Columbia	84,792	81,301	80,694	80,618	80,937	80,678	80,450	79,802	78,648	77,111	71,889
Florida	1,720,930	1,789,925	1,861,592	1,932,131	1,981,407	2,040,763	2,111,188	2,176,222	2,242,212	2,294,077	2,337,633
Georgia	1,107,994	1,126,535	1,151,687	1,177,569	1,207,186	1,235,304	1,270,948	1,311,126	1,346,761	1,375,980	1,401,291
Hawaii	167,488	169,493	171,708	174,747	177,448	180,410	183,795	187,180	187,653	189,887	188,069
Idaho	214,615	214,932	220,840	225,680	231,668	236,774	240,448	243,097	245,252	244,403	244,722
Illinois	1,794,916	1,797,355	1,821,407	1,848,166	1,873,567	1,893,078	1,916,172	1,943,623	1,973,040	1,998,289	2,011,530
Indiana	960,994	954,165	954,525	956,988	960,630	965,633	969,022	977,263	982,876	986,836	989,001
Iowa	478,200	478,486	483,652	491,363	494,839	498,519	500,440	502,343	502,941	501,054	498,214
Kansas	426,596	430,864	437,034	445,390	451,536	457,614	460,838	463,008	466,293	468,687	472,353
Kentucky	637,627	630,688	636,401	646,024	655,041	655,265	657,642	659,821	656,089	669,322	655,687
Louisiana	786,683	783,025	784,757	794,128	797,985	800,560	797,933	797,366	793,296	776,813	768,734
Maine	212,902	213,775	215,149	216,400	216,453	216,995	212,601	213,569	213,593	212,579	211,051
Maryland	688,947	698,806	715,176	736,238	751,850	772,638	790,938	805,544	818,583	830,744	841,671
Massachusetts	823,428	825,588	834,314	846,155	859,948	877,726	893,727	915,007	933,898	949,006	962,317
Michigan	1,582,785	1,576,785	1,584,431	1,593,561	1,603,610	1,599,377	1,614,784	1,641,456	1,685,714	1,702,717	1,720,287
Minnesota	726,950	739,553	756,374	773,571	793,724	810,233	821,693	835,166	847,204	853,621	856,455
Mississippi	503,326	502,020	502,417	504,127	506,668	505,907	505,962	506,272	503,967	504,792	502,379
Missouri	806,639	807,934	816,558	842,965	859,357	866,378	878,541	889,881	900,517	910,613	913,494
Montana	152,191	151,265	152,974	155,779	160,011	163,009	164,341	165,547	164,627	162,335	159,988
Nebraska	269,434	270,920	274,081	279,552	282,414	285,097	287,100	289,744	291,967	292,681	291,140
Nevada	176,474	186,834	201,316	211,810	222,974	235,800	250,747	265,041	282,131	296,621	311,061
New Hampshire	169,413	171,696	172,785	177,138	181,247	185,360	189,319	194,171	198,308	201,629	204,713
New Jersey	1,080,871	1,076,005	1,089,646	1,109,796	1,130,560	1,151,307	1,174,206	1,197,381	1,227,832	1,250,276	1,268,996
New Mexico	292,425	296,057	301,881	308,667	315,668	322,292	327,248	329,640	332,632	331,673	328,753
New York	2,573,715	2,565,841	2,598,337	2,643,993	2,689,686	2,733,813	2,766,208	2,813,230	2,843,131	2,861,823	2,877,143
North Carolina	1,083,156	1,080,744	1,086,871	1,097,598	1,114,083	1,133,231	1,156,767	1,183,090	1,210,108	1,236,083	1,254,821
North Dakota	118,809	117,816	117,825	118,376	118,734	119,127	119,288	119,100	120,123	118,572	114,927
Ohio	1,778,544	1,764,410	1,771,089	1,783,767	1,795,199	1,807,319	1,814,290	1,836,015	1,844,698	1,847,114	1,842,163
Oklahoma	580,426	578,580	579,087	588,263	597,096	604,076	609,718	616,393	620,695	623,681	628,492
Oregon	461,752	472,394	472,394	498,614	510,122	516,611	521,945	527,914	537,854	541,346	542,809
Pennsylvania	1,659,714	1,655,279	1,667,834	1,692,797	1,717,613	1,744,082	1,764,946	1,787,533	1,804,256	1,815,151	1,816,414
Rhode Island	133,585	135,729	138,813	142,144	143,798	145,676	147,487	149,799	151,324	153,321	154,785
South Carolina	615,774	616,177	622,112	627,470	640,464	643,696	648,725	645,586	652,816	659,273	664,600
South Dakota	126,910	127,329	129,164	131,576	134,573	142,825	143,482	144,685	143,331	142,443	132,495
Tennessee	821,580	819,660	824,595	833,651	855,231	866,557	881,425	893,770	904,818	893,044	905,454
Texas	3,283,707	3,328,514	3,382,887	3,464,371	3,541,769	3,608,262	3,677,171	3,748,167	3,828,975	3,891,877	3,945,367
Utah	431,119	438,554	446,652	456,430	463,870	471,365	474,675	477,121	481,812	482,957	481,176
Vermont	93,381	94,779	95,762	97,137	98,558	102,755	104,533	105,565	106,341	105,984	105,120
Virginia	982,393	985,346	998,601	1,016,204	1,031,925	1,045,471	1,060,809	1,079,854	1,096,093	1,110,815	1,124,022
Washington	790,918	810,232	839,709	869,327	896,475	915,952	938,314	956,572	974,504	991,235	998,053
West Virginia	335,912	327,540	322,389	320,249	318,296	314,383	310,511	307,112	304,052	301,419	297,530
Wisconsin	774,857	782,905	797,621	814,671	829,415	844,001	860,581	870,175	879,259	881,780	879,542
Wyoming	97,793	97,172	98,226	102,074	100,313	100,899	100,314	99,859	99,058	97,115	95,241
Bureau of Indian Affairs	—	—	—	—	—	—	—	—	—	—	50,125
Department of Defense dependents schools:											
Overseas schools	—	—	—	—	—	—	—	—	80,715	78,254	78,170
Domestic schools	—	—	—	—	—	—	—	—	—	—	—
Outlying areas											
American Samoa	11,764	12,258	12,463	13,365	13,994	14,484	14,445	14,576	14,766	15,214	15,372
Guam	26,041	26,493	26,391	28,334	30,077	30,920	32,185	32,960	33,393	32,444	32,222
Northern Marianas	6,079	6,101	6,449	7,096	8,086	8,188	8,429	8,809	9,041	9,246	9,498
Puerto Rico	661,693	651,225	644,734	642,392	637,034	631,460	621,121	627,620	618,861	617,157	613,862
Virgin Islands	23,492	21,193	21,750	22,346	22,887	22,752	23,126	22,737	22,385	22,136	20,976

See notes at end of table.

589

Enrollment in public elementary and secondary schools, by state or jurisdiction: Fall 1988 to fall 2002—Continued

State or jurisdiction	Fall 1999			Fall 2000			Fall 2001			Projected 2002 enrollment
	Total	Prekindergarten through grade 8[1]	Grades 9 to 12[2]	Total	Prekindergarten through grade 8[1]	Grades 9 to 12[2]	Total	Prekindergarten through grade 8[1]	Grades 9 to 12[2]	
1	13	14	15	16	17	18	19	20	21	22
United States	46,857,149	33,488,378	13,368,771	47,203,539	33,688,302	13,515,237	47,687,871	33,952,003	13,735,868	47,917,774
Alabama	740,732	538,687	202,045	739,992	538,634	201,358	737,294	535,684	201,610	735,102
Alaska	134,391	95,601	38,790	133,356	94,442	38,914	134,358	94,897	39,461	136,005
Arizona	852,612	623,561	229,051	877,696	640,566	237,130	922,180	671,658	250,522	928,624
Arkansas	451,034	317,714	133,320	449,959	318,025	131,934	449,805	317,925	131,880	447,511
California	6,038,590	4,336,688	1,701,902	6,140,814	4,407,825	1,732,989	6,248,610	4,479,950	1,768,660	6,324,871
Colorado	708,109	506,568	201,541	724,508	516,566	207,942	742,145	529,156	212,989	743,987
Connecticut	553,993	403,913	150,080	562,179	406,445	155,734	570,228	410,017	160,211	570,552
Delaware	112,836	80,274	32,562	114,676	80,801	33,875	115,555	81,274	34,281	116,394
District of Columbia	77,194	59,917	17,277	68,925	53,686	15,239	75,392	57,951	17,441	71,183
Florida	2,381,396	1,725,493	655,903	2,434,821	1,759,902	674,919	2,500,478	1,797,414	703,064	2,512,316
Georgia	1,422,762	1,044,030	378,732	1,444,937	1,059,983	384,954	1,470,634	1,075,195	395,439	1,480,548
Hawaii	185,860	133,250	52,610	184,360	132,293	52,067	184,546	131,881	52,665	187,105
Idaho	245,136	168,822	76,314	245,117	170,421	74,696	246,521	171,423	75,098	248,076
Illinois	2,027,600	1,462,234	565,366	2,048,792	1,473,939	574,853	2,071,391	1,484,207	587,184	2,078,416
Indiana	988,702	699,221	289,481	989,267	703,277	285,990	996,133	711,471	284,662	996,674
Iowa	497,301	335,919	161,382	495,080	333,804	161,276	485,932	329,670	156,262	488,004
Kansas	472,188	325,818	146,370	470,610	323,227	147,383	470,205	322,426	147,779	466,317
Kentucky	648,180	458,826	189,354	665,850	471,442	194,408	654,363	473,499	180,864	641,883
Louisiana	756,579	548,019	208,560	743,089	546,575	196,514	731,328	536,951	194,377	732,412
Maine	209,253	148,774	60,479	207,037	145,709	61,328	205,586	143,864	61,722	205,191
Maryland	846,582	607,125	239,457	852,920	609,093	243,827	860,640	610,907	249,733	866,348
Massachusetts	971,425	706,251	265,174	975,150	702,575	272,575	973,140	699,496	273,644	975,497
Michigan	1,725,639	1,244,586	481,053	1,720,626	1,222,482	498,144	1,730,668	1,222,763	507,905	1,785,908
Minnesota	854,034	580,363	273,671	854,340	577,766	276,574	851,384	573,028	278,356	846,434
Mississippi	500,716	365,357	135,359	497,871	363,907	133,964	493,507	361,648	131,859	492,990
Missouri	914,110	618,758	265,352	912,744	644,803	267,941	909,792	642,513	267,279	911,074
Montana	157,556	107,490	50,066	154,875	105,226	49,649	151,947	102,721	49,226	151,820
Nebraska	288,261	197,014	91,247	286,199	195,486	90,713	285,095	194,653	90,442	283,568
Nevada	325,610	239,625	85,985	340,706	250,721	89,985	356,814	262,473	94,341	363,775
New Hampshire	206,783	146,854	59,929	208,461	147,124	61,337	206,847	144,489	62,358	206,754
New Jersey	1,289,256	953,766	335,490	1,313,405	967,719	345,686	1,341,656	971,934	369,722	1,356,374
New Mexico	324,495	228,592	95,903	320,306	224,879	95,427	320,260	225,036	95,224	323,656
New York	2,887,776	2,033,748	854,028	2,882,188	2,029,456	852,732	2,872,132	2,017,342	854,790	2,887,555
North Carolina	1,275,925	934,725	341,200	1,293,638	945,470	348,168	1,315,363	955,965	359,398	1,318,475
North Dakota	112,751	74,968	37,783	109,201	72,421	36,780	106,047	70,454	35,593	104,602
Ohio	1,836,554	1,296,450	540,104	1,835,049	1,293,646	541,403	1,830,985	1,286,632	544,353	1,830,227
Oklahoma	627,032	446,719	180,313	623,110	445,409	177,701	622,139	445,997	176,142	611,488
Oregon	545,033	378,474	166,559	546,231	379,283	166,948	551,480	381,695	169,785	552,119
Pennsylvania	1,816,716	1,262,181	554,535	1,814,311	1,257,824	556,487	1,821,627	1,254,692	566,935	1,841,516
Rhode Island	156,454	113,520	42,934	157,347	113,545	43,802	158,046	112,783	45,263	161,217
South Carolina	666,780	483,725	183,055	677,411	493,226	184,185	691,078	499,982	191,096	692,003
South Dakota	131,037	89,590	41,447	128,603	87,838	40,765	127,542	86,982	40,560	126,830
Tennessee	916,202	664,393	251,809	909,161	668,123	241,038	925,030	674,638	250,392	928,795
Texas	3,991,783	2,895,853	1,095,930	4,059,619	2,943,047	1,116,572	4,163,447	3,016,214	1,147,233	4,166,333
Utah	480,255	329,185	151,070	481,485	333,149	148,336	484,677	338,013	146,664	484,246
Vermont	104,559	72,276	32,283	102,049	70,320	31,729	101,179	69,299	31,880	100,943
Virginia	1,133,994	817,143	316,851	1,144,915	815,748	329,167	1,163,091	826,184	336,907	1,181,476
Washington	1,003,714	694,750	308,964	1,004,770	694,367	310,403	1,009,200	696,257	312,943	1,010,515
West Virginia	291,811	203,475	88,336	286,367	201,199	85,168	282,885	199,803	83,082	281,438
Wisconsin	877,753	596,439	281,314	879,476	594,740	284,736	879,361	591,804	287,557	874,803
Wyoming	92,105	61,654	30,451	89,940	60,148	29,792	88,128	59,093	29,035	87,824
Bureau of Indian Affairs	49,076	37,450	11,626	46,938	35,746	11,192	46,476	35,021	11,455	—
Department of Defense dependents schools:										
Overseas schools	[3] 108,035	90,498	17,537	73,581	59,299	14,282	73,212	58,750	14,462	—
Domestic schools	—	—	—	34,058	30,581	3,477	32,283	28,825	3,458	—
Outlying areas										
American Samoa	15,477	11,899	3,578	15,702	11,895	3,807	15,897	11,911	3,986	—
Guam	32,951	24,151	8,800	32,473	23,698	8,775	31,992	23,133	8,859	—
Northern Marianas	9,732	7,634	2,098	10,004	7,809	2,195	10,479	8,015	2,464	—
Puerto Rico	613,019	447,204	165,815	612,725	445,463	167,262	604,177	438,053	166,124	—
Virgin Islands	20,866	14,821	6,045	19,459	13,906	5,553	18,780	13,421	5,359	—

—Not available.

[1] Includes elementary unclassified.

[2] Includes secondary unclassified.

[3] Includes both overseas and domestic schools.

NOTE: Some data have been revised from previously published figures.

SOURCE: U.S. Department of Education, National Center for Education Statistics, The NCES Common Core of Data (CCD), "State Nonfiscal Survey of Public Elementary/Secondary Education," 1988–89 through 2001–02, and *Projections of Education Statistics to 2013.* (This table was prepared July 2003.)

Percentage distribution of enrollment in public elementary and secondary schools, by race/ethnicity and state or jurisdiction: Fall 1991 and fall 2001

State or jurisdiction	Percentage distribution, fall 1991						Percentage distribution, fall 2001					
	Total	White [1]	Black [1]	Hispanic	Asian or Pacific Islander	American Indian/ Alaska Native	Total	White [1]	Black [1]	Hispanic	Asian or Pacific Islander	American Indian/ Alaska Native
1	2	3	4	5	6	7	8	9	10	11	12	13
United States	**100.0**	**67.4**	**16.4**	**11.8**	**3.4**	**1.0**	**100.0**	**60.3**	**17.2**	**17.1**	**4.2**	**1.2**
Alabama	100.0	62.8	35.5	0.3	0.5	0.9	100.0	60.5	36.5	1.5	0.8	0.7
Alaska	100.0	66.9	4.4	2.2	3.9	22.6	100.0	60.4	4.7	3.6	5.9	25.5
Arizona	100.0	62.4	4.2	25.0	1.5	6.9	100.0	51.3	4.7	35.3	2.1	6.6
Arkansas	100.0	74.5	24.0	0.6	0.6	0.3	100.0	71.1	23.3	4.2	0.9	0.5
California	100.0	44.5	8.6	35.3	10.8	0.8	100.0	35.0	8.4	44.5	11.2	0.9
Colorado	100.0	74.9	5.2	16.6	2.3	1.0	100.0	66.8	5.7	23.3	3.0	1.2
Connecticut	100.0	74.3	12.8	10.4	2.2	0.2	100.0	69.2	13.8	13.7	3.0	0.3
Delaware	100.0	67.3	27.8	3.1	1.6	0.2	100.0	59.6	31.1	6.6	2.4	0.3
District of Columbia	100.0	4.0	89.5	5.3	1.1	#	100.0	4.6	84.4	9.4	1.6	#
Florida	100.0	61.2	24.2	12.9	1.6	0.2	100.0	52.5	24.9	20.4	1.9	0.3
Georgia	100.0	60.7	37.9	0.6	0.8	#	100.0	53.8	38.2	5.5	2.4	0.2
Hawaii	100.0	23.9	2.6	5.2	67.9	0.3	100.0	20.3	2.4	4.5	72.3	0.4
Idaho	100.0	92.6	0.3	4.9	0.8	1.3	100.0	85.4	0.8	11.2	1.3	1.3
Illinois	100.0	65.4	21.4	10.3	2.8	0.1	100.0	59.0	21.2	16.2	3.5	0.2
Indiana	100.0	86.4	10.9	1.9	0.7	0.1	100.0	83.0	11.8	3.9	1.0	0.2
Iowa	100.0	94.0	2.9	1.4	1.4	0.4	100.0	89.6	4.1	4.0	1.7	0.5
Kansas	100.0	84.6	8.1	4.7	1.7	0.9	100.0	77.8	8.9	9.8	2.2	1.3
Kentucky	100.0	89.8	9.4	0.2	0.5	#	100.0	87.7	10.3	1.1	0.7	0.2
Louisiana	100.0	52.7	44.7	1.0	1.2	0.4	100.0	48.7	47.8	1.6	1.3	0.7
Maine	100.0	98.3	0.5	0.2	0.8	0.2	100.0	96.2	1.4	0.6	1.1	0.7
Maryland	100.0	60.4	33.2	2.5	3.6	0.3	100.0	52.4	37.2	5.4	4.6	0.4
Massachusetts	100.0	80.5	7.8	8.1	3.5	0.2	100.0	75.7	8.6	10.8	4.5	0.3
Michigan	100.0	78.2	17.2	2.4	1.3	1.0	100.0	73.4	20.0	3.6	2.0	1.0
Minnesota	100.0	89.9	3.6	1.4	3.2	1.8	100.0	82.0	7.0	3.8	5.2	2.0
Mississippi	100.0	48.3	50.7	0.1	0.5	0.4	100.0	47.3	51.0	0.9	0.7	0.2
Missouri	100.0	82.5	15.7	0.8	0.9	0.2	100.0	79.0	17.5	2.0	1.2	0.3
Montana	100.0	88.4	0.4	1.3	0.7	9.2	100.0	85.9	0.6	1.9	1.0	10.6
Nebraska	100.0	89.4	5.5	2.9	1.1	1.1	100.0	81.8	6.9	8.2	1.6	1.6
Nevada	100.0	73.2	9.0	12.1	3.7	2.0	100.0	54.5	10.3	27.4	6.1	1.7
New Hampshire	100.0	97.0	0.8	1.0	1.0	0.2	100.0	95.0	1.2	2.1	1.5	0.2
New Jersey	100.0	64.4	18.6	12.2	4.7	0.1	100.0	59.4	17.9	16.0	6.6	0.2
New Mexico	100.0	41.2	2.3	45.3	0.9	10.4	100.0	34.3	2.4	51.0	1.1	11.3
New York	100.0	59.4	20.1	15.8	4.4	0.3	100.0	54.8	19.9	18.6	6.2	0.4
North Carolina	100.0	66.4	30.2	0.9	1.0	1.6	100.0	60.0	31.3	5.2	1.9	1.5
North Dakota	100.0	91.2	0.7	0.6	0.7	6.8	100.0	88.7	1.1	1.3	0.8	8.1
Ohio	100.0	83.6	14.1	1.3	0.9	0.1	100.0	80.1	16.7	1.9	1.2	0.1
Oklahoma	100.0	73.5	10.0	3.0	1.1	12.4	100.0	63.7	10.8	6.5	1.5	17.5
Oregon	100.0	88.1	2.4	4.9	2.9	1.8	100.0	79.1	3.0	11.5	4.2	2.2
Pennsylvania	100.0	82.2	13.2	2.9	1.7	0.1	100.0	77.7	15.3	4.8	2.1	0.1
Rhode Island	100.0	82.7	6.5	7.2	3.1	0.4	100.0	73.4	8.1	14.8	3.2	0.6
South Carolina	100.0	57.7	41.1	0.5	0.6	0.1	100.0	54.7	41.7	2.4	1.0	0.2
South Dakota	100.0	90.6	0.5	0.6	0.7	7.6	100.0	86.2	1.3	1.4	1.0	10.2
Tennessee	100.0	76.6	22.2	0.3	0.7	0.1	100.0	71.8	24.8	2.1	1.2	0.2
Texas	100.0	49.0	14.3	34.4	2.1	0.2	100.0	40.9	14.4	41.7	2.8	0.3
Utah	100.0	91.9	0.7	4.0	1.9	1.4	100.0	84.7	1.0	9.9	2.8	1.5
Vermont	100.0	97.9	0.6	0.3	0.7	0.6	100.0	95.8	1.2	1.0	1.5	0.5
Virginia	100.0	72.6	23.7	1.0	2.6	0.1	100.0	62.8	27.1	5.5	4.3	0.3
Washington	100.0	81.4	4.2	6.1	5.8	2.5	100.0	73.5	5.4	10.9	7.5	2.6
West Virginia	100.0	95.5	3.9	0.2	0.4	0.1	100.0	94.5	4.4	0.4	0.6	0.1
Wisconsin	100.0	85.2	8.8	2.7	2.1	1.3	100.0	80.1	10.2	5.0	3.4	1.4
Wyoming	100.0	89.6	0.9	6.0	0.7	2.8	100.0	87.3	1.4	7.2	0.9	3.2
Bureau of Indian Affairs	—	—	—	—	—	—	100.0	0.0	0.0	0.0	0.0	100.0
Department of Defense dependents schools												
Overseas schools	—	—	—	—	—	—	100.0	61.6	19.1	9.3	9.1	1.0
Domestic schools	—	—	—	—	—	—	100.0	51.6	25.8	18.5	3.5	0.6
Outlying areas												
American Samoa	100.0	0.0	0.0	0.0	100.0	0.0	100.0	0.0	0.0	0.0	100.0	0.0
Guam	100.0	10.3	1.6	0.3	87.8	0.0	100.0	1.5	0.3	0.2	97.9	0.1
Northern Marianas	100.0	0.1	0.0	0.0	99.9	0.0	100.0	0.4	0.1	0.0	99.5	0.0
Puerto Rico	—	—	—	—	—	—	100.0	0.0	0.0	100.0	0.0	0.0
Virgin Islands	100.0	0.9	86.8	11.8	0.5	0.0	—	—	—	—	—	—

—Not available.

#Rounds to zero.

[1] Excludes persons of Hispanic origin.

NOTE: Percentage distribution based upon students for whom race/ethnicity was reported, which may be less than the total number of students in the state. Detail may not sum to totals due to rounding.

SOURCE: U.S. Department of Education, National Center for Education Statistics, The NCES Common Core of Data (CCD), "State Nonfiscal Survey of Public Elementary/ Secondary Education," 1991–92 and 2001–02. (This table was prepared September 2003.)

Selected statistics on enrollment, teachers, graduates, and dropouts in public school districts enrolling more than 15,000 students, by state: 1990, 2000, and 2001

Name of district, by state	State	Enrollment, fall 1990	Enrollment, fall 2000	Enrollment, fall 2001	White, non-Hispanic	Minority Total	Black, non-Hispanic	Hispanic	Asian/Pacific Islander	American Indian/Alaska Native	Number of classroom teachers, fall 2001	Pupil/teacher ratio, fall 2001	Total number of staff, fall 2001	Student/staff ratio, fall 2001	Dropouts Total	Grade 9	Grade 10	Grade 11	Grade 12	Number of high school graduates, 2000–01[2]	Number of schools, fall 2001
1	2	3	4	5	6	7	8	9	10	11	12	13	14	15	16	17	18	19	20	21	22
Districts with more than 15,000 students	†	16,751,144	19,977,378	20,268,269	42.1	57.9	25.3	25.6	6.3	0.7	1,196,540	16.9	2,305,608	8.8	—	—	—	—	—	—	29,080
Baldwin County	AL	17,479	22,656	23,062	81.0	19.0	16.7	1.5	0.4	0.4	1,523	15.1	2,919	7.9	3.6	2.4	3.5	4.9	4.5	1,057	46
Birmingham City	AL	41,536	37,843	37,154	2.5	97.5	96.4	0.8	0.3	#	2,307	16.1	4,459	8.3	2.3	2.5	2.5	2.4	2.0	1,800	92
Huntsville City	AL	23,945	22,832	22,762	52.5	47.5	42.6	2.1	2.4	0.5	1,541	14.8	2,816	8.1	1.9	2.5	2.2	1.6	1.0	1,390	48
Jefferson County	AL	40,664	40,726	40,396	74.1	25.9	24.2	1.1	0.4	#	2,477	16.3	4,595	8.8	4.9	3.3	5.3	5.8	5.5	2,429	62
Madison County	AL	13,861	15,675	16,075	79.2	20.8	13.8	1.1	0.6	#	937	17.2	1,761	9.1	4.2	2.9	4.6	6.4	3.4	795	24
Mobile County	AL	67,203	64,976	63,846	46.5	53.5	50.3	0.7	1.8	0.8	4,043	15.8	7,527	8.5	5.0	5.1	5.7	4.9	4.2	3,391	102
Montgomery County	AL	35,956	33,267	33,140	24.0	76.0	73.9	0.6	1.3	0.1	2,145	15.5	4,053	8.2	4.6	2.3	4.7	5.8	6.1	1,305	61
Shelby County	AL	16,089	20,129	20,768	84.9	15.1	11.5	2.3	1.0	0.2	1,374	15.1	2,606	8.0	3.1	2.4	2.6	3.5	4.0	1,012	34
Tuscaloosa County	AL	14,426	15,666	15,653	74.7	25.3	24.0	0.8	0.5	#	960	16.3	1,887	8.3	3.6	2.0	4.9	7.2	4.9	755	28
Anchorage	AK	42,300	49,526	49,767	61.7	38.3	8.8	6.0	10.4	13.1	2,813	17.7	5,596	8.9	9.3	5.9	9.2	9.5	13.3	2,441	98
Fairbanks North Star Borough	AK	14,961	15,659	15,385	71.4	28.6	8.1	3.8	3.2	13.4	891	17.3	1,768	8.7	10.5	9.7	12.1	12.7	7.0	802	34
Amphitheater Unified	AZ	13,835	16,857	16,985	62.5	37.5	3.3	29.3	2.7	2.2	867	19.6	1,790	9.5	4.1	2.5	2.4	3.4	6.3	947	22
Cartwright Elementary	AZ	14,369	17,746	19,451	14.2	85.8	7.5	76.4	0.8	1.1	954	20.4	2,021	9.6	†	†	†	†	†	†	22
Chandler Unified	AZ	14,853	21,703	23,383	58.3	41.7	5.6	31.0	3.5	1.6	1,171	20.0	2,187	10.7	3.1	3.8	2.3	3.4	2.9	1,021	25
Deer Valley Unified	AZ	11,008	27,158	28,678	82.5	17.5	2.8	11.0	2.9	0.9	1,525	18.8	2,933	9.8	5.0	4.0	4.0	6.8	5.8	1,320	29
Gilbert Unified	AZ	15,898	29,188	31,276	80.2	19.8	3.0	12.6	3.4	0.8	1,709	18.3	3,336	9.4	2.5	1.4	1.5	3.1	4.3	1,817	33
Kyrene Elementary	AZ	10,863	19,446	19,119	72.6	27.4	3.6	15.0	7.0	1.8	1,046	18.3	1,907	10.0	†	†	†	†	†	†	26
Mesa Unified	AZ	62,470	73,587	74,808	65.4	34.6	2.9	25.2	2.1	3.7	3,698	20.2	7,657	9.8	4.1	2.6	5.3	5.0	3.3	4,014	89
Paradise Valley Unified	AZ	26,698	34,882	35,451	77.8	21.2	2.9	14.8	2.5	1.1	1,846	19.2	3,268	10.8	4.6	2.8	3.3	6.1	6.6	2,136	46
Peoria Unified	AZ	20,846	32,608	35,171	72.6	27.4	4.7	18.7	2.9	1.1	1,833	19.2	3,231	10.9	5.1	3.9	4.1	7.1	6.4	1,990	36
Phoenix Union High	AZ	18,182	22,192	22,479	15.4	84.6	10.6	69.2	1.7	3.1	1,247	18.3	2,615	8.7	12.5	9.3	12.1	14.4	16.1	3,534	14
Scottsdale Unified	AZ	19,741	26,958	27,479	83.1	16.9	2.0	10.7	3.1	1.1	1,560	17.6	2,648	10.4	1.6	1.5	1.2	2.1	1.8	1,708	34
Tucson Unified	AZ	56,177	61,869	62,104	52.9	47.1	6.6	33.4	3.0	4.1	3,442	18.0	7,307	8.5	6.1	6.5	6.0	6.8	5.2	3,308	121
Washington Elementary	AZ	22,446	24,723	24,811	55.0	45.0	6.2	32.4	3.0	3.4	1,441	17.2	2,793	8.9	†	†	†	†	†	†	32
Little Rock	AR	25,813	25,502	25,367	26.4	73.6	68.7	3.2	1.5	0.2	1,890	13.4	3,887	6.5	4.4	2.8	4.5	4.4	6.5	1,285	54
Pulaski County Special	AR	21,495	18,657	18,735	61.6	38.4	36.0	1.4	0.7	0.3	1,270	14.7	2,681	7.0	7.3	7.2	6.3	6.7	9.8	861	36
ABC Unified	CA	20,972	22,303	22,301	13.1	86.9	9.9	36.8	40.0	0.3	1,014	22.0	1,950	11.4	†	†	†	†	†	1,545	30
Alum Rock Union Elementary	CA	16,078	15,835	15,075	4.6	95.4	2.2	72.5	19.9	0.8	765	19.7	1,307	11.5	†	†	†	†	†	†	25
Alvord Unified	CA	14,853	17,664	18,130	30.7	69.3	5.7	58.0	5.2	0.4	804	22.6	1,388	13.1	†	†	†	†	†	843	18
Anaheim Elementary	CA	14,972	22,275	22,426	9.4	90.6	1.9	82.3	6.2	0.2	1,017	22.1	1,838	12.2	†	†	†	†	†	†	23
Anaheim Union High	CA	23,086	29,363	30,258	27.3	72.7	3.4	52.6	16.2	0.5	1,227	24.7	2,325	13.0	†	†	†	†	†	3,345	21
Antelope Valley Union High	CA	10,937	19,056	19,748	43.4	56.6	19.6	31.5	4.3	1.2	827	23.9	1,562	12.6	†	†	†	†	†	3,152	10
Antioch Unified	CA	13,045	20,018	20,613	48.3	51.7	14.3	25.5	10.6	1.3	993	20.8	1,579	13.1	†	†	†	†	†	1,116	22
Bakersfield City Elementary	CA	24,911	27,674	27,998	19.1	80.9	13.5	64.4	1.9	1.1	1,511	18.5	2,868	9.8	†	†	†	†	†	†	43
Baldwin Park Unified	CA	15,878	17,473	17,944	3.3	96.7	1.2	88.0	7.2	0.2	820	21.9	1,495	12.0	†	†	†	†	†	732	22
Bellflower Unified	CA	9,917	14,935	15,321	26.3	73.7	17.3	47.7	8.4	0.4	681	22.5	1,172	13.1	†	†	†	†	†	785	15
Burbank Unified	CA	12,057	16,170	16,204	52.3	47.7	2.5	37.8	7.0	0.4	785	20.7	1,440	11.3	†	†	†	†	†	1,027	20
Cajon Valley Union Elementary	CA	26,852	19,059	18,896	62.8	37.2	7.0	26.0	3.0	1.2	887	21.3	1,701	11.1	†	†	†	†	†	†	28
Capistrano Unified	CA	13,505	45,074	46,756	72.9	27.1	1.5	19.1	6.1	0.4	2,116	22.1	3,687	12.7	†	†	†	†	†	2,528	49
Chaffey Joint Union High	CA	23,257	19,851	20,738	33.5	66.5	10.6	49.2	6.1	0.6	868	23.9	1,556	13.3	†	†	†	†	†	3,682	9
Chino Valley Unified	CA	23,224	31,763	32,481	40.7	59.3	4.9	42.9	11.0	0.5	1,432	22.7	2,466	13.2	†	†	†	†	†	1,777	31
Chula Vista Elementary	CA	16,415	23,132	23,865	19.5	80.5	5.0	61.2	13.7	0.6	1,224	19.5	2,112	11.5	†	†	†	†	†	†	39
Clovis Unified	CA	27,585	32,717	33,418	60.7	39.3	3.5	20.8	14.1	0.9	1,510	22.1	2,910	11.5	†	†	†	†	†	1,927	36
Colton Joint Unified	CA	17,209	31,037	33,044	18.6	81.4	9.7	67.7	3.4	0.6	1,095	21.0	1,790	12.9	†	†	†	†	†	896	25
Compton Unified	CA	23,036	30,999	31,820	0.3	99.7	31.5	67.1	1.0	0.1	1,374	23.2	2,831	11.2	†	†	†	†	†	798	39
Conejo Valley Unified	CA	12,227	20,999	21,247	74.5	25.5	1.4	16.1	7.3	0.7	988	21.5	1,764	12.0	†	†	†	†	†	1,425	29
Corona-Norco Unified	CA	16,058	37,487	39,614	43.7	56.3	6.0	43.7	6.0	0.6	1,878	21.1	3,173	12.5	†	†	†	†	†	2,080	38
Cupertino Union Elementary	CA	15,418	15,670	15,575	31.7	68.3	1.7	12.1	53.9	0.6	737	21.1	1,194	13.0	†	†	†	†	†	†	24
Desert Sands Unified	CA	21,973	23,500	24,582	37.0	63.0	4.2	56.4	2.0	0.4	1,150	21.4	1,977	12.4	†	†	†	†	†	1,321	27
Downey Unified	CA	27,246	21,474	21,887	16.8	83.2	2.1	73.7	7.0	0.4	960	22.8	1,729	12.7	†	†	†	†	†	1,377	22
East Side Union High	CA	14,663	24,282	23,665	16.1	83.9	4.6	40.5	38.4	0.4	1,068	22.2	1,793	13.2	†	†	†	†	†	4,484	18
Elk Grove Unified	CA	20,227	47,736	49,970	36.6	63.4	19.2	18.3	24.5	1.4	2,422	20.6	4,369	11.4	†	†	†	†	†	2,607	53
Escondido Union Elementary	CA	12,656	19,312	19,782	38.1	61.9	3.0	53.8	4.0	1.1	1,012	19.6	1,815	10.9	†	†	†	†	†	†	21
Fairfield-Suisun Unified	CA	20,227	22,263	22,517	35.7	64.3	22.4	23.4	15.0	1.4	1,086	20.7	1,743	12.9	†	†	†	†	†	1,144	27
Folsom-Cordova Unified	CA	12,656	16,277	16,987	69.7	30.3	8.8	11.3	9.6	0.6	794	21.4	1,463	11.6	†	†	†	†	†	872	30

See notes at end of table.

Selected statistics on enrollment, teachers, graduates, and dropouts in public school districts enrolling more than 15,000 students, by state: 1990, 2000, and 2001—Continued

Name of district, by state	State	Enrollment, fall 1990	Enrollment, fall 2000	Enrollment, fall 2001	White, non-Hispanic	Minority Total	Black, non-Hispanic	Hispanic	Asian/Pacific Islander	American Indian/Alaska Native	Number of classroom teachers, fall 2001	Pupil/teacher ratio, fall 2001	Total number of staff, fall 2001	Student/staff ratio, fall 2001	Dropouts Total	Grade 9	Grade 10	Grade 11	Grade 12	Number of high school graduates, 2000-01[2]	Number of schools, fall 2001
1	2	3	4	5	6	7	8	9	10	11	12	13	14	15	16	17	18	19	20	21	22
Fontana Unified	CA	27,043	37,244	38,930	12.2	87.8	9.4	75.9	2.0	0.5	1,789	21.8	3,347	11.6	—	—	—	—	—	1,667	35
Fremont Unified	CA	27,172	31,078	30,691	36.5	63.5	4.2	13.9	44.8	0.6	1,451	21.2	2,313	13.3	—	—	—	—	—	1,829	41
Fresno Unified	CA	71,500	79,007	81,058	19.2	80.8	11.8	50.5	17.8	0.7	3,859	21.0	7,453	10.9	—	—	—	—	—	3,530	99
Fullerton Joint Union High	CA	12,729	15,165	15,500	31.7	68.3	2.4	46.1	19.6	0.3	556	27.9	1,098	14.1	—	—	—	—	—	2,692	8
Garden Grove Unified	CA	37,969	48,742	49,809	18.7	81.3	1.2	50.0	29.8	0.3	2,154	23.1	4,104	12.1	—	—	—	—	—	2,614	66
Glendale Unified	CA	25,459	30,329	30,314	58.1	41.9	1.1	22.9	17.7	0.2	1,421	21.3	2,710	11.2	—	—	—	—	—	1,948	32
Grossmont Union High	CA	18,647	23,639	23,989	66.1	33.9	7.4	19.8	4.9	1.8	994	24.1	1,945	12.3	—	—	—	—	—	4,198	15
Hacienda La Puente Unified	CA	23,267	24,646	25,282	10.0	90.0	2.9	69.5	17.2	0.4	1,175	21.5	2,142	11.8	—	—	—	—	—	1,322	37
Hayward Unified	CA	19,122	24,205	24,199	16.7	83.3	15.4	46.1	21.1	0.7	1,215	19.9	2,007	12.1	—	—	—	—	—	1,163	33
Hemet Unified	CA	12,811	17,451	18,169	60.2	39.8	4.0	32.8	1.9	1.0	856	21.2	1,560	11.6	—	—	—	—	—	922	20
Hesperia Unified	CA	13,113	15,360	15,683	55.3	44.7	6.4	36.2	1.5	0.7	706	22.2	1,347	11.6	—	—	—	—	—	817	19
Inglewood Unified	CA	16,355	17,295	17,796	0.6	99.4	41.0	57.6	0.8	0.1	790	22.5	1,418	12.6	—	—	—	—	—	572	19
Irvine Unified	CA	20,735	23,961	24,412	55.4	44.6	2.3	6.9	34.9	0.5	1,042	23.4	1,880	13.0	—	—	—	—	—	1,734	34
Jurupa Unified	CA	15,419	19,839	20,017	30.9	69.1	4.8	61.8	2.1	0.4	937	21.4	1,691	11.8	—	—	—	—	—	836	24
Kern Union High	CA	20,183	29,333	29,788	42.8	57.2	8.0	44.3	4.0	0.9	1,282	23.2	2,600	11.5	—	—	—	—	—	5,626	22
Lake Elsinore Unified	CA	11,000	17,178	17,769	55.4	44.6	4.5	35.8	3.3	0.9	784	22.7	1,489	11.9	—	—	—	—	—	994	20
Lancaster Elementary	CA	11,248	14,433	15,278	35.9	64.1	26.1	33.5	3.6	0.9	715	21.4	1,334	11.5	†	†	†	†	†	†	18
Lodi Unified	CA	23,954	27,339	27,855	59.7	40.3	7.1	29.2	3.4	0.6	1,437	19.4	2,559	10.9	—	—	—	—	—	1,408	42
Long Beach Unified	CA	71,342	93,694	96,488	17.3	82.7	19.5	46.7	16.1	0.3	4,581	21.1	9,123	10.6	—	—	—	—	—	4,396	90
Los Angeles Unified	CA	625,086	721,346	735,058	9.6	90.4	12.4	71.4	6.3	0.3	36,115	20.4	76,112	9.7	—	—	—	—	—	27,579	663
Lynwood Unified	CA	15,469	18,237	18,786	0.3	99.7	11.2	85.9	2.4	0.1	712	26.4	1,608	11.7	—	—	—	—	—	781	15
Madera Unified	CA	13,728	15,957	16,397	20.0	80.0	3.4	75.2	1.3	0.1	773	21.2	1,412	11.6	—	—	—	—	—	762	19
Manteca Unified	CA	13,356	16,877	17,309	51.0	49.0	5.6	33.0	9.5	1.5	756	22.9	1,577	11.0	—	—	—	—	—	1,064	23
Modesto City Elementary	CA	17,405	18,740	19,158	31.8	68.2	5.6	53.3	8.4	1.0	923	20.8	1,642	11.7	†	†	†	†	†	†	27
Montebello Unified	CA	32,938	34,794	35,379	3.0	97.0	0.4	92.3	4.2	0.1	1,506	23.5	2,633	13.4	—	—	—	—	—	1,601	29
Moreno Valley Unified	CA	29,064	32,730	33,295	25.4	74.6	23.5	44.8	5.8	0.4	1,612	20.7	2,949	11.3	—	—	—	—	—	1,605	33
Mt Diablo Unified	CA	32,840	36,648	36,824	60.5	39.5	4.9	21.8	12.3	0.4	1,800	20.5	2,940	12.5	—	—	—	—	—	2,180	56
Napa Valley Unified	CA	13,705	21,658	21,919	56.8	43.2	2.1	35.2	4.0	1.9	1,056	20.8	1,974	11.1	—	—	—	—	—	898	35
Newport-Mesa Unified	CA	16,434	21,777	21,658	54.3	45.7	1.2	38.4	5.8	0.3	1,141	19.0	2,298	9.4	—	—	—	—	—	1,245	31
Norwalk-La Mirada Unified	CA	22,000	23,724	23,610	18.8	81.2	4.7	68.1	8.1	0.3	1,135	20.8	1,970	12.0	—	—	—	—	—	1,190	29
Oakland Unified	CA	52,095	54,863	53,545	5.7	94.3	45.0	31.1	17.7	0.5	2,853	18.8	5,398	9.9	—	—	—	—	—	1,660	100
Oceanside City Unified	CA	17,034	20,046	20,983	31.9	68.1	11.4	47.8	8.2	0.7	1,377	19.6	2,019	13.4	—	—	—	—	—	1,030	26
Ontario-Montclair Elementary	CA	21,033	23,900	24,300	10.8	89.2	5.6	80.0	3.2	0.4	1,121	21.4	2,219	11.1	†	†	†	†	†	†	31
Orange Unified	CA	25,224	31,097	31,689	44.2	55.8	3.1	40.4	11.8	0.5	1,506	21.0	2,860	11.1	—	—	—	—	—	1,840	42
Oxnard Elementary	CA	12,212	16,249	16,507	10.3	89.7	3.2	82.8	3.1	0.6	770	21.4	1,332	12.4	†	†	†	†	†	†	20
Oxnard Union High	CA	11,512	14,552	15,149	25.0	75.0	3.9	60.8	9.7	0.6	781	19.4	1,175	12.9	—	—	—	—	—	2,470	9
Pajaro Valley Joint Unified	CA	16,355	19,864	19,863	21.7	78.3	0.6	75.4	1.4	0.9	903	22.0	2,039	9.7	—	—	—	—	—	993	30
Palm Springs Unified	CA	14,427	20,847	21,532	29.6	70.4	5.2	60.8	3.6	0.8	1,074	20.0	1,891	11.4	—	—	—	—	—	848	24
Palmdale Elementary	CA	12,855	20,853	21,777	26.5	73.5	20.6	49.1	3.5	0.3	1,027	21.2	1,822	12.0	†	†	†	†	†	†	24
Paramount Unified	CA	13,000	16,862	17,060	3.6	96.4	11.8	81.0	3.5	0.1	805	21.2	1,382	12.3	—	—	—	—	—	578	18
Pasadena Unified	CA	21,802	23,559	23,447	15.4	84.6	28.6	52.2	2.8	1.0	1,133	20.0	2,223	10.5	—	—	—	—	—	955	31
Placentia-Yorba Linda Unified	CA	21,438	26,046	26,121	60.5	39.5	1.7	28.5	9.1	0.2	1,187	22.0	2,132	12.3	—	—	—	—	—	1,538	30
Pomona Unified	CA	26,918	34,479	35,070	8.0	92.0	8.9	76.0	6.2	0.9	1,594	22.0	2,837	12.4	—	—	—	—	—	1,342	39
Poway Unified	CA	24,662	32,532	32,507	68.4	31.6	3.1	18.7	9.5	0.3	1,506	21.6	2,698	12.0	—	—	—	—	—	2,235	30
Redlands Unified	CA	16,002	19,411	19,892	47.1	52.9	8.0	33.2	10.7	1.0	921	21.6	1,513	13.2	—	—	—	—	—	1,302	30
Rialto Unified	CA	19,794	29,283	29,283	10.4	89.6	25.5	60.0	2.5	1.6	1,331	22.0	2,390	12.3	—	—	—	—	—	1,277	21
Riverside Unified	CA	31,326	38,124	39,688	40.4	59.6	10.2	44.2	4.2	1.0	1,803	22.0	3,394	11.7	—	—	—	—	—	2,113	44
Rowland Unified	CA	17,000	17,500	17,500	7.6	92.4	4.9	58.3	28.6	0.6	810	21.6	1,688	10.4	—	—	—	—	—	1,076	26
Sacramento City Unified	CA	49,557	52,734	53,418	23.4	76.6	22.2	27.3	25.5	1.6	2,471	21.6	4,793	11.1	—	—	—	—	—	2,334	79
Saddleback Valley Unified	CA	25,130	35,199	35,166	69.2	30.8	2.1	17.9	10.4	0.4	1,624	21.6	2,652	13.2	—	—	—	—	—	2,026	37
San Bernardino City Unified	CA	40,589	52,031	54,166	18.9	81.1	20.4	56.2	3.4	1.1	2,512	21.6	4,992	10.8	—	—	—	—	—	1,897	65
San Diego City Unified	CA	121,152	141,804	141,599	26.6	73.4	15.5	39.7	17.6	0.6	7,501	18.9	14,375	9.9	—	—	—	—	—	6,534	182
San Francisco Unified	CA	61,688	59,979	58,566	10.5	89.5	15.5	21.6	51.9	0.4	3,274	17.9	4,924	11.9	—	—	—	—	—	3,514	113
San Jose Unified	CA	29,630	33,015	32,309	29.5	70.5	3.3	50.3	15.3	1.6	1,620	19.9	2,698	12.0	—	—	—	—	—	1,830	57
San Juan Unified	CA	47,690	50,266	51,383	73.9	26.1	6.7	11.2	6.0	2.2	2,488	20.6	4,925	10.4	—	—	—	—	—	3,345	86
San Ramon Valley Unified	CA	16,119	20,742	21,000	78.9	21.1	1.6	4.1	14.7	0.7	981	21.4	1,784	11.8	—	—	—	—	—	1,396	29
Santa Ana Unified	CA	45,964	60,643	61,909	3.7	96.3	0.8	91.7	3.7	0.1	2,845	21.8	5,297	11.7	—	—	—	—	—	2,330	54
Simi Valley Unified	CA	18,262	21,181	21,379	71.0	29.0	1.6	18.8	7.4	1.2	981	21.8	1,758	12.2	—	—	—	—	—	1,151	28

See notes at end of table.

Selected statistics on enrollment, teachers, graduates, and dropouts in public school districts enrolling more than 15,000 students, by state: 1990, 2000, and 2001—Continued

Name of district, by state	State	Enrollment, fall 1990	Enrollment, fall 2000	Enrollment, fall 2001	White, non-Hispanic	Total	Black, non-Hispanic	Hispanic	Asian/Pacific Islander	American Indian/Alaska Native	Number of classroom teachers, fall 2001	Pupil/teacher ratio, fall 2001	Total number of staff, fall 2001	Student/staff ratio, fall 2001	Total	Grade 9	Grade 10	Grade 11	Grade 12	Number of high school graduates, 2000–01	Number of schools, fall 2001
1	2	3	4	5	6	7	8	9	10	11	12	13	14	15	16	17	18	19	20	21	22
Stockton City Unified	CA	32,687	37,573	39,213	13.5	86.5	14.9	47.4	21.3	2.9	1,956	20.0	3,570	11.0	—	—	—	—	—	1,244	47
Sweetwater Union High	CA	27,894	35,330	37,175	15.6	84.4	4.6	67.5	11.9	0.6	1,750	21.2	3,062	12.1	—	—	—	—	—	4,322	25
Temecula Valley Unified	CA	7,596	18,980	20,258	68.6	31.4	4.8	18.2	7.1	1.4	991	20.4	1,702	11.9	—	—	—	—	—	1,035	22
Torrance Unified	CA	19,645	24,118	24,555	44.6	55.4	3.8	17.1	33.6	0.9	1,216	20.2	2,152	11.4	—	—	—	—	—	1,804	30
Tustin Unified	CA	10,831	16,963	17,863	39.4	60.6	3.0	44.4	15.0	0.3	810	22.1	1,385	12.9	—	—	—	—	—	861	26
Vacaville Unified	CA	12,593	15,148	15,163	63.1	36.9	8.3	20.3	6.9	1.3	783	19.4	1,373	11.0	—	—	—	—	—	990	19
Vallejo City Unified	CA	19,049	20,270	20,034	17.5	82.5	34.3	21.3	26.1	0.8	918	21.8	1,960	10.2	—	—	—	—	—	1,136	28
Ventura Unified	CA	15,383	17,527	17,632	55.0	45.0	2.5	36.6	3.8	1.2	778	22.7	1,494	11.8	—	—	—	—	—	1,039	29
Visalia Unified	CA	21,309	23,989	24,579	41.4	58.6	2.6	48.5	6.8	0.6	1,164	21.1	2,124	11.6	—	—	—	—	—	1,264	32
Vista Unified	CA	18,489	27,651	28,018	43.8	56.2	6.6	43.4	5.6	0.6	1,301	21.5	2,518	11.1	—	—	—	—	—	1,879	27
Walnut Valley Unified	CA	12,613	14,849	15,005	20.7	79.3	4.9	18.6	55.8	0.1	674	22.3	1,175	12.8	—	—	—	—	—	1,330	16
West Contra Costa Unified	CA	31,292	34,499	34,667	16.1	83.9	31.4	34.7	17.6	0.2	1,762	19.7	3,151	11.0	—	—	—	—	—	1,635	63
William S Hart Union High	CA	10,278	17,001	18,410	66.1	33.9	2.8	22.8	7.0	0.5	771	23.9	1,362	13.5	—	—	—	—	—	2,351	13
Academy 20	CO	10,986	17,628	18,137	85.9	14.1	3.7	5.8	3.7	1.0	1,115	16.3	2,112	8.6	—	—	—	—	—	1,081	26
Adams-Arapahoe	CO	25,897	30,453	31,528	37.0	63.0	22.3	35.5	4.3	0.9	1,678	18.8	3,481	9.1	—	—	—	—	—	1,032	51
Boulder Valley	CO	21,502	27,508	27,963	79.5	20.5	2.3	12.7	5.4	0.7	1,705	16.4	3,418	8.2	—	—	—	—	—	1,651	58
Cherry Creek	CO	29,210	42,320	44,228	74.9	25.1	10.1	8.2	6.3	0.4	2,579	17.2	5,101	8.7	—	—	—	—	—	2,644	52
Colorado Springs	CO	30,009	32,699	32,808	68.7	31.3	9.6	17.5	2.9	1.3	1,938	16.9	3,714	8.8	—	—	—	—	—	1,822	64
Denver County	CO	59,013	70,847	72,361	20.9	79.1	19.7	54.9	3.3	1.2	4,376	16.5	8,928	8.1	—	—	—	—	—	2,585	134
Douglas County	CO	13,125	34,918	38,054	89.1	10.9	1.5	5.5	3.2	0.6	2,206	17.3	4,274	8.9	—	—	—	—	—	1,696	56
Greeley	CO	11,657	15,998	16,527	52.2	47.8	1.2	45.0	1.0	0.6	955	17.3	1,747	9.5	—	—	—	—	—	807	32
Jefferson County	CO	76,275	87,703	88,460	81.1	18.9	1.6	13.1	3.3	0.9	4,724	18.7	9,846	9.0	—	—	—	—	—	5,145	166
Littleton	CO	15,524	16,516	16,590	87.6	12.4	1.7	7.4	2.8	0.6	927	17.9	1,820	9.1	—	—	—	—	—	1,157	27
Mesa County Valley	CO	17,024	19,688	20,040	82.5	17.5	0.9	14.6	1.0	1.0	1,154	17.4	2,312	9.1	—	—	—	—	—	1,085	40
Northglenn-Thornton	CO	20,838	30,079	31,544	67.5	32.5	2.3	24.1	4.9	1.2	1,672	18.9	3,418	9.2	—	—	—	—	—	1,593	46
Poudre	CO	18,589	24,052	24,412	81.8	18.2	1.8	12.3	3.1	1.1	1,417	17.2	2,820	8.7	—	—	—	—	—	1,449	47
Pueblo City	CO	18,364	17,636	17,738	40.3	59.7	2.4	54.9	0.6	1.8	1,050	16.9	2,008	8.8	—	—	—	—	—	950	41
St. Vrain Valley	CO	15,070	19,620	20,736	72.7	27.3	0.9	22.8	2.7	0.9	1,158	17.9	2,129	9.7	—	—	—	—	—	1,037	37
Bridgeport	CT	19,687	22,432	22,796	10.8	89.2	43.1	42.5	3.4	0.2	1,435	15.9	2,766	8.3	11.2	9.4	11.4	15.2	9.8	752	36
Hartford	CT	25,418	22,543	22,276	5.8	94.2	40.2	52.9	1.0	0.1	1,643	13.6	3,564	6.3	11.5	15.5	10.6	8.5	5.8	615	36
New Haven	CT	17,881	19,549	20,200	12.0	88.0	56.2	30.2	1.6	#	1,376	14.7	3,251	6.2	6.4	7.0	5.5	7.4	5.2	738	49
Stamford	CT	11,574	14,791	15,053	45.2	54.8	26.8	23.1	4.8	0.1	1,244	12.1	2,127	7.1	3.9	2.4	1.9	4.1	3.2	817	22
Waterbury	CT	13,323	16,282	16,762	33.7	66.3	25.5	38.4	1.9	0.5	1,188	14.1	2,115	7.9	3.9	4.5	5.0	3.1	2.0	564	28
Christina	DE	17,872	19,882	19,755	52.8	47.2	35.5	7.9	3.7	0.2	1,305	15.1	2,614	7.6	5.9	7.2	6.5	4.4	4.5	925	28
Red Clay Consolidated	DE	14,551	15,827	15,777	52.9	47.1	29.4	14.0	3.6	0.2	951	16.6	1,753	9.0	5.3	6.1	6.1	5.4	3.0	741	28
District of Columbia	DC	80,694	68,925	68,449	4.6	95.4	84.4	9.4	1.6	#	4,951	13.8	11,391	6.0	—	—	—	—	—	2,808	165
Alachua County	FL	26,305	29,712	29,679	54.8	45.2	37.9	4.2	2.8	0.2	1,639	18.1	4,040	7.3	7.2	7.5	7.3	6.4	7.4	1,425	61
Bay County	FL	21,827	25,755	26,068	80.3	19.7	15.9	1.6	1.9	0.3	1,511	17.3	3,309	7.9	1.9	1.8	1.4	2.3	2.0	1,205	44
Brevard County	FL	56,503	70,597	71,781	79.1	20.9	14.1	4.9	1.6	0.3	3,914	18.3	7,950	9.0	2.6	4.1	2.6	2.1	0.7	3,572	109
Broward County	FL	161,101	251,129	262,055	39.3	60.7	36.4	21.2	2.9	0.3	12,763	20.5	25,038	10.5	2.0	2.2	1.8	2.0	1.8	10,644	244
Charlotte County	FL	13,030	17,170	17,322	85.6	14.4	8.4	4.2	1.4	0.4	908	19.1	2,131	8.1	4.0	3.1	3.3	5.1	4.9	1,041	24
Citrus County	FL	11,697	15,199	15,238	90.6	9.4	4.6	3.2	1.2	0.4	926	16.5	1,991	7.7	3.5	3.2	3.9	3.2	3.9	766	25
Clay County	FL	21,925	28,115	29,063	83.9	16.1	10.0	3.8	2.1	0.2	1,620	17.9	3,392	8.6	3.0	4.1	2.1	2.8	2.3	1,502	32
Collier County	FL	20,850	34,203	36,521	54.1	45.9	11.4	33.2	1.1	0.2	1,930	18.9	4,541	8.0	4.9	5.1	5.0	5.2	4.4	1,526	51
Duval County	FL	111,142	125,846	127,392	49.4	50.6	43.5	4.1	2.8	0.2	6,478	19.7	11,526	11.1	9.7	10.7	8.3	8.2	11.1	4,950	178
Escambia County	FL	42,950	45,012	44,807	57.8	42.3	37.1	1.7	2.7	0.8	2,480	18.1	5,278	8.5	2.9	3.4	2.8	2.5	3.0	2,030	84
Hernando County	FL	12,831	17,215	17,944	84.7	15.3	7.4	6.8	0.8	0.3	994	18.1	2,363	7.6	2.2	2.8	1.8	1.9	1.6	841	23
Hillsborough County	FL	124,337	164,311	169,789	50.5	49.5	24.0	23.1	2.1	0.2	9,975	17.0	19,650	8.6	3.1	4.6	2.6	2.5	1.5	7,734	219
Indian River County	FL	11,683	14,979	15,423	73.6	26.4	14.2	10.7	1.1	0.4	797	19.4	1,759	8.8	3.7	1.8	3.0	4.0	2.1	699	27
Lake County	FL	21,065	29,293	30,689	55.9	44.1	33.0	8.9	1.2	0.3	1,605	19.1	3,589	8.6	5.2	4.2	4.7	6.0	4.9	1,347	52
Lee County	FL	43,240	58,401	60,718	65.7	34.3	15.0	17.8	1.2	0.3	3,064	19.8	6,439	9.4	5.1	7.6	6.2	6.4	6.9	2,661	78
Leon County	FL	27,241	32,050	31,855	55.9	44.1	40.2	1.9	1.9	0.1	1,774	18.0	4,089	7.8	3.5	3.6	3.7	3.0	8.1	1,594	60
Manatee County	FL	26,207	36,569	38,282	68.8	31.2	13.0	16.0	0.9	0.3	2,102	18.2	4,782	8.0	5.5	5.5	5.6	6.2	3.6	1,516	74
Marion County	FL	29,577	38,562	39,350	68.8	31.2	18.0	8.8	0.8	0.3	2,261	17.4	5,215	7.5	4.4	4.5	4.5	4.4	7.1	1,782	64
Martin County	FL	11,692	16,308	16,798	74.6	25.4	10.6	13.6	1.0	0.3	907	18.5	1,881	8.9	0.6	0.9	0.5	0.3	0.6	800	28
Miami-Dade County	FL	292,023	368,625	375,836	10.8	89.2	30.3	57.6	1.0	0.1	19,043	19.7	37,469	10.0	6.3	6.2	5.1	5.9	8.7	16,213	363
Okaloosa County	FL	26,140	30,344	30,903	80.3	19.7	13.0	3.5	2.7	0.5	1,706	18.1	3,570	8.7	4.3	3.1	3.3	4.3	7.1	1,832	50

See notes at end of table.

Selected statistics on enrollment, teachers, graduates, and dropouts in public school districts enrolling more than 15,000 students, by state: 1990, 2000, and 2001—Continued

Name of district, by state	State	Enrollment, fall 1990	Enrollment, fall 2000	Enrollment, fall 2001	White, non-Hispanic	Minority Total	Black, non-Hispanic	Hispanic	Asian/ Pacific Islander	American Indian/ Alaska Native	Number of classroom teachers, fall 2001	Pupil/ teacher ratio, fall 2001	Total number of staff, fall 2001	Student/ staff ratio, fall 2001	Dropouts Total	Grade 9	Grade 10	Grade 11	Grade 12	Number of high school graduates, 2000–01[2]	Number of schools, fall 2001
1	2	3	4	5	6	7	8	9	10	11	12	13	14	15	16	17	18	19	20	21	22
Orange County	FL	102,672	150,681	157,433	42.6	57.4	28.9	24.5	3.6	0.4	8,946	17.6	19,092	8.2	5.9	7.6	5.1	4.5	4.9	6,650	184
Osceola County	FL	19,514	34,566	37,779	47.3	52.7	9.5	40.5	2.5	0.2	1,709	22.1	4,164	9.1	5.2	4.1	4.6	5.9	7.8	1,552	48
Palm Beach County	FL	105,712	153,871	160,223	48.3	51.7	30.0	19.0	2.2	0.5	8,678	18.5	17,624	9.1	3.0	3.0	3.9	2.3	2.3	6,938	193
Pasco County	FL	33,891	49,704	52,675	86.4	13.6	4.0	8.1	1.1	0.3	2,987	17.6	6,787	7.8	5.4	5.1	6.0	4.9	5.7	2,057	66
Pinellas County	FL	92,976	113,027	114,583	71.9	28.1	19.1	5.6	3.1	0.3	6,480	17.7	13,932	8.2	5.0	6.1	5.1	3.9	3.5	4,996	169
Polk County	FL	64,579	79,477	81,207	62.5	37.5	23.2	13.2	1.0	0.2	4,851	16.7	10,482	7.7	6.9	6.0	6.1	7.1	9.4	3,440	142
Saint Johns County	FL	12,080	20,090	20,954	86.3	13.7	10.2	2.3	1.1	0.2	1,156	18.1	2,467	8.5	2.8	2.2	3.0	1.9	3.6	994	34
Saint Lucie County	FL	22,224	29,540	30,590	56.9	43.1	29.8	11.7	1.2	0.4	1,934	15.8	4,254	7.2	2.1	2.4	1.7	1.9	1.5	1,155	42
Santa Rosa County	FL	15,708	22,633	23,233	90.6	9.4	5.5	1.9	1.4	0.6	1,265	18.4	2,283	10.2	2.4	3.6	3.9	2.9	3.7	1,077	37
Sarasota County	FL	26,881	35,533	37,147	80.5	19.5	9.7	8.1	1.4	0.3	1,937	19.2	4,308	8.6	3.5	3.6	3.9	2.9	3.7	1,817	48
Seminole County	FL	48,831	60,869	62,786	69.1	30.9	13.9	13.7	3.0	0.3	3,394	18.5	6,602	9.5	1.0	0.9	1.0	1.0	1.2	3,329	72
Volusia County	FL	48,342	61,557	62,599	73.3	26.7	15.4	9.9	1.1	0.2	3,806	16.4	8,292	7.5	1.7	1.3	1.8	1.8	1.8	3,004	92
Atlanta City	GA	60,714	58,230	56,586	6.8	93.2	89.2	3.1	0.8	0.1	3,742	15.1	7,277	7.8	21.9	19.9	19.0	21.4	30.2	1,828	97
Bibb County	GA	24,378	24,739	24,675	27.2	72.8	70.8	0.9	0.9	0.1	1,449	17.0	3,049	8.1	12.6	17.8	11.8	19.2	11.8	820	42
Chatham County	GA	34,044	35,344	34,681	30.4	69.6	65.6	2.0	1.8	0.2	2,164	16.0	4,100	8.5	11.3	13.4	11.6	10.5	7.4	1,191	49
Cherokee County	GA	16,086	26,043	27,110	89.0	11.0	3.7	6.0	1.1	0.2	1,676	16.2	3,202	8.5	5.0	1.0	3.3	5.5	13.6	1,214	31
Clayton County	GA	34,754	46,930	48,232	19.3	80.7	68.8	7.2	4.6	0.1	2,556	18.9	5,829	8.3	9.1	9.2	8.8	8.9	9.8	1,700	49
Cobb County	GA	69,441	95,781	98,338	63.0	37.0	25.0	8.1	3.6	0.1	6,388	15.4	12,074	8.1	3.8	2.9	4.0	4.2	4.3	5,223	96
Columbia County	GA	14,096	18,756	19,149	81.6	18.4	13.2	1.9	3.2	0.1	1,128	17.0	2,342	8.2	5.1	4.9	5.1	5.4	5.3	1,016	24
Coweta County	GA	10,430	16,766	17,515	72.9	27.1	23.9	2.5	0.7	0.1	1,103	15.9	2,319	7.6	3.5	4.2	3.1	3.3	3.1	706	23
DeKalb County	GA	74,108	95,958	97,501	12.1	87.9	77.5	6.5	3.8	0.1	6,417	15.2	12,889	7.6	7.6	7.8	6.8	7.5	7.4	4,073	129
Dougherty County	GA	18,482	17,489	16,710	15.8	84.2	83.2	0.5	0.4	0.1	1,042	16.0	2,401	7.0	11.4	13.1	12.0	10.0	8.4	645	26
Douglas County	GA	14,002	16,799	18,101	68.3	31.7	27.0	3.2	1.3	0.2	1,058	17.1	2,182	8.3	3.1	3.4	6.5	5.9	6.0	776	25
Fayette County	GA	13,105	19,590	20,318	79.2	20.8	15.1	2.6	3.0	0.1	1,380	14.7	2,556	7.9	2.1	1.6	2.9	2.0	2.1	1,374	24
Forsyth County	GA	7,742	17,131	18,860	93.1	6.9	0.5	5.4	0.8	0.2	1,220	15.5	2,407	7.8	4.9	3.8	4.6	6.3	7.2	652	21
Fulton County	GA	41,195	68,583	69,841	47.5	52.5	39.0	7.0	5.9	0.1	4,639	15.1	9,210	7.6	5.2	4.8	4.8	5.4	4.7	3,298	77
Gwinnett County	GA	63,930	110,075	116,339	60.2	39.8	18.1	12.2	8.9	0.5	7,598	15.3	13,725	8.5	1.5	1.4	1.5	1.5	1.7	5,913	86
Hall County	GA	13,738	20,330	21,115	70.9	29.1	5.8	22.0	0.9	0.4	1,222	17.3	2,304	9.2	4.7	1.1	4.4	6.0	8.2	754	29
Henry County	GA	10,929	23,601	25,503	73.8	26.2	21.7	2.5	1.9	0.1	1,432	17.8	2,888	8.8	6.1	1.2	7.2	6.7	4.4	1,079	28
Houston County	GA	16,249	21,529	22,189	63.2	36.8	32.4	2.5	1.7	0.2	1,472	15.1	2,885	7.7	5.9	6.0	5.8	6.2	4.4	1,097	34
Muscogee County	GA	30,038	32,916	32,910	35.2	64.8	60.5	2.9	1.3	0.4	2,075	15.9	4,718	7.0	6.8	6.9	6.8	6.7	8.5	1,430	51
Paulding County	GA	7,604	16,587	18,048	87.0	13.0	10.7	1.7	0.4	0.2	1,098	16.4	2,114	8.5	5.7	6.0	6.2	6.0	12.5	581	21
Richmond County	GA	33,660	35,424	35,104	27.1	72.9	69.7	2.0	1.0	0.1	2,143	16.4	4,507	7.8	6.1	5.5	6.6	6.0	6.5	1,418	55
Hawaii Dept of Education	HI	171,309	184,360	184,546	20.3	79.7	2.4	4.5	72.3	0.4	11,007	16.8	19,463	9.5	5.7	3.9	5.8	6.2	7.8	10,102	279
Boise City Independent	ID	14,802	26,598	26,778	89.0	11.0	1.6	5.8	3.1	0.5	1,508	17.8	2,767	9.7	9.0	7.1	10.2	10.6	8.0	1,740	53
Meridian Junction	ID		23,854	25,226	92.6	7.4	1.2	3.7	2.2	0.3	1,285	19.6	2,244	11.2	5.0	4.5	4.4	5.5	6.0	1,408	36
City of Chicago	IL	408,714	435,261	437,418	9.5	90.5	51.3	35.8	3.2	0.2	24,064	18.2	28,430	15.4	16.8	19.9	17.2	15.7	11.4	14,091	599
Community Unit 300	IL	7,670	23,173	24,347	71.0	29.0	4.3	21.8	2.5	0.5	1,383	17.6	1,884	12.9	3.4	1.6	3.7	1.5	4.5	941	22
Indian Prairie	IL	16,212	18,762	18,961	77.6	22.4	7.0	4.8	10.4	0.2	1,091	15.2	1,313	14.4	0.9	0.1	0.6	0.9	2.1	1,114	30
Naperville	IL	17,378	18,961	19,596	81.8	18.2	2.6	3.1	12.4	0.1	1,313	15.4	1,279	14.4	1.0	0.1	0.5	0.9	2.7	1,279	21
Peoria	IL	15,583	15,724	15,721	38.4	61.6	56.7	1.9	2.9	0.1	1,285	14.1	1,285	12.2	11.9	11.2	10.2	14.6	12.0	836	45
Rockford	IL	27,726	27,399	27,691	52.9	47.1	31.3	11.1	3.6	1.1	1,712	16.2	2,086	13.3	7.6	7.5	7.1	6.1	9.7	1,221	53
Schaumburg	IL		15,575	15,354	65.1	34.9	7.0	11.5	16.2	0.2	966	15.9	1,154	13.3	†	†	†	†	†	†	27
School District 46	IL	27,255	36,767	37,998	47.1	52.9	9.7	39.8	3.2	0.2	2,331	16.3	2,702	14.1	3.7	2.1	5.3	3.9	3.6	1,872	51
Springfield	IL	15,813	15,387	15,454	62.0	38.0	34.8	1.8	1.3	0.1	978	15.8	1,191	13.0	1.5	0.8	1.6	2.8	1.2	844	36
Waukegan	IL	12,116	15,510	16,242	11.7	88.3	22.9	63.0	2.3	0.1	842	19.3	994	16.3	2.5	0.8	4.1	2.7	3.0	625	24
Evansville-Vanderburgh SC	IN	22,918	22,875	22,936	83.0	17.0	15.4	0.7	0.7	0.2	1,472	15.6	2,935	7.8	—	—	—	—	—	1,402	43
Fort Wayne Community	IN	31,611	31,843	32,081	63.5	36.5	26.5	7.1	2.2	0.7	1,806	17.8	3,635	8.8	—	—	—	—	—	1,595	55
Gary Community SC	IN	26,620	19,206	18,282	0.3	99.7	98.2	1.3	0.1	0.1	1,022	17.9	2,850	6.4	—	—	—	—	—	861	38
Indianapolis	IN	48,140	41,008	41,195	33.1	66.9	59.9	6.5	0.4	0.1	2,679	15.4	5,323	7.7	—	—	—	—	—	1,464	92
MSD Lawrence Township	IN	11,066	15,692	15,992	63.5	36.5	30.2	4.1	2.1	0.1	914	17.5	2,055	7.8	—	—	—	—	—	850	19
South Bend Community SC	IN	21,425	21,536	21,603	50.6	49.4	36.5	11.0	1.3	0.5	1,346	16.0	3,077	7.0	—	—	—	—	—	1,123	38
Vigo County SC	IN	16,982	16,545	16,474	91.4	8.6	6.8	0.6	1.1	0.1	995	16.6	2,000	8.2	—	—	—	—	—	1,003	30
Cedar Rapids	IA	16,988	17,780	17,606	85.4	14.6	10.0	2.1	2.1	0.5	1,108	15.9	2,207	8.0	2.5	2.3	2.7	3.2	1.9	1,047	33
Davenport	IA	17,841	16,874	16,656	74.1	25.9	16.4	6.1	2.3	1.1	1,135	14.7	2,093	8.0	3.4	2.0	3.8	3.3	4.7	861	33
Des Moines Independent	IA	30,514	32,435	32,010	69.6	30.4	15.3	9.8	4.5	0.7	2,276	14.1	4,478	7.1	6.4	7.0	7.0	6.7	4.4	1,652	61
Blue Valley	KS	9,432	17,111	18,022	90.5	9.5	2.8	1.7	4.8	0.3	1,200	15.0	2,242	8.0	0.7	0.1	0.3	1.1	1.5	1,167	28

See notes at end of table.

Selected statistics on enrollment, teachers, graduates, and dropouts in public school districts enrolling more than 15,000 students, by state: 1990, 2000, and 2001—Continued

Name of district, by state	State	Enrollment, fall 1990	Enrollment, fall 2000	Enrollment, fall 2001	Percentage distribution of enrollment, by race, fall 2001 — White, non-Hispanic	Minority — Total	Minority — Black, non-Hispanic	Minority — Hispanic	Minority — Asian/Pacific Islander	Minority — American Indian/Alaska Native	Number of classroom teachers, fall 2001	Pupil/teacher ratio, fall 2001	Total number of staff, fall 2001	Student/staff ratio, 2001	Percent dropouts from grades 9-12, 2000-01[1] — Total	Grade 9	Grade 10	Grade 11	Grade 12	Number of high school graduates, 2000-01[2]	Number of schools, fall 2001
1	2	3	4	5	6	7	8	9	10	11	12	13	14	15	16	17	18	19	20	21	22
Kansas City	KS	21,948	21,173	21,217	22.6	77.4	50.8	22.6	3.5	0.5	1,544	13.7	2,955	7.2	6.7	4.3	8.5	8.3	6.4	896	42
Olathe	KS	14,868	20,703	21,564	86.1	13.9	5.6	4.6	3.3	0.5	1,482	14.6	2,784	7.7	2.0	0.1	1.6	2.7	3.6	1,260	38
Shawnee Mission	KS	30,563	30,765	30,381	86.3	13.7	5.1	5.2	2.9	0.5	1,964	15.5	3,808	8.0	2.1	0.7	1.8	2.8	3.2	2,245	54
Wichita	KS	46,847	48,228	48,852	51.5	48.5	23.4	17.0	5.5	2.6	3,095	15.8	5,800	8.4	8.0	5.6	7.9	8.3	11.0	2,218	92
Fayette County	KY	32,083	33,130	33,799	70.3	29.7	23.3	3.6	2.7	0.1	2,413	14.0	4,903	6.9	6.2	7.2	5.2	4.9	7.2	1,673	65
Jefferson County	KY	91,450	96,860	93,516	62.5	37.5	34.3	1.8	1.3	0.1	5,374	17.4	13,508	6.9	6.7	5.8	7.7	8.4	4.8	5,140	172
Ascension Parish School Board	LA	13,001	15,038	15,159	67.1	32.9	29.6	2.5	0.4	0.4	1,038	14.6	2,053	7.4	6.2	8.0	5.7	5.4	5.3	787	21
Bossier Parish SB	LA	17,804	18,797	18,595	66.0	34.0	29.7	2.6	1.5	0.2	1,134	16.4	2,342	7.9	6.2	8.0	7.0	4.8	8.9	988	36
Caddo Parish SB	LA	51,375	45,119	44,859	35.8	64.2	62.6	0.6	0.7	0.2	3,013	14.9	6,696	6.7	10.6	9.8	9.9	9.8	14.0	2,243	74
Calcasieu Parish SB	LA	32,917	32,261	31,644	65.1	34.9	32.6	0.6	0.6	0.2	2,189	14.6	4,377	7.0	9.6	5.7	6.2	5.7	14.0	1,896	59
East Baton Rouge Parish SB	LA	61,669	54,246	52,350	26.0	74.0	71.1	0.8	2.0	#	3,567	14.7	7,182	7.3	9.6	9.5	9.7	10.5	8.5	2,835	106
Jefferson Parish SB	LA	58,177	50,891	50,766	38.4	61.6	48.8	8.0	4.2	0.5	3,399	14.9	7,075	7.2	8.6	12.6	12.0	10.6	7.1	2,433	85
Lafayette Parish SB	LA	29,403	28,931	29,310	59.0	41.0	38.4	1.1	1.3	0.2	1,936	15.1	3,574	8.2	8.6	10.9	9.4	5.9	7.3	1,620	44
Lafourche Parish SB	LA	16,173	15,165	15,085	72.0	28.0	21.9	1.0	1.0	3.7	1,143	13.2	2,183	6.9	5.5	4.9	6.7	6.1	4.5	844	28
Livingston Parish SB	LA	16,310	19,723	19,853	93.6	6.4	5.5	0.6	0.2	0.1	1,251	15.9	2,362	8.4	5.0	1.3	7.5	9.0	0.5	1,023	36
Orleans Parish SB	LA	82,925	77,610	73,185	3.8	96.2	93.0	1.2	2.0	0.1	4,552	16.1	8,808	8.3	11.4	13.9	9.0	6.9	14.6	3,450	130
Ouachita Parish SB	LA	17,667	17,479	17,760	71.8	28.2	27.0	0.7	0.5	0.1	1,236	14.4	2,511	7.1	8.4	8.4	7.5	6.9	9.3	826	53
Rapides Parish SB	LA	24,765	23,467	22,996	54.0	46.0	43.1	0.5	0.9	1.1	1,574	14.6	3,235	7.0	6.9	6.4	5.2	6.7	6.9	1,295	33
Saint Landry Parish SB	LA	17,213	15,457	15,327	44.5	55.5	54.6	0.5	0.2	0.1	1,072	14.3	2,190	7.1	6.1	6.7	7.3	7.3	6.0	797	38
Saint Tammany Parish SB	LA	27,522	32,392	32,834	81.4	18.6	16.0	1.5	0.9	0.1	2,275	14.4	4,623	8.0	8.0	8.5	9.0	8.5	9.0	1,800	51
Tangipahoa Parish SB	LA	16,724	18,197	18,075	54.2	45.8	44.3	0.4	0.4	0.5	1,080	16.7	2,252	8.6	8.6	6.4	9.0	9.9	7.6	948	37
Terrebonne Parish SB	LA	21,116	19,774	19,401	62.0	38.0	27.7	1.0	1.3	8.1	1,405	13.8	2,728	7.1	9.9	10.5	9.2	9.9	9.7	1,102	42
Anne Arundel County	MD	65,011	74,491	75,081	74.3	25.7	20.1	2.5	2.9	0.3	4,440	16.9	7,940	9.5	4.5	4.1	4.9	5.2	3.8	4,344	119
Baltimore City	MD	108,663	99,859	97,817	10.2	89.8	88.0	0.9	0.6	0.3	6,303	15.5	10,660	9.2	12.5	12.6	13.0	12.0	12.4	4,342	177
Baltimore County	MD	86,737	106,898	107,212	59.7	40.3	33.7	1.0	4.0	0.5	6,857	15.6	13,023	8.2	2.9	2.8	2.8	3.3	2.8	6,553	170
Calvert County	MD	10,398	16,170	16,651	82.2	17.8	15.7	1.0	0.9	0.2	963	17.3	1,865	8.9	4.0	3.5	3.8	3.3	5.5	972	25
Carroll County	MD	21,835	27,528	28,127	95.4	4.6	2.4	0.9	1.1	0.2	1,582	17.8	2,752	10.2	2.3	1.4	2.0	2.6	3.3	1,739	41
Cecil County	MD	12,868	15,905	16,095	91.0	9.0	6.3	1.7	0.7	0.2	1,000	16.1	1,808	8.9	3.6	2.7	3.8	4.3	3.9	807	31
Charles County	MD	18,708	23,468	24,001	57.1	42.9	37.5	2.1	2.4	1.0	1,352	17.8	2,415	9.9	3.5	3.2	4.1	3.8	2.8	1,509	34
Frederick County	MD	26,848	36,885	38,022	85.5	14.5	9.1	2.9	2.2	0.5	2,320	16.4	4,174	9.1	3.0	1.7	2.8	4.3	4.8	2,294	57
Harford County	MD	31,500	39,520	39,966	80.1	19.8	14.8	2.4	2.4	0.3	2,526	15.8	4,242	9.4	2.0	1.7	3.7	3.5	3.5	2,285	51
Howard County	MD	29,949	44,946	46,257	68.7	31.3	17.8	2.9	10.4	0.3	3,107	14.9	5,816	8.0	1.8	1.7	2.3	2.3	2.1	2,916	68
Montgomery County	MD	103,757	134,180	136,895	47.4	52.6	21.1	17.2	13.9	0.3	8,662	15.8	17,211	8.0	3.2	2.3	1.9	2.2	1.8	7,993	193
Prince George's County	MD	108,868	133,723	135,039	10.3	89.7	77.4	8.6	3.2	0.5	8,067	16.7	15,310	8.8	3.1	4.0	2.8	2.4	3.3	7,428	196
Saint Mary's County	MD	12,549	15,151	15,482	76.7	23.3	18.8	1.8	2.2	0.5	954	16.2	1,648	9.4	3.2	2.5	3.7	2.7	3.8	847	27
Washington County	MD	17,778	19,782	19,961	88.5	11.5	8.5	1.6	1.2	0.2	1,329	15.0	2,294	8.7	4.0	4.2	4.1	4.0	3.8	1,213	46
Boston	MA	60,543	63,024	62,141	14.7	85.3	47.5	28.4	8.9	0.4	5,466	11.4	10,462	5.9	8.1	11.0	5.8	8.7	7.5	3,239	134
Brockton	MA	14,529	16,791	16,755	41.3	58.7	43.3	11.4	3.0	0.9	1,432	11.7	2,530	6.6	5.7	6.0	7.1	6.3	2.5	707	25
Lowell	MA	13,488	15,989	15,162	44.3	55.7	4.7	20.5	30.5	#	1,333	11.4	2,267	6.7	9.8	11.9	10.2	6.6	9.9	566	29
Lynn	MA	11,914	15,318	15,248	41.9	58.1	15.3	28.9	13.8	0.2	1,061	14.4	1,911	8.0	3.9	3.6	5.3	3.8	2.4	723	30
Springfield	MA	24,194	26,526	25,091	23.0	77.0	29.1	45.3	2.4	0.2	—	—	—	—	8.0	9.1	7.8	7.7	7.0	1,173	49
Worcester	MA	21,066	25,828	25,826	51.5	48.5	11.2	28.7	8.0	0.6	2,336	11.1	4,229	6.1	6.3	6.5	4.7	6.5	7.5	1,123	50
Ann Arbor	MI	14,199	16,539	16,772	68.9	31.1	15.6	3.2	11.8	0.5	964	17.4	2,003	8.4	—	—	—	—	—	1,157	33
Dearborn City	MI	13,380	17,129	18,439	94.7	5.3	2.1	1.8	0.9	0.3	1,052	17.5	2,207	8.3	—	—	—	—	—	1,008	30
Detroit City	MI	168,116	162,194	166,675	3.5	96.5	90.8	4.5	0.9	0.3	9,053	18.4	20,147	8.3	—	—	—	—	—	6,068	265
Flint City	MI	27,601	25,625	22,218	19.1	80.9	75.9	2.5	0.5	2.0	1,381	16.1	2,855	7.8	—	—	—	—	—	752	46
Grand Rapids City	MI	26,250	22,803	22,803	31.8	68.2	41.8	22.7	1.7	2.0	1,428	16.0	2,890	7.9	—	—	—	—	—	788	96
Lansing Public	MI	21,350	17,610	17,372	39.8	60.2	39.4	14.5	5.1	1.2	1,057	16.4	2,176	8.0	—	—	—	—	—	689	44
Livonia	MI	16,373	18,347	19,678	92.6	7.4	3.2	1.7	2.2	0.3	996	19.8	2,213	8.9	—	—	—	—	—	1,274	36
Plymouth-Canton Community Schools	MI	14,955	16,518	16,671	84.6	15.4	4.2	1.7	9.0	0.5	830	20.1	1,804	9.2	—	—	—	—	—	1,044	24
Utica Community	MI	23,960	27,786	28,304	90.5	9.5	1.3	2.6	5.1	0.5	1,512	18.7	3,077	9.2	—	—	—	—	—	1,792	42
Anoka-Hennepin	MN	34,524	41,314	41,419	90.0	10.0	3.7	1.6	3.6	1.1	2,229	18.6	4,274	9.7	4.0	0.4	1.8	4.6	9.5	2,439	59
Minneapolis	MN	36,763	48,834	48,155	26.6	73.4	43.9	11.1	14.3	4.1	3,311	14.5	6,254	7.7	13.7	9.6	14.3	15.4	16.9	1,999	144
Osseo	MN	19,483	22,017	22,041	72.7	27.3	14.2	2.5	9.7	0.8	1,283	17.2	2,547	8.7	—	—	—	—	—	1,304	30
Rochester	MN	13,897	15,929	16,030	79.2	20.8	8.5	3.4	8.5	0.4	872	18.4	1,519	10.6	4.0	2.4	3.7	5.4	4.9	1,067	37
Rosemount-Apple Valley-Eagan	MN	17,029	28,330	28,364	87.3	12.7	4.8	2.1	5.2	0.5	1,701	16.7	3,099	9.2	1.8	0.4	1.1	2.1	3.8	1,784	37

See notes at end of table.

Selected statistics on enrollment, teachers, graduates, and dropouts in public school districts enrolling more than 15,000 students, by state: 1990, 2000, and 2001—Continued

Name of district, by state	State	Enrollment, fall 1990	Enrollment, fall 2000	Enrollment, fall 2001	Percentage distribution of enrollment, by race, fall 2001						Number of classroom teachers, fall 2001	Pupil/ teacher ratio, fall 2001	Total number of staff, fall 2001	Student/ staff ratio, fall 2001	Percent dropouts from grades 9–12, 2000–01 [1]					Number of high school graduates, 2000–01 [2]	Number of schools, fall 2001
					White, non-His-panic	Total	Black, non-His-panic	His-panic	Asian/ Pacific Islander	American Indian/ Alaska Native					Total	Grade 9	Grade 10	Grade 11	Grade 12		
1	2	3	4	5	6	7	8	9	10	11	12	13	14	15	16	17	18	19	20	21	22
St Paul	MN	32,366	45,115	44,194	31.9	68.1	25.2	10.5	30.6	1.8	3,000	14.7	6,611	6.7	8.8	2.6	5.1	9.1	18.0	2,268	125
South Washington County	MN	11,260	14,953	15,138	88.5	11.5	4.1	2.7	4.2	0.6	915	16.5	1,758	8.6	2.7	0.1	0.6	2.6	7.6	1,061	22
Desoto County	MS	13,470	19,812	20,920	78.9	21.1	17.5	2.6	0.9	0.2	1,082	19.3	2,211	9.5	2.1	0.3	4.4	4.7	#	874	24
Jackson Public	MS	33,546	31,351	31,436	4.4	95.6	95.0	0.3	0.3	0.1	1,870	16.8	4,409	7.1	4.9	5.7	4.4	4.7	4.4	1,203	60
Rankin County	MS	12,824	15,013	15,292	77.6	22.4	21.0	0.7	0.6	0.1	919	16.6	1,752	8.7	2.1	2.0	1.7	2.4	2.7	733	23
Columbia	MO	12,786	16,178	16,547	73.8	26.2	19.5	2.1	4.2	0.4	1,267	13.1	2,340	7.1	4.7	1.5	4.2	7.1	6.6	941	30
Fort Zumwalt R-11	MO	10,110	16,521	17,281	94.6	5.4	3.4	1.1	0.8	0.1	1,052	16.4	2,091	8.3	2.7	1.8	3.6	4.0	1.3	952	21
Francis Howell	MO	13,391	19,497	19,390	93.0	7.0	4.3	1.1	1.2	0.5	1,134	17.1	2,100	9.2	2.1	1.1	3.1	2.8	1.8	1,240	23
Hazelwood	MO	16,985	18,855	19,327	46.5	53.5	51.6	0.8	1.0	0.1	1,165	16.6	2,408	8.0	3.4	2.5	3.6	4.3	3.3	1,231	25
Kansas City	MO	34,486	37,298	38,558	14.3	85.7	71.9	11.5	2.0	0.3	2,568	15.0	4,642	7.5	6.7	8.8	7.1	5.3	2.7	1,214	88
North Kansas City	MO	15,732	17,258	17,247	85.6	14.4	5.8	5.0	2.8	0.7	1,201	14.4	2,300	7.5	3.7	2.4	2.5	5.0	5.4	1,091	31
Parkway	MO	21,542	20,433	20,525	73.0	27.0	17.3	1.5	8.1	0.2	1,225	16.8	2,452	8.4	1.8	0.7	1.5	2.6	2.6	1,454	28
Rockwood	MO	15,608	21,203	21,644	83.7	16.3	12.6	0.9	2.6	0.1	1,325	16.3	2,397	9.0	2.4	1.2	3.4	2.7	2.5	1,408	29
Saint Louis City	MO	43,284	44,412	43,969	15.9	84.1	81.5	1.1	1.3	0.1	3,453	12.7	6,478	6.8	9.4	11.1	9.9	8.7	5.4	1,490	123
Springfield	MO	23,631	24,630	24,647	89.8	10.2	5.3	2.2	2.0	0.6	1,534	16.1	2,838	8.7	5.4	4.8	4.8	9.6	6.1	1,513	56
Lincoln	NE	27,986	31,354	31,581	84.4	15.6	6.6	4.2	3.5	1.3	2,320	13.6	4,385	7.2	6.5	1.0	5.7	8.1	11.4	1,927	66
Millard	NE	16,764	19,160	19,329	94.0	6.0	1.7	1.8	2.2	0.3	1,249	15.5	2,324	8.3	1.6	#	0.9	1.8	3.7	1,431	34
Omaha	NE	41,699	45,197	45,782	50.7	49.3	31.5	14.6	1.7	1.5	3,100	14.8	6,369	7.2	9.9	11.8	10.2	9.0	7.4	2,244	83
Clark County	NV	121,959	231,655	245,659	47.7	52.3	13.9	30.5	7.0	0.8	12,514	19.6	20,573	11.9	6.1	3.9	1.7	5.6	15.0	9,594	275
Washoe County	NV	38,466	56,268	58,532	63.8	36.2	3.6	24.3	5.7	2.6	3,570	16.4	7,192	8.1	4.3	2.1	0.9	5.7	9.6	2,669	95
Manchester	NH	14,604	17,407	17,438	85.7	14.3	3.8	7.6	2.4	0.4	1,105	15.8	1,885	9.3	7.5	6.2	6.3	9.2	9.2	1,140	22
Camden City	NJ	19,497	17,517	17,430	1.3	98.7	55.9	40.7	1.9	0.2	1,599	10.9	3,485	5.0	33.3	52.8	27.9	22.5	13.5	564	33
Elizabeth City	NJ	15,266	19,674	20,014	12.5	87.5	24.3	60.9	2.4	#	1,829	10.9	3,420	6.3	6.3	7.3	7.8	4.0	4.3	1,010	26
Jersey City	NJ	28,585	31,347	31,493	9.4	90.6	36.9	39.3	13.6	0.8	2,576	12.2	5,146	6.1	6.1	7.1	6.9	5.9	3.3	1,433	39
Newark City	NJ	48,433	42,150	42,241	8.6	91.4	59.8	30.7	0.8	0.1	3,567	11.8	7,278	5.8	5.8	6.5	6.5	7.7	5.1	1,723	76
Paterson City	NJ	22,109	24,629	25,446	6.2	93.8	38.5	52.8	2.5	#	2,140	11.9	3,726	6.8	14.2	16.8	17.9	8.6	6.2	974	36
Tom's River Regional	NJ	16,002	17,621	18,050	90.6	9.4	3.1	4.1	2.2	0.1	1,149	15.7	2,118	8.5	3.0	0.7	2.9	4.2	4.7	1,257	17
Albuquerque	NM	88,295	85,276	87,201	38.9	61.1	3.8	50.6	2.0	4.7	5,847	14.9	11,353	7.7	8.6	9.5	9.3	9.0	5.8	4,547	138
Las Cruces	NM	19,216	22,185	22,414	29.3	70.7	2.3	66.5	1.1	0.9	1,682	13.3	3,290	6.8	5.4	6.5	6.0	4.6	4.1	1,281	37
Brentwood Unified	NY	11,749	15,565	16,144	17.6	82.4	22.4	58.1	1.9	0.1	1,020	15.8	2,070	7.8	2.1	#	2.3	3.3	2.9	799	17
Buffalo City	NY	47,235	45,721	44,849	27.5	72.5	58.1	11.7	1.2	1.4	3,511	12.8	6,400	7.0	6.5	1.2	1.6	2.1	2.3	1,308	76
New York City	NY	944,113	1,066,516	1,049,831	15.3	84.7	34.4	37.9	12.2	0.4	65,804	16.0	129,139	8.1	6.5	9.6	8.4	11.5	5.7	39,577	1218
Rochester City	NY	32,705	36,294	36,235	15.3	84.8	64.8	19.1	1.8	0.2	3,169	11.4	5,709	6.3	9.9	9.9	8.4	14.6	6.6	925	62
Sachem CSD	NY	15,187	14,948	15,137	91.0	9.0	1.0	4.8	3.1	0.1	1,122	13.5	1,901	8.0	1.7	0.1	0.4	4.2	2.7	865	15
Syracuse City	NY	22,432	23,015	22,796	44.2	55.8	46.3	6.9	1.5	1.1	1,837	12.4	4,003	5.7	5.5	4.0	4.7	8.6	6.8	524	35
Yonkers City	NY	18,621	26,237	26,447	19.8	80.2	30.0	44.4	5.7	0.2	1,899	13.9	4,002	6.6	1.9	2.3	1.9	4.2	1.9	952	39
Alamance-Burlington	NC	10,322	20,729	21,318	61.5	38.5	26.9	9.9	1.4	0.3	1,374	15.5	2,455	8.7	6.7	6.5	7.1	7.1	7.7	916	33
Buncombe County	NC	22,026	24,708	24,762	88.2	11.8	7.5	3.2	0.7	0.5	1,531	16.2	3,071	8.1	6.1	5.6	5.1	6.7	4.5	1,306	39
Cabarrus County	NC	12,853	19,115	20,183	77.7	22.3	15.2	5.6	1.1	0.4	1,310	15.4	2,417	8.4	4.9	5.0	6.1	3.5	4.7	986	25
Catawba County Schools	NC	12,770	16,250	16,379	77.7	22.3	8.1	4.8	7.2	0.2	1,017	16.1	1,922	8.5	6.5	5.6	6.7	8.7	5.2	854	22
Charlotte-Mecklenburg	NC	77,069	103,336	106,312	44.7	55.3	43.6	6.8	4.4	0.5	6,927	15.3	13,897	7.6	7.4	8.0	7.6	6.3	7.2	4,723	137
Cumberland County	NC	44,612	50,850	51,434	42.1	57.9	49.0	5.5	1.6	1.7	3,245	15.9	6,235	8.2	4.8	7.6	6.0	4.6	2.5	2,702	83
Davidson County	NC	16,426	19,136	19,248	95.1	4.9	2.7	1.3	0.7	0.3	1,136	16.9	2,101	9.2	6.8	7.9	8.1	5.9	5.0	990	28
Durham	NC	18,517	29,728	30,574	30.8	69.2	59.0	8.4	2.4	0.2	2,140	14.3	3,670	8.3	4.8	4.8	6.2	4.7	3.7	1,395	44
Forsyth County	NC	37,625	44,769	45,707	50.8	49.2	37.6	7.6	1.3	0.7	3,146	14.5	5,367	8.5	5.2	4.9	5.1	7.1	7.8	2,207	68
Gaston County	NC	29,631	30,603	30,973	74.5	25.5	20.5	4.1	0.4	0.9	1,832	16.9	3,656	8.5	7.1	5.8	6.7	4.3	5.6	1,395	52
Guilford County	NC	24,575	63,417	64,546	48.2	51.8	42.9	5.1	2.5	0.4	4,047	15.9	7,971	8.1	8.0	6.7	8.4	5.2	3.8	3,078	101
Harnett County	NC	11,890	16,338	16,577	59.6	40.4	32.2	6.9	0.4	0.9	1,056	15.7	2,055	8.8	4.6	4.9	5.1	4.3	5.1	697	25
Iredell-Statesville	NC	10,610	17,253	17,839	73.9	26.1	18.3	5.1	1.1	0.4	1,024	17.4	2,029	8.8	6.8	5.8	8.4	8.8	8.2	835	32
Johnston County	NC	14,647	21,334	22,425	67.8	32.2	22.6	8.9	0.4	0.3	1,529	14.7	2,939	7.6	6.0	4.4	6.7	8.2	6.6	893	31
Nash-Rocky Mount	NC	11,653	18,342	18,307	39.3	60.7	55.0	4.2	1.1	0.3	1,243	14.7	2,431	7.9	7.9	5.8	7.9	7.4	3.9	897	27
New Hanover County	NC	19,090	21,792	21,792	64.1	35.9	29.8	1.9	1.6	1.2	1,431	15.2	2,984	7.3	5.6	4.4	4.5	5.3	6.6	1,170	35
Onslow County	NC	18,605	20,984	21,176	64.1	35.9	28.8	4.3	1.2	0.2	1,335	15.9	2,757	7.7	5.1	5.0	4.7	5.9	5.1	1,132	33
Pitt County	NC	17,669	20,040	20,528	43.7	56.3	51.8	3.1	1.2	0.2	1,285	16.0	2,474	8.3	5.0	5.5	7.8	8.7	8.2	973	32
Randolph County	NC	13,572	17,271	17,738	86.9	13.1	6.0	6.0	0.6	0.2	1,071	16.0	2,141	8.3	7.0	6.5	8.3	7.7	5.2	797	27
Robeson County	NC	23,251	23,911	23,998	21.2	78.8	31.7	3.6	0.3	43.1	1,490	16.1	3,083	7.8	10.9	10.4	14.3	10.2	7.4	959	41

See notes at end of table.

Selected statistics on enrollment, teachers, graduates, and dropouts in public school districts enrolling more than 15,000 students, by state: 1990, 2000, and 2001—Continued

Name of district, by state	State	Enrollment, fall 1990	Enrollment, fall 2000	Enrollment, fall 2001	White, non-His-panic	Minority Total	Black, non-His-panic	His-panic	Asian/ Pacific Islander	American Indian/ Alaska Native	Number of classroom teachers, fall 2001	Pupil/ teacher ratio, fall 2001	Total number of staff, fall 2001	Student/ staff ratio, fall 2001	Dropouts Total	Grade 9	Grade 10	Grade 11	Grade 12	Number of high school grad-uates, 2000–01[2]	Number of schools, fall 2001
1	2	3	4	5	6	7	8	9	10	11	12	13	14	15	16	17	18	19	20	21	22
Rowan-Salisbury	NC	16,403	20,472	20,823	70.3	29.7	23.5	4.6	1.3	0.3	1,364	15.3	2,624	7.9	5.8	4.9	6.0	6.8	5.6	1,005	30
Union County	NC	12,864	22,862	24,152	74.9	25.1	17.7	6.4	0.7	0.3	1,452	16.6	2,845	8.5	5.0	4.3	6.0	5.3	4.4	1,059	33
Wake County	NC	64,266	98,950	101,756	61.5	38.5	28.5	5.6	4.1	0.3	6,408	15.9	11,804	8.6	4.0	4.3	4.2	3.9	3.5	5,140	120
Wayne County	NC	13,653	19,279	19,267	48.8	51.2	44.6	5.4	1.1	0.2	1,233	15.6	2,476	7.8	5.2	4.5	5.4	6.0	5.0	1,025	31
Akron City	OH	33,213	31,464	29,676	48.8	51.2	48.4	0.8	1.9	0.1	2,549	11.6	5,553	5.3	6.4	6.6	5.0	6.3	7.9	1,520	62
Cincinnati City	OH	50,394	46,562	42,774	25.9	74.1	72.5	0.7	0.8	0.1	3,167	13.5	5,871	7.3	5.0	8.5	7.6	7.0	5.0	1,247	76
Cleveland City	OH	68,924	75,684	72,199	18.8	81.2	71.3	8.9	0.7	0.4	6,619	10.9	12,352	5.8	19.6	20.1	20.0	18.5	19.0	1,880	125
Columbus City	OH	63,956	64,511	64,833	34.8	65.2	60.5	2.2	2.2	0.2	4,437	14.9	7,981	8.1	10.1	10.9	9.1	9.9	10.5	2,569	146
Dayton City	OH	28,000	23,522	20,547	27.2	71.4	70.4	1.0	0.4	0.1	1,437	14.3	2,921	7.0	1.4	1.9	1.5	0.9	0.5	843	42
Lakota Local SD	OH	9,356	14,659	15,498	88.3	11.7	5.7	1.7	4.2	0.1	982	15.8	1,940	8.0	0.5	#	0.7	0.9	0.4	920	17
South-Western City	OH	16,605	19,216	20,369	83.0	17.0	10.7	4.2	1.8	0.3	1,235	16.5	2,336	8.7	7.5	9.0	5.6	6.8	8.3	859	32
Toledo City	OH	40,126	37,738	36,495	45.6	54.4	46.6	7.0	0.7	0.1	2,686	13.6	4,811	7.6	7.8	8.9	8.1	6.5	6.7	1,728	66
Edmond	OK	13,041	17,064	17,481	83.9	16.1	7.5	2.5	2.6	3.5	1,034	16.9	1,852	9.4	3.1	2.5	3.8	2.3	5.2	1,165	22
Lawton	OK	17,727	17,338	17,034	51.0	49.0	31.4	9.0	2.2	6.4	1,072	15.9	2,159	7.9	2.8	1.1	3.8	3.4	2.9	996	38
Moore	OK	16,630	18,101	18,378	71.6	28.4	4.9	5.0	4.0	14.5	1,148	16.0	1,976	9.3	5.3	3.6	6.5	6.8	4.4	1,194	27
Oklahoma City	OK	36,038	39,750	40,240	30.4	69.6	36.7	24.6	2.7	5.6	2,637	15.3	5,089	7.9	12.5	19.0	10.3	10.3	4.4	1,448	97
Putnam City	OK	18,071	19,506	19,442	65.2	34.8	19.6	7.3	4.3	3.6	1,227	15.9	2,022	9.6	6.7	10.2	6.3	5.8	2.2	1,114	27
Tulsa	OK	40,732	42,812	42,302	43.1	56.9	35.6	11.3	1.3	8.6	2,793	15.1	5,963	7.1	9.6	10.5	9.4	9.4	8.8	1,866	84
Beaverton	OR	24,874	33,600	34,699	71.4	28.6	3.0	11.6	13.1	0.9	1,640	21.2	3,214	10.8	5.6	2.6	4.3	7.8	8.2	1,924	50
Eugene	OR	17,904	18,432	18,476	83.0	17.0	2.9	6.3	5.2	2.6	850	20.7	1,770	10.4	3.2	2.6	3.0	3.8	2.3	1,221	48
Hillsboro	OR	—	18,315	18,519	68.9	31.1	1.8	21.9	6.8	0.6	894	20.7	1,997	9.3	4.4	2.8	3.0	2.8	4.4	937	30
North Clackamas	OR	12,403	14,876	15,274	84.1	15.9	1.8	5.8	7.5	0.9	771	19.8	1,451	10.5	4.4	1.4	3.4	7.2	6.4	849	27
Portland	OR	53,042	53,141	52,908	60.4	39.6	16.6	10.0	10.7	2.3	3,016	17.5	5,749	9.2	11.9	9.6	10.9	13.1	14.7	2,704	107
Salem/Keizer	OR	27,756	35,108	36,163	73.1	26.9	1.5	20.3	3.4	1.6	1,705	21.2	3,461	10.4	7.5	3.4	5.9	6.6	15.3	1,854	65
Allentown City	PA	13,519	16,424	16,174	35.1	64.9	15.4	47.1	2.2	0.2	853	19.0	1,623	10.0	3.9	2.3	2.7	6.2	6.1	755	23
Central Bucks	PA	10,286	17,305	17,924	95.2	4.8	1.5	1.0	2.3	#	990	18.1	1,935	9.3	1.4	0.1	0.3	2.4	2.9	1,026	20
Philadelphia City	PA	190,978	201,190	197,083	15.9	84.1	65.4	13.5	5.0	0.2	10,686	18.4	24,981	7.9	9.2	6.8	9.9	10.7	11.6	9,362	263
Pittsburgh	PA	39,896	38,560	37,612	39.9	60.1	58.0	0.5	1.5	0.1	2,789	13.6	5,490	6.9	6.7	4.6	7.2	7.5	8.7	2,062	91
Reading	PA	11,965	15,487	16,726	25.2	74.8	15.7	57.9	1.2	#	903	18.5	1,739	9.6	13.0	7.3	16.4	17.2	14.5	522	19
Providence	RI	20,908	26,937	27,159	16.3	83.7	22.6	51.6	8.7	0.9	1,712	15.9	2,992	9.1	10.3	12.9	10.9	7.6	7.6	1,083	54
Aiken County	SC	23,964	25,147	24,433	61.2	38.8	35.4	2.5	0.7	0.3	1,549	15.8	1,802	13.6	3.1	3.0	2.8	3.6	1.8	1,118	39
Beaufort County	SC	12,525	16,721	17,038	46.7	53.3	43.4	8.8	0.9	0.4	1,222	13.9	1,360	12.5	3.4	2.0	3.0	5.4	4.7	682	24
Berkeley County	SC	27,392	26,635	26,836	59.4	40.6	36.6	2.4	1.7	0.4	1,761	15.2	2,068	13.0	4.0	3.6	4.8	4.2	3.7	1,278	35
Charleston County	SC	43,667	44,767	43,516	39.0	61.0	57.4	2.3	1.2	0.5	3,046	14.3	3,492	12.5	2.8	3.1	3.4	2.3	1.7	1,600	75
Dorchester	SC	13,737	16,678	17,004	68.8	31.2	28.0	1.4	1.2	0.3	1,079	15.8	1,272	13.4	3.5	3.7	4.3	3.4	2.0	805	16
Greenville County	SC	51,471	59,875	61,268	66.2	33.8	27.7	4.4	1.6	0.3	3,982	15.4	4,732	12.9	2.2	2.2	4.3	2.4	1.5	2,788	94
Horry County	SC	24,085	29,894	29,283	69.3	30.7	26.9	1.8	1.1	0.3	2,025	14.5	2,458	12.9	1.9	1.5	1.9	2.6	1.8	1,327	42
Lexington #01	SC	11,204	17,285	17,866	89.3	10.7	7.1	1.8	1.1	0.3	1,272	14.0	1,464	12.2	1.8	1.5	2.5	1.9	1.2	871	20
Pickens County	SC	14,298	15,938	16,170	88.5	11.5	8.8	1.6	0.8	0.1	1,068	15.1	1,213	13.3	4.7	5.9	4.3	4.2	3.7	654	25
Richland #01	SC	27,071	27,061	26,408	19.4	80.6	78.2	1.6	0.7	0.1	2,090	12.6	2,529	10.4	5.1	5.1	4.6	3.4	3.2	1,109	48
Richland #02	SC	12,792	17,409	18,213	41.4	58.6	52.7	3.2	2.5	0.2	1,231	14.8	1,436	12.7	3.7	2.4	5.5	2.9	4.1	974	21
York County	SC	12,690	14,925	15,304	59.1	40.9	35.1	2.4	1.6	1.7	977	15.7	1,146	13.4	1.6	7.3	1.5	1.3	3.8	609	23
Sioux Falls	SD	16,120	19,097	19,386	86.4	13.6	4.5	3.5	2.1	3.5	1,227	15.8	2,209	8.8	4.8	0.9	4.7	5.9	8.2	1,160	41
Hamilton County	TN	22,874	39,915	40,514	—	—	—	—	—	—	2,669	15.2	5,050	8.0	6.4	4.5	7.2	3.6	7.9	1,765	80
Knox County	TN	50,429	51,944	51,866	—	—	—	—	—	—	3,588	14.5	6,518	8.0	2.4	#	0.7	3.4	6.9	2,434	89
Memphis City	TN	106,223	113,730	115,992	—	—	—	—	—	—	7,155	16.2	12,853	9.0	9.2	7.7	8.9	10.3	11.0	3,791	174
Montgomery County	TN	17,532	23,339	24,256	—	—	—	—	—	—	1,537	15.8	2,904	8.4	3.5	2.1	2.1	5.5	5.3	861	30
Nashville-Davidson	TN	67,452	67,689	67,689	—	—	—	—	—	—	4,700	14.4	8,313	8.1	8.8	8.6	9.2	10.0	7.3	2,468	123
Rutherford County	TN	18,228	25,356	26,826	—	—	—	—	—	—	1,693	15.8	2,668	10.1	1.5	1.5	2.1	2.9	3.9	1,459	34
Shelby County	TN	37,605	46,972	44,547	—	—	—	—	—	—	2,517	17.7	4,835	9.2	3.0	0.9	1.3	2.5	7.0	2,490	46
Sumner County	TN	19,650	22,347	22,755	—	—	—	—	—	—	1,510	15.1	2,803	8.1	5.0	1.9	3.0	6.3	10.8	1,367	38
Williamson County	TN	11,502	19,545	20,257	—	—	—	—	—	—	1,248	16.2	2,364	8.6	1.4	0.3	0.3	1.4	3.9	1,289	30
Abilene ISD	TX	18,217	18,118	17,737	56.6	43.4	11.8	30.0	1.2	0.4	1,342	13.2	2,653	6.7	5.2	4.5	5.3	5.3	6.1	963	39
Aldine ISD	TX	41,372	52,520	53,332	8.8	91.2	33.7	54.7	2.8	0.1	3,574	14.9	7,698	6.9	5.1	4.9	4.6	4.9	6.4	2,003	65
Alief ISD	TX	29,774	42,151	43,697	8.9	91.1	36.9	39.4	14.7	0.1	2,692	16.2	5,421	8.1	4.2	3.1	4.1	3.9	5.9	1,813	91
Amarillo ISD	TX	27,374	28,908	29,205	51.0	49.0	10.9	35.3	2.6	0.2	1,984	14.7	3,761	7.8	4.2	2.5	4.4	4.7	5.8	1,470	51

See notes at end of table.

Selected statistics on enrollment, teachers, graduates, and dropouts in public school districts enrolling more than 15,000 students, by state: 1990, 2000, and 2001—Continued

Name of district, by state	State	Enrollment, fall 1990	Enrollment, fall 2000	Enrollment, fall 2001	Percentage distribution of enrollment, by race, fall 2001						Number of classroom teachers, fall 2001	Pupil/teacher ratio, fall 2001	Total number of staff, fall 2001	Student/staff ratio, fall 2001	Percent dropouts from grades 9–12, 2000–01 [1]					Number of high school graduates, 2000–01 [2]	Number of schools, fall 2001
					White, non-Hispanic	Total (Minority)	Black, non-Hispanic	Hispanic	Asian/Pacific Islander	American Indian/Alaska Native					Total	Grade 9	Grade 10	Grade 11	Grade 12		
1	2	3	4	5	6	7	8	9	10	11	12	13	14	15	16	17	18	19	20	21	22
Arlington ISD	TX	44,958	58,866	60,222	44.6	55.4	21.6	26.4	6.9	0.5	4,042	14.9	8,100	7.4	7.6	7.3	6.2	7.6	10.2	2,843	75
Austin ISD	TX	65,797	77,816	77,684	32.5	67.5	15.0	49.6	2.6	0.2	5,304	14.6	10,451	7.0	5.6	3.7	6.3	6.0	7.4	3,619	111
Beaumont ISD	TX	18,684	20,696	20,799	23.8	76.2	64.1	9.2	2.7	0.2	1,493	13.9	2,967	7.0	6.7	6.2	8.4	4.8	7.8	997	36
Birdville ISD	TX	18,466	21,246	21,784	70.0	30.0	4.7	19.0	5.9	0.4	1,408	15.5	2,725	8.0	1.4	1.0	1.5	1.9	1.7	1,151	33
Brownsville ISD	TX	34,906	40,898	42,573	2.0	98.0	0.1	97.6	0.2	#	2,912	14.6	6,734	6.3	3.7	3.4	4.6	3.0	4.0	2,011	50
Carrollton-Farmers Branch ISD	TX	16,234	24,134	25,002	38.7	61.3	11.1	36.3	13.3	0.6	1,685	14.8	3,155	7.9	3.6	2.8	3.0	3.1	6.3	1,589	39
Clear Creek ISD	TX	22,372	29,875	31,048	69.6	30.4	6.8	14.0	9.2	0.3	1,983	15.7	3,623	8.6	2.4	1.6	2.2	2.2	4.0	1,980	33
Conroe ISD	TX	23,288	34,928	36,775	74.3	25.7	5.1	18.1	2.1	0.5	2,396	15.3	4,925	7.5	2.5	1.8	3.0	2.6	3.1	2,137	44
Corpus Christi ISD	TX	41,881	39,138	39,450	21.3	78.7	5.6	71.7	1.1	0.3	2,429	16.2	5,168	7.6	6.5	5.4	7.0	6.3	7.9		64
Cypress-Fairbanks ISD	TX	41,196	63,497	67,562	56.4	43.6	10.3	25.1	8.0	0.2	4,453	15.2	8,964	7.5	5.4	4.6	6.3	5.1	1.6	3,673	57
Dallas ISD	TX	135,320	161,548	163,562	7.2	92.8	34.3	56.8	1.3	0.4	10,562	15.5	19,837	8.2	5.8	4.6	6.3	5.6	6.3	6,008	226
Ector County ISD	TX	26,993	26,831	26,996	37.5	62.5	5.3	56.1	0.6	0.5	1,802	15.0	3,570	7.6	6.2	4.5	8.6	4.9	9.4	1,506	42
Edinburg ISD	TX	13,685	22,005	22,976	2.9	97.1	0.2	96.8	0.2	#	1,523	15.1	3,441	6.7	5.8	3.8	5.0	4.9	5.5	944	34
El Paso ISD	TX	64,092	62,325	62,844	14.5	85.5	4.6	79.3	1.3	0.3	4,163	15.1	8,503	7.4	3.1	2.0	2.4	3.1	6.5	3,065	88
Fort Bend ISD	TX	36,270	53,999	56,186	35.8	64.2	28.3	18.7	17.1	0.1	3,459	16.2	6,977	8.1	6.9	6.9	7.0	5.6	5.5	3,376	58
Fort Worth ISD	TX	69,163	79,661	80,597	20.1	79.9	29.7	48.1	1.9	0.1	5,024	16.0	10,148	7.9	6.9	2.9	4.9	3.6	8.4	3,259	143
Galena Park ISD	TX	15,593	18,885	19,346	13.8	86.2	17.0	67.1	1.9	0.1	1,326	14.6	2,612	7.4	2.0	1.3	2.0	1.6	6.2	1,008	23
Garland ISD	TX	37,978	50,312	52,391	44.8	55.2	9.6	31.0	6.6	0.2	3,239	16.2	6,041	8.7	5.3	4.1	5.3	6.0	3.8	2,553	67
Goose Creek ISD	TX	17,654	18,003	18,330	38.8	61.2	17.0	42.6	1.1	0.6	1,157	15.8	2,381	7.7	4.1	1.8	4.6	5.0	6.2	961	26
Grand Prairie ISD	TX	16,482	20,257	20,965	30.2	69.8	14.4	50.5	4.1	0.8	1,408	14.9	2,574	8.1	#	#	5.3	6.0	6.5	950	32
Harlingen Consolidated ISD	TX	13,805	15,857	16,146	12.0	88.0	0.7	86.6	0.7	0.1	1,029	15.7	2,395	6.7	8.0	4.6	5.3	5.1	4.9	822	24
Houston ISD	TX	194,435	208,462	210,950	9.6	90.4	31.3	56.1	3.0	0.1	12,097	17.4	30,589	6.9	2.0	5.8	14.3	5.0	8.7	7,632	299
Humble ISD	TX	19,560	24,684	25,322	70.7	29.3	10.6	15.3	3.2	0.9	1,694	14.9	3,375	7.5	2.0	0.3	1.2	3.8	3.0	1,604	29
Hurst-Euless-Bedford ISD	TX	18,733	19,203	19,540	64.0	36.0	10.0	15.7	9.4	0.5	1,276	15.3	2,498	7.8	2.0	1.7	2.7	3.3	3.0	1,194	31
Irving ISD	TX	23,509	29,097	30,096	29.0	71.0	13.3	52.0	5.2	0.3	2,123	14.2	3,826	7.9	4.2	3.0	4.2	4.6	5.6	1,221	37
Judson ISD	TX	13,145	16,603	17,160	32.7	67.3	25.6	38.7	2.7	0.7	1,179	14.6	2,465	7.0	3.8	1.9	2.4	4.5	8.8	785	21
Katy ISD	TX	19,507	34,503	37,554	69.7	30.3	6.1	18.0	6.1	#	2,547	14.7	4,802	7.8	1.2	1.1	0.9	1.0	1.8	2,018	39
Keller ISD	TX	8,212	17,083	18,396	80.1	19.9	4.4	9.5	5.6	0.6	1,049	17.5	1,928	9.5	2.6	1.9	2.5	3.4	4.0	873	23
Killeen ISD	TX	22,131	29,687	30,536	36.5	63.5	40.6	17.9	4.3	0.5	2,105	14.5	4,621	6.6	3.2	1.2	2.5	2.3	6.7	1,281	44
Klein ISD	TX	26,220	32,376	34,223	57.7	42.3	13.4	21.0	7.6	0.3	2,162	15.8	4,506	7.6	2.7	1.4	2.6	3.4	5.0	2,033	32
La Joya ISD	TX	8,523	17,641	18,992	0.4	99.6	0.4	99.0	#	#	1,184	16.0	2,733	6.9	8.6	5.0	10.0	6.4	15.4	640	21
Lamar Consolidated ISD	TX	12,335	15,159	16,242	37.0	63.0	13.3	48.0	1.6	0.4	1,080	15.0	2,337	6.9	4.6	3.9	4.2	3.0	6.0	793	31
Laredo ISD	TX	23,304	22,547	23,656	0.7	99.3	0.7	98.0	0.1	0.1	1,445	16.4	3,467	6.8	6.1	4.6	6.7	3.0	11.3	998	29
Leander ISD	TX	5,419	14,499	15,603	77.1	22.9	4.3	15.2	2.9	0.5	1,099	14.2	2,021	7.7	2.6	1.2	0.6	2.0	6.0	694	17
Lewisville ISD	TX	20,776	39,096	40,953	73.2	26.8	7.6	13.3	5.4	0.3	2,809	14.6	4,771	8.6	1.4	0.6	0.9	2.0	2.5	1,951	52
Lubbock ISD	TX	30,786	39,026	28,933	39.5	60.5	14.8	44.2	1.2	0.2	2,780	13.7	3,722	7.8	3.8	1.7	3.0	2.9	6.6	1,795	58
Mansfield ISD	TX	7,570	14,888	16,866	66.5	33.5	15.3	13.9	3.9	0.4	1,104	14.7	2,073	8.1	2.6	1.7	2.9	3.8	2.2	731	19
McAllen ISD	TX	18,432	21,747	22,469	9.4	90.6	0.5	88.4	1.7	#	1,530	15.3	3,455	6.5	5.9	4.6	7.5	4.9	7.4	1,196	32
Mesquite ISD	TX	25,920	32,334	33,246	45.8	54.2	19.0	22.6	3.9	0.4	2,053	16.2	4,063	8.2	3.7	2.7	4.1	4.0	4.7	1,806	36
Midland ISD	TX	21,082	20,522	20,755	45.4	54.6	9.6	43.1	1.0	0.4	1,386	15.0	2,780	7.5	5.5	4.0	6.3	6.7	5.7	1,274	
North East ISD	TX	39,909	50,875	53,218	48.0	52.0	6.7	39.5	2.6	0.3	3,549	15.0	7,137	7.0	2.0	1.1	3.1	2.3	3.3	3,014	67
Northside ISD	TX	50,229	63,739	66,000	34.7	65.3	6.7	56.1	2.3	0.1	4,352	15.2	9,424	7.0	3.3	2.3	2.8	2.9	5.8	3,582	85
Pasadena ISD	TX	37,643	42,577	43,477	24.1	75.9	5.6	66.8	3.3	0.2	2,707	16.1	5,403	8.0	6.4	5.1	5.2	6.8	9.7	1,900	54
Pflugerville ISD	TX	6,482	14,545	15,259	47.3	52.7	18.0	26.1	8.0	0.5	1,025	14.9	1,699	9.0	1.9	1.2	1.6	1.8	3.2	869	21
Pharr-San Juan-Alamo ISD	TX	16,563	22,537	23,826	1.3	98.7	0.2	98.4	0.1	0.1	1,506	15.8	3,512	6.8	6.7	4.4	8.1	7.6	8.1	1,079	34
Plano ISD	TX	32,555	47,161	49,091	66.8	33.2	7.7	10.8	14.4	0.3	3,528	13.9	6,077	8.1	0.8	0.4	0.3	0.9	1.9	2,520	64
Richardson ISD	TX	35,138	35,138	35,245	44.7	55.3	23.5	22.5	9.0	0.3	2,445	14.4	4,236	8.3	2.3	1.6	2.4	1.8	3.6	1,886	55
Round Rock ISD	TX	28,398	31,536	32,667	64.8	35.2	8.5	18.8	7.6	0.3	2,349	13.9	4,623	7.1	2.3	2.1	2.0	2.2	2.6	1,860	42
San Angelo ISD	TX	16,488	16,092	15,689	45.7	54.3	6.5	46.5	0.3	0.1	982	16.0	1,912	8.2	4.1	2.1	4.0	7.0	7.2	980	28
San Antonio ISD	TX	60,161	57,273	57,462	6.3	93.7	9.6	83.2	0.4	0.1	3,659	15.7	7,740	7.4	7.6	6.7	8.3	7.0	9.1	2,500	104
Socorro ISD	TX	14,350	26,711	28,268	9.1	90.9	1.2	91.8	0.4	0.2	1,651	17.1	3,280	8.6	3.2	2.2	3.1	3.3	4.8	1,308	29
Spring Branch ISD	TX	23,661	31,659	32,578	37.6	62.4	6.4	27.3	6.5	0.1	2,150	15.2	4,581	7.1	3.3	3.5	3.4	2.3	3.3	1,688	49
Spring ISD	TX	18,537	23,034	24,529	34.4	65.6	28.8	37.6	6.1	0.2	1,619	15.1	3,472	7.1	3.2	1.9	2.8	3.7	5.4	1,237	26
Tyler ISD	TX	16,182	16,626	16,880	34.4	65.6	35.9	28.4	1.0	#	1,165	14.5	2,301	7.3	4.6	2.7	5.7	4.9	6.0	916	30
United ISD	TX	12,553	27,556	29,096	2.7	97.3	0.2	96.6	0.4	0.1	1,866	15.6	4,317	6.7	8.9	7.1	8.5	10.1	12.0	1,331	35
Waco ISD	TX	14,304	15,433	15,502	18.8	81.2	38.0	42.6	0.4	0.2	1,054	14.7	2,182	7.0	2.6	1.9	2.1	2.7	3.2	623	34
Wichita Falls ISD	TX	15,011	15,013	15,293	59.9	40.1	17.2	19.9	2.4	0.7	1,129	13.6	2,178	7.0	6.0	3.1	4.5	3.0	3.9	890	35
Ysleta ISD	TX	49,974	46,394	46,811	8.0	92.0	2.3	88.7	0.4	0.6	2,987	15.7	6,011	7.8	6.0	3.1	4.5	6.3	11.5	2,754	59

See notes at end of table.

Selected statistics on enrollment, teachers, graduates, and dropouts in public school districts enrolling more than 15,000 students, by state: 1990, 2000, and 2001—Continued

Columns 6–11 = Percentage distribution of enrollment, by race, fall 2001. Columns 16–20 = Percent dropouts from grades 9–12, 2000–01[1].

Name of district, by state	State	Enrollment, fall 1990	Enrollment, fall 2000	Enrollment, fall 2001	White, non-Hispanic	Minority Total	Black, non-Hispanic	Hispanic	Asian/Pacific Islander	American Indian/Alaska Native	Number of classroom teachers, fall 2001	Pupil/teacher ratio, fall 2001	Total number of staff, fall 2001	Student/staff ratio, fall 2001	Dropouts Total	Grade 9	Grade 10	Grade 11	Grade 12	Number of high school graduates, 2000–01[2]	Number of schools, fall 2001
1	2	3	4	5	6	7	8	9	10	11	12	13	14	15	16	17	18	19	20	21	22
Alpine	UT	38,852	47,117	48,296	91.2	8.8	0.5	6.0	1.8	0.5	2,057	23.5	2,984	16.2	2.0	0.5	1.0	2.3	4.2	2,893	58
Davis	UT	55,558	59,578	59,366	90.1	9.9	1.3	6.1	2.0	0.5	2,701	22.0	5,227	11.4	1.8	0.3	0.6	0.9	5.1	4,205	83
Granite	UT	78,554	71,328	72,082	74.8	25.2	1.4	16.1	6.5	1.2	3,423	21.1	5,753	12.5	7.1		4.8	8.9	13.8	4,337	98
Jordan	UT	64,991	73,158	73,494	91.8	8.2	0.5	5.2	2.0	0.4	3,072	23.9	5,709	12.9	4.4	2.4	3.5	4.5	7.1	4,901	81
Nebo	UT	16,393	21,094	22,159	92.5	7.5	0.3	5.3	0.7	1.2	898	24.7	1,642	13.5	1.4	0.1	0.7	1.3	3.5	1,247	31
Salt Lake City	UT	24,766	25,367	25,161	53.9	46.1	4.1	30.3	9.7	2.0	1,239	20.3	2,785	9.0	9.0	5.2	6.7	10.0	14.4	1,305	42
Washington	UT	13,264	18,374	18,963	90.1	9.9	0.4	5.8	1.5	2.2	835	22.7	1,531	12.4	2.5	0.1	1.8	3.1	5.4	1,236	30
Weber	UT	25,425	27,783	27,917	91.8	8.2	0.9	5.5	1.4	0.4	1,227	22.8	2,124	13.1	1.7	0.1	0.9	2.2	3.7	1,913	40
Arlington County	VA	14,825	18,870	19,109	41.5	58.5	14.2	34.3	9.9	0.1	1,802	10.6	3,307	5.8	2.6	3.3	2.2	2.7	2.0	963	32
Chesapeake City	VA	29,533	37,645	38,010	61.4	38.6	34.7	1.6	2.0	0.3	2,598	14.6	5,361	7.1	3.4	3.7	2.9	3.2	3.7	2,297	46
Chesterfield County	VA	44,480	51,212	52,726	70.7	29.3	23.0	3.0	2.7	0.5	3,544	14.9	6,397	8.2	4.5	5.3	4.2	3.6	4.7	3,166	59
Fairfax County	VA	128,766	156,412	160,584	59.0	41.0	10.5	14.0	16.0	0.3	12,310	13.0	22,874	7.0	2.8	2.2	2.5	2.8	3.7	10,514	198
Hampton City	VA	21,383	23,290	23,192	36.3	63.7	59.0	2.4	1.9	0.3	1,749	13.3	3,217	7.2	2.7	2.2	2.7	2.8	3.5	1,357	37
Hanover County	VA	11,328	16,611	17,192	88.4	11.6	9.6	0.8	1.1	0.2	1,243	13.8	2,041	8.4	0.4	0.2	0.3	0.3	1.0	961	20
Henrico County	VA	32,638	41,655	42,928	58.9	41.1	34.7	2.2	3.9	0.3	2,781	15.4	4,823	8.9	2.3	1.6	2.4	1.9	2.5	2,428	66
Loudoun County	VA	14,485	31,804	34,571	76.3	23.7	8.5	8.1	6.9	0.2	2,192	15.8	4,283	8.1	1.8	3.1	1.0	1.7	3.1	1,591	56
Newport News City	VA	28,925	33,008	32,907	36.6	63.4	55.8	4.2	2.5	0.9	2,338	14.1	4,510	7.3	5.3	3.1	4.1	4.3	5.5	1,675	47
Norfolk City	VA	36,541	37,349	37,006	28.0	72.0	67.4	2.4	2.0	0.2	2,755	13.4	4,975	7.4	6.8	5.2	6.2	4.4	4.7	1,268	59
Portsmouth City	VA	18,405	16,473	16,844	28.2	71.8	69.9	1.0	0.8	0.2	1,151	14.6	2,608	6.5	5.1	5.0	6.5	5.0	1.5	783	29
Prince William County	VA	41,888	54,646	58,017	58.0	42.0	24.1	12.8	4.5	0.5	3,320	17.5	6,304	9.2	2.8	4.8	4.7	1.9	7.3	3,014	74
Richmond City	VA	27,021	27,237	26,840	6.9	93.1	90.8	1.7	0.6	0.1	2,078	12.9	3,709	7.2	3.1	3.0	2.8	3.7	0.5	1,083	63
Spotsylvania County	VA	12,227	18,876	20,280	77.8	22.2	17.0	3.1	1.8	0.3	1,368	14.8	2,536	8.0	2.4	1.9	2.7	2.6	3.3	1,006	29
Stafford County	VA	12,555	21,124	22,635	76.2	23.8	17.9	3.4	2.2	0.3	1,402	16.1	2,600	8.7	3.1	2.3	2.3	3.7	3.0	1,362	24
Virginia Beach City	VA	70,266	76,586	75,970	62.0	38.0	28.0	4.0	5.6	0.3	5,213	14.6	9,665	7.9	5.2	4.6	4.5	6.7	5.3	4,458	85
Bellevue	WA	14,748	15,431	15,510	69.3	30.7	2.8	7.5	20.1	0.4	860	18.0	1,847	8.4	—	—	—	—	—	1,066	34
Bethel	WA	11,669	16,260	16,260	73.9	26.1	9.2	5.8	9.2	1.8	784	20.7	1,686	9.6	—	—	—	—	—	859	26
Edmonds	WA	18,868	22,067	22,089	74.6	25.4	4.5	5.8	13.3	1.8	1,102	20.0	2,270	9.7	—	—	—	—	—	1,086	42
Everett	WA	15,343	18,683	18,943	77.5	22.5	4.2	6.1	10.3	1.8	874	21.7	1,861	10.2	—	—	—	—	—	843	34
Evergreen (Clark)	WA	14,810	21,650	22,556	83.3	16.7	3.9	4.7	7.3	1.0	1,196	18.9	2,304	9.9	—	—	—	—	—	1,027	37
Federal Way	WA	18,168	22,623	22,636	61.7	38.3	12.4	8.9	15.6	1.4	1,118	20.3	2,293	9.9	—	—	—	—	—	1,103	33
Highline	WA	16,208	18,024	17,752	48.8	51.2	13.0	15.5	20.4	2.3	898	19.8	1,940	9.2	—	—	—	—	—	945	33
Kent	WA	21,027	26,535	26,670	68.8	31.2	9.5	6.8	13.7	1.2	1,404	19.0	2,886	9.2	—	—	—	—	—	1,500	43
Lake Washington	WA	23,050	23,662	23,050	80.5	19.5	2.2	5.0	11.4	0.9	1,183	20.1	2,396	9.9	—	—	—	—	—	1,465	49
Northshore	WA	17,511	20,255	20,184	83.0	17.0	2.1	5.1	8.7	1.1	994	20.3	2,034	9.9	—	—	—	—	—	1,322	34
Puyallup	WA	15,100	19,757	19,468	84.4	15.6	3.4	4.6	5.9	1.7	994	19.6	1,961	9.9	—	—	—	—	—	1,078	33
Seattle	WA	43,593	47,575	47,449	40.1	59.9	23.1	10.8	23.4	2.6	2,652	17.9	5,658	8.4	—	—	—	—	—	2,448	129
Spokane	WA	29,186	31,725	31,518	86.3	13.7	4.5	2.7	2.8	3.6	1,756	18.0	3,649	8.6	—	—	—	—	—	155	69
Tacoma	WA	30,169	34,093	34,146	55.8	44.2	21.0	8.4	12.6	2.2	1,804	18.9	3,799	9.0	—	—	—	—	—	1,440	74
Vancouver	WA	16,423	21,892	22,155	79.9	20.1	4.4	8.9	4.7	2.1	1,125	19.7	2,522	8.8	—	—	—	—	—	1,156	38
Kanawha County	WV	34,284	29,250	28,616	87.5	12.5	11.0	0.4	1.1	0.1	1,950	14.7	3,668	7.8	5.6	4.3	6.6	6.0	5.7	1,698	75
Green Bay Area	WI	18,048	20,104	20,320	73.0	27.0	3.6	9.7	9.0	4.7	1,394	14.6	2,549	8.0	2.9	0.1	0.1	1.8	9.8	1,292	36
Kenosha	WI	16,219	20,099	20,553	72.0	28.0	13.5	12.6	1.5	0.4	1,379	14.9	2,371	8.7	2.1	1.4	3.4	2.6	2.8	1,276	40
Madison Metropolitan	WI	23,214	25,087	24,893	62.4	37.6	18.5	8.3	10.1	0.7	2,070	12.0	3,936	6.3	3.5	2.0	3.4	4.7	4.4	1,589	52
Milwaukee	WI	92,784	97,985	97,762	18.3	81.7	60.3	16.1	4.3	1.0	5,980	16.3	13,651	7.2	10.5	12.3	10.4	9.5	8.3	3,446	208
Racine	WI	21,904	21,102	21,265	59.1	40.9	25.6	13.8	1.2	0.3	1,340	15.9	2,496	8.5	4.9	3.9	3.5	6.7	6.2	1,196	36

—Not available.

† Not applicable.

Rounds to zero.

[1] Alaska, Arizona, Colorado, Idaho, Illinois, Maryland, New Jersey, South Dakota, Tennessee, Virginia, Vermont, and Wisconsin reported data on an alternative July through June cycle, rather than the specified October through September cycle.

[2] Includes regular and other high school diplomas.

NOTE: Total enrollment, staff, and teacher data in this table reflect totals reported by school districts and may differ from data derived from summing school level data to school district aggregates. SB=School board. SC=School corporation. ISD=Independent school district. Detail may not sum to totals due to rounding.

SOURCE: U.S. Department of Education, National Center for Education Statistics, The NCES Common Core of Data (CCD), "Public Elementary/Secondary School Universe Survey," 2001–02. (This table was prepared September 2003.)

Enrollment, poverty, and federal funds for the 100 largest school districts: Selected years, 1999–2000 to 2003–04

Column groupings: columns 8–11 = "Revenues by source of funds, in thousands, 2000–01"; columns 12–17 = "Revenue for selected federal programs, in thousands, 2000–01"; columns 18–21 = "Title I allocations for 2003–04, in thousands".

Name of district, by enrollment size	State	Rank order	Enrollment, fall 2001	5- to 17-year-old population, 1999–2000	5- to 17-year-old population below the poverty level, 1999–2000	Poverty rate of 5- to 17-year-olds, 1999–2000	Total	Federal	Federal as a percent of total	Federal revenue per student, 2000–01[1]	Title I, basic and concentration grants	School lunch	Vocational education	Drug-free schools	Eisenhower math and science	Special education	Basic grants	Concentration grants	Targeted grants	Education finance incentive grants
1	2	3	4	5	6	7	8	9	10	11	12	13	14	15	16	17	18	19	20	21
New York City	NY	1	1,049,831	1,401,412	395,260	28.2	12,051,996	1,016,645	8.4	953	466,662	251,945	12,679	[2] 14,595	[2] 9,819	129,675	406,595	92,504	154,133	116,468
Los Angeles Unified	CA	2	735,058	864,520	244,330	28.3	6,386,075	601,387	9.4	834	[2] 163,730	178,598	11,951	[2] 7,979	[2] 3,904	65,246	176,594	40,890	73,208	59,111
City of Chicago	IL	3	437,418	541,318	134,339	24.8	3,799,647	634,099	16.7	1,457	167,383	138,958	10,248	4,351	4,164	55,785	121,134	13,421	48,623	43,220
Miami-Dade County	FL	4	375,836	413,461	90,311	21.8	2,897,334	264,099	9.1	716	81,604	79,073	9,383	2,454	1,673	21,134	57,964	13,421	22,691	17,707
Broward County	FL	5	262,055	279,888	39,297	14.0	1,961,930	130,969	6.7	522	27,894	36,550	2,690	1,711	699	20,126	25,388	5,879	8,759	6,835
Clark County	NV	6	245,659	248,469	33,284	13.4	1,595,417	72,498	4.5	314	15,815	22,435	2,304	890	1,523	15,168	21,241	4,918	5,815	5,815
Houston Independent	TX	7	210,950	230,872	59,937	26.0	1,565,924	168,123	10.7	806	61,574	54,366	[2] 5,094	2,148	1,584	10,932	43,814	9,765	15,769	16,028
Philadelphia City	PA	8	197,083	285,308	68,005	23.8	1,732,140	238,677	13.8	1,186	91,332	47,960	2,353	2,968	794	[2] 0	63,462	14,694	24,266	29,844
Hawaii	HI	9	184,546	217,604	26,931	12.4	1,682,332	140,953	8.4	765	18,584	30,149	2,705	3,411	594	16,678	20,696	4,245	5,812	5,342
Hillsborough County	FL	10	169,789	183,190	30,295	16.5	1,276,144	151,250	11.9	921	30,323	30,285	4,478	1,049	1,308	20,604	19,777	4,579	6,559	5,118
Detroit City	MI	11	166,675	219,474	62,441	28.5	1,535,965	187,226	12.2	1,154	97,196	30,991	1,728	594	722	11,200	69,532	16,484	21,995	26,727
Dallas Independent	TX	12	163,562	183,471	45,134	24.6	1,159,569	116,635	10.1	722	39,083	39,819	1,571	848	497	7,192	31,470	7,496	11,191	11,043
Fairfax County	VA	13	160,584	177,545	8,775	4.9	1,587,591	52,036	3.3	333	6,906	11,538	2,065	1,566	529	16,652	6,865	1,589	1,860	2,079
Palm Beach County	FL	14	160,223	164,965	24,457	14.8	1,222,275	115,449	9.4	750	21,776	22,847	2,114	660	900	16,145	15,698	3,635	5,105	3,984
Orange County	FL	15	157,433	158,771	36,751	23.1	1,141,204	72,903	6.4	484	19,867	20,458	951	996	[2] 678	16,294	15,829	3,665	5,152	4,020
San Diego City Unified	CA	16	141,599	161,585	24,402	15.1	1,282,638	100,393	7.8	708	[2] 27,868	26,702	[2] 1,283	[2] 1,572	362	12,661	27,053	6,173	9,084	7,334
Montgomery County	MD	17	136,895	156,662	9,843	6.1	1,490,614	49,428	3.3	368	8,395	10,717	1,089	883	845	11,393	8,708	2,016	2,438	2,028
Prince George's County	MD	18	135,039	148,744	14,053	9.0	1,131,113	68,276	6.0	511	12,708	22,389	845	845	690	10,152	12,431	2,865	3,745	3,284
Duval County	FL	19	127,392	146,906	22,446	15.1	874,119	72,860	8.3	579	20,084	20,154	1,283	1,061	224	14,408	14,735	3,412	4,762	3,716
Gwinnett County	GA	20	116,339	116,906	7,582	6.5	947,384	26,473	2.8	240	[2] 2,577	8,691	2,360	2,428	724	[2] 4,119	5,768	1,335	1,491	1,459
Memphis City	TN	21	115,990	130,899	31,873	24.3	836,473	91,379	10.9	803	27,495	29,593	2,747	2,635	537	8,148	20,392	4,722	6,790	7,917
Pinellas County	FL	22	114,583	132,179	19,170	14.5	928,424	65,046	7.0	575	17,672	15,371	2,462	712	457	15,154	12,340	2,857	3,908	3,050
Baltimore County	MD	23	107,212	133,111	10,117	7.6	994,600	45,662	4.6	427	[2] 10,110	10,057	883	512	391	9,406	9,266	2,146	2,637	2,220
Charlotte-Mecklenburg	NC	24	106,312	123,499	15,648	12.7	957,824	44,048	4.6	426	11,042	11,042	[2] 1,344	[2] 717	377	[2] 4,845	10,841	2,510	3,348	3,401
Wake County	NC	25	101,756	112,455	10,440	9.3	781,557	34,846	4.5	352	[2] 5,258	8,694	[2] 839	2,417	225	[2] 7,892	7,148	1,655	2,032	2,064
Cobb County	GA	26	98,338	105,956	7,126	6.7	812,872	22,469	2.8	235	3,229	5,383	323	2,415	1,597	[2] 4,808	5,426	1,256	1,393	1,359
Baltimore City	MD	27	97,817	119,659	26,525	22.2	968,038	144,514	14.9	1,447	43,092	25,433	2,634	1,933	1,039	14,803	29,643	6,467	8,445	7,802
Milwaukee	WI	28	97,762	123,452	29,624	24.0	1,026,302	120,838	11.8	1,233	47,221	19,817	2,327	[2] 1,152	[2] 230	12,309	34,198	6,549	9,412	11,311
De Kalb County	GA	29	97,501	120,958	16,800	13.9	866,312	44,148	5.1	460	[2] 8,397	20,263	[2] 468	2,838	536	[2] 3,758	11,298	2,616	3,462	3,827
Long Beach Unified	CA	30	96,488	104,485	30,580	29.3	741,740	86,028	11.6	918	[2] 25,194	21,983	990	2,935	268	6,280	21,934	5,079	7,277	5,875
Jefferson County	KY	31	93,516	120,605	17,729	14.7	751,351	68,121	9.1	703	[2] 4,592	17,238	2,444	2,362	328	[2] 4,998	12,689	2,938	3,986	4,600
Jefferson County	CO	32	88,460	99,899	5,565	5.6	654,384	21,852	3.3	249	5,702	4,257	476	405	183	5,978	4,184	822	1,050	1,088
Albuquerque	NM	33	87,201	103,097	18,516	18.0	581,963	46,613	8.0	549	15,613	11,895	583	453	490	8,209	11,805	2,733	3,730	4,117
Polk County	FL	34	81,207	87,019	16,229	18.6	529,403	46,444	8.8	584	12,880	16,979	1,346	439	586	7,686	10,602	2,438	3,263	2,546
Fresno Unified	CA	35	81,058	115,763	32,182	27.8	697,240	74,544	10.7	944	[2] 24,416	20,756	1,266	2,866	515	7,032	23,293	5,394	7,761	6,266
Fort Worth Independent	TX	36	80,797	87,894	21,534	24.5	569,803	59,595	10.5	748	21,212	15,775	1,023	953	480	5,303	15,051	3,485	4,835	4,484
Austin Independent	TX	37	77,684	85,866	14,804	17.2	666,389	48,514	7.3	623	11,548	13,572	731	925	206	6,657	10,396	2,407	3,176	2,858
Virginia Beach City	VA	38	75,970	86,272	7,335	8.5	546,938	37,194	6.8	486	6,177	4,318	750	330	250	7,824	5,688	1,316	1,460	1,569
Anne Arundel County	MD	39	75,081	90,553	5,863	6.5	665,211	25,684	3.9	345	5,211	8,455	578	316	183	8,255	5,336	1,167	1,275	988
Mesa Unified	AZ	40	74,808	82,203	3,448	10.0	472,497	29,904	6.3	406	6,956	5,428	936	336	356	5,787	6,124	1,340	1,435	1,392
Jordan	UT	41	73,494	82,485	3,448	4.2	412,130	22,273	5.4	304	2,907	2,239	645	368	376	5,201	2,239	0	0	0
Orleans Parish	LA	42	73,185	87,243	32,716	37.5	504,519	72,239	14.3	931	29,877	22,984	1,681	798	451	3,687	23,461	4,887	7,029	6,645
Denver County	CO	43	72,361	83,997	16,421	19.5	591,513	51,990	8.8	734	15,808	12,033	740	1,256	248	5,420	12,176	2,760	3,726	4,453
Cleveland Municipal	OH	44	72,199	98,234	33,175	33.8	727,063	114,030	15.7	1,507	[2] 36,285	16,820	3,763	1,240	636	11,613	27,162	6,300	9,058	11,414
Granite	UT	45	72,082	76,139	6,350	8.3	378,915	32,588	8.6	457	6,283	8,195	657	487	161	5,412	5,088	1,558	1,180	1,360
Brevard County	FL	46	71,781	79,992	9,882	12.4	408,361	34,247	8.4	485	8,874	6,498	655	250	527	9,277	6,431	1,489	1,802	1,406
Fulton County	GA	47	69,841	80,860	6,754	8.4	741,195	18,836	2.5	275	[2] 3,941	7,744	[2] 344	2,298	543	[2] 2,876	5,194	1,203	1,327	1,293
District Of Columbia	DC	48	68,449	82,396	22,906	27.8	1,042,261	114,876	11.0	1,667	21,128	18,112	3,416	1,428	246	6,564	24,781	5,738	8,115	6,278
Nashville-Davidson County	TN	49	67,689	88,634	14,971	16.9	478,466	41,062	8.6	607	11,718	12,055	1,482	2,452	367	6,959	9,794	2,268	3,013	3,355
Cypress-Fairbanks Independent	TX	50	67,562	65,662	4,030	6.1	471,506	14,629	3.1	230	2,535	4,661	220	660	182	4,505	2,828	0	662	513
Northside Independent	TX	51	66,000	70,886	9,023	12.7	459,615	31,791	6.9	499	5,395	8,836	503	303	303	6,278	6,332	1,466	1,728	1,438
Columbus City	OH	52	64,833	75,127	18,604	24.8	644,401	54,583	8.5	846	[2] 20,582	13,412	1,754	451	451	5,862	15,360	3,557	4,851	5,928
Guilford County	NC	53	64,546	72,193	10,072	14.0	470,931	28,255	6.0	446	5,601	11,555	2,942	2,367	161	[2] 5,661	6,922	1,603	1,952	1,982
Mobile County	AL	54	63,846	80,547	18,150	22.5	397,173	51,304	12.9	790	[2] 16,880	15,004	2,389	248	527	9,601	11,524	2,668	3,629	3,801
El Paso Independent	TX	55	62,844	65,027	21,389	32.9	429,357	52,186	12.2	837	19,507	14,367	1,008	543	543	3,892	16,625	3,638	4,743	4,394
Seminole County	FL	56	62,786	69,544	6,773	9.7	408,336	23,988	5.9	394	5,854	5,340	418	278	246	5,736	4,742	1,038	1,111	867

See notes at end of table.

Enrollment, poverty, and federal funds for the 100 largest school districts: Selected years, 1999–2000 to 2003–04—Continued

Column groups: columns 8–11 = "Revenues by source of funds, in thousands, 2000–01"; columns 12–17 = "Revenue for selected federal programs, in thousands, 2000–01"; columns 18–21 = "Title I allocations for 2003–04, in thousands".

Name of district, by enrollment size	State	Rank order	Enrollment, fall 2001	5- to 17-year-old population, 1999–2000	5- to 17-year-old population below the poverty level, 1999–2000	Poverty rate of 5- to 17-year-olds, 1999–2000	Total	Federal	Federal as a percent of total	Federal revenue per student, 2000–01 student[1]	Title I, basic and concentration grants	School lunch	Vocational education	Drug-free schools	Eisenhower math and science	Special education	Basic grants	Concentration grants	Targeted grants	Education finance incentive grants
1	2	3	4	5	6	7	8	9	10	11	12	13	14	15	16	17	18	19	20	21
Volusia County	FL	57	62,599	68,205	10,291	15.1	445,841	32,723	7.3	532	10,161	8,487	806	345	272	7,666	7,386	1,616	1,917	1,496
Boston	MA	58	62,141	84,513	25,062	29.7	911,851	58,100	6.4	922	24,029	9,662	1,565	539	774	8,913	25,522	5,584	7,851	8,517
Tucson Unified	AZ	59	62,104	76,730	13,868	18.1	422,137	43,838	10.4	709	11,850	11,193	1,394	347	407	7,742	9,944	2,176	2,795	2,969
Santa Ana Unified	CA	60	61,909	63,711	15,590	24.5	462,602	41,938	9.1	692	7,251[2]	14,414	889	609[2]	214[2]	4,978	11,032	2,554	3,391	2,738
Greenville County	SC	61	61,268	70,408	9,430	13.4	481,652	28,500	5.9	476	6,016	7,880	1,220	249	240	8,212	6,791	1,572	1,885	2,316
Lee County	FL	62	60,718	63,418	9,508	15.0	462,222	36,503	7.9	625	7,271	9,202	925	194	296	6,920	6,129	1,419	1,695	1,323
Arlington Independent	TX	63	60,222	64,370	8,561	13.3	401,736	20,864	5.2	354	3,093	7,954	399	476	200	4,555	5,965	1,381	1,597	1,310
Davis	UT	64	59,366	60,634	3,291	5.4	315,011	23,856	7.6	400	3,719	5,645	885	181	151	4,187	2,087	0	531	590
San Francisco Unified	CA	65	58,566	81,169	13,393	16.5	462,344	37,149	8.0	619	11,647[2]	9,935	530[2]	901[2]	387[2]	41	11,698	2,560	3,030	2,447
Washoe County	NV	66	58,532	60,862	7,144	11.7	370,823	21,744	5.9	391	3,067	5,664	482	243	255	5,347	4,531	1,049	1,161	799
Prince William County	VA	67	58,017	60,195	3,829	6.4	457,000	13,685	3.0	250	1,721	4,236	471	204	204	4,399	2,978	0	689	719
San Antonio Independent	TX	68	57,462	64,022	22,550	35.2	494,681	65,198	13.2	1,138	22,610[2]	20,215	1,152	795[2]	532	4,165	18,210	3,983	5,107	4,750
Atlanta City	GA	69	56,586	66,131	22,888	34.6	794,993	57,368	7.2	985	23,751[2]	13,558	1,007[2]	472[2]	472[2]	3,190	20,953	4,585	5,653	6,460
Fort Bend Independent	TX	70	56,186	58,910	4,331	7.4	376,222	12,204	3.2	226	2,571	3,191	420	216	164	3,190	3,114	0	743	580
San Bernardino City Unified	CA	71	54,166	56,982	20,457	35.9	400,126	40,277	10.1	774	14,938[2]	14,602	545	175	327	4,798	14,898	3,421	4,725	3,815
Oakland Unified	CA	72	53,545	71,490	21,404	29.9	491,702	51,521	10.5	939	14,398[2]	13,796	964	655[2]	383[2]	5,086	16,591	3,660	5,092	4,112
Sacramento City Unified	CA	73	53,418	62,170	18,286	29.4	448,894	53,753	12.0	1,019	16,829	11,758	837	822	460	4,930	16,308	3,568	4,242	3,425
Aldine Independent	TX	74	53,332	51,942	11,474	22.1	392,734	36,947	9.4	703	8,372	15,330	545	565	346	4,659	8,060	1,866	2,343	2,042
North East Independent	TX	75	53,218	58,613	6,165	10.5	402,805	19,521	4.8	384	3,215	6,275	317	277	221	4,867	4,315	0	1,086	860
Portland	OR	76	52,908	60,504	8,144	13.5	478,812	45,548	9.5	857	11,697	12,099	773	2,630	394	3,150	8,100	1,772	1,971	2,609
Chesterfield County	VA	77	52,726	55,914	3,412	6.1	366,758	14,345	3.9	280	2,249	2,382	636	278	190	5,349	2,651	0	596	616
Pasco County	FL	78	52,675	51,380	7,887	15.4	371,878	30,182	8.1	607	6,461	8,390	373	206	237	7,139	5,484	1,200	1,312	1,024
Garland Independent	TX	79	52,391	55,127	4,837	8.8	322,791	17,453	5.4	347	2,790	5,751	317	208	185	3,844	3,365	0	815	638
East Baton Rouge Parish	LA	80	52,350	78,965	15,718	19.9	405,651	44,635	11.0	823	12,626	14,821	1,347	387	177	5,740	10,137	2,347	3,120	2,950
Knox County	TN	81	51,866	61,722	8,459	13.7	317,457	19,808	6.2	381	5,726	6,101	121	290[2]	241[2]	6,212	5,610	1,299	1,522	1,555
Cumberland County	NC	82	51,434	54,989	7,456	13.6	341,141	26,540	7.8	584	7,274[2]	10,931	895[2]	234[2]	302[2]	4,191[2]	6,785	1,571	1,903	1,933
San Juan Unified	CA	83	51,383	57,056	7,456	18.0	416,226	29,715	8.7	528	5,656	5,593	325	732	143	4,624	5,665	1,312	1,478	1,193
Jefferson Parish	LA	84	50,766	85,029	16,487	19.4	351,463	40,329	11.5	792	12,863	12,356	888	1,021	421	4,687	10,656	2,467	3,305	3,124
Elk Grove Unified	CA	85	49,970	50,345	7,845	15.6	432,181	19,613	4.5	411	3,819	6,397	278	127	162	3,494	6,156	1,425	1,653	1,335
Garden Grove Unified	CA	86	49,809	54,569	10,304	18.9	354,087	29,750	8.4	610	12,925	10,354	416	225	416	3,838	8,010	4,218	2,314	1,868
Anchorage	AK	87	49,767	55,838	4,421	7.9	388,725	41,802	10.8	844	6,552	5,791	844	670[2]	341[2]	5,160	5,306	1,105	1,985	1,907
Plano Independent	TX	88	49,091	54,438	2,705	5.0	445,512	10,341	2.3	219	1,077	2,016	254	194	131	3,880	1,897	0	396	297
Wichita	KS	89	48,852	58,228	9,476	16.3	355,775	35,563	10.0	737	11,051	8,603	582[2]	393	257[2]	2,892	8,060	1,866	2,291	3,347
Alpine	UT	90	48,296	49,039	3,178	6.5	237,143	13,208	5.6	280	3,326	3,337	446	131	123	3,014	2,032	0	513	569
Clayton County	GA	91	48,232	51,195	7,691	15.0	354,154	23,082	6.5	492	3,235[2]	10,094	233[2]	201[2]	157[2]	3,427	5,908	1,368	1,541	1,519
Minneapolis	MN	92	48,155	58,982	13,685	23.2	614,522	42,807	7.0	877	14,261	13,049	77	381	384	4,092	11,154	2,855	3,374	4,436
Seattle	WA	93	47,449	61,734	7,796	12.6	480,775	39,196	8.2	824	11,238	6,343	588	573[2]	345	4,590	7,120	2,630	1,606	1,925
Ysleta Independent	TX	94	46,811	44,503	13,138	29.5	320,105	35,933	11.2	775	11,190	11,088	728	184	309	2,942	9,860	2,157	2,704	2,396
Capistrano Unified	CA	95	46,756	56,434	3,462	6.1	324,189	10,449	3.2	232	1,790	2,182	118	200	136	3,627	2,473	0	557	450
Howard County	MD	96	46,257	51,295	2,283	4.5	426,630	10,664	2.5	237	1,369	1,618	292	150	96	3,730	1,997	0	0	0
Omaha	NE	97	45,782	58,810	8,980	15.3	342,561	35,715	10.4	790	10,215	9,524	924	394	351	5,242	7,482	1,732	2,140	2,777
Forsyth County-Winston Salem	NC	98	45,707	52,728	7,738	14.7	339,299	21,347	6.3	477	—	6,565	—	—	294	—	5,301	1,227	1,374	1,396
Caddo Parish	LA	99	44,859	50,084	13,612	27.2	322,918	31,880	9.9	707	9,993	9,407	969	264	0[2]	4,593	8,780	2,033	2,636	2,492
Buffalo City	NY	100	44,849	56,189	22,052	39.2	553,335	68,983	12.5	1,509	24,231	13,853	740	318	7,103	7,103	21,028	4,869	6,778	4,578

—Not available.

[1] Federal revenue per student is based on fall enrollment collected by the Bureau of the Census.

[2] Data are for 1999–2000.

SOURCE: U.S. Department of Education, National Center for Education Statistics, The NCES Common Core of Data (CCD), "National Public Education Financial Survey," 2000–01, and the U.S. Department of Commerce, "Survey of Local Government Finances." (This table was prepared September 2003.)

Enrollment of 3-, 4-, and 5-year-old children in preprimary programs, by level and control of program and attendance status: Selected years, October 1965 to October 2001

[In thousands]

Year and age	Total population, 3 to 5 years old	Enrollment by level and control						Enrollment by attendance		
		Total	Percent enrolled	Nursery school		Kindergarten		Full-day	Part-day	Percent full-day
				Public	Private	Public	Private			
1	2	3	4	5	6	7	8	9	10	11
Total, 3 to 5 years old										
1965	12,549	3,407 (87)	27.1 (0.7)	127	393	2,291	596	—(—)	—	—(—)
1970	10,949	4,104 (71)	37.5 (0.7)	332	762	2,498	511	698 (36)	3,405	17.0 (0.8)
1975	10,185	4,955 (71)	48.7 (0.7)	570	1,174	2,682	528	1,295 (47)	3,659	26.1 (1.0)
1980	9,284	4,878 (69)	52.5 (0.7)	628	1,353	2,438	459	1,551 (51)	3,327	31.8 (1.0)
1985	10,733	5,865 (78)	54.6 (0.7)	846	1,631	2,847	541	2,144 (62)	3,722	36.6 (0.9)
1987	10,872	5,931 (78)	54.6 (0.7)	819	1,736	2,842	534	2,090 (62)	3,841	35.2 (0.9)
1988	10,993	5,978 (87)	54.4 (0.8)	851	1,770	2,875	481	2,044 (68)	3,935	34.2 (1.0)
1989	11,039	6,026 (87)	54.6 (0.8)	930	1,894	2,704	497	2,238 (70)	3,789	37.1 (1.0)
1990	11,207	6,659 (82)	59.4 (0.7)	1,199	2,180	2,772	509	2,577 (71)	4,082	38.7 (0.9)
1991	11,370	6,334 (84)	55.7 (0.7)	996	1,828	2,967	543	2,408 (69)	3,926	38.0 (1.0)
1992	11,545	6,402 (85)	55.5 (0.7)	1,073	1,783	2,995	550	2,410 (69)	3,992	37.6 (1.0)
1993	11,954	6,581 (86)	55.1 (0.7)	1,205	1,779	3,020	577	2,642 (72)	3,939	40.1 (1.0)
1994[1]	12,328	7,514 (86)	61.0 (0.7)	1,848	2,314	2,819	534	3,468 (80)	4,046	46.2 (0.9)
1995[1]	12,518	7,739 (87)	61.8 (0.7)	1,950	2,381	2,800	608	3,689 (81)	4,051	47.7 (0.9)
1996[1]	12,378	7,580 (90)	61.2 (0.7)	1,830	2,317	2,853	580	3,562 (83)	4,019	47.0 (0.9)
1997[1]	12,121	7,860 (87)	64.9 (0.7)	2,207	2,231	2,847	575	3,922 (85)	3,939	49.9 (0.9)
1998[1]	12,078	7,788 (87)	64.5 (0.7)	2,213	2,299	2,674	602	3,959 (85)	3,829	50.8 (0.9)
1999[1]	11,920	7,844 (86)	65.8 (0.7)	2,209	2,298	2,777	560	4,154 (86)	3,690	53.0 (0.9)
2000[1]	11,858	7,592 (86)	64.0 (0.7)	2,146	2,180	2,701	565	4,008 (85)	3,584	52.8 (0.9)
2001[1]	11,899	7,602 (87)	63.9 (0.7)	2,164	2,201	2,724	512	3,940 (85)	3,662	51.8 (0.9)
3 years old										
1965	4,149	203 (24)	4.9 (0.6)	41	153	5	4	—(—)	—	—(—)
1970	3,516	454 (28)	12.9 (0.8)	110	322	12	10	142 (16)	312	31.3 (3.1)
1975	3,177	683 (33)	21.5 (1.0)	179	474	11	18	259 (22)	423	37.9 (2.6)
1980	3,143	857 (36)	27.3 (1.1)	221	604	16	17	321 (24)	536	37.5 (2.4)
1985	3,594	1,035 (41)	28.8 (1.1)	278	679	52	26	350 (27)	685	33.8 (2.2)
1987	3,569	1,022 (41)	28.6 (1.1)	264	703	24	31	378 (28)	644	37.0 (2.3)
1988	3,719	1,027 (45)	27.6 (1.2)	298	678	24	26	369 (30)	658	35.9 (2.5)
1989	3,713	1,005 (45)	27.1 (1.2)	277	707	3	18	390 (31)	615	38.8 (2.6)
1990	3,692	1,205 (45)	32.6 (1.2)	347	840	11	7	447 (31)	758	37.1 (2.2)
1991	3,811	1,074 (44)	28.2 (1.2)	313	702	38	22	388 (30)	687	36.1 (2.3)
1992	3,905	1,081 (44)	27.7 (1.1)	336	685	26	34	371 (29)	711	34.3 (2.3)
1993	4,053	1,097 (45)	27.1 (1.1)	369	687	20	20	426 (31)	670	38.9 (2.3)
1994[1]	4,081	1,385 (48)	33.9 (1.2)	469	887	19	9	670 (38)	715	48.4 (2.1)
1995[1]	4,148	1,489 (49)	35.9 (1.2)	511	947	15	17	754 (40)	736	50.6 (2.1)
1996[1]	4,045	1,506 (51)	37.2 (1.3)	511	947	22	26	657 (39)	848	43.7 (2.1)
1997[1]	3,947	1,528 (51)	38.7 (1.3)	643	843	25	18	754 (41)	774	49.4 (2.1)
1998[1]	3,989	1,498 (51)	37.6 (1.3)	587	869	27	14	735 (40)	763	49.1 (2.1)
1999[1]	3,862	1,505 (50)	39.0 (1.3)	621	859	13	12	773 (41)	732	51.3 (2.1)
2000[1]	3,929	1,541 (51)	39.2 (1.3)	644	854	27	16	761 (41)	779	49.4 (2.1)
2001[1]	3,985	1,538 (51)	38.6 (1.3)	599	901	14	23	715 (40)	823	46.5 (2.1)
4 years old										
1965	4,238	683 (42)	16.1 (1.0)	68	213	284	118	—(—)	—	—(—)
1970	3,620	1,007 (38)	27.8 (1.1)	176	395	318	117	230 (21)	776	22.8 (1.9)
1975	3,499	1,418 (41)	40.5 (1.2)	332	644	313	129	411 (27)	1,008	29.0 (1.7)
1980	3,072	1,423 (40)	46.3 (1.3)	363	701	239	120	467 (28)	956	32.8 (1.8)
1985	3,598	1,766 (45)	49.1 (1.3)	496	859	276	135	643 (35)	1,123	36.4 (1.7)
1987	3,597	1,717 (45)	47.7 (1.3)	431	881	280	125	548 (32)	1,169	31.9 (1.7)
1988	3,598	1,768 (50)	49.1 (1.4)	481	922	261	104	519 (35)	1,249	29.4 (1.8)
1989	3,692	1,882 (51)	51.0 (1.4)	524	1,055	202	100	592 (37)	1,290	31.4 (1.8)
1990	3,723	2,087 (48)	56.1 (1.3)	695	1,144	157	91	716 (38)	1,371	34.3 (1.6)
1991	3,763	1,994 (48)	53.0 (1.3)	584	982	287	140	667 (37)	1,326	33.5 (1.7)
1992	3,807	1,982 (49)	52.1 (1.3)	602	971	282	126	632 (36)	1,350	31.9 (1.7)
1993	4,044	2,178 (50)	53.9 (1.2)	719	957	349	154	765 (39)	1,413	35.1 (1.6)
1994[1]	4,202	2,532 (51)	60.3 (1.2)	1,020	1,232	198	82	1,095 (45)	1,438	43.2 (1.6)
1995[1]	4,145	2,553 (50)	61.6 (1.2)	1,054	1,208	207	84	1,104 (45)	1,449	43.3 (1.6)
1996[1]	4,148	2,454 (52)	59.2 (1.3)	1,029	1,168	180	77	1,034 (46)	1,420	42.1 (1.6)
1997[1]	4,033	2,665 (50)	66.1 (1.2)	1,197	1,169	207	92	1,161 (47)	1,505	43.5 (1.6)
1998[1]	4,002	2,666 (49)	66.6 (1.2)	1,183	1,219	210	53	1,179 (48)	1,487	44.2 (1.6)
1999[1]	4,021	2,769 (48)	68.9 (1.2)	1,212	1,227	207	122	1,355 (49)	1,414	48.9 (1.6)
2000[1]	3,940	2,556 (49)	64.9 (1.3)	1,144	1,121	227	65	1,182 (49)	1,374	46.2 (1.6)
2001[1]	3,927	2,608 (49)	66.4 (1.2)	1,202	1,121	236	49	1,255 (48)	1,354	48.1 (1.6)
5 years old[2]										
1965	4,162	2,521 (55)	60.6 (1.3)	18	27	2,002	474	—(—)	—	—(—)
1970	3,814	2,643 (40)	69.3 (1.1)	45	45	2,168	384	326 (24)	2,317	12.3 (0.9)
1975	3,509	2,854 (33)	81.3 (0.9)	59	57	2,358	381	625 (32)	2,228	21.9 (1.1)
1980	3,069	2,598 (29)	84.7 (0.9)	44	48	2,183	322	763 (34)	1,835	29.4 (1.3)
1985	3,542	3,065 (31)	86.5 (0.9)	73	94	2,519	379	1,151 (42)	1,914	37.6 (1.3)
1987	3,706	3,192 (32)	86.1 (0.9)	124	152	2,538	378	1,163 (43)	2,028	36.4 (1.3)
1988	3,676	3,184 (34)	86.6 (0.9)	72	170	2,590	351	1,155 (47)	2,028	36.3 (1.4)
1989	3,633	3,139 (34)	86.4 (0.9)	129	132	2,499	378	1,255 (48)	1,883	40.0 (1.5)
1990	3,792	3,367 (31)	88.8 (0.8)	157	196	2,604	411	1,414 (47)	1,953	42.0 (1.3)
1991	3,796	3,267 (33)	86.0 (0.9)	100	143	2,642	382	1,354 (47)	1,913	41.4 (1.4)
1992	3,832	3,339 (33)	87.1 (0.9)	135	127	2,688	390	1,408 (47)	1,931	42.2 (1.4)
1993	3,857	3,306 (34)	85.7 (0.9)	116	136	2,651	403	1,451 (48)	1,856	43.9 (1.4)
1994[1]	4,044	3,597 (32)	88.9 (0.8)	359	194	2,601	442	1,704 (50)	1,893	47.4 (1.3)
1995[1]	4,224	3,697 (34)	87.5 (0.8)	385	226	2,578	507	1,830 (51)	1,867	49.5 (1.3)
1996[1]	4,185	3,621 (36)	86.5 (0.9)	290	202	2,652	477	1,870 (53)	1,750	51.7 (1.4)
1997[1]	4,141	3,667 (34)	88.5 (0.8)	368	219	2,616	465	2,007 (53)	1,660	54.7 (1.4)
1998[1]	4,087	3,624 (33)	88.7 (0.8)	442	211	2,437	535	2,044 (53)	1,579	56.4 (1.4)
1999[1]	4,037	3,571 (34)	88.4 (0.8)	376	212	2,557	426	2,027 (52)	1,544	56.8 (1.4)
2000[1]	3,989	3,495 (34)	87.6 (0.9)	359	206	2,447	484	2,065 (52)	1,431	59.1 (1.4)
2001[1]	3,987	3,456 (35)	86.7 (0.9)	363	179	2,474	440	1,970 (52)	1,485	57.0 (1.4)

—Not available.

[1] Data collected using new procedures. May not be comparable with figures prior to 1994.

[2] Enrollment data include only those students in preprimary programs.

NOTE: Data are based on sample surveys of the civilian noninstitutional population. Although cells with fewer than 75,000 children are subject to wide sampling variation, they are included in the table to permit various types of aggregations. Detail may not sum to totals due to rounding. Standard errors appear in parentheses.

SOURCE: U.S. Department of Education, National Center for Education Statistics, *Preprimary Enrollment*, various years; and U.S. Department of Commerce, Bureau of the Census, Current Population Survey (CPS), October 1980 through October 2001, unpublished tabulations. (This table was prepared October 2002.)

603

Children 3 to 21 years old served in federally supported programs for the disabled, by type of disability: Selected years, 1976–77 to 2001–02

Type of disability	1976–77	1980–81	1989–90	1990–91	1991–92	1992–93	1993–94	1994–95	1995–96	1996–97	1997–98	1998–99	1999–2000	2000–01	2001–02
1	2	3	4	5	6	7	8	9	10	11	12	13	14	15	16
	Number served in thousands														
All disabilities	3,694	4,144	4,594	4,710	4,875	5,036	5,216	5,378	5,573	5,730	5,903	6,055	6,190	6,296	6,407
Specific learning disabilities	796	1,462	2,047	2,129	2,232	2,351	2,408	2,489	2,579	2,649	2,725	2,789	2,830	2,843	2,846
Speech or language impairments	1,302	1,168	971	985	996	994	1,014	1,015	1,022	1,043	1,056	1,068	1,078	1,084	1,084
Mental retardation	961	830	547	535	537	518	536	555	570	579	589	597	600	599	592
Emotional disturbance	283	347	380	390	399	400	414	427	438	445	453	462	468	473	476
Hearing impairments	88	79	57	58	60	60	64	64	67	68	69	70	70	70	70
Orthopedic impairments	87	58	48	49	51	52	56	60	63	66	67	69	71	72	73
Other health impairments	141	98	52	55	58	65	82	106	133	160	190	221	254	292	337
Visual impairments	38	31	22	23	24	23	24	24	25	25	25	26	26	25	25
Multiple disabilities	—	68	86	96	97	102	108	88	93	98	106	106	111	121	127
Deaf-blindness	—	3	2	1	1	1	1	1	1	1	1	2	2	1	2
Autism and traumatic brain injury	—	—	—	—	5	19	24	29	39	44	54	67	80	94	118
Developmental delay	—	—	—	—	—	—	—	—	—	—	4	12	19	28	45
Preschool disabled [1]	—	—	381	390	416	450	486	519	544	552	564	568	582	592	612
	Percentage distribution of children served														
All disabilities	100.0	100.0	100.0	100.0	100.0	100.0	100.0	100.0	100.0	100.0	100.0	100.0	100.0	100.0	100.0
Specific learning disabilities	21.5	35.3	44.6	45.2	45.8	46.7	46.2	46.3	46.3	46.2	46.2	46.1	45.7	45.2	44.4
Speech or language impairments	35.2	28.2	21.1	20.9	20.4	19.7	19.4	18.9	18.3	18.2	17.9	17.6	17.4	17.2	16.9
Mental retardation	26.0	20.0	11.9	11.4	11.0	10.3	10.3	10.3	10.2	10.1	10.0	9.9	9.7	9.5	9.2
Emotional disturbance	7.7	8.4	8.3	8.3	8.2	7.9	7.9	7.9	7.9	7.8	7.7	7.6	7.6	7.5	7.4
Hearing impairments	2.4	1.9	1.2	1.2	1.2	1.2	1.2	1.2	1.2	1.2	1.2	1.2	1.1	1.1	1.1
Orthopedic impairments	2.4	1.4	1.0	1.0	1.0	1.0	1.1	1.1	1.1	1.2	1.1	1.1	1.1	1.1	1.1
Other health impairments	3.8	2.4	1.1	1.2	1.2	1.3	1.6	2.0	2.4	2.8	3.2	3.6	4.1	4.6	5.3
Visual impairments	1.0	0.7	0.5	0.5	0.5	0.5	0.5	0.4	0.4	0.4	0.4	0.4	0.4	0.4	0.4
Multiple disabilities	—	1.6	1.9	2.0	2.0	2.0	2.1	1.6	1.7	1.7	1.8	1.8	1.8	1.9	2.0
Deaf-blindness	—	0.1	#	#	#	#	#	#	#	#	#	#	#	#	#
Autism and traumatic brain injury	—	—	—	—	0.1	0.4	0.5	0.5	0.7	0.8	0.9	1.1	1.3	1.5	1.8
Developmental delay	—	—	—	—	—	—	—	—	—	—	0.1	0.2	0.3	0.4	0.7
Preschool disabled [1]	—	—	8.3	8.3	8.5	8.9	9.3	9.7	9.8	9.6	9.6	9.4	9.4	9.4	9.6
	Number served as a percent of total enrollment [2]														
All disabilities	8.3	10.1	11.3	11.4	11.6	11.8	12.0	12.2	12.4	12.6	12.8	13.0	13.2	13.3	13.4
Specific learning disabilities	1.8	3.6	5.0	5.2	5.3	5.5	5.5	5.6	5.8	5.8	5.9	6.0	6.0	6.0	6.0
Speech or language impairments	2.9	2.9	2.4	2.4	2.4	2.3	2.3	2.3	2.3	2.3	2.3	2.3	2.3	2.3	2.3
Mental retardation	2.2	2.0	1.3	1.3	1.3	1.2	1.2	1.3	1.3	1.3	1.3	1.3	1.3	1.3	1.2
Emotional disturbance	0.6	0.8	0.9	0.9	0.9	0.9	1.0	1.0	1.0	1.0	1.0	1.0	1.0	1.0	1.0
Hearing impairments	0.2	0.2	0.1	0.1	0.1	0.1	0.1	0.1	0.1	0.1	0.1	0.2	0.1	0.1	0.1
Orthopedic impairments	0.2	0.1	0.1	0.1	0.1	0.1	0.1	0.1	0.1	0.1	0.1	0.1	0.2	0.2	0.2
Other health impairments	0.3	0.2	0.1	0.1	0.1	0.2	0.2	0.2	0.3	0.4	0.4	0.5	0.5	0.6	0.7
Visual impairments	0.1	0.1	0.1	0.1	0.1	0.1	0.1	0.1	0.1	0.1	0.1	0.1	0.1	0.1	0.1
Multiple disabilities	—	0.2	0.2	0.2	0.2	0.2	0.2	0.2	0.2	0.2	0.2	0.2	0.2	0.3	0.3
Deaf-blindness	—	#	#	#	#	#	#	#	#	#	#	#	#	#	#
Autism and traumatic brain injury	—	—	—	—	#	#	0.1	0.1	0.1	0.1	0.1	0.1	0.2	0.2	0.2
Developmental delay	—	—	—	—	—	—	—	—	—	—	#	#	#	0.1	0.1
Preschool disabled [1]	—	—	0.9	0.9	1.0	1.1	1.1	1.2	1.2	1.2	1.2	1.2	1.2	1.3	1.3

—Not available.

Rounds to zero.

[1] Includes preschool children 3–5 years served under Chapter I and IDEA, Part B. Prior to 1987–88, these students were included in the counts by disability condition. Beginning in 1987–88, states were no longer required to report preschool children (0–5 years) by disability condition.

[2] Based on the total enrollment in public schools, kindergarten through 12th grade, including a relatively small number of prekindergarten students.

NOTE: Includes students served under Chapter I and Individuals with Disabilities Education Act (IDEA), formerly the Education of the Handicapped Act. Prior to October 1994, children and youth with disabilities were served under the Individuals with Disabilities Education Act, Part B, and Chapter 1 of the Elementary and Secondary Education Act. In October 1994, Congress passed the Improving America's Schools Act in which funding for children and youth with disabilities was consolidated under IDEA, Part B. Data reported in this table for years prior to 1993–94 include children ages 0–21 served under Chapter 1. Counts are based on reports from the 50 states and the District of Columbia only (i.e., figures from outlying areas are not included). Increases since 1987–88 are due in part to new legislation enacted in fall 1986, which mandates public school special education services for all disabled children ages 3 through 5, in addition to age groups previously mandated. Some data have been revised from previously published figures. Detail may not sum to totals due to rounding.

SOURCE: U.S. Department of Education, Office of Special Education and Rehabilitative Services, *Annual Report to Congress on the Implementation of The Individuals with Disabilities Education Act*, various years, and unpublished tabulations; and National Center for Education Statistics, *Statistics of Public Elementary and Secondary School Systems,* various years, and The NCES Common Core of Data (CCD), "State Nonfiscal Survey of Public Elementary/Secondary Education," 1989–90 through 2001–02. (This table was prepared July 2003.)

Percentage distribution of disabled persons 6 to 21 years old receiving education services for the disabled, by educational environment and type of disability: United States and outlying areas, 1999–2000 and 2000–01

Type of disability	All environ- ments	Regular school, outside regular class			Separate public school facility	Separate private school facility	Public residential facility	Private residential facility	Homebound/ hospital placement
		Less than 21 percent	21–60 percent	More than 60 percent					
1	2	3	4	5	6	7	8	9	10
					1999–2000				
All persons, 6 to 21 years old	**100.0**	**47.3**	**28.3**	**20.3**	**1.9**	**1.0**	**0.4**	**0.3**	**0.5**
Specific learning disabilities	100.0	45.3	37.9	15.8	0.4	0.3	0.1	0.1	0.2
Speech or language impairments	100.0	87.5	6.7	5.3	0.2	0.2	#	#	0.1
Mental retardation	100.0	14.1	29.5	50.5	4.1	0.9	0.4	0.2	0.4
Emotional disturbance	100.0	25.8	23.4	32.8	7.5	5.5	1.5	2.0	1.5
Hearing impairments	100.0	40.3	19.3	24.5	5.4	1.6	8.0	0.6	0.2
Orthopedic impairments	100.0	44.4	21.9	27.7	3.5	0.7	0.1	0.1	1.6
Other health impairments	100.0	44.9	33.2	17.2	0.9	0.7	0.1	0.2	2.7
Visual impairments	100.0	49.1	19.5	17.7	4.6	1.1	6.5	0.9	0.6
Multiple disabilities	100.0	11.2	18.8	43.0	15.0	6.8	1.3	1.4	2.5
Deaf-blindness	100.0	14.8	10.1	39.7	13.8	3.4	12.2	4.2	1.7
Autism	100.0	20.7	14.5	49.9	7.9	5.4	0.2	1.1	0.5
Traumatic brain injury	100.0	31.0	26.6	31.6	2.6	4.6	0.4	0.9	2.3
Developmental delay	100.0	44.7	29.7	24.2	0.8	0.2	#	#	0.3
					2000–01				
All persons, 6 to 21 years old	**00.0**	**6.5**	**9.8**	**19.5**	**1.9**	**1.1**	**0.4**	**0.3**	**0.5**
Specific learning disabilities	100.0	44.3	40.3	14.4	0.3	0.3	0.1	0.1	0.2
Speech or language impairments	100.0	85.6	8.4	5.1	0.2	0.6	#	#	0.1
Mental retardation	100.0	13.2	29.1	51.7	4.2	0.9	0.3	0.2	0.4
Emotional disturbance	100.0	26.8	23.4	31.8	7.7	5.4	1.6	2.0	1.3
Hearing impairments	100.0	42.3	20.0	22.5	4.4	1.9	8.3	0.6	0.2
Orthopedic impairments	100.0	46.4	23.4	24.3	3.5	0.7	0.1	0.1	1.6
Other health impairments	100.0	45.1	33.9	16.7	0.8	0.8	0.2	0.2	2.4
Visual impairments	100.0	50.5	20.1	16.0	4.7	1.2	5.9	0.9	0.7
Multiple disabilities	100.0	12.1	16.0	45.5	14.6	6.9	1.3	1.3	2.3
Deaf-blindness	100.0	18.1	9.9	34.2	14.5	4.5	12.5	4.4	1.9
Autism	100.0	24.3	15.3	46.4	7.2	5.2	0.3	0.9	0.4
Traumatic brain injury	100.0	32.3	27.9	29.4	2.8	4.2	0.3	0.9	2.2
Developmental delay	100.0	46.4	29.9	22.3	0.6	0.4	#	0.1	0.2

\# Rounds to zero.

NOTE: Data by disability condition are only reported for 6- to 21-year-old students. Detail may not sum to totals due to rounding.

SOURCE: U.S. Department of Education, Office of Special Education and Rehabilitative Services, *Annual Report to Congress on the Implementation of The Individuals with Disabilities Education Act*, and unpublished tabulations. (This table was prepared July 2003.)

Number and percent of children served under Individuals with Disabilities Education Act, Part B, by age group and state or jurisdiction: Selected years, 1990–91 to 2001–02

State or jurisdiction	Ages 3 to 21						Ages 3 to 5			
	1990–91	1999–2000	2000–201	2001–02	Disabled students as a percent of public school enrollment, 2001–02[1]	Percent change, ages 3 to 21, 1990–91 to 2001–02	1990–91	1999–2000	2000–01	2001–02
1	2	3	4	5	6	7	8	9	10	11
United States	4,760,999	6,190,235	6,295,816	6,407,418	13.4	34.6	440,661	581,997	592,087	612,084
Alabama	94,945	99,733	99,828	96,477	13.1	1.6	7,498	7,316	7,554	7,526
Alaska	14,745	17,495	17,691	18,017	13.4	22.2	1,813	1,633	1,637	1,678
Arizona	57,235	93,333	96,442	100,886	10.9	76.3	4,936	9,076	9,144	9,906
Arkansas	47,835	60,864	62,222	63,969	14.2	33.7	5,274	9,031	9,376	9,504
California	469,282	640,815	645,287	657,671	10.5	40.1	40,489	58,491	57,651	58,456
Colorado	57,102	76,858	78,715	80,083	10.8	40.2	4,894	8,059	8,202	8,581
Connecticut	64,562	74,722	73,886	74,016	13.0	14.6	6,142	7,275	7,172	7,390
Delaware	14,294	16,287	16,760	17,295	15.0	21.0	1,579	1,641	1,652	1,875
District of Columbia	6,290	9,348	10,559	12,456	16.5	98.0	411	560	374	436
Florida	236,013	356,198	367,335	379,609	15.2	60.8	16,387	29,363	30,660	32,590
Georgia	101,997	164,374	171,292	178,239	12.1	74.7	7,333	15,922	16,560	17,709
Hawaii	13,169	22,964	23,951	23,526	12.7	78.6	1,273	1,860	1,919	1,930
Idaho	22,017	29,112	29,174	29,100	11.8	32.2	3,129	3,626	3,591	3,650
Illinois	239,185	287,475	297,316	306,355	14.8	28.1	26,122	27,689	28,787	29,664
Indiana	114,643	151,599	156,320	161,519	16.2	40.9	8,937	14,499	15,101	16,347
Iowa	60,695	71,970	72,461	73,084	15.0	20.4	6,329	5,599	5,580	5,487
Kansas	45,212	60,036	61,267	61,873	13.2	36.9	4,308	7,334	7,728	8,135
Kentucky	79,421	91,521	94,572	98,146	15.0	23.6	11,008	15,897	16,372	17,747
Louisiana	73,663	96,632	97,938	99,325	13.6	34.8	7,541	9,671	9,957	10,061
Maine	27,987	35,139	35,633	36,580	17.8	30.7	2,895	3,954	3,978	4,230
Maryland	91,263	111,711	112,077	112,426	13.1	23.2	10,409	9,750	10,003	10,614
Massachusetts	154,616	165,013	162,216	150,003	15.4	3.0	17,014	14,568	14,328	13,070
Michigan	166,927	213,585	221,456	226,061	13.1	35.4	14,963	19,236	19,937	20,887
Minnesota	80,896	107,860	109,880	110,964	13.0	37.2	10,529	11,366	11,522	11,804
Mississippi	60,934	62,359	62,281	62,196	12.6	2.1	5,704	6,812	6,944	6,902
Missouri	101,955	134,950	137,381	141,524	15.6	38.8	4,889	10,683	11,307	12,222
Montana	17,138	19,039	19,313	19,262	12.7	12.4	1,934	1,614	1,635	1,687
Nebraska	32,761	42,577	42,793	43,864	15.4	33.9	2,961	3,707	3,724	3,896
Nevada	18,440	35,703	38,160	40,227	11.3	118.2	1,742	3,664	3,676	3,976
New Hampshire	19,658	28,597	30,077	30,270	14.6	54.0	2,077	2,193	2,387	2,452
New Jersey	181,319	214,875	221,715	228,844	17.1	26.2	17,190	16,058	16,361	16,716
New Mexico	36,037	52,346	52,256	52,225	16.3	44.9	2,247	5,115	4,970	5,145
New York	307,458	434,347	441,333	440,232	15.3	43.2	26,353	50,140	51,665	53,313
North Carolina	123,126	173,067	173,067	186,972	14.2	51.9	10,700	17,361	17,361	19,010
North Dakota	12,504	13,612	13,652	13,627	12.8	9.0	1,374	1,283	1,247	1,294
Ohio	205,440	236,200	237,643	238,547	13.0	16.1	12,487	19,341	18,664	19,075
Oklahoma	65,653	83,149	85,577	87,801	14.1	33.7	5,359	6,077	6,393	6,714
Oregon	55,149	73,531	75,204	76,129	13.8	38.0	3,581	6,387	6,926	7,227
Pennsylvania	219,428	233,273	242,655	249,731	13.7	13.8	23,156	21,161	21,477	21,885
Rhode Island	21,076	29,895	30,727	31,816	20.1	51.0	2,112	2,651	2,614	2,692
South Carolina	77,765	103,153	105,922	110,037	15.9	41.5	8,346	11,352	11,775	11,967
South Dakota	14,987	16,246	16,825	16,931	13.3	13.0	2,366	2,267	2,286	2,244
Tennessee	104,898	126,732	125,863	126,245	13.6	20.4	7,536	10,690	10,699	11,132
Texas	350,636	493,850	491,642	492,857	11.8	40.6	30,955	36,079	36,442	37,244
Utah	47,747	54,957	53,921	54,570	11.3	14.3	4,565	5,899	5,785	5,922
Vermont	12,263	14,073	13,623	13,886	13.7	13.2	1,200	1,391	1,237	1,293
Virginia	113,971	157,995	162,212	170,518	14.7	49.6	11,791	14,023	14,444	15,145
Washington	85,395	116,235	118,851	120,970	12.0	41.7	11,409	11,623	11,760	11,881
West Virginia	43,135	50,314	50,333	50,136	17.7	16.2	3,630	5,409	5,445	5,332
Wisconsin	86,930	121,209	125,358	127,035	14.4	46.1	12,213	13,934	14,383	14,574
Wyoming	11,202	13,307	13,154	13,286	15.1	18.6	1,571	1,667	1,695	1,867
Bureau of Indian Affairs	6,997	12,913	8,448	8,571	18.4	22.5	1,092	386	338	266
Outlying areas	39,445	63,981	70,670	71,440	10.5	81.1	3,937	6,750	8,168	7,845
American Samoa	363	703	697	813	5.1	124.0	48	55	48	64
Guam	1,750	2,230	2,267	2,368	7.4	35.3	198	195	205	218
Northern Marianas	411	568	569	590	5.6	43.6	211	48	53	52
Palau	459	123	131	169	(2)	-63.2	45	11	10	13
Puerto Rico	35,129	58,740	65,504	65,874	10.9	87.5	3,345	6,274	7,746	7,378
Virgin Islands	1,333	1,617	1,502	1,626	8.7	22.0	90	167	106	120

[1] Percent of students that are disabled is based on the enrollment in public schools, prekindergarten through 12th grade.

[2] Public school was not reported.

NOTE: Prior to 1994, children and youth with disabilities were served under the Individuals with Disabilities Education Act IDEA, Part B, and Chapter 1 of the Elementary and Secondary Education Act. In October 1994, Congress passed the Improving America's Schools Act in which funding for children and youth with disabilities was consolidated under (IDEA), Part B. Data reported in this table for years prior to 1994 include children served under Chapter 1. Some data revised from previously published figures.

SOURCE: U.S. Department of Education, Office of Special Education and Rehabilitative Services, Annual Report to Congress on the Implementation of The Individuals with Disabilities Education Act, various years, and unpublished tabulations, and the National Center for Education Statistics, The NCES Common Core of Data (CCD), "State Nonfiscal Survey of Public Elementary/Secondary Education," 2001–02. (This table was prepared July 2003.)

Number of gifted and talented students in public elementary and secondary schools, by sex and state: 2000

State	Total	Male	Female	Gifted and talented as a percent of total enrollment, by sex		
				Total	Male	Female
1	2	3	4	5	6	7
United States	**2,926,034**	**1,419,729**	**1,506,305**	**6.3**	**6.0**	**6.7**
Alabama	25,437	13,264	12,173	3.5	3.5	3.5
Alaska	5,574	2,868	2,706	4.2	4.2	4.2
Arizona	46,638	21,892	24,746	10.5	9.5	11.4
Arkansas	55,851	28,296	27,555	6.4	6.3	6.5
California	411,363	199,627	211,736	6.9	6.5	7.3
Colorado	45,701	22,567	23,134	6.5	6.2	6.7
Connecticut	17,470	8,415	9,055	3.3	3.1	3.5
Delaware	6,100	2,866	3,234	5.4	4.9	5.9
District of Columbia	—	—	—	—	—	—
Florida	105,341	53,936	51,405	4.4	4.4	4.5
Georgia	113,036	54,421	58,615	8.0	7.5	8.5
Hawaii	11,957	5,109	6,848	6.6	5.4	7.8
Idaho	9,204	4,640	4,564	3.8	3.7	3.9
Illinois	126,063	61,073	64,990	6.3	5.9	6.7
Indiana	62,670	28,872	33,798	6.3	5.7	7.0
Iowa	39,453	19,281	20,172	8.1	7.7	8.6
Kansas	14,952	8,231	6,721	3.3	3.5	3.0
Kentucky	71,773	33,830	37,943	11.5	10.5	12.6
Louisiana	24,548	12,337	12,211	3.4	3.4	3.5
Maine	11,668	5,780	5,888	5.4	5.2	5.6
Maryland	100,487	46,773	53,714	12.0	10.9	13.1
Massachusetts	11,263	5,275	5,988	1.2	1.1	1.3
Michigan	61,896	30,171	31,725	3.6	3.4	3.8
Minnesota	61,555	30,304	31,251	7.3	7.0	7.6
Mississippi	27,873	13,369	14,504	5.6	5.3	6.0
Missouri	30,494	15,710	14,784	3.4	3.5	3.4
Montana	8,642	4,232	4,410	5.6	5.3	5.9
Nebraska	31,555	15,318	16,237	11.3	10.7	11.9
Nevada	11,583	5,958	5,625	3.5	3.5	3.4
New Hampshire	3,829	1,841	1,988	1.7	1.6	1.9
New Jersey	99,418	47,300	52,118	7.8	7.3	8.4
New Mexico	12,107	6,644	5,463	3.8	4.1	3.6
New York	94,915	45,931	48,984	3.3	3.1	3.5
North Carolina	125,536	59,621	65,915	10.0	9.3	10.8
North Dakota	2,613	1,279	1,334	2.4	2.3	2.5
Ohio	101,656	50,432	51,224	5.5	5.3	5.7
Oklahoma	84,467	40,904	43,563	13.9	13.1	14.7
Oregon	41,668	21,754	19,914	7.7	7.8	7.6
Pennsylvania	88,483	45,861	42,622	4.9	4.9	4.9
Rhode Island	3,400	1,548	1,852	2.2	1.9	2.4
South Carolina	66,546	30,470	36,076	9.9	8.9	11.0
South Dakota	4,370	2,267	2,103	3.4	3.4	3.3
Tennessee	27,032	12,688	14,344	3.0	2.7	3.3
Texas	351,068	167,049	184,019	9.0	8.3	9.7
Utah	13,707	6,555	7,152	2.9	2.7	3.1
Vermont	1,191	563	628	1.1	1.0	1.2
Virginia	116,914	56,724	60,190	10.3	9.7	10.9
Washington	44,412	21,260	23,152	4.5	4.2	4.8
West Virginia	6,021	3,232	2,789	2.1	2.2	2.1
Wisconsin	84,872	40,636	44,236	10.0	9.3	10.7
Wyoming	1,659	753	906	1.9	1.6	2.1

—Not available.

NOTE: Detail may not sum to totals due to rounding.

SOURCE: U.S. Department of Education, Office of Civil Rights, "OCR Elementary and Secondary Survey: 2000." (This table was prepared October 2003.)

High school graduates compared with population 17 years of age, by sex of graduates and control of school: Selected years, 1869–70 to 2002–03

[Numbers in thousands]

School year	Population 17 years old [1]	High school graduates						Graduates as a ratio of 17-year-old population
		Total [2]	Sex		Control		
			Male	Female	Public [3]	Private [4]	
1	2	3	4	5	6	7	8
1869–70	815	16	7	9	—	—	2.0
1879–80	946	24	11	13	—	—	2.5
1889–90	1,259	44	19	25	22	22	3.5
1899–1900	1,489	95	38	57	62	33	6.4
1909–10	1,786	156	64	93	111	45	8.8
1919–20	1,855	311	124	188	231	80	16.8
1929–30	2,296	667	300	367	592	75	29.0
1939–40	2,403	1,221	579	643	1,143	78	50.8
1947–48	2,261	1,190	563	627	1,073	117	52.6
1949–50	2,034	1,200	571	629	1,063	136	59.0
1951–52	2,086	1,197	569	627	1,056	141	57.4
1953–54	2,135	1,276	613	664	1,129	147	59.8
1955–56	2,242	1,415	680	735	1,252	163	63.1
1956–57	2,272	1,434	690	744	1,270	164	63.1
1957–58	2,325	1,506	725	781	1,332	174	64.8
1958–59	2,458	1,627	784	843	1,435	192	66.2
1959–60	2,672	1,858	895	963	1,627	231	69.5
1960–61	2,892	1,964	955	1,009	1,725	239	67.9
1961–62	2,768	1,918	938	980	1,678	240	69.3
1962–63	2,740	1,943	956	987	1,710	233	70.9
1963–64	2,978	2,283	1,120	1,163	2,008	275	76.7
1964–65	3,684	2,658	1,311	1,347	2,360	298	72.1
1965–66	3,489	2,665	1,323	1,342	2,367	298	76.4
1966–67	3,500	2,672	1,328	1,344	2,374	298	76.3
1967–68	3,532	2,695	1,338	1,357	2,395	300	76.3
1968–69	3,659	2,822	1,399	1,423	2,522	300	77.1
1969–70	3,757	2,889	1,430	1,459	2,589	300	76.9
1970–71	3,872	2,938	1,454	1,484	2,638	300	75.9
1971–72	3,973	3,002	1,487	1,515	2,700	302	75.6
1972–73	4,049	3,035	1,500	1,535	2,729	306	75.0
1973–74	4,132	3,073	1,512	1,561	2,763	310	74.4
1974–75	4,256	3,133	1,542	1,591	2,823	310	73.6
1975–76	4,272	3,148	1,552	1,596	2,837	311	73.7
1976–77	4,272	3,152	1,548	1,604	2,837	315	73.8
1977–78	4,286	3,127	1,531	1,596	2,825	302	73.0
1978–79	4,327	3,101	1,517	1,584	2,801	300	71.7
1979–80	4,262	3,043	1,491	1,552	2,748	295	71.4
1980–81	4,212	3,020	1,483	1,537	2,725	295	71.7
1981–82	4,134	2,995	1,471	1,524	2,705	290	72.4
1982–83	3,962	2,888	1,437	1,451	2,598	290	72.9
1983–84	3,784	2,767	—	—	2,495	272	73.1
1984–85	3,699	2,677	—	—	2,414	263	72.4
1985–86	3,670	2,643	—	—	2,383	260	72.0
1986–87	3,754	2,694	—	—	2,429	265	71.8
1987–88	3,849	2,773	—	—	2,500	273	72.0
1988–89	3,842	2,744	—	—	2,459	285	71.4
1989–90	3,505	2,589	—	—	2,320	269	73.9
1990–91	3,418	2,493	—	—	2,235	258	72.9
1991–92	3,399	2,478	—	—	2,226	252	72.9
1992–93	3,449	2,480	—	—	2,233	247	71.9
1993–94	3,443	2,464	—	—	2,221	243	71.6
1994–95	3,636	2,520	—	—	2,274	246	69.3
1995–96	3,640	2,518	—	—	2,273	245	69.2
1996–97	3,792	2,612	—	—	2,358	254	68.9
1997–98	4,008	2,704	—	—	2,439	265	67.5
1998–99	3,918	2,759	—	—	2,486	273	70.4
1999–2000	4,057	2,831	—	—	2,554	277	69.8
2000–01	4,006	2,852	—	—	2,569	283	71.2
2001–02 [5]	4,052	2,917	—	—	2,630	287	72.0
2002–03 [5]	—	2,986	—	—	2,685	301	—

—Not available.

[1] Derived from *Current Population Reports,* Series P-25. For years 1869–70 through 1989–90, 17-year-old population is an estimate of the October 17-year-old population based on July data. Data for 1990–91 and later years are October estimates prepared by the Census Bureau.

[2] Includes graduates of public and private schools.

[3] Data for 1929–30 and preceding years are from *Statistics of Public High Schools* and exclude graduates from high schools that failed to report to the Office of Education.

[4] For most years, private school data have been estimated based on periodic private school surveys.

[5] Public high school graduates based on state estimates.

NOTE: Includes graduates of regular day school programs. Excludes graduates of other programs, when separately reported, and recipients of high school equivalency certificates. Some data have been revised from previously published figures. Detail may not sum to totals due to rounding.

SOURCE: U.S. Department of Education, National Center for Education Statistics, *Annual Reports of the Commissioner of Education,* 1870 through 1910; *Biennial Survey of Education in the United States,* 1919–20 through 1949–50; *Statistics of State School Systems, Statistics of Public Elementary and Secondary School Systems; Statistics of Nonpublic Elementary and Secondary Schools;* 1959 through 1980, The NCES Common Core of Data (CCD); State Nonfiscal Survey, 1981 through 2001, and *Projections of Education Statistics to 2013.* (This table was prepared September 2003.)

Public high school graduates, by state or jurisdiction: Selected years, 1969–70 to 2002–03

State or jurisdiction	1969–70	1979–80	1980–81	1985–86	1990–91	1995–96	1999–2000 [1]	2000–01	Projected 2001–02, graduates	Projected 2002–03, graduates	Percent change, 1990–91 to 2002–03
1	2	3	4	5	6	7	8	9	10	11	12
United States	2,588,639	2,747,678	2,725,285	2,382,616	2,234,893	2,273,109	2,553,844	2,568,956	2,630,130	2,684,920	20.1
Alabama	45,286	45,190	44,894	39,620	39,042	35,043	37,819	37,082	37,260	36,850	–5.6
Alaska	3,297	5,223	5,343	5,464	5,458	5,945	6,615	6,812	6,790	7,160	31.2
Arizona	22,040	28,633	28,416	27,533	31,282	30,008	38,304	46,773	44,830	47,610	52.2
Arkansas	26,068	29,052	29,577	26,227	25,668	25,094	27,335	27,100	26,890	27,410	6.8
California	260,908	249,217	242,172	229,026	234,164	259,071	309,866	315,189	326,140	331,730	41.7
Colorado	30,312	36,804	35,897	32,621	31,293	32,608	38,924	39,241	41,160	41,650	33.1
Connecticut	34,755	37,683	38,369	33,571	27,290	26,319	31,562	30,388	32,610	32,980	20.9
Delaware	6,985	7,582	7,349	5,791	5,223	5,609	6,108	6,614	6,600	6,770	29.6
District of Columbia [2]	4,980	4,959	4,848	3,875	3,369	2,696	2,695	2,808	2,760	2,560	–24.0
Florida	70,478	87,324	88,755	83,029	87,419	89,242	106,708	111,112	120,050	120,340	37.7
Georgia	56,859	61,621	62,963	59,082	60,088	56,271	62,563	62,499	65,520	67,100	11.7
Hawaii	10,407	11,493	11,472	9,958	8,974	9,387	10,437	10,102	10,140	10,000	11.4
Idaho	12,296	13,187	12,679	12,059	11,961	14,667	16,170	15,941	16,090	15,940	33.3
Illinois	126,864	135,579	136,795	114,319	103,329	104,626	111,835	110,624	117,430	120,570	16.7
Indiana	69,984	73,143	73,381	59,817	57,892	56,330	57,012	56,172	56,350	56,460	–2.5
Iowa	44,063	43,445	42,635	34,279	28,593	31,689	33,926	33,774	33,580	34,290	19.9
Kansas	33,394	30,890	29,397	25,587	24,414	25,786	29,102	29,360	29,840	29,850	22.3
Kentucky	37,473	41,203	41,714	37,288	35,835	36,641	36,830	36,957	34,890	34,360	–4.1
Louisiana	43,641	46,297	46,199	39,965	33,489	36,467	38,430	38,314	37,910	37,710	12.6
Maine	14,003	15,445	15,554	13,006	13,151	11,795	12,211	12,654	12,620	12,950	–1.5
Maryland	46,462	54,270	54,050	46,700	39,014	41,785	47,849	49,222	50,490	51,520	32.1
Massachusetts	63,865	73,802	74,831	60,360	50,216	47,993	52,950	54,393	55,590	55,250	10.0
Michigan	121,000	124,316	124,372	101,042	88,234	85,530	97,679	96,515	104,550	110,610	25.4
Minnesota	60,480	64,908	64,166	51,988	46,474	50,481	57,372	56,581	59,090	59,980	29.1
Mississippi	29,653	27,586	28,083	25,134	23,665	23,032	24,232	23,748	23,510	23,380	–1.2
Missouri	55,315	62,265	60,359	49,204	46,928	49,011	52,848	54,138	54,050	54,890	17.0
Montana	11,520	12,135	11,634	9,761	9,013	10,139	10,903	10,628	10,640	10,740	19.2
Nebraska	21,280	22,410	21,411	17,845	16,500	18,014	20,149	19,658	20,330	20,250	22.7
Nevada	5,449	8,473	9,069	8,784	9,370	10,374	14,551	15,127	15,800	12,940	38.1
New Hampshire	8,516	11,722	11,552	10,648	10,059	10,094	11,829	12,294	12,480	12,950	28.7
New Jersey	86,498	94,564	93,168	78,781	67,003	67,704	74,420	76,130	78,290	82,320	22.9
New Mexico	16,060	18,424	17,915	15,468	15,157	15,402	18,031	18,199	17,580	17,650	16.4
New York	190,000	204,064	198,465	162,165	133,562	134,401	141,731	141,884	144,820	146,030	9.3
North Carolina	68,886	70,862	69,395	65,865	62,792	57,014	62,140	63,288	66,100	68,310	8.8
North Dakota	11,150	9,928	9,924	7,610	7,573	8,027	8,606	8,445	8,060	8,030	6.0
Ohio	142,248	144,169	143,503	119,561	107,484	102,098	111,668	111,281	109,220	113,610	5.7
Oklahoma	36,293	39,305	38,875	34,452	33,007	33,060	37,646	37,458	36,510	36,280	9.9
Oregon	32,236	29,939	28,729	26,286	24,597	26,570	30,151	29,939	31,140	31,630	28.6
Pennsylvania	151,014	146,458	144,645	122,871	104,770	105,981	113,959	114,436	116,150	118,980	13.6
Rhode Island	10,146	10,864	10,719	8,908	7,744	7,689	8,477	8,603	8,900	9,080	17.3
South Carolina	34,940	38,697	38,347	34,500	32,999	30,182	31,617	29,742	31,450	33,140	0.4
South Dakota	11,757	10,689	10,385	7,870	7,127	8,532	9,278	8,881	8,950	8,800	23.5
Tennessee	49,000	49,845	50,648	43,263	44,847	43,792	41,568	40,642	42,240	43,580	–2.8
Texas	139,046	171,449	171,665	161,150	174,306	171,844	212,925	215,316	219,340	228,510	31.1
Utah	18,395	20,035	19,886	19,774	22,219	26,293	32,501	31,036	30,720	30,280	36.3
Vermont	6,095	6,733	6,424	5,794	5,212	5,867	6,675	6,856	7,040	6,820	30.9
Virginia	58,562	66,621	67,126	63,113	58,441	58,166	65,596	66,067	66,630	71,620	22.6
Washington	50,425	50,402	50,046	45,805	42,514	49,862	57,597	55,081	57,470	58,490	37.6
West Virginia	26,139	23,369	23,580	21,870	21,064	20,335	19,437	18,440	17,110	17,230	–18.2
Wisconsin	66,753	69,332	67,743	58,340	49,340	52,651	58,545	59,341	60,260	61,730	25.1
Wyoming	5,363	6,072	6,161	5,587	5,728	5,892	6,462	6,071	6,160	6,000	4.7
Bureau of Indian Affairs	—	—	—	—	—	—	—	—	—	—	—
Department of Defense dependents schools:											
Overseas schools	—	· —	—	—	—	2,674	2,642	2,621	—	—	—
Domestic schools	—	—	—	—	—	—	560	568	—	—	—
Outlying areas											
American Samoa	[3] 367	—	—	608	597	719	698	722	—	—	—
Guam	972	—	—	840	1,014	987	1,406	1,371	—	—	—
Northern Marianas	—	—	—	—	273	325	360	361	—	—	—
Puerto Rico	24,917	—	—	31,597	29,329	29,499	30,856	30,154	—	—	—
Virgin Islands	[3] 432	—	—	1,044	981	937	1,060	966	—	—	—

—Not available.

[1] Revised from previously published data.

[2] Beginning in 1985–86, graduates from adult programs are excluded.

[3] Data are for 1970–71.

NOTE: Data include graduates of regular day school programs, but exclude graduates of other programs and persons receiving high school equivalency certificates. Some data have been revised from previously published figures.

SOURCE: U.S. Department of Education, National Center for Education Statistics, *Statistics of Public Elementary and Secondary Schools,* various years, and The NCES Common Core of Data (CCD), "State Nonfiscal Survey of Public Elementary/Secondary Education," 1986–87 through 2001–02, and *Projections of Education Statistics to 2013.* (This table was prepared July 2003.)

Public high school graduates and dropouts, by race/ethnicity and state or jurisdiction: 2000–01

State or jurisdiction	High school graduates, by race/ethnicity, 2000–01						Percent of 9th to 12th graders who dropped out during 2000–01, by race/ethnicity [1]					
	Total	White, non-Hispanic	Black, non-Hispanic	Hispanic	Asian or Pacific Islander	American Indian/ Alaska Native	Total	White, non-His-panic	Black, non-His-panic	Hispanic	Asian or Pacific Islander	American Indian/ Alaska Native
1	2	3	4	5	6	7	8	9	10	11	12	13
United States [2,3]	2,568,194	1,782,327	336,074	296,783	126,861	26,151	—	—	—	—	—	—
Alabama	37,082	24,073	11,986	238	348	437	4.1	4.2	4.0	5.5	2.5	2.6
Alaska	6,812	4,678	246	173	429	1,286	8.2	6.3	11.4	11.0	8.6	12.7
Arizona	46,773	—	—	—	—	—	10.9	7.1	13.9	16.8	5.0	17.0
Arkansas	27,100	20,454	5,697	528	302	119	5.3	4.8	6.5	8.6	3.7	7.5
California	315,189	139,228	22,474	103,795	46,958	2,734	—	—	—	—	—	—
Colorado	39,241	30,684	1,681	5,321	1,250	305	—	—	—	—	—	—
Connecticut	30,388	23,429	3,369	2,563	961	66	3.0	2.0	5.3	7.0	1.8	3.7
Delaware [3]	6,479	4,400	1,661	208	195	15	4.2	3.6	5.3	7.5	2.2	2.4
District of Columbia	2,808	117	2,401	215	72	3	—	—	—	—	—	—
Florida	111,112	66,205	23,608	17,943	3,068	288	4.4	3.5	5.9	5.6	2.4	3.9
Georgia	62,499	39,353	19,795	1,281	1,988	82	7.2	5.7	9.4	9.4	3.7	6.2
Hawaii	10,102	1,917	177	441	7,534	33	5.7	6.3	7.1	6.3	5.5	9.3
Idaho	15,941	14,541	70	973	224	133	5.6	—	—	—	—	—
Illinois	110,624	79,210	15,498	10,855	4,889	172	6.0	3.5	12.9	10.4	2.7	6.4
Indiana	56,172	49,794	4,358	1,304	621	95	—	—	—	—	—	—
Iowa	33,774	31,618	678	582	684	212	2.7	2.3	7.3	9.1	2.3	10.4
Kansas	29,360	25,220	1,844	1,323	702	271	3.2	2.6	5.4	7.6	2.1	5.6
Kentucky	36,957	33,421	2,995	232	269	40	4.6	4.5	6.5	4.6	2.7	0.0
Louisiana	38,314	21,873	15,046	509	678	208	8.3	6.5	10.8	8.8	4.8	9.7
Maine	12,654	12,295	84	79	121	75	3.1	3.1	3.6	2.6	4.5	5.9
Maryland	49,222	28,726	16,155	1,708	2,488	145	4.1	3.2	5.9	3.7	1.6	4.7
Massachusetts	54,393	43,704	4,222	3,845	2,517	105	3.4	2.6	6.0	7.9	3.9	3.2
Michigan	96,515	79,452	12,060	2,139	1,989	875	—	—	—	—	—	—
Minnesota	56,581	50,714	1,840	916	2,468	643	4.0	2.9	12.3	12.7	5.5	15.1
Mississippi	23,748	12,297	11,158	87	190	16	4.6	3.8	5.6	3.6	1.8	3.9
Missouri	54,138	45,716	6,824	711	753	134	4.2	3.9	6.2	7.4	2.6	5.4
Montana	10,628	9,629	33	169	108	689	4.2	3.5	5.2	8.5	3.6	11.0
Nebraska	19,658	17,619	827	762	311	139	4.0	2.9	10.9	12.2	3.8	13.9
Nevada	15,127	10,348	1,201	2,331	998	249	5.2	4.0	6.8	8.0	6.8	4.4
New Hampshire	12,294	—	—	—	—	—	5.4	5.2	9.5	11.6	4.3	7.8
New Jersey	76,130	49,647	11,507	9,402	5,370	204	2.8	1.6	5.7	5.6	1.0	12.0
New Mexico	18,199	7,587	426	7,954	236	1,996	5.3	3.6	5.3	6.7	2.4	5.9
New York	141,884	94,355	20,594	16,317	10,124	494	3.8	2.1	6.3	7.2	2.9	6.5
North Carolina	63,288	43,119	16,810	1,264	1,334	761	6.3	5.4	7.6	10.6	4.6	11.7
North Dakota	8,445	7,923	47	54	48	373	2.2	1.5	3.9	3.2	3.2	10.0
Ohio [3]	110,861	96,206	11,645	1,378	1,509	123	3.9	3.0	9.2	8.9	2.4	7.6
Oklahoma	37,458	26,066	3,243	1,492	751	5,906	5.2	4.6	7.9	10.6	3.9	4.8
Oregon [3]	29,732	25,782	604	1,629	1,269	448	5.3	4.5	11.7	11.5	4.4	8.4
Pennsylvania	114,436	96,931	11,915	2,961	2,567	62	3.6	2.7	7.4	8.9	2.9	5.7
Rhode Island	8,603	6,977	546	769	273	38	5.0	3.9	8.5	10.2	5.8	8.4
South Carolina	29,742	—	—	—	—	—	3.3	3.0	3.8	3.8	1.2	6.4
South Dakota	8,881	8,358	41	65	83	334	3.9	2.6	6.3	8.7	3.9	20.6
Tennessee	40,642	—	—	—	—	—	4.3	—	—	—	—	—
Texas	215,316	109,634	28,295	69,595	7,218	574	4.2	2.5	5.4	6.1	2.2	5.0
Utah	31,036	28,209	184	1,527	768	348	3.7	3.2	7.9	9.0	4.9	8.3
Vermont	6,856	—	—	—	—	—	4.7	4.7	7.0	7.5	2.5	7.0
Virginia	66,067	45,339	14,930	2,342	3,311	145	3.5	2.8	4.9	6.4	2.4	6.3
Washington	55,081	43,686	2,157	3,495	4,675	1,068	4.0	—	—	—	—	—
West Virginia	18,440	17,573	665	54	131	17	4.2	4.2	5.2	7.3	0.6	14.3
Wisconsin	59,341	52,835	2,835	1,557	1,567	547	2.3	1.4	9.8	6.5	2.4	5.7
Wyoming	6,071	5,578	53	279	63	98	6.4	5.8	16.9	11.6	5.4	14.1
Bureau of Indian Affairs	—	—	—	—	—	—	—	—	—	—	—	—
Department of Defense dependents schools:												
Overseas schools [3]	2,119	1,160	422	175	362	0	—	—	—	—	—	—
Domestic schools [3]	535	194	117	199	25	0	—	—	—	—	—	—
Outlying areas												
American Samoa	722	0	0	0	722	0	1.9	0.0	0.0	0.0	1.9	0.0
Guam [3]	1,349	24	3	3	1,319	0	11.4	6.9	4.3	13.6	11.3	10.0
Northern Marianas	361	1	0	0	360	0	6.1	0.0	0.0	0.0	6.1	0.0
Puerto Rico	30,154	0	0	30,154	0	0	1.0	0.0	0.0	1.0	0.0	0.0
Virgin Islands	966	5	875	79	4	3	3.9	9.4	3.5	8.5	0.0	0.0

—Not available.

[1] Alabama, Alaska, Florida, Hawaii, Illinois, Maryland, New Jersey, Oklahoma, Tennessee, Vermont, and Puerto Rico reported data on an alternative July through June cycle, rather than the specified October through September cycle for dropout data.

[2] U.S. total includes estimates for nonreporting states, based on 2000 12th-grade enrollment racial/ethnic distribution reported by state.

[3] Data differ slightly from figures reported in other tables due to varying reporting practices for racial/ethnic survey data.

SOURCE: U.S. Department of Education, National Center for Education Statistics, The NCES Common Core of Data (CCD) "Local Education Agency Universe Survey Dropout and Completion Data File: School Year 2000–01," Version 1a; and unpublished data. (This table was prepared October 2003.)

Percent of high school dropouts (status dropouts) among persons 16 to 24 years old, by sex and race/ethnicity: Selected years, April 1960 to October 2001

Year	Total				Male				Female			
	All races	White, non-Hispanic	Black, non-Hispanic	Hispanic origin	All races	White, non-Hispanic	Black, non-Hispanic	Hispanic origin	All races	White, non-Hispanic	Black, non-Hispanic	Hispanic origin
1	2	3	4	5	6	7	8	9	10	11	12	13
1960[1]	27.2 —	— —	— —	— —	27.8 —	— —	— —	— —	26.7 —	— —	— —	— —
1967[2]	17.0 —	15.4 —	28.6 —	— —	16.5 —	14.7 —	30.6 —	— —	17.3 —	16.1 —	26.9 —	— —
1968[2]	16.2 —	14.7 —	27.4 —	— —	15.8 —	14.4 —	27.1 —	— —	16.5 —	15.0 —	27.6 —	— —
1969[2]	15.2 —	13.6 —	26.7 —	— —	14.3 —	12.6 —	26.9 —	— —	16.0 —	14.6 —	26.7 —	— —
1970[2]	15.0 —	13.2 —	27.9 —	— —	14.2 —	12.2 —	29.4 —	— —	15.7 —	14.1 —	26.6 —	— —
1971[2]	14.7 —	13.4 —	23.7 —	— —	14.2 —	12.6 —	25.5 —	— —	15.2 —	14.2 —	22.1 —	— —
1972	14.6 (0.3)	12.3 (0.3)	21.3 (1.1)	34.3 (2.2)	14.1 (0.4)	11.6 (0.4)	22.3 (1.6)	33.7 (3.2)	15.1 (0.4)	12.8 (0.4)	20.5 (1.4)	34.8 (3.1)
1973	14.1 (0.3)	11.6 (0.3)	22.2 (1.1)	33.5 (2.2)	13.7 (0.4)	11.5 (0.4)	21.5 (1.5)	30.4 (3.2)	14.5 (0.4)	11.8 (0.4)	22.8 (1.5)	36.4 (3.2)
1974	14.3 (0.3)	11.9 (0.3)	21.2 (1.0)	33.0 (2.1)	14.2 (0.4)	12.0 (0.4)	20.1 (1.5)	33.8 (3.0)	14.3 (0.4)	11.8 (0.4)	22.1 (1.5)	32.2 (2.9)
1975	13.9 (0.3)	11.4 (0.3)	22.9 (1.1)	29.2 (2.0)	13.3 (0.4)	11.0 (0.4)	23.0 (1.6)	26.7 (2.8)	14.5 (0.4)	11.8 (0.4)	22.9 (1.4)	31.6 (2.9)
1976	14.1 (0.3)	12.0 (0.3)	20.5 (1.0)	31.4 (2.0)	14.1 (0.4)	12.1 (0.4)	21.2 (1.5)	30.3 (2.9)	14.2 (0.4)	11.8 (0.4)	19.9 (1.4)	32.3 (2.8)
1977	14.1 (0.3)	11.9 (0.3)	19.8 (1.0)	33.0 (2.0)	14.5 (0.4)	12.6 (0.4)	19.5 (1.5)	31.6 (2.9)	13.8 (0.4)	11.2 (0.4)	20.0 (1.4)	34.3 (2.8)
1978	14.2 (0.3)	11.9 (0.3)	20.2 (1.0)	33.3 (2.0)	14.6 (0.4)	12.2 (0.4)	22.5 (1.5)	33.6 (2.9)	13.9 (0.4)	11.6 (0.4)	18.3 (1.3)	33.1 (2.8)
1979	14.6 (0.3)	12.0 (0.3)	21.1 (1.0)	33.8 (2.0)	15.0 (0.4)	12.6 (0.4)	22.4 (1.5)	33.0 (2.8)	14.2 (0.4)	11.5 (0.4)	20.0 (1.3)	34.5 (2.8)
1980	14.1 (0.3)	11.4 (0.3)	19.1 (1.0)	35.2 (1.9)	15.1 (0.4)	12.3 (0.4)	20.8 (1.5)	37.2 (2.7)	13.1 (0.4)	10.5 (0.4)	17.7 (1.3)	33.2 (2.6)
1981	13.9 (0.3)	11.3 (0.3)	18.4 (0.9)	33.2 (1.8)	15.1 (0.4)	12.5 (0.4)	19.9 (1.4)	36.0 (2.6)	12.8 (0.4)	10.2 (0.4)	17.1 (1.2)	30.4 (2.5)
1982	13.9 (0.3)	11.4 (0.3)	18.4 (1.0)	31.7 (1.9)	14.5 (0.4)	12.0 (0.4)	21.2 (1.5)	30.5 (2.7)	13.3 (0.4)	10.8 (0.4)	15.9 (1.3)	32.8 (2.7)
1983	13.7 (0.3)	11.1 (0.3)	18.0 (1.0)	31.6 (1.9)	14.9 (0.4)	12.2 (0.4)	19.9 (1.5)	34.3 (2.8)	12.5 (0.4)	10.1 (0.4)	16.2 (1.3)	29.1 (2.6)
1984	13.1 (0.3)	11.0 (0.3)	15.5 (0.9)	29.8 (1.9)	14.0 (0.4)	11.9 (0.4)	16.8 (1.4)	30.6 (2.8)	12.3 (0.4)	10.1 (0.4)	14.3 (1.2)	29.0 (2.6)
1985	12.6 (0.3)	10.4 (0.3)	15.2 (0.9)	27.6 (1.9)	13.4 (0.4)	11.1 (0.4)	16.1 (1.4)	29.9 (2.8)	11.8 (0.4)	9.8 (0.4)	14.3 (1.2)	25.2 (2.7)
1986	12.2 (0.3)	9.7 (0.3)	14.2 (0.9)	30.1 (1.9)	13.1 (0.4)	10.3 (0.4)	15.0 (1.3)	32.8 (2.7)	11.4 (0.4)	9.1 (0.4)	13.5 (1.2)	27.2 (2.6)
1987	12.6 (0.3)	10.4 (0.3)	14.1 (0.9)	28.6 (1.8)	13.2 (0.4)	10.8 (0.4)	15.0 (1.3)	29.1 (2.6)	12.1 (0.4)	10.0 (0.4)	13.3 (1.2)	28.1 (2.6)
1988	12.9 (0.3)	9.6 (0.3)	14.5 (1.0)	35.8 (2.3)	13.5 (0.4)	10.3 (0.5)	15.0 (1.5)	36.0 (3.2)	12.2 (0.4)	8.9 (0.4)	14.0 (1.4)	35.4 (3.3)
1989	12.6 (0.3)	9.4 (0.3)	13.9 (1.0)	33.0 (2.2)	13.6 (0.5)	10.3 (0.5)	14.9 (1.5)	34.4 (3.1)	11.7 (0.4)	8.5 (0.4)	13.0 (1.3)	31.6 (3.1)
1990	12.1 (0.3)	9.0 (0.3)	13.2 (0.9)	32.4 (1.9)	12.3 (0.4)	9.3 (0.4)	11.9 (1.3)	34.3 (2.7)	11.8 (0.4)	8.7 (0.4)	14.4 (1.3)	30.3 (2.7)
1991	12.5 (0.3)	8.9 (0.3)	13.6 (0.9)	35.3 (1.9)	13.0 (0.4)	8.9 (0.4)	13.5 (1.4)	39.2 (2.7)	11.9 (0.4)	8.9 (0.4)	13.7 (1.3)	31.1 (2.7)
1992[3]	11.0 (0.3)	7.7 (0.3)	13.7 (0.9)	29.4 (1.9)	11.3 (0.4)	8.0 (0.4)	12.5 (1.3)	32.1 (2.7)	10.7 (0.4)	7.4 (0.4)	14.8 (1.4)	26.6 (2.6)
1993[3]	11.0 (0.3)	7.9 (0.3)	13.6 (0.9)	27.5 (1.8)	11.2 (0.4)	8.2 (0.4)	12.6 (1.3)	28.1 (2.5)	10.9 (0.4)	7.6 (0.4)	14.4 (1.3)	26.9 (2.5)
1994[3]	11.4 (0.3)	7.7 (0.3)	12.6 (0.8)	30.0 (1.2)	12.3 (0.4)	8.0 (0.4)	14.1 (1.1)	31.6 (1.6)	10.6 (0.4)	7.5 (0.4)	11.3 (1.0)	28.1 (1.7)
1995[3]	12.0 (0.3)	8.6 (0.3)	12.1 (0.7)	30.0 (1.1)	12.2 (0.4)	9.0 (0.4)	11.1 (1.0)	30.0 (1.6)	11.7 (0.4)	8.2 (0.4)	12.9 (1.1)	30.0 (1.7)
1996[3]	11.1 (0.3)	7.3 (0.3)	13.0 (0.8)	29.4 (1.2)	11.4 (0.4)	7.3 (0.4)	13.5 (1.2)	30.3 (1.7)	10.9 (0.4)	7.3 (0.4)	12.5 (1.1)	28.3 (1.7)
1997[3]	11.0 (0.3)	7.6 (0.3)	13.4 (0.8)	25.3 (1.1)	11.9 (0.4)	8.5 (0.4)	13.3 (1.2)	27.0 (1.6)	10.1 (0.4)	6.7 (0.4)	13.5 (1.1)	23.4 (1.6)
1998[3]	11.8 (0.3)	7.7 (0.3)	13.8 (0.8)	29.5 (1.1)	13.3 (0.4)	8.6 (0.4)	15.5 (1.2)	33.5 (1.6)	10.3 (0.4)	6.9 (0.4)	12.2 (1.1)	25.0 (1.6)
1999[3]	11.2 (0.3)	7.3 (0.3)	12.6 (0.8)	28.6 (1.1)	11.9 (0.4)	7.7 (0.4)	12.1 (1.1)	31.0 (1.6)	10.5 (0.4)	6.9 (0.4)	13.0 (1.1)	26.0 (1.5)
2000[3]	10.9 (0.3)	6.9 (0.3)	13.1 (0.8)	27.8 (1.1)	12.0 (0.4)	7.0 (0.4)	15.3 (1.2)	31.8 (1.6)	9.9 (0.3)	6.9 (0.4)	11.1 (1.0)	23.5 (1.5)
2001[3]	10.7 (0.3)	7.3 (0.3)	10.9 (0.7)	27.0 (1.1)	12.2 (0.4)	7.9 (0.4)	13.0 (1.1)	31.6 (1.6)	9.3 (0.3)	6.7 (0.4)	9.0 (0.9)	22.1 (1.4)

—Not available.

[1] Based on the April 1960 decennial census.

[2] White and Black include persons of Hispanic origin.

[3] Because of changes in data collection procedures, data may not be comparable with figures for earlier years.

NOTE: All races includes other racial/ethnic groups not shown separately. "Status" dropouts are 16- to 24-year-olds who are not enrolled in school and who have not completed a high school program regardless of when they left school. People who have received GED credentials are counted as high school completers. All data except for 1960 are based on October counts. Data are based upon sample surveys of the civilian non-institutionalized population. Standard errors appear in parentheses.

SOURCE: U.S. Department of Commerce, Bureau of the Census, Current Population Survey (CPS), unpublished tabulations; and U.S. Department of Education, National Center for Education Statistics, *Dropout Rates in the United States, 2001.* (This table was prepared October 2002.)

Number of students with disabilities exiting special education, by basis of exit, age, and type of disability: United States and outlying areas, 2000–01

Age and type of disability	Total exiting special education	Graduated with diploma	Received a certificate of attendance	Reached maximum age [1]	No longer receives special education	Died	Moved, known to continue	Moved, not known to continue	Dropped out [2]
1	2	3	4	5	6	7	8	9	10
Age group									
14 to 21 and over	582,791	173,523	33,427	5,959	70,448	1,791	148,031	59,940	89,672
14	64,541	17	29	5	15,438	245	34,655	10,897	3,255
15	71,433	77	34	4	16,583	312	35,087	12,219	7,117
16	81,222	1,170	213	8	14,995	337	32,715	12,743	19,041
17	121,070	42,432	4,668	48	12,790	336	25,024	11,194	24,578
18	144,146	79,878	12,914	777	7,390	262	13,831	7,293	21,801
19	66,264	37,095	8,789	418	2,298	137	4,576	3,258	9,693
20	19,258	8,286	3,418	904	620	77	1,450	1,429	3,074
21 and over	14,857	4,568	3,362	3,795	334	85	693	907	1,113
Type of disability for 14- to 21-year-olds and over									
All disabilities	582,791	173,523	33,427	5,959	70,448	1,791	148,031	59,940	89,672
Specific learning disabilities	340,511	117,645	14,813	1,558	41,069	580	79,863	33,692	51,291
Mental retardation	67,062	16,735	11,820	2,472	2,729	380	16,536	5,791	10,599
Emotional disturbance	94,794	15,032	2,342	579	8,038	169	34,806	13,721	20,107
Speech or language impairments	23,267	4,685	579	97	10,582	32	3,734	1,673	1,885
Multiple disabilities	9,686	2,742	1,184	652	420	249	2,678	775	986
Other health impairments	27,763	8,815	905	107	5,691	202	6,351	2,717	2,975
Hearing impairments	6,503	2,747	604	76	605	14	1,340	517	600
Orthopedic impairments	5,882	2,295	403	123	775	101	1,107	441	637
Visual impairments	2,498	1,161	170	35	219	25	516	178	194
Autism	2,563	740	422	215	157	15	649	216	149
Deaf-blindness	182	54	27	10	7	10	44	17	13
Traumatic brain injury	2,080	872	158	35	156	14	407	202	236

[1] The upper age mandate for providing special education and related services as defined by state law, practice, or court order.

[2] Dropped out is defined as the total who were enrolled at some point in the reporting year, were not enrolled at the end of the report year, and did not exit through any of the other bases described. This category includes dropouts, runaways, GED recipients, expulsions, status unknown, and other exiters.

SOURCE: U.S. Department of Education, Office of Special Education and Rehabilitative Services, *Annual Report to Congress on the Implementation of The Individuals with Disabilities Education Act, 2002,* and unpublished tabulations. (This table was prepared July 2003.)

Private elementary and secondary enrollment, teachers, and schools, by orientation of private schools and selected school characteristics: Fall 1999

Selected school characteristic	Kindergarten to 12th-grade enrollment				Teachers				Schools			
	Total	Catholic	Other religious	Non-sectarian	Total	Catholic	Other religious	Non-sectarian	Total	Catholic	Other religious	Non-sectarian
1	2	3	4	5	6	7	8	9	10	11	12	13
Total	**5,162,684**	**2,511,040**	**1,843,580**	**808,063**	**395,317**	**149,600**	**152,915**	**92,801**	**27,223**	**8,102**	**13,232**	**5,889**
Standard error	25,410	4,787	24,799	5,428	2,881	210	2,759	722	239	24	228	68
Level of school												
Elementary	2,831,372	1,814,676	750,026	266,669	187,833	100,565	58,386	28,882	16,530	6,707	6,843	2,981
Secondary	806,639	607,682	112,132	86,825	62,737	41,301	10,586	10,849	2,538	1,114	718	707
Combined	1,524,673	88,682	981,422	454,569	144,746	7,734	83,943	53,070	8,155	282	5,672	2,201
School enrollment												
Less than 50	196,309	5,497	128,007	62,806	26,329	769	15,898	9,662	7,565	172	5,031	2,362
50 to 149	716,129	149,542	385,184	181,403	71,676	12,543	36,431	22,702	7,738	1,408	4,280	2,050
150 to 299	1,424,018	767,888	496,825	159,306	102,457	45,928	38,371	18,157	6,571	3,450	2,364	757
300 to 499	1,228,631	720,044	357,479	151,109	84,086	41,439	26,627	16,020	3,219	1,876	946	397
500 to 749	805,490	477,806	215,910	111,774	54,078	26,057	15,964	12,057	1,352	805	360	187
750 or more	792,106	390,264	260,177	141,666	56,691	22,864	19,624	14,203	778	391	250	136
Percent minority students												
None	291,838	61,442	212,771	17,624	25,578	4,053	19,613	1,912	4,012	415	3,228	368
1 to 9 percent	2,282,659	1,216,054	806,530	260,075	164,869	72,015	64,951	27,903	9,219	3,737	4,149	1,332
10 to 29 percent	1,360,769	589,224	433,044	338,502	115,605	37,070	37,304	41,231	6,435	1,733	2,702	1,999
30 to 49 percent	414,323	190,783	139,742	83,798	32,424	11,471	10,994	9,959	2,455	604	1,007	844
50 percent or more	813,095	453,537	251,494	108,064	56,841	24,991	20,053	11,797	5,103	1,613	2,145	1,345
Community type												
Central city	2,540,516	1,293,629	870,219	376,668	189,984	76,118	71,244	42,622	10,825	3,737	4,550	2,538
Urban fringe/large town	2,051,094	1,022,949	714,090	314,056	155,436	59,815	58,053	37,568	10,359	3,142	4,725	2,492
Rural/small town	571,074	194,463	259,272	117,340	49,897	13,667	23,619	12,611	6,040	1,223	3,958	859

NOTE: Includes special education, vocational/technical education, and alternative schools. Includes only schools that offer first or higher grade. Excludes prekindergarten students. Detail may not sum to totals due to rounding.

SOURCE: U.S. Department of Education, National Center for Education Statistics, "Private School Universe Survey, 1999–2000." (This table was prepared September 2001.)

Private elementary and secondary schools, enrollment, teachers, and high school graduates, by state: 1991 to 1999

State	Schools		Enrollment[1]								Teachers		High school graduates	
	1999[2]	Standard error	Fall 1991		Fall 1993		Fall 1997		Fall 1999		Fall 1999	Standard error	1998–99	Standard error
			Enrollment	Standard error	Enrollment	Standard error	Enrollment	Standard error	Enrollment	Standard error				
1	2	3	4	5	6	7	8	9	10	11	12	13	14	15
United States[3] ...	27,223	238.6	4,889,545	26,471	4,836,442	12,875	5,076,118	15,549	5,162,684	25,410	395,317	2,881	273,025	2,054
Alabama	374	21.6	69,441	8,390	72,630	4,724	72,486	682	73,352	2,527	5,934	170	4,324	194
Alaska	69	1.6	5,520	543	5,884	0	6,253	220	6,172	63	572	51	245	8
Arizona	276	4.4	39,460	(4)	41,957	0	44,991	652	44,060	428	3,319	63	2,399	39
Arkansas	192	14.0	22,792	(4)	29,011	3,995	26,645	290	26,424	1,233	2,075	90	1,320	86
California	3,318	27.8	613,068	16,643	569,062	1,987	609,506	3,730	619,067	1,533	43,159	503	28,097	253
Colorado	339	5.5	57,352	11,374	53,732	7,798	52,563	1,109	52,142	397	4,353	115	2,470	79
Connecticut	348	5.7	67,374	(4)	70,198	1,875	69,293	494	70,058	224	6,879	87	5,141	142
Delaware	96	2.7	22,803	(4)	22,308	0	24,193	911	22,779	303	1,784	28	1,151	18
District of Columbia	89	4.4	17,776	322	15,854	0	16,671	155	16,690	701	1,898	31	1,231	83
Florida	1,545	79.1	205,600	2,988	233,743	3,789	273,628	2,359	290,872	8,152	22,929	776	12,866	279
Georgia	592	31.4	96,683	4,078	97,726	3,586	107,065	1,477	116,407	4,157	10,677	591	6,819	317
Hawaii	130	1.5	36,306	(4)	30,537	0	33,300	350	32,193	169	2,475	23	2,533	31
Idaho	94	2.0	6,644	(4)	8,019	0	9,635	203	10,209	96	790	29	459	8
Illinois	1,354	11.8	301,374	1,158	293,038	794	298,620	1,101	299,871	1,365	19,589	142	16,652	122
Indiana	677	13.9	99,450	7,004	91,986	0	105,358	1,836	105,533	1,461	7,362	198	4,597	133
Iowa	265	4.8	51,431	(4)	50,602	211	50,138	520	49,565	446	3,545	46	2,693	69
Kansas	237	16.7	35,077	(4)	37,045	0	40,573	363	43,113	1,731	3,166	158	2,071	64
Kentucky	368	17.0	65,990	(4)	58,058	0	70,731	413	75,084	1,927	5,478	193	3,997	191
Louisiana	434	12.8	139,248	(4)	145,512	4,036	141,633	696	138,135	1,982	9,206	113	8,716	296
Maine	139	4.6	14,854	(4)	16,999	0	17,187	292	18,287	133	1,760	51	2,050	43
Maryland	701	36.9	113,774	(4)	112,481	0	129,898	937	144,131	4,700	12,152	288	7,596	329
Massachusetts	694	13.1	126,006	3,419	126,744	1,362	127,105	1,103	132,154	508	12,497	149	9,632	192
Michigan	1,012	13.9	187,095	710	187,741	0	187,940	1,538	179,579	1,554	11,771	179	9,114	167
Minnesota	530	8.7	93,404	2,401	86,051	0	90,400	918	92,795	1,047	6,467	129	4,010	114
Mississippi	207	9.1	58,757	1,377	58,655	1,564	54,529	457	51,369	1,357	3,884	106	3,649	159
Missouri	576	7.2	116,440	1,884	117,466	616	119,534	964	122,387	1,076	9,105	114	6,851	170
Montana	90	2.0	9,644	(4)	9,111	0	8,341	220	8,711	88	740	37	395	23
Nebraska	237	4.2	39,673	(4)	39,564	0	40,943	320	42,141	415	2,963	67	2,303	74
Nevada	80	1.3	8,482	(4)	10,723	0	12,847	241	13,926	81	973	24	639	6
New Hampshire	171	5.7	18,712	1,330	18,386	0	21,143	297	23,383	193	2,208	72	1,894	46
New Jersey	905	14.1	209,913	8,195	195,921	0	205,126	1,535	198,631	785	15,496	198	11,072	339
New Mexico	182	3.5	23,236	(4)	20,007	0	19,251	534	23,055	195	1,992	73	1,361	46
New York	1,981	22.0	498,668	7,158	473,119	4,776	467,520	1,821	475,942	1,227	37,190	404	26,314	338
North Carolina	588	37.1	63,255	5,224	69,000	1,803	88,127	1,260	96,262	3,775	8,962	422	4,256	160
North Dakota ..	55	1.3	7,518	(4)	7,577	0	7,332	72	7,148	97	545	12	448	20
Ohio	974	11.2	269,064	13,362	246,805	3,480	251,543	1,528	254,494	1,694	16,165	134	13,394	173
Oklahoma	179	11.0	34,025	9,317	25,837	3,584	27,675	345	31,276	1,049	2,727	83	1,635	49
Oregon	347	12.4	30,918	1,003	34,092	0	44,290	1,364	45,352	1,287	3,473	92	2,376	75
Pennsylvania ..	1,964	51.8	359,440	6,920	342,298	4,260	343,191	4,401	339,484	2,954	24,453	848	18,002	414
Rhode Island ..	127	3.0	21,242	(4)	23,153	0	25,597	195	24,738	127	1,961	26	1,404	56
South Carolina	326	19.0	46,086	2,013	51,600	1,819	56,169	700	55,612	2,506	4,912	281	2,915	202
South Dakota ..	83	2.6	10,539	(4)	9,575	0	9,794	143	9,364	232	743	24	442	19
Tennessee	533	39.9	82,969	2,953	84,538	2,909	84,651	746	93,680	3,519	7,921	265	6,717	162
Texas	1,281	52.6	170,670	472	211,337	7,591	223,294	1,703	227,645	7,260	19,777	410	9,988	353
Utah	78	1.4	9,836	(4)	9,793	0	12,653	201	12,614	114	1,091	29	792	42
Vermont	122	4.9	8,351	(4)	9,107	0	10,823	196	12,170	199	1,361	65	1,273	57
Virginia	582	34.2	80,887	1,872	84,438	4,584	98,307	1,071	100,171	4,171	9,389	248	5,010	178
Washington	494	8.8	66,556	2,798	70,205	1,858	76,956	1,462	76,885	519	5,697	144	3,262	48
West Virginia ..	151	11.8	12,908	(4)	13,539	0	14,640	225	15,895	974	1,486	151	883	96
Wisconsin	991	16.6	142,339	220	141,762	0	143,577	1,748	139,455	1,828	10,025	241	5,525	168
Wyoming	41	1.4	1,840	(4)	1,919	0	2,593	110	2,221	45	241	28	41	5

[1] Excludes prekindergarten enrollment.

[2] The estimates for 1999 were computed using a different procedure from that used prior to 1997–98.

[3] NCES employed an area frame sample to account for noninclusion of schools at the national level. However, caution should be exercised in interpreting state by state characteristics since the samples were not designed to produce such numbers.

[4] Insufficient data to compute a standard error.

NOTE: Includes special education, vocational/technical education, and alternative schools. Standard errors for states are root mean squared errors to correct for bias in model based estimates. Tabulation includes only schools that offer first or higher grade. Some data have been revised from previously published figures. Detail may not sum to totals due to rounding.

SOURCE: U.S. Department of Education, National Center for Education Statistics, "Private School Universe Survey,1999–2000;" and *Indirect State-Level Estimation for the Private School Survey, 1999.* (This table was prepared August 2001.)

Revenues for public elementary and secondary schools, by source and state or jurisdiction: 2000–01

State or jurisdiction	Total, in thousands	Federal			State		Local and intermediate		Private [1]	
		Amount, in thousands	Per student	Percent of total	Amount, in thousands	Percent of total	Amount, in thousands	Percent of total	Amount, in thousands	Percent of total
1	2	3	4	5	6	7	8	9	10	11
United States	$400,919,024	$29,086,413	$616	7.3	$199,146,586	49.7	$163,479,177	40.8	$9,206,847	2.3
Alabama	4,812,302	453,817	613	9.4	2,881,224	59.9	1,227,512	25.5	249,749	5.2
Alaska	1,370,271	215,921	1,619	15.8	782,348	57.1	333,592	24.3	38,410	2.8
Arizona	5,797,151	616,976	703	10.6	2,525,390	43.6	2,506,856	43.2	147,929	2.6
Arkansas	2,812,169	260,705	579	9.3	1,676,138	59.6	820,201	29.2	55,125	2.0
California	51,007,510	4,159,513	677	8.2	31,392,549	61.5	14,929,920	29.3	525,528	1.0
Colorado	5,349,899	299,576	413	5.6	2,222,083	41.5	2,576,924	48.2	251,315	4.7
Connecticut	6,460,491	276,427	492	4.3	2,553,180	39.5	3,527,302	54.6	103,583	1.6
Delaware	1,112,519	87,904	767	7.9	732,599	65.9	277,769	25.0	14,247	1.3
District of Columbia ...	1,042,711	115,527	1,676	11.1	†	†	918,793	88.1	8,391	0.8
Florida	17,866,868	1,599,259	657	9.0	8,695,213	48.7	6,917,556	38.7	654,841	3.7
Georgia	12,191,113	783,487	542	6.4	5,963,337	48.9	5,249,268	43.1	195,020	1.6
Hawaii	1,682,330	140,951	765	8.4	1,511,317	89.8	9,105	0.5	20,957	1.2
Idaho	1,593,966	128,646	525	8.1	977,438	61.3	461,605	29.0	26,278	1.6
Illinois	18,217,079	1,421,519	694	7.8	6,124,183	33.6	10,301,826	56.6	369,551	2.0
Indiana	9,033,180	464,489	470	5.1	4,833,954	53.5	3,477,771	38.5	256,967	2.8
Iowa	3,954,178	248,689	502	6.3	1,943,708	49.2	1,556,878	39.4	204,902	5.2
Kansas	3,597,726	231,473	492	6.4	2,198,216	61.1	1,074,216	29.9	93,820	2.6
Kentucky	4,509,893	448,073	673	9.9	2,702,932	59.9	1,258,841	27.9	100,047	2.2
Louisiana	5,060,133	580,356	781	11.5	2,497,875	49.4	1,921,174	38.0	60,729	1.2
Maine	1,934,178	153,100	739	7.9	863,295	44.6	880,399	45.5	37,384	1.9
Maryland	7,846,891	477,463	560	6.1	2,928,715	37.3	4,178,103	53.2	262,611	3.3
Massachusetts	10,148,498	511,198	524	5.0	4,420,622	43.6	5,052,863	49.8	163,816	1.6
Michigan	16,358,532	1,116,374	649	6.8	10,603,606	64.8	4,276,902	26.1	361,649	2.2
Minnesota	7,873,549	370,648	434	4.7	4,765,802	60.5	2,497,149	31.7	239,951	3.0
Mississippi	2,903,534	400,804	805	13.8	1,607,126	55.4	804,183	27.7	91,421	3.1
Missouri	7,102,501	491,233	538	6.9	2,661,904	37.5	3,680,122	51.8	269,242	3.8
Montana	1,140,168	131,299	848	11.5	542,692	47.6	418,700	36.7	47,477	4.2
Nebraska	2,307,804	168,036	587	7.3	805,419	34.9	1,210,412	52.4	123,937	5.4
Nevada	2,393,494	122,360	359	5.1	683,605	28.6	1,497,331	62.6	90,198	3.8
New Hampshire	1,714,147	77,365	371	4.5	884,875	51.6	712,119	41.5	39,788	2.3
New Jersey	15,967,075	628,834	479	3.9	6,669,858	41.8	8,351,731	52.3	316,652	2.0
New Mexico	2,426,705	338,213	1,056	13.9	1,725,551	71.1	316,268	13.0	46,674	1.9
New York	34,266,171	1,961,653	681	5.7	15,818,051	46.2	16,187,387	47.2	299,080	0.9
North Carolina	9,262,181	670,380	518	7.2	6,144,449	66.3	2,216,699	23.9	230,653	2.5
North Dakota	767,798	102,697	940	13.4	299,089	39.0	324,794	42.3	41,216	5.4
Ohio	16,649,361	1,007,370	549	6.1	7,187,325	43.2	7,840,209	47.1	614,457	3.7
Oklahoma	4,034,825	410,681	659	10.2	2,386,216	59.1	1,035,597	25.7	202,332	5.0
Oregon	4,564,408	336,992	617	7.4	2,566,099	56.2	1,528,766	33.5	132,551	2.9
Pennsylvania	17,053,891	1,107,854	611	6.5	6,443,673	37.8	9,176,463	53.8	325,901	1.9
Rhode Island	1,545,675	90,634	576	5.9	652,723	42.2	781,753	50.6	20,566	1.3
South Carolina	5,459,399	446,838	660	8.2	2,941,097	53.9	1,873,403	34.3	198,061	3.6
South Dakota	885,229	107,532	836	12.1	312,880	35.3	438,651	49.6	26,167	3.0
Tennessee	5,711,950	524,351	577	9.2	2,532,336	44.3	2,493,439	43.7	161,824	2.8
Texas	30,469,570	2,656,951	654	8.7	12,855,241	42.2	14,246,504	46.8	710,874	2.3
Utah	2,745,656	204,939	426	7.5	1,608,249	58.6	867,784	31.6	64,683	2.4
Vermont	1,035,679	60,523	593	5.8	732,563	70.7	226,175	21.8	16,418	1.6
Virginia	9,313,330	520,773	455	5.6	3,939,548	42.3	4,649,755	49.9	203,253	2.2
Washington	8,058,875	625,231	622	7.8	5,072,388	62.9	2,101,004	26.1	260,253	3.2
West Virginia	2,375,788	243,131	849	10.2	1,450,453	61.1	654,155	27.5	28,049	1.2
Wisconsin	8,327,255	418,472	476	5.0	4,424,429	53.1	3,295,254	39.6	189,099	2.3
Wyoming	803,414	69,176	769	8.6	403,020	50.2	317,995	39.6	13,223	1.6
Outlying areas										
American Samoa	58,262	45,822	2,918	78.6	10,551	18.1	1,801	3.1	89	0.2
Guam	—	—	—	—	—	—	—	—	—	—
Northern Marianas	55,164	17,619	1,761	31.9	37,230	67.5	255	0.5	60	0.1
Puerto Rico	2,331,691	671,870	1,097	28.8	1,658,907	71.1	98	#	815	#
Virgin Islands	165,801	28,256	1,452	17.0	0	0.0	137,400	82.9	146	0.1

—Not available.

† Not applicable.

Rounds to zero.

[1] Includes revenues from gifts, and tuition and fees from patrons.

NOTE: Excludes revenues for state education agencies. Detail may not sum to totals due to rounding.

SOURCE: U.S. Department of Education, National Center for Education Statistics, The NCES Common Core of Data (CCD), "National Public Education Financial Survey," 2000–01. (This table was prepared July 2003.)

Current expenditures for public elementary and secondary education, by state or jurisdiction: Selected years, 1969–70 to 2000–01

[In thousands]

State or jurisdiction	1969–70	1979–80	1980–81	1985–86	1989–90	1990–91	1991–92	1992–93	1993–94
1	2	3	4	5	6	7	8	9	10
United States	**$34,217,773**	**$86,984,142**	**$94,321,093**	**$137,164,965**	**$188,229,359**	**$202,037,752**	**$211,210,190**	**$220,948,052**	**$231,542,764**
Alabama	422,730	1,146,713	1,393,137	1,761,154	2,275,233	2,475,216	2,465,523	2,610,514	2,809,713
Alaska	81,374	377,947	476,368	818,219	828,051	854,499	931,869	967,765	1,002,515
Arizona	281,941	949,753	1,075,362	1,649,832	2,258,660	2,469,543	2,599,586	2,753,504	2,911,304
Arkansas	235,083	666,949	709,394	1,085,943	1,404,545	1,510,092	1,656,201	1,703,621	1,782,645
California	3,831,595	9,172,158	9,936,642	15,040,898	21,485,782	22,748,218	23,696,863	24,219,792	25,140,639
Colorado	369,218	1,243,049	1,369,883	2,018,579	2,451,833	2,642,850	2,754,087	2,919,916	2,954,793
Connecticut	588,710	1,227,892	1,440,881	2,144,094	3,444,520	3,540,411	3,665,505	3,739,497	3,943,891
Delaware	108,747	269,108	270,439	391,558	520,953	543,933	572,152	600,161	643,915
District of Columbia ...	141,138	298,448	295,155	406,910	639,983	647,901	677,422	670,677	713,427
Florida	961,273	2,766,468	3,336,657	5,092,668	8,228,531	9,045,710	9,314,079	9,661,012	10,331,896
Georgia	599,371	1,608,028	1,688,714	2,979,980	4,505,962	4,804,225	4,856,583	5,273,143	5,643,843
Hawaii	141,324	351,889	395,038	575,456	700,012	827,579	884,591	946,074	998,143
Idaho	103,107	313,927	352,912	492,092	627,794	708,045	760,440	804,231	859,088
Illinois	1,896,067	4,579,355	4,773,179	6,066,390	8,125,493	8,932,538	9,244,655	9,942,737	10,076,889
Indiana	809,105	1,851,292	1,898,194	2,851,080	4,074,578	4,379,142	4,544,829	4,797,946	5,064,685
Iowa	527,086	1,186,659	1,337,504	1,644,359	2,004,742	2,136,561	2,356,196	2,459,141	2,527,434
Kansas	362,593	830,133	958,281	1,423,225	1,848,302	1,938,012	2,028,440	2,224,080	2,325,247
Kentucky	353,265	1,054,459	1,096,472	1,434,962	2,134,011	2,480,363	2,709,623	2,823,134	2,952,119
Louisiana	503,217	1,303,902	1,767,692	2,333,748	2,838,283	3,023,690	3,188,024	3,199,919	3,309,018
Maine	155,907	385,492	401,355	688,673	1,048,195	1,070,965	1,121,360	1,217,418	1,208,411
Maryland	721,794	1,783,056	1,937,159	2,634,209	3,894,644	4,240,862	4,362,679	4,556,266	4,783,023
Massachusetts	907,341	2,638,734	2,794,762	3,403,505	4,760,390	4,906,828	5,035,973	5,281,067	5,637,337
Michigan	1,799,945	4,642,847	5,196,249	6,184,767	8,025,621	8,545,805	9,156,501	9,532,994	9,816,830
Minnesota	781,243	1,786,768	1,900,322	2,637,722	3,474,398	3,740,820	3,936,695	4,135,284	4,328,093
Mississippi	262,760	756,018	716,878	1,058,301	1,472,710	1,510,552	1,536,295	1,600,752	1,725,386
Missouri	642,030	1,504,988	1,643,258	2,277,576	3,288,738	3,487,786	3,611,613	3,710,426	3,981,614
Montana	127,176	358,118	380,092	567,901	641,345	719,963	751,710	785,159	822,015
Nebraska	231,612	581,615	629,017	911,983	1,233,431	1,297,643	1,381,290	1,430,039	1,513,971
Nevada	87,273	281,901	287,752	495,147	712,898	864,379	962,800	1,035,623	1,099,685
New Hampshire	101,370	295,400	340,518	522,604	821,671	890,116	927,625	972,963	1,007,129
New Jersey	1,343,564	3,638,533	3,648,914	5,735,895	8,119,336	8,897,612	9,660,899	9,915,482	10,448,096
New Mexico	183,736	515,451	560,213	808,036	1,020,148	1,134,156	1,212,189	1,240,310	1,323,459
New York	4,111,839	8,760,500	9,259,948	13,686,039	18,090,978	19,514,583	19,781,384	20,898,267	22,059,949
North Carolina	676,193	1,880,862	2,112,417	2,991,747	4,342,826	4,605,384	4,660,027	4,930,823	5,145,416
North Dakota	97,895	228,483	254,197	379,470	459,391	460,581	491,293	511,095	522,377
Ohio	1,639,805	3,836,576	4,149,858	5,856,999	7,994,379	8,407,428	9,124,731	9,173,393	9,612,678
Oklahoma	339,105	1,055,844	1,193,373	1,740,981	1,905,332	2,107,513	2,268,958	2,442,320	2,680,113
Oregon	403,844	1,126,812	1,292,624	1,662,372	2,297,944	2,453,934	2,626,803	2,849,009	2,852,723
Pennsylvania	1,912,644	4,584,320	4,955,115	6,750,520	9,496,788	10,087,322	10,371,796	10,944,392	11,236,417
Rhode Island	145,443	362,046	395,389	569,935	801,908	823,655	865,898	934,815	990,094
South Carolina	367,689	997,984	1,006,088	1,708,603	2,322,618	2,494,254	2,564,949	2,690,009	2,790,878
South Dakota	109,375	238,332	242,215	360,832	447,074	481,304	518,156	553,005	584,894
Tennessee	473,226	1,319,303	1,429,938	1,990,889	2,790,808	2,903,209	2,859,755	3,139,223	3,305,579
Texas	1,518,181	4,997,689	5,310,181	9,642,812	12,763,954	13,695,327	14,709,628	15,121,655	16,193,722
Utah	179,981	518,251	587,648	906,484	1,130,135	1,235,916	1,296,723	1,376,319	1,511,205
Vermont	78,921	189,811	224,901	346,164	546,901	599,018	606,410	616,212	643,828
Virginia	704,677	1,881,519	2,045,412	3,183,707	4,621,071	4,958,213	4,993,480	5,228,326	5,441,384
Washington	699,984	1,825,782	1,791,477	2,702,652	3,550,819	3,906,471	4,259,048	4,679,698	4,892,690
West Virginia	249,404	678,386	754,889	1,164,882	1,316,637	1,473,640	1,503,980	1,626,005	1,663,868
Wisconsin	777,288	1,908,523	2,035,879	2,893,797	3,929,920	4,292,434	4,597,004	4,954,900	5,170,343
Wyoming	69,584	226,067	271,153	488,616	509,084	521,549	545,870	547,938	558,353
Outlying areas									
American Samoa	—	—	—	14,997	21,838	24,946	26,972	23,636	25,161
Guam	16,652	—	—	78,545	101,130	116,406	132,494	161,477	160,797
Northern Marianas	—	—	—	12,556	20,476	26,822	32,498	38,784	32,824
Puerto Rico	—	—	713,000	842,827	1,045,407	1,142,863	1,207,235	1,295,452	1,360,762
Virgin Islands	—	—	—	76,751	128,065	119,950	121,660	120,510	120,556

See notes at end of table.

Current expenditures for public elementary and secondary education, by state or jurisdiction: Selected years, 1969–70 to 2000–01—Continued

[In thousands]

State or jurisdiction	1994–95	1995–96	1996–97	1997–98	1998–99	1999–2000[1]	2000–01
1	11	12	13	14	15	16	17
United States	**$243,877,582**	**$255,106,683**	**$270,174,298**	**$285,485,370**	**$302,876,294**	**$323,888,508**	**$348,170,327**
Alabama	3,026,287	3,240,364	3,436,406	3,633,159	3,880,188	4,176,082	4,354,794
Alaska	1,020,675	1,045,022	1,069,379	1,092,750	1,137,610	1,183,499	1,229,036
Arizona	3,144,540	3,327,969	3,527,473	3,740,889	3,963,455	4,288,739	4,632,539
Arkansas	1,873,595	1,994,748	2,074,113	2,149,237	2,241,244	2,380,331	2,505,179
California	25,949,033	27,334,639	29,909,168	32,759,492	34,379,878	38,129,479	42,908,787
Colorado	3,232,976	3,360,529	3,577,211	3,886,872	4,140,699	4,401,010	4,758,173
Connecticut	4,247,328	4,366,123	4,522,718	4,763,653	5,075,580	5,402,836	5,693,207
Delaware	694,473	726,241	788,715	830,731	872,786	937,630	1,027,224
District of Columbia	666,938	679,106	632,952	647,202	693,712	780,192	830,299
Florida	11,019,735	11,480,359	12,018,676	12,737,325	13,534,374	13,885,988	15,023,514
Georgia	6,136,689	6,629,646	7,230,405	7,770,241	8,537,177	9,158,624	10,011,343
Hawaii	1,028,729	1,040,682	1,057,069	1,112,351	1,143,713	1,213,695	1,215,968
Idaho	951,350	1,019,594	1,090,597	1,153,778	1,239,755	1,302,817	1,403,190
Illinois	10,640,279	10,727,091	11,720,249	12,473,064	13,602,965	14,462,773	15,658,682
Indiana	5,243,761	5,493,653	6,055,055	6,234,563	6,697,468	7,110,930	7,548,487
Iowa	2,622,510	2,753,425	2,885,943	3,005,421	3,110,585	3,264,336	3,430,885
Kansas	2,406,580	2,488,077	2,568,525	2,684,244	2,841,147	2,971,814	3,258,807
Kentucky	2,988,892	3,171,495	3,382,062	3,489,205	3,696,331	3,837,794	4,047,392
Louisiana	3,475,926	3,545,832	3,747,508	4,029,139	4,264,981	4,391,189	4,485,878
Maine	1,281,706	1,313,759	1,372,571	1,433,175	1,510,024	1,604,438	1,704,422
Maryland	5,083,380	5,311,207	5,529,309	5,843,685	6,165,934	6,545,135	7,041,586
Massachusetts	6,062,303	6,435,458	6,846,610	7,381,784	7,948,502	8,564,039	9,272,387
Michigan	10,440,206	11,137,877	11,686,124	12,003,818	12,785,480	13,994,294	14,243,597
Minnesota	4,622,930	4,844,879	5,087,353	5,452,571	5,836,186	6,140,442	6,531,198
Mississippi	1,921,480	2,000,321	2,035,675	2,164,592	2,293,188	2,510,376	2,576,457
Missouri	4,275,217	4,531,192	4,775,931	5,067,720	5,348,366	5,655,531	6,076,169
Montana	844,257	868,892	902,252	929,197	955,695	994,770	1,041,760
Nebraska	1,594,928	1,648,104	1,707,455	1,743,775	1,821,310	1,926,500	2,067,290
Nevada	1,186,132	1,296,629	1,434,395	1,570,576	1,738,009	1,875,467	1,978,480
New Hampshire	1,053,966	1,114,540	1,173,958	1,241,255	1,316,946	1,418,503	1,518,792
New Jersey	10,776,982	11,208,558	11,771,941	12,056,560	12,874,579	13,327,645	14,773,650
New Mexico	1,441,078	1,517,517	1,557,376	1,659,891	1,788,382	1,890,274	2,022,093
New York	22,989,629	23,522,461	24,237,291	25,332,735	26,885,444	28,433,240	30,884,292
North Carolina	5,440,426	5,582,994	5,964,939	6,497,648	7,097,882	7,713,293	8,209,954
North Dakota	534,632	557,043	577,498	599,443	625,428	638,946	668,814
Ohio	10,030,956	10,408,022	10,948,074	11,448,722	12,138,937	12,974,575	13,893,495
Oklahoma	2,763,721	2,804,088	2,990,044	3,138,690	3,332,697	3,382,581	3,750,542
Oregon	2,948,539	3,056,801	3,184,100	3,474,714	3,706,044	3,896,287	4,112,069
Pennsylvania	11,587,027	12,374,073	12,820,704	13,084,859	13,532,211	14,120,112	14,895,316
Rhode Island	1,050,969	1,094,185	1,151,888	1,215,595	1,283,859	1,393,143	1,465,703
South Carolina	2,920,230	3,085,495	3,296,661	3,507,017	3,759,042	4,087,355	4,492,161
South Dakota	612,825	610,640	628,753	665,082	696,785	737,998	796,133
Tennessee	3,540,682	3,728,486	4,145,380	4,409,338	4,638,924	4,931,734	5,170,379
Texas	17,572,269	18,801,462	20,167,238	21,188,676	22,430,153	25,098,703	26,546,557
Utah	1,618,047	1,719,782	1,822,725	1,916,688	2,025,714	2,102,655	2,250,339
Vermont	665,559	684,864	718,092	749,786	792,664	870,198	934,031
Virginia	5,750,318	5,969,608	6,343,768	6,736,863	7,137,419	7,757,598	8,335,805
Washington	5,138,928	5,394,507	5,587,803	5,987,060	6,098,008	6,399,885	6,782,127
West Virginia	1,758,557	1,806,004	1,847,560	1,905,940	1,986,562	2,086,937	2,157,568
Wisconsin	5,422,264	5,670,826	5,975,122	6,280,696	6,620,653	6,852,178	7,249,081
Wyoming	577,144	581,817	591,488	603,901	651,622	683,918	704,695
Outlying areas							
American Samoa	28,643	30,382	33,780	33,088	35,092	42,395	40,642
Guam	161,434	158,303	156,561	168,716	—	—	—
Northern Marianas	45,008	44,037	53,140	56,514	50,450	49,832	46,569
Puerto Rico	1,501,485	1,667,640	1,740,074	1,981,603	2,024,499	2,086,414	2,257,837
Virgin Islands	122,094	122,286	122,188	131,315	146,474	135,174	125,252

—Not available.

[1] Data revised from previously published figures.

NOTE: Beginning in 1980–81, expenditures for state administration are excluded. Detail may not sum to totals due to rounding.

SOURCE: U.S. Department of Education, National Center for Education Statistics, *Statistics of State School Systems;* and The NCES Common Core of Data (CCD), "National Public Education Financial Survey," 1985–86 through 2000–01. (This table was prepared August 2003.)

Total and current expenditure per pupil in public elementary and secondary schools: Selected years, 1919–20 to 2001–02

School year	Expenditure per pupil in average daily attendance				Expenditure per pupil in fall enrollment [1]				
	Unadjusted dollars		Constant 2001–02 dollars [2]		Unadjusted dollars		Constant 2001–02 dollars [2]		Annual percent change in current expenditure
	Total expenditure	Current expenditure	Total expenditure	Current expenditure	Total expenditure	Current expenditure	Total expenditure	Current expenditure	
1	2	3	4	5	6	7	8	9	10
1919–20	$64	$53	$598	$499	$48	$40	$448	$373	—
1929–30	108	87	1,129	903	90	72	935	747	—
1931–32	97	81	1,197	1,002	82	69	1,014	848	—
1933–34	76	67	1,026	908	65	57	871	771	—
1935–36	88	74	1,140	963	74	63	964	815	—
1937–38	100	84	1,240	1,043	86	72	1,065	896	—
1939–40	106	88	1,348	1,123	92	76	1,168	973	—
1941–42	110	98	1,257	1,124	94	84	1,077	962	—
1943–44	125	117	1,275	1,196	105	99	1,074	1,008	—
1945–46	146	136	1,425	1,332	124	116	1,214	1,135	—
1947–48	205	181	1,567	1,388	179	158	1,368	1,212	—
1949–50	260	210	1,959	1,583	231	187	1,738	1,404	—
1951–52	314	246	2,132	1,668	275	215	1,867	1,461	—
1953–54	351	265	2,326	1,755	312	236	2,068	1,560	—
1955–56	387	294	2,565	1,950	354	269	2,345	1,783	—
1957–58	447	341	2,792	2,129	408	311	2,546	1,941	—
1959–60	471	375	2,856	2,275	440	350	2,668	2,125	—
1961–62	517	419	3,066	2,484	485	393	2,877	2,331	—
1963–64	559	460	3,228	2,660	520	428	3,004	2,475	—
1965–66	654	538	3,651	3,003	607	499	3,390	2,788	—
1967–68	786	658	4,121	3,449	732	612	3,833	3,209	—
1969–70	955	816	4,505	3,849	879	751	4,147	3,544	—
1970–71	1,049	911	4,707	4,087	970	842	4,352	3,778	6.6
1971–72	1,128	990	4,884	4,286	1,034	908	4,479	3,931	4.0
1972–73	1,211	1,077	5,039	4,483	1,117	993	4,648	4,135	5.2
1973–74	1,364	1,207	5,213	4,614	1,244	1,101	4,753	4,207	1.7
1974–75	1,545	1,365	5,315	4,695	1,423	1,257	4,896	4,325	2.8
1975–76	1,697	1,504	5,454	4,831	1,563	1,385	5,022	4,449	2.9
1976–77	1,816	1,638	5,514	4,972	1,674	1,509	5,081	4,581	3.0
1977–78	2,002	1,823	5,697	5,186	1,842	1,677	5,240	4,770	4.1
1978–79	2,210	2,020	5,749	5,256	2,029	1,855	5,279	4,827	1.2
1979–80	2,491	2,272	5,717	5,214	2,290	2,088	5,255	4,794	–0.7
1980–81	[3] 2,742	2,502	[3] 5,641	5,146	[3] 2,529	2,307	[3] 5,203	4,746	–1.0
1981–82	[3] 2,973	2,726	[3] 5,630	5,161	[3] 2,754	2,525	[3] 5,215	4,781	0.7
1982–83	[3] 3,203	2,955	[3] 5,816	5,365	[3] 2,966	2,736	[3] 5,385	4,968	3.9
1983–84	[3] 3,471	3,173	[3] 6,077	5,556	[3] 3,216	2,940	[3] 5,630	5,147	3.6
1984–85	[3] 3,722	3,470	[3] 6,271	5,847	[3] 3,456	3,222	[3] 5,822	5,429	5.5
1985–86	[3] 4,020	3,756	[3] 6,583	6,150	[3] 3,724	3,479	[3] 6,099	5,698	5.0
1986–87	[3] 4,308	3,970	[3] 6,901	6,360	[3] 3,995	3,682	[3] 6,400	5,898	3.5
1987–88	[3] 4,654	4,240	[3] 7,159	6,522	[3] 4,310	3,927	[3] 6,630	6,040	2.4
1988–89	5,109	4,645	7,512	6,829	4,738	4,307	6,966	6,333	4.8
1989–90	5,550	4,980	7,789	6,988	5,174	4,643	7,262	6,515	2.9
1990–91	5,885	5,258	7,830	6,996	5,486	4,902	7,300	6,522	0.1
1991–92	6,074	5,421	7,832	6,989	5,629	5,023	7,257	6,476	–0.7
1992–93	6,281	5,584	7,853	6,981	5,804	5,160	7,257	6,451	–0.4
1993–94	6,492	5,767	7,912	7,029	5,996	5,327	7,307	6,492	0.6
1994–95	6,725	5,989	7,967	7,095	6,208	5,529	7,355	6,550	0.9
1995–96	6,962	6,147	8,029	7,090	6,443	5,689	7,431	6,562	0.2
1996–97	7,300	6,393	8,186	7,169	6,764	5,923	7,585	6,642	1.2
1997–98	7,703	6,676	8,487	7,354	7,142	6,189	7,868	6,819	2.7
1998–99	8,118	7,013	8,792	7,595	7,533	6,508	8,158	7,048	3.4
1999–2000	8,592	7,394	9,044	7,782	8,033	6,912	8,455	7,276	3.2
2000–01	9,197	7,898	9,360	8,037	8,589	7,376	8,742	7,507	3.2
2001–02 [3]	9,553	8,203	9,553	8,203	8,922	7,661	8,922	7,661	2.1

—Not available.

[1] Data for 1919–20 to 1953–54 are based on school–year enrollment.

[2] Based on the Consumer Price Index, prepared by the Bureau of Labor Statistics, U.S. Department of Labor, adjusted to a school–year basis.

[3] Estimated.

NOTE: Beginning in 1980–81, state administration expenditures are excluded from both "total" and "current" expenditures. Beginning in 1988–89, extensive changes were made in the data collection procedures. Some data have been revised from previously published figures.

SOURCE: U.S. Department of Education, National Center for Education Statistics, *Statistics of State School Systems; Revenues and Expenditures for Public Elementary and Secondary Education;* The NCES Common Core of Data (CCD), "National Public Education Financial Survey, 1987–88 through 2000–01"; and *Projections of Education Statistics to 2013.* (This table was prepared August 2003.)

Total and current expenditures per pupil in fall enrollment in public elementary and secondary education, by function and state or jurisdiction: 2000–01

State or jurisdiction	Total	Current expenditures, capital expenditures, and interest on school debt												Capital outlay[1]	Interest on school debt
		Current expenditures													
		Total	Instruction	Support services								Food services	Enterprise operations[2]		
				Total	Students[3]	Instructional[4]	General administration	School administration	Operation and maintenance	Student transportation	Other support services				
1	2	3	4	5	6	7	8	9	10	11	12	13	14	15	16
United States	$8,589	$7,376	$4,539	$2,528	$368	$337	$151	$415	$719	$298	$241	$293	$16	$998	$215
Alabama	6,718	5,885	3,629	1,854	263	220	154	360	509	248	100	402	0	719	114
Alaska	10,492	9,216	5,300	3,603	581	499	163	526	1,182	347	305	266	46	1,129	147
Arizona	7,752	5,278	3,012	1,915	353	151	92	290	603	202	224	351	0	2,060	414
Arkansas	6,224	5,568	3,400	1,856	259	232	201	332	488	197	147	311	0	530	127
California	8,088	6,987	4,343	2,379	284	405	56	485	657	170	321	259	7	1,036	64
Colorado	7,836	6,567	3,755	2,574	261	287	93	422	666	200	645	215	23	934	335
Connecticut	11,609	10,127	6,469	3,286	554	352	206	553	932	460	229	282	91	1,247	235
Delaware	10,258	8,958	5,448	3,102	405	129	99	501	988	489	491	408	0	1,178	122
District of Columbia	15,078	12,046	5,982	5,726	1,190	1,307	329	532	1,286	782	299	339	0	2,671	361
Florida	7,512	6,170	3,600	2,270	312	381	70	373	668	263	204	300	0	1,180	162
Georgia	8,176	6,929	4,394	2,178	316	352	92	422	546	262	188	352	5	1,122	125
Hawaii	7,466	6,596	3,973	2,236	478	256	180	402	625	117	178	387	0	646	225
Idaho	6,365	5,725	3,511	1,963	326	225	145	339	543	267	119	250	0	516	124
Illinois	9,170	7,643	4,565	2,826	464	315	250	403	807	340	247	251	0	1,288	240
Indiana	9,124	7,630	4,700	2,623	335	244	138	431	831	418	225	308	0	855	638
Iowa	7,865	6,930	4,059	2,353	448	347	196	362	614	215	173	306	211	818	116
Kansas	7,624	6,925	4,061	2,543	389	308	254	428	724	272	168	321	0	466	234
Kentucky	6,445	6,079	3,725	2,033	234	295	179	350	533	304	139	320	0	252	114
Louisiana	6,727	6,037	3,638	2,003	245	268	141	330	565	323	131	396	0	552	138
Maine	9,096	8,232	5,506	2,446	262	251	163	455	798	371	146	280	0	679	185
Maryland	9,317	8,256	5,057	2,790	355	444	78	536	682	402	292	250	159	966	95
Massachusetts	9,953	9,509	6,307	2,866	452	323	185	415	872	399	220	336	0	185	259
Michigan	9,829	8,278	4,832	3,196	520	390	190	514	873	341	369	250	0	1,223	328
Minnesota	9,137	7,645	4,748	2,580	266	439	214	322	692	416	231	317	0	1,144	348
Mississippi	5,755	5,175	3,126	1,712	216	216	160	296	505	225	94	336	1	455	125
Missouri	7,673	6,657	4,039	2,327	310	292	207	399	678	315	125	291	0	786	230
Montana	7,208	6,726	4,150	2,303	327	258	205	356	700	294	163	266	8	408	74
Nebraska	8,298	7,223	4,504	2,184	286	271	277	367	657	197	129	286	249	922	152
Nevada	7,893	5,807	3,628	1,995	221	231	94	415	567	232	235	185	0	1,693	393
New Hampshire	8,245	7,286	4,733	2,317	466	209	247	407	624	315	48	236	0	801	158
New Jersey	12,485	11,248	6,668	4,240	972	361	318	596	1,140	627	226	274	66	1,048	188
New Mexico	7,371	6,313	3,511	2,496	621	282	189	367	632	303	102	302	4	952	106
New York	11,938	10,716	7,274	3,150	353	297	227	445	977	524	326	292	0	922	301
North Carolina	7,633	6,346	4,024	1,964	331	217	127	420	493	223	154	358	0	1,105	181
North Dakota	6,716	6,125	3,645	1,973	219	187	301	297	558	285	126	299	208	523	69
Ohio	8,668	7,571	4,428	2,879	412	460	194	446	718	339	310	263	1	932	165
Oklahoma	6,516	6,019	3,483	2,149	377	189	171	320	703	198	191	322	64	437	60
Oregon	8,531	7,528	4,424	2,844	478	326	123	471	656	319	471	239	21	768	236
Pennsylvania	9,640	8,210	5,127	2,775	382	295	249	361	848	399	241	293	16	1,047	382
Rhode Island	9,663	9,315	6,007	3,067	704	358	144	471	796	392	203	240	0	175	173
South Carolina	8,089	6,631	3,968	2,299	437	402	87	399	599	203	172	340	25	1,270	188
South Dakota	7,453	6,191	3,671	2,196	324	274	209	321	625	218	226	307	16	1,118	144
Tennessee	6,875	5,687	3,664	1,743	193	307	110	295	552	197	91	280	0	992	196
Texas	8,046	6,539	3,952	2,260	317	363	108	359	727	172	215	326	0	1,206	301
Utah	5,578	4,674	3,024	1,369	169	197	47	281	446	141	89	246	35	764	141
Vermont	9,914	9,153	5,930	2,973	626	312	226	599	731	292	188	246	3	610	151
Virginia	8,418	7,281	4,493	2,503	343	445	110	431	718	338	118	283	2	972	165
Washington	8,073	6,750	4,007	2,415	472	311	154	327	668	265	217	221	108	1,035	289
West Virginia	8,083	7,534	4,629	2,467	253	203	194	412	796	500	109	438	0	511	38
Wisconsin	9,595	8,243	5,109	2,872	388	425	214	426	731	334	356	261	0	1,036	316
Wyoming	8,693	7,835	4,738	2,833	456	314	161	466	853	333	250	262	3	756	101
Outlying areas															
American Samoa	2,935	2,588	1,054	1,028	432	176	32	118	159	36	73	507	0	347	0
Guam	—	—	—	—	—	—	—	—	—	—	—	—	—	—	—
Northern Marianas	5,684	4,655	3,774	599	59	10	486	0	31	7	6	282	0	1,029	0
Puerto Rico	3,790	3,685	2,577	760	116	47	63	0	366	70	98	348	0	73	31
Virgin Islands	6,913	6,437	4,037	2,056	362	205	299	402	458	222	108	307	37	477	0

—Not available.

[1] Includes expenditures for property and for building and alterations completed by school district staff or contractors.

[2] Includes expenditures for operations funded by sales of products or services (e.g., school bookstore or computer time).

[3] Includes expenditures for health, attendance, and speech pathology services.

[4] Includes expenditures for curriculum development, staff training, libraries, and media and computer centers.

NOTE: Excludes expenditures for state education agencies. "0" indicates none or less than $0.50. Some data have been revised from previously published figures. Detail may not sum to totals due to rounding.

SOURCE: U.S. Department of Education, National Center for Education Statistics, The NCES Common Core of Data (CCD), "National Public Education Financial Survey," 2000–01. (This table was prepared August 2003.)

619

Number of public school districts and public and private elementary and secondary schools: Selected years, 1869–70 to 2001–02

School year	Regular public school districts[1]	Public schools[2]					Private schools[2,3]		
		Total, all schools[4]	Total, schools with reported grade spans[5]	Schools with elementary grades		Schools with secondary grades	Total[4]	Schools with elementary grades	Schools with secondary grades
				Total	One-teacher				
1	2	3	4	5	6	7	8	9	10
1869–70	—	116,312	—	—	—	—	—	—	—
1879–80	—	178,122	—	—	—	—	—	—	—
1889–90	—	224,526	—	—	—	—	—	—	—
1899–1900	—	248,279	—	—	—	—	—	—	—
1909–10	—	265,474	—	—	—	212,448	—	—	—
1919–20	—	271,319	—	—	—	187,948	—	—	—
1929–30	—	248,117	—	238,306	148,712	23,930	—	9,275	3,258
1931–32	—	245,941	—	—	143,445	—	—	—	—
1933–34	—	242,929	—	236,236	138,542	24,714	—	9,992	3,327
1935–36	—	237,816	—	—	130,708	—	—	—	—
1937–38	119,001	229,394	—	221,660	121,178	25,467	—	9,992	3,327
1939–40	117,108	226,762	—	—	113,600	—	—	11,306	3,568
1941–42	—	222,660	—	—	107,692	—	—	—	—
1945–46	101,382	—	—	160,227	86,563	24,314	—	9,863	3,294
1947–48	94,926	—	—	146,760	75,096	25,484	—	10,071	3,292
1949–50	83,718	—	—	128,225	59,652	24,542	—	10,375	3,331
1951–52	71,094	—	—	123,763	50,742	23,746	—	10,666	3,322
1953–54	63,057	—	—	110,875	42,865	25,637	—	11,739	3,913
1955–56	54,859	—	—	104,427	34,964	26,046	—	12,372	3,887
1957–58	47,594	—	—	95,446	25,341	25,507	—	13,065	3,994
1959–60	40,520	—	—	91,853	20,213	25,784	—	13,574	4,061
1961–62	35,676	—	—	81,910	13,333	25,350	—	14,762	4,129
1963–64	31,705	—	—	77,584	9,895	26,431	—	—	4,451
1965–66	26,983	—	—	73,216	6,491	26,597	17,849	15,340	4,606
1967–68	22,010	—	94,197	70,879	4,146	27,011	—	—	—
1970–71	17,995	—	89,372	65,800	1,815	25,352	—	14,372	3,770
1973–74	16,730	—	88,655	65,070	1,365	25,906	—	—	—
1975–76	16,376	88,597	87,034	63,242	1,166	25,330	—	—	—
1976–77	16,271	—	86,501	62,644	1,111	25,378	19,910	16,385	5,904
1978–79	16,014	—	84,816	61,982	1,056	24,504	19,489	16,097	5,766
1979–80	15,929	87,004	—	—	—	—	—	—	—
1980–81	15,912	85,982	83,688	61,069	921	24,362	20,764	16,792	5,678
1982–83	15,824	84,740	82,039	59,656	798	23,988	—	—	—
1983–84	15,747	84,178	81,418	59,082	838	23,947	[6]27,694	[6]20,872	[6]7,862
1984–85	—	84,007	81,147	58,827	825	23,916	—	—	—
1985–86	—	—	—	—	—	—	[6]25,616	[6]20,252	[6]7,387
1986–87	[7]15,713	83,455	82,190	60,784	763	23,389	—	—	—
1987–88	[7]15,577	83,248	81,416	59,754	729	23,841	[6]26,807	[6]22,959	[6]8,418
1988–89	[7]15,376	83,165	81,579	60,176	583	23,638	—	—	—
1989–90	[7]15,367	83,425	81,880	60,699	630	23,461	—	—	—
1990–91	[7]15,358	84,538	82,475	61,340	617	23,460	[6]24,690	[6]22,223	[6]8,989
1991–92	[7]15,173	84,578	82,506	61,739	569	23,248	[6]25,998	[6]23,523	[6]9,282
1992–93	[7]15,025	84,497	82,896	62,225	430	23,220	—	—	—
1993–94	[7]14,881	85,393	83,431	62,726	442	23,379	[6]26,093	[6]23,543	[6]10,555
1994–95	[7]14,772	86,221	84,476	63,572	458	23,668	—	—	—
1995–96	[7]14,766	87,125	84,958	63,961	474	23,793	27,686	25,153	10,942
1996–97	[7]14,841	88,223	86,092	64,785	487	24,287	—	—	—
1997–98	[7]14,805	89,508	87,541	65,859	476	24,802	27,402	24,915	10,779
1998–99	[7]14,891	90,874	89,259	67,183	463	25,797	—	—	—
1999–2000	[7]14,928	92,012	90,538	68,173	423	26,407	27,223	24,685	10,693
2000–01	[7]14,859	93,273	91,691	69,697	411	27,090	—	—	—
2001–02	[7]14,559	94,112	92,696	70,516	408	27,468	—	—	—

—Not available.

[1] Includes operating and nonoperating districts.

[2] Schools with both elementary and secondary programs are included under elementary schools and also under secondary schools.

[3] Data for most years are partly estimated.

[4] Includes regular schools and special schools not classified by grade span.

[5] Includes elementary, secondary, and combined elementary/secondary schools.

[6] These data are from sample surveys and should not be compared directly with the data for earlier years.

[7] Because of expanded survey coverage, data are not directly comparable with figures prior to 1986.

SOURCE: U.S. Department of Education, National Center for Education Statistics, *Annual Reports of the Commissioner of Education,* 1870 through 1910; *Biennial Survey of Education in the United States,* 1919–20 through 1949–50; *Statistics of State School Systems,* 1959–60 through 1967–68; *Statistics of Public Elementary and Secondary School Systems,* 1970–71 through 1980–81; *Statistics of Nonpublic Elementary and Secondary Schools,* 1970–71 through 1979–80; *Private Schools in American Education;* Schools and Staffing Survey (SASS), "Private School Questionnaire," 1987–88 and 1990–91; *Private School Universe Survey,* 1991–92 through 1999–2000; and The NCES Common Core of Data (CCD), 1982–83 through 2001–02. (This table was prepared July 2003.)

Public elementary and secondary schools, by type of school: 1967–68 to 2001–02

Year	Total, all public schools	Schools with reported grade spans										Combined elementary/ secondary schools [5]	Other schools [6]
		Total	Elementary schools				Secondary schools						
			Total [1]	Middle schools [2]	One-teacher schools	Other elementary schools	Total [3]	Junior high [4]	3-year or 4-year high schools	5-year or 6-year high schools	Other sec-ondary schools		
1	2	3	4	5	6	7	8	9	10	11	12	13	14
1967–68	—	94,197	67,186	—	4,146	63,040	23,318	7,437	10,751	4,650	480	3,693	—
1970–71	—	89,372	64,020	2,080	1,815	60,125	23,572	7,750	11,265	3,887	670	1,780	—
1972–73	—	88,864	62,942	2,308	1,475	59,159	23,919	7,878	11,550	3,962	529	2,003	—
1974–75	—	87,456	61,759	3,224	1,247	57,288	23,837	7,690	11,480	4,122	545	1,860	—
1975–76	88,597	87,034	61,704	3,916	1,166	56,622	23,792	7,521	11,572	4,113	586	1,538	1,563
1976–77	—	86,501	61,123	4,180	1,111	55,832	23,857	7,434	11,658	4,130	635	1,521	—
1978–79	—	84,816	60,312	5,879	1,056	53,377	22,834	6,282	11,410	4,429	713	1,670	—
1980–81	85,982	83,688	59,326	6,003	921	52,402	22,619	5,890	10,758	4,193	1,778	1,743	2,294
1982–83	84,740	82,039	58,051	6,875	798	50,378	22,383	5,948	11,678	4,067	690	1,605	2,701
1983–84	84,178	81,418	57,471	6,885	838	49,748	22,336	5,936	11,670	4,046	684	1,611	2,760
1984–85	84,007	81,147	57,231	6,893	825	49,513	22,320	5,916	11,671	4,021	712	1,596	2,860
1986–87	83,455	82,190	58,801	7,452	763	50,586	21,406	5,142	11,453	4,197	614	1,983	[7] 1,265
1987–88	83,248	81,416	57,575	7,641	729	49,205	21,662	4,900	11,279	4,048	1,435	2,179	[7] 1,832
1988–89	83,165	81,579	57,941	7,957	583	49,401	21,403	4,687	11,350	3,994	1,372	2,235	[7] 1,586
1989–90	83,425	81,880	58,419	8,272	630	49,517	21,181	4,512	11,492	3,812	1,365	2,280	[7] 1,545
1990–91	84,538	82,475	59,015	8,545	617	49,853	21,135	4,561	11,537	3,723	1,314	2,325	2,063
1991–92	84,578	82,506	59,258	8,829	569	49,860	20,767	4,298	11,528	3,699	1,242	2,481	2,072
1992–93	84,497	82,896	59,676	9,152	430	50,094	20,671	4,115	11,651	3,613	1,292	2,549	1,601
1993–94	85,393	83,431	60,052	9,573	442	50,037	20,705	3,970	11,858	3,595	1,282	2,674	1,962
1994–95	86,221	84,476	60,808	9,954	458	50,396	20,904	3,859	12,058	3,628	1,359	2,764	1,745
1995–96	87,125	84,958	61,165	10,205	474	50,486	20,997	3,743	12,168	3,621	1,465	2,796	2,167
1996–97	88,223	86,092	61,805	10,499	487	50,819	21,307	3,707	12,424	3,614	1,562	2,980	2,131
1997–98	89,508	87,541	62,739	10,944	476	51,319	21,682	3,599	12,734	3,611	1,738	3,120	1,967
1998–99	90,874	89,259	63,462	11,202	463	51,797	22,076	3,607	13,457	3,707	1,305	3,721	1,615
1999–2000	92,012	90,538	64,131	11,521	423	52,187	22,365	3,566	13,914	3,686	1,199	4,042	1,474
2000–01	93,273	91,691	64,601	11,696	411	52,494	21,994	3,318	13,793	3,974	909	5,096	1,582
2001–02	94,112	92,696	65,228	11,983	408	52,837	22,180	3,285	14,070	3,917	908	5,288	1,416

—Not available.

[1] Includes schools beginning with grade 6 or below and with no grade higher than 8.

[2] Includes schools with grade spans beginning with 4, 5, or 6 and ending with grade 6, 7, or 8.

[3] Includes schools with no grade lower than 7.

[4] Includes schools with grades 7 and 8 or grades 7 through 9.

[5] Includes schools beginning with grade 6 or lower and ending with grade 9 or above.

[6] Includes special education, alternative, and other schools not classified by grade span.

[7] Because of revision in data collection procedures, figures not comparable to data for other years.

SOURCE: U.S. Department of Education, National Center for Education Statistics, *Statistics of State School Systems;* 1967–68 and 1975–76; *Statistics of Public Elementary and Secondary Day Schools,* 1970–71, 1972–73, 1974–75, and 1976–77 through 1980–81; and The NCES Common Core of Data (CCD), "Public Elementary/Secondary School Universe Survey," 1982–83 through 2001–02. (This table was prepared April 2003.)

Public elementary and secondary schools, by type and state or jurisdiction: 1990–91 to 2001–02

State or jurisdiction	Total, all schools, 1990–91	Total, all schools, 1995–96	Total, all schools, 2000–01	Number of schools, 2001–02			Combined elementary/secondary[3]				Other[4]	Alternative[5]	Special education[5]	One-teacher schools[5]
				Total	Elementary[1]	Secondary[2]	Total	Pre-kindergarten, kindergarten, or 1st grade to grade 12	Other schools ending with grade 12	Other combined schools				
1	2	3	4	5	6	7	8	9	10	11	12	13	14	15
United States	**84,538**	**87,125**	**93,273**	**94,112**	**65,228**	**22,180**	**5,288**	**2,784**	**2,001**	**503**	**1,416**	**5,483**	**1,987**	**408**
Alabama	1,297	1,319	1,517	1,526	917	401	207	134	54	19	1	76	28	0
Alaska	498	495	515	522	193	92	237	222	9	6	0	33	2	24
Arizona	1,049	1,133	1,724	1,815	1,173	459	133	71	42	20	50	78	13	7
Arkansas	1,098	1,098	1,138	1,153	717	420	16	4	7	5	0	5	0	0
California	7,913	7,876	8,773	8,916	6,435	2,058	421	344	59	18	2	1,127	122	52
Colorado	1,344	1,486	1,632	1,667	1,188	385	77	32	37	8	17	90	22	2
Connecticut	985	1,045	1,248	1,246	877	217	151	120	22	9	1	203	30	0
Delaware	173	181	191	199	135	43	9	5	3	1	12	10	14	0
District of Columbia	181	186	198	198	130	47	5	4	1	0	16	6	10	0
Florida	2,516	2,760	3,316	3,419	2,241	451	727	311	386	30	0	180	131	3
Georgia	1,734	1,763	1,946	1,969	1,589	339	41	17	21	3	0	28	1	0
Hawaii	235	246	261	279	204	57	17	15	1	1	1	1	3	2
Idaho	582	618	673	688	418	232	38	25	11	2	0	68	11	11
Illinois	4,239	4,142	4,342	4,351	3,197	983	138	61	52	25	33	132	264	2
Indiana	1,915	1,924	1,976	1,980	1,419	456	75	26	43	6	30	73	39	0
Iowa	1,588	1,556	1,534	1,521	1,045	428	38	1	37	0	10	37	10	5
Kansas	1,477	1,487	1,430	1,431	996	424	2	1	1	0	9	0	0	0
Kentucky	1,400	1,402	1,526	1,459	1,010	346	85	19	64	2	18	173	12	0
Louisiana	1,533	1,470	1,530	1,540	1,028	329	165	102	56	7	18	117	31	0
Maine	747	726	714	711	533	163	15	11	4	0	0	0	3	7
Maryland	1,220	1,276	1,383	1,385	1,089	256	28	15	9	4	12	65	50	0
Massachusetts	1,842	1,850	1,905	1,908	1,452	330	121	31	25	65	5	38	5	0
Michigan	3,313	3,748	3,998	3,984	2,739	851	158	74	62	22	236	214	175	11
Minnesota	1,590	2,157	2,362	2,408	1,276	753	157	46	72	39	222	555	228	4
Mississippi	972	1,011	1,030	1,037	587	319	116	68	47	1	15	59	0	0
Missouri	2,199	2,256	2,368	2,380	1,567	644	124	42	77	5	45	84	62	1
Montana	900	894	879	871	509	362	0	0	0	0	0	5	2	78
Nebraska	1,506	1,411	1,326	1,307	903	345	48	47	0	1	11	0	58	93
Nevada	354	423	511	531	386	126	10	2	6	2	9	37	14	11
New Hampshire	439	460	526	472	377	95	0	0	0	0	0	0	0	0
New Jersey	2,272	2,279	2,410	2,430	1,883	455	11	2	5	4	81	18	83	0
New Mexico	681	721	765	793	557	200	36	24	10	2	0	58	15	2
New York	4,010	4,149	4,336	4,351	3,119	937	151	79	54	18	144	86	26	1
North Carolina	1,955	1,985	2,207	2,234	1,749	377	81	19	46	16	27	77	20	0
North Dakota	663	613	579	569	331	204	34	33	1	0	0	0	31	5
Ohio	3,731	3,865	3,916	3,912	2,716	948	143	58	43	42	105	48	32	5
Oklahoma	1,880	1,830	1,821	1,824	1,223	589	2	0	1	1	10	3	1	1
Oregon	1,199	1,216	1,273	1,300	962	284	49	33	15	1	5	75	12	13
Pennsylvania	3,260	3,182	3,252	3,251	2,388	795	56	17	23	16	12	13	12	2
Rhode Island	309	310	328	333	265	64	4	3	0	1	0	5	4	0
South Carolina	1,097	1,095	1,127	1,145	844	281	18	7	7	4	2	17	7	1
South Dakota	802	824	769	762	461	276	15	7	8	0	10	32	6	33
Tennessee	1,543	1,563	1,624	1,646	1,223	344	70	37	30	3	9	24	20	0
Texas	5,991	6,638	7,519	7,761	5,077	1,780	887	435	426	26	17	860	133	2
Utah	714	735	793	791	510	246	16	4	8	4	19	53	19	4
Vermont	397	384	393	392	277	69	46	37	8	1	0	2	61	3
Virginia	1,811	1,889	1,969	2,090	1,482	406	48	29	15	4	154	150	59	0
Washington	1,936	2,124	2,305	2,233	1,413	617	165	72	48	45	38	256	82	8
West Virginia	1,015	877	840	822	597	196	21	10	5	6	8	24	11	0
Wisconsin	2,018	2,037	2,182	2,212	1,558	589	65	22	36	7	0	164	12	0
Wyoming	415	410	393	388	263	112	11	6	4	1	2	24	1	15
Bureau of Indian Affairs	—	—	189	189	106	26	56	49	3	4	1	0	0	[6] 26
Department of Defense dependents schools:														
Domestic schools	—	—	71	70	58	7	5	2	2	1	0	0	0	0
Overseas schools	—	171	156	154	105	38	11	11	0	0	0	0	0	0
Outlying areas														
American Samoa	30	31	31	31	24	6	0	0	0	0	1	0	1	0
Guam	35	35	38	38	34	4	0	0	0	0	0	0	0	0
Northern Marianas	26	24	29	29	24	4	0	0	0	0	1	0	0	0
Puerto Rico	1,619	1,561	1,543	1,538	917	379	201	4	8	189	41	25	29	0
Virgin Islands	33	34	36	36	24	11	2	0	0	0	1	0	2	0

—Not available.

[1] Includes schools beginning with grade 6 or below and with no grade higher than 8.

[2] Includes schools with no grade lower than 7.

[3] Includes schools beginning with grade 6 or below and ending with grade 9 or above.

[4] Includes schools not classified by grade span.

[5] Schools are also included under elementary, secondary, combined, or other as appropriate.

[6] Data are for 1998–99.

SOURCE: U.S. Department of Education, National Center for Education Statistics, The NCES Common Core of Data (CCD), "Public Elementary/Secondary School Universe Survey," 1990–91 through 2001–02. (This table was prepared April 2003.)

Public elementary schools, by grade span, average school size, and state or jurisdiction: 2001–02

State or jurisdiction	Total, all elementary schools	Total, all regular elementary schools [1]	Schools, by grade span						Average number of students per school [2]	
			Prekindergarten, kindergarten, or 1st grade to grades 3 or 4	Prekindergarten, kindergarten, or 1st grade to grade 5	Prekindergarten, kindergarten, or 1st grade to grade 6	Prekindergarten, kindergarten, or 1st grade to grade 8	Grades 4, 5, or 6 to 6, 7, or 8	Other grade spans	All elementary schools	Regular elementary schools [1]
1	2	3	4	5	6	7	8	9	10	11
United States	65,228	64,181	4,870	23,189	14,003	5,327	11,983	5,856	477	482
Alabama	917	907	87	306	171	71	195	87	479	481
Alaska	193	192	0	27	111	21	17	17	332	332
Arizona	1,173	1,143	58	222	333	301	155	104	518	524
Arkansas	717	717	99	148	246	6	130	88	378	378
California	6,435	6,273	175	1,937	2,459	739	934	191	624	638
Colorado	1,188	1,182	33	549	246	47	231	82	415	416
Connecticut	877	816	85	326	129	80	155	102	468	473
Delaware	135	133	49	30	6	3	32	15	524	528
District of Columbia	130	130	8	22	74	10	13	3	385	385
Florida	2,241	2,240	32	1,405	174	62	458	110	758	759
Georgia	1,589	1,587	35	922	84	14	384	150	664	665
Hawaii	204	203	3	59	111	6	24	1	574	577
Idaho	418	415	36	94	173	20	63	32	359	361
Illinois	3,197	3,092	322	746	461	731	526	411	439	450
Indiana	1,419	1,407	75	604	378	29	253	80	458	460
Iowa	1,045	1,043	97	346	232	15	218	137	286	287
Kansas	996	996	77	287	274	106	175	77	294	294
Kentucky	1,010	993	50	461	169	91	193	46	431	437
Louisiana	1,028	1,003	100	319	194	78	222	115	456	462
Maine	533	531	71	103	76	110	94	79	248	249
Maryland	1,089	1,052	18	632	128	23	217	71	546	559
Massachusetts	1,452	1,442	204	474	216	91	235	232	431	431
Michigan	2,739	2,727	233	1,114	405	147	529	311	413	413
Minnesota	1,276	1,116	113	324	404	56	206	173	405	448
Mississippi	587	587	81	111	130	43	127	95	523	523
Missouri.	1,567	1,555	122	516	335	105	297	192	379	380
Montana	509	506	18	67	224	120	50	30	173	174
Nebraska	903	890	0	0	558	251	68	26	187	189
Nevada	386	379	7	179	98	21	62	19	658	666
New Hampshire	377	377	51	112	51	47	75	41	368	368
New Jersey	1,883	1,869	273	532	221	258	346	253	483	484
New Mexico	557	548	30	208	140	10	111	58	369	372
New York	3,119	3,114	245	1,150	580	114	620	410	601	601
North Carolina	1,749	1,740	63	976	66	109	419	116	534	536
North Dakota	331	331	9	40	197	49	22	14	177	177
Ohio	2,716	2,699	398	811	605	127	516	259	411	413
Oklahoma	1,223	1,223	64	332	184	303	223	117	341	341
Oregon	962	937	2	496	186	78	188	12	383	389
Pennsylvania	2,388	2,388	294	867	518	84	447	178	473	473
Rhode Island	265	264	27	108	43	4	45	38	405	405
South Carolina	844	843	66	396	81	23	220	58	562	562
South Dakota	461	458	19	111	102	117	82	30	178	179
Tennessee	1,223	1,218	138	419	136	194	245	91	503	505
Texas	5,077	4,994	533	1,945	770	108	1,126	595	541	548
Utah	510	510	19	100	332	4	40	15	532	532
Vermont	277	241	14	24	111	66	15	47	216	240
Virginia	1,482	1,469	46	814	154	13	305	150	538	541
Washington	1,413	1,338	74	509	435	60	225	110	437	454
West Virginia	597	594	83	192	146	40	102	34	310	312
Wisconsin	1,558	1,507	120	656	238	100	308	136	356	360
Wyoming	263	262	14	61	108	22	40	18	190	191
Bureau of Indian Affairs	106	106	7	4	23	64	3	5	227	227
Department of Defense dependents schools:										
Domestic schools	58	58	14	17	4	2	11	10	462	462
Overseas schools	105	105	8	18	51	9	17	2	481	481
Outlying areas										
American Samoa	24	24	1	0	0	21	1	1	496	496
Guam	34	34	0	24	0	0	7	3	680	680
Northern Marianas	24	24	0	0	12	0	1	11	271	271
Puerto Rico	917	885	6	1	873	0	27	10	306	305
Virgin Islands	24	24	0	1	22	0	1	0	441	441

[1] Excludes special education and alternative schools.
[2] Average for schools reporting enrollment data.

NOTE: Includes schools beginning with grade 6 or below and with no grade higher than 8. Excludes schools not reported by grade level, such as some special education schools for the disabled.

SOURCE: U.S. Department of Education, National Center for Education Statistics, The NCES Common Data (CCD), "Public Elementary/Secondary School Universe Survey," 2001–02. (This table was prepared April 2003.)

Public secondary schools, by grade span, average school size, and state or jurisdiction: 2001–02

State or jurisdiction	Total, all secondary schools	Total, all regular secondary schools[1]	Schools, by grade span							Vocational schools[2]	Average number of students per school[3]	
			Grades 7 to 8 and 7 to 9	Grades 7 to 12	Grades 8 to 12	Grades 9 to 12	Grades 10 to 12	Other spans ending with grade 12	Other grade spans		All secondary schools	Regular secondary schools[1]
1	2	3	4	5	6	7	8	9	10	11	12	13
United States	22,180	18,382	3,285	3,302	615	13,391	679	217	691	1,023	718	807
Alabama	401	302	27	99	10	220	31	6	8	76	661	684
Alaska	92	71	19	23	1	47	1	1	0	2	490	601
Arizona	459	418	84	49	6	307	6	2	5	18	691	726
Arkansas	420	399	49	198	4	96	44	2	27	19	432	434
California	2,058	1,272	334	237	33	1,418	13	7	16	0	959	1,472
Colorado	385	317	51	64	12	248	3	2	5	7	631	719
Connecticut	217	174	29	14	3	166	3	1	1	17	853	947
Delaware	43	36	12	1	2	28	0	0	0	5	1,004	1,015
District of Columbia	47	44	11	2	0	30	0	0	4	0	458	471
Florida	451	416	16	42	20	357	3	4	9	36	1,515	1,598
Georgia	339	322	12	4	6	309	3	1	4	0	1,155	1,205
Hawaii	57	56	13	9	0	33	0	0	2	0	1,119	1,136
Idaho	232	163	46	54	5	103	19	0	5	10	441	561
Illinois	983	787	164	68	26	612	13	37	63	26	669	786
Indiana	456	396	72	94	4	253	3	1	29	29	779	813
Iowa	428	395	61	89	1	265	8	2	2	0	415	439
Kansas	424	424	67	85	2	263	7	0	0	0	409	409
Kentucky	346	262	34	70	5	233	3	0	1	10	607	745
Louisiana	329	291	60	45	162	52	1	1	8	8	696	738
Maine	163	136	23	12	1	125	1	0	1	27	524	524
Maryland	256	186	21	5	12	185	26	2	5	26	1,143	1,325
Massachusetts	330	272	34	38	13	236	3	2	4	45	855	904
Michigan	851	694	100	91	25	562	18	4	51	45	684	779
Minnesota	753	461	66	265	31	260	63	29	39	12	444	676
Mississippi	319	224	37	70	10	172	22	1	7	86	644	644
Missouri	644	565	60	193	7	332	26	14	12	61	539	547
Montana	362	358	185	0	0	175	1	0	1	0	176	177
Nebraska	345	345	33	202	0	99	11	0	0	0	341	341
Nevada	126	94	18	20	4	77	1	5	1	3	869	1,091
New Hampshire	95	95	17	0	0	76	1	0	1	0	716	716
New Jersey	455	394	68	36	7	318	8	3	15	51	956	1,029
New Mexico	200	164	38	41	3	108	5	0	5	0	561	653
New York	937	832	98	158	13	595	22	0	51	25	942	989
North Carolina	377	355	19	9	4	330	4	2	9	7	978	1,018
North Dakota	204	197	14	131	3	49	4	1	2	7	238	238
Ohio	948	866	174	133	37	578	11	2	13	72	731	732
Oklahoma	589	589	108	1	0	393	66	3	18	0	347	347
Oregon	284	242	36	33	14	193	5	2	1	0	668	759
Pennsylvania	795	707	101	159	10	399	32	10	84	82	882	891
Rhode Island	64	48	8	2	0	49	3	0	2	11	878	1,001
South Carolina	281	228	29	20	8	200	13	7	4	40	946	950
South Dakota	276	262	91	2	0	180	2	0	1	4	168	171
Tennessee	344	314	32	32	4	262	10	0	4	23	820	831
Texas	1,780	1,445	333	193	18	1,173	11	10	42	25	749	897
Utah	246	203	84	31	8	50	60	1	12	0	831	987
Vermont	69	54	7	23	0	38	0	0	1	14	624	635
Virginia	406	335	31	10	41	260	7	2	55	48	1,061	1,122
Washington	617	446	121	62	27	312	41	20	34	11	607	796
West Virginia	196	145	30	23	3	105	13	6	16	34	550	619
Wisconsin	589	486	75	53	5	401	21	24	10	1	524	621
Wyoming	112	95	33	7	5	59	7	0	1	0	332	371
Bureau of Indian Affairs	26	26	1	8	0	17	0	0	0	0	344	344
Department of Defense dependents schools:												
Domestic schools	7	7	2	0	1	4	0	0	0	0	545	545
Overseas schools	38	38	2	23	1	12	0	0	0	0	472	472
Outlying areas												
American Samoa	6	5	0	0	0	6	0	0	0	1	656	720
Guam	4	4	0	0	0	4	0	0	0	0	2,215	2,215
Northern Marianas	4	4	1	1	0	2	0	0	0	0	979	979
Puerto Rico	379	358	187	28	1	7	147	1	8	14	597	603
Virgin Islands	11	8	6	0	0	4	1	0	0	1	791	973

[1] Excludes vocational, special education, and alternative schools.
[2] Vocational schools are also included under appropriate grade span.
[3] Average for schools reporting enrollment data.

NOTE: Includes schools with no grade lower than 7. Excludes schools not reported by grade level, such as some special education schools for the disabled.

SOURCE: U.S. Department of Education, National Center for Education Statistics, The NCES Common Core of Data (CCD), "Public Elementary/Secondary School Universe Survey," 2001–02. (This table was prepared April 2003.)

States requiring testing for initial certification of teachers, by skills or knowledge assessment: 1990 and 2002

State	Assessment for certification, 1990				Assessment for certification, 2002				
	Basic skills exam	Subject matter exam	Knowledge of teaching exam	Assessment of teaching performance	Basic skills exam	Subject matter exam	General knowledge exam	Knowledge of teaching exam	Assessment of teaching performance
1	2	3	4	5	6	7	8	9	10
Alabama					(1)	(2)		(2)	X
Alaska					X				
Arizona	X		X			X		X	X
Arkansas		X	X		X	X		X	X
California	X	X			X	(3)			
Colorado	X			X		X			
Connecticut	X	X		X	X	X			
Delaware	X				X				
District of Columbia	X	X			X	X			X
Florida		X	X	X	X	X	X	X	X
Georgia		X		X	X	X			
Hawaii	X	X	X		X	X		X	
Idaho		X	X						
Illinois		X	X		X	X			
Indiana	X	X	X		X	X	X	X	
Iowa	X	X	X	X					
Kansas	X		X					X	
Kentucky				X	(1)				X
Louisiana	X	X	X		X	X	X	X	X
Maine	X	X	X	X	X		X	X	
Maryland	X	X	X		X	X		X	X
Massachusetts		(4)				(4)			
Michigan					X	X	(5)		
Minnesota	X				X	X		X	
Mississippi		X	X	X	X			X	
Missouri		X			(1)	X		(6)	
Montana	X		X		X				
Nebraska	X				X				
Nevada	X	X	X		X	X		X	
New Hampshire	X				X	X			
New Jersey		X				X	(7)		X
New Mexico	X		X	X	X	X		X	
New York	X		X				X	X	
North Carolina				X	(1)	X			
North Dakota					(1)		X	X	
Ohio [8]		X	X			X		X	X
Oklahoma					X	X	X	(9)	X
Oregon	X	X	X	X	X	X			(10)
Pennsylvania	X	X	X		X	X	X	X	
Rhode Island [11]	X		X	X			X		
South Carolina			X	X	X	X		X	X
South Dakota [12]					X	X			X
Tennessee				X	(13)	X		X	X
Texas [14]		X	X			X		X	
Utah								(15)	
Vermont					X				
Virginia	X	X	X	X	X	X	X		
Washington			X		(1)				
West Virginia	X	X		X	X	X		X	X
Wisconsin	X				X				
Wyoming									

[1] For admission to teacher education program.
[2] Institution's exit exam.
[3] Subject matter exam or completion of an approved subject matter program.
[4] In 1990, test required for foreign language, bilingual, and English as a Second Language. In 2002, two-part exam covers communication and literacy skills and the subject matter knowledge for the certificate.
[5] Elementary certificate exam (subject-area exam).
[6] If no subject knowledge assessment is designated.
[7] For elementary education.
[8] Test requirements in 1990 set by school districts.
[9] Required for standard certificate.
[10] For Oregon graduates.
[11] Principles of Learning Teaching Test (K-6) or (7–12).
[12] Required within the institutional program requirements.
[13] Basic skills exams in reading, math, and writing are covered in the Praxis Pre-professional Skills Test.
[14] Screening for admission to a teacher preparation program includes college level skills in reading, oral and written communication, critical thinking, and mathematics.
[15] Entry year requirement.

SOURCE: Council of Chief State School Officers, "State Education Indicators, 1990;" and National Association of State Directors of Teacher Education and Certification, "The NASDTEC Manual 2002: Manual on Certification & Preparation of Educational Personnel in the United States & Canada." (This table was prepared August 2002.)

Public and private elementary and secondary teachers, enrollment, and pupil to teacher ratios: Selected years, fall 1955 to fall 2002

Year	Elementary and secondary teachers, in thousands			Elementary and secondary enrollment, in thousands			Elementary and secondary pupil/teacher ratio		
	Total	Public	Private	Total	Public	Private	Total	Public	Private
1	2	3	4	5	6	7	8	9	10
1955	1,286	1,141	[1] 145	35,280	30,680	[1] 4,600	27.4	26.9	[1] 31.7
1960	1,600	1,408	[1] 192	42,181	36,281	[1] 5,900	26.4	25.8	[1] 30.7
1965	1,933	1,710	223	48,473	42,173	6,300	25.1	24.7	28.3
1970	2,292	2,059	233	51,257	45,894	5,363	22.4	22.3	23.0
1971	2,293	2,063	[1] 230	51,271	46,071	[1] 5,200	22.4	22.3	[1] 22.6
1972	2,337	2,106	[1] 231	50,726	45,726	[1] 5,000	21.7	21.7	[1] 21.6
1973	2,372	2,136	[1] 236	50,446	45,446	[1] 5,000	21.3	21.3	[1] 21.2
1974	2,410	2,165	[1] 245	50,073	45,073	[1] 5,000	20.8	20.8	[1] 20.4
1975	2,453	2,198	[1] 255	49,819	44,819	[1] 5,000	20.3	20.4	[1] 19.6
1976	2,457	2,189	268	49,478	44,311	5,167	20.1	20.2	19.3
1977	2,488	2,209	279	48,717	43,577	5,140	19.6	19.7	18.4
1978	2,479	2,207	272	47,635	42,550	5,085	19.2	19.3	18.7
1979	2,461	2,185	[1] 276	46,651	41,651	[1] 5,000	19.0	19.1	[1] 18.1
1980	2,485	2,184	301	46,208	40,877	5,331	18.6	18.7	17.7
1981	2,440	2,127	[1] 313	45,544	40,044	[1] 5,500	18.7	18.8	[1] 17.6
1982	2,458	2,133	[1] 325	45,165	39,566	[1] 5,600	18.4	18.6	[1] 17.2
1983	2,476	2,139	337	44,967	39,252	5,715	18.2	18.4	17.0
1984	2,508	2,168	[1] 340	44,908	39,208	[1] 5,700	17.9	18.1	[1] 16.8
1985	2,549	2,206	343	44,979	39,422	5,557	17.6	17.9	16.2
1986	2,592	2,244	[1] 348	45,205	39,753	[1] 5,452	17.4	17.7	[1] 15.7
1987	2,631	2,279	352	45,487	40,008	5,479	17.3	17.6	15.6
1988	2,668	2,323	[1] 345	45,430	40,189	[1] 5,242	17.0	17.3	[1] 15.2
1989	2,734	2,357	377	45,741	40,543	5,198	16.7	17.2	13.8
1990	2,753	2,398	[1] 355	46,451	41,217	[1] 5,234	16.9	17.2	[1] 14.7
1991	2,787	2,432	355	47,322	42,047	5,275	17.0	17.3	14.9
1992	2,822	2,459	[1] 363	48,145	42,823	[1] 5,322	17.1	17.4	[1] 14.7
1993	2,870	2,504	366	48,813	43,465	5,348	17.0	17.4	14.6
1994	2,926	2,552	[1] 374	49,609	44,111	[1] 5,498	17.0	17.3	[1] 14.7
1995	2,978	2,598	380	50,502	44,840	5,662	17.0	17.3	14.9
1996	3,054	2,667	[1] 387	51,375	45,611	[1] 5,764	16.8	17.1	[1] 14.9
1997	3,134	2,746	388	51,968	46,127	5,841	16.6	16.8	15.1
1998	3,221	2,830	[1] 391	52,476	46,539	[1] 5,937	16.3	16.4	[1] 15.2
1999	3,306	2,911	395	52,875	46,857	6,018	16.0	16.1	15.2
2000	3,332	2,941	[1] 390	53,366	47,204	[1] 6,162	16.0	16.0	[1] 15.8
2001	3,388	2,998	390	53,890	47,688	[1] 6,202	15.9	15.9	[1] 15.9
2002[2]	3,369	2,983	385	54,158	47,918	6,241	16.1	16.1	16.2

[1] Estimated.
[2] Projected.

NOTE: Data for teachers are expressed in full-time equivalents. Data for private schools includes kindergarten and a relatively small number of nursery school teachers and students. Ratios for public schools reflect totals reported by states and differ from totals reported for schools by states or school districts. Some data have been revised from previously published figures. Detail may not sum to totals due to rounding.

SOURCE: U.S. Department of Education, National Center for Education Statistics, *Statistics of Public Elementary and Secondary Day Schools*, 1955–56 through 1984–85; The NCES Common Core of Data (CCD), "State Nonfiscal Survey of Public Elementary/Secondary Education," 1985–86 through 2001–02 surveys; and *Projections of Education Statistics to 2013*. (This table was prepared October 2003.)

Estimated average annual salary of teachers in public elementary and secondary schools: 1959–60 to 2002–03

School year	Current dollars					Constant 2002–03 dollars		
	All teachers	Elementary teachers	Secondary teachers	Earnings per full-time employee working for wages or salary [1]	Ratio of average teachers' salary to earnings per full-time employee	All teachers	Elementary teachers	Secondary teachers
1	2	3	4	5	6	7	8	9
1959–60	$4,995	$4,815	$5,276	$4,632	1.08	$30,959	$29,844	$32,701
1961–62	5,515	5,340	5,775	4,928	1.12	33,415	32,354	34,990
1963–64	5,995	5,805	6,266	5,373	1.12	35,399	34,278	37,000
1965–66	6,485	6,279	6,761	5,838	1.11	37,013	35,838	38,589
1967–68	7,423	7,208	7,692	6,444	1.15	39,751	38,600	41,192
1969–70	8,626	8,412	8,891	7,334	1.18	41,587	40,555	42,864
1970–71	9,268	9,021	9,568	7,815	1.19	42,489	41,356	43,864
1971–72	9,705	9,424	10,031	8,334	1.16	42,951	41,708	44,394
1972–73	10,174	9,893	10,507	8,858	1.15	43,283	42,087	44,700
1973–74	10,770	10,507	11,077	9,647	1.12	42,067	41,040	43,267
1974–75	11,641	11,334	12,000	10,420	1.12	40,933	39,854	42,196
1975–76	12,600	12,280	12,937	11,218	1.12	41,377	40,326	42,483
1976–77	13,354	12,989	13,776	11,991	1.11	41,436	40,304	42,746
1977–78	14,198	13,845	14,602	12,823	1.11	41,283	40,257	42,458
1978–79	15,032	14,681	15,450	13,822	1.09	39,965	39,031	41,076
1979–80	15,970	15,569	16,459	15,086	1.06	37,463	36,523	38,611
1980–81	17,644	17,230	18,142	16,517	1.07	37,094	36,224	38,141
1981–82	19,274	18,853	19,805	17,863	1.08	37,299	36,484	38,326
1982–83	20,695	20,227	21,291	18,946	1.09	38,399	37,531	39,505
1983–84	21,935	21,487	22,554	19,874	1.10	39,248	38,446	40,355
1984–85	23,600	23,200	24,187	20,815	1.13	40,636	39,947	41,647
1985–86	25,199	24,718	25,846	21,727	1.16	42,173	41,368	43,256
1986–87	26,569	26,057	27,244	22,642	1.17	43,500	42,662	44,605
1987–88	28,034	27,519	28,798	23,698	1.18	44,073	43,263	45,274
1988–89	29,564	29,022	30,218	24,651	1.20	44,426	43,612	45,409
1989–90	31,367	30,832	32,049	25,643	1.22	44,989	44,221	45,967
1990–91	33,084	32,490	33,896	26,791	1.23	44,992	44,184	46,096
1991–92	34,063	33,479	34,827	27,990	1.22	44,885	44,115	45,892
1992–93	35,029	34,350	35,880	29,036	1.21	44,760	43,892	45,847
1993–94	35,737	35,233	36,566	29,778	1.20	44,511	43,884	45,544
1994–95	36,675	36,088	37,523	30,568	1.20	44,407	43,696	45,434
1995–96	37,642	37,138	38,397	31,518	1.19	44,370	43,776	45,260
1996–97	38,443	38,039	39,184	32,735	1.17	44,058	43,595	44,907
1997–98	39,351	39,008	39,945	34,269	1.15	44,308	43,922	44,977
1998–99	40,550	40,097	41,303	35,893	1.13	44,881	44,380	45,715
1999–2000	41,827	41,326	42,571	37,718	1.11	44,996	44,457	45,796
2000–01	43,400	42,937	44,028	39,272	1.11	45,141	44,660	45,794
2001–02	44,683	44,308	45,246	—	—	45,667	45,284	46,243
2002–03	45,822	45,658	46,119	—	—	45,822	45,658	46,119

—Not available.

[1] Calendar-year data from the U.S. Department of Commerce have been converted to a school-year basis by averaging the two appropriate calendar years in each case. Beginning in 1992–93, data are wage and salary accruals per full-time-equivalent employee.

NOTE: Constant 2002–03 dollars based on the Consumer Price Index, prepared by the Bureau of Labor Statistics, U.S. Department of Labor. Some data have been revised from previously published figures.

SOURCE: National Education Association, *Estimates of School Statistics*, 1959–60 through 2002–03; and unpublished data. (Copyright © 2003 by the National Education Association. All rights reserved.); and U.S. Department of Commerce, Bureau of Economic Analysis, *National Income and Product Accounts*, 1959–60 through 2002–03. (This table was prepared August 2003.)

Estimated average annual salary of teachers in public elementary and secondary schools, by state: Selected years, 1969–70 to 2002–03

State	Current dollars							Constant 2002–03 dollars						Percent change, 1989–90 to 2002–03 in constant dollars
	1969–70	1979–80	1989–90	1999–2000	2000–01	2001–02	2002–03	1969–70	1979–80	1989–90	1999–2000	2000–01	2001–02	
1	2	3	4	5	6	7	8	9	10	11	12	13	14	15
United States	$8,626	$15,970	$31,367	¹$41,827	¹$43,400	¹$44,683	¹$45,822	$41,587	$37,463	$44,989	$44,996	$45,141	$45,667	1.9
Alabama	6,818	13,060	24,828	36,689	37,069	37,194	38,246	32,870	30,637	35,610	39,468	38,556	38,013	7.4
Alaska	10,560	27,210	43,153	46,462	48,123	49,418	49,685	50,911	63,831	61,893	49,982	50,054	50,506	−19.7
Arizona	8,711	15,054	29,402	36,902	37,167	39,973	¹ 40,894	41,997	35,315	42,170	39,698	38,658	40,853	−3.0
Arkansas	6,307	12,299	22,352	33,386	34,641	¹ 36,962	¹ 37,753	30,407	28,852	32,059	35,915	36,031	37,776	17.8
California	10,315	18,020	37,998	47,680	52,480	54,348	¹ 56,283	49,730	42,273	54,499	51,292	54,585	55,545	3.3
Colorado	7,761	16,205	30,758	38,163	39,184	40,659	¹ 41,275	37,416	38,015	44,115	41,054	40,756	41,555	−6.4
Connecticut	9,262	16,229	40,461	51,780	52,693	53,551	¹ 54,362	44,653	38,071	58,032	55,703	54,807	54,730	−6.3
Delaware	9,015	16,148	33,377	44,435	47,047	48,363	50,772	43,462	37,881	47,872	47,801	48,935	49,428	6.1
District of Columbia ...	10,285	22,190	38,402	47,076	48,704	47,049	50,763	49,585	52,055	55,079	50,642	50,658	48,085	−7.8
Florida	8,412	14,149	28,803	36,722	38,230	39,275	39,465	40,555	33,192	41,311	39,504	39,764	40,140	−4.5
Georgia	7,276	13,853	28,006	41,023	42,216	44,073	45,533	35,078	32,497	40,168	44,131	43,910	45,044	13.4
Hawaii	9,453	19,920	32,047	40,578	40,052	42,615	44,464	45,574	46,730	45,964	43,652	41,659	43,554	−3.3
Idaho	6,890	13,611	23,861	35,547	37,450	39,591	40,148	33,217	31,930	34,223	38,240	38,952	40,463	17.3
Illinois	9,569	17,601	32,794	46,486	47,847	49,435	51,289	46,133	41,290	47,036	50,008	49,767	50,524	9.0
Indiana	8,833	15,599	30,902	41,850	43,311	44,195	45,097	42,585	36,593	44,322	45,020	45,049	45,168	1.7
Iowa	8,355	15,203	26,747	35,678	36,479	38,230	38,921	40,280	35,664	38,362	38,381	37,943	39,072	1.5
Kansas	7,612	13,690	28,744	34,981	35,901	37,093	38,123	36,698	32,115	41,227	37,631	37,341	37,910	−7.5
Kentucky	6,953	14,520	26,292	36,380	36,589	37,951	38,981	33,521	34,062	37,710	39,136	38,057	38,787	3.4
Louisiana	7,028	13,760	24,300	33,109	33,615	36,328	¹ 36,878	33,883	32,279	34,853	35,617	34,964	37,128	5.8
Maine	7,572	13,071	26,881	35,561	36,373	37,300	38,121	36,505	30,663	38,555	38,255	37,832	38,122	−1.1
Maryland	9,383	17,558	36,319	44,048	45,963	48,251	49,677	45,236	41,189	52,091	47,385	47,807	49,314	−4.6
Massachusetts	8,764	17,253	34,712	46,580	48,649	50,293	52,043	42,252	40,473	49,786	50,109	50,601	51,401	4.5
Michigan	9,826	19,663	37,072	49,044	51,317	¹ 52,676	¹ 54,071	47,372	46,127	53,171	52,759	53,376	53,836	1.7
Minnesota	8,658	15,912	32,190	39,802	42,212	42,194	¹ 42,833	41,741	37,327	46,169	42,817	43,906	43,123	−7.2
Mississippi	5,798	11,850	24,292	31,857	31,954	33,295	¹ 34,555	27,953	27,799	34,841	34,270	33,236	34,028	−0.8
Missouri	7,799	13,682	27,094	35,656	36,715	37,996	38,826	37,600	32,096	38,860	38,357	38,188	38,833	−0.1
Montana	7,606	14,537	25,081	32,121	33,249	34,379	35,754	36,669	34,102	35,973	34,554	34,583	35,136	−0.6
Nebraska	7,375	13,516	25,522	33,237	34,175	36,236	37,896	35,556	31,707	36,605	35,755	35,546	37,034	3.5
Nevada	9,215	16,295	30,590	¹ 39,390	¹ 40,443	¹ 40,764	¹ 41,795	44,426	38,226	43,874	42,374	42,066	41,662	−4.7
New Hampshire	7,771	13,017	28,986	37,734	38,301	39,915	¹ 40,519	37,465	30,536	41,574	40,593	39,838	40,794	−2.5
New Jersey	9,130	17,161	35,676	52,015	52,268	53,192	54,166	44,017	40,257	51,169	55,955	54,365	54,364	5.9
New Mexico	7,796	14,887	24,756	32,554	33,785	36,440	36,687	37,585	34,923	35,507	35,020	35,140	37,243	3.3
New York	10,336	19,812	38,925	51,020	51,500	52,000	52,600	49,831	46,476	55,829	54,885	53,566	53,145	−5.8
North Carolina	7,494	14,117	27,883	39,404	41,480	42,680	43,076	36,129	33,117	39,992	42,389	43,144	43,620	7.7
North Dakota	6,696	13,263	23,016	29,863	30,891	32,253	33,210	32,282	31,113	33,011	32,125	32,130	32,963	0.6
Ohio	8,300	15,269	31,218	41,436	42,764	44,029	45,452	40,015	35,819	44,775	44,575	44,480	44,999	1.5
Oklahoma	6,882	13,107	23,070	31,298	34,499	34,744	34,854	33,179	30,747	33,089	33,669	35,883	35,509	5.3
Oregon	8,818	16,266	30,840	42,336	44,989	46,081	47,600	42,512	38,158	44,233	45,543	46,794	47,096	7.6
Pennsylvania	8,858	16,515	33,338	48,321	49,528	50,599	51,800	42,705	38,742	47,816	51,982	51,515	51,713	8.3
Rhode Island	8,776	18,002	36,057	47,041	¹ 48,474	¹ 49,758	¹ 51,076	42,310	42,230	51,716	50,605	50,419	50,854	−1.2
South Carolina	6,927	13,063	27,217	36,081	37,938	39,923	41,279	33,396	30,644	39,037	38,814	39,460	40,802	5.7
South Dakota	6,403	12,348	21,300	29,071	30,265	31,295	32,416	30,869	28,967	30,550	31,273	31,479	31,984	6.1
Tennessee	7,050	13,972	27,052	36,328	37,431	38,515	39,677	33,989	32,776	38,800	39,080	38,933	39,363	2.3
Texas	7,255	14,132	27,496	37,567	38,361	39,232	40,001	34,977	33,152	39,437	40,413	39,900	40,096	1.4
Utah	7,644	14,909	23,686	34,946	36,441	¹ 37,414	¹ 38,413	36,852	34,975	33,972	37,593	37,903	38,238	13.1
Vermont	7,968	12,484	29,012	37,758	38,253	39,240	41,603	38,414	29,286	41,611	40,618	39,788	40,104	#
Virginia	8,070	14,060	30,938	38,744	40,175	¹ 41,731	43,152	38,906	32,983	44,374	41,679	41,787	42,650	−2.8
Washington	9,225	18,820	30,457	41,043	42,137	43,464	44,949	44,475	44,149	43,684	44,152	43,828	44,421	2.9
West Virginia	7,650	13,710	22,842	35,009	35,888	36,751	38,508	36,881	32,162	32,762	37,661	37,328	37,560	17.5
Wisconsin	8,963	16,006	31,921	41,153	42,122	42,232	42,871	43,211	37,548	45,783	44,271	43,812	43,162	−6.4
Wyoming	8,232	16,012	28,141	34,127	34,678	37,837	37,876	39,687	37,562	40,362	36,712	36,069	38,670	−6.2

\# Rounds to zero.

¹ Data estimated by the National Education Association.

NOTE: Constant 2002–03 dollars are based on the Consumer Price Index prepared by the Bureau of Labor Statistics, U.S. Department of Labor. The price index does not account for different rates of change in the cost of living among states. Some data have been revised from previously published figures.

SOURCE: National Education Association, *Estimates of School Statistics*, 1969–70 through 2002–03. (Copyright © 2003 by the National Education Association. All rights reserved.) (This table was prepared August 2003.)

Federal on-budget funds for education, by agency: Selected fiscal years, 1970 to 2003

[In thousands of current dollars]

Agency	1970	1975	1980	1985	1990	1995	2000	2001	2002	2003[1]
1	2	3	4	5	6	7	8	9	10	11
Total	$12,526,499	$23,288,120	$34,493,502	$39,027,876	$51,624,342	$71,639,520	$85,944,203	$94,846,476	$109,361,491	$124,736,574
Department of Education	4,625,224	7,350,355	13,137,785	16,701,065	23,198,575	31,403,000	34,106,697	36,562,025	46,324,352	57,442,854
Department of Agriculture	960,910	2,219,352	4,562,467	4,782,274	6,260,843	9,092,089	11,080,031	11,329,740	12,033,544	12,756,018
Department of Commerce	13,990	38,967	135,561	55,114	53,835	88,929	114,575	134,654	130,660	90,100
Department of Defense	821,388	1,009,229	1,560,301	3,119,213	3,605,509	3,879,002	4,525,080	5,417,621	5,438,182	5,244,192
Department of Energy	551,527	764,676	1,605,558	2,247,822	2,561,950	2,692,314	3,577,004	3,885,773	3,992,886	4,086,914
Department of Health and Human Services	1,796,854	3,675,225	5,613,930	5,322,356	7,956,011	12,469,563	17,670,867	20,540,411	22,875,705	25,406,660
Department of Housing and Urban Development	114,709	52,768	5,314	438	118	1,613	1,400	1,600	1,600	1,500
Department of the Interior	190,975	300,191	440,547	549,479	630,537	702,796	959,802	1,092,588	1,186,213	1,231,006
Department of Justice	15,728	61,542	60,721	66,802	99,775	172,350	278,927	431,220	454,933	477,201
Department of Labor	424,494	1,103,935	1,862,738	1,948,685	2,511,380	3,967,914	4,696,100	5,193,100	5,865,100	6,082,500
Department of State	59,742	89,433	25,188	23,820	51,225	54,671	388,349	390,068	487,097	404,127
Department of Transportation	27,534	52,290	54,712	82,035	76,186	135,816	117,054	153,682	162,208	135,259
Department of the Treasury	18	1,118,840	1,247,463	290,276	41,715	49,496	83,000	88,000	163,000	195,000
Department of Veterans Affairs	1,032,918	4,402,212	2,351,233	1,289,849	757,476	1,324,382	1,577,374	1,802,342	2,122,289	2,653,341
Other agencies and programs										
ACTION	†	7,081	2,833	1,761	8,472	†	†	†	†	†
Agency for International Development	88,034	78,896	176,770	198,807	249,786	290,580	332,500	488,600	521,500	570,500
Appalachian Regional Commission	37,838	45,786	19,032	4,745	93	10,623	7,243	9,560	15,767	14,800
Barry Goldwater Scholarship and Excellence in Education Foundation ...	†	†	†	†	1,033	3,000	3,000	3,000	3,000	3,000
Corporation for National and Community Service	†	†	†	†	†	214,600	386,000	452,000	404,000	516,000
Environmental Protection Agency	19,446	33,875	41,083	60,521	87,481	125,721	98,900	125,400	163,900	171,600
Estimated education share of federal aid to the District of Columbia	33,019	55,487	81,847	107,340	104,940	78,796	127,127	147,093	166,057	174,400
Federal Emergency Management Agency	290	290	1,946	1,828	215	170,400	14,894	23,778	8,376	8,600
General Services Administration	14,775	22,532	34,800	†	†	†	†	†	†	†
Harry S Truman Scholarship fund	†	†	−1,895	1,332	2,883	3,000	3,000	2,000	4,000	3,000
Institute of American Indian and Alaskan Native Culture and Arts Development	†	†	†	†	4,305	13,000	2,000	4,000	4,000	5,000
Institute of Museum and Library Services ..	†	†	†	†	†	†	166,000	172,000	219,000	171,000
James Madison Memorial Fellowship Foundation	†	†	†	†	191	2,000	7,000	3,000	2,000	2,000
Japanese-United States Friendship Commission	†	†	2,294	2,236	2,299	2,000	3,000	3,000	3,000	3,000
Library of Congress	29,478	63,766	151,871	169,310	189,827	241,000	299,000	315,000	397,000	399,000
National Aeronautics and Space Administration	258,366	197,901	255,511	487,624	1,093,303	1,757,900	2,077,830	2,406,036	2,320,469	2,361,100
National Archives and Records Administration	†	†	†	52,118	77,397	105,172	121,879	148,175	219,000	294,000
National Commission on Libraries and Information Science	†	449	2,090	723	3,281	1,000	2,000	1,000	2,000	2,000
National Endowment for the Arts	340	4,754	5,220	5,536	5,577	9,421	10,048	10,442	11,109	11,350
National Endowment for the Humanities	8,459	63,955	142,586	125,671	141,048	151,727	100,014	105,709	97,731	106,093
National Science Foundation	295,628	535,294	808,392	1,147,115	1,588,891	2,086,195	2,955,244	3,338,936	3,491,851	3,642,115
Nuclear Regulatory Commission	†	7,093	32,590	30,261	42,328	22,188	12,200	12,100	10,700	12,900
Office of Economic Opportunity	1,092,410	16,619	†	†	†	†	†	†	†	†
Smithsonian Institution	2,461	5,509	5,153	7,886	5,779	9,961	25,764	28,723	36,761	35,799
United States Arms Control Agency	100	†	661	395	25	†	†	†	†	†
United States Information Agency	8,423	9,405	66,210	143,007	201,547	294,800	†	†	†	†
United States Institute of Peace	†	†	†	†	7,621	12,000	13,000	15,000	15,000	16,000
Other agencies	1,421	5,949	990	432	885	500	300	9,100	7,500	6,645

† Not applicable.

[1] Estimated, except for U.S. Department of Education, which are actual numbers.

NOTE: To the extent possible, amounts reported represent outlays, rather than obligations. Some data have been revised from previously published data. Detail may not sum to totals because of rounding. Negative amounts occur when program receipts exceed outlays.

SOURCE: U.S. Department of Education, National Center for Education Statistics, compiled from data appearing in U.S. Office of Management and Budget, *Budget of the U.S. Government, Appendix,* fiscal years 1972 to 2004; National Science Foundation, *Federal Funds for Research and Development,* fiscal years 1970 to 2003; and unpublished data obtained from various federal agencies. (This table was prepared April 2004.)

Federal on-budget funds for education, by level or other educational purpose, agency, and program:
Selected fiscal years, 1970 to 2003
[In thousands of current dollars]

Level or educational purpose, agency, and program	1970	1975	1980	1985	1990[1]	1995[2]	2000[3]	2001[4]	2002[5]	2003[6]
1	2	3	4	5	6	7	8	9	10	11
Total, all programs	$12,526,499	$23,288,120	$34,493,502	$39,027,876	$51,624,342	$71,639,520	$85,944,203	$94,846,476	$109,361,491	$124,736,574
Elementary/secondary education programs	5,830,442	10,617,195	16,027,686	16,901,334	21,984,361	33,623,809	43,790,783	48,530,061	52,754,118	59,655,670
Department of Education[7]	2,719,204	4,132,742	6,629,095	7,296,702	9,681,313	14,029,000	20,039,563	22,862,445	25,246,185	30,749,304
Education for the disadvantaged	1,339,014	1,874,353	3,204,664	4,206,754	4,494,111	6,808,000	8,529,111	8,647,199	9,247,725	11,253,024
Impact aid program[8]	656,372	618,711	690,170	647,402	816,366	808,000	877,101	1,040,425	1,125,056	1,097,047
School improvement programs[9]	288,304	700,470	788,918	526,401	1,189,158	1,397,000	2,549,971	2,925,237	3,809,953	6,752,890
Indian education	†	40,036	93,365	82,328	69,451	71,000	65,285	77,791	103,935	115,864
English Language Acquisition	21,250	92,693	169,540	157,539	188,919	225,000	362,662	362,662	414,132	565,126
Special education	79,090	151,244	821,777	1,017,964	1,616,623	3,177,000	4,948,977	5,809,009	7,000,092	8,490,699
Vocational and adult education	335,174	655,235	860,661	658,314	1,306,685	1,482,000	1,462,977	2,262,234	1,777,695	1,942,716
Education Reform - Goals 2000[10]	†	†	†	†	†	61,000	1,243,479	1,737,888	1,767,597	531,938
Department of Agriculture	760,477	1,884,345	4,064,497	4,134,906	5,528,950	8,201,294	10,051,278	10,140,527	10,836,407	11,614,372
Child nutrition programs[11]	299,131	1,452,267	3,377,056	3,664,561	4,977,075	7,644,789	9,554,028	9,561,027	10,253,932	11,414,372
Agricultural Marketing Service—commodities[12]	341,597	248,839	388,000	336,502	350,441	400,000	400,000	400,000	399,935	15,000
Special milk program	83,800	122,858	159,293	15,993	18,707	(11)	(11)	(11)	(11)	(11)
Estimated education share of Forest Service permanent appropriations	35,949	60,381	140,148	117,850	182,727	156,505	97,250	179,500	182,540	185,000
Department of Commerce	†	†	54,816	†	†	†	†	†	†	†
Local public works program—school facilities[13]	†	†	54,816	†	†	†	†	†	†	†
Department of Defense	143,100	264,500	370,846	831,625	1,097,876	1,295,547	1,485,611	1,475,014	1,439,818	1,511,066
Junior R.O.T.C.	12,100	12,500	32,000	55,600	39,300	155,600	210,432	217,053	239,026	252,438
Overseas dependents schools	131,000	252,000	338,846	613,437	864,958	855,772	904,829	906,044	833,992	872,800
Domestic schools[8]	†	†	†	162,588	193,618	284,175	370,350	351,917	366,800	385,828
Department of Energy[14]	200	300	77,633	23,031	15,563	12,646	†	†	†	†
Energy conservation for school buildings[15]	†	†	77,240	22,731	15,213	10,746	†	†	†	†
Pre-engineering program	200	300	393	300	350	1,900	†	†	†	†
Department of Health and Human Services[16]	167,333	683,885	1,077,000	1,531,059	2,396,793	5,116,559	6,011,036	6,958,027	7,365,761	7,589,057
Head Start[17]	†	403,900	735,000	1,075,059	1,447,758	3,534,000	5,267,000	6,199,812	6,536,977	6,667,533
Payments to states for AFDC work programs[18]	†	†	†	†	459,221	953,000	15,000	4,000	16,489	16,500
Social Security student benefits[19]	167,333	279,985	342,000	456,000	489,814	629,559	729,036	754,215	812,295	905,024
Department of the Interior	140,705	220,392	318,170	389,810	445,267	493,124	725,423	890,497	945,264	982,061
Mineral Leasing Act and other funds: Payments to states—estimated education share	12,294	27,389	62,636	127,369	123,811	18,750	24,610	34,680	62,325	70,432
Payments to counties—estimated education share	16,359	29,494	48,953	59,016	102,522	37,490	53,500	57,060	68,504	88,712
Indian Education: Bureau of Indian Affairs schools	95,850	141,056	178,112	177,265	192,841	411,524	466,905	488,418	503,819	512,292
Johnson-O'Malley assistance[20]	16,080	22,251	28,081	25,675	25,556	24,359	17,387	16,998	17,113	16,908
Education construction	†	†	†	†	†	†	161,021	292,341	292,503	292,717
Education expenses for children of employees, Yellowstone National Park	122	202	388	485	538	1,000	2,000	1,000	1,000	1,000
Department of Justice	8,237	9,822	23,890	36,117	65,997	128,850	224,800	380,600	408,400	436,100
Vocational training expenses for prisoners in federal prisons	2,720	3,039	4,966	8,292	2,066	3,000	1,000	2,000	7,000	8,000
Inmate programs[21]	5,517	6,783	18,924	27,825	63,931	125,850	223,800	378,600	401,400	428,100
Department of Labor	420,927	1,097,811	1,849,800	1,945,268	2,505,487	3,957,800	4,683,200	5,189,000	5,859,000	6,071,000
Job Corps[22]	†	175,000	469,800	604,748	739,376	1,029,000	1,256,000	1,369,000	1,467,000	1,511,000
Training programs—estimated funds for education programs[23]	420,927	922,811	1,380,000	1,340,520	1,766,111	2,928,800	3,427,200	3,820,000	4,392,000	4,560,000
Department of Transportation[24]	45	50	60	60	46	62	188	215	400	635
Tuition assistance for educational accreditation—Coast Guard personnel[25]	45	50	60	60	46	62	188	215	400	635
Department of the Treasury	†	847,139	935,903	273,728	†	†	†	†	†	†
Estimated education share of general revenue sharing:[26] State[27]	†	475,224	525,019	†	†	†	†	†	†	†
Local	†	371,915	410,884	273,728	†	†	†	†	†	†
Tuition assistance for educational accreditation—Coast Guard personnel[25]	†	†	†	†	†	†	†	†	†	†
Department of Veterans Affairs[28]	338,910	1,371,500	545,786	344,758	155,351	311,768	445,052	487,422	487,490	525,420
Noncollegiate and job training programs[29]	281,640	1,249,410	439,993	224,035	12,848	†	†	†	†	†
Vocational rehabilitation for disabled veterans[30]	41,700	73,100	87,980	107,480	136,780	298,132	438,635	479,817	487,490	525,420
Dependents' education[31]	15,570	48,990	17,813	13,243	5,723	5,961	6,417	7,605	—	—
Service members occupational conversion and training act of 1992[32]	†	†	†	†	†	7,675	†	†	†	†

See notes at end of table.

Federal on-budget funds for education, by level or other educational purpose, agency, and program: Selected fiscal years, 1970 to 2003—Continued

[In thousands of current dollars]

Level or educational purpose, agency, and program	1970	1975	1980	1985	1990[1]	1995[2]	2000[3]	2001[4]	2002[5]	2003[6]
1	2	3	4	5	6	7	8	9	10	11
Other agencies:										
Appalachian Regional Commission[33]	33,161	41,667	9,157	4,632	93	2,173	2,588	5,922	6,522	6,900
National Endowment for the Arts[34]	†	3,686	4,989	4,399	4,641	7,117	6,002	5,839	5,800	8,842
Arts in education	†	3,686	4,989	4,399	4,641	7,117	6,002	5,839	5,800	8,842
National Endowment for the Humanities[35]	20	149	330	321	404	997	812	1,063	511	413
Office of Economic Opportunity[36]	1,072,375	16,619	†	†	†	†	†	†	†	†
Head Start[37]	325,700	†	†	†	†	†	†	†	†	†
Other elementary and secondary programs[38]	42,809	16,612	†	†	†	†	†	†	†	†
Job Corps[39]	144,000	†	†	†	†	†	†	†	†	†
Youth Corps and other training programs[40]	553,368	7	†	†	†	†	†	†	†	†
Volunteers in Service to America (VISTA)[41]	6,498	†	†	†	†	†	†	†	†	†
Other programs:										
Estimated education share of federal aid to the District of Columbia	25,748	42,588	65,714	84,918	86,579	66,871	115,230	133,490	152,560	160,500
Postsecondary education programs	**$3,447,697**	**$7,644,037**	**$11,115,882**	**$11,174,379**	**$13,650,915**	**$17,618,137**	**$15,008,715**	**$14,938,278**	**$22,964,177**	**$29,319,632**
Department of Education[7]	1,187,962	2,089,184	5,682,242	8,202,499	11,175,978	14,234,000	10,727,315	9,840,748	17,056,188	22,706,436
Student financial assistance[42]	†	†	3,682,789	4,162,695	5,920,328	7,047,000	9,060,317	10,160,986	12,577,937	14,092,384
Federal Direct Student Loan Program[43,44]	†	†	†	†	†	840,000	-2,862,240	255,162	97,304	5,115,949
Federal Family Education Loan Program[44,45]	2,323	111,087	1,407,977	3,534,795	4,372,446	5,190,000	2,707,473	-2,404,824	2,342,829	1,216,003
Higher education	1,029,131	1,838,066	399,787	404,511	659,492	871,000	1,530,779	1,462,478	1,687,173	1,930,342
Facilities—loans and insurance[44]	114,199	16,292	-19,031	5,307	19,219	-6,000	-2,174	-957	1,993	-5,702
College housing loans[44,46]	†	†	14,082	-164,061	-57,167	-46,000	-41,886	-30,654	-36,933	-31,590
Educational activities overseas	774	1,881	3,561	1,838	82	†	†	†	†	†
Historically Black Colleges and Universities Capital Financing, Program Account[47]	†	†	†	†	†	†	150	195	197	133
Gallaudet College and Howard University	38,559	111,971	176,829	229,938	230,327	292,000	291,060	340,103	330,807	336,261
National Technical Institute for the Deaf[48]	2,976	9,887	16,248	27,476	31,251	46,000	43,836	58,259	54,881	52,656
Department of Agriculture	†	6,450	10,453	17,741	31,273	33,373	30,676	82,437	88,764	93,626
Agriculture Extension Service, Second Morrill Act payments to agricultural and mechanical colleges and Tuskegee Institute[49]	†	6,450	10,453	17,741	31,273	33,373	30,676	82,437	88,764	93,626
Department of Commerce	8,277	14,973	29,971	2,163	3,312	3,487	3,800	3,954	4,160	4,200
Sea Grant Program[50]	†	1,886	3,123	2,163	3,312	3,487	3,800	3,954	4,160	4,200
Merchant Marine Academy[51]	6,160	10,152	14,809	†	†	†	†	†	†	†
State marine schools[51]	2,117	2,935	12,039	†	†	†	†	†	†	†
Department of Defense[52]	322,100	379,800	545,000	1,041,700	635,769	729,500	1,147,759	1,299,169	1,485,552	1,569,079
Tuition assistance for military personnel	57,500	86,800	(53)	77,100	95,300	127,000	263,303	346,458	401,498	426,536
Service academies[54]	78,700	86,200	106,100	196,400	120,613	163,300	212,678	241,187	245,786	264,670
Senior R.O.T.C.[55]	108,100	116,500	(53)	354,000	193,056	219,400	363,461	387,091	471,867	494,195
Professional development education[55]	77,800	90,300	(53)	414,200	226,800	219,800	308,317	324,433	366,401	383,678
Department of Energy[14]	3,000	3,000	57,701	19,475	25,502	28,027	†	†	†	†
University laboratory cooperative program	3,000	3,000	2,800	6,500	9,402	8,552	†	†	†	†
Teacher development projects[56]	†	†	1,400	†	†	†	†	†	†	†
Graduate traineeship programs[57]	—	—	—	—	—	—	†	†	†	†
Energy conservation for buildings— higher education[15]	†	†	53,501	12,705	7,459	7,381	†	†	†	†
Minority honors vocational training[58]	†	†	†	150	†	†	†	†	†	†
Honors research program[58]	†	†	†	120	6,472	2,221	†	†	†	†
Students and teachers[59]	†	†	†	†	2,169	9,873	†	†	†	†
Department of Health and Human Services[16]	981,483	1,686,650	2,412,058	516,088	578,542	796,035	954,190	1,360,554	1,567,367	1,698,087
Health professions training programs[60]	353,029	599,350	460,736	212,200	230,600	298,302	340,361	681,062	818,056	882,396
Indian health manpower[61]	†	†	7,187	5,577	9,508	27,000	16,000	29,000	34,000	35,000
National Health Service Corps scholarships	†	1,206	70,667	2,268	4,759	78,206	33,300	43,000	46,200	46,300
National Institutes of Health training grants[62]	†	154,875	176,388	217,927	241,356	380,502	550,220	589,704	650,686	715,789
National Institute of Occupational Safety and Health training grants	8,088	7,182	12,899	8,760	10,461	11,660	14,198	17,699	18,358	18,558
Alcohol, drug abuse, and mental health training programs[63]	118,366	83,727	122,103	43,617	81,353	†	†	†	†	†
Health teaching facilities	†	353	3,078	739	505	365	110	89	67	44
Social Security postsecondary students' benefits[64]	502,000	839,957	1,559,000	25,000	†	†	†	†	†	†
Department of Housing and Urban Development[44]	114,199	-55,418	†	†	†	†	†	†	†	†
College housing loans[44,46]	114,199	-55,418	†	†	†	†	†	†	†	†

See notes at end of table.

Federal on-budget funds for education, by level or other educational purpose, agency, and program: Selected fiscal years, 1970 to 2003—Continued

[In thousands of current dollars]

Level or educational purpose, agency, and program	1970	1975	1980	1985	1990[1]	1995[2]	2000[3]	2001[4]	2002[5]	2003[6]
1	2	3	4	5	6	7	8	9	10	11
Department of the Interior	31,749	50,844	80,202	125,247	135,480	159,054	187,179	149,391	185,849	205,545
Shared revenues, Mineral Leasing Act and other receipts— estimated education share	6,949	15,480	35,403	71,991	69,980	82,810	98,740	58,580	89,614	107,665
Indian programs:										
Continuing education[65]	9,380	13,311	16,909	24,338	34,911	43,907	57,576	63,044	68,340	70,109
Higher education scholarships	15,420	22,053	27,890	28,918	30,589	32,337	30,863	27,767	27,895	27,771
Department of State	30,850	50,347	†	†	2,167	3,000	319,000	316,800	385,000	299,000
Educational exchange[66]	30,850	50,347	†	†	—	†	319,000	316,800	385,000	299,000
Mutual educational and cultural exchange activities	30,454	50,300	†	†	—	†	303,000	300,800	361,000	276,000
International educational exchange activities	396	47	†	†	—	†	16,000	16,000	24,000	23,000
Russian, Eurasian, and East European Research and Training[67]	†	†	†	†	2,167	3,000	†	†	†	†
Department of Transportation[24]	11,197	11,885	12,530	55,569	46,025	59,257	60,300	80,500	78,700	90,200
Merchant Marine Academy[51]	†	†	†	19,898	20,926	30,850	34,000	49,000	43,000	50,000
State marine schools[51]	†	†	†	19,777	8,269	8,980	7,000	7,000	7,000	7,000
Coast Guard Academy[25]	9,342	9,780	10,000	11,857	12,074	13,500	15,500	15,200	17,700	18,800
Postgraduate training for Coast Guard officers[68]	1,655	1,855	2,230	3,499	4,173	5,513	2,500	6,900	7,200	8,800
Tuition assistance to Coast Guard military personnel[25]	200	250	300	538	582	414	1,300	2,400	3,800	5,600
Department of the Treasury	†	268,605	296,750	†	†	†	†	†	†	†
General revenue sharing—estimated state share to higher education[26,27]	†	268,605	296,750	†	†	†	†	†	†	†
Coast Guard Academy[25]	†	†	†	†	†	†	†	†	†	†
Postgraduate training for Coast Guard officers[68]	†	†	†	†	†	†	†	†	†	†
Tuition assistance to Coast Guard military personnel[25]	†	†	†	†	†	†	†	†	†	†
Department of Veterans Affairs[28]	693,490	3,029,600	1,803,847	944,091	599,825	1,010,114	1,132,322	1,314,920	1,634,799	2,127,921
Vietnam-era veterans:[69]	638,260	2,840,600	1,579,974	694,217	46,998	†	†	†	†	†
College student support	†	†	1,560,081	679,953	39,458	†	†	†	†	†
Work-study	†	†	19,893	14,264	7,540	†	†	†	†	†
Service persons college support[70]	18,900	74,690	46,617	35,630	8,911	†	†	†	†	†
Post-Vietnam veterans[71]	†	†	922	82,554	161,475	33,596	3,958	4,000	2,227	3,260
All-volunteer-force educational assistance:[72]	†	†	†	196	269,947	868,394	984,068	1,129,264	1,385,109	1,861,613
Veterans[73]	†	†	†	†	183,765	760,390	876,434	993,271	1,236,125	1,700,424
Reservists[74]	†	†	†	196	86,182	108,004	107,634	135,993	148,984	161,189
Veteran dependents' education[75]	36,330	114,310	176,334	131,494	100,494	95,124	131,296	167,939	233,819	249,048
Payments to state education agencies[76]	†	†	†	†	12,000	13,000	13,000	13,717	13,644	14,000
Other agencies:										
Appalachian Regional Commission[33]	4,105	2,545	1,751	—	—	2,741	2,286	2,025	7,258	6,000
National Endowment for the Humanities[35]	3,349	25,320	56,451	49,098	50,938	56,481	28,395	30,581	30,000	39,538
National Science Foundation	42,000	60,283	64,583	60,069	161,884	211,800	389,000	432,000	415,000	454,000
Science and engineering education programs	37,000	60,283	64,583	60,069	161,884	211,800	389,000	432,000	415,000	454,000
Sea Grant Program[50]	5,000	†	†	†	†	†	†	†	†	†
United States Information Agency[77]	8,423	9,405	51,095	124,041	181,172	260,800	†	†	†	†
Educational and cultural affairs[66]	†	†	49,546	21,079	35,862	13,600	†	†	†	†
Educational and cultural exchange programs[78]	†	†	†	101,529	145,307	247,200	†	†	†	†
Educational exchange activities, international	†	†	1,549	1,433	3	†	†	†	†	†
Information center and library activities[79]	8,423	9,405	†	†	†	†	†	†	†	†
Other programs:										
Barry Goldwater Scholarship and Excellence in Education Foundation[80]	†	†	†	—	1,033	3,000	3,000	3,000	3,000	3,000
Estimated education share of federal aid to the District of Columbia	5,513	10,564	13,143	15,266	14,637	9,468	11,493	13,199	12,539	13,000
Harry S Truman Scholarship fund[44,81]	†	†	-1,895	1,332	2,883	3,000	3,000	2,000	4,000	3,000
Institute of American Indian and Alaskan Native Culture and Arts Development[82]	†	†	†	—	4,305	13,000	2,000	4,000	4,000	5,000
James Madison Memorial Fellowship Foundation[83]	†	†	†	—	191	2,000	7,000	3,000	2,000	2,000
Other education programs	**$964,719**	**$1,608,478**	**$1,548,730**	**$2,107,588**	**$3,383,031**	**$4,719,655**	**$5,484,571**	**$5,880,007**	**$6,297,697**	**$6,584,678**
Department of Education[7]	630,235	1,045,659	747,706	1,173,055	2,251,801	2,861,000	3,223,355	3,293,355	3,396,823	3,435,182
Administration	47,456	108,372	187,317	284,900	328,293	404,000	458,054	551,681	531,259	548,318
Libraries[84]	108,284	225,810	129,127	85,650	137,264	117,000	†	†	†	†
Rehabilitative services and disability research	473,091	709,483	426,886	798,298	1,780,360	2,333,000	2,755,468	2,730,254	2,852,170	2,871,797
American Printing House for the Blind	1,404	1,994	4,349	4,230	5,736	7,000	9,368	10,531	12,925	14,875

See notes at end of table.

Federal on-budget funds for education, by level or other educational purpose, agency, and program:
Selected fiscal years, 1970 to 2003—Continued

[In thousands of current dollars]

Level or educational purpose, agency, and program	1970	1975	1980	1985	1990[1]	1995[2]	2000[3]	2001[4]	2002[5]	2003[6]
1	2	3	4	5	6	7	8	9	10	11
Trust funds and contributions[44]	†	†	27	−23	148	†	465	889	469	192
Department of Agriculture	135,637	220,395	271,112	336,375	352,511	422,878	444,477	454,576	469,373	472,720
Extension Service	131,734	215,523	263,584	325,986	337,907	405,371	424,174	432,476	447,473	450,520
National Agricultural Library	3,903	4,872	7,528	10,389	14,604	17,507	20,303	22,100	21,900	22,200
Department of Commerce	1,226	2,317	2,479	†	†	†	†	†	†	†
Maritime Administration:										
Training for private sector employees[51]	1,226	2,317	2,479	†	†	†	†	†	†	†
Department of Health and Human Services[16]	24,273	31,653	37,819	47,195	77,962	138,000	214,000	243,000	276,200	307,900
National Library of Medicine	24,273	31,653	37,819	47,195	77,962	138,000	214,000	243,000	276,200	307,900
Department of Housing and Urban Development	†	†	†	†	†	†	†	†	†	†
Urban mass transportation—managerial training grants[85]	†	†	†	†	†	†	†	†	†	†
Department of Justice	5,546	42,818	27,642	25,517	26,920	36,296	34,727	29,120	23,433	25,301
FBI National Academy	2,066	5,100	7,234	4,189	6,028	12,831	22,479	22,198	18,958	18,824
FBI Field Police Academy	2,500	5,254	7,715	10,220	10,548	11,140	11,962	6,644	4,366	6,477
Narcotics and dangerous drug training	980	1,152	2,416	83	850	325	286	278	109	—
National Institute of Corrections[86]	†	31,312	10,277	11,025	9,494	12,000	†	†	†	†
Department of State	20,672	28,113	25,000	23,791	47,539	51,648	69,349	73,268	102,097	105,127
Foreign Service Institute	15,857	20,750	25,000	23,791	47,539	51,648	69,349	73,268	102,097	105,127
Center for Cultural and Technical Interchange[66]	4,815	7,363	†	†	†	†	†	†	†	†
Department of Transportation[24]	3,964	11,877	10,212	3,785	1,507	650	700	495	591	600
Highways training and education grants[87]	2,418	3,250	3,412	1,500	—	—	—	—	—	—
Maritime Administration:										
Training for private sector employees[51]	†	†	†	1,135	1,507	650	700	495	591	600
Urban mass transportation—managerial training grants[85]	1,546	2,627	500	1,150	†	†	†	†	†	†
Federal Aviation Administration[88]										
Air traffic controllers second career program[89]	—	6,000	6,300	—	—	—	—	—	—	—
Department of the Treasury	18	3,096	14,584	16,160	41,488	48,000	83,000	88,000	163,000	195,000
Federal Law Enforcement Training Center[90]	18	3,096	14,584	16,160	41,488	48,000	83,000	88,000	163,000	195,000
Other agencies:										
ACTION[91]	†	7,045	2,833	1,761	8,472	†	†	†	†	†
Estimated education funds[92]	†	7,045	2,833	1,761	8,472	†	†	†	†	†
Agency for International Development	88,034	78,896	99,707	141,847	170,371	260,408	299,000	452,000	480,000	526,000
Education and human resources	61,570	58,349	80,518	115,104	142,801	248,408	299,000	452,000	480,000	526,000
American schools and hospitals abroad	26,464	20,547	19,189	26,743	27,570	12,000	†	†	†	†
Appalachian Regional Commission[32]	572	1,574	8,124	113	†	5,709	2,369	1,613	1,987	1,900
Corporation for National and Community Service[91]	†	†	†	†	†	214,600	386,000	452,000	404,000	516,000
Estimated education funds[92]	†	†	†	†	†	214,600	386,000	452,000	404,000	516,000
Federal Emergency Management Agency[93]	290	290	281	405	215	170,400	14,894	23,778	8,376	8,600
Estimated architect/engineer student development program[94]	40	40	31	155	200	—	—	—	—	—
Estimated other training programs[95]	250	250	250	250	15	—	—	450	380	600
Estimated disaster relief[96]	—	—	—	—	—	170,400	14,894	23,328	7,996	8,000
General Services Administration										
Libraries and other archival activities[97]	14,775	22,532	34,800	†	†	†	†	†	†	†
Institute of Museum and Library Services[84]	†	†	†	†	†	†	166,000	172,000	219,000	171,000
Japanese-United States Friendship Commission[98]	†	†	2,294	2,236	2,299	2,000	3,000	3,000	3,000	3,000
Library of Congress	29,478	63,766	151,871	169,310	189,827	241,000	299,000	315,000	397,000	399,000
Salaries and expenses	20,700	48,798	102,364	130,354	148,985	198,000	247,000	260,000	342,000	354,000
Books for the blind and the physically handicapped	6,195	11,908	31,436	32,954	37,473	39,000	46,000	49,000	50,000	42,000
Special foreign currency program	2,273	2,333	3,492	4,621	10	†	†	†	†	†
Furniture and furnishings	310	727	14,579	1,381	3,359	4,000	6,000	6,000	5,000	3,000
National Aeronautics and Space Administration										
Aerospace education services project	350	600	882	1,800	3,300	5,923	6,800	6,832	6,569	†
National Archives and Records Administration[99]										
Libraries and other archival activities	†	†	†	52,118	77,397	105,172	121,879	148,175	219,000	294,000
National Commission on Libraries and Information Science[100]	†	449	2,090	723	3,281	1,000	2,000	1,000	2,000	2,000
National Endowment for the Arts[34]	340	1,068	231	1,137	936	2,304	4,046	4,603	5,309	2,508
National Endowment for the Humanities[35]	5,090	38,486	85,805	76,252	89,706	94,249	70,807	74,065	67,220	66,141

See notes at end of table.

633

Federal on-budget funds for education, by level or other educational purpose, agency, and program: Selected fiscal years, 1970 to 2003—Continued

[In thousands of current dollars]

Level or educational purpose, agency, and program	1970	1975	1980	1985	1990[1]	1995[2]	2000[3]	2001[4]	2002[5]	2003[6]
1	2	3	4	5	6	7	8	9	10	11
Smithsonian Institution	2,461	5,509	5,153	7,886	5,779	9,961	25,764	28,723	36,761	35,799
Museum programs and related research	2,261	4,203	3,254	4,665	690	3,190	18,000	21,000	29,000	27,000
National Gallery of Art extension service	200	300	426	675	474	771	764	723	761	799
Woodrow Wilson International Center for Scholars	†	1,006	1,473	2,546	4,615	6,000	7,000	7,000	7,000	8,000
U.S. Information Agency—Center for Cultural and Technical Interchange[66]	†	†	15,115	18,966	20,375	34,000	†	†	†	†
U.S. Institute of Peace[101]	†	†	†	—	7,621	12,000	13,000	15,000	15,000	16,000
Other programs:										
Estimated education share of federal aid for the District of Columbia	1,758	2,335	2,990	7,156	3,724	2,457	404	404	958	900
Research programs at universities and related institutions[102]	**$2,283,641**	**$3,418,410**	**$5,801,204**	**$8,844,575**	**$12,606,035**	**$15,677,919**	**$21,660,134**	**$25,498,130**	**$27,345,499**	**$29,176,593**
Department of Education[103]	87,823	82,770	78,742	28,809	89,483	279,000	116,464	565,477	625,156	551,932
Department of Agriculture	64,796	108,162	216,405	293,252	348,109	434,544	553,600	652,200	639,000	575,300
Department of Commerce	4,487	21,677	48,295	52,951	50,523	85,442	110,775	130,700	126,500	85,900
Department of Defense	356,188	364,929	644,455	1,245,888	1,871,864	1,853,955	1,891,710	2,643,438	2,512,812	2,164,047
Department of Energy	548,327	761,376	1,470,224	2,205,316	2,520,885	2,651,641	3,577,004	3,885,773	3,992,886	4,086,914
Department of Health and Human Services	623,765	1,273,037	2,087,053	3,228,014	4,902,714	6,418,969	10,491,641	11,978,830	13,666,377	15,811,616
Department of Housing and Urban Development	510	2,650	5,314	438	118	1,613	1,400	1,600	1,600	1,500
Department of the Interior	18,521	28,955	42,175	34,422	49,790	50,618	47,200	52,700	55,100	43,400
Department of Justice	1,945	8,902	9,189	5,168	6,858	7,204	19,400	21,500	23,100	15,800
Department of Labor	3,567	6,124	12,938	3,417	5,893	10,114	12,900	4,100	6,100	11,500
Department of State	8,220	10,973	188	29	1,519	23	†	†	†	†
Department of Transportation	12,328	28,478	31,910	22,621	28,608	75,847	55,866	72,472	82,517	43,824
Department of the Treasury	†	†	226	388	227	1,496	†	†	†	†
Department of Veterans Affairs	518	1,112	1,600	1,000	2,300	2,500	†	†	†	†
ACTION	†	36	†	†	†	†	†	†	†	†
Agency for International Development	†	†	77,063	56,960	79,415	30,172	33,500	36,600	41,500	44,500
Environmental Protection Agency	19,446	33,875	41,083	60,521	87,481	125,721	98,900	125,400	163,900	1/1,600
Federal Emergency Management Agency	†	†	1,665	1,423	†	†	†	†	†	†
National Aeronautics and Space Administration	258,016	197,301	254,629	485,824	1,090,003	1,751,977	2,071,030	2,399,204	2,313,900	2,361,100
National Science Foundation	253,628	475,011	743,809	1,087,046	1,427,007	1,874,395	2,566,244	2,906,936	3,076,851	3,188,115
Nuclear Regulatory Commission	†	7,093	32,590	30,261	42,328	22,188	12,200	12,100	10,700	12,900
Office of Economic Opportunity	20,035	†	†	†	†	†	†	†	†	†
U.S. Arms Control and Disarmament Agency	100	†	661	395	25	†	†	†	†	†
Other agencies	1,421	5,949	990	432	885	500	300	9,100	7,500	6,645

† Not applicable.
—Not available.

[1] Excludes $4,440,000,000 for federal support for medical education benefits under Medicare in the U.S. Department of Health and Human Services. Is not included in the total because data before fiscal year 1990 are not available. This program has existed since Medicare began, but was not available as a separate budget item until FY 90.

[2] Excludes $7,510,000,000 for federal support for medical education benefits under Medicare. See footnote 1.

[3] Excludes $8,020,000,000 for federal support for medical education benefits under Medicare. See footnote 1.

[4] Excludes $8,030,000,000 for federal support for medical education benefits under Medicare. See footnote 1.

[5] Excludes $8,000,000,000 for federal support for medical education benefits under Medicare. See footnote 1.

[6] Estimated. Data for the U.S. Department of Education are actual numbers and those for the other agencies are estimates. Excludes $7,800,000,000 for federal support for medical education benefits under Medicare. See footnote 1.

[7] The U.S. Department of Education was created in May 1980. It formerly was the Office of Education in the U.S. Department of Health, Education, and Welfare.

[8] Domestic Schools formerly called Section 6 of public law 81–874 (the former Impact Aid statute) was funded and administered by the U.S. Department of Education during 1951–1981. This program allowed the Secretary to make arrangements for the education of children who resided on federal property when no suitable local school district could or would provide for the education of these children. Since 1981, the provision was funded by the Department of Defense and in 1994, when public law 81–874 was repealed, the Department of Defense was authorized to fund and administer similar provisions.

[9] School Improvement programs include many programs. Some of these are No Child Left Behind, 21st Century Community Learning Centers, Class Size Reduction, Charter Schools, and Safe and Drug-Free Schools. Some of these programs will be transferred out of the School Improvement programs in fiscal year 2004.

[10] This program created a national framework for education reform and meeting the National Education Goals. This program included the School-To-Work Opportunities program which initiated a national system to be administered jointly by the U.S. Departments of Education and Labor. Programs in the Education Reform program have been transferred to the School Improvement program or discontinued in FY 2002. Amounts in this program reflect balances that are spending out from prior-year appropriations.

[11] Starting in FY 94, the Special Milk program was included in the Child Nutrition program.

[12] These commodities are purchased under Section 32 of the Act of August 24, 1935, for use in the child nutrition programs.

[13] This program assisted in the construction of public facilities, such as vocational schools, through grants or loans. No funds have been appropriated for this account since FY 77, and it was completely phased out in FY 84.

[14] The U.S. Department of Energy was created in 1977. It formerly was the Energy Research and Development Administration and before that the Atomic Energy Commission. No funds were designated for any of the education programs listed in this table in FYs 96 and 97.

[15] This program was established in 1979. Funds were first appropriated for this program in FY 80.

[16] The U.S. Department of Health and Human Services was part of the U.S. Department of Health, Education, and Welfare until May 1980.

[17] The Head Start program was formerly in the Office of Economic Opportunity, and funds were appropriated to the U.S. Department of Health, Education, and Welfare, Office of Child Development, beginning in 1972.

[18] This program was created by the Family Support Act of 1988. It provides funds for the Job Opportunities and Basic Skills Training program. This activity is being replaced by Temporary Assistance for Needy Families program.

[19] After age 18, benefits terminate at the end of the school term or in 3 months, whichever is less.

[20] This program provides funding for supplemental programs for eligible American Indian students in public schools.

[21] This program finances the cost of academic, social, and occupational education courses for inmates in federal prisons.

[22] The Job Corps program was formerly in the Office of Economic Opportunity, and funds were appropriated to the U.S. Department of Labor beginning in 1971 and 1972.

[23] Some of the work and training programs included in this program were in the Office of Economic Opportunity and were transferred to the U.S. Department of Labor in 1971 and 1972. Beginning in FY 94, the School-to-Work Opportunities program is included. This program is administered jointly by the U.S. Departments of Education and Labor.

[24] The U.S. Department of Transportation was created in 1967.

[25] This program was transferred from the U.S. Department of the Treasury to the U.S. Department of Transportation in 1967. This program was transferred to the U.S. Department of Homeland Security in March of 2003.

[26] This program was established in FY 72 and closed in FY 86.

[27] The states' share of revenue-sharing funds could not be spent on education in FYs 81–86.

[28] The U.S. Department of Veterans Affairs, formerly the Veterans Administration, was created in March 1989.

[29] This program provides educational assistance allowances in order to restore lost educational opportunities to those individuals whose careers were interrupted or impeded by reason of active military service between January 31, 1955, and January 1, 1977.

U.S. Department of Education appropriations for major programs, by state or jurisdiction: Fiscal year 2002

[In thousands]

State or jurisdiction	Total	Grants for the disadvantaged [1]	Block grants to states for school improvement [2]	School assistance in federally affected areas [3]	Vocational and adult education [4]	Education for the handicapped [5]	Bilingual education [6]	Indian education	Degree-granting institutions [7]	Student financial assistance [8]	Rehabilitation services [9]
1	2	3	4	5	6	7	8	9	10	11	12
Total, 50 States and D.C. [10]	$48,115,250	$11,610,496	$5,121,926	$1,001,820	$1,806,499	$8,117,386	$401,333	$97,133	$1,936,921	$15,525,227	$2,496,510
Total, 50 States, D.C., other activities, and outlying areas	51,216,195	12,179,000	6,132,017	1,135,500	1,880,000	8,335,533	664,269	97,133	1,982,761	16,213,374	2,596,608
Alabama	837,161	180,633	84,873	2,886	34,156	131,754	1,298	1,777	70,195	275,920	53,670
Alaska	239,489	40,751	26,768	96,065	5,507	25,537	659	9,936	11,928	12,968	9,369
Arizona	974,015	206,534	87,273	141,947	31,458	124,460	12,343	11,390	19,541	293,192	45,878
Arkansas	486,394	116,885	56,074	724	20,415	81,158	1,201	327	25,093	151,773	32,745
California	5,935,156	1,775,451	626,349	74,848	220,164	871,465	117,281	6,552	159,384	1,829,357	254,305
Colorado	579,686	117,501	61,205	10,887	22,165	105,255	5,272	678	22,169	208,310	26,242
Connecticut	431,276	120,217	53,008	7,175	17,129	98,734	3,903	0	11,641	100,107	19,363
Delaware	127,188	32,035	26,856	105	6,840	23,677	547	0	5,808	21,926	9,394
District of Columbia	421,190	39,388	26,238	1,330	6,531	12,527	619	0	264,691	57,061	12,805
Florida	2,516,757	568,540	239,317	10,901	95,115	444,031	25,124	54	63,789	950,692	119,194
Georgia	1,289,018	365,498	149,709	18,481	53,066	217,559	8,017	0	63,142	339,259	74,287
Hawaii	210,019	39,125	26,944	39,208	8,741	28,740	1,598	0	15,790	39,193	10,677
Idaho	223,169	42,748	28,484	6,197	9,758	38,811	1,148	451	6,676	74,484	14,413
Illinois	1,862,798	486,619	215,368	19,526	73,377	372,310	19,791	104	63,592	517,420	94,691
Indiana	943,985	178,766	87,502	1,375	40,163	188,609	3,172	0	27,665	356,142	60,591
Iowa	455,866	73,488	45,328	519	19,184	90,455	1,723	190	25,968	169,510	29,502
Kansas	438,762	95,004	46,888	17,948	17,518	79,204	2,461	817	20,970	132,682	25,270
Kentucky	708,787	180,425	81,863	975	31,844	120,397	1,364	0	27,419	216,125	48,377
Louisiana	900,512	244,575	109,136	6,063	36,662	132,554	1,729	842	44,305	278,910	45,734
Maine	228,772	47,052	29,151	2,474	8,626	41,600	500	128	10,843	73,187	15,210
Maryland	695,146	174,723	79,460	6,779	28,832	145,430	3,994	175	35,415	181,907	38,432
Massachusetts	1,103,236	248,595	100,196	882	31,099	210,073	7,173	71	37,395	421,478	46,275
Michigan	1,563,844	476,324	195,920	3,690	63,300	286,636	5,225	3,541	38,428	400,848	89,932
Minnesota	721,090	130,292	72,880	10,657	27,103	142,619	4,506	3,562	23,838	263,733	41,901
Mississippi	639,938	148,694	71,353	3,433	23,301	85,734	817	398	34,359	232,886	38,963
Missouri	933,574	188,420	95,766	17,504	37,546	167,294	2,265	68	28,458	340,407	55,846
Montana	240,333	40,162	32,353	38,325	7,622	26,818	500	3,194	17,857	62,417	11,087
Nebraska	286,611	48,051	33,564	19,330	10,961	55,183	1,482	738	10,777	89,409	17,116
Nevada	197,031	47,127	28,746	3,772	9,887	47,044	3,678	750	4,156	38,692	13,180
New Hampshire	178,638	31,120	28,099	10	8,235	35,715	500	0	5,908	58,282	10,768
New Jersey	1,119,026	290,615	124,130	18,371	44,511	267,367	13,235	52	25,961	281,655	53,128
New Mexico	477,065	95,348	44,193	78,419	13,443	67,533	4,185	7,799	23,557	121,331	21,257
New York	4,006,226	1,153,073	417,115	18,388	108,181	568,844	36,818	1,504	79,294	1,485,274	137,676
North Carolina	1,160,770	252,444	117,978	11,917	51,666	225,458	6,710	3,662	63,266	348,150	79,519
North Dakota	191,176	30,653	27,627	27,181	5,966	19,403	500	1,552	10,972	57,991	9,330
Ohio	1,756,397	388,143	183,184	3,826	73,891	316,705	4,940	0	44,796	627,997	112,915
Oklahoma	694,245	142,767	71,092	35,202	25,742	107,165	2,251	22,020	41,558	208,330	38,117
Oregon	497,455	120,717	52,733	2,522	20,752	94,899	3,931	2,458	13,900	154,478	31,065
Pennsylvania	1,874,804	456,344	198,732	3,373	74,870	310,465	6,911	0	52,502	656,160	115,446
Rhode Island	206,149	39,112	26,838	3,045	8,976	33,312	1,376	0	6,117	77,181	10,194
South Carolina	704,228	163,830	72,324	3,500	29,684	128,180	1,899	61	40,957	217,923	45,870
South Dakota	317,630	32,346	28,202	41,516	6,518	23,220	500	3,197	8,211	164,459	9,462
Tennessee	858,850	174,444	86,815	2,840	39,117	169,552	2,244	0	39,366	284,816	59,596
Texas	3,784,243	1,038,704	420,208	73,025	143,780	665,244	55,393	339	122,549	1,078,826	186,177
Utah	394,568	52,665	35,314	8,237	16,964	76,667	2,946	1,191	12,874	164,132	23,576
Vermont	149,116	27,085	26,396	263	5,694	18,865	500	139	7,180	53,339	9,656
Virginia	1,424,688	200,137	99,402	39,264	42,929	200,047	5,256	26	44,550	734,024	59,054
Washington	834,721	178,444	86,924	47,833	33,122	159,029	7,190	4,538	33,453	239,519	T244,670
West Virginia	360,629	91,057	43,886	4	14,763	56,964	500	0	23,642	104,664	25,148
Wisconsin	804,604	169,398	85,778	10,992	34,165	157,236	3,658	2,345	39,522	250,052	51,458
Wyoming	129,221	28,427	26,327	8,088	5,403	19,845	500	509	5,493	26,650	7,980
Other activities											
Indian Tribe (Set-Aside)	241,786	77,769	34,104	0	14,750	84,525	5,000	0	0	0	25,638
Other	1,300,891	77,650	795,766	131,582	19,591	22,579	252,594	0	0	0	1,128
Outlying areas											
American Samoa	27,681	9,391	6,974	0	407	6,309	1,107	0	320	2,091	1,081
Guam	45,820	8,369	10,620	0	830	13,971	1,417	0	1,663	7,087	1,863
Marshall Islands	376	0	0	0	0	0	0	0	376	0	0
Micronesia	16,519	0	0	0	1,677	0	0	0	1,951	12,891	0
Northern Mariana Islands	18,606	4,304	3,696	0	586	4,836	719	0	1,723	1,596	1,147
Palau	952	0	0	0	0	0	0	0	952	0	0
Puerto Rico	1,408,824	378,979	149,379	1,859	34,801	77,140	2,017	0	36,796	660,854	67,000
Virgin Islands	39,489	12,042	9,553	239	859	8,787	82	0	2,058	3,628	2,240

[1] Title I, formerly called Chapter 1, Education Consolidation and Improvement Act of 1981, includes Grants to Local Education Agencies, Basic, Concentration, Targeted, and Education Finance Incentive Grants; Reading First State grants; Even Start; Migrant Education grants, Neglected and Delinquent Children grants; and Comprehensive School Reform Grants.

[2] Title VI, formerly called Chapter 2, Education Consolidation and Improvement Act of 1981, includes Teacher Quality State Grants; 21st Century Community Learning Centers; Educational Technology State Grants; State Grants for Innovation Programs; State Assessments, including No Child Left Behind; Education for the Homeless Children and Youth; Rural and Low-Income Schools Program; Small, Rural School Achievement Program, Fund for the Improvement of Education--Comprehensive School Reform; Safe and Drug-Free Schools and Communities State Grants; and State Grants for Community Services for Expelled or Suspended Students.

[3] Includes Impact Aid—Basic Support Payments; Impact Aid—Payments for Children with Disabilities; Impact Aid Construction; and Impact Aid Payments for Federal Property.

[4] Includes Vocational Education State Grants; State Grants for Incarcerated Youth Offenders; English Literacy and Civics Education State Grants, Tech-Prep Education; and and Adult Education State Grants.

[5] Includes Special Education—Grants to States, Preschool Grants, and Grants for Infants and Families with Disabilities.

[6] Includes Language Assistance State Grants.

[7] Includes Institutional Aid to Strengthen Higher Education Institutions serving significant numbers of low-income students; Other Special Programs for the Disadvantaged; Cooperative Education; Fund for the Improvement of Postsecondary Education; Fellowships and Scholarships; and annual interest subsidy grants for facilities construction.

[8] Includes Pell Grants, Leveraging Educational Assistance Partnership, formerly the State Student Incentive Grants, Federal Supplemental Educational Opportunity Grants, Federal Work-Study, Guaranteed Student Loans interest subsidies; and Federal Perkins Loans-Capital Contributions.

[9] Includes Rehabilitation Services--Vocational Rehabilitation Grants to States; Supported Employment State Grants; Client Assistance State Grants; and Independent Living State Grants; Services for Older Blind Individuals; Protection and Advocacy for Assistive Technology; Protection and Advocacy for Assistive Technology; and Protection and Advocacy of Individual Rights.

[10] Total excludes other activities and outlying areas.

NOTE: Data reflect revisions to figures in the *Budget of the United States Government, Fiscal Year 2004*. Detail may not sum to totals due to rounding.

SOURCE: U.S. Department of Education, National Center for Education Statistics, based on unpublished tabulations from the Office of Management and Budget. (This table was prepared August 2003.)

Appropriations for Title I, No Child Left Behind Act of 2001, by type of appropriation and state or jurisdiction: Fiscal years 2001 and 2002

[In thousands]

State or jurisdiction	Title I total, fiscal year 2001 [1]	Title I, fiscal year 2002 [1]		State Agency Programs					State Grants for Innovative Programs, fiscal year 2002	State Assessments, fiscal year 2002
		Total	Title I, grants to local education agencies [2]	Neglected and Delinquent	Migrant	Comprehensive School Reform	Even Start	Reading First State Grants		
1	2	3	4	5	6	7	8	9	10	11
Total, 50 States and DC [3]	$9,234,677	$11,610,496	$9,910,729	$46,785	$382,120	$216,439	$218,227	$836,195	$376,802	$360,192
Total, 50 States, DC, other activities, and outlying areas	9,654,721	12,179,000	10,350,000	48,000	396,000	235,000	250,000	900,000	385,000	387,000
Alabama	148,053	180,633	154,939	760	2,725	3,397	3,224	15,587	5,715	6,227
Alaska	32,644	40,751	29,752	236	6,855	622	1,128	2,159	1,912	3,558
Arizona	156,266	206,534	173,247	1,695	6,462	3,721	3,708	17,700	6,801	6,840
Arkansas	94,914	116,885	97,237	408	5,183	2,147	2,023	9,886	3,445	4,946
California	1,367,077	1,775,451	1,448,834	3,889	127,546	30,997	31,210	132,975	46,714	29,379
Colorado	90,926	117,501	96,385	400	7,517	2,156	2,042	9,002	5,549	6,133
Connecticut	94,206	120,217	104,127	1,060	3,021	2,359	2,258	7,393	4,271	5,412
Delaware	25,040	32,035	27,674	211	306	558	1,128	2,159	1,912	3,558
District of Columbia	30,026	39,388	34,870	82	441	709	1,128	2,159	1,912	3,322
Florida	458,720	568,540	476,520	2,396	22,925	10,679	10,381	45,639	18,654	13,534
Georgia	280,608	365,498	313,331	2,020	8,713	6,779	6,815	27,838	10,873	9,140
Hawaii	29,060	39,125	33,672	117	745	705	1,128	2,759	1,912	3,849
Idaho	33,438	42,748	32,795	141	4,572	719	1,128	3,392	1,912	4,059
Illinois	388,845	486,619	430,679	1,923	2,352	9,521	9,333	32,810	16,363	12,240
Indiana	144,460	178,766	152,669	1,092	5,208	3,603	3,285	12,908	7,952	7,490
Iowa	61,192	73,488	62,956	342	1,682	1,458	1,296	5,753	3,766	5,127
Kansas	77,350	95,004	73,139	352	11,864	1,674	1,575	6,400	3,621	5,045
Kentucky	150,394	180,425	152,146	778	7,218	3,314	3,226	13,743	5,035	5,843
Louisiana	209,730	244,575	213,134	897	2,427	4,697	4,202	19,217	6,233	6,520
Maine	39,672	47,052	37,942	142	4,385	843	1,128	2,612	1,912	3,899
Maryland	135,565	174,723	153,984	2,140	528	3,372	3,354	11,345	6,927	6,911
Massachusetts	198,384	248,595	220,646	1,267	1,789	4,900	4,691	15,301	7,618	7,302
Michigan	385,697	476,324	420,800	508	8,615	9,019	8,908	28,474	13,288	10,504
Minnesota	106,118	130,292	112,965	184	2,376	2,671	2,418	9,679	6,613	6,734
Mississippi	135,686	148,694	130,431	506	1,369	3,043	2,239	11,106	3,943	5,227
Missouri	154,202	188,420	163,744	1,048	1,631	3,675	3,414	14,909	7,307	7,126
Montana	31,678	40,162	34,294	98	960	741	1,128	2,941	1,912	3,683
Nebraska	40,930	48,051	37,640	222	5,174	864	1,128	3,024	2,302	4,300
Nevada	35,433	47,127	40,691	162	226	884	1,128	4,037	2,528	4,428
New Hampshire	24,051	31,120	26,874	258	144	558	1,128	2,159	1,912	3,912
New Jersey	229,339	290,615	257,022	1,877	2,050	5,750	5,489	18,427	10,525	8,944
New Mexico	75,147	95,348	82,193	363	872	1,748	1,781	8,391	2,611	4,474
New York	899,236	1,153,073	1,027,699	3,219	9,544	21,829	22,331	68,451	23,836	16,460
North Carolina	193,160	252,444	214,423	943	7,008	4,679	4,651	20,740	9,840	8,557
North Dakota	23,612	30,653	26,530	56	223	558	1,128	2,159	1,912	3,474
Ohio	331,418	388,143	341,108	2,981	2,486	7,623	7,050	26,895	14,736	11,322
Oklahoma	111,795	142,767	122,629	321	2,026	2,654	2,600	12,536	4,531	5,559
Oregon	97,037	120,717	94,339	1,819	13,003	2,146	2,015	7,396	4,307	5,432
Pennsylvania	383,931	456,344	399,600	857	10,473	8,948	8,354	28,111	15,158	11,560
Rhode Island	30,152	39,112	34,250	418	70	769	1,128	2,478	1,912	3,717
South Carolina	122,528	163,830	142,364	1,225	540	2,985	3,077	13,640	5,146	5,906
South Dakota	24,476	32,346	27,405	232	822	558	1,128	2,201	1,912	3,591
Tennessee	148,692	174,444	152,480	634	535	3,385	3,038	14,373	7,071	6,993
Texas	804,201	1,038,704	862,758	2,456	57,843	18,042	18,597	79,007	29,441	19,625
Utah	42,385	52,665	43,651	510	1,750	965	1,128	4,662	3,518	4,987
Vermont	20,936	27,085	22,382	325	613	479	1,128	2,159	1,912	3,443
Virginia	150,677	200,137	174,347	445	799	3,830	3,800	16,916	8,816	7,978
Washington	142,891	178,444	142,699	697	15,580	3,256	3,031	13,182	7,733	7,367
West Virginia	79,851	91,057	81,033	369	84	1,791	1,652	6,128	2,076	4,172
Wisconsin	141,009	169,398	149,747	1,247	619	3,552	3,116	11,118	7,090	7,004
Wyoming	21,835	28,427	23,956	457	219	509	1,128	2,159	1,912	3,382
Other activities										
Indian Tribe Set-Aside	58,200	77,769	70,821	800	0	1,648	0	4,500	0	1,850
Other non-state allocations	43,800	77,650	7,500	0	10,000	9,400	23,250	27,500	0	17,000
Outlying areas										
American Samoa	6,131	9,391	7,453	0	0	173	337	1,428	511	351
Guam	5,275	8,369	6,646	0	0	149	300	1,274	1,098	754
Northern Marianas	3,047	4,304	3,541	0	0	84	160	519	344	236
Puerto Rico	293,154	378,979	333,296	415	3,880	6,811	7,273	27,305	5,503	6,108
Virgin Islands	10,438	12,042	10,014	0	0	295	453	1,279	742	509

[1] Formerly Chapter 1.
[2] Includes Basic, Concentration, Targeted, and Education Finance Incentive Grants.
[3] Total excludes other activities and outlying areas.

NOTE: Detail may not sum to totals due to rounding.

SOURCE: U.S. Department of Education, Budget Service, Elementary, Secondary, and Vocational Education Analysis Division, unpublished data. (This table was prepared February 2004.)

U.S. Department of Agriculture obligations for child nutrition programs, by state or jurisdiction: Fiscal years 2001 and 2002

[In thousands of dollars]

State or jurisdiction	Total, fiscal year 2001	Fiscal year 2002							
		Total	Special milk	School lunch [1]	School breakfast	State administrative expenses	Commodities and cash in lieu of commodities [2]	Child and adult care	Summer food service
1	2	3	4	5	6	7	8	9	10
United States [3]	$9,850,516	$10,454,599	$16,031	$5,891,898	$1,530,047	$123,695	$863,527	$1,779,169	$250,232
Alabama	188,798	205,383	60	119,677	30,112	2,410	16,699	32,285	4,141
Alaska	27,620	29,019	3	16,775	3,062	484	2,037	6,349	309
Arizona	190,658	208,023	143	120,080	29,649	2,518	14,008	39,484	2,141
Arkansas	115,880	128,857	18	68,106	21,366	1,548	12,225	23,726	1,869
California	1,311,014	1,365,946	848	818,610	203,936	15,637	92,325	216,756	17,835
Colorado	94,502	99,553	160	56,241	10,600	1,413	9,674	20,694	772
Connecticut	77,202	83,609	444	50,129	10,917	996	10,107	9,744	1,271
Delaware	26,152	27,651	51	12,714	3,265	491	2,202	7,618	1,311
District of Columbia	27,254	27,637	7	15,782	4,269	391	2,084	3,337	1,768
Florida	549,725	588,488	107	345,143	91,908	6,340	41,497	86,338	17,155
Georgia	388,150	417,171	31	230,785	72,767	4,563	32,819	65,480	10,727
Hawaii	41,550	44,288	7	28,312	6,413	617	3,738	4,485	716
Idaho	39,429	42,232	200	26,048	4,921	557	4,484	4,435	1,587
Illinois	394,928	420,517	2,821	246,156	39,665	4,892	35,428	82,169	9,386
Indiana	162,632	169,058	310	99,308	21,579	1,995	16,653	26,351	2,862
Iowa	86,194	90,401	117	50,150	10,358	1,178	12,047	15,798	710
Kansas	92,062	100,688	142	49,427	13,690	1,352	7,800	27,022	1,256
Kentucky	172,602	181,022	101	100,947	34,076	2,060	15,399	23,815	4,626
Louisiana	257,882	266,681	53	145,959	45,833	3,268	20,067	45,311	6,190
Maine	35,012	36,626	132	18,428	4,212	620	3,412	9,038	784
Maryland	144,485	152,958	484	80,324	21,803	1,905	12,702	30,957	4,782
Massachusetts	168,642	176,126	528	87,304	22,164	2,376	17,384	41,093	5,277
Michigan	256,410	273,536	867	155,233	40,650	3,294	25,491	44,583	3,418
Minnesota	163,298	170,145	973	74,604	16,956	2,537	16,365	55,913	2,796
Mississippi	174,190	183,955	6	105,405	36,401	2,078	13,638	22,309	4,117
Missouri	181,440	196,356	454	109,072	30,418	2,321	15,164	32,425	6,502
Montana	30,694	31,116	42	14,837	3,325	560	2,750	8,953	648
Nebraska	66,353	69,936	120	32,697	6,348	1,126	7,747	21,124	773
Nevada	45,780	50,750	158	32,598	8,048	554	5,062	3,098	1,232
New Hampshire	21,020	21,790	193	12,055	2,362	361	3,673	2,703	444
New Jersey	198,074	213,929	895	127,122	19,159	2,407	18,499	37,951	7,898
New Mexico	112,499	116,532	15	53,437	16,468	1,664	6,389	32,812	5,748
New York	725,309	752,058	1,045	422,849	94,611	8,699	59,823	125,532	39,500
North Carolina	313,708	334,418	142	176,069	54,254	3,891	27,969	66,855	5,238
North Dakota	24,693	24,700	94	10,758	2,099	507	2,381	8,494	367
Ohio	281,647	309,168	897	173,506	39,411	3,526	34,377	51,744	5,707
Oklahoma	152,974	165,803	69	82,928	27,285	2,156	12,670	38,415	2,279
Oregon	104,742	109,563	129	56,958	18,735	1,520	8,227	22,708	1,285
Pennsylvania	295,622	310,925	782	181,447	40,065	3,365	30,104	41,516	13,647
Rhode Island	29,452	33,256	98	18,609	4,203	470	2,955	5,975	946
South Carolina	177,022	186,778	8	107,367	33,586	2,057	15,831	21,034	6,895
South Dakota	29,572	30,069	43	16,332	3,534	505	3,294	5,701	658
Tennessee	203,768	219,997	26	123,308	33,893	2,568	19,993	34,975	5,234
Texas	996,566	1,083,349	92	628,606	203,416	11,373	76,241	139,927	23,694
Utah	81,088	86,923	73	45,129	7,151	1,278	8,827	22,329	2,136
Vermont	15,737	16,370	75	8,006	2,307	352	1,640	3,679	311
Virginia	185,141	189,315	263	113,552	28,457	1,523	19,344	22,319	3,857
Washington	165,839	178,065	291	97,480	24,035	2,187	15,764	35,312	2,996
West Virginia	73,220	78,085	34	40,232	14,451	1,017	6,645	13,997	1,619
Wisconsin	136,667	139,920	1,360	77,282	10,225	1,838	16,142	30,419	2,654
Wyoming	15,617	15,858	23	7,879	1,629	351	1,733	4,085	159
Other activities									
Administrative costs	6,226	3,078	0	0	0	0	3,078	0	0
Department of Defense dependents schools	7,635	7,293	0	6,197	33	0	1,063	0	0
Outlying areas	183,831	193,252	2	120,200	30,818	2,431	13,187	18,549	8,065
American Samoa	0	0	0	0	0	0	0	0	0
Guam	5,366	5,637	0	3,931	1,252	213	168	73	0
Northern Marianas	0	0	0	0	0	0	0	0	0
Puerto Rico	172,359	181,180	0	112,275	29,209	1,970	12,512	17,826	7,389
Trust Territories	560	0	0	0	0	0	0	0	0
Virgin Islands	5,546	6,434	2	3,994	357	247	508	650	676
Undistributed [4]	255,883	131,888	1,468	7,658	(19,895)	6,181	54,533	33,013	48,931

[1] Special Meal Assistance program is combined with "School Lunch" program.

[2] Commodities are based on preliminary food orders for fiscal year 2001.

[3] Excludes other activities, outlying areas, and undistributed.

[4] Undistributed amount reflects the difference between preliminary state earnings reports and federal obligations as of September 30, 2002. Undistributed amount under school lunch includes obligations for American Samoa and the Northern Marianas Islands.

NOTE: Data are based on obligations as reported September 30, 2002. Detail may not sum to totals due to rounding.

SOURCE: U.S. Department of Agriculture, Food and Nutrition Service, Budget Division, unpublished data. (This table was prepared July 2003.)

637

U.S. Department of Health and Human Services allocations for Head Start and enrollment in Head Start, by state or jurisdiction: Fiscal years 1999 to 2002

State or jurisdiction	1999		2000		2001		2002	
	Head Start allocations (in thousands)	Head Start enrollment [1]	Head Start allocations (in thousands)	Head Start enrollment [2]	Head Start allocations (in thousands)	Head Start enrollment [3]	Head Start allocations (in thousands)	Head Start enrollment [4]
1	2	3	4	5	6	7	8	9
United States [5]	$4,021,476	729,697	$4,546,132	761,844	$5,346,145	804,598	$5,627,581	810,472
Alabama	71,983	15,263	82,414	15,823	95,374	16,498	100,154	16,529
Alaska	8,786	1,281	9,738	1,297	11,656	1,586	12,104	1,839
Arizona	62,444	11,127	73,697	11,882	89,629	12,865	96,913	13,297
Arkansas	43,449	10,097	48,379	10,316	57,381	10,818	61,024	10,930
California	554,366	86,459	642,512	95,280	758,591	97,667	801,430	98,687
Colorado	46,602	9,135	52,226	9,333	61,805	9,826	65,716	9,872
Connecticut	37,906	6,825	41,674	6,857	47,931	7,207	49,985	7,224
Delaware	8,873	2,126	9,820	2,119	11,831	2,243	12,286	2,231
District of Columbia	19,201	3,279	20,926	3,345	23,203	3,343	24,091	3,403
Florida	169,996	30,792	195,696	32,389	236,056	34,657	252,370	35,610
Georgia	112,040	21,121	126,281	21,580	151,340	23,140	161,740	23,414
Hawaii	15,786	2,799	18,199	2,916	21,166	3,073	21,977	3,073
Idaho	14,121	2,266	16,098	2,387	20,158	2,890	21,663	3,347
Illinois	192,580	35,211	214,965	37,767	248,855	39,805	259,780	39,619
Indiana	65,226	13,057	72,467	13,323	85,241	14,256	88,667	14,145
Iowa	36,038	7,003	40,714	7,235	47,381	7,689	49,495	7,620
Kansas	32,958	7,000	37,061	7,447	44,951	7,897	47,909	8,013
Kentucky	76,409	15,281	85,198	15,701	99,054	16,419	103,473	16,190
Louisiana	100,196	20,703	110,318	20,975	128,484	21,969	135,048	22,136
Maine	18,695	3,618	20,378	3,631	24,770	3,958	26,661	4,002
Maryland	54,966	9,626	61,920	9,968	71,713	10,487	74,929	10,527
Massachusetts	78,544	12,094	85,917	12,250	99,675	13,004	104,182	13,040
Michigan	171,121	33,422	186,842	33,769	215,873	35,112	225,290	35,269
Minnesota	51,740	9,630	56,401	9,715	65,523	10,164	69,643	10,331
Mississippi	117,375	25,091	129,843	25,455	149,606	26,624	155,259	26,742
Missouri	78,622	16,191	93,475	16,574	108,305	17,718	113,256	17,646
Montana	13,839	2,678	15,267	2,703	18,944	2,971	20,117	2,982
Nebraska	23,890	4,518	26,660	4,571	32,142	4,982	34,580	5,252
Nevada	11,484	2,035	12,369	2,035	18,367	2,694	19,786	2,754
New Hampshire	9,114	1,425	9,838	1,425	12,388	1,632	12,861	1,632
New Jersey	94,945	14,443	104,743	14,567	120,245	15,329	125,176	15,262
New Mexico	35,363	7,108	38,374	7,135	45,919	7,618	49,185	7,749
New York	304,283	45,040	342,136	46,805	398,522	48,952	418,239	49,493
North Carolina	93,979	17,394	104,684	17,808	124,580	18,991	132,667	19,202
North Dakota	10,561	2,002	11,973	2,042	15,750	2,287	16,036	2,307
Ohio	178,271	36,454	196,684	38,261	226,942	38,072	236,999	38,081
Oklahoma	54,422	12,217	61,555	12,655	72,190	13,228	76,910	13,460
Oregon	40,118	5,480	46,071	5,771	54,785	9,129	57,105	9,199
Pennsylvania	165,674	29,124	181,844	29,650	209,346	31,104	219,115	30,986
Rhode Island	15,330	2,817	17,378	2,952	20,412	3,150	21,184	3,150
South Carolina	56,280	11,207	64,060	11,604	74,963	12,184	78,507	12,248
South Dakota	12,708	2,485	14,045	2,587	17,513	2,925	18,079	2,827
Tennessee	81,387	14,753	92,040	15,747	107,146	16,344	112,344	16,507
Texas	299,891	58,173	361,846	63,171	429,075	67,572	454,292	67,664
Utah	23,185	4,679	27,840	5,079	35,858	5,403	36,270	5,527
Vermont	9,691	1,438	10,514	1,438	12,553	1,573	13,023	1,573
Virginia	66,246	12,243	74,487	12,652	89,890	13,612	95,366	13,772
Washington	69,601	9,831	78,359	10,287	92,257	11,106	97,247	11,167
West Virginia	36,062	7,043	39,842	7,144	46,713	7,590	48,625	7,650
Wisconsin	67,582	13,113	72,177	12,953	83,337	13,478	86,941	13,489
Wyoming	7,546	1,500	8,187	1,468	10,760	1,757	11,882	1,803
Other activities								
Migrant programs	178,122	38,132	206,391	31,607	246,905	33,355	257,815	33,850
Support activities	—	†	—	†	—	†	210,255	†
American Indian/Alaska Native programs	130,191	21,237	144,768	22,391	171,289	23,632	181,794	23,837
Outlying areas	**172,634**	**40,889**	**205,616**	**41,812**	**240,376**	**43,650**	**259,125**	**44,290**
Puerto Rico	155,526	33,470	185,563	34,393	216,476	35,894	234,304	36,920
Pacific Territories	10,297	5,989	12,356	5,989	14,381	6,209	14,943	6,209
Virgin Islands	6,811	1,430	7,697	1,430	9,519	1,547	9,878	1,161

—Not available.

† Not applicable.

[1] The distribution of enrollment by age was: 6 percent were 5 years old and over; 59 percent were 4-year-olds; 31 percent were 3-year-olds; and 4 percent were under 3 years of age. Handicapped children accounted for 13 percent in Head Start programs. The racial/ethnic composition was: American Indian/Alaska Native, 3 percent; Hispanic, 27 percent; Black, 35 percent; White, 31 percent; and Asian, 3 percent.

[2] The distribution of enrollment by age was: 5 percent were 5 years old and over; 56 percent were 4-year-olds; 33 percent were 3-year-olds; and 6 percent were under 3 years of age. Handicapped children accounted for 13 percent in Head Start programs. The racial/ethnic composition was: American Indian/Alaska Native, 3 percent; Hispanic, 29 percent; Black, 35 percent; White, 30 percent; Asian, 2 percent; and Hawaiian/Pacific Islander, 1 percent.

[3] The distribution of enrollment by age was: 4 percent were 5 years old and over; 54 percent were 4-year-olds; 35 percent were 3-year-olds; and 7 percent were under 3 years of age. Handicapped children accounted for 13 percent in Head Start programs. The racial/ethnic composition was: American Indian/Alaska Native, 4 percent; Hispanic, 30 percent; Black, 34 percent; White, 30 percent; Asian, 2 percent, and Hawaiian/Pacific Islander, 1 percent.

[4] The distribution of enrollment by age was: 5 percent were 5 years old and over; 52 percent were 4-year-olds; 36 percent were 3-year-olds; and 7 percent were under 3 years of age. Handicapped children accounted for 13 percent in Head Start programs. The racial/ethnic composition was: American Indian/Alaska Native, 3 percent; Hispanic, 30 percent; Black, 33 percent; White, 28 percent; Asian, 2 percent, and Hawaiian/Pacific Islander, 1 percent.

[5] Excludes other activities and outlying areas.

NOTE: Detail may not sum to totals due to rounding.

SOURCE: U.S. Department of Health and Human Services, Office of Human Development Services. (This table was prepared July 2003.)

Average reading, mathematics, and science literacy scores of 15-year-olds, by sex and country: 2000

Country	Reading literacy			Mathematics literacy			Science literacy		
	Total	Male	Female	Total	Male	Female	Total	Male	Female
1	2	3	4	5	6	7	8	9	10
OECD total [1]	499 (2.0)	485 (2.3)	514 (2.0)	498 (2.1)	504 (2.6)	493 (2.3)	502 (2.0)	502 (2.5)	503 (2.0)
OECD average [2]	500 (0.6)	485 (0.8)	517 (0.7)	500 (0.7)	506 (1.0)	495 (0.9)	500 (0.7)	501 (0.9)	501 (0.8)
Australia	528 (3.5)	513 (4.0)	546 (4.7)	533 (3.5)	539 (4.1)	527 (5.1)	528 (3.5)	526 (3.9)	529 (4.8)
Austria	507 (2.4)	495 (3.2)	520 (3.6)	515 (2.5)	530 (4.0)	503 (3.7)	519 (2.6)	526 (3.8)	514 (4.3)
Belgium	507 (3.6)	492 (4.2)	525 (4.9)	520 (3.9)	524 (4.6)	518 (5.2)	496 (4.3)	496 (5.2)	498 (5.6)
Canada	534 (1.6)	519 (1.8)	551 (1.7)	533 (1.4)	539 (1.8)	529 (1.6)	529 (1.6)	529 (1.9)	531 (1.7)
Czech Republic	492 (2.4)	473 (4.1)	510 (2.5)	498 (2.8)	504 (4.4)	492 (3.0)	511 (2.4)	512 (3.8)	511 (3.2)
Denmark	497 (2.4)	485 (3.0)	510 (2.9)	514 (2.4)	522 (3.1)	507 (3.0)	481 (2.8)	488 (3.9)	476 (3.5)
Finland	546 (2.6)	520 (3.0)	571 (2.8)	536 (2.2)	537 (2.8)	536 (2.6)	538 (2.5)	534 (3.5)	541 (2.7)
France	505 (2.7)	490 (3.5)	519 (2.7)	517 (2.7)	525 (4.1)	511 (2.8)	500 (3.2)	504 (4.2)	498 (3.8)
Germany	484 (2.5)	468 (3.2)	502 (3.9)	490 (2.5)	498 (3.1)	483 (4.0)	487 (2.4)	489 (3.4)	487 (3.4)
Greece	474 (5.0)	456 (6.1)	493 (4.6)	447 (5.6)	451 (7.7)	444 (5.4)	461 (4.9)	457 (6.1)	464 (5.2)
Hungary	480 (4.0)	465 (5.3)	496 (4.3)	488 (4.0)	492 (5.2)	485 (4.9)	496 (4.2)	496 (5.8)	497 (5.0)
Iceland	507 (1.5)	488 (2.1)	528 (2.1)	514 (2.3)	513 (3.1)	518 (2.9)	496 (2.2)	495 (3.4)	499 (3.0)
Ireland	527 (3.2)	513 (4.2)	542 (3.6)	503 (2.7)	510 (4.0)	497 (3.4)	513 (3.2)	511 (4.2)	517 (4.2)
Italy	487 (2.9)	469 (5.1)	507 (3.6)	457 (2.9)	462 (5.3)	454 (3.8)	478 (3.1)	474 (5.6)	483 (3.9)
Japan	522 (5.2)	507 (6.7)	537 (5.4)	557 (5.5)	561 (7.3)	553 (5.9)	550 (5.5)	547 (7.2)	554 (5.9)
Korea, Republic of	525 (2.4)	519 (3.8)	533 (3.7)	547 (2.8)	559 (4.6)	532 (5.1)	552 (2.7)	561 (4.3)	541 (5.1)
Luxembourg	441 (1.6)	429 (2.6)	456 (2.3)	446 (2.0)	454 (3.0)	439 (3.2)	443 (2.3)	441 (3.6)	448 (3.2)
Mexico	422 (3.3)	411 (4.2)	432 (3.8)	387 (3.4)	393 (4.5)	382 (3.8)	422 (3.2)	423 (4.2)	419 (3.9)
Netherlands [3]	— (—)	517 (4.8)	547 (3.8)	— (—)	569 (4.9)	558 (4.6)	— (—)	529 (6.3)	529 (5.1)
New Zealand	529 (2.8)	507 (4.2)	553 (3.8)	537 (3.1)	536 (5.0)	539 (4.1)	528 (2.4)	523 (4.6)	535 (3.8)
Norway	505 (2.8)	486 (3.8)	529 (2.9)	499 (2.8)	506 (3.8)	495 (2.9)	500 (2.8)	499 (4.1)	505 (3.3)
Poland	479 (4.5)	461 (6.0)	498 (5.5)	470 (5.5)	472 (7.5)	468 (6.3)	483 (5.1)	486 (6.1)	480 (6.5)
Portugal	470 (4.5)	458 (5.0)	482 (4.6)	454 (4.1)	464 (4.7)	446 (4.7)	459 (4.0)	456 (4.8)	462 (4.2)
Spain	493 (2.7)	481 (3.4)	505 (2.8)	476 (3.1)	487 (4.3)	469 (3.3)	491 (3.0)	492 (3.5)	491 (3.6)
Sweden	516 (2.2)	499 (2.6)	536 (2.5)	510 (2.5)	514 (3.2)	507 (3.0)	512 (2.5)	512 (3.5)	513 (2.9)
Switzerland	494 (4.3)	480 (4.9)	510 (4.5)	529 (4.4)	537 (5.3)	523 (4.8)	496 (4.4)	500 (5.7)	493 (4.7)
United Kingdom	523 (2.6)	512 (3.0)	537 (3.4)	529 (2.5)	534 (3.5)	526 (3.7)	532 (2.7)	535 (3.4)	531 (4.0)
United States	504 (7.1)	490 (8.4)	518 (6.2)	493 (7.6)	497 (8.9)	490 (7.3)	499 (7.3)	497 (8.9)	502 (6.5)
Non-OECD countries									
Brazil	396 (3.1)	388 (3.9)	404 (3.4)	334 (3.7)	349 (4.7)	322 (4.7)	375 (3.3)	376 (4.8)	376 (3.8)
Latvia	458 (5.3)	432 (5.5)	485 (5.4)	463 (4.5)	467 (5.3)	460 (5.6)	460 (5.6)	449 (6.4)	472 (5.8)
Liechtenstein	483 (4.1)	468 (7.3)	500 (6.8)	514 (7.0)	521 (11.5)	510 (11.1)	476 (7.1)	484 (10.9)	468 (9.3)
Russian Federation	462 (4.2)	443 (4.5)	481 (4.1)	478 (5.5)	478 (5.7)	479 (6.2)	460 (4.7)	453 (5.4)	467 (5.2)

—Not available.

[1] Refers to the mean of the data values for all OECD countries, to which each country contributes equally, regardless of the absolute size of the student population of each country.

[2] Refers to the average for OECD countries as a single entity, to which each country contributes in proportion to the number of 15-year-olds enrolled in its schools.

[3] Response rate is too low to ensure comparability with other countries.

NOTE: Scales were designed to have an average score of 500 points, and standard deviation of 100. Standard errors appear in parentheses.

SOURCE: Organization for Economic Cooperation and Development (OECD), *Program for International Student Assessment (PISA), Knowledge and Skills for Life, 2000.* (This table was prepared August 2002.)

Percentage distribution of 15-year-olds at selected reading literacy proficiency levels, by country: 2000

Country	Mean score	Percentage distribution at levels of proficiency					
		Below level 1[1]	Level 1[2]	Level 2[3]	Level 3[4]	Level 4[5]	Level 5[6]
1	2	3	4	5	6	7	8
OECD total[7]	499 (2.0)	6.2 (0.4)	12.1 (0.4)	21.8 (0.4)	28.6 (0.4)	21.8 (0.4)	9.4 (0.4)
OECD average[8]	500 (0.6)	6.0 (0.1)	11.9 (0.2)	21.7 (0.2)	28.7 (0.2)	22.3 (0.2)	9.5 (0.1)
Australia	528 (3.5)	3.3 (0.5)	9.1 (0.8)	19.0 (1.1)	25.7 (1.1)	25.3 (0.9)	17.6 (1.2)
Austria	507 (2.4)	4.4 (0.4)	10.2 (0.6)	21.7 (0.9)	29.9 (1.2)	24.9 (1.0)	8.8 (0.8)
Belgium	507 (3.6)	7.7 (1.0)	11.3 (0.7)	16.8 (0.7)	25.8 (0.9)	26.3 (0.9)	12.0 (0.7)
Canada	534 (1.6)	2.4 (0.3)	7.2 (0.3)	18.0 (0.4)	28.0 (0.5)	27.7 (0.6)	16.8 (0.5)
Czech Republic	492 (2.4)	6.1 (0.6)	11.4 (0.7)	24.8 (1.2)	30.9 (1.1)	19.8 (0.8)	7.0 (0.6)
Denmark	497 (2.4)	5.9 (0.6)	12.0 (0.7)	22.5 (0.9)	29.5 (1.0)	22.0 (0.9)	8.1 (0.5)
Finland	546 (2.6)	1.7 (0.5)	5.2 (0.4)	14.3 (0.7)	28.7 (0.8)	31.6 (0.9)	18.5 (0.9)
France	505 (2.7)	4.2 (0.6)	11.0 (0.8)	22.0 (0.8)	30.6 (1.0)	23.7 (0.9)	8.5 (0.6)
Germany	484 (2.5)	9.9 (0.7)	12.7 (0.6)	22.3 (0.8)	26.8 (1.0)	19.4 (1.0)	8.8 (0.5)
Greece	474 (5.0)	8.7 (1.2)	15.7 (1.4)	25.9 (1.4)	28.1 (1.7)	16.7 (1.4)	5.0 (0.7)
Hungary	480 (4.0)	6.9 (0.7)	15.8 (1.2)	25.0 (1.1)	28.8 (1.3)	18.5 (1.1)	5.1 (0.8)
Iceland	507 (1.5)	4.0 (0.3)	10.5 (0.6)	22.0 (0.8)	30.8 (0.9)	23.6 (1.1)	9.1 (0.7)
Ireland	527 (3.2)	3.1 (0.5)	7.9 (0.8)	17.9 (0.9)	29.7 (1.1)	27.1 (1.1)	14.2 (0.8)
Italy	487 (2.9)	5.4 (0.9)	13.5 (0.9)	25.6 (1.0)	30.6 (1.0)	19.5 (1.1)	5.3 (0.5)
Japan	522 (5.2)	2.7 (0.6)	7.3 (1.1)	18.0 (1.3)	33.3 (1.3)	28.8 (1.7)	9.9 (1.1)
Korea, Republic of	525 (2.4)	0.9 (0.2)	4.8 (0.6)	18.6 (0.9)	38.8 (1.1)	31.1 (1.2)	5.7 (0.6)
Luxembourg	441 (1.6)	14.2 (0.7)	20.9 (0.8)	27.5 (1.3)	24.6 (1.1)	11.2 (0.5)	1.7 (0.3)
Mexico	422 (3.3)	16.1 (1.2)	28.1 (1.4)	30.3 (1.1)	18.8 (1.2)	6.0 (0.7)	0.9 (0.2)
New Zealand	529 (2.8)	4.8 (0.5)	8.9 (0.5)	17.2 (0.9)	24.6 (1.1)	25.8 (1.1)	18.7 (1.0)
Norway	505 (2.8)	6.3 (0.6)	11.2 (0.8)	19.5 (0.8)	28.1 (0.8)	23.7 (0.9)	11.2 (0.7)
Poland	479 (4.5)	8.7 (1.0)	14.6 (1.0)	24.1 (1.4)	28.2 (1.3)	18.6 (1.3)	5.9 (1.0)
Portugal	470 (4.5)	9.6 (1.0)	16.7 (1.2)	25.3 (1.0)	27.5 (1.2)	16.8 (1.1)	4.2 (0.5)
Spain	493 (2.7)	4.1 (0.5)	12.2 (0.9)	25.7 (0.7)	32.8 (1.0)	21.1 (0.9)	4.2 (0.5)
Sweden	516 (2.2)	3.3 (0.4)	9.3 (0.6)	20.3 (0.7)	30.4 (1.0)	25.6 (1.0)	11.2 (0.7)
Switzerland	494 (4.3)	7.0 (0.7)	13.3 (0.9)	21.4 (1.0)	28.0 (1.0)	21.0 (1.0)	9.2 (1.0)
United Kingdom	523 (2.6)	3.6 (0.4)	9.2 (0.5)	19.6 (0.7)	27.5 (0.9)	24.4 (0.9)	15.6 (1.0)
United States	504 (7.1)	6.4 (1.2)	11.5 (1.2)	21.0 (1.2)	27.4 (1.3)	21.5 (1.4)	12.2 (1.4)
Non-OECD countries							
Brazil	396 (3.1)	23.3 (1.4)	32.5 (1.2)	27.7 (1.3)	12.9 (1.1)	3.1 (0.5)	0.6 (0.2)
Latvia	458 (5.3)	12.7 (1.3)	17.9 (1.3)	26.3 (1.1)	25.2 (1.3)	13.8 (1.1)	4.1 (0.6)
Liechtenstein	483 (4.1)	7.6 (1.5)	14.5 (2.1)	23.2 (2.9)	30.1 (3.4)	19.5 (2.2)	5.1 (1.6)
Russian Federation	462 (4.2)	9.0 (1.0)	18.5 (1.1)	29.2 (0.8)	26.9 (1.1)	13.3 (1.0)	3.2 (0.5)

[1] Less than 335 score points. Although students at this level may have the technical capacity to read, they have serious difficulties in using reading literacy as an effective tool to advance knowledge.

[2] Between 335 and 407 score points. Indicates an ability to locate a single piece of information, identify the main theme of a text, or make a simple connection with everyday knowledge.

[3] Between 408 and 480 score points. Indicates an ability to locate straightforward information, make low-level inferences, work out what a well-defined part of a text means, and use some outside knowledge to understand it.

[4] Between 481 and 552 score points. Indicates an ability to locate multiple pieces of information, make links between different parts of a text, and relate it to familiar everyday knowledge.

[5] Between 553 and 625 score points. Indicates an ability to locate embedded information, construe meaning from nuances of language, and critically evaluate a text.

[6] Above 625 score points. Indicates an ability to manage information that is difficult to find in unfamiliar texts, show detailed understanding of such text, and evaluate critically and build hypotheses.

[7] Refers to the mean of the data values for all OECD countries, to which each country contributes equally, regardless of the absolute size of the student population of each country.

[8] Refers to the average for OECD countries as a single entity, to which each country contributes in proportion to the number of 15-year-olds enrolled in its schools.

NOTE: Mean score was designed to have an average of 500 points, and a standard deviation of 100. Standard errors appear in parentheses. Detail may not sum to totals due to rounding.

SOURCE: Organization for Economic Cooperation and Development, Program for International Student Assessment (PISA), *Knowledge and Skills for Life, 2000*. (This table was prepared August 2002.)

Average 8th-grade mathematics scores, by content areas, average time spent studying out of school, and country: 1999

Country	Average achievement scale score						Distribution of daily out-of-school study time in mathematics, with mean mathematics scores					
	Mathematics overall	Fractions and number sense	Geometry	Algebra	Data representation, analysis and probability	Measurement	No time		Less than 1 hour		One hour or more	
							Percent	Mean score	Percent	Mean score	Percent	Mean score
1	2	3	4	5	6	7	8	9	10	11	12	13
International average	487 (0.7)	487 (0.7)	487 (0.7)	487 (0.7)	487 (0.7)	487 (0.7)	10 (0.1)	455 (1.7)	50 (0.2)	495 (0.8)	40 (0.2)	486 (0.9)
Australia	525 (4.8)	519 (4.3)	497 (5.7)	520 (5.1)	522 (6.3)	529 (4.9)	15 (1.0)	493 (6.3)	63 (1.1)	537 (5.0)	22 (1.0)	515 (6.3)
Belgium (Flemish)	558 (3.3)	557 (3.1)	535 (4.1)	540 (4.6)	544 (3.8)	549 (4.0)	3 (0.8)	476 (21.8)	50 (1.0)	573 (3.8)	47 (1.2)	550 (3.1)
Bulgaria	511 (5.8)	503 (6.6)	524 (5.9)	512 (5.1)	493 (6.1)	497 (6.6)	12 (1.2)	494 (9.5)	45 (1.3)	516 (5.5)	43 (1.7)	521 (7.9)
Canada	531 (2.5)	533 (2.5)	507 (4.7)	525 (2.4)	521 (4.5)	521 (2.4)	11 (0.8)	527 (5.2)	61 (1.0)	542 (2.8)	28 (1.0)	510 (3.3)
Chile	392 (4.4)	403 (4.9)	412 (5.4)	399 (4.3)	429 (3.8)	412 (4.9)	17 (0.8)	384 (5.9)	54 (0.7)	400 (4.7)	29 (1.0)	394 (7.1)
Chinese Taipei	585 (4.0)	576 (4.2)	557 (5.8)	586 (4.4)	559 (5.1)	566 (3.4)	31 (1.3)	529 (4.8)	44 (0.8)	604 (3.5)	25 (1.0)	627 (4.7)
Cyprus	476 (1.8)	481 (3.0)	484 (4.6)	479 (1.6)	472 (4.6)	471 (4.0)	9 (0.6)	425 (7.2)	51 (1.1)	496 (2.7)	40 (1.1)	469 (2.4)
Czech Republic	520 (4.2)	507 (4.8)	513 (5.5)	514 (4.0)	513 (5.9)	535 (5.0)	12 (1.0)	525 (9.2)	68 (1.3)	528 (4.6)	20 (1.1)	493 (5.2)
England	496 (4.1)	497 (3.8)	471 (4.2)	498 (4.9)	506 (8.0)	507 (3.8)	— (—)	— (—)	— (—)	— (—)	— (—)	— (—)
Finland	520 (2.7)	531 (3.8)	494 (6.0)	498 (3.1)	525 (3.8)	521 (4.7)	7 (0.6)	506 (8.1)	85 (0.8)	525 (2.5)	8 (0.7)	486 (6.8)
Hong Kong, SAR [1]	582 (4.3)	579 (4.5)	556 (4.9)	569 (4.5)	547 (5.4)	567 (5.8)	25 (1.2)	552 (6.1)	51 (0.9)	591 (3.9)	24 (1.1)	600 (4.8)
Hungary	532 (3.7)	526 (4.2)	489 (4.3)	536 (4.1)	520 (5.9)	538 (3.5)	4 (0.4)	497 (9.9)	71 (1.0)	540 (3.6)	25 (1.1)	514 (5.0)
Indonesia	403 (4.9)	406 (4.1)	441 (5.1)	424 (5.7)	423 (4.4)	395 (5.1)	10 (0.8)	396 (8.4)	38 (1.0)	405 (5.6)	51 (1.4)	406 (5.4)
Iran, Islamic Republic	422 (3.4)	437 (4.5)	447 (2.9)	434 (4.9)	430 (6.0)	401 (4.7)	3 (0.3)	375 (14.1)	22 (0.8)	425 (3.7)	75 (1.0)	427 (3.7)
Israel [2]	466 (3.9)	472 (4.4)	462 (5.4)	479 (4.5)	468 (5.1)	457 (5.1)	8 (0.6)	436 (11.3)	48 (1.1)	491 (4.2)	44 (1.4)	454 (4.3)
Italy	479 (3.8)	471 (5.0)	482 (5.6)	481 (3.6)	484 (4.5)	501 (5.0)	5 (0.5)	400 (9.5)	39 (1.2)	488 (4.5)	57 (1.3)	482 (4.0)
Japan	579 (1.7)	570 (2.6)	575 (5.1)	569 (3.3)	555 (2.3)	558 (2.4)	26 (1.2)	558 (3.8)	54 (0.9)	586 (2.0)	20 (0.9)	585 (2.5)
Jordan	428 (3.6)	432 (3.2)	449 (7.1)	439 (5.3)	436 (7.8)	438 (4.4)	8 (0.6)	374 (9.8)	33 (0.8)	441 (4.6)	60 (1.0)	445 (4.3)
Korea, Republic of	587 (2.0)	570 (2.7)	573 (3.9)	585 (2.7)	576 (4.2)	571 (2.8)	34 (1.0)	560 (2.6)	45 (0.7)	598 (2.0)	21 (0.9)	610 (4.1)
Latvia (Latvian-speaking schools) [2]	505 (3.4)	496 (3.7)	522 (5.6)	499 (4.3)	495 (4.8)	505 (3.5)	3 (0.4)	480 (13.8)	58 (1.3)	516 (4.1)	40 (1.3)	493 (4.1)
Lithuania [2]	482 (4.3)	479 (4.3)	496 (5.8)	487 (3.7)	493 (3.6)	467 (4.0)	3 (0.5)	417 (15.8)	68 (1.4)	486 (4.4)	29 (1.3)	483 (5.3)
Macedonia, Republic of	447 (4.2)	437 (4.7)	460 (6.1)	465 (4.0)	442 (6.2)	451 (5.2)	6 (0.4)	429 (9.2)	49 (1.1)	461 (4.6)	45 (1.2)	448 (4.1)
Malaysia	519 (4.4)	532 (4.7)	497 (4.4)	505 (4.8)	491 (4.0)	514 (4.6)	2 (0.2)	(3) (3)	28 (0.9)	523 (6.5)	71 (1.0)	519 (4.2)
Moldova	469 (3.9)	465 (4.2)	481 (5.0)	477 (3.7)	450 (5.7)	479 (4.9)	8 (0.7)	452 (7.6)	48 (1.4)	476 (4.1)	44 (1.6)	473 (5.0)
Morocco	337 (2.6)	335 (3.6)	407 (2.2)	353 (4.7)	383 (3.5)	348 (3.5)	13 (0.9)	324 (8.0)	29 (0.9)	341 (6.6)	58 (1.5)	350 (3.2)
Netherlands	540 (7.1)	545 (7.1)	515 (5.5)	522 (7.7)	538 (7.9)	538 (5.8)	8 (1.1)	559 (14.0)	78 (1.3)	546 (6.7)	14 (1.5)	507 (12.2)
New Zealand	491 (5.2)	493 (5.0)	478 (4.2)	497 (4.7)	497 (5.0)	496 (5.3)	14 (0.9)	444 (6.7)	66 (1.2)	507 (5.3)	20 (1.2)	480 (6.6)
Philippines	345 (6.0)	378 (6.3)	383 (3.4)	345 (5.8)	406 (3.5)	355 (6.2)	5 (0.4)	288 (13.2)	42 (0.8)	363 (6.2)	53 (0.8)	347 (6.7)
Romania	472 (5.8)	458 (5.7)	487 (6.4)	481 (5.2)	453 (4.7)	491 (4.9)	9 (0.7)	417 (7.7)	25 (1.5)	457 (6.2)	66 (1.8)	494 (5.4)
Russian Federation	526 (5.9)	513 (6.4)	522 (6.0)	529 (4.9)	501 (4.8)	527 (6.0)	6 (0.5)	483 (10.0)	49 (1.3)	537 (6.7)	45 (1.5)	530 (5.2)
Singapore	604 (6.3)	608 (5.6)	560 (6.7)	576 (6.2)	562 (6.2)	599 (6.3)	5 (0.5)	562 (10.7)	34 (1.0)	612 (7.6)	61 (1.1)	604 (5.7)
Slovak Republic	534 (4.0)	525 (4.8)	527 (7.3)	525 (4.6)	521 (4.6)	537 (3.3)	6 (0.6)	535 (8.3)	70 (0.8)	542 (3.9)	23 (0.9)	513 (4.7)
Slovenia	530 (2.8)	527 (3.7)	506 (6.2)	525 (2.9)	530 (4.2)	523 (3.7)	8 (0.7)	530 (7.7)	63 (1.1)	541 (3.3)	29 (1.0)	511 (4.1)
South Africa	275 (6.8)	300 (6.0)	335 (6.6)	293 (7.7)	356 (3.8)	329 (4.8)	10 (0.8)	241 (14.1)	37 (0.7)	293 (8.6)	53 (1.1)	273 (7.9)
Thailand	467 (5.1)	471 (5.3)	484 (4.4)	456 (4.9)	476 (4.0)	463 (6.2)	6 (0.4)	424 (5.6)	45 (1.1)	459 (5.8)	49 (1.2)	482 (5.8)
Tunisia	448 (2.4)	443 (2.8)	484 (4.4)	455 (2.7)	446 (5.1)	442 (3.1)	7 (0.5)	439 (5.3)	27 (0.8)	452 (3.4)	66 (0.9)	450 (2.9)
Turkey	429 (4.3)	430 (4.3)	428 (5.7)	432 (4.6)	446 (3.3)	436 (6.5)	6 (0.6)	398 (7.1)	41 (1.0)	422 (4.4)	52 (1.4)	448 (4.7)
United States	502 (4.0)	509 (4.2)	473 (4.4)	506 (4.1)	506 (5.2)	482 (3.9)	15 (1.1)	466 (4.8)	58 (0.7)	514 (4.0)	27 (1.1)	505 (4.5)

—Not available.

[1] SAR=Special Administrative Region.

[2] Countries not meeting all International Association for the Evaluation of Educational Achievement's sampling specifications.

NOTE: Data are for 8th-grade or equivalent in most countries. Possible scores range from 1 to 1,000. Standard errors appear in parentheses. Detail may not sum to totals due to rounding.

SOURCE: International Association for the Evaluation of Educational Achievement, Third International Mathematics and Science Study, 1999, *TIMSS 1999 International Mathematics Report*, by Ina V.S. Mullis et al. Copyright © 2000 International Association for the Evaluation of Educational Achievement (IEA). (This table was prepared May 2001.)

Pupils per teacher in public and private elementary and secondary schools, by level of education and country: Selected years, 1985 to 2001

Country	Elementary						Junior high schools (lower secondary)						Senior high schools (upper secondary)					
	1985	1990	1996	1999	2000	2001	1985	1990	1996	1999	2000	2001	1985	1990	1996	1999	2000	2001
1	2	3	4	5	6	7	8	9	10	11	12	13	14	15	16	17	18	19
Australia	[1]13.8	—	18.1	17.3	17.3	17.0	—	—	—	[2]13.7	—	—	3.2	—	—	[2]10.8	—	—
Austria	11.3	11.6	12.7	14.5	—	14.3	9.2	7.7	9.2	9.6	—	9.8	15.2	12.4	8.5	10.0	—	9.9
Belgium	—	—	—	13.9	15.0	13.4	—	—	—	—	—	—	—	—	—	—	—	—
Canada	18.1	17.1	17.0	18.7	18.1	18.3	16.0	15.5	20.0	18.7	18.1	18.4	16.0	15.3	19.5	20.0	19.5	17.2
Denmark	12.7	11.2	11.2	10.6	10.4	10.0	10.2	9.3	10.1	11.6	11.4	11.1	14.8	13.3	12.1	13.2	14.4	13.9
France	—	—	19.5	19.6	19.8	19.5	—	—	—	12.9	14.7	13.5	—	—	—	12.7	10.4	11.2
Germany[3]	20.7	20.3	20.9	21.0	19.8	19.4	16.9	14.6	16.0	16.4	15.7	15.7	23.7	21.0	13.1	12.4	13.9	13.7
Ireland	—	—	22.6	21.6	21.5	20.3	—	—	—	15.9	15.2	—	7.2	8.3	—	—	—	—
Italy	12.8	10.7	11.2	11.3	11.0	10.8	9.6	8.5	10.8	10.3	10.4	9.9	10.8	10.7	9.8	10.2	10.2	10.4
Japan	—	[1]20.8	19.7	21.2	20.9	20.6	—	18.6	16.2	17.1	16.8	16.6	—	16.2	15.6	14.1	14.0	14.0
Netherlands	20.2	19.2	20.0	16.6	16.8	17.2	12.7	12.4	—	—	—	—	—	—	—	—	—	—
New Zealand	20.1	19.1	22.0	20.5	20.6	19.6	—	—	18.1	19.8	19.9	18.7	—	—	14.1	12.8	13.1	12.8
Norway	—	—	—	12.6	11.6	11.6	—	—	—	10.1	9.9	9.3	—	—	—	9.9	9.7	9.2
Portugal	—	—	—	—	12.1	11.6	—	—	—	—	10.4	9.9	—	—	—	—	7.9	8.0
Spain	26.8	21.2	18.0	15.4	14.9	14.7	21.4	18.8	17.8	—	—	—	15.3	14.8	14.2	—	—	—
Sweden	11.6	10.6	12.7	13.3	12.8	12.4	10.8	10.2	12.2	13.3	12.8	12.4	13.1	11.9	15.2	15.5	15.2	16.6
Turkey	31.1	30.6	—	30.0	30.5	29.8	41.3	48.4	—	—	—	—	11.0	12.1	—	16.1	14.0	17.2
United Kingdom	19.7	22.0	21.3	22.5	21.2	20.5	—	18.5	16.0	17.4	[2]17.6	[2]17.3	11.1	13.9	15.3	[2]12.4	[2]12.5	[2]12.3
United States	17.0	15.6	16.9	16.3	15.8	16.3	16.5	15.9	17.5	16.8	16.3	17.0	16.2	15.8	14.7	14.5	14.1	14.8

—Not available.

[1] Public schools only.

[2] Includes only general programs.

[3] Data for 1985 are for the former West Germany.

SOURCE: Organization for Economic Cooperation and Development (OECD), *Education at a Glance,* selected years 1985 to 2001; and previously unpublished tabulations. (This table was prepared September 2003.)

Average 8th-grade science scores, by content areas, average time spent studying out of school, and country: 1999

Country	Overall science scores	Earth science	Life science	Physics	Chemistry	Environmental and resource issues	Scientific inquiry and the nature of science	No time Percent	No time Mean score	Less than 1 hour Percent	Less than 1 hour Mean score	One hour or more Percent	One hour or more Mean score
1	2	3	4	5	6	7	8	9	10	11	12	13	14
International average	488 (0.7)	488 (0.9)	488 (0.7)	488 (0.9)	488 (0.8)	488 (0.7)	488 (0.7)	14 (0.2)	462 (1.2)	49 (0.2)	495 (1.0)	36 (0.2)	486 (1.0)
Australia	540 (4.4)	519 (6.1)	530 (4.4)	531 (6.3)	520 (5.0)	530 (6.3)	535 (4.9)	21 (1.4)	510 (6.6)	65 (1.4)	553 (4.4)	14 (0.8)	533 (6.9)
Belgium (Flemish)	535 (3.1)	533 (3.5)	535 (4.6)	530 (3.5)	508 (3.3)	513 (3.5)	526 (4.9)	14 (1.1)	537 (8.7)	55 (1.2)	543 (4.0)	31 (1.4)	520 (3.9)
Bulgaria	518 (5.4)	520 (5.7)	514 (6.9)	505 (5.8)	527 (5.7)	483 (6.4)	479 (5.6)	17 (1.6)	505 (8.7)	38 (1.2)	523 (6.7)	45 (1.5)	528 (7.0)
Canada	533 (2.1)	519 (3.7)	523 (3.8)	521 (3.8)	521 (5.4)	521 (3.5)	532 (5.1)	20 (1.0)	525 (4.1)	62 (0.9)	541 (2.3)	18 (0.7)	515 (4.4)
Chile	420 (3.7)	435 (7.0)	431 (3.7)	428 (5.6)	435 (5.2)	449 (4.8)	441 (4.7)	17 (0.7)	415 (4.9)	53 (0.8)	431 (4.7)	30 (1.0)	417 (5.4)
Chinese Taipei	569 (4.4)	538 (3.0)	550 (3.3)	552 (3.9)	563 (4.3)	567 (4.0)	540 (4.9)	38 (1.3)	530 (5.7)	42 (0.9)	588 (4.4)	20 (0.9)	607 (4.7)
Cyprus	460 (2.4)	459 (5.4)	468 (3.8)	459 (2.9)	470 (4.6)	475 (4.3)	467 (4.6)	18 (0.7)	425 (6.6)	57 (0.9)	474 (3.1)	25 (1.0)	461 (5.0)
Czech Republic	539 (4.2)	533 (6.9)	544 (4.1)	526 (4.2)	512 (5.2)	516 (5.7)	522 (5.7)	18 (1.1)	529 (7.0)	62 (1.2)	546 (4.5)	20 (1.1)	530 (5.0)
England	538 (4.8)	525 (3.9)	533 (6.2)	528 (4.5)	524 (5.5)	518 (5.8)	538 (5.1)	— (—)	— (—)	— (—)	— (—)	— (—)	— (—)
Finland	535 (3.5)	520 (5.5)	520 (4.0)	520 (4.4)	535 (4.5)	514 (7.1)	528 (4.0)	8 (0.8)	514 (9.7)	84 (0.9)	541 (3.5)	8 (0.6)	511 (10.8)
Hong Kong, SAR [1]	530 (3.7)	506 (4.3)	516 (5.5)	523 (4.9)	515 (5.2)	518 (4.9)	531 (2.8)	39 (1.3)	513 (4.2)	48 (1.0)	543 (4.0)	13 (0.6)	539 (6.6)
Hungary	552 (3.7)	560 (3.9)	535 (4.0)	543 (4.3)	548 (4.7)	501 (6.6)	526 (5.9)	6 (0.6)	505 (8.6)	49 (1.2)	558 (4.0)	45 (1.3)	554 (4.0)
Indonesia	435 (4.5)	431 (6.4)	448 (3.6)	452 (5.5)	425 (3.9)	489 (4.8)	446 (4.3)	13 (0.8)	432 (6.7)	40 (0.9)	442 (4.9)	47 (1.1)	435 (5.9)
Iran, Islamic Republic	448 (3.8)	459 (5.2)	437 (3.7)	445 (5.7)	487 (4.1)	470 (5.5)	446 (5.3)	3 (0.3)	432 (16.0)	29 (1.0)	453 (4.1)	68 (1.1)	451 (4.6)
Israel [2]	468 (4.9)	472 (5.2)	463 (4.0)	484 (5.3)	479 (4.7)	458 (4.0)	476 (8.3)	17 (0.8)	449 (7.8)	60 (1.1)	487 (4.6)	23 (1.1)	450 (6.5)
Italy	493 (3.9)	502 (5.9)	488 (4.6)	480 (4.1)	493 (4.8)	491 (5.4)	489 (4.6)	7 (0.7)	435 (8.6)	48 (1.4)	501 (4.3)	45 (1.4)	498 (4.3)
Japan	550 (2.2)	533 (6.2)	534 (5.4)	544 (2.9)	530 (3.1)	506 (5.5)	543 (2.8)	39 (1.4)	535 (3.2)	50 (1.2)	560 (2.3)	12 (0.7)	555 (7.5)
Jordan	450 (3.8)	446 (3.5)	448 (4.1)	459 (3.6)	483 (5.5)	476 (6.0)	440 (5.5)	7 (0.5)	396 (9.2)	37 (1.0)	466 (5.0)	56 (1.1)	465 (3.7)
Korea, Republic of	549 (2.6)	532 (2.7)	528 (3.6)	544 (5.1)	523 (3.7)	523 (4.5)	545 (7.3)	45 (0.8)	527 (2.9)	42 (0.7)	564 (3.1)	13 (0.6)	578 (4.6)
Latvia (Latvian-speaking schools) [2]	503 (4.8)	495 (5.4)	509 (3.9)	495 (3.9)	490 (3.7)	493 (5.2)	495 (4.7)	9 (0.6)	480 (9.9)	66 (1.0)	509 (5.4)	25 (1.0)	496 (6.3)
Lithuania [2]	488 (4.1)	476 (4.4)	494 (4.6)	510 (4.3)	485 (4.6)	458 (5.1)	483 (6.4)	10 (0.9)	456 (8.2)	66 (1.2)	493 (4.8)	25 (1.2)	494 (4.9)
Macedonia, Republic of	458 (5.2)	464 (4.2)	468 (4.9)	463 (6.0)	481 (6.1)	432 (4.2)	464 (3.6)	3 (0.3)	428 (15.3)	25 (1.0)	453 (5.9)	72 (1.2)	470 (5.3)
Malaysia	492 (4.4)	491 (4.2)	479 (5.4)	494 (4.1)	485 (3.5)	502 (4.4)	488 (4.5)	4 (0.3)	460 (10.6)	36 (1.1)	493 (5.1)	60 (1.2)	495 (4.9)
Moldova	459 (4.0)	466 (4.2)	477 (3.9)	457 (5.5)	451 (5.6)	444 (6.2)	471 (3.8)	7 (0.6)	439 (10.8)	29 (1.0)	460 (5.8)	63 (1.2)	467 (4.2)
Morocco	323 (4.3)	363 (3.3)	347 (2.8)	352 (4.2)	372 (4.8)	396 (5.1)	391 (4.2)	14 (0.8)	323 (12.4)	35 (1.2)	330 (4.9)	51 (1.7)	335 (6.4)
Netherlands	545 (6.9)	534 (7.2)	536 (7.2)	537 (6.5)	515 (6.4)	526 (8.5)	534 (6.5)	6 (0.8)	530 (11.6)	80 (1.5)	555 (6.4)	15 (1.3)	507 (12.9)
New Zealand	510 (4.9)	504 (5.8)	501 (5.6)	499 (4.7)	503 (4.9)	503 (5.2)	521 (6.8)	18 (1.1)	472 (6.8)	66 (1.2)	528 (4.8)	15 (1.0)	491 (7.7)
Philippines	345 (7.5)	390 (5.0)	378 (6.7)	393 (6.3)	394 (6.5)	391 (7.6)	403 (5.5)	5 (0.4)	294 (14.4)	41 (0.8)	365 (9.7)	54 (0.9)	348 (7.7)
Romania	472 (5.8)	475 (5.5)	475 (6.0)	465 (6.8)	481 (6.1)	473 (6.6)	456 (5.5)	16 (0.9)	451 (8.4)	36 (1.0)	479 (7.8)	48 (1.3)	484 (5.6)
Russian Federation	529 (6.4)	529 (5.1)	517 (6.5)	529 (6.3)	523 (8.0)	495 (6.6)	491 (4.9)	5 (0.4)	494 (8.4)	34 (1.3)	534 (7.1)	61 (1.3)	536 (6.4)
Singapore	568 (8.0)	521 (7.3)	541 (7.2)	570 (6.7)	545 (8.3)	577 (8.3)	550 (5.9)	7 (0.6)	507 (13.2)	38 (1.1)	573 (9.9)	55 (1.2)	573 (7.1)
Slovak Republic	535 (3.3)	537 (4.3)	535 (6.2)	518 (4.1)	525 (4.9)	512 (4.5)	507 (3.9)	8 (0.7)	521 (7.5)	67 (1.2)	539 (3.7)	25 (1.2)	532 (4.8)
Slovenia	533 (3.2)	541 (4.3)	521 (3.9)	525 (4.4)	509 (5.4)	519 (4.5)	513 (4.3)	10 (0.8)	526 (6.7)	52 (1.1)	546 (3.7)	38 (1.1)	521 (4.2)
South Africa	243 (7.8)	348 (8.9)	289 (7.3)	308 (6.7)	350 (8.5)	350 (8.5)	329 (6.4)	15 (1.8)	211 (14.0)	39 (1.1)	269 (11.1)	47 (1.3)	237 (8.7)
Thailand	482 (4.0)	470 (3.9)	508 (4.5)	475 (4.2)	439 (4.3)	507 (3.0)	462 (4.2)	8 (0.5)	455 (4.8)	50 (1.1)	480 (4.8)	42 (1.2)	493 (5.2)
Tunisia	430 (3.4)	442 (2.7)	441 (5.0)	425 (6.3)	439 (3.7)	462 (5.0)	451 (3.4)	13 (0.8)	438 (8.2)	39 (0.9)	434 (5.3)	48 (1.0)	425 (2.8)
Turkey	433 (4.3)	435 (4.6)	444 (4.5)	441 (4.0)	437 (5.0)	461 (3.6)	445 (6.3)	6 (0.5)	409 (12.9)	44 (0.9)	433 (4.0)	51 (1.2)	444 (4.4)
United States	515 (4.6)	504 (4.2)	520 (4.1)	498 (5.5)	508 (4.8)	509 (6.4)	522 (4.3)	24 (1.4)	495 (6.4)	60 (1.3)	532 (4.6)	16 (0.8)	502 (5.9)

—Not available.

[1] SAR=Special Administrative Region.

[2] Countries not meeting all International Association for the Evaluation of Educational Achievement's sampling specifications.

NOTE: Data are for 8th-grade or equivalent in most countries. Possible scores range from 1 to 1,000. Detail may not sum to totals due to rounding. Standard errors appear in parentheses.

SOURCE: International Association for the Evaluation of Educational Achievement, Third International Mathematics and Science Study 1999, TIMSS 1999 International Science Report, by Michael O. Martin et al. Copyright © 2000. International Association for the Evaluation of Educational Achievement (IEA). (This table was prepared June 2001.)

Number of bachelor's degree recipients per 100 persons of the theoretical age of graduation, by sex and country: Selected years, 1989 to 2000

Country	Men and women							Men					Women				
	1989	1990	1992	1995	1996	1999	2000	1989	1990	1992	1995	1996	1989	1990	1992	1995	1996
1	2	3	4	5	6	7	8	9	10	11	12	13	14	15	16	17	18
Australia	19.6	—	28.5	34.9	36.0	27.0	36.3	18.9	—	23.7	27.6	28.9	21.1	—	33.6	42.7	43.3
Austria	6.6	7.7	—	9.8	10.5	12.0	16.0	7.6	8.5	—	10.6	11.4	5.5	6.8	—	8.9	9.6
Belgium [1]	16.5	17.1	—	—	15.9	17.8	—	18.9	19.5	—	—	16.7	14.1	14.7	—	—	15.2
Canada	—	—	32.2	31.8	31.9	29.3	27.9	—	—	27.6	26.4	26.5	—	—	37.6	37.4	37.4
Czech Republic	—	—	—	—	—	10.8	13.6	—	—	—	—	—	—	—	—	—	—
Denmark	12.9	15.0	22.3	28.5	28.0	—	9.2	11.5	13.3	17.7	25.1	23.1	14.4	16.9	27.2	31.9	33.0
Finland	16.9	17.1	—	22.2	23.9	33.9	36.3	17.1	17.0	—	22.0	22.4	16.6	17.1	17.9	22.3	25.6
France	13.8	14.9	—	—	—	24.9	24.6	13.7	14.7	—	—	—	13.9	15.1	—	—	—
Germany [2]	13.2	12.9	—	16.2	16.1	16.0	19.3	16.1	15.7	—	18.2	18.2	10.1	10.0	—	14.0	13.5
Hungary	—	—	—	—	—	26.9	—	—	—	—	—	—	—	—	—	—	—
Iceland	—	—	—	—	—	28.9	33.2	—	—	—	—	—	—	—	—	—	—
Ireland	16.4	17.4	17.8	21.2	25.5	26.0	31.2	31.9	17.5	17.9	19.9	24.6	—	17.3	17.7	22.7	26.4
Italy	8.9	9.2	—	11.8	12.6	16.0	18.1	9.1	9.3	—	10.8	11.4	8.7	9.0	—	12.9	13.8
Japan	—	22.1	23.2	22.8	22.9	29.0	30.9	—	31.5	31.9	30.4	30.7	—	12.4	14.0	14.9	14.9
Korea, Republic of	—	—	—	—	—	27.1	—	—	—	—	—	—	—	—	—	—	—
Mexico	—	—	—	—	—	11.2	—	—	—	—	—	—	—	—	—	—	—
Netherlands	10.2	8.0	17.6	22.0	19.6	33.5	—	12.3	9.4	17.3	20.6	18.2	7.9	6.5	17.8	23.4	21.1
New Zealand	36.1	15.3	17.2	24.7	30.8	37.3	—	16.6	15.4	16.9	20.9	26.2	15.5	15.1	17.4	28.6	35.4
Norway	24.6	27.5	19.0	23.0	27.4	33.9	—	18.1	19.1	14.5	17.2	20.2	31.7	36.3	23.7	28.9	34.8
Portugal	—	7.6	—	14.6	15.7	—	—	—	5.9	—	10.8	11.3	—	9.3	—	18.3	20.2
Spain	17.7	18.6	—	24.0	26.1	30.3	—	14.6	15.3	—	19.6	21.5	21.0	22.0	—	28.6	31.0
Sweden	13.0	12.2	14.1	15.5	19.1	27.2	28.1	11.1	10.5	11.8	14.0	15.1	15.1	14.0	16.4	17.0	23.3
Switzerland	7.7	7.7	—	9.1	9.3	20.5	10.4	10.1	10.3	—	11.4	11.5	5.3	5.1	—	6.8	7.2
Turkey	6.0	6.1	6.1	7.0	—	9.6	—	7.3	7.5	7.5	8.6	—	4.6	4.5	4.6	5.2	—
United Kingdom	—	—	20.4	31.6	34.4	36.8	37.5	—	—	21.0	30.3	32.7	—	—	19.8	32.9	36.2
United States	27.3	28.6	27.4	33.2	34.7	33.2	33.2	25.5	26.2	24.6	29.3	30.6	29.2	31.1	30.3	37.3	38.9

—Not available.

[1] Data for Flemish Belgium only.

[2] Data for 1989 are for the former West Germany.

NOTE: The graduation rate relates the number of people with bachelor's degrees to the number of people in the population at the typical age of graduation. Data for 1999 and 2000 reflect a reclassification of degree levels and may not be comparable to figures for earlier years.

SOURCE: Organization for Economic Cooperation and Development, *Education at a Glance 2002*, and previously unpublished tabulations. (This table was prepared August 2003.)

Percent of bachelor's degrees awarded in science, by field and country: Selected years, 1985 to 2000

Country	All science degrees					Natural sciences					Mathematics and computer science					Engineering				
	1985	1990	1995	1999	2000	1985	1990	1995	1999	2000	1985	1990	1995	1999	2000	1985	1990	1995	1999	2000
1	2	3	4	5	6	7	8	9	10	11	12	13	14	15	16	17	18	19	20	21
Australia	—	—	19.3	19.4	21.1	—	—	9.9	7.0	7.6	—	—	3.8	4.5	5.1	—	—	5.6	7.9	8.5
Austria	16.8	19.6	21.1	26.0	25.7	5.0	5.3	6.0	6.3	5.0	4.1	5.2	5.3	3.2	3.4	7.7	9.0	9.9	16.5	17.3
Belgium [1]	—	—	—	25.3	—	4.6	—	—	6.1	—	1.7	—	—	2.3	—	—	—	—	17.0	—
Canada	17.1	16.4	16.7	19.7	20.0	4.9	6.0	6.5	8.2	8.1	4.5	4.2	3.8	4.0	4.3	7.7	6.2	6.4	7.5	7.6
Czech Republic	—	—	—	29.3	29.5	—	—	—	3.8	4.2	—	—	—	3.0	8.4	—	—	—	22.5	16.9
Denmark	—	—	—	—	10.5	6.3	4.4	2.5	—	6.8	—	—	—	—	3.1	16.2	21.7	17.0	—	0.6
Finland	39.3	33.5	37.2	33.2	32.2	7.7	4.1	4.0	0.6	3.9	6.3	5.9	6.9	2.4	3.3	25.3	23.4	26.3	30.2	24.9
France	—	—	—	27.1	30.1	—	—	—	—	12.2	—	—	—	—	5.5	—	—	—	12.5	12.5
Germany [2]	23.8	31.3	31.6	33.5	31.7	5.0	7.2	6.7	6.9	6.4	2.3	3.5	5.2	5.2	4.9	16.5	20.5	19.7	21.4	20.3
Hungary	—	—	—	17.3	12.6	—	—	—	1.1	1.1	—	—	—	1.3	1.2	—	—	—	14.9	10.4
Iceland	—	—	—	13.6	16.5	—	—	—	6.1	6.0	—	—	—	2.6	4.0	—	—	—	4.9	6.5
Ireland	28.8	34.1	32.3	25.8	29.3	12.8	14.1	16.9	8.8	11.5	4.0	6.3	4.7	7.1	7.2	12.0	13.7	10.7	10.0	10.6
Italy	19.5	19.7	19.5	27.6	27.5	8.1	7.6	6.8	6.0	5.9	3.1	3.9	3.8	3.4	3.2	8.3	8.3	8.9	18.2	18.4
Japan	22.7	23.5	22.8	18.9	18.9	2.4	2.4	3.4	—	—	—	—	—	—	—	20.3	21.0	19.3	18.9	18.9
Korea, Republic of	—	—	—	36.7	36.9	—	—	—	6.3	6.3	—	—	—	4.5	4.3	—	—	—	25.9	26.3
Mexico	—	—	—	22.9	23.0	—	—	—	2.1	2.2	—	—	—	7.0	6.7	—	—	—	13.8	14.1
Netherlands	21.8	21.1	—	16.5	16.2	8.5	7.1	—	3.2	3.2	1.2	1.6	1.6	1.7	1.9	12.1	12.4	—	11.6	11.1
New Zealand	20.5	19.5	—	18.6	17.8	11.7	8.2	—	12.1	11.2	5.5	5.5	—	1.6	1.9	3.3	5.8	3.2	5.0	4.7
Norway	—	12.9	16.8	12.8	11.6	2.5	2.1	3.1	0.8	0.7	1.8	0.6	0.5	2.8	3.4	—	10.2	13.2	9.3	7.5
Poland	—	—	—	16.5	16.7	—	—	—	2.1	2.7	—	—	—	1.8	2.0	—	—	—	12.6	12.0
Portugal	—	—	15.0	—	17.5	6.5	6.7	2.2	—	1.7	—	—	2.8	—	3.6	—	10.5	9.9	—	12.2
Spain	13.9	15.0	18.2	21.0	22.7	5.5	5.7	4.3	4.8	5.3	1.3	2.6	4.5	3.9	4.3	7.0	6.7	9.4	12.3	13.1
Sweden	15.4	24.0	26.4	25.0	27.7	2.6	4.1	3.9	3.6	3.7	1.6	4.7	5.5	3.0	3.7	11.3	15.2	17.0	18.4	20.3
Switzerland	20.2	23.0	22.3	25.1	25.1	10.3	11.2	10.4	6.5	6.0	2.1	3.7	3.7	1.8	1.8	7.9	8.1	8.3	16.8	17.3
Turkey	23.0	20.6	20.9	24.2	24.1	3.6	4.6	5.1	7.1	7.4	1.6	2.1	2.7	3.7	3.6	17.8	13.8	13.1	13.4	13.1
United Kingdom	—	—	—	28.9	28.5	—	—	—	9.8	12.5	—	—	—	6.4	5.8	—	—	—	12.7	10.2
United States	21.7	16.9	—	17.4	17.1	6.3	5.1	—	7.2	6.6	5.5	4.0	3.3	3.3	3.9	9.8	7.8	6.7	6.9	6.6

—Not available.

[1] Data for the Flemish Belgium only.

[2] Data for 1985 are for the former West Germany.

SOURCE: Organization for Economic Cooperation and Development, previously unpublished tabulations. (This table was prepared May 2003.)

645

Foreign students enrolled in institutions of higher education in the United States and outlying areas, by continent, region, and selected countries of origin: Selected years, 1980–81 to 2001–02

Continent, region, and country	1980–81		1985–86		1990–91		1995–96		1998–99		1999–2000		2000–01		2001–02	
	Number	Per-cent	Number	Per-cent	Number	Per-cent	Number	Per-cent	Number	Per-cent	Number	Per-cent	Number	Per-cent	Number	Per-cent
1	2	3	4	5	6	7	8	9	10	11	12	13	14	15	16	17
Total	311,880	100.0	343,780	100.0	407,530	100.0	453,787	100.00	490,933	100.0	514,723	100.0	547,867	100.0	582,996	100.0
Africa	38,180	12.2	34,190	9.9	23,800	5.8	20,844	4.59	26,222	5.3	30,292	5.9	34,217	6.2	37,724	6.5
Eastern Africa	6,260	2.0	6,730	2.0	7,590	1.9	7,596	1.67	10,189	2.1	11,559	2.2	13,516	2.5	15,331	2.6
Central Africa	1,130	0.4	1,540	0.4	1,650	0.4	1,346	0.30	1,413	0.3	1,775	0.3	1,859	0.3	1,972	0.3
North Africa	7,310	2.3	5,980	1.7	4,540	1.1	3,422	0.75	4,151	0.8	4,525	0.9	5,184	0.9	5,593	1.0
Southern Africa	1,480	0.5	2,360	0.7	2,840	0.7	2,657	0.59	2,956	0.6	3,247	0.6	3,304	0.6	3,443	0.6
West Africa	22,000	7.1	17,580	5.1	7,180	1.8	5,818	1.28	7,513	1.5	9,176	1.8	10,346	1.9	11,385	2.0
Nigeria	17,350	5.6	13,710	4.0	3,710	0.9	2,093	0.46	2,876	0.6	3,602	0.7	3,820	0.7	4,499	0.8
Asia	94,640	30.3	156,830	45.6	229,830	56.4	259,893	57.27	275,076	56.0	280,146	54.4	302,058	55.1	324,812	55.7
East Asia	51,650	16.6	80,720	23.5	146,020	35.8	166,717	36.74	177,141	36.1	180,146	35.0	189,371	34.6	196,813	33.8
China	2,770	0.9	13,980	4.1	39,600	9.7	39,613	8.73	51,001	10.4	54,466	10.6	59,939	10.9	63,211	10.8
Hong Kong	9,660	3.1	10,710	3.1	12,630	3.1	12,018	2.65	8,735	1.8	7,545	1.5	7,627	1.4	7,757	1.3
Japan	13,500	4.3	13,360	3.9	36,610	9.0	45,531	10.03	46,406	9.5	46,872	9.1	46,497	8.5	46,810	8.0
Korea, Republic of	6,150	2.0	18,660	5.4	23,360	5.7	36,231	7.98	39,199	8.0	41,191	8.0	45,685	8.3	49,046	8.4
Taiwan	19,460	6.2	23,770	6.9	33,530	8.2	32,702	7.21	31,043	6.3	29,234	5.7	28,566	5.2	28,930	5.0
South and Central Asia	14,540	4.7	25,800	7.5	42,370	10.4	45,401	10.00	52,602	10.7	58,148	11.3	71,765	13.1	86,131	14.8
India	9,250	3.0	16,070	4.7	28,860	7.1	31,743	7.00	37,482	7.6	42,337	8.2	54,664	10.0	66,836	11.5
Pakistan	2,990	1.0	5,440	1.6	7,730	1.9	6,427	1.42	5,905	1.2	6,107	1.2	6,948	1.3	8,644	1.5
South East Asia	28,450	9.1	50,310	14.6	41,440	10.2	47,774	10.53	45,333	9.2	41,852	8.1	40,916	7.5	41,868	7.2
Indonesia	3,250	1.0	8,210	2.4	9,520	2.3	12,820	2.83	12,142	2.5	11,300	2.2	11,625	2.1	11,614	2.0
Malaysia	6,010	1.9	23,020	6.7	13,610	3.3	14,015	3.09	11,557	2.4	9,074	1.8	7,795	1.4	7,395	1.3
Philippines	—	—	3,920	1.1	4,270	1.0	3,127	0.69	2,864	0.6	3,143	0.6	3,139	0.6	3,295	0.6
Singapore	—	—	3,930	1.1	4,500	1.1	4,098	0.90	4,030	0.8	4,250	0.8	4,166	0.8	4,141	0.7
Thailand	6,550	2.1	6,940	2.0	7,090	1.7	12,165	2.68	12,489	2.5	10,983	2.1	11,187	2.0	11,606	2.0
Europe	25,330	8.1	34,310	10.0	49,640	12.2	67,358	14.84	73,809	15.0	78,485	15.2	80,584	14.7	81,579	14.0
Eastern Europe	1,670	0.5	1,770	0.5	4,780	1.2	18,032	3.97	23,131	4.7	25,731	5.0	27,674	5.1	29,591	5.1
Western Europe	23,660	7.6	32,540	9.5	44,860	11.0	49,326	10.87	50,674	10.3	52,754	10.2	52,910	9.7	51,988	8.9
France	—	—	3,680	1.1	5,630	1.4	5,710	1.26	6,241	1.3	6,877	1.3	7,273	1.3	7,401	1.3
Germany [1]	3,310	1.1	4,730	1.4	7,000	1.7	9,017	1.99	9,568	1.9	9,800	1.9	10,128	1.8	9,613	1.6
Greece	3,750	1.2	4,440	1.3	4,360	1.1	3,365	0.74	2,847	0.6	2,782	0.5	2,768	0.5	2,599	0.4
Spain	—	—	1,740	0.5	4,300	1.1	4,809	1.06	4,195	0.9	4,337	0.8	4,156	0.8	4,048	0.7
United Kingdom	4,440	1.4	5,940	1.7	7,300	1.8	7,799	1.72	7,765	1.6	7,990	1.6	8,139	1.5	8,414	1.4
Latin America	49,810	16.0	45,480	13.2	47,580	11.7	47,253	10.41	55,436	11.3	62,098	12.1	63,634	11.6	68,358	11.7
Caribbean	10,650	3.4	11,100	3.2	12,610	3.1	10,737	2.37	11,884	2.4	13,828	2.7	14,423	2.6	13,879	2.4
Central America	12,970	4.2	12,740	3.7	15,950	3.9	14,220	3.13	15,455	3.1	16,854	3.3	16,764	3.1	18,826	3.2
Mexico	6,730	2.2	5,460	1.6	6,740	1.7	8,687	1.91	9,641	2.0	10,607	2.1	10,670	1.9	12,518	2.1
South America	26,190	8.4	21,640	6.3	19,020	4.7	22,296	4.91	28,097	5.7	31,416	6.1	32,447	5.9	35,653	6.1
Brazil	—	—	2,840	0.8	3,900	1.0	5,497	1.21	8,052	1.6	8,600	1.7	8,846	1.6	8,972	1.5
Colombia	—	—	4,010	1.2	3,180	0.8	3,462	0.76	5,041	1.0	6,277	1.2	6,765	1.2	8,068	1.4
Venezuela	11,750	3.8	7,040	2.0	2,890	0.7	4,456	0.98	5,133	1.0	5,125	1.0	5,217	1.0	5,627	1.0
Middle East	84,710	27.2	52,720	15.3	33,420	8.2	30,563	6.74	32,836	6.7	34,897	6.8	36,858	6.7	38,545	6.6
Iran	47,550	15.2	14,210	4.1	6,260	1.5	2,628	0.58	1,660	0.3	1,885	0.4	1,844	0.3	2,216	0.4
Jordan	6,140	2.0	6,590	1.9	4,320	1.1	2,222	0.49	2,039	0.4	2,074	0.4	2,187	0.4	2,417	0.4
Lebanon	6,770	2.2	7,090	2.1	3,900	1.0	1,554	0.34	1,315	0.3	1,582	0.3	2,005	0.4	2,435	0.4
Saudi Arabia	10,440	3.3	6,900	2.0	3,590	0.9	4,191	0.92	4,931	1.0	5,156	1.0	5,273	1.0	5,579	1.0
Turkey	—	—	2,460	0.7	4,080	1.0	7,678	1.69	9,377	1.9	10,100	2.0	10,983	2.0	12,091	2.1
North America [2]	14,790	4.7	16,030	4.7	18,950	4.6	23,644	5.21	23,302	4.7	24,128	4.7	25,888	4.7	27,039	4.6
Canada	14,320	4.6	15,410	4.5	18,350	4.5	23,005	5.07	22,746	4.6	23,544	4.6	25,279	4.6	26,514	4.5
Oceania	4,180	1.3	4,030	1.2	4,230	1.0	4,202	0.93	4,228	0.9	4,676	0.9	4,624	0.8	4,852	0.8
Stateless [3]	240	0.1	190	0.1	80	#	30	#	28	#	7	#	10	#	87	#

—Not available.
Rounds to zero.

[1] Data for 1980–81 and 1985–86 are for West Germany (Federal Republic of Germany before unification).
[2] Excludes Mexico and Central America, which are included with Latin America.
[3] Home country unknown or undeclared.

NOTE: Totals and subtotals include other countries not shown separately. Data are for "nonimmigrants," i.e., students who have not migrated to this country. Detail may not sum to totals due to rounding.

SOURCE: Institute of International Education, "Open Doors," various years. (Latest edition copyright © 2002 by the Institute of International Education. All rights reserved.) (This table was prepared July 2003.)

Total public direct expenditures on education as a percentage of the gross domestic product, by level and country: Selected years, 1985 to 2000

Country	All institutions [1]					Primary and secondary institutions					Higher education institutions				
	1985	1990	1995	1999	2000	1985	1990	1995	1999	2000	1985	1990	1995	1999	2000
1	2	3	4	5	6	7	8	9	10	11	12	13	14	15	16
Average for year	5.3	4.9	4.9	5.1	5.2	3.7	3.5	3.4	3.5	3.5	1.1	1.0	0.9	1.2	1.2
Average for countries reporting data for all years	5.4	5.2	5.3	5.6	5.4	3.7	3.7	3.6	3.7	3.6	1.1	1.1	1.1	1.4	1.4
Australia	5.4	4.3	4.5	5.0	5.1	3.5	3.2	3.2	3.8	3.9	1.7	1.0	1.2	1.2	1.2
Austria	5.6	5.2	5.3	6.3	5.8	3.7	3.6	3.8	4.1	3.8	1.0	1.0	0.9	1.7	1.4
Belgium [2]	6.3	4.8	5.0	5.5	5.2	4.0	3.4	3.4	3.5	3.4	1.0	0.8	0.9	1.5	1.3
Canada	6.1	5.4	5.8	5.7	5.5	4.1	3.7	4.0	3.5	3.3	2.0	1.5	1.5	1.9	2.0
Czech Republic	—	—	4.8	4.4	4.4	—	—	3.4	3.0	3.0	—	—	0.7	0.8	0.8
Denmark	6.2	6.2	6.5	8.1	8.4	4.7	4.4	4.2	4.8	4.8	1.2	1.3	1.3	2.4	2.5
Finland	5.8	6.4	6.6	6.2	6.0	—	4.3	4.2	3.8	3.6	—	1.2	1.7	2.1	2.0
France	—	5.1	5.8	6.0	5.8	—	3.7	4.1	4.2	4.1	—	0.8	1.0	1.1	1.0
Germany [3]	4.6	—	4.5	4.7	4.5	2.8	—	2.9	3.0	3.0	1.0	—	1.0	1.1	1.1
Greece	—	—	3.7	3.6	3.8	—	—	2.8	2.4	2.7	—	—	0.8	1.1	0.9
Hungary	—	5.0	4.9	4.7	4.9	—	3.5	3.3	2.9	3.1	—	0.8	0.8	0.9	1.0
Iceland	—	4.3	4.5	—	6.0	—	3.3	3.4	—	4.7	—	0.6	0.7	—	1.1
Ireland	5.6	4.7	4.7	4.3	4.4	4.0	3.3	3.3	3.1	3.0	0.9	0.9	0.9	1.2	1.3
Italy	4.7	5.8	4.5	4.5	4.6	3.2	4.1	3.2	3.2	3.2	0.6	1.0	0.7	0.8	0.8
Japan	—	3.6	3.6	3.5	3.6	—	2.9	2.8	2.7	2.7	—	0.4	0.4	0.5	0.5
Korea, Republic of	—	—	3.6	4.1	4.3	—	—	3.0	3.2	3.3	—	—	0.3	0.6	0.7
Luxembourg	—	—	4.3	—	—	—	—	4.2	—	—	—	—	0.1	—	—
Mexico	—	3.2	4.6	4.4	4.9	—	2.2	3.4	3.1	3.4	—	0.7	0.8	0.8	0.9
Netherlands	6.2	5.7	4.6	4.8	4.8	4.1	3.6	3.0	3.1	3.2	1.5	1.6	1.1	1.3	1.3
New Zealand	—	5.5	5.3	6.3	7.0	—	3.9	3.8	4.8	4.9	—	1.2	1.1	1.2	1.7
Norway	5.1	6.2	6.8	7.4	6.7	4.0	4.1	4.1	4.3	3.9	0.7	1.1	1.5	2.0	1.7
Poland	—	—	5.2	5.2	5.2	—	—	3.3	3.6	3.8	—	—	0.8	0.8	0.8
Portugal	—	—	5.4	5.7	5.7	—	—	4.1	4.2	4.2	—	—	1.0	1.0	1.0
Russian Federation	—	—	3.4	[4]3.0	3.0	—	—	1.9	—	1.7	—	—	0.7	—	0.5
Spain	3.6	4.2	4.8	4.5	4.4	2.9	3.2	3.5	3.3	3.1	0.4	0.7	0.8	0.9	1.0
Sweden	—	5.3	6.6	7.7	7.4	—	4.4	4.4	5.1	4.9	—	1.0	1.6	2.1	2.0
Switzerland	4.9	5.0	5.5	5.5	5.4	4.0	3.7	4.1	4.0	3.9	0.9	1.0	1.1	1.2	1.2
Turkey	—	3.2	2.2	4.0	3.5	—	2.3	1.4	2.9	2.4	—	0.9	0.8	1.1	1.1
United Kingdom	4.9	4.3	4.6	4.7	4.8	3.1	3.5	3.8	3.3	3.4	1.0	0.7	0.7	1.1	1.0
United States	4.7	5.3	5.0	5.2	5.0	3.2	3.8	3.5	3.5	3.5	1.3	1.4	1.1	1.4	1.1

—Not available.

[1] Includes preprimary and other expenditures not classified by level.

[2] Data are for Flemish Belgium only.

[3] Data for 1985 are for the former West Germany.

[4] Data are for 2000.

NOTE: Direct public expenditure on educational services includes both amounts spent directly by governments to hire educational personnel and to procure other resources, and amounts provided by governments to public or private institutions, or households. Figures for 1985 also include transfers and payments to private entities, and thus are not strictly comparable with later figures. Some data revised from previously published figures.

SOURCE: Organization for Economic Cooperation and Development (OECD), *Education Database; Annual National Accounts*, Vol. 1, 1997; and *Education at a Glance*, 2000 through 2003. (This table was prepared September 2003.)

Public libraries, books and serial volumes, library visits, and reference transactions, by state: Fiscal year 2001

State	Number of public libraries, excluding branches	Number of books and serial volumes[1] (in thousands)	Number of books and serial volumes per capita	Library visits per capita[2]	Circulation per capita	Public library reference transactions per capita[3]	State	Number of public libraries, excluding branches	Number of books and serial volumes[1] (in thousands)	Number of books and serial volumes per capita	Library visits per capita[2]	Circulation per capita	Public library reference transactions per capita[3]
1	2	3	4	5	6	7	1	2	3	4	5	6	7
United States	9,129	767,055	2.8	4.3	6.5	1.1							
Alabama	207	8,801	2.0	2.8	3.6	0.6	Missouri	150	18,716	3.7	4.4	7.6	1.2
Alaska	86	2,264	3.6	4.5	5.8	0.5	Montana	79	2,625	2.9	3.9	5.3	0.6
Arizona	35	8,760	1.7	4.1	6.5	0.9	Nebraska	272	6,004	4.6	5.1	8.6	0.8
Arkansas	43	5,497	2.1	2.8	4.1	0.6	Nevada	23	4,382	2.2	3.9	5.1	0.7
California	179	67,219	1.9	3.9	5.0	1.1	New Hampshire	229	5,572	4.6	4.7	7.1	0.7
Colorado	116	11,071	2.6	6.4	10.4	1.4	New Jersey	309	31,035	3.7	5.0	5.9	0.9
Connecticut	194	14,109	4.1	6.1	8.4	1.1	New Mexico	80	4,132	2.6	3.5	4.9	0.7
Delaware	37	1,468	1.9	3.5	5.8	0.7	New York	750	78,546	4.4	5.9	7.2	1.8
District of Columbia	1	2,472	4.3	3.5	2.1	2.1	North Carolina	76	15,916	2.0	3.6	5.4	0.9
Florida	72	29,826	1.8	3.6	5.0	1.5	North Dakota	82	2,158	3.9	4.0	7.1	0.7
Georgia	57	15,143	1.9	3.2	4.6	0.9	Ohio	250	47,088	4.1	6.3	13.8	1.6
Hawaii	1	3,195	2.6	4.6	5.6	0.8	Oklahoma	115	6,316	2.2	4.7	5.4	0.7
Idaho	106	3,577	3.1	5.5	7.7	0.7	Oregon	125	8,476	2.7	5.9	12.2	0.8
Illinois	629	41,620	3.7	5.4	7.4	1.5	Pennsylvania	459	28,061	2.3	3.3	4.7	0.8
Indiana	239	22,145	3.9	5.9	11.1	1.3	Rhode Island	48	3,997	3.8	5.4	6.3	0.8
Iowa	537	11,450	4.0	5.1	8.7	0.7	South Carolina	41	8,260	2.1	3.6	4.5	1.1
Kansas	321	10,438	4.7	5.5	9.6	1.2	South Dakota	126	2,835	4.8	5.5	8.0	0.9
Kentucky	116	7,891	2.0	3.4	5.2	0.5	Tennessee	184	10,080	1.8	3.0	3.9	0.7
Louisiana	65	10,850	2.4	2.9	4.1	1.0	Texas	540	35,725	1.8	2.9	4.2	0.9
Maine	273	5,891	4.9	4.9	6.9	0.8	Utah	70	6,064	2.7	5.2	11.0	1.4
Maryland	24	15,323	3.0	5.0	9.0	1.4	Vermont	188	2,731	4.7	5.2	6.7	0.7
Massachusetts	371	30,465	4.8	(4)	7.2	0.9	Virginia	90	18,659	2.6	4.2	7.9	1.1
Michigan	381	27,188	2.7	4.0	5.2	0.8	Washington	65	17,003	2.9	4.7	9.6	1.4
Minnesota	140	14,414	(4)	(4)	(4)	(4)	West Virginia	97	4,920	2.7	3.4	4.4	0.8
Mississippi	49	5,615	2.0	2.9	3.2	0.5	Wisconsin	379	18,647	3.5	5.7	9.2	1.0
							Wyoming	23	2,415	4.9	5.4	7.6	0.8

[1] Some data are different from other tables due to a different population base.

[2] The total number of persons entering the library for any purpose during the year.

[3] A reference transaction is an information contact which involves the knowledge, use, recommendations, interpretation or instructions in the use of one or more information sources by a member of the library staff.

[4] Data not shown because response rate is less than 70 percent.

NOTE: Data include imputations for nonresponse.

SOURCE: U.S. Department of Education, National Center for Education Statistics, *Public Libraries in the United States: FY 2001. (This table was prepared August 2003.)*

Average grade that the public would give public schools in their community and in the nation at large: 1974 to 2003

Year	All adults		No children in school		Public school parents		Private school parents	
	Nation	Local community	Nation	Local community	Nation	Local community	Nation	Local community
1	2	3	4	5	6	7	8	9
1974	—	2.63	—	2.57	—	2.80	—	2.15
1975	—	2.38	—	2.31	—	2.49	—	1.81
1976	—	2.38	—	2.34	—	2.48	—	2.22
1977	—	2.33	—	2.25	—	2.59	—	2.05
1978	—	2.21	—	2.11	—	2.47	—	1.69
1979	—	2.21	—	2.15	—	2.38	—	1.88
1980	—	2.26	—	—	—	—	—	—
1981	1.94	2.20	—	2.12	—	2.36	—	1.88
1982	2.01	2.24	2.04	2.18	2.01	2.35	2.02	2.20
1983	1.91	2.12	1.92	2.10	1.92	2.31	1.82	1.89
1984	2.09	2.36	2.11	2.30	2.11	2.49	2.04	2.17
1985	2.14	2.39	2.16	2.36	2.20	2.44	1.93	2.00
1986	2.13	2.36	—	2.29	—	2.55	—	2.14
1987	2.18	2.44	2.20	2.38	2.22	2.61	2.03	2.01
1988	2.08	2.35	2.02	2.32	2.13	2.48	2.00	2.13
1989	2.01	2.35	1.99	2.27	2.06	2.56	1.93	2.12
1990	1.99	2.29	1.98	2.27	2.03	2.44	1.85	2.09
1991	2.00	2.36	—	—	—	—	—	—
1992	1.93	2.30	1.92	—	1.94	2.73	1.85	—
1993	1.95	2.41	1.97	2.40	1.97	2.48	1.80	2.11
1994	1.95	2.26	1.95	2.16	1.90	2.55	1.86	1.90
1995	1.97	2.28	1.98	2.25	1.93	2.41	1.81	1.85
1996	1.93	2.30	1.91	2.22	2.00	2.56	1.80	1.86
1997	1.97	2.35	1.99	2.27	2.01	2.56	1.99	1.87
1998	1.93	2.41	1.92	2.36	1.96	2.51	1.81	2.20
1999	2.02	2.44	2.03	2.42	1.97	2.56	—	—
2000	1.98	2.47	1.94	2.44	2.05	2.59	—	—
2001	2.01	2.47	2.00	2.42	2.04	2.66	—	—
2002	2.08	2.44	2.08	2.40	2.06	2.61	—	—
2003	2.11	2.41	2.09	2.32	2.16	2.57	—	—

—Not available.

NOTE: Average based on a scale where A=4, B=3, C=2, D=1, and F=0.

SOURCE: Phi Delta Kappa, Phi Delta Kappan "The Annual Gallup Poll of the Public's Attitudes Toward the Public Schools," selected years 1974–2003. (This table was prepared August 2003.)

Items most frequently cited by the general public as a major problem facing the local public schools: Selected years, 1970 to 2003

Problem	Percent																		
	1970	1975	1980	1985	1989	1990	1991	1992	1993	1994	1995	1996	1997	1998	1999	2000	2001	2002	2003
1	2	3	4	5	6	7	8	9	10	11	12	13	14	15	16	17	18	19	20
Lack of discipline	18	23	26	25	19	19	20	17	15	18	15	15	15	14	18	15	15	17	16
Lack of financial support	17	14	10	9	13	13	18	22	21	13	11	13	15	12	9	18	15	23	25
Fighting/violence/gangs	—	—	—	—	—	—	—	9	13	18	9	14	12	15	11	11	10	9	4
Use of drugs	11	9	14	18	34	38	22	22	16	11	7	16	14	10	8	9	9	13	9
Standards/quality of education	—	—	—	—	—	—	—	—	—	8	4	—	8	6	2	5	—	—	4
Large schools/overcrowding	—	10	7	5	8	7	9	9	8	7	3	8	8	8	8	12	10	17	14
Lack of respect	—	—	—	—	—	—	—	—	—	3	3	2	—	2	2	2	—	—	—
Lack of family structure/problems of home life	—	—	—	—	—	—	—	—	—	5	3	4	—	—	—	—	—	—	—
Crime/vandalism	—	—	—	—	—	—	—	—	—	4	2	3	—	2	5	5	—	—	—
Getting good teachers	12	11	6	10	7	7	11	5	5	3	2	3	3	5	4	4	6	8	5
Parents' lack of interest	3	2	6	3	6	4	7	5	4	3	2	—	—	2	4	4	—	—	—
Poor curriculum/standards	6	5	11	11	8	8	10	9	9	3	2	3	—	1	2	2	—	—	—
Pupils' lack of interest/truancy	—	3	5	5	3	6	5	3	4	3	2	5	6	5	2	—	—	—	—
Integration/segregation/racial discrimination	17	15	10	4	4	5	5	4	4	3	2	2	—	—	—	—	—	—	—
Management of funds/programs	—	—	—	—	—	—	—	—	—	—	2	—	—	—	—	—	—	—	—
Moral standards	—	—	—	2	3	3	3	4	3	—	—	—	—	2	2	—	—	—	—
Low teacher pay	—	—	—	2	4	6	4	3	3	—	—	—	—	2	2	4	—	—	4
Teachers' lack of interest	—	—	6	4	4	4	2	2	—	—	—	—	—	—	—	—	—	—	—
Drinking/alcoholism	—	—	2	3	4	4	2	2	—	—	—	—	—	—	—	—	—	—	—
Lack of proper facilities	11	3	2	1	1	2	—	—	—	—	—	—	—	—	—	—	—	—	—

—Not available.

NOTE: Respondents were permitted to select multiple or no major problems.

SOURCE: Phi Delta Kappa, *Phi Delta Kappan* "The Annual Gallup Poll of the Public's Attitudes Toward the Public Schools," selected years 1970–2003. (This table was prepared August 2003.)

Labor force status of 1980 to 2002 high school dropouts, by sex and race/ethnicity: Selected years, October 1980 to October 2002

Year, sex, and race or ethnicity	Dropouts		Dropouts in civilian labor force [1]				Dropouts not in labor force	
	Number (in thousands)	Percent of total	Number, (in thousands)	Labor force participation rate	Unemployed		Number, (in thousands)	Percent of population
					Number, (in thousands)	Unemployment rate		
1	2	3	4	5	6	7	8	9
All dropouts [2]								
1980	739	100.0	471	63.7 (2.4)	149	31.6 (3.0)	268	36.3 (2.4)
1985	612	100.0	413	67.5 (2.8)	147	35.6 (3.4)	199	32.5 (2.8)
1990	405	100.0	280	69.0 (3.5)	90	32.3 (4.3)	125	31.0 (3.5)
1995	604	100.0	409	67.7 (2.9)	121	29.6 (3.5)	195	32.3 (2.9)
1996	496	100.0	289	58.4 (3.5)	80	27.6 (4.2)	206	41.6 (3.5)
1997	502	100.0	302	60.2 (3.5)	77	25.4 (4.0)	200	39.8 (3.5)
1998	505	100.0	308	60.9 (3.5)	87	28.2 (4.1)	197	39.1 (3.5)
1999	524	100.0	300	57.3 (3.4)	78	26.1 (4.0)	224	42.7 (3.4)
2000	515	100.0	350	68.0 (3.3)	99	28.1 (3.8)	165	32.0 (3.3)
2001	506	100.0	324	64.0 (3.4)	116	35.9 (4.3)	182	36.0 (3.4)
2002	401	100.0	271	67.7 (3.7)	81	29.8 (4.4)	129	32.3 (3.7)
Men								
1980	422	57.1	305	72.3 (3.0)	93	30.5 (3.6)	117	27.7 (3.0)
1985	321	52.5	261	81.3 (3.2)	98	37.5 (4.4)	60	18.7 (3.2)
1990	215	53.1	173	80.2 (4.2)	63	36.2 (5.6)	42	19.8 (4.2)
1995	339	56.1	251	74.0 (3.7)	72	28.7 (4.4)	88	26.0 (3.7)
1997	289	57.6	207	71.8 (4.2)	42	20.3 (4.5)	81	28.2 (4.2)
1998	257	50.9	164	63.9 (4.8)	31	19.0 (4.8)	93	36.1 (4.8)
1999	243	46.4	162	66.8 (4.8)	42	25.8 (5.5)	81	33.2 (4.8)
2000	295	57.3	220	74.4 (4.1)	54	24.5 (4.6)	76	25.6 (4.1)
2001	298	58.9	198	66.5 (4.4)	68	34.2 (5.4)	100	33.5 (4.4)
2002	214	53.4	149	69.5 (5.0)	35	23.4 (5.5)	65	30.5 (5.0)
Women								
1980	317	42.9	166	52.4 (3.9)	56	33.7 (5.1)	151	47.6 (3.9)
1985	291	47.5	152	52.2 (4.3)	49	32.2 (5.5)	139	47.8 (4.3)
1990	190	46.9	107	56.3 (5.5)	28	26.1 (6.5)	83	43.7 (5.5)
1995	265	43.9	157	59.5 (4.6)	49	30.9 (5.7)	107	40.5 (4.6)
1997	213	42.4	95	44.4 (5.4)	35	36.6 (7.9)	119	55.6 (5.4)
1998	248	49.1	143	57.8 (5.0)	56	38.7 (6.5)	105	42.2 (5.0)
1999	282	53.8	139	49.2 (4.7)	37	26.4 (6.0)	143	50.8 (4.7)
2000	220	42.7	131	59.4 (5.3)	45	34.2 (6.6)	90	40.6 (5.3)
2001	207	40.9	126	60.6 (5.4)	48	38.6 (6.9)	82	39.4 (5.4)
2002	187	46.6	122	65.6 (5.5)	46	37.6 (7.0)	64	34.4 (5.5)
White [3]								
1980	580	78.5	392	67.6 (2.7)	106	27.0 (3.1)	188	32.4 (2.7)
1985	458	74.8	330	72.1 (3.0)	116	35.2 (3.8)	128	27.9 (3.0)
1990	303	74.8	211	69.8 (4.0)	56	26.3 (4.6)	92	30.2 (4.0)
1995	448	74.2	312	69.8 (3.3)	85	27.2 (3.9)	135	30.2 (3.3)
1997	386	76.9	250	64.8 (3.9)	51	20.5 (4.1)	136	35.2 (3.9)
1998	384	76.0	257	67.0 (3.8)	63	24.5 (4.3)	127	33.0 (3.8)
1999	377	71.9	227	60.3 (4.0)	54	23.6 (4.5)	150	39.7 (4.0)
2000	384	74.6	280	73.0 (3.6)	70	24.9 (4.1)	104	27.0 (3.6)
2001	401	79.2	273	68.1 (3.7)	89	32.4 (4.5)	128	31.9 (3.7)
2002	281	70.1	188	67.0 (4.5)	48	25.6 (5.1)	93	33.0 (4.5)
Black [3]								
1980	146	19.8	73	50.0 (6.2)	40	(4) (4)	73	50.0 (6.2)
1985	132	21.6	69	52.3 (6.8)	30	(4) (4)	63	47.7 (6.8)
1990	86	21.2	56	65.3 (8.5)	30	(4) (4)	30	34.7 (8.5)
1995	109	18.0	66	61.0 (7.7)	27	(4) (4)	42	39.0 (7.7)
1997	90	17.9	41	45.1 (9.0)	22	(4) (4)	49	54.9 (9.0)
1998	98	19.4	46	47.2 (8.7)	23	(4) (4)	52	52.8 (8.7)
1999	118	22.5	59	50.0 (7.9)	20	(4) (4)	59	50.0 (7.9)
2000	111	21.5	58	51.9 (8.1)	27	(4) (4)	53	48.1 (8.1)
2001	85	16.8	42	49.9 (9.3)	21	(4) (4)	43	50.1 (9.3)
2002	79	19.7	55	69.8 (8.9)	27	(4) (4)	24	30.2 (8.9)
Hispanic [5]								
1980	91	12.3	60	65.9 (7.4)	17	(4) (4)	31	34.1 (7.4)
1985	106	17.3	73	68.9 (7.9)	33	(4) (4)	33	31.1 (7.9)
1990	67	16.5	32	(4) (4)	10	(4) (4)	35	(4) (6.7)
1995	174	28.8	119	68.6 (6.7)	35	29.3 (8.0)	55	31.4 (6.7)
1997	121	24.1	88	73.1 (8.0)	15	17.4 (8.1)	32	26.9 (8.0)
1998	120	23.8	82	68.5 (8.5)	22	27.1 (9.8)	38	31.5 (8.5)
1999	119	22.7	85	71.4 (8.3)	10	12.0 (7.0)	34	28.6 (8.3)
2000	101	19.6	62	61.1 (9.7)	22	(4) (4)	39	38.9 (9.7)
2001	119	23.5	84	70.6 (8.3)	27	32.6 (10.2)	35	29.4 (8.3)
2002	94	23.4	62	66.5 (9.7)	23	(4) (4)	31	33.5 (9.7)

[1] The labor force includes all employed persons plus those seeking employment. The labor force participation rate is the percentage of persons either employed or seeking employment. The unemployment rate is the percent of persons in the labor force who are seeking employment.

[2] Persons 16 to 24 years old who dropped out of school in the 12-month period ending in October of years shown.

[3] Includes persons of Hispanic origin.

[4] Data not shown where base is less than 75,000.

[5] Persons of Hispanic origin may be of any race.

NOTE: Data are based upon sample surveys of the civilian noninstitutional population. Includes dropouts from any grade, including a small number from elementary and middle schools. Even though the standard errors are large, smaller estimates are shown to permit users to combine categories in various ways. Detail for the above race and Hispanic-origin groups will not sum to totals because data for the "other races" group are not presented and Hispanics are included in both the White and Black population groups. Some data have been revised from previously published figures. Standard errors appear in parentheses. Detail may not sum to totals due to rounding.

SOURCE: U.S. Department of Labor, Bureau of Labor Statistics, *College Enrollment of High School Graduates*, selected years 1980 to 2002. (This table was prepared March 2004.)

Unemployment rate of persons 16 years old and over, by age, sex, race/ethnicity, and educational attainment: 2000, 2001, and 2002

Sex, race/ethnicity, and educational attainment	Percent unemployed, 2000 [1]				Percent unemployed, 2001 [1]				Percent unemployed, 2002 [1]			
	16- to 24-year-olds [2]			25 years old and over	16- to 24-year-olds [2]			25 years old and over	16- to 24-year-olds [2]			25 years old and over
	Total	16 to 19 years	20 to 24 years		Total	16 to 19 years	20 to 24 years		Total	16 to 19 years	20 to 24 years	
1	2	3	4	5	6	7	8	9	10	11	12	13
All persons												
All education levels	9.3 (0.1)	13.1 (0.3)	7.2 (0.2)	3.0 (#)	10.6 (0.1)	14.7 (0.3)	8.3 (0.2)	3.7 (#)	12.0 (0.2)	16.5 (0.3)	9.7 (0.2)	4.6 (#)
Less than high school completion ..	15.1 (0.3)	15.6 (0.4)	13.8 (0.6)	6.3 (0.2)	16.7 (0.3)	17.3 (0.4)	15.3 (0.6)	7.2 (0.2)	18.4 (0.4)	19.0 (0.4)	17.0 (0.6)	8.4 (0.2)
High school completion, no college	9.4 (0.3)	11.6 (0.5)	8.4 (0.3)	3.4 (0.1)	10.7 (0.3)	13.3 (0.5)	9.5 (0.3)	4.2 (0.1)	12.6 (0.3)	15.9 (0.6)	11.1 (0.3)	5.3 (0.1)
Some college, no degree	5.5 (0.2)	6.7 (0.5)	5.1 (0.2)	2.9 (0.1)	6.4 (0.2)	8.1 (0.6)	6.0 (0.2)	3.5 (0.1)	7.7 (0.2)	9.2 (0.6)	7.3 (0.3)	4.8 (0.1)
Associate degree	3.3 (0.4)	— (—)	3.3 (0.4)	2.3 (0.1)	4.5 (0.5)	— (—)	4.4 (0.5)	2.9 (0.1)	7.2 (0.6)	— (—)	7.1 (0.6)	4.0 (0.1)
Bachelor's degree or higher	4.3 (0.3)	— (—)	4.3 (0.3)	1.7 (#)	5.7 (0.4)	— (—)	5.7 (0.4)	2.3 (0.1)	5.8 (0.4)	— (—)	5.8 (0.4)	2.9 (0.1)
Men												
All education levels	9.7 (0.2)	14.0 (0.4)	7.3 (0.2)	2.8 (#)	11.4 (0.2)	16.0 (0.4)	9.0 (0.2)	3.6 (0.1)	12.8 (0.2)	18.1 (0.5)	10.2 (0.2)	4.7 (0.1)
Less than high school completion ..	14.9 (0.4)	16.5 (0.5)	11.7 (0.6)	5.4 (0.2)	17.1 (0.4)	18.7 (0.6)	14.2 (0.7)	6.4 (0.2)	18.7 (0.5)	20.8 (0.6)	15.1 (0.7)	7.8 (0.2)
High school completion, no college	9.2 (0.3)	11.6 (0.6)	8.2 (0.4)	3.4 (0.1)	10.8 (0.4)	13.1 (0.8)	9.9 (0.4)	4.3 (0.1)	12.7 (0.4)	16.4 (0.8)	11.3 (0.4)	5.4 (0.1)
Some college, no degree	5.7 (0.3)	7.3 (0.8)	5.3 (0.3)	2.7 (0.1)	7.0 (0.3)	9.2 (0.9)	6.5 (0.4)	3.4 (0.1)	8.1 (0.4)	9.8 (0.9)	7.8 (0.4)	4.7 (0.1)
Associate degree	3.3 (0.6)	— (—)	3.1 (0.6)	2.3 (0.2)	5.4 (0.8)	— (—)	5.3 (0.8)	3.1 (0.2)	8.0 (0.9)	— (—)	7.6 (0.9)	4.3 (0.2)
Bachelor's degree or higher	4.4 (0.6)	— (—)	4.5 (0.6)	1.5 (0.1)	6.7 (0.7)	— (—)	6.7 (0.7)	2.2 (0.1)	6.9 (0.7)	— (—)	7.0 (0.7)	3.0 (0.1)
Women												
All education levels	8.9 (0.2)	12.1 (0.4)	7.1 (0.2)	3.2 (0.1)	9.6 (0.2)	13.4 (0.4)	7.5 (0.2)	3.7 (0.1)	11.1 (0.2)	14.9 (0.4)	9.1 (0.3)	4.6 (0.1)
Less than high school completion ..	15.3 (0.5)	14.5 (0.5)	18.4 (1.1)	7.8 (0.3)	16.0 (0.5)	15.5 (0.6)	17.6 (1.1)	8.6 (0.3)	17.9 (0.5)	17.0 (0.6)	20.7 (1.1)	9.5 (0.3)
High school completion, no college	9.5 (0.4)	11.5 (0.7)	8.5 (0.4)	3.5 (0.1)	10.5 (0.4)	13.4 (0.8)	9.1 (0.5)	4.0 (0.1)	12.3 (0.4)	15.4 (0.8)	10.9 (0.5)	5.1 (0.1)
Some college, no degree	5.3 (0.3)	6.3 (0.6)	4.9 (0.3)	3.0 (0.1)	5.9 (0.3)	7.3 (0.7)	5.5 (0.3)	3.6 (0.1)	7.3 (0.3)	8.8 (0.8)	6.8 (0.4)	5.0 (0.2)
Associate degree	3.3 (0.6)	— (—)	3.4 (0.6)	2.4 (0.1)	3.9 (0.6)	— (—)	3.9 (0.6)	2.7 (0.2)	6.7 (0.8)	— (—)	6.6 (0.8)	3.7 (0.2)
Bachelor's degree or higher	4.2 (0.4)	— (—)	4.2 (0.4)	1.8 (0.1)	5.0 (0.5)	— (—)	5.0 (0.5)	2.3 (0.1)	5.1 (0.5)	— (—)	5.0 (0.5)	2.8 (0.1)
White, non-Hispanic												
All education levels	7.4 (0.2)	10.4 (0.3)	5.5 (0.2)	2.4 (#)	8.6 (0.2)	11.7 (0.3)	6.7 (0.2)	3.0 (#)	9.8 (0.2)	13.5 (0.3)	7.7 (0.2)	3.9 (#)
Less than high school completion ..	12.7 (0.4)	12.6 (0.4)	13.2 (0.9)	5.2 (0.2)	13.9 (0.4)	13.8 (0.4)	14.3 (0.9)	5.8 (0.2)	15.6 (0.4)	15.4 (0.5)	16.4 (1.0)	7.5 (0.3)
High school completion, no college	7.2 (0.3)	9.0 (0.5)	6.3 (0.3)	2.8 (0.1)	9.0 (0.3)	10.4 (0.6)	8.3 (0.4)	3.5 (0.1)	10.5 (0.3)	13.2 (0.7)	9.2 (0.4)	4.5 (0.1)
Some college, no degree	4.5 (0.4)	5.3 (0.6)	4.2 (0.2)	2.5 (0.1)	5.2 (0.2)	6.7 (0.6)	4.8 (0.3)	3.1 (0.1)	6.3 (0.3)	8.0 (0.6)	5.8 (0.3)	4.2 (0.1)
Associate degree	3.1 (0.5)	— (—)	3.0 (0.5)	2.0 (0.1)	4.4 (0.6)	— (—)	4.3 (0.6)	2.4 (0.1)	6.0 (0.6)	— (—)	5.6 (0.6)	3.5 (0.1)
Bachelor's degree or higher	3.9 (0.4)	— (—)	4.0 (0.4)	1.5 (0.1)	5.4 (0.4)	— (—)	5.4 (0.4)	2.0 (0.1)	5.3 (0.4)	— (—)	5.2 (0.4)	2.7 (0.1)
Black, non-Hispanic												
All education levels	18.5 (0.5)	24.9 (1.0)	15.3 (0.6)	5.4 (0.1)	20.7 (0.6)	29.8 (1.1)	16.4 (0.6)	6.2 (0.2)	22.7 (0.6)	30.1 (1.2)	19.3 (0.7)	7.7 (0.2)
Less than high school completion ..	29.7 (1.2)	28.5 (1.4)	32.2 (2.1)	10.5 (0.6)	33.0 (1.2)	33.7 (1.5)	31.8 (2.0)	11.9 (0.6)	35.0 (1.3)	34.9 (1.6)	35.2 (2.2)	13.6 (0.6)
High school completion, no college	18.6 (0.9)	23.9 (1.9)	16.7 (1.0)	6.5 (0.3)	19.5 (0.9)	27.1 (2.1)	17.0 (1.0)	7.5 (0.3)	22.6 (1.0)	28.0 (2.0)	20.7 (1.1)	8.8 (0.3)
Some college, no degree	10.0 (0.8)	12.1 (2.2)	9.6 (0.9)	4.2 (0.3)	12.2 (0.9)	16.4 (2.6)	11.4 (0.9)	5.0 (0.3)	14.6 (1.0)	15.7 (2.6)	14.4 (1.0)	6.9 (0.3)
Associate degree	6.7 (1.9)	— (—)	6.8 (2.0)	3.5 (0.4)	8.3 (2.1)	— (—)	8.4 (2.1)	4.8 (0.4)	13.3 (2.4)	— (—)	13.6 (2.5)	6.0 (0.5)
Bachelor's degree or higher	5.9 (1.5)	— (—)	6.1 (1.5)	2.5 (0.2)	7.5 (1.7)	— (—)	7.6 (1.7)	2.6 (0.2)	4.9 (1.4)	— (—)	5.0 (1.5)	4.2 (0.3)
Hispanic origin [3]												
All education levels	10.3 (0.4)	16.6 (0.8)	7.5 (0.4)	4.4 (0.1)	11.1 (0.4)	17.7 (0.8)	8.1 (0.4)	5.3 (0.1)	12.9 (0.4)	20.0 (0.9)	9.9 (0.4)	6.1 (0.1)
Less than high school completion ..	14.1 (0.6)	19.9 (1.1)	9.5 (0.7)	6.2 (0.3)	14.8 (0.6)	20.0 (1.1)	10.8 (0.7)	7.4 (0.3)	16.7 (0.7)	22.9 (1.2)	12.2 (0.8)	7.7 (0.3)
High school completion, no college	8.9 (0.6)	12.5 (1.4)	7.8 (0.7)	3.9 (0.2)	9.4 (0.6)	16.4 (1.6)	7.2 (0.6)	4.5 (0.2)	11.4 (0.7)	17.3 (1.6)	9.5 (0.7)	5.9 (0.3)
Some college, no degree	6.3 (0.7)	10.5 (1.8)	5.1 (0.7)	3.3 (0.3)	7.4 (0.7)	9.3 (1.7)	6.8 (0.8)	3.8 (0.3)	8.6 (0.8)	11.9 (2.0)	7.9 (0.8)	5.7 (0.4)
Associate degree	2.1 (1.1)	— (—)	2.2 (1.1)	2.8 (0.4)	1.6 (0.8)	— (—)	1.7 (0.8)	3.8 (0.5)	7.5 (1.9)	— (—)	6.9 (1.8)	5.0 (0.5)
Bachelor's degree or higher	3.9 (1.4)	— (—)	4.0 (1.4)	2.2 (0.3)	5.3 (1.5)	— (—)	5.3 (1.5)	3.6 (0.3)	8.4 (1.9)	— (—)	8.5 (1.9)	3.4 (0.3)

—Not available.
Rounds to zero.

[1] The unemployment rate is the percent of individuals in the labor force who are not working and who made specific efforts to find employment sometime during the prior 4 weeks. The labor force includes both employed and unemployed persons.

[2] Excludes persons enrolled in school.

[3] Persons of Hispanic origin may be of any race.

NOTE: Some data have been revised from previously published figures. Standard errors appear in parentheses.

SOURCE: U.S. Department of Labor, Bureau of Labor Statistics, Office of Employment and Unemployment Statistics, previously unpublished tabulations of annual averages from the Current Population Survey. (This table was prepared May 2003.)

Labor force participation of persons 16 years old and over, by highest level of education, age, sex, and race/ethnicity: 2002

Age, sex, and race/ethnicity	Labor force participation rate [1]						Employment/population ratio [2]					
	Total	Less than high school completion [3]	High school completer	College			Total	Less than high school completion [3]	High school completer	College		
				Some college, no degree	Associate degree	Bachelor's degree or higher				Some college, no degree	Associate degree	Bachelor's degree or higher
1	2	3	4	5	6	7	8	9	10	11	12	13
16 to 19 years old [4]	47.4 (0.4)	39.6 (0.5)	67.0 (0.8)	57.7 (1.0)	— (—)	— (—)	39.6 (0.4)	32.0 (0.4)	56.4 (0.9)	52.4 (1.0)	— (—)	— (—)
Men	47.5 (0.5)	40.0 (0.6)	70.3 (1.1)	55.0 (1.5)	— (—)	— (—)	38.9 (0.5)	31.7 (0.6)	58.7 (1.2)	49.6 (1.5)	— (—)	— (—)
Women	47.3 (0.5)	39.0 (0.7)	63.9 (1.2)	59.9 (1.3)	— (—)	— (—)	40.3 (0.5)	32.4 (0.6)	54.0 (1.2)	54.6 (1.4)	— (—)	— (—)
White, non-Hispanic	52.0 (0.5)	44.3 (0.6)	70.1 (1.0)	61.3 (1.2)	— (—)	— (—)	45.0 (0.5)	37.5 (0.6)	60.8 (1.0)	56.4 (1.2)	— (—)	— (—)
Black, non-Hispanic	35.8 (1.0)	28.4 (1.1)	56.3 (2.3)	45.0 (3.4)	— (—)	— (—)	25.0 (0.9)	18.5 (1.0)	40.5 (2.3)	37.9 (3.3)	— (—)	— (—)
Hispanic	44.0 (1.0)	36.4 (1.2)	67.6 (2.3)	58.3 (3.4)	— (—)	— (—)	35.2 (1.0)	28.0 (1.1)	55.8 (2.5)	51.5 (3.5)	— (—)	— (—)
20 to 24 years old [4]	76.4 (0.3)	69.4 (0.7)	80.5 (0.4)	72.3 (0.5)	85.3 (0.9)	82.7 (0.7)	69.0 (0.3)	57.7 (0.8)	71.5 (0.5)	67.0 (0.5)	79.2 (1.0)	77.9 (0.8)
Men	80.7 (0.5)	81.6 (1.1)	86.9 (0.7)	72.3 (0.9)	89.0 (1.5)	83.8 (1.4)	72.5 (0.5)	69.3 (1.3)	77.0 (0.8)	66.7 (0.9)	82.2 (1.8)	78.0 (1.6)
Women	72.1 (0.5)	54.0 (1.5)	73.4 (0.9)	72.2 (0.8)	82.0 (1.2)	82.0 (1.2)	65.6 (0.5)	42.8 (1.5)	65.4 (1.0)	67.3 (0.9)	76.6 (1.9)	77.9 (1.3)
White, non-Hispanic	79.1 (0.3)	70.6 (1.2)	83.3 (0.5)	74.2 (0.5)	87.5 (1.0)	85.9 (0.7)	73.1 (0.3)	59.0 (1.3)	75.6 (0.6)	69.8 (0.6)	82.7 (1.1)	81.4 (0.8)
Black, non-Hispanic	68.6 (1.1)	56.6 (2.8)	73.1 (1.7)	66.5 (1.9)	85.7 (3.8)	74.7 (4.1)	55.4 (1.2)	36.6 (2.7)	58.0 (1.9)	57.0 (2.0)	73.8 (4.8)	70.7 (4.3)
Hispanic	76.3 (0.8)	73.6 (1.5)	79.9 (1.4)	74.5 (1.8)	78.1 (4.3)	79.8 (3.9)	68.8 (0.9)	64.7 (1.6)	72.3 (1.5)	68.6 (1.9)	72.8 (4.6)	73.4 (4.3)
25 and older	67.2 (0.1)	44.4 (0.3)	64.2 (0.2)	71.2 (0.2)	77.1 (0.3)	78.6 (0.2)	64.1 (0.1)	40.6 (0.2)	60.8 (0.2)	67.7 (0.2)	74.1 (0.3)	76.3 (0.2)
Men	75.9 (0.2)	57.2 (0.5)	74.5 (0.3)	78.3 (0.4)	84.3 (0.5)	84.0 (0.3)	72.3 (0.2)	52.7 (0.5)	70.5 (0.3)	74.6 (0.4)	80.7 (0.6)	81.4 (0.3)
Women	59.4 (0.2)	32.5 (0.4)	55.3 (0.3)	64.9 (0.4)	71.7 (0.5)	73.0 (0.3)	56.6 (0.2)	29.4 (0.4)	52.4 (0.3)	61.7 (0.4)	69.1 (0.5)	71.0 (0.3)
White, non-Hispanic	66.4 (0.1)	36.1 (0.3)	62.1 (0.2)	69.1 (0.3)	76.8 (0.3)	78.0 (0.2)	63.9 (0.1)	33.3 (0.3)	59.4 (0.2)	66.2 (0.3)	74.1 (0.3)	75.9 (0.2)
Black, non-Hispanic	67.6 (0.4)	39.9 (0.9)	68.2 (0.7)	77.3 (0.8)	79.0 (1.2)	82.8 (0.8)	62.3 (0.4)	34.5 (0.9)	62.2 (0.7)	71.9 (0.9)	74.2 (1.3)	79.3 (0.8)
Hispanic	71.0 (0.4)	61.3 (0.6)	74.1 (0.7)	80.6 (0.9)	80.8 (1.4)	83.2 (0.9)	66.6 (0.4)	56.6 (0.6)	69.7 (0.7)	76.1 (1.0)	76.8 (1.5)	80.4 (1.0)

—Not available.

[1] Percent of the civilian population who are employed or seeking employment.
[2] Number of persons employed as a percent of civilian population.
[3] Includes persons reporting no school years completed.
[4] Excludes persons enrolled in school.

NOTE: Standard errors appear in parentheses.

SOURCE: U.S. Department of Labor, Bureau of Labor Statistics, Office of Employment and Unemployment Statistics, previously unpublished tabulations from the Current Population Survey. (This table was prepared May 2003.)

Median annual income of year-round, full-time workers 25 years old and over, by highest level of educational attainment and sex: 1990 to 2001

Sex and year	Total	Elementary/secondary			College						
		Less than 9th grade	9th to 12th grade, no completion[1]	High school completion (includes equivalency)[2]	Some college, no degree[3]	Associate degree[4]	Bachelor's or higher degree[5]				
							Total[5]	Bachelor's[6]	Master's[4]	Professional[4]	Doctorate[4]
1	2	3	4	5	6	7	8	9	10	11	12
	Current dollars										
Men											
1990	$30,733 (—)	$17,394 (—)	$20,902 (—)	$26,653 (—)	$31,734 (—)	— (—)	$42,671 (—)	$39,238 (—)	— (—)	— (—)	— (—)
1991	31,613 (—)	17,623 (—)	21,402 (—)	26,779 (—)	31,663 (—)	$33,817 (—)	45,138 (—)	40,906 (—)	$49,734 (—)	$73,996 (—)	$57,187 (—)
1992	32,057 (120)	17,294 (—)	21,274 (—)	27,280 (175)	32,103 (—)	33,433 (—)	45,802 (—)	41,355 (304)	49,973 (—)	76,220 (—)	57,418 (—)
1993	32,359 (124)	16,863 (—)	21,752 (—)	27,370 (204)	32,077 (—)	33,690 (—)	47,740 (—)	42,757 (536)	51,867 (—)	80,549 (—)	63,149 (—)
1994	33,440 (246)	17,532 (453)	22,048 (319)	28,037 (322)	32,279 (300)	35,794 (430)	49,228 (707)	43,663 (633)	53,500 (854)	75,009 (3,040)	61,921 (1,619)
1995	34,551 (275)	18,354 (545)	22,185 (342)	29,510 (358)	33,883 (517)	35,201 (535)	50,481 (312)	45,266 (510)	55,216 (973)	79,667 (2,582)	65,336 (2,188)
1996	35,622 (150)	17,962 (594)	22,717 (414)	30,709 (184)	34,845 (456)	37,131 (435)	51,436 (303)	45,846 (458)	60,508 (945)	85,963 (3,317)	71,227 (3,362)
1997	36,678 (149)	19,291 (629)	24,726 (466)	31,215 (171)	35,945 (293)	38,022 (774)	53,450 (755)	48,616 (851)	61,690 (771)	85,011 (4,253)	76,234 (3,611)
1998	37,906 (291)	19,380 (600)	23,958 (547)	31,477 (169)	36,934 (291)	40,274 (539)	56,524 (421)	51,405 (349)	62,244 (847)	94,737 (12,105)	75,078 (2,507)
1999	40,333 (144)	20,429 (444)	25,035 (535)	33,184 (388)	39,221 (581)	41,638 (459)	60,201 (439)	52,985 (722)	66,243 (690)	100,000 (37,836)	81,687 (3,953)
2000	41,059 (156)	20,789 (376)	25,095 (436)	34,303 (457)	40,337 (312)	41,952 (460)	61,868 (303)	56,334 (573)	68,322 (1,506)	99,411 (20,832)	80,250 (2,446)
2001	41,617 (104)	21,361 (235)	26,209 (251)	34,723 (299)	41,045 (214)	42,776 (561)	62,223 (279)	55,929 (335)	70,899 (687)	100,000 (—)	86,965 (3,013)
Women											
1990	21,372 (—)	12,251 (—)	14,429 (—)	18,319 (—)	22,227 (—)	— (—)	30,377 (—)	28,017 (—)	— (—)	— (—)	— (—)
1991	22,043 (—)	12,066 (—)	14,455 (—)	18,836 (—)	22,143 (—)	25,000 (—)	31,310 (—)	29,079 (—)	34,949 (—)	46,742 (—)	43,303 (—)
1992	23,139 (159)	12,958 (—)	14,559 (—)	19,427 (176)	23,157 (—)	25,624 (—)	32,304 (—)	30,326 (294)	36,037 (—)	46,257 (—)	45,790 (—)
1993	23,629 (166)	12,415 (—)	15,386 (—)	19,963 (173)	23,056 (—)	25,883 (—)	34,307 (—)	31,197 (310)	38,612 (—)	50,211 (—)	47,248 (—)
1994	24,399 (165)	12,430 (427)	15,133 (328)	20,373 (158)	23,514 (327)	25,940 (295)	35,378 (280)	31,741 (314)	39,457 (606)	50,615 (2,154)	51,119 (2,888)
1995	24,875 (160)	13,577 (490)	15,825 (293)	20,463 (162)	23,997 (274)	27,311 (428)	35,259 (313)	32,051 (273)	40,263 (556)	50,000 (2,532)	48,141 (2,373)
1996	25,808 (131)	14,414 (559)	16,953 (333)	21,175 (143)	25,167 (267)	28,083 (526)	36,461 (296)	33,525 (437)	41,901 (564)	57,624 (3,635)	56,267 (3,300)
1997	26,974 (134)	14,161 (492)	16,697 (335)	22,067 (148)	26,335 (291)	28,812 (660)	38,038 (481)	35,379 (295)	44,949 (837)	61,051 (4,737)	53,038 (3,626)
1998	27,956 (199)	14,467 (429)	16,482 (322)	22,780 (254)	27,420 (271)	29,924 (513)	39,786 (408)	36,559 (305)	45,283 (760)	57,565 (1,705)	57,796 (1,881)
1999	28,844 (216)	15,098 (492)	17,015 (298)	23,061 (279)	27,757 (369)	30,919 (318)	41,747 (275)	37,993 (614)	48,097 (862)	59,904 (4,479)	60,079 (3,130)
2000	30,327 (138)	15,798 (327)	17,919 (434)	24,970 (236)	28,697 (364)	31,071 (307)	42,706 (439)	40,415 (284)	50,139 (735)	58,957 (3,552)	57,081 (2,999)
2001	31,356 (91)	16,691 (255)	19,156 (359)	25,303 (132)	30,418 (186)	32,153 (231)	44,776 (367)	40,994 (231)	50,669 (328)	61,748 (3,976)	62,123 (2,228)
	Constant 2001 dollars										
Men											
1990	$41,644 (—)	$23,569 (—)	$28,322 (—)	$36,115 (—)	$43,000 (—)	— (—)	$57,820 (—)	$53,168 (—)	— (—)	— (—)	— (—)
1991	41,106 (—)	22,915 (—)	27,829 (—)	34,821 (—)	41,171 (—)	$43,972 (—)	58,693 (—)	53,190 (—)	$64,669 (—)	$96,217 (—)	$74,360 (—)
1992	40,465 (151)	21,830 (—)	26,854 (—)	34,435 (221)	40,523 (—)	42,202 (—)	57,816 (—)	52,202 (384)	63,081 (—)	96,212 (—)	72,478 (—)
1993	39,659 (152)	20,667 (—)	26,659 (—)	33,545 (250)	39,314 (—)	41,291 (—)	58,510 (—)	52,403 (657)	63,568 (—)	98,721 (—)	77,396 (—)
1994	39,961 (294)	20,951 (541)	26,348 (381)	33,504 (385)	38,574 (359)	42,774 (514)	58,828 (845)	52,178 (756)	63,933 (1,021)	89,636 (3,633)	73,996 (1,935)
1995	40,151 (320)	21,329 (633)	25,781 (397)	34,293 (416)	39,375 (601)	40,906 (622)	58,663 (363)	52,602 (593)	64,165 (1,131)	92,579 (3,000)	75,925 (2,543)
1996	40,208 (169)	20,275 (670)	25,642 (467)	34,663 (208)	39,331 (515)	41,911 (491)	58,058 (342)	51,748 (517)	68,298 (1,067)	97,030 (3,744)	80,397 (3,795)
1997	40,471 (164)	21,286 (694)	27,283 (514)	34,443 (189)	39,663 (323)	41,954 (854)	58,978 (833)	53,644 (939)	68,070 (851)	93,803 (4,693)	84,119 (3,984)
1998	41,185 (316)	21,056 (652)	26,030 (594)	34,200 (184)	40,129 (316)	43,758 (586)	61,413 (457)	55,852 (379)	67,628 (920)	102,932 (13,152)	81,572 (2,724)
1999	42,875 (153)	21,717 (472)	26,613 (569)	35,275 (412)	41,693 (618)	44,262 (488)	63,995 (467)	56,324 (768)	70,418 (733)	106,303 (40,221)	86,835 (4,202)
2000	42,227 (160)	21,381 (387)	25,809 (448)	35,279 (470)	41,485 (321)	43,146 (473)	63,628 (312)	57,937 (589)	70,266 (1,549)	102,240 (21,425)	82,534 (2,516)
2001	41,617 (104)	21,361 (235)	26,209 (251)	34,723 (299)	41,045 (214)	42,776 (561)	62,223 (279)	55,929 (335)	70,899 (687)	100,000 (—)	86,965 (3,013)
Women											
1990	28,959 (—)	16,600 (—)	19,551 (—)	24,822 (—)	30,118 (—)	— (—)	41,161 (—)	37,963 (—)	— (—)	— (—)	— (—)
1991	28,662 (—)	15,689 (—)	18,796 (—)	24,492 (—)	28,792 (—)	32,507 (—)	40,712 (—)	37,811 (—)	45,444 (—)	60,778 (—)	56,307 (—)
1992	29,208 (201)	16,357 (—)	18,378 (—)	24,523 (222)	29,231 (—)	32,345 (—)	40,777 (—)	38,280 (371)	45,489 (—)	58,390 (—)	57,800 (—)
1993	28,960 (203)	15,216 (—)	18,857 (—)	24,467 (212)	28,258 (—)	31,722 (—)	42,047 (—)	38,235 (380)	47,323 (—)	61,539 (—)	57,907 (—)
1994	29,157 (197)	14,854 (510)	18,084 (392)	24,346 (189)	28,099 (391)	30,998 (353)	42,277 (335)	37,931 (375)	47,151 (724)	60,485 (2,574)	61,088 (3,451)
1995	28,907 (186)	15,777 (569)	18,390 (340)	23,780 (188)	27,886 (318)	31,737 (497)	40,974 (364)	37,246 (317)	46,789 (646)	58,104 (2,942)	55,943 (2,758)
1996	29,131 (148)	16,270 (631)	19,136 (376)	23,901 (161)	28,407 (301)	31,699 (594)	41,155 (334)	37,841 (493)	47,296 (637)	65,043 (4,103)	63,511 (3,725)
1997	29,764 (148)	15,626 (543)	18,424 (370)	24,349 (163)	29,059 (321)	31,792 (728)	41,972 (531)	39,038 (326)	49,598 (924)	67,365 (5,227)	58,524 (4,001)
1998	30,374 (216)	15,718 (466)	17,908 (350)	24,751 (276)	29,792 (294)	32,513 (557)	43,228 (443)	39,721 (331)	49,200 (826)	62,545 (1,852)	62,796 (2,044)
1999	30,662 (230)	16,050 (523)	18,087 (317)	24,514 (297)	29,506 (392)	32,868 (338)	44,378 (292)	40,388 (653)	51,128 (916)	63,679 (4,761)	63,865 (3,327)
2000	31,190 (142)	16,248 (336)	18,429 (446)	25,681 (243)	29,514 (374)	31,955 (316)	43,921 (451)	41,565 (292)	51,566 (756)	60,635 (3,653)	58,705 (3,084)
2001	31,356 (91)	16,691 (255)	19,156 (359)	25,303 (132)	30,418 (186)	32,153 (231)	44,776 (367)	40,994 (231)	50,669 (328)	61,748 (3,976)	62,123 (2,228)
	Number of persons with income (in thousands)										
Men											
1990	44,406 (269)	2,250 (74)	3,315 (89)	16,394 (188)	9,113 (145)	— (—)	13,334 (172)	7,569 (133)	— (—)	— (—)	— (—)
1991	44,199 (268)	1,807 (66)	3,083 (86)	15,025 (181)	8,034 (136)	2,899 (84)	13,350 (172)	8,456 (140)	3,073 (86)	1,147 (53)	674 (41)
1992	44,752 (269)	1,815 (66)	3,009 (85)	14,722 (179)	8,067 (137)	3,203 (88)	13,937 (175)	8,719 (142)	3,178 (87)	1,295 (56)	745 (43)
1993	45,873 (271)	1,790 (66)	3,083 (86)	14,604 (179)	8,493 (140)	3,557 (92)	14,346 (177)	9,178 (145)	3,131 (87)	1,231 (55)	808 (45)
1994	47,566 (273)	1,895 (68)	3,057 (86)	15,109 (182)	8,783 (142)	3,735 (95)	14,987 (181)	9,636 (148)	3,225 (88)	1,258 (55)	868 (46)
1995	48,500 (324)	1,946 (72)	3,335 (93)	15,331 (196)	8,908 (151)	3,926 (101)	15,054 (194)	9,597 (157)	3,395 (94)	1,208 (56)	853 (47)
1996	49,764 (340)	2,041 (76)	3,441 (99)	15,840 (207)	9,173 (159)	3,931 (105)	15,339 (204)	9,898 (165)	3,272 (96)	1,277 (60)	893 (51)
1997	50,807 (343)	1,914 (74)	3,548 (100)	16,225 (209)	9,170 (159)	4,086 (107)	15,864 (207)	10,349 (169)	3,228 (96)	1,321 (61)	966 (53)
1998	52,381 (347)	1,870 (73)	3,613 (101)	16,442 (210)	9,375 (161)	4,347 (111)	16,733 (212)	11,058 (174)	3,414 (98)	1,264 (60)	998 (53)
1999	53,062 (348)	1,993 (75)	3,295 (97)	16,589 (211)	9,684 (164)	4,359 (111)	17,142 (214)	11,142 (175)	3,725 (103)	1,267 (60)	1,008 (54)
2000	54,065 (351)	1,968 (75)	3,354 (97)	16,834 (213)	9,792 (164)	4,729 (115)	17,387 (216)	11,395 (177)	3,680 (102)	1,274 (60)	1,038 (54)
2001	54,013 (351)	2,207 (79)	3,503 (100)	16,314 (209)	9,494 (162)	4,714 (115)	17,780 (218)	11,479 (177)	3,961 (106)	1,298 (61)	1,041 (55)
Women											
1990	28,636 (235)	847 (46)	1,861 (67)	11,810 (163)	6,462 (123)	— (—)	7,655 (133)	4,704 (106)	— (—)	— (—)	— (—)
1991	29,474 (237)	733 (42)	1,819 (67)	10,959 (157)	5,633 (115)	2,523 (78)	7,807 (135)	5,263 (112)	2,025 (70)	312 (28)	206 (23)
1992	30,346 (240)	734 (42)	1,659 (64)	11,039 (158)	5,904 (118)	2,655 (80)	8,355 (139)	5,604 (115)	2,192 (73)	334 (29)	225 (24)
1993	30,683 (240)	765 (43)	1,576 (62)	10,513 (154)	6,279 (121)	3,067 (86)	8,483 (140)	5,735 (116)	2,166 (73)	323 (28)	260 (25)
1994	31,379 (242)	696 (41)	1,675 (64)	10,785 (156)	6,256 (121)	3,210 (88)	8,756 (142)	5,901 (118)	2,174 (73)	398 (31)	283 (26)
1995	32,673 (276)	774 (45)	1,763 (68)	11,064 (168)	6,329 (128)	3,336 (93)	9,406 (155)	6,434 (129)	2,208 (77)	421 (33)	283 (27)
1996	33,549 (290)	750 (46)	1,751 (71)	11,363 (177)	6,582 (136)	3,468 (99)	9,636 (163)	6,689 (137)	2,213 (79)	413 (34)	322 (30)
1997	34,624 (294)	791 (48)	1,765 (71)	11,475 (177)	6,628 (136)	3,538 (100)	10,427 (169)	7,173 (141)	2,448 (83)	488 (37)	318 (30)
1998	35,628 (297)	814 (48)	1,878 (73)	11,613 (178)	7,070 (140)	3,527 (100)	10,725 (172)	7,288 (143)	2,639 (87)	468 (37)	329 (31)
1999	37,091 (302)	886 (50)	1,883 (73)	11,824 (180)	7,453 (144)	3,804 (104)	11,242 (176)	7,607 (146)	2,818 (89)	470 (37)	346 (31)
2000	37,762 (304)	930 (52)	1,950 (75)	11,789 (180)	7,391 (144)	4,118 (108)	11,584 (178)	7,899 (148)	2,823 (90)	509 (38)	353 (32)
2001	38,228 (306)	927 (51)	1,869 (73)	11,690 (179)	7,283 (143)	4,190 (109)	12,269 (183)	8,257 (151)	3,089 (94)	531 (39)	392 (34)

—Not available.

[1] Includes 1 to 3 of years high school for 1990.

[2] Includes 4 years of high school for 1990, and equivalency certificates for the other years.

[3] Includes 1 to 3 years of college and associate degrees for 1990.

[4] Not reported separately for 1990.

[5] Includes 4 or more years of college for 1990.

[6] Includes 4 years of college for 1990.

NOTE: Data for 1992 and later years are based on 1990 Census counts; prior years are based on 1980 counts. Standard errors appear in parentheses. Detail may not sum to totals due to rounding.

SOURCE: U.S. Department of Commerce, Bureau of the Census, Current Population Reports, Series P-60, "Money Income of Households, Families, and Persons in the United States," "Income, Poverty, and Valuation of Noncash Benefits," selected years; and Series P-60, "Money Income in the United States," selected years. (This table was prepared August 2003.)

A

A to Z Teacher Stuff, 5994
A&F Video's Art Catalog, 6212
A&L Fund Raising, 2843
A&M University, 411
A+ Enterprises, 2844
A-V Online, 5774
AAA Teacher's Agency, 193
AACE, 4708
AACE Careers Update, 4425
AACRAO Data Dispenser, 4317
AACS Newsletter, 4112
AACSB Newsline, 4113
AACTE Briefs, 3484
AAEE Job Search Handbook for Educators, 3913
AAHE Bulletin, 4114
AASA Bulletin, 4318
AATF National Bulletin, 4502
ABC Feelings Adage Publications, 4730
ABC School Supply, 5226
ABC Toon Center, 5896
ABC-CLIO, 3755, 3963, 4073, 4092
ABC-CLIO Schools, 6158
ABDO Publishing Company, 4731
AC Montessori Kids, 1537
ACCESS ERIC, 1
ACCT Advisor, 4319
ACE Fellows Program, 3297, 3619
ACF Office of Public Affairs, 4393
ACI & SEV Elementary School, 1451
ACJS Today, 4115
ACSI Teachers' Convention, 654
ACT, 5775, 6233, 6235
ACT Success, 5730
ACTFL Newsletters, 4503
ACTION, 2
ACTIVITY, 4637
ADA Update, 4320
ADE Bulletin, 4504
ADP Lemco, 5227
AE Finley Foundation, 2677
AECT, 3307
AEE and Kendall/Hunt Publishing Company, 3428, 3437, 3475
AEJMC, 695
AEL, Inc., 51, 4158, 4226
AFCENT Elementary & High School, 1538
AFL-CIO, 2866, 3301
AFL-CIO Guide to Union Sponsored Scholarships, Awards & Student Aid, 2866
AFS Intercultural Programs USA, 4155
AGC/United Learning, 5155
AGS, 4732
AGS/Lake Publishing Company, 4903
AIMS Education Foundation, 4733
AIMS Multimedia, 5414
AISES, 676
ALA Editions Catalog, 4544
ALISE, 3308
AM Educational Publishing, 4107
AMX Corporation, 5776
APCO, 5228
ART New England Summer Workshops, 3620
ASBO International Annual Meetings and Exhibits, 157
ASC Electronics, 5777
ASCA Counselor, 4455
ASCD, 163, 699, 4761

ASCD Annual Conference & Exhibit Show, 655
ASCD Update, 4116
ASHA, 683
ASPIRA Association, 3
ASQ, 3298
ASQ Annual Koalaty Kid Conference, 3298
ASQC, 5946
ASRS of America, 5474
ASSC Newsletter, 4117
ATEA Journal, 3485
AV Guide Newsletter, 4118
AVA Update, 4321
AVKO Dyslexia Research Foundation, 5075
AZLA/MPLA Conference, 656
Abbotsholme School, 1539
Abcteach, 5992
Abdul Hamid Sharaf School, 1452
Abe Wouk Foundation, 2378
Abell Foundation, 2491
AbleNet, 5229
Ablex Publishing Corporation, 4734
About Education Distance Learning, 6185
About Education Elementary Educators, 6021
About Parenting/Family Daycare, 6010
Abquaiq Academy, 1453
Academe, 4119
Academia Cotopaxi American International School, 1296
Academic Alliances, 3260
Academic Programs Office, 3036
Academic Software Development Group, 6146
Academic Travel Abroad, 222
Academic Year & Summer Programs Abroad, 3732
Academy for Educational Development, 4, 3430, 3448, 6040
Academy of Applied Science, 362
Academy of Criminal Justice Services, 4115
Academy-English Prep School, 1540
Accelerated Math, 5778, 6112
Accelerated Reader, 5779, 6140
Accountability Reporting and Research, 3207
Accounter Systems USA, 5230
Accounting & Financial Management Services, 2878
Accounting, Personnel & School Finance Unit, 3255
Accreditation & Curriculum Services Department, 3097
Accreditation & Standards Division, 3153
Accreditation Fact Sheet, 4322
Accredited Institutions of Postsecondary Education, 3733, 4015
Accu-Cut Systems, 5231
Accu-Weather, 6147
AccuLab Products Group, 6148
AccuNet/AP Multimedia Archive, 6156
AccuWeather, Inc., 6156
Accuracy Temporary Services Incorporated, 837
Achelis Foundation, 2609
Ackworth School, Ackworth, 1541
Acorn Naturalists, 4735
Action Alliance for Virginia's Children and Youth, 592
Action in Teacher Education, 3486
Active Child, 4736
Active Learning, 4737
Active Parenting Publishers, 4738, 803

Active Parenting Publishing, 5156
Activities and Strategies for Connecting Kids with Kids: Elementary Edition, 3734
Activities and Strategies for Connecting Kids with Kids: Secondary Edition, 3735
Actrix Systems, 5780
Add Vantage Learning Incorporated, 838
Adden Furniture, 5475
Addison-Wesley Publishing Company, 4739
Administration & Financial Management Center, 3004
Administrative & Financial Services, 3105
Administrative Information Report, 4323
Administrative Services, 3233
Administrative Services Office, 3059, 3101
Admission Officer's Handbook for the New SAT Program, 6234
Admixture Division, 5595
Adolescence, 4456, 4638
Adolescent Pregnancy Prevention Clearinghouse, 4016
Adolph Coors Foundation, 2359
Adrian & Jessie Archbold Charitable Trust, 2610
Adult Extended Learning Office, 3060
Adult Services, 2538
Adult/Continuing Education, 6143
Advance Family Support & Education Program, 4740
Advance Infant Development Program, 839
Advance Products Company, 5415
Advance Program for Young Scholars, 5
Advanced Keyboard Technology, Inc., 5329
Advantage Learning Systems, 6067, 6227
Adventures Company, 5618
Advisory & Distribution Committee Office, 2704
Advocate, 4120
Advocates for Language Learning Annual Meeting, 657
Aegon USA, 2492
Aero Gramme, 4121
Aerospace Education Foundation, 363
Aerospace Industries Association of America, 194
Aetna Foundation, 2366
African Studies Center, University of Pennsylvania, 6066
African-American Institute, 380
Agency Support, 3118
Agency for Instructional Technology, 391, 3261, 4719
Agency for Instructional Technology/AIT, 5157
Agency for International Development, 223
Agenda: Jewish Education, 4122
Aguirre International Incorporated, 840
Ahmanson Foundation, 2276
Aid for Education, 2845
Air Rights Building, 2494
Air Technologies Corporation, 5476
Airomat Corporation, 5232
Airspace USA, 5233
Aisha Mohammed International School, 1966
Aiyura International Primary School, 1090
Ake Panya International School, 1091
Akron Community Foundation, 2692
Al Ain English Speaking School, 1454
Al Bayan Bilingual School, 1455
Al Khubairat Community School, 1456
Al Rabeeh School, 1457
Al-Nouri English School, 1458

Al-Worood School, 1459

Alabama Business Education Association, 411

Alabama Department of Education, 2917, 2918, 2919, 2920, 2921, 2922, 2923, 2925, 2926, 2927, 2928

Alabama Department of Rehabilitation Services, 2924

Alabama Education Association, 412

Alabama Library Association, 413

Alabama State Department of Education, 2916

Alarion Press, 4741

Alaska Association of School Librarians, 414

Alaska Business Education Association, 415

Alaska Commission on Postsecondary Education, 2929

Alaska Department of Education, 2930, 2932, 2934

Alaska Department of Education & Early Development, 2931

Alaska Department of Education & Early Development, 2929

Alaska Department of Education & Energy Developmnt, 2933

Alaska Department of Education Bilingual & Bicultural Education Conference, 3299

Alaska Department of Labor & Workforce Development, 2935

Alaska Library Association, 416

Albania Tirana International School, 1967

Albert & Ethel Herzstein Charitable Foundation, 2764

Albert Whitman & Company, 4742

Alcoa Foundation, 2726

Alcohol & Drug Prevention for Teachers, Law Enforcement & Parent Groups, 6036

Alconbury Elementary School, 1542

Alconbury High School, 1543

Alex & Marie Manoogian Foundation, 2526

Alexander M Patch Elementary School, 1544

Alexander M Patch High School, 1545

Alexander Muss High School Israel, 1968

Alexandra House School, 1030

Alfa Aesar, 5619

Alfred M Barbe High School, 492

Alfred P Sloan Foundation, 2611

Alfred T Mahan Elementary School, 1546

Alfred T Mahan High School, 1547

Alice Tweed Tuohy Foundation, 2277

All American Scoreboards, 5416

All Art Supplies, 5234, 6213

All Sports, 2846

Allen Communications, 5781

Allen County Public Library, 2461

Alliance for Parental Involvement in Education, 6, 4256

Alliance for Schools That Work, 7

Alliance for Technology Access, 392

Alliance for Technology Access Conference, 392

Alliance for Technology Access/Hunter House, 3754

Allied Video Corporation, 5158

Alltech Electronics Company, 5782

Allyn & Bacon, 4743

Alma Industries, 5477

Almaty International School, 1969

Alotau International Primary School, 1092

Alpha Publishing Company, 4744

Alternative Education Resource Organizations, 4121

Altman Foundation, 2612

Altschul Group Corporation, 5159

Alumni Newsletter, 4668

Amberg Elementary School, 1548

Ambrit Rome International School, 1549

Ambrose Monell Foundation, 2613

Ambrose Video Publishing Inc, 5160

Amelia Earhart Intermediate School, 1093

Ameren Corporation, 2570

Ameren Corporation Charitable Trust, 2570

America Taking Action, 5897

America for the Art, 3998, 4054

American School, 1970

American Academy Larnaca, 1422

American Academy of Arts & Sciences Bulletin, 4578

American Academy of Pediatrics, 8

American Alliance for Health, Phys. Ed. & Dance, 4606

American Alliance for Health, Physical Education, Recreation and Dance, 342

American Art Clay Company, 6214

American Art Therapy Association, 329

American Assembly/Collegiate Schools of Business, 4113

American Assn. of State Colleges & Universities, 4354

American Association School Administrators National Conference on Education, 658

American Association for Career Education, 4425

American Association for Chinese Studies, 381

American Association for Counseling & Development, 214

American Association for Employment in Education Annual Conference, 659

American Association for Employment in Education, 659, 3771, 3913

American Association for Higher Education, 4114

American Association for Higher Education: Annual Assessment Conference, 660

American Association for Higher Education: Learning to Change Conference, 661

American Association for Higher Education: Summer Academy, Organizing for Learning, 662

American Association for State & Local History, 4745

American Association for Vocational Instructional Materials, 9

American Association of Christian Schools, 4112

American Association of Colleges for Teacher Education-Directory, 663, 3262, 3421

American Association of Colleges for Teacher Ed., 3274, 3421, 3484

American Association of Collegiate Registrars, 154, 3300, 3860, 4317

American Association of French Teachers, 664

American Association of Higher Education, 3260

American Association of Physics Teachers, 665, 4658

American Association of School Administrators, 155, 666, 4746, 3357, 3404, 3547, 3835, 3837, 3885, 4318, 4369, 4417, 5801, 6032, 6035

American Association of School Librarians National Conference, 667

American Association of Schools & Departments of Journalism, 298

American Association of Sex Educators, 4488

American Association of Sex Educators, Counselors & Therapists Conference, 668

American Association of Sex Educators, Counsel ors & Therapists, 211

American Association of Specialized Colleges, 10

American Association of Teachers of French, 299, 4502

American Association of University Professors, 4119

American Association of University Women, 649

American Associations for Higher Education, 660, 661, 662

American Biology Teacher, 4648

American Board of Master Educators, 355

American Business Communication Association, 11, 300

American Business Directories, 3852, 3902, 4019, 4041, 4108

American Business Directories, Inc., 3881

American Camping Association, 669

American Camping Association National Conference, 669

American Chemical Society, 5620

American Choral Directors Association, 4583

American College Testing, 6235, 4637

American College-Greece, 1550

American College-Sofia, 1423

American Collegiate Institute, 1460

American Community School, 1461

American Community School-Abu Dhabi, 1462

American Community School-Beirut, 1463

American Community School-Cobham, 1551

American Community School-Egham, 1552

American Community School-Hillingdon, 1553

American Community Schools, 1554

American Community Schools-Athens, 1555

American Consulate General Karachi, 2144

American Consulate General Lahore, 1189

American Cooperative School, 1297, 1971

American Cooperative School of Tunis, 1972

American Council for Drug Education, 12

American Council on Education, 13, 448, 670, 3297, 3619, 3829, 4123, 4190, 6242

American Council on Education Annual Meeting, 670

American Council on Education Library & Information Service, 448

American Council on Education for Journalism, 301

American Council on Education: GED Testing Service, 4123

American Council on Industrial Arts Teacher Education, 330

American Council on Rural Special Education, 14

American Council on Schools and Colleges, 15

American Council on the Teaching of Foreign Languages Annual Conference, 302, 671

American Council on the Teaching of Foreign Lang., 4503, 4519

American Counseling Association, 212, 672, 4455, 4467, 4468, 4469, 4472, 4478, 4482, 4485, 4487, 4489, 4495

Publisher Listings Appear in Bold

American Counseling Association Annual Convention, 672

American Dance Therapy Association, 331

American Driver & Traffic Safety Education Association, 356

American Econo-Clad Services, 6076

American Education Finance Association, 156, 673

American Education Finance Association Annual Conference & Workshop, 673

American Educational Research Association, 674, 3263, 3743, 4174, 4175

American Educational Research Journal, 3487

American Educational Studies Association, 675, 3264

American Educator, 3488

American Elementary & High School, 1298

American Embassy Accra, 1068

American Embassy Algiers, 1992

American Embassy Bratislava, 2016

American Embassy School, 1973

American Embassy School of New Delhi, 1974

American Embassy School-Reykjavik, 1556

American Express Company, 2614

American Express Foundation, 2614

American Federation of Teachers, 16, 3488

American Federation of Teachers Biennial Convention & Exhibition, 3301

American Foam, 5235

American Forest Foundation, 4982

American Foundation Corporation, 2693

American Foundation for Negro Affairs, 3265

American Friends Service Committee, 224

American Guidance Service, 4747

American Historical Association, 3987

American Home Economics Association, 5126

American Honda Foundation, 2823

American Indian Science & Engineering Society Annual Conference, 676

American Institute for Foreign Study, 3732

American Institute of Physics, 4748

American International School, 1464

American International School of Nouakchott, 1975

American International School-Abu Dhabi, 1465

American International School-Abuja, 1976

American International School-Bamako, 1977

American International School-Bolivia, 1299

American International School-Bucharest, 1424

American International School-Budapest, 1425

American International School-Carinthia, 1557

American International School-Chennai, 1978

American International School-Costa Rica, 1979

American International School-Cyprus, 1426

American International School-Dhaka, 1031, 1094

American International School-Florence, 1558

American International School-Freetown, 1980

American International School-Genoa, 1559

American International School-Guangzhou, 1095

American International School-Israel, 1466

American International School-Johannesburg, 1032

American International School-Kingston, 1981

American International School-Krakow, 1427

American International School-Kuwait, 1467

American International School-Lesotho, 1982

American International School-Libreville, 1983

American International School-Lincoln Buenos Aires, 1300

American International School-Lisbon, 1560

American International School-Lome, 1984

American International School-Lom, 1033

American International School-Lusaka, 1985

American International School-Mozambique, 1986

American International School-Muscat, 1468

American International School-N'Djamena, 1987

American International School-Nouakchott, 1988

American International School-Riyadh, 1469

American International School-Rotterdam, 1561

American International School-Salzburg, 1562

American International School-Vienna, 1428, 1563

American International School-Zambia, 1034

American International Schools, 841

American Jewish Congress, 225

American Journal of Education, 4124

The American Legion, 4001

American Libraries, 4545

American Library Association, 316, 667, 677, 4545, 4546, 4563

American Library Association Annual Conference, 677

American Locker Security Systems, 5556

American Mathematical Society, 678, 4575

American Montessori Society, 17, 4422

American Montessori Society Conference, 679

American Musicological Society, 332

American Nicaraguan School, 1989

American Nuclear Society, 4749

American Overseas School-Rome, 1564

American Physiological Society, 4750

American Plastics Council, 5236

American Playground Corporation, 5731

American Psychological Association Annual Conference, 680

American Public Health Association, 681

American Public Health Association Annual Meeting, 681

American Public Human Services Association, 18, 4266

American Samoa Department of Education, 1990

American Scholar, 4125

American School, 1301

American School & University - Who's Who Directory & Buyer's Guide, 3861

American School & University Magazine, 4324

American School Board Journal, 4325, 3290

American School Counselor Association, 213

American School Directory, 3736

American School Foundation AC, 1302

The American School Foundation of Monterrey, 1419

American School Foundation-Guadalajara, 1303

American School Foundation-Monterrey, 1304

American School Health Association, 19, 4189, 4216

American School Health Association's National School Conference, 682

American School Honduras, 1991

American School of Bucharest, 1429

American School of Kinshasa, 1035

American School of Warsaw, 249

American School of the Hague, 1565

American School-Algiers, 1992

American School-Antananarivo, 1993

American School-Asuncion, 1994

American School-Barcelona, 1566

American School-Belo Horizonte, 1305

American School-Bilbao, 1567

American School-Bombay, 1096

American School-Brasilia, 1306

American School-Campinas, 1307

American School-Doha, 1470

American School-Dschang, 1995

American School-Durango, 1308

American School-Guangzhou (China), 1097

American School-Guatemala, 1309, 1996

American School-Guayaquil, 1310

American School-Japan, 1098

American School-Kuwait, 1471

American School-Laguna Verde, 1311

American School-Las Palmas, 1568

American School-Lima, 1312

American School-London, 1569

American School-Madrid, 1570

American School-Milan, 1571

American School-Niamey, 1997

American School-Pachuca, 1313

American School-Paris, 1572

American School-Port Gentil, 1998

American School-Puebla, 1314

American School-Puerto Vallarta, 1315

American School-Recife, 1316

American School-Santo Domingo, 1945

American School-Tampico, 1317

American School-Tangier, 1036

American School-Tegucigalpa, 1999

American School-Torreon, 1318

American School-Valencia, 1573

American School-Warsaw, 2000

American School-Yaounde, 1037, 2001

American School-the Hague, 1574

American Schools Association of Central America, Columbia-Caribbean and Mexico, 226

American Secondary Education, 4639

American Society for Training & Development, 3422

American Society for Training and Development Information Center, 3266

American Society for Training-Development International Conference, 3302

American Society for Training/Development-Trai ning Video, 3422

American Society of Civil Engineers, 6041

American Society of Educators, 4559, 4714

American Society of International Law, 227

American Sociological Review, 4669

American Speech-Language-Hearing Association, 303, 683, 3267

American Sports Education Institute, 343

American Students & Teachers Abroad, 4126

American Swing Products, 5732
American Technical Education Association, 684, 3485
American Technical Publishers, 4751
American Textbook Council, 382
American Time & Signal Company, 5417
American Trade Schools Directory, 4094
American Water Works Association, 4752
American for the Art, 3996, 3997, 4053
American-British Academy, 1472
American-Nicaraguan School, 2002
American-Scandinavian Foundation, 2867, 4444
American-Scandinavian Foundation Magazine, 4444
Ameritech Foundation, 2435
Amherst Regional High School, 503
Amman Baccalaureate School, 1473
Amoco Galeota School, 2003
Ampersand Press, 4753
Amsco School Publications, 4754
Amusing and Unorthodox Definitions, 3737
An Overview of the World Wide Web, 3553
Analog & Digital Peripherals, 3538
Anatolia College, 1575
Anatomical Chart Company, 5237
Anchor Audio, 5161, 6077
Anchor Pad, 5947
Anchor Pad Products, 5783, 5947
Andersen Corporation, 2550
Andersen Elementary & Middle School, 2004
Andersen Foundation, 2550
Anderson's Bookshops, 4755
Andrew W Mellon Foundation, 2615
Angeles Group, 5478
Angels School Supply, 5238
Anglican International School-Jerusalem, 1474
Anglo American School, 1319
Anglo Colombian School, 1320
Anglo-American School, 1321
Anglo-American School-Moscow, 1576
Anglo-American School-St. Petersburg, 1577
Ankara Elementary & High School, 1475
Annenberg Foundation, 2727
Annenberg/CPB Project, 4756
Annual Academic-Vocational Integrated Curriculum Conference, 685
Annual Building Championship Schools Conference, 3303
Annual Challenging Learners with Untapped Potential Conference, 686
Annual Conductor's Institute of South Carolina, 3621
Annual Conference on Hispanic American Education, 687
Annual Convention, 3304
Annual Effective Schools Conference, 688
Annual Ethics & Technology Conference, 689
Annual Microcomputers in Education Conference, 690
Annual NCEA Convention & Exposition, 691
Annual New England Kindergarten Conference, 3305
Annual Register of Grant Support, 3957
Annual Report & Notes from the Field, 4127
Annual State Convention of Association of Texas Professional Educators, 3306
Annual Summer Institute for Secondary Teachers, 3622

Annual Technology & Learning Conference, 692
Ansbach Elementary School, 1578
Ansbach High School, 1579
Anthro Corporation Technology Furniture, 5479
AnthroNotes, 4649, 4670
Anthropology Outreach Office, 4670
Anti-Defamation League, 5050
Antofagasta International School, 1322
Antwerp International School, 1580
Anzoategui International School, 2005
Aoba International School, 1099
Aol@School, 5239
Appalachia Educational Laboraory, 623
Appalachian State University, 4617
Appalachian State University, College of Education, 4629
Apple Computer, 5784, 3287
Apple Education Grants, 3287
AppleSeeds, 4671
Applebaum Foundation, 2387
Applied Business Technologies, 5948
Applied Data & Technology Unit, 3256
Applied Mathematics Program, 6113
Applied Technology & Adult Learning, 3043
Applied Technology Education Services, 3220
Appraisal: Science Books for Young People, 4650
Appropriate Inclusion and Paraprofessionals, 3423
Aprovecho Institute, 228
Aquinas College, 1946
Arab Unity School, 1476
Arbor Scientific, 5621
Arcadia Foundation, 2728
Architectural Precast, 5480
Arco/Macmillan, 3962
Area Cooperative Educational Services, 842
Argonner Elementary School, 1581
Arizona Association of Independent Academic Schools, 417
Arizona Department of Education, 2260, 2262, 2266, 2267, 2268, 2936
Arizona Governor's Committee on Employment of People with Disabilities, 2261
Arizona Library Association, 418, 656
Arizona School Boards Association, 419
Arizona State University, 330, 690, 4391, 4507, 4612
Arkansas Business Education Association, 422
Arkansas Department of Education, 2937, 2939, 2940
Arkansas Department of Education: Special Education, 2938
Arkansas Education Association, 423
Arkansas Library Association, 424
Arkansas School Study Council, 4117
Armada Art Inc., 5240
Armada Art Materials, 5240
Armenia QSI International School-Yerevan, 2006
Arnold Bernhard Foundation, 2616
Arnold Grummer, 6215
Arrillaga Foundation, 2278
Arrowmont School of Arts & Crafts, 6216
Art & Creative Materials Institute, 6217
Art Education, 4579
Art Image Publications, 4757
Art Instruction Schools, 6218

Art Materials Catalog, 5241
Art Supplies Wholesale, 5242, 5234, 6213
Art Visuals, 4758
Art to Remember, 2847, 5243, 6219
ArtSketchbook.com, 6220
Artix, 5244
Arts & Activities, 4580
Arts & Entertainment Network, 5418
Arts Education Policy Review, 4581
Arts Institutes International, 6221
Arts Management in Community Institutions: Sum mer Training, 3489
Arts Scholarships, 2868
Arundel School, 1038
Arusha International School, 1039
Arvin Foundation, 2462
Ascom Timeplex, 5785
Ashgabat International School, 1100
Ashland Incorporated Foundation, 2477
Asian American Curriculum Project, 317, 4759
AskERIC, 5891
AskSam Systems, 5949
Asmara International Community School, 1040
Asociacion Colegio Granadino, 1323
Asociacion Escuelas Lincoln, 1324
Aspen Group International,Inc, 1002
Aspen Publishers, 4445
Aspen Publishing, 2831, 4012, 4445
Aspen Publishing, Inc., 3959, 4167, 4338, 4373, 4378, 4446, 4448
Aspira of Penna, 843
Assessing Student Performance, 3424
Assessment & Evaluation, 3160
Assessments & Accountability Branch Delaware Department of Education, 2971
Assessories by Velma, 5245
Assistance to States Division, 2879
Assistant Commissioner's Office, 3021
Assistant Superintendent & Financial Services, 2917
Assistive Technology Clinics, 5076
Assn for Childhood Educational International, 632
Assn. for Legal Support of Alternative Schools, 4308
Assn. for Supervision & Curriculum Dev. (ASCD), 4063
Assn. for Supervision & Curriculum Development, 4116
Assn. of Private Schools for Exceptional Children, 4239
Assocation of Christian Schools International, 654
Associated Grantmakers of Massachusetts, 2506
Associated Schools Project Network, 229
Associated Schools Project in Education for International Co-operation, 3738
Associates for Renewal in Education, 449
The Association For Science Teacher Education, 698
Association for Advancement of Behavior Therapy Annual Convention, 693
Association for Advancement of Computing in Education, 324, 364, 393
Association for Asian Studies, 230
Association for Behavior Analysis, 694
Association for Behavior Analysis Annual Convention, 694
Association for Canadian Studies in the US, 231

Association for Career and Technical Education, 394, 3532

Association for Childhood Education International Annual Conference, 632

Association for Childhood Education International, 4402, 4421

Association for Community Based Education, 3739, 4134

Association for Community-Based Education Directory of Members, 20, 3739

Association for Continuing Higher Education Directory, 824, 3425

Association for Disabled Students, 21

Association for Education in Journalism and Mass Communication Convention, 695

Association for Educational Communications & Technology, 4095, 5162

Association for Educational Communications & Technology Annual Convention, 395, 3307

Association for Educational Communications & Tech., 4095

Association for Experiental Education, 3508

Association for Experiential Education, 4060, 4436, 4605

Association for Experiential Education Annual Conference, 633

Association for Gender Equity Leadership in Education, 22

Association for Individually Guided Education, 484

Association for Institutional Research, 357

Association for Integrative Studies, 23

Association for International Practical Training, 232

Association for Library & Information Science Education Annual Conference, 318, 3308

Association for Measurement & Evaluation in Counseling & Development, 214

Association for Persons with Severe Handicaps Annual Conference, 696

Association for Play Therapy, 24, 697

Association for Play Therapy Conference, 697

Association for Play Therapy Newsletter, 4457

Association for Refining Cross-Cultured International, 844

Association for Science Education Teachers, 365

Association for Science Teacher Education, 698, 4760

Association for Supervision & Curriculum, 25, 699, 4761, 655

Association for Supervision & Curriculum Develop., 4347

Association for Suppliers of Printing & Publishing Technologies, 195

Association for Technology Educators, 559

Association for Volunteer Administration, 4321

Association for World Travel Exchange, 233

Association for the Advancement of International Education, 700

Association for the Care of Children's Health, 26

Association for the Education of Gifted Underachieving Students Conference, 701

Association for the Study of Higher Education Annual Meeting, 702

Association of American Colleges & Universitie s Annual Meeting, 703

Association of American Colleges & Universities, 703, 4225

Association of American International Colleges & Universities, 234

Association of American Publishers, 4762

Association of American Schools of Brazil, 235

Association of American Schools of Central America, 236

Association of American Schools of South America, 237

Association of Boarding Schools, 27

Association of British Schools in Spain, 238

Association of California School Administrators, 4384

Association of Christian Schools International, 239, 845

Association of College & Research Libraries, 3435

Association of Commonwealth Universities, 2824, 2825, 3752

Association of Community College Trustees, 704, 4319

Association of Departments of English, 4504

Association of Educational Publishers, 721, 4160

Association of Educational Therapists, 215

Association of Educators in Private Practice, 28

Association of Experiential Education, 4588

Association of International Educators, 240

Association of International Schools in Africa, 241

Association of Orthodox Jewish Teachers of the New York Public Schools, 4128

Association of Orthodox Jewish Teachers of the NY, 4128

Association of School Business Officials International, 157

Association of School Business Officials Int'l, 3884, 4370, 5963

Association of Science-Technology Centers Dimensions, 366, 705, 4651

Association of Science-Technology Centers Incorp., 705

Association of Teacher Educators, 3268

Association of Teachers of Latin American Studies, 4690

Aston Publications, 4443

Astronauts Memorial Foundation, 3721

Astronomical Society of the Pacific, 4667

Astronomy to Go, 5622

Asuncion Christian Academy, 1430

At-Risk Resources, 5246

At-Risk Students: Identification and Assistance Strategies, 3567

Atheneum Books for Children, 4763

Athens College, 1582

Athletic Director, 4600

Athletic Management, 4601

Athletic Training, 4602

Athletics Administration, 4603

Atkinson Foundation, 2279

Atlanta International School, 2007

Atlanta-Fulton Public Library, 2403

Atlantic Fitness Products, 5557

Atlas Track & Tennis, 5247

Atran Foundation, 2617

Attention, 4458

Attention Deficit Disorder Association, 29

Auburn University at Montgomery Library, 2250

Audio Forum, 5248

Audio Visual Products Division, 5173

Audio Visual/Video Products, 5434

Audrey Hillman Fisher Foundation, 2729

Auerbach Central Agency for Jewish Education Incorporated, 846

Augsbury College, 3626

Australian Press-Down Under Books, 4764

Australian Vice-Chancellors' Committee, 1279

Austrian Institute, 2211

Authentic Jane Williams' Home School Market Guide, 3740

Autodesk Retail Products, 5950

Auxiliary Services, 3131

Avcom Systems, 5951

Avenida Deputado Cristovan Chiaradia 120, 1305

Aviano Elementary School, 1583

Aviano High School, 1584

Aviation Information Resources, 196

Avon Books, 4765

Awakening Brilliance: How to Inspire Children to Become Successful Learners, 3741

Awards and Recognition Association, 30, 642, 4272

Awards for University Administrators and Librarians, 2824

Awards for University Teachers and Research Workers, 2825

Awesome Library, 5898, 5995, 6110

Awiley Company, 4766

Awty International School, 2008

Aylmer Press, 6074

Azerbaijan Baku International School, 2009

B

BCI Burke Company, 5733

BEPS 2 Limal International School, 1585

BGS Systems, 5786

BKS Publishing, 4031

BLINKS.Net, 6161

BLS Tutorsystems, 5787

BUILD Sucess Through the Values of Excellence, 5163

Babenhausen Elementary School, 1586

Bad Kissingen Elementary School, 1587

Bad Kreuznach Elementary School, 1588

Bad Kreuznach High School, 1589

Bad Nauheim Elementary School, 1590

Badge-A-Minit, 5249

Badminton School, 1591

Bag Lady School Supplies, 5250

Baghdad International School, 1477

Bahrain Bayan School, 1478

Bahrain Elementary & High School, 1479

Bahrain School, 1480

Baker & Taylor, 6078

Baku International School, 2010

Balance Sheet, 3490

Balboa Elementary School, 1325

Balboa High School, 1326

Bale Company, 5251

Bali International School, 1101

Ball Brothers Foundation, 2011

Ball State University, 3623

Ballad of an EMail Terrorist, 5892
Ballantine/Del Rey/Fawcett/Ivy, 4767
Bamberg Elementary School, 1592
Bamberg High School, 1593
Banda School, 1041
Bandung Alliance International School, 1102
Bandung International School, 1103
Bangalore International School, 1104
Bangkok Patana School, 1105
Bangor Cork Company, 5252
Banjul American Embassy School, 2012
Bank Of America Private Bank, 2803
Bank Street College of Education, 5082
Bank of America Center, 2280
BankAmerica Foundation, 2280
Barbara Cox Anthony Foundation, 2424
Barco Products, 5558
Barker College, 1327
Barr Media/Films, 5419
Barron's Educational Series, 4768
Barrow Hills School, 1594
Basics Plus, 847
Baton Rouge Area Foundation, 2483
Baumgarten's, 5253
Baumholder High School, 1595
Bavarian International School, 1596
Bayer Corporation, 2730
Bayer/NSF Award for Community
    Innovation, 3288
Baylor College of Medicine, 4769
Beacon Education Management, 848
Beacon Hill School, 1106
Beatrice P Delany Charitable Trust, 2618
Beazley Foundation, 2800
Bechtel Group Corporate Giving Program,
    2281
Bedales School, 1597
Bedford School, 1598
Bedgebury School, 1599
Beech Tree Books, 4770
Before You Can Discipline, 4459
Before the School Bell Rings, 3426
Beijing BISS International School, 1107
Belair School, 1947
Belgium Antwerp International School, 1600
Belgrano Day School, 1328
BellSouth Foundation, 2404
Belson Manufacturing, 5734
Benedict Foundation for Independent
    Schools, 2388
Benjamin & Roberta Russell Educational and
    Charitable Foundation, 2251
Benjamin Franklin International School, 1601
Bentley College, 4688
Benwood Foundation, 2756
Bergwall Productions, 5164
Berlin International School, 1602
Berlin Potsdam International School, 1603
Bermuda High School, 1948
Bermuda Institute-SDA, 1949
Bernard Osher Foundation, 2282
Berne University, 3662
Best Manufacturing Sign Systems, 5254
Best-Rite, 5255
Better Chance, 31
Better Teaching, 3491
Between Classes-Elderhostel Catalog, 4129
Beverly Celotta, 849
Beyond Tracking: Finding Success in
    Inclusive Schools, 3427
Beyond Words, 4505, 4615
Beyond the Bake Sale, 3742
Bibliographic Information Center, 2782

Bienvenue Annual Conference, 634
Big Chalk-The Education Network, 5899
Bilingual Research Journal, 4506
Bilingual Review Press, 4507
Bilingue School Isaac Newton, 1329
Bilkent University Preparatory
    School-Bilkent International School, 1481
BillHarley.com, 6134
Bingham Academy Ethiopia, 2013
Binney & Smith, 5256
Biographical Membership Directory, 3743
Birmingham Public Library, 2252
Bishkek International School, 2014
Bishop Anstey Junior School, 1950
Bishop Mackenzie International Schools,
    1042
Bishop's School, 1482
Bitburg Elementary School, 1604
Bitburg High School, 1605
Bitburg Middle School, 1606
Bjorn's International School, 1607
Black Butterfly Children's Books, 4771
Black Cultural Center, 95
Black Forest Academy, 1608
Black History Month, 5257
Blackboard Resurfacing Company, 5258
Blaine Window Hardware, 5559
Blake Books, 4772
Blanton & Moore Company, 5481
Blaustein Building, 2501
Bleacherman, M.A.R.S., 5560
Blind School, 3140
Bloxham School, 1609
Blue Coat School, 1610
Bluegrass Regional Recycling Corporation,
    850
Bluestocking Press, 3740, 4773
Bluestocking Press Catalog, 4773
Blumenfeld Education Newsletter, 4130
Board, 3492, 4326
Bob Hope Primary School, 1108
Bob's Big Pencils, 5259
Bobbing Software, 5952
Bobit Publishing Company, 4285
Bodman Foundation, 2619
Boeblingen Elementary School, 1611
Boettcher Foundation, 2360
Bogor Expatriate School, 1109
Boise Public Library, 2432
Boletin, 4672
Bonn International School, 1612
Bontang International School, 1110
Book It!/Pizza Hut, 5260
Book of Metaphors, Volume II, 3428
Booklist, 4546
Books for All Times, 4170
Booth-Bricker Fund, 2484
Bordeaux International School, 1613
Borden, 5261
Borenson & Associates, 5319
Borham Library, 2273
Borroughs Corporation, 5482
Bosnia-Herzegovina QSI International
    School-Sa rajevo, 2015
Boston Foundation, 2507
Boston Globe Foundation II, 2508
Boston Public Library, 2509
Bowling Green State University, 4639
Boyce Enterprises, 6162
Boyds Mill Press, 4774
Boys-Viva Supermarkets Foundation, 2283
Bradley Foundation, 2405
Brady Office Machine Security, 5483

Braeburn High School, 1043
Braeburn School, 1044
Bratislava American International School,
    2016
Brent International School-Manila, 1111
Brent School, 1112
Bretford Manufacturing, 5484
Bricker's International Directory, 3862
BridgeWater Books, 4775
Brief Legal Guide for the Independent
    Teacher, 3429
Bright Ideas Charter School, 4776
**Brighton Academy/Foundation of Human
    Understanding**, 4131
Brighton Times, 4131
Brillantmont International School, 1614
Bristol-Myers Squibb Foundation, 2620
British Aircraft Corp School, 1483
British American Educational Foundation,
    242
British American School, 1330
British Council School-Madrid, 1615
British Embassy Study Group, 1484
British International School, 1113
British International School Cairo, 1045
British International School-Istanbul, 1485
British Kindergarten, 1616
British Primary School, 1617
British Primary School-Stockholm, 1618
British School Manila, 1114
British School-Amsterdam, 1619
British School-Bern, 1620
British School-Brussels, 1621
British School-Costa Rica, 1331
British School-Lom, 1046
British School-Muscat, 1115
British School-Netherlands, 1622
British School-Oslo, 1623
British School-Paris, 1624
British School-Rio de Janeiro, 1332
British School-Venezuela, 1333
British Yeoward School, 1047
Brixey, 5485
Broadhurst Primary School, 1048
Brochure of American-Sponsored Overseas
    Schools, 4132
Brodart Automation, 6093
Brodart Company, Automation Division,
    5486, 6079
Broderbund Software, 5788
Bromsgrove School, 1625
Bronx Zoo, 5058
Brooke House College, 1626
Brookhouse Preparatory School, 1049
Brown & Benchmark Publishers, 4777
Brunch Bunch, 5900
Brussels American School, 1627
Brussels English Primary School, 1628
Bryanston School, 1629
Bryant Junior High School, 422
Bryant University, 4710
Bryant and Stratton College, 3624
Buckstaff Company, 5487
Buckswood Grange International School,
    1630
Budgets & Planning, 3191
Buenos Aires International Christian
    Academy, 1334
Buffalo & Erie County Public Library, 2621
Buffalo State College, 4392
Buhl Foundation, 2731
Buhl Optical Company, 5420
Building Leadership Bulletin, 4327

Publisher Listings Appear in Bold

Building Life Options: School-Community Collaborations, 3430
Bulgaria Anglo-American School-Sofia, 2017
Bull HN Information Systems, 5953
Bulletin Boards for Busy Teachers, 5789
Bulman Products, 5262
Bunting & Lyon, 3846
Bureau for At-Risk Youth Guidance Channel, 4778
Bureau of Electronic Publishing, 5954
Bureau of National Affairs, 2911
Burkel Equipment Company, 5561
Burlington Northern Foundation, 2765
Burma International School Yangon, 2018
Burnett Foundation, 2766
Burns Family Foundation, 2019
Burton D Morgan Foundation, 2694
Bush Foundation, 2551
Business & Science Division, 2487
Business & Sciences Department, 2265
Business Education Association of Metro New York, 546
Business Education Forum, 4328
Business Information Division, 2761
Business Publishers, 4779, 4407, 4447, 4633, 4703
Business Services Office, 2982
Business Teachers Association of New York State, 547
Business, Economics & Law, 2665
Business, Science & Documents, 2393
Business, Science & Technology Department, 2806
Business-Education Insider, 4133
BusyCooks.com, 5901
Butzbach Elementary School, 1631
Bydee Art, 5263
Byron Elementary School, 1632
Bytes of Learning Incorporated, 6068

C

C-SPAN Classroom, 5421
C-Thru Ruler Company, 5264
C/O Ann T Keiser, 2512
C/O Bank South N.A., 2410
C/O BellSouth Corporation, 2404
C/O Boston Safe Deposit & Trust Company, 2510
C/O Brookhill Corporation, 2354
C/O Chemical Bank, 2622
C/O Dexter Shoe Company, 2490
C/O Emmet, Marvin & Martin, 2642
C/O Emrys J. Ross, 2302
C/O Fiduciary Resources, 2292
C/O First Manhattan Company, 2659
C/O First National Bank of Maryland, 2493
C/O Foundations of the Milken Families, 2323
C/O Fulton, Duncombe & Rowe, 2613
C/O Gibney, Anthony & Flaherty, 2663
C/O JPMorgan Private Bank, 2646
C/O Jay L. Owen, 2449
C/O Melton Bank N.A., 2745
C/O Michael Bienes, 2400
C/O NationsBank of Georgia, 2409
C/O Patterson, Belknap, Webb & Tyler, 2653
C/O U.S. Trust Company of New York, 2669

C/O UMB Bank, N.A., 2573
C/S Newsletter, 3493
CA Monitor of Education, 4248
CAE Software, 6114
CARE, 243
CASE Currents, 4329
CASE Directory of Advancement Professionals in Education, 3744
CASE Newsletter, 4330
CASE in Point, 4331
CASIO, 5422
CASL Software, 5790
CASPR, 5423
CBE Report, 4134
CCAS Newsletter, 4582, 4652
CCI/Crosby Publishing, 4700
CCU Software, 5791
CCV Software, 5792
CD Publications, 2848
CD Publictions, 3786
CDE Books & Videos, 2942
CDE Press, 3778
CDS International, 244
CEA Forum, 4508
CEDS Communique, 4135
CEM Corporation, 5623
CHADD, 706
CHADD: Children & Adults with Attention Deficit/Hyperactivity Disorder, 32, 706
CHEM/Lawrence Hall of Science, 5265
CIV International School-Sophia Antipolis, 1633
CLEARVUE/eav, 4780
CMP Media, 4722
CNC Software, 6174
COLLEGESOURCE, 4017
CORD Communications, 5266
CPM Educational Program, 851
CRAFT House Corporation, 5711
CRS, 5955
CTB/McGraw-Hill, 6207
CUNY Teacher Incentive Program, 2869
Cabell Publishing, 3914
Cabell Publishing Company, 3745, 3863, 3915, 3916, 3917, 4018
Cabell's Directory of Publishing Opportunities in Education, 3914
Cabell's Directory of Publishing Opportunities in Accounting, 3915
Cabell's Directory of Publishing Opportunities in Economics & Finance, 3916
Cabells Directory of Publishing Opportunities in Educational Curriculum & Methods, 3745
Cabells Directory of Publishing Opportunities in Educational Psychology and Administration, 3863, 3917, 4018
Cable in the Classroom, 4700, 5424
Cadet Gray: Your Guide to Military Schools-Mil itary Colleges & Cadet Programs, 3746
Cairo American College, 1050, 1486
Calculators, 4781
Calcutta International School Society, 1116
Caldwell Flores Winters, 852
Caleb C & Julia W Dula Educational & Charitable Foundation, 2622
Califone International, 5267
California Biomedical Research Association, 367
California Business Education Association, 426

California Classical Association-Northern Section, 427
California Community Foundation, 2284
California Council for Adult Education, 3309
California Department of Education, 2941, 2944, 2945, 2946, 2947, 2948, 2949, 2951
California Department of Education Catalog, 2942
California Department of Special Education, 2943
California Foundation for Agriculture in the C lassroom, 428
California Kindergarten Association, 3310
California Kindergarten Association Annual Conference, 3310
California Library Association, 429
California Reading Association, 430
California School Boards Association, 3311, 4332
California School Library Association, 431
California Schools Magazine, 4332
California State University, 4483
California State University - Long Beach, 4682
California State University, Dept. of History, 388
California Teachers Association, 432
California Weekly Explorer, 4673
California Weekly Reporter, 4673
Callaway Foundation, 2406
Calliope, 4674
Calpe College International School, 1634
Caltex American School, 1117
Camberwell Grammar School, 1118
Cambridge Development Laboratory, 5793
Cambridge High School, 1487
Cambridge University Press, 4782, 4540
Campion School, 1635
Campus America, 5956
Canadian Academy, 1119
Canadian Association of Independent Schools, 245
Canadian Association of Second Language Teachers, 6072
Canadian College Italy-The Renaissance School, 1636
Canadian School-India, 1120
Canadian Valley Vo Tech, 94
Canberra Grammar School, 1121
Candlewick Press, 4783
Cannon Foundation, 2678
Canon USA, 5425
Capital Cities-ABC Corporate Giving Program, 2623
Capitol Christian School, 1951
Capstone Press, 4784
Captiol Publications, 4276, 4453
Cardinal Industries, 5268
Career & Lifelong Learning, 3225
Career & Technical Education, 3061, 3180
Career & Vocational Counseling Directory, 4019
Career Book, 3918
Career Development Activities for Every Classroom, 3919
Career Development for Exceptional Individuals, 4426
Career Education News, 4427
Career Evaluation Systems, 853
Career Guidance Foundation, 3787, 4017
Career Guide to Professional Associations Directory of Organizations, 3920

Career Information Center; 13 Volumes, 3921
Career Technology & Adult Learning, 3046
Careers Bridge Newsletter, 4428
Careers Conference, 3312
Careers Information Officers in Local
  Authorities, 3922
**Careers Research & Advisory
  Centre/Hobsons Pub.**, 3922
**Careers/Consultants Consultants in
  Education**, 3737, 3756, 3780, 3788, 3853
Careers/Consultants in Education Press, 4785
Cargill Foundation, 2552
Caribbean American School, 2020
Caribbean International School, 1335
Caribbean-American School, 2021
Carl & Lily Pforzheimer Foundation, 2624
Carl Vinson Institute of Government, 4696
Carmel School-Hong Kong, 1122
Carnegie Corporation of New York, 2625
Carnegie Foundation for the Advancement of
  Teaching, 854
Carney Sandoe & Associates, 855
Carolina Biological Supply Co., 4084
Carolina Biological Supply Company, 5624
Carolina Lawson Ivey Memorial Foundation,
  2253
Carolrhoda Books, 4786
Carousel Productions, 5269
Carpets for Kids Etc..., 5488
Carrie Estelle Doheny Foundation, 2285
Carson-Dellosa Publishing Company, 4787
Carter/Tardola Associates, 856
Carus Corporate Contributions Program,
  2436
Casa Montessori Internationale, 1123
Casa del Pueblo Community Program, 246
Casablanca American School, 1051
Cascade School Supplies, 5270
Cascais International School, 1637
Case Western Reserve University, 4528
Castelli Elementary School, 1638
Castelli International School, 1639
Casterton School, 1640
Catalog Card Company, 6080
Catalog of Federal Domestic Assistance,
  3958
Catalog of Federal Education Grants, 3959
Catalyst for Change, 4136
Catholic Library Association, 4547
Catholic Library World, 4547
Catholic Medical Mission Board, 247
Caulastics, 5426
Cavina School, 1052
Caxton College, 1641
Cebu International School, 1124
Cedar Rapids Public Library, 2472
Cedrus, 5165
Celebrate Diversity, 5271
Celebrate Earth Day, 5272
Center Academy, 1642
Center Enterprises, 5273
Center Focus, 4137
**Center for Adult Learning & Education
  Credentials**, 4186
Center for Adult Learning and Educational
  Credentials, 33
Center for Appalachian Studies & Services
  Annual Conference, 707
Center for Applications of Psychological
  Type Biennial Education Conference, 708
Center for Applied Linguistics, 304
Center for Civic Education, 34

Center for Continuing Education of Women
  Newsletter, 4138
Center for Critical Thinking and Moral
  Critique Annual International, 635
Center for Education Studies, 382
Center for Educational Innovation, 857
Center for Educational Leadership Trinity
  University, 3625
Center for Educational Outreach and
  Innovation, 6163
Center for Educational Policy Studies, 35
Center for Educational Technologies, 396
Center for Equity and Excellence in
  Education, 5077
Center for Gifted Education and Talent
  Development Conference, 709
Center for Global Education, 3626
Center for Image Processing in Education,
  3627
**Center for Information &
  Communication**, 647
Center for Instructional Services, 3493
Center for International Development,
  2249
**Center for International Ed./University of
  TN**, 3969
Center for Learning, 5078, 5274
The Center for Learning, 5078
Center for Learning Connections, 3628
Center for Occupational Research &
  Development, 3629
Center for Parent Education Newsletter, 4139
Center for Peak Performing Schools, 3303
Center for Play Therapy, 187, 3630, 4788,
  4032
Center for Play Therapy Fall Conference,
  3313
Center for Play Therapy Summer Institute,
  825
**Center for Professional Development &
  Services**, 858, 3701
Center for Research on the Context of
  Teaching, 5079
Center for Research on the Education of
  Students Placed at Risk, 5080
Center for Resource Management, 859
Center for Rural Education and Small
  Schools Annual Conference, 710
Center for Rural Studies, 3269
Center for School Assessment & Research,
  3005
**Center for Science & Technology
  Education**, 3396
Center for Social Organization of Schools,
  5081
Center for Strategic & International Studies,
  248
Center for Teacher/Learning Math, 4570
Center for Teaching International Relations,
  5275
Center for Teaching/Learning Math, 4566
Center for Technology & School Change,
  3720
Center for Technology in Education, 5082
Center for U.N. Studies, GPO Box 2786,
  3481
**Center for the Future of Teaching &
  Learning**, 3548
Center for the Study of Reading, 5083

**Center for the Study of Small/Rural
  Schools**, 5084, 796, 3567, 3574, 3576,
  3578, 3580, 3590, 3591, 3596, 3600, 3601,
  3602, 3604, 3607, 3608, 3609, 3611, 3612,
  3613, 3614
Center for the Teaching of the Americas,
  4672
Center of Concern, 4137
Center on Disabilities Conference, 711
Center on Education and Work, 3312,
  3439, 3937
Center on Families, Schools, Communities &
  Children's Learning, 5085
Center on Human Policy, 36
Center on Organization & Restructuring of
  Schools, 5086
Central American Resource Center, 4090
**Central Bureau for Educational Visits &
  Exchanges**, 3800
Central Java Inter-Mission School, 1125
Central Primary School, 1126
Central Regional Educational Laboratory,
  4789
Central States Conference on the Teaching
  of Foreign Languages, 3314
Central and Eastern European Schools
  Association, 249
Centre International De Valbonne, 1643
Centro Cultural Brazil-Elementary School,
  1336
Centroplex Branch Grants Collection,
  2485
Century Consultants, 5957
Certification & Accreditation, 3047
Certification and Accreditation Programs
  Directory, 3923
Challenger Center for Space Science
  Education, 5625
Champlin Foundations, 2749
Chancery Software, 5920
Chancery Student Management Solutions,
  6081
Chandra X-ray Observatory Center, 5902
Change, 4140
Character Education, 5166, 6039
Character Education Evaluation Tool Kit,
  3747
Character Education Kit: 36 Weeks of
  Success: Elementary Edition, 3748
Character Education Partnership, 3432,
  3465, 3468, 3474, 3568, 3584, 3747, 3794,
  3831, 3832, 3864, 3865, 3866, 3871, 3873,
  3879, 3896, 4214
Character Education Questions & Answers,
  3864
Character Education Resource Guide, 3865
Character Education: Making a Difference,
  3568
Character Education: Restoring Respect &
  Responsibility in our Schools, 3569
Character Education: The Foundation for
  Teacher Education, 3866
Chariot Software Group, 5794
Charitable & Crown Investment - 323,
  2574
Charles & Ellora Alliss Educational
  Foundation, 2553
Charles A Frueauff Foundation, 2269
Charles C Thomas, Publisher, 3868
Charles Scribner & Sons, 4790
Charles Stewart Mott Foundation, 2527
Charleston County Library, 2752
Charters-Ancaster School, 1644

Chas. E. Petrie Comapny, 2858
The Chase Manhattan Bank, 2618
Chase Manhattan Corporation Philanthropy
    Department, 2626
Chatlos Foundation, 2389
Chauncey & Marion Deering McCormick
    Foundation, 2437
Chemtrol, 5562
Cherrydale Farms, 5903, 6024
Cheshire Corporation, 5427
Chiang Mai International School, 1127
Chicago Board of Trade, 4791
Chicago Community Trust, 2438
Chicago Principals Association Education
    Conference, 3315
Chief Counsel, 3173, 3208
Chief Manufacturing, 5428
Chief Manufacturing, Inc., 3412
Chief of Staff Bureau, 3025
Chief of Staff Office, 3174
Child Care Information Exchange, 180
Child Development, 4391
Child Like Consulting Limited, 860
Child Psychiatry & Human Development,
    4460
Child Study Journal, 4392
Child Welfare, 4461
Child Welfare League of America, 4461
Child and Adolescent Social Work Journal,
    4462
Child and Youth Care Forum, 4640
Child's Play Software, 5795
Childcraft Education Corporation, 5276
Childhood Education Association
    International, 636
Children Today, 4393
Children and Families, 4394
Children's Book Council, 4792
**Children's Defense Fund Education &
    Youth Develop.**, 4016
Children's Educational Opportunity
    Foundation, 861
Children's Factory, 5489
Children's Furniture Company, 5490
Children's Hospital, 5076
Children's House, 1645
Children's Literature Festival, 829
Children's Literature in Education, 4411
Children's Press, 4793
Children's Press/Franklin Watts, 4794
**Children's Science Book Review
    Committee**, 4650
Children's Television Workshop, 4795
Childrens Youth Funding Report, 2848
Childs Consulting Associates, 862
Childswork/Childsplay, 5277
Chime Time, 4796
China Books & Periodicals, 3942
Chinese American International School, 2022
Chinese International School, 1128
Chinese Universities & Colleges, 3749
Chip Taylor Communications, 5167
Chisholm, 5429
Chittagong Grammar School, 1129
Choice, 4548
Choices Education Project, 4797
Choosing Your Independent School in the
    United Kingdom & Ireland, 3750
Choral Journal, 4583
Choristers Guild, 712
Choristers Guild's National Festival &
    Directors' Conference, 712

Christian A Johnson Endeavor Foundation,
    2627
Christian Literacy Association, 4616
Christian Literacy Outreach, 4616
Christy-Houston Foundation, 2757
Chroma, 5278
Chroma-Vision Sign & Art System, 5279
ChronTrol Corporation, 5626
Chronicle Financial Aid Guide, 3960
Chronicle Guidance Publications, 3960,
    4096, 4501
Chronicle Vocational School Manual, 4096
Chronicle of Higher Education, 4429
Chrysler Corporate Giving Program, 2528
Churchill Media, 5168
Cirriculum Research and Development
    Group, 5087
Cisco Educational Archives, 3570
Cite Scolaire International De Lyon, 1646
Citibank of Florida Corporate Giving
    Program, 2390
Citizenship Through Sports and Fine Arts
    Curriculum, 5280
CitraRaya International Village, 1267
**City University of NY, Instructional
    Resource Ctr.**, 4520
Civic Practices Network, 37
Civil Rights, 2880
Clarence E Mulford Trust, 2489
Clarence Manger & Audrey Cordero Plitt
    Trust, 2493
Claridge Products & Equipment, 5281
Claris Corporation, 5796
Clark-Winchcole Foundation, 2494
Classic Modular Systems, 5627
Classroom, 863
The Classroom, 5915
Classroom Connect, 3316, 3631
Classroom Direct, 5797
Classroom Exchange, 5890
Classroom Notes Plus, 4509
Classroom Strategies for the English
    Language Learner, 4033
Classroom Teacher's Guide for Working
    with Paraeducators, 3571, 3751
Claude R & Ethel B Whittenberger
    Foundation, 2433
Clavier, 4584
Clay Foundation, 2814
Clearing House: A Journal of Educational
    Research, 4141, 4333
Clearinghouse for Immigrant Education, 38
Clearinghouse for Midcontinent
    Foundations, 2571
Clemson University, 4479, 4644, 5122
Cleveland H Dodge Foundation, 2628
Clinical Play Therapy Videos:
    Child-Centered Developmental &
    Relationship Play Therapy, 3572
**Clonlara Home Based Education
    Programs**, 805, 4172
Clonlara School Annual Conference Home
    Educato rs, 805
Close Up Publishing, 4798
Close-Up Foundation, 358
Closing the Achievement Gap, 3431
Closing the Gap, 713
Clowes Fund, 2463
Coalition of Essential Schools, 864
Cobblestone, 4675
Cobblestone Publishing, 4657, 4671, 4674,
    4675, 4677, 4679
Cobham Hall, 1647

Coca-Cola Foundation, 2407
Cochabamba Cooperative School, 1337
Cognitive Concepts, 4799
Colegio Abraham Lincoln, 1338
Colegio Albania, 2023
Colegio Alberto Einstein, 1339
Colegio Americano De Guayaquil, 1340
Colegio Anglo Colombiano, 1341
Colegio Bilingue Juan Enrigue, 1342
Colegio Bolivar, 1343
Colegio Columbo Britanico, 1344
Colegio Corazon de Maria, 2024
Colegio De Parvulos, 2025
Colegio Del Buen Pastor, 2026
Colegio Del Sagrado Corazon, 2027
Colegio Ecole, 1648
Colegio Espiritu Santo, 2028
Colegio Gran Bretana, 1345
Colegio Granadino, 1346
Colegio Inmaculada, 2029
Colegio Inmaculada Concepcion, 2030
Colegio Interamericano de la Montana, 1347
Colegio Internacional-Carabobo, 2031
Colegio Internacional-Caracas, 2032
Colegio Internacional-Puerto La Cruz, 2033
Colegio International-Meres, 1649
Colegio International-Vilamoura, 1650
Colegio Jorge Washington, 1348
Colegio Karl C Parrish, 1349
Colegio La Inmaculada, 2034
Colegio La Milagrosa, 2035
Colegio Lourdes, 2036
Colegio Madre Cabrini, 2037
Colegio Maria Auxiliadora, 2038
Colegio Marista, 2039
Colegio Marista El Salvador, 2040
Colegio Mater Salvatoris, 2041
Colegio Montelibano, 1350
Colegio Notre Dame Nivel, 2042
Colegio Nuestra Senora de La Caridad, 2043
Colegio Nuestra Senora de La Merced, 2044
Colegio Nuestra Senora de Lourdes, 2045
Colegio Nuestra Senora de Valvanera, 2046
Colegio Nuestra Senora del Carmen, 2047
Colegio Nuestra Senora del Pilar, 2048
Colegio Nuestra Senora del Rosario, 2049
Colegio Nuestra Sra del Rosario, 2050
Colegio Nueva Granada, 1351
Colegio Padre Berrios, 2051
Colegio Parroquial San Jose, 2052
Colegio Peterson SC, 1352
Colegio Ponceno, 2053
Colegio Puertorriqueno de Ninas, 2054
Colegio Reina de Los Angeles, 2055
Colegio Rosa Bell, 2056
Colegio Sacred Heart, 2057
Colegio Sagrada Familia, 2058
Colegio Sagrados Corazones, 2059
Colegio San Agustin, 2060
Colegio San Antonio, 2061
Colegio San Antonio Abad, 2062
Colegio San Benito, 2063
Colegio San Conrado (K-12), 2064
Colegio San Felipe, 2065
Colegio San Francisco De Asis, 2066
Colegio San Gabriel, 2067
Colegio San Ignacio de Loyola, 2068
Colegio San Jose, 2069
Colegio San Juan Bautista, 2070
Colegio San Juan Bosco, 2071
Colegio San Luis Rey, 2072
Colegio San Marcus, 1353
Colegio San Miguel, 2073

Colegio San Rafael, 2074
Colegio San Vicente Ferrer, 2075
Colegio San Vicente de Paul, 2076
Colegio Santa Clara, 2077
Colegio Santa Cruz, 2078
Colegio Santa Gema, 2079
Colegio Santa Rita, 2080
Colegio Santa Rosa, 2081
Colegio Santa Teresita, 2082
Colegio Santiago Apostol, 2083
Colegio Santisimo Rosario, 2084
Colegio Santo Domingo, 2085
Colegio Santo Nino de Praga, 2086
Colegio Santos Angeles Custod, 2087
Colegio Ward, 1354
Colegio de La Salle, 2088
Coleman Foundation, 2439
Colgate University, 4205
Collective Publishing Service, 5934
College Athletic Administrator, 4601
College Board, 359, 2870, 4800
The College Board, 4006
College Board Guide to High Schools, 4068
College Board News, 4463
College Board Publications, 5169, 326,
  3451, 3769, 3774, 3961, 4020, 4021, 4027,
  4068, 4463, 4464, 4465, 6211, 6234, 6236,
  6237, 6238, 6239, 6241, 6244
College Board Review, 4464
College Board/SAT, 5798
College Bound, 865
College Costs and Financial Aid Handbook,
  3961
College Du Leman International School, 1651
College English Association, 4508
College Entrance Examination Board, 866
College Financial Aid Annual, 3962
College Handbook, 4020
College Handbook Foreign Student
  Supplement, 4021
College International-Fontainebleau, 1652
College Lycee Cevenol International, 1653
College Times, 4465
College Transfer Guide, 4022
College of Education, 710
College of the Ozarks, 3632
College-Bound Seniors, 6236
CollegeChoice, StudentChoice, 6237
Collins & Aikman Floorcoverings, 5282
Collins Foundation, 2720
Colloquoy on Teaching World Affairs, 4676
Colombo International School, 1130
Colony High School, 415
Colorado Association of Libraries, 435
Colorado Association of School Executives
  Conference, 3317
Colorado Business Educators, 436
Colorado Community College &
  Occupational Education System, 437
Colorado Congress of Parents, Teachers &
  Students, 438
Colorado Department of Education, 2952,
  2953, 2954, 2955, 2956, 2957, 2958, 2959
Colorado Education Association, 439
Colorado Library Association, 440
Colorado Library Association Conference,
  830
Colorado State University, 4438
Colorado Time Systems, 5735
Coloring Concepts, 4801
Columbia Cascade Company, 5283
Columbia University Teachers College,
  3487

Columbia University's Biosphere 2 Center,
  5628
**Columbia University, School of Library
  Sciences**, 4557
Coming Up Short? Practices of Teacher
  Educators Committed to Character, 3432
Commandant Gade Special Education
  School, 2089
Committee for Education Funding, 3880
Committee on Continuing Education for
  School Personnel, 3270
Commonwealth Foundation, 2495
Commonwealth Universities Yearbook, 3752
Communicating for Agriculture, 250
Communication Disorders Quarterly, 4510
Communication: Journalism Education
  Today, 4511
Communications Services, 3026, 3192
Communique, 4466
Community Affairs Division, 2448
Community College Exemplary Instructional
  Programs, 4023
Community College Services, 3161
Community Colleges Division, 3013
Community Connections, 867
Community Foundation for Jewish
  Education, 868
Community Foundation for Southeastern
  Michigan, 2529
Community Foundation of Greater Flint,
  2530
Community Foundation of Greater New
  Haven, 2367
Community Foundation of New Jersey, 2594
Community Outreach Services, 3081
Community Outreach and Education for the
  Arts Handbook, 4051
Community Playthings, 5491
Community Relations & Special Populations,
  3006
Community United Methodist School, 2090
Commuter Perspectives, 4142
Compaq Computer Corporation, 5945
Comparative Guide to American Colleges for
  Students, Parents & Counselors, 4024
Compendium of Tertiary & Sixth Forum
  Colleges, 4069
Compensatory Education & Support
  Services, 3048
Compensatory Education Office, 3162
Compensatory Education Program, 2881
Competency-Based Framework for
  Professional Development of Certified
  Health Specialists, 3433
Complete Guide to Work, Study & Travel
  Overseas, 3924
Complete Learning Disabilities Directory,
  3753
Composition Studies Freshman English
  News, 4512
Comprehensive Health Education
  Foundation, 4802
CompuServe Information Services, 149
Computer City Direct, 5799
Computer Friends, 5800
Computer Learning Foundation, 4803
Computer Literacy Press, 4804
Computer Prompting & Captioning
  Company, 5170
Computer Resources, 5958
Computer Science Department, 5151
Computer Using Educators, Inc (CUE), 397

Computer and Web Resources for People
  with Disabilities, 3754
Computers on Campus National Conference,
  714
Comstock Foundation, 2808
Concept Media, 5171
Concepts to Go, 4805
Concern-America Volunteers, 251
Concordia International School-Shanghai,
  1131
Conference Daily Newspaper Online, 5801
Conference for Advancement of
  Mathematics Teaching, 715
Conference on Information Technology, 716
Conferencing with Students & Parents Video
  Series, 3573
Conflict Resolution Strategies in Schools,
  3574
Congressional Quarterly, 4806
Connect, 3633
Connecticut Business Education Association,
  441
Connecticut Department of Education, 2961
Connecticut Early Childhood Unit, 2962
Connecticut Education Association, 442
Connecticut Educational Media Association,
  443
Connecticut Governor's Committee on
  Employment of the Handicapped, 2963
Connecticut Library Association, 806
Connecticut Mutual Financial Services, 2368
Connecticut School Library Association, 444
Connecticut Valley Biological Supply
  Company, 5629
Connecting Link, 869
Connection, 4334
Connelly Foundation, 2732
Conover Company, 870, 3575
Conrad N Hilton Foundation, 2585
Consider a Christian College, 4070
Consortium for School Networking, 398
Consortium on Reading Excellence, 871
Constitutional Rights Foundation, 39
Construction Specialties, 5498
Constructive Playthings, 5736
Consulting Psychologists Press, 3669
Consumer Relations, 6121
Contact Center, Inc., 352
Contact East, 5563
Contemporary Education, 4143
Contemporary World Issues: Public
  Schooling in America, 3755
Continental Film, 5492
Continental Press, 4807
Continental School (Sais British), 1488
Continuing Education, 3209
Continuing Education Guide, 3867
Continuing Education Press, 3981, 3984,
  4014, 4034, 4035, 4036, 4037, 4038, 4039,
  4040, 4045, 4052
Continuous Learning Group Limited
  Liability Company, 872
Contracting Out: Strategies for Fighting
  Back, 3434
Cooke Foundation, 2425
Cooper Industries Foundation, 2767
Cooperative International Pupil-to-Pupil
  Program, 252
Cooperative Learning Strategies, 3576
Copenhagen International School, 1654
Cord Foundation, 2586
Cordell Hull Foundation for International
  Education, 253

Core Services, 3226
Corlan Products, 5299
Cornocopia of Concise Quotations, 3756
Corporate Design Foundation, 873
Corporate University Enterprise, 874
Corpus Christi State University, 2768
Costa Rica Academy, 1355
Cotopaxi Academy, 1356
Cottonwood Press, 4808
Council for Advancement & Support of Education, 40, 3744, 4147
Council for Advancement and Support of Educati on, 717
Council for Aid to Education, 875
Council for Educational Development and Research, 3757, 5088
Council for Exceptional Children, 41, 4809
The Council for Exceptional Children, 46, 50, 182, 260, 406, 718, 3272, 3286, 3457, 3498, 3523, 3526, 3531, 3785, 3951, 4135, 4148, 4150, 4177, 4180, 4184
Council for Exceptional Children Annual Convention, 718
Council for Indian Education, 383
Council for International Exchange of Scholars, 2232, 6044
Council for Jewish Education, 42
Council for Learning Disabilities, 637, 3271, 4220, 4221
Council of Administrators of Special Education, 3272
Council of British Independent Schools in the European Communities-Members Directory, 254, 638, 3925
Council of Chief State School Officers, 158, 3877
Council of Colleges of Arts & Sciences, 4582, 4652
Council of Education Facility Planners-Interna tional, 255
Council of Graduate Schools, 43, 3768
Council on Foreign Relations, 256
Council on Hemisphere Affairs, 257
Council on International Educational Exchange, 258, 634, 4299, 6043
Council on Islamic Education, 259
Council on Library Technical Assistants, 319
Council on Occupational Education, 876
Council on Postsecondary Accreditation, 44
Council-Grams, 4513
Counseling & Values, 4467
Counseling Association, 216
Counseling Today, 4468
Counselor Education & Supervision, 4469
Counselor's Handbook for the SAT Program, 6238
Counterforce, 4514
Counterpoint, 4144, 5493
Country Day, 2091
Country Day School, 1357
Cowles Charitable Trust, 2629
Crandon Institute, 1358
Creating High Functioning Schools : Practice and Research, 3868
Creating Quality Reform: Programs, Communities and Governance, 3869
Creating Schools of Character Video Series, 3577
Creating the Quality School, 3870
Creative Artworks Factory, 5284
Creative Child & Adult Quarterly, 4145
Creative Classroom, 4412
Creative Classroom Publishing, 4412

Creative Competitions, Inc., 136
Creative Education Foundation, 4204
Creative Educational Surplus, 5285
Creative Learning Consultants, 877
Creative Learning Systems, 878
Creative Outdoor Designs, 5737
Creative Teaching Press, 4810
Creative Urethanes, Children's Creative Response, 4292
Creativity Research Journal, 4146
Cricket Magazine Group, 4811
Crisis Management in Schools, 3578
Critical Issues in Urban Special Education: The Implications of Whole-School Change, 3634
Critical Thinking Video Set, 3579
Critical and Creative Thinking in the Classroom, 3635
Crizmac Art & Cultural Education Materials Inc, 5286
Croatia American International School-Zagreb, 2092
Croner Publications, 4094
Cronin Foundation, 2531
Croughton High School, 1655
Crow Canyon Archaeological Center, 5630
Crown Mats & Matting, 5287
Crystal Productions, 5172
Crystal Trust, 2375
Cuisenaire Company of America, 5631
Cullen Foundation, 2769
Cultural Education, 3124
Cummings Elementary School, 1132
Current, 5387
Current Openings in Education in the USA, 4430
Current Reviews for Academic Libraries, 4548
Currents, 4147
Curriculm Associates, 3289
Curriculum & Instructional Leadership Branch, 2944
Curriculum Alignment: Improving Student Learning, 3580
Curriculum Associates, 4812, 6201
Curriculum Brief, 3494
Curriculum Center - Office of Educational Services, 3636
Curriculum Development & Textbooks, 3210
Curriculum, Assessment & Accountability Services, 3027
Curriculum, Assessment & Professional Development, 3211
Curriculum, Assessment and Technology, 3212
Curriculum, Instruction & Professional Development, 3141
Curtis Marketing Corporation, 5738
Curundu Elementary School, 1359
Curundu Junior High School, 1360
Cut & Paste, Master Teacher, 3495
CyberStretch By Jazzercise, 5494
Cyborg Systems, 5959

D

DC Division of Special Education, 2975
DC Heath & Company, 4813
DCDT Network, 4148
DECA Dimensions, 4149
DISCOVER Science Program, 5632

DLD Times, 4150
DLM Teaching Resources, 4814
DOS/Administrative Officer, 2017
DSM Engineered Plastics Company, 5607
Da-Lite Screen Company, 5495
Dade Community Foundation, 2391
Dahle USA, 5288
Daisy Marquis Jones Foundation, 2630
Dakar Academy, 1053
Daktronics, 5430
Dalat School, 1133
Dale J Bellamah Foundation, 2606
Dallas International School, 2093
Dallas Public Library, 2770
Dan Murphy Foundation, 2286
Danforth Foundation, 2572
Danube International School, 1656
Darmstadt Elementary School, 1657
Darmstadt Junior High School, 1658
Darryl L Sink & Associates, 3637
Darwin College, 641
Data & Technology, 3072
Data Command, 5802
Data Management, 3073
Data Trek, 6082
Datacad, 3581
Datasearch Group, 4707
David & Lucile Packard Foundation, 2287
Davidson & Associates, 5803
Davis Publications, 4595
Dawn Publications, 4815
Dawson Education Cooperative, 879
Dawson Education Service Cooperative, 880
Dayton Foundation, 2695
De Blijberg, 1659
De Paul University, 4512
DeBourgh Manufacturing Company, 5564
DeFoe Furniture 4 Kids, 5496
DeVry University, 3638
DeWitt Wallace-Reader's Digest Fund, 2631
Dean Close School, 1660
Dean Foundation for Little Children, 2510
Decar Corporation, 5497
Decision Line, 4151
Decision Sciences Institute, 4151
DecoGard Products, 5498
Defense Information Systems Agency, 6013
Defense Language Institute-English Language Branch, 2233
Dekko Foundation, 2464
Delaware Business Education Association, 445
Delaware Department of Education, 2972
Delaware Department of Education: Administrati ve Services, 2973
Delaware Library Association, 446
Delaware State Education Association, 447
Delcastle High School, 445
Dell Computer Corporation, 5804
Dellora A & Lester J Norris Foundation, 2440
Delmar Thomson Learning, 3639
Delta Biologicals, 5633
Delta Biologicals Catalog, 5634
Delta Education, 4816
Demco, 6083
Denver Foundation, 2361
Department Management Services Branch, 2945
Department of CCTE, Teachers College/Communication, 4713
Department of Construction Technology, 3658

Department of Defense, Office of Dependent Schools, 2245, 3947
Department of Education, 2884, 2888, 2890, 2894, 2902, 2903, 2904, 2962
Department of Education/1175 Main Building, 2878
Department of Education/3005 Main Building, 2889
Department of Education/3028 Mary E. Switzer Bldg., 2905
Department of Education/3042 Mary E. Switzer Bldg., 2879
Department of Education/3086 Mary E. Switzer Bldg., 2900
Department of Education/3153 Main Building, 2887
Department of Education/3181 Main Building, 2885
Department of Education/3530 Mary E. Switzer Bldg., 2906
Department of Education/4000 Portals Building, 2882
Department of Education/4090 Mary E. Switzer Bldg., 2914
Department of Education/4100 Portals Building, 2897
Department of Education/4181 Main Building, 2899
Department of Education/4200 Portals Building, 2907
Department of Education/4300 Portals Building, 2896
Department of Education/4500 Portals Building, 2908, 2909, 2910
Department of Education/5082 Mary E. Switzer Bldg., 2895
Department of Education/5102 Regional Office Bldg., 2901
Department of Education/Mary E. Switzer Building, 2880
Department of Education/Regional Office Bldg., 2883
Department of Education/Regional Office Building, 2832
Department of Individuals & Family Syudies, 4398
Department of Library Science, 829
Department of State, 2135
Depco, 3640, 6164
Depco- Millennium 3000, 5431
Deputy Commissioner, 3089
Deputy Superintendent, 2918
Deputy Superintendent Office, 3163
Design Science, 6117
Designer Artwear I, 5289
Designing & Implementing a Leadership Academy in Character Education, 3871
Designs for Learning, 881
Deskbook Encyclopedia of American School Law, 3872
Desktop Presentations & Publishing, 4152
Destination College: Planning with the PSAT/NMSQT, 6239
Detecto Scale Corporation, 5635
Detroit Edison Foundation, 2532
Developer, 4335
Developing a Character Education Program, 3873
Development Education: A Directory of Non-Governmental Practitioners, 3874
Development and Alumni Relations Report, 4153
Dewey Decimal Classification, 6084

Dexheim Elementary School, 1661
Dexter Educational Toys, 5290
Dexter Educational Toys, Inc., 5290
Dhahran Academy International School Group, 1489
Dhahran Central School, 1490
Dhahran Hills School, 1491
Diagnostic Reading Inventory for Bilingual Students in Grades K-8, 4061
Diagnostic Reading Inventory for Primary and Intermediate Grades K-8, 4062, 6202
Dial Books for Young Readers, 4817
Dialog Information Services, 6165
Dick Blick Art Materials, 5291
Dickson Company, 5636
Dickson Foundation, 2679
Didax Educational Resources, 4818
Different Books, 4154
Digest of Supreme Court Decisions, 3758
Digital Divide Network, 5805, 6193
Digital Equipment Corporation, 5806
Dillon Foundation, 2441
Dimensions of Early Childhood, 181
Dinah-Might Activities, 4819
Dinocardz Company, 4820
Dinorock Productions, 5292
Direct Instructional Support Systems, 882
Directions, 4155
Directory for Exceptional Children, 3759
Directory of Catholic Schools & Colleges in the UK, 3760
Directory of Catholic Special Educational Programs & Facilities, 3761
Directory of Central Agencies for Jewish Education, 3762
Directory of Central America Classroom Resources, 4090
Directory of Chief Executive Officers of United Methodist Schools, Colleges & Universities, 3875
Directory of College Cooperative Education Programs, 3763
Directory of Curriculum Materials Centers, 3435
Directory of ERIC Information Service Providers, 3764
Directory of Educational Contests for Students K-12, 3963
Directory of English Language Schools in Japan Hiring English Teachers, 3926
Directory of Financial Aid for Women, 3964
Directory of Graduate Programs, 3765
Directory of Indigenous Education, 3766
Directory of Institutional Projects Funded by Office of Educational Research, 3965
Directory of International Grants & Fellowships in the Health Sciences, 3966
Directory of International Internships Michigan State University, 3927
Directory of International Internships: A World of Opportunities, 3767
Directory of Manufacturers & Suppliers, 4046
Directory of Member Institutions and Institutional Representatives, 3768
Directory of Members of the Association for Library and Information Science Education, 4047
Directory of Organizations in Educational Management, 3876
Directory of Overseas Educational Advising Centers, 3769
Directory of Play Therapy Training, 4025

Directory of Postsecondary Institutions, 3770
Directory of Public Elementary and Secondary Education Agencies, 4071
Directory of Public School Systems in the United States, 3771
Directory of Public Vocational-Technical Schools & Institutes in the US, 4097
Directory of Resources & Exchange Programs, 3772
Directory of Schools, Colleges, and Universities Overseas, 3928
Directory of State Education Agencies, 3877
Directory of Vocational-Technical Schools, 4098
Directory of Work and Study in Developing Countries, 3929
Directory of Youth Exchange Programs, 3773
Disability Compliance for Higher Education, 4156
Disability Determination Division, 2919
Disability Rights Education & Defense Fund, 45
Discipline Techniques you can Master in a Minute Video Series, 3582
Discovery Education, 5155
Discovery Enterprises, Ltd., 4972
Discovery Networks, 5432
Discovery Toys, 5293
Discrimination Law Update, 4336
Diskovery Educational Systems, 5960
Disney Educational Productions, 5294
Disney Juvenile Publishing, 4821
Disney Press, 4821
Dissertation Fellowships in the Humanities, 2871
Distance Education & Training Council, 3273
Distance Education Database, 6166
Distance Learning Directory, 3436
District of Columbia Business Education Association, 450
District of Columbia Department of Education, 2976
District of Columbia Library Association, 451
Div. of Marsh Lumber Company, 5347
Diversified Learning, 4427
Diversity 2000, 4157
Diversity, Accessibility and Quality, 3774
A Division Lerner Publications Group, 4913
Division for Children with Communication Disorders Newsletter, 4395
Division for Early Childhood, 182
Division for Learning Disabilities, 46
Division for Learning Support: Equity & Advocacy, 3249
Division for Research, 5089
Division of Administrative Services, 3244
Division of Business Services, 3049
Division of Carriage Industries, 5596
Division of Compensatory Education, 3044
Division of Education Services, 3102
Division of Information-Technology Support, 3098
Division of Instruction, 3090
Division of International Special Education & Services, 260
Division of Janitex Rug Service Corporation, 5751
A Division of Lerner Publishing Group, 4786
Division of Library Services, 3014
Division of Student Leadership Services, 593

 Publisher Listings Appear in Bold

Division of USA McDonald Corporation, 5528

Division of West Coast Chain Manufacturing Co., 5328

A Divisions of Lerner Publishing Group, 5000

Dixie Art Supplies, 5295

Doha College-English Speaking, 1492

Doha English Speaking School, 1493

Doha Independent School, 1494

Dominic Press, 4822

Dominican Child Development Center, 2094

Don Johnston Developmental Equipment, 5807

Don't Miss Out: The Ambitous Students Guide to Financial Aid, 3967

Donald K. Olson & Associates, 5637

Donald W Reynolds Foundation, 2587

Dorado Academy, 2095

Dorling Kindorley Company, 4823

Doron & Associates, 4152

Doron Precision Systems, 5961

Dover Court Prep School, 1134

Dover Publications, 4824

Dow Corning Corporation, 5565

Down-To-Earth Books, 4281

Downside School, 1662

Dr. Anthony A Cacossa, 883

Dr. CC & Mabel L Criss Memorial Foundation, 2582

Dr. Labush's Links to Learning, 6028

Dr. Playwell's Game Catalog, 5296

Dr. Scholl Foundation, 2442

Dragonfly, 4413

Dramatics, 4585

Dranetz Technologies, 5638

Draper, 5297

Draw Books, 5298

Dresden International School, 1663

Dresher Foundation, 2496

Dri-Dek Corporation, 5566

Drug Information & Strategy Clearinghouse, 47

Dukane Corporation, 5173

Duke Endowment, 2680

Dulaney Brown Library, 2717

Duluth Public Library, 2554

Dupont Company, 5299

Durable Corporation, 5300

Dutch Mill Bulbs, 2849

Dutton Children's Books, 4825

Dwight School, 2096

DynEd International, 4826

E

E-900 First National Bank Building, 2551

E-S Sports Screenprint Specialists, 2850

E-Z Grader Company, 3539

E-Z Grader Software, 3539

E.L. Cord Foundation Center For Learning Literacy, 2586

ECC International School, 1664

EDUCAUSE, 399, 719, 6167, 4701, 4702

EDUCAUSE Quarterly, 4701

EDUCAUSE Review, 4702

EF Educational Tours, 48

EL Wiegand Foundation, 2588

EME Corporation, 6115

EPIE Institute, 4109

EPPA Consulting, 884

ERD, 5505

ERIC Clearinghouse for Science, Math & Environ mental Education, 368

ERIC Clearinghouse for Social Studies Educatio n, 384

ERIC Clearinghouse on Assessment & Evaluation, 49

ERIC Clearinghouse on Counseling & Student Services, 217, 4470

ERIC Clearinghouse on Disabilities and Gifted Education, 50

ERIC Clearinghouse on Educational Management, 159, 3876

ERIC Clearinghouse on Elementary & Early Child hood Education, 188

ERIC Clearinghouse on Languages and Linguistic s, 160, 305

ERIC Clearinghouse on Reading, English & Communication, 349

ERIC Clearinghouse on Rural Education & Small Schools, 51

ERIC Clearinghouse on Teaching and Teacher Education, 3274

ERIC Clearinghouse on Urban Education, 52

ERIC Document Reproduction Service, 3772

ERIC/CRESS Bulletin, 4158

ERS Spectrum, 4337

ESP Publishers, Inc., 4064

ETA - Math Catalog, 4827

ETA Cuisenaire, 6022

ETR Associates, 4828

EVAN-Motor Corporation, 4829

EWI, 3642

EZ Grader, 5301

Eagle Education Fund, 4159

Eagle Forum, 4159

Early Advantage, 5174

Early Childhood Council, 3164

Early Childhood Education, 3142

Early Childhood Education Journal, 4396

Early Childhood Report: Children with Special Needs and Their Families, 4397

Early Childhood Research Quarterly, 4398

Early Childhood Today, 4399

Early Ed, 5302

Early Start-Fun Learning, 4830

Early Years, 4424

Earn & Learn: Cooperative Education Opportunities, 3930

Earth Education: A New Beginning, 4081

Earth Foundation, 4831

Earthkeepers, 4082

East Asia Regional Council of Overseas Schools, 261

East Baton Rouge Parish Library, 2485

East Bay Educational Collaborative, 885

East Central Educational Service Center, 886

Easter Seals, 53

Easter Seals Communications, 53

Eastern Illinois University School of Technology, 3641

Eastern Montana College Library, 2580

EasyLobby, 5996

Ebsco Subscription Services, 6085

Echolab, 5433

Ecole Active Bilingue, 1665

Ecole Active Bilingue Jeannine Manuel, 1666

Ecole D'Humanite, 1667

Ecole Des Roches & Fleuris, 1668

Ecole Flamboyant, 1952

Ecole Lemania, 1669

Ecole Nouvelle Preparatoire, 1670

Ecole Nouvelle de la Suisse Romande, 1671

Economics Press, 3528

EdIndex, 5929

EdPress News, 4160

Eden Hall Foundation, 2733

Edge Learning Institute, 887

edhelper.com, 5905

Edinburgh American School, 1672

Edison Schools, 888

Edison Welding Institute, 3642

Editorial Projects in Education, 4832

Edmark, 4833

Edmark Corporation, 5808, 6119

Edmonds School Building, 768

Edmund Scientific - Scientifics Catalog, 5639

Edna McConnell Clark Foundation, 2632

Edradour School, 1673

Edron Academy-Calz Al Desierto, 1361

EduQuest, An IBM Company, 5809

Educare, 2097

Educate@Eight, 4414

Educating for Character, 3878

Educating for Character: How Our Schools Can Teach Respect and Responsibility, 3879

Educating for Employment, 4431

Education, 4161

Education & Treatment of Children, 3496

Education Advisory Group, 183

Education Alternatives, Inc. (EAI), 7

Education Budget Alert, 3880

Education Center, 4834

Education Commission of the States, 54

Education Concepts, 889

Education Conference, 3318

Education Daily, 4338

Education Data, 890

Education Department, 5303

Education Development Center, 55, 891

Education Digest, 4162

Education Extension, 56

Education Funding, 3074

Education Funding Research Council, 3989, 4344, 4385, 4386

Education Grants Alert, 4446

Education Hotline, 4163

Education Index, 3540

Education Information Services, 2234, 2240, 3934, 4430

Education Information Services which Employ Americans, 2234

Education Information Services/Instant Alert, 2236, 2246, 3497, 3776, 3945, 3946

Education Jobs, 4432

Education Management Consulting LLC, 892

Education Management Corporation, 6221

Education Management Services, 5606

Education Minnesota, 512

Education Newsline, 4164

Education Now and in the Future, 4165

Education Personnel Update, 4339

Education Program Support, 2932

Education Programs & Services, 2964

Education Quarterly, 4166

Education Services, 2262

Education Sourcebook: Basic Information about National Education Expectations and Goals, 3775

Education Station, 5904

Education Technology Conference, 720

Education Technology News, 4703

Education Technology Office, 3028

Education USA, 4167

Education Update, 4168
Education Week, 4169, 5885
Education World, 5906
Education in Focus, 4170
Education of Special Populations & Adults, 3213
Education, Training and Research Associates, 57
Educational & Psychological Measurement, 4471
Educational Activities, 5810
Educational Administration Quarterly, 4340
Educational Administration Resource Centre Database, 3541
Educational Computer Systems Group, 5806
Educational Consultants Directory, 3881
Educational Consultants of Oxford, 893
Educational Credential Evaluators, 894
Educational Data Center, 5962
Educational Data Service, 895
Educational Dealer-Buyers' Guide Issue, 3882
Educational Directories, 3838, 3839, 3911
Educational Directories Unlimited, Inc., 6057
Educational Equipment Corporation of Ohio, 5304
Educational Equity Concepts, 58
Educational Film & Video Locator, 4099
Educational Forum, 4171
Educational Foundation of America, 2826
Educational Freedom Spotlight On Homeschooling, 4172
Educational Horizons, 4173
Educational Impressions, 3903
Educational Information & Resource Center, 896, 5090
Educational Information Services, 2235, 3446, 3820, 3821, 3822, 3939, 3940, 3941, 3948, 4434
Educational Innovations, 3082
Educational Institutions Partnership Program, 6013
Educational Leadership, 4063
Educational Leadership Institute, 3275
Educational Marketer, 4835
Educational Media Association of New Jersey, 539
Educational Placement Service, 6031
Educational Placement Sources-Abroad, 3776
Educational Placement Sources-US, 2236, 3497
Educational Press Association of America, 4836
Educational Productions, 4837
Educational Products, 5640
Educational Products Information Exchange Institute, 5091
Educational Publishing Summit: Creating Managi ng & Selling Content, 721
Educational Rankings Annual, 3777
Educational Register, 59
Educational Research Analysts, 4230
Educational Research Forum, 4174
Educational Research Service, 5092, 4337
Educational Researcher, 4175
Educational Resources, 897, 5811
Educational Resources Catalog, 3778
Educational Resources Information Ctr./Access ERIC, 3764
Educational Screen, 4118
Educational Services, 2953

Educational Services Company, 898
Educational Services for Children & Families, 3015
Educational Specialties, 899
Educational Staffing Program, 2237
Educational Structures, 6168
Educational Summit, 3643
Educational Support Programs, 3037
Educational Systems for the Future, 900
Educational Teaching Aids, 4838
Educational Technology, 4704
Educational Technology Center, 400
Educational Technology Design Consultants, 901
Educational Technology Publications, 3536
Educational Testing Service, 902, 5093, 6240, 5142
Educational Testing Service/Library, 6228
Educational Theatre Association, 334, 722, 4585, 4593, 4597
Educational Theatre Association Conference, 722
Educational Theory, 4176
Educational Video Group, 5175
Educator's Desk Reference: A Sourcebook of Educational Information & Research, 3779
Educator's Scrapbook, 3780
Educators Guide to FREE Computer Materials and Internet Resources, 3781
Educators Guide to FREE Family and Consumer Education Materials, 4072
Educators Guide to FREE Films, Filmstrips and Slides, 3782
Educators Guide to FREE Guidance Materials, 4026
Educators Guide to FREE HPER Materials, 4059
Educators Guide to FREE Multicultural Material, 3783
Educators Guide to FREE Science Materials, 4083
Educators Guide to FREE Social Studies Materials, 4091
Educators Guide to FREE Videotapes-Elementary/ Middle School Edition, 3904
Educators Guide to FREE Videotapes-Secondary Edition, 3905
Educators Progress Service, 4839, 3449, 3781, 3782, 3783, 3801, 3802, 3904, 3905, 3906, 4026, 4059, 4072, 4080, 4083, 4091
Educators Publishing Service, 4840
Educators for Social Responsibility, 4183
Edumate-Educational Materials, 4841
Edusystems Export, 903
eduverse.com, 3551
Edward E Ford Foundation, 2497
Edward John Noble Foundation, 2633
Edward R. Murrow High School, 546
Edward W Hazen Foundation, 2634
Edwin Gould Foundation for Children, 2635
Edwin H. Benz Company, 5641
Effective Schools Products, 904
Effective Strategies for School Reform, 3644
Effective Training Solutions, 905
Efficacy Institute, 906
eFundraising, 6025
efundraising.com, 5908
Eiki International, 5434
Eisenhower National Clearinghouse, 5910

Eisenhower National Clearinghouse for Mathemat ics and Science Education, 325, 369
El Abra School, 1362
El Paso Community Foundation, 2771
El Plantio International School Valencia, 1674
El Pomar Foundation, 2362
El-Hi Textbooks and Serials in Print, 3784
Ela Beach International School, 1135
Elaine E & Frank T Powers Jr Foundation, 2636
Elderhostel, 4129
Electro-Steam Generator Corporation, 5642
Electronic Book Catalog, 5305
Electronic Bookshelf, 6086
Electronic Learning, 4341, 4705
Electronic School, 4706
Electronic Specialists Inc., 5812
Electronics Industries Alliance/CEA, 3645
Elementary & High School, 1421
Elementary & Secondary Education, 2882, 3016
Elementary Education Professional Development School, 3646
Elementary School Center for Advocacy & Policy on Behalf of Children, 189
Elementary School Guidance & Counseling, 4472
Elementary School Journal, 4415
Elementary Secondary Bilingual & Research Branch, 2883
Elementary Teacher's Ideas and Materials Workshop, 4416
Elementary Teachers Guide to FREE Curriculum Materials, 3906
Elementary, Middle & Secondary Education, 3125
Elementary, Secondary & Vocational Analysis, 2884
Eleven Principals of Effective Character Educa tion, 3583
Eleven Principles of Effective Character Educa ion, 3584
Eli Lilly & Company Corporate Contribution Program, 2465
Ellerslie School, 1675
Ellis, 4842
Ellison Educational Equipment, 5306
Ellwood Foundation, 2772
Elmer & Mamdouha Bobst Foundation, 2637
Elmer Holmes Bobst Library, NYU, 2637
Elmo Manufacturing Corporation, 5435
Elsternwick Campus-Wesley College, 1136
Embassy of Japan, 3935
Embracing an Inclusive Society: The Challenge for the New Millennium, 723
Embracing the Child, 5909
Emco Maier Corporation, 3647
Emergency Librarian, 4549
Emerging Technology Consultants, 907, 4105
Emirates International School, 1495
Employment Opportunities, 4433
Employment Training Center, Community College, 462
Emporia State University, 108
Encyclopaedia Britannica, 4843
Endura Rubber Flooring, 5307
Energy Concepts, 3648, 5349
Energy Learning Center, 4844
Engineering Steel Equipment Company, 5499
English Education, 4515

English Help, 5911, 6144
English Journal, 4516
English Junior School, 1676
English Kindergarten, 1677
English Leadership Quarterly, 4517
English Montessori School, 1678
English School, 1363
English School-Fahaheel, 1496
English School-Helsinki, 1679
English School-Kuwait, 1497
English School-Los Olivos, 1680
English Speaking School, 1498
English Teaching Fellow Program, 197
English as a Speech Language Video Series, 5176
English for Specific Purposes, 4518
English in Asia: Teaching Tactics for New English Teachers, 3931
Enid & Crosby Kemper Foundation, 2573
Enka Okullari-Enka Schools, 1499
Enoch Pratt Free Library, 2498
EnrollForecast: K-12 Enrollment Forecasting Program, 5963
Enrollment Management Report, 4342
Environmental Systems Research Institute, 5813
Environments, 5500
ePALS.com, 5890
Epie Institute, 908
Episcopal Cathedral School, 2098
Epistemological Engineering, 909
Epson America, 5964
Equitable Foundation, 2638
Equity & Access Office, 3181
Equity 2000, 326
Equity Clearinghouse, 60
Erie County Library System, 2734
eSchool News, 4729
Escola Americana do Rio de Janeiro, 1364
Escola Maria Imaculada, 1365
Escole Tout Petit, 2099
Escuela Anaco, 1366
Escuela Beata Imelda, 2100
Escuela Bella Vista, 2101
Escuela Bilingue Santa Barbara, 1367
Escuela Bilingue Valle De Sula, 1368
Escuela Campo Alegre, 2102
Escuela Campo Alegre-Venezuela, 2103
Escuela Caribe Vista School, 2104
Escuela International Sampedrana, 1369
Escuela Las Morochas, 2105
Escuela Las Palmas, 1370
Escuela Nuestra Senora Del Carmen, 2106
Escuela Superior Catolica, 2107
Esmet, 5567
Essential Learning Products, 4845
Estes-Cox Corporation, 5643
Ethical Issues in Experiential Education, 3437
Ethnic Arts & Facts, 4846
Etowah High School, 459
Eugene & Agnes E Meyer Foundation, 2379
Eugene McDermott Foundation, 2773
Europa Publications, 3956, 3992
European Business & Management School, 1681
European Council of International Schools, 639, 2238, 3932, 3812
European School Culham, 1682
European School-Brussels I, 1683
European School-Italy, 1684
Eva L & Joseph M Bruening Foundation, 2696
Evan-Moor Corporation, 4847

Evangelical Christian Academy, 1685
Evangelical School for the Deaf, 2108
Evanston Public Library, 2443
Evansville-Vanderburgh School Corporation, 4219
Evelyn & Walter Haas Jr Fund, 2288
Everbrite, 5416
Eversan Inc., 5814
Everyday Learning Corporation, 4848
Everything You Need for Reading, 4064
Evo-Ora Foundation, 2263
Ewing Halsell Foundation, 2774
Ex-Cell Metal Products, 5568
Examiner Corporation, 910
Excell Education Centers, 911
Excellence in Teaching Cabinet Grant, 3289
Exceptional Child Education Resources, 3498
Exceptional Children, 4177
Exceptional Children Education Resources, 3785
The Exchange, 2499, 2505
Executive Deputy Superintendent, 2991
Executive Office & External Affairs, 2946
Executive Session, 4343
Executive Summary Sets, 3883
Exercise Exchange, 4617
Exploratorium, 4849
Extensions - Newsletter of the High/Scope Curriculum, 3499
External Affairs, 3007
External Relations, 3083
Extra Editions K-6 Math Supplements, 4850
Exxon Education Foundation, 2775
Eye on Education, 3585

F

F(G) Scholar, 4851
FIOCES, 3811
FMJ/PAD.LOCK Computer Security Systems, 5965
FOTODYNE, 5644
FPMI Communications, 912
FR Bigelow Foundation, 2555
FRS National Teacher Agency, 2239
FUTUREKIDS School Technology Solutions, 6186
Faces, 4677
Facilities Network, 5569
Facing History & Ourselves, 61
Facts On File, 3976, 3977
Facts on File, 4852
Faculty Exchange Center, 3933
Faculty Exchange Center Directory and House Exchange Supplement, 3933
Faculty, Staff & Administrative Openings in US Schools & Colleges, 4434
Fahy-Williams Publishing, 3882
Fair-Play Scoreboards, 5436
Fairgate Rule Company, 5308
Faisalabad Grammar School, 1137
Faith Academy, 1138
Fajardo Academy, 2109
Falcon School, 1431
Family & School Support, 3227
Family Centered Learning Alternatives, 62
Family Reading Night Kit, 5309
Family Relations, 4473
Family Services Report, 3786

Family Therapy: The Journal of the California Graduate School of Family Psychology, 4474, 4641
Farmington High School, 441
Farny R Wurlitzer Foundation, 2444
Farrar, Straus & Giroux, 4853
Fascinating Folds, 5310
Fase Productions, 5177
Fastech, 3649
Faye McBeath Foundation, 2817
Federal Assistance, 3143
Federal Program Services, 2954
Federal Programs, 2939
Federal Research Report, 4447
Federal Resources for Educational Excellence, 3550
Federal Student Aid Information Center, 4009
Federal/Special/Collaboration Services, 3154
Feistritzer Publishing, 3525
Fellowships in International Affairs-A Guide to Opportunities in the US & Abroad, 3968
Fellowships, Scholarships and Related Opportunities, 3969
Feltwell Elementary School, 1686
Festo Corporation, 3650, 5437
Fibersin Industries, 5570
Field Services, 3214
Field Services Branch, 2947
Fifty State Educational Directories, 3787
Filette Keez Corporation/Colorworks Diskette Organizing System, 6087
Films for Humanities & Sciences, 5178
FinAid, 6047
Finance & Administrative Services, 2965
Finance & Management, 3198
Finance & Support Services, 2992
Financial & Information Services, 3017
Financial & Personnel Services, 3132
Financial Aid for Research & Creative Activities Abroad, 3970
Financial Aid for Study Abroad: a Manual for Advisers & Administrators, 3971
Financial Conditions & Aids Payment, 3075
Financial Management Team, 3228
Financial Resources for International Study, 3972
Financial Resources for International Study, 3973
Financing Graduate School, 3974
Finishing Strong: Your Personal Mentoring & Planning Guide for the Last 60 Days of Teaching, 3438
First Bank System Foundation, 2556
First District Resa, 913
First Step Systems, 5645
First Steps/Concepts in Motivation, 5179
First Tennessee Bank, 2759
First Union University, 2681
First Years, 4854
Fiscal Services & Quality Control, 3022
Fisher Publishing Company, 3789
Fisher Scientific Company, 5646
Fisher Scientific/EMD, 5647
Fiskars Corporation, 5311
Fisons Instruments, 5648
Fitchburg State College, Education Department, 4618
Flagler Foundation, 2801
Flagpole Components, 5571
Flagship Carpets, 5501
Fleetwood Group, 5502
Flexi-Wall Systems, 5572

Flinn Foundation, 2264
Flinn Scientific, 5649
Flo-Pac Corporation, 5573
Florida Association for Media in Education, 453
Florida Atlantic University-Multifunctional Resource Center, 5094
Florida Business Education Association, 454
Florida Department of Education, 2980
Florida Education Association, 455, 4178
Florida Elementary School Principals Association Conference, 3319
Florida Library Association, 456
Florida School Administrators Association Summer Conference, 3320
Florida State University, 357
Florida Teaching Profession-National Association, 457
Florida Vocational Association Conference, 3321
Floyd Beller - Wested, 3766
Flute Talk, 4586
Focus, 4178, 4678
Focus on Autism, 4179
Focus on Learning Problems in Math, 4566
Focus on Research, 4180
Focus on School, 4073
Focus on the SAT: What's on it, How to Prepare & What Colleges Look For, 6241
Foellinger Foundation, 2466
Follett Software Company, 6088
Fondren Foundation, 2776
Footsteps, 4679
Forbes Custom Publishing, 4855
Ford Family Foundation, 2721
Ford Foundation, 2639
Ford Motor Company Fund, 2533
Fordham Equipment Company, 5503
Foreign Faculty and Administrative Openings, 3934
Foreign Faculty and Administrative Openings, 2240
Foreign Language Annals, 4519
Foreign Student Service Council, 262, 4181
Foreign Students School, 1371
Forestry Supplies, 5650
Formac Distributing, 4856
Fort Clayton Elementary School, 1372
Fort Kobbe Elementary School, 1373
Fortune Education Program, 4182
Forum, 4183
Forum for Reading, 4618
Fory Hays State University, 486
Foster Foundation, 2809
Foundation & Corporate Grants Alert, 4448
Foundation Center, 2827, 3975
Foundation Center-Carnegie Library of Pittsbur gh, 2735
Foundation Center-District of Columbia, 2380
Foundation Center-San Francisco, 2289
Foundation Collection, 2735
Foundation Collection/Ivan Allen Department, 2403
Foundation Grants to Individuals, 3975
Foundation for Critical Thinking, 3651, 724
Foundation for Critical Thinking Regional Workshop & Conference, 724
Foundation for Educational Innovation, 914
Foundation for Exceptional Children: Focus, 4184
Foundation for Library Research, 6089

Foundation for Student Communication, 63
Foundation for the Carolinas, 2682
Foundation for the Mid South, 2566
Foundation for the National Capitol Region, 2381
Foundations Focus, 2290
Four Rivers Software Systems, 5574
Four State Regional Technology Conference, 3652
Fox Laminating Company, 5312
Fraboom, 5913
France-Merrick Foundation, 2499
Frances & Benjamin Benenson Foundation, 2640
Francis H Clougherty Charitable Trust, 2291
Frank Schaffer Publications, 4857, 5651, 4409
Frankfurt International School, 1687
Franklin County Public Schools, 609
Franklin Learning Resources, 5305
Franklin Watts, 4858
Fred B & Ruth B Zigler Foundation, 2486
Frederiksborg Gymnasium, 1688
Free Money for College: Fifth Edition, 3976
Free Money for Foreign Study: A Guide to 1,000 Grants for Study Abroad, 3977
Free Spirit Publishing, 4859
Free Stuff for Canadian Teachers, 6003
Free Teaching Aids.com, 3552
Freedom & Enterprise, 4680
Freedoms Foundation at Valley Forge, 4678
Freewill Baptist School, 2110
Freitas Foundation, 2292
French International School, 1139
French-American International School, 2111
Frey Foundation, 2534
Frey Scientific, 5652
Friendly Systems, 5575
Friends Council on Education, 64, 4269
Friends School, 1689
Frist Foundation, 2758
Fritz B Burns Foundation, 2293
Frog Publications, 4860
Frost & Jacobs, 2712
Fukuoka International School, 1140
Fulbright News, 4185
Fulbright Teacher Exchange, 2241
Fulbright and Other Grants for USIA Graduate Study Abroad, 3978
Fund Your Way Through College: Uncovering 1,100 Opportunities in Aid, 3979
Fund for New Jersey, 2595
FundRaising.Com, 5894
Fundacion Colegio Americano de Quito, 1374
Fundcraft Publishing, 2859
Funding & Information Resource Center, 2347
Funding Information Center, 2472, 2813
Fundraising USA, 2851
Funny School Excuses, 3788
Future Graph, 4851
Future Music Oregon, 333
Future of Rural Education, 5180

GE Capitol Modular Space, 5576
GED Items, 4186
GED Testing Service, 6242
GMAT Success, 6243
GPN Educational Media, 5181
GPN Year 2005 Literacy Catalog, 5181
GTE Educational Network Services, 5867
GTE Foundation, 2828
Gaeta Elementary & Middle School, 1690
Gale Group, 3777, 3810, 3859
Gale Research, 6157, 3923, 4008
GameTime, 5739
Games2Learn, 5816
Gangs in Our Schools: Identification, Response, and Prevention Strategies, 5182
Ganley's Catholic Schools in America, 3789
Garden International School, 1141
Gared Sports, 5740
Gareth Stevens, 4861
Garmisch Elementary School, 1691
Gates Foundation, 2363
Gateway Learning Corporation, 5817
Gaylord Brothers, 6090
Geelong Grammar School-Glamorgan, 1142
Geilenkirchen Elementary School, 1692
Geist, 5966
Geist Manufacturing, 5966
Gelnhausen Elementary School, 1693
General Administrative Services, 2920
General Audio-Visual, 5438
General Board of Higher Education & Ministry/UMC, 3660, 3796, 3875
General Counsel, 2921, 3193
General Motors Foundation, 2535
General Robotics Corporation, 6179
Geneva English School, 1694
Geography: A Resource Guide for Secondary Schools, 4092
George & Mary Kremer Foundation, 2872
George D Robinson School, 2112
George Dehne & Associates, 915
George F Baker Trust, 2641
George F Cram Company, 5313
George Foundation, 2777
George Frederick Jewett Foundation, 2294
George Gund Foundation, 2698
George I Alden Trust, 2829
George Link Jr Foundation, 2642
George Washington School, 1375
George Washington University, 4523, 4531, 5077, 5120
Georgetown American School, 2113
Georgia Association of Educators, 458
Georgia Business Education Association, 459
Georgia Department of Education, 2981
Georgia Library Association, 460
Georgia Parents & Teachers Association, 461
Georgia QSI International School-Tbilisi, 2114
Georgia Southern University, 827
Geothermal Education Office, 370
German Academic Exchange Service (DADD), 6045
German Historical Institute, 3980
German Swiss International School, 1143
German-American Scholarship Guide-Exchange Opportunities for Historians and Social Scientist, 3980
Gershowitz Grant and Evaluation Services, 2830
Gerstung/Gym-Thing, 5741
GetQuizzed, 6194

G

GAMCO Educational Materials, 5815
GAR Foundation, 2697

Getting Funded: The Complete Guide to Writing Grant Proposals, 3981
Gheens Foundation, 2478
Gibson Tech Ed, 6169
Giessen Elementary School, 1695
Giessen High School, 1696
Gift-in-Kind Clearinghouse, 5314
Gifted Child Society, 65
Gifted Child Society Conference, 725
Gifted Child Society Newsletter, 4187
Gilbert & Jaylee Mead Family Foundation, 2382
Gimnazija Bezigrad, 1432
Girls Incorporated, 66
Gladys & Roland Harriman Foundation, 2643
Gladys Brooks Foundation, 2644
Glen Products, 5577
Glencoe/Div. of Macmillan/McGraw Hill, 4862
Glenunga International High School, 1144
Global Computer Supplies, 5967
Global Learning, 263
Global Learning Corporation, 6020
Global Occupational Safety, 5578
Global Press, 3931
Global Schoolhouse, 3544, 5914
Glynn Christian School, 2115
Goethe House New York, 4863
Gold Medal Products, 2852
Gold's Artworks, 5315
Golden Artist Colors, 5316
Good Hope School-Kowloon, 1145
Good Hope School-St. Croix, 2116
Good Shepherd School, 2117
Good Sports, 5504
Goodheart-Willcox Publisher, 4864
Gordon & Mary Cain Foundation, 2778
Goroka International School, 1146
Government & Business Services, 2686
Government & Public Affairs Office, 225
Government Documents, 2252, 2723
Government Relations, 3076, 3165
Governmental Policy Branch, 2948
Grace & Franklin Bernsen Foundation, 2715
Grace Baptist Academy, 2118
Grad. School Library & Info. Science, 4558
Graduate & Undergraduate Programs & Courses in Middle East Studies in the US, Canada, 3790
Graduate Programs for Professional Educators, 3653
Graduate Record Examinations Program/ ETS, 3765
Graduate Scholarship Book, 3982
Grafco, 5505
Grafenwoehr Elementary School, 1697
Graffiti Gobbler Products, 5579
Grammer, 5506
Grand Canyon University College of Education, 3654
Grand Rapids Foundation, 2536
Grange School, 1376
Grant & Resource Center of Northern California, 2295
Grant Opportunities for US Scholars & Host Opportunities for US Universities, 3983
Grant Writing Beyond The Basics: Proven Strate gies Professionals Use To Make Proposals Work, 3984
Grantmanship Center, 3857
Grants & Awards Available to American Writers, 3985

Grants Administration Branch, 2977
Grants Management Association, 2514
Grants Register, 3986
Grants Resource Center, 2525, 2711
Grants and Awards for K-12 Students: 80 Sources of Funding, 2831
Grants and Contracts Handbook, 3884
Grants and Contracts Service, 2832
Grants for School Districts Monthly, 4449
Grants, Fellowships, & Prizes of Interest to Historians, 3987
Grantsmanship Center, 2833
Grantsmanship Center Magazine, 4450
Graphic Arts Education & Research Foundation, 198
Graphic Arts Technical Foundation, 199
Graphix, 5317
Grayce B Kerr Fund, 2500
Great Adventure Tours, 5653
Great Classroom Management Series, 3586
Great Classroom Management Video Series, 3587
Great Source Catalog, 4074
Great Source Education Group, 4074, 5337
Green Fund, 2645
Greene & Associates, 5818
Greengates School, 1377
Greenhaven Press, 4865
Greensteds School, 1054
Greenville Foundation, 2296
Greenwillow Books, 4866
Greenwood Garden School, 1698
Greeting Tree, 5507
Gressco, 5508
Gressco Ltd., 5508, 5490
Grey House Publishing, 3753
Grolier, 5819
Grolier Interactive, 6170
Grolier Multimedial Encyclopedia, 5318
Grolier Publishing, 4867, 4793, 4858, 5318, 6170
Grounds for Play, 5742
Grover Hermann Foundation, 2445
GrowSmartBrains.com, 6189
Gryphon House, 4868
Gstaad International School, 1699
Guam Adventist Academy, 2119
Guam Department of Education, 2120
Guam High School, 2121
Guam S Elementary & Middle School, 2122
Guamani School, 2123
Guidance Associates, 5183
Guidance Channel, 4778, 4893, 5257, 5271, 5272, 5296, 5402, 5409
Guide to Department of Education Programs, 3988
Guide to Educational Opportunities in Japan, 3935
Guide to Federal Funding for Education, 3989, 4344
Guide to Geekdom, 6195
Guide to International Exchange, Community Service & Travel for Persons with Disabilities, 3791
Guide to Schools and Departments of Religion and Seminaries, 3792
Guide to Summer Camps & Schools, 3793
Guide to Vocational and Technical Schools East & West, 4100
Guide to the College Board Validity Study Service, 6244
Guided Discoveries, 5654

Guidelines for Contracting with Private Providers for Educational Services, 3885
Guidelines for Effective Character Education Through Sports, 3794
The Guidence Channel, 5277
Guild Notes Bi-Monthly Newswletter, 3500
Gulf English School, 1500

H

H Wilson Company, 5509
H&H Enterprises, 5580
H.W. Wilson Company, 3540
HACH Company, 5655
HAZ-STOR, 5581
HEATH Resource Center, 67
HJ Heinz Company Foundation, 2736
HN & Frances C Berger Foundation, 2297
HON Company, 5510
HOST/Racine Industries, 5582
HR on Campus, 4345
HW Buckner Charitable Residuary Trust, 2376
Haagsche School Vereeniging, 1700
Habara School, 1501
Hagedorn Fund, 2646
Haggar Foundation, 2779
Hainerberg Elementary School, 1701
Hako Minuteman, 5583
Hall Family Foundation, 2574
Hall of the States, Suite 419, 90
Halvorsen Tunner Elementary and Middle School, 1702
Hamilton Electronics, 5439
Hamilton Library, 2431
Hampton Public Library, 2802
Hanau High School, 1703
Hanau Middle School, 1704
Handbook of Private Schools, 3795
Handbook of United Methodist-Related Schools, Colleges, Universities & Theological Schools, 3796
Handling Chronically Disruptive Students at Risk Video Series, 3588
Hands-On Equations, 5319
Hands-On Prints, 4869
HappyTeachers.com, 6196
Harare International School, 1055
Harcourt Brace Jovanovich, 178
Hardcourt Religion Publishers, 4870
Harmonic Vision, 6127, 6223
Harold Alfond Trust, 2490
Harold KL Castle Foundation, 2426
HarperCollins, 4024
Harrington Software, 5968
Harrisville Designs, 5320
Harrow School, 1705
Harry & Grace Steele Foundation, 2298
Harry A & Margaret D Towsley Foundation, 2537
Hartford Foundation for Public Giving, 2369
Hartford Square North, 2370
Harvard College Guide to Grants, 3990
Harvard Education Letter, 4188
Harvard Graduate School of Education, 400, 3397, 3634, 3644, 3655, 3656, 3674, 3680, 3703, 3712, 4537
Harvard Institute for School Leadership, 3655
Harvard Seminar for Superintendents, 3656
Harvest Christian Academy, 2124
Hasbro Children's Foundation, 2647

Hatherop Castle School, 1706
Hawaii Business Education Association, 462
Hawaii Department of Education, 2983
Hawaii Education Association, 463
Hawaii Library Association, 464
Hawaii State Teachers Association, 465
Hawaiian Electric Industries Charitable Foundation, 2427
Haworth, 5511
Haws Corporation, 5584
Hayes School Publishing, 5321
Hazelden Educational Materials, 4871
Head of The Class, 6133
Health & Social Work, 4475
Health Connection, 5184
Health Occupations Students of America, 200
Health Outreach Project, 916
Health in Action, 4189
Hearlihy & Company, 3589
Heathkit Educational Systems, 5656
Hebron School-Lushington Hall, 1147
Heidelberg High School, 1707
Heidelberg Middle School, 1708
Heifner Communications, 6171
Heinemann, 4872
Heldref Publications, 3507, 3516, 4140, 4141, 4207, 4208, 4333, 4348, 4581, 4604, 4654, 4661, 4685, 4692, 6252
Hellenic College-London, 1709
Hellenic-American Education Foundation Athens College-Psychico College, 1710
Heller, 5549
Helping Your Child Succeed in Elementary School, 4417
Helsingin Suomalainen, 1711
Henry & Ruth Blaustein Rosenberg Foundation, 2501
Henry Ford Centennial Library, 2538
Henry Holt & Company, 4873
Henry Holt Books for Young Readers, 4874
Henry J Kaiser Family Foundation, 2299
Henry Luce Foundation, 2648
Henry S Wolkins Company, 5322
Herbert H & Grace A Dow Foundation, 2539
Herbert H. Lamson Library, 2593
Heritage Foundation, 4133, 4168
Herman Goldman Foundation, 2649
Herrick Foundation, 2540
Hess Foundation, 2650
Het Nederlands Lyceum, 1712
Het Rijnlands Lyceum, 1713
Hiawatha Education Foundation, 2557
Hidden America, 3797
High School Journal, 4642
High School Reform Conference, 726
High Touch Learning, 4875
High/Scope Educational Research Foundation, 4876, 3499
Higher & Professional Education, 3126
Higher Education & National Affairs, 4190
Higher Education Center, 5095
Higher Education Consortium, 917
Higher Education Directory, 3798
Higher Education Management Office, 3062
Higher Education Opportunities for Women & Minorities: Annotated Selections, 3799
Higher Education Publications, 3798
Higher Education/Postsecondary Office, 3175
Highlands Program, 918
Highlights for Children, 4400, 4418
Highsmith Company, 6091
Hillcrest International School, 1148
Hillcrest Secondary School, 1056

Hillhouse Montessori School, 1714
Hiroshima International School, 1149
Hispanic Yearbook-Anuario Hispano, 3886
History Department, 2621
History Happens, 6137
History Matters Newsletter, 4681
History Teacher, 4682
History of Education Quarterly, 4191
History of Science Society, 371
Hitachi Foundation, 2383
Hitting the High Notes of Literacy, 727
Hoagies Gifted Education Page, 5999
Hoagies' Gifted Education Page, 6026
Hobart Institute of Welding Technology, 3657
Hobby Foundation, 2780
Hoechst Celanese Foundation, 2596
Hogar Colegio La Milagrosa, 2125
Hohenfels Elementary School, 1715
Hohenfels High School, 1716
Hokkaido International School, 1150
Holiday House, 4877
Holmwood House, 1717
Holocaust Resource Center, 4157
Holometrix, 5657
Home & Building Control, 5585
Home & Professional Products Group, 5261
Home from Home (Educational Exchange Programs), 3800
Homeschooler's Guide to FREE Teaching Aids, 3801
Homeschooler's Guide to FREE Videotapes, 3802
Homeschooling Marketplace Newsletter, 4192
HomeworkSpot, 5916
Hon Foundation, 2300
Honeywell, 5585
Honeywell Foundation, 2597
Hong Kong International School, 1151
Hooked on Phonics Classroom Edition, 5323
Hoosier Science Teachers Association Annual Meeting, 807
Hoover Foundation, 2699
Hoover's, 4878
Horace W Goldsmith Foundation, 2651
Horn Book, 4879
Horn Book Guide, 4879
Hort School: Conference of the Association of American Schools, 640
Houghton Mifflin Books for Children, 4880
Houghton Mifflin Company, 6014
Houghton Mifflin Company: School Division, 4881
Houston Endowment, 2781
Houston Public Library, 2782
How to Create a Picture of Your Ideal Job or Next Career, 3936
How to Find Out About Financial Aid & Funding, 3991
How to Plan and Develop a Career Center, 3439, 3937
How to Raise Test Scores, 3440
Howard Elementary School, 1378
Howard Greene Associates, 919
Howard University, 4211
Howell Playground Equipment, 5658
Hubbard Scientific, 5659
Hubbell, 5820
Hugh & Hazel Darling Foundation, 2301
Human Kinetics Publishers, 4607, 4614
Human Relations Media, 5185

Human Resource Development, 3182
Human Resources, 224
Human Resources Center, 68
Human Resources Office, 2940, 3077
Human Resources and Administration, 2885
Human Services, 2966
Human-i-Tees, 2853
Humanities Software, 6069
Hummel Sweets, 2854
Huntley Pascoe, 920
Huntsville Public Library, 2254
Hutchinson United School District #308, 484
Hvitfeldtska Gymnasiet, 1718
Hyams Foundation, 2511
Hyde & Watson Foundation, 2598
Hydrus Galleries, 5324
Hyperion Books for Children, 4882

I

IA O'Shaughnessy Foundation, 2558
IBM Corporate Support Program, 2652
IBN Khuldoon National School, 1502
ICA Quarterly, 4476
IDRA Newsletter, 4193
IEA Reporter, 4194
IIE Academic Year Abroad, 3803
IIE Passport: Short Term Study Abroad, 5186
ILA Reporter, 4550
INFOCOMM Tradeshow, 728
INSIGHTS Visual Productions, 5187
INTELECOM Intelligent Telecommunications, 5188
IPA Newsletter, 4346
IREX, 277
ISM Independent School Management, 3529
ISS Directory of Overseas Schools, 3804
ITP South-Western Publishing, 3490
ITP South-Western Publishing Company, 4883
Idaho Department of Education, 2989
Idaho Education Association, 466, 4194
Idaho Library Association, 467
Idea Factory, 4884
iEARN USA, 5917
Ikego Elementary School, 1152
Ilford, 6224
Illesheim Elementary and Middle School, 1719
Illinois Affiliation of Private Schools for Exceptional Children, 469
Illinois Assistant Principals Conference, 3322
Illinois Association of School Business Officials, 470
Illinois Business Education Association, 471
Illinois Citizens' Education Council, 472
Illinois Department of Education, 2993, 2999
Illinois Education Association, 473
Illinois Library Association, 474, 808
Illinois Library Association Conference, 808
Illinois Principals Professional Conference, 3323
Illinois Resource Center, 3324
Illinois Resource Center Conference of Teachers of Linguistically Diverse Students, 3324
Illinois School Boards Association, 3325

Publisher Listings Appear in Bold

Illinois School Library Media Association, 475

Illinois State Board of Education, 3000

Illinois State University, 4362

Illinois Vocational Association Conference, 809

Impact Publications, 3938

Improvement & Assistance Branch Delaware Department of Education, 2974

Improving Learning and Teaching, 652

Improving Parent/Educator Relationships, 3590

Improving Student Performance, 729

Improving Student Thinking in the Content Area, 3591

In Focus, 6172

In Search of Character, 5189

In-Box Master Teacher, 3501

Incirlik Elementary School, 1503

Incirlik High School, 1504

Inclusion Guide for Handling Chronically Disruptive Behavior, 3805

Inclusion: The Next Step, 3441

Inclusion: The Next Step the Video Series, 3592

Inclusive Education Programs, 4195

Incorporating Multiple Intelligences into the Curriculum and into the Classroom: Elementary, 3806

Incorporating Multiple Intelligences into the Curriculum and into the Classroom: Secondary, 3807

Increasing Student Achievement in Reading, Wri ting, Mathematics, Science, 730

Independent Bonn International School, 1720

Independent Education Consultants Association, 731, 4198

Independent Living, 69

Independent Scholar, 4196

Independent School, 4419, 4643

Independent School District #709, 4284

Independent Schools Association of the Southwest-Membership List, 161, 3808

Independent Schools Association of the Southwest, 3808

Independent Schools Information Service, 1721, 3750

Independent Study Catalog, 3809

Index of Majors and Graduate Degrees, 4027

India American Embassy School-New Delhi, 2126

India American International School-Bombay, 2127

Indian University, 4191

Indiana Association of School Business Officials, 476

Indiana Business Education Association, 477

Indiana Cash Drawer, 5821

Indiana Department of Education, 3008, 3010

Indiana Library Federation, 478

Indiana School Boards Association Annual Conference, 3326

Indiana State Teachers Association, 479

Indiana State University, School of Education, 4143

Indiana University, School of Library Science, 4556

Indiana University, Social Studies Dev. Center, 384

Indiana University-Purdue University of Indianapolis, IUPUI, 3658

Indiana University-Purdue University/Indianapolis, 4522

Indianapolis Foundation, 2467

Indianhead School, 1153

Industrial Teacher Education Directory, 4101

Industrial Training Institute, 3659

Industry Reference Handbooks, 3810

Infant School-House #45, 1505

InfoUse, 6138

Infocus: A Newsletter of the University Continuing Education Association, 3502

Information & Telecommunications Services, 2984

Information Access Company, 6092

Information Career Opportunities Research Center, 3926

Information Center on Education, 5096

Information Central, 3849

Information Design, 5969

Information Exchange, 5097

Information Literacy: Essential Skills for the Information Age, 4102

Information Searcher, 4707

Information Services, 3108, 2607

Information Systems, 2967

Information Technology & Libraries, 4551

Information Today, 4715

Informativo, 4451

Infusing Brain Research, Multi-Intelligence, Learning Styles and Mind Styles, 732

Ingenuity Works, 5822

Ingraham Dancu Associates, 921

Ingraham Memorial Fund, 2302

Innova Corporation, 5660

Innovating Worthy Projects Foundation, 2392

Innovative Higher Education, 4197

Innovative Learning Group, 922

Innovative Programming Systems, 923

Innovator, 3503

Innsbruck International High School, 1722

Inquiry in Social Studies: Curriculum, Research & Instruction, 4683

Insect Lore, 5325, 5661

Insight, 924, 4198

Insights Visual Productions, 5662

Inst Tecnologico De Estudios, 1379

Insta-Foam Products, 5586

Instant Access: Critical Findings from the NRC/GT, 733

Institut Alpin Le Vieux Chalet, 1723

Institut Auf Dem Rosenberg, 1724

Institut Chateau Beau-Cedre, 1725

Institut Le Champ Des Pesses, 1726

Institut Le Rosey, 1727

Institut Montana Bugerbug-American Schools, 1728

Institut Monte Rosa, 1729

Institute for Academic Excellence, 925

Institute for Chemical Education, 4885

Institute for Child Development, 5921, 6000

Institute for Development of Educational Activities, 70, 926

Institute for Earth Education, 372, 4081, 4082, 4086, 4087

Institute for Educational Leadership, 71, 4886

Institute for Global Ethics, 927

Institute for Research in Learning Disabilitie s, 5098

Institute for Social Science Research/UCLA Archive, 3327

Institute of Cultural Affairs, 264

Institute of Higher Education, 3660

Institute of Int'l Education Overseas Employment, 3545

Institute of International Education, 265, 2248, 3749, 3803, 3973, 5186, 6048, 6049

Instron Corporation, 5663

Instruction Division, 3050

Instruction Office, 3183

Instructional Design, 5823

Instructional Materials Laboratory, 5099

Instructional Programs, 3063

Instructional Resources Corporation, 5190

Instructional Services, 2922, 2985

Instructional Services Division, 3106, 3221, 3250

Instructor, 4420, 5824

Instrumentalist, 4587

Integrated Research, 3517

Integrated/Thematic Curriculum and Performance Assessment, 734

Integrating Information Technology for the, 6197

Integrating Technology into the Classroom Vide o Series, 3593

Intel Science Talent Search Scolarship, 2873

IntelliTools, 4887

Intellimation, 4888

Inter-American Academy, 2128

Inter-Community School, 1730

Inter-Regional Center, 266

Intercultural Development Research Association, 4193

Intercultural Press, 4889

Interface Network, 928

Interlocken, 201

Interlocken Center for Experiential Learning, 201

Intermedia, 5191

Internal Administration, 3194

Internal Operations, 3215

International Academy, 1731

International Alliance of Teacher Scholars, 3337

International Association for Continuing Education & Training, 267

International Association for Continuing Education, 3454, 3455, 3867

International Association for Social Science Information Service & Technology, 3327

International Association for the Exchange of Students for Technical Experience, 268

International Association of Counseling Services, 218

International Association of Pupil Personnel Workers, 162

International Association of School Librarians hip, 320

International Association of Students in Economics & Business Management, 269

International Association of Teachers of English as a Foreign Language, 641

International Awards Market, 642

International Baccalaureate North America, 270

International Baccalaureate Organization, 271

International Biographical Centre/Melrose Press, 3814

International Center for Leadership in Education, 929

International Centre for Distance Learning, 6166

International Christian School, 1154

International Clearinghouse for the Advancement of Science Teaching, 3594

International College Spain, 1732
International Community School, 1155, 1506
International Community School-Abidjan, 2129
International Community School-Addis Ababa, 1057
International Conference, 643
International Congress Secretariat, 644
International Congress for School Effectiveness & Improvement, 644
International Council for Health, Physical Education and Recreation, 344
International Council of Scientific Unions Committee on Science Teaching, 373
International Council on Education for Teaching, 3276
International Curriculum Management Audit Center, 3661
International Development Intern Program, 223
International Dyslexia Association, 306
International Dyslexia Association Annual Conference, 645
International Education, 4199
International Educational Exchange, 272, 2886
International Educator, 4435
International Educators Cooperative, 2242
International Elementary School-Estonia, 1433
International Exhibit, 646
International Federation of Organizations for School Correspondence/Exchange, 3811
International Foundation Directory, 3992
International Graduate School, 3662
International Graphic Arts Education Association, 202, 273
International Headquarters, 6085
International High School-Yangon, 2130
International Historic Films, 5192
International Honor and Professional Association, 3318
International Institutional Services, 274
International Journal of Instructional Media, 3504
International Journal of Play Therapy, 4477
International Journal of Qualitive Studies in Education, 4200
International Listening Association Annual Convention, 647
International Management Institute, 1733
International Monetary Fund, 275
International Montessori Society, 4235
International Oceanographic Foundation, 4666
International Opportunities Program, 6042
International Performance Improvement Conferen ce Expo, 735
International Personnel Management Association, 4367
International Physicians for the Prevention of Nuclear War, 276
International Preparatory School, 1380, 1734
International Reading Association, 350, 802, 4619, 4630, 4631
International Reading Association Annual Convention, 648
International Research & Exchange Board, 3983
International Research and Exchange Board, 6050
International Research and Exchanges Board, 277

International Rotex, 5970
International Scholarship Book: The Complete Guide to Financial Aid, 3993
International School Beverweerd, 1735
International School Manila, 1156
International School Nido de Aguilas, 1381
International School of Choueifat, 1507
International School of Panama, 640
International School of Port-of-Spain, 2131
International School of the Sacred Heart, 1157
International School-Aberdeen, 1736
International School-Algarve, 1737
International School-Amsterdam, 1738
International School-Aruba, 1953
International School-Bangkok, 1158
International School-Basel, 1739
International School-Beijing, 1159
International School-Belgrade, 1434
International School-Bergen, 1740
International School-Berne, 1741
International School-Brussels, 1742
International School-Budapest, 1435
International School-Cartagena, 1743
International School-Conakry, 2132
International School-Curacao, 1744, 1954
International School-Curitiba, 1382
International School-Dakar, 2133
International School-Dusseldorf, 1745
International School-Eastern Seaboard, 1160
International School-Eerde, 1746
International School-Estonia, 1436
International School-Fiji, 1161
International School-Friuli, 1747
International School-Geneva, 1748
International School-Grenada, 2134
International School-Hamburg, 1749
International School-Hannover Region, 1750
International School-Havana, 2135
International School-Helsinki, 1751
International School-Ho Chi Minh City, 1162
International School-Iita, 1752
International School-Islamabad, 2136
International School-Kenya, 1058
International School-Kuala Lumpur, 1163
International School-La Paz, 1383
International School-Lae, 1164
International School-Latvia, 1437
International School-Lausanne, 1753
International School-Le Chaperon Rouge, 1754
International School-London, 1755
International School-Lyon, 1756
International School-Manila, 1165
International School-Moshi, 1059
International School-Naples, 1757
International School-Nice, 1758
International School-Ouagadougou, 2137
International School-Panama, 1384
International School-Paphos, 1438
International School-Paris, 1759
International School-Penang-Uplands, 1166
International School-Phnom Penh, Cambodia, 1167
International School-Phnom Penh-Cambodia, 1168
International School-Port of Spain, 2138
International School-Prague, 1439
International School-Pusan, 1169
International School-Sfax, 2139
International School-Singapore, 1170
International School-Sotogrande, 1760
International School-Stavanger, 1761

International School-Stockholm, 1762
International School-Stuttgart, 1763
International School-Tanganyika, 1060
International School-Trieste, 1764
International School-Turin, 1765
International School-Ulaanbaatar, 1171
International School-Venice, 1766
International School-West Indies, 1955
International School-Yangon, 2140
International School-Zug, 1767
International Schools Association, 930
International Schools Directory, 3812
International Schools Services, 278, 293, 2237, 3804, 4242
International Schule-Berlin, Potsdam, 1768
International Secondary School-Eindhoven, 1769
International Society for Business Education, 279
International Society for Performance, 72, 735, 3515
International Society for Technology in Education, 401
International Society for Technology in Education, 4711
International Software, 6095
International Studies & Programs, 3767
International Studies Association, 280
International Study Telecom Directory, 3813
International Symposium, 649
International Teachers Service, 1440
International Technology Education Association Conference, 650
International Technology Education Association, 408, 3494, 4726
International Thespian Society, 334
International Trombone Association, 651
International Trombone Festival, 651
International Visual Literacy Association, 4634
International Volunteer, 4201
International Who's Who in Education, 3814
International Workcamp Directory, 3815
International Workshops, 3663
International Yearbook of Education: Education in the World, 3816
Internationale Schule Frankfurt-Rhein-Main, 1770
Internet Resource Directory for Classroom Teachers, 4103
Interskolen, 1771
Interstate Coatings, 5587
Intertec Publishing, 3861, 4324
Intervention in School and Clinic, 3505
Introlink, 5834
Iowa Business Education Association, 480
Iowa Council Teachers of Math Conference, 3328
Iowa Department of Education, 3018, 3017
Iowa Educational Media Association, 481
Iowa Library Association, 482
Iowa Public Television, 3019
Iowa Reading Association Conference, 3329
Iowa School Administrators Association Annual Convention, 3330
Iowa School Boards Association, 3331
Iowa State Education Association, 483
Iowa State University, 481
Irene E & George A Davis Foundation, 2512
Iron Mountain Forge, 5743
Island Drafting & Technical Institute, 3664
Island School, 1172

Istanbul International Community School, 1508
It Starts in the Classroom, 4202
Italic Handwriting Series-Book A, 4034
Italic Handwriting Series-Book B, 4035
Italic Handwriting Series-Book C, 4036
Italic Handwriting Series-Book D, 4037
Italic Handwriting Series-Book E, 4038
Italic Handwriting Series-Book F, 4039
Italic Handwriting Series-Book G, 4040
Italic Letters, 4052
Itawamba Community College, 518
Iteachk, 736
Ivanhoe Grammar School, 1173
Izmir American Institute, 2141
Izmir Elementary & High School, 1509

J

J Bulow Campbell Foundation, 2408
J Weston Walch, Publisher, 4890
J&A Handy-Crafts, 5326
J&Kalb Associates, 931
J. Burrow & Company, 1864
J.A. Sexauer, 5588
J.W. McCormick Post Office & Courthouse, 3058
JCB/Early Childhood Education Consultant Service, 932
JCH International, 5744
JESNA, 73
JI Foundation, 2653
JJ Jones Consultants, 933
JK Gholston Trust, 2409
JL Bedsole Foundation, 2255
JN Darby Elementary School, 1174
JP Associates Incorporated, 934
JP Morgan Charitable Trust, 2654
JP Morgan Services, 2376
JR Holcomb Company, 5440
JR Hyde Foundation, 2759
JVC Professional Products Company, 5441
Jacaranda Designs, 4891
Jackson Senior High School, 522
Jackson-Hinds Library System, 2567
Jacksonville Public Library, 2393
Jakarta International School, 1175
James & Abigail Campbell Foundation, 2428
James G Boswell Foundation, 2303
James G Martin Memorial Trust, 2513
James Graham Brown Foundation, 2479
James Irvine Foundation, 2304
James M Johnston Trust for Charitable and Educational Purposes, 2502
James R Dougherty Jr Foundation, 2783
James S Copley Foundation, 2305
James S McDonnell Foundation, 2575
Janet Hart Heinicke, 935
Janice Borla Vocal Jazz Camp, 3665
January Productions, 5193
Japan International School, 1176
Japanese American Cultural Center, 844
Jarrett Publishing Company, 4892
Jason Project, 5918
Jay Klein Productions Grade Busters, 5971
JayJo Books, 4893
Jaypro, 5745
Jaypro Sports, 5745
Jeddah Preparatory School, 1510
Jefferson Center for Character Education, 4296

Jefferson Community College, 489
Jefferson State Community College, 3666
Jeffress Memorial Trust, 2803
Jessie B Cox Charitable Trust, 2514
Jessie Ball duPont Fund, 2394, 4127
Jewish Education Service of North America, 73, 3762, 4122
Jewish Educators Assembly, 74
Jewish Foundation for Education of Women, 2874, 2868, 2869, 2871, 2877, 4007
Jewish Labor Committee, 4668
Jewish Teachers Association, 75
Jiffy Printers Products, 5327
Job Bulletin, 6032
Jobs Clearinghouse, 4436
Jobs for California Graduates, 936
Jobs in Russia & the Newly Independent States, 3938
John & Mary Franklin Foundation, 2410
John Dewey Society for the Study of Education & Culture, 76
John F Kennedy Center for the Performing Arts, 335
John F Kennedy International School, 1061, 1772
John F Kennedy School-Berlin, 1773
John F Kennedy School-Queretaro, 2142
John H & Wilhelmina D Harland Charitable Found ation, 2411
John Jewett & H Chandler Garland Foundation, 2306
John McGlashan College, 1177
John McLaughlin Company, 937
John McShain Charities, 2737
John S & James L Knight Foundation, 2834
John W Anderson Foundation, 2468
John W Kluge Foundation, 2503
John Wiley & Sons, 4894
Johns Hopkins University, 5080, 5081
Johnson & Johnson Associates, 938
Johnsonite, 5664
Jolani School, 463
The Jones Center For Families, 2271
JonesKnowledge.com, 6173
Joppenhof/Jeanne D'arc Clg, 1774
Jordan American Community School, 2143
Joseph & Edna Josephson Institute, 939
Joseph & Rae Gann Charitable Foundation, 2395
Joseph B Whitehead Foundation, 2412
Joseph Drown Foundation, 2307
Jossey-Bass Publishers, 3424, 3462, 3472, 3887, 3890, 4766
Jostens Learning Corporation, 5825, 5972
Joukowsky Family Foundation, 2655
Journal for Research in Mathematics Education, 4567
Journal for Specialists in Group Work, 4478
Journal of Adolescent & Adult Literacy, 4619
Journal of American History, 4684
Journal of At-Risk Issues, 4479, 4644
Journal of Basic Writing, 4520
Journal of Behavioral Education, 4203
Journal of Child and Adolescent Group Therapy, 4480
Journal of Children's Communication Development, 4521
Journal of Classroom Interaction, 3506
Journal of College Admission, 4481
Journal of College Science Teaching, 4653
Journal of Computers in Math & Science, 4568

Journal of Computing in Childhood Education, 4708
Journal of Cooperative Education, 4437
Journal of Counseling and Development, 4482
Journal of Creative Behavior, 4204
Journal of Curriculum & Supervision, 4347
Journal of Curriculum Theorizing, 4205
Journal of Disability Policy Studies, 4206
Journal of Drug Education, 4483
Journal of Early Intervention, 4401
Journal of Economic Education, 3507, 4685
Journal of Education for Business, 4348
Journal of Education for Library and Information Sciences, 4552
Journal of Educational Research, 4207
Journal of Educational Technology Systems, 4709
Journal of Emotional and Behavioral Disorders, 4484
Journal of Employment Counseling, 4485
Journal of Environmental Education, 4604, 4654
Journal of Experiential Education, 3508, 4588, 4605
Journal of Experimental Education, 4208
Journal of Geography, 4686
Journal of Humanistic Education and Development, 4486
Journal of Information Systems Education, 4710
Journal of Law and Education, 4209
Journal of Learning Disabilities, 4210
Journal of Multicultural Counseling & Development, 4487
Journal of Negro Education, 4211
Journal of Physical Education, Recreation and Dance, 4606
Journal of Positive Behavior Interventions, 4212
Journal of Recreational Mathematics, 4569
Journal of Research and Development in Education, 4213
Journal of Research in Character Education, 4214
Journal of Research in Childhood Education, 4402, 4421
Journal of Research in Rural Education, 4215
Journal of Research in Science Teaching, 4655
Journal of Research on Computing in Education, 4711
Journal of School Health, 4216
Journal of Sex Education & Therapy, 4488
Journal of Special Education, 4217
Journal of Special Education Technology, 4712
Journal of Student Financial Aid, 3994
Journal of Teaching Writing, 4522
Journal of Teaching in Physical Education, 4607
Journal of Urban & Cultural Studies, 4218
Journal of Vocational Education Research, 4438
Journal on Excellence in College Teaching, 3509
Journalism Education Association, 307, 737, 3510
Journalism Quarterly, 4523
Journey Education, 5826
Joy Carpets, 5512
Joyce Foundation, 2446
Jubail British Academy, 1511

Jules & Doris Stein Foundation, 2308
Julia R & Estelle L Foundation, 2656
Julio R Gallo Foundation, 2309
July in Rensselaer, 3667
Jumeirah English Speaking School, 1512
Jump Start Math for Kindergartners, 6005
JuneBox.com, 5919
Junior Achievement, 4895
Just 4 Teachers, 5912
Justrite Manufacturing Company, 5665

K

K'nex Education Division, 3668
K-12 District Technology Coordinators, 4104
K-6 Science and Math Catalog, 4084
KI, 5513
KIDSNET, 3907
KIDSNET Media Guide and News, 3907
KLM Bioscientific, 5666
KSJ Publishing Company, 3950
Kabira International School, 1062
Kaeden Corporation, 4896
Kaiserslautern Elementary School, 1775
Kaiserslautern High School, 1776
Kaiserslautern Middle School, 1777
Kaleidoscope, 3669, 4219
Kaludis Consulting Group, 940
Kanawha County Public Library, 2815
Kane/Miller Book Publishers, 4897
Kansai Christian School, 1178
Kansas Association of School Librarians, 485
Kansas Business Education Association, 486
Kansas City Public Library, 2576
Kansas City School District, 657
Kansas Department of Education, 3023
Kansas Division of Special Education, 3024
Kansas Education Association, 487
Kansas Library Association, 488
Kansas School Boards Association
    Conference, 3332
Kansas State University, 307, 737, 3510
**Kansas State University/College of
    Education**, 14
Kansas United School Administrators
    Conference, 3333
Kaohsiung American School, 1179
Karachi American Society School, 2144
Karl C Parrish School, 1385
Karnak Corporation, 5589
Karol Media, 5194
Kathleen Price and Joseph M Bryan Family
    Foundation, 2683
Kean College of New Jersey, 3270
Keep America Beautiful, 4898
Kellems Division, 5820
Kellett School, 1180
Ken Cook Education Systems, 5827
Ken Haycock and Associates, 4549
Ken-a-Vision Manufacturing Company, 5667
Kenan Center, 2687
Kendale Primary International School, 1778
Kendall-Hunt Publishing Company, 4899
Kennedy Center Alliance for Arts Education,
    335
Kennedy-King College, 319
Kenneth T & Eileen L Norris Foundation,
    2310
Kensington Microwave, 5828
Kensington School, 1779
Kensington Technology Group, 5514

Kent H. Smith Library, 2708
Kent State University, 3670, 4552
Kentland Foundation, 2804
Kentucky Association of School
    Administrators, 941
Kentucky Business Education Association,
    489
Kentucky Department of Education, 3029,
    3026, 3032
Kentucky Library Association, 490
Kentucky School Boards Association
    Conference, 3334
Kentucky School Media Association, 491
Kentucky School Superintendents
    Association Meeting, 3335
Kentucky State University, 3671
Kepro Circuit Systems, 5668
Kestrel Manor School, 1063
Kettering Fund, 2700
Kewaunee Scientific Corporation, 5669
Key-Bak, 5328
Keyboard Instructor, 5329
Keystone Schoolmaster Newsletter, 4349
Khartoum American School, 1064
Kid Keys 2.0, 6015
Kids Percussion Buyer's Guide, 5330
Kids at Heart & School Art Materials, 5331
KidsAstronomy.com, 6154
KidsCare Childcare Management Software,
    3542
Kidstamps, 5332
Kidstuff Playsystems, 5746
Kiev International School, 1441
Kigali International School, 1065
Kilmer Square, 2595
Kilmore International School, 1181
Kimball Office Furniture Company, 5515
Kimbo Educational, 5195
Kinabalu International School, 1182
Kinder Magic, 6016
King Fahad Academy, 1780
King Faisal School, 1513
King George V School, 1183
King's College, 1781, 553
Kingsgate English Medium Primary School,
    1066
Kingston Press Services, Ltd., 4524
Kingsway Academy, 1956
Kisumu International School, 1067
Kitakyushu International School, 1184
Kitzingen Elementary School, 1782
Kleine Brogel Elementary School, 1783
Kleiner & Associates, 942
Kluwer Academic/Human Sciences Press,
    4197, 4203, 4277, 4396, 4411, 4460, 4462,
    4480, 4640
Knex Education, 5333, 5670
Knex Education Catalog, 5333, 5670
Knowledge Adventure, 4900, 6005, 6015
Knowledge Unlimited, 4901, 5362
Koc School, 1514
Kodaikanal International School, 1185
Kodaly Teaching Certification Program, 3672
Koffler Sales Company, 5671
Komodo Dragon, 5672
Kompan, 5747
Kongeus Grade School, 2145
Kool Seal, 5590
Kooralbyn International School, 1186
Koret Foundation, 2311
Kowloon Junior School, 1187
Kraus International Publications, 4902
Kreonite, 5673

Kresge Foundation, 2541
Kruger & Eckels, 5674
Kulas Foundation, 2701
Kuwait English School, 1515
Kyoto International School, 1188

L

LA Steelcraft Products, 5748
**LASPAU (Latin America Scholarship
    Program)**, 4451
LAUNCH, 77
LCD Products Group, 6181
LD Forum, 4220
LDSystems, 5591
LEGO Data, 5675
LG Balfour Foundation, 2515
LINC, 402
LINX System, 5676
LMS Associates, 4562
LRP Publications, 4144, 4153, 4156, 4195,
    4295, 4342, 4345, 4352, 4353, 4372, 4375,
    4376, 4379, 4390, 4397, 4431, 4500
LSBA Quarter Notes, 4350
La Chataigneraie International School, 1784
La Maddalena Elementary School, 1785
Lab Safety Supply, 5677
Lab Volt Systems, 3673, 5678
Lab-Aids, 5679
Lab-Volt, 5467
Labconco Corporation, 5680
Labelon Corporation, 5442
Labor Department Building, 2963
Lahore American School, 1189
Lajes Elementary School, 1786
Lajes High School, 1787
Lake Education, 4903
Lakenheath Elementary School, 1788
Lakenheath High School, 1789
Lakenheath Middle School, 1790
Lakeside Manufacturing, 5681
Lakeview Corporate Center, 2392
Lakewood Publications, 4387
Lancing College, 1791
Landmark Editions, 4904
Landscape Structures, 5749
Landstuhl Elementary and Middle School,
    1792
Lane Family Charitable Trust, 2312
Lane Science Equipment Company, 5682
Langensheidt Publishing, 4905
Language & Speech, 4524
Language Arts, 4525
Language Schools Directory, 4041
Language Travel Magazine, 6053
Language, Speech & Hearing Services in
    School, 4526
Lanna International School Thailand, 1190
Lapis Technologies, 5829
Las Vegas-Clark County, 2589
Laser Learning Technologies, 5830
Lasy USA, 5683
Laubach LitScape, 4620
Laubach Literacy Action, 4065, 4620,
    4621, 4622
Laubach Literacy Action Directory, 4065
Lauri, 5334
Law of Teacher Evaluation: A
    Self-Assestment Handbook, 3442
Lawrence A Heller Associates, 943
Lawrence Erlbaum Associates, 4146

Lawrence Hall Youth Services, 469
Lawrence Hall of Science, 4906
Lawrence Productions, 5831
LePAC NET, 6093
Leadership and the New Technologies, 3674
Leadership for Lifelong Learning, 3413
Leadership: Rethinking the Future, 5196
Leading Educational Placement Sources in the US, 3939
Leading to Change, 3887
League for Innovation in the Community College, 716
Leap Frog Learning Materials, 4907
Learner-Centered, 652
Learning & The Enneagram, 3675
Learning Channel, 5443
Learning Company, 5832
Learning Connection, 4908
Learning Disabilities Association of America, 78, 653, 4909
Learning Disability Quarterly, 4221
Learning Independence Through Computers, 402
Learning Links, 4910
Learning Materials Workshop, 3676, 5335
Learning Needs Catalog, 5336
Learning Point Magazine Laboratory, 4222
Learning Power and the Learning Power Workbook, 5337
Learning Research and Development Center, 5100
Learning Resources Center, 2685
Learning Resources Network, 4608
Learning Results Services Bureau, 3030
Learning Services, 3119
Learning ShortCuts, 3543
Learning Station/Hug-a-Chug Records, 5444
Learning Team, 6149
Learning Technologies, 5684
Learning Unlimited Network of Oregon, 4223
Learning Well, 5338, 5445
Learning Workshop.com, 5942
Learning for All Seasons, 4253
Learning for Life, 3443
LearningGate, 5926
Lee & Low Books, 4911
Lee Metal Products, 5516
Legal & Audits Branch, 2949
Legal Basics: A Handbook for Educators, 3817, 3888
Legal Issues and Education Technology, 3889
Legal Notes for Education, 4351
Legislation & Congressional Affairs, 2887
Leica Microsystems EAD, 5685
Leighton Park School, 1793
Leightronix, 5446
Leipzig International School, 1794
Leland Fikes Foundation, 2784
Lennen Bilingual School, 1795
Leo A Myer Associates/LAMA Books, 4912, 4255
Leon Lowenstein Foundation, 2657
Leona Group, 944
Lerner Publishing Group, 4913
Lesley University, 3305, 3372
Lesson Plan Search, 5922
Lesson Plans and Modifications for Inclusion and Collaborative Classrooms, 3818
Lesson Plans and Modifications for Inclusion a nd Collaborative Classrooms, 3595
Lesson Plans for Character Education: Elementary Edition, 3819

Lesson Plans for Integrating Technology into the Classroom: Secondary Edition, 4075
Lesson Plans for Problem-Based Learning, Elementary Edition, 3908
Lesson Plans for Problem-Based Learning: Secondary Edition, 4076
Lesson Plans for the Substitue Teacher: Elementary Edition, 3444
Lesson Plans for the Substitute Teacher: Secondary Edition, 4077
Lesson Plans, Integrating Technology into the Classroom: Elementary Edition, 3909
lessonplanspage.com, 5923
Lettie Pate Evans Foundation, 2413
Levi Strauss Foundation, 2313
Levittown Public Library, 2658
Lexia Learning Systems, 6203
Leys School, 1796
Leysin American School, 1797
Liaison Bulletin, 4224
Liberal Education, 4225
Libra Publishers, 4456, 4474, 4638, 4641
Libraries & Culture, 4553
Libraries Unlimited, 4049, 4050
Libraries Unlimited Academic Catalog, 4048
Libraries, Archives & Museums, 2933
Library Bureau, 5517
Library Collections, Acquisitions & Technical Services, 4554
Library Corporation, 6094
Library Corporation, Sales & Marketing, 5833
Library Development & Services, 3051
Library District, 2589
Library Issues: Briefings for Faculty and Administrators, 4555
Library Programs, 2888
Library Quarterly, 4556
Library Resources & Technical Services, 4557
Library Services, 2581
Library Services Division, 3251
Library Store, 5518
Library Trends, 4558
Library-Reference Department, 2768
Liceo Pino Verde, 1386
Life Lab Science Program, 5101
Life Skills Training, 3445
Life Technologies, 5686
LifeWay Church Resources, 4294
A Lifetime of Color, 5384
Lifeworld of Leadership, 3890
Light Machines, 3677
Lil' Fingers, 6012
Lilly Conference on College Teaching, 3336
Lilly Conferences on College and University Teaching, 3337
Lilly Endowment, 2469
Limassol Grammar-Junior School, 1442
Limon School, 1387
Lincoln Community School, 1068
Lincoln International Academy, 1388
Lincoln International School of Uganda, 1069
Lincoln International School-Kampala, 2146
Lincoln International School-Uganda, 1070
Lincoln School, 1191, 2147
Lincoln-Marti Schools, 2148
Lincolnshire, 2591
Linden Tree Children's Records & Books, 4914
Lingo Fun, 6095
LinguiSystems, 6204
Link, 4226

LinkNet, 5834
Linkage, 945
Linray Enterprises, 5339
Lisle-Interaction, 4227
List Industries, 5592
List of Over 200 Executive Search Consulting Firms in the US, 3940
List of Over 600 Personnel & Employment Agencies, 3941
List of Over 70 Higher Education Association, 3820
List of Regional, Professional & Specialized Accrediting Association, 3446
List of State Boards of Higher Education, 3821
List of State Community & Junior College Board Offices, 3822
Listening Library, 4915
Literacy Advocate, 4621
Literacy Volunteers of America National Conference, 738
Little Family Foundation, 2516
Little People's Learning Center, 2149
The Little Red School House, 5893
Little School House, 2150
Little Tikes Company, 5519
Little, Brown & Company, 4916
Live Wire Media, 6037
LiveText Curriculum Manager, 6198
Living in China: A Guide to Studying, Teaching & Working in the PRC & Taiwan, 3942
Livorno Elementary School, 1798
Livorno High School, 1799
Lloyd A Fry Foundation, 2447
Loans and Grants from Uncle Sam, 3995
Loctite Corporate Contributions Program, 2370
Lodestar Books, 4917
Loew-Coenell, 5340
Logal Software, 6116
Logical Systems, 946
Logos School of English Education, 1443
London Central High School, 1800
Longstreth, 5341
Longview Foundation for Education in World Affairs/International Understanding, 2805
Longwood Foundation, 2377
Look Inside the SAT I: Test Prep from the Test Makers Video, 6245
Looking at Schools: Instruments & Processes for School Analysis, 3891
Lorentz International School, 1801
Los Angeles Educational Alliance for Restructu ring Now, 947
Lothrop, Lee & Shepard Books, 4918
Louis & Anne Abrons Foundation, 2659
Louis Calder Foundation, 2371
Louisana State Department of Education, 3039
Louise H & David S Ingalls Foundation, 2702
Louise M Davies Foundation, 2314
Louise Taft Semple Foundation, 2703
Louisiana Association of Business Educators, 492
Louisiana Association of Educators, 493
Louisiana Association of School Business Officials, 494
Louisiana Children's Research Center for Development & Learning, 948
Louisiana Department of Education, 3038, 3042

Louisiana Library Association, 495
Louisiana Scholar's College, 5
Louisiana School Boards Association, 4350
Louisiana School Boards Association
  Conference, 3338
**Louisiana State University, Dept. of
  Curriculum**, 4596, 4655
**Louisiana State University, School of
  Dentistry**, 3345
**Louisiana State University/Dept. of
  Kinesiology**, 4613
Louisville Free Public Library, 2480
Love to Teach, 5342
Lowell Berry Foundation, 2315
Loyola University, 689
Luanda International School, 2151
Lucasey Manufacturing Company, 5520
Luke B Hancock Foundation, 2316
Lundia, 5521
Lusitania International College Foundation,
  1802
Lutheran Education Association, 79, 739,
  4291
Lutheran Education Association Convention,
  739
Lutheran Parish School, 2152
Lycee Francais De Belgique, 1803
Lycee International-American Section, 1804
Lyce International-American Section, 1805
Lynde & Harry Bradley Foundation, 2818
Lyndhurst Foundation, 2760
Lynne Rienner Publishing, 4919, 3968
Lyon Electric Company, 5687
Lyon Metal Products, 5522
Lyra, 5343

M

M&M Mars Fundraising, 2855
M.E. Sharpe, Inc., 5010
M.I. Smart Program, 6160
MARCIVE, 6096
MATRIX: A Parent Network and Resource
  Center, 80
MAYTC Journal, 4571
MCM Electronics, 5447
MD Anderson Foundation, 2785
MDR School Directory, 3823
MEA Today, 4228
MECC, 5835
METCO, 4250
MHS, 4920
MISCO Computer Supplies, 5973
MJ Murdock Charitable Trust, 2810
MK & Company, 949
MMI-Federal Marketing Service, 5750
MPC Multimedia Products Corp, 5197
MPI School & Instructional Supplies, 5344
MPR Associates, 950
**MSU: Dean's Office of Int'l Studies and
  Programs**, 3927
MacMillan Children's Books, 4921
MacMillan Guide to Correspondence Study,
  3447
MacMillan Publishing Company, 3447,
  3733, 3779, 3792, 3921, 4015, 4763, 4790
MacMillan Reference, 4922
Mackay School, 1389
Macmillan/McGraw-Hill School Division,
  4923
Macro Press, 4924

Magazine of History, 4687
Magi Educational Services Incorporated, 951
Magna Awards, 3290
Magna Plan Corporation, 5448
Magna Publications, 4925, 769, 3870
Magnet Source, 5688
Magnetic Aids, 5345
Magyar British International School, 1444
Mailer's Software, 5346
Main Street Foundations: Building
  Community Te ams, 5198
Maine Association of School Libraries, 496
Maine Business Education Association, 497
Maine Department of Education, 3045
Maine Education Association, 498
Maine Library Association, 499
Maine Principals Association Conference,
  3339
Maine State Library, 5097
Mainstream, 203
Maintaining Safe Schools- School Violence
  Alert, 4352
Maintenance, 5593
Major Educational Resources Corporation,
  4926
Makassar International School, 1192
Malacca Expatriate School, 1193
Malpass Foundation, 2542
Malvern College, 1806
Mamopalire of Vermont, 5836
Management & Finance Office, 3039
Management Concepts, 952
Management Information Systems, 3084
Management Services, 2889, 3166
Management Simulations, 953
Management Systems & Technology
  Services Division, 2978
Management, Budget & Planning, 2955
Managing Info Tech in School Library
  Media Center, 4049
Managing Media Services Theory and
  Practice, 4050
Managing School Business, 4353
Managing Students Without Coercion, 3596
Mannheim Elementary School, 1807
Mannheim High School, 1808
Manor School, 2153
Maranatha Christian Academy, 2154
Marbrook Foundation, 2559
MarcoPolo, 403
Marcraft International Corporation, 3678
Margaret Danyers College, 1809
Margaret E Oser Foundation, 2317
Margaret Hall Foundation, 2481
Margaret K McElderry Books, 4927
Margaret L Wendt Foundation, 2660
Mari, 4928
Marian Baker School, 1390
Marin Community Foundation, 2318, 2290
Marion I & Henry J Knott Foundation, 2504
Marist Brothers International School, 1194
Mark Twain Elementary School, 1810
Market Data Retrieval, 3823, 3892
Market Data Retrieval-National School
  Market Index, 3892
Marketing Education Resource Center, 954
Marketing Recreation Classes, 4608
Marquette University Memorial Library,
  2819
Marriner S Eccles Foundation, 2794
Marsh Industries, 5347
Marsh Media, 5199
Marshmedia, 5199

Martha Holden Jennings Foundation, 2704
Martin De Porress, 548
Maru A Pula School, 1071
Mary A Crocker Trust, 2319
Mary Hillman Jennings Foundation, 2738
Mary Jo Williams Charitable Trust, 2474
Mary Owen Borden Memorial Foundation,
  2599
Mary Ranken Jordan & Ettie A Jordan
  Charitable Foundation, 2577
Mary Reynolds Babcock Foundation, 2684
Maryland Center for Career and Technology
  Education, 3679
Maryland Department of Education, 3052,
  3055
Maryland Educational Media Organization,
  500
Maryland Educational Opportunity Center,
  955
Maryland Elco Incorporated Educational
  Funding Company, 956
Maryland Library Association, 501
Maryland State Teachers Association, 502
Marymount International School-Rome, 1811
Marymount International School-United
  Kingdom, 1812
Marymount School, 1391
Mason Associates, 957
**Massachusetts Bay Community College
  Press**, 4023
Massachusetts Business Educators
  Association, 503
Massachusetts Department of Education,
  3056
Massachusetts Department of Educational
  Improvement, 3057
Massachusetts Elementary School Principals
  Association Conference, 3340
Massachusetts Home Learning Association
  Newsletter, 4229
Massachusetts Library Association, 504
Massachusetts School Boards Association
  Meeting, 3341
Massachusetts Teachers Association, 505
Master Bond, 5594
Master Builders, 5595
Master Teacher, 3597, 3431, 3438, 3441,
  3444, 3453, 3473, 3479, 3480, 3482, 3483,
  3492, 3495, 3501, 3513, 3518, 3519, 3521,
  3533, 3534, 3569
Master Woodcraft, 5348
Master Woodcraft Inc., 740
MasterTeacher, 4929
Mastercam, 6174
Mateflex-Mele Corporation, 5523
Material Science Technology, 5349
Math Notebook, 4570
MathSoft, 4930
MathStories.com, 6124
MathType, 6117
The Mathemagician, 6126
Mathematica, 5974, 6118
Mathematical Association of America, 327
Mathematics & Computer Education, 4571
Mathematics Teacher, 4572
Mathematics Teaching in the Middle School,
  4573
Matrix Media Distribution, 958
Matrix Newsletter, 4713
Matthew C Perry Elementary School, 1195
Matthew C Perry Middle & High School,
  1196
Mattlidens Gymnasium, 1813

Matworks, 5751
Maurice Amado Foundation, 2320
Mayenne English School, 1814
McCamish Foundation, 2414
McConnell Foundation, 2321
McCracken Educational Services, 4931
McCune Foundation, 2739
McDonnell Douglas Foundation, 2578
McGraw Hill Children's Publishing, 4932
McGraw Hill School Division, 3555
McGraw-Hill Educational Resources, 5837
McGraw-Hill Foundation, 2661
McGregor Fund, 2543
McKenzie Group, 959
McKesson Foundation, 2322
McNeese State University, 4716
Mead Corporation Foundation, 2705
Meadows Foundation, 2786
Measurement, 960
Measurement & Evaluation in Counseling
    and Development, 4489
Measurement Learning Consultants, 961
Medart, 5596
Media & Methods Magazine, 4559, 4714
Media Management & Magnetics, 5975
Media Marketing Group, 4097, 4098
Media Projects, 5200
Media and American Democracy, 3680
Medianet/Dymaxion Research Limited, 6097
Mediterranean Association of International
    Schools, 281
Medtronic Foundation, 2560
Meeting the Tide of Rising Expectations, 741
Meiji Techno America, 5689
Mel Bay Publications, 4933
Mel Gabler's Newsletter, 4230
Melkonian Educational Institute, 1445
**Membership Services American Library
    Association**, 4544
Memo to the President, 4354
Memorial Library, 2821
Mental Edge, 3543
Mentone Boys Grammar School, 1197
Mentoring Teachers to Mastery, 3598
Menwith Hill Estates & Middle School, 1815
Mercantile Bank, 2577
Mercedes College, 1198
Merck Company Foundation, 2600
Merit Audio Visual, 6175
Merit Software, 6175
Merlyn's Pen: Fiction, Essays and Poems by
    America's Teens, 4527
Merriam-Webster, 4934
Merrimack Education Center, 962, 5102
Mervin Bovaird Foundation, 2716
Methodist Ladies College, 1199
**Metro International Program Services of
    New York**, 4185
Metrologic Instruments, 5690
Metropolitan Atlanta Community
    Foundation, 2415
Metropolitan School, 1392
Meyer Memorial Trust, 2722
Miami University, 3336, 3509, 4473
Michigan Association for Media in
    Education, 507
Michigan Association of Elementary and
    Middle School Principals Conference,
    3342
Michigan Association of School
    Administrators, 508
Michigan Department of Education, 3064,
    3069

Michigan Education Association, 509
Michigan Education Council, 963
Michigan Elementary & Middle School
    Principals Association, 510
Michigan Library Association, 511
Michigan School Boards Association Fall
    Leadership Conference, 3343
Michigan Science Teachers Association
    Annual Conference, 3344
Michigan State University, 702, 6051
Michigan State University Libraries, 2544
**Michigan State University, College of
    Education**, 5113
MicroAnalytics, 5976
MicroLearn Tutorial Series, 5977
Micrograms Publishing, 6017
Microsoft Corporation, 5524, 5838
Mid-Atlantic Regional Educational
    Laboratory, 5103
**Mid-Continent Regional Educational
    Laboratory**, 5104, 60
**Mid-South Educational Research
    Association**, 3345, 4278
Midas Consulting Group, 964
**Middle East Studies Association of North
    America**, 3790
Middle Grades Education in an Era of
    Reform, 3448
Middle School Teachers Guide to FREE
    Curriculum Materials, 3449
Middle School: Why and How, 5201
Middle States Council for the Social Studies
    Annual Regional Conference, 3346
Midnight Play, 6128
Midwest Publishers Supply, 5350
Midwestern Regional Educational
    Laboratory, 5105
Mildred Weedon Blount Educational and
    Charitab le Foundation, 2256
Milken Family Foundation, 2323
Mill Creek Foundation, 2416
Millbrook Press, 4935
Miller Electric Manufacturing Company,
    3681
Miller Freeman, 3399
Miller Multiplex, 5351, 5525
Miller, Cook & Associates, 965
Millersville University, 3682
Millfield School, 1816
Mills Bee Lane Memorial Foundation, 2417
Milton Roy Company, 4936
Mimosa Publications, 4937
MindTwister Math, 6119
Mindplay, 6006
Minneapolis Foundation, 2561
Minneapolis Public Library, 2562
Minnesota Business Educators, 513
Minnesota Congress of Parents, Teachers &
    Students, 514
Minnesota Department of Children, Families
    & Learning, 3078
Minnesota Department of Education, 3079
Minnesota Education Update, 4231
Minnesota Leadership Annual Conference,
    3347
Minnesota Library Association, 515
Minnesota School Administrators
    Association, 3348
Minnesota School Boards Association,
    516, 3347
Minnesota School Boards Association
    Annual Meeting, 3349

Minority Student Guide to American
    Colleges, 3824
Minsk International School, 1200
Miracle Recreation Equipment Company,
    5752
Miranda Lux Foundation, 2324
Miss Jackie Music Company, 4599
Mississippi Advocate For Education, 517
Mississippi Business Education Association,
    518
Mississippi Department of Education,
    3085, 3081, 3082, 3083, 3084, 3087, 3088
Mississippi Employment Security
    Commission, 3086
Mississippi Library Association, 519
Mississippi Power Foundation, 2568
Missouri Association of Elementary School
    Principals, 520
Missouri Association of Secondary School
    Principals, 521
Missouri Business Education Association,
    522
Missouri Congress of Parents & Teachers,
    523
Missouri Department of Education, 3091,
    3089, 3090, 3093, 3094, 3095, 3096, 4232
Missouri LINC, 5106
Missouri Library Association, 524
Missouri Library Association Conference,
    826
Missouri National Education Association
    Conference, 525, 3350
Missouri School Boards Association Annual
    Meeting, 3351
Missouri Schools, 4232
Missouri State Teachers Association, 526
Missouri State Teachers Association
    Conference, 3352
Misty City Software, 5839
Mitchell Foundation, 2257
Mitinet/Marc Software, 6098
Mitsubishi Professional Electronics, 5449
Mobility International USA, 3791
Model Classroom, 966
Model Technologies, 4938
Modern American School, 1393
Modern Educational Systems, 967
Modern Language Association Annual
    Conference, 742
Modern Language Journal, 4528
Modern Red Schoolhouse Institute, 968
Modern School Supplies, 5691
ModuForm, 5526
ModuForm, Inc., 5526
Modular Hardware, 5597
Mohammed Ali Othman School, 1516
Mohon International, 5692
Mombasa Academy, 1072
Momentum, 4233
Mondo Publishing, 4939
Money for Film & Video Artists, 3996, 4053
Money for International Exchange in the
    Arts, 3997
Money for Visual Artists, 3998, 4054
Monkton Combe School, 1817
Monsanto Company, 5352
Monsanto Fund, 2579
Montana Association of County School
    Superintendents, 527
Montana Association of Elementary School
    Principals Conference, 3353
Montana Association of School Librarians,
    528

Montana Business Education Association, 529

Montana Department of Education, 3099, 3097, 3098, 3100

Montana Education Association, 4228

Montana High School Association Conference, 819

Montana Library Association, 530

Montana Office of Public Instruction, 4234

Montana School Boards Association, 969

Montana Schools, 4234

Montana State Library, 2581

Montessori House of Children, 2155

Montessori LIFE, 4422

Montessori Observer, 4235

Montgomery Intermediate Unit 23, 970

Monti Parioli English School, 1818

Moody Foundation, 2787

Moore Express, 971

Moore Foundation, 2470

Moravian School, 2156

Moreguina International Primary School, 1201

Morehead State University, 3683

Morgan Buildings, Pools, Spas, RV's, 5527

Morning Glory Press, 4940

Morris & Gwendolyn Cafritz Foundation, 2384

Morrison Christian Academy, 1202

Morrison School Supplies, 5353

Morrocoy International, 2157

Mosaica Education, 972

Motivating Students in the Classroom Video Ser ies, 3599

Mougins School, 1819

Mount Carmel Elementary School, 2158

Mount Hagen International School, 1203

Mount Saint Agnes Academy, 1957

Mountain Plains Library Association, 579

Mountainside Publishing Company, 4555

Mountainview School, 1820

Mpulse Maintenance Software, 3684

Mrs. Glosser's Math Goodies, 6123

Mt Zaagham International School, 1204

Multi-Video, 5450

MultiMedia Schools, 4715

Multicorp, 973

Multicultural Education: Teaching to Diversity, 3600

Multicultural Educations: Valuing Diversity, 5202

Multimedia - The Human Body, 6120

Multimedia and Videodisc Compendium for Education and Training, 4105

Multnomah County Library, 2723

Munich International School, 1821

Murray International School, 1205

Murree Christian School, 1206

Museum Products Company, 5693

Museum Stamps, 6222

Music Ace 2, 6223

Music Education Research Council, 3295

Music Educators Journal, 4589

Music Educators Journal and Teaching Music, 4590

Music Educators National Conference, 743

Music Teacher Find, 6129

Music Teachers Association National Conference, 744

Music Teachers Guide to Music Instructional Software, 4055

Music Teachers National Association, 336, 5107, 744, 4051, 4055, 4057

Music and Guitar, 6130

Music for Little People, 4941

Music, Art, Sociology & Humanities, 2562

Musikgarten, 3685

Mussoorie International School, 1207

Myra Foundation, 2690

N

N&N Publishing Company, 4942

NAAEE Member Services Office, 745

NABE News, 4529

NACAC Bulletin, 4490

NACDA, 4603

NAEA News, 4591

NAEIR Advantage, 4236

NAFSA Newsletter, 4237

NAFSA's Guide to Education Abroad for Advisers & Administrators, 3825

NAFSA: Association of International Educators, 3825, 3971, 4237

NAFSA: National Association of International Educators, 746

NAIEC Newsletter, 4238

NAME National Office, 754

NAPNSC Accrediting Commission for Higher Education, 4322

NAPSEC News, 4239

NASA Educational Workshop, 3686

NASA Headquarters, 4947

NASDTEC Knowledge Base, 3450

NASFAA Newsletter, 4452

NASILP Journal, 4530

NASP Publications, 4943

NASPA Forum, 4355

NASSP Bulletin, 4645

NASW Job Link: The Social Work Employment Line, 204

NASW News, 4491

NCR Corporation, 5840

NCRTL Special Report, 3511

NCS Marketing, 5978

NCS Pearson, 5925, 6168

NCSIE Inservice, 3512

NCSS Summer Professional Development Programs, 3687

NCTM Educational Materials, 4944

NCTM News Bulletin, 4574

NEA Almanac of Higher Education, 3826

NEA Foundatrion for tHe Improvement of Educati on, 5108

NEA Higher Education Advocate, 4240

NEA Today, 4241

NEWSLINKS, 4242

NHSA Journal, 4403

NJEA Review, 4243

NREA News, 4244

NSSEA Essentials, 784

NSTA, 3686

NSTA Award for Principals, 3291

NSTA Awards, 3292

NSTA Educational Workshops, 747

NSTA Reports!, 4656

NTID at Rochester Institute of Technology, 4252

NUVO, Ltd., 5203

NY School Boards, 4356

NYCTeachers.com, 6001

NYPER Publications, 4300, 4320, 4336, 4339, 4343, 4359, 4366

NYSTROM, 4945

Nadeen Nursery & Infant School, 1517

Naden Scoreboards, 5451

Nagoya International School, 1208

Nalge Company, 5694

Names Unlimited, 5354

Naples Elementary School, 1822

Naples High School, 1823

Narrabundah College, 1209

Narrative Press, 4946

Nasco, 5355, 5356, 5357

Nasco Arts & Crafts Catalog, 5355

Nasco Early Learning & Afterschool Essential C atalogs, 5356

Nasco Math Catalog, 5357

Nashville Public Library, 2761

Nat'l Assn. for Creative Children & Adults, 4145

Nat'l Assn. for Exchange of Industrial Resources, 4236

Nat'l Association for College Admission Counseling, 752, 4481, 4490

Nat'l Association of Elementary School Principals, 4363

Nat'l Association of Secondary School Principles, 4323

Nat'l Health Education Credentialing, 3433

National Academy Foundation, 748

National Academy Foundation Annual Institute for Staff Development, 748

National Academy Press, 3461, 4085, 5700

National Academy of Education, 81, 2835

National Accrediting Commission of Cosmetology, Arts and Sciences, 4245

National Accrediting Commission of Cosmetology, 4245

National Aeronautics & Space Administration, 4947

National Alliance for Safe Schools, 82

National Alliance of Black School Educators, 749, 4246, 114

National Art Education Association, 337, 750, 4579, 4591

National Art Education Association Annual Convention, 750

National Assn. of Industrial Teacher Educators, 4101

National Assn. of Secondary School Principals, 4645

National Assn. of Self-Instructional Language, 4530

National Assn. of State Directors of Special Ed., 4224

National Assn. of Student Financial Aid Admin., 4452

National Assn. of Student Personnel Administrators, 4355

National Association for Asian and Pacific American Education, 83

National Association for Bilingual Education, 308, 751, 4506, 4529

National Association for College Admission Counseling Conference, 752

National Association for Developmental Education, 84

National Association for Girls and Women in Sports, 345

National Association for Girls and Women in Sports Yearly Conference, 753

National Association for Industry-Education Cooperation, 85

National Association for Industry-Education Co-op, 4238, 5121

National Association for Legal Support of Alternative Schools, 86
National Association for Multicultural Education, 754
National Association for Music Education, 338, 4589, 4590, 4598
National Association for Research in Science Teaching, 374
National Association for Sport & Physical Education News, 4609
National Association for Sport & Physical Ed., 4600, 4609
National Association for Supervision and Curriculum Development, 163
National Association for Women in Education Directory, 3827
National Association for Year-Round Education, 87, 755, 3830
National Association for the Education of Young Children, 190
National Association of Academic Advisors for Athletics, 346
National Association of Biology Teachers, 375, 756, 4648
National Association of Boards of Education, 88
National Association of Catholic School Teachers, 89
National Association of Christian Educators, 4164
National Association of Elementary School Principals Conference, 164, 191, 757
National Association of Elementary School Principa, 3715
National Association of Federal Education Prog ram Administrators, 165
National Association of Federally Impacted Schools, 90
National Association of Hebrew Day School PTA'S, 4258
National Association of Independent Schools, 758, 4419, 4643
National Association of Media and Technology Centers, 404
National Association of Principals of Schools for Girls Directory, 166, 3893
National Association of Principals/Girls Schools, 3893
National Association of Private Schools for Exceptional Children Conference, 167, 759
National Association of School Psychologist Directory, 4028
National Association of School Psychologists, 219, 760, 4028, 4466, 4496, 4943
National Association of Schools of Music, 339
National Association of Science Teachers, 4665
National Association of Secondary School Principals Annual Convention and Exposition, 168, 3354
National Association of Social Workers, 220, 4475, 4491, 4497, 4498, 4499
National Association of State Boards of Education Conference, 91, 3355
National Association of State Boards of Education, 4334
National Association of State Directors of Teacher Education & Certification, 169, 3277
National Association of State Scholarship and Grant Program Survey Report, 3999

National Association of State Scholarship Programs, 3999
National Association of Student Activity Advisers, 92
National Association of Student Councils, 93
National Association of Student Financial Aid Administrators Directory, 170, 4000
National Association of Student Financial Aid Administrators, 761, 810
National Association of Student Personnel Administrators, 171
National Association of Substance Abuse Trainers & Educators, 221
National Association of Teachers' Agencies, 205, 762, 2243, 3943
National Association of Trade & Industrial Instructors, 94
National Athletic Trainers' Association, 347, 4602
National Black Alliance for Graduate Level Education, 95
National Black Child Development Institute, 763, 5109
National Business Education Association, 206, 360, 4328
National Career Development Association Conference, 3356
National Catholic Education Association Annual Convention & Exposition, 764
National Catholic Educational Association, 96, 691, 764, 3761, 4233
National Center for Community Education, 3278
National Center for Construction Education & Research, 3688
National Center for ESL Literacy Education, 351
National Center for Education Statistics, 2890, 3770
National Center for Fair & Open Testing, 6246
National Center for Improving Science Education, 5110
National Center for Learning Disabilities, 97
National Center for Montessori Education Conference, 765
National Center for Research in Mathematical Sciences Education, 5111
National Center for Research in Vocational Education, 5112
National Center for Research on Teacher Learning, 5113
National Center for Research on Teacher Education, 3511
National Center for Science Education, 376, 4660
National Center for Science Teaching & Learning, 4948, 5114
National Center for Teaching Thinking, 3635
National Center for the Study of Privatization in Education, 5115
National Center on Education & the Economy, 974, 5116
National Center on Education in the Inner Cities, 5117
National Child Labor Committee, 5118
National Clearinghouse for Alcohol & Drug Information, 5119
National Clearinghouse for Bilingual Education Newsletter, 4531
National Clearinghouse for Bilingual Education, 5120

National Clearinghouse for Commuter Programs, 4142
National Clearinghouse for Information on Business Involvement in Education, 5121
National Coalition for Sex Equity in Education, 4492
National Coalition for Sex Equity in Education, 766
National Coalition of Advocates for Students, 98
National Coalition of Alternative Community Schools, 99, 767
National Coalition of Independent Scholars, 100, 4196
National Coalition of Title 1-Chapter 1 Parents Conference, 768
National Commission for Cooperative Education, 101, 3763
National Communication Association, 4533
National Computer Systems, 3689, 5979
National Conference Logistics Center, 791
National Conference on Education, 3357
National Conference on Parent Involvement, 102
National Conference on Standards and Assessment, 3358
National Conference on Student Services, 769
National Congress for Educational Excellence, 103
National Congress on Aviation and Space Education, 770
National Contact Hotline, 352
National Council for Black Studies, 104
National Council for Geographic Education, 3359, 4686
National Council for History Education, 3360, 4681
National Council for Social Studies Annual Conference, 3361
National Council for the Accreditation of Teacher Education, 3279
National Council for the Social Studies, 385, 4949, 3687, 4093, 4691, 4694, 4695, 4697, 6248
National Council of Administrative Women in Education, 172
National Council of English Teachers Conference, 3362
National Council of Higher Education, 105, 771
National Council of Independent Schools' Associations, 2244
National Council of State Directors of Adult Education, 173
National Council of State Supervisors of Music, 2936
National Council of States on Inservice Education, 3512
National Council of Teachers of Mathematics Annual Meeting, 3363
National Council of Teachers of English, 309, 3364, 4950, 3362, 4509, 4513, 4516, 4517, 4525, 4534, 4539
National Council of Teachers of Mathematics, 328, 3365, 4567, 4572, 4573, 4574, 4577, 4944
National Council of Urban Education Associatio ns, 106
National Council on Alcoholism & Drug Abuse, 772
National Council on Disability, 2891
National Council on Economic Education, 4951

National Council on Measurement in Education, 107
National Council on Rehabilitation Education, 108
National Council on Student Development, 109
National Council on US-Arab Relations, 282
National Dance Association, 4610
National Data Bank for Disabled Student Services, 174
National Directory of Children, Youth & Families Services, 3828
National Directory of Internships, 3944
National Dissemination Center for Children with Disabilities, 110
National Dropout Prevention Center, 5122
National Dropout Prevention Center/Network Conference, 773
National Early Childhood Technical Assistance System, 184, 5123
National Education Association, 111, 3280
National Education Association (NEA), 105, 106, 112, 113, 126, 308, 356, 771, 774, 3366, 3423, 3434, 3757, 3826, 4240, 4241, 4282, 4306, 5088, 5095
National Education Association Annual Meeting, 3366
National Education Association Student Program, 112
National Education Association of New Mexico, 543
National Education Association of New York, 549, 4120
National Education Association, New Hampshire, 4249
National Education Association-Retired, 113, 774
National Education Policy Institute, 114
National Education Service Center, 4432
National Educational Computing Conference, 3367
National Educational Service, 115, 3456, 5377
National Educational Systems, 185
National Enneagram Institute at Milton Academy, 3675
National Evaluation Systems, 975
National Faculty Forum, 4357
National Faculty of Humanities, Arts & Sciences, 4357
National Federation of Modern Language Teacher s Association, 310
National Federation of State High School Assoc., 5280
National Film Board, 5204
National Forum of Instructional Technology Journal, 4716
National Foundation for Dyslexia, 311, 6229
National Geographic School Publishing, 4952, 5205
National Geographic Society, 4953
National Guide to Educational Credit for Training Programs, 3829
National Guild of Community Schools of the Arts, 340, 775, 4404, 4592
National Guild of Community Schools of the Arts, 3489, 3500, 4404, 4433, 4592
National Head Start Association, 186, 3690, 4954, 4394, 4403
National Head Start Association Annual Conference, 776
National Heritage Academies, 976
National Homeschool Association, 116, 4247

National Homeschool Association Newsletter, 4247
National Information Center for Educational Media, 5124, 6176
National Information Center for Educational Media, 5774
National Institute for School and Workplace Safety Conference, 175, 777
National Institute for Science Education, 377
National Institute for Staff & Organizational Dev., 646
National Institute of Art and Disabilities, 341
National Institute of Child Health and Human Development, 2892
National Institute on Disability and Rehabilitation Research, 405
National Institutes of Health, 3966
National Instruments, 5695
National Lekotek Center, 117
National Library of Education, 3478
National Middle School Association, 118, 361, 3281, 3368
National Middle School Association's Annual Conference and Exhibition, 3368
National Monitor of Education, 4248
National Multicultural Institute, 723
National Network for Early Language Learning (NELL), 312
National Network of Learning Disabled Adults, 119
National Occupational Information Coordinating Committee Conference, 3369
National Optical & Scientific Instruments, 5696
National Organization on Disability, 120
National Parent-Teacher Association Annual Convention & Exhibition, 778
National Professional Resources, 3458, 3556
National Reading Styles Institute, 977
National Reading Styles Institute Conference, 779
National Reference Directory of Year-Round Education Programs, 3830
National Registration Center for Study Abroad, 283, 4493
National Research Center on English Learning and Achievement, 313
National Research Center on the Gifted & Talented, 5125
National Resource Center on Self-Care & School-Age Child Care, 5126
National Rural Education Annual Convention, 780
National Rural Education Association, 781, 780, 3522, 4244, 4280, 4368
National School Board Association, 3889
National School Boards Annual Conference, 782
National School Boards Association, 121, 692, 828, 4325, 4388
National School Boards Association Annual Conference & Exposition, 3370
National School Boards Association Library, 5127
National School Conference Institute, 783, 685, 686, 687, 688, 726, 730, 732, 734, 801, 3358, 3398, 3711
National School Public Relations Association, 122, 3894, 4202, 4358, 4364
National School Safety Center, 176, 5128, 4288

National School Safety and Security Services, 978
National School Services, 3477
National School Supply & Equipment Association, 784
National School Supply & Equipment Association, 3895
National Schools Community for Economic Education, 4680
National Schools of Character, 3896
National Schools of Character: Best Practices and New Perspectives, 3831
National Schools of Character: Practices to Adopt & Adapt, 3832
National Science Foundation, 2836, 3294
National Science Resources Center, 5129
National Science Teachers Association, 378, 747, 3291, 3292, 3296, 4413, 4653, 4656, 4659, 4663, 4664
National Science Teachers Association Area Convention, 3371
National Society for Experiential Education, 123, 785, 3833, 3944
National Society for the Study of Education, 124
National Staff Development Council, 3282, 4335
National Standards for Dance Education News, 4610
National Student Assistance Conference, 786
National Student Exchange, 125
National Student Program, 126
National Study of School Evaluation, 6205, 6247, 729
National Survey of Course Offerings and Testing in Social Studies K-12, 6248
National Teachers Clearinghouse, 207
National Teachers Hall of Fame, 3293
National Teaching Aids, 5358, 5753
National Telemedia Council, 127
National Textbook Company, 4955
National Training Aids, 5464
National Trust for Historic Preservation: Office of Education Initiatives, 2893
National Women's History Network, 4699
National Women's History Project, 4956
National Women's History Project Annual Conference, 787
National Women's Student Coalition, 128
National Women's Studies Association, 129, 3283
National Writing Project, 4957, 4535
National Youth-At-Risk Conference, 827
Native American Homeschool Association, 130
Natrona County Public Library, 2822
Nazarene Christian School, 2159
Near East-South Asia Council of Overseas Schools, 284
Nebraska Department of Education, 3103, 3104
Nebraska Library Association, 531
Nebraska School Boards Association Annual Conference, 820
Nebraska State Business Education Association, 532
Nebraska State Education Association, 533
Need A Lift?, 4001
Nepal Lincoln School, 2160
NetLingo Internet Directory, 4106
NetLingo The Internet Dictionary, 5841
NetOp, 6188
NetZero, 5842

Network, 4358
Neubruecke Elementary School, 1824
Neuchatel Junior College, 1825
Neumade Products Corporation, 5452
Nevada Department of Education, 3107
Nevada Library Association, 534
Nevada State Education Association, 535
Nevco Scoreboard Company, 5453
New Braunfels General Store International, 5754
New Canaan Publishing Company, 4958
New Century Education Corporation, 5843
New England Association of Schools and Colleges, 3834
New England Association of Schools and Colleges, 3834
New England History Teachers Association, 386
New England Journal of History, 4688
New England Kindergarten Conference, 3372
New England League of Middle Schools, 3373
New England Library Association, 506
New English School, 1518
New Hampshire Business Education Association, 536
New Hampshire Charitable Foundation, 2592
New Hampshire Department of Education, 3109, 3108
New Hampshire Division of Instructional Services, 3110
New Hampshire Education Association, 537
New Hampshire Educator, 4249
New Hampshire Library Association, 538
New Haven Free Library, 444
New Hermes, 5359
New Horizons, 4493
New Images, 4250
New International School of Thailand, 1210
New Jersey Department of Education, 3112
New Jersey Department of Education: Finance, 3113
New Jersey Division of Special Education, 3114
New Jersey Education Association, 540, 4243
New Jersey Education Law Report, 4439
New Jersey Library Association, 541
New Jersey School Boards Association, 4361
New Jersey School Boards Association Annual Meeting, 811
New Jersey State Department of Education, 542, 4166
New Jersey State Library, 3115
New Learning Technologies, 788
New Mexico Business Education Association, 544
New Mexico Department of Education, 3120
New Mexico Department of School-Transportation & Support Services, 3121
New Mexico Highlands University, 5149
New Mexico Junior College, 109
New Mexico Library Association, 545
New Mexico School Boards Association Conference Annual Meeting, 3374
New Mexico State Library, 2607
New Orleans Public Library, 2487
New Press, 4959
New School Rome, 1826
New York Department of Education, 3127, 3125, 3126

New York Education Personnel Update, 4359
New York Foundation, 2662
New York Library Association, 550
New York School Board Association, 3304
New York School Superintendents Association Annual Meeting, 3375
New York Science Teachers Association Annual Meeting, 3376
New York State Council of Student Superintendents Forum, 812
New York State School Boards Association, 4356
New York State United Teachers, 4251
New York State United Teachers Conference, 3377
New York Teacher, 4251
New York Teachers Math Association Conference, 3378
New York Times, 6141
New York University, 4515
Newbridge Discovery Station, 5360
Newbridge Jumbo Seasonal Patterns, 5361
Newfound Regional High School, 536
News & Views, 4689
News N' Notes, 4252
News World Communications, 5063
News for You, 4622
NewsBank, 4960
NewsCurrents, 5362
Newton College, 1827
Nile C Kinnick High School, 1211
Nishimachi International School, 1212
No Child Left Behind, 2894
NoRad Corporation, 6177
Noel/Levitz Centers, 979
Non-Credit Learning News, 4253
Non-Profit Resource Center/Pack Memorial Library, 2685
Norco Products, 5528
Nord Family Foundation, 2706
Nordic Software, 6007
Norra Reals Gymnasium, 1828
North American Association for Environmental Education, 131, 387, 3379
North American Association of Educational Negotiators News, 132, 4254
North American Montessori Teachers' Association, 789
North American Professional Driver Education Association, 133
North American Students of Cooperation, 134
North Carolina Association for Career and Technical Education Conference, 3380
North Carolina Association for Career and Technical Education, 551
North Carolina Association of Educators, 552
North Carolina Business Education Association, 553
North Carolina Department of Education, 3133, 3131, 3132, 3135
North Carolina Department of Instructional Services, 3134
North Carolina Department of Public Instructio n, 554
North Carolina Library Association, 555
North Carolina School Administrators Conference, 3381
North Central Association Annual Meeting, 3382
North Central Association Commission on Accred., 3382
North Central Association of Colleges & Schools, 3653

North Central Conference on Summer Schools, 3383
North Central Regional Educational Laboratory, 5130, 4222, 6199
North Dakota Business and Office Education Association, 556
North Dakota Department of Education, 3136, 3139
North Dakota Department of Public Instruction Division, 3137
North Dakota Education Association, 557
North Dakota Library Association, 558
North Dakota State Board for Vocational & Technical Education, 3138
North Dakota Vocational Educational Planning Conference, 821
North South Books, 4961
Northeast Conference at Dickinson College, 3384
Northeast Conference on the Teaching of Foreign Languages, 3384
Northeast Foundation for Children, 3476
Northeast Regional Center for Drug-Free Schools & Communities, 5131
Northeast Regional Christian Schools Internati onal Association, 813
Northeast Teachers Foreign Language Conference, 3385
Northeast and Islands Regional Educational Laboratory, 5132
Northeastern Illinois University, 84
Northeastern University, 5085
Northern Arizona University, 3691
Northern California Comprehensive Assistance Center, 433
Northern California Grantmakers, 2325
Northern Illinois University, 298, 314, 470
Northern Mariana Islands Department of Education, 2161
Northern Trust Company Charitable Trust, 2448
Northlands Day School, 1394
Northside Primary School, 1073
Northwest Association of Schools & Colleges Annual Meeting, 135, 3386
Northwest International Education Association, 285
Northwest Regional Educational Laboratory, 3387, 5133, 4165
Notices of the American Mathematical Society, 4575
Notre Dame High School, 2162
Nova, 5529
Nsansa School, 1074
Nuestra Senora de La Altagracia, 2163
Nuestra Senora de La Providencia, 2164
Number2.com, 6145
Numont School, 1829
Nursery Schools & Kindergartens Directory, 3902
Nystrom, Herff Jones, 4962

O

O'Flynn Consulting, 6002, 6136
OASCD Journal, 4360
OASES, 548
OCLC Forest Press, 6084
Oak House School, 1830
Oakham School, 1831
Oakstone Publishing, 3847, 3854, 3872

Oakstone Publishing, Inc., 4351, 4365, 4377
Occupational Programs in California Community Colleges, 4255
Oceanic Cablevision Foundation, 2429
Octameron Associates, 2875, 3930, 3967, 3995
Odyssey, 4657
Odyssey of the Mind, 136
Office of Accountability, 3087
Office of Bilingual Education and Minority Language Affairs, 2895
Office of Career Services, 3990
Office of District of Columbia Affairs, 452
Office of Elementary and Secondary Education, 3176
Office of Field, Curriculum & Instruction Services, 3167
Office of Finance, 3184
Office of Indian Education, 2896
Office of Juvenile Justice and Delinquency Prevention, 177
Office of Learning Programs Development, 3031
Office of Library Development & Services, 4231
Office of Management & Budget, 3958
Office of Migrant Education, 2897
Office of Overseas Schools, 2898
Office of Overseas Schools, Department of State, 4132
Office of Proposal Entry, 2527
Office of Public Affairs, 2899
Office of Research Reporting, 2892
Office of School Management, 3065
Office of Special Education Programs, 2900
Office of State Coordinator of Vocational Education for Disabled Students, 2968
Office of Student Financial Assistance Programs, 2901
Office of Vocational Education, 3040
Office of the Comptroller, 3177
Office of the Deputy Superintendent, 3009
Office of the State Director for Career & Technical Education, 2986
Office of the Superintendent, 3066
Official Guide to the SAT II: Subject Tests, 6249
Ohaus Corporation, 5697
Ohio Association of School Business Officials, 560
Ohio Association of Secondary School Administrators, 561
Ohio Bell Telephone Contribution Program, 2707
Ohio Business Teachers Association, 3388
Ohio Department of Education, 3144, 3140, 3141, 3142, 3143, 3145, 3146, 3147, 3148, 3149, 3150, 3151, 3152
Ohio Library Council, 562
Ohio Library Council Trade Show, 814
Ohio Public School Employees Association Convention, 3389
Ohio School Boards Association Capital Conference & Trade Show, 815
Ohio Secondary School Administrators Association Fall Conference, 3390
Ohio State Library Foundation Center, 2708
Ohio State University, 368, 369, 4526, 4628, 5114
Ohio State University, College of Education, 4305
Ohio University, 4486
Okinawa Christian School, 2165

Okinawa Christian School International, 1213
Oklahoma City University, 2717
Oklahoma Curriculum Development, 4360
Oklahoma Department of Career and Technology Education, 3155
Oklahoma Department of Education, 3156, 3153, 3154, 3157, 3158, 3159
Oklahoma Department of Education; Financial Services, 3157
Oklahoma Education Association, 563
Oklahoma Library Association, 564
Oklahoma School Boards Association & School Administrators Conference, 3391
Oklahoma State University-Stillwater, 56
Old Dominion University, 365
Ome Resa, 980
Omnicor, 5410
Omnigraphics, 3775
OnLine Educator, 5844
One Commerce Square, 2740
One Hand Typing and Keyboarding Resources, 6192
One Hundred Ways Parents Can Help Students Achieve, 3835
One Mellon Bank Center, 2741
One-On-One with the SAT, 6250
Online Computer Systems, 5845
OnlineLearning.net, 3557
Oosting & Associates, 981
Open Classroom, 2166
Opening List in US Colleges, Public & Private Schools, 3945
Opening List of Professional Openings in American Overseas Schools, 3946
Operation Crossroads Africa, 286
Operations & School Support, 3216
Operations Department, 3100
Oporto British School, 1832
Opportunities Industrialization Centers International, 287
Options Publishing, 4963
Options in Learning, 4256
Oranatics Journal, 4593
Orange Cherry Software, 6099
Orators & Philosophers: A History of the Idea of Liberal Education, 3451
Oregon Association of Student Councils, 565
Oregon Community Foundation, 2724
Oregon Department of Education, 3168, 3160, 3161, 3162, 3163, 3164, 3165, 3166, 3167, 3169, 3170, 3171, 3172
Oregon Education Association, 566
Oregon Educational Media Association, 567
Oregon Federation of Teachers, 568
Oregon Library Association, 569
Oregon School Boards Association Annual Convention, 3392
Orff-Schulwerk Teacher Certification Program, 3692
Organization of American Historians, 4964, 4684
Organization of American States, 288, 1418
Organization of Virginia Homeschoolers, 594
Organizations of American History, 4687
Orlando Public Library-Orange County Library System, 2396
Osaka International School, 1214, 2167
Osaka YMCA International High School, 1215
Osan Elementary School, 1216
Osan High School, 1217
Oscoda Plastics, 5530

Oslo American School, 1833
Otto Bremer Foundation, 2563
Our Children: The National PTA Magazine, 4257
Our Lady of Mercy School, 1395
Outback Play Centers, 5755
Outcome-Based Education: Making it Work, 3601
Outcomes & Assessment Office, 3185
Outdoor Education Association, 137
Outeiro de Polima-Arneiro, 1893
Outreach Department, 4749
Overseas American-Sponsored Elementary and Secondary Schools, 3836
Overseas Children's School, 1218
Overseas Employment Info- Teachers, 3565, 6075
Overseas Employment Info-Teachers, 6030
Overseas Employment Opportunities for Educators, 2245, 3947
Overseas Employment Services, 3928
Overseas Family School, 1219
Overseas School of Colombo, 1220
Overview of Prevention: A Social Change Model, 3602
Owens Community College, 3693, 559
Owens-Corning Foundation, 2709

P

P. Lambda Theta, Int'l Honor & Professional Assn., 4173
PACER Center, 138, 3452
PASCO Scientific, 5698
PBS TeacherSource, 5846, 3559
PBS Video, 5206
PCTE Bulletin, 4532
PEN American Center, 3985
PF Collier, 4965
PICS Authentic Foreign Video, 5207
PRO-ED, 4966, 4029
PTA National Bulletin, 4258
PTA in Pennsylvania, 4259
Pacific Harbour International School, 1221
Pacific Northwest Council on Languages Annual Conference, 3393
Pacific Northwest Library Association, 321, 468, 822
Pacific Regional Educational Laboratory, 5134
Pacific Telesis Group Corporate Giving Program, 2326
Pagestar, 3558
Paideia Group, 3694
Pakistan International School-Peshawar, 1519
Palache Bilingual School, 2168
Palisades Educational Foundation, 2663
Palmer Foundation, 2449
Palmer Snyder, 5531
Pamela Joy, 982
Pamela Sims & Associates, 3695, 3741
Pan American Christian Academy, 1396
Pan American School-Bahia, 1397
Pan American School-Costa Rica, 1398
Pan American School-Monterrey, 1399
Pan American School-Porto Alegre, 1400
Panama Canal College, 1401
Panasonic Communications & System Company, 5454
Panic Plan for the SAT, 6251
Panterra American School, 1834

Paoli Publishing, 3824
Paradigm Lost: Reclaiming America's Educational Future, 3837
Paraeducator's Guide to Instructional & Curricular Modifications, 3513
Paragon Furniture, 5532
Parek Stuff, 5770
Parent Educational Advocacy Training Center, 5135
The Parent Institute, 3491, 4405, 4423, 4636, 4646, 4647
Parent Involvement Facilitator: Elementary Edition, 3910
Parent Involvement Facilitator: Secondary Edition, 4078
Parent Link, 5847
Parent Training Resources, 3452
Parenting Press, 4967
Parents Make the Difference!, 4423
Parents Make the Difference!: School Readiness Edition, 4405
Parents Rights Organization, 139
Parents Still Make the Difference!, 4646
Parents Still Make the Difference!: Middle School Edition, 4647
Parents as Teachers National Center, 790, 4260, 5136
Parents, Let's Unite for Kids, 140
Paris American Academy, 1835
Parlant Technologies, 5980
Parlant Technology, 5847
Parsifal Systems, 983
Partners in Learning Programs, 5363
Pasir Ridge International, 1222
Passing Marks, 4261
Patrick Henry Elementary School, 1836
Patterson's American Education, 3838
Patterson's Elementary Education, 3911
Patterson's Schools Classified, 3839
Paul & Mary Haas Foundation, 2788
Paul H Rosendahl, PHD, 984
Pawling Corporation, 5533
Paying Less for College, 4002
Peace Corp, 2169
Peak School, 1223
Pearson Education, 3982, 3993
Pearson Education Communications, 3869
Pearson Education Technologies, 5364
Peel Productions, 5298
Peerless Sales Company, 5534
Penco Products, 5598
Penguin USA, 4968
Peninsula Community Foundation, 2327
Pennsylvania Assn. of Secondary School Principals, 4349
Pennsylvania Council for the Social Studies, 3394, 4689, 4693
Pennsylvania Council of Teachers of English, 4532
Pennsylvania Department of Education, 3178, 3173, 3174, 3175, 3176, 3177, 3514
Pennsylvania Education, 3514
Pennsylvania Home Schoolers Newsletter, 4262
Pennsylvania Library Association, 570
Pennsylvania PTA, 4259
Pennsylvania School Boards Association Annual Meeting, 3395
Pennsylvania School Librarians Association, 571
Pennsylvania Science Teachers Association, 3396

Pennsylvania State Education Association, 572, 4263
Pennsylvania State University, 3646, 3723, 4669
Pennsylvania State University-Workforce Education & Development Program, 3696
Pentel of America, 5365
Penton Overseas, 5208
People United for Rural Education, 141
People to People International, 289
Peopleware, 5848
Percussion Marketing Council, 5330
Perfect PC Technologies, 985
Perfection Learning, 4969, 5032
Perfection Learning Corporation, 4969
Performa, 986
Performance Improvement Journal, 3515
Performance Learning Systems, 3697
Performance Resource Press, 3605, 5189, 5214, 5382
Pergamon Press, Elsevier Science, 4554
Perma Bound Books, 4970
Permagile Industries, 5599
Permanent School Fund, 3217
Perot Foundation, 2789
Perse School, 1837
A Personal Planner & Training Guide for the Substitute Teacher, 3730
Personal Planner & Traning Guide for the Paraeducator Video Set, 3603
Personal Planner and Training Guide for the Paraprofessional, 3453
Personalized Software, 6008
Personalizing the Past, 4971
Personnel Services, 2987, 3145
Persons as Resources, 3840
Perspective, 4690
Perspectives for Policymakers, 4361
Perspectives on History Series, 4972
Peter D & Eleanore Kleist Foundation, 2397
Peter Li Education Group, 4374
Peter Loring/Janice Palumbo, 2521
Peter Norton Family Foundation, 2328
Peterhouse, 1075
Peterson's Competitive Colleges, 3841
Peterson's Grants for Graduate and Postdoctoral Study, 4003
Peterson's Guide to Four-Year Colleges, 3842, 4004
Peterson's Guide to Independent Secondary Schools, 4079
Peterson's Guide to Professional Degree Programs in the Visual Arts, 4056
Peterson's Guide to Two-Year Colleges, 3843
Peterson's Guides, 3809, 3841, 3842, 3843, 3844, 3848, 3862, 3972, 3974, 4002, 4003, 4004, 4005, 4011, 4013, 4056, 4070, 4079, 4088, 4100, 5730
Peterson's Regional College Guides, 3844
Peterson's Sports Scholarships and College Athletic Programs, 4005
Pew Charitable Trusts, 2740
Peyton Anderson Foundation, 2418
Peytral Publications, 4973
Phelps Publishing, 4974
Phi Delta Kappa, 290
Phi Delta Kappa Educational Foundation, 4264, 3426, 3427, 3442, 3463, 3469, 3616, 3758
Phi Delta Kappa International, 3661, 3817, 3888
Phil Hardin Foundation, 2569
Philip H Corboy Foundation, 2450

Phillip Roy Multimedia Materials, 6038
Phillips Broadband Networks, 5849
Phoenix Films/BFA Educ Media/Coronet/MII, 5209
Phoenix Learning Group, 5209
Phoenix Learning Resources, 4975
Phoenix Learning Resources Conference, 831
Phoenix Public Library, 2265
Phonics Institute, 4623
Phuket International Preparatory School, 1224
Phyllis A Beneke Scholarship Fund, 2816
Physical Education Digest, 4611
Physical Educator, 4612
Physics Teacher, 4658
Piano Workshop, 3698
Picture Book Learning Volume-1, 4042
Pike Publishing Company, 3470
Pin Man, 5366
Pine Peace School, 2170
Pinewood Schools of Thessaloniki, 1838
Pioneer New Media Technologies, 5850
Pittsburg State University, 3699, 3652
Pittsburgh Office And Research Park, 2733
Place in the Woods, 3797, 4154, 4560, 4625
Planning & Changing, 4362
Planning & Evaluation Service, 2902
Planning for Higher Education, 4265
Planning, Research & Evaluation, 2994
Planning, Results & Information Management, 3053
PlayConcepts, 5367
PlayDesigns, 5756
Playground Environments, 5757
Playnix, 5758
Playworld Systems, 5759
Pleasant Company Publications, 4976
Plough Foundation, 2762
Plymouth State College, 2593
Pocket Books/Paramount Publishing, 4977
Poetry Alive, 987
Polaroid Corporation, 5851
Polaroid Education Program, 3700
Policy & Planning, 3010, 3195
Policy & Practice, 4266
Policy, Assessment, Research & Information Systems, 3234
Policy, Planning & Management Services, 2903
Polk Brothers Foundation, 2451
Polyform Products Company, 5368
Ponce Baptist Academy, 2171
Popondetta International School, 1225
Population Connection, 4978, 4267
Population Educator, 4267
Population Institute, 291
Pordenone Elementary School, 1839
Porter Athletic Equipment Company, 5760
Porter Sargent Publishers, 3793, 3795, 3851
Porter Sargent Publishers, Inc., 3759
Post Secondary Educational Assistance, 988
Postcard Geography, 5928
Postsecondary Services, 3067
Power Industries, 5852
Power of Public Engagement Book Set, 3845
PowerSchool, 5993
Powr-Flite Commercial Floor Care Equipment, 5600
Practical Handbook for Assessing Learning Outcomes in Continuing Education, 3454
Prahram Campus-Wesley College, 1226

Prairie High School, 436
Prakken Publications, 4110, 4162, 4721
Pre-K Today, 4406
Prentice Hall School Division, 4979
Prentice Hall School Division - Science, 4980
Prentice Hall/Center for Applied Research in Education, 4981
Prescott Anglo American School, 1402
President's Council on Physical Fitness & Sports, 348
Presidential Awards for Excellence in Mathematics and Science Teaching, 3294
Presidential Classroom, 5210, 5369
Pressley Ridge School, 3496
Preventing School Failure, 3516, 6252
Prevention Researcher, 3517
Prevention Service, 989
PrimaryGames.com, 6029
Prime Technology Corporation, 6113
Prince Charitable Trust, 2452
Princeton Educational Publishers, 4416
Princeton Review, 990
Princeton University, 63
Principal, 4363
Principal Communicator, 4364
A Principal's Guide to Creating and Building Climate for Inclusion, 3731
The Principals' Center, 3643
Principals' Center Spring Institute Conference, 3397
Principles of Good Practice in Continuing Education, 3455
Printing Industries of America, 208
Priority Computer Services, 991
Priory School, 1840
Prism Computer Corporation, 992
Private Education Law Report, 4365
Private English Junior School, 1446
Private Independent Schools, 3846
Private School Law in America, 3847
Private School, Community & Junior College Four Year Colleges & Universities, 3948
Pro Libra, 322
Pro-Ed, 4408, 4484, 4494
Pro-Ed., Inc., 3505, 4179, 4206, 4210, 4212, 4217, 4271, 4274, 4510
ProCoat Products, 5601
ProLiteracy Worldwide, 353
Proactive Leadership in the 21st Century, 3897
Problem Solving Concepts, 6150
Process of Elimination - a Method of Teaching and Learning Basic Grammar, 4043
Procter & Gamble Fund, 2710
Professional Computer Systems, 993
Professional Development & Licensing, 3116
Professional Development Institute, 994
Professional Development Institutes, 3701
Professional Development Workshops, 3702
Professional Learning Communities at Work, 3456
Professional Office Instruction & Training, 420
Professional Responsibility Office, 3128
Professional Services, 2923, 3158
Professional Technical Education, 3169
Professional Vision Master Teacher, 3518
Professor Master Teacher, 3519
Professor Weissman's Software, 5370
Profiles, 995
Programs & Accountability, 2995

Programs for Preparing Individuals for Careers in Special Education, 3457
Programs for the Improvement of Practice, 2904
Progressive Publishing Company, 3520
Progressive Teacher, 3520
Project Innovation, 4161
Project Innovation of Mobile, 4626
Project Learning Tree, 4982
Project Zero Classroom, 3703
Proliteracy Volunteers of America, 727
Prophecy Elementary School, 2172
Providence Public Library, 2750
Proxima Corporation, 6178
Prudential Foundation, 2601
Prudential Plaza, 2601
Prufrock Press, 4983
Psychological Assessment Resources, 6209, 6230
Psychological Corporation, 178, 6253
Psychometric Affiliates, 6254
Public Education Alert, 4268
Public Education Association, 4268
Public Education Fund Network, 5137
Public Employment Law Notes, 4366
Public Library of Cincinnati, 2711
Public Personnel Management, 4367
Public Relations Starter Pacs Notebook, 3898
Public Relations Student Society of America, 142
Public School Finance, 2956
Public Schools USA: A Comparative Guide to School Districts, 3848
Public Service Company of Oklahoma Corporate Giving Program, 2718
Public Welfare Foundation, 2385
Publishers' Development Corporation, 4580
Puerto Rico Department of Education, 2173
Puffin Books, 4984
Pumpkin Masters, 5371
Puppets on the Pier, 5372
Purdue University, Department of English, 4543
Purdy-Kresge Library, 2548
Pure Gold Teaching Tools, 6131
Pusan American School, 1227
Pusan Elementary & High School, 1228
Put Reading First: The Research Building Blocks For Teaching Children To Read, 4044
Pyramid Educational Consultants, 996

Q

QED's State School Guides, 3899
QEG, 4269
QSI International School-Bratislava, 1447
QSI International School-Chisinau, 2174
QSI International School-Ljubljana, 1448
QSI International School-Phuket, 1229
QSI International School-Skopje, 2175
QSI International School-Tbilisi, 1449
QSI International School-Vladivostok, 2176
QSI International School-Yerevan, 1450
QSI International School-Zhuhai, 1230
QSP, 2856
QUIN: Quarterly University International News, 4270
Quadrus, 2299

Quality Education Data, 4985, 5138, 3899, 4104, 4111
Quality Education Development, 997
Quality Industries, 5761
Quality School, 3604
Quality School Teacher, 3458
Quantum, 4659
Quantum Performance Group, 998
Quantum Technology, 6151
Quarry Bay School, 1231
Quarterly Journal of Speech, 4533
Quarterly Review of Doublespeak, 4534
Quarterly of the NWP, 4535
Queen Elizabeth School, 1841
Queens College, 1958
Queens College the English School, 1842
Quest, 4613
Quest Aerospace Education, 5699
Quetzal Computers, 5853
Quick-Source, 4107
QuickTips, 3560
Quickset International, 5455
Quill Corporation, 5981
Quill and Scroll, 4536
Quinlan Publishing, 4287, 4449
Qwik-File Storage Systems, 5373

R

RB5X: Education's Personal Computer Robot, 6179
RC Musson Rubber Company, 5374
RCA Rubber Company, 5375
RCM Capital Management Charitable Fund, 2329
RD & Joan Dale Hubbard Foundation, 2608
RHL School, 3561
RIF Newsletter, 4624
RISO, 5535
RJ Maclellan Charitable Trust, 2763
RJ McElroy Trust, 2473
RLS Groupware, 5854
RMF Products, 5456
RR Bowker, 4986
RR Bowker Reed Reference, 3784, 4099
RR Bowker, Reed Reference, 3957
RTI-Research Technology International, 5457
RW Fair Foundation, 2790
Rabat American School, 1076
Rabaul International School, 1232
Rack III High Security Bicycle Rack Company, 5602
Radio Shack, 5855
Rahmaniah-Taif-Acad International School, 1520
Rainbow Development Center, 2177
Rainbow Educational Media Charles Clark Company, 5211
Rainbow Educational Video, 5212
Rainbow Elementary School, 1843
Rainbow Learning Institute, 2178
Rainbow School, 2179
Raintree/Steck-Vaughn, 4987
Ralph M Parsons Foundation, 2330
Ramstein Elementary School, 1844
Ramstein High School, 1845
Ramstein Intermediate School, 1846
Ramstein Junior High School, 1847
Rand McNally, 4988
Random House, 4989

Random House/Bullseye/Alfred A Knopf/Crown Boo ks for Young Readers, 4990
Ras Al Khaimah English Speaking School, 1521
Ras Tanura School, 1522
Rathdown School, 1848
Rauland Borg, 5982
Read, America!, 4560, 4625
Reading & O'Reilley, 5412
Reading & O'Reilly: The Wilton Programs, 5213
Reading Improvement, 4626
Reading Psychology, 4627
Reading Recovery Council of North America, 354
Reading Research Quarterly, 4628
Reading Research and Instruction, 4629
Reading Teacher, 4630
Reading Today, 4631
Reading is Fundamental, 5376
Ready to Read, Ready to Learn, 4066
Real SAT's, 6255
Realtime Learning Systems, 5854
Rebus, 999, 3702
Reclaiming Children and Youth, 4271
Recognition & Supervision of Schools, 2996
Recognition Review, 4272
Reconnecting Youth, 5377
Recorded Books, 4991
Recording for the Blind & Dyslexic, 4632
Records Consultants, 1000
Recreation Creations, 5762
Recreation Equipment Unlimited, 5458
Recruiting Fairs for Overseas Teaching, 2246
Recruiting New Teachers, 3284
Red Ribbon Resources, 5378
Rediker Administration Software, 5983
Redland School, 1403
Redleaf Press, 4992
Reed Reference Publishing Company, 4986
Reference Department, 2750, 2755
Reference Desk Books, 4993, 3746
Reference Service Press, 3964, 3970, 3991
Reference Services, 2798
Regenstein Foundation, 2453
Region 10: Education Department, 3238
Region 1: Education Department, 3058
Region 2: Education Department, 3129
Region 3: Education Department, 3179
Region 5: Education Department, 2997
Region 6: Education Department, 3218
Region 7: Education Department, 3092
Region 9: Education Department, 2950
Regional Laboratory for Educational Improvement of the Northeast, 5139
Regional Learning Service of Central New York, 1001
Regional Services Centers, 3032
Regional Spotlight, 4273
Regionale Internationale School, 1849
Registration Bulletin, 6256
Regulus Communications, 4103
Rehabilitation Counseling Bulletin, 4494
Rehabilitation Services, 2924
Rehabilitation Services Administration, 2905
Rehabilitation Services Division, 3054, 3104
Reinventing Your School Board, 1002
Relearning by Design, 1003
Reliance Plastics & Packaging, 5459
Religious Education Association of the US & Canada, 143
Remedial and Special Education, 4274

Renaissance Educational Associates, 4275
Renaissance Educator, 4275
Renaissance Graphic Arts, 5379
Renaissance Learning, 5309, 5778, 5779, 5857, 6067, 6112, 6140
Renaissance Learning and School Renaissance Inst., 6231
Renew America, 144
Report on Education Research, 4276
Report on Literacy Programs, 4633
Report on Preschool Programs, 4407
Reports of the National Center for Science Education, 4660
Republic Storage Systems Company, 5603
Requirements for Certification of Teachers & Counselors, 3459
Research & Development Office, 3041
Research Assessment Management, 1004
Research Department, 5090
Research Technology International, 5536
Research for Better Schools, 5140, 3891
Research for Better Schools Publications, 3460
Research in Higher Education, 4277
Research in the Schools, 4278
Research in the Teaching of English, 4537
Research to Practice Division, 2906
Research, Accountability & Professional, 3245
Research, Advocacy & Legislation/Council of LaRaza, 3858
Research, Study, Travel, & Work Abroad, 3949
Residential Schools, 3080
Resolution Technology, 5460
Resource Booklet for Independent Music Teachers, 4057
Resource Development, 3186
Resources for Teaching Elementary School Science, 5700
Resources for Teaching Middle School Science, 3461
Restructuring Curriculum Conference, 3398
Restructuring in the Classroom, 3462
Retaining Great Teachers, 3521
Retention in Education Today for All Indigenous Nations, 791
Revolution Revisited: Effective Schools and Systemic Reform, 3463
Reydon School for Girls, 1404
Rheometrics, 5701
Rhetoric Review, 4538
Rhode Island Association of School Business Officials, 573
Rhode Island Department of Education, 3187, 3180, 3181, 3182, 3183, 3184, 3185, 3186, 3188, 3189, 3190
Rhode Island Educational Media Association, 574
Rhode Island Foundation, 2751
Rhode Island Library Association, 575
Rhode Island National Education Association, 576
Rhythms Productions, 4994
Rich Foundation, 2419
Richard & Helen DeVos Foundation, 2545
Richard C Owen Publishers, 4995
Richard E Byrd Elementary School, 1233
Richard H Driehaus Foundation, 2454
Richard King Mellon Foundation, 2741
Richardton High School, 556
Richmond Public Library, 2806
Rider College, 3346

Rift Valley Academy, 1077
Right on Programs, 6100
Rikkyo School in England, 1850
Riordan Foundation, 2331
Riverdeep Interactive Learning, 5336, 5930, 6073, 6125, 6155
Riverside Publishing Company, 4996
Riverside School, 1851
Robert & Polly Dunn Foundation, 2420
Robert D Edgren High School, 1234
Robert E Nelson Associates, 1005
Robert G & Anne M Merrick Foundation, 2505
Robert G Friedman Foundation, 2398
Robert McNeel & Associates, 3704
Robert Morgan Vocational Tech., 454
Robert R McCormick Tribune Foundation, 2455
Robert Sterling Clark Foundation, 2664
Robinson Barracks Elementary School, 1852
Robinson School, 2180
RobotiKits Direct, 5461
Rochester Public Library, 2665
Rock Hill Communications, 5055
Rock Paint Distributing Corporation, 5380
Rock and Roll Hall of Fame, 3622
RockHill Communications, 4728
Rockford Systems, 3705
Rockwell International Corporation Trust, 2742
Roeper Institute, 4279
Roeper Review: A Journal on Gifted Education, 4279
Rogers Family Foundation, 2517
Rollin M Gerstacker Foundation, 2546
Rome International School, 1853
Ronald S Lauder Foundation, 2666
Rookey Associates, 1006
Room 108, 6027
Roosevelt Roads Elementary School, 2181
Roosevelt Roads Middle & High School, 2182
Root Learning, 1007
Roots & Wings Educational Catalog-Australia for Kids, 4997
Roppe Corporation, 5763
Rosall School, 1854
Rose Electronics, 5856
Rosemead, 1855
Rosen Publishing Group, 4998
Rosslyn Academy, 1078
Rota Elementary School, 1856
Rota High School, 1857
Roudybush Foreign Service School, 1858
Routledge/Europa Library Reference, 4999
Roy and Christine Sturgis Charitable and Educa tional Trust, 2270
Royal Barney Hogan Foundation, 2332
Ruamrudee International School, 1235
Rugby School, 1859
Runestone Press, 5000
Runnymede College School, 1860
Rural Educator-Journal for Rural and Small Schools, 3522, 4368
Rural Educator: Journal for Rural and Small Schools, 4280
Russ Bassett Company, 5537
Ruth & Vernon Taylor Foundation, 2364
Ruth Eleanor Bamberger and John Ernest Bamberger Memorial Foundation, 2795
Rygaards International School, 1861

S

S&S Arts & Crafts, 5381
S&S Worldwide, 5381
S'Portable Scoreboards, 5462
SAP Today, 3605, 5214
SARUT, 5702
SAT Math Flash, 6210
SAT Services for Students with Disabilities, 6257
SAT Success, 6258
SCI Technologies, 6152
SCOTVIC: S McDonald, Principal, 4069
SEAL, 6180
SERVE, 5141, 792, 4410
SERVE Conference, 792
SH & Helen R Scheuer Family Foundation, 2667
SH Cowell Foundation, 2333
SIGI PLUS, 5142
SIM International, 2013
SIMBA Information, 4835
SKOLE: A Journal of Alternative Education, 4281
SLEP Program Office, 6208
SNAP-DRAPE, 5538
SNEA Impact: The Student Voice of the Teaching Profession, 4282
SOLINET, Southeastern Library Network, 6101
SONY Broadcast Systems Product Division, 5463
SSMart Newsletter, 4576
STAR Reading & STAR Math, 5857
STN Media Company Inc., 4289
SUNY College at Oswego, 3706
SVE & Churchill Media, 5858
SVE: Society for Visual Education, 5215
Sacramento Regional Foundation, 2334
Saddleback Educational, 5001
Safe & Drug Free Catalog, 5382
Safe Day Education, 5931
Safe Schools America, 179
Safe-T-Rack Systems, 5703
SafeKids.Com, 5932
SafeSpace Concepts, 5002
Safety Forum, 4283
Safety Play, 5764
Safety Society, 4283
Safety Storage, 5604
Sage Publications, 5003, 4471
Saigon South International School, 1236
Saint Anthony School, 2183
Saint Eheresas Elementary School, 2184
Saint Francis Elementary School, 2185
Saint George's School, 1405
Saint John's School, 2186
Saint John's School, Puerto Rico, 2187
Saint Paul Foundation, 2564
Saints Peter & Paul High School, 2188
Sakura of America, 5383
Sally Foster Gift Wrap, 2857
Salsbury Industries, 5605
Salt Lake City Public Library, 2796
Saltus Cavendish School, 1959
Salzburg International Preparatory School, 1862
Sam Houston State University, 832
Samaritan Rehabilitation Institute, 2261
Samoa Baptist Academy, 2189
Samuel & May Rudin Foundation, 2668
Samuel N & Mary Castle Foundation, 2430

Samuel Roberts Noble Foundation, 2719
Samuel S Fels Fund, 2743
San Bernadino City Unified School District, 4261
San Carlos & Bishop McManus High School, 2190
San Diego Foundation, 2335
San Diego State University, 700
San Francisco Foundation, 2336
San Francisco State University, 427
San Juan Select - Structures, 3562
San Vincente Elementary School, 2191
Sanaa International School, 1523
Sancta Maria International School, 1237
Sandford English Community School, 1079
Sanford Corporation, 5384
Sanford- A Lifetime of Color, 6135
Santa Barbara Control Systems, 5562
Santa Barbara Foundation, 2337
Santa Barbara School, 2192
Santa Cruz Cooperative School, 1406
Santa Margarita School, 1407
Santiago Christian School, 2193
Santillana Publishing, 5004
Sapelo Foundation, 2421
Sarah Scaife Foundation, 2744
Sargent-Welch Scientific Company, 5704
Satellite Educational Resources Consortium, 5143
Satellites and Education Conference, 816
Saudi Arabian International British School, 1524
Saudi Arabian International School-Dhahran, 1525
Saudi Arabian International School-Riyadh, 1526
Saudia-Saudi Arabian International School, 1527
Sax Arts and Crafts, 5385
Sax Visual Art Resources, 5385
Scantron Corporation, 5984
Schiller Academy, 1863
Schiller Center, 145
Scholarship America, 2876
Scholarship Handbook, 4006
Scholarships for Emigres Training for Careers in Jewish Education, 4007
Scholarships in the Health Professions, 2877
Scholarships, Fellowships and Loans, 4008
Scholastic, 5005, 4341, 4399, 4406, 4420, 4705, 5824
Scholastic Testing Service, 6259
School Administrator, 4369
School Arts, 4058
School Assistance Division, 2907
School Book Fairs, 5006
School Bulletin, 4284
School Bus Fleet, 4285
School Business Affairs, 4370
School Counselor, 4495
School Cruiser, 5859
School Development & Information, 3229
School Equipment Show, 793
School Executive, 4371
School Finance, 2998, 3146
School Finance & Data Management, 2934
School Financial Resources & Management, 3252
School Food Service, 3147
School Food Services Administration, 3188
School Foodservice & Nutrition, 4286
School Foodservice Who's Who, 3849
School Guide, 3850

School Guide Publications, 3850, 4022
School Identifications, 2858
School Improvement, 3159
School Improvement & Assessment Services, 2999
School Improvement & Performance Center, 3011
School Improvement Programs-Drug Free Schools & Communities Division, 2908
School Improvement Programs-Equity and Educational Excellence Division, 2909
School Improvement Programs-School Effectivene ss Division, 2910
School Law Briefings, 4372
School Law Bulletin, 4287
School Law News, 4373
School Library Journal, 4561
School Library Media Activities Monthly, 4562
School Library Media Quarterly, 4563
School Management Accountability, 3122
School Management Study Group, 1008
School March by Public Priority Systems, 1009
School Mate, 5386
School Memories Collection, 2859
School Planning & Management, 4374
School Program Quality, 3068
School Promotion, Publicity & Public Relations: Nothing but Benefits, 3900
School Psychology Review, 4496
School Renaissance Model, 3563, 6225
School Safety, 4288
School Science & Mathematics Association, 4576
School Transportation News, 4289
School Zone, 4290
School at Tembagapura, 1238
School for the Deaf, 3148
School of Education, 313
School of Interdisciplinary Studies, 23
School of Music, 3707, 333
School of the Good Shepherd, 2194
School-Wide Stratigies for Retaining Great Tea chers, 3606
SchoolArts Davis Publications, 4594
SchoolArts Magazine, 4595
SchoolHouse, 5860
SchoolJobs.com, 6034
SchoolMatters, 5387
SchoolTech Forum, 3399
Schools & Colleges Directory, 4060
Schools Abroad of Interest to Americans, 3851
Schools Industrial, Technical & Trade Directory, 4108
Schools for the Deaf & Blind, 3222
Schools of England, Wales, Scotland & Ireland, 1864
Schools-Business & Vocational Directory, 3852
Schoolwide Discipline Strategies that Make a Difference in Teaching & Learning, 3901
Schutz American School, 1080
Schweinfurt American Elementary School, 1865
Schweinfurt Middle School, 1866
Science Activities, 4661
Science First, 5724
Science Inquiry Enterprises, 5007
Science Instruments Company, 5705
Science News Magazine, 4662
Science Scope, 4663

Science Service, 379
Science Source, 5706, 5676
Science Teacher, 4664
Science and Children, 4665
Science for All Children; A Guide to
  Improving Science Education, 4085
Science for Kids, 6009
Science for Today & Tomorrow, 5707
Science, Social Science, 2812
Scientific Laser Connection, Incorporated,
  5708
Scientific Learning, 5144
Scots PGC College, 1239
Scott & McCleary Publishing Company,
  5008, 4043, 4061, 4062
Scott Foresman Company, 5009
Scott Resources/ Hubbard Scientific, 5464
Scott Sign Systems, 5388
Scott Sign Systems, Inc., 5393
Scott and McCleary Publishing Co., 6202
Scratch-Art Company, 5389
Screen Works, 5539
Sea Bay Game Company, 5390
Sea Frontiers, 4666
Seaman Nuclear Corporation, 5861
Search Associates, 3285
Sears-Roebuck Foundation, 2456
Seattle Foundation, 2811
Seattle Public Library, 2812
Secondary Teachers Guide to FREE
  Curriculum Materials, 4080
Section 504 Compliance Advisor, 4375
**Security National Bank & Trust
  Company**, 2816
Sega Youth Education & Health Foundation,
  2338
Seisen International School, 1240
Semarang International School, 1241
Sembach Elementary School, 1867
Sembach Middle School, 1868
Seminar Information Service, 3464
Senior Researcher Award, 3295
Sensa of New Jersey, 1010
Seoul Academy, 1242
Seoul British School, 1243
Seoul Elementary School, 1244
Seoul Foreign School, 1245
Seoul High School, 1246
Service Civil International, 292
Service-Learning and Character Education:
  One Plus One is More Than Two, 3465
Servicemaster, 5606
Services for Education, 3199
Services for Individuals with Hearing Loss,
  3257
Seth Sprague Educational and Charitable
  Foundation, 2669
Seton Identification Products, 5391
Sevenoaks School, 1869
Seventh Day Adventist, 2195
Sevilla Elementary & Junior High School,
  1870
Sexual Assault and Harassment on Campus
  Conference, 794
Sexuality Information & Education Council
  of the US, 146
Shain/Shop-Bilt, 5709
Shanghai American School, 1247
Shape Elementary School, 1871
Shape High School, 1872
Shape International School, 1873
Shapes, Etc., 5392
Shaping the Future, 4291

Sharing Space, 4292
Sharjah English School, 1528
Sharjah Public School, 1529
Sharp Electronics Corporation, 6181
Sharpe Reference, 5010
Shatin College, 1248
Shatin Junior College, 1249
Sheffield Plastics, 5607
Shekou International School, 2196
Sheldon Lab Systems, 5710
Sherborne School, 1874
Sherman Fairchild Foundation, 2372
Shirley Handy, 1011
Shirley Lanham Elementary School, 1250
Shore Fund, 2745
Shreve Memorial Library, 2488
Shure Brothers, 5465
Sid W Richardson Foundation, 2791
Sidcot School, 1875
Sidney Kreppel, 1012
Sidney Stern Memorial Trust, 2339
Siebert Lutheran Foundation, 2820
Sierra Bernia School, 1876
Sifundzani School, 1081
Sigma Tau Delta, 314
Sign Product Catalog, 5393
Signet Classics, 5011
Sigonella Elementary & High School, 1877
Sigtunaskolan Humanistiska Laroverket,
  1878
Silver Moon Press, 5012
Simon & Schuster Children's Publishing,
  5013
Simon & Schuster Interactive, 6128
Singapore American School, 1251
Sir Harry Johnston Primary School, 1082
Sir James Henderson School, 1879
Sirsi Corporation, 6102
Site-Based Management, 3607
Skagerak Gymnas, 1880
Skilcraft, 5711
Skills Bank Corporation, 5862
SkillsUSA Champions, 4440
Skullduggery Kits, 5712
Skulls Unlimited International, 5713
SkyLight, 798
Skylight Professional Development, 3440
Slate Newsletter, 4539
**The Slater/ Langston Community
  Complex**, 449
Sleek Software Corporation, 5863
Slovak Republic QSI International School of
  Bratislava, 2197
Slovenia QSI International School-Ljubljana,
  2198
Slow Learning Child Video Series, 5216
Small Fry Originals, 5394
Smart Family Foundation, 2373
Smartstuff Software, 5864
Smith Elementary School, 1881
**Smithsonian Anthropology Outreach
  Office**, 4649
Smithsonian Institution, 4624, 6055
Smithsonian Institution/Office of Elementary
  & Secondary Education, 5145
Social Education, 4691
Social Issues Resources Series, 5014, 6103
Social Science & History Department, 2498
Social Science Education Consortium, 5015
Social Sciences Department, 2396, 2584
Social Sciences Reference, 2509
Social Sciences/Humanities, 2544
Social Studies, 4692

Social Studies Journal, 4693
Social Studies Professional, 4694
Social Studies School Service, 5016
Social Studies and the Young Learner, 4695
Social Work Research Journal, 4497
Social Work in Education, 4498
SocialWork, 4499
Society for Applied Learning Technology,
  4717, 720, 788
**Society for College and University
  Planning (SCUP)**, 4265
Society for Developmental Education, 736
Society for History Education, 388
Society for Research in Child Development,
  795, 5146
Society for Visual Education, 5865
Society for the Advancement of Education,
  147
**Society for the Advancement of Good
  English**, 4514
Society of Automotive Engineers, 5714
Society of School Librarians International,
  323
SofterWare, 5866
Sol & Clara Kest Family Foundation, 2340
Sollars Elementary School, 1252
Solutions Skills, 1013
Sonoma State University Annual
  Conference, 3400
SourceView Software International, 5985
South Carolina Department of Education,
  3196, 3191, 3192, 3193, 3194, 3195, 3197
South Carolina Education Association, 577
South Carolina Library Association, 578
South Carolina Library Association
  Conference, 3401
South Carolina State Library, 2753
South Dakota Community Foundation, 2754
South Dakota Department of Education,
  3198, 3199, 3202
South Dakota Department of Education &
  Cultural Affairs, 3200
**South Dakota Dept of Education &
  Cultural Affairs**, 3201
South Dakota Education Association, 580
South Dakota Library Association, 581
South Dakota State Historical Society, 3201
South Dakota State Library, 2755
South Island School, 1253
South Pacific Academy, 2199
South Putnam High School, 477
Southeast Regional Center for Drug-Free
  Schools & Communities, 5147
Southeastern Library Association, 421, 425
Southern Association Colleges & Schools,
  3402
Southern Association of Colleges & Schools,
  595
Southern Early Childhood Annual
  Convention, 3403
Southern Early Childhood Association,
  181, 3403
Southern Illinois University Carbondale,
  3729
Southern Illinous University, 471
Southern Peru Staff Schools-Peru, 2200
Southern Polytechnic State University, 3708
Southern Precision Instruments Company,
  5715
Southern Regional Education Board,
  5148, 4273
Southern Sport Surfaces, 5608
Southland Instruments, 5716

Southlands English School, 1882
Southwest Association College and
    University Housing Officers, 832
Southwest Comprehensive Regional
    Assistance Center-Region IX, 5149
Southwest Educational Development
    Laboratory Letter, 4293
Southwest Florida Community Foundation,
    2399
Southwest Independent Schools Association,
    148
Southwest Plastic Binding Corporation, 5395
Southwestern Educational Development
    Laboratory, 5150
Southwestern Oklahoma State University,
    3709
Space Day, 5935
Spacemaster Systems, 5540
Spacesaver Corporation, 5541
Spangdahlem Elementary School, 1883
Spangdahlem Middle School, 1884
Special Collections-Grants, 2580
Special Education, 3000, 3055, 3069, 3149,
    3170, 3203
Special Education & Rehabilitation Services,
    5017
Special Education Division, 3093
Special Education Law Monthly, 4376
Special Education Law Update, 4377
Special Education Leadership, 4294
Special Education News, 5936
Special Education Office, 3202
Special Education Report, 4378
Special Education Service Agency, 1014
Special Education Services, 2925, 3042
Special Educator, 4295
Special Instructional Services, 3033
Special Interest Group for Computer Science
    Education, 5151
Special Libraries, 4564
Special Libraries Association, 4046, 4564,
    4565
Special Needs Office, 3189
Special Programs, 2266
Special Services, 2957
SpecialNet, 5867
Specialist, 4565
Specialized Programs, 3001
Specialized Programs Branch, 2951
Specialized Solutions, 3710
Spectronics Corporation, 5717
Spectrum Corporation, 5396
Speech Bin, 5018
Speedball Art Products Company, 5397
Spencer Foundation, 2457
Spencerian Office Plaza, 5147
Spitz, 5718
Spokane Public Library, 2813
Spoken Arts, 5217
Sponge Stamp Magic, 5398
Sport Court, 5765
Sport Floors, 5766
Sportfield Elementary School, 1885
Sportmaster, 5767
Sports Management Group, 1015
Sports Media, 6139
Sports Shoes & Apparel, 2860
Sprint Foundation, 2475
St. Albans College, 1408
St. Andrew's College, 1886
St. Andrew's School, 1960
St. Andrew's Scots School, 1409

St. Andrews International School-Bangkok,
    1254
St. Anne's Parish School, 1961
St. Anne's School, 1887
St. Anthony's International College, 1888
St. Barnabas College, 1083
St. Catherine's British School, 1889
St. Catherine's School, 1410
St. Christopher School, 1890
St. Christopher's School, 1255
St. Clare's Oxford, 1891
St. Croix Christian Academy, 2201
St. Croix Country Day School, 2202
St. Croix Moravian School, 2203
St. Croix SDA School, 2204
St. David's Center, 2727
St. David's School, 1892
St. Dominic's International School, 1893
St. Dominic's Sixth Form College, 1894
St. George's College, 1411
St. Georges English School, 1895
St. Georges School, 1896
St. Georges School-Switzerland, 1897
St. Gerard's School, 1898
St. Helen's School, 1899
St. Hilda's College, 1412
St. John School, 1413
St. John's College, 1962
St. John's International School, 1256, 1900
St. Joseph High School, 2205
St. Joseph International School, 1257
St. Joseph's International Primary School,
    1258
St. Louis Public Schools, 4428
St. Margaret's British School-Girls, 1414
St. Mark's College, 1259
St. Martin's Press, 3986
St. Mary's Catholic High School, 1530
St. Mary's International School, 1260
St. Mary's School, 1084, 1901
St. Maur International School, 1261
St. Michael's College, 3385
St. Michael's International School, 1262
St. Michael's School, 1902
St. Patrick School, 2206
St. Paul's College, 1085
St. Paul's Methodist College, 1963
St. Paul's School, 1415
St. Pauls School, 1416
St. Peter & Paul Elementary School, 2207
St. Peter's School, 1417
St. Stephen's International School, 1263
St. Stephen's School, 1903
St. Xavier's Greenherald School, 1264
Stack the Deck Writing Program, 5019
Stackhouse Athletic Equipment Company,
    5768
Stackpole-Hall Foundation, 2746
Staedtler, 5399
Staff Development & Technical Assistance,
    3135
Staff Development Workshops & Training
    Sessions, 3711
Stan D. Bird's WhizBang Thang, 5997
Standards & Certification Division, 3111
Standards and Accountability: Their Impact
    on Teaching and Assessment, 3712
Stanford University, 5079
Star News, 4296
Starr Foundation, 2670
State Board Relations & Legal Services, 3012
**State Board of Education, Planning &
    Research**, 4297

State Library, 2958
State Library of North Carolina, 2686
State Mutual Book & Periodical Service,
    3760
State Public Library System, 2988
State Services Division District of Columbia,
    2979
State Street Foundation, 2518
Statewise: Statistical & Research Newsletter,
    4297
Stavenger British School, 1904
Stearley Heights Elementary School, 1265
Steelcase Foundation, 2547
Stenhouse Publishers, 5020
Steve Wronker's Funny Business, 2861
Stewart Howe Alumni Service of New York,
    1016
Story Teller, 5021
Storytelling for Educational Enrichment The
    Magic of Storytelling, 3713
Stover School, 1905
Stowe School, 1906
Straight Scoop News Bureau, 5937
Strake Foundation, 2792
Strategic Planning for Outcome-Based
    Education, 3608
Strategies for Educational Change, 1017
Street Scenes, 4298
Strengthening the Family: An Overview of a
    Hol istic Family Wellness Model, 3609
Student Affairs Today, 4379
Student Aid News, 4453
Student Development, 3150
Student Development Services, 3002
Student Financial Assistance, 3070
Student Guide, 4009
Student Help and Assistance Program to
    Educati on, 2400
Student Instructional Services, 2926
Student Services, 3235
Student Services & Instructional Services,
    3246
Student Services Office, 3171
Student Software Guide, 5868
Student Transportation Systems, 5976
Student Travels Magazine, 4299
Students Forum, 149
Students with Disabilities Resources, 711
Students-at-Risk Video Series, 3610
Studies in Art Education, 4596
Studies in Australia, 6056
Studies in Second Language Acquisition,
    4540
Study & State Film Library, 3139
Study Abroad, 4010
StudyAbroad.com, 6058
Subscription Department, 4429
**Subsidiary of the Reader's Digest
    Association**, 2856
Suburban Superintendents Conference, 3404
Success for All Foundation, 1018
Sudbury Foundation, 2519
Sullivans Elementary School, 1266
Sultan's School, 1531
Sulzburger & Graham Publishing, 3920
Sulzer Family Foundation, 2458
Summer Institute in Siena, 3714
Summer Programs for School Teams, 3715
Summer School, 3383
Summerfield School SRL, 1907
Summerhill School, 1908
Summing It Up: College Board Mathematics
    Assessment Programs, 6211

Summit Learning, 5022
Summit Vision, 150
Sun Microsystems, 5869
Sunbeam, 2208
Sunburst Technology, 5023, 6120
Sunburst/Wings for Learning, 5870
Sundance Publishing, 5024
Sunland Lutheran School, 1964
Sunny View School, 1909
Sunshine School, 1532
Sunship Earth, 4086
Sunship III, 4087
Superintendent, 2927
Superintendent/School Board Relationships, 3611
Superintendents Only, 4380
Superintendents Only Master Teacher, 4381
Superintendents Work Conference, 3405
Supplemental Instruction, Supervisor Workshops, 3716
Support Programs & Quality Results Division, 3258
Support Services, 2267, 3197
Support Services Bureau on Learning, 3034
Support Systems International Corporation, 5871
Surabaya International School, 1267
Surfside Software, 5872
Sutton Park School, 1910
Sutton Valence School, 1911
Swans School, 1912
Swedes Systems - HAGS Play USA, 5769
Swift Instruments, 5466, 5719
Sylvan Learning Systems, 5400
Synergistic Systems, 5025
Synergy Learning, 3633
Synsor Corporation, 5542
Syracuse University, 4102
Syria Damascus Community School, 2209
System Works, 5609
Systems & Computer Technology Services, 5986
Szekely Family Foundation, 2341

T

T-Shirt People/Wearhouse, 2862
TACS/WRRC, 5152
TAM Connector, 4718
TASA, 5026
TASIS Hellenic International School, 1913
TASIS The American School in England, 1914
TCF Foundation, 2565
TECHNOS Quarterly for Education & Technolgy, 4719
TED Newsletter, 3523
TEDA International School-Tianjin, 1268
TEDCO, 5720
TENTEL Corporation, 5610
TERC, 5153
TESOL Journal: A Journal of Teaching and Classroom Research, 3524, 4541
TESOL Quarterly, 4542
TESS: The Educational Software Selector, 4109
THE Institute & Knowvation, 3717
THE Journal, 4382, 4720
TIYM Publishing, 3886
TL Clark Incorporated, 5027
TMC/Soundprints, 5028

TOEFL Test and Score Manual, 6260
TQM: Implementing Quality Management in Your School, 3612
TUV Product Service, 3718
Tab Products Company, 5543
Tabubil International School, 1269
Taegu Elementary & High School, 1270
Taipei American School, 1271
Taking the SAT I: Reasoning Test, 6261
Taking the SAT II: The Official Guide to the SAT II: Subject Tests, 6262
Tambourine Books, 5029
Tandy Leather Company, 5401
Tanglin Trust Schools, 1272
Tapion School, 1965
Target Vision, 5873
Tarsus American College and SEV Primary, 1533
Tashkent International School, 2210
Taunus International Montessori School, 1915
Taylor & Francis Books, 4999
Taylor & Francis Publishers, 5030
Taylor Law Update, 4300
Teach Overseas, 293
Teach in Great Britain, 1916
Teacher & Administrative Preparation, 3071
Teacher Appreciation, 5402
Teacher Certification & Professional Education, 2959
Teacher Education & Certification, 3003, 3035, 3151
Teacher Education & Certification Office, 3190
Teacher Education Division, 3286
Teacher Education Institute, 3719
Teacher Education Reports, 3525
Teacher Education and Special Education, 3526
Teacher Educators Association, 3406
Teacher Exchange, Off. of International Education, 272, 2886
Teacher Ideas Press Libraries Unlimited, 3466
Teacher Link: An Interactive National Teleconference, 796
Teacher Magazine, 3527
Teacher Support Software, 6070
Teacher Universe, 5874
Teacher$ Talk, 4301
Teacher's Friend Publications, 5031
Teacher's Guide to Classroom Management, 3528
Teacher's Video Company, 5218
Teacher-Created Materials, 3467
TeacherWeb, 5940
Teachers & Writers Collaborative, 315
Teachers Association in Instruction Conference, 3407
Teachers College, Columbia University, 52, 3405
Teachers College-Columbia University, 6163
Teachers College: Columbia University, 3720
Teachers Curriculum Institute, 1019
The Teachers Employment Network, 3564
Teachers Insurance and Annuity Association, 4301
Teachers Service Association, 1020
Teachers Store, 5403
Teachers as Educators of Character: Are the Nations Schools of Education Coming Up Short?, 3468

Teachers as Heros, 3613
Teachers as Leaders, 3469
Teachers in Publishing, 3470
Teachers in Touch, 3529
Teachers of English to Speakers of Other Languages Convention and Exhibit, 294, 797
Teachers of English to Speakers of Other Languages, 3524, 4541, 4542
Teachers' Committee on Central America, 389
Teachers@Work, 6033
TeachersZone.Com, 5939
Teaching & Learning, 3230
Teaching & Learning Division, 2969
Teaching About Islam & Muslims in the Public School Classroom, 3471
Teaching Children Mathematics, 4577
Teaching Education, 3530
Teaching Elementary Physical Education, 4614
Teaching Exceptional Children, 3531
Teaching Georgia Government Newsletter, 4696
Teaching Journal, 4597
Teaching K-8 Magazine, 4424
Teaching Music, 4598
Teaching Opportunities in Latin America for US Citizens, 1418
Teaching Our Youngest-A Guide for Preschool Teachers and Child Care and Family Providers, 3912
Teaching Overseas, 3950
Teaching and Learning, 3204
Teaching as the Learning Profession: Handbook of Policy and Practice, 3472
Teaching for Intelligence Conference, 798
Teaching for Intelligent Behavior, 3614
Teaching for Results, 3473
Teaching in Austria, 2211
Teaching is A Work of Heart, 5941
Tech Directions, 4721
Tech Directions-Directory of Federal & Federal and State Officials Issue, 4110
Tech Ed Services, 1021
Tech World, 5467
Technical & Adult Education Services, 3247
Technical Education Research Centers, 1022
Technical Education Systems, 5468
Techniques-Connecting Education and Careers, 3532
Technolink Corporation, 5875
Technology & Learning, 4722, 6111
Technology & Learning Schooltech Exposition & Conference, 799
Technology & Media Division, 406
Technology Pathfinder for Administrators Master Teacher, 4383, 4723
Technology Pathfinder for Teachers, 4724
Technology Pathfinder for Teachers Master Teacher, 3533, 4725
Technology Student Association, 407, 800
Technology Student Conference, 800
Technology Teacher, 4726
Technology Training for Educators, 3721
Technology and Children, 408
Technology and Learning Conference, 828
Technology in 21st Century Schools, 801
Technology in Education Newsletter, 4727
Technology in Public Schools, 4111
Technology, Reading & Learning Difficulties Conference, 802

Teen Court: An Alternative Approach to Juvenil e Justice, 5219
TekData Systems Company, 6104
Tektronix Foundation, 2725
Telaire Systems, 5721
Telemetrics, 409
Telex Communications, 5469
Telluride Newsletter, 4302
Temple Christian School, 2212
Temple University, 5117
Ten Speed Press, 3936
Tennessee Association of Secondary School Principals, 582
Tennessee Department of Education, 3205, 3203, 3204, 3206
Tennessee Education, 4303
Tennessee Library Association, 583
Tennessee School Board Bulletin, 4304
Tennessee School Boards Association, 584, 4304
Tennessee School Boards Association Conference, 3408
Tennessee Technical University, 675
Tepromark International, 5544
Tesco Industries, 5545
Tesseract Group, 1023
Test Collection, 6228
TestSkills, 6263
Testing Miss Malarky, 6206
Tests: a Comprehensive Reference for Psycholog y, Education & Business, 4029
Texas A & M University- Commerce, 4136
Texas A&M University, College of Education, 4627
Texas Association of Secondary School Principals, 585
Texas Classroom Teachers Association, 833, 5938
Texas Department of Education, 3219, 3208, 3210, 3211, 3212, 3213, 3214, 3215, 3216, 3217
Texas Education Agency, 715, 3207, 3209
Texas Instruments, 5404, 6121
Texas Library Association, 586
Texas Library Association Conference, 834
Texas Middle School Association Conference, 3409
Texas School Boards Association Conference, 3410
Texas State Teachers Association, 3411
Texas Vocational Home Economics Teachers Association Conference, 835
Texwood Furniture, 5546
Thai-Chinese International School, 1273
Their Best Selves: Building Character Education and Service Learning Together, 3474
Theme Connections, 5032
Theory Into Practice, 4305
Theory and Research in Social Education, 4697
Theory of Experiential Education, 3475
Ther-A-Play Products, 5033
Thessaloniki International High School & Pinewood Elementary School, 1917
Think Before You Punch: Using Calculators on the New SAT I and PSAT/NMSQT, 6264
Think Quest, 6132
Think Quest Library of Entries, 5924
Thirty-Four Activities to Promote Careers in Special Education, 3951
This Active Life, 4306

Thomas & Dorothy Leavey Foundation, 2342
Thomas & Irene Kirbo Charitable Trust, 2401
Thomas D Buckley Trust, 2583
Thomas J Emery Memorial, 2712
Thomas Jefferson School, 1918
Thompson Publishing Group, 2402
Thomson Learning, 5034
Three Forks High School, 529
Three M Center, 6105
Three M Library Systems, 6105
Three M Visual Systems, 5470
Three Mellon Bank Center, 2744
Three R'S for Teachers: Research, Reports & Reviews, 4307
Three Rs Master Teacher, 3534
3M Austin Center, 5470
Thrust for Educational Leadership, 4384
Tidbits, 4308
Tiffin Systems, 5611
Tiger Foundation, 2671
Tigoni Girls Academy, 1086
Timbertop Campus, 1274
Time Cruiser Computing Corporation, 5859
Time to Teach, Time to Learn: Changing the Pace of School, 3476
Time-Life Books, 5035
Times Mirror Foundation, 2343
Timken Foundation of Canton, 2713
Timken-Sturgis Foundation, 2344
Timothy Anderson Dovetail Consulting, 1024
Tiny Thought Press, 5036
Tips for Reading Tutors, 4067
Tirana International School-Albania, 2213
Tisch Foundation, 2672
Title I Handbook, 4385
Title I Monitor, 4386
Today's Catholic Teacher, 3535
Today's School Psychologist, 4500
Together Inc., 5366
Tom & Frances Leach Foundation, 2691
Tom Snyder Productions, 5037, 5471, 5876
Tooling University, 3722
Tools to Help Youth, 5220
Tooltron Industries, 5722
Top Colleges for Science, 4088
Top Quality School Process (TQSP), 3477
Topics in Early Childhood Special Education, 4408
Topog-E Gasket Company, 5612
Tor Books/Forge/SMP, 5038
Tot-Mate by Stevens Industries, 5547
Total Quality Schools Workshop, 3723
Totline Newsletter, 4409
Touraine Paints, 5613
Tower City Center, 2701
Toyota Tapestry Grants for Teachers, 3296
Toyota USA Foundation, 2345
Traill Preparatory School, 1275
Training & Development Programs, 2911
Training & Presentations, 3412
Training Magazine, 4387
Training Research Journal: The Science and Practice of Training, 3536
Training Video Series for the Professional School Bus Driver, 5221
Training Video Series for the Substitute Teacher, 3615
Training of Trainers Seminar, 803
Transitions Abroad, 3924, 3955
Transitions Abroad Publishing, 4309
Transitions Abroad: The Guide to Learning, Living, & Working Abroad, 4309

Transnational Industries, 5718
Trapeze Software, 5987
Travelers Group, 2673
Treasury of Noteworthy Proverbs, 3853
Triarco Arts & Crafts, 5405
Tricycle Press, 5039
Trident Technical College, 824
Trinity Christian School, 2214
Triops, 5723
Tripp Lite, 5877
Trippense Planetarium Company, 5724
Troll Associates, 5040
Troll Book Fairs, 2863
Tru-Flex Recreational Coatings, 5613
True Basic, 5878
True Colors, 5222
Trull Foundation, 2793
Truman High School, 4511
Trumpet Club, 5041
Trust to Reach Education Excellence, 2837
Trustees of the Ayer Home, 2520
Tudor Publishing Company, 6018
Tufloc Group, 5567
Tularosa High School, 544
Tull Charitable Foundation, 2422
Turkmenistan Ashgabat International School, 2215
Turn-the-Page Press, 5042
Turrell Fund, 2602
Turst Funds Incorporated, 2346
TutorList.com, 5943
Twenty First Century Schools Council, 3172
Twenty First Century Teachers Network, 6191
Twenty First Century Teachers Network: The McG uffey Project, 410
Twenty-Third Publications, 5048

U

U.N. Educational, Scientific & Cultural Assn., 4010, 4089
U.N. Non-Governmental Liaison Service, 3874
U.S. Department of Education, 405
U.S. National Center for Education Statistics, 5879
U.S. Office of Educational Research & Improvement, 3965
U.S. Office of Postsecondary Education, 3799
U.S. Public School Universe Database, 5879
U.S. Section, 210
U.S. Student Programs Division, 3978
UCLA Statistical Consulting, 5154
UMI, 6106
UN Educational, Scientific & Cultural Assn., 3816
UN Educational, Scientific & Cultural Association, 3773
UNESCO, 229
UNESCO Associated Schools Project Network, 3738
UNESCO Sourcebook for Out-of-School Science & Technology Education, 4089
UNI Overseas Recruiting Fair, 817, 2247
UNL-Independent Study High School, 532
US Bank, 2582
US Chapter, 279
US Civil Service Commission, San Antonio Area, 2233

US College-Sponsored Programs Abroad, 2248

US Department of Defense Dependents Schools, 2912

US Department of Education, 2913, 2881, 3988, 6046

US Department of Education, Region VIII, 4414

US Department of Education: Office of Educational Research & Improvement, 3478

US Department of Education: Region VIII, 2960

US Department of State, 2898

US Department of State International, 6062

US Department of State, Office Overseas Schools, 3836

US Government Printing Office, 3949, 4126

US Information Agency, 197

US National Center for Education Statistics, 4071

US Supreme Court Education Cases, 3854

US West Foundation, 2365

USA CityLink Project, 5880

USA Today, 5043

USA Today Financial Aid for College, 4011

USC Summer Superintendents' Conference, 804

USCEA, 4844

Ukarumpa High School, 1276

Ukraine Kiev International School-An American Institution, 2216

Ultimate Early Childhood Music Resource, 4599

Ultra Play Systems, 5770

Understanding and Relating To Parents Professionally, 3479

Unifex Professional Maintenance Products, 5590

Unilab, 5725

Union Carbide Foundation, 2838

Union Pen Company, 2864

Unisys, 5881

United Airlines Foundation, 2459

United Art and Education, 5241

United Nations Development Program, 295

United Nations International School, 2217

United Nations International School-Hanoi, 1277

United Nations Nursery School, 1919

United States Institute of Peace, 2839

United States Steel Foundation, 2747

United States-Japan Foundation, 2840

United Student Aid Funds Newsletter, 4454

United Transparencies, 5223

United World College-Adriatic, 1920

United World College-Atlantic, 1921

United World College-SE Asia, 1278

Universal American School, 1534

Universe in the Classroom, 4667

University Continuing Education Association, 3413, 3502

University Products, 5548, 6107

University Research, 1025

University Research Company, 5988

University Vacancies in Australia, 1279

University del Sagrado Corazon, 2218

University of Alaska, Conference & Special Events, 3299

University of Alaska-Anchorage Library, 2259

University of Alberta, 3541

University of Arizona, 4538

University of Arkansas at Little Rock, 3724

University of California, 5265

University of California, Berkeley, 4957, 5112

University of California, Los Angeles, 5154

University of Central Florida, 3725

University of Chicago, 4124

University of Chicago Press, 3459, 5146

University of Colorado, 128

University of Colorado-Denver, School of Education, 4171

University of Connecticut, 709, 733, 5125

University of Denver, 5275

University of Florida, 4760

University of Georgia, College of Education, 3486, 4213

University of Georgia-Instructional Technology, 1026

University of Hawaii, 2431, 2986

University of Houston-University Park, 3506

University of Illinois, 11, 300, 5083

University of Illinois at Urbana, 188, 4176

University of Iowa, 4536, 5207

The University of Kansas, 5098

University of Maine, College of Education, 4215

University of Maryland, 49, 174, 3594, 6146

University of Massachusetts at Boston, 4218

University of Michigan, 4518

University of Michigan Association, 3503

University of Michigan-Dearborn Center for Corporate & Professional Development, 3726

University of Minnesota, 35, 6052

University of Minnesota, Office in Education, 4270

University of Missouri, 301, 2571, 4415

University of Missouri-Columbia, 5099

University of Missouri-Kansas City, 3716

University of Nebraska at Omaha, 3314

University of New Mexico, 390, 836

University of North Carolina, 4642

University of North Carolina at Chapel Hill, 3570

University of North Carolina at Greensboro, 217

University of North Carolina, School of Education, 152

University of North Carolina-Charlotte, 4683

University of North Texas, 187, 825, 3313, 3572, 3630, 4025, 4788

University of Northern Iowa, 817, 2247

University of Notre Dame, 3994

University of Oklahoma, 5084

University of Oregon, 159

University of Pennsylvania, 6060

University of Phoenix Online, 6187

University of Pittsburgh, 280, 5100, 6059

University of Siena-S/American Universities, 3714

University of South Alabama, 2258

University of South Carolina, 714

University of South Carolina Law School, 4209

University of South Carolina, College of Education, 3530

University of Southern California, 6061

University of Southern California, School of Ed., 804

University of Tennessee, 582, 4199, 4303

University of Texas at Austin/Univ. of Texas Press, 4553

University of Vermont, College of Agriculture, 3269

University of Wisconsin, 4885

University of Wisconsin - Oshkosh, 4635

University of Wisconsin, Milwaukee, 4340

University of Wisconsin-Madison, 2821, 3919, 5111

University of the Pacific, 4551

Unschoolers Network, 4310

Updating School Board Policies, 4388

Uplinc, 1027

Upstart Books, 5044

Urban & Field Services, 3117

Urban & Teacher Education, 3094

Urban Information, 2770

Uruguayan American School, 1420, 2219

Uruguayan American School-Montevideo, 2220

Useful Learning, 5045

Uskudar American Academy, 1535

Utah Department of Education, 3220, 3221, 3222

Utah Education Association, 587

Utah Library Association, 588

Utah Office of Education, 3223

Utah Office of Education; Agency Services Division, 3224

Uzbekistan Tashkent International School, 2221

V

VEWAA Newsletter, 4441

VGM Career Books, 3918

VGM Career Books/National Textbook Company, 3952

VGM's Careers Encyclopedia, 3952

VIDYA Books, 5046

VIP Views, Ideas & Practical Solutions, 4389

VSBA Newsletter, 4311

VV Cooke Foundation Corporation, 2482

Vacation-Work Publishers, 3929

Vajont Elementary School, 1922

Valenti Builders, 2460

Valenti Charitable Foundation, 2460

Valiant, 6182

Vanguard Crafts, 5406

Varitronics Systems, 5472

Velan, 5989

Venezuela Colegio Internacional-Carabobo, 2222

Venezuela Escuela Campo Alegre, 2223

Venezuela International School-Caracas, 2224

Ventura County Community Foundation, 2347

Ventura Educational Systems, 5882

Verdala International School, 1923

Vermont Community Foundation, 2797

Vermont Department of Education, 3231, 3225, 3226, 3227, 3228, 3229, 3230

Vermont Department of Libraries, 2798

Vermont Education Association, 589

Vermont Library Association, 590

Vermont School Boards Association, 4311

Vermont Special Education, 3232

Vernier Software, 6183
Verona Elementary School, 1924
Vibrac Corporation, 5726
Vicenza Elementary School, 1925
Vicenza High School, 1926
Vicenza International School, 1927
Victoria Foundation, 2603
Video Project, 5224
Videodiscovery, 6153
Vienna Christian School, 1928
Vienna International School, 1929
Vientiane International School, 1280
Views & Visions, 4442
Viking Children's Books, 5047
Vilseck Elementary School, 1930
Vilseck High School, 1931
Vincent-Curtis, 59, 3855
Vincent-Curtis Educational Register, 3855
Violen School, International Department, 1932
Virgin Island Montessori School, 2225
Virgin Islands Department of Education, 2226
Virginia A Ostendorf, 3436
Virginia ASCD, 3416
Virginia Alliance for Arts Education, 596
Virginia Association for Health, Physical Education, Recreation & Dance, 597
Virginia Association for Supervision and Curriculum Development, 598
Virginia Association for the Education of the Gifted, 599
Virginia Association of Elementary School Principals Conference, 600, 3414
Virginia Association of Independent Schools-Conference, 601, 3415
Virginia Association of Independent Schools, 602
Virginia Association of School Superintendents, 603
Virginia Association of School Business Officials, 604
Virginia Association of School Personnel Administrators, 605
Virginia Centers for Community Education, 3236
Virginia Congress of Parents & Teachers, 606
Virginia Consortium of Administrators for Education of the Gifted, 607
Virginia Council for Private Education, 608
Virginia Council of Administrators of Special Education, 609
Virginia Council of Teachers of Mathematics, 610
Virginia Council on Economic Education, 611
Virginia Department of Education, 3237, 3233, 3234, 3235, 3236
Virginia Education Association, 612
Virginia Educational Media Association, 613
Virginia Educational Research Association, 614
Virginia Educators Annual Conference, 3416
Virginia Foundation for Educational Leadership, 2807
Virginia High School League, 615
Virginia Library Association, 616
Virginia Middle School Association, 617
Virginia School Boards Association, 618
Virginia School Boards Association Conference, 3417
Virginia Secondary & Middle School Committee, 595

Virginia Student Councils Association, 619
Virginia Vocational Association, 620
Visible Ink Press/Gale Research, 3979
Vision, 4410
Vision 23, 5048
Visions in Action, 296
Visual Literacy Review & Newsletter, 4634
Viziflex Seels, 5883
Vocational & Adult Education, 2914, 3095
Vocational & Career Education, 3152
Vocational & Educational Services for Disabled, 3130
Vocational Biographies, 4030
Vocational Education, 2928, 3123, 3206
Vocational Education Division, 2990
Vocational Evaluation & Work Adjustment Assn., 4441
Vocational Industrial Clubs of America, 4440
Vocational Prgs. for the Disabled & Disadvantaged, 2968
Vocational Rehabilitation, 2935, 3096
Vocational Rehabilitation Services, 3020
Vocational Technical Education, 3088
Vocational Technological Education, 2268
Vocational Training News, 4443
Vocational-Technical School Systems, 2970
Vogelweh Elementary School, 1933
Voices in the Hall: High School Principals at Work, 3616
Volkel Elementary School, 1934
Volunteers for Peace, 591, 3815, 4201
Voyager Expanded Learning, 192, 6232

W

W Brooks Fortune Foundation, 2471
W Dale Clark Library, 2584
W. C. Heller & Company, 5549
WA-ACTE Career and Technical Exhibition for Career and Technical Education, 823
WCER Highlights, 4312
WESTLAW, 5990
WH Freeman & Company, 5049
WIDS-Worldwide Instructional Design System, 5823
WLN, 6108
WM Keck Foundation, 2348
WORLD OF DIFFERENCE Institute, 5050
WSRA Journal, 4635
Wachovia Financial Center, 2834
Wadsworth Publishing School Group, 5051
Wagner Spray Tech Corporation, 5614
Wagner Zip-Change, 5407
Walker & Company, 5052
Walker And Company, 6206
Walker Display, 5408
Wall Street Journal - Classroom Edition, 4698
Walter & Elise Haas Fund, 2349
Walter & Leona Dufresne Foundation, 2434
Walter S Johnson Foundation, 2350
Walton Family Foundation, 2272
Walworth Barbour American International School in Israel, 1536
Warner-Lambert Charitable Foundation, 2604
Warren P & Ava F Sewell Foundation, 2423
Warren Publishing House, 5053
Washington Association for Career & Tech Education, 823
Washington Counseletter, 4501

Washington DC Department of Education, 2915
Washington Department of Education, 3239
Washington Department of Education; Instruction Program, 3240
Washington Department of Education; Commission on Student Learning Administration, 3241
Washington Department of Education; Executive Services, 3242
Washington Department of Education; School Business & Administrative Services, 3243
Washington Education Association, 621
Washington International School, 2227
Washington Library Association, 622
Washington Post Company Educational Foundation, 2386
Washington State Convention & Trade Center, 3367
Washington State University, 4314
Washoe County Library, 2590
Waterford Institute, 5884
Waterford-Kamhlaba United World College, 1087
Waterfront Books, 5054
Watson Institute for International Studies, 4797
Wausau Tile, 5771
Wavelength, 3617, 3727
Wayne & Gladys Valley Foundation, 2351
Wayne State University, 2548
We Care Child Development Center, 2228
Wear Proof Mat Company, 5772
Weaver Instructional Systems, 6071
Web Connection, 5885
Web Feet Guides, 4728, 5055
Web Work Shops, 3566
Websense, 6184
Weingart Foundation, 2352
Welcome to Teaching and our Schools, 3480
Weld Foundation, 2521
Wellesley College, 1281
Welligent, 6004
Wellness Reproductions, 5409
Wells Fargo Foundation, 2353
Wesley International School, 1282
Wesleyan Academy, 2229
West Aurora Public Schools, District 129, 4290
West Educational Publishing, 5056
West Group, 5990
West Virginia Department of Education, 3248, 3244, 3245, 3246, 3247
West Virginia Education Association, 624
West Virginia Library Association, 625
WestEd, 434
WestEd: Focus, 4313
Westark Community College, 2273
Western Academy of Beijing, 1283
Western Association of Colleges & Employers, 209
Western Association of Schools and Colleges, 3856
Western History Association, 390
Western History Association Annual Meeting, 836
Western Illinois University, 4476
Western Journal of Black Studies, 4314
Western Massachusetts Funding Resource Center, 2522
Western Michigan University, 373, 3344
Western Psychological Services, 5057

Westinghouse Electric Corporation, 2841
Westinghouse Foundation, 2841
Weston Woods Studios, 5225
Westwing School, 1935
Westwood International School, 1088
Westwood Press, 3504
Wetzel Elementary School, 1936
Wewak International Primary School, 1284
What Works and Doesn't With at Risk
    Students, 4031
What's New Magazine, 3537
What's Working in Parent Involvement, 4636
Wheelit, 5550
Whirlpool Foundation, 2549
Whitaker Newsletters, 4439
White Office Systems, 5551
White Plains Public Library, 2674
Whitney Brothers Company, 5552
Who's Who in the Social Studies Annual
    Directory, 4093
Whole Nonprofit Catalog, 3857
Wholesale Educational Supplies, 5473
Wichita Public Library, 2476
Wids Learning Design System, 3728
Wiegand Center, 2588
Wiesbaden Middle School, 1937
Wikki Stix One-of-a-Kind Creatables, 5410
Wilbur D May Foundation, 2354
Wild Goose Company, 5727
Wilderness Education Association, 151
Wildlife Conservation Society, 5058, 5303
Wildlife Supply Company, 5728
Wilf Family Foundation, 2605
William & Flora Hewlett Foundation, 2355
William A Ewing & Company, 1028
William C & Theodosia Murphy Nolan
    Foundation, 2274
William C Bannerman Foundation, 2356
William E Schrafft & Bertha E Schrafft
    Charita ble Trust, 2523
William K. Bradford Publishing Company,
    6122
William Morrow & Company, 5059
William Penn Foundation, 2748
William R Kenan Jr Charitable Trust, 2687
William Randolph Hearst Foundation, 2675
William T & Marie J Henderson Foundation,
    2799
William T Grant Foundation, 2676
William T Sampson, 1421
**Williamsburg-James City County Public
    Schools**, 604
Williamson Publishing Company, 3953
Wilmar, 5615
Wilson Language Training, 5411
Wilton Art Appreciation Programs, 5412
Windhoek International School, 1089
Winnebago Software Company, 6109
Winning Federal Grants: A Guide to the
    Government's Grant-Making Process,
    4012
Winning Money for College: The High
    School Student's Guide to Scholarships,
    4013
Winsted Corporation, 5553
Winston Derek Publishers, 5060
Winston-Salem Foundation, 2688
Winthrop Rockefeller Foundation, 2275
Wiremold Company, 5886
Wisconsin Association of School Boards,
    3418
Wisconsin Association of School District
    Administrators Conference, 3419

Wisconsin Center for Education Research,
    4312
Wisconsin College System Technical, 3253
Wisconsin Department of Education,
    3249, 3250, 3251, 3252
Wisconsin Department of Public Instruction,
    3254
Wisconsin Education Association Council,
    626
Wisconsin Educational Media Association,
    627
Wisconsin Library Association, 628
Wisconsin School Administrators
    Association Conference, 3420
Wisconsin Technical College System
    Foundation, 5887
Wisconsin Technical College System
    Foundation, 1029
Wisconsin Vocational Association, 4442
Wisconsin Vocational Association
    Conference, 818
Witt Company, 5616
Wm. C. Brown Communications, 6142
wNet School, 6023
Wolfe Associates, 2714
Wolfert Van Borselen, 1938
Wolfram Research, 5061, 5974, 6118
Wolverine Sports, 5773
Women Educators, 152
Women's Educational & Industrial Union,
    153
Women's History Network News, 4699
Women's International League for Peace &
    Freed om, 210
Women's Job Search Handbook, 3953
Wood Designs, 5554
WoodKrafter Kits, 5729
Woodstock Corporation, 2524
Woodstock School, 1285
Worcester Public Library, 2525
Word Associates, 5888, 5977
Worden Company, 5555
Wordware Publishing, 6019
WorkSafeUSA, 5944
Workforce Education and Development, 3729
Workforce Preparation: An International
    Perspective, 3954
Working Holidays: The Complete Guide to
    Finding a Job Overseas, 3955
Working Together: A Guide to
    Community-Based Educational
    Resources, 3858
Workman Publishing, 5062
Worksop College, 1939
World & I, 5063
**World Affairs Council of North
    California**, 4676
**World Associaiton for Symphonic Bands
    & Ensembles**, 643
World Association of Publishers,
    Manufacturers & Distributors, 297
World Association of Publishers,
    Manufacturers & Distributors, 5064
World Bank, 5065
World Book Educational Products, 5066
World Classroom, 6020
**World Council for Curriculum &
    Instruction**, 3840
**World Council for Gifted & Talented
    Children**, 4315
World Eagle, 5067
World Education Services, 6063
World Exchange Program Directory, 3481

World Geography Web Site, 6158
World Gifted, 4315
World Resources Institute, 5068
World Wide Arts Resources, 6064
World of Learning, 3859, 3956
World of Play Therapy Literature, 4032
WorldCom Foundation, 403
WorldTeach, 2249
WorldView Software, 6159
WorldWide Classroom, 3813
Worlddidac, 297, 5064
Worldwide Headquaters, 6165
Worms Elementary School, 1940
Worth Publishers, 5069
Worthington Family Foundation, 2374
Wright Group, 5070
Wright State University, Lake Campus,
    3388
Write Now: A Complete Self Teaching
    Program for Better Handwriting, 4045
Write Now: A Complete Self-Teaching
    Program Fo or Better Handwriting, 4014
Write Source Educational Publishing House,
    5071
Writing Lab Newsletter, 4543
Wuerzburg Elementary School, 1941
Wuerzburg High School, 1942
Wuerzburg Middle School, 1943
Wyoming Department of Education, 3259,
    3255, 3256, 3257, 3258
Wyoming Education Association, 629
Wyoming Library Association, 630
Wyoming School Boards Association, 631

X

Xerox Foundation, 2842
Xiamen International School, 1286

Y

Y&H Soda Foundation, 2357
Yakistan International School-Karachi, 2230
Yew Chung Shanghai International School,
    1287
Yogyakarta International School, 1288
Yokohama International School, 1289
Yokota East Elementary School, 1290
Yokota High School, 1291
Yokota West Elementary School, 1292
Yonggwang Foreign School, 1293
You Can Handle Them All, 3482
You Can Handle Them All Discipline Video
    Series, 3618
Young Audiences Newsletter, 4316
Young Explorers, 5413
Your Personal Mentoring & Planning Guide
    for the First 60 Days of Teaching, 3483
Your School and the Law, 4390
Youth for Understanding (YFU), 6065

Z

Z Smith Reynolds Foundation, 2689
ZDNet, 6190
Zama Junior High & High School, 1294
Zaner-Bloser K-8 Catalog, 5072

Zellerbach Family Fund, 2358
Zep Manufacturing, 5617
Zephyr Press, 5073
Zion Academy, 2231
ZooBooks, 5074
ZooBooks/Wildlife Education. Ltd., 5074
Ztek Company, 5889
Zukeran Elementary School, 1295
Zurich International School, 1944

Alabama

Alabama Business Education Association, 411

Alabama Education Association, 412

Alabama Library Association, 413

Alabama State Department of Education, 2916

Assistant Superintendent & Financial Services, 2917

Association for Science Teacher Education Science Annual Meeting, 698

Auburn University at Montgomery Library, 2250

Benjamin & Roberta Russell Educational and Charitable Foundation, 2251

Birmingham Public Library, 2252

Carolina Lawson Ivey Memorial Foundation, 2253

Deputy Superintendent, 2918

Disability Determination Division, 2919

FPMI Communications, 912

General Administrative Services, 2920

Huntsville Public Library, 2254

Inter-Regional Center, 266

JL Bedsole Foundation, 2255

Jefferson State Community College, 3666

Mildred Weedon Blount Educational and Charitab le Foundation, 2256

Mitchell Foundation, 2257

National Council for Geographic Education Annual Meeting, 3359

Post Secondary Educational Assistance, 988

Rehabilitation Services, 2924

Student Instructional Services, 2926

Superintendent, 2927

University of South Alabama, 2258

Alaska

Alaska Association of School Librarians, 414

Alaska Business Education Association, 415

Alaska Commission on Postsecondary Education, 2929

Alaska Department of Education Administrative Services, 2930

Alaska Department of Education & Early Development, 2931

Alaska Department of Education Bilingual & Bicultural Education Conference, 3299

Alaska Library Association, 416

Community Connections, 867

Education Program Support, 2932

Libraries, Archives & Museums, 2933

School Finance & Data Management, 2934

Special Education Service Agency, 1014

University of Alaska-Anchorage Library, 2259

Arizona

AZLA/MPLA Conference, 656

American Council on Industrial Arts Teacher Education, 330

Annual Academic-Vocational Integrated Curriculum Conference, 685

Annual Challenging Learners with Untapped Potential Conference, 686

Annual Conference on Hispanic American Education, 687

Annual Effective Schools Conference, 688

Annual Microcomputers in Education Conference, 690

Arizona Association of Independent Academic Schools, 417

Arizona Department of Education, 2260

Arizona Governor's Committee on Employment of People with Disabilities, 2261

Arizona Library Association, 418

Arizona School Boards Association, 419

Center for Image Processing in Education, 3627

Conference on Information Technology, 716

Council of Education Facility Planners-Interna tional, 255

Education Services, 2262

Evo-Ora Foundation, 2263

Flinn Foundation, 2264

High School Reform Conference, 726

Increasing Student Achievement in Reading, Wri ting, Mathematics, Science, 730

Infusing Brain Research, Multi-Intelligence, Learning Styles and Mind Styles, 732

Integrated/Thematic Curriculum and Performance Assessment, 734

National Council of State Supervisors of Music, 2936

National Network of Learning Disabled Adults, 119

National School Conference Institute, 783

North Central Association Annual Meeting, 3382

Northern Arizona University, 3691

Phoenix Public Library, 2265

Professional Office Instruction & Training, 420

Restructuring Curriculum Conference, 3398

Special Programs, 2266

Staff Development Workshops & Training Sessions, 3711

Technology in 21st Century Schools, 801

Tesseract Group, 1023

Vocational Technological Education, 2268

Arkansas

Arkansas Business Education Association, 422

Arkansas Department of Education, 2937

Arkansas Department of Education: Special Education, 2938

Arkansas Education Association, 423

Arkansas Library Association, 424

Charles A Frueauff Foundation, 2269

Children's Educational Opportunity Foundation, 861

Dawson Education Cooperative, 879

Dawson Education Service Cooperative, 880

Dimensions of Early Childhood, 181

Federal Programs, 2939

Roy and Christine Sturgis Charitable and Educa tional Trust, 2270

Southern Early Childhood Annual Convention, 3403

The Jones Center For Families, 2271

University of Arkansas at Little Rock, 3724

Walton Family Foundation, 2272

Westark Community College, 2273

William C & Theodosia Murphy Nolan Foundation, 2274

Winthrop Rockefeller Foundation, 2275

California

Advance Infant Development Program, 839

Aguirre International Incorporated, 840

Ahmanson Foundation, 2276

Alice Tweed Tuohy Foundation, 2277

Alliance for Technology Access Conference, 392

American Honda Foundation, 2823

Arrillaga Foundation, 2278

Asian American Curriculum Project, 317

Assessing Student Performance, 3424

Association for Play Therapy, 24

Association for Play Therapy Conference, 697

Association for Refining Cross-Cultured International, 844

Association for the Advancement of Internation al Education, 700

Association of Educational Therapists, 215

Atkinson Foundation, 2279

BankAmerica Foundation, 2280

Bechtel Group Corporate Giving Program, 2281

Bernard Osher Foundation, 2282

Boys-Viva Supermarkets Foundation, 2283

CPM Educational Program, 851

Caldwell Flores Winters, 852

California Biomedical Research Association, 367

California Business Education Association, 426

California Classical Association-Northern Section, 427

California Community Foundation, 2284

California Council for Adult Education, 3309

California Department of Education, 2941

California Department of Education Catalog, 2942

California Department of Special Education, 2943

California Foundation for Agriculture in the C lassroom, 428

California Kindergarten Association Annual Conference, 3310

California Library Association, 429

California Reading Association, 430

California School Boards Association Conference, 3311

California School Library Association, 431

California Teachers Association, 432

Carnegie Foundation for the Advancement of Teaching, 854

Carrie Estelle Doheny Foundation, 2285

Center for Civic Education, 34

Center for Critical Thinking and Moral Critique Annual International, 635

Center for Research on the Context of Teaching, 5079

Center on Disabilities Conference, 711

Classroom Connect, 3316, 3631

Coalition of Essential Schools, 864

College Bound, 865

Computer Using Educators, Inc (CUE), 397

Concern-America Volunteers, 251

Consortium on Reading Excellence, 871

Constitutional Rights Foundation, 39

Council on Islamic Education, 259
Creative Learning Systems, 878
Curriculum & Instructional Leadership
    Branch, 2944
Dan Murphy Foundation, 2286
Darryl L Sink & Associates, 3637
David & Lucile Packard Foundation, 2287
Department Management Services Branch,
    2945
Disability Rights Education & Defense Fund,
    45
Education, Training and Research
    Associates, 57
Effective Training Solutions, 905
Epistemological Engineering, 909
Evelyn & Walter Haas Jr Fund, 2288
Excell Education Centers, 911
Executive Office & External Affairs, 2946
Field Services Branch, 2947
Foundation Center-San Francisco, 2289
Foundation for Critical Thinking, 3651
Foundation for Critical Thinking Regional
    Workshop & Conference, 724
Foundations Focus, 2290
Francis H Clougherty Charitable Trust, 2291
Freitas Foundation, 2292
Fritz B Burns Foundation, 2293
George Frederick Jewett Foundation, 2294
Geothermal Education Office, 370
Governmental Policy Branch, 2948
Grant & Resource Center of Northern
    California, 2295
Grantsmanship Center, 2833
Greenville Foundation, 2296
HN & Frances C Berger Foundation, 2297
Harry & Grace Steele Foundation, 2298
Henry J Kaiser Family Foundation, 2299
Hon Foundation, 2300
Hugh & Hazel Darling Foundation, 2301
Ingraham Memorial Fund, 2302
International Association for Social Science
    Information Service & Technology, 3327
International Conference, 643
James G Boswell Foundation, 2303
James Irvine Foundation, 2304
James S Copley Foundation, 2305
Jobs for California Graduates, 936
John Jewett & H Chandler Garland
    Foundation, 2306
Joseph & Edna Josephson Institute, 939
Joseph Drown Foundation, 2307
Jules & Doris Stein Foundation, 2308
Julio R Gallo Foundation, 2309
Kaleidoscope, 3669
Kenneth T & Eileen L Norris Foundation,
    2310
Koret Foundation, 2311
Lane Family Charitable Trust, 2312
Legal & Audits Branch, 2949
Levi Strauss Foundation, 2313
Life Lab Science Program, 5101
Lilly Conferences on College and University
    Teaching, 3337
Los Angeles Educational Alliance for
    Restructu ring Now, 947
Louise M Davies Foundation, 2314
Lowell Berry Foundation, 2315
Luke B Hancock Foundation, 2316
MATRIX: A Parent Network and Resource
    Center, 80
MK & Company, 949
MPR Associates, 950
Margaret E Oser Foundation, 2317

Marin Community Foundation, 2318
Mary A Crocker Trust, 2319
Matrix Media Distribution, 958
Maurice Amado Foundation, 2320
McConnell Foundation, 2321
McKesson Foundation, 2322
Midas Consulting Group, 964
Milken Family Foundation, 2323
Miranda Lux Foundation, 2324
National Academy of Education, 81, 2835
National Association for Asian and Pacific
    American Education, 83
National Association for Year-Round
    Education Annual Conference, 87, 755
National Center for Research in Vocational
    Education, 5112
National Center for Science Education, 376
National Coalition of Independent Scholars,
    100
National Institute of Art and Disabilities, 341
National School Safety Center, 176, 5128
National Women's History Project Annual
    Conference, 787
Northern California Comprehensive
    Assistance Center, 433
Northern California Grantmakers, 2325
Pacific Telesis Group Corporate Giving
    Program, 2326
Pamela Joy, 982
Peninsula Community Foundation, 2327
Perfect PC Technologies, 985
Peter Norton Family Foundation, 2328
Prism Computer Corporation, 992
RCM Capital Management Charitable Fund,
    2329
Ralph M Parsons Foundation, 2330
Region 9: Education Department, 2950
Research Assessment Management, 1004
Restructuring in the Classroom, 3462
Riordan Foundation, 2331
Royal Barney Hogan Foundation, 2332
SH Cowell Foundation, 2333
Sacramento Regional Foundation, 2334
San Diego Foundation, 2335
San Francisco Foundation, 2336
Santa Barbara Foundation, 2337
School Identifications, 2858
SchoolTech Forum, 3399
Scientific Learning, 5144
Sega Youth Education & Health Foundation,
    2338
Seminar Information Service, 3464
Shirley Handy, 1011
Sidney Stern Memorial Trust, 2339
Society for History Education, 388
Sol & Clara Kest Family Foundation, 2340
Sonoma State University Annual
    Conference, 3400
Specialized Programs Branch, 2951
Sports Management Group, 1015
Szekely Family Foundation, 2341
Teacher-Created Materials, 3467
Teachers Curriculum Institute, 1019
Teachers Service Association, 1020
Teachers in Publishing, 3470
Teachers' Committee on Central America,
    389
Teaching About Islam & Muslims in the
    Public School Classroom, 3471
Tech Ed Services, 1021
Technology, Reading & Learning
    Difficulties Conference, 802
Thomas & Dorothy Leavey Foundation, 2342

Times Mirror Foundation, 2343
Timken-Sturgis Foundation, 2344
Toyota USA Foundation, 2345
Turst Funds Incorporated, 2346
UCLA Statistical Consulting, 5154
USC Summer Superintendents' Conference,
    804
Ventura County Community Foundation,
    2347
WM Keck Foundation, 2348
Walter & Elise Haas Fund, 2349
Walter S Johnson Foundation, 2350
Wayne & Gladys Valley Foundation, 2351
Weingart Foundation, 2352
Wells Fargo Foundation, 2353
WestEd, 434
Western Association of Colleges &
    Employers, 209
Wilbur D May Foundation, 2354
William & Flora Hewlett Foundation, 2355
William A Ewing & Company, 1028
William C Bannerman Foundation, 2356
Y&H Soda Foundation, 2357
Zellerbach Family Fund, 2358

Colorado

ACSI Teachers' Convention, 654
Adolph Coors Foundation, 2359
Annual Building Championship Schools
    Conference, 3303
Assistive Technology Clinics, 5076
Association for Experiential Education
    Annual Conference, 633
Association of Christian Schools
    International, 239, 845
Boettcher Foundation, 2360
Colorado Association of Libraries, 435
Colorado Association of School Executives
    Conference, 3317
Colorado Business Educators, 436
Colorado Community College &
    Occupational Education System, 437
Colorado Congress of Parents, Teachers &
    Students, 438
Colorado Department of Education, 2952
Colorado Education Association, 439
Colorado Library Association, 440
Colorado Library Association Conference,
    830
Denver Foundation, 2361
Distance Learning Directory, 3436
EDUCAUSE, 399, 719
Education Commission of the States, 54
Educational Services, 2953
El Pomar Foundation, 2362
Equity Clearinghouse, 60
Federal Program Services, 2954
Gates Foundation, 2363
Journal of Experiential Education, 3508
Management, Budget & Planning, 2955
Mid-Continent Regional Educational
    Laboratory, 5104
National Rural Education Annual
    Convention, 780
National Women's Student Coalition, 128
Public School Finance, 2956
Quality Education Data, 5138
Reinventing Your School Board, 1002
Rural Educator-Journal for Rural and Small
    Schools, 3522

Ruth & Vernon Taylor Foundation, 2364
Special Services, 2957
State Library, 2958
Teacher Certification & Professional
 Education, 2959
Teacher Ideas Press Libraries Unlimited,
 3466
US Department of Education: Region VIII,
 2960
US West Foundation, 2365

Connecticut

A&L Fund Raising, 2843
Aetna Foundation, 2366
All Sports, 2846
Area Cooperative Educational Services, 842
Center for Gifted Education and Talent
 Development Conference, 709
Community Foundation of Greater New
 Haven, 2367
Connecticut Business Education Association,
 441
Connecticut Department of Education, 2961
Connecticut Early Childhood Unit, 2962
Connecticut Education Association, 442
Connecticut Educational Media Association,
 443
Connecticut Governor's Committee on
 Employment of the Handicapped, 2963
Connecticut Library Association, 806
Connecticut Mutual Financial Services, 2368
Connecticut School Library Association, 444
Datacad, 3581
Education Programs & Services, 2964
Educational Foundation of America, 2826
Finance & Administrative Services, 2965
Hartford Foundation for Public Giving, 2369
Howard Greene Associates, 919
Human Services, 2966
Information Systems, 2967
Instant Access: Critical Findings from the
 NRC/GT, 733
International Journal of Instructional Media,
 3504
Loctite Corporate Contributions Program,
 2370
Louis Calder Foundation, 2371
MarcoPolo, 403
Modern Educational Systems, 967
National Association of Teachers' Agencies
 Conference, 205, 762
National Research Center on the Gifted &
 Talented, 5125
Office of State Coordinator of Vocational
 Education for Disabled Students, 2968
QSP, 2856
Religious Education Association of the US &
 Canada, 143
Sherman Fairchild Foundation, 2372
Smart Family Foundation, 2373
Steve Wronker's Funny Business, 2861
Summer Institute in Siena, 3714
Teaching & Learning Division, 2969
Union Carbide Foundation, 2838
Union Pen Company, 2864
Vocational-Technical School Systems, 2970
Worthington Family Foundation, 2374
Xerox Foundation, 2842

Delaware

Assessments & Accountability Branch
 Delaware Department of Education, 2971
Crystal Trust, 2375
Delaware Business Education Association,
 445
Delaware Department of Education, 2972
Delaware Department of Education:
 Administrati ve Services, 2973
Delaware Library Association, 446
Delaware State Education Association, 447
HW Buckner Charitable Residuary Trust,
 2376
Improvement & Assistance Branch Delaware
 Department of Education, 2974
International Reading Association, 350
International Reading Association Annual
 Convention, 648
JCB/Early Childhood Education Consultant
 Service, 932
Longwood Foundation, 2377
Pyramid Educational Consultants, 996
Teachers in Touch, 3529

District of Columbia

AACTE Briefs, 3484
ACE Fellows Program, 3297, 3619
ACTION, 2
AFL-CIO Guide to Union Sponsored
 Scholarships, Awards & Student Aid, 2866
ASPIRA Association, 3
Abe Wouk Foundation, 2378
Academic Alliances, 3260
Academic Travel Abroad, 222
Academy for Educational Development, 4
Accounting & Financial Management
 Services, 2878
Agency for International Development, 223
American Association for Higher Education:
 Ann ual Assessment Conference, 660
American Association for Higher Education:
 Lea rning to Change Conference, 661
American Association for Higher Education:
 Sum mer Academy, Organizing for
 Learning, 662
American Association of Colleges for
 Teacher Education-Directory, 663, 3262,
 3421, 3421
American Association of Collegiate
 Registrars & Admissions Officers, 154,
 3300
American Council on Education, 13
American Council on Education Annual
 Meeting, 670
American Council on Education Library &
 Information Service, 448
American Driver & Traffic Safety Education
 Association, 356
American Educational Research Association,
 674, 3263
American Educator, 3488
American Federation of Teachers, 16
American Federation of Teachers Biennial
 Convention & Exhibition, 3301
American Jewish Congress, 225
American Psychological Association Annual
 Conference, 680

American Public Health Association Annual
 Meeting, 681
American Public Human Services
 Association, 18
American Society of International Law, 227
Annual NCEA Convention & Exposition, 691
Appropriate Inclusion and Paraprofessionals,
 3423
Assistance to States Division, 2879
Associates for Renewal in Education, 449
Association for Canadian Studies in the US,
 231
Association for Community-Based
 Education, 20
Association of American Colleges &
 Universitie s Annual Meeting, 703
Association of Boarding Schools, 27
Association of Community College Trustees
 Conference, 704
Association of International Educators, 240
Association of Science-Technology Centers
 Incorporated Conference, 366, 705
Building Life Options: School-Community
 Collaborations, 3430
Casa del Pueblo Community Program, 246
Center for Adult Learning and Educational
 Credentials, 33
Center for Applied Linguistics, 304
Center for Strategic & International Studies,
 248
Character Education: Making a Difference,
 3568
Civil Rights, 2880
Coming Up Short? Practices of Teacher
 Educators Committed to Character, 3432
Compensatory Education Program, 2881
Consortium for School Networking, 398
Contracting Out: Strategies for Fighting
 Back, 3434
Cooperative International Pupil-to-Pupil
 Program, 252
Council for Advancement & Support of
 Education, 40
Council for Advancement and Support of
 Educati on, 717
Council for Educational Development and
 Research, 5088
Council of Chief State School Officers, 158
Council of Graduate Schools, 43
Council on Hemisphere Affairs, 257
Council on Postsecondary Accreditation, 44
DC Division of Special Education, 2975
Distance Education & Training Council, 3273
District of Columbia Department of
 Education, 2976
District of Columbia Library Association,
 451
ERIC Clearinghouse on Languages and
 Linguistic s, 160, 305
ERIC Clearinghouse on Teaching and
 Teacher Education, 3274
Educational Leadership Institute, 3275
Elementary Secondary Bilingual & Research
 Branch, 2883
Elementary, Secondary & Vocational
 Analysis, 2884
Eleven Principles of Effective Character
 Educa ion, 3584
Embracing an Inclusive Society: The
 Challenge for the New Millennium, 723
English Teaching Fellow Program, 197
Eugene & Agnes E Meyer Foundation, 2379
Foreign Student Service Council, 262

Geographic / Florida

Foundation Center-District of Columbia, 2380

Foundation for Educational Innovation, 914

Foundation for the National Capitol Region, 2381

Gilbert & Jaylee Mead Family Foundation, 2382

Grants Administration Branch, 2977

Grants and Contracts Service, 2832

HEATH Resource Center, 67

Higher Education Center, 5095

Hitachi Foundation, 2383

Human Resources and Administration, 2885

Infocus: A Newsletter of the University Continuing Education Association, 3502

Institute for Educational Leadership, 71

Intel Science Talent Search Scolarship, 2873

International Association for Continuing Education & Training, 267

International Educational Exchange, 272, 2886

International Monetary Fund, 275

International Research and Exchanges Board, 277

International Symposium, 649

Journal of Economic Education, 3507

Kaludis Consulting Group, 940

Kennedy Center Alliance for Arts Education, 335

Legislation & Congressional Affairs, 2887

Library Programs, 2888

Management Systems & Technology Services Division, 2978

Mathematical Association of America, 327

McKenzie Group, 959

Middle Grades Education in an Era of Reform, 3448

Morris & Gwendolyn Cafritz Foundation, 2384

NAFSA: National Association of International Educators, 746

NASW Job Link: The Social Work Employment Line, 204

NCSS Summer Professional Development Programs, 3687

NEA Foundatrion for tHe Improvement of Educati on, 5108

National Alliance of Black School Educators Conference, 749

National Association for Bilingual Education, 308, 751

National Association for Multicultural Education, 754

National Association for the Education of Young Children, 190

National Association of Boards of Education, 88

National Association of Federally Impacted Schools, 90

National Association of Independent Schools Conference, 758

National Association of Private Schools for Exceptional Children Conference, 167, 759

National Association of Social Workers, 220

National Association of Student Financial Aid Administrators, 170

National Association of Student Financial Aid Administrators, 761, 810

National Association of Student Personnel Administrators, 171

National Black Child Development Institute, 763, 5109

National Catholic Education Association Annual Convention & Exposition, 764

National Catholic Educational Association, 96

National Center for ESL Literacy Education, 351

National Center for Education Statistics, 2890

National Center for Improving Science Education, 5110

National Clearinghouse for Bilingual Education, 5120

National Coalition of Title 1-Chapter 1 Parents Conference, 768

National Council for Social Studies Annual Conference, 3361

National Council for the Accreditation of Teacher Education, 3279

National Council of Higher Education, 105, 771

National Council of State Directors of Adult Education, 173

National Council of Urban Education Associatio ns, 106

National Council on Disability, 2891

National Council on Measurement in Education, 107

National Council on US-Arab Relations, 282

National Dissemination Center for Children with Disabilities, 110

National Education Association, 111, 3280

National Education Association Annual Meeting, 3366

National Education Association Student Program, 112

National Education Association-Retired, 113, 774

National Education Policy Institute, 114

National Institute on Disability and Rehabilit ation Research, 405

National Network for Early Language Learning (NELL), 312

National Occupational Information Coordinating Committee Conference, 3369

National Organization on Disability, 120

National Science Resources Center, 5129

National Student Program, 126

National Trust for Historic Preservation: Office of Education Initiatives, 2893

No Child Left Behind, 2894

North American Association for Environmental Education, 131, 387, 3379, 3379

Office of Bilingual Education and Minority Language Affairs, 2895

Office of District of Columbia Affairs, 452

Office of Indian Education, 2896

Office of Juvenile Justice and Delinquency Prevention, 177

Office of Migrant Education, 2897

Office of Overseas Schools, 2898

Office of Public Affairs, 2899

Office of Special Education Programs, 2900

Office of Student Financial Assistance Programs, 2901

Organization of American States, 288

Planning & Evaluation Service, 2902

Policy, Planning & Management Services, 2903

Population Institute, 291

Practical Handbook for Assessing Learning Outcomes in Continuing Education, 3454

President's Council on Physical Fitness & Sports, 348

Preventing School Failure, 3516

Principles of Good Practice in Continuing Education, 3455

Programs for the Improvement of Practice, 2904

Public Education Fund Network, 5137

Public Welfare Foundation, 2385

Rehabilitation Services Administration, 2905

Renew America, 144

Research for Better Schools, 5140

Research to Practice Division, 2906

Resources for Teaching Middle School Science, 3461

School Assistance Division, 2907

School Improvement Programs-Drug Free Schools & Communities Division, 2908

School Improvement Programs-Equity and Educational Excellence Division, 2909

School Improvement Programs-School Effectivene ss Division, 2910

Science Service, 379

Service-Learning and Character Education: One Plus One is More Than Two, 3465

Smithsonian Institution/Office of Elementary & Secondary Education, 5145

State Services Division District of Columbia, 2979

Teacher Education Reports, 3525

Teachers as Educators of Character: Are the Nations Schools of Education Coming Up Short?, 3468

Their Best Selves: Building Character Education and Service Learning Together, 3474

Training & Development Programs, 2911

Twenty First Century Teachers Network: The McG uffey Project, 410

US Department of Education, 2913

US Department of Education: Office of Educational Research & Improvement, 3478

United States Institute of Peace, 2839

University Continuing Education Association Annual Conference, 3413

Visions in Action, 296

Washington DC Department of Education, 2915

Washington Post Company Educational Foundation, 2386

Florida

American Council on Schools and Colleges, 15

American Education Finance Association, 156

American Education Finance Association Annual Conference & Workshop, 673

American Sports Education Institute, 343

Applebaum Foundation, 2387

Association for Institutional Research, 357

Association of American Schools of South America, 237

Benedict Foundation for Independent Schools, 2388

Center for Applications of Psychological Type Biennial Education Conference, 708

Chatlos Foundation, 2389

Child Like Consulting Limited, 860

Citibank of Florida Corporate Giving Program, 2390
Dade Community Foundation, 2391
Florida Association for Media in Education, 453
Florida Atlantic University-Multifunctional Resource Center, 5094
Florida Business Education Association, 454
Florida Department of Education, 2980
Florida Education Association, 455
Florida Elementary School Principals Association Conference, 3319
Florida Library Association, 456
Florida School Administrators Association Summer Conference, 3320
Florida Teaching Profession-National Association, 457
Florida Vocational Association Conference, 3321
George & Mary Kremer Foundation, 2872
History of Science Society, 371
Innovating Worthy Projects Foundation, 2392
Jacksonville Public Library, 2393
Jessie Ball duPont Fund, 2394
John Dewey Society for the Study of Education & Culture, 76
John S & James L Knight Foundation, 2834
Joseph & Rae Gann Charitable Foundation, 2395
National Center for Construction Education & Research, 3688
National Congress on Aviation and Space Education, 770
National Institute for School and Workplace Safety Conference, 175, 777
Orlando Public Library-Orange County Library System, 2396
Peter D & Eleanore Kleist Foundation, 2397
Professional Development Institute, 994
Robert G Friedman Foundation, 2398
Sexual Assault and Harassment on Campus Conference, 794
Solutions Skills, 1013
Southwest Florida Community Foundation, 2399
Specialized Solutions, 3710
Student Help and Assistance Program to Educati on, 2400
Teacher Education Institute, 3719
Thomas & Irene Kirbo Charitable Trust, 2401
Thompson Publishing Group, 2402
University of Central Florida, 3725

Georgia

Action in Teacher Education, 3486
American Association for Vocational Instructio nal Materials, 9
Atlanta-Fulton Public Library, 2403
Aviation Information Resources, 196
BellSouth Foundation, 2404
Bradley Foundation, 2405
CARE, 243
Callaway Foundation, 2406
Coca-Cola Foundation, 2407
Connecting Link, 869
Council of Administrators of Special Education, 3272
Council on Occupational Education, 876
First District Resa, 913
Georgia Association of Educators, 458

Georgia Business Education Association, 459
Georgia Department of Education, 2981
Georgia Library Association, 460
Georgia Parents & Teachers Association, 461
Health Outreach Project, 916
Highlands Program, 918
J Bulow Campbell Foundation, 2408
JK Gholston Trust, 2409
John & Mary Franklin Foundation, 2410
John H & Wilhelmina D Harland Charitable Found ation, 2411
Joseph B Whitehead Foundation, 2412
Lettie Pate Evans Foundation, 2413
Logical Systems, 946
McCamish Foundation, 2414
Metropolitan Atlanta Community Foundation, 2415
Mill Creek Foundation, 2416
Mills Bee Lane Memorial Foundation, 2417
NAAEE Member Services Office, 745
National Center for Montessori Education Conference, 765
National Council for Black Studies, 104
National Youth-At-Risk Conference, 827
Peyton Anderson Foundation, 2418
Progressive Teacher, 3520
Rich Foundation, 2419
Robert & Polly Dunn Foundation, 2420
Safe Schools America, 179
Sapelo Foundation, 2421
School of Music, 3707
Southeastern Library Association, 421, 425
Southern Association Colleges & Schools, 3402
Southern Polytechnic State University, 3708
Southern Regional Education Board, 5148
Training of Trainers Seminar, 803
Tull Charitable Foundation, 2422
University of Georgia-Instructional Technology, 1026
Warren P & Ava F Sewell Foundation, 2423

Hawaii

Barbara Cox Anthony Foundation, 2424
Business Services Office, 2982
Cirriculum Research and Development Group, 5087
Cooke Foundation, 2425
Harold KL Castle Foundation, 2426
Hawaii Business Education Association, 462
Hawaii Department of Education, 2983
Hawaii Education Association, 463
Hawaii Library Association, 464
Hawaii State Teachers Association, 465
Hawaiian Electric Industries Charitable Founda tion, 2427
Information & Telecommunications Services, 2984
Instructional Services, 2922, 2985
James & Abigail Campbell Foundation, 2428
Oceanic Cablevision Foundation, 2429
Office of the State Director for Career & Technical Education, 2986
Pacific Regional Educational Laboratory, 5134
Paul H Rosendahl, PHD, 984
Samuel N & Mary Castle Foundation, 2430
State Public Library System, 2988
University of Hawaii, 2431

Idaho

Boise Public Library, 2432
Claude R & Ethel B Whittenberger Foundation, 2433
Idaho Department of Education, 2989
Idaho Education Association, 466
Idaho Library Association, 467
Moore Express, 971
Northwest Association of Schools & Colleges Annual Meeting, 135, 3386
Pacific Northwest Library Association, 321, 468, 822, 822
Vocational Education Division, 2990
Walter & Leona Dufresne Foundation, 2434

Illinois

American Academy of Pediatrics, 8
American Art Therapy Association, 329
American Association of French Teachers Conference, 664
American Association of School Librarians National Conference, 667
American Association of Schools & Departments of Journalism, 298
American Association of Teachers of French, 299
American Business Communication Association, 11, 300
American Library Association, 316
American Library Association Annual Conference, 677
Ameritech Foundation, 2435
Annual Ethics & Technology Conference, 689
Awards and Recognition Association, 30
Career Evaluation Systems, 853
Carus Corporate Contributions Program, 2436
Center for the Study of Reading, 5083
Chauncey & Marion Deering McCormick Foundation, 2437
Chicago Community Trust, 2438
Chicago Principals Association Education Conference, 3315
Coleman Foundation, 2439
Community Foundation for Jewish Education, 868
Council on Library Technical Assistants, 319
Curriculum Center - Office of Educational Services, 3636
DeVry University, 3638
Dellora A & Lester J Norris Foundation, 2440
Dillon Foundation, 2441
Directory of Curriculum Materials Centers, 3435
Dr. Scholl Foundation, 2442
ERIC Clearinghouse on Elementary & Early Child hood Education, 188
Easter Seals Communications, 53
Eastern Illinois University School of Technology, 3641
Educational Specialties, 899
Energy Concepts, 3648
Evanston Public Library, 2443
Executive Deputy Superintendent, 2991
Farny R Wurlitzer Foundation, 2444
Finance & Support Services, 2992

Grand Canyon University College of Education, 3654

Grover Hermann Foundation, 2445

How to Raise Test Scores, 3440

Illinois Affiliation of Private Schools for Exceptional Children, 469

Illinois Assistant Principals Conference, 3322

Illinois Association of School Business Officials, 470

Illinois Business Education Association, 471

Illinois Citizens' Education Council, 472

Illinois Department of Education, 2993

Illinois Education Association, 473

Illinois Library Association, 474

Illinois Library Association Conference, 808

Illinois Principals Professional Conference, 3323

Illinois Resource Center Conference of Teachers of Linguistically Diverse Students, 3324

Illinois School Boards Association, 3325

Illinois School Library Media Association, 475

Illinois Vocational Association Conference, 809

Improving Student Performance, 729

Independent Schools Association of the Central States, 161

Innovative Learning Group, 922

Institute of Cultural Affairs, 264

International Awards Market, 642

International Council on Education for Teaching, 3276

International Graphic Arts Education Association, 202, 273

Janice Borla Vocal Jazz Camp, 3665

Joyce Foundation, 2446

Kodaly Teaching Certification Program, 3672

Lloyd A Fry Foundation, 2447

Lutheran Education Association, 79

Lutheran Education Association Convention, 739

Management Simulations, 953

Midwestern Regional Educational Laboratory, 5105

National Association for Developmental Education, 84

National Council of English Teachers Conference, 3362

National Council of Teachers of English Annual Convention, 309, 3364

National Lekotek Center, 117

National Society for the Study of Education, 124

North American Professional Driver Education Association, 133

North Central Regional Educational Laboratory, 5130

Northern Trust Company Charitable Trust, 2448

Orff-Schulwerk Teacher Certification Program, 3692

Palmer Foundation, 2449

Philip H Corboy Foundation, 2450

Planning, Research & Evaluation, 2994

Polk Brothers Foundation, 2451

Prince Charitable Trust, 2452

Programs & Accountability, 2995

Recognition & Supervision of Schools, 2996

Regenstein Foundation, 2453

Region 5: Education Department, 2997

Requirements for Certification of Teachers & Counselors, 3459

Richard H Driehaus Foundation, 2454

Robert E Nelson Associates, 1005

Robert R McCormick Tribune Foundation, 2455

Rockford Systems, 3705

School Improvement & Assessment Services, 2999

Sears-Roebuck Foundation, 2456

Sigma Tau Delta, 314

Society for Research in Child Development, 795, 5146

Specialized Programs, 3001

Spencer Foundation, 2457

Student Development Services, 3002

Sulzer Family Foundation, 2458

Teaching for Intelligence Conference, 798

Top Quality School Process (TQSP), 3477

United Airlines Foundation, 2459

Valenti Charitable Foundation, 2460

Wavelength, 3617, 3727

Workforce Education and Development, 3729

Indiana

Administration & Financial Management Center, 3004

Agency for Instructional Technology, 391, 3261

Allen County Public Library, 2461

American Association of Specialized Colleges, 10

American Camping Association National Conference, 669

Art to Remember, 2847

Arvin Foundation, 2462

Association for Educational Communications & Technology Annual Convention, 395, 3307

Ball State University, 3623

Before the School Bell Rings, 3426

Beyond Tracking: Finding Success in Inclusive Schools, 3427

C/S Newsletter, 3493

Center for Professional Development & Services, 858

Center for School Assessment & Research, 3005

Clowes Fund, 2463

Community Relations & Special Populations, 3006

Dekko Foundation, 2464

ERIC Clearinghouse for Social Studies Educatio n, 384

ERIC Clearinghouse on Reading, English & Communication, 349

East Central Educational Service Center, 886

Education Conference, 3318

Educational Services Company, 898

Eli Lilly & Company Corporate Contribution Program, 2465

External Affairs, 3007

Foellinger Foundation, 2466

Hoosier Science Teachers Association Annual Meeting, 807

Indiana Association of School Business Officials, 476

Indiana Business Education Association, 477

Indiana Department of Education, 3008

Indiana Library Federation, 478

Indiana School Boards Association Annual Conference, 3326

Indiana State Teachers Association, 479

Indiana University-Purdue University of Indianapolis, IUPUI, 3658

Indianapolis Foundation, 2467

International Curriculum Management Audit Center, 3661

International Listening Association Annual Convention, 647

John W Anderson Foundation, 2468

July in Rensselaer, 3667

Law of Teacher Evaluation: A Self-Assestment Handbook, 3442

Lilly Endowment, 2469

Moore Foundation, 2470

National Educational Service, 115

National Student Exchange, 125

Office of the Deputy Superintendent, 3009

Phi Delta Kappa, 290

Piano Workshop, 3698

Priority Computer Services, 991

Professional Computer Systems, 993

Professional Development Institutes, 3701

Professional Learning Communities at Work, 3456

Revolution Revisited: Effective Schools and Systemic Reform, 3463

School Improvement & Performance Center, 3011

State Board Relations & Legal Services, 3012

Teachers Association in Instruction Conference, 3407

Teachers as Leaders, 3469

Voices in the Hall: High School Principals at Work, 3616

W Brooks Fortune Foundation, 2471

Wilderness Education Association, 151

Iowa

Book of Metaphors, Volume II, 3428

Cedar Rapids Public Library, 2472

Center for Learning Connections, 3628

Community Colleges Division, 3013

Division of Library Services, 3014

Educational Services for Children & Families, 3015

Elementary & Secondary Education, 2882, 3016

Ethical Issues in Experiential Education, 3437

Financial & Information Services, 3017

Gershowitz Grant and Evaluation Services, 2830

Iowa Business Education Association, 480

Iowa Council Teachers of Math Conference, 3328

Iowa Department of Education, 3018

Iowa Educational Media Association, 481

Iowa Library Association, 482

Iowa Public Television, 3019

Iowa Reading Association Conference, 3329

Iowa School Administrators Association Annual Convention, 3330

Iowa School Boards Association, 3331

Iowa State Education Association, 483

Janet Hart Heinicke, 935

National Association of Media and Technology Centers, 404

Noel/Levitz Centers, 979

People United for Rural Education, 141

Profiles, 995

RJ McElroy Trust, 2473

Theory of Experiential Education, 3475
UNI Overseas Recruiting Fair, 817
Vocational Rehabilitation Services, 3020

Kansas

American Council on Rural Special
  Education, 14
Assistant Commissioner's Office, 3021
Association for Individually Guided
  Education, 484
Board, 3492
Center for Rural Education and Small
  Schools Annual Conference, 710
Character Education: Restoring Respect &
  Responsibility in our Schools, 3569
Classroom Teacher's Guide for Working
  with Paraeducators Video Set, 3571
Closing the Achievement Gap, 3431
Conferencing with Students & Parents Video
  Series, 3573
Creating Schools of Character Video Series,
  3577
Critical Thinking Video Set, 3579
Cut & Paste, Master Teacher, 3495
Depco, 3640
Discipline Techniques you can Master in a
  Minute Video Series, 3582
Education Data, 890
Educational Resources, 897
Eleven Principals of Effective Character
  Educa tion, 3583
Finishing Strong: Your Personal Mentoring
  & Planning Guide for the Last 60 Days of
  Teaching, 3438
Fiscal Services & Quality Control, 3022
Four State Regional Technology Conference,
  3652
Great Classroom Management Series, 3586
Great Classroom Management Video Series,
  3587
Handling Chronically Disruptive Students at
  Risk Video Series, 3588
In-Box Master Teacher, 3501
Inclusion: The Next Step, 3441
Inclusion: The Next Step the Video Series,
  3592
Institute for Research in Learning Disabilitie
  s, 5098
Integrating Technology into the Classroom
  Vide o Series, 3593
Journalism Education Association, 307, 737,
  3510, 3510
Kansas Association of School Librarians, 485
Kansas Business Education Association, 486
Kansas Department of Education, 3023
Kansas Division of Special Education, 3024
Kansas Education Association, 487
Kansas Library Association, 488
Kansas School Boards Association
  Conference, 3332
Kansas United School Administrators
  Conference, 3333
Lesson Plans and Modifications for Inclusion
  a nd Collaborative Classrooms, 3595
Lesson Plans for the Substitue Teacher:
  Elementary Edition, 3444
Mary Jo Williams Charitable Trust, 2474
Master Teacher, 3597
Mentoring Teachers to Mastery, 3598

Motivating Students in the Classroom Video
  Ser ies, 3599
National Council on Rehabilitation
  Education, 108
National Teachers Hall of Fame, 3293
Paraeducator's Guide to Instructional &
  Curricular Modifications, 3513
Personal Planner & Traning Guide for the
  Paraeducator Video Set, 3603
Personal Planner and Training Guide for the
  Paraprofessional, 3453
Pittsburg State University, 3699
Professional Vision Master Teacher, 3518
Professor Master Teacher, 3519
Retaining Great Teachers, 3521
School-Wide Stratigies for Retaining Great
  Tea chers, 3606
Sprint Foundation, 2475
Students-at-Risk Video Series, 3610
Teaching for Results, 3473
Technology Pathfinder for Teachers Master
  Teacher, 3533
Three Rs Master Teacher, 3534
Training Video Series for the Substitute
  Teacher, 3615
Understanding and Relating To Parents
  Professionally, 3479
Welcome to Teaching and our Schools, 3480
Wichita Public Library, 2476
You Can Handle Them All, 3482
You Can Handle Them All Discipline Video
  Series, 3618
Your Personal Mentoring & Planning Guide
  for the First 60 Days of Teaching, 3483

Kentucky

Ashland Incorporated Foundation, 2477
Bluegrass Regional Recycling Corporation,
  850
Chief of Staff Bureau, 3025
Curriculum, Assessment & Accountability
  Services, 3027
EPPA Consulting, 884
Education Technology Office, 3028
Gheens Foundation, 2478
James Graham Brown Foundation, 2479
Kentucky Association of School
  Administrators, 941
Kentucky Business Education Association,
  489
Kentucky Department of Education, 3029
Kentucky Library Association, 490
Kentucky School Boards Association
  Conference, 3334
Kentucky School Media Association, 491
Kentucky School Superintendents
  Association Meeting, 3335
Kentucky State University, 3671
Learning Results Services Bureau, 3030
Louisville Free Public Library, 2480
Margaret Hall Foundation, 2481
Morehead State University, 3683
Office of Learning Programs Development,
  3031
Regional Services Centers, 3032
Southeast Regional Center for Drug-Free
  Schools & Communities, 5147
Special Instructional Services, 3033
Support Services Bureau on Learning, 3034
VV Cooke Foundation Corporation, 2482

Louisiana

Academic Programs Office, 3036
Advance Program for Young Scholars, 5
Basics Plus, 847
Baton Rouge Area Foundation, 2483
Booth-Bricker Fund, 2484
East Baton Rouge Parish Library, 2485
Educational Support Programs, 3037
Fred B & Ruth B Zigler Foundation, 2486
Louisiana Association of Business
  Educators, 492
Louisiana Association of Educators, 493
Louisiana Association of School Business
  Officials, 494
Louisiana Children's Research Center for
  Development & Learning, 948
Louisiana Department of Education, 3038
Louisiana Library Association, 495
Louisiana School Boards Association
  Conference, 3338
Management & Finance Office, 3039
Mid-South Educational Research Association
  Annual Meeting, 3345
National Association of Substance Abuse
  Trainers & Educators, 221
New Orleans Public Library, 2487
Office of Vocational Education, 3040
Research & Development Office, 3041
Shreve Memorial Library, 2488
Special Education Services, 2925, 3042

Maine

Applied Technology & Adult Learning, 3043
Clarence E Mulford Trust, 2489
Council on International Educational
  Exchange, 258
Division of Compensatory Education, 3044
Harold Alfond Trust, 2490
Information Exchange, 5097
Institute for Global Ethics, 927
Maine Association of School Libraries, 496
Maine Business Education Association, 497
Maine Department of Education, 3045
Maine Education Association, 498
Maine Library Association, 499
Maine Principals Association Conference,
  3339

Maryland

ACCESS ERIC, 1
Abell Foundation, 2491
Aegon USA, 2492
Aid for Education, 2845
American Association of Physics Teachers
  National Meeting, 665
American Dance Therapy Association, 331
American Speech-Language-Hearing
  Association, 303, 683, 3267, 3267
Association for Childhood Education
  International Annual Conference, 632
Association for International Practical
  Training, 232
Association for Persons with Severe
  Handicaps Annual Conference, 696

Beverly Celotta, 849
CHADD: Children & Adults with Attention Deficit/Hyperactivity Disorder, 32, 706
Career Technology & Adult Learning, 3046
Center for Research on the Education of Students Placed at Risk, 5080
Center for Social Organization of Schools, 5081
Certification & Accreditation, 3047
Childhood Education Association International, 636
Childrens Youth Funding Report, 2848
Clarence Manger & Audrey Cordero Plitt Trust, 2493
Clark-Winchcole Foundation, 2494
Commonwealth Foundation, 2495
Compensatory Education & Support Services, 3048
District of Columbia Business Education Association, 450
Division of Business Services, 3049
Dr. Anthony A Cacossa, 883
Dresher Foundation, 2496
Drug Information & Strategy Clearinghouse, 47
ERIC Clearinghouse on Assessment & Evaluation, 49
Educational Systems for the Future, 900
Edward E Ford Foundation, 2497
Enoch Pratt Free Library, 2498
France-Merrick Foundation, 2499
Grayce B Kerr Fund, 2500
Henry & Ruth Blaustein Rosenberg Foundation, 2501
Hummel Sweets, 2854
Instruction Division, 3050
International Association for the Exchange of Students for Technical Experience, 268
International Association of Pupil Personnel Workers, 162
International Clearinghouse for the Advancement of Science Teaching, 3594
International Dyslexia Association, 306
International Dyslexia Association Annual Conference, 645
International Performance Improvement Conferen ce Expo, 735
International Society for Performance Improvement, 72
James M Johnston Trust for Charitable and Educational Purposes, 2502
John W Kluge Foundation, 2503
Learner-Centered, 652
Learning Independence Through Computers, 402
Library Development & Services, 3051
Longview Foundation for Education in World Affairs/International Understanding, 2805
Mainstream, 203
Marion I & Henry J Knott Foundation, 2504
Maryland Center for Career and Technology Education, 3679
Maryland Department of Education, 3052
Maryland Educational Media Organization, 500
Maryland Educational Opportunity Center, 955
Maryland Elco Incorporated Educational Funding Company, 956
Maryland Library Association, 501
Maryland State Teachers Association, 502

National Association of School Psychologists Annual Convention, 219, 760
National Clearinghouse for Alcohol & Drug Information, 5119
National Council for the Social Studies, 385
National Data Bank for Disabled Student Services, 174
National Institute of Child Health and Human Development, 2892
National School Public Relations Association, 122
National School Supply & Equipment Association, 784
National Women's Studies Association, 129, 3283
Performance Improvement Journal, 3515
Planning, Results & Information Management, 3053
Robert G & Anne M Merrick Foundation, 2505
School Equipment Show, 793
Success for All Foundation, 1018
T-Shirt People/Wearhouse, 2862
Teacher Magazine, 3527
Teaching as the Learning Profession: Handbook of Policy and Practice, 3472
University Research, 1025

Massachusetts

ART New England Summer Workshops, 3620
Annual New England Kindergarten Conference, 3305
Associated Grantmakers of Massachusetts, 2506
Beacon Education Management, 848
Boston Foundation, 2507
Boston Globe Foundation II, 2508
Boston Public Library, 2509
Carney Sandoe & Associates, 855
Center on Families, Schools, Communities & Children's Learning, 5085
Civic Practices Network, 37
Clearinghouse for Immigrant Education, 38
Corporate Design Foundation, 873
Critical Issues in Urban Special Education: The Implications of Whole-School Change, 3634
Critical and Creative Thinking in the Classroom, 3635
Dean Foundation for Little Children, 2510
E-S Sports Screenprint Specialists, 2850
EF Educational Tours, 48
Education Development Center, 55, 891
Educational Placement Sources-US, 3497
Educational Register, 59
Educational Technology Center, 400
Effective Strategies for School Reform, 3644
Efficacy Institute, 906
Excellence in Teaching Cabinet Grant, 3289
Facing History & Ourselves, 61
George I Alden Trust, 2829
Harvard Institute for School Leadership, 3655
Harvard Seminar for Superintendents, 3656
Hyams Foundation, 2511
International Physicians for the Prevention of Nuclear War, 276
Irene E & George A Davis Foundation, 2512
James G Martin Memorial Trust, 2513

Jessie B Cox Charitable Trust, 2514
KidsCare Childcare Management Software, 3542
LG Balfour Foundation, 2515
Leadership and the New Technologies, 3674
Learning & The Enneagram, 3675
Linkage, 945
List of Regional, Professional & Specialized Accrediting Association, 3446
Little Family Foundation, 2516
Massachusetts Business Educators Association, 503
Massachusetts Department of Education, 3056
Massachusetts Department of Educational Improvement, 3057
Massachusetts Elementary School Principals Association Conference, 3340
Massachusetts Library Association, 504
Massachusetts School Boards Association Meeting, 3341
Massachusetts Teachers Association, 505
Media and American Democracy, 3680
Meeting the Tide of Rising Expectations, 741
Merrimack Education Center, 962, 5102
NASDTEC Knowledge Base, 3450
National Association of State Directors of Teacher Education & Certification, 169, 3277
National Coalition of Advocates for Students, 98
National Commission for Cooperative Education, 101
National Evaluation Systems, 975
National Teachers Clearinghouse, 207
New England History Teachers Association, 386
New England Kindergarten Conference, 3372
New England League of Middle Schools, 3373
New England Library Association, 506
Pennsylvania School Librarians Association, 571
Polaroid Education Program, 3700
Principals' Center Spring Institute Conference, 3397
Project Zero Classroom, 3703
Recruiting New Teachers, 3284
Region 1: Education Department, 3058
Regional Laboratory for Educational Improvement of the Northeast, 5139
Rogers Family Foundation, 2517
Standards and Accountability: Their Impact on Teaching and Assessment, 3712
State Street Foundation, 2518
Sudbury Foundation, 2519
TERC, 5153
TUV Product Service, 3718
Technical Education Research Centers, 1022
Time to Teach, Time to Learn: Changing the Pace of School, 3476
Timothy Anderson Dovetail Consulting, 1024
Trustees of the Ayer Home, 2520
Uplinc, 1027
Weld Foundation, 2521
Western Massachusetts Funding Resource Center, 2522
William E Schrafft & Bertha E Schrafft Charita ble Trust, 2523
Women's Educational & Industrial Union, 153
Woodstock Corporation, 2524
Worcester Public Library, 2525

Michigan

AVKO Dyslexia Research Foundation, 5075
Accuracy Temporary Services Incorporated, 837
Adult Extended Learning Office, 3060
Alex & Marie Manoogian Foundation, 2526
Association for Asian Studies, 230
Association for Behavior Analysis Annual Convention, 694
Association for Gender Equity Leadership in Education, 22
Association for the Study of Higher Education Annual Meeting, 702
Charles Stewart Mott Foundation, 2527
Childs Consulting Associates, 862
Chrysler Corporate Giving Program, 2528
Clonlara School Annual Conference Home Educato rs, 805
Community Foundation for Southeastern Michigan, 2529
Community Foundation of Greater Flint, 2530
Cronin Foundation, 2531
Detroit Edison Foundation, 2532
Effective Schools Products, 904
Extensions - Newsletter of the High/Scope Curriculum, 3499
Ford Motor Company Fund, 2533
Frey Foundation, 2534
General Motors Foundation, 2535
Grand Rapids Foundation, 2536
Harry A & Margaret D Towsley Foundation, 2537
Henry Ford Centennial Library, 2538
Herbert H & Grace A Dow Foundation, 2539
Herrick Foundation, 2540
Higher Education Management Office, 3062
Innovator, 3503
Instructional Programs, 3063
International Council of Scientific Unions Committee on Science Teaching, 373
Kresge Foundation, 2541
Leona Group, 944
Malpass Foundation, 2542
McGregor Fund, 2543
Michigan Association for Media in Education, 507
Michigan Association of Elementary and Middle School Principals Conference, 3342
Michigan Association of School Administrators, 508
Michigan Department of Education, 3064
Michigan Education Association, 509
Michigan Education Council, 963
Michigan Elementary & Middle School Principals Association, 510
Michigan Library Association, 511
Michigan School Boards Association Fall Leadership Conference, 3343
Michigan Science Teachers Association Annual Conference, 3344
Michigan State University Libraries, 2544
NCRTL Special Report, 3511
National Center for Community Education, 3278
National Center for Research on Teacher Learning, 5113
National Conference on Parent Involvement, 102
National Heritage Academies, 976

National Homeschool Association, 116
National Student Assistance Conference, 786
North American Students of Cooperation, 134
Office of School Management, 3065
Office of the Superintendent, 3066
Postsecondary Services, 3067
Professional Development Workshops, 3702
Rebus, 999
Richard & Helen DeVos Foundation, 2545
Rollin M Gerstacker Foundation, 2546
SAP Today, 3605
School Program Quality, 3068
Steelcase Foundation, 2547
Student Financial Assistance, 3070
Teacher & Administrative Preparation, 3071
University of Michigan-Dearborn Center for Corporate & Professional Development, 3726
Wayne State University, 2548
Whirlpool Foundation, 2549

Minnesota

Alliance for Schools That Work, 7
Andersen Foundation, 2550
Bush Foundation, 2551
Cargill Foundation, 2552
Center for Educational Policy Studies, 35
Center for Global Education, 3626
Charles & Ellora Alliss Educational Foundation, 2553
Closing the Gap, 713
Communicating for Agriculture, 250
Data & Technology, 3072
Data Management, 3073
Designs for Learning, 881
Duluth Public Library, 2554
Education Funding, 3074
Education Minnesota, 512
Emerging Technology Consultants, 907
Examiner Corporation, 910
FR Bigelow Foundation, 2555
Financial Conditions & Aids Payment, 3075
First Bank System Foundation, 2556
Graduate Programs for Professional Educators, 3653
Hiawatha Education Foundation, 2557
Higher Education Consortium, 917
Human Resources Office, 2940, 3077
IA O'Shaughnessy Foundation, 2558
INFOCOMM Tradeshow, 728
Innovative Programming Systems, 923
Insight, 924
Marbrook Foundation, 2559
Medtronic Foundation, 2560
Minneapolis Foundation, 2561
Minneapolis Public Library, 2562
Minnesota Business Educators, 513
Minnesota Congress of Parents, Teachers & Students, 514
Minnesota Department of Children, Families & Learning, 3078
Minnesota Department of Education, 3079
Minnesota Leadership Annual Conference, 3347
Minnesota Library Association, 515
Minnesota School Administrators Association, 3348
Minnesota School Boards Association, 516
Minnesota School Boards Association Annual Meeting, 3349

National Computer Systems, 3689
Otto Bremer Foundation, 2563
PACER Center, 138
Parent Training Resources, 3452
Residential Schools, 3080
Saint Paul Foundation, 2564
Scholarship America, 2876
TCF Foundation, 2565
Training & Presentations, 3412

Mississippi

Community Outreach Services, 3081
Educational Consultants of Oxford, 893
Educational Innovations, 3082
External Relations, 3083
Foundation for the Mid South, 2566
JJ Jones Consultants, 933
Jackson-Hinds Library System, 2567
Management Information Systems, 3084
Mississippi Advocate For Education, 517
Mississippi Business Education Association, 518
Mississippi Department of Education, 3085
Mississippi Employment Security Commission, 3086
Mississippi Library Association, 519
Mississippi Power Foundation, 2568
Office of Accountability, 3087
Phil Hardin Foundation, 2569
Vocational Technical Education, 3088

Missouri

Advocates for Language Learning Annual Meeting, 657
Ameren Corporation Charitable Trust, 2570
American Council on Education for Journalism, 301
Clearinghouse for Midcontinent Foundations, 2571
College of the Ozarks, 3632
Danforth Foundation, 2572
Deputy Commissioner, 3089
Division of Instruction, 3090
Enid & Crosby Kemper Foundation, 2573
Hall Family Foundation, 2574
Instructional Materials Laboratory, 5099
James S McDonnell Foundation, 2575
Kansas City Public Library, 2576
Mary Ranken Jordan & Ettie A Jordan Charitable Foundation, 2577
McDonnell Douglas Foundation, 2578
Missouri Association of Elementary School Principals, 520
Missouri Association of Secondary School Principals, 521
Missouri Business Education Association, 522
Missouri Congress of Parents & Teachers, 523
Missouri Department of Education, 3091
Missouri LINC, 5106
Missouri Library Association, 524
Missouri Library Association Conference, 826
Missouri National Education Association Conference, 525, 3350

Missouri School Boards Association Annual Meeting, 3351
Missouri State Teachers Association, 526
Missouri State Teachers Association Conference, 3352
Monsanto Fund, 2579
Montana Association of School Librarians, 528
National Council on Alcoholism & Drug Abuse, 772
Parents Rights Organization, 139
Parents as Teachers National Center, 790, 5136
People to People International, 289
Region 7: Education Department, 3092
Senior Researcher Award, 3295
Special Education Division, 3093
Supplemental Instruction, Supervisor Workshops, 3716
Urban & Teacher Education, 3094
Vocational & Adult Education, 2914, 3095
Vocational Rehabilitation, 2935, 3096

Montana

Accreditation & Curriculum Services Department, 3097
Council for Indian Education, 383
Division of Information-Technology Support, 3098
Eastern Montana College Library, 2580
Montana Association of County School Superintendents, 527
Montana Association of Elementary School Principals Conference, 3353
Montana Business Education Association, 529
Montana Department of Education, 3099
Montana High School Association Conference, 819
Montana Library Association, 530
Montana School Boards Association, 969
Montana State Library, 2581
Operations Department, 3100
Parents, Let's Unite for Kids, 140

Nebraska

Administrative Services Office, 3059, 3101
Central States Conference on the Teaching of Foreign Languages, 3314
Division of Education Services, 3102
Dr. CC & Mabel L Criss Memorial Foundation, 2582
National Contact Hotline, 352
National Federation of Modern Language Teacher s Association, 310
Nebraska Department of Education, 3103
Nebraska Library Association, 531
Nebraska School Boards Association Annual Conference, 820
Nebraska State Business Education Association, 532
Nebraska State Education Association, 533
Rehabilitation Services Division, 3054, 3104
Thomas D Buckley Trust, 2583
W Dale Clark Library, 2584

Nevada

Administrative & Financial Services, 3105
Conrad N Hilton Foundation, 2585
Cord Foundation, 2586
Donald W Reynolds Foundation, 2587
EL Wiegand Foundation, 2588
Las Vegas-Clark County, 2589
National Conference on Standards and Assessment, 3358
Nevada Department of Education, 3107
Nevada Library Association, 534
Nevada State Education Association, 535
Washoe County Library, 2590

New Hampshire

Academy of Applied Science, 362
Center for Resource Management, 859
Information Services, 3108
Interlocken Center for Experiential Learning, 201
International Graduate School, 3662
Iteachk, 736
Lincolnshire, 2591
New Hampshire Business Education Association, 536
New Hampshire Charitable Foundation, 2592
New Hampshire Department of Education, 3109
New Hampshire Division of Instructional Services, 3110
New Hampshire Education Association, 537
New Hampshire Library Association, 538
Plymouth State College, 2593
Sports Shoes & Apparel, 2860
Standards & Certification Division, 3111

New Jersey

A+ Enterprises, 2844
AAA Teacher's Agency, 193
Association for the Care of Children's Health, 26
Association for the Education of Gifted Underachieving Students Conference, 701
Committee on Continuing Education for School Personnel, 3270
Community Foundation of New Jersey, 2594
Education Management Consulting LLC, 892
Educational Data Service, 895
Educational Information & Resource Center, 896, 5090
Educational Media Association of New Jersey, 539
Educational Publishing Summit: Creating Managi ng & Selling Content, 721
Educational Summit, 3643
Educational Testing Service, 902, 5093
Foundation for Student Communication, 63
Fund for New Jersey, 2595
Fundraising USA, 2851
Gifted Child Society, 65
Gifted Child Society Conference, 725
Global Learning, 263
Hoechst Celanese Foundation, 2596
Honeywell Foundation, 2597

Hyde & Watson Foundation, 2598
International Schools Services, 278
Lab Volt Systems, 3673
M&M Mars Fundraising, 2855
Mary Owen Borden Memorial Foundation, 2599
Mason Associates, 957
Merck Company Foundation, 2600
Middle States Council for the Social Studies Annual Regional Conference, 3346
National Coalition for Sex Equity in Education, 766
New Jersey Department of Education, 3112
New Jersey Department of Education: Finance, 3113
New Jersey Division of Special Education, 3114
New Jersey Education Association, 540
New Jersey Library Association, 541
New Jersey School Boards Association Annual Meeting, 811
New Jersey State Department of Education Resource Center, 542
New Jersey State Library, 3115
Odyssey of the Mind, 136
Outdoor Education Association, 137
Performance Learning Systems, 3697
Pro Libra, 322
Professional Development & Licensing, 3116
Prudential Foundation, 2601
Relearning by Design, 1003
Sensa of New Jersey, 1010
Strategies for Educational Change, 1017
Teach Overseas, 293
Teacher's Guide to Classroom Management, 3528
Telemetrics, 409
Training Research Journal: The Science and Practice of Training, 3536
Troll Book Fairs, 2863
Turrell Fund, 2602
Urban & Field Services, 3117
Victoria Foundation, 2603
Warner-Lambert Charitable Foundation, 2604
Wilf Family Foundation, 2605

New Mexico

Agency Support, 3118
American Indian Science & Engineering Society Annual Conference, 676
Dale J Bellamah Foundation, 2606
Learning Services, 3119
National Association for Legal Support of Alternative Schools, 86
National Coalition of Alternative Community Schools, 99, 767
National Council on Student Development, 109
National Education Association of New Mexico, 543
National Information Center for Educational Media, 5124
New Mexico Business Education Association, 544
New Mexico Department of Education, 3120
New Mexico Department of School-Transportation & Support Services, 3121
New Mexico Library Association, 545

New Mexico School Boards Association Conference Annual Meeting, 3374
New Mexico State Library, 2607
RD & Joan Dale Hubbard Foundation, 2608
School Management Accountability, 3122
Southwest Comprehensive Regional Assistance Center-Region IX, 5149
Western History Association, 390
Western History Association Annual Meeting, 836

New York

Achelis Foundation, 2609
Adrian & Jessie Archbold Charitable Trust, 2610
African-American Institute, 380
Alfred P Sloan Foundation, 2611
Alliance for Parental Involvement in Education, 6
Altman Foundation, 2612
Ambrose Monell Foundation, 2613
American Association for Chinese Studies, 381
American Council for Drug Education, 12
American Educational Research Journal, 3487
American Express Foundation, 2614
American Montessori Society, 17
American Montessori Society Conference, 679
American-Scandinavian Foundation, 2867
Andrew W Mellon Foundation, 2615
Annual Convention, 3304
Arnold Bernhard Foundation, 2616
Arts Management in Community Institutions: Sum mer Training, 3489
Arts Scholarships, 2868
Association for Advancement of Behavior Therapy Annual Convention, 693
Association for World Travel Exchange, 233
Atran Foundation, 2617
Beatrice P Delany Charitable Trust, 2618
Better Chance, 31
Bienvenue Annual Conference, 634
Bodman Foundation, 2619
Bristol-Myers Squibb Foundation, 2620
British American Educational Foundation, 242
Bryant and Stratton College, 3624
Buffalo & Erie County Public Library, 2621
Business Education Association of Metro New York, 546
Business Teachers Association of New York State, 547
CDS International, 244
CUNY Teacher Incentive Program, 2869
Caleb C & Julia W Dula Educational & Charitable Foundation, 2622
Capital Cities-ABC Corporate Giving Program, 2623
Carl & Lily Pforzheimer Foundation, 2624
Carnegie Corporation of New York, 2625
Catholic Medical Mission Board, 247
Center for Education Studies, 382
Center for Educational Innovation, 857
Center for Technology in Education, 5082
Center on Human Policy, 36
Chase Manhattan Corporation Philanthropy Department, 2626

Christian A Johnson Endeavor Foundation, 2627
Classroom, 863
Cleveland H Dodge Foundation, 2628
College Board, 359, 2870
College Entrance Examination Board, 866
Competency-Based Framework for Professional Development of Certified Health Specialists, 3433
Cordell Hull Foundation for International Education, 253
Council for Aid to Education, 875
Council for Jewish Education, 42
Council on Foreign Relations, 256
Cowles Charitable Trust, 2629
Cultural Education, 3124
Daisy Marquis Jones Foundation, 2630
DeWitt Wallace-Reader's Digest Fund, 2631
Delmar Thomson Learning, 3639
Dissertation Fellowships in the Humanities, 2871
ERIC Clearinghouse on Urban Education, 52
Edison Schools, 888
Edna McConnell Clark Foundation, 2632
Education Index, 3540
Educational Equity Concepts, 58
Educational Products Information Exchange Institute, 5091
Edward John Noble Foundation, 2633
Edward W Hazen Foundation, 2634
Edwin Gould Foundation for Children, 2635
Elaine E & Frank T Powers Jr Foundation, 2636
Elementary School Center for Advocacy & Policy on Behalf of Children, 189
Elementary, Middle & Secondary Education, 3125
Elmer & Mamdouha Bobst Foundation, 2637
Epie Institute, 908
Equitable Foundation, 2638
Equity 2000, 326
Eye on Education, 3585
Festo Corporation, 3650
Ford Foundation, 2639
Foundation Center, 2827
Frances & Benjamin Benenson Foundation, 2640
George Dehne & Associates, 915
George F Baker Trust, 2641
George Link Jr Foundation, 2642
Girls Incorporated, 66
Gladys & Roland Harriman Foundation, 2643
Gladys Brooks Foundation, 2644
Green Fund, 2645
Guild Notes Bi-Monthly Newswletter, 3500
Hagedorn Fund, 2646
Hasbro Children's Foundation, 2647
Henry Luce Foundation, 2648
Herman Goldman Foundation, 2649
Hess Foundation, 2650
Higher & Professional Education, 3126
Hitting the High Notes of Literacy, 727
Horace W Goldsmith Foundation, 2651
Human Resources Center, 68
Human-i-Tees, 2853
IBM Corporate Support Program, 2652
Independent Living, 69
Information Center on Education, 5096
Institute of International Education, 265
International Association of Students in Economics & Business Management, 269
International Baccalaureate North America, 270

International Center for Leadership in Education, 929
International Institutional Services, 274
Island Drafting & Technical Institute, 3664
J&Kalb Associates, 931
JI Foundation, 2653
JP Associates Incorporated, 934
JP Morgan Charitable Trust, 2654
Jewish Education Service of North America, 73
Jewish Educators Assembly, 74
Jewish Foundation for Education of Women, 2874
Jewish Teachers Association, 75
Joukowsky Family Foundation, 2655
Julia R & Estelle L Foundation, 2656
Leon Lowenstein Foundation, 2657
Levittown Public Library, 2658
Life Skills Training, 3445
Literacy Volunteers of America National Conference, 738
Louis & Anne Abrons Foundation, 2659
MacMillan Guide to Correspondence Study, 3447
Magi Educational Services Incorporated, 951
Margaret L Wendt Foundation, 2660
Martin De Porress, 548
McGraw-Hill Foundation, 2661
Modern Language Association Annual Conference, 742
Mosaica Education, 972
NCSIE Inservice, 3512
National Academy Foundation Annual Institute for Staff Development, 748
National Association for Industry-Education Cooperation, 85
National Center for Learning Disabilities, 97
National Center for the Study of Privatization in Education, 5115
National Center on Education & the Economy, 974, 5116
National Child Labor Committee, 5118
National Clearinghouse for Information on Business Involvement in Education, 5121
National Council of Administrative Women in Education, 172
National Education Association of New York, 549
National Guild of Community Schools of the Arts Conference, 340, 775
National Reading Styles Institute, 977
National Reading Styles Institute Conference, 779
National Research Center on English Learning and Achievement, 313
New York Department of Education, 3127
New York Foundation, 2662
New York Library Association, 550
New York School Superintendents Association Annual Meeting, 3375
New York Science Teachers Association Annual Meeting, 3376
New York State Council of Student Superintendents Forum, 812
New York State United Teachers Conference, 3377
New York Teachers Math Association Conference, 3378
Northeast Regional Center for Drug-Free Schools & Communities, 5131
Operation Crossroads Africa, 286
Orators & Philosophers: A History of the Idea of Liberal Education, 3451

Palisades Educational Foundation, 2663
Phoenix Learning Resources Conference, 831
Princeton Review, 990
ProLiteracy Worldwide, 353
Professional Responsibility Office, 3128
Public Relations Student Society of America, 142
Quality Education Development, 997
Quality School Teacher, 3458
Quantum Performance Group, 998
Region 2: Education Department, 3129
Regional Learning Service of Central New York, 1001
Robert Sterling Clark Foundation, 2664
Rochester Public Library, 2665
Ronald S Lauder Foundation, 2666
Rookey Associates, 1006
SH & Helen R Scheuer Family Foundation, 2667
SUNY College at Oswego, 3706
Samuel & May Rudin Foundation, 2668
Scholarships in the Health Professions, 2877
Seth Sprague Educational and Charitable Foundation, 2669
Sexuality Information & Education Council of the US, 146
Sidney Kreppel, 1012
Society for the Advancement of Education, 147
Starr Foundation, 2670
Stewart Howe Alumni Service of New York, 1016
Superintendents Work Conference, 3405
Teachers & Writers Collaborative, 315
Teachers College: Columbia University, 3720
Tiger Foundation, 2671
Tisch Foundation, 2672
Travelers Group, 2673
United Nations Development Program, 295
United States-Japan Foundation, 2840
Vocational & Educational Services for Disabled, 3130
White Plains Public Library, 2674
William Randolph Hearst Foundation, 2675
William T Grant Foundation, 2676

North Carolina

AE Finley Foundation, 2677
Auxiliary Services, 3131
Cannon Foundation, 2678
Cisco Educational Archives, 3570
Dickson Foundation, 2679
Duke Endowment, 2680
ERIC Clearinghouse on Counseling & Student Services, 217
Financial & Personnel Services, 3132
First Union University, 2681
Foundation for the Carolinas, 2682
Kathleen Price and Joseph M Bryan Family Foundation, 2683
Mary Reynolds Babcock Foundation, 2684
Master Woodcraft Inc., 740
Measurement, 960
Musikgarten, 3685
National Association of Principals of Schools for Girls, 166
National Early Childhood Technical Assistance System, 184, 5123
National Society for Experiential Education Conference, 123, 785

Non-Profit Resource Center/Pack Memorial Library, 2685
North Carolina Association for Career and Technical Education Conference, 3380
North Carolina Association for Career and Technical Education, 551
North Carolina Association of Educators, 552
North Carolina Business Education Association, 553
North Carolina Department of Education, 3133
North Carolina Department of Instructional Services, 3134
North Carolina Department of Public Instructio n, 554
North Carolina Library Association, 555
North Carolina School Administrators Conference, 3381
Paideia Group, 3694
Poetry Alive, 987
SERVE, 5141
SERVE Conference, 792
Staff Development & Technical Assistance, 3135
State Library of North Carolina, 2686
William R Kenan Jr Charitable Trust, 2687
Winston-Salem Foundation, 2688
Women Educators, 152
Z Smith Reynolds Foundation, 2689

North Dakota

ATEA Journal, 3485
American Technical Education Association Annual Conference, 684
Myra Foundation, 2690
North Dakota Business and Office Education Association, 556
North Dakota Department of Education, 3136
North Dakota Department of Public Instruction Division, 3137
North Dakota Education Association, 557
North Dakota Library Association, 558
North Dakota State Board for Vocational & Technical Education, 3138
North Dakota Vocational Educational Planning Conference, 821
Study & State Film Library, 3139
Tom & Frances Leach Foundation, 2691

Ohio

Akron Community Foundation, 2692
American Association for Employment in Education Annual Conference, 659
American Educational Studies Association, 675, 3264
American Foundation Corporation, 2693
American School Health Association, 19
American School Health Association's National School Conference, 682
Analog & Digital Peripherals, 3538
Association for Disabled Students, 21
Association for Integrative Studies, 23
Association for Technology Educators, 559
Balance Sheet, 3490
Blind School, 3140
Brief Legal Guide for the Independent Teacher, 3429

Burton D Morgan Foundation, 2694
Center for Learning, 5078
Creative Learning Consultants, 877
Curriculum, Instruction & Professional Development, 3141
Dayton Foundation, 2695
Direct Instructional Support Systems, 882
E-Z Grader Software, 3539
ERIC Clearinghouse for Science, Math & Environ mental Education, 368
Early Childhood Education, 3142
Edison Welding Institute, 3642
Education Concepts, 889
Educational Theatre Association Conference, 722
Eisenhower National Clearinghouse for Mathemat ics and Science Education, 325, 369
Emco Maier Corporation, 3647
Eva L & Joseph M Bruening Foundation, 2696
Fastech, 3649
Federal Assistance, 3143
GAR Foundation, 2697
George Gund Foundation, 2698
Gold Medal Products, 2852
Hearlihy & Company, 3589
Hobart Institute of Welding Technology, 3657
Hoover Foundation, 2699
Industrial Training Institute, 3659
Institute for Development of Educational Activities, 70, 926
International Thespian Society, 334
Journal on Excellence in College Teaching, 3509
Kent State University, 3670
Kettering Fund, 2700
Kulas Foundation, 2701
Lilly Conference on College Teaching, 3336
Louise H & David S Ingalls Foundation, 2702
Louise Taft Semple Foundation, 2703
Marketing Education Resource Center, 954
Martha Holden Jennings Foundation, 2704
Mead Corporation Foundation, 2705
Music Teachers Association National Conference, 744
Music Teachers National Association, 336, 5107
National Black Alliance for Graduate Level Education, 95
National Career Development Association Conference, 3356
National Center for Science Teaching & Learning, 5114
National Council for History Education Conference, 3360
National Middle School Association, 118, 361, 3281, 3281
National Middle School Association's Annual Conference and Exhibition, 3368
National School Safety and Security Services, 978
National Staff Development Council, 3282
Nord Family Foundation, 2706
North American Montessori Teachers' Association, 789
Ohio Association of School Business Officials, 560
Ohio Association of Secondary School Administrators, 561
Ohio Bell Telephone Contribution Program, 2707

Ohio Business Teachers Association, 3388
Ohio Department of Education, 3144
Ohio Library Council, 562
Ohio Library Council Trade Show, 814
Ohio Public School Employees Association Convention, 3389
Ohio School Boards Association Capital Conference & Trade Show, 815
Ohio Secondary School Administrators Association Fall Conference, 3390
Ohio State Library Foundation Center, 2708
Ome Resa, 980
Owens Community College, 3693
Owens-Corning Foundation, 2709
Personnel Services, 2987, 3145
Procter & Gamble Fund, 2710
Public Library of Cincinnati, 2711
Reading Recovery Council of North America, 354
Root Learning, 1007
School Finance, 2998, 3146
School Food Service, 3147
School March by Public Priority Systems, 1009
School for the Deaf, 3148
Student Development, 3150
Students Forum, 149
Summit Vision, 150
Teacher Education & Certification, 3003, 3035, 3151, 3151
Thomas J Emery Memorial, 2712
Timken Foundation of Canton, 2713
Today's Catholic Teacher, 3535
Tooling University, 3722
Vocational & Career Education, 3152
Wolfe Associates, 2714

Oklahoma

Accreditation & Standards Division, 3153
At-Risk Students: Identification and Assistance Strategies, 3567
Center for the Study of Small/Rural Schools, 5084
Conflict Resolution Strategies in Schools, 3574
Cooperative Learning Strategies, 3576
Crisis Management in Schools, 3578
Curriculum Alignment: Improving Student Learning, 3580
Education Extension, 56
Federal/Special/Collaboration Services, 3154
Grace & Franklin Bernsen Foundation, 2715
Improving Parent/Educator Relationships, 3590
Improving Student Thinking in the Content Area, 3591
Managing Students Without Coercion, 3596
Mervin Bovaird Foundation, 2716
Multicultural Education: Teaching to Diversity, 3600
National Association of Trade & Industrial Instructors, 94
National Rural Education Association Annual Convention, 781
Oklahoma City University, 2717
Oklahoma Department of Career and Technology Education, 3155
Oklahoma Department of Education, 3156
Oklahoma Department of Education; Financial Services, 3157

Oklahoma Education Association, 563
Oklahoma Library Association, 564
Oklahoma School Boards Association & School Administrators Conference, 3391
Outcome-Based Education: Making it Work, 3601
Overview of Prevention: A Social Change Model, 3602
Professional Services, 2923, 3158
Public Service Company of Oklahoma Corporate Giving Program, 2718
Quality School, 3604
Retention in Education Today for All Indigenous Nations, 791
Samuel Roberts Noble Foundation, 2719
School Improvement, 3159
Site-Based Management, 3607
Southwest Independent Schools Association, 148
Southwestern Oklahoma State University, 3709
Strategic Planning for Outcome-Based Education, 3608
Strengthening the Family: An Overview of a Hol istic Family Wellness Model, 3609
Superintendent/School Board Relationships, 3611
TQM: Implementing Quality Management in Your School, 3612
Teacher Link: An Interactive National Teleconference, 796
Teachers as Heros, 3613
Teaching for Intelligent Behavior, 3614
www.positivepins.com, 2865

Oregon

Aprovecho Institute, 228
Assessment & Evaluation, 3160
Collins Foundation, 2720
Community College Services, 3161
Compensatory Education Office, 3162
Deputy Superintendent Office, 3163
ERIC Clearinghouse on Educational Management, 159
Early Childhood Council, 3164
Ford Family Foundation, 2721
Future Music Oregon, 333
Government Relations, 3076, 3165
Interface Network, 928
International Society for Technology in Education, 401
Management Services, 2889, 3166
Measurement Learning Consultants, 961
Meyer Memorial Trust, 2722
Mpulse Maintenance Software, 3684
Multnomah County Library, 2723
National Parent-Teacher Association Annual Convention & Exhibition, 778
North American Association of Educational Negotiators, 132
Northwest Regional Educational Laboratory, 3387, 5133
Office of Field, Curriculum & Instruction Services, 3167
Oregon Association of Student Councils, 565
Oregon Community Foundation, 2724
Oregon Department of Education, 3168
Oregon Education Association, 566
Oregon Educational Media Association, 567
Oregon Federation of Teachers, 568

Oregon Library Association, 569
Oregon School Boards Association Annual Convention, 3392
Pacific Northwest Council on Languages Annual Conference, 3393
Prevention Researcher, 3517
Professional Technical Education, 3169
Student Services Office, 3171
TACS/WRRC, 5152
Tektronix Foundation, 2725
Twenty First Century Schools Council, 3172

Pennsylvania

Alcoa Foundation, 2726
American Foundation for Negro Affairs, 3265
American Friends Service Committee, 224
American Musicological Society, 332
Annenberg Foundation, 2727
Arcadia Foundation, 2728
Aspira of Penna, 843
Attention Deficit Disorder Association, 29
Audrey Hillman Fisher Foundation, 2729
Auerbach Central Agency for Jewish Education Incorporated, 846
Bayer Corporation, 2730
Bayer/NSF Award for Community Innovation, 3288
Buhl Foundation, 2731
Chief of Staff Office, 3174
Connelly Foundation, 2732
Dutch Mill Bulbs, 2849
Eden Hall Foundation, 2733
Education & Treatment of Children, 3496
Elementary Education Professional Development School, 3646
Erie County Library System, 2734
Foundation Center-Carnegie Library of Pittsbur gh, 2735
Friends Council on Education, 64
Graphic Arts Technical Foundation, 199
HJ Heinz Company Foundation, 2736
Higher Education/Postsecondary Office, 3175
International Association of School Librarians hip, 320
International Studies Association, 280
John McShain Charities, 2737
K'nex Education Division, 3668
Lawrence A Heller Associates, 943
Learning Disabilities Association of America International Conference, 78, 653
Learning Research and Development Center, 5100
Mary Hillman Jennings Foundation, 2738
McCune Foundation, 2739
Mid-Atlantic Regional Educational Laboratory, 5103
Millersville University, 3682
Montgomery Intermediate Unit 23, 970
National Association for Research in Science Teaching, 374
National Association of Catholic School Teachers, 89
National Center on Education in the Inner Cities, 5117
Northeast Conference on the Teaching of Foreign Languages, 3384
Northeast Regional Christian Schools Internati onal Association, 813
Office of Elementary and Secondary Education, 3176

Office of the Comptroller, 3177
Opportunities Industrialization Centers International, 287
Parsifal Systems, 983
Pennsylvania Council for the Social Studies Conference, 3394
Pennsylvania Department of Education, 3178
Pennsylvania Education, 3514
Pennsylvania Library Association, 570
Pennsylvania School Boards Association Annual Meeting, 3395
Pennsylvania Science Teachers Association, 3396
Pennsylvania State Education Association, 572
Pennsylvania State University-Workforce Educat ion & Development Program, 3696
Pew Charitable Trusts, 2740
Prevention Service, 989
Region 3: Education Department, 3179
Research for Better Schools Publications, 3460
Richard King Mellon Foundation, 2741
Rockwell International Corporation Trust, 2742
SIGI PLUS, 5142
Samuel S Fels Fund, 2743
Sarah Scaife Foundation, 2744
Satellites and Education Conference, 816
Search Associates, 3285
Shore Fund, 2745
Stackpole-Hall Foundation, 2746
Total Quality Schools Workshop, 3723
United States Steel Foundation, 2747
Westinghouse Foundation, 2841
What's New Magazine, 3537
William Penn Foundation, 2748
Women's International League for Peace & Freed om, 210

Rhode Island

American Mathematical Society, 678
Career & Technical Education, 3061, 3180
Champlin Foundations, 2749
East Bay Educational Collaborative, 885
Equity & Access Office, 3181
Human Resource Development, 3182
Instruction Office, 3183
Northeast and Islands Regional Educational Laboratory, 5132
Office of Finance, 3184
Outcomes & Assessment Office, 3185
Providence Public Library, 2750
Resource Development, 3186
Rhode Island Association of School Business Officials, 573
Rhode Island Department of Education, 3187
Rhode Island Educational Media Association, 574
Rhode Island Foundation, 2751
Rhode Island Library Association, 575
Rhode Island National Education Association, 576
School Food Services Administration, 3188
Special Needs Office, 3189
Teacher Education & Certification Office, 3190

South Carolina

Annual Conductor's Institute of South Carolina, 3621
Association for Continuing Higher Education Directory, 824, 3425
Association for Education in Journalism and Mass Communication Convention, 695
Budgets & Planning, 3191
Charleston County Library, 2752
Communications Services, 3026, 3192
Computers on Campus National Conference, 714
General Counsel, 2921, 3193
Internal Administration, 3194
National Dropout Prevention Center, 5122
National Dropout Prevention Center/Network Conference, 773
Policy & Planning, 3010, 3195
Sally Foster Gift Wrap, 2857
Satellite Educational Resources Consortium, 5143
Society of School Librarians International, 323
South Carolina Department of Education, 3196
South Carolina Education Association, 577
South Carolina Library Association, 578
South Carolina Library Association Conference, 3401
South Carolina State Library, 2753
Support Services, 2267, 3197
Teaching Education, 3530

South Dakota

Finance & Management, 3198
John McLaughlin Company, 937
Mountain Plains Library Association, 579
Services for Education, 3199
South Dakota Community Foundation, 2754
South Dakota Department of Education & Cultural Affairs, 3200
South Dakota Education Association, 580
South Dakota Library Association, 581
South Dakota State Historical Society, 3201
South Dakota State Library, 2755
Special Education Office, 3202

Tennessee

American Board of Master Educators, 355
Association for Library & Information Science Education Annual Conference, 318, 3308
Benwood Foundation, 2756
Center for Appalachian Studies & Services Annual Conference, 707
Christy-Houston Foundation, 2757
Frist Foundation, 2758

Institute of Higher Education, 3660
JR Hyde Foundation, 2759
Lyndhurst Foundation, 2760
Mental Edge, 3543
Modern Red Schoolhouse Institute, 968
Nashville Public Library, 2761
Oosting & Associates, 981
Plough Foundation, 2762
RJ Maclellan Charitable Trust, 2763
School Memories Collection, 2859
Special Education, 3000, 3055, 3069, 3069, 3149, 3170, 3203
Teaching and Learning, 3204
Tennessee Association of Secondary School Principals, 582
Tennessee Department of Education, 3205
Tennessee Library Association, 583
Tennessee School Boards Association, 584
Tennessee School Boards Association Conference, 3408
Vocational Education, 2928, 3123, 3206, 3206

Texas

Accountability Reporting and Research, 3207
Add Vantage Learning Incorporated, 838
Albert & Ethel Herzstein Charitable Foundation, 2764
Annual State Convention of Association of Texas Professional Educators, 3306
Apple Education Grants, 3287
Burlington Northern Foundation, 2765
Burnett Foundation, 2766
Center for Educational Leadership Trinity University, 3625
Center for Occupational Research & Development, 3629
Center for Play Therapy, 187, 3630
Center for Play Therapy Fall Conference, 3313
Center for Play Therapy Summer Institute, 825
Chief Counsel, 3173, 3208
Children's Literature Festival, 829
Choristers Guild's National Festival & Directors' Conference, 712
Clinical Play Therapy Videos: Child-Centered Developmental & Relationship Play Therapy, 3572
Conference for Advancement of Mathematics Teaching, 715
Continuing Education, 3209
Cooper Industries Foundation, 2767
Corpus Christi State University, 2768
Cullen Foundation, 2769
Curriculum Development & Textbooks, 3210
Curriculum, Assessment & Professional Development, 3211
Curriculum, Assessment and Technology, 3212
Dallas Public Library, 2770
Education of Special Populations & Adults, 3213
Educational Technology Design Consultants, 901
El Paso Community Foundation, 2771
Ellwood Foundation, 2772
Eugene McDermott Foundation, 2773
Ewing Halsell Foundation, 2774
Exxon Education Foundation, 2775

Field Services, 3214
Fondren Foundation, 2776
GTE Foundation, 2828
George Foundation, 2777
Gordon & Mary Cain Foundation, 2778
Haggar Foundation, 2779
Health Occupations Students of America, 200
Hobby Foundation, 2780
Houston Endowment, 2781
Houston Public Library, 2782
Internal Operations, 3215
International Exhibit, 646
Intervention in School and Clinic, 3505
James R Dougherty Jr Foundation, 2783
Journal of Classroom Interaction, 3506
LAUNCH, 77
Learning for Life, 3443
Leland Fikes Foundation, 2784
MD Anderson Foundation, 2785
Meadows Foundation, 2786
Moody Foundation, 2787
Multicorp, 973
National Association of Academic Advisors for Athletics, 346
National Athletic Trainers' Association, 347
National Congress for Educational Excellence, 103
National Educational Systems, 185
Operations & School Support, 3216
Paul & Mary Haas Foundation, 2788
Permanent School Fund, 3217
Perot Foundation, 2789
Psychological Corporation, 178
RW Fair Foundation, 2790
Records Consultants, 1000
Region 6: Education Department, 3218
Sid W Richardson Foundation, 2791
Southwest Association College and University Housing Officers, 832
Southwestern Educational Development Laboratory, 5150
Special Interest Group for Computer Science Education, 5151
Storytelling for Educational Enrichment The Magic of Storytelling, 3713
Strake Foundation, 2792
Texas Association of Secondary School Principals, 585
Texas Classroom Teachers Association Conference, 833
Texas Department of Education, 3219
Texas Library Association, 586
Texas Library Association Conference, 834
Texas Middle School Association Conference, 3409
Texas School Boards Association Conference, 3410
Texas State Teachers Association, 3411
Texas Vocational Home Economics Teachers Association Conference, 835
Trull Foundation, 2793
Voyager Expanded Learning, 192

UK

International Association of Teachers of English as a Foreign Language, 641
International Trombone Festival, 651

Utah

Applied Technology Education Services, 3220
Marriner S Eccles Foundation, 2794
Ruth Eleanor Bamberger and John Ernest Bamberger Memorial Foundation, 2795
Salt Lake City Public Library, 2796
School Management Study Group, 1008
Schools for the Deaf & Blind, 3222
Utah Education Association, 587
Utah Library Association, 588
Utah Office of Education, 3223
Utah Office of Education; Agency Services Division, 3224

Vermont

Career & Lifelong Learning, 3225
Center for Rural Studies, 3269
Connect, 3633
Core Services, 3226
Family & School Support, 3227
Financial Management Team, 3228
Learning Materials Workshop, 3676
Northeast Teachers Foreign Language Conference, 3385
School Development & Information, 3229
Teaching & Learning, 3230
Vermont Community Foundation, 2797
Vermont Department of Education, 3231
Vermont Department of Libraries, 2798
Vermont Education Association, 589
Vermont Library Association, 590
Vermont Special Education, 3232
Volunteers for Peace, 591
William T & Marie J Henderson Foundation, 2799

Virginia

ASCD Annual Conference & Exhibit Show, 655
Action Alliance for Virginia's Children and Youth, 592
Administrative Services, 3233
Aerospace Education Foundation, 363
Aerospace Industries Association of America, 194
American Alliance for Health, Physical Education, Recreation and Dance, 342
American Association School Administrators National Conference on Education, 658
American Association of School Administrators Annual Convention, 155, 666
American Association of Sex Educators, Counselors & Therapists Conference, 668
American Association of Sex Educators, Counselors & Therapists, 211
American Council on the Teaching of Foreign Languages Annual Conference, 302, 671
American Counseling Association, 212
American Counseling Association Annual Convention, 672
American International Schools, 841
American School Counselor Association, 213

American Society for Training and Development Information Center, 3266
American Society for Training-Development International Conference, 3302
American Society for Training/Development-Trai ning Video, 3422
Annual Technology & Learning Conference, 692
Association for Advancement of Computing in Education, 324, 364, 393, 393
Association for Career and Technical Education, 394
Association for Measurement & Evaluation in Counseling & Development, 214
Association for Science Education Teachers, 365
Association for Supervision & Curriculum Development Annual Conference, 25, 699
Association for Suppliers of Printing & Publishing Technologies, 195
Association of School Business Officials International, 157
Association of Teacher Educators, 3268
Beazley Foundation, 2800
Better Teaching, 3491
Center for Equity and Excellence in Education, 5077
Close-Up Foundation, 358
Corporate University Enterprise, 874
Council for Exceptional Children, 41
Council for Exceptional Children Annual Convention, 718
Council for Learning Disabilities, 637, 3271
Counseling Association, 216
Curriculum Brief, 3494
Division for Early Childhood, 182
Division for Learning Disabilities, 46
Division for Research, 5089
Division of International Special Education & Services, 260
Division of Student Leadership Services, 593
ERIC Clearinghouse on Disabilities and Gifted Education, 50
Education Technology Conference, 720
Educational Research Service, 5092
Electronics Industries Alliance/CEA, 3645
Exceptional Child Education Resources, 3498
Flagler Foundation, 2801
Grants and Awards for K-12 Students: 80 Sources of Funding, 2831
Graphic Arts Education & Research Foundation, 198
Hampton Public Library, 2802
Independent Education Consultants Association Conference, 731
Ingraham Dancu Associates, 921
International Association of Counseling Services, 218
International Council for Health, Physical Education and Recreation, 344
International Society for Business Education, 279
International Technology Education Association Conference, 650
Jeffress Memorial Trust, 2803
Johnson & Johnson Associates, 938
Kentland Foundation, 2804
Magna Awards, 3290
Management Concepts, 952
Miller, Cook & Associates, 965
Music Educators National Conference, 743
NASA Educational Workshop, 3686

NSTA Award for Principals, 3291
NSTA Awards, 3292
NSTA Educational Workshops, 747
National Art Education Association, 337
National Art Education Association Annual
  Convention, 750
National Association for College Admission
  Counseling Conference, 752
National Association for Girls and Women in
  Sports Yearly Conference, 753
National Association for Girls and Women in
  Sports, 345
National Association for Music Education,
  338
National Association for Supervision and
  Curriculum Development, 163
National Association of Biology Teachers
  Conference, 375, 756
National Association of Elementary School
  Principals Conference, 164, 191, 757, 757
National Association of Federal Education
  Prog ram Administrators, 165
National Association of Schools of Music,
  339
National Association of Secondary School
  Principals Annual Convention and
  Exposition, 168, 3354
National Association of State Boards of
  Education Conference, 91, 3355
National Association of Student Activity
  Advisers, 92
National Association of Student Councils, 93
National Business Education Association,
  206, 360
National Conference on Education, 3357
National Council of Teachers of
  Mathematics Annual Meeting, 3363
National Council of Teachers of
  Mathematics Conference, 328, 3365
National Foundation for Dyslexia, 311
National Head Start Association, 186, 3690
National Head Start Association Annual
  Conference, 776
National Resource Center on Self-Care &
  School-Age Child Care, 5126
National School Boards Annual Conference,
  782
National School Boards Association, 121
National School Boards Association Annual
  Conference & Exposition, 3370
National School Boards Association Library,
  5127
National Science Foundation, 2836
National Science Teachers Association, 378
National Science Teachers Association Area
  Convention, 3371
Native American Homeschool Association,
  130
New Learning Technologies, 788
Octameron Associates, 2875
Organization of Virginia Homeschoolers, 594
Parent Educational Advocacy Training
  Center, 5135
Policy, Assessment, Research & Information
  Systems, 3234
Presidential Awards for Excellence in
  Mathematics and Science Teaching, 3294
Printing Industries of America, 208
Programs for Preparing Individuals for
  Careers in Special Education, 3457
Richmond Public Library, 2806
Schiller Center, 145
Service Civil International, 292

Southern Association of Colleges & Schools,
  595
Student Services, 3235
Suburban Superintendents Conference, 3404
Summer Programs for School Teams, 3715
TED Newsletter, 3523
TESOL Journal: A Journal of Teaching and
  Classroom Research, 3524
Teacher Education Division, 3286
Teacher Education and Special Education,
  3526
Teacher Educators Association, 3406
Teachers of English to Speakers of Other
  Languages Convention and Exhibit, 294,
  797
Teaching Exceptional Children, 3531
Techniques-Connecting Education and
  Careers, 3532
Technology & Media Division, 406
Technology Student Association, 407
Technology Student Conference, 800
Technology and Children, 408
Technology and Learning Conference, 828
Toyota Tapestry Grants for Teachers, 3296
Trust to Reach Education Excellence, 2837
US Department of Defense Dependents
  Schools, 2912
Virginia Alliance for Arts Education, 596
Virginia Association for Health, Physical
  Education, Recreation & Dance, 597
Virginia Association for Supervision and
  Curriculum Development, 598
Virginia Association for the Education of
  the Gifted, 599
Virginia Association of Elementary School
  Principals Conference, 600, 3414
Virginia Association of Independent
  Schools-Conference, 601, 3415
Virginia Association of Independent Schools,
  602
Virginia Association of School
  Superintendents, 603
Virginia Association of School Business
  Officials, 604
Virginia Association of School Personnel
  Administrators, 605
Virginia Centers for Community Education,
  3236
Virginia Congress of Parents & Teachers, 606
Virginia Consortium of Administrators for
  Education of the Gifted, 607
Virginia Council for Private Education, 608
Virginia Council of Administrators of
  Special Education, 609
Virginia Council of Teachers of
  Mathematics, 610
Virginia Council on Economic Education,
  611
Virginia Department of Education, 3237
Virginia Education Association, 612
Virginia Educational Media Association, 613
Virginia Educational Research Association,
  614
Virginia Educators Annual Conference, 3416
Virginia Foundation for Educational
  Leadership, 2807
Virginia High School League, 615
Virginia Library Association, 616
Virginia Middle School Association, 617
Virginia School Boards Association, 618
Virginia School Boards Association
  Conference, 3417
Virginia Student Councils Association, 619

Virginia Vocational Association, 620

Washington

Child Care Information Exchange, 180
Comstock Foundation, 2808
Edge Learning Institute, 887
Education Advisory Group, 183
Family Centered Learning Alternatives, 62
Foster Foundation, 2809
Huntley Pascoe, 920
Kleiner & Associates, 942
MJ Murdock Charitable Trust, 2810
Marcraft International Corporation, 3678
Model Classroom, 966
National Educational Computing
  Conference, 3367
Northwest International Education
  Association, 285
Region 10: Education Department, 3238
Robert McNeel & Associates, 3704
Seattle Foundation, 2811
Seattle Public Library, 2812
Spokane Public Library, 2813
WA-ACTE Career and Technical Exhibition
  for Career and Technical Education, 823
Washington Department of Education, 3239
Washington Department of Education;
  Instruction Program, 3240
Washington Department of Education;
  Commission on Student Learning
  Administration, 3241
Washington Department of Education;
  Executive Services, 3242
Washington Department of Education;
  School Business & Administrative
  Services, 3243
Washington Education Association, 621
Washington Library Association, 622

West Virginia

Appalachia Educational Laboraory, 623
Center for Educational Technologies, 396
Clay Foundation, 2814
Continuous Learning Group Limited
  Liability Company, 872
Division of Administrative Services, 3244
ERIC Clearinghouse on Rural Education &
  Small Schools, 51
Institute for Earth Education, 372
Kanawha County Public Library, 2815
National Alliance for Safe Schools, 82
Phyllis A Beneke Scholarship Fund, 2816
Research, Accountability & Professional,
  3245
Student Services & Instructional Services,
  3246
Technical & Adult Education Services, 3247
West Virginia Department of Education, 3248
West Virginia Education Association, 624
West Virginia Library Association, 625

Wisconsin

ASQ Annual Koalaty Kid Conference, 3298

Association of Educators in Private Practice, 28
Careers Conference, 3312
Carter/Tardola Associates, 856
Center on Organization & Restructuring of Schools, 5086
Conover Company, 870, 3575
Division for Learning Support: Equity & Advocacy, 3249
Educational Credential Evaluators, 894
Edusystems Export, 903
Faye McBeath Foundation, 2817
How to Plan and Develop a Career Center, 3439
Institute for Academic Excellence, 925
Instructional Services Division, 3106, 3221, 3250, 3250
International Workshops, 3663
Library Services Division, 3251
Lynde & Harry Bradley Foundation, 2818
Marquette University Memorial Library, 2819
Middle School Teachers Guide to FREE Curriculum Materials, 3449
Miller Electric Manufacturing Company, 3681
National Center for Research in Mathematical Sciences Education, 5111
National Conference on Student Services, 769
National Institute for Science Education, 377
National Registration Center for Study Abroad, 283
National Telemedia Council, 127
North Central Conference on Summer Schools, 3383
Performa, 986
School Financial Resources & Management, 3252
Siebert Lutheran Foundation, 2820
University of Wisconsin-Madison, 2821
Wids Learning Design System, 3728
Wisconsin Association of School Boards Annual Conference, 3418
Wisconsin Association of School District Administrators Conference, 3419
Wisconsin College System Technical, 3253
Wisconsin Department of Public Instruction, 3254
Wisconsin Education Association Council, 626
Wisconsin Educational Media Association, 627
Wisconsin Library Association, 628
Wisconsin School Administrators Association Conference, 3420
Wisconsin Technical College System Foundation, 1029
Wisconsin Vocational Association Conference, 818

Wyoming Education Association, 629
Wyoming Library Association, 630
Wyoming School Boards Association, 631

Wyoming

Accounting, Personnel & School Finance Unit, 3255
Applied Data & Technology Unit, 3256
Natrona County Public Library, 2822
Services for Individuals with Hearing Loss, 3257
Support Programs & Quality Results Division, 3258
Wyoming Department of Education, 3259

Arts

A&F Video's Art Catalog, 6212
ART New England Summer Workshops, 3620
Alarion Press, 4741
All Art Supplies, 6213
American Academy of Arts & Sciences Bulletin, 4578
American Art Clay Company, 6214
American Art Therapy Association, 329
American Dance Therapy Association, 331
American Musicological Society, 332
Annual Conductor's Institute of South Carolina, 3621
Annual Summer Institute for Secondary Teachers, 3622
Arnold Grummer, 6215
Arrowmont School of Arts & Crafts, 6216
Art & Creative Materials Institute, 6217
Art Education, 4579
Art Image Publications, 4757
Art Instruction Schools, 6218
Art Visuals, 4758
Art to Remember, 6219
ArtSketchbook.com, 6220
Arts & Activities, 4580
Arts Education Policy Review, 4581
Arts Institutes International, 6221
Choral Journal, 4583
Choristers Guild's National Festival & Directors' Conference, 712
Clavier, 4584
Coloring Concepts, 4801
Community Outreach and Education for the Arts Handbook, 4051
Creative Teaching Press, 4810
Crizmac Art & Cultural Education Materials Inc, 5286
Dover Publications, 4824
Dramatics, 4585
ERIC Clearinghouse for Social Studies Education, 384
Educational Theatre Association Conference, 722
Flute Talk, 4586
Future Music Oregon, 333
Graphic Arts Education & Research Foundation, 198
Graphix, 5317
Harmonic Vision, 6127
Instrumentalist, 4587
International Conference, 643
International Thespian Society, 334
International Trombone Festival, 651
International Workshops, 3663
Italic Letters, 4052
Janice Borla Vocal Jazz Camp, 3665
Journal of Experiential Education, 4588
July in Rensselaer, 3667
Kennedy Center Alliance for Arts Education, 335
Kodaly Teaching Certification Program, 3672
Mel Bay Publications, 4933
Midnight Play, 6128
Mondo Publishing, 4939
Money for Visual Artists, 3998
Museum Stamps, 6222
Music Ace 2, 6223
Music Educators Journal, 4589
Music Educators Journal and Teaching Music, 4590

Music Educators National Conference, 743
Music Teacher Find, 6129
Music Teachers Association National Conference, 744
Music Teachers Guide to Music Instructional Software, 4055
Music Teachers National Association, 336
Music and Guitar, 6130
Musikgarten, 3685
NAEA News, 4591
National Art Education Association, 337
National Art Education Association Annual Convention, 750
National Association for Music Education, 338
National Association of Schools of Music, 339
National Council of State Supervisors of Music, 2936
National Guild of Community Schools of the Arts, 340
National Guild of Community Schools of theArts Conference, 775
National Institute of Art and Disabilities, 341
National Standards for Dance Education News, 4610
Oranatics Journal, 4593
Orff-Schulwerk Teacher Certification Program, 3692
Peterson's Guide to Professional Degree Programs in the Visual Arts, 4056
Phelps Publishing, 4974
Piano Workshop, 3698
Pure Gold Teaching Tools, 6131
Resource Booklet for Independent Music Teachers, 4057
Rhythms Productions, 4994
School Arts, 4058
SchoolArtsDavis Publications, 4594
SchoolArts Magazine, 4595
Studies in Art Education, 4596
Teaching Journal, 4597
Teaching Music, 4598
Ultimate Early Childhood Music Resource, 4599
http://library.thinkquest.org, 6132
http://members.truepath.com/headoftheclass, 6133
www.sanford-artedventures.com, 6135
www.songs4teachers.com, 6136

Civics & Government

AppleSeeds, 4671
Boletin, 4672
Center for Civic Education, 34
Children's Book Council, 4792
Choices Education Project, 4797
Cobblestone, 4675
Colloquoy on Teaching World Affairs, 4676
Congressional Quarterly, 4806
Directory of Central America Classroom Resources, 4090
ERIC Clearinghouse for Social Studies Education, 384
Educators Guide to FREE Social Studies Materials, 4091
Facts on File, 4852
Focus, 4678
Footsteps, 4679
Frog Publications, 4860

Goethe House New York, 4863
Greenhaven Press, 4865
Hands-On Prints, 4869
High Touch Learning, 4875
Horn Book Guide, 4879
Houghton Mifflin Books for Children, 4880
Houghton Mifflin Company: School Division, 4881
Hyperion Books for Children, 4882
Jacaranda Designs, 4891
Keep America Beautiful, 4898
Knowledge Unlimited, 4901
Lynne Rienner Publishing, 4919
Media and American Democracy, 3680
Middle States Council for the Social Studies Annual Regional Conference, 3346
NASDTEC Knowledge Base, 3450
NCSS Summer Professional Development Programs, 3687
National Council for Social Studies Annual Conference, 3361
National Council for the Social Studies, 385
National Council for the Social Studies, 4949
National Survey of Course Offerings and Testing in Social Studies K-12, 6248
National Women's History Project, 4956
National Women's History Project Annual Conference, 787
New Press, 4959
NewsBank, 4960
Organization of American Historians, 4964
Pennsylvania Council for the Social Studies Conference, 3394
Perspectives on History Series, 4972
Phi Delta Kappa Educational Foundation, 4264
Population Connection, 4978
Rand McNally, 4988
Roots & Wings Educational Catalog-Australia for Kids, 4997
Routledge/Europa Library Reference, 4999
Sharpe Reference, 5010
Social Issues Resources Series, 5014
Social Science Education Consortium, 5015
Social Studies School Service, 5016
USA Today, 5043
VIDYA Books, 5046
WORLD OF DIFFERENCE Institute, 5050
West Educational Publishing, 5056
Western History Association Annual Meeting, 836
Who's Who in the Social Studies Annual Directory, 4093
Winston Derek Publishers, 5060
World & I, 5063
World Bank, 5065
World Book Educational Products, 5066
World Eagle, 5067
World Resources Institute, 5068
Worth Publishers, 5069
www.ushistory.com, 6137

Economics

American Educational Studies Association, 675
Bluestocking Press Catalog, 4773
Chicago Board of Trade, 4791
Freedom & Enterprise, 4680
Junior Achievement, 4895

National Council on Economic Education, 4951

English

ABDO Publishing Company, 4731
AGS, 4732
Accelerated Reader, 5779
American Educational Studies Association, 675
Amsco School Publications, 4754
Australian Press-Down Under Books, 4764
Ballantine/Del Rey/Fawcett/Ivy, 4767
Barron's Educational Series, 4768
Beech Tree Books, 4770
Black Butterfly Children's Books, 4771
Bluestocking Press Catalog, 4773
BridgeWater Books, 4775
Brown & Benchmark Publishers, 4777
Capstone Press, 4784
Carolrhoda Books, 4786
Center for Critical Thinking and Moral Critique Annual International, 635
Center for Education Studies, 382
Center for Learning, 5078
Charles Scribner & Sons, 4790
Children's Book Council, 4792
Children's Literature Festival, 829
Children's Press, 4793
Chime Time, 4796
Cottonwood Press, 4808
Creative Teaching Press, 4810
Cricket Magazine Group, 4811
Dial Books for Young Readers, 4817
Disney Press, 4821
Dover Publications, 4824
Dutton Children's Books, 4825
DynEd International, 4826
ERIC Clearinghouse on Reading, English & Communication, 349
Education Center, 4834
Education Development Center, 891
Ellis, 4842
Encyclopaedia Britannica, 4843
Essential Learning Products, 4845
Evan-Moor Corporation, 4847
Farrar, Straus & Giroux, 4853
First Years, 4854
Formac Distributing, 4856
Foundation for Critical Thinking, 3651
Foundation for Critical Thinking Regional Workshop & Conference, 724
Frank Schaffer Publications, 4857
Frog Publications, 4860
Games2Learn, 5816
Gareth Stevens, 4861
Greenwillow Books, 4866
Henry Holt Books for Young Readers, 4874
Hitting the High Notes of Literacy, 727
Holiday House, 4877
Increasing Student Achievement in Reading, Writing, Mathematics, Science, 730
International Reading Association Annual Convention, 648
Journalism Education Association, 737
Kane/Miller Book Publishers, 4897
Lake Education, 4903
Landmark Editions, 4904
Learning Connection, 4908
Learning Links, 4910
Lee & Low Books, 4911

Lerner Publishing Group, 4913
Linden Tree Children's Records & Books, 4914
Literacy Volunteers of America National Conference, 738
Lodestar Books, 4917
Lothrop, Lee & Shepard Books, 4918
MacMillan Children's Books, 4921
Macmillan/McGraw-Hill School Division, 4923
Margaret K McElderry Books, 4927
Mari, 4928
Media and American Democracy, 3680
Millbrook Press, 4935
Mondo Publishing, 4939
Narrative Press, 4946
National Center for ESL Literacy Education, 351
National Council of Teachers of English, 4950
National Writing Project, 4957
New Canaan Publishing Company, 4958
North South Books, 4961
PF Collier, 4965
Perfection Learning Corporation, 4969
Phoenix Learning Resources Conference, 831
Picture Book LearningVolume-1, 4042
Pocket Books/Paramount Publishing, 4977
Random House/Bullseye/Alfred A Knopf/Crown Books for Young Readers, 4990
Rhythms Productions, 4994
Riverside Publishing Company, 4996
Scholastic, 5005
School Book Fairs, 5006
Scott Foresman Company, 5009
Signet Classics, 5011
Silver Moon Press, 5012
Simon & Schuster Children's Publishing, 5013
Stack the Deck Writing Program, 5019
Sundance Publishing, 5024
TMC/Soundprints, 5028
Theme Connections, 5032
Tor Books/Forge/SMP, 5038
Tricycle Press, 5039
Troll Associates, 5040
Trumpet Club, 5041
Turn-the-Page Press, 5042
Upstart Books, 5044
Useful Learning, 5045
Viking Children's Books, 5047
Warren Publishing House, 5053
Winston Derek Publishers, 5060
Writing Lab Newsletter, 4543
Zaner-Bloser K-8 Catalog, 5072

Foreign Language

AATF National Bulletin, 4502
ACTFL Newsletters, 4503
Advocates for Language Learning Annual Meeting, 657
Alaska Department of Education Bilingual & Bicultural Education Conference, 3299
American Association for Chinese Studies, 381
American Association of French Teachers Conference, 664
American Association of Teachers of French, 299

American Council on the Teaching of Foreign Languages, 302
American Council on the Teaching of Foreign Languages Annual Conference, 671
Asian American Curriculum Project, 317
Barron's Educational Series, 4768
Bienvenue Annual Conference, 634
Bilingual Research Journal, 4506
Bilingual Review Press, 4507
CEA Forum, 4508
Center for Applied Linguistics, 304
Central States Conference on the Teaching of Foreign Languages, 3314
Directory of Central America Classroom Resources, 4090
DynEd International, 4826
ERIC Clearinghouse on Languages and Linguistics, 160
ERIC Clearinghouse on Languages and Linguistics, 305
Edumate-Educational Materials, 4841
Elementary Secondary Bilingual & Research Branch, 2883
Ellis, 4842
Foreign Language Annals, 4519
Frog Publications, 4860
Illinois Resource Center Conference of Teachers of Linguistically Diverse Students, 3324
International Association of Teachers of English as a Foreign Language, 641
International Educational Exchange, 2886
Kane/Miller Book Publishers, 4897
Learning Connection, 4908
Lee & Low Books, 4911
Modern Language Association Annual Conference, 742
Mondo Publishing, 4939
National Association for Bilingual Education, 308
National Association for Bilingual Education, 751
National Center for ESL Literacy Education, 351
National Clearinghouse for Bilingual Education Newsletter, 4531
National Federation of Modern Language Teachers Association, 310
National Network for Early Language Learning (NELL), 312
Northeast Conference on the Teaching of Foreign Languages, 3384
Northeast Teachers Foreign Language Conference, 3385
Office of Bilingual Education and Minority Language Affairs, 2895
Pacific Northwest Council on Languages Annual Conference, 3393
SLEP Program Office, 6208
Santillana Publishing, 5004
Studies in Second Language Acquisition, 4540
TESOL Journal: A Journal of Teaching and Classroom Research, 4541
TESOL Quarterly, 4542
TOEFL Test and Score Manual, 6260
Teachers of English to Speakers of Other Languages Convention and Exhibit, 797

Geography

African-American Institute, 380
American Association for Chinese Studies, 381
American Association for State & Local History, 4745
American Educational Studies Association, 675
Art Visuals, 4758
Asian American Curriculum Project, 4759
Association for Refining Cross-Cultured International, 844
Association for the Advancement of International Education, 700
Center for Appalachian Studies & Services Annual Conference, 707
Choices Education Project, 4797
Colloquoy on Teaching World Affairs, 4676
Council for Indian Education, 383
Dinah-Might Activities, 4819
Directory of Central America Classroom Resources, 4090
Ethnic Arts & Facts, 4846
Geography: A Resource Guide for Secondary Schools, 4092
Goethe House New York, 4863
Hands-On Prints, 4869
High Touch Learning, 4875
Ingenuity Works, 5822
International Schools Association, 930
Jacaranda Designs, 4891
Kane/Miller Book Publishers, 4897
Keep America Beautiful, 4898
Langenseheidt Publishing, 4905
Lerner Publishing Group, 4913
NYSTROM, 4945
National Council for Geographic Education Annual Meeting, 3359
National Geographic School Publishing, 4952
National Geographic Society, 4953
New England History Teachers Association, 386
North South Books, 4961
Population Connection, 4978
Rand McNally, 4988
Roots & Wings Educational Catalog-Australia for Kids, 4997
Routledge/Europa Library Reference, 4999
Sharpe Reference, 5010
Social Science Education Consortium, 5015
Teachers' Committee on Central America, 389
VIDYA Books, 5046
Western History Association, 390
World & I, 5063
World Bank, 5065
World Book Educational Products, 5066
World Eagle, 5067
World Resources Institute, 5068

History

Alarion Press, 4741
Alumni Newsletter, 4668
American Association for Chinese Studies, 381
American Association for State & Local History, 4745

American Educational Studies Association, 675
American Sociological Review, 4669
AnthroNotes, 4649
AnthroNotes, 4670
AppleSeeds, 4671
Art Visuals, 4758
Asian American Curriculum Project, 4759
Bluestocking Press Catalog, 4773
Boletin, 4672
California Weekly Explorer, 4673
Calliope, 4674
Center for Education Studies, 382
Center for Learning, 5078
Choices Education Project, 4797
Cobblestone, 4675
Colloquoy on Teaching World Affairs, 4676
Council for Indian Education, 383
Dinocardz Company, 4820
Editorial Projects in Education, 4832
Educators Guide to FREE Social Studies Materials, 4091
Ethnic Arts & Facts, 4846
Faces, 4677
Facts on File, 4852
Goethe House New York, 4863
History Matters Newsletter, 4681
History of Science Society, 371
Jacaranda Designs, 4891
Lerner Publishing Group, 4913
Middle States Council for the Social Studies Annual Regional Conference, 3346
NYSTROM, 4945
National Council for History Education Conference, 3360
National Council on Economic Education, 4951
National Women's History Project, 4956
National Women's History Project Annual Conference, 787
New England History Teachers Association, 386
New Press, 4959
Organization of American Historians, 4964
Pennsylvania Council for the Social Studies Conference, 3394
Personalizing the Past, 4971
Perspectives on History Series, 4972
Pleasant Company Publications, 4976
Routledge/Europa Library Reference, 4999
Runestone Press, 5000
Sharpe Reference, 5010
Social Science Education Consortium, 5015
Society for History Education, 388
Teachers' Committee on Central America, 389
VIDYA Books, 5046
WORLD OF DIFFERENCE Institute, 5050
Western History Association, 390
Western History Association Annual Meeting, 836
Who's Who in the Social Studies Annual Directory, 4093
World & I, 5063
www.ushistory.com, 6137

Mathematics

AIMS Education Foundation, 4733
Accelerated Math, 5778
Advantage Learning Systems, 6227

American Mathematical Society, 678
Association for Advancement of Computing in Education, 364
Association for Science Teacher Education Science Annual Meeting, 698
Association of Science-Technology Centers, 366
Conference for Advancement of Mathematics Teaching, 715
Didax Educational Resources, 4818
ERIC Clearinghouse for Science, Math & Environmental Education, 368
ETA - Math Catalog, 4827
Education Development Center, 891
Eisenhower National Clearinghouse for Mathematics and Science Education, 325
Eisenhower National Clearinghouse for Mathematics and Science Education, 369
Equity 2000, 326
Everyday Learning Corporation, 4848
Extra Editions K-6 Math Supplements, 4850
F(G) Scholar, 4851
Focus on Learning Problems in Math, 4566
Games2Learn, 5816
Increasing Student Achievement in Reading, Writing, Mathematics, Science, 730
Ingenuity Works, 5822
Iowa Council Teachers of Math Conference, 3328
Journal for Research in Mathematics Education, 4567
Journal of Computers in Math & Science, 4568
Journal of Recreational Mathematics, 4569
K'nex Education Division, 3668
K-6 Science and Math Catalog, 4084
Lawrence Hall of Science, 4906
Math Notebook, 4570
MathSoft, 4930
Mathematical Association of America, 327
Mathematics & Computer Education, 4571
Mathematics Teacher, 4572
Mathematics Teaching in the Middle School, 4573
Mimosa Publications, 4937
NCTM Educational Materials, 4944
NCTM News Bulletin, 4574
National Council of Teachers of Mathematics Annual Meeting, 3363
National Council of Teachers of Mathematics, 328
National Council of Teachers of Mathematics Conference, 3365
Notices of the American Mathematical Society, 4575
Options Publishing, 4963
SAT Math Flash, 6210
SSMart Newsletter, 4576
Summing It Up: College Board Mathematics Assessment Programs, 6211
Summit Learning, 5022
Teaching Children Mathematics, 4577
WH Freeman & Company, 5049
Wolfram Research, 5061
Word Associates, 5888

Reading & Language Arts

ABC Feelings Adage Publications, 4730

ADE Bulletin, 4504
AGS, 4732
Accelerated Reader, 5779
Advantage Learning Systems, 6227
Australian Press-Down Under Books, 4764
Beyond Words, 4505
Brown & Benchmark Publishers, 4777
Carolrhoda Books, 4786
Carson-Dellosa Publishing Company, 4787
Center for Learning, 5078
Christian Literacy Outreach, 4616
Classroom Notes Plus, 4509
Classroom Strategies for the English Language Learner, 4033
Cognitive Concepts, 4799
Concepts to Go, 4805
Conover Company, 870
Continental Press, 4807
Cottonwood Press, 4808
Council-Grams, 4513
Counterforce, 4514
Creative Teaching Press, 4810
Curriculum Associates, 4812
Diagnostic Reading Inventory for Bilingual Students in Grades K-8, 4061
Diagnostic Reading Inventory for Primary and Intermediate Grades K-8, 4062
Diagnostic Reading Inventory for Primary and Intermediate Grades K-8, 6202
Dinah-Might Activities, 4819
Dominic Press, 4822
DynEd International, 4826
ERIC Clearinghouse on Reading, English & Communication, 349
English Education, 4515
English for Specific Purposes, 4518
Essential Learning Products, 4845
Everything You Need for Reading, 4064
Exercise Exchange, 4617
Formac Distributing, 4856
Forum for Reading, 4618
Frog Publications, 4860
Games2Learn, 5816
Gareth Stevens, 4861
Getting Funded: The Complete Guide to Writing Grant Proposals, 3981
Greenwillow Books, 4866
Henry Holt Books for Young Readers, 4874
Hidden America, 3797
Higher Education & National Affairs, 4190
Hitting the High Notes of Literacy, 727
Increasing Student Achievement in Reading, Writing, Mathematics, Science, 730
International Reading Association, 350
International Reading Association Annual Convention, 648
Iowa Reading Association Conference, 3329
Italic Handwriting Series-Book A, 4034
Italic Handwriting Series-Book B, 4035
Italic Handwriting Series-Book C, 4036
Italic Handwriting Series-Book D, 4037
Italic Handwriting Series-Book E, 4038
Italic Handwriting Series-Book F, 4039
Italic Handwriting Series-Book G, 4040
Journal of Adolescent & Adult Literacy, 4619
Journal of Basic Writing, 4520
Kaeden Corporation, 4896
Language Arts, 4525
Language Schools Directory, 4041
Laubach LitScape, 4620
Laubach Literacy Action Directory, 4065
Lauri, 5334
Learning Connection, 4908

Literacy Volunteers of America National Conference, 738
Mari, 4928
McCracken Educational Services, 4931
National Contact Hotline, 352
National Council of English Teachers Conference, 3362
National Council of Teachers of English, 309
National Council of Teachers of English Annual Convention, 3364
National Reading Styles Institute Conference, 779
National Writing Project, 4957
News for You, 4622
Options Publishing, 4963
PF Collier, 4965
PRO-ED, 4966
Phoenix Learning Resources, 4975
Phoenix Learning Resources Conference, 831
Phonics Institute, 4623
Picture Book Learning Volume-1, 4042
Prentice Hall School Division, 4979
Process of Elimination - a Method of Teaching and Learning Basic Grammar, 4043
Put Reading First: The Research Building Blocks For Teaching Children To Read, 4044
RIF Newsletter, 4624
Rand McNally, 4988
Reading Improvement, 4626
Reading Psychology, 4627
Reading Recovery Council of North America, 354
Reading Research Quarterly, 4628
Reading Research and Instruction, 4629
Reading Teacher, 4630
Reading Today, 4631
Ready to Read, Ready to Learn, 4066
Recorded Books, 4991
Rhythms Productions, 4994
Scott & McCleary Publishing Company, 5008
Social Studies School Service, 5016
Sundance Publishing, 5024
TASA, 5026
Tambourine Books, 5029
Technology, Reading & Learning Difficulties Conference, 802
Tips for Reading Tutors, 4067
Useful Learning, 5045
WSRA Journal, 4635
Warren Publishing House, 5053
Word Associates, 5888
Workman Publishing, 5062
Wright Group, 5070
Write Now: A Complete Self Teaching Program for Better Handwriting, 4045
Write Now: A Complete Self-Teaching Program Foor Better Handwriting, 4014
Write Source Educational Publishing House, 5071

Science

AGS, 4732
AIMS Education Foundation, 4733
Academy of Applied Science, 362
Acorn Naturalists, 4735
American Association of Physics Teachers National Meeting, 665
American Biology Teacher, 4648

American Indian Science & Engineering Society Annual Conference, 676
American Institute of Physics, 4748
American Nuclear Society, 4749
American Water Works Association, 4752
Ampersand Press, 4753
Annenberg/CPB Project, 4756
Arbor Scientific, 5621
Association for Advancement of Computing in Education, 364
Association for Science Education Teachers, 365
Association for Science Teacher Education Science Annual Meeting, 698
Association for Science Teacher Education, 4760
Association of Science-Technology Centers, 366
Association of Science-Technology Centers Incorporated Conference, 705
Bayer/NSF Award for Community Innovation, 3288
Baylor College of Medicine, 4769
Blake Books, 4772
California Biomedical Research Association, 367
Center for Educational Policy Studies, 35
Children's Television Workshop, 4795
Coloring Concepts, 4801
Dawn Publications, 4815
Delta Education, 4816
Dinocardz Company, 4820
Dorling Kindorley Company, 4823
Dover Publications, 4824
ERIC Clearinghouse for Science, Math & Environmental Education, 368
EVAN-Motor Corporation, 4829
Earth Education: A New Beginning, 4081
Earth Foundation, 4831
Earthkeepers, 4082
Education Development Center, 891
Eisenhower National Clearinghouse for Mathematics and Science Education, 325
Eisenhower National Clearinghouse for Mathematics and Science Education, 369
Energy Concepts, 3648
Geothermal Education Office, 370
Glencoe/Div. of Macmillan/McGraw Hill, 4862
History of Science Society, 371
Hoosier Science Teachers Association Annual Meeting, 807
ITP South-Western Publishing Company, 4883
Idea Factory, 4884
Increasing Student Achievement in Reading, Writing, Mathematics, Science, 730
Institute for Chemical Education, 4885
Institute for Earth Education, 372
International Council of Scientific Unions Committee on Science Teaching, 373
John Wiley & Sons, 4894
K'nex Education Division, 3668
K-6 Science and Math Catalog, 4084
Lawrence Hall of Science, 4906
Macro Press, 4924
Michigan Science Teachers Association Annual Conference, 3344
Milton Roy Company, 4936
Model Technologies, 4938
Music for Little People, 4941
NASA Educational Workshop, 3686
NSTA Educational Workshops, 747

National Aeronautics & Space Administration, 4947
National Association for Research in Science Teaching, 374
National Association of Biology Teachers, 375
National Association of Biology Teachers Conference, 756
National Center for Science Education, 376
National Center for Science Teaching & Learning/Eisenhower Clearinghouse, 4948
National Congress on Aviation and Space Education, 770
National Geographic School Publishing, 4952
National Geographic Society, 4953
National Institute for Science Education, 377
National Science Foundation, 2836
National Science Resources Center, 5129
National Science Teachers Association, 378
National Science Teachers Association Area Convention, 3371
NewsBank, 4960
North American Association for Environmental Education, 387
Nystrom, Herff Jones, 4962
Pennsylvania Science Teachers Association, 3396
Prentice Hall School Division - Science, 4980
Project Learning Tree, 4982
SSMart Newsletter, 4576
Science Inquiry Enterprises, 5007
Science Service, 379
Science for All Children; A Guide to Improving Science Education, 4085
Scott Foresman Company, 5009
Sunship Earth, 4086
Sunship III, 4087
TMC/Soundprints, 5028
Top Colleges for Science, 4088
UNESCO Sourcebook for Out-of-School Science & Technology Education, 4089
Wadsworth Publishing School Group, 5051
Wildlife Conservation Society, 5058
ZooBooks, 5074

Special Education

American Speech-Language-Hearing Association Annual Convention, 683
Association for Disabled Students, 21
Association for Persons with Severe Handicaps Annual Conference, 696
Attention Deficit Disorder Association, 29
CASE Newsletter, 4330
CASE in Point, 4331
CHADD: Children & Adults with Attention Deficit/Hyperactivity Disorder, 32
Career Development for Exceptional Individuals, 4426
Center on Disabilities Conference, 711
Center on Human Policy, 36
Closing the Gap, 713
Communication Disorders Quarterly, 4510
Council for Exceptional Children Annual Convention, 718
Council for Learning Disabilities International Conference, 637
Council for Learning Disabilities, 3271
Council of Administrators of Special Education, 3272
Counterpoint, 4144

DLD Times, 4150
Different Books, 4154
Disability Compliance for Higher Education, 4156
Disability Determination Division, 2919
Disability Rights Education & Defense Fund, 45
Division for Learning Disabilities, 46
ERIC Clearinghouse on Disabilities and Gifted Education, 50
Early Childhood Report: Children with Special Needs and Their Families, 4397
Easter Seals Communications, 53
Education Development Center, 891
Focus on Research, 4180
Illinois Affiliation of Private Schools for Exceptional Children, 469
Inclusive Education Programs, 4195
International Dyslexia Association, 306
International Dyslexia Association Annual Conference, 645
Intervention in School and Clinic, 3505
Journal of Disability Policy Studies, 4206
Journal of Learning Disabilities, 4210
Journal of Special Education, 4217
LAUNCH, 77
LD Forum, 4220
Learning Disabilities Association of America, 78
Learning Disabilities Association of America International Conference, 653
Learning Disabilities Association of America, 4909
Learning Disability Quarterly, 4221
Learning Independence Through Computers, 402
Lesson Plans for Integrating Technology into the Classroom: Secondary Edition, 4075
Liaison Bulletin, 4224
LinguiSystems, 6204
National Center for Learning Disabilities, 97
National Council on Disability, 2891
National Foundation for Dyslexia, 311
National Foundation for Dyslexia, 6229
National Institute of Art and Disabilities, 341
National Institute on Disability and Rehabilitation Research, 405
National Network of Learning Disabled Adults, 119
National Organization on Disability, 120
Office of Special Education Programs, 2900
Office of State Coordinator of Vocational Education for Disabled Students, 2968
PRO-ED, 4966
Recording for the Blind & Dyslexic, 4632
Rehabilitation Services, 2924
Roots & Wings Educational Catalog-Australia for Kids, 4997
SAT Services for Students with Disabilities, 6257
Society for Visual Education, 5865
Special Education & Rehabilitation Services, 5017
Special Education Law Update, 4377
Special Education Leadership, 4294
Special Education Report, 4378
Special Education Services, 2925
Special Educator, 4295
Speech Bin, 5018
Synergistic Systems, 5025
Web Feet Guides, 5055
www.specialednews.com, 5936

Technology

AV Guide Newsletter, 4118
Agency for Instructional Technology, 391
Agency for Instructional Technology, 3261
Aid for Education, 2845
American Technical Education Association Annual Conference, 684
American Technical Publishers, 4751
American Trade Schools Directory, 4094
Annual Ethics & Technology Conference, 689
Annual Microcomputers in Education Conference, 690
Annual Technology & Learning Conference, 692
Appalachia Educational Laboraory, 623
Apple Education Grants, 3287
Association for Advancement of Computing in Education, 324
Association for Advancement of Computing in Education, 364
Association for Advancement of Computing in Education, 393
Association for Career and Technical Education, 394
Association for Educational Communications & Technology: Membership Directory, 4095
Association for Educational Communications & Technology, 395
Association for Educational Communications & Technology Annual Convention, 3307
Association of Science-Technology Centers Incorporated Conference, 705
Bayer/NSF Award for Community Innovation, 3288
Center for Educational Technologies, 396
Chronicle Vocational School Manual, 4096
Classroom, 863
Closing the Gap, 713
Commuter Perspectives, 4142
Computer Learning Foundation, 4803
Computer Literacy Press, 4804
Computer Using Educators, Inc (CUE), 397
Computers on Campus National Conference, 714
Conference on Information Technology, 716
Consortium for School Networking, 398
Curriculum Brief, 3494
Directory of Public Vocational-Technical Schools & Institutes in the US, 4097
Directory of Vocational-Technical Schools, 4098
EDUCAUSE, 399
Education Technology Conference, 720
Educational Technology Center, 400
Educators Guide to FREE Computer Materials and Internet Resources, 3781
Electronic Learning, 4341
Electronic Specialists Inc., 5812
Emerging Technology Consultants, 907
Four State Regional Technology Conference, 3652
Guide to Vocational and Technical Schools East & West, 4100
Indiana University-Purdue University of Indianapolis, IUPUI, 3658
Industrial Teacher Education Directory, 4101
Information Literacy: Essential Skills for the Information Age, 4102
Ingenuity Works, 5822

IntelliTools, 4887
International Association for Social Science
    Information Service & Technology, 3327
International Society for Technology in
    Education, 401
International Technology Education
    Association Conference, 650
Internet Resource Directory for Classroom
    Teachers, 4103
Journal of Computers in Math & Science,
    4568
K-12 District Technology Coordinators, 4104
Leadership and the New Technologies, 3674
Learning Independence Through Computers,
    402
MarcoPolo, 403
Maryland Center for Career and Technology
    Education, 3679
Mathematics & Computer Education, 4571
Michigan Association for Media in
    Education, 507
Millersville University, 3682
Multimedia and Videodisc Compendium for
    Education and Training, 4105
National Association of Media and
    Technology Centers, 404
National Computer Systems, 3689
National Educational Computing
    Conference, 3367
NetLingo The Internet Dictionary, 5841
New Learning Technologies, 788
Pittsburg State University, 3699
Quick-Source, 4107
Robert McNeel & Associates, 3704
SUNY College at Oswego, 3706
School Executive, 4371
School of Music, 3707
SchoolTech Forum, 3399
Schools Industrial, Technical & Trade
    Directory, 4108
Southwestern Oklahoma State University,
    3709
Specialized Solutions, 3710
Sunburst Technology, 5023
TESS: The Educational Software Selector,
    4109
THE Journal, 4382
Tech Directions-Directory of Federal &
    Federal and State Officials Issue, 4110
Technology & Learning Schooltech
    Exposition & Conference, 799
Technology & Media Division, 406
Technology Pathfinder for Administrators
    Master Teacher, 4383
Technology Student Association, 407
Technology Student Conference, 800
Technology and Children, 408
Technology and Learning Conference, 828
Technology in 21st Century Schools, 801
Technology in Public Schools, 4111
Telemetrics, 409
Tom Snyder Productions, 5037

Associations & Organizations

ACCESS ERIC , 1
http://ericec.org
ASPIRA Association , 3
www.aspira.org
Academic Travel Abroad , 222
www.academic-travel.com/ata
Academy for Educational Development , 4
www.aed.org
Academy of Applied Science , 362
www.aas-world.org
Action Alliance for Virginia's Children and Youth, 592
www.vakids.org
Advance Program for Young Scholars , 5
www.nsula.edu/scholars
Aerospace Education Foundation , 363
www.aef.org
Aerospace Industries Association of America , 194
www.aia-aerospace.org
African-American Institute , 380
www.aaionline.org
Agency for Instructional Technology , 391
www.ait.net
Alabama Business Education Association , 411
http://abea2000.tripod.com
Alabama Education Association , 412
www.myaea.org
Alabama Library Association , 413
www.akla.org/akasl/home.com
Alaska Library Association , 416
www.akla.org
Alliance for Technology Access Conference , 392
www.ataccess.org
American Academy of Pediatrics , 8
www.aap.org
American Alliance for Health, Physical Educat ion, Recreation and
Dance, 342
www.aahperd.org
American Art Therapy Association , 329
www.arttherapy.org
American Association for Chinese Studies , 381
www.ccny.cuny.edu/aacs
American Association for Vocational Instructi nal Materials, 9
www.aavim.com
American Association of Collegiate Registrars & Admissions
Officers, 154
www.aacrao.org
American Association of School Administrators , 155
www.aasa.org
American Association of Sex Educators, Counse ors & Therapists,
211
www.aasect.org
American Association of Teachers of French , 299
www.frenchteachers.org
American Council on Education , 13
www.acenet.edu
American Council on Education Library & Information Service,
448
www.acenet.edu
American Council on Rural Special Education , 14
www.ksu.edu/acres
American Council on Schools and Colleges , 15
www.corpmgttrust.com
American Council on the Teaching of Foreign Languages, 302
www.actfl.org/
American Counseling Association , 212
www.counseling.org
American Dance Therapy Association , 331
www.adta.org
American Driver & Traffic Safety Education Association, 356
http://144.80.48.9/adtsea/default.aspx

American Federation of Teachers , 16
www.aft.org
American Friends Service Committee , 224
www.afsc.org
American Jewish Congress , 225
www.ajcongress.org
American Library Association , 316
www.ala.org
American Montessori Society , 17
www.amshq.org
American Musicological Society , 332
www.ams-net.org
American Public Human Services Association , 18
www.aphsa.org
American School Counselor Association , 213
www.schoolcounselor,org
American School Health Association , 19
www.ashaweb.org
American Schools Association of Central America,
Columbia-Caribbean and Mexico, 226
www.tri-association.org
American Society of International Law , 227
www.asil.org
American Speech-Language-Hearing Association , 303
www.asha.org
Appalachia Educational Laboraory , 623
www.ael.org
Arizona School Boards Association , 419
www.azsba.org
Asian American Curriculum Project , 317
www.asianamericanbooks.com
Associated Schools Project Network , 229
http://portal.unesco.org
Association for Advancement of Computing in Education, 324
www.aace.org
Association for Advancement of Computing in Education, 393
www.aace.org
Association for Asian Studies , 230
www.aasianst.org
Association for Canadian Studies in the US , 231
www.acsus.org
Association for Career and Technical Educatio , 394
www.acteonline.org
Association for Educational Communications & Technology, 395
www.aect.org/
Association for Gender Equity Leadership in Education, 22
www.agele.org
Association for Institutional Research , 357
www.airweb.org
Association for Integrative Studies , 23
www.muohio.edu
Association for International Practical Training, 232
www.aipt.org
Association for Library & Information Science Education, 318
www.alise.org
Association for Play Therapy , 24
www.a4pt.org
Association for Science Education Teachers , 365
http://theaste.org
Association for Supervision & Curriculum Development, 25
www.ascd.org
Association for Suppliers of Printing & Publishing Technologies,
195
www.npes.org
Association for Technology Educators , 559
www.rwc.uc.edu/obta
Association of American International Colleges & Universities,
234
www.aaicu.org
Association of American Schools of Central America, 236
www.american-schools.com.mx
Association of American Schools of South America, 237
www.aassa.com

Association of British Schools in Spain , 238
www.nabss.org
Association of Christian Schools Internationa , 239
www.acsi.org
Association of Educational Therapists , 215
www.aetonline.org
Association of Educators in Private Practice , 28
www.aepp.org
Association of International Educators , 240
www.nafsa.org
Association of International Schools in Afric , 241
www.aisa.or.ke
Association of School Business Officials International, 157
http://asbointl.org
Association of Science-Technology Centers , 366
www.astc.org
Aviation Information Resources , 196
www.airapps.com
Awards and Recognition Association , 30
www.ara.org
Better Chance , 31
www.betterchance.org
British American Educational Foundation , 242
www.baef.org
CDS International , 244
www.cdsintl.org
CHADD: Children & Adults with Attention Deficit/Hyperactivity
Disorder, 32
www.chadd.org
California Business Education Association , 426
www.cbeaonline.org
California Classical Association-Northern Section, 427
http://userwww.sfsu.edu/~barbaram/cca.htm
California Foundation for Agriculture in the lassroom, 428
www.cfaitc.org
California Library Association , 429
www.cla-net.org
California Reading Association , 430
www.californiareads.org
California School Library Association , 431
www.schoolibrary.org
California Teachers Association , 432
www.cta.org
Canadian Association of Independent Schools , 245
www.cais.ca
Catholic Medical Mission Board , 247
www.cmmb.org
Center for Applied Linguistics , 304
www.cal.org
Center for Civic Education , 34
www.civiced.org
Center for Education Studies , 382
www.historytextbooks.org
Center for Educational Technologies , 396
www.cet.edu
Center for Play Therapy , 187
www.coe.unt.edu./cpt/prosindex.html
Center for Strategic & International Studies , 248
www.csis.org
Central and Eastern European Schools Association, 249
www.ceesa.org
Child Care Information Exchange , 180
www.ccie.com
Civic Practices Network , 37
www.cpn.org
Clearinghouse for Immigrant Education , 38
www.mcas1.org
Close-Up Foundation , 358
www.closeup.org
College Board , 359
www.collegeboard.org
Colorado Association of Libraries , 435
www.cal-webs.org

Colorado Library Association , 440
www.coloradoea.org
Communicating for Agriculture , 250
www.selfemployedcountry.com
Computer Using Educators, Inc (CUE) , 397
www.cue.org
Concern-America Volunteers , 251
www.concernamerica.org
Connecticut Educational Media Association , 443
www.ctcema.org
Consortium for School Networking , 398
www.cosn.org
Constitutional Rights Foundation , 39
www.crf-usa.org
Cordell Hull Foundation for International Education, 253
http://payson.tulane.edu/cordellhull
Council for Advancement & Support of Educatio , 40
www.case.org
Council for Exceptional Children , 41
www.cec.sped.org
Council for Indian Education , 383
www.cie-mt.org
Council of British Independent Schools in the European
Communities, 254
www.cobisec.org
Council of Chief State School Officers , 158
www.ccsso.org
Council of Education Facility Planners-Intern tional, 255
www.cefpi.com
Council on Foreign Relations , 256
www.cfr.org
Council on Hemisphere Affairs , 257
www.coha.org
Council on International Educational Exchange , 258
www.ciee.org
Council on Islamic Education , 259
www.cie.org
Council on Postsecondary Accreditation , 44
www.cgsnet.org
Counseling Association , 216
www.counseling.org
Delaware Library Association , 446
www.dla.lib.de.us
Dimensions of Early Childhood , 181
www.southernearlychildhood.org
Disability Rights Education & Defense Fund , 45
www.dredf.org
District of Columbia Business Education Association, 450
www.dcla.org
Division of Student Leadership Services , 593
www.vaprincipals.org
EDUCAUSE , 399
www.educause.edu
EF Educational Tours , 48
www.eftours.com
ERIC Clearinghouse on Assessment & Evaluation , 49
www.ericae.net
ERIC Clearinghouse on Disabilities and Gifted Education, 50
www.cec.sped.org/ericec.htm
ERIC Clearinghouse on Educational Management , 159
www.eric.uoregon.edu
ERIC Clearinghouse on Elementary & Early Chil hood Education,
188
www.ericeece.org
ERIC Clearinghouse on Languages and Linguisti s, 160
www.cal.org
ERIC Clearinghouse on Languages and Linguisti s, 305
www.cal.org/ericcll/
ERIC Clearinghouse on Rural Education & Small Schools, 51
www.ael.org/eric
ERIC Clearinghouse on Urban Education , 52
http://eric-web.tc.columbia.edu
East Asia Regional Council of Overseas School , 261
www.earcos.org

Easter Seals Communications , 53
www.easterseals.com
Education Advisory Group , 183
www.eduadvisory.com
Education Commission of the States , 54
www.ecs.org
Education Development Center , 55
http://main.edc.org
Education Extension , 56
www.okstate.edu/education/outreach
Education Minnesota , 512
www.educationminnesota.org
Education, Training and Research Associates , 57
www.etr.org
Educational Equity Concepts , 58
www.edequity.org
Educational Media Association of New Jersey , 539
www.emanj.org
Educational Register , 59
www.vincentcurtis.com
Educational Technology Center , 400
http://edetc1.harvard.edu
Eisenhower National Clearinghouse for Mathema ics and Science
Education, 325
www.enc.org
Eisenhower National Clearinghouse for Mathema ics and Science
Education, 369
www.enc.org
Equity 2000 , 326
www.collegeboard.org
Equity Clearinghouse , 60
www.mcrel.org
Facing History & Ourselves , 61
www.facinghistory.org
Florida Association for Media in Education , 453
www.floridamedia.org
Florida Education Association , 455
www.feaweb.org
Foundation for Student Communication , 63
www.princeton.edu/~fscint
Future Music Oregon , 333
http://darkwing.uoregon.edu/~fmo
Georgia Business Education Association , 459
www.georgiagbea.org
Georgia Parents & Teachers Association , 461
www.georgiapta.org
Geothermal Education Office , 370
http://geothermal.marin.org
Gifted Child Society , 65
www.gifted.org
Girls Incorporated , 66
www.girlsinc.org
Graphic Arts Education & Research Foundation , 198
www.npes.org
Graphic Arts Technical Foundation , 199
www.gatf.org
HEATH Resource Center , 67
www.heath.gwu.edu
Hawaii Business Education Association , 462
www.geocites.com
Hawaii Library Association , 464
www.hlaweb.org
Hawaii State Teachers Association , 465
www.hsta.org
Health Occupations Students of America , 200
www.hosa.org
History of Science Society , 371
www.hssonline.org
Idaho Education Association , 466
www.idahoea.org
Idaho Library Association , 467
www.idaholibraries.org

Illinois Affiliation of Private Schools for Exceptional Children,
469
www.iapsec.org
Illinois Education Association , 473
www.ila.org
Illinois Library Association , 474
www.ila.org
Illinois School Library Media Association , 475
www.islma.org
Independent Schools Association of the Central States, 161
www.isacs.org
Indiana Association of School Business Officials, 476
www.indiana-asbo.org
Indiana Business Education Association , 477
http://ind-ibea.org
Indiana Library Federation , 478
www.ilfonline.org
Indiana State Teachers Association , 479
www.istain.org
Institute for Earth Education , 372
www.eartheducation.org
Institute for Educational Leadership , 71
www.iel.org
International Association for Continuing Education & Training,
267
www.iacet.org
International Association for the Exchange of Students for
Technical Experience, 268
www.iaeste.org
International Association of Counseling Services, 218
www.iacsinc.org
International Association of School Librarian hip, 320
www.ias-slo.org
International Baccalaureate North America , 270
www.ibo.org
International Baccalaureate Organization , 271
www.ibo.org
International Council for Health, Physical Education and
Recreation, 344
www.ichpersd.org
International Dyslexia Association , 306
www.interdys.org
International Graphic Arts Education Association, 202
www.igaea.org
International Graphic Arts Education Association, 273
www.igaea.org
International Physicians for the Prevention of Nuclear War, 276
www.ippnw.org
International Reading Association , 350
www.reading.org
International Research and Exchanges Board , 277
www.irex.org
International Schools Services , 278
www.iss.edu
International Society for Performance Improvement, 72
www.ispi.org
International Society for Technology in Education, 401
www.iste.org
International Thespian Society , 334
www.edta.org
Iowa Library Association , 482
www.iowalibraryassociation.org
Iowa State Education Association , 483
www.isea.org
Jewish Education Service of North America , 73
www.jesna.org
Jewish Educators Assembly , 74
wwww.jewisheducators.org
John Dewey Society for the Study of Education & Culture, 76
www.johndeweysociety.org
Journalism Education Association , 307
www.jea.org
Kansas Business Education Association , 486
www.ksbea.org

Kansas Education Association , 487
www.knea.org
Kansas Library Association , 488
http://skyways.lib.ks.us.kla
Kennedy Center Alliance for Arts Education , 335
www.kennedy-center.org/education/kcaaen
Kentucky Library Association , 490
www.kylibasn.org
Kentucky School Media Association , 491
www.kysma.org
Learning Disabilities Association of America , 78
www.ldanatl.org
Learning Independence Through Computers , 402
www.linc.org
Louisiana Association of Educators , 493
www.lae.org
Louisiana Library Association , 495
www.llaonline.org
Lutheran Education Association , 79
www.lea.org
MATRIX: A Parent Network and Resource Center , 80
www.matirxparents.org
Maine Association of School Libraries , 496
www.maslibraries.org
Maine Library Association , 499
http://mainelibraries.org
MarcoPolo , 403
www.marcopolo-education.org
Martin De Porress , 548
www.mdp.org
Maryland Educational Media Organization , 500
www.tcps.md.us
Maryland Library Association , 501
www.mdlib.org
Massachusetts Library Association , 504
www.masslib.org
Massachusetts Teachers Association , 505
www.massteacher.org
Mathematical Association of America , 327
www.maa.org
Mediterranean Association of International Schools, 281
www.mais-web.org
Michigan Association for Media in Education , 507
www.mame.gen.mi.us
Michigan Library Association , 511
www.mla.lib.mi.us
Minnesota Business Educators , 513
http://mbei.gen.mn.us
Minnesota Library Association , 515
www.mnlibraryassociation.org
Minnesota School Boards Association , 516
www.mnmsba.org
Mississippi Library Association , 519
www.misslib.org
Missouri Association of Secondary School Principals, 521
www.moassp.org
Missouri Library Association , 524
http://molib.org
Missouri National Education Association , 525
www.mnea.org
Missouri State Teachers Association , 526
www.msta.org
Montana Association of County School Superintendents, 527
www.sammt.org/macss
Montana Library Association , 530
www.mtlib.org
Music Teachers National Association , 336
www.mtna.org
NASW Job Link: The Social Work Employment Lin , 204
www.socialworkers.org
National Academy of Education , 81
www.nae.nyu.edu
National Alliance for Safe Schools , 82
www.safeschools.org

National Art Education Association , 337
www.naea-reston.org
National Association for Bilingual Education , 308
www.nabe.org
National Association for Girls and Women in Sports, 345
www.aahperd.org/nagws
National Association for Industry-Education Cooperation, 85
www2.pcom.net/naiec
National Association for Music Education , 338
www.menc.org
National Association for Supervision and Curriculum
Development, 163
www.ascd.org
National Association for Year-Round Education , 87
www.NAYRE.org
National Association for the Education of Young Children, 190
www.naeyc.org
National Association of Academic Advisors for Athletics, 346
www.nfoura/org
National Association of Biology Teachers , 375
www.nabt.org
National Association of Boards of Education , 88
www.ncea.org
National Association of Elementary School Principals, 164
www.naesp.org
National Association of Elementary School Principals, 191
www.naesp.org
National Association of Federally Impacted Schools, 90
www.sso.org/nafis/
National Association of Media and Technology Centers, 404
www.namtc.org
National Association of Private Schools for Exceptional Children,
167
www.napsec.com
National Association of School Psychologists , 219
www.masponline.org
National Association of Schools of Music , 339
www.arts-accredit.org/nasm.htm
National Association of Secondary School Principals, 168
http://nasspcms.principals.org
National Association of Social Workers , 220
www.naswdc.org
National Association of State Boards of Education, 91
www.nasbe.org
National Association of State Directors of Special Education, 169
www.nasdse.org
National Association of Student Activity Advisers, 92
http://nasccms.principals.org/s_nasc
National Association of Student Financial Aid Administrators, 170
www.nasfaa.org
National Association of Student Personnel Administrators, 171
www.naspa.org/
National Association of Teachers' Agencies , 205
www.jobsforteachers.com
National Athletic Trainers' Association , 347
www.nata.org
National Business Education Association , 206
www/nbea.org
National Business Education Association , 360
www.nbea.com
National Catholic Educational Association , 96
www.ncea.org
National Center for Learning Disabilities , 97
www.ncld.org
National Center for Science Education , 376
www.ncseweb.org
National Coalition of Advocates for Students , 98
www.ncasboston.org
National Coalition of Alternative Community Schools, 99
www.ncacs.org
National Coalition of Independent Scholars , 100
www.ncis.org
National Commission for Cooperative Education , 101
www.co-op.edu

National Council for Black Studies , 104
www.nationalcouncilforblackstudies.com
National Council for the Social Studies , 385
www.ncss.org
National Council of Higher Education , 105
www.nea.org/he/nche
National Council of State Directors of Adult Education, 173
www.ncsdae.org
National Council of Teachers of English , 309
www.ncte.org
National Council of Teachers of Mathematics , 328
www.nctm.org
National Council of Urban Education Associati ns, 106
www.nea.org/ncueahome
National Council on Measurement in Education , 107
www.ncme.org
National Council on Student Development , 109
www.wjcac.com/directory
National Data Bank for Disabled Student Services, 174
www.inform.umd.edu/
National Dissemination Center for Children with Disabilities, 110
www.nichey.org
National Early Childhood Technical Assistance Center, 184
www.nectas.unc.edu
National Education Association , 111
www.nea.org
National Education Association Student Progra , 112
www.nea.org
National Education Association of New Mexico , 543
www.nea-nm.org
National Education Association-Retired , 113
www.nea.org/retired
National Education Policy Institute , 114
www.nabse.org
National Educational Service , 115
www.nesonline.com
National Guild of Community Schools of the Arts, 340
www.nationalguild.org
National Head Start Association , 186
www.nhsa.org
National Institute for School and Workplace Safety, 175
www.nisws.com
National Institute for Science Education , 377
www.wcer.wisc.edu/nise
National Institute of Art and Disabilities , 341
www.niadart.org
National Institute on Disability and Rehabili ation Research, 405
www.ed.gov/about/offices/list/osers/nidrr
National Lekotek Center , 117
www.lekotek.org
National Middle School Association , 118
www.nmsa.org
National Middle School Association , 361
www.nmsa.org
National Network for Early Language Learning (NELL), 312
www.educ.iastate.edu/nnell/
National Network of Learning Disabled Adults , 119
www.nifl.gov/nalld/resource.html
National Organization on Disability , 120
www.nod.org
National Registration Center for Study Abroad , 283
www.nrcsa.com
National Research Center on English Learning and Achievement,
313
www.cela.albany.edu
National School Boards Association , 121
www.nsba.org
National School Public Relations Association , 122
www.nspra.org
National School Safety Center , 176
www.nssc1.org
National Science Teachers Association , 378
www.nsta.org

National Society for Experiential Education , 123
www.nsee.org
National Student Exchange , 125
www.buffalostate.edu/~nse
National Student Program , 126
www.nea.org
National Telemedia Council , 127
http://danenet.wicip.org/ntc/
National Women's Studies Association , 129
www.nwsa.org
Native American Homeschool Association , 130
www.expage.com/page/nahomeschool
Near East-South Asia Council of Overseas Schools, 284
www.nesacenter.org
Nebraska Library Association , 531
www.nol.org/home/nla
Nebraska State Education Association , 533
www.nsea.org
Nevada Library Association , 534
www.nevadalibraries.org
Nevada State Education Association , 535
www.nsea.nv.org
New Hampshire Business Education Association , 536
rhill@newfound.k12.nh.us
New Hampshire Education Association , 537
www.neanh.org
New Hampshire Library Association , 538
www.state.nh.us/nhla
New Jersey Education Association , 540
www.njea.org
New Jersey State Department of Education Resource Center, 542
www.state.nj.us/education
North American Association for Environmental Education, 131
www.naaee.org
North American Association for Environmental Education, 387
http://naaee.org
North American Association of Educational Negotiators, 132
www.naen.org/
North American Students of Cooperation , 134
www.nasco.coop
North Carolina Association for Career and Technical Education,
551
www.ncacte.org
North Carolina Association of Educators , 552
www.ncae.org
Northern California Comprehensive Assistance Center, 433
www.wested.org/cs/we/view/pj/224
Northwest Association of Schools & Colleges , 135
www2.boisestate.edu/nasc
Odyssey of the Mind , 136
www.odysseyofthemind.com
Office of Juvenile Justice and Delinquency Prevention, 177
www.ojjdp.ncjrs.org
Oklahoma Education Association , 563
www.okea.org
Oregon Educational Media Association , 567
www.teleport.com
Organization of Virginia Homeschoolers , 594
www.vahomeschoolers.org
PACER Center , 138
www.pacer.org
Pacific Northwest Library Association , 321
www.pnla
Pacific Northwest Library Association , 468
www.iapsec.org
Parents Rights Organization , 139
www.educational-freedom.org
Parents, Let's Unite for Kids , 140
www.pluk.org
Pennsylvania School Librarians Association , 571
www.plsa.org
Pennsylvania State Education Association , 572
www.psea.org

People to People International , 289
www.ptpi.org
Phi Delta Kappa , 290
www.pdkintl.org
President's Council on Physical Fitness & Sports, 348
www.fitness.gov
Printing Industries of America , 208
www.gain.net
Pro Libra , 322
www.prolibra.com
ProLiteracy Worldwide , 353
www.proliteracy.org
Psychological Corporation , 178
www.hbem.com
Public Relations Student Society of America , 142
www.prssa.org
Reading Recovery Council of North America , 354
www.readingrecovery.org
Renew America , 144
www.sol.crest.org/enviroment/renew_america
Rhode Island Educational Media Association , 574
www.ri.net
Rhode Island National Education Association , 576
www.neari.org
Safe Schools America , 179
www.safeschoolsamerica.com
Schiller Center , 145
www.schiller.org
Science Service , 379
www.sciserv.org
Sexuality Information & Education Council of the US, 146
www.siecus.org
Sigma Tau Delta , 314
www.english.org
Society of School Librarians International , 323
http://facon.jmu.edu/~ramseyil/sslihome.htm
South Carolina Library Association , 578
www.scla.org
Summit Vision , 150
www.summit-vision.com
Teach Overseas , 293
www.iss.edu
Teachers & Writers Collaborative , 315
www.twc.org
Teachers of English to Speakers of Other Languages, 294
www.tesol.org
Technology & Media Division , 406
www.tamcec.org
Technology Student Association , 407
www.tsaweb.org
Technology and Children , 408
www.iteawww.org
Telemetrics , 409
www.telemetrics.com
Tennessee School Boards Association , 584
www.tsba.net
Texas Library Association , 586
www.txla.org
Twenty First Century Teachers Network: The Mc uffey Project,
410
www.21ct.org/
United Nations Development Program , 295
www.undp.org
Vermont Library Association , 590
www.vermontlibraries.org
Virginia Association for the Education of the Gifted, 599
www.vagifted.org
Virginia Association of Independent Schools , 602
www.vais.org
Virginia Association of School Personnel Administrators, 605
www.aaspa.org
Virginia Congress of Parents & Teachers , 606
www.vapta.org

Virginia Council for Private Education , 608
www.vcpe.org
Virginia Council of Administrators of Special Education, 609
www.vcase.org
Virginia Council on Economic Education , 611
www.vcee.org
Virginia Educational Media Association , 613
www.vema.gan.va.us
Virginia School Boards Association , 618
www.vsba.org
Visions in Action , 296
www.visionsinaction.org
Volunteers for Peace , 591
www.vfp.org
Voyager Expanded Learning , 192
www.voyagerlearning.com
WestEd , 434
www.WestEd.org
Western Association of Colleges & Employers , 209
wwww.wace.net
Western History Association , 390
www.unm.edu/~wha
Wilderness Education Association , 151
www.weainfo.org
Wisconsin Educational Media Association , 627
www.wemaonline.org
Women's Educational & Industrial Union , 153
www.weiu.org
Women's International League for Peace & Free om, 210
www.wilpf.org

Conferences & Trade Shows

ACSI Teachers' Convention , 654
www.acsi.org
ASCD Annual Conference & Exhibit Show , 655
www.ascd.org
AZLA/MPLA Conference , 656
www.azla.org
American Association School Administrators National Conference
on Education, 658
www.aasa.org
American Association for Employment in Education Annual
Conference, 659
www.aaee.org
American Association for Higher Education: An ual Assessment
Conference, 660
www.aahe.org
American Association for Higher Education: Le rning to Change
Conference, 661
www.aahe.org
American Association for Higher Education: Su mer Academy,
Organizing for Learning, 662
www.aahe.org
American Association of Colleges for Teacher Ed Annual Meeting
and Exhibits, 663
www.aacte.org
American Association of French Teachers Conference, 664
www.frenchteachers.org/convention
American Association of Physics Teachers National Meeting, 665
www.aapt.org
American Association of School Administrators Annual
Convention, 666
www.aasa.org
American Association of School Librarians National Conference,
667
www.ala.org/aasl
American Association of Sex Educators, Counselors & Therapists
Conference, 668
www.aasect.org
American Camping Association National Conference, 669
www.acaamps.org

American Council on Education Annual Meeting , 670
  www.acenet.edu/meeting/index.cfm
American Council on the Teaching of Foreign Languages Annual Conference, 671
  www.actfl.org
American Counseling Association Annual Convention, 672
  www.counseling.org
American Education Finance Association Annual Conference & Workshop, 673
  www.aefa.cc
American Educational Research Association Annual Meeting, 674
  www.aera.net
American Indian Science & Engineering Society Annual Conference, 676
  www.aises.org
American Library Association Annual Conferenc , 677
  www.ala.org
American Mathematical Society , 678
  www.ams.org
American Montessori Society Conference , 679
  www.amshq.org
American Psychological Association Annual Conference, 680
  www.apa.org/convention05
American Public Health Association Annual Meeting, 681
  www.apha.org/meetings
American School Health Association's National School Conference, 682
  www.ashaweb.org
American Speech-Language-Hearing Association Annual Convention, 683
  www.asha.org
American Technical Education Association Annual Conference, 684
  www.ateaonline.org
Annual Academic-Vocational Integrated Curriculum Conference, 685
  www.nscinet.com
Annual Ethics & Technology Conference , 689
  www.ethicstechconference.org
Annual Microcomputers in Education Conference , 690
  mec.asu.edu
Annual NCEA Convention & Exposition , 691
  www.ncea.org
Annual Technology & Learning Conference , 692
  www.nsba.org
Association for Advancement of Behavior Therapy Annual Convention, 693
  www.aabt.org
Association for Behavior Analysis Annual Convention, 694
  www.abainternational.org
Association for Childhood Education International Annual Conference, 632
  www.acei.org
Association for Education in Journalism and Mass Communication Convention, 695
  www.aejmc.org/convention
Association for Experiential Education Annual Conference, 633
  www.aee.org
Association for Persons with Severe Handicaps Annual Conference, 696
  www.tash.org
Association for Play Therapy Conference , 697
  www.a4pt.org
Association for Science Teacher Education Science Annual Meeting, 698
  www.aste.chem.pitt.edu
Association for Supervision & Curriculum Development Annual Conference, 699
  www.ascd.org
Association for the Advancement of Internatio al Education, 700
  www.aaie.org
Association for the Education of Gifted Underachieving Students Conference, 701
  www.aegus1.org

Association for the Study of Higher Education Annual Meeting, 702
  www.ashe.ws/index.htm
Association of American Colleges & Universiti s Annual Meeting, 703
  www.aacu-edu.org
Association of Community College Trustees Conference, 704
  www.acct.org
Association of Science-Technology Centers Incorporated Conference, 705
  www.astc.org
Bienvenue Annual Conference , 634
  www.ciee.org
CHADD: Children & Adults with Attention Deficit/Hyperactivity Disorder, 706
  www.chadd.org
Center for Appalachian Studies & Services Annual Conference, 707
  www.cass.etsu.edu/
Center for Critical Thinking and Moral Critique Annual International, 635
  www.criticalthinking.org
Center for Gifted Education and Talent Development Conference, 709
  www.gifted.uconn.edu
Center for Play Therapy Summer Institute , 825
  www.centerforplaytherapy.com
Center for Rural Education and Small Schools Annual Conference, 710
  www.coe.ksu.edu/CRESS/conference.html
Center on Disabilities Conference , 711
  www.csun.edu/cod
Childhood Education Association International , 636
  wwwacei.org
Choristers Guild's National Festival & Directors' Conference, 712
  www.choristersguild.org
Clonlara School Annual Conference Home Educat rs, 805
  www.clonlara.org
Closing the Gap , 713
  www.closingthegap.com
Computers on Campus National Conference , 714
  www.rcce.sc.edu/coc
Conference for Advancement of Mathematics Teaching, 715
  www.tea.state.tx.us
Conference on Information Technology , 716
  www.league.org
Council for Advancement and Support of Educat on, 717
  www.case.org
Council for Exceptional Children Annual Convention, 718
  www.cec.sped.org
Council for Learning Disabilities International Conference, 637
  www.cldinternational.org
Council of British Independent Schools in the European Communities Annual Conference, 638
  www.cobisec.org
EDUCAUSE , 719
  www.educause.edu
Education Technology Conference , 720
  www.salt.org
Educational Publishing Summit: Creating Manag ng & Selling Content, 721
  www.edpress.org
Educational Theatre Association Conference , 722
  www.edta.org
Embracing an Inclusive Society: The Challenge for the New Millennium, 723
  www.nmci.org
European Council of International Schools , 639
  www.ecis.org
Foundation for Critical Thinking Regional Workshop & Conference, 724
  www.criticalthinking.org
Gifted Child Society Conference , 725
  www.gifted.org

High School Reform Conference , 726
www.nscinet.com
Hitting the High Notes of Literacy , 727
www.literacyvolunteers.org
Hort School: Conference of the Association of American Schools,
640
www.isp.edu.pa
INFOCOMM Tradeshow , 728
www.chiefmfg.com
Illinois Library Association Conference , 808
www.ila.org
Improving Student Performance , 729
www.nsse.org
Increasing Student Achievement in Reading, Wr ting,
Mathematics, Science, 730
www.nscinet.com
Independent Education Consultants Association Conference, 731
www.IECAonline.com
Infusing Brain Research, Multi-Intelligence, Learning Styles and
Mind Styles, 732
www.nscinet.com
Instant Access: Critical Findings from the NRC/GT, 733
www.gifted.uconn.edu
Integrated/Thematic Curriculum and Performanc Assessment, 734
www.nscinet.com
International Association of Teachers of English as a Foreign
Language, 641
www.iatefl.org
International Awards Market , 642
www.ara.org
International Conference , 643
www.wasbe.org/en/conferences/index.html
International Congress for School Effectiveness & Improvement,
644
www.icsei.net
International Dyslexia Association Annual Conference, 645
www.interdys.org
International Exhibit , 646
www.nisod.org
International Listening Association Annual Convention, 647
www.bsu.edu/cics
International Performance Improvement Confere ce Expo, 735
www.ispi.org
International Reading Association Annual Convention, 648
www.reading.org
International Symposium , 649
www.aauw.org
International Technology Education Association Conference, 650
www.iteawww.org
International Trombone Festival , 651
www.trombone.net
Iteachk , 736
www.iteachk.com
Journalism Education Association , 737
www.jea.org/
Learner-Centered , 652
www.iut2000.org
Learning Disabilities Association of America International
Conference, 653
www.ldaamerica.org
Lutheran Education Association Convention , 739
www.lea.org
Meeting the Tide of Rising Expectations , 741
www.nasdtec.org
Missouri Library Association Conference , 826
www.mlnc.com/~mla/
Music Educators National Conference , 743
www.menc.org
Music Teachers Association National Conferenc , 744
www.mtna.org
NAAEE Member Services Office , 745
www.naaee.org
NSTA Educational Workshops , 747
www.nsta.org/programs/new

National Academy Foundation Annual Institute for Staff
Development, 748
www.naf-education.org
National Alliance of Black School Educators Conference, 749
www.nabse.org
National Art Education Association Annual Convention, 750
www.naea-reston.org
National Association for Bilingual Education , 751
www.nabe.org
National Association for College Admission Counseling
Conference, 752
www.nacac.com
National Association for Girls and Women in Sports Yearly
Conference, 753
www.aahperd.org/nagws/nagws
National Association for Multicultural Education, 754
www.inform.umd.edu/name
National Association for Year-Round Education Annual
Conference, 755
www.NAYRE.org
National Association of Biology Teachers Conference, 756
www.nabt.org
National Association of Elementary School Principals Conference,
757
www.naesp.org
National Association of Independent Schools Conference, 758
www.nais.org
National Association of Private Schools for Exceptional Children
Conference, 759
www.napsec.com
National Association of School Psychologists Annual Convention,
760
www.nasponline.org
National Association of Teachers' Agencies Conference, 762
www.jobsforteachers.com
National Black Child Development Institute Annual Conference,
763
www.nbcdi.org
National Catholic Education Association Annual Convention &
Exposition, 764
www.ncea.org
National Coalition for Sex Equity in Educatio , 766
www.ncsee.org
National Conference on Student Services , 769
www.magnapubs.com
National Congress on Aviation and Space Education, 770
www.cap.af.mil
National Council of Higher Education , 771
www.nea.org
National Council on Alcoholism & Drug Abuse , 772
www.ncada-stl.org
National Dropout Prevention Center/Network Conference, 773
www.dropoutprevention.com
National Education Association-Retired , 774
www.nea.org/retired
National Guild of Community Schools of the Arts Conference, 775
www.nationalguild.org
National Head Start Association Annual Conference, 776
www.nhsa.org
National Institute for School and Workplace Safety Conference,
777
www.nisws.com/
National Rural Education Association Annual Convention, 781
www.nrea.net
National School Conference Institute , 783
www.nscinet.com
National School Supply & Equipment Association, 784
www.nessa.org
National Society for Experiential Education Conference, 785
www.nsee.org
National Women's History Project Annual Conference, 787
www.nwhp.org
New Learning Technologies , 788
www.salt.org

North American Montessori Teachers' Association, 789
www.montessori-namta.org/
Parents as Teachers National Center Conference, 790
www.patnc.org
Retention in Education Today for All Indigenous Nations, 791
www.conferencepros.com
SERVE Conference , 792
www.serve.org
Satellites and Education Conference , 816
www.sated.org/eceos
Sexual Assault and Harassment on Campus Conference, 794
www.ed.mtu.edu/safe
Teacher Link: An Interactive National Teleconference, 796
cssrs.ou.edu
Teachers of English to Speakers of Other Languages Convention
and Exhibit, 797
www.tesol.org
Teaching for Intelligence Conference , 798
www.iriskylight.com
Technology & Learning Schooltech Exposition & Conference, 799
www.SchoolTechExpo.com
Technology Student Conference , 800
www.tsawww.org
Technology and Learning Conference , 828
www.nsba.org
Technology in 21st Century Schools , 801
www.nscinet.com
Technology, Reading & Learning Difficulties Conference, 802
www.trld.com
Texas Library Association Conference , 834
www.txla.org
Training of Trainers Seminar , 803
www.activeparenting.com
UNI Overseas Recruiting Fair , 817
www.uni.edu/placement/overseas
WA-ACTE Career and Technical Exhibition for Career and
Technical Education, 823
www.wa-acte.org

Consultants

Association for Refining Cross-Cultured International, 844
www.arcint.com
Association of Christian Schools Internationa , 845
www.acsi.org
Beacon Education Management , 848
www.beaconedu.com
Center for Professional Development & Service , 858
www.pdkintl.org
Childs Consulting Associates , 862
www.childs.com
Classroom , 863
www.classroominc.org
Conover Company , 870
www.conovercompany.com
Continuous Learning Group Limited Liability Company, 872
www.clg-online.com
Council on Occupational Education , 876
www.council.org
East Central Educational Service Center , 886
www.ecesc.k12.in.us
Edison Schools , 888
www.edisonschools.com
Education Concepts , 889
www.ed-concepts.com
Education Development Center , 891
www.edc.org
Education Management Consulting LLC , 892
www.edmgt.com
Educational Credential Evaluators , 894
www.ece.org

Educational Information & Resource Center , 896
www.eirc.org
Educational Systems for the Future , 900
www.esf-protainer,com
Educational Technology Design Consultants , 901
www.etdc.com/html/about_us.html
Effective Training Solutions , 905
www.trainingsucess.com
Efficacy Institute , 906
www.efficacy.org
Examiner Corporation , 910
www.xmn.com
FPMI Communications , 912
www.fmpi.com
Institute for Development of Educational Activities, 926
www.idea.com
Institute for Global Ethics , 927
www.globalethics.org
Interface Network , 928
info@leaderEd.com
John McLaughlin Company , 937
www.mclaughlincompany.com
Kaludis Consulting Group , 940
www.kcg.com
Leona Group , 944
www.leonagroup.com
Linkage , 945
www.linkageinc.com
Magi Educational Services Incorporated , 951
www.westchesterinst.org
Management Concepts , 952
www.managementconcepts.com
Marketing Education Resource Center , 954
www.mark-ed.com
Mosaica Education , 972
www.mosaicaeducation.com
National Heritage Academies , 976
www.heritageacademies.com
National Reading Styles Institute , 977
www.nrsi.com
National School Safety and Security Services , 978
www.schoolsecurity.org
Performa , 986
www.performainc.com
Poetry Alive , 987
www.poetryalive.com
Relearning by Design , 1003
www.relearning.org
School March by Public Priority Systems , 1009
www.schoolmatch.com
Special Education Service Agency , 1014
www.isbe.net
Success for All Foundation , 1018
www.successforall.net
Tesseract Group , 1023
www.tesseractgroup.org
University of Georgia-Instructional Technolog , 1026
http//itechl.coe.uga.edu
Uplinc , 1027
www.uplinc.com
William A Ewing & Company , 1028
www.members.aol.com/ewingo

Financial Resources

AFL-CIO Guide to Union Sponsored Scholarships, Awards &
Student Aid, 2866
www.unionplus.org
Abell Foundation , 2491
www.abell.org
Achelis Foundation , 2609
fdncenter.org/grantmaker/achelis-bodman

Adolph Coors Foundation , 2359
www.adolphcoors.org
Aegon USA , 2492
www.aegonins.com
Aetna Foundation , 2366
www.aetna.com/foundation/
Aid for Education , 2845
cdpublications.com
Akron Community Foundation , 2692
www.akroncommunityfdn.org
Albert & Ethel Herzstein Charitable Foundation, 2764
www.herzsteinfoundation.org
Alcoa Foundation , 2726
www.alcoa.com
All Sports , 2846
www.graduationshirts.com
Allen County Public Library , 2461
www.acpl.lib.in.us
Altman Foundation , 2612
www.altmanfoundation.org
Ambrose Monell Foundation , 2613
www.monellvetlesen.org
Ameren Corporation Charitable Trust , 2570
www.ameren.com
American Express Foundation , 2614

www.home3.americanexpress.com/corp/philanthropy/contacts.asp
American Honda Foundation , 2823
www.hondacorporate.com/community
American-Scandinavian Foundation , 2867
www.amscan.org
Ameritech Foundation , 2435
www.ntlf.com
Andrew W Mellon Foundation , 2615
www.mellon.org
Annenberg Foundation , 2727
www.annenbergfoundation.org
Arizona Department of Education , 2260
www.ade.state.az.us
Art to Remember , 2847
www.arttoremember.com
Arts Scholarships , 2868
www.jfew.org
Ashland Incorporated Foundation , 2477
www.ashland.com
Associated Grantmakers of Massachusetts , 2506
www.agmconnect.org
Atlanta-Fulton Public Library , 2403
www.af.public.lib.ga.us
Auburn University at Montgomery Library , 2250
www.aumnicat.aum.edu
Awards for University Teachers and Research Workers, 2825
www.devry.edu
Bayer Corporation , 2730
www.bayerus.com/about/community/
Beazley Foundation , 2800
www.beazleyfoundation.org
BellSouth Foundation , 2404
www.bellsouthfoundation.org
Birmingham Public Library , 2252
www.bplonline.org/resources/subjects/gov/deault
Boettcher Foundation , 2360
www.boettcherfoundation.org
Boise Public Library , 2432
www.boisepubliclibrary.org
Boston Foundation , 2507
www.tbf.org
Boston Globe Foundation II , 2508
www.bostonglobe.com/community/foundation/partner.stm
Boston Public Library , 2509
www.bpl.org
Bristol-Myers Squibb Foundation , 2620
www.bms.com

Buffalo & Erie County Public Library , 2621
www.buffalolib.org/libraries/central
Burton D Morgan Foundation , 2694
www.bdmorganfdn.org
Bush Foundation , 2551
www.bushfoundation.org
CUNY Teacher Incentive Program , 2869
www.jfew.org
California Community Foundation , 2284
www.calfund.org
Cannon Foundation , 2678
www.thecannonfoundationinc.org
Cargill Foundation , 2552
www.cargill.com
Carnegie Corporation of New York , 2625
www.carnegie.org
Carrie Estelle Doheny Foundation , 2285
www.dohenyfoundation.org
Cedar Rapids Public Library , 2472
www.crlibrary.org
Champlin Foundations , 2749
www.fdncenter.org/grantmaker/champlin
Charles A Frueauff Foundation , 2269
www.frueauffoundation.com
Charles Stewart Mott Foundation , 2527
www.mott.org
Charleston County Library , 2752
www.ccpl.org
Chatlos Foundation , 2389
www.chatlos.org
Chicago Community Trust , 2438
www.cct.org
Childrens Youth Funding Report , 2848
cdpublications.com
Christian A Johnson Endeavor Foundation , 2627
www.csuohio.edu/uored/funding/johnson.htm
Claude R & Ethel B Whittenberger Foundation , 2433
www.whittenberger.org
Cleveland H Dodge Foundation , 2628
www.chdodgefoundation.org
Clowes Fund , 2463
www.clowesfund.org
Coca-Cola Foundation , 2407
www.thecoca-colacompany.com
Coleman Foundation , 2439
www.colemanfoundation.org
College Board , 2870
www.collegeboard.org
Collins Foundation , 2720
www.collinsfoundation.org
Community Foundation for Southeastern Michigan, 2529
www.cfsem.org
Community Foundation of Greater Flint , 2530
www.cfgf.org
Community Foundation of Greater New Haven , 2367
www.cfgnh.org
Community Foundation of New Jersey , 2594
www.cfnj.org
Connelly Foundation , 2732
www.connellyfdn.org
Conrad N Hilton Foundation , 2585
www.hiltonfoundation.org
Cooke Foundation , 2425
www.hawaiicommunityfoundation.org
Cooper Industries Foundation , 2767
www.cooperindustries.com
Cord Foundation , 2586
www.unr.edu/cll
Corpus Christi State University , 2768
www.library.ci.corpus-christi.tx.us
Cullen Foundation , 2769
www.cullenfdn.org
Dade Community Foundation , 2391
www.dadecommunityfoundation.org

Daisy Marquis Jones Foundation , 2630
  www.dmjf.org
Dallas Public Library , 2770
  www.dallaslibrary.org
Danforth Foundation , 2572
  www.orgs.muohio.edu/forumscp/indez.html
David & Lucile Packard Foundation , 2287
  www.packard.org
Dayton Foundation , 2695
  www.daytonfoundation.org
Denver Foundation , 2361
  www.denverfounation.org
Detroit Edison Foundation , 2532
  www.my.dteenergy.com
Dissertation Fellowships in the Humanities , 2871
  www.jfew.org
Donald W Reynolds Foundation , 2587
  www.dwreynolds.org
Dr. Scholl Foundation , 2442
  www.drschollfoundation.com
Dresher Foundation , 2496
  www.jdgraphicdesign.com/dresher/dresherfoundation/
Duke Endowment , 2680
  www.dukeendowment.org
Duluth Public Library , 2554
  www.duluth.lib.mn.us
Dutch Mill Bulbs , 2849
  www.dutchmillbulbs.com
Eastern Montana College Library , 2580
  www.msubillings.edu/library
Eden Hall Foundation , 2733
  www.edenhallfdn.org
Edna McConnell Clark Foundation , 2632
  www.emcf.org
Education Services , 2262
  www.ade.state.az.us/edservices
Educational Foundation of America , 2826
  www.efaw.org
Edward E Ford Foundation , 2497
  www.eeford.org
Edward W Hazen Foundation , 2634
  www.hazenfoundation.org
El Paso Community Foundation , 2771
  www.epcf.org
El Pomar Foundation , 2362
  www.elpomar.org
Enoch Pratt Free Library , 2498
  www.pratt.lib.md.us
Erie County Library System , 2734
  www.ecls.lib.pa.us
Eugene & Agnes E Meyer Foundation , 2379
  www.meyerfoundation.org
Eva L & Joseph M Bruening Foundation , 2696
  www.fmscleveland.com/bruening
Evanston Public Library , 2443
  www.evanston.lib.il.us
Exxon Education Foundation , 2775
  www.exxon.mobile.com
FR Bigelow Foundation , 2555
  www.frbigelow.org
Faye McBeath Foundation , 2817
  www.fayemcbeath.org
Flinn Foundation , 2264
  www.flinn.org
Foellinger Foundation , 2466
  www.foellinger.org
Ford Family Foundation , 2721
  www.tfff.org
Ford Foundation , 2639
  www.fordfound.org
Ford Motor Company Fund , 2533
  www.ford.com
Foundation Center , 2827
  www.fdncenter.org

Foundation Center-Carnegie Library of Pittsbu gh, 2735
  www.clpgh.org/clp/Foundation
Foundation Center-District of Columbia , 2380
  www.fdncenter.org/washington/index.jhtml
Foundation Center-San Francisco , 2289
  www.fdncenter.org
Foundation for the Carolinas , 2682
  www.fftc.org
Foundation for the Mid South , 2566
  www.fndmidsouth.org
Foundation for the National Capitol Region , 2381
  www.cfncr.org
Foundations Focus , 2290
  www.marincf.org
Fred B & Ruth B Zigler Foundation , 2486
  www.ziglerfoundation.org
Frey Foundation , 2534
  www.freyfdn.org
Frist Foundation , 2758
  www.fristfoundation.org
Fund for New Jersey , 2595
  www.fundfornj.org
GAR Foundation , 2697
  www.garfdn.org
GTE Foundation , 2828
  www.gte.com
General Motors Foundation , 2535
  www.gm.com/company/gmability/philanthropy
George Foundation , 2777
  www.thegeorgefoundation.org
George Gund Foundation , 2698
  www.gundfdn.org
George I Alden Trust , 2829
  www.aldentrust.org
Gladys Brooks Foundation , 2644
  www.gladysbrooksfoundation.org
Gold Medal Products , 2852
  www.gmpopcorn.copm
Grace & Franklin Bernsen Foundation , 2715
  www.bernsen.org
Grand Rapids Foundation , 2536
  www.grfoundation.org
Grantsmanship Center , 2833
  www.tgci.com
HJ Heinz Company Foundation , 2736
  www.heinz.com/jsp/foundation.jsp
Hagedorn Fund , 2646
  www.fdncenter.org/grantmaker/hagedorn/
Hampton Public Library , 2802
  www.hampton.va.us
Harold KL Castle Foundation , 2426
  www.castlefoundation.org
Hasbro Children's Foundation , 2647
  www.hasbro.org
Hawaiian Electric Industries Charitable Found tion, 2427
  www.hei.com/heicf/heicf.html
Henry & Ruth Blaustein Rosenberg Foundation , 2501
  www.blaufund.org
Henry Ford Centennial Library , 2538
  www.dearborn.lib.mi.us/aboutus/adult.htm
Henry J Kaiser Family Foundation , 2299
  www.kff.org
Henry Luce Foundation , 2648
  www.hluce.org
Herbert H & Grace A Dow Foundation , 2539
  www.hhdowfdn.org
Hess Foundation , 2650
  www.hess.com
Hitachi Foundation , 2383
  www.hitachi.org
Honeywell Foundation , 2597
  www.honeywell.com/about/foundation.html
Houston Endowment , 2781
  www.houstonendowment.org

Houston Public Library , 2782
   www.hpl.lib.tx.us/hpl/hplhome
Human-i-Tees , 2853
   www.humanitees.com
Huntsville Public Library , 2254
   www.hpl.lib.al.us/
Hyams Foundation , 2511
   www.hyamsfoundation.org
Hyde & Watson Foundation , 2598
   www.fdncenter.org/grantmaker/hydeandwatson
Indianapolis Foundation , 2467
   www.indyfund.org
Intel Science Talent Search Scolarship , 2873
   www.sciserv.org
Irene E & George A Davis Foundation , 2512
   www.davisfdn.org
JL Bedsole Foundation , 2255
   www.jlbedsolefoundation.org
Jackson-Hinds Library System , 2567
   www.jhlibrary.com
Jacksonville Public Library , 2393
   www.neflin.org/members/libraries/jackspub.htm
James Graham Brown Foundation , 2479
   www.jgbf.org
James S McDonnell Foundation , 2575
   www.jsmf.org
Jeffress Memorial Trust , 2803
   www.wm.edu/grants/opps/jeffress.htm
Jessie B Cox Charitable Trust , 2514
   www.hemenwaybarnes.com/selectsrv/jbcox/cox.html
Jessie Ball duPont Fund , 2394
   www.dupontfund.org
Jewish Foundation for Education of Women , 2874
   www.jfew.org
John S & James L Knight Foundation , 2834
   www.knightfdn.org
Joseph B Whitehead Foundation , 2412
   www.jbwhitehead.org
Joseph Drown Foundation , 2307
   www.jdrown.org
Joukowsky Family Foundation , 2655
   www.joukowsky.org
Joyce Foundation , 2446
   www.joycefdn.org
Julia R & Estelle L Foundation , 2656
   www.oisheifdt.org
Kanawha County Public Library , 2815
   www.kanawha.lib.wv.us
Kansas City Public Library , 2576
   www.kclibrary.org
Kenneth T & Eileen L Norris Foundation , 2310
   www.norrisfoundation.org
Koret Foundation , 2311
   www.koretfoundation.org
Kresge Foundation , 2541
   www.kresge.org
Kulas Foundation , 2701
   www.fdncenter.org/grantmaker/kulas/
Las Vegas-Clark County , 2589
   www.lvccld.org
Lettie Pate Evans Foundation , 2413
   www.lpevans.org
Levi Strauss Foundation , 2313
   www.levistrauss.com
Levittown Public Library , 2658
   www.nassaulibrary.org/levtown/
Lilly Endowment , 2469
   www.lillyendowment.org
Lloyd A Fry Foundation , 2447
   www.fryfoundation.org
Longview Foundation for Education in World
Affairs/International Understanding, 2805
   www.fdncenter.org/grantmaker/longview/index.html

Louis Calder Foundation , 2371
   www.louiscalderfdn.org
Louisville Free Public Library , 2480
   www.lfpl.org
Luke B Hancock Foundation , 2316
   www.fdcenter.org/grantmaker/hancock
Lynde & Harry Bradley Foundation , 2818
   www.bradleyfdn.org
Lyndhurst Foundation , 2760
   www.lyndhurstfoundation.org
MJ Murdock Charitable Trust , 2810
   www.murdock-trust.org
Margaret Hall Foundation , 2481
   www.margarethallfoundation.org
Marin Community Foundation , 2318
   www.marincf.org
Marion I & Henry J Knott Foundation , 2504
   www.knottfoundation.org
Marquette University Memorial Library , 2819
   www.marquette.edu/library/
Martha Holden Jennings Foundation , 2704
   mhjf.org
Mary A Crocker Trust , 2319
   www.mactrust.org
Mary Owen Borden Memorial Foundation , 2599
   www.fdncenter.org/grantmaker/borden/index.htm
Mary Reynolds Babcock Foundation , 2684
   www.mrbf.org
McConnell Foundation , 2321
   www.mcconnellfoundation.org
McCune Foundation , 2739
   www.mccune-db.mccune.org
McGregor Fund , 2543
   www.mcgregorfund.org
McKesson Foundation , 2322
   www.mckesson.com/foundation.html
Meadows Foundation , 2786
   www.mfi.org
Medtronic Foundation , 2560
   www.medtronic.com
Merck Company Foundation , 2600
   www.merck.com
Metropolitan Atlanta Community Foundation , 2415
   www.atlcf.org
Meyer Memorial Trust , 2722
   www.mmt.org
Michigan State University Libraries , 2544
   www.lib.msu.edu
Milken Family Foundation , 2323
   www.mff.org
Minneapolis Foundation , 2561
   www.minneapolisfoundation.org
Minneapolis Public Library , 2562
   www.mplib.org
Miranda Lux Foundation , 2324
   ww.mirandalux.org
Mississippi Power Foundation , 2568
   www.southerncompany.com/mspower/edufound
Monsanto Fund , 2579
   www.monsanto.com/monsanto/about_us/monsanto_fund
Montana State Library , 2581
   www.msl.state.mt.us/
Moody Foundation , 2787
   www.moodyf.org
Morris & Gwendolyn Cafritz Foundation , 2384
   www.cafritzfoundation.org
Multnomah County Library , 2723
   www.multcolib.org
Nashville Public Library , 2761
   www.library.nashville.org
National Science Foundation , 2836
   www.nsf.gov
Natrona County Public Library , 2822
   www.library.natrona.net

New Hampshire Charitable Foundation , 2592
   www.nhcf.org
New Mexico State Library , 2607
   www.stlib.state.nm.us
New York Foundation , 2662
   www.nyf.org
Non-Profit Resource Center/Pack Memorial Library, 2685
   www.buncombecounty.org
Nord Family Foundation , 2706
   www.nordff.org
Northern Trust Company Charitable Trust , 2448
   www.ntrs.com
Octameron Associates , 2875
   www.octameron.com
Oregon Community Foundation , 2724
   www.ocfl.org
Orlando Public Library-Orange County Library System, 2396
   www.ocls.lib.fl.us
Otto Bremer Foundation , 2563
   www.fdncenter.org/grantmaker/bremer/
Peninsula Community Foundation , 2327
   www.pcf.org
Pew Charitable Trusts , 2740
   www.pewtrusts.com
Phil Hardin Foundation , 2569
   www.philhardin.org
Philip H Corboy Foundation , 2450
   www.corboydemetrio.com
Phoenix Public Library , 2265
   www.phxlib.org
Plymouth State College , 2593
   www.plymouth.edu/psc/library
Polk Brothers Foundation , 2451
   www.polkbrosfdn.org
Prince Charitable Trust , 2452
   www.fdncenter.org/grantmaker/prince/chicago.html
Providence Public Library , 2750
   www.provlib.org
Prudential Foundation , 2601
   www.prudential.com
Public Library of Cincinnati , 2711
   www.cincinnatilibrary.org
Public Welfare Foundation , 2385
   www.publicwelfare.org
RJ McElroy Trust , 2473
   www.mcelroytrust.org
Ralph M Parsons Foundation , 2330
   www.rmpf.org
Rhode Island Foundation , 2751
   www.rifoundation.org
Richard King Mellon Foundation , 2741
   fdncenter.org/grantmaker/rkmellon/
Richmond Public Library , 2806
   www.richmondpubliclibrary.org
Riordan Foundation , 2331
   www.riordanfoundation.org
Robert R McCormick Tribune Foundation , 2455
   www.rrmtf.org
Robert Sterling Clark Foundation , 2664
   www.rsclark.org
Rochester Public Library , 2665
   www.rochester.lib.ny.us/central
Rollin M Gerstacker Foundation , 2546
   www.tamu.edu/baum/gerstack.html
SH Cowell Foundation , 2333
   www.shcowell.org
Sacramento Regional Foundation , 2334
   www.sacregfoundation.org
Saint Paul Foundation , 2564
   www.saintpaulfoundation.org
Salt Lake City Public Library , 2796
   www.slcpl.lib.ut.us
Samuel N & Mary Castle Foundation , 2430
   www.fdncenter.org

Samuel Roberts Noble Foundation , 2719
   www.noble.org
Samuel S Fels Fund , 2743
   www.samfels.org
San Diego Foundation , 2335
   www.sdfoundation.org
San Francisco Foundation , 2336
   www.sff.org
Santa Barbara Foundation , 2337
   www.sbfoundation.org
Sarah Scaife Foundation , 2744
   www.scaife.com
Scholarship America , 2876
   dollarsforscholars.org
Scholarships in the Health Professions , 2877
   www.jfew.org
School Identifications , 2858
   www.schoolidents.com
School Memories Collection , 2859
   www.schoolmemories.com
Seattle Foundation , 2811
   www.seattlefoundation.org
Seattle Public Library , 2812
   www.spl.org
Shreve Memorial Library , 2488
   www.shreve-lib.org
Siebert Lutheran Foundation , 2820
   www.siebertfoundation.org
South Carolina State Library , 2753
   www.state.sc.us/scsl/
South Dakota Community Foundation , 2754
   www.sdcommunityfoundation.org
South Dakota State Library , 2755
   www.sdstatelibrary.com
Southwest Florida Community Foundation , 2399
   www.floridacommunity.com
Spencer Foundation , 2457
   www.spencer.org
Spokane Public Library , 2813
   www.spokanelibrary.org
Starr Foundation , 2670
   www.fdncenter.org/grantmaker/starr
State Library of North Carolina , 2686
   www.statelibrary.dcr.state.nc.us
State Street Foundation , 2518
   www.statestreet.com
Steelcase Foundation , 2547
   www.steelcase.com
Steve Wronker's Funny Business , 2861
   www.swfb.net/swfb.htm
Sudbury Foundation , 2519
   www.sudburyfoundation.org
TCF Foundation , 2565
   www.tcfexpress.com
Tektronix Foundation , 2725
   www.tek.com
Thompson Publishing Group , 2402
   www.thompson.com or www.grantsandfunding.com
Tiger Foundation , 2671
   www.tigerfoundation.org
Times Mirror Foundation , 2343
   www.timesmirrorfoundation.org
Toyota USA Foundation , 2345
   www.toyota.com/foundation
Trull Foundation , 2793
   www.trullfoundation.org
Trust to Reach Education Excellence , 2837
   http://tree.principals.org
Tull Charitable Foundation , 2422
   www.tullfoundation.org
Turrell Fund , 2602
   www.fdncenter.org/grantmaker/turrell
Union Pen Company , 2864
   www.unionpen.com

United States Institute of Peace , 2839
  www.usip.org
United States Steel Foundation , 2747
  www.psc.uss.com/usxfound
United States-Japan Foundation , 2840
  www.us-jf.org
University of Alaska-Anchorage Library , 2259
  www.lib.uaa.alaska.edu/
University of Hawaii , 2431
  www.libweb.hawaii.edu/uhmlib
University of South Alabama , 2258
  http://library.southalabama.edu
University of Wisconsin-Madison , 2821
  www.grants.library.wisc.edu
Ventura County Community Foundation , 2347
  www.vccf.org
Vermont Community Foundation , 2797
  www.vermontcf.org
Vermont Department of Libraries , 2798
  www.dol.state.vt.us
Victoria Foundation , 2603
  www.victoriafoundation.org
W Dale Clark Library , 2584
  www.omahapubliclibrary.org
WM Keck Foundation , 2348
  www.wmkeck.org
Walter & Elise Haas Fund , 2349
  www.haassr.org
Walter S Johnson Foundation , 2350
  www.wsjf.org
Walton Family Foundation , 2272
  www.wffhome.com
Washoe County Library , 2590
  www.washoe.lib.nv.us/
Wayne State University , 2548
  www.lib.wayne.edu
Weingart Foundation , 2352
  www.weingartfnd.org
Wells Fargo Foundation , 2353
  www.wellsfargo.com
Western Massachusetts Funding Resource Center , 2522
  www.diospringfield.org/wmfrc.html
Westinghouse Foundation , 2841
  www.westinghousenuclear.com
White Plains Public Library , 2674
  www.whiteplainslibrary.org
Wichita Public Library , 2476
  www.wichita.lib.ks.us
William & Flora Hewlett Foundation , 2355
  www.hewlett.org
William Penn Foundation , 2748
  www.williampennfoundation.org
William Randolph Hearst Foundation , 2675
  www.hearstfdn.org
William T Grant Foundation , 2676
  www.wtgrantfoundation.org
Winston-Salem Foundation , 2688
  www.wsfoundation.org
Worcester Public Library , 2525
  www.worcpublib.org
Xerox Foundation , 2842
  www.xerox.com
Z Smith Reynolds Foundation , 2689
  www.zsr.org
www.positivepins.com , 2865
  www.thepinman-pins.com

Government Agencies

Accountability Reporting and Research , 3207
  www.tea.state.tx.us

Administrative Services Office , 3059
  www.michigan.gov
Administrative Services Office , 3101
  www.nde.state.ne.us/ADSS/index.html
Adult Extended Learning Office , 3060
  www.michigan.gov
Alabama State Department of Education , 2916
  www.alsde.edu
Alaska Commission on Postsecondary Education , 2929
  www.state.ak.us/acpc
Alaska Department of Education & Early Development, 2931
  www.educ.state.ak.us
Applied Technology Education Services , 3220
  www.usoe.k12.ut.us
Arkansas Department of Education , 2937
  http://arkedu.state.ar.us
Arkansas Department of Education: Special Education, 2938
  http://arkedu.state.ar.us
Assessment & Evaluation , 3160
  www.ode.state.or.us
Assistant Commissioner's Office , 3021
  www.ksbe.state.ks.us
California Department of Education , 2941
  www.cde.ca.gov
Career & Technical Education , 3061
  www.michigan.gov
Career & Technical Education , 3180
  www.ridoe.net
Colorado Department of Education , 2952
  www.cde.state.co.us
Communications Services , 3026
  www.kde.state.ky.us
Connecticut Department of Education , 2961
  www.state.ct.us/sdel
Delaware Department of Education , 2972
  www.doe.state.de.us
Delaware Department of Education: Administrat ve Services, 2973
  www.doe.state.de.us
Division for Learning Support: Equity & Advocacy, 3249
  www.dpi.state.wi.us
Equity & Access Office , 3181
  www.ridoe.net
Financial & Information Services , 3017
  www.state.ia.us/educate
Florida Department of Education , 2980
  www.firn.edu/doe/
Georgia Department of Education , 2981
  www.gadoe.org
Hawaii Department of Education , 2983
  www.k12.hi.us
Higher Education Management Office , 3062
  www.michigan.gov
Human Resource Development , 3182
  www.ridoe.net
Idaho Department of Education , 2989
  www.sde.state.id.us
Illinois Department of Education , 2993
  www.isbe.state.il.us
Indiana Department of Education , 3008
  www.doe.state.in.us
Information Services , 3108
  www.ed.state.nh.us
Instruction Office , 3183
  www.ridoe.net
Instructional Programs , 3063
  www.michigan.gov
Instructional Services Division , 3250
  www.dpi.state.wi.us
Iowa Department of Education , 3018
  www.state.ia.us/educate
Kansas Department of Education , 3023
  www.ksbe.state.ks.us
Kentucky Department of Education , 3029
  www.kde.state.ky.us

Libraries, Archives & Museums , 2933
www.energy.state.ak.us
Library Services Division , 3251
www.dpi.state.wi.us
Louisiana Department of Education , 3038
www.doe.state.la.us
Maine Department of Education , 3045
www.state.me.us/education
Management & Finance Office , 3039
www.doe.state.la.us
Maryland Department of Education , 3052
www.msde.state.md.us
Massachusetts Department of Education , 3056
www.doe.mass.edu
Michigan Department of Education , 3064
www.michigan.gov/mde
Minnesota Department of Children, Families & Learning, 3078
cfl.state.mn.us
Minnesota Department of Education , 3079
www.education.state.mn.us
Mississippi Department of Education , 3085
www.mde.k12.ms.us
Mississippi Employment Security Commission , 3086
www.mesc.state.ms
Missouri Department of Education , 3091
www.dese.state.mo.us
Montana Department of Education , 3099
www.opi.state.mt.us
National Council of State Supervisors of Music, 2936
http://ade.state.az.us/
National Council on Disability , 2891
www.ncd.gov/
National Institute of Child Health and Human Development, 2892
www.nichd.nih.gov
National Trust for Historic Preservation: Office of Education
Initiatives, 2893
www.nationaltrust.org
Nebraska Department of Education , 3103
www.nde.state.ne.us
Nevada Department of Education , 3107
www.nsn.k12.nv.us
New Hampshire Department of Education , 3109
www.state.nh.us/doe
New Jersey Department of Education , 3112
www.state.nj.us/education
New Jersey Department of Education: Finance , 3113
www.state.nj.us/education
New Jersey State Library , 3115
www.njstatelib.org
New Mexico Department of Education , 3120
www.sde.state.nm.us
New York Department of Education , 3127
www.nysed.gov
No Child Left Behind , 2894
www.ed.gov/nclb
North Carolina Department of Education , 3133
www.ncpublicschools.org
North Dakota Department of Education , 3136
www.state.nd.us/espb
North Dakota Department of Public Instruction Division, 3137
www.dpi.state.nd.us/dpi/index.htm
Office of Elementary and Secondary Education , 3176
www.pde.state.pa.us
Office of Finance , 3184
www.ridoe.net
Office of Overseas Schools , 2898
www.state.gov
Office of School Management , 3065
www.michigan.gov
Office of Special Education Programs , 2900
www.ed.gov./offices/osers/idea/index.htm
Office of the State Director for Career & Technical Education,
2986
www.hawaii.edu/cte

Office of the Superintendent , 3066
www.michigan.gov
Ohio Department of Education , 3144
www.ode.state.oh.us
Oklahoma Department of Education , 3156
http://sde.state.ok.us
Oregon Department of Education , 3168
www.ode.state.or.us
Outcomes & Assessment Office , 3185
www.ridoe.net
Pennsylvania Department of Education , 3178
www.teaching.state.pa.us
Policy, Assessment, Research & Information Systems, 3234
www.pen.k12.va.us
Postsecondary Services , 3067
www.michigan.gov
Region 10: Education Department , 3238
www.ed.gov
Regional Services Centers , 3032
www.kde.state.ky.us
Rehabilitation Services , 2924
www.rehab.state.al.us
Rehabilitation Services Division , 3104
www.bocrehab.state.ne.us
Research to Practice Division , 2906
www.ed.gov/offices/osers/osef
Resource Development , 3186
www.ridoe.net
Rhode Island Department of Education , 3187
www.ridoe.net
School Finance , 3146
www.ode.state.ohio.us/foundation/www_.html
School Financial Resources & Management , 3252
www.dpi.state.wi.us
School Food Services Administration , 3188
www.ridoe.net
School Program Quality , 3068
www.michigan.gov
South Carolina Department of Education , 3196
www.state.sc.us
South Dakota Department of Education & Cultural Affairs, 3200
www.state.sd.us/deca/
South Dakota State Historical Society , 3201
www.state.sd.us/deca/
Special Education , 3000
www.isbe.net
Special Education , 3170
www.ode.state.or.us
Special Needs Office , 3189
www.ridoe.net
Teacher & Administrative Preparation , 3071
www.michigan.gov
Teacher Education & Certification Office , 3190
www.ridoe.net
Teaching and Learning , 3204
www.state.tn.us/education
Tennessee Department of Education , 3205
www.state.tn.us/education
Texas Department of Education , 3219
www.sbec.state.tx.us
US Department of Education , 2913
www.ed.gov
US Department of Education: Region VIII , 2960
www.ed.gov
Utah Office of Education , 3223
www.usoe.k12.ut.us
Utah Office of Education; Agency Services Division, 3224
www.usoe.k12.ut.us
Vermont Department of Education , 3231
Vermont.gov
Virginia Department of Education , 3237
www.pen.k12.va.us
Vocational & Adult Education , 3095
www.dese.state.mo.us

Vocational Education Division , 2990
www.sde.state.id.us
Vocational Rehabilitation , 2935
www.labor.state.ak.us/dur/home.htm
Washington Department of Education , 3239
www.k12.wa.us
West Virginia Department of Education , 3248
www.wvde.state.wv.us
Wisconsin College System Technical , 3253
www.board.tec.wi.us
Wisconsin Department of Public Instruction , 3254
www.dpi.state.wi.us
Wyoming Department of Education , 3259
www.k12.wy.us

Professional Development

AACTE Briefs , 3484
www.aacte.org
ACE Fellows Program , 3297
www.acenet.edu
ACE Fellows Program , 3619
www.acenet.edu/programs/fellows
ART New England Summer Workshops , 3620
www.massart.edu/at_massart/academic_prgms/continuing/
ASQ Annual Koalaty Kid Conference , 3298
www.asq.org
ATEA Journal , 3485
www.ateaonline.org
Academic Alliances , 3260
www.aahe.org
Agency for Instructional Technology , 3261
www.ait.net
American Association of Colleges for Teacher Education, 3262
www.aacte.org
American Association of Colleges for Teacher Education-Directory, 3421
www.aacte.org
American Association of Collegiate Registrars & Admissions Officers, 3300
www.aacrao.org
American Educational Research Association , 3263
www.aera.net
American Educational Studies Association , 3264
www.uakron.edu/aesa
American Federation of Teachers Biennial Convention & Exhibition, 3301
www.aft.org
American Society for Training-Development International Conference, 3302
www.astd.org/astd/conferences/about_conferences
American Speech-Language-Hearing Association , 3267
www.asha.org
Annual Conductor's Institute of South Carolin , 3621
www.conductorsinstitute.com
Annual Convention , 3304
www.nyssba.org
Annual New England Kindergarten Conference , 3305
www.lesley.edu
Annual State Convention of Association of Texas Professional Educators, 3306
www.atpe.org
Annual Summer Institute for Secondary Teacher , 3622
www.rockhall.com/programs/institute.asp
Apple Education Grants , 3287
www.apple.com
Appropriate Inclusion and Paraprofessionals , 3423
www.nea.org
Arts Management in Community Institutions: Su mer Training, 3489
www.nationalguild.org

Association for Continuing Higher Education Directory, 3425
charleston.net/org/ache/
Association for Educational Communications & Technology Annual Convention, 3307
www.aect.org/Events/default.htm
Association for Library & Information Science Education Annual Conference, 3308
www.alise.org
Association of Teacher Educators , 3268
www.ate1.org/pubs/home.cfm
At-Risk Students: Identification and Assistance Strategies, 3567
cssrs.ou.edu
Ball State University , 3623
www.bsu.edu/cast/itech
Bayer/NSF Award for Community Innovation , 3288
www.bayernsfaward.com
Before the School Bell Rings , 3426
www.pdkintl.org
Better Teaching , 3491
www.parent-institute.com
Beyond Tracking: Finding Success in Inclusive Schools, 3427
www.pdkintl.org
Board , 3492
www.masterteacher.com
Book of Metaphors, Volume II , 3428
www.kendallhunt.com
Bryant and Stratton College , 3624
www.bryantstratton.edu
California School Boards Association Conference, 3311
www.csba.org
Careers Conference , 3312
www.cew.wisc.edu
Center for Educational Leadership Trinity University, 3625
http://carme.cs.trinity.edu/education/index.asp
Center for Global Education , 3626
www.augsburg.edu/global
Center for Image Processing in Education , 3627
www.evisual.org
Center for Learning Connections , 3628
www.learningconnections.org
Center for Occupational Research & Developmen , 3629
www.cord.org
Center for Play Therapy , 3630
www.centerforplaytherapy.com
Center for Play Therapy Fall Conference , 3313
www.centerforplaytherapy.com
Center for Rural Studies , 3269
crs.uvm.edu
Character Education: Making a Difference , 3568
www.character.org
Character Education: Restoring Respect & Responsibility in our Schools, 3569
www.masterteacher.com
Cisco Educational Archives , 3570
www.sunsite.unc.edu/cisco/cisco-home
Classroom Connect , 3316
www.classroom.com
Classroom Connect , 3631
www.classroom.com
Classroom Teacher's Guide for Working with Paraeducators Video Set, 3571
www.masterteacher.com
Clinical Play Therapy Videos: Child-Centered Developmental & Relationship Play Therapy, 3572
www.centerforplaytherapy.com
Closing the Achievement Gap , 3431
www.masterteacher.com
College of the Ozarks , 3632
www.cofo.edu
Coming Up Short? Practices of Teacher Educators Committed to Character, 3432
www.character.org
Conferencing with Students & Parents Video Series, 3573
www.masterteacher.com

Conflict Resolution Strategies in Schools , 3574
  cssrs.ou.cdu
Connect , 3633
  www.synergylearning.org
Conover Company , 3575
  www.conovercompany.com
Contracting Out: Strategies for Fighting Back , 3434
  www.nea.org
Cooperative Learning Strategies , 3576
  cssrs.ou.edu
Council for Learning Disabilities , 3271
  www.cldinternational.org
Council of Administrators of Special Educatio , 3272
  www.casecec.org
Creating Schools of Character Video Series , 3577
  www.masterteacher.com
Crisis Management in Schools , 3578
  cssrs.ou.edu
Critical Issues in Urban Special Education: The Implications of Whole-School Change, 3634
  www.gse.harvard.edu/~ppe
Critical Thinking Video Set , 3579
  www.masterteacher.com
Curriculum Alignment: Improving Student Learning, 3580
  cssrs.ou.edu
Curriculum Center - Office of Educational Services, 3636
  www.oes.siu.edu
Cut & Paste, Master Teacher , 3495
  www.masterteacher.com
Darryl L Sink & Associates , 3637
  www.dsink.com
Datacad , 3581
  www.datacad.com
DeVry University , 3638
  www.devry.edu
Delmar Thomson Learning , 3639
  www.delmar.com
Depco , 3640
  www.depcoinc.com
Discipline Techniques you can Master in a Minute Video Series, 3582
  www.masterteacher.com
Distance Education & Training Council , 3273
  www.detc.org
E-Z Grader Software , 3539
  www.ezgrader.com
ERIC Clearinghouse on Teaching and Teacher Education, 3274
  www.aacte.org
Eastern Illinois University School of Technology, 3641
  www.eiu-edu/~tech1
Edison Welding Institute , 3642
  www.ewi.org
Education Conference , 3318
  www.pilambda.org
Educational Leadership Institute , 3275
  www.iel.org
Effective Strategies for School Reform , 3644
  www.gse.harvard.edu/~ppe
Electronics Industries Alliance/CEA , 3645
  www.CEMAweb.org
Elementary Education Professional Development School, 3646
  www.ed.psu/pds
Eleven Principals of Effective Character Educ tion, 3583
  www.masterteacher.com
Eleven Principles of Effective Character Educ ion, 3584
  www.character.org
Emco Maier Corporation , 3647
  www.emcomaier-usa.com
Energy Concepts , 3648
  www.energy-concepts-inc.com
Ethical Issues in Experiential Education , 3437
  www.kendallhunt.com
Excellence in Teaching Cabinet Grant , 3289
  www.curriculumassociates.com

Extensions - Newsletter of the High/Scope Curriculum, 3499
  www.highscope.org
Eye on Education , 3585
  www.eyeoneducation.com
Fastech , 3649
  www.fastechinc.net
Festo Corporation , 3650
  www.festo-usa.com
Finishing Strong: Your Personal Mentoring & Planning Guide for the Last 60 Days of Teaching, 3438
  www.masterteacher.com
Foundation for Critical Thinking , 3651
  www.criticalthinking.org
Four State Regional Technology Conference , 3652
  www.pittstate.edu
Grand Canyon University College of Education , 3654
  www.ncahigherlearningcommission.org
Great Classroom Management Series , 3586
  www.masterteacher.com
Great Classroom Management Video Series , 3587
  www.masterteacher.com
Guild Notes Bi-Monthly Newswletter , 3500
  www.nationalguild.org
Handling Chronically Disruptive Students at Risk Video Series, 3588
  www.masterteacher.com
Harvard Institute for School Leadership , 3655
  www.gse.harvard.edu/~ppe
Harvard Seminar for Superintendents , 3656
  www.gse.harvard.edu/~ppe
Hearlihy & Company , 3589
  www.hearlihy.com
Hobart Institute of Welding Technology , 3657
  www.welding.org
How to Plan and Develop a Career Center , 3439
  www.cew.wisc.edu
How to Raise Test Scores , 3440
  www.skylightedu.com
Illinois Assistant Principals Conference , 3322
  http://ipa.vsat.net
Illinois Principals Professional Conference , 3323
  http:ipa.vsat.net
Improving Parent/Educator Relationships , 3590
  cssrs.ou.edu
Improving Student Thinking in the Content Are , 3591
  cssrs.ou.edu
In-Box Master Teacher , 3501
  www.masterteacher.com
Inclusion: The Next Step , 3441
  www.masterteacher.com
Inclusion: The Next Step the Video Series , 3592
  www.masterteacher.com
Indiana University-Purdue University of Indianapolis, IUPUI, 3658
  www.engr.iupui.edu/cnt
Industrial Training Institute , 3659
  www.trainingrus.com
Infocus: A Newsletter of the University Continuing Education Association, 3502
  www.nucea.edu
Institute of Higher Education , 3660
  www.gbhem.org/highed.html
Integrating Technology into the Classroom Vid o Series, 3593
  www.masterteacher.com
International Association for Social Science Information Service & Technology, 3327
  www.iassistdata.org/conferences
International Council on Education for Teaching, 3276
  www.nl.edu
International Curriculum Management Audit Center, 3661
  www.pdkintl.org
International Graduate School , 3662
  www.berne.edu

International Workshops , 3663
www.internationalworkshops.org
Intervention in School and Clinic , 3505
www.proedinc.com
Island Drafting & Technical Institute , 3664
www.islanddrafting.com
Janice Borla Vocal Jazz Camp , 3665
www.janiceborlavocaljazzcamp.org
Jefferson State Community College , 3666
www.jeffstateonline.com
Journal of Classroom Interaction , 3506
www.coe.uh.edu
Journal of Economic Education , 3507
www.heldref.org
Journal of Experiential Education , 3508
www.aee.org
Journal on Excellence in College Teaching , 3509
http://ject.lib.muohio.edu/
Journalism Education Association , 3510
www.jea.org/
K'nex Education Division , 3668
www.knexeducation.com
Kent State University , 3670
www.tech.kent.edu
Kentucky State University , 3671
www.kysu.edu
Lab Volt Systems , 3673
www.labvolt.com
Law of Teacher Evaluation: A Self-Assestment Handbook, 3442
www.pdkintl.org
Leadership and the New Technologies , 3674
www.gse.harvard.edu/~ppe
Learning Materials Workshop , 3676
www.learningmaterialswork.com
Learning for Life , 3443
www.learning-for-life.org
Lesson Plans and Modifications for Inclusion nd Collaborative
Classrooms, 3595
www.masterteacher.com
Lesson Plans for the Substitue Teacher: Elementary Edition, 3444
www.masterteacher.com
Life Skills Training , 3445
www.LifeSkillsTraining.com
Light Machines , 3677
www.Imcorp.com/_vti_bin/shtml.exe/search/index.html
Lilly Conference on College Teaching , 3336
www.muohio.edu/lillyconference/
Lilly Conferences on College and University Teaching, 3337
www.iats.com
Managing Students Without Coercion , 3596
cssrs.ou.edu
Marcraft International Corporation , 3678
www.eclassrooms.net
Master Teacher , 3597
www.masterteacher.com
Media and American Democracy , 3680
www.gse.harvard.edu/~ppe
Mental Edge , 3543
www.learningshortcuts.com
Mentoring Teachers to Mastery , 3598
www.masterteacher.com
Michigan School Boards Association Fall Leadership Conference,
3343
www.masb.org
Middle School Teachers Guide to FREE Curriculum Materials,
3449
www.freeteachingaids.com
Miller Electric Manufacturing Company , 3681
www.millerwelds.com
Millersville University , 3682
www.millersv.edu
Minnesota Leadership Annual Conference , 3347
www.mnmsba.org

Minnesota School Administrators Association , 3348
wwwmnasa.org
Missouri National Education Association Conference, 3350
www.mo.nea.org
Morehead State University , 3683
www.morehead-st.edu/colleges/science/iet
Motivating Students in the Classroom Video Se ies, 3599
www.masterteacher.com
Mpulse Maintenance Software , 3684
www.mpulsecmms.com
Multicultural Education: Teaching to Diversit , 3600
cssrs.ou.edu
Musikgarten , 3685
www.musikgarten.org
NASA Educational Workshop , 3686
www.nsta.org/programs/new.htm
NASDTEC Knowledge Base , 3450
www.nasdtec.org
NCRTL Special Report , 3511
www.ncrtb.msu.edu
NSTA Award for Principals , 3291
www.nsta.org
National Association of Secondary School Principals Annual
Convention and Exposition, 3354
www.nasspconvention.org
National Association of State Boards of Education Conference,
3355
www.nasbe.org
National Association of State Directors of Teacher Education &
Certification, 3277
www.nasdtec.org
National Center for Community Education , 3278
www.nccenet.org
National Center for Construction Education & Research, 3688
www.nccer.org
National Computer Systems , 3689
www.ncs.com
National Conference on Education , 3357
www.aasa.org
National Conference on Standards and Assessment, 3358
www.nscinet.com
National Council for Geographic Education Annual Meeting, 3359
www.nege.org
National Council for History Education Conference, 3360
www.history.org/nche
National Council for the Accreditation of Teacher Education, 3279
www.ncate.org
National Council of English Teachers Conference, 3362
www.ncte.org
National Council of Teachers of Mathematics Annual Meeting,
3363
www.nctm.org
National Council of Teachers of English Annual Convention, 3364
www.ncte.org
National Council of Teachers of Mathematics Conference, 3365
www.nctm.org
National Education Association , 3280
www.nea.org
National Education Association Annual Meeting, 3366
www.nea.org
National Educational Computing Conference , 3367
www.neccsite.com
National Head Start Association , 3690
www.nhsa.org
National Middle School Association , 3281
www.nmsa.org
National Middle School Association's Annual Conference and
Exhibition, 3368
www.nmsa.org
National Staff Development Council , 3282
www.nsdc.org
National Teachers Hall of Fame , 3293
www.nthf.org

National Women's Studies Association , 3283
www.nwsa.org
New England Kindergarten Conference , 3372
www.lesley.edu/kc
New England League of Middle Schools , 3373
www.nelms.org
North American Association for Environmental Education, 3379
www.naaee.org
North Carolina Association for Career and Technical Education Conference, 3380
www.ncacte.org
North Central Association Annual Meeting , 3382
www.ncacasi.org
North Central Conference on Summer Schools , 3383
www.conted.ufuc.edu
Northeast Conference on the Teaching of Foreign Languages, 3384
www.dickinson.edu/nectfl
Northern Arizona University , 3691
www.nau.edu/~ifwfd/aztec
Northwest Association of Schools & Colleges Annual Meeting, 3386
www2.idbsu.edu/nasc
Orators & Philosophers: A History of the Idea of Liberal Education, 3451
www.collegeboard.org
Outcome-Based Education: Making it Work , 3601
cssrs.ou.edu
Overview of Prevention: A Social Change Model , 3602
cssrs.ou.edu
Owens Community College , 3693
www.owens.cc.oh.us
Pacific Northwest Council on Languages Annual Conference, 3393
www.isu.edu/~nickcrai/pncfl
Paideia Group , 3694
http://hometown.aol.com/paideiapgi/webpage.html
Pamela Sims & Associates , 3695
www.pamelasims.com
Paraeducator's Guide to Instructional & Curricular Modifications, 3513
www.masterteacher.com
Parent Training Resources , 3452
www.pacer.org
Pennsylvania Council for the Social Studies Conference, 3394
www.pcss.org
Pennsylvania State University-Workforce Educa ion & Development Program, 3696
www.ed.psu.edu/wfed
Performance Improvement Journal , 3515
www.ispi.org
Personal Planner & Traning Guide for the Paraeducator Video Set, 3603
www.masterteacher.com
Personal Planner and Training Guide for the Paraprofessional, 3453
www.masterteacher.com
Pittsburg State University , 3699
www.pittstate.edu
Presidential Awards for Excellence in Mathematics and Science Teaching, 3294
www.ehr.nsf.gov
Preventing School Failure , 3516
www.heldref.org
Prevention Researcher , 3517
www.TPRonline.org
Professional Development Institutes , 3701
www.pdkintl.org
Professional Development Workshops , 3702
www.rebusinc.com
Professional Learning Communities at Work , 3456
www.nesonline.com
Professional Vision Master Teacher , 3518
www.masterteacher.com
Professor Master Teacher , 3519
www.masterteacher.com

Project Zero Classroom , 3703
www.gse.harvard.edu/~ppe
Quality School , 3604
cssrs.ou.edu
Quality School Teacher , 3458
www.nprinc.com
Recruiting New Teachers , 3284
www.rnt.org/channels/clearinghouse
Research for Better Schools Publications , 3460
www.rbs.org
Resources for Teaching Middle School Science , 3461
www.si.edu/nsrc
Restructuring in the Classroom , 3462
www.josseybass.com
Retaining Great Teachers , 3521
www.masterteacher.com
Revolution Revisited: Effective Schools and Systemic Reform, 3463
www.pdkintl.org
Robert McNeel & Associates , 3704
www.rhino3d.com
Rockford Systems , 3705
www.rockfordsystems.com
Rural Educator-Journal for Rural and Small Schools, 3522
www.colostate.edu
SUNY College at Oswego , 3706
www.oswego.edu
School-Wide Stratigies for Retaining Great Te chers, 3606
www.masterteacher.com
Seminar Information Service , 3464
www.seminarinformation.com
Service-Learning and Character Education: One Plus One is More Than Two, 3465
www.character.org
Site-Based Management , 3607
cssrs.ou.edu
Sonoma State University Annual Conference , 3400
www.criticalthinking.org
South Carolina Library Association Conference , 3401
www.scla.org
Southern Association Colleges & Schools , 3402
www.saes.org
Southern Early Childhood Annual Convention , 3403
www.seca50.org
Southern Polytechnic State University , 3708
www.spsu.edu/oce
Southwestern Oklahoma State University , 3709
www.swosu.edu
Specialized Solutions , 3710
www.specializedsolutions.com
Standards and Accountability: Their Impact on Teaching and Assessment, 3712
www.gse.harvard.edu/~ppe
Strategic Planning for Outcome-Based Educatio , 3608
cssrs.ou.edu
Strengthening the Family: An Overview of a Ho istic Family Wellness Model, 3609
cssrs.ou.edu
Students-at-Risk Video Series , 3610
www.masterteacher.com
Suburban Superintendents Conference , 3404
www.aasa.org
Summer Institute in Siena , 3714
www.sienamusic.org
Summer Programs for School Teams , 3715
www.naesp.org
Superintendent/School Board Relationships , 3611
cssrs.ou.edu
Superintendents Work Conference , 3405
www.conference.tc.columbia.edu
Supplemental Instruction, Supervisor Workshop , 3716
www.umkc.edu/cad

TESOL Journal: A Journal of Teaching and Classroom Research, 3524
www.tesol.edu
THE Institute & Knowvation , 3717
www.thejournal.com/institute
TQM: Implementing Quality Management in Your School, 3612
cssrs.ou.edu
TUV Product Service , 3718
www.tuvglobal.com
Teacher Magazine , 3527
www.edweek.org
Teacher-Created Materials , 3467
www.teachercreated.com
Teachers College: Columbia University , 3720
www.tc.columbia.edu/~academic/ctsc
Teachers as Educators of Character: Are the Nations Schools of
Education Coming Up Short?, 3468
www.character.org
Teachers as Heros , 3613
cssrs.ou.edu
Teachers as Leaders , 3469
www.pdkintl.org
Teaching for Intelligent Behavior , 3614
cssrs.ou.edu
Teaching for Results , 3473
www.masterteacher.com
Techniques-Connecting Education and Careers , 3532
www.acteonline.org
Technology Pathfinder for Teachers Master Teacher, 3533
www.masterteacher.com
Technology Training for Educators , 3721
www.amfcse.org
Tennessee School Boards Association Conferenc , 3408
www.tsba.net
Their Best Selves: Building Character Education and Service
Learning Together, 3474
www.character.org
Theory of Experiential Education , 3475
www.kendallhunt.com
Three Rs Master Teacher , 3534
www.masterteacher.com
Today's Catholic Teacher , 3535
www.catholicteacher.com
Tooling University , 3722
www.toolingu.com
Total Quality Schools Workshop , 3723
www.ed.psu.edu/ctqs/index.html
Toyota Tapestry Grants for Teachers , 3296
www.nsta.org/programs/tapestry
Training & Presentations , 3412
www.chiefmfg.com
Training Video Series for the Substitute Teacher, 3615
www.masterteacher.com
Understanding and Relating To Parents Professionally, 3479
www.masterteacher.com
University of Arkansas at Little Rock , 3724
www.ualr.edu/~autocad
University of Central Florida , 3725
www.distrib.ucf.edu
University of Michigan-Dearborn Center for Corporate &
Professional Development, 3726
www.umich.edu
Virginia Association of Elementary School Principals Conference,
3414
www.vaesp.org
Virginia Association of Independent Schools-Conference, 3415
www.vais.org
Virginia School Boards Association Conference , 3417
www.vsba.org
Voices in the Hall: High School Principals at Work, 3616
www.pdkintl.org
Wavelength , 3617
www.wavelengthinc.com

Wavelength , 3727
www.wavelengthinc.com
Welcome to Teaching and our Schools , 3480
www.masterteacher.com
What's New Magazine , 3537
www.media-methods.com
Wids Learning Design System , 3728
www.wids.org
Wisconsin Association of School Boards Annual Conference, 3418
www.wasb.org
Workforce Education and Development , 3729
www.siu.edu/~wed01/OCDP/OCDPFrame.htm
You Can Handle Them All , 3482
www.masterteacher.com
You Can Handle Them All Discipline Video Series, 3618
www.masterteacher.com
Your Personal Mentoring & Planning Guide for the First 60 Days
of Teaching, 3483
www.masterteacher.com
http://www.gsn.org , 3544
www.gsn.org
www.learningpage.com , 3554
www.sitesforteachers.com

Publications

A Personal Planner & Training Guide for the Substitute Teacher,
3730
www.masterteacher.com
A Principal's Guide to Creating and Building Climate for
Inclusion, 3731
www.masterteacher.com
AAEE Job Search Handbook for Educators , 3913
www.aaee.org
AAHE Bulletin , 4114
www.aahebulletin.com
AASA Bulletin , 4318
www.aasa.org
AATF National Bulletin , 4502
www.frenchteachers.org
ACCT Advisor , 4319
www.acct.org
ACJS Today , 4115
www.acjs.org
ADE Bulletin , 4504
www.ade.org
ALA Editions Catalog , 4544
www.ala.org
Academe , 4119
www.aaup.org
Academic Year & Summer Programs Abroad , 3732
www.aifs.com
Accreditation Fact Sheet , 4322
www.napnsc.org
Activities and Strategies for Connecting Kids with Kids:
Elementary Edition, 3734
www.masterteacher.com
Activities and Strategies for Connecting Kids with Kids:
Secondary Edition, 3735
www.masterteacher.com
Agenda: Jewish Education , 4122
www.jesna.org
American Biology Teacher , 4648
www.nabt.org
American School Directory , 3736
www.asd.com
American Students & Teachers Abroad , 4126
www.access.gpo.gov
American Trade Schools Directory , 4094
ww.croner.com
American-Scandinavian Foundation Magazine , 4444
www.amscan.org

Annual Register of Grant Support , 3957
   www.bowker.com
Annual Report & Notes from the Field , 4127
   www.dupontfund.org
AnthroNotes , 4649
   www.nmnsi.edu/anthro
AppleSeeds , 4671
   www.cobblestonepub.com
Arts & Activities , 4580
   www.artsandactivities.com
Arts Education Policy Review , 4581
   www.heldref.org
Association for Play Therapy Newsletter , 4457
   www.a4pt.org
Association of Science-Technology Centers Dimensions, 4651
   www.astc.org
Athletic Training , 4602
   www.nata.org
Athletics Administration , 4603
   www.nacda.com
Attention , 4458
   www.chadd.org
Awakening Brilliance: How to Inspire Children to Become
Successful Learners, 3741
   www.pamelasims.com
Before You Can Discipline , 4459
   www.masterteacher.com
Between Classes-Elderhostel Catalog , 4129
   www.elderhostel.org
Beyond the Bake Sale , 3742
   www.masterteacher.com
Bilingual Research Journal , 4506
   www.nabe.org
Board , 4326
   www.masterteacher.com
Booklist , 4546
   www.ala.org/booklist
Building Leadership Bulletin , 4327
   www.ipa.vsta.net
CASE Directory of Advancement Professionals in Education, 3744
   www.case.org
CEA Forum , 4508
   www.as.ysu.edu/~english/cea/forum1.htm
COLLEGESOURCE , 4017
   www.collegesource.org
Cabell's Directory of Publishing Opportunities in Education, 3914
   www.cabells.com
Cabell's Directory of Publishing Opportunities in Accounting,
3915
   www.cabells.com
Cabell's Directory of Publishing Opportunitie in Economics &
Finance, 3916
   www.cabells.com
Cabells Directory of Publishing Opportunities in Educational
Curriculum & Methods, 3745
   www.cabells.com
Cabells Directory of Publishing Opportunities in Educational
Psychology and Administration, 3863
   www.cabells.com
Cabells Directory of Publishing Opportunities in Management,
3917
   www.cabells.com
Cabells Directory of Publishing Opportunities in Educational
Psychology and Administration, 4018
   www.cabells.com
Cable in the Classroom , 4700
   www.ciconline.org
Calliope , 4674
   www.cobblestonepub.com
Career Development Activities for Every Classroom, 3919
   www.cew.wisc.edu
Center Focus , 4137
   www.coc.org

Certification and Accreditation Programs Directory, 3923
   www.galcgroup.com
Change , 4140
   www.heldref.org
Character Education Evaluation Tool Kit , 3747
   www.character.org
Character Education Kit: 36 Weeks of Success: Elementary
Edition, 3748
   www.masterteacher.com
Character Education Questions & Answers , 3864
   www.character.org
Character Education Resource Guide , 3865
   www.character.org
Character Education: The Foundation for Teacher Education, 3866
   www.character.org
Child Development , 4391
   www.asu.edu
Child Psychiatry & Human Development , 4460
   www.wkpa.nl
Child and Adolescent Social Work Journal , 4462
   www.wkpa.nl
Child and Youth Care Forum , 4640
   www.wkpa.nl
Children and Families , 4394
   www.nhsa.org
Children's Literature in Education , 4411
   www.wkpa.nl
Chinese Universities & Colleges , 3749
   www.iie.org
Choice , 4548
   www.ala.org/acrl/choice
Chronicle Financial Aid Guide , 3960
   www.chronicleguidance.com
Chronicle Vocational School Manual , 4096
   www.chronicleguidance.com
Classroom Notes Plus , 4509
   www.ncte.org
Classroom Strategies for the English Language Learner, 4033
   www.masterteacher.com
Classroom Teacher's Guide for Working with Paraeducators, 3751
   www.masterteacher.com
Cobblestone , 4675
   www.cobblestonepub.com
College Board Guide to High Schools , 4068
   www.collegeboard.org
College Board News , 4463
   www.collegeboard.org
College Board Review , 4464
   www.collegeboard.org
College Costs and Financial Aid Handbook , 3961
   www.collegeboard.org
College Handbook , 4020
   www.collegeboard.org
College Times , 4465
   www.collegeboard.org
Commonwealth Universities Yearbook , 3752
   www.acu.ac.uk
Communication Disorders Quarterly , 4510
   www.proedinc.com
Communique , 4466
   www.nasponline.org
Community Outreach and Education for the Arts Handbook, 4051
   www.mtaa.org
Commuter Perspectives , 4142
   www.umd.edu/NCCP
Complete Guide to Work, Study & Travel Overseas, 3924
   www.transitionsabroad.org
Complete Learning Disabilities Directory , 3753
   www.greyhouse.com
Computer and Web Resources for People with Disabilities, 3754
   www.ataccess.org
Council for Educational Development and Research Directory,
3757
   www.nea.org

Council of British Independent Schools in the European Communities-Members Directory, 3925
www.cobisec.org
Council-Grams , 4513
www.ncte.org
Counterpoint , 4144
www.lrp.com
Creating High Functioning Schools : Practice and Research, 3868
www.ccthomas.com
Creating the Quality School , 3870
www.magnapubs.com
Creative Classroom , 4412
www.creativeclassroom.com
Creativity Research Journal , 4146
www.erlbaum.com
DECA Dimensions , 4149
www.deca.org
Designing & Implementing a Leadership Academy in Character Education, 3871
www.character.org
Developing a Character Education Program , 3873
www.character.org
Development and Alumni Relations Report , 4153
www.lrp.com
Diagnostic Reading Inventory for Bilingual Students in Grades K-8, 4061
www.scottmccleary.com
Diagnostic Reading Inventory for Primary and Intermediate Grades K-8, 4062
www.scottmccleary.com
Digest of Supreme Court Decisions , 3758
www.pdkintl.org
Directory for Exceptional Children , 3759
www.portersargent.com
Directory of Central Agencies for Jewish Education, 3762
www.jesna.org
Directory of Chief Executive Officers of United Methodist Schools, Colleges & Universities, 3875
www.gbhem.org/highed.html
Directory of College Cooperative Education Programs, 3763
www.co-op.edu
Directory of Financial Aid for Women , 3964
www.rspfunding.com
Directory of Indigenous Education , 3766
www.wested.org
Directory of International Grants & Fellowships in the Health Sciences, 3966
www.nih.gov/fic
Directory of International Internships Michigan State University, 3927
www.isp.msu.edu
Directory of International Internships: A World of Opportunities, 3767
www.isp.msu.edu
Directory of Manufacturers & Suppliers , 4046
www.sla.org
Directory of Members of the Association for Library and Information Science Education, 4047
www.alise.org
Directory of Organizations in Educational Management, 3876
www.eric.uoregon.edu
Directory of Overseas Educational Advising Centers, 3769
www.collegeboard.org
Directory of Play Therapy Training , 4025
www.centerforplaytherapy.com
Directory of Postsecondary Institutions , 3770
www.ed.pubs/
Directory of Public School Systems in the United States, 3771
www.aaee.org
Directory of Resources & Exchange Programs , 3772
www.erds.com
Directory of State Education Agencies , 3877
www.ccsso.org

Disability Compliance for Higher Education , 4156
www.lrp.com/ed
Diversity, Accessibility and Quality , 3774
www.collegeboard.org
Don't Miss Out: The Ambitous Students Guide t Financial Aid, 3967
www.octameron.com
Dragonfly , 4413
www.nsta.org
Dramatics , 4585
www.etassoc.org
EDUCAUSE Quarterly , 4701
www.educause.edu
EDUCAUSE Review , 4702
www.educause.edu
ERIC Clearinghouse on Counseling & Student Services, 4470
ericcass.uncg.edu
ERS Spectrum , 4337
www.ers.org
Early Childhood Education Journal , 4396
www.wkpa.nl
Early Childhood Report: Children with Special Needs and Their Families, 4397
www.lrp.com
Early Childhood Today , 4399
www.scholastic.com
Earn & Learn: Cooperative Education Opportunities, 3930
www.octameron.com
Earth Education: A New Beginning , 4081
www.eartheducation.org
Earthkeepers , 4082
www.eartheducation.org
EdPress News , 4160
www.edpress.org
Educate@Eight , 4414
www.ed.gov
Educating for Character , 3878
www.masterteacher.com
Educating for Character: How Our Schools Can Teach Respect and Responsibility, 3879
www.character.org
Educating for Employment , 4431
www.lrp.com/ed
Education , 4161
www.rcassel.com
Education Budget Alert , 3880
www.cef.org
Education Digest , 4162
www.eddigest.com
Education Hotline , 4163
www.edweek.org
Education Now and in the Future , 4165
www.nwrel.org
Education Sourcebook: Basic Information about National Education Expectations and Goals, 3775
www.omnigraphics.com
Education Technology News , 4703
www.bpinews.com
Education Update , 4168
www.heritage.org
Education Week , 4169
www.edweek.org
Educational & Psychological Measurement , 4471
www.sagepub.com
Educational Freedom Spotlight On Homeschoolin , 4172
www.clonlara.org
Educational Horizons , 4173
www.pilambda.org
Educational Leadership , 4063
www.ascd.org
Educational Rankings Annual , 3777
www.galegroup.com
Educational Resources Catalog , 3778
www.cde.ca.gov/cdepress

Educational Theory , 4176
www.ed.uiuc.edu/educational-theory
Educators Guide to FREE Computer Materials and Internet Resources, 3781
www.freeteachingaids.com
Educators Guide to FREE Family and Consumer Education Materials, 4072
www.freeteachingaids.com
Educators Guide to FREE Films, Filmstrips and Slides, 3782
www.freeteachingaids.com
Educators Guide to FREE Guidance Materials , 4026
www.freeteachingaids.com
Educators Guide to FREE HPER Materials , 4059
www.freeteachingaids.com
Educators Guide to FREE Multicultural Materia , 3783
www.freeteachingaids.com
Educators Guide to FREE Science Materials , 4083
www.freeteachingaids.com
Educators Guide to FREE Social Studies Materials, 4091
www.freeteachingaids.com
Educators Guide to FREE Videotapes-Elementary Middle School Edition, 3904
www.freeteachingaids.com
Educators Guide to FREE Videotapes-Secondary Edition, 3905
www.freeteachingaids.com
Electronic School , 4706
www.electronic-school.com
Elementary School Guidance & Counseling , 4472
www.counseling.org
Elementary Teachers Guide to FREE Curriculum Materials, 3906
www.freeteachingaids.com
Employment Opportunities , 4433
www.nationalguild.org
English Journal , 4516
www.ncte.org
English Leadership Quarterly , 4517
www.ncte.org
Enrollment Management Report , 4342
www.lrp.com
Everything You Need for Reading , 4064
www.espbooks.com
Exceptional Children Education Resources , 3785
www.cec.sped.org/bk/catalog/journals.htm
Executive Summary Sets , 3883
www.masterteacher.com
Faces , 4677
www.cobblestonepub.com
Family Services Report , 3786
cdpublications.com
Federal Research Report , 4447
www.bpinews.com
Fellowships in International Affairs-A Guide to Opportunities in the US & Abroad, 3968
www.rienner.com
Financial Aid for Research & Creative Activities Abroad, 3970
www.rspfunding.com
Financial Aid for Study Abroad: a Manual for Advisers & Administrators, 3971
www.nafsa.org
Financial Resources for International Study , 3973
www.iie.org
Focus , 4678
www.ffvf.org
Focus on Autism , 4179
www.proedinc.com
Footsteps , 4679
www.cobblestonepub.com
Forum , 4183
www.esrnational.org
Free Money for College: Fifth Edition , 3976
www.factsonfile.com
Free Money for Foreign Study: A Guide to 1,000 Grants for Study Abroad, 3977
www.factsonfile.com

Freedom & Enterprise , 4680
www.nsccc.org
Fulbright and Other Grants for USIA Graduate Study Abroad, 3978
www.iie.org
Ganley's Catholic Schools in America , 3789
www.ganleyscatholicschool.com
German-American Scholarship Guide-Exchange Opportunities for Historians and Social Scientist, 3980
www.ghi-dc.org
Getting Funded: The Complete Guide to Writing Grant Proposals, 3981
www.cep.pdx.edu
Gifted Child Society Newsletter , 4187
www.gifted.org
Graduate & Undergraduate Programs & Courses in Middle East Studies in the US, Canada, 3790
www.acls.org
Grant Opportunities for US Scholars & Host Opportunities for US Universities, 3983
www.irex.org
Grant Writing Beyond The Basics: Proven Strat gies Professionals Use To Make Proposals Work, 3984
www.cep.pdx.edu
Grants & Awards Available to American Writers, 3985
www.pen.org
Grants Register , 3986
www.vhpsva.com
Grants, Fellowships, & Prizes of Interest to Historians, 3987
www.theaha.org
Grantsmanship Center Magazine , 4450
www.tgci.com
Great Source Catalog , 4074
www.greatsource.com
Guide to Educational Opportunities in Japan , 3935
www.embjapan.org
Guide to Federal Funding for Education , 4344
www.grantsandfunding.com
Guide to International Exchange, Community Service & Travel for Persons with Disabilities, 3791
www.miusa.org
Guide to Summer Camps & Schools , 3793
www.portersargent.com
Guidelines for Contracting with Private Providers for Educational Services, 3885
www.aasa.org
Guidelines for Effective Character Education Through Sports, 3794
www.character.org
HR on Campus , 4345
www.lrp.com
Handbook of Private Schools , 3795
www.portersargent.com
Handbook of United Methodist-Related Schools, Colleges, Universities & Theological Schools, 3796
www.gbhem.org/highed.html
Harvard College Guide to Grants , 3990
www.ocs.fas.harvard.edu
Harvard Education Letter , 4188
www.edletter.org
Health & Social Work , 4475
www.socialworkers.org
Health in Action , 4189
www.ashaweb.org
Helping Your Child Succeed in Elementary School, 4417
www.aasa.org
Higher Education Directory , 3798
www.hepinc.com
Hispanic Yearbook-Anuario Hispano , 3886
www.tiym.com
History Matters Newsletter , 4681
www.history.org/nche
Homeschooler's Guide to FREE Teaching Aids , 3801
www.freeteachingaids.com

Homeschooler's Guide to FREE Videotapes , 3802
www.freeteachingaids.com
How to Find Out About Financial Aid & Funding , 3991
www.rspfunding.com
How to Plan and Develop a Career Center , 3937
www.cew.wisc.edu
IDRA Newsletter , 4193
www.idra.org
IEA Reporter , 4194
www.idahoea.org
IIE Academic Year Abroad , 3803
www.iiebooks.org
ILA Reporter , 4550
www.ila.org
IPA Newsletter , 4346
www.ipa.vsta.net
ISS Directory of Overseas Schools , 3804
www.iss.edu
Inclusion Guide for Handling Chronically Disruptive Behavior,
3805
www.masterteacher.com
Inclusive Education Programs , 4195
www.lrp.com/ed
Incorporating Multiple Intelligences into the Curriculum and into
the Classroom: Elementary, 3806
www.masterteacher.com
Incorporating Multiple Intelligences into the Curriculum and into
the Classroom: Secondary, 3807
www.masterteacher.com
Index of Majors and Graduate Degrees , 4027
www.collegeboard.org
Industry Reference Handbooks , 3810
www.galegroup.com
Information Searcher , 4707
www.infosearcher.com
Innovative Higher Education , 4197
www.wkpa.nl
Insight , 4198
www.IECAonline.com
Instructor , 4420
www.scholastic.com/instructor
International Foundation Directory , 3992
www.europapublications.co.uk
International Journal of Play Therapy , 4477
www.a4pt.org
International Journal of Qualitive Studies in Education, 4200
www.tandF.co.uk/journals
International Study Telecom Directory , 3813
www.worldwide.edu
International Volunteer , 4201
www.vfp.org
International Workcamp Directory , 3815
www.vfp.org
Italic Handwriting Series-Book A , 4034
www.cep.pdx.edu
Italic Handwriting Series-Book B , 4035
www.cep.pdx.edu
Italic Handwriting Series-Book C , 4036
www.cep.pdx.edu
Italic Handwriting Series-Book D , 4037
www.cep.pdx.edu
Italic Handwriting Series-Book E , 4038
wwww.cep.pdx.edu
Italic Handwriting Series-Book F , 4039
www;.cep.pdx.edu
Italic Handwriting Series-Book G , 4040
www.cep.pdx.edu
Italic Letters , 4052
www.cep.pdx.edu
Jobs Clearinghouse , 4436
www.aee.org
Jobs in Russia & the Newly Independent States , 3938
www.impactpublications.com

Journal for Research in Mathematics Education , 4567
www.nctm.org
Journal of Adolescent & Adult Literacy , 4619
www.reading.org
Journal of At-Risk Issues , 4479
www.dropoutprevention.org
Journal of At-Risk Issues , 4644
www.dropoutprevention.org
Journal of Behavioral Education , 4203
www.wkpa.nl
Journal of Child and Adolescent Group Therapy , 4480
www.wkpa.nl
Journal of College Admission , 4481
www.nacac.com
Journal of College Science Teaching , 4653
www.nsta.org
Journal of Creative Behavior , 4204
www.cef-cpsi.org
Journal of Curriculum & Supervision , 4347
www.ascd.org/framejcs.html
Journal of Disability Policy Studies , 4206
www.proedinc.com
Journal of Education for Business , 4348
www.heldref.org
Journal of Educational Research , 4207
www.heldref.org
Journal of Emotional and Behavioral Disorders , 4484
www.proedinc.com
Journal of Environmental Education , 4604
www.heldref.org
Journal of Experiential Education , 4588
www.aee.org
Journal of Experiential Education , 4605
www.aee.org
Journal of Experimental Education , 4208
www.heldref.org
Journal of Geography , 4686
www.ncge.org
Journal of Learning Disabilities , 4210
www.proedinc.com
Journal of Positive Behavior Interventions , 4212
www.proedinc.com
Journal of Research in Character Education , 4214
www.character.org
Journal of Research in Rural Education , 4215
www.umaine.edu
Journal of Research on Computing in Education , 4711
www.iste.org
Journal of School Health , 4216
www.ashaweb.org
Journal of Sex Education & Therapy , 4488
www.aasect.org
Journal of Special Education , 4217
www.proedinc.com
K-12 District Technology Coordinators , 4104
www.qeddata.com
K-6 Science and Math Catalog , 4084
www.carolina.com
KIDSNET Media Guide and News , 3907
www.kidsnet.org
Language & Speech , 4524
www.kingstonepress.com
Language Arts , 4525
www.ncte.org
Laubach LitScape , 4620
www.laubach.org
Laubach Literacy Action Directory , 4065
www.laubach.org
Leading to Change , 3887
www.josseybass.com
Learning Point Magazine Laboratory, 4222
www.ncrel.org
Legal Basics: A Handbook for Educators , 3817
www.pdkintl.org

Legal Basics: A Handbook for Educators , 3888
www.pdkintl.org
Lesson Plans and Modifications for Inclusion and Collaborative Classrooms, 3818
www.masterteacher.com
Lesson Plans for Character Education: Elementary Edition, 3819
www.masterteacher.com
Lesson Plans for Integrating Technology into the Classroom: Secondary Edition, 4075
www.masterteacher.com
Lesson Plans for Problem-Based Learning, Elementary Edition, 3908
www.masterteacher.com
Lesson Plans for Problem-Based Learning: Secondary Edition, 4076
www.masterteacher.com
Lesson Plans for the Substitute Teacher: Secondary Edition, 4077
www.masterteacher.com
Lesson Plans, Integrating Technology into the Classroom: Elementary Edition, 3909
www.masterteacher.com
Liberal Education , 4225
www.aacu-edu.org
Libraries Unlimited Academic Catalog , 4048
www.lu.com
Library Collections, Acquisitions & Technical Services, 4554
www.elsvier.com
Library Issues: Briefings for Faculty and Administrators, 4555
www.libraryissues.com
Library Trends , 4558
www.edfu.lis.uiuc.edu/puboff
Lifeworld of Leadership , 3890
www.josseybass.com
Link , 4226
www.ael.org
Literacy Advocate , 4621
www.laubach.org
Living in China: A Guide to Studying, Teaching & Working in the PRC & Taiwan, 3942
www.chinabooks.com
Loans and Grants from Uncle Sam , 3995
www.octameron.com
Looking at Schools: Instruments & Processes for School Analysis, 3891
www.rbs.org
Magazine of History , 4687
www.oah.org
Maintaining Safe Schools- School Violence Alert, 4352
www.lrp.com/ed
Managing Info Tech in School Library Media Center, 4049
www.lu.com
Managing Media Services Theory and Practice , 4050
www.lu.com
Managing School Business , 4353
www.lrp.com
Mathematics Teacher , 4572
www.nctm.org
Mathematics Teaching in the Middle School , 4573
www.nctm.org
Media & Methods Magazine , 4559
www.media-methods.com
Media & Methods Magazine , 4714
www.media-methods.com
Memo to the President , 4354
www.aascu.org
Merlyn's Pen: Fiction, Essays and Poems by America's Teens, 4527
www.merlynspen.com
Momentum , 4233
www.ncea.org
Money for Film & Video Artists , 3996
www.artsusa.org
Money for Film & Video Artists , 4053
www.artsusa.org

Money for International Exchange in the Arts , 3997
www.artsusa.org
Money for Visual Artists , 3998
www.artsusa.org
Money for Visual Artists , 4054
www.artsusa.org
Montessori LIFE , 4422
www.amshq.org
Montessori Observer , 4235
www.wdn.com/trust/ims
MultiMedia Schools , 4715
www.infotoday.com
Multimedia and Videodisc Compendium for Education and Training, 4105
www.emergingtechnology.com
Music Educators Journal , 4589
www.menc.org
Music Educators Journal and Teaching Music , 4590
www.menc.org
Music Teachers Guide to Music Instructional Software, 4055
www.mtna.org
NABE News , 4529
www.nabe.org
NACAC Bulletin , 4490
www.nacac.com
NAEA News , 4591
www.naea-reston.org
NAEIR Advantage , 4236
www.freegoods.com
NAFSA Newsletter , 4237
www.nafsa.org
NAFSA's Guide to Education Abroad for Advisers & Administrators, 3825
www.nafsa.org
NAIEC Newsletter , 4238
www2.pcom.net/naiec
NCTM News Bulletin , 4574
www.nctm.org
NEA Almanac of Higher Education , 3826
www.nea.org
NEA Higher Education Advocate , 4240
www.nea.org
NEA Today , 4241
www.nea.org
NEWSLINKS , 4242
www.iss.edu
NREA News , 4244
www.colostate.edu
NSTA Reports! , 4656
www.nsta.org
NY School Boards , 4356
www.nyssba.org
National Accrediting Commission of Cosmetology, Arts and Sciences, 4245
www.naccas.org
National Alliance of Black School Educators (NABSE), 4246
www.nabse.org
National Clearinghouse for Bilingual Education Newsletter, 4531
www.ncbe.gwu.edu
National Coalition for Sex Equity in Education, 4492
www.ncsee.org
National Directory of Internships , 3944
www.nsee.org
National Guild of Community Schools of the Arts, 4404
www.nationalguild.org
National Guild of Community Schools of the Arts, 4592
www.nationalguild.org
National Monitor of Education , 4248
www.e-files.org
National Reference Directory of Year-Round Education Programs, 3830
www.nayre.org

National School Supply & Equipment Associatio
Membership/Buyers' Guide Directory, 3895
   www.nssea.org
National Schools of Character , 3896
   www.character.org
National Schools of Character: Best Practices and New
Perspectives, 3831
   www.character.org
National Schools of Character: Practices to Adopt & Adapt, 3832
   www.character.org
National Society for Experiential Education , 3833
   www.nsee.org
National Standards for Dance Education News , 4610
   www.aahperd.org/nda
Need A Lift? , 4001
   www.EMBLEM.legion.org
NetLingo Internet Directory , 4106
   www,netlingo.com
Network , 4358
   www.nspra.org
New Horizons , 4493
   www.nrcsa.com
News & Views , 4689
   www.pcss.org
News for You , 4622
   www.laubach.org
Odyssey , 4657
   www.odysseymagazine.com
One Hundred Ways Parents Can Help Students Achieve, 3835
   www.aasa.org
Oranatics Journal , 4593
   www.etassoc.org
Our Children: The National PTA Magazine , 4257
   www.pta.org
PTA in Pennsylvania , 4259
   www.papta.org
Paradigm Lost: Reclaiming America's Educational Future, 3837
   www.aasa.org
Parent Involvement Facilitator: Elementary Edition, 3910
   www.masterteacher.com
Parent Involvement Facilitator: Secondary Edition, 4078
   www.masterteacher.com
Parents Make the Difference! , 4423
   www.parent-institute.com
Parents Make the Difference!: School Readiness Edition, 4405
   www.parent-institute.com
Parents Still Make the Difference! , 4646
   www.parent-institute.com
Parents Still Make the Difference!: Middle Sc ool Edition, 4647
   www.parent-institute.com
Parents as Teachers National Center , 4260
   www.patnc.org
Pennsylvania State Education Association , 4263
   www.psea.org
Phi Delta Kappa Educational Foundation , 4264
   www.pdkintl.org
Phonics Institute , 4623
   www.readingstore.com
Physical Education Digest , 4611
   www.pedigest.com
Picture Book Learning Volume-1, 4042
   www.picturebooklearning.com
Planning & Changing , 4362
   http://coe.ilstu.edu/eafdept/pandc.htm
Planning for Higher Education , 4265
   www.scup.org/phe
Policy & Practice , 4266
   www.aphsa.org
Population Educator , 4267
   www.populationeducation.org
Power of Public Engagement Book Set , 3845
   www.masterteacher.com
Principal Communicator , 4364
   www.napra.org

Private Independent Schools , 3846
   www.buntingandlyon.com
Proactive Leadership in the 21st Century , 3897
   www.masterteacher.com
Process of Elimination - a Method of Teaching and Learning
Basic Grammar, 4043
   www.scottmccleary.com
Public Education Alert , 4268
   www.pea-online.org
Public Relations Starter Pacs Notebook , 3898
   www.masterteacher.com
Put Reading First: The Research Building Blocks For Teaching
Children To Read, 4044
   www.edpubs.org
QED's State School Guides , 3899
   www.qeddata.com
Quantum , 4659
   www.nsta.org
Quarterly Journal of Speech , 4533
   www.natcom.org
Quarterly Review of Doublespeak , 4534
   www.ncte.org
Quarterly of the NWP , 4535
   www.writingproject.org
Ready to Read, Ready to Learn , 4066
   www.edpubs.org
Reclaiming Children and Youth , 4271
   www.proedinc.com
Recognition Review , 4272
   www.ara.org
Recording for the Blind & Dyslexic , 4632
   www.rfbd.org
Rehabilitation Counseling Bulletin , 4494
   www.proedinc.com
Remedial and Special Education , 4274
   www.proedinc.com
Report on Literacy Programs , 4633
   www.bpinews.com
Report on Preschool Programs , 4407
   www.bpinews.com
Reports of the National Center for Science Education, 4660
   www.ncseweb.org
Research in Higher Education , 4277
   www.wkpa.nl
Research, Study, Travel, & Work Abroad , 3949
   www.access.gpo.gov
Resource Booklet for Independent Music Teachers, 4057
   www.mtna.org
Rhetoric Review , 4538
   http://members.aol.com/sborrowman/rr/html
Roeper Review: A Journal on Gifted Education , 4279
   www.roeperreview.org
Rural Educator-Journal for Rural and Small Schools, 4368
   www.colostate.edu
Rural Educator: Journal for Rural and Small Schools, 4280
   www.colostate.edu
Scholarship Handbook , 4006
   www.collegeboard.org
Scholarships for Emigres Training for Careers in Jewish
Education, 4007
   www.jfew.org
Scholarships, Fellowships and Loans , 4008
   www.galegroup.com
School Administrator , 4369
   www.aasa.org
School Executive , 4371
   www.media-methods.com
School Guide , 3850
   schoolguides.com
School Law Briefings , 4372
   www.lrp.com
School Library Journal , 4561
   www.slj.com

School Promotion, Publicity & Public Relations: Nothing but Benefits, 3900
www.masterteacher.com
School Psychology Review , 4496
www.nasponline.org
School Safety , 4288
www.nssc1.org
School Transportation News , 4289
www.stnonline.com
SchoolArts Davis Publications, 4594
www.davis-art.com/
Schools & Colleges Directory , 4060
www.aee.org
Schools Abroad of Interest to Americans , 3851
www.portersargent.com
Schoolwide Discipline Strategies that Make a Difference in Teaching & Learning, 3901
www.masterteacher.com
Science Activities , 4661
www.heldref.org
Science Scope , 4663
www.nsta.org
Science Teacher , 4664
www.nsta.org
Science and Children , 4665
www.nsta.org
Science for All Children; A Guide to Improving Science Education, 4085
www.si.edu/nsrc
Secondary Teachers Guide to FREE Curriculum Materials, 4080
www.freeteachingaids.com
Section 504 Compliance Advisor , 4375
www.lrp.com/ed
Shaping the Future , 4291
www.lea.org
SkillsUSA Champions , 4440
www.skillsusa.org
Slate Newsletter , 4539
www.ncte.org
Social Education , 4691
www.ncss.org
Social Studies Journal , 4693
www.pcss.org
Social Studies Professional , 4694
www.ncss.org
Social Work Research Journal , 4497
www.socialworkers.org
Social Work in Education , 4498
www.socialworkers.org
SocialWork , 4499
www.socialworkers.org
Society for Applied Learning Technology , 4717
www.salt.org
Southwest Educational Development Laboratory Letter, 4293
www.sedl.org
Special Education Law Monthly , 4376
www.lrp.com/ed
Special Educator , 4295
www.lrp.com
Student Affairs Today , 4379
www.lrp.com
Student Travels Magazine , 4299
www.ciee.org
Studies in Second Language Acquisition , 4540
www.indiana.edu/~ssla
Sunship Earth , 4086
www.eartheducation.org
Sunship III , 4087
www.eartheducation.org
Superintendents Only , 4380
www.masterteacher.com
Superintendents Only Master Teacher , 4381
www.masterteacher.com

TECHNOS Quarterly for Education & Technolgy , 4719
www.technos.net
TESOL Journal: A Journal of Teaching and Classroom Research, 4541
www.tesol.edu
TESOL Quarterly , 4542
www.tesol.com
THE Journal , 4382
www.thejournal.com
THE Journal , 4720
www.thejournal.com
Teaching Children Mathematics , 4577
www.nctm.org
Teaching Journal , 4597
www.etassoc.org
Teaching K-8 Magazine , 4424
www.teachingk-8.com
Teaching Music , 4598
www.menc.org
Teaching Our Youngest-A Guide for Preschool Teachers and Child Care and Family Providers, 3912
www.edpubs.org
Tech Directions , 4721
www.eddigest.com
Technology & Learning , 4722
www.techlearning.com
Technology Pathfinder for Administrators Master Teacher, 4383
www.masterteacher.com
Technology Pathfinder for Administrators Master Teacher, 4723
www.masterteacher.com
Technology Pathfinder for Teachers , 4724
www.masterteacher.com
Technology Pathfinder for Teachers Master Teacher, 4725
www.masterteacher.com
Technology Teacher , 4726
www.iteawww.org
Technology in Public Schools , 4111
www.qeddata.com
Tests: a Comprehensive Reference for Psycholo y, Education & Business, 4029
www.proedinc.com
Theory Into Practice , 4305
www.coe.ohio-state.edu
This Active Life , 4306
www.nea.org/retired
Three R'S for Teachers: Research, Reports & Reviews, 4307
www.masterteacher.com
Tips for Reading Tutors , 4067
www.edpubs.org
Title I Handbook , 4385
www.TitleIonline.com
Title I Monitor , 4386
www.TitleIonline.com
Today's School Psychologist , 4500
www.lrp.com/ed
Topics in Early Childhood Special Education , 4408
www.proedinc.com
Totline Newsletter , 4409
www.frankschaffer.com
Transitions Abroad: The Guide to Learning, Living, & Working Abroad, 4309
www.transitionsabroad.com
Universe in the Classroom , 4667
www.astrosociety.org
VIP Views, Ideas & Practical Solutions , 4389
www.masterteacher.com
Vincent-Curtis Educational Register , 3855
www.vincentcurtis.com
Vision , 4410
www.serve.org
Vocational Biographies , 4030
www.vocbio.com
Washington Counseletter , 4501
www.chronicleguidance.com

Web Feet Guides , 4728
www.webfeetguides.com
WestEd: Focus , 4313
www.WestEd.org
What Works and Doesn't With at Risk Students , 4031
www.literacyfirst.com
What's Working in Parent Involvement , 4636
www.parent-institute.com
Working Holidays: The Complete Guide to Finding a Job
Overseas, 3955
www.transitionsabroad.org
World of Learning , 3859
www.galegroup.com
World of Play Therapy Literature , 4032
www.centerforplaytherapy.com
Write Now: A Complete Self Teaching Program for Better
Handwriting, 4045
www.cep.pdx.edu
Write Now: A Complete Self-Teaching Program F or Better
Handwriting, 4014
www.cep.pdx.edu
Writing Lab Newsletter , 4543
www.owl.english.purdue.edu/lab/newsletter/index.html
Your School and the Law , 4390
www.lrp.com/ed
eSchool News , 4729
www.eschoolnews.com

Publishers

ABC Feelings Adage Publications , 4730
www.abcfeelings.com
ABDO Publishing Company , 4731
www.abdopub.com
AIMS Education Foundation , 4733
www.aimsedu.org
Acorn Naturalists , 4735
www.acornnaturalists.com
Active Parenting Publishers , 4738
www.activeparenting.com
Alarion Press , 4741
www.alarion.com
American Association of School Administrators , 4746
www.aasa.org
American Nuclear Society , 4749
www.aboutnuclear.com
American Technical Publishers , 4751
www.go2atp.com
Ampersand Press , 4753
www.ampersandpress.com
Art Visuals , 4758
www.members.tripod.com
Asian American Curriculum Project , 4759
www.asianamericanbooks.com
Association for Supervision & Curriculum Development, 4761
www.ascd.org
Awiley Company , 4766
www.josseybass.com
Barron's Educational Series , 4768
www.barronseduc.com
Bluestocking Press Catalog , 4773
www.bluestockingpress.com
Bureau for At-Risk Youth Guidance Channel , 4778
www.at-risk.com
Business Publishers , 4779
www.bpinews.com
CLEARVUE/eav , 4780
www.clearvue.com
Cambridge University Press , 4782
www.cup.cam.ac.uk
Capstone Press , 4784
www.capstonepress.com

Carolrhoda Books , 4786
www.lernerbooks.com
Center for Play Therapy , 4788
www.centerforplaytherapy.com
Children's Book Council , 4792
www.cbcbooks.org
Children's Press , 4793
publishing.grolier.com
Choices Education Project , 4797
www.choices.edu
Cognitive Concepts , 4799
www.cogcon.com
College Board , 4800
www.collegeboard.org
Coloring Concepts , 4801
www.coloringconcepts.com
Computer Learning Foundation , 4803
www.computerlearning.org
Computer Literacy Press , 4804
www.complitpress.com
Continental Press , 4807
www.continentalpress.com
Cottonwood Press , 4808
www.cottonwoodpress.com
Council for Exceptional Children , 4809
www.cec.sped.org
Creative Teaching Press , 4810
www.creativeteaching.com
Curriculum Associates , 4812
www.curriculumassociates.com
Dial Books for Young Readers , 4817
www.penguinputnam.com
Didax Educational Resources , 4818
www.didaxinc.com
DynEd International , 4826
www.dyned.com
ETA - Math Catalog , 4827
www.etauniverse.com
ETR Associates , 4828
www.etr.org
Edmark , 4833
www.edmark.com
Educational Productions , 4837
www.edpro.com
Educational Teaching Aids , 4838
www.etauniverse.com
Educators Progress Service , 4839
www.freeteachingaids.com
Educators Publishing Service , 4840
www.epsbooks.com
Ellis , 4842
www.ellis.com
Encyclopaedia Britannica , 4843
www.britannica.com
Ethnic Arts & Facts , 4846
www.ethnicartsnfacts.com
Exploratorium , 4849
www.exploratorium.edu
Facts on File , 4852
www.factsonfile.com
Forbes Custom Publishing , 4855
www.forbescp.com
Frog Publications , 4860
www.frog.com
Gareth Stevens , 4861
garethstevens.com
Goodheart-Willcox Publisher , 4864
www.goodheartwillcox.com
Grolier Publishing , 4867
www.publishing.grolier.com
Gryphon House , 4868
www.ghbooks.com
Horn Book Guide , 4879
http://www.hbook.com

Houghton Mifflin Books for Children , 4880
www.hmco.com
Institute for Chemical Education , 4885
ice.chem.wisc.edu
IntelliTools , 4887
www.intellitools.com
Intercultural Press , 4889
www.interculturalpress.com
J Weston Walch, Publisher , 4890
www.walch.com
JayJo Books , 4893
www.jayjo.com
Kaeden Corporation , 4896
www.kaeden.com
Kane/Miller Book Publishers , 4897
www.kanemiller.com
Keep America Beautiful , 4898
www.kab.org
Kendall-Hunt Publishing Company , 4899
www.kendallhunt.com
Knowledge Adventure , 4900
www.education.com
Knowledge Unlimited , 4901
www.newscurrents.com
Langenseheidt Publishing , 4905
www.hammondmap.com
Lawrence Hall of Science , 4906
www.lawrencehallofscience.org
Learning Disabilities Association of America , 4909
www.ldaamerica.org
Learning Links , 4910
www.learinglinks.com
Lee & Low Books , 4911
www.leeandlow.com
Lerner Publishing Group , 4913
www.lernerbooks.com
Listening Library , 4915
www.listeninglib.com
Lynne Rienner Publishing , 4919
www.fireflybooks.com
MHS , 4920
www.mhs.com
Magna Publications , 4925
www.magnapubs.com
Mari , 4928
www.mariinc.com
MasterTeacher , 4929
www.masterteacher.com
MathSoft , 4930
www.mathsoft.com
McCracken Educational Services , 4931
www.mccrackened.com
Mel Bay Publications , 4933
www.melbay.com
Millbrook Press , 4935
www.millbrookpress.com
Mondo Publishing , 4939
www.mondopub.com
Morning Glory Press , 4940
www.morningglorypress.com
NASP Publications , 4943
www.naspionline.org
NCTM Educational Materials , 4944
www.nctm.org
Narrative Press , 4946
www.narrativepress.com
National Council of Teachers of English , 4950
www.ncte.org
National Geographic Society , 4953
www.nationalgeographic.com
National Head Start Association , 4954
www.nhsa.org
National Women's History Project , 4956
www.nwhp.org

National Writing Project , 4957
www.writingproject.org
New Canaan Publishing Company , 4958
www.newcanaanpublishing.com
Options Publishing , 4963
www.optionspublishing.com
Organization of American Historians , 4964
www.oah.org
PRO-ED , 4966
www.proedinc.com
Parenting Press , 4967
www.ParentingPress.com
Penguin USA , 4968
www.penguinputnam.com
Perfection Learning Corporation , 4969
www.fireflybooks.com
Perspectives on History Series , 4972
www.ushistorydocs.com
Peytral Publications , 4973
www.peytral.com
Phelps Publishing , 4974
www.phelpspublishing.com
Population Connection , 4978
www.populationconnection.org
Prufrock Press , 4983
www.prufrock.com
Quality Education Data , 4985
www.qeddata.com
Raintree/Steck-Vaughn , 4987
www.steck-vaughn.com
Redleaf Press , 4992
www.redleafpress.org
Richard C Owen Publishers , 4995
www.rcowen.com
Riverside Publishing Company , 4996
www.riverpub.com
Roots & Wings Educational Catalog-Australia for Kids, 4997
www.rootsandwingscatalog.com/ www.australiaforkids.com
Routledge/Europa Library Reference , 4999
www.reference.routlege-ny.com
Runestone Press , 5000
www.lernerbooks.com
SafeSpace Concepts , 5002
www.safespaceconcepts.com
Sage Publications , 5003
www.fireflybooks.com
Scholastic , 5005
www.scholastic.com
Scott & McCleary Publishing Company , 5008
www.scottmccleary.com
Sharpe Reference , 5010
www.mesharpe.com
Simon & Schuster Children's Publishing , 5013
www.simonsayskids.com
Social Science Education Consortium , 5015
www.ssecinc.org
Social Studies School Service , 5016
www.socialstudies.com
Stenhouse Publishers , 5020
www.stenhouse.com
Story Teller , 5021
www.thestoryteller.com
Summit Learning , 5022
www.summitlearning.com
Sunburst Technology , 5023
www.sunburst.com
Sundance Publishing , 5024
www.sindancepub.com
TL Clark Incorporated , 5027
www.tlclarkinc.com
TMC/Soundprints , 5028
www.soundprints.com
Tom Snyder Productions , 5037
www.tomsynder.com

Turn-the-Page Press , 5042
www.turnthepage.com
Upstart Books , 5044
www.hpress.highsmith.com
WORLD OF DIFFERENCE Institute , 5050
www.adl.org
Walker & Company , 5052
www.walkerbooks.com
Waterfront Books , 5054
www.waterfrontbooks.com
Web Feet Guides , 5055
www.webfeetguides.com
Western Psychological Services , 5057
www.wpspublish.com
Wildlife Conservation Society , 5058
www.wcs.com
World & I , 5063
www.worldandi.com
World Eagle , 5067
www.worldeagle.com
Wright Group , 5070
www.wrightgroup.com
Zaner-Bloser K-8 Catalog , 5072
www.zaner-bloser.com
Zephyr Press , 5073
www.zephyrpress.com
ZooBooks , 5074
www.zoobooks.com

Research Centers

AVKO Dyslexia Research Foundation , 5075
www.avko.org
Center for Equity and Excellence in Education , 5077
www.ceee.gwu.edu
Center for Learning , 5078
www.centerforlearning.org
Center for Research on the Education of Students Placed at Risk,
5080
www.csos.jhu.edu
Center for the Study of Small/Rural Schools , 5084
cssrs.ou.edu
Cirriculum Research and Development Group , 5087
www.hawaii.edu/crdg
Council for Educational Development and Research, 5088
www.nea.org
Educational Research Service , 5092
www.ers.org
Higher Education Center , 5095
www.nea.org
Learning Research and Development Center , 5100
www.lrdc.pitt.edu
Life Lab Science Program , 5101
www.lifelab.org
Mid-Atlantic Regional Educational Laboratory , 5103
www.temple.edu/lss
NEA Foundatrion for tHe Improvement of Educat on, 5108
www.nife.org
National Black Child Development Institute , 5109
www.nbcdi.org
National Center for Research in Vocational Education, 5112
http://vocserve.berkeley.edu
National Center on Education & the Economy , 5116
www.ncee.org
National Clearinghouse for Alcohol & Drug Information, 5119
health.org
National Clearinghouse for Bilingual Educatio , 5120
www.ncbe.gwu.edu
National Clearinghouse for Information on Business Involvement
in Education, 5121
www2.pecom.net/naiec

National Dropout Prevention Center , 5122
www.dropoutprevention.org
National Early Childhood Technical Assistance System, 5123
www.nectas.unc.edu
National Information Center for Educational Media, 5124
www.nicem.com
National Science Resources Center , 5129
www.nsrconline.org
North Central Regional Educational Laboratory , 5130
www.ncrel.org
Northeast and Islands Regional Educational Laboratory, 5132
www.lab.brown.edu
Northwest Regional Educational Laboratory , 5133
www.nwrel.org
Parent Educational Advocacy Training Center , 5135
www.peatc.org
Parents as Teachers National Center , 5136
www.patnc.org
Quality Education Data , 5138
www.qeddata.com
SERVE , 5141
www.serve.org
Scientific Learning , 5144
www.scientificlearning.com
Southwestern Educational Development Laboratory, 5150
www.sedl.org
TACS/WRRC , 5152
http://interact.uoregon.edu/wrrc/wrrc.html
TERC , 5153
www.terc.edu

School Supplies

ADP Lemco , 5227
www.adplemco.com
AGC/United Learning , 5155
www.discoveryed.com
AIMS Multimedia , 5414
www.aimsmultimedia.com
ASRS of America , 5474
www.elecompack.com
AbleNet , 5229
www.ablenet.com
Accu-Cut Systems , 5231
www.accucut.com
Active Parenting Publishing , 5156
www.activeparenting.com
Adden Furniture , 5475
www.addenfurniture.com
Air Technologies Corporation , 5476
www.airtech.net
Airomat Corporation , 5232
www.airomat.com
Airspace USA , 5233
www.airspacesolutions.com
All American Scoreboards , 5416
www.allamericanscoreboards.com
All Art Supplies , 5234
www.allartsupplies.com
Allied Video Corporation , 5158
www.alliedvd.com
Ambrose Video Publishing Inc , 5160
www.ambrosevideo.com
American Foam , 5235
www.bfoam.com
American Locker Security Systems , 5556
www.americanlocker.com
American Plastics Council , 5236
www.plastics.org
American Playground Corporation , 5731
www.american-playground.com

American Swing Products , 5732
www.americanswing.com
Anatomical Chart Company , 5237
www.anatomical.com
Anchor Audio , 5161
www.anchoraudio.com
Angeles Group , 5478
www.angeles-group.com
Angels School Supply , 5238
www.angelschoolsupply.com
Anthro Corporation Technology Furniture , 5479
www.anthro.com
Aol@School , 5239
www.school.aol.com
Arbor Scientific , 5621
www.arborsci.com
Armada Art Materials , 5240
www.armadaart.com
Art Materials Catalog , 5241
www.unitednow.com
Art Supplies Wholesale , 5242
www.allartsupplies.com
Art to Remember , 5243
www.arttoremember.com
Artix , 5244
www.artix.bc.ca
Astronomy to Go , 5622
www.astronomytogo.com
Audio Forum , 5248
www.audioforum.com
BUILD Sucess Through the Values of Excellence , 5163
cssrs.ou.edu
Badge-A-Minit , 5249
www.badgeaminit.com
Bale Company , 5251
www.bale.com
Baumgarten's , 5253
www.baumgartens.com
Best Manufacturing Sign Systems , 5254
www.bestsigns.com
Best-Rite , 5255
www.bestrite.com
Binney & Smith , 5256
www.crayola.com
Blaine Window Hardware , 5559
www.blainewindow.com
Blanton & Moore Company , 5481
www.blantonandmoore.com
Brodart Company, Automation Division , 5486
www.brodart.com
Buckstaff Company , 5487
www.buckstaff.com
C-Thru Ruler Company , 5264
www.CThruRuler.com
CASPR , 5423
www.caspr.com
CHEM/Lawrence Hall of Science , 5265
www.lawrencehallofscience.org
Cable in the Classroom , 5424
www.ciconline.org
Califone International , 5267
www.califone.com
Carolina Biological Supply Company , 5624
www.carolina.com
Carpets for Kids Etc... , 5488
www.carpetforkids.com
Center for Learning , 5274
www.centerforlearning.org
Challenger Center for Space Science Education, 5625
www.challenger.org
Character Education , 5166
cssrs.ou.edu
Chemtrol , 5562
www.chemtrolcontrol.com

Chief Manufacturing , 5428
www.chiefmfg.com
Children's Furniture Company , 5490
www.gressco.com
Childswork/Childsplay , 5277
www.childswork.com
Chip Taylor Communications , 5167
www.chiptaylor.com
Chroma , 5278
www.chromaonline.com
Citizenship Through Sports and Fine Arts Curriculum, 5280
www.nfhs.org
Claridge Products & Equipment , 5281
www.claridgeproducts.com
Classic Modular Systems , 5627
www.dct.com/cms
College Board Publications , 5169
www.collegeboard.org
Collins & Aikman Floorcoverings , 5282
www.powerbond.com
Colorado Time Systems , 5735
www.coloradotime.com
Columbia Cascade Company , 5283
www.timberform.com
Computer Prompting & Captioning Company , 5170
www.cpcweb.com
Concept Media , 5171
www.conceptmedia.com
Contact East , 5563
www.contacteast.com
Continental Film , 5492
www.continentalfilm.com
Crizmac Art & Cultural Education Materials In , 5286
www.crizmac.com
Crow Canyon Archaeological Center , 5630
www.crowcanyon.org
Crown Mats & Matting , 5287
www.crown-mats.com
Crystal Productions , 5172
www.crystalproductions.com
CyberStretch By Jazzercise , 5494
www.jazzercize.com
Da-Lite Screen Company , 5495
www.da-lite.com
Dahle USA , 5288
www.dahleusa.com
Daktronics , 5430
www.daktronics.com
Delta Biologicals , 5633
www.deltabio.com
Delta Biologicals Catalog , 5634
www.deltabio.com
Depco- Millennium 3000 , 5431
www.depcoinc.com
Detecto Scale Corporation , 5635
www.detectoscale.com
Dick Blick Art Materials , 5291
www.dickblick.com
Discovery Toys , 5293
www.discoverytoyslink.com/elizabeth
Dixie Art Supplies , 5295
www.dixieart.com
Draper , 5297
www.draperinc.com
Draw Books , 5298
www.drawbooks.com
Dri-Dek Corporation , 5566
www.dri-dek.com
Early Advantage , 5174
www.earlyadvantage.com
Education Department , 5303
www.wcs.com
Educational Video Group , 5175
www.evgonline.com

Edwin H. Benz Company , 5641
www.benztesters.com
Electro-Steam Generator Corporation , 5642
www.electrosteam.com
Ellison Educational Equipment , 5306
www.ellison.com
English as a Speech Language Video Series , 5176
www.masterteacher.com
Estes-Cox Corporation , 5643
www.esteseducator.com
Fair-Play Scoreboards , 5436
www.fair-play.com
Family Reading Night Kit , 5309
www.renlearn.com
Fascinating Folds , 5310
www.fascinating-folds.com
Festo Corporation , 5437
www.festo-usa.com
Fiskars Corporation , 5311
www.fiskars.com
Fordham Equipment Company , 5503
www.fordhamequip.com
Forestry Supplies , 5650
www.forestry-suppliers.com
Fox Laminating Company , 5312
www.foxlam.com
Future of Rural Education , 5180
cssrs.ou.edu
GPN Year 2005 Literacy Catalog , 5181
www.gpn.unl.edu
GameTime , 5739
www.gametime.com
Gangs in Our Schools: Identification, Response, and Prevention
Strategies, 5182
cssrs.ou.edu
Gared Sports , 5740
www.garedsports.com
Gold's Artworks , 5315
www.goldsartworks.20m.com
Golden Artist Colors , 5316
www.goldenpaints.com
Grafco , 5505
www.grafco.com
Grammer , 5506
www.grammerusa.com
Graphix , 5317
www.grafixarts.com
Greeting Tree , 5507
www.greetingtree.com
Gressco Ltd. , 5508
www.gressco.com
Grounds for Play , 5742
www.groundsforplay.com
Guidance Associates , 5183
www.guidanceassociates.com
H Wilson Company , 5509
www.hwilson.com
HAZ-STOR , 5581
www.hazstor.com
Hands-On Equations , 5319
www.borenson.com
Harrisville Designs , 5320
www.harrisville.com
Haworth , 5511
www.haworth.com
Haws Corporation , 5584
www.hawsco.com
Hayes School Publishing , 5321
www.hayespub.com
Health Connection , 5184
www.healthconnection.org
Henry S Wolkins Company , 5322
www.wolkins.com

Hooked on Phonics Classroom Edition , 5323
www.hop.com
Howell Playground Equipment , 5658
www.primestripe.com
Hydrus Galleries , 5324
www.hydra9.com
IIE Passport: Short Term Study Abroad , 5186
www.iiebooks.org
In Search of Character , 5189
www.pronline.net
Insect Lore , 5325
www.insectlore.com
Insect Lore , 5661
www.insectlore.com
Intermedia , 5191
www.intermedia-inc.com
International Historic Films , 5192
www.ihffilm.com
J&A Handy-Crafts , 5326
www.jacrafts.com
Jaypro , 5745
www.jaypro.com
Joy Carpets , 5512
www.joycarpets.com
Justrite Manufacturing Company , 5665
www.justritemfg.com
Ken-a-Vision Manufacturing Company , 5667
www.ken-a-vision.com
Kensington Technology Group , 5514
www.kensington.com
Kewaunee Scientific Corporation , 5669
www.kewaunee.com
Key-Bak , 5328
www.keybak.com
Keyboard Instructor , 5329
www.keyboardinstructor.com
Kids Percussion Buyer's Guide , 5330
www.playdrums.com
Kidstamps , 5332
www.kidstamps.com
Kidstuff Playsystems , 5746
www.fun-zone.com
Knex Education Catalog , 5333
www.knexeducation.com
Knex Education Catalog , 5670
www.knexeducation.com
Koffler Sales Company , 5671
www.kofflersales.com
Kompan , 5747
www.kompan.com
LA Steelcraft Products , 5748
www.lasteelcraft.com
LDSystems , 5591
www.bottompump.com
LINX System , 5676
www.thesciencesource.com
Lab-Aids , 5679
www.lab-aids.com
Leadership: Rethinking the Future , 5196
cssrs.ou.edu
Learning Materials Workshop , 5335
www.learningmaterialswork.com
Learning Needs Catalog , 5336
www.learningneeds.com
Learning Station/Hug-a-Chug Records , 5444
www.learningstationmusic.com
Learning Technologies , 5684
www.starlab.com
Lee Metal Products , 5516
www.leemetal.com
Library Bureau , 5517
www.librarybureau.com
Library Store , 5518
www.thelibrarystore.com

Loew-Coenell , 5340
www.loew-cornell.com
Love to Teach , 5342
www.lovetoteach.com
MCM Electronics , 5447
www.mcmelectronics.com
MPC Multimedia Products Corp , 5197
www.800-pickmpc.com
Magna Plan Corporation , 5448
www.visualplanning.com
Magnet Source , 5688
www.magnetsource.com
Magnetic Aids , 5345
www.magneticaids.com
Main Street Foundations: Building Community T ams, 5198
cssrs.ou.edu
Marsh Industries , 5347
www.marsh-ind.com
Marshmedia , 5199
www.marshmedia.com
Master Bond , 5594
www.masterbond.com
Mateflex-Mele Corporation , 5523
www.mateflex.com
Material Science Technology , 5349
www.energy-concepts-inc.com
Media Projects , 5200
www.mediaprojects.org
Meiji Techno America , 5689
www.meijitechno.com
Microsoft Corporation , 5524
www.microsoft.com
Middle School: Why and IIow , 5201
cssrs.ou.edu
Midwest Publishers Supply , 5350
www.mps-co.com
ModuForm , 5526
www.moduform.com
Morgan Buildings, Pools, Spas, RV's , 5527
www.morganusa.com
Multicultural Educations: Valuing Diversity , 5202
cssrs.ou.edu
Museum Products Company , 5693
www.museumproducts.net
Naden Scoreboards , 5451
www.naden.com
Nasco Arts & Crafts Catalog , 5355
www.eNASCO.com
Nasco Early Learning & Afterschool Essential atalogs, 5356
www.eNasco.com
Nasco Math Catalog , 5357
www.nascofa.com
National Optical & Scientific Instruments , 5696
www.nationaloptical.com
National Teaching Aids , 5358
www.hubbardscientific.com
National Teaching Aids , 5753
www.hubbardscientific.com
Neumade Products Corporation , 5452
www.neumade.com
Nevco Scoreboard Company , 5453
www.nevco.com
New Hermes , 5359
www.newhermes.com
NewsCurrents , 5362
www.newscurrents.com
Norco Products , 5528
www.norcoproducts.com
Nova , 5529
www.novadesk.com
Oscoda Plastics , 5530
www.oscodaplastics.com
Outback Play Centers , 5755
www.outbackplaycenters.com

PASCO Scientific , 5698
ww.pasco.com
Paragon Furniture , 5532
www.paragoninc.com
Pearson Education Technologies , 5364
www.pearsonedtech.com
Penco Products , 5598
www.pencoproducts.com
Pentel of America , 5365
www.pentel.com
Phoenix Films/BFA Educ Media/Coronet/MII , 5209
www.phoenixlearninggroup.com
Pin Man , 5366
www.thepinmanok.com
PlayDesigns , 5756
www.playdesigns.com
Playworld Systems , 5759
www.playworldsystems.com
Polyform Products Company , 5368
www.sculpey.com
Porter Athletic Equipment Company , 5760
www.porter-ath.com
Powr-Flite Commercial Floor Care Equipment, 5600
www.powrflite.com
Presidential Classroom , 5210
www.presidentialclassroom.org
Presidential Classroom , 5369
www.presidentialclassroom.org
ProCoat Products , 5601
www.procoat.com
Professor Weissman's Software , 5370
www.math911.com
Puppets on the Pier , 5372
www.puppetdream.com
RC Musson Rubber Company , 5374
www.mussonrubber.com
RMF Products , 5456
www.rmfproducts.com
Rainbow Educational Media Charles Clark Company, 5211
www.rainbowedumedia.com
Reconnecting Youth , 5377
www.nesonline.com
Red Ribbon Resources , 5378
ww.redribbonresources.com
Renaissance Graphic Arts , 5379
www.printmaking-materials.com
Research Technology International , 5536
www.ritco.com
Resources for Teaching Elementary School Science, 5700
www.si.edu
RobotiKits Direct , 5461
www.robotikitsdirect.com
Rock Paint Distributing Corporation , 5380
www.handyart.com
SNAP-DRAPE , 5538
www.snapdrape.com
Safe & Drug Free Catalog , 5382
www.pronline.net
Safety Play , 5764
www.mindspring.com
Sakura of America , 5383
www.gellyroll.com
Salsbury Industries , 5605
www.mailboxes.com
Sanford Corporation , 5384
www.sanfordcorp.com
Sax Visual Art Resources , 5385
www.saxfcs.com
Science Source , 5706
www.thesciencesource.com
Scientific Laser Connection, Incorporated , 5708
www.slclasers.com
Scott Resources/ Hubbard Scientific , 5464
www.hubbardscientific.com

Scott Sign Systems , 5388
  www.scottsigns.com
Scratch-Art Company , 5389
  www.scratchart.com
Screen Works , 5539
  www.thescreenworks.com
Servicemaster , 5606
  www.servicemaster.com
Seton Identification Products , 5391
  www.seton.com
Sign Product Catalog , 5393
  www.scottsigns.com
Skulls Unlimited International , 5713
  www.skullsunlimited.com
Slow Learning Child Video Series , 5216
  www.masterteacher.com
Society of Automotive Engineers , 5714
  www.sae.org
Southern Precision Instruments Company , 5715
  www.flash.net/spico
Spacesaver Corporation , 5541
  www.spacesaver.com
Spectronics Corporation , 5717
  www.spectroline.com
Speedball Art Products Company , 5397
  www.speedballart.com
Sport Court , 5765
  www.sportcourt.com
Stackhouse Athletic Equipment Company , 5768
  www.stackhouseathletic.com
Staedtler , 5399
  www.staedtler-usa.com
Swift Instruments , 5466
  www.swiftmicroscope.com
Sylvan Learning Systems , 5400
  www1.sylvan.net
TEDCO , 5720
  www.tedcotoys.com
Teacher's Video Company , 5218
  www.teachersvideo.com
Tech World , 5467
  www.labvolt.com
Technical Education Systems , 5468
  www.tii-tech.com
Teen Court: An Alternative Approach to Juveni e Justice, 5219
  cssrs.ou.edu
Telex Communications , 5469
  www.telex.com
Texas Instruments , 5404
  www.ti.com
Texwood Furniture , 5546
  www.texwood.com
Tiffin Systems , 5611
  www.tiffinmetal.com
Tom Snyder Productions , 5471
  www.tomsnyder.com
Tools to Help Youth , 5220
  www.communityintervention.com
Tooltron Industries , 5722
  www.tooltron.com
Training Video Series for the Professional School Bus Driver, 5221
  www.masterteacher.com
Triops , 5723
  www.triops.com
Trippense Planetarium Company , 5724
  www.sciencefirst.com
True Colors , 5222
  cssrs.ou.edu
Unilab , 5725
  www.unilabinc.com
University Products , 5548
  www.universityproducts.com

Video Project , 5224
  www.videoproject.org
Wausau Tile , 5771
  www.wausautile.com
Wear Proof Mat Company , 5772
  www.notracks.com
Wholesale Educational Supplies , 5473
  www.discountav.com
Wikki Stix One-of-a-Kind Creatables , 5410
  www.wikkistix.com
Wildlife Supply Company , 5728
  www.wildco.com
Wilton Art Appreciation Programs , 5412
  www.wiltonart.com
Winsted Corporation , 5553
  www.winsted.com
Young Explorers , 5413
  www.youngexplorers.com

Software, Hardware & Internet Resources

A-V Online , 5774
  www.nicem.com
ACT , 5775
  www.act.org
Accelerated Math , 5778
  www.renlearn.com
Accelerated Math , 6112
  www.renlearn.com
Accelerated Reader , 5779
  www.renlearn.com
Accelerated Reader , 6140
  www.renlearn.com
AccuNet/AP Multimedia Archive , 6156
  www.ap.accuweather.com
Advantage Learning Systems , 6067
  www.renlearn.com
Alcohol & Drug Prevention for Teachers, Law Enforcement & Parent Groups, 6036
  www.nodrugs.com
Anchor Audio , 6077
  www.anchoraudio.com
Anchor Pad , 5947
  www.anchorpad.com
Anchor Pad Products , 5783
  www.anchorpad.com
Applied Mathematics Program , 6113
  www.primetechnology.net
AskSam Systems , 5949
  www.asksam.com
BLINKS.Net , 6161
  www.blinks.net
Brodart Company, Automation Division , 6079
  www.brodart.com
Bulletin Boards for Busy Teachers , 5789
  www.geocities.com/VisionTeacherwv/
Cambridge Development Laboratory , 5793
  www.edumatch.com
Campus America , 5956
  www.campus.com
Center for Educational Outreach and Innovatio , 6163
  www.tc.columbia.edu
Century Consultants , 5957
  www.centuryltd.com
Chancery Student Management Solutions , 6081
  www.chancery.com
Chariot Software Group , 5794
  www.chariot.com
College Board/SAT , 5798
  http://sat.org/
Computer Friends , 5800
  www.cfriends.com

Conference Daily Newspaper Online , 5801
  www.aasa.org
Depco , 6164
  www.depcoinc.com
Dewey Decimal Classification , 6084
  www.oclc.org/fp
Digital Divide Network , 5805
  www.digitaldividenetwork.org
Diskovery Educational Systems , 5960
  www.diskovery.com
Doron Precision Systems , 5961
  www.doronprecision.com
EDUCAUSE , 6167
  www.educause.edu
EME Corporation , 6115
  www.emescience.com
Educational Activities , 5810
  www.edact.com
Educational Placement Service , 6031
  www.teacherjobs.com
Educational Structures , 6168
  www.ncspearson.com
Electronic Specialists Inc. , 5812
  www.elect-spec.com
Eversan Inc. , 5814
  www.eversan.com
Follett Software Company , 6088
  www.fsc.follett.com
Games2Learn , 5816
  www.games2learn.com
Gateway Learning Corporation , 5817
  www.hop.com
Geist , 5966
  www.geistmfg.com
Gibson Tech Ed , 6169
  www.gibsonteched.com
Grolier Interactive , 6170
  http://publishing.grolier.com
Harmonic Vision , 6127
  www.harmonicvision.com
Information Design , 5969
  www.idesigninc.com
Ingenuity Works , 5822
  www.ingenuityworks.com
Instructional Design , 5823
  www.wids.org
Instructor , 5824
  www.scholastic.com/instructor
Job Bulletin , 6032
  www.aasa.org
Journey Education , 5826
  www.journeyed.com
Jump Start Math for Kindergartners , 6005
  www.knowledgeadventure.com
Kensington Microwave , 5828
  www.kensington.com
LePAC NET , 6093
  www.brodart.com
Learning Company , 5832
  www.learningcompanyschool.com
Library Corporation , 6094
  www.tlcdelivers.com
Live Wire Media , 6037
  www.livewiremedia.com/
MARCIVE , 6096
  www.marcive.com
Mamopalire of Vermont , 5836
  www.bethumpd.com
Mastercam , 6174
  www.mastercamedu.com
MathType , 6117
  www.mathtype.com
Mathematica , 5974
  www.wolfram.com

Mathematica , 6118
  www.wolfram.com
Media Management & Magnetics , 5975
  www.computersupplypeople.com
Medianet/Dymaxion Research Limited , 6097
  www.medianet.ns.ca
Merit Audio Visual , 6175
  www.merutsoftware.com
MicroLearn Tutorial Series , 5977
  www.wordassociates.com
Micrograms Publishing , 6017
  www.micrograms.com
Midnight Play , 6128
  www.simonandschuster.com
MindTwister Math , 6119
  www.edmark.com
Mindplay , 6006
  www.mindplay.com
Multimedia - The Human Body , 6120
  www.sunburst.com
Music Teacher Find , 6129
  www.MusicTeacherFind.com
Music and Guitar , 6130
  www.nl-guitar.com
NCS Marketing , 5978
  www.ncspearson.com
National Information Center for Educational Media, 6176
  www.nicem.com
NetLingo The Internet Dictionary , 5841
  www.NetLingo.com
NetZero , 5842
  www.netzero.com
New Century Education Corporation , 5843
  www.ncecorp.com
New York Times , 6141
  www.nytimes.com/learning
Nordic Software , 6007
  www.nordicsoftware.com
OnLine Educator , 5844
  faldo.atmos.uiuc.edu/CLA
Orange Cherry Software , 6099
  www.orangecherry.com
PBS TeacherSource , 5846
  www.pbs.org/teachersource
Parent Link , 5847
  www.parlant.com
Phillip Roy Multimedia Materials , 6038
  www.philliproy.com
Proxima Corporation , 6178
  www.proxima.com
Pure Gold Teaching Tools , 6131
  www.puregoldteachingtools.com
RB5X: Education's Personal Computer Robot , 6179
  www.edurobot.com
Right on Programs , 6100
  www.rightonprograms.com
SCI Technologies , 6152
  www.scitechnologies.com
SOLINET, Southeastern Library Network , 6101
  www.solinct.net
STAR Reading & STAR Math , 5857
  www.renlearn.com
SVE & Churchill Media , 5858
  www.svemedia.com
School Cruiser , 5859
  www.epals.com
SchoolHouse , 5860
  www.encarta.msn.com/schoolhouse/maincontent.asp
Science for Kids , 6009
  www.scienceforkids.com
Sharp Electronics Corporation , 6181
  www.sharplcd.com
Sirsi Corporation , 6102
  www.sirsi.com

Sleek Software Corporation , 5863
www.sleek.com
Smartstuff Software , 5864
www.smartstuff.com
SofterWare , 5866
www.softerware.com
Support Systems International Corporation , 5871
www.fiberopticcableshop.com
Teacher Support Software , 6070
www.tssoftware.com
Teacher Universe , 5874
www.teacheruniverse.com
Teachers@Work , 6033
www.teachersatwork.com
TekData Systems Company , 6104
www.tekdata.com
Tom Snyder Productions , 5876
www.tomsnyder.com
Trapeze Software , 5987
www.trapezesoftware.com
True Basic , 5878
www.truebasic.com
Ventura Educational Systems , 5882
www.venturaes.com
WESTLAW , 5990
www.westlaw.com
Web Connection , 5885
www.edweek.org
Websense , 6184
www.websense.com
William K. Bradford Publishing Company , 6122
www.wkbradford.com
Winnebago Software Company , 6109
www.winnebago.com
Word Associates , 5888
www.wordassociates.com
Ztek Company , 5889
www.ztek.com
ePALS.com , 5890
www.epals.com
http://futurekids.com , 6186
www.futurekids.com
http://www.crossteccorp.com , 6188
www.crossteccorp.com
www.fundraising.com , 5998

Teaching Opportunities Abroad

AC Montessori Kids , 1537
www.acmontessorikids.com
ACI & SEV Elementary School , 1451
www.aci.k12.tr
Academia Cotopaxi American International School, 1296
www.cotopaxi.k12.ec
Ake Panya International School , 1091
www.akepanya.co.th
Al Bayan Bilingual School , 1455
www2.kems.net/users/bbs
Al-Worood School , 1459
www.alworood.sch.ae
Alconbury Elementary School , 1542
www.alco-hs.odedodea.edu/aes
Alexander Muss High School Israel , 1968
www.amhsi.com
Almaty International School , 1969
www.state.gov/www/about_state/schools/oalmaty.html
Ambrit Rome International School , 1549
www.ambrit-rome.com
American School , 1970
www.amschool.org
American College-Greece , 1550
www.acg.edu

American College-Sofia , 1423
www.acs.acad.bg
American Collegiate Institute , 1460
www.aci.k12.tr
American Community School , 1461
www.acs.edu.lb
American Community School-Abu Dhabi , 1462
www.acs.sch.ae
American Community School-Beirut , 1463
www.acs.edu.lb
American Community School-Cobham , 1551
www.acs-england.co.uk
American Community School-Egham , 1552
www.acs-england.co.uk
American Community School-Hillingdon , 1553
www.acs-england.co.uk
American Community Schools-Athens , 1555
www.acs.gr
American Cooperative School , 1971
www.acslp.org
American Cooperative School of Tunis , 1972
www.acst.net
American Embassy School , 1973
www.serve.com/aesndi
American Embassy School-Reykjavik , 1556
www.state.gov/m/a/os/1438.htm
American International School-Abu Dhabi , 1465
www.aisa.sch.ae
American International School-Bamako , 1977
www.aisbmali.org
American International School-Bolivia , 1299
www.aisb.edu.bo
American International School-Bucharest , 1424
www.aisb.ro
American International School-Budapest , 1425
www.aisb.hu
American International School-Chennai , 1978
www.aisch.org
American International School-Costa Rica , 1979
www.cra.ed.cr
American International School-Cyprus , 1426
www.aisc.ac.cy
American International School-Dhaka , 1031
www.ais-dhaka.net
American International School-Dhaka , 1094
www.ais-dhaka.net
American International School-Florence , 1558
www.aisfitaly.org
American International School-Genoa , 1559
www.space.tin.it/internet/elrosser
American International School-Guangzhou , 1095
www.aisgz.edu.cn
American International School-Johannesburg , 1032
www.aisj-jhb.com
American International School-Krakow , 1427
www.aisk.kompit.com.pl
American International School-Kuwait , 1467
www.aiskuwait.org
American International School-Lesotho , 1982
www.aisl.lesoff.co.za
American International School-Lincoln Buenos Aires, 1300
www.lincoln.edu.ar
American International School-Lisbon , 1560
www.ecis.org/aislisbon/index.html
American International School-Lome , 1984
www.membres.lycos.fr
American International School-Lusaka , 1985
www.aislusaka.org
American International School-Muscat , 1468
www.taism.com
American International School-Riyadh , 1469
www.aisr.org
American International School-Rotterdam , 1561
www.aisr.nl

American International School-Salzburg , 1562
www.ais.salzburg.at
American International School-Vienna , 1428
www.ais.at
American International School-Vienna , 1563
www.ais.at
American International School-Zambia , 1034
www.aesl.sch.zm
American Nicaraguan School , 1989
www.ans.edu.ni
American Overseas School-Rome , 1564
www.aosr.org
American School , 1301
www.amschool.edu.sv
American School Foundation AC , 1302
www.asf.edu.mx
American School Foundation-Monterrey , 1304
www.asfm.edu.mx
American School of the Hague , 1565
www.ash.nl
American School-Antananarivo , 1993
www.asa.blueline.mg
American School-Asuncion , 1994
www.asa.edu.py
American School-Barcelona , 1566
www.a-s-b.com
American School-Bilbao , 1567
www.saranet.es/asb
American School-Bombay , 1096
www.asbindia.org
American School-Brasilia , 1306
www.eabdf.br
American School-Doha , 1470
www.asdqatar.org
American School-Guangzhou (China) , 1097
www.aisgz.edu.cn
American School-Guatemala , 1309
www.colegioamericanoguatemula.com
American School-Guatemala , 1996
www.cag.edu.gt
American School-Japan , 1098
www.asij.ac.jp
American School-Kuwait , 1471
www.ask.edu.kw/index1
American School-Las Palmas , 1568
www.aslp.org
American School-London , 1569
www.asl.org
American School-Madrid , 1570
www.amerschmad.org
American School-Milan , 1571
www.asmilan.org
American School-Paris , 1572
www.asparis.org
American School-Puerto Vallarta , 1315
www.americanschool-pv.com.mx
American School-Recife , 1316
www.ear.com
American School-Tampico , 1317
www.ats.edu.mx
American School-Torreon , 1318
www.cat.mx
American School-Valencia , 1573
www.ecis.org/valencia
American School-Warsaw , 2000
www.asw.waw.pl
American-Nicaraguan School , 2002
www.ans.edu.ni
Amman Baccalaureate School , 1473
www.arabia.com/ABS
Anatolia College , 1575
www.anatolia.edu.gr
Anglo-American School-Moscow , 1576
www.aas.ru

Antofagasta International School , 1322
www.ais.cl
Antwerp International School , 1580
www.ais-antwerp.be
Anzoategui International School , 2005
www.anaco.net
Ashgabat International School , 1100
www.qsi.org
Asociacion Colegio Granadino , 1323
www.granadino.com
Asociacion Escuelas Lincoln , 1324
www.lincoln.edu.ar
Atlanta International School , 2007
www.aischool.org
Awty International School , 2008
www.awty.org
Azerbaijan Baku International School , 2009
www.qsi.org
BEPS 2 Limal International School , 1585
www.beps.com
Bahrain Bayan School , 1478
www.bayan.edu.bh
Baku International School , 2010
www.qsi.org
Bali International School , 1101
www.bdg.centrin.net.id/~bis
Bandung Alliance International School , 1102
www.baisedu.org
Bangkok Patana School , 1105
www.patana.com
Banjul American Embassy School , 2012
www.baes.gm
Barrow Hills School , 1594
www.haslemere.com
Bavarian International School , 1596
www.bis-school.com
Beacon Hill School , 1106
www.asioonline.net.hk/beacon
Bedales School , 1597
www.bedales.org.uk
Bedford School , 1598
www.bedfordschool.beds.org.uk/info/contac
Beijing BISS International School , 1107
www.biss.com.cn
Belgium Antwerp International School , 1600
www.ais-antwerp.be
Benjamin Franklin International School , 1601
www.bfis.org
Berlin International School , 1602
www.berlin-international-school.de
Berlin Potsdam International School , 1603
www.bpis.de
Bilkent University Preparatory School-Bilkent International
School, 1481
www.bupsbis.bilkent.edu.tr
Bishkek International School , 2014
www.qsi.org
Black Forest Academy , 1608
www.bfacademy.com
Bloxham School , 1609
www.bloxhamschool.com
Blue Coat School , 1610
www.bluecoatschool.org
Bonn International School , 1612
www.bis.bonn.org
Bordeaux International School , 1613
http://bordeaux-intl-school.com
Bosnia-Herzegovina QSI International School-S rajevo, 2015
www.qsi.org
Brent International School-Manila , 1111
www.brentmanila.edu.ph
Brent School , 1112
www2.mozcom.com/~brent

Brillantmont International School , 1614
www.brillantmont.ch
British Primary School , 1617
www.britishprimary.com
British School-Brussels , 1621
www.britishschool.be
British School-Lom , 1046
www.bsl.tg
British School-Netherlands , 1622
www.britishschool.nl
British School-Paris , 1624
www.ecis.org
Bromsgrove School , 1625
www.bromit.demon.co.uk
Brussels English Primary School , 1628
www.beps.com
Buckswood Grange International School , 1630
www.buckswood.co.uk
Buenos Aires International Christian Academy , 1334
www.baica.com
Bulgaria Anglo-American School-Sofia , 2017
www.geocities.com/angloamericanschool
CIV International School-Sophia Antipolis , 1633
www.civissa.org
Cairo American College , 1050
www.cac.edu.eg
Cairo American College , 1486
www.cac.edu.eg
Camberwell Grammar School , 1118
www.asap.unimelb.edu.au/asa/directory/data/342
Canadian Academy , 1119
www.canacad.ac.jp/canacad/welcome.html
Canadian College Italy-The Renaissance School , 1636
www.ccilanciano.com
Canadian School-India , 1120
www.canschoolindia.org
Canberra Grammar School , 1121
www.cgs.act.edu.au
Carmel School-Hong Kong , 1122
www.carmel.edu.hk
Casablanca American School , 1051
www.cas.ac.ma
Castelli International School , 1639
www.pcg.it/CIS
Cebu International School , 1124
www2.mozcom.com/~cisram
Central Java Inter-Mission School , 1125
www.geocities.com
Chinese American International School , 2022
www.cie-cais.org
Chinese International School , 1128
www.cis.edu.hk
Colegio Bolivar , 1343
www.colegiobolivar.edu.co
Colegio Gran Bretana , 1345
www.colgranbret.edu.co
Colegio Internacional-Carabobo , 2031
www.aassa.com
Colegio Internacional-Caracas , 2032
www.cic-caracas.org
Colegio Internacional-Puerto La Cruz , 2033
www.ciplc.net
Colegio Karl C Parrish , 1349
www.kcparrish.edu.co
Colegio Nueva Granada , 1351
www.cng.edu
College Du Leman International School , 1651
www.cdl.ch
Colombo International School , 1130
www.cis.lk
Concordia International School-Shanghai , 1131
www.ciss.com.cn
Copenhagen International School , 1654
www.cis-edu.dk

Council for International Exchange of Scholar , 2232
www.cies.org
Country Day School , 1357
www.cds.ed.cr
Croatia American International School-Zagreb , 2092
www.asz.tel.hr/asz
Dakar Academy , 1053
www.dakaracademy.com
Dallas International School , 2093
http://dis.pvt.k12.tx.us
Danube International School , 1656
www.danubeschool.at
Dresden International School , 1663
www.dresden-is.de
Dwight School , 2096
www.dwight.edu
Ecole Active Bilingue Jeannine Manuel , 1666
www.eabjm.com
Emirates International School , 1495
www.eischool.com
English Montessori School , 1678
www.emeg.home.ml.org
Enka Okullari-Enka Schools , 1499
www.enkaschools.com
Episcopal Cathedral School , 2098
www.episcopalcathedralschool.com
Escuela Bella Vista , 2101
www.ebv.org.ve
Escuela Campo Alegre , 2102
www.eca.com.ve
European Business & Management School , 1681
www.ebms.edu
European Council of International Schools , 2238
www.ecis.org
Evangelical Christian Academy , 1685
http://ourworld.compuserve.com/homepages/eca_madrid
Faith Academy , 1138
www.faith.edu.ph
Frankfurt International School , 1687
www.fis.edu
French-American International School , 2111
www.fais-ihs.org
Fukuoka International School , 1140
www.worldwide.edu/japan/fukuoka
Fulbright Teacher Exchange , 2241
www.grad.usda.gov
Fundacion Colegio Americano de Quito , 1374
www.fcaq.k12.ec
Garden International School , 1141
www.gardenschool.edu.my
Geneva English School , 1694
www.geneva-english-school.ch
Georgetown American School , 2113
www.geocities.com/Athens/Atlantis/6811
Goroka International School , 1146
www.ieapng.com
Grange School , 1376
www.grange.cl
Gstaad International School , 1699
www.gstaadschool.ch
Guam Adventist Academy , 2119
www.tagnet.org/gaa
Harare International School , 1055
www.his.ac.zw
Harvest Christian Academy , 2124
www.harvestministries.net
Hellenic College-London , 1709
www.rmplc.co.uk/eduweb/sites/hellenic
Hellenic-American Education Foundation Athens
College-Psychico College, 1710
www.haef.gr
Hiroshima International School , 1149
http://hiroshima-is.ac.jp

Hokkaido International School , 1150
http://his.ac.jp
Hong Kong International School , 1151
www.hkis.edu.hk
Hvitfeldtska Gymnasiet , 1718
www.hvitfeldt.educ.goteborg.se
Independent Bonn International School , 1720
www.ibis-school.com
Independent Schools Information Service , 1721
www.isis.org.uk
India American Embassy School-New Delhi , 2126
www.serve.com/aesndi
India American International School-Bombay , 2127
www.ashindia.org
Institut Le Rosey , 1727
www.rosey.ch
Institut Montana Bugerbug-American Schools , 1728
www.montana.zug.ch
Inter-American Academy , 2128
www.acig.k12.ec
Inter-Community School , 1730
www.icsz.ch
International Christian School , 1154
www.ics.edu.hk
International College Spain , 1732
www.icsmadric.com
International Community School , 1155
www.ICSBangkok.com
International Community School-Abidjan , 2129
www.icsa.ac.ci
International Community School-Addis Ababa , 1057
www.icsaddisababa.org
International Elementary School-Estonia , 1433
www.online.ee/~iese
International Management Institute , 1733
www.timi.edu
International Preparatory School , 1380
www.tipschool.com
International Preparatory School , 1734
www.tipschool.com
International School Manila , 1156
www.ismanila.com
International School Nido de Aguilas , 1381
www.nido.cl
International School of Choueifat , 1507
www.iscad-sabis.net/
International School of Port-of-Spain , 2131
www.isps.edu.tt
International School of the Sacred Heart , 1157
http://iac.co.jp/~issh3
International School-Aberdeen , 1736
www.isa.abdn.sch.uk
International School-Amsterdam , 1738
www.isa.nl
International School-Bangkok , 1158
www.isb.ac.th
International School-Beijing , 1159
www.isb.bj.edu.cn
International School-Belgrade , 1434
www.isb.co.yu
International School-Bergen , 1740
www.isb.gs.hl.no
International School-Berne , 1741
www.isberne.ch
International School-Brussels , 1742
www.isb.be
International School-Curacao , 1744
www.isc.an
International School-Dusseldorf , 1745
www.isdedu.com
International School-Eastern Seaboard , 1160
www.ise.ac.th
International School-Estonia , 1436
www.online.ee/~iese

International School-Fiji , 1161
www.internationalschool.fj
International School-Hamburg , 1749
www.ish.intrasat.org
International School-Hannover Region , 1750
www.is-hr.de
International School-Helsinki , 1751
www.ish.edu.hel.fi
International School-Ho Chi Minh City , 1162
www.ishcmc.com
International School-Islamabad , 2136
www.isoi.edu.pk
International School-Kenya , 1058
www.isk.ac.ke
International School-Kuala Lumpur , 1163
www.iskl.edu.my
International School-Latvia , 1437
www.isl.edu.lv
International School-Lausanne , 1753
www.isl.ch
International School-London , 1755
www.islondon.com
International School-Manila , 1165
www.ismanila.com
International School-Moshi , 1059
www.ecis.org
International School-Naples , 1757
www.intschoolnaples.it
International School-Ouagadougou , 2137
http://iso.htmlplanet.com
International School-Panama , 1384
www.isp.edu.pa
International School-Paris , 1759
www.isparis.edu
International School-Phnom Penh, Cambodia , 1167
www.cambodia-web.net/education.ispp
International School-Phnom Penh-Cambodia , 1168
www.ispp.edu.kh
International School-Port of Spain , 2138
www.isps.edu.tt
International School-Prague , 1439
www.isp.cz
International School-Pusan , 1169
www.ispusan.co.kr
International School-Singapore , 1170
www.iss.edu.sg
International School-Sotogrande , 1760
www.sis.ac
International School-Stavanger , 1761
www.iss.stavager.rl.no
International School-Stockholm , 1762
www.intsch.se
International School-Stuttgart , 1763
www.ecis.org/iss
International School-Tanganyika , 1060
www.istafrica.com
International School-Trieste , 1764
www.geocities.com/athens/oracle/1329
International School-Ulaanbaatar , 1171
www.mongol.nct/inschool
International Schule-Berlin, Potsdam , 1768
www.shuttle.de/p/isbp
Internationale Schule Frankfurt-Rhein-Main , 1770
www.isf-net.de
Interskolen , 1771
www.interskolen.com
Island School , 1172
www.island.edu.hk
Istanbul International Community School , 1508
www.iics.k12.tr
Ivanhoe Grammar School , 1173
www.igs.vic.edu.au
JN Darby Elementary School , 1174
www.darby-es.pac.odedodea.edu

Jakarta International School , 1175
www.jisedu.org
John F Kennedy International School , 1772
wwwjfk.ch
John F Kennedy School-Berlin , 1773
www.jfks.de
Jordan American Community School , 2143
www.acsamman.edu.jo
Kabira International School , 1062
www.kabiraschool.com
Karl C Parrish School , 1385
www.kcparrish.edu.co
Kendale Primary International School , 1778
www.diesis.com/kendale
Kestrel Manor School , 1063
www.kestrelmanorschool.com
Kiev International School , 1441
www.qsi.org
Kilmore International School , 1181
www.kilmore.vic.edu.au
King's College , 1781
www.kingsgroup.com/idik
Koc School , 1514
www.kocschool.k12.tr
Kodaikanal International School , 1185
www.kis.ernet.in
Kooralbyn International School , 1186
www.isd.com.au/schools/q7209
Kyoto International School , 1188
www.kyoto-is.org
Leighton Park School , 1793
www.leightonparkreading.sch.uk
Leipzig International School , 1794
www.intschool-leipzig.com
Leys School , 1796
www.theleys.cambs.sch.uk
Leysin American School , 1797
www.las.ch
Lincoln Community School , 1068
www.lincoln.edu.gh
Lincoln International Academy , 1388
www.lintac.com
Lincoln International School of Uganda , 1069
www.lincoln.ac.ug
Lincoln International School-Uganda , 1070
www.lincoln.ac.ug
Lincoln School , 1191
www.lsnepal.com
Lincoln-Marti Schools , 2148
www.lincolnmarti.com
Logos School of English Education , 1443
www.hlogos.ac.cy
Lycee International-American Section , 1804
www.lycee-intl-american.org
Lyce International-American Section , 1805
http://lycee-intl-american.org
Makassar International School , 1192
www.crosswinds.net\-mischool
Malvern College , 1806
www.malcol.org
Mannheim Elementary School , 1807
www.mann-es.odedodea.edu
Marian Baker School , 1390
www.marianbakerschool.com
Marist Brothers International School , 1194
www.marist.ac.jp
Maru A Pula School , 1071
www.map.ac.bw
Marymount International School-United Kingdom , 1812
www.marymount.kingston.sch.uk
Mentone Boys Grammar School , 1197
www.mentonegs.vic.edu.au
Methodist Ladies College , 1199
www.mlc.vic.edu.au

Monkton Combe School , 1817
www.monktoncombesschool.com
Morrison Christian Academy , 1202
www.morrison.mknet.org
Morrocoy International , 2157
www.geocities.com/minaspov
Mougins School , 1819
www.mougins-school.com
Munich International School , 1821
www.mis-munich.de
Nagoya International School , 1208
www.nisjapan.net
National Association of Teachers' Agencies , 2243
www.jobsforteachers.com
Nepal Lincoln School , 2160
www.lsnepal.com
Nishimachi International School , 1212
www.nishimachi.ac.jp
Okinawa Christian School International , 1213
www.ocsi.org
Osaka International School , 1214
www.senri.ed.jp
Overseas Family School , 1219
www.ofs.edu.sg
Overseas School of Colombo , 1220
www.osc.lk
Pan American Christian Academy , 1396
www.paca.com.br
Pan American School-Costa Rica , 1398
www.pas.edu.mx
Pasir Ridge International , 1222
prschool@bpp.mega.net.id
Peace Corp , 2169
www.peacecorps.gov
Puerto Rico Department of Education , 2173
www.de.gobierno.pr
Pusan American School , 1227
www.210.107.81.252
QSI International School-Bratislava , 1447
www.qsi.org
QSI International School-Ljubljana , 1448
www.qsi.org
QSI International School-Phuket , 1229
www.phuketschl.com
QSI International School-Tbilisi , 1449
www.qsi.org
QSI International School-Zhuhai , 1230
www.qsi.org
Rabat American School , 1076
www.ras.edu.ac.ma
Riverside School , 1851
www.riverside.ch
Robinson School , 2180
www.geocities.com
Roosevelt Roads Elementary School , 2181
www.netdial.caribe.net
Roosevelt Roads Middle & High School , 2182
www.antilles.odedodea.edu
Ruamrudee International School , 1235
www.rism.ac.th
Rugby School , 1859
www.rugby-school.co.uk
Runnymede College School , 1860
www.runnymede-college.com
Saigon South International School , 1236
www.web.cybercon.com/SSIS
Saint John's School , 2186
www.stjohns.edu.gu
Sanaa International School , 1523
www.qsi.org
Santa Cruz Cooperative School , 1406
www.sccs.edu.bo
Schiller Academy , 1863
www.schiller-academy.org.uk

Schweinfurt American Elementary School , 1865
www.schw-es.odedodea.edu
Scots PGC College , 1239
www.scotspgc.qld.edu.au
Seisen International School , 1240
www.seisen.com
Seoul Academy , 1242
www.uriel.net/~unicorn
Seoul Foreign School , 1245
www.sfs-h.ac.kr
Shanghai American School , 1247
www.saschina.org
Shekou International School , 2196
www.sis.org
Sidcot School , 1875
www.sidcot.org.uk
Sigtunaskolan Humanistiska Laroverket , 1878
www.sshl.se
Singapore American School , 1251
www.sas.edu.sg
Sir James Henderson School , 1879
www.sirjameshenderson.com
Slovak Republic QSI International School of Bratislava, 2197
www.qsi.sk
Slovenia QSI International School-Ljubljana , 2198
www.qsi.org
St. Andrew's Scots School , 1409
www.sanandres.esc.edu.ar
St. Andrews International School-Bangkok , 1254
www.st-andrews.ac
St. Catherine's School , 1410
www.redeseducacion.com.ar
St. George's College , 1411
www.stgeorge.com.ar
St. John's International School , 1900
www.stjohns.be
St. Mark's College , 1259
www.stmarkscollege.com.au
St. Stephen's International School , 1263
www.sis.edu
St. Stephen's School , 1903
www.ststephens.it
Sutton Park School , 1910
www.suttonpoark.ie
Syria Damascus Community School , 2209
www.syria-guide.com/school/dcs
TASIS Hellenic International School , 1913
www.tasis.com
TASIS The American School in England , 1914
www.tasis.com
TEDA International School-Tianjin , 1268
www.tistschool.org
Taipei American School , 1271
www.tas.edu.tw
Tanglin Trust Schools , 1272
www.tts.edu.sg
Tarsus American College and SEV Primary , 1533
www.tac.k12.tr
Thessaloniki International High School & Pinewood Elementary School, 1917
www.users.otenet.gr/~pinewood
Tirana International School-Albania , 2213
www.qsi.org
UNI Overseas Recruiting Fair , 2247
www.uni.edu/placement/overseas
United Nations International School , 2217
www.unis.org
United Nations International School-Hanoi , 1277
www.unishanoi.org
United World College-SE Asia , 1278
www.uwcsea.edu.sg
University Vacancies in Australia , 1279
www.avcc.edu.au

Uruguayan American School , 1420
www.uas.edu.uy
Uruguayan American School-Montevideo , 2220
www.uas.edu.uy
Uskudar American Academy , 1535
www.uaa.k12.tr
Venezuela Escuela Campo Alegre , 2223
www.internet.ve/eca
Venezuela International School-Caracas , 2224
www.cic-caracus.org
Verdala International School , 1923
www.verdala.org
Vienna Christian School , 1928
www.vienna-christian-sch.org
Vienna International School , 1929
www.vis.ac.at
Vientiane International School , 1280
www.vis.laopdr.com
Virgin Islands Department of Education , 2226
www.networkvi.com/education
Walworth Barbour American International School in Israel, 1536
www.american.hasharon.k12.il
Washington International School , 2227
www.wis.edu
Wesley International School , 1282
www.weleyinterschool.org
Western Academy of Beijing , 1283
www.wab.edu
Windhoek International School , 1089
www.wis.edu.na
Woodstock School , 1285
www.woodstock.ac.in
WorldTeach , 2249
www.worldteach.org
Xiamen International School , 1286
www.xischina.com
Yakistan International School-Karachi , 2230
www.isk.edu.pk
Yew Chung Shanghai International School , 1287
www.ycef.com
Yokohama International School , 1289
www.yis.ac.jp
Zukeran Elementary School , 1295
www.oki-dso.odedodea/okinawa/schools/zes/zes.html
Zurich International School , 1944
www.zis.ch

Testing Resources

A&F Video's Art Catalog , 6212
www.aandfvideo.com
Admission Officer's Handbook for the New SAT Program, 6234
www.collegeboard.org
Advantage Learning Systems , 6227
www.advlearn.com
All Art Supplies , 6213
www.allartsupplies.com
American Art Clay Company , 6214
www.amaco.com
American College Testing , 6235
www.act.org
Arnold Grummer , 6215
www.arnoldgrummer.com
Arrowmont School of Arts & Crafts , 6216
www.arrowmont.org
Art & Creative Materials Institute , 6217
www.acminec.org
Art Instruction Schools , 6218
www.artists-ais.com
Art to Remember , 6219
www.arttoremember.com

ArtSketchbook.com , 6220
  www.artsketchbook.com
CTB/McGraw-Hill , 6207
  www.ctb.com
College-Bound Seniors , 6236
  www.collegeboard.org
CollegeChoice, StudentChoice , 6237
  www.collegeboard.org
Counselor's Handbook for the SAT Program , 6238
  www.collegeboard.org
Curriculum Associates , 6201
  www.curriculumassociates.com
Destination College: Planning with the PSAT/NMSQT, 6239
  www.collegeboard.org
Diagnostic Reading Inventory for Primary and Intermediate Grades
K-8, 6202
  www.scottmccleary.com
Focus on the SAT: What's on it, How to Prepare & What
Colleges Look For, 6241
  www.collegeboard.org
Guide to the College Board Validity Study Service, 6244
  www.collegeboard.org
Lexia Learning Systems , 6203
  www.lexialearning.com
LinguiSystems , 6204
  www.linguisystems.com
Look Inside the SAT I: Test Prep from the Test Makers Video,
6245
  www.collegeboard.org
Museum Stamps , 6222
  www.museumstamps.com
Music Ace 2 , 6223
  www.harmonicvision.com
National Study of School Evaluation , 6205
  www.nsse.org
National Study of School Evaluation , 6247
  www.nsse.org
Official Guide to the SAT II: Subject Tests, 6249
  www.collegeboard.org
One-On-One with the SAT , 6250
  www.collegeboard.org
Preventing School Failure , 6252
  www.heldref.org
Psychological Assessment Resources , 6209
  www.parinc.com
Psychological Assessment Resources , 6230
  www.parinc.com
Real SAT's , 6255
  www.collegeboard.org
Registration Bulletin , 6256
  www.collegeboard.org
SAT Services for Students with Disabilities, 6257
  www.collegeboard.org
Scholastic Testing Service , 6259
  www.ststesting.com
Summing It Up: College Board Mathematics Assessment
Programs, 6211
  www.collegeboard.org
TOEFL Test and Score Manual , 6260
  www.collegeboard.org
Taking the SAT I: Reasoning Test , 6261
  www.collegeboard.org
Taking the SAT II: The Official Guide to the SAT II: Subject
Tests, 6262
  www.collegeboard.org
TestSkills , 6263
  www.collegeboard.org
Testing Miss Malarky , 6206
  www.walkerbooks.com
Think Before You Punch: Using Calculators on the New SAT I
and PSAT/NMSQT, 6264
  www.collegeboard.org

Educators Resource Directory

Online Database

Educators Resource Directory is available in Print and in an Online Databases. Subscribers to the **Online Database** can access their subscription Internet and do customized searches that instantly locate needed resources of information. It's never been faster or easier to locate just the right resource. Whether you're searching for Professional Resources or information about Teaching Abroad, the information you need is only a click away with **Educators Resource Directory – Online Database**.

Visit www.greyhouse.com and explore the subscription site free of charge or call (800) 562-2139 for more information.

Education Resources

The Comparative Guide to American Elementary & Secondary Schools, 2004/05

The only guide of its kind, this award winning compilation offers a snapshot profile of every public school district in the United States serving 1,500 or more students – more than 5,900 districts are covered. Organized alphabetically by district within state, each chapter begins with a Statistical Overview of the state. Each district listing includes contact information (name, address, phone number and web site) plus Grades Served, the Numbers of Students and Teachers and the Number of Regular, Special Education, Alternative and Vocational Schools in the district along with statistics on Student/Classroom Teacher Ratios, Drop Out Rates, Ethnicity, the Numbers of Librarians and Guidance Counselors and District Expenditures per student. As an added bonus, *The Comparative Guide to American Elementary and Secondary Schools* provides important ranking tables, both by state and nationally, for each data element. For easy navigation through this wealth of information, this handbook contains a useful City Index that lists all districts that operate schools within a city. These important comparative statistics are necessary for anyone considering relocation or doing comparative research on their own district and would be a perfect acquisition for any public library or school district library.

"This straightforward guide is an easy way to find general information. Valuable for academic and large public library collections." –ARBA

2,400 pages; Softcover ISBN 1-59237-047-0, $125.00

The Complete Learning Disabilities Directory, 2005/06

The Complete Learning Disabilities Directory is the most comprehensive database of Programs, Services, Curriculum Materials, Professional Meetings & Resources, Camps, Newsletters and Support Groups for teachers, students and families concerned with learning disabilities. This information-packed directory includes information about Associations & Organizations, Schools, Colleges & Testing Materials, Government Agencies, Legal Resources and much more. For quick, easy access to information, this directory contains four indexes: Entry Name Index, Subject Index and Geographic Index. With every passing year, the field of learning disabilities attracts more attention and the network of caring, committed and knowledgeable professionals grows every day. This directory is an invaluable research tool for these parents, students and professionals.

"Due to its wealth and depth of coverage, parents, teachers and others… should find this an invaluable resource." -Booklist

900 pages; Softcover ISBN 1-59237-092-6, $145.00 ◆ Online Database $195.00 ◆ Online Database & Directory Combo $280.00

To preview any of our Directories Risk-Free for 30 days, call (800) 562-2139 or fax to (518) 789-0556

Sedgwick Press
Health Directories

The Complete Directory for People with Disabilities, 2005

A wealth of information, now in one comprehensive sourcebook. Completely updated for 2005, this edition contains more information than ever before, including thousands of new entries and enhancements to existing entries and thousands of additional web sites and e-mail addresses. This up-to-date directory is the most comprehensive resource available for people with disabilities, detailing Independent Living Centers, Rehabilitation Facilities, State & Federal Agencies, Associations, Support Groups, Periodicals & Books, Assistive Devices, Employment & Education Programs, Camps and Travel Groups. Each year, more libraries, schools, colleges, hospitals, rehabilitation centers and individuals add *The Complete Directory for People with Disabilities* to their collections, making sure that this information is readily available to the families, individuals and professionals who can benefit most from the amazing wealth of resources cataloged here.

"No other reference tool exists to meet the special needs of the disabled in one convenient resource for information." –Library Journal

1,200 pages; Softcover ISBN 1-59237-054-3, $165.00 ♦ Online Database $215.00 ♦ Online Database & Directory Combo $300.00

The Complete Directory for People with Chronic Illness, 2005/06

Thousands of hours of research have gone into this completely updated 2005/06 edition – several new chapters have been added along with thousands of new entries and enhancements to existing entries. Plus, each chronic illness chapter has been reviewed by an medical expert in the field. This widely-hailed directory is structured around the 90 most prevalent chronic illnesses – from Asthma to Cancer to Wilson's Disease – and provides a comprehensive overview of the support services and information resources available for people diagnosed with a chronic illness. Each chronic illness has its own chapter and contains a brief description in layman's language, followed by important resources for National & Local Organizations, State Agencies, Newsletters, Books & Periodicals, Libraries & Research Centers, Support Groups & Hotlines, Web Sites and much more. This directory is an important resource for health care professionals, the collections of hospital and health care libraries, as well as an invaluable tool for people with a chronic illness and their support network.

"A must purchase for all hospital and health care libraries and is strongly recommended for all public library reference departments." –ARBA

1,200 pages; Softcover ISBN 1-59237-081-0, $165.00 ♦ Online Database $215.00 ♦ Online Database & Directory Combo $300.00

The Complete Mental Health Directory, 2004

This is the most comprehensive resource covering the field of behavioral health, with critical information for both the layman and the mental health professional. For the layman, this directory offers understandable descriptions of 25 Mental Health Disorders as well as detailed information on Associations, Media, Support Groups and Mental Health Facilities. For the professional, *The Complete Mental Health Directory* offers critical and comprehensive information on Managed Care Organizations, Information Systems, Government Agencies and Provider Organizations. This comprehensive volume of needed information will be widely used in any reference collection.

"... the strength of this directory is that it consolidates widely dispersed information into a single volume." –Booklist

800 pages; Softcover ISBN 1-59237-046-2, $165.00 ♦ Online Database $215.00 ♦ Online & Directory Combo $300.00

Older Americans Information Directory, 2004/05

Completely updated for 2004/05, this Fifth Edition has been completely revised and now contains 1,000 new listings, over 8,000 updates to existing listings and over 3,000 brand new e-mail addresses and web sites. You'll find important resources for Older Americans including National, Regional, State & Local Organizations, Government Agencies, Research Centers, Libraries & Information Centers, Legal Resources, Discount Travel Information, Continuing Education Programs, Disability Aids & Assistive Devices, Health, Print Media and Electronic Media. Three indexes: Entry Index, Subject Index and Geographic Index make it easy to find just the right source of information. This comprehensive guide to resources for Older Americans will be a welcome addition to any reference collection.

"Highly recommended for academic, public, health science and consumer libraries..." –Choice

1,200 pages; Softcover ISBN 1-59237-037-3, $165.00 ♦ Online Database $215.00 ♦ Online Database & Directory Combo $300.00

To preview any of our Directories Risk-Free for 30 days, call (800) 562-2139 or fax to (518) 789-0556

The Complete Directory for Pediatric Disorders, 2004/05

This important directory provides parents and caregivers with information about Pediatric Conditions, Disorders, Diseases and Disabilities, including Blood Disorders, Bone & Spinal Disorders, Brain Defects & Abnormalities, Chromosomal Disorders, Congenital Heart Defects, Movement Disorders, Neuromuscular Disorders and Pediatric Tumors & Cancers. This carefully written directory offers: understandable Descriptions of 15 major bodily systems; Descriptions of more than 200 Disorders and a Resources Section, detailing National Agencies & Associations, State Associations, Online Services, Libraries & Resource Centers, Research Centers, Support Groups & Hotlines, Camps, Books and Periodicals. This resource will provide immediate access to information crucial to families and caregivers when coping with children's illnesses.

"Recommended for public and consumer health libraries." –Library Journal

1,200 pages; Softcover ISBN 1-59237-045-4, $165.00 ◆ Online Database $215.00 ◆ Online Database & Directory Combo $300.00

The Complete Directory for People with Rare Disorders, 2002/03

This outstanding reference is produced in conjunction with the National Organization for Rare Disorders to provide comprehensive and needed access to important information on over 1,000 rare disorders, including Cancers and Muscular, Genetic and Blood Disorders. An informative Disorder Description is provided for each of the 1,100 disorders (rare Cancers and Muscular, Genetic and Blood Disorders) followed by information on National and State Organizations dealing with a particular disorder, Umbrella Organizations that cover a wide range of disorders, the Publications that can be useful when researching a disorder and the Government Agencies to contact. Detailed and up-to-date listings contain mailing address, phone and fax numbers, web sites and e-mail addresses along with a description. For quick, easy access to information, this directory contains two indexes: Entry Name Index and Acronym/Keyword Index along with an informative Guide for Rare Disorder Advocates. The Complete Directory for People with Rare Disorders will be an invaluable tool for the thousands of families that have been struck with a rare or "orphan" disease, who feel that they have no place to turn and will be a much-used addition to the reference collection of any public or academic library.

"Quick access to information… public libraries and hospital patient libraries will find this a useful resource in directing users to support groups or agencies dealing with a rare disorder." –Booklist

726 pages; Softcover ISBN 1-891482-18-1, $165.00

The Directory of Drug & Alcohol Residential Rehabilitation Facilities, 2004

This brand new directory is the first-ever resource to bring together, all in one place, data on the thousands of drug and alcohol residential rehabilitation facilities in the United States. *The Directory of Drug & Alcohol Residential Rehabilitation Facilities* covers over 1,000 facilities, with detailed contact information for each one, including mailing address, phone and fax numbers, email addresses and web sites, mission statement, type of treatment programs, cost, average length of stay, numbers of residents and counselors, accreditation, insurance plans accepted, type of environment, religious affiliation, education components and much more. It also contains a helpful chapter on General Resources that provides contact information for Associations, Print & Electronic Media, Support Groups and Conferences. Multiple indexes allow the user to pinpoint the facilities that meet very specific criteria. This time-saving tool is what so many counselors, parents and medical professionals have been asking for. *The Directory of Drug & Alcohol Residential Rehabilitation Facilities* will be a helpful tool in locating the right source for treatment for a wide range of individuals. This comprehensive directory will be an important acquisition for all reference collections: public and academic libraries, case managers, social workers, state agencies and many more.

"This is an excellent, much needed directory that fills an important gap…" –Booklist

300 pages; Softcover ISBN 1-59237-031-4, $135.00

To preview any of our Directories Risk-Free for 30 days, call (800) 562-2139 or fax to (518) 789-0556

Universal Reference Publications
Statistical & Demographic Reference Books

The Value of a Dollar 1860-2004, Third Edition

A guide to practical economy, *The Value of a Dollar* records the actual prices of thousands of items that consumers purchased from the Civil War to the present, along with facts about investment options and income opportunities. This brand new Third Edition boasts a brand new addition to each five-year chapter, a section on Trends. This informative section charts the change in price over time and provides added detail on the reasons prices changed within the time period, including industry developments, changes in consumer attitudes and important historical facts. Plus, a brand new chapter for 2000-2004 has been added. Each 5-year chapter includes a Historical Snapshot, Consumer Expenditures, Investments, Selected Income, Income/Standard Jobs, Food Basket, Standard Prices and Miscellany. This interesting and useful publication will be widely used in any reference collection.

"Recommended for high school, college and public libraries." –ARBA

600 pages; Hardcover ISBN 1-59237-074-8, $135.00

Working Americans 1880-1999
Volume I: The Working Class, Volume II: The Middle Class, Volume III: The Upper Class

Each of the volumes in the *Working Americans 1880-1999* series focuses on a particular class of Americans, The Working Class, The Middle Class and The Upper Class over the last 120 years. Chapters in each volume focus on one decade and profile three to five families. Family Profiles include real data on Income & Job Descriptions, Selected Prices of the Times, Annual Income, Annual Budgets, Family Finances, Life at Work, Life at Home, Life in the Community, Working Conditions, Cost of Living, Amusements and much more. Each chapter also contains an Economic Profile with Average Wages of other Professions, a selection of Typical Pricing, Key Events & Inventions, News Profiles, Articles from Local Media and Illustrations. The *Working Americans* series captures the lifestyles of each of the classes from the last twelve decades, covers a vast array of occupations and ethnic backgrounds and travels the entire nation. These interesting and useful compilations of portraits of the American Working, Middle and Upper Classes during the last 120 years will be an important addition to any high school, public or academic library reference collection.

"These interesting, unique compilations of economic and social facts, figures and graphs will support multiple research needs. They will engage and enlighten patrons in high school, public and academic library collections." –Booklist

Volume I: The Working Class ◆ 558 pages; Hardcover ISBN 1-891482-81-5, $145.00
Volume II: The Middle Class ◆ 591 pages; Hardcover ISBN 1-891482-72-6; $145.00
Volume III: The Upper Class ◆ 567 pages; Hardcover ISBN 1-930956-38-X, $145.00

Working Americans 1880-1999 Volume IV: Their Children

This Fourth Volume in the highly successful *Working Americans 1880-1999* series focuses on American children, decade by decade from 1880 to 1999. This interesting and useful volume introduces the reader to three children in each decade, one from each of the Working, Middle and Upper classes. Like the first three volumes in the series, the individual profiles are created from interviews, diaries, statistical studies, biographies and news reports. Profiles cover a broad range of ethnic backgrounds, geographic area and lifestyles – everything from an orphan in Memphis in 1882, following the Yellow Fever epidemic of 1878 to an eleven-year-old nephew of a beer baron and owner of the New York Yankees in New York City in 1921. Chapters also contain important supplementary materials including News Features as well as information on everything from Schools to Parks, Infectious Diseases to Childhood Fears along with Entertainment, Family Life and much more to provide an informative overview of the lifestyles of children from each decade. This interesting account of what life was like for Children in the Working, Middle and Upper Classes will be a welcome addition to the reference collection of any high school, public or academic library.

600 pages; Hardcover ISBN 1-930956-35-5, $145.00

Working Americans 1880-2003 Volume V: Americans At War

Working Americans 1880-2003 Volume V: Americans At War is divided into 11 chapters, each covering a decade from 1880-2003 and examines the lives of Americans during the time of war, including declared conflicts, one-time military actions, protests, and preparations for war. Each decade includes several personal profiles, whether on the battlefield or on the homefront, that tell the stories of civilians, soldiers, and officers during the decade. The profiles examine: Life at Home; Life at Work; and Life in the Community. Each decade also includes an Economic Profile with statistical comparisons, a Historical Snapshot, News Profiles, local News Articles, and Illustrations that provide a solid historical background to the decade being examined. Profiles range widely not only geographically, but also emotionally, from that of a girl whose leg was torn off in a blast during WWI, to the boredom of being stationed in the Dakotas as the Indian Wars were drawing to a close. As in previous volumes of the *Working Americans* series, information is presented in narrative form, but hard facts and real-life situations back up each story. The basis of the profiles come from diaries, private print books, personal interviews, family histories, estate documents and magazine articles. For easy reference, *Working Americans 1880-2003 Volume V: Americans At War* includes an in-depth Subject Index. The *Working Americans* series has become an important reference for public libraries, academic libraries and high school libraries. This fifth volume will be a welcome addition to all of these types of reference collections.

600 pages; Hardcover ISBN 1-59237-024-1; $145.00 Five Volume Set (Volumes I-V), Hardcover ISBN 1-59237-034-9, $675.00

The Asian Databook: Statistics for all US Counties & Cities with Over 10,000 Population

This is the first-ever resource that compiles statistics and rankings on the US Asian population. *The Asian Databook* presents over 20 statistical data points for each city and county, arranged alphabetically by state, then alphabetically by place name. Data reported for each place includes Population, Languages Spoken at Home, Foreign-Born, Educational Attainment, Income Figures, Poverty Status, Homeownership, Home Values & Rent, and more. Next, in the Rankings Section, the top 75 places are listed for each data element. These easy-to-access ranking tables allow the user to quickly determine trends and population characteristics. This kind of comparative data can not be found elsewhere, in print or on the web, in a format that's as easy-to-use or more concise. A useful resource for those searching for demographics data, career search and relocation information and also for market research. With data ranging from Ancestry to Education, *The Asian Databook* presents a useful compilation of information that will be a much-needed resource in the reference collection of any public or academic library along with the marketing collection of any company whose primary focus in on the Asian population.

1,000 pages; Softcover ISBN 1-59237-044-6 $150.00

The Hispanic Databook: Statistics for all US Counties & Cities with Over 10,000 Population

Previously published by Toucan Valley Publications, this second edition has been completely updated with figures from the latest census and has been broadly expanded to include dozens of new data elements and a brand new Rankings section. The Hispanic population in the United States has increased over 42% in the last 10 years and accounts for 12.5% of the total US population. For ease-of-use, *The Hispanic Databook* presents over 20 statistical data points for each city and county, arranged alphabetically by state, then alphabetically by place name. Data reported for each place includes Population, Languages Spoken at Home, Foreign-Born, Educational Attainment, Income Figures, Poverty Status, Homeownership, Home Values & Rent, and more. Next, in the Rankings Section, the top 75 places are listed for each data element. These easy-to-access ranking tables allow the user to quickly determine trends and population characteristics. This kind of comparative data can not be found elsewhere, in print or on the web, in a format that's as easy-to-use or more concise. A useful resource for those searching for demographics data, career search and relocation information and also for market research. With data ranging from Ancestry to Education, *The Hispanic Databook* presents a useful compilation of information that will be a much-needed resource in the reference collection of any public or academic library along with the marketing collection of any company whose primary focus in on the Hispanic population.

"This accurate, clearly presented volume of selected Hispanic demographics is recommended for large public libraries and research collections."-Library Journal

1,000 pages; Softcover ISBN 1-59237-008-X, $150.00

The Comparative Guide to American Suburbs, 2005

The Comparative Guide to American Suburbs is a one-stop source for Statistics on the 2,000+ suburban communities surrounding the 50 largest metropolitan areas – their population characteristics, income levels, economy, school system and important data on how they compare to one another. Organized into 50 Metropolitan Area chapters, each chapter contains an overview of the Metropolitan Area, a detailed Map followed by a comprehensive Statistical Profile of each Suburban Community, including Contact Information, Physical Characteristics, Population Characteristics, Income, Economy, Unemployment Rate, Cost of Living, Education, Chambers of Commerce and more. Next, statistical data is sorted into Ranking Tables that rank the suburbs by twenty different criteria, including Population, Per Capita Income, Unemployment Rate, Crime Rate, Cost of Living and more. *The Comparative Guide to American Suburbs* is the best source for locating data on suburbs. Those looking to relocate, as well as those doing preliminary market research, will find this an invaluable timesaving resource.

"Public and academic libraries will find this compilation useful...." – Booklist

1,700 pages; Softcover ISBN 1-59237-004-7, $130.00

To preview any of our Directories Risk-Free for 30 days, call (800) 562-2139 or fax to (518) 789-0556

Ancestry in America: A Comparative Guide to Over 200 Ethnic Backgrounds

This brand new reference work pulls together thousands of comparative statistics on the Ethnic Backgrounds of all populated places in the United States with populations over 10,000. Never before has this kind of information been reported in a single volume. Section One, Statistics by Place, is made up of a list of over 200 ancestry and race categories arranged alphabetically by each of the 5,000 different places with populations over 10,000. The population number of the ancestry group in that city or town is provided along with the percent that group represents of the total population. This informative city-by-city section allows the user to quickly and easily explore the ethnic makeup of all major population bases in the United States. Section Two, Comparative Rankings, contains three tables for each ethnicity and race. In the first table, the top 150 populated places are ranked by population number for that particular ancestry group, regardless of population. In the second table, the top 150 populated places are ranked by the percent of the total population for that ancestry group. In the third table, those top 150 populated places with 10,000 population are ranked by population number for each ancestry group. These easy-to-navigate tables allow users to see ancestry population patterns and make city-by-city comparisons as well. Plus, as an added bonus with the purchase of *Ancestry in America*, a free companion CD-ROM is available that lists statistics and rankings for all of the 35,000 populated places in the United States. This brand new, information-packed resource will serve a wide-range or research requests for demographics, population characteristics, relocation information and much more. *Ancestry in America: A Comparative Guide to Over 200 Ethnic Backgrounds* will be an important acquisition to all reference collections.

"This compilation will serve a wide range of research requests for population characteristics
… it offers much more detail than other sources." –Booklist

1,500 pages; Softcover ISBN 1-59237-029-2, $225.00

Weather America, A Thirty-Year Summary of Statistical Weather Data and Rankings

This valuable resource provides extensive climatological data for over 4,000 National and Cooperative Weather Stations throughout the United States. *Weather America* begins with a new Major Storms section that details major storm events of the nation and a National Rankings section that details rankings for several data elements, such as Maximum Temperature and Precipitation. The main body of *Weather America* is organized into 50 state sections. Each section provides a Data Table on each Weather Station, organized alphabetically, that provides statistics on Maximum and Minimum Temperatures, Precipitation, Snowfall, Extreme Temperatures, Foggy Days, Humidity and more. State sections contain two brand new features in this edition – a City Index and a narrative Description of the climatic conditions of the state. Each section also includes a revised Map of the State that includes not only weather stations, but cities and towns.

"Best Reference Book of the Year." –Library Journal

2,013 pages; Softcover ISBN 1-891482-29-7, $175.00

Profiles of America: Facts, Figures & Statistics for Every Populated Place in the United States

Profiles of America is the only source that pulls together, in one place, statistical, historical and descriptive information about every place in the United States in an easy-to-use format. This award winning reference set, now in its second edition, compiles statistics and data from over 20 different sources – the latest census information has been included along with more than nine brand new statistical topics. This Four-Volume Set details over 40,000 places, from the biggest metropolis to the smallest unincorporated hamlet, and provides statistical details and information on over 50 different topics including Geography, Climate, Population, Vital Statistics, Economy, Income, Taxes, Education, Housing, Health & Environment, Public Safety, Newspapers, Transportation, Presidential Election Results and Information Contacts or Chambers of Commerce. Profiles are arranged, for ease-of-use, by state and then by county. Each county begins with a County-Wide Overview and is followed by information for each Community in that particular county. The Community Profiles within the county are arranged alphabetically. *Profiles of America* is a virtual snapshot of America at your fingertips and a unique compilation of information that will be widely used in any reference collection.

A Library Journal Best Reference Book   "An outstanding compilation." –Library Journal

10,000 pages; Four Volume Set; Softcover ISBN 1-891482-80-7, $595.00

The Environmental Resource Handbook, 2004

The Environmental Resource Handbook, now in its second edition, is the most up-to-date and comprehensive source for Environmental Resources and Statistics. Section I: Resources provides detailed contact information for thousands of information sources, including Associations & Organizations, Awards & Honors, Conferences, Foundations & Grants, Environmental Health, Government Agencies, National Parks & Wildlife Refuges, Publications, Research Centers, Educational Programs, Green Product Catalogs, Consultants and much more. Section II: Statistics, provides statistics and rankings on hundreds of important topics, including Children's Environmental Index, Municipal Finances, Toxic Chemicals, Recycling, Climate, Air & Water Quality and more. This kind of up-to-date environmental data, all in one place, is not available anywhere else on the market place today. This vast compilation of resources and statistics is a must-have for all public and academic libraries as well as any organization with a primary focus on the environment.

"…the intrinsic value of the information make it worth consideration by libraries with
environmental collections and environmentally concerned users." –Booklist

1,000 pages; Softcover ISBN 1-59237-030-6, $155.00 ◆ Online Database $300.00

To preview any of our Directories Risk-Free for 30 days, call (800) 562-2139 or fax to (518) 789-0556

America's Top-Rated Cities, 2004

America's Top-Rated Cities provides current, comprehensive statistical information and other essential data in one easy-to-use source on the 100 "top" cities that have been cited as the best for business and living in the U.S. This handbook allows readers to see, at a glance, a concise social, business, economic, demographic and environmental profile of each city, including brief evaluative comments. In addition to detailed data on Cost of Living, Finances, Real Estate, Education, Major Employers, Media, Crime and Climate, city reports now include Housing Vacancies, Tax Audits, Bankruptcy, Presidential Election Results and more. This outstanding source of information will be widely used in any reference collection.

"The only source of its kind that brings together all of this information into one easy-to-use source. It will be beneficial to many business and public libraries." –ARBA

2,500 pages, 4 Volume Set; Softcover ISBN 1-59237-038-1, $195.00

America's Top-Rated Smaller Cities, 2004

A perfect companion to *America's Top-Rated Cities*, *America's Top-Rated Smaller Cities* provides current, comprehensive business and living profiles of smaller cities (population 25,000-99,999) that have been cited as the best for business and living in the United States. Sixty cities make up this 2004 edition of *America's Top-Rated Smaller Cities*, all are top-ranked by Population Growth, Median Income, Unemployment Rate and Crime Rate. City reports reflect the most current data available on a wide-range of statistics, including Employment & Earnings, Household Income, Unemployment Rate, Population Characteristics, Taxes, Cost of Living, Education, Health Care, Public Safety, Recreation, Media, Air & Water Quality and much more. Plus, each city report contains a Background of the City, and an Overview of the State Finances. *America's Top-Rated Smaller Cities* offers a reliable, one-stop source for statistical data that, before now, could only be found scattered in hundreds of sources. This volume is designed for a wide range of readers: individuals considering relocating a residence or business; professionals considering expanding their business or changing careers; general and market researchers; real estate consultants; human resource personnel; urban planners and investors.

"Provides current, comprehensive statistical information in one easy-to-use source... Recommended for public and academic libraries and specialized collections." –Library Journal

1,100 pages; Softcover ISBN 1-59237-043-8, $160.00

Crime in America's Top-Rated Cities, 2000

This volume includes over 20 years of crime statistics in all major crime categories: violent crimes, property crimes and total crime. *Crime in America's Top-Rated Cities* is conveniently arranged by city and covers 76 top-rated cities. *Crime in America's Top-Rated Cities* offers details that compare the number of crimes and crime rates for the city, suburbs and metro area along with national crime trends for violent, property and total crimes. Also, this handbook contains important information and statistics on Anti-Crime Programs, Crime Risk, Hate Crimes, Illegal Drugs, Law Enforcement, Correctional Facilities, Death Penalty Laws and much more. A much-needed resource for people who are relocating, business professionals, general researchers, the press, law enforcement officials and students of criminal justice.

"Data is easy to access and will save hours of searching." –Global Enforcement Review

832 pages; Softcover ISBN 1-891482-84-X, $155.00

The American Tally, 2003/04   Statistics & Comparative Rankings for U.S. Cities with Populations over 10,000

This important statistical handbook compiles, all in one place, comparative statistics on all U.S. cities and towns with a 10,000+ population. *The American Tally* provides statistical details on over 4,000 cities and towns and profiles how they compare with one another in Population Characteristics, Education, Language & Immigration, Income & Employment and Housing. Each section begins with an alphabetical listing of cities by state, allowing for quick access to both the statistics and relative rankings of any city. Next, the highest and lowest cities are listed in each statistic. These important, informative lists provide quick reference to which cities are at both extremes of the spectrum for each statistic. Unlike any other reference, *The American Tally* provides quick, easy access to comparative statistics – a must-have for any reference collection.

"A solid library reference." –Bookwatch

500 pages; Softcover ISBN 1-930956-29-0, $125.00

To preview any of our Directories Risk-Free for 30 days, call (800) 562-2139 or fax to (518) 789-0556

Grey House Publishing
Business Directories

The Directory of Business Information Resources, 2005

With 100% verification, over 1,000 new listings and more than 12,000 updates, this 2005 edition of *The Directory of Business Information Resources* is the most up-to-date source for contacts in over 98 business areas – from advertising and agriculture to utilities and wholesalers. This carefully researched volume details: the Associations representing each industry; the Newsletters that keep members current; the Magazines and Journals - with their "Special Issues" - that are important to the trade, the Conventions that are "must attends," Databases, Directories and Industry Web Sites that provide access to must-have marketing resources. Includes contact names, phone & fax numbers, web sites and e-mail addresses. This one-volume resource is a gold mine of information and would be a welcome addition to any reference collection.

"This is a most useful and easy-to-use addition to any researcher's library." –The Information Professionals Institute

2,500 pages; Softcover ISBN 1-59237-050-0, $195.00 ♦ Online Database $495.00

Nations of the World, 2005 A Political, Economic and Business Handbook

This completely revised edition covers all the nations of the world in an easy-to-use, single volume. Each nation is profiled in a single chapter that includes Key Facts, Political & Economic Issues, a Country Profile and Business Information. In this fast-changing world, it is extremely important to make sure that the most up-to-date information is included in your reference collection. This 2005 edition is just the answer. Each of the 200+ country chapters have been carefully reviewed by a political expert to make sure that the text reflects the most current information on Politics, Travel Advisories, Economics and more. You'll find such vital information as a Country Map, Population Characteristics, Inflation, Agricultural Production, Foreign Debt, Political History, Foreign Policy, Regional Insecurity, Economics, Trade & Tourism, Historical Profile, Political Systems, Ethnicity, Languages, Media, Climate, Hotels, Chambers of Commerce, Banking, Travel Information and more. Five Regional Chapters follow the main text and include a Regional Map, an Introductory Article, Key Indicators and Currencies for the Region. New for 2004, an all-inclusive CD-ROM is available as a companion to the printed text. Noted for its sophisticated, up-to-date and reliable compilation of political, economic and business information, this brand new edition will be an important acquisition to any public, academic or special library reference collection.

"A useful addition to both general reference collections and business collections." –RUSQ

1,700 pages; Print Version Only Softcover ISBN 1-59237-051-9, $145.00 ♦ Print Version and CD-ROM $180.00

The Grey House Performing Arts Directory, 2005

The Grey House Performing Arts Directory is the most comprehensive resource covering the Performing Arts. This important directory provides current information on over 8,500 Dance Companies, Instrumental Music Programs, Opera Companies, Choral Groups, Theater Companies, Performing Arts Series and Performing Arts Facilities. Plus, this edition now contains a brand new section on Artist Management Groups. In addition to mailing address, phone & fax numbers, e-mail addresses and web sites, dozens of other fields of available information include mission statement, key contacts, facilities, seating capacity, season, attendance and more. This directory also provides an important Information Resources section that covers hundreds of Performing Arts Associations, Magazines, Newsletters, Trade Shows, Directories, Databases and Industry Web Sites. Five indexes provide immediate access to this wealth of information: Entry Name, Executive Name, Performance Facilities, Geographic and Information Resources. *The Grey House Performing Arts Directory* pulls together thousands of Performing Arts Organizations, Facilities and Information Resources into an easy-to-use source – this kind of comprehensiveness and extensive detail is not available in any resource on the market place today.

"Immensely useful and user-friendly ... recommended for public, academic and certain special library reference collections." –Booklist

1,500 pages; Softcover ISBN 1-59237-023-3, $185.00 ♦ Online Database $335.00

Research Services Directory, 2003/04 Commercial & Corporate Research Centers

This Ninth Edition provides access to well over 8,000 independent Commercial Research Firms, Corporate Research Centers and Laboratories offering contract services for hands-on, basic or applied research. *Research Services Directory* covers the thousands of types of research companies, including Biotechnology & Pharmaceutical Developers, Consumer Product Research, Defense Contractors, Electronics & Software Engineers, Think Tanks, Forensic Investigators, Independent Commercial Laboratories, Information Brokers, Market & Survey Research Companies, Medical Diagnostic Facilities, Product Research & Development Firms and more. Each entry provides the company's name, mailing address, phone & fax numbers, key contacts, web site, e-mail address, as well as a company description and research and technical fields served.

"An important source for organizations in need of information about laboratories, individuals and other facilities." –ARBA

1,400 pages; Softcover ISBN 1-59237-003-9, $395.00 ♦ Online Database (includes a free copy of the directory) $850.00

To preview any of our Directories Risk-Free for 30 days, call (800) 562-2139 or fax to (518) 789-0556

The Directory of Venture Capital Firms, 2005

This edition has been extensively updated and broadly expanded to offer direct access to over 2,800 Domestic and International Venture Capital Firms, including address, phone & fax numbers, e-mail addresses and web sites for both primary and branch locations. Entries include details on the firm's Mission Statement, Industry Group Preferences, Geographic Preferences, Average and Minimum Investments and Investment Criteria. You'll also find details that are available nowhere else, including the Firm's Portfolio Companies and extensive information on each of the firm's Managing Partners, such as Education, Professional Background and Directorships held, along with the Partner's E-mail Address. *The Directory of Venture Capital Firms* offers five important indexes: Geographic Index, Executive Name Index, Portfolio Company Index, Industry Preference Index and College & University Index. With its comprehensive coverage and detailed, extensive information on each company, *The Directory of Venture Capital Firms* is an important addition to any finance collection.

> *"The sheer number of listings, the descriptive information provided and the outstanding indexing make this directory a better value than its principal competitor, Pratt's Guide to Venture Capital Sources. Recommended for business collections in large public, academic and business libraries." —Choice*

1,300 pages; Softcover ISBN 1-59237-062-4, $450.00 ◆ Online Database (includes a free copy of the directory) $889.00

The Directory of Mail Order Catalogs, 2005

Published since 1981, this 2005 edition features 100% verification of data and is the premier source of information on the mail order catalog industry. Details over 12,000 consumer catalog companies with 44 different product chapters from Animals to Toys & Games. Contains detailed contact information including e-mail addresses and web sites along with important business details such as employee size, years in business, sales volume, catalog size, number of catalogs mailed and more. Four indexes provide quick access to information: Catalog & Company Name Index, Geographic Index, Product Index and Web Sites Index.

> *"This is a godsend for those looking for information." —Reference Book Review*

1,700 pages; Softcover ISBN 1-59237-066-7 $250.00 ◆ Online Database (includes a free copy of the directory) $495.00

The Directory of Business to Business Catalogs, 2005

The completely updated 2005 *Directory of Business to Business Catalogs*, provides details on over 6,000 suppliers of everything from computers to laboratory supplies… office products to office design… marketing resources to safety equipment… landscaping to maintenance suppliers… building construction and much more. Detailed entries offer mailing address, phone & fax numbers, e-mail addresses, web sites, key contacts, sales volume, employee size, catalog printing information and more. Jut about every kind of product a business needs in its day-to-day operations is covered in this carefully-researched volume. Three indexes are provided for at-a-glance access to information: Catalog & Company Name Index, Geographic Index and Web Sites Index.

> *"An excellent choice for libraries… wishing to supplement their business supplier resources." —Booklist*

800 pages; Softcover ISBN 1-59237-064-0, $165.00 ◆ Online Database (includes a free copy of the directory) $325.00

Thomas Food and Beverage Market Place, 2005

Thomas Food and Beverage Market Place is bigger and better than ever with thousands of new companies, thousands of updates to existing companies and two revised and enhanced product category indexes. This comprehensive directory profiles over 18,000 Food & Beverage Manufacturers, 12,000 Equipment & Supply Companies, 2,200 Transportation & Warehouse Companies, 2,000 Brokers & Wholesalers, 8,000 Importers & Exporters, 900 Industry Resources and hundreds of Mail Order Catalogs. Listings include detailed Contact Information, Sales Volumes, Key Contacts, Brand & Product Information, Packaging Details and much more. *Thomas Food and Beverage Market Place* is available as a three-volume printed set, a subscription-based Online Database via the Internet, on CD-ROM, as well as mailing lists and a licensable database.

> *"An essential purchase for those in the food industry but will also be useful in public libraries where needed. Much of the information will be difficult and time consuming to locate without this handy three-volume ready-reference source." —ARBA*

8,500 pages, 3 Volume Set; Softcover ISBN 1-59237-058-6, $495.00 ◆ CD-ROM $695.00 ◆
CD-ROM & 3 Volume Set Combo $895.00 ◆ Online Database $695.00 ◆ Online Database & 3 Volume Set Combo, $895.00

To preview any of our Directories Risk-Free for 30 days, call (800) 562-2139 or fax to (518) 789-0556

The Grey House Safety & Security Directory, 2005

The Grey House Safety & Security Directory is the most comprehensive reference tool and buyer's guide for the safety and security industry. Arranged by safety topic, each chapter begins with OSHA regulations for the topic, followed by Training Articles written by top professionals in the field and Self-Inspection Checklists. Next, each topic contains Buyer's Guide sections that feature related products and services. Topics include Administration, Insurance, Loss Control & Consulting, Protective Equipment & Apparel, Noise & Vibration, Facilities Monitoring & Maintenance, Employee Health Maintenance & Ergonomics, Retail Food Services, Machine Guards, Process Guidelines & Tool Handling, Ordinary Materials Handling, Hazardous Materials Handling, Workplace Preparation & Maintenance, Electrical Lighting & Safety, Fire & Rescue and Security. The Buyer's Guide sections are carefully indexed within each topic area to ensure that you can find the supplies needed to meet OSHA's regulations. Six important indexes make finding information and product manufacturers quick and easy: Geographical Index of Manufacturers and Distributors, Company Profile Index, Brand Name Index, Product Index, Index of Web Sites and Index of Advertisers. This comprehensive, up-to-date reference will provide every tool necessary to make sure a business is in compliance with OSHA regulations and locate the products and services needed to meet those regulations.

"Presents industrial safety information for engineers, plant managers, risk managers, and construction site supervisors..." –Choice

1,500 pages, 2 Volume Set; Softcover ISBN 1-59237-067-5, $225.00

The Grey House Homeland Security Directory, 2005

This updated edition features the latest contact information for government and private organizations involved with Homeland Security along with the latest product information and provides detailed profiles of nearly 1,000 Federal & State Organizations & Agencies and over 3,000 Officials and Key Executives involved with Homeland Security. These listings are incredibly detailed and include Mailing Address, Phone & Fax Numbers, Email Addresses & Web Sites, a complete Description of the Agency and a complete list of the Officials and Key Executives associated with the Agency. Next, *The Grey House Homeland Security Directory* provides the go-to source for Homeland Security Products & Services. This section features over 2,000 Companies that provide Consulting, Products or Services. With this Buyer's Guide at their fingertips, users can locate suppliers of everything from Training Materials to Access Controls, from Perimeter Security to BioTerrorism Countermeasures and everything in between – complete with contact information and product descriptions. A handy Product Locator Index is provided to quickly and easily locate suppliers of a particular product. Lastly, an Information Resources Section provides immediate access to contact information for hundreds of Associations, Newsletters, Magazines, Trade Shows, Databases and Directories that focus on Homeland Security. This comprehensive, information-packed resource will be a welcome tool for any company or agency that is in need of Homeland Security information and will be a necessary acquisition for the reference collection of all public libraries and large school districts.

"Compiles this information in one place and is discerning in content. A useful purchase for public and academic libraries." –Booklist

800 pages; Softcover ISBN 1-59237-057-8, $195.00 ◆ Online Database (includes a free copy of the directory) $385.00

The Grey House Transportation Security Directory & Handbook, 2005

This brand new title is the only reference of its kind that brings together current data on Transportation Security. With information on everything from Regulatory Authorities to Security Equipment, this top-flight database brings together the relevant information necessary for creating and maintaining a security plan for a wide range of transportation facilities. With this current, comprehensive directory at the ready you'll have immediate access to: Regulatory Authorities & Legislation; Information Resources; Sample Security Plans & Checklists; Contact Data for Major Airports, Seaports, Railroads, Trucking Companies and Oil Pipelines; Security Service Providers; Recommended Equipment & Product Information and more. Using the *Grey House Transportation Security Directory & Handbook*, managers will be able to quickly and easily assess their current security plans; develop contacts to create and maintain new security procedures; and source the products and services necessary to adequately maintain a secure environment. This valuable resource is a must for all Security Managers at Airports, Seaports, Railroads, Trucking Companies and Oil Pipelines.

800 pages; Softcover ISBN 1-59237-075-6, $195

International Business and Trade Directories, 2003/04

Completely updated, the Third Edition of *International Business and Trade Directories* now contains more than 10,000 entries, over 2,000 more than the last edition, making this directory the most comprehensive resource of the worlds business and trade directories. Entries include content descriptions, price, publisher's name and address, web site and e-mail addresses, phone and fax numbers and editorial staff. Organized by industry group, and then by region, this resource puts over 10,000 industry-specific business and trade directories at the reader's fingertips. Three indexes are included for quick access to information: Geographic Index, Publisher Index and Title Index. Public, college and corporate libraries, as well as individuals and corporations seeking critical market information will want to add this directory to their marketing collection.

"Reasonably priced for a work of this type, this directory should appeal to larger academic, public and corporate libraries with an international focus." –Library Journal

1,800 pages; Softcover ISBN 1-930956-63-0, $225.00 ◆ Online Database (includes a free copy of the directory) $450.00

To preview any of our Directories Risk-Free for 30 days, call (800) 562-2139 or fax to (518) 789-0556

Sports Market Place Directory, 2005

For over 20 years, this comprehensive, up-to-date directory has offered direct access to the Who, What, When & Where of the Sports Industry. With over 20,000 updates and enhancements, the *Sports Market Place Directory* is the most detailed, comprehensive and current sports business reference source available. In 1,800 information-packed pages, *Sports Market Place Directory* profiles contact information and key executives for: Single Sport Organizations, Professional Leagues, Multi-Sport Organizations, Disabled Sports, High School & Youth Sports, Military Sports, Olympic Organizations, Media, Sponsors, Sponsorship & Marketing Event Agencies, Event & Meeting Calendars, Professional Services, College Sports, Manufacturers & Retailers, Facilities and much more. *The Sports Market Place Directory* provides organization's contact information with detailed descriptions including: Key Contacts, physical, mailing, email and web addresses plus phone and fax numbers. Plus, nine important indexes make sure that you can find the information you're looking for quickly and easily: Entry Index, Single Sport Index, Media Index, Sponsor Index, Agency Index, Manufacturers Index, Brand Name Index, Facilities Index and Executive/Geographic Index. For over twenty years, *The Sports Market Place Directory* has assisted thousands of individuals in their pursuit of a career in the sports industry. Why not use "THE SOURCE" that top recruiters, headhunters and career placement centers use to find information on or about sports organizations and key hiring contacts.

1,800 pages; Softcover ISBN 1-59237-077-2, $225.00 ◆ CD-ROM $479.00

Sedgwick Press
Hospital & Health Plan Directories

The Directory of Hospital Personnel, 2005

The Directory of Hospital Personnel is the best resource you can have at your fingertips when researching or marketing a product or service to the hospital market. A "Who's Who" of the hospital universe, this directory puts you in touch with over 150,000 key decision-makers. With 100% verification of data you can rest assured that you will reach the right person with just one call. Every hospital in the U.S. is profiled, listed alphabetically by city within state. Plus, three easy-to-use, cross-referenced indexes put the facts at your fingertips faster and more easily than any other directory: Hospital Name Index, Bed Size Index and Personnel Index. *The Directory of Hospital Personnel* is the only complete source for key hospital decision-makers by name. Whether you want to define or restructure sales territories... locate hospitals with the purchasing power to accept your proposals... keep track of important contacts or colleagues... or find information on which insurance plans are accepted, *The Directory of Hospital Personnel* gives you the information you need – easily, efficiently, effectively and accurately.

"Recommended for college, university and medical libraries." -ARBA

2,500 pages; Softcover ISBN 1-59237-065-9 $275.00 ◆ Online Database $545.00 ◆ Online Database & Directory Combo, $650.00

The Directory of Health Care Group Purchasing Organizations, 2005

This comprehensive directory provides the important data you need to get in touch with over 800 Group Purchasing Organizations. By providing in-depth information on this growing market and its members, *The Directory of Health Care Group Purchasing Organizations* fills a major need for the most accurate and comprehensive information on over 800 GPOs – Mailing Address, Phone & Fax Numbers, E-mail Addresses, Key Contacts, Purchasing Agents, Group Descriptions, Membership Categorization, Standard Vendor Proposal Requirements, Membership Fees & Terms, Expanded Services, Total Member Beds & Outpatient Visits represented and more. Five Indexes provide a number of ways to locate the right GPO: Alphabetical Index, Expanded Services Index, Organization Type Index, Geographic Index and Member Institution Index. With its comprehensive and detailed information on each purchasing organization, *The Directory of Health Care Group Purchasing Organizations* is the go-to source for anyone looking to target this market.

"The information is clearly arranged and easy to access...recommended for those needing this very specialized information." –ARBA

1,000 pages; Softcover ISBN 1-59237-091.8, $325.00 ◆ Online Database, $650.00 ◆ Online Database & Directory Combo, $750.00

The HMO/PPO Directory, 2005

The HMO/PPO Directory is a comprehensive source that provides detailed information about Health Maintenance Organizations and Preferred Provider Organizations nationwide. This comprehensive directory details more information about more managed health care organizations than ever before. Over 1,100 HMOs, PPOs and affiliated companies are listed, arranged alphabetically by state. Detailed listings include Key Contact Information, Prescription Drug Benefits, Enrollment, Geographical Areas served, Affiliated Physicians & Hospitals, Federal Qualifications, Status, Year Founded, Managed Care Partners, Employer References, Fees & Payment Information and more. Plus, five years of historical information is included related to Revenues, Net Income, Medical Loss Ratios, Membership Enrollment and Number of Patient Complaints. *The HMO/PPO Directory* provides the most comprehensive information on the most companies available on the market place today.

"Helpful to individuals requesting certain HMO/PPO issues such as co-payment costs, subscription costs and patient complaints. Individuals concerned (or those with questions) about their insurance may find this text to be of use to them." -ARBA

600 pages; Softcover ISBN 1-59237-057-8, $275.00 ◆ Online Database, $495.00 ◆ Online Database & Directory Combo, $600.00

To preview any of our Directories Risk-Free for 30 days, call (800) 562-2139 or fax to (518) 789-0556